D1472825

The Dictionary of Art · volume eleven

The Dictionary of Art

CONSULTING EDITOR Hugh Brigstocke

EDITOR Jane Turner

11

Ferrara

TO

Gainsborough

GROVE

An imprint of Oxford University Press

Oxford University Press

Oxford   New York
Auckland   Bangkok   Buenos Aires   Cape Town   Chennai
Dar es Salaam   Delhi   Hong Kong   Istanbul   Karachi   Kolkata
Kuala Lumpur   Madrid   Melbourne   Mexico City   Mumbai   Nairobi
São Paulo   Shanghai   Taipei   Tokyo   Toronto

Copyright © 1996 by Oxford University Press
Published by Oxford University Press, Inc.
198 Madison Avenue, New York, New York 10016
www.oup-usa.org

ISBN 0-19-517068-7

The Dictionary of Art, edited by JANE TURNER, was published in thirty-four volumes
in 1996 by Macmillan Publishers Limited

Text keyboarded by Wearset Limited, Sunderland, England
Database management by Pindar plc, York, England
Imagesetting by William Clowes Limited, Suffolk, England
Printed and bound by China Translation and Printing Services Ltd. , Hong Kong

Contents

General Abbreviations

The abbreviations employed throughout this dictionary, most of which are listed below, do not vary, except for capitalization, regardless of the context in which they are used, including bibliographical citations and for locations of works of art. The principle used to arrive at these abbreviations is that their full form should be easily deducible, and for this reason acronyms have generally been avoided (e.g. Los Angeles Co. Mus. A. instead of LACMA). The same abbreviation is adopted for cognate forms in foreign languages and in most cases for plural and adjectival forms (e.g. A.= Art, Arts, Arte, Arti etc). Not all related forms are listed below. Occasionally, if a name, for instance of an artists' group or exhibiting society, is repeated within the text of one article, it is cited in an abbreviated form after its first mention in full (e.g. The Pre-Raphaelite Brotherhood (PRB) was founded...); the same is true of archaeological periods and eras, which are abbreviated to initial letters in small capitals (e.g. In the Early Minoan (EM) period...). Such abbreviations do not appear in this list. For the reader's convenience, separate full lists of abbreviations for locations, periodical titles and standard reference books and series are included as Appendices A–C in vol. 33.

A.	Art, Arts	Anthropol.	Anthropology	Azerbaij.	Azerbaijani
A.C.	Arts Council	Antiqua.	Antiquarian, Antiquaries	B.	Bartsch [catalogue of Old Master prints]
Acad.	Academy	app.	appendix		
AD	Anno Domini	approx.	approximately	b	born
Add.	Additional, Addendum	AR	Arkansas (USA)	BA	Bachelor of Arts
addn	addition	ARA	Associate of the Royal Academy	Balt.	Baltic
Admin.	Administration			bapt	baptized
Adv.	Advances, Advanced	Arab.	Arabic	BArch	Bachelor of Architecture
Aesth.	Aesthetic(s)	Archaeol.	Archaeology	Bart	Baronet
Afr.	African	Archit.	Architecture, Architectural	Bask.	Basketry
Afrik.	Afrikaans, Afrikaner	Archv, Archvs	Archive(s)	BBC	British Broadcasting Corporation
A.G.	Art Gallery				
Agrar.	Agrarian	Arg.	Argentine	BC	Before Christ
Agric.	Agriculture	ARHA	Associate of the Royal Hibernian Academy	BC	British Columbia (Canada)
Agron.	Agronomy			BE	Buddhist era
Agy	Agency	ARIBA	Associate of the Royal Institute of British Architects	Beds	Bedfordshire (GB)
AH	Anno Hegirae			Behav.	Behavioural
A. Inst.	Art Institute	Armen.	Armenian	Belarus.	Belarusian
AK	Alaska (USA)	ARSA	Associate of the Royal Scottish Academy	Belg.	Belgian
AL	Alabama (USA)			Berks	Berkshire (GB)
Alb.	Albanian	Asiat.	Asiatic	Berwicks	Berwickshire (GB; old)
Alg.	Algerian	Assist.	Assistance	BFA	Bachelor of Fine Arts
Alta	Alberta (Canada)	Assoc.	Association	Bibl.	Bible, Biblical
Altern.	Alternative	Astron.	Astronomy	Bibliog.	Bibliography, Bibliographical
a.m.	ante meridiem [before noon]	AT&T	American Telephone & Telegraph Company	Biblioph.	Bibliophile
Amat.	Amateur	attrib.	attribution, attributed to	Biog.	Biography, Biographical
Amer.	American	Aug	August	Biol.	Biology, Biological
An.	Annals	Aust.	Austrian	bk, bks	book(s)
Anatol.	Anatolian	Austral.	Australian	Bkbinder	Bookbinder
Anc.	Ancient	Auth.	Author(s)	Bklore	Booklore
Annu.	Annual	Auton.	Autonomous	Bkshop	Bookshop
Anon.	Anonymous(ly)	Aux.	Auxiliary	BL	British Library
Ant.	Antique	Ave.	Avenue	Bld	Build
Anthol.	Anthology	AZ	Arizona (USA)	Bldg	Building

Bldr	Builder	Chin.	Chinese	Cur.	Curator, Curatorial, Curatorship
BLitt	Bachelor of Letters/Literature	Christ.	Christian, Christianity	Curr.	Current(s)
BM	British Museum	Chron.	Chronicle	CVO	Commander of the [Royal]
Boh.	Bohemian	Cie	Compagnie [French]		Victorian Order
Boliv.	Bolivian	Cinema.	Cinematography	Cyclad.	Cycladic
Botan.	Botany, Botanical	Circ.	Circle	Cyp.	Cypriot
BP	Before present (1950)	Civ.	Civil, Civic	Czech.	Czechoslovak
Braz.	Brazilian	Civiliz.	Civilization(s)	$	dollars
BRD	Bundesrepublik Deutschland [Federal Republic of Germany (West Germany)]	Class.	Classic, Classical	*d*	died
		Clin.	Clinical	d.	denarius, denarii [penny, pence]
		CO	Colorado (USA)		
Brecons	Breconshire (GB; old)	Co.	Company; County	Dalmat.	Dalmatian
Brez.	Brezonek [lang. of Brittany]	Cod.	Codex, Codices	Dan.	Danish
Brit.	British	Col., Cols	Collection(s); Column(s)	DBE	Dame Commander of the Order of the British Empire
Bros	Brothers	Coll.	College		
BSc	Bachelor of Science	collab.	in collaboration with, collaborated, collaborative	DC	District of Columbia (USA)
Bucks	Buckinghamshire (GB)			DDR	Deutsche Demokratische Republik [German Democratic Republic (East Germany)]
Bulg.	Bulgarian	Collct.	Collecting		
Bull.	Bulletin	Colloq.	Colloquies		
bur	buried	Colomb.	Colombian	DE	Delaware (USA)
Burm.	Burmese	Colon.	Colonies, Colonial	Dec	December
Byz.	Byzantine	Colr	Collector	Dec.	Decorative
C	Celsius	Comm.	Commission; Community	ded.	dedication, dedicated to
C.	Century	Commerc.	Commercial	Democ.	Democracy, Democratic
c.	*circa* [about]	Communic.	Communications	Demog.	Demography, Demographic
CA	California	Comp.	Comparative; compiled by, compiler	Denbs	Denbighshire (GB; old)
Cab.	Cabinet			dep.	deposited at
Caerns	Caernarvonshire (GB; old)	Concent.	Concentration	Dept	Department
C.A.G.	City Art Gallery	Concr.	Concrete	Dept.	Departmental, Departments
Cal.	Calendar	Confed.	Confederation	Derbys	Derbyshire (GB)
Callig.	Calligraphy	Confer.	Conference	Des.	Design
Cam.	Camera	Congol.	Congolese	destr.	destroyed
Cambs	Cambridgeshire (GB)	Congr.	Congress	Dev.	Development
can	canonized	Conserv.	Conservation; Conservatory	Devon	Devonshire (GB)
Can.	Canadian	Constr.	Construction(al)	Dial.	Dialogue
Cant.	Canton(s), Cantonal	cont.	continued	diam.	diameter
Capt.	Captain	Contemp.	Contemporary	Diff.	Diffusion
Cards	Cardiganshire (GB; old)	Contrib.	Contributions, Contributor(s)	Dig.	Digest
Carib.	Caribbean	Convalesc.	Convalescence	Dip. Eng.	Diploma in Engineering
Carms	Carmarthenshire (GB; old)	Convent.	Convention	Dir.	Direction, Directed
Cartog.	Cartography	Coop.	Cooperation	Directrt	Directorate
Cat.	Catalan	Coord.	Coordination	Disc.	Discussion
cat.	catalogue	Copt.	Coptic	diss.	dissertation
Cath.	Catholic	Corp.	Corporation, Corpus	Distr.	District
CBE	Commander of the Order of the British Empire	Corr.	Correspondence	Div.	Division
		Cors.	Corsican	DLitt	Doctor of Letters/Literature
Celeb.	Celebration	Cost.	Costume	DM	Deutsche Mark
Celt.	Celtic	Cret.	Cretan	Doc.	Document(s)
Cent.	Centre, Central	Crim.	Criminal	Doss.	Dossier
Centen.	Centennial	Crit.	Critical, Criticism	DPhil	Doctor of Philosophy
Cer.	Ceramic	Croat.	Croatian	Dr	Doctor
cf.	confer [compare]	CT	Connecticut (USA)	Drg, Drgs	Drawing(s)
Chap., Chaps	Chapter(s)	Cttee	Committee	DSc	Doctor of Science/Historical Sciences
		Cub.	Cuban		
Chem.	Chemistry	Cult.	Cultural, Culture	Dut.	Dutch
Ches	Cheshire (GB)	Cumb.	Cumberland (GB; old)	Dwell.	Dwelling
Chil.	Chilean			E.	East(ern)

EC	European (Economic) Community	figs	figures	Heb.	Hebrew
Eccles.	Ecclesiastical	Filip.	Filipina(s), Filipino(s)	Hell.	Hellenic
Econ.	Economic, Economies	Fin.	Finnish	Her.	Heritage
Ecuad.	Ecuadorean	FL	Florida (USA)	Herald.	Heraldry, Heraldic
ed.	editor, edited (by)	*fl*	*floruit* [he/she flourished]	Hereford & Worcs	Hereford & Worcester (GB)
edn	edition	Flem.	Flemish	Herts	Hertfordshire (GB)
eds	editors	Flints	Flintshire (GB; old)	HI	Hawaii (USA)
Educ.	Education	Flk	Folk	Hib.	Hibernia
e.g.	*exempli gratia* [for example]	Flklore	Folklore	Hisp.	Hispanic
Egyp.	Egyptian	fol., fols	folio(s)	Hist.	History, Historical
Elem.	Element(s), Elementary	Found.	Foundation	HMS	His/Her Majesty's Ship
Emp.	Empirical	Fr.	French	Hon.	Honorary, Honourable
Emul.	Emulation	frag.	fragment	Horiz.	Horizon
Enc.	Encyclopedia	Fri.	Friday	Hort.	Horticulture
Encour.	Encouragement	FRIBA	Fellow of the Royal Institute of British Architects	Hosp.	Hospital(s)
Eng.	English	FRS	Fellow of the Royal Society, London	HRH	His/Her Royal Highness
Engin.	Engineer, Engineering			Human.	Humanities, Humanism
Engr., Engrs	Engraving(s)	ft	foot, feet	Hung.	Hungarian
		Furn.	Furniture	Hunts	Huntingdonshire (GB; old)
Envmt	Environment	Futur.	Futurist, Futurism	IA	Iowa
Epig.	Epigraphy	g	gram(s)	ibid.	*ibidem* [in the same place]
Episc.	Episcopal	GA	Georgia (USA)	ICA	Institute of Contemporary Arts
Esp.	Especially	Gael.	Gaelic		
Ess.	Essays	Gal., Gals	Gallery, Galleries	Ice.	Icelandic
est.	established	Gaz.	Gazette	Iconog.	Iconography
etc	*etcetera* [and so on]	GB	Great Britain	Iconol.	Iconology
Ethnog.	Ethnography	Gdn, Gdns	Garden(s)	ID	Idaho (USA)
Ethnol.	Ethnology	Gdnr(s)	Gardener(s)	i.e.	*id est* [that is]
Etrus.	Etruscan	Gen.	General	IL	Illinois (USA)
Eur.	European	Geneal.	Genealogy, Genealogist	Illum.	Illumination
Evangel.	Evangelical	Gent.	Gentleman, Gentlemen	illus.	illustrated, illustration
Exam.	Examination	Geog.	Geography	Imp.	Imperial
Excav.	Excavation, Excavated	Geol.	Geology	IN	Indiana (USA)
Exch.	Exchange	Geom.	Geometry	in., ins	inch(es)
Excurs.	Excursion	Georg.	Georgian	Inc.	Incorporated
exh.	exhibition	Geosci.	Geoscience	inc.	incomplete
Exp.	Exposition	Ger.	German, Germanic	incl.	includes, including, inclusive
Expermntl	Experimental	G.I.	Government/General Issue (USA)	Incorp.	Incorporation
Explor.	Exploration			Ind.	Indian
Expn	Expansion	Glams	Glamorganshire (GB; old)	Indep.	Independent
Ext.	External	Glos	Gloucestershire (GB)	Indig.	Indigenous
Extn	Extension	Govt	Government	Indol.	Indology
f, ff	following page, following pages	Gr.	Greek	Indon.	Indonesian
		Grad.	Graduate	Indust.	Industrial
F.A.	Fine Art(s)	Graph.	Graphic	Inf.	Information
Fac.	Faculty	Green.	Greenlandic	Inq.	Inquiry
facs.	facsimile	Gr.-Roman	Greco-Roman	Inscr.	Inscribed, Inscription
Fam.	Family	Gt	Great	Inst.	Institute(s)
fasc.	fascicle	Gtr	Greater	Inst. A.	Institute of Art
fd	feastday (of a saint)	Guat.	Guatemalan	Instr.	Instrument, Instrumental
Feb	February	Gym.	Gymnasium	Int.	International
Fed.	Federation, Federal	h.	height	Intell.	Intelligence
Fem.	Feminist	ha	hectare	Inter.	Interior(s), Internal
Fest.	Festival	Hait.	Haitian	Interdiscip.	Interdisciplinary
fig.	figure (illustration)	Hants	Hampshire (GB)	intro.	introduced by, introduction
Fig.	Figurative	Hb.	Handbook	inv.	inventory

Inven.	Invention
Invest.	Investigation(s)
Iran.	Iranian
irreg.	irregular(ly)
Islam.	Islamic
Isr.	Israeli
It.	Italian
J.	Journal
Jam.	Jamaican
Jan	January
Jap.	Japanese
Jav.	Javanese
Jew.	Jewish
Jewel.	Jewellery
Jord.	Jordanian
jr	junior
Juris.	Jurisdiction
KBE	Knight Commander of the Order of the British Empire
KCVO	Knight Commander of the Royal Victorian Order
kg	kilogram(s)
kHz	kilohertz
km	kilometre(s)
Knowl.	Knowledge
Kor.	Korean
KS	Kansas (USA)
KY	Kentucky (USA)
Kyrgyz.	Kyrgyzstani
£	libra, librae [pound, pounds sterling]
l.	length
LA	Louisiana (USA)
Lab.	Laboratory
Lancs	Lancashire (GB)
Lang.	Language(s)
Lat.	Latin
Latv.	Latvian
lb, lbs	pound(s) weight
Leb.	Lebanese
Lect.	Lecture
Legis.	Legislative
Leics	Leicestershire (GB)
Lex.	Lexicon
Lg.	Large
Lib., Libs	Library, Libraries
Liber.	Liberian
Libsp	Librarianship
Lincs	Lincolnshire (GB)
Lit.	Literature
Lith.	Lithuanian
Liturg.	Liturgical
LLB	Bachelor of Laws
LLD	Doctor of Laws
Lt	Lieutenant
Lt-Col.	Lieutenant-Colonel
Ltd	Limited

m	metre(s)
m.	married
M.	Monsieur
MA	Master of Arts; Massachusetts (USA)
Mag.	Magazine
Maint.	Maintenance
Malay.	Malaysian
Man.	Manitoba (Canada); Manual
Manuf.	Manufactures
Mar.	Marine, Maritime
Mason.	Masonic
Mat.	Material(s)
Math.	Mathematic
MBE	Member of the Order of the British Empire
MD	Doctor of Medicine; Maryland (USA)
ME	Maine (USA)
Mech.	Mechanical
Med.	Medieval; Medium, Media
Medic.	Medical, Medicine
Medit.	Mediterranean
Mem.	Memorial(s); Memoir(s)
Merions	Merionethshire (GB; old)
Meso-Amer.	Meso-American
Mesop.	Mesopotamian
Met.	Metropolitan
Metal.	Metallurgy
Mex.	Mexican
MFA	Master of Fine Arts
mg	milligram(s)
Mgmt	Management
Mgr	Monsignor
MI	Michigan
Micrones.	Micronesian
Mid. Amer.	Middle American
Middx	Middlesex (GB; old)
Mid. E.	Middle Eastern
Mid. Eng.	Middle English
Mid Glam.	Mid Glamorgan (GB)
Mil.	Military
Mill.	Millennium
Min.	Ministry; Minutes
Misc.	Miscellaneous
Miss.	Mission(s)
Mlle	Mademoiselle
mm	millimetre(s)
Mme	Madame
MN	Minnesota
Mnmt, Mnmts	Monument(s)
Mnmtl	Monumental
MO	Missouri (USA)
Mod.	Modern, Modernist
Moldav.	Moldavian

Moldov.	Moldovan
MOMA	Museum of Modern Art
Mon.	Monday
Mongol.	Mongolian
Mons	Monmouthshire (GB; old)
Montgoms	Montgomeryshire (GB; old)
Mor.	Moral
Morav.	Moravian
Moroc.	Moroccan
Movt	Movement
MP	Member of Parliament
MPhil	Master of Philosophy
MS	Mississippi (USA)
MS., MSS	manuscript(s)
MSc	Master of Science
MT	Montana (USA)
Mt	Mount
Mthly	Monthly
Mun.	Municipal
Mus.	Museum(s)
Mus. A.	Museum of Art
Mus. F.A.	Museum of Fine Art(s)
Music.	Musicology
N.	North(ern); National
n	refractive index of a medium
n.	note
N.A.G.	National Art Gallery
Nat.	Natural, Nature
Naut.	Nautical
NB	New Brunswick (Canada)
NC	North Carolina (USA)
ND	North Dakota (USA)
n.d.	no date
NE	Nebraska; Northeast(ern)
Neth.	Netherlandish
Newslett.	Newsletter
Nfld	Newfoundland (Canada)
N.G.	National Gallery
N.G.A.	National Gallery of Art
NH	New Hampshire (USA)
Niger.	Nigerian
NJ	New Jersey (USA)
NM	New Mexico (USA)
nm	nanometre (10^{-9} metre)
nn.	notes
no., nos	number(s)
Nord.	Nordic
Norm.	Normal
Northants	Northamptonshire (GB)
Northumb.	Northumberland (GB)
Norw.	Norwegian
Notts	Nottinghamshire (GB)
Nov	November
n.p.	no place (of publication)
N.P.G.	National Portrait Gallery
nr	near

Nr E.	Near Eastern	Per.	Period	Ptg(s)	Painting(s)
NS	New Style; Nova Scotia (Canada)	Percep.	Perceptions	Pub.	Public
		Perf.	Performance, Performing, Performed	pubd	published
n. s.	new series			Publ.	Publicity
NSW	New South Wales (Australia)	Period.	Periodical(s)	pubn(s)	publication(s)
NT	National Trust	Pers.	Persian	PVA	polyvinyl acetate
Ntbk	Notebook	Persp.	Perspectives	PVC	polyvinyl chloride
Numi.	Numismatic(s)	Peru.	Peruvian	Q.	quarterly
NV	Nevada (USA)	PhD	Doctor of Philosophy	4to	quarto
NW	Northwest(ern)	Philol.	Philology	Qué.	Québec (Canada)
NWT	Northwest Territories (Canada)	Philos.	Philosophy	*R*	reprint
		Phoen.	Phoenician	*r*	*recto*
NY	New York (USA)	Phot.	Photograph, Photography, Photographic	RA	Royal Academician
NZ	New Zealand			Radnors	Radnorshire (GB; old)
OBE	Officer of the Order of the British Empire	Phys.	Physician(s), Physics, Physique, Physical	RAF	Royal Air Force
				Rec.	Record(s)
Obj.	Object(s), Objective	Physiog.	Physiognomy	red.	reduction, reduced for
Occas.	Occasional	Physiol.	Physiology	Ref.	Reference
Occident.	Occidental	Pict.	Picture(s), Pictorial	Refurb.	Refurbishment
Ocean.	Oceania	pl.	plate; plural	*reg*	*regit* [ruled]
Oct	October	Plan.	Planning	Reg.	Regional
8vo	octavo	Planet.	Planetarium	Relig.	Religion, Religious
OFM	Order of Friars Minor	Plast.	Plastic	remod.	remodelled
OH	Ohio (USA)	pls	plates	Ren.	Renaissance
OK	Oklahoma (USA)	p.m.	post meridiem [after noon]	Rep.	Report(s)
Olymp.	Olympic	Polit.	Political	repr.	reprint(ed); reproduced, reproduction
OM	Order of Merit	Poly.	Polytechnic		
Ont.	Ontario (Canada)	Polynes.	Polynesian	Represent.	Representation, Representative
op.	opus	Pop.	Popular	Res.	Research
opp.	opposite; opera [pl. of opus]	Port.	Portuguese	rest.	restored, restoration
OR	Oregon (USA)	Port.	Portfolio	Retro.	Retrospective
Org.	Organization	Posth.	Posthumous(ly)	rev.	revision, revised (by/for)
Orient.	Oriental	Pott.	Pottery	Rev.	Reverend; Review
Orthdx	Orthodox	POW	prisoner of war	RHA	Royal Hibernian Academician
OSB	Order of St Benedict	PRA	President of the Royal Academy	RI	Rhode Island (USA)
Ott.	Ottoman			RIBA	Royal Institute of British Architects
Oxon	Oxfordshire (GB)	Pract.	Practical		
oz.	ounce(s)	Prefect.	Prefecture, Prefectural	RJ	Rio de Janeiro State
p	pence	Preserv.	Preservation	Rlwy	Railway
p., pp.	page(s)	prev.	previous(ly)	RSA	Royal Scottish Academy
PA	Pennsylvania (USA)	priv.	private	RSFSR	Russian Soviet Federated Socialist Republic
p.a.	per annum	PRO	Public Record Office		
Pak.	Pakistani	Prob.	Problem(s)	Rt Hon.	Right Honourable
Palaeontol.	Palaeontology, Palaeontological	Proc.	Proceedings	Rur.	Rural
		Prod.	Production	Rus.	Russian
Palest.	Palestinian	Prog.	Progress	S	San, Santa, Santo, Sant', São [Saint]
Pap.	Paper(s)	Proj.	Project(s)		
para.	paragraph	Promot.	Promotion	S.	South(ern)
Parag.	Paraguayan	Prop.	Property, Properties	s.	solidus, solidi [shilling(s)]
Parl.	Parliament	Prov.	Province(s), Provincial	Sask.	Saskatchewan (Canada)
Paroch.	Parochial	Proven.	Provenance	Sat.	Saturday
Patriarch.	Patriarchate	Prt, Prts	Print(s)	SC	South Carolina (USA)
Patriot.	Patriotic	Prtg	Printing	Scand.	Scandinavian
Patrm.	Patrimony	pseud.	pseudonym	Sch.	School
Pav.	Pavilion	Psych.	Psychiatry, Psychiatric	Sci.	Science(s), Scientific
PEI	Prince Edward Island (Canada)	Psychol.	Psychology, Psychological	Scot.	Scottish
Pembs	Pembrokeshire (GB; old)	pt	part	Sculp.	Sculpture

SD	South Dakota (USA)	suppl., suppls	supplement(s), supplementary	Urb.	Urban
SE	Southeast(ern)	Surv.	Survey	Urug.	Uruguayan
Sect.	Section	SW	Southwest(ern)	US	United States
Sel.	Selected	Swed.	Swedish	USA	United States of America
Semin.	Seminar(s), Seminary	Swi.	Swiss	USSR	Union of Soviet Socialist Republics
Semiot.	Semiotic	Symp.	Symposium		
Semit.	Semitic	Syr.	Syrian	UT	Utah
Sept	September	Tap.	Tapestry	v	verso
Ser.	Series	Tas.	Tasmanian	VA	Virginia (USA)
Serb.	Serbian	Tech.	Technical, Technique	V&A	Victoria and Albert Museum
Serv.	Service(s)	Technol.	Technology	Var.	Various
Sess.	Session, Sessional	Territ.	Territory	Venez.	Venezuelan
Settmt(s)	Settlement(s)	Theat.	Theatre	Vern.	Vernacular
S. Glam.	South Glamorgan (GB)	Theol.	Theology, Theological	Vict.	Victorian
Siber.	Siberian	Theor.	Theory, Theoretical	Vid.	Video
Sig.	Signature	Thurs.	Thursday	Viet.	Vietnamese
Sil.	Silesian	Tib.	Tibetan	viz.	videlicet [namely]
Sin.	Singhala	TN	Tennessee (USA)	vol., vols	volume(s)
sing.	singular	Top.	Topography	vs.	versus
SJ	Societas Jesu [Society of Jesus]	Trad.	Tradition(s), Traditional	VT	Vermont (USA)
Skt	Sanskrit	trans.	translation, translated by; transactions	Vulg.	Vulgarisation
Slav.	Slavic, Slavonic			W.	West(ern)
Slov.	Slovene, Slovenian	Transafr.	Transafrican	w.	width
Soc.	Society	Transatlant.	Transatlantic	WA	Washington (USA)
Social.	Socialism, Socialist	Transcarpath.	Transcarpathian	Warwicks	Warwickshire (GB)
Sociol.	Sociology	transcr.	transcribed by/for	Wed.	Wednesday
Sov.	Soviet	Triq.	Triquarterly	W. Glam.	West Glamorgan (GB)
SP	São Paulo State	Tropic.	Tropical	WI	Wisconsin (USA)
Sp.	Spanish	Tues.	Tuesday	Wilts	Wiltshire (GB)
sq.	square	Turk.	Turkish	Wkly	Weekly
sr	senior	Turkmen.	Turkmenistani	W. Midlands	West Midlands (GB)
Sri L.	Sri Lankan	TV	Television		
SS	Saints, Santi, Santissima, Santissimo, Santissimi; Steam ship	TX	Texas (USA)	Worcs	Worcestershire (GB; old)
		U.	University	Wtrcol.	Watercolour
SSR	Soviet Socialist Republic	UK	United Kingdom of Great Britain and Northern Ireland	WV	West Virginia (USA)
St	Saint, Sankt, Sint, Szent			WY	Wyoming (USA)
Staffs	Staffordshire (GB)	Ukrain.	Ukrainian	Yb., Y.-b.	Yearbook, Year-book
Ste	Sainte	Un.	Union	Yem.	Yemeni
Stud.	Study, Studies	Underwtr	Underwater	Yorks	Yorkshire (GB; old)
Subalp.	Subalpine	UNESCO	United Nations Educational, Scientific and Cultural Organization	Yug.	Yugoslavian
Sum.	Sumerian			Zamb.	Zambian
Sun.	Sunday	Univl	Universal	Zimb.	Zimbabwean
Sup.	Superior	unpubd	unpublished		

A Note on the Use of the Dictionary

This note is intended as a short guide to the basic editorial conventions adopted in this dictionary. For a fuller explanation, please refer to the Introduction, vol. 1, pp. xiii–xx.

Abbreviations in general use in the dictionary are listed on pp. vi–xi; those used in bibliographies and for locations of works of art or exhibition venues are listed in the Appendices in vol. 33.

Alphabetization of headings, which are distinguished in bold typeface, is letter by letter up to the first comma (ignoring spaces, hyphens, accents and any parenthesized or bracketed matter); the same principle applies thereafter. Abbreviations of 'Saint' and its foreign equivalents are alphabetized as if spelt out, and headings with the prefix 'Mc' appear under 'Mac'.

Authors' signatures appear at the end of the article or sequence of articles that the authors have contributed; in multipartite articles, any section that is unsigned is by the author of the next signed section. Where the article was compiled by the editors or in the few cases where an author has wished to remain anonymous, this is indicated by a square box (□) instead of a signature.

Bibliographies are arranged chronologically (within section, where divided) by order of year of first publication and, within years, alphabetically by authors' names. Abbreviations have been used for some standard reference books; these are cited in full in Appendix C in vol. 33, as are abbreviations of periodical titles (Appendix B). Abbreviated references to alphabetically arranged dictionaries and encyclopedias appear at the beginning of the bibliography (or section).

Biographical dates when cited in parentheses in running text at the first mention of a personal name indicate that the individual does not have an entry in the dictionary. The presence of parenthesized regnal dates for rulers and popes, however, does not necessarily indicate the lack of a biography of that person. Where no dates are provided for an artist or patron, the reader may assume that there is a biography of that individual in the dictionary (or, more rarely, that the person is so obscure that dates are not readily available).

Cross-references are distinguished by the use of small capital letters, with a large capital to indicate the initial letter of the entry to which the reader is directed; for example, 'He commissioned Leonardo da Vinci . . .' means that the entry is alphabetized under 'L'.

F
[continued]

Ferrara. Italian city in Emilia-Romagna, situated on the delta of the River Po. It was the centre of a flourishing court under the Este family from the 13th century to the 16th (*see* ESTE (i)). A noted example of early Renaissance urban planning, it was also the centre of a distinctive school of painting and of tapestry-weaving. The city, which now has *c.* 155,000 inhabitants, is divided into two distinct sections, medieval to the south and Renaissance to the north.

1. History and urban development. 2. Art life and organization. 3. Centre of tapestry production. 4. Buildings.

1. HISTORY AND URBAN DEVELOPMENT.

(i) Introduction. Ferrara lies on the left bank of a subsidiary channel running south from the Po, known as the Po di Ferrara, at the point where this divides into the Po di Volano and the Po di Primaro. The city originated on the right bank within this divide, centred on the cathedral of S Giorgio, built in the 7th century AD (altered). In 986 Ferrara was placed under the rule of Tedaldo, Count of Modena and Canossa (988–1012), son of Emperor Otto I, who built Castel Tedaldo (destr. 1608) on the left bank. In 1106 the relics of the city's patron saints, George and Maurelius, Bishop of Voghenza and Ferrara (*d* 644), were brought to the cathedral. After the death of Matilda of Canossa in 1115 Ferrara became a free comune, and the centre of the city was transferred to the left bank of the river, the cathedral being refounded in 1132–5 during the domination of the Adelardi family on the Piazza Maggiore (now the Piazza Trento e Trieste), the main market-place and site of the open-air law court (*see* §4(i) below).

Ferrara was a centre of strife between the Guelph (papal) and Ghibelline (imperial) factions, but from 1242, when Azzo II (*reg* 1215–22; 1240–64) established control of the city with Venetian help, it was ruled by the Este family, who remained in power until 1598. A Venetian representative, Visdomino, was retained there. Ferrara was papal territory, but the Este family were made papal vicars, subject to the payment of the *census vicariatus*. Alberto (*reg* 1361–93) obtained other privileges after a pilgrimage to Rome in 1391, commemorated by a statue and inscription on the cathedral façade. He also founded the university.

In the long period of peace under Alberto's heir, his young son Niccolo III (*reg* 1393–1441), the city achieved international importance, the ecumenical Council of Ferrara in 1438 providing the most significant testimony to Niccolo's reputation as a mediator. The Este family retained and increased their power and prestige through a mixture of political astuteness and advantageous marriages, but the disastrous war with Venice waged from 1482 to 1484 by Ercole I (*reg* 1471–1505) and Ercole's subsequent intrigues to regain lost territory were partly responsible for encouraging the invasion of Italy by the French king Charles VIII. Francophile policies were continued by Alfonso I (*reg* 1505–34), and the Calvinist sympathies of Renée of France (1510–75), wife of Ercole II (*reg* 1534–59), created further discord between the increasingly powerful papacy and the Este family. After the death without a legitimate heir of Alfonso II (*reg* 1559–97), the troops of Pope Clement VIII occupied Ferrara. Cesare (*reg* 1597–1628) moved the court to Modena, and under the papal legates Ferrara entered a period of obscurity, not helped by the silting of the Po delta. Between 1796 and 1815 the city was occupied by Napoleonic troops.

(ii) Medieval. Medieval Ferrara developed along the left bank of the river, with the Via Ripagrande (Via Carlo Mayr) running for nearly a mile downstream from the castle. This street was later to be used for the races held on the feast of St George (23 April) and as the beginning of the processional route used by visitors arriving by water (e.g. Lucrezia Borgia in 1502). The parallel Via delle Volte retains its medieval aspect in its narrow arched and cobbled length, as does the Via S Romano, which is flanked by narrow arcades. The latter connects the Via Ripagrande with the Piazza Maggiore.

Apart from the cathedral, Ferrara is largely the creation of the Este family from the mid-13th century. The subsoil of the city is essentially reclaimed marshland, and it is significant that one device used by Borso (*reg* 1450–71) was the *paraduro*, a wattle fence used in land reclamation. Many buildings required pile foundations. Brick, usually from Lugo or Mellara, was the normal building material, although stone was brought from Verona (from where most of the masons came) or from Istria, across the Adriatic. Flooring was often of terracotta, sometimes glazed or painted, or *batudo*, an amalgam of crushed marble. External decoration usually consisted of moulded terracotta friezes and cornices, some of which were made in Modena. Exteriors were normally painted, sometimes with figures, more often with geometric and heraldic designs.

The first important Este building was the Palazzo del Corte (now the Palazzo Comunale), begun by Azzo II in 1242 at the west end of the Piazza Maggiore facing the cathedral. In 1283 the Torre de Rigobello (destr. 1593), a clock-tower facing down the square, was built by Obizzo I (*reg* 1264–93). In 1385 Niccolo II (*reg* 1361–88) founded the large, imposing moated fortress (Castello Vecchio or Estense; see fig. 1) that still dominates the city, on what was then its northern edge. The castle was linked to the Corte by a corridor, the Via Coperta, in 1471 (raised 1499), and the two formed the focus of court life until the Este family left Ferrara, although Alberto rebuilt Castel Tedaldo and Niccolò III built the Castello Nuovo (1425–35, destr. 1562) on the riverbank downstream. It was in the Corte that Pope Eugenius IV was entertained during the Council of Ferrara.

Alberto built the Palazzo Schifanoia (*see* §4(ii) below) south-east of the city centre and the villa of Belfiore to the north. Belfiore was continued by Niccolò III, who added near by the church and monastery of S Maria degli Angeli. Both buildings were linked to the city by a poplar-lined avenue (Via dei Piopponi, Via degli Angeli, Corso Vittorio Emanuele, Corso Ercole d'Este). Niccolò III also built

the most famous Este *delizia* (palace), the great villa of Belriguardo (destr.) *c.* 15 km south-east of Ferrara.

(iii) Renaissance and later. Under Leonello (*reg* 1441–50) the first elements of architectural decoration in the new Renaissance style were introduced in the *volta del Cavallo*, an arch to support Niccolò Baroncelli's bronze equestrian statue of *Niccolò III*, begun in 1443 (destr. 1796). This pedestal has been attributed to Leon Battista Alberti, who judged the competition for the statue, but there is no documentary foundation for this claim, nor for the claim that he designed the cathedral bell-tower (1451–1596), which was continued by Borso d'Este. Borso extended the city by enclosing an area to the east, the Addizione Borsiana, but his most important building was the Certosa (1452–61) to the north-east, parts of which have been incorporated into the city cemetery. A richly decorated palace was also built there for his own use.

In the late 15th century under Ercole I, Ferrara was transformed and enlarged. In preparation for his marriage in 1473 a series of balconies, one adorned with medallions representing the *Twelve Caesars*, was added to the Torre de Rigobello to provide better viewpoints in the main square. A raised platform supported by a columnar arcade was built along the side of the cathedral. For the first 20 years of his rule Ercole concentrated on the Corte, which by the time of his death had been transformed into a

1. Ferrara, Castello Estense, begun 1385; the towers were modified in 1570

worthy ducal residence by his architects Pietro de Benvenuti (*fl* 1458–84) and Biagio Rossetti. The Corte included the Cortile Grande, with an external staircase built in 1479 by Benvenuti; the court chapel, which possessed one of the finest choirs in Europe; and a garden court overlooked by guest rooms and the duke's private apartments and studio. The private rooms were connected by the Camere Dorate, a series of gilded state rooms (built 1479–81), to the Sala Grande (50×16 m), where the most important court festivals and theatrical entertainments were held. Beneath the Sala Grande was an arcade of 25 columns with shops, but they were both destroyed by fire in 1532, only a fragment surviving. The Sala dalle Commedie was the first purpose-built Renaissance theatre (1503), but Ercole died before it was finished. In the Castello Vecchio apartments were prepared for the duchess (1477), who had a garden to the north across the moat, with a pavilion surmounted by a statue of *Hercules*. This survived until 1655, when it was cleared away to allow the Via degli Angeli to extend to the castle moat, but it was described in detail by Ercole's eulogist Giovanni Sabadino degli Arienti (*d* 1510). In the town Rossetti also began the Palazzo di Lodovico il Moro (now the Museo Nazionale Archeologico), which he left unfinished in 1503, with a fine arcaded cortile.

In 1492 Ercole and Rossetti began the extension north of the city, later known as the Addizione Erculea. A defensive moat was dug to enclose the Certosa, S Maria degli Angeli, Belfiore and the Barco, the ducal hunting park, all of which had been damaged in the war with Venice. A circuit of walls was begun (completed by Alfonso I and his successors). Rossetti built the first part of the walls and is generally credited with the overall plan of the Addizione, but it was done in consultation with Ercole, who took a close personal interest in all his projects. Some of the roads in the Addizione already existed, but the layout of the straight, wide streets and the Piazza Nuova (now the Piazza Ariostea), surrounded by arcaded palaces, was an important advance in town planning. Some of the palaces located on the principal crossroads survive, notably the Palazzo dei Diamanti (begun 1493 by Rossetti, remodelled 1565; damaged 1943; *see* ROSSETTI, BIAGIO, fig. 1), which is atypically faced in marble (diamond-shaped blocks) rather than brick. Particularly pious towards the end of his life, Ercole founded fourteen new monasteries or churches and contributed to the cost of nine others, but not all survive. S Francesco (1227) was partly rebuilt by Rossetti in 1494 and its bell-tower added in 1605.

Ferrara's population, estimated at *c.* 38,000 in 1500, did not expand to fill the new extension. After disastrous earthquakes in 1570 resources were concentrated on repairing damage, including the raising of Castello Vecchio by Alessandro Balbi. Giovanni Battista Aleotti refaced the Palazzo Bentivoglio with stone rustication, scrolls and trophies, and between 1579 and 1594 he and Balbi added a fourth storey to the cathedral bell-tower. Under the rule of the papal legates from 1598 the only substantial building work was the pentagonal fortress built in 1608, including the site of the Castel Tedaldo (moat filled in 1858, fortress destr. 1859) by Aleotti, who also added a floor to the Palazzo del Ragione in 1603 and in 1610 designed a new façade for the Palazzo del Paradiso, an Este palace of 1391

that was the seat of the university from 1586 until 1962. In the 17th century, however, Ferrara became important in the development of theatre design and scenery: the seating arrangement of the Teatro della Sala Grande, built in 1602, anticipated that of a modern opera house, the seats ranked according to the structure of society. In addition, Aleotti for the first time incorporated into the stage a system of six simultaneously moving pairs of wings. Rebuilt in 1660, the theatre burnt down in 1679. Growth of the city was contained until the 20th century, when it expanded beyond its walls; it suffered heavy bomb damage in World War II.

BIBLIOGRAPHY
G. Sabadino degli Arienti: *De triumphis religionis* [*c.* 1500]; ed. W. Gundersheimer as *Art and Life at the Court of Ercole I d'Este* (Geneva, 1972)
A. Frizzi: *Memorie riguardanti per la storia di Ferrara*, 4 vols (Ferrara, 1791–1809/*R* 1848)
F. Bonasera: *Forma veteris urbis Ferrariae* (Florence, 1965)
L. Chiappini: *Gli Estensi* (Varese, 1967)
B. Zevi: *Biagio Rossetti* (Turin, 1970)
W. Gundersheimer: *Ferrara: The Style of a Renaissance Despotism* (Princeton, 1972)
C. Rosenberg: 'The Erculean Addition to Ferrara: Contemporary Reactions and Pragmatic Considerations', *Acta: Conference on the Early Renaissance: Binghamton, NY, 1978*, pp. 51–3
F. Bocchi: 'La "Terranova" da campagna a città', *La corte e lo spazio: Ferrara Estense*, i (Rome, 1982), pp. 167–92
T. J. Tuohy: *Studies in Domestic Expenditure at the Court of Ferrara, 1451–1505: Artistic Patronage and Princely Magnificence* (diss., U. London, 1982), pp. 257–63 [palace reconstruction]
P. Ravenna: *Le Mura di Ferrara* (Modena, 1985)
T. J. Tuohy: *Herculean Ferrara, Ercole d'Este (1471–1505) and the Invention of a Ducal Court* (Cambridge, 1995)

2. ART LIFE AND ORGANIZATION. Most Ferrarese art production was centred on the Este court. Exceptions included Nicholaus and other sculptors working on the cathedral (*see* §4(i) below), and Carlo Bononi and Guercino, whose careers would have been very different if the Este court had not left Ferrara in 1598. The large numbers of religious paintings produced to decorate the churches, many of which had been built by the Este family, were, however, often commissioned by patrons not directly involved with the court, and as religious art has survived better than court art an imbalance has been created. The great period of Ferrarese art production coincided with the Este ascendancy in the 15th and 16th centuries.

Obizzo I (*reg* 1264–93) suppressed the guilds in 1287, and no important painter emerged in the 14th century. Antonio Alberti depicted scenes from the Council of Ferrara in the Palazzo del Paradiso after 1438, and other painters working for the Este family in the mid-15th century included Rogier van der Weyden (*see* WEYDEN, VAN DER, (1)), Piero della Francesca, Jacopo Bellini (*see* BELLINI, (1)) and PISANELLO, whose portraits and medals provide the most evocative images of the court of Leonello d'Este. The first important painter of Ferrara was COSIMO TURA, who can be considered as the founder of the school of Ferrara. His most important followers were FRANCESCO DEL COSSA and ERCOLE DE' ROBERTI, although they both produced some of their most important work in Bologna, as did Lorenzo Costa (i). Lodovico Mazzolino specialized in highly detailed, small-scale paintings, but the influence of manuscript illumination was characteristic of the early Ferrarese school, and even large paintings were very detailed. Influenced by Ercole I's penitential mood, Ferrarese art at the end of the 15th century suffered a fallow period, represented by the bleak images of Michele di Luca dei Coltellini, Gian Francesco de' Maineri and Domenico Panetti (1460–1512).

In the early 16th century Ferrara was renowned for artillery personally produced by Alfonso I. The duchy was under constant threat, and the Duke was unable to indulge in serious artistic patronage until after the death of Pope Julius II in 1513. Then he commissioned mythological scenes for his rooms in the Via Coperta from Giovanni Bellini (*Feast of the Gods*; 1514; Washington, DC, N.G.A.) and Titian (*Bacchus and Ariadne*; 1523; London, N.G.; *see* TITIAN, fig. 4) in Venice, and the main influences on 16th-century Ferrarese painting became the Venetians, notably Giorgione, and Raphael. The most significant painters of the time include Battista and Dosso Dossi, GAROFALO, Ortolano, GIROLAMO DA CARPI, Giuseppe Mazzuoli, Camillo Filippi and his son Sebastiano II, and SCARSELLINO, whose works survive in many churches, including S Paolo, S Domenico and S Francesco. The Ferrarese school came to a triumphant conclusion with the elegant large-scale works of Carlo Bononi (e.g. S Maria in Vado).

A court environment required particular services of painters. The Salone dei Mesi painted by Cossa and others in the Palazzo Schifanoia (*see* §4(ii) below) depicting activities at the court of Borso d'Este is the only surviving example of a common type of decoration. Many rooms at Belfiore and Belriguardo were painted with courtly scenes (destr.). The production of dynastic and courtly images of record was an important task of court painters. The complex astrological programme of the Salone dei Mesi may have been unusual, but Ferrara was an important centre for the production of tarot cards. Ephemeral work was also required of painters. Theatrical performances were a regular feature of Ferrarese court life after 1487, and Dosso Dossi painted scenery for the plays of Ludovico Ariosto, de' Roberti designed triumphal arches, Tura painted tournament costumes, Carpi painted carriages, and many painters were involved in the decoration of *bucintori*, the state barges that navigated the Po, as well as marriage chests, bridal beds and cradles. Carnival masks from Ferrara were much in demand in Milan and Rome. Ferrara's reputation as a centre for theatrical performance reached new heights after the 1560s, when Cornelio Bentivoglio I staged ever more spectacular jousts and musical dramas, which were continued by his son Enzo (*see* BENTIVOGLIO, (3) and (4)).

Sculptors were also required to produce ephemera for state visits or weddings, but the normal sculptural material was terracotta, as in the rest of Emilia, and life-size, free-standing groups, particularly of the *Lamentation*, were common; Ludovico de Castellani (*fl* 1456–1505) and Alfonso Lombardi both made such groups. Terracotta or cast stucco were used in interior decoration: the Sala degli Stucchi in the Palazzo Schifanoia is the only surviving example, but Tura's chapel at Belriguardo and a room at the Palazzo della Certosa (both destr.) had similar rich decoration. Although the equestrian statue of *Niccolò III* (1443–51) by the Florentine NICCOLÒ BARONCELLI and his assistant DOMENICO DI PARIS, the first bronze equestrian statue of the Renaissance, was destroyed in 1796

together with another bronze statue of *Borso d'Este* (1454), an over life-size bronze *Crucifixion* group by these sculptors survives in the cathedral. Alfonso Lombardi worked in terracotta and marble, mostly in Bologna. Antonio Lombardo of Venice carved the finest marble reliefs in Ferrara, which were perhaps intended for Alfonso I's 'camerino di alabastro' (1506–16; Florence, Bargello; St Petersburg, Hermitage).

Wood inlay (intarsia) and carving (intaglio) was provided by Arduino da Baisio (*fl* 1406–53) and the brothers Christoforo Canozzi da Lendinara (*d* 1491) and Lorenzo Canozzi da Lendinara (*d* 1477), who decorated *studioli* for Leonello and Borso d'Este. Stefano de Donabona (*fl* 1472–1503) made inlaid doors for Ercole I and carved the architectural elements of the Camere Dorate. Tapestry was an important element of palace decoration, and most Ferrarese painters furnished designs (*patroni*; *see* §3 below). Under Borso, Ferrara was an important centre for manuscript illumination, and his Bible (1455–61; Modena, Bib. Estense, MS. V.G. 12–13, lat. 422–3) was one of the most expensive books produced in Italy (*see* BIBLE OF BORSO D'ESTE). Illuminators included Taddeo Crivelli, Franco dei Russi and Guglielmo Giraldi.

Ferrarese art is widely dispersed. In 1598 Cardinal Pietro Aldobrandini removed many paintings to Rome, and Cesare d'Este removed most of the collections to Modena. In 1746 Augustus III of Poland acquired many of the best Este pictures (Dresden, Gemäldegal. Alte Meister). During the Napoleonic period most religious institutions were suppressed and their paintings gathered together to form the nucleus of the Pinacoteca Nazionale in the Palazzo dei Diamanti. The collection of Ferrarese paintings assembled by Marchese Giovanni Battista Costabili was dispersed during the 19th century. An important exhibition of Ferrarese painting was held in the city in 1933. Giovanni Boldini, who was active in Paris in the late 19th century, was born in Ferrara; there is a Museo Boldini in the Palazzo Massari.

BIBLIOGRAPHY

G. Baruffaldi: *Vite de' pittori e scultori ferraresi* [*c*. 1697–1722]; ed. G. Boschini, 2 vols (Ferrara, 1844–6)

G. Campori: 'I miniatori degli Estensi', *Atti & Mem. RR. Deput. Stor. Patria Prov. Moden. & Parm.*, vi (1872), pp. 142–274

——: 'L'arazzeria Estense', *Atti & Mem. RR. Deput. Stor. Patria Prov. Moden. & Parm.*, viii (1876), pp. 415–80

A. Venturi: 'I primordi del rinascimento artistico a Ferrara', *Riv. Stor. It.*, i (1884), pp. 591–631

G. Campori: *Gli artisti italiani e stranieri negli stati Estensi* (Modena, 1885)

A. Venturi: 'L'arte ferrarese nel periodo di Borso d'Este', *Riv. Stor. It.*, ii (1885), pp. 689–749

——: 'L'arte ferrarese nel periodo di Ercole d'Este', *Atti & Mem. Regia Deput. Stor. Patria Prov. Romagna*, n. s. 2, vi (1888), pp. 350–422; vii (1889), pp. 368–412

G. Gruyer: *L'Art ferrarais à l'époque des princes d'Este*, 2 vols (Paris, 1897)

E. G. Gardner: *The Painters of the School of Ferrara* (London, 1911)

La pittura ferrarese del rinascimento (exh. cat., Ferrara, Pin. N., 1933)

R. Longhi: *Officina ferrarese* (Rome, 1934)

A. Venturi, ed.: *La bibbia di Borso d'Este* (Milan, 1937)

S. Zamboni: *Pittori di Ercole I d'Este* (Milan, 1975)

THOMAS TUOHY

3. CENTRE OF TAPESTRY PRODUCTION. The collection of northern European tapestries owned by the Este family was already large by 1436, when the family began to follow the lead of the Gonzaga in Mantua in hiring French and Flemish master weavers to care for them, to

weave new tapestries and to act as liaisons with northern workshops for larger commissions. Tapestry patronage varied in tenor with political events and with each succeeding ruler. The first Flemish weavers were hired under Niccolò III d'Este, Marquess of Ferrara, who had bought many prestigious northern sets. Jacomo de Flandria de Angelo (*fl* 1436) is the first mentioned, hired apparently to repair tapestries. He was joined by another master, Pietro di Andrea di Fiandra (*fl* 1441–71), in 1441. Rinaldo Boteram (pseud. di Gualtieri; *fl* 1438–81) from Brussels, one of the most famous northern weavers in Italy during the 15th century, may have already worked for Niccolò before he set up shop in Siena in 1438.

It was apparently Niccolò's son, Leonello d'Este, however, who first encouraged the weaving of new tapestries in the city on a large scale. In 1444, probably because of the rich tapestry displays planned for his second marriage to Maria of Aragon, Leonello not only bought and borrowed many sets but also attracted many master weavers including Boteram, who, although he moved to Mantua in 1448, continued to serve as a go-between for court orders of larger tapestries from the north for over 30 years. Another important master, Livinus Gilii de Burgis (*fl* 1444–after 1473), also arrived in 1444 and worked in Ferrara, except for a short period in Florence (1455–7), until he went to Milan in 1463; he returned briefly to Ferrara in 1473. None of the tapestries woven in Ferrara for Leonello or the many more woven for his successor, Borso d'Este, has survived, but documents indicate that most were small pieces such as altar frontals, bench-backs and bed covers and hangings, often of precious materials and from cartoons by the city's finest painters, particularly Cosimo Tura. The Paris master Renaud de Maincourt (pseud. Rainaldo de Man Curta; *fl* 1451–7) was in Ferrara briefly in 1457, the year another French weaver, Rubinetto di Francia (*fl* 1457–84), began working there. Giovanni Lattres of Arras (*fl* 1461–7; *d* by 1471) is also documented mainly in Ferrara, except for a brief stay in Venice between 1462 and 1464. Giovanni Mille (*fl* 1464–5) and Rinaldo Grue (*fl* 1464–71), two weavers from Tournai (now in Belgium), arrived in Ferrara in 1464; in 1470 Rigo d'Alemagna (*fl* 1470–74) arrived and was most active under Borso's successor, Ercole I d'Este. The only 15th-century Ferrarese tapestries to survive are two versions of a *Pietà* (*c.* 1475–6; Lugano, Col. Thyssen–Bornemisza, and Cleveland, OH, Mus. A.) woven by Rubinetto di Francia from a cartoon by Tura, which illustrate the high quality of both design and weaving that must have characterized Ferrarese production in this period.

During the later rule of Ercole I and under the great painting patron Alfonso I d'Este, there was a hiatus in Ferrarese tapestry production, until it was revived under Ercole II d'Este. The brothers Giovanni Karcher (*fl* 1517–62) and NICOLAS KARCHER had possibly been active in Ferrara by 1517, mainly repairing tapestries. In 1536 Ercole II sent Nicolas to Brussels to recruit eight weavers, including JAN ROST, to establish a proper court factory. Another northern weaver, Gerardo Slot (*fl* 1537–42), is documented working independently at the court at this time. Ercole began commissioning ambitious sets of large tapestries from these masters as an integral part of his extensive redecorating programme for his palace and other

residences. Among those who painted the cartoons were the Dossi brothers, Giulio Romano, Girolamo da Carpi, Leonardo da Brescia (*fl* 1544; *d* 1598) and Garofalo. Only a few of these tapestries survive, including the remains of the five *Metamorphoses* (*c.* 1544–5; two tapestries, Paris, Louvre; fragments, priv. cols) after cartoons by Battista Dossi, and seven *Pergoline* (*c.* 1556–9; one tapestry and two fragments, Paris, Mus. A. Déc.) from cartoons by Leonardo da Brescia. A series of eight *Stories of SS George and Maurelius* woven by Karcher's workshop for Ferrara Cathedral from cartoons (1550–53) by Garofalo, Camillo Filippi and Luca d'Olanda (*fl* 1536–54) is *in situ*.

During the reign of Alfonso II d'Este, tapestry production again declined. Giovanni Karcher's son Luigi Karcher (*d* 1580), who was a painter as well as a weaver, inherited the Karcher workshop in 1562. His major surviving work is a tapestry of the *Marriage of the Virgin* from a cartoon by Camillo Filippi and his son Sebastiano Filippi II for the *Life of the Virgin* cycle in Como Cathedral (1569–70; *in situ*). After Luigi's death tapestry weaving effectively ended in Ferrara.

BIBLIOGRAPHY

G. Campori: *L'arazzeria Estense* (Modena, 1876/*R* Sala Bolognese, 1980)

A. Venturi: 'Le arti minori a Ferrara nella fine del sec. XV: L'arazzeria', *L'Arte*, xii (1909), pp. 207–10

M. Viale Ferrero: *Arazzi italiani del cinquecento* (Milan, 1963), pp. 18–22, 45, 50–51

C. Adelson: 'The Decoration of Palazzo Vecchio in Tapestry: The *Joseph Cycle* and Other Precedents for Vasari's Decorative Campaigns', *Atti del convegno Vasariano: Arezzo, 1981*, pp. 170–73

N. Forti Grazzini: *L'arazzo ferrarese* (Milan, 1982); review by C. Adelson in *Burl. Mag.*, cxxvii (1985), pp. 307–8

Arazzi del cinquecento a Como (exh. cat., ed. N. Forti Grazzini; Como, Cathedral, 1986), pp. 57–60

CANDACE J. ADELSON

4. BUILDINGS.

(i) Cathedral. Dedicated to S Giorgio, the cathedral was built originally in the 7th century on the right bank of the river (the building survives, altered, *see* ITALY, fig. 7). After the acquisition of the relics of SS George and Maurelius in 1106, and prompted by the allegiance to Rome of Bishop Landolfus, a new site on the left bank was designated in 1132, and the building begun before 1135. The five-aisled basilica, a symbol of the emergent city-state, was dedicated in 1146. However, only the lower sections of the façade and the outer south wall up to the level of the cornice are of this period. The screen façade was completed in the 14th and 15th centuries, and the interior was remodelled in the 17th.

The large, two-storey porch-portal on the west façade is the work of the sculptor NICHOLAUS, whose name appears in a laudatory inscription dated 1135 on the tympanum (see fig. 2). He was probably also responsible for the two-storey Porta dei Mesi (now dismantled) on the south side of the nave facing the old market square. Its appearance can be reconstructed from descriptions and from fragments (two lions and two griffins) preserved *in situ* and in the Museo del Duomo (the tympanum fragment, *Eve Nursing Cain and Abel* and the *Labours of the Months*, the last possibly by a pupil of Benedetto Antelami). The tympanum of the main portal bears an exceptionally large relief of an equestrian *St George Slaying the Dragon*, while on the lintel are carved scenes of the *Infancy of*

2. Ferrara Cathedral, west façade, tympanum and lintel of main portal, 1135

Christ. Represented on the jambs are four prophets holding scrolls and, at the top, on either side of the doorway, the *Annunciation*. The inventive iconographic programme of both portals also includes references to the Crusades (the *St George* and the crusader figures once on the Porta dei Mesi) and to civil and legal concerns (e.g. the lions, atlantids and knotted columns of the double-storey porches, which have been associated with the tradition of the Throne of Solomon). The griffins and other fantastic animals derived from Byzantine and Islamic sources illustrate the wide range of visual models employed for this work. The arcaded bell-tower, begun in the 15th century, shows the style of Alberti.

BIBLIOGRAPHY

A. K. Porter: *Lombard Architecture*, ii (New Haven, 1917), pp. 404–18

D. Robb: 'Niccolò: A North Italian Sculptor of the Twelfth Century', *A. Bull.*, xii (1930), pp. 374–420

T. Krautheimer-Hess: 'The Original Porta dei Mesi and the Art of Niccolò', *A. Bull.*, xxvi (1944), pp. 152–74

G. H. Crichton: *Romanesque Sculpture in Italy* (London, 1954)

S. A. Zavin: *Ferrara Cathedral Façade* (diss., New York, Columbia U., 1972)

C. Gnudi: 'Il Maestro di Mesi dei Ferrara e la lunetta di San Mercuriale di Forlì', *Symposium. The Year 1200: Metropolitan Museum of Art, New York, 1975*, pp. 469–96; repr. in *Paragone*, 317–19 (1976), pp. 3–14

A. M. Romanini, ed.: *Atti del seminario internazionale di Ferrara. Nicholaus e l'arte del suo tempo: Ferrara, 1981*, 3 vols [includes articles by C. Verzar Bornstein and G. Zanichelli]

E. Kain: *The Sculpture of Nicholaus and the Development of a North Italian Romanesque Workshop*, Dissertatione zur Kunstgeschichte, xxiv (Vienna, 1986)

C. Verzar Bornstein: *Portals and Politics in the Early Italian City State: The Sculpture of Nicholaus in Context* (Parma, 1988)

CHRISTINE VERZAR

(ii) Palazzo Schifanoia. The palazzo, located in the south-eastern section of Ferrara just within the Renaissance city walls, owes its present shape to four separate building campaigns undertaken by members of the Este family. According to the Ferrarese chronicler Ugo Caleffini, the palazzo first built by Alberto V in 1385 was a small, single-storey edifice. In 1391 Alberto enlarged the building to twice its original length and by a third of its depth. He also connected it internally to an adjoining building on the eastern side, raised the main floor to accommodate a sunken cellar and added a large loggia to the back of the palazzo at the western end. A general idea of the composition of the rooms is conveyed through an inventory of the palazzo's contents made in 1436. The rooms were named after their decoration: 'deli alifanti, dele donzeli et cimeri, di san zorzo, dale pigne and dale rode' (elephants, maidens and crests, St George, pines and wheels). Borso d'Este began extensive remodelling of the palazzo some time after 1465. The earliest document is dated 28 February 1468, and building work appears to have been finished by the end of 1469. He added a *piano nobile* at the second-storey level (above the former main floor), extended a staircase from the garden to the new *piano nobile*, added an elaborate marble doorframe to the main entrance and repainted the decorative geometric frescoes on the façade of the building. Three of the rooms decorated for Borso are still extant: the Sala degli Stemmi, the Sala degli Stucchi and the Salone dei Mesi. In 1493 Ercole I enlarged the palazzo to the east and transformed its 'medieval' appearance by replacing the merloned roofline with an oversized,

3. Ferrara, Palazzo Schifanoia, Salone dei Mesi, *Aries, Taurus, Gemini*, frescoes on the eastern wall by Francesco del Cossa, before 1470

classically inspired terracotta cornice. Until the late 16th century the Palazzo Schifanoia was used by the Este family both as a suburban retreat and as a lodging house for important visitors. In 1438, during the Council of Ferrara, Demetrius (*d* 1460), brother of Emperor John VII Palaiologos (*reg* 1425–48), was housed there; in 1468 three of the Sforza brothers stayed there, and in 1471 the Venetian ambassador and his family were placed there. In 1482, however, Cardinal Francesco Gonzaga wrote to his *camerario*, Giovan Francesco Strata, saying that he preferred not to be put up at the Schifanoia because it was a long way from the centre and stuffy in winter. In 1538 the palazzo became the residence of the retired Archbishop of Ravenna, Cardinal Benedetto Accolti. Since the 18th century it has served as a tobacco processing plant, a granary, an asylum for deaf-mutes and as a music school. It was given the status of civic museum in 1897.

The internal decoration of the Palazzo Schifanoia has suffered greatly through neglect, abuse and inexpert restorations carried out early in the 19th century. The Sala degli Stemmi contains remains of a series of frescoed medallions with the Este coat of arms and the personal imprese of Borso d'Este. Most of the frescoes have disappeared, but the massive and highly elaborate stucco frieze (*c.* 2.5 m high) containing six sculpted, polychrome, nearly life-size, seated figures of the *Virtues* set within shallow niches has survived. The decoration was begun by Domenico di Paris and Bongiovanni di Geminiano some time after April 1467 and was finished before the end of 1469. The room was apparently used as an audience chamber. It has been suggested that Borso d'Este, when seated on his throne in this room, would have been seen as the embodiment of the missing virtue of Justice.

The Salone dei Mesi, although severely damaged and with little more than half of the frescoes surviving, is the major monument of 15th-century Ferrarese art. The room measures 24×11×7.5 m. The walls are divided by painted grisaille pilasters into eighteen sections. Six sections are frescoed with jousting scenes and cityscapes; the remaining twelve are dedicated to the months of the year; hence the name of the room. They run chronologically anti-clockwise and are divided into three horizontally superimposed zones. The upper section of each panel illustrates the triumphal procession of the pagan god or goddess of the month following the list provided by the ancient Roman astrological poet Marcus Manilius (*Astronomica*, ii, 439–47). The pictorial models for these gods were drawn primarily from the text and illustrations of the late medieval mythographic handbooks. The middle zone shows the zodiacal sign of each month surrounded by three astrological demi-gods, called decans after their function of dividing the 30° of each astrological month into three segments of 10°. The representation of the decan-gods were probably drawn from a contemporary manuscript containing a severely edited version of the Latin translation of Abu Ma'shar's *Introductorium in astronomiam*, made by Hermannus Dalmata [Georgius Zotori Zapari Fenduli]. The lowest zone of the panels contains scenes of daily life at the court of Borso d'Este.

Two contemporary documents mention the decoration of the Salone dei Mesi: the first is a letter to Borso d'Este from Francesco del Cossa dated 25 March 1470, in which he identifies himself as the author of the three panels on the eastern wall (the zodiacal months of Aries, Taurus and Gemini; see fig. 3); this also provides a *terminus ante quem* for the *salone*. The second is a payment for work done before 16 September 1473 to Baldassare d'Este for having 'touched up' 36 portrait busts of the Duke. The authorship of the other frescoes in the *salone* has remained the subject of fierce debate: proposed candidates include Ercole de'

Roberti, Antonio Cicognara, Cosimo Tura, Ettore d'Antonio de' Bonacossi (*d* 1522), the Master of the Occhi Spalancati, the Master of the Occhi Ammiccanti, the Master of Ercole and the mysterious Vicino da Ferrara.

BIBLIOGRAPHY

F. Avventi: *Descrizione dei dipinti di Cosimo Tura detto Cosmè ultimamente scoperti nel Palazzo Schifanoia in Ferrara nell'anno 1840* (Bologna, 1840)

A. Venturi: 'Gli affreschi del Palazzo di Schifanoia in Ferrara secondo recenti pubblicazioni e nuove ricerche', *Atti & Mem. Reale Deput. Stor. Patria Prov. Romagna*, 3rd ser., iii (1885), pp. 381–414

——: 'Ein Brief des Francesco del Cossa', *Kunstfreund*, ix (1885), pp. 129–34

A. Warburg: 'Italienische Kunst und internationale Astrologie im Palazzo Schifanoia zu Ferrara', *L'Italia e l'arte straniera. Atti del X Congresso internazionale di storia dell'arte: Roma, 1912*, pp. 178–93

G. Bargellesi: *Palazzo Schifanoia: Gli affreschi nel Salone dei Mesi in Ferrara* (Bergamo, 1945)

P. d'Ancona: *I mesi di Schifanoia in Ferrara: Con una notizia sul restauro di Cesare Gnudi* (Milan, 1954)

R. Longhi: *Opere complete di Roberto Longhi*, v (Florence, 1956), pp. 37–9, 48–51, 99–102, 137–8, 182–4

C. Rosenberg: 'Francesco del Cossa's Letter Reconsidered', *Mus. Ferrar.: Boll. Annu.*, v/vi (1975–6), pp. 11–15

S. Macioce: 'La *Borsiade* di Tito Vespasiano Strozzi e la "Sala dei Mesi" di Palazzo Schifanoia', *Annu. Ist. Stor. A.*, n. s. 2 (1982–3), pp. 3–13

K. Lippincott: *The Frescoes of the Salone dei Mesi in the Palazzo Schifanoia in Ferrara: Style, Iconography and Cultural Context* (diss., U. Chicago, 1987)

R. Varese, ed: *Atlante di Schifanoia* (Modena, 1989)

K. Lippincott: 'The Iconography of the Salone dei Mesi and the Study of Latin Grammar in Fifteenth-century Ferrara', *La Corte di Ferrara e il suo mecenatismo, 1441–1598*, ed. M. Pade, L. Waage Petersen and D. Quarta (Modena, 1990), pp. 93–109

KRISTEN LIPPINCOTT

Ferrara, Costanzo da. *See* COSTANZO DA FERRARA.

Ferrara, Girolamo da. *See* CARPI, GIROLAMO DA.

Ferrara, Jackie (*b* Detroit, MI, 17 Nov 1929). American sculptor and draughtswoman. She had no formal art education but from an early age enjoyed making useful domestic furniture, such as shelves and cupboards. After moving to live and work in New York in 1952, she became involved in the arts in various ways, taking classes in leatherwork and pottery and, through her job at the Henry Street Settlement, coming into contact with dance and theatre. In the 1960s she attended performances and Happenings at the Judson Gallery and Judson Church and herself performed in two of Claes Oldenburg's Happenings (1962 and 1965), which influenced her. At this time she was making various sorts of sculpture. She began making the work for which she became known in the 1970s. It typically comprises wooden pyramidal/ziggurat-type constructions, made by stacking horizontally layered steps. An early mature work is *Hollow Core Pyramid* (plywood, 0.61×0.61×0.61 m, 1974; Glen Ridge, NJ, Levy priv. col.), for which the inspiration was an unwrapped mummy, which she found intensely 'beautiful, haunting and evocative'; she wanted her own work to have a similar quality. Other early works for which she is known include *Curved Pyramid* (0.99×1.52×0.46 m) and *Stacked Pyramid* (2.60×3.96×1.20 m; both treated fir, 1973; New York, Michael Klein Inc.). *Stacked Pyramid* was her first outdoor work. Her many large-scale public works include *Castle Clinton: Tower and Bridge* (cedar, 0.33×0.61×0.36 m, 1979; New York, Battery Park) and *Meeting Place* (1989; Seattle, WA, Convention and Trade Cent.), a lobby area of concrete and slate floor, with steps and platform, and concrete and steel seating. All these works are characterized by Ferrara's meticulous craftsmanship and their reference to generic types of non-Western building, such as those of Mesoamerica and Egypt, and to geometric form. Works by Ferrara are in the collections of the County Museum of Art, Los Angeles, MOMA, New York, and the Louisiana Museum, Humlebæk.

BIBLIOGRAPHY

Drawings: June/July 1977 (New York, 1977)

Jackie Ferrara (exh. cat., text by M. R. Klein; Amherst, U. MA, U.Gal.; San Francisco, CA, A. Inst. Gals; 1980)

CECILE JOHNSON

Ferrari, de'. Italian family of artists. (1) Gregorio de' Ferrari and his father-in-law, Domenico Piola, were responsible for decorating some of the largest and most prestigious palaces and churches in Genoa in the 1670s and 1680s—a successful partnership that continued with their sons (2) Lorenzo de' Ferrari and Paolo Gerolamo Piola. Another of Gregorio's sons, Giuseppe de' Ferrari (*d* 1768), was a restorer and also a painter, though less renowned than his father and brother. A signed canvas by him of the *Virgin and Child Adored by SS Mauro and Sebastian* (Calizzano, S Mauro) is a pastiche of the sweet putti and *sfumato* style of Gregorio and of the more smoothly polished and academic figures of Lorenzo.

(1) Gregorio de' Ferrari (*b* Porto Maurizio, Imperia, 12 April 1647; *d* Genoa, 26 Jan 1726). Painter. He came to Genoa to study law but devoted his time and energy to painting. He studied with Domenico Fiasella from *c.* 1664–9, and in this period he may have painted scenes in the style of Giovanni Andrea de' Ferrari, Fiasella and Giovanni Battista Casone. He assisted Fiasella on the altarpiece *St Clare Repulsing the Saracens* (1667; Montoggio, parish church). Probably after the death of Fiasella in 1669, Gregorio went to Parma, perhaps accompanied by Giovanni Battista Merano and Andrea Sighizzi (*d* 1684), from whom he may have acquired his skill in *quadratura* design. In Parma he abandoned the monumentality of Fiasella's art, and began to develop a softer, more lyrical manner. He made an oil copy (Genoa, Mus. Accad. Ligustica B.A.) of Correggio's frescoes in the dome of Parma Cathedral. Two paintings, the *Rest on the Flight into Egypt* and the *Virgin with St Jerome and the Magdalene* (both untraced), apparently copies after Correggio, are mentioned by Ratti (see Soprani) as the property of Anton Raphael Mengs. During his years in Parma, Gregorio may have exchanged ideas with Giovanni Battista Gaulli, Merano and Giovanni Andrea Carlone. The paintings executed after his return (*c.* 1671) to Genoa suggest the influence of these artists and are distinguished by the graceful elongations and vertical spiral movement of the figures, which resemble those sculpted by Filippo Parodi and Bernardo Schiaffino. They became more undulating and more tightly modelled by the end of the century. Two canvases inspired by Correggio, *St Francis Comforted by an Angel* and *Rest on the Flight into Egypt* (both Genoa, S Siro), are dated to *c.* 1674–5. Domenico Piola is said to have admired Gregorio's work so much that in 1674 he gave his daughter to Gregorio for a wife. The marriage encouraged a harmonious working relationship, which contributed to the prestige of the Casa Piola workshop, founded in the 1660s (*see* PIOLA). In S Siro, Genoa, Piola painted a vault, the *Glory of St Gaetano* (1674), and in 1676 he received payment for the adjoining vault, the *Glory of St Andrew Avellino*, frescoed by Gregorio in 1676–7.

In 1681 Gregorio painted *St Clare Repulsing the Saracens* (Imperia-Oneglia, parish church), a dramatic work, with flickering light and twisting draperies. Around 1686–7 he also worked in Turin, where he painted two ovals in the Palazzo Reale, *Jupiter Crowning Mars* and *Jupiter and Fame*, and two oval decorations in the Palazzo del Pozzo della Cisterna.

In the 1680s, with Sighizzi as *quadraturista*, Gregorio frescoed several ceilings in the Palazzo Balbi Senarega, Genoa. The brilliant and delicate sketch (Oberlin Coll., OH, Allen Mem. A. Mus.) that he made for the allegorical figures and architectural decoration in a room provides further evidence of his prowess in composing intricate *quadratura* designs. In 1682 he was commissioned to paint two canvases (*St Lawrence* and *St Stephen*) in SS Annunziata. During the French bombardment of the city, Piola and Gregorio worked in the Villa Gropallo, where Gregorio frescoed an *Allegory of Time* with a frieze of the *Four Seasons* in the large drawing-room. Gregorio next frescoed two vaults in the Palazzo Rosso (*Spring* and *Summer*; competed 1688) to accompany two rooms frescoed by Piola. By 1689 Gregorio had also frescoed the Brignole Sale drawing-room with the *Myth of Phaëthon* and painted a small cupola fresco in the chapel (both destr.). In these frescoes Piola and Gregorio worked within a similar ornamental structure, but Piola usually delineated each figure clearly, whereas Gregorio delighted in arranging twisting, elongated figures to soar through space in a swirl of arms, legs and draperies, as in the *Allegory of Summer* (see fig. 1). The two artists worked together again at the Palazzo Granello, Genoa, where Gregorio frescoed two rooms with *Cupid and Psyche* and *Neptune and Amphitrite* in a style close to that of the frescoes in the Palazzo Rosso. Around 1690 he also frescoed the large vault in SS Giacomo e Filippo, Genoa, with an *Assumption of the Virgin* (destr.; known through photographs), and designed the surrounding *quadratura*, which was frescoed by Francesco Costa (1672–1740). This vision of the Virgin, soaring diagonally towards God the Father and viewed from below by serpentine figures on balconies, inspired the commander of the French fleet, Jacques Bailli de Noailles, to ask Gregorio to work in Marseille.

Accompanied by his son Lorenzo, Gregorio worked for two years in Marseille (1692–4), painting decorative frescoes and canvases. A payment in 1694 from the Durazzo family for a design for a silver chandelier indicates that he had by then returned to Genoa. That year he also received a commission to fresco the vault of S Paolo in Campetto (destr.), where he depicted the *Glory of St Paul*, portraying the saint surrounded by angels and virtues. At the turn of the century he possibly painted the *Death of St Scholastica* (*c.* 1700; Genoa, Pal. Reale) and the *Virgin and Souls in Purgatory* (Porto Maurizio, S Leonardo), which was paid for in 1703. From 1700 to 1705 he restored Andrea Ansaldo's dome in SS Annunziata; his style is evident in many of the dome's figures, but the compartmentalized design was Ansaldo's. The *Triumph in the*

1. Gregorio de' Ferrari: *Allegory of Summer* (completed 1688), fresco, Palazzo Rosso, Genoa

Name of the Baptist (Sestri Ponente, S Giovanni Battista) and the altarpiece with characteristic elongated figures, *St Vincent Ferrer and Child with Other Saints* (Taggia, S Domenico), are datable on stylistic grounds to after 1700.

Towards the end of his career, and perhaps stimulated by the work of Gaetano Zumbo and Angelo de Rossi (1671–1715), Gregorio turned to modelling and colouring papier-mâché and plaster figures. His paintings of this time used a smaller figure scale, and were often caprices, set in landscapes with architecture (e.g. the *Pool of Bethesda*, priv. col., see Newcome, 1979, p. 145). His method of constructing his paintings little by little is particularly visible in the panoramic setting and varied figure scale of such a late work as *Moses Striking the Rock* (1690s; Genoa, Pal. Rosso) and the *Virgin of Lepanto* (Genoa, priv. col., see Newcome, 1979, p. 147), on which his son Lorenzo assisted. Gregorio's last fresco decoration was for the cupola, apse and chapels in SS Camillo e Croce, Genoa. Most of these frescoes, including the *Triumph of the True Cross* in the octagonal cupola, were designed and painted by Gregorio with the help of his son Lorenzo between 1715 and 1726. Drawings (New York, Met.; Genoa, Pal. Rosso; Chicago, IL, A. Inst.) show that Gregorio also planned the lunette in the apse, *Heraklios Carrying the Cross to Jerusalem.*

Like Piola, Gregorio supplied designs for a variety of media. He may have supplied drawings (*c.* 1678–80; Florence, Uffizi) for Filippo Parodi's Morosini tomb in the church of S Nicolò da Tolentino in Venice, and his designs

2. Gregorio de' Ferrari: *Juno and Argus*, pen and brown wash, heightened with white, on brown paper, 261×235 mm, *c.* 1680 (Florence, Galleria degli Uffizi)

for frontispieces include a portrait of Francesco Invrea (doge from 1693 to 1695) engraved by Martial Desbois (1630–*c.* 1700). Other drawings are of mythological subjects (see fig. 2). His skill in composing intricate *quadratura* designs was passed on to his students, Francesco Costa (1672–1740), Imperiale Bottini and (2) Lorenzo de' Ferrari.

BIBLIOGRAPHY

R. Soprani: *Vite* (1674); ed. C. G. Ratti (1768–9), ii, pp. 109–18
Y. de Masi: *La vita e l'opera di Gregorio de' Ferrari* (Genoa, 1945)
A. Griseri: 'Per un profilo di Gregorio de' Ferrari', *Paragone*, vi/67 (1955), pp. 22–46
E. Gavazza: 'Contributo a Gregorio de' Ferrari', *A. Ant. & Mod.*, 24 (1963), pp. 326–36
Disegni di Gregorio de' Ferrari (exh. cat., Genoa, Pal. Rosso, 1963)
Dipinti di Gregorio de' Ferrari (exh. cat., Genoa, Pal. Rosso, 1965)
A. Griseri: *Gregorio de' Ferrari* (Milan, 1966)
L. Puccio: 'Sensibilità settecentesca di Gregorio de' Ferrari', *Boll. Ligustico Stor. & Cult. Reg.*, xix/3–4 (1967), pp. 101–18
——: 'Frescanti genovesi a Palazzo Centurione in Fossatello', *Boll. Ligustico Stor. & Cult. Reg.*, xxi/1–4 (1969), pp. 113–30
L. Puccio Canepa: 'Ascendenze di Gregorio de' Ferrari', *Boll. Ligustico Stor. & Cult. Reg.*, xxiv/1–4 (1972), pp. 69–82
Genoese Baroque Drawings (exh. cat. by M. Newcome, Binghamton, SUNY; Worcester, MA, A. Mus.; 1972), nos 92–100
M. Newcome-Schleier: *Maestri genovesi dal cinque al settecento*, Biblioteca di disegni, x (Florence, 1976), nos 27–9
M. Newcome: 'Notes on Gregorio de' Ferrari and the Genoese Baroque', *Pantheon*, xxxvii/2 (1979), pp. 142–9
——: 'Un tempio di Nettuno', *Prospettiva* [Florence], xxiii (1980), pp. 79–82
G. Gruitrooy: 'Three Bozzetti by Gregorio de' Ferrari and some Related Documents', *Burl. Mag.*, cxxviii (1986), pp. 666–70
——: *Gregorio de'Ferrari* (Berlin, 1987)
Disegni genovesi dal XVI al XVIII secolo (exh. cat. by M. Newcome, Florence, Uffizi, 1989), nos 80–82
E. Gavazza, F. Lamera and L. Magnani: *La pittura in Liguria: Il secondo seicento* (Genoa, 1990)

Kunst in der Republik Genoa (exh. cat. by M. Newcome, Frankfurt am Main, Schirn Ksthalle, 1992), nos 87–91

(2) Lorenzo de' Ferrari (*b* Genoa, 14 Nov 1680; *d* Genoa, 28 July 1744). Painter, son of (1) Gregorio de' Ferrari. He was the grandson of Domenico Piola and evolved an independent style based on his grandfather's and father's work. He studied by making copies after the work of Guido Reni and Anthony van Dyck (Soprani), and at the age of 12 he accompanied his father to Marseille, where he worked as his assistant. He probably also assisted Gregorio in the restoration of Andrea Ansaldo's dome in SS Annunziata, Genoa. Lorenzo's early work was influenced by the graceful, elongated figures, spiralling movement and elaborate *quadratura* of his father. He also responded to the more academic and balanced style of Genoese artists who had worked in Rome with Carlo Maratti and Giovanni Battista Gaulli, such as Paolo Girolamo Piola, and Domenico Parodi. In his ceiling decoration he often used formulae established by the Casa Piola, such as pairs of *ignudi* and corner ornament.

Lorenzo's earliest dated work is a frontispiece, *Allegory in Honour of Doge Lorenzo Centurione*, engraved by Maximilian Joseph Limpach (*fl* early 18th century) in 1717. The complexity of this allegorical scene and its fully developed figure style indicate that Lorenzo was highly skilled when he began to work with his father on the decoration of SS Camillo e Croce, Genoa. Here he painted an altarpiece, *SS Nicholas, Matthew and Lucy* (*c.* 1715–20), in a style deeply indebted to Gregorio, with whom he also collaborated on the decoration of the cupola, the *Triumph of the Holy Cross* (1715–26). Lorenzo painted the lunette fresco, *Heraklios Carrying the Cross to Jerusalem*, simplifying the designs of his father, and he painted other scenes in a balanced academic style, with tight brushwork. In 1720–22 he painted an altarpiece, *Virgin and Child with SS Joseph, Ignatius Loyola and Francis Xavier* (Tosse, SS Ignazio e Francesco Saverio). In 1724, on the death of P. G. Piola, he completed frescoes in the nave of S Marta, Genoa. Other frescoes of the 1720s include a vault in the Palazzo Pallavicini–Podesta–Bruzzo (see Gavazza, 1965, figs 12–14), where the ornamental stucco figures, designed by P. G. Piola, were executed by Francesco Biggi (1668–1736). A number of datable works stress the variety of his activities in the 1720s, which included designing the ornamental structure erected in the Gesù, Genoa, to celebrate the canonization of SS Luigi Gonzaga and Stanislao Kotska in 1726.

Lorenzo's frescoes of stories of Aeneas in the Palazzo Sauli, Genoa (see Gavazza, 1965, figs 27, 29–31) may be dated on stylistic grounds to 1730–34, before a two-month visit to Rome in 1734. In Rome he admired the work of Sebastiano Conca, Marco Benefial and Agostino Masucci; on the return journey he stopped briefly in Florence, where he met Ignazio Enrico Hugford. Although this trip to Rome was very brief, it seems to have changed his style, and he developed a more intricate, Rococo manner. No trace remains of the elaborate structures erected in Genoa Cathedral to celebrate the canonization of Catherine Fieschi Adorno in 1736, but the frescoes with Giovanni Battista Natali (1698–1765) in the gallery of the Palazzo Spinola, Genoa (1736), where the centre medallion shows

Venus and Bacchus with Cupid, demonstrate this new festive style.

Four highly illusionistic cupolas decorated by Lorenzo in the Gesù, Genoa, with figures in the style of Domenichino, may be dated on stylistic grounds to the same period as the vault frescoes (see Gavazza, 1965, figs 62–5) in the Palazzo Gio Carlo Doria, Genoa, which were painted to celebrate a Doria marriage that took place in 1738. Lorenzo's last work is the splendid Galleria d'Oro in the Palazzo Spinola, Genoa; it is an ornate, Rococo fantasy, where brilliantly coloured frescoes of the story of Aeneas are placed into an intricate pattern of gilt stuccos and mirrors. Lorenzo's many academic figure drawings account for the success of his complex decorative schemes, and many of his studies of the individual figures have survived, among them the beautiful and precisely modelled black-chalk drawing, *Helmeted Woman Seated with a Lion* (Genoa, Mus. Accad. Ligustica B.A.).

BIBLIOGRAPHY
DBI
R. Soprani: *Vite* (1674); ed. C. G. Ratti (1768–9), ii, pp. 263–71
Y. de Masi: *La vita e l'opera di Lorenzo de' Ferrari* (Genoa, 1945)
E. Gavazza: 'Lorenzo de' Ferrari, tra Arcadia e neoclassicismo', *Commentari*, iv (1963), pp. 268–88
——: *Lorenzo de' Ferrari* (Milan, 1965)
Genoese Baroque Drawings (exh. cat. by M. Newcome, Binghamton, SUNY; Worcester, MA, A. Mus; 1972), nos 141–6
M. Newcome-Schleier: *Maestri genovesi dal cinque al settecento*, Bibioteca di disegni, x (Florence 1976), no. 40
E. Gavazza: 'Il momento della grande decorazione', *Dal Seicento al primo Novecento*, ii of *La pittura a Genova e in Liguria* (Genoa, 1987), pp. 185–276
M. Newcome: 'Lorenzo de' Ferrari Revisited', *Paragone*, cxx/335 (1978), pp. 62–79
E. Mattiauda: 'Un documento per la Pala di Lorenzo de' Ferrari a Tosse', *Boll. Ligustico Stor. & Cult. Reg.*, xxxii–xxxiii (1980–81), pp. 49–53
M. Newcome-Schleier: 'Dessins de l'école génoise dans les collections publiques', *Rev. Louvre*, iii (1985), pp. 211–12
Disegni genovesi dal XVI al XVIII secolo (exh. cat. by M. Newcome, Florence, Uffizi, 1989), nos 106–10
Kunst in der der Republik Genoa (exh. cat. by M. Newcome, Frankfurt am Main, Schirn Ksthalle, 1992), nos 119–20

For further bibliography *see* (1) above.

M. NEWCOME

Ferrari [de Ferrari; Deferrari], **Defendente** (*b* Chivasso, nr Turin; *fl* Piedmont, *c.* 1500–35). Italian painter. It has been established through connoisseurship that he trained in the workshop of GIOVANNI MARTINO SPANZOTTI, who, after his move to Chivasso *c.* 1502, dominated painting in western Piedmont for some 30 years. Many of the works previously thought to have been by Spanzotti are now attributed to Defendente. The polyptych of the *Virgin and Child with Saints* (*c.* 1505; Biella, S Sebastiano) is clearly deeply indebted to Spanzotti, yet Defendente's *Virgin Enthroned with Saints* (1505–7; Turin Cathedral), which is surrounded by 18 small panels depicting legends of SS Crispin and Crispianus, shows that he was also influenced by the highly ornamental qualities of Late Gothic art, a northern European style that persisted in the area around Turin into the early years of the 16th century. Defendente's elaboration of that style is again apparent in his nocturnal *Nativity* (before 1508; Cambridge, MA, Fogg), and it can also be seen in a succeeding group that includes a *Nativity* (1510; Turin, Mus. Civ. A. Ant.) that is almost a miniature version of the earlier one.

It is harder to trace consistent traits in Defendente's art between *c.* 1508 and 1530. His triptych depicting a *Nativity with Saints* (1511; Avigliana, S Giovanni) was followed by a *Christ among the Doctors* (Turin, Mus. Civ. A. Ant.; a copy by Giovanni Battista Giovenone provides a *terminus ante quem* of 1513) and another group of works is closely similar in style. These paintings, while still reflecting Defendente's earlier work, indicate a response to the new art of the Renaissance. The spacious landscape background of the *Baptism* (1508–13; Turin Cathedral) suggests central Italian influence. This confluence of Gothic traditions and Renaissance art can also be seen in the *Assumption of the Virgin*, painted for the Confraternity of the Holy Shroud at Ciriè, near Turin. An inscription on the predella indicates who commissioned it and when it was painted: *Hoc opus feceru[n]t fieri mercatores lanor[um] Ciricaci 1516*.

Around 1520, a particularly fruitful period, Defendente painted the beautiful *Nativity* (1518; Riggisberg, Abegg-Stift.) and the *Penitent St Jerome* (1520; see fig.), which is distinguished by its nocturnal landscape. In these years he appears to have concentrated mainly on small works, searching for an emotional intensity that does not feature in his large altarpieces. The harsh elements in his style were abandoned in favour of more fluid brushstrokes and the creation of soft, dense highlights. This explains the disparity between works such as the delightful small

Defendente Ferrari: *Penitent St Jerome*, tempera on panel, 430×280 mm, 1520 (Turin, Museo Civico d'Arte Antica)

triptych portraying the *Adoration of the Magi* at the centre and the *Nativity* and *Deposition* on either side (1523; Turin, Gal. Sabauda) and the large *Adoration*, perhaps of slightly later date, that repeats the composition, enriching it with elaborate Renaissance architecture. In 1523 Defendente also provided drawings for the choir-stalls in S Gerolamo at Biella.

In the following years Defendente was equally prolific, though few of the works from this period can be securely dated. It seems that his workshop expanded and he himself repeated earlier compositions. In 1526 he made two replicas of subjects painted many years earlier: a copy (1526; Amsterdam, Rijksmus.) of Raphael's *Orléans Madonna* (Chantilly, Mus. Condé) and a *Christ among the Doctors* (1526; Stuttgart, Württemberg. Landesmus.). Spanzotti too had treated these subjects: his *Christ among the Doctors* was painted before 1513 (Turin, Mus. Civ. A. Ant.); his copy of the *Orléans Madonna* (Baltimore, MD, Walters A.G.) is not dated.

Defendente's paintings of the late 1520s seem to reveal the presence of a very skilful assistant, called the 'Pseudo-Giovenone' by Romano (1970). The most convincing example of their collaboration is the *Virgin and Child with St Anne* (1528; Amsterdam, Rijksmus.). Another of Defendente's late works, a monumental winged polyptych depicting the *Adoration of the Child with Saints* (1531; Ranvuso, nr Turin, S Antonio), is supported by a document of 1530, which refers to the work's artist having been commissioned to provide this for the community at Moncalieri. Despite its late date the work does not introduce any new stylistic elements and indeed seems less subtle, refined and aristocratic in style than Defendente's earlier works. He continued to work until at least 1535, the date that appears on the *Virgin Enthroned between SS Crispin and Crispinianus* (Avigliana, Turin, S Giovanni).

BIBLIOGRAPHY
A. M. Brizio: *La pittura in Piemonte dall'età romanica al cinquecento* (Turin, 1942), pp. 45–64, 195–201
B. Berenson: *Italian Pictures of the Renaissance: Central Italian and North Italian Schools*, 3 vols (London, 1968), pp. 101–6
G. Romano: *Casalesi del cinquecento: L'avvento del manierismo in una città padana* (Turin, 1970), pp. 11–12
——: 'Orientamenti della pittura casalese da G. M. Spanzotti alla fine del cinquecento', *Quarto congresso di antichità e d'arte della Società Piemontese d'Archeologia e Belle Arti: Casale Monferrato, 1974*, pp. 289–98
Soprintendenza alle gallerie e alle opere d'arte del Piemonte: Recuperi e nuove acquisizioni (exh. cat., ed. G. Romano; Turin, Gal. Sabauda, 1975)
Opere d'arte a Vercelli e nella sua provincia: Recuperi e restauri, 1968–1976 (exh. cat., ed. F. Mazzini; Vercelli, Mus. Civ. Borgogna, 1976), pp. 23–4, 134–5

RICCARDO PASSONI

Ferrari, Ettore (*b* Rome, 25 March 1845; *d* Rome, 19 Aug 1929). Italian sculptor, painter and politician. He was the son of the sculptor and patriot Filippo Ferrari (1819–97), who both taught him to sculpt and imparted to him a passion for Republican politics. In 1868 he won a biennial scholarship to study at the Accademia Nazionale di San Luca in Rome, where he remained until 1872. During this period he rebelled against the classicism of the Roman Academy by interpreting the Baroque style and employing Romantic subject-matter in such works as *Jacopo Ortis* (terracotta, 0.2×1.5×2.35 m; Rome, Accad. N. S Luca). His combination of historical themes and the dynamism

of a style influenced by Bernini was not well received in academic circles in Italy.

In 1880 Ferrari received his first public commission when, after being awarded first prize for sculpture in the Esposizione Nazionale in Turin for his *Cum Spartaco pugnavit* (Rome, G.N.A. Mod.), he won the competition for the monument to *Victor-Emanuel II*, erected on the Riva degli Schiavoni in Venice in 1887 (*in situ*). The same year he became a member of a masonic lodge where he reached the highest office of Grand Master. In the 1880s he abandoned the themes of the heroic Risorgimento, developing a natural style of his own. In 1882 he was elected a deputy for the Sinistra Repubblicana (Republican Left) and was re-elected until 1892. From this time he completed a number of monuments to politicians and heroes of the Italian Risorgimento (particularly to Giuseppe Garibaldi) in such Italian cities as Ancona, Milan, Pavia, Rome, Vicenza, Venice and Verona. Among the most significant are those in Rome: to *Giordano Bruno* (1889; *in situ*) in the Campo dei Fiori and to *Giuseppe Mazzini*, commissioned in 1902 but not erected on the Aventine Hill until 1949 due to the hostility expressed by the Catholic and Monarchist factions. He also painted landscapes of the Roman Campagna in watercolour and oils, many of which were done during his association with Venticinque della Campagna Romana, a group of Roman landscape painters.

BIBLIOGRAPHY
B. Mantura: 'Ettore Ferrari: Sculture tra il 1867 e il 1889', *Capitolium*, xlix (1974), pp. 41–50
Ettore Ferrari 1845–1929 (exh. cat. by B. Mantura and P. Rosazza Ferraris, Milan, Pal. Cult. Lat., 1988–9)

PIETRO ROCCASECCA

Ferrari, Eusebio (*fl* Vercelli, 1508; *d* after 18 Sept 1526). Italian painter and ?architect. He is first documented in Gaudenzio Ferrari's commission for the polyptych depicting scenes from the *Life of St Anne*, for which he agreed to act as guarantor; although this suggests that he was already a mature artist, his style was based on the new elements introduced by Gaudenzio Ferrari, later the leading artist in Vercelli. This can be seen in Eusebio Ferrari's *Adoration of the Child Jesus* (1505–10; priv. col.), created at the same time as his frescoed grotesques in the Palazzo Verga at Vercelli. On a trip to Rome (*c.* 1505) Gaudenzio Ferrari encountered the style formulated in central Italy by Perugino and others and was possibly accompanied by Eusebio. Eusebio's greatest work, his triptych of the *Adoration of the Child Jesus with Saints* (?*c.* 1519; Mainz, Altertmus. & Gemäldegal.), shows traces of a greater familiarity with the Lombard style of art, with Bramantino and the works created by Pedro Fernández in the Po Valley but also with the style of painting introduced by Leonardo da Vinci. Ferrari did not achieve so much in his *Virgin and Child with Saints* (1519; Turin, Museo Civ. A. Ant.) or the *Mystic Marriage of St Catherine* (1520s; Turin, Gal. Sabauda). Eusabio Ferrari has been postulated (Romano) as the architect of the church of S Sebastiano at Biella, one of the most important examples of Piedmontese architecture and clearly influenced by Bramante.

BIBLIOGRAPHY
G. Romano: 'Eusebio Ferrari e gli affreschi cinquecenteschi di Palazzo Verga a Vercelli', *Prospettiva* [Florence], 33–6 (1983–4), pp. 135–44

Ferrari, Gaudenzio (*b* Valduggia, nr Vercelli, 1475–80; *d* Milan, 3 Jan 1546). Italian painter and sculptor. He probably received his training at Varallo at the beginning of the 1490s, a lively period in the town's artistic life, when extensive works were being carried out at the sacromonte (*see* SACROMONTE). His master was Gian Stefano Scotto (*fl* 1508), none of whose works has as yet been identified but who, judging from the early work of his pupil, may have been influenced by Lombard artists. Gaudenzio's early works, such as a painting on panel of the *Crucifixion* (Varallo, Mus. Civ. Pietro Calderini), were influenced by the poetic art of Bramantino and by the northern Italian classicizing style of the Milanese painter Bernardo Zenale. His early, but self-assured, *Angel of the Annunciation* (*c.* 1500; Vercelli, Mus. Civ. Borgogna), painted for the Convento delle Grazie, Vercelli, suggests that these sources were soon enriched by his response to the tender Renaissance style of Pietro Perugino (active at the Certosa di Pavia, 1496–9). Gaudenzio is also recorded at Vercelli in the first known documentary reference to him, the contract for a polyptych commissioned by the Confraternità di Sant'Anna in 1508, with Eusebio Ferrari acting as guarantor. There remain four paintings of scenes from the *Life of St Anne and God the Father* (Turin, Gal. Sabauda) and two of the *Annunciation* (London, N.G.). In these works Gaudenzio's style is more controlled, possibly as a result of a journey to central Italy in *c.* 1505.

In 1513 Gaudenzio painted a cycle of frescoes showing scenes from the *Passion* on the dividing wall of S Maria delle Grazie, Varallo. Giovanni Martino Spanzotti had painted a similar cycle in S Bernardino, Ivrea, a century earlier. The frescoes are rich in strikingly realistic detail and convey emotion with passionate intensity; here Gaudenzio created new forms to express human emotions and attitudes. In the second decade of the 16th century he painted a series of great polyptychs in the area around Novara. A polyptych at Arona shows, in the upper register, *God Blessing SS Ambrose and Felinus, Jerome and Gratianus* and, in the lower, the *Nativity with SS Catherine and Barbara, Gaudentius and Peter Martyr*, with *Christ and the Apostles* on the predella (1511; Arona, S Maria). An altar (1514–21) in the church of S Gaudenzio, Novara, shows a *Nativity* in the upper register with a divided *Annunciation* to either side of it and a *Virgin and Child with Saints* below, flanked by *SS Peter and John the Baptist* and *Agabus and Paul*. The predella is devoted to *Legends of St Gaudentius*. In the second altar Gaudenzio conveys emotion with ease and grace, predominantly through rich and emotionally expressive colour.

It is harder to trace Gaudenzio's career over the next decade. By 1517 work had resumed on the chapels of the sacromonte at Varallo, where between *c.* 1520 and 1526 he was responsible for such masterpieces as the chapel of the Crucifixion (XXXVIII) (*see* SACROMONTE, fig. 1) and the chapel of the Adoration of the Magi (V). He combined painting with life-size statues of polychrome terracotta and created a radically new rendering of scenes from the Passion. The sculptures, which are startlingly realistic, are arranged as though on a stage and blend with illusionistic and dramatically expressive frescoes. At the same time Gaudenzio started painting and gilding the great wooden altarpiece created by Giovanni Angelo del Mayno for the

Sanctuary of the Assumption at Morbegno, with scenes from the *Life of the Virgin and Christ*. The beautiful polyptych of the *Holy Sacrament* (Isola Bella, Mus. Borromeo) must have been painted by 1531.

Gaudenzio's work was done over a wide geographical area, but it was at Vercelli that he achieved his greatest success. Between 1529 and 1532 he painted an altar, the *Virgin of the Oranges*, and frescoed scenes from the *Life of Mary Magdalene*, a *Crucifixion* (see fig.) and scenes from the *Life of the Virgin* in the church of S Cristoforo, Vercelli. The powerful *Crucifixion*, or the harmonious and spirited *Assumption of the Virgin*, demonstrate Gaudenzio's high level of achievement in portraying sacred subjects. The psychological power of the protagonists is remarkable, as successful here as in his smaller paintings.

At this point Gaudenzio began working more regularly in Lombardy, starting with his ethereal, visionary frescoes

Gaudenzio Ferrari: *Crucifixion*, fresco, 1529–32 (Vercelli, S Cristoforo)

of *Angel Musicians* (1534–6) for the dome of the sanctuary of S Maria delle Grazie at Saronno, where he succeeded the recently deceased Bernardino Luini. The contract was drawn up in Milan, where Gaudenzio lived from 1539 until his death and where he opened a workshop that carried out the city's main private commissions. In the frescoes at Saronno, and in his later work in Milan, Gaudenzio's art took a new direction; he placed greater emphasis on a more theatrical language of gesture and expression, and he drew closer to the prevailing style of Milanese Mannerism. This emphasis on drama is developed in works such as the *Martyrdom of St Catherine* (Milan, Brera) and the frescoes for S Maria della Pace, now transferred on to canvas, depicting scenes from the *Life of St Anne* and scenes from the *Life of the Virgin* (1545; Milan, Brera), which are among the most impressive works of his final years. Gaudenzio was an influential artist and a series of cartoons (Turin, Accademia) suggests the existence of a school of artists who kept his style alive throughout the rest of the century.

BIBLIOGRAPHY

G. P. Lomazzo: *Trattato de l'arte della pittura* (Milan, 1584)
Mostra di Gaudenzio Ferrari (exh. cat., ed. A. M. Brizio and others; Vercelli, Mus. Borgogna, 1956)
G. Testori: *Il gran teatro montano: Saggi su Gaudenzio Ferrari* (Milan, 1965)
V. Viale: *Gaudenzio Ferrari* (Turin, 1969)
C. Debiaggi: 'Nuovi apporti e alcune precisazioni sulla scultura lignea di Gaudenzio', *Studi gaudenziani* (Biella, 1977), pp. 9–28
Gaudenzio Ferrari e la sua scuola: I. Cartoni cinquecenteschi dell'Accademia Albertina (exh. cat., ed. G. Romano; Turin, Accad. Albertina, 1982)
F. M. Ferro: 'Gaudenzio a Romagnano Sésia', *Paragone*, xxxiv/401–3 (1983), pp. 72–80
G. Romano: 'Eusebio Ferrari e gli affreschi cinquecenteschi di Palazzo Verga a Vercelli', *Prospettiva*, xxxiii–xxxvi (1983–4), pp. 135–44
F. M. Ferro: 'Un'ancona milanese di Gaudenzio', *Paragone*, xxxvi/419–23 (1985), pp. 157–63
G. Romano: 'Gerolamo Giovenone, Gaudenzio Ferrari e gli inizi di Bernardino Lanino: Testimonianze d'archivio e documenti figurativi', *Bernardino Lanino e il cinquecento a Vercelli*, ed. G. Romano (Turin, 1986), pp. 13–62

RICCARDO PASSONI

Ferrari, Giovanni Andrea de' (*b* Genoa, *c.* 1598; *d* Genoa, 25 Dec 1669). Italian painter. He was a prolific easel painter who painted many altarpieces and, with Gioacchino Assereto and Orazio de' Ferrari, created a lyrical, richly coloured manner that influenced the later development of the Genoese Baroque. He studied with Bernardo Castello (ii), then with Bernardo Strozzi; he adopted Strozzi's manner so completely that his pictures were confused with those of his master. Some of these compositions survive, but they can usually be distinguished from Strozzi's by a thinner application of paint, expressive van Dyckian heads, tapered hands and tightly rolled drapery sleeves.

With few exceptions, such as the allegorical figures of *Justice* and *Temperance* painted as part of a series for the Palazzo Ducale, Genoa (*in situ*), to which Andrea Ansaldo and Domenico Fiasella also contributed, Giovanni Andrea's work consists of religious subjects. His earliest known dated pictures are *Birth of the Virgin* (1616; Genoa, Nostra Signora del Rimedio) and small canvases of the *Life of the Virgin* (1619; Genoa, Figlie di S Giuseppe, Conservatory), where the figures, with swollen foreheads, profiles and circular eyes, emphasize the close working

relationship with Strozzi; there is nevertheless a new interest in direct and tender naturalism. In the 1620s Giovanni Andrea painted several large canvases with scenes from the lives of the saints and drew on varied stylistic sources. The deep space, architectural backgrounds and tight grouping of the figures in the *St Thomas Preaching to the King of India* (1624; Genoa, S Fede) and the *Charity of St Antonino* (1628; Montoggio, S Giovanni Decollato) suggest the influence of Ansaldo. The *Birth of the Virgin* (1632; Voltri, S Ambrogio) sets the religious scene in the context of everyday life within an intimate, warmly lit interior, rich in still-life details. It conveys emotion with subtlety, and both this painting and the *Guardian Angel* (1632; Santa Margherita Ligure, S Margherita d'Antiochia) suggest the artist's response to the sweetness of Castello.

In 1634 Giovanni Andrea was made a member of the Accademia di S Luca in Rome, but there is no record of his being in Rome. His interest and skill in precisely painted still-life details and rich fabrics demonstrate not only the influence of Ansaldo and Fiasella but also that of van Dyck and Cornelius and Lucas de Wael, Flemish artists who were active in Genoa in the 1620s. These aspects are further visible in dated paintings of the 1630s, such as the lunette painting the *Miracle of St Bridget* (commissioned 1634; Genoa, Mus. Accad. Ligustica B.A.), the sumptuous *Madonna of the Rosary with SS Dominic and Catherine* (1635; Varazze, S Domenico) and the *Carmine Madonna with St Simon Stock* (1635; Alássio, church of the Carità). There are few dated pictures to establish a chronology after the 1630s, yet the figures in the dated *Calling of Peter and Andrew* (1650; Piacenza, S Maria della Pace) suggest that his work remained fairly consistent. He moved away from the mannerisms of Strozzi and Ansaldo and is most successful in his refined and psychologically subtle biblical narratives, such as *Esau Selling his Birthright* (Genoa, Mus. Accad. Ligustica B.A.), through which he contributed to the poetic, neo-Venetian images of his pupils. Without family obligations, and one of the few artists to stay in Genoa, he devoted much attention to his students, among whom were Valerio Castello (ii), Giovanni Battista Merano and possibly Giovanni Benedetto Castiglione.

BIBLIOGRAPHY

R. Soprani: *Vite* (1674), pp. 255–9; ed. C. G. Ratti (1768–9), i, pp. 266–71
G. V. Castelnovi: 'La prima metà del seicento: Dall'Ansaldo a Orazio de Ferrari', *La pittura a Genova e in Liguria*, ii (Genoa, 1971, rev. 1987), pp. 90–96, 135–8
Genoese Baroque Drawings (exh. cat. by M. Newcome, Binghamton, SUNY; Worcester, MA, M. Mus.; 1972), cat. nos 39–41 [with bibliog.]
V. Belloni: *Pittura genovese del seicento*, ii (Genoa, 1974), pp. 7–19
M. Newcome: 'Notes on Three Drawings in the Palazzo Rosso', *Master Drgs*, xxiii–xxiv/2 (1985–6), pp. 204–7
F. R. Pesenti: *La pittura in Liguria, artisti del primo seicento* (Genoa, 1986), pp. 307–32 [with illus.]
Genova nell'età barocca (exh. cat., ed. E. Gavazza and G. R. Terminiello; Genoa, Pal. Spinola and Pal. Reale, 1992)
Kunst in der Republik Genua, 1528–1815 (exh. cat., Frankfurt am Main, Schirn Ksthalle, 1992)

M. NEWCOME

Ferrari, Juan Manuel (*b* Montevideo, 21 May 1874; *d* Buenos Aires, 31 Oct 1916). Uruguayan sculptor. He received his first sculptural lessons at the workshop of his father, the Italian sculptor Juan Ferrari (1836–1918), followed by a brief period at the Escuela Nacional de Bellas Artes in Buenos Aires in 1888. From 1890 he studied in Rome under Ettore Ferrari (thought by some to have been a relation) and Ercole Rosa, winning first prize for sculpture in 1892. On returning to Montevideo in 1897 he established a workshop as well as a course in visual arts at the University of Uruguay. By the time he moved to Buenos Aires in 1910, his reputation as a sculptor specializing in monumental work was firmly established in Uruguay and Argentina.

While still living abroad Ferrari created sculptures of the human figure influenced by Auguste Rodin's use of voids and striking contrasts of light, such as *Prometheus Chained* (1893; Montevideo, Av. Agraciada). On his return to Latin America he made numerous full-length figures on a small scale such as *The San Román Café Owner* (1896) and *Diógenes Héquet* (*c.* 1896) (both Montevideo, Mus. N.A. Plást.), busts and monumental works such as *Monument to General San Martín's Liberation Army* (1914; Mendoza, Argentina, Cerro de la Gloria) and the monument to General Juan Antonio Lavalleja, *Carbine on his Back and Sabre in Hand* (1902; Minas, Plaza Mayor). In 1915 he completed a life-size memorial sculpture dedicated

to Arturo Santa-Anna (Montevideo, Buceo cemetery), in which he masterfully summarized his development.

UNPUBLISHED SOURCES

Montevideo, Mus. N. A. Plást. [B. Parallada: *Monografía sobre Juan Manuel Ferrari*]

BIBLIOGRAPHY

J. P. Argul: *Las artes plásticas del Uruguay* (Montevideo, 1966); rev. as *Proceso de las artes plásticas del Uruguay* (Montevideo, 1975)

ANGEL KALENBERG

Ferrari, Luca (*b* Reggio Emilia, 17 Feb 1605; *d* Padua, 8 Feb 1654). Italian painter. The sources (Tiraboschi) maintain that he was a pupil of Guido Reni, but to judge from the style of his earliest surviving works—the *Miracle of Giovanni Francesco Vincenzo* and the *Miracle of Laura di Correggio* (both *c.* 1626–7; Reggio Emilia, Madonna della Ghiara)—which show no hint of Reni's influence, he was more likely to have trained in his home town alongside the artists Leonello Spada, Alessandro Tiarini and Carlo Bononi, who in the 1610s and 1620s were decorating the basilica of the Madonna della Ghiara. He may well be the Luca who is mentioned in a Modenese document of 1627 as having assisted Tiarini. In 1635 he was documented in Padua, where he was a member of the 'Fraglia dei pittori'

Luca Ferrari: *Death of Cleopatra*, oil on canvas, 1.45×1.70 m, *c.* 1644–8 (Modena, Galleria e Museo Estense)

for two years and where he worked on the large canvas depicting *St Dominic Imploring the Virgin to End the Plague* (1635; Padua, Cassa di Risparmio) and other works on canvas (e.g. altarpieces painted in 1642 in S Francesco and S Tommaso) and in fresco (e.g. the funerary chapel (1640) of the de Lazara family at Conselve). His knowledge of 16th-century Venetian painting was fundamental in helping him to lighten the weighty vigour of Emilian naturalism and to adopt paler, more luminous colours. The decoration of the basilica of the Madonna della Ghiara was finished in this new style (1644–8), and he executed important paintings for the churches of Reggio Emilia (e.g. the *Wedding at Cana* and the *Baptism*, both in S Pietro). In 1650 he was again documented in the vicinity of Padua, where he was working on the frescoes for the Villa Selvatico (now Emo Capodilista) at Battaglia Terme and for the Villa Barbarigo at Noventa Vincentina. These decorations are airy and light-hearted in an almost 18th-century manner. He also specialized in the execution of large-scale canvases depicting historical subjects (see fig.), mythological subjects, such as the two *Scenes from the Iliad* that were once in the d'Este Villa Pisani (now Venice, Pal. Pisani–Moretta) and in small-scale cabinet paintings and altarpieces, in particular the *Deposition* (1652; Padua, Basilica of S Antonio) and the *Miracle of St Anthony* (1653; Este, Church of the Battuti). His last documented commission was the decoration of the ceiling of S Tommaso Cantauriense in Padua (*in situ*), which displays a more complex perspective and the clashing of different light sources. His spectacular style, which in later works was sometimes marred by forced effects, won him much fame, numerous imitators and a lasting influence on successive generations of Venetian painters.

BIBLIOGRAPHY

M. Boschini: *La carta del navigar pittoresco* (Venice, 1660), pp. 553, 560
G. Tiraboschi: *Notizie de' pittori, scultori, architetti e incisori . . .* (Modena, 1786), pp. 202–5
Maestri della pittura del seicento emiliano (exh. cat., ed. F. Arcangeli, M. Calvesi and G. C. Cavalli; Bologna, Pal. Archiginnasio, 1959), pp. 136–8
C. Donzelli and G. M. Pilo: *I pittori del seicento veneto* (Florence, 1967), pp. 168–70
F. d'Arcais: 'La decorazione della villa Rezzonico-Barbarigo a Noventa Vincenta', *A. Ven.*, xxi (1968), pp. 182–90
R. Pallucchini: *La pittura veneziana del '600* (Milan, 1981), pp. 217–22
A. Coccioli Mastroviti: 'Luca Ferrari', *La pittura in Italia: Il seicento*, ed. M. Gregori and E. Schleier (Milan, 1988, rev. 1989), ii, p. 737
M. Ferretti: 'Due dipinti "fuori contesto" all'Osservanza di Bologna', *Prospettiva*, lvii–lx (1989–90), pp. 55–65

DANIELE BENATI

Ferrari, Orazio de' (*bapt* Voltri, 22 Aug 1606; *d* Genoa, 1657). Italian painter. He was a prolific artist who painted mainly religious subjects, which included many pictures of saints and devotional altarpieces. His most characteristic works show the scene set across the foreground and illuminated against a dark background. His figures have well-defined, often exaggerated facial expressions, nervous contours and multiple pockets of shadow. They are sometimes close to Gioacchino Assereto's muscular figures, inspired by Rubens, as in the dramatic *Seizure of Samson* (*c.* 1650; Ascoli Piceno, Pin. Civ.), or are more tender and introspective, suggesting the devotional piety of Giovanni Andrea de' Ferrari. His brushwork is loose

and open, and this vivacity is also apparent in his drawings (examples in Vienna, Albertina; Genoa, Pal. Rosso) in which heavy washes approximate his rich *sfumato*, and the dot-and-dash pen outlines correspond to the elusive contours in his paintings. Orazio worked under Andrea Ansaldo in the 1620s, and the ornate fabrics and metalwork in his paintings are reminiscent of his master; his compositions, however, generally lack Ansaldo's background perspectives and bright colour.

Orazio's first documented work is the *Martyrdom of St Sebastian* (1630; Voltri, SS Nicolò ed Erasmo). In 1631 he married Ansaldo's niece, and the next dated works are his restoration of Ansaldo's *St Lucy* (1639; Voltri, S Erasmo) and the naturalistic and warmly lit *St Sebastian with SS Biagio and Roch* (1639; Loano, S Giovanni Battista). It has been suggested (Pesenti, p. 433) that his response to Caravaggesque naturalism indicates that he travelled to Naples *c.* 1638, but this remains unclear. His dated works of the 1640s include the *Last Supper* (1641; Genoa, Nostra Signora del Monte), the *Virgin and Child with St Felix of Cantalice* (1643; Arenzano, SS Nazario e Celso), similar to a composition by Bernardo Strozzi (Genoa, S Caterina di Portoria), and the monumental *St James Consecrating St Peter Martyr* (1647; Genoa, oratory of S Giacomo della Marina) and *Virgin and Child with SS John and Joseph* (1648; Genoa, S Maria in Consolazione). In the *Last Supper* of 1641, and the related, yet more austere *Last Supper* in S Siro, Genoa, Orazio uncharacteristically creates a sense of space by an elaborate architectural perspective reminiscent of Ansaldo.

In the early 1650s Orazio worked at Menton and Monaco. He is recorded in Monaco in 1651 and 1652, when he received from Prince Grimaldi Honoré II (*d* 1662) the collar of the Order of S Michel, and again in 1654. He painted biblical scenes on canvas for the Grimaldi family and frescoed an open gallery in the Palazzo Grimaldi at Monaco with the *Labours of Hercules* (repainted). Other dated works of the 1650s are the *Nativity with St Francis* (1653; Genoa, Albergo dei Poveri) and the *Death of St Joseph* (1654; Sestri Levante, S Maria di Nazareth). In 1655–7 he painted a series of canvases of the *Life of Anania* (Genoa, S Bartolomeo degli Armeni), who received from Christ an image of the *Volto Santo*. These are among his richest works and convey the psychological reactions of many figures, warmly and naturalistically observed. His frescoes, mentioned by Ratti, are little known; the churches of S Vito and S Andrea in Genoa have been destroyed, while frescoes of the *Life of St Andrew Avellino* in S Siro, Genoa, may have been repainted. Orazio died in the plague.

BIBLIOGRAPHY

R. Soprani: *Vite* (1674), pp. 219–21; ed. C. G. Ratti (1768), pp. 286–9
G. V. Castelnovi: 'La prima metà del seicento: Dall'Ansaldo a Orazio de Ferrari', *La pittura a Genova e in Liguria*, ii (Genoa, 1971, rev. 1987), pp. 142–3 [with bibliog.]
L. Alfonso: 'Andrea Ansaldo e Orazio de Ferrari', *La Berio*, ii–iii (1973), pp. 79–83
V. Belloni: *Pittura genovese del seicento*, ii (Genoa, 1974), pp. 25–40
F. R. Pesenti: *La pittura in Liguria: Artisti del primo seicento* (Genoa, 1986), pp. 433–87 [with illus.]
Genova nell'età barocca (exh. cat., ed. E. Gavazza and G. R. Terminiello; Genoa, Pal. Spinola and Pal. Reale, 1992)

Kunst in der Republik Genua, 1528–1815 (exh. cat., Frankfurt am Main, Schirn Ksthalle, 1992)

M. NEWCOME

Ferrari [Ferreriusz; Ferri], **Pompeo** (*b* ?Rome, *c.* 1660; *d* Rydzyna, 15 May 1736). Italian architect, active in Poland. Only two of Ferrari's works dating from his period in Italy are known, a design for a monastery (1678) and a scheme for a palace (1681): both were awarded prizes by the Accademia di S Luca, Rome. He was brought to Poland by the governor of Poznań, Stanislav Leszczyński, son and heir to Rafal, King of Poland. It was for them that Ferrari planned the reconstruction of the royal palace in Leszno (destr. 1707) and rebuilt (*c.* 1700) the west wing of the castle in Rydzyna. Also for them, he drew up a plan (after 1707) for the church of the Czech Brothers of St John in Leszno. He settled permanently on the Leszczyński estates in Rydzyna, where in 1703 he married Anna Rozyna Eitner. Ferrari's works include the parish churches at Obrzyck (1714–28) and Wschów (1720–26). At Gostyń he completed (1726–8) the Philippine church begun by Jan Catenacci in 1675, a building on a centralized plan that was inspired by S Maria della Salute, Venice, and with an octagonal drum and dome. For the Cistercians he designed churches at Owiński (1720–28) and Lad, near Konin (1728–35). He rebuilt (1723–32) the archbishop's palace (altered in the 19th century) at Poznań and designed the chapel (1727–30) of Archbishop Teodor Potocki at Gniezno Cathedral. He also introduced to the Wielkopolska (Greater Poland) region a hitherto unknown system for organizing building work using firms of contractors. He was the leading Italian architect in Poland at the turn of the 17th century. His entire creative output is connected with the Wielkopolska region, where his centralized churches, with their elliptical domes strongly influenced by Francesco Borromini, are an important feature. The political setback of his patron, however, whose rule over Poland (1704–9) proved to be a brief interim in the reign of Augustus II, prevented him from obtaining major secular commissions, and his non-ecclesiastical work was limited to rebuilding existing houses. In his later schemes the strong influence of Guarino Guarini is apparent.

BIBLIOGRAPHY

W. Dalbor: *Pompeo Ferrari, 1660–1736* (Warsaw, 1938)

A. Cipriani, P. Marconi and E. Valerini: *I disegni di architettura dell'Archivo storico dell'Accademia di San Luca* (Rome, 1974)

A. Kusztelski: 'Twórczość Pompeo Ferrariego: Rewizja stanu badań i nowe ustalenia' [The creative output of Pompeo Ferrari: a reassessment of the state of research and new conclusions], *Sztuka 1 poł. XVIII wieku: Materiały sesji Stowarzyszenia Historyków Sztuki: Rzeszów, 1978* [Polish art of the first half of the 18th century: proceedings of the symposium of the Association of Art Historians], pp. 137–50

E. Kręglewska-Foksowicz: *Sztuka Leszna* [Leszno's art] (Poznań, 1982)

ANDRZEJ ROTTERMUND

Ferrata, Ercole (*b* Pelsoto [now Pellio Inferiore], nr Como, 1610; *d* Rome, 11 April 1686). Italian sculptor. He was apprenticed at an early age to the sculptor Tommaso Orsolino (*fl* 1616–?1674) of Genoa and was in Naples by 1637, when he is recorded as a marble-worker in the Corporazione di Scultori e Marmori. He remained in Naples for about nine years, during which time he carved several statues, including life-size ones of *St Andrew, St Thomas* and two members of the D'Aquino family kneeling in prayer (1641–6; S Maria la Nova, chapel of S Giacomo della Marca) as well as decorative and garden sculpture for villas of the nobility. Some of this work was done in collaboration with Cosimo Fanzago.

In 1646 Ferrata travelled to L'Aquila, where he supplied sculptural decoration for a chapel in S Maria di Roio and a sandstone statue for the façade of a small oratory dedicated to St Anthony of Padua. In the same year he travelled to Rome with Virgilio Spada, who introduced him to Bernini. Bernini employed Ferrata to carve the marble reliefs of two pairs of putti carrying medallions with papal portraits and two pairs of putti carrying keys (1647) as decoration for the pilasters in the nave of St Peter's.

Between 1647 and 1654 Ferrata collaborated with Bernini in Rome on the decoration of St Peter's, on the redecoration of the crypt in S Francesca Romana (S Maria Nuova), for which he carved a marble oval relief (*c.* 1649) representing the saint with an angel holding a book, and on the tomb in S Maria sopra Minerva of *Cardinal Domenico Pimentel* (*d* 1653), for which he carved three over life-size relief figures of the cardinal kneeling in prayer accompanied by Faith and Wisdom. During the same period he assisted Algardi with the large marble relief of the *Encounter of Leo the Great and Attila* (1646–53; Rome, St Peter's) and collaborated with Domenico Guidi on the execution, from Algardi's design, of the marble high altar (1651–5), S Nicola da Tolentino, Rome. Here Ferrata carved the life-size statue of *St Nicola* in the niche above the altar and the relief of *God the Father* in the tympanum of the aedicula. Algardi regarded Ferrata as one of his most important assistants, and Ferrata was one of the four who inherited the contents of the master's studio, including many terracotta models.

From 1654 Ferrata carved or modelled sculpture for most of the major architectural or sculptural projects in Rome. These include the decoration (1660–72) of S Agnese in Agone, for which he carved the over life-size marble relief of the *Martyrdom of St Emerenziana* and the over life-size marble statue of *St Agnes on the Pyre* (begun 1660; see fig.), and the decoration (1662–5) of the nave of S Maria in Vallicella (Chiesa Nuova), for which he modelled several angels and allegorical figures in stucco after designs by Pietro da Cortona. Ferrata's stylistic development in Rome can be divided into three periods. In the 1650s and early 1660s his style was strongly influenced by that of Algardi. His *St Agnes on the Pyre* resembles Algardi's *St Mary Magdalene* (*c.* 1628; Rome, S Silvestro al Quirinale, Cappella Bandini). Both statues have similar contrapposto poses and agitated draperies that reflect the ecstasy of martyrdom. The *St Agnes* has flamboyant features derived from Bernini, such as the wind-blown cloak flying behind the saint's shoulder and the carved flames of the pyre, which give the statue a painterly quality. After 1665 Ferrata's work became more severely classicizing, and all extravagant flourishes were suppressed. In works such as the large marble statue of the *Angel Carrying the Cross* (1668–9; Rome, Ponte S Angelo) and the life-size statue of *Faith* (1665–70; Rome, S Giovanni dei Fiorentini, Falconieri Chapel), the figures have strong contrapposto poses, and the drapery is designed to emphasize the form beneath.

Ercole Ferrata: *St Agnes on the Pyre*, marble, over life-size, begun 1660 (Rome, S Agnese in Agone)

In the last 15 years or so of his life Ferrata's work became extremely planar. The over life-size figure of Eternity on the tomb of *Cardinal Bonelli* (before 1674; Rome, S Maria sopra Minerva) is designed so that the head, shoulders and hips are twisted into the same plane. This flatness is more exaggerated in the under life-size marble figure of Time on the tomb of *Monsignor Giulio del Cornu* (before 1686; Rome, Gesù e Maria) and in the marble relief of *St Romano on his Bier* (1685–6), placed beneath the high altar of Nepi Cathedral. Also in this late period Ferrata produced the marble statue of *St Elizabeth* (1679–83) for the altar of Cardinal Friedrich von Hessen's mortuary chapel in Breslau (now Wrocław) Cathedral. This was a reworking of his design for *St Agnes on the Pyre* and one of his most important independent commissions.

Ferrata ran an important studio, where he trained a number of sculptors, including Melchiorre Caffa, Giovanni Battista Foggini, Carlo Andrea Marcellini and Camillo Rusconi. In addition, from 1667 he and Ciro Ferri instructed young Florentine artists studying in Rome at the Accademia Fiorentina under the sponsorship of Cosimo III, Grand Duke of Tuscany. Though financially successful, Ferrata was not a first-rate designer: he either imitated Algardi or used designs provided by his leading pupil, Caffa. At Caffa's death in 1667, Ferrata completed his pupil's most important commissions, the relief of the *Martyrdom of St Eustace* (1660–72; Rome, S Agnese in

Agone) and the *Charity of St Thomas of Villanova* (1662–71; Rome, A Agostino, Pamphili Chapel).

BIBLIOGRAPHY

F. Baldinucci: *Notizie* (1681–1728); ed. F. Ranalli (1845–7)
L. Pascoli: *Vite* (1730–36), i, pp. 237–47
V. Golzio: *Seicento e settecento* (Turin, 1950, rev. 2/1960), pp. 209–15
R. Wittkower: *Gian Lorenzo Bernini: The Sculptor of the Roman Baroque* (London, 1955, rev. 2/1961), pp. 20, 34
L. Montalto: 'Ercole Ferrata e le vicende litigiose del basso rilievo di Sant'Emerenziana', *Commentari*, viii (1957), pp. 47–68
A. Nava-Cellini: 'Contribuito al periodo napoletano di Ercole Ferrata', *Paragone*, xii/137 (1961), pp. 37–44
M. Weil: *The History and Decoration of the Ponte S Angelo* (University Park, 1974), pp. 81–4, 145–7
R. Preimesberger and M. Weil: 'The Pamphili Chapel in Sant'Agostino', *Röm. Jb. Kstgesch.*, xv (1975), pp. 183–98
J. Montagu: *Alessandro Algardi*, i (New Haven, 1985), pp. 46–8, 208–11, 216–17 [with extensive bibliog.]
——: *Roman Baroque Sculpture: The Industry of Art* (New Haven, 1989)

MARK S. WEIL

Ferrazzi, Ferruccio (*b* Rome, 15 March 1891; *d* Rome, 8 Dec 1978). Italian painter and sculptor. He began as an assistant to his sculptor father, Stanislao Ferrazzi (*d* 1943), and attended the Scuola Libera del Nudo (1905–8) and from 1908 studied under Max Roeder (1866–1947) at the Istituto di Belle Arti in Rome. Success came early when *The Hearth* (1910; Rome, G.N.A. Mod.), influenced by Giovanni Segantini, was bought by the state at the Esposizione Universale, Rome (1911). He assimilated French influences in Paris in 1913, adopting freer brushwork and shaped canvases and roughening his sculptures' surfaces (e.g. *The Lovers*, clay, 1915; destr.; see Ragghianti, pl. 30). In 1916 he visited Montreux, where he discovered the work of Cézanne. Ferrazzi subsequently destroyed many early works and embarked on a rich period of classicism, with such Ingresque nudes as *Merry Life No. 2* (1922; Rome, Pal. Braschi). Mannerist fantasy infused the portrayal of his wife as a Madonna in *Nocturnal Festival* (1921–3; priv. col., see Ragghianti, pl. 107), which established Ferrazzi's maturity within the Scuola Romana. A series of psychologically piercing portraits followed, introducing a crystalline symbolism, while he won international recognition when *Tragic Voyage* (1925; Pittsburgh, PA, Carnegie Mus. A.) was exhibited in New York in 1926. In the later 1920s Ferrazzi painted increasingly frenzied and disturbing symbolic animal subjects at Casalaccio di Tivoli. Official commissions followed his appointment as Professor of Decoration at the Accademia di San Luca in Rome in 1929. These included the lengthy *Apocalypse* mosaic project (1933–54; Acqui, Ottolenghi Mausoleum). The horrors of World War II and his father's death sparked a psychological crisis that resulted in nightmarish images (e.g. *Years of Horror—The Room*, 1943–6; priv. col., see Ragghianti, pl. 200), but he subsequently resumed mural painting, producing, for example, encaustics for S Benedetto, Rome (*Life of St Benedict*; 1949).

BIBLIOGRAPHY

C. L. Ragghianti, J. Recupero and N. C. Ferrazzi: *Ferruccio Ferrazzi* (Rome, 1974)

MATTHEW GALE

Ferreira, Gaspar (*fl* Coimbra, 1718–61). Portuguese architect, builder and designer. His name is first recorded in 1718 at Coimbra as master of works for the university and responsible for planning its buildings over the large area under its control. He directed the construction of the magnificent University Library (1718–25), including the great bookcases, a work of superb quality (designer unknown). He was self-taught, and in carrying out the plans and designs sent from Lisbon he acquired the knowledge that is reflected in his later work. He was renowned in the provincial region of Beira, where he encouraged the use of architectural forms closer to those employed in the centres of Coimbra and Lisbon. He advised on the restoration of Viseu Cathedral, where he designed the organ case (1720), the twin retables of *St John* and *St Peter* and the pulpits (all 1721), inspired by the bookcases of the Coimbra University Library. His designs for the scheme at the Misericórdia, Mangualde (*c.* 1722), although harmonious, still retain provincial elements. His plans for the university tower at Coimbra (1728) were rejected, although he was responsible for supervising the project after designs sent from Lisbon.

The high technical quality of Ferreira's work led in 1731 to commissions from the wealthy canons of Santa Cruz, Coimbra. In 1732 he returned to Viseu, where he supervised the remodelling of the high altar of the cathedral after the designs (1729) by Santos Pacheco de Lima. He also designed furnishings for the cathedral at Viseu, including the choir-stalls, in exotic wood and partly gilded (1733–4), which are similar to the design (1726) of those in Oporto Cathedral by Luis Pereira da Costa and Miguel Marques and which are a fine example of Joanine wood-carving; their attribution is facilitated by their similarity to the episcopal throne of Guarda Cathedral. Ferreira also worked for the Sta Maria Cistercian nunnery at Arouca, carrying out improvements to the dormitories and designing a new repository (*c.* 1735); and it is possible that he supervised the building of the convent church (1704–18), after the design by Carlos Gimac, in which the hard local granite is softened by the use of delicate mouldings. In 1737, perhaps through his work for the same hospital of charity at Mangualde, he was commissioned to build the Misericórdia at Sta Comba, Dão.

From 1737 he executed the plans by Carlos Mardel for the great cloister of Sta Clara-a-Nova, Coimbra, an extensive work that probably occupied him for several years. He collaborated on the remodelling of the convent at Lorvão (1742–61). Between 1752 and 1754 he was working on the reconstruction of the façade of the hospital at Montemor-o-Velho, where he combined existing elements with details, such as the more evolved and elegant design for the portal-window, that are given particular delicacy by the use of the local white limestone. For Sta Clara-a-Nova, Coimbra, he supervised the building of the elegant Baroque portal (1761) to a design of Central European origin by Carlos Mardel. The skill of this provincial master of works is evident in his ability to interpret plans for architectural projects that had been commissioned by the state in Lisbon.

BIBLIOGRAPHY
A. Nogueira Goncalves: *Inventário artístico de Portugal: Cidade de Coimbra* (Lisbon, 1947), pp. 82–3, 105–6
Distrito de Coimbra (Lisbon, 1953), pp. 139, 194–5, 198
R. C. Smith: *Cadeirais de Portugal* [Choir-stalls of Portugal] (Lisbon, 1968), pp. 60–61
P. Dias: *Mosteiro de Arouca* (Coimbra, 1980), pp. 19–20

A. Alves: 'A actividade de Gaspar Ferreira em terras do interior beirão' [The activity of Gaspar Ferreira in the Beira region], *Mundo A.*, vi (1982), p. 217
Coimbra, arte e história (Oporto, 1983)
N. Correia Borges: *História da arte em Portugal: Do barroco ao rococó*, ix (Lisbon, 1986), pp. 26–7
Coimbra e região (Lisbon, 1987), pp. 74–5, 182
ANTÓNIO FILIPE PIMENTEL

Ferreira, Jesús Reyes. *See* REYES FERREIRA, JESÚS.

Ferreira, Simão (*b* Coimbra; *fl* 1588–1607). Portuguese silver- and goldsmith. A *carta de privilégio* dated 21 March 1588 and signed by the rector of Coimbra University granted him the privileges enjoyed by professors and students of the university. Another document (Coimbra, Registo Câmara Mun.) of the Municipality of Coimbra appointed 'Simão Ferreira, silversmith and resident in the city of Coimbra' to make 'all things necessary' for its chapel and for the churches in that diocese and in those of Oporto and Lamego. Two magnificent pieces by him survive in the chapel of Coimbra University (with relevant documents in the University archive recording the commissions and the expenses involved): an imposing lamp, completed in October 1597, and a fine jewelled chalice in silver gilt, which he undertook to execute in a letter of 28 August 1601. Other pieces commissioned from him by the University—two jewelled crowns, a monstrance, two thuribles, an incense boat, another lamp and a holy-water stoup, all executed between 1593 and 1606—have not survived. From later inventories it is known that many of these works were melted down in the second half of the 18th century. On the basis of the technical and stylistic quality of his surviving work, however, Ferreira can be identified as one of the most important Portuguese master silver- and goldsmiths of the late 16th century and early 17th.

BIBLIOGRAPHY
A. Vasconcelos: *Real Capela da Universidade de Coimbra* (Coimbra, 1908), pp. 102, 129
J. M. Teixeira de Carvalho: 'Ourives de Coimbra', *Instituto*, lxviii (1921), pp. 195–202
L. Costa: *Artistas portugueses* (Oporto, 1922)
V. Correia and A. N. Gonçalves: *Cidade de Coimbra* (1947), ii of *Inventário artístico de Portugal* (Lisbon, 1943–)
MARIA LEONOR D'OREY

Ferrer (Garcia), Rafael (Pablo Ramón) (*b* Santurce, Puerto Rico, 1933). Puerto Rican painter and sculptor. In 1952 he entered Syracuse University, NY, to study for a liberal arts degree and there began to paint, influenced by the Cubist works of Picasso and Braque. After only 18 months he went to the Universidad de Puerto Rico, where he studied painting under the French Surrealist painter Eugenio Granell (*b* 1912). Through Granell, Ferrer became acquainted with Dada and Surrealism and in 1953 was introduced by him to André Breton and Wilfredo Lam, and to the writer Benjamin Peret in Paris. After three months in Paris he went to New York, where he worked as a drummer while continuing to paint. He returned to Puerto Rico in 1960 and the following year had a controversial two-man show with the Puerto Rican painter Rafael 'Chafo' Villamil at the museum of the Universidad de

Puerto Rico, near Mayaguez. By this time he had abandoned painting in favour of sculpting in wood, steel and other materials.

In 1966 Ferrer moved to Philadelphia and soon met Robert Morris (ii), Richard Serra and the American sculptor Italo Scanga (*b* 1932). In December 1968 he made several *Leaf Pieces*, consisting simply of piles of leaves, in various New York galleries, including the Leo Castelli Gallery (see 1973 exh. cat., p. 10). The following year he produced his *Hay, Grease, Steel* and *Ice Pieces* (see 1971 exh. cat.) for the *Anti-Illusion/Procedures/Materials* show at the Whitney Museum of American Art in New York. These ephemeral works caused him to be associated with the Process art movement, a label he later rejected. In 1972 he put on a show at the Pasadena Art Museum, CA, which included the work *Madagascar*, the first of several that referred to specific geographical locations. Later installations, under titles such as *Celebes, Patagonia, Sudan*, were made from various materials and objects, including animal skins, kayaks and explorers' equipment. The *Deseo* show at the Contemporary Arts Center, Cincinnati, OH (1973), included works of this type (see 1973 exh. cat.). After 1978 Ferrer abandoned installations and returned to painting.

BIBLIOGRAPHY

Rafael Ferrer: Enclosures (exh. cat. by S. Prokopoff, Philadelphia, U. PA., Inst. Contemp. A., 1971)
Deseo: An Adventure, Rafael Ferrer (exh. cat. by C. Ratcliff, Cincinnati, Contemp. A. Cent., 1973)
Rafael Ferrer (exh. cat. by S. Prokopoff, Boston, ICA, 1978)

Ferreri, Marco [Ferrari d'Antonio d'Agrate]. *See* AGRATE, MARCO D'.

Ferretti, Giovanni Domenico [Giovan Domenico; Giandomenico] (*b* Florence, 15 June 1692; *d* 18 Aug 1768). Italian painter. He was the son of the goldsmith Antonio di Giovanni da Imola and Margherita di Domenico Gori. His mother's family, which included her brother, the antiquarian ANTONIO FRANCESCO GORI, was extremely influential in Florence and proved very important for Ferretti. In the first years of his life he lived in Imola, where he was sent to study (1708) with the local painter Francesco Chiusuri. After the family moved to Florence, Ferretti was taught there by Tommaso Redi and Sebastiano Galeotti. Later he spent five years in Bologna, an important centre for the practice and teaching of academic painting, where, in the workshop of Felice Torelli, his work acquired its characteristic style.

On returning to Florence in 1715, Ferretti frescoed the ceiling of S Chiara, the scenes of which are practically illegible. Two years later he became a member of the Accademia del Disegno. Between 1718 and 1719, thanks to the protection of Cardinal Ulisse Gozzadini, Ferretti obtained several commissions in Bologna and Imola. At the latter he decorated the cupola of the cathedral with images of the patron saints, *Cassian, Peter Chrysologus, Projectus* and *Maurelius*. Back in Florence he produced two canvases for the church of the Impruneta (1721–2) and an oval painting for the Badia of Castiglion Fiorentino showing the *Ecstasy of St Teresa of Avila with St Catherine of Siena* (1723), which is the only signed and dated work

surviving from the early part of his career. Among the most important works of his youthful period are the decoration of the ceiling of a *salone* in the Palazzo Nonfinito (Strozzi) in Florence (1715–20) and the ceiling of the great staircase of the Palazzo Amati-Cellesi in Pistoia (1721), which shows the strong influence of the cycle painted by Sebastiano Ricci in the Palazzo Marucelli-Fensi (1706–7). The airy quality of Ricci's compositions, however, is interpreted in the light of Ferretti's own Emilian training. Ferretti went on to develop his interest in the *bozzetto* (oil sketch), a form particularly congenial to him.

In 1725 Ferretti frescoed some rooms in the Villa Puccini near Pistoia; by this time he had clearly achieved a distinctive, personal approach to style and the rhythmic composition of figures. From about 1728, if not before, he worked for the *arazzeria* or tapestry workshop of Gian Gastone, the Grand Duke of Tuscany (*reg* 1723–37), for which several payments are listed. He undertook to design a tapestry representing *Water*, in collaboration with Lorenzo del Moro (1677–1735), who executed the decorative friezes and also assisted him in other projects during the following years. The *Rape of Europa* (Florence, Uffizi; see fig.) was probably the modello for the cartoon of a tapestry, which was never finished, and which had been intended to hang beside those of *Fire* by Giuseppe Grisoni and of *Air* by Vincenzo Meucci (1694–1766).

The increased number of Ferretti's commissions and academic honours accompanied his growing reputation in Florence. In 1731 he became one of the Dodici Maestri di Pittura at the Florentine Accademia, and in the following year he became Console of the same institution, a post he retained almost until his death. In the 1730s he produced some of his most important works for numerous Florentine churches. In 1734 he finished the decoration of the choir and apse of the Badia church, with the *Martyrdom of St Stephen* and the *Assumption and Coronation of the Virgin*. In collaboration with Mauro Soderini (*b* 1704), formerly his colleague in the Torelli workshop in Bologna, Ferretti completed two decorative cycles (1736–7). The first was for the oratory of the Madonna della Quercia at Le Cure (near Florence), in which Rinaldo Botti (*c.* 1650–*c.* 1740) also participated; this was lost at the end of the 18th century, when the building was modernized. The second cycle, painted with Meucci also, is in S Domenico al Maglio in Florence. In the same year the Archbishop of Florence, Giuseppe Montelli, commissioned from a group of painters the decoration of his private chapel, S Salvatore al Vescovado. Ferretti was responsible for the apse with the *Adoration of the Shepherds* and the cupola with *God the Father Blessing*.

Ferretti's fame also extended outside Florence. In Pistoia he painted the work that is considered his masterpiece, the frescoes in the church of SS Prospero e Filippo (1731–46). His collaborators were Lorenzo del Moro and Pietro Anderlini (1687–*c.* 1755), who painted the *quadratura* passages. These paintings, which are outstanding for their complexity and monumentality, represent the moment of the artist's fullest maturity, having absorbed the influence of Ricci and translated the solidity learnt from his Emilian masters into airy and elegant forms. In 1741, for the chapel of S Giuseppe in Florence Cathedral, he

Giovanni Domenico Ferretti: *Rape of Europa*, oil on canvas, 2.05×1.46 m, *c.* 1728 (Florence, Galleria degli Uffizi)

painted the canvas of the *Death of St Joseph*; and in the refectory of the convent of the SS Annunziata he produced frescoes depicting scenes from the *Life of Christ*. Ferretti's sureness of technique is manifested not only in his large religious compositions but also in such secular paintings as the frescoed allegorical scenes in the Sala delle Stagioni in the Palazzo Sansedoni at Siena. His various series of *Harlequinades* (1742) were undoubtedly influenced by the presence of Goldoni in Florence that year. In these the treatment of the still-lifes and the naturalistic details reflect the influence of the Bolognese painter Giuseppe Maria Crespi, which can, in fact, already be seen in some of the artist's early works.

In the last phase of his career Ferretti produced several elaborate paintings, which in some places show a decline in quality and a few concessions to academic taste. Among these were the *Martyrdom of St Bartholomew* for SS Ranieri e Luigi in S Giuliano Terme (near Pisa), and the *Adoration of the Magi* in S Paolino, Florence. In 1755 he worked on the last great decorative project of his life, the frescoes for S Maria del Carmine in Florence. The work was carried out in several stages. First he decorated the chapels of St Lucy and the Ascension with frescoes of *St Mary Magdalene de' Pazzi and Angels* and *St Andrea Corsini and Angels*. Three years later, on the inner façade of the church, he painted four pictures framed by stucco decorations, show- ing the *Blessed Angelico Mazzinghi and the Venerable Arcangiolo Paoli with Groups of Angels*. The cycle also includes a grandiose canvas depicting the *Deposition*, which was to have been placed in the chapel of St Jerome, but the rather uneven quality of the painting betrays the participation of assistants. This was the only work to escape the disastrous fire of 1771 that destroyed the rest. Ferretti died while working on the canvas of the *Virgin Giving the Scapular to St Simeon Stock* for the central nave of the church, and the work was left for his pupil Alessandro Masini to complete.

BIBLIOGRAPHY

L. Berti: 'Inediti di Giovan Domenico Ferretti', *Commentari*, i (1950), pp. 105ff

The Disguises of Harlequin by G. D. Ferretti (exh. cat. by E. A. Maser, Lawrence, U. KS, Spencer Mus. A., 1956)

E. A. Maser: *Giovanni Domenico Ferretti* (Florence, 1968)

G. Edwald: 'Alcuni ritratti di ignoti del tardo barocco fiorentino', *Ant. Viva*, xiii (1974), pp. 36–9

E. A. Maser: 'Addenda ferrettiana', *Kunst des Barock in der Toskana*, by K. Langheit and others (Munich, 1976), pp. 383–94

M. Gregori: 'Per il periodo giovanile di Giovan Domenico Ferretti', *Kunst des Barock in der Toskana*, by K. Langheit and others (Munich, 1976), pp. 367–80

G. Leoncini: 'Giovanni Domenico Ferretti: Contributi alla ritrattistica fiorentina del settecento', *Paragone*, cccxxix (1977), pp. 58–72

M. Chiarini: 'La pittura del settecento in Toscana', *La pittura in Italia: Il settecento*, ed. G. Briganti, i (Milan, 1989), pp. 275–321

S. M. Trkulja: 'Ferretti, Giovan Domenico', *La pittura in Italia: Il settecento*, ed. G. Briganti, ii (Milan, 1989), pp. 716–17

ENRICA BANTI

Ferrey, Benjamin (*b* Christchurch, Hants, 1 April 1810; *d* London, 22 Aug 1880). English architect. As a boy he made drawings of Christchurch Priory and Wimborne Minster. By 1826 he was a pupil of A. C. Pugin, for whom he measured and drew medieval buildings in England and Normandy, and with whose son, A. W. N. Pugin, he became friendly. In 1832 or 1833 Ferrey entered the office of William Wilkins, where he worked on the drawings for the National Gallery, London. From 1834 to 1836 he was in partnership in Bloomsbury with Thomas Larkins Walker (*d* 1860). He was commissioned by Sir George Gervis, Baronet, to lay out his estate at Bournemouth (1834–6) with a hotel (now Royal Bath Hotel) and villas (mostly destr. 1900–20). He soon developed an extensive practice, in which he showed an eclectic and versatile approach to style.

In 1841 Ferrey became Honorary Architect to the Diocese of Bath and Wells. He restored many old churches in that diocese and elsewhere (including Wells Cathedral in 1846), sometimes well, sometimes with too little sensitivity. He built *c.* 70 new churches, mostly in a correct Gothic Revival style (e.g. St Stephen's, Rochester Row, London), but a few in the Norman Revival, such as St Nicholas (1842–4), East Grafton, Wilts; his attempt to vault the nave in stone here led to disaster when the first bay crushed a visiting clergyman. He also designed numerous schools and parsonages. He had an extensive country-house practice, one of his chief commissions being the rebuilding of Wynnstay, Clwyd, after a fire in 1858, in French Renaissance Revival style. His public buildings included town halls at Luton (1846) and Dorchester (1847–8), the Dorset County Hospital (1839–56) and St Peter's College (1847–50), Saltley, Birmingham. He opposed the use of foreign Gothic Revival styles and of polychromy. His son Edmund Benjamin Ferrey (1846–1900) practised with him for ten years. He was a genial and popular man. In 1839 he became one of the first Fellows of the Institute of British Architects; he was twice Vice-President and in 1870 received its Gold Medal.

WRITINGS

Antiquities of the Priory Church of Christchurch, Hants (London, 1834) [text by W. Brayley]
Recollections of A. N. Welby Pugin and his Father, Augustus Pugin (London, 1861); eds C. Wainwright and J. Wainwright (London, 1978)

BIBLIOGRAPHY

DNB
'Benjamin Ferrey, F.S.A., Past Vice-President', *Trans. RIBA*, xxx (1879–80), pp. 219–21
Obituary, *Builder*, xxxix (1880), pp. 281–3

PETER HOWELL

Ferrez, Marc (*b* Rio de Janeiro, 1843; *d* Rio de Janeiro, 1923). Brazilian photographer. He trained as a photographer with Franz Keller (1835–90), from Mannheim, Germany, and worked as a photographer in Rio de Janeiro, before joining the photographic firm of Leuzinger. In 1865 he opened his own studio. He specialized in photographs of landscapes and shipping, as in *View of Rio de Janeiro with Corcorada and Sugarloaf* (*c.* 1875; see Fabian and Adam, pp. 134–5), but was also one of the first photographers of the Indian population of the Amazon region. In 1876 he exhibited his material—which was also of ethnological interest—at the *Exhibition of the Century* in Philadelphia, PA, winning the gold medal. In 1904, at the World's Fair in St Louis, MO, he was the only photographer to win a gold medal. In 1907 he opened the first picture-house in Rio de Janeiro and concentrated his attention on the new technical possibilities.

For illustration *see* PHOTOGRAPHY, fig. 12.

BIBLIOGRAPHY
E. Billeter: *Fotografie Lateinamerika* (Zurich and Berne, 1981)
R. Fabian and H. C. Adam: *Frühe Reisen mit der Kamera* (Hamburg, 1981), pp. 133–62

ERIKA BILLETER

Ferri, Ciro (*b* Rome, ?1634; *d* Rome, 13 Sept 1689). Italian painter, sculptor, architect and draughtsman. He was the most gifted pupil of Pietro da Cortona, and his style, in frescoes, easel paintings and drawings, remained a remarkably true interpretation of the latter's Roman Baroque; Pascoli wrote of Ferri: 'No pupil followed Cortona's style more closely than Ciro; none so nearly approached the beauty of his art, and the originality of his invention.' The work of the two artists is at times so close that attributions, especially among their drawings, have often been confused. In his designs for sculpture, architecture and decorative ornament, Ferri was indebted to both Cortona and Bernini. Ferri's art was important in spreading the decorative style of the Roman Baroque to Florence and to other cities.

1. ROME, FLORENCE AND BERGAMO, BEFORE 1669. About 1650 Ferri's father, Giovanni Stefano Ferri, a Genoese woodworker, sent him to study under Pietro da Cortona, in whose studio he remained for about ten years and learnt the principles of art, partly by copying Classical statues and Renaissance paintings. Ciro Ferri formed a close friendship with Cortona, and their collaboration meant that, early in his career, Ferri was involved in the major decorative commissions of the time. In 1656–7, with fellow pupils Lazzaro Baldi and Guglielmo Cortese, he worked under Cortona on the decoration of the Galleria di Alessandro VII in the Palazzo del Quirinale, Rome, for which he painted *Cyrus Freeing the Israelites* (*bozzetto*, Rome, Pal. Barberini). In the same period, recommended by Cortona, he worked with Cortese on the frescoed lunettes in the chapel of the Holy Sacrament in S Marco, which was redecorated between 1653 and 1657 on the orders of Niccolò Sagredo. Ferri's style, from these early works onwards, derived closely from that of Cortona, who delegated to him the task of completing the cartoons for the mosaics of *God the Father in Glory* (1657–9) for the cupola of the second bay of the right aisle in St Peter's, Rome. The two lunette frescoes on which he collaborated with Cortese in the Cesi Chapel in S Prassede may also date from this period, though an alternative dating to the early 1660s has also been suggested (Davis).

In 1659 Ferri left for Florence, because in July of that year Cortona decided to entrust him with the completion of the fresco decoration for the unfinished Sala di Apollo, one of the Planetary rooms in the Palazzo Pitti, Florence, the decoration of which had been commissioned by Ferdinando II de' Medici (*see* FLORENCE, §IV, 9). Cortona had worked on these rooms from 1641 to 1647 but had since been overburdened with papal commissions in Rome. He probably planned the entire work, including the stuccos, judging by the large number of his surviving drawings (Florence, Uffizi) and by contemporaneous sources. He may also have painted some of the figures on the ceiling. Yet the lunettes, showing *Julius Caesar Listening to an Account of Historic Deeds*, *Virgil Reading his Poem to Augustus*, *Justinian Ordering Old and Superseded Law Books to be Burnt* and *Alexander Reading the Poetry of Homer*, were painted by Ferri (1659–61), working from cartoons that he had prepared in Rome with the advice and approval of Cortona. Two years later Ferri returned to Florence to decorate the Sala di Saturno (1663–5). It is not clear whether he prepared the cartoons in Rome, under the supervision of Cortona, or independently in Florence. It is beyond doubt that all the work—the central ceiling fresco with the *Apotheosis of the Prince*, the four lunettes featuring episodes from the lives of ancient rulers and the frescoes of the *Muses* in the pendentives—were executed in strict adherence to Cortona's manner, though they do not quite achieve his imaginative brilliance and vitality. Ferri's drawings for this project, among them a compositional study (Düsseldorf, Kstmus.) and figure studies in red and black chalk (Rome, Gab. N. Stampe) are stylistically close to those by Cortona, yet his forms are less boldly modelled, his lines more sinuous and repetitive.

During his stay in Florence, Ferri also completed a series of paintings for Tuscan churches, among them the *Immaculate Conception with Four Saints* (1660) for S Francesco in Cortona (untraced) and various canvases for the Medici, Corsini and Gerini galleries, including *Alexander Reading the Poetry of Homer* (Florence, Pitti). He also designed an *Allegory of the Medici Family* (cartoon, England, priv. col., see Turner, 1979, fig. 8), engraved by François Spierre in 1664 for Abbate Giovanni Rimbaldesi.

Ferri left Florence in 1664 and travelled to Bergamo, where he painted a cycle of frescoes (1665–7) in the church of S Maria Maggiore. Meanwhile he also worked independently, producing easel paintings for Florentine patrons, such as Grand Duchess Vittoria della Rovere, for whom he may have painted the *Vestal Virgins Tending the Sacred Flame* (?c. 1666–7; Rome, Gal. Spada). It was his intention to go to Venice to improve his use of colour through a study of Venetian painting, though it is uncertain if this wish were fulfilled.

2. ROME, 1669–89. Ferri returned to Rome on the death of Pietro da Cortona in 1669 to complete the latter's unfinished commissions, the most important of which were the cartoons for the mosaics in the first bay of the right aisle of St Peter's. Cortona had begun work on these in 1668 but had finished only the drawings for the cupola; Ferri designed the figures of *Patriarchs*, *Prophets* and *Sibyls* in the spandrels and lunettes (finished 1674). He completed (*c.* 1673–4) the vault fresco begun by Cortona in 1668 in the Gavotti Chapel in S Nicolo Tolentino, for which he himself also designed a marble reliquary-sarcophagus beneath the altar (1676). Between 1667 and 1674 he completed the high altar in S Giovanni dei Fiorentini, begun by Cortona and continued by Borromini.

In 1670 Ferri was awarded one of the most prestigious commissions of the age—to decorate the cupola of S Agnese in Agone in Piazza Navona, Rome. This had to be completed before the Holy Year of 1675 and was to portray *God the Father in Glory*. The work did not go smoothly: Ferri was perhaps inhibited by the difficulty of planning an entire composition on his own or perhaps feared comparison with Giovanni Battista Gaulli's brilliantly coloured and spirited *Virtues* (1666–72) in the pendentives. The project was eventually completed in 1689 by Ferri's obscure pupil Sebastiano Corbellini, in a stiff and hesitant style.

Although Ferri continued to paint (e.g. *Erminia and the Shepherds*, early 1670s; Rome, Gal. Doria-Pamphili), from the early 1670s onwards he devoted more of his energies to preparatory drawings for sculpture, architecture, engravings and ornamental works. Among his most elaborate projects was the chapel of S Sebastiano (1672) in S Sebastiano fuori le Mura, where he created a rich design of coloured marbles and an altar elaborated by gilt bronze and amethyst. He also designed the ciborium (1673) for the high altar of the Chiesa Nuova. His renown increased in the artistic circles of Rome, and in 1673 Cosimo III, Grand Duke of Tuscany, anxious to improve Florentine sculpture, turned to him to found an academy at the Palazzo Madama in Rome, where young Florentine artists could study. At the Accademia Fiorentina Ferri instructed both sculptors and painters in drawing; Ercole Ferrata taught sculpture. Ferri's most promising pupil, Giovanni Battista Foggini, spread the decorative style of the Roman Baroque to Florence.

Ferri's great skill in designing motifs to be made in bronze, stucco or wood earned him numerous commissions, and he began to devote his time almost exclusively to preparatory design. His most significant project in this field, commissioned by Cosimo III, was the renovation (1675–85) of the choir chapel in S Maria Maddalena dei Pazzi in Florence, which incorporated decorative tondi (1676–9) by Pier Francesco Silvani and his own painted altarpiece (1684; Madrid, Real Acad. S Fernando). Other commissions were the cover for the font in S Giovanni in Fonte, Rome, from Innocent X (1679); the four statues in gilded bronze (1687–9) for the altar of S Ignazio in Il Gesù, Rome; the altar (*c.* 1682) of S Stefano in the church of the Cavalieri, Pisa; a bronze reliquary (*c.* 1687–9) in the co-cathedral of St John, La Valletta, Malta; and, finally, another commission from Cosimo III, the 14 tondi, in white and blue glazed terracotta, of the Stations of the Cross, originally in the garden of the convent of S Pietro d'Alcantara near the Villa dell'Ambrogiana, Montelupo (three, Montelupo, SS Quirico e Lucia all'Ambrogiana; one, London, V&A). These were carried out in 1685 according to Ferri's designs by students at the Accademia Fiorentina: Anton Francesco Andreozzi, Francesco Ciaminghi (*d* 1736), Giuseppe Piamontini and Camillo Cateni (*c.* 1662–1732).

Whereas Ferri's sculpture and architecture show him achieving a successful synthesis of the decorative styles of Cortona and Bernini, which became widely influential, in the painting of these years he developed a more serious, classical style, which suggests the influence of Carlo Maratti, as in the frescoes of *c.* 1680 or earlier featuring the allegories of *Spring*, *Autumn* (see fig.) and *Winter* on three ceilings in the Villa Falconieri at Frascati. Towards the end of the 1670s he designed one of the tapestries commemorating the significant events of Urban VIII's life

Ciro Ferri: *Allegory of Autumn*, fresco, *c.* 1680 or earlier (Frascati, Villa Falconieri)

and woven in the Barberini tapestry factory. His subject was *Urban VIII Repairing the Walls of Rome* (preparatory drawings, Rome, Gab. N. Stampe, and Windsor Castle, Royal Lib.), for which Pietro Lucatelli (*c.* 1634–1710), another Cortona pupil, made the enlarged cartoon (Berlin, Kupferstichkab.).

From 1681 to 1687 Ferri was Principal of the Accademia di S Luca, of which he had become a member in 1657. In his last years he specialized in designing ephemera, as for example his designs (Berlin, Kupferstichkab.; Florence, Uffizi) for a firework machine for a celebration held in the Piazza Navona to commemorate the capture of Buda from the Turks (engraved by Nicolas Dorigny in 1686). He concentrated especially on designs for ceremonial carriages, including that (Düsseldorf, Kstmus.) for the arrival in Rome on 8 January 1687 of Lord Palmer, Earl of Castlemaine, as ambassador to the Holy See; and another for Rinaldo d'Este, who had come to Rome on 28 October 1688 for nomination as a cardinal. He also made designs for engraving, among them the frontispiece (Rome, Gab. N. Stampe) for *La tesi dell'Abate Jo. Francesco Gomez* (1677) by Pietro Aguila.

BIBLIOGRAPHY

F. S. Baldinucci: *Vite* (1725–30); ed. A. Matteoli (1975), pp. 135–50

L. Pascoli: *Vite* (1730–36), i, pp. 171–6

Cortoneschi a Roma (exh. cat., Rome, Gal. N. A. Ant., 1956) [entries by L. Bianchi]

B. Canestro Chiovenda: 'Ciro Ferri e G. B. Gaulli e la cupola della chiesa di S Agnese in Piazza Navona', *Commentari*, x (1959), pp. 16–23

N. Wiberal: 'Contributo alle ricerche sul cortonismo in Roma: I pittori della galleria di Alessandro VII nel palazzo del Quirinale', *Bol. A.*, xlv/2 (1960), pp. 123–65

K. Noehles: 'Das Tabernakel des Ciro Ferri in der Chiesa Nuova zu Rom', *Miscellanea Bibliothecae Hertzianae*, xvi (Munich, 1961), pp. 429–36

K. Lankheit: *Florentinische Barockplastik: Kunst am Hofe der letzten Medici* (Munich, 1962)

I. Faldi: *I cartoni per gli arazzi Barberini della serie di Urbano VIII* (Rome, 1967)

W. Vitzthum: 'Inventar eines Sammelbandes des späten Seicento mit Zeichnungen von Pietro da Cortona und Ciro Ferri', *Studies in Renaissance and Baroque Art Presented to Anthony Blunt* (London, 1967), pp. 113–16

U. Schlegel: 'Ciro Ferri scultore', *Berlin Mus.*, xix/1 (1969), pp. 37–42

H. W. Kruft: 'A Reliquary by Ciro Ferri in Malta', *Burl. Mag.*, cxii (1970), pp. 629–5

K. Noehles: 'Der Hauptaltar von Santo Stefano in Pisa: Cortona, Ferri, Silvani, Foggini', *Giessen. Beitr. Kstgesch.*, i (1970), pp. 87–123

J. Montagu: 'A Bozzetto in Bronze by C. Ferri', *Jb. Hamburg. Kstsamml.*, xviii (1973), pp. 119–24

The Twilight of the Medici: Late Baroque Art in Florence, 1670–1743 (exh. cat., Detroit, MI, Inst. A., 1974)

M. Campbell: *Pietro Cortona at the Pitti Palace: A Study of the Planetary Rooms and Related Projects* (Princeton, 1977)

Disegni di Pietro da Cortona e Ciro Ferri dalle collezioni del Gabinetto Nazionale delle Stampe (exh. cat. by M. Giannatiempo, Rome, Gab. N. Stampe, 1977); rev. by N. Turner in *Prospettiva*, xvii (1979), pp. 74–7

M. Fagiolo dell'Arco and S. Carandini: *Effimero barocco* (Rome, 1977)

H. W. Kruft: 'Another Sculpture by Ciro Ferri in Malta', *Burl. Mag.*, cxxiii (1981), pp. 26–9

G. Fusconi: 'Per la storia della scultura lignea in Roma: Le carozze di Ciro Ferri per due ingressi solenni', *Antol. B. A.*, 21–2 (1984), pp. 80–97

B. Davis: *The Drawings of Ciro Ferri* (New York and London, 1986)

SIMONETTA PROSPERI VALENTI RODINÒ

Ferrini, Benedetto [Benedetto da Firenze] (*fl* 1453; *d* Bellinzona [now Switzerland], 1 Oct 1479). Italian architect and military engineer. He was one of the first architects in 15th-century Milan to abandon Gothic forms and to introduce elements of the Florentine Renaissance. Although his activity in the service of the dukes of Milan, Francesco Sforza (*see* SFORZA, (1)) and Galeazzo Maria Sforza, is confirmed by numerous documents, very few buildings survive that can be ascribed to Ferrini. In 1461, he was sent to Venice to work on the palace bought by Francesco Sforza, but the attribution to Ferrini of the façade fragment of the so-called Ca' del Duca at Venice can no longer be sustained. His name has, however, been more securely linked with parts of Milan Castle, which he converted (1472–6) into a residence equipped for the requirements of a Renaissance prince. There, he worked on the Corte Ducale with its extensive apartments, and he designed a courtyard arcade with flanking pilasters in the Florentine manner. He was responsible for planning the entire decoration of the Cappella Ducale, and he worked on the Rocchetta, which was used as the state treasury.

In 1471 Ferrini designed and built the Cappella dei Sette Santi in Milan Cathedral, but it has not been identified. Two years later he built the choir of S Maria del Monte at Sacro Monte di Varese (Lombardy), with three apses set out in trefoil plan and a crossing articulated by pilasters supporting an entablature. Documents show that he worked on many ducal castles, including Abbiategrasso

(1469), Vigevano (1471) and Soncino (1473; all in Lombardy), and on the fortifications at Savona in Liguria (1472), but the majority of these either cannot be identified or are lost. A surviving example of Ferrini's military architecture is the Rocca di Sasso Corbaro (1479) in Bellinzona (Switzerland), a castle distinguished by its unusual geometric plan.

BIBLIOGRAPHY

E. Motta: 'I castelli di Bellinzona sotto il dominio degli Sforza', *Boll. Svizzera It.* (1890), pp. 181–219

J. R. Spencer: 'The Ca' del Duca in Venice and Benedetto Ferrini', *J. Soc. Archit. Hist.*, xxix (1970), pp. 3–8

M. Verga Bandirali: 'Documenti per Benedetto Ferrini ingegnere ducale sforzesco, 1453–1479', *A. Lombarda*, 60 (1981), pp. 49–102

L. Patetta: *L'architettura del quattrocento a Milano* (Milan, 1987)

A. E. WERDEHAUSEN

Ferriss, Hugh (*b* St Louis, MO, 12 July 1889; *d* New York, 29 Jan 1962). American architect, draughtsman and theorist. He graduated in architecture in 1911 from Washington University, St Louis, where the teaching was Beaux-Arts oriented. In 1912 he moved to New York where he worked as a draughtsman in the large office of Cass Gilbert until 1915, when he launched his career as a freelance delineator. Although his first jobs were mostly illustrations or advertisements for newspapers or magazines, by the early 1920s finished perspective renderings, particularly of skyscrapers and other commercial architecture, became his principal work. Working in carbon pencil, he perfected a rich and dramatic chiaroscuro technique that exaggerated the monumental qualities of structures, suppressing ornament and detail and reducing buildings to the profound power of their simple mass. This abstraction of building forms, which had great influence on subsequent architecture by others, began with a series of 'zoning envelope' studies, which Ferriss did in 1922 with Harvey Wiley Corbett; these illustrated how the maximum building volumes permitted by New York's setback zoning laws of 1916 could be incrementally refined into finished building designs.

In 1929 Ferriss published his best-known book, *The Metropolis of Tomorrow*. Organized as a three-part thesis, the book examines contemporary skyscraper design, predicts future trends, then proposes a vision of urban Utopia—a rationalized skyscraper city of monumental towers, widely separated and positioned hierarchically in a geometric and symbolic city plan. In his text he charged that the contemporary city suffered from a total lack of planning and warned that architects must preserve human values in the face of inexorable urban growth. Although it was published just after the Wall Street crash, whose effects disillusioned Ferriss about capitalist cities, the book was received enthusiastically, and he was extolled as the USA's principal prophet of the urban future.

From the mid-1930s Ferriss's practice and stature in the architectural establishment grew steadily. He often served as official delineator and design consultant on large projects such as the World's Fair, New York (1936–9), and the United Nations headquarters in New York (1946–9). In 1940 he travelled across the USA sketching outstanding structures built in the previous decade. He was particularly attracted to factories, research centres and bridges, and to the great new hydroelectric dams of the

Tennessee Valley and western states. Many of these drawings were exhibited and later collected in his second book, *Power in Buildings* (1953). Although he was a licensed architect, Ferriss elected to 'build' only on paper. Yet like other great architectural delineators he created a compelling and influential two-dimensional reality.

For illustration *see* ARTIST'S HOUSE, fig. 6.

WRITINGS

The Metropolis of Tomorrow (New York, 1929/*R* 1986 with essay and appendices by C. Willis)
Power in Buildings (New York, 1953)

BIBLIOGRAPHY

J. Ferriss Leich: *Architectural Visions: The Drawings of Hugh Ferriss* (New York, 1980)

CAROL WILLIS

Ferro, Gregorio (*b* Santa Maria de Lamas, La Coruña, 1744; *d* Madrid, 1812). Spanish painter and illustrator. He served in the Benedictine monastery of S Martín Pinario, Santiago de Compostela, and his artistic talents won him the protection of the sculptor Felipe de Castro. Ferro moved to Madrid, where he won several prizes at the Real Academia de Bellas Artes de S Fernando in the 1760s. He was named Academico de Mérito in 1781 and began to work for the court in 1783. He had an aptitude for spectacular and grandiose compositions, which can be seen in his large paintings of religious scenes, such as the altarpiece of the *Holy Family*, painted for S Francisco el Grande, Madrid, or *St Augustine and Child* for the church of the monastery of La Encarnación in Madrid. He also painted canvases for the monastery of S Rosendo in Celanova (untraced) and for the cathedral of Santiago de Compostela as well as painting portraits and historical scenes (e.g. *Charles III Giving the Order for the Declaration of War against England*, 1788; Pontevedra, Mus. Pontevedra). Ferro also executed plates for the Academia de Lengua's edition (1780) of *Don Quixote* and for prints of religious subjects.

Ferro followed the style of Anton Raphael Mengs accurately but unimaginatively, but his paintings also show a familiarity with the work of Velázquez and other Spanish Baroque painters. In 1804 he became Director General of the Real Academia, after competing for the post with Goya.

BIBLIOGRAPHY

A. Cotarelo: 'Gregorio Ferro', *Ultreya* (1919)
R. Iglesia: 'Gregorio Ferro, pintor (1744–1812): Apuntes para su biografía', *Bol. Soc. Esp. Excurs.*, xxxv (1927), pp. 21–42
Marqués de Lozoya: 'El dietario de Gregorio Ferro', *Correo Erud.* (1940)
F. J. Sánchez Cantón: *Escultura y pintura del siglo XVIII: Francisco Goya*, A. Hisp., xvii (Madrid, 1965)

JUAN J. LUNA

Ferrotype. *See under* PHOTOGRAPHY, §I.

Ferrucci. Italian family of artists. Its members came from Fiesole and were active in Tuscany and elsewhere in Italy from the 15th century to the 17th. The most distinguished were the sculptor (1) Francesco di Simone Ferrucci, the sculptor and architect (2) Andrea di Piero Ferrucci and the sculptor (3) Francesco Ferrucci. Francesco di Simone was an eclectic artist who never developed a stable style of his own. He was an accomplished stone-carver and

elegant decorator but lacked a sure grasp of figure construction. A skilful carver, Andrea di Piero's speciality lay in large marble complexes combining architecture, statues and reliefs. As an architect he worked on Florence Cathedral, of which he was *capomaestro* from 1512 until his death. Francesco devoted himself to porphyry-carving, mostly working for the Medici family.

BIBLIOGRAPHY

Thieme–Becker

C. von Fabriczy: 'Die Bildhauerfamilie aus Fiesole', *Jb. Kön.-Preuss. Kstsamml.*, xxix (1908), suppl., pp. 1–28 [doc.]

(1) Francesco di Simone Ferrucci [Fiesolano; da Fiesole] (*b* Fiesole, 1437; *d* Florence, 24 March 1493). Sculptor. Francesco was probably trained by his father, Simone di Nanni Ferrucci (*b* 1402), and was decisively influenced by Desiderio da Settignano and Andrea del Verrocchio. Vasari named him among the pupils of Verrocchio, and it is possible that in the 1470s he assisted the master. He matriculated in the Arte dei Maestri di Pietra e di Legname, the Florentine sculptors' guild, in 1463 and established a workshop in Florence in 1466. By 1470, when he first submitted a *catasto* (land registry declaration), he was married and owned a house in Florence. He does not mention that house in his 1480 *catasto*, but lists another, purchased in 1474. Sometime between 1470 and 1480 he also acquired land near Pistoia.

Between 1460 and 1466 Francesco was employed making decorative carvings for the Badia at Fiesole, and from 1467 to 1478 he worked with his brother Bernardo Ferrucci (*b* 1447) at the convent of SS Annunziata, Florence, where they carved a marble cover for the tomb of Saracino Pucci (1469; untraced). No work by Francesco or Bernardo can be identified at SS Annunziata, but two doorframes in the transept of the Badia at Fiesole and possibly the design of a lavabo in the vestibule of the sacristy of the same church, for the carving of which Gregorio di Lorenzo received payment in 1461, can be attributed to Francesco. The doorframes in the Badia follow closely the decorative repertory and the figural types of Desiderio da Settignano.

Other documents record payments to Francesco for the execution of a holy water stoup (1466) for S Maria in Peretola, near Florence (*in situ*); the carving of the tomb of *Lemmo Balducci* (fragments, Florence, S Egidio) for the hospital of S Matteo, Florence (probably 1471–2), of which Balducci was the founder, and five columns for an altar in the hospital (1472); the execution of an indeterminable work for Prato Cathedral (1476); architectural carving in S Petronio, Bologna (1480); the delivery of a Holy Sacrament tabernacle that he made for the Sisters of S Maria di Monteluce, outside Perugia (1483; *in situ*); and the execution of a marble ciborium on commission from Cardinal Carlo de' Medici for Prato Cathedral (1487). In 1491 Francesco submitted a design (untraced) for the façade of Florence Cathedral, and in 1491 and 1492 he purchased marble from the Opera of the cathedral. Of the recorded projects, only the holy water stoup at Peretola and the Holy Sacrament tabernacle at Monteluce remain intact. The latter shows Francesco borrowing from both Desiderio da Settignano (the figure of the *Blessing Christ Child* is based on one that Desiderio made in the 1460s for his sacramental tabernacle in S Lorenzo, Florence) and

Verrocchio (the paired angels elaborate Verrocchio types, as seen especially in the monument to *Cardinal Niccolò Forteguerri*, started in 1476–7; Pistoia Cathedral). Of the tomb of *Balducci* (disassembled and transferred in 1785 to S Egidio) only a profile portrait of the deceased, a garland frieze and the base with two lion heads and coupled balusters in low relief, survive. The ciborium for Prato Cathedral (dismembered 1638) is also fragmentary, the principal piece being a *Blessing Christ Child* (Prato, Mus. Opera Duomo).

A single signed work by Francesco exists: the marble tomb of *Alessandro Tartagni* (?1477–80; Bologna, S Domenico; see fig.), who died in 1477. This demonstrates that by the late 1470s Francesco's figure and drapery style had changed markedly under the influence of Verrocchio. The seated figures of *Virtues* in the middle zone, with their inflated drapery, are clearly inspired by Verrocchio's style of that period (i.e. late 1470s), although the form of the decorative vocabulary of the monument, in particular the sarcophagus, derive from Desiderio's tomb of *Carlo Marsuppini* (1460s; Florence, Santa Croce). Vasari mentions a tomb of *Pietro Minerbetti* (*d* 1482) in S Pancrazio, Florence, of which only a marble relief of two angels

holding the arms of the Minerbetti family (Detroit, MI, Inst. A.) survives.

A marble relief of a birth and death scene (Florence, Bargello) has been attributed to Francesco but is usually associated with Verrocchio's workshop. Whether the relief belonged to the tomb of *Francesca Tornabuoni* (*d* 1473), as is claimed on the strength of a statement by Vasari in his *Vita* of Verrocchio, and how much Verrocchio had to do with its design are uncertain. But the relief bears the carving method seen in Francesco's portrait of *Balducci* and monument of *Tartagni*, and it may have been executed by him or under his direct supervision. Among other attributions to Francesco, the most notable are the tombs of *Barbara Manfredi* (*d* 1466; Forlì, S Mercuriale); *Vianesio Albergati the elder*, (*c.* 1481; Bologna, S Francesco); *Gian Francesco Oliva* (*d* 1478) and his wife, *Marsibilia Trinci* (*d* 1485), both in the convent of S Francesco at Monte-fiorentino, Province of Pesaro (probably 1485 or shortly after); and three marble reliefs of the *Virgin and Child* (Raleigh, NC Mus. A; London, V&A; Kansas City, MO, Nelson–Atkins Mus. A.). A drawing in Stockholm (Nmus.) is probably a study by Francesco for the *Tartagni* monument before its final design was decided; several designs for altars (London, V&A; Florence, Uffizi; Paris, Louvre) are attributed to him; and a group of sheets (divided between museums in Berlin, Chantilly, Dijon, Hamburg, London, New York and Paris), for the most part of about the same size and nearly all with sketches on both sides, once known as the 'Verrocchio Sketchbook', is generally regarded as from a sketchbook by Francesco and his workshop. Many of these sheets have inscriptions (of *ricordi*, drafts of letters, or accounts, not evidently related to the sketches), and three have dates (1487 and 1488); varying in style and quality, with certain motifs repeated frequently, the sketches suggest the probable intervention of apprentices or assistants drawing from workshop models.

BIBLIOGRAPHY

G. Vasari: *Vite* (1550, rev. 2/1568); ed. G. Milanesi (1878–85)

A. Venturi: 'Francesco di Simone Fiesolano', *Archv. Stor. A.*, v (1892), pp. 371–86

G. Gronau: 'Das sogenannte Skizzenbuch des Verrocchio', *Jb. Kön.-Preuss. Kstsamml.*, xvii (1896), pp. 65–72

A. E. Popham and P. Pouncey: *Italian Drawings in the Department of Prints and Drawings in the British Museum: The Fourteenth and Fifteenth Centuries*, i (London, 1950), pp. 38–40

J. Pope-Hennessy: *Catalogue of Italian Sculpture in the Victoria and Albert Museum*, i (London, 1964), pp. 170–76

C. Seymour jr: *Sculpture in Italy, 1400–1500*, Pelican Hist. A. (Harmonds-worth, 1966), pp. 149, 152–3

U. Middeldorf: *Sculptures from the Samuel H. Kress Collection: European Schools, XIV–XIX Century* (London, 1976), pp. 30–31

P. G. Pasini: 'La cappella dei conti Oliva', *Il Convento di Montefiorentino: Atti del convegno, 29 agosto 1979* (Studi Montefeltrani–Serie Atti dei Convegni, II) (San Leo, 1982), pp. 97–125

Italian Renaissance Sculpture in the Time of Donatello (exh. cat., ed. A. P. Darr; Detroit, MI, Inst. A., 1985), pp. 213–17

(2) Andrea di Piero (di Marco) Ferrucci [da Fiesole] (*b* Fiesole, 1465; *d* Florence, after 25 Oct 1526). Sculptor and architect, first cousin once removed of (1) Francesco di Simone Ferrucci. According to Vasari, he learnt the rudiments of his art from Francesco and completed his training under Michele Maini from Fiesole, of whom nothing else is known. His style was rooted in the realistic tradition of the late 15th century. As he matured it was

Francesco di Simone Ferrucci: marble tomb of *Alessandro Tartagni*, *c.* 1477–80 (Bologna, S Domenico)

Andrea di Piero Ferrucci: altarpiece of the *Crucifixion*, marble, h. 3.66 m, probably 1490s (London, Victoria and Albert Museum)

carry it through. The centrepiece, a life-size *Baptism* in high relief, owes nothing to Benedetto, however, and is one of Andrea's most important surviving sculptures. Also probably from the 1490s, but undocumented, are a marble ciborium and a large marble altarpiece of the *Crucifixion* (both London, V&A; see fig.), which before 1859 were in the former convent of S Girolamo, outside Fiesole. Andrea specialized in large marble altar complexes, combining architecture, statues and reliefs. His model for these appears to have been Andrea Sansovino's Corbinelli Altarpiece (*c.* 1486) in Santo Spirito, Florence, with its tripartite division, in the manner of a triumphal arch, with statues in niches in the main zone, and narrative reliefs above and below.

From at least 1508 Andrea was employed by the Opera of Florence Cathedral, from which, in 1512, he purchased a house in the Borgo Pinti and which, on 16 December 1512, appointed him *capomaestro* of the cathedral, an office he held until the end of his life. In 1508 he was engaged to work on the balustrade for one of the eight sides of the drum of the cupola; in 1512–13 he executed an over life-size marble statue of *St Andrew* for one of the tribune piers. This figure, with its exaggerated pose and awkward proportions, reveals an insecure knowledge of the structure of the human body but an attentiveness to texture and detail in the treatment of hair and flesh. In the handling of the drapery Andrea achieved impressive pictorial effects, emphasizing the softness and texture of the fabric. These bear out Vasari's description of Andrea's art as the outgrowth of a skill acquired through the carving of foliage and aided by a sense of judgement derived from the study of nature, but without the benefit of a sound grounding in drawing.

In 1514 Andrea was commissioned to make a statue of *St Peter* for another tribune pier, though he failed to execute the work and the commission was transferred to Baccio Bandinelli. In 1519 Andrea was engaged on a major project outside Tuscany: a marble altarpiece commissioned by Tamás Bakócz, Cardinal and Archbishop of Esztergom in Hungary, for the Cardinal's chapel in Esztergom Cathedral (*in situ*). This has been much mutilated: three statues that originally stood in niches in the middle zone have disappeared, and two of them have been replaced with modern statues. Other sculptures (mainly a relief of the *Annunciation*, reliefs of the *Evangelists* and a portrait of the kneeling *Cardinal Bakócz*) have been restored. In 1521–2 Andrea was again working in Florence Cathedral, carving the life-size marble commemorative bust of *Marsilio Ficino* for a wall niche next to the Porta dei Canonici. In 1522 he also executed the marble bust of the Florentine chancellor, *Marcello Virgilio Adriani*, for his cenotaph (Florence, S Francesco al Monte alle Croci). In 1524 he was commissioned by Antonia Vespucci to design the tomb of her husband, *Antonio Strozzi*, for S Maria Novella, the execution of which he left to his pupils Silvio Cosini, who carved the statue of the Virgin, and Tommaso di Pietro Boscoli (1503–74), who carved the two angels. On 29 March 1524 Michelangelo engaged Andrea as *capomaestro* of S Lorenzo, to direct the work on the tombs in the Medici Chapel. Among other undocumented works by Andrea are a life-size wooden *Crucifix* in S Felicità, Florence, and a smaller one in S Maria

modified, but only slightly, by the classical trends of the 16th century. Vasari claimed that Andrea worked in the church of the Innocenti at Imola and later in Naples and Rome, but this cannot be substantiated. He was in Naples in 1487, according to his father's *portata dell'estimo*. He may have lived there for several years, possibly engaged on different projects for King Ferdinand I through his promotion by the King's architect and military engineer, Antonio di Giorgio Marchesi (1451–1522) from Settignano, whose daughter he married; but the only certain work he made for Naples, a marble altar (destr. 1757) for the Brancacci Chapel in S Maria Annunziata, was paid for much later, in 1508. Although Andrea is documented as temporarily in residence at Naples in June 1508, by that time he was already in the service of the Opera of Florence Cathedral, and it appears that all his documented works, whether for patrons in Tuscany or elsewhere, were executed in Florence.

The earliest of his documented works are a marble altarpiece with a ciborium for Fiesole Cathedral (*in situ*), commissioned from him in 1488 but not completed until 1492–3, and a marble baptismal font for Pistoia Cathedral (*in situ*), which he executed in 1497–9 with the assistance of Jacopo d'Andrea del Maza, possibly after designs by Benedetto da Maiano. Benedetto had originally been engaged to do the work but died (1497) before he could

Primerana, Fiesole (probably early works), and two marble *Angels* bearing candelabra, installed in Volterra Cathedral, flanking the reliquary tomb (1522) of *St Octavian*.

BIBLIOGRAPHY

G. Vasari: *Vite* (1550, rev. 2/1568); ed. G. Milanesi (1878–85), iv, pp. 475–86

A. Venturi: *Storia* (1901–40), x/1, pp. 179–87

P. Bacci: 'Documenti su Benedetto da Maiano e Andrea da Fiesole relativi al 'fonte battesimale' del duomo di Pistoia', *Riv. A.*, ii (1904), pp. 271–84

J. Balogh: 'La cappella Bakócz di Esztergom', *Acta Hist. A. Acad. Sci. Hung.*, iii (1956), pp. 1–98 (70, 133–5)

J. Pope-Hennessy: *Catalogue of Italian Sculpture in the Victoria and Albert Museum*, i (London, 1964), pp. 179–82

DARIO A. COVI

(3) Francesco [Cecco] **(di Giovanni) Ferrucci (i)** [del Dadda; di Taddeo; del Tadda] (*b* Fiesole or Florence, 1497; *d* Florence, 29 May 1585). Sculptor, great nephew of (1) Francesco di Simone Ferrucci. The son of the stone-carver Giovanni Ferrucci (*b* 1461), he was trained in the family workshop in Fiesole. Under the patronage of Grand Duke Cosimo I de' Medici he was instructed in the virtually lost art of porphyry-carving and is renowned for commissions in this medium that came almost exclusively from the Medici family. Throughout his career he was also active as an architectural and ornamental carver in Florence, Carrara, Loreto and Naples.

In 1555, following a design by Giorgio Vasari, Ferrucci carved the porphyry fountain, surmounted by Andrea del Verrocchio's bronze *Putto with Dolphin*, for the courtyard of the Palazzo Vecchio, Florence. In 1560 he signed a porphyry relief of the *Head of Christ* (Prague, Rudolphinum); several versions of this composition exist, and a *Head of the Virgin* (untraced) may have been its pendant. The *Christ* provides the stylistic comparison against which a large porphyry portrait relief of *Cosimo I de' Medici* (after 1569; London, V&A) is attributed to him, and this is the finest of his portrait reliefs. Further portraits of *Cosimo I* and his wife, *Eleanora de Toledo*, and a signed *Cosimo il vecchio* (all Florence, Pal. Medici–Riccardi) may be those described by Vasari; another group of reliefs of other members of the Medici family (Florence, Bargello) are attributed to him, but their inferior carving suggests that they are probably workshop productions. He is reported to have sculpted two portraits of *Girolamo Savonarola*, one in the round (both untraced), and he carved the tomb of *Giovanni Francesco Vegio* (*d* 1554) in the Camposanto in Pisa.

Between *c*. 1570 and 1581, with assistance from his son Romolo Ferrucci (*d* 1621), Ferrucci carved the porphyry statue of *Justice* surmounting the antique granite column erected in 1566 in the Piazza Santa Trinita, Florence, to commemorate Cosimo I's victory over Republican exiles at the Battle of Montemurlo (1537). The work received a mixed critical reception, despite the considerable technical achievement of carving the monumental figure. A number of heads of *Alexander the Great* (Florence, Uffizi; Bargello; Mus. Opificio Pietre Dure) have been associated with his workshop. His own porphyry *Self-portrait* for his tomb in S Girolamo in Fiesole (transferred 1854 to Fiesole Cathedral) was carved in 1576.

BIBLIOGRAPHY

Thieme–Becker

G. Vasari: *Vite* (1550, rev. 2/1568); ed. G. Milanesi (1878–85), iv, pp. 475–87

D. Di Castro Moscati: 'The Revival of the Working of Porphyry in Sixteenth-century Florence', *Apollo*, cxxvi (1987), pp. 242–8

ANTONIA BOSTRÖM

Ferrucci, Francesco (ii) (*fl* Florence, 1589–1612). Italian craftsman. He was probably a member of the FERRUCCI family of sculptors and masons. He was active in the Galleria dei Lavori, the Medici Grand Ducal manufactory in Florence (*see* FLORENCE, §III, 2(i)), and was one of the first Florentine artisans to attempt the difficult technique of pietra dura mosaic. He is known through documents of the late 16th century and early 17th relating to certain works using this technique. He is first mentioned in 1589 as carving letters in lapis lazuli for the coats of arms of Tuscan cities for the Cappella dei Principi, Florence. In 1597 he produced a portrait in soft stone of *Cosimo I* (Florence, Mus. Opificio Pietre Dure), based on an oil painting by Domenico Passignano. Ferrucci's supremacy in stone mosaic portraiture was such that he was commissioned to make portraits of *Henry IV, King of France*, a wedding gift from Marie de' Medici to her bridegroom, and of *Ferdinando I* (both untraced). The last recorded work that Ferrucci did for the Medici was the pietra dura pavement (*in situ*) of the chapel of SS Annunziata, Florence, commissioned by Ferdinando I at the end of the 16th century and still under construction in 1611–12.

BIBLIOGRAPHY

A. M. Giusti, P. Mazzoni and A. Pampaloni Martelli: *Il Museo dell'Opificio delle Pietre Dure a Firenze* (Milan, 1978), nos 39, 456

D. Di Castro Moscati: 'The Revival of the Working of Porphyry in Sixteenth-century Florence', *Apollo*, cxxvi (1987), pp. 242–8

A. M. Giusti: *Tesori di pietre dure a Firenze: Itinerario per i musei e i luoghi d'arte* (Milan, 1989)

ANNAMARIA GIUSTI

Ferstel, Heinrich von (*b* Vienna, 7 July 1828; *d* Vienna, 14 July 1883). Austrian architect. He was a member of the second generation of historicist architects in Vienna, who continued and developed the pioneering work of such architects as Karl Rösner, Eduard Van der Nüll and August von Siccardsburg. These three, who represented the Romantic period of early historicism in Austria, were Ferstel's teachers from 1848 to 1850 at the Akademie der Bildenden Künste in Vienna, and VAN DER NÜLL & SICCARDSBURG in particular were important early influences. After leaving the academy, Ferstel joined the architectural firm of his uncle Friedrich Stache (1814–95), whom he assisted until 1853 in building castles and country houses for the high nobility in Bohemia. Domestic architecture continued to play an important part in his work. Before long, however, he was winning major architectural competitions, such as the international competition (1855) for the Votivkirche (1856–79; see fig.) in Vienna.

Built to commemorate the rescue of Emperor Francis Joseph (*reg* 1848–1916) from an assassination attempt in 1853, the new church was to be the only religious building on what became the Ringstrasse. It was also the first serious example of neo-Gothic architecture on an international level in Austria. The basic basilica design, with transept, is accompanied by four octagonal chapels and a chevet. Twin towers with elaborate spires flank the front

Heinrich von Ferstel: Votivkirche, Vienna, 1856–79

centred on the equestrian statue of Prince Carl Schwarzenberg, represented the most perfect urban achievement of Viennese historicism. Of the four buildings designed by Ferstel for the square, the palace (1863–9) for Archduke Ludwig Viktor was the most prominent.

At the same time, Ferstel was vying for important public commissions on the new Ringstrasse, and he produced designs for the great architectural competitions of the 1860s, including the Exchange (1863), the Parliament building (1865) and the Hofmuseen Imperial Museums (1867), none of which was realized. In 1866, thanks to his friendship with the art historian Rudolf von Eitelberger (1817–85), Ferstel received the commission for the Österreichisches Museum für Kunst und Industrie (now Österreichisches Museum für Angewandte Kunst). It was modelled on the South Kensington Museum (now Victoria and Albert Museum) in London, and Ferstel's design was based mainly on the Renaissance brick architecture of northern Italy. A large central palazzo court was adorned with elegant two-storey arcades and covered with a glass roof. The museum was intended to represent the historicist ideal of the *Gesamtkunstwerk*, and its exhibits and decoration were meant to stimulate contemporary artistic production. Ferstel later added the much simpler brick Kunstgewerbeschule (1873–7) to the museum.

The most famous work of Ferstel's later years is the Universität (1873–84). A new university had been planned since 1854, with Van der Nüll & Siccardsburg the commissioned architects. They originally designed a neo-Gothic university complex on the site of the Votivkirche, and when the church was planned they adapted their scheme, designing a range of 'medieval' university buildings behind it. As the architect of the Votivkirche, Ferstel strongly objected to this project, which he thought would lessen the monumental character of his church. In 1869 he was appointed university architect, but he could proceed only after a suitable site had been found (1870) on the former parade ground next to the church. The idea of a complex was rejected, so Ferstel had to develop a monolithic building to house all four faculties, lecture and ceremony halls, library and offices: an unprecedented task. To design an effective ground-plan, he freely adopted the system of Late Antique *thermae*, which allowed him a satisfactory grouping of large architectural masses. The exterior was designed in a blend of French and Italian Renaissance forms. In its exaggerated use of Renaissance elements, however, the university marks the end of the purist period of Viennese historicism and anticipates the taste for excess and grandeur that dominated for the rest of the century.

of the building. The entire church is a remarkably mature variation on the typical French Gothic cathedral, enriched with elements of German Gothic. The Votivkirche thus marks a turning-point in the development of Viennese historicism. It rejects the stylistic synthesis of the early, Romantic historicism, which was then still dominant, in favour of the Renaissance revival of the 1860s. Yet Ferstel also designed one of the main works of early historicism in Vienna, when he won, against Theophilus Hansen and Van der Nüll & Siccardsburg, the closed competition for the Bank and Börsengebäude (1855–60) in the heart of the city. Instead of the usual brick, Ferstel used expensive stone, which revealed the decorative richness and wealth of invention in his architecture, as well as his high artistic and technical standards.

In the 1860s Ferstel's buildings reflected either the Romantic or neo-Renaissance style, according to their social and aesthetic function. In his designs for private architecture Ferstel promoted the detached house based on those he had seen on a visit to England in 1851. He designed a number of these in a rather picturesque neo-Gothic style, but very few were built, the Viennese tradition of the huge city *Zinspalast* (block of flats) being too strong for such innovations. However, Ferstel's ideas were realized on the outskirts of Vienna, at Währing and Döbling, where the 'cottage' district of small villas with little gardens was constructed in 1872. More important, however, was Ferstel's design for the Schwarzenbergplatz. The square,

WRITINGS

with R. von Eitelberger: *Das bürgerliche Wohnhaus und das Wiener Zinshaus* (Vienna, 1860)

BIBLIOGRAPHY

R. von Eitelberger: *Ferstel und die Votivkirche*, Gesammelte kunsthistorische Schriften, i (Vienna, 1879), p. 277
M. von Ferstel: 'Die neue k. k. Universität in Wien', *Allg. Bauztg Abbild.*, lix (1894)
N. Wibiral: *Heinrich von Ferstel und der Historismus in der Baukunst des 19. Jahrhunderts* (diss., U. Vienna, 1952)
Österreichisches biographisches Lexikon, i (Graz and Cologne, 1957)
H. -R. Hitchcock: *Architecture: Nineteenth and Twentieth Centuries*, Pelican Hist. A. (Harmondsworth, 1958, 4/1977/R 1978), pp. 70, 213–14

N. Wibiral and R. Mikula: *Heinrich von Ferstel*, Die Wiener Ringstrasse: Bild einer Epoche, viii/3 (Wiesbaden, 1974)
Heinrich von Ferstel: Bauten und Projekte für Wien (exh. cat., ed. R. Kassal-Mikula; Vienna, Hist. Mus.; Vienna, Hermesvilla; 1983)

SUSANNE KRONBICHLER-SKACHA

Ferster [**Förster**], **Hans** (*fl* 1634–53; *d* 1653). German architect, active in Sweden. He worked in Stockholm from 1634, completing the church of St Jakob and enlarging St Gertrude's, the German church (both 1634–43). He was also responsible for the small parish and castle church (1638–40) in Tyresö, outside Stockholm, but his main achievement was the monumental, copper-roofed (later slated) Kristine church (1642–*c*. 1665; completed posthumously) at Falun in Dalecarlia. In addition he may have worked at Tyresö Castle and organized the building of Jakobsdal Castle, both near Stockholm, and he was engaged in the construction of private houses and official buildings in Stockholm. Ferster is regarded as a master of vaulting: his churches in Stockholm and Falun are characterized by their fine patterns of stylized Late Gothic design, employing star and net vaulting derived from the cellular vaults typical of east Prussia. They are basically Gothic in appearance, with polygonal choir walls, wall buttresses, tall, rounded, mullioned windows and medieval-looking towers crowned by Gothic spires or Renaissance lanterns. Only the latter features and such decorative traits as angle quoins, mouldings and consoles under the vaults show more contemporary forms. The exteriors are in brick with stone details, the bricks in the Kristine church in Falun being arranged in an elaborate pattern of rhomboids. Ferster's work may be considered representative of post-Gothic architecture. In Sweden the clash between consciously upheld traditional forms and those of Palladian or contemporary French origin is illustrated by the Swedish Crown's overlapping promotion of Ferster's Gothic church in Falun and the Palladian cathedral church (*c*. 1660–1702) by Nicodemus Tessin (i) at Kalmar in Småland. It was Ferster's style of building, however, that exerted a prolonged influence on many minor builders and craftsmen in Sweden.

BIBLIOGRAPHY
B. Flodin: *Murmästaren Hans Ferster: Verksamheten i Sverige, 1634–1653* [The master mason Hans Ferster: activity in Sweden, 1634–1653] (Lidingö, 1974) [Ger. summary]

TORBJÖRN FULTON

Ferté, Denis-Pierre-Jean Papillon de La. *See* PAPILLON DE LA FERTÉ, DENIS-PIERRE-JEAN.

Fertőd [formerly Eszterháza]. Town in Győr–Sopron County, western Hungary, 27 km south-east of Sopron. It is the site of the Esterházy Palace, the largest Rococo building of its kind in Hungary. The original manor house, which is the core of the building, was constructed in 1721 by Anton Erhard Martinelli. Between 1764 and 1784 Prince Miklós Esterházy (*see* ESTERHÁZY, §I(3)) extended it on the basis of his own plans, although Melchior Hefele was the architect chiefly involved in its rebuilding. Several architects, including Miklós Jakoby, collaborated on the project. The park was created in Baroque style and is also credited to Esterházy, although after his death it fell into

disrepair. Parts of the building were damaged in 1944–5, and restoration was carried out in 1958–9.

The elevation of the main building is a three-storey central block of eleven bays, the three central bays of which have an additional storey and project slightly. The ground floor is banded, and the balconied storeys above are articulated by giant pilasters. Two wings of the same elevation as the central block extend out, forming a large *cour d'honneur*, the inner angles of which are curved. The court is closed off at its front end by balconied wings of one storey with blind arcades and by an ornate Rococo wrought-iron gate adorned with vases. A fountain of a cherub with a dolphin is in the centre of the courtyard. Six bays of the garden façade project towards the extensive formal gardens designed in the French manner. The grounds originally had a music house (destr.) where Joseph Haydn was resident composer and Kapellmeister from 1761. There was also a Chinese house, hermitage, puppet theatre and picture gallery (all destr.). On the ground floor the Sala Terrena (one of 126 rooms) has a ceiling frescoed (1766) by Josef Ignaz Mildorfer (*see* HUNGARY, fig. 16). Johann Basilius Grundmann (1726–98) executed a fresco of *Apollo on the Chariots of the Sun* in the banquet hall on the first floor; the room also contains sculptures of the *Four Seasons* by Johann Joseph Rössler. The chapel has frescoes by Mildorfer. After years of neglect, the interior of the palace was restored by Zsigmond Babics at the end of the 19th century.

BIBLIOGRAPHY
L. Fülep, ed.: *A magyarországi művészet története* [The history of art in Hungary], 2 vols (Budapest, 1956, rev. 1970)
A. Kampis: *The History of Art in Hungary* (London, 1966)
L. Németh: *A Concise History of Hungarian Art* (Budapest, 1976); Eng. trans. by E. Hoch (Budapest, 1976)
M. Sallay: *The Esterházy Palace at Fertőd* (Budapest, 1979)
D. Dercsényi: *Historical Monuments and their Protection in Hungary* (Budapest, 1984)

BARBRA RUCKRIEGEL EGERVÁRY

Fesch, Joseph (*b* Ajaccio, Corsica, 3 Jan 1763; *d* Rome, 13 May 1839). French cardinal and collector of Swiss–Italian origin. He was the half-brother of Letizia Ramolino Bonaparte (1750–1836), mother of the future Emperor Napoleon I, to whom Fesch was close in age. Between *c*. 1796 and his death in 1839 he formed one of the largest private collections of paintings of the early 19th century.

Fesch studied at the seminary in Aix-en-Provence, later becoming Archdeacon of Ajaccio. He was favourable to Revolutionary ideas and took the constitutional oath in 1791, opposing the partisans of Corsican independence (Corsica had been ceded to France by Genoa in 1768). In 1793 he was obliged to escape to France and temporarily left the priesthood. During Napoleon's campaigns in Italy (1796–8) Fesch became, through his offices, a supplier to the French army: his wealth and his love for painting can be dated from this time. No doubt he profited from his nephew's situation and from plundering by French soldiers; his first acquisitions were given him by a terrified Ferdinando III, Grand Duke of Tuscany, from his own fine collection. However, he also frequented public sales and dealers.

Fesch returned to Paris in 1800 and began to acquire paintings at an extraordinary rate. He returned to religious life in 1802 and was made Archbishop of Lyon and then Cardinal of S Lorenzo-in-Lucina. From 1803 to 1806 he was French Ambassador in Rome, replacing the collector François Cacault, and when he returned to Paris in 1806 he was appointed Grand Almoner of France. He used his considerable income to augment his collection, taking advantage of the dispersal of a number of other collections to acquire (probably with the help of the dealer Jean-Baptiste-Pierre Le Brun) French, Dutch and Flemish paintings, as well as Italian works from some of the great Roman patrician families. In 1812, however, he quarrelled with the Emperor about his loyalty to Pius VII and lost his position, retiring to his diocese in Lyon before settling in August 1815 permanently with his sister in Rome, where he died; he did not resign from his archbishopric.

Fesch's residence in Rome was the Palazzo Falconieri in the Via Giulia, where he displayed his finest pieces; he also rented other dwellings in which he stored the rest of his huge collection. The antique and modern sculptures, which were difficult to transport and which he subsequently gave up collecting, as well as a number of apparently second-rate paintings that he had left in Paris, were sold at auction in Paris and London in 1816, 1817, 1819 and 1824. In Rome he led the life of an exile of limited resources, dividing his time between pious activities and the search for new paintings.

According to the inventory drawn up at his death (Rome, Archv Cent. Stato), Fesch's collection then comprised nearly 16,000 works; the high proportion of copies and mediocre works, mostly a result of their having been acquired in bulk, was possibly also associated with his plan to found a school for priests, with branches in Paris and Rome, that would provide an artistic education. However, there were also many masterpieces, including Giotto's *Dormition of the Virgin*, Fra Angelico's *Last Judgement* and Rembrandt's *Preaching of John the Baptist* (all Berlin, Gemäldegal.); Gabriel Metsu's *Sleeping Hunter* and Nicolas Poussin's *Dance to the Music of Time* (both London, Wallace); and Mantegna's *Agony in the Garden* and a Raphael *Crucifixion* (both London, N.G.). His tastes were fairly conventional, and his coverage of most periods of art history is notable mainly for its thoroughness. His awareness of the Italian 'Primitives' and of 17th-century art was influenced by Jean-Baptiste Séroux d'Agincourt and other members of the French legation in Rome. Apart from Watteau (paintings now in London, Wallace), he showed little interest in 18th-century French painting, nor, apart from family portraiture, in contemporary work; nor, unlike his nephew Lucien Bonaparte, in Spanish painting. His own portrait was sculpted by Antonio Canova in 1807–8 (marble; Ajaccio, Mus. Fesch).

In his will Fesch divided his collection into two unequal parts, leaving copies, sketches, portraits and 'some original paintings from each of the schools and some sculptures of the Crucifixion' to the Institut des Etudes, Ajaccio, which he had founded (work on the building started after his death). His heir was Joseph Bonaparte, who was initially hostile to these bequests but, after long negotiations with the town of Ajaccio, eventually sent 1000 objets d'art and 300 other paintings to be divided between various Corsican communes. The Musée Fesch, Ajaccio, was opened in 1852 and contains an overwhelming majority of Italian paintings: about 40 'Primitives' from the 14th century in Umbria and Rimini, including a 14th-century triptych of the *Calvary*, the *Adoration of the Magi* and the *Vision of the Blessed Claire of Rimini* that is one of the major works of the early period of the Rimini school, and others from the 14th and 15th centuries, including Bernardo Daddi's *Bishop Saint*, Sandro Botticelli's *Virgin and Child*, Giovanni Boccati's *Virgin with Angels* and Cosimo Tura's *Virgin and Saints*. The several hundred works from the 17th and 18th centuries include paintings by Giovanni Battista Gaulli, Andrea Pozzo, Corrado Giaquinto, Poussin and an astonishing series of Neapolitan still-lifes (e.g. *Still-life with a Monkey*, attributed to Giovanni Battista Ruoppolo, and *Still-life with a Skate* by Giuseppe Recco).

The Grande Galerie, consisting of about 3300 of the finest paintings in Fesch's collection, was sold at auction in Rome between 1843 and 1845; the most important of these was the double sale of 1845, first of Flemish, Dutch, German and French works (including Adriaen van de Velde's *Flight of Jacob*, Meindert Hobbema's *View of Holland* and two paintings of the *Virgin and Child* by Jan van Eyck), then of Italian paintings (including Vincenzo Foppa's *Adoration of the Magi* and Ercole de' Roberti's *Israelites Gathering Manna*; both London, N.G.), covered by a single catalogue published that year. Some paintings were acquired by the Bonaparte family and by collectors such as Samuel Woodburn, Walter Davenport Bromley, Bernard Mancel (1798–1872) and Spiridon *père*; most, however, were sold to dealers. The rest of this unrivalled collection was sold off in lots of 50 or 100 paintings a day, by size.

BIBLIOGRAPHY

Abbé Lyonnet: *Le Cardinal Fesch, archevêque de Lyon, primat des Gaules*, 2 vols (Lyon, 1841)

Galerie de feu S. E. le cardinal Fesch: Catalogue raisonné des tableaux de cette galerie, accompagné de notices historiques et analytiques … par George, Commissaire-Expert du Musée Royal du Louvre (sale cat., Rome, 17–18 March 1845)

Abbé Vanel: 'Deux Livres de comptes du cardinal Fesch, archevêque de Lyon', *Bull. Hist. Dioc. Lyon*, iv (1922); v (1923)

A. Latreille: *Napoléon et le Saint-Siège (1801–1808): L'Ambassade du cardinal Fesch à Rome* (Paris, 1935)

J. Thuillier: 'Les Tableaux du Cardinal-oncle', *L'Oeil*, xxxiv (1957), pp. 32–41

D. Carrington: 'Cardinal Fesch, a Grand Collector', *Apollo*, lxxxvi (1967), pp. 346–57

F. Haskell: *Rediscoveries in Art: Some Aspects of Taste, Fashion and Collecting in England and France* (London, 1976, 2/1980)

D. Thiébaut: *Ajaccio, musée Fesch: Les Primitifs italiens* (Paris, 1987)

DOMINIQUE THIÉBAUT

Feselen [Feselein], **Melchior** (*b* ?Nördlingen, *c.* 1495; *d* Ingolstadt, 10 April 1538). German painter. A family named Feselen is documented in Nördlingen at the beginning of the 16th century. The account-books of Unsere-Liebe-Frau-Kirche in Ingolstadt, the only source for Feselen's life, mention him as living in the town as an independent painter in 1521. In 1522 he was paid for an altarpiece and a panel painting, and he is again entered in 1528 and 1533. He would have received his basic training in Nördlingen, thus being influenced by Hans Schäufelein. Before settling in Ingolstadt, he clearly went to Passau: the first work that can be confirmed as his, a winged altar (1520) at Schloss Haidenburg near Passau, reveals Schäufelein's teaching in the figure types of the standing saints on the reverse and the taut disposition of their robes. The scenes on the front, however, *St Elizabeth Distributing Alms* and *St Roch Being Cured by an Angel*, show the influence of Wolf Huber—then working on the *St Anne* altar (1515–21) for Feldkirch—in the imaginative buildings and in landscapes, the form and expressiveness of which link Feselen with the Danube school.

In Ingolstadt, Feselen enjoyed a privileged position as the town's foremost painter. What survives of the many altars and small panels painted between 1522 and 1524 for local patrons shows him developing a less ambitious manner of painting, one nonetheless tied to popular taste and animated in its narrative, with a happy juxtaposition of figures and landscape. Later, still working from Ingolstadt, he received more important court commissions. He contributed, alongside Altdorfer and other leading painters, to the cycle of historical paintings commissioned by Duke William IV of Bavaria: the *Scene from Porsenna's Siege of Rome* is marked 1529, and *Julius Caesar's Siege of the City of Alesia* 1533 (both Munich, Alte Pin.). (A third picture from this series, once in Stockholm, is untraced.) These are remarkable works, derivative of Altdorfer, yet somewhat dry, being full of closely packed but unresolved details. On the other hand, parts of an altar from 1531 (*Adoration of the Magi* and *Burial and Assumption of Mary*, both Ingolstadt, Bayer. Armeemus.; other parts in various priv. cols), probably painted for the new Schloss Neuburg an der Donau belonging to Elector Otto Henry of the Palatinate, indicate renewed familiarity with the work of Wolf Huber: large, even hefty figures with heads characteristic of Huber's head studies (1522; Vienna, Ksthist. Mus.) and of his later works. Nothing has survived of the wall paintings that Feselen supposedly executed in 1536 at Neuburg.

BIBLIOGRAPHY
NDB; Thieme–Becker
G. M. Richter: 'Melchior Feselen: Ein Beitrag zur Geschichte der oberdeutschen Kunst im XVI. Jahrhundert', *Oberbayer. Archv*, liv (1909), pp. 191ff, 226ff
G. Mammel: *Albrecht Altdorfers 'Nachfolger' in Altbayern und die Landschaft als Bildgegenstand* (diss., U. Erlangen, 1951), pp. 34ff
P. Strieder: 'Melchior Feseleins Marienaltar von 1531', *Münchn. Jb. Bild. Kst*, n.s. 2, xii (1961), pp. 184–91
G. Goldberg: *Die Alexanderschlacht und die Historienbilder des bayerischen Herzogs Wilhelm IV und seiner Gemahlin Jacobea für die Münchner Residenz* (Munich, 1983), pp. 34–40

JANEZ HÖFLER

Feshin, Nikolay (Ivanovich) (*b* Kazan', 8 Dec 1881; *d* Los Angeles, 5 Oct 1955). Russian painter, active mainly in the USA. He trained in his father's gilding and joinery workshop, which produced iconostases. In 1901–8 he studied at the Higher Artistic School of the Academy of Arts, St Petersburg; the last two years were spent in the studio of Il'ya Repin. The figure composition of his diploma painting *Woman Cutting Cabbages* (1908–9; St Petersburg, Acad. A., Sci. Res. Mus.), which depicts the preparation of cabbages for the winter, is of a lively folkloric nature. From 1910 to the early 1920s Feshin revealed himself as a master of psychologically sensitive portraits saturated with colour, such as those of *Varya Adoratskaya* (1914) and *T. A. Popova* (1917; both Kazan', Mus. F.A. Tatarstan). He was an accomplished colourist: he used bold, bright colours that seemed to be lit from

within, and at the same time he knew how to extract enchanting effects from the harmonious combination of subdued tones in a restrained golden-ochre of silver-lilac range. In a series of genre pictures, which remained in sketch form, he produced memorable depictions of the drama of the revolutionary period, for example *Famine* (1921) and *Uprising in the Rear of Kolchak's Troops* (1923; both Kazan', Mus. F.A. Tatarstan).

In 1923 Feshin settled in the USA, where he took advantage of his fame as a portraitist and created a series of memorable portraits of Russian cultural leaders, renowned emigrants (e.g. of the sculptor *Sergey Konyonkov*, charcoal and chalk, 1929; Moscow, Konyonkov Mus.) and the American élite. He dedicated a series of expressive painted and drawn cycles to his impressions as a traveller, depicting American Indians, Mexican peasants and natives from the island of Bali. The most important works from his American period are kept in Feshin's museum in Santa Fe, New Mexico.

BIBLIOGRAPHY
P. Dul'sky: *N. I. Feshin* (Kazan', 1921)
H. Cracken: *Nicolai Feshin* (New York, 1961)
Nikolay Feshin (Leningrad, 1965) [with plates]
N. I. Feshin: Dokumenty, pis'ma, vospominaniya o khudozhnike [N. I. Feshin: documents, letters and recollections about the artist] (Leningrad, 1975)

SVETLANA M. CZERWONNAJA

Festetits, Samuel, Graf von (*b* 1806; *d* 1862). Austrian collector. A wealthy landowner, he lived primarily in Vienna, where he was part of the circle of the medallist Johann Daniel Böhm (1794–1865) and the dealer Georg Plach. As an art patron, he was a founding member *c.* 1850 of the Österreichische Kunstverein. His collection consisted mostly of paintings, drawings and prints by Italian, Netherlandish, Dutch and German Old Masters (e.g. Jacob van Ruisdael's *Wooded Landscape*; Vienna, Österreich. Mus. Kst & Ind.), which were acquired from such major collections as that of Balthasar Speth in Munich and those of Adamovic, Graf Georg Apponyi, Baranowsky, Hess, Lechi and Böhm in Vienna. In addition, he also bought important pictures from Italy, including a 14th-century altarpiece from a vestry in Lucca. The collection was sold in 1859 (Vienna, Artaria & Altmann, 7 March) and included 162 paintings. Plach appears to have acquired all of the remaining pictures, although more than 40 paintings from the collection entered the gallery of Herren Gsell, which was sold in 1872. Most of Festetits's collection of drawings was acquired by Dräxler von Carin and, much later, entered the collection of Klinkosch. Clairmont and Duchâteau in Paris acquired virtually all of the prints from Festetits's collection. In 1884 paintings that had remained with Graf Andor de Festetits were sold at auction (Amsterdam, Roos, 22–23 Jan).

BIBLIOGRAPHY
T. von Frimmel: *Lexikon der Wiener Gemäldesammlungen*, i (Munich, 1913), pp. 352–87
F. Lugt: *Marques* (1921), p. 163, no. 926

Festoon. Carved, moulded or painted ornament representing a chain or loop of fruit, flowers or leaves, suspended at both ends and often represented as bound with ribbons. It is sometimes distinguished from a swag, which may be defined as a piece of cloth or drapery hung in the same shape and also widely used as a decorative device in architecture and decoration. The device originated in Classical antiquity, when festoons of real fruit were hung between the skulls of slaughtered sacrificial animals and the sacrificial instruments. Later the festoon was applied as carved decoration to temple friezes and became part of the repertory of motifs used in secular architecture. The device has been widely applied in revivals of the classical style in architecture, interior decoration and, particularly from the 17th century, as an ornament on furniture, carpets, pottery and plate. Its forms are always slightly altered according to the prevailing taste and range from rich and elaborate clustered festoons of the Baroque period to the light and flowing festoons of the Neo-classical. In the Renaissance the festoon became one of the chief decorative motifs; instead of animal skulls or bucrania, ribbons, rosettes, masks and figures were incorporated into the design. The festoon was also popular during the Neo-classical period and was a frequent decorative feature of interiors by Robert Adam (i).

BIBLIOGRAPHY

F. S. Meyer: *Systematisch geordnetes Handbuch der Ornamentik* (Leipzig, 1888); Eng. trans. as *A Handbook of Ornament* (New York and London, n.d.)
P. Lewis and G. Darley: *Dictionary of Ornament* (London, 1986), pp. 128–9

Festos. *See* PHAISTOS.

Festsaal [Ger.: 'festival hall']. Largest room in a German castle or abbey, used for ceremonial occasions.

Fesulis, Andrea de. *See* ANDREA DA FIESOLE.

Feszl, Frigyes (*b* Pest [now Budapest], 20 Feb 1821; *d* Budapest, 25 July 1884). Hungarian architect. After studying under József Hild and Mihály Pollack in Hungary, he enrolled in 1839 at the Akademie der Bildenden Künste, Munich, where he was taught by Leo von Klenze, Friedrich von Gärtner and Friedrich Bürklein. Between 1840 and 1844 he worked in Bürklein's studio and afterwards went on a study tour of Germany, northern Italy, Switzerland, France and Austria. From 1845 to 1854 he formed a partnership with Lipót Kauser (1818–77) and Károly Gerster (1819–67) in Pest. A characteristic work of the partnership is the Balassovits House (1848–9), 57 Váci Street, Pest, built in the RUNDBOGENSTIL. For houses he designed Feszl frequently commissioned interior wall paintings on heroic nationalist themes, for example in the Heckenast Villa (*c.* 1850), Pilismarót, which was surrounded by an impressive Romantic garden. He built the Kochmeister Villa, 71 Budakeszi Road, Budapest (1852; with L. Kauser and K. Gerster), in the style of a timber-framed Swiss cottage. His striving for a recognizably Hungarian Romantic architecture is best expressed in the Vigadó Concert Hall (1860–64; interior altered after 1945), Budapest. This one- and two-storey building in the *Rundbogenstil* combines ornamentation in Moorish and Byzantine Revival styles with Hungarian decorative motifs, including reliefs of dancing peasants. Feszl's later buildings show a retreat from Romantic historicism, for example in

the Vicarage and Grammar School (1873–4), Nagymező Street, and the Mayer House (1883–4), 36 Bajza Street, both in Budapest. Among his many unexecuted designs are a Gothic Revival Parliament Building (1845), Budapest, an urban plan (1871; both Budapest, Hung. N. Archvs) for Budapest, and designs for the town hall (drawings 1872; Budapest, Hung. Mus. Archit.) of Nagykanizsa, the Art Hall (1874), Budapest, and the parish church (1884; both Budapest, Hung. N. Archvs), Köbánya, Budapest. His fantasy drawings for a 'Hungarian Memorial' (Budapest, Hung. Mus. Archit.) are remarkable examples of his use of metaphorical images. They show a ruinous ledge upheld by peasant figures: a probable reference to Hungary's lost War of Independence (1848–9).

BIBLIOGRAPHY

F. Vámos: 'Adalékok Feszl Frigyes építészetéhez és munkásságához' [Comments on the life and art of Frigyes Feszl], *Építés-Építészettudomány*, xvi (1984), pp. 109–38
Feszl Frigyes, 1821–1884 (exh. cat., ed. D. Komarik; Budapest, Hung. Mus. Archit., 1984)

ÁKOS MORAVÁNSZKY,
KATALIN MORAVÁNSZKY-GYÖNGY

Fête champêtre [Fr.: 'rural festival']. Term used to describe the depiction of figures enjoying pleasures in an open-air setting. The mood is frequently one of reverie, the figures appearing to be affected by the beauty of the pastoral landscape and, often, by music. Women, generally unclothed or partly clothed in early examples, may be nymphs, muses or general personifications of love; men, usually clothed, are often shepherds or courtiers and are shown under love's spell, attempting to woo their partners. The theme can first be identified in 16th-century Italian art, notably in Venice in the paintings of Giorgione and Titian, although the term *fête champêtre* was not applied at the time. Its development can be traced through to the 18th century when a variant, known as the *fête galante* (Fr.: 'courtship party'), practised principally by French artists (notably Antoine Watteau, Nicolas Lancret and Jean-Baptiste Pater), gained popularity as a genre. Subsequently, from the early 19th century the term *fête champêtre* was increasingly applied to the earlier Italian works and to the theme as a whole.

1. Precursors. 2. 16th–17th centuries. 3. 18th century. 4. Revival: mid-19th century–early 20th.

1. PRECURSORS. The precursors of the *fête champêtre* are medieval and early Renaissance manuscript illuminations, panel paintings and cassoni, tapestries and engravings that show lords and ladies in enclosed gardens, whiling away the time in pleasurable pursuits of love, music-making and dancing. The images, sometimes seen as visual counterparts to chivalric poems, are usually secular variations on the themes of the Garden of Eden or the Virgin in an enclosed bower or garden. Often accompanied by sumptuous banquets, they are either allegories of the Three Ages or the Senses or are representations of escape from the realities of the world (the Plague is often depicted as raging outside the walls). For example, in *The Seignorial Life (Courtly Life)* (*c.* 1500; Paris, Mus. Cluny), a set of French tapestries, the garden is a setting for a life in exquisite quarantine devoted to the pursuit of pleasure.

Here, a noble lady bathes while being serenaded by a woman on a lute and a man on a wind instrument.

2. 16TH–17TH CENTURIES. The cultivated and artificial worlds of the medieval period gave way to more natural ones in 16th-century Venetian and northern Italian art, in which figures are no longer sheltered but are situated in more open countryside. In the Renaissance period the writings of the Greeks and Romans, for example Theocritus' *Idylls*, the Philostratos family's *Imagines* and Virgil's *Eclogues*, were read for their descriptions of bucolic landscapes, which became the settings for the paintings of Giorgione, Titian, Dosso Dossi and others. The landscapes are often generalized, though sometimes identifiable as areas of the Venetian hinterland, and contain a repertory of figures taken from Classical sources. The *Concert champêtre* (c. 1510; Paris, Louvre; see fig. 1), originally thought to be a late work of Giorgione's but later more generally accepted as an early painting by his pupil Titian, displays the essential characteristics of the *fête champêtre*. Here, the figures—although having Classical connotations—are not readily identifiable. The two nude women are possibly muses or spirits of either poetry or music, unseen by the clothed men. The setting is an idyllic, open countryside, and musical instruments are present (one of the men plays a lute and one of the women holds

a recorder). There is a general air of lassitude and reverie, and a pervading pagan sensuality. Rather than gallant courtship, a poetic union of Man and Nature is implied, suggested by the integration of the human forms with the shapes of the landscape in a manner similar to the structures of musical rhythm. *Concert champêtre* is a visual counterpart to a passage of lyric poetry recalling the 'sacred groves' of such writers as Theocritus. The men in such paintings, clothed in contemporary dress, may represent the actual patrons for whom the works were commissioned or, more generally, the new humanistic Renaissance patron absorbed in the pleasures of Classical literature and music and in pantheistic communion with the natural world. The women, therefore, may be seen either as personifications of the Renaissance ideal of feminine beauty or as symbolic of the forces that spur creativity. A study of Classical art and poetry and a reading of ancient writers who integrated the natural and spiritual worlds were considered essential to a gentleman's education in the 15th and 16th centuries, as was the ability to play a musical instrument. Such paintings as *Concert champêtre* seem to reflect these humanist interests, functioning as visual metaphors for the creative Renaissance spirit.

Giorgione and Titian were the most skilled in capturing a mood of creative union between the Classical and

1. ? Giorgione or Titian: *Concert champêtre*, oil on canvas, 1.10×1.38 m, c. 1510 (Paris, Musée du Louvre)

contemporary worlds. Titian's *Bacchanal of the Andrians* (*c.* 1523–5; Madrid, Prado; *see* TITIAN, fig. 5), based on an event described in the *Imagines*, is a more active and boisterous version of the *fête champêtre*. Characteristically, nude and clothed figures intermingle; there is stress on the relaxing pleasures of music, dance, drink and the immersion in a beautiful landscape; and—most typical of the *fête champêtre*—the pagan world becomes tangible. Other Italian practitioners of the *fête champêtre* and its allegorical variations in the 16th century include Lorenzo Lotto, Dosso Dossi (e.g. the *Three Ages of Man*, *c.* 1518–20; New York, Met.; *see* DOSSI, (1), fig. 1) and Palma Vecchio, to whom is attributed *A Concert* (*c.* 1515–20; England, priv. col.; *see* Rylands, p. 128).

In the 17th century the *fête champêtre* was given a more direct treatment, notably through the depiction of festive occasions. The theme was taken up by several northern European painters, primarily Rubens. No longer reliant on Classical allegory, the *fête champêtre* was altered to reflect the manners and morals of the privileged classes. The pursuit of love, accompanied by music, continued to be important, although figures are usually clothed and settings are more closely identifiable, often as country estates or more formal, urban gardens. The gallant poems of courtship by such English Cavalier poets as Robert Herrick and such French poets as Tristan l'Hermite were influential. Scenes often depict fully fledged banqueting-parties or hunting-parties, accompanied by a suite of musicians rather than one or two lute- or flute-players. Space and figures are more animated, the lighting more dramatic and colours more resonant, in keeping with the Baroque style. The identities of figures, as well as their relationships with one another, are less ambiguous, freeing the images somewhat from their symbolic context. The medieval theme of the 'garden of love' was revived and updated for 17th-century tastes; however, there was also an interest in some of the more erotic myths painted by Renaissance artists and translated from the Greek or Latin by Renaissance writers.

Rubens's best-known work in this genre is the *Garden of Love* (*c.* 1634; Madrid, Prado), the title of which—typical of *fêtes champêtres*—was given only later (in this case, in the 18th century). The figures dominate the landscape, and the *fête champêtre* theme is less easily placed in an idyllic Arcadia. Even in *Rustic Couple Embracing* (Munich, Alte Pin.) and *Flemish Kermesse* (1635–8; Paris, Louvre), earthier depictions of the theme, the emphasis appears to be on a more immediate sensual gratification; in the latter painting, Rubens took a typical Flemish country dance and fashioned it into a slightly less civilized version of the *Garden of Love*. Paintings of groups enjoying themselves alfresco were popular with buyers in the Netherlands and Flanders in the 17th century, often as relaxing alternatives to the more intellectually taxing paintings of historical and religious themes. Besides Rubens, other northern European artists who produced versions of the *fête champêtre*, although in a less animated way, include David Vinckboons (e.g. *Merry Company in the Open Air*, 1610; Vienna, Akad. Bild. Kst.), Louis de Caulery (*fl* 1594–1620) (e.g. *Banquet in the Park*; Poznań, N. Mus.) and the engraver Abraham Bosse (e.g. *Springtime*; Paris, Bib. N., Cab. Est.).

3. 18TH CENTURY. The theme of the *fête champêtre* came to be associated with the French Rococo, reflecting a particular way of life among French nobility. Antoine Watteau was most instrumental in this, his paintings dealing with the inconsistencies, uncertainties and vagaries of human relationships (*see* WATTEAU, (1)). His metaphor was the theatre (especially the *commedia dell'arte*), with its costumed actors and actresses suggesting the 'play-acting' of real life. He was taught by Claude Gillot, who contributed to the development of the genre, and may also have been influenced by the themes of love and courtship in the plays of Florent Carton Dancourt (1661–1725). Watteau's unreal settings of formal French gardens recall those of the cloistered medieval 'gardens of love' more than they do those of the 16th-century Venetian *fêtes champêtres*. Equally as importantly, he drew on the traditions of the 17th century. A chalk drawing (1708–9; Paris, Mus. A. Déc.) of an embracing couple in Rubens's *Flemish Kermesse* shows his appreciation of the Flemish artist's sensuality, although his version is characteristically restrained and poignant.

In 1712 Watteau submitted four paintings as *morceaux d'agrégation* for acceptance into the Académie Royale de Peinture et de Sculpture. One of these, *The Foursome* (*c.* 1712; San Francisco, CA, de Young Mem. Mus.; *see* fig. 2), depicts a garden with two seated women and a seated man, the three regarding a Pierrot-like figure in white with a guitar slung over his hip. Typical of Watteau's paintings, the figures are immersed in a world of courtly etiquette and are thin, pale and hesitant—almost trembling. Conversation appears limited, the figures scarcely interact, and one has his face turned away from the viewer. The subject-matter—or lack of it—puzzled the members of the Académie, as it did not easily fit into any prescribed category. Watteau was allowed to choose the subject of his *morceaux de réception*, which he delivered in 1717. The painting, *Pilgrimage to the Isle of Cythera* (Paris, Louvre; *see* WATTEAU, fig. 3; version, Berlin, Schloss Charlottenburg), was the culmination of his particular style and choice of subject-matter and was registered by the Académie as 'une feste galante'. The term *fête galante* thus became applied to the whole body of his work and of that of his followers in the 18th century.

Variants of the *fête champêtre*, Watteau's paintings contain scenes of banqueting, music-parties or dancing. Full of restrained action and psychological subtleties, they depict a code of behaviour popular in the last years of the reign of Louis XIV (*reg* 1643–1715). His *fêtes galantes* never achieved a particularly high place in the hierarchy of paintings at the Académie and consequently had few imitators. In France only NICOLAS LANCRET (e.g. *Conversation galante*, *c.* 1719; London, Wallace) and JEAN-BAPTISTE PATER (e.g. *Fair at Bezons*, late 1720s; New York, Met.) faithfully practised the genre. Of the two, Lancret was less of a direct imitator, his paintings enriched with greater detail and a livelier narrative than Watteau's. After the deaths of Lancret and Pater, the *fête galante* declined in popularity in France, although it continued to be reproduced on porcelain services. From the mid-18th century François Boucher's coy and sweet paintings of 'shepherds' and 'shepherdesses' were loose variations of the theme (e.g. *Interrupted Sleep*, 1750; New York, Met.).

2. Antoine Watteau: *The Foursome, c.* 1712 (San Francisco, CA, M. H. de Young Memorial Museum)

Similarly, all seriousness was removed from Jean-Honoré Fragonard's versions of the *fête galante* (e.g. *Progress of Love* series, 1771–2; New York, Frick). Outside France, *fête galante* themes were popular with such artists as Antoine Pesne in Germany, Pierre-Antoine Quillard in Portugal and Philip Mercier in England. In Italy, Giuseppe Zais and Giandomenico Tiepolo painted scenes set in parks or gardens featuring elegantly dressed ladies and gentlemen dancing the minuet or engaged in 'love games'.

4. REVIVAL: MID-19TH CENTURY–EARLY 20TH. In the 19th century Ernest Meissonier and Narcisse Diaz were two of the few painters to revive the *fête galante* theme. Although Diaz was a member of the Barbizon school of landscape painting, several of his works of the 1830s and 1840s depict, in a thick impastoed manner, groups of women or lovers reclining in glades, dreamily and pensively listening to the 'music' of nature; musical instruments are present, although not actually played (e.g. *Elegant Society in a Park*, ?1830s; Reims, Mus. St-Denis). It was Manet, however, who painted the most innovative depictions of figures enjoying themselves in outdoor settings. He not only updated the 16th-century *fête champêtre* by dispensing with mythology, allegory and ambiguity but also reinvented the 18th-century *fête galante* by divesting it of polite social intercourse and modest intention.

Déjeuner sur l'herbe (1863; Paris, Mus. d'Orsay; *see* MANET, EDOUARD, fig. 1), for example, depicts two nude women and two clothed men, as in Titian's *Concert champêtre*, yet they are obviously recognizable as contemporary Parisians rather than nymphs or humanist intellectuals. Other elements of the *fête champêtre* and *fête galante* are present: a leafy park, a stream and a picnic with a still-life of fruit. However, the models are self-conscious, aware of the viewer's presence rather than being lost in a 'garden of love'. In one sense Manet's *fête* can be seen as a detached rendering of an artist's outing with his models. Though using various Renaissance sources for the painting, including the *Concert champêtre* itself, he reworked them in a manner suitable to the objective spirit he thought central to the 'modern world', with its uncompromising factualness and its anti-aesthetic ideas. Several of his other paintings, including *Music in the Tuileries Gardens* (1862; London, N.G.; see fig. 3), adapt the *fête champêtre* and *fête galante* to a bustling urban setting.

Renoir particularly admired Watteau's paintings and portrayed happier versions of the theme of the *fête galante* using his friends as models (e.g. the *Luncheon of the Boating Party*, 1880–81; Washington, DC, Phillips Col.). Monet deliberately paid homage to Manet—and through him Giorgione and Titian—in his own *Déjeuner sur l'herbe*

3. Edouard Manet: *Music in the Tuileries Gardens*, oil on canvas, 762×1181 mm, 1862 (London, National Gallery)

(begun 1865; unfinished; fragment of main canvas, Paris, Mus. d'Orsay; study 1865, Moscow, Pushkin Mus. F.A.). Manet's *Déjeuner sur l'herbe*, challenging as it did notions of 'appropriate' subject-matter, also fascinated such artists as Cézanne, who painted a psychologically disquieting work of the same title (1870–71; priv. col.; see L. Venturi: *Cézanne: Son art, son oeuvre*, Paris, 1936/*R* San Francisco, 1989, ii, pl. 107). Picasso's version (*'Déjeuner sur l'herbe' after Manet*, 1960; Paris, Mus. Picasso) was part of his extended examination of the artist's relationship with his model. Matisse's *Luxe, calme et volupté* (1904–5; Paris, Mus. d'Orsay) and *Joy of Life* (1905–6; Merion Station, PA, Barnes Found.; *see* MATISSE, HENRI, fig. 1) express the contented harmony of Man with Nature, the inspiration behind the first paintings of the *fête champêtre* theme over 300 years earlier.

BIBLIOGRAPHY

P. Fehl: 'The Hidden Game: A Study of the *Concert champêtre* in the Louvre', *J. Aesth. & A. Crit.*, xvi/2 (1957), pp. 153–68
L. Baldass: *Giorgione* (London, 1965)
P. F. Watson: *The Garden of Love in Tuscan Art of the Early Renaissance* (Philadelphia and London, 1979)
R. Tomlinson: *La Fête galante: Watteau et Marivaux*, Histoire des idées et critique littéraire, 194 (Geneva, 1981)
I. Ember: *Music in Painting: Music as a Symbol in Renaissance and Baroque Painting* (Budapest, 1984)
D. Posner: *Antoine Watteau* (London, 1984)
M. Roland Michel: *Watteau: An Artist of the Eighteenth Century* (London, 1984)
Watteau, 1684–1721 (exh. cat. by M. M. Grasselli and P. Rosenberg, Washington, DC, N.G.A.; Paris, Grand Pal.; Berlin, Schloss Charlottenburg; 1984–5)
R. C. Cafritz, L. Gowing and D. Rosand: *Places of Delight: The Pastoral Landscape* (Washington, DC, 1988)
R. L. Herbert: *Impressionism: Art, Leisure and Parisian Society* (New Haven and London, 1988)
Titian: Prince of Painters (exh. cat., ed. S. Biadene; Venice, Doge's Pal.; Washington, DC, N.G.A.; 1990–91)
Nicolas Lancret, 1690–1743 (exh. cat. by M. Tavener Holmes, New York, Frick; Fort Worth, TX, Kimbell A. Mus.; 1991–2)
E. Goodman: *Rubens: The Garden of Love as 'Conversatie à la mode'*, Oculi: Studies in the Arts of the Low Countries, iv (Amsterdam and Philadelphia, 1992)
P. Rylands: *Palma Vecchio*, Cambridge Stud. Hist. A. (Cambridge, 1992)
S. Fermor: 'Movement and Gender in Sixteenth-century Italian Painting', *The Body Imaged*, ed. K. Adler and M. Pointon (Cambridge, 1993), pp. 129–45

KIRK MARLOW

Fetherstonhaugh, Sir Matthew (*b* ?Newcastle upon Tyne, 1714; *d* London, 18 March 1774). English politician, patron and collector. The son of a Newcastle merchant, in 1746 he inherited the estates of his cousin, stated to be worth £400,000. That year he married Sarah Lethieuller, of an influential Huguenot family, and in fulfilment of his cousin's will secured a baronetcy. He was elected to the Royal Society in 1752; for nearly 20 years he was an MP, first for Morpeth (1755–61) and then for Portsmouth (1762–74).

In 1747 Fetherstonhaugh acquired the estate of Uppark, W. Sussex, NT, the decoration of which was to become a major preoccupation, although the exterior of the house (built by William Talman *c.* 1690) was not altered. In 1754–8 a London town house in Whitehall was built for Fetherstonhaugh to designs by James Paine. Earlier, in 1749–52, he had with his wife and a number of their relations made an extensive Grand Tour. During their long sojourn in Rome in 1751, he commissioned paintings

from Joseph Vernet, Charles-François de Lacroix and Pompeo Batoni, the last of whom supplied the paired *Personification of Purity of Heart* and *Personification of Meekness* and a series of half-length portraits, including *Sir Matthew Fetherstonhaugh* and *Sarah, Lady Fetherstonhaugh* (all Uppark). (How these and other sets of pictures by such artists as Luca Giordano, Francesco Zuccarelli and Arthur Devis were divided between Fetherstonhaugh's houses is not clear.) A pair of scagliola table-tops was acquired from the Florentine scagliola-maker Pietro Belloni, and after his return Fetherstonhaugh bought contemporary English furniture. His acquisitions, which survive substantially intact at Uppark (despite the fire of 1990), offer a remarkable insight into the taste of a discriminating *nouveau riche* collector of the mid-18th century. Fetherstonhaugh appears in Joshua Reynolds's *Travesty of the School of Athens* (Dublin, N.G.).

BIBLIOGRAPHY

A. Coleridge: 'Georgian Cabinet Makers at Uppark', *Connoisseur*, clxvi (1967), pp. 74–9, 157–63
Uppark, NT Guidebook (London, 1983)
A. M. Clark: *Pompeo Batoni: A Complete Catalogue of his Works with an Introductory Text*, ed. E. P. Bowron (Oxford, 1985), nos 154–63, 168–9

FRANCIS RUSSELL

Fetti [Feti], Domenico (*b* ?Rome, 1588 or 1589; *d* Venice, 16 April 1623). Italian painter. He is best known for his small-scale paintings illustrating the *Parables* (1618–21), painted in Mantua while he was court painter to Ferdinando Gonzaga. He was also a fine portrait painter. The great traditions of 16th-century Venetian art were his inspiration, yet he created a highly original, modern style in broadly handled paintings that glow with warm Venetian colour and vibrant light. Light was of paramount importance to him, and the radiant angel that features in many pictures, for example in *Jacob's Dream* (Vienna, Ksthist. Mus.), represents light itself. A sense of melancholy pervades his art, its recurrent themes being visions, dreams and scenes of lamentation.

1. LIFE AND WORK.

(i) Rome, to 1614. Fetti was first taught by his father, Pietro, and later studied with Andrea Commodi (1560–1638) and after 1604 with Lodovico Cigoli. Among his first works was a portrait of *Filippo Neri* (1610; untraced), commissioned by the oratory of Filippo Neri in Rome. Ferdinando Gonzaga, then a Cardinal in Rome, also received paintings from him in 1611, among them perhaps *St Mary of Egypt* and *St Jerome* (London, Hampton Court, Royal Col.). In 1613, when Ferdinando became the 6th Duke of Mantua and returned to take up residence there, Fetti continued to work for him. His *Repentance of St Peter* (Vienna, Ksthist. Mus.) and *David* (Nuremberg, Akad. Bild. Kst.) are among works that may date from this period. Another important early work is the *Ecce homo* (Florence, Uffizi), which pays homage to Cigoli's celebrated painting of that title (Florence, Pitti); it is probably the picture that Ferdinando presented to Cosimo II de' Medici in 1618.

In Rome, Fetti may have been attracted by the small-scale, realistic genre scenes by painters from northern Europe, and by the work of Carlo Saraceni, whose lyrical style was indebted both to Caravaggio and to Adam

Elsheimer. After completing the altarpiece *Angels Worshipping the Image of the Virgin and Child* (Baltimore, MD, Walters A.G.) for S Lorenzo in Damaso, Rome, Fetti followed the Duke to Mantua, probably in the early months of 1614.

(ii) Mantua, 1614–22. Ferdinando's generosity enabled Fetti to take his family to Mantua: his father and sister Giustina, who was a painter and an Ursuline nun (Sister Lucrina), were followed by his brother Vincenzo, who became a priest and was possibly also a painter. Fetti's first paintings in Mantua were for churches, the most successful of them a lunette for the chapel of the Palazzo della Ragione, Mantua, showing the *Virgin and Child with SS Anselm and Carlo Borromeo* (Mantua, Admin. Ist. Gonzaga). In Mantua his style matured rapidly. He became a superintendent of the Gonzaga collection and was deeply influenced by its riches, responding in his own art to a wide variety of sources. His *David* (1614–15; St Petersburg, Hermitage; on dep. Moscow, Pushkin Mus. F.A.) treats a Caravaggesque theme, yet the drawing and colour suggest an awareness of Emilian and Venetian painting. Another portrayal of *David* (*c.* 1614–15; Dresden, Gemäldegal.) and *Moses and the Burning Bush* (*c.* 1615–17; Vienna, Ksthist. Mus.) are deeply influenced by the colour and figure style of Rubens, who had preceded Fetti at the Gonzaga court. He was also attracted by the silvery light and landscape backgrounds of Veronese, who inspired his *Agony in the Garden* (1616–17; Prague, N.G., Šternberk Pal).

1. Domenico Fetti: *Melancholy* (second version), oil on canvas, 1.71×1.28 m, *c.* 1618 (Paris, Musée du Louvre)

Around 1617 Fetti painted a meditative *Mary Magdalene* (Rome, Gal. Doria-Pamphili), inspired by Correggio's *Magdalene Reading* (destr.); a copy, perhaps by his sister, is in the Royal Collection at Hampton Court. His *Melancholy* (1618; Venice, Accad.; version, Paris, Louvre; see fig. 1), a more explicit rendering of the themes that had begun to absorb him, shows a Magdalene-like figure, lush and voluptuous, gloomily contemplating a skull. She is surrounded by objects symbolizing man's intellectual and creative activities, among them a brush and palette. Yet the skull suggests the futility of these concerns, and the painting is an allegory of *vanitas*.

From 1616 to 1617 *Fetti* began to be overwhelmed with commissions for series of pictorial cycles. Two decorative panels with the imprese of Ferdinando Gonzaga (Mantua, priv. cols, see Safarik, 1985, figs 9–10) are all that survive of a much larger scheme, possibly from the Salone del Crogiulo in the Palazzo Ducale. The complex motifs of sphinxes, garlands and putti are Mannerist in feeling and were inspired by 16th-century decorative friezes.

In 1618 Fetti painted the series of *Eleven Apostles* and *Christ Blessing* (Mantua, Pal. Ducale), a work of great expressive freedom. Four scenes from the *Passion* (all Florence, Gal. Corsini) date from the same period: *Christ Crowned with Thorns* and the *Mocking of Christ* suggest the influence of Caravaggio moderated by a north European realism, while the *Agony in the Garden* was influenced by the art of Domenico Tintoretto and the Bassano family; the *Entombment of Christ* is a copy, perhaps painted in Fetti's workshop.

The monumental *Miracle of the Loaves and Fishes* (1618–19; Mantua, Pal. Ducale; see fig. 2), formerly on the end wall of the refectory in the convent of St Ursula in Mantua, is one of Fetti's great achievements of this period. Inspired by the art of Tintoretto, it attains a virtuoso freedom of handling that makes it particularly expressive and innovative.

Fetti was highly valued by the Gonzaga court and enjoyed substantial earnings. On 30 November 1620 the Duke presented him with a house in the Aquila quarter of Mantua. In 1621 Fetti made his first recorded journey to Venice, though he may have been there previously, perhaps in 1619 to see the comedy *La Venetiana*, dedicated to him by Giovanni Battista Andreini. Around 1620 he received his most demanding commission as a court painter, for a vast series of paintings celebrating the Gonzaga family to be hung at the top of the Galleria della Mostra in the Palazzo Ducale and consisting of 23 figures interspersed with 18 small putti. The only surviving works from this ambitious project are two historical portraits, one perhaps of *Francesco II Gonzaga* (Veltrusy Castle), the other probably of *Federico II Gonzaga* (Vienna, Ksthist. Mus.). A pair of over life-size paintings, both entitled *Poet* (*c.* 1620–21; sold London, Christie's, 13 Dec 1985, lot 89; Stockholm, Nmus.), are thought to have been part of a series of nine, probably intended for a room in the Appartamento del Paradiso at the Nova Domus, a palace within the Mantuan court precincts designed by Luca Fancelli.

Fetti's last major ducal commission was for a cycle of pictures illustrating the *Parables* (1618–21). This at first decorated the Grotta Isabelliana but was moved while

2. Domenico Fetti: *Miracle of the Loaves and Fishes*, oil on canvas, 3.30×8.45 m, 1618–19 (Mantua, Palazzo Ducale)

Fetti was still court painter to the Appartamento del Paradiso. The pictures were hung high, between the ceiling and the wooden wainscot. Ten of the originals are known: the *Mote and the Beam* (ex-Althorp House, Northants; version, York, C.A.G.), the *Sower* (Prague, N.G., Zbraslav Castle), the *Blind Leading the Blind*, the *Unmerciful Servant*, the *Good Samaritan*, the *Marriage Feast*, the *Lost Sheep*, the *Lost Silver*, the *Prodigal Son* and the *Wicked Husbandmen* (all Dresden, Gemäldegal. Alte Meister). Workshop copies survive of the *Pearl of Great Price* (Vienna, Ksthist. Mus.) and *Dives and Lazarus* (Washington, DC, N.G.A.), the latter possibly made by his sister, while the *Hidden Treasure* (New York, E. V. Thaw priv. col., see Michelini, 1955, fig. 144) is perhaps a workshop copy retouched by Fetti. The series attracted much attention, and numerous copies were made, many of them almost certainly in Fetti's workshop. The paintings are his most original works, showing the parables as events in everyday life, enriched with lively genre detail and revealing a tender concern for humanity. Many have expressive landscape settings. His emphasis on conveying religious truths with clarity and simplicity is in keeping with the doctrinal spirit of the Counter-Reformation.

In his portraits Fetti revived Venetian traditions that had been established by Domenico Tintoretto and Leandro Bassano. Direct and spontaneous, they often show the sitters with prized objects, as in the *Portrait of a Man with Gold Jug and Book* (c. 1620–21; Rohrau, Schloss), possibly depicting the artist's friend Niccolò Avellani; among his other celebrated portraits is that of the actor *Francesco Andreini* (1621–2; St Petersburg, Hermitage). The monochrome lunette *Margherita Gonzaga Receiving the Model of the Church of St Orsola from the Architect Antonio Maria Viani* (1619–20; Mantua, Pal. Ducale) is the only survivor of four paintings that once hung high up in the niches of the church of S Orsola, Mantua.

(iii) Venice, 1622–3. On 28 August 1622 Fetti attended a football game in Mantua with the painter Gabriele Balestrieri. They quarrelled violently, and Fetti had to leave for Venice, from where, on 10 September, he wrote to

Ferdinando Gonzaga to justify his sudden departure. In Venice he enjoyed the patronage of Giorgio Contarini dagli Scrigni, who was also the patron of Carlo Saraceni. Fetti's brother Vincenzo conveyed his paintings back and forth between Venice and Mantua.

Fetti's fine *Martyrdom of SS Fermo and Rustico* (Hartford, CT, Wadsworth Atheneum), distinguished by its warm and direct realism and by the rich colour and expressive effects of light, probably dates from 1622. The landscape setting seems to be derived from the country outside Verona, where the saints were martyred, suggesting that Fetti knew the area and had contacts with Veronese patrons. It was almost certainly during his stay in Venice that he painted four scenes from the *Life of Tobias*, of which *Tobias and the Angel* (Dresden, Gemäldegal. Alte Meister) and *Tobias Cures his Blind Father* (St Petersburg, Hermitage) survive. *Tobit Finds the Dead Israelite* and *Tobit and Tobias Bury the Dead Israelite* (both untraced) are known through engravings by Quirin Boel (1620–68); among the copies of the former, the best was probably that in the Kaiser-Friedrich Museum, Berlin (destr.).

In his late Venetian works Fetti developed a new lyricism, exemplified in the elegiac, windswept *Flight into Egypt* (Vienna, Ksthist. Mus.) and in *St Simeon* (New York, Suida Manning priv. col., see Spike, 1980, no. 22). The latter has a sweetly sentimental aura that seems to foreshadow Rococo taste; perhaps Fetti's last painting, it is a devout tribute to the patron saint of the Venetian parish of S Simeone Grande, in which he lived.

2. WORKSHOP PRACTICE. Fetti's father and sister are known to have been active in the busy workshop he set up in Mantua; Pietro Fetti's *Self-portrait* (Florence, Uffizi) shows his style to have been similar to that of his son but rougher and drier. Other painters documented there are a certain Monsù Michel, almost certainly identifiable with Michele Mattei of Burgundy, who worked with Fetti in 1620 on the decorations for the Galleria della Mostra in the Palazzo Ducale, Mantua. The records also mention the names of some pupils, Veronese by birth or adoption,

including Giovanni Battista Barca (*c.* 1594–1650) and Dionisio Guerri (1601–*c.* 1630). The latter almost certainly painted *Christ in the Desert Served by Angels* (Providence, RI Sch. Des., Mus. A.), which was based on Fetti's prototype (sold Milan, Finarte, 25 Nov 1976, lot 90).

The most important of Fetti's pupils was (?Camillo) Motta, who according to 19th-century sources painted the *St John the Evangelist* in the Ognissanti Church and the *St Eligius with Angels* in S Maria della Carità, both in Mantua. These paintings serve as a point of departure for reconstructing Motta's life and work and also suggest that he may have been Fetti's principal collaborator. The strongly contrasting chiaroscuro common to both the above paintings reappears identically in some of his copies of works by Fetti, such as the *Assumption* (Munich, Alte Pin.), the *Salvator mundi* (Lovere, Gal. Accad. B.A. Tadini) and the *Martyrdom of SS Fermo and Rustico* (Milan, priv. col., see Michelini, 1955, p. 136, fig. 149).

BIBLIOGRAPHY

G. Baglione: *Vite* (1642); ed. V. Mariani (1935), pp. 155, 158

G. Cadioli: *Descrizione delle pitture, sculture ed architetture che si osservano nella città di Mantova* (Mantua, 1763), pp. 14, 16–18, 29, 37, 40, 43, 45, 50, 52, 55, 60, 65, 71–6, 81, 83

A. Luzio: *La Galleria dei Gonzaga venduta all'Inghilterra nel 1627–28* (Milan, 1913)

M. Endres Soltmann: *Domenico Fetti* (diss., U. Munich, 1914)

R. Oldenbourg: *Domenico Fetti* (Rome, 1921)

M. Marangoni: 'Domenico Fetti', *Dédalo*, iii (1922–3), pp. 695–710, 777–92

J. Wilde: 'Zum Werke des Domenico Fetti', *Jb. Ksthist Samml. Wien*, n. s., x (1936), pp. 211–19

L. Ozzòla: 'Domenico Fetti nella Galleria di Mantova', *Emporium*, cviii (1948), pp. 137–42

P. Michelini: 'Domenico Fetti a Venezia', *A. Ven.*, ix (1955), pp. 123–37

P. Askew: 'Fetti's *Martyrdom* at the Wadsworth Atheneum', *Burl. Mag.*, ciii (1961), pp. 245–52

——: 'The Parable Paintings of Domenico Fetti', *A. Bull.*, xliii (1961), pp. 21–45

E. Marani and C. Perina: 'Domenico Fetti', *Mantova: Le arti*, iii (Mantua, 1965), pp. 454–65, 491–502

J. Lehmann: *Domenico Fetti: Leben und Werk des römischen Malers* (diss., U. Frankfurt am Main, 1967)

C. Boselli: *Nuove fonti per la storia dell'arte: L'archivio dei conti Gambara presso la Civica Biblioteca Queriniana di Brescia*, i: *Il carteggio* (Venice, 1971), pp. 63–6, 81

C. Tellini Perina: 'Inediti del seicento veneto: Fetti, Bassetti, Liberi', *A. Ven.*, xxv (1971), pp. 276–80

J. T. Spike: *Italian Baroque Paintings from New York Private Collections* (Princeton, 1980)

E. A. Safarik: 'Domenico Fetti 1983', *Accademia Nazionale Virgiliana: Il seicento nell'arte e nella cultura* (Cinisello Balsamo, 1985), pp. 47–52

——: *Domenico Fetti* (Milan, 1990)

E. A. SAFARIK

Feuchère, Jean-Jacques (*b* Paris, 26 Aug 1807; *d* Paris, 25 July 1852). French sculptor, painter, decorative artist and collector. Son of the chaser Jacques-François Feuchère (*d* 1828) and a pupil of Jean-Pierre Cortot and Claude Ramey, he first exhibited at the Salon of 1831. Over the ensuing decade he won the reputation, later shared with his pupil Jean-Baptiste Klagmann (1810–67), of leader in the small-scale, domestic sculpture industry. He modelled statuettes in a variety of historical styles, though he preferred a Renaissance idiom, working for bronze-casters such as M. Vittoz (*fl c.* 1840) and Victor Paillard (*fl* 1840–51), and producing models for the goldsmith François-Désiré Froment-Meurice (1802–55). One of his early Romantic subjects, a seated figure of *Satan* brooding after

his expulsion from paradise, went through numerous editions from *c.* 1833 (bronze cast, 1850; Los Angeles, CA, Co. Mus. A.), its Michelangelo-inspired posture prefiguring Jean-Baptiste Carpeaux's *Ugolino* (bronze version; Paris, Mus. d'Orsay) and Auguste Rodin's *Thinker* (bronze version; Paris, Mus. Rodin). Feuchère contributed to many of the sculptural projects of the July Monarchy: a marble relief of the *Crossing of the Bridge at Arcola* (1834) for the Arc de Triomphe; a statue of *St Theresa* (1837–9) for La Madeleine; three allegorical figures in bronze (1838) for the fountains in the Place de la Concorde; and designs for 12 Victories for Napoleon's funeral car (1840). He was a member of the hashish-smoking circle of the Hôtel Pimodan; Charles Baudelaire, a fellow member, regretted Feuchère's sacrifice of his talent to commercialism. However, at his early death, the sculptor was found to have sunk his considerable earnings in a remarkable private art collection, including paintings by Leonardo, Raphael and other Italian masters, as well as paintings by various Dutch masters and contemporary French artists.

BIBLIOGRAPHY

Lami

J. Janin: *Notice sur J. Feuchère* (Paris, 1853)

Romantics to Rodin (exh. cat., ed. P. Fusco and H. W. Janson; Los Angeles, Co. Mus. A., 1980)

H. Hawley: 'Some Intimate Sculptures of Feuchère', *Bull. Cleveland Mus. A.*, lxviii/3 (1981), pp. 75–83

P. Ward-Jackson: 'A.-E. Carrier-Belleuse, J.-J. Feuchère and the Sutherlands', *Burl. Mag.*, cxxvii (1985), pp. 147–53

PHILIP WARD-JACKSON

Feucht, Jacob. *See* FACHT, JACOB.

Feuchtmayer [Faichtmayer; Feichtmayr]. German family of artists. (1) Franz Joseph Feuchtmayer was a sculptor and stuccoist from Wessobrunn who worked principally for the Cistercian monastery of Salem in southern Germany. His brother (2) Johann Michael Feuchtmayer was a painter. Franz Joseph's elder son (3) Joseph Anton Feuchtmayer took over his father's workshop at Salem and became one of the most important German Rococo sculptors and stuccoists of the 18th century. His younger brother Gervasius Feuchtmayer (1697–1740) was a conventual at Salem and worked as a polychromer of wooden sculpture.

BIBLIOGRAPHY

Thieme–Becker

A. Czerny: *Kunst und Kunstgewerbe im Stifte St Florian* (Linz, 1886)

G. Hager: 'Die Bautätigkeit und Kunstpflege in Kloster Wessobrunn und die Wessobrunner Stukkatoren', *Oberbayer. Archiv Vaterländ. Gesch.*, xlviii (1893–4), pp. 195–512

H. Sauer: 'Archivalien zu Joseph Anton Feuchtmayer: Schaffen—Familie—Umkreis', *Z. Gesch. Oberrheins*, xciv (1946), pp. 382–457

H. Schnell and U. Schedler: *Lexikon der Wessobrunner Stukkatoren* (Munich, 1987)

(1) Franz Joseph Feuchtmayer (*bapt* Wessobrunn, 9 March 1660; *d* Mimmenhausen, 25 Dec 1718). Sculptor and stuccoist. He probably trained with his stepfather Johann Pöllandt (before 1632–1721). He lived at first in Linz and later in Schongau, working mainly in Upper Austria, until in 1708 he became head of the sculpture workshop at Salem and moved to nearby Mimmenhausen. From 1694 to around 1705 he executed carving for altars in the church of the Benedictine monastery at Seitenstetten. This work shows the influence of Giovanni Battista Carlone II, with whom Feuchtmayer is said to have worked in Linz and elsewhere. In 1697 he made carvings for the choir-stalls in the church of the Benedictine house at Einsiedeln. From 1706 Feuchtmayer was producing sculpture for Salem: in 1706–7 he made figures (destr.) for the façade of the prelacy and in 1707 executed stuccowork in the Wessobrunn style, with rich acanthus work and numerous groups of putti, for the abbot's residence. From 1708 he worked on his masterpiece, the Kaisersaal at Salem. This has 16 over life-size statues of emperors, 14 busts of popes and 4 life-size allegorical groups over the doorways. Although these sculptures are rather stiff in appearance, they betray an Italian influence. Feuchtmayer's later works include the funerary monument of *Anton Egon, Prince of Fürstenberg* in the chapel of Schloss Heiligenberg (1716) and the choir-stalls in the monastery church at Weingarten (from 1716). These last were completed by his son (3) Joseph Anton Feuchtmayer.

BIBLIOGRAPHY

H. Sauer: *Herkunft und Anfänge des Bildhauers Joseph Anton Feuchtmayer* (diss., U. Leipzig, 1932), pp. 9–21

W. Boeck: *Joseph Anton Feuchtmayer* (Tübingen, 1948), pp. 53–73

P. Zinsmaier: 'Notizen zur Kunstgeschichte des Bodenseeraumes', *Freiburg. Diöz.-Archv*, lxxiii (1953), pp. 200–08

A. Kaspar: 'Das Weingartener Chorgestühl', *Z. Württemberg. Landesgesch.*, xiii (1954), pp. 320–23

(2) Johann Michael Feuchtmayer (*bapt* Wessobrunn, 17 April 1666; *d* Konstanz, 15 Oct 1713). Painter, brother of (1) Franz Joseph Feuchtmayer. His first known activity was at Baumgartenberg in 1697. In 1701–7 he painted altarpieces for the monastic church at Hofen (Friedrichshafen). An altarpiece of *St Idda Visiting a Church by Night* (1706; Bauen, parish church) was probably intended for that saint's chapel in the monastery at Fischingen. In 1707 he was active painting ceiling frescoes and overdoors at the monastery of St Florian, and in 1712 he painted altarpieces for the chapel of St Maria Victoria at Salem. His paintings display a strong North Italian influence. In colouring, composition and treatment of the human figure they come very close to the Baroque work of Johann Michael Rottmayr.

BIBLIOGRAPHY

F. S. Meidinger: *Historische Beschreibung der kurfürstlichen Haupt- und Residenzstädte in Niederbaiern, Landshut und Straubing* (Landshut, 1787), pp. 382ff

F. A. Riof: 'Die Geschichte des Klosters Hofen und der Reichsstadt Buchhorn', *Schr. Ver. Gesch. Bodensees & Umgebung*, xxii (1893), pp. 13–70

J. Neuknecht: *Baumgartenberg* (Salzburg, 1968)

H. Gasser: 'Das Hochaltargemälde von Bauen: Ein bedeutendes Werk süddeutscher Barockmalerei', *Unsere Kstdkml.*, xxxii (1981), pp. 386–9

(3) Joseph Anton Feuchtmayer (*b* Linz, 3 June 1696; *d* Mimmenhausen, 2 Jan 1770). Sculptor and stuccoist, son of (1) Franz Joseph Feuchtmayer. He was one of the most original German sculptors of the 18th century. His eccentric and highly expressive figure style restricted the number of patrons willing to employ him, however, and led to the destruction of a number of his works in the 19th century. In addition to his role as head of the sculpture workshop at Salem, he acted as art adviser to the abbots and thus influenced the planning of monastic and ecclesiastical buildings at Salem and its dependencies.

1. TRAINING AND EARLY WORK, TO *c.* 1730. Around 1708 Joseph Anton Feuchtmayer moved with his father

to Mimmenhausen near the monastery of Salem. His first training was probably gained in the elder Feuchtmayer's workshop, and in 1714 he is recorded as collaborating on altars for Salem. The following year he was in Augsburg, and his knowledge of anatomy, unusual for a South German sculptor of the period, suggests that he may have attended the academy there. His earliest documented and almost complete, preserved sculptures are the slightly under life-size wooden figures of saints on the choir-stalls at the monastery church of Weingarten (1720–24). These draped figures arranged in great C-shaped and S-shaped curves, with a strong contrast between the angular, brittle carving of the draperies and the softly modelled flesh, betray the influence of his father's work. In the slightly earlier figure of an *Angel Playing a Lute* (wood, *c.* 1719; Karlsruhe, Bad. Landesmus.) the contrast between the qualities of the drapery and the body of the figure is even greater. In a figure of the *Virgin* (wood, 1725; Berlin, Skulpgal.) the drapery is wafer-thin, and the subtle curves of the body beneath can be seen clearly. While working at Weingarten Feuchtmayer met the stuccoist Diego Francesco Carlone and possibly also Donato Frisoni (1683–1735). His early stucco ceilings at Salem (1721 and 1726) and in the Heiliggeistkirche in Berne (1728–9) are in a delicate Régence style close to the designs of Frisoni. The rather nobler ceiling at the chapel of the grange in Bachhaupten (1729–30) shows Carlone's influence more strongly.

Feuchtmayer's early work is typified by the cycles of stucco figures, some over life-size, that he made for Schloss Kissleg (1726) and for the abbey church of St Peter (1728–31) in the Black Forest, the latter his first large-scale commission. The figures give a strong impression of spontaneity in their handling. The cleanly finished heads of those at Kissleg are in the tradition of Carlone; those at St Peter's are more freely modelled and expressive. These early figures have elongated proportions and ascetic bodies. Their wildly flowing draperies show the additional influence of Swabian Late Gothic sculpture. While they demonstrate to the full the creative possibilities of rapidly modelled stucco, Feuchtmayer consistently carried over these qualities into his work in other materials, giving many of his statues a weird, half-decayed appearance.

2. SALEM AND NEUBIRNAU, *c.* 1730–*c.* 1755. From 1730 Feuchtmayer worked continuously for the monastery at Salem, where his large workshop, free from guild restrictions, was engaged in numerous artistic tasks. He made statues for the lower gate and stables, as well as a great fountain for the courtyard and several altars for the abbey church. Much of this work is now ruined or destroyed. In 1730–34 he collaborated with Carlone at Einsiedlen, and in 1734–8 he was working at Engelberg, where he executed the high altar in a classical aedicular form. He may be said to have reached his mature figure style with the over life-size stucco statue of *Diogenes* (see fig. 1) executed in 1736 for the stairwell at Schloss Maurach. In this work the *figura serpentinata* typical of his earlier statuary is employed not only for aesthetic reasons, but also in order to relate the figure to its axial position in the narrow space that it occupies. The half-naked figure shows Feuchtmayer's interest in the expressive possibilities of

1. Joseph Anton Feuchtmayer: *Diogenes*, stucco, over life-size, 1736 (Überlingen, Schloss Maurach)

played a decisive role in the appointment of Johann Caspar Bagnato as architect at the Salem abbey church in 1755, and he seems to have been responsible for the decoration of the main portal on the lakeside façade and for the architectural sculpture on the tower at Neubirnau. The interior (see fig. 2) is dominated by his scagliola and polished stucco altars. Sculptural decoration is concentrated on the complex, elliptically planned high altar, Feuchtmayer's first with a fully developed architectural canopy (rearranged 1790). The figure sculpture has an expressiveness carried to the point of grotesque ugliness. The choir altars are reduced to monumental Rococo cartouches, their white stucco figures of saints contrasting with realistically coloured landscape reliefs and flesh-coloured putti. A gallery decorated with busts of saints and apostles, mostly by Feuchtmayer's assistants, runs round the interior of the church. It is probably the most important such ensemble produced in South Germany in the 18th century.

3. LATE WORKS, AFTER *c.* 1755. In 1755 Feuchtmayer competed for the commission to decorate the altars at Ottobeuren. The designs of Johann Michael Feichtmayer were, however, preferred to his. It was at this time that his late style was developing. It was seen for the first time in the life-size wooden figures of *St Wendelin* and *St Blasius* that Feuchtmayer added to the two aedicular altars in the nave chapels at Neubirnau in 1757. These late figures have less movement in their poses than his earlier statues, the bodies are more close-knit, the drapery more voluminous and the features more stereotyped. Important late works were the high altars in the abbey church at Beuron, decorated with an *Assumption* (1760; destr.), and that in the Franciscan church at Überlingen. The greatest of Feuchtmayer's late works, undertaken from 1761, were the choir-stalls, confessional and façade relief for the abbey church of St Gall. The relief work shows, like his late statues, a moderated dynamism but a concentration of expression. In his last years Feuchtmayer, influenced by French classicism, perhaps through the engravings of François de Neufforge, experimented with designs for altars in the form of obelisks, though none was carried out. His later executed altars are, however, characterized by a return to classical forms such as the simple aedicula. He continued to prepare designs for works at Salem, but received no further commissions until the year before his death.

Feuchtmayer's busy workshop was staffed by journeymen from Wessobrunn and also the Tyrol. Among the better-known sculptors who worked with him were Franz Anton Dirr and Johann Georg Dirr and Johann Wieland. Around 400 drawings by Feuchtmayer and his workshop survive (Konstanz, Städt. Wessenberg-Gemäldegal.; St Gall, Stift.-Bib.; Stuttgart, Staatsgal.; Berlin, Kstbib.), ranging from compositional sketches to presentation drawings. Although models as well as drawings were important in the evolution of his works only one of these terracotta *bozzetti* is known—a signed model of a bishop (Überlingen, Städt. Mus.). Feuchtmayer's designs for altars, cartouches etc were published in series of engravings, among them *Simetria deren fünf Saulen-ordnungen in Älteren vorgestelt*, printed *c.* 1750 in Augsburg.

the human body, and the features display his preference for the weird and grotesque. Further important decorative commissions followed: in 1737–9 the chapel of Schloss Mainau, in 1740 Merdingen parish church, and in 1741–3 the chapel at Schloss Meersburg. The figures on the altars in all these schemes form an integral part of the architecture and decoration, their extreme postures echoing the architectonic forms.

The 1740s were occupied for Feuchtmayer with large-scale commissions for Salem: in 1743 he worked at Scheer parish church and in 1747 at the former church of the Cistercian house at Habstahl. The stucco ceilings at Habstahl show the rocaille features combined with architectural fragments, busts and putti, that are typical of Feuchtmayer's decorative work of this decade. His most ambitious undertaking of this period, however, was the pilgrimage church at nearby Neubirnau. With the loss of much of his work at Salem this must be considered his surviving masterpiece.

In 1748–50 Feuchtmayer seems to have exerted a strong influence on the architecture of Neubirnau. The colossal external order of Ionic pilasters and the treatment of the corners of the interior, where the spatial composition is blurred and then resolved, bear the mark of his hand. He

2. Joseph Anton Feuchtmayer and others: interior of the pilgrimage church of Neubirnau, near Konstanz, 1748–50

NDB

BIBLIOGRAPHY

H. Sauer: *Herkunft und Anfänge des Bildhauers Joseph Anton Feuchtmayer* (diss., U. Leipzig, 1932)
H. Ginter: *Kloster Salem* (Karlsruhe, 1934)
H. Sauer: 'Das Werk Joseph Anton Faichtmayers: Ein Überblick', *Oberrhein. Kst*, vi (1936), pp. 201–55
W. Boeck: *Joseph Anton Feuchtmayer* (Tübingen, 1948)
P. Zinsmaier: 'Neue Beiträge aus Salemer Archivalien zu Joseph Anton Feuchtmayer', *Z. Gesch. Oberrheins*, n. s. lix (1950), pp. 147–80
W. Boeck: *Feuchtmayers Meisterwerke* (Tübingen, 1963)
B. Bushart: *Der Genius Joseph Anton Feuchtmayers* (Friedrichshafen, 1980)
W. Boeck: *Der Bildhauer, Altarbauer und Stukkator Joseph Anton Feuchtmayer* (Friedrichshafen, 1981)
U. Knapp: *Die Wallfahrtskirche Birnau: Planungs- und Baugeschichte* (Friedrichshafen, 1989)
——: 'Entwurf und Kopie: Zeichnungen Joseph Anton Feuchtmayers und seiner Werkstatt zum Hochaltar in der Heersburger Schlosskapelle', *Z. Dt. Ver. Kstwiss.*, 43 (1989), pp. 37–71
——: *Salem: Die Gebäude des ehemaligen Zisterzienserabtei und ihre Ausstattungen* (in preparation)

ULRICH KNAPP

Feuerbach, Anselm (*b* Speyer, 12 Sept 1829; *d* Venice, 4 Jan 1880). German painter and draughtsman. He received his first art lessons from the anatomical draughtsman at the University of Freiburg where his father, Joseph Anselm Feuerbach, lectured in Classical philology and archaeology. In 1845 he enrolled at the Düsseldorf Akademie where he studied under Wilhelm Schadow. Though adept at academic drawing, he was urged by Schadow to simplify his rather unresolved and crowded compositional sketches and concentrate on a few figures. In 1848 he moved to Munich where he made copies after Old Master paintings in the Alte Pinakothek, being especially impressed by the work of Rubens. Though eventually studying at the Munich Akademie, he saw the landscape painter Carl Rahl as his real mentor. Works such as *Landscape with a Hermit Returning Home* (1848–9; Karlsruhe, Staatl. Ksthalle) combine the rich mood of the Munich landscape tradition with subject-matter more typical of the Düsseldorf school.

In May 1850 Feuerbach moved to the Academie in Antwerp to study under Gustaf Wappers, and in 1851 went on to Paris, drawn by admiration for the work of Thomas Couture, whose *Romans of the Decadence* (1847; Paris, Mus. d'Orsay) he copied (1852; Freiburg im Breisgau, Augustinermus.). Feuerbach's *Hafiz Outside the Drinking House* (1852; Mannheim, Städt. Ksthalle) also

Anselm Feuerbach: *Plato's Symposium*, oil on canvas, 2.95×5.98 m, 1869 (Karlsruhe, Staatliche Kunsthalle)

reflects his admiration for Couture in its Classical setting and costumes and sense of material luxury. In Paris Feuerbach made copies from works in the Louvre, especially those of Veronese, Rubens and Delacroix, and came to feel that he had attained a new maturity, as is indeed suggested in his intense and self-confident *Self-portrait* of 1851–2 (Karlsruhe, Staatl. Ksthalle). He now expressed scorn for the laborious and pedantic academicism of German art, contrasting it with the genius and spontaneity of the great tradition of Italy and France. In the *Death of Aretino* (1854; Basle, Kstmus.), an accomplished painting strongly influenced by Veronese, Feuerbach declared his allegiance to this tradition.

Early in 1854 debts and other difficulties drove Feuerbach back to Germany. His father had died in 1851 and for the rest of his life he was dependent on the financial and moral support of his stepmother. In the hope of receiving portrait commissions, he took a studio in Karlsruhe. There he found a patron in the Regent (later Grand Duke) Frederick of Baden to whom he successfully applied for a stipend to enable him to go to Venice to make a copy of a work by Titian; he eventually chose to copy the *Assumption of the Virgin* of 1518 in the church of the Frari (copy, 1855; Karlsruhe, Staatl. Ksthalle). While original compositions from this period, such as *Musical Poetry* (1855–6; Karlsruhe, Staatl. Ksthalle), were closely allied to Renaissance models, Feuerbach also responded to the landscape of Italy in free studies intended for later use as backgrounds for history paintings, such as *Waterfall* (1855; Mannheim, Städt. Ksthalle).

In the autumn of 1856 Feuerbach left Venice and travelled via Bologna to Rome, which remained his principal place of residence for the rest of his life. During the summers he sketched in and around the city; works such as *Study from the Baths of Caracalla in Rome* (1858; Hamburg, Ksthalle) reveal his enthusiastic response to the heat and light of the south. Despite problems of both

money and health—bouts of syphilis-related illness plagued him to the end of his life—Feuerbach drew moral support from contact with the circle of German artists in Rome, including Arnold Böcklin and Reinhold Begas. He was, however, most bound to Rome in his attachment to Nanna Risi, a cobbler's wife whom he met in 1860 and in whom he saw the embodiment of the Classical ideal of womanhood; she became his model and shortly afterwards his mistress (until 1865). Feuerbach painted her in religious roles, as in *Virgin and Child with St John the Baptist and Musical Angels* (1859–60; Dresden, Gemäldegal. Neue Meister), as Classical heroines such as *Iphigenia* (1862; Darmstadt, Hess. Landesmus.), and in several portraits such as *Nanna* (1861; Karlsruhe, Staatl. Ksthalle). Her presence gave new conviction to Feuerbach's emulation of both Classical and Renaissance models; in particular it gave him confidence to add a new interest in mood and psychology to the traditional concern for form.

Throughout his first years in Rome, Feuerbach was engaged in plans for the composition *Plato's Symposium* (1869; Karlsruhe, Staatl. Ksthalle; see fig.), loosely based on an engraving of 1648 by Pietro Testa. Feuerbach was primarily concerned with the psychological forces at play, as revealed in expression, gesture and pose. The essential solemnity of the occasion—in contrast to Testa's version—is emphasized by the restrained movements of even the festive group entering at the left and by the cool grey, green and blue tones used for costumes and setting. Negative criticism of both these elements when the work was exhibited in Munich in 1869 led Feuerbach to produce a second version (1873; Berlin, Alte N.G.) enlivened with brighter and more varied colours, additional decoration and an altogether more theatrical air in the spirit of Hans Makart; this too had little success on its exhibition in 1874 in Vienna.

Feuerbach's capacity for more lively large-scale composition, drawing on Baroque rather than Renaissance models, was revealed in *Battle of the Amazons* (1872; Nuremberg, Stadtmus. Fembohaus) and in *Fall of the Titans* painted for the ceiling of the Great Hall of the Akademie in Vienna (1874–80; installed 1892, *in situ*). His last large-scale composition, the decorative friezes painted for the Nuremberg Chamber of Commerce in the newly built Palace of Justice, point to his real skills in achieving a balance between solemnity and festivity, warm and cool colouring, and type and individual, especially in the scene of *Emperor Ludwig Bestowing Privileges on the Citizens of Nuremberg* of 1878, *in situ*.

WRITINGS
Ein Vermächtnis von Anselm Feuerbach, ed. H. Feuerbach (Vienna, 1882)

BIBLIOGRAPHY
J. Allgeyer: *Anselm Feuerbach* (Bamberg, 1894; Berlin, 1904)
G. J. Kern and H. Uhde-Bernays: *Anselm Feuerbachs Briefe an seine Mutter* (Berlin, 1911)
H. Feuerbach: *Ihr Leben in ihren Briefen*, ed. H. Uhde-Bernays (Berlin, 1912)
E. Voigtländer: *Anselm Feuerbach: Versuch einer Stilanalyse* (Leipzig, 1912)
H. Uhde-Bernays: *Feuerbach* (Leipzig, 1922)
C. Neumann: *Der Maler Anselm Feuerbach* (Heidelberg, 1929)
H. Uhde-Bernays: *Feuerbach: Beschreibender Katalog seiner sämtlichen Gemälde* (Munich, 1929)
U. Christoffel: *Anselm Feuerbach* (Munich, 1944)
E. Waldmann: *Anselm Feuerbach* (Berlin, 1944)
E. Kühnemann: *Zu Anselm Feuerbachs reifem Stil* (diss., U. Cologne, 1948)
J. Lauts and W. Zimmermann: *Anselm Feuerbach* (Staatl. Ksthalle cat., Karlsruhe, 1961)
W. Zimmermann, ed.: *Anselm Feuerbach: Gemälde und Zeichnungen aus der Staatlichen Kunsthalle* (Karlsruhe, 1961; 1978)
M. Arndt: *Die Zeichnungen Anselm Feuerbachs* (diss., U. Bonn, 1968)
Anselm Feuerbach, 1829–1880: Gemälde und Zeichnungen (exh. cat., Karlsruhe, Staatl. Ksthalle, 1976)

ELIZABETH CLEGG

Feuerstein, Bedřich (*b* Dobrovice, 15 Jan 1892; *d* Prague, 10 May 1936). Czech architect, painter and stage designer. He graduated in architecture (1917) from the Technical University, Prague, and in 1921 he received a scholarship to the Ecole du Louvre in Paris. In 1922 he became a member of Devětsil, the group of avant-garde writers, artists and architects centred on the figure of Karel Teige. He also joined the Architects' Club. His early work was influenced by Cubism and classicism, but his most significant building was the crematorium (1921–3; with Bohumil Sláma) at Nymburk, a fundamental work of Czech architectural Purism composed of dramatic white cylinders and slabs, with a row of massive columns and ceremonial steps along the main façade. All his designs were strictly tectonic; he aimed for the creation of a new style inspired by the Neo-classical Empire style. During the first half of the 1920s he also worked as a stage designer in Prague, creating a range of designs in the spirit of poetic Purism; examples include sets for the National Theatre (1921–2), Prague. From 1924 to 1926 he worked in Paris for the Perret brothers and from 1926 to 1930 he worked in Tokyo with Antonin Raymond, where he was responsible for designing the Embassy of the USSR (1928) and St Luke's Hospital (1928–30). After his return to Czechoslovakia he worked mainly in stage design. Although he built comparatively little in Czechoslovakia, his judgement and awareness of developments abroad made him one of the real initiators of Czechoslovak avant-garde design.

BIBLIOGRAPHY
Bedřich Feuerstein (Prague, 1936)
Bedřich Feuerstein (exh. cat. by A. Masaryková, Prague, 1967)
'Bedřich Feuerstein', *Tschechische Kunst der 20er und 30er Jahre: Avantgarde und Tradition* (exh. cat. by J. Hilmera, J. Machalický and R. Sedláková; Darmstadt, Ausstellhallen Mathildenhöhe, 1988–9), pp. 60–64
Devětsil: Czech Avant-Garde Art, Architecture and Design of the 1920s and 1930s (exh. cat., ed. R. Švácha; Oxford, MOMA; London, Des. Mus.; 1990)
'Bedřich Feuerstein', *Český kubismus 1909–1925* (exh. cat. by Z. Lukeš, Düsseldorf, Kstver.; Prague, N. G.; 1991–92), pp. 244–5
The Art of the Avant-Garde in Czechoslovakia 1918–1938 (exh. cat., ed. J. Anděl; Valencia, IVAM Cent. Julio Gonzalez, 1993)

RADOMÍRA SEDLÁKOVÁ

Feure, Georges de [Sluijters, Georges Joseph van; Feuren, Georges van] (*b* Paris, 6 Sept 1868; *d* Paris, 26 Nov 1928). French designer and painter. Son of a Dutch architect and a Belgian mother, he started out as an actor, costumier and then interior decorator in Paris. In 1894 at the Galerie des Artistes Modernes he exhibited watercolours and paintings of a moderate Symbolist style, typically depicting women in a manner reminiscent of Aubrey Beardsley's work. Capturing the essence of the feminine spirit became his trademark. With Eugène Gaillard and Edouard Colonna he was selected by Siegfried Bing, founder of the Galeries de l'Art Nouveau, to design rooms for his Pavilion Bing at the Exposition Universelle, Paris (1900). De Feure's carpets, glassware and furniture designs (*see* ART NOUVEAU, fig. 2) for the boudoir and toilette were based on the theme of woman, emphasizing delicate lines and elegant sensuality. He later left Bing's gallery and, as an independent designer, created *vide-poche* furniture, which contained hidden marquetry compartments. This furniture suggested notions of secrecy and coquetry, themes that de Feure pursued throughout his career.

BIBLIOGRAPHY
'Le Mobilier de Georges de Feure', *A. & Déc.*, ii (1908), pp. 115–32
F. Borsi and E. Godoli: *Paris 1900* (New York, 1977)

CHARLOTTE MOSER

Fevère [Lefebvre; Fèvre], **Pietro** [Pierre] (*b* Antwerp, 1579; *d* Florence, 1669). Flemish tapestry-weaver. He was working in Paris in 1619, when he was invited by Cosimo II, Grand Duke of Tuscany, to go to Florence to assist in the revival of tapestry-weaving. Fevère, who knew both the high- and low-warp techniques, was given a workshop in the Palazzo Vecchio. In 1630, after the death of Jacopo Ebert Van Asselt (*fl* 1621–30), head weaver of the Arazzeria Medicea—the Medici tapestry factory—Fevère was named head weaver and moved to the larger workshops at S Marco. His sons Giovanni (*d* 1700), Francesco, Andrea, Filippo (*d* after 1677) and Jacopo worked with him.

Under his tutelage, the Arazzeria Medicea enjoyed a period of revived activity. The numerous large tapestries woven in his workshops include seven of the ten tapestries of the *Seasons and the Hours* (1641–3); five of the seven *Stories of St Paul* (1646; destr.); two of the five-piece *Story of Tobias* (1648; destr.); five of the twelve-piece *Story of Alexander* (1651; destr.); pieces of the *Life of Moses* (1650s); and *Stories of Grand Duke Cosimo I de' Medici* (1654–65; all surviving examples Florence, Sopr. B. A. & Storici Col.).

The fame of Fevère's work prompted Cardinal Mazarin to recall him to Paris to set up a workshop and bring new momentum to French weaving. With the approval of Ferdinand II, Grand Duke of Tuscany, Fevère made a brief trip to France between 1647–8 and 1650 and was named Tapissier du Roi on 13 September 1648; he apparently left his son Giovanni to direct the workshop there. On 26 February 1655 Pietro and Giovanni were accorded lodging in the Louvre and Fevère had to return to Paris to accept it on their behalf. On 3 July 1655, perhaps as incentive to keep Fevère in France, Louis XIV commanded that a larger workshop be constructed for the family in the Tuileries gardens. Fevère, however, returned to Florence, possibly almost immediately. Giovanni, who remained in Paris, founded one of the important dynastic workshops at the Gobelins (*see* GOBELINS, §2) at its institution in 1662.

Late in his career, Fevère initiated the practice of systematically weaving portable, high-warp tapestry replicas of favourite paintings from the Grand Ducal picture gallery, including the *Virgin and Child with SS Anne, Joseph and John the Baptist* after Rubens (1652); a *Virgin and Child* after Raphael and the *Holy Family* after Andrea del Sarto (1660; all Florence). Possibly following this Florentine example, this genre of virtuoso weaving subsequently became common in many other European tapestry factories.

BIBLIOGRAPHY

R.-A. Weigert: *French Tapestry* (Newton, MA, 1962), p. 179
Chefs-d'oeuvre de la Tapisserie Parisienne 1597–1662 (exh. cat. by J. Coural, Versailles, Château, Orangerie, (1967), p. 18
Palazzo Vecchio: Committenza e collezionismo mediceo (exh. cat., ed. Paola Barocchi, Florence, Pal. Vecchio, 1980), pp. 108–12
M. Chiarini: *Sustermans: Sessant'anni alla corte dei Medici* (exh. cat., Florence, Pitti, 1983), p. 44, no. 23

CANDACE J. ADELSON

Feyen-Perrin, (François-Nicolas-)Auguste (*b* Bey-sur-Seille, 12 April 1829; *d* Paris, 14 Oct 1888). French painter, draughtsman and printmaker. His older brother Eugène (1815–1908) was a painter, who persuaded their father to let Auguste pursue a similar career and served as his first teacher in Nancy. Auguste furthered his studies in Paris with Martin Drolling, Léon Cogniet and Adolphe Yvon. In Drolling's atelier Feyen-Perrin began a lifelong friendship with Jules Breton. He exhibited in the open Salon of 1848, and in 1853 and 1855, as 'Auguste Feyen'. From 1857 he became 'Feyen-Perrin', probably to distinguish himself from his brother, who was also a frequent Salon participant as 'Perrin'.

Influenced by the 1848 Revolution, Feyen-Perrin's first paintings were of peasants, and throughout his career he returned to rural subjects, making a speciality of fisherfolk scenes from Cancale, Roscroft and the isle of Batz in Brittany. In 1857 he sent the *Barque of Charon* (Nancy, Mus. B.-A.) to the Salon and often exhibited mythological and religious subjects thereafter. Quotations from Dante accompanied some early works, but from 1868 Feyen-Perrin almost invariably listed as his inspiration verse by his friend Paul-Armand Silvestre, a prolific poet, story-writer and art critic. Silvestre was also portrayed as one of the figures in Feyen-Perrin's important realist composition

for the 1863 Salon, the *Anatomy Lesson* (Tours, Mus. B.-A.), which depicted with stark Davidian lighting France's most celebrated surgeon, Dr Velpeau (1795–1867), teaching in La Charité hospital. The picture may have influenced Thomas Eakins's the *Gross Clinic* (1875; Philadelphia, PA, Thomas Jefferson U., Medic. Col.). Feyen-Perrin was a successful portraitist, painting, among others, Alphonse Daudet (Salon of 1876; untraced).

Feyen-Perrin was a progressive force in artistic politics: in 1871 the Commune secretly elected him, with Courbet, to a provisional committee of artists; and in 1873 he joined the group that organized the first Impressionist exhibition the following year, though he did not participate in that show. Instead he exhibited annually at the Salon etchings, lithographs and drawings as well as paintings. He received the Légion d'honneur in 1878. By his own admission Feyen-Perrin aimed at 'une bonne moyenne' (happy compromise): he was a representative French artist of the second half of the 19th century, successful and competent, but lacking in originality or distinctive flair.

BIBLIOGRAPHY

P. G. Hamerton: 'Examples of Modern Etching, XVII: A. Feyen-Perrin: "A Sailor's Infancy"', *Portfolio* [London] (1873), pp. 65–6
R. Ménard: 'Feyen-Perrin', *L'Art en Alsace-Lorraine* (1876), pp. 413–14
A. M. de Bélina: *Nos peintres dessinés par eux-mêmes* (Paris, 1883), pp. 217–19
Exposition des oeuvres de Feyen-Perrin (exh. cat., intro. J. Breton; Paris, Ecole N. Sup. B.-A., 1889)
E. C. Parry: '"The Gross Clinic" as Anatomy Lesson and Memorial Portrait', *A. Q.* [Detroit], xxxii (1969), pp. 373–91
The Realist Tradition: French Painting and Drawing, 1830–1900 (exh. cat. by G. P. Weisberg, Cleveland, OH, Mus. A., 1981), pp. 180–81, 288

JAMES P. W. THOMPSON

Feyerabend, Sigmund (*b* Heidelberg, 1527–8; *d* Frankfurt am Main, 1590). German publisher and woodblock-cutter. He was the son of the painter and blockcutter Ägidius Feyerabend and his wife, Anna Brentlein (*d* 1568), daughter of a rabbi in Mainz. After an apprenticeship with Jörg Breu (ii) in Augsburg, begun on 19 July 1540, Feyerabend spent some time in Italy and perhaps also in Mainz. In 1559 he settled in Frankfurt am Main, where he married the same year and acquired citizenship in 1560. After working as a block cutter and possibly also as a designer of book illustrations, he soon turned to the business side of publishing, which he managed with considerable success and, judging from numerous lawsuits, with shrewdness. He employed almost all the printers in Frankfurt am Main and attracted the best book illustrators in the country, foremost among them Virgil Solis from Nuremberg and Jost Amman from Zurich. One of his most successful collaborations with Solis resulted in a magnificent picture Bible in Martin Luther's translation (1560). After Solis's death (1562), Amman became the most important illustrator for Feyerabend, who published his famous *Kunstbüchlein* (1580), for which he also wrote the preface. Amman's woodcuts for Feyerabend's German edition of Flavius Josephus' *Jewish Antiquities* (1569) later attracted the attention of the young Rubens, who made numerous copies. Amman also produced the only portrait of Feyerabend in a woodcut (1569; B. 371), copied by Johann Sadeler I in an engraving (1587; Hollstein, no. 596).

Feyerabend's importance lies in his activity as a publisher. His dominance of the Frankfurt book trade (and that of his firm) lasted for 50 years and came to an end only with the death of his younger son, Charles-Sigismond (1579–1609). It was in no small part due to Feyerabend that Frankfurt's role as a publishing centre, particularly of illustrated books, continued well into the 18th century.

BIBLIOGRAPHY

Hollstein: *Ger.*

A. von Bartsch: *Le Peintre-graveur* (1803–21) [B.]

H. Pallmann: *Sigmund Feyerabend: Sein Leben und seine geschäftlichen Verbindungen* (Frankfurt am Main, 1881)

F. H. Meyer: 'Der Verleger Sigmund Feyerabend', *Archv Gesch. Dt. Bhand.*, xiv (1891), pp. 114–34

W. K. Zülch: *Frankfurter Künstler, 1223–1700* (Frankfurt am Main, 1935/R 1967), pp. 358–9 [expresses anti-Semitic sentiments]

J. Kirchner, ed.: *Lexikon des Buchwesens*, i (1952), p. 242

E. H. G. Klöss: 'Der Frankfurter Drucker-Verleger Weigand Han und seine Erben: Ein Beitrag zur Geschichte des Frankfurter Buchgewerbes im 16. Jahrhundert', *Archv Gesch. Bwsn.*, ii (1960), pp. 309–74

KRISTIN LOHSE BELKIN

Fez [Arab. Fās; Fr. Fès]. City in northern Morocco. The role of Fez as a city of artisans and commerce was assured by its location in the midst of a fertile and well-watered undulating region at the crossroads of the east–west passage from the Atlantic Ocean through the Taza Gap to Algeria with the north–south route from the Mediterranean Sea to the Sahara. The oldest Islamic foundation in Morocco, Fez preserves the monuments, souks, craft traditions and commerce of a pre-modern Islamic city. It also enjoys considerable religious and intellectual importance owing to the presence of the Qarawiyyin Mosque and University. UNESCO has funded the elaboration of a master plan for the city to help solve the problem of conserving a competitive, modern urban centre within a city museum.

In AD 789 Idris I (*reg* 789–93), eponym of the Idrisids (*reg* 789–926), a local Shi'ite dynasty, founded the city of Fez (Arab. *madinat fās*) on the east bank of the wadi Fas, a tributary of the Jebou River; in 809 Idris II (*reg* 793–828) founded a new city known as the 'Alid (Arab. *al-'aliyya*) opposite it on the west bank and built his palace there. In 817–18, following a riot at Córdoba, families of Andalusian refugees (Arab. *andalusiyyin*) established themselves in the city of Idris I. A short time later, refugees from Kairouan (Arab. *qarawiyyin*) in Tunisia were welcomed in the city of Idris II, which appears to have had a more civilized and Arabized character than its older, more Berber neighbour. The precise plan of the two first settlements on either side of the river can no longer be reconstituted, but they were located at the bottom of the Fez basin. With the decline of the Idrisids, Fez became a stake in the wars between the Fatimid dynasty (*reg* 909–72 in Tunisia) and the Umayyad dynasty of Spain (*reg* 756–1031).

Fez enjoyed a period of prosperity and expansion under the Almoravids (*reg* 1056–1147), although their capital was at Marrakesh. In 1069 the Almoravid ruler Yusuf ibn Tashufin (*reg* 1061–1106) took Fez, unified the two districts within one wall and constructed a fortress (Arab. *qasaba*) to the west. The Almoravid fortress seems to have been located on the site of the present kasba of the Filala to the west of the city. The west bank, better irrigated than the east bank, was enlarged and developed from the base of the valley towards the citadel. The two principal streets of the medina still follow this east–west direction. The west bank thus evolved rapidly, while the east bank became the domain of more modest artisans.

The Almohads (*reg* 1130–1269) entered Fez in 1146 and razed the Almoravid fortress and ramparts, which were soon re-erected. Fez remained the economic, intellectual and artistic centre of northern Morocco as a result of commerce between Spain and the central Maghrib, although the Almohads also preferred Marrakesh. The line of the early 13th-century ramparts has hardly changed, and the eight Almohad gates are still in place. The centre of the city included the mosque of the Qarawiyyin quarter, the tomb of Idris II, the market for precious goods (Arab. *qaysāriyya*) and the souk. A second, less important centre seems to have been located between the bridges over the wadi Fas and the mosque of the Andalusiyyin quarter to the east. These centres were linked to the gates by an irregular system of streets, for the sloping ground rendered all regular urbanistic schemes impractical. The city walls originally enclosed vast empty areas, and the city was able to expand within its walls until the 20th century.

Fez again became the capital of a realm in the middle of the 13th century, when it was taken by the Marinids (*reg* 1196–1549). The period of Marinid rule was the most splendid in the history of the city. The old quarters were embellished with numerous edifices, notably madrasas and mosques. In 1276 the Marinids created a new quarter *ex nihilo* on the plateau that dominates the old city from the west. Called the White City (Arab. *al-madinat al-baydā'*), it quickly became known as New Fez (Arab. *fās al-jadid*) in contrast to Old Fez (Arab. *fās al-bāli*). This city has a regular plan within a double wall. The palaces in the southwest (which still exist) were placed next to the administrative quarter in the north-west, which had its own congregational mosque. Further to the east extended the medina of New Fez, with streets intersecting at right angles to the principal north–south axis, souks, caravanserais (Arab. *funduq*), baths and mosques. The Jewish quarter (Arab. *mallah*), another Marinid creation, lies to the south of New Fez.

The Marinid period was followed by more than two centuries of troubles, interrupted only by a short period of prosperity at the end of the 16th century. In 1641, when the city was conquered by the Berber confederation of the Dila, the citizens appealed for help to the 'Alawi sharifs (*reg* from 1631), who established power there in 1666. Under the 'Alawis, Fez had many changes of fortune: al-Rashid (*reg* 1664–72) devoted himself actively to its embellishment, Isma'il as-Samin (*reg* 1672–1727) ignored it in favour of Meknès, and 'Abdallah (*reg* 1729–35) made it his capital, causing widespread destruction in his struggle to gain power. The majority of 'Alawi sovereigns undertook major constructions, although the urban character of the double city was hardly modified. Al-Rashid rebuilt the walls of Old Fez and constructed the kasba of the Shararda (Cherarda) to the north. 'Abdallah had the Dar al-Dabibagh (1729), a new kasba, erected about 5 km to the south-west, incidentally destroying the principal gates of Fez. Neither of these kasbas was ever integrated in the city. In the second half of the 19th century, the empty land between Old Fez and New Fez was filled with palaces and gardens. The surrounding hills received sumptuous habitations, notably in the south-west of Old Fez. At the beginning of the 20th century, the empty land between the Almohad rampart and the actual city was used for schools, playing fields and residences. During the French Protectorate (1912–56), a separate new city was created to the south-west; it did not modify the existing urban structures and continues to expand.

The oldest and most venerable of the many celebrated monuments in Fez is the Qarawiyyin (Karaouine) Mosque. Although its foundation goes back to the 9th century and its minaret to the 10th, its present form dates from the Almohad renovation of the mosque in 1134–43. It is one of the largest mosques of Morocco, measuring 82×68 m. The prayer-hall has 10 aisles parallel to the qibla wall, each with 21 bays. The line of central bays is covered with a series of richly decorated *muqarnas* cupolas, from which hang several bronze chandeliers made from bells captured from the Christians in Spain. The minbar, probably made in Córdoba and presented to the mosque in 1144, is a masterpiece of medieval Islamic woodwork: its triangular sides are decorated with deeply carved small panels and marquetry strapwork in a pattern generated from eight-pointed stars (*see* ISLAMIC ART, §VII, 1(iii)). Other fine woodwork includes the *'anaza* (1289), an auxiliary mihrab in a grille in the court façade of the prayer-hall. Although its exterior surface is heavily weathered, the interior preserves its inlaid interlace decoration and kufic inscriptions (*see* ISLAMIC ART, §VII, 2(i)). Behind the qibla wall of the mosque lie several annexes, including a library and a small triangular oratory to which bodies were brought before burial (Arab. *jāmi' al-janā'iz, jamaa el-gnaiz*, Fr. *mosquée des morts*). Under the Sa'dian dynasty (*reg* 1511–1659), the small court was embellished with two pavilions (see fig.) modelled on those in the Patio de los Leones at the Alhambra in Granada (*see* GRANADA, fig. 4). Under the Almoravids the mosque became a centre of learning that was the core of an important Islamic university. The Andalusiyyin (Andalous) Mosque, also founded in the 9th century and given a minaret in the 10th, is largely a creation of the Almohad period. The plan is a reduced version of that of the Qarawiyyin Mosque. The mosque preserves several important bronze bell lamps as well as a wooden minbar of the 10th century.

Madrasas were first built in Fez under the Marinids, and several fine examples are preserved. The Saffarin (1271), Sahrij (1321), Saba'iyyin (early 14th century), 'Attarin (1323–5; *see* ISLAMIC ART, fig. 61) and Misbahiyya (1347) madrasas are all located relatively near the Qarawiyyin Mosque. The Fez al-Jadid (1320) and the Bu 'Inaniyya (1350–55; *see* MADRASA, fig. 2) madrasas are situated further to the west; each is distinguished by a minaret. In general they are small buildings with a central court containing a basin, a hall for prayer and instruction, chambers for students and faculty, and latrines. The Bu 'Inaniyya is exceptional in having a congregational mosque. The buildings are notable for their refined decoration in carved plaster and wood and glazed tile (*see* ISLAMIC ART, §II, 6(iv)(b)). The immense Sharratin (Cherratine) Madrasa (1670), replacing an earlier structure, has poor and

Fez, Qarawiyyin Mosque, renovated 1134–43; court, with pavilion added in the early 17th century

monotonous decoration in comparison to the decorative programmes of the Marinid period.

Other buildings, including several caravanserais, monumental fountains and ancient palaces (transformed into commercial centres open to the public), have parts dating to the 16th and 17th centuries, although the architectural conservatism of the city makes it impossible to establish exact dates on stylistic grounds. The most venerated monument is the tomb of Idris II and the adjacent hospice (Arab. *zāwiya*). Although it was founded in the Idrisid period, the present structure dates only from the 18th century. The Batha Palace (19th century), converted during the Protectorate into a museum of the arts and traditions of Fez and its region (Mus. Dar Batha), preserves many features of Hispano-Moresque secular architecture.

Fez has been a noted centre for the production of textiles and leather goods since the Middle Ages. The Fez style of embroidery is done in counted cross-stitch in red or blue silk on cotton. The designs are largely geometric or geometricized vegetal patterns and have been used, at least since the 18th century, for cushion covers, curtains and towels (*see* ISLAMIC ART, §VI, 2(iii)(b)). A more elaborate type of embroidery is couched in gold and silver thread on velvet or leather. Many traditional textile techniques have been preserved in the production of the traditional wedding costumes of Fez: silk-weaving on draw looms, for example, was still practised in the 1980s to make sashes and belts. The tanneries of Fez, with their open dye vats, are one of the most picturesque, if malodorous, sights in the city.

BIBLIOGRAPHY

Enc. Islam/2: 'Fās'
C. Terrasse: *Médersas du Maroc* (Paris, [1927])
E. Lévi-Provençal: 'La Fondation de Fès', *An. Inst. Etud. Orient. U. Alger*, iv (1938), pp. 23–52
H. Terrasse: *La Mosquée des Andalous à Fès* (Paris, [1942])
R. Le Tourneau: *Fès avant le Protectorat* (Rabat, 1949)
H. Terrasse: *La Mosquée al-Qaraouiyin à Fès* (Paris, 1968)
J. Revault, L. Golvin and A. Amahane: *Les Palais et demeures de Fès*, 2 vols (Paris, 1985–9)
E. Wirth: 'La Médina de Fès en tant que modèle de la ville musulmane traditionnelle', *Géographie humaine*, vol. of *La Grande Encyclopédie du Maroc* (in preparation)

MARIANNE BARRUCAND

Fialetti, Odoardo (*b* Bologna, 1573; *d* Venice, 1638). Italian painter and printmaker. He was apprenticed in Bologna to Giovanni Battista Cremonini (*d* 1610) and after a short period in Rome moved to Venice, where he entered Tintoretto's workshop. By 1596 he was listed as a printmaker and from 1604 to 1612 is recorded as a member of the Venetian Fraglia dei Pittori. His work, although it reveals hints of the Carracci and the influence of Flemish art, remains within the tradition of late Mannerism. His works for Italian churches include *St Agnes* (Venice, S Nicolò da Tolentino) and scenes from the *Life of St Dominic* (Venice, SS Giovanni e Paolo, sacristy), which can be dated to the first decade of the 17th century. Four portraits of doges and a picture of the *Sala del Collegio* (London, Hampton Court, Royal Col.), which shows a session of the Doge's council, demonstrate Fialetti's interest in portraiture and in combining *vedute* with elements of genre.

Fialetti was a prolific engraver, and his *c.* 250 prints unite Mannerist elegance with the straightforward realism of the Carracci. Some reproduce works of Polidoro da Caravaggio, Tintoretto and Pordenone; others are of his own invention. In 1608 he collaborated with Palma Giovane on *Il vero modo et ordine per dissegnar tutte le parti et membra del corpo humano* (B. 198–207), which was intended to instruct the professional artist in how to draw the body and thereby introduced a new kind of manual to Venice. There followed a series of hunting scenes (*c.* 1610; B. 34–6), landscapes (B. 185–97), *Tritons and Nereids* (B. 24–9), the *Sport of Love* (1617; B. 6–19) and a series of *Habits of Religious Orders* (1626; B. 66–141).

BIBLIOGRAPHY
Bolaffi
C. Donzelli and G. M. Pilo: *I pittori del seicento veneto* (Florence, 1967), pp. 177–8
R. Pallucchini: *La pitture veneziana del seicento* (Milan, 1981), i, pp. 80–81
S. Buffa: *Italian Artists of the Sixteenth Century (1983)*, 38 [XVII/v] of *The Illustrated Bartsch*, ed. W. Strauss (New York, 1978–) [B.]
'Venice after 1600', *Italian Etchers of the Renaissance and Baroque* (exh. cat., ed. S. Welshreed; Boston, MA, Mus. F.A., 1989), pp. 248, 251

FELICIANO BENVENUTI

Fiamberti, Tommaso (*fl* 1498; *d* Cesena, between 7 Sept 1524 and 21 Jan 1525). Italian sculptor. Originally from Campione, Lake Lugano, he was mainly active in Cesena, where he is first documented in 1498. Commissions there for marble statues for the cathedral (1510) and for a chapel entrance arch at S Francesco (1513) apparently went unexecuted. His one certain independent work is the signed funerary monument of *Luffo Numai* (1509; Ravenna, S Francesco). This work of architectural and decorative sculpture, with polychrome stone inlay and rich classical *rinceau* decoration in high relief, suggests familiarity with Pietro Lombardo's work in Venice. Pilasters carved in the same style testify to Fiamberti's role in an earlier documented monument to *Luffo Numai* (1502; Forlì, S Maria dei Servi, also called S Pellegrino), in which he collaborated with a fellow Lombard, Giovanni Ricci (1440/50–after 1523), his partner from *c.* 1498 to 1508. The precise division of labour in this monument, however, remains controversial. The Forlì monument has formed the basis for many attributions of figural reliefs to Fiamberti, as well as for his identification (De Nicola) as the MASTER OF THE MARBLE MADONNAS (*see* MASTERS, ANONYMOUS, AND MONOGRAMMISTS, §I), but subsequent scholarship has cast doubt on these attributions, and the full range of Fiamberti's style remains problematical.

BIBLIOGRAPHY
Thieme–Becker
G. De Nicola: 'Tommaso Fiamberti: Il Maestro delle Madonne di Marmo', *Rass. A.*, ix (1922), pp. 73–81
J. Balogh: 'Uno sconosciuto scultore italiano presso il Re Mattia Corvino', *Riv. A.*, xv (1933), pp. 272–97
J. Pope-Hennessy: *Catalogue of Italian Sculpture in the Victoria and Albert Museum*, i (London, 1964), pp. 151–2
U. Middeldorf: 'An *Ecce homo* by the Master of the Marble Madonnas', *Album Amicorum J. G. van Gelder* (The Hague, 1973), pp. 234–6
G. Viroli: *La Pinacoteca Civica di Forlì* (Forlì, 1980), pp. 48–9
G. Gentilini: entry in *La Misericordia di Firenze: Archivio e raccolta d'arte* (Florence, 1981), cat. 58, pp. 248–9

ALISON LUCHS

Fiamminghini, i. *See* ROVERE, DELLA (ii).

Fiammingo [di Pietro Cili], **Adriano** (*fl* Florence, 1600–43). Flemish painter, active in Italy. Filippo Baldinucci briefly mentioned him as a landscape painter working in Florence. He is identifiable with the Adriano di Pietro Cili, probably from Siel, who appears in the records of the Accademia del Disegno first in 1600, when he matriculated while in the studio of Lodovico Cigoli, and then in subsequent years. His recorded works consist of six documented but untraced landscape paintings with figures by Cigoli (*DBI*) and two drawings (Florence, Uffizi, see 1986 exh. cat.). According to Baldinucci, his landscape manner, with its 'rich backgrounds, painted minutely in luminous greens and blues', greatly influenced draughtsmen and painters, especially Cristofano Allori and Valerio Marucelli (*fl* 1589–1620). A *Landscape with Tobias and the Angel* (Florence, priv. col., see 1986 exh. cat., no. 1.63) is attributed to him, and his style is reflected in the backgrounds of paintings by Cigoli, such as the *St Mary Magdalene* of 1605, and by Allori, such as the *St John the Baptist in the Desert* (both Florence, Pitti). He introduced a Flemish delicacy of line, colour and composition to the distinctive landscape style developed by painters, printmakers and draughtsmen in 17th-century Florence.

BIBLIOGRAPHY
DBI
F. Baldinucci: *Notizie* (1681–1728); ed. F. Ranalli (1845–7), iii, p. 723

Il seicento fiorentino: Arte a Firenze da Ferdinando I a Cosimo III (exh. cat., ed. P. Bigongiari and M. Gregori; Florence, Pal. Strozzi, 1986), ii, p. 131, no. 2.77; iii, p. 29

MILES L. CHAPPELL

Fiammingo, Giovanni. *See* VASANZIO, GIOVANNI.

Fiammingo, Paolo [Franck, Pauwels] (*b* ?Antwerp, *c.* 1540; *d* 1596). Flemish painter and draughtsman, active in Italy. He was registered in the Antwerp Guild of St Luke in 1561. By 1573 he was in Venice and an assistant in Tintoretto's workshop, where he specialized in landscape backgrounds (e.g. the paintings, 1579–80, for the church of S Rocco). From 1580 Paolo produced several series of paintings for the German banker and patron Hans Fugger (e.g. the *Nine Planets*, 1592; Munich, Alte Pin.). Paolo remained based in Venice, where he eventually opened a successful studio. As was customary, he made preparatory drawings for his landscape and figure compositions, sometimes pasting two together to change a design (e.g. the *Temptation of Christ*, *c.* 1596; New Haven, CT, Yale U. A.G.). Although he painted many religious pictures, his reputation was based on a particular type of mythological fantasy derived from the example of Giorgione. He gave a Venetian softness and grace to the theme of Classical demigods in a landscape, and his dreamlike landscapes anticipate the Italianate Flemish school later associated with Paul Bril and Jan Breughel the elder, for example the late *Landscape with Mythological Figure* (1592–6; London, N.G.) or *Acqua* (1580; known from two copies, both Rome, Mus. Capitolino). The latter is one of the *Four Triumphs of the Elements* (Valencia, Colegio del Patriarca) commissioned by Fugger. Paolo's masterpieces in this field are the four stunning *Allegories of Love* (*c.* 1585; all Vienna, Ksthist. Mus.), comprising *Amore letheo*, the

Punishment of Love, *Reciprocated Love* (see fig.) and *Love in the Golden Age*, the latter two of which became rapidly known through prints by Agostino Carracci (B. 119–20).

BIBLIOGRAPHY
A. von Bartsch: *Le Peintre-graveur* (1803–21) [B.]
E. Haverkamp-Begemann: 'Pauwels Franck—alias Paolo Fiammingo—als tekenar', *Bull. Rijksmus. Amsterdam*, x (1962), pp. 68–75
S. Mason Rinaldi: 'Appunti per Paolo Fiammingo', *A. Veneta*, xix (1965), pp. 95–107
——: 'Nuove opere di Paolo Fiammingo', *A. Veneta*, xxiv (1970), pp. 224–30
B. W. Meijer: 'Paolo Fiammingo Reconsidered', *Meded. Ned. Inst. Rome*, xxxvii (1975), pp. 117–30
S. Mason Rinaldi: 'Paolo Fiammingo', *Saggi & Mem. Stor. A.*, xi (1978), pp. 47–80, pls 163–88 [cat. rais.]
E. Fučíková and L. Konečný: 'Einige Bemerkungen zur *Gesichts-Allegorie* von Paolo Fiammingo und zu seinen Aufträgen für die Fugger', *A. Ven.*, xxxvii (1983), pp. 67–76
B. W. Meijer: 'Paolo Fiammingo tra indigeni e "forestieri" a Venezia', *Prospettiva*, xxxii (1983), pp. 20–32

□

Fiasella, Domenico [il Sarzana] (*b* Sarzana, 12 Aug 1589; *d* Genoa, 19 Oct 1669). Italian painter. He was the son of Giovanni Fiasella, a silversmith. At the age of 11 he studied briefly with Aurelio Lomi (1556–1622), who was in Genoa from 1597 to 1604, and then with Giovanni Battista Paggi. Around 1607 he left for Rome, where he copied paintings by Raphael and frequented the Accademia del Nudo. His painting of a *Nativity* (untraced) was admired by Guido Reni when it was on view for a celebration in S Maria della Scala, Rome (Soprani). Consequently Domenico Passignano and Giuseppe Cesari Arpino (1568–1640) asked him to work with them, and the Marchese Vincenzo Giustiniani commissioned paintings from him.

Paolo Fiammingo: *Reciprocated Love*, oil on canvas, 2.17×2.46 m, *c.* 1585 (Vienna, Kunsthistorisches Museum)

After about ten years in Rome, Fiasella returned to Sarzana, perhaps in 1616 when he painted an altarpiece, *Virgin and Child with St Lazzaro* (Sarzana, S Lazzaro). The heavy figures, precise modelling and strong lighting in this, his earliest dated painting, show that he had both learnt the classical language of Roman art and absorbed the naturalism and *sfumato* of Paggi, Passignano and the followers of Caravaggio. The painting is stylistically close, particularly in its hard contours, to other early works. These include two paintings, the *Raising of the Widow's Son of Nain* and the *Healing of the Blind Man of Jericho* (Sarasota, FL, Ringling Mus. A.), that are attributed to one or other of the Carracci in the Giustiniani inventories and that may have been painted in Rome. Another early work is *Supper in the House of Simon* (*c.* 1616; Genoa, Pal. Reale), inspired by a picture of the same subject by Lodovico Cigoli (1596; Rome, Pal. Doria-Pamphili).

Between 1616 and 1618 Fiasella went to Genoa, where he settled. His first Genoese commission was for decorative frescoes of scenes from the story of Esther in the Palazzo Patrone, then the Palazzo di Giacomo Lomellini (see fig. and Pesenti, pls 220–39). There is a possibility that these were painted in collaboration with Giovanni Battista Carlone (i). The Lomellini family then commissioned vault medallions and four canvases, the *Marriage at Cana*, the *Marriage of the Virgin*, the *Rest on the Flight into Egypt* and a *Baptism* (all Genoa, Pal. Bianco) for their church, SS Annunziata del Vastato, Genoa. The clarity of Fiasella's early style is close to that of Carlone, who had also trained in Rome and whose imagery Fiasella shared. Both artists also enjoyed long careers.

The clarity, detail, colour and classical figures in Fiasella's early compositions continued in paintings of the 1620s. These also show a response to the robust figure style, painterly surfaces and brilliant reds and golds of Rubens and Anthony van Dyck, as, for example, in *Prudence* (Genoa, Pal. Ducale), *St Ursula with the Holy Family* (1624; S Quirico, parish church) and *SS Apollonia, Lucy and Barbara* (1626; Sarzana, S Maria Assunta).

With the death of Paggi in 1629 and the departure of Bernardo Strozzi and Giovanni Benedetto Castiglione by the mid-1630s, painting in Genoa was dominated by Fiasella and his workshop. In the 1630s he painted a number of monumental altarpieces, including *Virgin and Child with St Bernardino and Salvator of Horta* (1630; Sarzana, S Francesco), the richly coloured *Assumption of the Virgin* (1632; Genoa, Nostra Signora del Monte) and *Virgin with SS Catherine of Alexandria and John the Baptist* (1634; Camogli, parish church). Between 1635 and 1637 he worked at Mantua. During these years he also followed the tradition of his father and the Carlone family by making designs for sculpture, among them a bronze *Virgin as Queen of Genoa*, cast by Giovanni Battista Bianco (*d* 1657), for the high altar of S Lorenzo, Genoa, and the same subject carved in stone by Domenico Scorticone (*d* 1650) for a niche in the Porta della Pila in Genoa, both pieces datable shortly after the 1637 proclamation defining the Virgin as 'Patrona, Signora e Regina della città di tutta la repubblica'. He also designed frontispieces, including one for the *Leggi delle compere di St Giorgio* (Genoa, 1634), another for *Il genio ligure* (Rome, 1650), engraved by

Domenico Fiasella: *Esther before Ahasuerus* (*c.* 1619), fresco, Palazzo Patrone, Genoa; possibly painted in collaboration with Giovanni Battista Carlone (i)

C. Bloemart (*b* 1603) in Rome, and another for *La Grillaia* by Angelico Aprosio (Naples, 1668).

Fiasella remained active until 1667. He was a prolific artist, who painted for Genoese patrons in Naples, Messina and Spain. His narrative scenes painted in the 1650s, like those of Carlone, have a Baroque vigour inspired by Castiglione, yet otherwise his work after the 1630s shows little stylistic development, as can be seen from the following examples: the *Virgin and Child with St John the Baptist Appearing to St Bernardino* (1643; Piacenza, S Vincenzo), the *Martyrdom of St Andrew* (1653; Sarzana Cathedral), the *Virgin and Child with SS Bernardino and Francis* (1659; Lerici, S Francesco) and *St Clare Repulsing the Saracens* (1667; Montoggio, parish church).

Fiasella's school provided a place for artists such as Pierre Puget and Castiglione to exchange ideas, and his talent as a teacher can be seen in the quality of his students, who included Valerio Castello, Domenico Piola and Gregorio de' Ferrari. His influence is detectable in various ways; his knowledge of Rubens and van Dyck was transmitted to his students Giovanni Andrea Podesta and Giovanni Battista Merano, and the naturalistic drawings of heads by his pupil Francesco Merano attest to Fiasella's expertise in portraiture. Fiasella's monumental figures, and smooth, closed brushstrokes differ sharply from the painterly, neo-Venetian art of his Genoese contemporaries, yet his drawing style is sometimes close to that of Giovanni Andrea de' Ferrari and Giovanni Battista Carlone (i); his drawings include figure studies in black chalk, such as the *Virgin and Child* (Florence, Uffizi), and compositional studies in pen and brown ink, such as *St Andrew Adoring the Cross* (Genoa, Pal. Rosso). There are occasional echoes of his sharp lighting and Rubensian figures in paintings by Orazio de' Ferrari. His pupil and brother-in-law, Giovanni Battista Casone (1609–after 1681), kept his style alive through the 1670s.

BIBLIOGRAPHY
R. Soprani: *Vite* (1674), pp. 245–53; ed. C. G. Ratti (1768–9), pp. 224–39
Genoese Masters: Cambiaso to Magnasco, 1550–1750 (exh. cat. by B. S. Manning and R. Manning, Dayton, OH, A. Inst.; Sarasota, FL,

Ringling Mus. A.; Hartford, CT, Wadsworth Atheneum; 1962–3), cat. nos 31–3

V. Belloni: *Pittura genovese del seicento* (Genoa, 1969), pp. 181–207

L. Alfonso: 'Domenico Fiasella detto il Sarzana', *La Berio*, xi (1971), pp. 38–44

G. V. Castelnovi: 'La pittura nella prima metà del seicento dall'Ansaldo a Orazio DeFerrari', *Dal seicento al primo novecento*, ii of *La pittura a Genova e in Liguria*, ed. C. B. Dufour and others (Genoa, 1971, rev. 2/1987)

P. Donati: *Domenico Fiasella: 'Il Sarzana'* (Genoa, 1974)

E. Gavazza: *La grande decorazione a Genova* (Genoa, 1974)

F. R. Pesenti: *La pittura in Liguria: Artisti del primo seicento* (Genoa, 1986), pp. 231–306 [full bibliog.; colour pls]

Domenico Fiasella (exh. cat. by P. Donati, Genoa, Pal. Reale, 1990)

M. NEWCOME

Fibre art. Collective term, coined in the 1970s, for creative, experimental fibre objects. A wide range of techniques is used, often in combinations that encompass both traditional (e.g. felting, knotting) and modern (e.g. photographic transfer) practices. The eclectic range of materials includes many not previously associated with textiles, such as paper, wood, iridescent film, nylon mesh and wire.

The first experimental work was done during the 1920s and 1930s by such artists as Anni Albers (*see* ALBERS, (2)) and GUNTA STÖLZL (*see* TAPESTRY, fig. 14) in Germany. Equally innovative work was produced in the 1940s and 1950s by Trude Guermonprez (*d* 1975), Luba Kreje (*b* 1925), Lenore Tawney (*b* 1925), Loja Saarinen (1879–1968), Dorothy Liebes (1897–1972), Marianne Strengell (*b* 1909) and others. These artists were concerned with natural and manmade materials, vibrant colours, formal pattern-making and texture derived from construction. By the 1960s a new direction in tapestry was replacing the tradition of the painter's cartoon woven by artisans, although that was still practised. Inspired by the decade's concern for freedom, revolution and primitive vigour, a second generation of fibre artists began to define and expand their ideas. Loom-woven hangings gave way to variously constructed pieces for display on the floor, on pedestals or hung from the ceiling. These included shaped, woven sisal work with an emphasis on form (e.g. by MAGDALENA ABAKANOWICZ in Poland; *see* TAPESTRY, fig. 15); floor pieces made of wrapped and stitched modular units (e.g. by Sheila Hicks of the USA; see fig.); cascading wrapped and knitted components (Claire Zeisler (1903–91), USA); large objects of such unusual fibres as rope (Françoise Grossen (*b* 1943), Switzerland); shaped tapestry weave (Herman Scholten (*b* 1932), Netherlands); synthetic materials, newsprint and raffia in basketry (Ed Rossbach (*b* 1914), USA); and ceiling-hung concentric layers of slit tapestry (Jagoda Buic (*b* 1930), from the former Yugoslavia).

In the 1970s and early 1980s there was intense activity by a third generation of artists. Continuing experimentation, together with a general maturation of style, resulted in huge, dynamic works. At the same time there was renewed interest in loom-woven and loom-controlled work and contemporary application of traditional techniques. There was a continued exploration of materials and techniques and a flowering of three-dimensional form. Fibre art was designed for use in architectural spaces (e.g. public buildings) and also in landscapes, and fibrous

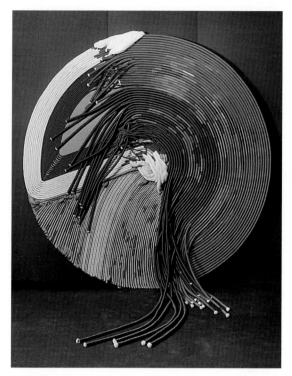

Sheila Hicks: *L'Epouse préférée occupe ses nuits*, wrapping, nylon, silk, gold and linen threads, diam. 4.06 m, 1972 (Paris, private collection)

materials were used to create sculpture and painting. Examples from this period include outdoor work in twisted paper in large plaited forms (Neda Alhilali (*b* 1938), USA); ritualistic objects made of twisted paper tapes (Dominic DiMare (*b* 1932), USA); needle techniques on cloth (Emilia Bohdziewicz (*b* 1941), Poland); combinations of knitting and plaiting (Ann Sutton (*b* 1935), England); basketry work of morning glory vines, leaves and milkweed manipulated in tapestry weave (John McQueen (*b* 1943), USA); mended sheet and shirt environments (Sheila Hicks); plaited horsehair and gesso panels (Olga de Amaral (*b* 1932), Colombia); free spatial forms on textile reliefs (Peter Jacobi (*b* 1935) and Ritzi Jacobi (*b* 1941), Germany); a mural of warp-face repp, space-dyed warp with shaped polyurethane weft, mixing wool, jute and cotton (Lia Cook (*b* 1942), USA); a double plain-weave that becomes a three-dimensional construction (Warren Seelig (*b* 1946), USA); and interwoven cotton strands (Masakazu Kobayashi (*b* 1944), Japan).

During the 1980s a fourth generation of artists widened their approach even further. Some traditional methods were revived and used in combination with new technology. There was an incredible expansion of form, driven by the insistence on art as a vehicle for ideas. The wide range of techniques is reflected in such diverse works as the loom-woven hangings of Sheila Hicks; the *shibori* indigo dyeing of Shihoko Fukomoto (*b* 1945, Japan); the story-telling quilts in painted and pieced fabric of Faith Ringgold (USA); the wood, fabric and rope banners of Inese Malitis (*b* 1959) and Ivars Malitis (*b* 1956, Latvia); the non-functional baskets of Ed Rossbach; the pressed, hammered, dyed and painted rayon of Lia Cook; the computerized weaving of abstract imagery of Cynthia Schira (*b* 1934, USA); the fibre optic weaving of Peggy Osterkamp (*b* 1940, USA); and by Hideho Tanaka (*b* 1942, Japan), sisal and stainless steel elements that absorb, reflect and transmit light.

BIBLIOGRAPHY

A. Albers: *On Weaving* (Middletown, CT, 1965)
I. Emery: *The Primary Structures of Fabrics* (Washington, DC, 1966)
M. Constantine and J. L. Larsen: *Beyond Craft: The Art Fabric* (New York, 1973, rev. Tokyo, 2/1986)
——: *The Art Fabric: Mainstream* (New York, 1973, rev. Tokyo, 2/1986)
A. Kuenzi: *La Nouvelle Tapisserie* (Geneva, 1973)
E. Rossbach: *Baskets as Textile Art* (New York, 1973)
J. L. Larsen, A. Bühler, B. Solyom, G. Solyom: *The Dyer's Art: Ikat, Batik, Plangi* (New York, 1976)
J. L. Larsen and B. Freudenheim: *Interlacing: The Elemental Fabric* (Tokyo and New York, 1986)
Frontiers in Fiber: The Americans (exh. cat. by M. Constantine and L. Reuter, Grand Forks, N. Dakota Mus. A., 1988)
Restless Shadows: Japanese Fibreworks (exh. cat., London, Goldsmiths' Gal., 1991)

MILDRED CONSTANTINE

Fibreglass. Term commonly used to describe glassfibre reinforced plastic, also known as glassfibre reinforced polyester or GRP. It is a light but strong and durable material, and, unlike most plastics (*see also* PLASTIC, §1), its use involves low-level technology, making it accessible as an artist's material, although its major uses are commercial and industrial.

The first stage in the manufacture of fibreglass involves the addition of a catalyst to crystic polyester resins, unsaturated, liquid forms of polyester (*see* RESIN, §2). The resulting solid plastic is, however, fairly brittle and thus is reinforced by glassfibre to give a composite material of greatly increased strength. Glassfibre consists of thinly drawn out molten glass, cooled rapidly to produce a continuous filament of exceptional tensile strength. It is made into rovings, a loosely spun thread and tape, as well as into woven tissue, chopped strand mat and woven rovings, all in thin, flexible sheets. These are embedded in the resin while it is liquid and become saturated and surrounded by it. Carbon fibre and 'Kevlar', a brand of para-aramid fibre, are also used to reinforce the resin and may be used in combination with glassfibre where even greater strength and impact resistance is required.

There are two basic methods of employing fibreglass, from which its artistic use has generally been adapted. The first is casting: after being activated by its catalyst, the syrupy liquid resin is painted or poured into a mould. The inclusion of glassfibre in the resin allows the production of large, but lightweight castings by using only a thin coating of the mould. When set, the casting retains the form and texture of the mould; a very smooth finish can be produced by this method. Casting is particularly suitable for figurative sculpture or at least works with a detailed form. Complex sculptures are cast in pieces and are then assembled with epoxy resin adhesive or additional applications of GRP materials. GRP is also a useful material for the production of moulds; because of its strength, slight flexibility and capacity to reproduce detailed features it is particularly suited to large moulds, where ease of handling is an important consideration and the production

Fibreglass and epoxy resin sculpture by Mark Boyle: *Holland Park Avenue Study*, 2.38×2.38×1.14 m, 1967 (London, Tate Gallery)

of clean castings presents difficulties. Concrete and artificial stone can be cast in fibreglass moulds, as well as the material itself. The alternative method is to build up layers of resin-impregnated glassfibre cloth on to an armature or framework. This method has various commercial and industrial uses but is limited as a sculptural technique to abstract compositions.

Experimentation with fibreglass as a sculptural medium occurred soon after it was first introduced (*see* PLASTIC, §2 (iii)). It was used, for example, by MARK BOYLE in his sculptures of urban terrain (e.g. *Holland Park Avenue Study*, 1967; London, Tate; see fig.). The theme of life-size polychrome figures, sometimes shocking or humorous, has frequently been used as a subject, and it was employed by such Pop artists as Allen Jones (e.g. *Hatstand, Table, Chair*, 1969; Aachen, Neue Gal.). The initial enthusiasm for fibreglass as an artist's medium has not, however, been maintained, and its main use remains commercial and industrial, for example boat building and the manufacture of racing car bodies.

Polyester resins can also be cast or modelled without glassfibre additions, usually for smaller objects. Known as cold cast resin metals, they can be filled with inert materials, pigments or powdered metals to give finely detailed castings that closely resemble other materials, particularly metals. They are used for mass-produced decorative sculptures and for such items as reproduction armour for theatrical costumes. They are also increasingly employed by sculptors for the production of limited editions, as the use of cold cast resins is less expensive than that of other materials, such as plaster, employed in traditional methods of reproducing sculpture. 'Clear embedding' resin, a type of polyester that cannot be used for glassfibre laminations, has also been employed by sculptors, notably by Fernandez

Arman (*b* 1928): *Torse aux gants* (1967; Cologne, Wallraf-Richartz-Mus.) is his best-known work in this medium. Although easy to employ, GRP and related cold cast polyester resins involve materials that can be unpleasant to use and that give rise to some health and safety considerations (*see* PLASTIC, §3). These are sufficient reasons to deter some artists from using them.

BIBLIOGRAPHY

J. W. Mills: *The Techniques of Casting for Sculpture* (London, 1967, 2/1990)
E. Lucie-Smith: *Arte oggi: dall' espressionismo astratto all' iperrealismo* (Milan, 1976); Eng. trans. as *Art Today* (Oxford, 1977, 2/1983)
Polyester Resin, Glassfibre, Cold Cast Resin Metals, Clear Embedding Resins (Reading and London, 1989)
Crystic Polyester Handbook (Wollaston, 1990)
The Strand Guide to Glassfibre (Wollaston, [1990]) [booklet]

JONATHAN STEPHENSON

Ficherelli, Felice [il Riposo] (*b* San Gimignano, 30 Aug 1603; *d* Florence, *bur* 5 March 1660). Italian painter. His most original works were easel pictures, for private collectors, often of cruel and violent subjects, which he interpreted with a morbid sensuality and ambiguous tenderness. He was brought to Florence when very young by the collector Conte Alberto Bardi (*d* 1632), who arranged for him to study with Jacopo da Empoli and to copy works by Andrea del Sarto. Ficherelli's clear compositions and luminous drapery, which remain evident throughout his career, reflect this training. In the early 1630s he was attracted by the delicate *sfumato* effects of Francesco Furini and developed a style close to that of Cecco Bravo; his works of this period include the *Sacrifice of Isaac* (Florence, priv. col., for illustration see Gregori, 1968, p. 26) and the *Martyrdom of St Agatha* (priv. col., see Cantelli, fig. 338). There followed in the late 1630s *Tarquin and Lucretia*, which is known in several versions (e.g. Rome, Accad. N. S Luca), the theatrical *Julia Receiving the Bloodstained Garments of Pompey* (Genoa, priv. col., see 1986 exh. cat., pl. 1.208), an *Allegory of Patience* (Florence, Bigongiari priv. col., see Gregori, 1974, fig. 23) and *Antiochus and Stratonica* (Auckland, C.A.G.). His altarpieces of the 1650s, among them the *Vision of St Filippo Neri* (1657–9; Florence, Certosa del Galluzzo, Pin.), are his only securely dated works and return to the clarity of Empoli, while his last works, such as *Lot and his Daughters* (Dublin, N.G.), are characterized by a new softness and freedom. His nickname, il Riposo, derived from his retiring nature.

BIBLIOGRAPHY

F. Baldinucci: *Notizie* (1681–1728); ed. F. Ranalli (1845–7)
M. Gregori: 'Felice Riposo', *Comma*, iii (1968) pp. 23–28
——: 'A Cross-section of Florentine Seicento Painting: The Piero Bigongiari Collection', *Apollo*, c/151 (1974), pp. 218–29
G. Cantelli: *Repertorio della pittura fiorentina del seicento* (Fiesole, 1983), pp. 78–9 [with bibliog.]
Il seicento fiorentino: Arte a Firenze da Ferdinando I a Cosimo III, 3 vols (exh. cat., Florence, Pal. Strozzi, 1986), i, pp. 382–8; iii, pp. 87–8
W. Balzano: 'Ficherelli, Felice', *La pittura italiana: Il seicento*, ed. R. Contini and C. Ginetti, ii (Milan, 1989), p. 739 [with bibliog.]

ELISA ACANFORA

Ficino, Marsilio (*b* Figline Valdarno, nr Florence, 19 Oct 1433; *d* Florence, 1499). Italian philosopher and writer. After studying the humanistic disciplines, medicine and philosophy in Florence, he embarked on the study of Platonism, sponsored by Cosimo de' Medici and later

Lorenzo. He translated the complete works of Plato into Latin (published 1484) and also wrote elaborate commentaries on some of the dialogues. His interpretation of Plato was Neo-Platonic, heavily based on Plotinus, whose *Enneads* he also translated and commented upon. Always concerned to stress the compatibility of Platonism with Christianity, in 1473 he became a priest. The 'Platonic Academy', which he led and inspired, was not a formal institution but rather a circle of friends who shared a common enthusiasm for Platonic philosophy.

As a Platonist, Ficino distrusted the plastic arts because they belonged to the ephemeral world of appearances rather than to the eternal and unchangeable realm of ideas. Nonetheless, he regarded the artist as a symbol of man's creative power and of his ability to transcend and perfect the natural world (*Theologia platonica*, XIII.iii; see Chastel). This conception both reflected and contributed to the increased dignity accorded to artists in the Renaissance.

In his Latin commentary on Plato's *Symposium* (1469), Ficino explained his concept of beauty as a reflection of the divine splendour in the created world and expounded his doctrine of love as a means of rising to the suprasensible world of ideas and ultimately attaining union with God. These notions, usually in a watered-down version, reached a wide popular audience in the 16th century and can be found in vernacular lyric poetry, as well as in many artistic and literary treatises. Michelangelo was in contact with Ficino and his circle in his youth and used many of the philosopher's ideas about beauty, love and divine frenzy in his poetry. Giovanni Paolo Lomazzo's *Idea del tempio della pittura* (1590) also reflects the influence of Ficino's account of beauty in his *Symposium* commentary.

Gombrich drew attention to the fact that Ficino was a friend and correspondent of Lorenzo di Pierfrancesco de' Medici, a patron of Botticelli and owner of the *Primavera* (Florence, Uffizi; *see* BOTTICELLI, SANDRO, fig. 2), and claimed that the main theme of the painting was a visual realization of the philosophical ideas expressed in a letter from Ficino to Lorenzo (*Opera*, vol. i, p. 805), in which he used Venus as a symbol of the virtue of *humanitas* (civilization and culture). Panofsky and Saxl argued that Ficino's discussion of melancholy (*De vita*, I.v, vi; III.ii, xi, xii, xxii) was one of the sources for Albrecht Dürer's engraving *Melencolia I* (*see* DÜRER, (1), fig. 9).

Ficino is depicted, together with Cristoforo Landino and Angelo Poliziano, in the foreground of Domenico Ghirlandaio's *Zachariah in the Temple* (Florence, S Maria Novella). Vasari recorded (*Vite*, 2/1568, ed. G. Milanesi (1878–85), vol. iii, p. 49) that there was another portrait of Ficino in Benozzo Gozzoli's *Meeting of the Queen of Sheba and King Solomon* (Pisa, Camposanto), but due to the poor condition of the fresco, he is no longer identifiable.

WRITINGS

Commentarium in Convivium Platonis, de amore, in Plato: *Opera omnia* (Florence, 1469; Fr. trans., Paris, 1956; Eng. trans., Columbia, MO, 1944, rev. Dallas, 2/1985)
Opera omnia, 2 vols (Basle, 1576/*R* Turin, 1962)

BIBLIOGRAPHY

E. Panofsky and F. Saxl: *Dürers 'Melencolia I': Eine Quellen- und Typengeschichtliche Untersuchung* (Leipzig, 1923), pp. 32–54, 104–20
P. O. Kristeller: *The Philosophy of Marsilio Ficino* (New York, 1943/*R* Gloucester, MA, 1964)

E. H. Gombrich: 'Botticelli's Mythologies: A Study in the Neo-Platonic Symbolism of his Circle', *J. Warb. & Court. Inst.*, viii (1945), pp. 7–60; rev. in E. H. Gombrich: *Symbolic Images: Studies in the Art of the Renaissance* (London, 1972, 3/1985), pp. 31–81

A. Chastel: *Marsile Ficin et l'art* (Geneva, 1954/R 1975 [with bibliog. suppl.])

Il lume del sole: Marsilio Ficino medico dell'anima (exh. cat., Figline Valdarno, Vecchio Pal. Com., 1984)

P. O. Kristeller: 'Marsilio Ficino and his Work after Five Hundred Years', *Marsilio Ficino e il ritorno di Platone*, ed. G. C. Garfagnini, i (Florence, 1986), pp. 15–196 [with bibliog.]

JILL KRAYE

Ficoroni, Francesco de (*b* Lugnano nel Lazio, 1664; *d* Rome, 1 Feb 1747). Italian scholar, archaeologist and antique collector. His studies and his major writings were devoted to ancient art, and were closely linked with the objects he collected throughout his life. These formed an important collection which earned him great fame, but which was dispersed after his death. It contained small objects and rarities including mirrors, graffiti, lead seals, coins, cameos, lockets and tesserae. The most important piece was undoubtedly the famous Ficoroni Cist from Praeneste (*c.* 325–*c.* 300 BC; Rome, Villa Giulia; *see* ETRUSCAN, §VI and fig. 34). One of Ficoroni's most important studies, published in Rome in 1745, was devoted to his native village, identified with the ancient Labicum. Another of his principal works, *Le vestigia e rarità di Roma* (1744), was also concerned with topographical matters. Ficoroni was elected correspondent of the Academy of Inscriptions and member of the Royal Academies of Paris and London and the Accademia Peloritana of Messina. He founded the Colonia Esquilina degli Inculti.

WRITINGS

Osservazione sopra l'antichità di Roma descritte nel diario italico publicato dal P. Bernard Montfaucon (Rome, 1709)

Le memorie più singulari di Roma (Rome, 1730)

Dei tali ed altri strumenti lusori degli antichi (Rome, 1734)

Le maschere sceniche e le figure comiche degli antichi romani (Rome, 1736)

Arcus Trajano dicatus Beneventi: Porta aurea dictus (Rome, 1739)

Descrizione di tre particolari statue scopertesi in Roma l'anno 1739 (Rome, 1739)

I piombi antichi (Rome, 1740)

Le vestigia e rarità di Roma ricercate e spiegate (Rome, 1744)

LUCA LEONCINI

Ficquet, Etienne (*b* Paris, 13 Sept 1719; *d* Paris, 11 Dec 1794). French engraver. On his mother's side he was the grandson of a goldsmith, which may have encouraged him to take up engraving. In 1736 he was a pupil of Georg Friedrich Schmidt (1712–75), and later he joined the workshop of Jacques-Philippe Lebas. About 1740 he engraved 34 mediocre portraits for a collection of portraits of famous people (Pognon and Bruand, nos 2–28, 30–36) being put together by the print publisher Odieuvre. He very soon came to specialize in small-scale portrait engravings after other artists' works: paintings, drawings or even other engravings. The hallmarks of his work were the great precision and attention to detail that he gave to his small plates, and his ability to reproduce, by means of multiple and dense incisions, the nuances of large-scale portrait engravings.

In the 1750s Ficquet was given the opportunity of consolidating his technique in the course of engraving, after drawings by François Eisen, 99 portraits (PB 47–145) to illustrate the *Vies des peintres flamands, allemands et hollandais* by Jean-Baptiste Descamps (Paris, 1753–64). From then on, Ficquet's work consisted mainly of portraits, usually intended as book illustrations; in 1761 they included *Jean de La Fontaine* (PB 154) and *Charles Eisen* (PB 155, 157) for the Fermiers Généraux edition of La Fontaine's *Contes*; *Pierre Corneille* (1765; PB 159) after Charles Le Brun for Voltaire's edition of Corneille's *Collected Plays*; and *Marcus Tullius Cicero* (1771; PB 149). Ficquet received commissions to execute other portraits, such as that of *Françoise d'Aubigné, Marquise de Maintenon* (1759) after Pierre Mignard, for the Dames de Saint-Cyr. His portraits of writers were generally decorated with borders designed and engraved by Pierre-Philippe Choffard.

It seems, however, that Ficquet seldom executed engravings in order to build up a stock. Despite his undeniable public success, he never managed to become independent of the book publishers so as to exploit his talent financially, particularly as his conscientious nature led him endlessly to modify and rework his plates, consigning more effort to each work than the fee would reward. He died penniless during the French Revolution.

BIBLIOGRAPHY

Portalis–Beraldi

L. E. Faucheux: *Catalogue raisonné de toutes les estampes qui forment les oeuvres gravés d'E. Ficquet, P. Savart, J.-B. de Grateloup et J.-B.-S. de Grateloup* (Paris, 1864)

E. Pognon and Y. Bruand: *Inventaire du fonds français: Graveurs du dix-huitième siècle*, Paris, Bib. N., Cab. Est. cat., ix (Paris, 1962), pp. 120–64 [PB]

CHRISTIAN MICHEL

Fidelle, Isidor Coridon. *See* FOLKEMA, JACOB.

Fiedler, Konrad (*b* Oederan, Saxony, 23 Sept 1841; *d* 3 June 1895). German philosopher. He gained a doctorate in Law, and, possessing a private income, he devoted himself to the theory of art. Impressed by Hans von Marées, whom he met in 1866–7 in Rome and whom he subsequently subsidized, Fiedler developed a general theory of the visual arts, adapting elements in current Neo-Kantian philosophy. In the first place, he contended that the external world and the mind cannot 'in the last analysis' be set over against each other as two kinds of thing that are known independently of each other. This may be interpreted either as the modest view that everything we say about the world must be said from some standpoint, or as a form of radical solipsism, which holds that the objects of our knowledge are just our own experiences. While some of Fiedler's formulations, particularly in his major work, *Über den Ursprung der künstlerischen Tätigkeit* (1887), suggest he held the extreme view, his final position in *Drei Bruchstüke* seems to be that the opposition in our ordinary experience between the viewing mind and subjects in the world makes us unable to grasp the underlying unity of mind and matter.

In the second place, Fiedler set out to eliminate the privileged position of language as the medium of mental life. In denying that there was anything mental that is not at the same time physical and involving the senses, he was denying that there was any possibility of thought that had no sensory vehicle, and that no such vehicle, not even words, could make present to us the complete sensory character of what it represented. Our mental grasp of the world is developed in one way through language and in another through visual formulation; each is as much a feat of ordering and a matter of knowledge as the other. In order to develop our visual grasp we must extract the specifically visual manifestations of objects from our global experience of them. This notion was influenced and developed by his close friend, the sculptor ADOLF VON HILDEBRAND, who in *Das Problem der Form in den bildenden Kunst* (1893) held that our ordinary visual experience of the world is shot through with a sensation of eye and head movements: these were only neutralized for objects far enough away for the lines of sight from the two eyes to be virtually parallel. The three-dimensionality of forms can only be realized artistically, therefore, when presented as if they were constituted by objects seen at a distance. This is most fully demonstrated in classical shallow relief, where the cues of contour, overlap, scale and cast shadow are used to define objects only when their dominant and space revealing aspects lie parallel to the plane of the relief or painting. Represented in this way objects make up a continuous configuration across the surface, which, though incompatible with literal spatial relations, is not perceived to be so.

The third feature of Fiedler's thought was his distinguishing the theory of art, which he connected with knowledge or cognition, from aesthetics, which for him was represented by Immanuel Kant's *Kritik der Urteilskraft* (1790) and was concerned with beauty, taste, and subjective responses to the world. Fiedler insisted that art was parallel to conceptual knowledge, although he also purged art of other interests in a manner reminiscent of the way Kant purged the pure judgement of taste from other interests or involvements.

WRITINGS

Über die Beurteilung von Werken der bildenden Kunst (Leipzig, 1876; Eng. trans., 1949/*R* 1957)
'Moderner Naturalismus und künstlerische Wahrheit', *Wissenschaftliche Beilage der Leipziger Zeitung* (Leipzig, 1881)
Über den Ursprung der künstlerischen Tätigkeit (Leipzig, 1887)
Schriften über Kunst, ed. H. Konnerth, 2 vols (Munich, 1913–14/*R* 1971)

BIBLIOGRAPHY

H. Konnerth: *Die Kunsttheorie Konrad Fiedlers: Eine Darlegung der Gesetzlichkeit der bildenden Kunst* (Munich, 1909)
B. Croce: 'La teoria dell'arte come pura visibilità', *Nuovi saggi di Estetica* (Bari, 1920), pp. 235–57
G. Jachmann, ed.: *Hildebrands Briefwechsel mit Konrad Fiedler* (Dresden, 1927)
W. Hoffman: *Grundlagen der modernen Kunst* (Stuttgart, 1961), pp. 229–31
M. Podro: 'The Parallel of Linguistic and Visual Formulation in the Writing of Konrad Fiedler', *Filosofia* (1961), pp. 628–40
H. Faensen: *Die bildnerische Form: Die Kunstauffassungen Konrad Fiedlers, Adolf von Hildebrands und Hans von Marees* (Berlin, 1965)
L. Dittmann: *Stil–Symbol–Struktur: Studien zu Kategorien der Kunstgeschichte* (Munich, 1967)
M. Podro: *The Manifold in Perception: Theories of Art from Kant to Hildebrand* (Oxford, 1972)

MICHAEL PODRO

Field, Erastus Salisbury (*b* Leverett, MA, 19 May 1805; *d* Leverett, 28 June 1900). American painter. He studied with Samuel F. B. Morse in New York during the winter of 1824–5. On his return to the rural isolation of Leverett, he painted his earliest known work, the portrait of his grandmother *Elizabeth Billings Ashley* (Springfield, MA, Mus. F.A.). His career as an itinerant portrait painter began in 1826, most of his commissions coming through a network of family associations in western Massachusetts and Connecticut. The portraits of 1836–40 are considered his best. From 1841 he lived mainly in New York, where he expanded his subject-matter to include landscapes and American history pictures. There he presumably studied photography, for on his return to Massachusetts he advertised himself as a daguerreotypist. His few portraits painted after 1841 are copied from his own photographs and lack the expressive characterization and decorative power of his earlier work. From 1865 to 1885 his paintings were based primarily on biblical and patriotic themes. The *Historical Monument of the American Republic* (1867–88; Springfield, MA, Mus. F.A.) stands alone in American folk art in size (2.82×3.89 m), scope and imaginative vision. Inspired by plans for a national celebration of the centennial of the USA in 1876, Field painted an architectural fantasy of eight towers linked by railway bridges and trains at the tops, with the history of the USA in low-relief sculpture on the exterior surfaces of the towers. Field added two more towers to the painting in 1888 and thereafter retired.

BIBLIOGRAPHY

Somebody's Ancestors: Paintings of Primitive Artists of the Connecticut Valley (exh. cat. by F. B. Robinson, Springfield, MA, Mus. F.A., 1942)
M. Black: 'Erastus Salisbury Field, 1805–1900', *American Folk Painters of Three Centuries* (exh. cat., ed. T. Armstrong and J. Lipman; New York, Whitney, 1980)
Erastus Salisbury Field, 1805–1900 (exh. cat. by M. Black, Springfield, MA, Mus. F.A., 1984)

RICHARD C. MÜHLBERGER

Field, George (*b* Berkhamsted, Herts, ?1777; *d* Isleworth, 28 Sept 1854). English chemist and writer. He was the leading colour chemist of his day in Britain, refining new dyes and pigments and supplying artists' materials. His *Chromatography* (1835) was the standard English text on pigments and their use until the 1880s. The work opens with a historical survey of the role and development of colour in art from ancient times onwards. He concluded that the potential to make full use of colour came last, both in the work of individual painters and that of specific schools. Having dealt with their expressive and symbolic powers, he attempted a scientific explanation of colours. He suggested that they were the result of the mixture of 'oxidizing' and 'hydrogenizing' rays, colours being, in fact, oxides of hydrogen. The bulk of the book, however, is devoted to individual colours and their different tones, qualities and applications. In his extensive speculative writings Field set out a theory of analogy between colour, line, sound, language and the structure of the universe. His ideas can be regarded as an attempt to reconcile materialism and idealism and to transform academic lore into what he termed an 'aesthetical science'. He was friendly with many artists, and among those who subscribed to his books were John Constable, J. M. W. Turner, William Etty, David Wilkie and Samuel F. B. Morse. Owen Jones employed his theories of colour harmony in the decoration (1851) of the Crystal Palace in London and reiterated them in *The Grammar of Ornament* (1856). Field was also closely involved in schemes to promote the British school and his colour writings were used by the

Pre-Raphaelite painters. Later writers such as David Ramsay Hay (1796–1866) looked to Field's ideas as the basis of design reform, and Hay summarized them in *The Science of Beauty* (Edinburgh and London, 1856).

WRITINGS

Chromatics, or an Essay on the Analogy and Harmony of Colours (London, 1817)
Chromatography, or a Treatise on Colours and Pigments and of their Powers in Painting (London, 1835)
Outlines of Analogical Philosophy, 2 vols (London, 1839)
Rudiments of the Painter's Art (London, 1850)

BIBLIOGRAPHY

DNB
R. D. Hartley: *Artists' Pigments, 1600–1835* (London, 1970)
D. Brett: 'The Aesthetical Science: George Field and the "Science of Beauty"', *A. Hist.*, ix (1986), pp. 336–50 [with full writings list]
George Field and his Circle: From Romanticism to the Pre-Raphaelite Brotherhood (exh. cat. by J. Gage, Cambridge, Fitzwilliam, 1989)

DAVID BRETT

Field, R(obert) N(ettleton) (*b* Bromley, Kent, 3 March 1899; *d* Auckland, 18 Feb 1987). English painter, sculptor, potter and teacher, active in New Zealand. He studied from 1919 to 1924 at the Royal College of Art in London, where he first became interested in the modern movement in painting and experimented with direct carving. In 1925 he emigrated to New Zealand to take up a position at the King Edward Technical College, Dunedin. There he proved an influential teacher. He established the Six and Four Art Club, partly in response to the English 7 & 5 Society, and inspired several students who were to become leading New Zealand painters, notably Colin McCahon and M. T. Woollaston.

Mostly small-scale, Field's work was experimental and helped to free art in New Zealand from representational values. Paintings such as *Christ at the Well of Samaria* (1929; Wellington, Mus. NZ, Te Papa Tongarewa) were striking for their pure colour and pointillist brushwork. Carvings such as *Wahine* (1933–4; Dunedin, NZ, Pub. A.G.) expressed an interest in materials for their own sake and were true to the original shape and nature of stone. After 1934 he concentrated on pottery, producing mainly tall, high-shouldered forms. In 1945 he became head of the first ceramic training centre in New Zealand at Avondale College, Auckland, and continued to promote studio pottery until after his retirement in 1960.

BIBLIOGRAPHY

M. Dunn: 'Robert Nettleton Field 1925–32', *Bull. NZ A. Hist.*, i (1972), pp. 1–11
A. K. C. Petersen: *R. N. Field: The Dunedin Years* (exh. cat., Palmerston North, Manawatu A.G., 1989)

A. K. C. PETERSEN

Field, Robert (*b* ?London, *c.* 1769; *d* Kingston, Jamaica, 9 Aug 1819). English painter and engraver, active in North America. He studied drawing at the Royal Academy Schools, London, in 1790. His three documented British mezzotint portraits after others' originals include that of *John Lewis* (*c.* 1793; London, Richmond Pub. Lib.). In 1794 he moved to the USA as part of the influx of British artists. Field spent 14 years working as a successful miniaturist in Baltimore, MD, Philadelphia, PA, Washington, DC, and Boston, MA. He was patronized by, among others, George and Martha Washington and several signatories of the Declaration of Independence. Field's works

combined the painterly Georgian manner with the pragmatic, linear style of traditional American portraiture.

In 1808 he left the USA for Halifax, NS, a city then enjoying great affluence as a British military base. While known only as a miniaturist in America, Field produced more than 50 major oil portraits, such as *Bishop Charles Inglis* (1810; London, N.P.G.), during his eight-year stay in Canada. He also produced and published an engraving of *Lt General John Coape Sherbrooke* (1816; Ottawa, N. Archvs) loosely based on his full-length portrait of *c.* 1815. Field's sophisticated images of Nova Scotia's gentry are relatively consistent in approach and intent. However, his paintings are more conservative than their British prototypes and their sobriety is typically North American. Field's formal and symbolic devices often reflect his admiration for Gilbert Stuart. By 1814 he had insufficient portrait commissions and, after briefly operating a stationery business, he moved to Jamaica in 1816, leaving only one recorded portrait from the West Indies.

BIBLIOGRAPHY

H. Piers: *Robert Field: Portrait Painter in Oils, Miniature and Water-colours and Engraver* (New York, 1927)
Robert Field, 1769–1819 (exh. cat., ed. S. Paikowsky; Halifax, A.G. NS, 1978)

SANDRA PAIKOWSKY

Fielding. English family of artists. The portrait and landscape painter Nathan Theodore Fielding (*fl* 1775–1819) was the father of six artists. He exhibited at the Royal Academy for the first time in 1799 and at the Society of Painters in Water-Colours in 1815. The family moved around England: in 1788 they were in Acton (London), and from 1794 to 1799 they lived in Durham; by 1800 they were back in London and then in 1804 they moved to the Lake District, first living at Ambleside and then at Keswick. Such moves were presumably an attempt to capture the market for picturesque landscape and were not unusual among this class of painter. Fielding sr painted small canvases of the Cumberland scenery, which his sons then copied. After his wife died *c.* 1806–7, Fielding moved with his children to Manchester and then to London. He was described in 1809 as 'a veteran artist whose old heads in the manner of [Balthasar] Denner are purchased at high prices by the admirers of that master' (Roget, p. 258). Two paintings by him (sold Sotheby's, London, 13 July 1988; illus. in cat.) are dated 1781 and 1782 and represent views near Sowerby Bridge, W. Yorks. They suggest a provincial skill in bird's-eye views and local topography. It is difficult to unravel the Fielding oeuvre, as the family were close collaborators, and all the brothers as well as one daughter, Amelia (*b* 1785), were painters.

(1) Theodore Henry Adolphus Fielding (*b* Yorkshire, 1781; *d* Croydon, 11 July 1851). Painter, printmaker, drawing-master and writer. He was the eldest son of Nathan Theodore Fielding. In 1819 he married Mary Ann Walton (*fl* 1821–35), daughter of James Walton, with whom he later produced *A Picturesque Tour of the English Lakes* (1821). Mary Ann was an accomplished watercolourist who was elected a member of the Society of Painters in Water-Colours in 1821. Theodore was a capable artist and writer, engraving his own work and providing descriptive text. *Picturesque Illustrations of the River Wye* (1821) contains texts and aquatints (after drawings by (3) Copley Fielding) by Theodore.

In 1823 Theodore joined his younger brothers (4) Thales Fielding and (5) Newton Fielding in Paris to work on Baron Isidore-Justin-Severin Taylor's *Voyages pittoresques et romantiques dans l'ancienne France* (1820–63). From 1817 the brothers shared a house in London; their students there included William Callow, Charles Bentley, J. W. Edge (1785–1834), Edouard Soulier and Ruskin. Most of these students probably benefited more from Copley than Theodore, as the latter moved to Croydon in 1826 to take up a lucrative post as drawing-master at the East India Company College at Addiscombe. During the last 20 years of his life he published several important treatises on painting and conservation.

WRITINGS

Synopsis of Practical Perspective, Linear and Aerial (London, 1829)
On the Theory of Painting (London, 1830, 2/1835, 3/1836)
On Painting in Oil and Water Colours, for Landscape and Portraits (London, 1839)
The Art of Engraving, with Various Modes of Operation . . . Illustrated with Specimens of the Different Styles of Engravings (London, 1841)
The Knowledge and Restoration of Old Paintings . . . (London, 1847)

(2) Frederick Felix Ferdinand Raffael Fielding (*b* Yorkshire, *c.* 1784; *d* London, 1853). Painter and lawyer, brother of (1) Theodore Henry Adolphus Fielding. The second son of Nathan Theodore Fielding, he exhibited landscape subjects at the Liverpool Academy in 1811, at the Carlisle Academy in 1824 and at the Royal Academy in 1826. He appears to have worked primarily in watercolour, though a competent topographical view of Cumberland in oils (Carlisle, Mus. & A.G.) reveals that, like all his brothers, he also worked in that medium. He was admitted to Gray's Inn in 1827 and was called to the Bar in 1832. He continued to paint as an amateur.

(3) (Anthony Van Dyck) Copley Fielding (*b* Sowerby Bridge, W. Yorks, 1787; *d* Worthing, W. Sussex, 2 March 1855). Painter, brother of (1) Theodore Henry Adolphus Fielding. The third son of Nathan Theodore Fielding, he was named after van Dyck and John Singleton Copley. He was the best known and most prolific of the Fielding brothers and was highly proficient, particularly in watercolour. Copley first worked closely with his father, travelling with him to Liverpool in 1807 and then to Wales in 1808. Their works of 1804 were said to be indistinguishable. He studied with John Varley in 1810 and exhibited at the Society of Painters in Water-Colours for the first time that year. He maintained a lifelong relationship with the Society, acting as treasurer from 1813, secretary from 1815 and president (elected 1831). He married Susannah Gisborne, Varley's sister-in-law, in 1813 and from 1816 divided his time between Brighton and London. He made frequent sketching tours, exhibiting many hundreds of views at the Water-Colour Society in the course of his life.

Technically, he was the most impressive of the brothers, with an ability to paint large-scale exhibition watercolours (for example, the *Ruins of Rievaulx Abbey, Yorkshire*; 1839; London, V&A). He won a gold medal at the Paris Salon of 1824, although he was the only Fielding brother who never visited France. His work after 1830 tends to consist of studio reworking, and there is a degree of slavishness and repetition to his later production that has marred his reputation; correspondence with his dealer, Colnaghi, towards the end of his life suggests he was more than willing to adapt apparently 'naturalistic' depictions to suit patrons' requirements.

(4) Thales Fielding (*b* Yorkshire, 1793; *d* London, 20 Dec 1837). Painter and drawing-master, brother of (1) Theodore Henry Adolphus Fielding. The fourth son of Nathan Theodore Fielding, Thales went to work in Paris in 1821 or spring 1822. He was employed, with his brother Newton, by the publisher J. F. d'Ostervald. He was in Paris for at least a year before the name Fielding is first mentioned in the journal of Delacroix. *Macbeth and the Witches* (exh. Salon 1824; untraced) was much admired by Stendhal and may have some connection with the lithograph of the same subject that Delacroix executed soon after. Delacroix and Thales painted each other's portraits (respectively: *c.* 1824, Paris, priv. col.; exh. RA 1827, untraced), probably in the studio that Thales occupied in 1824 until his departure for England in October, when Delacroix took it over. It was presumably on the Fieldings' advice that Delacroix visited London in 1825, at which time he described Thales, who acted as guide, as 'le meilleur enfant possible'. Thales possessed an impressionistic, fluid watercolour technique, which he applied extensively to figure subjects as well as landscapes (for example, *Hop Picking*; 1831; New Haven, CT, Yale Cent. Brit. A.; and *Crossing Solway Sands*; n.d.; U. Manchester, Whitworth A.G.). In 1836 he was appointed instructor at the Military Academy, Woolwich.

(5) Newton (Limbird Smith) Fielding (*b* Durham, 1797; *d* Paris, 1856). Printmaker, painter, instructor and writer, brother of (1) Theodore Henry Adolphus Fielding. The youngest of the Fielding brothers, Newton divided his life between London and Paris, marrying a French woman in 1833. He arrived in Paris in late 1821 or early 1822 and worked with his brother Thales for the publisher J. F. d'Ostervald. He acquired a considerable reputation for small-scale, brightly coloured and delicately worked watercolours of animals and birds in landscape. While this genre was very much his own invention, it owed much to the sporting tradition of the Alken family (much admired in France), to natural history in the manner of Thomas Bewick and to the literary tradition of Aesop and La Fontaine (e.g. *Ducks*, 1849, London, V&A; and the *Fox and the Crow*, 1827, Paris, Louvre). His work became well known through his lithographed albums (e.g. *Croquis par Newton Fielding*; Paris and London, 1829). He enjoyed the friendship of Delacroix and the dealer Charles Schroth and in 1827 was employed as drawing-master to the family of King Louis-Philippe. Between 1831 and 1833 he shared a studio with William Callow. The two artists collaborated, Callow painting landscapes and Newton introducing staffage. Lacking the secure posts occupied by his brothers Theodore and Thales, he suffered hardship towards the end of his life when the market for instruction manuals had been flooded both in Britain and France.

WRITINGS

How To Sketch from Nature: Or Perspective and its Application (London, ?1852, 2/1856)

UNPUBLISHED SOURCES

Paris, Bib. N. [Typescript of *Notes conçernant la famille de Newton Fielding*, inf. collected by Newton's grandson]

BIBLIOGRAPHY

J. L. Roget: *A History of the Old Water-colour Society* (London, 1891) [much inf., esp. on Copley]

H. Mallalieu: 'Raffael Revealed', *Ant. Collct.*, xx/5 (1985), p. 35 [account of the second brother's life]

M. Pointon: *The Bonington Circle: English Watercolour and Anglo-French Landscape, 1790–1855* (Brighton, 1985)

MARCIA POINTON

Fiennes, Celia (*b* Newton Toney, Wilts, 7 June 1662; *d* Hackney, London, 10 April 1741). English writer. In the course of 1697 and 1698 this maiden lady, an indefatigable and observant sightseer, rode through every English county, ostensibly to visit spas for her health, keeping a racy, if artless, journal. Her observations are of great value to art historians. As granddaughter of William, 1st Viscount Saye and Sele, she had the entrée to numerous great houses and is therefore a valuable source for their appearance and contents. Her taste was for the up-to-date, the 'artificial', 'neat' or 'commodious', for example sash windows; and she disliked such old-fashioned buildings as the Rows at Chester. Lichfield Cathedral was 'a stately structure but old'. Having a Puritan family background, she could be shocked by 'the immodesty of the pictures' at Burghley House, Cambs, 'especially in my Lord's apartment'. But her favourite painter was Antonio Verrio, 'the best hand in England' despite his nudes, whereas Raphael's tapestry cartoons at Hampton Court (now London, V&A) were only 'curious pictures of the Scriptures'. What she most admired in any artefact was verisimilitude: altarpieces in which the canopy or the satin 'looked just like real' or the stone weeder-woman at Woburn mistaken for 'a real living body'.

UNPUBLISHED SOURCES

Broughton Castle, Oxon [Manuscripts with full accounts of the journeys of 1697 and 1698, and short accounts of other journeys between 1682 and 1712]

BIBLIOGRAPHY

E. Griffiths, ed.: *Through England on a Side Saddle in the Time of William and Mary* (London, 1888) [the first printed edn of the journals, inc. and inaccurately transcribed]

J. Parkes: *Travel in England in the Seventeenth Century* (Oxford, 1925)

C. Morris, ed.: *The Journeys of Celia Fiennes* (London, 1947, rev. 1949)

E. Moir: *The Discovery of Britain: The English Tourists, 1540–1840* (London, 1964)

C. Morris, ed.: *The Illustrated Journeys of Celia Fiennes* (Exeter, 1982, rev. 3/1988) [slightly abbreviated but with new editorial matter]

CHRISTOPHER MORRIS

Fiennes de Clinton, Edward. *See* CLINTON, EDWARD FIENNES DE.

Fieravanti, Aristotele di. *See* FIORAVANTI, ARISTOTELE.

Fieravino, Francesco. *See* MALTESE, FRANCESCO.

Fierro, Pancho [Francisco] (*b* Lima, 1810; *d* Lima, 28 July 1879). Peruvian painter. A mulatto (of mixed parentage), he was self-taught and was probably illiterate (his paintings remained unsigned, and their titles were possibly added later). He became the leading *costumbrista* artist in Peru, with watercolours that recorded the people and events of the transitional phase between the colonial and Republican periods, although the fact that he portrayed not only established types and traditions but also figures from the early modern era, set him apart from other *costumbrista* artists. His works were usually characterized by their gentle caricature, and it has been suggested that some paintings were influenced by the works of Goya. His technique involved laying down a basic pencil sketch, which was then built up with a series of brightly coloured washes; the drawing often lacked proportion, perspective and shape, although outlines were usually eloquent and lively. The figure depicted was identifiable by the inclusion of details indicating his trade or status (e.g. *Friar Tomato*, n.d.; Lima, Mus. A.). Fierro's prolific output amounted to *c.* 1200 watercolours, *c.* 238 of which were owned by the contemporaneous Peruvian *costumbrista* writer Ricardo Palma (collection acquired in 1954 by the Municipalidad de Lima Metropolitana). The largest collection outside Peru is probably the 78 watercolours (St Petersburg, Mus. Ethnog.) bought by Leopold Schrenk, a Russian scientist sent by Tsar Nicholas I to Peru in 1854. Fierro exerted considerable influence both during his career and into the 20th century, when such leading Indigenist artists as José Sabogal took an interest in his work.

BIBLIOGRAPHY

J. Sabogal: *Pancho Fierro* (Lima, 1945)

J. A. de Lavalle and W. Lang: *Pintura contemporánea*, Colección arte y tesoros del Perú, i (Lima, 1975), pp. 32–7

Exposición de acuarelas Pancho Fierro (exh. cat., Lima, Mun. Lima Met., 1986)

T. Muñoz-Najar: 'Pancho en Rusia', *Caretas* [Lima] (1994), pp. 54–6

W. IAIN MACKAY

Fiesole, Andrea da. *See* ANDREA DA FIESOLE.

Fiesole, Jérôme de [Girolamo da]. *See* JÉRÔME DE FIESOLE.

Fiesole, Mino da. *See* MINO DA FIESOLE.

Fiesole, Silvio da. *See* COSINI, SILVIO.

Fieubet, Gaspard de (*b* Toulouse, 1626; *d* Grosbois, Doubs, 1694). French administrator, patron and financier. He was a royal treasurer noted for his probity; in 1671 he was appointed Councillor of State and chancellor to Queen Maria-Theresa (wife of Louis XIV). His first house in Paris was a mansion in the Place Royale (now 20, Place des Vosges), built in 1607; he had it altered and refurbished by Charles Chamois, who also rebuilt for him a house in the Rue de la Bûcherie. In 1676 Fieubet commissioned Jules Hardouin Mansart to build, or rather to rebuild for him a house on the Quai des Célestins. Even taking into account previous alterations to the house, the style of the future architect of Versailles appears uncertain. The ceilings were decorated with panels by Eustache Le Sueur, depicting the *Story of Tobias* (fragments, Paris, Louvre; Grenoble, Mus. Grenoble). In 1686 Fieubet retired to the Camaldolese Monastery at Grosbois.

BIBLIOGRAPHY

G. Brice: *Description nouvelle de ce qu'il y a de plus remarquable dans la ville de Paris*, ii (Paris, 1685, rev. 1752/*R* 1971), pp. 301, 486, 493

J.-A. Dulaure: *Nouvelle description des environs de Paris* (Paris, 1786), p. 308

Nouveau dictionnaire historique (Caen and Lyon, 1789)

G. Tallemant des Réaux: *Historiettes*, ii (Paris, 1834–5, rev. 1932/*R* 1960–61), p. 23

E. Bonnaffé: *Dictionnaire des amateurs français du XVIIème siècle* (Paris, 1884), p. 106

J. Hillairet: *Evocation du vieux Paris*, i (Paris, 1952), p. 45

M.-A. Férault: 'Charles Chamois: Architecte parisien', *Bull. Mnmtl*, cxlviii (1990), p. 125

PIERRE CHALEIX

Fieve, Carlos Luis Ribera y. *See* RIBERA (ii), (2).

Figari, Pedro (*b* Montevideo, 29 June 1861; *d* Montevideo, 24 July 1938). Uruguayan painter, writer, lawyer and politician. He showed artistic inclinations from childhood but completed a degree in law in 1886; his appointment as a defence counsel for the poor brought him into contact with social issues that later informed his art. In the same year he studied briefly with the academy-trained Italian painter Godofredo Sommavilla (1850–1944), married and left for Europe, where he came into contact with Post-Impressionism. On his return to Uruguay he became actively involved in journalism, law and politics and also fostered the creation of the Escuela de Bellas Artes. During the course of his life he published a number of books that reflected his broad interests in art, art education and legal matters. He was a member of the Uruguayan Parliament, president of the Ateneo of Montevideo (1901) and director of the Escuela Nacional de Artes y Oficios (1915).

In 1921 Figari moved to Buenos Aires in order to devote himself completely to painting. Working in oil on cardboard he created figurative compositions as arrangements of colour, reconstructing rather than documenting the Uruguayan scene; the geography, gaucho life, the celebrations, symbolic rituals and carnivals of the local black community. He continued to expand on this subject-matter while living in Paris from 1925 to 1933 in works painted from memory, which gained him broader recognition as a painter. Works such as *Call to Prayer* (1922), *Burial* (*c.* 1924; Montevideo, Mus. N.A. Plást.) and *Creole Dance* (*c.* 1925; New York, MOMA; *see* URAGUAY, fig. 3) both typify his work at its best. In 1930 he was awarded the Grand Prize in the *Exposición del centenario* in Montevideo, and on his return to Uruguay in 1933 he was appointed artistic adviser to the Ministry of Public Education.

WRITINGS

El crimen de la calle Chaná (Montevideo, 1896)

Plan general de la organización de la enseñanza industrial (Montevideo, 1917)

Arte, estética, ideal (Paris, 1920)

El arquitecto (Paris, 1928)

Historia Kiria (Paris, 1930)

BIBLIOGRAPHY

J. L. Borges: *Figari* (Buenos Aires, 1930)

L. V. Anastasía, A. Kalenberg and J. M. Sanguinetti: *El caso Almeida* (Montevideo, 1976)

A. Kalenberg: 'Pedro Figari: El escenario americano', *América: Mirada interior* (exh. cat., Bogotá, Bib. Luis-Angel Arango, 1985)

Seis maestros de la pintura uruguaya (exh. cat., ed. A. Kalenberg; Buenos Aires, Mus. N. B.A., 1987), pp. 57–82

ANGEL KALENBERG

Figdor, Albert (*b* Baden, nr Vienna, 16 May 1843; *d* Vienna, 22 Feb 1927). Austrian collector. During the late 19th century he assembled an extensive collection of approximately 6000 works of art, primarily from the medieval and Renaissance periods, most of which were in an excellent state of preservation. His collection was considered to be one of the most comprehensive in Austria before World War II. As well as simple but skilfully crafted objects for domestic and ecclesiastical use, there were pieces of higher quality, including metalwork, ivories, tapestries and ecclesiastical objects. The collection was particularly noted for its fine chairs. The paintings represented the major European schools, with the greatest concentration on the period from the 15th century to the early 16th. The most significant painting was Hieronymus Bosch's *Vagabond* (*c.* 1510; Rotterdam, Mus. Boymans–van Beuningen; *see* BOSCH, HIERONYMUS, fig. 6). After Figdor's death in 1927, his niece and heiress Margarete Becker-Walz was forbidden by a newly enacted Austrian law to export and sell the collection, except in its entirety. She eventually sold its entire contents to the art dealer Gustav Nebehay (1881–1935), who negotiated a deal whereby approximately 4000 works were sold and the remainder donated, as the Dr Albert Figdor-Stiftung, to the Kunsthistorisches Museum, Vienna, and to the Museen der Stadt Wien. Most of the works in the Stiftung were of Austrian origin, including a doll's house that was modelled after a patrician household. The most valuable part of this donation was a suite of medieval furniture originally from Schloss Annaberg in the Tyrol. A bronze statue of the *Flagellation* (*c.* 1614; Vienna, Ksthist. Mus.) by Adriaen de Vries had formerly belonged to Rudolf II, Holy Roman Emperor. Public sales of the collection took place in 1930 in Vienna (Cassirer, Artaria and Glückselig: 11–13 June [furnishings, paintings, tapestries, decorative arts and ecclesiastical objects]) and in Berlin (Cassirer, Artaria and Glückselig: 29–30 Sept [decorative arts and sculpture]).

BIBLIOGRAPHY

L. Baldass: 'Die Gemälde der Sammlung Figdor', *Pantheon*, x (1929), pp. 82–3, 465–72

H. Tietze: 'The Figdor Foundation in Vienna', *Burl. Mag.*, lv (1929), pp. 309–10

F. Eckhardt: 'The Sale of the Dr Albert Figdor Collection, Vienna', *Apollo*, xi (1930), pp. 355–9

□

Figini and Pollini. Italian architectural partnership formed in Milan in 1929 by Luigi Figini (*b* Milan, 27 Jan 1903; *d* Milan, 15 March 1984) and Gino Pollini (*b* Rovereto, 13 Jan 1903). They met while studying at the Scuola Superiore di Architettura del Politecnico, Milan; Figini graduated in 1926 and Pollini, who was also a musician and poet, the following year. Both were founder-members of GRUPPO 7; its four-part manifesto (1926–7) laid the foundations of Italian *Razionalismo* (*see* RATIONALISM (ii)). They both also became active members of CIAM from 1930.

The first works of Figini and Pollini were temporary pavilions designed for various decorative art exhibitions. An early example was the Casa Elettrica (1930; with Gruppo 7), built for the Società Edison at the 4th Biennale in Monza, with interiors by Guido Frette and Adalberto Libera, and kitchen design by Piero Bottoni. Conceived as a display space for electrical appliances, its clean efficient look and extensive use of glass established the basic syntax of many subsequent Rationalist designs. Another famous example was the artist's house at the 5th Triennale in

Milan (1933). Presented as a modern version of a Pompeian villa, this building has been seen as one of the most successful attempts to synthesize national and international tendencies in modern architecture, a concern central to Gruppo 7.

Other early works of Figini and Pollini in Milan included the remodelling of the Bar Craja (1930) and the De Angeli-Frua office building (1931–2), both with Luciano Baldessari; the elegant and airy interior of the former, overlooking Piazza Farrari, became the gathering point for the Milanese avant-garde. The firm also produced an entry for the Palazzo del Littorio competition (1934; with BBPR Architectural Studio and Luigi Danusso) for the National Fascist Party headquarters in Rome and a project for an addition to the Brera Academy (1935; with Giuseppe Terragni and Pietro Lingeri; unexecuted). Both projects are representative of northern Italian *Razionalismo* at its best. In the latter, the long slab block was entirely glazed on the north side while the south side, facing the garden, was rhythmically articulated through a subtle layering of concrete frames and screens.

In 1933 Figini and Pollini met the industrialist Adriano Olivetti and from then on the bulk of their work was in the service of the Olivetti firm. They prepared a master plan (1934) for the Olivetti village at Ivrea and designed an industrial complex, built in four stages between 1934 and 1957 (see fig.). The central office building displayed the continuous glazed wall that became a hallmark of Olivetti buildings around the world. They also designed a child care centre (1939–40), whose heavier proportions and use of local materials partly reflected the autarchic policies of the time; workers' housing (1940); and a social

services centre (1954–7). Olivetti himself promoted regional development in Italy, and a master plan for the Valle d'Aosta was drawn up by Figini and Pollini (1935; with BBPR Architectural Studio, Piero Bottoni and others) but never implemented (*see* BBPR ARCHITECTURAL STUDIO). Their last work of this period, the Corbusian Villa Manusardi (1942), Cartabbia, displayed a strong sensitivity to site conditions, with its brick vaulting and exposed stonework.

After World War II, the work of Figini and Pollini took a different direction. Their elegant office and residential block (1947–8) in Via Broletto, Milan, might be described as a summation of Rationalist themes that opened the way to a period of great freedom and experimentation. In Milan the huge INA-Casa housing estate (1951; with Gio Ponti) and two churches, Madonna dei Poveri (1952–4) and SS Giovanni e Paolo (1964), are most representative of this later phase. The churches employed complex hexagonal geometries and display rich surface articulations in marked contrast to the stringent discipline of earlier work. This new direction was also evident in the Olivetti social services centre, Ivrea, and in the elaborate brickwork of the block of flats (1956) in Via Circo, Milan. These works date from the so-called Neo-Liberty phase in Italian architecture when the principles of the International Style were being questioned for a presumed indifference to history.

While actively engaged in design, Pollini also taught architecture: from 1936 to 1968 at the Politecnico, Milan, and from 1969 to 1978 at the University of Palermo, where he designed the new Science Department (1972–82; with Vittorio Gregotti and G. Caronia). In 1985,

Figini and Pollini: Olivetti industrial complex, Ivrea, 1934–57

shortly after Figini's death, the firm of Figini and Pollini was awarded a gold medal by the city of Milan.

WRITINGS

L. Figini: *L'elemento verde e l'abitazione* (Milan, 1950)
G. Pollini: *Elementi di architettura* (Milan, 1966)

BIBLIOGRAPHY

E. Gentili-Tedeschi: *Figini e Pollini* (Milan, 1959)
C. Blasi: *Figini e Pollini* (Milan, 1963)
J. Ryckwert: 'Figini and Pollini', *Archit. Des.*, xxxvii (1967), pp. 369–78
G. Ciucci: 'Ivrea ou la communauté des clercs', *Archit. Aujourd'hui*, 18 (1976), pp. 7–12
D. P. Doordan: *Building Modern Italy: Italian Architecture, 1914–1936* (New York, 1988)
V. Savi: *Figini e Pollini: Architetture, 1927–1989* (Milan, 1990)

LIBERO ANDREOTTI

Figino, (Giovan) Ambrogio (*b* Milan, 1548; *d* Milan, 11 Oct 1608). Italian painter and draughtsman. A pupil of Giovanni Paolo Lomazzo, he was one of the most important artists working in Milan during the second half of the 16th century. His career, however, is poorly documented. His chief achievement, both in quantity and quality, was as a draughtsman, but he was also a very able portrait painter, highly popular with the nobility. His earliest known work is in fact a portrait of *Angelo Dannona*, signed and dated 1570 (London, Christie's, 28 June 1974, lot 61). The courtly style of his portraits is evident in two other surviving works: *Lucio Foppa* (*c.* 1585; Milan, Brera), shown in a noble and dignified pose, proudly attired in elegant shining armour against a dark background, and the *Portrait of a Member of the Cavalcabò Family* (*c.* 1580; Rome, Pal. Venezia). Here the subject is depicted in a half-length pose, turned three-quarters towards the right, his hand boldly placed on his hip. His gaze is deep and penetrating, his attitude courtly. Figino's portraiture received praise from illustrious contemporaries such as Torquato Tasso and Giambattista Marino and other less well-known poets including Gregorio Comanini, Gherardo Borgogni and Giuliano Goselini. However, most of his documented portraits are untraced.

Apart from his lifelong interest in portraiture, Figino's other interests are documented by about 430 sheets of drawings. The most important collections of these are in the Galleria dell'Accademia, Venice (162 sheets), the Royal Collection, Windsor Castle (118 sheets), and the Pierpont Morgan Library, New York (19 sheets). Through this prolific and eclectic production Figino's development can be followed from his first anatomical studies to his last agitated compositions. The early work includes studies after Leonardo and anatomical drawings done in the workshop of Lomazzo, who owned many of Leonardo's drawings. Around 1576–7 Figino travelled to Rome, where he diligently copied the work of Raphael and Michelangelo's Sistine Chapel ceiling and *Last Judgement*. He also sketched the antique statues in the courtyard of the Belvedere del Vaticano, especially the *Apollo Belvedere*, the Belvedere *Torso* and the Belvedere *Antinous* (all Rome, Vatican, Mus. Pio-Clementino). Other drawings by Figino include studies for heads and portraits, figures, mythological subjects and preparatory sketches for paintings. Outstanding in the last category are a great number of small sketches, often on both *recto* and *verso*, that are rich in variations and pentiments, for example studies for *St*

Ambrogio Figino: studies for *St Sebastian*, pen and brown ink, 213×143 mm, *c.* 1586 (Venice, Galleria dell'Accademia)

Sebastian (see fig.). Twenty or thirty of these may appear on the same sheet, crowded together and almost overlapping, documenting the genesis and construction of Figino's compositions.

About 15 of the drawings in this group are sketches for paintings in Milanese churches: the *Agony in the Garden* (Milan, S Maria Passione), *St Matthew and the Angel* (Milan, S Raffaele) and the *Virgin and Child Crushing the Serpent* (Milan, S Antonio Abate), all datable to *c.* 1586. Although executed in a severe style, the paintings are calm and balanced, containing strong echoes of Raphael and Michelangelo. In the *Virgin and Child with St John the Evangelist and the Archangel Michael* (*c.* 1588; Milan, Brera), the approach is cooler and more intellectual. This is still more evident in the *St Ambrose on Horseback* (1590; Milan, Castello Sforzesco), with its air of arrested drama and violence. The horse is frozen in a sudden rearing motion that slows and obstructs the furious rush of the punitive cavalcade.

In June 1590, at the peak of his career, Figino was commissioned to paint the shutters of the new organ in Milan Cathedral. These were completed in 1595. Two of the panels, depicting the *Resurrection* and the *Crossing of the Red Sea*, were destroyed during World War II but can be reconstructed from surviving photographs and from Figino's preparatory studies. The *Nativity* and another *Crossing of the Red Sea* are, however, still *in situ*. The signed and dated *Jupiter and the Heifer* (1599; Pavia, Pin. Malaspina), painted for the Holy Roman Emperor Rudolf II, shows a marked Mannerist refinement. The elegant figure of Juno recalls the work of Francesco Salviati, while that of Jupiter shows the influence of Pellegrino Tibaldi. Figino's secular works include the new genre of still-life (e.g. the *Still-life with Peaches*, c. 1596; Bergamo, Lorenzelli priv. col., see Ciardi, 1968, p. 225) and reveal a timely study of the recent experiments by Vincenzo Campi and Fede Galizia (*see* STILL-LIFE).

Figino's last phase was characterized by the crowded and heavy compositions of the *Birth of the Virgin* (Milan, S Antonio Abate), the *Pietà* and scenes from the *Life of St Benedict* (Milan, S Vittore al Corpo) and the *St George* (Rho, Santuario della Madonna dei Miracoli), all *c*. 1603–5. Finally, the *Coronation of the Virgin* (*c*. 1605) on the ceiling of S Vittore al Corpo, surrounded by rich gold and white stucco decoration, is the only known example of Figino's work as a fresco painter. In 1605 Figino moved to Turin, where he enjoyed continued success and directed works on the Grande Galleria of the Palazzo Reale of Charles-Emanuel I. His works in Turin remain untraced. He returned suddenly to Milan shortly before his death.

BIBLIOGRAPHY

R. Longhi: 'Ambrogio Figino e due citazioni al Caravaggio', *Paragone*, v/55 (1954), pp. 36–8
A. E. Popham: 'On a Book of Drawings by Ambrogio Figino', *Bib. Humanisme & Ren.*, 20 (1958), pp. 266–76
R. P. Ciardi: 'Giovan Ambrogio Figino e la cultura artistica milanese tra il 1550 e il 1580', *A. Lombarda*, vii (1962), pp. 73–84
J. H. Turnure: 'The Late Style of Ambrogio Figino', *A. Bull.*, xlvii/1 (1965), pp. 35–55
R. Longhi: 'Anche Ambrogio Figino sulla soglia della "natura morta"', *Paragone*, xviii/209 (1967), pp. 18–22
R. P. Ciardi: *Giovane Ambrogio Figino* (Florence, 1968)
P. Pouncey: 'Studies by Figino for his St Matthew Altarpiece', *Master Drgs* (1968), pp. 253–4
R. P. Ciardi: 'Addenda Figiniana', *A. Lombarda*, xvi (1971), pp. 267–74
M. L. Gatti Perer: 'Un ciclo inedito di disegni per la Beatificazione di Alessandro Sauli', *A. Lombarda*, xix/40 (1974), pp. 9–86
S. Coppa: 'Due opere di Ambrogio Figino in una donazione del 1637', *A. Lombarda*, 47–8 (1977), pp. 143–4
A. Perissa Torrini: 'Tre disegni inediti di Giovan Ambrogio Figino', *Prospettiva*, 40 (1985), pp. 75–81
——: *Galleria dell'Accademia di Venezia: Disegni del Figino* (1987), iv of *Catalogo dei disegni antichi* (Milan)

ANNALISA PERISSA TORRINI

Figueiredo, Cristóvão de (*fl* 1515–43). Portuguese painter. He was a pupil of Jorge Afonso and worked with Garcia Fernandes and Gregório Lopes, though each of their styles was personal and independent. He was one of the most esteemed painters of his time and received many royal commissions, but it is not known if he was ever officially appointed court painter. He is known to have made drawings for other artists, and in 1537 he was commissioned to make cartoons for tapestries that were to be woven in Flanders.

Figueiredo probably collaborated on the paintings for the high altar of the church of the convent of Jesus, Setúbal, dedicated to the *Life of Christ* and the *Life of the Virgin*, with paintings of Franciscan saints (1525–30; Setúbal, Mus. Setúbal). It is also probable that between *c*. 1510 and 1515 he collaborated on the paintings with scenes of the *Passion*, commissioned by Eleanor, daughter of the King of Spain, for Nossa Senhora do Pópulo, Caldas da Rainha (*in situ*).

Figueiredo's most important works include the paintings (all 1520–30) with scenes of the *Passion* for the high altar of Santa Cruz, Coimbra, commissioned by Manuel I. These include *Calvary* and *Ecce homo* (Coimbra, Santa Cruz, Sacristy), the latter showing the influence of both Albrecht Dürer, through an engraving of the same subject in the *Large Passion* series (1511), and Quinten Metsys, through a triptych (central *Crucifixion*, fragment exists; *Flagellation*; *Ecce homo*; all Coimbra, Mus. N. Machado de Castro) that Manuel I had acquired in Flanders and which since 1517 had been in the chapter house of the convent of S Clara in Coimbra. Figueiredo freely interpreted the *Ecce homo* by Metsys in his panel of the same subject, and to these combined sources he applied a low viewpoint, giving perspective of great originality. Other paintings by Figueiredo for the altar of Santa Cruz include the *Discovery* and *Exaltation of the Holy Cross* (Coimbra, Mus. N. Machado de Castro) and *Deposition* (Lisbon, Mus. N. A. Ant.). This last magnificent work shows a naturalistic treatment of the flora, and the donors are fine examples of contemporary Portuguese portraiture. The two tondi on Christ's tomb depict Old Testament scenes, *Jeremiah Cast into the Dungeon* and *Jonah and the Whale*, precursors of the central subject of the *Deposition*.

Figueiredo's other important commission between 1533 and 1537 was for three altarpieces for the Franciscan monastery of Ferreirim, of which eight panels exist, devoted to the *Life of Christ* and the *Life of the Virgin* (*in situ*). All these panels indicate the collaboration of Fernandes, especially in those dedicated to the *Life of the Virgin*, but the scenes of the *Passion of Christ*, including the *Road to Calvary*, *Crucifixion* and *Pietà*, demonstrate many characteristics of Figueiredo's style and again show in particular the influence of Dürer and Metsys. Figueiredo's triptych of the *Infante St Dom Fernando* (1538–9; untraced) was painted for the monastery at Batalha (commissioned by Queen Eleanor).

BIBLIOGRAPHY

A. Gusmão: *Os primitivos e a renascença in arte portuguesa: Pintura* (Lisbon, 1950), pp. 252–3
L. Reis-Santos: *Cristóvão de Figueiredo* (Lisbon, 1960)

DAGOBERTO L. MARKL

Figueroa, Leonardo de (*b* Utiel, Cuenca, ?1650; *d* Seville, *bur* 10 April 1730). Spanish architect. He trained as a mason before going *c*. 1670–75 to Seville, where all his major works were executed. His first major work was the façade and courtyard of the Hospital de los Venerables, which he took over from Juan Domínguez in 1687. The façade, in a narrow street, has a triple arcade at ground-floor level. The first floor features a niche flanked by columns with ornately figured shafts, capped by a curved open-topped pediment twisted inwards like a plant stem. The patio is arcaded at ground-floor level, with large flat-headed windows at the upper floor protected by balustrades. Brick pilasters marking off the bays recall Juan de Herrera's usage. From 1691 to 1709 Figueroa rebuilt the *Mudéjar* church of La Magdalena (formerly the convent of S Pablo), raising the height of the nave above that of the aisles and piercing each bay with a large clerestory window on either side. Above the crossing he set a dome on an octagonal drum and topped it with an undulating lantern, the whole picked out externally with polychrome tiles. The external walls are articulated by sober pilasters again in the manner of Herrera, which contrast with the angle lesenes surmounted by foliated brackets over *pinjantes*. Figueroa also made use of Fray Juan Ricci's undulant order on the entablature and split pediment of the central bell gable (where he also employed solomonic columns) and on the internal cornices of the dome and lantern, while in the cloister he featured undulant pilasters. Split pediments and solomonic columns are even applied to the little dormer windows that appear over the transepts.

The largest church with which Figueroa was involved was S Salvador, which he completed in 1696–1701, after a succession of architects had worked on an earlier design of unknown authorship. The horizontally stressed elevation is adapted from Sebastiano Serlio, and various structural and stylistic devices appear retardataire, but Figueroa's intervention is unmistakable in such idiosyncratic details as the interruption of the nave entablatures by the apexes of the nave arcade. The centralized plan for S Luis (1699–1731) bears a close resemblance to Carlo Rainaldi's design (1652) for S Agnese in Piazza Navona, Rome, while the door details resemble those devised by Francesco Borromini for the same church. However, many features of the stylistic vocabulary are Figueroa's, including the polychrome tiles that roof the dome and the use of brickwork with the vertical joints suppressed and the horizontal ones exaggerated by recession. Columns are featured with solomonic twists in the upper shaft but foliate decoration covering the lower part. Italian High Baroque volumetry is thus clad with Sevillian ornament. The sacramental chapel of S Catalina (1721), on a rectangular plan, has a bulbous octagonal turret and spire covered with glazed polychrome tiles.

From 1722 Figueroa completed the façade, main doorway, central courtyard and chapel of the Colegio (now Palacio) de S Telmo, which had been started in 1671 (*see* SPAIN, fig. 8). The elevation is of two main storeys in Figueroa's characteristic brickwork, articulated by panelled stone pilasters. The main doorway in the centre is in white stone, three storeys high and designed like a retable, decked out with statues representing the arts and sciences taught at the college. A semicircular balcony projects at first-floor level, supported by four atlantids. This exuberance is eschewed in Figueroa's last work, the renovation (1724) of the main court of the convent of La Merced (now the Museo de Bellas Artes), where academic restraint prevails. The manuscript of Figueroa's unpublished book on his professional experiences and artistic theories has been lost. His manner was continued after his death mainly by his son Ambrosio de Figueroa (1700–75).

BIBLIOGRAPHY

E. Llaguno y Amrola: *Notícias*, iv (1829)
A. Sancho Corbacho: *Arquitectura barroca sevillana del siglo XVIII* (Madrid, 1952)
G. Kubler: *Arquitectura de los siglos XVII y XVIII*, A. Hisp., xiv (Madrid, 1957)
G. Kubler and M. Soria: *Art and Architecture in Spain and Portugal and their American Dominions*, Pelican Hist. A. (Harmondsworth, 1959)
E. V. González: 'La arquitectura española del siglo XVIII', *Arte español del siglo XVIII*, J. C. Aznar, J. L. Morales y Marin and E. V. González (Madrid, 1984)

☐

Figueroa, Pedro José (*b* Bogotá, after *c*. 1750; *d* Bogotá, 1838). Colombian painter. Like the painters who had worked in the region during the colonial period, he specialized in portraits and religious paintings and displayed a preference for a frontal treatment of the human figure and for heavy draperies as backdrops. Nevertheless his work was distinguished by indications of atmosphere, customs and politics, which established the terms for the development of painting in Colombia during the 19th century. The portraits he painted after 1812 of the national hero, *Simón Bolívar* (e.g. Bogotá, Mus. N.), combined the solemnity and showiness of his attire with an understated and almost naive manner. His most important religious work, the *Trinity* (Bogotá Cathedral), is characterized by a pictorial economy and delicacy.

Figueroa's importance as the outstanding transitional figure between Colombia's colonial and republican periods can be measured by the influence that he exercised through his studio, where the most important Colombian painters of the 19th century received their artistic education. His sons Miguel Figueroa, Celestino Figueroa and José Santos Figueroa, as well as Luis García Hevia and José Manuel Groot, were among his pupils.

BIBLIOGRAPHY

G. Giraldo Jaramillo: *La miniatura, la pintura y el grabado en Colombia* (Bogotá, 1980), pp. 44, 53–4, 59, 96, 163–4, 178, 181, 267, 291, 349
E. Barney Cabrera: *Historia del arte colombiano*, ix (Bogotá, 1983)

EDUARDO SERRANO

Figurine. Small three-dimensional figure. In practice the term is often used interchangeably with STATUETTE, though it can be considered more appropriate in cases where the small figure is not free-standing but part of a larger, utilitarian artefact, such as a candelabra or mirror; where it is mass-produced or merely rudimentary; and where it does not relate to the forms and proportions of comparable large-scale sculpture.

☐

Fijałkowski, Stanisław (*b* Zdołbunów, Polesie, 4 Nov 1922). Polish painter and printmaker. He studied under Władysław Strzemiński at the Higher School of Fine Arts, Łódź (1946–51). Although he trained as a printmaker, the artistic production of his first ten years consisted of paintings. His earliest works were compositions dealing with the periphery of pure visual construction and poetic metaphor, in which the multiplicity of meanings of objects represented brings to mind the influence of Surrealism. In the 1960s he returned to printmaking, and his works in this area, especially the engravings, were either studies for paintings or simplified final versions of works that had begun as paintings. At the same time he abandoned the Surrealist poetic for a system of symbolic signs reduced to the simplest abstract forms located in the 'ideal' space of a neutral background.

Fijałkowski's work is related to esoteric traditions and theories of archetypes. He regarded his most significant influences as the teaching of Władysław Strzemiński and the theories of Carl Gustav Jung. The symbolism of the circle, square and triangle is allied to the numerical symbolism of Pythagoras and of the cabbala, and numbers appear in his works either directly or in the form of numerical relations of rhythms, colours and forms. The titles of his works refer to fundamental cultural texts—the Bible, the Talmud, the *Divina Commedia*—or to works in cultural theory (e.g. by Ernst Cassirer and Umberto Eco); often the title is the date on which the work was begun, in which case it is recorded in the artist's diary, which also records the development of the composition. Among the best-known works are the series *Motorways* (artist's col.) and the *Talmud* (artist's col.), begun in the 1970s.

BIBLIOGRAPHY

B. Kowalska: *Polska awangarda malarska, 1945–1970* [Polish avant-garde painting, 1945–1970] (Warsaw, 1975)

Stanisław Fijałkowski: Malarstwo, grafika [Stanisław Fijałkowski: paintings, prints] (exh. cat., ed. U. Czartoryska and A. Wesołowska; Łódź, Office A. Exh., 1978)

Présences polonaises (exh. cat., ed. D. Bozo and R. Stanisławski; Paris, Pompidou, 1983), pp. 272–3

EWA MIKINA

Fiji [Viti]. Archipelago of *c.* 300 islands (*c.* 100 inhabited) to the east of Vanuatu and to the north-west of Tonga. Fiji is composed of high volcanic islands, low atolls and combinations of both types. The group lies in the path of the prevailing south-east trade winds and is subject to frequent tropical cyclones. The two main islands of Viti Levu (Great Fiji) and Vanua Levu (Great Land) have thickly forested eastern slopes and dry western slopes. All the islands, except those of raised limestone and the atolls, are fertile. There are extensive reef systems, notably in the eastern Lau islands, with rich marine resources. The art of Fiji has been fairly well studied and illustrated (see bibliography). Examples of Fijian art are held by many museums throughout the world, particularly good collections being held by the Fiji Museum, Suva, Fiji; the Peabody Museum, Salem, MA; the National Museum of Natural History, Washington, DC; the Museum of Archaeology and Anthropology, Cambridge University; and the Museum für Völkerkunde, Berlin.

1. Introduction. 2. Men's art. 3. Women's art.

1. INTRODUCTION. Until the formalization of political borders in the 19th century, the area comprised a number of chiefdoms, whose political and military fortunes waxed and waned and whose boundaries fluctuated accordingly. At the time of European settlement in the 19th century, the inhabitants were not a homogenous population. Rather, they had cultural affinities with the peoples of Tonga, Samoa, Vanuatu, New Caledonia and elsewhere. The name Fiji is derived from the Tongan pronunciation (Fisi) of the first part of Viti Levu. Even the classification of Fiji within Melanesia or Polynesia is problematic: while the populations of the coastal areas and islands are 'Polynesian', relating to Tonga and Samoa, those of the interior of the main islands are 'Melanesian', having affinities with Vanuatu and New Caledonia. With no pidgin lingua franca, the language of Bau, one of the main centres of indigenous political power in the 19th century, has been officially adopted as standard Fijian.

The Fiji area was settled *c.* 1500 BC by makers of Lapita pottery who arrived from the west. The period up to the late 18th century was one of successive migrations, movements and local developments that produced a heterogenous population, divided into autochthonous 'land' clans and immigrant chiefly clans. It was not until the early 19th century that regular contact was established between islanders and Western visitors. Trade in sandalwood and *bêche-de-mer*, for Chinese markets, flourished briefly in the first quarter of the 19th century, when the only settlers were beachcombers and castaways. In the 1830s missionaries arrived, and, by the early 1870s, after a series of mass conversions, most Fijians except those in the interior of the main islands were nominally Christian. In 1874, the year when the most influential chiefs voluntarily ceded Fiji to Britain, European settlement had reached *c.* 2000 (compared to *c.* 100,000 Fijians). The importation of indentured labour from India brought *c.* 60,000 people from the subcontinent; by World War II, Fiji–Indians outnumbered indigenous Fijians: in 1992 the populations were roughly equal. Fiji gained independence in 1970 and became a republic after two bloodless coups in 1987.

Some Fijians were encountered, and objects collected, in Tonga in the late 18th century. The first collections of Fijian art and artefacts derive from the early 19th century. Since this period there have been major cultural upheavals yet also considerable continuity. This is apparent both in aspects of social organization and in artistic traditions, with late 20th-century art including 'traditional' items made not only for the craft market but also for local use, and fine-quality replicas of 19th-century pieces, as well as tourist art products, of which plastic 'grass' skirts are but one example. Fijians have no term translatable as 'art' but classify indigenous manufactured things as either *iyau* ('valuables', goods suitable for presentation) or *iyaya* (equipment, tools, household items). A significant aspect of valuables is whether they are made by men or women. In general, men worked with hard materials, such as wood, ivory and stone, while women used soft materials, such as bark, leaves and clay.

2. MEN'S ART. Most art produced by Fijian men has been in wood. Where the best stands of tropical hardwoods were to be found, clans of specialist carpenters (*matai*) produced not only house components but also sculptures, bowls, canoes, drums, weapons, headrests and ornaments, either for use within the chiefdom or in competitive exchanges (*solevu*) with other chiefdoms. Men of non-carpenter clans in these locations might also be skilled carpenters and assist in major works. Before European contact, the main tools were stone-bladed adzes, stone or shell burins and sharkskin rasps. Metal axes, plane blades, chisels, gouges, saws and drills were introduced by Europeans. Acceleration in the speed with which the dense-grained tropical hardwoods could be worked led during the 19th century to an increase in the scale and number of artefacts, especially canoes. Several carpenter clans continued to work with wood in the 1990s, notably the Lemaki of Kabara and the Jiafau of Vulaga, Lau, both of Samoan–Tongan origin.

In contrast to the art traditions of most Polynesian and Melanesian cultures, human-figure sculptures were comparatively rare in Fiji, and information on them is limited. They were used in temples or as part of temple architecture (see Clunie, 1986, pp. 165–8). Several are shaped as suspension hooks for offerings. Whatever their original purpose, such images ceased to be produced after Christian conversion in the late 19th century. Typologically, there are two general categories. The first type are wooden images between 200 and 1400 mm high, often less than finely finished and yet characterized by a certain sculptural vigour. These were collected from various parts of Fiji and have more in common with sculptures from New Caledonia and Vanuatu than with those from the Cook Islands, New Zealand or elsewhere in Polynesia. The second type are smaller, more finely finished and mostly of sperm-whale ivory, although some are of wood, and are thought to have been made either in Tonga or by Tongan craftsmen working for Fijian chiefs.

Wood bowls and vessels of various kinds are well represented in museum collections, and some continue to be made for local use and for sale. Three general categories may be identified. The first kind were for such pre-Christian priestly rituals as the preparation, drinking and libation-pouring of *yaqona* (an infusion of the root of the pepper, *Piper methysticum*, with water), and for anointing and libation with coconut oil. These are shallow dishes in anthropomorphic, zoomorphic or botanical form; some have a circular dish on a geometrically shaped pedestal. They are often finely finished with a rich patina from handling and from the *yaqona* or oil with which they were filled. A number of human-figure priest's *yaqona* dishes survive (see fig. 1; see also Oldman, 1943, pl. 69; Clunie, 1986, no. 130). Five fine bowls are in the form of a duck with outstretched wings (Hobart, Tasman. Mus. & A.G.; Norwich, U. E. Anglia, Sainsbury Cent.; Suva, Fiji Mus.). As with figure sculptures, these elaborate dishes ceased to be made after Christian conversion.

In contrast, large circular one-piece bowls with four or more legs (*tanoa*) have continued to be produced and used into the 1990s. Considered to be a Samoan or Tongan introduction to Fiji of recent pre-contact times, they are used for public state rituals, when *yaqona* is prepared as an offering to be drunk by the chief or senior person present. In the early 1990s the right to carve these bowls resided with the carpenters of Kabara, Lau, many of whom trace their ancestry to Samoa. *Tanoa* are classified as a valuable and are useful exchange items that move throughout the region, and even as far as Tonga. As with most important wood items, *tanoa* are made from *vesi* (*Intsia bijuga*), which is regarded as the best wood and is associated with chiefs and all that is straight and strong. Those *tanoa* for use before the most important chiefs or dignitaries have a long coir cord decorated with white cowrie shells, which is stretched towards the chief during the mixing of the drink. Bowls in the form of a turtle, with or without legs, are also occasionally used for *yaqona* preparation. The third variety of vessel, food bowls and trays, continued to be made in outer-island areas. Notable among them is the large oval *papasia*, which is superior to aluminium bowls for pounding root vegetables.

1. Fijian priest's *yaqona* dish in human form, wood, h. 267 mm, collected 1840 (London, British Museum)

Canoe-building was one of the carpenters' most important tasks, and 18th- and 19th-century Fijian sailing vessels were among the most efficient and seaworthy in the Pacific. While simple dugouts were made for river use, elegant single-outrigger and double-hulled canoes were the means of inter-island transport. The finest were made of *vesi*, and the various hull and superstructure components were lashed together with coir cordage. Sea-going canoes could sail in either direction by moving the base of the triangular sail from one end of the hull to the other ('shunting' technique). By the mid-19th century a large number of Fijian double-hulled vessels (*drua*) were plying Fijian and Tongan waters, some over 30 m long and capable of carrying over 100 passengers. Small 6–12 m outrigger canoes have continued to be used in Lau.

Fijian drums (*lali*) are of gong form and resemble truncated canoe hulls, being 1–2 m long. A pair of *lali*, one larger than the other, stand beside village ceremonial grounds (*rara*), where they are used for signalling purposes by being beaten with softwood mallets. Miniature versions (*lalinimeke*) are played held on the lap to accompany dances.

A wide range of wooden clubs were made prior to the cessation of indigenous warfare in the 1870s. A warrior's full equipment included a short throwing club with bulbous head, a hand club *c.* 1 m long with a shaped and engraved head and a long spear with an intricately barbed point. Some clubs have exquisite engravings, and those with chiefly associations may have whale ivory inlay. Bows were also made but were steadily replaced by muskets during the 19th century. The headrest (*kali*) was perhaps the most elegant of domestic equipment. These were cut from wood or bamboo and could take several forms, sometimes having separate legs lashed on with coir. They were used by high-status people to protect the elaborate coiffure that was common before missionary notions of cleanliness encouraged a close-cropped style. The centralization of chiefdoms in the 19th century, together with an increased supply of sperm-whale teeth from European traders, led to a development in the range and quantity of ornaments and chiefly regalia. Breastplates and necklaces were made with ivory and shell components, some circular in form, others being composed of split sections of whale tooth. Plain pearl-shell discs were mounted with flat ivory sections to create imposing plates 200–250 mm across (see fig. 2). The more complex examples are considered to be early to mid-19th century work of Tongan or Samoan specialists based in Fiji. Although the presentation whale's tooth (*tabua*), with a cord tied to each end, might occasionally be hung around the neck of someone engaged in a presentation, it is normally held in the hands by those speaking during an exchange.

2. Fijian breastplate, whale ivory and pearl shell, w. 263 mm, *c.* 1820–40 (University of Cambridge, Museum of Archaeology and Anthropology)

The building of chiefs' houses and tall spirit-houses or temples was coordinated by senior carpenters. A range of square, rectangular, circular and oval house types was built in different parts of Fiji, most having large posts, elaborate roof structures and walls and thatching of reeds, grass or bamboo. Decoration was minimal, although white cowries adorned the ridge-pole of chiefs' houses and temples.

3. WOMEN'S ART. Women in many parts of Fiji were skilled in the manufacture of decorated bark cloth (*masi*), mats and fibre skirts, and in basketry and net-making. Pottery was also made by the women of particular clans in a variety of locations, and tattoo was a female practice in many areas. The basic bark cloth of Fiji differed little from that of other parts of Polynesia. The use of stencils to apply designs was, however, unique to Fiji. Stencils made from leaves were cut in a variety of intricate patterns, and red–brown and black dye was rubbed over them on to the white cloth ground. Design styles and techniques varied from area to area and changed over time (for example, in the 1990s the stencils were made from X-ray film), but cloth has continued to be decorated in this way, and different areas produce distinct styles. Designs from Vatulele feature open patterns in red and black; Cakaudrove cloth has large black triangles and lozenges; Moce cloth has detailed red-and-black styles and Namuka-i-Lau cloth is characterized by very detailed, mostly black, decoration. Bark cloth was formerly used for men's loincloths, bedding and mosquito curtains, and for robes, seats and beds for high-status people or for those undergoing rites of passage and other rituals. It has continued to have ritual and exhange uses but has also become one of the leading items in a growing handicraft market. Besides the various kinds of stencilled cloth, two other types have continued to be made. *Gatu vaka Viti* are large sheets decorated with a combination of stencilling and rubbing techniques and are hung at weddings and used as burial shrouds. *Gatu vakaToga* are also enormous sheets (up to 80 m long and 5 m wide) that are decorated with a rubbing technique attributed originally to Tonga. These are made in eastern Fiji by groups of women representing a family, clan, village or chiefdom, and, after presentation, the sheets are cut into smaller sections for distribution to the recipients, who will use them in further presentations or for ritual clothing, seats or bedding.

Plaited pandanus-leaf or sedge mats were made in most areas of Fiji for household and ritual use. Some had patterns worked in with black-dyed strands and were used as special ritual seats and beds. Mats were, and are, presentation valuables, and performed many similar functions to bark cloth. They were integral to many ceremonies. Late 20th-century presentation mats were decorated with bright border designs in multicoloured yarns called *kula*. (This term actually refers to the red feathers formerly used to decorate the borders of fine mats in eastern Fiji and Samoa.) When laid on the ground at a wedding, edge to edge, these mats form a dazzling carpet of colour. A variety of baskets and fans were once made in great numbers from coconut and pandanus leaves, some designs worked in black. Some continue to be made for practical purposes, while others are made solely for the handicraft market. Until Christianization, women's clothing consisted of a fibre skirt (*liku*) in a variety of sizes, colours and styles.

The earliest surviving artefacts from Fiji are potsherds. By the 19th century there were a number of centres of pottery manufacture, using coiling or slab-building techniques. The specialist female potters of Kadavu, Nadroga, Nasilai, Malake and Levuka (Lakeba) are well known, although by the end of the 20th century only a few continued to practise their craft, working mostly for the handicraft market; hemispherical *yaqona* bowls have continued to be made in Nadroga. The most elaborate pots are the 19th-century drinking vessels made in south-east Viti Levu, which take such forms as turtles, citrus fruits, canoes, whales' teeth or sometimes a combination of these. Pots were not glazed, in the strict sense of the term, but were rubbed immediately after firing with *makadre* resin, which imparted a glossy brown waterproof varnish.

In contrast to Samoa, where it was confined to men, tattoo was restricted to women in 19th-century Fiji. In many areas adolescent girls were tattooed by female experts about the hips, genitals and mouth: patterns varied but were usually detailed. Whether the design systems resembled those on bark cloth or club engravings is difficult to establish. In the late 20th century men and women had simple healing tattoos, applied to ease injured or aching joints.

BIBLIOGRAPHY

T. Williams: *The Islands and their Inhabitants*, i of *Fiji and the Fijians*, ed. G. S. Rowe (London, 1858/*R* Suva, 1982)

J. Hornell: *The Canoes of Polynesia, Fiji, and Micronesia* (1936), i of *Canoes of Oceania* by A. C. Haddon and J. Hornell, Bishop Mus. Special Pubn, xxvii (Honolulu, 1936)

W. O. Oldman: *Polynesian Artifacts: The Oldman Collection Illustrated and Described* (Wellington, 1943, rev. 2/1953)

K. E. Larsson: *Fijian Studies* (Göteborg, 1960)

T. Barrow: *Art and Life in Polynesia* (Wellington and London, 1972)

G. S. Troxler: *Fijian Masi: A Traditional Art Form* (Greensboro, 1972)

F. Clunie: *Fijian Weapons and Warfare* (Suva, 1977)

S. Kooijman: *Tapa on Moce Island, Fiji: A Traditional Handicraft in a Changing Society*, Meded. Rijksmus. Vlkenknd., xxi (Leiden, 1977)

'*Artificial Curiosities': Being an Exposition of Native Manufactures Collected on the Three Pacific Voyages of Captain James Cook, R.N.*, Bishop Mus. Special Pubn, lxv (exh. cat. by A. L. Kaeppler, Honolulu, Bishop Mus., 1978)

R. Ewins: *Fijian Artefacts: The Tasmanian Museum and Art Gallery Collection* (Hobart, 1982)

——: *Mat Weaving in Gau*, Fiji Mus. Special Pubn, 3 (Suva, 1982)

Domodomo (1983–7)

F. Clunie: *Yalo i Viti—Shades of Fiji: A Fiji Museum Catalogue* (Suva, 1986)

J. Roth and S. Hooper, eds: *The Fiji Journals of Baron Anatole von Hügel, 1875–1877* (Suva, 1990)

STEVEN HOOPER

Fijt, Jan. *See* FYT, JAN.

Filālī. *See* 'ALAWI.

Filangieri, Gaetano, Prince of Satriano (*b* Naples, 1824; *d* Naples, 1892). Italian museum founder, director and writer. He was active in political life in his youth; after 1870, becoming increasingly distrustful of the unified Italian state, he devoted himself to the defence of Neapolitan interests. He served as a city councillor and was engaged in controversies over local cultural policy. He travelled to London, Paris and Vienna gathering ideas to help realize his dream of founding museums of art and industry in Naples; he hoped to regenerate Neapolitan taste and production through educating artists and craftsmen to integrate the major and minor arts. Having organized an exhibition of Neapolitan industrial art in 1877, he was among those appointed in 1878 to a commission for the establishment of a permanent museum of industrial art in the city. The Museo Artistico Industriale, which opened in 1882, was founded to collect ancient and modern examples of the decorative arts, including ceramics and furniture; it was also intended as a training ground for modern production, taking account of local needs. Filangieri wrote the museum's regulations, also laying out a plan for the course of studies. Compared with similar European museums, for example the South Kensington Museum, London (now V&A and Sci. Mus.), the Museo Artistico Industriale was innovative in its affiliation with trade schools, hence introducing new machines and manufacturing processes in its teaching methods. Filangieri was its director from 1882 to 1892. However, the synthesis of museum, schools and workshops proved impractical because of the South's economic underdevelopment. The museum was later absorbed into the Istituto Statale d'Arte di Napoli Filippo Palizzi, where the Museo Artistico delle Ceramiche (housing some of Filangieri's original collection) was opened in 1982 as a centenary celebration.

Concurrently Filangieri was involved in instigating the Museo Civico Gaetano Filangieri, which he founded in 1882 (having stipulated in 1881 that his fortune would be left to the city of Naples on condition that he was director of the museum for life). It was opened in 1888, in a building that conserved the 15th-century Palazzo Cuomo, which was dismantled and rebuilt on a site near by to make way for the new Via Duomo. The original façade of the Palazzo was retained and the interior reconstructed in a Renaissance Revival style with decorations designed by Filangieri; the work was executed by furniture-makers and potters from the Museo Artistico Industriale. The nature of the complete collection can be deduced only from Filangieri's catalogue of 1888, as two-fifths of it was destroyed during World War II. What remains nevertheless reflects his taste for Neapolitan decorative arts, including arms, ceramics, glass, coins and medals; there are also some notable paintings by such artists as Francesco Solimena, Luca Giordano and Massimo Stanzione.

Filangieri also edited a six-volume collection of *Documenti per la storia, le arti e le industrie delle provine napoletane* (1883–91). This monumental work, together with other essays he wrote on art history, reveals his adherence to positivist methods and his conscientious search for reliable documents from which to reconstruct the city's history, with ample attention to the applied arts.

WRITINGS

Il Museo Artistico-Industriale in Napoli: Relazione di Gaetano Filangieri Principe di Satriano con una ministeriale e lo statuto (Naples, 1879)

'Di una testa di cavallo in bronzo già di casa Maddaloni in Via Sedile di Nilo ora al Museo Nazionale di Napoli', *Archv Stor. Prov. Napolet.*, viii (1882), pp. 407–20

ed.: *Museo Artistico-Industriale e Scuole-Officine di Napoli: Statuto e regolamento generale e relazione per gli anni 1882–1883* (Naples, 1883)

ed.: *Documenti per la storia, le arti e le industrie delle provine napoletane*, 6 vols (Naples, 1883–91)

'Di un dipinto finora attribuito ad Antonio Solario detto "Lo Zingaro"', *Archv Stor. Prov. Napolet.*, ix (1884), pp. 91–103

'Mastro Giovanni Normando agonista ed architetto', *Archv Stor. Prov. Napolet.*, ix (1884), pp. 286–300
'Nuovi documenti intorno la famiglia, le case e le vicende di Lucrezia d'Alagno', *Archv Stor. Prov. Napolet.*, xi (1886), pp. 65–138, 330–99
Catalogo del Museo Civico Gaetano Filangieri Principe di Satriano (Naples, 1888)

BIBLIOGRAPHY

F. Acton: *Il Museo Civico 'Gaetano Filangieri Principe di Satriano'* (Naples, 1974)
Il sogno del principe: Il Museo Artistico Industriale di Napoli: La ceramica tra otto e novecento (exh. cat., ed. E. Alamaro; Faenza, Pal. Espos., 1984)
N. Barrella: 'Il Museo Civico Gaetano Filangieri di Napoli tra il 1882 e il 1892: Dalla politica culturale di un principe una lezione per il presente', *Museologia*, 18 (1985), pp. 27–45
——: *Il Museo Filangieri* (Naples, 1988)

GIOVANNA CASSESE

Filarete [Antonio di Pietro Averlino] (*b c.* 1400; *d c.* 1469). Italian sculptor, architect and theorist. According to Vasari, he trained in the studio of Lorenzo Ghiberti, but he developed a personal style that was relatively independent of Florentine influence. His *Trattato di architettura* was the first Renaissance architectural treatise to be written in vernacular Italian and illustrated with drawings and was an important work in the development of Renaissance architectural theory.

1. Sculpture. 2. Architectural works. 3. The *Trattato di architettura*.

1. SCULPTURE. Filarete is first recorded in 1433 in Rome, where he attended the coronation of the Emperor Sigismund. Presumably the same year he was commissioned by Pope Eugenius IV to design and execute the bronze door of the main porch of the old St Peter's (inscribed and dated, 1445; *see* ROME, fig. 11). The unsettled political conditions during the pontificate of Eugenius IV (1431–47) and the depiction of events during 1438–42 in the small, friezelike reliefs have led to the supposition (Spencer, 1978) that Filarete was not continuously engaged on the door and at one point was given a change of programme. The two wings of the door each consist of three rectangular fields of different size with large figures (see fig. 1); between these are smaller figural friezes. Pope Paul V later removed the doors (1619) to the central porch of the new St Peter's, where narrow rectangular fields were added above and below. The figures portrayed in the main fields are: Christ enthroned giving his blessing (top left); Mary enthroned (top right); St Paul (middle left); St Peter with Eugenius IV kneeling at his feet being given the keys (middle right); the martyrdom of St Paul (bottom left); and the martyrdom of St Peter (bottom right). The small friezelike figures in the relief between the main fields portray events from the pontificate of Eugenius IV. Antique and contemporary portraits, mythological scenes and animals are inserted in the acanthus tendrils.

The juxtaposition of Classical and Early Christian elements is a remarkable feature of the door, which is one of the earliest examples of Roman Renaissance sculpture. The division of the door into fields of different sizes, for example, departs from traditional medieval practice and also differs from Ghiberti's doors in the Baptistery at Florence, following instead such Classical models as the bronze doors of the Pantheon. At the same time, the combination of large seated figures with more detailed scenes on a significantly smaller scale reveals links with

1. Filarete: bronze doors (*c.* 1433–45), St Peter's, Rome

Early Christian diptychs of the time of the Consulate (Seymour). The scheme is intended to portray the primacy of the Roman Catholic Church and the Papacy, with its seat in Rome, in both its spiritual and temporal aspect. Indeed the Roman Church is depicted as the legitimate successor to the Roman Empire. The iconography of Christ, Mary, Peter and Paul in the principal fields follows Early Christian traditions, while the depiction of the crucifixion of St Peter on a mountain between two pyramids, the Castel Sant'Angelo and a tree, shows a mixture of various medieval and contemporary interpretations of the tradition of the crucifixion 'inter duas metas'. Stylistically the influence of the Classical world is visible not in the treatment of perspective (as in Ghiberti and Donatello), but in such detailed motifs as the disciples' clothing, the architecture and topographical reconstructions of the city of Rome, the acanthus tendrils and the profiles of Caesar and mythological scenes taken from Ovid's *Metamorphoses*.

During his time in Rome, Filarete also produced the statue of *A Rider* (inlaid with bronze, gold and enamel, 380×360×145 mm, signed, *c.* 1440–45; Dresden, Skulp-samml.), which was a copy of the equestrian statue of *Marcus Aurelius*. This is the earliest surviving small Renaissance bronze and the earliest known copy of an ancient sculpture. In 1448 Filarete was accused of stealing relics and had to flee Rome; the *Trattato* implies that he spent 1449 in Venice. In the same year he was commissioned by the town of Bassano del Grappa to execute a processional cross (silver on wood, plated with gold leaf, 490×370 mm, 1449; Bassano del Grappa, Mus. Civ.) recalling 14th-century prototypes and clearly showing the influence of Ghiberti. A signed plaque with an allegorical scene (bronze, 855×135 mm; St Petersburg, Hermitage) also dates from *c.* 1450. Later sculptural works include a statuette of *Hector on Horseback* (bronze, 255×255×125 mm, 1456; Madrid, Mus. Arqueol. N.) and a plaque with his *Self-portrait* (bronze, 88×67 mm, *c.* 1460; Milan, Mus. Civ. Milano).

2. ARCHITECTURAL WORKS. In 1451 Filarete accepted an invitation from Duke Francesco Sforza (*see* SFORZA, (1)) to move to Milan, where he started a new career as architect and architectural theorist. He stayed in Milan until 1465, his most important work there being the Ospedale Maggiore, commissioned by Sforza in 1456 with the object of uniting the city's many small hospitals into a single complex. After recurrent difficulties with the hospital management, local building workers and perhaps also with Sforza himself, Filarete resigned his post as building superintendent in 1465, when only a small part of the project had been completed. His successors, Guiniforte Solari (1429–81) and later Giovanni Antonio Amadeo, continued the construction but with a partial change of design. Further alterations in the 17th and 18th centuries mean that the only parts of the present building built to Filarete's design are the south cross-shaped hall with its four courts and accompanying façades. However, in his *Trattato*, Filarete gave detailed information about his project (see fig. 2). His planned layout was completely axio-symmetrical: two large, cruciform halls, each embraced by four small courts, would have flanked a central

court, with a church in the middle. The cruciform halls were to contain the beds, located according to the patients' illness and sex, all with a direct view of the altar, which was to stand under the domed crossing of the four arms.

The cruciform layout of the beds and the excellent ventilation and drainage system meant that the Ospedale Maggiore was the most advanced hospital of the age, for both organization and hygiene. Its design was immediately imitated in Pavia, Brescia and Parma, and subsequently throughout Europe. The origins of this type of hospital have been variously explained. The hospitals at Florence and Siena, which Filarete studied at the request of his patron in 1456, before he started planning, can at best have served as models for the technical and organizational aspects, since their layout is entirely different. It has been argued that the type evolved under Pope Nicholas V and then developed into the hospitals of Pavia and Mantua (Luca Fancelli), the chronological precedence of which is disputed; Quadflieg on the other hand traces the cruciform hall back to Islamic hospitals. Leverotti and Patetta refer to a document indicating that Filarete's design was influenced by a hospital project initiated by Cosimo de' Medici, which is attributed to Alberti or Bernardo Rossellino. The Ospedale Maggiore marks a turning-point in 15th-century Lombard architecture for here, for the first time, an architectural vocabulary is used that is influenced by the Florentine Renaissance, for example in the columned arcades of the courts and façades.

Another important commission Filarete received was for the new cathedral (1455–7) at Bergamo. However, due to extensive rebuilding in the 17th century, the only record of his work is a drawing in the *Trattato*: it shows an aisleless church with side chapels and a dominant cupola over the crossing flanked by four pointed towers. Francesco Sforza also recommended Filarete for appointment as building superintendent for the two largest schemes in Milan, the cathedral works and the Castello Sforzesco. However, Filarete immediately withdrew from these latter projects following disagreements with local artists. After a dispute with Sforza, Filarete left Milan *c.* 1465 and moved back to Florence, where he was received into Piero de' Medici's circle.

3. THE 'TRATTATO DI ARCHITETTURA'. During his time in the service of Francesco Sforza, Filarete wrote his

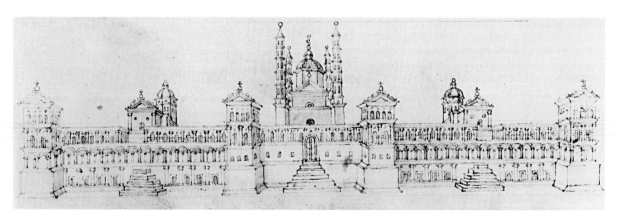

2. Filarete: façade of the Ospedale Maggiore, Milan, commissioned 1456; drawing from his *Trattato di architettura* (1461–4)

Trattato di architettura (1461–4), which remained unpublished until the late 19th century. Filarete's original manuscript has been lost, but several copies have survived. Of these it is generally agreed that the Codex Magliabechianus copy (Florence, Bib. N. Cent., MS. ii. i. 140) is the closest to Filarete's original. Although the treatise was first dedicated to Francesco Sforza, a further, reworked copy was produced for Piero de' Medici, with the addition of a key chapter in praise of the Medici family as patrons. The *Trattato* is substantially different in both spirit and form from the Classical prototype of Vitruvius and from Alberti's *De re aedificatoria* (1452). It is written as a court dialogue between the architect and his patron, and it contains a novelistic account of a town being founded by a rich prince.

Filarete's most significant contribution to Renaissance architectural theory lies in his remarks on the origin of architecture and its anthropomorphic proportions, planning stage method and finally in his project for the ideal town of Sforzinda. Like Vitruvius, Filarete traced the origin of architecture to primordial dwellings, but he gave the analysis a Christian slant by identifying Adam as the first architect. As the prototype of humanity, Adam is also seen as originating the proportions of columns. The proportions of the vertical supports in the first human habitation, which were subsequently developed into columns, therefore already correspond to those of the human body, and the anthropomorphic proportions of architecture are established in the first human dwelling. The human head becomes the basic unit for all measurements; starting from three average human sizes, Filarete develops the doctrine of the three orders of architecture (Doric, Ionic and Corinthian), exactly inverting that of Vitruvius: the Doric column is nine, the Ionic seven and the Corinthian eight heads high. Filarete is concerned only with a difference in proportion between the individual orders, not with any difference in detailing, as occurs in Vitruvius and Alberti. In his accompanying illustrations the Vitruvian descriptions of the form of capitals are interchanged. Filarete follows Vitruvius in deriving the basic geometrical units, the circle and square, from the proportions of the human body. Thanks to Filarete and subsequently Francesco di Giorgio Martini (MSS *c.* 1470–80), anthropomorphism, and its attendant doctrine of proportion as an integral part of architectural theory, were thus given more importance than at any time since Vitruvius.

Filarete's differentiation between the three stages of planning was significant for subsequent architectural practice in the Renaissance. The first stage, the 'congetto' or 'disegno in di grosso' (the sketch-plan), is followed by the 'disegno proporzionato' (the scale drawings squared up by the use of coordinate grids); finally, there is the 'disegno rilevato' or 'modello' (the wooden scale model illustrating the scheme). Above all, the gridded scale drawing, which for the first time set out the design and the completed building in a firmly defined dimensional relationship in all its parts, constituted an important innovation. The emphasis on theoretical design, and its clear definition in relation to the execution of a building, associates Filarete, like Alberti, with a higher social status for the architect, who is now seen as a humanistic scientist and courtier.

The relationship of the architect to his princely patron is another dominant theme in the treatise, especially evident in the description of the founding of Sforzinda, the first ideal town of the Renaissance to be planned and illustrated in detail. In Filarete's narrative, shortly after building is started, a Golden Book is found with a description in Greek of the city's ancient predecessor, which the prince then orders to be reconstructed. Sforzinda is planned as an octagonal central town with a radial network of streets, in the middle of which is the principal square with the cathedral, the Palazzo Signorile and adjoining markets. Two further squares with public and commercial buildings adjoin the central square. The parish churches and monastery churches are placed in the main thoroughfares. Filarete gives no specific location for the many other individual buildings mentioned. Following Vitruvius and Alberti he divides the various buildings, descriptions and plans of which form a substantial part of the account of Sforzinda, into public and private constructions; the former are then subdivided into religious and secular. Filarete also makes a further historical distinction between contemporary and ancient buildings. The designs for both groups are fantastic and utopian in form and style and are in marked contrast to contemporary built architecture. Against the background of the still medieval architecture of 15th-century Milan there is a sense of a continuous polemic against Gothic architecture and its pointed arches, which Filarete sets against the good architecture of antiquity that serves as a model for the buildings of Sforzinda.

WRITINGS

J. R. Spencer, ed.: *Filarete, Treatise on Architecture: Being the Treatise by Antonio di Piero Averlino, Known as Filarete*, 2 vols (New Haven, 1965)

A. M. Finoli and L. Grassi, eds: *Filarete: Trattato di architettura*, 2 vols (Milan, 1972)

BIBLIOGRAPHY

GENERAL

W. von Oettingen: *Über das Leben und die Werke des A. Averlino genannt Filarete* (Leipzig, 1888)

M. Lazzaroni and A. Munoz: *Filarete scultore e architetto del secolo XV* (Rome, 1908)

'Il Filarete: Atti del corso di specializzazione "Antonio Averlino detto il Filarete"', *A. Lombarda*, xii (1973)

SCULPTURE

V. Rakint: 'Une Plaquette du Filarete au Musée de l'Ermitage', *Gaz. B.-A.*, lxvi (1924), pp. 157–66

H. Keutner: '*Hektor zu Pferde*: Eine Bronzestatuette von Antonio Averlino Filarete', *Studien zur toskanischen Kunst: Festschrift für Ludwig H. Heydenreich* (Munich, 1963), pp. 139–56

P. Foster: 'Per il disegno dell'Ospedale Maggiore di Milano', *A. Lombarda*, xviii (1973), pp. 1–22

U. Nilgen: 'Filaretes Bronzetür von St Peter: Zur Interpretation von Bild und Rahmen', *Actas del XXIII Congreso internacional de historia del arte, Granada, 1973*, iii, pp. 569–85

C. Seymour: 'Some Reflections on Filarete's Use of Antique Visual Sources', *A. Lombarda*, xxxviii–xxxix (1973), pp. 36–47

C. Lord: 'Solar Imagery in Filarete's Doors to Saint Peter's', *Gaz. B.-A.*, lxxxvii (1976), pp. 143–50

J. R. Spencer: 'Filarete's Bronze Doors at St Peter's: A Cooperative Project with Complications of Chronology and Technique', *Collaboration in Italian Renaissance Art*, ed. J. T. Paoletti and W. S. Sheard (New Haven, 1978), pp. 33–57

——: 'Filarete the Medallist of the Roman Emperors', *A. Bull.*, xli/4 (1979), pp. 550–61

N. Gramaccini: 'Die Umwertung der Antike: Zur Rezeption des Marc Aurel', *Mittelalter und Renaissance, Natur und Antike* (exh. cat., Frankfurt am Main, Liebieghaus, 1985–6), pp. 51–83

R. Coppel: 'A Newly-discovered Signature and Date for Filarete's *Hector*', *Burl. Mag.*, 129 (1987), pp. 802–10

E. Parlato: 'Il gusto all'antica di Filarete scultore', *Da Pisanello alla nascita dei Musei Capitolini: L'Antico a Roma alla vigilia del Rinascimento* (exh. cat., Rome, Mus. Capitolino, 1988), pp. 115–34

P. Cannata: 'Le placchette del Filarete', *Stud. Hist. A.*, 22 (1989), pp. 35–53

ARCHITECTURE AND ARCHITECTURAL THEORY

L. Firpo: *La città ideale del Filarete* (Turin, 1954)

P. Tigler: *Die Architekturtheorie des Filarete* (Berlin, 1963)

J. Onians: 'Alberti and Filarete: A Study in their Sources', *J. Warb. & Court. Inst.*, xxxiv (1971), pp. 96–114

L. Grassi: *Lo 'Spedale dei Poveri' del Filarete: Storia e restauro* (Milan, 1972)

S. Lang: 'Sforzinda, Filarete and Filelfo', *J. Warb. & Court. Inst.* (1972), pp. 391–7

H. Saalman: 'Early Renaissance Architectural Theory and Practice in Antonio Filarete's *Trattato di Architettura*', *A. Bull.*, xli/1 (1979), pp. 89–106

L. Giordano: 'Il trattato del Filarete e l'architettura lombarda', *Les Traités d'architecture de la Renaissance. Actes du colloque: Tours, 1981*, pp. 115–28

F. Leverotti: 'Ricerche sulle origini dell'Ospedale Maggiore di Milano', *Archv Stor. Lombardo*, 10th ser., vi (1981), pp. 77–113

E. Quadflieg: *Filaretes Ospedale Maggiore in Mailand: Zur Rezeption islamischen Hospitalwesens in der italienischen Frührenaissance* (Cologne, 1981)

M. Rossi: 'I contributi del Filarete e dei Solari alla ricerca di una soluzione del duomo di Milano', *A. Lombarda*, lx (1981), pp. 15–23

L. Patetta: *L'architettura del quattrocento a Milano* (Milan, 1987)

A. E. WERDEHAUSEN

Fildes, (Samuel) Luke (*b* Liverpool, 18 Oct 1844; *d* London, 27 Feb 1927). English painter and illustrator. He first studied art at the Mechanics Institute in Liverpool and at the nearby Warrington School of Art. In 1863 he won a scholarship that enabled him to study at the South Kensington Art School in London and subsequently at the Royal Academy Schools. By the late 1860s he was earning money as an illustrator for such popular periodicals as the *Cornhill Magazine* and *Once a Week*.

Fildes's illustration *Houseless and Hungry*, which appeared as a wood-engraving in the first issue of the *Graphic* (4 Dec 1869), a socially conscious weekly, was the turning-point of his career. The engraving depicts homeless paupers queuing outside the casual ward of a workhouse. When it was shown to Charles Dickens by John Everett Millais, the author commissioned Fildes to illustrate his novel *The Mystery of Edwin Drood*. The unfinished book was published posthumously in 1870 with a set of 12 illustrations by Fildes.

In 1874 at the Royal Academy, Fildes exhibited *Applicants for Admission to a Casual Ward* (1874; Egham, U. London, Royal Holloway & Bedford New Coll.; see fig.), a painting based on the *Houseless and Hungry* illustration. The success of this work, with its forceful social message and dark-toned realism, established Fildes, along with Frank Holl (ii) and Hubert von Herkomer, as a leader of the social realist school in England that flourished during the 1870s. Fildes's sympathy for the poor reflects his origins; he was brought up by his grandmother Mary Fildes, an active political reformer who was seriously wounded in 1819 at the Peterloo Massacre near Manchester. Other social subjects by Fildes include *The Widower* (exh. RA 1876; Sydney, A.G. NSW), the *Return of the Penitent* (exh. RA 1879; Cardiff, City Hall) and *The Doctor* (exh. RA 1891; London, Tate). The last painting, set in a humble dwelling, shows a mortally ill child attended by a concerned physician with the distraught parents in the background. The sombre pathos of this work sparked an enormous popular response, and the engraving after it published by Agnew in 1892 was extremely successful.

Luke Fildes: *Applicants for Admission to a Casual Ward*, oil on canvas, 1.37×2.44 m, 1874 (Egham, University of London, Royal Holloway and Bedford New College)

After a trip to Venice in 1874 with his bride Fanny (*fl* 1873–83; *d* 1927), an artist and the sister of the painter Henry Woods (1846–1921), Fildes began to paint a series of Venetian subjects, which he exhibited at the Royal Academy during the 1880s; his most successful work of this type was an *Alfresco Toilette* (exh. RA 1889; Port Sunlight, Lady Lever A.G.). Popular for their vibrant colour and pretty women, these sentimental Venetian genre scenes offer a startling contrast to his paintings of social distress and poverty.

By 1890 the bulk of Fildes's work was almost exclusively portraiture, and his large and fashionable clientele included royalty. Among his royal commissions were portraits of the *Princess of Wales* (exh. RA 1894), *Edward VII* (exh. RA 1902; *see* REGALIA, fig. 2) and *George V* (1912) (all British Royal Col.). The financial rewards of portrait painting enabled the artist to commission a Queen Anne style house (1875–7) from Richard Norman Shaw, which was built at 11 Melbury Road, Kensington, London. Elected ARA in 1879, Fildes gained full membership in 1887 and was active in Academy affairs. He was knighted in 1906 and made KCVO in 1918. The contents of his studio were auctioned at Christie's, London, on 24 June 1927.

BIBLIOGRAPHY

W. W. Fenn: 'Our Living Artists: Luke Fildes, A.R.A.', *Mag. A.*, iii (1880), pp. 49–52

D. C. Thomson: 'The Life and Work of Luke Fildes, R.A.', *A. Annu.* (1895), pp. 1–3

L. V. Fildes: *Luke Fildes, R.A.: A Victorian Painter* (London, 1968)

B. Myers: 'Studies for *Houseless and Hungry* and the *Casual Ward* by Luke Fildes, R.A.', *Apollo*, cxxiv/952 (1982), pp. 36–43

Hard Times (exh. cat. by J. Treuherz, Manchester, C.A.G., 1987–8)

LEE M. EDWARDS

Filgueiras Lima, João (*b* Rio de Janeiro, 10 Jan 1932). Brazilian architect. He graduated in architecture from the Federal University of Rio de Janeiro (1955) and worked in various offices including the Retirement and Pensions Institute for Bankers in Rio de Janeiro (1952–8 and 1961–2). He then worked with Oscar Niemeyer on several projects in Brasília (1962–70) including the Faculty of Science (1963), University of Brasília, and Ministry of Defence (1970). Filgueiras Lima became one of the most sculpturally expressive architects in Brazil, but his work was also characterized by a commitment to the use of advanced industrial technology, particularly prefabrication, which he studied on a visit to the USSR, Poland and East Germany (1963). Major projects using structural prefabricated reinforced concrete include the Administrative Centre of Bahia (1973), Salvador, comprising several long, low-rise buildings curving round the contours, elevated on columns and designed as a series of modular boxes to allow for infinite extension. In the Central Administration of Bahia (CAB) chapel (1974), his curved plan was roofed by prefabricated concrete columns with flared tops, arranged in a dramatic, ascending helicoidal form. In the Hospital for Locomotive Disorders (1976), Brasília, he used precast Vierendeel girders, with octagonal cut-outs, to enclose and support the wards; these were stacked like boxes in a staggered form to provide terraces. Later projects included the medium- and maximum-security prisons (1986) in Rio de Janeiro. He also used lightweight prefabricated reinforced concrete for basic sanitation, in schools and health clinics, for passenger shelters, city furniture and small bridges. In 1978, based on the principles of this work, the Prefecture of Salvador set up a factory producing lightweight prefabricated sections to provide sanitation in the city's shanty towns; a similar organization was set up in Rio de Janeiro in 1984.

WRITINGS

Escola transitória (Brasília, 1984)

Fábrica de escolas (Rio de Janeiro, 1984)

BIBLIOGRAPHY

'João Filgueiras Lima, arquiteto', *Módulo*, 57 (1980), pp. 78–93

'Modern Brazilian Architecture', *Process: Archit.*, 17 (1980), pp. 98–111 [special issue]

REGINA MARIA PROSPERI MEYER

Filibe. *See* PLOVDIV.

Filiger [Filliger], **Charles** (*b* Thann, Alsace, 28 Nov 1863; *d* Brest, 11 Jan 1928). French painter and engraver. He studied in Paris at the Académie Colarossi. He settled in Brittany in 1889, where he was associated with Gauguin and his circle at Pont-Aven, but he remained a mystic and a recluse. The Breton setting, with its stark landscape and devout peasant inhabitants, provided fertile ground for the development of Filiger's mystical imagery and deliberate archaisms. Filiger's friend, the painter Emile Bernard, characterized Filiger's style as an amalgam of Byzantine and Breton popular art forms. The hieratic, geometric quality and the expressionless faces in his gouaches of sacred subjects such as *Virgin and Child* (1892; New York, A. G. Altschul priv. col., see 1979–80 exh. cat., p. 71) reveal Filiger's love of early Italian painting and the Byzantine tradition. Evident too in the heavy outlines and flat colours of his work are the cloisonnism of the Pont-Aven school and the influence of Breton and Epinal popular prints. Filiger's landscapes, such as *Breton Shore* (1893; New York, A. G. Altschul priv. col.), share with Gauguin's paintings an abstract, decorative quality and rigorous simplification.

In 1903 Filiger began a series of watercolours, *Chromatic Notations* (projects for stained glass), in which a figure, usually a Madonna (e.g. *Head of the Virgin, on a Yellow Ground*; Paris, Pompidou) or a stylized portrait is placed on a decorative, faceted background within an oval or polygonal frame. These geometric compositions were inspired by the theory of sacred measures developed in the German monastery of Beuron and brought back to the Pont-Aven circle by Paul Sérusier and Jan Verkade. Like most of Filiger's works, they are small in scale. His work was seen often in Paris, for example in the Salon des Indépendants in 1889 and the Salon de la Rose + Croix in 1892, organized in part by Filiger's long-standing patron, Count Antoine de la Rochefoucauld. Filiger collaborated with Rémy de Gourmont on engravings to illustrate the periodical *L'Ymagier* (1894–6). The poets Alfred Jarry and André Breton were particularly impressed with Filiger's mystical images. After 1899 he withdrew completely from Parisian artistic life.

BIBLIOGRAPHY

A. Jarry: 'Filiger', *Mercure France*, n. s. 57 (1894)

Neo-Impressionists and Nabis in the Collection of A. G. Altschul (exh. cat., ed. R. L. Herbert; New Haven, CT, Yale U. A.G., 1965), p. 74

M.-A. Anquetil: *Trois peintres mystiques du groupe de Pont-Aven: Charles Filiger, Jan Verkade, Mögens Ballin* (diss., U. Paris IV, 1974)

W. Jaworska: *Gauguin and the Pont-Aven School* (Greenwich, CT, 1974), pp. 159–69

R. Pincus-Witten: *Occult Symbolism in France* (New York, 1976), pp. 124–8

Post-Impressionism: Cross-currents in European Painting (exh. cat., London, RA, 1979–80), p. 71

TAUBE G. GREENSPAN

Filigree. Metalwork decoration in which fine precious metal wires, usually gold or silver, are delicately soldered in an openwork pattern. It is used especially in jewellery and the ornamentation of other small objects (*see* METAL, §V, 3 and MIGRATION PERIOD fig. 1).

□

Filipepi, Alessandro. *See* BOTTICELLI, SANDRO.

Filippi. Italian family of painters. Its members were active mainly in Ferrara in the 16th century. Sebastiano Filippi I (*b* Lendinara; *d* Ferrara, 19 Dec 1523) was the father of (1) Camillo Filippi, who was the father of (2) Sebastiano Filippi II and Cesare Filippi (*b* Ferrara, 1536; *d* 1602).

(1) Camillo Filippi (*b* Ferrara, *c.* 1500; *d* Ferrara, 1574). He was trained by Battista Dossi and Girolamo da Carpi. In 1537 he collaborated with the latter on the decoration of the Delizia di Voghiera, a project on which he was also joined by Garofalo, who strongly influenced him, and Biagio Pupini. His early *Baptism* (Rovigo, Accad. Concordi) shows the influence of both Battista Dossi and Garofalo, but the inspiration derived from the former is undermined by a stale and rigid adherence to the ideals expressed by Raphael. In the 1540s Filippi was engaged in a series of decorative projects with Girolamo da Carpi, at the Castello Estense, Ferrara (1541), in the Residenza della Montagnola, Copparo (1545; destr.), and again at the Castello Estense, Ferrara (1548). In 1550 he painted the altarpiece depicting the *Resurrection with Saints* (ex-S Barnaba, Ferrara; fragments in Ferrara, Pin. N.). The predella depicts the *Beheading of Pope Sixtus II* (priv. col.) and was formerly attributed to Camillo's son Cesare, as was the altarpiece. Displaying a typically diluted classicism, it is modelled on scenes in the contemporary series of cartoons for the tapestries in Ferrara Cathedral depicting scenes from the *Lives of SS George and Maurelius*, created in collaboration with Garofalo. Together with Girolamo da Carpi, Camillo painted frescoes of *Muses* in the Palazzo Fabiani Freguglia, Ferrara. The sedate classicism that characterizes the frescoes executed with da Carpi is enlivened in the *Adoration of the Magi* (1560s; Polesine, nr Ferrara, convent of S Antonio), painted after his son Sebastiano's return from Rome around 1553, as can be deduced from the stylistic debt it owes not only to Girolamo da Carpi and Garofalo but also to Sebastiano. The influence of Michelangelo, which is apparent in the figure types of the *Annunciation* (Ferrara, S Maria in Vado), again stems from his link with Sebastiano, although Camillo's adaptations also take account of the style of Vasari, Girolamo Siciolante and Francesco Salviati, recent works by whom were to be found in Bologna.

BIBLIOGRAPHY

Thieme–Becker

A. Mezzetti: *Dosso e Battista ferraresi* (Ferrara, 1965)

——: *Girolamo da Ferrara detto da Carpi* (Ferrara, 1977)

J. Bentini: 'Precisazioni sulla pittura a Ferrara nell'età di Alfonso II', *L'impresa di Alfonso II: Saggi e documenti sulla produzione artistica a Ferrara nel secondo cinquecento*, ed. J. Bentini and L. Spezzaferro (Bologna, 1987), pp. 71–136

(2) Sebastiano Filippi II [il Bastianino] (*b* Ferrara, *c.* 1532; *d* Ferrara, 23 Aug 1602). Son of (1) Camillo Filippi. He was trained by his father in a classical style linked to Battista Dossi and Dosso Dossi and Garofalo. Sebastiano collaborated with his father on such works as the *Adoration of the Magi* (*c.* 1560; Modena, Gal. & Mus. Estense), in which the group to the right depicting the Holy Family can be attributed to him. The *Virgin in Glory with SS Peter and Paul* (Vigarano Pieve, parish church), possibly an earlier work, is still closely linked to Battista Dossi's Raphaelesque style but tempered by Sebastiano's contacts with Girolamo da Carpi.

Sebastiano's decoration of the Palazzina di Marfisa, Ferrara, begun in 1559, shows the influence of grotesque painting and the classicism of Girolamo da Carpi, with echoes of Michelangelo and Parmigianino. His *St Jerome* (Ferrara, church of the Madonnina) recalls particularly Michelangelo's *Jeremiah* on the ceiling of the Sistine Chapel (Rome, Vatican). In a series of small paintings datable to the 1570s, such as the *Nativity of the Virgin, Adoration of the Shepherds* and the *Assumption* (all Ferrara, Pin. N.), a new feeling of warmth gently modulates the influences from Michelangelo, Parmigianino and Raphael. Sebastiano's *Virgin and Child in Glory with SS Barbara and Catherine* (Ferrara Cathedral), from the same period, was inspired by Raphael's *St Cecilia* (Bologna, Pin. N.) but also displays structural similarities with the work of Ortolano, Dosso Dossi and Girolamo da Carpi. In the *Annunciation* (Ferrara, Pin. N.) the more recent model of Pellegrino Tibaldi is used to modify ideas derived from Michelangelo.

Around 1565 Sebastiano went to Rome, where he was deeply impressed by Michelangelo's paintings in the Sistine Chapel. The resulting change in his painting can be seen in the *Last Judgement*, painted for S Cristoforo della Certosa, Ferrara, by comparing it with its companion piece, the *Transfiguration* (both Milan, Brera, on loan to Rovello Porro, parish church), which he painted with his father; this reveals the difference in quality between the two artists. In the tempera paintings of the *Prophets* and *Archangels* that surround the two altarpieces (both after 1570) in S Cristoforo della Certosa, Ferrara, the underlying Michelangelesque quality is strengthened by elements derived from Tibaldi and Dosso Dossi, recalling the latter's decorations in the Magno Palazzo of the Castello del Buonconsiglio, Trent. These paintings by Sebastiano show a new awareness of colour, which is even more marked in his *St Christopher*, also in the Certosa. Based on Titian's *St Christopher* (Venice, Doge's Pal.), it demonstrates the indefinite contours and painterly handling of Titian's late works.

The frescoes of allegorical subjects in the Castello Estense at Ferrara, datable to after the earthquake of 1570, are in a more emphatically Mannerist style, probably as a result of Sebastiano's familiarity with Giulio Romano's decoration of the Palazzo del Te, Mantua. In subsequent works, however, the tendency towards the dissolution of form becomes increasingly apparent. Sebastiano's great fresco of the *Last Judgement* (1577–80; Ferrara Cathedral) is a dramatic reinterpretation of Michelangelo's prototype, dissolving the shapes in a misty atmosphere. Other works from his later period continue this trend, immersing Michelangelo's sculptural forms in the liquid, melting colour of Titian's late paintings to achieve the extraordinary 'unfinished' quality of such works as the *Resurrection* and *Annunciation* (both Ferrara, S Paolo), painted after 1590. The strikingly modern effect he obtained by manipulating the paint with his fingers (a method favoured also by Titian) influenced 17th-century Venetian artists, including Girolamo Forabosco and Sebastiano Mazzoni.

BIBLIOGRAPHY

G. Baruffaldi: *Vite de' pittori e scultori ferraresi* (Ferrara, c. 1697–1722); ed. G. Boschini (Ferrara, 1844–6)
G. Gruyer: *L'Art ferrarais à l'époque des princes d'Este* (Paris, 1897)
C. Savonuzzi: 'Sebastiano Filippi detto il Bastianino', *A. Figurativa*, iii/1–4 (1947), pp. 85–94
F. Arcangeli: *Il Bastianino* (Ferrara, 1963)
G. Frabetti: *Manieristi a Ferrara* (Ferrara, 1972)
——: *L'autunno dei manieristi a Ferrara* (Ferrara, 1978)
M. A. Novelli: 'Dipinti ferraresi nei depositi dell'Alte Pinakothek di Monaco', *Cultura figurativa ferrarese tra XV e XVI secolo: In memoria di Giacomo Bargellesi* (Venice, 1981)
Bastianino e la pittura a Ferrara nel secondo '500 (exh. cat., ed. J. Bentini; Ferrara, Gal. Civ. A. Mod., 1985)
J. Bentini: 'Precisazioni sulla pittura a Ferrara nell'età di Alfonso II', *L'impresa di Alfonso II: Saggi e documenti sulla produzione artistica a Ferrara nel secondo cinquecento*, ed. J. Bentini and L. Spezzaferro (Bologna, 1987), pp. 71–136

UGO RUGGERI

Filippi, Giovanni Maria (*b* Dasindo, nr Stenico, *c.* 1560; *d* Moravia, after 1626). Italian architect, sculptor and master builder. His earliest known work is the main doorway (1586) of the parish church at Dasindo. The architraves in this church are also attributed to him. Filippi spent some time in Rome and then was invited to Prague by Rudolf II, Holy Roman Emperor, who in March 1602 appointed him director of building works at Hradčany Castle, the imperial palace, succeeding Giovanni Gargiolli, who had left the imperial service in 1598. In Prague, Filippi worked alongside Joseph Heintz (i) for almost seven years. On 23 March 1604 Filippi submitted an estimate for the continuation of building works begun at Hradčany Castle under Gargiolli, and later that year he acted as a technical adviser in building disputes with Prague burghers. Between 1606 and 1609 he remodelled the Kaiserhaus in Plzeň.

In 1607 Filippi asked the Emperor to double the annual pension that he received in addition to his salary, and his request was granted in January 1608. In 1610 Filippi was ennobled, and in the same year he spent several months in Italy. At some stage between 1609 and 1611 he was in Munich, where he built two doorways (destr.) for the Residenz and signed them. In July 1611 Filippi went to Innsbruck in order to carry out an inspection of the palace there for the Emperor. He also went to northern Italy in either 1609 or 1613, when he prepared designs for the collegiate church at Arco.

On his return to Prague in 1612, Matthias had succeeded his brother Rudolf II as Holy Roman Emperor, and he took Filippi as an architect on to his own staff. Filippi then designed the monumental catafalque for the deceased emperor in Prague Cathedral. In early 1613 he submitted a 'design . . . for the structure planned at the royal palace in Prague' (Krčálová, 1964). Matthias decided that the structure in question—possibly the Matthias Gate (1614), previously ascribed to Vincenzo Scamozzi—should be started as soon as possible. At the same time he permitted Filippi to go to Italy to bring his family back to Prague.

It is not known when Filippi returned to Prague, but he was dismissed from imperial service in December 1616 following a dispute with the builder's clerk Jacob Hübel (*fl* 1604–19), who had accused him of the unlawful appropriation and sale of building materials. Filippi appears to have remained in Prague after 1616 and is recorded in Brno in March 1617 as a master builder. In 1626 he was appointed official state architect of Liechtenstein by Prince Charles, in which capacity he was presumably concerned, among other projects, with building plans in Lednice (Eisgrub), Valtice (Feldsberg) and Vranov, near Brno. He is not recorded after this.

All evidence of Filippi's work in Prague, Bohemia and Moravia is speculative. He may perhaps be credited with the design of the pilgrimage church of St Mary (?1613–23) at Stará Boleslav (Altbunzlau), which was built by Jacopo de Vaccani. The design of Prague Town Hall (built from 1617 with the participation of Pietro Piscina) has also been ascribed to Filippi, as well as the doorways (1617) of the chapel of St Roch, Strahov, and of St Thomas (1614 and 1617). However, no documentary evidence of Filippi's participation in these buildings has yet been found. The only buildings known to be by Filippi, on which art-historical judgement may be made, are the catafalque for Rudolf II and the collegiate church at Arco, which show Filippi as the practitioner of a comparatively pure classical style in the manner of Palladio. Filippi's obvious proximity to the architectural ideas of Joseph Heintz (i) has also made it hitherto impossible to distinguish between their work.

BIBLIOGRAPHY

Thieme–Becker
E. Bortolotti: 'L'architetto della chiesa collegiata di Arco', *Ricordo del VII congresso della Lega Nazionale: Arco, 1900*, pp. 86–7
Z. Winter: *Řemeslnictvo a živnosti XVI. věku v Čechách, 1526–1620* [Crafts and small businesses of the 16th century in Bohemia, 1526–1620], v (Prague, 1909), pp. 75–7
K. Chytil: 'Vincenzo Scamozzi v Čechách a jeho brana na Hradě Pražském' [Vincenzo Scamozzi in Bohemia and his gate at Prague Castle], *Roč. Kruhu Pěstování Dějin Umění, 1922* (1923), pp. 20–50
G. Gerola: 'Artisti trentini all'estero', *Omaggio della Società per gli Studi Trentini alla XIX Riunione della Società Italiana per il Progresso delle Scienze in Trento* (Trento, 1930), p. 11
S. Weber: *Artisti trentini ed artisti che operarono nel Trentino* (Trento, 1933), p. 117
J. Krčálová: 'Il Palladianesimo in Cecoslovacchia e l'influsso del Veneto sull'architettura ceca', *Boll. Cent. Int. Stud. Archit. Andrea Palladio*, vi (1964), pp. 89–110
J. Zimmer: 'Iosephus Heinzius architectus cum antiquis comparandus: Příspěvek k poznání rudolfinské architektury mezi lety, 1590–1612' [Contribution to the understanding of Rudolfine architecture, 1590–1612], *Umění*, xvii (1969), pp. 217–46
——: *Hofkirche und Rathaus in Neuburg/Donau: Die Bauplanungen von 1591 bis 1630* (Weissenhorn, 1971), pp. 37ff, 53
H. Haupt: 'Fürst Karl I. von Liechtenstein, Obersthofmeister Kaiser Rudolfs II. und Vizekönig von Böhmen: Hofstaat und Sammeltätigkeit', *Edition der Quellen aus dem Liechtensteinischen Hausarchiv*, i (Vienna, 1983), pp. 43, 235
V. Cazzaniga: *Arco: Itinerario storico-turistico della 'Busa'*, La Conca d'Oro del Trentino (Arco, 1986), pp. 161–73

P. Preiss: *Italští umělci v Praze* [Italian artists in Prague] (Prague, 1986), pp. 63–104

JÜRGEN ZIMMER

Filippini. *See* ORATORIANS.

Filippo di Matteo Torelli. *See* TORELLI, FILIPPO DI MATTEO.

Filippo [Philip] **Neri** (*b* Florence, 21 July 1515; *d* Rome, 26 May 1595; *can* 12 May 1622; *fd* 26 May). Italian saint and Church reformer. The son of a Florentine notary, he lived in Rome from 1534, becoming involved in various religious movements, including the confraternity Trinità dei Pellegrini, which he helped found in 1548. Ordained as a priest in 1551, he became chaplain of S Girolamo della Carità, where he assembled a group of men from diverse social backgrounds to study scripture and aid the ill. He was made rector of S Giovanni dei Fiorentini in 1564 and there began a community of secular priests, which developed into the Congregation of the Oratory (*see* ORATORIANS).

The congregation gained official recognition in 1575 when Gregory XIII granted them the church of S Maria in Vallicella. The Oratorians encouraged research into the Early Christian Church, the values of which inspired their own. Antonio Bosio's *Roma sotterranea* (Rome, 1632) provided information, based on early sources, of the catacombs and tombs of martyrs; Pompeo Ugonio's *Historia delle stationi* (Rome, 1588), also inspired by Neri, described the Roman basilicas before the restorations of Sixtus V. The *Annales ecclesiastici* (Rome, 1588–1607) by Cesare Baronio (1538–1607) were conceived to fulfil a need, identified by Neri, for a history of the Church that was accessible to a wide public.

S Maria in Vallicella was rebuilt as the Chiesa Nuova, under the direction of Neri, between 1575 and 1593. The plan, which was based on that of Il Gesù, was by Matteo da Città di Castello (?1525–1590s); the nave and side chapels were completed between 1577 and 1582. A second building phase began in 1586, when the nave was enlarged, aisles added and the chapels consequently altered. The building, under Neri's close supervision, followed the model of S Giovanni dei Fiorentini, whose architect, Giacomo della Porta, was, with Martino Longhi (i) the elder, put in charge of the building.

The image of the Virgin was central to the church's decorative programme. In this period devotion to the Rosary was widespread, and Marian themes were popular as part of the polemic of the Counter-Reformation. Caravaggio's *Deposition* (1602–4; Rome, Pin. Vaticana), painted for the Cappella Vittrice, was indebted to the symbolism and iconography of catacomb paintings known to the artist through the copies made by Ciacconio. His *St Matthew* (Berlin, Kaiser-Friedrich Mus., destr.) illustrates the Filippine concepts of *umiltà* and *semplicità*. The artists involved in the decoration of the lateral chapels attempted, as Neri wished, to portray a religious event and at the same time to communicate to the faithful a quiet faith and optimism; this is evident in Federico Barocci's *Visitation* (1583–6) and the *Presentation of the Virgin* (1593–1603; both *in situ*). Filippo wished the vault to remain plain; nonetheless he was interested in the subjects of the altarpieces and wished them to show those mysteries of the Rosary that pertained to the Virgin. Unlike the Jesuits, the Oratorians did not create new artistic forms, but they did believe strongly in the intellectual power of images.

BIBLIOGRAPHY

L. Ponnelle and L. Bordet: *Filippo Neri e la società romana del suo tempo* (Florence, 1931)
C. Gasbarri, ed.: 'Filippo Neri', *Bibliotheca Sanctorum*, v (Rome, 1964), cols 760–89
H. E. Smither: *A History of Oratorio. I. The Oratorio in the Baroque Era: Italy, Vienna, Paris* (Chapel Hill, 1977)
J. Connors: *Borromini and the Roman Oratory* (New York, 1980)
A. Zuccari: 'La politica culturale dell'Oratorio romano nella seconda metà del cinquecento', *Stor. A.*, xli (1981), pp. 72–112
T. Troy: 'Expressive Aspects of Caravaggio's First Inspiration of Saint Matthew', *A. Bull.*, lxvii/4 (1985), pp. 636–52

DONATELLA GERMANÒ SIRACUSA

Filippuccio, Memmo di. *See* MEMMO DI FILIPUCCIO.

Filitosa. Bronze Age monumental ritual centre and fortified complex in the valley of the Taravo, 6 km from the sea in southern Corsica. The area was known as a source of antiquities for many years before excavations by Roger Grosjean in 1954–9 (never fully published) uncovered an extensive area of fortifications and occupation on the low hill that forms the centre of the site. The excavations demonstrated a sequence extending from the Neolithic period through the Bronze Age (5th to 2nd millennia BC) to the 'Torrean' phase of the Late Bronze–Early Iron Age (*c.* 1200–600 BC), equivalent to the Nuragic culture of Sardinia.

The site, on a small rocky hill, has discontinuous Cyclopean walling enclosing an area roughly 135×45 m. Extensive use was made of the natural outcrops in building the walls. In addition to the house foundations, the dominant features are two subcircular tower-like constructions, the 'Monument central' and the 'Monument ouest'. The first contained six complete and thirty-eight fragmentary statue menhirs set on and around the revetting wall. In the interior was a small circular chamber, apparently for cult use. In the second tower were found the remains of a dry-stone-walled round building 15 m in diameter, with a narrow entrance on the uphill side, leading to a cella-like central room with a domed vault. Fine pottery was found in it (Sartène, Mus. Dépt. Préhist. Corse).

The thirteen complete stelae or statue menhirs (*in situ*) found at or near Filitosa, together with the two from nearby Tappa, comprise one of the largest groups of such finds known and thus contribute considerably to the body of knowledge about Copper and Bronze Age (3rd and 2nd millennia BC) sculpture and carving. They are all anthropomorphic, some having exaggeratedly large heads with deeply pecked holes for eyes and, in a few cases, lateral holes (believed to be for the insertion of horns to represent horned helmets). Statue menhir Filitosa V is remarkable for its depiction of a long sword and dagger; usually only one or the other is shown. The depiction of these weapons suggests a later date than that of most statue menhirs. Radiocarbon dates indicate prolonged usage of the site.

See also PREHISTORIC ART, §II, 5(vi).

BIBLIOGRAPHY
R. Grosjean: 'Filitosa et son contexte archéologique', *Mnmts Piot*, lii/1 (1961) [whole issue]
——: *Filitosa: Haut lieu de la Corse préhistorique* (Sartène, 1975)

A. F. HARDING

Filla, Emil (*b* Chropyně, Moravia [now Czech Republic], 4 April 1882; *d* Prague, 6 Oct 1953). Czech painter, printmaker, sculptor, writer and collector. After a short period at a business school and in an insurance office in Brno, he became a student at the Academy of Fine Arts in Prague (1903). In 1904 he won the Academy's first prize. At the end of the year he set out on a lengthy journey to Germany, the Netherlands, Belgium, France and Italy. He became absorbed in the Old Masters, especially Rembrandt. His own style passed from Post-Impressionism to a more expressive dominance of colour. In 1907 he took part in the first exhibition of The Eight (*see* EIGHT, THE, (i)) with a programme painting, the *Reader of Dostoyevsky* (Prague, N.G., Trade Fair Pal.), partly influenced by the Munch exhibition in Prague in 1905. At the same time the picture is a very personal manifesto reflecting the *Angst* and scepticism of his generation. At the second exhibition of The Eight in 1908, he included paintings of the country around Dubrovnik. He moved to Prague, and in 1909, the year he visited Paris, he painted his expressive *Red Ace* (Prague, N.G., Trade Fair Pal.), on the strength of which he was admitted to the MÁNES UNION OF ARTISTS. In 1911 he edited several issues of *Volné směry*, in which he promoted Cubism and published reproductions of Picasso's works that he had seen in Paris. Following negative reaction from his readers and from the leaders of the association he and various of his friends withdrew from Mánes and founded the Group of Plastic Artists in May of that year, oriented primarily towards Cubism. He did not himself produce genuinely Cubist work until the end of 1912, when he somewhat arbitrarily combined various phases of Cubism as he had observed them in the work of Picasso, Braque and others (e.g. *Two Women*, 1912; Brno, Morav. Gal.). In 1913 he created his first Cubist sculptures (e.g. *Head*, bronze, h. 370 mm, 1912; Prague, N.G., Zbraslav Castle).

In 1914 Filla and his wife visited Paris but left for neutral Holland on the outbreak of war, living for almost a year in Rotterdam, where he painted Cubist still-lifes, such as *Still-life with Tray* (see fig.), similar to Picasso's in style but enriched by his acquaintance with 17th-century Dutch still-lifes. Filla moved to Amsterdam in 1915 and became a member of the Maffia group, the Czech-Slovak political resistance movement abroad. He met Theo van Doesburg, made contact with DE STIJL and exhibited at various exhibitions, including one staged by the group DE SPHINX at Leiden (1917). He founded the magazine *Michel im Sumpff* in 1917 for German deserters from the front, and when World War I ended he moved to The Hague to become Secretary at the Czechoslovak Embassy, returning to Prague at the beginning of 1920. His most striking Cubist works were painted in the Netherlands. During the 1920s he developed the aesthetics of Synthetic Cubism (*see* CUBISM) and once again became a member of Mánes. In 1925 he designed paintings on glass for the Czechoslovak Pavilion at the Exposition Internationale des Arts

Emil Filla: *Still-life with Tray*, oil on canvas, 718×548 mm, 1914 (Brno, Moravian Gallery)

Décoratifs et Industriels Modernes in Paris. About 1928 he moved towards a more lyrical Cubism with elements of Surrealism, subsequently painting a number of still-lifes with white as the dominant colour. In 1930 Filla expressed his views on artists such as El Greco and Honoré Daumier in his book *Otázky a úvahy*. At the beginning of the 1930s the influence of Surrealism on his figurative painting and especially his sculptures was intensified. He participated in *Poesie 1932*, a large international exhibition in Prague that announced the arrival of Surrealism in Bohemia.

An apparent break in Filla's work occurred in 1935 when—partly under the influence of Picasso but also deriving from his studies of Scythian art and Renaissance bronzes, about which he wrote specialist studies—he returned to themes of animals and human combat. His figurative, expressively eruptive style pointed to the growing threat of Nazi hegemony in Europe, as in *Tropical Night* (1938; Prague, N.G., Trade Fair Pal.). In 1939 he started work on a cycle of paintings on motifs from the ballads of the 19th-century Czech poet, K. J. Erben, creating universal parables of good and evil in which he underlined the threat to human values. He was arrested by the Germans on 1 September 1939 and spent the war in Buchenwald concentration camp, returning to his country in broken health in May 1945. The first post-war exhibition by the Mánes Union of Artists was devoted to Filla, with the foreword to the catalogue written by Vincenc Kramář. Filla was appointed a professor at the Academy of Applied Arts in Prague, in charge of the workshop for monumental painting. From June 1946 he produced genre paintings on themes reminiscent of Holland in the style of Cubo-Expressionism. The government placed at his disposal one wing of Peruc castle in northern Bohemia, where he installed part of the collection of Chinese art, Renaissance bronzes, African sculptures and Czech folk art that he had zealously collected before the war. Using Chinese ink almost exclusively, he produced large paintings on paper on motifs of Czech and Slovak folk-songs, striving to combine the tradition of European sensual painting and Chinese brush technique. In the early 1950s he started using coloured Chinese inks to paint narrow horizontal landscapes in the Bohemian Středohoří district, a hilly area around Peruc, reminiscent of the Chinese countryside. He established contact with Josef Sudek, who took photographs at Peruc. Although Filla strove to understand Communist cultural policy, since he hoped for a change in this area after 1945, his own work was not recognized owing to his defence of Cubism, which was officially regarded as 'bourgeois formalism'.

WRITINGS

Otázky a úvahy [Questions and considerations] (Prague, 1930)

Kunst und Wirklichkeit: Erwägungen eines Malers (Prague, 1936) [selection of studies]

Problém renesance a drobná plastika [The problem of the Renaissance and miniature sculpture] (Prague, 1938)

Rembrandt (Prague, 1939)

O výtvarném umění [On fine art] (Prague, 1948)

Jan van Goyen: Úvahy o krajinářství [Jan van Goyen: reflections on landscape painting] (Prague, 1957)

BIBLIOGRAPHY

V. Kramář: *Umění Emila Filly a Antonína Procházky* [The art of Emil Filla and Antonín Procházka] (Opava, 1932)

——: *Emil Filla, jeho význam a dílo* [Emil Filla, his importance and work] (Brno 1932)

Dílo Emila Filly [The work of Emil Filla] (Brno, 1936)

A. Matějček: *Emil Filla* (Prague, 1938)

Svět Emila Filly [The world of Emil Filla] (exh. cat. by V. Lahoda, Prague, Mun. Gal., 1987)

1909–1925 Kubismus in Prag (exh. cat., ed. J. Švestka and T. Vlček; Düsseldorf, Kstver., 1991) [incl. V. Lahoda: 'Herwarth Walden und Emil Filla', pp. 74–7, and 'Emil Filla', pp. 126–35]

VOJTĚCH LAHODA

Fillet. Narrow, flat, raised moulding used to give emphasis in architecture. The term is employed, for example, for the ridges (stria) between the flutes of an Ionic column, for the ribbon-like ornament between the echinus and necking of a column and for the uppermost step of a cornice. *See also* MOULDING, §II.

□

Fillia [Colombo, Luigi] (*b* Revello, 4 Oct 1904; *d* Turin, 1 Feb 1936). Italian painter, sculptor and writer. He moved to Turin and in 1922 began his literary career by contributing to a booklet of poems entitled *1+1+1=1 Dinamite* (Turin, 1922). He started painting as a self-taught artist, using his mother's surname as a pseudonym. In 1923 he founded the Turin Futurist group, whose other later adherents included the Bulgarian-born painter and architect Nicolay Diulgheroff (1901–82) and the Italian sculptor Mino Rossi (1904–63), with the publication of the manifesto *Futurista torinese—Sindacati artistici*. Through this group he assumed an important role in the 'second Futurism' (*see* FUTURISM, §1).

The inspiration for Fillia's earliest paintings was 'mechanical life', which he portrayed by abstracting from the subject using geometrical forms and a lively range of colours. He was clearly aware not only of the work of Giacomo Balla and Fortunato Depero, but also of the contemporary Constructivist art promoted in the periodicals *Cercle et carré* (*see* CERCLE ET CARRÉ) and *Esprit nouveau*. Through Enrico Prampolini, Fillia made contact with the Cercle et Carré group during a series of extended stays in Paris (1928, 1929, 1930 and 1932); he worked in Paris during these visits and exhibited there with Prampolini in 1932. In 1928 he took part in the Venice Biennale and in 1929 he had a one-man show in the Galleria Codebò in Turin. No longer fascinated by mechanical representations, during these years he concentrated in his paintings on forms and symbols conveying a kind of metaphysical spirituality, as in *The Lovers* (1929; Rome, G.N.A. Mod.).

In 1929 Fillia helped usher in a new phase of Futurism as a signatory of the *Manifesto dell'aeropittura futurista* (*see* AEROPITTURA). He devoted himself mainly to this style in his later paintings, creating landscapes and works on religious themes that reveal some links with the approach of the Novecento Italiano group. He was involved in many other spheres of activity: at the Esposizione Internazionale held in Turin in 1928, for example, he decorated the Futurist pavilion designed by Prampolini, and for the same event, together with Alberto Sartoris, Filippo Tommaso Marinetti and P. A. Saladin, he organized the *Prima mostra dell'architettura futurista*. He also published numerous literary and theatrical works and founded several journals; the most prestigious of these were *Stile futurista* (1934), on which he collaborated with Enrico Prampolini, and *Ambienti della nuova architettura* (1935).

BIBLIOGRAPHY

Fillia e l'avanguardia futurista negli anni del fascismo (exh. cat., ed. S. Evangelisti; Milan, Gal. Philippe Davreio, 1986)

Fillia: Fra immaginario meccanico e primordio cosmico (exh. cat. by E. Crispolti, Cuneo, Mus. Civ., 1988)

DANIELA DE DOMINICIS

Filling station. *See* SERVICE STATION.

Filliou, Robert (*b* Sauve, Gard, 17 Jan 1926; *d* les Eyzies-de-Tayac-Sireuil, nr Périgueux, 2 Dec 1987). French performance artist, conceptual artist and writer. He studied economics and science at the University of California at Los Angeles from 1948 to 1951, but he was self-taught as an artist. Having first worked as a playwright during the second half of the 1950s, in 1960 he presented the first of his performances incorporating poetry. By 1962 he was involved with the FLUXUS movement; sharing his fellow artists' distaste for marketable art objects, he not only continued to create performances and other ephemeral works but also involved himself in conceptual gestures such as the foundation of a 'République Géniale'. He made films and videos, sent enigmatic objects through the post as a form of correspondence art and worked against traditional ideas about the individuality of the artist by working collaboratively with others: in 1964 he and Joachim Pfeufer created the Poïpoïdrome, a group researching 'permanent creation' and the 'principle of equivalence', and in 1965 he and George Brecht founded La Cédille Qui Sourit (a shop and studio) at Villefranche-sur-Mer. While he worked in a variety of media, the form taken by any work was the one deemed most appropriate in embodying a particular idea. One of his major works, for instance, is a huge painting, *Research into the Origin*

(3×90 m, 1974; Lyon, Mus. St Pierre A. Contemp.), which carries, in handwritten script with notes and cross-references, a multitude of references and citations from scientific studies demonstrating the necessity of 'permanent creation'.

WRITINGS

Ample Food for Stupid Thought (New York, 1965)
with G. Brecht: *Games at the Cedilla, or the Cedilla Takes Off* (New York, 1967)
Teaching and Learning as Performance Arts (Cologne, 1970) [with texts by George Brecht, John Cage, Allan Kaprow and others]

BIBLIOGRAPHY

Das immerwährende Ereignis zeigt: Robert Filliou/The Eternal Network Presents: Robert Filliou/La Fête permanente présente: Robert Filliou (exh. cat. by J. Büchner and others, Hannover, Sprengel Mus.; Paris, Mus. A. Mod. Ville Paris; Berne, Ksthalle; 1984) [parallel Ger., Eng. and Fr. texts]
Le Poïpoïdrome de Robert Filliou et Joachim Pfeufer (Nantes, 1990)
For further bibliography *see* FLUXUS.

VANINA COSTA

Filloeul, Pierre (*b* Abbeville, 1696; *d* Paris, after 1754). French printmaker. He was the son of the engraver Gilbert Filloeul (1644–1714). He was his father's pupil (and not, as is sometimes claimed, that of Jacques-Philippe Lebas). His oeuvre extends from 1731 to 1754 and numbers *c.* 150 prints. He sometimes sold his works himself, but his principal publishers were Nicolas Larmessin, Pierre Roguié and Michel Odieuvre, who in 1738 brought out his *Recueil des portraits de rois de France* (60 plates). Beside portraits, including those of *Anne-Geneviève de Bourbon* (Pognon and Bruand, no. 120), *Anne-Marie-Louise d'Orléans, Duchesse de Montpensier* (PB 119) and *Stanislav I Leszczyński* (PB 2), Filloeul engraved illustrations for Jean de La Fontaine's *Contes* (PB 3–12) and for Charles-Jean-François Hénault's *Le Nouvel Abrégé chronologique de l'histoire de France* (1744). Between 1737 and 1755 he engraved 32 plates of insects, fish and birds for the *Spectacles de la nature* (PB 41–80) of Abbé Noël-Antoine Pluche and 19 pieces for the *Recueil d'oiseaux, insectes et animaux* (PB 100–118), mostly after Hieronymus van Kessel. Filloeul was also responsible for a series (6 plates) of *Singeries* (PB 88–93) after Christophe Huet and a *Livre de différents caractères de têtes* (PB 13–40) after Antoine Watteau, 27 plates of which appeared in 1734. In this he tried to imitate charcoal solely by means of line engraving, using an etched outline and finishing with a burin. He also reproduced some of Jean-Siméon Chardin's compositions, such as the *Knucklebones* (PB 86) and the *House of Cards* (PB 144). But he was above all the interpreter of Jean-Baptiste Pater, after whom he engraved many amorous scenes, including *Les Amants heureux* (PB 126), *La Courtisane amoureuse* (PB 6), *L'Amour et le badinage* (PB 125), *La Belle Bouquetière* (PB 123) and *Le Cocu battu et content* (PB 8).

BIBLIOGRAPHY

E. Pognon and Y. Bruand: *Inventaire du fonds français: Graveurs du dix-huitième siècle*, Paris, Bib. N., Cab. Est. cat., ix (Paris, 1962), pp. 179–203 [PB]

VÉRONIQUE MEYER

Filomarino, Ascanio, Cardinal [Archbishop of Naples] (*b* Naples *c.*1580; *d* Naples, 1666). Italian ecclesiastic, patron and collector. He came from an ancient and noble family, but his mother was a commoner, so that as a young man he suffered from the contempt of the Neapolitan aristocracy. In 1625 he went to Rome, where he joined the entourage of the Barberini family. He was made Archbishop of Naples by Urban VIII in 1641.

His years in Rome formed Filomarino's artistic taste. He responded to the new developments in Roman art between 1625 and 1640, and admired the painters patronized by Cardinal Francesco Barberini; his main preference was for those artists who, in the 1630s, were reviving the warmth and colour of Venetian painting, such as Pietro da Cortona and Nicolas Poussin. He owned three pictures by Poussin (untraced), engraved by Jean-Honoré Fragonard (Saint Non), and an early work by Pietro da Cortona (untraced), all in a classicizing Venetian style. The francophile Cardinal Francesco had also patronized Simon Vouet and Valentin de Boulogne, and Filomarino owned a *St Agnes*, a *Virgin* and twelve canvases of *Angels Bearing Symbols of the Passion* (two in Naples, Capodimonte) by Vouet, and seven pictures, among them a *Sacrifice of Isaac* (*c.* 1630; Montreal, Mus. F.A.) and portraits of himself and of *Scipione Filomarino* (untraced), by Valentin. He also bought pictures by the most celebrated Bolognese painters, e.g. Annibale Carracci's *Three Maries at the Sepulchre* (St Petersburg, Hermitage) and works (untraced) by Domenichino, Francesco Albani and Guido Reni. An unidentified work by Caravaggio was probably acquired out of homage to the latter's fame. Filomarino's admiration for Francesco Borromini's church of S Carlino alle Quattro Fontane, Rome, led him to commission Borromini to design an altar for his family chapel in the church of SS Apostoli, Naples.

On his return to Naples in 1642, Filomarino, bitterly resenting his earlier treatment by the nobles, was determined to dominate both them and the viceroy, and to uphold vigorously the privileges of the Church. He wished to stress the magnificence of his family and his authority and in 1646–7 encouraged the swift completion of the decoration of the chapel in SS Apostoli. Here the main panels of the altar are mosaic copies of paintings by Guido Reni, while a relief of putti is by François Du Quesnoy. Giuliano Finelli and Andrea Bolgi, both of whom had trained in Rome, and Giulio Mencaglia (*d* 1649), a classical sculptor working in Naples, executed the sculptural decoration. The chapel may have provided an important stimulus to the development of a classical tradition in Neapolitan sculpture. Filomarino's most interesting commission as a patron of architecture was the restoration of the Archbishop's palace, in a severely classical style. Giovanni Lanfranco painted the altarpiece in the palace chapel, which includes a portrait of Filomarino.

Filomarino's collection was important for the development of Neapolitan painting. The influence of Poussin, already apparent in the 1630s, increased during the 1640s. In the 1650s and 1660s Luca Giordano and Francesco di Maria may have been stimulated by the works in Filomarino's collection. Di Maria's portrait of the Cardinal is in the Galleria Corsini, Florence.

BIBLIOGRAPHY

R. de Saint Non: *Voyage pittoresque à Naples et en Sicilie* (Paris, 1829), i, p. 201
R. Ruotolo: 'Aspetti del collezionismo napoletano: Il Cardinale Filomarino', *Antol. B.A.*, 1 (1977), pp. 71–7

C. Fiorillo: 'Francesco Di Maria', *Napoli Nob.*, xxii/5–6 (1983), pp. 183–209

RENATO RUOTOLO

Filonov, Pavel (Nikolayevich) (*b* Moscow, 20 Jan 1883; *d* Leningrad [now St Petersburg], 3 Dec 1941). Russian painter, graphic artist and poet. He came from a working-class background; orphaned in childhood, he moved to St Petersburg, where he earned money through embroidery, house painting, restoring buildings and icons, and other tasks such as retouching photographs and making posters and wrappers for goods (a practical apprenticeship he never forgot). His interest in drawing and painting developed through copying, making portraits and the close study of human and animal anatomy. He entered the Academy of Arts, St Petersburg (1908) with difficulty but he left without graduating; his only important teacher was L. E. Dmitriyev-Kavkazsky (1849–1916), with whom he studied privately. Largely self-taught, he was a man of considerable intellectual powers.

Filonov's earliest mature work dates from 1909–10, notably *A Hero and his Fate* (oil on canvas; St Petersburg, Rus. Mus.). Subsequently, partly for financial reasons, he generally painted in watercolour or oil on paper. He wandered extensively through Russia, the Near East and western Europe. From 1910 to 1914 he exhibited regularly with the UNION OF YOUTH and he met and collaborated with the leaders of Russian literary Futurism, including Vladimir Mayakovsky, Velimir Khlebnikov and Aleksey Kruchonykh, but Filonov's modernism was essentially his own. It was rooted in Russian folk and primitive art (*see* NEO-PRIMITIVISM), in medieval Russian wall painting, in the linear manner of Dürer, the teeming imaginations of Bosch and Bruegel, the heightened, crowded realism of works by Vasily Surikov and Konstantin Savitsky and in the fragmented textures of the work of the Symbolist Mikhail Vrubel'.

Pavel Filonov: *Workers*, watercolour, 460×505 mm, 1925 (Erevan, State Picture Gallery of Armenia)

In 1913 Filonov came to public attention as co-designer with I. Shkol'nik (1882–1926) of Mayakovsky's play *Vladimir Mayakovsky: Tragediya*. During the four years until he was called up into the army (1916) Filonov was at the height of his powers, involved in a wide range of activities. His paintings were executed according to his principle of *sdelannost'* (a neologism: 'madeness' or 'craftedness'), which involved unremitting hard work on the art object leading to an extraordinarily detailed, crystalline, iridescent, apparently unstructured painterly texture (e.g. *Workers*, 1925; see fig.); inspiration was discounted, craftsmanship exalted and the aim was the cognition of all qualities of the object, visible and invisible, down to its last atom. Filonov proclaimed his ideas in many manifestos, of which *Sdelannyye kartiny* ('Made paintings'; 1914) was an early example. A second major principle, *mirovoy rastsvet* ('universal flowering'), signalled a shift from his earlier apocalyptic, haunted manner, with its agonizingly flayed human figures, towards images of organic growth and radiance. In 1915 he published a long and extraordinarily obscure poetic work, *Propeven' o prorosli mirovoy* ('The chant of universal flowering'), with his own illustrations. This was highly praised by Khlebnikov, who incorporated Filonov memorably into his own prose work *Ka* (1916) as an artist 'already at war, only a war to conquer time, not space', and whose *Izbornik stikhov, 1907–14* ('Selected poems, 1907–14'; St Petersburg, 1914) was designed by Filonov. This is a landmark in modern book illustration, in which Filonov turned individual letters into pictograms and fused word and image into a primitive and modern synthesis. In the same year his austere drawings for the Futurist miscellany *Rykayushchiy Parnas* ('Roaring Parnassus') supposedly caused almost the entire edition to be confiscated for indecency.

Filonov welcomed the Revolution of 1917 and he was for a short time in charge of the ideological section of Ginkhuk (*see* INKHUK). His lectures and proclamations became bellicose, as he battled equally against both academic and 'proletarian' art in support of his method, 'analytic art', which was to operate through 'madeness' in any of several modes (the primitive, the abstract, the hyper-real, often disconcertingly juxtaposed). Believing true art belonged to the people, Filonov no longer sold nor even signed his works and would not allow a one-man exhibition abroad nor the writing of a monograph about him; he lived a life of ascetic self-denial. Pupils began spontaneously to seek him out, and in 1925 he formalized the situation by establishing his 'Collective of Masters of Analytic Art', the Filonov school (Rus. Filonovtsy). This loosely knit group exhibited in 1927 and was commissioned to illustrate an ambitious edition of the Finnish epic *Kalevala* (pubd 1933), a complex undertaking by a team of 14 artists working collectively. Among them were Alisa Poret, M. D. Tsibasov and Tatyana Glebova. The Filonov school was a formative experience even for artists who subsequently reacted against it and was a significant phenomenon in Leningrad cultural life, influencing, among others, the poet N. Zabolotsky (1903–58).

Even before the *Kalevala*, however, the tide had turned against Filonov: a major retrospective exhibition was hung in the Russian Museum in Leningrad (1929–30) but never opened to the public; the press was hostile. From the early

1930s his position became precarious. Few works are datable to the last decade of his life, but neither his craftsmanship nor his sense of mission diminished. He died during the Siege of Leningrad (in which he was a fire-watcher). Despite his stature as a luminary of Russian Modernism, Filonov was reduced to a figure of myth. However, since the mid-1960s his work (mostly in St Petersburg, Rus. Mus.) has been gradually rediscovered and his writings published, and since the mid-1980s his work has been exhibited in Russia and elsewhere.

WRITINGS

Sdelannyye kartiny [Made paintings] (St Petersburg, 1914)
Propeven' o prorosli mirovoy [The chant of universal flowering] (Petrograd, 1915)

BIBLIOGRAPHY

J. Kříž: *Pavel Nikolajevič Filonov* (Prague, 1966)
V. Marcadé: *Le Renouveau de l'art pictural russe* (Lausanne, 1971)
J. E. Bowlt: 'Pavel Filonov: An Alternative Tradition?', *A.J.* [New York], xxxiv/3 (1975), pp. 208–16
——: 'Pavel Filonov: His Painting and Theory', *Rus. Rev.*, iii (1975), pp. 282–92
E. Kovtun: 'Iz istorii russkogo avangarda (P. N. Filonov)' [From the history of the Russian avant-garde (P. N. Filonov)], *Yezhegodnik rukopisnogo otdela Pushkinskogo doma na 1977 god* [Yearbook of the manuscript section of the Institute of Russian Literature, 1977], pp. 216–26
Rus. Lit., xi/3 (1982) [special issue devoted to Filonov]
T. N. Glebova: 'Souvenirs sur Filonov', *Cah. Mus. N. A. Mod.*, xi (1983), pp. 118–23
R. R. Milner-Gulland: '"Masters of Analytic Art": Filonov, his School and the *Kalevalà*', *Leonardo*, xvi/1 (1983), pp. 21–7
N. Misler and J. E. Bowlt, eds: *Pavel Filonov: A Hero and his Fate* (Austin, 1983) [trans. of Filonov's writings, with biog., commentaries and illus.]
P. N. Filonov: Zhivopis'. Grafika. Iz sobraniya Gosundarstvennogo Russkogo Muzeya [P. N. Filonov: Painting. Graphics. From the collection of the State Russian Museum] (exh. cat., Leningrad, Rus. Mus., 1988)
Filonov (exh. cat., Paris, Pompidou, 1989–90)

ROBIN MILNER-GULLAND

Filotesio, Nicola. *See* COLA DELL'AMATRICE.

Finch, Alfred William (*b* Brussels, 28 Nov 1854; *d* Helsinki, 1930). Belgian painter and potter. He studied painting at the Académie Royale des Beaux-Arts et Ecole des Arts Décoratifs in Brussels from 1878 to 1880. He was a founder-member of Les XX (*see* ⟨VINGT⟩, LES), a group of 20 avant-garde artists who held annual exhibitions of paintings and decorative arts between 1884 and 1895. Initially Finch painted land- and seascapes in the Impressionist style. In 1887—after Seurat and Camille Pissarro exhibited with Les XX—Finch adopted their divisionist painting technique. An early work in the Neo-Impressionist style, the *Race Course at Ostende* (1888; Helsinki, Athenaeum A. Mus.), shows his unfamiliarity with this new technique. His subsequent proficiency is evident in the work *English Coast at Dover* (1891; Helsinki, Athenaeum A. Mus.), which also makes use of a border constructed of divisionist dots, a device he borrowed from Seurat. Finch came to excel at rendering the atmospheric effect of the damp climate of the Channel coast—his main subject—through the use of widely spaced dots in related colour values. Finch served as a liaison between Les XX and the contemporary British art world. He invited Whistler to participate in the first exhibition of Les XX in Brussels in 1884. In return Whistler arranged for Finch to exhibit with the Society of British Artists in London in 1887 and 1888.

In 1886 and 1891 Finch visited England, where he was exposed to the tenets of the English Arts and Crafts Movement, and by the early 1890s he had turned his artistic focus to ceramics. Anna Boch (1848–1936), a fellow member of Les XX, invited Finch to the Boch Frères factory at La Louvière, Belgium. From 1890 to 1893 he worked as a decorator, applying Neo-Impressionist methods of painting to the decoration of ceramics; this was a new direction for the factory, which at the time was producing pastiches of the Delft, Sèvres and Isnik styles. He continued working as a painter and potter and in 1891 opened his own pottery at Forges-Chimay, France.

In 1897 a Swede, Count Louis Sparre (1863–1964), saw Finch's ceramics in Brussels and invited him to Finland to establish a ceramics division at the Iris factory in Porvoo. Finch brought the ideas of the English Arts and Crafts Movement and the Belgian Art Nouveau style to Finland. His ceramics for Iris are characterized by painted or incised abstract, wavy patterns, applied dots painted in slip and boldly coloured glazes. Iris ceramics were made to be sold in S. Bing's L'Art Nouveau and Julius Meier-Graefe's La Maison Moderne in Paris. A large two-handled bowl incised with a wave-like pattern around the rim and decorated with green and blue slips and carefully placed white slip dots (*c.* 1900; London, V&A) bears the monogram of La Maison Moderne.

After the closure of the Iris factory in 1902, Finch became head of the ceramics department at the Central School of Industrial Design in Helsinki where he experimented with high-temperature glazes on stoneware. He continued painting and in 1904 organized the first exhibition, in Helsinki, of Franco-Belgian Impressionist works in Finland, thus instigating a new Finnish school of painting. He also helped found the SEPTEM GROUP, which exhibited from 1912 to 1928.

BIBLIOGRAPHY

Neo-Impressionism (exh. cat. by R. L. Herbert, New York, Guggenheim, 1968)
Art Nouveau Belgique (exh. cat., Brussels, Pal. B.-A., 1980)
Belgian Art, 1880–1914 (exh. cat., New York, Brooklyn Mus., 1980)

JOELLEN SECONDO

Finch, Heneage, 4th Earl of Aylesford (*b* 4 July 1751; *d* 21 Oct 1812). English patron, collector and amateur artist. In 1767 he attended Christ Church, Oxford, where he met George Beaumont and learnt to draw under the tutelage of John Baptist Malchair. He went to Rome before 1776 and developed an interest in architecture, making drawings of St Peter's Cathedral and the Pantheon, among other buildings (drawings at Packington Hall, Warwicks). He also assembled a good collection of Old Master drawings and produced and collected etchings in the style of Rembrandt, but he was never skilled as a painter, nor did he collect paintings. His antiquarian interests led to his election as a member of the Society of Dilettanti in 1776. He succeeded to the earldom the following year. From 1784 the Italian architect JOSEPH BONOMI assisted him with new designs and decorations for Packington Hall. The resulting designs mirrored Aylesford's antiquarian interests and were among the earliest examples of Neo-classical interiors in Europe. In the Pompeian Gallery, for example, Bonomi used N. Ponce's *Description des Bains de*

Titus (Paris, 1786) to provide him with an archaeologically exact model. This was the first room of its kind, an advance on the Etruscan-style decoration by Robert Adam at Osterley House, London, and by James Wyatt at Heveningham Hall, Suffolk. Aylesford intended his Pompeian Gallery to provide an appropriate setting for his collection of Etruscan vases, and the room's furnishings included Klismos chairs that may predate those of Thomas Hope. The Pompeian Gallery was completed by John Francis Rigaud before 1810.

Bonomi's major contribution to Packington Hall was the stark church (1789–90) in its grounds—one of the earliest examples of the Greek Revival in Europe. Aylesford seems to have masterminded this commission, and he may also have intervened more directly. His drawings reveal an obsession with the Greek Doric order and with a form of cross-vaulted roof springing from columns; both of these unusual features can be found in the church interior. Bonomi's unprecedented design owed a great deal therefore to Aylesford's own interests.

BIBLIOGRAPHY

Colvin

F. Lugt: *Marques* (1921), no. 58

M. Binney: 'Packington Hall, Warwickshire, II: A Seat of the Earl of Aylesford', *Country Life*, cxlviii (16 July 1970), pp. 162–6

——: 'Packington Hall, Warwickshire, III: A Seat of the Earl of Aylesford', *Country Life*, cxlviii (23 July 1970), pp. 226–9

——: 'A Pioneer Work of Neo-classicism: The Church at Great Packington, Warwickshire', *Country Life*, cl (8 July 1971), pp. 110–15

D. Fitz-Gerald: 'A Gallery after the Antique: Some Reflections on "The Age of Neo-classicism"', *Connoisseur*, clxxxi (1972), pp. 2–13

SHEARER WEST

Find, Ludvig (Frederik) (*b* Vamdrup, Jutland, 16 May 1869; *d* Copenhagen, 24 Nov 1945). Danish painter. He began his art training in 1885, studying at the Kongelige Danske Kunstakademi in Copenhagen from 1886 to 1888. In 1888 he studied at the Artists' Study School under Frans Schwartz (1850–1917), and in 1900 he was a pupil of Kristian Zahrtmann. Though trained in a realistic tradition, Find sought to break away from it after seeing an exhibition in Copenhagen in 1888 that included work by Gauguin and Monet. He was also influenced by French Symbolism through his friendship with Mogens Ballin, who was connected to the circle around Gauguin and who was a member of the Nabis. Find travelled to Italy in 1893–4, where he studied early Renaissance art. These various influences can be seen in his work of the 1890s, particularly in a *Young Man: The Norwegian Painter Thorvald Erichsen* (1897; Copenhagen, Hirschsprungske Saml.), for which he was awarded a bronze medal at the Exposition Universelle in Paris in 1900. During a study trip to Paris in 1902 he developed a renewed interest in the Impressionists, especially Renoir, and the Neo-Impressionists Bonnard and Vuillard. At the same time he married, and from then on his family and their environment served as his range of motifs in a more liberated naturalism, where the decorative and pictorial elements of the painting complement each other in pure, light colours, as in *Hanne and her Mother* (1905; Esbjerg, Kstpav.). Find also painted portraits, including portraits of children, illustrated children's books, and he worked with ceramics and tin as a designer.

BIBLIOGRAPHY

M. Bodelsen: *Maleren Ludvig Find* [The painter Ludvig Find] (Copenhagen, 1943)

K. Varnedoe: *Northern Light: Nordic Art at the Turn of the Century* (New Haven and London, 1988), pp. 76–7

CLAUDINE STENSGAARD NIELSEN

Finden. English family of engravers. William Finden (*b* London, 1787; *d* London, 20 Sept 1852) and his brother Edward Francis Finden (*b* London, 30 April 1791; *d* London, 9 Feb 1857) studied under the engraver James Mitan (1776–1822) and became specialists in small-scale book illustration, at first working for such publishers as John Sharpe (*fl* 1801–30) but later building up their own business. They were much in demand for the minutely detailed plates carried by annuals and keepsakes, for which there was a vogue in the 1820s; the plates were engraved on steel, and large numbers could be printed. The first and most successful of their ventures was *Finden's Illustrations of the Life and Works of Lord Byron* (1833–4). A series of publications followed, but their ambitious folio *Finden's Royal Gallery of British Art* (1838–49) came at a time when the fashion for such works was faltering. William Finden also engraved a few large prints issued singly, for example after David Wilkie and Edwin Henry Landseer. His last large plate, the *Crucifixion* after William Hilton, was bought for £1470 by the Art-Union of London and distributed to subscribers.

BIBLIOGRAPHY

DNB; O'Donoghue; Thieme–Becker

J. R. Abbey: *Life in England in Aquatint and Lithography, 1770–1860* (London, 1953/R San Francisco, 1991)

——: *Travel in Aquatint and Lithography, 1770–1860* (London, 1956/R San Francisco, 1991)

A. Dyson: *Pictures to Print: The Nineteenth-century Engraving Trade* (London, 1984)

B. Hunnisett: *An Illustrated Dictionary of British Steel Engravers* (London, 1989), pp. 32–5

DAVID ALEXANDER

Finelli, Giuliano (*b* Carrara, 13 Dec 1601 or 12 Dec 1602; *d* Rome, 16 Aug 1653). Italian sculptor. He received his earliest artistic training and his gift for handling marble from his uncle, a stonecutter in the quarries at Carrara. In 1611 he accompanied his uncle to Naples, and there he entered the workshop of Michelangelo Naccherino, one of the most prominent Neapolitan sculptors. In 1622 he moved to Rome and almost immediately came to the attention of Gianlorenzo Bernini, who made him one of his principal studio assistants. In that capacity Finelli participated in a number of Bernini's most important projects of the 1620s. The young sculptor's virtuosity in carving marble and his facility in using the drill to achieve pictorial effects are nowhere more evident than in his contributions to Bernini's group *Apollo and Daphne* (1622–4; Rome, Gal. Borghese; see BERNINI, (2), fig. 1). The delicately carved twigs and roots that spring from Daphne's hands and feet are the work of Finelli. By 1629 his association with Bernini had come to an end, and he established himself as an independent artist with his marble statue of *St Cecilia* (1629–30) for the choir of S Maria di Loreto, Rome. While generically akin to Bernini's *St Bibiana* (1624–6; Rome, S Bibiana), Finelli's statue departs from Bernini's dynamic conception and is reserved and more classicizing in style, closer to Alessandro Algardi's stucco Saints in S Silvestro al Quirinale and to Pietro da Cortona's painted Saints in S Bibiana.

Finelli also distinguished himself as a talented sculptor of marble portrait busts, as is exemplified by his *Michelangelo Buonarroti the Younger* of 1630 (Florence, Casa Buonarroti), a work of vivid characterization, masterly carving and Baroque vitality. He helped to popularize a type of funerary effigy that had first appeared in Rome *c.* 1570 and in which the deceased is shown bust- or half-length, with hands joined in prayer, turning towards the altar. In his bust of *Cardinal Giulio Antonio Sartorio* (*c.* 1633–4; Rome, S Giovanni in Laterano) Finelli depicted the Cardinal as if kneeling behind a prie-dieu, with joined hands resting in front of him. By introducing a cushion on the ledge of the bust's niche, the truncation of the figure is screened and appears natural, and this illusionism is heightened by the bold movement of the figure towards the altar and the lively surface treatment of the marble. The most dynamic example of this type is Finelli's bust of *Cardinal Domenico Ginnasi* of 1640, which adorns that prelate's tomb (Rome, S Lucia alle Botteghe Oscure). Although directly based on Algardi's *Giovanni Garzia Mellini* (1638; Rome, S Maria del Popolo), as a drawing by Finelli in Besançon (Mus. B.-A. & Archéol.) proves, the Ginnasi bust surpasses Algardi's work in its immediacy of presentation, devotional fervour and convincing illusionism.

In 1634 Finelli turned his attention to Naples, lured there by the promise of patronage and protection from the Viceroy and after receiving the commission for marble statues of *St Peter* and *St Paul* for the entrance of the chapel of the Tesoro in the cathedral. Before completing these large and boldly conceived statues in 1639–40, he received his largest and single most important commission in 1637: a series of 13 bronze statues of saints for the interior of the chapel of the Tesoro. In 1638 he settled in Naples and spent the next ten years engaged on this project. The statues reveal at once Finelli's powers of invention in terms of variety of pose, expression and modelling, and his eclectic borrowings from Bernini, Algardi, Giovanni Lanfranco and Jusepe de Ribera.

Among Finelli's numerous other Neapolitan works, his funerary portraits of the Viceroy and his consort, *Manuel de Acevedo y Zuñiga* and *Leonor Maria de Guzmán* of *c.* 1635–7 (Salamanca, church of the Agustinas Descalzas) are of particular importance. They mark further developments to the effigy-in-prayer type, but they also demonstrate how Finelli embraced a specifically Neapolitan type of funerary statue, first conceived by Naccherino, in which the deceased appears life-size and full-length, genuflecting towards the altar.

Although he began his career in Bernini's shadow, Giuliano Finelli emerged to become one of Italy's most capable sculptors of the first half of the 17th century. He contributed fundamentally to the development of the activated effigy-in-prayer, and he was a seminal figure in the evolution of Baroque sculpture in Naples.

BIBLIOGRAPHY
Thieme–Becker
G. B. Passeri: *Vite* (1679); ed. J. Hess (1934), pp. 245–56
L. Pascoli: *Vite*, ii (1730–36), pp. 423–36
B. De Dominici: *Vite* (1742–3), iii, pp. 158–63
A. Muñoz: 'Il gruppo di *Apollo e Dafne* e la collaborazione di G. Finelli col Bernini', *Vita A.*, ix (1913), pp. 33–44
L. Bruhns: 'Das Motiv der ewigen Anbetung in der römischen Grabplastik des 16., 17. und 18. Jahrhunderts', *Röm. Jb. Kstgesch.*, iv (1940), pp. 253–432
R. Mormone: *Le sculture di G. Finelli nel tesoro di S Gennaro a Napoli* (Naples, 1956)
R. Wittkower: *Art and Architecture in Italy, 1600–1750*, Pelican Hist. A. (Harmondsworth, 1958, rev. 3/1982), pp. 305–6, 314–15
A. Nava Cellini: 'Un tracciato per l'attività ritrattistica di Giuliano Finelli', *Paragone*, xi/131 (1960), pp. 9–30
——: 'La scultura dal 1610 al 1656', *Storia di Napoli* (Cava dei Tirreni and Naples, 1967–78) v, pp. 783–825
R. Pastorelli: 'Giuliano Finelli', *Civiltà del seicento a Napoli* (exh. cat., ed. S. Cassani; Naples, Capodimonte, 1984), ii, pp. 192–6
G. Giotto Borrelli: 'Note per uno studio sulla tipologia della scultura funeraria a Napoli nel seicento', *Stor. A.*, liv (1985), pp. 141–56
J. Montagu: *Alessandro Algardi*, 2 vols (New Haven and London, 1985)

STEVEN F. OSTROW

Fini, Léonor (*b* Buenos Aires, 30 Aug 1908; *d* Paris, 18 Jan 1996). French painter, stage designer and illustrator of Argentine birth. She grew up in Trieste, Italy. Her first contact with art was through visits to European museums and in her uncle's large library, where she gleaned her earliest knowledge of artists such as the Pre-Raphaelites, Aubrey Beardsley and Gustav Klimt. She had no formal training as an artist. Her first one-woman exhibition took place in Paris in 1935 and resulted in friendships with Paul Eluard, Max Ernst, René Magritte and Victor Brauner, bringing her into close contact with the Surrealists; her sense of independence and her dislike of the Surrealists' authoritarian attitudes kept her, however, from officially joining the movement. Nevertheless her works of the late 1930s and 1940s reflect her interest in Surrealist ideas. She also participated in the major international exhibitions organized by the group.

Fini's almost mystical appreciation for the latent energy residing in rotting vegetation and her interest in nature's cycles of generation and decay can be seen in works such as *Os Ilyaque* (*c.* 1948; ex-West Dean House, W. Sussex; see Chadwick, no. 152) and *Sphinx regina* (1946; priv. col., see Chadwick, no. 154), which also reveal the influence of German Romantic and Symbolist painters. Her works are meticulously painted, their surfaces built with layers of small and carefully modulated brushstrokes. From the 1960s her work displayed a consistent set of obsessional, recurring themes: provocative nymphets, languid nudes and the ubiquitous sphinx-like cats that mediate between the human and the bestial. The elaborate rituals and mysterious sexual dramas first evident in Fini's work of the late 1930s continued to play a dominant role.

Fini's work for the theatre included costumes and sets for George Balanchine's *The Crystal Palace* (1945), Racine's *Bérénice* for Jean-Louis Barrault (1955), a production of Wagner's *Tannhäuser* at the Paris Opéra (1963) and Jean Genet's *Le Balcon* (1969). Among her numerous illustrations are drawings for editions of *Juliette* (Rome, 1944) by the Marquis de Sade, *Aurélia* (Monaco, 1960) by Nerval, *Les Fleurs du mal* (Paris, 1964) by Baudelaire and *Romeo and Juliet* (Nice, 1979) by Shakespeare.

BIBLIOGRAPHY
A. Moravia and others: *Léonor Fini* (Rome, 1945)
M. Brion: *Léonor Fini et son oeuvre* (Paris, 1955)
X. Gauthier: *Léonor Fini* (Paris, 1973)

W. Chadwick: *Women Artists and the Surrealist Movement* (London, 1985)
Léonor Fini (exh. cat., Paris, Pal. Luxembourg, 1986)

WHITNEY CHADWICK

Finial. Crowning ornament on the point of a spire or pinnacle.

Finiguerra, Maso [Tommaso] (*b* Florence, March 1426; *d* Florence, *bur* 24 Aug 1464). Italian goldsmith, niellist and draughtsman. Son of the goldsmith Antonio, he trained under his father and possibly under Lorenzo Ghiberti, but he was soon established as an independent master. A sulphur cast made by Finiguerra was recorded in 1449, and in 1452 he was paid for a pax decorated with enamel and niello for the Florentine Baptistery. In 1456 he enrolled as a goldsmith in the Arte della Seta, and in 1457 he entered into partnership with Piero di Bartolomeo Sali. Between 1457 and 1462 he and his partner made a pair of candlesticks for S Jacopo, Pistoia, and from 1461 to 1464 he received payments from Cino di Filippo Rinuccini for jewellery and objects made of gold. Before February 1464 he designed five figures, whose heads were painted by Alesso Baldovinetti, for two intarsia panels for the north sacristy in Florence Cathedral. These panels, showing the *Annunciation* and *St Zenobius between SS*

Maso Finignerra: *Coronation of the Virgin*, niello on silver pax, 1452 (Florence, Museo Nazionale del Bargello)

Eugenio and Crescenzo, were executed by his brother-in-law, Giuliano da Maiano. Maso left 14 volumes of drawings, various sulphur casts and some sketches, over which his heirs held protracted disputes.

Finiguerra was already famous in the 15th century, when he was praised as a goldsmith, niellist and master draughtsman. Vasari recorded that Maso 'drew much and very well', but Cellini stated that he always used Antonio Pollaiuolo's designs. Cellini's testimony has been used to deny Maso any real artistic ability, but documentary evidence has reinforced Vasari's judgement. Reconstruction of Finiguerra's oeuvre must begin with his only documented work, the designs for the intarsia panels in the north sacristy. It has been convincingly suggested that he was responsible for designing Giuliano da Maiano's intarsia of the *Annunciation*, formerly on a door of the abbey at Fiesole (Berlin, Tiergarten, Kstgewmus.). The close stylistic connection between these intarsia works and the niello of the *Coronation of the Virgin* on a pax (1452; Florence, Bargello; see fig.; *see also* NIELLO PRINT, §2 and fig.) formerly in the Baptistery confirms that this niello must have been the principal decoration of the pax for which Maso was paid in 1452. The *Coronation* is a masterpiece of refinement, in which Maso was clearly influenced by Fra Filippo Lippi's ornate style. Because of this, Maso has been credited with many nielli in Lippi's style, known through sulphur casts or paper impressions and noteworthy for their high artistic quality and wide range of subject-matter (e.g. Paris, Louvre; London, BM). A niello of the *Crucifixion* (Florence, Bargello) is stylistically close to the earliest group of these nielli and can be dated before the *Coronation* because of its debt to Ghiberti. The numerous copies of a later niello of the *Crucifixion* (Washington, DC, N.G.A.), which shows Pollaiuolo's influence, prove that Maso's works were very popular.

The successive influences of Ghiberti, Fra Filippo Lippi and Pollaiuolo can also be traced in the drawings that have been attributed to Finiguerra since Vasari's day; these are probably the works mentioned in the artist's will. Most are figure studies (Florence, Uffizi), but there are also some larger and more animated compositions such as *The Flood* (Hamburg, Ksthalle) and *Moses on Mt Sinai* (London, BM), which were made into prints in the 15th century. Most of the drawings were executed by tracing the outline in pen and delicately shading with the brush, a technique that produced effects similar to those of niello. The Colvin Chronicle (London, BM) cannot be considered Maso's work, although its author must have had access to his drawings.

Vasari attributed the invention of engraving to Finiguerra. He claimed that this technique originated in Maso's habit of checking his work as it progressed by taking sulphur casts from the nielli and then paper impressions from the casts. This is supported by the fact that besides the niello of the *Coronation of the Virgin*, there are also two sulphur casts (London, BM; Paris, Louvre) and a paper impression (Paris, Bib. N.). This, however, does not imply that Maso engraved metal plates with the exclusive aim of producing prints.

BIBLIOGRAPHY

Thieme–Becker
G. Vasari: *Vite* (1550, rev. 2/1568); ed. G. Milanesi (1878–85), iii, p. 287

O. H. Giglioli: 'Maso Finiguerra', *Miscellanea di storia dell'arte in onore di Igino Benvenuto Supino* (Florence, 1933), pp. 375–95

A. M. Hind: *Nielli. . .in the British Museum* (London, 1936), pp. 9–13

A. Blum: *Les Nielles du Quattrocento* (Paris, 1950), pp. 11–14

J. Goldsmith Phillips: *Early Florentine Designers and Engravers* (Cambridge, MA, 1955), pp. 3–56

E. Möller: 'Maso Finiguerra', *Bib. Humanisme & Ren.*, xxi (1959), pp. 185–9

B. Degenhart and A. Schmitt: *Corpus der italienischen Zeichnungen, 1300–1450*, i (Berlin, 1968), pp. 599–618, 662–5

Early Italian Engravings from the National Gallery of Art (exh. cat. by J. Levenson, K. Oberhuber and J. Sheehan, Washington, DC, N.G.A., 1973), pp. 1–11

K. Oberhuber: 'Vasari e il mito di Maso Finiguerra', *Il Vasari storiografo ed artista. Atti del congresso internazionale nel IV centenario della morte: Firenze, 1974*, pp. 383–93

D. Carl: 'Documenti inediti su Maso Finiguerra e la sua famiglia', *An. Scu. Norm. Sup. U. Pisa*, xiii/2 (1983), pp. 507–54

M. Haines: *La sacrestia delle messe nel duomo di Firenze* (Florence, 1983), pp. 165–75

Disegni italiani del tempo di Donatello (exh. cat. by L. Bellosi and A. Angelini, Florence, Uffizi, 1986), pp. 10, 72–111

M. Collareta and A. Capitanio, eds: *Oreficeria sacra italiana*, Florence, Bargello cat. (Florence, 1990)

MARCO COLLARETA

Fink, Larry [Laurence] (*b* New York, 11 March 1941). American photographer. He studied photography privately with Lisette Model and with Alexey Brodovitch (1898–1971). In 1974 he began to photograph the élite at benefit galas and fashionable nightclubs in New York, for example *Benefit, the Museum of Modern Art, June 1977* (see Fink, 1984, p. 23). After he moved to rural Martin's Creek, PA, in 1980, his photography of social celebrations focused on the unmannered directness of his neighbours at family parties, such as *Pat Sabatine's Twelfth Birthday Party, May 1981* (see Fink, 1984, pp. 76–7, 79), and county fairs. His use of a hand-held flash sharply lit the faces of his subjects, and, with the high contrast that he favoured in his developing, the fleeting animation of his subjects' gestures and expressions was intensified.

PHOTOGRAPHIC PUBLICATIONS
Social Graces (Millerton, 1984)

BIBLIOGRAPHY
Mirrors and Windows: American Photography Since 1960 (exh. cat., ed. J. Szarkowski; New York, MOMA, 1978)

American Images: New Work by Twenty Contemporary Photographers (exh. cat., ed. R. Danese; Washington, DC, Corcoran Gal. A., 1979)

MARY CHRISTIAN

Finkelstein, Nathan I. *See under* HANSON, TOMKIN, FINKELSTEIN.

Finland, Republic of [Suomi; Swed. Finnland]. Nordic European country, bordered to the north by Norway, to the east by the Russian Federation, to the south by the Gulf of Finland and to the west by the Gulf of Bothnia and Sweden (see fig. 1). The population is *c.* 5 million (1995 estimate), and the capital city is Helsinki (Swed. Helsingfors). It is the fifth largest country in Europe, with hundreds of thousands of glacial lakes and extensive forests separating the majority of Finland's population—clustered along the southern and western coasts—from the arctic wilderness and tundra of Lapland to the north. The country's history is interwoven with that of Sweden, of which it was a part from Viking times until 1809, and more recently with that of Russia. Both powerful neighbours tried to dominate the Finns, whose art developed

1. Map of Finland; those sites with separate entries in this dictionary are distinguished by CROSS-REFERENCE TYPE

as an assertion of separateness and independence as well as an affirmation of cultural identity.

I. Introduction. II. Architecture. III. Painting and graphic arts. IV. Sculpture. V. Interior decoration. VI. Furniture. VII. Ceramics. VIII. Glass. IX. Metalwork. X. Jewellery. XI. Textiles. XII. Vernacular arts. XIII. Patronage, collecting and dealing. XIV. Museums, libraries and photographic collections. XV. Historiography.

I. Introduction.

Wandering tribes of uncertain origin settled in Finland around the time of Christ; crusades introduced Christianity and opened trade routes about 1000 years later. Clerics from Britain, Germany and Sweden brought education and erected such medieval monuments as the stone churches in the Åland Islands (Fin. Ahvenanmaa) and the 13th-century cathedrals at Turku (Swed. Åbo) and Porvoo

(Swed. Borgå). Finland provided soldiers for Swedish imperial armies and timber for western Europe, and Swedish was the official language for education and government, while the use of the distinctive native tongue was neither sanctioned nor encouraged (the country remains bilingual). Ceded to Russia in 1809, Finland was an autonomous duchy until independence in 1917, which was followed by a short civil war the following year. The Finnish language, along with music and all the arts, became a symbol of defiance against increasing Russian influence and repression in the late 19th century. Those artists trained in Düsseldorf and Paris abandoned their continental styles and turned for inspiration to the native landscape and folk mythology, frequently with reference to the national epic, the *Kalevala* (1835), compiled by Elias Lönnrot, while architects rebelled against Russian Neoclassicism by creating their own National Romantic style, employing the humble and characteristically Finnish materials of wood and granite. Finnish pavilions at world fairs and buildings by ALVAR AALTO (*see* §II, 3 below) demonstrated the newly independent country's position at the forefront of industrial and architectural design despite its geographic isolation and agrarian economy.

In 1939 Finland refused to accede to Stalin's territorial demands and was invaded by the USSR. In the Russo-Finnish War that followed (1939–41), Finland's vastly outnumbered defence forces managed to resist the Soviet Red Army and to maintain the country's sovereignty but at a terrible cost in lives. From 1941 to 1944 Finland fought a second and predictably disastrous war with the Soviet Union to recover territory lost in the Russo-Finnish War. New towns had to be planned and housing constructed for a fifth of the population, relocated from Soviet-conquered Karelia; fortuitously, however, onerous treaty reparations forced Finland to restructure its economy totally, giving a prominent role to design alongside industry and technology, and after centuries of poverty the country became wealthy. Having seemingly achieved an ideal harmony between art and industry, Finland has played a leading role in the development of modern design.

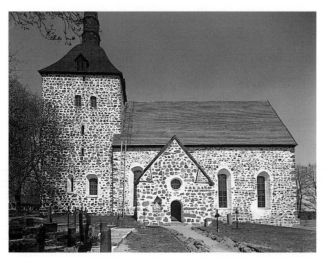
2. Granite church, Sund, Åland Islands, *c.* 1280–1300

Such sophistication and thorough urbanization notwithstanding, nature remains the chief inspiration for Finnish art.

BIBLIOGRAPHY
O. Okkonen: *Suomen taiteen historia* [History of Finnish art] (Porvoo, 1955)
S. Ringbom, ed.: *Konsten i Finland: Från medeltid til nutid* [Art in Finland: from the Middle Ages to the present day] (Helsinki, 1978, rev. 1987)
Apollo, cxv/243 (1982) [issue devoted to art in Finland]
J. Lintinen and others: *Finnish Vision: Modern Art, Architecture and Design* (Helsinki, 1983)
S. Sarajas-Korte, ed.: *Ars: Suomen taide* [Ars: the art of Finland], 6 vols (Helsinki, 1987–90)
M. Valkonen: *Finnish Art over the Centuries* (Helsinki, 1992)
R. Nikula: *Architecture and Landscape: The Building of Finland* (Helsinki, 1993)
WILLIAM MORGAN

II. Architecture.

1. Before 1618. 2. 1618–1809. 3. After 1809.

1. BEFORE 1618. Medieval Finland was sparsely populated, and permanent settlements were only to be found in the south and along the west coast. Because Finland had large coniferous tracts, it is natural that timber was the material used for most churches, town houses and rural buildings. Its perishability, however, has meant that only insignificant fragments have survived. Nevertheless, since timber architecture in Finland was not greatly affected by either the Reformation or the Renaissance, it is possible that many simple building types from later periods reflect the plans and traditions of medieval buildings. One example is the megaron house design, which has a single room and a door in the gable. The actual buildings that have survived from the medieval period, however, comprise a fragmentary collection of monuments, including 75 stone churches, 15 stone sacristies (the designs of which may have been based on those of timber churches), 5 castles, a few castle ruins and some late medieval manor houses.

Although many of the forms used in Finland in the medieval period were derived from other parts of Europe, they were given a distinctively Finnish character. One reason for this was that, whereas in many other countries brick was a cheap material used for the construction of walls, with decorative details being carved from soft sandstone or limestone, in Finland the natural stone was granite. As this was much harder to carve, it was generally used for walls, while brick was reserved for the details of windows and door openings. Some of Finland's oldest masonry buildings are located in the Åland Islands (Fin. Ahvenanmaa): six churches of red granite, built in the second half of the 13th century (see fig. 2). All had imposing west towers, which may originally have been built as defence towers. The prototypes of these would have been found on the Swedish island of Gotland, among other places (*see* SWEDEN, §II, 1). The church in the town of Hattula, south-east of Tampere (Swed. Tammerfors), was built *c.* 1370–1420 and is entirely of brick, a rare example of its period.

Turku (Swed. Åbo) on the south-west coast was an important centre in the medieval period. Among important buildings constructed at the time were the cathedral, consecrated in 1300 (*see* TURKU, §3 and fig. 2); the castle situated at the mouth of the River Aura, built in 1280, and with fortifying walls erected in 1310–20; the town hall (built 1320s); and the guildhalls and several merchants' town houses, built slightly later. The cathedral and the castle were begun by Swedish masons, but by the beginning of the 14th century the work had probably been taken over by craftsmen from Tallinn (now in Estonia), which during the 14th and 15th centuries was a Finnish centre for contacts with masons' lodges elsewhere in northern Europe. This wider contact partly influenced the design of churches in Finland; many of those built after the beginning of the 14th century lacked west towers, although some may originally have had free-standing or attached bell-towers that have not survived. Most Finnish churches from the 14th century on were constructed as hall churches (a type common in the Baltic region), having a rectangular plan, with aisles of equal height to the nave (see HALL CHURCH). Most of the churches built in the 14th century are in the south-west of the country and reflect the influence of the cathedral in nearby Turku. The castle in Turku was equally significant, particularly those parts built after a fire in 1365. The design of the vaulted, double-naved King's Hall and the interior of the chapel (c. 1400), with its four star vaults supported on a slender limestone pillar, appear to reflect contacts with MALBORK CASTLE in East Prussia (now Poland), the principal stronghold of the Teutonic Order. Turku Castle became one of the largest in Scandinavia and one of the seats of power of the Swedish king.

In the period from the beginning of the 15th century until the Reformation in the 1520s, there appears to have been building activity not only along the south-west coast but also in the interior province of Häme (Swed. Tavastland). During this time the wide and elongated shapes of Baltic hall churches were perfected in these areas. The cross-vault was developed into the star vault, following patterns in East Prussia, and the rich network of ribs was seen in its most magnificent form in the vaulting of chancels (e.g. the hall church in Kemiö (Swed. Kimito), 50 km south-east of Turku). Many churches acquired high, pointed red-brick gables that created striking visual contrasts when whitewashed niches were added. The origins for these contrasting designs may have come from similar structures in Denmark and northern Germany. The patterns, which varied from region to region, often featured crosses, circles and bands related to such holy configurations as the numbers of the Apostles (twelve) and the Trinity (three). Elaborate examples date from the late 15th century and the early 16th. The designs of gables were also different in each area, according to the particular schools of masons and builders that flourished on the south coast, on the west coast and in Häme.

Secular buildings of the 15th century also used brick extensively. The castles in Turku and Hämeenlinna (Swed. Tavastehus), south-east of Tampere, were enlarged (the latter being expanded between 1370 and 1450 and, again, between 1480 and 1520), and in both cases brick was used over greater areas than usual. One of the most important fortifications of the period is the castle of Olavinlinna (Swed. Olofsborg), which, as part of Finland's defence system, was constructed in 1475 in the province of Savo (Swed. Savolax) on the border with Russia. Built on a rock in the middle of a lake (part of a waterway system that constituted the only traversable route through the wilderness), the exterior of the castle was dominated by its five round canon towers, of which only three survive.

The Reformation of the 1520s resulted in an abrupt cessation of religious building. In 1527 the Swedish king Gustav I (reg 1523–60) was granted full powers to appropriate the Church's land and to confiscate its treasures. Thus the foundations of the Church's economy were destroyed, and all construction of a religious nature was suspended. While there are no surviving ecclesiastical structures from the period between 1520 and 1660, royal castles and fortresses continued to be built in brick and stone. Between 1556 and 1563, when Gustav's son John (later John III; reg 1568–92) was Duke of Finland, the castle in Turku was partly transformed from a late medieval fortification into a Renaissance palace. The building had outlived its function as a defensive construction and was redesigned; an upper storey was added, with large halls with plain wooden roofs and windows in the outer walls. Two staircases in the courtyard, built according to German patterns by Jakob Richter from Freiburg, Saxony, led directly up to the halls. Painters, carpenters, masons and sculptors were brought from Germany and the Netherlands (e.g. the Netherlandish sculptor Antonius Timmerman (d 1592), who went to Finland in 1556) to work on the interiors (see §V below). The influence of their early Renaissance style spread to the design of the stone houses that some noblemen had built on their estates near Turku.

BIBLIOGRAPHY

N. E. Wickberg: Byggnadskonst i Finland [Finnish architecture] (Helsinki, 1959; Eng. trans., 1965)

J. M. Richards: 800 Years of Finnish Architecture (London and Vancouver, 1978)

S. Sarajas-Korte, ed.: Ars: Suomen taide [Ars: the art of Finland], i–ii (Helsinki, 1987–8)

R. Nikula: Architecture and Landscape: The Building of Finland (Helsinki, 1993), pp. 9–39

M. Hiekkanen: The Stone Churches of the Medieval Diocese of Turku: A Systematic Classification and Chronology (Helsinki, 1994)

CARL JACOB GARDBERG

2. 1618–1809.

(i) 1618–c. 1750. The Thirty Years War (1618–48) led to the emergence of Lutheran Sweden as one of Europe's great powers. Contacts with European art and architecture opened up, and the increasing wealth of the nobility meant that architecture flourished, with the Renaissance giving way to the Baroque. Finland gained little from the new continental climate, however, since the Finnish nobility preferred to build and dwell close to the centre of power in Stockholm. Finnish architecture focused instead on churches and civic buildings. During the 17th century wooden churches were erected in Finland, with stylistic variations between regions. In the south-west, where medieval traditions were still strong, churches with rectangular plans and steep span roofs were built. In Ostrobothnia, further north, high west towers were added to the rectangular plan, also according to local medieval tradition. Here the main technical innovation involved reinforcing the side walls with hollow blockwork pillars. Completely new ideals were represented by Latin cross churches, which from 1690 onwards emerged in different parts of the country but mainly in the south-west, the lake district,

3. School building at Kokkola, Ostrobothnia, designed in Stockholm, 1693

Ostrobothnia and south-east Finland. These were usually initiated by the gentry and probably all depended on the same model, the Katarinakyrka in Stockholm, built as an ideal Protestant church (1656–82) by Jean De la Vallée. Separate belfries crowned by octagonal lanterns were developed along with the cruciform church. Stone churches were also built during this period, using traditional rectangular hall-church plans without apses. The manor church of Askainen (Swed. Askais), north of Turku, built by Herman Fleming (1619–77) in 1653 forms an exception, with a separate gallery for the owner. The pitched roof with a slight Dutch curve at the edges and whitewashed brick walls differ from traditional Finnish architecture.

The Baroque manor house was also a foreign innovation in Finland. Louhisaari (Swed. Villnäs), with its steep curved hip roof built by Herman Fleming in 1655 in connection with the church of Askainen, shows the influence of Dutch Palladianism both in the exterior and the interior. The whitewashed brick three-storey building has a strictly symmetrical façade with a slight concentration towards the main axis. Only the sandstone framing of the main portal shows a Baroque aesthetic. The architect of Louhisaari and Askainen remains unknown. Louhisaari signals the beginning of large-scale architectural planning, with flanking identical side wings and a garden facing an axial avenue. Timber manor houses have not survived, but documentation shows continental influence in the planning.

Demands for regular urban planning initiated a process of urbanization. A number of new towns were founded, especially during the reign of Per Brahe, governor of Finland (1637–40 and 1648–51). A university, the Academia Aboensis, was founded in Turku in 1640. The ideal urban plan was a regular town of squares with broad streets surrounded by customs walls. Public buildings such as town halls and barracks were placed around a central market square, and prospects were formed by single-storey timber houses placed along the streets, with covered gateways leading to enclosed courtyards. Many projected

towns were never constructed. Only Turku and Viipuri (Swed. Viborg; now Vyborg, Russia) had more than 1000 inhabitants, who in reality lived mainly in unpainted timber houses. Nevertheless, the 'typical' Finnish wooden town was created during the 'Great Power' era (see fig. 3).

The Nordic Wars of 1700–21 and 1742–3 brought an end to the 'Great Power' era. Vast areas in the east were lost to Russia in the peace of 1721, and the new border had immediate architectural consequences in Hamina (Swed. Fredrikshamn), founded in 1723, which became the substitute for Viipuri, now on the Russian side of the border (see VYBORG). Hamina was the only town in the Swedish kingdom to follow the plan of a star with streets radiating from the city centre. The town, which was surrounded by bastions and garrisons, was planned by Axel von Löwen (1686–1772). While official building activity was concentrated on repairing the damages of war, Turku employed the first town architect in Finland, the German Samuel Berner (d 1761). His main achievement was the town hall with a bell-tower (1735–6) in Turku, representing a change from late Baroque to Neo-classicism. The growth of a more 'enlightened' architecture was shown by the distribution of model drawings for civic building with modern solutions such as the 'Carolinian plan' and a manorial roof that had developed from Italian lanterned roofs.

(ii) c. 1750–1809. During the period of rebuilding and optimism that followed the peace of 1743, architectural taste began to favour French classicism. Academic tendencies competed with retrospective local traditions, especially in church architecture. In 1759 it was decreed that all churches financed by collection money should have their plans examined by the Office of Public Works and Buildings in Stockholm. Wooden churches still formed distinct geographical groups, but the importance of individual church builders and church-building families increased. In south-west Finland medieval traditions continued. Famous church builders were Antti Piimänen (1714–75), Mikael Piimänen (1748–1820) and Matti Åkerblom (1740–1819). Cruciform churches in Ostrobothnia were developed and perfected by Matti Hakola (1703–62), Antti Hakola (1704–78) and Matti Honka (1703–77). On both sides of the Russian border a special double cruciform church with a steep pyramidal roof was developed from the model of the Ulrika Eleonora Church in Hamina (Swed. Fredrikshamn), built in 1730–31 by Henrik Schultz and rebuilt 1748–51 by Arvi Junkkarinen as the Elizabeth Church, with no evidence of Russian influence.

The loss of Hamina in the peace treaty of 1743 resulted in the greatest architectural achievement under Swedish rule during the 18th century: the creation of Suomenlinna (Swed. Sveaborg; Viapori from 1808 to 1918), an island fortress off Helsinki (Swed. Helsingfors) and a base for the navy, built in 1748–91. The initiator and chief planner was CARL AUGUST EHRENSVÄRD. The fortress stretched over 6 islands, and a total of 35 buildings was included in the fortification system, strengthened by granite walls facing the sea. The Grand Court (from 1750) on Susisaari (Swed. Vargö) was the first monumental square to introduce late Baroque principles in Finland. The commandant's lodge was flanked by lower wings in a 'false perspective', where a couple of buildings formed a semi-circle to enclose the courtyard at the wider end. The navy courtyard, by CARL HÅRLEMAN, was richest in classicist articulation. Loviisa (Swed. Lovisa), a town founded in 1746 close to the Russian border, formed part of the same fortification project as Viapori. Its plan, by Ehrensvärd, proposed a new ideal town influenced by French classicism. Both varied and unified in conception, its outlines followed the lines of the shore or surrounding bastions; its buildings were painted red. Water was used aesthetically in both artificial and natural surroundings. Increasing use of mansard roofs narrowed street vistas. Squares varied in number and size: usually the main square was dominated by two-storey town halls in stone crowned with bell-towers.

There was an increase in the centralized control of architecture. In 1747 Carl Hårleman, as superintendent, had suggested that all public buildings should be approved by the Office of Public Works and Buildings, and a Rococo classicism was widely disseminated through his model drawings. The publication of plans for model buildings by Carl Wijnblad (1705–68) had a similar unifying influence, with their detailed advice on building both in stone and wood. The invention of a wood-saving tiled stove with an intricate system of flues by Carl Johan Cronstedt and Fabian Wrede (1724–95) in 1767 had a remarkable effect on the standard of living. Turku and Viapori both served as architectural models. Christian Fredrik Schröder (1722–89) was appointed town architect in Turku, and although not particularly original he became important because of his large and varied production. In addition to stone buildings in Turku, he designed a number of manor houses in south-west Finland, most importantly the manor houses belonging to ironmills such as Fagervik in southern Uusimaa, built from 1762 to 1773. Here the *corps de logis*, a yellow stone building with two main floors and a mansard roof, has a refined Rococo interior with a Chinese parlour and antique decorations. The building is surrounded by the works and a street lined with blacksmiths' houses designed by Schröder in 1775. An English landscape garden includes a church, a Chinese pavilion and a vast, utilitarian orchard. Although there was an increasing interest in aesthetic (as opposed to strictly utilitarian) gardens around 1750, the English landscape garden was an innovation brought to Finland through Viapori only after 1780.

As residential towns became more important than fortifications, there was an increasing variation in colour and style. Classicism thrived together with a somewhat stricter Neo-classicism. The façades of timber were covered with even boarding imitating stone buildings, with pilasters and profiled window frames and fillets. Yellow façades became more popular. In 1776 Superintendent C. F. ADELCRANTZ decreed that all public buildings were to be built in stone, a ruling intended to save timber that was little obeyed. More attention was paid to architectural design and artistic quality. The Appeal Court in Vaasa (Swed. Vasa), designed by Adelcrantz (1780–87), became the main representative of French classicism in Finland, with a rusticated ground-floor and a projection with colossal Tuscan pilasters crowned by a pediment flanked by obelisks. The two floors of whitewashed brick ended in a steep mansard roof. The facing park (1781–6) shows the increasing interest in parks and promenades.

Church building continued to struggle between official control and local vernacular traditions. On both sides of the Russian border the double cruciform wooden church was perfected under Johan Salonen (*b* 1738; *d* early 1800s) and his son Matti Salonen (1761/2–1823). Jacob Rijf (1753–1803) was the first apprentice from Finland to attend the architectural school of the Akademi for de Fria Konsterna in Stockholm. Descended from an Ostrobothnian church-building family, he managed to produce congenial solutions. He designed mainly wooden churches on both sides of the Gulf of Bothnia. The Office of Public Works and Buildings aimed for uniformity in church building. One exception was the stone church of Hämeenlinna, built 1792–8, which imitated the Pantheon in Rome with a circular plan and a hemispherical dome. Designed to royal command by Louis Jean Desprez, it differs from the Pantheon, however, in using an exaggerated Piranesian 'ultradoric' portico.

The Academy Building (1802–15) in Turku, designed by Carl Christopher Gjörwell (1766–1837) and surveyed by Carlo Bassi (1772–1840), was the last major architectural achievement in Finland during the Swedish regime. A strict façade in the style of simplified Swedish Neo-classicism hides a complex grouped around two inner courtyards. In contrast to the façade, the basilical festival hall, including apse and music gallery, and the entrance halls in the main axis are richly decorated. Polished red-granite columns carry a stuccoed barrel vault, further supported by flying buttresses. At the inauguration in 1817, however, the bust of the Russian tsar was placed in the apse instead of that of the Swedish king, for in 1808 the fortress of Viapori had surrendered, and after 1809 Finland became an autonomous Grand Duchy under Russia.

BIBLIOGRAPHY

C. Wijnblad: *Ritningar på fyratio wåningshus af sten och trettio af träd* [Plans for forty dwelling houses of stone and thirty of timber] (Stockholm, 1755–6)

G. Nikander, ed.: *Herrgårdar i Finland* [Manor houses in Finland], 3 vols (Helsinki, 1928–9)

C. J. Gardberg: 'Stadsplan och byggnadsskick i Borgå intill år 1834' [Urban planning and building practice in Borgå until 1834], *Svenska Littsällsk. Finland*, 328 (1950), pp. 57–207

L. Pettersson: 'Die Problematik der Doppelkreutzkirchen von Hamina', *Sitzungsberichte der Finnischen Akademie der Wissenschaften: Helsinki, 1959*, pp. 169–208

C. J. Gardberg: 'Från reformationen till stora ofreden: Byggnadskonst' [From the Reformation to the great discord: architecture], *Konsten i Finland*, ed. S. Ringbom (Helsinki, 1978, rev. 1987), pp. 60–72

——: 'Från freden i Nystad till 1809: Byggnadskonst och miljö' [From the peace in Nystad to 1809: architecture and environment], *Konsten i Finland*, ed. S. Ringbom (Helsinki, 1978, rev. 1987), pp. 89–105

L. Pettersson: 'National and International Features of the Old Wooden Church Architecture in Finland', *Abacus* (1979), pp. 11–55

H. Lilius: 'Kaupunkirakentaminen, 1617–1856' [Town building, 1617–1856], *Suomen kaupunkilaitoksen historia* [The history of Finnish civic institutions], i: *Keskiajalta 1870-luvulle* [From the Middle Ages to the 1870s] (Vantaa, 1981), pp. 303–88

——: *Suomalainen puukaupunki: Trästaden i Finland—The Finnish Wooden Town* (Rungsted Kyst, 1985)

O. af Hällström: *Sveaborg—Viapori—Suomenlinna: The Island Fortress off Helsinki* (Rungsted Kyst, 1986)

L. Pettersson: 'Templum Saloense: Pohjalaisen tukipilarikirkon arvoitus/ An Early Ostrobothnian Block-pillar Church and its Background' *Fin. Fornminnesfören. Tidskr./Suomen Muinaist. Aikak.*, xc (1987) [whole issue]

S. Sarajas-Korte, ed.: *Ars: Suomen taide* [Ars: the art of Finland], ii (Helsinki, 1988) [extensive coverage of architecture]

L. Pettersson: *Suomalainen puukirkko* [The Finnish wooden church] (Helsinki, 1992)

R. Nikula: *Architecture and Landscape: The Building of Finland* (Helsinki, 1993), pp. 41–65

ÅSA RINGBOM

3. AFTER 1809. As part of the Russification programme that began in 1809, Tsar Alexander moved the capital of the Grand Duchy of Finland from the medieval city of Turku (Swed. Åbo) to Helsinki (Swed. Helsingfors) and imported such architects as Carl Ludwig Engel, Carlo Bassi (1772–1840) and Louis-Tullius-Joachim Visconti to lay out towns and design key civic buildings. As Controller of Public Works, Engel created government structures, churches and town-plans that did much to give Finland a remarkably sophisticated public face. Engel designed classical plans for Helsinki and Turku (typically following one of many fires that destroyed much of Finland's wooden house townscape), as well as Helsinki Cathedral (1830–40; *see* HELSINKI, fig. 1), centrepiece of a monumental square defined by his Senate House (1812–21) and buildings for Helsinki University (1828–45; *see* ENGEL, CARL LUDWIG, figs 1 and 2).

The development of Finnish nationalism, with its revival and encouragement of indigenous artistic traditions, challenged the 'foreign' Neo-classicism of the Russian rulers. Abandoning the pastel stuccoed façades of their Swedish and Russian past, tough, hard-to-work granite was consciously employed as a metaphor of Finnish strength and stubbornness; appropriately, Finnish architects enthusiastically adapted the round arches and heavy masonry of American architect H. H. Richardson. Also influenced by Louis Sullivan, the English Arts and Crafts Movement and avant-garde continental styles, landmarks of this turn-of-the-century NATIONAL ROMANTICISM include the Kansallismuseo or National Museum of Finland (by GESELLIUS, LINDGREN, SAARINEN, 1902–11) and the National Theatre (by Onni Tarjanne, 1902), both in Helsinki, and the cathedral of St John in Tampere (by LARS SONCK, 1902–7), the tower of which was inspired by the medieval church at Finström in the Åland Islands. SELIM LINDQVIST, meanwhile, was chiefly influenced by the Viennese *Jugendstil*. Eliel Saarinen's Helsinki Railway Station (1904–14; for illustration *see* SAARINEN, (1)), itself a powerful symbol of aesthetic and economic independence, is less dependent on Finnish vernacular sources and employed reinforced concrete in its vaulted ceilings.

Modernism, and particularly the work of ALVAR AALTO, quickly eclipsed the brief 1920s revival of classicism, for example in J. S. Sirén's Parliament Building in Helsinki (1927–31; *see* SIRÉN, (1)) and the Atrium Apartments (1927) in Turku by ERIK BRYGGMAN. Eliel Saarinen's second-place finish in the competition for the Chicago Tribune Tower brought worldwide acclaim, but it also led to his emigration to the USA. Aalto's tuberculosis sanatorium (1929–33), Paimio (*see* INTERNATIONAL STYLE, fig. 1), and the city library (1927–35), Viipuri (now Vyborg, Russia), put Finland in the mainstream of the International Style, although Bryggman, Aalto's partner on the design of the Turku Fair in 1929 and sole designer of the Finnish

Pavilion at the Exposition Internationale Coloniale, Maritime et d'Art Flamand held in Antwerp in 1930, was an equally respected exponent of the modern aesthetic. As Aalto became increasingly famous abroad, his work became ever more personal and more 'Finnish'. After World War II, when architecture elsewhere was experimenting with new materials and technology, Aalto's civic centre for Säynätsalo (1952; *see* AALTO, ALVAR, fig. 2) was a seemingly modest, human-scaled exercise in brick and wood. It barely competes with the trees of its forest setting, yet it achieves a dignity and monumentality that make it one of the masterpieces of 20th-century architecture.

Aalto dominated Finnish architecture until his death in 1976, but partly owing to Finland's tradition of relying on competitions for almost all new public buildings, such designers as AARNE ERVI, VILJO REVELL, AARNO RUUSUVUORI, Aulis Blomstedt (*see* BLOMSTEDT, (2)), and Kaija Sirén and Heikki Sirén (*see* SIRÉN, (2)) developed an evolutionary Functionalism suited to the Finnish natural and cultural landscape; all were involved in the new garden city of Tapiola (Swed. Hagalund), near Helsinki, one of the most successful new towns anywhere. Otaniemi (Swed. Otnäs) Institute of Technology (see fig. 4), close to Tapiola, sums up post-war Finnish architecture, with the expressionistic main building (1964) by Aalto, the modernist chapel (1957) by the Siréns and the idiosyncratic, cavelike student centre (1966) by REIMA PIETILÄ, an architect–poet known as much for his metaphysical explorations of the language of architecture as for his buildings. Pietilä and his wife Raili created two major works in Tampere, the free-form Kaleva Church (1966) and the copper-domed, granite-walled public library (1986), known as 'Metso' because its coiled shape recalls a ruffed grouse.

Efforts to solve Finland's housing shortage were finally realized in the 1970s (a fifth of the country's population had been repatriated from lands taken by the USSR during World War II), but the result was many blocks of flats in the bland and sometimes bleak Social Democratic style of the time. Nevertheless, at the end of the 20th century the always fertile Modernist tradition was being revived by the so-called Helsinki school, for example in Gullichsen, Kairamo & Vormala's addition (1989) to the Stockmann Department Store in Helsinki, with its references to Aalto, Le Corbusier, Louis I. Kahn and other 20th-century masters; the early Modernist spirit is especially strong in the same partnership's Itäkeskus Tower and Commercial Centre (1987), Helsinki. At the same time, Arto Sipinen's respectful homage to Aalto in the Tapiola Cultural Centre (1989) and at Mica Moraine (1993), the lyrical evocation of rocks and lakes by the Pietiläs (and which is the residence outside Helsinki of the Finnish president), demonstrate the range and vitality of late 20th-century architecture in a country where the art of building is the highest calling. The Finnish obsession with light as both function and metaphor is demonstrated in the churches of JUHA LEIVISKÄ at Myyrmäki in Vantaa (Swed. Vanda) (1984) and Männistö in Kuopio (1993).

Five student architects, using the name MONARK, won the competition for the Finnish Pavilion at the World's Fair in Seville in 1992; comprised of two separate buildings, an organic–sculptural one of wood and a more

4. Alvar Aalto and others: Otaniemi Institute of Technology buildings, near Tapiola Garden City, begun 1950s

formal block of steel, Finland's official presence at Seville expressed the dualities of a technologically and economically developed state created by a forest people. The competition system, which professionally enfranchises so many young designers, was shaken by a controversial contest in 1993 for a national museum of contemporary art for Helsinki, in which American architect Steven Holl, one of four invited foreign contestants, was declared the winner. Nevertheless, Finland continued to produce an abundance of architectural talent. Mikko Heikkinen (*b* 1949) and Markku Komonen (*b* 1945), who achieved prominence with their winning design (1988) for Heureka, the Finnish Science Centre at Vantaa, emerged as the leading firm of the early 1990s with such notable modernist works as Rovaniemi Airport (1992), the European Film College (1993) at Ebeltoft, Denmark, and the small, reliquary-like Finnish Embassy (1994) in Washington, DC. The chancery is constructed from the traditional materials of wood, copper and granite; symbolizing the Finns' intimate relationship with nature, it is sensitively and quietly part of its wooded site.

BIBLIOGRAPHY
A. Salokorpi: *Modern Architecture in Finland* (London, 1970)
P. D. Pearson: *Alvar Aalto and the International Style* (New York, 1978)
Nordic Classicism, 1910–1930 (exh. cat., ed. S. Paavilainen; Helsinki, Mus. Fin. Archit., 1982)
I. Okkonen and A. Salokorpi: *Suomalainen arkkitehtuuri 1900-luvulla* [Finnish architecture of the 1900s] (Helsinki, 1985)
M. Quantrill: *Reima Pietilä* (New York, 1985)
V. Helander and S. Rista: *Suomalainen rakennustaide* [Modern architecture in Finland] (Helsinki, 1987)
J. Moorhouse and others: *Helsingin jugendarkkitehtuuri, 1895–1915/Helsinki Jugendstil Architecture, 1895–1915* (Helsinki, 1987)
J. Kautto, I. Holmila and J. Turtiainen, eds: *Suomalaista kaupunkiarkkitehtuuria/Finnish Town Planning and Architecture* (Helsinki, 1990)
P. Korvenmaa: *The Work of Architects: The Finnish Association of Architects, 1892–1992* (Helsinki, 1992)
S. Poole: *New Finnish Architecture* (New York, 1992)
R. Nikula: *Architecture and Landscape: The Building of Finland* (Helsinki, 1993), pp. 67–155
WILLIAM MORGAN

III. Painting and graphic arts.

1. Before *c*. 1840. 2. After *c*. 1840.

1. BEFORE *c*. 1840. Two significant rock paintings from the late Stone Age have been discovered in Finland: one in the south, which is geometric in design and painted in ochre, and the other in the north, which depicts animal forms. Examples of painted wood from the Viking era have not survived. During the medieval period Finnish painting was confined to secco wall painting, practised under the direction of the Catholic Church. Paintings survive in about 40 medieval churches, although some have been damaged and others insensitively restored; few Romanesque paintings have survived. The oldest paintings (*c*. late 13th century) are on the Åland Islands (Fin.

Ahvenanmaa) and show important influences from Sweden (which in turn had been derived from German models). Examples include the paintings of saints in Sund Church and the paintings in the churches at Lemland and Jomala.

The most important series of paintings, however, dates from the 15th century through to the early 16th. The mainly anonymous painters of the MÄLARDAL SCHOOL were active in Sweden and Finland from *c.* 1400 to *c.* 1470, producing wall paintings in the Gothic *Schöne Stil*; in the late 15th century a number of important vaulted churches were built in southern and south-west Finland and were decorated in the realist Late Gothic style. Influences came mainly from northern Germany via the Mälaren area of Sweden; Albert the painter from Sweden and the TIERP SCHOOL were particularly influential. Representative artists of the latter include Peter Henriksson, active in Finland *c.* 1470–90, whose work includes *St Peter* (1470–71; Kalanti Church), although his connection with the school is still subject to conjecture. Their subject-matter was influenced by the *Biblia pauperum* and *Speculum humanae salvationis* (*see* BIBLE, §I, 3(ii)). The colours are richer than in earlier works, and their theological programme can be clearly discerned. The paintings (*c.* 1510–22) in the Franciscan church at Rauma (Swed. Raumo) are influenced by Albert the painter and his school, while those in the churches of western Uusimaa, such as Espoo (Swed. Esbo), Inkoo (Swed. Ingå) and Siuntio (Swed. Sjundeå) are in turn influenced by those at Rauma; the *Dance of Death* (*c.* 1510–22) at Inkoo is particularly interesting.

Because of their sheer profusion the great series of paintings (1510–22) at Hattula and Lohja (Swed. Lojo) churches are considered among the most important: both series—the best preserved in Finland—are informed by the same theological background and concentrate on the depiction of people. Stylistically they differ from contemporary works and from each other, with the influence of Albert being traceable at Lohja. Few medieval glass paintings have survived, and illustrated missals and prayerbooks survive only in a few churches. It is known, nevertheless, that book illustration was practised in the Brigittine convent of Naantali (Swed. Nådendal).

Both ecclesiastical and secular painting from the Reformation to the early 17th century are extremely scarce. However, all the walls of the church of Isokyrö in Ostrobothnia bear paintings from the mid-16th century commissioned by the former court preacher Jacob Sigfridsson Geet. The paintings use few colours and are modelled on woodcuts by, among others, Hans Brosamer. The paintings by Ulf the painter at the gatekeeper's lodge at Turku (Åbo) Castle, which date from *c.* 1530, are among the few secular paintings to have survived from the period. They have late medieval and Renaissance features and depict a battle scene and a knight and his lady in a style similar to German art of the time. The only important work from the early 17th century is a portrait (1611) of the historian *Johann Messenius* by Cornelius Arendtz in Oulu (Swed. Vleåborg) Cathedral. Another important form to develop in the post-Reformation period was the epitaph. The earliest surviving example is the Jussoila epitaph in Rauma Church, which dates from 1572 and depicts the *Crucifixion*. During the 17th century epitaphs

were increasingly commissioned by the bourgeoisie and the aristocracy as well as the church. They were generally painted on wood, although Elin Fleming's epitaph (commissioned from Rostock in 1603) in Tenhola (Swed. Tenala) Church is carved in limestone. Allegories and morality subjects were also painted, often based on the ideology of the Counter-Reformation. The centre of ecclesiastical painting was Ostrobothnia, where exceptional work was produced by, among others, Lars Gallenius (*c.* 1658–1753).

Most secular painting in the 17th and 18th centuries took the form of portraiture. The Åbo Akademi (founded 1640) was an important artistic centre, employing a drawing master and producing painters of altarpieces and portraits. Jochim Neiman (*d* 1672) was a major portrait painter, and his students included Abraham Myra (*d* 1684). Other notable exponents of the form were Diedrich Möllerum (1642–1702) and Jochim Kröger and Anders Ulich (*fl* 1688–98) from Turku. The most important 18th-century portrait painter, Isak Wacklin (1720–58), was virtually the only representative of the Rococo style in Finland. The most prolific painter of this period was the Swedish-born NILS SCHILLMARK, who, in addition to portraits and figure paintings, produced landscapes and still-lifes in a style comparable to contemporary Swedish Neo-classicism.

5. Mikael Toppelius: *Samson Fighting with the Lion* (1775), wall painting, Haukipudas Church

Finland's first known woman painter was Margareta Capsia (1682–1759), who produced portraits and ecclesiastical paintings. Other notable 18th-century figures included Johan N. Backman (1706–65) and Johan Alm (1728–1810). Mikael Toppelius (1734–1821) was a major ecclesiastical painter, participating in the painting of the church at Turku Castle in the mid-18th century as well as producing impressive work at other churches (e.g. *Samson Fighting with the Lion*, 1775; Haukipudas Church; see fig. 5). He generally painted with distemper directly on wood, using subjects derived from the Bible as well as from Matthaus Merian (i), Hans Brosamer and Rubens. His somewhat clumsy rendering of Baroque influences gives his work a certain piety and charm. The most important painters of the early 19th century were the Romantic ALEXANDER LAURÉUS, who treated nationalist folk themes, and GUSTAF WILHELM FINNBERG, who produced history paintings and portraits and was the most gifted colourist of the Romantic period in Finland. Even after 1809, however, Finnish art remained dominated by Swedish influences, albeit at a private rather than an institutional level. Both Finnberg and Lauréus studied in Stockholm; Lauréus settled there, and Finnberg was also forced to return to Sweden later in his career in order to be able to support himself as an artist.

BIBLIOGRAPHY

L. Wennervirta: 'Goottilaista monumentaalimaalausta Länsi-Suomen ja Ahvenanmaan kirkoissa' [Gothic monumental painting in the churches of western Finland and Åland], *Fin. Fornminnesfören. Tidskr./Suomen Muinmuist. Aikak.*, xxxviii/1 (1930)
K. K. Meinander: *Porträtt i Finland före 1840-talet* [The portrait in Finland before 1840], i and ii (Helsinki, 1931)
O. A. Nygren: *Helgonen i Finlands medeltidskonst* [Saints in Finnish medieval art] (Helsinki, 1945)
——: *Gudsmodersbilden i Finlands medeltidskonst* [Images of the Virgin in Finnish medieval art] (Helsinki, 1951)
R. Pylkkänen: *Lohjan kirkko: Lisiä Lohjan pitäjänkertomukseen* [Lohja church: addenda to the chronicle of Lohja parish] (Lohja, 1959)
R. Mähönen: 'Kirkkomaalari Mikael Toppelius' [The church-painter Mikael Toppelius], *Fin. Fornminnesfören. Tidskr./Suomen Muinmuist. Aikak.*, lxxviii (1975)
S. Ringbom: 'Allegori och legend i några barocktavlor' [Allegory and legend in some Baroque paintings], *Taidehist. Tutkimuksia/Ksthist. Stud.*, ii (1976), pp. 119–34
S. Sarajas-Korte, ed.: *Ars: Suomen taide* [Ars: the art of Finland], i (Helsinki, 1987), pp. 310–81
B. von Bonsdorff: 'Kuvataide 1600- ja 1700-luvulla' [The visual arts in the 17th and 18th centuries], *Ars: Suomen taide* [Ars: the art of Finland], ed. S. Sarajas-Korte, ii (Helsinki, 1988), pp. 256–319

KAARINA PÖYKKÖ, KALEVI PÖYKKÖ

2. AFTER *c*. 1840. In the mid-19th century, Finnish art was given a fresh impetus by a general national awakening that began around this time, and for about a century the nationalist movement attempted, with varying degrees of success, to dominate Finnish art politics (*see* NATIONAL ROMANTICISM). Of decisive importance was the foundation in 1846 of the Finnish Art Association (Suomen Taideyhdistys). As the country's only art institution, founded by university professors, it acted more as an academy and began through elementary training and exhibitions to direct the artistic life of the country (*see* §XIII below). In its efforts to stimulate interest in the native land the nationalist project concentrated primarily on landscape. *Finland framställd i teckningar* (Finland in pictures), a book of lithographs edited and with texts by

Z. Topelius, appeared between 1845 and 1852, with illustrations by contemporary artists and amateurs. During the 1850s the brothers Magnus von Wright and Ferdinand von Wright (*see* WRIGHT, VON) also depicted idyllic Finnish landscapes, although their best work was the scientifically accurate depiction of birds. The first Finnish painter to gain international recognition was WERNER HOLMBERG, who from 1853 studied in Düsseldorf. Holmberg's ambitious aim was to create a Finnish school of landscape painting, and his works, which began as Romantic and moved towards a poetic realism, placed him among the best of the Nordic landscape painters. History painting was also supported by the nationalist movement: when ROBERT WILHELM EKMAN returned from studying in Stockholm, he was commissioned to paint two series of frescoes, the *Baptism of the Finnish People* and the *First Finnish Translation of the Bible* (1845–54), narrating the cultural history of the country for the chancel of Turku Cathedral. He also began to paint idealized and ethnographical paintings of ordinary people and, at the end of the 1850s, started painting subjects from the *Kalevala* epic.

From the 1860s the depiction of reality acquired increasing importance. Initially lyricism and idealism dominated, and paintings were based on outdoor sketches. Inspired by Holmberg's example, young landscape painters continued to travel to Düsseldorf, including HJALMAR MUNSTERHJELM, BERNDT LINDHOLM, FANNY CHURBERG (exceptional among Finnish landscape painters of the time, although her paintings were not generally understood until the emergence of Expressionism after 1910) and VICTOR WESTERHOLM. Among figure painters, on the other hand, Paris provided the main stimulus from the 1850s. The paintings of Thomas Couture exerted considerable influence in Finland, and the country's first figure painter of international standing was ALBERT EDELFELT, who went to Paris in 1874. With his portrait of *Louis Pasteur* (1885; Paris, Mus. d'Orsay) he became the best-known Finnish artist of his time; his skills were in demand in Europe's royal courts, and he helped develop artistic contacts between France and Finland.

In the 1880s *plein-air* painting became popular, prompting the emergence of two distinct styles. The first of these was a version of naturalism, which HELENE SCHJERFBECK and other women began to adopt at the beginning of the decade. The young Axel Gallén (later AKSELI GALLEN-KALLELA) also adhered to the style in his painting *Old Woman with a Cat* (1885; Turku, A. Mus.), while EERO JÄRNEFELT, who had studied in Russia and France, sought a profound form of realism. The second style to develop from the trend for *plein-air* painting was Impressionism, although this style was not yet fully understood in Finland; its closest adherent was Victor Westerholm, following his visit to Paris in 1888. From the 1890s, in what came to be seen as the golden age of Finnish art, Symbolism was harnessed by young nationalist artists and, as the dominance of the nationalists increased, the *Kalevala* again became a source of inspiration. Gallen-Kallela started painting subjects from the epic as early as 1889 and made trips to northern Karelia in 1890 and 1892 to gather material for his work. This initiated 'Karelianism', the nationalist enthusiasm for Karelia (where the ancient poems that formed the *Kalevala* had been gathered), and the Finnish identity became associated with the region. During the early 1890s many artists visited Karelia, and broad mountain landscapes became a favourite subject, treated in an ornamental style partly influenced by Japanese woodcuts. Particular attention was devoted to the winter landscape, regarded as particularly characteristic of Finland. This was treated in a lyrical and ornamental style, for example by PEKKA HALONEN (e.g. *Wilderness, Karelian Landscape*, 1899; Turku, A. Mus.; see fig. 6), who is regarded as the most national Finnish landscape painter of his time. Victor Westerholm depicted rivers in the snow in a more epic manner influenced by Symbolism. Idealized depictions of folk life were also popular: authenticity and humour were brought to the genre *c*. 1900 by JUHO RISSANEN, himself of humble origins.

At the beginning of the 20th century, Symbolism, which had hitherto been overshadowed by nationalism, came to the fore. HUGO SIMBERG in particular, with his fairy-tale

6. Pekka Halonen: *Wilderness, Karelian Landscape*, oil on canvas, 1.10×0.55 m, 1899 (Turku, Art Museum)

images, came to be regarded as among the outstanding Finnish artists of the period. His frescoes the *Wounded Angel*, the *Garden of Death* and *Bearers of the Garland of Life* (completed 1907) in Tampere Cathedral, which dwell on the subjects of life and death, were widely acclaimed. Despite the new educational opportunities available to Finnish artists, however, the socialists' rise to power in the first election of the single-chamber Parliament in 1907 shattered the idealistic faith that pro-Finnish artists had in the people, and national idealism suffered a blow. This mood was intensified by the disappointing reception given to a Finnish group of artists at the Salon d'Automne in Paris the following year, and the nationalist dominance of the art world gave way to the Swedish-speaking opposition, which emphasized the importance of following Paris. The most prominent artist around this time, following the death of Albert Edelfelt in 1905, was MAGNUS ENCKELL, who had spent time in Paris and who moved from an ascetic Symbolism to a use of brighter colours. A major new influence was the English-born ALFRED WILLIAM FINCH, who had moved from Belgium to Finland in 1897, bringing with him ideas from the Arts and Crafts Movement and from Art Nouveau. An exhibition (Helsinki, Athenaeum A. Mus.) of the work of Edvard Munch in 1909 was also highly influential. These figures revolutionized the use of bright colour in Finnish art *c*. 1910 and prompted enthusiasm for Post-Impressionism and Neo-Impressionism. The SEPTEM GROUP, founded by Finch, Enckell, Yrjö Ollila (1887–1932), Mikko Oinonen (1883–1956), Juho Rissanen, Ellen Thesleff and Verner Thomé (1878–1953), was in the vanguard of the new styles, while a number of younger artists were already experimenting with Fauvism.

During the economic boom at the time of World War I, the influence of Expressionism and Cubism, as well as of the Russian avant-garde, began to be felt, and colours again became more subdued. TYKO KONSTANTIN SALLINEN became a leading figure, although his Expressionist style met with some resistance. In 1917 the NOVEMBER GROUP was formed around him, advocating a form of nationalist Expressionism and establishing itself as a successor to the Septem group. Finland's independence in 1917 and the brief civil war that followed accentuated differences of opinion. New trends were seen as an attempt to undermine the basic values of society and, despite its incipient urbanization, Finland was still an agrarian society, full of doubts and prejudices concerning urban culture. The position of older artists and of patriotic critics was strengthened, and artistic innovation was further hampered by the young republic's limited resources and by the economic depression of the 1930s.

In this atmosphere of antipathy to modernism, the Russian avant-garde in particular was seen as dangerously revolutionary. Nevertheless the liberal opposition gained strength in the 1930s, and modernism managed to gain strength in Turku through Edwin Lydén (1879–1956), who had discovered abstract art during the 1920s in Germany. The most important figure in Turku, however, was OTTO MÄKILÄ, who embraced Surrealism in paintings that demonstrated an awareness of the French tradition of colourism. The art of the by now reclusive Helene Schjerfbeck, which had been revitalized by a one-woman aquatint and drypoint. Indeed graphic art came to be one of the most respected aspects of Finnish art internationally.

The 1960s was perhaps the most dynamic decade in the history of Finnish art, as the country prospered and the government became increasingly involved in the arts. At the start of the decade there was much enthusiasm for Abstract Expressionism, which, although short-lived, spread quickly throughout the country, as shown in the works of such artists as Lauri Ahlgrén (b 1929). As Finnish artists attempted to catch up with international art trends, particularly those of the USA, so Nouveau Réalisme emerged, mixed with elements of Dadaism, Surrealism and Pop art in the work of such artists as JAAKKO SIEVÄNEN. Ismo Kajander (b 1939) incorporated objets trouvés in his assemblages and KAUKO LEHTINEN daringly juxtaposed different materials and textures in his paintings. Important influences came from Paris, but the exhibitions of the Moderna Museet in Stockholm were also an important source of inspiration. Further stimuli came from the worldwide youth movement, burgeoning with the generation of the post-war population boom, as well as American underground movements and protest against the Vietnam War. The demand for increased social involvement rapidly evoked a response: Kimmo Kaivanto (b 1932), particularly in his graphic work, cultivated themes of pacifism and environmentalism, while Harro Koskinen (b 1945) went to the greatest extremes to undermine traditional values; he was convicted in court of defaming the Finnish coat of arms, with his work entitled *Pig Coat of Arms*, and of blasphemy, with his work *Pig Messiah*. This politicization of art continued into the early 1970s, waning later in the decade.

While it used to be typical of small countries such as Finland that only one artistic style could be dominant at any one time, the situation changed as a result of the broadening public interest in art and an improvement in conditions for artists. By the 1990s Finnish art had come to reflect the wide range of approaches that characterize modern Western art.

BIBLIOGRAPHY

J. Boulton Smith: *Modern Finnish Painting and Graphic Art* (London, 1970, rev. Helsinki, 1985)
Finskt, 1900 (exh. cat., Stockholm, 1971); Fr. trans. as *Finlande, 1900: Peinture, architecture, arts décoratifs* (Brussels, 1974)
S. Ringbom, ed.: *Konsten i Finland: Från medeltid til nutid* [Art in Finland: from the Middle Ages to the present day] (Helsinki, 1978, rev. 1987)
K. Varnedoe: *Northern Light: Realism and Symbolism in Scandinavian Painting, 1880–1910* (New York, 1982)
'Art in Finland', *Apollo* (May 1982) [whole issue]
J. Lintinen and others: *Finnish Vision: Modern Art, Architecture and Design* (Helsinki, 1983)
Dreams of a Summer Night (exh. cat., ed. L. Ahtola-Moorhouse, C. T. Edam and B. Schreiber; London, Hayward Gal., 1986)
S. Sarajas-Korte, ed.: *Ars: Suomen taide* [Ars: the art of Finland], iii–vi (Helsinki, 1989–90)
Kuvataiteilijat, 1991 [Dictionary of Finnish artists, 1991] (Helsinki, 1991)
M. Valkonen: *The Golden Age: Finnish Art, 1850–1907* (Helsinki, 1992)

AIMO REITALA

IV. Sculpture.

1. Before 1618. 2. 1618–c. 1880. 3. After c. 1880.

1. BEFORE 1618. The earliest sculpture to have been discovered in Finland is a large elk's head carved in wood, dating from c. 5900 BC, which was found at Rovaniemi in

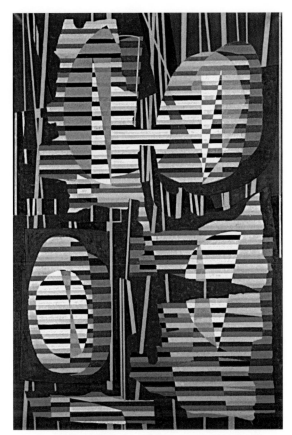

7. Sam Vanni: *Helsinki*, oil on canvas, 1.75×1.15 m, 1966 (Helsinki, Amos Anderson Museum of Art)

exhibition in 1917, became increasingly refined. ELLEN THESLEFF was likewise a lyrical colourist who produced paintings, prints and drawings throughout a particularly long creative life. Graphic art also became more popular in the early 20th century, especially in Helsinki and Turku during the 1930s, when cooperation between graphic artists increased and influences were sought in Scandinavia.

While artistic life remained vigorous during World War II, as a result of its isolation Finland was increasingly left behind in international art trends. The most notable reflection of the atmosphere and vision of the future during the war years were the *Finlandia* frescoes (*Finland Awakens* and *Finland Builds*), painted in 1943 by Lennart Segerstrale (1892–1975) for the Bank of Finland in Helsinki. In the immediate post-war period there was a return to Expressionism, pioneered by AIMO KANERVA in such works as *Yellow Meadow* (1945; Helsinki, City A. Mus.). Although Concrete art was resisted at first, it was adopted in Finland with unusual success in the 1950s and has continued to attract support. Purely abstract art was strongly represented by SAM VANNI, in such works as *Helsinki* (1966; see fig. 7), by Juhana Blomstedt (b 1937) and by LARS-GUNNAR NORDSTRÖM, who also introduced screenprinting to Finland. The profile of graphic arts was raised through the work of PENTTI LUMIKANGAS and PENTTI KASKIPURO, who were outstanding in their use of northern Finland. Animal heads were also used during the Stone Age to decorate weapons and utensils, but during the Bronze Age and Early Iron Age most items were imported from the Baltic area. Archaeological finds from the Viking period (9th and 10th centuries) demonstrate trade relations with central Sweden, while during the 11th century the importance of Gotland as an agent of Baltic trade increased. The influence of Sweden and the Baltic is also discernible in medieval Finnish sculpture, as individual works were imported from these areas. However, it is impossible accurately to chart changes in artistic styles on the basis of these works, and using stylistic features to date them is also difficult, as new styles often reached Finland via circuitous routes and after long delays. About 800 sculptures survive in Finland from the medieval period and, with few exceptions, they are all of wood and are all ecclesiastical, comprising crucifixes, images of the Virgin and the saints, and altar screens. Those wood-carvers active in Finland came from Sweden or from the Baltic cities: Conradus Pictor is documented as being active in Turku (Åbo) in the early 14th century, and his name suggests he was of German origin (none of his carvings has survived); the style of the work of the Master of Lieto, active in Turku in the first half of the 14th century, indicates that he may have been trained in Gotland, although it is possible that he was local. Only one wood-carver is known for certain to have been Finnish: the Master of Sääksmäki, who was active in the mid-15th century. In determining the origin of medieval Finnish wood-carvings, analysis of the timber itself has been an important tool: Finnish carvings were made from birch-wood, while the workshops of the Baltic cities used other woods (e.g. oak in Lübeck).

The earliest-known medieval wood-carving in Finland is the *Virgin* of Korppoo (Swed. Korpo), which appears to have been made in the Rhineland at the beginning of the 13th century, although opinions as to its origin have varied: stylistically the work has affinities with French sculptural decorations at Chartres Cathedral. The statue of *St Olaf* from Rusko Church (Turku, Prov. Mus.) has been dated to the late 13th century; this Norwegian saint was one of the most popular in Scandinavia throughout the medieval period. The work is attributed to the Master of Väte from Gotland, and stylistically there are links with German wood-carving. The works of another Gotland wood-carver, the Master of Bunge, however, reflect French style, and this artist is believed either to have been French or to have studied in France and to have been active in the first half of the 14th century; the *Virgin of Nousiainen* (Helsinki, N. Mus.) is attributed to his workshop. The figure's charming, asymmetrical and uncon-strained movement and the deep, elegant folds of her robe suggest French models.

The work of the Master of Lieto is of particular interest; over 20 wood-carvings have been attributed to him or his school, including a *Virgin and Child* (c. 1330; Turku, Prov. Mus.; see fig. 8). The figure's face and smile are Gothic in style, but the symmetry of the drapery is more old-fashioned. In the handling of the face, the Master of Lieto's equestrian statue of *St Martin of Tours* from Raisio (Swed. Reso) Church (Helsinki, N. Mus.) is reminiscent of the Master of Bunge's *Virgin of Nousiainen*, but the

8. Master of Lieto: *Virgin and Child*, wood, 0.54×1.12×0.44 m, *c.* 1330 (Turku, Provincial Museum)

depiction of the body and horse in the former work is markedly clumsier. One of the best examples of medieval Finnish art is the triptych reredos of *St Barbara* at Kalanti, sculpted by the Dominican Master Francke from Ham-burg. It appears to have been commissioned in 1412 by Bishop Magnus Tavast for Turku Cathedral. The central section shows the *Death, Assumption* and *Coronation* of the Virgin, executed according to Master Francke's sketches. The wings of the reredos bear paintings of the martyrdom of St Barbara.

In the early 15th century the decorative Gothic *Schöne Stil* reached the Nordic countries from Lübeck, the centre of wood-carving in the Baltic area; statues and altar screens were exported to Finland and Sweden, with many also reaching Finland via Tallinn. The monumental equestrian statue of *St George* (*c.* 1483 or 1487) in Stockholm Cathe-dral by the German wood-carver Bernt Notke became the model for statues of St George in, among others, the rural churches of Hattula and Hollola, while the realistic human head in Turku Cathedral is believed actually to have been made in Notke's workshop. The Reformation and administrative reorganization of the early 16th century brought great change to Finnish artistic life, notably with the economic impoverishment of the Church and the closing of the monasteries. Not until the 17th century, during Sweden's period of greatest power, did sculpture once more achieve prominence.

BIBLIOGRAPHY
K. K. Meinander: 'Medeltida altarskap och träsniderier i Finland' [Medieval reredos and wood-carvings in Finland], *Fin. Fornminnesfören. Tidskr./Suomen Muinmuist. Aikak.*, xxiv (1908)
C. A. Nordman: 'Medeltida skulptur i Finland' [Medieval sculpture in Finland], *Fin. Fornminnesfören. Tidskr./Suomen Muinmuist. Aikak.*, lxii (1964)
R. Pylkkänen: *Sancta Barbara* (Helsinki, 1966)
I. Racz and R. Pylkkänen: *Art Treasures of Medieval Finland* (Helsinki, n.d.)
T. Riska: 'Keskiajan puunveisto ja maalatut alttarikaapit' [Medieval wood-carving and painted altar screens], *Ars: Suomen taide* [Ars: the art of Finland], i, ed. S. Sarajas-Korte (Helsinki, 1987), pp. 182–225

TIMO KEINÄNEN

2. 1618–*c.* 1880. Very little sculpture was produced in Finland during this period for, although the country remained politically and culturally integrated with Sweden until 1809, it was very impoverished and isolated from the rest of Europe. Moreover, while wood for carving was abundant, stone suitable for sculpture had largely to be imported. What sculpture there was consisted mostly of funerary monuments and church sculpture, produced in the 17th century when Sweden was at the height of its political and economic power. Typically the work was carried out by foreign (most likely German) sculptors, as resources in Finland did not provide for the training of native artists.

The work of Arent Passer (*c.* 1560–1637) and his workshop in Tallinn (now in Estonia) is particularly noteworthy. While he is best known for his work in Tallinn Cathedral, in Finland his limestone monument to *Arvid Tönnesson Wildeman and Anna Hansdotter Björnram* (early 17th century) in Pernaa (Swed. Pernå) Church is of great interest; Wildeman (governor of Viipuri Castle, then in Finnish Karelia but now part of Russia) and his wife are sculpted in shallow relief, rich in classical allusions, in a manner typical of the Renaissance monumental style throughout northern Europe. Strapwork decoration, however, points to its later date stylistically, despite the old-fashioned clothing of the governor's wife. Equally splendid is the monument in Turku Cathedral to *Åke Tott* (1678; see fig. 9) by Peter Schultz (1647–89). Situated over the graves of Tott and his wife Christina Brahe (both devoted servants of King Gustav II Adolf of Sweden), it is a typical Baroque work, full of movement; it was executed in black and white marble, which was imported to Finland at great expense.

Thereafter little sculpture was either executed in Finland or imported until the isolated examples of work produced by Erik Cainberg (1771–1816). Cainberg went to Stockholm in 1790 in order to attend the Royal Academy of Fine Arts; he became an apprentice to the celebrated Johan Tobias Sergel, winning a prize in 1795 and in 1798 becoming Sergel's associate. From this period dates his well-executed medallion bust of *Jacob Riff* (plaster, 1799), one copy of which is in the Athenaeum Museum in

9. Peter Schultz: marble monument to *Åke Tott*, 1678, Turku Cathedral

Helsinki (Swed. Helsingfors) and the other in Sweden (Skellefteå Church). Cainberg later travelled to Rome on a six-year stipend, returning to Scandinavia in 1809. His subsequent works are among the first sculptural expressions of a Finnish nationalism that had begun to grow in the late 18th century. Notable among these are a number of plaster bas-reliefs executed in Turku, such as *Väinämöinen Playing the Kantele* (*c.* 1816; Turku, Old University Building), which depicts the Orphic seer of the *Kalevala* in a somewhat inappropriate Neo-classical idiom, acquired during Cainberg's studies in Stockholm and Rome. For much of the 19th century Cainberg's alliance of nationalist subject-matter to a Neo-classical style remained a problematic legacy for sculptors in Finland, such as WALTER MAGNUS RUNEBERG and Johannes Tanken (1849–83). A particularly influential figure during this period was the Swedish sculptor CARL ENEAS SJÖSTRAND, who made the first public monument in Finland to honour a public figure, *Henrik Gabriel Porthan* (1859; Turku). Sjöstrand taught at the Finnish Art Association (Suomen Taideyhdistys) in Helsinki and sent his students to Copenhagen, which was dominated at that time by Bertel Thorvaldsen's Neo-classical spirit. It was not until near the end of the 19th century that the influence of Neo-classicism on Finnish sculpture began to wane.

BIBLIOGRAPHY
S. Ringbom, ed.: *Konsten i Finland: Från medeltid til nutid* [Art in Finland: from the Middle Ages to the present day] (Helsinki, 1978, rev. 1987), pp. 82–4, 152–64

S. Sarajas-Korte, ed.: *Ars: Suomen taide* [Ars: the art of Finland], ii (Helsinki, 1988), pp. 257–66; v (Helsinki, 1990), pp. 60–75
N. Kent: *The Triumph of Light and Nature* (London, 1992), pp. 100–02

NEIL KENT, MICHAEL TUCKER

3. AFTER *c*. 1880. Towards the end of the 19th century new influences began to modify the classicism that had dominated for so long. A romantic, Renaissance-inspired sense of realism, for example, informed the works of Robert Stigell (1852–1907), such as *The Archer* (1887; Helsinki, Athenaeum A. Mus.), while Emil Wikström (1864–1942) pursued a more naturalistic but equally purposeful mood in such portrait busts as that of *Akseli Gallen-Kallela* (bronze, 1886; Helsinki, Athenaeum A. Mus.; see fig. 10). Gallen-Kallela was the leading figure in the renaissance of folk-inspired creativity that occurred towards the turn of the century and worked in a wide variety of media (*see* GALLEN-KALLELA, AKSELI). The expressive textures of his *Defence of the Sampo* (relief carving in wood, 1895; Helsinki, Gallen-Kallela Mus.) struck a ruggedly primitivistic note, in sharp contrast to both Stigell's late-Renaissance inclinations and the international Art Nouveau lyricism of VILLE VALLGREN. Whether creating free-standing sculptures or works of applied art, Vallgren epitomized a *fin-de-siècle* sweetness and musicality. The forms of his Havis Amanda Fountain (granite and bronze, 1905–8; Helsinki, Market Square) were created in what for Vallgren was an unusually large (and successful) scale; the work was acclaimed at the Paris Salon of 1907 before being reassembled in Helsinki.

At the end of the century the attempt to find a truly Finnish form of expression in sculpture focused largely on developing the primitivistic qualities of Gallen-Kallela's *Defence of the Sampo*. Eemil Halonen (1875–1950) established his reputation with six wood reliefs of subjects from folk life (e.g. *Man with Reindeer*; Helsinki, Athenaeum A. Mus.) that he carved for the Finnish Pavilion at the Exposition Universelle in Paris in 1900. In 1903–4 he pioneered the use of granite sculpture—which soon became a major feature of Nordic sculpture—with six decorative figures made for a firm in Viipuri. The sense of national identity that Halonen and Gallen-Kallela instilled into their wood-carvings found immediate and forceful echoes among a variety of sculptors. The ornamentation on the soapstone façade of the Pohjola Insurance Company Building (1900–01), Helsinki, is typical; here Hilda Flodin (1877–1958) used the motifs of bears, squirrels, pine-cones and primitive masks to create a rhythmically balanced effect. Equally remarkable is Emil Wikström's imposing granite *Bear* (1905–10) outside the main entrance of the National Museum of Finland in Helsinki.

Although a subtle classicism was still evident early in the 20th century in the work of such artists as Felix Nylund (1878–1940), public work was initially dominated by an increasingly stern NATIONAL ROMANTICISM. The sculpture of Wikström assumed particular importance, as in the gigantic stylized figures (completed 1914; for illustration *see* SAARINEN, (1)) made to flank the main entrance of Eliel Saarinen's new railway station in Helsinki. Following Finland's independence from Russia, National Romanticism continued its celebration of primal folk feelings, notably in the wood-carvings of Hannes Autere (1888–1967) in the 1920s, which extended the legacy of Gallen-Kallela and Halonen. Eventually, classically based monumental sculpture reasserted itself, in the aftermath of the struggle for independence and the civil war of 1918. Notable examples include the many commissions of WÄINÖ AALTONEN, such as the initially scandalous nude sculpture of the great athlete Paavo Nurmi, *Paavo Nurmi Running* (bronze, 1925; versions outside the Olympic Stadium, Helsinki, and in Turku).

Felix Nylund's *Three Smiths* (bronze, 1932; Helsinki, Old University House Square) epitomizes the social realism of much Nordic sculpture of the 1930s, while modernist experiments in laminated wood by Alvar Aalto foreshadowed the integration of applied and pure art principles that characterizes much of the most interesting sculpture from the 1950s onwards. The pioneering efforts of, among others, Aalto's friend Maire Gullichsen to bring modernist ideas and art to Finland initially met with considerable opposition. Nevertheless by the 1950s Finnish modernism was well established both at home and internationally. Distinctions between pure and applied art gradually became less and less meaningful: the glass vases that Timo Sarpaneva (*b* 1926) created in the 1950s exhibited clear sculptural qualities long before the artist decided (in 1964) to sever his connection with the vessel as a form and to make pure sculpture in glass. Also outstanding were the refined wooden bowls made by Tapio Wirkkala, whose elegantly simplified forms later exerted a decisive influence on the early development of KAIN TAPPER. Tapper is often considered the most 'Nordic' of contemporary sculptors working in a Daoist, primitivist manner,

10. Emil Wikström: *Akseli Gallen-Kallela*, bronze, 1886 (Helsinki, Athenaeum Art Museum)

and his later works recall the animism of Finnish prehistoric sculpture as well as Brancusi's synthesis of Eastern and Western sensibilities.

From the 1960s there was considerable diversity of sculptural activity: while the mixed media forms of Laila Pullinen (b 1933) were inspired by both Hellenism and the Italian Baroque, the large wooden constructions of Mauno Hartman (b 1930) evoke a northern dreamspace of fantastic, totemic proportions. Heated public debate surrounded the modernist, non-figurative monumental work of Eila Hiltunen (e.g. *Sibelius* monument, 1967; Helsinki), HARRY KIVIJÄRVI, Hannu Sirén (e.g. *STOA*, steel, 1981–4; Helsinki East Centre) and Veikko Hirvimäki; the antithesis to such monumentalism, however, is found in the intimate fragility of the environmental art of Martti Aiha (b 1952) and the forest and lakeside figures of Olavi Lanu (b 1952), sculpted from organic materials. The multi-media 'social sculpture' of the performance group Jack Helen & Brut incorporates an eclectic, colourful range of shamanic elements, while a more rationalist, albeit poetic ethos informs the motorized and boxed sand sculptures of Osmo Valtonen (b 1929). Southern-inflected classicism and totemic elements combine in the refined primitivism of the non-figurative marble pieces of Tom Ogle (b 1938), reminiscent of Barbara Hepworth, while the enduring links between pure and applied art have been developed in the textile work of Maija Lavonen and Kirsti Rantanen.

BIBLIOGRAPHY

A. Krohn, ed.: *Art in Finland: Survey of a Century* (Helsinki, 1953)
S. Saarikivi: 'The Modern Sculpture of Finland', *Introduction to Finland*, ed. G. Stenius (Helsinki, 1963)
G. Schildt: *Modern Finnish Sculpture* (London, 1970)
J. B. Smith: *The Golden Age of Finnish Art: Art Nouveau and the National Spirit* (Helsinki, 1975, rev. 1985)
L. Ahtola-Moorhouse: 'A Review of Finnish Sculpture, 1910–80', *Suomalaista veistotaidetta* [Finnish sculpture], ed. S. K. Oy and W. S. Oy (Porvoo and Helsinki, 1980)
J. Mallander: 'Finland', *Northern Poles: Breakaways and Breakthroughs in Nordic Painting and Sculpture of the 1970s and 1980s*, ed. T. Bløndal (Copenhagen, 1986), pp. 173–271
Nordic Concrete Art, 1907–1960 (Helsinki, 1988)
M. Tucker: *Dreaming with Open Eyes: The Shamanic Spirit in Twentieth-century Art and Culture* (London, 1992)

MICHAEL TUCKER

V. Interior decoration.

The medieval tradition of furniture fixed to the walls continued into the 16th century, although in the Renaissance, marked by the restoration of Turku (Swed. Åbo) Castle (1530s) and the repair of Viipuri (now Vyborg, Russia) Castle (c. 1540–50), doors were cased and walls and ceilings were panelled, a stylistic feature that was also reflected in the construction of carved wooden cupboards and chests. The craftsmen employed at Turku Castle were principally German Balts, and they brought with them a Germanic version of the Renaissance. Interior decoration in the 16th century also employed various textiles. At their best they might be imported tapestries, as in Turku Castle, or Nordic-made 'wallpaper'—wall, table and bench curtains. A peculiarly Finnish interior textile was the *ryijy*, which was used as a blanket in both beds and sledges (*see* §XI below). In some cases walls were also decorated with paintings, as at Turku Castle in the 1530s and 1540s. With the exception of a few Renaissance ceramic ovens, fires provided internal heating. Expensive window glass was used only in the most important rooms; pigs' bladders were used elsewhere. Rooms were lit mainly by candles in iron candlesticks and chandeliers.

In the Baroque décor of the late 17th century and the early 18th century fixed benches were replaced by chairs that were still placed close to the walls. Narrative, often biblical, paintings or ornaments and painted wallpapers were fixed separately to the wall. Representations of pomegranates on textiles and embossed leather, as well as painted fabric wall hangings of this period, have survived from Finnish country houses. Towards the end of the Baroque an aristocratic home might be lit by a crystal chandelier, formed with pieces shaped like oak leaves. Iron lamps, however, were still more common, and iron and bronze candlesticks began to become common at this time. Large brass candlesticks were generally used as wall lights, of which one variation became general in the decoration of churches in the 18th century.

In the Rococo dark-toned interiors gave way to paler, painted surfaces. Walls were either partially covered with panelling to the level of the windowsill or were covered entirely. The bare sections of the wall were dressed with painted fabric wall hangings or paintings, the subjects of which reflected the pastoral tastes of the time (see fig. 11). The use of framed wall hangings became more frequent in the 18th century as guild painters proliferated in Finland, and mechanically decorated hangings began to be manufactured. The most magnificent mansions had stoves imported from Germany, the Netherlands or Sweden, with the straight-flued Central European type dominant until the mid-18th century, but fireplaces or ovens bricked into the form of stoves were the norm.

In the Gustavian period furniture did not differ in principle from the Rococo except in its paler colours and straighter lines. Painted wall hangings featured landscapes and buildings or illusions of ancient Rome, Greece or Egypt. Paper wall hangings became even more widespread, as did mechanically printed wallpapers. Rooms were made lighter with the enlargement of windows and the use of uncoloured window glass, and with the lightening of colour schemes. The use of glass chandeliers, imported mainly from Sweden, spread (at least for important rooms). New seating arrangements, for example conversation groups around gaming- or tea-tables, were introduced.

The Empire style made little impact in Finland, and the general impression of interiors remained one of late Gustavian mahogany and pastel colours. It was not until the second quarter of the 19th century that the Biedermeier style initiated the idea of integrated furniture, and the custom of placing furniture next to the walls was finally abandoned. During the Rococo Revival in the mid-19th century, along with the other revivalist styles of the period, each room could have specialized furnishing: for example, Neo-classical for the main rooms, Baroque Revival for the dining-room, Renaissance Revival for the study and gentlemen's rooms, and a different style again for the bedrooms.

At the end of the 19th century extensively furnished rooms with thick velvet curtains and coverings were superseded by the lighter Art Nouveau style. At its most

11. Salon interior from Jakkorila Manor, Porvoo, with hunting, pastoral and allegorical wall and ceiling paintings, by Johan Bromander of Stockholm, 1763–5 (Helsinki, National Museum of Finland)

distinguished, the Finnish Art Nouveau interior was designed in every detail by the architect: fixed furnishings, furniture, lighting, stoves and even textiles. The *ryijy* was revived, either as an independent wall hanging or as a combined wall hanging and bench cover. By the 1920s the majority of Art Nouveau stylistic features had disappeared or become simplified. An essential change in interiors came about through the gradual change in towns to central heating and to electric lighting. By the 1930s the spirit of Functionalism demanded a return to individual pieces of furniture. Functionalism was initially the interior style of public buildings, with the majority of homes still furnished with adaptations of historical styles. A decrease in the size of accommodation brought about by urbanization was apparent, particularly after World War II. The new architecture of towns and private housing was based mainly on standard designs in which the architect specified the use of different rooms.

Finnish design in the 1950s dictated simplified, open furnishing and single-coloured wall surfaces, with works of art and crafts carefully positioned on them. The interiors of the 1960s were freer and more colourful. The natural effects of stone and wood were striven for, and large windows that took up the entire wall brought nature closer to the living space. The comparative smallness of city flats and rooms meant that standard items of furniture, such as dining-tables and chairs, sofas, and bed and bedside-table combinations, were often used. As television became more widespread, communal aerials for whole blocks of flats necessitated the placement of the television close to the aerial socket, bringing Finnish homes into further conformity. The interiors of the 1970s were dominated by the sofa. It was only in the 1980s that blocks of flats were designed with less standard, cube-shaped rooms, and this freer, more lively architecture liberated interior design.

BIBLIOGRAPHY

E. Jutikkala and G. Nikander, eds: *Suomen kartanot ja suurtilat* [Finnish mansions and great estates], ii (Helsinki, 1941)

C. Gardberg: 'Åbo slott under den äldre vasatiden' [Åbo Castle during the time of the Vasa dynasty], *Fin. Fornminnesfören. Tidskr./Suomen Muinmuist. Aikak.*, lx (1959)

H. Hyvönen: 'Kustavilaisen ajan sisustaminen ja Suomessa toimineet puuseppämestarit vuosina 1772–1809' [Interior furnishings at the time of Gustav and master-carpenter employment in Finland, 1772–1809], *Heinolan Kaupunginmus. Julkaisuja*, 1 (1992), pp. 66–133

——: 'Keisarillista loistoa ja hillittyä porvarillista charmia' [Imperial splendour and the understated charm of the bourgeoisie], *Heinolan Kaupunginmus. Julkaisuja*, 3 (1994), pp. 17–27

VI. Furniture.

1. BEFORE 1774. Medieval furniture in Finland was based on built-in benches and beds; only tables, chests and possibly the chair used by the head of the household were movable. Some surviving guild tables, with detachable tops, are typical of the medieval tradition, with legs

carved from a triple-rooted trunk and decorated with ball-like plant motifs (e.g. Helsinki, N. Mus.; Turku, Prov. Mus.). Joiners, active in Finland from the 14th century, made both furniture and carved ecclesiastical decoration. A few Romanesque–Gothic cupboards, misericords and pews survive, while certain 16th-century pulpits (e.g. church pulpit, Hattula Church, nr Hämeenlinna; 1550) illustrate the traditional skills of carver–joiners.

In the Renaissance, panelling and upholstery were introduced. In the early 17th century members of the Finnish aristocracy began to build castles and mansions in imitation of Swedish palaces, which precipitated a greater variety of furniture in the houses of the nobility, the clergy and the middle classes. The first guild of joiners was established in Turku (Swed. Åbo) in 1633. Finnish furniture was powerfully influenced by German and Dutch Renaissance styles. The legs of chairs and tables were turned and were united by stretchers. Cupboards were architectural in design, with panelled doors. Most furniture was made of oak, pine or birch, and upholstery was generally either of leather or embroidered textiles. The characteristic square-framed Renaissance chair survived in the vernacular tradition until the 19th century.

Baroque stylistic influences came both from Stockholm, itself strongly influenced by France, and from the more domestic Anglo-Dutch version. Chairs and tables were mainly in the Anglo-Dutch style, but cupboards and chests followed both north German and Dutch models. The French Baroque was simplified by Finnish furniture-makers; the most imposing pieces were imported from Sweden or the Continent. Most furniture was still made from oak, but for carved work such softer woods as birch or pine were preferred. Chairs were generally upholstered in leather, but sometimes richly embossed and gilt leather, Italian velvet, damask and tapestry were used on luxury furniture. The expanding European trade with India introduced a fashion for cane seat and chair backs. The second Finnish guild of joiners was founded in Viipuri in 1668.

Following the return of many Finnish aristocrats and artisans who had fled to Sweden during the Great Northern War (1700–21), stylistic influences in furniture came from England, and in 1731, to protect craftsmen, the Swedish authorities imposed an import duty on English furniture. Chairs, tables and sofas followed the English Queen Anne style, with curvilinear splat-backs and cabriole legs. This style, in particular the cabriole leg, remained popular throughout the Period of Freedom (1720–72). Native woods were often stained to imitate expensive imported timbers; however, the majority of masterworks, chiefly wardrobes, were made from pine veneered with oak. The country's third guild of joiners was established in Helsinki (Swed. Helsingfors) in 1747.

Rococo influences were transmitted to Finland only with the renovation of the Royal Palace in Stockholm in the 1750s. At the same time records of French chairs began to appear in the estate inventories of the Finnish aristocracy. The number of furniture-makers' guilds increased by two: Loviisa (Swed. Lovisa) in 1754 and Pori (Swed. Björneborg) in 1764. The guilds were slower to accept new styles for apprentices' masterwork than their customers were; however, by 1763, a Rococo-style walnut

cabinet with curved drawers and feet had been approved. Finnish furniture-makers favoured simplified versions of French and English Rococo designs, executed in birch or pine, veneered with oak, alder or walnut. Fashionable chair-frames were often painted in imitation of French and English taste, and there was a limited use of gilded and japanned finishes. Leather continued to be used for upholstery, but silk fabrics or specially woven tapestries were increasingly employed. The use of striped or checked linen fabrics in upholstery was imitated from Sweden.

2. 1774 AND AFTER. The Gustavian style first appeared in Finland in a master craftsman's work of 1775, a rectangular bureau with an English-style cylinder front. From the early 1780s rectangular furniture was generally known as 'new-style'. French influence is seen in Finnish shield-back chairs, but after the outbreak of the French Revolution in 1789 furniture models were sought from England. Marquetry decoration, seen for example in a design of 1783 (Helsinki, N. Archvs; see fig. 12) by Johan Åberg (1747–1820), was previously rare but became firmly established in the Gustavian period. From the 1790s the use of mahogany veneer and brass decorations became widespread and is found in many masterworks of the late Gustavian period.

In the late 18th century and the early 19th six more guilds were established: Oulu (Swed. Uleåborg; 1781); Vaasa (Swed. Vasa; 1784); Tammisaari (Swed. Ekenäs; 1787); Hämeenlinna (Swed. Tavastehus; 1806); Pori

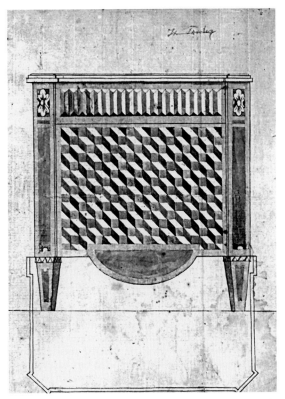

12. Design for a Gustavian bureau with marquetry decoration by Johan Åberg, 1783 (Helsinki, National Archives)

(1824); and Hamina (Swed. Fredrikshamn; 1826). With the exception of Hämeenlinna all the guilds were located in coastal harbours, and they formed important centres for training local craftsmen. Following Finland's annexation to Russia in 1809, there was an increased tendency for journeymen to travel eastwards, especially to St Petersburg, where a small colony of Finnish master craftsmen was established.

The Empire style never achieved widespread popularity in Finland. Its use was restricted to a few public buildings, for example the interior of Helsinki University. The majority of furniture-makers continued to work in a Gustavian idiom. The Empire style is most clearly discernible in the design of Finnish mirrors and also, in a simplified form, in some chairs, sofas and chests-of-drawers. Drawing-room furniture was generally painted in pale colours, sometimes white with marbling effects. Elegant gilt-bronze mounts, an essential feature of Empire style cabinetwork, were frequently replaced by carved and gilded or cast plaster ornaments. Sphinx and griffin ornaments were painted black.

The Biedermeier style became widely popular. The elegant Karl Johan style of Sweden, the heavier carved German style or the English Regency style (notably in cane-seated chairs) are apparent in work by some Turku and Helsinki furniture-makers, but it was the influence of St Petersburg, heavier and tending more towards the late Empire style, with carved volutes and palmette decorations, that was dominant. The St Petersburg influence is clearly seen in the work of the prolific furniture-maker Carl Petter Sundqvist, who made a series of drawings of Biedermeier furniture during his apprenticeship in St Petersburg (Turku, City Archive; 1827–8), after which he worked in Turku from 1831 to 1845. The emergence of complete furnishing schemes in this period altered Finnish furniture manufacture. Rooms had previously been equipped with furniture provided by different specialist workshops, with seat furniture being supplied by chairmakers, chests-of-drawers and cupboards by joiners, and mirrors by other firms. Now, comprehensive cabinetmakers were able fully to furnish a house.

Historical revival styles appeared in Finnish furniture from around 1830. Although some Gothic Revival features can be discerned from the late 1820s, the style never became popular, except for garden furniture. Finnish furniture-makers embraced the Rococo Revival style even more strongly than the Biedermeier. Alongside the persistent use of the Gustavian style, it became the dominant style of the 19th century, deriving inspiration from St Petersburg furniture and from such English patterns as the balloon-back chair. Chairs were generally stuffed with horsehair and were covered in strong single-colour or large-patterned fabrics.

Guilds were abolished in 1868 in Finland, and in 1879 full freedom of trade was instituted, resulting in an increase in factory production. Many large businesses either manufactured pieces themselves or ordered their furniture from subcontractors, or they imported furniture from St Petersburg. The ebonized salon Neo-classicism of Napoleon III, dining-room Baroque Revival and the Renaissance Revival style were all disseminated through these big industrial workshops. The most important of these were owned by Richard Heimberger in Helsinki (1860–1906) and Nikolai Boman in Turku (1871–1950s), and the best-known workshop of the period was Billnäs, founded in 1890, which manufactured American-style office furniture. Many of the larger firms had their own showrooms or warehouses in St Petersburg, Moscow and Tallinn.

Much Finnish Art Nouveau furniture was designed by leading architects: Eliel Saarinen (see SAARINEN, (1)), for example, designed furniture for Boman's workshop. Many architects insisted on controlling the design of furniture for houses that they had built. The first business to specialize solely in Art Nouveau furniture and ceramics was the Iris Factory (1897–1902), established in Porvoo (Bergå) by the painter Count Louis Sparre (1863–1964) and the potter and painter ALFRED WILLIAM FINCH. The enterprise was short-lived, and of greater significance were such firms as Boman and John Paischeff of Helsinki (1889–1931), which made architect-designed furniture. By the 1920s the Art Nouveau style had largely disappeared. Such furniture factories as the Asko Firm, set up in Lahti in 1918, manufactured simplified versions of 19th-century styles, including the English Chippendale style.

The Functional style of the late 1920s and the 1930s heralded the end of the 19th-century concept of integrated furniture, as the function of each piece now determined its form. In 1927 ALVAR AALTO experimented with the use of wood in his competition entry for the Viipuri City Library (completed 1935) and in 1929 he made curved plywood armchairs for the tuberculosis sanatorium, Paimio. His furniture was designed for particular architectural settings but in such a way that it could be mass produced and placed in other interiors. Finnish Functionalism was characterized by three basic furniture types: Aalto's laminated wood furniture; factory-made but architect-designed tubular metal furniture (which Aalto, too, had designed in the 1920s); and rectangular factory furniture. In 1927 the first Finnish furniture fair was held in Helsinki. In 1932 Asko was the first factory to produce Functionalist furniture.

Finnish design won international acclaim at the Milan Triennale in 1933, consolidated at the World's Fair of 1939 in New York. Furniture design of the 1940s had as its starting-point the idea of 'beautiful utility'. The Artek Firm, founded by Aalto in 1935, was at the forefront in creating carefully designed utility furniture. The Finnish designs that received so many international prizes in the 1950s, were, however, no longer popular in the 1960s with Finnish customers, who considered them élitist. Some Finnish designers earned international fame for their experiments in materials other than wood: for example Eero Aarnio (b 1932), with his 'Globe' and 'Pastille' plastic chairs for Asko; Antti Nurmesniemi (b 1927), with his experiments in leather; or Yrjö Kukkapuro (b 1933), with his 'Karuselli' and 'Saturnus' chairs. From the 1970s leading Finnish factories concentrated increasingly on the manufacture of self-assembly kit furniture.

BIBLIOGRAPHY

R. Nickander: 'Åbo snickarskrå' [The furniture trade in Åbo], *Kulturen* (1935–6), pp. 43–78
L. Bäcksbacka: 'Helsingfors snickare och snickarskrå' [Helsingfors furniture-makers and the furniture trade], *Fin. Mus.*, lx (1953), pp. 73–105
R. Pylkkänen: *Vanhat tuolimme* [Old Finnish chairs] (Porvoo, 1965, rev. 3/1974)

R. Miestamo: *The Form and Substance of Finnish Furniture* (Lahti, 1981)

Alvar Aalto: Furniture (exh. cat., ed. J. Pallasmaa; Helsinki, Mus. Fin. Archit., 1984)

H. Hyvönen: *Snickarämbetet i Lovisa, 1755–1966* [The furniture guild of Lovisa, 1755–1966] (Loviisa, 1987)

——: 'Finländsk snickarmästare anslutna till snickarämbetet i Stockholm pa 1700-talet' [Finnish master furniture-makers attached to the furniture guild of Stockholm in the 1700s], *Fin. Mus.*, xcv (1988), pp. 74–100

——: 'En nygotisk predikstol' [A neo-Gothic pulpit], *Fin. Mus.*, xcvii (1990), pp. 113–5

M. Supinen: *A. B. Iris: Suuri yritys* [A. B. Iris: great endeavour] (Sulkava, 1993)

H. Hyvönen: 'Suomessa toimineet puuseppämestarit vuosina 1810–1830' [Master-carpenter employment in Finland, 1810–1830], *Heinolan Kaupungimus. Julkaisuja*, 3 (1994), pp. 28–73

VII. Ceramics.

Knowledge of medieval Finnish ceramics is generally restricted to fragments of thrown pottery and a few hand-shaped ecclesiastical candlesticks found in southern Finland. Among the first recorded potters, who mainly came from Germany at the beginning of the Renaissance, was Abraham von Wittenberg, who worked for the court of John, Duke of Finland (later John III; *reg* 1568–92), in Turku (Swed. Åbo) Castle in the 1560s making wares and tiled stoves. The first Finnish guild of potters was established in Viipuri in 1668 and the second in Turku in 1738. Artisan ceramics were thrown, coarse, red earthenwares; in the west of Finland they followed the Swedish tradition and in the east the Russian tradition. At the beginning of the 18th century the aristocracy began to import faience and porcelain, mainly from Sweden and Germany. In 1762 the first tin-glazed earthenwares were made at the Hertonäs Oäkta Porcelain Factory (1762–1846) and later at the Alberga Faience Factory (1798–1861/2), both near Helsinki.

In the early 19th century eight ceramic factories were founded in Finland, of which the Fortuna Faience Factory (1814–66) manufactured stoneware industrial ceramics, and the Suotniemi Faience and Porcelain Factory (1841–94) in Suotniemi, Karelia, then in eastern Finland (now Russia), made faience. The latter was directed by the Austrians Albert Chobotsky, Fredrik Chobotsky and Nicolaus Chobotsky, and later by the Englishman Gregory Holden (*b* 1814), who introduced the English Rococo Revival style and transfer-printing to the factory. Suotniemi exported its products to Russia as well as serving a small, domestic market. The range of wares included transfer-printed dinner services, brightly coloured, marbled or sandy-coloured coffee services, decorative items and even walking-stick tops. Design and decoration followed foreign revivalist styles. Suotniemi contributed almost 90% of the ceramic output in Finland until the 1870s. Its later rival was the Wilhelm Andstén's Dutch Tile and Faience Factory (1842–1922) in Helsinki, which manufactured mainly ceramic tiles but also some ornamental ceramics. It was the first Finnish ceramic factory to manufacture artists' sculptures, such as a small statuette (1885) of the Finnish national poet Johan Ludvig Runeberg (1804–77) by his son Walter Magnus Runeberg. As the Art Nouveau style developed, ceramic stoves were designed by such leading architects as Eliel Saarinen and such artists as Akseli Gallen-Kallela. In the 19th century Finnish ceramic factories were largely stove manufacturers. The Rakkolanjoki Ceramics Factory (1877–1932) on the Karelian isthmus produced stoves until the introduction of central heating. Other wares were side products, and only a few factories in addition to Suotniemi departed from this craft tradition. Of these, the most important were Granfors (1841–65) and Bennvik (1856–60), both in north-west Finland, which produced mainly Rococo Revival designs made from moulds imported from Denmark. The Notsjö Porcelain Factory (1862–78) operated in conjunction with the Nuutajärvi Glassworks and was the second Finnish factory to manufacture faience.

In 1873 the Arabia Porcelain Factory in Helsinki (Swed. Helsingfors) was established as a subsidiary of the Swedish Rörstrand Factory, and it became the leading Finnish ceramics factory for the domestic and Russian markets. In the early period, it followed Rörstrand's styles and decoration. Porcelain was manufactured there from 1877. Arabia's first independent designs date from 1893, when the manufacture of majolica also began. The most important artist was the Swedish-born potter Thure Öberg (1871-1935), who was the factory's artistic director and who produced some distinguished Art Nouveau vases.

In 1897 the painter Count Louis Sparre (1863–1964) invited ALFRED WILLIAM FINCH to start and manage the Iris Factory in Porvoo (Borgå). In addition to making furniture, the factory produced red-clay, utilitarian wares in English-studio-type workshops. It attempted to create new forms of industrial wares based on vernacular designs. The factory was closed in 1902 after financial failure.

In the 20th century Finnish ceramics were generally associated with the Arabia Porcelain Factory. In 1932 the factory set up an independent art department for studio potters, which was directed until 1948 by the potter Kurt Ekholm (1907–75). This marked a breakthrough in Finnish art ceramics, the success of which was confirmed by the gold medal won by Toini Muona (1904–87) at the first Milan Triennale in 1933. In 1945 the industrial designer Kaj Franck (1911–89) was brought into the design department of the factory to produce designs for everyday utilitarian wares. The strength of his 'Kilta' tableware, produced in 1952, was its simple, functional form, and it soon became standard everyday ware in Finnish homes.

Finnish design was at the forefront of its field in the 1950s, when the Arabia potters attained international fame, collecting most of the awards at the Milan Triennales. Kaj Franck received numerous awards including the Compasso d'Oro prize in 1957 for his design work. The porcelain wares with pierced rice decoration (*c*. 1955; London, V&A; see fig. 13) developed by Friedl Holzer-Kjellberg (1905–93) represent a period in Arabia's production that was strongly characterized by the creative influence of Chinese porcelain, which is also seen in the coloured glazes of Toini Muona and the porcelain of Aune Siimes (1909–64). The wares produced in Finland during the 1950s were based on simple, geometric forms with abstract decoration that towards the end of the decade gave way to more fluid designs and luxurious decoration. In the 1960s Arabia returned to a more traditional concept of the dinner service. The first of these were 'Talvikki' by Raija Uosikkinen (*b* 1923) and 'Valencia' by Ulla Procopé (1921–68).

13. Porcelain dish with pierced rice decoration, designed by Friedl Holzer-Kjellberg, diam. 128 mm, made by the Arabia Porcelain Factory, Helsinki, c. 1955 (London, Victoria and Albert Museum)

There was no real tradition of ceramic sculpture in Finland: some factories, such as the Wilhelm Andstén's Dutch Tile and Faience Factory, had made sculptures in the 19th century, and the sculptors Ville Vallgren and Wäinö Aaltonen had experimented with reproducing their sculptures in ceramics; the German-born Angelica von Sivers had made a few sculptures at the Rakkolanjoki Ceramics Factory. Michael Schilkin (d 1962) was the first of the Arabia artists to produce ornamental human and animal statuettes and the factory's first public ornamental ceramic panels, stamped in relief. After him, the tradition was continued by such artists as Rut Bryk (b 1916), Francesca Mascitti Lindh (b 1931), Birger Kaipiainen (1915–88) and Toini Muona.

In 1975 Arabia and Rörstrand merged, and Arabia began to specialize in stoneware. At the same time the activities of the art department were restricted, and the majority of the artists who worked there were made redundant. The merger was unsuccessful and ended in 1977. Arabia's uncertain position and the new, more critical attitude of the consumer towards craft ceramics brought a group of small industrial companies and workshops into existence in the 1970s. The most important was Pentik, founded in northern Finland in 1971, which boasted two ex-Arabia ceramic artists, Anja Winqvist (b 1934) and Peter Winqvist (b 1941). As well as crockery, Pentik attempted to manufacture art ceramics. The important Swedish potter Henrik Allert (b 1937) was among the artists who were employed by Pentik. Outside the factories, small ceramic communities evolved during the 1970s, the most important of which were Pot Viapori (1973) in Helsinki and the Seenat Firm (1976) near Helsinki, both of which favoured a direct return to a national identity in ceramic production.

BIBLIOGRAPHY

E. Klinge: Unikate finnischer Künstler: Keramik (Düsseldorf, 1982)
H. Hyvönen: Suomalaista keramiikkaa [Finnish ceramics] (Porvoo, 1983)
——: 'Die Fayencefabrik Nuutajärvi', Suom. Mus., xci (1984), pp. 53–70
M. Kumela, K. Paatero and K. Rissanen: Arabia (Helsinki, 1987)
Scandinavian Ceramics and Glass in the Twentieth Century (exh. cat. by J. H. Opie, London, V&A, 1989)
H. Hyvönen: 'Suotniemi: Suomen ensimmäinen fajanssitehdas' [Suotniemi: Finland's first faience factory], Heinolan Kaupungimus. Julkaisuja, 2 (1993)
M. Supinen: A. B. Iris: Suuri yritys [A. B. Iris: great endeavour] (Sulkava, 1993)

HEIKKI HYVÖNEN

VIII. Glass.

Three phases are discernible in the manufacture of Finnish glass. The first is the so-called *Waldglas* period. The products, manufactured from indigenous materials, were mainly window glass and such utilitarian items as green and brown bottles, beer glasses, bowls and pots. Goblets and bottles with trailed decoration were among the better-quality *Waldglas* products. Around 1681 Gustav Jung (c. 1650–95) founded the first glassworks on the south-western coast of Finland at Uusikaupunki (Swed. Nystad), where glass was produced until 1685; only fragments have survived. Some high-quality, gilded, opal glass was produced at the end of the 18th century by the Åvik Factory at Somero (1748–1833) and the Mariedal Factory at Sipoo (Swed. Sibbo) (1779–1824).

The second phase began in the mid-19th century when the Nuutajärvi Glassworks, which had been founded in 1793 in the village of Nuutajärvi, became the leading Finnish glassworks. It employed Belgian, French, German and Swedish blowers and glasscutters. Among Nuutajärvi's new models were high-quality engraved, filigree and cut glass. The designs were similar to or direct copies of those wares manufactured by Swedish, German and French factories. The manufacture of bottles and jars became mechanized in the 19th century, and pressed glass was introduced in 1851.

The third phase began in the early 20th century with the development of modern Finnish design. Nuutajärvi is considered the innovator in this field, for it was there that the first competition for a new set of designs for domestic glass was held in 1905. The winner was the architect Walter Jung (1879–1946) with his Art Nouveau design. Since then nearly all Finnish glass designers have been active in other areas of design, such as architecture, furniture and textiles. At the Riihimäki Glassworks (1910–89) art glass was produced, as well as window and container glass. A central figure there was the designer and teacher Arttu Brummer (1891–1951), and such designers as Henry Ericsson (1898–1933) and Gunnel Nyman (1909–48) also produced designs at Riihimäki during the 1920s and 1930s. Like their Swedish counterparts, they often used heavy, clear metal with inserted air bubbles to decorate much of their work. Alvar Aalto created some of the best examples of modern Finnish glass; his famous 'Savoy' vases (1936) were made by Karhula Glassworks (founded 1890).

After World War II Saara Hopea (1925–85), who was also known for her work in silver, and Tapio Wirkkala (1915–85), whose work ranged from clear, colourless objects (e.g. 'Tokio' vase, 1955; London, V&A; see fig. 14) to coloured glass, began to produce their designs. During the 1950s and 1960s Wirkkala, Kaj Franck (1911–89) and Timo Sarpaneva (b 1926) received international recognition. Coloured glass was designed in the 1960s by such artists as Helena Tynell (b 1918) and Nanny Still (b 1926).

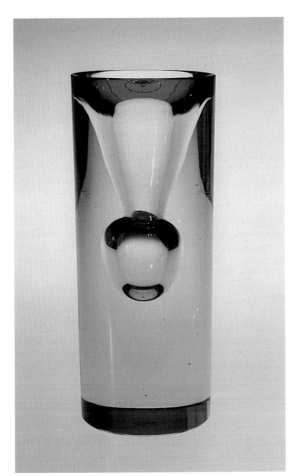

14. 'Tokio' glass vase designed by Tapio Wirkkala, h. 225 mm, made by the Iittala Glassworks, 1955 (London, Victoria and Albert Museum)

In the late 20th century Oiva Toikka (*b* 1931), Inkeri Toikka (*b* 1931), Heikki Orvola (*b* 1943), Kerttu Nurminen (*b* 1943), Valto Kokko (*b* 1933), Markku Salo (*b* 1954) and Brita Flander (*b* 1957) all created art glass as well as designs for mass-production. In 1988 the most important glass factories, Iittala (founded 1881) and Nuutajärvi, merged to form the Iittala–Nuutajärvi Co. From 1992 this was owned by Hackman & Co. From the early 1990s the Nuutajärvi trademark was used solely for art glass.

BIBLIOGRAPHY

V. Annala: *Suomen lasiteollisuus* [The Finnish glass industry], 3 vols (Helsinki, 1931–48)

S. Kopisto: *Lasia Suomen kansallismuseon kokoelmista* [Glass from the collections of the National Museum of Finland] (Helsinki, 1978)

R. Ahtokari: *Suomen lasiteollisuus, 1681–1981* [The Finnish glass industry, 1681–1981] (Helsinki, 1981)

A. Löfberg: *Suomen lasinpuhaltajat, 1748–1860* [Finnish glassblowers, 1748–1860] (Riihimäki, 1981)

Nuutajärvi: Kartano ja lasipruuki [Nuutajärvi: mansion and glassworks] (exh. cat., Helsinki, N. Mus., 1983)

M. Kahma and K. Koivisto: *The Modern Spirit: Glass from Finland* (Helsinki, 1985)

Suomen lasi elää [Finnish glass lives] (exh. cat., Riihimäki, Fin. Glass Mus., 1986)

Scandinavian Ceramics and Glass in the Twentieth Century (exh. cat. by J. H. Opie, London, V&A, 1989)

T. Poutasuo, ed.: *Nuutajärvi: 200 vuotta suomalaista lasia* [Nuutajärvi: 200 years of Finnish glass] (Tampere, 1993)

SIRKKA KOPISTO

IX. Metalwork.

Early pieces are often difficult to identify with any certainty as having been made in Finland because of a lack of hallmarks (not introduced until 1485) and because of their similarity to Swedish objects. The earliest known Finnish goldsmith, documented as Petrus Aurifaber, worked in Turku (Swed. Åbo) in 1371. In the Middle Ages the strongest influences on goldsmiths' work were the Catholic Church, the main patron of goldsmiths, and the trade of the Hanseatic League, which together brought Finland within the bounds of Western culture. Two examples of medieval silver are a Romanesque chalice at Porvoo (Swed. Borgå) Cathedral and the Gothic 'Ejby' chalice at Turku Cathedral.

Examples of Renaissance metalwork are rare, and such objects as spoons and a few beakers, tankards, scoops, goblets and ecclesiastical pieces that do survive are modest. Ornamentation was generally limited to simple engraved decoration, cast buttons and gilding. Plant and animal motifs, initial letters and family crests were used as decoration. Both Finnish and Swedish goldsmiths were influenced by German work at this time.

Between 1618 and 1721 Finnish silverware, compared to continental pieces, remained simple, although it is evident that some talented gold- and silversmiths were active. The formation in the early 17th century of a goldsmiths' guild based on the German model is evidence of international influence. From the second half of the 17th century Finnish silverware was clearly influenced in style by German Baroque silver yet it also became increasingly similar to Swedish models. The most typical Finnish Baroque silver objects are tankards, beakers, bowls, candlesticks, goblets and rat-tail spoons. From the 1680s iron candlesticks and chandeliers were produced, and some bronze chandeliers were imported from Sweden. Around ninety goldsmiths were active in Finland during the Baroque period, of whom the best known are Axel Hansson Båga (*fl* 1677–88) of Turku, Anders Bruse (*fl* 1678–83) of Oulu (Swed. Uleåborg) and Johan Grummellier (*fl* 1682–1701) of Viipuri (Swed. Viborg). The main centres of production were in Turku and Viipuri; a strong Baltic influence is visible in the work of Viipuri goldsmiths.

The Great Northern War (1700–21) disrupted production of metalwork in Finland until the end of the 1740s. Few pieces—mostly spoons, beakers, tumblers and ecclesiastical objects—survive from the early 18th century.

The Rococo style dominated metalworking between 1750 and 1770, a period of high-quality production. Influences came mainly, via Sweden, from France. Newfound prosperity caused an increase in the consumption of coffee and tea, as well as the development of towns and country houses, all of which stimulated demand for goldsmiths' wares. The best Finnish goldsmiths continued to work in Turku. Work in Viipuri, which had been ceded to Russia in 1721, remained old-fashioned and was influenced by St Petersburg. The most prominent goldsmith of the time was Nils Enberg (1723–79), and another representative of the Rococo style was Simon Gustaf Lydeman (1736–1806). An increasing number of coffee- and teapots, cream jugs and sugar bowls have survived from this period, although the majority are still tumblers and spoons.

From 1770 to 1800 the GUSTAVIAN STYLE dominated. Initially this style influenced only ornamentation: during the 1770s it was normal to find, for example, a Gustavian string of pearls decorating the rim of a Rococo-style object. In the 1780s, however, such Gustavian forms as cylindrical coffeepots, columnar candlesticks and urn-shaped sugar bowls and cream jugs became fashionable. Finnish silver of the 1790s typically features ball feet and mouldings on the galleries. New art forms introduced at this time include cruets with glass bottles, salts with glass vessels and stemmed beakers. The best goldsmiths of the period were Carl Fredrik Borgström (1755–1809) and Anton Christian Levon (1756–1817), both working in Turku.

During the war of 1808–9 and in the ensuing period, there was a decline in metalwork production. The introduction of the Empire style to Finland was thus delayed. This style persisted in Finnish goldsmiths' work to the end of the 1820s (see fig. 15), and its features were based on traditional Swedish examples. The focus of metalworking also began to move from Turku to the new capital, Helsinki (Swed. Helsingfors). The most prolific and best goldsmith of the Empire period was Carl Anton Carlborg (1770–1827) of Turku; prolific and talented goldsmiths also flourished in Helsinki and Porvoo at this time. After Finland's independence from Sweden, the old triple crown hallmark was changed to a single crown, and the use of date letters, with 'A' marking 1810, was introduced.

After 1820 Finnish metalwork received its stylistic influences almost exclusively from St Petersburg, where increasing numbers of Finns went as apprentices. On completing their training some of them returned to Finland, bringing with them the newest features of the Biedermeier style (c. 1825–45). In silverwork, the predominant feature of Finnish Biedermeier is the barrel form. Ornamentation is dominated by a band of forced oval

15. Silver sugar casket by Carl Anton Carlborg, h. 190 mm, made in Turku, 1824 (Helsinki, private collection)

blisters around the object's lower edge and punched chains of flowers and leaves. Figures deriving from the Empire style, such as the lyre, dolphins and swans, were often used on bases or stems. The most prolific goldsmith of the period was Olof Robert Lundgren (1794–1882) of Turku. A number of good goldsmiths, notably Roland Mellin (1803–67), were active in Helsinki.

In the second half of the 19th century metalwork was dominated by revivalist styles, of which the most important was the Rococo Revival. In Finland this remained influential almost to the end of the century, and silver in this style continues to be manufactured occasionally. The Renaissance, Baroque and Gustavian Revival styles appeared as isolated instances, often muddled with each other. The disbandment of the goldsmiths' guild in 1868 and the extension of freedom of trade in 1879 greatly influenced Finnish metalwork, and the first industrial metalworking companies were established at the end of the century. The most important examples of metalwork in the Art Nouveau style were designed by such leading artists and architects as E. O. W. Ehrström (1881–1934), Walle Rosenberg (1891–1919), Louis Sparre (1863–1964), VILLE VALLGREN, Jarl Eklund (1876–1962) and Max Frelander (1881–1949); Finnish production did not, however, reach high standards in this period. By the 1950s Finnish metalwork achieved international recognition with the silver designs of Tapio Wirkkala (1915–85) and Bertel Gardberg (b 1916).

BIBLIOGRAPHY
E. Helenius-Lehto: 'Mästare och mästerstycken i Åbo guldsmedskrå, 1713–1886' [Masters and masterpieces of Åbo goldsmithing, 1713–1886], Kulthist. Åb. (1933), pp. 71–116
T. Borg: Guld- och silversmeder i Finland, 1371–1873 [Gold- and silversmiths of Finland, 1371–1873] (Helsinki, 1935)
R. Pylkkänen: Gammalt silversmide i Finland [Antique silversmithing of Finland] (Helsinki, 1947)
R. Fagerström: Suomalaista hopeaa [Finnish silver] (Helsinki, 1983)

X. Jewellery.

Although Finnish metalwork can be documented with certainty to the medieval period, it was only in 1787 that hallmarks were extended to small objects. From that date it is thus possible to identify an increasing amount of jewellery hallmarked by Finnish goldsmiths. The surviving Finnish medieval pieces are, with a few exceptions, modest and of simple design. Expensive jewellery with large gemstones is uncommon.

In the medieval period the influence of the Catholic Church on jewellery is shown in the choice of depicting religious subjects, particularly in rings (e.g. Helsinki, N. Mus.); with the instigation of the Reformation in 1527, however, these subjects were discarded. At the same time the trade of the Hanseatic League brought both stylistic influences and ready-made jewellery to Finland. Foreign goldsmiths came to Finland as a result of this trade; their influence on the preparation of jewels was decisive. In the Renaissance the upper classes used jewellery extensively. Such powerful women as the Polish princess Catherine Jagiellon (1526–83), Duke John's wife, and Sofia Gyllenhielm (1550–83) owned extensive collections of jewellery; part of Catherine's collection was in fact of Polish origin, and Gyllenhielm is known to have imported jewels from as far afield as Italy. The pomander of Liuksiala (Helsinki,

N. Mus.) is the most important piece to have survived from this period.

Few items of jewellery survive from the period beginning in 1600. The pearl necklaces favoured during the Baroque were easily broken, and the fashionable gold brooches were melted down. In the second half of the 18th century rock crystal set in silver or tin was commonly used in Finnish jewellery. The Empire style, with its emphasis on the use of gold, was one of the best periods in Finnish jewellery-making; one of the best Empire goldsmiths was Elias Lindstedt (1771–1813), whose oeuvre includes a very fine gold necklace (Helsinki, N. Mus.).

Finnish objects of vertu, in common with other decorative arts, remained similar to their Swedish counterparts until 1809, when Finland was ceded to Russia. In the Biedermeier period Russian features were dominant in Finnish jewellery, a development that was encouraged by the apprenticeship of a number of Finnish jewellers in St Petersburg; some returned to Finland, some stayed in Russia. Peter Carl Fabergé employed a number of Finnish jewellers, foremost among them Henrik Wigström (1862–1930). In Finland the influence of St Petersburg revealed itself mainly as a stylistic feature. At the end of the 19th century the Art Nouveau style dominated Finnish design but had little impact on objects of vertu. Kalevala jewellery, associated with the firm of Kalevala Koru (founded 1937), Helsinki (Swed. Helsingfors), was based on medieval pieces and has been revived in modern times. In the 1960s abstract designs for jewellery by Björn Weckström (*b* 1935), executed by Lapponia Jewellery Ltd, Helsinki, attracted international attention.

BIBLIOGRAPHY
J. Haycraft: *Finnish Jewellery and Silverware* (Helsinki, 1969)
R. Fagerström: *Suomalaisia antiikkikoruja* [Finnish antique jewellery] (Helsinki, 1989)

RAIMO FAGERSTRÖM

XI. Textiles.

Many Finnish textiles, including embroidery, lace, woven fabrics and *ryijy*s, trace their roots to the medieval and Renaissance periods. Patterns and techniques spread from the top down, that is to say, from the upper class to ordinary people. Designs of various periods were then interpreted in an individual manner, and by the 18th and 19th centuries many textiles became typical folk art products. The nuns of the Brigittine convents, notably the one founded in Naantali (Swed. Nådendal) in 1438, had an important role in this process. They produced various textiles and, as part of the medieval aristocracy, they were also patrons of the arts. Indeed, the earliest evidence for the existence of the Nordic wool textiles, the *raanu*, *täkänä* and *ryijy*, is in the documents of Naantali convent, the medieval castles of Turku (Swed. Åbo), Häme (Swed. Tavastland) and Viipuri (Swed. Viborg), manors and parsonages.

The traditional geometric check and stripe patterns are best preserved in the *raanu*, a type of coverlet that in the late 20th century was also made around Lyngenfjord in Lapland. Woven on a warp-weighted loom, it was originally a fairly fine, twill-weave fabric, but it turned into a heavier, weft-faced tabby fabric in the later peasant tradition.

The *täkänä* was a medieval woollen double cloth with patterns based on the confronting peacocks, lions etc of early Near Eastern silks. A few examples have survived in ecclesiastical vestments (e.g. Helsinki, N. Mus.). The 19th-century folk version, on the other hand, takes its motifs from contemporary fabrics, in particular the stars, crosses and flowers of linen damasks, which at first were naturalistic and subsequently became stylized.

The *ryijy* is the best-known Finnish textile. It is a knotted pile fabric with a continuous weft that was used, pile down, on beds and during sleigh and boat journeys. Early *ryijy*s were probably plain, but weft stripes and checks were used by the 16th century; bright colours were then used for the ground fabric, but the pile was usually white, grey or black in imitation of a fleece.

The *ryijy* remained an upper-class object until the 17th century, when a more colourful and decorated form developed. These later examples are double-pile fabrics, the patterned ground having a short pile, usually woven with a fine wool, that was intended to be seen, while the underside remained coarser and more shaggy. The motifs reflect those used in Turkish fabrics and in pattern books; they include flower vases, animal and human figures, trees, wreaths, crowns and geometrical chessboard and fish-net patterns. Wedding *ryijy*s, in particular, were decorated with initials and the year (see fig. 16). Folk *ryijy*s include heart, tulip, acanthus and rose designs, which can be traced to particular areas through their imagery (*see also* §XII below). Their high period lasted about a hundred years from the mid-18th century.

16. Woollen wedding *ryijy*, 200×140 mm, 1817 (Helsinki, National Museum of Finland)

In the 19th century industrial production largely super-seded craftwork, but at the end of the century there was a counter-reaction, and the techniques and patterns of folk textiles were rediscovered. This phenomenon was part of the national awakening that occurred in Finland as in other European countries and led to the foundation of a number of influential institutions. Museums were set up, the collections of which were to provide inspiration for designers. The Finnish Association for Applied Arts, founded in 1875, and the Friends of Finnish Handicrafts, founded in 1879—both situated in Helsinki (Swed. Helsingfors)—contributed to the development of Finnish textile art. The Central School of Applied Arts, Helsinki, renamed the University of Industrial Arts, assumed an important place in the teaching of textiles. The Friends of Finnish Handicrafts began to collect old patterns and to distribute them to weavers. It also held design competitions in which, at the turn of the century, many of the country's leading artists and architects took part, among them Akseli Gallen-Kallela, Count Louis Sparre (1863–1964) and Eliel Saarinen. In their studios the textiles that initiated the development of modern art textiles in Finland were created. The Friends of Finnish Handicrafts works in cooperation with artists and make studio textiles, from *ryijy*s and other woven fabrics to such embroideries as flags and church vestments. Of the many teaching establishments, a notable example is Fredrika Wetterhoff's Kotiteollisuusopisto (handicraft school) in Hämeenlinna (Swed. Tavastehus), founded in 1885 to give traditionally grounded but artistically sound instruction.

After World War II, Finnish art textiles developed in a more geometric and abstract direction. For example, the traditional smooth pile of the *ryijy* was sometimes replaced by one of different lengths and of linen and silk in addition to wool. The significance of colour was also exploited. *Ryijy*s were designed by Eva Brummer (*b* 1901), Uhra Simberg-Ehrström (1914–79) and Kirsti Ilvessalo (*b* 1920) (e.g. of 1954; London, V&A). Laila Karttunen (1895–1981) and Eva Anttila (1894–1993) produced modern versions of *täkänä* pictorial hangings. The work of Dora Jung (1906–80)—*täkänä*s, *ryijy*s and ecclesiastical textiles—represents a high point of Finnish handicraft; Jung was also known for her linen damask designs for the Tampella Factory, which were awarded the Grand Prix in the Milan Triennale of 1957. Trained designers became more common in factories in the 1950s; Timo Sarpaneva (*b* 1926), working for the Porin Puuvillatehdas (Pori (Swed. Björneborg) Cotton Mill), was among the first, although he was better known as a glass artist. The work of the textile artists Marjatta Metsovaara (*b* 1927) and Irma Kukkasjärvi (*b* 1941) should also be mentioned, as should the printed textiles of Maija Isola (*b* 1927), Vuokko Nurmesniemi (*b* 1930) and Marimekko, the fabric and clothing company founded by Armi Ratia (1912–79).

BIBLIOGRAPHY

U. T. Sirelius: *Suomen ryijyt* [Finnish *ryijy*s] (Helsinki, 1924)
O. Mäki: *Taide ja työ* [Finnish designers of today] (Porvoo, 1954)
U. Hård af Segersted: *Suomen taideteollisuus* [History of Finnish applied art] (Helsinki, 1969)
R. Pylkkänen: *The Use and Traditions of Medieval Rugs and Coverlets in Finland* (Helsinki, 1974)
E. H. Beer: *Scandinavian Design: Objects of a Life Style* (Toronto, 1975)
L. R. Pylkkänen: 'Finland', *Needlework: An Illustrated History*, ed. H. Bridgeman and E. Drury (London, 1978), pp. 251–58
P. Sihvo: *Tradition und Volkskunst in Finnland* (Helsinki, 1978)
T. Sarantola and others: *Kirkkotekstiilit* [Ecclesiastical textiles] (Pieksämäki, 1986)

SIRKKA KOPISTO

XII. Vernacular arts.

Several diverse regions can be distinguished. In the north popular decorative traditions were influenced by ecological conditions and available resources, such as the horn and bone household goods, scored with geometric and plant motifs, made by the Saami. These features also distinguish vernacular decoration in northern Finland, where bone- and horn-carving characteristically comprises zigzag lines, rhomboids and hatched fields; many of these elements resemble prehistoric ornament. Finland's extensive coniferous forests have not particularly influenced the decoration of its vernacular art, although wood naturally dominates in house construction and furnishing. Birch was valued for openwork carving, and wooden dishes of Finnish spruce were distributed to the Baltic towns in the Middle Ages.

A distinct east–west difference is characteristic of vernacular art in Finland. In the Karelian border areas, influences from further east, especially from the Orthodox Church, dominated for centuries. Eastern Finnish everyday goods tended to be plainer than those of the west Finnish and Ostrobothnian farmers, who decorated their farming implements, tools, vehicles and interiors. Finnish popular art, particularly that of interior fittings, was richer and more varied in the western provinces. The introduction of fireplaces and chimneys in the coastal areas as early as the 16th century brought more spacious, smoke-free rooms, the fittings of which were influenced by Western styles: for a time after the mid-18th century, south-west Finland was almost a Swedish province in this respect.

Medieval traditions survived in many decorative forms and furniture types, such as long tables for farmhouses, with medieval band decoration and shallow-carved patterns, and the characteristic block chairs or chest chairs, which lost their connections with Renaissance types only in the 18th century. Wooden spoons and cheese moulds with carved basketry patterns and wall-knots, and other kinds of knot motif (e.g. Helsinki, N. Mus.), were typical of the western provinces of Satakunta and Häme (Swed. Tavastland). The wall-knot with four corner loops, a symbolic motif that represents an ability to hold a secret, is known in Finland and Sweden as the '[coat of] arms of St Hans [John the Baptist]'. Such simple motifs, prophylactic in intent to avert bad luck, are found in popular decoration and on all types of useful goods in the North Sea lands, Scandinavia and the Baltic area. They form a durable underlying stratum in vernacular art. Their symbolic meaning has not been satisfactorily elucidated, but objects associated with weddings and marriage were probably decorated to bring good luck. Fine, painstakingly made engagement presents were given to the bridegroom's family as part of the bride's dowry: furniture (*see also* §V above), chests, a pair of decorative chairs and the colourful knotted pile rugs and spreads (*ryijy*s; see fig. 16 above).

Finnish *ryijy*s, with their bright primary colours and combination of geometric and vegetal motifs (*see* §XI above), are linked in form and style to some of the west Norwegian *åkle* ('bedspread') and *rutevev* ('square patterned weaving') tapestries, made with the warp-weighted loom. The Finnish rugs, however, have a different and, to some extent, older decorative vocabulary: the wall-knot and swastika are motifs known from textiles in the Oseberg ship burial (9th century; Oslo, U. Oldsaksaml.), in which individual motifs float freely between the processional figures. The west Norwegian *rutevev* are akin to the Finnish rugs, although the technique is different and there is a wider range of motifs. *Ryijy*s, which developed most fully in the late Baroque period, are considered among the finest products of Finnish vernacular art. Although they differ slightly from west Norwegian and Swedish textiles in their combinations of motifs, it would appear that in their medieval form they represent an influence from the other Nordic lands. In the 16th century such bedspreads were used in town houses and on the larger farms, while folk production started first in west Finland and later in Ostrobothnia. The most distinctive *ryijy*s, by virtue of their strong, clearly defined forms and colours, come from the Satakunta and Häme areas (e.g. Helsinki, N. Mus.; Tampere, Häme Mus.).

Geometric motifs with an apparent symbolic meaning may be traced to prehistory. The pentagram and swastika, for example, endured as protective motifs until more recently. The latter, originally probably a sun symbol, also obtained a symbolic meaning in the medieval Church, representing Christ and the four Evangelists. Geometric wood-carving designs against a Gothic background often take the form of skilfully executed rosettes. The oldest wooden objects were unpainted and covered with carved decoration. Decorative painting as such, with typical Renaissance and Baroque flower motifs, began at the end of the 18th century; colour was used sparingly at first in domestic interiors. In inland areas, the most elaborate decorative painting in the 19th century appeared on the women's headdress caskets for churchgoing.

Collecting boxes for the poor, known as 'pauper sculptures', were placed outside churches in many central Finnish country towns. The custom pre-dated the Reformation, and after the 1530s, when the representation of saints was forbidden, these figures were legitimized with the names of Lazarus or the blind beggar Bartimaeus. Most were made to standard forms, intended to inspire charity, such as the invalid with a wooden leg, but the figures have an expressive intensity that grants them an interest beyond their status as folk art.

The last great florescence of Finnish wood-carving, decorative painting and weaving occurred in the first half of the 19th century. *Ryijy* weaving and the wearing of traditional dress survived in scattered areas until the early 20th century, when the production of household goods and other forms of handicraft was systematically revived. Finnish home craftwork is extensive and well organized. Textile design seems to have a fresher relation to the brightly coloured forms of vernacular art than its counterparts in Sweden and Norway, which remain more subservient to established interpretations of tradition.

BIBLIOGRAPHY

Y. Heikel: *Allmogekonst i det svenska Finland* [Peasant art in Swedish Finland] (Helsinki, 1934)

I. Rácz and N. Valonen: *Suomen kansantaiteen aarteita* [Treasures of Finnish folk art] (Helsinki, 1963; Eng. trans., 1969)

N. Valonen: 'Folkkonsten i Finland' [Folk art in Finland], *Nordisk folkkonst* [Nordic folk art], ed. S. Svensson (Lund, 1972), pp. 58–76

R. Pylkkänen: *The Use and Traditions of Medieval Rugs and Coverlets in Finland* (Helsinki, 1974)

P. Sihvo: *Tradition und Volkskunst in Finnland* (Helsinki, 1978)

M. Leppo: *Vaivasukot: Finnish Pauper-sculptures* (Helsinki, 1980)

NILS GEORG BREKKE

XIII. Patronage, collecting and dealing.

While Finland was under Swedish rule (until 1809), patronage of the arts was very limited, as the wealthy aristocracy was very much orientated towards Stockholm; most aspiring artists also went to study in Stockholm, and many subsequently settled there. A few collections of art were assembled during this period, however. At one time it was thought that such collections, particularly in the 17th century, consisted almost exclusively of portraits, but research in the late 20th century revealed that some manors and castles, such as the residence of the Creutz family at Pernaja (Swed. Pernå), contained broader collections of art. Towards the end of the period of Swedish rule, various Finnish government officials also acquired important collections of Swedish and central European paintings.

In the 19th century, the awakening nationalist movement highlighted the need for an active artistic life in Finland to promote a sense of cultural identity. As a result, in 1846 the Finnish Art Association (Suomen Taideyhdistys) was founded in Helsinki (Swed. Helsingfors). The Association initiated a collection and organized exhibitions of Finnish art as well as giving grants to students and artists. From 1863 the Association was partly funded by the State. Collecting also became more widespread during the 19th century, and exhibitions in Helsinki and Turku (Swed. Åbo) were largely based on private collections. The notable collection of paintings formed by O. W. Klinckowstrom (1778–1850) later became the basis of the Finnish Art Association, while other notable collectors in Helsinki included F. Cygnaeus, A. Mannerheim and C. J. Walleen; outside the capital notable figures included N. H. Pinello in Turku and L. de Nicolay in Viipuri (Swed. Viborg). Private collectors also played a decisive part in the expansion of the Athenaeum Art Museum in the late 19th century through donations; notable figures in this respect include Viktor Hoving (1846–1976) and H. F. Antell (1847–93), whose collections (donated in 1878 and 1893 respectively) included Finnish paintings and works by contemporary French artists.

In the late 19th century and the early 20th, among individual patrons Gustaf Adolf Serlachius (1830–1901) and his nephew Gösta Serlachius (1876–1942) both supported Akseli Gallen-Kallela; Gösta Serlachius also patronized the sculptors Emil Wikström and Hannes Autere and acted as Helene Schjerfbeck's dealer. In 1933 he established the Serlachius Art Foundation. Other significant private collectors in the early 20th century included Paul Sinebrychoff (1859–1917), Autere and Hjalmar Linder (1862–1921), who primarily collected Old Masters during the 1920s, and Karl Hedman (1864–1931), who bought Finnish and other European paintings to display at the Pohjanmaan Museo in Vaasa (Swed. Vasa). The brothers Ernst Dahlström (1846–1924) and Magnus

Dahlström (1859–1924) in Turku also collected art and helped finance the building of Turku Art Museum (Turun Taidemuseo) in 1904, while Amos Anderson (1878–1961), together with Salomo Wuorio (1857–1938) and Gösta Serlachius, funded the building of the Art Exhibition Hall (Taidehalli) in Helsinki as well as founding the Amos Anderson Museum of Art, which was opened in 1965 (*see* §XIV below). In the early 20th century there was also a marked increase in gallery activity, particularly during the economic boom at the time of World War I. Notable dealers of this period include Sven Strindberg, Leonard Bäcksbacka and Ivar Hörhammer, but the most renowned figure was Gösta Stenman (1888–1947), whose interests ranged from Old Masters to radical modern art and who acted as an adviser to Karl Hedman. Stenman was particularly important in supporting the work of Helene Schjerfbeck, acting as the artist's agent for many years.

In the public domain, attempts were made gradually to develop Finland's artistic organizations once independence had been achieved. In 1939 the Finnish Art Association's drawing school, art collections and foundations were merged to become the independent Finnish Academy of Art (Suomen Taideakatemian Säätiö), which received direct government funding. The Academy not only supported the Athenaeum Art Museum, which was merged with the Finnish National Gallery in 1990 (*see* §XIV below), but also funded a school, which later became the Academy of Fine Arts (Kuvataideakatemia), as well as providing grants to artists and funding acquisitions. Art administration was reformed in 1967, when the Arts Council of Finland was founded, along with committees overseeing different art forms. The State Art Committee also purchased works of art for public buildings. Private individuals remained important in the development of the arts. During the 1980s collecting expanded, partly as a means of investment, while the number of galleries also increased dramatically, with a particular focus on contemporary art.

BIBLIOGRAPHY

A. Lindström: *Paul ja Fanny Sinebrychoffin taidekokoelmat* [The art collections of Paul and Fanny Sinebrychoff] (Helsinki, 1974)

B. von Bonsdorff: 'Amos Andersons mecenatskap och hans museer' [Amos Anderson's patronage and his museum], *Ksthist. Tidskr.*, lvii/3–4 (1988), pp. 124–8

B. Nummelin: 'Bröderna Dahlström: Åbos konstmecenater' [The Dahlström brothers: Art patrons in Åbo], *Ksthist. Tidskr.*, lvii/3–4 (1988), pp. 129–32

J. Ervamaa: 'Kuvataide autonomian ajalla' [The visual arts during the period of autonomy], *Ars: Suomen taide* [Ars: the art of Finland], ed. S. Sarajas-Korte, iii (Helsinki, 1989), pp. 74–103

B. Arell: 'Helene Schjerfbeck and her Art Dealer Gösta Serlachius', *Helene Schjerfbeck* (exh. cat., ed. L. Ahtola-Moorhouse; Helsinki, N.G., 1992), pp. 91–103

TIMO KEINÄNEN, MARJA SUPINEN

XIV. Museums, libraries and photographic collections.

The central institution for museums of cultural history in Finland is the National Board of Antiquities (Museovirasto), which administers the National Museum of Finland (Suomen Kansallismuseo) in Helsinki (Swed. Helsingfors). The Board is responsible for the preservation of ancient monuments and for all archaeological excavations in the country, as well as for the care of historical buildings.

The National Museum was conceived in 1916 after various state-owned and private cultural history collections, formed in the latter half of the 19th century, were gathered together in one building. The Museum also has important non-European collections, for instance from the Finno-Ugrian culture in Siberia, from Alaska and from the Mesa Verde culture in Colorado, USA. The principal art museum in Finland is the Athenaeum Art Museum (Ateneumin Taidemuseo) in Helsinki, which from 1990 was incorporated with the Finnish National Gallery (Valtion Taidemuseo). The collections were begun as early as 1849 and focus principally on Finnish art from the 18th century onwards; there are also significant collections of foreign art, housed separately in the Museum of Foreign Art (Ulkomaisen Taiteen Museo), and of contemporary art, housed in the Museum of Contemporary Art (Nykytaiteen Museo), both of which are also administered by the National Gallery. From 1979 the state began to build up a system aimed at providing 15 regional art museums throughout the country, and from 1989 larger museums maintained by local authorities and foundations received a statutory state grant.

Many museums have benefited from donations from private collectors (*see* §XIII above), and in some cases museums have been founded on the basis of private collections or financial support. The Serlachius Art Foundation, for example, established by Gösta Serlachius (1876–1942) in 1933, supports the Serlachius Art Museum (Gösta Serlachius Taidemuseo) in Mänttä, and the Amos Anderson Museum of Art (Amos Andersonin Taidemuseo) in Helsinki is also named after its founder, while the Sara Hildén Art Museum (Sara Hildénin Taidemuseo) in Tampere (Swed. Tammerfors) was opened in 1979 with an extensive collection of contemporary Finnish and foreign art donated by the Sara Hildén Foundation.

There are *c*. 30 art libraries in Finland, most of them in art museums and educational institutions. The Finnish National Gallery houses the Central Art Archives, which contain important collections of photographs (50,000 colour transparencies and 30,000 black-and-white photographs); the Gallery's library also contains 32,000 books and exhibition catalogues. The best-organized art library is at the University of Industrial Arts (Taideteollinen Korkeakoulu) in Helsinki, with collections including over 30,000 printed documents, 300 periodical titles and 21,000 transparencies, while the most important architectural library, at the Museum of Finnish Architecture (Suomen Rakennustaiteen Museo) in Helsinki, has more than 25,000 books and catalogues and an archive containing 25,000 slides and 70,000 prints. There are more than 200,000 documents in the Museum's collection of original architectural drawings. Also noteworthy are the libraries of the departments of history of art at Helsinki University, the Åbo Akademi in Turku (Swed. Åbo) and Jyväskylä University.

BIBLIOGRAPHY

A. T. Huovinen, ed.: *Finnish Museums* (Helsinki, 1979)

Suomen tieteellisten kirjastojen opas/Vetenskapliga bibliotek i Finland [Guide to research libraries and information services in Finland] (Helsinki, rev. 8/1989) [with inf. key and names of libs in Eng.]

Nordiska konstbibliotek/Pohjoismaisia taidekirjastoja [Nordic art libraries] (Helsinki, 1991) [with inf. key in Eng.]

C. J. GARDBERG, KARI VÄHÄPASSI

XV. Historiography.

While antiquarianism and descriptions of monuments appeared in Finland from the 17th century, art historiography only truly began in the 19th century in connection with romantic antiquarianism. Medieval castles and churches were studied from the 1850s, while the study of medieval paintings was initiated by Emil Nervander (1840–1914). The study of more recent art was pioneered by Carl Gustav Estlander (1847–1910), whose history of modern art was published in 1867, while Eliel Aspelin (1847–1917) wrote monographs and published the first history of Finnish art (1891). The first major figure in Finnish art historiography, however, was Johan Jakob Tikkanen (1857–1930), whose study (1889) of the mosaics of the basilica of S Marco, Venice, brought him international fame. In 1897 he was appointed to the first (albeit initially temporary) professorship of art history at Helsinki (Swed. Helsingfors) University, an appointment that was made permanent in 1919. His most eminent successor was Lars Pettersson (1918–93), who concentrated on the study of Finnish wooden churches and stressed the objectivity of scholarly practice.

In 1926 another major history of Finnish art was edited by the critic Ludvig Wennervirta (1882–1959), and increased interest in the subject brought about the establishment of a new department of art history at the Åbo Akademi in Turku (Swed. Åbo). Lars-Ivar Ringbom (1901–71), who taught there from 1925 to 1968, was succeeded by his son Sixten Ringbom (1935–92), an internationally renowned scholar whose studies included 14th-century devotional images and Nordic stone architecture of c. 1900. Since 1967 and 1986, respectively, departments of art history at the universities of Jyväskylä and Turku have contributed to the study of art in Finland. A major new contribution was made to Finnish art historiography of the late 20th century by the six-volume history of Finnish art Ars: Suomen taide ('Ars: the art of Finland', 1987–90), which was edited by Salme Sarajas-Korte (b 1925), and to which most notable Finnish art historians contributed. Contemporary Finnish art history has made use of most of the modern theoretical approaches including iconography, history of ideas, social history and women's studies.

BIBLIOGRAPHY

C. G. Estlander: De bildande konsternas historia från slutet av adertonde århundradet till 1867 [History of the fine arts from the end of the 18th century to 1867] (Stockholm, 1867)

E. Aspelin: Suomalaisen taiteen historia pääpiirteissään [The principles of Finnish art history] (Helsinki, 1891)

L. Wennervirta, ed.: Finlands konst från förhistorisk tid till våra dagar [Finland's art from prehistoric times to the present day] (Helsinki, 1927)

S. Ringbom: Art History in Finland before 1920 (Helsinki, 1986)

AIMO REITALA

Finlay, Ian Hamilton (b Nassau, Bahamas, 28 Oct 1925). Scottish sculptor, graphic artist and poet. Brought up in Scotland, he briefly attended Glasgow School of Art and first made his reputation as a writer, publishing short stories and plays in the 1950s. In 1961 he founded the Wild Hawthorn Press with Jessie McGuffie and within a few years had established himself internationally as Britain's foremost concrete poet (see CONCRETE POETRY).

His publications also played an important role in the initial dissemination of his work as a visual artist. As a sculptor, he has worked collaboratively in a wide range of materials, having his designs executed as stone-carvings, as constructed objects and even in the form of neon lighting.

In 1966 Finlay and his wife, Sue, moved to the hillside farm of Stonypath, south-west of Edinburgh, and began to transform the surrounding acres into a unique garden, which he named Little Sparta. He revived the traditional notion of the poet's garden, arranging ponds, trees and vegetation to provide a responsive environment for sundials, inscriptions, columns and garden temples. As the proponent of a rigorous classicism and as the defender of Little Sparta against the intrusions of local bureaucracy, he insisted on the role of the artist as a moralist who comments sharply on cultural affairs. The esteem won by Finlay's artistic stance and style is attested by many important large-scale projects undertaken throughout the world. The 'Sacred Grove', created between 1980 and 1982 at the heart of the Kröller-Müller Sculpture Park, Otterlo, is one of the most outstanding examples of Finlay's work outside Little Sparta.

BIBLIOGRAPHY

Ian Hamilton Finlay (exh. cat., ACGB, 1977)

S. Bann: 'A Description of Stonypath', J. Gdn Hist., i/2 (1981), pp. 113–44

Y. Abrioux: Ian Hamilton Finlay: A Visual Primer (Edinburgh, 1985) [illustrated selection of work]

STEPHEN BANN

Finnberg, Gustaf [Kustaa] **Wilhelm** (b Parainen, 21 Nov 1784; d Stockholm, 28 June 1833). Finnish painter. He passed the Handicraft Painters Guild apprentice examination in Turku in 1805. He spent the years 1806 to 1820 in Stockholm, where he studied at the Konstakademi (1806–8 and 1810–14), and where he had the opportunity to study the work of Rembrandt. He was also influenced by the Romantic tendencies of later 18th-century English art, through the mediation of two Swedish artists who had studied in England and subsequently taught at the Royal School of Art: the portrait painter Carl Fredrik von Breda and the landscape painter Elias Martin. Finnberg hoped for a career as a history painter, but most of the works he produced in Stockholm were the portraits with which he made his living. Finnberg's portraits, for example Marie Sophie Aminoff (c. 1822; Finland, priv. col., see 1984 exh. cat., p. 37), are striking for their penetrating analysis of facial expression as a record of the sitter's character. Finnberg also painted miniatures, such as Portrait of a Lady (watercolour, 1810s; Uddevalla, Bohusläns Mus.), and city- and landscapes, such as Arsenalsgatan (before 1825; Stockholm, priv. col., see 1984 exh. cat., p. 24), dating from before 1825.

Finnberg returned to Turku at the beginning of the 1820s and worked there and in the aristocratic mansions and churches of the surrounding countryside until 1827. The only surviving example of his history painting is a series of 13 scenes depicting Christ and the Apostles (1822; Kemiö Church, nr Turku). In its emotional content and depth of colour it is an excellent example of the power of Finnberg's vision and reveals the impact of the works by Rembrandt that Finnberg had seen earlier. Finnberg was above all a colourist, and his rich and expressive painting style was unusual at that time, particularly in Scandinavia.

Finnberg's career in Finland came to an end when his studio and all the work in it was destroyed in the fire of 1827 that almost completely engulfed Turku. He moved immediately afterwards to Stockholm, where he spent the last six years of his life working in reduced circumstances, though still producing such fine portraits as that of *Maria Elizabeth Lundgren* (1828; Göteborg, Kstmus.).

BIBLIOGRAPHY

L. Wennervirta: *Kustaa Wilhelm Finnberg: Suomen taiteen uranuurtajia* [Kustaa Wilhelm Finnberg: a pioneer of Finnish art] (Porvoo, 1943), pp. 95–260

Gustaf Wilhelm Finnberg: 200-vuotismuistonäyttely [Gustaf Wilhelm Finnberg: 200th anniversary exhibition] (exh. cat., ed. L. Peltola and S. Sinisalo; Helsinki, Sinebrychoff A. Col., 1984)

S. Sinisalo: *Varhaista romantiikkaa: G. W. Finnberg* [Early romanticism in Finland: G. W. Finnberg], A. Suom. Taide, iii (1989), pp. 54–7, 64–70

SOILI SINISALO

Finoglia [Finoglio], **Paolo Domenico** (*b* Orta di Atella or Naples, *c.* 1590; *d* Conversano, 1645). Italian painter. He signed himself *Neapolitanus* and probably trained in Naples under the late Mannerist painter Ippolito Borghese (*d* 1627). Borghese's influence, though lasting, was not as strong as that of Caravaggio, whose art Finoglia came to admire. His work before 1626 is exemplified by the ten lunettes representing the *Founders of Religious Orders* in the Sala Capitolare (1620–*c.* 1626) of the Certosa di S Martino, Naples, which demonstrate his accomplished blending of late Mannerist and Caravaggesque styles. The *Circumcision* (1626), also in the Sala Capitolare, reveals the strong influence of Battistello Caracciolo, as does Finoglia's first important work in fresco, the decoration of the chapel of S Martino in the Certosa di S Martino with scenes from the *Life of St Martin* (*c.* 1632), which were provided to accompany Caracciolo's altarpiece of *St Martin* (1622–6) already in the chapel. Caracciolo's influence was lasting, observable later in the *Baptism of St Celsus* (*c.* 1635; Pozzuoli Cathedral). The precious late Mannerist rendering of details, combined with Caravaggesque effects of light, is seen again in the various versions of the *Immaculate Conception* (1629–30; Naples, S Lorenzo Maggiore; Airola, Annunziata; Montesarchio, S Francesco; Lille, Mus. B.-A.) and also in the *Virgin with SS Margaret, Bernard and Anthony of Padua* (1634; Naples, SS Bernardo e Margherita a Fonseca), the *Bride of the Sacred Canticles* and the *Annunciation* (both Airola, Annunziata).

During this period Finoglia was also working for rich private clients; he acted as a copyist and art dealer in association with Tommaso della Vigna and Tiberio Mazzucco, and he painted mythological scenes for the Cáson de Buen Retiro in Madrid. His most important aristocratic patron was Giangirolamo II Acquaviva d'Aragona, Conte di Conversano and a landowner in one of the richest provinces of Naples. It was probably on his invitation, *c.* 1635, that Finoglia moved to Apulia, where he worked until his death in Conversano and Monopoli, while maintaining constant links with Neapolitan artistic life. His work for Acquaviva included the cycle of the *Ten Scenes from the 'Gerusalemme liberata'* (*c.* 1635–45; Conversano, Mus. Civ.), one of the most important 17th-century

pictorial interpretations of Torquato Tasso's poem, commissioned for Acquaviva's castle at Conversano. Finoglia also decorated the church of SS Cosma e Damiano, founded in Conversano in 1635 by Acquaviva and his wife, Isabella Filomarino. Finoglia's signed works there are the *St Dominic*, the *Baptism of Valerian* and the *Martyrdom of St Januarius*. These, like the *Baptism of St Celsus* in Pozzuoli Cathedral, show the influence of Agostino Beltrano and Artemesia Gentileschi. Other works, such as the *Miracle of St Anthony* and the *Virgin with St Rose of Viterbo*, were obviously done with the help of assistants. Finoglia planned the fresco decoration for the ceiling of the church, and also for the ceiling of the Conte's nuptial chamber, but these projects were cut short by the imprisonment of his patron on political grounds in 1643. Finoglia nonetheless continued to work in Conversano, for example on the *SS Benedict and Blaise* for the monastery of S Benedetto, and in Monópoli, where he painted a *Virgin with SS Eligius and Tryphon*, for the church of S Angelo.

After Finoglia's death many unfinished commissions were completed by his followers, including most notably the unknown artist whose style has been identified in the *Virgin with St Rose of Viterbo* and in small lateral canvases in the chapels and some parts of the vault of SS Cosma e Damiano. The same hand can be seen in the *Annunciation* (Conversano, S Maria all' Isola), in the *Holy Family* and the *Virgin with SS Roch and Sebastian* (Conversano, church of the Paolotti), and in the *Immaculate Conception* (Tricase, S Maria della Serra). The style of these works suggests a possible connection with Francesco Guarino and other painters in the Neapolitan tradition who were working in Apulia at that time.

BIBLIOGRAPHY

Thieme–Becker

B. de Dominici: *Vite* (1742–5), iii, pp. 115–16

G. A. Galante: *Guida sacra della città di Napoli* (Naples, 1872); ed. N. Spinosa and others (Naples, 1985), pp. 101, 115, 124, 153, 157, 242, 265, 272, 274, 281–2, 284, 287–8

A. de Rinaldis: *La pittura del seicento nell'Italia meridionale* (Verona, 1929), pp. 24–5, pls 30–31

F. Marangelli: 'Paolo Finoglio attraverso i documenti', *Archv Stor. Pugl.*, i–iv (1967), pp. 195–210

R. Causa: *La pittura del seicento a Napoli dal naturalismo al barocco* (1972), v of *Storia di Napoli* (Cava dei Tirreni, 1967–78), pp. 934–6, 977

Painting in Naples, 1606–1705: From Caravaggio to Giordano (exh. cat., ed. C. Whitfield and J. Martineau; Naples, Capodimonte; London, RA; Washington, DC, N.G.A.; 1982–3), pp. 157–60

Civiltà del seicento a Napoli, 2 vols (exh. cat., ed. S. Cassani; Naples, Capodimonte, 1984), i, pp. 139–42, 272–5

Pintura napolitana de Caravaggio a Giordano (exh. cat., ed. A. E. Pérez Sánchez; Madrid, Pal. Villahermosa, 1985), pp. 136–41

RICCARDO LATTUADA

Finot, Louis (*b* Bar-sur-Aube, 10 July 1864; *d* Toulon, 16 May 1935). French art historian and archaeologist. He became interested in the history of India and in Sanskrit literature while working at the Bibliothèque Nationale in Paris, and this led to his first publication, *Lapidaires indiens*. In 1898 he became Director of the new Mission Archéologique of Indochina in Saigon, later known as the Ecole Française d'Extrême-Orient. In the following years he travelled throughout Indochina, organizing an inventory of historical monuments, establishing a library and a museum for the archaeological mission at Saigon, which was later transferred to Hanoi, and creating the *Bulletin de l'Ecole Française d'Extrême-Orient* in 1901. In 1904 he was appointed to a chair of the Collège de France and to the Ecole de Paris. He resumed directorship of the Ecole Française d'Extrême-Orient in 1930 for 17 years, and his name was given to the school's archaeological museum in Hanoi. His publications included important work on the epigraphy of Indochina.

WRITINGS
Lapidaires indiens (Paris, 1895)
Notes d'épigraphie indochinoise (Hanoi, 1916)

BIBLIOGRAPHY
H. Maspero: Obituary, *Rev. A. Asiat.*, ix (1935), pp. 121–2

Finsler, Hans (*b* Zurich, 7 Dec 1891; *d* Zurich, 1972). German photographer and teacher. He studied architecture at the Technische Hochschule in Munich (1909–14), later studying art history (1914–18). In 1922 he became librarian at the Kunstgewerbeschule in Halle, where he also taught art history. While there he developed his 'object photography', teaching a class in it from 1927 to 1932. From this period date photographs such as *Ceramic Tubing* (*c.* 1929; see exh. cat., p. 84). In 1932 he became head of the photography department at the Kunstgewerbeschule in Zurich, where he remained until 1958, and where he was an important influence on René Burri and Werner Bischof.

WRITINGS
Mein Weg zur Photographie (Zurich, 1971)

BIBLIOGRAPHY
Avant Garde Photography in Germany, 1919–1939 (exh. cat., ed. V. D. Coke; San Francisco, CA, Mus. A., 1980–81), p. 84

ERIKA BILLETER

Finson, Louis [Finsonius, Ludovicus] (*b* Bruges, *c.* 1580; *d* Amsterdam, 1617). Flemish painter. He was the son of the painter Jacques Fynson (*d* before 1609) and trained in his father's studio in Bruges; the influence of Netherlandish Mannerism is strong in his work. At some time early in the 17th century he travelled to Italy; he was certainly in Naples by 1608 and may also have previously spent some time in Rome. It is not certain whether he was a pupil of Caravaggio, but he is known to have copied many of Caravaggio's works and to have owned at least two of his paintings, one of which was the *Madonna of the Rosary* (Vienna, Ksthist. Mus.), which Finson bought with Abraham Vinck (1580–1621), perhaps as early as 1607. After 1612 Finson visited Spain and then France, arriving in Marseille early in 1613. He was already a painter of considerable repute and continued to enjoy much success in Provence and to command large sums for his paintings. From Marseille he was called to Aix-en-Provence by Nicolas-Claude Fabri de Peiresc, who commissioned from him a series of portraits and altarpieces. For the cathedral of St Sauveur in Aix, Finson executed the *Incredulity of St Thomas* (*in situ*). He was later commissioned to paint an altarpiece for the main altar of St Trophime in Arles. In 1614 Finson travelled to Montpellier and then to Paris; arriving there early in 1615, he painted a *Circumcision* (version, Paris, St Nicolas-des-Champs). He returned to the Netherlands the following July.

Finson's art is Italianized, yet it retains many elements of his Flemish training. He was instrumental in introducing Caravaggism to Provence at an early date; his works such as *St Mary Magdalene in Ecstasy* (Marseille, Mus. B.-A.), which is a copy of a Caravaggio painting, were themselves much copied. His own compositions display all the realism, tragic monumentality and powerful chiaroscuro effects of Caravaggesque work, though the elements of Flemish Mannerism set him apart from the main circle of Caravaggist painters.

BIBLIOGRAPHY
La Peinture en Provence au XVIIe siècle (exh. cat., ed. P. de Chennevières-Pointel; Marseille, Mus. B.-A., 1978), pp. 66–74
B. Nicolson: *The International Caravaggesque Movement* (London, 1979), pp. 47–8
M. Marini: 'La Giuditta del 1607: Un contributo a Caravaggio e a Louis Finson', *Ultimo Caravaggio e la cultura artistica a Napoli, in Sicilia e a Malta*, ed. M. Calvesi (Syracuse, 1987), pp. 59–80

Fiocco, Giuseppe (*b* Giacciano, nr Rovigo, 16 Nov 1884; *d* Padua, 6 Oct 1971). Italian art historian and teacher. He was the first historian, in the modern sense, of Venetian art, although his interests extended to all aspects of European art, including Impressionism and contemporary art. He took his degree in literature at the University of Bologna and then specialized in the history of art at the Scuola di Specializzazione di Adolfo Venturi in Rome. In 1926 he held the chair of art history at the University of Florence and in 1929 at the University of Padua, where he remained until 1956 and founded a flourishing centre of scholarship. As Director, from 1954–71, of the Fondazione Giorgio Cini Istituto di Storia dell'Arte in Venice, he gave the institution an international reputation. His scholarly output was vast, in books and articles in specialist journals, and in 1947 he was president of the editorial board of *Arte veneta*. He wrote, among other things, on the relationship between the Veneto and Tuscany in the Renaissance and on Mantegna, Palladio, Giorgione and Veronese. He contributed to the discovery of a series of minor painters, and also to the reassessment of such artists as Francesco Guardi. He was also interested in architecture, to which he brought all the vitality and modernity of his taste, and worked on the origins of Venetian art, which he identified in the culture of Palaeo-Christian Ravenna.

WRITINGS
Francesco Guardi (Florence, 1923)
L'arte di Andrea Mantegna (Bologna, 1927, 2/1959)
Paolo Veronese (Bologna, 1928, 2/1934)
Le influenze bizantine in Italia (Milan, 1929)
Giorgione (Bergamo, 1941, 2/1948)
Francesco Guardi: L'angelo Raffaele (Turin, 1958)

BIBLIOGRAPHY
R. Pallucchini: 'G. Fiocco', *A. Ven.*, xxv (1971), pp. 300–01
A. Chastel and others: 'In memoria di G. Fiocco', *Saggi & Mem. Stor. A.*, 8 (1972), pp. 9–21 [incl. complete list of writings]

FRANCO BERNABEI

Fioravanti [di Fieravanti], **Aristotele** [Aristotile da Bologna] (*b* Bologna, 1415–20; *d* Moscow, 1485–6). Italian engineer and architect, active also in Russia. The son of a local mason, Fieravante di Ridolfo (*c.* 1390–1430), Aristotele initially worked as a goldsmith. He secured notoriety as an engineer in 1455 first for transporting the campanile known as the Torre della Mangione (destr. 1825) of S

Maria del Tempio, Bologna, to a new site 18 m away, then for straightening the leaning campanile (destr. 18th century) of S Biagio, Cento, and finally for straightening the leaning campanile of S Angelo, Venice, which collapsed directly afterwards. In 1458 he moved with his family from Bologna to Milan, where he entered the service of Francesco I Sforza, Duke of Milan. After being sent to Mantua in 1459 to straighten another tower, he worked for the Duke as a hydraulic engineer, repairing a canal near Parma (from 1459) and constructing others near Cremona (from 1460) as well as one (from 1462) from the River Crostolo (between Parma and Reggio Emilia). He also worked as a military engineer inspecting fortifications, in which capacity he is mentioned in Filarete's *Trattato di architettura* (1461–4). Fioravanti returned to Bologna in 1464, and in the following year he was appointed the city architect and engineer. In 1467 he was invited by Matthias Corvinus to Hungary to prepare defences against the Turks, and he is reputed to have built a bridge over the Danube. In 1471 he visited Rome in order to transport the Vatican obelisk to the square in front of Old St Peter's, a task abandoned almost immediately at Pope Paul II's death. (The project was eventually undertaken by Domenico Fontana in 1586.)

Fioravanti returned to Bologna, where he was almost certainly involved in the design of the new façade of the Palazzo del Podestà. A model is said to have been prepared in 1472, but execution was delayed until 1484–94 and conducted by Francesco Fucci di Dozza (*fl* 1478–94) and Marsilio Infrangipani (*fl* 1469–1517). The façade, one of the most innovative and overtly *all'antica* designs of the 15th century, faces S Petronio and dominates Bologna's main square. It is organized as two storeys: a massive ground storey arcade rusticated with faceted masonry (each block embellished with a rosette) and articulated with Corinthian half columns, and an upper storey set back to allow for a balcony arranged with round-arched windows and ornamental Corinthian pilasters. The immediate model for the façade, which recalls such imperial prototypes as the Colosseum, was undoubtedly the Benediction Loggia (early 1460s; destr.) in front of Old St Peter's, Rome, which was still under construction when Fioravanti was called to Rome in 1471.

In 1475 Fioravanti left his family in Bologna and moved to Moscow, where in 1475–9 he rebuilt the cathedral of the Dormition (Uspensky) in the Kremlin for Ivan III (see fig.). The cathedral was intended for major state ceremonies, including the coronation of the tsar. It had already been substantially reconstructed (from 1472) by local builders when in 1474 it was partly destroyed in an earthquake. Fioravanti began work afresh by replacing the previous foundations with new and much deeper ones, and he made every effort to ensure the building's structural stability, using specially hardened lightweight bricks and iron tie-rods for the vaults. The layout of the building was dictated by Russian tradition and was required to be modelled in particular on the cathedral of the Dormition (rebuilt 1185–9) in Vladimir-Suzdal'. It is organized as a four-bay nave and aisles, with groin vaults and a typical five-domed arrangement at the east end, which terminates in a row of chapels. The main innovations of the tall interior are in the omission of galleries in order to give an

Aristotele Fioravanti: cathedral of the Dormition, Moscow, view from the south-east, 1475–9

airy and uncluttered effect, in the uniformity of bay size in both nave and aisles and in the use at the west end of four cylindrical piers resembling columns, which were once capped with Corinthian capitals (defaced 17th century). The building's most conspicuous elevation, that facing south, was given an imposing but severe stone-faced façade divided into four equal arched bays by tall pilasters rising through a traditional band of blind arcades with ornamental colonnettes.

BIBLIOGRAPHY

L. Beltrami: *Vita di Aristotile da Bologna* (Bologna, 1912)
V. Snegiryov: *Aristotel' Fioravanti i perestroyka moskovskogo Kremlya* [Aristotele Fioravanti and the reconstruction of the Moscow Kremlin] (Moscow, 1935)
C. De Angelis and P. Nanelli: 'La facciata del Palazzo del Podestà a Bologna', *A. Lombarda*, 44–5 (1976), pp. 79–82
S. Tugnoli Pattaro: 'Le opere bolognesi di A. Fioravanti', *A. Lombarda*, 44–5 (1976), pp. 35–70

DAVID HEMSOLL

Fiore, Jacobello del. *See* JACOBELLO DEL FIORE.

Fiorentino, Francesco. *See* FRANCISCUS ITALUS.

Fiorentino, Niccolò di Giovanni. *See* NICCOLÒ DI GIOVANNI FIORENTINO.

Fiorentino, Pier Maria. *See* SERBALDI DA PESCIA, PIER MARIA.

Fiorentino, Rosso. *See* ROSSO FIORENTINO.

Fiorenzo di Lorenzo (di Cecco di Pascolo) (*b* Perugia, *c.* 1445; *d* Perugia, early Feb 1522). Italian painter and architect. The earliest reliable document to mention him is dated 20 May 1463, when he was appointed in place of his father, Lorenzo di Cecco, to vote for the Capitano del Popolo. Between 1463 and 1469 his name appears on the register of painters of Perugia. In 1470 he was treasurer of the painters' guild, and in 1472 he was elected its prior for November–December. On 9 December that year the Sylvestrine monks of S Maria Nuova, Perugia, commissioned him to paint a double-sided polyptych (Perugia, G.N. Umbria) for the main altar of their church; he did not complete it until 1493. From the tenor of the contract and the substantial sum agreed—225 ducats—it appears that Fiorenzo was then considered the best of the young painters working in Perugia. In 1476, while the plague was becoming increasingly rampant, he painted a fresco of the *Madonna of Mercy* (Perugia, G.N. Umbria; see fig.) for the hospital of S Egidio (destr.), Perugia. Originally signed and dated, the work is badly damaged but remains of fundamental importance for understanding the art of Fiorenzo's early maturity. While its subject is characteristic of local plague banners, its style is directly related to Florentine art of the same period, for example in its use of the perspective device of square paving stones. Other elements recall the ambience of the Rossellini brothers and Andrea del Verrocchio, especially the motif of the angels flying overhead.

In the following years Fiorenzo executed numerous works in Perugia. Evidently in very comfortable economic circumstances, he played an important role in the political and administrative life of the city. In 1487 he signed and dated the painted decoration of the wooden niche for S Francesco al Prato (Perugia, G.N. Umbria), which probably once held a statue of the saint. The lunette depicts the *Virgin and Child* surrounded by cherubim and two angels. On the lateral piers are *SS Peter and Paul*, and in small tondi in the predella are *St Bonaventure, St Anthony of Padua, St Bernardino* and *St Louis of Toulouse*. Various ornamental motifs, some in relief, appear inside the niche and on the side walls. Stylistically this work shows Fiorenzo's interest in the art of Antoniazzo Romano (in the monumentality of the poses) and also of Bernardino Pinturicchio; his own style is quite recognizable, however, through a certain dryness of the contour and through his fastidious manner of painting entirely with the tip of the brush, which suggests that he had close connections with the art of illumination.

The same characteristics can be seen in Fiorenzo's polyptych for S Maria Nuova, which departs considerably from the commission of 1472, eventually being executed between 1487 and 1493. For a fee of 130 florins, the new contract stipulated a single unified surface, with the *Virgin and Child* to be painted on the central panel, *St Peter, St Benedict, John the Evangelist* and the *Blessed Paolo Bigazzini* on the sides, the *Annunciation with Saints* on the pilasters and the *Eternal Father with Saints* in the cusps. This work confirms the stylistic tendencies apparent in the niche, but while forms reminiscent of Antoniazzo and echoes of the style of the so-called Master of the Gardner Annunciation (now identified as Piermatteo d'Amelia) prevail in the central part, the side panels—perhaps the last to be painted—show very clear signs of the influence of Pietro Perugino.

These three works, plus a frescoed *Crucifixion* for S Maria di Monteluce, Perugia, documented to 1491 but so heavily repainted as to be almost illegible, are all that can be reliably assigned to Fiorenzo. None of his other securely documented works survives, and several of the attributions to him remain unsubstantiated. Works that can be most reasonably assigned to him on the basis of stylistic comparisons include the *Virgin and Child with St Jerome* (Boston, MA, Isabella Stewart Gardner Mus.); a fresco of the *Crucifixion with Saints* (1492; Montelabbate, S Maria); a fresco of the *Virgin and Child and the Mystic Marriage of St Catherine* (1498; ex-S Giorgio dei Tessitori, Perugia; Perugia, G.N. Umbria); three panels depicting *SS Digna and Emerita, St Anthony Abbot* and *St Catherine* (Perugia, G.N. Umbria); *St Peter* (Hannover, Niedersächs. Landesmus.); the *Wounded Christ and the Chalice* (Perugia, Fratticciola Selvatica priv. col.); and *St Sebastian with a Donor* (Aix-en-Provence, Mus. Granet).

The *Virgin and Child* (Paris, Mus. Jacquemart-André), strongly reminiscent of Verrocchio and usually assigned to the young Perugino, may belong to Fiorenzo's career before 1476. Some of the *tavolette* depicting miracles of S Bernardino (1475; Perugia, G.N. Umbria), especially the scenes of the *Resurrection of the Stillborn Child* and the *Captain of Tornano Attacked by Cut-throats and Restored by the Saint*, show notable points of contact with the almost caricature-like figures in the step of the niche for S Francesco al Prato. The triptych of *Justice* (Perugia, G.N.

Fiorenzo di Lorenzo: *Madonna of Mercy*, detached fresco, 2.90×1.85 m, 1476 (Perugia, Galleria Nazionale dell'Umbria)

Umbria), painted for the confraternity of S Andrea, Perugia, has been reattributed, on documentary evidence, to Bartolomeo Caporali and Sante di Apollonio del Celandro (*d* 1486).

Fiorenzo's activity as an architect has been little studied. In 1490 he prepared a drawing (ex-Perugia, Osp. Misericordia) in two separate parts for the windows, festoons, cornices and fireplaces in the *piano nobile* of the building (now the Palazzo dell'Università Vecchia, Perugia), which a bull of Pope Sixtus IV designated as the seat of the *studium*. Two stonecutters, Mariotto di Pace and Bartoccio di Paolo, were engaged to execute the individual parts. In 1491 a payment to Fiorenzo was recorded for the design of letters carved into the architrave of the building's transomed, double-lighted windows. Fiorenzo therefore played a role in the planning of those stylistic details that characterize one of the most important Renaissance buildings in Perugia. From the study of these details considerable correspondences in taste emerge, not only with the *tavolette* of S Bernardino, but also with some contemporary palazzi in Pienza and Rome, for example the Palazzo Venezia. Another building in Perugia with the same type of window, the house owned by the Cavalieri di Malta at the end of Via dei Priori (now Via S Francesco), was restored in 1484.

Fiorenzo di Lorenzo was a figure of major importance in the panorama of Perugian art between 1470 and 1490. He strongly influenced the painting and manuscript illumination of the years just before Perugino's style acquired predominance. Research remains to be done on Fiorenzo's relationships with other artists of the time, notably Bartolomeo Caporali, Pietro di Galeotto di Ercolano, Sante di Apollonio, Ludovico di Angelo Mattioli (*fl* 1481–1522), Niccolò del Priore (*fl* 1470–1501) and Orlando Merlini (*fl* 1501–10). His brother Bernardino (*fl* 1484–1511) was also a painter and possibly also his collaborator.

BIBLIOGRAPHY

B. Orsini: *Guida al forestiere per l'augusta città di Perugia* (Perugia, 1784), p. 312
A. Mariotti: *Lettere pittoriche perugine* (Perugia, 1788), pp. 80–82, 210, 230
S. Siepi: *Descrizione topologica–istorica della città di Perugia* (Perugia, 1822), p. 792
C. F. von Rumohr: *Italienische Forschungen* (Berlin, 1827), pp. 320–24
M. Guardabassi: *Indice–guida dei monumenti pagani e cristiani riguardanti l'istoria e l'arte esistenti nella provincia dell'Umbria* (Perugia, 1872), pp. 216–29
G. B. Cavalcaselle and J. A. Crowe: *Storia della pittura in Italia*, ix (Florence, 1902), pp. 143–58
J. C. Graham: *The Problem of Fiorenzo di Lorenzo* (Rome, 1903)
S. Weber: *Fiorenzo di Lorenzo* (Strasbourg, 1904)
W. Bombe: *Geschichte der Peruginer Malerei* (Berlin, 1912), pp. 122–43
A. Venturi: *Storia*, vii/2 (Milan, 1913), pp. 567–85
U. Gnoli: *Pittori e miniatori dell'Umbria* (Spoleto, 1923), pp. 112–17
R. van Marle: *Italian Schools*, xiv (1933), pp. 122–43
F. Zeri: 'Il Maestro dell'Annunciazione Gardner', *Boll. A.*, xxxviii (1953), pp. 125–7, 233
F. Santi: *La Galleria Nazionale dell'Umbria: Dipinti, sculture ed oggetti dei secoli XV–XVI* (Rome, 1985), pp. 65–76
F. Todini: *La pittura umbra: Dal duecento al primo cinquecento* (Milan, 1989), i, pp. 67–9; ii, pp. 478–89
M. Bury: 'Bartolomeo Caporali: A New Document and its Implications', *Burl. Mag.*, cxxxii (1990), pp. 469–75

P. SCARPELLINI

Fiori, Mario dei. *See* MARIO DEI FIORI.

Fiorillo, Johann Dominicus (*b* Hamburg, 13 Oct 1748; *d* Göttingen, 10 Sept 1821). German painter and art historian. He trained as a painter at the academy in Bayreuth before continuing his education in Rome under Pompeo Batoni and Giuseppe Bottani from 1761 to 1765. He then worked in Bologna, becoming a member of the Accademia di Belle Arti in 1769, the year he returned to Germany. He was court painter in Brunswick from 1769 to 1781, after which he moved to Göttingen, where he taught drawing and executed the *Delivery of Briseis* (1783; Bremen, priv. col.). In 1785, he began his association with the Georg-August-Universität in Göttingen, where he was charged initially with the care of the Kupferstichkabinett; by 1796 he also ran the painting gallery. His research on these collections, his lectures and writings such as *Geschichte der zeichnenden Künste von ihrer Wiederaufblebung bis auf den neuesten Zeiten* influenced a generation of students, earning him the rank of Professor in 1813 and membership of the academies of Augsburg, Vienna, Munich, Kassel and Paris. Fiorillo's writing followed the tradition of Luigi Lanzi, emphasizing the compilation of information at the expense of interpretive synthesis. However, the breadth of his interests, the range of sources upon which he drew for his multi-volume histories and his critical approach to those sources proved inspirational for Count Karl Friedrich von Rumohr, August Kestner and Wilhelm Heinrich Wackenroder.

WRITINGS

Über die Groteske (Göttingen, 1791)
Geschichte der zeichnenden Künste von ihrer Wiederaufblebung bis auf den neuesten Zeiten, 5 vols (Göttingen, 1798–1808)
Geschichte der zeichnenden Künste in Deutschland und den Vereinigten Niederlanden, 4 vols (Hannover, 1815–20)

BIBLIOGRAPHY

ADB; *NDB*; Thieme–Becker
W. Waetzoldt: *Deutsche Kunsthistoriker* (Leipzig, 1921–4/*R* Berlin, 1965), i, pp. 287–92
H. Dilly: *Kunstgeschichte als Institution* (Frankfurt am Main, 1979), pp. 174–83

ROBERT E. McVAUGH

Fire-dog. *See under* FIREPLACE FURNISHINGS.

Firenze, Andrea da. *See* ANDREA DA FIRENZE (i) and (ii).

Firenze, Desiderio da. *See* DESIDERIO DA FIRENZE.

Firenze, Michele da. *See* MICHELE DA FIRENZE.

Fireplace furnishings. Hearth accessories comprising fire-backs, andirons (also called fire-dogs), log forks and tongs for feeding the fire, plus a pair of bellows and a curfew for controlling it. Fire-backs are heavy cast-iron plates that protect the rear of the fireplace. Early examples often display simple decorative motifs (*see* ENGLAND, fig. 84), but during the 17th century elaborate armorial compositions and allegorical scenes with neat floral borders became common. Anne of Cleves House Museum, Lewes, E. Sussex, contains a collection of backs cast in the Sussex Weald foundries.

Andirons or fire-dogs stand on the hearth-stone and are intended to support burning logs. They are made in pairs and consist of an ornamental front standard with a horizontal billet bar behind. Sturdy wrought- and cast-iron andirons with heraldic devices were common in medieval interiors, but from the early 17th century, brass ormolu and silver standards (examples at Ham House, Surrey, NT; Knole, Kent, NT) elaborately styled in the fashion of the day became popular. The most luxurious gilt-bronze andirons, ornamented with cupids, beasts, Chinamen, foliated and floral forms or fantastic animals symbolizing fire, such as dragons and salamanders, were made in the 18th century by such Parisian bronziers as Jacques Caffiéri, Philippe Caffiéri and Thomire (examples at Waddesdon Manor, Bucks, NT). As wood-burning fireplaces continued to be used in the USA well into the 19th century, many distinctive cast-brass and *paktong* (Chin.: artificial silver alloy of 20% nickel with brass) andirons of excellent quality were made, notably in Charleston, SC.

Bellows, used to blow up or fan a fire, were sometimes lavishly decorated with carving, marquetry, oriental japanning or penwork and even overlaid with silver, needlework or stumpwork. Standing bellows of box design, worked by a pump handle, and wheel-operated bellows were introduced as labour-saving contraptions in the early 19th century. A curfew is a hoodlike brass cover, often with repoussé decoration, that was placed over the embers on the hearth at night to make the fire safe. Most extant examples date from the late 17th century, as they were superseded by wire spark guards.

With the adoption of coal burning in England during the early 18th century, fire-dogs were replaced by grates. These were at first designed as free-standing baskets with a cast-iron backplate, cheeks, barred front and a pair of standards (similar to andirons). The usual material was wrought-iron, possibly with a brass apron and posts, but later bright steel and *paktong* grates became popular. After *c.* 1750 hob-grates, Bath or Venetian stoves and register grates, which were built into the fireplace opening and reduced smoke problems, became available. Contemporary furniture patternbooks by Chippendale and William Ince and John Mayhew (*c.* 1736–1811) feature designs for grates, while William and John Welldon's *The Smith's Right Hand* (1765) and William Glossop's *The Stove-Grate Maker's Assistant* (1771) contain numerous illustrations of modern grates.

Robert Adam and other leading Neo-classical architects renowned for creating unified room schemes naturally took a keen interest in chimney furniture, and Adam's drawings (London, Soane Mus.) include many delicate designs for grates. Chimney-pieces in the main reception rooms at houses where he worked, such as Mersham-le-Hatch, Kent, Osterley Park House, London (see fig.), Newby Hall, N. Yorks, and Croome Court, Hereford & Worcs, were intended to be impressive, with bright steel grates, *en suite* fenders, sets of fire-irons and elegant mantelpiece garnitures.

One of the most accomplished Neo-classical smiths who worked with Adam at Harewood House, W. Yorks, Newby Hall and Nostell Priory, W. Yorks, was Maurice Tobin (*d* 1773) of Leeds. He and his successor, John Rodgers, occasionally marked their work with a name stamp. During the 18th century fire-irons were supplied in sets consisting of a poker, shovel and tongs, possibly

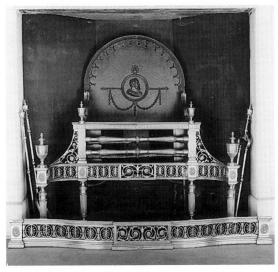

Fireplace furnishings comprising stove grate (w. 1.15 m), fender (w. 1.42 m) and fire-irons, *paktong* and cast-iron, designed by Robert Adam for the drawing-room at Osterley Park House, London, *c.* 1773 (London, Victoria and Albert Museum)

with a rook and hearth broom. They were normally kept propped up in a corner of the fireplace rather than, as earlier, suspended from hooks on the wall or provided with a stand, later known as a fireside companion. Coal was kept in a box or a metal coal-scuttle. In the 18th century these receptacles were brought into a room by a servant when the fire needed to be fed, but after about 1800 they remained by the hearth. Surviving japanned sheet-iron examples are of bucket or sarcophagus form with lids and sometimes liners; copper scuttles and wooden boxes became popular in the 19th century.

Chimney- or fire-boards were employed to close gloomy fireplace openings during the summer. They were both practical and decorative since by sealing off the space, soot and draughts were excluded; many were covered with wallpaper, painted to represent a vase of flowers, a grate or a decorative design related to the room scheme. Four splendid Neo-classical examples painted by Bagio Rebecca (1735–1808) in 1769 for Audley End, Essex, survive, and there is another important group at Osterley Park House.

Bills in country-house archives contain many payments to founders and smiths for chimney furniture, but few firms signed their work. Some of the most illustrious Regency designs were by George Bullock, while an anthology of plainer register stoves and grates was published in the trade catalogue of M. & G. Skidmore (1811; London, V&A). The Carron Iron Co. of Falkirk, Central, founded in 1759, was the most successful firm to mass-produce fire-grates and stoves. Its complete archive (Edinburgh, Scot. Record Office) documents its relationship with Adam and includes a number of manuscript designs; like the Coalbrookdale Iron Co., it sometimes marked its work. Falkirk Museum houses the entire collection of the former Carron Co. Museum, including many castings and trade catalogues. The firm continued to reproduce traditional patterns well into the 20th century; in fact, many foundries, notably Thomas Elsley & Co., London, produced high-quality copies of Georgian chimney furniture.

Mention should also be made of trivets, which support a pot or kettle near the fire. They generally have pierced brass tops and either stood on the hearth or were hung on the top bar of the grate. A cat is a six-armed stand of either turned wood or iron placed next to the fire to keep a plate of muffins or toast warm.

See also CHIMNEY-PIECE.

BIBLIOGRAPHY

R. Edwards: *Dictionary of English Furniture* (London, 1954)
H. Kauffman: *Early American Hand Irons and Other Fireplace Accessories* (New York, 1972)
G. de Bellaigue: *The James A. De Rothschild Collection at Waddesdon Manor* (London, 1974)
B. Rauchenburg: 'A School of Charleston, South Carolina Brass Andirons', *J. Early S. Dec. A.*, v (1979), pp. 26–75
The Fashionable Fireplace, 1660–1840 (exh. cat. by C. G. Gilbert and A. Wells-Cole, Leeds, Temple Newsam House, 1985)

CHRISTOPHER GILBERT

Firmian. Austrian family of patrons. One of the oldest Tyrolean noble families, they were based from 1473 to 1824 at Mezzocorona, near Trent (now in Italy), being hereditary marshals to the bishops of Trent from 1478. In 1526 they were raised to the imperial rank of Reichsfreiherr. The marriage of Franz Wilhelm von Firmian to Magdalena von Thun in 1678 advantageously allied them to another leading family of the region. Franz Alphons von Firmian, one of the sons of this marriage, took the Tyrol-born painter Paul Troger into the family's service when young and sent him on his artistic training in Venice. Franz Alphons became a Reichsgraf when this imperial title was conferred on the family in 1728. His brother Leopold Anton Eleutherius von Firmian (*b* Munich, 27 May 1679; *d* Salzburg, 22 Oct 1744) began his career as a page with Johann Ernst von THUN-HOHENSTEIN, Archbishop of Salzburg, having an education in Rome, and subsequently rose through various church appointments to become himself Archbishop of Salzburg in 1727. His rule here was overshadowed by his pointless expulsion of Protestants, forcing countless citizens of Salzburg to leave their homes in 1731–2, and it marked the end of distinguished archiepiscopal patronage in Salzburg. However, he brought in the Viennese court architect Antonio Galli-Bibiena to complete (1732) Schloss Klesheim, started by his predecessors to the designs of Johann Bernhard Fischer von Erlach, and also in Salzburg in 1732 built the Kapitelschwemme, modelled on the Trevi Fountain in Rome, with sculptures by Joseph Anton Pfaffinger (1684–1758). He later commissioned the building of Schloss Leopoldskron (1736), south of Salzburg, to the designs of the Benedictine architect Bernard Stuart. The Archbishop's court painter from 1728 was the Tyrolean Jacob Zanusi (1679–1742).

The Archbishop's nephew Franz Lactanz, Graf Firmian (*b* Trent, 1712; *d* Mezzocorona, 6 March 1786), was himself a painter and engraver (21 engravings in Innsbruck, Ubib.), trained by Paul Troger and enjoying the special support of his uncle. He housed his large art collection (destr. 19th century) in the Schloss Leopoldskron, which he had inherited. Franz Lactanz's brother Karl Joseph, Graf Firmian (*b* Mezzocorona, 6 Aug 1716; *d* Milan,

20 July 1782), received a comprehensive education in Innsbruck, Salzburg and Leiden and travelled at length in Italy and France before becoming a diplomat. He was Austrian ambassador in Naples in 1753 and imperial governor in Milan from 1759. Here he was able not only to administer reforms in Lombardy in the spirit of Emperor Joseph II but also to undertake many cultural activities such as helping to found the Brera library in Milan. An amateur painter like his brother, he gave special support to Johann Joachim Winckelmann and Angelica Kauffman and employed Martin Knoller as his court painter in Milan.

BIBLIOGRAPHY

C. von Wurzbach: *Biographisches Lexikon des Kaiserthums Oesterreich*, iv (Vienna, 1858), pp. 232–3
F. Martin: *Salzburgs Fürsten der Barockzeit* (Salzburg, 1952), pp. 177–97

JOHANNES RAMHARTER

Firmin-Didot, Ambroise. *See* DIDOT, (2).

First Gothic. *See* EARLY GOTHIC.

Firthaler [Firtaler; Viertaler; Virtaler; Virtler], **Barthlmä** [Bartholomä, Bartlme] (*fl c.* 1500–51). Austrian architect. He is thought to have been the son of Andre Firthaler of Innichen (now San Candido, South Tyrol), and he worked mainly in Tyrol and Carinthia. His earlier buildings, for example the castle chapel at Stein, Upper Carinthia (1505), still have simple star vaults, but in the following years his style was increasingly influenced by so-called *Astwerkgotik* motifs, which imitate branch and foliate forms. In the church built by Andre Firthaler at Wahlen (now Valle San Silvestro) in 1512, Barthlmä created a vault covered with flat, curving plaster ribs in the form of plant *rinceaux*. The ribs are no longer constructional, weight-bearing elements but have a purely decorative function. In the middle of each bay the ribs form a flower-like sexfoil, in the centre of which is an elaborate rosette instead of a boss. These sexfoil rib patterns are typical of Barthlmä's work and are found in the churches he built at Achornach (now Acereto; 1512–19), Prettau (now Predoi; 1524), St Martin at Ahrn (now San Martino, Valle Aurina) and Oberwielenbach (now Vila di Sopra; 1523), in the chapel of the auxiliary saints in the collegiate church of SS Candidus and Corbinian at Innichen (1524) and in St Michael at Lienz (vault 1531). The culmination of his artistic activity is represented by the churches of St Andreas, Laas (1515–35), Unsere Liebe Frau, Kötschach (1514–42), and Maria-Schnee at Maria Luggau (1515–44; only the tower survives). The thin plaster ribs spread plantlike over the whole vault, resembling fine, densely woven basketwork. In his last work, the Rainkirche in Welsberg (now Monguelfo; 1551), he further loosened the configurations of ribs, covering the vault with an ivy-like network of gnarled *rinceaux*. Firthaler's tomb is in the chancel of Laas Church.

BIBLIOGRAPHY

K. Atz: *Kunstgeschichte von Tirol und Vorarlberg* (Innsbruck, 1909), p. 493
K. Ginhart: *Die bildende Kunst in Österreich: Gotische Zeit* (Innsbruck, 1938)
E. Egg: *Kunst in Tirol* (Innsbruck, Vienna and Munich, 1970), p. 106
N. Nussbaum: *Deutsche Kirchenbaukunst der Gotik* (Cologne, 1985), pp. 282, 288

VERENA BEAUCAMP

Firuzabad [anc. Gur, Ardashir-Khurrah; Pers. Fīrūzā-
bād]. Site of Sasanian city in south-west Iran, just outside
the modern town of Firuzabad. It was planned by Ardashir
I (*reg c.* AD 224–41), the founder of the Sasanian dynasty
(*see* SASANIAN); its ancient name Ardashir-Khurrah means
'glory of Ardashir'. The walls of the city form a perfect
circle, within which is a circular inner core, probably
containing the public buildings, surrounded by radiating
streets dividing the city into 20 sectors. The pattern
continued into the countryside, resulting in an intricate
web of paths with the city at its centre.

Ardashir built his fortress, Qal'a-i Dukhtar, well away
from the city, on a crag commanding the road from Shiraz
to Firuzabad and thence to the Persian Gulf. The strongly
fortified structure was built in the early 3rd century AD,
when Ardashir was still nominally a Parthian vassal. It was
constructed of rough stone and mortar and still stands to
a considerable height. It is defended by a massive set of
outer curtain walls and has an elaborate system of wells
securing the water. It is built on three levels, a low entrance
level with winding ramps, an outer courtyard surrounded
by rooms serving as a barracks, and an upper terrace with
an impressive set of reception rooms. These consist of a
monumental iwan serving both as a reception hall and as
an entrance to a large domed chamber, the dome resting
on squinches above a square room. This combination of

iwan and domed chamber became a standard feature of
Sasanian palatial architecture.

Ardashir's elegant garden palace was built within a
walled enclosure on the plain outside the city some time
after Qal'a-i Dukhtar. The great arched entrance iwan
looked out on to a lake, circular like the city, and led to a
series of three great domed chambers, running across the
width of the building. Behind was a domestic unit consisting of a courtyard with smaller iwans and a row of rooms.
The whole was a balanced symmetrical building, the
severity of which was relieved by engaged columns and
buttresses on the outer walls and stucco cavetto cornices
above the doors and niches. These were copied from the
ruins of the Achaemenid palaces at PERSEPOLIS and serve
as a reminder of Ardashir's claim to be the heir of the
Achaemenids.

In addition to establishing a new order of monumental
architecture and urban planning, Ardashir revitalized rock
carving. Perhaps his most remarkable relief is beside the
Sasanian road, which winds along the mountain adjacent
to the Firuzabad plain. In a frieze 18 m long, carved in a
delicately modelled low relief, Ardashir and two companions are shown defeating three Parthian knights, among
whom can be identified the Parthian king Artabanus V
(*reg c.* 213–24). The scene is shown as three separate
contests. In the lead is Ardashir, who has unhorsed and
killed the King. Following him is his son Shapur (see fig.),

Firuzabad, detail from the jousting relief, recording the Sasanian defeat of the Parthians, the second Sasanian knight identified as Crown
Prince Shapur I, early 3rd century AD

whose lance has toppled the Parthian Grand Vizier and his horse, while the third Sasanian has swept his Parthian opponent off his horse and is clasping him in his arms. As well as symbolically recording the Sasanian defeat of the Parthian army in the Battle of Hormuzdegan in *c.* 224, this relief depicts how the Parthian and Sasanian heavy cavalry fought with long jousting lances and were able to maintain their seats despite the lack of stirrups by using carefully constructed saddles with clamps at the front to hold the thighs and a high cantle at the back. Differences in the armour of the two nations are carefully recorded: the Parthians used banded armour, while the Sasanians had chain-mail shirts. Each knight is identified by his distinctive family crest or device, embossed on helmets and on the horses' caparisons. A second relief carved beside the road as it crosses the river on a fine stone bridge illustrates Ardashir's investiture by the god Ahura Mazda.

See also IRAN, ANCIENT, §§II, 3 and IV.

BIBLIOGRAPHY

L. Vanden Berghe: *Archéologie de l'Iran ancien* (Leiden, 1959)
R. Ghirshman: *Iran: Parthians and Sassanians* (London, 1962)
E. Porada: *Ancient Iran* (London, (1965)
D. Huff: 'Qal'a-ye Dukhtar bei Firuzabad: Ein Beitrag zur sasanidischen Palastarchitektur', *Archäol. Mitt. Iran*, iv (1971), pp. 127–71
V. Lukonin: *From the Seleucids to the Sassanids* (1971), ii of *Persia* (London)
G. Herrmann: *The Iranian Revival*, The Making of the Past (Oxford, 1977)
D. Huff: 'Ausgrabungen auf Qal'a-ye Dukhtar bei Firuzabad, 1976', *Archäol. Mitt. Iran*, xi (1978), pp. 117–47
G. Herrmann: 'The Art of the Sasanians', *The Arts of Persia*, ed. R. W. Ferrier (New Haven, 1989), pp. 60–79

G. HERRMANN

Fisac (Serna), Miguel (*b* Daimiel, Ciudad Real, 29 Sept 1913). Spanish architect. His work is characterized by an attempt to implant northern European organicism into the local tradition and to apply it to religious architecture. His first buildings were in line with the monumentalist Classicism that dominated the architecture of Spain after the Civil War, but in the late 1940s organicism claimed his allegiance, and the Institutos Laborales de Daimiel (1951), Ciudad Real, and Almendralejo (1952), Badajoz, represent an adaptation of the foreign contribution in their use of autochthonous language and of local materials and techniques. An increased interest in the integration of building into landscape is evident in, for example, the Instituto de Enseñanza Media de Málaga (1954). Fisac's most influential contribution, however, was in his work on churches. It developed from, for example, the Colegio Apostólico de Arcas Reales (1952) in Valladolid, with convergent spaces built on symmetrical axes, steep upward curving in the roof and overhead lighting or lighting in elevated side strips, through Nuestra Señora de la Coronación (1958) in Vitoria, which has asymmetrical spaces, with curved, smooth, opaque walls that contrast with right-angled, textured and perforated walls, to S Ana (1963), Moratalaz, and Santa Cruz (1967), La Coruña, which are characterized by transverse ground-plans that favour participatory worship; in their construction reinforced concrete predominates. Fisac's experiments with hollow pieces of concrete in bone or organic shapes appeared in the roofing of naves and in creating the overhead lighting in the Centro de Estudios Hidrográficos de Madrid (1959), among other uses.

BIBLIOGRAPHY

J. Vellés and S. C. Velasco: *Miguel Fisac y la arquitectura religiosa* (Madrid, 1966)
D. Fullaondo: *Miguel Fisac* (Madrid, 1972)
M. C. Morales: *La arquitectura de Miguel Fisac* (Ciudad Real, 1979)

JORDI OLIVERAS

Fischel, Oskar (*b* Danzig [now Gdańsk, Poland], 10 July 1870; *d* London, 27 June 1939). German art historian. He studied art history at Königsberg (now Kaliningrad) and under Georg Gottfried Dehio at Strasbourg, where he obtained his doctorate in 1896 with a dissertation on Raphael's drawings. In 1900–01 he worked on the collection of engravings at the Wallraf-Richartz-Museum in Cologne, and later the holdings of the Lipperheidische Kostümbibliothek in Berlin. In 1914 he qualified as a university lecturer at Berlin University with a study on the fine arts and the stage, and in 1923 he was appointed Associate Professor of Art History. In Berlin, Fischel introduced the innovative idea of holding classes in front of original works of art in the Kaiser-Friedrich-Museum (destr.) to supplement the university lectures. He also taught at the Staatliche Kunstschule and Max Reinhardt's school of drama and gave public lectures and radio talks. His interest in the theatre gave rise to a plan to found a theatre museum in Berlin. Fischel was not able to realize the plan himself, but his ideas made an influential contribution to a theatrical exhibition in Magdeburg in 1927. He also studied film as an art form and as a medium of public education. Although his interests were wide-ranging, his most important achievement in the field of art history was the fundamental insight into Raphael's work that he formulated in numerous papers. Fischel died in London, fleeing from the Nazi regime.

WRITINGS

Tizian (Stuttgart, 1904, rev. 5/1924)
Die Meisterwerke des Kaiser-Friedrich-Museums zu Berlin (Munich, 1912)
Raphaels Zeichnungen, 8 vols (Berlin, 1913–41)
'Raffaello Santi', *Thieme–Becker*, xxix (1935), pp. 433–46
Raphael, 2 vols (London, 1948)
Raphael (Berlin, 1962)

BIBLIOGRAPHY

Oskar Fischel: Verzeichnis seiner Schriften (Cologne, 1962)

EDWIN LACHNIT

Fischer. Austrian family of artists.

(1) (Josef) Vincenz Fischer (*b* Schmidham bei Griesbach, 3 April 1729; *d* Vienna, 26 Oct 1810). Painter. He studied at the Akademie der Bildenden Künste in Vienna in 1749 and 1765. After travelling to Italy in 1753 to study, he worked briefly in Bavaria, then settled permanently in Vienna. He painted a series of frescoes and altarpieces in Austria, Hungary, Moravia and Bohemia, but also worked as a painter of historical subjects, painting small mythological and allegorical works. Among the most important frescoes for which he was solely responsible is the ceiling painting, in the temple of Diana at Schloss Laxenburg, of *Agamemnon Hunting* (1763; preparatory sketch, Vienna, Belvedere). Fischer was often employed in a specialist capacity to paint architectural elements, including the architectonic framework for frescoes by Franz Anton

Maulbertsch in the Kammerkapelle at the Hofburg in Vienna, and in the summer refectory at the monastery at Louka (now Czech Republic). In 1760 he became a member of the Akademie in Vienna and in 1764 was appointed professor of architecture, optics and perspective. He contributed to the series of pictures depicting famous events supervised by Martin Mijtens I, painting the architectural parts of the large ceremonial paintings such as *Coronation of Joseph II as Emperor* (Vienna, Schloss Schönbrunn). In his small landscape and architectural paintings, which depicted scenes from Greek and Roman history, and in such late altarpieces as *St Stephen* (1778; Oradea, Romania, cathedral), he increasingly adopted a classicizing style, attempting to combine late Baroque compositions with a refined linear style.

BIBLIOGRAPHY

K. Garas: *Franz Anton Maulbertsch, 1724–96* (Budapest and Vienna, 1960)

E. Baum: *Katalog der Österreichischen Barockmuseums im Unteren Belvedere in Wien* (Vienna, 1980)

KLÁRA GARAS

(2) Georg [Jiří] Fischer (*b* Vienna, 15 Dec 1768; *d* Prague, 9 Oct 1828). Architect and teacher, son of (1) Vincenz Fischer. He studied at the Akademie der Bildenden Künste, Vienna, and in 1785 he took up a position as draughtsman in the Royal and Imperial General Court Building Directorate. From 1788 he worked as principal quantity surveyor in the building department in Innsbruck and from 1792 at the Royal and Imperial Court Quantity Surveying Division in Vienna. In 1796 he was appointed chief quantity surveyor in the building department in Prague, and in 1803 he became professor of architecture at the Czech Polytechnic in Prague, where he trained numerous outstanding pupils in architecture and building. In 1811 he was appointed building director in the Department of Building for all of Bohemia. His most important works included the restoration (1804) of the Prague Belvedere in the Castle Park, the adaptation (1804–5) of the Jesuit seminary at no. 240/1, Husova Street, and the rebuilding (1807–12) of the former Hibernian House (refitted as an exhibition hall in the 1940s) in Republic Square, Prague. He also collaborated between 1816 and 1824 on the rebuilding of the church of St Gothard in Bubeneč, Prague, and the piarist church of the Holy Cross in Na Příkope, Prague.

BIBLIOGRAPHY

C. Jelinek: *Das ständisch–polytechnische Institut zu Prag* (Prague, 1856), p. 202

P. Toman: *Slovník českých výtvarných umělců* [Dictionary of Czech visual artists] (Prague, 1947)

YVONNE JANKOVÁ

Fischer, Johann Georg (*b* Marktoberdorf, Swabia, 21 Jan 1673; *d* Füssen, 26 April 1747). German architect. He worked as a foreman under his uncle, the architect JOHANN JAKOB HERKOMMER, in building the church of St Mang (1701–17) at Füssen. During 1710–20 he was president of the Füssen guild of masons. He did not begin to design buildings until past the age of 40: in 1717, after Herkommer's death, he took over the construction of the Innsbruck parish church, the St Jakobskirche (now the cathedral). Although several critics (e.g. Hammer, Krapf) doubted or underrated Fischer's contribution to this work,

stylistic and archival investigation (e.g. Hörtnagel) suggests that in 1717–18 he significantly modified Herkommer's original plan of the church. The nave is divided into three bays and surmounted by shallow domes. The third bay is prolonged by semicircular transverse niches, which are surmounted by similar domes, and the square choir is effectively emphasized by the light falling from the high drummed dome. Fischer also designed many smaller buildings, mainly chapels and village churches in Swabia and a few in the Tyrol. These include the cemetery chapel at Kisslegg (begun 1721) and the cemetery church of St Sebastian at Füssen (1721); among his parish churches are those at Bernbeuren (1721), St Andrew at Rosshaupten (1723–9), St Ulrich at Unterpinswang (1725–9), St Mary at Leeder (1730; unexecuted) and the former collegiate and castle church (now the parish church) at Wolfegg (1723). He also designed the chapel of the Five Wounds at Rieden (begun 1725), the Gymnasium at Dillingen (1723), the pilgrimage church of St Michael at Berchtholdshofen (1727) and the Cistercian collegiate church of the Assumption and St John the Baptist at Stams (1729–32).

BIBLIOGRAPHY

M. Hauttmann: *Geschichte der kirchlichen Baukunst in Bayern, Schwaben und Franken, 1550–1780* (Munich, 1921)

H. Hammer: 'Zur Frage der Baumeister der Innsbrucker Stadtpfarrkirche', *Tirol. Heimatbl.*, 11–12 (1938), pp. 345–8

H. Hörtnagel: 'Von den Baumeistern der St. Jakobs-Pfarrkirche zu Innsbruck', *Tirol. Heimatbl.*, 16 (1938), pp. 275–6

J. Weingartner: *Die Kirchen Innsbrucks* (Innsbruck, 1950)

R. Rauth: 'Johann Georg Fischer von Füssen als Baumeister des neuen Schlosses in Kisslegg', *Das Münster*, iv (1951), pp. 236 ff

H. Dussler: *Der Allgäuer Barockbaumeister Johann Jakob Herkommer* (Kempten, 1956)

J. Sauermost: *Der Allgäuer Barockbaumeister Johann Georg Fischer* (diss., U. Augsburg, 1969)

M. Krapf: *Johann Jakob Herkommer und das Phänomen der Chorkuppel der Domkirche St Jakob zu Innsbruck: Festschrift Johanna Gritsch* (Innsbruck, 1973)

BRIGITTE SCHNEIDER

Fischer, Johann Martin (*b* Bebele, near Füssen, Allgäu, 2 Nov 1740; *d* Vienna, 17 April 1820). Austrian sculptor and teacher. He was a poor peasant's son who was apprenticed to a village sculptor in the Allgäu region. He then worked in Vienna for ten years as an assistant to the sculptors Anton Tabota (1724–76), Jakob Christoph Schletterer (1699–1774) and Franz Xaver Messerschmidt. At the same time he studied at the Akademie der Bildenden Künste. His first independent works, dating from the mid-1770s, include a statue of *Mucius Scaevola* (marble, 1773) for Schönbrunn Park, and two side altars (1775–6) for the cathedral in Pécs. It was not until the 1780s that Fischer became a recognized and sought-after artist in Vienna. His oeuvre is very varied: working in metal and stone, he created figures of saints, such as the *Four Evangelists* (sandstone, 1781) for the high altar of the Michaelerkirche, as well as park statues and sculptures for buildings and tombs. Later his output of portraits and fountain statues increased in number and importance. To support his membership application to the Akademie der Bildenden Künste in 1785, he submitted an *écorché* figure, demonstrating his interest in anatomy. The following year he began to teach at the Akademie, starting as Professor of Anatomy and assistant in the sculpture class; he became Professor of Sculpture in 1806, succeeding Franz Anton Zauner, and was elected Director of the Akademie in 1815.

Fischer was one of those late 18th-century artists who, while professing their adherence to Neo-classicism, could not repudiate their late Baroque training. His attachment to this tradition enlivened portraits, such as the bust of *Bishop Heinrich Joseph Kerens* on the latter's tomb in St Pölten Cathedral (metal, 1792–4), that were in themselves austerely executed. His statues reveal the heritage of Georg Raphael Donner but also the influence of Messerschmidt, as shown by a comparison of Messerschmidt's Elisäus Fountain (1770; Vienna, Savoysches Damenstift) with Fischer's Joseph and Leopold fountains in the Graben in Vienna (metal, 1804). Fischer's interest in anatomy led him to write two books (1804 and 1806) on the subject.

BIBLIOGRAPHY

Thieme–Becker

M. Poch-Kalous: *Johann Martin Fischer* (Vienna, 1949)

Klassizismus in Wien: Architektur und Plastik (exh. cat., Vienna, Hist. Mus., 1978), pp. 78–9, 143–5, 148, 152–5, 157

MARIA PÖTZL-MALIKOVA

Fischer, Johann Michael (*b* Burglengenfeld, Oberpfalz, 18 Feb 1692; *d* Munich, 6 May 1766). German architect. He was one of the most creative architects of the late Baroque and Rococo in southern Germany, known primarily for his churches. In these he explored two basic antithetical concepts of Western ecclesiastical design: the traditional longitudinal arrangement of the church for liturgical procession in contrast to the ideal centralized church, and the gradual revealing of sacred space in contrast to its presentation as a complete whole. In four decades of building, Fischer worked to resolve these antitheses by interconnecting large, single spaces immediately visible in their entirety to smaller, ancillary spaces experienced as fragments, by combining centralized and longitudinal axes and by integrating curvilinear with rectilinear form.

1. Training and early work, to 1734. 2. Centralized churches, 1734–40. 3. Monastic churches of the 1740s. 4. Late work, 1750 and after.

1. TRAINING AND EARLY WORK, TO 1734. Trained as a mason by his father, Fischer's journeyman years began in 1712 and took him through Bohemia, Moravia and Austria. In 1718 he settled in Munich, where he worked under the City Mason Johann Mayr (1677–1731) and Johann Baptist Gunetzrhainer (1692–1763), fulfilling commissions for the Wittelsbach Elector Maximilian II Emanuel. In 1723 he became a citizen of Munich and master mason; he subsequently became court architect under Duke Clemens Franz of Bavaria, Freising Prince-Bishop Theodor Johann, and Clemens August, Elector-Archbishop of Cologne. The inscription on his monument in the Frauenkirche, Munich, says he built 32 churches, 23 monasteries and many palaces. Most of the ecclesiastical buildings are documented, but the secular work is scarcely known.

Fischer began his independent career in 1727 with projects for a new Premonstratensian convent church at Osterhofen-Altenmarkt on the River Danube and the Hieronymite votive church of St Anna am Lehel in the outskirts of Munich, commissioned by Electress Maria Amalia of Wittelsbach. At Osterhofen Fischer was required to use the foundations of the old church, which had partially collapsed, and to connect the new structure to the convent as the earlier church had been. He centralized the longitudinal nave imposed on him at Osterhofen and just as readily lengthened the central space of his design for St Anna am Lehel. For Osterhofen he used convex corners, sculpted wall piers, oval chapels and a coved barrel vault to lend the nave a centralizing character. The curvilinear chapels and convex balconies on either side of the nave, hollowed out between the deep piers and brightly lit by huge windows, create a field of luminous vertical spaces bordering the volume of the nave. At St Anna am Lehel (completed 1733; see fig. 1a), Fischer extended the centralized octagon by juxtaposing a circular vestibule and choir. He maintained the integrity of the oval vault over the octagon by permitting it to extend into, and partially cut away, the smaller vaults over vestibule and choir. Eight wall piers, arranged to emphasize the cardinal directions, create tall slots of space around the octagon. In these early independent projects, Fischer integrated longitudinal with centralized spaces and contrasted the clear geometry of central figures with luminous chapel shafts. The impact of his architectural intentions is intensified in both interiors by the ornate stucco and frescoes of the brothers Egid Quirin Asam and Cosmas Damian Asam.

Another church of this period, that for the Augustinian monastery at Diessen on the Ammersee (1732–9), has a façade that is a stiff version of the type Fischer later employed time and again: a colossal order rising from a tall base frames a convex centre, while the vertical accent established by the central door and large window above is continued through a pediment, which is sharply recessed and broken to continue the ascending line into an elegantly curved gable with a central niche. Inside, Fischer created a unitary space by transforming the traditional Latin-cross basilica. As at Osterhofen, he attached a wall-pier nave directly to the choir. Cross arches and an elaborate frame around the vault fresco lock the three middle bays of the nave into a unit. Shallow, widely separated wall piers produce vertical slots of space along the flanks, rather than distinct chapels. The restrained architecture of the interior is animated by a rich stucco programme by the brothers Franz Xaver Feichtmayer (i) and Johann Michael Feichtmayer, with sculpture by Johann Baptist Straub.

2. CENTRALIZED CHURCHES, 1734–40. Once the masonry shell of Diessen was in place (1734), Fischer went on to design three centralized churches in rapid succession. In them he explored geometries of plan and the orchestration of space and light to create a unified whole. For the parish and pilgrimage church of Maria Schnee (1734–51) at Aufhausen, near Regensburg, he bracketed an irregular octagon with a rectangular vestibule and almost square choir, establishing an entrance–altar axis (for illustration *see* ORATORIANS). The narrow diagonals of the octagon contain chapels below with balconies above, creating corners that consist of partially revealed deep spaces. Fischer transformed this more conventional vocabulary into a strikingly singular work for the Augustinian church (1736–9; destr. 1945) in Ingolstadt. Here the

centralized nave was entered directly, rather than through a vestibule (1b); oval chapels with balconies are set diagonally at the corners, and the smaller choir was a square with bevelled corners. Curves dominated the main space, in oval corner chapels, the outward curve of north and south walls, the eight concave wall piers and the concave coves over the pier arches that supported a pendentive dome. More than 20 years later, at Rott am Inn (*see* §4 below), Fischer explored a more elaborate version of this integrated clustering of independently vaulted and lit centralized spaces.

The foundations and façade of Fischer's project (1735) for the Confraternity church of the Order of St Michael at Berg am Laim, near Munich, were begun in 1737 under the direction of Municipal Architect Philip Jakob Kögl-sperger (1707–*c.* 1755). When Fischer assumed control in 1739, he modified the design to an arrangement of four partial spaces placed along a longitudinal axis, incorporating an oval vestibule, octagonal nave, rectangular presbytery with bevelled corners and an oval choir, each supporting separate vaults (1c). Columns and entablature unite the various spaces, assisted by the elaborate decorations of Johann Baptist Zimmermann, Johann Baptist Straub and Ignaz Günther among others.

3. MONASTIC CHURCHES OF THE 1740s. The walls of the former Cistercian monastery church at Fürstenzell were already in place when Fischer took over the project in 1740. His new plans focused on the interior and façade, and by the end of that year some of the vaults were already constructed. The façade (completed 1744) is drawn into the vertical by two towers and the succession of door, window and niche set into its convex centre. Inside, the church was simply designed, with shallow, widely spaced wall piers supporting a barrel vault in the nave, as do the straight walls of the narrower choir. Piers with paired pilasters and flat entablature, together with shallow lunettes, emphasize the planar character of the interior. The slight curve of the balconies between the piers and the rounded corners of the nave to east and west, which continue into the vault cove, are partially successful efforts to animate the space. Within this reduced setting the stucco by Johann Baptist Modler (1700–74) and Johann Georg Funk (*d* 1772), the fresco by Johann Jakob Zeiller and the main altar by Johann Baptist Straub dominate the architecture.

In the 1740s Fischer began major Benedictine monastery churches at Zwiefalten and Ottobeuren. New monastery buildings had been erected at Zwiefalten (from 1668), but the choir of the Romanesque church was razed in 1738, and in the following year the local builders Josef Schneider and Martin Schneider began a new church. The size of the commission outstripped their abilities, however, and the project was passed to Fischer in 1741 with the foundations of the choir, the north and south towers flanking it and the transept already in place. He completed the building in 1754; the interior decoration was concluded in 1785. The barrel-vaulted nave and choir are almost equal in length, separated by a slightly projecting transept, with a dome over the crossing. The breadth of the nave is emphasized by four chapels with convex balconies slotted between the wall piers, while the solid walls of the choir

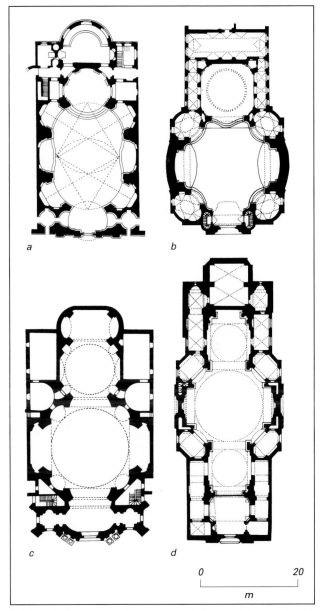

a   *b*

c   *d*

0   20
|_____|
m

1. Johann Michael Fischer: church plans: (a) St Anna am Lehel, near Munich, completed 1733; (b) Augustinian church at Ingolstadt, 1736–9 (destr.); (c) St Michael, Berg am Laim, begun 1737; (d) Benedictine church at Rott am Inn, 1759–63

emphasize its narrowness. Fischer employed variations of paired columns as the architectural leitmotif relating façade to interior and the different parts of the interior to one another. Colossal columns in grey ashlar on the façade are transformed inside to columns of marbled stucco with gilt capitals supporting segments of strongly projecting entablature; variations in the pairing of the columns characterize and interconnect the interior spaces. The white ground of the architecture is enhanced by the rich colour of Franz Joseph Spiegler's frescoes, Johann Michael Feichtmayer's stucco and Johann Joseph Christian's sculpture.

2. Johann Michael Fischer: interior of Ottobeuren monastery church, from 1748 (begun by others)

In 1748 Fischer was commissioned to build the church at Ottobeuren, the configuration of which had already been established. For the façade, Fischer employed a monumental version of the type he had designed at Diessen, Berg am Laim and Fürstenzell: two towers contained a convex centre, where columns framed a door, window and pediment recessed in the middle to continue the vertical accent into the elaborate gable above. Inside, the expansive dimensions of the Greek-cross plan created voluminous spaces flooded with light from huge windows; the pendentive dome over the crossing was met by slightly smaller pendentive domes in nave and choir, emphasizing the processional axis, while colossal columns and pilasters in marbled stucco underscored the monumental scale of the interior (see fig. 2; for further discussion see OTTOBEUREN).

4. LATE WORK, 1750 AND AFTER. Two other monastic commissions mark the beginning and end of Fischer's work in the 1750s, the first being the Anastasia Chapel (1750–58) attached to the monastery church of Benediktbeuren. Although attached to the north of the church choir, the chapel gives the impression of being an independent building. The elevations of the oval plan consist of single pilasters and large windows; a vault with tall lunettes covers the interior. The stucco of this light-flooded, jewel-like space is by Johann Michael Feichtmayer, the fresco by Johann Jakob Zeiller and the sculpture by Ignaz Günther.

The second commission, the former Benedictine monastery church (1759–63) at Rott am Inn, has a plain façade that masks one of Fischer's most complex and beautiful creations. The central figure of the longitudinal interior (see GERMANY, fig. 8) is an octagon with unequal sides and openings, supporting a circular dome. A rectangular domed space to the west stands between octagon and vestibule, its flanks opening through broad arches to chapels and balconies resembling those in the octagon. A similar rectangle to the east contains the choir, with balconies placed above the side walls. Behind it, balancing the vestibule in plan but not seen from inside the church, is the sacristy.

These centralized spaces create a longitudinal sequence from entrance to altar (see fig. 1d above), which Fischer both amplified and countered. Working with paired pilasters rather than columns, as he had for most of his large churches, he placed four pairs to the east and west sides of the octagon to stress the longitudinal axis, another four to the north and south of the cross axis and a final four to establish the far corners of the entrance and choir rectangles, relating this longitudinal axis back to the octagon.

Chapels and balconies produce a layering of spatial zones that augment the centralized spaces and axes, while the dominant white of the interior amplifies the full light from two tiers of large windows. Frescoes by Matthaus Günther, stucco by Jakob Rauch and Franz Xaver Feichtmayer (ii) and sculpture by Ignaz Günther and Josef Matthias Götz create an ensemble in dazzling colour that provides a counterpoint to the sharp-edged precision of the architecture (see also IGNAZ GÜNTHER, fig. 2).

Other commissions of the 1750s may have included work (1750–52) on the castle in Neuhaus am Inn; a tight block with two parallel gabled roofs perched on a tall base, it is a late work, architecturally modest and one of the few secular projects associated with his name. Three plans survive for the parish church of St George (1751–3) in Bichl, in which centralized spaces are again arranged in a longitudinal sequence: a rectangular vestibule with rounded ends opens to a larger, virtually square nave with diagonal niches in the corners and a smaller square choir with bevelled corners. Corner pilasters carry the pendentive dome. Fischer joined square spaces for other modest commissions, for example the pilgrimage and parish church (1755) in Sigmertshausen, which consists of two square units with bevelled corners: a larger one with a barrel vault for the nave and a smaller one with a flat pendentive dome for the choir.

Fischer's ability to provide simple churches with scale and dignity was matched by his ingenuity at solving complex problems. The monastery church (begun 1763) at Altomünster had to accommodate the Brigittine nuns and monks separately at the same services, remain accessible to the lay community, occupy a narrow, steep site and retain both the choir (1617) in the east and the Romanesque tower foundations in the west. For the lay congregation, Fischer provided a tall octagon with a flat dome placed behind the narrow façade. This opens to a rectangle with diagonal niches in the corners covered by a low-slung vault supporting the nuns' choir above. Behind the raised, deep choir, and elevated above it, is the monks' choir. A passageway runs from the entrance around the octagon and rectangle to the choir, effectively separating the outer walls from the free-standing, centralized spaces within and providing access to the different parts of the church. The combined use of centralized and longitudinal spaces in both unorthodox and traditional arrangements at Altomünster epitomizes Fischer's innovative ability to design within contemporary ecclesiastical conventions of form and arrangement.

BIBLIOGRAPHY

A. Feulner: 'Johann Michael Fischers Risse für die Klosterkirche in Ottobeuren', *Münchn. Jb. Bild. Kst*, viii (1913), pp. 46–62

——: 'Unbekannte Bauten Johann Michael Fischers', *Münchn. Jb. Bild. Kst*, xi (1914–15), pp. 41–66

M. Hauttmann: *Geschichte der kirchlichen Baukunst in Bayern, Schwaben und Franken, 1550–1780* (Munich, 1921), pp. 168–85

N. Lieb: 'Der Münchener Barockbaumeister Johann Michael Fischer und seine Familie', *Bl. Bayer. Landesver. Familienknd.*, xvi (1938), pp. 97–107

——: 'Johann Michael Fischer: Das Leben eines bayerischen Baumeisters im 18. Jahrhundert', *Münchn. Jb. Bild. Kst*, n. s., xiii (1938–9), pp. 142–53

H. Ernst: *Der Raum bei Johann Michael Fischer* (diss., U. Munich, 1950)

N. Lieb: *Barockkirchen zwischen Donau und Alpen* (Munich, 1953)

F. Hagen-Dempf: *Der Zentralbaugedanke bei Johann Michael Fischer* (Munich, 1954)

O. Freiermuth: 'Die Wandpfeilerkirchen im Werke des Johann Michael Fischer', *Das Münster*, viii (1955), pp. 320–32

B. Rupprecht: *Die bayerische Rokoko-Kirche* (1959), v of *Münchener historische Studien*, ed. M. Spindler (Kallmünz, 1955–)

H.-R. Hitchcock: *Rococo Architecture in Southern Germany* (London, 1968), pp. 175–208

H. Ernst: 'Zur Himmelsvorstellung im späten Barock, besonders bei Johann Michael Fischer', *Z. Bayer. Landesgesch.*, xxxv (1972), pp. 266–93

A. Laing: 'Central and Eastern Europe', *Baroque and Rococo: Architecture and Decoration*, ed. A. Blunt (New York, 1978), pp. 241–52
D. Hundt: *Johann Michael Fischer* (Freilassing, 1981)
N. Lieb: *Johann Michael Fischer: Baumeister und Raumschöpfer im späten Barock Süddeutschlands* (Regensburg, 1982)

CHRISTIAN F. OTTO

Fischer, József (*b* Budapest, 12 April 1901; *d* Budapest, 23 Feb 1995). Hungarian architect, urban planner and theorist. He studied (1915–19) at the State Architecture High School, Budapest, taking his master builder examination in 1926. His entry in the design competition for the Imperial Baths (1924), Budapest, demonstrated his Modernist leanings, which he elaborated in articles for the avant-garde periodicals *Munka* (Hung.: work) and *Tér és Forma* (Hung.: space and form). After the Hungarian affiliate of CIAM was formed (1929) under the leadership of Farkas Molnár, Fischer became one of its most active members and one of the most important pioneers of Functionalism in Hungary. The Hungarian group, which existed for nine years, worked within CIAM's overall focus on the need for affordable housing. Their utopian architectural and urban designs were illustrated by the collective house, Kolház (1931), and the collective town, Kolváros (1932), but in practice the group's members were primarily able to build only villas and residential blocks. Fischer's architecture combines various Modernist influences with his own individual style. His early works are strictly geometric, while the later work includes increasingly rich formal elements. His cube-like villa (1932) on Csatárka Street, Budapest, is flat-roofed, two-storey and white-plastered, with sensitively proportioned openings cut into the flat façade to create tension. The Villa Hoffman (1934) on Szépvölgyi Street, Budapest, is a simple prism with an outwardly projecting semi-cylindrical stairwell that is supported by slender concrete columns on sloping ground. Examples of his later style include the four-storey Rege Hotel (1940) and the Gyopár Hotel (1942) on Szabadság Hill in Buda. They are curved in form, and natural stone surfaces appear on the façades next to the plastered surfaces. After World War II, as the president of the Government Committee for Building and the City Public Works Council, Fischer helped draw up plans for the Budapest region. He was on the editorial board of *Tér és Forma* from 1942 to 1948 and was elected to the international leadership of the CIAM in 1947. After the political changes in 1948 he retired.

WRITINGS
Regular contributions to *Tér és Forma* (1928–48)

BIBLIOGRAPHY
E. Gábor: *A CIAM magyar csoportja* [The Hungarian CIAM group] (Budapest, 1972)
N. Pámer: *Magyar építészet a két világháboru kösött* [Hungarian architecture between the two World Wars] (Budapest, 1987)

ÁKOS MORAVÁNSZKY,
KATALIN MORAVÁNSZKY-GYŐNGY

Fischer, Karl von (*b* Mannheim, 19 Sept 1782; *d* Munich, 12 Feb 1820). German architect and teacher. He began his architectural career as an apprentice (1796–9) to the Munich Court Architect Maximilian von Verschaffelt and then went to Vienna to complete his studies at the academy there. He showed great promise when very young and was already active as an architect while still a student. He submitted a design for the projected national theatre in Munich (1802; unexecuted) and from Vienna he designed and directed the building of the Prinz-Carl-Palais (completed 1803; Königinstrasse, Munich), a monumental classical structure.

Between 1806 and 1809 Fischer undertook extensive travels in Italy and France. He spent the winter of 1808–9 in Italy, studying in particular the architecture of the Renaissance and of Palladio. He returned to Munich (1809) to become professor at the Akademie der Bildenden Künste and soon attracted the attention of Ludwig, Crown Prince of Bavaria (later King Ludwig I), an enthusiastic architectural patron, who appointed him Königlicher Oberbaurat (1809). Together they set out to transform Munich into a fitting capital for the new kingdom of Bavaria (created 1806). Working closely with the landscape designer Friedrich Ludwig von Sckell, Fischer prepared a comprehensive urban plan (1808–12) for the city, which influenced its development throughout the 19th century. He was directly responsible for the planning and layout of the Maxvorstadt suburb, with the elegant Briennenstrasse as its main axis. His most successful work was the circular Karolinenplatz (begun 1810; much altered), surrounded by 12 grand palaces for Bavarian aristocrats. His work was greatly admired at the time; the influential art critic and collector Sulpiz Boisserée described the area around the Karolinenplatz as the 'Fischer quarter' in a letter to Goethe. The fate of Fischer's Hof- und Nationaltheater (1811–18), at the time the largest public opera house in Western Europe, unfortunately typified his later career. The theatre burnt down in 1823 and was rebuilt by Leo von Klenze with slight alterations (completed 1825). Klenze had arrived in Munich in 1816 and within a short time he had replaced Fischer as Crown Prince Ludwig's favourite architect. The Prince took great delight in playing off his architects against each other. Klenze was almost instantly appointed Court Architect. Many of Fischer's ideas and designs were subsequently adopted and realized by Klenze. As early as 1809–10 Fischer had prepared plans for the Königsplatz with the Glyptothek, a sculpture gallery, as its centrepiece. In the final competition (1816) for the Glyptothek, however, Klenze's design won and was executed (1816–30). Similarly, Fischer's project (1810) for the Walhalla, a commemorative temple of famous Germans, was finally designed and executed by Klenze (designed 1816–21; built 1830–42).

Many of Fischer's other projects fared no better. His idea (1810) for a triumphal arch in Munich, the Karlstor, was finally realized in Friedrich von Gärtner's Siegestor (1843–52). Fischer's plans for the Palais Leuchtenberg, Munich, were taken up (1816) by Klenze using some of his original designs, while for the Königsbau (1826–35) of the Residenz, Munich, Klenze used Fischer's drawings of the Palazzo Pitti, Florence, as a source of inspiration. Fischer's premature death at the age of 38 was as much to blame for his unrealized potential as the volatility of his patron. Today, however, Fischer is regarded as the most important architect in the reign of King Maximilian I Joseph (*reg* 1799–1825) of Bavaria. His early buildings were influenced by the Baroque but his work soon assumed a strong and elegant classicism. Above all, his urban planning schemes had a strong impact on the architectural development and character of Munich. As a teacher at the Akademie der Bildenden Künste he was influential, his pupils including such prominent architects as Friedrich von Gärtner.

BIBLIOGRAPHY

H. Schindler: *Karl von Fischer (1782–1820): Ein Architekt des Klassizismus* (diss., Munich, Tech. U., 1951)
O. Hederer: *Karl von Fischer: Leben und Werk* (Munich, 1960)
Karl von Fischer, 1782–1820 (exh. cat. by W. Nerdinger and others, Munich, Neue Pin., 1982)
D. Watkin and T. Mellinghoff: *German Architecture and the Classical Ideal, 1740–1840* (London, 1987)

CLAUDIA BÖLLING

Fischer, Lili (*b* Priwall, nr Travemünde, 1947). German performance artist. From 1966 to 1973 she studied at the Hochschule für Bildende Künste in Hamburg. In the mid-1970s she began to design performances and record them in book or script form. Her performances were rituals involving the audience as active participants and were characteristically conducted with theatrical verve and a great sense of humour. They involved sensual experience (e.g. smells, in *Luggage of Scents*, 1988) and frequently incorporated herbs or spices. The *Conference of Plants with Choice of the Peace Plant* (see 1983 exh. cat.), performed in Oslo, Kiel, Bonn, Marseille and Hamburg in 1981–3, required every audience member to bring a plant from which they used extracts for gargling, for facial steam baths and for hand and foot massages. The event culminated in the audience's election of one plant as the 'peace plant'. A number of Fischer's performances commented on activities traditionally associated with women (e.g. *Sewing Aerobics* (1986)). Her work generally comprised live events, subsequently documented by portfolios with photographs, drawings and reports, or the use of cupboards or containers in which she placed specimens and props.

BIBLIOGRAPHY

Lili Fischer: Die Pflanzenkonferenzen mit Wahl des Friedenskrauts Drehbuch Oslo/Kiel/Marseille/Hamburg (exh. cat., foreword H. R. Leppien; Oslo, Unge Kstnernes Samfund; Kiel, Mus. Sophienblatt; Bonn, Gal. Philomene Magers; and elsewhere 1981–3)
E. von Radziewsky: 'Lili Fischer: Teekonvent, Quarkideen und Wattschlag', *Die Zeit*, 30 (20 July 1984)
Lili Fischer: Hausgeister (exh. cat., Heidelberg, Kstver.; Koblenz, Kstver.; 1988)

NINA LÜBBREN

Fischer, Theodor (*b* Schweinfurt, 28 May 1862; *d* Munich, 25 Dec 1938). German architect and teacher. He studied architecture at the Technische Hochschule, Munich, before working for Paul Wallot on the Reichstag in Berlin (1884–94). On returning to Munich, he worked for Gabriel von Seidl and started his own practice. In 1893 Fischer was appointed head of the new planning office in Munich, shaping the developing outskirts of the city and erecting his first public buildings, a series of schools influential throughout Germany, for example a school at Elisabethplatz, Munich (1902–4). He resigned in 1901 to devote time to his expanding practice and to teaching, first at the Technische Hochschule, Stuttgart, and in 1908 at the Technische Hochschule, Munich, where he was the first to teach city planning. He was a founder-member of the Deutscher Werkbund in 1907, serving as its first president, and he designed the central hall at the group's exhibition in Cologne in 1914. Between 1900 and 1930 he built numerous schools, civic buildings, churches, the extension to the University of Jena (1904–8), museums at Kassel (1908–11) and Wiesbaden (1912–15), private houses and some progressive public housing, including a housing scheme for factory workers at Gmindersdorf, near Reutlingen.

Towards the end of the 1920s Fischer accommodated Modernist influence by stripping his buildings down to essentials, which left the largest of his late works, such as his workers' hostel in Munich (1926), somewhat austere. His only building after 1933 was a brewery extension, and he suffered the indignity of seeing an ideology to which he had contributed exploited politically, for at the turn of the century he had been among the keenest proponents of the HEIMATSTIL, a South-German movement equivalent to the English Arts and Crafts Movement. It is probably due to the associations imposed on Heimatstil by the Nazis that Fischer's reputation suffered in post-war Germany.

Fischer's work does not fit architectural categories easily. His buildings are mainly of heavy, traditional construction, although he was also a pioneer in the use of reinforced concrete, for example the garrison church at Ulm (1908–11). Although he based his decoration and iconography on numerous sources and periods, he developed them with sufficient originality to achieve an overall unity. He opposed academic classicism but borrowed details and even large elements from Renaissance sources. The portico of the Kunstgebäude in Stuttgart (1910), for example, is a reinterpretation of Brunelleschi's Ospedale degli Innocenti, Florence. He held classical beliefs about proportion and consciously composed façades with regulating lines, but he disliked excessive symmetry and in his planning schemes pursued a type of picturesque irregularity promoted by Camillo Sitte. Fischer was adept at planning odd-shaped and sloping sites, the particularities of which he would skilfully and sensitively exploit, disposing building elements in a hierarchical manner to produce rich and apparently natural spatial sequences. He was also influential as the teacher of Erich Mendelsohn, Hugo Häring, Otto Bartning and Ernst May. Bruno Taut, J. J. P. Oud and Paul Bonatz were assistants in his office, and Le Corbusier worked for him in 1910, later writing that he found Fischer's work more memorable than any other German work he had then seen.

BIBLIOGRAPHY

R. Pfister: *Theodor Fischer* (Munich, 1968)
G. Albers: 'Theodor Fischer und die Münchner Stadtentwicklung bis zur Mitte unseres Jahrhunderts', *Bauen in München, 1890–1950*, ed. G. Albers (Munich, 1980), pp. 6–25
W. Nerdinger: 'Theodor Fischer', *Archit. Rev.*, clxxx (1986), pp. 61–5
——: *Theodor Fischer; Architekt und Städtebauer* (Berlin, 1988) [pubd in conjunction with exh.]
P. Blundell Jones: 'Theodor Fischer', *Architects' J.*, clxxxix/15 (1989), pp. 38–45, 48–55

PETER BLUNDELL JONES

Fischer von Erlach. Austrian family of architects. (1) Johann Bernhard Fischer von Erlach (the honorific was granted by the emperor in 1696 when Fischer was ennobled) was the son of Johann Baptist Fischer, a sculptor and decorator active in Graz, near the Austrian border with Italy. Johann Bernhard became the last great architect of the Renaissance and Baroque periods, occupying a central role in the buildings of the imperial court circle in Vienna. His eclectic approach was adopted as the official style of the Habsburg court. His second son, (2) Joseph Emanuel Fischer von Erlach, was trained by his father as his successor and completed his unfinished work after his death.

BIBLIOGRAPHY
A. Ilg: *Die Fischer von Erland* (Vienna, 1895)

(1) Johann Bernhard Fischer von Erlach (*b* Graz, 20 July 1656; *d* Vienna, 5 April 1723). He was a strikingly original architect, who synthesized the work of the leading Italian High Baroque architects of the previous generation, such as Gianlorenzo Bernini, Francesco Borromini and Pietro da Cortona, the late Baroque of his near contemporary Carlo Fontana and the early classicism of Jean Baptiste Mathey. His contribution to the culture of his time results from this synthesis, and the empire, which quickly gained strength after the defeat of the Turks in 1683, provided a welcome setting for him to realize his ideas. It is primarily for this idea of synthesis, and not as 'the father of Austrian Baroque', that Fischer should be remembered.

1. Training and early work, before 1692. 2. Mature and late work, 1692 and after.

1. TRAINING AND EARLY WORK, BEFORE 1692. In either 1671 or 1674 Prince Eggenberg, a patron of Fischer's father, was responsible for sending the young man to Rome, where he trained as a sculptor. Fischer's interests soon turned towards architecture and antiquity. His contemporaries in Rome were of the generation after Bernini, whose influence was still strongly felt. It was at this time that Fischer became interested in developing a systematic formulation of plans and building types. He was helped by Philipp Schor (*b* 1646), a member of a Tyrolean family of artists, for whom he worked as a 'scolar' and 'practicant'. Schor's father, Johann Paul Schor, had worked in Bernini's studio, and Fischer may have had access to Bernini's drawings. He also assimilated the advanced examples of French art that were then easily accessible in Rome through the Académie de France, and he was familiar with the academic and antiquarian circle centred on Queen Christina of Sweden, who was resident in Rome.

Fischer's first works were small in scale. He designed medals (1679 and 1682) of Charles II of Spain (*reg* 1665–1700) and his queen, Marie-Louise, for the Spanish Ambassador, the 7th Marqués del Carpio. When the Marqués was appointed viceroy in Naples (1684), Philipp Schor was summoned there, and the young Fischer went with him but returned to Austria shortly afterwards. By spring 1687 he was in Vienna, where he received further encouragement from the Eggenbergs and two commissions from the Emperor Leopold I. These were the restoration and completion (1687–97) with stucco decorations of Ferdinand II's mausoleum in Graz and a shared role with Lodovico Ottavio Burnacini over the alteration and the sculptural decoration of the *Trinity Column* in

Vienna (for alteration *see* BURNACINI, LODOVICO OTTAVIO). Soon afterwards Fischer was appointed architectural tutor to the Crown Prince Joseph and was thus closely associated from the beginning of his career with the imperial family and especially with Joseph I (*reg* 1705–11), who appointed him to his 'German' (i.e. xenophobic) court administration and later even acted as godfather to Fischer's eldest son. Fischer, with his Roman training, had returned home at the ideal moment, as there was a growing nationalist feeling, supported by the imperial court, that commissions should go to German rather than Italian or French artists. The climax of Fischer's immediate close association with the Emperor and his political ideals was the series of festive props designed and constructed for Joseph's coronation as King of Rome in 1690.

As early as 1688 Fischer was proclaiming his aspirations and abilities as an imperial architect with his ideal project for an imperial hunting-lodge symbolically placed on the heights of Schönbrunn, where the view extends across Vienna to Hungary, which had then just been annexed. The scheme, begun only in 1696 (*see* §2(i) below), which he took up again in his book *Entwurff einer historischen Architektur* (1721), has the hallmarks of a huge academy project, and it was unmistakably conceived as a rival project to Versailles in France, but with Habsburg iconography. The entrance court with its two pillars of Hercules (symbolizing the Emperor's claim to be regarded as a second Hercules for his prowess) and successive fountains, gardens, a grotto, ramps and terraces lead up to an oval plateau with a pool around which the splendid buildings of the 'hunting-lodge' are grouped. Fischer returned to the idea in 1704, turning it into a presentation piece for Frederick I of Prussia. His first architectural commissions to be built, however, came to him from the aristocracy rather than the Emperor and from families related by marriage to his father's old patron Prince Eggenberg, the Liechtensteins and the Althanns. The Belvedere (1687–90; destr.) for the garden of the palace near Vienna of John Adam Andreas, Prince of Liechtenstein, was only a garden building, but it shows Fischer's brilliance in handling architectural elements. The easy treatment of the building with its concave centre culminating in a great central arch, up to which lead two curving flights of steps, shows an Italian lightness of touch and virtuosity. The treatment of the Ionic order and the window architraves in particular clearly point to the repertory of form of Bernini's followers. Fischer also worked (*c*. 1688) at the Liechtenstein estates in Moravia (now part of the Czech Republic), designing the stables at Eisgrub (now Lednice) and the Sala Terrena at nearby Schloss Feldsberg (now Valtice).

For the Althann family, Fischer first designed the Ahnensaal or ancestral gallery (1688–93) at Schloss Frain an der Thaya (now Vranov nad Dyjí, Hungary). It is a free-standing oval building dramatically sited at the edge of a steep cliff. Between each pair of windows is a niche housing a statue and flanked by pilasters. The dome is pierced by ten large oval windows and has frescoes (completed 1695) by Johann Michael Rottmayr. Fischer was also commissioned to build the Gartenpalais Althann (1690–93; destr.) at Rossau, near Vienna. Here he designed an oval central element with four diagonally placed wings, an X-shaped structure that inspired imitations in Austria until the late 18th century; it was proposed by Germain Boffrand in his unexecuted first designs for Malgrange (1712) in Lorraine and is best known in Filippo Juvarra's version at Stupinigi (1729–35), near Turin. The combination of a cylindrical central element (whether round, oval or of composite form) with regularly shaped wings was a recurrent theme in Fischer's work.

2. MATURE AND LATE WORK, 1692 AND AFTER. The second part of Fischer's career began in 1692. Although he continued to make important and much imitated design solutions for secular buildings, he built a number of important churches and published a history of architecture, combined with designs for his own buildings and a quantity of ideal plans.

(i) Secular commissions. (ii) Ecclesiastical buildings. (iii) Writings.

(i) Secular commissions. In 1692, with the commission for the Palais Strattmann (1692–3; later Palais Windischgrätz; destr.), Fischer secured his first foothold as an architect in Vienna itself. The building has always been considered important in the development of the Baroque façade in the city of Vienna and in Austria as a whole, while at the same time being cited as proof of Fischer's eclecticism. The façade in fact seems too richly varied and decorated, almost like an apprentice piece. Only the projecting end bays appear regular or normal; each has two bays divided in Palladian style into a basement, *piano nobile* and attic bound together by a colossal order and entablature, with a parapet crowned by statues. In contrast, the five central bays are more lavishly decorated. The doorway is designed with Roman richness, as is the middle window complete with balcony above it. The *piano nobile* is furnished with its own order of double pilasters below a strongly emphasized attic, developed in garden-front style with cartouches below and ornate pediments above the windows and double-herm pilasters. The effect of the unequal decorative treatment is eclectic, due to the delight taken in working out the attic storey of the central part in sculptural terms. Even though skilful play is made with the illusion of depth in the façade, there is a lack of logic determining the whole façade and the break between the more detailed middle section and the colossal order on the sides.

In its layout the Stadtpalais (*c.* 1695–1700; now the Ministry of Finance) of Prince Eugene of Savoy, with its seven bays (extended to twelve bays in 1703) grouped around two doorways, certainly is linked to previous Viennese models. In the way that Fischer has improved the type, however, as well as in the differences between it and possible models by Palladio and by Bernini's Palazzo Chigi-Odescalchi (begun 1664), Rome, the independence of his architectural thinking is increasingly evident. The strong emphasis placed on the sculptured decorative elements, the window pediments and the doorways with their extremely pronounced consoles, surmounting balconies and vases is part of the new independence. This shift of emphasis lends animation to the façade, necessarily restrained because of the narrowness of the street. Elsewhere, in the special field of religious architecture and particularly in designing *maisons de plaisance*, the severity is lifted by the sculptural conception of the building itself. The staircase hall (*Treppenhaus*) of Prince Eugene's palace

is an extraordinary *tour de force*. It has an imperial staircase with the landing supported by muscular atlantids. While Prince Eugene's palace was being erected, Fischer was finally allowed to build at Schönbrunn (begun 1696, not completed; for further discussion *see* VIENNA, §V, 7(ii)), but the scale was relatively small, and the building was subsequently drastically altered inside and out for Maria-Theresa.

The influence of Bernini's universal model for Baroque 'palazzo' architecture, the Palazzo Chigi-Odescalchi, can be seen even more clearly in the Stadtpalais Batthyány (1699–1706; now the Palais Schönborn), which in turn served as a model for the Baroque palace generally in Vienna, even directly influencing Fischer's chief rival, JOHANN LUKAS VON HILDEBRANDT, particularly with its tapering pilasters. Again, although relatively few changes have been made (the central range is two bays shorter, the basement has two storeys and there is an attic storey below the entablature instead of two main floors), the execution and artistic treatment produce an entirely new result. Yet again, sculptural elements are mainly responsible for the transformation. These include vases placed in tall (Piedmontese-influenced) oval niches above the doorcases flanking the central gateway, reliefs above the windows of the *piano nobile* and richly shaped capitals adorning tapering pilasters, anticipating for the first time forms of the Régence style in the manner of Jean Berain I.

Other masterpieces of Fischer's palace architecture in his later period are the Bohemian Court Chancellery (1708–14), the Palais Trautson (*c.* 1710–16; see fig. 1) conceived as a detached palace to be viewed from all sides, both in Vienna; and the Clam-Gallas Palace in Prague (1707–13; now the Municipal Archives; for further discussion *see* BRAUN, MATYÁŠ BERNARD). The common characteristics of these works are a clearly defined basement with shallow rustication, an emphasized *piano nobile* with Roman Baroque pediments (alternately triangular and segmental), central pediments, the vertical thrust of the façade reinforced by the use of framed attic windows pushing up against the entablature, and a powerful entablature surmounted by balustrading or a plinth and statues. The reversion to the standard Roman design features adopted by Bernini's successors is also accompanied by the use of the Palladian pediment motif decorated with sculpture in the proper temple manner. The apparently tight pattern nonetheless allows enough scope for variations, leading at the Clam-Gallas Palace to the strongly emphasized projecting end bays, reminiscent of another Roman model, Borromini's unrealized scheme for the Palazzo Pamphili (1647) on the Piazza Navona. One of Fischer's final works was the Hofbibliothek, part of the Hofburg, Vienna (*see* VIENNA, §V, 5(i) and fig. 16), which was under consideration from 1716 but built posthumously (1723–36) and modified in execution by Fischer's son (2) Joseph Emanuel Fischer von Erlach.

There is a clear distinction in Fischer's work between his palace designs, which concentrate heavily on the composition of the façade, and the architecture of his villas and *maisons de plaisance*. His designs are in the tradition of the tempietti based on the virtuoso Roman tombs that can be seen at their best in Giovanni Battista Montana's engravings (first published 1624–36). Fischer's

1. Johann Bernhard Fischer von Erlach: Palais Trautson, Vienna, *c.* 1710–16

variations, however, are enriched by his virtuosity in shaping the plan, combining regular geometric shapes (circle, oval, triangle, square and hexagon) in symmetrical compositions. Over such complex but regular plans, Fischer created richly moulded, almost sculptured buildings that may be regarded as brilliant examples of his architectural composition. One example is the garden building (1694) based on three squares and three ovals for the park at Klesheim, a commission from the Archbishop of Salzburg, which appears externally to have three façades, each with a central outward-curving projection.

These garden buildings were the intermediate stage directly preceding the working out of Fischer's formula for villa architecture. Actual buildings in this category, such as Schloss Engelhartstetten (*c.* 1693) or the Gartenpalais Schlick-Eckhardt (*c.* 1695), are not as significant as the unrealized ideal plans taken up again in *Entwurff einer historischen Architektur*. Moreover, if it were purely a question of noting the incorporation of a round or oval main building into a larger complex, then it would have to be pointed out, as is the case with comparable Baroque inventions of complex building types (e.g. the X-shaped plan of the Gartenpalais Althann), that this was a preoccupation of Baroque architects all over Europe. What distinguishes Fischer is his ability to provide solutions that integrated the finest architectural achievements of Michelangelo and Bernini more than any other architect before him.

(ii) Ecclesiastical buildings. The special tradition of religious architecture was an ideal field for Fischer, combining architectural virtuosity with pomp and iconographical content. His principal churches were in Salzburg and Vienna. He had begun working in Salzburg (*see* SALZBURG, §1(ii)) for its Archbishop and Primate of Germany, Johann Ernst von Thun-Hohenstein, in 1693, with a court stable and a riding school, but the following year he was commissioned to design for Salzburg the Dreifaltigkeitskirche (1694) and two years later the Kollegienkirche, commissions that had a crucial effect on Baroque architecture in southern Germany, particularly for religious buildings. Other commissions for churches and a hospital in Salzburg followed until the Archbishop's death in 1709, when his successor turned to other architects. The Dreifaltigkeitskirche (completed 1698) is built upon a plan of two ovals at right angles to each other, one representing the nave, the other the concave façade (see fig. 2), which recalls Borromini's church of S Agnese (1653–5) in the Piazza Navona, Rome. Also Roman is the combination of façade, twin towers and dome. The oval nave anticipates the design of Fischer's later Karlskirche, Vienna, and underlines his liking for stereometrically neat shapes. His Roman experience enabled him to create quite naturally something that until then had been largely alien to church architecture in the German lands.

In the Kollegienkirche (1696–1707), a much larger and more monumental commission, Fischer proposed a completely novel solution. By shifting the crossing dome west, the traditional Latin cross was given a more regular shape, recalling Renato Rosati's S Carlo ai Catinari (begun 1612) in Rome and Jacques Le Mercier's church of the Sorbonne (1635–48), Paris. This solution made it possible for the

2. Johann Bernhard Fischer von Erlach: Dreifaltigkeitskirche, Salzburg, 1694–8

internal elevations and the layout of the side chapels to become symmetrical. The liturgically necessary nave and the architecturally ideal concept of a centralized, symmetrical form were thus brilliantly combined and, in Fischer's work, executed with an unprecedented logic. Overall, the church inspired two imitations within fifteen years, at Weingarten Abbey and Einsiedeln Abbey. With the Kollegienkirche, Fischer made a greater contribution to Baroque architecture than he did with his palaces or even his *maisons de plaisance*. His masterpiece, however, was the Karlskirche in Vienna (begun 1715; *see* AUSTRIA, fig. 6; for further discussion *see also* VIENNA, §V, 2). This unparalleled work encompassed the whole spectrum of Fischer's knowledge and interests and was full of iconographical significance for Emperor Charles VI, whose votive church it was. Thus, for example, the great Trajanic columns flanking the entrance bear reliefs depicting scenes from the life of St Carlo Borromeo, to whom the church is dedicated, the themes of which are Constancy and Fortitude. The columns also symbolize both the Pillars of Hercules (i.e. the Straits of Gibraltar), suggesting the history of the empire and Charles VI's claim to the throne of Spain; and the two pillars in the porch of the Temple of Solomon in Jerusalem, Jachin and Boaz (which may also mean Constancy and Fortitude), thus presenting Charles VI as the new Solomon, following through Fischer's derivation of architecture from Jerusalem in his *Entwurff einer historischen Architektur*.

(iii) Writings. Fischer's *Entwurff einer historischen Architektur*, presented to Charles VI in manuscript and proof form in 1712 and first printed in Vienna in 1721, is a major work of European architectural history. Like his buildings, Fischer's published work profits from and convinces by means of the wide scope of his knowledge and information and his great ability to summarize and synthesize. The book is also a form of self-promotion, including in Book IV Fischer's own works and projects, and in Book V specimens of urns and vases, an art category that he loved to design. These sections, however, are only a continuation of historical description covering all civilizations. The section on vases begins with the Bronze Sea, the huge water tank in the Temple of Solomon (*see* JERUSALEM, §II, 1(ii)), and the book itself describes the origins of architecture as in Jerusalem, serving as a corrective to Vitruvianism and enriching the historical perspective. His fascination with pictorial material relating to the Far Eastern and Oriental world, history and 'curiosities' is reflected in Book III, which deals with 'a few buildings by the Arabs and Turks, and also new Persian, Siamese, Chinese and Japanese building'. In this extension of the consideration of architectural history into regions and civilizations outside Europe, Fischer established a pattern of a scope and thoroughness hitherto unknown. He also took over a tradition, current at least since Pirro Ligorio, of the architectural reconstruction of ancient, predominantly Roman, buildings. The reconstruction of the architecture of ancient Rome in its formal and typological richness corresponded to Fischer's actual task of creating modern imperial architecture in Vienna. Reconstructions such as those of Trajan's Forum, the Domus Aurea or even the Naumachia Domitiani are reflected in modern terms, often with specific quotations, in schemes and buildings such as Schönbrunn and the Karlskirche, the two principal official monuments of the empire under Leopold I, Joseph I and Charles VI.

WRITINGS

Entwurff einer historischen Architektur (Vienna, 1721, 2/1725/R Farnborough, 1964; Eng. trans. of 2nd edn, 1730)

BIBLIOGRAPHY

D. Frey: *Johann Bernhard Fischer von Erlach: Eine Studie über seine Stellung in der Entwicklung der Wiener Palastfassade* (Vienna, 1923)
H. V. Lanchester: *Fischer von Erlach* (London, 1924)
H. Sedlmayr: *Fischer von Erlach der Ältere* (Munich, 1925)
B. Grimschitz: *Wiener Barockpaläste* (Vienna, 1944)
F. Hagen-Dempf: *Die Kollegienkirche in Salzburg* (Vienna, 1949)
E. Passmore: 'Fischer von Erlach, Architect to a Monarchy', *RIBA J.*, lviii (1951), pp. 452–75
D. Frey: 'J. B. Fischer von Erlach', *Jb. Kstgesch. Bundesdkmlamt.*, i (1955)
H. Haselberger-Blaha: 'Die Triumphtore Bernhard Fischers von Erlach', *Wien. Jb. Kstgesch.*, xvii (1955), pp. 63–85
G. Kunoth: *Die historische Architektur Fischers von Erlach* (Düsseldorf, 1956)
H. Sedlmayr: *Johann Bernhard Fischer von Erlach* (Vienna and Munich, 1956)
W. Buchowiecki: *Der Barockbau der ehemaligen Hofbibliothek in Wien, ein Werk J. B. Fischers von Erlach* (Vienna, 1957)
J. J. Morper: 'Schrifttum zum Fischer von Erlach', *Das Münster*, 1–2 (1957), pp. 49–51
F. D. Fergusson: 'St. Charles' Church, Vienna: The Iconography of its Architecture', *J. Soc. Archit. Historians*, xxix/4 (1970), pp. 318–26
A. Aurenhammer: *J. B. Fischer von Erlach* (London, 1973)
W. Schaber: 'Meisterwerke der Barockarchitektur: Johann Bernhard Fischer von Erlach und Salzburg', *Die Weltkunst*, lv/14 (1985), pp. 1982–5
E. Harris: *British Architectural Books and Writers* (Cambridge, 1990), pp. 194–6

WERNER OECHSLIN

(2) Joseph Emanuel Fischer von Erlach (*b* Vienna, 13 Sept 1693; *d* Vienna, 29 June 1742). Son of (1) Johann Bernhard Fischer von Erlach. He received his basic training from his father. He first presented himself to the Viennese aristocracy as a connoisseur of the most modern architecture with his illustrated work *Prospekte und Abrisse einiger Gebäude von Wien* (1713). Having been granted an unlimited scholarship for travel by Emperor Charles VI, at the end of 1713 Fischer went first to Rome, where among other things he purchased medals for the imperial numismatic collection. There too his father's connections gave him the necessary contacts, both in the learned circle of archaeologists, historians and engineers and among the aristocracy. It is probable that he went on to Naples. In 1717 he was in Paris, studying the most recent achievements of European architecture; his later work as an architect is indicative of his study under Robert de Cotte, the Director of the Académie Royale d'Architecture and Premier Architecte du Roi. Fischer continued the mathematical and technical side of his education with further periods of study in the Netherlands and England and through personal contact with such noted authorities as John Theophilus Désaguiliers (1683–1744) in London and Wilhelm Jakob van s'Gravesande (1688–1742) in the Netherlands.

An engineer with comprehensive training, Fischer included in his interests not only architecture but also the development of the steam engine; he built the first one to be sited in continental Europe at Kassel in 1721–2, for Charles, Landgrave of Hesse-Kassel. The steam engine built by the engineer Isaak Potter in 1722 for the mine at Königsberg (now Kaliningrad) was made to work only as a result of Fischer's pioneering innovations. His first work (1722–3) in Vienna was also in connection with the construction of a steam engine in the gardens of Prince Adam Franz Schwarzenberg (1680–1732) to provide power for his water display. In 1724 he installed the water supply, pumping station and goods lift at the abbey of Göttweig near Krems. From 1732 to 1736 he was commissioned by the Hofkammer to build steam engines and to undertake other engineering work of a technical nature for the mines in upper Hungary, where he also took on the role of builder and general contractor. His success brought him fame and recognition, and his work improved the finances of the state as well as his own. After confirmation of his status as a noble and his appointment to the Imperial Council in 1724, he was made a baron (1735).

Fischer had been trained purposely by his father to succeed him as an architect, and immediately on his return to Vienna at the end of 1722 he was appointed Imperial Court Architect. This was also to ensure the continuation of imperial projects under construction that had been designed by his father, who was already mortally ill. Various alterations to his father's designs can, however, be observed in all these buildings: at the court stables in the more pronounced sectioning off, corresponding to the main line of the neighbouring planned new Hofburg complex (from 1722), following the main direction already initiated by his father; at the Karlskirche (*see* AUSTRIA, fig. 6) in the high French dome, as well as in the interior decoration and furnishings (completed 1737; *see also*

VIENNA, §V, 2). In the Hofbibliothek (from 1723) also, he proposed alterations that are evident in only a few details in the interior. The side wings towards the Josefsplatz were not executed until later, in an altered form.

In terms of urban planning these buildings were conceived as belonging to the larger complex created by the Hofburg (*see* VIENNA, §V, 5 and fig. 15); as Imperial Court Architect Fischer produced three proposals for this, which can be reconstructed only partially. His plan for the Hofburg (1722–6) proposed a broadly new treatment of the axial relationships: essentially the palace would have been laid out in the form of two large adjoining courtyards, with a newly built Hofkapelle standing in the middle of the smaller one. Construction of the wing comprising the Reichskanzlei, which formed one long side of the larger courtyard, began in 1726, with Fischer supplanting as architect Johann Lukas von Hildebrandt, his counterpart at the court office, who had been involved with the scheme from 1723. The façade of the Reichskanzleitrakt, which is indebted equally to French classicism and to local tradition for its design, illustrates how Fischer had assimilated modern architectural thinking in this example of imperial architecture on the grand scale. While the first intention was that on the side facing the city there should be a staggered backdrop reminiscent of a stage set, with a semicircular *cour d'honneur* recessed into it, in the second set of plans the dimensions were adjusted to suit the existing site conditions; in the final version (1726) a uniformly structured form for the façade, the Michaelerfront, was created from the various built masses (see fig.). Construction work to these plans had not reached the halfway point when it was broken off, and it was not restarted in line with Fischer's scheme until 1889 (completed 1893 by Ferdinand Kirschner, 1821–96). The Winterreitschule (1729–35; now the Spanish Riding School) was built on the southern flank of the Michaelerfront. It is characterized by classical coolness and severity, with a lack of a striving for dynamic effect in the interior.

Fischer's contribution to the design of Klosterneuburg Abbey was another large building project that came to him through the Imperial Office of Works. The building in 1730, under the direction of Graf Gundacker Ludwig Joseph von Althann, Surveyor of the Imperial Works and Fischer's most influential protector, of an imperial residence within Klosterneuburg Abbey (already under construction), was based on Donato-Felice Allio's designs, but the building's grandeur was enhanced, and there was a stronger emphasis on the secular areas. These alterations were reflected externally in a reordering of the storeys and projecting bays, the introduction of cupolas and a nobler structuring of the façade. Allio implemented Fischer's innovations in his individual style.

For such major buildings as the Landständische Akademie (1730) in Vienna, the Ritterakademie (*c.* 1725) in Liegnitz (now Legnica) and the army pensioners' hospitals in Budapest (before *c.* 1727) and Prague (*c.* 1730), central planning by the Imperial Office of Works is generally assumed to have been in the person of Fischer, the more so as the iconological programme for these state buildings was also drawn up by Johann Konrad Albrecht von Albrechtsburg (1682–1751), a well-educated humanist

Joseph Emanuel Fischer von Erlach: the Michaelerfront, Hofburg, Vienna; engraving by Salomon Kleiner (Vienna, Österreichische Nationalbibliothek)

who was favoured for his invention of allegorical programmes concerning court buildings in particular. The so-called Albrechtkodex, which offers a list of these arrangements, is generally taken as a sign of Fischer's involvement. On the other hand, it can be objected, for example, that in the case of the hospital in Prague there is documentary evidence of plans by Kilian Ignaz Dientzenhofer, and in the case of the one in Budapest of plans by the Imperial Court Master Builder Erhard Martinelli; by the 1990s a study to define their respective contributions was still outstanding. Research has in fact considerably reduced the number of schemes that had traditionally been assigned to Fischer (including the imperial law courts (c. 1726), Hetzhaus (1735), Vizedomamt (1737) and the Stiftskirche (1739), all in Vienna, and Schloss Seelowitz in Moravia), but the following can be ascribed to him with certainty: the extension (from 1723) to the Gartenpalais Schwarzenburg, Vienna, including the reconstruction of the Kuppelsaal, striking internally and externally, and the decoration and furnishing of some interiors; the main building (1730) of Schloss Eckartsau, Lower Austria; and one of his masterpieces, the Gartenpalais Althann (1730) at Ungargasse, Vienna, for Graf Gundacker Ludwig Joseph von Althann. His masterly assimilation of new achievements in Western Europe turned this perfect example of structured space, with its numerous garden buildings, into the most modern garden layout in the late Baroque period of Vienna.

A number of town houses have been attributed to Fischer, but there is no documentary evidence to support such claims. Of these houses, only the Palais Rauchmiller

(c. 1735) at Neuer Markt, Vienna, survives. The others are known only through Salomon Kleiner's engraved views, so that it cannot be established whether they were ever built. His design (1735) for a palace for Albrecht, the creator of the decorative programmes, is known not to have been realized. Kleiner's view of the Palais Kinsky, Vienna, shows only slight changes to the shapes of the windows when compared to the actual structure, now confirmed as the work of Domenico Martinelli. In the work that Fischer carried out in the 1730s, the forms became gradually hard and rigid and began to be isolated from the wall pattern. The sober style of his late work finally sought to present the pure geometric surface as an expression of functional architecture, as for example in the extension (1735) to the Johannes Nepomuk Hospital, Vienna, as well as in the exterior walls of Grossweikersdorf parish church (1727), Lower Austria; Fischer's architectural rationalism seemed to increase with the size of the project.

Fischer occupied a position of special importance as a designer of sculptural and decorative work. Just as the tombs made for Starhemberg (before 1730; Vienna, Schottenkirche), Schlick (1723; Prague Cathedral), Sachsen-Zeitz (1725; Bratislava Cathedral) and Wolff (1722; Wrocław, St Elisabeth) used the motif of the wall obelisk already repeatedly used by his father, with only the Trautson tomb (1721; Vienna, Michaelerkirche) presenting a more or less original solution, so too were the reconstruction of the Josephsäule (1725), in the Hoher Markt, Vienna, and the Mariazell Gnadenaltar (1726; Mariazell pilgrimage church) based on his father's ideas.

On the other hand, in the Monument of Reconciliation in Raab (1731; now Györ) and the similarly constructed tomb of *John Nepomuk* (1729) in Prague Cathedral, Italian and French models were incorporated in the elaborate composition, and in the former an ark of the covenant and latter a sarcophagus is positioned in such a way as to make it seem almost suspended. While Joseph Emanuel Fischer von Erlach may not have been endowed with his father's imaginative powers and incomparable talent in manipulating architectural forms on a monumental scale, he was nevertheless a stylistically literate architect, well able to exploit both current foreign trends and native art traditions in the expression of Austrian imperial pomp.

WRITINGS

Prospekte und Abrisse einiger Gebäude von Wien, daselbst gezeichnet von Joseph Emanuel Fischer von Erlach (Vienna, 1713)

BIBLIOGRAPHY

J. Schmidt: 'Fischer von Erlach der Jüngere', *Mitt. Ver. Gesch. Stadt Wien* (1933)

H. Sedlmayr: *Johann Bernhard Fischer von Erlach* (Vienna and Munich, 1956/rev. 1976)

T. Zacharias: *Joseph Emanuel Fischer von Erlach* (Vienna and Munich, 1960)

P. Voit: 'Die Kunst Josef Emanuel Fischer von Erlachs und seine unbekannten Werke in Ungarn', *Actes du XXIIe congrès international d'histoire de l'art: Budapest 1967*, ii, pp. 131–40

F. Matsche: *Die Kunst im Dienst der Staatsidee Kaiser Karls VI* (Berlin and New York, 1981)

W. G. Rizzi: *Zum Stand der Forschung über Joseph Emanuel Fischer von Erlach*, Frühneuzeit-Studien, iii (Vienna, 1995)

W. GEORG RIZZI

Fischetti, Fedele (*b* Naples, 30 March 1732; *d* Naples, 25 Jan 1792). Italian painter and draughtsman. Born into a family of Neapolitan painters, he first worked in the bottega of Gennaro Borrello, whose daughter he married in 1753. He may have visited Rome during the 1750s (see 1979–80 exh. cat., p. 145), which would explain the moderated classical rethinking of the contemporary Rococo style that is evident in his early work. He executed works on sacred subjects, mainly of mediocre quality, for many Neapolitan churches during the period 1759–66. Among these are the canvases for the church of the Spirito Santo, including the *Presentation of the Virgin*; the *Birth of the Virgin* for S Maria in Portico; two canvases for S Maria la Nuova; and the frescoes for the nave vault of S Caterina da Siena.

In the mature and late periods of his career Fischetti was a brilliant decorator, as seen in his fresco cycles for the villas and palaces of the Neapolitan nobility and for the Bourbon court of Ferdinand IV. The artist attempted to reconcile the characteristics of late Baroque decoration with the new demands of formal clarity imposed by the court, using a lightened colour scheme. From the end of the 1770s and throughout the following decade he produced allegorical, mythological and historical frescoes, including those for the Palazzo Fondi; *Alexander of Aragon's Entry into Naples* for the *salone* of the Palazzo Maddaloni; and the *Dream of Alexander the Great* and other scenes for the gallery of the Palazzo Casacalenda (now the Palazzo Reale di Capodimonte). Between 1778 and 1781 he worked in the royal palace of Caserta, where he produced the frescoes of the *Four Seasons* and the related *Golden Age*. In 1784 Fischetti frescoed the Palazzo

Doria-d'Angri, where he adopted the courtly and classical decorative styles of such northern European painters as Heinrich Füger and Angelica Kauffman, who were then active in Rome. Stylistically very close to these frescoes is the canvas representing *Caesar and Cleopatra* (1780s; Bellavista, nr Naples, Bellucci Sessa priv. col.).

In this period Fischetti also began working, alongside Giuseppe Bonito, for the Accademia del Disegno in Naples, and he collaborated with such architects as Ferdinando Fuga and Mario Gaetano Gioffredo, but especially with Luigi Vanvitelli and Carlo Vanvitelli (1739–1821). Meanwhile he continued to paint religious works for Neapolitan churches, such as the *Crucifixion* (1780) for the Annunziata. He also executed frescoes in the church of the Annunziata in Capua. Whereas in his work for ecclesiastical patrons Fischetti's style is sometimes sterile, suffocated by late Mannerist influence, in his secular subjects he developed an aptitude for sophisticated naturalistic scenes, skilfully executed with a sense of colour derived from French painting.

Around 1789 Fischetti was engaged at the Palazzo Cellammare in Naples on a grandiose fresco of *Apollo and the Muses*. From 1790 to 1791 he decorated the gallery in the casino at San Leucio with frescoes of the *Triumph of Bacchus and Ariadne* and other scenes from the life of Bacchus, which were painted as a virtual hymn to life and to carefree sensuality. In this late phase of his career the artist was repetitive in his rationalistic approach and had lost his earlier freshness.

Fischetti produced a number of drawings during his career; these are remarkable for the excellent quality of execution and the fineness of line (e.g. *Allegory of the Golden Age*, *c.* 1778–9; New York, Scholz col.; other examples Naples, Soc. Stor. Patria, and New York, Cooper-Hewitt Mus.). He also executed cartoons, such as those for a series of tapestries representing the story of *Cupid and Psyche* (*c.* 1781) for the royal palace of Caserta (cartoons untraced; tapestries, Naples, Pal. Reale); and those (after 1781) for the tapestries of the *salone* of the casino at Carditello (cartoons untraced; tapestries, Naples, Mus. N. S Martino and Capodimonte). A younger relative of Fischetti was the decorative painter Fedele Alessandro Fischetti, who worked in a similar style (Causa Picone, 1968–9).

Bolaffi

BIBLIOGRAPHY

P. Orlandi: *Abecedario pittorico* (Florence, 1788), col. 1410

P. Sigismondo: *Descrizione di Napoli*, i (Naples, 1788), p. 224

C. T. Dalbono: *Storia della pittura in Napoli e in Sicilia dalla fine del 1600 a noi* (Naples, 1859), pp. 37, 42, 46ff

O. Ferrari: *Arazzi italiani del sei e settecento* (Milan, 1968), pp. 43–4, 105–8

M. Causa Picone: 'I disegni della Società Napoletana di Storia Patria', *Archv Stor. Prov. Napoletane*, n.s. 2, vii–viii (1968–9), p. 157

N. Spinosa: 'La pittura napoletana da Carlo a Ferdinando IV di Borbone', *Storia di Napoli*, viii (Naples, 1971), pp. 504, 516–18, 543–5

Civiltà del '700 a Napoli, 1734–1799, 2 vols (exh. cat. by R. Causa and others, Naples, Capodimonte; Naples, Pal. Reale; Naples, Villa Pignatelli; and elsewhere; 1979–80), i, pp. 145–7, 282–5, 363, 398–9; ii, p. 435

N. Spinosa: *Pittura napoletana del settecento dal Rococò al Classicismo* (Naples, 1986) [with full bibliog.]

M. Pisani: 'Una famiglia di pittori: I Fischetti', *Napoli Nob.*, 3rd ser., xxvii (1988), pp. 112–21

A. Spinosa: 'Fischetti, Fedele', *La pittura in Italia: Il settecento*, ed. G. Briganti, ii (Milan, 1990), p. 718

RAFFAELLA BENTIVOGLIO-RAVASIO

Fischinger, Oskar W. (*b* Gelnhausen, nr Frankfurt am Main, 22 June 1900; *d* Los Angeles, 31 Jan 1967). American painter and film maker of German birth. From 1914 to 1920 he had various apprenticeships in architecture, engineering and organ building. In 1920 he began to experiment with film using hand-drawn black-and-white abstract designs. His first four 'studies', set to musical recordings, were made between 1921 and 1924 and shown in Munich and Düsseldorf in 1925. These were animated abstract films using wax mouldings and involving a wax-cutting machine that Fischinger specially designed. In 1926 he moved to Berlin, where he remained for the next ten years. By 1927 he was working with Fritz Lang producing science fiction special effects while continuing his own film making. After the creation of sound on film he produced films such as *Study No. 7* (1930–31), a three minute black-and-white abstract film set to Brahms's *Hungarian Dance No. 5*.

Due to Nazi persecution in Germany, Fischinger decided to leave and to accept a contract with Paramount Studios in Hollywood, CA, in 1936. After artistic differences, he left for MGM in 1937 and for similar reasons left Walt Disney's studio in 1939. In 1947 he created *Motion Painting No. 1*, an abstract colour film using oil on perspex, and this was awarded the Grand Prix at the Exposition Internationale at Brussels the following year. From the late 1930s onwards Fischinger began to concentrate on abstract painting, which had previously been only an adjunct to his film making. His varied style ranged from the organic forms of *Swirls* (1947; Long Beach, CA, Mus. A.) to more geometrical works such as *Mosaic No. 2* (1952; Pasadena, CA, Norton Simon Mus.).

BIBLIOGRAPHY
Fischinger: A Retrospective of Paintings and Films (exh. cat. by G. Nordland, Denver, CO, Gal. 609, 1980)

Fischl, Eric (*b* New York, 9 March 1948). American painter, draughtsman and printmaker. After completing his BFA at the California Institute of Arts in Valencia, CA, in 1972, he taught from 1974 to 1978 at the Nova Scotia College of Art and Design in Halifax, NS. In 1978 he returned to New York and began to produce paintings in a naturalistic style of uncomfortably intimate scenes of middle-class suburban existence and burgeoning sexuality, as in *Master Bedroom* (1983; Los Angeles, CA, Mus. Contemp. A.), in which a nearly naked girl in hair-curlers kneels on a double bed with her arms around a large dog. By depicting the figures larger than life, he placed the viewer in the role of a child, exaggerating the psychological force of the situations by presenting them as if retrieved from memory. The historical lineage proposed by critics for the bravura technique of these works includes the paintings of Manet, Balthus and Edward Hopper, but the clear reliance on photography suggests a debt to the Photorealism of the 1960s. Perhaps to counter the misapprehension of his pictures as Neo-Expressionist, in the mid-1980s Fischl exaggerated their formal quality by fragmenting the image on to a series of separate panels overlapping at different angles, as in *Portrait of a Dog* (1987; New York, MOMA), a solution already explored in his six-part colour etching the *Year of the Drowned Dog* (1983; see exh. cat., p. 43).

BIBLIOGRAPHY
Eric Fischl: Scenes before the Eye (exh. cat. by C. W. Glenn and L. Barnes, Long Beach, CA State U., A. Mus.; Berkeley, U. CA, A. Mus.; Honolulu, Contemp. A. Cent. and elsewhere; 1986–7)
P. Schjeldahl: *Eric Fischl* (New York, 1988)

MARCO LIVINGSTONE

Fisco, Claude (Antoine) (*b* Leuven, 22 Jan 1736; *d* Erps-Kwerps, nr Leuven, 10 Jan 1825). Flemish engineer and architect. After completing his studies at the military academy in Brussels, he began a career as an engineer in 1766, making charts and drawing plans for military fortifications, bridges and roads. On 23 May 1772 he was appointed engineer to the city of Brussels and later became director of the municipal academy. In 1775 he designed the cool, harmonious Place des Martyrs, his most important architectural work. The classical Doric façades show, in the architrave and the bucrania of the frieze, the direct influence of the pattern books of Jacopo Vignola. Before the Place Royale was built, the Place des Martyrs was the first grandly conceived classical piece of town planning in Brussels. Although Fisco presented various designs for the Place Royale from 1775, the government gave this important commission to the Parisian architects Barnabé Guimard and Jean-Benoit-Vincent Barré, to the great humiliation of both Fisco and the court architect Laurent Benoît Dewez. Thereafter Fisco returned to military service and politics. He ended his career as city architect in Leuven (1804–07).

BIBLIOGRAPHY
BNB; Thieme–Becker
G. des Marez: 'La Place Royale à Bruxelles: Genèse de l'oeuvre, sa conception et ses auteurs', *Mem. Acad. Royale Belgique: Cl. B.-A.*, i (1923), pp. 6, 8, 21–5, 73–4
J. O'Donnell: 'Claude Fisco, ingénieur et architecte, 1736–1825', *Cah. Bruxell.*, xviii (1974), pp. 115–27
J. Sterckx: 'Het Martelarenplein in Brussel', *Mnmt & Landschappen*, v/1 (1986), pp. 36–50

J.-P. ESTHER

Fishbourne. English harbour village in West Sussex, 3 km west of Chichester. It is the site of a Roman palace excavated (1961–9) by B. W. Cunliffe. After occupation as a base for military stores from the time of the Roman invasion in AD 43 to *c.* 50, a substantial masonry house was built (*c.* 60–65) with a peristyle courtyard and a bath suite. This 'proto-palace' was decorated with painted plaster, stucco, *opus sectile*, mosaics and Corinthian columns, exceptional luxury in Britain at that date. It was far surpassed, however, by the magnificent palace built *c.* 75, which incorporated the known part of the proto-palace. It had four colonnaded wings arranged round a rectangular peristyle garden (100×76 m); the north and east wings had suites of rooms grouped around internal courtyards. The monumental entrance in the middle of the east wing led across the garden courtyard, through an avenue of hedges, trees and fountains formally laid out, to the central audience chamber (*triclinium*) in the west wing of state-rooms. A corridor nearly 100 m long ran along the back of this range. Much of the southern part of the complex remains unexcavated under modern buildings. The excavated remains are, however, under cover and include a museum.

The palace was decorated with materials and craftsmanship of the highest quality, including black-and-white geometric mosaics, wall veneers of imported coloured marble and wall paintings in the Pompeian style. Its owner was clearly of aristocratic rank; Cunliffe suggested that it belonged to Tiberius Claudius Cogidubnus, the British client king mentioned by Tacitus (*Agricola* xiv.2). The palace stood for over two centuries during which time it underwent several modifications, involving in particular the replanning of the north wing, effectively as a separate house. Polychrome mosaics were laid there in the 2nd century; one of them was preserved almost complete, and has a cupid riding a dolphin in the central medallion, and capricorns and seahorses in half circles. The palace was destroyed by fire during further alterations in the late 3rd century.

BIBLIOGRAPHY

B. Cunliffe: *Excavations at Fishbourne, 1961–1969*, Soc. Antiqua. London Res. Rep., xxvi, 2 vols (Leeds, 1971)

T. F. C. BLAGG

Fisher. English family of sculptors. Richard Fisher (*b* 1690) was a self-taught sculptor working in Ripon from *c.* 1715. He worked for the first Lord Walpole at Wolterton Hall, Norfolk, in 1737–8, and then at Castle Howard, N. Yorks, in 1741. He had established himself in York Minster Yard by 1746, and he may have been related to John Fisher the elder (Fisher of York; 1736–1804), the outstanding English sculptor working outside London in the second half of the 18th century and the founder of a family business that continued his high standards of craftsmanship through four generations, often making it difficult to attribute particular works to individual hands.

John Fisher the elder began his career in London, but he was persuaded to move to York by Thomas Watson-Wentworth, 1st Marquess of Rockingham, who was impressed by the two marble statuettes that Fisher exhibited at the Free Society of Artists in 1761: *Our Saviour with the Cross* (York Minster) and *Jupiter* (York, Yorks Mus.). Fisher subsequently produced marble chimney-pieces for Rockingham's country house, Wentworth Woodhouse, S. Yorks. His finest works can be ranked alongside the best monuments by Joseph Nollekens and John Bacon (i), for example the marble statue of *Sir George Saville* (*d* 1784; marble, York Minster) and the marble figure of *Hygeia* that commemorates *John Dealtry* (1773; York Minster). Fisher's output was prolific: between 1764 and his death in 1804 at least 66 monuments were produced, in which finely carved reliefs and figures are combined with coloured marbles and an abundance of decorative ornament in the style of the architects James and Robert Adam. He also produced busts, chimney-pieces and marble tops for Chippendale sideboards (the latter for the Gallery at Harewood House, W. Yorks).

John Fisher the elder worked in partnership with his brother Samuel Fisher (*fl* 1771–80) until 1780 and took his son John Fisher the younger (1760–1839) as an apprentice in 1785. Despite near-bankruptcy in 1795, the family business survived into later generations through John Fisher the elder's other sons William Fisher (?1777–1815) and Samuel Fisher (*d* 1812) and the three sons of John Fisher the younger: John Fisher (*b* 1786), Charles Fisher (1790–1861) and Richard Fisher (1786–1819). Other sculptors of the same family name were active in York in this period and may also be relatives.

BIBLIOGRAPHY

Gunnis

C. Myerscough: 'The Fishers of York: A Family of Sculptors', *York Historian*, vii (1986), pp. 46–59

JULIUS BRYANT

Fisher, Alvan [Alvin] (*b* Needham, MA, 9 Aug 1792; *d* Dedham, MA, 13 Feb 1863). American painter. Soon after he left the tutelage of John Ritto Penniman (*c.* 1782–1841), he began to paint genre landscapes such as *Winter in Milton, Massachusetts* (1815; Montclair, NJ, A. Mus.), which depicts a man on a horse-drawn sleigh enjoying the beauty of a fresh New England snowfall. In this work the artist seems more concerned with presenting an image of peacefulness than with the specific identification of the site. Despite its early date, the painting suggests the influence of Claude Lorrain as well as 17th-century Dutch winter scenes.

Although Fisher regularly accepted portrait commissions, his work demonstrates an appreciation of and continual commitment to the depiction of East Coast scenery. He was one of America's earliest landscape painters and an important member of the Hudson River school. Fisher travelled extensively: by 1820 he had sketched along the Connecticut River valley and at Niagara Falls. The tiny figures in the foreground of *Niagara Falls* (1820; Washington, DC, N. Mus. Amer. A.) add anecdotal interest and emphasize the majestic size of the Falls. However, Fisher preferred picturesque sites in New England and often made return trips there.

In 1825 Fisher travelled to Europe visiting England, France, Switzerland and Italy. On his return in 1826 he established a studio in Boston and quickly became a leading figure in the city's artistic community. From 1827 he exhibited landscapes regularly at the Boston Athenaeum. He also exhibited in New York, Philadelphia, PA, Washington, DC, and as far west as Natchez, MS.

As early as the mid-1830s Fisher had explored the White Mountains and the coast of Maine, expanding the scenic vocabulary of the Hudson River school; for example, in *The Notch* (1834; Harvard, MA, Fruitlands Mus.) the artist manipulated the lighting and exaggerated the cloud formations to achieve a dramatic composition. The cyclonic sky effects reveal the probable influence of Turner, whose work Fisher had seen in London and whose landscape prints he collected. Despite his productivity, critical acclaim and financial success Fisher was quickly forgotten after his death.

BIBLIOGRAPHY

M. M. Swan: 'The Unpublished Notebooks of Alvan Fisher', *Antiques*, lxviii/2 (1955), pp. 126–9
R. C. Vose jr: 'Alvan Fisher, 1792–1863: American Pioneer in Landscape and Genre', *CT Hist. Soc. Bull.*, xxvii/4 (1962), pp. 97–117
F. B. Adelson: *Alvan Fisher (1792–1863): Pioneer in American Landscape Painting* (diss., New York, Columbia U., 1982)
——: 'An American Snowfall: Early Winter Scenes by Alvan Fisher', *A. VA*, xxiv/3 (1983–4), pp. 2–9
——: 'Alvan Fisher in Maine: His Early Coastal Scenes', *Amer. A. J.*, xviii/3 (1986), pp. 63–73

—: 'Home on La Grange: Alvan Fisher's Lithographs of Lafayette's Residence in France', *Antiques*, cxxxiv/1 (1988), pp. 152–7

FRED B. ADELSON

Fisher, Edward (*b* Dublin, 18 Nov 1730; *d* London, after 1781). Irish engraver, active in England. He may have studied mezzotint engraving under James McArdell, as he later published some of McArdell's plates. He was working in London by 1757, the date of four mezzotint plates for C. N. Jenty's *Essay on . . . the Human Structure*. Fisher's first dated portraits appeared in 1758, and in 1759 he engraved his first plate after Reynolds, whose paintings were the basis for 28 of his total of some 66 portraits: of his 18 exhibits at the Society of Artists (1761–76), 14 were after Reynolds, the best known being *Garrick between Tragedy and Comedy* (1762; see Chaloner Smith, no. 20). In that year Horace Walpole remarked of the Irish-born mezzotint engravers in London: 'Houston, McArdell and Fisher have already promised by their works to revive the beauty of mezzotint.' James Northcote called Fisher 'that most exact and laborious artist, of whom Mr Reynolds used to say, that he was injudiciously exact', a fault which has been detected in such prints as the full-length portrait of *Lady Sarah Bunbury* (1766; CS 6). Among Fisher's last prints are a set of ten characters from Oliver Goldsmith's *Vicar of Wakefield* (CS 64), engraved from his own drawings and published by Robert Sayer and Bennett in 1776.

BIBLIOGRAPHY
DNB; Strickland; Thieme–Becker
H. Walpole: *A Catalogue of Engravers* (London, 1762, 2/1786), p. 245
J. Northcote: *The Life of Sir Joshua Reynolds*, i (1813, rev. 1818), p. 64
J. Chaloner Smith: *British Mezzotinto Portraits*, ii (London, 1879), pp. 485–510 [CS]
A. Graves: *The Society of Artists of Great Britain (1760–1791): The Free Society of Artists (1761–1783)* (London, 1907), p. 93
C. E. Russell: *English Mezzotint Portraits and their States: Catalogue of Corrections of and Additions to Chaloner Smith's 'British Mezzotinto Portraits'*, ii (London, 1926), pp. 107–11

DAVID ALEXANDER

Fisker, Kay (Otto) (*b* Copenhagen, 14 Feb 1893; *d* Copenhagen, 21 June 1965). Danish architect, designer and writer. As early as 1915 he collaborated with Aage Rafn in the competition for the railway stations on the island of Bornholm. The project was a brilliant artistic paraphrase of local architectural tradition, liberated from academic convention as well as provincial sentimentality. From 1909 to 1920 he studied at the Arkitektskole of the Kunstakademi in Copenhagen. He worked in Sweden in 1916–17 as a colleague of Sigurd Lewerentz and Gunnar Asplund. From the early 1920s he undertook a large-scale architectural practice in which substantial projects such as state-supported housing developments played an essential part. His large housing blocks, for example Hornbækhus (1923), Copenhagen, were well-proportioned, traditionally constructed multiple-bayed buildings with a minumum of classical elements of style. For the Exposition Internationale des Arts Décoratifs et Industriels Modernes in Paris (1925), Fisker designed the Danish pavilion in a cubism of severe brickwork. The trend towards the refined prismatic block in smooth brickwork was further elaborated in the unrealized project for the Danish Students' House (1928) in Paris. The breakthrough for this all-round, easily adaptable, almost timeless architectural form

came with the first prizewinning projects from 1931 for the University of Århus, in collaboration with C. F. Møller and Povl Stegmann, and the municipal hospital in Århus. Fisker was in partnership with C. F. Møller from 1929 to 1943, after which the latter carried on with the building of the university alone in accordance with the original plan for the project.

Until the building trade was industrialized and use of concrete components became widespread, Fisker's interpretation of modernism had a great influence on Danish architecture. Starting with compact blocks of masonry with pitched roofs, he created a continuous series of characteristic examples of his interpretation of the functionalist tradition: these included the large-scale housing developments of Vestersøhus (1939; see DENMARK, fig. 5), and Dronningegården (1944), the house for Mødrehjælpen, the national council for unmarried mothers (1954) and Voldparken School (1956), all in Copenhagen, all demonstrating variations of the same theme. Fisker's block of flats (1957) for the Hansaviertel in Berlin is not, however, typical of his style. Nor is the 15-storey prefabricated housing block (1958) in Brøndbyvester near Copenhagen. The last projects in which Fisker was personally involved included the Danish Institute in Rome (designed 1961–3, inaugurated 1967). Although Fisker was highly receptive to foreign influences, they were always modified by his strongly artistic temperament. He took a cautious view of modernism as a style and regarded it rather as an ethical obligation. In his opinion, architecture should reflect regional characteristics dependent on cultural traditions, local materials and climatic conditions. Fisker thus felt himself heir to a Danish tradition in the sphere of functional architecture whose exponents included Gottlob Bindesbøll, J. D. Herholdt (1818–1902), P. V. Jensen-Klint and Ivar Bentsen. In his eyes the combination of objectivity and moderation had helped to curb the excesses of both historicism and modernism. The result of this was a consistently high standard in Fisker's work, in which even modest assignments were stamped with his sure sense of quality, often with artistic finesse. Fisker regarded such non-Danish architects as Heinrich Tessenow, C. F. Voysey and the Chicago school as contemporaries working on the same lines.

As well as his work as a creative and highly productive architect, Fisker was active in other fields, including applied art and book production. Between 1936 and 1952 he took charge of fitting the interiors of a number of Danish passenger ships, such as the work on the DFDS Company's *Kronprinsesse Ingrid* (1947). From 1919 to 1927 he edited the periodical *Arkitekten* and redesigned its typography in a refined classical style. In 1919 he was a member of the teaching staff of the Arkitektskole of the Kunstakademi in Copenhagen, as a lecturer in house building (from 1924) and as professor (from 1936 to 1963).

WRITINGS
with F. R. Yerbury: *Modern Danish Architecture* (London, 1927)
with K. Millech: *Danske Arkitekturstrømninger, 1850–1950* [Trends in Danish architecture] (Copenhagen, 1951)

BIBLIOGRAPHY
S. E. Rasmussen: *Nordische Baukunst* (Berlin and Copenhagen, 1940)
H. E. Langkilde: *Arkitekten Kay Fisker* (Copenhagen, 1960)
'Det Danske Institut i Rom', *Arkitektur DK*, xiv/4 (1970), pp. 148–58

Nordisk klassicism/Nordic Classicism, 1910–1930 (exh. cat., ed. S. Paavilainen; Helsinki, Mus. Fin. Archit., 1982)
Archithese, 4 (1985) [issue containing numerous articles on Fisker and a bibliog.]

JØRGEN SESTOFT

Fister, Hans. *See* PFISTER, HANS.

Fitalis [Phytalis]. Greek family of sculptors, painters and architects. The brothers Ioannis Fitalis (*b* Tinos, ?1827), Georgios Fitalis (*b* Tinos, 1830; *d* 1901), Lazaros Fitalis (*b* Tinos, 1831; *d* 1909) and Markos Fitalis (*b* Tinos, 1834; *d* 1884 or 1901) all left Tinos at an early age to study at the Royal School of Fine Arts in Athens. In 1860 they opened a sculpture workshop, the Andriantopoieion, in which they produced mainly busts and statues for monuments and tombstones. It was headed by Georgios and Lazaros, who drew their inspiration from Classical models as well as from the ideas of Canova, which Lazaros had probably acquired in his earlier travels to Rome. The imposing statue of *Patriarch Gregory V* (1872; U. Athens), executed by Georgios, shows sculptural eloquence in its combination of richly detailed Baroque-style drapery with solid authoritative stature. Ioannis, who studied architecture at the Technical School in Athens (1844–6), worked with Lysandros Kaftantzoglou on the National Technical University buildings; he later worked on the island of Syros. Markos was primarily involved in painting and decorative projects, although he was also a sculptor. Ioannis worked mainly as an architect in Athens and Syros.

BIBLIOGRAPHY
S. Lydakes: *E ellenes glyptes* [The Greek sculptors] (Athens, 1981), pp. 37–51, 488–91
C. Christou and M. Koumvakali-Anastasiadi: *Modern Greek Sculpture, 1800–1940* (Athens, 1982), pp. 38–42, 169–72

EVITA ARAPOGLOU

Fitzalan, Henry, 12th Earl of Arundel (*b* 23 April 1512; *d* London, 24 Feb 1580). English statesman, patron and collector. Named after Henry VIII and educated at Cambridge, he was Deputy Governor at Calais from 1540 to 1544, Lord Chamberlain from 1546 to 1550 and a member of the Council of Regency under Edward VI in 1547. In 1551 he was briefly imprisoned, due to the hostility of John Dudley, Duke of Northumberland. Feigning initial support for the succession of Lady Jane Grey, Arundel became a key figure in the accession of Mary I in 1553 and became Lord High Steward in her household, an appointment renewed under Elizabeth I.

In 1549 Arundel had acquired a house in London off the Strand, later known as Arundel House (destr.). This was formerly the London residence of the bishops of Bath and Wells; he was thus one of many Tudor courtiers to benefit from the confiscation and forced sale of episcopal properties in London. Arundel House—later the setting for the renowned collection formed by the Earl's great-grandson, Thomas Howard, 2nd Earl of Arundel (*see* HOWARD (i), (1))—appears as an informal grouping of 16th-century ranges around a court in Wenzel Hollar's engravings of 1646. The extent of the 12th Earl's building work at this house is uncertain, as the previous secular owner, Sir Thomas Seymour (?1508–49), is said to have built extensively there. Arundel was probably responsible for the construction of a new gallery and lodgings at Arundel Castle, W. Sussex, as recorded by Tierney (1834). The chief building associated with Arundel, however, was Nonsuch Palace (destr.), Surrey, begun by Henry VIII in 1538, which was sold to him by Mary I in 1557. He mounted a huge entertainment for Queen Elizabeth there in 1559. It is doubtful that Arundel did any more there, however, than build the top or cupola of the gatehouse of the inner court and place his insignia on this feature and the outer gatehouse.

The contents of Nonsuch during Arundel's time there are of prime significance in the history of English art collecting, though the chief source—an inventory (1590) drawn up for John, 1st Baron Lumley (*see* LUMLEY), his son-in-law and heir—does not always make it possible to separate the contributions of the two men. The collection had a bias towards Flemish works and portraits. Arundel almost certainly acquired works by Hans Holbein (ii) directly from the royal collection; these included the fragment of the cartoon (London, N.P.G.) for the lost wall painting at Whitehall Palace, London, the portrait of *Christina of Denmark, Duchess of Milan* (London, N.G.) and a series of portrait drawings (Windsor Castle, Berks, Royal Lib.; *see* HOLBEIN, (3), fig. 5). He may also have bought those paintings listed in 1590 as works by Antonis Mor, Dürer and Jan van Scorel. His own portrait is recorded as the work of 'the famous painter Steven' (probably Steven van der Meulen); different derivations of this exist, the principal one being a half-length at Naworth Castle, Cumbria. Arundel's collection of books also formed, with Lumley's, part of the holdings that passed through crown ownership and are in the British Library, London; some volumes are marked with Arundel's signature and are said to have been deliberately gathered together in order to preserve works from monastic libraries that were threatened with dispersal after the dissolution of the monasteries in the 1530s and 1540s. In 1564 Arundel resigned his court offices and spent 1566–7 in Italy, largely at Padua. He was imprisoned in 1571–2 for supporting his son-in-law, Thomas Howard, 4th Duke of Norfolk (1536–72), in a conspiracy on behalf of Mary, Queen of Scots, and afterwards retired completely from court life.

UNPUBLISHED SOURCES
London, BL, Royal MSS 17. A. IX [life of Arundel]
DNB

BIBLIOGRAPHY
M. A. Tierney: *History of the Castle and Town of Arundel, with the Biography of its Earls* (London, 1834)
L. Cust: 'The Lumley Inventories', *Walpole Soc.*, vi (1917–18) [whole issue]
J. Dent: *The Quest for Nonsuch* (London, 1962/1970/*R* Sutton, 1981)
H. M. Colvin, ed.: *The History of the King's Works*, iv (London, 1982)

MAURICE HOWARD

FitzGerald, Desmond (*b* Nassau, 20 May 1846; *d* Brookline, MA, 22 Sept 1926). American engineer, patron and collector. He was educated in Providence, RI, in Paris and at the Phillips Academy in Andover, MA. He studied engineering and in 1873 became superintendent of the western division of the Boston waterworks, where he was instrumental in bringing about the sanitation of the water supply.

FitzGerald had studied sculpture in Paris as a young boy, and his love of art manifested itself in the creation of a collection of contemporary works by American, Dutch, Norwegian, Spanish, and in particular, French artists. He was an early friend of Claude Monet and owned numerous works by him, including *Mme Monet and Child* (1875), *Fishing Boats at Etretat, Hills of Vétheuil on the Seine* (1880) and *Sunset on the Seine: Winter Effect* (1880). Other Impressionist artists whose works appeared in his collection included Auguste Renoir, Edgar Degas, Camille Pissarro and Alfred Sisley. FitzGerald was an admirer and friend of the American painter W. Dodge Macknight (1860–1950); he owned over 300 works by this artist, built a gallery in his home in Brookline, MA, to house the collection and in 1916 published a study, *Dodge Macknight, Water Color Painter* (privately printed). FitzGerald's gallery also exhibited paintings by such American artists as Julian Alden Weir, Charles Herbert Woodbury (1864–1940), John Singer Sargent, John Joseph Enneking, Childe Hassam, John H. Twachtman, Edmund C. Tarbell, Maurice B. Prendergast and Alexander Robinson (1867–1938). His taste was for landscapes (in watercolour and pastel) of rural beauty or wilderness that responded to his love of the outdoors and the American West. His gallery was open to the public, and during the early decades of the 20th century it was a popular gathering place in Boston for art lovers and tourists. On FitzGerald's death the collection was dispersed at auction.

UNPUBLISHED SOURCES

Washington, DC, Smithsonian Inst., Archvs Amer. A. [Dodge Macknight papers, 1888–1950]

DAB

BIBLIOGRAPHY

Important Paintings by the Impressionists: The FitzGerald Collection (exh. cat., New York, Amer. A. Gals, 1927)

C. Troyen: *The Boston Tradition: American Paintings from the Museum of Fine Arts, Boston* (New York, 1980)

J. O'Reilly: 'Knight of Nights', *Condé-Nast Traveler*, xxvii (Sept 1992), pp. 128–33

LILLIAN B. MILLER

FitzGerald, Lionel LeMoine (*b* Winnipeg, 17 March 1890; *d* Winnipeg, 5 Aug 1956). Canadian painter. He attended evening classes at A. S. Kezthelyi's Art School in Winnipeg (1909) and studied at the Art Students League, New York (1921–2). He worked as a commercial artist in Winnipeg from 1922 to 1924 before joining the Winnipeg School of Art in 1924; he became its principal in 1929 and held that position until 1949, although he stopped teaching in 1947. In 1932 he was invited to become a member of the GROUP OF SEVEN and in the following year, when the group officially disbanded, he became a founder-member of the Canadian Group of Painters.

FitzGerald's work, ranging across landscape, still-life and figure painting and drawing, is characterized by a precise depiction of space, light and volume, as in *Doc Snyder's House* (1931) or *From an Upstairs Window, Winter* (1948; Ottawa, N.G.). His meticulous working procedure and self-critical perfectionism led him to produce only a small number of paintings, his work being most widely known through watercolours and drawings, some of them executed in a delicate variant of pointillism, for example *FitzGerald's Garden* (watercolour, 1946; Winnipeg, A.G.) or *Still-life with Reflector* (pen and ink, 1948; Toronto, A.G. Ont.). His work can properly be described as 'regional', in

that his usual subjects were people he knew and familiar landscapes and cityscapes in and around Winnipeg.

BIBLIOGRAPHY

Lionel LeMoine FitzGerald (1890–1956): The Development of an Artist (exh. cat., texts P. E. Bovey and A. Davis; Winnipeg, A.G., 1978)

Lionel LeMoine FitzGerald: His Drawings and Watercolours (exh. cat., text M. Callahan; Edmonton, Alta., A.G., 1982)

For further bibliography *see* GROUP OF SEVEN.

DAVID BURNETT

Fitz-James Stuart y Falcó, Jacobo, 17th Duque de Alba. *See* ALBA, (2).

Fitz-James Stuart y Silva, Carlos Miguel, 14th Duque de Alba. *See* ALBA, (1).

Fitzwilliam, Richard, 7th Viscount Fitzwilliam of Merrion (*b* Richmond, Surrey, 1 Aug 1745; *d* London, 4 Feb 1816). Irish collector. He was educated at Trinity Hall, Cambridge, where he was painted by Joseph Wright of Derby (Cambridge, Fitzwilliam), and began collecting music manuscripts. He subsequently studied the harpsichord in Paris with Jacques Duphly and travelled in the Low Countries, Italy and Spain (1772). He inherited his wealth from his mother, Catherine (*d* 1786), who was the eldest daughter and principal heir of Sir Matthew Decker, an Amsterdam merchant who around 1700 had purchased paintings in Antwerp for James Brydges, 1st Duke of Chandos. The Chandos collection was sold at auction in 1747, and Fitzwilliam was later to acquire two of the paintings—Gerrit Dou's *The Schoolmaster* and Willem van Mieris's *Market Stall* (both Cambridge, Fitzwilliam).

Fitzwilliam's estates were at Mount Merrion, near Dublin, and in 1776 he took his seat in the Irish House of Lords, although he was to spend most of his life in London and Paris. In 1784 he helped inaugurate the Handel Commemoration in Westminster Abbey as a director of the Concerts of Antient Musick. He was elected FRS in 1789. Between 1790 and 1806 he was MP for Wilton, Wilts, where his cousin and sole executor, George Augustus Herbert, 11th Earl of Pembroke, lived. In 1811 his *Letters of Atticus* were published anonymously in London.

Fitzwilliam bequeathed his important collections of music, illuminated manuscripts, prints (particularly rich in examples by Rembrandt), his library and 144 paintings to the University of Cambridge. Some of these paintings he had inherited, but others, which included Titian's *Venus and a Lutenist*, Veronese's *Hermes, Herse and Aglauros* and Palma Vecchio's *Venus and Cupid*, he purchased in London in 1800 after the sale of the Orléans collection. His bequest (1816) formed the nucleus of the Fitzwilliam Museum, the building of which began in 1837 to designs by George Basevi.

DNB

BIBLIOGRAPHY

C. Winter: *The Fitzwilliam Museum, Cambridge* (London, 1958), pp. 2–5

The Dutch Connection (exh. cat., ed. P. Woudhuysen; Cambridge, Fitzwilliam, 1988)

DAVID E. SCRASE

Fixative. Adhesive or consolidant applied to a friable pigment coating in order to fix it to the substrate or prevent crumbling. The aim of using a fixative is to provide increased strength with minimal change in appearance.

Most adhesives that can be applied in low viscosity have been used. Solvent-applied resins, such as dammar, mastic and shellac, were commonly employed by artists. Polysaccharides, gum arabic and *funori* (a seaweed extract) have been used in water solutions. Polysaccharides will cross-link and become insoluble by reaction with many pigments used. It is unlikely that appreciable amounts of fixative can be removed from a treated surface without harming the pigment layer.

The problems of stabilizing pigment surfaces have not been solved. Early attempts on wall paintings using wax and casein caused severe changes in colour and are almost impossible to remove. Wax causes dirt accumulation and further disfigurement of the image, while calcium caseinate shrinks, removing the surface layer. Agar-agar applied in solution (with polyvinyl alcohol) gels then shrinks while drying, causing damage to the surface. Fixatives are increasingly being chosen to provide only the minimum reinforcement necessary to hold the particles of pigment in place. Polymers, such as the cellulose derivatives carboxymethyl cellulose and methyl cellulose, tend to be poor formers of film and therefore create poor optical contact between particles and support. This retains the matt appearance of the surface and avoids the saturation of the colours. Alternatively, the adhesive, for example parylene, can be applied as a vapour that condenses to form a polymer film without disturbing the surface.

See also CONSOLIDANT.

BIBLIOGRAPHY
R. J. Gettens and G. L. Stout: *Painting Materials* (New York, 1966)
E. F. Hansen, E. T. Sdaoff and R. Lowinger: *A Review of Problems Encountered in the Consolidation of Paint on Ethnographic Wood Objects and Potential Remedies*, Preprints of the Triennial Meeting of the International Council of Museums Conservation Committee (Dresden, 1990), pp. 163–8
C. V. Horie: *Materials for Conservation: Organic Consolidants, Adhesives and Coatings* (London, 1990)

C. V. HORIE

Fjaestad, Gustaf (Edolf) (*b* Stockholm, 22 Dec 1868; *d* Arvika, 7 July 1948). Swedish painter, printmaker and designer. He trained at the Royal Academy of Arts in Stockholm in 1891–2. Subsequently he studied with Bruno Liljefors and Carl Larsson, assisting them with such decorative schemes as Larsson's fresco at the Nationalmuseum, Stockholm (1896). In 1897 he moved to the Arvika district of Värmland, where he worked together with his wife, Maja (1873–1961), as painter, craftsman and cabinetmaker, and gathered around him a circle of artists who became known as the Racken group. He first achieved public recognition at the Stockholm Artists Union exhibition in 1898 with some of his snow landscapes, which were an immediate popular success and were often reproduced. He had his first one-man exhibition in Stockholm in 1908, and his paintings were well received when exhibited in Berlin in 1914 and in London in 1927.

Fjaestad's speciality was the winter landscape. The approach he adopted in such early works as *Evening Sun in Early Winter* (1894) and *Winter Moonlight* (1895; both Stockholm, Nmus.) changed little thereafter. He was particularly fond of painting hoar-frost on trees and ice (e.g. *Hoar-frost on Ice*, 1901; Stockholm, Thielska Gal.).

The composition of Fjaestad's landscapes became increasingly stylized under the influence of Art Nouveau. In such works as *Winter Evening by a River* (1907; Stockholm, Nmus.), the abstract patterns created by light reflecting off rippling water became the principal subject. He also created a personal form of Pointillism from a pattern of dots or lines, which allowed him to transfer motifs from his oil paintings unchanged on to textiles, done in cooperation with his wife. Fjaestad also made woodcuts, influenced by Japanese prints.

BIBLIOGRAPHY
A. Fjaestad: *Gustaf och Maja Fjaestad: Ett konstnärspar* (Karlstad, 1981)
Dreams of a Summer Night (exh. cat., ACGB, 1986)

TORSTEN GUNNARSSON

Fjell, Kai (Breder) (*b* Skoger, 2 March 1907; *d* Oslo, 10 Jan 1989). Norwegian painter. After studying at the painting school in Drammen, he moved to Oslo, where he studied at the Håndverks- og Kunstindustriskole (1927–9) and for three months at the Kunstakademi, where he found the teaching meaningless. During this period he met his future wife, Ingeborg Helene Holt, who constantly modelled for him. A dark palette and a melancholy mood with symbolic undertones characterize his earliest work. The exhibition *Nyere Tysk Kunst* ('Recent German art') in Kunstnernes Hus in Oslo in 1932, which included works by Paul Klee, Franz Marc and Emil Nolde, fundamentally altered his ideas of artistic freedom. His one-man exhibition at Kunstnernes Hus in 1937 was a sensation. The paintings presented a rich diversity of human emotions and attitudes, and there was talk of a new Edvard Munch in connection with Fjell's approach to his subjects. There were disturbing themes of violence and death, manifested through expressive brushstrokes and saturated colours, as well as poetic paintings with glittering, clear colours. Common to all the works was their spontaneity and tendency towards Surrealism. From this exhibition the National Gallery in Oslo took two paintings of 1936. The *Calf Gets up* (1936; Oslo, N.G.) is symbolic, with its representation of spring and the beginning of life, of Fjell's own artistic endeavour, while *Homage by the Models* shows a mysterious group of dematerialized female figures that represent different levels of reality around the dead artist. The painting plays with the ideas of the cycles of life and death and the roles of the woman-model and the man-artist.

After cultivating ornamental and folkloric references verging on orientalism, Fjell moved towards cooler colours and more stringent formal contemplation, maintaining a varied subject-matter, as in *Crucifixion* (1946; Oslo, Kommunes Kstsaml.). During this period he represented Norway at the Venice Biennale (1952). He also produced monumental decorations, for example in Regjeringsbygget (Government Office Building; 1958) and in the departure lounge (1965–8) of Fornebo Airport, both in Oslo, stage decorations (e.g. for Ibsen's *Peer Gynt*, 1955), many imaginative drawings with flying, sure lines, especially as illustrations (e.g. for Rolf Stenersen's *Spinn efter Rimbaud*, Oslo, 1946), pastels and prints (e.g. *Mother and Child*, lithograph, before 1949; Oslo, N.G.); all were based on the same psychological insights as the paintings. Fjell, with diminished eyesight and in poor health, produced mostly watercolours and pastels in his last years. His wife helped him to depict his favourite subjects: his childhood on his parents' farm, nature, women (e.g. *Untitled*, 1987; priv. col., see 1990 exh. cat., p. 46) and thoughts about life and death. A memorial exhibition was held at Kunstnernes Hus in 1990.

BIBLIOGRAPHY

NKL

P. Gauguin: *Kai Fjell* (Oslo, 1944)

E. Egeland: *Kai Fjell* (Oslo, 1977)

H. Koefod: *Kai Fjell: Tegninger* [Kai Fjell: drawings] (Oslo, 1978)

S. Rajka: 'En folkekjær "postmodernist"' [A popular 'postmodernist'], *Vi ser på kst* [We look at art], 1 (1987), pp. 8–11 [interview with artist]

Kai Fjell (exh. cat., article S. O. Hoff; Oslo, Kstnernes Hus, 1990) [with Eng. trans.]

SUSANNE RAJKA

Flabellum. *See under* SCHEIBENKREUZ.

Flachat, Eugène (*b* Nîmes, April 1802; *d* Arcachon, 18 July 1873). French engineer. He was trained by his half-brother Stéphane Flachat (1800–84) and together they designed and built some of the first parts of the French railway network, including the Saint-Germain Railway (1835) and the Paris-Versailles-Rive Droite Railway (1836). In 1844 Flachat designed the Paris-Le Pecq Atmospheric Railway. Shortly afterwards he was appointed engineer to both the Ouest and Midi railway companies, becoming Chief Engineer on their amalgamation in 1857, and he was responsible for the design and execution of numerous railway bridges and viaducts, many in cast iron, on the routes to Paris from the west and south of France. Best remembered for the prominent role he played in developing wide-span iron construction techniques in France, his most important work was the 40-m span shed (1851–3) at the Gare Saint-Lazare, Paris. The use of rolled-iron plates in the trusses permitted a span of unprecedented width and stability. Although contemporary accounts differed, it seems to have been the success of this structure that led Napoleon III to order the demolition of the first, masonry pavilion of Victor Baltard's central markets, Les Halles, in Paris and order a competition for a new design to be built in iron and glass. Baltard won the competition, but Flachat's biographer maintained that the markets as finally built by Baltard were largely derived from Flachat's competition project (see Malo). Another of Flachat's designs involved the use of iron piles to consolidate the foundations of the central tower of Bayeux Cathedral, which was collapsing under the weight of an 18th-century cupola. Flachat was prominent in organizing and promoting the engineering profession in France independently of government training, and he was a founder and the first president of the Société des Ingénieurs Civils en France (1848), re-elected seven times before his retirement in 1859.

BIBLIOGRAPHY

DBF

L. Malo: *Notice sur Eugène Flachat* (Paris, 1873)

'Obsèques de M. Eugène Flachat', *Mém & C.-R. Soc. Ingén. Civ. France*, 22 (1873), pp. 263–8

B. Lemoine: *Les Halles de Paris* (Paris, 1980), pp. 28–30

F. Steiner: *French Iron Architecture*, Studies in the Fine Arts: Architecture (Ann Arbor, 1984), pp. 80–88

B. Lemoine: *L'Architecture du fer: France, XIXe siècle* (Seyssel, 1986)

KAREN BOWIE

Flack, Audrey (*b* New York, 30 May 1931). American painter, draughtswoman and sculptor. She studied at Yale University, New Haven, CT (1952) and at the Institute of Fine Arts, New York University (1953), where she was influenced by Abstract Expressionism. Her first solo exhibition was in 1959 at the Roko Gallery, New York. In the early 1970s, in her first mature works, she drew on family-album photographs and then photographs from magazines of public figures. Her concern for prevailing feminist issues was revealed in the well-known *Gray Border* series (1975–6), in which she concentrated on several feminized still-lifes painted in a Photorealist style. In large-scale paintings she manipulated stereotypes of art and femininity. A luminous spatial maze of intricately ordered objects appears in such works as *Leonardo's Lady* (1.88×2.03 m, 1975; New York, MOMA), in which a perfect pink rose, an art-historical treatise, lipstick, a Baroque-style statuette of a *Cupid*, costume jewellery, nail-varnish and other equally lustrous objects float above a picture plane that is never clearly defined. From the early 1980s Flack made large-scale indoor and outdoor sculptures based on female deities, imaginary and Classical. Examples of her work are in numerous private and public collections, notably the Australian National Gallery, Canberra, the Metropolitan Museum of Art, New York, and the National Museum of Women in the Arts, Washington, DC.

WRITINGS

Audrey Flack on Painting (New York, 1981)

BIBLIOGRAPHY

Breaking the Rules: Audrey Flack (exh. cat., ed. T. Gouma-Peterson; Los Angeles, UCLA, Wight A.G.; Youngstown, OH, Butler Inst. Amer. A.; Washington, DC, N. Mus. Women A.; Louisville, KY, Speed A. Mus.; 1992–3)

□

Flagg, Ernest (*b* Brooklyn, NY, 6 Feb 1857; *d* New York, 10 April 1947). American architect. He had no formal architectural education in the USA and spent his early career in partnership with his father and brother, engaged in land and building speculation in New York. This experience led Flagg's cousin, Cornelius Vanderbilt II, to provide financial support for his education at the Ecole des Beaux-Arts in Paris (1888–90). There he studied in the atelier of Paul Blondel and was joined by Walter B. Chambers (1866–1945), with whom he travelled and later formed a loosely structured partnership.

While studying in Paris, Flagg acquired a broad knowledge of the theory and practice of architecture during the early years of the Third Republic (1871–1900). From the writings of the mid-century theorist Charles Blanc, Flagg learned the concept of *parti* or 'the logical solution of the problem from his [the architect's] dual standpoint as constructor and artist'. This concept reconciled in the 1890s the disparate objectives that had characterized 19th-century architectural theory and design: art and science, aesthetics and technology, intuition and reason. On his return in 1891 Flagg advanced the cause of Beaux-Arts architecture in the USA by helping to found the Society of Beaux-Arts Architects along with Charles Follen McKim, William A. Boring (1858–1937) and Walter Chambers. He also joined with such other Ecole alumni as John

M. Carrère and Thomas Hastings in promoting Beaux-Arts theory and practice. An ardent opponent of the World's Columbian Exposition buildings of 1893 in Chicago, he vigorously denied that they reflected genuine Beaux-Arts principles and called upon architects to formulate a national style that would be 'architectural' and not 'archaeological'.

Based on the notion of *parti*, Flagg developed in 40 years' architectural practice an approach that stressed academic classicism, idealism and ceremonial planning. He designed each work according to the special needs of its building type. Such institutions as the Corcoran Gallery of Art (1892–7), Washington, DC, St Luke's Hospital (1892–7) in New York and the US Naval Academy (1896–1908) at Annapolis, MD, promoted academic classicism and idealism. His domestic architecture, however, was considerably freer. There he often employed a hybrid of Colonial Revival and 'modern French Renaissance' styles, in the belief that such buildings would advance the 19th-century search for a national style of architecture as a logical evolution from historical precedents. He synthesized these styles in his Alfred Corning Clark house (1898–1900; destr.), Riverside Drive, New York, as well as in his own town house (1905–7; destr.) at 109 East 40th Street, New York, and his country house (1898–9; 1907–9), Stone Court, on Staten Island, NY.

Some of his most inventive works were his commercial and utilitarian buildings, which combined French aestheticism with structural rationalism, conveying a reasoned approach to architecture as decorated structure. The Singer Loft Building (1902–4) in New York is a celebrated example. Its discrete use of metal, terracotta and glass, according to a method advocated by Eugène-Emmanuel Viollet-le-Duc and his followers, enclosed a skeletal steel frame. Moreover the Scribner Building (1912–13) at 597 Fifth Avenue, New York, with its opulent iron storefront, demonstrated clear affinities with French commercial buildings. Flagg's Singer Tower (building, 1896–8; tower, 1906–8; destr. 1967–8) at 149 Broadway was the first of the needle-like skyscrapers that were to characterize the spectacular New York skyline of the 1920s and 1930s. On its completion, this 47-storey skyscraper became the world's tallest building. It was a pragmatic demonstration of Flagg's solution to zoning reform: a tower, set back and restricted to a quarter of its site, that could rise indefinitely. Yet the design of the Singer Tower was a less successful solution than the Singer Loft Building was to the problem of enclosing a structural steel frame.

Flagg is widely regarded as the 'father of the modern model tenement' in the USA for his light-court plan, published in 1894, which replaced the notorious 'dumbbell' plan. The plan was first realized in his Alfred Corning Clark Buildings (1896–98; destr.), New York. He was also an ingenious inventor, with 30 registered US patents largely related to house construction techniques. After World War I, Flagg combined an interest in small house design and construction with a study of Greek principles of proportion. Forming a tenuous alliance between theory and practice, he used a module, fixed at 3 feet 9 inches (1.14 m), and a system of proportional relationships he claimed were derived from Greek principles. He designed, in response to post-war housing shortages, houses that were economical to construct and even possible for the user to build. His designs for small stone houses, which reflected regional and vernacular characteristics, were employed across the country, and his Staten Island houses, which included Bowcot (1916–18) and House-on-the-Wall or Wallcot (1918–22), were among his most imaginative.

A rugged individualist generally mistrusted for his personal conduct, Flagg did not achieve professional recognition until 1911 when he was elected to the American Institute of Architects. His importance lies in his advancement of the cause of French classicism in the USA, which challenged a generation of architects to reject archaeological revivalism in favour of a reasoned approach to design through the adoption of Beaux-Arts principles, and in his efforts to achieve height and density reform for skyscrapers and improve housing for the urban poor.

WRITINGS

'The Ecole des Beaux-Arts', *Archit. Rec.*, iii (1894), pp. 302–13, 419–28; iv (1894), pp. 38–43
'Influence of the French School on Architecture in the United States', *Archit. Rec.*, iv (1894), pp. 210–28
'The New York Tenement-house Evil and its Cure', *Scribner's Mag.*, xvi (1894), pp. 108–17
'American Architecture as Opposed to Architecture in America', *Archit. Rec.*, x (1900), pp. 178–90
Small Houses: Their Economic Design and Construction (New York, 1922)

BIBLIOGRAPHY

H. W. Desmond: 'The Works of Ernest Flagg', *Archit. Rec.*, xi (1902), pp. 1–104
O. F. Semsch: *A History of the Singer Building Construction: Its Progress from Foundation to Flag Pole* (New York, 1908)
J. P. Ford: *Slums and Housing*, 2 vols (Cambridge, MA, 1936)
M. Bacon: *Ernest Flagg: Beaux-Arts Architect and Urban Reformer* (New York, 1986)

MARDGES BACON

Flags and standards. Devices consisting of pieces of fabric attached to poles. Depending on the size and shape of a flag, it can be called a banner, gonfanon, guidon, pennon, standard, streamer or vexillum, though these terms are not always used consistently. The modern definition of a banner is an approximately square flag displaying the arms of its owner, while a standard is an elongated, tapering flag with a rounded or split end, showing a badge or badges, sometimes a crest and a motto (see fig. 1). Formerly used as military cognizances, heraldic banners and standards are now used only for ceremonial purposes. The term standard, however, is used flexibly to include not only fabric flags of various sizes and shapes but also three-dimensional devices—also called vexilloids—displayed as symbols of authority or carried in organized warfare as cognizances and rallying points in battle.

Of the parts of a flag, the pole is called the stave, its tip the finial and the metal mounting at the bottom end the ferrule. The surface of the cloth is the field, the part nearest to the stave the hoist and the opposite edge the fly. A distinction should be made between flags permanently attached to their staves and flags that can be hoisted on masts or poles by means of a lanyard. In English no specific terms are in use for these two types; in German the first is called *Fahne*, the latter *Flagge*. The *Fahne* cannot usually be replaced without a ceremony, but the *Flagge* is

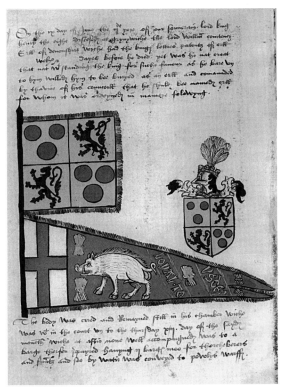

1. Banner, standard and arms of Lord William Courtenay (*d* 1511); miniature from the funeral collections of Sir Thomas Wriothesley, 1505–34 (London, British Museum, Add. MS. 45131)

replaceable at any time, when it has become unusable or unsuitable.

The fabric used for a flag has to be light enough to fly easily in the wind; if available silk is preferred, but linen and cotton have also been used extensively. Man-made fibres have become popular because of their durability. The designs displayed on the flag's field can be painted, embroidered, sewn or applied in any combination of these techniques.

From the earliest times flags have had special, often sacral character in representing authority or a body of men involved in warfare. Though the outward appearance of these symbols has changed over the centuries, there is still a mystique attached to them that manifests itself in the special code and etiquette used in encountering and handling them. The use of flags is minutely regulated in domestic and international relations; the respect to be paid to one's own or any other country's flag is of great importance in almost all societies and can be set aside only in the service of a higher principle, such as using freedom of speech as justification for the burning of a flag.

1. 'True' flags. 2. Vexilloid standards.

1. 'TRUE' FLAGS. The earliest representations of 'true' flags—pieces of fabric of more or less rectangular shape attached to an upright pole—are found on Chinese tile reliefs of chariots and horsemen of the Eastern Han period (AD 25–220). These depict small, probably silk rectangles

laterally attached to lances carried by horsemen; short split streamers flutter from the flags' upper corners. Practically identical in shape—narrow rectangles with twin streamers, sometimes differing in colour from the flag—are lance flags depicted in battle scenes on 7th-century AD murals excavated from 1946 in the Sogdian city of Pendzhikent, near Samarkand, and on the gold ewer of the so-called Treasure of Attila (Vienna, Ksthist. Mus.) found at Nagyszentmiklos, Hungary, in 1791.

(i) Chinese. (ii) Japanese. (iii) Islamic. (iv) Ancient Roman, Byzantine and Ostrogothic. (v) European, from the Middle Ages.

(i) Chinese. Flags are mentioned in Chinese sources of *c.* 500 BC, but nothing is known about their shape at this date. Although the cavalry flags of the Han period (206 BC–AD 220) are shown as rectangular with streamers, and rectangular flags, usually with three streamers spaced apart on the fly, are documented for the Song period (960–1279), the larger flags were typically of triangular shape, with flamelike jagged edges in contrasting colours. Their colour schemes were often based on those of the cardinal directions of Chinese cosmology: red for the south, black for the north, blue for the east, white for the west and yellow for the centre of the world. As early as the Han period a properly equipped Chinese army had banners, uniforms and horses in each of its five sections that corresponded with these directional colours. The four small triangular flags in a fanlike arrangement attached to the backs of actors representing warlords and generals in the Chinese theatre are relics from military practice of the late Ming period (1368–1644), when officers and even troopers, for example the first and the last man in a squadron, wore small flags in the units' colours strapped to their backs; these dorsal devices were probably introduced from Japan (*see* §(ii) below). In the second half of the 19th century an official flag for China—yellow with the imperial emblem of the five-clawed dragon and the flaming pearl—was adopted under European pressure. It was of the traditional triangular shape but was changed to the European rectangular form in 1890.

(ii) Japanese. In ancient Japan the earliest flag was a long streamer, *hata-jirushi*, mounted on a cross-bar like an elongated Roman vexillum (*see* §(iv) below). As an alternative to three-dimensional *ō-uma-jirushi* standards (*see* §2 below), the less spectacular but easier to handle *shihan* was used. This was a large fabric flag, almost square in shape. The cloth was attached to the stave by a sleeve or by evenly spaced fabric loops. A short horizontal bar set at right angles to the top of the stave kept the fabric spread out to make its *mon* (heraldic family emblems) or other cognizances clearly visible even without wind. A lesser standard of the same construction was the *nobori*; it was of a very long rectangular shape, often four or five times high as it was wide. Bearers of *nobori* in battle scenes are shown holding the stave in their left hand but grasping with their right a line attached to the top of the 3–4.5 m-high shaft in order to steady it. At the beginning of the Azuchi-Momoyama period (1568–1600) a more efficient way of carrying a personal device, or *sashimono*, was introduced by attaching it to the back of the bearer's cuirass (see fig. 2). The stave of the *sashimono* was slipped through a hinged bracket at the level of the shoulder

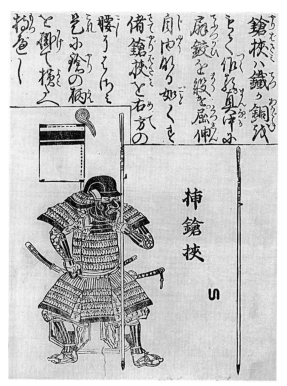

2. *Sashimono* carried by a samurai; woodcut from *Tanki yoryaku: Hikoben* [Manual: how to arm a warrior], 158×225 mm (Yedo, 1837) (New York, Metropolitan Museum of Art)

The Crusader states adopted colour coding of their own; the banners of the Kingdom of Jerusalem were white and those of the principality of Antioch red. After his victory over Bohemund VI, Prince of Antioch, in 1271, Baybars pointed out that his yellow banners had overcome Bohemund's red ones.

Islamic banners often displayed a combination of Koranic inscriptions, pious phrases and geometric and arabesque designs, as on the square example with lappets along the lower edge (Burgos, Real Monasterio de las Huelgas, Mus. Telas & Preseas) said to have been captured when Spanish forces defeated the Almohads at the Battle of Las Navas de Tolosa in 1212. Shield-shaped banners (Turk. *sanjak*) were made throughout the Mediterranean lands under the control of the Ottoman dynasty (*reg* 1281–1924); they were often decorated with a representation of *dhu'l-faqār*, the two-bladed sword of the Prophet. Banners were used not only in battle but were also carried by groups of pilgrims to Mecca, as for example a silk banner made in North Africa in 1683 (Cambridge, MA, Sackler Mus.). The crescent (Arab. *hilāl*) and star, used in the West to symbolize the Islamic world from the 15th century, were not adopted as official symbols in the Islamic world itself until the end of the 18th century.

(iv) Ancient Roman, Byzantine and Ostrogothic. The Roman standard that comes closest to the modern idea of a flag is the vexillum, a square piece of cloth hanging from a horizontal bar attached to a stave. The vexillum was mainly a cavalry ensign carried by the *vexillarius*. The sole surviving example of a Roman vexillum (St Petersburg, Hermitage) was found in Egypt, probably as a grave find. It measures around 500 sq. mm and is of linen dyed scarlet, painted with the image of Victory standing on a globe. At the lower edge there are the remains of a fringe. The famous labarum of Constantine the Great was such a vexillum. It was imperial purple, bore three portraits of the emperor and his two children and was topped by the chi-rho monogram of Christ, possibly within a laurel wreath. It appeared in this form from AD 312, after Constantine's victories over his rival, Maxentius, at Saxa Rubra and the Milvian Bridge. According to the Greek church historian Eusebios of Caesarea, it was inspired by Constantine's vision of a flaming cross in the heavens (*In hoc signo vinces*) and the appearance of Christ in a dream on the eve of the Battle of the Milvian Bridge.

The exact shape of the flags carried by the Romanized Germanic tribes of the Migration period (*c.* AD 375–500), who contributed to the fall of the Roman Empire, is not known. In all probability the white-and-gold banner of Theodoric, King of the Ostrogoths (*reg* AD 475–526), and the green-and-gold banner of his opponent, Odoacar, were of vexillum shape. Theodoric's banner was also reported to have had small bells attached to make its position known even in battle.

(v) European, from the Middle Ages. The earliest medieval flag borne in Europe was the gonfanon (Old High Ger. *gund*: 'battle'; *fano*: 'cloth'; see fig. 3). It was a rectangle of fabric attached to the stave by one of its narrow sides, usually by means of rings or loops. The fly was either cut into three or more lappets or had streamers sewn on separately. For a sturdier attachment of these streamers

blades and set into a socket in the small of the back, thus leaving both hands free to fight: the Japanese sword was designed for a two-handed grip, and the other favourite weapon of the samurai, the bow, also required the use of both hands. *Sashimono* were mostly of the *nobori* type, but could also be three-dimensional. The *sashimono* seems to have been introduced from America: its close resemblance to the Mexican *tlahuitztli* and *pantli* (*see* §2 below) and its relatively late appearance (1573) in Japan, 50 years after the Spanish conquest of Mexico, makes transfer across the Pacific likely.

(iii) Islamic. Armies in the Muslim world carried rectangular flags laterally attached to a lance or stave, often with a row of short lappets along the fly edge or with a streamer at the upper corner, as shown in several illustrations of a copy (Paris, Bib. N., MS. arabe 5847) of al-Hariri's *Maqamat* ('Assemblies'), produced at Baghdad in 1237. Another type of flag consisted of two ribbon-like streamers tied to a lance, as depicted on an unusual silver coin minted at Damascus *c.* AD 695 (see Nicolle, 1982, p. 8; Nicolle, 1986, p. 20).

Many reports circulated about the banners used by the Prophet Muhammad, their names and their colours. Colour symbolism became important under the late Islamic dynasties. The Umayyads (*reg* 661–750) used white, and the Abbasids (*reg* 750–1258) used black, while the Kharijites and some Shi'ites, who denied the caliphs' authority, sometimes used red and green respectively. The banners of the Mamluk sultan Baybars (*reg* 1260–77) were yellow.

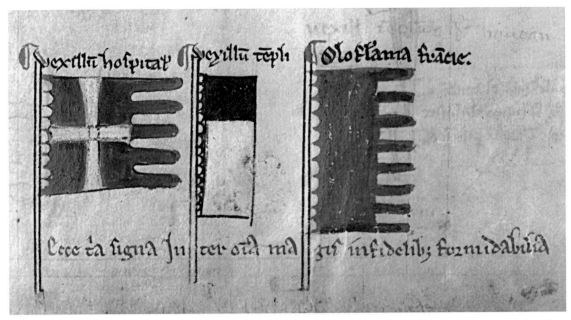

3. *Beauséant* of the Knights Templar, flanked by the gonfanon of the Hospitallers and the oriflamme of France, miniature by Matthew Paris from his *Chronica majora*, 55×120 mm, 1235–59 (Cambridge, Corpus Christi College, MS. 16, fol. 141)

the cloth's hem is often shown reinforced by a braided ribbon or an applied strip of fabric. Originally gonfanons seem to have been insignia of rank, without charges or devices, borne by high-ranking nobles and territorial overlords in command of larger military units. In the Holy Roman Empire major territorial fiefs were transferred by the ceremonial handing over of such a flag, gonfanon or banner (*Bannerlehen*). The earliest representation of this ceremony is found in a mosaic (*c.* AD 796–800; Rome, Lateran Pal.) showing St Peter handing a gonfanon with triple lappets to Charlemagne, thus investing him with the Empire. It was a pious belief that this particular gonfanon of red silk, patterned with small golden rosettes or roundels, was the original oriflamme, the sacred banner of the French kings, although the oriflamme of Louis VI (*reg* 1108–37) is reported to have had five lappets. The oriflamme was kept at Saint-Denis Abbey, near Paris, in peacetime and carried into battle until 1415, when it was lost at the Battle of Agincourt.

Banners of gonfanon shape with three lappets, but mounted on a horizontal crossbar, vexillum style, are now carried as ecclesiastic processional banners. In medieval warfare, however, they could be wheeled into battle flying from a tall mast mounted on a cart and sometimes accompanied by a signal bell. First recorded in Milan (1039) as a moveable, fortified rallying point in battle, such carts also came into use north of the Alps: in 1088 at the Battle of Pleichfeld in Germany; in 1138 at the Battle of the Standard at Northallerton, N. Yorks; in 1214 at Bouvines; and, apparently for the last time in war, at Strasbourg in 1336. The banner of St Kilian (Würzburg, Mainfränk. Mus.) is thought to have been hoisted on such a cart in 1266. This type of cart is still used in historical parades.

In the Bayeux Tapestry (Bayeux, Mus. Tap.), which records the Battle of Hastings (1066), more than twenty flags of gonfanon type, with three to five streamers, are depicted. They are rather small in size and of uniform shape, including the two that fly over the Saxon host. Only one flag in the tapestry is of an entirely divergent type; it is semicircular, with nine attached *flammulae* (flamelike lappets), and bears the device of a bird. It has been suggested that this could be one of the famous raven banners of the Viking sea-kings, carried as an heirloom by one of William I's followers. Viking raven standards (the raven was the bird sacred to Odin, ruler of battle) are recorded as early as AD 878 in the *Anglo-Saxon Chronicle* and as late as the reign of King Sverre of Norway (1184–1202).

Three of the gonfanons in the Bayeux Tapestry have crosses as devices, among the earliest examples of this Christian symbol on flags. In the First Crusade (1096–9) the *signum commune* of the crusaders was the cross, of any colour, borne on their clothing on the right shoulder and probably also on their flags. To achieve some semblance of order among the armies from all over Western Europe, it was agreed in the Treaty of Gisors (13 Jan 1188) that on the Third Crusade (1189–92) the French crusaders should wear red crosses, Englishmen white and Flemings green. This idea of colour coding was probably influenced by existing Islamic practices (*see* §(iii) above), which the crusaders had encountered during the First Crusade and the Second (1145–9).

The banner, a cloth of either square or upright rectangular shape bound to a lance shaft, became the most common form of flag in Europe from the 13th century. Although less ostentatious in shape than the gonfanon, it was ideal for the display of heraldic charges, which by then had come into universal use. A most intriguing interplay is evident between heraldic charges and the use of flags (*see* HERALDRY, §II, 1). Some very old arms of such territorial overlords as the kings of Aragon (or, four pallets gules) or those of the kings of Hungary (barry of eight, gules and argent) are clearly derived from the striped fabrics of banners. Even the royal arms of France (azure, semy of fleurs-de-lis or) resemble a brocade fabric pattern transferred to a shield. Similarly, the arms of many Italian city republics and Swiss cantons are based on the banners of the militias under which their citizen soldiers marched and fought, long before their communities found it necessary to adopt heraldic arms. On the other hand, since the gonfanon indicated territorial overlordship in the feudal system—and its use predated heraldic shield charges—a banner might display a device totally different from the personal arms of the lord. One of the frequently cited examples is the banner of Simon de Montfort, Earl of Leicester (?1208–65): per pale indented, gules and argent; his shield bore gules, a lion queue fourchée argent. A similar case existed with the Knights Templar, who carried white shields with red crosses but whose sacred banner, *Beauséant* (see fig. 3 above), was white with a black chief (Fr. *chef*: 'head'; 'chief') Significantly, in the trial of the Templars (1307) one of the crimes they were charged with was that of worshipping a mysterious black head. This seems to have been a malicious attempt to distort into a heresy the reverence the Templars paid to the *Beauséant* and is reminiscent of the accusation by the Latin church father Tertullian (*c.* AD 150–230) that the Roman legionaries idolatrously worshipped their eagle standards. The introduction of armorial charges on banners also raised the question about the proper position of these charges. In general, heraldic figures should be arranged facing the stave when the flag is flying, although this was awkward when a banner was hung and a lion, for example, would appear lying on his back.

Within large armies it became necessary to distinguish specific ranks of commanders: the easiest and most distinctive way to regulate this was the assignation of flags of specific shapes and sizes. From the 13th century a small triangular flag (pennon) attached to a lance became the mark of a knight. Commanders of larger units that contained a substantial number of knights with their retainers were entitled to a large square or rectangular banner, thus becoming knights banneret. These banners were carried by a trusted follower, man-at-arms or even another knight, not by the knight banneret himself. As a battlefield promotion a feudal lord could ceremoniously cut off the point of a knight's triangular pennon in order to square it into a banner. From the 15th century it also became customary in Western Europe—especially England, France and Burgundy—for knights banneret and nobles of higher rank to have very elongated, tapering standards, often with a split end. In France the banner as well as the standard would generally display the owner's arms, the heraldic charges adjusted accordingly.

In England during the late Plantagenet and Tudor periods, it was only the banner that showed the arms; the standard bore the crest, badges and motto (see fig. 1 above). It had a special panel at the hoist displaying the Cross of St George (argent, a cross gules) to indicate that its owner was English. The field was divided lengthwise

in the owner's livery colours and bore his crest and/or badges and his motto, the last usually placed on two bends towards the split tip of the fly. The size of English standards was strictly regulated: the king's standard to be carried in battle was 8–9 yards long (7.31–8.22 m); a duke's was 7 yards (6.4 m), 'the end to be split'; an earl's 6 yards (5.4 m); a baron's 5 yards (4.57 m); a knight banneret's 4.5 yards (4.11 m); and a knight bachelor's 4 yards (3.65 m); these probably refer to the measurement of standards flown from masts in the camp. A smaller tapering flag permitted to all armigers was the guidon. It was two-thirds the size of the standard but had a rounded tip. Its hoist panel displayed the bearer's arms, and its tail (queue) section was neutrally coloured and diapered. The standard's popularity waned after the Tudor period; in 1906 the Cross of St George was removed, because the standard was considered to be an English domestic flag, and therefore the nationality of the owner was understood. The St George's Cross was replaced by the owner's arms, and the field showed three representations of the badge or the crest and two badges separated by two bends, on which the motto was placed.

The English armies of the Hundred Years War (1337–1453) fought not only under the royal banner with the quarterly arms of France—whose inclusion into the English royal arms was one of the reasons for the wars—and England but also under the banner of St George (argent, a cross gules), St Edmund (azure, three crowns or), St Edward the Confessor (azure, a cross flory between five doves or) and the Holy Trinity. The banner of St George seems to have been used first by Edward I on his Crusade to Acre from 1270 to 1274.

Within the Holy Roman Empire there were about a dozen great principalities, but there were also hundreds of semi-independent, democratic, free city states and territories owned by almost independent feudal barons. With city militias and men-at-arms of local lords abounding, there was a proliferation of military ensigns but no regulated system for their use. Although there was a recognized difference between a banner and a *Fähnlein*, the latter roughly the equivalent of a standard, even a banner did not have to be rectangular, and the shape of the *Fähnlein* of one city militia might be deliberately quite different from that of a neighbouring town. The smallest type of flag, borne on a knight's lance or flown from a ship's mast, was the *Wimpel*. In the 10th century, under the Holy Roman Emperors Henry I the Fowler (*reg* AD 919–36) and Otto I the Great (*reg* 936–73), the main banner of the German host was a vexillum with the image of St Michael, its patron saint. The imperial banner in use until the early 13th century was a red gonfanon, carried by the emperors of the Holy Roman Empire as the successors of Charlemagne. About 1230 Frederick II introduced the *Reichsfahne*, a golden banner with the black eagle of the Empire. The eagle, a direct descendant of the *aquila* of the Roman legions, was interpreted as the 'arms' of ancient Rome (see §2 below). The earliest representation of the eagle banner shows it deeply forked, and similarly swallow-tailed flags were carried as imperial ensigns for centuries; one late example of its use was in the funeral procession (1558) of the Emperor Charles V.

German and Swiss city militias usually had one main banner (Ger. *Hauptbanner*; Swi. *Panner*), to be carried when the entire force went out on campaign, and one or more *Fähnlein* for smaller detachments. Their archers' units often carried a *Fähnlein* with a crossbow emblem added. From the early 14th century many banners and *Fähnlein* in the Empire bore a long streamer, the *Schwenkel*, usually at the upper corner of the fly, either cut from the flag's cloth itself or separately attached. As a variant, a fess or the horizontal arm of a cross as charge on the field could become elongated into a *Schwenkel*. Such a *Schwenkel*, especially a red one, called *Blutzagel* ('blood tail'), was considered a special mark of distinction, and it created a great deal of consternation when after the Battle of Murten (1476) René II, Duke of Lorraine, cut off the *Schwenkel* from the *Panneren* of his Swiss allies with his sword. In his opinion, and according to French custom, he was upgrading the banners into 'true' banners, but the magistrates of the German-Swiss cities thus 'honoured' took a dim view of this gesture. Several of the returning victorious hosts had to sew their *Schwenkel* back on before they were allowed to re-enter their home towns. The *Panner* of Zurich with its resewn red *Schwenkel* still exists (see Bruckner and Bruckner, p. 87).

Flags captured by the enemy are usually better known than those of the victors. The ensigns taken in battle are preserved and recorded as trophies, but the victors' own flags have been permitted to disintegrate and disappear unrecorded. At the Battle of Tannenberg (1410) the victorious Poles deposited the 46 captured banners of the defeated Teutonic Knights as trophies in Kraków Cathedral; they were recorded and illustrated in the *Banderia Pruthenorum* by Jan Długosz (see Ekdahl, 1976), which shows 16 *Schwenkel* of diverse shape and design. No trace remains of the Polish flags that were at Tannenberg.

In Italy during the 14th and 15th centuries two special variants of flag design were in use. In addition to the universally rectangular banners, with or without a *Schwenkel*, large armorial standards of elongated triangular shape are found with a long, free-flying streamer attached for only about a quarter of the length of the standard. These streamers were favoured by the fiercely anti-imperial Guelph cities and usually bore the charges of the house of Anjou: azure semy of fleurs-de-lis, a label gules. Another banner shape characteristic for Italy has a fly stepped in three or four stages, a form that prevents the banner cloth from dragging on the ground when marching with the banner shouldered.

In the 15th century Burgundy differed from all other countries in the military use of flags: in its ordinance of 1473 it had developed the regulation of flags within its army to a point reached again only in the Age of Absolutism, in the 17th and 18th centuries. Although the highest-ranking commanders were permitted to display their personal banners, and auxiliary and allied contingents fought under banners as well as standards of their own design, the units of the standing army had tapering standards and guidons for cavalry, rectangular banners for infantry and ribbon-like banderolles for all units smaller than a squadron. The almost square *grandes bannières* (1.52×1.21 m) were emblazoned with the multiquartered full Burgundian arms; lesser banners were 1.2×0.91 m.

The tapering *grands étendards* for the élite corps of the ducal Grand Guard and the Archers' Guard, as well as those for the 20 *companies d'ordonnance* of the regular army, were about 900 mm wide and around 2.75 m long. The four squadrons of each *companie* bore guidons, and the smallest units, *escouades*, carried banderolles. *Companie* standards had deeply split ends, and guidons were sharply pointed at the tips. Banners and standards were edged with company blue-and-white fringes, the ducal livery colours. The *companies d'ordonnance* bore standards of uniform pattern, but each in a different regimental colour. At the hoist was a panel with the image of the unit's patron saint in a quatrefoil frame, while the field was inscribed with the device JE LAY EMPRINS ('I have dared') of Charles the Bold, 4th Duke of Burgundy, and strewn with his badges of the firesteel and crossed ragged staves. The squadron guidons and the banderolles or *cornettes* repeated the same pattern. Archers' ensigns replaced the ragged staves with crossed arrows. The small pennons in the company colours worn by squadron commanders as crests on top of their helmets were peculiar to Burgundy. The flags of the Burgundian army are particularly well known because there are not only existing ordinance records but surviving flags as well. These were taken in battle during the Swiss–Burgundian Wars (1476–7), mostly at Grandson and Murten, and are reverently kept in Swiss town halls and local museums. Many more are depicted in beautifully illustrated manuscripts (*Fahnenbücher*) at Berne, Biel, Fribourg, St Gall, Glarus, Lucerne, Schwyz, Solothurn and Zurich. All Burgundian flags were of the highest artistic quality, painted in the workshops of such artists as Dieric Bouts I, Pierre Coustain, Jean Hennecart and Hugo van der Goes (see 1969 exh. cat.). After the death of Charles the Bold in the Battle of Nancy (1477), the badge of the crossed ragged staves continued to be displayed on the flags of his son-in-law and successor, Maximilian of Austria (later Emperor Maximilian I). In 1482 his son, Philip the Fair, became Duke of Burgundy, and in 1494 he married Joanna the Mad of Spain. He took with him the badge of the 'Burgundian Cross', which was then displayed on Spanish flags and continues to be used in a simplified form as the state flag of Florida and that of several Florida counties.

Small flags have been attached to fanfares and trumpets since the 15th century. Although purely ornamental, they follow the pattern of banners, on occasion even including a *Schwenkel*, as seen in Uccello's *Rout of San Romano* (1450–59; London, N.G.; Paris, Louvre; Florence, Uffizi).

Until the end of the 15th century banners had remained relatively small, usually not more than 1.5 sq. m, but in the early 16th century the German *Landsknechte*, foot soldiers (mostly pikemen and halberdiers), developed a type of flag of extraordinary size (h. *c.* 3 m) that could be seen through the dense forest of pikes. In order to make these huge masses of cloth manageable, they were cut into almost semicircular shape. *Landsknechte* units of around 300–500 men that had a flag of their own were therefore called *Fähnlein*. *Landsknechte* and other mercenary units without any binding loyalties except to their commanders and among themselves swore an oath of loyalty to their flag. When the unit was disbanded, the *Fähnlein* was ceremoniously torn to pieces and distributed to the men as keepsakes. Of the still surviving ceremonies of swearing-in recruits, the most spectacular and tradition-bound is the *Fahneneid* of the Papal Swiss Guard in Vatican City, Rome.

Flags mounted laterally on a lance shaft were originally designed for horsemen, whose rapid movement would extend the cloth to make it and its device visible. Foot soldiers, in particular if stationed in the centre of a pikemen's square, were restricted in movement; in order to show their banners—which in the days before uniforms were the main distinction between friendly and enemy forces—they had to wave them vigorously to display their cognizances continuously. Soon this practice developed into an art form called *Fahnenschwenken*, which became formalized and taught through manuals (see Heussler, 1615; Klett, 1679). The art survives in Switzerland, Germany, Belgium and Italy; especially famous events in Italy are the Palio of Siena and the Calcio of Florence.

From the mid-17th century the mercenary hordes of the Wars of Religion (1562–98) were gradually replaced with standing armies. From the 17th century even the terminology of flags changed: the term banner went out of use; square infantry flags became colours; and cavalry flags were divided into swallow-tailed guidons for dragoons and hussars and often square standards for heavy cavalry. For guard cuirassier regiments in Prussia and Russia even labarum-style standards surmounted by eagle finials were eventually introduced, while the Polish hussars, an élite corps of noblemen in the 17th century, had towering wings (a distant offshoot of Chinese dorsal flags; *see* §(i) above) mounted on the backplates of their cuirasses.

2. VEXILLOID STANDARDS. The earliest representations of military standards occur on such monuments of Predynastic Egypt as the Hunters' Palette (London, BM). Egyptian standards, as used until Roman times, were sculptures in the round, mounted on long poles and enhanced by fluttering streamers. Foremost among them were figures of animals with religious significance, such as the falcon of Horus or the jackal of Anubis (see fig. 4). The tribal standards of the Israelites mentioned in the Bible (Numbers 10:14–25) were clearly styled after the Egyptian model. Attributes of authority that amounted to vexilloid status were the ornamental ostrich-feather fans of the Pharaoh's court. Practically all other armies of the Ancient Near East also used three-dimensional standards, although most were of more abstract shapes than those of Egypt. Assyrian military standards were even mounted on chariots. The famous Royal Standard of Ur (*c*. 2600 BC; London, BM; *see* UR, fig. 2), however, is a misnomer; in spite of its war and peace iconography, it was probably the sound-box of a musical instrument.

The most widely known standards from antiquity are the *signa* of the Roman armies, the most famous of which are the eagles of the legions. Originally, according to Pliny, a legion had five standards: an eagle, a wolf, a minotaur, a horse and a boar. Gaius Marius in his reforms of the Roman armies (104 BC) made the eagle—as the bird sacred to Jupiter—the main standard. The eagle (*aquila*) in late Republican times was silver with a gilded thunderbolt in its claws; later it was made entirely of gold. There were also secondary standards, either for tactical units, such as the cohorts or maniples, or purely honorary. The charging boar of the Legio XX, stationed at Glevum (now Gloucester), or the capricorn—the zodiacal sign of Augustus—of Legio II Augusta were of the latter kind. The standard topped by a hand (*manus*) is thought to be the *signum* of the maniple and was supposed to be derived from a handful of straw tied to a spear shaft. The various decorative elements such as wreaths, discs and crescents (see fig. 5) attached to the staves were probably battle honours. In the imperial army a special standard was the *imago*, a medallion with the portrait of the emperor mounted on a stave; its bearer was the *imaginifer*. The eagle and the *imago* were in the charge of the first cohort of each legion.

The bearer of the eagle standard (*aquilifer*) was the senior standard-bearer (*signifer*). The distinguishing dress for *signifers* were hooded cloaks of lion- or bearskins worn over their armour. The staves of the *signa* bore iron ferrules with which they were planted into the ground when camp was set up. Short, hooked extensions on the lower shaft served as shoulder rests when carrying the *signa* on a march and as handgrips in planting or removing them. If a *signum* was stuck fast in the ground when

4. Standard bearers preceeding Pharaoh Narmer; relief from a votive palette (detail), greywacke, 420×640 mm, *c*. 3000 BC (Cairo, Egyptian Museum)

5. Roman standards; reverse of a bronze coin of Emperor Galba, diam. 28 mm, AD 68–9 (London, British Museum)

breaking camp, it was seen as a bad omen, and the men might refuse to move, waiting for a better omen. A legion's eagle was kept in a shrine in the centre of the camp and held in almost religious awe. The eagle's importance is indicated by the fact that a special campaign was launched into Germany in order to recover the three eagles lost by P. Quinctilius Varus in the Battle of Teutoburg Forest in AD 9. Napoleon deliberately harkened back to ancient Rome by introducing eagle standards for the French army in 1804. Contemporaneous with, and possibly inspired by, the standards of the Roman army are those of Celtic tribes; these often have animal images, especially boars, as sculpted on the Arch of Orange, France, or in the reliefs at Bormio, northern Italy.

A peculiar zoomorphic standard from ancient times was the *draco*, a windsock-like contraption of a metal head with open jaws and a fabric body that writhed in the wind like a live serpent (see fig. 6). Originally it was the tribal battle ensign of horse nomads from the east European steppes, the Sarmatians and Alani, who from AD 175 were hired into the Roman army as auxilliary cavalry. The showy *draco* standard, although originally strictly a cavalry ensign, had been adopted by the end of the 4th century as the *signum* of the cohort, carried by the *draconarius*. The *draco* was the inspiration for the battle standards of Uther Pendragon and King Arthur and was flown as the Wessex Dragon Standard at the Battle of Hastings in 1066.

A primitive forerunner of the *draco* was the *tös* of the Turkic nomads of the Central Asian steppes, who considered the wolf their totemic animal. This standard consisted of a wolf's skull with an attached skin mounted on a pole. Chinese sources of the Tang period (AD 618–907) mention that 'sacrifices are made to them four times a year' (see Esin, 1972). The Turkish horsetail standard (*tugh*) was not a true battle ensign but an insignia of rank: the numbers of *tugh* carried before a Turkish dignitary by his retainers indicated his status (e.g. 'Pasha of three horsetails'). Many *tugh* in European museums are embellished with a 'Turkish' crescent finial added by the captors. Standards made out of the tails of horses, wolves or leopards were ancient symbols of authority among the Eurasian steppe nomads;

Genghis Khan is known to have used a standard of nine yak tails (see Esin, 1972, pl. X).

The main banner of the Asian foes of late Rome and Byzantium, the Sasanian Persians, was a vexillum of leather spangled with jewels; it was supposed to be the apron of the legendary blacksmith Kawe, who raised the rebellion against the earlier dynasty of the Parthians and helped the Sasanians to the throne (AD 224). Other ensigns were three-dimensional standards comparable with the Roman *signa*; for example, the standard of the ruler of Fars consisted of a golden ball (the sun) and a silver crescent (the moon) above a pair of wings (the symbol of the deity Ahuramazda). In a rock-carving at Taq-i Bustan celebrating a victory of King Varham II (AD 276–93), the king is accompanied by the bearer of his T-shaped personal standard adorned with five large (presumably golden) pomegranates.

Standards were widely used in ancient India as indicated by the monumental reliefs at Bharhut (2nd century BC). The most common type is the parasol (*chattra*), a regal emblem used to show the presence of Siddhartha both as

6. *Draco* standard carried by a *draconarius*; miniature from the *Psalterium Aureum*, 152×65 mm, *c.* AD 890 (St Gall, Stifts-Bibliothek)

Prince Gautama before his renunciation and as the Buddha after his enlightenment. By extension the parasol is used in reliefs to indicate sites and monuments sanctified by the presence of the Buddha or his relics. The parasol recurs in many Buddhist reliefs, typically over stupas, sacred trees and images of the Buddha. The parasol was not, however, a specifically Buddhist device but rather one indicative of the nobility: kings, nobles and saints are often shown sheltered by parasols in reliefs and later miniature paintings; their attendants frequently carry fly-wisks (*cauri*), another trapping of the élite.

In China round or oval ceremonial fans (*tuan shan*) and parasols were carried as insignia of authority in the processions of high officials and emperors. Few, if any, examples of the long-handled ceremonial fan survive from the early periods. However, depictions in Han-period stone reliefs (2nd century AD) show that it was related to the hand-held rigid screen fan (*bian mian*), a common type made of feathers or of silk stretched over an oval or round frame. In the painting the *Palanquin Bearers* (Beijing, Pal. Mus.; for illustration *see* YAN LIBEN), attributed to the 8th-century AD artist Yan Liben, the emperor Taizong of the Tang dynasty is shown surrounded by palace ladies, two carrying large ceremonial fans and one a tall red parasol. Of much later date are two tall peacock-feather fans that flank the imperial seat in the main hall of the Yangxin dian, a residential palace of the Qing-dynasty Yongzheng Emperor (*reg* 1723–36) in the Forbidden City, Beijing (*see also* FAN, §II).

Triple-stacked parasols, probably derived from the parasol associated with the paraphernalia of Buddhism, were also an important part of ceremonial processions. They comprised brightly coloured and decorated textile cylinders or box shapes mounted on tall poles surmounted by ornate gilt finials. Screen and feather ceremonial fans, parasols and other vexilloids displayed in imperial processions of the Qing period (1644–1911) are shown in countless numbers in the horizontal scroll the *Wedding of the Guangxu Emperor* (after 1889; Beijing, Pal. Mus.).

In Japan warlords and generals had their standards (*uma-jirushi*) carried before them or planted at their command posts. Most standards were three-dimensional vexilloids, like the red parasol of Oda Nobunaga or the 'one thousand gourd' standard (a single large gilded gourd surmounting a tassel of small gourds, one for each victory gained) carried by his successor Toyotomi Hideyoshi. From 1566 the shogun Tokugawa Ieyasu (1543–1616) had a huge golden folding fan with the emblem of the rising sun as his *ō-uma-jirushi* (great standard) and a bronze disc pierced by a circular hole as his *ko-uma-jirushi* (lesser standard).

Standards were used in Mesoamerica from at least the 6th century AD. Best known are the Mexican Aztec standards made of colourful featherwork and called *tlahuitztli* (see fig. 7). These standards could be stationary religious signs, planted in the hand of a stone standard bearer at the foot of the temple pyramid, but most of them were military insignia. Those for military use were carried on the back by means of a ladder-like frame and held by shoulder straps across the chest. They came in a wide variety of extravagant shapes, ranging from the sun of quetzal feathers to the weaver's yarn rack. One of the

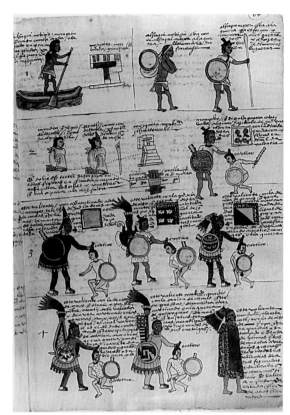

7. *Tlahuitztli* (top right and bottom left) and *pantli* (bottom right) carried by Aztec warriors; coloured drawing from the Codex Mendoza, *c*. 1535 (Oxford, Bodleian Library, MS. Arch. Selden. A. 1, fol. 64*r*)

highest-ranking was the *maxtla xiquipilli*, in the shape of the carry-all netbag used by the nomadic Chichimecs, as a nostalgic memorial to the early tribal history of the Aztecs, when they were still free-roaming hunters, before they settled in the Basin of Mexico. The *maxtla xiquipilli*—its net enhanced with gold wire and topped by a plume of precious quetzal feathers—was carried by the commander-in-chief of the Aztec armies in the fateful battle of Otumba (anc. Otumpan) following the *Noche Triste* (1 July 1520). It was its capture by Hernán Cortés that turned disaster into victory for the Spanish and signalled the end for the Aztec empire. The use of these dorsal standards was not limited to the Aztecs; they were borne by most Mesoamerican peoples. The hereditary foes of the Aztecs, the Tlaxcalans (Tlaxcaltecs), had four main standards for the four divisions of their army, the most famous being a crane with outspread wings and spangled with mirrors of black obsidian. Lower-ranking dorsal devices were *pantli*, oblong 'flags' of cloth and featherwork (see fig. 7). *Pantli* for the lowest ranks—officers commanding the smallest tactical unit of 20 men—were made only of stiff paper, a convention reflected in Aztec picture-writing where a paper *pantli* was the hieroglyph for the numeral 20. Parasols and huge feather fans also served as signs of rank (e.g. Maya feather fan; Vienna, Mus. Vlkerknd.; *see also* MESOAMERICA, PRE-COLUMBIAN, §IX, 3).

See also HERALDRY.

BIBLIOGRAPHY

The word 'Osprey' following a title indicates a book from the Osprey Men-at-Arms series.

GENERAL

L. Sickman and A. Soper: *The Art and Architecture of China*, Pelican Hist. A. (Harmondsworth, 1956, rev. 3/1968/*R* 1971)
S. Lloyd: *The Art of the Ancient Near East*, Praeger World of Art Series (New York, 1961)
M. E. L. Mallowan: *Early Mesopotamia and Iran* (New York, 1965)
J. N. Leonard: *Early Japan* (New York, 1968)
Die Burgunderbeute und Werke burgundischer Hofkunst (exh. cat., ed. F. Deuchler; Berne, Hist. Mus., 1969), pp. 89–166
R. A. Rorex and W. Fong: *Eighteen Songs of a Nomad Flute: The Story of Lady Wen Chi* (New York, 1974)
L. Artusi, S. Gabbrielli and F. Vaccaro: *Il calcio storico fiorentino* (Florence, 1976)
I. Bona: *The Dawn of the Dark Ages* (Budapest, 1976)
G. Azarpay: *Soghdian Painting: The Pictorial Epic in Oriental Art* (Berkeley and London, 1981)
Caves of the Thousand Buddhas (exh. cat. by R. Whitfield, A. Farrer, S. J. Vainker and J. Rawson, London, BM, 1989–90)

MILITARY

P. Amiot: *Art militaire des chinois, de Yong Tcheng* (Paris, 1772)
M. Murai: *Tanki yoryaku: Hikoben* [Manual: how to arm a warrior] (Yedo, 1837)
E. Seler: 'Altmexikanischer Schmuck und soziale und militärische Rangabzeichen', *Verhandlungen der Berliner Anthropologischen Gesellschaft: Berlin, 1889;* repr. in *Gesammelte Abhandlungen zur amerikanischen Sprach- und Altertumskunde*, ii (Graz, 1960), pp. 509–619
M. Jankovich: *Pferde, Reiter, Völkerstürme* (Munich, 1968); Eng. trans. as *They Rode into Europe* (London, 1971)
G. R. Watson: *The Roman Soldier* (Ithaca, 1969)
G. Webster: *The Roman Imperial Army* (New York, 1969)
M. Grant: *The Army of the Caesars* (New York, 1974)
P. Connolly: *The Roman Army* (London, 1975)
——: *Hannibal and the Enemies of Rome* (London, 1978)
D. Miller: *The Swiss at War, 1300–1500*, Osprey (London, 1979)
M. Simkins: *The Roman Army from Hadrian to Constantine*, Osprey (London, 1979)
S. R. Turnbull: *Samurai Armies, 1550–1615*, Osprey (London, 1979)
T. Wise: *Ancient Armies of the Middle East*, Osprey (London, 1981)
D. Nicolle: *The Armies of Islam, 7th–11th Centuries*, Osprey (London, 1982)
T. Wise: *Armies of the Carthaginian Wars, 265–146 BC*, Osprey (London, 1982)
N. Michael: *Armies of Medieval Burgundy, 1364–1477*, Osprey (London, 1983)
D. Nicolle: *Armies of the Ottoman Turks, 1300–1774*, Osprey (London, 1983)
——: *Italian Medieval Armies, 1300–1500*, Osprey (London, 1983)
T. Wise: *The Wars of the Roses*, Osprey (London, 1983)
D. Nicolle: *Arthur and the Anglo-Saxon Wars*, Osprey (London, 1984)
M. Simkins: *The Roman Army from Caesar to Trajan*, Osprey (London, 1984)
I. Heath: *The Vikings*, Osprey (London, 1985)
D. Nicolle: *Saladin and the Saracens: Armies of the Middle East, 1100–1300*, Osprey (London, 1986)
P. Wilcox: *Rome's Enemies (3): Parthians and Sassanid Persians*, Osprey (London, 1986)
P. Cornish: *Henry VIII's Army*, Osprey (London, 1987)
R. Hassig: *Aztec Warfare*, The Civilization of the American Indian Series (Norman, OK, 1988)

HERALDRY

A. Demmin: *Waffenkunde* (Leipzig, 1893)
A. C. Fox-Davies: *A Complete Guide to Heraldry* (London, 1909/*R* London and New York, 1978)
O. Neubecker: *Heraldry: Sources, Symbols and Meaning* (New York, 1976)
British Heraldry from its Origins to c. 1800 (exh. cat., ed. R. Marks and A. Payne: London, BM, 1978), pp. 31–41
R. Dennys: *Heraldry and the Heralds* (London, 1982)

T. Woodcock and J. M. Robinson: *The Oxford Guide to Heraldry* (Oxford, 1988)

MONOGRAPHS AND SPECIALIST STUDIES

RDK
S. Heussler: *Neues künstliches Fahnenbüchlein* (Nuremberg, 1615)
A. Klett: *Kleine Fahnenschule* (Nuremberg, 1679)
H. de Walden: *Banners, Standards and Badges from a Tudor Manuscript in the College of Arms (MS I 2)* (London, 1904)
J. P. Vogel: 'The Sacrificial Posts of Īsāpur', *Archaeol. Surv. India Annu. Rep.* (1910–11), pp. 40–48
D. R. Bhandarkar: 'Excavations at Besnagar', *Archaeol. Surv. India Annu. Rep.* (1913–14), pp. 186–226
R. P. Dayal: 'A Note on the Lālā Bhagat Pillar', *J. United Prov. Hist. Soc.*, iv (1930), pp. 38–41
J. S. P. Tatlock: 'The Dragons of Wessex and Wales', *Speculum*, viii (1933), pp. 223–35
A. S. Altekar: 'Three Maukhari Inscriptions of Yupas: Krita Year 295', *Epig. Ind.*, xxiii (1935), pp. 42–52
J. N. Banerjea: 'Indian Votive and Memorial Columns', *J. Ind. Soc. Orient. A.*, v (1937), pp. 13–20
O. Neubecker: *Fahnen und Flaggen* (Leipzig, 1939)
A. Bruckner and B. Bruckner: *Schweizer Fahnenbuch* (St Gall, 1942)
G. C. Miles: 'Mihrab and 'Anazah: A Study in Early Islamic Iconography', *Archaeologia Orientalia in Memoriam Ernst Herzfeld* (Locust Valley, NY, 1952), pp. 156–71
I. O. Evans: *Flags of the World* (New York, 1970)
H. Horstmann: *Die Rechstzeichen der europäischen Schiffe im Mittelalter* (Bremen, 1971)
E. Esin: 'Tös and Monçuk: Notes on Turkish Flag-pole Finials', *Cent. Asiat. J.*, xvi (1972), pp. 14–36
W. Denny: 'A Group of Silk Islamic Banners', *Textile Mus. J.*, iv (1974), pp. 67–81
W. Smith: *Flags through the Ages and across the World* (New York, 1975)
S. Ekdahl: *Die 'Banderia Pruthenorum' des Jan Dlugosz* (Gottingen, 1976)
H. Nickel: 'Dorsal Devices: Polish Hussards, Wings, Japanese *sashimono* and Aztec *tlahuitztli*', *Report: VIII Congress of the International Association of Museums of Arms and Military History: Warsaw, 1978*; also as 'Über Rückenstandarten', (1979), pp. 97–106
K. Ross: *Codex Mendoza: Aztec Manuscript* (Fribourg, 1978)
T. Wise: *Flags of the Napoleonic Wars*, 2 vols, Osprey (London, 1978)
——: *Military Flags of the World* (New York, 1978)

HELMUT NICKEL

Flahaut, Charles-Claude. *See* ANGIVILLER, Comte d'.

Flamboyant style. Architectural term referring to the sinuous, flickering patterns found in French tracery from the 14th century to the early 16th. By extension, it has come to designate French Late Gothic architecture in general, thus corresponding to English Perpendicular and German *Spätgotik* ('Late Gothic') or *Sondergotik*. The term appears to have come into general usage in the 19th century in the writings of, for example, Jules Michelet and Louis Gonse.

The sinuous lines of Flamboyant may have resulted automatically from the juxtaposition of geometric forms, seen, for example, in the mid-13th-century transept rose windows of Notre-Dame, Paris, and in the choir of St Urbain, Troyes, or they may be derived from Islamic architectural motifs. Flamboyant tracery patterns are formed of three basic shapes, which began to appear in the second half of the 13th century: the tightly pointed ogee arch, the tadpole-shaped mouchette and the leaf-shaped soufflet. Unlike geometric tracery, the arcs of these motifs were struck from multiple centres, placed outside as well as inside the unit. The use of such rigorously conceived window tracery in France was delayed until the end of the 14th century (e.g. in the western nave chapels of Amiens Cathedral), and the forms persisted to the 1520s, when rounded shapes regained popularity.

Although the analysis of tracery patterns has provided art historians with a useful descriptive tool, the term 'Flamboyant' is obviously somewhat limited if it is applied solely to the design of windows, and an appreciation of French Late Gothic architecture should also include a study of ground-plans, space and articulation. Ground-plans tend to be simplified and streamlined: the use of the double ambulatory, for example, became rare (St Séverin, Paris, begun 1450, is an exception). East ends are often angular, based on a triangle (e.g. Caudebec-en-Caux, Normandy, 1426–1515), hexagons (e.g. La Madeleine, Troyes, 1495–1508) or a combination of a trapezoid and a rectangle (e.g. St Etienne, Beauvais, c. 1500; St Jean-au-Marché, Troyes, begun 1520). The limited space of a cramped urban site may have been significant in the use of flat east ends and internalized, rather than projecting, buttresses (e.g. St Nicolas, Troyes, begun 1526). The fusion of spaces that had already characterized Rayonnant was additionally emphasized in Flamboyant, chapel spaces often flowing directly into the ambulatory in a series of interlocked polygonal cells (e.g. La Madeleine, Troyes, and Brienne-le-Château in Champagne, begun early 16th century, where interlocked hexagons resemble a honeycomb).

French Late Gothic designers employed several different types of elevation, ranging from the steep, three-storey elevation of St Maclou, Rouen, to an equally slender two-storey section at SS Gervais and Protais, Paris (begun

Flamboyant style tracery screens, Notre-Dame, Louviers, nave from the south, begun 1411

1494). There are massive squat buildings still with a clerestory (e.g. St Nizier, Troyes, begun c. 1500) and hall structures with three vaulted vessels of equal height (e.g. Sainte-Savine, Aube, begun early 16th century). The elimination of the capital allowed the supports to continue directly into the ribs and arches, producing a unified, seamless space. Alternative methods of articulation developed: one where the sharpened mouldings of the ribs and arches continued directly into the piers ('continuous mouldings'; e.g. St Germain, Amiens, c. 1500), and one where these mouldings were engulfed by the surfaces of the pier ('disappearing' or 'dying mouldings'; e.g. Saint-Nicolas de Port, 1495–1514, and St Etienne du Mont, Paris, begun 1492). In some buildings they were either combined (e.g. Notre-Dame, Cléry, nr Orléans, begun 1429) or used side by side (e.g. St Séverin, Paris). They both express the fact that in a multi-storey vaulted structure no single point (represented by the capital) can separate the role of the supporting member (the pier) from that of the supported (the arch or the rib). A similar fusion of previously separate elements is evident in the articulation of exteriors. On the transept façades of the cathedrals of Sens and Beauvais, Martin Chambiges fused the staircase turret with the buttress to form a richly decorated, polygonal framing device for the central bay of the façade.

Existing side by side in Flamboyant are the desire to achieve a new kind of visual clarity or logic, based on systems of articulation that go beyond the use of the Classical orders, and the desire to confound the beholder through the use of various kinds of illusionistic tricks. Pier bases provided an ideal opportunity for virtuoso performances in design and stonecutting. They often have multiple levels, with the more important elements placed closer to the pavement, expressing the hierarchy of the main transverse arches and ribs. The illusion is sometimes given that abstract, geometric form can exist within the inert mass of the stone, emerging as an angle here or there: this is particularly true of compositions based on rotated squares or polygons. The same kind of composition can provide visual links between the form of a pier base, a pilaster or a pinnacle. The fantastic dimension of Flamboyant is often achieved through organic forms, foliage or animals. The absence of capitals can lend organic appearance to the entire building; at St Merri, Paris (1515–52), for example, the pier base mouldings seem to grow from the sides of the pier like fungus from a tree trunk.

The inventiveness and whimsy of Flamboyant are expressed particularly forcefully in liturgical furniture (tombs, screens etc) and in exterior articulation. At the church of Brou, Bourg-en-Bresse, the fantasy of design of the choir-screen, balustrade and tombs contrasts with the cold rationality of the overall interior, with its system of continuous mouldings (for illustration see BROU, PRIORY CHURCH). The choir-screen of La Madeleine, Troyes, provides an example of a small-scale structure that seems to defy the laws of gravity, since the uprights that divide it into three bays do not rest on the ground. The structural daring of the screen and its luxuriant decoration contrast sharply with the smoothly rounded, massive pier forms of the choir. The whole composition, like so many churches of the late 15th century and early 16th, is illuminated by warm coloured light from stained glass of deeply saturated colours.

Although French Late Gothic designers tended to be somewhat more conservative in their approach to vault forms than their counterparts in England and in the areas corresponding to present-day Poland, Germany and the Czech and Slovak Republics, there were some exotic experiments. Particularly common was the addition of tiercerons and liernes to make star-shaped patterns with the points of intersection marked by pendant keystones (e.g. Cadouin Abbey cloister). Suspended wheel-like forms are also found (e.g. SS Gervais and Protais, Paris; Senlis Cathedral; St Etienne, Beauvais). Perhaps the most beautiful Flamboyant vaults are those that adapt the sinuous petal-like forms of window tracery (e.g. Beauvais Cathedral, chapels to the west of the transept).

Although Flamboyant exterior articulation is derived to some extent from Rayonnant, for example in the two-dimensional gables intersected by balustrades and the multiplicity of fine lines, important new forms appear. The mass of the building is sometimes dissolved in screens of tracery, often including startling effects of unsupported uprights (e.g. Albi Cathedral; Notre-Dame, Louviers, begun 1411; see fig.). The niche is a particularly important element in exterior articulation; with its elaborate base and canopy, it exists in its own right, with or without a statue. The limited space-enclosing capacity of the niche provided a link between monumental architecture and small-scale contemporary works in which it also appeared, such as the Angers Apocalypse tapestries (Angers, Château, Col. Tap.).

Although this discussion has concentrated on the unifying elements of Flamboyant, the prevailing political and economic climate (depopulation, the Black Death, the Hundred Years War) was not propitious for building, and linear stylistic developments are generally hard to detect. Apparently contradictory solutions often existed side by side: for example, in the rural churches of southern Champagne, where, in the late 15th century and early 16th, churches with soaring clerestories (e.g. St Jean-au-Marché, Troyes) were being built at the same time as massive squat structures, often without a clerestory (e.g. Sainte-Savine).

The rich historiography of Flamboyant can be summarized under three categories. Just as with High Gothic, early attempts to understand the style concentrated on the question of origins, but whereas the key element in High Gothic was defined as a structural one (the rib vault), the key to Flamboyant was identified as the double curved arch and the origins of the ogee were pursued. Since early examples of double curved tracery can be found in England, the question of regional origins has been hotly debated (Saint-Paul, Enlart, Tamir), and Flamboyant has had the misfortune (as far as the French are concerned) of being incorrectly labelled an English style.

A second misfortune for Flamboyant was the attempt to discover a moral, ethical or morphological basis for the understanding of style. Ruskin and his followers saw the lacy, non-structural inventions of Flamboyant (e.g. the tower of St Ouen at Rouen) as examples of the violation of the principle of truth to materials. Foçillon's morphological framework for the understanding of Gothic also brought pejorative conclusions: Flamboyant was seen as a decadent phase in which the harmonious relationship between structure and articulation was lost.

Later scholars pointed to the shortcomings of the approach to architecture based on theories of morality (Watkin) and attempted to establish a more objective intellectual framework (Białostocki), often based on a dialectic (Frankl, Sanfaçon). The key to this interpretation depends on the ability to understand the design formulae of a named master mason within the documented historical context (Bucher, Shelby, Murray). Such studies demonstrate that Late Gothic designers were frequently indebted to High Gothic and Rayonnant prototypes but that they also worked to achieve a new unity of structure, space and articulation.

BIBLIOGRAPHY

C. Enlart: *Manuel d'archéologie française depuis les temps mérovingiens jusqu'à la renaissance*, 3 vols (Paris, 1902–16)
A. Saint-Paul: 'L'Architecture française et la guerre de cent ans', *Bull. Mnmt*, lxxii (1908), pp. 5–40, 269–302
M. H. Tamir: 'The English Origin of the Flamboyant Style', *Gaz. B.-A.*, 6th ser., xxix (1946), pp. 257–68
P. Frankl: *The Gothic: Literary Sources and Interpretations through Eight Centuries* (Princeton, 1960)
J. Białostocki: 'Late Gothic: Disagreements about the Concept', *J. Brit. Archaeol. Assoc.*, xxix (1966), pp. 76–105
F. Cali: *L'Ordre flamboyant et son temps: Essai sur le style gothique du XIVe au XVIe siècle* (Paris, 1967)
H. Foçillon: *The Art of the West*, ii (London, 1969)
R. Sanfaçon: *L'Architecture flamboyante en France* (Quebec, 1972)
L. Shelby: *Gothic Design Techniques: The Fifteenth Century Design Booklets of Mathes Roriczer and Hanns Schmuttermayer* (Carbondale, 1977)
D. Watkin: *Morality and Architecture* (Oxford, 1977)
F. Bucher: *Architektor: The Lodge Books and Sketchbooks of Medieval Architects* (New York, 1979)
S. Murray: *Building Troyes Cathedral: The Late Gothic Campaigns* (Bloomington, 1987)

STEPHEN MURRAY

Flamen, Albert (*b* Bruges, *c.* 1620; *d* Paris, after 1693). Flemish etcher, engraver, draughtsman and painter, active in France. In 1648 he published a series of seven etchings to illustrate the Lord's Prayer (*Les Sept Demandes de l'oraison dominicale*). His oeuvre includes *c.* 600 etchings after his own designs, many of which are touched up with the burin or drypoint. Most of these constitute series published in small oblong books, often comprising 12 prints, and they reveal the influence of Jacques Callot. Flamen seems to have made many prints for Jacobus van Merlen (*fl* 1670), a member of the Antwerp family of engravers. Flamen's work consists primarily of series of fish, some parts dedicated to Nicolas Fouquet (e.g. B. 37–48), birds, mammals, landscapes (including views around Paris, ?1669, the Château de Longuetoise, B. 93–104, and others) and a set of moralizing emblems (1672; B. 130–41), one of the few dated works. Flamen's strength as an engraver lies in his use of picturesque elements. He may also have worked at the Gobelins. Apart from drawings and prints, he is known to have made paintings, although no works can be attributed to him with certainty. Possibly he can be identified with the 'A. Flament' who is documented in 1692 as 'peintre et dessinateur ordinaire de Monsieur, Frère du Roy'.

BIBLIOGRAPHY

Hollstein: *Dut. & Flem.*
A. von Bartsch: *Le Peintre-graveur* (1803–21), v [B.]
Quinze années d'acquisitions (exh. cat., Brussels, Bib. Royale Albert 1er, 1969), p. 262

'Flamen, Albert', *Dictionnaire des peintres belges du XIVe siècle à nos jours*, 3 vols (Brussels, 1994)

CHRISTIAN COPPENS

Flamen, Anselme (*b* St Omer, Pas-de-Calais, 2 Jan 1647; *d* Paris, 16 May 1717). French sculptor. A pupil of Gaspard Marsy, he studied at the Académie de France in Rome from 1675 to 1679. On his return he was employed to carve decorative stone sculptures on the façades of the château of Versailles, including a statue of *Erato* (1681–2; *in situ*). In 1681 he was received (*reçu*) as a member of the Académie Royale with an oval bas-relief of *St Jerome* (marble; Versailles, Notre-Dame). He assisted Marsy with a number of fountains and groups for the gardens at Versailles and after Marsy's death completed from his models the tomb of *Anne, Duc de Noailles* for St Paul, Paris (marble and bronze, 1683; destr.), and the group *Rape of Oreithyia by Boreas* for Versailles (marble, 1684–7; Paris, Louvre). He made numerous contributions to the royal building projects of the reign of Louis XIV, including a copy of the antique group *Faun with a Kid* (marble, 1685–6) and a statue of *Cyparissus* (marble, 1687) for the gardens at Versailles (both *in situ*), as well as stucco decoration for the Salon de l'Oeil de Boeuf (1701; *in situ*) within the palace and statues of *St Philip*, *St Bartholomew* and *St Irenaeus* (stone, 1707; *in situ*) for the exterior of the chapel.

Flamen contributed to the decoration of the church of the Invalides, Paris, with vigorous stone groups of *Prophets* in relief (1690–99; *in situ*) and a relief of an *Angel Carrying the Holy Ampulla* (1701–5; *in situ*). He also provided spirited works for the gardens of the château of Marly, Yvelines, including marble statues of *Diana* (1693; Paris, Louvre), *Callisto* (1696; Versailles, Château) and a *Companion of Diana* (1710–14; Versailles, Château). These works reveal a prolific artist of high technical ability whose early, vigorous, classicizing style evolved into the livelier and lighter Rococo idioms of the early 18th century.

BIBLIOGRAPHY

Lami; Souchal

J. Guiffrey: *Comptes des Bâtiments du Roi sous le règne de Louis XIV*, 5 vols (Paris, 1881–1901)

F. Souchal: 'Anselme Flamen, "natif de Saint-Omer", sculpteur du roi', *Gaz. B.-A.*, xci (1978), pp. 49–71

T. Hedin: 'Exemple d'une collaboration d'artistes: The partnership of Gaspard Marsy and Anselme Flamen, 1679–1681', *Gaz. B.-A.*, xcviii (1981), pp. 103–14

FRANÇOISE DE LA MOUREYRE

Flameng, François (*b* Paris, 6 Dec 1856; *d* Paris, 28 Feb 1923). French painter and draughtsman. He was the son and pupil of the engraver Leopold Flameng (1831–1911) and was taught by Alexandre Cabanel, Edmond Hédouin and Jean-Paul Laurens. He first exhibited at the Salon in 1873, working initially as a history and portrait painter. He produced several large historical compositions such as *Conquerors of the Bastille* (1881; Rouen, Mus. B.-A.), painted in an academic style characteristic of the Third Republic. He also worked as a decorative painter, producing nine panels for the great staircase of the Sorbonne in Paris depicting the foundation of the university and the history of French literature, for example *St Louis Delivering the Founding Charter to Robert de Sorbon* (1887) and *Moralists of the Court of Louis XIV: La Rochefoucauld and*

Molière (both *in situ*). He decorated the ceiling over the staircase in the Opéra Comique in Paris with paintings that owe something to Degas, such as *Tragedy* and *Dance* (1897; both *in situ*), but more to Boucher (*Comedy Pursuing the Vices*). He contributed to the design of the Salle des Fêtes at the Exposition Universelle in Paris in 1900 with three enormous compositions, *Silk and Wool*, the *Decorative Arts* and the *Chemical Industries* (all destr.). Flameng also produced ceiling paintings for the buffet at the Gare de Lyon (*in situ*) in Paris as well as wall and ceiling paintings for numerous public and private buildings, including the Hôtel des Invalides in Paris (now in Paris, Mus. Armée), the Grolier Club in New York and the Charitonenko Palace in Moscow (both *in situ*). In 1903 he collaborated with Léon Bonnat, P.-A.-J. Dagnan-Bouveret, Gustave Colin, Léon Glaize, Charles Lapostolet, Joseph Layraud and Tony Robert-Fleury on the decoration of the Salon des Arts in the Hôtel de Ville in Paris, contributing *Music*, a panel painted in a Symbolist style.

Flameng devoted himself almost exclusively to portrait painting in his later years, producing works with an 18th-century flavour such as *Mme Flameng, the Artist's Wife* (1893; Paris, Louvre). In 1894 he travelled to Russia, where his works were well received; Tsar Nicholas II bought four scenes from the life of Napoleon Bonaparte (1894–6; St Petersburg, Hermitage). *Mme Winterfeld* (1910; Nice, Mus. B.-A.) reveals his skill as a portrait painter, with its stylized grace of composition, latent eroticism (the model, covered in jewels, is voluptuously removing her glove) and fluidity of brushwork. Flameng also worked as an illustrator, producing 100 drawings for an edition of the complete works of Victor Hugo (Paris, 1886). He was appointed professor at the Ecole des Beaux-Arts in Paris in 1905 and became President of the Académie des Beaux-Arts in 1910.

BIBLIOGRAPHY

Thieme–Becker

Edouard-Joseph: *Dictionnaire biographique des artistes contemporains, 1910–1930*, ii (Paris, 1931), pp. 35–6

A. DAGUERRE DE HUREAUX

Flanagan, Barry (*b* Prestatyn, Clwyd, 18 Jan 1941). English sculptor and printmaker. He grew up in England and studied architecture briefly and then sculpture at Birmingham College of Art and Crafts between 1957 and 1958, and at St Martin's School of Art, London (1964–6). While a student he associated with dancers, poets and potters; he later stressed the importance of such temporary involvements. Alternating between abstract and figurative images and a variety of techniques, Flanagan maintained a consistently ironic attitude towards sculpture, an emphasis on the intrinsic qualities of the materials and an idiosyncratic lightness of touch that endowed the objects with a sense of vulnerability and impudence.

During the late 1960s Flanagan created temporary works of poured sand and draped cloth (e.g. *One Camion Sand Piece*, 1969; see 1969 Krefeld exh. cat., no. 18) and his own upright biomorphic forms made of stitched, dyed hessian filled with plaster and sand such as *aaing j gni aa* (1965; London, Tate). Their changeable forms, subject to the laws of gravity, make them inventive examples of the art form known as soft art. In their use of appropriated materials and improvisation they related to Arte Povera and were seen in the context of the art of Richard Serra, Richard Long, Eva Hesse and others in important group exhibitions, notably in 1969 in *When Attitudes Become Form*. After 1973 most of his works were free-standing, permanent objects. Initially lumps of quarried Hornton stone or marble were incised sparingly with spirals and simple drawings. Displayed on plinths that were often made of stacked blocks, and given such titles as *A Nose in Repose* (1977–9; London, Tate), these stones were part of the quizzical, iconic side of Flanagan's art, with references to Alfred Jarry's *Ubu Roi* (1896) and pataphysics, the 'science' of imaginary solutions.

The popularity and distinctiveness of Flanagan's work greatly increased when he began making sculptures of hares, the first, *Leaping Hare* (London, Waddington Gals), supported by a pyramid, cast in bronze in 1980. Other hares stood and adopted human attitudes as boxers or cricketers, and some were paired with an anonymous form, usually one of the hallmarks of the casting trade: an anvil

Barry Flanagan: *Hare on Helmet II*, bronze, 521×1260×610mm, 1981 (London, Tate Gallery)

or bell, or a helmet as in *Hare on Helmet II* (1981; London, Tate; see fig.). Flanagan's other favoured animals, the elephant, dog, cougar and horse, were equally primitive anatomically and yet anthropomorphically expressive even when enlarged to monumental scale. Later he worked from the life model. From 1970 Flanagan made prints whose animal and other themes related to his sculpture. *Welsh Cob* (linocut, 1983; see 1986 exh. cat., p. 27) was made as part of his preparatory studies for the life-size sculpture *Horse* (1983; artist's priv. col., see 1986 exh. cat., p. 10). In an abstract practice that began in 1981, he asked Italian carvers to enlarge and interpret in marble his casually twisted forms of soft clay. The results, such as *Carving No. 2* (1981; London, Tate), frequently had an eroticism equal to that of the animal sculptures and bronzes made of clay and wax. In 1987 he moved to Ibiza.

WRITINGS
'Sculpture Made Visible: Barry Flanagan in discussion with G. Baro', *Studio Int.*, clxxviii/915 (1969), p. 122

BIBLIOGRAPHY
Barry Flanagan: Object Sculptures (exh. cat., Krefeld, Mus. Haus Lange, 1969)
When Attitudes Become Form (exh. cat., Berne, Ksthalle; Krefeld, Kaiser Wilhelm Mus.; London, ICA; 1969)
Barry Flanagan: Sculpture, 1966–1976 (exh. cat. by C. Lampert, Eindhoven, Stedelijk Van Abbemus.; London, Serpentine Gal.; 1977) [cat. rev. for London exh.]
Barry Flanagan: Sculpture (exh. cat. by T. Hilton and M. Compton, Brit. Council Col., 1982)
Barry Flanagan: Sculptures (exh. cat. by C. Lampert, Paris, Pompidou, 1983)
Barry Flanagan: Prints, 1970–83 (exh. cat., ed. E. Knowles; London, Tate, 1986)
Barry Flanagan (exh. cat. by E. Juncosa and J. Thompson, Madrid, Fund. 'La Caixa', 1993)

CATHERINE LAMPERT

Flanders. *See* BELGIUM.

Flanders, Louis II, Count of. *See* LOUIS II, Count of Flanders.

Flandes, Juan de. *See* JUAN DE FLANDES.

Flandrin. French family of artists. Jean-Baptiste-Jacques Flandrin (1773–1838), an amateur painter who specialized in portraits, had seven children, of whom (1) Auguste Flandrin, (2) Hippolyte Flandrin and (3) Paul Flandrin became artists.

(1) (René-)Auguste Flandrin (*b* Lyon, 6 May 1801; *d* Lyon, 30 Aug 1842). Painter and printmaker. He attended the Ecole des Beaux-Arts in Lyon from 1817 to 1823, studying drawing and painting under Fleury Richard and Alexis Grognard (1752–1840). He produced engraved title-pages for musical romances and lithographic scenes of Lyon, such as the *Ruins of the Roman Aqueduct at Lyon* (1824; Paris, Bib. N.). In 1833 he moved to Paris, where he worked in Ingres's studio for a year. He then moved back to Lyon and in 1838 spent a few weeks in Rome. On his return, he set up a studio in Lyon where such artists as Louis Lamothe (1822–69) and Joseph Pognon studied. As well as landscape lithographs (e.g. *View of the Bridge at Beauregard on the Sâone*, 1834; Paris, Bib. N.), he also painted historical scenes, such as *Savonarola Preaching at S*

Miniato (1836; Lyon, Mus. B.-A.), and portraits, such as *Dr S. des Guidi* (1841; Lyon, Mus. B.-A.), which shows the influence of Ingres.

(2) Hippolyte(-Jean) Flandrin (*b* Lyon, 23 March 1809; *d* Rome, 21 March 1864). Painter and lithographer, brother of (1) Auguste Flandrin. He was initially discouraged from fulfilling his early wish to become an artist by Auguste's lack of success, but in 1821 the sculptor Denys Foyatier, an old family friend, persuaded both Hippolyte and Paul to train as artists. He introduced them to the sculptor Jean-François Legendre-Héral (1796–1851) and the painter André Magnin (1794–1823), with whom they worked copying engravings and plaster casts. After Magnin's death, Legendre-Héral took the brothers to the animal and landscape painter Jean-Antoine Duclaux (1783–1868). Hippolyte and Paul had both learnt the techniques of lithography from Auguste at an early age, and between the ages of 14 and 19 Hippolyte produced a number of lithographs, which he sold to supplement the family income. Many reflected his passion for military subjects (e.g. *Cossacks in a Bivouac, c.* 1825; Paris, Bib. N.). In 1826 the two brothers entered the Ecole des Beaux-Arts in Lyon, where Hippolyte studied under Pierre Révoil. Showing a precocious talent, he was soon advised to move to Paris, and having left the Ecole des Beaux-Arts in Lyon in 1829, he walked to the capital with his brother Paul; together they enrolled in the studio of Ingres. After several unsuccessful attempts, Hippolyte won the Grand Prix de Rome in 1832 with *Theseus Recognized by his Father* (1832; Paris, Ecole N. Sup. B.-A.), despite having suffered from cholera during the competition. His success was all the more spectacular given the general hostility to Ingres; Hippolyte was the first of his pupils to be awarded this prestigious prize.

Hippolyte arrived in Rome in 1833; Paul joined him there in 1834. After first working on such subjects as *Virgil and Dante in Hell* (1836; Lyon, Mus. B.-A.), Hippolyte developed a taste for religious works during this stay. From 1836 to 1837 he worked on *St Clare Healing the Blind* for the cathedral in Nantes, winning a first-class medal at the 1837 Salon, and in 1838 he painted

Hippolyte Flandrin: *Parting of the Red Sea*, oil on card, 485×570 mm, 1858; sketch for mural decoration for St Germain-des-Prés, Paris (Princeton, Princeton University, Art Museum)

Christ Blessing the Children (Lisieux, Mus. Vieux-Lisieux), which was exhibited at the 1839 Salon.

In 1838 Hippolyte returned to France; the following year he received a commission to decorate the Chapelle Saint-Jean of St Séverin in Paris with murals depicting the *Life of St John*. Unveiled in 1841, they won him the Croix de Chevalier. The encaustic painting technique resulted in a subdued colour scheme well suited to the Neo-classical austerity of the style. Soon after completing this project, he was one of several artists employed by the Duc de Luynes at the Château Dampierre; with Paul's assistance, he decorated its Great Hall with a series of semi-nude female figures in a graceful 'Etruscan' style. State commissions for murals continued; in 1842 he painted *St Louis Dictating his Laws* for the Chambre des Pairs of the Paris Sénat and began work on a series of biblical scenes for St Germain-des-Prés in Paris. The first, placed in the sanctuary, were executed between 1842 and 1846; the largest depict *Christ on the Road to Calvary* and the *Entry of Christ into Jerusalem*. Set on gold backgrounds, both pictures are highly dramatic despite the use of an emotionally restrained Neo-classical style. From 1846 to 1848 he decorated the Chapelle des Apôtres and the choir, also designing its stained-glass windows. From 1856 onwards he worked on the nave, work eventually finished after his death by Paul. This was the largest part of the commission, consisting of 20 separate panels showing scenes from the Old Testament and New Testament—the *Parting of the Red Sea* (see fig.), the *Annunciation*, the *Adoration of the Magi*, the *Crucifixion* etc—each surmounted by a prophet or other biblical figure. Though occasionally harking back to Giotto, Flandrin's work was chiefly influenced by Raphael. In 1864 he was also asked to decorate the transepts of the church; these were completed after his death by his pupil Sébastien Cornu.

By this time receiving more commissions than he could execute, Hippolyte was able to specialize in religious scenes; the revived popularity of large-scale church decoration in mid-19th-century Paris meant that there was no shortage of such work. In 1847 he had refused an offer to decorate St Vincent-de-Paul in Paris, in deference to his master Ingres, who had begun and then abandoned the project shortly before. It was then passed to François-Edouard Picot, but when the 1848 Revolution brought about a change in the Paris administration, the new mayor Armand Marast tried once again to persuade Flandrin to take up St Vincent-de-Paul. Finally a compromise was reached; Picot painted the choir and Flandrin the nave. The resulting works, executed from 1849 to 1853, largely consist of two friezes 39 m long and only 2.7 m high. Rather than break them up into smaller panels, Flandrin painted two processions of figures. On the one side are confessors, church doctors, martyred saints and apostles; on the other side are penitents, virgin saints and martyrs. Both friezes have a gold background, reminiscent of mosaics.

In 1853 Flandrin was elected a member of the Académie des Beaux-Arts; the following year he executed two allegorical murals of *Agriculture* and *Industry* for the Conservatoire National des Arts et Métiers in Paris. Returning to Lyon in 1855, he decorated St Martin d'Ainay as part of an overall restoration of the church. In 1857 he

was appointed professor at the Ecole des Beaux-Arts in Paris, and in 1863, though in poor health, he moved to Rome. Though primarily known as a religious painter, he also painted numerous portraits; early works, such as *Mme Vinet* (1841; Paris, Louvre), are cold but elegant. His portrait of *Emperor Napoleon III* (1861–2; Versailles, Château) was disliked by the sitter.

(3) (Jean-)Paul Flandrin (*b* Lyon, 28 May 1811; *d* Paris, 8 March 1902). Painter and lithographer, brother of (1) Auguste Flandrin and (2) Hippolyte Flandrin. Always very close to his brother Hippolyte, Paul followed much the same training, studying under Legendre-Héral, Magnin and Duclaux. Like Hippolyte, he was taught lithography by Auguste. He studied at the Ecole des Beaux-Arts in Lyon (1826–8) and in 1829 moved to Paris, where he enrolled in the studio of Ingres. The two brothers soon became Ingres's favoured pupils, and in 1832, the year that Hippolyte won the Prix de Rome, Paul won a prize for historical landscape, though he failed in the Prix de Rome competition the following year. Finding the separation from his brother painful, in 1834 he moved to join Hippolyte. Once in Rome, he soon discovered his vocation as a landscape painter. Ingres arrived as Director of the Académie de France in 1835, and Paul, among other artists, received a commission to make copies of the works in the Vatican. Although not a prizewinner, he was closely connected with the Villa Médici and often accompanied the students on their trips to the country. In 1837, fleeing a cholera epidemic in Rome, Paul and Hippolyte visited Padua, Venice, Verona, Mantua and other places. Joined by Auguste in 1838, the three brothers visited Livorno, Milan, Pisa and Florence.

Returning to France in 1839, Paul made his Salon debut that year with two landscapes, the *Sabine Mountains* (1838; Paris, Louvre) and *Nymphée* (1839; Angers, Mus. B.-A.), winning a second-class medal. In 1840 he helped Hippolyte decorate the Chapelle Saint-Jean of St Séverin in Paris, and in 1842 he was commissioned to decorate the Chapelle des Fonts-Baptismaux in the same church; he worked on this until 1845. He often travelled to Brittany, Dauphiné, Normandy and Provence in search of subjects, producing paintings such as the *Dauphiné Valley above Voreppe* (*c*. 1845; Aix-en-Provence, Mus. Granet). After helping Hippolyte on the decorations for St Paul in Nîmes (1847–9), he remained there to paint the landscape. His pictures are clearly in the classical tradition of Claude and Poussin; some, such as the melancholy *Solitude* (1857; Paris, Louvre), feature figures in antique dress.

State recognition of his work came in 1859 with a commission for the *Flight into Egypt* (1861; Orléans, Mus. B.-A.). In 1862 he painted with Corot and that year and the next worked at Fontainebleau on such landscapes as *At the Waterside* (1868; Bordeaux, Mus. B.-A.). During the Franco-Prussian War he stayed in Angers; in 1876, having lost his hard-won public esteem, he was forced to open a drawing school for girls. He received a commission to produce a cartoon for a tapestry for the Escalier Chagrin in the Sénat in 1878. Through much of the 1880s he worked outside Paris; he continued to paint until the end of the century, although his work was almost completely neglected—a neglect further compounded by the glittering reputation of his brother Hippolyte. Although Paul was not an innovator in the field of landscape painting, his canvases are invariably very appealing.

DBF

BIBLIOGRAPHY

J.-B. Poncet: *Hippolyte Flandrin* (Paris, 1864)
H. Delaborde: *Lettres et pensées d'Hippolyte Flandrin* (Paris, 1865)
M. De Montrond: *Hippolyte Flandrin* (Paris, 1865)
H. L. Sidney Lear: *A Christian Painter of the Nineteenth Century, Being the Life of Hippolyte Flandrin* (London, Oxford and Cambridge, 1875)
E. Montrosier: *Peintres modernes: Ingres, Hippolyte Flandrin, Robert-Fleury* (Paris, 1882), pp. 49–72
F. Bournand: *Trois artistes chrétiens: Michel-Ange, Raphael et Hippolyte Flandrin* (Paris, 1892), pp. 293–382
L. Masson: *Hippolyte Flandrin* (Paris, 1900)
G. Bodinier: *Un Ami angevin d'Hippolyte et Paul Flandrin: Correspondance de Victor Bodinier avec Hippolyte et Paul* (Angers, 1912)
M. Audin and E. Vial: *Dictionnaire des artistes et ouvriers d'art de la France: Lyonnais*, 2 vols (Paris, 1918)
Hippolyte, Auguste et Paul Flandrin: Une Fraternité picturale au XIXe siècle (exh. cat. by J. Foucart, B. Foucart and others, Paris, Mus. Luxembourg, 1984–5; Lyon, Mus. B.-A.; 1985) [full bibliog.]

Flandrin, Jules

Flandrin, Jules (*b* Corenc, nr Grenoble, 9 July 1871; *d* Corenc, May 1947). French painter, printmaker and draughtsman. While still at the Lycée de Grenoble he took courses in drawing and modelling. Abandoning his baccalauréat he joined a firm of printers in Grenoble in 1889 where he learnt the techniques of lithography while continuing his other art courses. Having done his military service he moved to Paris in 1893 and enrolled at the Ecole des Arts Décoratifs, which he attended during 1894. Late in 1894 he also enrolled at the Ecole des Beaux-Arts where, impressed by his ability, Gustave Moreau took him into his studio in 1895 even before he had passed the entrance examination. He remained there until Moreau's death in 1898 and also received encouragement and advice from Pierre Puvis de Chavannes at this time.

Flandrin first exhibited in 1896, at the Salon du Champ de Mars in Paris, with a number of paintings and lithographs. After becoming an associate member of the Société Nationale des Beaux-Arts in 1897, he exhibited paintings regularly, especially at the Salon des Indépendants and the Salon d'Automne, and he experimented with ceramics. His early paintings were portraits and also landscape works executed in luminous colour and depicting idyllic scenes such as *Valle d'Isère* (1904; Grenoble, Mus. Grenoble). In 1905 he first saw the Ballets Russes, which greatly impressed him and led to a number of paintings taken from the performances, such as *Les Sylphides* (see Marval, p. 165).

In the autumn of 1909 Flandrin made a short trip to Italy, visiting Venice, Florence and Rome. He exhibited at the Stafford Gallery in London in 1910 with the Neo-Impressionists and in 1912 exhibited in Berlin and Munich. In the same year he was decorated with the Légion d'honneur, an early recognition of his reputation. By this time his work was influenced by Maurice Denis and his synthetist ideas. Paintings such as *At the Fountain* (1913; Paris, Pompidou) showed him using simplified planes of unmodelled colour. He also employed duller colours, in keeping with the Nabi aesthetic that centred its colour spectrum on grey. This influence persisted throughout many of his later works.

After World War I, Flandrin took a studio on the Quai Saint-Michel, Paris, in the same block as that of Matisse and Albert Marquet, both of whom he knew from Moreau's studio. Having long been interested in tapestry, he founded the 'Atelier Grenoblois de Tapisserie de Haute Lisse' in Grenoble in 1920; it ran until 1923 when the financial cost became too great. During the 1920s he divided his time between Paris and Corenc and from 1926, between those two places and Italy. His paintings of this period show him at the height of his powers and still influenced by Denis, producing such works as *Landscape in the Outskirts of Biarritz* (1923; Lyon, Mus. B.-A.). In 1931 he settled in Grenoble and until the outbreak of World War II made regular trips to Paris. He concentrated on landscapes, outdoor scenes and still-lifes and, as in *Terrace of the Town Garden* (1932; Grenoble, Mus. Grenoble), often imbued these with a spiritual calm. Though friendly with the Fauves, he never allowed himself their expressive freedom in execution or use of colour. He also painted works for church interiors: from 1905 to 1928 he worked on a series of decorative panels for the church at Corenc and in 1931 he produced two panels for the church of St Bruno at Grenoble. In his last years he lost the compositional strength of his earlier works, as is apparent in such works as *Moonrise at Syracuse* (1942; Lyon, Mus. B.-A.).

DBF

BIBLIOGRAPHY

J. Marval: 'Les Danseurs de Flandrin', *A. Déc.* (April 1913), pp. 165–76
R. Huyghe and G. Bazin: *Histoire de l'art contemporain* (Paris, 1935/R New York, 1968), pp. 121–2
Hommage à Jules Flandrin (exh. cat. by M. Besset, Grenoble, Mus. Peint. & Sculp., 1972)

Flannagan, John B(ernard)

Flannagan, John B(ernard) (*b* Fargo, ND, 7 April 1895; *d* New York, 6 Jan 1942). American sculptor. An important proponent of modernism in America, he began studying painting in 1914 at the Minneapolis Institute of Arts. In New York he met the painter Arthur B. Davies, who suggested Flannagan try wood-carving. By 1927 Flannagan had abandoned both painting and wood-carving and, essentially self-taught, settled on direct carving in stone, although he did later experiment with metal casting. Flannagan preferred natural fieldstone to quarried material, favouring its rude and basic qualities. Similarly, he eschewed academic art, preferring simplified and abstracted forms. He chiselled as little as possible from the stones that he chose, seeking solely to release in his small-scale works the pantheistic image he believed existed in every rock. Often he made only shallow incisions to delineate his generalized animal and human figures. He dealt particularly with mother and child themes, such as *Woman and Child* (1932–3; Poughkeepsie, NY, Vassar Coll. A.G.), and with concepts of birth and rebirth, as seen in *Triumph of the Egg I* (1937; New York, MOMA).

Flannagan journeyed twice to Ireland in the early 1930s. On his return he spent seven months in a sanatorium recovering from alcoholism and depression. He continued to exhibit at New York galleries and in 1938 completed the *Gold Miner* for the Samuel Memorial in Fairmount Park, Philadelphia, PA, although he had been hurt in a car accident in 1936. Another car accident in 1939 left him severely injured, and he endured four operations that left him physically and emotionally debilitated. So great was his despair that, despite preparation for a forthcoming major retrospective exhibition, Flannagan took his own life in his New York studio.

WRITINGS
'The Image in the Rock', *Mag. A.*, xxxv (March 1942), pp. 90–95 [repr. in 1973 exh. cat.]
M. Flannagan, ed.: *Letters of John B. Flannagan* (New York, 1942)

BIBLIOGRAPHY
The Sculpture of John B. Flannagan (exh. cat., ed. D. C. Miller, intro. C. Zigrosser; New York, MOMA, 1942)
R. Forsyth: *John B. Flannagan: His Life and Works* (diss., Minneapolis, U. MN, 1965)
John B. Flannagan: Sculpture and Drawings from 1924–38 (exh. cat., intro. R. Forsyth; New York, Weyhe Gal.; Saint Paul, MN Mus. A.; 1973)

LAURETTA DIMMICK

Flat. *See* APARTMENT and TENEMENT BUILDING.

Flatman, Thomas (*b* London, 1635; *d* London, 8 Dec 1688). English miniature painter and poet. He was the son of a clerk in Chancery and entered the Inner Temple in 1658; he was called to the Bar in 1662. Among his earliest verses are lines prefixed to Sir William Sanderson's *Graphice* (1658), a work containing a description of the art of miniature painting, based on Edward Norgate's writings. It is not known whether Flatman received any practical instruction in this art, but his first miniatures (from 1661), for example the *Rev. Samuel Woodforde* (Cambridge, Fitzwilliam), show that he was acquainted with the work of Samuel Cooper. By this time he had entered the somewhat selfconscious artistic coterie of Charles Beale senior and his wife, the portrait painter Mary Beale. Flatman divided his career between writing poetry (in which his earnest religious temperament is revealed) and painting portraits in miniature. A versatile man, he was made a Fellow of the newly founded Royal Society in 1668. A number of his friends were leading clergymen, and many of his sitters were drawn from the Church and other intellectual circles.

Flatman's early miniatures are executed in a rather literal imitation of Cooper's style, but in his later works, exemplified by a *Self-portrait* (1673; London, V&A), he developed a freer and more brilliant manner. In these later portraits, which have a classical accent, he is second only to Cooper in the quality and force of his characterization.

WRITINGS
G. Saintsbury, ed.: *Minor Poets of the Caroline Period* (London, 1905–21/R 1968), iii, pp. 275–422

BIBLIOGRAPHY
J. Murdoch and others: *The English Miniature* (New Haven and London, 1981), pp. 148–53

GRAHAM REYNOLDS

Flatow, Louis Victor (*b* 1820; *d* London, 10 Nov 1867). British dealer. The son of a Prussian Jew, he arrived in England in 1835 and was naturalized British in 1863. He began his career dealing in dubious Old Masters but, after a short period as a chiropodist, became an important dealer in works by contemporary British artists, except members of the Pre-Raphaelite school. He combined a coarse and flamboyant nature with an acute entrepreneurial flair, more akin to that of an impresario than to the relatively more prosaic activities of Ernest Gambart, with

whom he is sometimes compared. Although believed to be illiterate (allegedly, the only word he could write was his own name, on cheques), he combined refinement of taste with a degree of financial genius. These attributes, combined with a congenial nature, made him a favourite with several artists, chiefly of the narrative school. These included George Elgar Hicks, whose *Changing Homes* (1862; London, Geffrye Mus.) was commissioned by Flatow, and William Powell Frith, who devoted considerable space to the dealer in his autobiography.

Flatow's most celebrated venture was the commission and purchase of Frith's *Railway Station* (1862; Egham, U. London, Royal Holloway & Bedford New Coll.), together with copyright, for £4500 (with an additional £750 for exhibition rights), which Flatow exhibited at a gallery at 7 The Haymarket and, afterwards, throughout Britain. The figure talking to the engine driver in the picture is the only known portrait of Flatow.

BIBLIOGRAPHY
W. P. Frith: *My Autobiography and Reminiscences*, ii (London, 1887), pp. 228–37
J. Maas: *Gambart: Prince of the Victorian Art World* (London, 1975), pp. 45–7, 135–9, 201–2

JEREMY MAAS

Flatware. *See* CUTLERY.

Flatz, (Johann) Gebhard (*b* Wolfurt, nr Bregenz, 11 June 1800; *d* Bregenz, 19 May 1881). Austrian painter. He studied at the Akademie der Bildenden Künste, Vienna, under Franc Kavčič and Anton Petter (1781–1858). In 1827, after a short period in Munich, he moved to Bregenz with his friend, the painter Liberat Hundertpfund (1806–78). In 1829 he and Hundertpfund moved to Innsbruck, where Flatz painted numerous portraits. In 1833 he went to Rome, where he remained for five years. His stay there and his meeting with Friedrich Overbeck were of great importance for his artistic development, as were the paintings of Fra Angelico and Raphael. He began to paint solely religious subjects in the manner of the NAZARENES. Paintings of the Virgin and Child are especially reminiscent of Overbeck; although rendered with great feeling and charm, they tend to be somewhat saccharine (e.g. *Virgin and Child*, 1858; Neuss, Clemens-Sels-Mus.). He briefly visited Innsbruck again but returned to Rome in 1840 with his pupil Jakob Fink (1821–46). In artistic and Catholic circles in Rome his reputation almost equalled that of Overbeck. After the Italian revolution of 1848–9, Flatz returned to Bregenz and executed numerous altarpieces and other paintings for local churches (e.g. two altar paintings, 1860 and 1869; Bregenz, St Antonius). A work of 1847, *Virgin and Child with St John* (sold Munich, Weinmüller, 27–9 June 1973; see Fuchs, p. 109) is painted as a tondo in the style of Raphael and Leonardo. He also painted commissions for patrons throughout Europe.

BIBLIOGRAPHY
Thieme–Becker
L. Welti: 'Förderung des Wolfurter "Nazareners" Gebhard Flatz durch seine Vorarlberger Landsleute', *Jb. Vorarlberg. Landesmusver.* (1967), pp. 146–8
D. Kocks: 'Ein nazarenisches Madonnenbild und seine Tradition', *Neusser Jb. Kst, Kultgew. & Heimatknd.* (1976), pp. 20–25
H. Fuchs: *Die österreichische Malerei des 19. Jahrhunderts*, suppl. vol. i (Vienna, 1978)

Die Nazarener in Österreich, 1809–1839: Zeichnungen und Druckgrafik (exh. cat., ed. C. Steinle and G. Fink; Graz, Neue Gal., 1979)

Flavin, Dan (*b* New York, 1 April 1933; *d* Riverhead, NY, 29 Nov 1996). American installation artist and painter. His father intended him to become a priest and from 1947 to 1952 he attended a seminary in Brooklyn, New York. In 1954 he studied at the University of Maryland Extension Program in Osan-Ni in Korea and in 1956 at the New College for Social Research in New York. He continued these art history studies in 1957–9 at Columbia University, New York, but was self-taught as an artist. His early work of the late 1950s and early 1960s was influenced by contemporary American art and included paintings with added objects, such as *Africa (To Seventy-two Negroes)* (1960; see 1969 exh. cat., p. 107), which incorporated a crushed metal can. Other works included poems and other texts set in gestural decorative designs, such as *My Dove, my Beautiful One, Arise, Arise* (1961; see 1969 exh. cat., p. 113), based on a poem by James Joyce. By 1961 Flavin had begun to make a number of Minimalist works using incandescent or fluorescent electric lights, such as *Icon I* (1961; see 1969 exh. cat., p. 125), which consisted of a monochrome painted wooden square with a fluorescent light mounted on the top edge. Both the title and the use of light bore religious connotations in the traditional association of light with the divine and sacred. He rapidly extended this technique into what became his mature style: installations, usually temporary, using white or coloured fluorescent light tubes, as well as a few autonomous and permanent works. The installation *Untitled (To Elizabeth and Richard Koshalek)* (1971; see 1973–4 exh. cat., p. 49), for example, which was installed at the Walker Art Center in Minneapolis, MN, consisted of a hall whose ceiling was covered by a rectilinear network of straight coloured tubes.

WRITINGS

' "… in daylight or cool white": An Autobiographical Sketch', *Artforum*, iv/4 (1965), pp. 20–24
'some other comments', *Artforum*, vi/4 (1967), pp. 20–25

BIBLIOGRAPHY

Fluorescent Light, Etc from Dan Flavin (exh. cat. by B. Smith, Ottawa, N.G.; Vancouver, A.G.; 1969)
Dan Flavin: Drei Installationen in fluoreszierendem Licht/Three Installations in Fluorescent Light (exh. cat. by M. Schneckenburger, E. Weiss and D. Ronte, Cologne, Wallraf-Richartz-Mus., 1973–4)
Neue Anwendungen Fluoreszierenden Lichts mit Diagrammen, Zeichnungen und Drucken von Dan Flavin (exh. cat. by J. Poetter and M. Deschamps, Baden-Baden, Staatl. Ksthalle, 1989)

☐

Flavitsky, Konstantin (Dmitriyevich) (*b* Moscow, 25 Sept 1830; *d* St Petersburg, 15 Sept 1866). Russian painter. He completed his studies at the Academy of Arts in St Petersburg in 1855. The influence of Karl Bryullov was central to Flavitsky's work. He combined the theatricality of academicism and the elegance of salon painting with a desire to observe a degree of realism in his subjects and to relate history to present events, thereby anticipating new developments in Russian history painting.

Christian Martyrs in the Colosseum (1862; St Petersburg, Rus. Mus.) is carefully composed, with notable similarities in composition to Karl Bryullov's the *Last Day of Pompeii*. Flavitsky's greatest achievement was his picture *Princess*

Tarakanova (1864; Moscow, Tret'yakov Gal.), which became one of the most popular 19th-century paintings in Russia. Its subject, Yelizaveta Tarakanova, had claimed to be the daughter of the Empress Elizabeth Petrovna and thus the rightful heir to the Russian throne. The adventuress, tricked into returning to Russia from Italy, was imprisoned in the Peter and Paul Fortress, where she died of tuberculosis. Flavitsky strengthened the melodramatic aspect of the subject by depicting her dying in a cell as it fills with flood water. This work was seen by those of liberal opinions as a denunciation of autocratic despotism.

BIBLIOGRAPHY

T. Gorina: *K. D. Flavitsky* (Moscow, 1955)

M. N. SOKOLOV

Flaxman, John (*b* York, 6 July 1755; *d* London, 9 Dec 1826). English sculptor, designer and teacher. He was the most famous English Neo-classical sculptor of the late 18th century and the early 19th. He produced comparatively few statues and portrait busts but devoted himself to monumental sculpture and became noted for the piety and humanity of his church monuments. He also had an international reputation based on his outline illustrations to the works of Homer, Aeschylus and Dante, which led him to be described by Goethe as 'the idol of all dilettanti'. More recently attention has focused on his models for pottery and silver, and he has emerged as an important pioneer in the development of industrial design.

1. Life and work. 2. Working methods and technique. 3. Critical reception and posthumous reputation.

1. LIFE AND WORK.

(i) Early work, to 1787. Flaxman was the son of a plaster-cast maker employed by both Louis-François Roubiliac and Peter Scheemakers (ii), and at an early age he showed great promise as a sculptor, exhibiting at the Royal Academy in 1771–3. He had entered the Royal Academy Schools in 1770 but failed to win a gold medal, which would have allowed him to travel to Italy. In 1775 he agreed to supply designs for ceramic medallions and plaques to Josiah Wedgwood, for whom his father had supplied casts, and for the next few years he seems to have tried to establish himself as a monumental sculptor while receiving regular work from Wedgwood. A group of remarkable early drawings (*c.* 1775–80; London, BM; Cambridge, Fitzwilliam) devoted to the tragic life of the poet Thomas Chatterton suggest that he had a strongly romantic side to his character. From an early age he showed an unusual interest, which he shared with his friend William Blake, in the art of the Middle Ages.

By the mid-1780s Flaxman had succeeded in establishing himself as a sculptor by executing the tomb of *Mrs Sarah Morley* in Gloucester Cathedral (marble, 1784), while also producing a number of designs for Wedgwood. It is clear that he found the work for Wedgwood onerous and unrewarding; nevertheless, some of his designs are remarkable. The *Apotheosis of Homer* relief (1778), for instance, which was adapted from an outline engraving of an ancient Greek vase in the collection of Sir William Hamilton for use on pots, chimney-pieces and plaques, has rarely been out of production. While most of his

Wedgwood designs are closely derived from the Antique, some, such as *Blind Man's Buff* (1782), show the influence of Florentine Renaissance art, while some pieces in the celebrated *Chess Set*, such as the bishop based on a figure on Wells Cathedral, are derived from English medieval sculpture. He also modelled a number of profile portraits for medallions in jasperware, such as *Captain James Cook* (*c.* 1779) and *Sarah Siddons* (1787). Flaxman provided Wedgwood with a wax relief of each design, which then became the property of the manufacturer, to be used without further reference to the artist, whose name would not appear on the final product.

(ii) 1787–94: Rome, the line drawings. In 1787, with money accumulated from his work for Wedgwood and his few commissions, Flaxman left for Rome, the goal of all sculptors of ambition. His time there was decisive for his career: by the time he returned to England he was an international celebrity with a number of important commissions awaiting him. For the first two years in Italy, however, although he filled his sketchbooks (London, V&A) with careful drawings from the Antique and from scenes observed in the streets of Rome, there was very little paid work. This changed in 1790, when he received a major commission, apparently on the recommendation of Canova, from Frederick Hervey, the eccentric Earl of Bristol and Bishop of Derry, for an over life-size marble group of the *Fury of Athamas* (marble; Ickworth, Suffolk, NT). Though competent, this is little more than an academic reworking of the *Laoköon* group, but there is individuality in the pathos of the figures. In 1792 he received what proved to be a more important commission, from Thomas Hope, for over a hundred drawings to illustrate Dante's *Divine Comedy*. They were engraved by Tommaso Piroli (?*c.* 1752–1824) in order that Hope, in Mrs Flaxman's bitter words, could 'give them away himself to the chosen few, whom he may think from their taste and virtue are entitled to them' (for illustration of Hope's Flaxman Room, at his gallery in London, *see* HOPE, (1)). Shortly afterwards Flaxman received further commissions from Mrs Georgiana Hare-Naylor (*d* 1806) to illustrate the Homeric epics *The Iliad* and *The Odyssey*, and from the Dowager Countess Spencer to illustrate the works of Aeschylus. Unlike the Dante engravings, which were not published until 1807, the engravings of these works were immediately made public, the former in 1793 and the latter in 1795.

Flaxman's drawings were unusual at the time for being conceived almost purely in terms of outline, though the dryness of the final engravings is as much due to Piroli as to Flaxman. The use of outline, which was derived from engravings after Greek vases, can be seen as an attempt by Flaxman to match the period of Homer with a comparably 'primitive' technique, just as he borrowed from 14th-century Italian art in order to give authenticity to his Dante illustrations. As George Romney wrote of the Homer engravings in 1793: 'they are outlines without shadow, but in the style of antient art. . . . They look as if they had been made in the age, when Homer wrote.' Flaxman, however, cited Roman sarcophagi as his models and seems to have conceived his drawings not as finished works but as ideas for relief sculptures that he intended to

execute on his return to England. The designs for *The Iliad* and *The Odyssey* caused an immediate sensation and were copied and pirated all over Europe. This success is partially accounted for by the fact that they were easy to trace or copy, making their imagery highly accessible. Their simplicity also made them easily adaptable to a variety of purposes; they appeared in every conceivable decorative setting throughout the 19th century. Improbably, the designs also seemed to be authentically 'antique', as Romney claimed, and to have recaptured the language of the dawn of art, although they reduce the Homeric epics to the proportions of domestic scenes and are unfailingly decorous in their treatment of emotion.

(iii) Work from 1794. Flaxman had received some commissions from England before he left Italy, including that for a large monument to *William Murray, 1st Earl of Mansfield*, for Westminster Abbey (marble, erected 1801; *see* ENGLAND, fig. 29). The design derives from papal tombs by Bernini and Canova, and it established Flaxman as the foremost monumental sculptor in England and thus a candidate for the monuments to British naval heroes to be erected in St Paul's Cathedral. Unfortunately, large monuments such as those to *Earl Howe* (marble, 1803–11) and *Lord Nelson* (marble, 1808–18) did not suit his gifts as a sculptor, which were at their best on a more intimate scale: his allegorical programmes were rather tame, and the weakness of his composition in three dimensions became apparent. Before he went to Italy, he had been taken up by the poet William Hayley, whose belief in the primacy of sentiment was more congenial to Flaxman than it had been to two of Hayley's other protégés, George Romney and William Blake. Hayley obtained for

1. John Flaxman: monument to *Dr Joseph Warton*, marble, 3.48×1.72 m, 1804 (Winchester Cathedral)

Flaxman a number of commissions for wall monuments in relief, including that to the scholar George Steevens (*c.* 1800–05; Poplar, St Matthias, on dep. Cambridge, Fitzwilliam), in which purity of outline is balanced gracefully against the warmth of engagement with the subject's personality. The monument to *Dr Joseph Warton* (see fig. 1), Headmaster of Winchester School, was conceived originally with the master and his pupils in Classical dress. They were finally shown in modern dress, but an antique clarity remains that is counterpointed by the unaffected naturalism of the boys, based on studies from life. Another early patron, Henry Philip Hope, commissioned a marble portrait bust for his chimney-piece (Copenhagen, Thorvaldsens Mus.); it was designed to be viewed frontally and thus avoids Flaxman's problems with multiple viewpoints.

Despite the success of his public monuments in an essentially Classical mode, Flaxman seems to have thought of himself increasingly as a Christian sculptor whose tomb figures were, in Allan Cunningham's words, 'all intended for the furtherance of devotion'. Without leaving the Church of England Flaxman had been for many years a devout Swedenborgian, and this expressed itself in his images of Redemption as the ascent of the soul to paradise, which is governed by angels who watch over man and ensure his passage to eternal life. Some of Flaxman's tombs show scenes of simple human affection, such as that to John and Susannah Phillimore, known as *Two Sisters in Affliction* (plaster model, 1804; London, U. Col.). Some show angels carrying a soul to heaven, as in the monument to *Agnes Cromwell*, inscribed *Come thou blessed* (1798–1800; Chichester Cathedral). In a number of cases they illustrate passages from the Lord's Prayer or the Acts of Mercy. The monument to *Harriet Baring*, for instance (1806–9; Micheldever, Hants, parish church), represents the deceased in low relief as Christian Virtue framed by a Gothic arch inscribed *Thy will be done*. The tomb of the Bromley family (Baginton, Warwicks, parish church) contains a virtually identical figure set against a Greek-type stele and is similarly inscribed.

Although Flaxman did no more work for Wedgwood after his first year in Italy, he continued to make designs for commercial use, including medals and, most notably, silverware for the firm of Rundell, Bridge & Rundell from 1805. His work for this firm included such spectacular pieces as the *Shield of Achilles* (silver gilt, 1817–21; Windsor Castle, Berks, Royal Col.) and the *National Cup* (1824–5; Windsor Castle, Berks, Royal Col.). His silverware, particularly his massive table ornaments, was favoured by the Prince Regent (later George IV).

2. WORKING METHODS AND TECHNIQUE. The popularity of Flaxman's smaller monuments and the large output of his studio inevitably led to the repetition of motifs and a standardization of finish, which perhaps came naturally to Flaxman, who had been involved in industrial production from his youth. After his return from Italy he appears to have confined himself almost entirely to making drawings and small plaster sketch models, leaving the working of the marble to studio assistants. The smoothly polished finish in favour at this period suited Flaxman's outline designs and could be achieved by assistants.

However, his practice of scaling-up with pointing machines from plaster models means that many of his works lack the coherence and presence appropriate to their size. He became aware of this problem towards the end of his career, and in order to work out the complex poses in three dimensions of the *Satan Overcome by St Michael* (1819–26; Petworth House, W. Sussex, NT) he made a full-scale model (plaster, London, U. Coll., Flaxman Gal.; see fig. 2). He produced a very large number of plaster models (the bulk of those surviving were presented to University College, London, by his sister-in-law Maria Denman in 1849; others are in London, Soane Mus.). These were probably used as much to aid potential patrons in their choice as for assistants to copy. Flaxman often exhibited them at the Royal Academy. Among his pupils and assistants was E. H. Baily, who completed the works left unfinished in his studio at his death.

2. John Flaxman: *Satan Overcome by St Michael*, plaster, 3.35 m, 1822 (London, University of London, University College, Flaxman Gallery)

**3. Critical reception and posthumous repu-
tation.** Flaxman ended his life as an eminent public
figure. He had been elected the first Professor of Sculpture
at the Royal Academy in 1810 and gave a series of
thoroughly planned lectures on the history of sculpture
and advice on such practical aspects of the art as drapery
modelling. His personal mildness was proverbial and was
seen by his contemporaries as entirely consonant with the
piety of his best-known sculptures. Though the reputation
of his outline designs continued to grow in Europe, he
confessed to Ludwig Schorn, a German admirer, that he
thought them overrated and less worthy of imitation than
nature. Yet it has been demonstrated (Symmons, 1984)
that these designs worked their way into the consciousness
of artists throughout Europe: not only of those of a
classicizing tendency such as Ingres, but also of those of
a seemingly opposite sensibility such as Géricault, Francisco Goya and many others. Flaxman's career as an artist–
designer established a pattern that was followed by others
later in the 19th century, including Alfred Gilbert in
England and Albert-Ernest Carrier-Belleuse in France. His
designs for silver remained influential throughout the
Victorian period, and many of his designs for Wedgwood
are still in production. Though his work is always distinguished, and his drawings and sculpture can be touching
in their humanity, his importance perhaps lies in the way
he brought together some of the seemingly contradictory
religious, artistic, commercial and technological trends of
his time.

WRITINGS
Lectures on Sculpture (London, 1829, rev. 1838)

BIBLIOGRAPHY
Gunnis
J. T. Smith: *Nollekens and his Times* (London, 1828), ii, pp. 434–53
A. Cunningham: *The Lives of the Most Eminent British Painters, Sculptors
    and Architects*, iii (London, 1830), pp. 274–367
W. G. Constable: *John Flaxman, 1755–1826* (London, 1927)
G. E. Bentley jr: *The Early Engravings of Flaxman's Classical Designs: A
    Bibliographical Study* (New York, 1964)
M. Whinney: *Sculpture in Britain, 1530–1830*, Pelican Hist. A. (London,
    1964, rev. 1975)
D. Irwin: *English Neoclassical Art* (London, 1966)
R. Rosenblum: *Transformations in Late Eighteenth Century Art* (Princeton,
    1967)
M. Whinney and R. Gunnis: *The Collection of Models by John Flaxman
    RA at University College London* (London, 1967)
R. N. Essick and J. La Belle, eds: *Flaxman's Illustrations to Homer* (New
    York, 1977)
N. Penny: *Church Monuments in Romantic England* (New Haven, 1977)
D. Irwin: *John Flaxman, 1755–1826: Sculptor, Illustrator, Designer*
    (London, 1979)
John Flaxman (exh. cat., ed. D. Bindman; London, RA, 1979)
John Flaxman: Mythologie und Industrie (exh. cat., ed. W. Hofmann;
    Hamburg, Ksthalle, 1979)
S. Symmons: *Flaxman and Europe: The Outline Illustrators and their
    Influence* (New York, 1984) [Garland thesis]

DAVID BINDMAN

Flechtheim, Alfred (*b* Münster, 1 April 1877; *d* London,
9 March 1937). German dealer. He came from a family of
grain merchants and began his career as one. His work
took him to Paris, where he became interested in art. In
1912 he was on the organizing committee of the Cologne
Sonderbund International Exhibition, which provided a
showpiece for radical contemporary art. In December
1913, encouraged by his friend Daniel-Henry Kahnweiler,
he decided to open an art gallery in Düsseldorf. Over the

next 20 years he established himself as the leading dealer
in contemporary art in Germany, with galleries in Düsseldorf, Cologne, Frankfurt and in Berlin, which became his
base from 1921 onwards. Flechtheim supported a number
of German artists, including, after 1925, George Grosz.
However, his business was always based around the
promotion of modern French art. Through Kahnweiler
he obtained pictures by Derain, Gris, Léger, Picasso and
Maurice de Vlaminck and promoted them successfully in
Germany. In 1921 he founded the periodical *Der Quer-
schnitt.* After the Nazi takeover of power Flechtheim
emigrated to England but he continued to promote
modern art, for example through the major exhibition,
Masters of French 19th-century Painting, held at the New
Burlington Galleries, London, in 1936.

BIBLIOGRAPHY
P. Mahlberg, ed.: *Beiträge zur Kunst des 19. Jahrhunderts und unserer Zeit*
    (Dusseldorf, 1913)
A. Vömel: 'Alfred Flechtheim, Kunsthändler und Verleger', *Imprimatur*,
    n.s., v (1967), pp. 90–113
Alfred Flechtheim: Sammler, Kunsthändler, Verleger (exh. cat., Düsseldorf,
    Kstmus., 1987)
P. Springer: 'Alfred Flechtheim: Ein Kunsthändler neuen Typs', *Avant-
    garde und Publikum*, ed. H. Junge (Cologne, Weimar and Vienna, 1992),
    pp. 79-92

MALCOLM GEE

Flegel, Georg (*b* Olmütz [Olomouc], Moravia, 1566;
d Frankfurt am Main, 1638). German painter. He was the
son of a shoemaker, and not being a Roman Catholic,
probably moved to Vienna after 1580, when the Counter-
Reformation began to take effect in Olmütz. In Vienna he
became the assistant of Lucas van Valckenborch I, whom
he subsequently followed to Frankfurt, then an important
centre for art dealing and publishing. He filled in staffage
in van Valckenborch's pictures of the seasons and portraits, inserting fruit, table utensils and flowers as still-life
set pieces. His faithful reproduction of flowers and fruit
drew on watercolours by Dürer, still-life painters from the
Netherlands living in Frankfurt, and botanical and zoological illustrations by Joris Hoefnagel, Pieter van der Borcht
IV and Carolus Clusius (1525–1609) then being published
in Frankfurt.

Between *c.* 1600 and 1627–30 Flegel produced 110
watercolours (Berlin, Kupferstichkab.; 31 destr., 1943–4)
depicting flowers, fruit and animals, and one *Self-portrait*
(1630; destr.). A double picture for a cupboard with
trompe-l'oeil still-lifes (Prague, N.G.) dates from *c.* 1610.
From 1611 he worked on pictures of tables set for meals,
for example the *Meal with Bunch of Flowers* (1630;
Stuttgart, Staatsgal.) and *Evening Meal* (1637; Frankfurt
am Main, Hist. Mus.). Depicted with precise factual
accuracy, free brushwork and a sometimes artistic use of
lighting effects, these are quite distinct from contemporary
Dutch and Flemish still-lifes in their static and unornamented presentation. Of Flegel's many still-lifes, only
those between 1635 and 1638 are dated (Cologne, Wallraf-
Richartz-Mus.; Frankfurt am Main, Städel. Kstinst.;
Prague, N.G.). His sons Friedrich (1597–1616) and Jacob
(*d* 1623) were his pupils (none of their work has survived),
as was Jacob Marrel in 1627.

BIBLIOGRAPHY
W. J. Müller: *Der Maler Georg Flegel und die Anfänge des Stillebens*
    (Frankfurt am Main, 1956)

Deutsche Maler und Zeichner des 17. Jahrhunderts (exh. cat., Berlin, Schloss Charlottenburg, 1966), pp. 13, 31–6, nos 15–23

W. J. Müller: 'Neuentdeckungen zum Werk des Georg Flegel', *Pantheon*, xxvi (1968), pp. 123–9

H. Seifertová: 'Georg Flegel Malíř *trompe l'œil*', *Umĕn í*, xxvi (1978), pp. 248–62

I. Bergström: 'Lucas van Valckenborch in Collaboration with Georg Flegel', *Tableau*, v (1983), pp. 320–27

Das Stilleben und sein Gegenstand (exh. cat., ed. I. Antonowa and others; Dresden, 1983), pp. 114–16

WOLFGANG J. MÜLLER

Flémal [Flémalle], **Bertholet** (*bapt* Liège, 23 May 1614; *d* Liège, 10 July 1675). Franco-Flemish painter and architect. He was born into a family of artists, and his first apprenticeship was probably in Liège with his father, Renier Flémal (*b* 1585), a painter of stained glass. Bertholet was later a pupil of Henri Trippet (*c.* 1600–74) before completing his training during the 1630s with Gérard Douffet. In 1638 Flémal went to Rome and on the return journey visited Florence and stayed for some time in Paris. He had returned to Liège by 1646. Flémal had a successful career there, painting for private collectors, but he was also commissioned to work for the many religious establishments. His patron was Canon Lambert de Liverloo, Chancellor to the Prince-Bishop of Liège. In addition, Flémal made designs for religious buildings and fittings as well as for his own house, but none of this architectural work has survived. In 1670 he was at the peak of his career. He was painter to the Prince-Bishop, Maximilian-Henry of Bavaria, and for Louis XIV of France he painted an allegory, *Religion Protecting France* (1670; destr. 1871), for the ceiling of the audience chamber at the Tuileries, Paris. In the same year he was appointed Professor at the Académie Royale in Paris. The Prince-Bishop made him a canonical prebendary of the collegiate church of St Paul at Liège.

Flémal's earliest known paintings seem to be *Alexander's Farewell* (Kassel, Schloss Wilhelmshöhe) and *Clelia's Flight* (Liverpool, Walker A.G.), two vigorous works marked by the influence of Poussin's followers, with whom Flémal would have had contact in Rome. The *Mysteries of the Old and New Testaments*, formerly in the Augustinian convent, and the *Sacrifice of Iphigenia*, carried out for the Hôtel Lambert (both Paris, Louvre), date from Flémal's Parisian period and are strongly influenced by French classicism.

Of the first works completed after Flémal's return to Liège, two paintings have been dated by Abry: a *Crucifixion* (1649; Liège, St Jean) and the *Adoration of the Magi* (1650; Liège, Cathedral). The *Expulsion of Heliodorus* and the *Death of Pyrrhus* (both Brussels, Mus. A. Anc.) date from the same period and incorporate the consistent elements of Flémal's work: a pronounced taste for classical architecture and an extreme tension. Taken as a whole, these early works are vigorous in style and often anecdotal in character, with little adjoining scenes full of figures and archaeological detail; there is a certain lack of skill in the drawing and the proportions, and the palette is warm and varied. The *Debate over the Blessed Sacrament* (Herve, St Jean Baptiste) and the portrait believed to be of *Gérard Douffet, his Wife and Bertholet Flémal* (Overijse, priv. col.; see Hendrick, p. 125, illus. 102) are the finest examples of

Bertholet Flémal: *Lamentation*, oil on canvas, 1.52×1.40 m, before 1668 (Orléans, Musée des Beaux-Arts)

this period and probably date from the late 1650s or early 1660s.

The *Adoration of the Shepherds* (*c.* 1665; Caen, Mus. B.-A.) and the remarkable *Lamentation* (before 1668; Orléans, Mus. B.-A.; see fig.) mark a new phase in Flémal's style. The number of figures is considerably reduced, and the compositions are clearer; in place of the warm and lively colours of the 1650s he gradually substituted a cool and subtle palette. This pursuit of a greater rigour reached its peak in two paintings: the *Lamentation* (Karlsruhe, Staatl. Ksthalle), remarkable for its simplicity and restrained emotion, and the *Finding of the True Cross* (1674; Liège, Sainte Croix), a painting of severe majesty, softened by the extreme refinement of its cool tones. Bertholet Flémal's art influenced the work of such artists as Renier de Lairesse (1612–67) and his son, Gérard de Lairesse, as well as several pupils, such as Jean-Gilles Delcour, Englebert Fisen (1655–1733) and Jean Guillaume Carlier.

BIBLIOGRAPHY

L. Abry: 'Bertholet Flémal', *Les Hommes illustres de la nation liégeoise*, ed. H. Helbig and S. Bormans (Liège, 1867)

L. Dewez: 'Un Maître liégeois du XVIIe siècle: Bertholet Flémalle (1614–1675)', *Vie wallonne*, viii (1927–8), pp. 129–48, 159–68

C. Bosson: *Bertholet Flémal Peintre et architecte liégeois, 1614–1675* (diss., U. of Liège, 1981)

——: 'L'Art de Bertholet Flémal à travers quelques oeuvres peu connues', *Cahier CACEF*, cxxvii (1987), pp. 13–16

J. Hendrick: 'Bertholet Flémal', *La Peinture au pays de Liège: XVIe, XVIIe et XVIIIe siècles* (Liège, 1987), pp. 127–46

J. Thuillier: 'Bertholet Flémal: Problèmes de catalogue et de chronologie, *Cahier CACEF*, cxxvii (1987), pp. 16–20

R. Jans: 'Bertholet Flémal et sa famille', *Bull. Inst. Archéol. Liège.*, ci (1989), pp. 73–110

CLAUDE BOSSON

Fleming, Hans (*b* Namur, *c.* 1545; *d* ?Kalmar, *c.* 1623). Flemish sculptor and master builder, active in Sweden. He worked in Sweden from the 1580s and is thought to be the master of the monument (1599) to *Magnus of Sweden* (1542–99), Duke of Östergötland, in the monastery church in Vadstena, and the monument (1598) to *Måns Ulfsparre* (*d* 1595) and his wife in the parish church of Kärda, Småland. Duke Magnus's memorial is a variation of the *tumba* type—a box-like monument with a sculptured effigy of the deceased on the lid, which protrudes and is carried by columns grouped around the structure. The effigy shows traces of original colouring. This monument type was repeatedly used during the 17th century. Fleming completed Vadstena Castle, with its two decorated gables (1605, 1620) that were probably influenced by the gable (1580s) of the Hall of State of the Royal Palace in Stockholm, attributed to Willem Boy. The Vadstena gables show a two-storey arrangement of pilasters, crowned by a broken-segment pediment and flanked by volutes, with female allegorical figures and warriors placed within niches and flanking the top structure.

BIBLIOGRAPHY

SVKL

S. Schéle: 'Hans Fleming eller Bernt von Münster?' [Hans Fleming or Bernt von Münster?], *Konsthist. Tidskr.*, xii (1943), pp. 30–37

G. Axel-Nilsson: *Dekorativ stenhuggarkonst i yngre vasastil* [Decorative sculpture in the later Vasa style] (Lund, 1950)

S. Schéle: 'Hans Fleming och Ulfsparregraven i Kärda kyrka' [Hans Fleming and the Ulfsparre monument in Kärda church], *Ksthist. Tidskr.*, xix (1950), pp. 46–8

R. Bennett: *Vadstena klosterkyrka, iii: Gravminnen* [Vadstena Abbey Church, iii: sepulchral monuments], Sveriges Kyrkor (Vadstena, 1985), pp. 15–22

TORBJÖRN FULTON

Flemming, Robert (*b c.* 1415; *d* Aug 1483). English writer and collector. He was the nephew of Richard Fleming, Bishop of Lincoln and founder of Lincoln College, Oxford. Robert is recorded at University College, Oxford, in 1430 and was elected Proctor in 1438, but he left Oxford in 1443 to pursue his studies abroad; in 1444 he matriculated at Cologne University, where he may have met the humanist William Gray, later Bishop of Ely. In 1446 he gained a degree in divinity at Padua, where he transcribed a copy of Cicero's *De officiis*, in a script influenced by humanist manuscripts. He attended the lectures of Guarino da Verona at Ferrara, gaining some knowledge of Greek. On his return to England he became Dean of Lincoln College in 1452 and chaplain to Henry VI by 1453. He was appointed to several posts in Rome from 1455, although he is not recorded there until the autumn of 1458. From 1462 to 1472, while residing in University College, Oxford, he made gifts of books to Lincoln College. While in Rome and Tivoli from 1473 until at least 1477, he became a friend of the humanist and papal librarian Bartolomeo Platina, returning to England in 1478. Flemming wrote Latin poems and epistles, of which only the volume of verse *Lucubratiunculae Tiburtinae* (Vienna, Österreich. Nbib., Cod. 2403), dedicated to Sixtus IV, survives; it includes descriptions of the Sistine Chapel and the Vatican library and praises Platina. Flemming made an important collection of books and manuscripts, many purchased in Italy, including Latin and Greek authors and translations by Leonardo Bruni, Guarino and others. Many of these were given to Lincoln College, where the surviving examples are annotated in Flemming's neat humanist hand.

BIBLIOGRAPHY

R. Weiss: *Humanism in England during the Fifteenth Century* (Oxford, 1941, rev. 3/1967), pp. 97–105

——: 'New Light on Humanism in England during the Fifteenth Century', *J. Warb. & Court. Inst.*, xiv (1951), pp. 21–33

A. B. Emden: *A Bibliographical Register of the University of Oxford to A.D. 1500* (Oxford, 1957), pp. 699–700

JEREMY GRIFFITHS

Flers, Camille (*b* Paris, 15 Feb 1802; *d* Annet-sur-Marne, 27 June 1868). French painter and pastellist. The son of a porcelain-maker, he first learnt painting in the studio of a porcelain decorator. After a period as a theatre decorator and a dancer, he became a pupil of the animal painter Joseph François Pâris (1784–1871). He devoted himself to landscape painting and became one of the precursors of *plein-air* painting. Referring to himself as a 'romantique-naturaliste', he was a member of the new Naturalist school of landscape painting that emerged in the 1830s in opposition to the official classicism of the Ecole des Beaux-Arts. He was one of the first to paint *sur le motif* (from life) in the forest of Fontainebleau, and he also made frequent visits to Barbizon, joining that group of artists known as 'le groupe de Marlotte'. His works consist largely of views of Normandy and the Paris environs; he concentrated on thatched cottages, farmyards, prairies, ponds and riverbanks. He made his début at the Salon in 1831 with a *View of the Village of Pissevache, Bas-Valais* and continued to exhibit there until 1863. His early style of the 1830s and 1840s is characterized by splashes of thick paint, a roughly textured paint surface, a bright palette and a range of lively tones, as in *Prairie* (1831; Paris, Resche). Between 1850 and 1860 he painted a series of images of rivers and ponds with boats and fishermen. These were executed in a style very close to that of Jules Dupré, with whom he was working at the time. The surface of these paintings is smooth, the touch even discrete with a dominantly light-coloured tonality, as in *Landscape: The Environs of Paris* (1854; Paris, Louvre). Flers was also noted for his pastels, which he exhibited at the Salon from 1843, especially in the 1840s. In 1846 he published his theories of drawing in pastel in the journal *L'Artiste*, and these did much to revive interest in the medium. In common with other artists associated with Barbizon, in the early 1860s Flers experimented with making clichés-verre.

WRITINGS

'Du pastel: De son application au paysage en particulier', *L'Artiste*, 4th ser., vii (1846), pp. 113–16

BIBLIOGRAPHY

Bellier de La Chavignerie-Auvray; *DBF*

P. Miquel: *Le Paysage français au XIXe siècle, 1824–1874: L'Ecole de la nature*, ii (Maurs-La-Jolie, 1975), pp. 142–57

L. Harambourg: *Dictionnaire des peintres paysagistes français au XIXe siècle* (Neuchâtel, 1985)

ATHENA S. E. LEOUSSI

Fletcher, Sir Banister (Flight) (*b* London, 15 Feb 1866; *d* London, 17 Aug 1953). English architect and writer. He was the elder son of Banister Fletcher (1833–99), an architect and surveyor, who became Professor of Architecture at King's College, London, in 1890. He studied at the Architectural Association, the Royal Academy Schools and University College in London and at the Ecole des Beaux-Arts in Paris. In 1884 he joined his father's office, becoming a partner in 1889; when his brother, Herbert

Phillips Fletcher (1872–1916), entered the partnership it became known as Banister Fletcher & Sons, under which name the practice continued for many years. As a designer, Fletcher was never in the first rank. His buildings, which included banks, churches, flats, houses and commercial work, reflect, if not obstrusively, the historicism then current. Only one, the Gillette factory (1937) on the Great West Road, Osterley, London, built when he was over 70, reveals sympathy with newer ideas. As a historian, his reputation rests firmly on *A History of Architecture*, which appeared to immediate acclaim in 1896. The first three editions were written jointly with his father; the next thirteen by him alone, ably supported by his office staff. Subsequent editions of this single-volume record of world architecture, although radically altered and expanded beyond recognition, are continuing evidence of his inspiration. Fletcher was also a barrister and an astute businessman closely associated with the City of London, serving as a Common Councillor for nearly 50 years, Master of the Carpenters' Company, and in 1918–19 Senior Sheriff. He was knighted in 1919.

WRITINGS

with B. Fletcher sr: *A History of Architecture . . . Being a Comparative View of the Historical Styles from the Earliest Period* (London, 1896, rev., enlarged 5/1905 as *A History of Architecture on the Comparative Method*, rev. 18/1975 by J. C. Palmes, rev. 19/1987 by J. Musgrove)

BIBLIOGRAPHY

DNB

W. Hanneford-Smith: *The Architectural Work of Sir Banister Fletcher* (London, 1934, rev., enlarged 2/1937)

M. S. Briggs: 'Sir Banister Fletcher: The Man and his Book', *J. London Soc.*, 322 (May 1954), pp. 19–26

JAMES PALMES

Flettner, Peter. *See* FLÖTNER, PETER.

Fleuron. Decorative motif in the shape of a formalized flower. In the Corinthian order it refers to the floral ornament on each face of the ABACUS of the capital.

□

Fleury (i). *See* SAINT-BENOÎT-SUR-LOIRE, ABBEY CHURCH.

Fleury (ii). *See* CHAMPFLEURY.

Fleury, Rohault de. *See* ROHAULT DE FLEURY.

Flicke, Gerlach (*b* Osnabrück; *d* London, Jan–Feb 1558). German painter, active in England. He probably moved to England *c.* 1545, and three signed and dated works by him survive. Of these, probably the earliest is a rather stiff and archaic portrait of *Archbishop Thomas Cranmer* (London, N.P.G.) in the style of Holbein, signed top right *Gerlacus flicus Germanus faciebat* and dated *Anno etatj 57 Julij 20*; the year does not appear but would be 1545 or 1546. Behind the sitter is a leaded window, with a looped red curtain to the right; Cranmer holds St Paul's Epistles and sits at a table covered with a Turkey carpet on which are other books and a paper. A number of related portraits of Cranmer use the same pattern. More fluent and distinguished is Flicke's *Portrait of an Unknown Nobleman*, traditionally identified as *William, Lord Grey of Wilton* (Edinburgh, N.G.), which is signed and dated 1547, the year in which Grey was knighted. The subject stands in the open air against a blue sky, a spray of blue columbines beside his right arm. Hervey, whose identification of the subject is persuasive, noted that this flower figures conspicuously as part of Grey's crest, described in the bill for his funeral. Hervey also attributed to Flicke a similar, undated, portrait of *Sir Peter Carew* (Edinburgh, N.G., on loan to London, Tower); like Grey, the subject wears a slit buff jerkin, white doublet and black plumed cap.

Flicke's third signed and dated work is a small double portrait of 1554, the *Self-portrait with 'Red Rover' Strangways* (77×115 mm; sold London, Sotheby's, 9 July 1975). In the 18th century this was seen by Horace Walpole at the house of Dr Thomas Monkhouse of Queen's College, Oxford. Flicke painted it while he and Strangways were in prison, perhaps in connection with Wyatt's rebellion against Queen Mary I's policy of submission to Spain and Rome. Above the self-portrait to the left, in Latin doggerel, the artist explains that it shows him as he was when he was a painter in the City of London and that it was painted from a mirror for his dear friends to remember him after his death. 'Red Rover', clearly a much younger man, was a gentleman-privateer who entered the service of Queen Elizabeth I and was killed in a sortie from Rouen in 1562. Flicke's English doggerel above 'Red Rover's' head begins: *Strangwish.thus strangely.depicted is One prisoner for thother hath done this*. Three further portraits in John Lumley's inventory of 1590, *The Red Velvet Book*, are listed as being by 'Garlicke'. One is a full-length of *Thomas, 1st Lord Darcy of Chiche*, said to have been signed and dated 1551, which was last seen in 1848 (ex-Irnham Hall, Lincs); a poor copy dated 1554, from Hengrave Hall in Suffolk, was sold in 1952 (untraced). The other two are a portrait of *Queen Mary*, presumed to be the one with a Lumley label in Durham Cathedral Library, and one of *Thomas Howard, 3rd Duke of Norfolk* (untraced).

Flicke was probably 'Garick the paynter' who was living in the City of London parish of St Mary Woolnoth in 1549, but he died in the parish of St Giles Cripplegate, which was popular with artists. In his will, where he is described as 'drawer', he names a wife Katherine, and a servant (apprentice) Harry Vauled, to whom he bequeathed land in Osnabrück and a book covered with white parchment.

BIBLIOGRAPHY

M. F. S. Hervey: 'Notes on a Tudor Painter: Gerlach Flicke', *Burl. Mag.*, xvii (1910), pp. 71–9

Connoisseur, xlv (1916), pp. 163–5

L. Cust: 'The Lumley Inventories', *Walpole Soc.*, vi (1918), pp. 22–3

E. Waterhouse: *Painting in Britain, 1530–1790*, Pelican Hist. A. (Harmondsworth, 1953, 4/1978), pp. 27, 338 n. 7

E. Auerbach: *Tudor Artists* (London, 1954), pp. 52, 71, 78, 87, 163

R. Strong: *The English Icon: Elizabethan and Jacobean Portraiture* (London, 1969), pp. 8, 77–81

MARY EDMOND

Flinck. Dutch family of artists and collectors. (1) Govaert Flinck, the son of a draper from Cleve (a Prussian territory in the 17th century), was a well-known pupil and follower of Rembrandt. He was a gifted painter, capable of producing work of considerable beauty, but his ambition and desire for success led him to paint superficially elegant works that lacked individual character and pandered to the tastes of the increasingly ostentatious and affluent Dutch merchant class of the 17th century. He also formed a small art collection, which was inherited by his son (2) Nicolaes Anthonis Flinck, who considerably augmented it, specializing in particular in drawings.

(1) Govaert Flinck (*b* Cleve, 25 Jan 1615; *d* Amsterdam, 2 Feb 1660). Painter and draughtsman. At the age of 14 he was apprenticed in Leeuwarden to the painter and Mennonite preacher Lambert Jacobsz. There Flinck met Jacob Backer, who had been in Jacobsz.'s studio since 1622. Many of Flinck's early works, especially his drawings, resemble those of Backer.

In 1633, after Flinck had acquired practical and technical skills with Jacobsz., he moved to Amsterdam, the financial and artistic centre of the northern Netherlands, to complete his training with Rembrandt. Flinck presumably worked in Rembrandt's studio for three years, setting up on his own in 1636, the date of his first known paintings, *Rembrandt as a Shepherd* (Amsterdam, Rijksmus.; on loan to the Rembrandthuis) and *The Shepherdess* (Brunswick, Herzog Anton Ulrich-Mus.), both of which demonstrate his artistic dependence on Rembrandt. While still under the influence of Rembrandt, he painted his first large-scale history picture, *Isaac Blessing Jacob* (*c.* 1638; Amsterdam, Rijksmus.; see fig. 1). This work, in which both the colouring and the composition are successfully worked out, justifiably created high expectations for the artistic future of the 23-year-old Flinck. Isaac is portrayed as a venerable figure on his death bed, giving his blessing to his illegitimate heir, Jacob. The subject was unusual within the context of the Rembrandt school, indicating that Flinck was striving for artistic independence. Yet this was not always the case: the composition of the *Annunciation to the Shepherds* (1639; Paris, Louvre) reflects Rembrandt's etching of the subject (1634; B. 44), but Flinck failed to capture the spiritual content of his master's work.

In the 1640s and 1650s Flinck, in common with many other Dutch painters, began to incorporate elements of Flemish style into his work. A note of fashionable elegance was introduced into his portraits in particular, as can be seen, for instance, in the double *Portrait of a Lady and a Gentleman* (1646; Karlsruhe, Staatl. Ksthalle). At the same time, in his history pictures, he adopted a range of colours that was more typically Flemish. This trend is discernible in the *Crucifixion* (1649; Basle, Kstmus.): though the composition can certainly be traced back to Rembrandt, the colouring is more similar to that of Flemish painting. In 1649 Flinck was also commissioned by Frederick William, Elector of Brandenburg (*reg* 1640–88), to paint the allegory of the *Birth (Death) of Prince William Hendrick*

1. Govaert Flinck: *Isaac Blessing Jacob*, oil on canvas, 1.17×1.41 m, *c.* 1638 (Amsterdam, Rijksmuseum)

III of Nassau (Potsdam, Neues Pal.), which was completed in 1650, after the Prince's death. This commission was carried out according to the then fashionable Baroque ideas, with pathos and routine skill; it satisfied Flinck's royal patron and was a milestone in the artist's successful career. The citizens of Amsterdam now thronged to have their portraits painted by him or at least to buy one of his history paintings. The current vogue for pomp and Baroque forms is also evident in Flinck's allegory of the *Mourning of Stadholder Frederick Henry* (1654; Amsterdam, Rijksmus.; see fig. 2), which depicts the grief of his widow, Amalia von Solms. The virtues of the Stadholder are commemorated in a large-scale painting originally intended for the Huis ten Bosch, the residence of the Orange family near The Hague.

In 1655 the new Amsterdam Stadhuis was completed, and Flinck, along with other leading history painters such as Ferdinand Bol, was commissioned to decorate its walls. Flinck's first commission was for the burgomaster's office, where his *Marcus Curtius Dentatus Refusing the Gifts of the Samnites* (1656; *in situ*) was intended to celebrate the virtues of incorruptibility. The large-scale composition, with its overt pathos, must have appealed to the taste of his contemporaries: it was artistically unchallenging and theatrically presented. It was installed opposite Bol's

Pyrrhus and Fabritius (1656; *in situ*; *see* BOL, FERDINAND, fig. 1). Flinck's initial success led to his being commissioned to paint another 12 monumental works for the town hall. Unfortunately, Flinck died suddenly four months after signing the contract giving him sole responsibility for the decoration of the town hall and before he had really started on this important commission. (Meanwhile Rembrandt's *Conspiracy of the Batavians under Claudius Civilis* (1662; Stockholm, Nmus.) was rejected.)

BIBLIOGRAPHY

Hollstein: *Dut. & Flem.*
A. Houbraken: *De groote schouburgh* (1718–21)
H. Gerson: *Het tijdperk van Rembrandt en Vermeer* [The age of Rembrandt and Vermeer] (Amsterdam, 1952)
Govaert Flinck: Der Kleefsche Apelles (exh. cat. by F. Gorissen, Cleve, Städt. Mus. Haus Koekkoek, 1965)
J. W. von Moltke: *Govaert Flinck, 1615–1660* (Amsterdam, 1965) [with cat. rais.]
J. Rosenberg, S. Slive and E. H. ter Kuile: *Dutch Art and Architecture, 1600–1800*, Pelican Hist. A. (Harmondsworth, 1966/R 1982), pp. 151–2
W. Sumowski: *Drawings of the Rembrandt School*, iv (New York, 1981)
——: *Gemälde der Rembrandt-Schüler*, ii (Landau, 1983), pp. 998–1151 [with comprehensive bibliog.]
——: 'Three Drawings by Govaert Flinck', *Essays in Northern European Art Presented to E. Haverkamp-Bergmann* (Doornspijk, 1983)
The Impact of a Genius: Rembrandt, his Pupils and Followers in the 17th Century (exh. cat. by A. Blankert and others, Amsterdam, Waterman Gal.; Groningen, Groninger Mus.; 1983), pp. 154–61

J. W. VON MOLTKE

(2) Nicolaes Anthonis Flinck (*b* Amsterdam, 1646; *d* Rotterdam, 1723). Collector, son of (1) Govaert Flinck. He became an orphan at the age of 14 and was subsequently raised by an uncle in Rotterdam. In 1663 he began law studies at Leiden University, and in 1669 he married the daughter of the mayor of Rotterdam, who introduced him into the best social circles. Flinck became a director of the East India Company and lived in a large town house on the Korte Hoogstraat, Rotterdam, which he decorated with his sizable art collection, part of which he had inherited from his father. Nicolaes also patronized the artist Adriaen van der Werff, who painted a ceiling in his house and a number of portraits for him. Flinck's collection included Classical sculpture, some of which he acquired from Jan Six and the 1st Duke of Buckingham, among others. However, Flinck concentrated mainly on collecting drawings by Dutch, Flemish and Italian artists: these included a number of views along the Amstel by Rembrandt, eight portraits from life by Anthony van Dyck, as well as drawings by Leonardo, Raphael, Giulio Romano and Baccio Bandinelli. Flinck also owned engravings, but in 1710 he abandoned collecting prints in preference to drawings. His taste and judgement were appreciated not only in the Netherlands but also in foreign countries; among the visitors to his collection were the Comte de Caylus. The year after Flinck's death, the 2nd Duke of Devonshire (*see* CAVENDISH, (2)) bought 500 drawings from the collection for 12,000 florins; most of these are still kept at Chatsworth House, Derbys, and form the nucleus of the collection of drawings formed by the Dukes of Devonshire (some sheets were sold at London, Christie's, on 3 July 1984 and 6 July 1987). After the death of the last of Flinck's three children, the remaining collection of 50 paintings, some lesser drawings and the engravings were sold at auction in Rotterdam on 4 November 1754.

2. Govaert Flinck: *Mourning of Stadholder Frederick Henry*, oil on canvas, 3.07×1.89 m, 1654 (Amsterdam, Rijksmuseum)

Drawings formerly in Flinck's collection are recognizable by the initial 'F' in black on the *recto* of the sheet.

BIBLIOGRAPHY

F. Lugt: *Marques* (1921), no. 959

P. Schatborn: 'Van Rembrandt tot Crozat: Vroege verzamelingen met tekeningen van Rembrandt', *Ned. Ksthist. Jb.*, xxxii (1981), pp. 1–54

Old Master Drawings from Chatsworth (exh. cat. by M. Jaffé, London, BM, 1993)

JANE SHOAF TURNER

Flindt [Flint; Flynt; Flynth; Vlyndt], **Paul, II** (*b* Nuremberg, *bapt* 6 Oct 1567; *d* Nuremberg, 1631 or later). German goldsmith, engraver and medallist. The son of the goldsmith Paul Flindt I (*fl* 1567; *d* 1582), he became a master in Nuremberg in 1601, after a lengthy stay in Vienna. A variant of his PF monogram was PVN, for Paul Vlindt Norimbergensis. Apart from a few lead plaques, only one securely attributable piece of his goldsmith work is known, an embossed oval gold-plated silver tray with figural motifs (1606; Moscow, Patriarch's Pal.). Although he maintained only a small workshop, Flindt exercised a major influence on the development of ornament in the goldsmith work of his time, especially through his serial engravings (over 200 sheets; 1592–1618; see 1985 exh. cat., nos 409–24, 461, 463–6) of all sorts of ornate pieces, garnished with ribbon- and band-ornament and rich figurative centres. These delicately shadowed, plastically modelled sheets, with their Mannerist motifs, created under the influence of Wenzel Jamnitzer, Jost Amman, Hendrick Goltzius and others, were taken by many goldsmiths as 'classical' models for their own work. It has been claimed that Flindt invented the embossing technique of copper-engraving, but this had already been practised before him, in Augsburg.

BIBLIOGRAPHY

ADB; *NDB*; Thieme–Becker

G. K. Nagler: *Monogrammisten* (1858–1920), iv, nos 2950–51, 3399, pp. 878–9, 982–3

E. W. Braun: 'Plaketten von Paul Flindt', *Archv Medaillen- & Plakettenknd.*, i (1913/14), pp. 21–6

Aufgang der Neuzeit (exh. cat., Nuremburg, Ger. Nmus., 1952), nos 37–41, 64

G. Irmscher: *Das Schweifwerk, Untersuchungen zu einem Ornamenttypus der Zeit um 1600 im Bereich ornamentaler Vorlageblätter* (diss., U. Cologne, 1978), pp. 74–91

Wenzel Jamnitzer und die Nürnberger Goldschmiedekunst, 1500–1700 (exh. cat., Nuremburg, Ger. Nmus., 1985), nos 68, 150, 409–24, 461, 463–6, *passim*

WERNER WILHELM SCHNABEL

Flint, Sir **William Russell** (*b* Edinburgh, 4 April 1880; *d* London, 30 Dec 1969). Scottish painter, printmaker and illustrator. After studying at Daniel Stewart's College, Edinburgh, he was apprenticed as a lithographic draughtsman and designer from 1894 to 1900 and studied part-time at the Royal Institute of Art, Edinburgh. He worked in London as a medical illustrator from 1900 to 1902, and then as a commercial artist, joining the staff of the *Illustrated London News* (1903–7). He illustrated limited editions of the classics, including Thomas Malory's *Morte d'Arthur* (London, 1910), Geoffrey Chaucer's *The Canterbury Tales* (London, 1912) and Homer's *The Odyssey* (London, 1924).

Flint established his reputation with watercolour landscapes of Scotland, France, Italy and Spain, many of them containing references to local customs, as in *Ascension Day, Catalonia* (Eton, Berks, Coll.). Having produced landscapes of Spain from 1921, he became particularly associated with figure studies of girls either nude or in Spanish costume. His delight in the female form also found expression in a book of caprices, *Models of Propriety* (London, 1951), and limited edition, signed colour reproductions of his watercolours became popular. In the 1920s and 1930s he also produced a number of drypoints, such as *Exits and Entrances* (1930; London, BM). He was made RA in 1933 and served as President of the Royal Society of Painters in Watercolours from 1936 to 1956; he was knighted in 1947.

BIBLIOGRAPHY

A. Palmer: *More than Shadows: A Biography of W. Russell Flint* (London, 1943)

R. Lewis: *Sir William Russell Flint, 1880–1969* (Edinburgh, 1980, rev. Newton Abbott, 1988)

THEO COWDELL

Flipart. French family of artists. The printmaker Jean-Charles Flipart (*b* Abbeville, *c.* 1683; *d* Paris, 23 May 1751), a pupil of Nicolas-Henry Tardieu, is known to have produced *c.* 15 engravings; he collaborated with many others on illustrated works, notably Jean-Baptiste de Monicart's *Versailles immortalisé* (1720–21). He trained his three sons as printmakers: (1) Jean-Jacques Flipart and Charles-François Flipart (1730–73) worked together on several portrait engravings for Bénigne Dujardin's and Gottfried Sellius's *L'Histoire générale des Provinces Unies* (1757); (2) Charles-Joseph Flipart, who settled in Spain, was active as both engraver and painter.

(1) Jean-Jacques Flipart (*b* Paris, 15 Feb 1719; *d* Paris, 9 July 1782). Printmaker. He was taught first by his father and then by Laurent Cars, who lived in the same house. Although he was considered to be one of Cars's more mediocre pupils, he nevertheless secured the patronage of Charles-Nicolas Cochin (ii), who in 1749 gave him two vignettes to engrave and, finding his work satisfactory, arranged for him to engrave the frontispiece drawn by René-Michel Slodtz for *La Fête publique donnée par la Ville de Paris à l'occasion du mariage du Dauphin en 1747* (Pognon and Bruand, no. 2), published in 1751 under the editorship of Jean-François Blondel. This engraving and a *Holy Family* (PB 9) after Giulio Romano established his reputation, and in 1755 he was approved (*agréé*) by the Académie Royale, but never presented his *morceau de réception*. In the 1750s he chiefly engraved illustrations after Cochin, who remained his friend and later gave him important prints to engrave, including a *Storm* (1765; PB 136) after Joseph Vernet.

From the 1760s onwards Flipart chiefly devoted himself to engraving paintings by Jean-Baptiste Greuze, including, in 1763, Greuze's *Self-portrait* (PB 127) and *Little Girl Winding Wool* (PB 128); in 1766 the *Dead Bird* (PB 139) and *Woman Knitting* (PB 129); and most notably, in 1767, the *Paralytic Tended by his Children* (PB 140). In 1770 Flipart produced the *Village Betrothal* (PB 143) and in 1777 the *Twelfth Night Cake* (PB 149). These plates, which were as profitable for the painter as for the engraver, were a great success with the public, Denis Diderot alone excepted. Flipart's remarkable talent as an etcher was not, however, put to its best use here; Greuze kept a close watch over the execution of the prints and demanded an excessive degree of finish which would have been more suited to line-engraving.

Flipart was in the habit of doing most of the work on his plates by etching, working them very densely and using as many as three bites, in order to eliminate as far as possible the white interstices. He used the burin only to emphasize the lines already made. This technique, which was all his own, made him one of the most celebrated engravers of large-scale subjects of his time. While during the years 1760–70 he continued to engrave some illustrations, he specialized chiefly in reproducing the most highly prized works of contemporary artists. Besides Cochin, Greuze and Vernet, he also made engravings after Carle Vanloo (e.g. the *Bear Hunt*, PB 145) and François Boucher (e.g. the *Tiger Hunt*, PB 146). At the time of Flipart's death, his studio was one of the most active in Paris.

BIBLIOGRAPHY

Portalis–Beraldi

C.-E. Gaucher: 'Éloge de Jean-Jacques Flipart, Graveur du Roi', *J. Paris* (3 Aug 1782)
E. Pognon and Y. Bruand: *Inventaire du fonds français: Graveurs du dix-huitième siècle*, Paris, Bib. N., Dept Est. cat., ix (Paris, 1962), pp. 203–44 [PB]
C. Michel: 'La Diffusion des gravures d'après Greuze', *Colloque Diderot et Greuze: Clermont-Ferrand, 1984*, pp. 39–49

CHRISTIAN MICHEL

(2) Charles-Joseph [Carlo Giuseppe] **Flipart** (*b* Paris, 9 Jan 1721; *d* Madrid, 2 Aug 1797). Engraver, painter and designer, brother of (1) Jean-Jacques Flipart. His father supervised his early artistic training. While in Paris, he met the Venetian painter Jacopo Amigoni, who may have encouraged him to go to Italy, as he moved there when still very young. He worked during the 1740s in the Venetian studio of the printmaker Joseph Wagner (1706–80), where he became acquainted with the splendid colouring and Baroque style of earlier and contemporary schools of painting. He also assimilated the descriptive and anecdotal richness of Pietro Longhi's style, combining it with the refinement of the French *fête galante*. He collaborated with Amigoni and probably followed him to Spain in 1747 to be his assistant at the Madrid court. When Amigoni died in 1752, Flipart completed the two allegorical tondi painted in Rococo style by the older artist for the Comedor de Gala in the Palacio de Aranjuez (*in situ*). At the same time he obtained commissions from the court circle, painting the *Surrender of Seville to St Ferdinand* (*c.* 1756) for the convent of the Visitación (now S Bárbara; *in situ*) and the *Immaculate Conception with SS Peter and Paul* (*c.* 1751; untraced) for the Hospital de los Italianos, both in Madrid. Ferdinand VI ordered two of his paintings, *St Ferdinand III* and *St Francis of Paola* (both *c.* 1752–8), to be sent to the Carmelite convent in Alba de Tormes (*in situ*).

In 1753 Flipart was appointed Pintor de Cámara and Abridor de Láminas ('plate engraver'). From then until shortly after the arrival of Corrado Giaquinto in June 1753 he directed work at the Real Fábrica de Tapices de S Bárbara. He also produced designs for the magnificent pietra dure tables (Madrid, Prado) made in the Buen Retiro workshop (*see* MADRID, §III, 3). There is evidence to suggest that he was more active as an engraver than as a painter, but few of his works survive, and documents

testifying to his life and work are scarce. He painted various portraits in the prevailing international style, for instance *Portrait of a Lady* (Madrid, Prado). His paintings show the free brushwork, the colouring and the creative and compositional formulae of a follower of Amigoni. However, despite the obvious dependence on his master, his work also reveals some individuality.

BIBLIOGRAPHY

A. Folco Zambelli: 'Contributo a Carlo Giuseppe Flipart', *A. Ant. & Mod.*, 18 (1962), pp. 186–99
J. J. Luna: 'Introducción al estudio de Charles-Joseph Flipart en España', *Homenaje a Don Antonio Domínguez Ortíz* (Madrid, 1981)

JUAN J. LUNA

Flitcroft, Henry (*b* 30 Aug 1697; *d* Hampstead, London, 25 Feb 1769). English architect. He grew up in the Office of Works community at Hampton Court, where his father was a labourer, and from 1711 he trained as a joiner. The turning-point in his career came when Richard Boyle, 3rd Earl of Burlington, noticed his drawing ability and employed him as a draughtsman and surveyor during the early 1720s. Many of the finished copies of the Earl's designs as well as the publication drawings for William Kent's *Designs of Inigo Jones* (1727) are in Flitcroft's elegant hand. Through Burlington's patronage Flitcroft entered the Office of Works in 1726. For 20 years he held the key post of Clerk of Works at Whitehall, Westminster and St James's before being promoted to the posts of Master Carpenter (1746–9), Master Mason (1748–58) and finally Comptroller (1758–69). Although overshadowed as a designer by Kent and later by Chambers, he proved a conscientious administrator with a sound practical knowledge of building. A colleague wrote that 'in our Office such a man is very necessary upon almost every occasion'. These qualities must have commended him to his private clients for whom almost all his architectural work was undertaken. Most were leading members of the political establishment whom he probably met through his official duties; they included Prince William Augustus, Duke of Cumberland, to whom he acted as architectural tutor (1733–7).

Many of Flitcroft's commissions involved remodelling existing houses or providing new stables and offices, for example St Giles House, Dorset (1740–44), Cumberland Lodge, Windsor Great Park (*c.* 1742–4), Wimpole Hall, Cambs (1742–55), Woburn Abbey, Beds (1747–61), and Milton House, Northants (1749–51). New houses included Stivichall Hall, Warwicks (1755–6; destr. from 1928), and in London a villa for Henry Hoare the younger at Clapham (1753–4; destr. 1853) and Kingston House, Knightsbridge (*c.* 1750; destr. 1937); all three had a central block linked to balancing office pavilions by screen walls containing garden gates. He also built three churches—St Giles-in-the-Fields, London (1731–4), St Olave's, Southwark, London (1738–9; destr. 1926), and Wimpole church, Cambs (1748–9)—and a number of houses in London.

Flitcroft's early training under Burlington brought him first-hand exposure to the designs of Palladio and Inigo Jones and these remained the dominant influence on his work. He was arguably the Earl's most faithful disciple and many of his elevations exhibit that austere Neoclassical quality that is the hallmark of the Burlington style.

One of Flitcroft's favourite devices was the Venetian window with blind roundels or rectangular panels flanking the head of the central opening, particularly used as a central feature with a Diocletian window above and rusticated doorway below. Flitcroft was especially successful as an interior decorator after the manner of Kent and Jones. He created magnificent suites of apartments at Wentworth Woodhouse, S. Yorks (1737–64), and Woburn (c. 1754–61) and designed furniture in the style of Kent for Wentworth Woodhouse, Wimpole and Ditchley Park, Oxon. Ceilings, doorcases and chimney-pieces followed examples by Jones although a lighter Rococo spirit infects some of his later carving and plasterwork.

Flitcroft also achieved some reputation as a designer of garden buildings; his Pantheon at Stourhead, Wilts (1753–4), is an original adaptation of an antique model, while the follies known as Alfred's Tower (1762) at Stourhead and Hoober's Stand, Wentworth Woodhouse, display an unexpectedly dramatic quality. Flitcroft designed a number of ornamental bridges, the most celebrated being his Great Bridge at Virginia Water, Surrey (c. 1750; destr.), a spectacular single-span timber arch based on a design by Palladio.

Above all a metropolitan architect working close to the fount of English Palladianism, Flitcroft was able to employ the leading London craftsmen and, if his designs lack originality, his work reveals an unfailing professionalism and accomplishment.

For illustration see ASSEMBLY ROOMS.

Colvin

BIBLIOGRAPHY

G. Scott Thomson: 'Woburn Abbey: Rebuilding 1747–61', *Family Background* (London, 1949)
R. Bearman: 'A Lost Warwickshire Country House: Stivichall Hall', *Warwicks Hist.*, i/3 (1970), pp. 12–18
K. Woodbridge: *Landscape and Antiquity: Aspects of English Culture at Stourhead, 1718 to 1838* (Oxford, 1970)
H. M. Colvin, ed.: *The History of the King's Works*, v (London, 1976)
G. Jackson-Stops: *Wimpole Hall, Cambridgeshire* (London, 1979)
J. E. Allan: 'Wentworth Woodhouse', *Archaeol. J.*, cxxxvii (1980), pp. 393–6

JULIET WEST

Flock and tinsel prints. Collective term for a type of woodcut to which powdered wool (flock) or tinsel (small fragments of metal) was applied. Such prints are rare. The technique was developed to imitate a patterned velvet in texture and appearance, its French and German names reflecting its appearance: *empreinte veloutée, Samt-Teigdrucke.* Of the seven examples of flock prints (including one duplicate) recorded by Hind, at least five were printed in red. It is not certain how flock prints were produced, but the process was probably as follows. The surface of the paper was first prepared to look like a textile web by the impression of an actual textile on the paper. The paper was then varnished or, alternatively, the textile was coated with varnish before its application to the paper. A woodblock carrying the image cut in relief was coated with a paste or glue and impressed on to the prepared paper. Flock was sprinkled, probably through a sieve, over the impression while the paste was still wet. The sheet was shaken to remove the flock from the unpasted areas. All the impressions known to Hind are south German and date to c. 1450–75: *St George* (Nuremberg, Ger. Nmus.),

St Barbara (Würzburg, Ubib.), the *Christ Child with Angels and Signs of the Passion* (Würzburg, Ubib.), *St Catherine* (Munich, Staatl. Graph. Samml.), *Christ on the Cross between the Virgin and St John* (Oxford, Ashmolean) and an *Allegorical Device, with Castle, Hind and Panther* (Munich, Staatl. Graph. Samml.).

Surviving examples of tinsel prints date from c. 1430–60. Small fragments of thin and sparkling metal and/or small quartz crystals were applied by paste or gum in addition to colour to embellish woodcuts. In the *Christ Child* (Munich, Staatl. Graph. Samml.; Schreiber, no. 810) and the *Man of Sorrows* (U. Hannover, Samml. Haupt.; s 868) gold tinsel is used to enhance a black background. A further category of print, which employed tin foil to elaborate decorative effect, is the theatrical tinsel print, a genre that flourished in Britain between c. 1814 and 1830. These engravings of contemporary actors and other popular figures could be purchased uncoloured ('plain') for a penny or coloured for two pennies. Male actors were particularly popular, often represented in a dramatic pose and wearing full or partial armour, allowing for a generous surface area of tinsel. The bright, primary colours and elaborate tinsel stencils were offset against a simple watercolour background, with the actor and publisher's name printed at the lower edge, and frequently mounted in a maplewood frame. The standard sheet size was 8×10 inches (200×250 mm). These were essentially popular prints and therefore anonymous, but the involvement of George Cruikshank has been suggested.

BIBLIOGRAPHY

W. L. Schreiber: *Manuel de la gravure sur bois et sur métal au XVe siècle*, 5 vols (Berlin, 1891–1910) [s]
W. L. Schreiber: *Die Meister der Metallschneidekunst nebst einem nach Schulen geordneten Katalog ihrer Arbeiten* (Strasbourg, 1926)
C. Dodgson: *Woodcuts of the XV Century in the Ashmolean Museum* (Oxford, 1929)
A. M. Hind: *An Introduction to a History of Woodcut*, 2 vols (London, 1935, 2/1963)
A. Griffiths: *Prints and Printmaking* (London, 1980)

LAURA SUFFIELD

Floding, Per Gustaf (*b* Lidköping, 3 March 1731; *d* Stockholm, 17 Oct 1791). Swedish printmaker, draughtsman and teacher. He learnt to draw as a youth in Stockholm and from 1747 studied engraving under Jean Eric Rehn. He produced several copperplate engravings for Carl Gustav Tessin's large collection of paintings, drawings and prints (Museum Tessinianum), and as a result he was awarded a scholarship to study at the Ecole des Beaux-Arts in Paris in 1755. He enrolled at the Ecole as a protégé of Tessin and Alexandre Roslin. He was taught drawing by Boucher, Louis-Michel van Loo, Joseph-Marie Vien and Roslin and engraving by Jacques-Philippe Lebas, Laurent Cars and Charles-Nicolas Cochin II. With François-Philippe Charpentier (1734–1817) he was among the earliest practitioners of aquatint or *gravure au lavis*, a means of reproducing pen-and-wash drawings, and executed five sheets (1762) in this technique. He did a large copperplate engraving of *Adolf Fredrik, Patron of the Arts*, after a drawing by Cochin (c. 1860). This was sent to Sweden and resulted in Floding's appointment in 1763 as His Majesty's Engraver and as *Garde des estampes* to Crown Prince Gustav (later Gustav III). In 1764 he returned to Sweden and in 1766 founded the Flodingska Gravyrskola, with Jakob Gillberg joining him as a teacher. The school eventually closed in 1778 owing to Floding's abrasive personality and his unpopularity with his students. In 1768 he was appointed professor and secretary at the Kungliga Akademi för de Fria Konsterna. In 1777 he was replaced as secretary and expelled from the membership of the academy as a result of his mismanagement of the post but was allowed to keep his professorship on the condition that his students would be treated more humanely. Floding was the foremost engraver in Sweden in the 18th century. One of his finest engravings is the portrait of *Gustav III* (1779). He also did a series of vignettes for the treatises of the Kungliga Vetenskapsakademi and several book plates. As his strength lay in copperplate engraving, his etchings are not of the same high quality.

BIBLIOGRAPHY
C. U. Palm: *Per Gustaf Floding och hans konstnärsskap* [Per Gustaf Floding and his artistry] (Stockholm, 1896)
G. W. Lundberg: *P. G. Floding: Le Graveur suédois* (Paris, 1932)
E. Hultmark, C. Hultmark and C. D. Moselius: *Svenska kopparstickare och etsare, 1500–1944* [Swedish copperplate engravers and etchers, 1500–1944] (Uppsala, 1944), pp. 101–3

A.-G. WAHLBERG

Florence [It. Firenze]. Italian city and capital of Tuscany. Situated on the banks of the River Arno *c.* 85 km east of Pisa and *c.* 230 km north of Rome, the city (population *c.* 450,000) lies in a basin surrounded by low hills. Florence is renowned as a centre of Italian art and architecture and for its role in the development of Renaissance art in the 15th century, particularly under the patronage of the Medici family.

I. History and urban development. II. Art life and organization. III. Centre of production. IV. Buildings. V. Institutions.

I. History and urban development.

1. Before *c.* AD 400. 2. *c.* AD 400–1282. 3. 1283–*c.* 1400. 4. *c.* 1400–1530. 5. 1531–1737. 6. After 1737.

1. BEFORE *c.* AD 400. The plain of the River Arno was first settled in the Neolithic era. In the 5th century BC the Etruscans established a settlement, not on the plain but on the nearby hill of Fiesole. A Roman colony, Florentia, was subsequently founded by Julius Caesar in the mid-1st century BC on the northern bank of the River Arno near its junction with the Mugnone. Following a typical castrum plan, a rectangular perimeter of brick-faced walls (*c.* 480×420 m) enclosed a regular grid of streets orientated to the cardinal directions and at an angle to the riverbank; this grid forms the core of the modern city. Four city gates, flanked by circular towers, stood astride the *cardo maximus* and *decumanus*, the principal north–south and east–west streets. The forum, the commercial and religious centre, stood in the middle of the town on the site of the present Piazza della Repubblica, where excavations have revealed the remains of the principal temple.

During the 1st and 2nd centuries AD, extramural development to the south and east along the river produced a zone of monumental public buildings, including two bath complexes, a theatre, a Temple of Isis and an amphitheatre, the oval form of which is preserved in the curving medieval streets west of Piazza Santa Croce. In AD 123 Emperor Hadrian re-routed the Via Cassia, one of the Roman trunk roads, to cross the Arno at Florence, and a stone bridge was probably constructed at about that time near the site of the present Ponte Vecchio. By the 2nd century AD the flourishing colony had a population of *c.* 10,000, and by the 4th century the inhabited area extended north of the walls to the present Piazza S Lorenzo, where the city's first Christian basilica, S Lorenzo, was consecrated as its cathedral by St Ambrose in AD 393. On the south side of the Arno, settlement radiated from the bridgehead where the main roads from Pisa and Arezzo converged, and by the early 5th century AD a Christian cemetery and church existed on the site of the present church of S Felicità.

BIBLIOGRAPHY
W. Paatz and E. Paatz: *Kirchen* (1940–54)
G. Maetzke: *Florentia* (Rome, 1941)
C. Hardie: 'The Origin and Plan of Roman Florence', *J. Roman Stud.*, lv (1965), pp. 122–40

2. *c.* AD 400–1282. As successive Gothic invasions wracked Tuscany in the 5th and 6th centuries, the settlement at Florence suffered demographic and economic decline. The bridge over the Arno was destroyed, and vulnerable peripheral areas of the city were abandoned. Nevertheless, during a period of relative peace, probably in the 5th century, the church of S Reparata, a large, three-aisled basilica, was constructed just inside the northern flank of the Roman walls on the site of the present cathedral. In the mid-6th century the Byzantine defenders of Florence built new fortifications enclosing a nucleus only about half the size of the Roman town, with massive Roman monuments used as defensive strongpoints linked by barricades. Towards the end of the 6th century, however, the settlement fell to the Lombards, becoming part of the Lombardic Duchy of Tuscany centred at Lucca. During Lombard domination in the 7th and 8th centuries the principal highway to Rome bypassed Florence, further contributing to its decline, but the continuity of urban life is attested by the foundation of new churches, including an octagonal Baptistery constructed probably in the 6th or 7th century. The Lombards also adapted Roman remains to their own uses: the Roman theatre to the west of Via dei Leoni, for example, became their fortress, with the addition of a tall watch-tower.

Tuscany became a Frankish province *c.* 775, and the Carolingian era marked the tentative beginnings of urban revival. A growing population and increasing prosperity in Florence were certainly among the motives for new city walls, probably constructed in the late 8th century or the early 9th. This circuit re-established the Roman perimeter on the east and west and incorporated a wedge of new settlement to the south. The bridge over the Arno was rebuilt, facilitating trade. When Florence became the administrative centre of its county in 854, a palace for the governing margrave was built just west of the Baptistery. Also at about this time, the remodelled S Reparata began to serve as the cathedral, and a canonry and bishop's palace were constructed near by. The church of S Michele in Orto, on the site of the present church of Orsanmichele, near the centre of the town, was probably also founded in the 9th century. The most important ecclesiastical foundation of the 10th century was the Benedictine abbey of

Beata Maria Virginis, known to Florentines simply as the Badia Fiorentina. The first large monastery within the city walls, it was founded in 978 by Willa, widow of Uberto, Margrave of Tuscany, and was lavishly endowed by her son, Count Ugo. The church was rebuilt in the 13th century.

By the beginning of the 11th century Florence had become an important trading centre for the fertile valleys of Tuscany; its population was then around 5000. Increasing commercial activity is evident from the first mention (1018) of a second market, still known as the Mercato Nuovo, which was established to supplement the single existing market-place on the site of the old Roman forum. The rate of church building also accelerated. New churches were founded (e.g. S Maria delle Vigne, 1094; later S Maria Novella; *see* §IV, 6 below), and many existing structures were remodelled, enlarged or entirely rebuilt, including the two surviving jewels of Florentine Romanesque architecture: S Miniato al Monte (*see* §IV, 7 and fig. 21 below) and the Baptistery (*see* §IV, 1(ii) and fig. 13 below). Matilda of Canossa, Countess of Tuscany (1046–1115), preferred Florence to the other cities of her realm, perhaps thereby encouraging its florescence, and new city walls have been attributed to her reign.

In 1115 Florence achieved de facto self-government with the establishment of a *comune* (confirmed by the Holy Roman Emperor in 1183), which protected the interests of the merchants who were by then developing the cloth industry, trade and money-lending activities that later brought such wealth to the city. Many aristocratic family clans took up residence in the city at this time; within its walls they built defensible family enclaves, threaded by narrow alleys and enclosing minuscule piazzas. The most characteristic feature of these urban strongholds was a lofty stone tower. Meanwhile, immigration of less powerful classes swelled the population of the suburbs. Under threat of attack by Frederick Barbarossa, Holy Roman Emperor, new city walls were speedily constructed in 1172–5 to enclose the unprotected suburbs north and south of the river. The course of this first circuit built by the *comune* remains legible in the sequence of streets that leads north from Ponte alla Carraia, turns east above S Lorenzo and south at Piazza S Pier Maggiore, forming three sides of a quadrilateral.

At the beginning of the 13th century, when the population had reached around 30,000, government by a Podestà (governing magistrate) replaced the *comune*, and the first guilds were formed (*see* §II, 1 below). At this time also there began a century of bitter political rivalries and feuds between the Guelph faction (who supported the papal cause) and the Ghibellines (who supported the Holy Roman Emperor). The city was characterized by dozens of fortified family enclave towers: by some estimates, 200 or more such towers, mostly packed densely within the Carolingian walls, had been constructed by the mid-13th century. Despite the continual disruptions to urban life caused by the factional disputes, however, trade and industry continued to flourish, and during a brief period of popular government ('Primo Popolo'; 1250–60), which enforced reductions in the height of towers, the first monumental civic building in Florence was constructed: the Palazzo del Popolo (now known as the Bargello and

housing the Museo Nazionale), built for the Capitano del Popolo, commander of the civic militia. Facing the Badia across Via del Proconsolo and incorporating a pre-existing tower, the fortress-like 13th-century block is distinguishable from later additions by its finely dressed stonework, executed in local brown limestone (*pietra forte*).

Expansion of the city continued, with settlements growing up ribbon-like along the highways outside the city gates. Magnets for further development were provided by the churches built in large open areas outside the city walls by the newly arrived mendicant orders: around 1220 the Dominicans acquired the church of S Maria Novella in the western suburbs (*see* §IV, 6 below) and began a long rebuilding campaign *c*. 1246, receiving communal subsidies to create public piazzas in front of each succeeding structure; the Franciscans established themselves at Santa Croce east of the city walls, building a modest church *c*. 1225 but by 1294/5 beginning construction of an enormous new church facing a large piazza (*see* §IV, 4 below); the Servites built a church (1250) to the northeast of the city walls that later became SS Annunziata (*see* §IV, 3 below); and on the southern side of the river (the Oltrarno) the Augustinians founded Santo Spirito (1250; rebuilt 15th century; *see* §3(ii) below), and the Carmelites built S Maria del Carmine (1268; mostly rebuilt 1782) on the fringes of the built-up area (they too received government aid in creating piazzas). The growing importance of the Oltrarno as an integral part of the city led to the construction of three additional bridges: Ponte alla Carraia (1220), Ponte alle Grazie (1237) and Ponte Santa Trìnita (1252).

By the mid-13th century the Florentine cloth industry was producing for markets all over Europe, and merchants were involved in a huge commercial and banking network; the city's gold florin, first minted at about this time, became the standard currency in Europe. Florence also began to extend her control over much of the surrounding territory, annexing smaller adjacent city states. The increasing wealth and power of the city was reflected in the layout of many new streets, both inside and outside the city walls on both sides of the river; for example, while there had previously been little order in the urban sprawl except for the central grid of the old Roman town, the straight and relatively wide swaths of the Via Maggio and Via dei Servi, both dating from the mid-13th century, exemplify new criteria of order and regularity in urban planning. The new streets in turn provided opportunities for further development, and construction of modest housing was fostered by many ecclesiastical institutions, which subdivided their lands into building lots (*casolaria*) typically no more than 5 or 6 m wide along the street. The *casolare* thus became the principal module of development outside the 12th-century walls.

BIBLIOGRAPHY

R. Davidsohn: *Forschungen zur Geschichte von Florenz*, 4 vols (Berlin, 1896–1908)

——: *Geschichte von Florenz*, 4 vols (Berlin, 1896–1927; Ital. trans., 8 vols, 1957–68)

F. Schevill: *History of Florence* (New York, 1936); rev. as *Medieval and Renaissance Florence*, 2 vols (New York, 1963)

W. Paatz and E. Paatz: *Kirchen* (1940–54)

G. Maetzke: 'Ricerche sulla topografia fiorentina nel periodo delle guerre goto-bizantine', *Rendi. Accad. N. Lincei, Cl. Sci. Mor., Stor. & Filol.*, 8th ser., iii (1948), pp. 97–112

W. Braunfels: *Mittelalterliche Stadtbaukunst in der Toskana* (Berlin, 1953)
U. Procacci: 'L'aspetto urbano di Firenze dai tempi di Cacciaguida a quelli di Dante', *Enciclopedia Dantesca*, ii (Rome, 1970), pp. 913–20
G. Fanelli: *Firenze: Architettura e città*, 2 vols (Florence, 1973) [vol. 2 contains numerous diagrams, maps, plans, photographs]
F. Sznura: *L'espansione urbana di Firenze nel dugento* (Florence, 1975)

PAULA SPILNER

3. 1283–*c.* 1400. Following war with Siena and continual struggles between Guelphs and Ghibellines, a second popular government ('Secondo Popolo') was set up in 1283 by the guilds. With the realization that once again extramural expansion had rendered Florence's fortifications obsolete, yet another circuit of walls was planned (begun 1299; completed 1333). This circuit enclosed all the monasteries and a huge area five times the size of the 12th-century walls, but the dramatic population decline of the 14th century meant that it was centuries before the new zone was fully developed. Construction was also begun on a new cathedral in 1296, and a new government building, the Palazzo dei Priori, the seat of the leaders of the guilds, was begun in 1299, symbolizing the civic values of the new political order in which the nobility were banned from holding office. By 1300 Florence was among the five largest cities in Europe, with a population of *c.* 100,000.

The 14th century, however, was a period of turmoil for Florence. A fire in 1304 destroyed hundreds of houses; there was famine in 1315–17; the Arno flooded in 1333, causing enormous damage; and the plague reached the city in 1348, resulting in a 60% decline in the population. These events led to acute difficulties in building works, including the slowing of progress on earlier projects, such as the Gothic churches of S Maria Novella and Santa Croce (consecrated 1443). Nevertheless the two principal hubs of the city became more clearly defined at this time as work continued on the new cathedral and government buildings. Much of the new cathedral by Arnolfo di Cambio had been completed by 1331 when relics presumed to be of the first bishop, St Zenobius (*d c.* 390), were found, and it was decided to extend the work to create a much larger church, for which the wool-merchants' guild (Arte della Lana) assumed responsibility. Work was initially concentrated on the campanile, begun by Giotto in 1334, and then continued on the cathedral by Francesco Talenti (from 1355; *see* §IV, 1(i) below). Several other works reinforced the identity of the cathedral district as the religious heart of the city: in 1336 the cathedral piazza (now Piazza del Duomo) was enlarged; in the 1350s the Loggia del Bigallo (now Museo del Bigallo) was built there for the charitable confraternity of the Misericordia; in 1363 it was forbidden to build jetties on houses around the piazza, the first of many such controls; and in 1366 several structures were demolished so that the cathedral apses could be built.

Meanwhile a civic hub was being developed around the fortress-like Palazzo dei Priori (now Palazzo Vecchio; *see* §IV, 8 and fig. 23 below), which stands on part of the site of the old Roman theatre and was first completed in 1302 but enlarged later in the century on an irregular, trapezoidal plan. It immediately became the administrative and political centre of the city. At the same time the adjacent piazza (now Piazza della Signoria) began to be opened up

specifically as a civic square, with no market functions; it was enlarged several times and was paved in the mid-14th century. In 1359 the Loggia della Mercanzia was built at the east end of the piazza to dispense justice over trade and guild matters. A few years later the Loggia dei Pisani was built on the west side and the Loggia dei Lanzi (or Loggia della Signoria; 1376–81) on the south side. The latter was built for ceremonial use by the Priori, and its arcade of semicircular arches anticipates Renaissance forms. The mint was built behind it and the whole area devoted to the agencies of the State.

The street linking the cathedral and the Palazzo dei Priori, the Via de' Calzaiuoli, which follows one of the old Roman roads, became the chief civic axis of the city. Along it, on the site of the old church of S Michele in Orto, was built the Orsanmichele (1336–1404; *see* §IV, 2 and fig. 16 below). This was a new grain market with two large, superimposed vaulted halls over an arcaded ground-floor, which by 1381 had been enclosed to form a sanctuary; this became an oratory for the trade guilds, all of whom had been involved in the project. The guilds were also important as founders and benefactors of hospitals. The cloth-merchants' guild (Calimala) built the hospital of Bonifazio, and the bankers' guild (Cambio) built the hospital of S Matteo; somewhat later the silk-workers' guild (Por S Maria) founded the Ospedale degli Innocenti (1419; *see* §(ii) below). Many such works were begun as a result of the 1348 plague.

Political and economic difficulties continued to occur during the period. The Florentine economy suffered a crisis in the 1340s when two of the most important banking families, the Peruzzi and the Bardi, became bankrupt; and the brief rule of Walter de Brienne, Duke of Athens, elected as Signore (1342–3), was ended by popular insurrection. Nevertheless the city's administrative structure was reorganized in 1343; instead of six *sestieri*, the new circuit of walls enclosed four *quartieri*, each subdivided into four smaller *gonfaloni*. Strong controls were also exerted by the city government over many aspects of development, chiefly as a reaction against acute congestion in the medieval nucleus. For example, the large zone enclosed by the new walls was to be developed in a rational manner, with broader, straighter streets: the original Roman grid, by then much modified by later encroachments, was considered the ideal model. A broadly radial pattern of new roads was established from the centre towards the city gates, together with a few major cross-axes, thus forming a roughly rectangular grid pattern with large areas of open space remaining. Existing open spaces were also enlarged, particularly in front of Santo Spirito, Santa Croce and S Maria Novella, where an important new public square was formed. Some streets in the old centre were also widened and jetties removed, while the process of paving continued throughout the central areas. Attempts were also made to impose greater discipline on new development by the alignment of façades and controls over facing materials and window types and sizes. Maximum heights were stipulated for new buildings, and the *comune* had the power compulsorily to demolish dangerous older structures, such as some of the fortress-towers. In 1349 a new agency, the Ufficiali delle Cinque Cose, took responsibility for most public works, including bridges, water supply, civic buildings and the city walls.

By 1400 three zones were clearly identifiable in the urban layout of Florence. The first was the original, densely developed core, irregularly superimposed on the Roman grid, with many fortified towers but with open space limited to the Piazza del Duomo and the Piazza della Signoria. The second zone included the area immediately surrounding the centre, originally just beyond the walls; this was also densely developed but with some squares, gardens and orchards. The third zone included the most recently enclosed areas beyond, developed only along the older radial routes and backed by large areas of gardens and orchards. The Oltrarno formed a small, compact zone south of the river, with some development along the Roman road; by this time there were four bridges linking it with the city centre.

Political unrest in the latter part of the 14th century, largely between the wealthy *borghesi* and the poorer artisans, culminated in the Ciompi revolt of 1378, when the wool-carders demanded the right to form a guild; this resulted briefly in direct popular representation in government. In 1382, however, a small number of wealthy merchant families succeeded in forming an oligarchic government, finally diminishing the political power of the guilds after nearly a century of dominance. By the beginning of the 15th century the population had recovered to *c.* 60,000; Arezzo was annexed in 1384, and in 1406 Florence conquered Pisa, signalling the final defeat of the Ghibellines and giving Florence control of an important seaport and extended opportunities for trade throughout the Mediterranean and to the Levant.

4. *c.* 1400–1530. In the early 1400s the Medici family began the final stage of its rise to power. One of the wealthiest families in Florence and one of the few to survive the banking crisis of the 1340s, the Medici were among the first Florentines to patronize the arts and humanist learning. At the same time, however, they were active supporters of the guilds and opponents of the oligarchy. Cosimo de' Medici (Il Vecchio) was exiled in 1433 but returned to popular acclaim in 1434 to become unofficial ruler as Lord of Florence ('Pater Patriae'). Medici patronage was a dominant factor in the development of Florence as the birthplace and cultural centre of the Italian Renaissance (*see* §II, 1 and 2 below).

The 15th century was marked by the complete reconfiguration of the medieval city of Florence as it became a centre of great wealth and power. In particular, the work of FILIPPO BRUNELLESCHI between 1418 and 1446 marked a decisive period in the development of both architecture and urban design. Brunelleschi's rational, structural approach was visionary, even revolutionary, by comparison with the earlier urban interventions of Giotto and Arnolfo, and it reached an unprecedented scale in the construction of the magnificent dome of the cathedral, built in 1420–36 (*see* §IV, 1(i)(a) and fig. 12 below). Quite different from any other tall structure in Florence, whether campanile or fortified tower, the dome dominated the entire city, acted as its symbol and asserted the power of its spiritual heart. Set in the middle of the urban fabric, the cathedral is best seen from a distance; the only important axial view within the city is from Via de' Servi, at the far end of which Brunelleschi laid out Piazza SS Annunziata to terminate the vista. His work at the Ospedale degli Innocenti (begun

1. Florence, Piazza SS Annunziata and Ospedale degli Innocenti by Filippo Brunelleschi, begun *c.* 1419

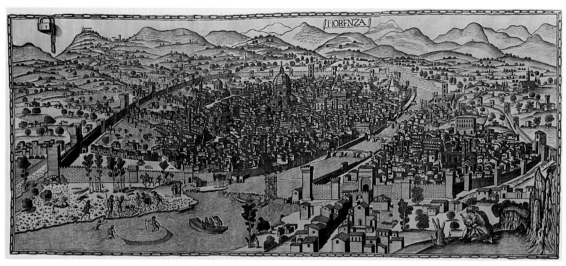

2. *Florence*, 'Pianta della Catena' view of the city, woodcut, attributed to Francesco Rosselli, 588×1315 mm, *c.* 1472 (Berlin, Kupferstichkabinett)

c. 1419) in that piazza is another masterpiece of the early Renaissance, its colonnade of semicircular arches developing forms seen earlier in the Loggia dei Lanzi but here made an essential part of the urban fabric (see fig. 1). Piazza SS Annunziata can be considered the first modern Florentine square. Topographical principles of design are equally clear at the Palazzo Pitti (*see* §IV, 9(i) below), which was built on a prominent terrace south of the Arno, with its façade aligned to the tower of Santo Spirito; probably begun *c.* 1457 it was built on an imposing scale by LUCA DI BONACCORSO PITTI as a demonstration of his wealth and power. The square created in front of it was the first in Florence to be related to a private house rather than a public building.

Under Medici rule, particularly that of Cosimo Il Vecchio (*reg* 1434–64), public building activity began to lose importance to the private sector. Particular architects became associated with individual patrons, for example MICHELOZZO DI BARTOLOMEO with the Medici and LEON BATTISTA ALBERTI with the Rucellai, who were second only to the Medici in wealth and influence, and a great age of palazzo building among the banking and merchant families began. The STROZZI built the finest such palace in the city (begun *c.* 1489), in the heart of the old quarter, designed and executed by Benedetto da Maiano, Giuliano da Sangallo and Cronaca; the Palazzo Strozzi (*see* ITALY, fig. 8) is grandiose, severe and monumental and was loosely based on the Palazzo dei Priori. Others included the Palazzo Medici (1444–60; now Palazzo Medici-Riccardi; for illustration *see* PALAZZO), built on the Via Larga (now Via Cavour) by Michelozzo; the Palazzo Rucellai (begun *c.* 1453), built to a design by Alberti (*see* ALBERTI, LEON BATTISTA, fig. 2); the Palazzo Antinori, perhaps by Giuliano da Sangallo; and the Palazzo Corsi by Michelozzo. These palaces transformed the districts immediately surrounding the old city centre, directly reflecting the wealth of the oligarchical clans that ruled the city. Because the banks and businesses of their owners remained in the medieval core of the city, they also marked the first separation between places of work and residence; the latter represented a new concept of the private palace as a self-contained entity. Their forbidding public façades contrast sharply with the light, refined design of their courtyards—private inner worlds surrounded by colonnades and loggias. In the same period some families began to build villas in the *contado*, the surrounding countryside. Most active again were the Medici, who eventually owned more than a dozen such houses (*see* §5 below); the most notable is Poggio a Caiano, rebuilt by Giuliano da Sangallo for Lorenzo the Magnificent in the mid-1480s (*see* POGGIO A CAIANO, VILLA MEDICI).

The de facto rule of Lorenzo the Magnificent (1469–92; *see* MEDICI, DE', (5)) marked the apogee of building activity by the families of Florence, which also included the patronage of churches. The Medici, for example, had earlier funded rebuilding work at S Lorenzo by Brunelleschi, his Old Sacristy (1419–29) being one of the earliest and purest monuments of the Renaissance (*see* §IV, 5 below). Later work at S Lorenzo by Michelozzo (and, subsequently, Michelangelo; see below) was also funded by the Medici, to the extent that it effectively became their own church. Medici patronage of nearby S Marco (built after 1452 by Michelozzo), where Cosimo Il Vecchio had established the first public library in Europe (*see* MEDICI, DE', (2); MICHELOZZO DI BARTOLOMEO, fig. 2), made this zone of the city the Medici quarter. Other notable church projects of the period included Santo Spirito, begun by Brunelleschi in 1436 and completed in 1483 (*see* RENAISSANCE, fig. 1; BRUNELLESCHI, FILIPPO, §I,1(viii) and fig. 3b), and major alterations to SS Annunziata, begun 1444 by Michelozzo and completed by Alberti *c.* 1470. The city centre was profoundly changed by these projects; it acquired a new, monumental character, much of which remains, particularly around the medieval nucleus. As a patron of all the arts, Lorenzo de' Medici was outstanding—although not unique—in stimulating the atmosphere for such extraordinary creative activity.

The Renaissance concept of the city and interest in its further beautification were also stimulated by progress in printing techniques, which, for the first time, allowed images of the city to be accurately committed to paper. The first important view was by Pietro del Massario (1469), while the well-known 'Pianta della Catena' view of *c.* 1472 (see fig. 2) is the first detailed attempt to portray the city within its natural context; it is no coincidence that the cathedral dome is shown precisely in the centre. The view represents a new way of seeing and understanding the urban form. Equally characteristic of an increasing sense of civic pride and cultural superiority are the minutely detailed descriptions of the city's wonders produced at about this time by such writers as Benedetto Dei.

Lorenzo de' Medici, whom the Pazzi family tried to assassinate in 1478, had his son Giovanni de' Medici made a cardinal at the age of 13 in 1489 (later Pope Leo X; *see* MEDICI, DE', (7)); the Medici bank failed before Lorenzo's death in 1492, however, and in 1494 his son Piero Il Fatuo (1472–1503) was forced to leave Florence after secretly surrendering the city to the French. A new republican government was set up, but in 1512 the Medici regained power. During the next few years they consolidated some of the urban projects of the previous century, establishing the Palazzo Medici as a rival to the Palazzo della Signoria (Palazzo dei Priori) as the city's seat of power. The Via Larga, on which the Palazzo Medici was situated, formed a direct continuation of the Via de' Calzaiuoli, the main urban axis, thus linking the Palazzo della Signoria, the cathedral and the Medici power-base in a single, direct line. In 1516–20 Antonio da Sangallo (*see* SANGALLO, (2)) completed the Piazza SS Annunziata—largely a Medici creation—with the Loggia dei Servi opposite Brunelleschi's loggia. Michelangelo enriched S Lorenzo, the Medici church, with the New Sacristy (begun 1519), which became the Medici funerary chapel, and with the Biblioteca Laurenziana (begun *c.* 1524), which housed the family's collection of manuscripts (*see* §IV, 5 below).

In 1529, after another brief republican interregnum, Florence was besieged by imperial forces; Michelangelo took charge of the fortifications and built a complex of new defences around S Miniato al Monte as well as extensive works to strengthen the city walls to the north. The siege lasted ten months and resulted in great destruction inside the city walls and in the surrounding area. Supported by both the Emperor and the Medici pope Clement VII (*see* MEDICI, DE (8)), the Medici finally returned to Florence in 1530, beginning 200 years of hereditary rule by the family.

5. 1531–1737. The rule of the unpopular Alessandro de' Medici (*reg* 1531–7), who was given the title Duke of Florence by the Emperor, was a period of political uncertainty in Florence, and few building works were undertaken. The construction of the huge Fortezza da Basso (1533–5) on the north-west flank of the city walls was symptomatic of the era: it was built not to defend the city from external aggression but as a base from which internal dissent could be crushed. Under Cosimo I (*reg* 1537–74; *see* MEDICI, DE', (14)), however, the introduction of policies for the reconstruction of Tuscan sovereignty transformed the city into the seat of an economically and culturally flourishing dukedom. Building works at this time were undertaken chiefly to serve the Medici court rather than the city as a whole, in order to

enhance and consolidate further their political and cultural power. The period is thus characterized essentially by works of order: the rebuilding of Ponte Santa Trìnita, the restoration of the Ponte Vecchio and the construction of the Uffizi.

Until 1540 the Medici had continued to reside at the family palace on Via Larga (now Villa Cavour), but in that year Cosimo I moved them into the Palazzo dei Priori, which became known as the Palazzo Ducale and was extensively remodelled by Giorgio Vasari (*see* §IV, 8 below). In 1550 they moved again, this time to the Palazzo Pitti across the Arno, which Eleonora Medici, wife of Cosimo I, had bought. As a result of these moves, several important urban works were undertaken that had a profound effect on the city centre. The Palazzo Pitti was enlarged (*see* §IV, 9 below) and became the focus of the courtly life of the capital, but the need for easy communication with the Palazzo Ducale (henceforth known as the Palazzo Vecchio) and the proliferation of bureaucracy led to the building of the Uffizi (from 1559; *see* §IV, 10 below) to house many government departments; this was one of the first buildings in Florence to be conceived as a piece of urban design (see fig. 3; *see also* VASARI, (1), fig. 6). Vasari, who became court architect, then also built the long Corridoio Vasariano connecting the Uffizi and the Palazzo Vecchio with the Ponte Vecchio and thence to the Palazzo Pitti, providing a secure, direct link between these two new poles of power. The whole focus of government in the city had thus altered, with nuclei on each side of the Arno.

Cosimo I also instigated many other works dedicated to enhancing the city's grandeur as a Medici fiefdom. Columns were erected in the piazzas of S Marco, Santa Trìnita and S Felice; the Via Maggio and Via Tornabuoni were widened and resurfaced; and the rebuilding of Ponte Santa Trìnita (*c.* 1570) by Bartolomeo Ammanati created, together with the Via Maggio, another significant link between the old city centre and the newly important districts of the Oltrarno. New loggias were erected at important points in the city's fabric: the Loggia del Pesce by Vasari in the Mercato Vecchio (*see* §5 and fig. 4 below), later moved to Piazza dei Ciompi; the Loggia del Mercato Nuovo (1547–51); and, later, the loggias of the Grana and S Maria Nuova. In 1571 the Jewish Ghetto, which had only two gates and was restricted by curfew, was formally established in a city block just north of the Mercato Vecchio. Consolidation of Medici power was also necessary well beyond the city walls; a programme of fortifications was undertaken in many dependent towns, including Pisa and Arezzo; LIVORNO was also restructured to become Florence's chief port on the Mediterranean. Wars with Siena, particularly in 1526, had necessitated works to Florence's own defences, especially across the Arno, but final victory over Siena in the period 1555–9 confirmed the Medici as absolute rulers of all Tuscany, and they were made grand dukes of Tuscany by the Emperor in 1569. Only Lucca remained as an independent city state.

Little work on churches was undertaken during the reign of Cosimo I, although the Jesuits arrived in Florence in 1546. Within existing churches, a new wave of austerity led to the removal of several choirs and the obliteration of some medieval wall paintings. Private palace building

3. Florence, courtyard of the Uffizi, by Giorgio Vasari, from 1560, with the Palazzo Vecchio and the dome of the cathedral beyond; depicted in a steel engraving by Giuseppe Vasi after a drawing by Giuseppe Zocchi

was chiefly confined to works by Cosimo's own courtiers and the favourites of his son Francesco de' Medici (later Francesco I). Examples are the palaces of the Grifoni, the Ramirez de Montalvo and the Almeni families. A new building type began to appear in the form of terraced houses for artisans, reflecting a new interest by the wealthy in land development, not only of their country estates but also within the city walls.

The courtly nature of Medici rule continued with Francesco I (*reg* 1574–87; *see* MEDICI, DE', (16); there was a renewed interest in the decorative frescoing of wall surfaces, such as that on the palazzo of Bianca Cappello, second wife of Francesco I, and a tendency towards highly mannerist detailing after the style of Michelangelo and Giulio Romano, with a parallel indulgence in capriccios in the form of gardens and grottoes. The reign of Ferdinando I (*reg* 1587–1609; *see* MEDICI, DE', (17)) is notable chiefly for the many important works of art commissioned for the Uffizi, but during this period Bernardo Buontalenti completed the Forte di Belvedere (1590–1600) above the Boboli Gardens at the Palazzo Pitti, built around the small villa at the highest point in the city. The villa had loggias on both principal façades to take advantage of views over the city and its southern hills. Few public works were necessary in this period. The Boboli Gardens were extended (*see* §IV, 9(iii) below), and new villas were built in the *contado* as part of a general reorganization of Medici lands. In 1599 Giusto Utens (*d c.* 1609) made a pictorial

record of all 14 Medici villas (Florence, Mus. Firenze com'era; see fig. 24 below); in addition to the Pitti and Poggio a Caiano villas, the most important were at PRATOLINO, La Peggio and Castello.

In the city itself, many older, medieval houses were modernized, often remodelled internally and refaced externally. Churches, too, were refurbished, often to provide space for a proliferation of private chapels. A new urban equilibrium was established within the city walls as the population stabilized at about 60,000 at the end of the 16th century. Much of the area enclosed by the walls remained undeveloped, with many gardens and orchards behind a narrow ribbon of housing along the radial routes. Stefano Bonsignori's depiction (Florence, Mus. Firenze com'era) of the city in 1584, a highly detailed aerial view based on a combination of axonometric and perspective projections, represents the record of a scientific age of enquiry and objectivity.

The reign of Cosimo II (*reg* 1609–21) represented a turning-point in the history of Florence and the beginning of a long period of decline. Mostly occupied with foreign policy, he was neither a strong character nor was he concerned with making his mark on the capital. By 1622 the population was *c.* 66,000, only a little more than it had been a century before. Farming was in crisis, with punitive levels of taxation, while the city's traditional cloth and silk industries continued to decline. Few urban works were therefore undertaken, although the chapel of the Princes by Matteo Nigetti at S Lorenzo was completed (*see* §IV, 5 below), and there were further works to the Palazzo Pitti and its gardens, both undertaken by the Parigi family, court favourites as architects and landscape designers; the palace was extended by the addition of three extra bays on each side after a competition in 1616 (see fig. 23 below). Further works of elaboration at the Pitti were executed by Ferdinando II and Cosimo III. The long reign of Ferdinando II (*reg* 1621–70; *see* MEDICI, DE', (22)) began with a famine in which 9000 died, and although the court remained the centre of social life, the city and its industries continued to decline. Few new buildings were instigated, although in the 1620s Cardinal Carlo de' Medici rebuilt SS Michele e Gaetano, and in 1627–31 the Badia Fiorentina was reconstructed. There is thus little important Baroque or Rococo architecture in Florence. In 1659 the Medici finally sold their original palace on Via Larga, another gesture symbolic of the family's decline; the Riccardi, who bought the palace, enlarged it between 1659 and 1694.

The wool and silk industries collapsed almost to the point of extinction during the reign of Cosimo III (*reg* 1670–1723). Although he was intelligent and well travelled, his court was a centre of luxury and decadence. His own religious fanaticism led to a rise in the fortunes of the religious houses, however. Many philanthropic works were undertaken, and the religious corporations (of which there were more than 100) also flourished. The only important building works were the grandiose Baroque Palazzo Corsini (1650–*c*. 1727) on the Arno and Palazzo Capponi (1698–1713), perhaps from a design by Carlo Fontana. The church of S Frediano in Cestello was rebuilt (1680–89) by Antonio Ferri (*d* 1716), as well as a number of Baroque chapels, including that of the Corsini (1675–83) at S Maria del Carmine. Much of the city's official year, though, was now given over to festivals of many kinds, to religious processions and firework displays. Following the death in 1737 of the dissolute Gian Gastone de' Medici, whose measures to reduce the national debt had driven many artists and architects away from Florence, the title of Grand Duke passed to the House of Lorraine.

6. AFTER 1737. By the time that power passed to the dukes of Lorraine, decline and corruption were widespread in Florence, and there were many abandoned estates. Francis, Grand Duke of Tuscany (*reg* 1737–65), revived the administration, and Tuscany was governed by a Council of Regency while Francis ruled *in absentia* as a benevolent despot. Similar policies were continued by his son Leopold (*reg* 1765–90; *see* HABSBURG-LORRAINE, (1)), and they effectively turned Florence into a modern city, albeit with the loss of its independence. Cultural life remained buoyant, however, and theatres flourished; there were eventually 20 in the city. The era of the Grand Tour also brought foreign visitors (*see* §II, 3 below) and an outpouring of guides, maps and *vedute*.

Leopold concentrated on agrarian reform, taking abandoned lands from the Church and giving rights to *contadini* (farm labourers). He also campaigned against the monasteries: 150 were suppressed in Tuscany, although 249 remained in Florence and 170 in the duchy beyond. Florence reverted to the status of a large market-town

with a princely court grafted on to it. Monasteries were converted to other uses, particularly after 1779; schools in each *quartiere* taught a basic free education to all. New chairs of jurisprudence, medicine and agronomy were established and the libraries enriched; and public gardens were opened at S Gallo and Le Cascine, a Medici park on the north bank of the Arno, west of the city centre. Among public health works, drainage was reordered and street paving continued, both funded by general taxation, while Piazza S Marco took its present form with a new church façade. Further modernization took place in the older palaces, a continuing reaction against the severity of medieval stonework.

In 1799 Napoleon invaded Tuscany, and the French occupied Florence until 1814. The administration was reordered on French lines, but all important decisions were taken in Paris. The 1810 census recorded a population of 73,000. Florence's municipal government in the Palazzo Vecchio took responsibility for all public works, schools and hospitals, and the city walls and bridges were restored. In 1808 Napoleon began to suppress the monasteries, resulting in many more buildings becoming available for new uses; some were converted into schools, hospitals or barracks, while others were sold. Grandiose renewal projects were prepared, chiefly by Giuseppe del Rosso (1760–1831), but few were executed, being far too ambitious for such a small city. The first large factory was built in 1810, while Elisa Bonaparte, Grand Duchess of Tuscany, indulged in further sumptuous works at the Palazzo Pitti.

In 1814 the house of Habsburg–Lorraine was restored to power in Florence and Tuscany; however the reign of Ferdinand III (*reg* 1814–24) did not reverse Napoleon's achievements, nor did that of his successor, Leopold II (*reg* 1824–59). In the latter period more public works were begun, some streets were widened and others cut. Via Larga was extended to the city walls, Via XXVII Aprile formed and Piazza dell'Indipendenza laid out. Much of the northern zone was developed, and two new iron bridges spanned the Arno, both outside the line of the city walls. Via de' Calzaiuoli was finally widened in the 1840s, after centuries of debate, to become the chief retail street of the city. The railway to Pisa was planned in 1838, the second in Italy; it was completed in 1848, the year in which the Rome–Pistoia line was terminated in Florence at a new station behind S Maria Novella.

In the mid-19th century the population increased from 81,000 in 1844 to 113,000 by 1859. New development took three principal forms: the filling-in of courtyards in the old centre; the construction of additional storeys on existing buildings; and the spread of new projects into undeveloped zones within the city walls. The latter included Barbano, centred on a new square, and Le Cascine. The northern part of the city contained major institutions such as hospitals and university buildings, while to the east, beyond Santa Croce, there were barracks and prisons. Architecture was dominated by historicism, and most new buildings were classical in style.

After the plebiscite of 1860, Tuscany became part of the new Kingdom of Italy, and a large programme of road works took place in Florence, partly to improve access to the station; thus Via Panzani, Via Cerretani and Via

Tornabuoni were widened. Santa Croce was completed with a new Gothic Revival façade by Niccola Matas in 1857–63, while the cathedral's façade was completed in 1887 by Emilio De Fabris. From 1865 to 1870 Florence was the capital of Italy; its population rapidly increased, only to fall again when the capital moved permanently to Rome. A plan for the city's growth was prepared by GIUSEPPE POGGI in 1864–77. It included new zones at Maglio and Mattonaia, and the scale of the proposals involved demolition of the city walls to facilitate expansion beyond; the city limits were thus extended much further. Poggi also designed Piazzale Michelangelo (1873), below S Miniato al Monte. With the destruction of the walls (1864–9), the city's spread became inevitable, although such zones as the Savonarola district were purely residential. Commuting to the centre became necessary, and in 1865 horse-bus services began.

Two projects of the late 19th century caused extensive destruction within the historic centre: in 1874 houses were cleared for new markets at S Lorenzo, and ten years later the Mercato Vecchio (see fig. 4) was removed and part of the Ghetto demolished to make way for the Piazza della Repubblica on the site of the Roman forum in the centre of the city. In association with these works, the entire zone between Via de' Calzaiuoli and Via Strozzi was rebuilt;

hundreds of medieval buildings were lost, including four churches.

Between 1895 and 1915 the population of Florence increased by 50,000, and 2000 terraced houses were built for the new working classes. A development plan of 1915 allowed the city to spread even further, and much expansion took place to the west (on both sides of the Arno) and to the north-east. Under the Fascist government there were further clearances near Santa Croce, but the chief monuments to the early modern era are the Berta municipal stadium (1932) by PIER LUIGI NERVI and the new S Maria Novella railway station (1935) by GIOVANNI MICHELUCCI and others. Industrial development was concentrated at Rifredi, north of the city. Much damage was inflicted in the German retreat of 1944, notably adjacent to the Ponte Vecchio; all other bridges were destroyed and later rebuilt.

Development after World War II spread in all directions on the plain, making Florence virtually contiguous with Prato. During the 20th century there was a progressive dilution of the identity of the city, which survived only in some quarters within the 1333 wall-line. Further material damage to the medieval and Renaissance heritage of Florence was experienced in 1966, when the River Arno flooded, and in 1993 when a bomb exploded in the Via dei Georgofili just to the west of the Uffizi, damaging the

4. Florence, Mercato Vecchio before its removal in the mid-1880s to form the Piazza della Repubblica, showing the 16th-century Loggia del Pesce by Giorgio Vasari (left); from a photograph by Gaetano Baccani, c. 1886 (Florence, Museo di Firenze com'era)

Uffizi itself, the Corridoio Vasariano, Palazzo Vecchio, Accademia Economica Agraria dei Georgofili and the deconsecrated church of S Stefano as well as several works of art. In both cases restoration work was undertaken with international support.

BIBLIOGRAPHY
F. L. del Migliore: *Firenze città nobilissima illustrata* (Florence, 1684)
E. Mazzanti and others: *Studi storici sul centro di Firenze* (Florence, 1889)
U. Pesci: *Firenze capitale, 1865–1870* (Florence, 1904)
G. Conti: *Firenze dai Medici ai Lorena: Storia, cronaca aneddotica, costumi* (Florence, 1909)
A. Mori and G. Boffito: *Firenze nelle vedute e nelle piante: Studio storico, topografico, cartografico* (Florence, 1926)
Stradario storico e amministrativo della città e del comune di Firenze (Florence, 1929)
W. Paatz and E. Paatz: *Kirchen* (1940–54)
M. Lopes Pegna: *Firenze dalle origini al medioevo* (Florence, 1962)
E. Detti: *Firenze scomparsa* (Florence, 1970)
M. Bucci and R. Bencini: *Palazzi di Firenze*, 4 vols (Florence, 1971–3)
L. Ginori Lisci: *I palazzi di Firenze nella storia e nell'arte* (Florence, 1972)
F. Borsi: *Firenze del cinquecento* (Rome, 1974)
A. Busignani and R. Bencini: *Le chiese di Firenze* (Florence, 1974–)
L. Benevolo: *Storia della città* (Rome and Bari, 1976)
J. R. Hale: *Florence and the Medici: The Pattern of Control* (London and New York, 1977)
La città del Brunelleschi (Florence, 1979)
G. Fanelli: *Firenze: La città nella storia d'Italia* (Rome and Bari, 1980) [comprehensive and well illustrated]

For further bibliography see §IV below.

RICHARD J. GOY

II. Art life and organization.

1. Before *c.* 1530. 2. *c.* 1530–*c.* 1800. 3. After *c.* 1800.

1. BEFORE *c.* 1530.

(i) Before *c.* 1400. (ii) *c.* 1400–*c.* 1530.

(i) Before c. *1400.* The art of Florence developed from the earliest distinctive Tuscan art, which was produced in the 13th century in Pisa and Lucca. The sculptor Nicola Pisano (i) demonstrated an understanding of Classical forms in the mid-13th century, and his son Giovanni Pisano carried into the Tuscan vernacular the latest developments of Gothic sculpture, creating figures of unprecedented naturalism. The sculptor's attention to the humanity of the figure can also be seen in the work of Pisan painters of the 12th and 13th centuries, especially that of Giunta Pisano, who clearly influenced other Tuscan artists, including the Master of the Bardi St Francis and Cimabue and, through him, Giotto and the early 14th-century Florentine painters.

The earliest surviving Florentine pictorial project of major proportions is the mosaic decoration of the internal dome of the Baptistery (begun *c.* 1225; see §IV, 1(ii)(b) below). Venetian participation is evident throughout the cycle, but Tuscan artists also seem to have worked on it. They created expressive, lively pictures with an emotional content dissociated from the Byzantine treatment of such themes. COPPO DI MARCOVALDO, the earliest identifiable Florentine artist, may have designed the central figure of Christ; it has a sense of volume also found in the panels depicting the Virgin and Child enthroned painted for the Servite churches in Siena (1261; Siena, S Maria dei Servi) and Orvieto (1265–70; Orvieto, Mus. Opera Duomo), sometimes attributed to Coppo.

Three gabled panels comparable to these panels, with attached decorative surrounds and depicting the Virgin and Child enthroned with other figures, were commissioned for the Florentine churches of S Maria Novella, Santa Trinita and Ognissanti in the late 13th and early 14th centuries. The panels show the development of naturalistic space and form in Florentine art, and while they are often called altarpieces, their use in the churches remains in question. The contract, signed by Duccio in 1285, for the panel for S Maria Novella, now known as the Rucellai *Madonna* (Florence, Uffizi), survives (see DUCCIO, §I, 2(i) and fig. 1). The term—'tavola'—used in the document for the work does not help to define its use, however, since from antiquity the word meant simply 'painted panel'; only later in the 14th century can it be shown to mean altarpiece. Neither does the contract record the panel's intended position. While such panels may have hung above altars or have decorated church walls, the evidence shows them only at the top of rood screens, for example the panel of the Virgin depicted in the fresco of the *Verification of the Stigmata* in the cycle of the *Life of St Francis* in the Upper Church at Assisi. In Duccio's Rucellai *Madonna*, and in the *Madonna and Child* (Florence, Uffizi) by CIMABUE, the Byzantine schema of depicting light on drapery with a network of gilded lines is retained. Giotto's treatment of light and form, however, was probably derived from the frescoes of Pietro Cavallini that he could have seen while working in Rome and from his observation of Gothic sculpture, including that of Arnolfo di Cambio, who carved figures for the façade of Florence Cathedral (*c.* 1300; now mainly Florence, Mus. Opera Duomo). In Giotto's narrative wall paintings, especially the frescoes (*c.* 1320) commissioned by the powerful banking families of the BARDI and Peruzzi for their chapels in Santa Croce, figures painted with dimension and monumentality are given dramatic expression. They exist within a naturalistic space, itself conceived with an awareness of the pattern created by forms across the surface of a picture (see GIOTTO, §I, 3(ii) and figs 7 and 8).

An approach similar to Giotto's is evident in the work of such contemporary painters as BERNARDO DADDI and the ST CECILIA MASTER (see MASTERS, ANONYMOUS, AND MONOGRAMMISTS, §I). These artists established the major preoccupations of Florentine painters in the centuries to come. Their attention to naturalism was encouraged by the subjects commissioned in the 14th century for churches of the Franciscan and Dominican orders, including Santa Croce and S Maria Novella. Depictions of people, places and events of only a few generations earlier, together with accessible representations of familiar stories, were commissioned for the large churches built for preaching to the laity of the expanding towns. While some scenes were based on traditional compositions, others, especially those concerning the orders' founders and early saints, had no precedent and gave artists scope for invention.

From the 13th century in churches throughout Florence, as in other Tuscan cities, there was an increased demand for religious panel painting, especially for the decoration of altars. The reasons for the emergence of the altarpiece are not clear; from the first decades of the 14th century, however, elaborate, multi-panelled structures with

5. Florence, Orsanmichele, relief attributed to Nanni di Banco: *Sculptors at Work*, marble, early 15th century

complicated carved wooden frames were produced by the most innovative Tuscan painters and woodworkers, directly influencing Florentine painting until the mid-15th century. Contracts show that clients often had a woodwork shape in mind when they employed a painter, and that they discussed with painters the holy figures to be depicted in the main panels of the work. The subject-matter of the narrative scenes, called 'stories' in the documents, that were to appear in the predella panels, is rarely mentioned in contracts and may have been left to the discretion of the painter.

Many of the earliest altarpieces for Florentine churches were made by artists from Florence's arch-rival, Siena; political differences did not prevent patrons in either city from employing painters from the other for major commissions. The Sienese artist Ugolino di Nerio, for example, was commissioned in the 1320s to paint a large work for the high altar of Santa Croce; it may have been the earliest polyptych produced for a Florentine altar. The guilds, presumably aware of the beneficial stimulation of outside talent, made it easy for foreign artists to work in Florence. Sculptors belonged to their own guild, which had minor status; by 1316, painters were members of the major Arte dei Medici e Speziali. Guilds themselves became important patrons of art (*see* GUILD, §3). From the early 14th century certain major guilds undertook the upkeep and embellishment of particular religious buildings, and all the guilds were involved in the restoration and decoration of Orsanmichele (see fig. 5; *see also* §IV, 2 below).

The taste for naturalism developed by the earliest Florentine painters waned in the third quarter of the 14th century, possibly in response to the plague in mid-century, and important commissions, such as the Strozzi Altarpiece (*c.* 1354–7) for S Maria Novella, were given to Andrea di Cione; in his work, and that of his brothers, figures were more iconic and space was more compressed than in earlier pictures (for further discussion and illustration *see* CIONE, (1)).

(ii) c. 1400–c. 1530. A renewed interest in Classical sources and naturalistic form emerged in the late 14th century and the early 15th. POGGIO BRACCIOLINI and a small group of Florentine humanists discovered in monasteries works by Cicero and other Classical authors that had been ignored for centuries (*see* HUMANISM, §1), and they developed a new script and style of book decoration specifically for use in reproducing Classical texts. The funding of large public projects by the civic authorities gave particular scope to sculptors, and in the first few decades of the 15th century DONATELLO, Lorenzo Ghiberti (*see* GHIBERTI, (1)) and NANNI DI BANCO created figures for the façades of the cathedral, the Loggia della Signoria (now Loggia dei Lanzi), Orsanmichele and the Baptistery that combine Classical simplicity and monumentality of form with naturalistic pose and modelling (see figs 15 and 17 below). The sculpture, much of which was just above street level, influenced painters, architects and other artists. Gentile da Fabriano cultivated a sumptuous naturalism, manifested in Florence in the altarpiece of the *Adoration of the Magi* (1423; Florence, Uffizi), painted for Palla Strozzi (*see* GENTILE DA FABRIANO, fig. 3; *see also* STROZZI, (1)). MASACCIO reanimated Giotto's monumental figures with a dramatic realism and, employing mathematical perspective, placed them in a convincing pictorial space. Filippo Brunelleschi created a new, classical architectural style (*see* §I, 3 above); LEON BATTISTA ALBERTI codified the artists' achievements in his theoretical treatise *De pictura* (1435); and Florence was established as the foremost centre of Renaissance culture in the 15th century.

Linear perspective, first demonstrated by Brunelleschi, revolutionized the treatment of space, and Florentine artists made creative use of the new technique. In the second third of the 15th century, Florentine artists of note—Lorenzo Ghiberti, Fra Angelico, Filippo Lippi, Paolo Uccello, Luca della Robbia, Domenico Veneziano and Andrea del Castagno—explored its possibilities, setting their figures in an environment that seemed to extend the real space of the viewer. In the final third of the century such artists as Antonio Pollaiuolo and Piero Pollaiuolo, Perugino, Sandro Botticelli, Filippino Lippi and Domenico Ghirlandaio created compositions in which elegant figures inhabited a space often defined by Classical monuments and physically bound on both frescoes and panels by decorative surrounds based on antique forms. These surrounds were developed in the mid-15th century as a new form of altarpiece structure reflecting the widespread interest in the Antique (*see* FRAME, §II). Gothic woodwork forms were eschewed in favour of Classical architectural elements. The new altarpieces were usually smaller than polyptychs and were composed of a rectilinear main panel over a predella; some were topped by pieces in the shape of a half tondo, but many surrounds consisted only of a simple architrave supported by columns. It is likely that sculptor-woodworkers were as influential as painters and their clients in developing the form. The earliest surviving antique-style carved surround is that made around 1432 for Fra Angelico's *Annunciation* altarpiece for S Domenico, Cortona (Cortona, Mus. Dioc.); an earlier painted surround can be seen in Masaccio's '*Trinity*' fresco (*c.* 1427) in S Maria Novella.

While there was no special artists' quarter in Florence, artistic methods were handed down in workshops in which master artists trained apprentices, who, together with other assistants, aided the master with projects. A clear account of workshop techniques and modes of operation is given in *Il libro dell'arte* (*c.* 1390) by CENNINO CENNINI. Since Cennini was a pupil of Agnolo Gaddi, who was the son of Giotto's assistant Taddeo Gaddi, the handbook can be taken to report the methods used in Giotto's shop and is a measure of the persistence of the tradition. The methods Cennini described, and the recipes he recorded, were employed into the 16th century. Workshop organization varied, however. The size of a shop depended on the personality and business requirements of individual artists, and the number of people employed might depend on the number and type of projects undertaken. Painting frescoes, for example, often required more assistance than the production of panels or altarpieces, and master painters were commonly required to transfer themselves, their assistants and their materials to a work site, often while retaining the main workshop in Florence.

The workshop tradition might have engendered stultified, conservative art, but in Florence that was not the case. The city's artists maintained a high degree of originality, and clients seem to have valued innovation. Giorgio Vasari (*see* VASARI, (1)) notes that the spirit of competition was important in the development of the best Florentine artists; in his account of the life of Perugino, he records that painters were spurred to creativity by a combination of critical attention, their natural industry and their eagerness for glory and honour. Originality is evident not only in style but also in the innovative use of materials, such as Luca della Robbia's use of glazed terracotta for sculpture, and in the organization of shops that offered diverse services. The workshop of ANDREA DEL VERROCCHIO, for example, produced sculpture in stone, bronze, silver and terracotta as well as panel paintings, and the absence of paintings that can be securely attributed to him suggests that he left an important part of the execution of panels to assistants. The POLLAIUOLO brothers were famous into the 16th century as masters of the skill most admired in Florence—design—and they were particularly praised for

it by Benvenuto Cellini. Their workshop produced sculpture, goldsmiths' work and painting in all media, as well as designs for embroidery, drawings and at least one print clearly for the use of other artists.

While Florentine workshops were usually competitive and individualistic, some projects required collaboration, and some artists specialized in cooperative work. MICHELOZZO DI BARTOLOMEO advised Ghiberti on bronze-casting and established a formal partnership with Donatello for the production of marble sculpture before becoming the chief architect of the Medici family. MASOLINO and Masaccio worked together on the frescoes in the Brancacci Chapel in S Maria del Carmine (*c.* 1427; see fig. 6), imaginatively unifying their different styles. Documents record that the projects for the sculptural decoration for the façades of the cathedral and the newly constructed Loggia della Signoria involved the joint efforts of painters, who designed the statues and reliefs, and sculptors, who realized the plans in stone. The chapel of the Cardinal of Portugal (second half of 15th century) in S Miniato al Monte is the supreme example of a successful collaboration by a large group of artists (see fig. 7; *see also* §IV, 7 below).

By the mid-15th century, the dominant mode of patronage had changed from corporate to personal, largely through the Medici family's expression of its power and immense wealth through patronage of the arts. The extent of Cosimo de' Medici's commissions, for example at S

6. Florence, S Maria del Carmine, Brancacci Chapel, fresco by Masaccio: *St Peter Healing with his Shadow*, c. 1427

7. Florence, S Miniato al Monte, Cardinal of Portugal's Chapel, second half of the 15th century

Lorenzo and S Marco, rivalled that of even the richest guilds (*see* MEDICI, DE', (2)). His son Piero commissioned works in painting and sculpture (*see* MEDICI, DE', (3)), and both men were responsible for the establishment of Florence as a centre of manuscript illumination (*see* VESPASIANO DA BISTICCI). Other patrons, mainly Medici supporters, followed suit on a smaller scale; Giovanni Rucellai employed Alberti to design his palace (begun *c.* 1453), family chapel (1464–7) in S Pancrazio and the façade (*c.* 1458–70) of S Maria Novella (see fig. 20 below). In the last quarter of the 15th century, Lorenzo the Magnificent styled himself more overtly as a prince, and his control of artistic life was unprecedented (*see* MEDICI, DE', (5)), although he acted personally as a collector rather than a commissioner of new work. The frescoes (*c.* 1478) by Domenico Ghirlandaio of scenes from the *Life of St Francis* in the Sassetti Chapel in Santa Trinita illustrate the new conditions; included among a large number of prominent portraits of the family is one showing Lorenzo himself standing next to FRANCESCO SASSETTI, manager of the Medici banking empire from 1463 (*see* ITALY, §XII, 4 and fig. 103).

The work of Florentine artists was highly regarded, and this is reflected in the payment they received for their work. Between 1400 and 1500 most painters trained in Florence seem to have been able to command higher fees than artists trained elsewhere. Lorenzo was thus able to use them as tools in his diplomacy, for example in securing a cardinalcy for his son Giovanni de' Medici, the future Pope Leo X. By the early 16th century, however, while Florentine artists continued to be in demand, those trained in other cities were equally sought after and well paid.

At the end of the 15th century, turbulent economic, political and social conditions and the preaching of GIROLAMO SAVONAROLA severely affected private patronage. The expulsion of the Medici family in 1494 led to the re-establishment of the republic, which initiated projects promoting the new regime, centred on the Palazzo della Signoria (now Palazzo Vecchio; *see* §IV, 8 below). Michelangelo was commissioned in 1501 to complete the colossal statue of *David* (Florence, Accad.), a traditional symbol of Florentine liberty (*see* MICHELANGELO, §I, 3; *see also* ITALY, fig. 54). Andrea Sansovino and Fra Bartolommeo were also hired, as were Leonardo and Michelangelo, who were commissioned to produce large frescoes of the *Battle of Anghiari* and the *Battle of Cascina* respectively. The frescoes (destr.) were never completed, but the cartoons of both were widely admired and strongly influenced contemporary Florentines. In the first decade of the 16th century, private patronage was revived on a more pious, sober note, as seen in the series of Madonnas painted by the newly arrived Umbrian artist, Raphael, and in the altarpieces of Fra Bartolommeo and ANDREA DEL SARTO. In the work of these artists extraneous details were eliminated, and monumental figures were represented in calm, balanced compositions that, together with contemporary achievements in Rome, came to be seen as defining a kind of classical perfection. With the return of the Medici in 1512, the sculptural and architectural embellishment of S Lorenzo was revived, principally under Michelangelo. At the same time, younger Florentine painters, chiefly ROSSO FIORENTINO and PONTORMO, began to develop particular aspects of High Renaissance style, contributing to the eclectic variety of styles now known as Mannerism.

BIBLIOGRAPHY

C. Cennini: *Il libro dell'arte* (MS.; *c.* 1390); trans. and notes by D. V. Thompson jr (New Haven, 1933/*R* New York, 1960)

L. B. Alberti: *De pictura* (MS.; 1435); ed. G. Papini (Lanciano, 1913)

N. di Bicci: *Le ricordanze* (MSS; 1453–75); ed. B. Santi (Pisa, 1976)

G. Vasari: *Vite* (1550, rev. 2/1568); ed. G. Milanesi (1878–85)

B. Cellini: *Trattato dell'oreficeria* and *Trattato della scultura* (MSS; begun 1565); ed. G. Milanesi (Florence, 1857)

P. Bacci: *Documenti toscani per la storia dell'arte*, ii (Florence, 1912)

H. Lerner-Lehmkuhl: *Zur Struktur und Geschichte des florentinischen Kunstmarktes im 15. Jahrhundert* (diss., U. Munich, 1936)

M. Wackernagel: *Der Lebensraum des Künstlers in der florentinischen Renaissance* (Leipzig, 1938; Eng. trans., Princeton, 1981)

R. Lopez: 'Hard Times and Investment in Culture', *The Renaissance: A Symposium*, ed. W. Ferguson (New York, 1953)

E. H. Gombrich: 'The Early Medici as Patrons of Art', *Italian Renaissance Studies*, ed. E. F. Jacob (London, 1960)

H. Hager: *Die Anfänge des italienischen Altarbildes: Untersuchungen zur Entstehungsgeschichte des toskanischen Hochaltarretabels* (Munich, 1962)

C. Gardner von Teuffel: *Studies of the Tuscan Altarpiece in the Fourteenth and Early Fifteenth Centuries* (diss., U. London, Courtauld Inst., 1974)

A. Thomas: *The Workshop Procedure of Fifteenth-century Florentine Artists* (diss., U. London, Courtauld Inst., 1976)

C. Gardner von Teuffel: 'The Buttressed Altarpiece: A Forgotten Aspect of Tuscan Fourteenth-century Altarpiece Design', *Jb. Berlin. Mus.*, xxi (1979), pp. 21–65

E. Skaug: 'Punch-marks—What Are they Worth? Problems of Tuscan Workshop Interrelationships in the Mid-fourteenth Century: The Ovile Master and Giovanni da Milano', *La pittura nel XIV e XV secolo. Il contributo dell'analisi tecnica alla storia dell'arte. Atti del XXIV congresso internazionale di storia dell'arte: Bologna, 1982*, iii, pp. 253–82

P. Burke: *The Italian Renaissance: Culture and Society in Italy* (Princeton, 1986)

F. W. Kent and P. Simons, eds: *Patronage, Art and Society in Renaissance Italy* (Oxford, 1987)
C. Hope: 'Altarpieces and the Requirements of Patrons', *Christianity and the Renaissance: Images and Religious Imagination in the Quattrocento*, ed. T. Verdon and J. Henderson (Syracuse, 1990)
B. Kempers: *Painting, Power and Patronage: The Rise of the Professional Artist in the Italian Renaissance* (London, 1992)
R. A. Goldthwaite: *Wealth and the Demand for Art in Italy* (London, 1993)
E. Borsook and F. Superbi Gioffredi: *Italian Altarpieces, 1250–1550: Function and Design* (Oxford, 1994)
M. Hollingsworth: *Patronage in Renaissance Italy* (London, 1994)
M. O'Malley: *The Business of Art: Contracts and Payment Documents for 14th- and 15th-century Altarpieces and Frescoes* (diss., U. London, 1994)
Painting and Illumination in Early Renaissance Florence, 1300–1450 (exh. cat., New York, Met., 1995)

MICHELLE O'MALLEY, CHRISTOPHER POKE

2. *c.* 1530–*c.* 1800.

(i) *c. 1530–c. 1600.* The events that led to the siege of 1529–30 and Alessandro de' Medici's appointment as Duke of Florence (*see* §I, 5 above) brought about a profound political, economic and cultural crisis in the city. Many emigrated, including Michelangelo in 1534, and the city's intellectual and artistic circles were dispersed. Alessandro was too concerned with securing his political position to occupy himself with matters of culture, but his successor, Cosimo I, introduced policies to promote the cultural and artistic prestige of Florence and Tuscany that soon gained considerable public support (*see* MEDICI, DE', (14)). The political and cultural organizations that emerged during this period, including the Accademia Fiorentina (founded 1542) and the Accademia del Disegno (founded 1563; *see* §V, 1 below), were to survive until the end of the Medici era. The celebrations in June 1539 for the marriage of Cosimo I and Eleonora, daughter of Pedro de Toledo, Viceroy of Naples (1484–1553), were evidence of improving political stability in Florence.

The success of Medici propaganda was manifested by the return (1553) of emigré writers, such as BENEDETTO VARCHI, and artists, including BACCIO BANDINELLI, BENVENUTO CELLINI (1545), BARTOLOMEO AMMANATI and Giorgio Vasari (*see* VASARI, (1)). The members of the Accademia Fiorentina, especially Varchi, were responsible for the elaboration of theories that were to have great influence on the development of linguistics, literature and visual arts in Florence and throughout Tuscany. The most active individual in the implementation of Medici cultural policy, however, was Vasari, who was appointed court architect and painter in 1554. In the next two decades he consolidated his position through important architectural projects, including the reconstruction and decoration of the Palazzo Vecchio into a representative residence for the head of state and the artistic supervision of the decorative work at the wedding in 1565 of the future Francesco I and Joanna of Austria (1547–78).

Medici propaganda achieved its triumphs not only as a result of its military successes but also through its many public foundations. In addition to the Accademia Fiorentina and Accademia del Disegno, various court manufacturing establishments were founded to produce, for example, tapestries (the Arazzeria Medicea, 1554; *see* §III, 3 below) and crystal glass (1569), and a foundry for light castings was modernized in 1556. The Biblioteca Laurenziana was opened to the public in 1571, and Cosimo established the basis of the Medici museum, creating an antiquities collection (1561–2) in the Palazzo Pitti that was independent of the rich collections at the Guardaroba in the Palazzo Vecchio; he also anticipated the building of the gallery at the Uffizi (*see* ITALY, §XIV). Artists active during the early part of his reign included JACOPO DA PONTORMO, whose figurative compositions, especially the *Last Judgement* (1546–56; destr. 1742) in the choir of S Lorenzo, were inspired by the work of Michelangelo, and AGNOLO BRONZINO, who was court portrait painter to Cosimo I (see fig. 8) and, with Vasari, was one of the founders of the Accademia del Disegno.

The reign of Francesco I (*reg* 1574–87; *see* MEDICI, DE', (16)) was marked by the development of goldsmithing, porcelain (*see* §III, 1 below) and crystal glass manufacture, for which Bernardo Buontalenti built the Casino de' Medici (1574; now the Palazzo della Corte d'Appello) in Piazza S Marco. Francesco's extensive collection of antiques, small bronzes, natural objects and watercolours depicting nature was originally housed at the *studiolo* (1570–73) in the Palazzo Vecchio (*see* STUDIOLO, fig. 2) and then in the Tribuna (*c.* 1580), an octagonal rotunda in the Uffizi. Numerous travellers, including Michel de Montaigne (1533–92), who visited in 1580, marvelled at the splendid gardens (1573–80; destr.) designed by Buontalenti for the Medici villa at Pratolino. The spectacles staged in the Teatro Mediceo, built in 1586 by Buontalenti on the top floor of the Uffizi, were influential in the development of opera. At the end of Francesco's reign Giambologna produced a bronze equestrian statue of *Grand Duke Cosimo I* (1587–93), which was placed in the Piazza della Signoria outside the Palazzo Vecchio (*see* GIAMBOLOGNA,

8. *Cosimo I in Armour* by Agnolo Bronzino, oil on canvas, 710×570 mm, 1543 (Florence, Galleria degli Uffizi)

fig. 6); it was replicated shortly afterwards in a version of *Francesco I* (1608) in Piazza SS Annunziata.

The Medici court was not the only stimulus in Florentine culture, however. Various brotherhoods and associations, both religious and lay, were highly active, and many individuals also collected and commissioned works of art. BERNARDO VECCHIETTI, for example, amassed an interesting collection after 1552 at his villa, Il Riposo, near Florence. This included drawings, cartoons and many models by Giambologna, whom Vecchietti sponsored between 1552 and 1566. He also organized an artists' workshop to provide for his own commissions. Niccolò Gaddi created a Galleria in which, as well as his collection of Italian and Dutch landscape drawings and watercolours of nature studies by JACOPO LIGOZZI, there were workshops specializing in the coloured stone used in the decoration of his ancestral chapel (1575–6) in S Maria Novella (*see* GADDI (ii), (2)). Il Riposo and the Galleria were meeting-places for art lovers and tourists alike.

The Medici court's role as the impetus for the city's cultural life was consolidated during the reign of Ferdinando I (*see* MEDICI, DE', (17)). Under a decree of 1588, all the court workshops were transferred to the Uffizi building and joined together in one uniform institution as the Galleria dei Lavori. In 1604 a workshop later known as the Opificio delle Pietre Dure (*see* §III, 2(i) below and ITALY, §VI, 3) was created within the framework of the Galleria, partly to meet the building requirements of the Cappella dei Principi in S Lorenzo (*see* §IV, 5 below), and it achieved international prominence in this craft. The studios of Giambologna and Jacques Bylivert were associated with the Galleria. Meanwhile, the sumptuous banquets that took place in 1600 during the marriage celebrations of Marie de' Medici and Henry IV, King of France, surpassed all the Medici's previous spectacles.

(ii) c. 1600–c. 1800. Ferdinando's collection contained two early paintings by Caravaggio of *Medusa* and *Bacchus* (both Florence, Uffizi), of which the former was given by Cardinal Francesco Maria del Monte in 1608. The Florentine artistic community, however, did not react to this stylistic innovation until considerably later, during the rule of Cosimo II (*reg* 1609–21; *see* MEDICI, DE', (19)); examples include *Still-life* (1625; Florence, Pitti) by JACOPO DA EMPOLI and Orazio Riminaldi's *Amore vincitore* (?first half of the 1620s; Florence, Pitti). The fashion for naturalistic painting that predominated at court was demonstrated by the visits of two painters from the school of Caravaggio: Giovanni Battista Caracciolo in 1617 and Gerrit van Honthorst *c.* 1620. Cosimo also admired naturalistic landscape painting, and Filippo Napoletano and Cornelis van Poelenburch worked at his court. At the same time, however, Jacques Callot, who was working in Florence between 1611–12 and 1621, represented the tradition of late Mannerism. Cardinal Giovanni Carlo de' Medici encouraged Salvator Rosa to work in Florence, where he established the Accademia dei Percossi, a lively meeting-place for poets, scientists and artists; both Rosa and Lorenzo Lippi were poets as well as painters, with a shared love of the burlesque.

The Baroque was first introduced at the court of Ferdinando II (*see* MEDICI, DE', (22)) when Cortona was commissioned in 1637 to decorate the state apartments at the Palazzo Pitti (*see* CORTONA, PIETRO DA, fig. 2; *see also* §IV, 9(ii) below), although only part of his scheme was implemented, with the help of CIRO FERRI. The Florentine artistic establishment, steeped in its own traditions, reacted with scepticism to the Roman innovations. This attitude was reflected in the endeavours of Carlo Roberto Dati (1619–76) and Giovanni Battista Brocchi, in 1646 and 1667 respectively, to continue Vasari's *Vite* with the cooperation of the Accademia del Disegno. The collections made by Cardinal Leopoldo de' Medici (*see* MEDICI, DE', (25)) and FILIPPO BALDINUCCI, who implemented the programme of the great Medici museum, were also intended to document Tuscan hegemony in contemporary culture.

This overtly apologetic concept of art history was modified under the influence of Cosimo III's universalistic ideas (*see* MEDICI, DE', (27)). Travels around Italy (especially Lombardy) in 1664 and to Germany, the Netherlands, France, England and Spain in 1667–9 introduced Cosimo and members of the family to other schools of art, and their purchases during their travels and after their return, particularly of Dutch and German paintings, further enriched the Medici museum. Cosimo's broader cultural policy was also demonstrated by the establishment of a Roman branch of the Accademia del Disegno in the Palazzo Madama (1673–86). Although this institution was short-lived, it played a major role in the artistic blossoming under the last Medici, with many of its pupils winning important posts in the Florentine court. GIOVANNI BATTISTA FOGGINI, for example, was appointed to two positions that had gained some importance during the reign of Ferdinando II, becoming first court sculptor (after 1687; see fig. 9) and court architect (1694). He supervised more than 100 artists at the Galleria dei Lavori, and his small bronzes were much sought after by collectors (*see* STATUETTE, §III). MASSIMILIANO SOLDANI took over the supervision of the Zecca, the grand-ducal mint, in 1682 and transformed it into a first-rate centre for medallion-making; Anton Domenico Gabbiani was known for his painterly decorative arts; and Livio Mehus was awarded the honorary title of Aiutante di Camera.

Other members of the Medici family were also notable patrons, including Francesco Maria de' Medici (1660–1711), who commissioned the Villa di Lappeggi (1700), near Grassina, and Grand Prince Ferdinando de' Medici (*see* MEDICI, DE, (28)), who financed many of the exhibitions held by the Accademia in the cloisters of SS Annunziata between 1680 and 1713. He also invited painters from Venice (e.g. Marco Ricci and Sebastiano Ricci) and Bologna (e.g. Giuseppe Maria Crespi). Significant initiatives were taken by Girolamo Ticciati, who wrote the first history of the Accademia del Disegno (1739); Francesco Maria Niccolò Gabburri, patron, author of *Le vite de pittori* (1719–41; Florence, Bib. N. Cent.) and Provveditore of the Accademia (1730–40); and Marchese Carlo Ginori (1702–57), who established a porcelain factory at Doccia in 1737. After the death of Cosimo III in 1723, however, the Medici's artistic circles disintegrated. The final, splendid gesture of the declining dynasty was in 1743, when the Medici art collection was bequeathed to

9. *Cardinal Leopoldo de' Medici* by Giovanni Battista Foggini, marble, h. 1.62 m, 1697 (Florence, Galleria degli Uffizi)

the city by Anna Maria Luisa de' Medici, Electress Palatine (*see* MEDICI, DE', (29)).

The creation of the Accademia di Belle Arti in 1784 and Luigi Lanzi's modernization of the Medici museum at the Uffizi from 1780 are evidence of renewed cultural life in Florence during the reign of Grand Duke Leopold (*see* HABSBURG-LORRAINE, (1)). Some of his overtly radical decisions, however, were responsible for great losses to the Tuscan cultural tradition, such as the recommendation issued in 1785 to remove from SS Annunziata all the offerings that had been gathered there over many centuries. As Constantino Bettini witnessed, 'there was a massacre of all the votive offerings, whether of wood, plaster or armour, which were stripped off the walls and thrown down. . .soon forming a huge, shapeless heap of heads, legs, arms and bodies'.

BIBLIOGRAPHY

K. Lenkheit: *Florentinische Barockplastik: Die Kunst am Hofe der letzten Medici, 1670–1743* (Munich, 1962)
J. Pope-Hennessy: *Italian High Renaissance and Baroque Sculpture* (London, 1963, rev. 3/1986)
E. Borsook: 'Art and Politics at the Medici Court: I. The Funeral of Cosimo de' Medici', *Mitt. Ksthist. Inst. Florenz*, xii (1965), pp. 31–54
L. Berti: *Il principe dello studiolo: Francesco I e la fine del rinascimento fiorentino* (Florence, 1967)
W. Prinz: *Die Sammlung der Selbstbildnisse in der Uffizien* (Berlin, 1971)
S. Rudolph: 'Mecenati a Firenze tra sei e settecento', *A. Illus.*, v (1972), pp. 228–37; vi (1973), pp. 213–28; vii (1974), pp. 279–98
The Twilight of the Medici: Late Baroque Art in Florence, 1670–1743 (exh. cat., ed. S. F. Rossen; Detroit, MI, Inst. A.; Florence, Pitti; 1974)
Omaggio a Leopoldo de' Medici (exh. cat., ed. A. Forlani Tempesti, A. M. Petrioli Tofani and S. Meloni Trkulja; Florence, Uffizi, 1975)
M. D. Davis: 'La galleria di sculture antiche di Cosimo I a Palazzo Pitti', *Le arti del principato mediceo* (Florence, 1980), pp. 31–54
C. W. Fock: 'Francesco I e Ferdinando I: I mecenati di pietre dure', *Le arti del principato mediceo* (Florence, 1980), pp. 317–63
Il primato del disegno (exh. cat., Florence, Pal. Strozzi, 1980)
Theater Art of the Medici (exh. cat. by A. R. Blumenthal, Hannover, NH, Dartmouth Coll., Hopkins Cent. A.G., 1980)
K. Langedijk: *The Portraits of the Medici, 15th–18th Centuries*, 3 vols (Florence, 1981–7)
F. Haskell and N. Penny: *Taste and the Antique: The Lure of Classical Sculpture, 1500–1900* (New Haven and London, 1982)
D. Heikamp: 'La galleria degli Uffizi descritta e disegnata', *Uffizi: Quattro secoli di una galleria. Atti del convegno internazionale di studi: Firenze, 1982*, ii, 461–88
K. Lankheit: *Die Modellsammlung der Porzellanmanufaktur Doccia: Ein Dokument italienischer Barockplastik* (Munich, 1982)
E. L. Goldberg: *Patterns in Late Medici Art Patronage* (Princeton, 1983)
M. Chappell: 'Florentine Baroque Art: Recent Studies and Some New Proposals', *SE Coll. A. Confer. Rev.*, x (1985), pp. 247–58
Il seicento fiorentino: Arte a Firenze da Ferdinando I a Cosimo III, 3 vols (exh. cat., ed. G. Guidi and others; Florence, Pal. Strozzi, 1986–7)
C. Cresti: *La Toscana dei Lorena: Politica del territorio e architettura* (Florence, 1987)
Z. Waźbiński: *L'Accademia medicea del disegno a Firenze nel cinquecento: Idea e istituzione* (Florence, 1987)

Z. WAŹBIŃSKI

3. AFTER *c.* 1800. Under French rule, especially that of Elisa Bonaparte, Grand Duchess of Tuscany (*see* BONAPARTE, (5)), the arts in Florence were dominated by such rigorously Neo-classical artists as PIETRO BENVENUTI (e.g. the *Oath of the Saxons*, 1809–12; Florence, Pitti); Luigi Sabatelli; PASQUALE POCCIANTI; Stefano Ricci (1765–1837); and, briefly, Antonio Canova (e.g. *Venus Emerging from the Bath*, 1804–12; Florence, Pitti). After the restoration of the Habsburgs, however, interest in the art of the Italian Primitives and the early Tuscan Renaissance, inspired by PURISMO, was renewed, especially in the work of LUIGI MUSSINI and Antonio Marini (1788–1861); the cultural debate was carried on in the journal *Antologia* (1821–3), founded by Giovan Pietro Vieusseux (1779–1863). Florence continued to attract cultured international tourism and was the residence of many foreigners, including Ingres from 1820 to 1824, the DEMIDOV family, the painter and art dealer William Blundell Spence, the American sculptors Hiram Powers, Horatio Greenough and Thomas Ball, and the collector Frederick Stibbert (1838–1906). The city's artistic life revolved around the Accademia di Belle Arti, where the teaching, formerly dominated by Neo-classicism, was led by the reformers of historical Romanticism (e.g. GIUSEPPE BEZZUOLI) and naturalism (e.g. LORENZO BARTOLINI and GIOVANNI DUPRÉ). The *Giornale del commercio* and *La Rivista* contained long articles on aesthetics, artists' studios and public works, such as the 28 statues (1837–56) of illustrious Tuscans for the portico of the Uffizi, and the Tribuna di Galileo (1841), designed by Giuseppe Martelli (1792–1876).

The richness and vivacity of artistic life in the mid-19th century were most visible in the antique shops and workshops of restorers, foundrymen, such as Clemente Papi (1802–75), sculptors, including Luigi Giovannozzi (1791–*c.* 1870) and Ottaviano Giovannozzi (*fl* 1820–48) from Settignano, and printers and cabinetmakers, such as Angiolo Barbetti (1803–80) and Luigi Frullini (1839–97). The establishment in 1845 of the Società Promotrice Fiorentina for the assistance of young artists, as an alternative to the Accademia, was an indication of the restlessness that led to the Risorgimento. The MAC-CHIAIOLI painters and their friends, including Giovanni Morelli and Edgar Degas, met at the Caffè Michelangelo. The Alinari and Brogi photographic studios were also established. In 1859 the Concorso Ricasoli was instituted as a competition for paintings and sculpture celebrating the Risorgimento, and the Esposizione Italiana was held in Florence in 1861 to celebrate the achievement of Italian unity (see fig. 10). From 1865 to 1870, when Florence was the capital of Italy, the liveliest cultural centres were the salons of Emilia Peruzzi (1827–1900), wife of the mayor Ubaldino Peruzzi (1822–91), and Fiorella Favard (*d* 1877). The disappointed hopes of the Risorgimento, the withdrawal from public activity of many prominent artists, such as GIOVANNI FATTORI, and the city's grave financial deficit blighted the following years, although the galleries of the Uffizi, Accademia and Bargello (established 1865) were reorganized, and Florence became the capital of the

antiques trade, through the activities of Stefano Bardini and Elia Volpi.

In the later 19th century the city recovered its prestige in the general renewal that came with Art Nouveau and a new impetus in the applied arts (e.g. maiolica by Galileo Chini and the Manifattura Cantagalli; glass by the Polloni, Quentin and De Matteis factories; artistic terracottas by the Manifattura di Signa) and with the presence of Gabriele D'Annunzio and numerous foreigners (e.g. Arnold Böcklin, Adolf von Hildebrand, Maurice Denis, Bernard Berenson and Herbert Horne). This revival was reflected in the review *Il marzocco*, the *Arte e fiori* exhibition (1897) and the later journals *Leonardo* (1903), *La voce* (1908) and Ardengo Soffici's *Lacerba* (1913). The Società Leonardo da Vinci di Scienze, Lettere ed Arti was founded in 1902, and an important exhibition on the Italian portrait was held in 1911. Two years later Filippo Tommaso Marinetti inaugurated the first Futurist exhibition in Florence.

The most important figure in official culture between the World Wars was Ugo Ojetti, who took part in all the initiatives of the Fascist period: the construction of the Palazzo delle Esposizioni (1922), where the annual spring exhibitions of the figurative arts and the craft exhibition (from 1931) were held; the establishment of the Galleria d'Arte Moderna in the Palazzo Pitti (1924); the initiation, in 1933, of the Maggio Musicale Fiorentino (with scenery and costumes by De Chirico); and the establishment of

10. Florence, Esposizione Italiana, 1861, the statue rotunda; pen and watercolour on paper, 280×420 mm (Florence, Uffizi, Gabinetto dei Disegni, Fondo Martelli, no. 5820A)

the Centro Studi sul Rinascimento. The Novecento Toscano movement also began; founded in 1927 in the studio of the painter Gianni Vagnetti (1898–1956), it followed the Novecento Italiano movement, established in Milan in 1922 to promote a return to classical figurative models and Italian cultural traditions.

Initiatives after World War II included the Mostra Biennale dell'Antiquariato and the Gallery of Graphic Art ('Il Bisonte'), which brought to Florence important artists from Italy and abroad. Painters working in Florence included Pietro Annigoni. The flood of 1966 caused grave damage to the city's artistic heritage, and in the next two decades the Centro di Restauro della Soprintendenza sponsored a series of initiatives for the restoration and recovery of works of art. The city also received numerous gifts from contemporary artists, notably the Della Ragione collection and donations by Alberto Magnelli, Corrado Cagli, Mirko and Marino Marini, intended for a museum of contemporary art. Further serious damage was caused by the explosion near the Uffizi in 1993; in addition to structural damage to buildings (see §I, 5 above), a small number of paintings were destroyed and several other works damaged, involving a renewed restoration effort that benefited from the expertise built up in the previous decades.

BIBLIOGRAPHY

P. E. Selvatico: *Dell'arte moderna a Firenze* (Milan, 1843)
W. B. Spence: *The Lions of Florence* (Florence, 1847, rev. 1852)
L'Esposizione Italiana del 1861: Giornale con incisioni e con gli atti ufficiali della commissione reale (1861–2)
J. Ruskin: *Mornings in Florence*, 2 vols (London, 1875–7)
U. Pesci: *Firenze capitale, 1865–1870* (Florence, 1904)
C. L. Dentler: *Famous Foreigners in Florence, 1400–1900* (Florence, 1964)
——: *Famous Americans in Florence* (Florence, 1976)
Gli Alinari: Fotografi a Firenze, 1852–1920 (exh. cat. by W. Settimelli and F. Zevi, Florence, Forte Belvedere, 1977)
L'Accademia di belle arti di Firenze, 1784–1984 (Florence, 1984)
F. Bagatti, G. Manghetti and S. Porto: *Futurismo a Firenze, 1910–1920* (Florence, 1984)
C. Del Bravo: 'Arte della restaurazione', *Le risposte dell'arte* (Florence, 1985), pp. 259–69
E. Spalletti: *Gli anni del Caffè Michelangelo, 1848–1861* (Rome, 1985)
Studi e ricerche di collezionismo e museografia: Firenze, 1820–1920 (Pisa, 1985)
A. Baldinotti and others: *La manifattura di signa* (Florence, 1986)
M. Bossi and L. Tonini, eds: *L'idea di Firenze* (Florence, 1989)
C. Costantini: *Firenze fra le due guerre: La pittura* (Florence, 1990)
M. Pratesi and G. Uzzani: *L'arte italiana del novecento: La Toscana* (Vicenza, 1991)

LIA BERNINI

III. Centre of production.

1. Porcelain. 2. Hardstones. 3. Tapestry.

1. PORCELAIN. A porcelain factory was in operation in the vicinity of the Palazzo Pitti during the reign of Francesco I. According to Vasari's *Vite*, it is believed to have originated *c*. 1565 with experiments by the court architect Bernardo Buontalenti. Production was first mentioned in 1575. The body employed was a soft-paste porcelain not unlike pottery from Iznik in Turkey and it possibly resulted from advice said to have been provided by a Levantine. Only 57 pieces of Medici porcelain have been recorded, and all but three, which are polychrome, are painted in underglaze blue of variable colour and control. Three main types of decoration were employed:

grotesque ornament derived from Italian maiolica, particularly the Raphaelesque type associated with the workshops of the Fontana and Patanazzi families in Urbino (*see* URBINO, §3); motifs borrowed from 15th-century as well as contemporary Chinese porcelains; and Ottoman styles based on 16th-century Iznik pottery. Forms derived from maiolica, metalwares and lapidary work included simple, deep dishes, but more typical were ewers, flasks (e.g. one of 1575–87; Paris, Louvre; *see also* ITALY, fig. 86) and cruets. Factory workmen included Flaminio Fontana (*fl* 1573–8) and Pier Maria da Faenza (*fl* 1580–89). Most pieces are marked with the dome of the cathedral of S Maria del Fiore and the letter F in underglaze blue. Production appears to have ended with Francesco's death (1587), but the presence in Florence in 1589 of the potter Niccolò Sisti (*fl c.* 1577–*c.* 1619) and the record in 1613 of porcelain tokens decorated with the Medici arms indicate continued, unofficial activity.

BIBLIOGRAPHY

Baron Davillier: *Les Origines de la porcelaine en Europe* (Paris, 1882)
G. Liverani: *Catalogo delle porcellane dei Medici* (Faenza, 1936)
J. Lessmann: 'Polychromes Medici-Porzellan', *Pantheon*, xxxiv (1976), pp. 280–87
G. Cora and A. Fanfani: *La porcellana dei Medici* (Milan, 1986)

CLARE LE CORBEILLER

2. HARDSTONES. Grand Duke Francesco I created a fashion for mosaics and intaglio works in hardstones and, taking a personal interest in experimentation with materials and techniques, fostered their production in Florence. In 1572 the Milanese brothers Ambrogio Caroni (*d* 1611) and Stefano Caroni (*d* 1611) moved to Florence, followed by Giorgio Gaffurri, the head of a Milanese workshop specializing in the engraving of rock crystal and pietre dure. Designed by such court-approved artists as Bernardo Buontalenti, sophisticated vases were decorated with gold and enamel work by the Florentine and north European goldsmiths whom Francesco I had gathered in the Casino de' Medici in Piazza S Marco, his private residence. Intarsia and pietre dure mosaics made at this time are mainly geometric in composition and give maximum prominence to the assortment of precious materials.

At the Galleria dei Lavori founded by Ferdinando I in 1588 (*see* §II, 2(i) above) the most prominent activity was the production of pietre dure. A predilection for ornamental and figurative themes prevailed, and the resulting mosaics are sophisticated examples of the use of hardstones to create 'stone paintings'. An opportunity to develop this technique was provided by the decoration of the Chapel of the Princes in S Lorenzo (*see* §IV, 5 below), a mausoleum with hardstone cladding and, at its centre, a small temple entirely in pietre dure with trimmings of precious metal. This work began under Ferdinando I in 1580–90 and continued for many years without being finished. The numerous craftsmen employed on the project executed the pietre dure mosaics following polychrome cartoons provided by such painters as Lodovico Cigoli, Bernardino Poccetti and Jacopo Ligozzi. The parts that were completed were dismantled and reused in various ways at the end of the 18th century (Florence, S Lorenzo; Florence, Pitti; Florence, Mus. Opificio Pietre Dure), though the decoration of the interior continued until the mid-19th century. Fully rounded statuettes, composed of various polychrome elements of pietre dure (Florence, Pitti) were also created for the chapel. This singular genre of 'mosaic sculpture', first produced in Florence at the end of the 16th century with the rock-crystal aedicula containing *Christ and the Woman of Samaria* (Vienna, Ksthist. Mus.), continued to be practised in the Florentine workshop alongside the other speciality of pietre dure mosaic.

During the 17th century Florentine mosaics were used to decorate sumptuous furnishings of various kinds, including table-tops, ebony cabinets, jewel caskets, clocks and reliquaries. The preferred subjects were compositions of flowers, fruit and birds. This fashion was inspired by the analytical naturalism of Jacopo Ligozzi, whose interest in botanical and zoological themes is reflected in the pietre dure ornamentation of a table (Florence, Uffizi; *see also* HARDSTONES, colour pl. I, fig. 1) and a chessboard (Florence, Pitti). Baroque taste continued to favour these subjects, enhancing the vivid polychrome effects with black marble backgrounds to create a greater decorative exuberance. The showy pietre dure is often accompanied by inlay work in rare woods and also by sculpted gilt-bronzes. Among the most important works produced in the 17th century are the great octagonal table (Florence, Uffizi), completed in 1649 after 18 years of work by a team of 12 craftsmen, and the contemporary cabinet of Ferdinando II (Florence, Uffizi).

During the long reign of Cosimo III, Florentine primacy in pietre dure was maintained due to the wealth of material and artistic resources lavished on the sumptuous creations so greatly prized by the European courts. The workshop was guided by GIOVANNI BATTISTA FOGGINI. After 1737 the grand ducal workshop under the new dynasty of Habsburg–Lorraine was engaged mainly on a series of over 60 stone pictures of figures (Vienna, Hofburg-Schauräume), commissioned by Grand Duke Francis for his residence in Vienna and drawn by Giuseppe Zocchi, the official draughtsman of the Galleria dei Lavori. During the reign of Leopold of Hapsburg–Lorraine the workshop's ornamental repertory was centred on sophisticated compositions of vases and still-lifes, used for table-tops and such luxurious objects as tobacco boxes, necklaces and jewel-cases, which were fashionable in the ensuing Napoleonic period. After 1814, however, the workshop began to feel the effect of the grand duchy's economic decline. It was frequently occupied in reusing and adapting existing works rather than in creating new ones; a huge amount of work and material, however, was absorbed between 1837 and 1850 on the monumental table of *Apollo and the Muses* (Florence, Pitti).

The end of the Grand Duchy of Tuscany in 1860 led to an irreversible crisis for the craft, which had always depended on court commissions. The workshop, renamed the Opificio delle Pietre Dure, came under the control of the Ministero dell'Istruzione Pubblica and opened its formerly exclusive production to public sale. From 1873 to 1923 it was directed by the painter Edoardo Marchionni (1837–1923), whose refined Liberty-style creations of the 1870s and 1880s were among the last original products of the workshop (e.g. Magnolia Table, Flower Vase with mosaics and reliefs, Great Vase with plant and animal motifs; all Florence, Mus. Opificio Pietre Dure). At the end of the 19th century the Opificio gradually shifted towards specializing in restoration of works of art.

See also ITALY, §§VI, 2–3 and X, 1(ii).

BIBLIOGRAPHY

A. Zobi: *Notizie storiche sull'origine e progressi dei lavori di commesso in pietre dure che si eseguiscono nell'I. e R. Stabilimento di Firenze* (Florence, 2/1853)
F. Rossi: *La pittura di pietra* (Florence, 1967)
A. M. Giusti, P. Mazzoni and A. Pampaloni Martelli: *Il Museo dell'opificio delle pietre dure a Firenze* (Milan, 1978)
U. Baldini, A. M. Giusti and A. Pampaloni Martelli: *La Cappella dei Principi e le pietre dure a Firenze* (Milan, 1979)
A. Gonzalez-Palacios: *Mosaici e pietre dure*, ii (Milan, 1981)
——: *Il Tempio del Gusto: Il Granducato di Toscana e gli stati settentrionali*, 2 vols (Milan, 1986)
Splendori di pietre dure: L'arte di corte nella Firenze dei Granduchi (exh. cat., ed. A. M. Giusti; Florence, Pitti, 1988–9)
A. M. Giusti: *Pietre Dure: Hardstones in Furniture and Decoration* (London, 1992)
A. Gonzalez-Palacios: *Il gusto dei principi*, 2 vols (Milan, 1993)

ANNAMARIA GIUSTI

3. TAPESTRY.

(i) Before 1554. (ii) 1554–*c*. 1600. (iii) After *c*. 1600.

(i) Before 1554. During the 15th century tapestries were imported into Florence from weavers and dealers in the south Netherlands and northern France. The major agent was the Medici Bank, the Bruges branch of which bought, commissioned or handled financial arrangements for tapestries. No tapestries traded through the Medici Bank, however, can be positively identified; a Netherlandish *verdure* with the Medici arms (Cleveland, OH, Mus. A.) was commissioned later, probably between *c*. 1513 and 1537.

At least two workshops of peripatetic northern tapestry-weavers are known to have been in operation in Florence at this time. Livinus Gilii de Burgis, primarily employed by the Este family in Ferrara, was permitted to weave enormous figured tapestries for the *ringhiera* of Florence's Palazzo Vecchio between 1455 and 1457, which were based on cartoons by Neri di Bicci and Vittorio Ghiberti. Between 1476 and 1480 the south Netherlandish master Giovanni di Giovanni produced works for Florence Cathedral. Little or nothing, however, remains of this production; a very small *Annunciation* (New York, Met.) is attributed to an early 16th-century Florentine workshop.

In 1545 Duke Cosimo I arranged for JAN ROST and NICOLAS KARCHER, two south Netherlandish master weavers, to establish workshops in Florence. Unlike his political rival Ercole II d'Este, who employed a workshop almost exclusively for his personal needs, Cosimo hoped to turn Florence into a centre of production for this luxury industry. He therefore assisted the workshops both economically and materially but stipulated in contracts (1546; Rost's renewed 1549; Karcher's renewed 1550) that they had to teach local apprentices the Netherlandish low-warp weaving technique and that their new equipment would revert to the Duke if they left Florence. Constant ducal orders were promised to supplement private commissions. In 1549 the weaver Francesco di Pacino (*fl* 1549) was also involved in the production of tapestries for the Duke.

Between 1546 and the end of 1553, 120 tapestries were woven in Florence for Cosimo I: 44 (42 extant) narrative pieces with fine sett and materials, including much silk and many metallic threads; and 76 (all destr.) heraldic covers of coarser wool and *filaticcio* (silk from broken cocoons), sometimes used for pack animals or carriages. The cartoons for the fine tapestries, which were mainly for the Palazzo Vecchio, were made by major Florentine painters. At first Cosimo asked AGNOLO BRONZINO to provide cartoons for three trial *portières* (1545–6; Florence, Sopr. B.A. & Storici Col.; *see also* TAPESTRY, fig. 8) for Rost and FRANCESCO SALVIATI to provide cartoons both for Karcher's trial altar tapestry of the *Lamentation* (1546) and for his *Ecce homo* (1547–9; both Florence, Uffizi). At the same time, Cosimo divided larger sets between the two weavers; a twenty-piece *Story of Joseph* series (1546–53; Florence, Sopr. B.A. & Storici Col.; Rome, Pal. Quirinale) from sixteen cartoons by Bronzino, three by Jacopo Pontormo and one by Salviati (see fig. 11), and ten *Grotesque 'spalliere'* (1546–?50; Florence, Sopr. B.A. & Storici Col., six on dep. London, It. Embassy) after Bacchiacca. Karcher wove a Moresque table carpet (Poggio a Caiano, Mus. Villa Medicea), from designs perhaps by Bronzino, and two additions (untraced) to a south Netherlandish *Story of Tobias* set owned by Cosimo I. Two *portières* of an *Allegory with the Medici–Toledo Arms* (1549–?50; Florence, Pitti), from cartoons by Benedetto Pagni da Pescia, were begun under Francesco di Pacino, but the second had to be completed in Karcher's workshop.

Salviati designed many private commissions in this period, including Karcher's *Resurrection* altar tapestry

11. Tapestry of *Joseph Explaining Pharoah's Dream of the Seven Fat and Seven Lean Kine*, wool, silk and metallic threads, 5.70×4.46 m; design and cartoon by Francesco Salviati, made in the workshop of Nicolas Karcher, Florence, 1548 (Florence, Soprintendenza per i Beni Artistici e Storici)

(c. 1546; Florence, Uffizi) for Benedetto Accolti, Cardinal of Ravenna, and Rost's *Meeting of Dante and Virgil* (c. 1547–9; Minneapolis, MN, Inst. A.; *see* ITALY, fig. 100). Nearly all the tapestries from this period are outstanding and distinguished by rich, innovative borders. The borders designed by Bronzino for the *Joseph* series are an Italian monumentalization of popular south Netherlandish garland models, but Bronzino's and Salviati's other border designs were inspired by such diverse sources as architecture, picture frames, East Asian carpets and the framing devices, combining cartouches and figures, of prints disseminated by the first Fontainebleau school in the 1540s. By the 1550s a distinctive and enduring Florentine approach to tapestry borders had developed, characterized by deft balancing of large, often crowded forms, strong plasticity—often working out from an architectonic framework with punctuating cartouches—and considerable visual humour. Although the Medici family had weavers at their service, they also continued to buy some south Netherlandish tapestries throughout the 16th century.

(ii) 1554–c. 1600. In 1554 Cosimo I used the equipment left by Karcher for a new, private ducal factory—now referred to as the Arazzeria Medicea. The reasons for this were doubtless both financial (the costly campaign against Siena combined with the famous masters' high fees) and practical (the slow production of truly fine tapestries compared with the numerous palaces and villas Cosimo had to decorate). At the new factory less complex designs with coarser sett and materials were executed, which lowered the cost and accelerated the rate of production. There were two workshops, headed by Benedetto di Michele Squilli (*fl* 1555–88) and Bastiano Sconditi (*fl* 1555–68).

Bronzino continued to design cartoons until 1557, but the temperament of the court architect and painter Giorgio Vasari was better suited to the increased pace projected by the Duke. After executing a few designs and possibly cartoons to accompany frescoed decorations in the Palazzo Vecchio, Vasari incorporated the production of tapestry cartoons into his workshop's well-organized decorating procedures. The Flemish painter JOANNES STRADANUS so excelled at this art that he soon became the official cartoonist for the workshops, designing his own compositions: for the Palazzo Vecchio they were biblical, historical and mythological (examples in Florence, Sopr. B.A. & Storici Col.; London, V&A; Paris, Mobilier N.); for rooms in the Villa Medici at Poggio a Caiano he designed 40 *Hunts* (1567–77; examples in Florence, Sopr. B.A. & Storici Col.; Pisa, Mus. N. S. Matteo; Siena, Pal. Reale); for Bianca Cappello, second wife of Francesco I, Grand Duke of Tuscany, he collaborated with Domenico d'Antonio Buti (c. 1550–90) on cartoons for five *Grotesques* (1572 and 1578; three, Paris, Mus. A. Déc.). Stradanus's cartoons are notable for their close observation of nature and characterizing detail and a keen sense of both decoration and humour. From late 1558 to 1574, the only set apparently woven for the Medici that was not designed by Stradanus was the *History of Florence* (1564; three, Florence, Sopr. B.A. & Storici Col.) for the Sala di Gualdrada in the Palazzo Vecchio from cartoons by Friedrich Sustris.

In 1575, the year after Cosimo I's death, Alessandro Allori, a favourite painter of Francesco I who had worked on tapestry cartoons under Bronzino, became the official cartonist at the Arazzeria Medicea. Allori was nearly as prolific as Stradanus, although his static figures and compositions are not as imaginative and humorous. His border designs follow Stradanus's in layout but are more formally structured. When Stradanus left Florence temporarily in 1576, Allori continued the *Hunts* for the Villa Medici. Allori's designs were, however, mainly for the Palazzo Pitti in Florence: mythological series included *Latona, Centaurs, Niobe, Phaëthon* and *The Seasons* (examples in Florence, Sopr. B.A. & Storici Col.). During this period more outside commissions were executed by the Arazzeria Medicea, and Allori's workshop painted cartoons for tapestries for the church of S Maria Maggiore in Bergamo (e.g. *Life of the Virgin*, 1582–6; *in situ*) and for the cathedral in Como. On Squilli's death (1588), Guasparri di Bartolomeo Papini (*d* 1621) became head weaver. After the succession (1587) of Ferdinando I, Grand Duke of Tuscany, who had been a cardinal, religious tapestries became more popular: Allori designed overdoors depicting the *Life of Christ* (1598–1600) and a *Passion* series (1592–1616; both Florence, Sopr. B.A. & Storici Col.) in collaboration with Lodovico Cigoli.

(iii) After c. 1600. During the first decades of the 17th century Cardinal Montalto was among the most assiduous patrons of the Arazzeria Medicea. After Allori's death (1607), Bernardino Poccetti made some cartoons for the Medici and for other private commissions. After Poccetti's death (1612), Michelangelo Cinganelli (1560–1635), who still worked in a basically 16th-century style, became the official painter for the Arazzeria (e.g. *Story of Phaëthon*, Florence, Sopr. B.A. & Storici Col.), although the Flemish painter Cornelis Schut I also painted two cartoons in 1628. The Flemish master Jacopo Ebert van Asselt (*fl* 1621; *d* 1630) became head weaver in 1621, and, although his son Pietro van Asselt (*fl* 1620–44) took over the family's separate workshop on Jacopo's death, PIETRO FEVÈRE, a Flemish weaver who favoured high-warp weaving—a new technique for Florence—became the next official head weaver. Fevère was the first to make tapestry copies of paintings in the Medici galleries (examples in Florence, Sopr. B.A. & Storici Col.). Under Fevère, and during the reign of Ferdinand II, the Medici commissions revived, and, following the death of Cinganelli (1635), such masters as Sigismondo Coccapani, Baccio del Bianco, Lorenzo Lippi, Giacinto Gimignani and Vincenzo Dandini painted cartoons for the factory.

After Fevère's death (1669), two head weavers, Giovanni Pollastri (*fl* 1655–?1673) and Bernardino van Asselt, Jacopo's son, who had inherited the family workshop (*fl* 1629–?1673), ran the factory. After their deaths, however, the hierarchy broke down: Stefano Termini (*fl* 1674–1703), Matteo Benvenuti (*fl* 1670–92), Niccolò Bartoli (*fl* 1671–7) and Bernardino Masi (*fl* 1671–87) continued to work in the low-warp technique, and pressure from them led Pietro Fevère's son Filippo Fevère (*fl* 1648–after 1677) to move to Venice. Stefano Termini's brother Giovan Battista Termini (*fl* 1673; *d* 1717), the only remaining high-warp weaver, finally went to Rome in 1684.

Both weaving and cartoons—including such work as architectural compositions and figures in niches (examples in Florence, Sopr. B.A. & Storici Col.)—were undistinguished for the next 20 years. When Giovan Battista Termini petitioned to return to the Arazzeria in 1703, he was made director and asked to re-establish high-warp weaving. His most important weaver was Leonardo Bernini (*fl* 1705–37); the low-warp weaver Vittorio Demignot (*d* 1742) from Turin also worked under Termini between 1716 and 1731. Termini abolished the then current archaic style of cartoon by introducing the work of the Baroque painter Giovanni Camillo Sagrestani (e.g. *Four Parts of the World*, 1715–26; Florence, Sopr. B.A. & Storici Col.).

Antonio Bronconi (*fl* 1700–32) became director after Termini's death (1717). Emulating contemporary workshop organization in France and Flanders, collaborative cartoons by specialists in different genres were painted: Lorenzo del Moro (*fl* 1725–34) made overall and ornamental designs, Girolamo Costner (*fl* 1721–6) painted landscapes, and Sagrestani and later also Matteo Bonechi painted figures (e.g. four *portières* of *The Elements*, 1725–32; Florence, Pitti). Between 1732 and 1737 Giovanni Francesco Pieri and, briefly (1737), Leonardo Bernini managed production. The largest projects of this period were the *Rape of Proserpina* (Florence, Sopr. B.A. & Storici Col.), from a cartoon by Giuseppe Grisone, and the *Fall of Phaëthon* (Florence, Sopr. B.A. & Storici Col.), from a cartoon by Vincenzio Meucci (1699–1766).

After the death (1737) of Gian Gastone, the last Medici grand duke, the Arazzeria was temporarily closed, and the following year one of the masters, Domenico del Rosso (*fl* 1736–68), left for Naples with a group of weavers. From 1740 tapestry-weaving was briefly revived under Francis, Grand Duke of Tuscany (1737–65; from 1745 Francis I, Holy Roman Emperor), who brought weavers from his workshop at the château of La Malgrange, near Nancy, to Florence. Commissions diminished, however, when he was called to defend the crown of his wife Maria-Teresa of Austria. In 1744 court payments ended. One of the last works of the Arazzeria Medicea was a half-length portrait of *Francis, Grand Duke of Tuscany* (1737; Florence, Pitti).

There is no record of tapestry-weaving in Florence from 1745 until 1902, when Count Federigo Niccola Marcelli (*fl* early 20th century) organized a private weaving school and workshop directed by Pia Cassigoli (*fl* 1902–15). The cartoons by Ezio Marzi (1875–1949/53) were inspired by 16th-century models but treated such current themes as the *Triumph of Work* or the *Genius of the Family*. In one series, five women symbolized different moments in history in different cities: for example *Abélard and Héloïse* for 12th-century Paris and the *Meeting of Romeo and Juliet* for Renaissance Verona. The workshop closed around 1915.

BIBLIOGRAPHY

C. Conti: *Ricerche storiche sull'arte degli arazzi in Firenze* (Florence, 1875/*R* 1983)

C. Rigoni: *Catalogo della R. Galleria degli arazzi* (Florence and Rome, 1884)

G. Poggi: 'La giostra medicea del 1475 e la "Pallade" del Botticelli', *L'Arte*, v (1902), pp. 71–7

J. A. F. Orbaan: *Stradanus te Florence* (Rotterdam, 1903)

A. Schiaparelli: *La casa fiorentina e i suoi arredi nei secoli XIV e XV* (Florence, 1908/R with suppl., 1983)

S. B.: 'Studio-Talk: Florence', *Int. Studio*, lvi (1915), pp. 285–8

R. Panichi: 'La "Marcelliana" scuola fiorentina di arazzi', *Vita A.*, viii (1915), pp. 44–8

D. Heikamp: 'Arazzi a soggetto profano su cartoni di Alessandro Allori', *Riv. A.*, xxxi (1956), pp. 105–55

——: 'La Manufacture de tapisserie des Médicis', *L'Oeil*, 164–5 (1968), pp. 22–31

——: 'Giovanni Stradanos Bildteppiche für den Palazzo Vecchio mit Darstellungen aus dem Leben der älteren Medici', *Mitt. Ksthist. Inst. Florenz*, xiv (1969), pp. 183–200

——: 'Die Arazzeria Medicea im 16. Jahrhundert: Neue Studien', *Münchn. Jb. Bild. Kst*, ser. 3, xxx (1969), pp. 33–74

A. Frezza: 'Influenze fiamminghe e originalità fiorentina nella storia dell'arazzeria medicea', *Rubens e Firenze* (Florence, 1979), pp. 229–48

D. Heikamp: 'Unbekannte Medici-Bildteppiche in Siena', *Pantheon*, xxxviii/4 (1979), pp. 376–82

C. Adelson: 'Bachiacca, Salviati, and the Decoration of the Sala dell'Udienza in Palazzo Vecchio', *Le arti del principato mediceo* (Florence, 1980), pp. 141–400

——: 'Cosimo I de' Medici and the Foundation of Tapestry Production in Florence', *Firenze e la Toscana dei Medici nell'Europa del cinquecento*, 3 vols (Florence, 1980), pp. 899–924

C. Adelson, A. Frezza and G. G. Bertelà: 'Arazzi', *Palazzo Vecchio: Committenza e collezionismo mediceo* (exh. cat., ed. P. Barocchi; Florence, Pal. Vecchio, 1980), pp. 43–116

C. Adelson: 'The Decoration of Palazzo Vecchio in Tapestry: The *Joseph* Cycle and Other Precedents for Vasari's Decorative Campaigns', *Atti del convegno vasariano: Arezzo, 1981*, pp. 145–77

A. Frezza: 'Documenti fiorentini per il parato di Clemente VIII', *Paragone*, xxxiii/391 (1982), pp. 56–74

C. Adelson: 'Florentine and Flemish Tapestries in Giovio's Collection', *Atti del convegno: Paolo Giovio, il rinascimento e la memoria: Como, 1983*, pp. 239–81

——: 'Three Florentine Grotesques in the Musée des Arts Décoratifs, Paris', *Bull. Liaison Cent. Int. Etud. Textiles Anc.*, lix–lx/1–2 (1984), pp. 54–60

——: 'Documents for the Foundation of Tapestry Weaving under Cosimo I de' Medici', *Renaissance Studies in Honor of Craig Hugh Smyth*, ed. A. Morrogh, ii (Florence, 1985), pp. 3–17

Gli arazzi della Sala dei Duecento: Studi per il restauro (exh. cat., Florence, Pal. Vecchio, 1985)

L. Meoni: 'Gli arazzieri delle "Storie della Creazione" medicee', *Boll. A.*, ser. 6, lviii (1989), pp. 57–66

C. Adelson: *The Tapestry Patronage of Cosimo I de' Medici: 1545–1553* (diss., New York U., 1990)

C. Adelson and R. Landini: 'The "Persian" Carpet in Charles Le Brun's *July* Was a 16th-century Florentine Table Tapestry', *Bull. Liaison Cent. Int. Etud. Textiles Anc.*, lxviii (1990), pp. 53–68

C. Adelson: *European Tapestry in the Minneapolis Institute of Arts* (Minneapolis, 1992)

——: 'On Benedetto Pagni da Pescia and Two Florentine Tapestries: The Allegorical "portiere" with the Medici–Toledo Arms', *Kunst des Cinquecento in der Toskana*, ed. M. Kämmerer (Munich, 1992), pp. 186–96

N. Forti Grazzini: *Il patrimonio artistico del Quirinale: Gli arazzi*, i (Rome and Milan, 1994), pp. 16–78

CANDACE J. ADELSON

IV. Buildings.

1. Cathedral buildings. 2. Orsanmichele. 3. SS Annunziata. 4. Santa Croce. 5. S Lorenzo. 6. S Maria Novella. 7. S Miniato al Monte. 8. Palazzo Vecchio. 9. Palazzo Pitti. 10. Uffizi.

1. CATHEDRAL BUILDINGS. Florence Cathedral (Duomo), whose great dome dominates the city, the tall campanile at its south-west corner, which balances the dome, and the Baptistery to the west—all set in the Piazza del Duomo in the centre of the city—form a remarkable group of polychrome marble buildings that demonstrates the traditions of Florentine art from the Romanesque period to the Renaissance. The immense programme of work on the cathedral in the 14th century and first half of the 15th was coordinated by the Opera del Duomo (cathedral works), which initiated the most prestigious artistic projects of the period. Many of the original works from the buildings, as well as models and equipment used in the planning and construction of the dome, are exhibited in the Museo dell'Opera del Duomo, which is on the site of the cathedral masons' workshops.

(i) Cathedral. (ii) Baptistery. (iii) Campanile. (iv) Cathedral works.

(i) Cathedral. Originally dedicated to S Reparata, the cathedral was rededicated to S Maria del Fiore in 1412. For many, it represents the beginning of the Renaissance period, with its soaring dome designed and executed in part by Filippo Brunelleschi, reflecting a rebirth of interest in Classical forms and methods of construction (see fig. 12).

(a) Architecture. (b) Sculpture. (c) Painting. (d) Stained glass. (e) Furnishings.

(a) Architecture. Excavations have shown that the first cathedral of Florence, probably dating from the 4th or early 5th century AD, was reconstructed in the 8th or 9th century and modified in the 11th, when the presbytery was raised over a large crypt, which contained a number of spolia. Shortly after 1294 work on a new cathedral was planned (begun 1296), and the old one was finally demolished in 1375. Responsibility for the new construction initially rested with the Florentine *comune* and the Bishop and Chapter.

The first master of the new cathedral was ARNOLFO DI CAMBIO, who died *c.* 1302. The extent to which his scheme was followed has been debated, but excavations indicate that he began work at the west and east ends simultaneously and that an eastern octagon was planned from the start. His church would have been shorter than the present building, however, and was probably intended to have a timber roof, with a wider central nave and relatively narrow aisles.

In 1331, when the presumed relics of St Zenobius (*d c.* 390), traditionally the first bishop of Florence, were found under the old crypt, it was decided to enlarge the original rebuilding project and to enlist financial help from all the major guilds, with the wool-merchants' guild (Arte della Lana) assuming control. Work was suspended in 1334, however, while the campanile was built (*see* §(iii)(a) below), but a fresco of *c.* 1342 (Florence, Mus. Bigallo) shows that the façade was by then partially built and that several bays of the aisle walls had been completed, presumably to Arnolfo's design.

Work resumed in 1355 under a new Master of Works, Francesco Talenti (*see* TALENTI, (1); *see also* GOTHIC, fig. 23), who made a wooden model (destr.) in May of that year in connection with defects in the chapels and windows of the cathedral. The old plans were modified in 1357 in order to accommodate the enlarged new project, and the first nave pier was founded; reference to a dome was also made for the first time, although Arnolfo's scheme probably incorporated such a feature. Discussions over the proportions of the cathedral, the form of the clerestory windows and of the drum that was to support the great dome, and whether the nave should have three or four bays, continued for a decade, and various designs were prepared before a definitive brick model (destr. 1421) was

12. Florence Cathedral, begun *c.* 1294; dome by Filippo Brunelleschi, 1420–36

approved in 1368. Andrea da Firenze, one of the committee members involved in these discussions, was at the same time decorating the Spanish Chapel at S Maria Novella, and his fresco there of the *Church Triumphant* depicts a vast building and dome very similar to the cathedral as finally built.

Between 1384 and 1410, the octagonal piers were built, the tribunes vaulted and the drum begun. A competition held in 1418 to decide the construction technique of the dome was won by Brunelleschi (with Lorenzo Ghiberti), with a proposal that avoided centering; one wooden model attributed to him survives (Florence, Mus. Opera Duomo). Brunelleschi then took sole control of the work, and the dome was completed in 1436; the lantern was built to Brunelleschi's design by Michelozzo di Bartolomeo and Bernardo Rossellino between 1446 and 1467. Apart from some exterior surfaces that still reveal the original brickwork beneath the marble casing, particularly at the base of the dome, the cathedral fabric was finally finished in the 19th century when a new Gothic-style façade was added (1871–87) by Emilio De Fabris to replace the original, incomplete work that was dismantled in 1587.

The completed building has a rib-vaulted nave of four bays (square in the main vessel, rectangular in the aisles); this leads to an eastern octagon the width of the nave, which is surrounded by three tribunes of identical design, each opening into five rectangular chapels. The church thus combines two Early Christian building types, the

basilica and the centralized martyrium. The Gothic nave has features in common with such Florentine churches as S Maria Novella (begun *c.* 1246) and Santa Croce (begun *c.* 1294; *see* §§6 and 4 below). The widely spaced main arcade is surmounted by a corbelled walkway that runs around the vault springers, continuing into the octagon, and the clerestory (like the drum of the dome) is pierced by oculi; the architectural elements are articulated in grey limestone. The octagonal, pointed dome is composed of two shells of herringbone brickwork, a Roman-derived technique that served to spread the weight evenly as the height increased. The shells are connected and strengthened by stone ribs; those at the angles concentrate the load on to the supporting piers, so that the dome can also be read as a cloister vault (*see* DOME, §§1 and 3, and VAULT). Brunelleschi's exedrae, which buttress the drum on its four free faces, are articulated by deep, shell-topped niches and coupled half-columns, while the lantern incorporates classical consoles, which also function as buttresses (for further discussion and illustrations *see* BRUNELLESCHI, FILIPPO, §I, 1(i) and (ix) and figs 1, 7 and 8).

BIBLIOGRAPHY

C. Guasti: *La cupola di Santa Maria del Fiore* (Florence, 1857)
——: *Santa Maria del Fiore: La costruzione della chiesa e del campanile* (Florence, 1887)
H. Saalman: 'Santa Maria del Fiore, 1294–1418', *A. Bull.*, xlvi (1964), pp. 471–500
G. Kreytenberg: *Der Dom zu Florenz: Untersuchungen zur Baugeschichte im 14. Jahrhundert* (Berlin, 1974)

G. Morozzi, F. Toker and J. Hermann: *Santa Reparata: L'antica cattedrale fiorentina* (Florence, 1974) [excav. reports]

F. Toker: 'Excavations below the Cathedral of Florence, 1965–1974', *Gesta*, xiv (1975), pp. 17–36

H. Saalman: *Filippo Brunelleschi: The Cupola of Santa Maria del Fiore* (London, 1980)

C. Pietramellara: *S Maria del Fiore a Firenze: I tre progetti* (Florence, 1984)

G. Rocchi and others: *S Maria del Fiore* (Milan, 1988)

(b) Sculpture. The new cathedral offered numerous opportunities for sculptural decoration on the exterior wall coverings, portals, finials and west façade, as well as the decoration of chapels and other interior spaces with altarpieces, free-standing monuments and single figures. Local painters played an important part in producing designs for sculpture, much of which was subsequently carried out by artists more skilled in carving marble, the main material used in the decoration of the complex. The exterior of the cathedral is distinguished by its use of local stone: white marble from Carrara, green from Prato and pink from Maremma. For reasons of preservation, many of the original furnishings and sculptural decoration from both the interior and exterior of the fabric are now housed in the Museo dell'Opera del Duomo.

The involvement of established Florentine workshops of the early 14th century in the first period of sculptural decoration on the cathedral exterior is particularly evident on the Porta del Campanile (south façade), where the date November 1310 appears on the *Annunciation*. The figure sculpture of the west façade was begun under the direction of Arnolfo di Cambio and continued in successive campaigns through the 14th and 15th centuries; but only a third of the façade was completed by 1587 when it was dismantled, and the sculpture removed to the interior of the cathedral or dispersed to surrounding palaces and gardens. A 16th-century drawing (Florence, Mus. Opera Duomo) by Bernardino Poccetti, literary descriptions and a fresco of *c.* 1342 (Florence, Mus. Bigallo) have enabled the main lines of the scheme to be reconstructed, although the details are disputed.

In contrast to the façade of Siena Cathedral (begun *c.* 1285), the façade sculpture at Florence Cathedral was subordinated to the architecture, with figures set in niches and around the portals in a coherent iconographic scheme. In the central tympanum was a seated *Virgin and Child*, probably flanked by *St Reparata* and *St Zenobius* and *Angels* (all Florence, Mus. Opera Duomo), with the reclining *Virgin of the Nativity* (Florence, Mus. Opera Duomo) in the left tympanum and the *Death of the Virgin* (ex-Berlin, Kaiser Friedrich Mus.) in the right; in a niche in the upper part of the façade was a statue of *Pope Boniface VII* (Florence, Mus. Opera Duomo). All these figures belong to the first campaign. After a break, work resumed in 1362; sculpture from this new phase (all Florence, Mus. Opera Duomo) includes a series of *Apostles* (1388) for the embrasures of the central portal; *Martyrs* and *Doctors of the Church* (1390s), including *SS Augustine and Gregory* by Niccolò di Piero Lamberti; a *St Barnabas* (1395) by Giovanni d'Ambrogio and four *Evangelists* for the niches between the portals. The last, executed from 1408–15 by DONATELLO, NANNI DI BANCO, Bernardo Ciuffagni and Niccolò di Piero Lamberti (for illustration *see* LAMBERTI), illustrate changing styles in sculpture in Florence at the

beginning of the 15th century. In 1415–16 Donatello also made a giant figure in white terracotta (untraced) for the upper part of the façade. The sculptures of the present polychrome façade, designed by Emilio De Fabris (1871–87), include statues of *St Reparata* and *St Zenobius* by Giovanni and Amalia Duprè, flanking the main portal. Augusto Passaglia (1838–1918) executed the bronze doors of the central and left portals in 1897 and 1903 respectively.

Such masters as GIOVANNI D'AMBROGIO, Niccolò di Piero Lamberti, Nanni di Banco and Donatello contributed to the Porta della Mandorla on the north side of the cathedral, begun in 1391 and completed *c.* 1423. The door surrounds, executed in the first phase, include musician angels in hexagons and the *Labours of Hercules* set among rich classicizing foliate decoration. The archivolts, with reliefs of angels holding scrolls, belong to the second phase, from 1404. The fine gable relief of the *Assumption of the Virgin* in a mandorla (1414–21) by Nanni di Banco is flanked by two low-relief heads of a prophet and prophetess and by small statues of prophets on the pinnacles, the former documented and the latter attributed to Donatello. Near by, on the buttress of the north tribune, stood life-size marble statues of *Isaiah* by Nanni di Banco (now inside the cathedral) and *David* by Donatello (Florence, Bargello), both commissioned in 1408.

In the interior of the cathedral there is much fine marble work, including the tomb of *Bishop Antonio d'Orso* (*d* 1320) by TINO DI CAMAINO, the Renaissance lavabos in the sacristies (*c.* 1438–40 and 1442–5) by Buggiano and the *Apostles* on the piers of the octagon, executed by various masters in the 16th century; but the marble singing-galleries (*cantorie*), carved by Donatello and Luca della Robbia during the 1430s and originally set up over the sacristy doors (now Florence, Mus. Opera Duomo), are the most notable pieces from the later period of decoration (*see* ROBBIA, DELLA, (1), fig. 1). The central octagonal choir, beneath the dome, was executed by BACCIO BANDINELLI from 1547 and completed by Giovanni Bandini.

For further discussion *see* §(e) below.

BIBLIOGRAPHY

G. Poggi: *Il duomo di Firenze: Documenti sulla decorazione della chiesa e del campanile tratti dall'archivio dell'opera*, 2 vols (Berlin, 1909/R Florence, 1988)

C. Seymour: 'The Younger Masters of the First Campaign of the Porta della Mandorla, 1391–1397', *A. Bull.*, xli (1959), pp. 1–17

R. Munman: 'The Evangelists for the Cathedral of Florence: A Renaissance Arrangement Recovered', *A. Bull.*, lxii (1980), pp. 207–17

J. Pope-Hennessy: *Luca della Robbia* (London, 1980)

M. Greenhalgh: *Donatello and his Sources* (London, 1982)

(c) Painting. Many artists, both foreign and Tuscan, produced paintings for the new cathedral as well as designs for sculpture and stained glass (*see* §(d) below). Although the original interior decoration is much altered, a number of paintings on panel and in fresco still remain on the walls and above the altar tables of the cathedral interior. The most significant of these are the fresco of *Dante Reading from the 'Divine Comedy'* (1465) by DOMENICO DI MICHELINO, the painted images of saints by Bernardo Daddi, Bicci di Lorenzo and Poppi, the *St Blaise Enthroned* (1408) by Rossello di Jacopo Franchi and the *St Joseph* altarpiece by Lorenzo di Credi. A number of fine paintings from the 15th and 16th centuries hang in the old sacristy

(Sagrestia dei Canonici). The walls of the north sacristy (Sagrestia delle Messe) are covered with elaborate, inlaid intarsia work thought to have been designed by, among others, Alesso Baldovinetti.

A number of illusionistic funeral monuments were painted in fresco. These include the two equestrian monuments to *Sir John Hawkwood* (1436) and *Niccolò da Tolentino* (1455–6), painted by Uccello and Andrea del Castagno respectively (*see* UCCELLO, PAOLO, fig. 1, and ANDREA DEL CASTAGNO, fig. 4). Uccello also painted the heads of prophets (1443) around the clock face on the interior of the façade. The inside of the dome, although no doubt originally planned by Brunelleschi to remain unpainted, was frescoed in 1573–4 by Giorgio Vasari and in 1578–9 by Federico Zuccaro, together with their workshops, with scenes from the *Last Judgement*.

BIBLIOGRAPHY
G. Poggi: *Il duomo di Firenze: Documenti sulla decorazione della chiesa e del campanile tratti dall'archivio dell'opera*, 2 vols (Berlin, 1909/*R* Florence, 1988)
M. Meiss: 'An Early Altarpiece from the Cathedral of Florence', *Bull. Met.*, n. s., xii (1954), pp. 302–17

ANABEL THOMAS

(d) Stained glass. The main windows of the cathedral date from the first half of the 15th century and combine the Renaissance style with traditional Gothic glazing techniques. Lorenzo Ghiberti designed the three oculi on the west front, with the *Assumption of the Virgin* (*c.* 1404) flanked by *St Lawrence* (1412) and *St Stephen* (1412). The eight oculi around the dome were designed by a remarkable combination of talents from 1438 to 1445: Donatello provided the *Coronation of the Virgin* and Paolo Uccello the *Nativity*, *Resurrection* and *Annunciation* (untraced), distinguished by pure colours and naturalism. Andrea del Castagno's *Deposition* is monumental and sculptural, while Ghiberti's mature style is seen in his *Presentation in the Temple*, *Agony in the Garden* and *Ascension*. Ghiberti completed the nave (the earliest four windows of which were made in 1394 by Antonio da Pisa) and apse with a unified design of tiers of prophets and saints under canopies, characterized by majestic scale and strong colours and imbued with great spirituality.

BIBLIOGRAPHY
A. Lane: 'Florentine Painted Glass and the Practice of Design', *Burl. Mag.*, xci (1949), pp. 43–8
G. Marchini: *Italian Stained Glass Windows* (London, 1957), pp. 43–52
L. Lee, G. Seddon and F. Stephens: *Stained Glass* (London, 1976), pp. 118–21

CAROLA HICKS

(e) Furnishings. Although the simple and solemn interior of the cathedral is devoid of superfluous ornament, it contains a variety of furnishings. Most notable are the sculptural artefacts at the east end. They include, in the central apse, Luca della Robbia's two free-standing *Kneeling Angels Holding Candlesticks* (1448) in enamelled terracotta above the altar and Lorenzo Ghiberti's shrine of *St Zenobius* with four low reliefs in bronze beneath it (1432–42; *see* GHIBERTI, (1), §I, 1(iv)). Over the north and south sacristies are Luca della Robbia's two large lunettes of the *Resurrection* (1443–4) and *Ascension* (1446–51) in enamelled terracotta. The bronze doors (1446–75) of the north sacristy, the result of a collaboration between Michelozzo

di Bartolomeo, Luca della Robbia and Maso di Bartolommeo, are decorated with ten reliefs, each framed by four heads of prophets.

The most important among the free-standing marble statues to be seen in the aisles are those originally designated for the old façade of the cathedral, notably Nanni di Banco's *Isaiah* (1408) and Bernardo Ciuffagni's *Isaiah* (completed 1427) in the south aisle. Among the marble busts commemorating famous philosophers and artists, also in the south aisle, are those of *Marsilio Ficino* (1521) by Andrea di Piero Ferrucci, *Giotto* (1490) by Benedetto da Maiano and *Filippo Brunelleschi* (1447–8) by Buggiano (for illustration *see* BUGGIANO). Brunelleschi was the only Florentine artist granted the honour of burial in the cathedral. Of special interest are Paolo Toscanelli's huge gnomon (1475) for solar observations, set in the pavement of the left apse, and the huge clock on the west wall above the central entrance. The latter shows the 24 hours of the day anticlockwise, beginning and ending at the bottom. It operates according to the '*hora italica*' system prevalent in Italy until the 18th century.

See also §(b) above.

BIBLIOGRAPHY
F. Bocchi: *Le bellezze di Firenze* (Florence, 1591)

YAEL EVEN

(ii) Baptistery. Most famous for its three sets of bronze doors (*see* §(c) below), the Baptistery is the oldest extant building in Florence. According to medieval Florentine tradition, it was a Roman temple of Mars and was dedicated to St John the Baptist in the early 4th century AD.

(a) Architecture. Excavations have revealed various floor-levels below the Baptistery's inlaid marble base (as well as a medieval cemetery in Piazza S Giovanni), and these fragments suggest that there was a building of some size on the site, possibly as early as the Roman period. The date of the present building is controversial, but it is now thought likely that it is a 6th- or 7th-century structure, although it has also been attributed to the 11th century: there was a consecration in 1059. The earliest reference to the church of St John the Baptist in Florence was in 897, but no specific description was given of its form or site. The present Baptistery certainly served as the city's cathedral during the 11th and 12th centuries, possibly during building work on the old church of S Reparata. The geometric facing was applied in this period, but the striped angle pilasters were added during the 13th century; the lantern dates from *c.* 1150.

The Baptistery, an octagonal structure with an internal dome that rises over 30 m above floor-level, was probably modelled on the Pantheon in Rome. The interior, with its marble decoration and rich mosaic work (*see* §(b) below), shows the influence of both medieval and Early Christian schemes. It is two-storey, with a rectangular eastern apse or *scarsella*, which replaced an earlier curved apse in the 11th century or early 13th century. The ground storey has coupled angle pilasters and free-standing Corinthian columns of granite supporting an entablature. The tripartite division of each side is repeated in the upper storey, which has a wall-passage fronted by an arcade carried on Ionic colonnettes and punctuated by Corinthian pilasters. The exterior (see fig. 13) is encased in geometric patterns of green-and-white marble, arranged in three registers, including an attic storey, which, with the pitched roof, masks the dome. The lowest level contains plain panels; the second carries blind arcades framing alternating pedimented and round-headed windows; and the attic storey has tripartite panels pierced in their centre by a small window and divided by Corinthian pilasters supporting an architrave. The blend of Romanesque and classicizing features contrasts strongly with the overall Gothic scheme of the nearby campanile (see fig. 12 above).

BIBLIOGRAPHY
A. Busignani and R. Bencini: *Il battistero di San Giovanni* (1988), iv of *Le chiese di Firenze* (Florence, 1974–)

ANABEL THOMAS

(b) Mosaics. Although there was no established tradition of mosaic work in medieval Florence, decorative schemes in this medium were begun at the Baptistery, the cathedral and S Miniato al Monte (*see* §IV, 7 below) in the 13th and 14th centuries. The Baptistery cycle is probably the most important. An inscription on the mosaics of the apse indicates that it was begun *c.* 1225 and, according to Giovanni Villani, the mosaics of the main vault were virtually completed by 1325. Documents indicate that the project was supervised by the cloth-merchants' guild (Arte di Calimala) and that its cost was met through special taxation and offerings on the feast day of St John the Baptist.

The programme presents an apocalyptic vision of history in which Christ presides in majesty at the *Last Judgement*, which fills three segments of the octagonal vault. The angelic hierarchy, scenes from *Genesis* and the lives of the patriarch *Joseph*, *Christ* and *St John the Baptist* are depicted in five superimposed zones in the remaining segments. Details show that the designers drew inspiration from a wide variety of sources, such as Early Christian decorative schemes, Tuscan panel paintings and even Byzantine and northern European manuscript illumination. The apse mosaics show eight patriarchs and prophets grouped around the *Lamb of God*, with *St John the Baptist* and the *Virgin and Child* enthroned at either side. A view that the figures were added in the late 13th century (see Demus) has been challenged on stylistic grounds (Klange, 1976).

The mosaics have been heavily restored so that it is difficult to ascertain the identity of the different masters. A document of 1301 referring to the dismissal of two fraudulent masters suggests that the guild officials may have tried to replace them with qualified mosaicists from Venice, or wherever else skilled artists could be found. According to Giorgio Vasari the work was carried out by Andrea Tafi (*fl c.* 1300–20) and his master, a Greek artist named Apollonius, who provided technical assistance and worked on the upper part of the vault. As mosaic work was an unfamiliar medium in medieval Florence, the suggestion that the Florentines sought advice on the technique may not be so far-fetched. A Roman or Venetian master may have begun work on the apse mosaics (Demus), and Venetian participation in the cycle is evident throughout, although Tuscan artists also seem to have been employed. The suggestion that Cimabue and Giotto

13. Florence, Baptistery, 6th or 7th century or possibly 11th century

worked here is not generally accepted, although Cimabue's followers probably executed some scenes (*see* CIMABUE, §1(ii)).

BIBLIOGRAPHY
G. Villani: *Cronica* (MS.; 14th century); ed. G. Aquilecchia (Turin, 1979)
G. Vasari: *Vite* (1550, rev. 2/1568); ed. G. Milanesi (1878–85), i, pp. 331–2
O. Demus: 'The Tribuna Mosaics of the Florence Baptistery', *Actes du VIe congrès international d'études byzantines: Paris, 1948*, ii, pp. 101–10
A. de Witt: *I mosaici del battistero di Firenze*, 5 vols (Florence, 1954–9)
I. Hueck: *Das Programm der Kuppelmosaiken in Florentiner Baptisterium* (Munich, 1962)
C. Ragghianti: 'Percorso di Giotto: I mosaici della cupola del battistero di Firenze', *Crit. A.*, xvi (1969), pp. 3–80
H. Wieruszowski: 'Art and the Commune at the Time of Dante', *Politics and Culture in Medieval Spain and Italy* (Rome, 1971), pp. 475–502
B. Klange: 'I mosaici della scarsella di San Giovanni a Firenze: L'iconografia', *Commentari*, xxvi (1975), pp. 248–58
——: 'I mosaici della scarsella di San Giovanni a Firenze: Problemi stilistici', *Commentari*, xxvii (1976), pp. 3–17

CATHERINE HARDING

(c) Doors. In 1329 the Arte di Calimala (the guild in charge of the Baptistery), abandoning an earlier plan to cover the wooden doors of the Baptistery with metal plates, decided to install new doors cast in bronze (now on the south side). Documents identify the designer as Andrea Pisano (*see* PISANO (ii), (1), §1). The doors, installed in 1336, were cast by the lost-wax process, with fire-gilt figures, background details and decorative motifs. The 28 rectangular fields contain reliefs, each within a quatrefoil frame, illustrating scenes from the *Life of St John the Baptist* and, in the lowest two rows, seated *Virtues*. In them Andrea succeeded in translating the narrative power of Giotto's paintings into sculpture (see fig. 14). The reliefs reveal the influence of northern Gothic art but also hint at the sculptor's future assimilation of the classical style in his work on the campanile (*see* §(iii)(b) below).

14. Florence, Baptistery, *The Visit of the Disciples*, by Andrea Pisano, bronze relief, 500×400 mm, detail from the south doors, 1329–36

In 1401 a competition was announced for a second set of bronze doors. The two finalists were Lorenzo Ghiberti and Filippo Brunelleschi; both entries, illustrating the *Sacrifice of Isaac*, are extant (Florence, Bargello). Ghiberti won the competition and was commissioned in 1403 to design doors with New Testament scenes. Installed in 1424 on the east side, these followed the scheme of the earlier doors, having twenty narratives and eight seated figures within quatrefoils (*see* GHIBERTI, (1), fig. 1). The enframing lattice is considerably richer than that of Pisano's doors, and the compositions are more closely coordinated with the quatrefoils.

In 1425 Ghiberti received the commission for the final set of doors. The Gothic quatrefoil and the distinction between the dark background and the gilt figures were this time abandoned; in contrast, the new doors had ten large, squarish, totally gilded reliefs, each containing several related Old Testament episodes. Through gilding, the use of Albertian perspective (*see* ALBERTI, LEON BATTISTA, §II, 1) and gradation of relief (diminishing as forms recede), Ghiberti achieved a convincing illusion of spatial depth and narrative continuity. The doors (completed 1452; *see* GHIBERTI, (1), fig. 4) made such a strong impression on the artist's contemporaries that his earlier set was transferred to the north entrance and the new

doors were installed on the east façade, facing the cathedral. According to Vasari, Michelangelo, in a play on the word *paradiso* (the area between a baptistery and a cathedral façade), claimed that Ghiberti's doors were worthy to be the 'Gates of Paradise'.

BIBLIOGRAPHY
I. Falk: *Studien zu Andrea Pisano* (Hamburg, 1940)
I. Falk and J. Lanyi: 'The Genesis of Andrea Pisano's Bronze Doors', *A. Bull.*, xxv (1943), pp. 132–53
R. Krautheimer: *Lorenzo Ghiberti*, 2 vols (Princeton, 1970)
B. Bearzi: 'La tecnica usata dal Ghiberti per le porte del battistero', *Lorenzo Ghiberti nel suo tempo. Atti del convegno internazionale di studi: Firenze, 1978*, i, pp. 219–22
U. Baldini, ed.: *Metodo e scienza: Operatività e ricerca nel restauro* (Florence, 1982), pp. 168–206 [cleaning and restoration of Gates of Paradise]
G. Kreytenberg: *Andrea Pisano und die toskanische Skulptur des vierzehnten Jahrhunderts* (Munich, 1984)
A. Moskowitz: *The Sculpture of Andrea and Nino Pisano* (Cambridge, 1986)

ANITA F. MOSKOWITZ

(iii) Campanile.

(a) Architecture. The campanile, or bell-tower, of Florence Cathedral (see fig. 12 above) was begun shortly after Giotto was elected Master of Works in April 1334. He died in 1337, but a design attributed to him survives (Siena, Mus. Opera Duomo). It shows a tower crowned by an octagonal spire, with window lights increasing in number from bottom to top and no statue niches; only the lowest zone corresponds to the completed tower. Work was continued during the 1340s by Andrea Pisano and finished in the late 1350s by Francesco Talenti, who increased the height of the storeys, thus enhancing the elegance and lightness of the structure; he also added a flat-topped belfry. The campanile is square in plan with octagonal corner buttresses. It is divided into horizontal zones: the lower ones are decorated with reliefs and statues (*see* §(b) below), while the upper and slightly narrower part of the tower is pierced on each of its four sides, first by two storeys of twin, two-light openings and, finally, in its uppermost storey, by a single great tripartite window. The campanile is 84 m high and, like the cathedral, is faced in white, green and pink marble.

(b) Sculpture. The programme for the sculpture of the campanile may well have been designed by Giotto before his death in 1337. It seems likely that the greater part of the early sculptural work was carried out under Andrea Pisano (*see* PISANO (ii), (1), §1), who was referred to as *capomaestro* (head of building works) in 1340. He does not appear in documents after 1342, the date of the Compagnia del Bigallo fresco (Florence, Mus. Bigallo), which shows the campanile partially built and the lower part faced in marble.

All the original sculpture is now in the Museo dell'Opera del Duomo, having been replaced on the campanile by replicas (see fig. 15). The six-sided reliefs of the lower storeys combine a number of narrative scenes and single figures to form a complex allegorical cycle, continuing and developing the one planned for the façade of the cathedral, the theme of which was the redemption of mankind through the intercession of the Virgin. The programme of the campanile illustrates the prophecy of redemption, represented by figures of sibyls, prophets and patriarchs, and man's preparation for life after death through his

15. Florence, cathedral campanile, west side showing replicas of statues by Donatello, 1420s and 1430s; originals now in Florence, Museo dell'Opera del Duomo

existence on earth, beginning with the *Creation of Adam and Eve* and continuing in personifications of the *Planets, Virtues, Liberal Arts* and *Seven Sacraments*. It is significant that the relief showing *Sculpture* suggests a new act of creation. The first sculptures to be completed were those on the south side, which faces towards the Via de' Calzaiuoli. The last work by Andrea Pisano was probably the scene of *Navigation* on the east side, although some scholars attribute some of the *Liberal Arts* to him. Luca della Robbia completed the series of *Liberal Arts* during the 1430s (*see* ROBBIA, DELLA, (1)).

Reference to the statues that were to be placed in niches above the reliefs was first made in 1415, when Bernardo Ciuffagni was allocated a figure of *Joshua*. This statue was reallocated to Donatello (*see* DONATELLO, §I) and finally completed by Nanni di Bartolo in 1420. Donatello completed two other figures during this period and collaborated with Nanni on the completion of the *Abraham and Isaac*, which was finished in 1421. In the early 1420s Donatello was working on three other statues, one of them being the *Zuccone*, which he was probably finishing during the 1430s after a brief absence in Siena. Some statues were repositioned in 1464 to make way for figures by Donatello and Nanni di Bartolo, and this resulted in some confusion over identification at a later date.

BIBLIOGRAPHY
A. Nardini: *Il campanile di Santa Maria del Fiore* (Florence, 1885)
G. Poggi: *Il duomo di Firenze: Documenti sulla decorazione della chiesa e del campanile tratti dall'archivio dell'opera*, 2 vols (Berlin, 1909/*R* Florence, 1988)
M. Trachtenberg: *The Campanile of Florence Cathedral* (New York, 1971)

A. Moskowitz: 'Trecento Classicism and the Campanile Hexagons', *Gesta*, xxii (1983), pp. 49–65

ANABEL THOMAS

(iv) Cathedral works. The decision in 1294 to build the new cathedral resulted in the establishment of the Opera del Duomo to oversee the cathedral works. It was funded largely by public monies and, until the advent of Medici patronage in the 15th century, it initiated and directed the most numerous, prestigious and challenging architectural and sculptural enterprises in and around Florence. Its members, the Operai, who all belonged to the Florentine wool-merchants' guild after 1331, supervised not only the cathedral works but also the work on the Loggia della Signoria (now Loggia dei Lanzi), the new wall around the Stinche prison, the papal apartment at S Maria Novella and the fortification of settlements in the Arno valley.

The scope of the programmes of work at the cathedral was enormous. During the first half of the 15th century alone, countless statues, stained-glass windows, altars, two singing-galleries (*cantorie*) and a set of bronze doors were commissioned, and the dome was constructed. Elected treasurers and notaries, a foreman and many skilled sculptors, glaziers, goldsmiths and painters were employed. Most projects were conceived as collaborative ventures. The four seated marble figures of *Evangelists* intended to flank the central entrance, for example (*see* §1(i)(b) above), were carved by Niccolò di Piero Lamberti, Nanni di Banco, Donatello and Bernardo Ciuffagni in seven years (1408–15; Florence, Mus. Opera Duomo). The dome, initially conceived with the enforced cooperation of Brunelleschi and Ghiberti, took 16 years to build (1420–36).

In order that such collaborations should hasten production and minimize costs, competition between potential or actual rivals was promoted. Luca Della Robbia (*see* ROBBIA, DELLA, (1)) and Donatello (*see* DONATELLO, §I), working together on the altar of St Paul (1439) or independently on the two singing-galleries (1431–9; Florence, Mus. Opera Duomo), vied for individual recognition. The allocation of equal stipends (but with bonuses for special accomplishments) further stimulated artists to excel, as did frequent evaluations of work in progress, sometimes announced as renewed contests. Ghiberti, who had designed cartoons for the stained glass of the façade and tribunes (1404–1420s), had to compete, once unsuccessfully, for the windows in the drum (designed 1443). Brunelleschi, whose model for the dome had been officially accepted (1420), had to submit further proposals for several sections of it (1423; 1425–26; 1436). This policy of reassessment and, if necessary, modification, enabled the Operai to control the workforce and to invite public opinion or even participation.

Since the primary goal was productivity, unity of style was sometimes sacrificed in the interest of speed. The Porta della Mandorla (1391–*c.* 1423) was assigned to artists of widely variable talent who were paid by the unit of carved marble. This same pragmatism is reflected in the use of an hour-glass to record the workers' presence on

site and in the rule that those working above ground must not descend more than once a day. Yet the Opera del Duomo played a key role in civic patronage for over a century and commissioned many works that are fundamental to the early Italian Renaissance.

BIBLIOGRAPHY
C. Seymour: 'The Younger Masters of the First Campaign of the Porta della Mandorla', *A. Bull.*, xli (1959), pp. 1–17
L. Becherucci and G. Brunetti: *Il Museo dell'Opera del Duomo a Firenze* (Florence, 1969)
Y. Even: 'The Sacristy Portals: Cooperation at the Florentine Cathedral', *Source: Notes Hist. A.*, vi (1987), pp. 7–13
——: 'Divide and Conquer: The Autocratic Patronage of the Opera del Duomo', *Source: Notes Hist. A.*, vii (1989), pp. 1–6
——: 'Lorenzo Ghiberti and Filippo Brunelleschi Reconsidered: Forced Alliances between Lifelong Adversaries', *Fides & Hist.*, xxii (1990), pp. 38–46
For further bibliography see entries on individual artists.

YAEL EVEN

2. ORSANMICHELE. Standing on the Via de' Calzaiuoli, midway between the ecclesiastical centre (the cathedral and Baptistery) and the secular centre (the Palazzo Vecchio and Piazza della Signoria), the church of Orsanmichele, a converted grain hall, marks the site where the nuns of S Michele originally had their convent and garden. There is a reference to the church of S Michele in Orto as early as the 9th century. The early history of the site shows that it

16. Florence, Orsanmichele, interior view, 1336–1404

assumed a number of different functions, both civic and ecclesiastical. The nuns ran a flourishing wool shop there, renowned both within and outside Florence, and during the late 12th century the building was used as a meeting-place for the governmental bodies that emerged during the early years of the *comune*. Churches were frequently used in this way before the erection of such new government buildings as the Bargello (originally the Palazzo del Popolo) and the Palazzo Vecchio. The dual character of Orsanmichele continued throughout the Gothic and Renaissance periods.

During the first half of the 13th century the convent gradually fell into a state of disrepair, and it was demolished in 1240 to make way for a market-square where grain was sold. Some 40 years later a loggia was built to house the grain market, perhaps to the design of Arnolfo di Cambio, and a painted image of the *Virgin* was set up on one of the interior pilasters. A company of singers known as the Laudesi was formed in 1291 to chant in front of this holy image, which from an early stage was renowned for performing miracles. Orsanmichele consequently became a pilgrimage site, a function that sometimes conflicted with the market. In June 1304 a fire destroyed the whole loggia, and although the image of the *Virgin* survived and was retrieved to be venerated once more in a temporary wooden shelter, it was only in 1336 that a decision was taken by the Signoria to rebuild the old loggia. The new building was to serve both as a grain market and as a place of worship. The wool-workers' guild was originally entrusted with sole responsibility for rebuilding the loggia, but it was later agreed that all the guilds should share this task. The architect is not documented. Vasari believed it to have been Taddeo Gaddi, working to a design by Arnolfo di Cambio; according to others Francesco Talenti, Neri di Fioravante (*fl* 1340–84) and Benci di Cione (*d* 1388) were responsible. It is known, however, that Andrea di Cione was commissioned to make the marble tabernacle inside (completed 1359/60) and that Bernardo Daddi was commissioned by the Laudesi in 1347 to produce a new painting of the *Virgin* and that this was placed within Andrea's tabernacle.

The sandstone exterior of the building clearly reflects the interior arrangement: three great rectangular spaces superimposed one upon another. The massive arches of the original ground-floor arcade, still visible despite having been filled in (see below), are typical of 13th-century and early 14th-century civic architecture in Italy. The ground-floor space was divided into two naves by two large, load-bearing piers, but the upper storeys were undivided, making them ideal for the storage and distribution of grain. By the time of the completion of the second storey in 1361, the Signoria had already determined to transfer the grain market elsewhere and to concentrate on the religious aspect of the site, but despite this the upper storeys were used for the grain trade until well into the 16th century, when Cosimo I decided to convert them to archives. The upper storeys subsequently housed the Società Dantesca, but a narrow staircase within the pier on the north-west corner of the building testifies to the original use, as does a corn-chute on one of the piers on the north side.

In the second half of the 14th century Simone Talenti (*see* TALENTI, (3)) was entrusted with the embellishment of the existing loggia arcade, at first leaving the spaces open with low parapets, allowing passers-by to see the holy image inside. By 1381, however, Talenti's delicate tracery in the upper part of the arches had been incorporated into a curtain wall, entirely filling in all but four of

17. Florence, Orsanmichele, niche figure of *St George* by Donatello, marble, *c.* 1414 (Florence, Museo Nazionale del Bargello)

the spaces and turning the open loggia of the grain market into an enclosed place of devotion (see fig. 16).

During the 14th-century work, a decision was made to decorate the exterior pilasters with large-scale statuary. It was not, however, until 1404, when the new building was completed, that the Signoria issued a firm decree to the guilds that the exterior niches should be completed. Seven major guilds and five of the fourteen minor ones were allotted niches. They were charged with financing and supervising the production of tabernacles and figures of their patron saints, in bronze for the major guilds and marble for the minor ones, which were to be finished within the space of ten years. The guilds that were not represented on the exterior were entrusted with tabernacles inside the church. This resulted in a period of activity lasting not ten, but twenty years, during which such leading sculptors as Donatello, Ghiberti, Nanni di Banco (see fig. 5 above) and NICCOLÒ DI PIERO LAMBERTI were entrusted with the decoration of individual guild niches. Competition between guilds and between individual artists engendered a highly creative, experimental and progressive series of works that significantly broadened the expressive scope of early Renaissance sculpture.

The most important figures are *St Mark* (1411–13; for the linen-drapers' guild), *St George* (c. 1414; for the armourers' guild; Florence, Bargello; see fig. 17) and the gilded bronze *St Louis of Toulouse* (c. 1418–22; Florence, Mus. Opera Santa Croce), all by Donatello (*see* DONATELLO, §I); *St John the Baptist* (c. 1412–16), *St Matthew* (1419; *see* GHIBERTI, (1), fig. 2) and *St Stephen* (1425–9; for the wool-workers' guild), all cast in bronze by Lorenzo Ghiberti; and *St Philip*, *Four Crowned Saints* (for illustration *see* NANNI DI BANCO) and *St Eligius*, all of disputed date, by Nanni di Banco. The tabernacles were also decorated with low reliefs that are themselves important in the development of early Renaissance sculpture, for example *St George and the Dragon* (c. 1416–17) by Donatello. In practice the church of Orsanmichele became the guild church of Florence and thus a powerful architectural statement in the context of the city's medieval and Renaissance history.

BIBLIOGRAPHY

P. Bargellini: *Orsanmichele a Firenze* (Milan, 1969)

A. Busignani and R. Bencini: *Quartiere di S Croce* (1982), iii of *Le chiese di Firenze* (Florence, 1974–)

G. Kreytenberg: 'Orsan Michele und die Florentiner Architektur um 1300', *Mitt. Ksthist. Inst. Florenz*, xxvii (1983), pp. 171–92

ANABEL THOMAS

3. SS ANNUNZIATA. In 1250 the small church of S Maria dei Servi was erected by the new Florentine mendicant order of Servites just outside the city walls at Cafaggio near the Porta Balla. The church, which became known as SS Annunziata after the miraculous image of the *Annunciation* frescoed on its interior rear wall (*see* SERVITES), was soon the site of a celebrated cult devoted to the Virgin. The ever-growing popularity of this image necessitated a series of new building campaigns, the most substantial of which occurred in 1264 and 1384. The 14th-century church was based on a typical basilican plan with a nave and two aisles divided by octagonal piers. Like Santa Croce, it had a T-shaped transept and a free-standing

monastic choir in the centre of the crossing behind a monumental screen wall.

The appearance of SS Annunziata was radically altered from 1444 by a series of major renovations initially planned and executed by Michelozzo. An Early Christian-style atrium (Chiostrino dei Voti) was constructed in front of the church and a marble tabernacle erected before the *Annunciation*. Transverse walls were placed between the nave piers and the outer walls, thereby transforming the aisles into a series of side chapels, and a large centralized addition with seven radiating chapels known as the tribune was built behind the high altar (for further discussion and plan of the church *see* MICHELOZZO DI BARTOLOMEO, §§1(ii), 3(ii) and fig. 4). At the same time the screen wall was dismantled, and a new circular choir, based on the one in the cathedral, was located within the tribune. Michelozzo was a conservative architect who drew heavily from both the Gothic tradition and Brunelleschi's newer Renaissance idiom. Like Brunelleschi's work, SS Annunziata was built using the traditional Florentine materials of *pietra serena* (dark-grey stone) and white plaster.

Michelozzo's elaborate building campaign was conceived under the aegis of the Medici family. Piero de' Medici was directly responsible for the tabernacle and its accompanying chapel, but he probably offered additional advice on the overall plan, the selection of the architect and the recruitment of other patrons for the newly formed chapels. Altogether, fourteen new patrons were needed: seven for the chapels of the nave and seven for the chapels encircling the tribune. As insufficient funds had been raised to complete the tribune, in 1449 Cosimo de' Medici and the prior of the monastery suggested to Ludovico II Gonzaga, 2nd Marquis of Mantua, that he finance its construction and that of the new choir. Ludovico finally agreed to bequeath to the church part of the military salary owed him by the Florentine community.

In 1455 construction of the tribune was halted at cornice level; it was resumed (1459–60) under the direction of Antonio di Ciaccheri Manetti, but the only progress made was the reinforcing of the pre-existing piers. Another ten years passed before continuation of the tribune was even considered. This time Ludovico Gonzaga intervened and assumed complete financial responsibility in exchange for the exclusive rights to the tribune and all of its chapels, and control over the artistic plans. He turned the project over (c. 1470) to Leon Battista Alberti, who modified Michelozzo's design by adding two additional radiating chapels, opening a grand triumphal arch between the nave and tribune, and covering the latter with a drum and dome patterned after ancient Roman mausolea. The loggia in front of the church was erected (1599–1604) by Giovanni Battista Caccini to Michelozzo's design, complementing the adjacent early Renaissance Ospedale degli Innocenti by Brunelleschi.

Early frescoes in the church include two (1453–7) by Andrea del Castagno in the north aisle chapels (*see* CASTAGNO, ANDREA DEL, §1(iv) and fig. 3); a series in the Chiostrino, including a *Nativity* (1462) by ALESSO BALDOVINETTI; the *Birth of the Virgin* (1513–14) by ANDREA DEL SARTO, who is buried in the church; the *Marriage of the Virgin* (1513) by FRANCIABIGIO; the *Visitation* (1516) by PONTORMO; and the *Assumption of the Virgin* (1517) by Rosso Fiorentino. In the 1580s the eastern chapel of the tribune was reconstructed by Giambologna as his own tomb, with fine bronze reliefs. During the 17th century a dazzling veil of Baroque decoration completely obliterated the earlier character of the interior; this decoration includes work by Matteo Nigetti, Giovanni Battista Foggini and BALDASSARE FRANCESCHINI ('Volterrano'), who produced the frescoes (1670–83) in the dome of the tribune.

BIBLIOGRAPHY
P. Tonini: *Il santuario della Santissima Annunziata di Firenze* (Florence, 1876)
L. Heydenreich: 'Die Tribuna der SS Annunziata in Florenz', *Mitt. Ksthist. Inst. Florenz*, iii (1932), pp. 268–85
W. Lotz: 'Michelozzos Umbau der SS Annunziata in Florenz', *Mitt. Ksthist. Inst. Florenz*, v (1937–40), pp. 402–22
L. M. Bulman: *Artistic Patronage at SS Annunziata, 1440–c. 1520* (diss., U. London, 1971)
H. Teubner: 'Das Langhaus der SS Annunziata in Florenz', *Mitt. Ksthist. Inst. Florenz*, xxii (1978), pp. 27–60
B. L. Brown: 'The Patronage and Building History of the Tribuna of SS Annunziata in Florence: A Reappraisal in Light of New Documentation', *Mitt. Ksthist. Inst. Florenz*, xxv (1981), pp. 59–146

BEVERLY LOUISE BROWN

4. SANTA CROCE. The church of Santa Croce was originally established as a Florentine place of worship for the Franciscan Order (*see* FRANCISCAN ORDER, §§I and III) by St Francis of Assisi at the beginning of the second decade of the 13th century. Building work on a modest fabric, remains of which are still visible under the existing pavement of the nave, was probably carried out before the saint's death in 1226. Certainly reference was made to the church of Santa Croce dei Minori in a papal bull of 1228. This first building thus pre-dated by a couple of decades the important Gothic reconstruction work carried out at the Dominican church of S Maria Novella on the other side of the city (*see* §6 below).

As a result of the rapid growth of the Franciscan Order during the 13th century, a second church was begun in 1252, and this in turn was probably incorporated into the enormous new project begun in 1294 or 1295. A dispute among the Franciscans over the size and grandeur of their places of worship had resulted in a split into two opposing groups, the Conventuali and the Spirituali, and the views of the former are reflected in the vast scale of the new Gothic church, with a length of some 115 m and a width (of nave and aisles) of about 38 m. Work on the new fabric progressed slowly, and the nave was not finished until the end of the 14th century. The church was finally consecrated in the presence of Pope Eugenius IV (*reg* 1431–47) in 1443, although the Gothic-style façade was added only in 1857–63 by Niccola Matas. The Piazza Santa Croce, provided to allow open-air preaching to the large congregations attracted to the order, remains one of Florence's most popular urban spaces.

The architectural style of Santa Croce, with pilasters, flattened acanthus-leaf capitals, pointed arches and windows, a strongly emphasized horizontal string-course gallery above the nave arcade and a spacious, simply bricked interior (see fig. 18), resembles the interior of the cathedral. Its architect has therefore traditionally been identified with Arnolfo di Cambio (*see* ARNOLFO DI

18. Florence, Santa Croce, interior of the nave, begun 1294 or 1295

CAMBIO, §3), who was Master of Works there. Unlike the vaulted cathedral, however, Santa Croce has an impressive trussed timber roof, which bears the dates 1341 and 1383. The east end is raised, a feature that is accentuated by the change of level in the continuous string-course gallery.

The T-shaped plan is similar to that of S Maria Novella, although at Santa Croce the regular spacing of the nave bays is continued to the east end and determines the width of the transepts. There is also a polygonal choir and many more small choir chapels, the proportions of which are not related to the nave and aisles. Exterior cornices at the east end mark out the individual chapels, which are separated inside by simple, unadorned piers. Similarly, the flat brick pilasters rising from the nave arcade capitals divide the nave walls into vertical sections, which are reflected in the truncated responds on the aisle walls. The low aisles, wide nave and horizontal roof timbers at Santa Croce increase the sense of horizontality given by the string-course gallery. The delicate octagonal piers of the arched Gothic portico on the north side of the church echo the more robust ones in the interior.

In the 15th century several notable architects worked at Santa Croce. The classically inspired Renaissance Pazzi Chapel (built 1442–c. 1465) by Brunelleschi (see BRUNEL-LESCHI, FILIPPO, §I, 1(v) and figs 5 and 6) contrasts very obviously with the first Gothic cloister on the south side, while a second, gracefully arched Renaissance cloister in *pietra serena* has been variously attributed to Brunelleschi and members of the Rossellino and da Maiano workshops. The Medici Chapel (1440s) at the end of the south transept was commissioned from Michelozzo by Cosimo de' Medici (see MICHELOZZO DI BARTOLOMEO, §3). Later, in the 16th century, the church underwent modernization when, in 1565–6, Giorgio Vasari removed the monks' choir or Ponte on the orders of Cosimo I and refurbished the existing side chapels, inserting the funerary monument to his contemporary Michelangelo.

In addition to Michelangelo, many great Italian writers, artists, musicians, historians and politicians were buried or commemorated in the church, among them Ghiberti, Galileo Galilei and Niccolò Machiavelli. Others include Leonardo Bruni (1369–1444), whose tomb (1444–51) was carved by Bernardo Rossellino, Francesco Nori (d 1478), whose tomb is by Antonio Rossellino (see ROSSELLINO, figs 1 and 2), and Carlo Marsuppini (1398–1453), with a tomb (c. 1453–60) by DESIDERIO DA SETTIGNANO. Notable later monuments include that of *Vittorio Alfieri* (1804–6) by Antonio Canova, and there is a Neo-classical monument to *Dante* (1829) by Stefano Ricci (1765–1837). Other important sculptural works include the *Tabernacle of the Annunciation* by Donatello (see DONATELLO, §I, 2(ii)) and the marble pulpit (completed 1485) by Benedetto da Maiano (for discussion and illustration see MAIANO, DA, (2), §1). There are also many important early frescoes and paintings in Santa Croce. Giotto painted those in the Bardi Chapel and the Peruzzi Chapel (both c. 1320; see GIOTTO, figs 7 and 8) and the polyptych in the Baroncelli Chapel. In addition, there are frescoes (after 1328) by Taddeo Gaddi in the Baroncelli Chapel, and the work of Bernardo Daddi and Agnolo Gaddi, among others, is also represented.

For further illustration see MONASTERY, fig. 11.

BIBLIOGRAPHY

W. Paatz and E. Paatz: *Kirchen* (1940–54)
R. Sciamannini: *La basilica di S Croce* (Florence, 1955)
J. White: *Art and Architecture in Italy, 1250 to 1400*, Pelican Hist. A. (Harmondsworth, 1966)
A. Busignani and R. Bencini: *Quartiere di S Croce* (1982), iii of *Le chiese di Firenze* (Florence, 1974–)

5. S LORENZO. The titular church of the Medici family, S Lorenzo is regarded by many as the quintessential Renaissance church. The rebuilding of the old Romanesque church of S Lorenzo, originally consecrated by St Ambrose in the 4th century, was largely carried out in the 15th century, with additions in the 16th and 17th. The Signoria gave permission for the enlargement of the existing church in 1418, and it has been argued that church officials were persuaded that the fabric should be extended in order to accommodate chapels for such families of standing as the Neroni, Ginori, Rondinelli, della Stufa, Nelli and Ciai. Although Filippo Brunelleschi was traditionally associated with the design of the new church, he is now thought to have designed only the Old Sacristy in the north-west corner, commissioned by Giovanni di Averardo de' Medici and the first part of the new fabric to be erected. The rest of the rebuilding work may have been conceived on the basis of his designs, but it is now thought more likely to have been carried out under the influence of such followers as Michelozzo (see discussion below).

Brunelleschi's Old Sacristy was commissioned in 1419 and mostly completed a decade later. Conceived as a cube surmounted by a hemispherical umbrella dome, with three small chapels—the central one open—ranged along one wall, the interior is regulated and articulated by a system of arches and roundels that interact with voids and flat surfaces (see BRUNELLESCHI, FILIPPO, §1(iv) and figs 2 and 3a). The void of the arched entrance to the small central chapel, which opens off the main space of the sacristy and has its own comparable square plan and dome, is balanced by the proportions and divisions of the opposite altar wall. The windows and wall articulation of the chapel in turn reflect the overall pattern of decoration in the sacristy, where a series of round-headed rectangular windows in the upper walls and open round windows in the dome is balanced by arched wall niches and decorated roundels set into the walls. A heavily defined entablature horizontally divides the wall surfaces of both sacristy and chapel. It is decorated with terracotta roundels of cherubs (c. 1433–43) by Donatello, who was responsible for much of the sacristy's decoration, including terracotta reliefs of the *Life of St John the Evangelist* (c. 1433–43), the chapel's titular saint, which are set in the pendentives beneath the main dome, and the bronze doors surmounted by terracotta reliefs either side of the small central chapel (see DONATELLO, §I, 2(ii)). The sacristy was designed as the funerary chapel of Giovanni di Averardo de' Medici, and at his death in 1429 his sons Cosimo de' Medici and Lorenzo de' Medici (1395–1440) contributed a considerable amount of money to S Lorenzo in order that masses should be said for his soul in the sacristy. The completion of this early phase of rebuilding thus clearly anticipated the leading role assumed by the Medici at S Lorenzo.

19. Florence, S Lorenzo, completed 1460s, interior of the nave looking east

By the mid-1430s a programme apparently existed for the uniform development of shallow chapels that were to follow the design of those already constructed in the sacristy and the adjoining transept. Cosimo was exiled from Florence in 1433–4, but a document dated June 1434 shows that a number of other individuals were interested in the continuation of building work at S Lorenzo, perhaps motivated by Cosimo's exile, since his absence would have weakened the Medici power base at the church. The 1434 document is particularly significant in that it makes no mention of Brunelleschi. Neither is he mentioned in relation to a decision by the Signoria the previous year to enlarge the piazza in front of S Lorenzo, nor in slightly later building accounts. It seems likely, therefore, that although Brunelleschi was clearly involved in the early stages of rebuilding and possibly even submitted a plan for the overall design, he was not the guiding influence in the overall execution of the church, where building work continued long after his death in 1446; it is now argued that Michelozzo, the architect favoured by the Medici family during the mid-15th century, probably played a leading part in its completion.

It was not until 1442 that the Medici intervened once more in the continuation of building work at S Lorenzo.

In that year Cosimo was involved in financial transactions with the Chapter in which it was agreed that he should have patronage over the entire transept of the new church, including the choir and high altar as well as the part of the remodelled fabric that included the remains of the old Romanesque church. The new church of S Lorenzo, designed on a Latin-cross plan and completed in the 1460s, reflects Renaissance preoccupations with balance and harmony. The exterior was never finished, but the rough façade clearly reflects the internal arrangement of a high central nave flanked by lower aisles and side chapels. Blind arcading on the lower level of the exterior measures out the dimensions of these internal chapels (which are exactly half the area of the square, domed aisle bays) while repeating the harmonious rhythms of aisle and nave arcading. The east end has a square central crossing, square choir and transepts, and square chapels grouped around the transepts.

The interior (see fig. 19) is articulated by bands of *pietra serena* stone that clearly define and demarcate the upper clerestory level as well as tracing the semicircular arches of the nave arcade, resting on classically inspired Corinthian columns. The bands of *pietra serena* reinforce the underlying 2:1 ratio that governs the proportions of both plan and elevation, the basic module being one side of the crossing square, to which the dimensions of choir, nave, aisles and chapels are related. Michelozzo's involvement in the work is supported by the architectural style of such details as the capitals in the nave and by the apparent decision to change the original undulating exterior chapel profiles to straight walls. It is significant that when in 1436 Brunelleschi submitted his design for Santo Spirito, the other great Florentine Renaissance church of the 15th century, it featured a series of curves on the exterior, reflecting the internal chapels.

Cosimo de' Medici was buried in S Lorenzo in 1464, his tomb designed by Verrocchio (1465–7). The Chapter subsequently gave his son Piero de' Medici permission to allocate those chapels that were still to be finished on the north side of the church to any citizens of his choice outside the Medici family. They were completed during the following two decades. By the last quarter of the 15th century the responsibility for the fabric and decoration of S Lorenzo lay firmly in the hands of the Medici and their supporters.

Medici patronage continued well into the 16th century, when Michelangelo was commissioned to design the façade (1516; unexecuted), the New Sacristy (1519–34) and the Biblioteca Laurenziana (begun c. 1524; see MICHELANGELO, §I, 4). The wooden model of the façade (1517; Florence, Casa Buonarotti) shows that Michelangelo was concerned with maintaining the unity of the existing church exterior. His design envisaged the continuation of the horizontal cornice bands and blind arcading still visible on the right nave, aisle and chapel exterior walls. The project remained unexecuted, however, when his attention was diverted to the New Sacristy, a funerary chapel for the Medici at the north-east corner of the church, which is regarded as one of the first and finest examples of Mannerism. It has been argued that the conservatism of Michelangelo's patrons, the Medici popes Leo X and Clement VII, demanded that the ground-plan should closely reflect that of Brunelleschi's Old Sacristy at the other end of the transept, but the agitated articulation of the internal walls marks a radical departure from the classical serenity of Brunelleschi's style. The Biblioteca Laurenziana, intended to house the family's collection of manuscripts, has an unconventional high vestibule dominated by a huge staircase (see MICHELANGELO, fig. 10), and a long, low reading-room (see LIBRARY, fig. 1). Work began in the mid-1520s under the patronage of Clement VII (see MEDICI, DE', (9)); like that on the New Sacristy, however, it was interrupted by the Medici family's exile in 1527 and again by Michelangelo's own permanent move to Rome in 1534. Building work at both sites was carried on by Giorgio Vasari and Bartolomeo Ammanati during the 1550s.

Medici hegemony at S Lorenzo was finally proclaimed in the building of the chapel of the Princes, begun by MATTEO NIGETTI to a revised design of Giovanni de' Medici during the early years of the 17th century. This grandiose mausoleum was executed during the 17th century and into the 18th, and it is the burial place of the Medici grand dukes. Designed as a vaulted, octagonal space entirely clad with dark-coloured marble and pietre dure (see §III, 2 above), it represents the Baroque ending

to a project originally conceived at the height of the Renaissance classical ideal.

The most important furnishings are the two pulpits (c. 1465–6; see DONATELLO, §I, 4; PULPIT, fig. 2) by Donatello and his pupils. In the opening between the Old Sacristy and the adjoining chapel is the double tomb of *Piero I and Giovanni de' Medici* (1472) by Verrocchio (see VERROCCHIO, ANDREA DEL, fig. 2). The New Sacristy contains the important tombs of *Giuliano de' Medici, Duke of Nemours* and *Lorenzo de' Medici, Duke of Urbino* (the 'Capitani') by Michelangelo (1524–34; see MICHELANGELO, §I, 3 and fig. 5). Notable paintings include the *Annunciation* (c. 1439) by Fra Filippo Lippi (see LIPPI (1), §I, 2).

BIBLIOGRAPHY
P. G. Conti: *La basilica di San Lorenzo* (Florence, 1940)
V. Herzner: 'Zur Baugeschichte von San Lorenzo in Florenz', *Z. Kstgesch.*, xxxvi (1974), pp. 89–115
I. Hyman: 'Notes and Speculations on S Lorenzo, Palazzo Medici and an Urban Project by Brunelleschi', *J. Soc. Archit. Historians*, xxxiv (1975), pp. 98–120
——: *15th-century Florentine Studies: The Palazzo Medici and a Ledger for the Church of San Lorenzo* (New York, 1976)
J. Ruda: 'A 1434 Building Programme for S Lorenzo in Florence', *Burl. Mag.*, cxx (1978), pp. 358–61
F. B. Saalman: 'S Lorenzo: The 1434 Chapel Project', *Burl. Mag.*, cxx (1978), pp. 361–4
H. Burns: 'S Lorenzo in Florence before the Building of the New Sacristy: An Early Plan', *Mitt. Ksthist. Inst. Florenz*, xxiii (1979), pp. 145–54
C. Elam: 'The Site and Early Building History of Michelangelo's New Sacristy', *Mitt. Ksthist. Inst. Florenz*, xxiii (1979), pp. 155–86
P. Roselli and O. Superchi: *L'edificazione della basilica di San Lorenzo* (Florence, 1980)
U. Baldini and B. Nardini: *Il complesso monumentale di San Lorenzo* (Florence, 1984)

6. S MARIA NOVELLA. The Dominican church of S Maria Novella was built on the site of a 10th-century chapel and of a later Romanesque church dedicated to S Maria delle Vigne (1094). St Dominic was in Bologna in 1219 and from there founded the Dominican convent in Florence (see DOMINICAN ORDER, §§I and III), acquiring the church of S Maria delle Vigne. It is not known when work was first begun on the new Gothic structure, although Dominican friars were documented as directing work there in 1246, and references had been made a few years earlier to the enlargement of the square to the east of the church; the reconstruction work was probably necessitated by larger congregations and the increasing numbers of pilgrims. Such circumstances may explain why the restrictions on size and height of churches laid down in the Dominican constitution were not observed. It is thought that in this first design the church was conventionally orientated, with its façade to the west, unlike the present façade that faces south. There were certainly opportunities for changes in design, since building work was interrupted during the mid-13th century when the monks ran out of funds. There was another burst of activity at the end of the 13th century, a new model for the church being mentioned in 1277. It seems likely that the existing choir and transepts were erected around that date, and work then progressed into the nave. Such details as the sculpting of the aisle capitals reveal a clear understanding of the work of the leading sculptor of the Gothic period, Andrea Pisano. The main structure was completed in 1360 by Jacopo Talenti (see TALENTI, (2)), who was

Master of Works between 1333 and his death in 1362. The bell-tower from the earlier structure was altered and incorporated during the early years of his activity.

The spacious, vaulted interior, orientated north–south, has a Latin-cross plan with a wide nave, high, narrow side aisles and a square sanctuary and square chapels at the north end. These features owe much to the architectural style of French Cistercian abbeys (*see* GOTHIC, §II, 1). Yet at S Maria Novella a change in design is evident in the development away from the narrow French nave towards a broader, lower central area. The equally proportioned spaces around the central crossing are also typical of the Italian Gothic development towards shorter transepts, closer in proportion to the nave bays. The decorative use of grey *pietra serena* on arches and vault-ribs against the white *intonaco* surfaces articulates the structure and emphasizes the sense of progression towards the altar that is created by the decreasing length of the nave bays closest to the square crossing. There is considerable controversy over the dating of various parts of the church, such as the Strozzi Chapel at the end of the left transept, which has been dated both to the 13th century and the mid-1340s. Andrea Pisano's influence on its construction has also been suggested. Some features of the church, notably the wide, round openings of the Chiostro Verde on the west side and the decorative blind arcading on the lower part of the façade, reflect the earlier Romanesque style.

Numerous changes were made to the fabric after the main building activity during the Gothic period, notably the addition of the classically inspired Renaissance façade (*c.* 1458–70; see fig. 20) by Alberti for Giovanni Rucellai (*see* ALBERTI, LEON BATTISTA, §III, 2(ii)(b)), with its green-and-white geometrical patterning and Rucellai *imprese*, mathematical proportions and innovative scroll forms, which were widely copied. Radical alterations were made to the aisle and transept chapels by Vasari in the 16th century, and the original deep choir-screen in the northern half of the nave, with integral chapels, known as the Ponte, was also removed at this time. As at Santa Croce, parts of the conventual complex underwent changes of use that were closely linked with the history of the Medici family. The convent chapter-room, now better known as the Spanish Chapel, which opens off the north side of the Chiostro Verde, was originally erected by Talenti in the mid-14th century not only for use by the friars of S Maria Novella but also as a central council chamber for all Dominicans in the province. Two centuries later, with the marriage of Eleonora of Toledo to Cosimo I de' Medici in 1539, a special dispensation was made for the chapter house to be used as a place of worship for the growing Spanish community in Florence. Its fresco decoration (1365; *see* ANDREA DA FIRENZE (i)) still bears witness, however, to its original purpose.

The church contains some notable works of art, among the earliest being the ceiling frescoes of *c.* 1270 and a Crucifix (*c.* 1300) by Giotto (*see* GIOTTO, §I, 3(iii) and fig. 10). Masaccio's *Trinity* (*c.* 1427) in the left aisle is remarkable for its early use of perspective (*see* MASACCIO, §I, 2(i) and fig. 5). The Strozzi Chapel contains frescoes (*c.* 1354–7) by Nardo di Cione and the Strozzi Altarpiece (*c.* 1354–7) by his brother Andrea (for discussion and illustration *see* CIONE, (1) and (2)). In the choir is the

20. Florence, S Maria Novella; lower part of façade before *c.* 1360, upper part by Leon Battista Alberti, *c.* 1458–70

important Tornabuoni fresco cycle (1485–90) by Ghirlandaio (*see* GHIRLANDAIO, (1), §I, 2(i)(b), and ITALY, fig. 30); and the chapel of Filippo Strozzi, which contains his tomb (1491–5) by Benedetto da Maiano, has a fresco cycle (completed 1502) by Filippino Lippi (*see* LIPPI, (2), §1(iv) and fig. 4). The frescoes (after 1447) in the Chiostro Verde were painted by Paolo Uccello in *terra verde*, which, along with earlier *terra verde* frescoes, gave the cloister its name. Other furnishings include a marble pulpit (1443–52) by Buggiano and a wooden Crucifix (*c.* 1410–15) by Brunelleschi in the Gondi Chapel (*see* CRUCIFIX, §3(ii) and fig. 5).

BIBLIOGRAPHY
G. Kiesow: 'Die gotische Südfassade von S Maria Novella in Florenz', *Z. Kstgesch.*, (1962), pp. 1ff
J. White: *Art and Architecture in Italy, 1250–1400*, Pelican Hist. A. (Harmondsworth, 1966)
K. G. Arthur: 'The Strozzi Chapel: Notes on the Building History of Sta Maria Novella', *A. Bull.*, lxv/3 (1983), pp. 367–86
A. M. Adorisio: 'Una precisazione sulla facciata gotica di Santa Maria Novella', *Ant. Viva*, xxvii/2 (1988), pp. 32–5

ANABEL THOMAS

7. S MINIATO AL MONTE. S Miniato is one of the oldest Benedictine churches in Tuscany. It stands on a hill south of the River Arno overlooking Florence and is not far from Piazzale Michelangelo. St Miniato was martyred in AD 250 during the persecutions of Emperor Decius (*reg* 249–51), and the origins of the church are traceable to early Carolingian times: in 783 Charlemagne donated several properties to the abbey of S Miniato for the repose of the soul of his bride Hildegarde. Later documents refer to a new construction, initiated by the Florentine bishop Hildebrand and supported financially by the Holy Roman Emperor Henry II and his wife Kunigunde. It was

consecrated by Hildebrand on 27 April 1018. The only remains of this building are a few stretches of wall near the crypt and probably some reused capitals. In the second half of the 11th century it was radically restructured in its present form: the recently built monastic complex is referred to in a decree (c. 1062) of Emperor Henry IV. It was not until the following century, however, that the work was completed.

The church has great architectural unity. Its broad basilican form is subdivided into a nave and two aisles, with a raised chancel terminating in a single semicircular apse (see fig. 21). The façade reflects the spaciousness of the interior. It consists of two orders faced with geometrically patterned green-and-white Prato marble intarsia in the Incrustation style, which was also used in the Florence Baptistery and at S Salvatore al Vescovado, in the Badia at Fiesole, and in the collegiate church of S Andrea at Empoli. The lower order at S Miniato has a blind arcade of five semicircular arches resting on Corinthian pilasters. These create a grave, tranquil rhythm, framing the entrance portals in a series of neatly defined geometric reflections. The upper part of the façade was probably begun in the 12th century and completed at the beginning of the 13th. Here the design is more broken up, though the decorative elements are articulated with classical clarity and proportion. In the centre, above the aedicule window that seems to derive from those of the Baptistery, is a 13th-century mosaic showing *Christ in Majesty with the Virgin and St Miniato*. The façade is crowned with a triangular pediment decorated with bichrome intarsia and two atlantids supporting the gable ends. At the summit stands an eagle with

a ball of wool in its claws—the symbol of the cloth-merchants' guild (Arte di Calimala), which contributed to the completion of the church.

The interior has elegant nave arcades supported by columns alternating with composite piers, which continue at the same height in the choir and as a blind arcade around the apse. The overall spatial conception reflects the Early Christian tradition, an impression reinforced by the exposed timber-trussed roof. Yet the composite piers support diaphragm arches in the Romanesque–Lombard style (one of the earliest constructions of this type south of the Appenines), creating a well-judged sequence of interruptions in the longitudinal axis. The rhythmic progression is interrupted by the chancel raised high above the crypt and reached by two flights of steps at the ends of the side aisles. Three great arches lead into the crypt, which has a groin vault supported on 36 miscellaneous monolithic columns. The geometric decoration of the type seen on the façade reappears on the interior nave walls. Here, however, a few additions and restorations were done in the 19th century. There are small round-arched windows in both the aisles and the clerestory.

Around 1297 a contemporary of Cimabue executed the great mosaic in the semi-dome of the apse, representing *Christ in Majesty with Symbols of the Evangelists, the Virgin and St Miniato*. Other internal embellishments were carried out during the Middle Ages: the inlaid pavement (completed 1207, according to an inscription in its first square); the pulpit; the choir-screen; Taddeo Gaddi's frescoes (partly destr.) in the crypt; and the scenes from the *Life of St Benedict* (c. 1387) by Spinello Aretino in the new sacristy.

Additions were also made during the Renaissance. The chapel of the Crucifix in the centre of the nave, in front of the entrance to the crypt, was commissioned in 1447–8 by Piero de' Medici, probably from Michelozzo, to hold the Crucifix of St John Gualberto, a Florentine nobleman. Its design, with a barrel vault supported on columns, shows a clear stylistic continuity with the architecture of the surrounding church. The so-called chapel of the Cardinal of Portugal (see fig. 7 above) is entered through a large coffered arch in the north aisle of the church. This monument is particularly representative of Florentine art of the second half of the 15th century, harmoniously combining architecture, sculpture and painting. The chapel was commissioned by King Alfonso V of Portugal in memory of his nephew James of Lusitania, Cardinal and Archbishop of Lisbon, who died in Florence on 15 December 1459. Its architecture, inspired by Brunelleschi, is attributed to Antonio di Ciaccheri Manetti, who was undoubtedly responsible for the inlaid pavement. The vault decoration is one of the masterpieces of Luca della Robbia, perhaps assisted by his brother Andrea. ALESSO BALDOVINETTI painted the lunettes and pendentives, but his major work is the panel painting of the *Annunciation* (1466–7), set in the recess under the arch of the left wall above the marble episcopal throne. On the opposite wall is the funeral monument of James of Lusitania, sculpted by Antonio Rossellino in 1461. This work is similar in plan to the monument to *Leonardo Bruni* executed in Santa Croce by Bernardo Rossellino, with the additional motif of marble curtains and, most notably, two graceful angels

21. Florence, S Miniato al Monte, interior looking east, second half of 11th century and later

that prefigure those of Verrocchio's monument to *Cardinal Niccolò Forteguerri* in Pistoia Cathedral. On the end wall, over the altar, is a copy of a panel painting, now in the Uffizi, of *SS Vincent, James and Eustace* by Antonio and Piero Pollaiuolo.

BIBLIOGRAPHY
F. Tarani: *La basilica di S Miniato al Monte* (Florence, 1909)
M. Salmi: 'Arte romanica fiorentina', *Arte*, xvii (1914), pp. 265–80, 369–78
L. Dami: 'La basilica di S Miniato al Monte', *Boll. A.* (1915), pp. 216–44
M. Salmi: *L'architettura romanica in Toscana* (Milan, 1926)
H. Beenken: 'Die Florentiner Inkrustationsarchitektur des XI. Jahrhunderts', *Z. Bild. Kst* (1926–7), pp. 221–30, 245–55
E. Anthony: *Early Florentine Architecture and Decoration* (Cambridge, 1927)
W. Horn: 'Romanesque Churches in Florence: A Study in their Chronology and Stylistic Development', *A. Bull.*, xxv (1943), pp. 112–31
W. Paatz and E. Paatz: *Kirchen*, iv (1952), pp. 211–94
P. Bargellini: *San Miniato al Monte: Kunst und Geschichte* (Florence, 1957)
F. Hartt, G. Corti and C. Kennedy: *The Chapel of the Cardinal of Portugal (1434–1459) at San Miniato in Florence* (Philadelphia, 1964)
P. Sanpaolesi: 'Sulla cronologia dell'architettura romanica fiorentina', *Studi di storia dell'arte in onore di Valerio Mariani* (Naples 1972), pp. 57–65
A. Busignani and R. Bencini: *Le chiese di Firenze*, i (Florence, 1974), pp. 217–58
B. Santi: *S Miniato* (Florence, 1976)
L. Zeppegno: *Le chiese di Firenze* (Rome, 1976), pp. 140–51
I. Moretti and R. Stopani: *La Toscana* (1982), v of *Italia Romanica*, 6 vols (Milan, 1978–84), pp. 119–25
M. C. Mendez Atanazio: *A arte em Florença no séc: XV e a capela do cardeal de Portugal* (Lisbon, 1983)

MARIO D'ONOFRIO

8. PALAZZO VECCHIO. Originally known as the Palazzo dei Priori and later as the Palazzo della Signoria and Palazzo Ducale, the 13th-century Palazzo Vecchio was built to house the Priori, the leaders of the guilds, following the establishment of the popular government in 1283. The site was probably chosen because of its proximity to their previous meeting-place, the church of S Piero Scheraggio (destr. 16th century). The new palace was an architectural statement of the new political order that followed the resolution of the fierce fighting between the Guelph and Ghibelline factions in the city (*see* §I, 3(i) above). Construction involved the demolition of a number of buildings formerly belonging to such families of the defeated Ghibelline faction as the Uberti and the Foraboschi, and the subsequent trapezoidal plan of the palace and its skewed façade largely resulted from the piecemeal acquisition of the building site. As the foundations were being laid in 1299, further houses in the vicinity were acquired and demolished in order to create a great piazza to the north (Piazza della Signoria) that would balance the open space on the west resulting from the levelling of the Uberti property. This occasional balancing of spaces continued throughout the first half of the 14th century, and as late as 1349 the decision was taken to demolish the church of S Romolo to the west of the palace in order to improve the square. The bell-tower (known as the *vacca* or 'cow') of the palace, which was considerably higher than the original Foraboschi tower on the same site, was a powerful symbol of the new government; it tolled warnings in times of unrest or danger and called citizens together to discuss matters of communal interest.

The palace was originally free-standing and extended only five bays along its northern flank, which was then the main front. It has been traditionally argued, although there is no precise documentation, that it was designed in the main by Arnolfo di Cambio. Construction was rapid, and the Priori were already installed in 1302, but such haste possibly contributed to later structural problems (see below). During the first half of the 14th century further property to the east was acquired so that the fabric could be expanded along the north front. These later developments are clearly visible in the variety of levels and openings on the north side, although some effort was made to achieve consistency through the use of string courses and a common window-line. The original walls were divided by narrow cornices into three horizontal sections of diminishing height. The robust, rusticated ashlar walls, constructed of blocks of stone quarried from the local Boboli hillside, were pierced by elegant Gothic windows with cusped double openings.

The Palazzo Vecchio (still the town hall of Florence) set the pattern for central Italian civic architecture during the 14th century. Its battlemented upper profile (see fig. 22), with deeply recessed supporting brackets decorated with the coats of arms of the Florentine *comune*, was typical of the fortification of secular buildings from the time of the free *comuni*. Warring factions within the early *comuni* often made it necessary for members of government to install themselves behind battlements and sturdy walls, with internal council chambers safely raised above the level of surrounding streets and squares. The Loggia dei Lanzi opposite the palace, erected during the late 14th century (*see* §I, 3(i) above) and originally known as the Loggia dei Priori or Loggia della Signoria, was used for public government ceremonies. Government officials often congregated on the raised platform (*aringhiera*) in front of the Palazzo Vecchio to hear public proclamations declaimed from the loggia. This structure therefore served as an open-air adjunct to the main government building.

The palace subsequently underwent many changes, both internally and externally. In the 15th century, when it was known as the Palazzo della Signoria, Michelozzo was charged with shoring up the internal courtyard and fortifying the tower, both of which were in danger of imminent collapse; the present courtyard is very different from the 13th-century original, where thick columns with bases and capitals in *pietra serena* lined each side. Michelozzo also carried out extensive alterations to many of the external windows and a number of the internal rooms. Some parts nevertheless remain in their earlier form, notably the ground-floor Sala d'Arme, with groin vaults supported by octagonal pilasters. In 1495, after the expulsion of the Medici, an enormous hall (later remodelled as the Salone del Cinquecento) was built by Cronaca for meetings of the new legislative body (Consiglio Maggiore) until its dissolution in 1530. Decorative schemes of the 15th century include the magnificent ceiling (1476–81) by Giuliano da Maiano and Benedetto da Maiano and frescoes (1482–4) by Ghirlandaio (*see* GHIRLANDAIO, (1), §I, 2(i)(b)) in the Sala dei Gigli; and intarsia work (1475–80) by Francione in the Sala dell'Udienza, where Francesco Salviati later produced important wall paintings (1543–5).

Between 1540 and 1550 the palace was used as the official residence of Cosimo I de' Medici and was called the Palazzo Ducale; during this period the Cappella di Eleonora was decorated by AGNOLO BRONZINO, court

22. Florence, Palazzo Vecchio, begun 1299, and Piazza della Signoria; from the *Death of Savonarola, c.* 1500 (Florence, Museo San Marco)

artist until 1555. The building became known as the Palazzo Vecchio only after Cosimo transferred his principal place of residence to the Palazzo Pitti on the other side of the River Arno in 1550 (*see* §9(i) below). Thereafter the Palazzo Vecchio was used only for government business. A particularly grandiose and ornate internal reconstruction was carried out under the direction of Vasari in 1555–72. Vasari decorated the courtyard in which Michelozzo had worked, designed and built the nearby great staircase rising to the Salone del Cinquecento, and planned an elaborate series of decorative schemes for the palace. The internal rooms reflect the individual tastes of various members of the Medici family: for example the *studiolo* of Cosimo's son Francesco I celebrates his interest in alchemy and the natural sciences (*see* MEDICI, DE', (16); for illustration *see* NALDINI, GIOVAN BATTISTA; *see also* STUDIOLO, fig. 2). Some of the schemes celebrate the triumphs of war and peace, the most splendid being in the Salone del Cinquecento, for which Vasari and his many collaborators painted 39 panels (1563–5) celebrating the power and glory of the Medici (*see* VASARI, GIORGIO, §I, 3(ii) and fig. 5; *see also* MEDICI, DE', (14), for illustration).

Thus, although it was conceived as a monument to a democratic government, the Palazzo Vecchio now bears witness to the power of Florence's best-known rulers, the Medici.

BIBLIOGRAPHY

G. Gargani: *Dell'antico Palazzo della Signoria fiorentina durante la repubblica* (Florence, 1872)
C. von Stegmann and H. von Geymuller: *The Architecture of the Renaissance in Tuscany* (Nuremberg, 1885)
A. Gotti: *Storia del Palazzo Vecchio in Firenze* (Florence, 1889)
J. White: *Art and Architecture in Italy, 1250–1400*, Pelican Hist. A. (Harmondsworth, 1966)
J. Paul: *Der Palazzo Vecchio in Florenz: Ursprung und Bedeutung seiner Form* (Florence, 1969)
G. Orlandi: *Il Palazzo Vecchio di Firenze* (Florence, 1977)
J. Cox-Rearick: *Bronzino's Chapel of Eleonora in the Palazzo Vecchio* (Berkeley, 1993)
R. Starn and L. Partridge: *Acts of Power: Three Halls of State in Italy, 1300–1600* (Berkeley, 1993)

9. PALAZZO PITTI. One of the largest palaces in Florence, the Palazzo Pitti is laid out on the slopes of the Boboli Hill, south of the Arno. It now houses the Galleria Palatina, the Galleria d'Arte Moderna, the Museo degli Argenti and other collections.

23. Florence, Palazzo Pitti, begun c. 1457; façade extended 1618–35 by the Parigi family

(i) Architecture. The palace was commissioned by LUCA
PITTI, who had owned the site (known as the Bogole)
from as early as 1418. It was probably begun c. 1457 and
was certainly well advanced by 1469 when the Pitti family
was already installed. By the latter date, however, Luca
Pitti had fallen from official favour, and the building work
seems to have been interrupted; it was certainly halted by
Pitti's death in 1472. It has been suggested that Brunelleschi produced the original design, consisting of seven bays
with three large ground-floor openings and heavy rustication on each of its three levels, which appears on the
predella of an altarpiece (Florence, Uffizi) from Santo
Spirito by Alessandro Allori. The Palazzo Pitti has traditionally been linked with the great new palace built for the
Medici family in Via Larga (now Via Cavour) in 1444–60.
Brunelleschi's plan for the latter was rejected in favour of
the less grandiose project put forward by Michelozzo, but
he may have subsequently offered similar designs to Luca
Pitti. The architect responsible for the actual construction
of the Palazzo Pitti is unknown, although some attempts
have been made to identify him with Luca Fancelli.

In 1550 the palace was bought from the Pitti family by
Eleonora de' Medici, wife of Cosimo I, and it became the
residence of the main branch of the Medici family; it was
connected with the Palazzo Vecchio and Uffizi by the
Corridoio Vasariano in 1565 (*see* §10 below). In 1560
Bartolomeo Ammanati was given instructions to enlarge
the building and construct a courtyard (*see* AMMANATI,
BARTOLOMEO, §2). He broke away from the contained
classicism of the earlier building and, under the Mannerist
influence of such contemporaries as Michelangelo and
Jacopo Vignola, introduced curiously shaped windows,

broken arches and a variety of rustication. At the same
time the surrounding land was developed to form one of
the first great Italian gardens (*see* §(iii) below). The garden
façade of the palace was arranged as an open loggia on the
first floor, giving a magnificent view over the grounds.

The palace was substantially altered under later members of the Medici family: from 1618 to 1635 the façade
was doubled in length by the PARIGI family (see fig. 23;
see also MEDICI, DE', (22)); and during the second half of
the 18th century, Ignazio Pellegrini added a great northern
wing and Gasparo Maria Paoletti created the Meridiana
wing (after 1776). The palace was finally completed in the
19th century with the construction of the southern wing,
the great internal staircase and the completion of the
Meridiana wing by PASQUALE POCCIANTI.

BIBLIOGRAPHY
F. Morandini: 'Palazzo Pitti: La sua costruzione e i successivi ingrandi-
menti', *Commentari*, i–ii (1965), pp. 35–46
P. Sanpaolesi: 'Il Palazzo Pitti e gli architetti fiorentini della discendenza
brunelleschiana', *Festschrift Ulrich Middledorf* (Berlin, 1968), pp. 124–
35
L. Ginori Lisci: *I palazzi di Firenze nella storia e nell'arte*, 2 vols (Florence,
1972)
M. Bucci and R. Bencini: *Palazzi di Firenze*, iv (Florence, 1973)

(ii) Decoration. The decoration of the palace began under
Ferdinand I de' Medici during the last years of the 16th
century. The first part to be decorated was the right wing,
which had been constructed by Ammanati for Cosimo I.
At the beginning of the 17th century much work took
place under Bernardino Poccetti, who painted the impressive *Battle of Bona and Prevesa* (c. 1608) in the Sala di Bona
(for illustration *see* LIVORNO), as well as a series of

grotesques inspired by the Antique in the small courtyard. A number of other artists, including Lodovico Cigoli, Cristofano Allori, Giovanni da San Giovanni and Baldassare Franceschini, took part in and continued the massive scheme of decoration begun by Poccetti—much of it glorifying the Medici.

Most of the existing interior decoration was carried out during the 17th and 18th centuries in the late Mannerist and Baroque styles. Artists from many parts of Italy came to Florence in the mid-17th century. Angelo Michele Colonna, Agostino Mitelli from Bologna and in particular Pietro da Cortona from Rome created elaborate scenographic decoration in fresco and stucco. The *Four Ages of Man* for the Sala della Stufa and the Planetary rooms were carried out by Cortona and his followers during the 1630s and 1640s, the latter completed in 1666 by Cortona's pupil CIRO FERRI. These magnificent flights of fantasy, full of allegories concerning the Medici and the glories of a mythical past, anticipated the grand style of Luca Giordano (*see* CORTONA, PIETRO DA, fig. 2). Many of the large-scale wall and ceiling decorations radically extended the apparent size of the court rooms through architectural and spatial illusionism.

Landscape views were later produced (e.g. by Salvator Rosa), mainly for the private rooms, where the interior decoration was continued under Ignazio Pellegrini, Jacopo Chiavistelli (1621–98) and Sebastiano Ricci, among others. Many of the smaller rooms were lined with silk tapestries and painted with elaborate architectural extensions and floating figures that anticipate the Rococo style of Giambattista Tiepolo. Some areas were also articulated by fine stucco mouldings, creating such dazzling small spaces as the oval Gabinetto and the Sala da Lavoro, or queen's music-room. In the later 18th century and early 19th, further projects took place; the Sala Bianca (1776–83) was decorated by Gasparo Maria Paoletti, and some rooms, such as the Sala d'Ercole, were decorated in the Neo-classical style during the early 19th century.

See also §(i) above and CACIALLI, GIUSEPPE.

BIBLIOGRAPHY
M. Chiarini: 'The Decoration of Palazzo Pitti in the Seventeenth and Eighteenth Centuries', *Apollo*, cvi (1977), pp. 178–89
K. A. Piacenti: 'The Summer Apartment of the Grand Dukes', *Apollo*, cvi (1977), pp. 190–97

ANABEL THOMAS

(iii) Boboli Gardens. The gardens of the Palazzo Pitti were designed on several levels with wild and cultivated vegetation, pools and fountains. They comprise two principal sections, the original one commissioned by Cosimo I de' Medici. In 1550 Niccolò Tribolo designed the waterworks and the basic lines of the central axis, which extends behind the Palazzo Pitti up to the Forte di Belvedere. After 1560 Bartolomeo Ammanati linked the palace and the garden by a courtyard and ramp. Bernardo Buontalenti created the fanciful tripartite Grotto Grande between 1583 and 1585 (*see* BUONTALENTI, BERNARDO, fig. 1); this contains frescoes by Bernardino Poccetti, a figure of *Venus* (*c.* 1565) by Giambologna and *Helen and Paris* sculpted by Vincenzo de' Rossi (1558–60; for illustration *see* ROSSI, VINCENZO DE'). On the exterior of the grotto is a group of *Adam and Eve* by Baccio Bandinelli, whose statue of *God the Father*, intended for the high altar of Florence Cathedral, was transformed into a figure of *Jupiter* and set in an adjacent rose garden. The Grotticina di Madama (*c.* 1584) contains marble goats by Giovanni Fancelli (*fl* 1568–86). Above the palace courtyard is the large

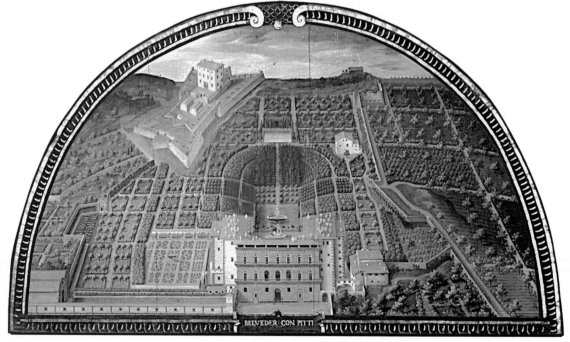

24. Florence, Boboli Gardens, begun *c.* 1550; depicted in lunette by Giusto Utens, tempera on canvas, 1.45×2.40 m, 1599–1602 (Florence, Museo di Firenze com'era)

Artichoke Fountain (1639–41) by Francesco Susini. This is set on the main axis of the palace and faces the stone amphitheatre (1599), which was built against the natural hollow of the rising hillside and was the site of many court festivities. Above the amphitheatre is the Neptune Fountain (1565–8) by Stoldo di Gino Lorenzi, and to the left is the Rococo Kaffehaus (1776) by Zanobi del Rosso (1724–87). By the walls of the Forte di Belvedere is a small casino and the Giardino del Cavaliere, a walled garden enclosing the Monkey Fountain by Pietro Tacca.

The second section of the garden, designed by Giulio Parigi and his son Alfonso, stretches down a slope to the Porta Romana gate. A magnificent cypress avenue lined with Classical statues leads to the Isolotto, a circular island surrounded by a moat, on which stands a replica of Giambologna's *Neptune* (original now Florence, Bargello) in the centre of the Ocean Fountain (1567–76). This section of the garden contains a rich collection of 18th-century genre statues. The areas flanking the avenue were formerly subdivided with mazes, flowerbeds and thickets for hunting birds.

When the *barco* (park) of Francesco I de' Medici at Pratolino was redesigned, many of the statues were sent to the Boboli Gardens. Tribolo's original design can be studied in one of 14 lunettes depicting the Medici villas in and around Florence (see fig. 24) by Giusto Utens (*d* before 19 April 1609). Despite minor planting changes and the reorganization of statues, the gardens remain largely intact, thus presenting a rare, extant example of a late Renaissance garden on this scale.

BIBLIOGRAPHY
G. Cambiagi: *Descrizione dell'imperiale giardino di Boboli* (Florence, 1757)
F. M. Soldini: *Descrizione del giardino di Boboli* (Florence, 1789)
F.Inghirami: *Description de l'imp. et r. palais Pitti et du r. jardin de Boboli* (Fiesole, 1832)
D. Heikamp: 'La grotta grande del giardino di Boboli', *Ant. viva*, iv (1965)
J. Chatfield and F. Gurrieri: *Boboli Gardens* (Florence, 1972)
Boboli 90. Transactions of the International Conference on the Protection and Use of the Garden: Florence, 1989

JUDITH CHATFIELD

10. UFFIZI. The Palazzo degli Uffizi houses the greatest collection of Florentine art and the State archives of Tuscany. Cosimo I de' Medici in 1559 commissioned the court architect, Giorgio Vasari, to design the palace, intending that it should house the public offices of the State—hence the name Uffizi, meaning offices (*see* VASARI, (1), §I, 3(iii) and fig. 6). By 1564 the part adjoining the Palazzo Vecchio was complete, and in 1565 Cosimo instructed Vasari to build the private passageway known as the Corridoio Vasariano linking the Palazzo Vecchio and Uffizi to the new Medici residence, the Palazzo Pitti on the far side of the River Arno. This was completed in a record five months. Vasari employed considerable engineering skill in overcoming the difficulties of building on sandy, unstable ground close to the river. He used iron to reinforce the building, which allowed him to insert large and frequent apertures, and he incorporated remains of the 11th-century Romanesque church of S Piero Scheraggio.

When Vasari died in 1574, the supervision of the work passed to BERNARDO BUONTALENTI and Alfonso di Santi Parigi (*d* 1590). The building was completed soon after 1580. Francesco I de' Medici (*see* MEDICI, DE', (16)) had the second storey of the palace remodelled to display the works of art belonging to the Medici family. Buontalenti completed the design of the Galleria and designed the Tribuna, the octagonal domed hall where the works of greatest value were kept. He also built the unusual side entrance known as the Porta delle Suppliche (*c.* 1580) and the theatre in the eastern part of the palace, where the Gabinetto dei Disegni is housed today.

The Uffizi occupies a U-shaped site between the Palazzo Vecchio and the Lungarno. Two long, narrow wings stand on either side of a narrow piazza and are linked by a short façade on the river-front, which is opened in a Venetian window on the ground-floor. The two wings are composed of long arcades supporting three upper storeys, and the façade is divided into regular units of three bays. Vasari's design elegantly frames and enhances the view both to the Palazzo Vecchio and to the river. The palace is built in Fossato stone, similar to the *pietra serena* that was used for many Florentine buildings. The Uffizi was the largest building project in Florence of its period and the first Florentine building to be conceived as a piece of urban design (see fig. 3 above). Modelled on Michelangelo's Biblioteca Laurenziana at San Lorenzo, it was intended as a faithful return to the principles of ancient architecture. It was also the first building designed as a museum, and its series of long, well-lit, interconnecting galleries served as a prototype for many subsequent museums and galleries.

See also MUSEUM, §I, and ITALY, §XIV, 2.

BIBLIOGRAPHY
Uffizi: Quattro secoli di una galleria. Atti del convegno internazionale di studi: Firenze, 1982
L. Berti, ed.: *Gli Uffizi: Storie e collezione* (Florence, 1983)

SARAH MORGAN

V. Institutions.

1. Accademia del Disegno. 2. Medici academy.

1. ACCADEMIA DEL DISEGNO. The Accademia was based on the Compagnia di S Luca (founded 1349), an association of artists of a religious character, and was constituted in 1563 largely at the instigation of Giorgio Vasari. Its numbers increased in 1571 when more artists broke away from the Arte dei Medici e Speziali (founded 13th century) and the masons' guild (founded 1236). The enlarged institution became the sole officially recognized professional body representing Florentine artists, and the school of art (*see* ACADEMY, §2). In its final legal form, established in 1585, it comprised the Compagnia and the Accademia *sensu stricto*, and it was administered on behalf of the court by a Luogotenente (lieutenant) drawn from a distinguished Florentine family. The Accademia survived in this form until it was replaced in 1784 by the Accademia di Belle Arti, founded by Leopold, Grand Duke of Tuscany.

The term 'academy' had been used formerly by Italian artists to describe their schools of art or their intellectual attitudes. Vasari extended its meaning to the whole Florentine scene (*see* §2 below). The new institution was modelled on the Accademia Fiorentina, which had been founded in 1542 through the transformation of the Accademia degli Umidi (1540) into an official institution.

After consultation with Florentine artists, including Agnolo Bronzino and Giovanni Angelo Montòrsoli, and members of the court, Vasari announced his plan on 24 May 1562 during the consecration of the chapel of St Luke in SS Annunziata, which Montòrsoli had offered to the artists of Florence. The Accademia's constitution, which was approved by the court on 13 January 1563, was shaped by VINCENZO BORGHINI, Prior of the Ospedale degli Innocenti (see fig. 25). For the first two years he acted as the Luogotenente, after which he continued to serve as the chief adviser on iconography. The Accademia's prestige in Florence was considerably enhanced by its organization of the memorial ceremony (14 July 1564) in honour of Michelangelo in S Lorenzo and the completion of extensive decorations for the Medici court, including the modernization of S Maria Novella and Santa Croce (1564–75), and the decorations for the wedding in 1565 of the future Francesco I and Joanna of Austria (1547–78).

Vasari's greatest success was the acquisition, with Cosimo I's support, of premises at the Cistercian monastery (destr.) in Borgo Pinti. The Accademia's school was housed there from 1568 to 1627, and lectures on mathematics and geometry were given as early as 1569 (*see* ITALY, §XVI, 2); the earliest surviving accounts date, however, from the first half of the 17th century. Young people learnt to draw by copying works of art and studying models from life. Exhibitions were staged at the monastery annually on 18 October, the feast of St Luke, the patron saint of artists. The theoretical principles on which the school was founded were discussed in its statutes, in *I tre primi libri . . . intorno agl'ornamenti che convengono a tutte le fabbriche che l'architettura compone* (1568; Venice, Bib. N. Marciana, MS. It. IV, 38) by Gherardo Spini and in Francesco Bocchi's *Eccellenza della statua del San Giorgio di Donatello* (Florence, 1584), which was dedicated to the Accademia.

The Accademia served as a model for the artists' associations and schools of art that emerged in Europe in the 17th and 18th centuries. Its vitality is indicated by the participation of its members in various competitions, for

25. *Presentation of the Statutes of the Accademia del Disegno by Vincenzo Borghini to Cosimo I de' Medici* (1609) by Bernardino Poccetti, fresco, Museo dell'Ospedale degli Innocenti, Florence

example for the façade of Florence Cathedral in 1635, and their contribution to the preservation of monuments of national importance and to the decree of 1601 that prohibited the export of works by the great masters (*see* ITALY, §XIII). The financial support of the Medici ensured that the Accademia's exhibitions (especially those held in 1681, 1706, 1715, 1724, 1729 and 1734) were of great artistic importance, and printed catalogues were issued on most occasions. From 1673 to 1686 a branch, modelled on the Ecole de France, was housed in the Palazzo Madama, Rome.

BIBLIOGRAPHY

G. Ticciati: *Notizie dell'Accademia del Disegno della città di Firenze dalla sua fondazione fino all'anno 1739* (MS.; London, BL, Ashburnham MS. 1035); ed. P. Fanfani in *Spigolatura michelangiolesca* (Pistoia, 1876), pp. 193–307

F. Boroni Salvadori: 'Le esposizioni d'arte a Firenze dal 1674 al 1767', *Mitt. Ksthist. Inst. Florenz*, xviii/1 (1974), pp. 1–166

T. Reynolds: *The Accademia del Disegno in Florence: Its Formation and Early Years* (diss., New York, Columbia U., 1974; microfilm, Ann Arbor, 1974)

The Twilight of the Medici: Late Baroque Art in Florence, 1670–1743 (exh. cat., ed. S. F. Rossen; Detroit, MI, Inst. A.; Florence, Pitti; 1974), pp. 19–24 [article by K. Lankheit]

C. Acidini: *Il disegno interrotto* (Florence 1980), pp. 13–183

C. Dempsey: 'Some Observations on the Education of Artists in Florence and Bologna during the Later Sixteenth Century', *A. Bull.*, lxii (1980), pp. 552–69

B. Laschke: 'Montorsolis Entwürfe für das Siegel der Accademia del Disegno in Florenz', *Mitt. Ksthist. Inst. Florenz*, xxxi/2–3 (1987), pp. 292–402

Z. Waźbiński: *L'Accademia Medicea del Disegno a Firenze nel cinquecento: Idea e istituzione*, 2 vols (Florence, 1987)

Z. WAŹBIŃSKI

2. MEDICI ACADEMY. Lorenzo the Magnificent developed lands at the Piazza S Marco (lands that his grandsire Cosimo had begun assembling in the 1450s, as Elam demonstrated) into a retreat with reception rooms as well as pleasant grounds. By 1480 the property was well-enough developed to show the Cardinal of Aragon its library and garden. Accounts by Benedetto Varchi and Vasari state that it was 'filled with antique and modern sculptures, in such a way that the loggia, the paths and all the rooms were adorned with good antique figures of marble, with paintings...from the hands of the best masters' (Vasari). According to them, young artists and aristocrats, including Michelangelo, were placed in the care of BERTOLDO DI GIOVANNI to study the examples of ancient art, forming a 'school and academy' that Pevsner defined as working to the 'first modern method'. As Bertoldo and Lorenzo died in 1491 and 1492 respectively, their involvement in the project would have been brief. The garden's contents were sacked in 1494 by French troops under Charles VIII.

Vasari's account, which appears only in the second edition (1568) of his *Vite*, has been questioned by some scholars, especially Chastel, noting that the inclusion of Niccolò Soggi (*c.* 1480–*c.* 1552), Lorenzo di Credi and Andrea Sansovino appears to be inaccurate. Chastel claimed that Vasari's description, which may be seen as a symbolic grafting of Domenico Ghirlandaio's pupils on to the Verrocchio workshop, was political in purpose, intended to create a prototype for the newly founded Accademia del Disegno (*see* §1 above) and to help secure the support of Cosimo I.

There is supporting evidence, however, for the existence of an educational instrument as described by Vasari and Varchi. As early as 1427 the humanist Poggio Bracciolini had used 'academy' precisely in the context of a villa containing sculptures that provided a place for contemplation (*see* ACADEMY, §1). Vasari continued to understand the same meaning. His writings show a fair knowledge of Bertoldo, whose chief contribution was to instruct Michelangelo in ways of looking at antique relief sculpture, as may be seen by a comparison of the former's *Battle* relief (Florence, Bargello) and the latter's *Battle of the Centaurs* (1492; Florence, Casa Buonarroti). Michelangelo's continued access to a Medici garden, whether at Piazza S Marco or in the Palazzo Medici, is indicated by a letter of 1494 to Adriano Fiorentino from his brother Amadeo with news of Michelangelo's escape 'from the garden'. Leonardo appears to have taken the idea of 'academy' to Milan, as the phrase 'Academia Leonardi Vinci' was applied to his workshop's knot-engravings. Pomponius Gauricus and Baccio Bandinelli were other early users of the term in an artistic context: Agostino dei Musi's engraving of 1531 shows Bandinelli and his 'academy' studying sculpture intently in a manner consistent with Vasari. The stress on the aristocratic nature of the enterprise by Vasari concurs with the belief of Leonardo and Bandinelli in the exalted calling of the artistic profession.

BIBLIOGRAPHY

G. Vasari: *Vite* (1550, rev. 2/1568); ed. G. Milanesi (1878–85), iv, pp. 256–9; vi, p. 201; vii, pp. 141–2

B. Varchi: *Orazione funerale di Benedetto Varchi fatta e recitata da lui pubblicamente nell'esequie di Michelagnolo Buonarroti* (Florence, 1564), pp. 21–2

K. Frey: *Michelangiolo Buonarroti: Quellen und Forschungen zu seiner Geschichte und Kunst* (Berlin, 1907), ii, pp. 45, 62–3

N. Pevsner: *Academies of Art, Past and Present* (Cambridge, 1940), pp. 1–66

A. Chastel: 'Vasari et la légende médicéenne: L'Ecole du jardin de Saint-Marc', *Studi vasariani. Atti del convegno internazionale per il IV centenario delle 'Vite' del Vasari: Firenze, 1950*, pp. 159–67

C. Elam: 'Il palazzo nel contesto della città', *Il Palazzo Medici–Riccardi di Firenze*, ed. G. Cherubini and G. Fanelli (Florence, 1990), pp. 44–57

J. D. Draper: *Bertoldo di Giovanni: Sculptor of the Medici Household* (Columbia, MO, and London, 1992)

JAMES DAVID DRAPER

Florence, Dukes of. *See* MEDICI, DE'.

Florensky, Pavel (Aleksandrovich) (*b* Yevlakh Halt, Transcaucasus, 21 Jan 1882; *d* Solovki Island, 15 Dec 1943). Russian priest, theologian and theorist. He studied mathematics at Moscow University in 1900–04 but after a spiritual crisis joined the seminary at the monastery of the Trinity and St Sergius at Sergiyev Posad and was ordained in 1911. In his youth he had been influenced by the aesthetic teachings of Lev Tolstoy, and between 1919 and 1922 he concentrated mainly on art theory. After the closure of the seminary he became part of the Commission on the Preservation of Monuments, presenting papers that include 'Church Rites as a Synthesis of the Arts' and 'The Iconostasis'. These were partially published in the magazine *Makovets* and were also circulated in manuscript form. He examined the symbolism of the Church in connection with the liturgy and particularly focused on the meaning of the iconostasis, where the saints are held to be a channel of grace. Some pages are devoted to colour symbolism.

The essay 'The Backward View' is linked with a series of lectures, 'The Analysis of Spaciousness in Works of Art', which he gave at the Vkhutemas in Moscow in 1922–4. In these he tried to combine his knowledge of geometry with concepts of spirituality and the psychology of perception. He argued that culture is revealed in the means by which space is organized; the backward view is God's as he looks down on earth. In 1933 he was arrested and sent to the concentration camp on Solovki.

WRITINGS

Sobraniye sochineniy [Collected works] (Paris, 1985)

BIBLIOGRAPHY

S. I. Fidel': *Ob ottse Pavle Florenskom* [On Father Pavel Florensky] (Paris, 1988)

V. S. TURCHIN

Florentia, Rafaelle de. *See* RAFFAELLINO DEL GARBO.

Florentin, Dominique. *See* BARBIERE, DOMENICO DEL.

Florentine mosaic. *See under* HARDSTONES and FLORENCE, §III, 2.

Florentinus, Franciscus. *See* FRANCISCUS ITALUS.

Florianus. *See* BLUEMNER, OSCAR.

Floridablanca, Conde de [Moñino, José] (*b* Murcia, 21 Oct 1728; *d* Seville, 30 Dec 1808). Spanish statesman, lawyer and patron. He was one of two chief legal advisers and criminal prosecutors for the crown in the 1760s and played a leading role in the investigations following the Squillache riots (1765) and the expulsion of the Jesuits. He successfully carried out a delicate mission to the Holy See between 1772 and 1776, and his energy, lucidity of mind and honesty made a favourable impression on other Spanish representatives in Rome. Charles III appointed him chief minister in February 1777, and he was subsequently ennobled. The post of First Secretary of State carried with it that of Protector of the Academia de S Fernando and, since Floridablanca continued in this appointment until he fell from power and was exiled in 1792, he had an important say in art policy for 16 years.

Floridablanca's principal concern was to raise the standard of arts and crafts in Spain as part of his wider efforts to strengthen the economy and international standing of his country. He approved the plan to reproduce major Spanish works of art in engraved form and seems to have given a personal impulse in 1778 to a series of engravings after the fresco cycle painted by Luca Giordano in the Casón of Buen Retiro in 1692. The ceiling frescoes representing an *Allegory of the Golden Fleece* and the *Labours of Hercules* (destr. 19th century) were painted along the upper part of the walls. Floridablanca took a personal interest in the paintings commissioned for the royal foundation and church of S Francisco el Grande in Madrid in the early 1780s, and in letters Francisco de Goya sensed that the Conde saw this as a competition between leading Spanish artists for future favours. Goya wrote to Floridablanca to explain the merits of his own picture of *St Bernardino Preaching* (1782–3; Madrid, Church of S

Francisco el Grande) and, since he highlighted its compositional ingenuity, he must have assumed some knowledge and appreciation of artistic conventions on the Conde's part.

Legislation introduced under Floridablanca had a major effect on the arts. He was against the restrictive practices of local guilds, and in 1782 it was decreed that guilds of carpenters and gilders should no longer prevent sculptors from applying the finish to their own statues; in 1786 a Royal Order permitted both foreign and Spanish artists to practise their art without let or hindrance wherever they pleased. He wanted to see improved standards of architecture and required the Academia de S Fernando to give formal approval for altarpieces or other works placed in churches; from 1787 only the Madrid Academia could declare that an architect was proficient and could practise. Finally, crafts were made honourable under Floridablanca, so that craft work no longer debarred an individual from claiming *hidalguía*, or high social status.

Floridablanca's personal taste remains an enigma. He lacked the means to cultivate a lavish life-style at the time of his embassy in Rome, but once he was prime minister he seems to have attached some importance to dress, and his red trousers and silk stockings were the subject of aristocratic ridicule. When Goya painted Floridablanca in his mid-50s in the *Conde de Floridablanca and Goya* (1783; Madrid, Banco Urquijó) the Conde certainly wore bright colours and silky materials. Apart from portraits, the only works we know that he commissioned were the decorations for his official residence in Madrid, now known as the Palacio de Godoy in the Plaza de la Marina Española; the building was used as the Naval Ministry in the 1920s. The decorations were planned and executed by Gregorio Ferro and José del Castillo between 1787 and 1792, but the decorative scheme was probably totally redone for Manuel Godoy, Prince de la Paz, when he took over the building in the 1790s. Paintings attributed in the 1930s to Ferro and Castillo are no longer visible in the Spanish government's Centre for Constitutional Studies, which now occupies the Palace.

In 1792 Floridablanca passed on his assessment of every aspect of government to his successor. He thought that the Academia de S Fernando might be incorporated into the ambitious Museum for the Sciences (now Museo del Prado). He was not at that juncture optimistic about practitioners in all the arts, believing that there were good Spanish architects, sculptors and engravers but that painting trailed behind and needed further stimulus.

BIBLIOGRAPHY

R. Iglesia: 'Gregorio Ferro, pintor (1742–1812): Apuntes para su biografía', *Bol. Soc. Esp. Excurs.*, xxxv (1927), pp. 21–41

C. Alcazar Molina: *El Conde de Floridablanca: Notas para su estudio* (Madrid, 1929)

A. Rumeu de Armes: *El testamento político del Conde de Floridablanca* (Madrid, 1962)

F. de Goya: Letters of 25 July 1781, 3 Nov 1784, 14 Jan 1785, in *Cartas a Martín Zapater*, ed. M. Agueda and X. de Salas (Madrid, 1982), nos 21, 58, 62

NIGEL GLENDINNING

Florigerio, Sebastiano [Sebastiano di Giacomo di Bologna da Conegliano] (*b* Conegliano, *c.* 1510; *d* Udine, between 1550 and 1564). Italian painter. According to Vasari, who mentioned him as Bastiano Florigorio, he was a pupil of Pellegrino da San Daniele. He is documented in Pellegrino's shop from 1523 and married his daughter in 1527. His earliest surviving paintings are the *Virgin and Child with SS Anne, Roch and Sebastian* and the lunette of *St John the Evangelist with SS Francis and Anthony* (both Venice, Accad.) from the altarpiece executed in 1524–5 for S Francesco, Conegliano. A large painting of the *Virgin and Child with SS George and John the Baptist* (1529; Udine, S Giorgio), probably his best known work, is closer to the style of Pordenone than to that of Pellegrino. From *c.* 1529 until 1533 he was in Padua, where he frescoed a *Pietà* (destr.) for the main altar of S Bovo and painted an altarpiece with the central panel depicting the *Pietà* (Rovigo, Accad. Concordi), the side panels *St Sebastian* and *St Roch* (both Padua, Mus. Civ.) and a predella of three panels: *SS Anthony and Prosdocimus* (Pordenone, priv. col.), signed and dated 1533, *St Daniel* (Venice, Calligaris priv. col.) and *St Justine* (untraced). The altarpiece was reassembled for the exhibition *Dopo Mantegna, Arte padovana e nel territorio nei secoli XV e XVI* (Padua, Pal. Ragione; 1976). He also executed frescoes (destr.) in the portico of the Palazzo del Capitano in Padua. Between 1538 and 1543 he was in Cividale. In 1543 he returned to Udine, where he probably remained until his death. Vasari attributed to him the portrait of *Raffaello Grassi* (Florence, Uffizi).

BIBLIOGRAPHY

G. Vasari: *Vite* (1550; rev. 2/1568); ed. G. Milanesi (1878–85), v, pp. 108–9

R. Marini: *Sebastiano Florigerio* (Udine, 1956)

M. Cosmacini: *Sebastiano Florigerio* (diss., U. Trieste, 1971)

G. Briganti, ed.: *La pittura in Italia: Il cinquecento* (Milan, 1988), p. 716

LUCA LEONCINI

Floris [Vriendt, de]. Flemish family of artists. The earliest known members of the family, then called de Vriendt, were active as masons in Brussels in the 15th century. One of them, Jan Florisz. de Vriendt, left his native town and settled in Antwerp *c.* 1450. His patronymic name 'Floris' became the usual family name for the next generations, although the original form 'de Vriendt' can still be found in official documents until the late 16th century. Jan Floris's grandson Cornelis Floris I (*d* 17 Sept 1538) had a mason's workshop in the Steenhouwersvest, Antwerp, where he specialized in cutting tombstones. Initially he was helped by the two eldest of his four sons, but later they all chose a more distinguished artistic profession: (1) Cornelis Floris II became a sculptor and an architect, (2) Frans Floris I a painter, Jan Floris a potter and Jacques Floris a painter of stained-glass windows. All four sons joined the Guild of St Luke in Antwerp. Before this, in 1533, their uncle Claudius Floris (*d* after 1548), the youngest brother of their father and presumably also the first teacher of Cornelis II, had also become a member of the Guild. No works by Claudius Floris survive, but his name occurs often in the Antwerp archives, for instance among the artists who restored and redecorated Antwerp Cathedral after the fire of 1533. In 1538 he was apparently already using Renaissance ornament motifs. That he may even have learnt them firsthand from a visit to Italy is suggested by the Italianate form of his name, 'Clauderio', which is sometimes given in documents.

BIBLIOGRAPHY

P. Rolland: 'La Famille Floris à Tournai', *32e Congrès Fédération archéologique et historique de Belgique: Antwerp, 1947*, i, pp. 294–317

(1) Cornelis Floris II (*b* Antwerp, *c.* 1513–14; *d* Antwerp, 20 Oct 1575). Sculptor and architect. The hypothesis (see Roggen and Withof) that he was the pupil of Jean Mone is contradicted by the fact that already in 1524 Mone had left Antwerp to become court sculptor to Margaret of Austria in Mechelen. According to his own testimony, Cornelis II was residing in Rome in 1538, when his father died. He then returned home to take care of his mother and younger brothers. He joined the Antwerp Guild of St Luke in 1539–40 and was also a member of the masons' guild. No works executed between 1539 and 1548 can be identified, years in which he presumably continued his father's workshop. However, he obviously intended to widen the scope of his artistic career and took an increasingly active part in the Guild: in 1547 and 1559 he served as its dean. During the first of his terms as dean, at the end of the guild year 1547–8, he embellished the guild register with grotesque initials (Antwerp, Stadsarchf). He used these ornaments profusely in his other works, and they became extremely popular in the decoration of several different art forms (e.g. architecture, sculpture, tapestries, metalwork, pottery etc).

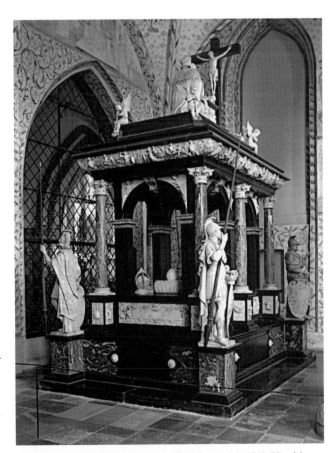

Cornelis Floris II: tomb of *Christian III of Denmark* (*c.* 1568–75), alabaster and marble, Roskilde Cathedral

Cornelis Floris's period of intense activity began *c.* 1548, with Hieronymus Cock's publication of his engraved series of *Vases* (Hollstein, nos 49–67). In 1549 Floris received the first of a series of commissions of funeral monuments for the Danish royal family, and it seems likely that he was also involved in the decorations for the triumphal entry of Philip II into Antwerp in April of that year. Like his brother Frans, whose participation in the event is documented, he bought a house early in 1550, presumably using his recent earnings. Floris's commissions for marble funeral monuments with alabaster statues came from foreign princes (e.g. *Christian III of Denmark*, *c.* 1568–75, Roskilde Cathedral, see fig.; *Albert I of Brandenberg*, *c.* 1569, Kaliningrad Cathedral), as well as from Flemish nobles (e.g. *Jean III, Comte de Mérode*, 1554; Geel, St Dimpnakerk). His designs for such monuments were popularized by the engravings published by Hieronymus Cock (*Veelderley niewe inuentien van antycksche sepultueren*, 1557). Other ornamental inventions of Floris were also engraved and published by Cock (*Veelderley veranderinghe van grotissen*, 1556). Among Floris's other surviving sculptures are such complex structures as the stone tabernacle (1550–52) of the St Leonarduskerk, Zoutleeuw (*see* BELGIUM, fig. 23), and the rood screen (1573) of Tournai Cathedral. These works were instrumental in spreading the Renaissance style throughout the Netherlands. Floris's style is based on the local south Netherlandish tradition of the early 16th century, enlivened by contact with the art of Renaissance Rome (for example the works of Andrea Sansovino) and possibly with the school of Fontainebleau (e.g. Primaticcio), especially in the artist's later years.

As an architect, Floris's most important and influential contributions were his designs for the portico (1557) of the Cologne Rathaus, for the new Stadhuis (1561–5) of Antwerp (*see* ANTWERP, fig. 9) and for the town house (1562–5; destr. 1816) of his brother Frans at Antwerp.

PRINTS

Veelderley veranderinghe van grotissen [Numerous varieties of grotesques] (Antwerp, 1556)
Veelderley niewe inuentien van antycksche sepultueren [Numerous new designs for antique sculpture] (Antwerp, 1557)

BIBLIOGRAPHY

Hollstein: *Dut. & Flem.*; Thieme–Becker
R. Hedicke: *Cornelis Foris und die Florisdekoration*, Studien zur niederländischen und deutschen Kunst im XVI Jahrhundert (Berlin, 1913)
P. Buschmann: 'Drawings by Cornelis Bos and Cornelis Floris', *Burl. Mag.*, xxix (1916), pp. 325–7
A. J. J. Delen: 'Un Dessin de Corneille Floris', *Rev. Belge Archéol. & Hist. A.*, ii (1932), pp. 322–4
A. Cosemans: 'Correspondentie van Cornelis Floris betreffende het Merodepraalgraf te Geel' [Correspondence from Cornelis Floris concerning the Merode funerary monument at Geel], *Rev. Belge Archéol. & Hist. A.*, v (1935), pp. 251–61
A. Corbet: 'Cornelis Floris en de bouw van het Stadhuis van Antwerpen' [Cornelis Floris and the building of the Antwerp Town Hall], *Rev. Belge Archéol. & Hist. A.*, vi (1936), pp. 223–64
J. Duverger: 'Cornelis Floris II en het Stadhuis te Antwerpen', *Gent. Bijdr. Kstgesch.*, vii (1941), pp. 37–72
D. Roggen and J. Withof: 'Cornelis Floris', *Gent. Bijdr. Kstgesch.*, viii (1942), pp. 79–171
——: 'Aanvullende nota's bij onze studie over Cornelis Floris' [Supplementary notes to our study of Cornelis Floris], *Gent. Bijdr. Kstgesch.*, ix (1943), pp. 133–6
H. Jonas: 'Vererblichkeit künstlerischer Begabung: Die Gebrüder Cornelis und Frans Floris de Vriendt, und ihr Künstlertum, eine kunsthistorische und genealogische Betrachtung', *Arch. Sippenforsch. & Verwandten Geb.*, xxxii (1966), pp. 408–14
S. Van Gelder: 'De Sacramentstoren van de Sint Leonarduskerk te Zoutleeuw', *Brabant. Flklore*, cxciv (1972), pp. 182–200
C. Van de Velde: 'The Grotesque Initials in the First Ligger and in the Busboek of the Antwerp Guild of Saint Luke', *Acta van het Internationaal Colloquium 'De Brabantse kunst rond het midden van de 16de eeuw en de wandtapijten van de Wawelburcht te Krakau'*: Brussels, *1972*, pp. 252–77
L. Smolderen: 'Le Tombeau de Charles le Téméraire', *Rev. Belge Archéol. & Hist. A.*, xlix/1 (1980–81), pp. 21–53
H. Honnens de Lichtenberg: 'Some Netherlandish Artists Employed by Frederick II', *Hafnia*, viii (1981), pp. 51–71
W. Aerts: 'Enkele aantekeningen in verband met de Sacramentstoren van Cornelis Floris in de Sint Leonarduskerk te Zoutleeuw' [A few notes in connection with Cornelis Floris's tabernacle for the St Leonarduskerk at Zoutleeuw], *Cornelis Floris Jb.* (1981), pp. 30–36
P. van Herck: 'Cornelis Floris, ontwerper van het doksaal in de kathedral te Doornik' [Cornelis Floris, designer of the rood screen in Tournai Cathedral], *Cornelis Floris Jb.* (1981), pp. 117–26
L. de Barsee and P. Baudouin: 'Cornelis de Vriendt de Jonge genaamd Floris, Antwerps beeldhouwer, ornamentist en bouwmeester (1514–1578)' [Cornelis de Vriendt the younger, called Floris, Antwerp sculptor, decorator and architect (1514–1578)], *Cornelis Floris Jb.* (1983), pp. 32–42
'Enno II en het mausoleum in de Grote Kerk van Emden', *Cornelis Floris Jb.* (1983), pp. 43–5
R. Steenmeyer: 'Twee stadhuizen van Vlissingen', *Cornelis Floris Jb.* (1983), pp. 80–97
A. Huysmans: 'De grafmonumenten van Cornelis Floris', *Rev. Belge Archéol. & Hist. A.*, lvi (1987), pp. 91–122

(2) Frans Floris I (*b* Antwerp, between 17 April 1519 and 1 Oct 1520; *d* Antwerp, 1 Oct 1570). Painter, draughtsman and etcher, brother of (1) Cornelis Floris II. He was one of the leading exponents of ROMANISM in Antwerp, and his history painting influenced a generation of Flemish artists. He was largely responsible for the introduction of studios organized in the Italian manner, with skilled assistants—a practice subsequently adopted by other Netherlandish artists, most notably Rubens.

1. LIFE AND WORK. Van Mander recorded that, as a young boy, Frans assisted his father in making bronze effigies for funeral monuments, but this cannot be substantiated. After his father's death, he switched to painting and became a pupil of Lambert Lombard in Liège, a surprising choice since there were many painters in Antwerp who could have taught him. However, it may have been the result of a friendship between Frans's brother Cornelis and Lombard, both of whom were in Rome *c.* 1538. It is also possible, although undocumented, that Frans trained as a painter in Antwerp before joining Lombard's studio.

Floris became a master in the Antwerp Guild of St Luke in 1539–40 and probably as early as 1541 or 1542 travelled to Rome, as his brother, and possibly his uncle Claudius, had done before him. While there, he drew copies of antique sculpture (e.g. the 'Roman Sketchbook', Basle, Bib. Öffentlicher Kstsamml., MS. U.iv.6–U.iv.29) and contemporary Italian paintings, including Michelangelo's work in the Sistine Chapel (the *Last Judgement* was unveiled in 1541), Raphael's decorations in the Vatican Loggie and the façade paintings on Roman palazzi by Polidoro da Caravaggio (e.g. Paris, Ecole N. Sup. B.-A.). An inscription on Giulio Bonasone's engraved portrait of Floris refers to him as a prominent member of the Netherlandish community in Rome. Floris also visited other Italian cities; in Mantua he copied Giulio Romano's frescoes in the Palazzo Ducale and the Palazzo del Te, and in Genoa it is likely that he saw Perino del Vaga's frescoes in the Palazzo

Doria. In 1543 Floris executed a triptych of *St Margaret* (Rome, priv. col., see Van de Velde, 1975, no. 1, fig. 1), commissioned by the del Bene family for the church of S Margherita Ligure, near Genoa. He remained in Italy until *c.* 1545 and was back in Antwerp by October 1547, when he married Clara Boudewijns, the daughter of an Antwerp goldsmith, and established his own studio in the city.

In 1549 Floris was commissioned by the city authorities to contribute to the decorations for the triumphal entry of Charles V and the Infante Philip into Antwerp. His work on the Arch of the Genoese, for which (according to van Mander) he painted seven life-size figures a day, for seven weeks, was highly praised and brought him to public attention. Some of these scenes are recorded in prints and one, *Victoria Surrounded by Prisoners and Trophies* (1552; Hollstein, no. 4), was etched by the artist himself.

By 1550 Floris was able to buy a house on the fashionable Meir, behind which he built his studio. His commissions came from the Church, secular authorities and private individuals. He produced a number of altarpieces for the guilds that were then installed in their chapels in the cathedral: the *Fall of the Rebel Angels* (1554; Antwerp, Kon. Mus. S. Kst.) was for the fencers' guild; the *Adoration of the Shepherds* (1567–8; Antwerp, Kon. Mus. S. Kst.; see fig. 1) for the gardeners' guild. The *Assumption of the Virgin* (1561–4) was executed for the cathedral's high altar but destroyed in the Iconoclastic Fury of 1566; Floris restored the triptych in 1567, but by 1581 it had disappeared from the church and was replaced by the artist's *Adoration of the Shepherds*, which remained

there until 1627 when Rubens's *Adoration of the Virgin* (*in situ*) was installed.

In 1571 a *Banquet of the Gods* was listed in an inventory of the Antwerp Stadhuis, although it is unclear whether it was transferred from the old building or in the new one designed by Cornelis Floris (1560–64). The contents of the Stadhuis were destroyed during the Spanish Fury of 1567 and replaced by paintings donated by local collectors; these donations included two other works by Frans Floris, a *Judgement of Solomon* (1547–56; Antwerp, Kon. Mus. S. Kst.) and a *Massacre of the Innocents* (untraced).

Many contemporary Antwerp collectors owned works by Floris, as is attested by 17th-century inventories. Niclaes Jongelinck, a rich merchant and tax collector, commissioned Floris to execute ten paintings of the *Labours of Hercules* (1554–5) for his house in the outskirts of Antwerp, and in 1556–7 he received seven paintings of the *Liberal Arts*. Although the *Hercules* series was still complete in the 18th century, only one work is now known, *Hercules and Antaeus* (Brussels, priv. col., see Van de Velde, 1975, no. 76, fig. 31); the *Liberal Arts* series was dispersed before the end of the 16th century, but one was rediscovered in the late 1980s (see fig. 2). (Cornelis Cort engraved both series, in 1563, Hollstein, nos 47–56, and 1565, Hollstein, nos 63–9, respectively.) These works by Floris exemplify the newly introduced genre of mythological and allegorical subject-matter—something Guicciardini recorded as largely due to Floris. Vasari shared Guicciardini's praise of the artist, though he stopped short of endorsing Floris's nickname of the 'Flemish Raphael'.

In Italy, Floris was known mainly through the medium of engravings, while in the Netherlands his fame was based on works that could be seen in several churches outside Antwerp. These included three triptychs for the great St Leonarduskerk at Zoutleeuw (all *in situ*), the *Seven Wounds of Christ* (*c.* 1555), the *Baptism of Christ* (*c.* 1558–60) and *Christ and the Repentant Sinners* (*c.* 1568), a pair of shutters for the memorial to Abbot Lucas Munnich in Ghent Cathedral and a triptych of the *Last Judgement* for Notre-Dame-de-la-Victoire in Brussels. The triptych of the *Crucifixion* for the Nieuwe Kerk, Delft (Arnstadt, Oberkirche, since the late 16th century), introduced Floris's art to the northern Netherlands, and van Mander recorded several examples of his work in private Dutch collections in such cities as Amsterdam and Middelburg. Floris also painted a number of strongly characterized portraits (e.g. *Portrait of a Man with a Falcon*, Brunswick, Herzog Anton Ulrich-Mus., and the *Portrait of a Woman with a Hound*, 1558; Caen, Mus. B.-A.).

The intensive activity of Floris's studio between *c.* 1555 and *c.* 1565 brought financial success, and in 1562–3 he built a magnificent house in a new quarter of the city with a spacious studio behind it (destr.). The street façade of the house was decorated with seven paintings imitating bronze sculptures in niches—personifications of the qualities required by the true artist: *Energy, Skill, Knowledge of Poetry, Knowledge of Architecture, Strength, Experience* and *Diligence*. Over the door was a large painting of *Pictura*. A series of 16th-century engravings by the Monogrammist TG (1576) and a drawing by Jan van Croes (*c.* 1700; Brussels, Bib. Royale Albert 1er) record the original

1. Frans Floris: *Adoration of the Shepherds*, oil on panel, 2.49×1.93 m, 1567–8 (Antwerp, Koninklijk Museum voor Schone Kunsten)

2. Frans Floris: *Awakening of the Arts after the End of the War*, oil on canvas, 1.57×2.38 m, 1556–7 (Ponce, Museo de Arte de Ponce)

appearance of the façade decoration, which had disappeared by the time the house was demolished in the early 19th century. According to van Mander, the cost of this house and Floris's lavish way of life and heavy drinking led to his downfall and death. All his possessions were publicly sold immediately after his death.

While Floris's work of *c.* 1545 frequently reflects his Italian studies and also has affinities with the work of Lambert Lombard and of Pieter Coecke van Aelst (e.g. in his use of changeant colours), his style later became increasingly monumental and the figures more convincingly placed in the composition. After 1560 his work became more Mannerist, and the sculptural handling of the figures gave way to a more painterly approach, even though the colours often tend towards the monochrome. The figures, perhaps because of contact with members of the school of Fontainebleau, become more elegant and the works generally more sophisticated, often with a somewhat melancholic air.

2. WORKING METHODS AND STUDIO. From the time of his return to Antwerp *c.* 1545, Floris organized his studio along the lines of those he had seen in Italy (e.g. that of Giulio Romano) and employed a considerable number of assistants (*see also* STUDIO, §II, 2). Van Mander, who knew several of Floris's pupils (e.g. Lucas de Heere, Frans Pourbus the elder and Ambrosius Francken), claimed that the artist had some 120 assistants, of whom he named 30. All seem to have joined Floris's studio after previous training. The young painters came from all over

the southern and northern Netherlands and from as far away as Cologne. One working method invented and developed by Floris was the use of study heads, life-size representations of heads of men and women that he painted in oil on panel. These he then put at the disposal of his assistants, either for literal transcription or for freer adaptations.

Floris's growing success from *c.* 1550 onwards and the increasing number of commissions he received meant that he had to rely heavily on his assistants, although their exact role is still unclear. Sometimes they painted figures using Floris's study heads, sometimes they added landscape backgrounds and sometimes they copied his compositions, either in paint or on paper, for reproductive engravers. Many such engravings after Floris's work were published in Antwerp, mostly by Hieronymus Cock. The plates were cut by some of the best engravers in the Netherlands (Philip Galle and Cornelis Cort in particular, but also Jan Wierix, Balthazar van den Bos, Pieter van der Heyden, Frans Huys, Dirck Volckertsz. Coornhert and Jan Sadeler I). The engravers worked mostly from preparatory drawings made from his paintings, presumably by Floris's assistants, and a number of such drawings still exist (e.g. *The Virtues*, engraved by Cornelis Cort, Hollstein, nos 75–82; Floris's designs in Berlin, Kupferstichkab., Brussels, Bib. Royale Albert 1er, and Vienna, Albertina). Some series were designed specifically for engraving (e.g. the *Five Senses*, 1560; Hollstein, nos 70–74). The exact part played by studio assistants in the creation of these preparatory drawings remains to be studied.

BIBLIOGRAPHY

Hollstein: *Dut. & Flem.*; *NBW*

G. Vasari: *Vite* (1550, rev. 2/1568); ed. G. Milanesi (1878–85), v, p. 441; vii, p. 585

L. Guicciardini: *Descrittione di . . . tutti i Paesi Bassi* (1567)

K. van Mander: *Schilder-boeck* ([1603]–1604)

C. Van de Velde: *Frans Floris (1519/20–1570): Leven en werken* (Brussels, 1975) [with early bibliog.]; reviews by K. G. Boon in *Burl. Mag.* cxix (1977), pp. 509–10; K. Renger in *Z. Kstgesch.*, xlii (1979), pp. 299–304

D. A. Iñíguez: 'Frans Floris, *La Virgen del Perdón* de la catedral de Méjico', *Archv Esp. A.* (1979), p. 439

H. Honnens de Lichtenberg: 'Some Netherlandish Artists Employed by Frederick II', *Hafnia*, vii (1981), pp. 51–71

C. L. Ragghianti: 'Fiamminghi del cinquecento in Toscana', *Crit. A.*, xlvi (1981), pp. 75–87

A. Lombard-Jourdan: '*Le Christ ailé*: Un Tableau inédit, au thème iconographique exceptionnel, monogrammé et daté 1562', *Gaz. B.-A.*, n. s. 5, xcviii (1981), pp. 28–32

L. Robijns: 'De herkomst van de verdwenen *Kruisigingstriptiek* van Frans Floris in de Sint-Martinuskerk te Aalst' [The return of the missing triptych of the *Crucifixion* by Frans Floris to the St-Martinuskerk in Aalst], *Archv. A. Lovan.* (1981), pp. 339–48

R. An der Heiden: 'Zur Wiederentdeckung eines verschollenen Gemäldes Frans Floris: *Gleichnis von den klugen und törichten Jungfrauen*', *Die Weltkunst*, liii (1983), pp. 1497–9

N. Bialler: 'Schilderachtige prenten (Picturesque Prints)', *Essays in Northern European Art Presented to Egbert Haverkamp-Begemann* (Doornspijk, 1983), pp. 33–7

J. Maldague: 'Michel-Ange et Pollaiuolo dans la *Chute des anges* (1554) de Frans Floris', *Jb.: Kon. Mus. S. Kst.* (1983), pp. 169–90

C. Van de Velde: 'Een studiekop van Frans Floris voor het Rubenshuis', *Cult. Jb. Stad Antwerpen* (1983), pp. 37–9

J. Maldague: 'Les Dessins de la *Chute de Phaéton* chez F. Floris et Michel-Ange', *Jb.: Kon. Mus. S. Kst.* (1984), pp. 173–88

F. Stampfle: 'The *Holy Kinship*: A Drawing in the Morgan Library Restored to Frans Floris', *Rubens and his World* (Antwerp, 1985), pp. 31–5

C. Van de Velde: 'The Painted Decoration of Floris's House', *Netherlandish Mannerism: Papers Given at a Symposium in the Nationalmuseum, Stockholm: 1984*, pp. 127–34

L. De Ren: 'De aankoop van zes schilderijen van Frans Floris door hertog Karel van Croij' [The purchase of six paintings by Frans Floris by Count Charles de Croij], *Jb.: Kon. Mus. S. Kst.* (1985), pp. 177–88

R. Grosshans: 'Ein Bild aus dem Umkreis des Frans Floris für die Gemäldegalerie', *Jb. Preuss. Kultbes.*, xxiii (1986), pp. 277–81

J. P. Guépin: '*Hercules belegerd door de Pygmeën*: Schilderijen van Jan van Scorel en Frans Floris naar een Icon van Philostratus' [*Hercules Besieged by Pygmies*: Paintings by Jan van Scorel and Frans Floris from an icon of Philostratus], *Oud-Holland*, cii (1988), pp. 155–73

C. King: 'Artes Liberales and the Mural Decoration of the House of Frans Floris', *Z. Kstgesch.* (1989), pp. 239–56

CARL VAN DE VELDE

Flosche, Daniel. *See* FRÖSCHL, DANIEL.

Flötner [Flettner], **Peter** (*b* Thurgau, 1485–96; *d* Nuremberg, 23 Nov 1546). German sculptor, medallist, cabinetmaker, woodcutter and designer. It has been conjectured on stylistic grounds that between 1515 and 1518 he was active in Augsburg and worked in Hans Daucher's workshop on the sculptural decoration (destr.) of the Fugger funerary chapel in St Anna. His early style was formed by the Italianism of Daucher and of Hans Burgkmair I and also by a journey to Italy in 1520–21. He was briefly active in Ansbach before arriving in 1522 in Nuremberg; there he was documented as master sculptor when receiving citizenship in August 1523. His earliest sculptural work in Nuremberg is thought to have been 22 capitals (early 1520s) for the renovated Rathaus (destr. 1945). The use of Italian Renaissance ornament, such as volutes decorated with acanthus leaves and fluting, represented a progressive

development, in contrast to Albrecht Dürer's Gothic-inspired architectural design of the Ehrenpforte. Flötner's first-hand study of Italian Renaissance architectural vocabulary is apparent in the ornamentation of the pilasters of the triangular fountain (1526) in the Markt at Mainz, commissioned by Cardinal Albrecht von Brandenburg. Most of the motifs he used, such as vases with arabesques of combined acanthus leaves and vine leaves extending into grotesque figures or dolphins, are derived from Lombard architectural works, such as the portals of the Certosa di Pavia.

Flötner's mature style is first seen in the Apollo Fountain (1532; Nuremberg, Stadtmus. Fembohaus; see fig.), which in its time was claimed to be the most modern fountain in Nuremberg. It was cast in bronze, probably by Hans Vischer or Pankraz Labenwolf (*see* LABENWOLF, (1)), with both of whom Flötner collaborated on various occasions, and was originally placed in the courtyard of the Herrenschiesshaus in Nuremberg. Apollo is depicted bow and arrow in hand, surrounded by putti riding on sea-creatures; this figure, which is based on Jacopo de' Barbari's engraving of *Apollo and Diana*, demonstrates in its formal clarity and slender proportions Flötner's understanding of Italian Renaissance classicism. A woodcut dated 1533 and signed P.F. (Dresden, Kupferstichkab.), which represents grotesques and dancing putti, is closely related to the Apollo

Peter Flötner: Apollo Fountain, bronze, 1532 (Nuremberg, Stadtmuseum Fembohaus)

Fountain in the lively treatment of the plump bodies of the putti.

Flötner's subsequent important commissions were for the interior decoration and furnishing of several noblemen's houses. Designs that survive in the form of woodcuts, such as the *Venetian Bedstead* (Hollstein, no. 69) and various versions of columns and capitals (Hollstein, nos 42–53) dating from the mid-1530s, reveal Flötner's architectural talents. He may have been responsible for the plans of the garden room of the Hirschvogel house (1534; destr. 1945); such features as Georg Pencz's illusionistic ceiling paintings, inspired by Giulio Romano's decorations in Mantua, testified to the extent to which Italian Renaissance innovations had been assimilated in Nuremberg. Flötner carved the wall panelling, the doorways and the stone chimney-piece, all of which displayed his lucid mature style, while a full understanding of the Classical architectural orders was reflected in the balanced arrangement of architrave, frieze and cornice, as well as in his much imitated use of grotesque ornament.

Flötner's fervent support of the Reformation was expressed in anti-Catholic woodcuts such as the *Pious Pilgrimage and Procession of Gluttonous Friars and Sisters from one Church Dedication Festival to Another to Get Indulgences* (c. 1530–35; Hollstein, no. 5). Other prints that mock the Roman Catholic Church include the *Triumphal Arch for Johann Eck* (Hollstein, no. 26) and the *New Passion of Christ* (Hollstein, no. 6), in which the Pope and other ecclesiastics are depicted as the scourgers of Christ. Flötner's talents as designer were applied to a multiplicity of objects, such as a set of 48 playing cards (Hollstein, no. 89) or the *Human Sundial* (c. 1535; Wolfenbüttel, Herzog August Bib., Hollstein, no. 40). His most successful application of the lessons learnt from Italian art is seen in his plaquette design, as in the plaquette depicting the story of *Ate and the Litae* (Santa Barbara, U. CA, A. Mus.), cast c. 1535–40 and based on passages from the Homeric epic the *Iliad*, which Flötner probably knew from Andrea Alciato's *Emblematum libellum*. With its deep space, subtly graduated relief and naturalistic details, in a manner reminiscent of Albrecht Altdorfer and the Danube school, combined with confident treatment of classical Italian concepts of human form, it demonstrates Flötner's mastery of landscape depiction.

In creating decorative sculpture Flötner's method was to prepare a drawing, from which he carved a model in stone or wood, subsequently cast in bronze or silver. The soapstone model of the *Triumph of a Sea-goddess* (c. 1537; Cambridge, MA, Busch-Reisinger Mus.) is a rare surviving example of such a model, which, together with a preliminary drawing (Brunswick, Herzog Anton Ulrich-Mus.) of the same subject and a bronze cast (Paris, Mus. A. Déc.) made by the goldsmith David Knopf (1520/21–1602), offers a valuable insight into Flötner's working methods. The most famous example of his work in the field of decorative arts is the Holzschuher covered goblet (c. 1540; Nuremberg, Ger. Nmus.), which he created in collaboration with the Nuremberg goldsmith MELCHIOR BAIER. Flötner carved bacchanalian scenes recalling his plaquettes into the coconut shell that forms the body of the goblet; the final is in the shape of a satyr pouring wine into a man's mouth, while round the stem winds a Bacchic rout, featuring amorous couples and copulating goats.

Flötner played a leading part in the dissemination of his interpretation of Classical architectural motifs and was also the first artist to introduce grotesque motifs into German Renaissance ornament. In 1546 Rudolff Wijffenbach published *Das Kunstbuch des Peter Flötner*, a compilation of 40 of Flötner's surviving woodcuts that contributed greatly to his influence on German artists working in other media; one such was Wenzel Jamnitzer, who drew on Flötner for many of his designs for goldsmith work.

For illustration of furniture by Flötner *see* CUPBOARD.

BIBLIOGRAPHY

Hollstein: *Ger.*; Thieme–Becker
R. Wijffenbach: *Das Kunstbuch des Peter Flötner* (1546; *R* Berlin, 1882)
J. von Sandrart: *Teutsche Academie* (1675–9); ed. A. R. Peltzer (1925), p. 74
K. Lange: *Peter Flötner: Ein Bahnbrecher der deutschen Renaissance auf Grund neuer Entdeckungen* (Berlin, 1897)
H. Röttinger: *Peter Flettners Holzschnitte* (Strasbourg, 1916)
E. F. Bange: *Peter Flötner* (Leipzig, 1926)
Peter Flötner und die Renaissance in Deutschland: Ausstellung anlässlich des 400. Todesjahres Peter Flötners (exh. cat., Nuremberg, 1946–7)
C. K. Kuhn: 'An Unknown Relief by Peter Flötner', *A. Q.* [Detroit], xvii (1954), pp. 109–13
W. Schwemmer: *Das Bürgerhaus in Nürnberg* (Tübingen, 1972)
M. Angerer: *Peter Flötners Entwürfe: Beiträge zum Ornament und Kunsthandwerk in Nürnberg in der 1. Hälfte des 16. Jahrhunderts* (diss., Munich, Ludwig-Maximilians-U., 1983)
J. Rasmussen: *Die Nürnberger Altarbaukunst der Dürerzeit* (Munich, 1983)
Nuremberg: A Renaissance City, 1500–1618 (exh. cat., by J. C. Smith, Austin, U., TX, Huntington A.G., 1983)
Gothic and Renaissance Art in Nuremberg, 1300–1550 (exh. cat., New York, Met.; Nuremberg, Ger. Nmus., 1986), pp. 435–54   □

Flower painting. Type of painting in which one or more flowers or plants are depicted. The subject is generally associated with STILL-LIFE painting. The painting of flowers has its antecedents in the HERBAL and 'scientific' depictions of plants. It began to emerge as a specialism in northern Europe in manuscripts produced in Bruges and Ghent in the 15th century, particularly those executed by the Master of Mary of Burgundy, whose paintings are surrounded by scattered naturalistic flowers or compartments with still-lifes; for example, the glass vase with some flowers in a folio in the Book of Hours of Engelbrecht of Nassau (c. 1485–90; Oxford, Bodleian Lib., MS. Douce 219, fol. 145v). This article discusses flower painting as a distinct genre in Western art. For its history in ancient and non-Western civilizations *see* CHINA, §V; EGYPT, ANCIENT, §VI, 1(ii); GREECE, ANCIENT, §VI, 1(ii); ISLAMIC ART, §I, 7; JAPAN, §II; KOREA, §I, 5; ROME, ANCIENT, §II, 5.

1. Symbolism. 2. History.

1. SYMBOLISM. The inclusion of flowers in religious paintings of the 16th century was almost entirely symbolic (*see* SYMBOL). In the Portinari Altarpiece, for example, the blue garden iris (a royal flower) may be taken as an attribute of the Virgin as Queen of Heaven; the orange lily (also a royal symbol) represents Christ as King of Heaven. (The white candidum lily was perhaps the most frequent allusion to the purity of the Virgin and almost

mandatory in depictions of the Annunciation.) Royalty is balanced by humility in the guise of violets, who hide their flowers behind their leaves and lie, like the Christ Child, on the ground. The transparent glass is perhaps a reference to the Virgin birth, the carnations, signifying incarnation, are beneath the columbines, representing the dove of the Holy Spirit. The vine in the pottery vase, together with the wheat, are clearly the bread and wine of the Eucharist. The symbolism of flowers, as it applies to secular 17th-century flower paintings, has been the subject of lively debate among historians; although it seems that Ambrosius Bosschaert I was probably not concerned with such associations in his work, nothing would have prevented an onlooker from choosing to read symbolic meanings in his bouquets. Certainly, Jan de Heem and his pupil, Abraham Mignon, were partial to a single wheat-ear as a symbol of Resurrection (John, 12:24).

It is generally agreed that the theme of VANITAS was a strong tradition in flower painting. Certain established conventions continued to be followed by artists, even after they themselves and their customers had ceased to take heed of the implied message. Once the Council of Trent (1545–63) had forbidden religious imagery of the traditional form, these 'hidden messages' may have taken on more importance. *Vanitas* dwelt on the brevity and insignificance of man's earthly life, urging him to ensure his entry to the eternal life thereafter by righteous, Christian conduct. The flower is clearly transitory, again with Biblical endorsement, and painters showed leaves eaten by insects and caterpillars representing man trapped in his humble earthly life, awaiting the transformation to the butterfly, traditionally associated, like birds, with the soul, freed to fly upward to heaven. Worms and flies awaited the earthly body below, and pearl-like dewdrops would not survive the rising of the sun. Where artists wished to emphasize the *vanitas* element, watches, hour-glasses, candles, soap-bubbles, skulls etc were also included; some artists may, however, simply have welcomed the challenge of painting a watch and bringing in another texture to contrast with petals and marble ledges.

Flowers also represented luxury; gardens were the preserve of the wealthy and were usually restricted to their estates. Only substantial houses in the cities had gardens and only small ones in countries where land was precious. The rarity of the cultivated blooms was reflected in the layout of gardens, whose primary function was to display flowers in the manner of an outdoor *Wunderkammer*. So closely related are the enthusiasm for gardening and the rise of flower painting that it is difficult to know whether the wealthy garden-owner commissioned the first flower painting as a record of his achievements or as a compensation for any horticultural failure, and whether he sought to prolong indefinitely the beauty of the costly and short-lived flowering; or whether the artist saw an opportunity and anticipated the demand. The numerous florilegia, for example that published by Emmanuel Sweert (1552–1612) in 1612, were produced primarily to sell the plants. Flower paintings may be compared with the ostentatious banquet still-lifes of the later 17th century, where silver-gilt tazze and jugs are juxtaposed with Venetian glass and exotic foods, fruit and flowers. The price of a finished work by

even so successful and highly-paid a specialist as Ambrosius Bosschaert the elder was probably exceeded by that of the flowers he depicted.

A conflict existed. The newly independent and increasingly prosperous Dutch, with a worldwide empire, sought to enjoy their wealth through gardens and costly flower paintings, yet they were urged to set no store by the vanities of this world. An excellent example of this conflict of meaning is the tulip, which became the object of intense speculation in the 1630s; bulbs changed hands at enormous prices before the market crashed in 1637, and artists were needed to record each new variety: Jacob Marrel and Judith Leyster both painted 'tulip books'. Nevertheless, the tulip's luxurious aspect is counterbalanced by its frequent appearance in emblem books as a symbol of folly and greed, and one must consider both possibilities when looking at flower paintings of the period.

2. HISTORY.

(i) Early 17th century. (ii) Late 17th century. (iii) 18th–20th centuries.

(i) Early 17th century. The first artists recognized as specialist flower painters were Jacques de Gheyn, Ambrosius Bosschaert I (see BOSSCHAERT, (1)), Roelandt Savery (see SAVERY, (2)) and Jan Breughel the elder (see BRUEGEL, (3)). Very little remains of de Gheyn's work, and his influence in the development of the genre is less easily detectable than others. His exquisite and much illustrated watercolour of three tulips with a snakeshead fritillary is dated 1600 (Paris, Fond. Custodia, Inst. Néer.). No dated oil painting by Bosschaert, Breughel or Savery is earlier than 1603, nor are there undated works stylistically datable to pre-1600, although a lost painting by Savery is said to be dated 1600. Correspondence of the late 1590s between Middelburg flower enthusiasts and Carolus Clusius, then Director of the Botanic Garden in Leiden, suggests that flower paintings were being executed. Dutch writers and theorists adhered to the idea of the hierarchy of subjects in art, with history painting at the top and still-life very much at the bottom. This view was not shared by many patrons; in 1606 no finer gift could be contrived for Marie de' Medici than a flower-piece by de Gheyn costing 600 guilders, and, later in the century, paintings by Daniel Seghers were given by the rulers of Flanders to other Catholic heads of state.

The work of Ambrosius Bosschaert the elder epitomizes the early flower-piece (see fig. 1). The vase is centrally placed; the composition is tightly contained in an oval, or what Bergström has called a radial composition; the lighting is even; and overlapping is minimal to show each flower in the manner of an early Dutch portrait, for which each sitter had paid a share. Insects enliven the scene. The accuracy in the depiction of each flower, whether costly or commonplace, recalls the spirit of Dürer's plant studies, manuscripts, the works of Jacopo Ligozzi and Joris Hoefnagel, and the entire concept of scientific naturalism and botanical study. Bosschaert's depiction is accurate in every detail and gives the impression of a brilliant and convincing bouquet arranged in a glass vase. However, taken as a whole, the painting is, of course, an illusion. The flowers are from different seasons and, with few

1. Flower painting by Ambrosius Bosschaert I, oil on copper, 550×390 mm, *c.* 1618 (Copenhagen, Statens Museum for Kunst)

unification, but there is a clear loosening of technique, so that individual brushstrokes become perceptible. His drawing on the prepared surface was rapid, and he did not feel obliged entirely to obliterate this pencil preparation. This relative loosening of technique went with the above greater freedom of composition and a livelier choice of attendant creatures, while shells remained a favourite motif. (The value of shells as collectables could exceed even that of flowers.) Van der Ast thus initiated ideas whose development transformed flower painting in the next generation. Bartholomeus Abrahamsz. Assteyn (1607–*c.* 1667), Johannes Baptista van Fornenburgh (*fl* 1608–*c.* 1649), Jan Baers (*d* 1641), Michiel Sweerts, Anthony Claesz. II (*c.* 1616–*c.* 1652) and, to some extent, Jacob Marrel may be associated with the Bosschaert dynasty.

In his achievements, van der Ast benefited from the influence of Roelandt Savery, a highly important and independent artist, who matured in the service of Emperor Rudolf II and joined the Utrecht Guild of St Luke in 1619. Savery's large set-pieces are similar to plates from florilegia, for example that engraved by Hendrick Hondius the elder after Elias Verhulst (1599); they teem with flowers and creatures brought to life by his painterly brushwork. His approach is brimming with Flemish vigour, even in the tightest detail, and the constraints of Bosschaert's compositional formulae and the serenity of mood are sacrificed for dramatic effect, achieved with strong chiaroscuro lighting. Some pigment darkening may be responsible for accentuating his already strong contrast and dark, defining outlines. There is, however, no evidence of this in one of his finest and best-preserved panels (1612; Vaduz, Samml. Liechtenstein), where the characterization of the mouse behind the love-in-the-mist (nigella) is a reminder of his skill as an animal painter. As with Bosschaert and van der Ast, the scale of Savery's work ranges from a small copper panel (168×139 mm) to a monumental bouquet of 1624 (1.30×0.80 m; Utrecht, Cent. Mus.). Christoffel van den Berghe's bouquet of 1617 (Philadelphia, PA, Mus. A.) shows the influence of Bosschaert and Savery and displays a competence that suggests other flower paintings by him remain to be discovered beyond the four known examples. Unlike Bosschaert, van den Berghe remained in Middelburg.

The work of Jan Breughel the elder is also fundamental to an understanding of flower painting. Such was the stature of Breughel in Europe that the new genre may be said to have gained prestige because he included it among his wide-ranging works. His technique was typically Flemish; whereas Bosschaert returned day after day to a tulip to build up a glazed perfection, where the evidence of hand and brush are gradually eliminated, Breughel 'draws' vigorously in paint with the brush in the manner of Rubens's oil studies: the colour is brilliant; the white ground provides great luminosity; and the whole is imbued with irrepressible vitality. This technical mastery, which allowed such speed of completion, is the sole explanation of the size of the autograph works. The large 'compendium' bouquets, often in wooden tubs (versions Amsterdam, Rijksmus., and Vienna, Ksthist. Mus.), may contain nearly 200 flowers from 40 species. Yet his miniaturist technique, learnt from his grandmother, Marie Bessemers

exceptions, this is true of all 17th- and 18th-century flower paintings. The artist relied on his drawings and watercolours, taken directly from individual flowers as they bloomed, to compose such imaginary bouquets. Licence was also taken on occasion with scale, lighting and the likelihood that such a large quantity of flowers and foliage could have been squeezed into the glass or vase.

Bosschaert's style was perpetuated by his three sons, Ambrosius the younger, Johannes and Abraham, and his young brother-in-law, BALTHASAR VAN DER AST, or, as aptly named by Bol (1962), the 'Bosschaert dynasty'. Their work shows that they benefited from inherited working drawings from Ambrosius the elder, none of which survive. Unlike the Bosschaerts, van der Ast enjoyed a long career and a large output (*c.* 200 works are known). He enlarged the compositional repertory with variations: a single tulip in a vase; a conventional vase of flowers; a combination of a vase or basket with shells and fruit; flowers and shells lying on a table top with a shell as the only container for some of the flowers; and new interior and exterior settings. A pair of small panels by van der Ast, once in the collection of Princess Amalia von Solms (now USA, priv. col., on loan to Washington, DC, N.G.A.), are thought to be the earliest example of the pairing of fruit and flowers as pendants. In contrast, he worked on large canvases equally successfully.

Van der Ast kept essentially to the glazing technique of Bosschaert with pearly, enamel effects and a subtle, tonal (*fl* 1537; *d* 1550), in youth, allowed him to achieve a level of detail that requires a magnifying glass to appreciate, for example his tondo surrounding Rubens's *Madonna and Child* with a garland with over 30 birds among the flowers (Paris, Louvre). Osias Beert I was an important contemporary still-life and flower painter at Antwerp, who also collaborated with Rubens, and whose works were confused with Breughel's until the 1930s. Beert's nephew and pupil was Frans Ykens. Six paintings by Georg Flegel, active in Frankfurt am Main, are reminiscent of the large Breughel and Savery bouquets, although his greatest contribution was in still-life painting. Another comparison is with the large painting on copper of 1627 (Amsterdam, priv. col.; see Mitchell, fig. 26) by Peter Binoit (1590/93–1632), a member of the circle of Isaak Soreau (1604–after 1638) and also active in nearby Hanau.

The Flemish sense of monumentality and the need for votive images in the Catholic world led naturally to the development of variations in wreaths, garlands and cartouches to surround the religious image. DANIEL SEGHERS, who became Breughel's pupil at Antwerp in 1611 and through whom he was reconverted to Catholicism, devoted the major part of his life to this end in the service of the Jesuit Order. As a result simple, secular, informal bouquets by Seghers are rare. Jan van Kessel II, Breughel's grandson, perpetuated the Breughel style and format into the late 17th century. Breughel's son by his first marriage, Jan Breughel the younger, is now recognized as an excellent flower painter in his own right (*see* BRUEGEL, (4)).

The diffusion of flower painting outside the Netherlands is typified by Jean-Michel Picart (*c.* 1600–1682), born at Antwerp but who became French by adoption. His oval bouquet (Cambridge, Fitzwilliam) is unthinkable without the example of Seghers. Jacques Linard was another prominent member of the Franco-Flemish colony of artists based at Saint-Germain-des-Prés. The close links between the southern Netherlands and Spain and the continual importation of paintings from the north for the court and nobility ensured that Juan de Arellano was soon painting garlands inspired by Seghers. Arellano's most distinguished works were of very large baskets filled with flowers to the bottom (e.g. Fort Worth, TX, Kimbell A. Mus.), painted as if 'shaken by a sudden gust of wind'. Seghers's work and his visit to Rome (1625–7) also inspired Mario de' Fiori, who interpreted the garland in his own Italianate manner, which, in turn, influenced Arellano. Their names, like that of JEAN-BAPTISTE MONNOYER in France and England, became familiar through large-scale production and diffusion to meet the demand for flower paintings, which had arisen not only because of their intrinsic qualities but also because of their decorative role in the elaborate interiors of the later 17th century and early 18th. In Antwerp this need was later met by the studios of the Verbruggen and Casteels families. Nicholaes van Verendael (1640–90), the most accomplished decorative flower painter of his generation, was an exception among Flemish-born artists in his lack of financial success.

(ii) Late 17th century. In this period the Dutch and Flemish traditions were unified through Jan de Heem I, whose name remains the best-known of all 17th-century still-life and flower painters (*see* HEEM, DE, (1)). Unlike Bosschaert, Breughel or Seghers, de Heem was as notable for his large-scale still-life banquet pieces as he was for flower painting. He trained with van der Ast, and his still-lifes are in the Haarlem tradition of Pieter Claesz. Having absorbed the Bosschaert tradition in his native Utrecht and having worked in Leiden, in 1636 de Heem moved to Antwerp and came under the influence of Seghers. De Heem took up garlands, cartouches and swags, skilfully adding fruits. His work is characterized by his mature technical perfection and brilliance of colour with characteristic strong reds and whites. The contrast between Bosschaert and this de Heem bouquet of the late 1640s is instructive: de Heem's stems flow freely; flower-heads thrust towards the on-looker; the vase casts a shadow on the shelf; and the trailing stems and a wheat-ear in front of the vertical face of the stone shelf are familiar repoussoir effects (see fig. 2). With the flowers placed to the back of the bouquet in half tone, these are all subtle devices to create depth. In flower painting the need to convince the onlooker that there is a space where this large bouquet can stand is fundamental to the illusion. In this context de Heem's sensitivity to light and atmosphere might be said to be the strongest legacy of his Dutch upbringing. His closest followers, as flower painters, were his son Cornelis de Heem (1631–95) and Abraham Mignon; the latter, at his best, rivals his teacher. Some scholars have judged a few paintings to be the result of collaboration between the two. The highly finished style of the tight brush dominated flower painting, although ABRAHAM VAN BEYEREN offered a contrasting softer and freer technique.

2. Jan de Heem: *Vase of Flowers*, oil on panel, 475×370 mm (Brussels, Musées Royaux des Beaux-Arts de Belgique)

Unsurprisingly, in the latter part of the century flower painting followed the fashion for increasing opulence that originated in France. WILLEM VAN AELST took up the S-curves and the elegance of colour and design, inherent in de Heem's work, and tempered his palette to cool French blues, greys and purples, helped in doing so by his stays in Paris (1645) and Italy (1649). A moulded marble top replaces the stone shelf, a silver vase his glass one, with an elaborate watch and ribbon to provide further notes of opulence and sophistication. In 18th-century France Nicolas de Largillierre and François Desportes were attentive not only to this source but also to the strong painterly qualities of Abraham van Beyeren and Jan Fyt. The possibilities of the baroque, eccentric bouquet were well explored by Simon Verelst. During his Italian stay, van Aelst was friendly with OTTO MARSEUS VAN SCHRIECK, whose outdoor settings in dark, forest floors show flowers, herbs, thistles and poisonous plants, abounding with snakes, toads, moths and insects, all carefully nurtured for study by the painter. The effect is one of drama and mild horror or fascination that impressed Matthias Withoos and van Aelst's pupil, the youthful RACHEL RUYSCH, who carried Dutch flower painting gloriously into the 18th century.

Jan van Huysum (see HUYSUM, VAN, (1)), who was the most successful flower painter in history, took the flowerpiece to its apogee (see fig. 3). He maintained the highest standard of finish—the smallest feather in the lining of a bird's nest bears scrutiny. He continued the lightening of the palette, apparent with Ruysch, and banished the dark

3. Flower painting by Jan van Huysum, oil on canvas, 800×600 mm, 1726 (London, Wallace Collection)

or neutral background, replacing it with inviting, verdant glimpses of the patron's estate, real or imaginary, with fine trees and statuary. He saw the colouristic and decorative potential of terracotta vases with putti in relief. Van Huysum's drawings show his rapid massing of contents in terms of light and shade; he instinctively avoided the overloading that sometimes threatened his principal follower, Jan van Os, and, in every aspect, displayed an unerring refinement of taste. The international influence of van Huysum was such that no thinking, conventional flower painter could take up the palette without awareness of him. Van Huysum's only direct pupil, Margareta Haverman (*fl c.*1716–30), went to Paris in the 1720s, a forerunner of those who were part of an exodus that took place in the later part of the century.

(*iii*) 18th–20th centuries. At the end of the 17th century, the focus of flower painting moved away from the Netherlands for the first time. Gerard van Spaendonck (*see* SPAENDONCK, VAN, (1)) led the way to Paris, followed by his younger brother, Cornelis, Pierre-Joseph Redouté, Georgius van Os and Jean van Dael, all of whom saw glittering patronage and a desire for flower paintings that could not be satisfied by French-born painters; Anne Vallayer-Coster is an exception to this generalization. The upheavals of the Revolution (1789–95) and war seemed to leave the advancement of botanical study and flower painting unscathed. Empress Joséphine's enthusiasm for gardens and flowers was indulged on an unprecedented scale by Napoleon, but very much in the tradition of royal and courtly support of flower painting. Spaendonck was not only the master of all formats from the 50 mm-diameter miniature to the large-scale Salon canvas, but of all media, too, including engraving. His role as a teacher was of great importance after his appointment to the Musée National d'Histoire Naturelle in 1780. Spaendonck's complete, specialist mastery of van Huysum's legacy of supreme skill was one side of his success; the other was the elegance and refinement of French taste.

Although the majority of van Spaendonck's followers were French, one of the best known was of Belgian birth, PIERRE-JOSEPH REDOUTÉ, whose fame outshone that of his master. Redouté's reputation derived from countless reproductions of the plates made from his original watercolours. His *Campanula* (1787; London, V&A; for illustration *see* REDOUTÉ, PIERRE-JOSEPH) was painted for a private patron, but the great majority of his vellums were single specimen studies destined for engraving to illustrate many books, of which *Les Liliacées* (1802–16) and *Les Roses* (1817–24) are the best known, and to contribute to *Les Vélins du Roi*, in succession to van Spaendonck. He also succeeded him as a teacher of major importance. At the museum, Redouté taught classes for 30 hours a week for 16 years and privately instructed both amateurs and professionals at his studio in Paris and at Fleury-sous-Meudon. Some of his pupils (e.g. Camille de Chantereine) became teachers in their turn, others his collaborators (e.g. Pancrace Bessa and Lesourd de Beauregard, his successor at the museum).

By the 18th century watercolour flower painting was established as a fitting accomplishment for aristocratic ladies. It had originally been the most expressive method

4. Flower painting by Jean-Siméon Chardin, oil on canvas, 452×371 mm, 1760–63 (Edinburgh, National Gallery of Scotland)

of botanical illustration in the hands of such artists as Joris Hoefnagel, de Gheyn, Giovanna Garzoni, Nicolas Robert and, later, Georg Dionysius Ehret, Ferdinand Bauer (1760–1826) and his brother Francis Bauer (1758–1840); it was also used by artists who accompanied the early plant-hunters (e.g. Jacques Le Moyne de Morgues, Maria Sibylla Merian and Francis Masson) for obvious practical reasons. In England Ehret wrote that 'had he divided himself in twenty parts, he would still have had his hands full'. What had been the preserve of the few became, in the 19th century, a popular pastime as did outdoor landscape sketching. From the Salon des Aquarellistes in Paris to the local horticultural society, exhibitions proliferated, as did instructional manuals, colouring books, sentimental flower books and botanical journals.

Pupils of both van Spaendonck and Redouté, and their contemporaries throughout Europe, found employment through the traditional links between fine flower painting and industry. Jakob Ber (1786–1863) equalled the achievements of his teacher van Spaendonck at the Sèvres Porcelain Factory, and his pupils succeeded him. The leading artist of the Viennese school, Johann Baptist Drechsler (1756–1811) began painting porcelain at 16 and rose to be Director of Porcelain Design at the Academy in Vienna by 1807, combining the roles of designer, easel painter and teacher. Many parallels to Drechsler's career may be cited in the textile industry. In some cases, to the detriment of his subsequent reputation, an artist's best work has remained in local museums or private collections; for example, the work of Jean-Georges Hirn (1777–1839) is little known today outside Colmar, France. One of the most important flower painters in France in the 19th century, ANTOINE BERJON, suffered the same fate until

1974 and has still to be properly appreciated. Lyon was the centre of the world's silk industry and therefore needed and encouraged flower draughtsmen and painters as designers for the weaver. Works by de Heem, Mignon and van Dael were collected by the museum in Lyon and a Salon des Fleurs opened in 1807, to help Lyonnais artists in their studies at the Ecole des Beaux-Arts. With Berjon as their inspiration and instructor, these artists formed the most prolific school of flower painting in France, if not Europe, and were inevitably champions of the Dutch and Flemish tradition. The influence of Lyon was, thus, far-reaching and enduring. In the second half of the 19th century there was little reason for the traditional approach to flower painting to lose its mass appeal. On the contrary, William Henry Hunt's birds'-nests and the bouquets of John Wainwright (fl 1859–69) seem a distant echo of van Huysum, and the tradition continues today.

However, other approaches were possible; and these derive from the work of JEAN-SIMÉON CHARDIN (see fig. 4). A centrally placed, simple Delft vase and small, contained bouquet of carnations, tuberoses and sweet peas, on a simple shelf where a few petals and a red carnation have fallen, seem at first glance to revive the format and serenity of Bosschaert in the age of Louis XV. Yet, clearly, the approach, the technique, the lighting, the mood were far ahead of their time, and, despite the contemporary praise for Chardin, he fell into a neglect that was only rectified in the mid-1840s. The most commanding flower painter in the second half of the 19th century was Henri Fantin-Latour (see FANTIN-LATOUR, (1)), who united the Vermeer-like quality of Chardin with

5. Henri Fantin-Latour: *Basket of Roses*, oil on canvas, 489×603 mm, 1890 (London, National Gallery)

6. Odilon Redon: *Wild Flowers*, pastel, 570×330 mm, *c*. 1912 (Paris, Musée du Louvre, Cabinet des Dessins)

a meticulous approach reminiscent of the early masters (see fig. 5). The achievements of Berjon, Fantin-Latour and Manet are inseparable from the example of Chardin. His immediate and more modest followers were Antoine Vollon and his son Alexis Vollon (1865–1945), Théodule Ribot, Philippe Rousseau and François Bonvin, although the latter rarely painted flowers. Hovering between Romanticism and Realism, between Delacroix and Courbet, these artists generally favoured an informal treatment of flowers in copper pots, often with books on the table, with the emphasis on painterliness, working from their own arrangements set up in the studio with some 'props' familiar from many appearances. Their painterly approach was not confined to France, of course. With William Merrit Chase, the American painter (of Danish origin) Emil Carlsen (1853–1932)—a keen student of Vollon's in the 1870s with a collection of his work—became the leading still-life painter of his period.

ODILON REDON was introduced to plants and flowers by the botanist Clavaud. Once again the botanist encouraged the flower painter, and, throughout his life, Redon was never happier than when in a garden or a garden studio. His flower paintings mostly belong to the post-1900 period, although he had painted them as early as the mid-1860s. In *Wild Flowers* (*c*. 1912; see fig. 6) he depicts field flowers with great intensity of colour. The Expressionist EMIL NOLDE must also be considered a flower painter. His series of sunflowers from 1926 (version,

Madrid, Mus. Thyssen-Bornemisza) are in direct homage to the work of van Gogh, while his watercolours were painted in the 1930s and 1940s, the period when he was banned from professional activity and materials were hard to acquire. For him, as for Redon and many other artists of the late 19th and 20th centuries, flower painting was often as much a form of relaxation or escape from the pressures of life as it was for their patrons.

BIBLIOGRAPHY

R. Warner: *Dutch and Flemish Flower and Fruit Painters of the XVIIth Centuries* (London, 1928, rev. Amsterdam, 1975)

J. G. van Gelder: 'Van blompot en blomglas', *Elsevier's Geïllus. Mdschr.*, lxvi (1936)

M.-L. Hairs: *Les Peintres flamands de fleurs au XVIIe siècle* (Brussels, 1955; rev. 1965)

I. Bergström: *Dutch Still-life Painting in the Seventeenth Century* (London, 1956)

M. Charageat: 'La Fleur dans la miniature du moyen-âge au 17ème siècle', *Jardin des Arts*, 54 (1959)

C. Sterling: *Still-life Painting from Antiquity to the Present Time* (Paris, 1959)

L. J. Bol: *The Bosschaert Dynasty* (Leigh-on-Sea, 1962)

M. Faré: *La Nature morte en France* (Paris, 1962)

La natura morta italiana (exh. cat., Naples, Pal. Real, 1964)

I. Bergström: *Maestros españoles de bodegones y floreros del siglo XVII* (Gothenberg, 1970)

W. H. Gerdts and R. Burke: *American Still-life Painting* (New York, 1971)

P. Mitchell: *European Flower Painters* (London, 1973/R Schiedam, 1981)

E. de Jongh: 'The Interpretation of Still-life Paintings: Possibilities and Limit', *Still-life in the Age of Rembrandt* (exh. cat., Auckland, C.A.G., 1982)

A Flowery Past: A Survey of Dutch and Flemish Paintings from 1600 until the Present (exh. cat. by S. Segal, Amsterdam, P. de Boer Gal.; 's Hertogenbosch, Nordbrabants Mus.; 1982)

A Prosperous Past: The Sumptuous Still-life in the Netherlands, 1600–1700 (exh. cat. by S. Segal, The Hague, Mauritshuis, 1988)

E. Hardoin-Fugier and E. Grafe: *French Flower Painting of the Nineteenth Century: A Dictionary* (London, 1989)

Flowers and Nature (exh. cat. by S. Segal, Osaka, Nabio Mus.; Tokyo, Station Gal.; Sydney, A.G. NSW; 1990)

P. Taylor: *The Flower Fadeth: Looking at Floral Still-lifes in Golden Age Holland* (diss., U. Cambridge, 1991)

Bouquets from the Golden Age (exh. cat., The Hague, Mauritshuis, 1992)

PETER MITCHELL

Flügelaltar. Altarpiece with movable wings (*see* ALTARPIECE, §2).

Flurer, Franz Ignaz (*bapt* Augsburg, 12 Aug 1688; *d* Graz, 25 June 1742). German painter. He trained (1701–6) with the Augsburg painter Johann Rieger (*fl* 1690; *d* 1730). By 1720 he was employed by Graf Ignaz Maria Attems (*d* 1732) to paint canvases and Baroque frescoes for his castles at Slovenska Bistrica (1720–21) and Brežice (1722–7), Slovenia, and at Gösting (1728–9; destr.), near Graz. He also painted frescoes for the Kursaal at Tobelbad (1732; *in situ*) and for a garden pavilion at Schloss Brunnsee (*Allegory of Agriculture*, 1733; *in situ*, rest.). His landscapes depict ports, travellers and Graf Attems's castles. His religious works were executed mainly for churches in Graz, including *St Giles* (1730–33) for the main altar in Graz Cathedral. His compositions were derived from those of the Augsburg painter Melchior Seidl (1657–1727) and from Annibale Carracci and Pietro da Cortona's frescoes in Rome; his landscapes were influenced by Italian art, especially that of the Venetians Marco Ricci and Luca Carlevaris, and by the Dutch painter Pieter Mulier (*c*. 1637–1701).

BIBLIOGRAPHY
Franz Ignaz Flurer (1688–1742): Ein Barockmaler in der Steiermark (exh. cat., ed. W. Steinböck, text U. Kraus-Müller; Graz, Steiermärk. Landesmus., 1982–3)

KSENIJA ROZMAN

Fluting. Decoration consisting of parallel concave channels (flutes). The Romans occasionally applied fluting in a fan or whorl design to marble or metal vessels (*see* ROME, ANCIENT, §IX, 1(iv)) and wavelike fluting (strigillation) to sarcophagi, but it has a much longer history in architecture, providing vertical emphasis on the shafts of columns and pilasters, especially those constructed in drums. The earliest instances are found in dynastic Egypt during the 3rd and 2nd millennia BC (e.g. step pyramid complex of Djoser (*reg c.* 2630–*c.* 2611 BC) at Saqqara; tomb of Ammenemes I (*reg c.* 1938–*c.* 1908 BC) at Beni Hasan; the Aten temple of Akhenaten (*reg c.* 1353–*c.* 1336 BC) at Karnak; and the portico of the shrine dedicated to Anubis at Deir el-Bahri, built by Queen Hatshepsut (*reg c.* 1479–*c.* 1458 BC)). The circumference of the shaft was divided into 8, 16, 20, 24 or more vertical facets; each facet was then slightly hollowed, forming a shallow flute that met its neighbour in a sharp edge (arris). Two or four of the facets, on orthogonal axes, might be left as flat surfaces and inscribed.

Two particular types of fluting developed in Archaic and Classical Greece in association with the Doric and Ionic orders respectively. Doric fluting (see fig. (a)) resembles the Egyptian, but the flute channels are concave quarter-circles in profile, producing more pronounced arrises. The number of flutes varied at first, from 12 (e.g. Assos, 6th century BC; now Behramkale, Turkey) to 24 ('Temple of Neptune', *c.* 460 BC, in the Sanctuary of Hera at Paestum), but it soon became fixed at 20 (*see* ORDERS, ARCHITECTURAL, §I, 1). Ionic fluting initially differed from the Doric only in the greater numbers of flutes: 36 or 40 (although the Naxian Column, *c.* 560 BC, at Delphi had 44). Later these were reduced to a standard 24 (sometimes to 20), and they were spaced apart with flat bands (fillets) between them, the width of the fillets being normally one-quarter that of the flutes. The flute channels were deepened in profile to a half-circle, terminating at both ends in semicircular 'caps', leaving the fillets in high relief (see fig. (b)). Vitruvius (IV.i.7) likened the effect to folds of matronly drapery. The fluting on Corinthian columns followed the Ionic model. It was customary to lay out and carve a sample section at the neck of the shaft, which was normally part of the capital block, before it was lifted into position. Doric columns would be given a matching template on the drum at the foot of the shaft as well. The fluting was then extended over the intervening drums when finishing the building as a whole.

By the Hellenistic period, on civic and domestic buildings the fluting was frequently rusticated: it was limited to the upper two-thirds of the shaft while the lower third—vulnerable to damage—was left plain (see fig. (c)), or simply faceted, sometimes made of a contrasting stone. Alternatively, the fluting of the lower third of Ionic and Corinthian column shafts could be cabled, the fillets continuing to the bottom but in low relief; the flutes between them were cut as solid convex mouldings (see fig. (d)). Roman taste introduced such additional embellishments as beading and darts between the caps of the

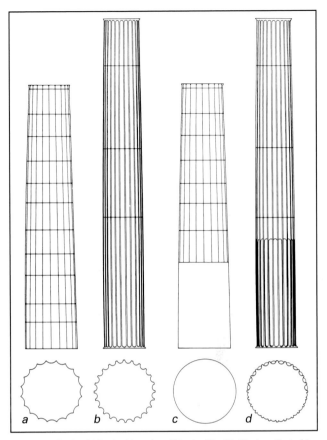

Fluting: (a) Doric; (b) Ionic; (c) rusticated Doric; (d) cabled Ionic or Corinthian

flutes. The fluting might also be twisted around the shaft in a spiral, as at the theatre (late 2nd century AD) at Sabratha (*see* ROME, ANCIENT, fig. 51). Roman methods changed from the Greek in that, as capitals and bases were made of separate blocks and shafts became increasingly monolithic, the fluting was no longer partially worked out on the ground but was done *in situ* after the column was erected.

Fluting in Renaissance and later architecture, although generally modelled on ancient types, is distinguished by some elaborate versions of cabling, shaped to resemble rope, ribbons or tassels, placed in bands at intervals up the shaft (e.g. the columns invented by PHILIBERT DE L'ORME) or stepped in a spiral (e.g. the columns (1815–17) designed by Benjamin Latrobe for the north and south wings of the Capitol building in Washington, DC).

BIBLIOGRAPHY
W. Stevenson Smith: *Art and Architecture of Ancient Egypt*, Pelican Hist. A. (Harmondsworth, 1958)
R. Martin: *Matériaux et techniques*, i of *Manuel d'archéologie grecque* (Paris, 1965), pp. 299–302
A. Claridge: 'Roman Methods of Fluting Corinthian Columns and Pilasters', *Città e architettura nella Roma imperiale*, Analecta Romana Istituti Danici Supplementum, x (Odense, 1983), pp. 119–28
D. Watkin: *A History of Western Architecture* (London, 1986)

A. CLARIDGE

Fluxus. Informal international group of avant-garde artists working in a wide range of media and active from the early 1960s to the late 1970s. Their activities included public concerts or festivals and the dissemination of innovatively designed anthologies and publications, including scores for electronic music, theatrical performances, ephemeral events, gestures and actions constituted from the individual's everyday experience. Other types of work included the distribution of object editions, correspondence art and concrete poetry. According to the directions of the artist, Fluxus works often required the participation of a spectator in order to be completed (*see* PERFORMANCE ART).

The name Fluxus, taken from the Latin for 'flow', was originally conceived by the American writer, performance artist and composer George Maciunas (1931–78) in 1961 as the title for a projected series of anthologies profiling the work of such artists as the composer La Monte Young, George Brecht, Yoko Ono (*b* 1933), Dick Higgins (*b* 1928), BEN, Nam June Paik and others engaged in experimental music, concrete poetry, performance events and 'anti-films' (e.g. Paik's imageless *Zen for Film*, 1962). In a manifesto of 1962 ('Neo-Dada in Music, Theater, Poetry, Art', in J. Becker and W. Vostell: *Happenings, Fluxus, Pop Art, Nouveau Réalisme*, Hamburg, 1965), Maciunas categorized this diversity under the broad heading of 'Neo-Dada' and stressed the interest shared by all the artists in manifesting time and space as concrete phenomena. Influences of Fluxus noted by Maciunas included John Cage's concrete music (1939) and intermedia event at Black Mountain College, NC (1952), with Merce Cunningham, Robert Rauschenberg and others; the Nouveaux Réalistes; the work of Ben; the concept art of Henry Flynt (*b* 1940); and Duchamp's notion of the ready-made.

The first of many Fluxus festivals, or Fluxconcerts, was organized by Maciunas in 1962 at the Museum Wiesbaden in Wiesbaden, Germany, to promote the anthology. The International Fluxus Festival of the Newest Music (festum fluxorum) consisted of 14 concerts, presenting musical and performance work by Joseph Beuys, Brecht, Cage, Alison Knowles (*b* 1933), Paik, Wim T. Schippers, Wolf Vostell, Robert Watts (1923–87), Young and others. Fluxconcerts—sometimes called *Aktionen*—also took place in Düsseldorf, Wuppertal, Paris, Copenhagen, Amsterdam, Nice, Stockholm and Oslo in 1962 and 1963. These events organized by Maciunas were influenced and paralleled by the independent activities of Young, Flynt, Robert Morris (ii) and others at Yoko Ono's studio in New York in 1961 and Brecht and Watts's Yam Festival in New York in 1963. All these artists were eventually associated with Maciunas and Fluxus, either through their collaboration on multiples, inclusion in anthologies, or participation in Fluxus concerts. The typical Fluxconcert consisted of a rapid series of performances of short events of scored actions and music. These events frequently consisted of physical performances representative of mundane activities, or music based on non-musical sound sources. They were often humorous and concerned with involving the audience, specifically to disrupt the expected conventions of musical and theatrical performance and spectatorship; their 'event scores' were characterized by reduction, repetition, improvisation and chance.

About nine major compilations of activities of Fluxus artists were planned. The first, entitled *Fluxus 1* (Wiesbaden and New York, 1964), was termed a yearbox, because of its unique wooden packaging. The contents included texts and objects by dozens of artists associated with the first Fluxfestival, such as Ay-O, Brecht, Stanley Brown, Robert Filliou, Ken Friedman (*b* 1949), Geoff Hendricks (*b* 1931), Higgins, Takehisa Kosugi, Jackson MacLow (*b* 1932), Takako Saito, Tomas Schmit, Ben and Emmett Williams (*b* 1925). The publication of collections of object-based works by artists associated with Fluxus and the documentation of Fluxconcerts soon became the focus of Maciunas's activities. Examples of these publications include: broadsides, such as *Fluxmanifesto on Fluxamusement* (edited by Maciunas in New York, 1965); the 11 irregularly published editions of the *Fluxus Newspaper* (New York, 1964–79); *Fluxyearbox 2* (1966–8, 1976); the Duchamp-inspired attaché case of objects entitled *Fluxkit* (New York, 1965–6); the *Fluxfilms* anthology (New York, 1966) and the *Fluxus Cabinet* (New Marlborough, MA, 1975–7). Perhaps most important of all of Maciunas's publishing activities remain the object multiples, conceived as inexpensive, mass-produced unlimited editions. These were either works made by individual Fluxus artists, sometimes in collaboration with Maciunas, or, most controversially, Maciunas's own interpretations of an artist's concept or score. Their purpose was to erode the cultural status of art and to help to eliminate the artist's ego.

Fluxus embraced many of the concepts and practices associated with the post-war avant-garde of western Europe and North America, including those of Lettrism, concrete poetry, concrete and random music, Happenings and conceptual art, as first described by Flynt during the late 1950s and early 1960s. Under the organization and direction of Maciunas, a specific programme of ideological goals was formulated and disseminated through a series of manifestos. The manifesto of 1963 exhorted the artist to 'purge the world of bourgeois sickness, "intellectual", professional and commercialized culture ... dead art, imitation, artificial art, abstract art, illusionistic art ... promote a revolutionary flood and tide in art, promote living art, anti-art, ... non art reality to be grasped by all peoples, not only critics, dilettantes and professionals'. The *Fluxmanifesto on Fluxamusement* used innovative typography and ready-made printed images to communicate the concept of the self-sufficiency of the audience, an art where anything can substitute for an art work and anyone can produce it.

BIBLIOGRAPHY

Happening und Fluxus: Materialen (exh. cat., ed. H. Sohm and H. Szeeman; Cologne, Kstver., 1970)
H. Ruhe: *Fluxus, the Most Radical and Experimental Art Movement of the Sixties* (Amsterdam, 1979)
J. Hendricks, ed.: *Addenda I* (New York, 1983)
Addenda II: The Gilbert and Lila Silverman Collection (exh. cat., ed. J. Hendricks; Pasadena, Baxter A.G., 1983)
B. Moore: *Fluxus I: A History of the Edition* (New York, 1985)
Fluxus: Selections from the Gilbert and Lila Silverman Collection (exh. cat. by C. Phillpot and J. Hendricks, New York, MOMA, 1988)
J. Hendricks: *Fluxus Codex* (New York, 1989)
E. Milman, ed.: 'Fluxus: A Conceptual Country', *Visible Language*, xxvi/1–2 (1992) [special issue]

MICHAEL CORRIS

Flynt [Flynth], Paul, II. *See* FLINDT, PAUL, II.

Fobsen, Jacob van. *See* ES, JACOB VAN.

Focillon, Henri(-Joseph) (*b* Dijon, 1881; *d* New Haven, CT, 3 March 1943). French art historian. He is regarded as the most significant French art theorist of the 20th century. As the son of an engraver, Victor-Louis Focillon (1849–1918), he was brought up with a knowledge of workshop techniques as well as with a circle of family friends that included Monet and Rodin. Focillon studied philology at the Ecole Normale Supérieure, Paris, then at Bourges and Chartres, and from 1913 worked for ten years in Lyon, where he became Professor of the History of Modern Art and at the same time Director of the Musée des Beaux-Arts. In 1918, he submitted his doctoral thesis on Piranesi to Paris University, where he worked from 1924, succeeding Emile Mâle in the chair of Medieval Archaeology at the Sorbonne. In 1925, he became Professor of the University's new Institut d'Art et du Moyen Age, where he trained a generation of French scholars. In 1938, he transferred to the Collège de France as Professor of Art History but in October of that year accepted a chair at Yale University, where he had already worked in 1934; in 1940, he became the first Senior Scholar in Residence at Dumbarton Oaks, Washington, DC, which had recently become part of Harvard University. Prevented by the war from ever returning to France, he regarded the USA as his second home.

Focillon's interests in art were eclectic, as demonstrated by the range of subjects on which he wrote. He was generally more concerned with the concept of formal analysis to account for the evolution of styles than in detailed studies of iconography; he never sought to separate the decorative from the fine arts but applied his insights to painting, engraving, drawing, stained glass, sculpture and architecture in order to demonstrate some of the common processes underlying their creation. He always retained a particular fascination with engraving (*Giovanni-Battista Piranesi*, 1918; *Maîtres de l'estampe*, 1930), a subject that influenced his critical interpretations of art through a special understanding of the significance of technique and medium. His first studies were of Classical antiquity, which he initially approached through inscriptions (*Inscriptions latines d'Afrique*, 1904). While at Lyon, he wrote about Cellini and Raphael, as well as the work of local artists. He then turned his attention to the arts of the East (*Hokusai*, 1914; *L'Art Bouddique*, 1921), developing an awareness of the links between East and West as explored by many artists. This led to work on the 19th century, which he regarded as the great era of French painting (*La Peinture au XIXe siècle*, 1927–8). By this point he was becoming increasingly interested in medieval art. His methodological study, *La Vie des formes* (1934), was both an approach to structuring such diverse material and an exploration of the nature of form in art, developing the theories of Adolf von Hildebrand, Heinrich Wölfflin and Aloïs Riegl; this has been widely translated and represents a major contribution to art theory. It was followed by perhaps his best-known work, *Art d'Occident* (1938), which traces the development of Romanesque and Gothic style. As well as these major works, he wrote many articles and reviews, including various aspects of literary history and philology; the bibliography of his published works contains 378 entries. He was not only a fine writer but also a most distinguished teacher, influential both in France and in the USA; he also undertook extensive lecture tours of Europe and North and South America.

WRITINGS
Giovanni-Battista Piranesi (Paris, 1918, rev. 1928)
La Peinture au XIXe et XXe siècles, 2 vols (Paris, 1927–8)
La Vie des formes (Paris, 1934); Eng. trans. by C. Beecher Hogan and G. Kubler (New York, 1948/*R* 1989)
Rembrandt (Paris, 1936)
Art d'Occident: Le moyen âge roman et gothique (Paris, 1938); Eng. trans. by D. King (London, 1963, rev. Oxford, 3/1986)
Collection Henri Focillon, 3 vols (Paris, 1952–5)

BIBLIOGRAPHY
Gaz. B.-A., n.s. 5, xxvi (1944) (volume dedicated to Focillon)
L. Grodecki, ed.: *Bibliographie Henri Focillon* (New Haven and London, 1963)

Fodor, Carel Joseph (*b* Amsterdam, 18 April 1801; *d* Amsterdam, 24 Dec 1860). Dutch collector and merchant. In 1820 he joined his father's coal merchant's business and from *c*. 1834 began to collect avidly. He started by buying paintings by 'modern' Dutch and Belgian artists, such as Barend Cornelis Koekkoek, Andreas Schelfhout, Willem Roelofs and Cornelis Springer, often paying very high prices. After 1850 Fodor became increasingly interested in the work of foreign artists, mainly French and German painters. He acquired work by, among others, Prosper Marilhat and a portrait after van Dyck by Gericault. His finest purchase was Ary Scheffer's *Christus Consolator* (1837; Amsterdam, Hist. Mus.), which he acquired for Dfl 24,806 from the Duc d'Orléans's sale in Paris in 1853 (*see* ORLÉANS, House of, (8)). Fodor also collected drawings and watercolours. Before 1851 these consisted mainly of Dutch, Flemish and Italian works of the 16th and 17th centuries; he then became interested in French watercolours of the 17th to 19th centuries. He kept no records of his acquisitions, but it is clear that he sometimes bought directly from the artists (on one occasion he returned a drawing to Jan Weissenbruch saying that he wanted only the finest works), as well as from dealers, auctions and exhibitions. From 1850 he was advised by the painter and dealer Arie Johannes Lamme (1812–1900), later the first director of the Boymans Museum, Rotterdam (1852). Fodor was appointed to a number of honorary posts and in 1854 helped the city of Amsterdam acquire Rembrandt's *Jewish Bride* (Amsterdam, Rijksmus.). Fodor left his entire collection to the city: the gift, fully catalogued by Lamme, comprised 151 paintings, 897 drawings and watercolours and 302 prints, together with Fodor's three houses on the Keizergracht, one of which was intended to house the collection as a museum. The first museum in Amsterdam, it was opened in 1863. After initial success, taste began to change, and, despite a brief revival of interest in the 1930s, it ceased to be popular. In 1948 the building became a museum of contemporary art, and the collection was transferred to the Amsterdam Historisch Museum, where it remains intact, a fine example of Dutch bourgeois taste in the mid-19th century.

BIBLIOGRAPHY
I. Hagenbeek-Fey: *Carel Joseph Fodor (Amsterdam, 1801–1860) en zijn schilderijen verzameling* (Amsterdam, 1975)
The Fodor Collection: Nineteenth-century French Drawings and Watercolors from Amsterdam's Historisch Museum (exh. cat., ed. W. Loos; Hamilton, NY, Colgate U.; Picker A. G.; New York, Baruch Coll. Gal.; Amsterdam, Hist. Mus.; 1985–6)

☐

Fogelberg, Bengt Erland (*b* Göteborg, 8 Aug 1786; *d* Trieste, 22 Dec 1854). Swedish sculptor and archaeologist. He studied from 1803 at the Kungliga Akademi för de Fria Konsterna, Stockholm, where he joined those who opposed its conservative method of education. He belonged to the influential circles in early 19th-century Swedish art and literature that promoted a more realistic style and Romantic subject-matter, in particular Old Norse themes. In 1818 Fogelberg successfully exhibited plaster sketches of *Odin*, *Thor* and *Frey* (Stockholm, Kun. Akad., on dep. Ulriksdal, nr Stockholm, Orangerie Mus.). They were the starting-points for Fogelberg's most celebrated monumental works, which were executed much later in marble (in a greatly revised state), commissioned by Karl XIV Johan (*reg* 1818–44): *Odin* was produced in 1830 and *Thor* and *Balder* in 1844 (all Ulriksdal, nr Stockholm, Orangerie Mus.). The works derive from antique sculptures, but in *Odin* and *Thor* Fogelberg conveyed in a personal way a realistic and slightly barbaric power that corresponded to the contemporary view of these figures as the Nordic equivalents of Jupiter and Mars.

Between 1817 and 1844 Fogelberg made important artistic contacts in France and Italy. Provided with a scholarship from the Kungliga Akademi för de Fria Konsterna, he travelled to Paris in 1820, where he studied sculpture with François-Joseph Bosio and drawing with Pierre Guérin. In 1821 he moved to Italy and remained in Rome for most of his life, making two short visits in 1845 and 1854 to Sweden, where he had been appointed Royal Sculptor and member of the Akademi in 1832. The powerful influence of antique art and the Neo-classicism of Canova and Bertel Thorvaldsen found expression above all in such classicizing works as *Paris with the Apple* (1824; Stockholm, Nmus.). He also executed a number of rough plaster sketches of portraits of Swedish historical personalities. Some of these were cast in bronze in large formats between 1853 and 1854, for example the elegant and vigorous *Karl XIV Johan on Horseback* (Stockholm, Södermalmstorg). His skill at characterization, which he developed in Rome, and his modern style make these works among the most significant and graceful of 19th-century Swedish sculptures. Fogelberg's work is best represented in the Göteborgs Konstmuseum and especially in the Nationalmuseum, Stockholm, which acquired in 1856 *c.* 70 sketches and models in plaster or terracotta from the artist's estate; several of them are now in the Orangerie Museum, Ulriksdal, near Stockholm. Fogelberg was also a skilful archaeologist who accumulated a considerable collection of antique medals and terracottas.

WRITINGS
Osservazioni d'arte fatte su i colossi di Monte Cavallo (Rome, 1843)

BIBLIOGRAPHY
C. Leconte: *L'Oeuvre de Fogelberg* (Paris, 1856)

SVKL

R. Josephson: 'Fogelberg's nordiska gudar' [Fogelberg's Nordic gods], *N. Mus. Ab.* (1922), pp. 83–125

PONTUS GRATE

Foggia, Nicola di Bartolomeo da. *See* NICOLA DI BARTOLOMEO DA FOGGIA.

Foggini, Giovanni Battista (*b* Florence, 25 April 1652; *d* Florence, 12 April 1725). Italian sculptor and architect. The foremost Florentine sculptor of the late Baroque period, he was first apprenticed to two painters successively but soon showed a greater propensity for sculpture. In 1673 he was sent by the young Grand Duke of Tuscany, Cosimo III de' Medici, to study in the newly instituted Accademia Fiorentina in Rome. There he remained for three years, studying under Ercole Ferrata, a sculptor of the second Baroque generation, and Ciro Ferri, a painter who was a close follower of Pietro da Cortona. His precocious ability at this period is demonstrated in a terracotta relief of the *Slaying of the Niobids* (Florence, Mus. Opificio Pietre Dure & Lab. Rest. Opere A.); a marble relief of the *Adoration of the Shepherds* (St Petersburg, Hermitage); and a bronze relief of the *Crucifixion* (Florence, Pitti), until recently ascribed to the court sculptor of the day, Ferdinando Tacca. These early works established his characteristic style, a novel late Baroque manner that changed little throughout his career.

On his return from Rome in 1676, Foggini immediately began to receive commissions for sculpture from the Medici court. A decade later he was appointed grand ducal sculptor, after the death of Tacca, and in 1694 became the court architect as well. From then until his death he was chiefly employed on commissions for the Medici, with Massimiliano Soldani as his only rival. Foggini supervised the grand ducal studio and foundry in Borgo Pinti, which was the centre for official bronze commissions, and also the Galleria dei Lavori (now the Opificio delle Pietre Dure; *see* FLORENCE, §III, 2(i)), the manufactory for works in hardstone inlay. He was a prolific and assured draughtsman, and approximately 400 of his designs (Florence, Uffizi; London, V&A; Paris, Louvre; Rome, Gal. N. Stampe) for sculpture, bronze statuettes, furniture and ornaments involving hardstones have survived. As Montagu has observed of these (see 1974 exh. cat.):

> It is their sculptural quality, the combination of hardstone with mounts which are not merely decorative but often sculptural works of art in their own right, playing a much more dominant role in the total ensemble, which characterizes the works made in this period, and distinguishes them from earlier products of the Florentine workshops, or the pieces made by Florentine craftsmen for the Gobelins in Paris.

Many of Foggini's designs were carved by GIUSEPPE ANTONIO TORRICELLI and resulted in some of the latter's best work.

The main projects from the earlier part of Foggini's career, involving both sculpture and architecture, were the reliefs in the Corsini Chapel of scenes from the *Life of St Andrea Corsini* (finished 1691; Florence, S Maria del Carmine; see fig.) and those in the Feroni Chapel (1691–3; Florence, SS Annunziata). His reliefs are very pictorial, betraying his training by followers of Pietro da Cortona and Alessandro Algardi, and are designed with strong, and

Giovanni Battista Foggini: *First Mass of St Andrea Corsini*, marble relief, finished 1691 (Florence, S Maria del Carmine, Corsini Chapel)

often contrasting, diagonals. The skies are frequently populated with mythological or Christian figures amid clouds and shafts of light. He also produced a tomb for *St Francis Xavier* (1691–7; Old Goa, Jesuit church of Bom Jesus) that was sent to Goa. His biographer, Baldinucci (p. 376), mentions 'gruppi e statuette e bassirilievi di bronzo di rara perfezione' between his descriptions of these two major projects, implying that most of Foggini's smaller, private commissions date from the 1680s or 1690s. Foggini also carved a series of busts of Florentine worthies (Manchester, C.A.G.) and several superb portraits of the Medici dynasty, such as his bust of *Cardinal Leopoldo de' Medici* (1697; Florence, Uffizi; *see* FLORENCE, §III, 2; other examples, London, V&A; Washington, DC, N.G.A.; Donaueschingen, Fürstenberg-Samml.).

Following Tacca's precedent, Foggini also modelled a number of two-figure groups, with mythological or allegorical subjects, for casting into bronze. These were often designed with a principal view in mind and constituted as pairs, as is the case with the *Abduction of Orithyia by Boreas* and the *Abduction of Proserpine by Pluto* (examples, Rome, Pal. Barberini; Toronto, A.G. Ont.). Foggini exploited the tensile strength of bronze to permit dramatically projecting limbs and exciting centrifugal compositions with irregular outlines. The drapery flows in soft, plastic ripples, conveying the sinuous lines of his sketches and the smooth touch of fingers and stylus on the wax models: the rippling folds catch the light and convey a sense of rapid movement, contrasting with the broad, bare areas of flesh. His many

pupils prolonged his style well past the middle of the 18th century and until the advent of Neo-classicism.

BIBLIOGRAPHY
F. S. Baldinucci: *Vite* (1725–30); ed. A. Matteoli (1975), pp. 373–90
K. Lankheit: 'Il giornale del Foggini', *Riv. A.*, xxxiv (1959), pp. 55–108
——: *Florentinische Barockplastik* (Munich, 1962), pp. 47–109
——: 'Eine Serie von "Uomini famosi" des florentinischen Barock', *Pantheon*, xxxix/1 (1971), pp. 22–39
The Twilight of the Medici: Late Baroque Art in Florence, 1670–1743 (exh. cat., ed. S. F. Rossen; Detroit, MI, Inst. A.; Florence, Pitti; 1974), pp. 48–78, nos 11–41
Florentine Baroque Bronzes (exh. cat. by C. Avery and C. Keeble, Toronto, Royal Ont. Mus., 1975), pp. 22–33
M. Davis, ed.: *Kunst des Barock in der Toskana: Studien zur Kunst unter den letzten Medici*, It. Forsch. Ksthist. Inst. Florenz, 3rd ser., ix (Munich, 1976)
Disegni di Giovan Battista Foggini (exh. cat. by L. Monaci, Florence, Uffizi, 1977)
K. Lankheit: *Die Modellsammlung der Porzellanmanufaktur Doccia*, It. Forsch. Ksthist. Inst. Florenz, 3rd ser., xii (Munich, 1982)
C. Avery: *Baroque Sculpture and Medals in the Art Gallery of Ontario: The Margaret and Ian Ross Collection* (Toronto, 1988), pp. 17–25, nos 2–4
Splendori di pietre dure: L'arte di corte nella Firenze dei Granduchi (exh. cat., ed. A. M. Giusti; Florence, Pitti, 1988–9)

CHARLES AVERY

Foggo. English family of painters. James Foggo (*b* London, 11 June 1790; *d* London, 14 Sept 1860) and his brother George Foggo (*b* London, 14 April 1793; *d* London, 26 Sept 1869) trained in Paris at the Ecole des Beaux-Arts under Jean-Baptiste Regnault. This may account for their determined pursuit of history painting in the Grand Manner, despite lack of support for such pictures in England. James returned to London in 1815 and established himself as a painter of historical, literary and biblical subjects, supplementing his income by teaching. George joined him in 1819, and they worked closely together until James's death in 1860. Both were keen to encourage national appreciation of art, and in 1837 they founded a society for free public access to museums, monuments and works of art, which attracted considerable support. They entered the competitions for fresco designs for the New Palace of Westminster between 1840 and 1843, although without success. Competent draughtsmen, they excelled in figure drawing. However, the size and monumentality of their paintings meant that few were sold. Their best-known works are the *People of Parga Burying their Dead* (1819; untraced) and the *Entombment* (1826), which became the altarpiece of the French Protestant Church of St-Martin's-le-Grand in London. After the death of his brother, George did little original work, devoting himself to the advancement of art. He also lithographed the Raphael Cartoons.

BIBLIOGRAPHY
Redgrave
Obituary, *A. J.* [London], vi (1860), p. 372 [James Foggo]
Obituary, *A. J.* [London], viii (1869), p. 360 [George Foggo]

JUSTINE HOPKINS

Fogolino, Marcello (*b* Vicenza, between 1483 and 1488; *d* after 1548). Italian painter and printmaker. The son of Francisco, a painter from Friuli, he was trained in Vicenza, in the workshop of Bartolomeo Montagna. Although he was in Venice between *c.* 1508 and 1516, it was Montagna's retardataire style belonging to the 15th century that proved the decisive influence in Fogolino's early works, for example the *Virgin and Child with Saints* (*c.* 1513–15; The

Hague, Mauritshuis). Between 1521 and 1524 he worked in Friuli, where his *St Francis with SS Daniel and John the Baptist* (*c.* 1522; Pordenone Cathedral), with its asymmetrical arrangement and bulky, powerfully modelled figure types, shows him responding quickly to Pordenone's dynamic style.

In 1527 Fogolino and his brother Matteo were banished from Venetian territory for their complicity in a murder. They settled in Trent until they were reprieved by the Venetians. Fogolino won extensive court patronage in Trent. At the Castel Buonconsiglio he collaborated with Girolamo Romanino and Giovanni Dosso on a fresco cycle (1531–2) for Prince–Bishop Bernard von Cles (1485–1539), and he was later involved in the production of triumphal decorations for the visits in 1536 and 1541 respectively of King Ferdinand and his elder brother, Emperor Charles V. Fogolino's work from this period continues to reflect his earlier formative experiences of Montagna and Pordenone, but it is modified by the influence of contemporary Roman artists increasingly apparent in the styles of Romanino and Dosso. In 1547 he executed frescoes depicting scenes from the *Life of Moses* for the Palazzo Vescovile, Ascoli Piceno. Fogolino also made a small number of refined drypoint engravings, for example the *Woman and Child beside a Classical Building* (Amsterdam, Rijksmus.). He is last recorded in Trent in 1548.

BIBLIOGRAPHY
L. Puppi: *Marcello Fogolino pittore e incisore* (Trent, 1966) [incl. full bibliog.]
F. Barbieri: *Pittori di Vicenza, 1480–1520* (Vicenza, 1981)

THOMAS NICHOLS

Fohr, Carl Philipp (*b* Heidelberg, 26 Nov 1775; *d* Rome, 29 June 1818). German painter and draughtsman. His first drawing lessons, from the age of 13, were from Friedrich Rottmann (1768–1816), the father of the painter Carl Rottmann. In 1810 the Darmstadt Court Councillor, Georg Wilhelm Issel, discovered Fohr sketching at Stift Neuberg near Heidelberg and, the following year, invited him to Darmstadt and provided encouragement and financial support. From 1813 Fohr carried out commissions for Grand Duchess Wilhelmina of Hesse, for whom he produced a *Sketchbook of the Neckar Region*, a collection of views and historical subjects (30 watercolours; 1813–14) and also a *Baden Sketchbook* (30 watercolours, 1814–15; both Darmstadt, Hess. Landesmus.). These far surpassed the usual level attained in this genre in their sharpness of detail, delicacy of colour and pictorial inventiveness. The Crown Princess granted him an annual pension of 500 guilders. From July 1815 to May 1816, Fohr was a student of landscape painting at the Kunstakademie in Munich, and it was here that his breakthrough into an independent and ingenious drawing style came about.

Formative influences on Fohr's work were the approach to landscape in the paintings of Joseph Anton Koch, Albrecht Dürer's prints and drawings (especially the drawings for the prayerbook of the Emperor Maximilian, known through the engravings of Nepomuk Strixner) and the writings of three leading Romantics: Friedrich de la Motte-Fouqué, Ludwig Tieck and Clemens Brentano. From September to October 1815 Fohr made a walking tour to the Tirol and northern Italy (including Padua, Verona and Venice) and, on the way back to Munich, stayed in Salzburg. His experience of the Alps and the Italian landscape cleansed his watercolour style of its provincial qualities, and in Salzburg he was introduced to oil painting by Domenico Quaglio and Ludwig Sigismund Ruhl. He also produced compositions related to works by de la Motte-Fouqué and Tieck and a particularly inventive set of illustrations to the *Niebelungenlied*. From 8 May to 18 October 1816 Fohr was in Heidelberg, where revolutionary Republican student circles made him more aware of the current strivings to create a mood of national unity. Fohr's portrait and landscape drawings from this summer and early autumn (e.g. the *Self-portrait*, Heidelberg, Kurpfälz. Mus.; see fig.) represent the first high point in his oeuvre.

On 18 October 1816 Fohr set off for Rome, arriving on 21 November and staying at the Casa Buti. He became friendly with several German artists, including Johann Anton Ramboux, and also made contact with the Nazarenes, especially the Protestants in the group, such as Julius Schnorr von Carolsfeld. Fohr never belonged to the inner Nazarene circle, however, and religious subjects remained peripheral to his concerns. In Spring 1817 Fohr worked in the Roman studio of Joseph Anton Koch. For a projected group portrait he made drawings of the German Nazarenes in the Café Greco (46 pencil drawings and 4 sketches, Heidelberg, Kurpfälz. Mus.). He went for long walks in the outskirts of Rome (Lake Nemi, Olevano, Tivoli) and made sketches as a basis for subsequent oil landscapes. Seven oil paintings have survived, of which

Carl Philipp Fohr: *Self-portrait*, pen and black ink and wash, 273×188 mm, 1816 (Heidelberg, Kurpfälzisches Museum)

the most accomplished is the *Landscape near Rocca Canterano in the Sabine Hills* (1818; priv. col., see 1968 Frankfurt am Main exh. cat., pl. 8). This combined observation of nature with an idealized treatment of the view and Romantic fairy-tale elements with realism. On 29 June 1818, while bathing in the Tiber with artist friends, Fohr drowned. The watercolours and drawings he left behind in Rome had a strong influence on artists such as Franz Horny and Ludwig Richter.

BIBLIOGRAPHY
K. Graf von Hardenberg and E. Schilling: *Carl Philipp Fohr: Leben und Werk eines deutschen Malers der Romantik* (Freiburg, 1925)
Carl Fohr, 1795–1818 und die Maler um ihn (exh. cat., Heidelberg, Kurpfälz. Mus., 1925)
A. von Schneider: *Carl Philipp Fohr: Skizzenbuch—Bildniszeichnungen deutscher Künstler in Rom* (Berlin, 1952)
Carl Philipp Fohr, 1795–1818 (exh. cat., Frankfurt am Main, Städel. Kstinst. & Städt. Gal., 1968)
Carl Philipp Fohr: Skizzenbuch der Neckargegend und badisches Skizzenbuch (exh. cat., Heidelberg, Kurpfälz. Mus., 1968)
J. C. Jensen: 'Zeichnungen von Carl Philipp Fohr aus der Zeit seines letzten Aufenthaltes in Heidelberg im Jahre 1816', *Aurora: Eichendorff Alm.*, xxix (1969), pp. 23–8

JENS CHRISTIAN JENSEN

Foil (i). Term used in tracery for any of several circular or nearly circular lobes that intersect in points (cusps) projecting inwards from an arc (*see* TRACERY, fig. 2). Three such lobes are a trefoil, four a quatrefoil etc.

Foil (ii). Thin leaf or sheet of gold, silver or other metal used to decorate works of art (*see* GILDING, §I, 1).

Fokke, Simon (*b* Amsterdam, 1 Sept 1712; *d* Amsterdam, 10 April 1784). Dutch draughtsman, printmaker and collector. His father was the surgeon and actor Arend Fokke. Simon became a pupil of Jan Caspar Philips (*c.* 1700–*c.* 1773) when he was 13, and although he had originally wanted to become an actor, on completing his apprenticeship with Philips in 1732 he chose a career as an artist. He soon developed a highly individual style as a printmaker and draughtsman. His interest in the theatre (he also designed stage scenery) may have contributed to the dramatic nature of many of his drawings and etchings. They are spontaneous, elegant and evocative and sometimes show the influence of Cornelis Troost. Fokke was inspired mainly by scenes of everyday life, however.

He was well known for his book illustrations, title pages and vignettes, most of which were commissioned by printers and booksellers. Good examples of his work are the plates in Jan Wagenaar's *De vaderlandsche historie* (1749–60) and his illustrations of Lucretia Wilhelmina van Merken's epic poem *David* (1767). In addition to his original work, he also copied drawings and paintings by such artists as Hendrick Avercamp, Nicolaes Berchem, Jusepe de Ribera, Cornelis Troost and Joseph Vernet. He possessed a fine collection of Italian, French and Dutch drawings and prints, which was auctioned in 1784. His brother-in-law was the famous actor and engraver Jan Punt. Fokke taught his sons Jan Fokke (1745–1812) and Arend Fokke (1755–1812), both of whom became well-known authors and artists. Arend drew mainly caricatures and wrote humorous books.

BIBLIOGRAPHY
Scheen; Thieme–Becker
E. de la Fontaine Verwey: *De illustratie van letterkundige werken in de XVIIIe eeuw: Bijdrage tot de geschiedenis van het Nederlandse boek* [The illustration of literary works in the XVIIIth century: contribution to the history of the Dutch book] (diss., U. Leiden, 1934)
Dutch Masterpieces from the Eighteenth Century: Paintings & Drawings, 1700–1800 (exh. cat., ed. E. R. Mandle; Minneapolis, MN, Inst. A.; Toledo, OH, Mus. A.; Philadelphia, PA, Mus. A.; 1971–2), pp. 45–6
'Simon Fokke: Tentoonstellingsberichten en ander nieuws' [Simon Fokke: exhibition information and other news], *Antiek*, xviii (1983–4), pp. 475–6

P. KNOLLE

Folchetti, Stefano (*b* San Ginesio; *fl* 1492–1513). Italian painter. The *Virgin and Child with Saints* (San Ginesio, Mus. Pin. Gentili) and the fresco of the *Madonna and Child* in SS Rosario, Amandola, both dated 1492, are his earliest known works. In 1494 he painted the *Virgin and Child with a Donor* (Urbisaglia, S Maria di Brusciano). The *Virgin and Child between the Blessed Liberatus da Loro and St Francis* (San Ginesio, Mus. Pin. Gentili) is datable within the 1490s. His painting basically reflects the style of Carlo Crivelli, probably transmitted through the influence of Crivelli's brother Vittore. Facial expressions tend to be accentuated in a grotesque manner, in keeping with Late Gothic decorative taste, which is also apparent in the costumes, especially in the conspicuous use of gold. His work is also influenced by the Sanseverino school, especially Lorenzo d'Alessandro (*c.* 1440–1503). Within the limits of Crivelli's style Folchetti pursued an interest in abstract, at times archaic, decorative patterning. The potentially expressive and dynamic forces of the lines are, however, tempered by a tendency to fall into a mechanical repetition of geometric formulae. In the *Virgin and Child* (1506; San Ginesio, S Gregorio) a growing interest in rendering volume signals a break from the hitherto rigorous attention to surface patterning, but the latter aspect prevails in Folchetti's fresco of the *Madonna and Child* in S Maria, Ronzano. In Urbisaglia the artist is represented by a *Pietà* (Chiesa della Maestà) and a triptych depicting the *Mystic Marriage of St Catherine with SS Peter and Lawrence* (1507; Collegiata di S Lorenzo), and in the Municipio, Sarnano, by a *Crucifixion* dated 1513. Other works by Folchetti can be found in Amandola, San Ginesio, Recanati Cathedral and Philadelphia, PA (Mus. A).

BIBLIOGRAPHY
P. Zampetti: *La pittura marchigiana da Gentile a Raffaello* (Venice, 1970), pp. 192–200
Lorenzo Lotto nelle Marche: Il suo tempo, il suo influsso (exh. cat., ed. P. dal Poggetto and P. Zampetti; Ancona, Il Gesu; S Francesco alle Scale; Loggia Mercanti; 1981)
Documenti dell'Abruzzo Teramano, i (Rome, 1983), pp. 359–60

MARIO ALBERTO PAVONE

Foley, John Henry (*b* Dublin, 24 May 1818; *d* London, 27 Aug 1874). Irish sculptor, active in England. He was the most important sculptor of mid-Victorian Britain. Although his close contemporary Alfred Stevens has eclipsed him in fame and reputation, Foley's achievements were more substantial and more influential on the sculptural mainstream. He was the son of a grocer and was educated at the Royal Dublin Society's art schools (*c.* 1831–4) and at the Royal Academy, London (1835–8). He first attracted attention at the Academy in 1840, with *Ino and*

Bacchus (plaster; Dublin, Royal Dublin Soc.), the mild eroticism of which showed the influence of Etienne-Maurice Falconet. Similar works by Foley in this genre were *Youth at the Stream* (1844; bronze version, 1851; Stratford-on-Avon, Bancroft Gdns) and *Innocence* (1847; Osborne House, Isle of Wight, Royal Col.). These idealized sculptures are delicately executed and elegantly attenuated, showing some Mannerist influence. The *Art-Union* (later *Art Journal*), Foley's most consistent critical champion, considered *Youth at the Stream* to be the most beautiful work at the Royal Academy exhibition of 1844 and in 1860 commissioned a statuette version of it in bronze; a Copeland porcelain version of *Innocence* was produced in 1847.

On the strength of these works, Foley was commissioned to execute for the Houses of Parliament marble statues of two 17th-century statesmen: *John Hampden* (1847) and *John Selden* (1854), works that showed his capacity to handle a more robust realism. His portrait statues subsequently tended to eclipse his works on imagined subjects, although he presented the *Elder Brother from Comus* (marble, 1860) to the Royal Academy as his diploma work, on election to full membership. After 1861 he stopped exhibiting there, owing to disagreements over the arrangement of his works; like John Gibson (i) he was dissatisfied with the inadequate space allocated to sculpture. However, such was his reputation that not exhibiting did not injure his career.

Foley was particularly admired for his technical excellence, unmatched by any of his contemporaries. It is significant that he was one of the few sculptors left unscathed by the criticisms of Francis Palgrave. Comparable work by William Calder Marshall, John Bell or William Theed is blander and adheres more to Neoclassical traditions, while Foley's work has greater vigour and originality; it reflects his statement to the Royal Academy Commission of 1863 that he placed 'no greater value on acquaintance with the best works of ancient times than with those of modern times'. Two portrait statues evince his admiration of French 18th-century sculpture: *Sir Charles Barry* (marble, 1860; London, Pal. Westminster), shows the architect working at the drawing-board, dressed in a loose wrapper similar to the dressing-gown worn by Jean-Antoine Houdon's *Voltaire Seated* (1778; versions, Paris, Mus. Comédie-Fr., St Petersburg, Hermitage); while the cross-legged pose and alertness of *Sir Benjamin Guinness* (1873; Dublin, St Patrick's Cathedral) show the influence of Louis-François Roubiliac's *George Frederick Handel* (1738; London, V&A).

Although Foley paid close attention to accuracy in costume, his portraits showed that the demands of meticulous sartorial realism need not be constricting; qualities of humanity emerge in his statues of two politicians, *John Fielden* (bronze, 1863; Todmorden, W. Yorks, Cent. Vale Park) and *Sidney, 1st Baron Herbert of Lea* (bronze, 1867; London, Waterloo Place). The latter's pensive pose was a major influence on a central public monument of the New Sculpture, Hamo Thornycroft's *General Gordon* (1888; London, Victoria Embankment Gdns). The bronze reliefs on the pedestal of the *Herbert* statue (e.g. the *Forging of an Armstrong Gun*) are notable for their vigorous realism. Another much admired work was *Henry, 1st Viscount*

Hardinge (bronze, 1858; Kent, priv. col.; see Read, 1982, p. 6), which, according to William Michael Rossetti, 'stands markedly at the head of British equestrian statues of any period'.

It is a reflection of Foley's status that he was the only sculptor to contribute two major sculptures to the Albert Memorial (completed 1876) in Kensington Gardens, London; these were the marble group *Asia* (1864–71) and the bronze statue of *Prince Albert*. The *Asia* group shows the allegorical figure of India mounted on an elephant; she is unveiling herself, an allusion to her continent's display of products at the Great Exhibition of 1851, and is flanked by figures representing the main Asian cultures, conveyed with their racial types and costumes. Foley was commissioned to execute the statue of *Prince Albert* following the death of Carlo Marochetti; the statue, unfinished at the time of Foley's death, was completed by his assistant Thomas Brock. Dressed in his Garter robe, the Prince is enthroned under a canopy in a pose that attempts to be both ideal and real, regal yet human (see fig.). The Great Exhibition handbook that he holds takes on biblical status. Characteristic care went into the positioning of the figure to maximize accessibility to the spectator far below. Both *Prince Albert* and *Asia* show greater conservatism than most of Foley's other works, possibly because of the importance of the commission and also because he thought that the sculpture should integrate with the whole monument. Another major late work by Foley was the monument to *Daniel O'Connell* (bronze, 1866–83; Dublin,

John Henry Foley: *Prince Albert*, bronze, h. 4.26 m, 1868–76 (London, Kensington Gardens)

O'Connell Street). Over 12 m tall, the monument consists of a statue of O'Connell, a drum relief of fifty figures led by an allegorical image of Erin, and four winged Victories at the base. Like *Prince Albert*, this work was completed after Foley's death by Brock. Foley's work is well represented in his native city through this and other works (e.g. statues of *Oliver Goldsmith*, bronze, 1864; Dublin, Trinity College; and *Prince Albert*, bronze, 1871), and there are nine original plaster models at the Royal Dublin Society.

Apart from Brock, Foley's many pupils included C. B. Birch, Francis John Williamson (1833–1920), Albert Bruce-Joy (1842–1924) and Mary Grant (1831–1908). Edmund Gosse, the man of letters who was a critic of the New Sculpture, saw the revival of British sculpture as taking place through Foley, and it is significant that Alfred Gilbert singled him out in his 1901 Royal Academy professorial lecture as 'a great man whose work. . .he had never ceased to admire for its prowess and for its fixed and steadfast purpose'.

BIBLIOGRAPHY
Gunnis

Report of the Commissioners Appointed to Inquire into the Present Position of the Royal Academy in Relation to the Fine Arts; Together with the Minutes of Evidence Presented to both Houses of Parliament (London, 1863)

W. M. Rossetti: *Fine Art, Chiefly Contemporary* (London and Cambridge, 1867)

W. C. Monkhouse: *The Works of J.H. Foley, Sculptor* (London, 1875)

S. A[tkinson]: *Arts and Industries in Ireland: 1. John Henry Foley, R.A.* (Dublin, 1882)

E. Gosse: 'The New Sculpture, 1879–94', *A. J.* [London] (1894), pp. 38–42

B. Read: 'John Henry Foley', *Connoisseur*, clxxxvi (1974), pp. 262–71

S. Bayley: *The Albert Memorial: The Monument in its Social and Architectural Context* (London, 1981)

B. Read: *Victorian Sculpture* (New Haven and London, 1982)

C. Avery and M. Marsh: 'The Bronze Statuettes of the Art Union of London: The Rise and Decline of Victorian Taste in Sculpture', *Apollo*, cxxi (1985), pp. 328–37

R. Dorment: *Alfred Gilbert* (New Haven and London, 1985)

MARK STOCKER

Foligno, Niccolò da. *See* NICCOLÒ DA FOLIGNO.

Folk architecture. *See* VERNACULAR ARCHITECTURE.

Folk Art. Term used broadly to describe those arts that exist outside the received canons of taste established by or on behalf of the leaders of a given society. Implicit in such a definition is the existence of a society that is sufficiently complex to permit more than one level of cultural activity to thrive. The art of the élite may be dominant, but it is usually a minority aesthetic. In countries or regions that have at some time formed part of larger political entities, the élite culture may have dwindled while the folk culture has developed as a symbol of nationalism. Folk art exists in clearly defined geographical regions among peoples with shared characteristics such as language or religion. Tradition usually provides some component, not only in terms of content, subject-matter or use but also in structure, craft techniques, tools and materials. Folk art is as inseparable from folk building (*see* VERNACULAR ARCHITECTURE) as it was inseparable from daily life. The 'applied' or 'decorative' arts (e.g. furniture) have their 'folk' equivalents (*see* FURNITURE, VERNACULAR).

Although the preceding paragraph might suggest that some unanimity exists concerning the nature of folk art and the nomenclature with which to discuss it, as Michael Owen Jones has observed, 'There is no consensus in definitions as to what folk art is, no criteria are exclusive and no distinguishing characteristics are consistently employed.' 'Folk', 'peasant', 'primitive' or 'naive' are some of the many 'labels' that have been appended to this level of artistic activity. No two are exactly synonymous, for while words such as 'primitive' have other associations, alternatives such as 'peasant' exclude art that is urban but not urbane. Furthermore, many of these words carry some sense of condescension.

Uncertainties over definition go back at least to the Prague *Congrès international des art populaires* held in 1928 under the auspices of the League of Nations. In 1950 the American magazine *Antiques* invited 13 'authorities' to answer the question 'What is American folk art?', a request that inspired definitions that were almost as numerous as the contributions. For Edith Halpert folk art was the art of the middle class, whereas for Janet MacFarlane and Louis C. Jones it belonged to the working class. For others it was, above all, 'non-academic'. Seven contributors considered folk art to be the work of highly trained craftsmen ('artisan painting', as Flexner termed it), while an equal number (frequently the same individuals) considered it to be the work of the untrained, a confusion arising partly from the numerous meanings of 'folk art' but also from the use of the phrase 'formal training' in which the writer identifies neither 'academic schooling', nor the potentially no less 'formal' craft training. E. P. Richardson was of the opinion that folk art was either the product of professional craftsmen or the work of untrained professionals. Many objected to the term 'folk art'.

Writing in 1967 (see Hansen), Robert Wildhaber, as a Swiss, was well qualified to recognize 'the many facets of folk art'. He concluded, with understandable caution, that folk art comprised 'articles decorated in traditional styles, associated with specific communities'. This seems reasonable as far as it goes, but it does not help in connection with 'free-standing' works, such as buildings, easel paintings or sculptures.

The diversity of opinion represented in these contributions may be partly attributed to their subjective approach, but even where a more historical and detached view has been attempted, questions of definition remained intractable. Clearly a more satisfactory epistemology is called for, one that incorporates this diversity within an underlying homogeneity. The main difficulty with a term such as folk art in a field that is in the process of establishing parameters is that many other aspects of 'creativity' are outside the confines of the patrician and polite arts. 'Outsider art' has indeed come to mean the work, mainly two-dimensional and pictorial, of those confined within their own preoccupations, some of whom have been or are sufficiently obsessional to have been confined in mental institutions. The interest in these 'outsiders' in ART BRUT, for example, is a post-Freudian phenomenon; it is 'an art without precedent or tradition' and, as such, is the antithesis of folk art. In George Melly's memorable phrase, 'outsider artists' are members of 'a tribe of one', the monads. In contrast, the folk artist is not an 'outsider' and neither is he necessarily a 'loner'. The folk artist is a member of a tradition. Further confusion arises with the 'artistic amusements' of aristocratic amateurs (in both the exact and inexact meaning of the word) whose circumstances might result in a 'tasteful' watercolour that may be 'naive' in execution but sophisticated in outlook. With the development of manufacturing and the availability of prepared canvases and oil paint in collapsible metal tubes, easel paintings were produced by persons from all walks of life and the 'Sunday painter' was born.

Perhaps in response to parallel difficulties, musicologists in Germany have advanced the 'production' and 'reception' theories as a way of examining folk music. Folk art could usefully be evaluated in this way. However, much of the folk art that has been preserved is the work of anonymous craftsmen and women, and this has resulted in greater attention being paid to 'reception' theories, since they are more easily studied from the available data. The 'production'-based approach is perhaps more relevant, even though it depends on the very limited documentation available concerning the makers. The often repeated, but seldom justified, assertion that folk art is the work of the untrained is one of the many results of this lack of documentation. A monument to the view that folk artists were self-taught 'hobbyists' is Sidney Janis's book *They Taught themselves* (1942). However, where authorship is known, it is evident that, more often than not, folk art is the product of a person professionally engaged in an appropriate or related craft or a person whose daily work encompassed a relevant craft—for instance a shepherd who worked wood from hedgerows.

The definition of the two words 'folk' and 'art' also produces imponderables. Does 'folk' encompass the whole of humanity, and, if so, why, of all the States in the American Union, is Kentucky so well known for being 'full of folks' (see 1977 exh. cat., p. 26)? Does 'art' in this context include architecture, painting, sculpture and the decorative arts? Would not each be better described as building, picture-making, carving and furnishing? These questions have been seriously and provocatively considered by Henry Glassie and Kenneth Ames in the USA. In discussing 'popular culture' Glassie referred to that which is fashionable and, therefore by definition, largely non-traditional, as, for example, the products of the mass media, the printing press or television. As such, 'popular culture' has come to be understood as distinct from *l'art populaire*, although there may be points at which they overlap. Thus, while Glassie drew no distinction between 'folk culture' (including building) and 'folk art', he saw clear distinctions between 'popular culture' and 'folk culture': 'Most of "folk art" is not folk because it is popular; the paintings made on velvet by young ladies in seminaries... for example.'

Although folk art is a visual language spoken outside patrician circles, it is not necessarily inimical to them. A case in point is the 18th-century Baroque style of southern central Europe, a version of which migrated north to Scandinavia, where it was translated into a curvilinear style of painting and relief-carving (the Gudbrandsdal school; see fig.), which, in turn, may relate to a debased version of the strapwork ornament of Viking times. Thus, suspended between two high cultures, a tension exists within

Folk art cupboard decorated with carved acanthus ornaments, from Skjåk, Gudbrandsdal, Norway, 1783 (Oslo, Kunstindustrimuseum)

this work that gives vibrance to a folk art that is not utterly outside other art-historical contexts.

It is Glassie's view that folk material may show great variation over geographical space and minor variations through time, an observation that provides a valuable antonym to 'high art', which has more often obeyed opposite laws. This interpretation corresponds to Ames's analogy of folk art with archaeology (see 1977 exh. cat.), in which 'tradition' is regarded as a characteristic of long duration over a relatively small geographical area, in contrast to 'horizon', in which a feature occurs for a limited duration over a wide geographical area. In the Western tradition, folk art is characteristically marked by tradition, whereas for high art 'horizon' is of greater importance.

On the other hand, Ames argued that folk art is non-professional and is therefore 'not so much simple as based on widely shared capabilities'— an ontogenous art. In the sense that most folk painters and sculptors define the world as they believe it to be (subjectively) rather than as they observe it to be (objectively), this view may be acceptable. However, most such artists also display remarkable technical accomplishment in their chosen craft—a craft that is itself part of a wide tradition. This knowledge, this expertise in the hand, is the result of generations of empirical experience transmitted by example and by word of mouth. It is a knowledge that results in a *traditional form* or construction, which may admit *innovation in content* or decoration. For this reason some authorities (e.g. J. Russell Harper) have preferred the more exact and more historical 'production' theories, clustered around the term 'VERNACULAR ART', to the vague requirements of an aesthetic 'reception'-based term such as 'folk art'.

BIBLIOGRAPHY

S. Janis: *They Taught themselves: American Primitive Painters of the Twentieth Century* (New York, 1942)
Antiques (May 1950), pp. 350–62
H. J. Hansen, ed.: *European Folk Art* (London, 1967)
H. Glassie: *Patterns in the Material Folk Culture of the Eastern United States* (Philadelphia, 1968)
J. Russell Harper: *A People's Art: Primitive, Naive, Provincial and Folk Painting in Canada* (Toronto and Buffalo, 1974)
H. W. Hemphill jr and J. Weissman: *Twentieth-century American Folk Art and Artists* (New York, 1974)
M. Owen Jones: *The Hand Made Object and its Maker* (Los Angeles, 1975)
J. Cuisenier: *French Folk Art* (Tokyo and New York, 1976)
Beyond Necessity: Art in the Folk Tradition (exh. cat. by K. L. Ames, Winterthur, DE, Du Pont Mus., 1977)
Outsider Art (exh. cat. by V. Musgrave and R. Cardinal, ACGB, 1979)
I. M. G. Quimby and S. T. Swank, eds.: *Perspectives on American Folk Art* (New York, 1980)
G. Melly: *A Tribe of One* (Yeovil, 1981)
J. Ayres: 'American Folk Art in Britain', *Clarion* (Fall 1982), pp. 34–9
O. Bihalji-Merin and N.-B. Tomašević, eds: *World Encyclopedia of Naive Art: A Hundred Years of Naive Art* (London, 1984)
In Another World: Outsider Art from Europe and America (exh. cat. by R. Malbert and D. Maclagan, ACGB, 1987)
Antiques (Jan 1989), pp. 272–87
J. Ayres: 'Folk Art', *Antiques* (March 1993), pp. 422–7

JAMES AYRES

Folkema, Jacob [Isidor Coridon Fidelle] (*b* Dokkum, 18 Aug 1692; *d* Amsterdam, *bur* 3 Feb 1767). Dutch printmaker and draughtsman. He was trained from an early age by his father Johannes Folkema, a goldsmith, and by Bernard Picart in Amsterdam. His earliest work is the engraving of the *Virgin and Child* (1707). He made mostly drawings and etchings but also one or two mezzotint portraits. He sometimes used the engraver's burin to work over areas in shadow. The majority of his 300 or so prints are portraits, topographical views, frontispieces, book illustrations or vignettes. He etched a number of miniature portraits painted by his sister Anna Folkema (1695–1768), who was also an engraver, and contributed prints to the *Dresden Gallery*, a collection of reproductive engravings after masterpieces from the picture collection in Dresden. Although he worked mostly after other artists' drawings and paintings, prints such as the illustrations to Cervantes (Amsterdam, 1731) are based on his own designs.

Scheen, p. 152

BIBLIOGRAPHY
CHRISTIAAN SCHUCKMAN

Follin, Bartolomeo (*b* Venice, 1730; *d* Warsaw, ?1808). Italian engraver. A student of the master engraver Marco Alvise Pitteri in Venice, and later of Lorenzo Zucchi in Dresden, he entered the service of the Margrave Friedrich at Bayreuth in 1760. There he engraved, among other things, a portrait of the Margrave painted by Francesco Pavona (1695–1777). In 1761 the Margrave named him a teacher at the Bayreuther Akademie, and soon after he sent him to Rome for further training under the guidance of Anton Raphael Mengs and Giovanni Battista Casanova, the latter a compatriot of Follin's who had established a notable practice in Dresden. In Rome, Follin assisted in promoting the new theories of Neo-classicism being advanced by Winckelmann and Mengs. He quickly became acquainted with Winckelmann, who commissioned drawings and engravings of ancient sculpture from him. Follin also engraved a portrait of Winckelmann himself, painted by Casanova. The engraving (Hermanin and Lavagnino, p. 141) is Neo-classical in nearly every detail. Winckelmann is seen in profile, rising cameo-style from a concave oval framed by a broad band with rosettes at each corner. Follin and Casanova further classicized Winckelmann's blunt features by endowing him with a mass of short curls reminiscent of an ancient conqueror or emperor. The idealized portrait head is cut just above the clavicle and placed so that the spectator looks up at the graceful curve of the bust. The depiction is clear and simple throughout; the engraver was nevertheless able to convey the different textures of flesh, hair and marble through his skilful engraving techniques. In 1763 Follin returned to Dresden, where he engraved the numerous paintings in the Gallery there. In 1766 he left Dresden to follow Count Friedrich von Brühl to Warsaw, where he worked in various divisions of the army as a drawing teacher and as an engraver. He also made engravings after portraits of the Polish royalty, aristocracy and intelligentsia, as well as reproducing paintings by Rubens, van Dyck, Batoni and others.

BIBLIOGRAPHY

Bolaffi; Thieme–Becker
F. Hermanin and E. Lavagnino: *Gli artisti italiani in Germania*, iii, *I pittori e gl'incisori* (Rome, 1943), pp. 140–43
A. Schulz: *Die Bildnisse J. J. Winckelmanns* (Berlin, 1953), p. 55

ALEXANDRA HERZ

Follot, Paul (*b* Paris, 17 July 1877; *d* Sainte-Maxime, nr St Tropez, 1941). French designer. He was a leading designer of furniture and interiors in the transition from Art Nouveau to ART DECO before World War I and in the subsequent popularization of the Art Deco style. He was a pupil of Eugène-Samuel Grasset in Paris, and his earliest designs, in the Gothic style, were published in *Art et Décoration*, the journal of design reform founded in 1887. From 1899 Follot was designing bronzes, jewellery and textiles for La Maison Moderne, the commercial outlet for Art Nouveau objects, and his interior design for a study, shown in 1904 at the first Salon of the Société des Artistes-Décorateurs, of which he was a founder-member, demonstrated his affinity with the prevailing curvilinear characteristics of Art Nouveau. Follot's design for a study shown at the same Salon in 1909 revealed a change towards simpler, more rectilinear forms inspired by the revival of Neo-classicism, which became characteristic of his style. He employed light woods, ornamented with carved and gilded fruits, garlands and cornucopias (e.g. chair, 1913; Paris, Mus. A. Déc.). Before 1914 he earned a reputation as a de luxe designer, working for private patrons as well as for commercial retailers of the highest quality. In 1911 Wedgwood commissioned designs from Follot, and the Pomona, Sylvia and Galbia ranges were put into production in 1919. In 1923 he was appointed head of the Atelier Pomone, the design studio of the Paris department store Le Bon Marché, and he designed the Pavilion Pomone for the Exposition Internationale des Arts Décoratifs et Industriels Modernes of 1925 in Paris.

In 1928 he was engaged to design furniture and interiors for the Modern Art Department of Waring & Gillow in London. Opposed to the austerity of modernism, Follot exhibited a sumptuous dining-room at the Salon des Artistes Décorateurs in 1929 and in 1935 designed a luxury suite on the liner *Normandie*.

DBF

BIBLIOGRAPHY

J. Rutherford: 'Paul Follot', *Connoisseur*, cciv (1980), pp. 86–91
A. Duncan: *Art Deco Furniture: The French Designers* (London, 1984)

CLAIRE BRISBY

Folly. Structure often, but not necessarily, towered, the functional utility of which—whether to form a landmark, house a gamekeeper or commemorate a racehorse—is subordinate to its creator's need for self-expression. The forms this might take are diverse and barely classifiable. The elegant Obelisk (h. 42.7 m) built by Mrs William Conolly of Castletown House, Co. Kildare, to a design by Richard Castle, in order to relieve local distress in the hard winter of 1739–40 is a folly, but so too is the giant statue of *Neptune* (*c.* 1749; much damaged) constructed of clinker from his brass foundry by the Quaker industrialist William Champion at Warmley (nr Bristol, Avon). The folly is essentially a West European phenomenon, a gesture of Romantic revolt, the mark of eccentric individuality and sometimes of spiritual malaise.

Such late 16th-century Italian gardens as PRATOLINO (created 1569–84; destr. 1819) had grotesque follies in the shape of huge titans carved from the rock by Giambologna, which fascinated English and French travellers: just before his death Henry, Prince of Wales (1594–1612), was planning another giant three times as large, with rooms in its head, for the garden created for him at Richmond (Surrey) by Salomon de Caus. Jacobean architecture was, however, so bizarre and turreted in its ordinary forms that it hardly supplied the necessarily repressive atmosphere to stimulate folly building on a wide scale. Association is a common element in folly building, but before a folly is created as a visible icon to an idealized history there must be a strong nostalgia for a lost national past. In 17th-century Sweden, where military victories had created a conscious national pride, this condition already existed; hence the setting of rune stones and pine trees on a prehistoric tumulus by Bengt Oxenstierna (1623–1702) at the edge of his formal garden of Rosersberg to create a Rune Hill. Each country tends to make folly icons that are significant to its own culture. In the late 18th century Gustav III nursed a project for a folly at Drottningholm in the shape of a Tartar Camp, which could have been devised only in a country bordering Russia. The Turkish Tent, to a design by Louis-Jean Desprez, that Gustav raised at Haga in 1785, and in which he actually held a privy council meeting, owed more to the French and English influences current in contemporary Swedish garden design. The same must be said of Desprez's Gothic Tower (1792) at Drottningholm.

In Britain it was only in the 18th century, with the acceptance of the regular horizontality of the Palladian style and with the security that had brought leisure, wealth and tedium, that follies proliferated. Where classical architecture is the norm, it is not easy to accept a classical park temple as a folly, even if it was built as such, because it is stylistically conformist. Towers were the true staple of folly architecture, from Sir John Vanbrugh's massive neo-medieval garden tower, the Belvedere (1717), at Claremont, Surrey, to the spindly folly built in 1935 (rest. 1989) by Sir Gerald Hugh Tyrwhitt-Wilson, 14th Baron Berners (1883–1950), on a hill outside Faringdon, Oxon. Whether built to improve the view or for the enjoyment of the spectator, the tower is essentially an expression of the Romantic sensibility, and, whatever the ostensible motive of the builder, such a folly registers an inescapable impact on the landscape and on local awareness.

Folly towers offer extraordinary variety: poetic Rococo-chinoiserie in the Culloden Tower (1746), perhaps designed by Daniel Garrett (*d* 1753), at Temple Lodge, Richmond (N. Yorks); rare Indian marbles in the Haldon Belvedere (or Lawrence Castle) near Exeter, Devon, built in 1788 by Sir Robert Palk (1717–98); and Portland cement for Peterson's Tower (1879–85; h. 66 m) built by Andrew Thomas Turton Peterson (1813–1906) at Sway, Hants. In 1890, on the site of the present Wembley Stadium, London, Sir Edward Watkin commissioned a cast iron tower that was to exceed the Eiffel Tower by 45 m and contain shops, Turkish baths and a winter garden. 'Watkin's Folly', as it was called, reached the first stage and then rusted, unvisited and forlorn; it was dismantled in 1907.

When folly towers were designed to be inhabited, the folly aspect was often intensified despite their utility. In Britain, France and Germany, the nations most deeply involved in the Romantic movement, such folly houses were built for the full indulgence of its spirit. Clytha Castle in Gwent, set on a wooded hill, has elegant rooms around a courtyard between three unmatching towers. According to an inscription, the building in 1790 by William Jones of Clytha House in the valley below 'was undertaken for the purpose of relieving a mind sincerely afflicted by the loss of a most excellent wife'. The Column House of François-Nicolas-Henry Racine, Baron de Moinville (1734–97), demonstrates the same self-indulgent melancholy and the owner's determination to enjoy nature while comfortably inhabiting an evocation of the ruined past (see fig.). It was built in 1780–81, perhaps to Moinville's own design (for amateurism is a theme of follies), in the DÉSERT DE RETZ, a stretch of rough woodland near Marly, west of Paris. This was not a Gothic folly but a classical one: a gigantic broken column, deeply fluted and concealing a five-storey house within its apparent wreck. The Schloss auf der Pfaueninsel (1794–6), Berlin, built by Johann Gottlieb Brendel for Frederick William II of Prussia, exemplifies another aspect of the folly, that of fantasy environment inspired by recent voyages of discovery. Inside, a luxurious suite of rooms is climaxed by the Tahiti Room: nature without and an even more exotic nature within.

Castles and castellated structures were very popular: the Ragged Castle (*c.* 1750), a rubble building with castellations by Thomas Wright (1711–86), survives in Great Badminton Park, Avon. Other common types of folly include castles, grotto and hermitage follies, tombs and garden follies. By their subterranean associations with the tomb all grotto-follies have a certain air of earthy melancholy, even when decorated with shells, pebbles and scraps of mirror (*see* GROTTO). The fashion for them spread to Britain from France and Italy early in the 17th century; the grotto (?1630) at Woburn Abbey (Beds), possibly by

Vue Perspective de la Colonne.

Folly house of François-Nicolas-Henry Racine, Baron de Moinville, in the Désert de Retz, 1780–81; from G.-L. Le Rouge: *Jardins anglo-chinois*, ii (Paris, 1776–87), cahier XIII, pl. 4 (London, British Library)

Isaac de Caux, is perfectly preserved. Alexander Pope created a grotto folly (*c.* 1718) under the public road at Twickenham and popularized the form in his letters. Another (1739) at Goldney House at Clifton, Bristol, has a biblical theme with a sculpted *Daniel in the Lion's Den* and a cascade of water falling into a pool. The domed grotto at Goodwood House, W. Sussex, created *c.* 1740 by ladies in the family of Charles Lennox, 2nd Duke of Richmond (1701–50), reproduced Rococo ornament faithfully in spar and shells, and the outstandingly delicate grotto (1736) in the East Pavilion at Mereworth Castle, Kent, is said by tradition to be the work of an invalid member of the family.

What shells were to grottoes, bark was to hermitage follies. Few built in this flammable material have survived, but Thomas Wright's Root House (*c.* 1750) still remains in Badminton Park. The bark Sanctuary of the Hermit Finch (1807) at Burley on the Hill, Leics, was burnt in 1965. A living hermit was an essential part of a correct hermitage folly. Some were paid £50 a year on condition that their hair was kept uncut, but at Merlin's Cave, designed in 1735 (destr.) for Queen Caroline (1683–1737) at Richmond Gardens (now Kew), William Kent made do with waxworks (for illustration *see* HERMITAGE).

The tomb itself provided another creative spur to the invention of follies, often with wit. Robert Watson, a master of foxhounds living at Larch Hill House, Coole, near Kilcock, Co. Meath, who claimed to believe that he would be reincarnated as a fox, built three dens of stone and earth (*c.* 1810) in the park for his subsequent accommodation; one of them is embattled and Gothic. Jack Fuller (1757–1834), a Sussex squire who built several follies on his estate, built a tomb for himself in the

churchyard at Brightling, E. Sussex, in the form of a pyramid (1811), in which he planned to be buried seated upright with wine and a roast fowl set beside him.

The compulsion towards the grotesque can take the shape of a folly garden. At Stancombe Park, Stinchcombe, Glos, tunnels (1840) provide the only access to a hidden lake, claustrophobically surrounded by flowers and trees. Two successive 19th-century Earls of Shrewsbury crammed such a variety of pagodas, temples, rockwork and bridges into the park at ALTON TOWERS that their creation spans the slender boundary between garden buildings and a folly garden. Temple Combe, Berks, has a genuine prehistoric stone circle, transported from Jersey in 1785 to make a Druid garden.

Although primarily European, follies were also built in the USA. Some 19th-century examples include Calvert Vaux's Belvedere Castle (1869) and Gothic Dairy (1870) in Central Park, New York, but the brilliant abstract creation (1921–54) at Watts, Los Angeles, by SIMON RODIA demonstrates that the folly adapts readily to 20th-century art forms.

BIBLIOGRAPHY
B. Jones: *Follies and Grottoes* (London, 1953, rev. 2/1974)
C. Lancaster: *Architectural Follies in North America* (Tokyo, 1960)
G. Headley and W. Meulenkamp: *Follies: A National Trust Guide* (London, 1986, rev. 1990)
G. Jellicoe and others, eds: *The Oxford Companion to Gardens* (Oxford, 1986), pp. 192–3

TIM MOWL

Foltz, Philipp von (*b* Bingen, 11 May 1805; *d* Munich, 5 Aug 1877). German painter. He received his early training from his father, the miniature painter Ludwig Foltz (i); his brother Ludwig Foltz (ii) (1809–67) became a builder and sculptor. In 1825 he entered the Munich Akademie der Bildenden Künste and studied under Peter Cornelius, whom he assisted with the frescoes in the Glyptothek (1820–30, destr. World War II). He afterwards executed frescoes of his own in the Hofgarten and the Königsbau of the Munich Residenz, which he decorated with scenes from the poems of Friedrich Schiller and Gottfried August Bürger. In 1835 he visited Italy and became an active member of the Ponte Molle Society. In Rome he was influenced more by his contemporaries August Riedel (1799–1883) and Léopold Robert than by the 15th-century Italian artists who had inspired the Nazarenes. In his history paintings of this period (e.g. *Departure of King Otto I from his Family*, 1832; Munich, Neue Pin.) he departed from the strict academic classicism of Cornelius and his circle in favour of a more romantic and painterly approach. This was also the hallmark of his very successful genre paintings of Alpine life.

In 1838 Foltz returned to Munich, where he executed a succession of religious and important historical compositions in an increasingly realistic manner. In 1851 he became professor of painting at the Munich Akademie, where he exercised a decisive influence on the new generation of students. In 1852 Maximilian II, King of Bavaria, engaged him to decorate the Maximilianum in Munich with scenes from German history. In 1865 he was appointed director of the Munich Pinakothek, where he was responsible for completely reorganizing the collection and embarked on a controversial programme of picture restoration. Due to ill-health he retired from public life in 1875.

BIBLIOGRAPHY
Thieme–Becker

COLIN J. BAILEY

Fomin. Russian family of architects and teachers. (1) Ivan Fomin was one of the leading exponents of classicism in 20th-century Russian architecture. His career spanned the revolution of 1917 but was at its most influential when his brand of classicism was adopted by the Soviet state, first as 'proletarian classicism' and later as Socialist Realism. His son (2) Igor' Fomin was a prolific executor of the approved classicist style, mainly in Leningrad (now St Petersburg).

(1) Ivan (Aleksandrovich) Fomin (*b* Oryol, 3 Feb [NS] 1872; *d* Moscow, 12 June 1936). He was a son of a postmaster and grew up in Riga. At his second attempt he was admitted to the Academy of Arts, St Petersburg, in 1894, but he was suspended for participating in student unrest. For a time he worked for the leading Russian exponent of Art Nouveau, Fyodor Shekhtel', in Moscow. He returned to the Academy in 1905, eventually finishing his diploma in architecture in 1909. His graduation prize was a study trip to Egypt, Italy and Greece. Although a convinced classicist from this period onwards, exemplified by his Polovtsev Mansion (1911–13), Petrograd (now St Petersburg), Fomin preserved his interest in the notion of *Gesamtkunstwerk* and experimented with garden city design, for example at Laspi (1916–17), a resort in the Crimea. He completed around 50 designs by 1917, including a station, a bank and a museum. Following the establishment of the Soviet state, Fomin formed a small group of classicist architects, including Aleksandr Gegello and Grigory Simonov (1893–1974), and elaborated an

architectural style he believed to be appropriate for the new political conditions. Early examples of the resulting 'red Doric' style, as it came to be known, include the designs (1919) for a Workers' Palace and the Korshch Theatre, both in Petrograd. Characterized by plain stone surfaces, colonnades, courtyards and regimented columns, the style establishes an atmosphere that is both severe and solemn. This adherence to a classicist architectural language led him, however, into confrontation with other architects, such as the Constructivists, who considered the work of Fomin and the Renaissance Revival architect Ivan Zholtovsky too symbolic of the pre-revolutionary world and not sufficiently forward-looking.

Undeterred, Fomin continued to develop his ideas into a complete theory of architectural design. The 'red Doric' was superseded by 'proletarian classicism', intended to be an architecture of 'pathos and heroism'. The basis for this new architectural style, Fomin argued, lay in the selective assimilation of classical elements, and his subsequent works were marked by a conscious rationalization of classical architecture and a logical continuation of ideas first explored in his concept of the 'red Doric'. A simplified classicism emerged in the 1920s, stripped bare of decoration, porticos and cornices, and repetitive and standardized in effect, but which harnessed the potential of modern construction technology and materials. Notable examples include the House of the Soviets (1924), Bryansk, the Industrial Bank (1925), Yekaterinburg, and the Polytechnic (1927–32), Ivanovo-Voznesensk. The most complete examples of his theory of 'proletarian classicism', however, are the headquarters building for the Moscow Soviet (see fig.) and the Dynamo Sports Club, both built in Moscow in 1928. They are paradoxical buildings, attempting to fuse classicist ideas with those of the Modern Movement. The main façades of both buildings are dominated by rhythmic, standardized elements. The paired columns, for example, which run for all but one of the six storeys, have neither plinths nor capitals and are separated by vertical runs of metal windows broken by bands of masonry at each floor level.

While within these projects the element of monumentality is subdued, Fomin found no difficulty in adapting himself to the new political conditions of the 1930s. As Socialist Realism became the officially approved artistic style, an architecture was demanded that was explicitly monumental and heroic. As the avant-garde Constructivists were losing the debate on the subject of history and continuity in architecture, Fomin proceeded in a series of projects in the mid-1930s to explore further the potential of classicism, which by this time was widely believed to be synonymous with a national architectural style. His contributions to Moscow's underground railway system, the Krasnyye Vorota (now Lermontovskaya) metro station (1935) and Ploshchad' Sverdlova (now Teatral'naya) metro station (1938), both possess a palatial, sombre quality with heavily sculpted marbled interiors and coffered ceilings. Although massive in character and built to impress with the latent potential and achievements of the Soviet system, they nevertheless respond to a human scale. However, his design (unexecuted; with P. V. Abrosimov (1900–61) and Mikhail Minkus) for the Ministry of Heavy Industry, Moscow, reveals the potentially disastrous conclusion of the pursuit of a heroic monumentality. It

Ivan Fomin: headquarters building for the Moscow Soviet, Moscow, 1928

envisaged a frighteningly large and superhuman complex of arches and columns, the scale of which is breathtaking, oppressive and disturbing. Such an image has inevitably led to comparisons of this type of architecture with the rationalized classicism, within the urban landscape, of Albert Speer, and Fomin's executed buildings are a better reflection of his desire to build a 'democratic and international architecture'. Fomin also taught at the Academy of Arts, Leningrad, and after 1933 in the studio of the Moscow Soviet.

WRITINGS
'Iz moyego tvorcheskogo opyta' [From my creative experiences], *Arkhit. SSSR*, v (1933), pp. 32–3
'Rekonstruktsiya klassiki: O stile nashey epokhi' [Classical reconstruction: on the style of our epoch], *Iskusstvo*, 19–20 (1933), p. 6

BIBLIOGRAPHY
M. Il'in: *Ivan A. Fomin* (Moscow, 1946)
M. Minkus and N. A. Pekareva: *Ivan Aleksandrovich Fomin* (Moscow, 1953)
S. O. Chan-Magomedov: *Pioniere der sowjetischen Architektur* (Dresden, 1983); Eng. trans. as S. O. Khan-Magemedov: *Pioneers of Soviet Architecture* (London, 1987), pp. 11, 19, 21, 64, 74
A. V. Ryabushin and I. V. Shishkina: *Sovetskaya arkhitektura* (Moscow, 1984), pp. 29, 45, 47, 52, 70
A. M. Shuravliev and A. V. Ikonnikov: *Arkhitektura sovetskoi rossii* (Moscow, 1987)
A. V. Ikonnikov: *Russian Architecture of the Soviet Period* (Moscow, 1988)

JONATHAN CHARNLEY

(2) Igor' (Ivanovich) Fomin (*b* Moscow, 3 Feb (NS) 1904). Son of (1) Ivan Fomin. From 1920 to 1924 he studied architecture at the Polytechnical Institute and from 1924 to 1926 at the Academy of Arts, Leningrad (now St Petersburg), under Andrey Belogrud and Vladimir Shchuko. His works in the late 1920s followed Constructivist principles: the Narvsky dispensary for textile workers (1927–30; with Lev Rudnev) and the school (1930), both on Stachek Prospekt, Leningrad. The House of Soviets of the Moscow District (1930–35; with V. G. Daugel), Leningrad, an asymmetrical composition, is dominated by a powerful cylindrical building housing the reception rooms. The latter are linked by tiers of galleries that encircle a small yard roofed with a glazed skylight. From 1929 to 1941 Fomin worked with Yevgeny Levinson in Leningrad, developing an original version of modernized 'reinforced-concrete classicism', close in spirit to the works of Auguste Perret. Their joint works include the Lensovet House apartment block (1931–4) on the embankment of the River Kaprovka and the classicist residential block (1931–9) on Petrovskaya Embankment. In the post-war years he continued the revival of St Petersburg classicism in such buildings as the administrative block (1946; with G. I. Aleksandrov), Surovsky Prospekt, and the Ploshchad' Vosstaniya metro station (1951–5), with V. V. Gankevich (1914–81) and B. N. Zhuravlyov (1910–71). In the 1970s he directed the planning of Leningrad State University, Petrodvorets (now Peterhof). From 1935 he taught in the architectural faculty of the I. E. Repin Institute, Leningrad.

BIBLIOGRAPHY
S. V. Vasil'kovsky: 'Tvorchestvo Y. A. Levinsona i I. I. Fomina' [The work of Y. A. Levinson and I. I. Fomin], *Arkhit. Leningrada*, i (1939)

A. V. IKONNIKOV

Fomison, Tony (*b* Christchurch, 12 July 1939; *d* Waitangi, 7 Feb 1990). New Zealand painter. After graduating in sculpture from the University of Canterbury in 1961, he began to paint seriously. He was involved professionally in archaeology, including recording early Maori rock drawings. In 1963 he travelled to Europe, returning to Christchurch in 1967. He extended his use of photographic sources for his work from the Old Masters to medical and often grotesque images, as in *No!* (Christchurch, NZ, McDougall A. G.). He moved to Auckland in 1973 and from then Polynesian culture and imagery dominated his work. From these sources he built up his distinctive symbolic vocabulary, for example in *Too Late* (1986; Rotorua, A. G.). In 1994 Fomison's work toured throughout New Zealand in the exhibition *Fomison: What Shall We Tell Them?*

BIBLIOGRAPHY

Tony Fomison: A Survey of his Paintings and Drawings from 1961 to 1979 (exh. cat. by J. Barr, Lower Hutt, NZ, Dowse A. G., 1979)

L. Strongman: *Tony Fomison: An Artist's Life* (MA thesis, U. Canterbury, 1990)

What Shall We Tell Them? (exh. cat., ed. I. Wedde; Wellington, NZ, C.A.G., 1994)

JIM BARR, MARY BARR

Fon. Kwa-speaking people, numbering *c.* one million, occupying the southern part of the Republic of Benin.

1. ROYAL ARTS. The Fon kingdom of Danhome (Dahomey) was founded at the beginning of the 17th century, and in its capital, Agbome (Abomey), there remain impressive kingly and princely palaces, ministers' homes, temples and artists' quarters. Since art was important to the state, kings were known as much for their encouragement of innovations in the arts as for their prowess on the field of battle. The former palace of the Fon kings Guezo (*reg* 1818–58) and Glele (*reg* 1858–89) has been converted into a museum (*see* BENIN REPUBLIC, §5). The original palace chambers, their colourful bas-reliefs intact, house important examples of the royal arts: thrones, memorial altars (*assen*), appliqué work showing the events of each king's reign, ministers' robes, staffs of office, memorial sculptures and jewellery. These art objects, and others that found their way into various European and American collections, show a rich diversity of forms and subjects.

One of the most famous Fon sculptures is the life-size iron statue of a warrior (Paris, Mus. de l'Homme; see fig.), the work of Akati Akpele Kendo (*fl* mid-19th century) of Mahi origins, who was brought to the capital by King Guezo during the northern wars. The sculpture represents Guezo in the guise of Gu, the Fon deity of war, smithing and iron. The figure once held a large sword and a gong raised in anticipation of battle. The sculpture originally formed part of a palace military shrine, where it was encircled with giant iron swords and machetes set upright in the floor, whose forms were echoed in the figure's crown. These knives and the warrior figure itself were commissioned by King Glele, soon after his enthronement, for the memorial ceremonies for his father King Guezo, in commemoration of the latter's victories over the Mahi people. While closely associated with Guezo, the work also incorporates important references to Glele. The wargod, Gu, was Glele's protective deity, and the large swords were not only an innovation of Glele's reign but also one of his most frequently used and distinctive emblems. Like many works of African art, this sculpture's symbolic grounding is multifarious, being memorials to both Guezo and Glele, a shrine figure to Gu and a war altar intended to assure victory in battle.

Fon statue of a warrior, iron, h. 1.65 m, 19th century (Paris, Musée de l'Homme)

Early descriptions of the court and extant Fon arts are evidence of numerous unique images. Early accounts (Forbes, Skertchly, Burton) describe such unusual works as a 2 m-high silver stork, a silver ostrich with real eggs under each wing, a 1.5 m-high silver tree, a crow, a sheep, a dog, a monkey climbing a tree, wooden representations of animals, birds and a fort, an iron figure of a man turning a windmill, a full-scale glass coach, two silver ships and a 6 m-long wooden model ship complete with sails. Although most of these works are now lost, many of the remaining examples demonstrate a similar innovative concern. A silver guinea-fowl (Paris, priv. col.), a silver elephant and buffalo (Paris, priv. col.) and a brass warrior figure (Paris, Mus. Dapper) are among the finest examples of Fon metal sculpture. They served as royal commemorative statues, and they were identified with the princely ancestral association, Nesuxwe. The elephant and buffalo were dedicated to King Guezo and were probably commissioned for memorial ceremonies. Like most of the royal arts, these works were displayed during the annual royal ceremonies and carried in a parade by the Nesuxwe priestesses, the king's daughters. These, and other silver and brass sculptures, are the works of the royal smithing family, Hontondji, whose workshop and residence has continued to be located opposite the palace.

Gigantic zoomorphic wooden king figures (Paris, Mus. de l'Homme) representing King Glele as a lion and King Behanzin (1891–4) as a shark also exemplify the concern for innovation in Fon art. Like the large iron warrior figure, these works served simultaneously as royal memorials and as power figures (*bo*), which were thought to aid victory in war. Both were the works of Sosa Dede (*fl* late 19th century), a court sculptor, said to be a son of King Agonglo (1789–97). These works, whose striking contrapposto postures and raised arm gestures suggest origins in European lion heraldry, may exemplify Fon interest in foreign art sources. The Fon also seem to have drawn on foreign imagery in their royal thrones, which show similarities with Asante models, and in their royal crowns, which seem to have been modelled on Yoruba examples.

2. OTHER ARTS. Innovation and diversity are also characteristics of other Fon sculpture in wood. There are several distinct types, including *bocio*, which are carved and set up outside the home in response to problems identified in the course of geomancy (*fa*). As surrogates for individual family members, they have a protective role in attracting potential harm to themselves. Carved both by sculpturally unskilled geomancers and by trained artists, these sculptures vary considerably in aesthetic quality. Most, however, emphasize polelike forms and simplified features and show considerable weathering. Another Fon figural tradition portrays the wives of Legba, the messenger deity. These sculptures are placed on altars constructed at entrances to compounds. Unlike the *bocio* figures, these works are carved in pairs by trained artists and display greater detailing of facial and other features.

A third Fon figural tradition in wood is characterized by the striking diversity of objects and materials that are aggregated on to them, including skulls, iron, rope, cords, feathers, gourds, shells, cloth and leaves. These sculptures are prepared by specialists called *botonon*, who are known for their manipulation of mystical powers. After purchasing an appropriate sculpture from the artist, the *botonon* incorporates the requisite materials into the carving to empower it. Some of the figures, which are bound with string or cord, serve to attack one's enemies, preventing them from causing harm. Other sculptures of this type draw upon the imagery and powers of nature: an attached dog's skull, for example, provides watchful vigilance; an owl's skull offers protection against sorcery. Such works are very private objects, their manufacture and means of power are kept secret, and the works themselves are rarely

brought out from the inner rooms. The prominent themes in these sculptures, of bondage, silencing, aggression and danger, reflect a concern with psychological power—power that can benefit even those of humble birth. As such they are foils to the more refined forms and warfare concerns of Fon royal art.

BIBLIOGRAPHY
F. E. Forbes: *Dahomey and the Dahomans*, 2 vols (London, 1851)
R. F. Burton: *A Mission to Gelele, King of Dahome*, 2 vols (London, 1864)
J. A. Skertchly: *Dahomey as It Is* (London, 1874)
M. J. Herskovits: *Dahomey: An Ancient West African Kingdom*, 2 vols (New York, 1938)
P. Mercier: *Les Asé du Musée d'Abomey*, col. cat. (Dakar, 1952)
——: 'The Fon of Dahomey', *African Worlds*, ed. D. Forde (London, 1954), pp. 210–34
A. Adandé: *Les Récades des rois du Dahomey*, Abomey, Mus. N. col. cat. (Dakar, 1962)
C. Merlo: *Un Chef d'oeuvre d'art nègre: 'Le Buste de la Prêtresse'* (Auvers-sur-Oise, 1966)
M. A. Glele: *Le Danxome: Du Pouvoir aja à la nation Fon* (Paris, 1974)
C. E. Adandé: *Les Grandes Teintures et les bas-reliefs du Musée d'Agbomè* (diss., U. N. Benin, 1977)
M. Adams: 'Fon Appliqued Cloths', *Afr. A.*, xiii/2 (1980), pp. 28–41, 87–8
R. F. Thompson: *Flash of the Spirit: African and Afro-American Art and Philosophy* (New York, 1983)
Asen: Iron Altars of the Fon People of Benin (exh. cat., ed. E. G. Bay; Atlanta, Emory U. Mus. A. & Archaeol., 1985)
S. P. Blier: 'King Glele of Danhomé—Part One: Divination Portraits of a Lion King and a Man of Iron', *Afr. A.*, xxiii/4 (1990), pp. 42–53, 93–4
——: 'King Glele of Danhomé—Part Two: Dynasty and Destiny', *Afr. A.*, xxiv/1 (1991), pp. 44–55, 101–3

SUZANNE PRESTON BLIER

Fondukistan. Buddhist sanctuary on a hill in the Ghorband Valley, Parvan Province, Afghanistan. The site was surveyed in 1936 and excavated in 1937 by the Délégation Archéologique Française en Afghanistan. The finds were divided between the Kabul Museum (sculptures and wall paintings) and the Musée Guimet, Paris (sculptures).

The sanctuary comprises a courtyard with a central stupa built of schist, surrounded by 12 niches of mudbrick and rammed earth, decorated with painted clay sculptures and wall paintings. The unbaked clay sculptures from Fondukistan were developed from Indian Gupta models and show only traces of the Hellenistic tradition of the north-west Indian subcontinent. The sculptures are quite similar to those of the late period from Tepe Sardar and a few other sites in Afghanistan and the north-west, such as Ushkar in Kashmir, and possibly inspired some later developments in eastern Central Asia. The formal characteristics of the sculptures from Fondukistan have even led some scholars to recognize in them a peculiarly moving formula of refined religious expression, in the manner of Late Gothic art. Whatever the aesthetic evaluation, it is clear that Fondukistan and the other cognate sites were able to synthetize Indian and Gandharan models with the same Sasanian formulae and patterns that later also influenced European medieval art.

The wall paintings are comparable with those of Bamiyan, especially Phase II of the most recent classification (*see* AFGHANISTAN, §II, 1(iii)), and also show very close Sasanian affinities. Those of niche E (including the famous Maitreya) are among the most representative paintings from pre-Islamic Afghanistan.

Unusually for a Buddhist sanctuary, the sculptures of the 'princely pair' in niche E were accompanied by two cinerary urns, one of which contained two drachms of the Sasanian monarch Khusrau II (*reg* AD 590–628). This provided a *terminus post quem* for the clay sculptures, but one of the coins was overstruck by an early Arab governor and is therefore dated AD 657. Other noteworthy pieces from Fondukistan include the 'pyre of Jyotishka's mother' from niche C and the images of niche D, of which the 'bejewelled Buddha' undoubtedly exhibits one of the most sophisticated iconographies of the period (*see* AFGHANI-STAN, §II, 1(ii)(d) and fig. 9).

The central stupa is presumably somewhat earlier than the niches. The structure is decorated with dwarf pilasters made of single blocks of stone, similar to those of Stupa 20 at Tepe Sardar, which also appears to be earlier than the unbaked clay sculptures of Fondukistan type from the same site.

BIBLIOGRAPHY

R. Ghirshman: *Les Chionites-Hephtalites*, Mém. Dél. Archéol. Fr. Afghan-istan, xiii (Cairo, 1948), pp. 28–32
J. Hackin: 'Le Monastère bouddhique de Fondukistân', in J. Hackin, J. Carl and J. Meunié: *Diverses recherches archéologiques en Afghanistan (1933–1940)*, Mém. Dél. Archéol. Fr. Afghanistan, viii (Paris, 1959), pp. 49–58
B. Rowland: *Art in Afghanistan: Objects from the Kabul Museum* (London, 1971), pp. 43–8
——: *The Art of Central Asia* (New York, 1974)
W. Ball and J. C. Gardin: *Archaeological Gazetteer of Afghanistan*, i (Paris, 1982), pp. 100–01 [extensive bibliog.]
D. Klimburg-Salter: *The Kingdom of Bāmiyān: Buddhist Art and Culture of the Hindu Kush* (Naples, 1989)
M. Taddei: 'The Bejewelled Buddha and the Mahiṣāsuramardinī: Religion and Political Ideology in Pre-Muslim Afghanistan', *South Asian Archaeology, 1989*, ed. C. Jarrige (Madison, 1992), pp. 457–64

MAURIZIO TADDEI

Fonduli [Fondulo]. Italian family of artists. (1) Giovanni Paulo Fonduli was probably the son of Fondulino de Fonduliis (*fl c.* 1444–9), a goldsmith and sculptor whose family had long-established ties with the district of Crema. Giovanni's brother Bartolomeo Fonduli (*fl* Vicenza, 1471–1505) also practised as a goldsmith. (2) Agostino Fonduli, son of Giovanni, was an architect as well as a sculptor, working throughout Lombardy and collaborating with Bramante in Milan.

☐

(1) Giovanni Paulo Fonduli [Fondulli, Fundulli, Fondulio; Giovanni da Crema, Giovanni da Cremona] (*fl* second half of 15th century). Sculptor. A contract dated 29 November 1469, written by Fonduli himself, has survived, stipulating the execution of three *all'antica* terracotta altarpieces for a church to be built in the Castello at Este. From Fonduli's handwriting and Venetian dialect, it can be deduced that he had had some education and that he had probably worked outside of Crema, in Padua. In a later contract of 3 March 1484, Fonduli agreed to create a bronze relief for the Paduan church of Il Santo. Terni de Gregory suggested that the relief may be extant in the church but attributed to another artist. Bronze was the medium preferred by Fonduli. His best-known work (also attributed to the MASTER 10.FF; *see* MASTERS, ANONYMOUS, AND MONOGRAMMISTS, §III), the bronze, partially gilded *Seated Goddess* (h. 204 mm; London, Wallace), signed 'OPUS IO/CRE', demonstrates his knowledge of antique sculpture. Based on an original ancient statue of *Andromeda* (Naples, Mus. Archeol. N.), it has been compared with Andrea Riccio's later images of female figures. In this work Fonduli combined naturalism with a characteristically Venetian taste for luxuriant forms, in order to create an image of the partially draped nude goddess that vies with the best of Riccio. Attributions of Fonduli's sculptures to Riccio are fairly common. The stylistic similarities between the two artists, combined with Fonduli's anticipation of the freer sculptural forms of the 16th century, suggest that he was the younger artist and perhaps Riccio's student. The multitude of variants on Fonduli's name may include the initials IO.F.F. (implying the Latin form of his name 'Johannes Fondulini Fondulus') found on several bronze Paduan plaquettes, for example the *Allegorical Scene* (h. 32 mm; London, V&A) and one set as a sword pommel (h. 76 mm; London, Wallace). Each plaquette reflects knowledge of the goldsmith's art, a knowledge Fonduli acquired in his father's workshop.

BIBLIOGRAPHY

W. Bode: *Die italienischen Bronzestatuetten der Renaissance* (Berlin, 1907)
W. Terni de Gregory: 'Giovanni da Crema and his "Seated Goddess"', *Burl. Mag.*, xcii (1950), pp. 158–61

ROBIN A. BRANSTATOR

(2) Agostino Fonduli [de' Fondulis; de Fondutis] [il Padovano] (*fl* 1483; *d* Crema, 1522). Sculptor and architect, son of (1) Giovanni Paulo Fonduli. He trained with his father in the Paduan circles of the followers of Donatello. In 1483 Agostino was in Milan, where he worked on the naturalistically painted terracotta *Pietà* group of 14 figures for the church of S Maria presso S Satiro, a work that was inspired both by Paduan Late Gothic naturalism and by the classicism of Andrea Mantegna. He also undertook a bust and panels for the lower frieze of the octagonal sacristy. These works, in which he was subjected to the artistic judgement of Bramante, are evidence of a well-matured Renaissance style. In 1484–6, together with his brother-in-law Giovanni di Domenico Battagio, Agostino worked on the Palazzo Landi (now Palazzo dei Tribunali) at Piacenza, producing busts and other decorations. In 1499 he was given the commission for the ceilings and other decoration for the Vimercati house (destr.), Crema, and he was present in 1501 for the valuation of the sculptural works executed for the façade of Crema Cathedral; his collaboration in the decoration of the Palazzo Fodri may also be associated with this visit. During 1502 Fonduli probably worked on a series of ten statues intended for the church of S Maria presso S Celso, Milan. In Crema again in 1510 he was commissioned to produce a tomb for the church of S Maddalena e Santo Spirito. The eight statues for this may perhaps be identified with those now in the parish church of S Martino at Palazzo Pignano, near Pandino, in which Paduan naturalism and the influence of Mantegna are combined with a classicism that derives from Bramante. Although inspired by Bramante, the architectural structure of S Maddalena e Santo Spirito (completed 1523) is also attributed to Fonduli, as are S Maria della Misericordia (1513–16) and SS Giacomo e Filippo (1517–51; rest. 1925), both in Castelleone (Cremona). Fonduli was the only Lombard sculptor collaborating with Bramante in Milan who could assure Bramante of a proper classical training. While remaining faithful to Bramante's teaching, as shown in his use of decoration in strict keeping with the architecture, he was able to provide an easy sense of balance in his personal interpretation of the monumentality that is typical of the Lombard sculptural tradition.

BIBLIOGRAPHY

M. Bandirali: 'Scheda per Agostino Fondulo scultore', *A. Lombarda*, iii/1 (1958), pp. 29–44

M. L. Ferrari: 'Il raggio di Bramante nel territorio cremonese: Contributi ad Agostino de Fonduli', *Studi bramanteschi: Atti del Congresso internazionale: Milan, Urbino and Rome, 1970*, pp. 223–32

S. Bandera Bistoletti: 'La "Pieta" di Agostino de' Fonduli in S Satiro nell'occasione del suo restauro', *A. Lombarda*, 86–7 (1988), pp. 71–82

M. Verga Bandirali: 'Contributo all ricostruzione di una fase cremasca nel percorso di Agostino Fondulo', *A. Lombarda*, 92–3 (1990), pp. 63–75

ADRIANO GHISETTI GIAVARINA

Fongario [da Fonghaia]**, Bernardino.** *See* FUNGAI, BERNARDINO.

Fonhave, Hinrik. *See* FUNHOF, HINRIK.

Fonseca, António Manuel da (*b* Lisbon, 1796; *d* Lisbon, 1890). Portuguese painter. He received his early training from his father, João Tomás da Fonseca (1754–1835), then studied at the Aula de Desenho (drawing class) at the Casa Pia, Lisbon, under Manuel da Rocha. In collaboration with his father he decorated in fresco the Palácio Quintela-Farrobo with mythological scenes, including the *Rape of the Sabines* and *Minerva and Cupid* (both 1822). In Rome between 1827 and 1834 he became a pupil of Vincenzo Camuccini and of Andrea Pozzi, and for his patron, Baron Quintela (1801–69), who became Conde de Farrobo in 1834, he made copies of earlier masters including Raphael, Domenichino and Carlo Dolci. In 1837 he was appointed professor of history painting at the Academia de Belas-Artes, Lisbon, a post he retained until 1863.

Though António Fonseca did not possess great talent and his training had been eclectic, he was the only erudite exponent of Neo-classical painting in Portugal. In 1903 the critic Ribeiro Arthur summarized his qualities at the Academia: 'His methods were archaic, but he was perhaps the best teacher at the Academia, and among his pupils were artists who were to become well known.' In 1843 he exhibited at the Academia the *Death of Afonso de Albuquerque* (1840; untraced) and his best-known work, *Aeneas Rescuing Anchises from Burning Troy* (1843; Mafra, Pal. N.). These were praised by Count Atanazy Raczyński for their composition and colouring, and they were, he said, the only works exhibited that could merit the title 'history painting'. Both paintings show the late influence of Jacques-Louis David, in particular *Aeneas*, a painting that belonged to the academic style of the previous generation, now considered old-fashioned. Fonseca's work had few followers in Portuguese art. He exhibited in 1855 at the Exposition Universelle, Paris, and in 1871 in Madrid. His decorative work included fresco scenes of allegories (1841–3; Lisbon, Pal. Necessidades), and for the Palácio Quintela-Farrobo, Lisbon, he painted seven panels with hunting scenes (1853). Between 1863 and 1868 he also exhibited at the Sociedade Promotora de Belas-Artes, Lisbon, and in 1880 at the centenary Camões Exhibition, Palácio de Cristal, Oporto, he showed works on the theme of Camões including *Luís de Camões Invoking the Muses* (1880; untraced). His work was collected by Ferdinand II, and he was appointed a

Pintor da Câmara Real and teacher to the royal princes. In 1862 he was elected to the Institut de France and in 1872 to the Real Academia de S Fernando, Madrid.

BIBLIOGRAPHY

A. Raczyński: *Les Arts en Portugal* (Paris, 1846), p. 94

J. A. Marques: *O quadro de Eneias* (Lisbon, n.d.)

L. Cordeiro: *Segundo livro da crítica* (Lisbon, 1872)

R. Arthur: *Arte e artistas contemporâneos* (Lisbon, 1903), p. 12

D. de Macedo: *Académicos e românticos* (Lisbon, 1950)

P. Soromenho: *O pintor lisboeta: A. M. Fonseca* (Lisbon, 1957)

J. A. França: *A arte em Portugal no século XIX*, i (Lisbon, 1966), pp. 248–54

LUCÍLIA VERDELHO DA COSTA

Fonseca, Gonzalo (*b* Montevideo, 2 July 1922; *d* Seravezza, Italy, 11 June 1997). Uruguayan painter and sculptor. He studied from 1942 under Joaquín Torres García and was one of the original members in 1944 of the TALLER TORRES GARCÍA, in whose mixed exhibitions he took part. In his sculptures and paintings alike he searched for a structured fixing of a recognizable motif, which he conceived as a kind of naturalism. From 1964 he concentrated solely on sculpture. He spent much of his career in the USA; one of his best-known sculptures is a concrete *Tower* (h. *c.* 13 m; Mexico City, Ruta de la Solidaridad) for the 1968 Olympic Games in Mexico City. He was also the creator of the first sidewalk sculpture in New York city; an unpolished marble column, *Votive Column* (1970) on East 70th Street, between Park Avenue and Madison Avenue. In 1990 he represented Uruguay at the Venice Biennale.

BIBLIOGRAPHY

J. P. Argul: *Las artes plásticas del Uruguay* (Montevideo, 1966); rev. as *Proceso de las artes plásticas del Uruguay* (Montevideo, 1975)

Uruguay: Gonzalo Fonseca (exh. cat. by A. Kalenberg, Montevideo, Mus. N. A. Plást., 1990)

Gonzalo Fonseca: Recent Works (exh. cat., ed. Karl Katz; New York, Jew. Mus., 1971)

ANGEL KALENBERG

Fonseca, Maria Inês Carmona Ribeiro da. *See* MENEZ.

Fonseca e Silva, Valentim da [Valentim, Mestre] (*b* Brazil, *c.* 1750; *d* Rio de Janeiro, 1813). Brazilian sculptor and wood-carver. His earliest surviving works, mainly commissioned from religious fraternities and all located in Rio de Janeiro, date from the late 1770s. His surviving work, typical of the transition from Baroque-Rococo to Neo-classicism, includes the carving on the main altar of the noviciate chapel of the church of Carmo and the altar of the church of S Francisco de Paula; the statues of *St John the Evangelist* and *St Matthew* (both Rio de Janeiro, Mus. Hist. N.); the two monumental candelabra in the monastery of S Bento; and the fountains das Marrecas, das Saracuras and do Lapidário in city squares. His most important work was the large-scale sculptural project that he planned for the Passeio Público in Rio de Janeiro, consisting of terraces with benches tiled with *azulejos* (glazed tiles), pavilions decorated by the painter Leandro Joaquim (1738–98), waterfalls, four flights of steps, statues of *Apollo*, *Diana*, *Jupiter* and *Mercury*, and an entrance gate with bas-reliefs and two pyramids or obelisks (1783). The whole scheme, of which much remains, constitutes a pioneering attempt to improve the conditions of life and leisure in that city.

BIBLIOGRAPHY

M. A. Porto Alegre: 'Iconografia brasileira', *Rev. Inst. Hist. & Geog. Bras.*, xix (1856)

N. Batista: 'Mestre Valentim', *Rev. SPAHN*, iv (1940)

ROBERTO PONTUAL

Fonseca y Acevedo, Alonso de, Archbishop of Toledo (*b* Santiago de Compostela, 1476; *d* Toledo, 4 Feb 1534). Spanish prelate and educator. The illegitimate son of Alfonso de Fonseca, Archbishop of Santiago, Fonseca studied at the University of Salamanca. In 1507 he succeeded his father as Archbishop of Santiago and in 1524 became Archbishop of Toledo, primate of Spain.

Fonseca was a prominent figure at the Spanish court of Charles V, serving as a member of the Council of State. Known for his humanistic concerns, he established university colleges in Salamanca and in his native Santiago. A supporter of Erasmus, he employed Juan de Vergara, Spain's leading Erasmian humanist, as his secretary. He was also a protector of Diego de Sagredo, whose treatise on Renaissance architectural theory, *Medidas del romano* (1526), was dedicated to the Archbishop and had considerable influence on his architectural taste. After its publication, Fonseca, once a patron of Juan de Alava, the architect responsible for reforms the prelate had ordered in the cloister of Santiago Cathedral, turned to the classicizing work of Alonso de Covarrubias and Diego de Siloé. These architects collaborated in the construction of the Colegio de Santiago el Cebedeo (?1519–28), Salamanca, and the Colegio Santiago el Mayor (from 1529), Santiago, Fonseca's two most important educational foundations. The Archbishop also commissioned Covarrubias to remodel his palace (begun after 1526) in Alcalá de Henares and the new Capilla de los Reyes Nuevos (1529–34), Toledo Cathedral. Fonseca's Renaissance tastes were also reflected in his patronage of Juan de Borgoña, from whom he commissioned retables for the Ursuline Convent, Salamanca (1529–31), and for the Capilla de los Reyes Nuevos, Toledo Cathedral (1531–3), and of Alonso Berruguete, who sculpted a retable (*c.* 1530–35) for the Colegio de Santiago el Cebedeo, which Fonseca had established in Salamanca.

BIBLIOGRAPHY

D. de Sagredo: *Medidas del romano* (1526); ed. F. Marías and A. Bustamante (Madrid, 1986), pp. 16, 25–6

J. M. Pita Andrade: 'Don Alonso de Fonseca y el arte del renacimiento', *Cuad. Estud. Gallegos*, xiii (1958), pp. 73–193

——: 'La huella de los Fonseca en Salamanca', *Cuad. Estud. Gallegos*, xiv (1959), pp. 209–32

'Realizaciones artísticas de Alonso de Fonseca', *Cuad. Estud. Gallegos*, xxiii (1968), pp. 29–44

RICHARD L. KAGAN

Fonson, Charles-Auguste (*b* Mons [Flem. Bergen], *bapt* 15 April 1706; *d* Mons, 13 March 1788). Belgian sculptor. He was the son of a sculptor and probably trained first with his father. All that is known of his work is his extensive contribution to the furnishing of the church of St Nicolas en Havré at Mons, on which he worked from 1755. He first executed the high altar; it is traditionally conceived, with a wood statue of *St Nicholas* in the centre and figures of angels in the clouds above. The wooden stalls are also by Fonson; those around the first north and south columns have panels carved with reliefs in a Rococo setting. The reliefs are rather flat and conventionally placed within their frames; the somewhat insipid figures show an imperfect mastery of anatomy and perspective. Their fine detail, however, displays Fonson's skill in handling wood. The reliefs of the other stalls are better, with a more convincing illusion of depth and a more classicizing style; but Fonson's work as a whole is lacking in vitality.

BIBLIOGRAPHY

BNB; Thieme–Becker

A. Mathieu: *Biographie montoise* (Mons, 1848)

E. Marchal: *La Sculpture et les chefs d'oeuvre de l'orfèvrerie belges* (Brussels, 1895), pp. 52–3

IRIS KOCKELBERGH

Font [Lat. *fons*: 'spring']. Object in which, or by which, baptism, the Christian rite of initiation, is practised. Evolving modes of liturgical practice, most notably the adoption of infant baptism (*see* §3 below), have resulted in widely varying physical forms and positioning within the church.

1. Introduction. 2. Early Christian. 3. Byzantine and medieval. 4. Renaissance. 5. Baroque and Neo-classical. 6. Modern.

1. INTRODUCTION. John the Baptist baptized people in the River Jordan, washing them clean of sin. Jesus, however, told his followers that they must be reborn through baptism: 'except a man be born of water and of the Spirit, he cannot enter into the kingdom of God' (John 3:5). Christian baptism is thus a ritual dying and rebirth as a new person, entering the tomb of death (or the womb, for the second time) and being resurrected to a new life, sharing in the experiences of Christ, who himself suffered death but was reborn. The font, therefore, is an item of liturgical furniture, but it is also a physical symbol, embodying the ideas of death and rebirth. Some of the earliest fonts that have been identified were shaped like a coffin or tomb; others, being circular, approximated more to the womb. The numbers six and eight are found in early baptismal architecture, in the shape of either the font or the BAPTISTERY that housed it; occasionally hexagonal and octagonal structures are combined. These represent the sixth and eighth days, on which Christ died (Friday) and was then reborn (Sunday), providing the source of the baptismal candidate's ultimate hope. Some large, round cistern fonts are a reminder that such symbols are not peculiar to Christianity but can be found in the Cauldron of Rebirth of Celtic myth (*see also* GUNDESTRUP CAULDRON). Many Italian baptisteries are octagonal, and in Gothic art, both medieval and modern revivals, fonts are frequently eight-sided. Some Christian traditions have long employed small bowls, perhaps raised on a column, for infant or adult baptism, while others immerse adult candidates in large tanks, set beneath the floor.

For a discussion of holy water stoups *see* CHURCH, §IV, 3.

BIBLIOGRAPHY

J. G. Davies: *The Architectural Setting of Baptism* (London, 1962)

A. Eljenholm Nichols: *Seeable Signs: The Iconography of the Seven Sacraments, 1350–1544* (Woodbridge, 1995)

JOHN THOMAS

2. EARLY CHRISTIAN. Baptism, as administered by both the Eastern and Western Churches in the first centuries of the Christian era, was by immersion, usually of adult converts during Holy Week or at Pentecost. Movable fonts might have been of wood, silver or other metal, while fixed fonts were of marble, dressed stone or

masonry, sometimes set into the floor of a separate BAPTISTERY (see fig. 1). The shallowness of most fonts (the water could rarely have been more than 500 mm deep) suggests that submersion was rarely practised. Forms and locations generally reflect the particular traditions of each area. The liturgical use of smaller vessels that sometimes appear alongside the main one is not clear. One interpretation is that they were used for the baptism of babies, but more probably they contained the oils used during the ceremony. Another widespread element was a ciborium, supported above the font on small columns or pilasters, from which curtains were hung, probably for use in the baptism of women, who were assisted by deaconesses during this rite. Normally the font was also provided with channels for filling and emptying, although in numerous cases these are absent and the vessel was filled manually. There are also many examples of two fonts placed alongside each other.

Symbolism concerning death and rebirth often governed the selection of types (see §1 above), such as the connotations of martyrdom that underlay cruciform fonts, which are recorded from the early 4th century at Tyre. Many of the earliest surviving fonts seem to be elliptical, circular or octagonal. The original elliptical font (early 4th century) in the baptistery at Aquileia was replaced by a hexagonal font, and this type was frequently found in the vast territory of the patriarchate of Aquileia. Various forms, of which the square and circle are the oldest, were used in the numerous baptisteries of Macedonia and Serbia; cruciform fonts were used mainly in the 6th century. The same situation is found in Greece, where examples may be octagonal, hexagonal or in the shape of a Maltese cross. Peculiar to Constantinople (now Istanbul) are large vessels of various forms carved from Proconnesian marble; many are conserved outside the Archaeological Museum, Istanbul. In Asia Minor, however, the prevalent type was rectangular with rounded sides (as also in Egypt and Nubia), usually set into the floor, or cruciform. The rectangular baptismal font of masonry lined with plaster in the meeting house (c. 240) at Dura Europos served as a model in Syria, especially with regard to its position in the apse rather than at the centre of the baptistery (see DURA EUROPOS, §4). This location was also selected in the Early Christian basilicas of Cyprus (e.g. 5th century; Kourion Cathedral). Alongside the canonical forms, some unusual shapes are recorded, especially in North Africa, including multi-lobed fonts and vessels decorated inside with precious mosaics. There are also distinctive forms with numerous steps in Spain.

Western baptismal fonts, which may be up to 5 m in diameter, are generally much larger than those of the East. Parallel with the evolution of the baptismal liturgy, in which the ceremony was gradually shortened, there were numerous cases, from Sardinia to Rome and Syria, in which fonts were altered internally to reduce their size. This can be seen as a prelude to the gradual introduction later of baptism by aspersion (see §3(i) below).

BIBLIOGRAPHY
W. M. Bedard: *The Symbolism of the Baptismal Font in Early Christian Thought* (Washington, DC, 1951)
E. Yarnold: *The Awe-inspiring Rites of Initiation: Baptismal Homilies of the Fourth Century* (Slough, 1971)

1. Early Christian cruciform and subsidiary fonts (4th century AD), baptistery of the North church, Avdat, Palestine

A. Khatchatrian: *Origine et typologie des baptistères paléochrétiens* (Mulhouse, 1982)

MARINA FALLA CASTELFRANCHI

3. BYZANTINE AND MEDIEVAL.

(i) Liturgical change. (ii) Materials. (iii) Font covers.

(i) Liturgical change. Changing baptismal practices are recorded as early as 578, when reference was made at the Council of Auxerre to baptisms taking place in villages rather than in the few baptisteries as formerly required by the Early Christian rite (see §2 above). Nor was the rite restricted to bishops, since Cuthbert, Archbishop of Canterbury (reg 740–58), ordered all priests to baptize regularly. By the 9th century, when Pope Leo IV (reg 847–55) recommended that every church should have a font, there was far less need for the baptism of adult converts in the Western Church. Infant baptism, which had always been practised sporadically, became increasingly important. In 789 Charlemagne ordered that all should be baptized when one year old; by 960 this had been reduced in England to 37 days, and from the 11th century the expected age was but a few days. Partial submersion, as is represented on an ivory bookcover (late 9th century; Metz, Mus. A. & Hist.), replaced the earlier practice of semi-immersion. It was to be many centuries before affusion was generally accepted, and then only within some traditions.

The manner in which the rite was administered similarly changed the physical requirements of the font. Few parish churches were able to provide a separate baptistery and the large *piscinae* or tanks necessary for mass adult baptism. Where such provision continued, however, notably in Italy, southern France and, to a lesser extent, Germany, tanks retained the scale of earlier examples but were positioned above ground (*see* BAPTISTERY, §3). The octagonal font (*c.* 1122–35) of Verona Cathedral, for example, is made from a solid block of marble. Each side measures approximately 1.2 m, and in the centre there is a small platform, resembling an ambo, which may have been intended to protect the bishop's vestments. There is a similar octagonal font (1246) in the baptistery at Pisa (*see* GUIDO DA COMO).

Various explanations have been suggested for a number of fonts that have small secondary basins at the side (e.g. *c.* 1200; Youlgreave, Derbys, All Saints), for example to wash off the chrism (baptismal oil) or, with a cover fitted, to serve as a locker for a chrism cruet. Three angular projections on the 14th-century font at St Michael, Sutton Bonnington (Notts), may have provided ledges for cruets or for book, salt and candle, all of which were sometimes linked symbolically with the rite. A late development appears to have been the insertion of a partition of stone or lead into the basin so that drippings from the child's body do not fall back into the holy water; the earliest French examples of such 'partitioned fonts' date from the 15th century.

(ii) Materials. Any suitably impermeable material might be used for medieval fonts. Stone employed included marble, sandstone, limestone and granite. Metal fonts might be bronze, lead or pewter. Silver fonts for royal baptisms are recorded, but none has survived. There are even rare examples of brick fonts (e.g. early 16th century; Chignal Smealy, Essex, St Nicholas).

(a) Stone and wood. It is difficult to date the earliest stone fonts in parish use. While there are some examples that reuse earlier worked stones, such as a Roman altar at Chollerton (Northumb.), there is no indication of when this may have been done. Dates between the 6th and 8th centuries have been suggested for a roughly shaped boulder (diam. *c.* 850 mm) at Old Radnor, Powys. The font of St Martin, Canterbury, which comprises 22 stones mortared together like bricks, has sometimes been claimed as of the 6th century, but some of the ornament arranged in three tiers is no earlier than the 12th century. Numerous unmounted tub fonts survive (e.g. Tangmere, W. Sussex, St Andrew), but their very simplicity creates problems of dating without the assistance of an inscription, as at Partrishow (*c.* 1060; Powys), or decoration, such as trumpet spirals and vine scrolls (?9th century; Deerhurst, Glos, St Mary).

Given the numbers of fonts that must have been required, it is necessary to consider the use of wooden fonts, probably with a lead lining to retain the holy water. Although the early 13th-century pine font at Alnö, near Sundsvall, based on stone models from Gotland (see below), is one of the few to have survived from before the end of the 15th century (e.g. Marks Tey, Essex, St Andrew), their usual early form may be surmised from the barrel-like fonts represented in baptism scenes on fonts (e.g. 1118; Liège, St Barthélemy; *see* RAINER OF HUY) and on a tapestry of the *Lives of SS Piatus and Eleutherius* (1402; Tournai Cathedral). The staves and hoops of a barrel are faithfully rendered on marble fonts (e.g. 11th century; Perpignan Cathedral), and cable moulding around the rim and base of 12th-century stone fonts

may be in imitation of rope. The bottom of the inscribed tub font (?11th century) of St Mary, Potterne (Wilts), is a separate stone sealed with lead, as might have sealed a wooden barrel.

The extensive rebuilding of parish churches in England during the 12th century led to the creation of many new fonts. Their decoration varies greatly, from simple dog-tooth designs (e.g. Lilstock Chapel, Somerset) to finely carved interlace and *rinceaux*, which sometimes develops into writhing snakes (e.g. Alphington, Devon, St Michael). The latter example also displays the common use of arcading (here interlaced) as a decorative element or to provide a setting for figures and scenes, such as the Virtues trampling Vices in trefoiled niches, with churches in the spandrels above, around the font (*c.* 1180) of St Peter, Southrop, Glos (*see also* ROMANESQUE, §III, 1(v)(a)). Most English tub fonts that may be dated to the 11th and 12th centuries are cylindrical, although some are rectangular or square, such as the 12th-century font at Holy Trinity, Lenton (Notts), upon which appear scenes from the *Resurrection*, divided by the arms of a cross, and two registers of elaborate arcades, with an angel standing inside each arch.

One consequence of the increasing importance of infant baptism was that fonts could be smaller and, for convenience, raised on a pedestal. At St Bonifatius, Freckenhorst, near Münster, the frieze of *Daniel in the Lions' Den* on the lower register of the tub font (1129; h. 1.26 m; diam. 1.17 m; *see* ROMANESQUE, §III, 1(ix)(b)) spills over into the low pedestal. Still greater height and more varied shapes could be achieved by inserting a shaft between the bowl and the base. At first shafts were plain or grooved, but the imaginative integration of the various elements that could be achieved is well displayed in the lion hunt on a granite font (*c.* 1200; h. 1.12 m) in Munkbrarup church (Schleswig), in which a man attacked by a lion on the bowl appears to be suspended above the arcade that decorates the shaft.

Many variations were introduced for the shallow bowl required by the new practices. Mounted fonts may be divided into tabular fonts, in which the bowl is hollowed out from a flat-based block, and cup fonts, in which the shape of the hollow is repeated on the underside. The simplest way of mounting the latter is as a chalice font. At St Cassian, Chaddesley Corbett (Hereford & Worcs; *c.* 1160–70), for example, the rim has a deep band of basketweave decoration, the shallow basin has a fearsome dragon emerging from dense interlace, the squat shaft is a rope coil, and more interlace covers the rounded pedestal.

Greater variety, however, was achieved in the 12th and 13th centuries by using multiple supports (either engaged or detached), with a central pedestal and slimmer legs at the corners or around the perimeter. Occasionally low supports were carved as lions (e.g. mid-13th century; Hohenkirchen Church; *see also* DENMARK, §IV, 1). Although greater numbers sometimes appear, such as the eight outer shafts supporting the square font at St Mary, South Wootton (Norfolk), the most numerous have four outer legs. This is characteristic of a series of richly decorated cup fonts in Cornwall, for example at St Petroc, Bodmin, where the bowl has deeply carved flowers, interlaced stems and knotted serpents. The shafts of the supporting legs are plain, but the capitals of the supporting legs are carved as winged heads.

This method of mounting is shared by two of the most extensive sequences of medieval fonts, the distribution of both of which appears to have been dependent on centralized production and water transport. During the 12th century many large fonts of bluish-black marble (*c.* 1.1 m square), elaborately carved with narrative scenes and decorative motifs that often cover each face of the basin, were exported from Tournai to France (e.g. Laon Cathedral), England (e.g. Lincoln Cathedral) and the regions in the south Netherlands accessible by water (e.g. Dondermonde, Onze Lieve Vrouwekerk; *see* ROMANESQUE, §III, 1(viii)). Certain iconographic themes appear on widely dispersed examples, such as the *Life of St Nicholas* (e.g. Winchester Cathedral; Zedelgem Church). Cruder, mostly circular fonts were also exported from Namur (*see* ROMANESQUE, §III, 1(viii)). The polished surface of south Netherlandish fonts was copied using English shelly limestones from Kent and Sussex (e.g. Ifield, St Margaret), but most especially at Purbeck, Dorset, where simple designs (initially square and later octagonal) were mass-produced throughout the late 12th century and the 13th. Decoration is mostly limited to blank arcades (e.g. Knapton, Norfolk, SS Peter and Paul), in which painted figures may have been placed. Another major centre of production in northern Europe was Gotland, where several workshops were active and from where fonts carved with biblical scenes and fantastic animals were exported across the Baltic (*see* ROMANESQUE, §III, 1(xi) and fig. 45; *see also* SWEDEN, §IV, 1). The round, early 13th-century font at Borby (Schleswig), for example, with reliefs of the *Nativity*, the *Magi before Herod* and the *Adoration of the Magi* and seated figures at the corners of its square base, closely resembles another at Sörup (also Schleswig).

The simplicity of Purbeck fonts was carried over into English freestone fonts in the later 13th century, although some interesting forms are found, such as the trefoiled arcade supporting the octagonal bowl at St John the Baptist, Barnack (Cambs). From the 14th century most fonts stood on a single pedestal. The panels of the bowl were often carved with tracery patterns directly related to the style of contemporary windows (e.g. early 14th century; Brailes, Warwicks, St George). Niches at first were empty, but these were soon filled with single figures, while registers of architectural settings on both the bowl and the pedestal were transformed by ogee arches and pinnacles in the most elaborate Late Gothic styles (e.g. early 15th century; Walsoken, Cambs, All Saints). These changes necessitated a great revival in figure sculpture and the reintroduction of narrative reliefs and symbolic motifs set within the panels. The latter frequently include the *Symbols of the Evangelists* and the *Instruments of the Passion* (e.g. Hastings, St Clement). An especially fine sequence of 28 octagonal fonts in East Anglia is decorated with the *Seven Sacraments*, while the eighth panel frequently has the *Baptism*, *Crucifixion* or *Last Judgement*. The delicate carving on these fonts would not have survived a long journey from the quarries of the East Midlands, and it is documented that the font of St Nicholas, East Dereham (Norfolk), was made there in 1468. Rich tracery and nodding ogees also appear on the fonts at St Ägidius, Wiedenbrück, near Münster (*c.* 1440), and Strasbourg Cathedral (1453; for discussion and illustration *see* DOTZINGER, JODOK).

(b) Metal. The high technical standards of Mosan and German metalworkers from the early 12th century encouraged the manufacture of bronze cauldron fonts, of which the best-known early example is in St Barthélemy, Liège (*see* BELGIUM, §IV, 1 and fig. 22; *see also* ROMANESQUE, §VI, 4(ii)(b)). In their simplest form these might have a plain bowl relieved by bands of inscriptions and stand on three gently curving legs (e.g. before 1216; Osnabrück Cathedral). The shallow bowl (*c.* 1220) in Bremen Cathedral, however, is more typical in its two registers of arcaded decoration and in the imaginative transformation of the legs into four men seated on lions. At Hildesheim Cathedral the kneeling male supporters represent the Rivers of Paradise (*c.* 1225; *see* HILDESHEIM, §1(ii)). Similar themes continued into the early 16th century. At St Blasiikirche, Münden, near Kassel, for example, the font made by Nicholaus von Stettin in 1392 has four male figures trampling dragons, which themselves rest on lions, while St George, with the dragon at his feet, is one of the four figures at Albersdorf, Schleswig (*c.* 1400). Among the fonts cast by Hinrich Klinghe (*fl* 1460–77), the bowl at Pilsum, Lower Saxony (1465), stands directly on figures with the heads of the Symbols of the Evangelists, while at the Alte Kirche, Pellworm, North Friesian Islands (1475), the figures are dressed as deacons. Chalice fonts with a central shaft were made from the late 13th century (*see* GOTHIC, §V, 4). Even this form, however, could be further elaborated by the use of supporters in fantastic guises, such as the four dragons that help support on their tails the round chalice font (1437) in the Marienkirche, Berlin. (For a further example and illustration *see* VISCHER, (1).)

The surviving numbers of English lead fonts in the form of a shallow tub would indicate that this may have been a common material, especially in the late 12th century and the early 13th. They were probably cast flat, using sand moulds taken from a wooden pattern, bent into a cylinder and soldered together, usually with four seams. Six fonts in Gloucestershire (e.g. *c.* 1150–75; Frampton-on-Severn, St Mary) were made from the same mould showing prominent figures alternating with foliage scrolls in an arcade (*see* ENGLAND, §IX, 2(i)). Lead fonts were made in France between the 12th and 15th centuries (*see* FRANCE, §IX, 2(i)). French manufacture has been suggested for an exceptional font (*c.* 1200; Brookland, St Augustine) with cycles of the *Labours of the Months* and *Signs of the Zodiac* arranged in two registers. The former theme also appears on the 12th-century font at Saint-Evroult-de-Montfort (Orne).

There is less evidence for the casting of pewter fonts, although there were important workshops in Bohemia from the early 15th century (*see* CZECH REPUBLIC, §VIII, 2, and fig. 31).

(iii) Font covers. Since the hallowed water might be left in the bowl for up to four weeks it was necessary to protect it from contamination or theft with covers and locks. Early flat oak lids and iron hinges were sometimes replaced in the later Middle Ages by openwork spires, as elaborate as any goldsmiths' work, which could be lifted clear by

pulleys and ensured the prominence of the font in any church setting. Although most English covers are of oak (e.g. Ufford, Suffolk, St Mary), bronze was sometimes used in the Netherlands and Germany, for example above Dietrich Molner of Erfurt's bronze font (1440) in St Katharinen, Brandenburg. Permanent structures were also built around and above the font, such as the stone corona

2. Stone font, oak canopy with polychromy (*c.* 1500), St Botolph, Trunch, Norfolk

(*c.* 1330–40) in St Mary, Luton, probably the oldest surviving example, the two-tiered, octagonal crown (*c.* 1500) that dominates the interior of St Botolph, Trunch (see fig. 2), and the unfinished, triangular ciborium (1470) in Ulm Minster.

BIBLIOGRAPHY

F. Bond: *Fonts and Font-covers* (London, 1908)
K. Noehles: *Die westfälischen Taufsteine des 12. und 13. Jahrhunderts* (Münster, 1952)
G. Randall: *Church Furnishing and Decoration in England and Wales* (London, 1980)
F. Nordström: *Medieval Baptismal Fonts: An Iconographic Study* (Umeå, 1984)

MARCHITA BRADFORD MAUCK

4. RENAISSANCE. In Italy it was still customary to place the font, usually a monolithic basin, with or without a pedestal, within a baptistery. In the early 15th century, however, a new type of font developed that was to become very popular in Italy in the following century and co-exist with the traditional type. This so-called Renaissance font is approached by a flight of steps, at the top of which is a polygonal, square or round basin, supported on a pedestal and covered by a lid. The side of the basin and the lid are usually ornamented.

The most influential design in the type's development was the new font (1416–31) for the Siena Baptistery, on which Lorenzo Ghiberti was commissioned to advise, with decoration by Ghiberti, Donatello, Jacopo della Quercia and others. This was innovative in its structure, with a lidless basin and a tabernacle, and in its combination of bronze and marble. The hexagonal basin bears six gilded bronze reliefs of the *Life of St John the Baptist*, separated by six free-standing bronze *Virtues* set in shallow marble niches. Gold and azure blue enamelled friezes and inscriptions decorate the rim of the basin and the steps. A cluster of columns in the middle of the basin supports the hexagonal marble tabernacle, which is fashioned after Florentine models. On five sides there is the figure of an *Apostle*, set within a niche, while on the sixth there is a small door, behind which are stored the baptismal ointments. Putti crown the corners of the tabernacle, and above these rise columns supporting a statue of *St John the Baptist*.

Elements of this new type were to appear in new commissions and as additions to existing fonts. In Massa Marittima Cathedral, for example, the font (1267) comprised a single block of marble (2.73×2.40×0.98 m), with reliefs by GIROLDO DA COMO, to which was added a tabernacle (1447) by Pagno di Lapo and Giovanni Rossellino (1417–*c.* 1496). Among the most important fonts with a tabernacle standing within the basin are the travertine font (1460) in the crypt of Pienza Cathedral, made by the school of Bernardo Rossellino; that made before 1484 by the workshop of Antonio Federighi for the chapel of S Giovanni Battista in Siena Cathedral; and the font (1502) made by Andrea Sansovino for the baptistery of Volterra Cathedral, which bears reliefs of *Hope*, *Faith*, *Justice*, *Charity* and the *Baptism*.

For bibliography *see* §5 below.

5. BAROQUE AND NEO-CLASSICAL. The sacrament of baptism was never a subject of controversy during the Reformation. The reformers were critical only of the manner in which baptism was performed: they insisted

that all participants should understand the nature of the liturgical act; the act must be performed in public; and it must be shorn of unnecessary religious ceremonies. As a result the development of the font was not directly influenced, although there was controversy about its actual placement in the church. According to the rules established by Carlo Borromeo, it might be placed in a specially built baptistery, in a separate chapel or, if there were no room for either possibility, the font could be placed at the entrance of the church following medieval tradition (*see* CHURCH, §II, 3(i)). This last solution was intended to underline baptism's symbolic meaning of entrance into the mysteries of the Church. In contrast, Jean Calvin (1509–64) stated that the font should stand close to the pulpit (*see* CHURCH, §II, 4).

The design of the font was still not entirely fixed. In early Reformation churches, shallow basins, which could be set directly on the altar table or in a frame next to the pulpit, continued to be regularly used. Stricter requirements were not established until the 17th century: the baptismal font should be made of a single piece of sandstone or marble set on a pedestal, although in poorer churches wood lined with copper or lead was more usual; richer churches could afford a silver font. Two main types continued to be made throughout the 17th and 18th centuries. The Renaissance type persisted particularly in England (e.g. *c.* 1663; Durham Cathedral), Spain and France, with a bowl on a slender pedestal set on a small flight of steps (*see* §4 above). The basin was generally round or polygonal and decorated with cherubs' heads, which sometimes also appeared on the rounded base. The other type was a small cast-metal basin, standing on a graceful foot or mounted against a wall or other surface. The basin, which gradually became larger during the 17th and 18th centuries in continental Europe, consisted of a receiving basin with a sacrarium underneath to catch the overflowing water. The baptismal font of Tréguier Cathedral in Brittany stands on six columns, with a seventh for the sacrarium.

Font covers, which had evolved during the late medieval period into decorative miniature towers in the form of a tabernacle or ark, were reduced under the influence of the Reformation to a flatter design, sometimes crowned with a lantern. Additionally, the whole font was sometimes encased (e.g. 1637; Cambridge, St Botolph) or placed under a bell-shaped cover, which in turn became a ciborium. There was a wide variation in the iconographic decoration from period to period. During the early Baroque, the iconography, which commonly featured St John the Baptist, Adam and Eve, the Baptism, Annunciation, Crucifixion and numerous eucharistic symbols, was still under Gothic and Renaissance influences. During the High and late Baroque, however, all iconographic scenes were excluded from the font, except for an occasional figure of Christ. The basin was smooth and undecorated or covered with ornaments, putti and garlands of fruit and flowers. The font of Tours Cathedral, for example, has a slender stem ornamented with leaves supporting a round basin with a band frieze and leaf decoration; it is crowned with a bell-shaped cover.

During the second half of the 18th century everything was reduced to as pure a form as possible, represented by the Wedgwood black basaltware font (1780) in Essendon Church (Herts). The font (*c.* 1763, by Robert Adam) in St Mary Magdalene, Croome d'Abitot (Hereford & Worcs), is made entirely of mahogany. The tall, fluted pedestal stands on three claw feet and supports a round basin ornamented with acanthus and winged cherubs' heads; the low cover is a later addition. The use of bronze became a striking characteristic of the period. Robert Adam's font (1772) in St Mary, Ruabon (Clwyd), alternates wood, bronze and marble in a pictorial fantasy. The pedestal is a wooden tripod tapering towards the base, with cut-out framework and lions' heads alternating with garlands. This supports a vase-shaped marble basin covered with a simple wooden lid. The last large fonts are encountered in the Neo-classical period. Richard Hayward's beautiful round marble font (1789) in St James, Bulkington (Warwicks), is ornamented with a classicizing relief of the *Baptism*. The basin rests on three small feet that stand on a strikingly massive pedestal of coloured marble, made from a Roman column drum.

BIBLIOGRAPHY

P. Saintenoy: *Prolégomènes à l'étude de la filation des formes des fonts baptismaux depuis les baptistères jusqu'au 16e siècle* (Brussels, 1892)

J. C. Wall: *Porches and Fonts* (London, 1912)

E. T. Green: *Baptismal Fonts Classified and Illustrated* (London, 1928)

R. Bauerreisz: *Fons sacer* (Munich, 1949)

H. Caspary: *Das Sakramentstabernakel in Italien bis zum Konzil von Trient: Gestalt, Ikonographie und Symbolik, kultische Funktion* (diss., Munich, Ludwig-Maximilians-U., 1964)

M. Whinney: *Sculpture in Britain, 1530–1830*, Pelican Hist. A. (Harmondsworth, 1964)

J. T. Paoletti: *The Siena Baptistry Font: A Study of an Early Renaissance Collaboration Program, 1416–1434* (New York and London, 1979)

IRIS KOCKELBERGH

6. MODERN. The first half of the 19th century may be said to mark the lowest point of the font's fortunes. In Catholic churches throughout continental Europe and in Protestant Anglican churches, fonts of all periods were left disused and forgotten, often filled with rubbish and moved to a remote corner of the church. Baptism in churches was usually administered using small bowls, ranging from elegant porcelain to cheap tin, which might be fixed to the pulpit when not in use or laid on the altar or communion table. The font or its substitute was often moved close to the other liturgical furnishings at the east end of the church (*see* CHURCH, §II, 4), following the 18th-century Protestant and Reformed practice of collecting all the liturgical functions within a single, central area. One reason for the decline of church fonts in several Christian traditions was the prevalence of domestic baptism, which was performed not in the church but at the place of birth, using whatever came to hand. The use of a baptismal bowl in church has been characteristic of some traditions, such as Methodism, since the 18th century.

Graphic records of the abuses of fonts and baptism exist in the writings of those associated with the Gothic Revival, notably the members of the Ecclesiological Society and A. W. N. Pugin, who fulminated against these practices in the 1840s and 1850s. They advocated the reinstatement of the font as a respectfully treated piece of liturgical furniture, restored to its traditional place at the rear of the church, preferably near the entrance. They also argued for the readoption of octagonal fonts as a return to the ancient symbol of the Resurrection (or 'regeneration', as the Ecclesiologists preferred). Pugin was particularly distressed by the abuses that he witnessed in Catholic churches on the Continent. His own designs, like those of other Gothic Revival architects, were often elaborately carved structures in the Decorated style (e.g. 1841–6; Cheadle, St Giles), with bowls set on wide pedestals, and the whole perhaps positioned on a stone footpace. Fonts based on Romanesque models were popular in Europe.

During the 1860s and 1870s British architects who had travelled abroad, notably in Italy, introduced the idea of a separate baptistery, translated into their native styles, although few of the resulting structures are truly independent. In some churches provision was also made from the 19th century for baptism by total or partial immersion. Large sunken tanks, generally supplied with running water, are most strongly associated with Baptist churches, which formerly had practised immersion in natural streams; a few examples were also placed in 19th-century Anglican churches.

Towards the end of the 19th century the historicist styles were augmented by the influence of the Arts and Crafts Movement and Art Nouveau (see fig. 3), often combining various media, including marble, stone, bronze and even hardstones. In many ways the fonts of the Modern Movement from about the late 1920s reproduce the forms of very early models, with a bowl or tub supported on a single pedestal or several such supports; other examples are pure prisms (circular or polygonal) that simply rise from the

3. Font by William Reynolds-Stephens, marble and bronze, 1904, St Mary the Virgin, Great Warley, Essex

floor. Many modern fonts are in free and varied forms that almost defy description or are of the utmost simplicity, such as the natural boulder installed in the baptistery of Coventry Cathedral. All the traditional materials have been used in the 20th century, with the notable addition of cast concrete, the plasticity of which enhances the formal possibilities. In many new churches the material is carefully chosen to complement the architectural design. The limestone font in St Wolfgang (1938–40, by Dominikus Böhm), Regensburg, for example, has a cover with small sculptures of the *Evangelists* by Hanns Rheindorf (*b* 1902). In St Anna (1954–6, by Rudolf Schwarz), Düren, the font is a covered bowl on legs and has a separate bowl (sacrarium) from which the water is sprinkled in the Roman rite. Hans Arp designed an inverted conical font for the Allerheiligenkirche (1950), Basle, by Hermann Baur (1894–1980), while Antonin Raymond's concrete font for St Anselm's (1950) in Tokyo is mounted on a tripod. Jean Bazaine's font for Sacré-Coeur (1951, by Maurice Novarina), Audincourt, is carved with writhing visceral forms that recall the understanding of the font as a symbol of the womb. Michael Warren supplied liturgical furniture in unseasoned Irish oak, including a font, for St Laurence O'Toole (1982, by Scott Tallon Walker), Baldoyle, Co. Dublin.

The Liturgical Movement, which evolved on the Continent in the early 20th century, emphasized the centrality and communal aspect of baptism, although the font might be placed variously in a central position or in a separate baptistery. During the late 1980s some Catholic and Anglican churches introduced immersion tanks for the initiation of adult converts, who may come from non-Christian traditions. It remains to be seen whether this is a late product of the Liturgical Movement or a short-lived fashion.

For bibliography *see* §§1 and 5 above.

JOHN THOMAS

Fontaine, Jacques-François-Joseph. *See* SWEBACH, JACQUES-FRANÇOIS.

Fontaine, Pierre-François-Léonard (*b* Pontoise, 20 Sept 1762; *d* Paris, 10 Oct 1853). French architect and writer. With his friend and collaborator, CHARLES PERCIER, he was one of the principal French architects of the 19th century and the best exponent of late Neo-classicism, or the EMPIRE STYLE. Born during the reign of Louis XVI, he died when Napoleon III was on the throne. Continuously, from 1800 to 1851, he held positions of the highest responsibility, supervising the construction of public buildings. As the architect to the government, he worked for Napoleon (*see* BONAPARTE, (1)), in Paris and at the châteaux of Saint-Cloud, Fontainebleau and Compiègne; he built the Arc de Triomphe du Carrousel (Louvre) and started the construction of the arcades in Rue de Rivoli (*see* PARIS, fig. 7). During the reigns of Louis XVIII and Charles X, he built the Chapelle Expiatoire, Rue d'Anjou, Paris, and supervised for a number of years the site of the Arc de Triomphe at the Etoile. For Louis-Philippe, Fontaine built at Neuilly, completed the Palais Royal and carried out restorations.

Fontaine was one of the most intelligent analysts of architecture in the first half of the 19th century. After his first encounter with Bonaparte at the end of 1799, he started to write a journal, which he maintained until his death, with the exception of an interval between 1833 and 1841, when he was writing *Mia vita* (unpublished), which records the events of his life before the beginning of the journal. The five volumes of Fontaine's *Journal*, believed lost in a fire at the store of the Louvre Library in 1871, were rediscovered in 1982 and purchased by the Library of the Ecole des Beaux-Arts in Paris. Its publication in 1987 fundamentally changed our understanding of the history of French architecture at the beginning of the 19th century.

1. TRAINING AND EARLY WORK, 1778–1800. Between 1778 and 1779, when Fontaine was 16, his father, a designer of fountains, took him to the site on the Isle-Adam, north of Paris, where he was employed on important hydraulic projects for the residence of the Prince de Conti (1734–1814). With his lively mind, curiosity and strong will, and after meeting there the architect André (*b* 1762), Fontaine decided to become an architect himself. A young draughtsman five years his senior, Jean-Thomas Thibaut (1757–1826), befriended him and taught him the rudiments of the profession. Their shared enthusiasm rapidly became fanatical; and after Fontaine had almost died of exhaustion on his return from an expedition on foot to Paris, where they visited an exhibition of drawings from the Prix de Rome, his father agreed that he should become an architect. In 1779 he started work in the studio of Antoine-François Peyre, where he remained for six years, during which time he met Charles Percier.

In 1785 the Académie de l'Architecture awarded Fontaine second prize in the Concours de Rome for his design of a 'Funerary Monument for the Sovereigns of a Great Empire'. The jury justified placing him second as a reprimand to those who concentrated on their draughtsmanship, giving 'to this aspect alone a degree of attention which can prove detrimental to the main purpose of their study' (Académie d'Architecture, *Correspondance des directeurs*, xv, p. 105). This judgement did not deter Fontaine from leaving to visit Italy in October 1785. 'Having little money' (*Mia vita*), he was admitted in 1787 with a bursary at the Académie de France in Rome. Percier arrived there in 1786, and they took an oath of friendship, 'without any noise or fuss, . . . but based on respect and confidence' (*Mia vita*); and they soon became known as 'the two Etruscans'. They made drawings for two works that were well received, the *Palais, maisons. . .à Rome* (1798) and the *Choix des plus célèbres maisons de plaisance de Rome* (1809).

The revolutionary events of 1789 and the ruin of his father precipitated Fontaine's return to Paris in 1790. In the 'terrible year of 1792', he took refuge in September in England, where he survived by producing decorative work, wallpapers, snuff-boxes and fans. Percier remained in Paris and was appointed director in charge of the scene painting of the Opéra. In December 1792 he invited Fontaine to join him, and for four years they worked on classical decorations, backdrops for the plays in vogue at the time, including *Horace* by Guillard and *Psyché* by Pierre-Gabriel Gardel. They were also involved in designing furniture for the cabinetmakers François-Honoré-Georges Jacob-Desmalter and Georges-Alphonse Jacob-Desmalter and restoring private residences. One of those they worked on

(1798–9), the house of M. Chauvelin in the Rue de la Victoire, was adjacent to the house of Josephine Bonaparte. She visited the restored house and expressed the wish to meet the two architects in order to propose that they refurbish Malmaison. They had become fashionable.

Fontaine and Percier were received at Malmaison on 31 December 1799 and presented to First Consul Bonaparte by the painter Jacques-Louis David. Fontaine has left a memorable record of the meeting in *Mia vita*. Napoleon asked David what had become of the works of art sent from Italy to France. 'Why not', he asked, 'put all those beautiful things there in the church, under the magnificent dome of the Invalides? It would be a tribute to the army which had brought about their conquest.' Fontaine was called upon to comment and wrote that he 'completely forgot the hero; [he] could see only a little man in a grey frock-coat, and in rather a sharp tone and without constructing sentences properly and with no premises [he] replied, "What effect could the *Apollo*, the *Venus* and the *Laokoon* have under the roof and dome of the Invalides? If we want to set up trophies in recognition of the army in their retirement home, let them be equal to the standards that the army itself took from the enemy"'. His words were effective; the colours marking each French victory appeared one after the other under the roof of the Invalides. On 6 January 1800, six days after the interview, Bonaparte commissioned Fontaine to redecorate the Invalides, and he and Percier worked on Malmaison from 1800 to 1802 (see fig.)

Pierre-François-Léonard Fontaine and Charles Percier: Napoleon's Library, Malmaison, 1800

2. OFFICIAL ARCHITECT, FROM 1801. On 24 December 1800 an attempt was made on Napoleon's life, as he was going to the Opéra. One of the consequences was that the architect of the Tuileries, Etienne-Chérubin Lecomte (?1766–1818), was removed from office, and on 18 January 1801 Fontaine was appointed architect to the government. 'I invest my confidence in you; try not to lose it', Bonaparte declared. Fontaine arranged for Percier to share the appointment, but Napoleon dealt only with Fontaine. The two architects now took over responsibility for the imperial palaces. In May 1804 Bonaparte became Emperor, and with increasing frequency he sought Fontaine's advice on important projects: the completion of the Madeleine (1806), the reorganization of the Terre-plein of the Pont Neuf, the covered and open-air markets, cemeteries and fountains of Paris. The Rue de Rivoli was begun, the Arc de Triomphe du Carrousel (Louvre) built 1806–7, and the question of linking the Louvre and Tuileries palaces generated a large number of projects (1809).

In 1805 Fontaine obtained a considerable budget for the completion of the Palais du Louvre and the façades of the Cour Carrée. Napoleon had hoped that it would be possible to complete the sides of the courtyard and to roof over those parts of the building still open to the elements. The Cour Carrée, however, had been begun with two different decorative systems: two façades, underway according to the plans of Pierre Lescot (from 1546), comprised two orders and an attic; the other two façades followed a design primarily by Claude Perrault (1667), comprising three orders crowned by a balustrade. Fontaine took the initiative to demolish the northern façade and to complete the courtyard in three orders, with the exception of the façade with the dome and sculptures by Jean Goujon (from 1547), which was half built and which he finished. The Emperor never supported Fontaine's desire to build a transverse wing separating the Louvre from the Tuileries in order to mask the non-alignment of the two palaces. This contentious issue led to the Emperor's remark, 'What is big is always beautiful. I am unable to take the decision to divide into two a space whose principal virtue should be its size' (*Journal*, p. 250).

Fontaine's influence on architecture in France derived from his achievements, his intimacy with Napoleon, from his post as architect to the government and from 1813 as Premier Architecte de l'Empereur—an appointment that gave him considerable power over all the buildings under construction—and also from the young architects who attended the studio he operated with Percier. He contributed to the diffusion throughout Europe of an acceptable classical style, now usually known as the Empire style. He had little taste for Romanticism; he did not appreciate the Gothic Revival style and disliked visible ironwork—he successfully opposed plans to build the Iéna and Invalides bridges in metal. Against the purism of the Emperor, who dreamt of a classical décor for Paris, Fontaine objected that plans and elevations of buildings should be determined by the nature of the project. Primarily a Neo-classical architect, he was not limited to the use of a classical vocabulary. He did not hesitate to criticize the Greek temple plan put forward by Alexandre-Pierre Vignon in 1807 for the Madeleine. Neither did he approve of the plan for an obelisk that Jean-François Thérèse Chalgrin

and Antoine-François Peyre submitted in 1809 for the Pont Neuf, giving preference instead to 'a tower similar to a belfry … like the towers of Malines, Strasbourg and others' (*Journal*, p. 354). The Renaissance Revival façades of the Rue de Rivoli (designed in 1802; *see* PARIS, fig. 7) anticipated by some 30 years the change in taste that was expressed through the buildings that formed the manifesto of the style: the Ecole des Beaux-Arts (1833) and the Bibliothèque Sainte-Geneviève (1843–50).

Percier's precise drawings have always been commended, but Fontaine also was an excellent architect and draughtsman, as is shown in his travel notebooks and hundreds of drawings (e.g. Paris, Louvre) and watercolours. After the withdrawal of Percier in 1814, he continued alone a career studded with remarkable achievements: the completion of the Palais Royal (1814–31); the restoration (1822; subsequent restorations) of the Théâtre-Français; the construction of the Galerie d'Orléans (1828–30; destr. 1930); the restoration, with the architect Alexandre Dufour (1760–1835), of the château of Versailles (1814–15); the construction of the Chapelle Expiatoire (1816–26); the restoration (1816) of the Elysée Palace for Charles-Ferdinand, Duc de Berry (1778–1820); the restoration and enlargement (1819–31; north wing remains) of the château of Neuilly for the Duc d'Orléans; the restoration (1824–33) of the château of Eu; the setting up of the Museum of Charles X at the Louvre (1825–30); and the St Ferdinand Chapel, or Notre Dame de la Compassion (1842–3), at Porte Maillot. Fontaine's one great regret was that he had been unable to realize his project for a palace for Napoleon's son, the King of Rome, on the Chaillot Hill (where the Trocadéro is today), a project for which he and Percier had worked out many designs between 1810 and 1814.

For further illustration *see* SPAIN, fig. 30.

WRITINGS

with C. Percier and C.-L. Bernier: *Palais, maisons et autres édifices modernes dessinés à Rome* (Paris, 1798, 3/1830/*R* Meisenheim, 1980)

Journal, 1799–1853, 2 vols (Paris, 1987)

with C. Percier: *Recueil de décorations intérieures comprenant tout ce qui a rapport à l'ameublement* (Paris, 1801, 4/1922/*R* Farnborough, 1971)

Description des cérémonies et des fêtes qui ont eu lieu pour le couronnement de LL MM Napoléon, empereur des Français et roi d'Italie, et Joséphine son auguste épouse. Recueil de décorations exécutées dans l'église Notre-Dame de Paris et au Champ-de-Mars, d'après les dessins et sous la conduite de Ch. Percier et P. F. L. Fontaine (Paris, 1807)

Choix des plus célèbres maisons de plaisance de Rome et de ses environs (Paris, 1809, 2/1813)

Description des cérémonies et des fêtes qui ont eu lieu pour le mariage de SM l'empereur Napoléon avec SAI l'archiduchesse Marie-Louise d'Autriche (Paris, 1810)

Arc de Triomphe des Tuileries érigé en 1806, d'après les dessins et sous la direction de MM Ch. Percier et P. F. L. Fontaine, architectes (Paris, 1827)

Résidences de souverains: Parallèle entre plusieurs résidences de souverains de France, d'Allemagne, de Suède, de Russie, d'Espagne et d'Italie (Paris, 1835)

Regular contributions to *Alm. Bât.* (1807–14, 1831–8)

BIBLIOGRAPHY

J. F. Michaud: *Biographie universelle* (Paris, 1856)

M. Fouche: *Percier et Fontaine*, ed. H. Laurens (Paris, 1907)

L. Hautecoeur: *Histoire de l'architecture classique en France*, v (Paris, 1953)

M.-L. Biver: 'Fontaine et Percier, amis légendaires', *Rev. Inst. Napoléon*, xciv (Jan 1965)

J.-M. Darnis: *Les Monuments expiatoires du supplice de Louis XVI et Marie-Antoinette sous l'Empire et la Restauration, 1812–30* (Paris, 1981)

H. J. Haassengier: *Das Palais du Roi de Rome auf dem Hügel von Chaillot* (Frankfurt am Main, 1983)

MAURICE CULOT

Fontainebleau. French town *c.* 65 km south-west of Paris in the département of Seine-et-Marne. It is famous for its royal château, and during the 16th century it became an important centre for tapestry production; it is also associated with a particularly elegant style of painting, sculpture, stuccowork and printmaking practised by artists commissined to decorate the Château (*see* FONTAINEBLEAU SCHOOL below).

1. Château. 2. Centre of tapestry production.

1. CHÂTEAU. This royal hunting-lodge was first mentioned in 1137 and became for nearly 350 years the chief palace of the kings of France, who were attracted by the hunting afforded by the Forêt de Bière. The present château dates from the rebuilding and enlargements (begun 1528) of Francis I (only one tower surviving of earlier work) and from the modifications undertaken by subsequent sovereigns until 1868. As a result of this piecemeal construction, Fontainebleau is a complex, irregular structure of different dates and styles.

(i) Before 1610. (ii) 1610 and after.

(i) Before 1610. In April 1528 Francis I (*see* VALOIS, (14)) commissioned GILLES LE BRETON for a programme of building (completed 1540) at Fontainebleau. The Cour de l'Ovale (see fig. 1a) was to be rebuilt using the old foundations and retaining the old keep, while a gallery, now the Galerie François I (1b), was to be constructed linking this with the Trinitarian abbey to the west, which was soon demolished and replaced by the Cour du Cheval Blanc (1c). This was named after a plaster cast (untraced) of the horse from a statue of *Emperor Marcus Aurelius* in Rome. Le Breton's work is simple, and the materials are local.

The first floor of the Cour de l'Ovale has a Corinthian order of flat pilasters, and the tall roof is pierced by large dormers with triangular pediments. A colonnade was added in 1541 and runs round most of the ground floor. The medieval gatehouse (now called the Porte Dorée; 1d) in the south-west corner was rebuilt in Renaissance style, based on the entrance to the ducal palace at Urbino. The north range of the Cour du Cheval Blanc survives almost unaltered and is of plastered rubble with brick dressings. Adjoining the Porte Dorée to the east is the vast Salle de Bal (1e; see below), designed (1541) by Sebastiano Serlio, and next to it in turn is the Chapelle St-Saturnin (1f), on the site of the original medieval chapel.

At the châteaux of Blois (1515) and Chambord (1519), Francis I had favoured a rich external decoration with the internal walls left bare for tapestry. At Fontainebleau, however, this was reversed: the façades are of an austere

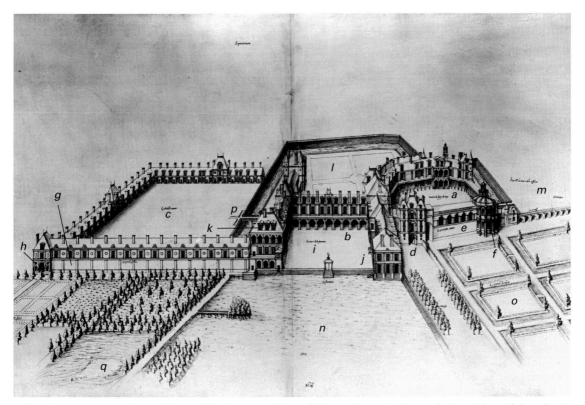

1. Fontainebleau, view from the south, begun 1528: (a) Cour de l'Ovale; (b) Galerie François I; (c) Cour du Cheval Blanc; (d) Porte Dorée; (e) Salle de Bal; (f) Chapelle St-Saturnin; (g) Galerie d'Ulysse; (h) Grotte des Pins; (i) Cour de la Fontaine; (j) Aile de la Belle Cheminée; (k) Appartements des Reines Mères; (l) Jardin de la Reine (now the Jardin de Diane); (m) site of the later Cour des Offices; (n) lake; (o) parterre (later, Parterre du Tibre); (p) site of the later horseshoe staircase; (q) formal gardens, later replaced by the Jardin Anglais; annotations added to a pen and ink drawing by Jacques Androuet Du Cerceau, 513×742 mm, *c.* 1570 (London, British Library)

simplicity, as the stone used was unsuitable for sculpture, while the interior received rich and permanent decoration. In 1530 ROSSO FIORENTINO was entrusted with the decorations of the interior, later joined (1532) by FRANCESCO PRIMATICCIO. Together they developed the style of the first FONTAINEBLEAU SCHOOL, in effect the first extensive and consistent display of Mannerism in northern Europe. Rosso died in 1540, but Primaticcio is known to have worked here as late as 1555, having been joined by NICOLÒ DELL'ABATE in 1552. The most complete interior surviving from Francis I's reign is the gallery bearing his name on the first floor of the block that joins the Cour de l'Ovale to the Cour du Cheval Blanc. Decorated by Rosso (c. 1533–40), like so much at Fontainebleau it has suffered from frequent readjustments and restorations. Each of the 14 piers between its windows is treated as a decorative unit, the lower part in walnut panelling carved by Francisco Scibec de Carpi and lightly gilded, the upper part containing a large fresco surrounded by an elaborate frame of stucco figures and strapwork ornament. Rosso's stucco figures (1535–7) are often in high relief and show the influence of Michelangelo, while the iconography of the paintings (1537–9) is extremely involved, representing in a cryptic manner the achievements of Francis I (see FRANCE, §V, 1 and fig. 43).

Another survival of Francis I's period now forms the upper storey of the Escalier du Roi. This was the bedroom (planned 1541; ceiling 19th century) of the Duchesse d'Etampes (see FRANCE, fig. 43, and PRIMATICCIO, FRANCESCO, fig. 1), designed by Primaticcio and containing frescoes of *Alexander the Great* set in stucco frames. Finally Primaticcio and dell'Abate were responsible for the decoration of the long Galerie d'Ulysse (begun c. 1542; destr. 1738; see fig. 1g; see also PRIMATICCIO, FRANCESCO, fig. 2), which formed the south range of the Cour du Cheval Blanc. The gallery was only half finished when Francis I died (1547), but its ceiling was decorated with grotesques and small panels of figures probably influenced by Perino del Vaga's chapel ceiling at the Palazzo Cancelleria, Rome. The only part of this wing to survive is the Grotte des Pins (1541–3; 1h), variously attributed to Serlio and Primaticcio, with a heavily rusticated façade decorated with atlantids, whose musculature is in part defined by the rustication. Serlio did begin the Salle de Bal (1541) and carried it up to the intended vault, but he was superseded by Primaticcio and dell'Abate, who completed it (1552–6) with a flat ceiling.

By the death of Francis I, Fontainebleau had acquired much of its present appearance: the Cour de l'Ovale, the Cour du Cheval Blanc and the gallery that joined them were all begun and mostly completed, while the Cour de la Fontaine (1i), with the Galerie François I to the north and a range of kitchen buildings ending in the Pavillon des Poêles to the west, was not. Catherine de' Medici commissioned Primaticcio (1568) to enclose the Cour de la Fontaine on the east by what became known as the Aile de la Belle Cheminée (1j). He produced what is perhaps the most distinguished façade in the whole palace, fusing French and Italian style with a double flight of steps against the central block between the end pavilions. It was to set the style for the whole Cour de la Fontaine. The buildings opposite the Aile de la Belle Cheminée, formerly

containing kitchens, were rebuilt as the Appartements des Reines Mères (1k), their façades (1565–8) also by Primaticcio. The reverse side of this wing fronts the Cour du Cheval Blanc, and its façade, by Le Breton, centred on a simple staircase (1556; dest. 1634) by de L'Orme.

Henry IV made considerable alterations and additions to Fontainebleau. He enclosed a new courtyard (begun 1599) to the north of the Galerie François I and Cour de l'Ovale around the Jardin de la Reine (1l; now the Jardin de Diane). The only part to survive contains the Galerie des Cerfs (interior repainted 1863) on the ground floor with the Galerie de Diane (interior destr. early 19th century) above. The Jardin de Diane is now named after the Fountain of Diana, the plinth of which bears bronze figures (1603) by Pierre Biard (see BIARD, (2)). The east side of the Cour de l'Ovale was made into the main entrance by straightening out the wings and bringing in a triumphal arch by Primaticcio, originally in the Cour du Cheval Blanc, and now crowned with a square dome. Further to the east Henry built the Cour des Offices (1m; 1606–9), designed by Rémy Collin (fl 1601–34), with one- and two-storey ranges around three sides of a quadrangle and its main entrance in the form of a heavily rusticated niche. Henry also refaced the south front of the Galerie François I and, by means of some remodelling, continued this more dignified architecture round to Le Breton's west front overlooking the Cour du Cheval Blanc.

Under Henry IV the decoration of the interior was entrusted to a team of artists, mostly French or Flemish, supervised by Martin Fréminet, Toussaint Dubreuil and Ambroise Dubois. Together they formed the second Fontainebleau school. The most important of their works to survive are the ceiling and high altar of the chapel of the Trinité (1608). Designed by Fréminet, the long vault, enriched with paintings set in stucco frames (1629) by BARTHÉLÉMY TREMBLAY, lends great magnificence to the chapel (for illustration see FRÉMINET, MARTIN). The Salle Ovale or Cabinet de Théagène (1606–9) shows the style of Dubois: the exquisite landscapes on the wainscot are contrasted with his large canvases above. Outstanding also was the huge fireplace that gave its name to the Aile de la Belle Cheminée, a great reredos of stone and marble, 7 m high and 6 m broad, which filled the entire space between the doors in the Grande Salle. This was the work of Matthieu Jacquet de Grenoble (d 1610) and took five years to achieve (1598–1603; dismantled 1725). Framed between coupled Corinthian columns, it contained the life-size equestrian statue of *Henry IV*, now in the Salon du Donjon.

Outside the château Henry IV created an island garden, the Jardin de l'Etang, in the lake (1n) in front of the Cour de la Fontaine, laid out as a *parterre de broderie* (1595; island destr. 1713). He also built a pavilion in the middle of the lake (rebuilt 1664; rest. c. 1811) and laid out the Parterre du Tibre (1o) south of the Cour de l'Ovale and the Cour des Offices. It was so called because of the statue and fountain at its centre.

(ii) 1610 and after. Louis XIII's major work at Fontainebleau was the addition of the magnificent horseshoe-shaped staircase (1632–4) in the Cour du Cheval Blanc (see figs 1p and 2 and STAIRCASE, fig. 4), designed by Jean Androuet Du Cerceau. When Louis XIV came to the

2. Fontainebleau, Cour du Cheval Blanc, with the staircase (1632–4) by Jean Androuet Du Cerceau against the façade (begun 1528) by Gilles Le Breton and the ends of the Aile François I (completed by 1540) to the left and Aile Louis XV (1738–50) to the right

throne (1643) Fontainebleau was by far the finest of his palaces. In 1685 he created the beautiful apartment with white and gold decoration in the Pavillon de la Porte Dorée for Mme de Maintenon, and he also enlarged his own bedroom (1714). Outside, Louis Le Vau redesigned the Parterre du Tibre (1662) and created an architectural cascade (largely destr. 1723) at the head of Henry IV's canal. Louis XV's reconstructions entailed the loss of the Belle Cheminée (1725) and some of Francis I's finest interiors, particularly the Galerie d'Ulysse, which was replaced (1738–50) by the Aile Louis XV, a block of apartments for members of the court, designed by Jacques Gabriel and completed to modified designs by his son Anges-Jacques Gabriel. Inside the Gros Pavillon, which replaced the Pavillon des Poêles, was the Cabinet du Conseil (1751; further additions 1772), its ceiling painted by François Boucher (1753) and its panelling by Amédée van Loo and Jean-Baptiste Pierre.

Louis XVI made considerable alterations to Fontainebleau (1785), including the addition of his own Petits Appartements and the redecoration of two of the rooms of his queen-consort, Marie-Antoinette. He ordered the sumptuous *meuble d'été*, which is today in her bedchamber. The Salon de Jeu, designed by Richard Mique, was in the fashionable Pompeian style. Overdoors in *trompe l'oeil* by Piat-Joseph Sauvage (1744–1818) and a ceiling painted by Jean-Simon Berthélemy completed the decor (1786). The same team created Marie-Antoinette's Boudoir, perhaps the most perfect piece of interior decoration in the whole

palace, where stucco reliefs over the doors complement the panelled walls painted with grotesques.

In 1804 Napoleon I, Emperor of the French, made his Throne Room in Louis XIV's bedchamber, substituting for the bed a throne designed by Charles Percier. It was in Louis XVI's Petits Appartements, however, that Napoleon made his most important redecorations (1808). The rooms retained most of the original fireplaces, panelling and architecture, into which framework were inserted new hangings and furniture in Empire style. In the grounds Napoleon commissioned (1810) Maximilien-Joseph Hurtault (1765–1824) to remodel the gardens south of the Aile Louis XV into a Jardin Anglais (see fig. 1q) and to restore the Jardin de Diane. Subsequent alterations at Fontainebleau were minor and included the great restoration, mostly by Jean Alaux (1786–1854), of the frescoes and the building (1857) of a new court theatre for Napoleon III in the Aile Louis XV, to designs by Hector-Martin Lefuel (1857). Under the Third Republic an enormous programme of restoration began (1924), largely funded by John D. Rockefeller jr, followed by a second campaign (1964–8), stimulated by André Malraux, which undertook, among other things, the very difficult further restoration of the Renaissance frescoes.

See also CHÂTEAU.

BIBLIOGRAPHY
P. Dan: *Trésor des merveilles de la maison royale de Fontaine-bleau* (Paris, 1642)
J. Aigoin: *Fontainebleau sous le Deuxième Empire* (Paris, 1931)
A. Bray: 'Les Origines de Fontainebleau', *Bull. Mnmtl*, lxxxxiv (1935), pp. 171–214

F. Herbet: *Le Château de Fontainebleau* (Paris, 1937)
A. Blunt: *Art and Architecture in France, 1500–1700*, Pelican Hist. A. (Harmondsworth, 1953, rev. 4/1982)
Y. Bottineau: 'La Cour de Louis XIV à Fontainebleau', *Bull. Soc. Etud. XVIIe Siècle* (1954)
P. Verlet: 'Le Boudoir de Marie-Antoinette à Fontainebleau', *A. France*, i (1961), pp. 159–68
Y. Bottineau: 'Précisions sur le Fontainebleau de Louis XVI', *Gaz. B.-A.* (1967), pp. 139–58
——: 'Le Château de Fontainebleau sous Louis XV', *Médec. France* (Dec 1972)
A. Chastel, ed.: 'La Galerie François I au Château de Fontainebleau: Le Programme, le système de la galerie', *Rev. A.* [Paris], xvi–xvii (1972), pp. 143–52
J. P. Samoyault: 'Le Château de Fontainebleau sous Napoléon I', *Médec. France* (1974)
J. Ehrmann: 'La Belle Cheminée de Fontainebleau', *Actes du colloque international sur l'art de Fontainebleau: Paris, 1975*, pp. 117–26
I. Dunlop: *Royal Palaces of France* (London, 1985), pp. 31–81
G. Jellicoe, S. Jellicoe, P. Goode and M. Lancaster, eds: *The Oxford Companion to Gardens* (Oxford and New York, 1986), pp. 193–5

IAN DUNLOP

2. CENTRE OF TAPESTRY PRODUCTION. Attempts have been made to see the tapestry workshop at Fontainebleau as the precursor of the French factories of the 17th century. The truth, in fact, seems somewhat more modest: the Fontainebleau workshop was similar to other temporary workshops installed in private residences by important figures to fulfil their personal requirements. Set up in the château of Fontainebleau by Francis I in 1540, the workshop had only a limited number of high-warp weavers. A dozen are known by name, all of them apparently of French origin, several also being owners of a workshop in Paris. Working under the Surintendant des Bâtiments, Philibert Babou de la Bourdaisière (1484–1557), they were paid on a daily rate by the King, who supplied them with the raw materials necessary to produce tapestries. It is therefore surprising to find no mention of tapestries from Fontainebleau among the 213 hangings listed in 1551 in the Garde Meuble; almost all of the tapestries listed were from Brussels.

Attributed to the workshop of Fontainebleau are a number of hangings, the designs of which reflect the Fontainebleau Mannerist style, although the possibility of their having been woven in Paris has not been ruled out. Only one set can be positively attributed to Fontainebleau, the renowned series of six tapestries (Vienna, Ksthist. Mus.) that reproduced part of the decoration by Rosso Fiorentino and Francesco Primaticcio for the Galerie François I in the château of Fontainebleau (*see* §1(i) above). The sumptuous hangings, woven with gold and silver thread, were executed from at least February 1540 to July 1547. The hangings are more than just a true copy; they are a transposition of the decoration of the gallery, replanned from the perspective of a tapestry. The shading is modified, the colouring is different, and the great freedom with which stucco and frescoes were combined in the gallery has been clarified and simplified in order to achieve a greater unity in the series of hangings. The tapestries also incorporate such *trompe l'oeil* architectural elements as wainscoting and beam ends to create a deliberately illusionistic effect. The work of adapting the decoration is attributed to Claude Baudoin and other painters who were entrusted with executing the tapestry cartoons. The date of the closure of the workshop at Fontainebleau is not known. The year 1547 is often mentioned, but according to a letter from Primaticcio (see Pressouyre, 1969) it could have been after 1565.

BIBLIOGRAPHY
S. Pressouyre: 'Les Fontes du Primatice à Fontainebleau', *Bull. Mnmtl* (1969), p. 226, n. 1
——: 'La Galerie François Ier au château de Fontainebleau: Le Témoignage des tapisseries', *Rev. A.* (1972), nos 16–17, pp. 106–11, 122–3
Rosso Fiorentino (exh. cat., ed. E. A. Caroll; Washington, DC, N.G.A., 1987–8)

ISABELLE DENIS

Fontainebleau school [Fr. Ecole de Fontainebleau]. Term that encompasses work in a wide variety of media, including painting, sculpture, stuccowork and printmaking, produced from the 1530s to the first decade of the 17th century in France. It evokes an unreal and poetic world of elegant, elongated figures, often in mythological settings, as well as incorporating rich, intricate ornamentation with a characteristic type of strapwork. The phrase was first used by Adam von Bartsch in *Le Peintre-graveur* (21 vols, Vienna, 1803–21), referring to a group of etchings and engravings, some of which were undoubtedly made at Fontainebleau in France (*see* FONTAINEBLEAU, §1). More generally, it designates the art made to decorate the château of Fontainebleau, built from 1528 by Francis I and his successors (*see* VALOIS, (14)), and by extension it covers all works that reflect the art of Fontainebleau. The principal artists of the school were ROSSO FIORENTINO, FRANCESCO PRIMATICCIO, NICOLÒ DELL'ABATE, ANTONIO FANTUZZI, ANTOINE CARON and, later, TOUSSAINT DUBREUIL, Ambroise Dubois and MARTIN FRÉMINET. With the re-evaluation of MANNERISM in the 20th century, the popularity of the Fontainebleau school has increased hugely. There has also been an accompanying increase in the difficulty of defining the term precisely.

1. Introduction. 2. First Fontainebleau school. 3. Second Fontainebleau school.

1. INTRODUCTION. When Francis I returned from his imprisonment in Madrid (1525–7) by the Holy Roman Emperor Charles V, he chose to live in and near Paris rather than in the Loire Valley as he had done in the first part of his reign. For that purpose he embarked on a large campaign of building residences in the Ile-de-France, beginning in 1527. His favourite residence became Fontainebleau, approximately 65 km south-east of Paris, where he owned a ruined medieval castle in the middle of excellent hunting grounds. The structure was rapidly rebuilt and expanded without great architectural distinction; however, for the interior the King decided on an ambitious programme of painted decoration to be executed in the Italian manner. Earlier in his reign he had attempted to attract well-known Italian artists to his court but had been turned down by both Raphael and Michelangelo. Leonardo had accepted his invitation in 1516, but, no longer able to paint, he died in 1519 near Amboise. In 1518 Andrea del Sarto was brought to France, but he returned to Florence the following year. The King was more successful with a younger generation of artists. It was probably partly on the advice of Pietro Aretino that he invited Rosso Fiorentino, who arrived in 1530 and

worked for him until his suicide in 1540. In 1532 Primaticcio arrived, a younger and still unproven artist sent from Mantua by Giulio Romano, who was too preoccupied with work to come himself. In 1553 Nicolò dell'Abate joined Primaticcio at Fontainebleau, where they were both active until their deaths in the early 1570s. After this time artistic activity was very reduced at Fontainebleau because of political instability and the Wars of Religion (1562–98). However, from 1595 activity resumed under Henry IV (*reg* 1589–1610) with a new group of artists who constituted what is sometimes called the second Fontainebleau school.

2. First Fontainebleau school.

(i) Work of Rosso and Primaticcio. (ii) Role of printmaking. (iii) Dispersion of artists from Fontainebleau. (iv) Influence. (v) Later developments. (vi) General character.

(i) Work of Rosso and Primaticcio. The first phase of work, which ended with Rosso's death in 1540, was the most innovative and complex. For practical reasons, the first projects executed were for the living-quarters of the King and his queen Eleanor and were entrusted not to Rosso but to Primaticcio. Initially this seems surprising, as Rosso was a much better-known artist and had arrived before Primaticcio. However, it is generally accepted that the reason for this apparent anomaly lay with Primaticcio's having brought with him a project for the Chambre du Roi that had been established by Giulio Romano in Mantua. Giulio was not only Raphael's heir—and therefore more authoritative than Rosso—but was also much more experienced in executing monumental decorations. Rosso and Primaticcio are often thought of as strongly contrasting artistic personalities, but in the 19th century critics frequently confused their works. This is significant if one is to understand the kind of currency that the term 'Fontainebleau school' has acquired. Indeed, at Fontainebleau the two artists were in close contact, and the younger Primaticcio perhaps learnt more from Rosso than is generally assumed. Although Primaticcio worked independently of Rosso, and each had a team of assistants from France and other countries, they worked closely together and collaborated on the decorative scheme for the Pavillon de Pomone (destr.) and the Galerie François I (1532–9). This complicates an assessment of their respective contributions to the most striking innovation of the 1530s at Fontainebleau: a type of decoration in which a combination of painting and stucco relief is placed above a high wainscoting.

Louis Dimier, in *Le Primatice* (Paris, 1900), proposed that the initiatives came from Rosso and that the Galerie François I was the one decisive work. The exuberant and original decoration of this extremely long and narrow room is still fairly well-preserved. The Chambre du Roi (1533–5), however, has been destroyed. Its decoration was carried out on the basis of a project designed by Giulio and apparently brought to France by Primaticcio; the walls were wainscoted up to about 2 m, and frescoes above depicted the *History of Psyche* encased in a rich framework of gilt stucco with subsidiary pictures. Here, the main elements of the characteristic Fontainebleau scheme were already in place. There is, of course, a long way between drawings for the project and the final execution. The

placement over high wainscoting, for instance, was certainly a decision made in relation to French habits, and it would not be clear from the drawing that the framework was to be in full stucco relief. Nor should one exaggerate the importance of this priority because the Galerie François I was surely already being planned while the Chambre du Roi was being decorated. Rosso may have been consulted about final decisions for the Chambre, and Primaticcio's expertise in stuccowork could have helped in planning the very complex scheme of the Galerie. Rather than individual responsibilities, what is important is that the work done at Fontainebleau, by transplanted Italian masters assisted by French, Italian and Flemish artists and craftsmen catering to French patrons, has a different appearance from comparable decorations in Italy. It is this new 'look'—hard as it may be to define—and the contacts between many artists of various nationalities gathered in a somewhat isolated place that are the basis of what can be called the Fontainebleau school.

The death of Rosso in 1540 marked a new phase in the art of Fontainebleau. Rosso's art was most often characterized by an extremely unconventional, bizarre and almost extravagant fantasy and a taste for the rare and unexpected that affected both his subject-matter and treatment of figures. Primaticcio, who had been trained in the discipline of Raphael transmitted through Giulio Romano, produced much more classicizing work. He became the uncontested leader of court art during the last years of Francis I's reign (1540–47), and when Rosso died he was in fact in Rome collecting antique sculptures for the King and making moulds of some of the best-known Classical works to have them cast in bronze at Fontainebleau. For this task he brought back with him the young Jacopo Vignola as a technical assistant. Other new arrivals from Italy, among them the Florentine goldsmith Benvenuto Cellini and the Bolognese architect and theorist Sebastiano Serlio, could only reinforce Primaticcio's classicizing tendencies. Cellini crafted the salt of Francis I (1540–43; Vienna, Ksthist. Mus.; *see* CELLINI, BENVENUTO, fig. 4) and secured his reputation as a significant bronze sculptor with the *Nymph of Fontainebleau* (?1543; Paris, Louvre) planned for the entrance gate of the château. He was set up in Paris rather than at Fontainebleau and had troubled relations with the French. It is difficult to say how much of an impact his rather unsuccessful stay made in France beyond the production of a handful of masterpieces.

For Primaticcio, these years were a time of astounding productivity. As well as the arduous task of supervising the making of casts (Fontainebleau, Château) of such antique sculptures as the *Laokoon* (Rome, Vatican, Mus. Pio-Clementino) and *Sleeping Ariadne*, he executed frescoes (early 1540s; part destr.) for the vestibule of the Porte Dorée, decorated the bedchamber of the Duchesse d'Etampes (1541–4) and much of the Galerie d'Ulysse (late 1540s; destr. 1738), the latter his largest and most complex painted decoration (*see* PRIMATICCIO, FRANCESCO, figs 1 and 2, and FRANCE, fig. 43). The most spectacular commission must have been a suite of baths known as the Appartement des Bains (1544–7; destr.), a series of six rooms for bathing and relaxation set up beneath the Galerie François I. In these rooms such masterpieces of the King's collection as Leonardo's *Virgin of the Rocks* (commissioned 1483; Paris, Louvre) and Andrea del Sarto's *Charity* (1518; Paris, Louvre; *see* SARTO, ANDREA DEL, fig. 3) were displayed, encased in stucco frameworks. The central room, with a small pool in the middle, was decorated with the story of *Jupiter and Callisto*, and apparently several murals had explicitly erotic content. This extraordinary ensemble can be understood as the synthesis of a strongly vernacular and medieval tradition of having public and princely baths on the one hand and a humanistic tradition of ancient Roman baths on the other. Although the rooms were destroyed, we have some records of the decoration through drawings and prints. While the subject-matter was partly playful, the style was in a grand antique manner.

(ii) Role of printmaking. The production of prints is one of the most original aspects of the Fontainebleau school, although it is not known exactly when or how it started. According to Vasari, engravings of Rosso's work were made in France while he was still alive. This seemed unlikely, although recent evidence appears to confirm it. Pierre Milan, possibly an Italian immigrant, was certainly making engravings in Paris by 1540. Rosso was in Rome before the city was sacked in 1527 and was deeply involved in printmaking, drawing compositions specifically to be engraved by Giovanni Jacopo Caraglio. In France he may have decided to renew this practice by collaborating with craftsmen in Paris. Etchings probably began to be made at Fontainebleau in 1542, a time when frenetic decorative activity was taking place. Antonio Fantuzzi, a painter from Bologna and one of Primaticcio's principal assistants, may have had the initiating role and was certainly the most

productive, along with Léon Davent, a professional print-maker, and Jean Mignon, a French painter employed at Fontainebleau. Prints executed there have a characteristic appearance: they are quickly made, experimental and apparently uncommercial in intention. Most reproduce compositions by Rosso, Primaticcio and Giulio Romano. Primaticcio himself, whatever his degree of involvement, must have at least tolerated this activity, since he surely controlled most of the drawings that were reproduced. Other artists at Fontainebleau, notably Geoffroy Dumon-stier and Domenico del Barbiere, produced prints of their own compositions. Printmaking at Fontainebleau seems to have lasted for only a few years. After 1545, when Fantuzzi produced fewer etchings, the character of the production changed, becoming more careful and com-mercial, and Luca Penni became the main provider of compositions. Eventually, the whole activity seems to have moved to Paris, possibly when Francis I died in 1547. Meanwhile, the production of burin engravings in Paris continued in the workshop of Pierre Milan, who employed René Boyvin, the plates made by the two being indistin-guishable at this time. Later, Boyvin signed his prints and continued to produce them at least until 1580. Most of the designs engraved by the Milan–Boyvin workshop were by Rosso (see fig. 1); by Léonard Thiry, Rosso's Flemish assistant at Fontainebleau, who worked in his master's style (e.g. the *Livre de la conqueste de la toison d'or*, probably done in the 1540s but not published by Boyvin until 1563); and by Penni, who apprenticed his son Lorenzo Penni (*fl c.* 1557) to Boyvin.

Printmaking made a major contribution to the Fontaine-bleau school. To a certain extent, the production of prints

1. Pierre Milan, after Rosso Fiorentino (completed by René Boyvin): *Nymph of Fontainebleau*, engraving, 307×517 mm, 1553 (Vienna, Graphische Sammlung Albertina)

balanced the stylistically diverse contributions to 16th-century French court art, giving it greater homogeneity than it would otherwise have had. More significantly, perhaps, prints—especially Fantuzzi's—were an important factor in the conversion of Rosso's monumental decorations into an ornamental style that could be applied to all kinds of works, from architecture to jewellery.

(iii) Dispersion of artists from Fontainebleau. Fontainebleau also functioned as a school in the more literal sense, in that it was the training-ground for many artists. Pierre Bontemps, a sculptor who worked at Fontainebleau in the late 1530s and probably finished his training there, was later employed on royal projects for many years. The marble *Monument for the Heart of Francis I* (1550–56; ex-Abbey of Les Hautes-Bruyères; Paris, Saint-Denis Abbey; for illustration *see* BONTEMPS, PIERRE) is a characteristic example of the Fontainebleau school, having strapwork ornament derived from Rosso and relief compositions with elongated, pliant and sensuous figures reminiscent of Primaticcio. It is unclear to what extent Bontemps himself was responsible for the figures, the architectural design in all likelihood being by Philibert de L'Orme. Even artists who arrived as fully trained professionals altered their manner when in contact with Rosso or Primaticcio. This must have been the case with Luca Penni, who worked with his brother-in-law Perino del Vaga in Genoa before coming to France. Although Penni first worked with Rosso, he was much more affected by Primaticcio, whose manner he adapted to his more ponderously Roman taste. *The Justice of Otto* (Paris, Louvre), the only painting generally accepted as by his hand, was thought in the 18th century to be by Primaticcio. Léonard Thiry, however, adopted Rosso's stylistic peculiarities and continued to produce many compositions in his manner for a decade after the master's death.

In many cases, artists who were of considerable repute then are little known today, for example Lorenzo Naldini, a Florentine sculptor who had considerable success in France, and the sculptor and painter Simon Le Roy (*fl* 1534–42), who had moved to Paris by 1542. When an actual work is identified, it can be disconcerting. The *Deposition* (originally Orléans Chapel at the Celestins; now Paris, Ste Marguerite) had long been attributed to Francesco Salviati (another Florentine painter who came to France, although little is known of his activity there) but has since been identified as a work by Charles Dorigny, a painter active at Fontainebleau under Primaticcio. Generally Florentine in character, with distant echoes of the work of Andrea del Sarto, it has little to do with what is generally thought of as characteristic of the Fontainebleau school. One cannot therefore assume that all those who worked at Fontainebleau practised what would be recognized as art of the Fontainebleau school; nevertheless, the great numbers of artists who participated in the programmes of decoration there undoubtedly played an important part in spreading the style. In the 1540s in particular there was a veritable diaspora of artists who had worked there. After Rosso's death several sculptors probably left because there was much less work for them. More dramatic changes were brought about by the death of Francis I in 1547. Henry II (*reg* 1547–59), his successor,

was much less attached to Fontainebleau, and artistic activity there during his reign was drastically reduced, with the result that a number of artists sought work elsewhere. The centre of gravity of artistic life moved to Paris. In addition, Henry was much less interested in painted decorations of the Italian type and rather more attracted to architecture and to sculptural decoration; he was also more inclined to patronize French artists.

(iv) Influence. The strong classicizing tendency of the 1540s was the dominant trend, although the more playful and fantastic art of Rosso was not forgotten. Jean Cousin *le père*, who moved from Sens to Paris probably shortly before 1540, was influenced by Fontainebleau. His production of the 1520s and 1530s is unknown, but works of the 1540s, especially his cartoons for tapestries depicting the *Life of St Mamas* (Langres Cathedral; Paris, Louvre; *see* COUSIN, (1), fig. 2), clearly echo the new classicizing style. Significantly, several etchings from his designs of the mid-1540s have long been considered as products of the Fontainebleau school. This would probably also have happened to *Eva Prima Pandora* if its attribution to Cousin had not always been perpetuated by his distant relatives who owned it until it entered the Musée du Louvre. François Clouet, whose court portraits betray his southern Netherlandish ancestry, also painted pictures in the Fontainebleau manner: for example, the *Bath of Diana* (Rouen, Mus. B.-A.) and the *Lady in her Bath* (?*Marie Touchet*) (*c.* 1570; Washington, DC, N.G.A.; for illustration *see* CLOUET, (2)). Such anonymous paintings as the *Toilet of Venus* (Paris, Louvre) combine borrowings from Rosso and Primaticcio almost as a deliberate demonstration of their compatibility and their validity as works of the Fontainebleau school. The few monumental painted decorations commissioned show the success of Fontainebleau: several rooms at the château of Ancy-le-Franc (Yonne) attributed to Primaticcio and dell'Abate; the 12 painted overmantels at the château of Ecouen (Val d'Oise) done for Anne, Duc de Montmorency; and the paintings of episodes from Virgil's *Aeneid* in the gallery of the north wing of the Grand Ecuyer of Claude Gouffier's château of Oiron (Deux-Sèvres) by Noël Jallier, an otherwise entirely unknown painter who was clearly aware of Fontainebleau but also, it seems, of recent developments in Rome.

In spite of these examples, painted murals of the type prominent in Italy did not become popular in France. During the reign of Henry II the authority of Primaticcio was reduced, and the French architects Philibert de L'Orme and Pierre Lescot controlled most royal patronage; they preferred sculpted decoration, which was more traditional in France. The impact of Fontainebleau was nevertheless considerable. The exuberant decoration of Lescot's façade of the Cour Carrée of the Palais du Louvre, with its exquisite figures in relief (1547–50) carved by Jean Goujon (for illustration *see* LESCOT, PIERRE), would be unthinkable without the example of Primaticcio. The fact that much of the sculptural decoration at Diane de Poitiers's château of Anet (Eure-et-Loire) was attributed to Jean Goujon points to a similar source of inspiration, even if the attribution itself is discredited. Indeed, the well-known statue of *Diana with a Stag* (ex-château of

Anet; Paris, Louvre), sometimes attributed to Goujon, with its graceful curves and tapering limbs, is the epitome of the Fontainebleau style. Domenico del Barbiere, who had worked at Fontainebleau, established a practice in Troyes and strongly inflected the great local sculptural tradition of Champagne towards the new court style.

(v) Later developments. The later works of Primaticcio have a slightly new character due partly to personal evolution and continued contacts with developments in Italy but also probably to the arrival in France in 1552 of Nicolò dell'Abate, a skilled painter from Modena who had already established his reputation in Italy. A virtuoso draughtsman and an original colourist, dell'Abate's Emilian training in the tradition of Correggio and Parmigianino prepared him for his new position as Primaticcio's almost exclusive executant for painting. Primaticcio's works of this time display bolder decorative schemes with complex perspective effects and a warmer, more lively and less classicizing manner, as in the decorations (1552–6) for the Galerie Henrie II (Salle de Bal) at Fontainebleau. Being less favoured by Henry II, he was able to work for others, especially the Guise family. For the residence of François de Lorraine, 2nd Duc de Guise (1519–63), in Paris (now Hôtel de Soubise) he decorated the chapel with a spectacular *Adoration of the Magi* (destr.) that filled the walls of the choir. Such paintings had limited impact outside immediate court circles, in part because they were not reproduced by printmakers. However, the charming but weak *Birth of Cupid* (New York, Met.), one of a group of paintings by anonymous masters, is in the style of the Fontainebleau school and is indebted to both Primaticcio and dell'Abate. The MASTER OF FLORA (*see* MASTERS, ANONYMOUS, AND MONOGRAMMISTS, §I), often considered to be the artist, is the result of an assemblage of works, the common authorship of which seems difficult to sustain. Dell'Abate himself produced independent paintings in France (e.g. the *Rape of Proserpina*; Paris, Louvre) that show that he was not impervious to Primaticcio's example, thus reinforcing the coherence of the Fontainebleau school. In paintings such as these and in destroyed decorations for Fontainebleau he also developed an original landscape style (for example *see* ABATE, NICOLÒ DELL', fig. 1). Antoine Caron is—with the exception of contemporary portrait painters—the first French artist with a substantial body of easel paintings. His tiny figures, gesticulating in a balletic manner, are reminiscent of dell'Abate's, but his art—especially his strange sense of colour—is his own, and he is the most typical artist working in the last decades of the reign of the Valois kings.

Catherine de' Medici assumed much power after the death of her husband Henry II in 1559, and Primaticcio once again became a favourite, succeeding de L'Orme as surveyor of the royal works. In this capacity he controlled not only buildings and their painted decoration but also the work of sculptors, notably those working on royal tombs. It was within this framework that Germain Pilon formed his mature style under Primaticcio's direct guidance, continuing the full impact of the art of Fontainebleau until 1590.

(vi) General character. The term 'Fontainebleau school' has been applied so loosely, referring to any 16th-century Italianate work with elongated forms, especially within a market-place eager to give a more precise appellation to mediocre anonymous products, that it can appear meaningless. Nevertheless, used more prudently it points to an important phenomenon: the creation of an original kind of court art in France under Francis I and its partial transformation and diffusion over the next 40 years. While its components may seem disparate to the scholar of Italian art, it must be remembered that for the French, who had come from a tradition of late Flamboyant work and *mille fleurs* tapestries, this must have seemed very new and highly classical in style. As has been noted, there were also such homogenizing factors as the production of prints and the training of artists at Fontainebleau. Other artists were instrumental in giving currency to the art of the court, principally the architect and engraver Jacques Androuet Du Cerceau (i) and the goldsmith and engraver Etienne Delaune. Through various channels, the art of Fontainebleau affected all areas of visual production, from monumental buildings to the design of jewellery. The decorative arts had always had an important tradition in France, and this continued, though with the adoption of the new style from Fontainebleau. While the Italian artists at court were occasionally occupied with the decorative arts, Jean Cousin (i)—although always designated as a painter—was in fact mostly occupied with projects for tapestries, stained-glass windows, Limoges enamels, luxury vessels and armoury for execution by various craftsmen. Thus, the 'Fontainebleau school' affected the whole visual environment of upper-class society.

To see this phenomenon as mere fashion belittles its importance. It has deep ideological implications. Through its origins and associations, what might be called the 'classicizing Mannerism' of the Fontainebleau school was very much a royal style. As such, it made royal power manifest and thereby reinforced it, contributing to a sense of national identity at a particularly important time in the history of France, when there was great instability. In that sense the phenomenon of the Fontainebleau school is an active element in the complex establishment of the modern or 'absolute' monarchy. On the other hand, display was a prime method of establishing prestige on the European stage, making luxury a necessity.

3. SECOND FONTAINEBLEAU SCHOOL. The Wars of Religion and the dynastic crisis caused by the death in 1589 of Henry III, last king of the Valois line, marked a caesura in French life. Once peace was restored by the new Bourbon king Henry IV, a deliberate effort was made to re-establish continuity as a marker of legitimacy. Painters had never entirely abandoned Fontainebleau; Henry IV undertook its vigorous rejuvenation, as well as that of a few others such as the château of Saint-Germain-en-Laye and the Palais du Louvre. An artist of great talent, Toussaint Dubreuil ensured real continuity by collaborating with Ruggiero de Ruggieri (*fl* 1557–97), one of Primaticcio's Italian assistants, who had become Premier Peintre to the King. Dubreuil's references to Primaticcio and the art of the great reigns of Francis I and Henry II are clear and deliberate. *Cybele Awakening Morpheus* (Fontainebleau, Château), for example, is a paraphrase of Primaticcio's composition in the vestibule of the Porte

2. *Gabrielle d'Estrées and her Sister, the Duchesse de Villars*, by an anonymous artist of the second Fontainebleau school, oil on panel, 0.96×1.25 m, end of the 16th century (Paris, Musée du Louvre)

Dorée. However, Dubreuil was a fertile and elegant composer in his own right who, like Primaticcio, did not execute the paintings himself. His decorative projects have all been destroyed, but his drawings and descriptions of them (Paris, Louvre and Ecole N. Sup. B.-A.; Amsterdam, Rijksmus.) show that he was inventive and original. Unfortunately, this heir to Primaticcio died prematurely in 1602. Concurrently with Dubreuil, Ambroise Dubois from Antwerp produced fluent, if less original, work. He is supposed to have arrived in France fully trained, but his art shows that he may have had close contact with the earlier Fontainebleau style. However, this may have been because Fontainebleau and Paris were requisite stops for northern European artists on their training journeys to Rome. Some did not feel it necessary to go further south. After Dubreuil's death Henry IV recalled Martin Fréminet from Italy, where he had spent several years. In Rome he had been particularly attentive to Michelangelo and had formed a vehement style with highly pliable figures that also recalls the art of such northern European artists as Bartholomäus Spranger, although it is difficult to know whether this was due to direct contacts or to an independent synthesis of similar elements. Fréminet's decoration (1606–19) of the chapel of the Trinity at Fontainebleau is the most important decorative ensemble surviving from the period (for illustration *see* FRÉMINET, MARTIN). His death in 1619, a few years before Rubens's execution of the cycle of paintings of the *Life of Marie de' Medici* (Paris, Louvre) for the Palais du Luxembourg, marked the end of an era.

During Henry IV's reign the deliberate return to the art of the earlier Fontainebleau school is strikingly felt in a series of erotic pictures, the most famous of which is *Gabrielle d'Estrées and her Sister, the Duchesse de Villars* (Paris, Louvre; see fig. 2), where the anonymous artist combined two earlier prototypes, François Clouet's *Lady in her Bath* and *Lady at her Dressing-table* (Worcester, MA, A. Mus.), for Henry's mistress. In this case, the sense of a second Fontainebleau school seems proclaimed in an almost programmatic way.

BIBLIOGRAPHY

L. de Laborde: *La Renaissance des arts à la cour de France*, 2 vols (Paris, 1850–55)

L. Dimier: *Le Primatice, peintre, sculpteur et architecte des rois de France* (Paris, 1900)

——: *French Painting in the Sixteenth Century* (London and New York, 1904)

S. Béguin: *L'Ecole de Fontainebleau: Le Maniérisme à la cour de France* (Paris, 1960)

W. M. Johnson: 'Les Débuts du Primatice à Fontainebleau', *Rev. A.*, 6 (1969)

H. Zerner: *L'Ecole de Fontainebleau: Gravures* (Paris, 1969; Eng. trans., London and New York, 1969)

Actes du colloque international sur l'art de Fontainebleau. L'Art de Fontaine-bleau: Paris, 1972

S. Béguin and others: 'La Galerie François Ier au château de Fontaine-bleau', *Rev. A.*, 16–17 (1972) [double issue]

L'Ecole de Fontainebleau (exh. cat., ed. S. Béguin; Paris, Grand Pal., 1972–3)

H. Zerner: *Italian Artists of the Sixteenth Century (1979)*, 32 [XVI/i] of *The Illustrated Bartsch*, ed. W. Strauss (New York, 1978–)

J.-J. Lévèque: *L'Ecole de Fontainebleau* (Neuchâtel, 1984)

Fontainebleau et l'estampe au XVIe siècle: Iconographie et contradictions (exh. cat. by K. Wilson-Chevalier, Nemours, Château Mus., 1985)

De Nicolò dell'Abate à Nicolas Poussin: Aux sources du classicisme, 1550–1650 (exh. cat., ed. B. Grinbaum; Meaux, Mus. Bossuet, 1988)

K. Wilson-Chevalier: 'Women on Top at Fontainebleau', *Oxford A. J.*, xvi/1 (1993), pp. 34–48

The French Renaissance in Prints from the Bibliothèque Nationale de France (exh. cat. by C. Buckingham and others, Los Angeles, UCLA, Grunwald Cent. Graph. A.; New York, Met.; 1994–5)

HENRI ZERNER

Fontana (i). Italian family of potters. The workshop founder, Guido Durantino (*d c.* 1576), was established as a potter in Urbino by 1519 and by 1553 had adopted the name Fontana. His three sons, Nicolo Fontana (*d* 1565), Camillo Fontana (*d* 1589) and Orazio Fontana (*c.* 1510–76), also took part in the business, as did Nicolo's son Flaminio Fontana (*fl* after 1576). The workshop was one of the most influential in the area during the 16th century.

Guido Durantino has been described as 'an artist of somewhat elusive personality' (Mallet), and it is still not certain whether as head of the workshop he confined his activities to the administration shop or was also a painter. The products of his studio include works dated between 1528 and 1542 and two important armorial services (both *c.* 1535) made for the Constable of France, Anne de Montmorency, and Cardinal Antoine Duprat; there are also indications that Guido's shop received commissions from Guidobaldo II, Duke of Urbino. Nicola di Gabriele Sbraghe (formerly incorrectly identified as Nicolò Pelli-pario; *see* URBINO, NICOLA DA) was one of at least six painters whose hand can be identified among the marked works from the Fontana shop, and it was here that Nicola painted his famous plate (1528; Florence, Bargello) de-picting *St Cecilia*. The workshop maintained consistently high, if diverse, artistic and technical levels, producing *istoriato* (*see* URBINO, fig. 2) and white-ground grotesque wares, as well as plain white ceramics and fired and unfired utilitarian items. The grotesque wares of the Patanazzi family provided some competition for the Fontana work-shop, and it can be difficult to differentiate between the products of the two shops between *c.* 1570 and 1585. Orazio Fontana probably began his career in his father's shop as a painter of *istoriato* wares, although his fame is attributable more to the appearance of his monogram on a number of pieces than to his talent as an artist. Seven pieces (including one formerly in Berlin, Schloss Charlot-tenburg; destr.) bear dates between 1541 and 1544 along with his monogram. The Berlin plate (inscribed 5 Nov 1542) typified Orazio's lively style, which has been de-scribed as 'far from impeccable and sometimes downright careless' (Mallet). His later career was highlighted by his service as master potter to the Duke of Savoy in 1564, a year before he established his own workshop in Urbino and provided maiolica to the Medici court in Florence (*see* CERAMICS, colour pl. I, fig. 1). Flaminio Fontana, the son

of Nicolo, carried on the family business until the late 16th century. He was involved with the Medicis' attempt to duplicate true East Asian porcelain and spent time in Florence supervising firings of the 'Medici porcelain' between 1573 and 1578.

BIBLIOGRAPHY

B. Rackham: 'The Maiolica Painter Guido Durantino', *Burl. Mag.*, lxxvii (1940), pp. 182–8

G. Liverani: 'Un piatto a Montpellier marcato da Orazio Fontana ed altri ancora', *Faenza*, xliii (1957), pp. 131–4

J. V. G. Mallet: 'In bottega di Maestro Guido Durantino in Urbino', *Burl. Mag.*, cxxix (1987), pp. 284–98

WENDY M. WATSON

Fontana (ii). Italian family of painters and draughtsmen. They were active mostly in Bologna and Rome. (1) Prospero Fontana was a leading Bolognese exponent of Mannerism. (2) Lavinia Fontana, his daughter and pupil, was the first woman artist to have commissions for large-scale and public works as well as portraiture.

(1) Prospero Fontana (*b* Bologna, 1512; *d* Bologna, 1597). He trained with Innocenzo da Imola, a follower of Raphael, and early in his career assisted the Mannerist painter Perino del Vaga on the decoration of the Palazzo Doria in Genoa. His contact with Mannerist artists contin-ued during his years as an assistant to Giorgio Vasari on projects in Rome and Florence. Despite this exposure to progressive influences, he continued to paint in an essen-tially conservative style in this period, as in the *Transfigu-ration with Saints* (1545; Bologna, S Domenico). From 1548 he moved between Rome and Bologna: in 1550 he executed frescoes of scenes from the *Life of Constantine* in the Palazzina della Viola, Bologna (*in situ*); in 1550–51 he supervised the decorations of the Vatican Belvedere, Rome, for Pope Julius III; and in 1551 he executed frescoes of *Virtues* and *Gods* in the Palazzo Bocchi, Bologna. Early in 1553 he was again in Rome, where he worked with Taddeo Zuccaro on the decorations (destr.) of the Villa Giulia. During this final period in Rome he also executed decorations for the loggia of the Palazzo di Firenze (*in situ*) for Balduino del Monte, brother of Julius III. Around 1560 he worked briefly with Primaticcio at Fontainebleau in France. His first convincing use of a Mannerist style occurs in such works of this period as the *Disputation of St Catherine* (*c.* 1560; Bologna, Madonna del Baraccano). He assisted Vasari again in 1563–5 on the decorations of the Palazzo Vecchio in Florence, and in 1565 he was admitted to the Florentine Accademia del Disegno. He followed the Mannerist style of Vasari until he settled in Bologna in the 1570s. There he responded to the appeals of Cardinal Gabriele Paleotti for artists to provide clear and persuasive religious works in keeping with the suggestions of the Council of Trent. The use of descriptive naturalism and convincing expression charac-terizes his late style, as in *St Alessio Distributing Alms* (1576; Bologna, S Giacomo Maggiore). His last important public commission dates from the late 1570s, when he contributed decorations for the rebuilt apse of S Pietro, Bologna (*in situ*). Although he continued to paint in the 1590s, Prospero failed to respond to the reform of Bolognese painting instigated by the Carracci family.

BIBLIOGRAPHY
Thieme–Becker
The Age of Correggio and the Carracci (exh. cat., Washington, DC, N.G.A.;
   New York, Met.; Bologna, Pin. N.; 1986), pp. 136–40
V. Fortunati Pietrantonio: *La pittura bolognese del '500* (Bologna, 1986)

(2) Lavinia Fontana (*b* Bologna, *bapt* 24 Aug 1552; *d*
Rome, 11 Aug 1614). Daughter of (1) Prospero Fontana.
She was trained by her father and followed his Mannerist
style. Her first recorded works, which date from 1575,
were small paintings for private devotion, such as the *Holy
Family* (Dresden, Gemäldegal.). By 1577 she had become
established as a portrait painter in Bologna. Works of this
date include the *Self-portrait at the Harpsichord* (Rome,
Gal. Accad. S Luca) and the portrait of *Senator Orsini*
(Bordeaux, Mus. B.-A.). Her portrait style reflects the
formality of central Italian models as well as the naturalistic
tendencies of the north Italian tradition. The elegantly
costumed Orsini is shown seated at a table, with a suite of
rooms opening behind him, a setting recalling such Florentine portraits of the 1530s as Agnolo Bronzino's *Bartolommeo Panciatichi* (Florence, Uffizi). Lavinia used a similar
setting for other portraits, including the *Gozzadini Family*
(1584; Bologna, Pin. N.). Female sitters are also shown in
elaborate dress, with particular attention paid to details of
embroidery and jewels, and they are often accompanied
by small dogs (e.g. Baltimore, Walters A.G.; Florence,
Pitti). In naturalism and treatment of detail her portraits
are comparable with those of her famous north Italian
predecessor, Sofonisba Anguissola (e.g. *Portrait of a
Woman*, 1557; Berlin, Gemäldegal.).

Although best known for her portraits, Lavinia also
painted mythological and religious subjects, one of her
most accomplished being the *Noli me tangere* (1581;
Florence, Uffizi; see fig.). The simplicity of the composition and its soft light and muted golden colours show the
influence of Correggio's painting of the same subject
(1520s; Madrid, Prado), which was then in Bologna. Her
incorporation of qualities typical of Correggio's work was
unusual among Bolognese artists at this date, before their
introduction by Annibale Carracci. Her first documented
public commission was in 1584, for the *Assumption of the
Virgin with SS Peter Crisologus and Cassian* (Imola, Pin.
Civ.), a work full of Venetian colour and light. In 1589
she painted another major altarpiece, the *Holy Family with
the Sleeping Christ Child* for the monastery of S Lorenzo
at the Escorial, Madrid (*in situ*), in a High Renaissance
classical style reminiscent of Sebastiano del Piombo. Her
response to progressive developments in Bolognese painting was tempered by her training in the Mannerist style of
her father, and the tension between the two modes is
evident in such works of the 1590s as the *Assumption of
the Virgin* (Pieve di Cento, Parrochiale) and the *Consecration to the Virgin* (Marseilles, Mus. B.-A.). The elaborate
Visit of the Queen of Sheba to Solomon (Dublin, N.G.) may
also date from this period.

Lavinia's work was introduced to Rome about 1600
with the *Vision of St Hyacinth* (Rome, S Sabina), commissioned by Girolamo Bernerio, Cardinal of Ascoli. The
success of this painting and the prospect of important
new patrons probably prompted her move there in 1603,
the year she received her most important public commission, for a large altarpiece depicting the *Martyrdom of St*

Lavinia Fontana: *Noli me tangere*, oil on canvas, 810×650 mm, 1581 (Florence,
Galleria degli Uffizi)

Stephen (destr. 1823) for the basilica of S Paolo fuori le
Mura, Rome. The painting is recorded in an engraving of
1611 by Jacques Callot (see J. Lieure: *Jacques Callot*, i,
Paris, 1924, no. 33). No major public commissions followed this, though she continued to work as a portrait
painter in Rome (e.g. *Head of a Young Man*; Rome, Gal.
Borghese). Among her last works are the full-length figures
of *SS Cecilia, Catherine, Clare and Agnes* for the pilasters
of the high altar of S Maria della Pace, Rome (*in situ*).
These were commissioned by Gaspare Rivaldi, whose
portrait by Lavinia is also in the church. One of the last of
the Late Mannerist painters, Lavinia was not a stylistic
innovator, but the range of subject-matter and format and
the number of works she produced is significant; hers is
the largest extant body of work by a woman artist active
before 1700. She had 11 children from her marriage in
1577 to Gian Paolo Zappi, a minor artist who had studied
with her father and became her agent.

BIBLIOGRAPHY
Thieme–Becker
R. Galli: *Lavinia Fontana, pittrice, 1552–1614* (Imola, 1940)
Women Artists, 1550–1950 (exh. cat. by L. Nochlin and A. Sutherland
   Harris; Los Angeles, CA, Co. Mus. A.; Austin, U. TX A. Mus.;
   Pittsburgh, PA, Carnegie; New York, Brooklyn Mus.; 1976–7)
E. Tufts: 'Lavinia Fontana, Bolognese Humanist', *Le arti a Bologna e in
   Emilia dal XVI al XVII secole/Receuils d'actes des Congrès internationaux
   d'histoire de l'art: Bologna, 1982*, pp. 129–34
V. Fortunati Pietrantonio: *La pittura bolognese del '500* (Bologna, 1986),
   pp. 727–75

The Age of Correggio and the Carracci (exh. cat. Washington, DC, N.G.A.; New York, Met.; Bologna, Pin. N.; 1986), pp. 132–5
M. T. Cantaro: *Lavinia Fontana bolognese* (Milan, 1989) [with full bibliog.]

□

Fontana (iii). Italian family of painters, draughtsmen and printmakers, active in Austria.

(1) Giovanni Battista Fontana (*b* Ala, nr Verona, 1524; *d* Innsbruck, 25 Sept 1587). His training was based on the works of such masters as Titian and Veronese, and his activity in Austria, documented from 1562, comprised substantial decorative projects and altarpieces, drawings and numerous engravings. In 1562 he and his brother (2) Giulio Fontana executed frescoes (destr.) in the chapel of Schloss Kaiser-Ebersdorf in Vienna; in 1573 he was in Innsbruck, where he settled and in 1575 became court painter to Archduke Ferdinand of Austria. In Innsbruck he created frescoes for the oratory of the Hofkirche; the spheristerion (1573); the Silberne Kapelle, built by Giulio Fontana, in which he executed 14 scenes of the *Passion* (1576); and a room in the castle (1578). A more important work was the decoration of the ceiling of the dining-hall of Schloss Ambras, illustrating *Allegories of the Zodiac, the Elements and the Planets* (1583–4; *in situ*). In 1576 Fontana painted the altarpiece for the Gotteshaus in Seefeld and in 1580 a portrait of the *Cardinal Archduke Andreas of Austria*; in 1582 he provided drawings for the catalogue of the collection of armour at Schloss Ambras. Seventy-eight etchings (1559–79) have been attributed (Bartsch) to Giovanni Battista Fontana, but they present considerable stylistic and technical disparities and are not always signed or initialled; possibly Giulio Fontana contributed to them. The engravings include prints of paintings by Titian, Veronese and Domenico Campagnola, as well as original designs by Giovanni Battista Fontana; in many cases he probably produced only the drawing. Of four additional folios (Passavant), that depicting the *Flight into Egypt* (1580), initialled B.F., has a freedom and immediacy of touch reminiscent of Campagnola's xylographs. In other copper engravings, however, Fontana used a fine point to render minute depictions: for example, a series of twenty-seven illustrations of the story of *Romulus and Remus* (1573; B. 24a–50), dedicated to the Archduke, and a series of seven sheets with the *Parables of Christ* (B. 4–10), set in picturesque landscapes of northern style, which are among his most convincing works.

(2) Giulio Fontana (*b* ?Verona; *fl* 1562–78). Brother of (1) Giovanni Battista Fontana. In 1562 he was working in Vienna, where, with his brother, he executed frescoes (destr.) in the chapel of Schloss Kaiser-Ebersdorf. He was in the Tyrol in 1576–8, commissioned by Archduke Ferdinand of Austria to produce a topographical map of the Iselberg and environs and to build the Silberne Kapelle beside the Hofkirche of Innsbruck. He is known as an engraver of Titian's works: his rendering of *Spain Succouring Religion* (1568) reproduces the version (untraced) painted for the Holy Roman Emperor Maximilian II; the *Battle of Cadore* (1569; see ICONOGRAPHY AND ICONOLOGY, fig. 4) was engraved from the canvas (destr. 1577) then in the Palazzo Ducale, Venice. Other known works include illustrations for books published in Venice: the *Trattato di scienza d'arme* (1568) by Cornelio Agrippa, with

figures in the text, and the *Vida de nuestra bendita señora Maria Virgen* (1569), with 38 engravings. Certain stylistic differences among the various engravings attributed to Giovanni Battista Fontana suggest that his brother Giulio may have participated to a considerable extent.

Bolaffi

BIBLIOGRAPHY

J. D. Passavant: *Le Peintre-graveur*, vi (Leipzig, 1860–64), pp. 182–3
M. Pittaluga: *L'incisione italiana nel cinquecento* (Milan, 1930)
E. Morpurgo: *Gli artisti italiani in Austria*, i (Rome, 1937)
Renaissance in Italien 16. Jahrhundert (exh. cat. by K. Oberhuber, Vienna, Albertina, 1966)
R. Brenzoni: *Dizionario di artisti veneti* (Florence, 1972)
H. Zerner: *Italian Artists of the 16th Century* (1979), 32 (XVI/1) of *The Illustrated Bartsch*, ed. W. Strauss (New York, 1978–)

MARIA CRISTINA CHIUSA

Fontana (iv). Italian family of engineers, architects, urban planners and building contractors. They were originally from the Swiss canton of Ticino. (2) Domenico Fontana and his elder brother (1) Giovanni Fontana founded an important building enterprise in Rome that had strong links with Pope Sixtus V (*reg* 1585–90), who conceived a far-sighted plan to refashion Rome as a world capital (*see* PERETTI, (1)). The Fontana workshop, where a third brother Marsilio Fontana and, later, their nephew Carlo Maderno worked, was responsible for many of the projects connected with this plan, and the Pope's urgency in proceeding with his schemes led Domenico to adopt a standardized architectural vocabulary. Although it did not exclude grandeur of conception, this had of necessity a limited formal range and simplified detailing, resulting in a prosaic, derivative classicizing effect that has been called the 'Style Sixtus V' (see Wittkower).

(1) Giovanni Fontana (*b* Melide, Lake Lugano, 1540; *d* Rome, 1614). He was primarily a hydraulic engineer and was a prominent member of the family workshop, directing its engineering works. One of his principal projects under Pope Sixtus V was the management of the Acqua Felice scheme (1587–90) in Rome, involving the improvement of the aqueduct, which was still under construction, and the erection at the north-east corner of Piazza S Bernardo of a monumental fountain known as Mostra dell'Acqua Felice or Fontana del Mosè (*in situ*) that was designed by his brother Domenico (elevation and ground-plan in *Della transportatione dell'obelisco vaticano* (1590), fol. 56r). The Via Pia (now Via XX Settembre), under which the water was further conveyed, also had to be levelled, and four additional fountains, the Quattro Fontane, were created at the Acqua Felice's intersection with Sixtus's new Via Sistina (now Via Quattro Fontane; *see* (2), §1(ii) below). During the pontificate of Sixtus V, Giovanni Fontana also built waterworks and fountains in Civitavecchia and with his brother executed hydraulic and other works in the Villa Mattei on the Celio hill in Rome. He was partly responsible for the hydraulic works (1603–21) for the water theatre at the Villa Aldobrandini in Frascati (*see* FRASCATI, fig. 1), which were begun under Clement VIII, and under Paul V he executed similar works for the villas of Torlonia (1607–10) and Mondragone (1613–14), Frascati, acquired by Paul V's nephew Cardinal Scipione Borghese. Giovanni Fontana succeeded his brother Domenico as chief architect to Clement VIII and Paul V after Domenico finally moved to Naples in 1596 (*see* (2), §1(iii) below), and he took over responsibility for building all the Fontana workshop's commissions. One of his most important late projects was directing construction of the Acqua Paola (1608–11), brought to Rome by Paul V. This was furnished with a monumental fountain on the Janiculum hill, designed by FLAMINIO PONZIO as an elaboration on the Mostra dell'Acqua Felice.

(2) Domenico Fontana (*b* Melide, Lake Lugano, 1543; *d* Naples, 28 June 1607). Brother of (1) Giovanni Fontana. He was one of the few Roman architects of the late 16th century who was famous in his own lifetime, owing mostly to his organizational and engineering feat in removing and re-erecting the ancient obelisk in St Peter's Square (*see* §1(ii) below). These organizational skills played a large part in making possible the realization of much of Pope Sixtus V's building programme.

1. Life and work. 2. Working methods and technique.

1. LIFE AND WORK.

(i) Early works, before 1585. Domenico Fontana's career as a constructional engineer began with practical building work. He completed courses of training in his birthplace and in Rome, where he is first recorded as a stuccoist in the early 1570s and then as a mason (1574). He worked with a group of compatriots, many of whom were related, and this group subsequently developed into a large workshop led by Domenico. His earliest experience as an architect dates from 1577–8, when he built a small mansion in the Piazza Pasquino for Cardinal Felice Peretti. This was his first contact with his principal patron, who later became Pope Sixtus V. In 1578 the Cardinal commissioned from him the large Villa Montalto on the Esquiline hill, near S Maria Maggiore, which was a complex of buildings with formal gardens and a huge vineyard (destr. 1862–89; site now occupied by the Stazione Termini); in 1579–81 Domenico built the casino at the villa and, during the next few years before Peretti was elected Pope in 1585, he constructed three avenues radiating from the villa gate near S Maria Maggiore to the casino. During the pontificate the villa was enlarged, and the central avenue was extended past the casino to the highest point within the walls of Rome; a new transverse axis was extended beyond the villa into the urban environment, which was restructured at the same time.

Another important early commission (1581) from the Cardinal was a chapel at S Maria Maggiore for relics of the crib of Bethlehem (*see* ROME, §V, 20). Constructed during the pontificate, the magnificently decorated Sistine Chapel contains the tombs of *Sixtus V* and *Pius V*, also designed by Fontana. In 1581–6 Domenico worked as the contractor and supervising architect for the façade of Giacomo della Porta's S Luigi dei Francesi, the first recorded undertaking of his workshop or architectural 'firm'.

(ii) Work for Sixtus V, 1585–91. Both Domenico Fontana and his workshop benefited when he acquired Roman citizenship in the first half of 1585 and his patron, who was elected Pope on 24 April, appointed him as papal

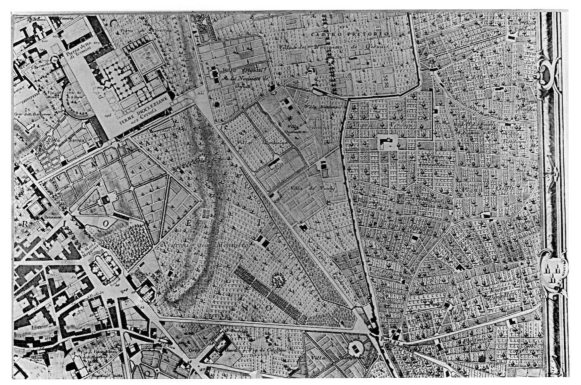

1. Domenico Fontana: urban-planning projects, including Villa Montalto, in the area of S Maria Maggiore, Rome, 1585–90; detail from Giovanni Battista Nolli: the *Pianta di Roma*, 1748 (Rome, Bibliotheca Hertziana), showing S Maria Maggiore at bottom left

architect; towards the end of that year Fontana also became a member of the Accademia di S Luca. His building activities for Sixtus included all major works for the Camera Apostolica (the papal board of works), which are well documented in surviving records (Rome, Archv Stato) as well as being described in both volumes of his *Della trasportatione dell'obelisco vaticano* (1590 and 1604). The works concentrated on the remodelling and rebuilding of the papal palaces of the Vatican, Lateran and Quirinal, together with extensive urban planning work aimed at improving the run-down Monti quarter in the south-eastern part of the city in order to encourage settlement and economic revival there (*see* ROME, §II, 3; *see also* PERETTI, (1)). The fundamental requirement for the Monti quarter was the provision of a water supply, which Gregory XIII had envisaged and which Sixtus at once took in hand. The Acqua Felice runs from the Alban Hills to the city by way of an aqueduct that incorporates some ancient remains and was the first new aqueduct to be built in the city since antiquity. Domenico Fontana was initially involved as an adviser on the project, and his brother Giovanni took over its management in 1587 (*see* §(1) above).

The Pope's urban-planning measures linked up with the ideas of his predecessors Pius IV and Gregory XIII and were part of an overall plan to make the principal religious sites of Rome more easily accessible to pilgrims. The Pope first turned his attention to the renewal of the infrastructure around the three centres of S Maria Maggiore, Piazza delle Terme (with S Maria degli Angeli) and the Lateran, and in 1585 he commissioned the Fontana workshop to carry out a comprehensive street-building programme with S Maria Maggiore at the centre of new axes (see fig. 1). The Via Sistina (or Strada Felice) was extended from the church north-west to the Trinità dei Monti (although intended to reach the Piazza del Popolo) and south-east to Santa Croce in Gerusalemme. It crossed three hills and was straight as a plumbline for 4 km and wide enough to take five carriages abreast. The Via Panisperna was also improved and straightened, and Sixtus had the Via Merulana (begun by Pius IV and continued by Gregory XIII) completed from S Maria Maggiore to the Lateran. In 1585–6 three further street axes marked the final limits of the Villa Montalto: the Via di Porta S Lorenzo (destr.), the present Via Marsala and the Via Viminale, and in 1587–9 a Lateran–Colosseum axis was created, making partial use of the ancient Via Maior. All these roads were laid out by Domenico Fontana regardless of any difficulties; he overcame all natural obstacles and tore down any ancient or medieval structures that stood in the way, while at the same time opening up some very fine views and perspectives.

Four ancient obelisks surmounted by crosses were also re-erected at important junctions of the new street system, and the removal of the first obelisk from its original position on the former Circus of Nero, south of St Peter's, to its present location in the centre of St Peter's Square is the achievement for which Domenico Fontana is best known. The operation, described in the first volume of his *Della trasportatione* (1590), took place between April and September 1586 and was a signal triumph. Sixtus V made Domenico a Cavaliere dello Speron d'Oro (knight of the golden spur) and Conte Palatino and conferred on

2. Domenico Fontana: Sistine Chapel (begun 1581), S Maria Maggiore, Rome; engraving from his *Della trasportatione dell'obelisco vaticano*, i (Rome, 1590), pl. 52, showing the lowering of the reliquary of the crib of Bethlehem into the chapel (London, British Museum)

him the status of a Roman patrician. Domenico's assistant in removing the Vatican obelisk was his nephew Carlo Maderno, who took charge of the erection of the next three obelisks: at the choir end of S Maria Maggiore (1587), in front of the transept façade of S Giovanni in Laterano (1588) and in the Piazza del Popolo (1589). These pagan monuments, converted to the service of Christianity, created new topographical motifs and drew attention to four of the seven principal churches of Rome. In 1587 Fontana and Maderno performed another technical *tour de force* by transporting the medieval altar of the crib in S Maria Maggiore to the newly erected Sistine Chapel (see fig. 2). In the same year they crowned Trajan's Column with a statue of *St Peter* and in 1588 that of Marcus Aurelius with a statue of *St Paul*. Finally, in 1589 they erected the monumental antique group of the *Dioscuri* in the Piazza di Montecavallo (now Piazza del Quirinale) at one end of the Via Pia, at the other end of which stands Michelangelo's Porta Pia.

Meanwhile Domenico Fontana's work on the three papal residences continued, the Lateran undergoing the most radical transformation. The medieval palace complex was replaced by a massive new building (1585–90) constructed around an inner courtyard (*see* ROME, §V, 15(i) and fig. 46). A two-storey benediction loggia (1588) was placed in front of the north transept of the church, adjacent to the new palace; and at the medieval papal chapel, Sancta Sanctorum, to the north-east of the palace, which was left isolated by the demolition works, he added a new structure to house the Scala Santa. In the Vatican, besides much remodelling of the old papal palace and the Castel Sant' Angelo, two new buildings were designed by Domenico Fontana (*see* ROME, §V, 14(iii)(a)): the Vatican Library, which cut across the middle of Bramante's long, terraced Cortile del Belvedere; and the Palazzo Sisto V, built on the east side of the Cortile S Damaso, starting from a third loggia wing begun under Gregory XIII. This cubic structure, towering above St Peter's Square, closes the vista of the Vatican complex of palaces on the eastern side. Fontana also worked as a technical consultant to Giacomo della Porta in the construction of the dome of St Peter's (1588–93). At the Palazzo del Quirinale he continued work on the new building, later completed by Maderno (*see* ROME, §V, 26), and he built the large portal (1589) of the Cancelleria.

When Sixtus V died, the Fontana workshop carried on the construction of the Palazzo Sisto V until 1591. A plan to transform the Colosseum into a factory for spinning wool, with living-quarters for the workers at an upper level, lapsed with the Pope's death, although Fontana already had 100 labourers and 70 wagons on site. A further commission from Sixtus V, a bridge over the River Tiber at Borghetto, north of Rome, was completed at the beginning of the reign of Clement VIII. This gave rise to a lawsuit against Domenico, who was accused in this and several other cases of having lined his pockets by using cheap building materials. The trial (1592–3) was above all an expression of envy and dislike of an architect and contractor who had been so favoured by Sixtus V.

(iii) Naples, 1592–1607. Having been invited by the Spanish viceroy to Naples, Domenico Fontana lived alternately there and in Rome from 1592 to 1596, when he finally settled in Naples. There he held the title of Ingegnere Maggiore del Regno di Napoli until his death in 1607. The firm in Rome was taken over by Maderno and Giovanni Fontana, the former probably acting as artistic director. In Naples, Domenico founded a new establishment with his son Giulio Cesare Fontana (*fl* 1593–1627) and the architectural engineer Bartolomeo Picchiatti; his projects there are noted in the second volume of his *Della trasportatione* (1604). As in Rome, he received mainly urban planning commissions during his career in Naples; notable examples include the improvement and enlargement of the Piazza del Castel Nuovo (1596; now part of the Piazza del Municipio) and the construction (1596–8) of the Strada di S Lucia (now Via Cesario Console–Via Nazario Sauro–part of Via Partenope) and the Strada Olivarez (now Via Cristoforio Colombo–Via Nuova Marina). His most important work in Naples was the Palazzo Reale (Piazza del Plebiscito). After a first stage of building in 1600–02, it was continued after Domenico's death by Giulio Cesare Fontana; in the 18th and 19th centuries it was considerably altered and

much enlarged. The plinth of the right-hand column of the left entrance bears the signature and title of Domenico Fontana, and he is proudly depicted in the frontispiece to his book.

2. WORKING METHODS AND TECHNIQUE. As a sober technocrat, Domenico Fontana was the ideal collaborator for an ambitious, though uninspired, patron such as Sixtus V, who pursued his comprehensive building projects with a considerable sense of urgency. In response to this pressure, Domenico built up an efficient and reliable architectural enterprise that assumed responsibility for planning and financing, organizing building sites and procuring materials, and for road building and surface engineering, as well as a great deal of the raw construction work, stuccowork, painting and site supervision. Other works were delegated to smaller contractors, workshops and craftsmen. In view of the volume of commissions and the size of his workshop, the design and execution of projects could not always have been carried out by Domenico alone, although the commissions were nominally addressed to him. In many cases Giovanni Fontana or Carlo Maderno directed projects, and they probably also had a share in designing. Thus no individual style, still less a stylistic evolution, can be discerned in their works. They adopted the simplest and most obvious solution to each situation as they found it, with artistic quality a secondary concern. One consequence of this approach was that the planning process was confined to the drawing-board, neglecting the third dimension. Street and road axes were designed without regard for the contours of the land, and more complex designs involving urban and garden planning did not take shape as a unity but fell into separate overlapping axial systems (e.g. Villa Montalto, Piazza delle Terme). Piazzas and courtyards were planned not as three-dimensional spaces but as spaces defined by façades (e.g. Lateran Palace); buildings were similarly designed not as three-dimensional forms but as a series of uniform façades folded back at the corners; such façades were built up extremely flatly, forming very angular abutments to each other (e.g. Sistine Chapel).

True to his unassuming style, Domenico Fontana drew on the Roman repertory for his vocabulary of forms. His building types were based on High Renaissance models, especially the Palazzo Farnese, Rome; in matters of architectural detail he was chiefly guided by Michelangelo and his followers, notably Giacomo della Porta and Giacomo del Duca and, to some extent, also by Jacopo Vignola. At the same time, some unorthodox simplifications appear, mostly based on contemporary models; for example, the reduced Doric frieze in the Lateran was influenced by della Porta and the smooth capitals of the Sistine Chapel by Michelangelo. In both Fontana's architectural and urban planning work the individual element was subordinated to the realization of the whole and to gains in decorative quality—characteristics paradoxically suggestive of the Baroque.

WRITINGS

D. Fontana: *Della trasportatione dell'obelisco vaticano e delle fabbriche di nostro signore papa Sisto V fatte dal cavalliere Domenico Fontana, architetto di sua santita*, i (Rome, 1590); ii (Naples, 1604); ed. A. Carugo, intro. P. Portoghesi (Milan, 1978)

BIBLIOGRAPHY

EARLY SOURCES

G. Baglione: *Vite* (1642); ed. V. Mariani (1935)
G. P. Bellori: *Vite* (1672); ed. E. Borea (1976)
F. S. Baldinucci: *Notizie* (1681–1728); ed. F. Ranalli (1845–7)
A. Bertolotti: *Artisti svizzeri in Roma nei secoli XV, XVI e XVII,* Richerche e studi negli archivi romani (Bellinzona, 1886)

GENERAL

R. Pane: *Architettura dell'età barocca in Napoli* (Naples, 1939), pp. 39–53
U. Donati: *Artisti ticinesi a Roma* (Bellinzona, 1942)
F. Castagnoli and others: *Topografia e urbanistica di Roma,* Storia di Roma xxii (Bologna, 1958), pp. 409–22, 517–19
R. Wittkower: *Art and Architecture in Italy, 1600–1750,* Pelican Hist. A. (Harmondsworth, 1958, rev. 1965, rev. 2/1973), pp. 26, 38
C. D'Onofrio: *Gli obelischi di Roma: Storia e urbanistica di una città dall'età al XX secolo* (Rome, 1967, rev. 3/1992)
S. Giedion: *Space, Time and Architecture: The Growth of a New Tradition* (Cambridge, MA, and London, 1967), pp. 75–106
F. Strazzullo: *Architetti e ingegneri napoletani dal '500 al '700* (Naples, 1969)
H. Hibberd: *Carlo Maderno and Roman Architecture, 1580–1630* (London, 1971)
A. Blunt: *Neapolitan Baroque and Rococo Architecture* (London, 1975)
R. Schiffmann: *Roma felix: Aspekte der städtebaulichen Gestaltung unter Papst Sixtus V* (Berne, 1985)
C. D'Onofrio: *Le fontane di Roma* (Rome, 1986)
D. R. Coffin: *Gardens and Gardening in Papal Rome* (Princeton, 1991), pp. 97–9, 142–5

SPECIALIST STUDIES

J. A. F. Orbaan: 'Dai conti di Domenico Fontana, 1585–1588', *Boll. A.,* vii (1913), pp. 419–24; viii (1914), pp. 59–71
A. Cametti: 'Una divisione di beni tra i fratelli Giovanni, Domenico e Marsilio Fontana', *Boll. A.,* xii (1918), pp. 170–84
T. W. Stürup: *Studien und Vorarbeiten zu Domenico Fontana: Frühwerke bis 1585* (diss., U. Vienna, 1940)
A. Muñoz: 'Domenico Fontana, architetto, 1543–1607', *Quad. Italo-Sviz.,* iii (1944)
A. Schiavo: 'Notizie biografiche sui Fontana', *Stud. Romani,* xix (1971), pp. 56–61
E. Guidoni, A. Marino and A. Lanconelli: 'I "Libri dei conti" di Domenico Fontana', *Stor. Città,* xl (1986), pp. 45–77; xliii (1987), pp. 86–104; xlviii (1988), pp. 98–104

ROME

G. Matthiae: 'La villa Montalto alle Terme', *Capitolium,* xiv (1939), pp. 139–47
K. Schwager: 'Zur Bautätigkeit Sixtus' V an S Maria Maggiore in Rom', *Misc. Bib. Hertz.* (1961), pp. 324–54
J. Wasserman: 'The Palazzo Sisto V in the Vatican', *J. Soc. Archit. Historians,* xxi (1962), pp. 26–35
——: 'The Quirinal Palace in Rome', *A. Bull.,* xlv (1963), pp. 205–44
J. Hess: 'La biblioteca vaticana: Storia della costruzione', *Kunstgeschichtliche Studien zu Renaissance und Barock,* 2 vols (Rome, 1967), i, pp. 143–52, 163–79
T. A. Marder: 'Sixtus V and the Quirinal', *J. Soc. Archit. Historians,* xxxvii (1978), pp. 283–94
H. Ost: 'Die Cappella Sistina in S Maria Maggiore', *Kunst als Bedeutungsträger: Gedenkschrift für Günter Bandmann* (Berlin, 1978), pp. 279–303
L. Spezzaferro: *La Roma di Sisto V,* Storia dell'arte italiana, III/v (Turin, 1983), pp. 363–405
C. L. C. E. Witcombe: 'Sixtus V and the Scala Santa', *J. Soc. Archit. Historians,* xliv (1985), pp. 368–79
L. Di Nuzzo: 'La progettazione sistina della piazza di S Giovanni in Laterano', *Stor. Città,* xl (1986), pp. 5–44
S. F. Ostrow: *The Sistine Chapel at S Maria Maggiore: Sixtus V and the Art of Counter-Reformation* (diss., Princeton U., NJ, 1987)
C. Benocci: 'Roma, Villa Mattei al Celio: Le sistemazioni cinque-seicentesche del giardino, di Giovanni e Domenico Fontana', *Stor. Città,* xlvi (1988), pp. 100–24
B. Burkart: *Der Lateran Sixtus V und sein Architekt Domenico Fontana* (diss., U. Bonn, 1989)
C. Pietrangeli, ed.: *Il palazzo apostolico lateranense* (Florence, 1991)
M. Quast: *Die Villa Montalto in Rom: Entstehung und Gestalt im Cinquecento* (Munich, 1991)
M. P. Sette and S. Benedetti, eds: 'Architetture per la città', *Stor. Archit.,* i (1992)
M. L. Madonna, ed.: *Roma di Sisto V: Le arti e la cultura* (Rome, 1993)

NAPLES

A. Miola: 'Cavagni contro Fontana: A proposito della reggia di Napoli', *Napoli Nob.,* i (1892), pp. 14–18, 89–91, 99–103
T. Colletta: 'Domenico Fontana a Napoli: I progretti urbanistici per l'area del porto', *Stor. Città,* xliv (1987), pp. 76–118
I. Di Resta: 'La maniera a Napoli: Il palazzo reale del Fontana', *L'architettura a Roma e in Italia, 1580–1621: Atti del XXIII congresso di storia dell'architettura: Roma, 1988,* ii, pp. 343–9

MATTHIAS QUAST

Fontana (v). Italian family of architects and engineers. They were distantly related to Domenico Fontana (*see* FONTANA (iv), (2)) and were mainly active in Rome. The family's fame was largely based on the work of (1) Carlo Fontana, who continued the traditions laid down by the great masters of the High Baroque (Bernini, Borromini, Pietro da Cortona) and passed them on to his students, who included Johann Bernhard Fischer von Erlach, Johann Lukas von Hildebrandt, Domenico Martinelli, Nicodemus Tessin (ii), James Gibbs and Filippo Juvarra. The essential conservatism of this tradition was particularly obvious in the work of (5) Mauro Fontana, which, although it does not offer genuine highlights or new directions for future development, nonetheless concludes the architectural mission of the family in a coherent and dignified fashion.

(1) Carlo Fontana (*b* Rancate, nr Como, 1638; *d* Rome, 1714). Fontana's first teacher in architecture was Giovanni Maria Bolino (*architetto-misuratore* to Virgilio Spada and Pope Alexander VII), to whom he was apprenticed about 1653 at the age of 15. He received additional training under Pietro da Cortona and was already an accomplished draughtsman when he assisted his master in

1. Carlo Fontana: high altar (1674), S Maria in Traspontina, Rome

the execution of the comprehensive project (1665–8) for the façade and piazza of S Maria della Pace, Rome. A decisive influence in his development was Giovanni Lorenzo Bernini, who employed him for about ten years and whom he assisted in the remodelling (1664–7) of the Palazzo Chigi in Piazza SS Apostoli, Rome, the building of the Scala Regia in the Vatican (1663), the Church of the Assumption in Ariccia and the enlargement (c. 1662–70) of the Chigi Palace facing it. To Carlo Rainaldi, with whom he collaborated on the projection and realization of the twin churches in the Piazza del Popolo, Rome (begun 1661), he soon revealed the potential of a competent rival.

Fontana's first major independent work was the façade (c. 1665) of S Biagio in Campitelli, Rome, where he effectively responded to the unfavourable visual conditions in the narrow street by the backward bending of the lateral compartments in the upper storey and the employment of a forced perspective for the framing devices of the main portal. The church was dismantled in 1929 and re-erected on the Piazza Capizucchi in 1940. The exiled Queen Christina of Sweden commissioned Carlo Fontana to construct the Teatro Tor di Nona (1669–71), and during this period he became greatly involved in scenographic designs for the Roman theatres, to which he referred later in his book *Tempio vaticano* (1694). Remarkably scenographic features are displayed by the interior decoration of S Marta in the Piazza Collegio Romano, Rome, which he enlarged (1670–74), employing above the altars the Berninian motif of angels holding picture frames. His first masterpiece, the tempietto altar (1674; see fig. 1) in S Maria in Traspontina, Rome, shows flying angels carrying the dome in the shape of a monumental crown. A second major work of this period is the remodelling (1670–74) of the drum and the construction of a dome for the cathedral in Montefiascone, which had been damaged by fire. The exterior view is dominated by unusually heavy ribs issuing from the corners of the octagon, which contrast with the concave contractions of the shell between them in a most unconventional fashion. Working outside Rome, he built or remodelled the country palace in S Quirico d'Orcia (1678–9) and the Villa Cetinale (1679–80) for Flavio and Mario Chigi respectively.

Fontana reached the first peak of his career in the 1680s, when he built the double-tiered, concave façade of S Marcello al Corso, Rome (see fig. 2). Articulated by full columns and pilasters, it is based on the principle of three layers stepped backwards and is set on concentric circles, the centre of which coincides with the first viewing point of the spectator, who approaches the front from the Via del Corso. In this period he also completed the Cappella Ginetti (1671–84) in S Andrea della Valle, Rome, adjusting his scheme to the predetermined shape of the chapel. He also constructed the Cappella Cibo (1682–4) in S Maria del Popolo, which had first been planned on concentric circles, on a cruciform plan with reduced arms at the sides and opposite the entrance. Its merit lies in the harmonious blending of polychrome marbles and the coordination of painting, sculpture and architecture to create the unified effect of a complete work of art. The Cappella Cibo was followed by the redecoration (1692–8) of the baptismal chapel in St Peter's. Fontana illuminated the chapel from

2. Carlo Fontana: façade of S Marcello al Corso, Rome, 1682–3

above by closing the radial window opposite the entrance and opening the vault with an oculus that receives its light indirectly from a window in the outer wall of the basilica. The cover in gilt bronze for the baptismal font is a decorative masterpiece. He also employed indirect lighting from hidden sources at the sides in the Cappella dell'Assunta (1685–7; destr.) of the Collegio Clementino, Rome. Fontana demonstrated his ability for large-scale planning in his project for the circular church of St Ignatius at Loyola, Spain, which is flanked by the arcaded rectangular courtyards of the Collegium Regium and for which he was invited to submit his plan (c. 1681). The building is remarkable for its scenographic setting in a valley flanked by mountains and the River Urola. Fontana's talent for creating such special effects is also demonstrated in his project for a church to be built in the Colosseum as a monument of the Church Triumphant (first version 1676–9; final version before 1700). Situated at the end of the arena, it would have appeared like a stage set, dramatically enframed by the surrounding ruins. Similar intentions are also discernible in the opening of the central niche of the monumental Fontana Paola on the Janiculum, Rome, to which Fontana also added a semicircular basin commissioned by Alexander VIII (reg 1689–91).

A distinguished work of the early 1690s is the barrel-vaulted hall (c. 1690–92, enlarged c. 1719) for the Biblioteca Casanatense, Rome, which was followed by projects (1691–1700) to adapt Bernini's Palazzo Ludovisi, Rome, for use as a papal Curia for Innocent XII. Fontana built a tripartite portico on the familiar lines of a triumphal arch and surmounted the façade with a belfry resting on an attic (1694–6). The semicircular courtyard, which he also designed, has been replaced by a modern structure. It was the tragedy of Fontana's career that his most complex and ambitious projects remained unrealized. This is true of his imaginative plan for a church in the Colosseum and his two projects (1690) for the enlargement of St Peter's Square, the second of which even envisaged a new layout for the entire Vatican Borgo, including the creation of a piazza behind the church. However, Fontana was well aware that neither of these projects had any chance of being realized during his lifetime, and he cited this as the justification for publishing his ideas. His second plan, however, did eventually serve as a basis for the creation in 1929 of the present Via della Conciliazione. Fontana also received commissions from abroad, but his major project (1696) for a Palais Liechtenstein at Landskron was rejected. The final period of his career was marked by a series of setbacks and frustrations. His project (1694) for the Jesuit Church at Frascati was built to a different plan, and the Teatro Tor di Nona was demolished for moral reasons by order of Pope Innocent XII immediately after its rebuilding (1695–7).

Fontana's last works in Rome under Clement XI include the portico-façade (1702) of S Maria in Trastévere and the drainage of S Teodoro al Palatino (1702–4), which he surrounded with a ditch and made more accessible by the addition of a small square, the shape of which repeats on a smaller scale what he had once envisaged for the area behind the Vatican basilica. During this period he was also responsible for the very ornate refurbishment (1702–8) of S Spirito dei Napolitani, the Cappella Albani in S Sebastiano (1706–12) and such utilitarian structures as the granary (1703–5) on the Piazza di Termini and the Casa Corezzionale (1703–4), a reformatory institution for juvenile delinquents attached to the Ospizio di S Michele. This work is a masterpiece, both architecturally and functionally, and attracted considerable attention soon after its construction, eventually earning Fontana a place in the history of modern prison building (see PRISON and fig.). For the enlargement of the Ospizio itself, he designed the church on a cruciform ground-plan between two symmetrically adjoining courtyards, a plan reminiscent of his project for the Jesuit College at Loyola. Unfortunately, only a little more than half of Fontana's scheme was executed (1708–14). His most elaborate works of the early 18th century were temporary structures, catafalques for Leopold I, Holy Roman Emperor (1705) and for Peter II, King of Portugal (1707; see fig. 3). Not only are these substantial re-elaborations of his first masterpiece, the tempietto altar of S Maria in Traspontina, but they also indicate his understanding and role in the development of a decorative style which led to the 'barochetto' or Roman Rococo.

Fontana was also a proficient and dedicated engineer. His judgement on the static safety of the drum and dome of St Peter's was requested in 1680 and considered convincing. He also demonstrated that he would have been able to save Bernini's structurally unsound bell-tower (destr. 1646) on the left of the façade. An expert in hydraulics, he repaired water conduits, including the Acqua Paola (1670–76). History and the architecture of ancient

3. Carlo Fontana: design for the catafalque of Peter II of Portugal in S Andrea in Portogallo, pen and grey wash, 477×277 mm, 1707 (Windsor, Windsor Castle, Royal Library)

times were of great interest to him. He produced schemes for the reconstruction of the Montecitorio area in Rome and the Borgo Vaticano. He also attempted to reconstruct the Pantheon and the Colosseum, believing them to be the most important structures of Roman antiquity and the equivalent of great contemporary buildings, among which the basilica of St Peter's would, for Fontana, always take first place.

Although he had distinguished himself as president (1686 and 1693–9) of the Accademia di S Luca, Fontana was humiliated by not being re-elected to the position after the turn of the century. His knowledge of Classical subjects is recorded in a number of publications, however, and the reputation that he enjoyed in his own time was eloquently expressed by Angelo Crescimbeni (1734–81), who referred in his obituary notice to Fontana's works as 'accomplishments which are all apt to make us realize the vastness of his talent, his enormous knowledge, and how much he distinguished himself from the other professionals of his time'.

WRITINGS
Palazzo Montecitorio (Rome, 1694, 2/1708)
Tempio Vaticano (Rome, 1694)
Utilissimo trattato delle acque correnti (Rome, 1696)
Anfiteatro Flavio (The Hague, 1725)

(2) Francesco (Antonio) Fontana (*b* Rome, 1668; *d* Castelgandolfo, 3 July 1708). Son of (1) Carlo Fontana. He trained under his father, and on 20 September 1693 he was nominated and elected Accademico di Merito at the Accademia di S Luca in Rome, obtaining membership on 10 January 1694. Francesco is best known for his church of SS Apostoli in Rome, begun in 1701 and completed after his death by his father (whose pupil he had been) and Niccoló Michetti. Erected on the restricted site of an Early Christian basilica, SS Apostoli emulates S Ignazio of the Collegio Romano. Its distinction, however, resides in an impression of spaciousness and splendour achieved by a thoughtfully balanced scheme of proportion and the skilful use of coloured marble. Francesco's second major building was the Dogana di Terra (1695), Rome, which incorporates the 11 colossal columns of the Hadrianeum into the articulative scheme of the main front of the new structure. The building has been altered in modern times but is known through 18th-century views. After this, it has been established (see Kelly, 1980) that he was in charge (1697–1701) of completing Ottaviano Mascherino's church of S Salvatore in Lauro, where he worked on the transept in conformity with Mascherino's original plan.

At the beginning of the 18th century Fontana provided the plan and a model for the abbey church in Fulda, and also attributed to him is the design of the centralized church of S Maria del Suffragio in Ravenna, begun in 1701 and comprising an octagonal main space opening on all sides into chapels. The excessively heavy coffered ceiling of S Pietro in Vincoli (1705) is one of Fontana's less successful works, but the delicately curved front of S Andrea in Portogallo (1705–6; now S Maria ad Nives) demonstrates a full understanding of the tradition established by Borromini and his followers, as well as Fontana's ability to solve problems of urban context. Like his father, Francesco was an expert in water engineering; in 1695 he was appointed Architetto dell'Acqua Felice under Innocent XII. When Carlo became Chief Architect of St Peter's in 1697, Francesco took over his father's former position as Revisore delle Misure. He also later followed in the footsteps of his other famous ancestor, Domenico Fontana (who had moved four obelisks in Rome while in the service of Sixtus V, 1585–90), when in 1704 he directed the raising of the Colonna Antonina, an enterprise that succeeded only on the second attempt in the following year. The column was destined to adorn the square in front of the Palazzo Ludovisi, which Carlo Fontana had expanded for the use of a papal Curia. Perhaps Francesco's chief merit, however, was in the able administration of the Accademia di S Luca and the influence he had on such students as Filippo Juvarra.

Adhering to the tenets of Late Baroque classicism, Francesco's major works approach the taste and grandeur of those of his father, even if they show less imagination. It would be wrong to call his work conservative or retardataire, however, for a significant element of 18th-century Roman architecture, the 'progressive' approach introduced by Borromini, was also strongly evident in his development, unfortunately cut short by his early death.

(3) Girolamo Fontana II (*b* Rancate, nr Como, *c*. 1668; *d* Frascati, 27 Sept 1701). Nephew of (1) Carlo Fontana. Together with his cousin (2) Francesco he trained under Carlo from *c*. 1685 to 1687 and assisted his uncle in the repair of the Acqua Felice, Rome. He seems to have begun an independent career in the service of the prestigious Colonna family, for whom he designed stage sets (*c*. 1690). These were based on a single-point perspective, and those employing urban motifs were characterized by an arched opening with a fountain at the end of the foreshortened view. Girolamo is known to have completed Antonio del Grande's famous gallery (begun *c*. 1654) in the Palazzo Colonna, Rome, between 1693 and 1703 (*see* DISPLAY OF ART, fig. 1). The work must already have been well advanced, but the free-standing columns that flank the entrances into the hall recall Girolamo's use of this motif in his stage sets.

Around 1700 Girolamo assisted his uncle in the restoration of the Acquedotto di Civitavecchia and also erected some buildings in the port at Anzio, most notably a small church for the sailors (S Antonio). His main work, however, is the remodelling and completion of the façade of S Pietro in Frascati (commissioned 1696). He took advantage of the site, which faced a square outside the city walls (destr.), to design a two-tiered front articulated by heavy columns in both storeys. The upper level is surmounted by a huge segmental pediment, a conscious allusion to Giacomo della Porta's nearby Villa Aldobrandini (1598–1603). Girolamo skilfully refashioned the existing bell-tower on the right-hand side and matched it with a similar one on the other side to create strong vertical accents. The façade (apart from the sculptural decoration) was essentially complete by 1700. Its somewhat conventional effect is due to the architect's desire to integrate his scheme with the existing structure in a style compatible with the local idiom. Girolamo lived just long enough to see his major work, and a wall fountain on the same square also requested from him, virtually finished.

(4) Carlo Stefano Fontana (*b c*. 1675; *d* Rome, 29 Oct 1740). Brother of (3) Girolamo II Fontana. He was an abbé of S Giovanni in Laterano, Rome, and took part early in his career in the Concorsi Clementini (the annual competition instituted by Pope Clement XI in 1702) at the Accademia di S Luca, coming second to Filippo Juvarra in 1705 with his design for a 'villa per tre personaggi'. He remodelled the nave of the upper church of S Clemente (*see* ROME, §V, 17(iii)(a)) during 1701–15 and was also responsible for the building's façade. The two-storey front is surmounted by a heavy triangular pediment and relates well to the atrium, which Carlo Stefano also designed. Other schemes by Carlo Stefano include refronting the 4th-century church of S Eusebio, Rome (1711), with a similar solution to that at S Clemente, and the restoration (1716–22; with Antonio Canevari) of the church of SS Giovanni e Paolo, Rome. He also designed the richly ornamented wooden ceiling of the cathedral at Velletri.

(5) Mauro Fontana (*b* Rome, 2 Jan 1701; *d* Rome, 17 July 1767). Son of (2) Francesco Fontana. His first known work was the high altar (1727; destr. 1833) of S Maria della Vittoria in Rome, a richly decorated niche for the venerated image of the Virgin with the Christ Child called 'della Vittoria' in allusion to the victory of the Catholic League over the Protestant Union in the Battle at the White Mountain in 1620. His career seemed initially to be promising and even advancing rapidly, when in 1728 he was invited to submit a project for SS Nome di Maria in Rome. The foundation of this church was connected with a victory over the Turks, who had besieged Vienna in 1683. In 1731 Mauro was appointed architect for its construction, one of the most important commissions of the period in Rome. He was removed in 1735, however, by the church's patron, Cardinal Lodovico Pico della Mirandola, who preferred a design by Antoine Derizet. It was only after the death of the cardinal in 1743 that Mauro was reappointed, and by that time only the decoration of the chapel of the high altar remained incomplete. Mauro's design again focused on the glorification of a representation of the Virgin and Child. Also flanked by columns, the chapel seems to look back to the lost altar of S Maria della Vittoria and, in the articulation of the interior, to his Cappella Cavallerini (1739) in S Carlo ai Catinari in Rome. The chapel in SS Nome di Maria is closely associated with the tradition of Carlo Fontana's chapels, which are all distinguished by the chromatic effects of their marble facing. Mauro's chief accomplishment was the church and convent of the Orsoline (1745–60; now the Accademia di S Cecilia). The building group contains the church of SS Giuseppe e Orsola, a sail-vaulted hall church of three bays, which has since been altered for the performances of the Accademia. The façade has a double order of giant pilasters to emphasize the entrance and to carry a powerful triangular pediment. In 1758 Mauro became a member of the Accademia di S Luca. Unfortunately, in 1760 he withdrew his acceptance piece (destr.), a project for the confessio of the high altar in S Giovanni in Laterano, Rome, for which Piranesi also prepared designs (New York, Columbia U., Avery Archit. & F.A. Lib.). Mauro's career climaxed in his election in 1761 as president of the Accademia di S Luca. In a sense a perpetuator of Carlo Fontana's workshop, Mauro lived and worked in his grandfather's house opposite the monastery of S Spirito alla Colonna Trajana (destr.).

UNPUBLISHED SOURCES

Rome, Accad. N. S Luca [MS. 51, fols 114*v*, 116*v*, 117, 118; MS. 52, fols 1, 4*v*, 6*v*, 28*v*, 29]
Rome, Archv Cent. Stato [*Ufficio 13 dei Notari Capitolini*, vol. 600, fols 202ff, 308ff, Ia; Collezione Piante e Mappe, Cartella no. 439]
Rome, Archv Vicariato [*S Lorenzo ai Monti, 39, Status Animarum, 1745–1753*, fols 26, 71, 110, 154, 171*v*, 190, 233, 308, 342*v*]

BIBLIOGRAPHY

Macmillan Enc. Architects; Thieme–Becker
A. Menichella: 'Carlo Fontana', *Vite de' pittori, scultori ed architetti moderni* (Rome, 1929), pp. 1005–25 [crit. edn of *Vite* of L. Pascoli]
E. Coudenhave-Erthal: *Carlo Fontana und die Architektur des römischen Spätbarocks* (Vienna, 1930)
——: 'Römisches Stadtbaudenken zum Ende des Seicento', *Festschrift für Hermann Egger* (Graz, 1933), pp. 95–103
U. Donati: *Artisti ticinesi a Roma* (Bellinzona, 1942)
E. Zocca: *La basilica dei SS Apostoli in Roma* (Rome, 1959)
A. Martini and M. L. Casanova: *SS Nome di Maria* (Rome, 1962), lxx of *Le chiese di Roma illustrate*, pp. 21–4, 31–5, 52–67
G. Matthiae: *S Maria della Vittoria* (Rome, 1965), lxxxiv of *Le chiese di Roma illustrate*, p. 40
H. Hager: 'Zur Planung und Baugeschichte der Zwillingskirchen auf der Piazza del Popolo: S Maria di Monte Santo und S Maria dei Miracoli in Rom', *Röm. Jb. Kstgesch.* (1967–8), p. 191
L. Pirotta: 'Francesco Fontana sostituito di Carlo Maratta nel principato dell'Accademia di S Luca', *Urbe*, xxxi/2 (1968), pp. 16–21
H. Hager: 'Carlo Fontana's Project for a Church in Honour of the *Ecclesia Triumphans* in the Colosseum, Rome', *J. Warb. & Court. Inst.*, xxxvi (1973), p. 319
A. Braham: *Funeral Decorations in Early Eighteenth-century Rome*, London, V&A cat., vii (London, 1975)
C. Elling: *Rome: The Biography of its Architecture from Bernini to Thorwaldsen* (Tübingen, 1975)
S. Jacob: *Italienische Zeichnungen der Kunstbibliothek Berlin: Architektur und Dekoration, 16. bis 18. Jahrhundert* (Berlin, 1975), pp. 156–8, pls 793–7
A. Braham and H. Hager: *Carlo Fontana: The Drawings at Windsor Castle* (London, 1977) [with extensive bibliog.]
H. Hager: 'Girolamo Fontana e la facciata della cattedrale di S Pietro a Frascati', *Commentari*, xxxviii (1977), pp. 77–92
L. Razza: *La basilica cattedrale di Frascati* (Frascati, 1979)
C. Kelly: *Ludovico Rusconi Sassi and Early Eighteenth-century Architecture in Rome* (diss., University Park, PA State U., 1980; microfilm, Ann Arbor, 1980)
A. Blunt: *Guide to Baroque Rome* (New York, 1982), pp. 22, 127, 248
S. Scott Munshower: 'Concorso Clementino of 1705', *Architectural Fantasy and Reality: Drawings from the Accademia Nazionale di S Luca in Rome, Concorsi Clementi, 1700–50* (exh. cat., ed. H. Hager and S. Scott Munshower; University Park, PA State U., Mus. A., 1982)
G. Delfini: *S Carlo ai Catinari* (Rome, 1985), n. s. cxvi of *Le chiese di Roma illustrate*, pp. 113ff
A. Buschow: *Kirchenrestaurierungen in Rom vor dem Hintergrund der päpstlichen Kunst- und Kulturpolitik in der ersten Hälfte des 18. Jahrhunderts* (diss., Bonn, Rhein. Friedrich-Wilhelms-U., 1987)
H. Hager: 'Carlo Fontana: Pupil, Partner, Principal, Preceptor', *The Artist's Workshop*, ed. P. Lukehart, Studies in the History of Art (Washington, DC, 1993), pp. 122–55

HELLMUT HAGER

Fontana, Annibale (*b* Milan, 1540; *d* Milan, 1587). Italian medallist, hardstone-engraver and sculptor. During the first half of his career, before 1570, he concentrated on making medals and on rock crystal engraving. From 1570 he turned increasingly to sculpture, especially that (from 1574) for the decoration of S Maria presso S Celso in Milan.

1. BEFORE 1570. He came from a family of Swiss origin, from Ticino, and was active mainly in Milan. According to Giovanni Paolo Lomazzo, his great friend, Fontana's early activity was mainly medal-making and engraving on rock crystal and hardstones (pietre dure). Based on references in Lomazzo, portrait medals of *Ferdinando Francesco D'Avalos* and *Lomazzo* (both Milan, Castello Sforzesco) have been attributed to Fontana. The latter, which dates from 1560–61, shows Lomazzo presented to Prudence and Fortune on the reverse. The medal dedicated to Avalos, who was governor of Milan from 1560, is more elaborate and of higher quality. It has been suggested (Rossi) that it reflects Bernardino Campi's painted portrait (untraced) of Avalos done in 1562, a possible *post quem* date for the medal. A medal of the philosopher *Ottaviano Ferrari* (Milan, Castello Sforzesco) with a bust of Aristotle on the reverse, also of this period, is ascribed to Fontana on the basis of a passage in a speech by the writer Francesco Cicereio (1521–96). The status and occupations of the subjects of these medals indicate that Fontana was in contact with patrons of high rank and with the intellectual circles of Milan. This is confirmed by his membership of the Accademia della Val di Blenio, also

mentioned by Lomazzo. Stylistically, the three medals derive from Leone Leoni and Jacopo da Trezzo I, and these influences continued in his work.

In addition to the three documented medals, there are four signed examples, probably also early (1557–60). The inscription ANN (Annibale) appears on the medal of the banker *Tommaso Marino* (Bergamo, Gal. Accad. Carrara), which is among Fontana's securely identified early works. This was probably made *c.* 1557, when Marino is documented in Milan. The date is supported by the fact that the medal is based on the portrait of Marino included in the *Crucifixion* (Fiesole, Badia), painted by Bernardino Campi in the 1550s. A medal of *Cristoforo Madruzzo* (Milan, Castello Sforzesco), Bishop of Trent and governor of Milan in 1556–7, is also signed ANN. The style of the portrait resembles that of the documented medals, while the reverse, of a type used in medals by other artists, may derive from existing plaques or medals. The inscription to Madruzzo as 'restorer of the state of Milan' indicates that it was executed in or before 1557. This medal is stylistically related to a silver medal of *Consalvo di Cordova* (Bergamo, Gal. Accad. Carrara), signed ANNIBAL, with a battle scene on the reverse, probably made in 1558–60. A silver medal of the *condottiere Giovan Battista Castaldi* (Milan, Castello Sforzesco), signed ANIB, once attributed to Annibale Borgognone (*fl* 1537–68), has been assigned to Fontana on the basis of stylistic affinities with the Ferrari and Consalvo di Cordova medals (Valerio, 1977).

Fontana's rock crystal engravings were in great demand by aristocratic patrons. Seven plaques with biblical scenes, engraved *c.* 1569 for Albert V, Duke of Bavaria (1550–79), were set in the ebony Albertine casket (Munich, Residenz). An oval crystal vase engraved with the *Story of Jason* and another with *Stories of Bacchus* (both Munich, Residenz) are attributed to Fontana (Heinz-Wied). He also seems to have provided designs for crystal engravings by the Saracchi brothers, including a rock crystal flask (Dresden, Grünes Gewölbe) for which there is a drawing by Fontana (Milan, Bib. Ambrosiana). The numerous crystal engravings attributed to Fontana are distinguished by a masterly use of space, with active figures showing the influence of Michelangelo mediated through that of Leoni.

2. 1570 AND AFTER. The first reference to Fontana as a marble sculptor dates from 1570, when he is documented in Palermo in connection with a valuation of reliefs by Vincenzo Gaggini (1527–95) for the portal of the cathedral there. His presence in Palermo is important evidence of his contact with the Gaggini family workshop and also supports the hypothesis that he visited Rome and saw work there by followers of Michelangelo, particularly Guglielmo della Porta.

Fontana returned to Milan by 1572 and two years later entered the service of the Fabbrica of S Maria presso S Celso. All his known work as a sculptor was made for this church and is well documented in its archives. He collaborated with Stoldo di Gino Lorenzi on the façade of the church. The quality of this work indicates that he was already experienced in the field of large-scale sculpture, although no earlier example by him is known. His first two statues for the façade were the prophets *Isaiah* and *Jeremiah* (1575–6), for the niches of the upper order. The

formal language of these works confirms the influence of Leoni and also of Pellegrino Tibaldi, and the severe devotional style clearly reflects the dictates of the Counter-Reformation. The statues of *Sibyls* (1577–9) reclining on the tympanum of the main portal, which have deep-cut drapery and expressive faces, derive from Michelangelo and della Porta. Fontana's collaboration with Lorenzi, who continued the tradition of the Florentine followers of Michelangelo, may have drawn him away from capricious manneristic features towards a severe classicism that was sometimes academic in character.

From 1580 to 1583 Fontana executed three large reliefs for the façade: the *Adoration of the Shepherds*, the *Presentation at the Temple* and the *Marriage at Cana*. A terracotta model for the *Adoration* relief survives (Washington, DC, N.G.A.; see fig. 1). The compositions have a vertical emphasis, with monumental figures in paired poses clearly derived from Michelangelo. Fontana next executed statues

1. Annibale Fontana: *Adoration of the Shepherds*, terracotta model, 1.09×0.57 m, *c.* 1580 (Washington, DC, National Gallery of Art)

of the *Assumption of the Virgin* and two *Angels* for the pinnacle. The contract of 1583 specified four angels, two praying and two singing. Only the latter were carved by him, however; the praying angels were completed to his design after his death by Milano Vimercati (*fl* 1577–93). Two wax models for the *Angels* (Cleveland, OH, Mus. A.; Los Angeles, CA., Co. Mus. A.) are rare surviving 16th-century examples in perishable material. The statue of the *Assumption* (see fig. 2), completed in 1584, remained on the pinnacle until 1620, when it was replaced with a copy by Andrea Prevosti (*fl* 1624–63). Fontana's statue, which was intended to be seen from far below, rising into open space in a whirling movement, is behind the main altar, where it conveys at least some sense of his grandiose vision. The *Assumption* also reflects a figure by Michelangelo, that of *Rachel* on the tomb of *Julius II* (Rome, S Pietro in Vincoli).

Fontana also worked on statues for the interior of the church, including *St John the Evangelist* (1583–7) for a niche to the right of the main altar and an *Assumption of the Virgin* (1583–6) for the altar of the Vergine dei Miracoli. In this second version of the *Assumption* the ascending movement is accentuated, and there is a more dramatic

treatment of drapery and gesture. Most notably, it is not on a plinth but poised on a cloud, apparently suspended in space, a bold solution that anticipates the ecstatic sacred images of Baroque sculpture. For the same altar in 1583 Fontana was commissioned to make two silver plaques, of the *Birth of the Virgin* and the *Death of the Virgin*. Terracotta models for both survive, as well as a series of preparatory drawings (Milan, Bib. Ambrosiana). Only the *Birth of the Virgin* was executed by Fontana; the *Death of the Virgin* was completed from his model after his death by Francesco Brambilla.

From 1574, when he joined its Fabbrica, Fontana's only documented work is for S Maria presso S Celso. The bronze decorations on the façade are no longer ascribed to him, however. Also rejected is the attribution to him of the bronze candelabras in the Certosa di Pavia, although he is documented at the Certosa in 1580, and drawings for the sacristy cupboards have been assigned to him (Bossaglia). The attribution to Fontana of the monument to *Bishop Malombra* (Milan, S Angelo), proposed by Vigezzi, has found no support.

BIBLIOGRAPHY

Thieme–Becker

G. P. Lomazzo: *Trattato dell'arte della pittura, scoltura e architettura* (Milan, 1584); ed. R. P. Ciardi (Florence, 1974)

——: *Rime* (Milan, 1587)

P. Morigia: *La nobiltà di Milano* (Milan, 1595; rev. 2/1619), pp. 471–2

P. P. Bosca: *De origine et statu Bibliothecae Ambrosianae* (Milan, 1672)

A. Venturi: *Storia* (1901–40), X/iii, pp. 466–82

E. Kris: *Meister und Meisterwerke der Steinschneidekunst in der italienische Renaissance* (Vienna, 1929)

S. Vigezzi: *La scultura lombarda nel cinquecento* (Milan, 1929)

E. Kris: 'Materialen zur Biographie des Annibale Fontana und zur Kunsttopographie der Kirche S Maria presso S Celso in Mailand', *Mitt. Ksthist. Inst. Florenz*, iii (1930), pp. 201–53

C. Baroni: 'Problemi di scultura manieristica lombarda', *Arti: Rass. Bimest. A. Ant. & Mod.*, v (1943), pp. 180–90

J. Pope-Hennessy: *Italian Renaissance Sculpture* (London, 1958), pp. 408–9

E. Spina Barelli: 'Disegni lombardi inediti nella Biblioteca Ambrosiana', *Vita e pensiero* (Milan, 1966)

R. Bossaglia: 'La scultura', *La Certosa di Pavia* (Milan, 1968), p. 68

O. Raggio: 'Alessandro Algardi e gli stucchi di Villa Pamphili', *Paragone*, 251 (1971), pp. 3–38

B. Heinz-Wied: 'Studi sull'arte della scultura in pietra dura durante il rinascimento: I fratelli Saracchi', *Ant. viva* (1973), pp. 37–58

A. P. Valerio: 'Annibale Fontana e il paliotto della Vergine dei Miracoli in Santa Maria presso San Celso', *Paragone*, 279 (1973), pp. 32–53

——: 'Annibale Fontana', *Il seicento lombardo* (exh. cat., Milan, Pal. Reale, 1973, pp. 15–16)

——: 'La medaglia a Milano, 1535–1565', *Omaggio a Tiziano* (exh. cat., Milan, Pal. Reale, 1977), pp. 132–51

F. Rossi: 'Medaglie', *I campi e la cultura artistica cremonese del cinquecento* (exh. cat., ed. M. Gregori; Cremona, Mus. Civ. Ala Ponzone, 1985), pp. 358–62

P. M. de Winter: 'Recent Accessions of Italian Renaissance Decorative Arts', *Bull. Cleveland Mus. A.*, lxxiii/4 (1986), pp. 163–9

Dizionario della chiesa ambrosiana, ii (Milan, 1988), pp. 1248–50 [entry by S. Gavazzi]

MARIA TERESA FIORIO

2. Annibale Fontana: *Assumption of the Virgin*, marble, 1584 (Milan, S Maria presso S Celso)

Fontana, Baldassare (*b* Chiasso, 26 July 1661; *d* Chiasso, 6 Oct 1733). Italian stuccoist and architect, active in Moravia and Poland. He was a pupil of Carlo Fontana and Antonio Raggi. Most of Baldassare Fontana's surviving works date from his early period in Moravia, including the decoration of the Archbishop's Palace in KROMĚŘÍŽ and his most important decorative work at the Norbertine monastery (1692, 1694, 1704–5) in Hradisko near Olomouc, in the residence (1693–4) at Hrubčice and in the

Norbertines' summer residence (1694–5) in Šebetov. In 1693 Fontana was invited to Poland for the first time by the church of St Clement in Wieliczka near Kraków to decorate the chapel of the Mnisze family. He returned to Poland in July 1695 to begin the most important work of his life: the decoration of the church of St Anna in Kraków, where he adorned the nave piers with swags and medallions and the high altar with saints and angels. He worked on this intermittently until 1704. Fontana's work at St Anna's also brought him other commissions from Polish patrons for interior decorations, both ecclesiastical and secular. These included the decoration (1697; 1699) of the Italian chapel at the Franciscan church in Kraków, the decoration (1699) of the church of the Order of St Clare in Stary Sącz, the decoration (1701) of the Romanesque church of St Andrew in Kraków, including the boat pulpit, and the *Confession of St Jacek Odrowąż* in the chapel at the Dominican monastery in Kraków. He also executed decoration in palaces near Barany and in Krzysztofory and in houses at Mariacki Square and Szczepańska Street, Kraków, where low-relief putti adorn a vaulted first-floor room. Fontana's most important secular work was the decoration at the residence in Uherčice. Other surviving work includes decorative work at the Franciscan friary in Uherské, Hradiště, and the decoration (*c.* 1708) at the residence in Buchlovice. Later works included decorations at the affiliated Norbertine church (completed 1731) in Kopeček, at the church and monastery (from 1724) of the Cistercians in Velehrad, in the residence at Brnenskie Ivanovice and at the affiliate (1725–34) of the Velehrad Monastery in Polešovice. Fontana frequently returned to Chiasso in the late autumn, moving back to Moravia in the spring to continue his work. His introduction of the style of Bernini into Poland and the Czech lands inspired at least three generations of sculptors, and in this part of Europe he is regarded as the greatest stuccoist of the late 17th and early 18th centuries.

BIBLIOGRAPHY

J. Pagaczewski: 'Geneza i charakterystyka sztuki Baltazara Fontany' [The origin and characteristics of Baldassare Fontana's art], *Roc. Kraków*, xxx (1938), pp. 3–48

M. Karpowicz: *Artisti ticinesi in Pologna nel '600* (Bellinzona, 1983), pp. 167–71, 175

——: *Baldassare Fontana, 1661–1733: Un berniniano ticinese in Moravia e Pologna* (Lugano, 1990)

ANDREW STOGA

Fontana, Franco (*b* Modena, 9 Dec 1933). Italian photographer. He began to take photographs in 1961 and had his first exhibition in 1968. Interested in the interplay of colours, he created an intensively vibrant and original language that he successfully used to explore diverse subjects, including urban landscape, portraiture, fashion, still-life and the nude. His work has been defined as intimately poised between abstraction and pragmatism, with later critics creating the label of 'Photographic Transavantgarde' for his style. He worked with 35 mm cameras, mostly on location: his studio, he claimed, was 'the world'.

PHOTOGRAPHIC PUBLICATIONS

Franco Fontana (Parma, 1976)
Presenzassenza (Monza, 1982)
Landscape Photography (New York, 1984)

BIBLIOGRAPHY

Subject: Landscape (exh. cat. by P. P. Preti, London, Phot. Gal., 1974)

MARGHERITA ABBOZZO HEUSER

Fontana, Lucio (*b* Rosario, Santa Fé, Argentina, 19 Feb 1899; *d* Comabbio, nr Varese, 7 Sept 1968). Italian painter, sculptor and theorist of Argentine birth. He moved with his family to Milan in 1905 but followed his father back to Buenos Aires in 1922 and there established his own sculpture studio in 1924. On settling again in Milan he trained from 1928 to 1930 at the Accademia di Brera, where he was taught by the sculptor Adolfo Wildt; Wildt's devotion to the solemn and monumental plasticity of the Novecento Italiano group epitomized the qualities against which Fontana was to react in his own work. Fontana's sculpture *The Harpooner* (gilded plaster, h. 1.73 m, 1934; Milan, Renzo Zavanella priv. col., see 1987 exh. cat., p. 118) is typical of his work of this period, with a dynamic nervousness in the thin shape of the weapon poised to deliver a final blow and in the coarse and formless plinth. Soon afterwards, together with other northern Italian artists such as Fausto Melotti, Fontana abandoned any lingering Novecento elements in favour of a strict and coherent form of abstraction. In 1934 he became a member of Abstraction–Création and went on to take part in the Corrente group's exhibitions.

In his early abstractions Fontana took a middle course between painting and sculpture by producing plaster reliefs and free-standing but essentially planar works in plaster or iron, for example *Abstract Sculpture* (iron, h. 625 mm, 1934; Turin, Gal. Civ. A. Mod.), in which a meandering but generally straight-edged line of metal describes a single plane. Fontana at this time used both flat, geometrically regular shapes and organic biomorphic forms with undulating contours suggestive of enlarged cells. There are other ambiguities and apparent inconsistencies in his work of the late 1930s: alongside his search for a geometric perfection he also produced an extensive group of ceramics in which figures or objects are suggested in a fragmented and violently disturbed form that draws attention to the manipulation of the clay by his hand, and especially by his thumb. In works such as *Horses* (1938; Duisburg, Lehmbruck-Mus.), some of which he produced in 1937 at the Sèvres factory in Paris, Fontana displayed his sympathy with the Neo-Expressionist currents that were emerging in the major cities of Italy as a reaction against the retrospective spirit of the Novecento.

During World War II Fontana returned to Argentina, where in 1946 he founded the Academia Altamira with the artists Jorge Romero Brest and Jorge Larco; together they collaborated on the *Manifiesto blanco* (Buenos Aires, 1946). In this text, which Fontana did not sign but to which he actively contributed, he began to formulate the theories that he was to expand as SPAZIALISMO, or Spatialism, in five manifestos from 1947 to 1952. He opted decisively for abstraction but hinted also at the need to take account of new techniques made possible by scientific progress. This text therefore marked the end for him not only of figurative art but also of a static, classical style of abstraction. He also questioned the traditional reliance in Western art on a flat support such as canvas or paper, proposing instead that the time had come for artists

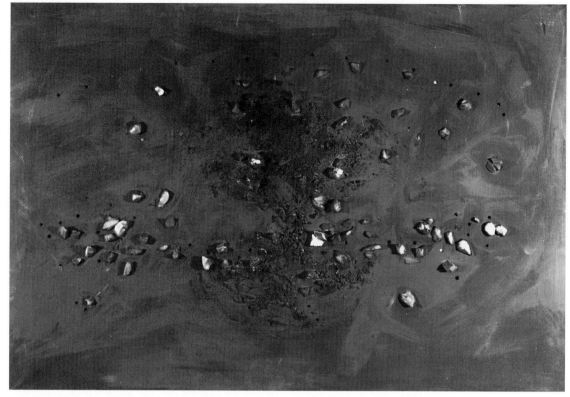

Lucio Fontana: *Spatial Concept*, oil on canvas with glass, 0.85×1.25 m, 1955 (Milan, Civico Museo d'Arte Contemporanea)

to work in three or rather four physical dimensions, since time also had to be added to the equation, in order to disturb the entire environment with their interventions.

Following his return to Italy in 1948 Fontana exhibited his first *Spatial Environment* (1949; Milan, Gal. Naviglio), which prefigured later international developments such as environmental art, performance art, land art and Arte Povera. This first temporary installation by Fontana consisted of a giant amoeba-like shape suspended in the void in a darkened room and bombarded by neon light, a material which was to be taken up by other artists in the 1960s. By their nature such works had an ephemeral life, but they were reconstructed for later exhibitions on the basis of documentary evidence provided by Fontana's drawings, by photographs and by first-hand accounts. Fontana's concern with environments led him also to collaborate in the early 1950s with the architect Luciano Baldessari on the design of several exhibition pavilions.

Fontana's concept of Spazialismo, as formulated in the texts that he published on his return to Italy, was based on the principle that in our age matter should be transformed into energy in order to invade space in a dynamic form. He applied these theories to a feverish, violent, subversive and radical production in which he synthesized the various elements of his art. He devised the generic title *Concetto spaziale* ('spatial concept') for these works and used it for almost all his later paintings. These can be divided into broad categories: the *Buchi* ('holes'), beginning in 1949, and the *Tagli* ('slashes'), which he instituted in the mid-1950s. In both types of painting Fontana assaulted the heretofore sacrosanct surface of the canvas, either by making holes in it or by slashing it with sharp linear cuts.

The *Buchi*, such as *Spatial Concept* (oil on paper mounted on canvas, 790×790 mm, 1952; Paris, Pompidou), continue to exploit the beauty of chance and accident seen earlier in Fontana's ceramics, and in this sense they bear comparison with other developments of the period such as *Art informel*, Tachism, Abstract Expressionism and action painting. In some works Fontana violated the surface not only by piercing it but by sticking irregularly shaped objects, such as bits of coloured glass, on the canvas in random configurations, as in *Spatial Concept* (1955; see fig.). The *Tagli*, such as *Spatial Concept—Expectations* (1959; Paris, Mus. A. Mod. Ville Paris), are clearer and more concise in form, but they are also generally asymmetrically and casually arranged. However many cuts are made into the canvas, the surface as a whole remains intact and two-dimensional, and, for all their apparent violence, these pictures continue to be displayed as conventional easel paintings. They form an important part of Fontana's contribution to CONTINUITÀ, which the artist joined in 1961.

Fontana applied similar techniques to sculptures such as *Spatial Concept* (painted iron, diam. 3 m, 1952; Turin, Gal. Civ. A. Mod.). The most successful of these works are those in which the incisions are made into a lumpy surface that retains the delightfully irregular and unpredictable character of soft organic materials such as wax or chalk even when cast in bronze. Other sculptures are more decisively three-dimensional, as in the case of imperfect and randomly shaped spheres such as *Nature* (1959–60; Otterlo, Rijksmus Kröller-Müller), in which visible gashes suggest sexual orifices or eruptions of volcanic activity. In sculptures of this type Fontana not only completely freed himself from the tyranny of two dimensions but created a balance between the idea and its physical manifestation. Among Fontana's last works are a series of *Teatrini* ('little theatres'; e.g. 1965; Paris, Pompidou), in which he returned to an essentially flat idiom by using backcloths enclosed within wings resembling a frame; the reference to theatre emphasizes the act of looking, while in the foreground a series of irregular spheres or oscillating, wavy silhouettes creates a lively shadow play. He was awarded the Grand Prize for Painting at the Venice Biennale of 1966.

WRITINGS
Primo manifesto dello spazialismo (Milan, 1947)
Secondo manifesto dello spazialismo (Milan, 1948)
Manifesto tecnico dello spazialismo (Milan, 1951)

BIBLIOGRAPHY
T. Sauvage: *Pittura italiana del dopoguerra* (Milan, 1957)
G. P. Giani: *Lucio Fontana* (Venice, 1958)
E. Crispolti: 'Carriera barocca di Fontana', *Il Verri*, iii/3 (1959), pp. 101–8
M. Tapié: *Devenir de Fontana* (Turin, 1961)
F. De Bartolomeis: *Segno antidisegno di Lucio Fontana* (Turin, 1967)
G. Ballo: *Fontana: Idea per un ritratto* (Turin, 1970)
Lucio Fontana: Concetti spaziali (Turin, 1970)
E. Crispolti: *Omaggio a Fontana* (Rome, 1971)
P. Fossati: *L'immagine sospesa* (Turin, 1971), pp. 168–78
G. Manganelli: *L'ironia teologica di Fontana* (Milan, 1978)
G. Ballo: *Lucio Fontana* (Rimini, 1982)
E. Crispolti: *Fontana: Catalogo generale*, 2 vols (Milan, 1986) [cat. rais.]
Lucio Fontana (exh. cat. by B. Blistène and others, Paris, Pompidou, 1987)
Lucio Fontana (exh. cat. by B. Blistène and others, Amsterdam, Stedel. Mus.; London, Whitechapel A.G.; 1988)
Lucio Fontana, 1899–1968 (exh. cat., Barcelona, Fund. Caixa Pensions, 1988)

RENATO BARILLI

Fontane, (Henri) Theodor [Théodore] (*b* Neuruppin, 30 Dec 1819; *d* Berlin, 20 Sept 1898). German writer. His reputation rests on his Realist novels of Berlin life, the first of which was published in 1878. His writings on art are earlier and occupy only a marginal position in his work as a whole. He had no training in art history, although his paternal grandfather, Peter Fontane (*fl* 1787–95), was a miniature painter who had served as drawing instructor to the children of Emperor Frederick William II of Prussia. From 1844 onwards he frequented the Berlin literary societies Tunnel über der Spree and Rütli, meeting such painters as Franz Kugler and Adolph Friedrich Erdmann Menzel and such writers as Friedrich Eggers, Hugo von Blomberg and August von der Heyden. Here and in his subsequent writings he defended the role of the non-specialist art critic that, like a number of the major European writers of the late 19th century, he himself assumed in the next two decades.

Fontane lived in London from 1855 to 1859. These years contributed significantly to his development as a journalist. He visited galleries and exhibitions, reporting on the Manchester Art Treasures Exhibition of 1857 in a series of 'Briefe aus Manchester' (*Die Zeit*, sum.–aut. 1857), in which he attempted to produce a concise history of English painting for German readers; he was especially

sympathetic to the work of the Pre-Raphaelites. After returning to Berlin, Fontane began to report regularly on the biennial exhibitions of the Akademie der Künste, first for the Viennese paper *Das Vaterland* and then for the daily press in Berlin. He covered all the exhibitions up to 1874, except for 1868 and 1870, in articles that focus on the subject-matter of individual pictures, providing valuable insight into the taste of a period of extensive artistic activity no longer represented fully in public collections. As he emerged as a novelist, after 1874 Fontane ceased to write on art, apart from the occasional book review.

WRITINGS
E. Gross, ed.: *Sämtliche Werke*, 30 vols (Munich, 1959–75) [xxiii/1 incl. 'Zwanzig Turnersche Landschaften in Marlborough House' (1857), pp. 25–9; 'Aus Manchester' (1860), pp. 51–161; 'Die diesjährige Kunstausstellung' (1862), pp. 165–251; 'Berliner Kunstausstellung' (1864), pp. 264–319; 'Berliner Kunstausstellung' (1866), pp. 345–89 [sw]
W. Keitel and H. Nürnberger, ed.: *Werke, Schriften und Briefe*, 19 vols (Munich, 1962–) [wsb]

BIBLIOGRAPHY
H. H. Reuter: *Fontane*, 2 vols (Munich, 1968)
W. Vogt: 'Fontane und die bildende Kunst', *sw*, xxiii/2 (Munich, 1970), pp. 185–97
S. Wüsten: 'Theodor Fontanes Gedanken zur historischen Architektur und bildenden Kunst und sein Verhältnis zu Franz Kugler', *Fontane Bl.*, 3 (1975), pp. 323–52
——: 'Zu kunstkritischen Schriften Fontanes', *Fontane Bl.*, 4 (1978), pp. 174–200
P.-K. Schuster: *Theodor Fontane: Effi Briest—Ein Leben nach christlichen Bildern* (Tübingen, 1978)
H. Streite-Buscher: 'Zur Kunst und Kunstgeschichte', wsb, iii/5 (Munich, 1986), pp. 821–31
W. Jung: *Bildergespräche: Zur Funktion von Kunst und Kultur in Theodor Fontanes 'L'Adultera'* (Stuttgart, 1991)

JOHN OSBORNE

Fontanesi, Antonio (*b* Reggio Emilia, 23 Feb 1818; *d* Turin, 17 April 1882). Italian painter, draughtsman and printmaker.

1. EARLY WORK AND LITHOGRAPHS, TO 1855. In 1832, at the age of 14, he began attending the local Scuola di Belle Arti where he was a pupil of Prospero Minghetti (1786–1853). Fontanesi's early work revealed his versatility: in the 1830s he produced tempera murals for several houses in Reggio Emilia, such as the Casa Zanichelli, Via S Filippo (*in situ*), and the Casa Ghinizzini, Via Emilia Santo Stefano (*in situ*), combining townscapes and architectural perspectives with friezes and medallions in an 18th-century manner. For the 1841–2 and 1845–6 theatre seasons he designed stage sets for performances of operas, including Verdi's *Nebuchadnezzar*, performed in the Teatro Comunale. Although he was appreciated in Reggio Emilia, Fontanesi resented the limited cultural climate, and shortly after his mother's death in 1845, he left for Turin. Probably stirred by the ideals of the contemporary Italian revolt against the Austrians, he then moved on to Milan, where he joined the forces of Garibaldi.

After the 1848 armistice Fontanesi sought refuge in Lugano, just across the Swiss border. Over the next two years he travelled round Switzerland, compiling an album of sketches (now Turin, Gal. Civ. A. Mod.). At the end of 1850 he settled in Geneva, where he set up a studio and soon began to establish himself both as a tutor (usually to the sons of the rich) and as an artist. Earlier works, such as *Morning: Herd Drinking* (1849; Reggio Emilia, Mus.

Civ. & Gal. A.), reveal that he was already painting with confidence and freedom, even to the point of mixing oils and tempera, a memory, perhaps, of his earlier practice in painting scenery for the stage. He soon came to be especially admired for his charcoal drawings, in which he was recognized as the equal of the Swiss artists François Diday and Alexandre Calame. Fontanesi also executed a number of lithographic views, both of landscapes and of town scenes. With the support of the dealer Victor Brachard, he found publishers for these, both in Geneva (Gruaz included them in the album *Musée Suisse*) and abroad (the printers Pilet and Cougnard commissioned two entire series, *Villa Eynard*, see cat. rais., pp. 82–92, and a *Stroll through Geneva*, see cat. rais., pp. 93–109, published in 1854). In all, 56 lithographs by Fontanesi are known, almost all from the 1850s; he returned to lithography only in 1880 with *Clouds* (Turin, Gal. Civ. A. Mod.).

2. LANDSCAPES AND ETCHINGS, 1855–66. In 1855 Fontanesi visited the Exposition Universelle in Paris and shortly afterward re-established contact with François Auguste Ravier (1814–95), an artist whose encouragement and intellectual stimulation were to be of importance for Fontanesi in the following years. After becoming a soldier again in 1859, when he took part in the second Italian War of Independence, Fontanesi returned to Geneva, where he remained until 1865, devoting himself to painting. Using nature merely as a source of basic inspiration, he developed his own original interpretation of the landscape, making each image the result of mental elaboration on what was observed. While the earlier landscape paintings from Geneva had been marked by a simple lyricism in the manner of Corot (e.g. the *Path in the Chestnut Grove*, 1850–55, Turin, Gal. Civ. A. Mod.), the work from his second stay in Geneva is much more complex both in technique and in expression. Paintings such as *Landscape with Cattle after Rain* (1861; Turin, Gal. Civ. A. Mod.) are vigorous in execution as befits the subtle, fleeting mood they seek to capture. Fontanesi's landscapes were usually poised between art and nature in the idealizing tradition of Claude Lorrain, encouraging the spectator to apply both his emotions and his intellect to the scene depicted. Fontanesi frequently reworked the motifs found in, or suggested by, reality, even in his drawings or etchings.

There are few definite dates for Fontanesi's etching activity, which appears to have begun before 1857, although it is known that he presented a group of etchings to his friend the Marchese Ferdinando di Breme, an influential patron of the arts, in the form of an album. His earliest plates were relatively simple celebrations of an idealized version of country life (see fig. 1), with settings recalling Liguria and Savoy; but Fontanesi soon moved on to technically complex scenes such as that of the *Little Hedonists* (1860–65), which combines a finely detailed foreground with a soft, smudged background and an effect of quivering silhouette in the branches and foliage as if

1. Antonio Fontanesi: *Fruit picking*, etching, 370×265 mm (Geneva, Cabinet des Estampes du Musée d'Art et d'Histoire)

seen against brilliant light. Fontanesi's ability to make light seem to emerge from the oxidized ground of the etching plate recalls his skill, as a painter, at making light glow through colour laid on a background prepared with gesso priming. It is possible that Fontanesi was influenced in his etching technique by his familiarity with the technique of *cliché-verre*, which he had begun to practise in 1863, probably at the instigation of Ravier. Fontanesi used *cliché-verre* again for work prepared during a trip to England: a dozen views of London (1866). In some of these, notably *Westminster Abbey*, he achieved his most expressive and vibrant use of light: it seems almost as though the very walls and towers of Westminster have become permeated by light, rather than the skies and shimmering ripples on the water. Most of Fontanesi's etchings are now in Turin (Gal. Civ. A. Mod.), Reggio Emilia (Mus. Civ. & Gal. A.), Milan (Castello Sforzesco) and Geneva (Mus. A. & Hist.).

3. LATE WORK, 1866–82. Returning to Italy from London, Fontanesi settled in Florence as a guest of the painter Cristiano Banti (1824–1904). Here the work of the Macchiaioli was of much greater significance for him than it had been on his earlier meetings with them in the mid-1850s. The *Market in Florence* (1867; Turin, Gal. Civ. A. Mod.) recalls Macchiaioli painting in its bold treatment of light and shade. Fontanesi was now appreciated in Italy not just as an artist but also as a teacher: in 1869 he was made professor of landscape painting at the Accademia Albertina in Turin, a post created specially for him. He began to paint the countryside around Turin and also took pupils from the Accademia out for *plein-air* sketching. Much of his best work from this time attempts to capture a particular atmosphere, as in *After the Rain* (c. 1870; Turin, Gal. Civ. A. Mod.; see fig. 2) and *April* (1873; Turin, Gal. Civ. A. Mod.), or the individual's feelings in a particular landscape setting, as in the first version of *Solitude* (1875; Reggio Emilia, Mus. Civ. & Gal. A.).

Following an Italian–Japanese agreement aimed at opening Japan to Western culture and thus to modernization, Fontanesi was selected to go to Tokyo to teach at the Academy. He stayed from 1876 to 1878, returning earlier than planned due to illness. Though still remembered as the founder of a flourishing school of Western painting, Fontanesi derived very little from Japanese art. On his return to Turin he went back to painting; he again took his students to sketch in the countryside where he expounded on the 'poetry' of the scene before them and urged them to recall the example of the work of Claude Lorrain. Particularly striking during Fontanesi's last years was his treatment of twilight, sunset and water, often in combination, as in a painting very reminiscent of J. M. W. Turner (whose work Fontanesi had seen in London), *Sunset on the River Po at S Mauro* (1878–81; Turin, Gal. Civ. A. Mod.). The virtuosity of Fontanesi's late work is especially evident in the sketchbooks (Turin, Gal. Civ. A. Mod.), where the character and the drama of a landscape or view of a town is frequently captured with a few brushstrokes.

BIBLIOGRAPHY
M. Calderini: *Antonio Fontanesi, pittore paesista* (Turin, 1909, 2/1925)
C. Carrà: *Antonio Fontanesi* (Rome, 1924)
Antonio Fontanesi, 1818–1882 (exh. cat., ed. M. Bernardi; Turin, Gal. Civ. A. Mod., 1932)

2. Antonio Fontanesi: *After the Rain*, oil on canvas, 732×535 mm, *c*. 1870 (Turin, Galleria Civica d'Arte Moderna)

M. Bernardi: *Antonio Fontanesi* (Milan, 1933)
Cinquanta opere di Antonio Fontanesi (exh. cat., ed. M. Bernardi; Turin, Gal. Gazzetta Popolo, 1947)
Antonio Fontanesi (exh. cat., ed. G. Briganti; Reggio Emilia, Soc. Casino, 1949)
M. Bernardi: *Antonio Fontanesi* (Turin, 1967)
Fontanesi e l'incisione (exh. cat., ed. A. Dragone; Tokyo, It. Cult. Inst., 1977)
Antonio Fontanesi: L'opera grafica (exh. cat., ed. A. Dragone; Turin, Pal. Chiablese; Piacenza, Gal. A. Mod. Ricci Oddi; Bologna, Mus. Civ. Risorgimento; 1979–80 [cat. rais.]
M. Iseki: *Pittore Fontanesi* (Tokyo, 1984)

ANGELO DRAGONE

Font de Gaume. Cave site in France, in the Beune Valley 1 km from Les Eyzies, Dordogne. It is one of the most famous and historically important sites for Palaeolithic cave art (*see also* PREHISTORIC EUROPE, §II, 1 and 2). The cave of Font de Gaume had been known and visited throughout history, but the paintings were found only in 1901 by Denis Peyrony, a few days after the discovery of art in the nearby cave of LES COMBARELLES. A description of the paintings, largely the work of the Abbé HENRI BREUIL, was published in 1910, but more figures have since been found, and the cleaning of the walls in the 1960s, together with continuing conservation work since then, has improved the visibility of many images.

The cave is *c*. 120 m long, with a ceiling up to 10 m high and a width of *c*. 1.5–3.0 m (for layout of cave *see* PREHISTORIC EUROPE, fig. 8). Some distance from the entrance

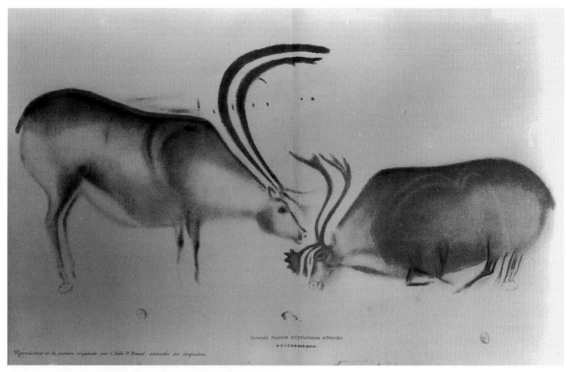

Font de Gaume, cave painting of reindeer, w. 2.45 m, Late Upper Palaeolithic period, *c.* 16,000–*c.* 12,000 BP; reconstruction drawing (original *in situ*)

is a constriction in the passage, which narrows to a width of 400 mm; formerly it was just 900 mm high. The main decorated gallery, which has three side passages, lies beyond. At its far end, to one side, stands a chamber with paintings of 12 bison together with horses and tectiform (hut-shaped) signs. The art of Font de Gaume is believed to be Magdalenian in date, attributable to Style III (*c.* 20,000–*c.* 16,000 BP) of the French scholar ANDRÉ LEROI-GOURHAN and especially to Style IV (*c.* 16,000–*c.* 12,000 BP). Bison figures dominate the cave as a whole; some are bichrome, red-and-brown or red-and-black, and they often exploit the bulging surface of the wall. Several form groups, arranged either in lines or facing each other; some have massive humps. Many figures combine painting and engraving, and scraping of the wall is sometimes used to accentuate anatomical details such as eyes, horns, or tusks on mammoths. In 1910, Breuil identified 80 bison, 40 horses (including a famous leaping horse), 23 mammoths, 17 reindeer or deer, 8 bovids, 4 caprids, 2 rhinoceroses (including a well-known red figure), 1 or 2 felines, 1 bear, 1 wolf, 1 human, 4 stencilled hand outlines, 19 tectiform signs and 5 or 6 other signs. To this list have been added 6 mammoths, 5 or 6 horses, 2 bison, 1 ibex, 1 reindeer, 4 tectiform signs, 2 other signs, and some dots and stripes—a total of about 230 figures. Some of the mammoths are highly realistic, detailed engravings; but by far the most famous image in the cave is a pair of painted reindeer with sweeping antlers, in which the male is bending to lick the female's head (see fig.).

BIBLIOGRAPHY

L. Capitan, H. Breuil and D. Peyrony: *La Caverne de Font-de-Gaume aux Eyzies (Dordogne)* (Monaco, 1910)
M. Sarradet: *Font-de-Gaume* (Périgueux, 1969)
J. Brunet and P. Vidal: 'Font-de-Gaume aux Eyzies: Les Derniers Travaux de conservation', *Archéologia*, clxi (1981), pp. 19–32 [fine colour pict.]
P. Daubisse and others: *La Grotte de Font-de-Gaume* (Périgueux, 1984)
A. Roussot: 'Grotte de Font-de-Gaume', *L'Art des cavernes* (Paris, 1984), pp. 129–34

PAUL G. BAHN

Fonte, Jacopo della. *See* JACOPO DELLA QUERCIA.

Fontebasso, Francesco (*b* Venice, 4 Oct 1707; *d* Venice, 31 May 1769). Italian painter, printmaker and draughtsman. He was one of the most prolific and well-known followers of Sebastiano Ricci, with whom he had his earliest training, and particularly of Giambattista Tiepolo. By the end of the 1720s he had studied in Rome (where he is documented in 1728) and Bologna (Oretti MS.); the influence of the forthright tenebrism of the Bolognese school is evident in his first independent works, such as the *Adoration of the Shepherds* (*c.* 1732; Burano, S Martino). Around 1730 he was in Udine, where he studied Tiepolo's frescoes in the cathedral and in the archbishop's palace, and during the next few years he came into direct contact with Tiepolo, perhaps in Venice. Ricci remained influential, and in 1731 Fontebasso was engraving, in Venice, the altarpiece of *St Gregory Interceding for Souls in Purgatory* that Ricci had painted for S Alessandro della Croce in Bergamo. Fontebasso's work, however, increasingly emulated that of Tiepolo, with a consequent lightening and freeing of his palette.

Fontebasso was adept at fresco. In 1734 he frescoed the two main portions of the ceiling of the church of the Gesuiti in Venice with the *Angels Appearing to Abraham*

Francesco Fontebasso: *Family of Darius before Alexander*, oil on canvas, 1.28×1.65 m, *c.* 1750 (Dallas, TX, Museum of Fine Art)

and *Elijah Carried to Heaven in a Chariot of Fire* (both *in situ*), and in 1736 he executed an ambitious fresco cycle in the church of the Annunziata in Trent, much of which was destroyed in World War II; there remain the apsidal vault frescoes, the *Fall of the Rebel Angels*, and two lunettes, the *Nativity* and the *Circumcision*. By the 1740s he was well established as a decorative frescoist and as a history painter and engraver.

Fontebasso's ambition to emulate Tiepolo extended to drawing (collections Venice, Mus. Correr; St Petersburg, Hermitage), where his original manner emulated Tiepolo's pen and wash technique, and to engraving, where his *Various Bacchanales and Historical Scenes* (1744) is the only Venetian series of etchings of his era from Tiepolo's *Capricci*. He also executed numerous illustrations for books, such as Venetian 'festival books', which display his originality to advantage. His most important frescoes were for the Barbarigo family, at the Palazzo Duodo, Venice (between 1743 and 1752), and at the Palazzo Barbarigo, Venice, where he frescoed a *Triumph of Venice* (1745). For the Palazzo Duodo he created decorations for six rooms, both on canvas (e.g. *Cleopatra's Banquet*, Newport, priv. col., see Magrini, 1988, fig. 54) and in fresco. Two ceiling frescoes, *Bacchus and Ariadne* and *Mount Olympus*, remain *in situ*; they display a marked influence of Tiepolo in technique and border on the plagiaristic in composition.

As a history painter, Fontebasso's works recall Ricci in composition but are enlivened by a busy brush and richly pleasing colours, as in the *Family of Darius before Alexander* (*c.* 1750; Dallas, TX, Mus. F.A.; see fig.). He became a founder-member, in 1755, of the Accademia Veneziana and was in demand throughout the Veneto. In 1759 he painted for Felice Alberti d'Enno, Prince Bishop of Trent, a cycle of pictures for the Castello del Buonconsiglio, Trent; among these were scenes from the *Life of Moses* (two *in situ*).

Fontebasso was invited to Russia in 1761 and worked at St Petersburg for Catherine II, Empress of Russia, painting many ceilings and decorations for the Imperial Palace (destr.). He also painted history paintings and portraits, such as that of a *Man Holding a Glass Eye* (St Petersburg, Hermitage), which almost certainly depicts the eye doctor Felix Tadini, another Italian expatriate. Fontebasso returned to Venice late in 1762 and until his death worked steadily on a number of projects, including a series of canvases for the chapel of S Pietro d'Alcantara, showing scenes from the saint's life, at S Francesco della Vigna, Venice, in 1765. He became President of the Accademia Veneziana in 1768.

UNPUBLISHED SOURCE

Bologna, Bib. Com. Archiginnasio, MS. B. 123–35.II [M. Oretti: *Notizie de' professori del disegno, cioè pittori, scultori ed architetti bolognesi e de' forestieri di sua scuola, c.* 1760]

BIBLIOGRAPHY

P. A. Orlandi and P. Guarienti: *Abecedario pittorico* (Venice, 1753), p. 189

J. Byam Shaw: 'The Drawings of Francesco Fontebasso', *A. Ven.*, viii (1954), pp. 317–25

R. Pallucchini: *Pittura veneziana del settecento* (Venice, 1960)

E. Martini: 'I dipinti di Francesco Fontebasso a Palazzo Duodo', *Not. Pal. Albani*, ii/1 (1973), pp. 50–56

M. Magrini: 'Alcune notizie su Francesco Fontebasso', *Atti Ist. Ven. Sci., Lett. & A.*, cxxxii (1974), pp. 285–98

L. Sester: 'Un gruppo di tempere inedite di Francesco Fontebasso', *Not. Pal. Albani*, vii/2 (1978), pp. 78–83

M. Magrini: *Francesco Fontebasso* (Venice, 1988)

The Glory of Venice: Art in the Eighteenth Century (exh. cat., ed. J. Martineau and A. Robison; London, RA; Washington, DC, N.G.A.; 1994–5)

JOHN WILSON

Fontenai [Fontenay], Abbé de [Bonafous, Louis-Abel] (*b* Castelnau-de-Brassac, Tarn, 3 or 4 May 1736; *d* Paris, 28 March 1806). French writer. He was the son of a lawyer; having been a pupil of the Jesuits, he joined that Order in 1752 but was never ordained priest. He became in his turn a teacher at Jesuit colleges, first at Albi and then at Tournon. When in 1762 the Jesuit Order was suppressed in France, he moved to Paris and became a writer, publishing under the name of Abbé de Fontenai and continuing to wear clerical dress. In 1777 he published a *Dictionnaire des Artistes* that was, as the author acknowledged in his preface, extremely derivative of Pierre-Jean Mariette's *Abécédario*. It differed from it, however, in that Fontenai also recounted the lives of some actors, dancers, musicians, watchmakers and other craftsmen. He expressly stated that the aims of the dictionary were to present worthy models for other artists to emulate; to outline the history of art for interested amateurs; and to give pleasure by including amusing anecdotes.

Fontenai also worked as a journalist, one of a reactionary tendency. Between 1779 and 1784 he edited the *Affiches, annonces et avis divers*, which he had founded; it was succeeded by the thrice-weekly *Journal général de France* (1785–91), which dealt primarily with the latest literary, economic and political events. Fontenai was essentially a prolific compiler of information, rather than an original thinker. In 1786 he produced an *Abrégé de la vie des peintres* and also published the greater part of the catalogue of the Galerie du Palais-Royal in Paris. This survey of the collections of the Ducs d'Orléans appeared in 57 instalments between 1786 and 1808. Between 1783 and 1790, as the fortunes of the Bourbon monarchy were declining, Fontenai produced *L'Illustre Destinée des Bourbons* in four volumes, a defence of the House of Bourbon that used selective historical examples to uphold the hereditary legitimacy of Louis XVI. During the Reign of Terror of the French Revolution he lived in hiding in Paris; emerging after the events of 18 Brumaire, he founded the *Journal général de la littérature, des sciences et des arts*, which continued to be published until June 1802. Fontenai went on to contribute to such diverse publications as a *Dictionnaire de l'élocution française* and an *Histoire universelle* (both 1802) and a *Dictionnaire géographique* (1803).

WRITINGS

Dictionnaire des artistes ou notice historique et raisonnée des architectes, peintres, graveurs, sculpteurs, musiciens, acteurs et danseurs, imprimeurs, horlogers et mécaniciens, 2 vols (Paris, 1777)

Journal général de France (Paris, 1785–91)

Abrégé de la vie des peintres (Paris, 1786)

Journal général de la littérature, des sciences et des arts (Paris, 1801–2)

BIBLIOGRAPHY

DBF

VALERIE MAINZ

Fontenay Abbey. Former Cistercian abbey in France, in the Racherie Valley, east of Montbard, Burgundy. The second daughter-house of Clairvaux, it was established by St Bernard himself in 1118. In 1130 growing numbers necessitated a move to a new site in the valley, where the first abbot, Godefroy de Rochetaillee (resigned 1132), provided temporary buildings and a chapel dedicated to St Paul. It was left to his successor, Guillaume de Spiriaco (1132–54), to construct a permanent church and begin the cloister ranges. These buildings still largely remain, the earliest surviving complex of buildings of the Clairvaux filiation.

The abbey church, built of limestone, was begun *c.* 1139 with money provided by Everard, Bishop of Norwich, who joined the community in that year; it was sufficiently complete to be consecrated in 1147. It is therefore the oldest, though not necessarily the most representative, of the surviving group of so-called Bernardine churches, the lost model for which was the new church at Clairvaux itself. At Fontenay (see fig.), the church demonstrates the impressive austerity of the Bernardine plan (a): a substantial nave of eight bays with an unstressed crossing; a short, low, two-bay, square-ended presbytery; low transepts with two rectangular chapels on each arm; and a low narthex (destr.) at the west end of the nave. Though simple in plan, the building was monumental in scale, with an overall length of 66 m and a width across the transepts of 30 m. The external elevation was severe, depending on its massing for effect.

Inside, there is no triforium or clerestory, only blank walling above the pointed nave arcades. The church is covered throughout with pointed barrel vaults, those in the aisles being constructed transversely to the main axis of the building. The vaults in the transepts and presbytery are much lower than those of the nave, which is the dominant space within the church, containing the choirs of both monks and lay brothers. Its design was economical but effective, with arcades of two unchamfered orders carried on rectangular piers with attached half-columns supporting the inner order and a plain pilaster on the inner face rising to a hollow-chamfered abacus. Articulation was provided by attached shafts rising from the abacus to a matching string course at the springing of the high vault, which was divided into bays by bold, unchamfered transverse arches. Similar articulation was provided in the two-bay presbytery and in the transepts. The presbytery was entered by a tall, wide arch springing from the same level as the nave arcades; similar arches gave access to the transepts. The inner transept chapels opened into the presbytery and provided the upper entrances to the monks' choir. The church at Fontenay has no wall passages, and access to the space over the transept chapel vaults was provided in the form of doors, high up in the arcade walls above the chapel entrances, which can only have been reached by ladder.

Work on the claustral ranges must have followed close on the completion of the church. While the church embodied Bernardine puritanism, the detailing of the cloister buildings clearly shows a softening of approach, best seen in the chapter house of *c.* 1150, vaulted in three aisles of three bays ((c); the easternmost bay has been demolished). Here, rib vaults were used for the first time, rising from clustered piers with octagonal capitals (for illustration, *see* CHAPTER HOUSE, fig. 2). The treatment of the piers effectively continues the linear accent of the vault ribs to ground level. A similar scheme was used for the day-room (d), which completes the east cloister range to the south of the chapter house, although here both circular and octagonal piers were employed, with simplified rib mouldings, indicative of the secondary status of the room. Of the remainder of the cloister ranges, only the warming house at the east end of the south range remains (e), but excavated footings indicate an east–west refectory with a kitchen at its west end (f and g), and a west range that did not abut the cloister but had an intervening yard or 'lane' for the use of the lay brothers (h). The inexact alignment of the west range might suggest that it pre-dates both the church and cloister, and it might be considered as one of Abbot Godefroy's 'temporary' buildings.

In contrast to the surviving cloister ranges, the contemporary cloister walks were barrel-vaulted and remain very much as originally built, apart from the demolition of a square washing fountain (*lavabo*; (i)), which projected into the garth from the south walk. Its offset position reflects the location of the original refectory door. The detailing of the cloister arcades is extremely simple. Each walk has eight bays divided by buttresses, and in each bay twin shafts with plain bell capitals and double, hollow-chamfered abaci carry paired, round arches within a larger arch. The spandrels are plain and unpierced, and the arcades are barely moulded. The only hint of a softer approach is found in the north walk, where the buttresses are carried by twin shafts matching those of the arcade itself (*see* MONASTERY, §I, 4 and fig. 4).

At the end of the 12th century the refectory was rebuilt on the developed Cistercian model with a north–south alignment. Its sole surviving bay indicates that it was lit by two tiers of deeply splayed twin lancets. A single pier of its central arcade survives, suggesting that the new building was roofed in two spans, closely comparable with the new refectory built at Fountains Abbey, England, in the early 1170s. As well as the claustral ranges, permanent service ranges were provided from the late 12th century, including the 'forge' (j), a guest house (k) and a dovecot (n). This last, the finest of all Cistercian service buildings, comprised the abbey mill and workshops in a two-storey structure of nine bays, the ground floor vaulted throughout with boldly chamfered rib vaults rising from circular piers.

The decline of the abbey began in the 16th century, with the Wars of Religion and the introduction of the commendatory system (1557); by the mid-18th century the buildings were in a ruinous condition. The abbey was sold in 1791 and became a paper mill; it was resold in 1906, when restorations were begun.

BIBLIOGRAPHY

L. Begule: *L'Abbaye de Fontenay et l'architecture cistercienne* (Paris, 1928)
P. Fergusson: *The Architecture of Solitude* (Princeton, 1984)
R. Stalley: *The Cistercian Monasteries of Ireland* (London, 1987)

GLYN COPPACK

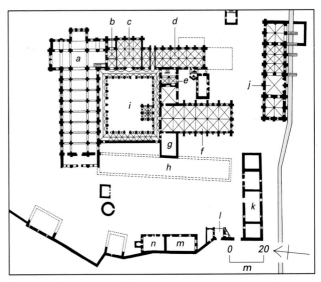

Fontenay Abbey, begun *c.* 1139, plan: (a) church; (b) sacristy; (c) chapter house; (d) day-room (below dormitory); (e) warming room; (f) refectory; (g) kitchen; (h) lay brothers' wing; (i) cloister with lavabo; (j) 'forge'; (k) guest house; (l) gate-house; (m) bake-house and brew-house; (n) dovecot

Fontes e Abrantes, Marquês de [Aires de Sá e Meneses, Rodrigo] (*b* Lisbon, 1676; *d* Lisbon, 1733). Portuguese diplomat and patron. He was at the court of Peter II of Portugal and was known as a connoisseur of painting, sculpture and, in particular, of architecture. He used his knowledge of geometry and mathematics to make designs for forts with regular ground-plans, although none of these plans or projects has survived. During the reign of John V he held the post of artistic adviser to the King, who sent him on an embassy to Rome, where he remained from 1712 to 1718, and where he carried out political and cultural commissions for the court. He was successful in his mission to persuade Clement XI to elevate the Royal Chapel (destr. 1755), Paço da Ribeira, Lisbon, to the status of a Patriarchal church in 1716. In that year the Marquês de Fontes was received in audience by the Pope and made a state entry into Rome, famous at the time for its magnificence. This is reflected in the carved allegories, alluding to Portuguese history and discoveries, on the magnificent Italian state coaches used in the entry (Belém, Mus. N. Coches).

It is probable that in Italy the Marquês de Fontes acquired information likely to be useful to the King during the years of planning that immediately preceded the building of the monastery-palace of Mafra; the architect Carlos Gimac (*b* Malta, ?1660; *d* ?1730) was part of his entourage during this period. Little is known of the Marquês's activities after his return to Portugal in 1718. He was a patron of the painter Francisco Vieira de Matlos, who mentioned having seen Dom Rodrigo sketch plans (untraced) for a palace. Before 1733 he built a small chapel, of which the architect is unknown, in the style of the 17th century in the cloister of the Augustinian convent of Nossa Senhora da Graça, Évora; this was intended as a funerary chapel for his wife, Dona Isabel de Lorena (*d* 1699).

BIBLIOGRAPHY
A. de Carvalho: *Dom João V e a arte do seu tempo* (Lisbon, 1962), pp. 241–2

JOSÉ FERNANDES PEREIRA

Fontevrault [Fontevraud] **Abbey.** Former abbey in Loiret, France. It was founded in 1100 by Robert d'Arbrissel (*c.* 1047–1117) and received a papal charter in 1106. Between 1189 and *c.* 1250 it was the dynastic burial church of the Plantagenet counts of Anjou (also kings of England). A joint house of monks and nuns, the abbey was suppressed in 1792 and the conventual buildings were mostly destroyed, although the Romanesque octagonal kitchen survives. Remaining buildings were converted to a prison, which closed in 1963. The 12th-century abbey church has a two-bay choir with an apse, ambulatory and three radiating chapels, and a transept with two bays and a chapel on each arm. The eastern parts are vaulted with barrel vaults, but the single-cell nave has four domed bays and a passage in the thickness of the wall (*see also* ROMANESQUE, fig. 25).

The church is best known as the repository of the tomb effigies of *Henry II, King of England,* his wife, *Eleanor of Aquitaine, Richard I* and *Isabella of Angoulême,* wife of King John (*reg* 1199–1216) and mother of Henry III. Like Joan (*d* 1199), daughter of Henry and Eleanor (1122–1204) and dowager queen of Sicily, Isabella (*d* 1246) was not interred in the royal cemetery but in the nuns' burial ground. Henry III had her body transferred to the royal mausoleum in 1254 and a new effigy created, in wood rather than stone but in a style clearly intended to match the three stone figures. The last familial burial was that of

Joan's son, *Raymond VII, Count of Toulouse* (*d* 1249), whose tomb effigy was discovered during excavations in the church. The heart of Henry III was interred at Fontevrault in 1289.

Although Eleanor made gifts to the abbey as early as 1152, and Henry II began making gifts while he was still Duke of Normandy and Count of Anjou, there is no evidence that Fontevrault was chosen to be the family necropolis before Henry's death at Chinon in 1189. It has been presumed that it was Eleanor, taking advantage of the location of the abbey only 25 km from Chinon, who played the major role in establishing the 'cemetery of kings', but Bienvenu pointed out that Eleanor was imprisoned in England until 1190 and suggested that Henry's donations over many years indicate that the decision was his. Eleanor did, however, retire there after Henry's death, and it was probably she, after the death of Richard in 1199, who commissioned the three remaining stone effigies. The stylistic closeness of the two male effigies suggests that they were the work of the same artist. Otherwise there are no close stylistic comparisons to be made.

The effigies themselves are important for the history of royal funerary images because those of *Henry II* (see fig.) and *Richard I* are among the earliest carved figures of recumbent kings to be shown in full regalia, including crowns, sceptres, gloves, swords and spurs. The effigy of *Eleanor* (*see* SARCOPHAGUS, fig. 4) shows no specific regalia other than her crown. In addition, she is shown holding a prayerbook rather than in the act of praying, and, unlike the two male figures, she is depicted as a living

Fontevrault Abbey, effigy of *Henry II, King of England,* limestone, *c.* 1200

person with eyes half closed. The details indicate that the images were part of a deliberate attempt to recreate the royal funeral ceremony introduced by the Plantagenets after their accession to the English throne. Thus, the effigy of *Henry II* closely follows the description of the royal burial by Benedict of Peterborough (*d* 1193). A specific association between royal consecration and burial was probably first established following the premature death in 1183 of the young Henry, the heir-apparent, since he was clothed for burial in the garments he had worn for his consecration.

The discovery of the fifth effigy, that of *Raymond VII of Toulouse*, adjacent to the north-west crossing pier, indirectly helps to locate the original royal tombs, as it explains the sculpted fragments and traces of painted heraldry found on the east face of the north-west crossing pier in 1910, as well as the sarcophagus containing the body of a count found by F. Lardier in 1638. Since it is known that Count Raymond was buried outside, but next to, the royal enclosure, the elaborate funerary crypt and chapel constructed for the Plantagenets must have occupied the north arm of the transept. Roger of Hoveden (*d* ?1201) stated that the burials were within the choir of the church, but the liturgical choir may well have included the transept arms. Certainly the report of Honorat Nicquet (stating that, before 1504, painted drapery forming the background of the image of the Virgin was seen against the big pier furthest from the altar on the north wall and perpendicular to the crossing pier) suggests that the royal tomb enclosure was placed in the north transept, whence the tombs had been displaced to the nave of the church in 1504. The only known images of the royal mausoleum date from after 1638, when a crypt for the burial of abbesses was excavated, and the royal tombs were reinstalled in the north transept. On the recommendation of experts, the four royal tombs were installed in 1992 in the eastern bay of the nave, even though the archaeological evidence leaves the precise original location in doubt.

BIBLIOGRAPHY

EARLY SOURCES

Benedict of Peterborough: *Chronicle of the Reigns of Henry II and Richard I* (1169–92; London, BL, Cotton MS. Julius A.xi); ed. W. Stubbs, Rolls Series, 49, ii (London, 1867), pp. 71–83

Roger of Hoveden: *Chronicles* (late 12th century; Oxford, Bodleian Lib., MS. Laud. 582); ed. W. Stubbs, Rolls Series, 51 (London, 1868–71), ii, p. 367

H. Nicquet: *Histoire de l'ordre de Font-Evraud* (Paris, 1642)

GENERAL

L. A. Bosseboeuf: *Fontevrault: Son histoire et ses monuments* (Tours, 1890), p. 71 [account by Lardier]

A. Erlande-Brandenburg: 'Le "Cimetière des rois" à Fontevrault', *Congr. Archéol. France*, cxxii (1964), pp. 482–92

T. S. R. Boase: 'Fontevrault and the Plantagenets', *J. Brit. Archaeol. Assoc.*, n.s. 2, xxxiv (1971), pp. 1–10

M. Mélot: *L'Abbaye de Fontevrault* (Paris, 1971)

A. Erlande-Brandenburg: 'La Sculpture funéraire vers les années 1200: Les Gisants de Fontevrault', *The Year 1200: A Symposium*, ed. J. Hoffeld, iii (New York, 1975), pp. 561–77

K. Bauch: *Das mittelalterliche Grabbild: Figürliche Grabmäler des 11. bis 15. Jahrhunderts in Europa* (Berlin and New York, 1976), pp. 54–6

J.-M. Bienvenu: 'Aliénor d'Aquitaine et Fontevraud', *Cah. Civilis. Méd.*, xxix (1986), pp. 15–27

Colloque international sur la figuration des morts dans la chrétienté médiévale jusqu'à la fin du premier quart du XIVe siècle: Fontevraud, 1988 [esp. articles by A. Erlande-Brandenburg, J.-R. Gaborit, M.-M. Gauthier and C. T. Woods]

A. Erlande-Brandenburg: 'La Mort du roi Henri II', *Bull. Soc. Amis Vieux Chinon*, ix (1989), pp. 125–33

C. de Maupeou: 'Présentation des gisants des Plantagenêts, abbaye de Fontevraud: l'Evolution de la présentation des gisants au XIXe et XXe siècle', *Monumental*, ii (1993), pp. 56–67

P. Prunet: 'Présentation des gisants des Plantagenêts, abbaye de Fontevraud: Etude préambule et projet', *Monumental*, ii (1993), pp. 51–55

WILLIAM W. CLARK

Font i Carreras, Augusto (*b* Barcelona, 1845; *d* Barcelona, 1924). Spanish Catalan architect, restorer and teacher. He studied at the Escuela Superior de Arquitectura in Madrid and then continued his preparation in Barcelona under Elías Rogent before becoming a professor in the city's newly created Escuela de Arquitectura (1871), teaching art history and design. With Rogent he specialized in the restoration of such great architectural ensembles as Tarragona Cathedral (1883), frequently using brick and generally adopting a historicist approach influenced by the rationalist theories of Viollet-le-Duc. Other noteworthy achievements include the reinforcement of the cupola of the basilica del Pilar in Saragossa and the construction of the *cimborio* of Barcelona Cathedral, in a perfect neo-Gothic style. Font i Carreras also built numerous mansions for the aristocracy and wealthy bourgeoisie of Catalonia and was responsible for the Palace of Fine Arts in the Exposició Universal (1888) in Barcelona. In the course of his successful career he also became an associate member of the Real Academia de Bellas Artes de S Fernando, Madrid, and in Barcelona was elected to membership of the Academia de S Jorge and the Academia de Ciencias y Artes; he was also President of the Asociacíon de Arquitectos de Cataluña and of the Comisión Provincial de Monumentos.

BIBLIOGRAPHY

B. Bassegoda: *Augusto Font y Carreras* (Barcelona, 1924)

P. Navascués and others: *Del neoclasicismo al modernismo* (Madrid, 1979)

A. Bonet and others: *La polémica ingenieros–arquitectos en España: Siglo XIX* (Madrid, 1985)

ALBERTO VILLAR MOVELLÁN

Fontpertuis, Vicomte de. *See* ANGRAN, LOUIS-AUGUSTE.

Fonvizin, Artur (Vladimirovich) (*b* Riga, 11 Jan 1883; *d* Moscow, 19 Aug 1973). Russian painter. The son of a German forester, he studied at the Moscow School of Painting, Sculpture and Architecture (1901–4) and private academies in Munich (1904–6). He took part in the Blue Rose exhibition (1907) and was a member of the Jack of Diamonds group and the Association of Artists of Revolutionary Russia (AKhRR). In 1922, 1924 and 1925 he exhibited with the Makovets group, which sought the rebirth of easel painting and developed a lyrical, expressionistic style. This was particularly important to Fonvizin's aesthetic, as was his contact with Mikhail Larionov, a friend from student days.

Fonvizin turned almost exclusively to watercolour at the end of the 1920s and became one of its most original exponents in 20th-century art. He employed extremely free, vibrant brushwork, sometimes with greatly diluted colour, and often made masterly use of tinted paper, creating a semi-fantastic world of quivering visions, centred around theatre and circus motifs. In his work the mirage-like free play of colour sometimes verges on abstraction. The majority of his series contain a large number of pictures, covering decades of work. Examples are the *Circus* series (1930s–1960s; Moscow, Tret'yakov Gal.; St Petersburg, Rus. Mus., and elsewhere), in which the dominant figure is a female rider emerging from the midst of magical effects of colour, and *Songs and Ballads* (1940–1950s; Moscow, Tret'yakov Gal., and elsewhere), based on motifs from old romantic songs. He produced large cycles of theatre portraits, which inextricably fuse the actor and the stage setting (e.g. *Actresses*, 1930s–1960s; Moscow, Tret'yakov Gal. and Bakhrushin Cent. Theat. Mus., and elsewhere). He often painted floral still-lifes and (predominantly in the 1960s) impressive Turneresque landscapes, and he was successful as an illustrator (e.g. for E. T. A. Hoffmann's *Klein Zaches* (1937; unpubd) and other works; sepia drawings, Moscow, Pushkin Mus. F.A.).

BIBLIOGRAPHY
G. Zagyanskaya: *A. V. Fonvizin* (Moscow, 1970)
A. V. Fonvizin, 1882–1973 (exh. cat., Moscow, Cent. House of Artists, 1984)

M. N. SOKOLOV

Foochou. *See* FUZHOU.

Footner, William (*b* London, 1799; *d* Montreal, 23 June 1872). Canadian architect of English birth. His background is unclear, but he was evidently trained in the Neo-classical style, probably in London, and emigrated to Canada in 1838. He settled in Sherbrooke, Quebec, where he completed his first major commission, the Court House (1841) in Sherbrooke, a Neo-classical brick building with a Doric portico. He subsequently moved to Montreal and appears in notarial records as an architect between September 1841 and February 1872. His masterpiece is the Bonsecours Market (1844–7), Rue des Commissaires, Montreal, a commission won by competition in 1842. Combining Greek Revival and Palladian styles, it was conceived as a multipurpose building to be used as a market, concert hall and offices of the city council. Its tin-covered dome crowns a long stone building, with central entrances and end wings. Facing the port, it has three storeys with a rusticated basement, hammer-dressed stone in the main part and channelled ashlar with radiating voussoirs at the wings. The city façade on Rue St-Paul is of two storeys, with a pediment over the entrance supported by six baseless cast-iron Doric columns. The dome is set on a high drum, with wood Ionic pilasters between arched windows. Few other buildings are attributed to him with any certainty.

BIBLIOGRAPHY
Macmillan Enc. Architects
N. Bosworth: *Hochelaga Depicta* (Montreal, 1839)
G. Pinard: *Montréal: Son histoire, son architecture*, 3 vols (Montreal, 1986–9)

DONNA MCGEE

Foppa, Cristoforo. *See* CARADOSSO.

Foppa, Vincenzo (*b* Bagnolo, nr Brescia, 1427–30; *d* Brescia, 1515–16). Italian painter and architect. He spent most of his painting career at Pavia, where he was patronized by the ruling Sforza family, the Dukes of Milan. Although many of his frescoes have been destroyed, his work in this medium prompted Filarete to name him among the greatest painters of his time, the only Lombard

to be so honoured. Foppa also worked at Genoa and Savona, but he spent most of his later years working at Brescia.

1. BEFORE 1480. He was the son of Giovanni Sandrino, a tailor from Bagnolo. Although it is not known where he trained, his early style has prompted suggestions that he may have visited Padua, Venice or Verona. In the *Virgin and Child with Angel Musicians* (Florence, I Tatti), probably his earliest work, the squat, compact figures of the angels appear alongside the more elegant, curvilinear figure of the Virgin, whose Gothic qualities may derive from the work of Stefano da Verona or Michelino da Besozzo. The silver-grey flesh tones remained characteristic of Foppa's painting throughout his career. However, in his first signed and dated work, the *Crucifixion* (1456; Bergamo, Accad. Carrara B.A.), such Gothic features have disappeared. The skilled use of perspective and the classical triumphal arch framing the scene are comparable to the work of Jacopo Bellini, Andrea Mantegna or Giovanni Donato da Montorfano. Other early works are the *Virgin and Child* (*c.* 1450; Milan, Castello Sforzesco), the *Dead Christ Supported by an Angel* (Milan, priv. col., see Torriti, p. 112) and the signed panel of *St Jerome* (Bergamo, Accad. Carrara B.A.). It has also been suggested, with less plausibility, that he may have provided cartoons for a series of stained-glass windows in Milan Cathedral, executed during the 1450s by Niccolò da Varallo (*b* 1420).

Foppa was in Pavia by 1458, having probably arrived there several years earlier. Although no record of his first works for the court at Pavia survive, he must have made a good impression. In June 1461, while he was working for the priors of Genoa Cathedral in the Cappella di S Giovanni Battista, the Milanese duke Francesco Sforza intervened on Foppa's behalf, asking the priors to treat him with greater respect. The chapel was left unfinished when Foppa returned to Pavia in 1462 and was completed by him only in 1471.

Most of Foppa's documented works of the 1460s, including a signed and dated altarpiece (1462) for the church of the Carmine in Pavia, are lost. Natale (1982) suggested that two panels of *St Paul* and *St Siro* (Minneapolis, MN, Inst. A.) may have come from this altarpiece. Foppa also executed frescoes of prophets (destr.) in the great cloister of the Certosa di Pavia and an altarpiece (untraced) for S Maria delle Grazie in Monza, commissioned by Galeazzo Maria Sforza in 1466.

In 1463 Francesco Sforza summoned Foppa to Milan with the promise of work. According to Filarete, Foppa frescoed the courtyard of the Medici Bank in Milan with the *Story of the Emperor Trajan*, along with portraits of Roman emperors and members of the Sforza family. Only a fragment of a *Young Boy Reading Cicero* (*c.* 1465; London, Wallace) survives from this fresco cycle. Two drawings of the *Justice of Trajan* (Berlin, Altes Mus.; Oxford, Ashmolean) have been tentatively associated with the project, but the Berlin drawing is pricked for direct transfer and it seems more likely that it was made for a small panel painting.

The fresco cycle of the *Life of St Peter Martyr* in the Portinari Chapel in S Eustorgio, Milan, was commissioned in the late 1460s by Pigello Portinari (*d* 1468), the representative of the Medici Bank in Milan. Despite the absence of documentation to confirm Foppa's hand in this work, the stylistic attribution is long-standing, and the connection between the artist and the patron is known to have been close. The frescoes demonstrate Foppa's ability to deal with perspective and architectural space on a large scale. The scene of *St Peter Martyr's Miracle at Narni* (see fig. 1) is set obliquely beneath a receding brick arch, with a miscellany of architectural motifs such as staircases, niches and crenellated walls behind the figures. The adjoining episode of the *Martyrdom of St Peter* takes place in an expansive landscape of forest, lake and mountains.

In 1467 Foppa asked Portinari for a letter of recommendation to Bianca Maria Sforza, Duchess of Milan, in order that he be accorded the rights and privileges of a citizen of Pavia and be permitted to buy property in the city. This was granted, and in 1468 he was made a member of the household of Galeazzo Maria Sforza, the new Duke of Milan. Despite this new status, he received little employment from the Duke before 1474. In 1469 he tried to obtain the commission to decorate the Camposanto in Pisa, but the task had already been assigned to Benozzo Gozzoli. By 1471 he was back in Genoa to complete the unfinished work in the cathedral, for which he received a further ten ducats.

Foppa probably returned to Brescia the following year, since a signed altarpiece dated 1472 was recorded by the 17th-century writer Bernardino Faini as having been in S Maria Maddalena in Brescia. He was back in Milan by July 1473, however, where he appraised the work of Stefano de Fedeli (*fl* 1472–81) in the ducal chapel of the Castello di Porta Giovia.

1. Vincenzo Foppa: *St Peter Martyr's Miracle at Narni* (*c.* 1468), fresco, Portinari Chapel, S Eustorgio, Milan

During the mid- to late 1470s Foppa worked in collaboration with the court artists Bonifacio Bembo and Zanetto Bugatto on several major projects in Pavia for Galeazzo Maria Sforza. In 1474 they agreed to provide an immense wooden altarpiece for the castle, which was to contain 200 holy relics and be decorated with appropriate images of saints. The work had to be halted after the Duke's murder in December 1476. It has been suggested that the panel of *SS Agnes and Catherine* (Baltimore, MD, Walters A.G.), in which the figures stand in a loggia-like architectural setting, may have formed part of this work. In 1476, at the request of the Pavian noblewoman Zaccarina Beccharia, the artists agreed to paint a rood screen (destr.) for the Franciscan church of S Giacomo fuori Pavia. The screen was to include 21 scenes from the life of Christ. Evidently there was a problem of integrating the artists' various styles, since the patron complained that the painters' work was not uniform.

Various devotional works have been dated to the second half of the 1470s. They include the half-length *Virgin and Child with an Apple* (Berlin, Gemäldegal.), the *Virgin and Child with a Book* (Milan, Castello Sforzesco), the *Virgin and Child* (Florence, I Tatti) and a signed *Adoration of the Christ Child* (ex-Fisher priv. col., Detroit; see Wittgens, pl. 68). The most impressive, however, is a polyptych (*c.* 1476; Milan, Brera), including the *Virgin and Child with Saints*, that was originally painted for the high altar in S Maria delle Grazie, Bergamo. It was dismantled in the 19th century and reconstructed, with incorrect additions, at the beginning of the 20th. In it, Foppa's style appears as a curious mixture: the old-fashioned gold ground behind the saints in the upper tier is replaced lower down by landscapes and innovative spatial and architectural designs, suggesting that while Foppa experimented with new styles, he was still willing to accommodate conservative Milanese tastes. Between 1477 and 1509 Foppa received payments for the decoration of the Averoldi Chapel in S Maria del Carmine, Brescia, for which he executed images of the *Evangelists* and the *Doctors of the Church*.

2. FROM 1480. During the early 1480s Foppa was working in Pavia. The Bottigella Altarpiece (Pavia, Pin. Malaspina), in which Silvestro Bottigella and his wife are shown kneeling before the enthroned Virgin, was probably executed before 1486. The continuing popularity of his traditional images of the Virgin and Child standing before a curtain or landscape is testified by the group of paintings of this subject dating from the 1480s (Milan, Mus. Poldi Pezzoli; New York, Met., see fig. 2; Philadelphia, PA, Johnson priv. col.; Florence, Uffizi). A detached fresco of the *Virgin and Child with SS John the Baptist and John the Evangelist* (Milan, Castello Sforzesco) from S Maria di Brera is dated 1485.

Also dating from this decade are various works representing St Sebastian, a subject perfectly suited to Foppa's ability to portray human anatomy. Among these are the detached fresco (Milan, Brera) from S Maria di Brera, Milan, and a wooden panel (Milan, Castello Sforzesco), in which the saint is shown in a contrapposto pose bound to an antique column, with the surrounding archers poised in such a way as to display a wide variety of musculature and movements. A small panel of *St Sebastian* (Florence,

2. Vincenzo Foppa: *Virgin and Child*, tempera and gold on panel, 438×324 mm, 1480s (New York, Metropolitan Museum of Art)

I Tatti), often attributed to Foppa, has been variously dated to the 1450s and the 1480s, although its colouring and hazily defined figures are uncharacteristic of Foppa's style.

Foppa had returned to Genoa by the end of the 1480s. In 1488 his associate Bertolino della Canonica was paid 15 lire on his behalf for figures of the martyrdom of St Sebastian for the altar of the Guild of St Sebastian, Genoa. In February 1489 Foppa was paid for an altarpiece (destr.) in the Doria Chapel in the Certosa di Rivarola outside Genoa. A surviving but ruined polyptych of the *Virgin and Child with Saints and a Donor* (Savona, Pin. Civ.) includes the name of the patron, Manfredi de Fornari, and the date 9 April 1489. The most important work produced during this stay in Liguria is the much damaged altarpiece for the oratory of S Maria di Castello, Savona (*in situ*), commissioned by Giuliano della Rovere (later Julius II) at a cost of 18,000 gold scudi. Although the three-tiered polyptych, which includes carved wooden figures in niches, was designed by Foppa in its entirety, he did not complete the work and had to be threatened with imprisonment before it was finally finished in August 1490. The figure of St John the Evangelist is signed by the local artist Louis Bréa.

In 1487 Foppa agreed to paint a chapel in S Piero in Gessate, Milan, for Ambrogio Griffi. The patron, an important member of the Sforza court, asked the Duke of

Milan, Ludovico Sforza (il Moro), to write to the authorities in Brescia and request that Foppa be persuaded to fulfil his contract. Despite this pressure, however, Foppa never even began work in the Griffi Chapel, which was eventually decorated by Bernardo Zenale and Bernardino Butinone.

Foppa seems to have decided to settle in Brescia permanently from 1489. In that year the city council granted him a yearly allowance of 100 lire on the condition that he would practise his art within the town. The agreement names him as an architect as well as a painter. In 1490 the grant was ratified, and Foppa was asked to fresco the newly built Loggetta in the main square of the town.

By May 1495, when the council decided to discontinue Foppa's salary, he may have already returned to Pavia. Documents from July 1497 to 1499 concern his work on an altarpiece (untraced) for S Maria Gualtieri, Pavia, in association with Giovanni Siro Cattaneo da Bermano (*fl* 1499–1506). Other paintings from this late period include the *Virgin and Child with SS Faustina and Giovita* (Brescia, Pin. Civ. Tosio-Martinengo), a portrait of *Francesco Brivio* (Milan, Mus. Poldi Pezzoli), the signed *Pietà* (ex-Kaiser-Friedrich Mus., Berlin, destr.), the *Adoration of the Magi* (London, N.G.), the *Annunciation* (Isola Bella, Mus. Borromeo) and *SS Bernardino and Anthony of Padua* (Washington, DC, N.G.A.). In the early 1500s Foppa was back in Brescia, and in 1514 he executed a double-sided banner (Brescia, Pin. Civ. Tosio-Martinengo) for the town of Orzinuovi outside Brescia. On one side is depicted the *Virgin and Child with SS Catherine and Bernardino* and on the other *SS Roch, Sebastian and George*.

BIBLIOGRAPHY

A. Filarete: *Tratatto di architettura* (1451–64); ed. A. M. Finoli and L. Grassi, 2 vols (Milan, 1972)

M. Caffi: 'Vincenzo Foppa da Brescia, pittore ed architetto', *Archv Stor. Lombardo*, v (1878), pp. 96–106

C. J. Ffoulkes and R. Maiocchi: *Vincenzo Foppa of Brescia, Founder of the Lombard School: His Life and Works* (London, 1909)

W. Suida: 'Studien zur lombardische Malerei des XV. Jahrhunderts', *Sonderabdruck aus den Monatsheften für Kunstwissenschaft* (Leipzig, 1909), pp. 477–783

——: 'Two Unknown Pictures by Vincenzo Foppa', *Burl. Mag.*, xlv (1924), pp. 210–11

R. Henniker-Heaton: 'An Unpublished Picture by Vincenzo Foppa', *A. Amer.*, xii (1925), pp. 196–9

A. Venturi: 'Anconetta di Vincenzo Foppa', *Arte*, xxxvii (1934), pp. 76–7

K. T. Parker: 'Vincenzo Foppa', *Old Master Drgs*, xiii (1938), pp. 6–8

F. Wittgens: *Vincenzo Foppa* (Milan, 1949)

E. K. Waterhouse: 'The Fresco by Vincenzo Foppa in the Wallace Collection', *Burl. Mag.*, xcii (1950), p. 177

S. Bottari: 'Una tavola di Vincenzo Foppa', *Commentari*, ii (1951), pp. 201–2

E. Sandberg-Vavalà: 'Vincenzo Foppa', *Burl. Mag.*, xciii (1951), pp. 134–5

C. Ragghianti: 'Il Foppa e le vetrerie del duomo di Milano', *Crit. A.*, vi (1954), pp. 520–43

——: 'Postilla foppesca', *Crit. A.*, ix (1955), pp. 285–92

P. Rotondi: *Vincenzo Foppa in Santa Maria di Castello a Savona* (Genoa, 1958)

E. Arslan: 'Vincenzo Foppa', *Storia di Brescia* (Brescia, 1963), ii, pp. 929–48

R. Cipriani, G. A. dell'Aqua and F. Russoli: *La Cappella Portinari in S Eustorgio a Milano* (Milan, 1963)

P. Torriti: 'Contributo a Vincenzo Foppa', *A. Lombarda*, viii (1963), pp. 112–13

S. Matalon: *Vincenzo Foppa* (Milan, 1965)

M. Delai Emiliani: 'Per la prospettiva "padana": Foppa revisitato', *A. Lombarda*, xvi (1971), pp. 117–36
G. Frangi: *Foppa: Lo stendardo di Orzinuovi* (Brescia, 1977)
J. Gitlin Bernstein: 'Science and Eschatology in the Portinari Chapel', *A. Lombarda*, n. s., xxvi/60 (1981), pp. 33–40
M. Natale: 'Vincenzo Foppa: San Siro; San Paolo', *Zenale e Leonardo: Tradizione e rinnovamento della pittura lombarda* (exh. cat., Milan, Mus. Poldi Pezzoli, 1982), pp. 90–93
A. Nova: 'I tramezzi in Lombardia fra XV e XVI secolo: Scene della Passione e devozione francescana', *Il francescanesimo in Lombardia: Storia e arte* (Milan, 1983), pp. 197–215
G. Scotti: 'Alcune ipotesi di lettura per gli affreschi della Cappella Portinari alla luce degli scritti di S Antonino vescovo di Firenze', *A. Lombarda*, n. s., xxviii/64 (1983), pp. 65–78
E. Samuels Welch: 'New Documents for Vincenzo Foppa', *Burl. Mag.*, cxxvii (1985), pp. 296–300
M. Gregori and others: *Pittura del cinquecento a Brescia* (Milan, 1986)
E. SAMUELS WELCH

Foppes van Essen, Jacob van. *See* ES, JACOB VAN.

Fora, del. Italian family of artists. The sculptor Giovanni (or Nanni) Miniato (1398–1479), a collaborator of Donatello, had three sons who were active in Florence as artists: Bartolomeo di Giovanni (di Miniato) del Fora (1442–94), (1) Gherardo di Giovanni (di Miniato) del Fora and (2) Monte di Giovanni (di Miniato) del Fora. The three brothers maintained a book workshop together from 1465 and continued to work together until 1476, when Bartolomeo left, seemingly for financial reasons. Since Gherardo and Monte often collaborated, their work is sometimes difficult to distinguish with complete confidence. Both were familiar with contemporary painting, but they had different interests. Gherardo was sensitive to an ordered arrangement of figures in space; he preferred his portraits to be inscrutable, and he liked to reproduce contemporary Florentine architecture faithfully. Monte's urban views, by comparison, were more imaginative and his portraits more expressive.

BIBLIOGRAPHY
G. Vasari: *Vite* (1550, rev. 2/1568); ed. G. Milanesi (1878–85)
E. Muntz: *La Bibliothèque de Mathias Corvin* (Paris, 1899)
P. d'Ancona: *La miniatura fiorentina dall'XI al XVI secolo*, 2 vols (Florence, 1914)
G. S. Martini: 'La bottega di un cartolaio fiorentino nella seconda metà del '400', *La Bibliofilia*, lviii (1956), supplement, pp. 5–82
M. Levi d'Ancona: *Miniatura e miniatori a Firenze dal XIV al XVI secolo* (Florence, 1962)
A. Garzelli: *La Bibbia di Federico da Montefeltro: Un'officina libraria fiorentina, 1477–1478* (Rome, 1977)
——: 'Arte del *Libro d'Ore* e committenza medicea, 1485–1536', *Atti del i congresso nazionale di storia dell'arte: Roma, 1978*, pp. 475–99
——: 'Sulla fortuna del Gerolamo mediceo del van Eyck nell'arte fiorentina del quattrocento', *Studi in onore di Roberto Salvini* (Florence, 1984), pp. 347–53
——: *Miniature fiorentine del rinascimento: Un primo censimento*, i–ii (Florence, 1985)
All'ombra del lauro: Documenti librari della cultura in età laurenziana (exh. cat., ed. A. Lenzuni; Florence, Bib. Medicea-Laurenziana, 1992)
Maestri e botteghe: Pittura a Firenze alla fine del quattrocento (exh. cat., Florence, Pal. Strozzi, 1993), pp. 106–8

(1) Gherardo di Giovanni (di Miniato) del Fora (*b* Florence, 1445; *d* Florence, 1497). Illuminator and painter. He was active from the early 1460s as an illuminator and also painted panels and frescoes; his large-scale work can be attributed only through a systematic analysis of the illumination that has been assigned to him by scholars in the 20th century. With his brothers he maintained a workshop (see Martini, 1956), from which the principal

religious and secular institutions of Florence commissioned illustrated books. Gherardo lived for many years as a lay brother in S Marco; he had literary and musical interests and frequented the bottegas of the most prestigious painters, from Bartolomeo della Gatta to Leonardo da Vinci. The salient characteristics of Gherardo's work in manuscripts, and sometimes in printed books, include the introduction of the Antique; an interest in portraiture and the peculiarities of architecture and landscape; the study of colour and light; the early introduction of Netherlandish elements in landscapes; and innovations in the layout of the page. He also introduced an unusual type of border, elegantly decorated *all'antica* with cameos, grotesques, mythological figures and candelabra drawn from engravings and sculpture. Other sculptural motifs include the tondo, reminiscent of Donatello, and the festoons with fruit and flowers in the style of the della Robbia family.

In works in which Gherardo collaborated with his brother (2) Monte di Giovanni del Fora, there is often a problem of identification, as in the refined iconography of the Bible (1488; Florence, Bib. Medicea-Laurenziana, MS. Plut. 17.15) illuminated for Matthias Corvinus. Gherardo's style is defined on the basis of the *Death of St Peter Martyr* (fol. 127) in the manuscript (Florence, Bargello, MS. 68) made for the hospital of S Maria Nuova, for which he was paid on 3 March 1477. Gherardo's background landscapes contain echoes of Netherlandish painting, with new uses of light and colour that often reflected ideas introduced by Leonardo. Among Gherardo's works in printed books, the most important is the copy of Pliny's *Natural History* (Oxford, Bodleian Lib., MS. Douce 310), illuminated for Filippo Strozzi and containing three important portraits of *King Ferdinand II*, a *Man with his Son* (in the incipit of the preface) and *Cristoforo Landino* (in the proem). In the borders are such mythological scenes as the *Triumph of Bacchus, Bacchus and Ariadne on Naxos, Mercury* and *Putti*. In Livy's *History of Rome* XXI–XXX (*c.* 1479; U. Valencia, Bib., MS. 763) are more representations of Bacchus and, on the frontispiece, two splendid studies of candelabra with Classical masks and festoons. In the *Works of Homer* (printed 1488; Naples, Bib. N., SQ XXIII K 22), folio 244 is decorated with cameos; while the firm lines and clear transition from light to dark in the full-page *Portrait of a Young Man* (fol. 2*v*) reveal a sympathetic interest in the style of Piero della Francesca. The last phase of Gherardo's taste for the Antique is represented in the extraordinary copy of Petrarch's *Trionfi* (Baltimore, MD, Walters A.G., MS. W.755), where the scenes are enclosed by forms that suggest worked gold. Particularly striking is the *Triumph of Death*, with an image of *Laura on her Deathbed with Bystanders* (fol. 30) in an architectural setting decorated with Classical low reliefs. A copy of Aratus' *Phaenomena* (Florence, Bib. Medicea-Laurenziana, MS. 89 sup. 43) contains depictions of themes closely linked with the text, prompting comparison with the painting of the *Combat of Love and Chastity* (London, N.G.).

Gherardo's large-format religious projects were undertaken for Florentine churches and convents. In a group of choir-books (Florence, S Lorenzo) Gherardo executed some of the miniatures: the large *Martyrdom of St Lawrence* (corale K, fol. 45), with its images of Castel S Angelo and the Torre delle Milizie, is notable. The exquisite arrangement of groups of bystanders and the background views of Florence, Pisa and Rome demonstrate Gherardo's skills. More of his religious miniatures are found in a Franciscan Breviary (London, BL, Add. MS. 29735), where the *Adoration of the Magi* (fol. 28*v*) and the *Invention of the True Cross* (fol. 127) are treated like sketches for a large painting. Another large work, produced with Monte, is the Missal for S Maria del Fiore (*c.* 1494), in which Gherardo depicted elaborate mythological figures in the borders of folio 8. One of his last large-format illustrations is the incipit page of Nicholas of Lyra's *Postilla* (1494–6; 7 vols; Lisbon, Arquiv. N.), commissioned by Manuel I of Portugal: here again, in *Pope Damasus I Receiving the Vulgate from St Jerome*, a Classical atmosphere is evoked by the image of the Colosseum. The sketchy style of the miniature recalls Gherardo's fresco of *Pope Martin V Conferring Privileges on the Hospital of S Maria Nuova* (1474; Florence, S Egidio).

Among the many Books of Hours to which Gherardo contributed, a notable example is the Book of Hours (Munich, Bayer. Staatsbib., Clm. 23639) commissioned by Lorenzo de' Medici. Its production was organized by Gherardo, who painted the most important scenes (other contributors included Francesco Rosselli and Giovanni Boccardi). Gherardo executed the *Deposition*, the *Raising of Lazarus* and *David Praying* in a painterly manner; this is the highest-quality manuscript of those he painted for Lorenzo de' Medici. The Psalter (Cambridge, Fitzwilliam, Add. MS. 37–1970), commissioned by another member of the Medici family, is outstanding for the elegantly coloured pages and the candelabra. In their compositional innovations and their renderings of architecture and landscape, these small masterpieces recall the very greatest masters of Renaissance painting.

BIBLIOGRAPHY

F. Zeri: 'I frammenti di un celebre *Trionfi della Castità*', *Diari di lavoro*, i (Bergamo, 1971), pp. 56–65
G. Bologna: *Miniature italiane della Biblioteca Trivulziana* (Milan, 1974)

(2) Monte di Giovanni (di Miniato) del Fora (*b* Florence, 1448; *d* between 3 Nov 1532 and 6 March 1533). Illuminator, painter and mosaicist, brother of (1) Gherardo di Giovanni del Fora. His extensive activity as a painter, mainly on panel, has yet to be reconstructed. A mosaic portrait of *St Zenobius* (1504; Florence, Mus. Opera Duomo) demonstrates his ability as a mosaicist; this is also mentioned in documents. His career began during the 1460s in a book workshop, collaborating with his two brothers. In Florence, Monte received commissions from the most prestigious religious orders (the cathedral, S Giovanni, the canons of S Lorenzo, the convents of S Marco and SS Annunziata, the Ospedale degli Innocenti, the Arcispedale di S Maria Nuova) and the most eminent families (the Medici, the Strozzi and Camillo Maria Vitelli); outside Florence he produced miniatures of high quality and great originality for the Primacy of Pisa and Aosta Cathedral and for the greatest European sovereigns, including Manuel I of Portugal and the King of Hungary, Matthias Corvinus. The influence of many painters can be seen in Monte's miniatures. From the late works of Fra Filippo Lippi, who introduced him to the study of drapery,

he learnt the use of hatching and a certain softness in the application of paint. From contemporary Netherlandish art he learnt such compositional solutions as the device of a picture within a picture. In his range of Classical and mythological themes, grotesques, cameos and themes from literary works on antique subjects, he was a precursor of Filippino Lippi. Among the most important features of Monte's work are the vast range of learned iconographic references, both religious and secular, and the innovative incorporation of references to the patron of the work. In short, Monte's illumination is characterized by its exuberant imagery, rich invention, sophisticated intellectual play and extremely versatile brushwork.

With Gherardo he illuminated the Missal of S Egidio (Florence, Bargello, MS. 67) for S Maria Nuova. This manuscript has been dated (Levi d'Ancona, 1962) to 1474–6, although this date is not without problems. The *Annunciation* (fol. 5*r*; partly by Gherardo) and the *Lamentation* (fol. 150*v*) are rich in innovations: studies of drapery and anatomy, a new use of colour and complex, imaginative Classical landscapes and urban vistas; in the borders are tondi with monochrome low reliefs recalling the work of Donatello. Among the manuscripts that Monte and Gherardo illuminated for Matthias Corvinus is a large Bible (Florence, Bib. Medicea-Laurenziana, MS. Plut. 15.17). The opening miniature (fol. 2*v*) shows *David Praying*, with related episodes including *Young David Gathering Stones from the Stream*, in which the image of David is reflected in the water like that of Narcissus gazing at his reflection. There are also portraits of three sovereigns, *Matthias Corvinus*, *Charles VIII* and an unidentified king. On the facing folio is a *Battle between Jews and Philistines* (fol. 3*r*). The borders of both pages are rich in iconographic details alluding to Matthias and in Classical references. Monte also dedicated a work by Didymus (the *Liber de spiritu sancto*, 1488; New York, Pierpont Morgan Lib., MS. 496) to Matthias Corvinus. The composition, including a portrait of *Matthias Corvinus and his Wife* (fol. 2*r*), is conceived as a great altar decorated with Classical low reliefs (e.g. *Apollo at the Castalia Spring* and *Apollo and Marsyas*) and other symbols of military, artistic and civic virtues referring to the King.

In 1496 Camillo Maria Vitelli commissioned the copy of Ptolemy's *Cosmographia* (Florence, Bib. N. Cent., MS. XIII.16), which has borders packed with Classical armoury, cameos and motifs partly taken from the ceiling of the Domus Aurea, Rome, extolling the military virtues of the client. A significant example of a type of coloured page introduced by Monte is found in the collection of musical texts by various authors (Florence, Bib. N. Cent., MS. Banco Rari 229), with a portrait of the musician *Johannes Martini* against a ruby-red background. In a copy of Nicholas of Lyra's *Postilla* (1494–6; Lisbon, Arquiv. N.), made for Manuel I of Portugal, Monte represented large architectural–sculptural structures, a large aedicula with portraits of *Matthias Corvinus*, wearing spectacles, and *Charles VIII of France*. Monochrome paintings with Classical subjects in the borders and elements derived from the Domus Aurea, are interspersed with religious subjects. Nicolò Valori's *Life of Lorenzo* (Florence, Bib. Medicea-Laurenziana, MS. Plut. 61.3) was illuminated for Lorenzo de' Medici; it includes a *View of Florence* and a tiny portrait of *Lorenzo* in the right border of the incipit page.

Florence Cathedral and S Giovanni were among Monte's ecclesiastical clients. His finest works include a Missal (Florence, Bib. Medicea-Laurenziana, MS. Edili 109), which Zanobi Moschini finished writing in 1493, in which Monte and Gherardo produced the miniature of the *Crucifixion with the Virgin and St John the Baptist* and a predella with the *Lamentation*; both these works show strong links with Jan van Eyck. The group of works produced in collaboration with Gherardo during the 1490s includes a manuscript (Florence, Bib. Medicea-Laurenziana, MS. Edili 109) written in 1493 and illuminated in 1494, in which the *Annunciation* (fol. 8) repeats the scheme of Monte's panel painting (Modena, Mus. Stor. & A. Med. & Mod.) on the same subject but with greater articulation of the spatial setting.

Documents reveal that from the 1490s to the end of his long career, Monte worked on a series of choir-books (damaged 1966; Florence, Mus. Opera Duomo). The enormous historiated initials include religious scenes and vigorous portraits. Here, Monte's mature style is characterized by a persistent interest in Netherlandish formulae and a growing attraction to the monumental compositions of Domenico Ghirlandaio. The sumptuous Missal (Rome, Vatican, Bib. Apostolica, Barb. Lat. 610) for the Baptistery of Florence was illuminated in 1510. Its pages (380×270 mm) contain a *St John the Baptist Enthroned*, above a *Dance of Salome*. Of great interest for its use of a picture within a picture is the *Last Supper* (fol. 185). Among the miniatures executed for Florence Cathedral (all Florence, Mus. Opera Duomo) in the first quarter of the 16th century are the *Adam and Eve in the Garden of Eden* (MS. D, fol. 2*v*), the *Baptism*, with portraits of contemporaries (MS. C 11, fol. 4), the *Annunciation* (MS. S, fol. 54), the *Nativity* (MS. S, fol. 114) and the *Marriage at Cana* (MS. C, fol. 71), with a view of Piazza S Marco, Florence, at sunset. Both with and without Gherardo, Monte illustrated Books of Hours for important weddings, in which he introduced structural and thematic ideas previously unknown in the repertories of other illuminators.

BIBLIOGRAPHY
A. Garzelli: 'Codici miniati della Biblioteca Laurenziana', *Crit. A.* (1975), 143, pp. 19–38; 144, pp. 25–40
——: 'Rogier van der Weyden, Hugo van der Goes, Filippo Lippi nella pagina di Monte', *Scritti in memoria di Mario Rotili* (Naples, 1984)
ANNAROSA GARZELLI

Forabosco, Girolamo (*b* Venice, 1605; *d* Padua, 23 Jan 1679). Italian painter. He was active in Padua and Venice, where he was enrolled in the Fraglia dei Pittori between 1634 and 1639 and paid taxes from 1640 to 1644. His early work, such as the portrait of the so-called *Menichina* (1624; Rome, Pal. Barberini), was influenced by that of Alessandro Varotari (Padovanino), who had revived the style of Titian. He also adopted compositional and formal schemes from Tiberio Tinelli, as in the *Portrait of a Woman* (Venice, Zattera priv. col., see Pallucchini, fig. 543). The large canvas of the *Miraculous Rescue* (1646; Malamocco, S Maria Assunta), commissioned by Giovanni Ventura as an ex-voto for his escape from a shipwreck, shows

Forabosco, unconstrained by the narrative and devotional character premises of the undertaking, creating a tender portrait group, distinguished by its spontaneity. The most striking quality of his work is its combination of physiognomic exactitude with free, fluid brushwork.

Several religious paintings date from between 1654 and 1660, such as the *Ecstasy of St Francis* and *St Magnus the Bishop Presenting the Model of the Church of St Zachariah* (both Venice, S Nicolò dei Tolentini). Portraits of this period include those of the *Doge Carlo Contarini* and his wife *Paolina Loredano* (1655–6; Venice, Brogliato-Bentivoglio priv. col., see Pallucchini, figs 546–7) and the portrait of a presumed *Courtesan* (Vienna, Ksthist. Mus.), painted either before 1659 or in 1662, the finest example of a remarkable group of similar female portraits.

Count Jan Humprecht Czernin von Chudenitz (*see* CZERNIN, (1)), Imperial Ambassador to Venice (1660–63), commissioned numerous works from Forabosco, among them *Joseph and Potiphar's Wife* (perhaps the one now in Rovigo, Accad. Concordi) and perhaps also *Angelica and Medoro* (Rome, priv. col., see Pallucchini, pl. xiv), which reveals a debt to Pietro della Vecchia. In his last 20 years Forabosco's bold brushwork gradually yielded to a more finished style, influenced by Emilian painters such as Reni, Albani and, especially, Guido Cagnacci, who was active in Venice *c.* 1650. To this period can be dated the *St Ursula* (New York, O'Connor Lynch priv. col.) and the *Allegory of Fame* (Rome, priv. col., see Safarik, fig. 14). Forabosco was considered one of the greatest Venetian painters of his time by Boschini but was later forgotten.

BIBLIOGRAPHY
M. Boschini: *La carta del navegar pitoresco* (Venice, 1660); ed. A. Pallucchini (Venice and Rome, 1966), pp. 541–4
E. A. Safarik: 'Per la pittura veneta del seicento: Girolamo Forabosco', *A. Illus.*, vi (1973), pp. 353–63
R. Pallucchini: *La pittura veneziana del seicento* (Milan, 1981), i, pp. 180–85; ii, figs 540–60
G. Vio: 'Per la datazione del "telero" del Forabosco a Malamocco', *A. Ven.*, xxxviii (1984), pp. 202–3
E. A. SAFARIK

Forain, Jean-Louis (*b* Reims, 23 Oct 1852; *d* Paris, 11 July 1931). French painter, printmaker and illustrator. Around 1860 he moved with his family to Paris, where he was taught by Jacquesson de la Chevreuse (1839–1903), Jean Baptiste Carpeaux and André Gill. He participated in the Franco-Prussian War (1870–71) and was a friend of the poets Paul Verlaine and Arthur Rimbaud; the latter is the presumed subject of a portrait (1874; priv. col., see 1982 exh. cat., no. 1) that may have influenced Manet's late portrait of *Mallarmé* (1876; Paris, Louvre). Forain first met Manet through his friendship with Degas in the early 1870s at the salon of Nina de Callias. He continued to associate with Manet, meeting the group of young Impressionists at the Café Guerbois and the Café de la Nouvelle Athènes. In 1878 Forain painted a small gouache, *Café Scene* (New York, Brooklyn Mus.), which probably influenced Manet's *Bar at the Folies-Bergère* (1881–2; London, Courtauld Inst. Gals).

In 1879 Forain was invited by Degas to join the fourth Impressionist exhibition, and he exhibited again with the Impressionists in the fifth (1880), sixth (1881) and eighth

Jean-Louis Forain: *Fisherman*, oil on canvas, 965×990 mm, 1884 (Southampton, City Art Gallery)

(1886) exhibitions, receiving favourable reviews from Huysmans, Félix Fénéon and Diego Martelli. He lightened his palette and employed the Impressionist methods of short brushstrokes and complementary colour juxtapositions to create some luminous *plein-air* paintings such as the *Race-track* (1884–5; Springfield, MA, Mus. F.A.) and the *Fisherman* (1884; Southampton, C.A.G.; see fig.). As Huysmans pointed out, one of Forain's most successful subjects was the Parisian woman, who appeared in many guises in the works of his Impressionist period (*c.* 1879–1900). Like Degas, who was his best friend and the greatest influence on him, Forain depicted scenes backstage at the Opéra and at the race-track as well as nudes in naturalistic interiors, often drawing from the same model with Degas. Unlike Degas, Forain exhibited at the Salon des Artistes Français, showing the *Buffet* (Paris, Féd. Mutualiste) in 1884 and the *Widower* (Paris, Louvre) in 1885. Both have more formal compositions, and the figures are solidly delineated, but they also demonstrate Forain's Impressionist principles in the low viewpoint and diagonal composition influenced by Japanese woodcuts, the freely brushed surfaces and the interest in the effects of light.

Forain's career as an illustrator began in 1876 when his first published drawing appeared on the cover of *Le Scapin*. He worked regularly for the *Courrier français* from 1887 and drew albums for *Le Figaro* in 1891: he worked on *Le Figaro* intermittently for the next 35 years. His drawings for the *Courrier français* made him famous, his captions so witty and biting that they were described as written in vitriol, and he was known as the 'Juvénal du *Figaro*'.

Forain began printmaking in the mid-1870s. In his first etching period (1875–90) his subjects were backstage views, café-concerts and the Folies-Bergère. He also etched illustrations to Huysmans's *Marthe* (1876) and *Croquis parisiens* (1880). In 1890 he took up lithography

with scenes of Parisian life, often several versions of the same subject, such as his six plates of the *Private Room*. He also created some memorable portraits in this medium such as the elegant *Colette Willy*, four brilliant portraits of *Renoir* and two of *Ambroise Vollard*. He resumed etching in 1902 but changed his subject-matter to concentrate on religious and courtroom subjects of great drama and deep feeling, expressed with bravura technique.

After 1900 Forain's painting style also underwent a change, both in technique and subject-matter. The latter change was the result of Forain's experience of the Dreyfus trials, which also prompted him to co-found, with CARAN D'ACHE, the weekly satirical journal *Psst!*, and his renewal of Christian faith in the company of his old friend Huysmans in 1900 at Ligugé: he began to paint biblical and law-court scenes and, in 1915, pictures inspired by World War I. The colours of his work became sombre, reflecting the expressive qualities of this new subject-matter. Among his most moving religious representations are the oil painting the *Prodigal Son* (1909; Boston, MA, Pub. Lib.) and the series of etchings on the same subject. Forain presented this as a contemporary drama of reconciliation, with the figures shown in contemporary dress and attitudes, rather than as a historical biblical scene. Forain's law-court scenes contrast the vulnerability of the defendant with the bored indifference or histrionic gestures of the lawyers, as in *Unwed Mother* ('Fille-mère', 1909; Bristol, Mus. & A.G.). His paintings were championed in 1910 by Octave Maus, resulting in a retrospective of over 400 works at the Musée des Arts Décoratifs, Paris, which revealed the scope of Forain's oeuvre and established him as a major artist.

In February 1915, aged 62, Forain joined the camouflage corps and later became a correspondent for *Le Figaro*, covering all phases of World War I with biting, satirical images of the futility of war. His palette later brightened and his figures became more fluidly rendered and less solid. Although continuing with religious and legal subjects, he returned to the theme of the dance in the oils *Tango* (1925; priv. col., see 1978 exh. cat., no. 58) and *Charleston* (1926; Washington, DC, N.G.A.) and the gouache *Cabaret* (1926; Boston, MA, Pub. Lib.), all virtuoso paintings conveying the jazz rhythms of the speak-easy.

Forain ended his career as President of the Société Nationale des Beaux-Arts, member of the Académie Française and Commandant de la Légion d'honneur. His work was admired by Degas, Manet and Cézanne, and a generation of social realists was influenced by his biting pictorial condemnations of injustice, greed, lust, stupidity and the horrors of war.

BIBLIOGRAPHY

J.-K. Huysmans: *L'Art moderne* (Paris, 1883)
M. Lehrs: 'Forain', *Graph. Kst*, xxxiv (1911), pp. 9–28
M. Guerin: J.-L. Forain: *Lithographe* (Paris, 1912) [cat. rais.]
H. Ghéon: 'Jean-Louis Forain', *A. & Déc.*, xxxiii (1913), pp. 1–12
G. Geffroy: 'Forain', *A. & Artistes*, xxi (1921), pp. 49–78
O. Maus: *Trente années de lutte pour l'art, 1884–1914* (Brussels, 1926)
C. Kunstler: *Forain* (Paris, 1931)
L. Vaillat: *En écoutant Forain* (Paris, 1931)
J. Sloane: 'Religious Influences on the Art of Jean-Louis Forain', *A. Bull.*, xxxiii (1941), pp. 199–207
J.-L. Forain: Peintre, dessinateur et graveur (exh. cat., Paris, Bib. N., 1952)
Forain (exh. cat., Williamstown, Clark A. Inst., 1963)

L. Browse: *Forain the Painter* (London, 1978)
Jean-Louis Forain, 1852–1931 (exh. cat., ed. J. Chagnaud-Forain, Y. Brayer and C. Richébé; Paris, Mus. Marmottan, 1978)
J. Bory: *Forain* (Paris, 1979)
Jean-Louis Forain, 1852–1931: Works from New England Collections (exh. cat., ed. A. Faxon; Framingham, Danforth Mus. A., 1979)
A. Faxon: *Jean-Louis Forain: A Catalog Raisonné of the Prints* (New York, 1982)
Jean-Louis Forain: Artist, Realist, Humorist (exh. cat., ed. A. Faxon; Washington, DC, Int. Exh. Found. 1982)

ALICIA CRAIG FAXON

Forbát [Füchsl], Fred [Alfréd] (*b* Pécs, 31 March 1897; *d* Stockholm, 23 May 1972). Architect, urban planner and teacher, of Hungarian birth, active in Germany. He studied at the Hungarian Imperial Joseph Technical University, Budapest, from 1914, and from 1918 at the Technische Hochschule, Munich, where he studied urban planning under Theodor Fischer. In 1920–22 he was employed in Weimar in Walter Gropius's office at the Bauhaus. There he designed the Bauhaussiedlung am Horn plan, which was shown in the Bauhaus exhibition (1923), as well as a three-storey studio building and a model house of standardized cast concrete elements that could be enlarged or reduced as required. All these designs reflected the rationalist spirit of the Bauhaus, with simple, geometric façades, flat roofs and functional emphasis. The influence of the De Stijl movement was also apparent in projecting corbels, consoles and strips. In 1923 Forbát founded the short-lived Neue Reklame Gestaltung enterprise with the Hungarian painter Sándor Bortnyik, then in 1924–5 he led a League of Nations housing project for Turkish refugees in Thessalonika.

In 1925 Forbát settled in Berlin, where he completed the Autohof am Botanischen Garten car park (1925), Lichterfelde, Berlin, a circular, windowless building with a stuccoed façade divided by red-brick pilasters that stood out spectacularly from the surrounding houses. After he had taken German citizenship in 1928, he opened his own design office in Berlin and concentrated on the development of low-cost housing. He was voted on to the committee, led by Bruno Taut, that advised the city on housing construction projects. In 1929–31 he participated with Gropius, Otto Bartning, Hugo Häring and Paul Rudolf Henning in Hans Scharoun's extensive housing development, Siemensstadt, in Charlottenburg, Berlin. Forbát's contribution comprised three blocks of flats on the eastern side of the site: Block 7 (1929) is strictly vertical, with five forcefully projecting stairwells; Block 6 (1930–31) has continuous loggias facing a large, internal grassed area, and a plain streetfront; while Block 6a (1930–31) is notable for the two different sizes of flats, 48 and 70 sq. m. Forbát's Mommsen Stadium (1929–30), in Eichamp, Berlin, has an elegant steel structure with curved stairs at each end of the stand. On the entrance façade the white-stuccoed horizontal bands contrast with the glazed stairwells and brick pilasters. In 1930 Forbát held an urban planning seminar at Johannes Itten's private school in Berlin. He also took part in the construction of the Haselhorst housing estate (1930–31) in Spandau, Berlin, for which Gropius had won the architectural competition in 1928. This was transformed by Forbát, under the increasingly poor economic conditions of the time, into a series of four-storey blocks, orientated east–west and

containing small one- to two-roomed flats of between 37 and 57 sq. m.

Forbát was active in the CIAM congress (1929) in Frankfurt am Main and subsequently became a member of the Hungarian branch of CIAM. Apart from the architectural problems of establishing uniformly well-orientated, healthy and economical housing, he was also concerned with socio-economic conditions. In the hope of realizing some of his progressive architectural ideas he spent 1932 in the USSR with Ernst May's group and helped plan the towns of Karaganda and Magnitogorsk. In 1933 he returned to Hungary, where he built a summer house (1936) on Mecsek Hill, Pécs, the lower walls of local stone, the upper part of reinforced concrete with a white-stuccoed façade. Another house (1936), Kölcsey Street, Pécs, also departs from the strict functionalist line, with its raw brick façade and forcefully projecting flat roof on the south side acting as a sun screen.

In 1938, being Jewish, Forbát was forced to emigrate. He settled in Lund, Sweden, where at first he worked (1938–42) with Sune Lindström (1906–89) on the design for the national housing estate network. Thereafter he concentrated on urban planning, producing a number of city plans including the general developmental plan for Landskrona (1945–50; with Harry Egler). In 1959–60 he was a professor of urban planning at the Technical University, Stockholm.

UNPUBLISHED SOURCES
Stockholm, Arkitmus. [memoirs, in Ger.]

WRITINGS
Byggnadslagen i Sverige [Building regulations in Sweden] (Munich and Berlin, 1957)

BIBLIOGRAPHY
Fred Forbát: Architekt und Stadtplaner (exh. cat., Darmstadt, Bauhaus-Samml., 1969)
N. Pámer: *Magyar építészet a két világháboru között* [Hungarian architecture between the two World Wars] (Budapest, 1986)
Wechselwirkungen (exh. cat., ed. H. Gassner; Kassel, Neue Gal., 1986)

ÁKOS MORAVÁNSZKY, KATALIN MORAVÁNSZKY-GYÖNGY

Forbes. English painters. (1) Stanhope Forbes and his Canadian-born wife, (2) Elizabeth Stanhope Forbes, were both closely linked with the NEWLYN SCHOOL. In 1899, ten years after their marriage, they founded the Newlyn Art School (closed 1938), situated in a small gallery by the sea in Newlyn.

(1) Stanhope (Alexander) Forbes (*b* Dublin, 18 Nov 1857; *d* Newlyn, Cornwall, 2 March 1947). He studied in London at the Lambeth School of Art (1874–6) and then at the Royal Academy Schools (1876–8). After this he studied under Léon Bonnat in Paris for two years and was much influenced by the rustic Realism of Jean-François Millet and Jules Bastien-Lepage. His early pictures, which he began to exhibit at the Royal Academy in 1878, are strongly French in style and are mostly scenes of peasant life in the Bastien-Lepage idiom. In 1881 he painted in Brittany with his friend Henry Herbert La Thangue, and in 1884 he and a group of artist friends 'discovered' the Cornish fishing village of Newlyn. Forbes settled there for the rest of his life, and he is generally regarded as the 'father' of the Newlyn school, although he was not the first to discover the village. In 1885 he exhibited *Fish Sale*

Stanhope Forbes: *Fish Sale on a Cornish Beach*, oil on canvas, 1.21×1.55 m, 1885 (Plymouth, City Museum and Art Gallery)

on a Cornish Beach (1885; Plymouth, City Mus. & A.G.; see fig.) at the Royal Academy. The picture was much admired and helped to arouse critical interest in the Newlyn group of painters. Forbes was also one of the founder-members of the New English Art Club in 1886. For a time he exhibited there but later turned against it, mainly because of his dislike of Walter Richard Sickert and his 'low life' followers. Forbes remained faithful to the Royal Academy, becoming an ARA in 1892 and an RA in 1910. He also remained faithful to Newlyn and to such scenes of village life as the *Village Philharmonic* (1888; Birmingham, Mus. & A.G.) and, probably his most famous picture, the *Health of the Bride* (1889; London, Tate). The latter was painted in the same year as his marriage to Elizabeth Armstrong (*see* (2) below). By this time Forbes was developing a distinctively English style of his own and had successfully absorbed the French influences of his youth. He continued to paint the same kind of subjects for the rest of his life, as in the *Drinking Place* (1900; Oldham, A.G.). In his later work his technique became bolder and his colours lighter, as in *The Pond* (1930, Newport, Gwent, Mus. & A.G.).

BIBLIOGRAPHY
A. Meynell: 'Newlyn', *A. J.* [London] (1889), pp. 98–101
W. Meynell: 'Mr. Stanhope A. Forbes, A.R.A.', *A. J.* [London] (1892), pp. 65–9
N. Garstin: 'The Work of Stanhope A. Forbes, A.R.A.', *The Studio*, xxiii (1901), pp. 81–8
L. Birch: *Stanhope Forbes and Elizabeth S. Forbes* (London, 1906)
C. L. Hind: 'The Art of Stanhope Forbes', *A. J.* [London] (1911) [Christmas issue]
Artists of the Newlyn School, 1880–1900 (exh. cat. by C. Fox and F. Greenacre, Newlyn, A.G.; Plymouth, City Mus. & A.G.; Bristol, Mus. & A.G.; 1979), pp. 53–90
Painting in Newlyn, 1880–1930 (exh. cat. by C. Fox and F. Greenacre, London, Barbican A.G., 1985), pp. 51–9, 108–14
C. Wood: *Paradise Lost: Paintings of the English Countryside, 1850–1914* (London, 1988)

CHRISTOPHER WOOD

(2) Elizabeth (Adela) Stanhope Forbes [née Armstrong] (*b* Kingston, Ont., 1859; *d* Newlyn, Cornwall, 1912). Wife of (1) Stanhope Forbes. She studied briefly at the South Kensington School of Art in London, then at the Art Students' League in New York (*c.* 1877–80), mainly under William Merritt Chase. After this she travelled around Europe with her mother, studied with Frank Duveneck and J. Frank Currier in Munich and spent several months in the artists' colony of Pont-Aven in Brittany. A *Zandvoort Fisher Girl* (1884; Penzance, Penlee House Mus. & A.G.) was painted while spending the summer in Zandvoort with a group of Chase's students. In 1885 she moved to Newlyn in Cornwall and became involved with the Newlyn school, marrying its leading practitioner, Stanhope Forbes, in 1889. A frequent subject of her paintings is children, for example *School Is Out* (1889; Penzance, Penlee House Mus. & A.G.), and, like the other Newlyn artists, her paintings are characterized by a *plein-air* naturalism. *Jean Jeanne Jeannette* (*c.* 1892; Manchester, C.A.G.) was inspired by a second trip to Brittany in 1891 and shows the influence of Jules Bastien-Lepage. A specially constructed mobile studio enabled Forbes to work from nature in all weathers. Her later paintings are more reminiscent of second-generation Pre-Raphaelites, depicting young girls, sometimes in medieval costume, in outdoor settings.

WRITINGS

King Arthur's Wood (Bristol and London, 1904) [with illus. by Forbes]

BIBLIOGRAPHY

E. B. S.: 'The Paintings and Etchings of Mrs Stanhope Forbes', *The Studio*, iv (1895), pp. 186–92
P. Dunford: *A Biographical Dictionary of Women Artists in Europe and America since 1850* (Philadelphia, 1989)

NINA LÜBBREN

Forbes, James Staats (*b* Aberdeen, 7 March 1823; *d* London, 5 April 1904). Scottish administrator and collector. Educated at Woolwich, London, in 1840 he entered the office of Isambard Kingdom Brunel as a draughtsman. In 1861 Forbes became General Manager of the London, Chatham and Dover Railway Co. and from 1873 to 1899 was Chairman of the company. In 1873 he unsuccessfully contested Dover at a by-election as a Liberal candidate. He combined a successful business career with the formation of a collection of about 4500 drawings and paintings, the importance of which lay in the large holding of 19th-century French and Dutch landscapes and genre scenes; these he often lent to public galleries in Britain and abroad. He collected in particular works by painters of the Barbizon school, including Théodore Rousseau, Charles-François Daubigny, Jules Dupré and Jean-François Millet, and owned such drawings by Jean-Baptiste-Camille Corot as *Ville d'Avray: The Pond, the House of M. Corot's Father and its Summer-house*. Among Dutch artists, he acquired examples of the work of Matthijs Maris, Anton Mauve and Jozef Israëls. He also bought landscapes by Richard Wilson, John Constable, for example *Dedham from Gun Hill* (1813; Stuttgart, Staatsgal.), and painters of the Norwich school, as well as genre scenes by Thomas Faed and Hubert von Herkomer. Forbes's collection was largely dispersed after his death, and 176 pictures were offered for sale at the Public Art Galleries, Brighton, in 1908.

DNB
BIBLIOGRAPHY

Obituary, *The Times* (6 April 1904)
A. Robaut: *L'Oeuvre de Corot* (Paris, 1905)
'The Grafton Gallery', *Athenaeum* (27 May 1905), p. 664
Selection from the Collection of the Late James Staats Forbes (exh. cat., London, Grafton Gals, 1905)
Pictures from the Collection of the Late J. Staats Forbes (exh. cat., Brighton, Pub. A. Gals, 1908)

ATHENA S. E. LEOUSSI

Forbes, Malcolm (Stevenson) (*b* New York, 19 Aug 1919; *d* 24 Feb 1990). American publisher and collector. In his position as Chairman and Editor-in-chief of the fortnightly American business magazine *Forbes*, he established one of the oldest corporate art collections in America in the 1950s when he began to acquire *objets d'art*

created by Peter Carl Fabergé: the collection contains over 300 pieces, including 12 Imperial Easter eggs. A man of eclectic tastes, and spurred by fond childhood memories, Forbes assembled a collection of 100,000 lead soldiers and over 500 tin clockwork toy boats. The Fabergé works and selected toys are displayed at the Forbes Magazine Galleries in New York with American presidential manuscripts and related historical memorabilia that Forbes believed 'better depict each [president] than the likenesses that abounded in their time'. Numbering over 3000 pieces, the collection is the finest of its kind in private hands.

The Forbes picture collection, predominantly conservative in flavour, features works by French 19th-century military painters, Victorian artists, Kinetic artists, American Realists and 19th- and 20th-century photographers. Forbes established the Musée des Ballons in Balleroy, France, which traces the history of ballooning from its beginning in 1783, and the Museum of Military Miniatures in Tangier, Morocco, which draws on the golden years of model soldier production in the late 19th century to present a collection of historical and educational interest.

BIBLIOGRAPHY

The Royal Academy (1837–1901) Revisited (exh. cat. by C. Forbes, New York, Met., 1975)
M. Kelly: *Highlights from the Forbes Magazine Collection* (New York, 1985)

MARGARET KELLY

Forbin, (Louis-Nicolas-Philippe-)Auguste, Comte de (*b* La Roque d'Anthéron, Bouches-du-Rhône, 19 Aug 1777; *d* Paris, 23 Feb 1841). French museum director, painter, printmaker, writer and military officer. He studied painting in Aix-en-Provence under Jean-Antoine Constantin, alongside his lifelong friend François-Marius Granet; further teachers included Jean-Jacques de Boissieu, Jean-Louis Demarne and, from 1796, Jacques-Louis David. He first exhibited at the Salon in that year. However, during the Empire he was chiefly celebrated as a soldier, writer and lover. He became Chamberlain and consort to Napoleon's sister, Pauline Bonaparte, Princess Borghese, and was decorated for his conduct in the Portuguese and Austrian campaigns. In 1810 *Charles Barimore*, the most successful of his four Orientalist novels, was a great sensation in Empire boudoirs. Forbin's most significant contributions to the history of art came when he returned to Paris after the restoration of the Bourbon monarchy in 1814.

Following his appointment in 1816 as Director of the Royal Museums, to succeed Vivant Denon, Forbin's first concern was to minimize the repatriation of works of art acquired by force during the Revolutionary and Napoleonic wars. In 1817 he embarked on a semi-official mission to Greece, Palestine, Egypt and Sicily, during which he acquired many ancient works for the royal collection. Moreover, his voluminous journals served him and other artists in illustrating his highly successful *Voyage dans le Levant en 1817 et 1818* (1819); this pictorial and literary account helped to establish an itinerary for the century's many published and painted accounts of travels to the Orient.

On his return from the East, Forbin restructured and expanded the Royal Museums. He created the Musée du Luxembourg in 1818 for the acquisition and display of works by living artists. The Musée Charles X, which opened in the Louvre in 1827, contained one of Europe's first official Egyptian collections. Forbin helped to choose, hire and direct the eight leading artists, including Ingres and Antoine-Jean Gros, who painted the Musée's cycle of ceiling paintings.

In addition to supervising the taking of casts of the Elgin Marbles in 1819 and acquiring the *Venus de' Milo* in 1821, Forbin bought diverse paintings of high quality, despite a highly polarized and politicized art world. He overcame the government's fear of the exiled Napoleon and of his court painter, David, when he acquired David's *Intervention of the Sabine Women*, *Leonidas at Thermopylae*, the *Coronation of Napoleon in Notre-Dame* (see DAVID, JACQUES-LOUIS, fig. 4) and the *Distribution of the Eagle Standards* in 1818. At the 1819 Salon, Forbin gave advantageous placement to Théodore Gericault's politically indelicate *Raft of the Medusa* (see GERICAULT THÉODORE, fig. 3); he then courageously argued for its acquisition, which came in 1825. Although he maintained his post until his death, his health had already begun to fail in 1828, when Alphonse de Cailleux took over many of his responsibilities.

Forbin was a painter of real talent and restrained ambitions, who exhibited in 11 Salons from 1796 to 1840. Contemporaries praised his landscapes, church interiors (e.g. *Interior of the Peristyle of a Monastery*, 1830; Paris, Louvre) and historical genre scenes for their effects of light. Today he is seen as an early Romantic and Orientalist. His *Ruins of Ascalon in Palestine* (Paris, Louvre), exhibited at the 1831 Salon, depicts a classical landscape in which soaring natural and architectural elements frame an Oriental figure standing before a view into deep space. Forbin gave this and other pictures to the Louvre; his works are also to be seen in many French provincial museums, as well as in private collections.

WRITINGS
Voyage dans le Levant en 1817 et 1818 (Paris, 1819)
Portefeuille du Comte de Forbin, directeur général des musées de France, contenant ses tableaux, dessins et esquisses les plus remarquables avec un texte rédigé par M. le comte de Marcellus (Paris, 1843)

BIBLIOGRAPHY
J.-M. Carré: *Voyageurs et écrivains français en Egypte*, i (Cairo, 1932, rev. 1956), pp. 196–205
P. Angrand: *Le Comte de Forbin et le Louvre en 1819* (Lausanne, 1972)
TODD B. PORTERFIELD

Force, Jean-Aimar Piganiol de la. *See* PIGANIOL DE LA FORCE, JEAN-AIMAR.

Forces Nouvelles. French group organized by the painter and critic Henri Héraut (*b* 1894), whose first exhibition, in April 1935 at the Galerie Billiet-Vorms in Paris, consisted of paintings by Héraut, Robert Humblot (1907–62), Henri Jannot (*b* 1909), Jean Lasne (1911–46), Alfred Pellan, Georges Rohner (*b* 1913) and Pierre Tal-Coat. Héraut, the eldest of the painters, hoped to establish a new aesthetic through the group and stated in his preface to the catalogue that since all modern movements, starting with Impressionism and Expressionism, had endangered art there was a need to return to drawing, tradition and nature. The group's concentration on nature was often manifested in their preference for still-lifes, such as Lasne's

Still-life (1939; Paris, Pompidou). Sensitive to the political situation in Europe, they rejected light-hearted subject-matter, often dwelling on disaster, as in Humblot's *Dead Child* (1936; priv. col., see exh. cat., pl. 11), and relied on a restricted dark palette, as in Héraut's *Othello* (1935; Rennes, Mus. B.-A. & Archéol.).

In January 1936 the first exhibition was held of the Salon de la Nouvelle Génération (Paris, Gal. Charpentier), founded by Héraut as an extension of Forces Nouvelles. The group's original members were joined by other painters such as Francis Gruber, Germaine Richier, Raymond-Jean Legueult (*b* 1898), André Fougeron and Jacques Despierre (*b* 1912). At the second Forces Nouvelles exhibition, held at the Galerie Billiet-Vorms in March 1936, Pellan and Tal-Coat were not present, although they still associated with the broader Salon de la Nouvelle Génération; the catalogue's preface was written by Eugenio d'Ors, who became one of the group's chief theorists, continuing Héraut's ideas. The last Salon de la Nouvelle Génération was held in 1938 at the Galerie Billiet-Vorms with 34 painters and sculptors, and the third Forces Nouvelles exhibition was held in 1939 at the Galerie de Berri in Paris, with only Héraut, Humblot, Jannot and Rohner. There were further Forces Nouvelles exhibitions until 1943, but its impetus was lost by 1939, and after World War II the artists pursued separate careers.

BIBLIOGRAPHY
Forces Nouvelles, 1935–1939 (exh. cat. by P. Vorms and others, Paris, Mus. A. Mod. Ville Paris, 1980)

□

Ford, Edward Onslow (*b* London, 27 July 1852; *d* London, 23 Dec 1901). English sculptor. He studied painting briefly in Antwerp and Munich before turning to sculpture in 1870. Although never officially attached to any one studio or school, he studied and worked as a sculptor in Munich for five years, sharing a studio with Edwin Roscoe Mullins (1848–1907). Returning to London in 1875, Ford set up as a portrait sculptor in marble and terracotta but did not receive his first public commission until 1881. This was the bronze monumental statue of *Sir Rowland Hill*, now standing in King Edward Street, London, in which his modelling brings life to the surfaces of an otherwise orthodox exercise. During these early years in England Ford displayed a taste for realism, encouraged by the work of Jules-Aimé Dalou and also taken up by William Hamo Thornycroft. The conventional appearance of his first works, however, may be due to his early dependence upon professional assistants.

Ford was inspired with wider ambitions by the stylistic renewal in English sculpture that was eventually termed the New Sculpture by Edmund Gosse in 1894; arising from the interest of the Aesthetic Movement in the pure and applied arts, it received enormous impetus from the early works of Alfred Gilbert. Its effect on Ford's work is first seen in his life-sized portrait of *Sir Henry Irving as Hamlet* (marble, 1883; London, Guildhall). Here the realism of an inevitably picturesque subject is no less important than its derivation from Michelangelo, indicating that the true subject was the state of mind of the sitter and that the seated figure is the embodiment of spiritual affliction.

Ford's true sympathy, however, was with Gilbert's poetic symbolism clothed in a naturalistic but fluid and expressive formal language. This is seen particularly in two works exhibited at the Royal Academy in 1886, *Folly* (see fig.) and *A Study*. These are not only the most satisfactory expressions of Ford's art but also among the purest expressions of the New Sculpture. The importance of *Folly* lies in the sculptor's rejection of orthodox iconography and classical canons of beauty in favour of a thin but ethereally beautiful adolescent female type, also in his use of enigmatic gesture to create a mood of invitation evoking many levels of response. Though the critics of the day could scarcely explain their reaction to this image, they recognized its quality. It established Ford's reputation and was purchased from the exhibition by the Chantrey Bequest. His use here of the statuette scale was in response to the call of the Art Workers' Guild for small-scale works of art for the home, while his use of the lost-wax process reflected Gilbert's practice and his determination to improve the technical quality of this format.

In *A Study* (bronze; Aberdeen, A.G.) Ford took up a theme introduced by Gilbert's *Study of a Head* (bronze, 1883; Cardiff, N. Mus.), a life-sized bust of a young girl. Despite its fidelity to nature Ford's bust, like Gilbert's, goes beyond portraiture to the investigation of the inner state of the sitter. However, where the wistful face of Gilbert's work speaks of individual experience, Ford's *Study* conveys the eternal, spiritual quality of youthful innocence, enhanced by a still more severe abstraction of volumes and outline.

Ford continued his experiments in the life-sized figure of *Peace* (bronze, 1887; Liverpool, Walker A.G.), exhibited at the Royal Academy in 1887, with its ingenuous pose and somnambulistic melancholy. The figure was widely circulated in statuette form.

Ford had been co-opted into the newly founded Art Workers' Guild in 1884, and in 1889 he was elected president of the National Association for the Advancement of Art and its Application to Industry. The interest of the Guild lay in the area between the pure and applied arts, an interest explored in Ford's bronze statuette of *The Singer* (London, Tate), exhibited at the Royal Academy in 1889. Although Gilbert, in his *Enchanted Chair* (1886, destr.; see R. Dorment, *Alfred Gilbert* (New Haven, 1985), pl. 27) and monuments, was already thinking along these lines, Ford was the first to exhibit the new hybrid as 'ideal' sculpture, paving the way for the mixed-media works of George Frampton in the 1890s. Such a step, no doubt made easier by Ford's informal training, nevertheless brought out a latent pictorialism in his sculpture. This tended to obscure the delicate subtlety of his earlier work and led him into unsuccessful attempts to rework Gilbert's medieval themes in mixed media. Though Ford occasionally returned to his earlier preoccupations in works such as *Echo* (marble, 1895; Port Sunlight, Lady Lever A.G.), his choice of themes became more conventional. Of his memorials, *General Gordon on a Camel* (bronze, 1887–90; Chatham, Royal Engin. Mus.) and the *Shelley Memorial* (marble figure on bronze and marble base, 1892–3; Oxford, U. Coll.) are both life-sized works distinguished by their expressive modelling and refreshingly unorthodox approach. As a portrait sculptor in bronze and marble Ford was equalled in his day only by Gilbert, but adhered more faithfully to the fact. His fluid, illusionistic modelling records his sitters with sympathetic warmth but also a high degree of realism. Among his best works in this genre are *James Lever sr* (marble, 1895; Port Sunlight, Lady Lever A.G.), *Sir John Millais* (bronze, 1897; London, N.P.G.) and *Sir George Henschel* (bronze, 1895; Edinburgh, N.P.G.). Ford's bust of *Queen Victoria* (marble, 1899; Windsor Castle, Berks, Royal Col.) is one of the most sympathetic records of the monarch in old age. Ford was elected ARA in 1888 and RA in 1895. However, prone to overwork, he died prematurely and in debt.

Edward Onslow Ford: *Folly*, bronze statuette, h. 698 mm, 1886 (London, Tate Gallery)

BIBLIOGRAPHY

W. Armstrong: 'E. Onslow Ford, ARA', *Portfolio* (1890), pp. 67–71
M. H. Dixon: 'Onslow Ford, ARA', *Mag. A.*, xv (1892), pp. 325–30
E. Gosse: 'The New Sculpture, 1879–1894', *A. J.* (London) (1894), pp. 202, 277–8, 281–2, 306–7
M. H. Dixon: 'Onslow Ford, RA', *A. J.* (London) (1898), pp. 294–7

——: 'Onslow Ford, RA: An Imaginative Sculptor', *Archit. Rev.*, viii (1900), pp. 257–63

M. H. Spielmann: *British Sculpture and Sculptors of To-day* (London, 1901)

F. Rinder: 'Edward Onslow Ford, RA', *A. J.* (London) (1902), pp. 59–62

M. H. Spielmann: 'E. Onslow Ford, RA: In Memoriam', *Mag. A.*, xxvi (1902), pp. 181–4

British Sculpture 1850–1914 (exh. cat., London, F.A. Soc., 1968)

F. Haskell: 'The Shelley Memorial', *Oxford A. J.*, i (1978), pp. 3–6

B. Read: *Victorian Sculpture* (New Haven, 1982)

S. Beattie: *The New Sculpture* (New Haven, 1983)

ANTHEA BROOK

Ford, Richard (*b* London, 21 April 1796; *d* Heavitree, Devon, 31 Aug 1858). English writer, collector and amateur artist. He was educated at Winchester and at Trinity College, Oxford. He went on the Grand Tour in 1818. In Naples he acquired what was said to be Correggio's original oil sketch for the fresco in the dome of Parma Cathedral (now considered to be a 17th-century copy), and in 1819 he published an account of the picture. By 1822 Ford had formed a collection of etchings by Parmigianino and Andrea Schiavone; in that year he produced 12 plates that he had etched from the originals in his possession, describing them as the 'first attempts of an amateur'.

In 1830 he went to Spain with his family. During his three years there he made over 500 drawings, which comprise the most complete pictorial record of Spanish cities and their monuments before the advent of photography. His drawings of Seville (see 1974 exh. cat., nos 35–51) show the Moorish walls and the beautiful 16th-century gateways that have subsequently been destroyed. Ford spent three winters in Seville, where he formed the nucleus of his collection of Spanish pictures.

On his return from Spain in 1833, Ford settled in Exeter, where he began to write an account of his Spanish experiences. The project was temporarily postponed, partly because he was enlarging an Elizabethan cottage he had bought at Heavitree, near Exeter, as well as redesigning its gardens in a Spanish style to include a Moorish tower (1838). With no room for his Spanish pictures in the small house, he sold them, explaining in a letter to his friend H. E. Addington, 'they. . .give me no pleasure and much expense and trouble. The pleasure is in *acquisition not in possession.*' The auction (9 June 1836) included seven paintings attributed to Murillo (e.g. *Two Franciscan Monks*; Ottawa, N.G.) and Zurbarán's *St Serapion* (Hartford, CT, Wadsworth Atheneum), which was sold for only £5 10s.

From 1836 Ford contributed a number of lengthy reviews to the *Quarterly Review*, several of them on Spanish subjects. This led the publisher John Murray to invite Ford to write the *Hand-book for Travellers in Spain*. Ford had optimistically estimated that it would take him six months, but he spent nearly five years on the project; his account of the pictures in the Prado ran to over 17,000 words. When the book finally appeared in 1845, it was an immediate success; with its wit and irony, it remains a valuable source-book. It was followed in 1846 by *Gatherings from Spain*, which was primarily written for the entertainment of ladies. While writing the *Hand-book*, Ford published a short life of Velázquez in the *Penny Cyclopaedia* (1843), which was recognized by Carlo Justi

as the best appreciation of that artist in the English language.

As a collector, Ford's taste was catholic and not confined to Spanish art. To the family collection of works by Richard Wilson he added drawings, prints and engravings, waxes and bronzes by Giambologna, porcelain figures from the Doccia factory and, after a visit to Rome in 1840, marble reliefs by Pierre-Etienne Monnot and a fine collection of Italian maiolica.

WRITINGS

Hand-book for Travellers in Spain, 2 vols (London, 1845); ed. I. Robertson (London, 1966)

Gatherings from Spain (London, 1846); ed. B. Ford (London, 1970)

R. E. Prothero, ed: *The Letters of Richard Ford* (London, 1905)

BIBLIOGRAPHY

G. Waagen: *Treasures of Art in Great Britain*, ii (London, 1854), pp. 223–6

B. Ford: 'Richard Ford's Articles and Reviews', *Book Hb.*, vii (1948), pp. 369–80 [full bibliog. of Ford's articles and reviews]

Richard Ford in Spain (exh. cat., ed. D. Sutton and B. Ford; London, Wildenstein & Co. Ltd, 1974) [incl. reprint of Ford's 'Life of Velázquez']

BRINSLEY FORD

Förderer, Walter Maria (*b* Laufen-Uhwiesen, 21 March 1928). Swiss sculptor and architect. He trained as a sculptor at the Kunstgewerbeschule in Basle and as an architect as an apprentice to Hermann Baur (1894–1980). In 1956 he founded his own practice with Rolf G. Otto (*b* 1924); from 1958 to 1964 he worked in partnership with Rolf G. Otto and Hans Zwimpfer (*b* 1930). In 1965 Förderer was appointed professor at the Staatliche Akademie der Bildenden Künste in Karlsruhe; from 1986 he was a professor at Stuttgart University. The Förderer, Otto and Zwimpfer partnership executed a series of important buildings for educational institutions in the early 1960s. The Wirtschaftshochschule (1959–63) in St Gall attempted to fuse architecture and art in a *Gesamtkunstwerk*, albeit one based on polarities. The organization of the complex, executed in exposed concrete, is strictly orthogonal, with vertical and horizontal layering and interpenetration of the individual buildings, nevertheless achieving an overall effect of plasticity. Förderer also pursued his ideas of spatial design in his churches, which he perceived as 'objects of necessary purposelessness'. All built within a brief period in the late 1960s, they form a stylistic unity (e.g. church of the Holy Cross in Chur, 1966–9; St Nicolas in Hérémence, Canton Wallis, 1967–71). The formal features of this architecture, which relate to the international movement of Brutalism, include an expressive handling of exposed concrete, cubic-sculptural structuring of the building and dramatic light contrasts. Förderer's buildings may be understood as 'walk-in sculptures' or spatial experiences. The recognition that his notions of space could not be expressed logically through architecture led him to return to sculpture in the late 1970s. From 1979 he began his 'Stereoscopic Boxes' and 'Stereoscopic Steles', offering peep-show-like openings on to 'illusionary rooms' into which one can only look rather than enter. Förderer made a variety of theoretical statements. *Bauen ein Prozess* (1968), which he published with Lucius Burckhardt (*b* 1925), falls within the discussion of Functionalism and postulates among other things a renunciation of 'thematic thinking' in precisely defined building tasks in favour of longer-term, flexible planning strategies.

WRITINGS

Kirchenbau von heute für morgen? Fragen heutiger Architektur und Kunst (Zurich, 1964)

with L. Burckhardt: *Bauen ein Prozess* (Teufen, 1968)

Entrückte Räume (exh. cat., Munich, Staatl. Antikensamml. and Glyptothek, 1988)

BIBLIOGRAPHY

M. Bächer: *Walter M. Förderer, Architektur—Skulptur* (Neuchâtel, 1975)

BRUNO MAURER

Fordwich, Viscount. *See* COWPER, GEORGE NASSAU CLAVERING.

Forest, Jean-Baptiste (*b* Paris, *c.* 1634; *d* Paris, 17 March 1712). French painter and dealer. He trained with his father, the landscape painter Pierre Forest (*d* 1675), and then in Rome under Pier Francesco Mola (ii). On his return journey to France, *c.* 1667–8, he is said to have made landscape drawings from nature in Provence and the Franche-Comté that must have been among the first of their type by a French artist. A delicate ink drawing of a *Fort* (Paris, Louvre), attributed to him, probably belongs to this series. He exhibited landscape paintings at the Salon of 1669 and in 1674 was received (*reçu*) as a member of the Académie Royale. As a Protestant he was expelled from the Académie in 1681 but re-admitted in 1699. An *Education of Bacchus* (Tours, Mus. B.-A.) has been attributed to him; the only other record of his paintings is an engraving of his *Mary Magdalene* by Jacobus Coelemans (1654–1731/2) in the Witt Collection. Contemporary commentators praised his work for its combination of the classical tradition of landscape painting with direct observation from nature, and he is known to have been sympathetic to the views of his friend Roger de Piles, the defender of colourism in the debate between the 'Rubénistes' and the 'Poussinistes' (*see* POUSSINISME and RUBENISME). Forest dealt in paintings, and an inventory taken at his death shows that he owned a large number of copies after such masters as Titian, Tintoretto, Veronese and Rubens. He was the brother-in-law of Charles de La Fosse and the father-in-law of Nicolas de Largillierre.

BIBLIOGRAPHY

Mariette

A.-J. Dézallier d'Argenville: *Abrégé de la vie des plus fameux peintres* (Paris, 1745–52, 2/1762), pp. 185–8

G. Wildenstein: 'Le Peintre Jean Forest, révélé par son inventaire après décès', *Gaz. B.-A.*, li (1958), pp. 243–54

THOMAS NICHOLS

Forestier. French family of bronze-founders. Etienne Forestier (*b* Paris, *c.* 1712; *d* Paris, 1768), who became a master bronze-founder in 1737, supplied bronze furniture mounts to Jean-François Oeben, André-Charles Boulle and Gilles Joubert. He cast Jean-Claude Chambellan Duplessis's models for bronzes on the Bureau du Roi by Oeben and Jean-Henri Riesener (1769; Paris, Louvre; *see* BUREAU, fig. 2). The Forestiers feature in the accounts of the Bâtiments du Roi from 1755 until the Revolution. After Etienne's death his widow and sons Etienne-Jean Forestier and Pierre-Auguste Forestier (*b* Paris, 1755; *d* Paris, 1835) continued the Parisian bronze-founding business from a workshop in the Rue Ste Avoie, Etienne-Jean

having become a master in 1764. Their customers included Louis-François de Bourbon, Prince de Conti. The Forestiers also appear frequently, particularly from 1784 to 1788, in the accounts of the Garde Meuble de la Couronne under the directorship of the sculptor Jean Hauré (*fl* 1744–96), regarding bronzework for King Louis XVI's and Queen Marie-Antoinette's various palaces. The Forestiers produced bronze furniture mounts, ornament for chimney-pieces (examples of 1781 and 1788; Versailles, Château) and for the banisters of the Hôtel du Garde-Meuble (1787) at Versailles (now 11, Rue des Reservoirs). The casting of the magnificent sphinx fire-dogs (1786; Versailles, Château) for Marie-Antoinette's Salon des Nobles at Versailles, designed by the sculptor Louis-Simon Boizot and gilded by Claude Galle, has been attributed to the Forestiers. Their collaborations with Pierre-Philippe Thomire included a folding screen at Compiègne (1786; Paris, Louvre), fire-dogs and wall lights, including two pairs with lions' heads for Louis XVI's Chambre du Roi at Saint-Cloud (1788; New York, Met.). After the Revolution Pierre-Auguste opened a shop supplying bronzework, sometimes employing the designs of Charles Percier and Pierre-François-Léonard Fontaine.

BIBLIOGRAPHY

F. J. B. Watson: *Wallace Collection: Catalogue of Furniture* (London, 1956)

G. de Bellaigue: *The James A. de Rothschild Collection at Waddesdon Manor*, 2 vols (London, 1974)

S. Eriksen: *Early Neo-classicism in France* (London, 1974)

H. Ottomeyer, P. Pröschel and others: *Vergoldete Bronzen* (Munich, 1986)

P. Verlet: *Les Bronzes dorés français du XVIIIe siècle* (Paris, 1987)

□

Forgery. Production of a counterfeit or fake object with the intention to deceive.

I. Introduction. II. Authentication techniques. III. The importance of forgery.

I. Introduction.

An art forgery can best be described as an object that departs from transiently agreed canons of AUTHENTICITY and is intended to deceive. A COPY, reproduction or imitation is not in itself an offence in law, except in the case of counterfeit money. Where prosecuting authorities can be persuaded to take action against art forgers, they usually proceed under the provisions covering business fraud in general, but the courts in many countries have traditionally shown leniency towards art forgers. Art forgery, therefore, involves neither a clear cut class of objects nor a readily defined offence in law (*see* ART LEGISLATION). Art-forgery scandals involve not just the forged objects but also the sale of such objects. The forger's skill lies not so much in the fabrication of the objects, which in practice may be quite pitiful, as in their promotion—the conjuring tricks and optical illusions of the art world. Often forgers succeed only because a critic, dealer, collector or curator passionately wants to believe in the forgeries, lured by the profit or status of an apparent art-world coup.

A few forgeries do live up to the stereotype of the brilliantly crafted object, made using the methods and materials of an earlier time, artificially aged and then restored so as to be as nearly as possible a physical

1. Forgery by Han van Meegeren of Johannes Vermeer: *Supper at Emmaus*, oil on canvas, 1.29×1.17 m, 1936–7 (Rotterdam, Museum Boymans–van Beuningen)

facsimile of an object from a previous era. However, a huge range of other objects that are knowingly misrepresented as they change hands are commonly lumped together as forgeries: copies, misattributed works, mechanical reproductions and works heavily restored or cobbled together from a miscellany of authentic and spurious parts. In the case of moulded or printed objects, the issue becomes even more complicated, since the original mould or printing surface, as well as any individual cast or impression, may also be copied, reproduced, restored or used without the authority of the artist to produce whole editions of objects, which may later be used fraudulently. The objects involved in forgery scandals therefore share as a characteristic only their departure from whatever has been agreed, by the standards of a particular market at a particular time, to comprise the canon of authenticity for objects of that type.

For separate discussions of forgery within specific civilizations *see* AFRICA, §X; CYCLADIC, §IV, 2; CYPRUS, §VI; EGYPT, ANCIENT, §XIX; ETRUSCAN, §IX; HELLADIC, §XI; INDIAN SUBCONTINENT, §XIV; ISLAMIC ART, §IX; MESOAMERICA, PRE-COLUMBIAN, §XI, 3; MINOAN, §XI; PACIFIC ISLANDS, §IV; and SOUTH AMERICA, PRE-COLUMBIAN, §IX, 3.

II. Authentication techniques.

1. Connoisseurship. 2. Historical evidence. 3. Technical examination.

1. CONNOISSEURSHIP. Traditional CONNOISSEURSHIP evolved both as a means of assessing quality and of separating authentic objects from imitations. It depends therefore not just on intuitive judgements of the aesthetic effect but also on skilful assessment of whether materials, processes of manufacture and aging and style look right, irrespective of whether or not they look pleasing. It has proved both notoriously flawed and stunningly revealing. Thus the forgery by HAN VAN MEEGEREN of the *Supper*

at Emmaus by Johannes Vermeer (1936–7; Rotterdam, Mus. Boymans–van Beuningen; see fig. 1) was greeted with adulation by the Vermeer scholar Abraham Bredius, to whom it appeared as confirmation of his theories about the development of Vermeer's painting, and as a rotten fake by the agent of the dealer JOSEPH DUVEEN. Similarly, the forgeries of Samuel Palmer by Tom Keating (1917–84), for example *Barn at Shoreham* (Bedford, Cecil Higgins A.G.), deceived distinguished museum officials but not other leading Palmer scholars.

The connoisseur's first concern has generally been to ensure that objects are the product of a certain period. However, many imitations were originally made in good faith in response to a reverence for the past: the forms of the early kingdoms of ancient Egypt were celebrated in the later kingdoms through the imitation of artefacts; for example the formal pose and costume of a tomb statue of Nenkheftka (*c.* 2400 BC) have been respectfully copied by the sculptor of the statue of Tjayasetimu (*c.* 630 BC; both limestone; London, BM). Similarly, the forms of an earlier era were replicated in the Kamakura period (AD 1185–1333) in Japan, bronze forms of the Shang period (*c.* 1600–*c.* 1100 BC) were revived in China during the Song (AD 960–1279), and those of ancient Greece lived on in ancient Rome. Only with a general fascination for the past in Ming-period China (AD 1368–1644), and with the revived reverence for the Classical world in Italy from the 15th century and in northern Europe mainly from the 18th, did respect for the forms of the past become consistently distinguished from respect for the actual relics. Coins, gems and Classical sculpture were promoted in Renaissance Italy as ancient artefacts rather than as contemporary imitations. But even in 18th-century Rome, authenticity was still not cherished as it is in the 20th-century art world. While many tourists were certainly the victims of flourishing forgery trades such as that which operated in Chiusi in the mid-19th century (*see* ETRUSCAN, §IX), such knowledgeable collectors as Charles Townley also showed what now seems a cavalier tolerance for tamperings with the original characteristics of the object, as seen in the drastic restoration by such practitioners as BARTOLOMEO CAVACEPPI.

Scope for art forgery expanded greatly in 19th-century Europe. Respect for the past at the beginning of the century extended to include the medieval past and by the end of the century had become a passion for the history of every culture, including those considered primitive. Such restorations as those of EUGÈNE-EMMANUEL VIOLLET-LE-DUC at Notre-Dame in Paris, which confused imitation and original, were increasingly attacked. At the same time, the growing taste for authenticity in relics of the past made the era from 1850 to 1940 a golden age for forgers, in which legendary practitioners remained undetected for years while substantial bodies of their work found their way on to the market and into the most prestigious collections. The earlier successes in particular were imitations of the Renaissance, for example the bas-reliefs and busts by Giovanni Bastianini, sculpture and paintings by ALCEO DOSSENA, the hundreds of illuminations by the still unidentified Spanish Forger (*fl* 1900–30), the metalwork of Reinhold Vasters (1827–1909; *see* SPITZER, FRÉDÉRIC), spotted only when more than a thousand of his designs were discovered in London at the Victoria and Albert Museum in the 1970s (see fig. 2), and the painted fabrications of Icilio Joni, cheerfully revealed in his picaresque memoirs. It was also the period when the clients of Lord Duveen and his confidential agent BERNARD BERENSON seem so consistently to have been deceived. Artefacts of every period and culture poured from the workshops. Few manuals for early 20th-century collectors fail to spare some pages for hints about the tricks of the trade, such as the turn-of-the-century practice of storing continental imitations of Louis XV and XVI furniture in London for a few months to accelerate patination of the wood by damp and fog before shipment to the USA.

Connoisseurship of the work of individual makers developed much earlier in China than in the West. However, in China, forgeries of the work of individuals are especially difficult to distinguish from the copies of the work of their masters that it was the duty of every artist to perfect, as stipulated by, among others, so early a master as Gu Kaizhi of the 4th–5th century AD. The skill of the forger was therefore much more highly respected, and the offence taken far less seriously, than in 20th-century Western society. Thus in the early 15th century Shen Zhou, founder of the Wu school of Chinese painting, refused to begrudge the myriad forgers of his work their rewards on the grounds that it hardly mattered, as the collectors were interested only in the monetary value of the pictures. The early 19th-century critic Wu Xiu declared that the very best works of the painter Dong Qichang, the

influential artist and theorist, were actually those painted by his leading imitators.

The first evidence of a comparable cult of the individual artist in the West appears in the early Roman era, when, according to Alsop, the Greek poet Phaedrus (15 BC–AD 50) warned against forgeries of the sculptures of Myron of Eleutherai and Praxiteles and the paintings of Zeuxis. This kind of homage became a preoccupation for connoisseurs as part of the revival of Classical values in Europe from the 15th century. However, whereas tales of indistinguishable copying of the work of the master by the pupil in China attest in part to a faith in the ability of the spirit of the work of one creator to be sustained by another, similar stories in the West are associated with the evolution of the idea of the artist as a solitary genius. So the deceptive copies or imitations of prints and Classical sculpture by earlier masters, such as those by the young Michelangelo (described in Vasari's *Vite*, 2/1568), of Raphael by Andrea del Sarto, or of Titian by Rubens, become a stock-in-trade of the legend of the early life of the master. Subsequently the market for forgeries of the work of individual masters by lesser painters has gone from strength to strength. Examples are the many 16th-century imitations in the Netherlands of the work of Hieronymus Bosch, the engraving of *Big Fish Eat Little Fish* (published by Hieronymous Cock in Antwerp in 1557; see 1990 exh. cat., no. 131). More recently, the 20th-century frenzy to invest in artistic genius has nourished such triumphs as van Meegeren's imitations of Vermeer, Tom Keating's fakes of artists from several different centuries and imitations by Elmyr de Hory (*fl* 1946–76) of such 20th-century painters as Raoul Dufy, Braque, Modigliani and Matisse. One of the latter's 'Matisse' drawings—*Lady with Flowers and Pomegranates* (1955)—was bought by the Fogg Art Museum, Cambridge, MA, but never exhibited.

The intimacy of the association between the market, forgery and connoisseurship is summed up in the person of Bernard Berenson, who vividly exemplifies how connoisseurship both helped to provoke the golden age of forgery and concurrently developed to become something of a restraint. His own expertise unquestionably set new standards in techniques of attribution of early Italian paintings in the first decades of the 20th century, while simultaneously being pressed into service to bamboozle major collectors over attribution and restoration (according to Secrest) and forgeries as well (according to Simpson). Similarly, a 12th-century connoisseur in China was known as 'advantage thrice' because of his skill in repeatedly using his reputation as a critic to sow confusion between the originals brought to him for an opinion and the copies he himself made from them (Fong). However, the development of connoisseurship in the early decades of the 20th century, spurred on by such attempts as those of GIOVANNI MORELLI to put the business of attribution on a scientific footing, reached a point where the study of art history seemed to consist in little else, but it nevertheless probably brought the forgery free-for-all to an end. A vast amount of forgery is still going on, but since the 1940s it has tended to be aimed mainly at less well-informed collectors and at the lower end of the art and antiques market, for example the mass production of plastic fake SCRIMSHAW. The forgeries of the pots of Bernard Leach,

2. Fake 'Renaissance' pendant by Reinhold Vasters, gold enamel and precious stones, h. 71 mm, *c.* 1880s (London, Victoria and Albert Museum)

3. Forgery by an imitator of Botticelli: *Madonna of the Veil*, tempera on panel, 882×458 mm, ?19th century (London, University of London, Courtauld Institute Galleries)

created an appropriate sheen by soaking their copies in water and laying them out to dry on lacquer twenty or thirty times a day for three months. Among passing references to numerous other dodges, Joni explained how a little spirit on the surface of tempera paint would induce a convincing craquelure while evaporating. The self-confessed forger of Old Master drawings Eric Hebborn (1934–96), who claimed in his autobiography (1991) to have flooded the market with hundreds of fake drawings over the years, published what amounted to a 'recipe book' for forgers in late 1995, a few months before his death in Rome under suspicious circumstances.

Stylistic criteria were most easily satisfied by simple copying. Alternatively, furniture and sculpture have often been dressed up by cobbling together miscellaneous parts, original and imitation, from a variety of sources. In rare instances this technique was also used for paintings, but much the commonest strategy has been to copy parts from many pictures into a new composition. Those that depended for success on this simple ruse include the 'Botticelli' *Madonna of the Veil* (?19th century; U. London, Courtauld Inst. Gals; see fig. 3), which was bought by Arthur Hamilton Lee, Viscount Lee of Fareham (1868–1947), and celebrated throughout the 1930s; the van Gogh forgeries sold by the art dealer Otto Wacker (*fl* 1927–32); the modest confections successfully marketed for decades by the Spanish Forger; and the portrait of *St Catherine* (*c.* 1975), apparently by Matthias Grünewald, that the Cleveland Museum of Art acquired in the late 1970s.

2. HISTORICAL EVIDENCE. Wherever possible the connoisseur will complement judgements about quality and age with historical evidence, which usually takes the form of comments that some object in a painting is either anachronistic or implausible, either in terms of date or form. The *Adoration of the Magi* (*c.* 1497–1500) by Andrea Mantegna and the *Annunciation* (*c.* 1465) by Dieric Bouts I, acquired by the J. Paul Getty Museum, Malibu, CA, have both been attacked on these grounds (among others), with claims that the fur in the Mantegna is, implausibly, ocelot and that the canopy in the *Annunciation* is of implausible construction. The charges have been vigorously defended, but for all the passion of the debates over such points they rarely resolve the issues. The evidence almost always seems to prove insufficient for a convincing consensus. Similarly, signatures, ceramic marks, hallmarks and inscriptions of all kinds are essential guides to what an object is supposed to be (*see* MARKS, §§2–5) but are generally too easily imitated to be useful for purposes of authentication. Very occasionally they betray slovenly forgeries, such as those of Jean-François Millet analysed by Herbert, or forgers who fall foul of technicalities of grammar or linguistics, for example the enamellers of the spurious masterpiece of medieval Middle Eastern glass, the Hope Goblet (?19th century; London, BM).

Of far more value in the case of major works is the record of PROVENANCE—the history of the ownership and display of the object. (It was the questionable nature of its provenance that raised doubts about the authenticity of the *Sea at Saintes Maries*, a painting that had previously been attributed to van Gogh; Otterlo, Rijksmus. Kröller-Müller.) Most works of great value have left in their wake

produced in 1980 during pottery classes in a gaol in Wolverhampton, survived only three months on the market before being recognized as such (London, Met. Police Hist. Mus.). In spite of some astonishing triumphs with museums, most of the minor successes, even of such stars as Tom Keating and Elmyr de Hory, seem to have been outside the limelight of the art market.

The snares laid by forgers for the connoisseur have remained remarkably consistent through the ages. Much time and effort have always been saved by adapting old works or using old materials—hence the surprising prices achieved for unused early 19th-century sketchbooks—but more often forgers just imitated appearances by a variety of procedures. Fong records how Wu Xiu, in early 19th-century China, wrote of forgers who persuaded ink to penetrate their paper in a convincing manner and then a litter of references in catalogues of sales and exhibitions, inventories and wills, and in memoirs and diaries. Such references are often complemented by marks, seals and labels on the object itself. A large component of the skill of scholars who choose to specialize in establishing canonical bodies of work for individual painters lies in knowing how to find and match up these two sets of evidence. The Chinese have considerably greater experience in this field too, since paintings from the earliest times accumulated artists' inscriptions, collectors' marks (*see* MARKS, §5) and colophons, expressions of confidence by earlier connoisseurs. In the case of later artists in the West, the family or scholars have often compiled virtually comprehensive lists of works: thus a would-be forger of Paul Klee will know that any informed potential buyer will be aware that the Paul Klee Stiftung in the Kunstmuseum, Berne, has comprehensive documentation of the artist's output. But, in general, a major work that has left no historical traces, or apparently ancient objects from unspecified archaeological sites, must always be highly suspect. Similarly, archaic objects or objects from a vanishing culture that come with a provenance that cannot be independently confirmed are a dubious INVESTMENT, and the more exceptional, the more dubious.

The first strategy of the forger against the evidence of provenance is to specify a source that cannot readily be researched because of political circumstances (a complication here is that such sources are also regularly specified for authentic works exported or excavated illegally from readily accessible countries). A second strategy is to duplicate a known work, risking the subsequent reappearance of the original: the forger, probably van Meegeren, of *The Procuress* by Dirck van Baburen (U. London, Courtauld Inst. Gals) took a cue from a painting glimpsed in the background of an authentic Vermeer. A few years later the original Baburen surfaced in the Isle of Wight. Few forgeries under such circumstances survive comparison with their originals, but sufficient artists have made replicas of their own work for there to be scope for helpfully protracted and acrimonious controversies. An artist's descendants generally appear to be a convincing source for authentic works but may not always have resisted the temptation to pay their relative the compliment of a little supplementary production. Thus Richard Bonington (1768–1835), who outlived his son Richard Parkes Bonington, seems to have completed for the market a number of unfinished watercolours. Jean-François Millet's grandson Jean Charles Millet (*fl* 1920–30) helped put numerous Millet drawings and prints on the market in the 1920s, for example the *Potato Gatherers* (lithograph; U. Manchester, Whitworth A.G.). Forgeries may come complete with suggestive links to known contacts of the artist, such as the inscription that spuriously connected Keating's fake Palmers to the perfectly genuine descendants of Palmer's friend Jane Kelly, or the hints that linked 2414 fake Corot paintings to the doctor who tended the artist in his last illness (e.g. *Nocturne* and *Saint-Brévin near Saint-Nazaire*; both U. Manchester, Whitworth A.G.).

3. TECHNICAL EXAMINATION. During the 20th century scientific techniques have increasingly been recruited to assist traditional connoisseurship and historical research. Microscopic inspection, which barely goes beyond traditional connoisseurship, is often decisive—for example in revealing stress-cracks round worm-holes made by drilling or even with a shotgun. Similarly, modern pigments, often finely ground by mechanical processes, may be unlike earlier pigments coarsely ground by hand. However, an enormous variety of more elaborate techniques is now also employed to reveal anomalies in processes of fabrication, in materials or in age (*see* TECHNICAL EXAMINATION, §I). X-rays have proved perhaps the most powerful tool in exposing hidden secrets of manufacture and repair. They were reputedly first employed in a court case in Berlin in 1929 to demonstrate that X-radiographs of Wacker's forgeries of van Gogh looked quite unlike those of authentic paintings by the artist. Similarly, ultraviolet illumination can reveal both artificial PATINA on marble (e.g. forged figurines; *see* CYCLADIC, §IV, 2), on repairs to ancient bronze and on recently applied oil paint on an original surface (*see* TECHNICAL EXAMINATION, §II, 2). Such techniques as gas laser spectrometry provide details of the elemental composition of materials from which molecular constituents and possible sources can be inferred. Other processes provide direct analysis of molecular components. Two techniques—radiocarbon dating and thermoluminescence (*see* TECHNICAL EXAMINATION, §VII, 1 and 2)—indicate the age of objects by measuring properties of their constituent materials that transform steadily through natural radioactive processes from around the time of manufacture. Radiocarbon dating is generally used for wood, bone, ivory, textiles, leather, parchment and paper; with ceramics the mineral clock is used for thermoluminescence dating based on the firing of the ceramic. Using dendrochronology, the tree-ring patterns of wooden panels can be compared with master patterns established from dated samples for woods of different types and areas (*see* TECHNICAL EXAMINATION, §VII, 3). There are problems with all these techniques, but, taken with other data, they often help to provide a consistent picture.

Such techniques have presented real difficulties for the forger. In some cases scientific evidence has been questioned, as in the dispute as to whether lead-tin yellow in the Georges de La Tour painting the *Fortune Teller* (?1620–30; New York, Met.) does or does not eliminate the possibility of mid-20th-century production (*see* PIGMENT, §IX). But generally, once scientific experts have pronounced, confession follows to settle the issue. Furthermore, new techniques keep appearing. The forger of Lord Lee's 'Botticelli' would no doubt have removed the 20th-century wire-drawn nail hidden embedded in the edge of an inner plank of the panel had he, or she, anticipated the intrusion of X-rays. An attractive option for the forger is to follow the example of de Hory and concentrate on contemporary work, so that anomalies are less obvious. Another possibility is to forge modest objects that may escape technical examination because the expense cannot be justified. Again, extensive research and scholarly investigation are unlikely to be available for objects that may have been excavated or exported illegally, and this murky market is copiously supplied with forgeries. Metalwork, especially if hand-modelled rather than cast, must remain a tempting field. If the constituent metals are carefully researched, there are few aging transformations for the forger to worry about. The authenticity of jewellery, vessels, coins and scientific instruments poses great difficulties for the connoisseur.

A more subtle strategy for the forger is to produce an object that satisfies initial tests, thus discouraging further tests. Van Meegeren, in planning his master forgery, the *Supper at Emmaus*, carefully anticipated such superficial technical criteria by cunningly using a medium of oil mixed with the newly available artificial resin Bakelite. The result was an enamel-like surface that, after rolling and baking, not only convincingly resembled the surface of a Vermeer but, vitally, would resist simple organic solvent tests in just the way to be expected of 300-year-old oil paint. Once subjected to proper analysis, his bizarre medium was revealed, but so convincing were the preliminary tests that no proper analysis took place until long after the painting had been purchased for the Museum Boymans–van Beuningen. More modest contemporary forgers may give their oil work a coating of gelatin, which also offers some resistance to the organic solvents commonly used by restorers in preliminary tests. As data about the material characteristics of major works of art steadily accumulate from routine conservation, and as non-destructive probes proliferate, the ambitious forger may seem to be ever more restricted. However, the buyer's capacity to be deceived, so that proper criteria are never brought to bear, remains undiminished, and never more so than when, for whatever reason, secrecy veils the processes of assessment.

III. *The importance of forgery.*

From a decorative point of view it does not matter at all if an object is a forgery. However, it certainly matters from a financial point of view. When a painting thought to be by Raoul Dufy turns out to be by Elmyr de Hory (e.g. *Promenade des Anglais, Nice*, 1962), its value immediately diminishes by perhaps a hundredfold, because the monetary value placed on works of art has more to do with financial conventions and a search for vehicles of credit than with aesthetics. Works of art have become investment items because, like banknotes, their value is guaranteed if their provenance, be it from an authorized mint or a recognized artist, has been established. For the purposes of an orderly economy, art or banknote forgeries need to be rejected because they distort the standards of rarity and quality on which values depend. But the loss of financial value of the forged Dufy has no more to do with its artistic qualities than has the loss of value of a banknote with the artistic quality of the forgery; artistic assessment aids authentication but has little bearing on financial value.

Forgeries may also confuse research, for example the forged Egyptian clay statuette (*c.* 1900) discovered in Rhodesia (now Zimbabwe) that was taken as evidence of early Egyptian presence in Africa (*see* EGYPT, §XIX). They are a contamination for the connoisseur who hopes to characterize the visual properties of a particular kind of work. In China, so prevalent was the tradition of copying that it is probably impossible in some cases to know whether certain pieces are actually the work of an ancient artist or whether, like the work of the Greek sculptor

Praxiteles, only the copies remain. For the student relying on works of art as evidence of matters incidental to aesthetics, forgeries bear false witness. This is perhaps most vividly exemplified by doctored photographs, because of the notion, deeply ingrained though surely discredited, that the camera cannot lie. The most disturbing examples are political, for instance the notorious Stalinist elimination of Leon Trotsky from the visual history of the Russian Revolution; more entertaining are the examples of spiritual manifestations, widely fabricated in the later 19th century, such as those decorating Georgiana Houghton's *Chronicles of the Photographs of Spiritual Beings* (London, 1882). A full account of the processes of forgery is available in the case of the Cottingley fairy photographs (1917; Leeds, U. Lib.; see fig. 4), in which cardboard cut-out fairies devised by two children from Cottingley, W. Yorks, were taken to be true manifestations of the spirit world by Arthur Conan Doyle (1859–1930), among many others (see 1990 exh. cat., pp. 87–90).

More fundamentally, art forgeries challenge assumptions about art: they reveal how relative assumptions about aesthetics and authenticity must be. They certainly undermine the stereotype of the artist as an individual endowed with special gifts that enable him or her to create works that in some way speak a universal language intelligible to those whose sensitivities have been trained. Accordingly, some may aspire to restore a work of art, by objective scientific means, to a canonical pristine form from which its elevated messages shine out as far as possible undulled by age or restoration. These assumptions are poignantly displayed when applied to 'primitive' art. The fabrication and use of sacred objects in nomadic, forest and desert cultures tend to offend every canon sacred to the art connoisseur: they are often made by groups rather than individuals; they are made to match an approved pattern rather than create a new form; they are meaningless to their makers except when used in a particular context and are not intended for visual contemplation in isolation; they may be reworked, repaired and used as long as possible and then discarded or destroyed. Nevertheless, the art market still seeks to transform these objects into commodities for exchange along with other works of art, assayable for authenticity in terms of origin and date and, of course, highly susceptible to forgery.

Art forgeries act as a reminder that the ostensible need to establish individual authorship seems as much a requirement of the market as of the refinement of an understanding of a universal aesthetic message. Copyists, collaborators, restorers and forgers can sometimes imitate, if not invent, works that aesthetically function very well. For example, Alpers raised the question of whether the notion of Rembrandt as an individual inventor is not a consciously contrived illusion, fostered by a circle of artists who were prepared to allow their own identities to remain in the background. The pure aesthetic experience to which the connoisseur aspires often seems suspiciously bound up with possession and exchange of art as property. In any case the canonical original condition of works of art is as inaccessible to a non-contemporary audience as the context in which 'primitive' artefacts were meaningful for their makers: hence the scope for restoration to become

4. Forged photograph of 'Alice and the Fairies', from the Cottingley fairy photographs, 1917 (Leeds, University of Leeds Library, Brotherton Collection)

so confused with forgery that the history of the transformations and interpretations of an object may be as meaningful as any original condition to which it can be returned. How fortunate then that, though values in art seem to be ever shifting and subject to socially driven change, forgery persists and so provides a consistent viewpoint from which to assess them.

BIBLIOGRAPHY
I. Joni: *Le memorie di un pittore di quadri antichi con alcune descrizioni sulla pittura a tempera e sul modo di fare invecchiare i dipinti e le donature* (Florence, 1932); Eng. trans. as *The Affairs of a Painter* (London, 1936)
R. Huyghe: 'Simple histoire de 2414 faux Corots', *Amour A.*, i/2 (1936), pp. 73–6
P. B. Coremans: *Van Meegeren's Faked Vermeers and de Hoochs: A Scientific Examination* (London, 1949)
R. L. Herbert: 'Les Faux Millet', *Rev. A.*, 21 (1973), pp. 56–65
S. J. Fleming: *Authenticity in Art* (London, 1975)
T. Keating, G. Norman and F. Norman: *The Fake's Progress* (London, 1977)
W. Voeklke and R. S. Wieck: *The Spanish Forger* (New York, 1978)
M. Secrest: *Being Bernard Berenson* (London, 1980)
C. Wright and D. de Marly: 'Fake?', *Connoisseur*, ccv (1980), pp. 22–5
W. Fong: 'The Problem of Forgeries in Chinese Painting', *Artibus Asiae*, xxv (1982), pp. 95–119
D. Dutton, ed.: *The Forger's Art* (Berkeley, 1983)
G. Norman: 'Mantegna's *Magi*: Fine Art or Forgery?', *The Times* (4 Dec 1985), p. 12
J. Alsop: 'The Faker's Art', *NY Rev. Bks* (23 Oct 1986), pp. 25–31
J. Bly, ed.: *Is it Genuine? How to Collect Antiques with Confidence* (Toronto, 1986)
M. Kaye: *Fake, Fraud or Genuine? Identifying Authentic American Antique Furniture* (Boston, 1987)
C. Simpson: *The Secret Partnership of Bernard Berenson and Joseph Duveen* (London, 1987)
S. Alpers: *Rembrandt's Enterprise: The Studio and the Market* (London, 1988)
Retaining the Original: Multiple Originals, Copies and Reproductions, Stud. Hist. A., xx (Washington, DC, 1989)
Fake? The Art of Deception (exh. cat., ed. M. Jones; London, BM, 1990)
E. Hebborn: *Drawn to Trouble: The Forging of an Artist, an Autobiography* (Edinburgh, 1991)
——: *Art Forger's Handbook* (Rome, 1995)

DAVID PHILLIPS

Fork. *See under* CUTLERY.

Forlati. Italian family. The architect (1) Ferdinando Forlati and his wife, the archaeologist (2) Bruna Forlati, collaborated in their work, making a significant contribution to the preservation of the architectural and archaeological heritage of the Veneto.

(1) Ferdinando Forlati (*b* Verona, 1 Nov 1882; *d* Venice, 18 July 1975). Architect and conservator. After graduating from Padua University as a civil engineer he became, in 1907, the architect of the Fine Arts and Monuments Department in Venice. In 1926 he was appointed Soprintendente in Trieste, where his major works included the restoration of S Giusto, the Roman forum and the medieval castle, where he introduced the new technique of injecting shots of concrete to consolidate a wall. He also helped to preserve the rarely considered regional architecture of Friuli and Istria. From 1935 to 1952 he served as Soprintendente in Venice, where he completed the restoration of the Ca' d'Oro and the basilican complex on Torcello; he also saved the Torre degli Anziani in the Palazzo Municipale, Padua, from demolition. After World War II, in which he organized the protection and removal of major works of art, he took part in the enormous task of reconstruction, energetically opposing the trend to demolish damaged buildings. His important achievements included his work at the church of the Eremitani, Padua, at Palladio's basilica and the cathedral in Vicenza, the spectacular straightening of the Palazzo dei Trecento, Treviso, and the restoration of the monuments on the island of San Giorgio, Venice. As Proto (official architect) of S Marco, Venice, he solved many of the building's technical problems and structural weaknesses. Throughout his career Forlati demonstrated great artistic sensibility, and he pioneered new techniques in the preservation of ancient monuments.

WRITINGS

intro.: *Mostra della ricostruzione degli edifici storici ed artistici danneggiati dalla guerra* (exh. cat., ed. R. Silviero; Treviso, Pal. Trecento, 1951), pp. 21–100
La basilica di San Marco attraverso i suoi restauri (Trieste, 1975)
S Giorgio Maggiore: Il complesso monumentale e i suoi restauri, 1951–1956 (Padua, 1977)

(2) Bruna Forlati [née Tamaro] (*b* Grumello del Monte, 31 Jan 1894; *d* Venice, 13 Feb 1987). Archaeologist and museum official. She graduated in Classical Philology in Genoa in 1915 and studied archaeology in Rome and Athens in 1916–20. In the following year she started to work for the Archaeological Office in Trieste, directing excavations both in the city and at the site of Nesactium (now Vizače, Croatia). She founded the Istrian Archaeological Museum in Pula. In 1929 Bruna married Ferdinando Forlati, and in 1936 she became director of the Museo Archeologico, Venice. From 1952 to 1961 she was Soprintendente for archaeology in the Veneto; of her many achievements, her excavations in Verona and Vicenza and the creation of new museums at Adria, Altino, Oderzo and Aquileia are particularly outstanding. From 1958 to 1969 Bruna lectured on Greek and Roman antiquities at Padua University. She was secretary of the National Association of Aquileia (1964–82), president of the Istrian Society of Archaeology and History and editor of its periodical (1967–86). Throughout her life Bruna was involved in both serious scholarship and the presentation of archaeological sites. Always very active and open to new developments and ideas, she had a great gift for establishing excellent relationships with colleagues, even in such delicate situations as the negotiations after World War II for the division of artistic property with the Yugoslav authorities.

WRITINGS

Pola et Nesactium, Iscriptiones Italiae, x/1 (Rome, 1947), pp. xxxv, 297
Il museo archeologico del Palazzo Reale di Venezia (Rome, 1953), pp. 1–80
Da Aquileia a Venezia (Milan, 1980) [pp.13–95]

ALBERTA FABRIS GRUBE

Forli, Ansuino da. *See* ANSUINO DA FORLÌ.

Forlì, Melozzo da. *See* MELOZZO DA FORLÌ.

Form. Term applied to such aspects of a work of art as internal organization and shape, often used with some degree of distinction from the subject-matter, content,

function and style of works of art. An analysis of form as a means of evaluating a work is called FORMALISM. Most of what we value within a work of art is due to relationships, and 'form' takes a leading part in our ideas about art. 'Form', however, is not simply relationship nor all a work of art's relationships. Rather, works have artistic form insofar as they constitute distinct artistic entities owing to relationships of their parts and aspects. 'Form', then, is primarily a constitutive idea, a term that has been given confusing usage over opposed connotations. This article outlines the different uses and connotations of 'form', now and in the past, and shows some of the ways in which it compares and contrasts as an idea with other related concepts in art.

1. Etymology and general meanings. 2. Contraries and correlatives. 3. Aesthetic principles of form.

1. ETYMOLOGY AND GENERAL MEANINGS. A single sentence by the anthropologist and art historian FRANZ BOAS indicates form's familiar variety: 'The general formal elements of. . .symmetry, rhythm and emphasis or delimitation of form. . .underlie all forms of ornamental art.' Three important variants appear here: first, form as an organizing principle (called arrangement, organization, structure); second, form as shape, figure or other disposition in space of whatever dimensions (accessible there by sight and other senses); third, form as kind or type. To these should be added a fourth variant: forms as canons, moulds or repeatable procedures by which sometimes groupings of the third type are generated. With the first pair of meanings we normally speak of a work of art 'having' form; with the latter pair of a work of art providing an 'instance of' a form. These four meanings will be referred to throughout this article. There is also another common usage, set apart from these: forms as distinguishable entities actually within works of art, which led HEINRICH WÖLFFLIN to complain of 'a fatal double meaning' in the word.

The Latin term *forma* shows a similar spread and has the implication of beauty, so it is perhaps better to consider this family of meanings through a more remote conceptual ancestor, the Greek term *eidos*. This originally had the sense of 'the look of a thing by means of which we recognize it', which, naturally, came to include a thing's perceptible and characteristic shape (as it is by visible contours that people like to distinguish and to identify particular things). The wider meaning in turn expanded to that of the characteristic nature of a thing—whether visual or not—and thereby into 'type', the class of things so characterized (Boas's third meaning). From the early sense of visual recognition down to the abstract sense of essence, this progression reveals a cognitive constant. On account of its *eidos*, a thing is recognized, known or intelligible to us as a distinct entity. This cognitive connotation of form is a recurring theme in the long tradition of Western AESTHETICS that stretches from Classical times to the present. It has been stressed—to good purpose or not—from St Augustine (354–430) to Immanuel Kant to varieties of modern formalism in order to diminish the artistic importance of sensuous qualities, though such is not its inevitable implication.

The later meanings of *eidos* also suggest internal relationships: the constitution, organization or ordering of a thing. The sovereign sense of 'form' as organization implies richer and more varied relationships of an entity to its parts or factors than does 'shape' alone. The foot of a pot, the arch in a doorway, the path through a garden, for example, are functional as well as spatial parts. Also form can exist in spatial and other relationships among physical shapes. For example, repetitive action with ensuing repetitions of similar shapes are striking formal characteristics of primitive handwork, which reappear in modern art. Again, the handling of the relationships of parts to each other or to the entire work—whether, say, their distinctness as parts is accentuated, or whether they flow into each other—has provided valuable form categories. Some form principles even deny literal shape.

A useful approach to form stems from one of the architects of *eidos*, ARISTOTLE, in his writings about nature. For Aristotle, the form of a thing is its 'formative' cause: what constitutes it as the entity it is. If the verb 'to form' is considered prior to the noun there is a better sense of its difference from such frequently used rough synonyms as 'organize', 'arrange', 'structure', 'design' or 'unify'. The particular artistic form of a work of art is therefore that set of relationships among its parts or aspects that form it, that is, that constitute it as an entity with an artistic nature. Its general forms (in the third sense) are the sets of relationships that constitute it as a work of art of given types. Since art is normally understood aesthetically (and 'aesthetic' is often taken in terms of form), many accounts of artistic form concern perceptible constitutive relationships and are influenced by psychological theories of the latter (*see also* PERCEPTION and PSYCHOLOGY AND ART).

This account of 'form' should not be taken as stating a commonplace. First, not all the important relationships among a work's parts are artistically constitutive of it as a particular work, nor as a work of art of a certain kind. For example, the temporal order of construction of a work, though artistically important, may not play a role in constituting the finished product as an entity. Second, works of art sometimes have the nature of aggregates, artistically characterized as unique and treasured entities by no greater 'relationship' than an enduring juxtaposition of parts, added to and altered at various times. Such rather formless communities are still understood as distinctive entities, e.g. old buildings and sites. With acquaintance the mind finds, or invents, valued relationships—but these did not constitute the thing. Here the sense of there being an entity may be more productive of relationships among parts than vice versa. The phenomenon of transparency demonstrates perceptually how two entities may be distinguishable without thereby being formed, or even shaped. We might therefore consider a requirement for a work having form (or being formed) that it has a nature through following (or at least being conformable to) organizing principles that relate its constituents. (An often prized sense of 'vitality' in works of art may then be expressed as that of a formative principle being perceptibly at work in them, or at least so imagined.) Some such principles are easily recognizable in many works: perspective, trabeation, opposition, light modulation, articulation, centrism and iteration are only some of a long list of form principles

that are more or less specifiable, figuring importantly under the fourth 'form' heading. Although very influential aesthetic traditions favour 'whole' things, not all formed artistic entities are wholes. For example, repeated 'infinite' patterns in tile or decorative work and fabric weaves do not entail whole, or even bounded or completable entities, yet they constitute characterized entities, are generated by describable formative principles and are enjoyed as such. They are therefore formed things, not mere aggregates.

2. CONTRARIES AND CORRELATIVES. A work of art may be 'lacking form' or appear 'formless'. These states depend on a degree of comparison, and what lacks form in one conception of a work of art, entity, part or relationship may have it in another. Western thought about art has long celebrated normative canons of form, sometimes praising (besides wholeness and vitality) such qualities as coherence, unity and completeness, though with diversity in accounts of such virtues and the means by which they are attained. These values are not, however, universally accepted or applicable. Any given ideal of form in art may be rejected. The very ideas of individuation, or even distinctive characterization of entities, may be neglected or devalued in art. Furthermore, wilful degrees of formlessness or resistance to form are found in the work of most artists, movements and epochs and have even been the main characteristic of some. Such ideas as 'the sublime' in nature, which developed in 18th-century European aesthetics, and 'emptiness' in Eastern philosophies (e.g. in Buddhism: Skt *sūnyatā* or Chin. *kong*), express some of these principles. The relatively unindividuated, fragmentary and unfinished have all been valued, along with partless unity. We should also note the importance of formlessness in setting off form, as well as the familiar perceptual interest people take in things relatively formless, as when looking at clear sky, sparkling light, into shadow or deep water. Finally, in the visual arts there is interest in the relationships between form and formlessness, for example as one emerges from the other or passes into it.

The states of being formed or formless are usually considered contraries, situated in opposed directions along scales that, like hot and cold, consist of relative degrees. But 'form', as described above, also names what the work of art thereby has or lacks. The term then occurs in another sort of contrast, one of correlative complements, implying distinction but with neither intrinsic opposition nor degree. For example, form has long been contrasted with 'matter' or materials: the factors put in relationship. Again, reference to a work's form may mark the means as opposed to the ends—'how' as against 'what'—especially to the uses or functions of the work. The former contrast is especially important, as in most cultures the ideas of art and artistry are based upon that of skilled and purposeful arrangement of materials into things. Artists are considered to be masters of traditional forms and, in modern times, to be makers of new ones.

As form has more than one general term of contrast, an understanding of a work's form will be affected by our understanding of its tacit or stated complement. For example, approaches to art titled 'formalist' may operate from either correlative. Where the implied contrast is material, formalism is a relative idea that must be specified by context, since, as noted above, the factors related may themselves be forms or formed things. It should be noted that contemporary science reveals the experiences of colour and brightness—the classic examples of pure matter for visual art—to be themselves complex 'formal' operations of the visual system. 'Form' and 'matter', besides being generally correlative terms, are therefore also relative ones, though to say this is to add little to Aristotle. It is a fallacy to suppose that this variety of formalism, as implying emphasis on relatively higher levels of form, thereby departs from immediate perception. For example, the series 'position', 'difference of position', 'change in such difference', 'rate of change of such acceleration' etc runs in a direction of increasingly abstract form but represents one of increasingly direct and easy sensation, as a ride in a vehicle would demonstrate. Parallel situations exist in the perception of art.

Where the contrast with 'form' is 'function' (for further discussion see FUNCTIONALISM), formalism is frequently taken to include, and even to feature, the correlative 'material' rather than to contrast with it. Since it is normal for practitioners of any productive activity to concentrate upon means and methods (as it is there that ways of working, and hence skill and artistry, lie), we should expect that among themselves artists would emphasize 'means', come to value them for their own sakes, even make them ends in themselves—although what we identify as form in an artefact is much affected by what we take to be its function. In art, as elsewhere, such value may become predominant, autonomous or even subversive of other values. By these means, the correlatives 'form' and 'function' have often in modern times been treated as antitheses. A less tractable set of aesthetic issues concerns the contrasts of form with 'content' in art: meaning, feeling, subject-matter etc. For example, in writing of the 'formal elements' of ornamental art, Boas intended a contrast with representational and symbolic elements. It is probably best to consider this as an instance of the second (form/function) distinction, in which an organized thing has the function of representing, symbolizing or expressing something mental, rather than as a third correlative, so long as we remember that function interacts with formal principle. The widespread tendency to treat this distinction as, basically, an instance of the first (form/matter) distinction generally proves mischievous.

3. AESTHETIC PRINCIPLES OF FORM. Art and its history, criticism, identification and teaching have developed specific form conceptions in the first sense, some rough-and-ready, others highly developed, for a variety of purposes. One is of providing a basis for form in the third and fourth classifications, though it must be emphasized that such classifications are often made according to other considerations, such as function. Some of these have been discussed above. The distinctions among, for example, plane, solid and envelope or container forms have been taken broadly to distinguish painting, sculpture and architecture or kinds of each. Another important use (including various efforts by Wölfflin and many others) is the formation of stylistic categories, explanatory of particular works, groups of works and even global differences via different 'senses of form' in art, culture or mentality.

Sometimes form conceptions are offered as replacements for those of style (for accounts of such employments see STYLE and similar headings).

BIBLIOGRAPHY
H. Wölfflin: *Kunstgeschichtliche Grundbegriffe* (Munich, 1915); Eng. trans. as *Principles of Art History* (London, 1932)
F. Boas: *Primitive Art* (Oslo, 1927)
H. Read: *The Meaning of Art* (London, 1931, rev. 1949)
H. Wölfflin: *Italien und das deutsche Formgefühl* (Munich, 1931); Eng. trans. as *The Sense of Form in Art: A Comparative Psychological Study* (New York, 1958)
S. Pepper: *Aesthetic Quality: A Contextualist Theory of Beauty* (New York, 1937)
L. Whyte, ed.: *Aspects of Form: A Symposium on Form in Nature and Art* (New Haven, 1952)
S. Langer: *Feeling and Form* (New York, 1953)
M. Beardsley: *Aesthetics: Problems in the Philosophy of Criticism* (New York, 1958)
G. Collier: *Form, Space, and Vision* (Englewood Cliffs, 1963, rev. 3/1972)
M. de Sausmarez: *Basic Design: The Dynamics of Visual Form* (London, 1964)
E. Gombrich: *Norm and Form: Studies in the Art of the Renaissance* (London, 1966)
M. Schapiro: 'On Perfection, Coherence, and Unity of Form and Content', *Art and Philosophy*, ed. S. Hook (New York, 1966), pp. 3–15
R. Venturi: *Complexity and Contradiction in Architecture* (New York, 1966)
R. Arnheim: *Toward a Psychology of Art* (Berkeley, 1967)
A. Ehrenzweig: *The Hidden Order of Art: A Study in the Psychology of Artistic Imagination* (London, 1967)
F. Peters: *Greek Philosophical Terms: A Historical Lexicon* (New York, 1967) [for *eidos*]
H. Osborne: *Aesthetics and Art Theory: A Historical Introduction* (London, 1968)
W. Tatarkiewicz: 'Form in the History of Aesthetics', *Dictionary of the History of Ideas: Studies of Selected Pivotal Ideas*, ed. P. Wiener, ii (New York, 1973), pp. 216–25
M. Finch: *Style in Art History: An Introduction to Theories of Style and Sequence* (Metuchen, 1974)
W. Tucker: *The Language of Sculpture* (London, 1974)
E. H. Gombrich: *The Sense of Order: A Study in the Psychology of Decorative Art* (Oxford, 1979)
D. Bohm: *Wholeness and the Implicate Order* (London, 1980)
D. Marr: *Vision* (San Francisco, 1982)
M. Podro: *The Critical Historians of Art* (New Haven, 1982)
D. Pole: *Aesthetics, Form and Emotion* (London, 1983)
W. Uttal: *On Seeing Forms* (Hillsdale, 1988)
J. Koenderink: *Solid Shape* (Cambridge, MA, 1990)

PATRICK MAYNARD

Forma. Italian group, founded in Rome in 1947. Its members included Pietro Consagra, Giulio Turcato, Piero Dorazio, Achille Perilli (*b* 1927), Antonio Sanfilippo (1923–80), Carla Accardi, Ugo Attardi (*b* 1923), Mino Guerrini and Concetto Maugeri. These artists played an important part in the development of Italian abstract art during the late 1940s and the 1950s. While influenced by contemporary ART INFORMEL, the work of Forma cannot be confined to any neat stylistic definition. Both Turcato and Dorazio experimented at this time with geometric abstraction, influenced in particular by the work of the Futurist Giacomo Balla. Turcato's paintings had a strong narrative element, as can be seen from *Political Gathering* (1950; Rome, Gal. Anna d'Ascanio), in which the bright red triangles have an obvious political significance. While Dorazio's work consisted of disciplined rhythmic patterns of interlocking shapes, other artists, such as the painters Accardi and Sanfilippo and the sculptor Consagra, concentrated on creating freer, more expressive works. During the 1950s Turcato, too, moved towards a more lyrical form of abstraction. As well as staging its own exhibitions (e.g. at the Art Club in Rome in 1947), Forma was involved in important international events, including the Venice Biennale of 1948 and the exhibition *Arte astratta e concreta in Italia*, held at the Galleria d'Arte Moderna in Rome in 1951. The group also made an important contribution to debate on art through its eponymous magazine. Its successor was the group CONTINUITÀ (founded 1961), which included Accardi, Consagra, Dorazio, Perilli and Turcato.

BIBLIOGRAPHY
Meister der Italienischen Moderne XIX: Forma 1, 1947–1987: Accardi, Attardi, Consagra, Dorazio, Guerrini, Maugeri, Perilli, Sanfilippo, Turcato (exh. cat. by B. Krimmel and others, Darmstadt, Inst. Mathildenhöhe, 1987–8)

CHRISTOPHER MASTERS

Formalism. Term for any approach to the arts, whether theoretical, critical or historical, that emphasizes the autonomy or primacy of formal qualities. In the case of painting, these qualities are usually understood to be compositional elements such as line, value, colour and texture: they can be distinguished from technique on the one hand and content on the other. Because compositional elements can be considered and enjoyed independently of the way in which a picture evokes the visible world, tells a story or expresses philosophical ideas, some formalists have argued that representation of any kind is incidental to art. They may be answered by those who insist that formal values, when elevated to objects of primary interest, in fact perform a kind of representation. The difficulties involved in the use of such terms helps explain why formalism has met with resistance in recent decades; at the same time, the issues that it attempts to address are so fundamental to art that it is bound to arouse perennial interest.

The origins of formalism are deeply rooted in ancient thought, in the belief for example that the universe is governed by numerical relationships, or in the notion of form as the intelligible quality of things, imposed upon or inherent in matter. Even in antiquity such ideas were applied to the arts: Aristotle understood art (*techne*) as a shaping process analogous to the processes of nature, while Vitruvius distinguished the design (*lineamenta*) of a building from its material existence. These applications were developed during the Renaissance. The humanist philosopher Benedetto Varchi, in a lecture (*Due lezzione*, Florence, 1550) on one of Michelangelo's sonnets, defined the task of the sculptor as the drawing-forth of the 'actual' from the 'potential' being. In the Enlightenment, with its concern for the psychological nature of knowledge, there arose the notion that the experience of a work of art as a work of art was neither purely sensual nor purely rational and that an 'aesthetic' experience could be distinguished from other kinds of experience. If in looking at a picture we are moved to religious insights, for example, we are not experiencing the picture aesthetically. Kant, on the other hand, in his *Critique of Judgment*, formulated the possibility of 'adherent' as well as 'pure' beauty and admitted that beauty could be a symbol of the good, that aesthetic experience could thus have a resonance in the realm of morality. Friedrich Schiller, pushing Kant's ideas towards Romanticism, emphasized the spiritually therapeutic nature of aesthetic experience, its capacity to reconcile the conflicting aspects of human nature and even to be an instrument of social and political reform.

Modern formalism evolved during the late 19th century and early 20th. An important impetus was given to this development by aestheticism, a broad-based cultural movement, in large part a reaction against the ills of modern industrial society. The literary and artistic movement known as Symbolism also played a part by emphasizing emotional expression above objective representation and stressing the integrity and autonomy of the work of art as object. The German essayist and critic KONRAD FIEDLER, who was inspired by Kant, developed a formalist theory that was adapted and popularized by his friend, the sculptor ADOLF VON HILDEBRAND. In Britain, similar ideas were broadcast in a more flamboyant fashion by James McNeill Whistler. The idea that a painting must succeed as an arrangement of compositional elements before it could succeed as representation was also central to the art of the Post-Impressionists and is found in a variety of forms in the writings of their critical supporters. Such ideas served the liberating impulses of MODERNISM, helping, as in the case of Kandinsky, to open the way for abstraction. They also informed much of the criticism that subsequently popularized 'modern art', most notably in the writings of ROGER FRY, CLIVE BELL and HERBERT READ during the first half of the 20th century. Later, the American critic CLEMENT GREENBERG developed a formalist definition of modernism in painting that was highly influential until the mid-1970s. In the meantime, formalism had also had a profound effect on the discipline of art history. Bernard Berenson, for example, invoked Hildebrand and Fry in giving a theoretical framework to his connoisseurship. The Viennese scholar ALOIS RIEGL and the Swiss HEINRICH WÖLFFLIN each sought to develop a systematic approach to the history of art that would, among other things, define the historical evolution of style as an autonomous and necessary process. Riegl made use of the notion of 'artistic will' (*Kunstwollen*) to establish the distinctive formal features of works of art as the products of something other than technique. Wölfflin believed that, ideally, the history of art could be written 'without names', that it could be reduced to purely impersonal and necessary processes. Although the conceptual foundations of these systems were soon disputed, they have continued to serve as points of reference for such scholars as Wilhelm Worringer, Hans Sedlmayr and Otto Pächt (1902–88). Wölfflin's critical terminology survived the obsolescence of his system and still enjoys currency even in the English-speaking world.

See also INTENTION, §2.

BIBLIOGRAPHY
W. Worringer: *Abstraktion und Einfühlung: Ein Beitrag zur Stilpsychologie* (Munich, 1908)
C. Bell: *Art* (London, 1913)
H. Wölfflin: *Kunstgeschichtliche Grundbegriffe* (Munich, 1915)
R. Fry: *Vision and Design* (London, 1920)
A. Riegl: *Gesammelte Aufsätze*, ed. K. Swoboda (Augsburg, 1929)
M. Podro: *The Manifold in Perception* (Oxford, 1972)
M. Lurz: *Heinrich Wölfflin: Biographie einer Kunsttheorie* (Worms, 1981)
M. Podro: *The Critical Historians of Art* (New Haven, 1982)
C. Greenberg: *Collected Essays*, 4 vols, ed. J. O'Brien (Chicago, 1986–93)
T. Eagleton: *Ideology of the Aesthetic* (London, 1989)
D. Summers: 'Form: Nineteenth-century Metaphysics and the Problem of Art-historical Description', *Crit. Inq.*, xv (1989), pp. 372–406

J. Crary: *Techniques of the Observer* (Cambridge, MA, 1990)

M. Olin: *Forms of Representation in Alois Riegl's Historiography* (University Park, PA, 1992)

M. Iverson: *Alois Riegl: Art History and Theory* (Cambridge, MA, 1993)

ROBERT WILLIAMS

Forment, Damián (*b* ?Valencia, *c.* 1480; *d* Santo Domingo de la Calzada, Logroño, 22 Dec 1540). Spanish sculptor. He is recorded in Valencia from 1500. In 1509 he moved to Saragossa to work on the main retable in the cathedral of Nuestra Señora del Pilar, which is modelled on the Gothic altarpiece in the cathedral of La Seo, Saragossa. The Pilar retable, one of Forment's noblest works, is made in alabaster and has three vertical sections surmounted by Gothic cresting and a central open section that houses the tabernacle (*sagrario*). The sculpture includes Forment's self-portrait and that of his wife, as well as reliefs on the base and main body depicting the *Presentation*, the *Assumption* and the *Birth of the Virgin* that show his knowledge of Renaissance art. In Saragossa, Forment also carved the main wooden retable (1511–24), which is Gothic in structure, in the church of S Pablo and that in the church of S Miguel de los Navarros (1518), for which he turned to Renaissance forms. His alabaster retable (1520–34) for the cathedral at Huesca is, however, modelled on his earlier Gothic retable at El Pilar. This work is mature in its masterful composition and expressive qualities. His alabaster retable (1527–9; heavily restored) in the monastery at Poblet, Tarragona, has three storeys, an ornamental cresting and seven vertical sections.

At the height of his career in 1539 Forment was commissioned to carve the wooden retable in the cathedral at S Domingo de la Calzada, a work that was completed by his assistants. Its structure and ornament reflect Castillian influence. The fragments of the tomb made by Forment in 1527 for *Juan de Lanuza* are in the Ayuntamiento, Alcañiz, Teruel. Forment introduced Renaissance forms to Aragon, assisted by a highly productive workshop. His work is characterized by fine decorative carving and the plasticity of the figures. With their shortened proportions and sense of realism they often recall a style of the late 1400s.

Ceán Bermúdez

BIBLIOGRAPHY

J. Martínez: *Discursos practicables del nobilísimo arte de la pintura* (MS. before 1682); 1st edn M. Nougués y Secail (Zaragoza, 1853–4); 3rd edn Julián Gállego (Barcelona, 1950)

Conde de la Vinaza: *Adiciones al Diccionario del Ceán Bermúdez* (Madrid, 1889)

R. del Arco: 'Datos sobre Damián Forment y su gran retablo de la Catedral de Huesca: Desposorios de Ursula Forment, hija suya', *Bol. Soc. Esp. Excurs.*, 23 (1915), pp. 10–21

A. Melon: 'Forment y el Monasterio de Poblet (1527–35)', *Rev. Archvs, Bib. & Mus.*, xxxvi (1917), pp. 276–302

J. Tramoyeres Blasco: 'El retablo de la Puridad, obra de Nicolás Falcó con la colaboración de los imagineros Pablo, Onofre y Damián Forment', *Archv A. Valenciano*, iv (1918), pp. 1–22

X. de Salas: 'Escultores renacientes en el Lavante español: Damián Forment en Barcelona, en Alcañiz, en Valencia', *An. & Bol. Mus. A. Barcelona*, I, 1 (1941), pp. 79–92; I, 2 (1942), pp. 35–87

M. Abizanda Broto: *Damián Forment, el escultor de la corona de Aragón* (Barcelona, 1942)

A. I. Souto Silva: *El retablo de San Miguel de los Navarros* (Saragossa, 1983)

MARGARITA ESTELLA

Formenton, Tommaso (*b* Vicenza, *c.* 1428; *d* 1492). Italian architect. The son of a local carpenter and presumably trained in the same profession, in 1467 he was appointed engineer to the city of Vicenza. Here, from 1481, he supervised the construction of loggia arcades (destr.; rebuilt by Palladio from 1549) around the city's Palazzo della Ragione (known as the Basilica), and he remained in charge of operations until 1491, when the work was almost complete. The design is known from early descriptions and images and from a few surviving fragments and remaining physical evidence. The two storeys of groin-vaulted loggia arcades, faced in pink and white stone and crowned with ornamental merlons, were built around three external sides of the existing palace, an enormous Late Gothic building (*c.* 1450–60; Domenico da Venezia) with an assembly hall covered by a vast keel roof occupying the entire upper storey. Formenton's design was evidently inspired by the Palazzo della Ragione in nearby Padua, a building of similar shape and size that had been fronted with new loggia arcades after 1420, although it was adapted to suit the Vicenza building's layout and Gothic style. The lower storey was arranged with broad round arches carried on squat columns, their spacing adjusted to accord with the unavoidable irregularities of the central building and the space restrictions of the site, while the upper storey was arranged with pointed arches in a doubled rhythm to match the windows of the assembly hall. Work was completed in 1494, but the loggias partly collapsed in 1496, soon after the installation of a staircase (1495–6), and were not rebuilt to the same design.

In 1484 Formenton was mentioned by the council of Brescia as 'architectus optimus' and as the designer of a new communal palace there, for which he personally delivered a large, spectacular model in 1489. The design is apparently lost. The existing palace, the magnificent Palazzo della Loggia (begun 1492), built in a radically classical style related to the works of Alberti in Mantua and the early works of Bramante in Milan, with massive arcades and applied orders, seems to have been based on an earlier design and is perhaps a development of an original project that had been commissioned in 1467. Formenton's scheme, which would have been very different in style, was presumably requested as a belated alternative and was perhaps intended for one of the other sites around the same piazza that were under consideration in 1489.

BIBLIOGRAPHY

B. Zamboni: *Memorie intorno alle pubbliche fabbriche più insigni della città di Brescia* (Brescia, 1778)

A. Magrini: 'Intorno Tommaso Formenton ingegnere vicentino nel secolo XV', *Archv Ven.*, iii (1872), pp. 38–59; iv (1872), pp. 37–58

G. G. Zorzi: 'Contribuzioni alla storia dell'arte vicentina nei secoli XV e XVI', *Miscellania di storia veneto-tridentina delle reale deputazione veneto-tridentina di storia patria*, ii (Venice, 1926), pp. 1–330

F. Barbieri: *Corpus palladianum II: La basilica palladiana di Vicenza* (Vicenza, 1968), pp. 28–32

D. Hemsoll: 'Bramante and the Palazzo della Loggia in Brescia', *A. Lombarda*, 86–7 (1988), pp. 167–79

G. Lupo: 'Platea magna communis Brixiae, 1433–1509', *La piazza, la chiesa, il parco*, ed. M. Tafuri (Milan, 1991), pp. 56–95

DAVID HEMSOLL

Formes. *See* ART ABSTRAIT.

Formigé, Jean-Camille (*b* Boussat, Gironde, 24 July 1845; *d* Montfermeil, 27 Aug 1926). French architect. He studied (1865–9) at the Ecole des Beaux-Arts, Paris, and had an important career in the Service des Edifices Diocésains, which he joined in 1876. He succeeded Charles Laisné as diocesan architect of Auch in 1879 and subsequently became architect of Meaux, Poitiers and Laval. He finally became inspecteur général adjoint in 1901. At the same time he worked for the Commission des Monuments Historiques. The various buildings he restored included the ancient abbey of Conques (begun 1878) and, in Poitiers, the churches of Notre-Dame-La-Grande, Ste Radegonde and St Hilaire Le Grand, as well as the Palais de Justice. He helped with the excavation (1881–2) of the ruins of Sanxay and restored the abbey of St-Savin-sur-Gartempe, the castle at Chauvigny (all Vienne) and the church at Poissy (Yvelines). Most of his work in the South of France involved the restoration or conservation of Romano-Gallic remains. He became a member of the Monuments Historiques in 1887 but resigned in 1892 when the commissioners were forbidden to work also as architects for the Commission. Formigé's work on new buildings in Paris included the Palais des Beaux-Arts et des Arts Libéraux at the Exposition Universelle of 1889, for which he won a prize, and the crematorium of Père-Lachaise (completed 1889; enlarged 1903–5). From 1884 to 1920 he was the architect to the Service des Promenades et Jardins in Paris and contributed significantly to the designs for the overground Métro. He was also architect-in-chief of the Conseil des Bâtiments Civils.

BIBLIOGRAPHY

David de Penarum, Roux et Delaire: *Les Architectes élèves de l'Ecole des beaux-arts* (Paris, 1895), p. 317

JEAN-MICHEL LENIAUD

Formists [Pol. *Formiści*]. Polish group of painters and sculptors that flourished between 1917 and 1922, from 1917 to 1919 known as the Polish Expressionists (Ekspresjoniści Polscy). A foretaste of the Formists' work appeared in the three *Wystawy niezależnych* ('Exhibitions of the Independents'; 1911–13) in Kraków, organized by the artists later to become leading Formists: the painter and stage designer Andrzej Pronaszko (1888–1961), his brother Zbigniew Pronaszko and Tytus Czyżewski, who all opposed Impressionism and favoured Cubism, Futurism and Expressionism. The Formists first exhibited in Kraków in 1917. Their aim was to find a new form and a new national style (they saw themselves as the Polish equivalent of the Italian Futurists and French Cubists) that was in part a continuation of the artistic ideology of the turn of the century (Polish modernism). A wide variety of artists took part in Formist exhibitions, including Stanisław Ignacy Witkiewicz, Leon Chwistek, the painter Tymon Niesołowski (1882–1965), August Zamoyski and the graphic artist Władysław Skoczylas (1883–1934), who later became the chief ideologist of national art.

The Formists published their own journal, *Formiści*, which appeared between 1919 and 1921 in Kraków. They collaborated with the circle of Polish Futurist poets and the Poznań-based group Revolt (Bunt). But the Formists lacked a clearly defined ideological and artistic programme. The theorists of Formism, firstly Zbigniew Pronaszko,

then Chwistek and Czyżewski and finally Chwistek's rival Witkiewicz, held diametrically opposed views on art, which largely contributed to the break-up of the group: first the Kraków section, then the Warsaw and Lwów branches. Another key factor in the disintegration of the group was the shift of position by some Formists to colourism. An attempt in 1927 by Warsaw-based Formists to revive the group came to nothing. The Formists were the first innovative group in Poland. However, the diversity of their stylistic experimentation meant that any continuation of Formism should really be sought in Polish Art Deco rather than in the subsequent work of the avant-garde.

BIBLIOGRAPHY

J. Pollakówna: *Formiści* [The Formists] (Wrocław, 1972)

H. Stępień: 'Formiści polscy' [The Polish Formists], *Polskie życie artystyczne w latach 1915–39* [Polish artistic life in the years 1915–39], ed. A. Wojciechowski (Wrocław, 1974)

WOJCIECH WŁODARCZYK

Formosa. *See* TAIWAN.

Formwork (i). The support for the total dead load of an arch, vault or dome during construction. *See* CENTERING.

Formwork (ii). Liner or form, made of steel, wood or plastics, into which liquid concrete is poured or pumped. *See* SHUTTERING.

□

Forner, Raquel (*b* Buenos Aires, 22 April 1902; *d* Buenos Aires, 10 June 1988). Argentine painter. She completed her studies at the Academia Nacional de Bellas Artes in Buenos Aires in 1923 and from 1929 to 1931 received tuition in Paris from Othon Friesz. In her choice of subject-matter she revealed a consistent concern with humanity and with the events of her time. During the Spanish Civil War (1936–9) she began to paint pictures in a powerful and dramatic style, inspired by the tragedies that have laid humanity waste, and often working in series, as in *The Drama* (1940–46; e.g. Buenos Aires, Mus. N. B.A.) and the closely related *See No Evil, Hear No Evil, Speak No Evil* (1939; Buenos Aires, Mus. Mun. A. Plást. Sívori), *The Rocks* (1947), *The Farce* (1948), *The Banners* (1952) and *Apocalypse* (1954); in the last of these, charred tree trunks, architecture in ruins and fantastic beings bear witness to a civilization in agony.

In 1958 Forner began work on *Space Series* and related pictures such as *Battle of Astral Beings II* (1961; Washington, DC, Kennedy Cent. Perf. A.) and the *Return of the Astronaut* (1969; Washington, DC, N. Air & Space Mus.), in which she related, with great imagination, the adventures and misadventures of a humanity hurled into the cosmic abyss. Her colours became vibrant and the surfaces of her paintings densely populated with interlaced figures undergoing metamorphosis at fantastic speed. The mythology created by Forner on the theme of humanity in space, both in these paintings and in several portfolios of lithographs, points towards the future and to hope for the moral improvement of humanity.

BIBLIOGRAPHY

Raquel Forner (exh. cat., essay P. Restany; Paris, UNESCO, 1977)

G. Whitelow: *Raquel Forner* (Buenos Aires, 1980)

NELLY PERAZZO

Forni, Ulisse (*b* Siena, *c*. 1820; *d* Florence, 1867). Italian restorer. He worked in Florence from 1845. He is known for his manual, published in 1866, in which he frequently disagreed with GIOVANNI SECCO-SUARDO. Although it lacks the clear presentation of the latter's work, Forni's handbook is nevertheless one of the most valuable manuals of 19th-century restoration. Apart from an over-extensive list of recipes and an inexact approach to bibliography and information, it reflects a more modern working context than Secco-Suardo's work and devotes much space to the restoration of medieval paintings, as well as dealing with different methods of rescuing, restoring and transferring wall paintings, probably based on advice provided by Gaetano Bianchi. Forni is known to have worked on Cosimo Rosselli's *Adoration of the Magi* (Florence, Uffizi) and Pontormo's *Venus* based on a cartoon by Michelangelo (Florence, Accad.).

WRITINGS
Manuale del pittore restauratore (Florence, 1866)

BIBLIOGRAPHY
G. Incerpi: 'Conservazione e restauro dei quadri degli Uffizi nel periodo lorenese', *Gli Uffizi: Quattro secoli di una galleria: fonti e documenti* (exh. cat., Florence, Uffizi, 1982), pp. 315–57
A. Conti: *Storia del restauro e della conservazione delle opere d'arte* (Milan, 1973, 2/1988), pp. 261–70, 354

ALESSANDRO CONTI

Fornovo, Giovanni Battista (*b* Parma, *c*. 1532; *d* 20 Nov 1585). Italian architect. He was in the service of Cardinal Alessandro Farnese from at least 1558, and worked with Jacopo Vignola on the Villa Farnese at Caprarola until 1562, when he was called to Piacenza to supervise the building of Vignola's Palazzo Farnese. Fornovo then entered the service of Ottavio Farnese, 2nd Duke of Parma and Piacenza, in which he remained for the rest of his life; he was, however, relieved of responsibility for the Palazzo Farnese in 1564. Fornovo's principal works were undertaken in Parma, where he designed the church of S Quintino (*c*. 1560), a longitudinal, aisleless church that demonstrates some of the characteristics of his work: an emphasis on verticality and an almost Gothic sense of structure in the lively outline of its external walls. His most important church, SS Annunziata, Parma, was begun in 1566; the dome was built from 1626 by Girolamo Rainaldi, then court architect, but closely followed Fornovo's design. The façade of SS Annunziata has an extremely tall, three-storey arched portico, articulated with orders, in a reworking of Alberti's S Andrea (begun 1470), Mantua; it is topped with an attic and pediment. The plan, based on a modified lateral oval, comprises two semicircular apses covered by ribbed semi-domes, with a rectangular, barrel-vaulted central space between. Five semicircular chapels radiate from each apse, creating an exceptional sense of centrifugal movement around the central core of the building. Externally, the convex projections of the chapels are balanced by concave walls above, set between tall buttresses; the resultant effect anticipates the Baroque plasticity of the drum of Francesco Borromini's S Andrea delle Fratte (1653–65), Rome. There are also echoes of the Romanesque in the rows of niches on the exterior chapel walls, which contrast with niched windows below and are derived from the work of Giulio Romano. The adjacent large Observantine cloister was begun at the same time as the church but was not completed until 1688. Fornovo may also have been involved in urban improvements in Parma in 1566, for which a drawing survives (Parma, Archv Stato).

BIBLIOGRAPHY
F. da Parma: *Memorie istoriche delle chiese e dei conventi dei frati minori dell'osservante, e riformata provincia di Bologna*, ii (Parma, 1760)
I. Affò: *Ricerche . . . intorno la chiesa, il convento, e la fabbrica della SS Annunziata di Parma* (Parma, 1796)
W. Lotz: 'Die ovalen Kirchenräume des Cinquecento', *Röm. Jb. Kstgesch.*, vii (1955), pp. 7–99
B. Adorni: 'SS Annunziata in Parma: Architetto G. B. Fornovo', *Archit.: Cron. & Stor.*, xv/5 (1969), pp. 332–41
——: *L'architettura farnesiana a Parma, 1545–1630* (Parma, 1974), pp. 48, 104–15
——: *L'architettura farnesiana a Piacenza, 1545–1600* (Parma, 1982), pp. 54, 196

BRUNO ADORNI

Forsberg, Nils, the elder (*b* Kätteryd, Skåne, 17 Dec 1842; *d* Helsingborg, 8 Nov 1934). Swedish painter. He came from a very poor background and trained initially as an artisan painter. He received his first artistic education at the Handicraft Association's school in Göteborg in the mid-1860s. In 1867 he was awarded a scholarship to visit the Exposition Universelle in Paris. He studied further at the Ecole des Beaux-Arts under Léon Bonnat, remaining in Paris for over 30 years. Like Gustaf Cederström Forsberg sought to renew Swedish history painting by investing it with techniques borrowed from French Realism. Another essential feature of his painting was the great social and moral commitment seen in such contemporary subjects as the *Family of Acrobats before the Circus Director* (1878; Göteborg, Kstmus.), which attacked child labour. Forsberg's biggest success was with the powerful *A Hero's Death* (1888; Stockholm, Nmus.), which was awarded a first-class gold medal at the Paris Salon of 1888. The subject derived from Forsberg's experiences in Paris during the Franco-Prussian War (1870–71), when he served as a hospital orderly. Forsberg worked for several years on the picture, studying every detail from models. The result was a painting of contemporary history, which united the effective figure grouping of academic tradition with the energetic brushwork of Realism and a moral commitment of his own. Forsberg's subsequent work never attained the same level. He moved back to Sweden in 1904 and lived in Helsingborg. Apart from portraits, his later output consisted mostly of history paintings, for example *Gustavus Adolphus before the Battle of Lützen* (1900; Göteborg, Kstmus.) and *Stenbock's Courier* (1910; Helsingborg, Vikingsberg Kstmus.). His son, Nils Forsberg the younger (*b* 1870), was also a painter.

WRITINGS
Mitt liv [My life] (Stockholm, 1929)

BIBLIOGRAPHY
G. Nordensvan: *Svensk konst och svenska konstnärer i det 19 århundradet* [Swedish art and Swedish artists in the 19th century], ii (Stockholm, 1928), pp. 223–4

TORSTEN GUNNARSSON

Forster, François (*b* Le Locle, Switzerland, 22 Aug 1790; *d* Paris, 24 June 1872). French engraver of Swiss birth. He came to Paris in 1805, studied with the engraver Pierre-Gabriel Langlois (1754–1810), and in 1813 entered the

Ecole des Beaux-Arts. He won the Deuxième Grand Prix de Rome for graphic art in 1809 and the Première Grand Prix in 1814 with the work *An Academy* (1814; Paris, Bib. N.). In 1828 he became a naturalized French citizen and in 1844 was elected to the Académie des Beaux-Arts. He was one of the most outstanding engravers of his time, producing prints from a wide variety of paintings. He went to Italy and made a number of plates from Renaissance masterpieces, for example *Christ in the Tomb* (1814; Paris, Bib. N.) after Andrea del Sarto, and the *Three Graces* (1841; Paris, Bib. N.) after Raphael. He also engraved the work of more contemporary artists: the *Sleep of Endymion* (1820; Paris, Bib. N.) after Anne-Louis Girodet (for illustration *see* GIRODET, fig. 1), and *Aeneas and Dido* (1828; Paris, Bib. N.) after Pierre Guérin. He also engraved a number of portraits, including *Wellington* (1818) after François Gérard, and *Queen Victoria* (1846; both Paris, Bib. N.) after Franz Xavier Winterhalter. Forster provided plates, after Achille Déveria, for Auguste de Chambure's *Napoléon et ses contemporains* (Paris, 1824) and for Ennio Quirino Visconti's *Iconographie ancienne* (Paris, 1823).

DBF

BIBLIOGRAPHY

H. Béraldi: *Les Graveurs du XIXe siècle*, vi (Paris, 1887), pp. 142–9
Inventaire du fonds français après 1800, Paris, Bib. N., Dépt. Est. cat., viii (Paris, 1954), pp. 114–16

☐

Forster, Georg (*b* Danzig [now Gdánsk, Poland], 26 Nov 1754; *d* Paris, 10 Jan 1794). German writer and politician. With his father he accompanied James Cook (1728–79) on his global voyage (1772–5). He was professor of Natural Sciences at Kassel and Vilna (1779–87) and became librarian at the University of Mainz in 1788. There he joined the Jacobin Club in 1792 and was one of the leaders of the radical Mainz Republic until the Prussian invasion in 1793; he died in exile.

Forster's philosophy epitomizes the 'anthropological turn' of the later Enlightenment. He was on close terms with Georg Christoph Lichtenberg and Johann Gottfried Herder and conducted the controversy with Kant on teleology and the philosophy of culture that underlies the second part of the latter's *Kritik der Urteilskraft* (Berlin, Liebau, 1790). He brought back from his global voyage an interest in the art and artefacts of non-European societies and applied these insights to European society, developing the concept of culture to describe the relation between intellectual and technical progress. Apart from this, his writings in art criticism are fairly unadventurous, his enthusiasm for the idealist aesthetics of Johann Joachim Winckelmann, Goethe and Schiller co-existing uneasily with his critique of philosophical idealism.

WRITINGS

Werke, 2 vols (Berlin and Weimar, 1968)

BIBLIOGRAPHY

H. Brunschwig: *La Crise de l'état prussien à la fin du XVIIIe siècle et la genèse de la mentalité romantique* (Paris, 1947); Eng. trans. by F. Jellinek as *Enlightenment and Romanticism in Eighteenth Century Prussia* (Chicago, 1974)
L. Uhlig: *Georg Forster: Einheit und Mannigfaltigkeit in seiner geistigen Welt* (Tübingen, 1967)

HOWARD CAYGILL

Förster, Hans. *See* FERSTER, HANS.

Förster, (Christian Friedrich) Ludwig, Ritter von (*b* Bayreuth, 8 Oct 1799; *d* Gleichenberg, 16 June 1863). Austrian architect, publisher and teacher. In 1818 he went to Vienna to study at the academy. Although Förster pursued an academic career at the academy, as a lecturer (1820–26) and professor of architecture (1842–5), his influence was due mainly to his great ability as a publisher and his untiring work on the urban reorganization of Vienna. In 1836 he founded the *Allgemeine Bauzeitung* (1836), one of the earliest 19th-century architectural journals. Given the rigid spirit of politics and the arts in Vienna at that time, the *Bauzeitung* was a bold enterprise, but it succeeded in establishing a long-desired contact with architectural trends in western Europe and in introducing historicist architecture in Vienna and throughout the Austro-Hungarian Empire. Förster's contribution to the planning of the expansion of Vienna also began in 1836, when he presented his first design. He continued to produce proposals for Vienna until the international competition in 1858, when his was one of the three main prizewinning projects together with those of Eduard Van der Null (with August von Siccardsburg) and Eduard Strache. The final plan received Imperial sanction in 1859 (*see* VIENNA, §II, 3). In his own architectural practice Förster concentrated on functional buildings and private houses. In 1839 he built one of the earliest factories in Vienna and in 1846 Förster invited the Danish architect Theophilus Hansen (*see* HANSEN, (2)) to join his office. The partnership that was formed contributed decisively to the development of early historicism in Vienna, especially by introducing rich ornamentation of Oriental (Förster) and Byzantine (Hansen) origin. In addition to several town and country houses, their most important works included the Protestant Gustav-Adolfkirche (1846–9) in Vienna, the competition project for the new parish church (1848) in Vienna-Altlerchenfeld and designs for competitions for the Vienna Arsenal and for a new city gate (both 1849). Hansen left the firm in 1852, but Förster continued to build in a similar rich style, for example in the synagogues in Vienna and Pest (1859), Hungary.

BIBLIOGRAPHY

H. von Förster and E. von Förster: 'Christian Friedrich Ludwig Ritter von Förster', *Allg. Bauztg Abbild.*, xxix (1864), p. 1
Österreichisches biographisches Lexikon, i (Graz and Cologne, 1957)
R. Wagner-Rieger: *Vom Klassizismus bis zur Secession*, Gesch. Stadt Wien, vii/3 (Vienna, 1973), pp. 142–5
——: *Theophil von Hansen*, Die Wiener Ringstrasse: Bild einer Epoche, viii/4 (Wiesbaden, 1980), pp. 28–38

SUSANNE KRONBICHLER-SKACHA

Forster, Thomas (*b* c. 1677; *d* London, after 1712). English draughtsman. Possibly a native of Northumberland, he worked in London and was one of the last notable portrait draughtsmen to work in the tradition of black lead, or plumbago, on vellum, a tradition established in England by such artists as David Loggan, John Faber and Robert White. His style, in portraits such as that of his wife, *Sarah Jennings* (1712; London, V&A), is more refined than theirs, distinguished by a greater appreciation of contour and a highly decorative approach to details such as curls of hair and wigs and folds of drapery, which do much to relieve the somewhat tired Baroque formulae of busts and half-lengths in common usage among contemporary miniaturists and draughtsmen. However, Forster's sitters were usually less important than those of Loggan or White. His work was seldom engraved, and he did not apparently practise as an engraver himself, which may account for his greater sensitivity as a draughtsman.

A number of Forster's sitters can be connected with James Butler, 2nd Duke of Ormonde, and with Ireland, but there is no evidence that Forster visited that country. Forster was perhaps also a topographer, for an elevation of the Banqueting House, London, is signed with his name. He may have been related to Charles Forster, who pursued what had become a rather old-fashioned technique of portraiture until c. 1717. The amateur Mary Blencowe (Blencow), daughter of the judge Sir John Blencowe (1642–1726), later Mrs Alexander Prescott of Thoby Priory, Essex, also displays Forster's influence in her portrait drawings.

BIBLIOGRAPHY

C. F. Bell and R. L. Poole: 'English Seventeenth Century Portrait Drawings in Oxford Collections', *Walpole Soc.*, xiv (1926), pp. 73–9

E. Croft-Murray and P. Hulton: *British Drawings: XVI and XVII Centuries*, London, BM cat., i (London, 1960), pp. 319–21

DAVID BLAYNEY BROWN

Förster, Wieland (*b* Dresden, 12 Feb 1930). German sculptor. From 1953 to 1958 he studied at the Hochschule für Bildende Künste in Dresden under the German sculptors Walter Arnold (*b* 1909) and Hans Steger (*b* 1923). He first met Fritz Cremer in 1956 and during the same period studied the portraiture of Marino Marini and Hans Wimmer, whose methods came to serve him as a guide. From 1959 to 1961 he was a graduate student of Cremer's at the Akademie der Künste der DDR in East Berlin. In 1962 he met the illustrator and painter Paul Eliasberg, who was living in Paris, and they became friends. After 1974 he was a member of the Akademie der Künste and ran a master's studio there.

The animating force in Förster's sculptural work is the interplay of natural forms and abstractions based on them: the egg shape, the cylinder, the ellipse and the cube. The search for the beauty and liveliness of volume is always present in his work. Major works in bronze by him that reflect both man's enjoyment of life and his sorrow and capacity for suffering include *Large Figure of a Bathing Woman* (1971; Halle, Staatl. Gal. Moritzburg), *Large Neeberg Figure* (1971–4; Altenburg, Staatl. Lindenau-Mus.) and *Man Grieving*, a memorial for the victims of the bombing of Dresden on 13 February 1945 (1985; Dresden, Skulpsamml.).

BIBLIOGRAPHY

C. Keisch: *Wieland Förster* (Dresden, 1977)

BARBARA BARSCH

Forstner, Leopold (*b* Leonfelden, Upper Austria, 2 Nov 1878; *d* Stockerau, nr Vienna, 5 Nov 1936). Austrian designer, painter and illustrator. He studied from 1899 to 1902 under Kolo Moser and Karl Karger (1848–1913) at the Kunstgewerbeschule in the Österreichisches Museum für Kunst und Industrie in Vienna, and in 1903 under Ludwig Herterich (1856–1932) at the Kunstakademie in Munich. He was represented at the 15th exhibition of the Vienna Secession in 1902 and produced woodcuts for *Ver*

Sacrum in 1903. He was co-founder of the Vereinigung Wiener Kunst im Hause; he designed the poster for the exhibition of 1903–4 and showed stained-glass windows, naturalistic watercolours of peasant types, and tapestry designs. He made numerous study trips to Germany, the Netherlands, Belgium and especially Italy, where he studied the work of glassmakers and mosaicists in Ravenna, Rome and Venice. From 1906 he worked intensively to revive the art of the mosaic, prepared the foundation of the Wiener Mosaik Werkstätte (trade licence 1908) and added his own glassworks in 1912. With the Wiener Werkstätte and the Wiener Keramik, Forstner's Wiener Mosaik Werkstätte was a main centre of the arts and crafts revival in the early 20th century, and novel in that both design and execution were by the same person. Composite mosaics of glass, marble, enamel, ceramics and metals were a speciality, winning Forstner numerous commissions in Vienna and throughout the Austro-Hungarian empire. He exhibited large-format mosaics at the *Kunstschau Wien* (1908), the *Internationale Kunstschau* of 1909 (e.g. *The Dance*, glass, mother-of-pearl and metal, 8.25×8.25 m, 1909; Vienna, Mus. Angewandte Kst) and the *Hagenbund* exhibition (1911). From 1906 to 1912 he produced mosaics designed by Rudolf Jettmar and stained-glass windows designed by Moser for the Kirche am Steinhof, Vienna. In 1908–10 he designed and executed the mosaic *Spring* in the dining-room at the Hotel Wiesler, Graz. In 1909–11 he produced the mosaic frieze, designed by Klimt, in the dining-room of the Palais Stoclet, Brussels. During World War I he made drawings in Albania and Macedonia (Vienna, Mus. Angewandte Kst; Mus. Vlkerknd.). In 1919 he founded the Edelglas- Mosaik- und Emailwerkstätte and the Edelglaswerke AG in Stockerau (closed in 1937), producing high-quality glass bowls, vases and services. Between 1929 and 1936 he taught at the Bundesgymnasium in Hollabrunn.

BIBLIOGRAPHY

Die Wiener Mosaikwerkstätte Leopold Forstner (exh. cat., ed. W. Mrazek; Vienna, Mus. Angewandte Kst, 1975–6)

W. Mrazek: *Leopold Forstner: Ein Maler und Materialkünstler des Wiener Jugendstils* (Vienna, 1981)

E. Lässig: *Leopold Forstner als christlicher Künstler des Jugendstils* (diss., U. Vienna, 1989)

SABINE KEHL-BAIERLE

Fort-Brescia, Bernardo. *See under* ARQUITECTONICA.

Fort Center. Site of a prehistoric village with complex earthworks, which flourished on the banks of Caloosahatchee River near Lake Okeechobee in south Florida, USA. By *c.* 450 BC the hunter–gatherer occupants had created a 9 m-wide, 350 m-diameter circular ditch to drain a vast garden plot. By *c.* AD 150 a more complex system of circular and radial ditches enclosed a ceremonial centre with two low, flat-topped mounds. On one of the mounds stood a charnel house in which bodies were prepared for placement on a roughly constructed wooden platform, standing in an artificial pond. The upper platform piers were elaborately carved to represent birds and felines (see fig.). At the collapse of this platform, *c.* AD 500, many of the 300 burial bundles were salvaged, placed on the former location of the charnel house and covered with a mound of sand. Several of these reburials were accompanied by

Fort Center, charnel platform pier with carved eagle effigy, wood, h. 1.57 m, w. 0.38 m, *c.* AD 150–500 (Gainesville, FL, University of Florida, Florida Museum of Natural History)

incised and stamped platform pipes of a style known as Hopewellian (*see* HOPEWELL MOUNDS), by ornaments carved of Appalachian minerals or by a few ceramic vessels (all Gainesville, U. FL, Florida Mus. Nat. Hist.) traded from sites related to the Hopewell culture in northern Florida. Nevertheless, the local sand-tempered, plain-surfaced ceramics and the style of the wooden carvings relate Fort Center to several dozen large and complex 'Big Circle' earthwork sites of the non-Hopewellian Belle Glades Tradition, found between the Everglades and sites along the Florida Keys, including KEY MARCO. At the time of European contact in the 16th century this area was occupied by Calusa Indians.

For further discussion of the indigenous art and architecture of the region *see* NATIVE NORTH AMERICAN ART.

BIBLIOGRAPHY

J. Milanich and C. Fairbanks: *Florida Archaeology* (New York, 1980)

W. Sears: *Fort Center: An Archaeological Site in the Okeechobee Basin* (Gainesville, 1982)

DAVID S. BROSE

Fort du Plessy, Claude Le. *See* LE FORT DU PLESSY, CLAUDE.

Forte, Luca (*b* Naples, *c.* 1615; *d* before 1670). Italian painter. He specialized in still-lifes, and although only a few of his signed or initialled works survive, he is nonetheless regarded as a main exponent of the genre. He is particularly significant for having introduced the naturalism of Caravaggio into still-life painting in Naples. His development was influenced by the work of contemporary specialists in Rome, such as Tommaso Salini, Giovanni Battista Crescenzi and Pietro Paolo Baonzi, and by the work of certain Spanish artists, especially Blas de Ledesma and Juan van der Hamen. De Dominici wrote of Forte as being older than Paolo Porpora (*b* 1617), which would place him at the very start of still-life painting in 17th-century Naples. There are few known facts about his life, but it is known that he was a witness in 1639 to the marriage contract of the Neapolitan painter Aniello Falcone. Forte must therefore have belonged to the artistic circle around Falcone, whose workshop served as a kind of academy of design as well as a school of life drawing between 1630 and 1640. The connection is confirmed by a 17th-century inventory of the Neapolitan palace of Ferrante Spinelli, Prince of Tarsia, which lists a picture in which Forte painted the flowers and fruit while Falcone was responsible for the figures.

The most important works for establishing Forte's stylistic chronology are the *Still-life with Tuberose and Crystal Goblet* (Rome, Pal. Corsini), a schematized and apparently early composition, and three signed canvases (Sarasota, FL, Ringling Mus. A.; ex-Matthiesen F.A., London; Marano di Castenaso, M. Pradelli priv. col., see 1982 exh. cat., p. 161), which are unanimously ascribed to the decade after 1640 and thus represent his middle period. In these works the composition is complex and articulated, the light is still and the contrasts between light and shadow marked; they are executed with minute attention to detail. Closely related are two small octagonal canvases of *Cherries, Strawberries and Other Fruit* and *Apples and Pears* (both Naples, Mus. N. Cer., on dep. Naples, Capodimonte). To this same period or very shortly after it are ascribed a pair of pendants featuring *Lemons, Lemon Trees and Landscape* and *Dried Fruit, Flowers and Landscape* (Florence, Leone Cei & Sons), in which landscape begins to play an important role. These are among the last attributable pictures and are masterpieces of delicacy and precision.

BIBLIOGRAPHY

B. de Dominici: *Vite* (1742–5), iii, p. 135

U. Prota Giurleo: 'Un complesso familiare di artisti napoletani del secolo XVII', *Napoli Riv. Mun.*, n. s. 2, lxxviii (1951), p. 26

R. Causa: 'Luca Forte e il primo tempo della natura morta napoletana', *Paragone*, xiii (1962), no. 145, pp. 41–8

——: *La natura morta a Napoli nel sei e settecento* (1972), v/2 of *Storia di Napoli* (Cava dei Tirreni, 1967–78), pp. 1005–9

Painting in Naples from Caravaggio to Giordano (exh. cat., ed. C. Whitfield and J. Martineau; London, RA, 1982), pp. 160–62
L. Salerno: *La natura morta italiana* (Rome, 1984), pp. 92–3, fig. 36
Civiltà del seicento a Napoli, 2 vols (exh. cat., ed. S. Cassani; Naples, Capodimonte, 1984–5), i, pp. 142–3, 278–82

ROBERTO MIDDIONE

Fortescue-Brickdale, (Mary) Eleanor (*b* Upper Norwood, Surrey, 25 Jan 1872; *d* Kensington, London, 10 March 1945). English illustrator, painter and designer. She entered the Royal Academy Schools, London, and won a prize for a mural design in 1897. She specialized in book illustration, in pen and ink and later in colour. Among her many commissions were illustrations to Tennyson's *Poems* (1905) and *Idylls of the King* (1911) and Browning's *Pippa Passes* (1908). She was particularly popular with the publishers of the lavishly illustrated gift-books fashionable in the Edwardian era. She exhibited regularly at the Royal Academy and the Royal Water-Colour Society. She took up stained-glass design (windows in Bristol Cathedral), which modified her style of illustration to flat areas of colour within black outlines. She also painted plaster figurines and designed bookplates.

Fortescue-Brickdale continued the Pre-Raphaelite tradition, reworking romantic and moralizing medieval subjects in naturalistic and often strong colour and elaborate detail. Her most important oil painting is *The Forerunner* (exh. RA 1920; Liverpool, Walker A.G.). For 40 years she occupied a studio at 11 (later 55) Holland Park Road, London, near the school founded in 1910 by her close friend Byam Shaw, where she taught. A representative group of her works on paper is in the Ashmolean Museum, Oxford.

BIBLIOGRAPHY
Centenary Exhibition of Works by Eleanor Fortescue-Brickdale (exh. cat. by G. L. Taylor, Oxford, Ashmolean, 1972–3)

GERALD TAYLOR

Fortin, Marc-Aurèle (*b* Sainte-Rose, nr Quebec, 14 March 1888; *d* Abitibi, Quebec, 2 March 1970). Canadian painter and etcher. From 1904 to 1908 he studied at the Ecole du Plateau in Montreal under the Canadian painter Ludger Larose and he also attended evening classes run by Larose and the Canadian painter Edmond Dyonnet (1859–1954) at the Monument National. He later studied at the Art Institute of Chicago and also in New York and Boston, working under Edmund C. Tarbell, Edward J. Finley Timmons (*b* 1882), John H. Vanderpoel and John White Alexander. Returning to Canada in 1914 he produced works influenced by the Barbizon school, such as *Line of the Côte Croche at Sainte-Rose* (*c.* 1915; Rouyn, Mr and Mrs J. P. Bonneville priv. col., see 1964 exh. cat., pl. 2).

From about 1920 to 1935, Fortin concentrated on landscapes and townscapes. Together with Adrien Hébert and others he was a member of the radical Montreal group of artists and writers, L'Arche. Some of his landscapes, such as *Landscape, Ahuntsic* (1920–35; Ottawa, N.G.), were executed in a simplified, almost naive style. Works such as *Landscape, Hochelaga* (1929; Ottawa, N.G.) showed the effects of the contemporary rapid industrialization on workers and their surroundings. In 1935 he travelled to Europe, painting in southern France and northern Italy, but he returned to Canada the same year to work in the Baie-Saint-Paul and Gaspé regions. He was made an Associate Member of the Royal Canadian Academy in 1942 and from then until 1957 he exhibited every two years at the L'Art Français Gallery in Montreal. His painting of this period, still of landscapes, used bright colours and showed a greater simplification of forms, as shown by *Landscape at Sainte-Rose* (*c.* 1950, Montreal, Mus. F.A.). In 1955 he was prevented from painting by an illness that led to the amputation of both legs; he did not resume until 1962.

BIBLIOGRAPHY
M. Barbeau: *Painters of Quebec* (Toronto, 1946), pp. 11–17
Fortin (exh. cat. by J.-R. Ostiguy, Ottawa, N.G., 1964)
B. Lord: *The History of Painting in Canada: Towards a People's Art* (Toronto, 1974), pp. 146–7

Fortini, Giovacchino (*b* Settignano, nr Florence, 1670; *d* Florence, 1736). Italian sculptor, medallist, architect and festival designer. He was a leading figure in the generation of sculptors trained in Florence after the dissolution of the Accademia Fiorentina in Rome (1686). Taught by Carlo Marcellini and Giuseppe Piamontini, he worked under Giovanni Battista Foggini on sculpture for the Feroni Chapel in SS Annunziata, Florence (1691–3), and the nave of SS Michele e Gaetano (1694–6). His principal sculptures are marble works for the high altar of SS Annunziata (1704–6) and portraits. His statues of *St Filippo Benizzi* and *St Giuliana Falconieri* for the Annunziata altar, with their animated balance and restrained intensity, are among the best of their date in Florence. Several portrait busts and reliefs, with an unsparingly detailed realism tempered by coolly imperious expression, have been attributed to him. The basis for these attributions is the signed marble effigy of *Baron Philipp Bertram Degenhard Joseph von Hochkirchen* (*d* 1703), shown reclining in armour and peruke (1701; tomb destr.; effigy in Cologne Cathedral). It is possible that he executed the Baron's tomb during a sojourn in Germany.

Fortini's portrait medals, among the finest of the period in invention, modelling and chasing, include one of *Marchese Fabio Feroni* (1702)—the terracotta bust of *Feroni* (Florence, Orlando Petreni priv. col.) is probably also Fortini's work—and two portrait medals dated 1717 and 1725 of the *Electress Palatine Anna Maria Luisa de' Medici* (e.g. 1717; Florence, Bargello). For the electress he also produced a small bronze group, the *Education of the Virgin* (1723; Cologne, Kstgewmus.). Perhaps because of a personal shift in interest to medals and small sculpture, which gave scope for his mastery of delicate detail, his later works in stone for Florentine and Portuguese churches show a decline in his ability to work on a large scale, as is evident in his *St Philip* (1732; Mafra, Basilica).

Fortini succeeded Giovanni Battista Foggini as Chief Court Architect to the Medici and was also one of the 12 masters of the Accademia del Disegno in Florence. He worked as a festival designer; a *St Sebastian* (Florence, Misericordia) in wood and gesso was probably made for the Grand Prince Ferdinando de' Medici for the saint's day in 1709. Fortini also prepared designs (two in Florence, Archv Stato; see Monaci) for the funeral service (14 Feb 1711) for Francesco Maria de' Medici in SS Annunziata.

BIBLIOGRAPHY

F. Schottmüller: 'Opere di Giovacchino Fortini', *Boll. A.*, xxvi (1932), pp. 201–8

R. Verres: 'Zu Giovacchino Fortini', *Pantheon*, xviii (1936), pp. 358–9

K. Lankheit: *Florentinische Barockplastik: Die Kunst am Hofe der letzten Medici, 1670–1743* (Munich, 1962), esp. pp. 88, 172, 175–8, 192–3, 226–7, Doc. 19 [early biog. by Gabburri, numerous illus.]

L. Monaci: 'Inediti Fogginiani', *Paragone*, xxv/289 (1974), pp. 55–6

The Twilight of the Medici: Late Baroque Art in Florence, 1670–1743 (exh. cat., Detroit, MI, Inst. A.; Florence, Pitti; 1974), pp. 29–30, 80–85

B. L. Brown: 'A Drawing and a Payment for a Silver Missal Cover by Fortini', *Burl. Mag.*, cxxiii (1981), pp. 29–30

La Misericordia di Firenze: Archivio e raccolta d'arte (Florence, 1981), pp. 207–8

E. Chini: *La chiesa e il convento dei Santi Michele e Gaetano a Firenze* (Florence, 1984), pp. 216–17, 220, 305–6

F. Vannel and G. Toderi: *La medaglia barocca in Toscana* (Florence, 1987), pp. 114–19

S. Bellisi: *Ant. Viva.*, xxxi (1992) [several articles]

Repertorio della scultura fiorentina del seicento e settecento (Turin, 1993)

ALISON LUCHS

Fortnum, C(harles) D(rury) E(dward) (*b* Hornsey, London, 2 March 1820; *d* Stanmore, Middx, 6 March 1899). English collector and writer. He was one of the leading European collectors and authorities on the decorative arts during the second half of the 19th century. His early adult life (1840–45) was spent in southern Australia where it is often supposed that he made his fortune in mining copper. At this stage Fortnum's interests lay in mineralogy and entomology. Two judicious marriages, both to cousins who had independently inherited fortunes made from the success of Fortnum & Mason in Piccadilly, London, provided a solid financial basis for his future activities as a collector.

Fortnum formed his distinguished collection of fine-art objects mainly during the 1850s and 1860s, while travelling in Europe, in the sale rooms and by exchanges with fellow collectors. His collection numbered over a thousand items, including works of Egyptian, Etruscan, Greek, Roman, East Asian, Italian and German origin. These were kept at his home, the Hill House, Stanmore, of which an invaluable photographic record dating from 1873 is preserved (Oxford, Ashmolean). The main strength of the collection were the bronzes (including medals and plaquettes), maiolica and finger-rings, although it also comprised paintings and sculpture, glassware and porcelain of some significance. Fortnum was primarily a connoisseur who put quality and historical significance before the random accumulation of choice objects.

Fortnum's achievements as a scholar were closely related to the strengths of his collection. His publications on the ceramics and bronzes in the South Kensington Museum (now the Victoria and Albert Museum) and the maiolica in the Ashmolean Museum, Oxford, together with his articles in *Archaeologia* and the *Archaeological Journal* on a variety of topics including finger-rings, seals and gems, remain standard works. He was elected Fellow of the Society of Antiquaries in 1858 and served as Vice-President (1886, 1891, 1894); he was also appointed Trustee of the British Museum in 1889. Although some objects from his collection were given to the British Museum, Oxford University became his chief beneficiary. The protracted negotiations over the loan and eventual gift of Fortnum's collection began in 1881 and led to a generous endowment in 1889, which resulted in the enlargement of the Ashmolean Museum. Fortnum also left several of his books and papers to Oxford, as well as a four-volume manuscript catalogue of his collection, which is an important source of information about collecting in the late 19th century.

WRITINGS

A Descriptive Catalogue of the Maiolica and Enamelled Earthenware of Italy: The Hispano Moresco, Persian, Damascus and Rhodian Wares in the South Kensington Museum (London, 1872)

A Descriptive Catalogue of the Bronzes of European Origin in the South Kensington Museum (London, 1876)

A Descriptive and Illustrated Catalogue of his [C. D. E. Fortnum's] Collection of Works of Antique, Renaissance and Modern Art (London, 1889)

A Descriptive Catalogue of the Maiolica and Enamelled Earthenware of Italy in the Ashmolean Museum, Oxford: Fortnum Collection (Oxford, 1897)

BIBLIOGRAPHY

DNB

J. V. G. Mallett: 'C. D. E. Fortnum and Italian Majolica of the Renaissance', *Apollo*, cviii (1978), pp. 396–404

G. Taylor and D. Scarisbrick: *Finger Rings from Ancient Egypt to the Present Day* (Oxford, 1978), pp. 5–21

——: 'Storico e storicismo: Fortnum, Cantagalli e Castellani', *Faenza*, lxiv (1978), pp. 37–47

R. F. Ovenell: *The Ashmolean Museum, 1683–1894* (Oxford, 1986), pp. 227, 243, 245–7, 256, 259–60

C. Lloyd: 'Two Large Plaquettes in Oxford from the Collection of C. D. E. Fortnum', *Stud. Hist. A.*, xxii (1989), pp. 207–24 [Center for Advanced Study in the Visual Arts Symposium Paper IX: National Gallery of Art, Washington, DC, 1989]

N. Penny: *Catalogue of European Sculpture in the Ashmolean Museum: 1540 to the Present Day* (Oxford, 1992)

CHRISTOPHER LLOYD

Fortoul, Hippolyte (*b* Digne, 4 Aug 1811; *d* Ems-les-Bains, 7 July 1856). French critic, art historian and administrator. In the 1830s he started on a career in journalism, while associating with a group of avant-garde artists that included Pierre-Jean David d'Angers and with such architects as Henri Labrouste, Félix-Jacques Duban and Louis Duc.

His closest friendship was with the architect Léon Vaudoyer, with whom he travelled extensively. Together they formulated the idea that the morphology of medieval and Renaissance buildings represents a record of the political and social attitudes of the past. As a critic for the liberal journals *Le Bon Sens*, *Revue britannique*, *Le National de 1834* and George Sand's *Revue indépendante*, Fortoul argued that art should be the instrument of social and political change. This idea was further developed on trips with Vaudoyer to England (1837) and Germany (1839), resulting in the publication of Fortoul's most important work, *De l'art en Allemagne*, an analysis of the historicist tendencies in contemporary German art and artistic theory.

Appointed Ministre de l'Instruction Publique et des Cultes under Napoleon III, he introduced reforms in both the administration and the architecture of educational establishments and places of worship. He set up a series of advisory and review committees, staffed largely by the architects he had supported in print in the 1830s: Vaudoyer, Léonce Reynaud, Eugène-Emanuel Viollet-le-Duc and later Labrouste were appointed to the Service des Edifices Diocésains. Founded in 1853, this oversaw all the work of building and restoring cathedrals, seminaries and bishops' palaces. Fortoul commissioned a plan for the rebuilding of the Sorbonne, Paris (shelved on his death), worked on by Vaudoyer and Duc; commissioned Viollet-le-Duc to design new university buildings at Clermont-Ferrand; and charged Duc with creating a model for *lycées* in France. The building in which he had the greatest involvement was the new cathedral (1852–93) at Marseille, designed by Vaudoyer (*see* VAUDOYER, (2), fig. 2). After his death, Fortoul's reputation declined rapidly, as his name was associated exclusively with the authoritarian and centralized curricular reforms of his period as Ministre de l'Instruction Publique.

WRITINGS

'Fronton du Panthéon', *Nouv. Minerve*, 10 (1837), pp. 433–41; also in *Le Panthéon, symbole des révolutions*, ed. B. Bergdoll (Paris, 1989), pp. 313–16

'Travaux exécutés à Paris par la liste civile, par l'état, par la ville', *Le National de 1834* (4 Jan 1840), pp. 1–2

De l'art en Allemagne, 2 vols (Paris, 1841)

Etudes d'archéologie et d'histoire, 2 vols (Paris, 1854)

G. Massa-Gille, ed.: *Journal d'Hippolyte Fortoul*, 2 vols (Geneva, 1979–89)

BIBLIOGRAPHY

P. Raphaël: 'Fortoul: Journaliste républicain et critique littéraire', *Nouv. Rev.*, 62 (1922), pp. 193–205, 298–312; 63 (1923), pp. 28–52

——: 'Fortoul: Critique d'art', *Révolution 1848*, 20 (1923–4), pp. 39–57

P. Raphaël and M. Gontard: *Un Ministre de l'instruction publique sous l'empire autoritaire: Hippolyte Fortoul, 1841–1856* (Paris, 1975)

B. Bergdoll: *Léon Vaudoyer: Historicism in the Age of Industry* (New York, 1994)

BARRY BERGDOLL

Fortress. *See* CASTLE, §I; *see also* MILITARY ARCHITECTURE AND FORTIFICATION.

Fortuny. Spanish family of artists and collectors, active also in Italy. During his brief but highly successful career (1) Mariano Fortuny y Marsal became one of the leading Spanish painters of the mid-19th century. His fame and fortune were primarily the result of his historical genre paintings. His son (2) Mariano Fortuny y Madrazo settled in Venice, where he worked first as a painter but went on to build a reputation as a fashion and theatre designer.

(1) Mariano (José Bernardo) Fortuny y Marsal (*b* Reus, 11 June 1838; *d* Rome, 21 Nov 1874). Painter and etcher. His work drew both on earlier Spanish art, especially the paintings and etchings of Goya, and on contemporary foreign works, notably the paintings of the Italian Macchiaioli and those of the French artist Ernest Meissonier.

1. REUS AND BARCELONA, 1838–57. Fortuny was orphaned at an early age. His paternal grandfather, Maria Fortuny i Baró (1782–1855), himself a frustrated artist, undertook the boy's education. In 1850 Fortuny attended drawing lessons in Reus, and then he studied watercolour and oil painting under the amateur painter Domingo Soberano; he also had lessons in the workshop of the silversmith and miniaturist Antonio Bassa. In September 1852 Fortuny went to Barcelona with his grandfather in search of new and broader horizons for his artistic training. In Barcelona, with the help of the sculptor Domingo Talarn (*fl c.* 1838–91), he obtained a small grant to study at the Escuela de Bellas Artes and entered the studio of the painter Claudio Lorenzale y Sugrañes (1814–89), an enthusiastic follower of the German painter Friedrich

1. Mariano Fortuny y Marsal: *Ramón Berenguer III Nailing the Ensign of St Eulàlia into Foix Castle*, oil on canvas, 1.18×0.90 m, 1850s (Barcelona, Real Accademia Catalana de Bellas Artes de San Jorge)

Overbeck. Fortuny was encouraged to work in Overbeck's idealizing manner, and his first drawings and sketches bear the traces of the linear purity of this style. A reaction against it, however, was encouraged by Fortuny's discovery of lithographs by Paul Gavarni, which he copied. (Fortuny started producing his own prints, mostly etchings, in the early 1860s.) Fortuny's individual style was first apparent in the painting *Cholera in Reus* (1850s; untraced, see Folch i Torres, pl. 20), where a contemporary situation is rendered in a manner both naturalistic and dramatic. Fortuny continued, however, to produce work in a more academic vein, treating both religious subjects, such as *St Paul at the Areopagus* (1850s; Barcelona, Mus. A. Mod.), and historical themes, such as *Ramón Berenguer III Nailing the Ensign of St Eulàlia into Foix Castle* (1850s; Barcelona, Real Acad. Cat. B.A.S Jorge; see fig. 1). Both works are rather cold and contrived, but they were well received, and with the second painting he won a scholarship, in 1857, to study in Rome.

2. ROME AND MOROCCO, 1858–70. In March 1858 Fortuny arrived in Rome, which he described as 'a great cemetery visited by foreigners'. He looked keenly, however, at the art of the Renaissance and Baroque periods, admiring especially the portrait of *Innocent X* by Diego Velázquez. He was also impressed by some of Raphael's frescoes in the Vatican but was disappointed by the work of Michelangelo. Fortuny's main aim at this time was to produce a series of small paintings in a more personal style

2. Mariano Fortuny y Marsal: *Curate's Office*, oil on canvas, 600×935 mm, 1867–70 (Barcelona, Museu d'Art Modern)

with mythological subjects. An opportunity to work in this direction occurred during the Spanish war with Morocco (1860), when Fortuny was sent to Morocco to record scenes of battle. This experience was the crucible in which his artistic personality took shape; the richness of the colour, the dazzling light and the exotic environment contributed to changing Fortuny's conception of painting, especially history painting. He now strove for freshness, realism and local detail, using vibrant colour and a freer and more spontaneous brushstroke to suggest movement through clearly defined shading. He produced lively pencil sketches, subtle watercolours and small oil paintings from which he developed splendid canvases such as the unfinished *Battle of Tetuán* (1862–4; Barcelona, Mus. A. Mod.) and the rather more conventional *Odalisque* (1862; Barcelona, Mus. A. Mod.), reminiscent of the work of Eugène Delacroix. A subsequent visit to Morocco (1862) provided further inspiration through the exotic splendour of the location. He produced his first etchings, a medium in which he was to excel, on Arab themes, ranging from the picturesque (e.g. *Arab Family*, 1862) to the tragic, with scenes in the spirit of Goya (*Moroccan Warrior Watching by a Corpse*, mid-1860s). The journey to Morocco decided his artistic direction; this was enriched by his short stay in Madrid on his way back to Rome, during which he studied earlier art in the Museo del Prado. He also made a short visit to Paris in order to study Horace Vernet's painting of the *Battle of Smalaha* in preparation for his own *Battle of Tetuán*, and he was strongly influenced by Delacroix's painting, the *Battle of Taillebourg*.

After Fortuny's return to Rome his style gained in fluency and virtuosity, delicacy of touch and dazzling

colour. His work began to attract imitators. He received a large number of commissions, and he was offered an advantageous business contract by the Parisian dealer Goupil, which brought him money and fame but which subjected his work to commercial taste. With the watercolour painting the *Young Count* (1862; Barcelona, Mus. A. Mod.), Fortuny embarked on a long series of 'frock-coat' (historical genre) subjects, influenced by the work of Giovanni Battista Tiepolo and Antoine Watteau. Such pictures came to be so popular that Fortuny had to continue to produce them. Nevertheless, they brought him international fame and money and gave rise to the style known as *Fortunismo*. Fortuny was, however, able to rise above the pettiness inherent in the genre to produce such works as the *Print Collector* (mid-1860s; Barcelona, Mus. A. Mod.) and the *Curate's Office* (1867–70; Barcelona, Mus. A. Mod.; see fig. 2). Such paintings were of small format, executed with a meticulous, virtuoso technique and based on observation of the natural world; they treated realistic subjects with a marked degree of frivolity and irony. In these works Fortuny may be seen to have continued the tradition of the *tableautin*, the small studio painting derived from the work of lesser Dutch masters of the 17th century and developed in France as a reaction to the emphasis and grandiloquence inherent in aspects of both Classicism and Romanticism. The major exponent of this tradition during Fortuny's time was the French artist Meissonier. Fortuny's personal contribution to the genre was an ability to produce the lively surface sensibility of the colourist. He had a sparkling technique and a passion for light, and he found exceptional satisfaction in the pictorial subject. This is certainly the case with the

Curate's Office. The subject of the picture had been inspired by Fortuny's visits to a curate's office in Madrid to make arrangements relating to his marriage in 1867 to Cecilia de Madrazo (daughter of the painter Federico de Madrazo). While in Madrid Fortuny had also been able to study at greater length the work of the great Spanish painters in the Museo del Prado, and he copied paintings by El Greco, Velázquez and, above all, Goya.

3. GRANADA AND ROME, 1870–74. Fortuny continued to be based in Rome until 1870, when he went to Paris. There he finished the *Curate's Office*, which enjoyed unprecedented success. (Théophile Gautier described it as 'a sketch by Goya continued and retouched by Meissonier'.) The political tension at that time between France and Spain, however, prompted him to move to Granada, where he remained for two years. In Granada he devoted himself to becoming a collector and to the revival of the applied arts. The luminous quality of his work from this time has been compared to that of the Macchiaioli painters in Italy, because of their shared technique based on broad areas of coloured shading. Fortuny did indeed admire Giovanni Boldini and was also close to Giovanni Fattori, Silvestro Lega and other Macchiaioli. In 1872 he paid another short visit to Morocco. On his return to Rome, where he was enthusiastically received, he became increasingly dissatisfied and melancholy. It seems from a letter that he wrote to Baron Davillier that he felt a strong need to free himself from the commercial trap in which he appeared to be caught: 'I want to have the pleasure of painting for myself. In this lies true painting.' His last works testify to his anxiety, especially in the strong emotional value inherent in the colour shading. His work during this time in Granada shows his interest in the natural world, which gained solidity in his final works painted in 1874 during his summer stay in Portici, near Naples, where the light and climate are so similar to those of Andalusia. Such paintings as *Naked Man on the Beach at Portici* (Madrid, Prado) suggest an imminent change of style. Fortuny's inveterate interest in the exotic also took a new turn towards 'Japanese' subjects, resulting in the charming picture *Fortuny's Children in the Japanese Room of his House* (1874; Madrid, Prado). Fortuny died within a short time of arriving back in Rome, according to some accounts as a result of malaria and to others of a stomach ailment contracted several years before.

WRITINGS

Fortuny: Sa Vie, son oeuvre, sa correspondance, ed. Baron Davillier (Paris, 1874)

BIBLIOGRAPHY

S. Sampere y Miquel: *Mariano Fortuny* (Barcelona, 1880)
J. Ysart: *Fortuny: Ensayo biográfico-artístico* (Barcelona, 1882)
F. Miquel y Badia: *Fortuny: Su vida y sus obras* (Barcelona, 1887)
J. Frances: *Fortuny y el fortunismo* (Madrid, 1929)
A. Mestres: *'La vicaria' de Fortuny* (Barcelona, 1929)
A. Maseras and C. Fages de Climent: *Fortuny, la mitad de una vida* (Madrid, 1932)
A. Maseras: *El pintor Fortuny* (Barcelona, 1936)
Fortuny (exh. cat., Barcelona, Pal. Virreina, 1940)
L. Gil Fillol: *Fortuny* (Barcelona, 1942)
——: *Mariano Fortuny: Su vida, su arte* (Barcelona, 1952)
J. Ciervo: *Mariano Fortuny: Fundador del colorido español* (Barcelona, 1959)
J. Folch i Torres: *Fortuny* (Reus, 1962)
J. de la Puente: *Mariano Fortuny* (Buenos Aires, 1964)
——: *Dibujo y grabado de Fortuny* (Madrid, 1970)
Primer centenario de la muerte de Fortuny (exh. cat., Barcelona, Mus. A. Mod., 1974)
E. Arias Angles: *Fortuny* (Madrid, 1979)
C. Gonzalez and C. Benito: *Fortuny* (Madrid, 1983)
Mariano Fortuny collezionista (exh. cat. by S. Fuso and S. Mescola, Venice, Mus. Fortuny, 1983)

ENRIQUE ARIAS ANGLES

(2) Mariano Fortuny y Madrazo (*b* Granada, 11 May 1871; *d* Venice, 2 May 1949). Designer, painter, etcher, photographer, son of (1) Mariano Fortuny y Marsal. When his father died prematurely in 1874, he and his family moved to Paris to join his uncle, the painter Raimundo Madrazo y Garreta. Through him, the young Fortuny met many famous artists and began to paint.

In 1889 the family moved to Venice, where Fortuny continued to paint, his most accomplished pictures being portraits in tempera of himself and his family (e.g. *Cecilia Fortuny*, 1928, and *Henriette Fortuny*, 1935; Venice, Mus. Fortuny); his skill as a draughtsman is apparent in his etchings. In 1893 he visited Bayreuth, and from then on Wagnerian themes dominated his painting. Fortuny's interests were wider than painting, however; he was fascinated equally by the past and by new technology. He collected contemporary photographs and himself became a photographer, specializing in wide-angle and colour prints (Venice, Mus. Fortuny) and evolving a system of indirect lighting. This led him to designing for the theatre, where he could use his many diverse talents. The Fortuny cupola, used to represent stage skies, was widely adopted by theatres, and he created many designs for the opera house La Scala, Milan (e.g. designs for *Tristan und Isolde*, 1901; Venice, Mus. Fortuny).

In 1892 Fortuny moved into the Palazzo Orfei (now the Museo Fortuny), a 13th-century Venetian palace that was his home and studio for the rest of his life. He returned to visit Paris, where his circle included the writer Marcel Proust and the composer Reynaldo Hahn (1875–1947). There in 1897 he met Henriette Negrin, his lifelong companion and collaborator. She went to live with him in Venice in 1902, but his family disapproved of the match, and it was 16 years before they finally married.

In 1906 Fortuny turned his attention to fashion and textile design. His most famous fashion creation was the 'Delphos' dress, initially a tea-gown for Henriette, which proved extremely popular and a lucrative source of income. Based on the *chiton*—a tunic worn by Classical Greek charioteers—it was made in silk that had been very finely pleated by a special process involving heated porcelain or copper tubes. Fortuny was not a couturier, but he continued to produce these dresses, with velvet capes to accompany them. Each garment was individually dyed in soft, glowing colours achieved almost exclusively by natural dyes. He rejected the constantly changing styles of commercial fashion; instead he saw dress as a timeless form of expression. In contrast to contemporary French fashion designers, he looked to history and exotic cultures, and his designs were derived from such eclectic sources as Japanese kimonos, Coptic tunics, North African and Arab garments, and medieval and ecclesiastical robes. Fortuny sought to re-create historic woven patterns, for example designs from the Italian Renaissance, by a revolutionary new printing process, using gold and silver metallic pigments. These were reproduced first on velvet and then with greater success on cotton, which is more absorbent. In 1921 he opened a textile factory (still operating in the late 20th century) on the Giudecca in Venice, producing printed cottons by industrial techniques. Fortuny suffered financial problems in the late 1930s, but he continued working until his death.

BIBLIOGRAPHY
Immagini e materiali del laboratorio Fortuny (exh. cat. by S. Fuso and S. Mescola, Venice, Mus. Fortuny, 1978) [Fortuny's photos]
A. -M. Deschodt: *Mariano Fortuny, un magicien de Venise* (Paris, 1979)
G. de Osma: *Mariano Fortuny: His Life and Work* (London, 1980)
Mariano Fortuny: Venise (exh. cat., ed. J. M. Tuscherer and G. de Osma; Lyon, Mus. Hist. Tissus, 1980; rev. Brighton, A.G. & Mus., 1980)
Mariano Fortuny collezionista (exh. cat. by S. Fuso and S. Mescola, Venice, Mus. Fortuny, 1983) [Fortuny's phot. col.]
Fortuny & Caramba (exh. cat. by S. Mescola and S. Fuso, Venice, Mus. Fortuny, 1987) [Fortuny's theatrical costumes]

RICHARD JEFFREE

Forum. Public place or market-place in a Roman town. Many of the town's main religious and administrative buildings were to be found there, such as the BASILICA, curia and comitium (*see* ROME, ANCIENT, §II, 1(i)(b)). The arrangement of the forum and its buildings is one of the most distinctive elements of Roman urban planning (*see* ROME, ANCIENT, §III, 2). It was usually placed at the intersection of two main streets, although the square itself was normally inaccessible to traffic. The Forum Romanum at Rome (see fig; *see also* ROME, §V, 1) has its origins in the 7th century BC and developed throughout the Republican period until a systematic remodelling, begun by Julius Caesar in 54 BC, was completed by Augustus (*reg* 27 BC–AD 14). A series of Imperial fora (*see* ROME, §V, 2) were built north of the Forum Romanum. They comprised the Forum Julium, Forum Augustum, the Templum Pacis of Vespasian and the Forum of Nerva and culminated in the Forum of Trajan, the greatest of all.

Many older fora were rebuilt or built anew on regular lines during the early Empire. The forum at Pompeii is a large open space (*c.* 120×30 m) dominated at the north by the late 2nd-century BC Temple of Jupiter. Attempts to regularize it had begun in the late 2nd century BC when a colonnade was built across the south (short) side of the forum, extending some way along the east side and in front of the basilica in the south-west corner (*see* POMPEII, fig. 3). On the west side was the colonnaded enclosure of the 2nd-century BC Temple of Apollo, and there was a *macellum* in the north-east corner. The forum developed rapidly in the course of the 1st century AD, when new public buildings were erected along its south and east side, and honorific statues filled the central part of the square. The two-storey colonnade of white limestone columns along the east side was still incomplete when the eruption of Vesuvius occurred in AD 79. Had it been completed, the result would have been a unified square of the Hellenistic type.

Vitruvius, writing between 27 and 23 BC, prescribed an oblong forum with sides in the ratio of 2:3 and an adjoining basilica (*On Architecture* V.i). Fora of this type have been found in many Republican and early Imperial towns such as Veleia in northern Italy and Glanum. During the 1st century AD this type of forum achieved its most developed form in the so-called 'tripartite forum'. This type has a temple, surrounded on three sides by colonnades, facing one of its short sides, while a basilica shuts off its other short side. Examples include those at Augst, Virunum as well as Lugdunum Convenarum (Saint-Bertrand-de-Comminges), while variations of the plan can be seen at Bavay, Trier (*see* TRIER, §1) and Paris. In provinces where the

Forum Romanum, Rome, viewed from the Palatine, 7th century BC–AD 14

army had a more dominant role, such as Mauretania or Britain, there is evidence that fora more closely followed the layout of the *principia* of military camps (*see* CASTRUM). The forum at Calleva Atrebatum (now Silchester), for example, has a square enclosure surrounded on three sides by shops and on the fourth by a basilica divided into three naves. Behind the basilica and opening off it is a curia on the main axis of the forum. The fora of Banasa, Volubilis and Sala in Mauretania were also built on the model of *principia*. At THAMUGADI the forum is a colonnaded enclosure with an apsed basilica on its east side and a curia and temple on its west. The old forum at Leptis Magna is less regular, having temple and basilica on adjacent sides. The Severan forum at Leptis, however, is surrounded on three sides by colonnades and dominated on the fourth by the large temple of the Severan family (*see* LEPTIS MAGNA, §1 and BASILICA, fig. 2). This arrangement is more immediately reminiscent of the Imperial fora at Rome, especially the twin apsed basilica placed transversely across the main axis of the forum in the manner of the Basilica Ulpia in the Forum of Trajan.

BIBLIOGRAPHY

P. von Blanckenhagen: 'The Imperial Fora', *J. Soc. Archit. Hist.*, xii (1954), pp. 21–6

P. Grimal: *Les Villes romaines* (Paris, 1954); trans. and enlarged by G. M. Woloch as *Roman Cities* (Madison, 1983)

A. Boethius: 'The Hellenized Italic Town', *The Golden House of Nero* (Ann Arbor, 1960), pp. 26–93

J. B. Ward-Perkins: 'From Republic to Empire: Reflections on the Early Provincial Architecture of the Roman West', *J. Roman Stud.*, lx (1970), pp. 1–19

R. Martin: 'Agora et forum', *Mél. Ecole Fr. Rome: Ant.*, lxxxiv (1972), pp. 903–33

J. B. Ward-Perkins: *Cities of Ancient Greece and Italy* (London, 1974)

W. L. MacDonald: *An Urban Appraisal* (1986), ii of *The Architecture of the Roman Empire* (New Haven and London, 1965–86)

P. Gros and M. Torelli: *Storia dell'urbanistica: Il mondo romano* (Rome and Bari, 1988)

F. B. SEAR

Foscari, Francesco, Doge of Venice (*b* Egypt, 1373/4; *reg* 15 April 1423–23 Oct 1457; *d* 1 Nov 1457). Venetian ruler and patron. He was the longest serving doge in the history of Venice. His reign was a period of constant warfare, during which Venice consolidated her hold on her mainland possessions and acquired further territory. His only surviving son, Jacopo Foscari (*c.* 1415-57), a celebrated humanist, was three times disgraced for alleged corruption. After his son's final banishment and death, Francesco was persuaded by a group of hostile nobles to abdicate. He died a week later and was given a full ducal burial in the church of S Maria Gloriosa dei Frari, Venice. His tomb monument (for illustration *see* BREGNO, (i)) in the same church, executed by members of the Bregno family, was erected at the instigation of his grandson Nicolò Foscari, probably in the 1480s. Its mixture of Gothic and Renaissance elements echoes the transitional character of public art and architecture during his reign.

Foscari was a popular doge, whose fondness for pageantry, jousts and tournaments gave his reign a spectacular, courtly air. A new wing of the Doge's Palace was begun in 1424, facing the Piazzetta and continuing the design of the 14th-century frontage on the Bacino di S Marco (*see* VENICE, §IV, 6(i)). The red and white diaper pattern on the upper walls may have been added in Foscari's time.

The culmination of the Piazzetta extension was the new entrance to the palace, the monumental, extravagantly carved, Gothic Porta della Carta, commissioned in 1438 from Giovanni and Bartolomeo Buon (*see* BUON (i)), but revealing the influence of Michelozzo di Bartolomeo in the form of its gable. The Porta della Carta led into a covered passageway, also begun in 1438, flanked on its south side by a staircase, the Scala Foscara (completed by 1453; destr. *c.* 1603), which is known from an engraving by Cesare Vecellio in his *Habiti antichi e moderni* (Venice, 1590). The eastward end of the new entrance passage was framed by a grand triumphal arch, now the lower storey of the so-called Arco Foscari, although originally it probably consisted only of a heavy round-arched opening in red and white striped marble, surmounted by a balustrade, with the Foscari arms in the spandrels. A similar arch is depicted in a mosaic of the *Death of the Virgin* (*c.* 1430-51) in the vault of the chapel of the Madonna dei Mascoli in S Marco, Venice.

About 1452 Doge Foscari began an enormous family palace, the Ca' Foscari, on a conspicuous bend in the Grand Canal, Venice. Although the building is emphatically Gothic in style, with borrowings from the Doge's Palace, the enthusiasm for humanist scholarship in Venice during his reign is suggested by such decorative features as the *all'antica* putti bearing the Foscari arms over the second-floor windows. A strikingly realistic portrait bust of *Foscari* in his old age, formerly part of the kneeling effigy (destr. 1797) on the Porta della Carta, is housed in the Doge's Palace. His likeness is also recorded in a fine ducal portrait (Venice, Correr), attributed to Lazzaro Bastiani.

BIBLIOGRAPHY

M. Sanudo the younger: *De origine, situ et magistratibus urbis Venetae, ovvero la città di Venezia (1493–1530)*; ed. A. Caracciolo Aricò (Milan, 1980)

A. da Mosto: *I dogi di Venezia nella vita pubblica e privata* (Milan, 1960), pp. 162–74

H. Trevor Roper: 'Doge Francesco Foscari', *The Horizon Book of the Renaissance*, ed. J. H. Plumb (London, 1961), pp. 273–80; also in *Renaissance Essays* (London, 1985), pp. 1–12

D. Pincus: *The Arco Foscari: The Building of a Triumphal Gateway in Fifteenth Century Venice* (New York and London, 1976)

A. Markham Schulz: 'The Sculpture of Giovanni and Bartolomeo Bon and their Workshop', *Trans. Amer. Philos. Soc.*, lxviii/3 (1978), pp. 1–81

S. Romano, ed.: *La Porta della Carta: I restauri* (Venice, 1979)

U. Franzoi, T. Pignatti and W. Wolters: *Il Palazzo Ducale di Venezia* (Treviso, 1990)

DEBORAH HOWARD

Foshan [Fatsan; Fo-shan]. Chinese city and surrounding area in the Pearl River (Zhu jiang) delta, Guangdong Province, 16 km south-west of Guangzhou (Canton). Foshan ('Buddha Hill') was a religious and commercial centre from the 10th century onwards.

The Foshan area is particularly known for the pottery of the town of SHIWAN. Archaeological excavations have shown that the area has one of the longest surviving pottery production traditions in China. Pottery of the Neolithic period (*c.* 6500–*c.* 1600 BC) has been unearthed, and graves of the Han period (206 BC–AD 220) have yielded detailed pottery models depicting everyday scenes, such as men at work in the rice fields, and pottery mortuary vessels. Tombs from subsequent periods contained other types of crematory jars and pottery burial objects.

Remains of kilns dating from the Tang period (AD 618–907) onwards have also been unearthed. The manufacture of everyday utensils goes back at least to the Tang, whereas the production of art pottery is somewhat later. Shiwan wares are made from a mixture of local clay and imported clay from Dongguan County on the other side of the Pearl River estuary. This combination is particularly suited to sculpture and the high relief designs characteristic of the area. Pottery production at Foshan was never under state control, and the potters were free to explore styles of the famous kilns of various periods and of ancient bronze vessels. As the forms and glazes of pots, bowls, vases and dishes often demonstrate, Shiwan potters are master imitators. They are also accomplished artists, especially in respect of pottery sculpture and miniature scenes. For centuries they have been inspired by the Cantonese opera, native to the Foshan area, and by popular religion and history when choosing characters to sculpt. The figures produced are naturalistic, but there is a marked tendency to exaggerate archetypal features. The lively expressions of the face and the warmth of the body are often emphasized by leaving these areas unglazed, setting them off against the glazed folds of the garments. Examples of miniature scenes, coloured and glazed ceramic reliefs depicting themes from mythology and figures from the Daoist pantheon, are visible on the roofs of Foshan's Zu ci miao (Ancestral Temple).

During the Ming (1368–1644) and Qing (1644–1911) periods the population of Foshan greatly increased, and the city became one of the main handicraft centres of China. Such diverse arts developed as silk-weaving and embroidery, manufacture of brass, tin and silver wares and papercutting. The artisans of Foshan have achieved a reputation for their ingenuity in turning waste materials into art products: in the making of papercuts, they have created a unique style by contrasting metal foil with coloured paper.

BIBLIOGRAPHY

'Gongyi ming cheng: Foshan' [A famous handicraft city: Foshan], *Xingfu huabao*, xxxix (Feb 1959), pp. 34–7

'Guangdong Foshan shijiao Lanshi Dong Han mu fajue baogao' [Report on the excavation of tombs of the Eastern Han dynasty at Lanshi outside Foshan, Guangdong Province], *Kaogu* [Archaeology] (1964), no. 9, pp. 448–57

'Guangdong Foshan shijiao Lanshi Tang zhi Ming mu fajue ji' [Notes on the excavation of tombs from the Tang period to the Ming period at Lanshi outside Foshan, Guangdong Province], *Kaogu* [Archaeology] (1965), no. 6, pp. 284–6

Shekwan Pottery (Hong Kong, 1977)

Shiwan tao zhan: Exhibition of Shiwan Wares (exh. cat., U. Hong Kong, Fung Ping Shan Mus., 1979)

Fan Wei: 'Foshan zumiao' [The Ancestral Temple of Foshan], *Wenwu tiandi* (1990), no. 3, pp. 42–3

BENT NIELSEN

Fossati. Swiss family of artists. They came from Morcote (Ticino), and members of the family worked both north and south of the Alps. From at least 1720 most had links with Venice, including the architect and engraver Giorgio Fossati (*b* Morcote, 1706; *d* Venice, 1778) and his brother (1) Davide Antonio Fossati. Giorgio's sons included the architect Carlo Giuseppe Fossati (*b* Venice, 1737) and the architect and painter Domenico Fossati (*b* Venice, 1743; *d* Venice, 14 Aug 1784). (2) Gaspare Trajano Fossati and Giuseppe Fossati (*b* Morcote, 5 July 1822; *d* Morcote, Feb 1891) were the grandsons of Carlo Giuseppe.

(1) Davide Antonio Fossati (*b* Morcote, 1708; *d* Venice, *c.* 1779). Painter and printmaker, active in Italy. Having moved to Venice in 1720, he frequented the studios of Vicenzo Maria Mariotti and Daniel Gran, with whom he collaborated on frescoes in the Villa Cornaro near Venice, the Palais Schwarzenberg (1723–4; *in situ*) and the Imperial Library (1726; *in situ*) in Vienna. After working in Pressburg (now Bratislava, 1728) and in St Martinsberg, near Raab (1729), he returned to Venice in 1730 and painted a ceiling fresco depicting *Apollo and Marsyas* (1730–31) in the Villa Pesaro, near Este. His prints included a notable series of 24 landscape views and capriccios with ruins (1743; Windsor Castle, Berks, Royal Col.) after paintings and drawings by Marco Ricci, etched with a fresh and direct stroke. After *c.* 1750 Fossati's creativity diminished considerably, and he acted mainly as an artistic adviser and expert.

Thieme–Becker

BIBLIOGRAPHY

D. Succi: *Da Carlevarijs ai Tiepolo: Incisori veneti e friulani del settecento* (Venice, 1983), pp. 170–77

DARIO SUCCI

(2) Gaspare Trajano Fossati (*b* Morcote, Ticino, 7 Oct 1809; *d* Morcote, 5 Sept 1883). Architect, great-great nephew of (1) Davide Antonio Fossati. He trained at the Accademia di Belle Arti di Brera, Milan, where he won a gold medal, and he studied ancient monuments in Rome. In 1833–7 he worked in St Petersburg, where he was appointed architect to the imperial court in 1836. In 1837 he travelled to Constantinople (now Istanbul) to build the new Russian Embassy (1838–45), a vast Neo-classical building prominently situated in Pera. He and his brother Giuseppe soon became the busiest architects in Constantinople, where they remained until 1858. Besides building churches, villas and embassies (e.g. the Dutch Embassy, completed 1855), they designed public buildings for the Ottoman government in a Neo-classical style reflecting the westernizing reforms of the time. The grandest of these was a large porticoed block (1846; destr. 1933) near Hagia Sophia that was intended for the Ottoman University but used as the Palace of Justice. From 1847 to 1849 the brothers undertook major structural repairs to, and redecoration of, Hagia Sophia for Sultan Abdülmecid (*reg* 1839–61), during which the Byzantine mosaic decoration was briefly uncovered. The mosaics were not included in the album published by Gaspare (1852; *see also* SALZENBERG, WILHELM), but the Fossati drawings (Bellinzona, Archv Cnt.) were published by Mango (1962). Despite inaccuracies they provide valuable information, particularly about mosaics destroyed since 1849.

WRITINGS

Aya Sophia Constantinople, as Recently Restored by Order of H.M. the Sultan Abdul Medjid (London, 1852)

with Giuseppe Fossati: *Rilievi storico-artistici sulla architettura bizantina dal IV al XV e fino al XIX secolo* (Milan, 1890)

BIBLIOGRAPHY

T. Lacchia: *I Fossati: Architetti del sultano di Turchia* (Rome, 1943)

C. Mango: *Materials for the Study of the Mosaics of St Sophia at Istanbul*, Dumbarton Oaks Studies, viii (Washington, DC, 1962) [with bibliog.]

C. Palumbo-Fossati: *I Fossati di Morcote* (Bellinzona, 1970)

Z. Çelik: *The Remaking of Istanbul: Portrait of an Ottoman City in the Nineteenth Century* (Seattle, 1986)

SEBASTIAN WORMELL

Fossen [Fossens], Jacob van. *See* ES, JACOB VAN.

Fossum. Swedish rock-carving site, east of Tanumshede (Bohuslän), dating from the 8th to the 6th century BC. The main panel (3×15 m; *see* PREHISTORIC EUROPE, fig. 34) features *c.* 130 carvings of varying sizes, mainly of warriors, ships, animals and cup-marks. The panel's compositional uniformity and stylistic homogeneity suggest that it may have been carved by a single artist. The absence of superimpositions also indicates that the site was worked for a short period of time. The panel is dominated by a group of warrior-like and phallic male figures, most of whom have rectangular bodies. Several carry swords of the Hallstatt type and axes, and they may represent priests or deities. Two figures carry spears and are hunting deer, while a third is shooting a bow. To the right of the main group is a composition unique in Scandinavian rock art, depicting three male figures holding sticks and dancing in a squatting position. Two of the figures are shown back to back above a cup-mark. To the far left of the panel is the figure of a female dancer with her hair tied in a ponytail. Her sex is denoted by a cup-mark. Few female figures are found in Scandinavian rock art, but almost all examples have cup-marks to indicate their sex. It has been suggested that cup-marks could be a female symbol in the male-dominated fertility cult of the Scandinavian Bronze Age, possibly of an aniconic female deity who could not be represented. In such a case, the female figures could be priestesses participating in the cult. The ships represented at Fossum have high sterns with stylized animal heads. A series of lines is used to indicate the crew. One ship has two phallic axemen on board. The panel also features carvings of foot soles, dogs, deer and circular designs with irregular attachments.

See also PREHISTORIC EUROPE, §V, 9.

BIBLIOGRAPHY

G. Burenhult: *Götalands hällristningar (utom Göteborgs och Bohuslän samt Dalsland)* [The rock carvings of Götaland], i (diss., U. Stockholm, 1980) [with Eng. summary]
S. Janson, E. B. Lundberg and U. Bertilsson: *Hällristningar och hällmålningar i Sverige* [Rock-carvings and rock paintings in Sweden] (Helsingborg, 1989)
J. Coles: *Images of the Past: A Guide Book to the Carvings and Other Monuments of Northern Bohuslän* (Uddevalla, 1990)

GÖRAN BURENHULT

Foster. English family of architects.

(1) John Foster I (*b* Liverpool, *c.* 1759; *d* Liverpool, 27 April 1827). He was the son of a Liverpool joiner and builder. He continued the family business at a time when the town was rapidly expanding and thereby made a large fortune; he was also in those years the most important architectural influence on the development of Liverpool. Like his friend William Roscoe, Foster was proud of Liverpool, seeing it as a modern Florence, its bankers and merchants as latter-day Medici.

About 1790 he succeeded Charles Eyes as Surveyor to the Liverpool Corporation, a post he held for over thirty years, and was also surveyor to the docks. He himself practised as an architect employing an elegant Neo-classical style influenced by James Wyatt, with whom he came into contact over the extension of the Liverpool Exchange (now the Town Hall) in 1787. Wyatt produced the designs for the reconstruction of its interior after a fire in 1795 and a scheme of improvements for the surrounding area, including the widening of Castle Street and the laying out of Exchange Flags, a new square, behind the Town Hall; Foster adapted and executed Wyatt's designs for all these projects. He was also a competent Gothic Revival architect and his chief surviving work in this style is the shell of St Luke's Church at the top of Bold Street, begun for the Liverpool Corporation in 1811.

(2) John Foster II (*b* Liverpool, *c.* 1787; *d* Birkenhead, 21 Aug 1846). Son of (1) John Foster I. He succeeded his father as Surveyor to the Liverpool Corporation and maintained the family's monopoly of public building in Liverpool until his retirement after the Municipal Reform Act of 1835. He trained as an architect in the London offices of James and Jeffry Wyatt before travelling abroad to study Greek architecture. In 1810 he accompanied Charles Robert Cockerell, Karl Haller von Hallerstein (architect to Ludwig I of Bavaria), Linck of Württemberg and Otto von Stackelberg of Estonia (1787–1837) on the expedition to Greece that discovered the marble sculptures at Aigina and the Temple of Apollo Epiurius at Barsai in the Peloponnese. Many of his drawings of Greek architecture survive in the Walker Art Gallery, Liverpool. On his return to Liverpool in 1814, Foster enriched the town with many fine public buildings, which were inspired by his studies of Greek architecture. His Custom House of 1828–35 (gutted 1941, destr.), an impressive domed building with an Ionic portico, was among the finest Greek Revival public buildings in England. St John's Market (1819–25; destr. 1965) was historically significant as the first large-scale covered market in England. Foster's most impressive surviving building is St James's Cemetery, a necropolis of Piranesian grandeur formed in a disused quarry in 1823–4. The mortuary chapel is a miniature Greek temple, while the Huskisson Memorial in the centre is a free interpretation of the choragic monument of Lysikrates in Athens.

BIBLIOGRAPHY

J. A. Picton: *Memorials of Liverpool*, i (London, 1873, rev. 1875), pp. 230, 470
P. Fleetwood-Hesketh: *Murray's Lancashire Architectural Guide* (London, 1955), pp. 88–9
J. M. Robinson: *The Wyatts* (Oxford, 1979), pp. 177–8

JOHN MARTIN ROBINSON

Foster, John (*bapt* Dorchester, MA, 10 Dec 1648; *d* Dorchester, 9 Sept 1681). American printer and print-maker. He was the son of early settlers in Massachusetts and graduated from Harvard College in 1667; he then taught in Dorchester (now South Boston), and about 1670 began making the earliest pictorial woodcuts in English-speaking North America. In 1675 he became the first letterpress printer in Boston and the second in New England. Foster's woodcut *Richard Mather* (*c.* 1670; Cambridge, MA, Harvard U., Houghton Lib.; *see* BOSTON fig. 4) is among the earliest of American portraits and perhaps the first in any medium by an artist born in English-speaking America. His *Map of New-England*,

'White Hills' version (1677; Boston, MA Hist. Soc.), which he adapted from a manuscript source (untraced), was the first map to be cut, printed and published north of Mexico. Despite their primitive quality, Foster's prints are strongly designed and show a keen awareness of Baroque style in the graphic arts. In addition to his work as a printer and printmaker, Foster took an interest in medicine, music, astronomy, meteorology, mathematics and possibly painting.

BIBLIOGRAPHY
R. Holman: 'Seventeenth-century American Prints', *Prints in and of America to 1850*, ed. J. D. Morse (Charlottesville, 1970), pp. 23–52

DAVID TATHAM

Foster, Myles Birket (*b* Tynemouth, Northumb., 4 Feb 1825; *d* Weybridge, Surrey, 27 March 1899). English painter, illustrator and collector. After a short and unsatisfactory period working in the family brewing business, he was able to convince his Quaker parents to allow him to pursue a career in art. He was apprenticed to a wood-engraver, Ebenezer Landells (1808–60), who recognized Foster's talent for drawing and set him to work designing blocks for engraving. Foster also provided designs for *Punch* and the *Illustrated London News*. In 1846 he set up on his own as an illustrator. The rustic vignettes of the seasons that he contributed to the *Illustrated London News* and its counterpart, the *Illustrated London Almanack*, established him as a charming interpreter of the English countryside and rural life and led to his employment illustrating similar themes in other publications. During the 1850s his designs were much in demand; he was called upon to illustrate volumes of the poetry of Longfellow, Sir Walter Scott and John Milton. His range was limited, however, and he was criticized for relying on the same rural imagery regardless of the nature of the text.

Foster's book illustration culminated in *Pictures of English Landscapes*, commissioned in 1858 by the engravers George Dalziel and Edward Dalziel and published in 1862. Intent on establishing himself as a watercolour painter, he stopped accepting further commissions for book illustrations in 1858. In 1859 he exhibited for the first time at the Society of Painters in Water-Colours in London. His initial bid for membership was rejected, but he became an associate the following year and achieved full membership in 1862. In his watercolours he developed further the themes of an idyllic rural England with which he had made a name for himself as an illustrator. Three characteristic early examples are *The Milkmaid* (1860; London, V&A), *The Hay Rick* (1862; New Haven, CT, Yale Cent. Brit. A.; see fig.) and *Lane Scene at Hambleden*, exhibited at the Society of Painters in Water-Colours in 1863 (London, Tate). His watercolour technique, with its reliance on stippling rather than broad washes, reflects his experience in designing for wood-engraving; but it also suggests an awareness of the watercolour styles of such popular contemporaries as William Henry Hunt and John Frederick Lewis. His work was appreciated as being Pre-Raphaelite in detail, without the harshness of colour and the unorthodox compositional formats that rendered the Pre-Raphaelites' work disturbing. Foster's watercolours proved even more popular than his illustrations. Each new work was eagerly awaited. Chromolithographs spread the

Myles Birket Foster: *The Hay Rick*, watercolour and bodycolour, 777×680 mm, 1862 (New Haven, CT, Yale Center for British Art)

popularity of his realistic but sanitized rustic images to an audience who could not afford the watercolours.

In 1860 Foster built an elaborate Tudor-style home, known as The Hill, in Witley, Surrey; this became a social centre for a group of artist friends including Fred Walker, Charles Keene and William Quiller Orchardson. Interior decoration was provided by Morris, Marshall, Faulkner & Co. Foster assembled an impressive collection of British art at The Hill, including works by J. M. W. Turner, William Henry Hunt, John Frederick Lewis (*The Hhareem*, 1850; London, V&A), Samuel Palmer and Edward Burne-Jones.

While rural England was the inspiration for much of his work, Foster travelled regularly on the Continent, gleaning material for publications and watercolours. In 1852 he journeyed down the Rhine, seeking subjects to illustrate an edition of Longfellow's *Hyperion*. Another tour through Belgium, Germany and Switzerland in 1854 provided material for *The Rhine and its Picturesque Scenery* (pubd 1856). In the 1870s he made a number of trips to Italy while engaged on a commission from a Lincoln corn merchant, Charles Seely, for 50 watercolours of Venice. Visits to Brittany resulted in a volume of 35 lithographs published by the artist in 1878.

In 1893 illness forced Foster to sell The Hill together with most of his collection of pictures. He moved to a smaller house in Weybridge, Surrey, where he continued to paint until his death.

BIBLIOGRAPHY
H. M. Cundall: *Birket Foster, RWS* (London, 1906)
F. Lewis: *Myles Birket Foster (1825–1899)* (Leigh-on-Sea, 1973)
J. Reynolds: *Birket Foster* (London, 1984)

SCOTT WILCOX

Foster, Sir **Norman** (*b* Manchester, 1 June 1935). English architect. He studied at the University of Manchester (1956–61) and Yale University, New Haven, CT (1961–2). Returning to London in 1963, he formed the practice Team 4 Architects with Richard Rogers, Su Rogers and his future wife, Wendy Ann Cheesman. His first major commission was a factory for Reliance Controls Ltd at Swindon (1967; with Richard Rogers), which was designed with an elegantly expressed steel structure. In 1967 the partnership ended and Norman and Wendy Foster established the firm Foster Associates. Early on he developed the theme of the 'serviced shed', the concept of a rapidly constructed, lightweight prefabricated envelope, with integrated structure and services and a highly adaptable interior. His principal works of this early period are the air-supported temporary office structure (1968) for Computer Technology Ltd, Hemel Hempstead, Herts, the Fred Olsen Ltd Amenity Centre (1969), Millwall Docks, London, the IBM Advance Head Office (1971), Cosham, Hants, and another building for Computer Technology Ltd (1971) at Hemel Hempstead. From 1968 to 1983 he also worked with R. Buckminster Fuller on several unexecuted projects using climate-controlled geodesic structures.

Foster's first major urban commission was the Willis Faber & Dumas head office (1974; for illustration *see* CURTAIN WALL (ii)) at Ipswich. The visual bulk of the building (accommodating 1300 people) is minimized by the use of a deep plan form that follows the irregular curves of the existing streetscape, the structure clad entirely in window-walls of reflective tinted glass. A characteristic of the design is the sky-lit atrium that houses a double bank of escalators linking the floors. These incorporate recreation into the working environment: thus two floors of office space are contained between two amenity floors—a swimming-pool at ground-level and a restaurant pavilion and garden at roof-level.

The idea of the well-serviced and precisely detailed shed is expressed most completely at the Sainsbury Centre for Visual Arts (1977; for illustration *see* SPACE-FRAME) at the University of East Anglia, Norwich, a gallery designed to house works of primitive and contemporary art. The building is an open-plan rectangular enclosure, fully glazed at both ends, formed by a steel space frame containing within its depth the building's mechanical services. The exterior cladding of both walls and roof consists of vacuum-formed superplastic aluminium panels sealed with neoprene gaskets, and lined inside with perforated aluminium louvres. These themes—a single arch structure, controlled natural light and a double skin structure—were again used at the Leichtathletikhalle (1982), Frankfurt am Main.

The structure of Foster's earlier 'serviced sheds' was generally concealed by the building's cladding system, resulting in a bland, often glazed façade. In his later works he used structure more expressively, for example in the Renault Distribution Centre (1984; for illustration *see* HIGH TECH), Swindon, a modular building with bright yellow structural masts supporting lightweight roof panels. One of his best-known works, the Hongkong & Shanghai Banking Corporation's headquarters (1981–5; see fig.) in Hong Kong, a heavily modelled composition of structure,

vertical services and different types of cladding panel, used an expressive form in an intensely urban context. His aim was to redesign and upgrade the conventional office tower in terms of spatial variety, the interpenetration of public and private space, and technical performance. The building is suspended from pairs of steel masts, which are connected up the building at five points by two-storey trusses from which the floors are hung. The semi-public banking hall is contained within a ten-storey atrium reached by escalators from a public pedestrian concourse running beneath the building. The spatial variety created by the staggered profile, varying floor clusters and progression from public to private space is clearly expressed on the exterior. Another important work was the new terminal building for London's third airport at Stansted, Essex (*see* ENGLAND, fig. 13), for which he carried out feasibility studies in 1981. Opened in 1991, the compact, fully glazed two-storey building is naturally lit and is significant for its low energy consumption.

In terms of building plans Foster's principal intention was to upgrade the quality of the internal environment, especially in the office workplace. Two recurring, formative themes appear: first, the introduction of natural light into a deep plan form, as with the buildings at Ipswich, the University of East Anglia, Hong Kong and Stansted; and second, the gradation of public to private space, as for example in the University of East Anglia and Hong Kong buildings. These features are combined with Foster's concern for townscape in his Carré d'Art (opened 1993), an art gallery and multi-media library sited next to the ancient Maison Carrée in Nîmes. An elegant, geometric structure in concrete, glass and steel, with half of its nine storeys placed underground, it exemplifies the best use of contemporary design in an historic environment. Foster also designed in 1981 a range of furniture, initially for his own office but later marketed, consisting of knock-down pieces freely adaptable to workplace requirements.

Although the factory-produced, jointed, interchangeable elements of which Foster's buildings are composed give them a superficial resemblance to those of his former partner Richard Rogers, Foster's work does not derive from the same Futurist–Expressionist base, nor can his buildings be interpreted as symbolic of a technological urban utopia. His concern lies essentially with the technology of materials and their assembly and, in terms of historical roots, his work finds inspiration both in 19th-century architectural engineering such as the Eiffel Tower, Paris, the Crystal Palace (destr.), London, and the Galleria Vittorio Emmanuele, Milan, and in such 20th-century constructions as the Apollo landing craft, American Airstream caravans and the crop-sprayers of the American plains.

Foster's search for clarity, precision and high performance in building components and their assembly often resulted in the application of technologies traditionally foreign to the building industry. For instance, aerospace technology was applied at the Sainsbury Centre in the superplastic cladding panels, and again in the floor panels of the Hongkong & Shanghai Bank. The junction between structure and glazing in the Renault building combines technology used in hovercraft skirts with long-distance lorry fixings. His interest in factory production, however,

Norman Foster: Hongkong & Shanghai Bank, Hong Kong, 1981–5

was essentially based round the craftsmanship of building rather than on methods of mass production. He was concerned not with the mere assembly of available components, like the car industry, but with the development of advanced materials technology and the production process in order to improve the performance of building components and the clarity of their assembly. This involves the fabrication and testing of an unusually large range of prototype components for each of his projects. His buildings, particularly in their enclosing outer skin, possess a logical simplicity and extreme refinement. This, together with the rigorous integration of structure, construction and services, gives them an elegance and precision seldom found outside the field of industrial design. In this sense he was regarded as one of the leading exponents of High-Tech architecture (*see* HIGH TECH), producing works of abstract beauty. In 1983 Foster became the youngest recipient for 58 years of the RIBA Gold Medal, and he was knighted in 1990.

BIBLIOGRAPHY

'High Tech to Appropriate: A View of Foster Associates' Approach to Appropriate Technology', *Archit. Des.*, xlvi/3 (1976), pp. 160–61
Foster Associates, intro. R. Banham (London, 1979)
'Foster Associates: The Architecture of the Near Future', *Space Des.*, ccx (1982), pp. 5–68 [special feature]
Norman Foster: Architect—Selected Works, 1962–84 (exh. cat., intro. C. R. Dodwell; U. Manchester, Whitworth A.G., 1984)
Foster Associates: Six Architectural Projects, 1975–1985 (exh. cat. by S. Esterson and A. Best, Norwich, U. E. Anglia, Sainsbury Cent., 1985)
F. Chaslin, F. Hervet and A. Lavalou: *Norman Foster* (Paris, 1986)
I. Lambot: *The New Headquarters of the Hongkong & Shanghai Banking Corporation: A Personal Folio of Photographs by Ian Lambot* (Hong Kong, 1986)
C. Davies: *High-Tech Architecture* (New York, 1988)
I. Lambot, ed.: *Foster Associates: Buildings and Projects* (London, 1989–)
S. Williams: *Hongkong Bank: The Building of Norman Foster's Masterpiece* (London, 1989)
I. Lambot, ed.: *Team 4 and Foster Associates: Buildings and Projects, 1964–1973* (London, 1991)

MICHAEL FORSYTH

Fothergill, John. See under BOULTON, MATTHEW.

Fotiades, Theodoros (*b* Ayios Theodoros, 1878; *d* Nicosia, 17 April 1952). Cypriot architect. He studied medicine for two years in Athens and then decided to enrol in architecture at the National Technical University. He graduated in 1904 and went to Alexandria, where he spent 15 years working as an architect on public projects in the city, apart from two years in Cyprus between 1914 and 1916. In 1920 he returned permanently to Cyprus and, during his working life there, he was employed by the ecclesiastical authorities, the Evcaf (Islamic Foundations Trust), several municipalities and many private clients. His early buildings were constructed in the neo-classical style that he had been taught in Athens. His schools, for example the Pancyprian Gymnasium (1922) and Phaneromeni Girls' School (1925), both in Nicosia, tended to be imposing and symmetrical, with pedimented gables at each end of the principal façade and an Ionic portico in the centre. The many private residences he designed incorporating neo-classical elements are characterized by stacked Ionic pilasters creating different planes in their placement across the façade. His more elaborate residences, such as the building now used as the State Gallery in Nicosia, have round balconies in one or two corners to offset the squareness of the plan and to mediate between the two principal façades. Fotiades was also a particularly successful exponent of the neo-Byzantine style of church building in Cyprus. After 1930 he taught himself to use reinforced concrete and, during the next two decades, he built many structures in the new material. These included public utilities such as shops and stoas, and the building housing the Ionic Bank and Cleopatra Hotel in Nicosia, constructed in the 1930s.

BIBLIOGRAPHY

I. Ionas: 'O Theodoros Fotiadis: Mia strophi stin istoria tis architektonikis stin Kypro' [Theodoros Fotiadis: A turning-point in the history of architecture in Cyprus], *Epitiris ton kendron epistimonikon erevnon*, xix (1992), pp. 759–74

MICHAEL GIVEN

Foucault, Michel (*b* Poitiers, 15 Oct 1926; *d* Paris, 25 June 1984). French critic. He was one of a small group of French philosophers and critics who achieved worldwide fame in the 1960s by offering a distinctively new perspective on the human sciences. Although these thinkers were generally grouped under the heading of Structuralism, Foucault himself frequently denied being a Structuralist. He was more a historian whose choice of subject-matter—the history of madness, the birth of the clinic, the history of sexuality—involved him in an unremitting critical examination of the discourse through which his subjects of study had, as he saw it, been constituted.

Foucault's major contribution to the history of art lies in the new attention he devoted to the issue of representation. In *Les Mots et les choses* (1966) he began his account of the relation between words and things from the Renaissance to the modern period with a brilliant analysis of Velázquez's painting *Las meninas*. This was explained as a kind of allegory of the process of representation itself as it was conceived in the 'classic age' of the 17th and 18th centuries, an interplay of different 'looks'. The painter Velázquez looks out at us, Foucault argued, but we also occupy the same viewing space as his sitters, the King and Queen of Spain, whose presence can be inferred from their appearance in the mirror opposite to us. This challenging interpretation of *Las meninas* gave rise to much controversy, and some of Foucault's basic assumptions were questioned by art historians such as the Americans Leo Steinberg and Jonathan Brown. But Foucault's text struck a responsive chord in the Belgian Surrealist painter René Magritte, who entered into correspondence with him. Ultimately this contact resulted in Foucault's charming essay, *Ceci n'est pas une pipe* (1973), which takes its title from Magritte's painting. Foucault was here able to sketch out, from a contemporary viewpoint, the implications of his theory of the variable relationship between linguistic signs and plastic elements in the history of Western art.

In reviewing the history of the various systems of confining the insane, the sick and the criminal, Foucault inevitably touched on the role of architecture in this process. In *Surveiller et punir* (1976) he devoted considerable attention to the plan by Jeremy Bentham (1748–1832) for his Panopticon, an ideal prison of a circular design, in which all inmates could be constantly surveyed from a central viewing position. Foucault implied that Bentham's penal regime of universal visibility has been realized in much of the mass architecture of the present century.

WRITINGS
Les Mots et les choses (Paris, 1966); Eng. trans. as *The Order of Things* (London, 1970)
Ceci n'est pas une pipe (Montpellier, 1973; Eng. trans., Berkeley, 1983)
Surveiller et punir (Paris, 1976); Eng. trans. as *Discipline and Punish* (Harmondsworth, 1977)

BIBLIOGRAPHY
D. Macey: *The Lives of Michel Foucault* (London, 1993)
D. Eribon: *Michel Foucault* (Paris, 1989; Eng. trans. of 1st edn, Cambridge, MA, 1991; 2/London, 1992)
J. Miller: *The Passion of Michel Foucault* (London, 1993)

STEPHEN BANN

Foucault, Nicolas-Joseph (*b* Paris, 8 June 1643; *d* Paris, 7 Feb 1721). French antiquary. He was educated by the Jesuits and, from 1674 to 1706, he held administrative posts successively in Montauban, Pau, Poitiers and Caen. Throughout his life he maintained an interest in art and archaeology, assembling, particularly during his stay in southern France, a fine collection of rare books and manuscripts, antique figures, medals and coins, most of which had been found in France. He began excavating in Montauban and in Languedoc, but it was in Normandy, while administrator of Caen, that he made his most significant discoveries. In 1703 at the village of Vieux near Caen he uncovered ruins of an ancient Roman town, Aregenua, including a gymnasium and baths, and established from inscriptions and coins found on the site that the town was inhabited up to the 4th century AD. Near Valognes, he also discovered the site of the ancient town of Alauna. Many of the finds from these excavations have, however, been dispersed and lost.

In old age Foucault was forced to sell off his collections. His library was sold and probably dispersed. His collection of antique bronzes was acquired by King Louis XV in 1727 and passed into the royal collection. Some pieces originally belonging to Foucault have been identified from a handwritten inventory of his collection.

BIBLIOGRAPHY
F. Baudry, ed.: *Mémoires de Nicolas-Joseph Foucault* (Paris, 1862)
E. Babelon and J.-A. Blanchet: *Catalogue des bronzes antiques de la Bibliothèque Nationale* (Paris, 1885), pp. xii–xxvi
M. Besnier: 'Histoire des fouilles de Vieux', *Mém. Soc. N. Antiqua. France*, 7th ser., lix (1909), pp. 225–335

Foucher, Alfred Charles Auguste (*b* Lorient, 21 Nov 1865; *d* Paris, 30 Oct 1952). French art historian and archaeologist. He qualified with an arts degree in 1888 and began postgraduate Sanskrit and Indian studies in 1891 at the Ecole Pratique des Hautes Etudes, Sorbonne University. His primary interest was in Buddhist legend and tradition, and the relationship between India and the Western Classical world. In 1895, after obtaining his doctorate and a lectureship at the university, he spent two years on a scientific mission in India, visiting museums and sites, taking photographs and collecting manuscripts, coins and sculpture. The information he gathered on the art and sites of Gandhara during this survey was presented as his *doctorat ès lettres* thesis in 1905.

In 1898 he helped to establish a permanent archaeological mission, the Ecole Française d'Extrême Orient. While stationed in Saigon as the mission's director (1904–7), he organized an archaeological expedition to Java. In May 1907 he was given charge of Indian language and literature at the Sorbonne. Later in that year he was appointed assistant director, and in 1914 director, of the Ecole Pratique des Hautes Etudes. In the next decade he spent most of his time abroad: as exchange professor at Columbia University, USA (1915–16), then as Director-General of the Archaeological Survey of India (1918–21), before establishing a new French archaeological mission in Afghanistan (1921–5). Following his survey of sites, Balkh (ancient Bactria), Kapisa (Begram) and Hadda were excavated. In 1925–6 he set up a Franco-Japanese institute in Tokyo, returning to France via Korea and China to resume teaching at the Sorbonne. Together with Sylvain Lévi and Emile Senart, he founded the Institut de Civilisation Indienne (1928). He was appointed professor with tenure (1929), retiring in 1936 to write up his accumulated research on India and Afghanistan. He was awarded the Légion d'honneur in 1951.

Foucher's pioneering work remains a primary key to Buddhist and Gandharan studies. His meticulous documentation of excavation and museum records was reinforced by extensive personal field surveys, and he is often the best source of contemporary information on archaeological sites. His theory that Seleucid Greek settlements in Afghanistan were the original source of Classical influence in Gandhara has been subsequently confirmed by the discovery of Ai Khanum and other Hellenistic remains in the region of the Oxus River (Amu Darya). His comprehensive analysis of Gandharan art and iconography is still unequalled, although certain details have been corrected by later research.

WRITINGS
Etude sur l'iconographie bouddhique de l'Inde d'après des documents nouveaux (Paris, 1900)
'Notes sur la géographie ancienne du Gandhâra', *Bull. Ecole Fr. Extrême-Orient*, i (1901), pp. 323–69 (*R* Hanoi, 1902; Eng. trans. by H. Hargreaves, Calcutta, 1915/*R* Varanasi, 1974)
Sur la frontière indo-afghane (Paris, 1901)
Etude sur l'iconographie bouddhique de l'Inde d'après des textes inédits (Paris, 1905; Eng. trans., abridged, Middletown, CT, 1963)
L'Art gréco-bouddhique du Gandhâra, 2 vols (Paris, 1905–18, rev. 1951)
Les Représentations de 'Jatakas' sur les bas-reliefs de Barhut (Paris, 1908)
'L'Origine grecque de l'image du Bouddha', *Bib. Vulgarisation Mus. Guimet*, xxxviii (1913), pp. 231–72
The Beginnings of Buddhist Art and Other Essays in Indian and Central Asian Archaeology (Paris and London, 1917)
Rapport préliminaire sur l'interprétation des peintures et sculptures d'Ajanta (Bombay, 1920)
with J. Marshall: *The Monuments of Sāñcī* (Calcutta, 1940)
La Vieille Route de l'Inde de Bactres à Taxila, Mém. Dél. Archéol. Fr. Afghanistan, i, 2 vols (Paris, 1942–7)
La Vie du Bouddha d'après les textes et les monuments de l'Inde (Paris, 1949)
Les Vies antérieures du Bouddha d'après les textes et les monuments de l'Inde (Paris, 1955)

BIBLIOGRAPHY
A. Merlin: 'Notice sur la vie et les travaux de M. Alfred Foucher', *Acad. Inscr. & B.-Lett.: C. R. Séances* (1954), pp. 457–66
L. Nehru: *Origins of the Gandhāran Style: A Study of Contributory Influences* (Delhi, 1989) [assessment of Foucher's theories on Gandharan art]

E. ERRINGTON

Foucou, Jean-Joseph (*b* Riez, Alpes de Haute-Provence, 7 June 1739; *d* Paris, 1815). French sculptor. He studied at the Ecole de Peinture et Sculpture in Marseille before entering the Paris studio of Jean-Jacques Caffiéri after

1760. In 1769 he won the Prix de Rome and joined the Ecole des Elèves Protégés before spending the years 1771 to 1775 at the Académie de France in Rome. On his return to Paris his work hesitated between two stylistic tendencies, as is illustrated on the one hand by the four Baroque reliefs of scenes from the *Life of St Louis* in the chapel of the Château Borély, Marseille (1772–8; *in situ*), or by the flamboyant bust of the dramatist *Jean-François Regnard* (marble, exh. 1779 Salon; Paris, Comédie-Fr., foyer), and on the other hand by the more modern, gently classicizing statue of a *Bacchante* (marble, 1777; versions, Marseille, Mus. B.-A., and Paris, Louvre), which was once erroneously attributed to Clodion.

Foucou's career began slowly, and his first attempt to become a full member of the Académie Royale in 1785 failed, though he was received (*reçu*) later the same year on submission of a second *morceau de réception*, a marble statuette of a *River God* (Paris, Louvre). His involvement in the decoration of Marie-Antoinette's dairy at Rambouillet, in conjunction with Pierre Julien and Claude Dejoux, brought him in 1787 the royal commission for a statue of the soldier *Bertrand Duguesclin* in the series of Illustrious Frenchmen devised by the Comte d'Angiviller (plaster, exh. 1789 Salon: marble, exh. 1799 Salon; Versailles, Château). This successful piece was a spirited pre-Romantic image of heroic action, mixed with the picturesque medievalism of the Troubadour style.

Foucou continued to work during the French Revolution; he was involved with the decoration of the Panthéon in 1792–3, and in 1796 he undertook restoration work for Alexandre Lenoir's Musée des Monuments Français. He exhibited regularly at the Salons between 1799 and 1814 and was involved, in a subordinate capacity, in the great building projects of the Empire (1804–14), including decorative sculpture for the Arc de Triomphe du Carrousel, Paris (1808), and for the Colonne de la Grande Armée, Place Vendôme, Paris (1806–10).

BIBLIOGRAPHY
Lami
Autour du néo-classicisme (exh. cat., Paris, Gal. Cailleux, 1973), no. 68

PHILIPPE DUREY

Foucquet [Fouquet]. French family of artists. Bernard Foucquet the elder had two sons who were active primarily in Sweden: the painter Jacques Foucquet (*fl* 1685–1704) and the sculptor Bernard Foucquet the younger (*b* 1640; *d* after 1711). While in France, Jacques was an officer and engineer in the employ of Louis XIV. He was influenced by Charles Le Brun's style, which was taught at the Académie Royale de Peinture et de Sculpture in Paris. In 1694 he was brought to Sweden, together with other French artists, by Nicodemus Tessin the younger to execute monumental historical and allegorical works in the newly built Royal Palace in Stockholm. His principal works there are the three central ceiling panels (1700–02) of the vault in the Gallery of Charles XI in the State Apartment in the north wing. The paintings in this gallery and in the adjoining Cabinet of Peace and Cabinet of War depict incidents in the war between Denmark and Sweden during the reign of Charles XI and the peace that followed. The King is represented dressed as a Roman military commander surrounded by a host of Classical gods and allegorical figures, and the whole scheme is continued in sculpted stuccowork groupings by René Chauveau, another French artist. Foucquet also did paintings in two other adjoining rooms of the same apartment: a series of allegorical scenes and a group of mythological subjects including *Cupid and Psyche* and *Venus and Mars*. His figures are rather heavy and his colours dense, the layout of the whole programme—including the frames and the sculptural decoration in the vaults—being inspired by French examples in the style of Le Brun, Jean Le Pautre and Jean Bérain I. Foucquet's whereabouts after his work in Stockholm are unknown.

Bernard the younger was brought to Sweden in 1696 by Nicodemus Tessin the younger, again to assist in the decoration of the Royal Palace in Stockholm. For the exterior he executed bronze lions, which were placed in front of the north façade; he also did other sculptures for the south façade. He sculpted groups of figures and ornamental decoration for the Gallery of Charles XI. In 1706 he returned to France, but he was back in Sweden the following year. One of his major commissions at this time was a bronze model (Stockholm, Kun. Husgerådskam.) for an unexecuted equestrian statue of *Charles XI* based on François Girardon's statue of *Louis XIV* (begun 1683; destr. 1792; fragment, Paris, Louvre). His style is essentially Baroque but with an element of classical restraint. He settled permanently in France in 1711 and died at an unknown date.

BIBLIOGRAPHY
SVKL
J. F. Böttiger: *Bernard Foucquet och gjuteriet på Bännarbanan* [Bernard Foucquet and the foundry at the Bannarbana] (Stockholm, 1916)
A. Lindblom: *Fransk barock- och rokokoskulptur i Sverige* (Uppsala, 1923)
R. Josephson: 'Bernard Foucquet, den svenska barockens monumentalskulptär', *Tidskr. Kstvet.*, xi (1927), pp. 89–106; xii (1928), pp. 1–13
M. Olsson, ed.: *Stockholms slotts historia* [The history of the palace in Stockholm], ii (Stockholm, 1940)

TORBJÖRN FULTON

Fougeron, André (*b* Paris, 1 Oct 1912). French painter and printmaker. He worked first as an apprentice draughtsman and then as an unskilled metalworker. Having attended evening classes, though otherwise self-taught, he took part in the first Maison de la Culture show in Paris in 1936. He exhibited several works at the Salon des Surindépendants in 1937, such as the *Spanish Martyr* (1937; artist's col., see 1981 exh. cat., p. 51), which showed his disgust with the Spanish Civil War (1936–9). The same year he exhibited at the important *L'Art cruel* show at the Galerie Billiet-Vorms in Paris. Organized by Jean Cassou, this was designed as a forum for politically-engaged art, especially that dealing with the Spanish conflict.

Fougeron was mobilized in 1938 and again in 1939, and he was taken prisoner before his demobilization in 1940. On his return to Paris he joined the Resistance, setting up a clandestine print works in 1941 from which he and his colleagues published journals such as *L'Université libre* and *Les Lettres françaises*. The following year he took charge of the Front National des Arts, helped by the French painter Edouard Goerg (1893–1969) and Edouard Pignon. After being taught by Jacques Villon, he also started to produce etchings in 1942, later producing five to illustrate Martial d'Auvergne's poem *Prière pour les déshérités* (Paris, 1944). In 1944, working with Joseph

Billiet, then Directeur des Beaux-Arts, he organized and took part in the Salon de la Libération at the Salon d'Automne in Paris, which was centred on the work of Picasso. From 1946 to 1950 he was secretary-general of the Union des Arts Plastiques, which was formed after the dissolution of the Front National des Arts. He had his first one-man show at the Galerie Billiet-Caputo in Paris in 1946.

Fougeron's works of the 1940s included such overtly political paintings as *Rue de Paris 43* (1943; see 1987 exh. cat., pl. 4), depicting France under the occupation, and executed in an expressive, realist style. There were also, especially in the later 1940s, many paintings on lighter subjects, such as domestic interiors and still-lifes, which showed the influence of Picasso, as in *Maternal Games* (1946; see 1973 exh. cat., no. 2). In 1953, together with the Russian painter Boris Taslitzki (*b* 1911) and Pignon, Fougeron organized the exhibition *De Marx à Staline* at the Maison de la Métallurgie in Paris. Designed to commemorate the 70th anniversary of Karl Marx's death, it included Fougeron's *French Peasants Defending their Land* (1953; see 1987 exh. cat., pl. 49), depicting resistance to American military bases in France, as well as works by Picasso, Léger and others. In many works of the 1950s he painted themes from the lives of workers, as in *Harvest by the Railway Track* (1959; see 1987 exh. cat., pl. 12), which reflected the technological development of modern life and agriculture. Together with landscapes and nudes, he continued these themes into the 1960s. At the outbreak of the Vietnam War, he painted *Vietnam 67* (1967; see 1973 exh. cat., no. 28), a powerful protest against the consequences of war, in a similar vein to that of his works from the Spanish Civil War period.

After the mid-1970s Fougeron's painting changed radically, though its social intent remained. *Humiliated Couple* (1974–5; see 1987 exh. cat., pl. 19), for example, was executed in a graphic, simplified linear style that was characteristic of this period. Many of the works of the 1970s were based on the art of Courbet, as in *Woman with Portraits* (1975–6; see 1987 exh. cat., pl. 72), which was composed from a collage of distinct images, another feature of these later paintings. His later works, such as the *Arrangement of the Large Louvre (Contemporary History Painting)* (1983–4; see 1987 exh. cat., pl. 50), use the same graphic style and, invariably, stencilled messages to address social problems such as Third World poverty, capitalist corruption and so on. Showing the influence of Pop art stylistically, they lack the impact of the earlier works and, by the obviousness of the messages, also lack subtlety. Fougeron's importance really lies in that period from the 1930s to the 1950s when a debate raged in France about the relation between art and politics, and when he firmly opted for an art of overt political commitment.

BIBLIOGRAPHY
J.-A. Cartier: 'A. Fougeron', *Documents*, vii (April 1955), pp. 1–16 [whole issue devoted to Fougeron]
N. N. Kalitna: *Fougeron* (Leningrad and Moscow, 1962)
André Fougeron (exh. cat. by E. Belachova, Moscow, Pushkin Mus. F.A., 1968)
J. Uhlitzsch: *André Fougeron* (Leipzig, 1970)
J. Rollin: *André Fougeron* (Berlin, 1972)
Fougeron (exh. cat. by P. Josse, Châteauroux, Salle Cordeliers, 1973)
Paris-Paris: Créations en France, 1937–1957 (exh. cat., Paris, Pompidou, 1981), pp. 206–12
André Fougeron: Pièces détachées, 1937–1987 (exh. cat. by Fougeron and others, Paris, Gal. Jean-Jacques Dutko, 1987)

Foujita, Tsugouharu [Fujita, Tsuguharu] (*b* Tokyo, 27 Nov 1886; *d* Zurich, 29 Jan 1968). French painter of Japanese birth. After graduating from the Tokyo School of Fine Arts in 1910, he went to France in 1913. Though associated with the Ecole de Paris he developed an individual style. He became an annual member of the Salon d'Automne in 1919 and a permanent member in the following year. Subsequently his reputation in Parisian artistic circles rose, established by such works as *My Studio* (1921; Paris, Mus. N.A. Mod.) and *Five Nudes* (1923; Tokyo, N. Mus. Mod. A.), where he used a thin, delicate line on a background of milk-white material, like the surface of porcelain; this style was particularly impressive in his cool, complaisant nudes. In 1929 he briefly returned to Japan, holding a successful one-man show in Tokyo. He left Paris in 1931 and travelled through South, Central and North America before returning to Japan in 1933. He was made a member of the Nikakai (Second Division Society) in the following year and painted several murals in Japan, including *Annual Events of Akita, Festivals of Miyoshi Shrine of Mt Taihei*, commissioned by Hirano Masakichi of Akita (Akita, Hirano Masakichi A. Mus.). He visited Paris in 1939 to 1940, painting *Still-life with Cat* (Tokyo, Bridgestone A. Mus.) and *Cats (Fighting)* (Tokyo, N. Mus. Mod. A.). In 1941 he left the Nikakai and was appointed to the Imperial Art Academy. He was also attached to the Navy and Army Ministries and used his excellent descriptive and compositional skills to depict war zones in China and South-East Asia. He was awarded the Asahi Culture Prize for the *Last Day of Singapore* (1942; Tokyo, N. Mus. Mod. A.) and other works. He went to the USA in 1949 and to Paris in the following year, taking French nationality in 1955 and becoming a Catholic convert, with the baptismal name of Léonard, in 1959. In 1966 he had the chapel of Notre-Dame-de-la-Paix built in Reims, and he devoted his last years to its design and its stained glass and murals.

BIBLIOGRAPHY
J. Selz: *Foujita* (Paris, 1981)
S. Buisson and D. Buisson: *La Vie et l'oeuvre de Léonard-Tsuguharu Foujita* (Paris, 1987)
J. Tanaka: *Hyōden Fujita Tsuguharu* [Fujita Tsuguharu, a critical biography] (Tokyo, 1988)

TORU ASANO

Foul-biting. Term used in etching when the ground collapses, allowing the acid to attack the plate underneath indiscriminately and uncontrollably so that when printed, there are dots or irregular areas. Foul-biting occurs when the ground is imperfect, the plate is left in the acid-bath too long or when the etched lines are drawn too close together.

Fould, Louis (*d* by 1860). French collector. His immense collection, which was universal in its scope, was displayed in a gallery on the Rue de Berry in Paris, and was catalogued by Anatole Chabouillet, Curator of medals and antiquities at the Bibliothèque Impériale. It numbered around 3000 items and included works of art from ancient Egypt, Greece and Rome, the Middle Ages and the Renaissance; Fould also owned Islamic metalwork, Chinese bronzes, enamels and porcelain. In 1860, at the sale (Paris, 4–27 June) following Fould's death, the Musée du Louvre, Paris, acquired almost the whole of Fould's collection of Egyptian antiquities, including the head of a colossal statue of *Osiris*. At the same time the Louvre also acquired a number of important works from other areas and periods; among them was a Greek marble statue of two fauns and a magnificent painting by David Teniers (ii), *Interior of a Tavern*, which Fould had purchased at the sale of the pictures of the Comtesse de Verrue.

BIBLIOGRAPHY

P. Burty: 'Vente de la collection Louis Fould', *Gaz. B.-A.*, n. s. 1, vii (1860), pp. 54–60, 119–23

A. Darcel: 'La Collection Louis Fould', *Gaz. B.-A.*, n. s. 1, vi (1860), pp. 266–93

M. A. Chabouillet: *Description des antiquités et objets d'art composant le cabinet de M. Louis Fould* (Paris, 1861)

E. Galichon: 'Description des antiquités composant le cabinet de M. L. Fould', *Gaz. B.-A.*, n. s. 1, xi (1861), pp. 231–40

□

Foulis, Robert (*b* Glasgow, 20 April 1707; *d* Edinburgh, 2 June 1776). Scottish printer and educator. He was of humble origin, but determined to become a printer. In 1739 he went to Paris where he purchased fine and rare books that he sold in London for a profit. Two years later he had established a bookshop in Glasgow and began to print with such success that in 1743 he was appointed printer to the university. Foulis's *Iliad* (1757) and *Odyssey* (1758) are among the finest examples of 18th-century typography. From 1751–3 he travelled in France and the Netherlands purchasing prints and over 350 paintings to provide the nucleus of the teaching collection of an academy of fine arts that he intended to establish in Glasgow on his return. The Foulis Academy (founded 1753) was housed in the university and financed by loans from Glasgow merchants. Tuition was free and the academy was the first to award scholarships for foreign study. It also held the first public art exhibition in Scotland (1761). A contemporary painting (Glasgow, Mitchell Lib.) attributed to David Allan shows students drawing, painting and modelling, but engraving was their principal activity as the sale of their prints was the only source of revenue. Foulis also established the Foulis Press, which published *The Raphael Bible* in 1770 at 2 guineas and *The Seven Cartoons of Raphael* in 1773 at 3 guineas. Individual prints were also sold including topographical views of Glasgow by Robert Paul (1739–70), a student in 1756. Unfortunately, with the exception of David Allan and James Tassie the medallist, few of the students were particularly talented. The Academy's finances, always precarious, received a severe setback in 1770 on the death of Archibald Ingram, one of the institution's supporters, whose executors recalled his capital, and in 1775 it was forced to close. The collection, which contained many paintings of doubtful attribution, was sold in London for a small sum. The Mitchell Library holds both original prints and student copies from the academy.

WRITINGS

A Catalogue of Pictures . . . by the Most Admired Masters of the Roman, Florentine, Parman, Bolognese, Venetian, Flemish and French Schools, 3 vols (London, 1774)

BIBLIOGRAPHY

DNB

H. Miles: 'Early Exhibitions in Glasgow: I (1761–1838)', *Scot. A. Rev.*, viii/3 (1962), pp. 26–30

D. and F. Irwin: *Scottish Painters at Home and Abroad, 1700–1900* (London, 1975)

DAVID RODGERS

Fountain. Sculptural or architectural structure that channels a spring or source of water and shapes it by means of jets or sprays, the water falling into one or more containers or basins.

I. Introduction. II. Antiquity. III. Islamic lands. IV. Western world.

I. Introduction.

Fountains may serve decorative or practical purposes and have, in a multitude of forms, been a feature of both public and private spaces since ancient times. They have been erected to celebrate technological advancement in a civilization, for example in the harnessing of water for public use; to serve as objects of religious significance or to commemorate events of historical importance; and to create poetic and theatrical displays.

Whereas the fountain is documented throughout the world, its absence from some areas is due to such factors as the lack of an adequate hydraulic system for its construction or, in terms of the fountain's decorative function, the prevalence of a different aesthetic for the display of water.

The latter has historically been the case in East Asia. An essential feature of Chinese landscaping has been the use of the reflective properties of clear, deep water, as in pools or ponds, where the water begins at and returns to an unseen source. Together with mountains, water in landscape painting symbolizes the harmony of nature as found in Daoist philosophy. The Great Fountains in China at the Yuanmingyuan summer palace near Beijing, which were commissioned by Emperor Qianlong (*reg* 1736–96) and devised by the French Jesuit Father Benoit, are a notable exception. Now ruined, the palace and gardens, often called the Chinese Versailles, featured Baroque fountains with obelisks jetting forth water. Japanese art tends to use water in its natural state although in more sensual and dynamic forms such as cascades, ravines, mountain streams or springs where the source is often revealed.

For further discussion of gardens in East Asia, *see* GARDEN, §VI, 1–3.

BIBLIOGRAPHY

F. Fanelli: *Fontaines et jets d'eau* (Paris, *c.* 1690)

G. Jellicoe and S. Jellicoe: *Water: The Use of Water in Landscape Architecture* (London, 1971)

M. Bring and J. Wayembergh: *Japanese Gardens* (New York, 1981)

E. T. Morris: *The Gardens of China* (New York, 1983)

C. A. Luchinat, ed.: *La fonte delle fonti: Iconologia degli artifizi d'acqua* (Florence, 1985)

G. Jellicoe and S. Jellicoe, eds: *The Oxford Companion to Gardens* (Oxford and New York, 1986), pp. 196–9

D. Jones, ed.: *Il teatro delle acque* (Rome, 1992)

C. W. Moore: *Water and Architecture* (New York, 1994)

II. Antiquity.

Evidence abounds for the existence of fountains in ancient Greece, although few survive. Typologies of fountains ranged from those with shafts, basins, niches and exedras to fountain-houses (*krenai*). Pausanias' *Guide to Greece* noted that every *polis* had 'water flowing down to a fountain . . .'. Fountains for public use are to be distinguished from those fountains and springs that were the objects of religious veneration; often connected with defence, the former were part of municipal works programmes, such as the aqueduct built to supply Athens in the late 6th century BC. One notable, elaborate fountain-house was the legendary nine-spouted Enneakrounos, possibly that found in the Athenian Agora, dating from the late 6th century BC. Rectangular in form, it had a central entrance and a shallow basin at each end. Contemporary vase-paintings are a source of study for the forms of fountain-houses, which had columnar porches and water flowing from taps on the rear or side walls. Ornament was minimal, usually featuring lion-head spouts in bronze or stone. Resembling small temples, these early Greek examples were simple utilitarian structures, determined by the character of the source and designed for the convenience of users (*see also* GREECE, ANCIENT, §II, 1(i)(b)).

Ritual fonts celebrating water sources and serving as sites for purification were dedicated to the gods. Particularly noteworthy was the Kastalian Spring at Delphi, sacred to Apollo. Shrines to Pan and local deities as well as to nymphs and muses adorned temple groves and garden sanctuaries, but they were also found in streets, agoras and other public places. An architecturally enclosed fountain, open to the sky, such as the fountain-house of Lower Peirene in the Corinthian Agora (*see* CORINTH, §1(iii)(a)) was both a sacred spring and city reservoir. Pausanias (*Guide to Greece*, II.iii.2–3) described Peirene as a 'spring ornamented with white marble and there have been made chambers like caves, out of which the water flows into an open-air well . . .'.

Fountains were often part of civic improvements, and those built under the Roman Empire (known as nymphaea) were complex structures dedicated to nymphs or serving as the termini of aqueducts (*see* ROME, ANCIENT, §III, 3). Like monumental architecture fountains could become elaborate works, as witness the two-tiered Nymphaeum of Trajan (2nd century AD) at Ephesos (*see* EPHESOS, §I, 2(i)). In the late 1st century BC Vitruvius discussed ways of conducting water via mechanical contrivances, water screws, organs and pumps. His published work (*On Architecture*) is crucial for an understanding of contemporary technology and was, of course, invaluable to his followers. Agrippa, as the organizer of Rome's water department in the 1st century BC, constructed aqueducts, some 500 fountains and 700 basins and pools for public use. Frontinus became Chief Commissioner of Water in AD 97, and his *De aquis urbis Romae* (AD 97) is a fundamental source of knowledge for all matters pertaining to the water supply of ancient Rome. Expertise in the use of a plethora of waterworks also informs Pliny the younger's description of the great variety found in his Tuscan villa: an 'ornamental pool . . . with its water falling from a height and foaming white when it strikes the marble . . . a fountain opposite plays and catches its water, throwing it high into the air . . . a fountain rises and disappears underground . . . and throughout can be heard the sound of running streams . . .' (*Letters*, V.vi).

Since few examples survive of the more than 1000 fountains from antiquity, many may be apprehended more readily from literary sources than from archaeological remains. Propertius cites the Theatre of Pompey (dedicated in 55 BC), the earliest and most magnificent theatre in Rome, in his *Elegies* (II.xxxii); both this and the complex of the Meta Sudans near the Arch of Constantine (AD 312) contain examples of nymphaea; representations of such nymphs as Egeria and Juturna were more modestly housed near groves and springs, and in later works river-gods were incorporated. Sculpted fountains drawn largely from mythological subjects adorned the peristyles and atria of great houses, while yet another fountain type is found on landscape frescoes of rustic shrines and seaside grottoes. Nowhere was water more celebrated than in Hadrian's Villa at Tivoli (AD 118–34; *see* TIVOLI, §2(i)). Channels of water flowed through the gardens; there were pools, grottoes, nymphaea, baths with fountain jets and watery enclaves that Hadrian built to recall the wonders of his eastern conquests. Of particular note were the Canopus canal and the Serapeum, a vast nymphaeum with fountains fed by an aqueduct.

BIBLIOGRAPHY

Frontinus: *On the Water Supply of Rome*
Pausanias: *Guide to Greece*
Vitruvius: *On Architecture*
B. Dunkley: 'Greek Fountain-buildings before 300 BC', *Brit. Sch. Athens*, xxxvi (1935–6), pp. 143–204
P. Grimal: *Les Jardins romains . . .* (Paris, 1943)
D. Kapossy: *Brunnenfiguren der hellenistischen und römischen Zeit* (Zurich, 1969)
F. Glaser: *Antike Brunnenbauten in Griechenland* (Vienna, 1983)

III. Islamic lands.

The Islamic world inherited the fountain traditions of the Late Antique Mediterranean region and of the Sasanian lands, developing new modes and reviving ancient mechanical devices. For example, al-Jazari designed fountains based on the automata of Hero of Alexandria that were able to set figures in motion by compressing air and to produce sounds that were emitted through trumpet and bird forms. The climate and hydrography of the Islamic regions governed the types of hydraulic systems used, and these ranged from canals, aqueducts and qanats to *norias* (water-driven water-raising machines) and *saqiyas* (animal-driven water-raising machines). One of the principal uses of fountains was in mosques, which always provided facilities for ritual washing before prayer. While some mosques had basins, others had fountains. An early example was the so-called Pharaoh's Tray (*c.* 850; Baghdad, Khan Mirjan), formerly in the Great Mosque at Samarra. This monolith, measuring over 3 m in diameter, has a single jet in the centre and a thin channel around the base to draw the overflow and direct it into a lower pool. Most Ottoman mosques of the 15th and 16th centuries contained fountains, also for ablution, and these were located either in the centre of the forecourt or in rows of spigots along the exterior (e.g. Istanbul, Sultan Ahmed Mosque; for illustration *see* ISLAMIC ART, fig. 66). Another type of fountain was the *sabil*, or public drinking-fountain. The structure usually comprised a grilled space open to the street, with spigots and/or troughs fed from reservoirs. Such fountains were found throughout Islamic lands. As in other cultures the provision of water was considered an act of God.

The use of fountains in palaces and gardens was for an entirely different purpose: the control and display of water—a scarce resource—was a prerogative of power. Umayyad palaces in Syria in the 8th century (e.g. Khirbat al-Mafjar, near Jericho) had courtyards with central tholos-type fountains. Gardens were often divided into four, symbolizing the four rivers of the Garden of Eden, and this and other garden patterns spread from the Eastern Mediterranean to the Iberian peninsula and to Kashmir and India (*see also* GARDEN, §IV, 2). At the Alhambra in Granada (*see* GRANADA, §III, 2) water symbolizes aesthetic delight, economic well-being and spiritual enlightenment. Channels run throughout the gardens, punctuated by reflecting pools and basins carved of marble in circular and hexagonal forms. These often enclose a single jet and are set in the midst of foliage and flora. Water is enhanced by polychrome faiences, local stones, *azulejos* (glazed tiles) and multicoloured pavements. The fourfold schema was used in the celebrated Court of the Lions, built in the 14th century by Muhammad V (*reg* 1354–91), which contains an enchanting fountain fed by small jets of water in each of the galleried sides of the courtyard. The basin (4 m in diameter) at the intersection of the two axes of the court is supported by 12 grey marble lions and bears an inscription praising the beauties of the palace and the plentitude of the water supply. Examples of Islamic sculptures of animals, designed as fountain heads or as basins, also exist in Spain, such as the basin in the form of an eagle found in Seville (AD 987; now Madrid, Mus. Arqueol. N.).

Similar uses of water to those in the Alhambra are found in Persian paradisal gardens, based on related patterns of irrigation with channels representing the four sacred rivers. A square tank at the central crossing, often marked by a pavilion, recalls the ideal of Paradise in the

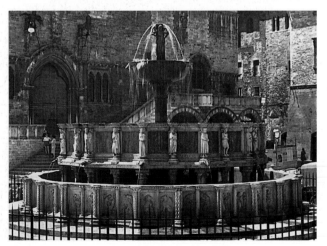

1. Fontana Maggiore (1277–8) by Nicola Pisano, Piazza Quattro Novembre, Perugia

gardens of the Koran, 'with gushing fountains . . . and rivers flowing beneath'. If these gardens are meditative in mood and designed for delectation, fountains in the East, in Kashmir, Srinagar and Lahore, are exuberant. Here, as in the West, fountains are often associated with places of worship (i.e. for ablutions in mosques). The Wafa Bagh (Garden of Fidelity; 1508–09) at Kabul had small jets and chutes of water, while in the gardens of Kashmir in the 17th century greater use of water was made, with pools and channels. Shah Jahan (*reg* 1627–58) added a black marble pavilion set in a rectangular pool surrounded by gravity-fed jets and waterfalls to the Shalimar Bagh at Srinagar (begun *c.* 1620 by Jahangir, *reg* 1605–27; *see* GARDEN, fig. 11), which is dominated by a central water channel. At the Shalimar Bagh (completed 1642; for illustration *see* LAHORE) at Lahore, also by Shah Jahan, the central terrace was designed to include 144 fountains; this is the best preserved of all Mughal gardens.

BIBLIOGRAPHY
L. Torres Balbás: 'Patios de crucero', *Al-Andalus*, xxiii (1958), pp. 171–92
D. Wilbur: *Persian Gardens* (Rutland, VT, 1962)
S. Crowe and S. Haywood: *The Gardens of Mughul India* (London, 1972)
O. Grabar: *The Alhambra* (Cambridge, MA, 1978)
E. B. Moynihan: *Paradise as a Garden in Persia and Mughal India* (New York, 1979)
J. Lehrman: *Earthly Paradise* (Berkeley, 1980)
Y. Tabbaa: 'Towards an Interpretation of the Use of Water in Islamic Courtyards and Courtyard Gardens', *J. Gdn Hist.*, vii (1987), pp. 197–220
——: 'The Medieval Islamic Garden: Typology and Hydraulics', *Garden History: Issues, Approaches, Methods*, ed. J. D. Hunt (Washington, DC, 1992), pp. 303–29

IV. Western world.

1. Medieval. 2. Renaissance. 3. Baroque. 4. Modern.

1. MEDIEVAL. In medieval European fountains associated with the Church, the representation of saints replaced that of nymphs, and the water basin itself was transformed into a baptismal font, as seen in manuscripts of the Soissons Gospels (9th century; Paris, Bib. N., MS. 8850, fol. 6*v*) and late medieval paintings. A compelling image of the fountain symbolizing Paradise is that in the Très Riches Heures (Chantilly, Mus. Condé, MS. 65, fol. 25*v*), begun by the Limbourg brothers in 1411–16 and completed by Jean Colombe (*c.* 1485–6), where it resembles a cathedral lantern. Its secular counterparts were the ornamental table fountains of Burgundian royalty and illustrations of fountains symbolizing love and youth in chivalric romances. Aspects of ancient gardens mingled with the marvels of their Muslim successors in the enlightened courts of southern Italy and Sicily, for example at pleasure pavilions near Palermo such as the Zisa (1165–7), with its famed Sala della Fontana. The fountain was often part of a subliminal Christian iconography, as in the *Lady with the Unicorn* series of tapestries (*c.* 1490; Paris, Mus. Cluny) and in the *Hunt of the Unicorn* tapestries (*c.* 1500; New York, Met.).

Civic fountains proliferated throughout the Mediterranean region and in central Europe, most fulfilling the practical needs of supplying water to the populace, serving as a trough for horses and as a meeting-place for the exchange of news and goods. Free-standing types com-

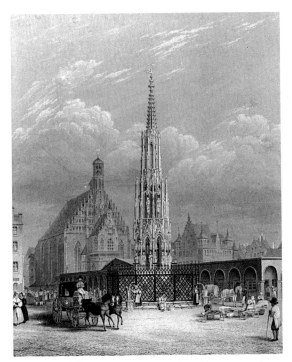

2. Schöner Brunnen (begun 1361), probably by Heinrich Parler, Marktplatz, Nuremberg

central niche flanked by personifications of eight Virtues. Notable monumental fountains outside Italy include the Schöner Brunnen (see fig. 2) in Nuremberg, probably by Heinrich Parler, built from 1361, and which at 18 m in height dominates the market place. The pyramidal Gothic form constitutes a compendium of the city and of Christian and pagan knowledge. Among the surfeit of sandstone sculptural forms are figures representing Emperor Charles IV, the seven imperial electors and nine heroes.

2. RENAISSANCE. During the Renaissance in Europe there was a shift of focus in fountain design towards virtuoso sculptural displays. Roman statues of river-gods, nymphs and marine creatures were integrated with architecturally designed basins. In these monumental free-standing forms, figures enact the tales of Ovid, allegorize political states and represent Christian saints, while embracing a central column (most frequently the water conduit). This new effusiveness was matched by an 'architecture' of water, as new inventions were incorporated to display either gentle streams, bubbling droplets, minuscule trickles or powerful jets. Whereas public fountains still served practical functions such as providing water for animals, Renaissance humanism spawned a new genre. Expanding needs coupled with the rediscovery of Frontinus's work spurred the building and renovation of Roman aqueducts, and each pope was successively challenged to improve the city's water supply.

Among the earliest Renaissance fountains are those at the château of Gaillon (destr. 1798), near Rouen, built for Cardinal Georges I d'Amboise. Shipped from Genoa in 1508, the court fountain (over 7 m high) heralded the beginning of the Renaissance in France. Known from Du

prised variations of circular, polygonal or quadrilobe basins raised on steps with water passing through a shaft, whereas wall fountains were often defined by niches. A strong local vernacular persists, distinguishing fountains in different regions: in Brittany, for example, religious statues in arched recesses preside over covered sources and projecting basins, often creating an ex-voto shrine and supposedly possessed of healing properties. Some fountains encapsulated the secular and Christian histories of the city in which they stood. The Gothic Fontana Maggiore (1277–8; see fig. 1) in Perugia comprises a veritable encyclopedia of the Middle Ages, with images divided among its three basins. Designed by Nicola Pisano (see PISANO (i), (1)) and inaugurated in 1278, it initiated a programme of urban renewal, thereby affirming the power and prosperity of the free Commune. Located in the heart of the city between the cathedral and the Palazzo dei Priori, its iconography is both religious and political, the sculpture (by, among others, Giovanni Pisano) depicting prophets, saints, the months of the year and the arts, the signs of the zodiac and stories from Genesis and the origins of Rome. Symbolic of both church and city, the fountain celebrates Perugia's autonomy and affirms its prosperity and grandeur.

Siena, a city blessed with an abundance of water, also possesses a fountain that constitutes a civic allegory. Jacopo della Quercia designed the Fonte Gaia (Fountain of Joy; 1414–19; restored 1868) with a quadrilateral basin, erected in the Campo opposite the Palazzo Pubblico. Panels include scenes of the Creation and the Expulsion and allusions to the founding of Siena; homage is rendered to the Virgin, who as the city's patron appears in the

3. Fountain of Neptune (1563) by Giambologna, Piazza Nettuno, Bologna

Cerceau's engravings, it consisted of an ornate shaft supporting two circular shells surmounted by a figure of *St John the Baptist*, the whole rising from an octagonal basin. Classified as a 'candelabra' type, the fountain was comparable to fountains in drawings by Jacopo Bellini and late 15th-century Italian prints. It was situated at the centre of the court of honour and contained abundant pagan and religious imagery connected with the Cardinal's spiritual missions. With its marine creatures and lactating Graces, the fountain also recalls that depicted in Francesco Colonna's *Hypnerotomachia Poliphili* (1499), a romance that became a popular source for antique-derived garden motifs. Italian 16th-century rivals were animated by humanistic allegorical programmes. Foremost are the fountains designed for the Medici's Villa di Castello, where similar forms are more artfully interpreted. Water issues from the mouth of *Antaeus* as he struggles with *Hercules* at the summit of Niccolò Tribolo's fountain (*c.* 1540; for illustration *see* TRIBOLO, NICCOLÒ) and springs from the tresses of the bronze *Venus* by GIAMBOLOGNA atop the Fountain of the Labyrinth in the garden of the adjacent Villa Petraia, near Florence.

Together with monumental sculpture, fountains became the nuclei of newly created town squares in Italy and northern Europe in the mid-16th century. The figure of Neptune, trident in hand, was an appropriate topos to reinforce maritime associations. The Fountain of Orion (1547–53) by GIOVANNI ANGELO MONTORSOLI, situated in the cathedral square of Messina, celebrates both the

4. Fountain of the Innocents (1549) by Jean Goujon, Place des Innocents, Paris

triumphal entry into the city of Charles V and the enhancement of the water supply. Recumbent river-gods of the Nile, Tigris, Tiber and the local Cumano—source of the fountain's water—are part of complex sculptural groupings culminating in the victorious figure of *Orion*, legendary founder of Messina. Facing the harbour is the marble Fountain of Neptune, also by Montorsoli. Built in 1554–7, it comprises an enormous statue of the sea god calming the Straits of Messina and ruling over personifications of the sea-monsters *Scylla* and *Charybdis*. The spirit of Michelangelo hovers over Bartolomeo Ammannati's Fountain of Neptune (*c.* 1560–75) in the Piazza della Signoria, Florence: sea nymphs languish on the basin's edge from which, in the words of Filippo Baldinucci, 'rises the great Colossus of Neptune, ten braccia high, standing on a chariot drawn by four sea-horses . . .'.

In Bologna, Giambologna's Fountain of Neptune (1563; see fig. 3) was the fulcrum of a programme of urban improvements in the city centre initiated by Pius IV. Inscriptions on the fountain's base confirm the links between Church and city, stating that the fountain, for public use, was the gift of the Pope, Cardinal and Papal Legate. The entire fountain may perhaps be interpreted as a paean to Pius IV symbolized by *Neptune*, who, with the Tridentine decrees, brought order out of chaos and calmed papal seas. Situated between the religious and civic centres, the fountain marks the virtual heart of the city. Other ancient deities expressed the glory of living monarchs in a new form, which has been characterized as the freestanding fountain with a raised central figure (see Wiles). At Fontainebleau both Cellini's unrealized colossal (16 m) Fountain of Mars (*see* CELLINI, BENVENUTO, §I, 3) and the *Hercules* (1541), attributed to Francesco Primaticcio, celebrated the virtues and deeds of Francis I. Similar allegorical fountains are found in English gardens, for example the Diana Fountain (1580s) at Nonsuch Palace, an encomium to Elizabeth I.

Variations of 'standard' Renaissance fountains are ubiquitous. The Pretoria Fountain (1550–75), by Francesco Camilliani (*d* 1586; enlarged by his son, CAMILLO CAMILLIANI), which occupies virtually the entire Piazza Pretoria in Palermo, is an early 'island' type, approached by bridge. Goethe described it as 'removed from the canons of good taste' and suggested that its existence may be due to deposits of various superior marbles used in 'niches from which [protrude] all sorts of animal heads . . . horses, lions, camels, elephants . . . Within this circular menagerie one is rather surprised to see a fountain . . . allowing people to draw the copiously flowing water' (*Italienische Reise*, 1816–17). As a vehicle for classically derived sculpture few fountains rival the Fountain of the Innocents in Paris (see fig. 4). Originally built at the junction of the Rue St Denis and the Rue aux Fers (now erected in the Place des Innocents), the fountain was designed by Jean Goujon in 1549 for the occasion of the triumphal entry into Paris of Henry II (*see* GOUJON, JEAN). It was rebuilt in the 18th century by Augustin Pajou as a free-standing structure. Unique in form, it combines components of tribune and temple, altar and tomb, open loggia and triumphal arch. Goujon created an allegory of water through his carved reliefs: nymphs emerge from the sea bearing urns (for illustration *see* GOUJON, JEAN), while cavorting putti and dolphins honour the Dauphin; Paris appears as the metaphorical ship of state in a fountain that also marks the amelioration of the city's water supply. Bernini was overwhelmed by the fountain, proclaiming it 'the most beautiful thing in Paris' (*Diary*, 1665).

More lavish displays of water were reserved for the gardens of private villas and châteaux, often the homes of the clergy. The programme was frequently designed to express the generosity of the patron and to ensure his renown, but principally to render praise to God. Nowhere was the play of waters more ingeniously contrived than at the Villa d'Este at Tivoli (*see* TIVOLI, §3). Conceived in 1550, it was begun a decade later for Cardinal Ippolito II d'Este of Ferrara. The iconographic programme of the gardens was created by PIRRO LIGORIO and focuses on the figure of Hercules. Emblems of eagles, ships, fleurs-de-lis and lactating sphinxes decorate the Alley of the Hundred Fountains, and Ligorio himself was responsible for designing the figure of *Rome* for the Fountain of Rometta and the nymphs for the Fountain of Tivoli, known also as the Oval Fountain. Other notable fountains in the gardens include the Fountain of Nature, containing a water organ, and the Fountain of the Owl and Birds, incorporating water-driven automata. At Bagnaia (*see* BAGNAIA, VILLA LANTE) water flows from the grottoes at the apex of the Villa Lante (1568–78), built for Cardinal Gianfrancesco Gambara, along a central axis to the Fountain of the Moors below, bearing the Cardinal's coat-of-arms. Nine statues of muses gaze at the Fountain of Pegasus, and further references to the golden age of Rome, in accord with Ovid's *Metamorphosis*, are abundant. The programme of the waterworks and fountains was the work of Tommaso Ghinucci.

3. BAROQUE. In the late 16th century the application of science to art to create an 'architecture' of water enabled water itself, rather than sculpture or structure, to become the medium for artistic expression. Fountains in the form of cascades and waterfalls appeared in the grounds of French châteaux and in the villas of Frascati. In the Villa Aldobrandini (1598–1603), designed by Giacomo della Porta, John Evelyn noted the water theatre with its 'Atlas spouting up the streame to an incredible height' (4–5 May 1645, *Diary, 1641–1705/6*, London, 1906). Elaborate mechanisms devised for a variety of water displays became the wonder of princely gardens, and the subjects portrayed were typically ancient myths combined with modern allegories. BERNARDO BUONTALENTI designed fantastic fountains and automata in 1589 for Francesco I de' Medici, Grand Duke of Tuscany, at his villa, PRATOLINO. This paradigmatic Mannerist garden marked the genesis of a type wherein water was manipulated in accordance with the devices of the Ancients. Water appeared in a series of *tableaux vivants*, and the whole was overseen by Giambologna's colossus, a personification of the *Apennines*, which controlled the flow of water through the gardens (*see* GIAMBOLOGNA). Complex installations were also made by Thomas Francini (1571–1651) and his brother Alexandre Francini (*d* 1648), summoned to France by Henry IV to build fountains and grottoes at Saint-Germain-en-Laye and Fontainebleau.

Technical understanding had been enhanced in 1589 with the publication of two important works: Giovanni Battista Aleotti's translation of Heron's *Pneumatica* and Bernardino Baldi's book on theatrical automata. Engravings of fountains appeared in numerous publications, but few were more instructive regarding intricate hydraulic contrivances than Salomon de Caus's *Les Raisons des forces movvantes* (1615; *see* CAUS, (1)). In a series of etchings the author illustrates machines and fountains that he designed (from 1613) for the Hortus Palatinus at Heidelberg. Mythological figures demonstrate theorems in mechanisms designed for the movement of water— pumps, water-clocks and water-organs—creating a type of pictorial scientific allegory.

In Rome the most significant building of monumental fountains since the time of Agrippa took place during the Baroque period. Bernini (*see* BERNINI, (2)) perfectly encapsulated the dynamic spirit of the age in fountains that are poetic dramas and theatrical spectacles. Freestanding monumental sculpture expanded in new directions in the fusion of stone and water. In his Triton Fountain (1642–3) in the Piazza Barberini, the sea-god emits a huge jet of water upwards, resulting in the unified ensemble of the whole structure (see fig. 5); disguised praise for Urban VIII's literary prowess and his enlightened rule enriches its symbolism. In the Four Rivers Fountain (1648–51; *see* MONUMENT, PUBLIC, fig. 2) in the Piazza Navona, Bernini created a masterpiece of artistry and engineering. At the centre of a triad of fountains that defines the piazza, four river-gods are depicted in marble; these representations of natural forces are countered by an obelisk, surmounted by a cross with the Pamphili dove, symbolizing the power of the Catholic Church as ruled by

5. Triton Fountain (1642–3) by Gianlorenzo Bernini, Piazza Barberini, Rome

Innocent X and representing a triumph of Christianity over paganism.

Fountains were a crucial means in 17th-century France of integrating the landscape with architecture. Although water was a major component of earlier château gardens, at Vaux-le-Vicomte innovations were introduced in 1656–61, featuring the Allée d'eau, with reflecting pools and fountains (*see* VAUX-LE-VICOMTE, §2). ANDRÉ LE NÔTRE, who designed these gardens, was soon to reach the apogee of his art at Versailles (*see* VERSAILLES, §2), where a shortage of water failed to prevent Louis XIV from creating the most extravagant waterworks in history. Celebrating the course of Apollo through the heavens from the rising to the setting of the sun, the fountains praised the glory of the Sun King. As the gardens became a *mise-en-scène*, the fountains were the primary source of diversion for the court. The hydraulics of many basins were the work of François de Francine (1617–88), who in 1651 had been made superintendent of the waters and fountains of France. He devised the display for the grotto of Thetis (completed 1668), a marvel of the palace at Versailles, and site of royal banquets, theatrical performances and court entertainments. Another notable example is the Bassin du Char d'Apollon (see fig. 6), which incorporates the gilded-lead group *Apollo in his Chariot* (1668–70) by JEAN TUBY. Schemes for bringing water to the château (which were both foolhardy and costly in lives) included the 'Machine de Marly' (1683), designed to raise water from the Seine and to conduct it by aqueduct to Versailles, and an unrealized plan (1684) to divert the waters of the Eure. Despite the difficulties, Versailles's gravity-defying jets and personifications of mythological figures became the ultimate symbols of absolute monarchy, the displays assuming a myriad of forms—crystal globes, sparkling atoms, sunburst rays, radiating sunflowers, forests of vertical jets—all enhanced by reflections in ponds and pools. Arches, towers, pyramids and beacons in geometric patterns were set within formal *parterres* against box hedges. Any doubts as to the subordination of nature to royal power were dispelled by Versailles: the triumph of art was seen in the manipulation of water, to be experienced in accordance with an itinerary written by Louis XIV and supplemented by that of Jean-Baptiste Colbert, the latter assuring that the monarch would witness the water plays, which were in fact turned off immediately the King was out of sight.

Imitations of the gardens of Versailles were created at royal residences throughout Europe. Nicodemus Tessin (*see* TESSIN, (2)), who met Le Nôtre in the 1680s, completed the park begun by his father Nicodemus Tessin

6. Bassin du Char d'Apollon (1668–70) by François de Francine, incorporating *Apollo in his Chariot* by Jean Tuby, château of Versailles

(i) at the royal palace of Drottningholm, near Stockholm, with *allées*, *parterres* and fountains comparable to those at Versailles; indeed Drottningholm was known as the 'Versailles of the north'. The Italian architect Giovanni Francesco Guerniero (1665–1745) created magnificent waterworks from 1701 for the park at Wilhelmshöhe, which eventually combined Italian Baroque and English landscape design with French planning. Most notable was a gigantic series of cascades—originally planned to cover a height of 200 m over a distance of 1000 m—inspired by a much smaller version at the Villa Aldobrandini in Frascati; however, the Wilhelmshöhe cascade was a third of the planned size. Unusual fountains such as the Celestial Globe and the Terrestrial Globe adorn the late 17th-century gardens of Het Loo (Appeldoorn Pal., Het Loo, Netherlands), probably designed by Daniel Marot I and which had 50 different types of waterworks. A surfeit of decoration characterizes the fountains of La Granja de SAN ILDEFONSO, built for Philip V of Spain in the 1720s. Of particular note is the Fountain of Perseus and Andromeda by RENÉ FRÉMIN. In the gardens of PETERHOF (begun 1715), designed for Peter I, the fountains, canals and statues rival those of Versailles, most notably in the Great Cascade (for illustration *see* PETERHOF) with its central (originally lead) sculpture *Samson Rends the Lion's Jaw* (later replaced by a bronze figure by Mikhail Kozlovsky),

in which a 20 m jet is forced out through the lion's jaw. Elements of Versailles merge with those of Tivoli in the Palazzo Reale (begun 1752) at Caserta (*see* CASERTA, PALAZZO REALE). Laid out by Martin Biancour (under the supervision of Luigi Vanvitelli) along a grand canal, a series of fountains was designed for the contemplation of Ovid's *Metamorphoses*, featuring the characters of *Diana* and *Actaeon*, *Venus* and *Adonis*, *Ceres*, *Juno* and *Aeolus* at the climax. The water feeding these fountains was transported to the park by a remarkable aqueduct 42 km long.

Situated in front of the Palazzo Poli in Rome, the Trevi is perhaps the most spectacular of all fountains (for illustration *see* SALVI, NICOLA). The present structure was begun by Nicola Salvi in 1732, although it was built on the site of an earlier fountain erected under Pope Nicholas V and demolished in 1640. A collaborator of Salvi was Giovanni Battista Maini, who created the central figure of *Oceanus*. Pietro Bracci (1700–73) also produced white marble statues for the fountain, although these were not put in place until the 1760s. The whole rests on a large rock basin and is framed by the bays of the façade of the Palazzo Poli; the visual impact of this, the most monumental of Rome's fountains, lies in the contrast between the figure of *Oceanus* amid rocks and torrential waters and the formality of the palace behind.

7. Fountain (1977–8) by Charles W. Moore, Piazza d'Italia, New Orleans

4. MODERN. As with the arts in general, revivals, whether classical, Baroque or Gothic, characterized fountain design in the 19th century. Fountains were often erected to mark urban improvements, as attention to the transformation of the urban fabric of many cities led to an increased focus on public works. In the largest cities new fountains accompanied the building or renewal of the infrastructure. In Paris, where Baron Georges-Eugène Haussmann's programme for the transformation of the city involved the creation of a new sewer system and waterworks, Louis-Tullius-Joachim Visconti (see VISCONTI (ii), (3)) adorned parks and squares with Renaissance Revival fountains such as the Louvois Fountain (1844), its four nymphs representing the four main rivers of France. This style proliferated as a paradigmatic model for the modern city fountain.

Friedrich Weinbrenner, a building inspector in Karlsruhe, designed fountains for the newly built city plazas, including that on the Marktplatz (1822–33; rebuilt 1955), a monument to Louis, Grand Duke of Baden. New heroes were used as subjects, as in the *Hermann and Dorothea* group (1863) in the Schlossgarten, in which the couple are romantically poised above a waterfall; the city's lively fountain tradition was later translated into strict genre types. To join the symbolism of light with that of water, Frédéric-Auguste Bartholdi added gas lamps to the conventional classical imagery of the cast-iron fountain he sent to the Philadelphia Centennial International Exhibition of 1876. Images of *Neptune* also continued to appear,

as with the fountain on the Schlossplatz in Berlin. Built in 1880, this aggregate of river allegories and putti surmounted by a bronze *Neptune* related to the naval policies of William II. Rome also witnessed a Renaissance revival with the Fountain of the Naiads (1870–1911) in the Piazza della Repubblica, for which Mario Rutelli (*b* 1859) provided sculptures (1901–11) of four bronze nymphs playing beneath a powerful hydraulic display that compensates for the somewhat inauthentic rhetoric. Within the city's districts, public drinking fountains were resurrected; ten were designed in 1927 by Pietro Lombardi, including the Pine Cone, a miniature copy from a Byzantine model, now in the Vatican Belvedere.

In the years after World War II water increasingly became a common element in civic spaces, although fountains were often less popular than waterfalls, waterwalls, pools or jets. They continued frequently to be linked with urban development schemes and came to play an important role in enhancing the increasingly dense environment, reflecting a concern with function as well as with aesthetic quality. There is laudable artistry in Lawrence Halprin's evocations of nature in the Lovejoy Fountain (1966–68) in the heart of Portland, OR. Water is manipulated by using the patterns of movement typical of mountain streams and waterfalls. The street setting transforms the fountain into a participatory theatre: ready access is of primary importance, and the water performs variously as a murmuring brook and a roaring torrent. This sense of intrigue with water in motion was reinforced

8. Carnival Fountain (1975–7) by Jean Tinguely, Theaterplatz, Basle

in the late 20th century by new technology such as the submersible pump, which eliminated the need for gravity, and computer-controlled programmes that recorded patterns of water and permitted an infinite variety of replays. Exploiting these inventions, Philip Johnson designed the fountain (1965) at the centre of Lincoln Plaza, New York, which dramatically uses cut-off points to catch the 16 m aerated spray at the top of its flight prior to a downpour of geometric patterns transformed into clouds of foam. Also by Johnson is a series of water gardens designed in 1975 as part of a project to create an agora in Fort Worth, TX. The gardens in turn evoke the experience of mountains, cascades, pools, forests, lakes and rivers. On a more modest scale Paley Park (Zion and Breen, 1968), a tiny oasis (14×30 m) in mid-Manhattan, New York, is a delightful shaded area with a rear water-wall that suggests the sound of the sea and blocks off the surrounding din of traffic and people.

Corporations have proved to be enlightened clients for experimentation in fountain design. In Dallas the 60-storey glass prism of Allied Bank Plaza (1986; now First Interstate Bank Tower) by I. M. Pei & Partners seems to float above Fountain Place, a plaza designed by the landscape designer Dan Kiley as a classical water garden with at its centre a fountain of 160 jets surrounded by rows of cypress trees interlaced by a grid of pathways; a micro-climate has been created within the six-acre area that serves to unify the entire district. Designed by Charles W. Moore, the Piazza d'Italia (1977–8; see fig. 7), in a deteriorating neighbourhood of New Orleans was commissioned to give identity to the Italian community and to celebrate its achievements. It incorporates a fountain based on a complex architectural conceit, focusing on a map of Italy, with Sicily, the origin of the local population, at the centre. References to Hadrian's maritime theatre at Tivoli and Post-modernist architectural vocabulary fuse with the local vernacular and with private allusions.

The abstract forms and industrial materials used in sculpture in the late 20th century also appear in contemporary fountains. Isamu Noguchi designed (1973–8) a toros-shaped fountain in the Philip A. Hart Plaza in Detroit. The fountain is an appropriate metaphor for the power of technology: a pylon 36.6 m high, made from twisted stainless steel, projects rings of jets both upwards and downwards into a granite rink. Electro-motors propel the scrap-iron sculptures in the pool of the Carnival Fountain in the Theaterplatz, Basle, designed in 1975–7 by JEAN TINGUELY (see fig. 8). With Niki de Saint Phalle he also produced the Stravinsky Fountain (1983) next to the Centre Georges Pompidou in Paris; its combination of aleatory and chromatic schemes and automated sound and motion effectively results in 'motorized collages', in which the sensuousness of Saint Phalle's figural sculpture contrasts with the hard edges of Tinguely's black metal mechanisms. In essence fountains in the late 20th century often became hybrids of artistic functions: they were frequently incorporated into much larger complexes; no longer simply set-pieces designed to inspire wonder, fountains more often were viewed as accessible components of the urban environment, inviting active participation. They also remained important vehicles for artistic expression and a vital form of public art.

BIBLIOGRAPHY

S. de Caus: *Les Raisons des forces movvantes* (Frankfurt am Main, 1615/*R* Amsterdam, 1973)

B. H. Wiles: *The Fountains of Florentine Sculptors* (Cambridge, MA, 1933)

A. Chapuis and E. Droz: *Les Automates* (Neuchâtel, 1948)

P. Underwood: 'The Fountain of Life in Manuscripts of the Gospels', *Dumbarton Oaks Pap.*, 5 (1950), pp. 41–138

C. D'Onofrio: *Le fontane di Roma* (Rome, 1957, rev. 3/1986)

G. Poisson: *Les Fontaines de Paris* (Paris, 1957)

D. R. Coffin: *The Villa d'Este at Tivoli* (Princeton, NJ, 1960)

W. Smith: 'Pratolino', *J. Soc. Archit. Hist.*, xx (1961), pp. 155–68

A. Dombrowski: *Deutsche monumentale Brunnen in Kaiserreich* (Hildesheim and New York, 1963)

H. V. Morton: *The Fountains of Rome* (London, 1966)

E.-E. Pfannschmidt: *Wasserspiele: Brunnen, Quellen und Fontänen* (Tübingen, 1967); Eng. trans. as *Fountains and Springs* (New York, 1969)

K. Hoffmann-Curtius: *Der Programm der Fontana Maggiore in Perugia* (Düsseldorf, 1968)

D. R. Coffin, ed.: *The Italian Garden* (Washington, DC, 1972)

H. Hansler: *Brunnen, Denkmale und Freiplastiken in Nürnberg* (Nuremberg, 1977)

N. Miller: *French Renaissance Fountains* (New York, 1977)

E. B. MacDougall, ed.: *Fons Sapientiae: Renaissance Garden Fountains* (Washington, DC, 1978)

R. Strong: *The Renaissance Garden in England* (London, 1979)

D. Boeminghaus: *Wasser im Stadtbild: Brunnen . . .* (Munich, 1980)

H. Hazlehurst: *Gardens of Illusion* (Nashville, TN, 1980)

G. Hoffmann: *Brunnen und Wasserspiele* (Stuttgart, 1980)

A. Monteil: *Der Tinguely-Brunnen in Basle* (Basle, 1980)

N. Miller: *Heavenly Caves: Reflections on the Garden Grotto* (New York, 1982)

'Place Debate: Piazza d'Italia', *Places*, i (1984), pp. 7–31

G. Weber: *Brunnen und Wasserkünste in Frankreich . . .* (Worms, 1985)

E. B. MacDougall, ed.: *Medieval Gardens* (Washington, DC, 1986)

S. Pedone: *La fontana Pretoria a Palermo* (Palermo, 1986)

J. Pinto: *The Trevi Fountain* (New Haven, 1986)

G. Brandenburger and others: *Denkmäler, Brunnen . . . in Karlsruhe, 1715–1945* (Karlsruhe, 1987)

A. Baur Brunnen: *Quellen des Leben und der Freude* (Munich and Vienna, 1989)

L. Cardelli, ed.: *Fontana di Trevi: La storia, il restauro* (Rome, 1991)

NAOMI MILLER

Fountaine, Sir Andrew (*b* Salle, Norfolk, 1676; *d* Narford, Norfolk, 4 Sept 1753). English collector and architect. He was the eldest son of Andrew Fountaine and Sarah Chicheley. In 1696 he was introduced to the court of William III and was knighted in 1698. In 1701 he accompanied Lord Macclesfield to carry the Act of Succession to the Elector of Hannover, whose gift of a silver-gilt salver remains in the family collection (priv. col., see 1985 exh. cat., p. 107). Fountaine then undertook the Grand Tour. He was initially interested in coins and medals, but among the few works of art acquired on this tour was his own youthful portrait in red chalk by Carlo Maratti (priv. col., see 1985 exh. cat., p. 93).

Fountaine had returned to London by the end of 1703. On his father's death in 1706, he inherited the estate and newly built hall at Narford, Norfolk, although he did not reside there until 1732–3. He embarked on a second Grand Tour of France and Italy, beginning in Paris in 1714, when he re-established himself as a favourite at the court of Cosimo III, Grand Duke of Tuscany. The painting of *Sir Andrew Fountaine and Friends in the Tribune* (1715; priv. col., see 1985 exh. cat., p. 95), by Giulio Pignatta (1684–1751), is an important early record of British travellers in the gallery that displayed the best of the Medici collection. Among the works of art Fountaine certainly acquired on this tour was a portrait medallion of himself by Antonio Francesco Selvi and a pastel portrait of *Cosimo III* (both

1715; priv. col., see 1985 exh. cat., pp. 95–6) by Domenico Tempesti (*c.* 1655–1737), both of which testify to his acceptance at Florence.

In 1725 Fountaine was made vice-chamberlain to Princess Caroline and later became tutor to her son Prince William, Duke of Cumberland. On 14 July 1727 he succeeded Sir Isaac Newton as Warden of the Mint. Fountaine was also a talented amateur architect: Robert Morris, in his *Essay in Defence of Ancient Architecture* (1728), called him a 'practitioner of architecture', coupling his name with those of his close friends Richard Boyle, 3rd Earl of Burlington, and Henry Herbert, 9th Earl of Pembroke (who, in 1747, commissioned a bust of Fountaine from Louis-François Roubiliac; Wilton House, Wilts). Vertue recorded that the gardens at Narford, which included an Ionic temple and an ornamental deer-house, were laid out in 'the best manner, wholly I believe by [Fountaine's] own direction'. Fountaine also appears to have designed the first Hamond's Charity School at neighbouring Swaffham in 1736 (Norwich, Norfolk Record Office, PD52/347), and Horace Walpole recorded that he designed 'a large ugly room' for Sir Matthew Decker at his house at Richmond Green, Surrey (*Walpole Soc.*, xvi (1928), p. 40).

In 1731–2 Fountaine held a sale of part of his collection. This included works attributed to van Dyck, Rembrandt, Rubens and Michelangelo. At this time he also suffered heavy losses, mainly of miniatures, in a fire at White's Chocolate-house in St James's Street, London, where he was storing part of his collection before removal to Narford. The earliest, incomplete, catalogue of paintings at Narford, dated 17 September 1738, is in the Fountaine family collection. This lists five of the canvases by Giovanni Antonio Pellegrini still at Narford Hall and also a portrait by Godfrey Kneller of *Richard Boyle, Lord Burlington* (untraced) over the chimney-piece, supporting the suggestion that at least some of the decorative scheme by Pellegrini was the gift of Lord Burlington.

Sir Andrew Fountaine's collection of maiolica at Narford Hall was described by Vertue as 'the most compleat collection of the kind in this part of Europe yet'. He began the collection in 1714 while on his second Grand Tour. An oval maiolica dish, moulded in relief, is from the Fontana workshop and of the type known to have been delivered direct to the Medici in 1588. This strengthens the impression that Fountaine acquired some of his maiolica direct from Cosimo III (London, V&A, 78–1885; see 1985 exh. cat., p. 103). The collection was greatly enlarged by Sir Andrew and his descendant, also Andrew Fountaine (*d* 1874), to include Henri II ware, Palissy ware, Nevers ware, Limoges enamels, ivory-carvings, honestone, rock crystal, Greek and Roman coins and ancient armour. It was dispersed at a sale in 1884.

BIBLIOGRAPHY

Colvin; *DNB*

J. Kemble: *State Papers and Correspondence Illustrative of the Social and Political State of Europe from the Revolution to the Accession of the House of Hanover* (London, 1857)

Fountaine Collection Sale Catalogues, London, Christie, Manson & Woods: 16–19 June 1884 [maiolica etc]; 7–10 July 1884 [prints and drgs]; 6 July 1894 [obj. of art]; 7 July 1894 [ptgs]; 22 April 1904 [porcelain etc]

Fountaine Collection Sale Catalogues, London, Sotheby, Wilkinson & Hodge: 11–14 June 1902 [books and MSS]; 21 June 1902 [engrs and drgs]

'The Note-books of George Vertue', *Walpole Soc.*, xxvi (1938), p. 120

B. Ford: 'Sir Andrew Fountaine: One of the Keenest Virtuosi of his Age', *Apollo*, cxxii (1985), pp. 352–63

Norfolk and the Grand Tour: Eighteenth-century Travellers Abroad and their Souvenirs (exh. cat. by A. W. Moore, Norwich, Castle Mus., 1985)

A. W. Moore: *Dutch and Flemish Painting in Norfolk: A History of Taste and Influence, Fashion and Collecting* (London, 1988)

——: 'The Fountaine Collection of Maiolica', *Burl. Mag.*, cxxx (1988), pp. 435–47

ANDREW W. MOORE

Fountain pen. *See* PEN, §3.

Fountains Abbey. Former Cistercian monastery near Ripon, N. Yorks.

1. HISTORY. According to Serlo of Kirkstall (*fl c.* 1205), Fountains Abbey was founded by Benedictine monks of St Mary's Abbey, York, who were dissatisfied with the discipline of their urban house. Thurstan (*reg* 1114–40), Archbishop of York, granted a site in Skeldale in 1132–3, and in the same year Fountains was admitted into the Cistercian Order by St Bernard of Clairvaux, who sent GEOFFROI D'AINAI to advise the monks. The land was well watered, both by the River Skell and by six springs, hence the name St Mary of the Springs, latinized to 'de Fontibus'. A fabric fund existed in 1135, the year that Hugh of York and Serlo joined the house. Their arrival seems to have been a turning-point in the abbey's fortunes. Grants of land towards the building of the church followed in 1140. A primitive wooden church was replaced in stone before 1147, when a fire led at least to a reflooring. Excavation of the first stone church has revealed an aisleless cruciform plan (l. *c.* 35 m) with a squared chancel, transept in echelon and a nave narrower than the choir entry. There was probably no marked crossing. This church lay on the site of the present crossing and south transept. Thicker foundations suggest that the chancel was vaulted. The early monastic layout had a cloister south of, and longer than, the nave, but otherwise a standard Benedictine arrangement with the addition of a large lay brothers' block along the west walk.

The early monastery prospered, and between 1137 and 1150 Fountains founded eight daughter houses. The fire of 1147 and the growth of the house dictated the replacement of the first stone church by the present structure (see §2 below). The reconstruction encompassed much of the house and has bequeathed a well-preserved monastic complex of *c.* 1150–1230, the largest British Cistercian ruin (for plan *see* MONASTERY, fig. 1).

Fountains was dissolved in 1539, after the penultimate Abbot, William of Thirsk, had been executed for opposing Henry VIII. A scheme to raise the church to cathedral status foundered, and Fountains passed in 1540 to Sir Richard Gresham (*d* 1549). Some of the abbey stone was used to build Fountains Hall in the late 16th century; and in 1768 William Aislabie (1700–81) incorporated the ruins into the landscaped park of STUDLEY ROYAL. Main restorations of the ruins took place between 1840 and 1854 under John Walbran (1817–69) and from 1966 to 1982 by the Department of the Environment.

2. ABBEY CHURCH. The present church, built of limestone quarried at the site soon after the fire of 1147,

repeated the stepped eastern termination of the first stone church on a larger scale, with an aisleless, two-bay chancel and transept arms with three eastern chapels. There is a full crossing, an aisled nave of 11 bays and a low narthex with a lean-to roof. The finished plan reflects that of the second church at CLAIRVAUX ABBEY. The surviving sections of the mid-12th-century church had barrel vaults over aisles and transept chapels, while the nave roof was wood. The church, which was finished c. 1160, was early enough to possess a low crossing tower, a feature later proscribed. The nave was divided internally by screens, the monk's choir being situated beneath the crossing and into the nave, while the seven western nave bays formed the lay brothers' choir. The choir and innermost transept chapels were subsequently replaced, and the upper west façade of the west front now has a single Late Gothic window.

The style is pointed Romanesque. The nave elevation has columnar piers, octagonal scalloped capitals and abaci, moulded pointed arches, a blank, unarticulated middle zone and round-headed clerestory windows rising from a continuous string course, with a second string course linking the window heads. Externally the bay divisions are marked by pilaster buttresses and a string course uniting the window heads. The most interesting feature is the aisle vaulting, transverse barrel vaults probably reflecting the Burgundian connections of English Cistercian architecture. The disjointed springing level of the arcade and aisle vault is masked by colonnettes with their own scallop capitals extending from the main pier, while the aisle responds are merely corbelled into the plain wall. These vaults probably reflect an earlier, simpler system at Rievaulx Abbey, while other motifs relate to contemporary north English work at Durham Cathedral and Selby Abbey. The transept chapels have twin windows topped by an oculus and a curious, dentilated, external gable motif.

The present choir was begun by John of York, Abbot in 1203–11, and completed by Abbot John of Kent by 1247, giving the church an internal length of 100.6 m. Five aisled bays led to a giant eastern transept, flat-faced to the east, called the chapel of the Nine Altars. The transept is two bays deep east–west, although the interior spaces north and south were undivided. Twin, full-height arches divide the central 'crossing' bay from the arms and frame the east wall, which now contains a voided Late Gothic window. Originally there were either triple stepped lancets or uniform lancets with a gable oculus. The choir elevation was two-storey, with arcades and clerestory, the latter with a wall passage. The piers alternated octagonal and clustered, thicker and thinner shafts alternating around a diamond-plan core. The piers supporting the giant entry arches into the Nine Altars chapel were also clustered, with coloured Nidderdale 'marble' shafts.

The choir aisle has a continuous trefoil dado arcade, the detached shafts all ribbed, and a triple-arched upper design, with a single lancet framed by colonnettes supporting the capitals of a high-stepped trefoil wall arcade. The asymmetrical side arches are curiously misshapen. The triple-shafted aisle responds stand above the dado arcade. The aisles swallowed the innermost transept chapel of the earlier church. The choir and aisles had quadripartite rib vaults. The height of the aisle roof and clerestory sill

1. Fountains Abbey, chapel of the Nine Altars, interior looking south, begun c. 1203

suggest principal buttresses beneath the lean-to roofs, although there is also evidence for exposed flyers. The high altar stood west of the entry arches to the Nine Altars chapel, although the monastic choir remained beneath the crossing and into the nave.

The chapel of the Nine Altars (see fig. 1) has sheer, narrow bays divided horizontally into three zones: a dado matching the choir aisles; tall lancets above, alternating with attenuated blind arches framed by colonnettes with mid-height shaft rings, creating a continuous sequence on three walls; and a clerestory of single lancets, corresponding with the choir clerestory, including the wall passage, framed within staggered trefoil arches similar to the aisles. The original vaults failed and were replaced with wooden roofs in 1483. Externally, the two ranges of windows are flanked by massive polygonal full-height buttresses, some strengthened in the 15th century. The nine altars that gave the chapel its name were arranged on a long step the full length of the transept in groups of three, each separated by a stone wall. The early 13th-century work at Fountains reveals sufficient stylistic links with contemporary work at Beverley Minster to suggest co-authorship.

Minor late medieval alterations and additions include the Perpendicular gable-end windows and the north transept tower, built by Huby, Abbot from 1495 to 1526, with stepped gabled buttresses and Perpendicular windows.

3. MONASTIC BUILDINGS. The claustral buildings of c. 1150–1240 are well preserved. The chapter house, with three richly moulded doors, had clustered marble piers

2. Fountains Abbey, west range of the cloister, ground-floor of the cellarium, late 12th century

and foliate and waterleaf capitals carrying vaults in three aisles. The early 13th-century refectory (l. *c.* 35 m) lies north–south against the south cloister walk in the English Cistercian manner, the end bridging the stream. All the kitchen offices survive. The two-storey west range, the cellarium, is the most celebrated of the monastic buildings at Fountains. The ground-floor (see fig. 2) was originally subdivided with the cellarer's stores, the outer parlour and, at the southern end, the lay brothers' refectory. Almost the whole interior is now thrown open, displaying a spectacular interior 100 m long, with 22 vaulted bays in two aisles. The simple quadripartite vaults spring directly from the piers, whose form derives directly from the ribs. The rough-stone webbing is exposed. The lay brothers' dormitory above has its own stair into the western nave and access to a southern reredorter block slung over another branch of the stream. Nearly all the other buildings survive, including the infirmary ranges, bakehouses, guest accommodation, mills, bridges and gates.

BIBLIOGRAPHY

Serlo of Kirkstall: *Narratio de fundatione monasterii de Fontibus* [*c.* 1205]; ed. J. R. Walbran and J. T. Fowler, *Memorials of the Abbey of St Mary's at Fountains*, i, Surtees Soc., xlii (1863), pp. 46–7

P. Draper: 'The Nine Altars at Durham and Fountains', *British Archaeological Association Conference Transactions: Medieval Art and Architecture at Durham Cathedral: Durham, 1977*, pp. 74–86

R. Gilyard Beer: *Fountains Abbey* (London, 1978)

R. Morris: *Cathedrals and Abbeys of England and Wales* (London, 1979)

P. Fergusson: *Architecture of Solitude: Cistercian Abbeys in Twelfth-century England* (Princeton, 1984)

R. Gilyard Beer and G. Coppack: 'Excavations at Fountains Abbey, North Yorkshire, 1979–80: The Early Development of the Monastery', *Archaeologia* [Soc. Antiqua. London], cviii (1986), pp. 147–88

C. Norton and D. Park, eds: *Cistercian Art and Architecture in the British Isles* (Cambridge, 1986) [articles by N. Coldstream, P. Fergusson and R. Halsey]

FRANCIS WOODMAN

Fouquet [Foucquet], **Jean** (*b* Tours, *c.* 1415–20; *d* Tours, before 8 Nov 1481). French painter and illuminator. He is regarded as the most important French painter of the 15th century and was responsible for introducing Italian Renaissance elements into French painting. Little is known of his life, and, apart from a signed self-portrait medallion (Paris, Louvre), his only authenticated work is the *Antiquités judaïques* (Paris, Bib. N., MS. fr. 247). A corpus of works by Fouquet has therefore been established on the basis of stylistic criteria, but its exact chronology is uncertain.

1. Life and work. 2. Influence.

1. LIFE AND WORK.

(i) Paintings and drawings. (ii) Manuscripts.

(i) Paintings and drawings. The earliest known work attributed to Fouquet (Pächt, 1974) is the painted portrait of *Gonella* (360×240 mm; Vienna, Ksthist. Mus.), the jester of Niccolo III d'Este (*reg* 1393–1441); a date of *c.* 1440 for the panel has been confirmed by dendrochronological analysis. The portrait conveys a sense of subdued verism. Despite certain Netherlandish features, such as the minute analysis of the details of the face, its French character is seen in the 'stereometric simplification' (Pächt), the rendering of the flesh, physiognomic details and the use of colour; infra-red analysis has also revealed that there are colour notations written in French (e.g. *blanc* on the left sleeve). The painter evidently made a quick sketch of the model and only subsequently applied colour. One tempting theory about Fouquet's training is that he was apprenticed in the Bourges workshops of Jacob de Littemont (*d c.* 1478), court painter of Charles VII, whose name suggests a south Netherlandish origin; this might explain the combination of Netherlandish and French traits seen in the portrait.

Fouquet may have gone to Rome as a member of the French delegation of 1446, possibly as court portrait painter, although he could have travelled there independently. In any case, he was there between 1446 and 1448 and was well enough known to paint the portrait of *Pope Eugenius IV* (*reg* 1431–47), which hung in the sacristy of the Dominican convent of S Maria sopra Minerva in Rome (untraced); it is mentioned by Antonio Filarete (J. Spencer: *Filarete's Treatise on Architecture*, Yale, 1965, p. 120), Francesco Florio (see Fiot) and Giorgio Vasari. The choice of a painter who was 'the image of youth' (Filarete) to portray the Pope may perhaps be explained by the fact that the Superior General of the convent, Tixier, was French (see Schwager). The central part of the portrait is known through an engraving in Onuphrius Panvinius' *Elogia et imagines accuratissime ad vivum aeneis typis delineatae* (Rome, 1568), although the 'two intimates' of the Pope described by Filarete are missing. Its novel conception, with the Pope shown in three-quarter view, his gaze directed at the spectator, and the modelling reminiscent of a bas-relief, must have made a lasting impression on contemporaries, and the portrait is said to have caused a sensation in Italy. It was painted on canvas, an unusual support for the period despite examples by Hugo van der Goes and Fra Angelico, suggesting that it was an urgent commission; and it may have been executed before the Pope's death on 23 February 1447. Fouquet probably painted other portraits in Rome.

The treatment of the human figure and the conception of spatial design seen in Fouquet's pictures suggest that he studied the work of contemporary Italian masters. Through the Dominicans of S Maria sopra Minerva, he could have met Fra Angelico, then working in the Vatican Palace on frescoes in the chapel of St Peter (1447), the chapel of St Lawrence (1448) and the chapel of Nicholas V (1448–9), and Filarete, who finished working on the bronze doors of St Peter's in August 1445. He also seems to have known the work of such artists as Masaccio, Paolo Uccello, Filippo Brunelleschi, Donatello and Jacopo Bellini, and he probably travelled to Florence and perhaps to Venice; he seems to have been influenced by Bellini's 'pointillist' technique in the use of gold and by details from his book of drawings (Paris, Louvre; *see* BELLINI, (1)). Both Bellini and Fouquet avoided a purely rational perspective, based on a single vanishing point, and developed a more empirical approach, in order to retain coherence of composition. This appears in the architectural recollections in Fouquet's pictures (the city of Rome, the Forum, St Peter's, details of cornices and capitals, etc), although he rarely made direct copies, always transforming his models.

By the end of 1448 Fouquet had returned to Tours, where he occupied 'a house with a piece of fallow land and a tower'; he married and pursued his profession there.

1. Jean Fouquet: *Etienne Chevalier and St Stephen*, tempera on panel, 960×880 mm, after 1452 (Berlin, Gemäldegalerie)

After 1452 he painted for ETIENNE CHEVALIER a diptych (the Melun diptych), showing the Treasurer being presented by his patron St Stephen to the Virgin, as well as a Book of Hours. The diptych was to be placed over the tomb of Etienne's wife Catherine Budé (d 1452) in Notre-Dame, Melun, and is essentially an intercessional picture. On the left wing (Berlin, Gemäldegal.; see fig. 1) Etienne Chevalier is depicted in prayer in his palace, shown with marble-covered walls incised with his name and title. The right panel (960×860 mm; Antwerp, Kon. Mus. S. Kst.) depicts another world: Heaven appears to open, revealing a supernatural vision of the Virgin as Queen of Heaven, her throne surrounded by seraphim and cherubim; she appears with breast uncovered, while the Christ Child points to Etienne with the forefinger of his left hand. The colours were originally stronger; the flesh of the Virgin and Child, rendered in greyish-white, creates an effect of extreme pallor, contrasting with the vivid unbroken reds and blues of the surrounding angels. The supernatural effect of the apparition is paradoxically reinforced by the realistic representation of the figures. Chevalier appears to pray before a sculpted image, and one scholar has noted a resemblance to reliefs by Antonio Rossellino.

Details of the Virgin's costume and comparison with authenticated representations (e.g. a drawing in Paris, Louvre) tend to confirm the tradition that the Virgin has the features of Agnès Sorel (d Feb 1450), mistress of Charles VII, although it has also been proposed that she reflects a portrait of Etienne's wife. At all events, the picture was conceived in a particular context towards a precise end. The picture of Chevalier was not an autonomous portrait, a relatively rare type at this time in France, nor did it form part of a triptych, as has sometimes been conjectured: the description by the historian Denys Godefroy, who saw the picture in its original location c. 1660, confirms that there were only two panels 'closing one upon the other'. Godefroy also described the frame, which had been lost by the beginning of the 18th century:

> The borders are covered inside with blue velvet embellished and enriched all around with plenty of Antique love-knots, separated from each other by even spaces and woven in a fine embroidery of gold and silver; on each side of these knots is a large E (Estienne), also in the Antique manner, all covered with small, fine pearls; and between the love knots are silver-gilt medals of medium size representing some sacred story, the figures of which are painted admirably well (*Remarques sur l'histoire de Charles VII* (Paris, 1661), p. 885).

The diptych was placed high above the tomb, making it difficult to see the medallions, which must have separated the two panels. Two of these medals have been identified. One bears a self-portrait of the artist, signed *Jo*[ann]*es Fouquet* (diam. 68 mm; Paris, Louvre); the other represents a scene from the *Legend of St Stephen* (ex-Schloss Köpenick, Berlin; destr. 1945). On the former Fouquet is shown frontally in gold against a plain black ground, his features drawn with the virtuosity of an engraver. The unusual technique seems to be his own invention, probably stimulated by the Early Christian gilded glass medallions that he could have admired in Rome (see 1981 exh. cat.), but he may also have sought the help of local goldsmiths such as his neighbour Jean Harenc of Tours.

Fouquet's portrait of *Charles VII* (860×710 mm; Paris, Louvre) is an intense psychological study, mercilessly revealing the truth of the face despite a certain idealism. The King is depicted half-length, in three-quarter view, and looks out from a niche through parted, light green curtains. He is identified by the inscription on the frame, which describes him as the TRES VICTORIEUX ROY DE FRANCE. The date has been disputed. An X-ray of the panel has revealed beneath the portrait the outlines of a Virgin and Child coinciding with those of the Melun diptych. This suggests that the portrait was executed in haste and that Fouquet lacked an empty panel; such urgency could be explained if this were an official portrait to commemorate a victory, as indicated by the epithet on the frame. There were many commissions (tapestries, commemorative medals etc.) to celebrate such victories as that at Formigny (15 April 1450) and even more the reconquest of Guyenne (1453), which ended the Hundred Years War; Fouquet's portrait could be one of these, perhaps for a service in an oratory. Since Fouquet was not the official painter to the King, the commission may have come from a member of the court, from Jacques Coeur, for example, or from Jean Bernard, Archbishop of Tours (d 1466), one of Fouquet's documented patrons, who could have obtained connections for him at court. Bernard's will mentions a commission from Fouquet for an altarpiece of the *Assumption* (untraced) for the church in Caudes (Indre-et-Loire).

Another portrait by Fouquet of Charles VII (d 1461), known through a copy made for Roger de Gaignières (Paris, Bib. N., Cab. Est., OA 14, fol. 3), must have dated from the end of the King's reign, because it showed him already suffering from a tumour of the jawbone. After Charles's death, Jacob de Littemont had Fouquet sought urgently to colour the death-mask; this commission reflects Fouquet's high reputation: it required a faithful and presentable image of the King to be laid on his coffin for public display during his funeral in Paris. The same year Fouquet was entrusted with making plans for scaffolds and other works for the performance of a mystery play for Louis XI's entry into Paris. Perhaps while in Paris, Fouquet may have drawn the silverpoint *Portrait of a Papal Legate* (198×135 mm; New York, Met.; copy, Windsor Castle, Berks, Royal Col.), inscribed 'a Roman legate of our Holy Father'.

The *Lamentation* ('Nouans *Pietà*'; 1.46×2.37 m) in the parish church at Nouans-les-Fontaines (Indre-et-Loire) is one of Fouquet's rare large-format panels. It is dated by some scholars to the end of his career, by others to c. 1455–60; arguments for the latter include some technical resemblances to the portrait of *Charles VII* and the rapidity of execution. Analysis of the paint layers during restorations has shown that the paint was 'carefully laid in layers of regular thickness using a binding material with a base of oil mixed with a variable quantity of eggs' (see 1980 exh. cat.), which has rekindled the debate.

Neither the name of the donor nor the provenance of the *Lamentation* is known, but several patrons have been proposed, including Jacques Maussabré (d 1498). The Maussabré family had a devotion to Our Lady of Pity and, being settled in the Nouans region, could have been responsible for commissioning the panel. The inscription on the frame emphasizes the patron's intentions, reading

The sculptural, monumental quality and the dignity of the figure are further accentuated by the background, which initially has an Italian Renaissance character but is actually composed of heraldic elements, for example the muzzled bears on the capitals holding the arms of Jouvenel des Ursins.

About 1468 Fouquet was cited by Francesco Florio, then living in Tours, as the author of fine *imagines sanctorum* (untraced) in Notre-Dame-la-Riche, Tours (see Fiot). In 1475 Fouquet was made Peintre du Roi. The following year he painted the canopy (destr.) for the entry into Tours of Alfonso V of Portugal (*reg* 1438–81). He was apparently not active after 1479.

(ii) Manuscripts. The Hours of Etienne Chevalier (see fig. 3), probably begun *c.* 1452, is Fouquet's finest work. The manuscript was cut up by an art dealer in Basle after he had acquired it in Paris at the end of the 18th century and is now dispersed and incomplete (40 miniatures in Chantilly, Mus. Condé, MS. 71; two in Paris, Louvre; and five leaves dispersed in Paris, Bib. N., MS. nouv. acq. lat. 1416; Upton House, Warwicks, NT, MS. 184; London, BL, Add. MS. 37421; Paris, Mus. Marmottan; and New York, Met.). A pair of leaves of the text has now been recovered, enabling the original arrangement of the gatherings to be deduced (Schaefer, de Hamel and Ribault). The arms and monogram (two Es separated by a dash) of Etienne Chevalier appear throughout the manuscript.

2. Jean Fouquet: *Guillaume Jouvenel des Ursins*, panel, 960×739 mm, *c.* 1460–65 (Paris, Musée du Louvre)

'He hath borne our griefs and carried our sorrows' (Isaiah 53.4) and 'For Christ also hath once suffered for sins, the just for the unjust' (I Peter 3.18); the script resembles that on Fouquet's self-portrait medallion in the Louvre. The intensity of the central group, which forms a compact, nearly square composition, is weakened by the figure of the donor with St James on the right and by the Holy Women in the background, and Fouquet perhaps added these figures swiftly at the patron's request. The original freshness of the colours and the free, rapid technique, illustrating Fouquet's virtuosity as a panel painter, have been revealed by cleaning.

The portrait of the Chancellor, *Guillaume Jouvenel des Ursins* (*c.* 1460–65; Paris, Louvre; see fig. 2), who died in 1472, is the most outstanding of Fouquet's later works (*see* JOUVENEL DES URSINS). The preparatory chalk drawing (267×195 mm; Berlin, Kupferstichkab.), a unique survival, was undoubtedly drawn rapidly from life. Fouquet indicated the future colour scheme with regard to the modelling and distribution of highlights by touches of chalk. Despite its apparent precision of detail, the drawing is dominated by the geometry of the composition. On the finished portrait, the opulent contours accentuate the prismatic modelling of the body. Fouquet transformed and idealized the details in order to convey their essential nature. He attempted to capture a timeless element in his model rather than record mere appearances; in this respect he resembled Petrus Christus rather than Jan van Eyck. The treatment of costume and pose gives an impression that the character of the sitter, a self-made man, is formed largely by his social rank and position (Pächt, 1940–41).

3. Jean Fouquet: *Adoration of the Magi*, detached miniature from the Hours of Etienne Chevalier, 162×117 mm, begun *c.* 1452 (Chantilly, Musée Condé, Château de Chantilly, MS. 71)

In this Book of Hours Fouquet employed reminiscences of his Italian travels to create environments that would have been unfamiliar to his readers; for example, Roman elements, coloured marbles and acanthus capitals are employed for the representation of *Christ before Pilate* (Chantilly, Mus. Condé). Through an attentive reading of the texts he provided, where possible, new interpretations of the sacred events, surrounding the characters with figures and settings drawn from everyday life. Most importantly, however, he created a new relationship between text and illustration. Renouncing the usual border of *rinceaux*, his miniatures often fill the page (especially those showing interior scenes, e.g. the *Annunciation of the Virgin's Death*, set in a chapel; Chantilly, Mus. Condé, MS. 71), and the beginning of the prayer is set below in *trompe l'oeil* on a claret-coloured band: the letters are painted to imitate relief, as if they were cast in copper gilt. Fouquet also employed a bipartite layout, as in the miniature of *St Martin Dividing his Cloak* (161×117 mm; Paris, Louvre). Here the *bas-de-page* forms an independent zone that complements the principal action: two angels hold open a diptych showing a small scene painted in two colours with gold, its frame surmounted by the initial letter of the prayer. Above, on a second level, suggesting a stage, the procession is led by St Martin on to a bridge towards the Grand Châtelet giving access to Paris. The miniature combines an empirical perspective that has a very wide

angle of vision with an effect of movement in depth. The depiction of the Seine, a bridge and the houses of the city is distinctive compared to earlier manuscripts, although Fouquet must have known the compositions of the Boucicaut Master, as he appears to have retouched a Book of Hours (London, BL, Add. MS. 16997) belonging to Etienne Chevalier that contained illuminations by that Master. Fouquet's *Martyrdom of St Apollonia* (Chantilly, Mus. Condé, MS. 71) shows a representation of a medieval theatre, which must have been inspired by visual impressions of mystery plays. His involvement with theatrical events is documented in 1461, but he doubtless participated on earlier projects; his sense of colour may have been stimulated by such productions, which provided opportunities for studying colours in movement and the play of light on costumes, and he probably also collaborated on costume designs and stage sets. Fouquet used dark blues, madder reds, lively yellows, all shades of green and a range of whites, but the inimitable aspect of his work is his use of gold, either applied with a brush in broad areas, like the polychrome on a statue, or in very fine hatching strokes of varied lengths and stippled, infinitely varying highlights. Comparable effects, including the transparent use of whites, are found in panels by Jacopo Bellini, especially in the *Virgin of Humility with the Donor, Lionello d'Este, Marchese di Ferrara* (*c.* 1441; Paris, Louvre).

The illuminations added by Fouquet to a Book of Hours belonging to the brother of the financier Simon de Varie (Malibu, CA, Getty Mus.; discovered by Marrow) are datable between 1465 and 1468 and are stylistically close to the Hours of Etienne Chevalier. They are notable for their purely heraldic or devotional, rather than narrative, character, showing Fouquet's capacity to respond to the requirements of a particular commission. One opening (fols 1*v*–2*r*) is arranged in diptych form and shows Simon de Varie in prayer before the Virgin and Child, his arms prominently displayed in the background. The illuminations are distinguished by the play of heraldic colours, the delicacy of the portraits and the bewitching fascination of the armorial paintings.

Towards the end of Charles VII's reign, Fouquet executed two large series of contemporary historical illuminations. The *Grandes Chroniques de France* (460×350 mm; Paris, Bib. N., MS. fr. 6465; *see* PARIS, fig. 2) traces the history of France from its beginnings to the time of Charles V. Decorated with 51 illuminations, this particular manuscript was almost certainly produced for the King. Different episodes are often represented in the same miniature, and the illuminations reveal Fouquet's knowledge of the city of Paris. Boccaccio's *Des Cas des nobles hommes et femmes* (390×290 mm; Munich, Bayer. Staatsbib., Clm. gall. 6), the 'Munich Boccaccio', was copied by Pierre Favre, parish priest of Aubervilliers, in 1458 for Laurent Girard (*b* ?1410–20), son-in-law of Etienne Chevalier and a high functionary of the treasury. The frontispiece illumination (fol. 2*v*) depicts the *Lit de Justice* (see fig. 4), the political trial of Jean, Duc de Alençon, held under Charles VII at Vendôme in 1458. It is both a representation of a specific event and an image composed of symbolic elements (Pächt, 1940–41) and shows a vision of contemporary society, which preserves

4. Jean Fouquet: *Lit de Justice*, frontispiece miniature from Boccaccio: *Des Cas des nobles hommes et femmes*, 390×290 mm, after 1458 (Munich, Bayerische Staatsbibliothek, Clm. gall. 6, fol. 2*v*)

the individuality of the figures represented. The miniatures provide a snapshot of the hierarchies of monarchy, but in the foreground Fouquet has taken care to depict the bourgeoisie, peasants and students—the marginal populace—as onlookers; the sergeants-at-arms are shown having trouble holding them back. A portrait of the painter is also included, denoting the point of departure for the perspective construction. The design is based on a lozenge, a shape that enabled Fouquet to suggest depth yet at the same time to unify the elements of the composition and symbolize France.

Among other works by Fouquet are eight illuminations executed in the first half of the 1460s in a small Book of Hours (108×80 mm; New York, Pierpont Morgan Lib., MS. M.834). The patron of the second series of miniatures in the book, painted by Jean Colombe, has been identified as Louise Chauvet, wife of Jean ROBERTET, secretary to Louis XI. Robertet was a curious figure, a rhetorical poet who enjoyed word play and subtle mottoes, which are found in both parts of the manuscript. Fouquet's section of the Book of Hours contains the motto 'S'IL AVIENT AR', thought to refer to another owner, possibly Antoine Raguier. Fouquet also contributed to the Book of Hours of Charles de France (182×136; Paris, Bib. Mazarine, MS. 473), Louis XI's brother.

Fouquet's only authenticated works are the illuminations in a copy of Flavius Josephus' *Les Antiquités judaïques* (430×285 mm; Paris, Bib. N., MS. fr. 247), which Jacques d'Armagnac, Duc de Nemours (*reg* 1461–77), inherited through his father Bernard from Jean, Duc de Berry. After d'Armagnac was arrested in 1476, the book passed into the library of Peter II, Duke of Bourbon, whose secretary was François Robertet, son of Jean Robertet. François wrote on the last page that nine of the illuminations were 'by the hand of the able painter and illuminator of King Louis XI, Jehan Foucquet, native of Tours'. The illuminations (eleven, however, not nine, a mistake of Robertet) were probably executed *c.* 1465, when Jacques d'Armagnac was in Tours; he probably gave specific instructions to Fouquet, who must have overpainted the arms of Jean, Duc de Berry, and chosen the scenes to be represented. These large miniatures (178×210 mm) reflect Fouquet's experience of larger-scale painting. The blurred, velvety drawing and the broad areas of colour make the summer light radiate in an airy, vaporous atmosphere. A transparent grey wash is used for virtuoso effects of aerial perspective, and eddies of dust are felt to fill the air. At a time when manuscript illumination was competing with printed books, Fouquet realized the essential difference between the two and produced a very elaborate layout that takes precise account of the text. The figures are multiplied and their scale in proportion to the setting reduced, resulting in truly epic paintings. An intense emotion prevails in the indecisive, murderous battles. To render the atmosphere of distant, Eastern lands Fouquet used local landscapes and architecture, but he transformed them by incorporating details described in the texts. For example to represent the Temple of Jerusalem, Tours Cathedral received a revetment of gold, and the city of Jericho is shown encompassed by the Loire and the hills of its right bank.

In 1469 Louis XI instituted the Order of St Michael, for which Fouquet made some armorial paintings (untraced). He also executed the copy of the Order's statutes intended for the King (205×150 mm; Paris Bib. N., MS. fr. 19819) and perhaps carried out other works as well. The single illumination of the manuscript, on the frontispiece, shows a session of the chapter of the Order presided over by Louis XI, with his favourite dog and an ermine in the foreground. Among the knights is the Order's secretary, Jean Robertet. Below, painted in gold, angels bearing the armour of St Michael present the collar of the Order, surmounted by the royal coat of arms. Two knights are debating; Louis XI appears to consider their discussion but mainly watches the dog. The use of white dominates the colour scheme of the miniature.

Four large illuminations, remnants of an oversized book on ancient history, the *Histoire ancienne jusqu'à César et faits des romains* (Paris, Louvre), represent the culmination of Fouquet's style. The compositions are even more monumental than the *Antiquités judaïques*, and the juxtaposition of planes staggered in depth (e.g. winding rivers, rows of trees) heralds the painting of the High Renaissance. Some scenes, such as that showing Pompey on a white horse, are reminiscent of wall painting. In adapting a monumental painting style to a small-scale format, Fouquet was able to offer his patrons unique works, impossible to attain in printed books. Some views of Rome certainly drawn by Fouquet but coloured by an assistant in a Titus Livius (Paris, Bib. N., MS. fr. 20071), especially the frontispiece, which was altered by overpainting by an owner of the book at the beginning of the 16th century (see 1981 exh. cat.), establish this evolution towards broad handling and a more developed style of landscape.

In 1472 Fouquet went to Blois to discuss with Mary of Cleves, Duchess of Orléans, a possible commission for a Book of Hours; two years later he received payment for another Book of Hours for the historian Philippe de Commynes (*c.* 1446–1511), and in the same year (1474) he executed, with the sculptor Michel Colombe, a model on parchment for the future tomb of Louis XI.

2. INFLUENCE. Fouquet seems to have had an important workshop, and his assistants, who included Pierre Hannes (*fl c.* 1455), must have added colour to illuminations drawn by the master himself. The workshop apparently continued after his death until the end of the 15th century, probably through his two sons Louis and François (both *b* after 1448), and many manuscripts echoing his style may have been produced in it. His influence was felt in the workshop of Jean Colombe in Bourges, who copied his illuminations, and in south-west France (e.g. Paoul Goybault), Savoy and Piedmont. The paintings of the Fontainebleau school and of Jean Clouet also reflect Fouquet's work, while Hans Holbein the younger appears to have known his portraits. In the 17th century evidence of his style was lost, but his memory began to be recovered in the 18th. It was only in the Romantic period, however, that Fouquet's work was resuscitated by such scholars as Gustav Waagen and the Comte de Bastard, who paved the way for the fundamental studies of Paul Durrieu.

BIBLIOGRAPHY

G. Vasari: *Vite* (1550, rev. 2/1568); ed. G. Milanesi (1878–85), ii, p. 461 [contains reference to Fouquet in Rome]

G. F. Waagen: *Kunstwerke und Künstler in England und Paris*, iii (Berlin, 1839), pp. 371–4

A. de Bastard and L. de Laborde: *Jehan Foucquet: Histoire de sa vie et appréciations de ses oeuvres* (Paris, 1864)

P. Durrieu: *Les Antiquités judaïques et le peintre Jean Fouquet* (Paris, 1908) [bibliog. to 1907]

M. J. Friedländer: 'Eine Bildnisstudie Jean Fouquets', *Jb. Kön.-Preuss. Kstsamml.*, xxxi (1910), pp. 127–30

T. Cox: *Jehan Foucquet, Native of Tours* (London, 1931)

H. Focillon: 'Le Style monumental de Jean Fouquet', *Gaz. B.-A.*, n. s. 5, xv (1936), pp. 17–32

K. Perls: *Jean Fouquet* (London and Paris, 1940)

O. Pächt: 'Jean Fouquet: A Study of his Style', *J. Warb. & Court. Inst.*, iv (1940–41), pp. 85–102

C. Jacques [Sterling]: *La Peinture française: Les Peintres du moyen âge* (Paris, 1941), pp. 36–42; cat. pp. 17–20

E. A. van Moé and P. Valéry: *Les Fouquet de la Bibliothèque Nationale* (Paris, 1943) [facs.]

Abbé Bourderioux: 'La *Pietà* de Nouans', *Bull. Soc. Archéol. Touraine*, xxix (1948), p. 383

Manuscrits à peintures en France: La Peinture des manuscrits gothiques (exh. cat. by J. Porcher, Paris, Bib. N., 1955), pp. 117–31

R. Fiot: 'Jean Fouquet à Notre-Dame-la-Riche de Tours', *Rev. A.* [Paris], x (1970), pp. 29–46 [contains refs to Fouquet by Francesco Florio]

K. Schwager: 'Über Jean Fouquet in Italien und sein verlorenes Porträt Papst Eugen IV', *Festschrift für Kurt Badt* (Cologne, 1970), pp. 206–34

C. Sterling and C. Schaefer: *Les Heures d'Etienne Chevalier de Jean Fouquet* (Paris, 1971; Eng. trans., London, 1972) [facs.]

C. Schaefer: *Recherches sur l'iconologie et la stylistique de l'art de Jean Fouquet* (Lille, 1972)

O. Pächt: 'Die Autorschaft des Gonella-Bildnisses', *Jb. Ksthist. Samml. Wien*, lxx (1974), pp. 39–88

C. Schaefer: 'Le Diptyque de Melun de Jean Fouquet', *Jb. Kon. Mus. S. Kst.* (1975), pp. 1–100

La Vie mystérieuse des chefs d'oeuvre: La Science au service de l'art (exh. cat. by M. Hours, Paris, Grand Pal., 1980)

C. Schaefer, C. de Hamel and J. Y. Ribault: 'Du Nouveau sur les Heures de E. Chevalier illustrées par J. Fouquet', *Gaz. B.-A.*, n. s. 5, xcviii (1981), pp. 193–200

Jean Fouquet (exh. cat. by N. Reynaud, Paris, Louvre, 1981)

E. König: *Französische Buchmalerei um 1450: Der Jouvenel-Maler, Der Maler des Genfer Boccaccio und die Anfänge Jean Fouquets* (Berlin, 1982)

G. Tournoy: 'Francisco Florio, nouvelliste italien', *Acta conventus neo-latini S. Andreani/Proceedings of the 5th International Congress of Neo-Latin Studies: St Andrews, 1982*, pp. 193–202

The Last Flowering: French Painting in Manuscripts, 1420–1530, from American Collections (exh. cat. by J. Plummer and G. Clark, New York, Pierpont Morgan Lib., 1982)

F. Avril: 'Le Destinataire des Heures "vie à mon désir": Simon de Varie', *Rev. A.* [Paris], 67 (1985), pp. 33–40

J. Marrow: 'Miniatures inédites de Jean Fouquet: Les Heures de Simon de Varie', *Rev. A.* [Paris], 67 (1985), pp. 7–32

F. Avril, T. Gousset and B. Guenée: *Les Grandes Chroniques de France* (Paris, 1987) [facs.]

Les Manuscrits à peinture en France, 1460–1520 (exh. cat. by F. Avril and N. Reynaud, Paris, Bib. N., 1993), pp. 130–51

C. Schaefer: *Jean Fouquet: Auf der Schwelle der Renaissance* (Dresden, 1994)

CLAUDE SCHAEFER

Fouquet [Foucquet], **Nicolas** (*bapt* Paris, 27 Jan 1615; *d* Pignerol [now Pinerolo, Piedmont], 22 March 1680). French finance minister, patron and collector. He was the son of François Fouquet (*d* 1640), a royal official who had formed a collection of medals and books much admired by the antiquary Nicolas-Claude Fabri de Peiresc. During the civil disturbances of the Fronde, Nicolas Fouquet was loyal to Cardinal Mazarin and became Procureur Général to the Parlement de Paris in 1650; in 1653 he became joint Surintendant des Finances to Louis XIV. From 20 February 1659 until his arrest on charges of treason on 5 September 1661, he held the latter post alone. His personal wealth, though much exaggerated by his detractors, was great. He followed the examples of Cardinal Richelieu and Cardinal Mazarin and became one of the foremost collectors and patrons in 17th-century France. He provided the model on which Louis XIV based the splendour of his own collecting and patronage.

Following the fashion set by Richelieu for owning great houses close to Paris, Fouquet acquired many properties, chief among them the châteaux of Saint-Mandé, on the outskirts of Paris, and VAUX-LE-VICOMTE, near Melun. He greatly enlarged the estate and the buildings at Saint-Mandé and assembled there a library of more than 27,000 books and manuscripts, as well as collections of medals, paintings and antique and modern statuary. In 1655 he sent his younger brother, the Abbé Louis Fouquet, to Rome to buy works of art. With the help of Nicolas Poussin, Louis bought paintings, sculpture and other items, which found their way to Saint-Mandé and Vaux. Much of the contemporary sculpture at Saint-Mandé was by Michel Anguier, who worked at the house from 1655 to 1658. Among his works were statues of *Hercules* and *Charity* (both untraced), the latter supposedly representing Mme Fouquet and her children. According to early sources, there were also 14 life-size statues of the *Gods of Olympus*, copied by Anguier from antique originals. Statues of *Leda* (New York, Met.) and *Amphitrite* (Toledo, OH, Mus. A.) may belong to this group. These, alternating with 33 bronze and marble busts, decorated Fouquet's newly built gallery. Among the curiosities of the collection at Saint-Mandé were two Egyptian sarcophagi (Paris, Louvre), then believed to contain the bodies of the pharaoh Cheops and his brother.

Fouquet's main achievement as a patron was the building of Vaux-le-Vicomte (1656–61), the most perfect example of a non-royal château built in France in the mid-17th century. The architect at Vaux was Louis Le Vau, the garden designer André Le Nôtre; the painter Charles Le Brun was in charge of the decoration, and the sculptors Anguier, Pierre Puget and François Girardon also worked there. Antoine Trummel, La Quintinie and the fountain-maker Claude Robillot worked in the gardens (*see* LE NÔTRE, ANDRÉ, fig. 1; *see also* GARDEN, §VIII, 4 (ii)), and Thibault Poissant furnished models for terms. It was the site on which what was later to be developed as the LOUIS XIV STYLE found its first integrated expression. The rapidly built house and much of the decoration at Vaux remain intact, but the lavish furnishings, pictures, movable sculptures, tapestries and other contents were, with the contents of Saint-Mandé, scattered after Fouquet's disgrace. Many pieces passed into the French royal collection. Others were sold at public auctions in Paris and at Saint-Mandé in 1665–6.

Among the items passing into the hands of Louis XIV were some of the splendid tapestries and carpets of gold and silk woven at Brussels, at Mortlake and at the factory established by Fouquet at Maincy, near Vaux, in 1658. A number of pictures from Fouquet's collection can be traced. These include Poussin's the *Israelites Gathering Manna in the Desert*, painted for Paul Fréart de Chantelou, and Veronese's *Susanna and the Elders* (both Paris, Louvre). Four paintings by Jacopo Bassano on the theme of the *History of Noah* (Paris, Louvre; Marseille, Mus. B.-A.; Bordeaux, Mus. B.-A.; and Nancy, Mus. B.-A.) may have been among the nine works by that artist owned by Fouquet. Fouquet's traceable sculptures include Puget's *Gallic Hercules* (Paris, Louvre), intended for Vaux but unfinished in 1661, and an antique bronze statue of *Antinous* (Potsdam, Schloss Sanssouci), as well as a set of 14 marble terms (Versailles, Château), once at Vaux and based on designs supplied by Poussin.

The team of artists, craftsmen and gardeners assembled by Fouquet for the construction and decoration of Vaux was taken over by Louis XIV and employed on royal projects by the Bâtiments du Roi, the most eminent among them becoming the leading figures in the development of the château of VERSAILLES. Similarly, the designers, weavers and half-finished tapestries at Maincy were moved in 1662 to the newly bought Hôtel des Gobelins in Paris, where they formed the nucleus of the new royal Gobelins factory (*see* GOBELINS, §2).

Although Fouquet has frequently been criticized for diverting the resources of the French state into projects for self-aggrandizement, in the *Défense* written at the time of his arrest he justified the splendours of his life-style and his enormously expensive building schemes by the need to retain the faith of creditors in the financial buoyancy of the Crown, without which the pressing needs of the exchequer could not have been met.

BIBLIOGRAPHY

E. Bonnaffé: *Les Amateurs de l'ancienne France: Le Surintendant Fouquet* (Paris and London, 1882)

——: *Dictionnaire des amateurs français au XVIIe siècle* (Paris, 1884)

U. V. Chatelain: *Le Surintendant Fouquet protecteur des lettres, des arts et des sciences* (Paris, 1905)

D. Dessert: *Fouquet* (Paris, 1987) [it is not certain that the portrait on the cover of this book is of Fouquet]

PATRICK LE CHANU

Fouquier [Foucquier], **Jacques** (*b* Antwerp, 1590–91; *d* Paris, 1659). Flemish painter and draughtsman, active in France. His first surviving painting is the *Winter Landscape* (1617; Cambridge, Fitzwilliam), a work in the manner of Jan Breughel I, who may have been his master. However, a drawing of a *River Scene* (Rotterdam, Mus. Boymans–van Beuningen), containing references to such Dutch landscape masters as Willem Buytewech and Esaias van de Velde (i), suggests that he may have trained in Holland. In 1614 he became a master in the artists' guild in Antwerp and in 1616 in that of Brussels. Soon afterwards he was in Heidelberg, working for Frederick V, the Elector Palatine: a *View from the Terrace of Heidelberg Castle* is known from two engravings of 1620. A *Mountainous Landscape with Huntsmen* (Nantes, Mus. B.-A.; see fig.) of the same year—a sweeping panorama with a bluish horizon—recalls the style of Josse de Momper II.

Fouquier's landscapes were much appreciated in France, where he settled in 1621; they were bought by many of the great collectors of the time, including Louis Phélypeaux de La Vrillière, Michel Particelli d'Hemery, Sieur d'Emery (*c.* 1595–1650), Jean-Baptiste Colbert and Richelieu. He is said to have collaborated with Rubens, and in 1626 he was commissioned by Louis XIII to paint views of French towns, as part of a scheme to decorate the Grande Galerie of the Louvre. Félibien stated that he visited Toulon and Aix but did very little work there. In 1641 he quarrelled with Poussin, who had been summoned to Paris to produce a new plan for the gallery. He was a forgotten

Jacques Fouquier: *Mountainous Landscape with Huntsmen*, oil on canvas, 1.18×1.99 m, 1620 (Nantes, Musée des Beaux-Arts de Nantes)

artist by the time he died. Apart from the works mentioned above, the *Landscape with Hunters* (1622; Cologne, Wallraf-Richartz-Mus.) is the only painting by Fouquier that can be precisely dated. But his style seems to have moved away from Dutch and Flemish models towards the Italianate classicism of Paul Bril and Claude. Indeed, one of his drawings, *Trees near a Pond* (Oxford, Ashmolean), was once attributed to Claude, and *Landscape with a Castle on the Mountain* (pen-and-ink and wash; Vienna, Albertina) is even closer to him in its sense of space and its handling of trees, leaves and rocks. Fouquier's finest drawing, *Wooded Landscape Crossed by a Stream* (Paris, Louvre), justifies Mariette's praise for the 'marvellous darkness and freshness' of his rendition of wood-hollows.

Fouquier's works were frequently engraved, notably by Jean Morin, Gabriel and Nicolas Pérelle, Arnold and Pieter de Jode, Alexander Voet (1613–89/90) and Ignatius van der Stock (*fl* 1660s). While his pupils, apart from Philippe de Champaigne, were of no consequence, Fouquier's synthesis of descriptive northern landscapes with the heroic landscape style developed in Rome had a strong impact on landscape painting in France in the first half of the 17th century.

BIBLIOGRAPHY

Mariette
A. Félibien: *Entretiens sur les vies et les ouvrages des plus excellens peintres anciens et modernes* (Paris, 1685–8, 2/1725/*R* London, 1967), iv, pp. 34, 416
W. Stechow: 'Drawings and Etchings by Jacques Fouquier', *Gaz. B.-A.*, n. s. 5, ii (1942), pp. 419–34

THIERRY BAJOU

Four, the. Scottish group of artists formed *c.* 1893 by CHARLES RENNIE MACKINTOSH, HERBERT MACNAIR and the sisters Margaret and Frances MACDONALD.

Four Arts Society of Artists [Rus. Obshchestvo Khudozhnikov '4 Iskusstva']. Soviet exhibiting society, active in Moscow from 1924 to 1932. The society was planned to include representatives of all 'Four Arts', painting, sculpture, graphics and architecture. Among its members were the painters Martiros Saryan and Konstantin Istomin (1887–1942), the graphic artists Pyotr Miturich, Lev Bruni and Vladimir Favorsky, the sculptor Aleksandr Matveyev and painters such as Pavel Kuznetsov and Kuz'ma Petrov-Vodkin, who had previously exhibited with the Blue Rose group. At different times the group included such architects as Ivan Zholtovsky, Aleksey Shchusev, Vladimir Shchuko and El Lissitzky, together with artists such as Ivan Klyun, Vladimir Lebedev (1891–1967) and the sculptor Vera Mukhina contributing to one or more of the society's four Moscow exhibitions (1925, 1926, 1928 and 1929).

The group believed that the various visual arts should cooperate in the construction of the new environment and realized several projects, including a house at Sochi, on the Black Sea, on which Zholtovsky and Kuznetsov collaborated. The group's declaration of 1929 stressed its commitment to 'painterly realism' and the achievements of the 'French school...that has most fully and thoroughly developed the fundamental properties of the art of painting'. It emphasized that subject-matter was chosen in accordance with purely artistic problems and asserted, 'A new form is important not for its resemblance to a living form, but for its harmony with the material from which it is made, i.e. the surface plane of the painting, colour-pigment, canvas etc.' In 1931 the group petitioned to join AKhRR, the Association of Artists of Revolutionary Russia, but in 1932 it was dissolved by the Decree on the Reconstruction of Literary and Artistic Organizations.

WRITINGS
'Four Arts Society of Artists: Declaration, 1929', *Russian Art of the Avant Garde: Theory and Criticism, 1902–1934*, ed. J. Bowlt (New York, 1976), pp. 281–4

BIBLIOGRAPHY
V. Perel'man, ed.: *Bor'ba za realism v izobrazitel'nom iskusstve 20-kh godov: Materialy, dokumenty, vospominaniya* [The battle for realism in the fine arts of the 1920s: materials, documents, reminiscences] (Moscow, 1962), pp. 230–35

CHRISTINA LODDER

Fourierism. Theory of social organization proposed by the French reformer Charles Fourier (1772–1837). It advocates a society based not on duty but on a collective harmony of the passions, which would allow the freedom of the individual to benefit society as a whole. Including, as it did, a vision of a new architecture to house the community, Fourierism had considerable influence on architects and builders as well as on writers. Fourier envisioned the regrouping of society into communities, or phalanges (phalanxes), of some 400 families (1600 to 1800 people), who were to share the results of their labours in proportion to the capital they had contributed to the community, the work they had carried out and their individual talents. Women and men were treated as equals.

The earliest engraving to depict one of these ideal communities was published on 28 June 1832, in the fifth issue of the periodical launched by the movement and entitled *Le Phalanstère*. The layout of the accommodation is similar to that of the château of Versailles, and the street gallery that provided access to the residential rooms and workshops resembles the Grande Galerie of the Louvre (opened to the public in 1793). Fourier viewed this street gallery as a two-storey construction: 'At ground-floor level, it comprises arcades laid out parallel to the building, as at the Palais Royal; over these arcades, above the ceiling of the lower gallery, is the first-floor gallery. This should continue the full height of the building and be illuminated by broad, high windows in the event that the apartments of the upper storeys open onto it; alternatively, it may stop to form a terrace for the upper storey... The street gallery is used for important meals and extraordinary meetings' (Considerant, 1848, p. 37). The gallery also provided shelter from the elements.

Several attempts were made to set up these communities, both in France and in the USA. They were unsuccessful, with the notable exception of the Familistère built at Guise between 1859 and 1870, on the initiative of Jean-Baptiste Godin (1817–88), an industrialist follower of Fourier. The business, which produced stoves, prospered as a community for about a century. The factory was located alongside three residential buildings. The latter are constructed successively on a plan close to Fourier's model, each surrounding a central courtyard enclosed by glass, and inside are apartments with access gained from galleries. They are still inhabited.

Fourier's philosophy also made an impression on César-Denis Daly, the founder and director of the first French magazine on architecture, the *Revue générale d'architecture et des travaux publics* (1840–87); on Henri Labrouste, the architect of the Bibliothèque Sainte-Geneviève (1839–51) and the Bibliothèque Nationale (1854–75), both in Paris; and on the lesser-known architect of the agricultural community at Saint-Firmin (Oise) of 1847, François Coignet, an entrepreneur of chemical products and disseminator of construction in 'artificial stone' (i.e. cement) during the 1850s. Théodore Labrouste, brother of Henri, and Eugène Laval (1818–69) were also influenced by the community model in their building of the municipal hospital (1858) at 200 Rue du Faubourg Saint-Denis in Paris, and the imperial homes for the aged at Vincennes and Vésinet (1859), both close to Paris. It was perhaps on hospital and townhouse building that the architectural influence of Fourierism was strongest, but Fourier's ideas have affected many social housing projects, including the Unité d'Habitation, also known as the Cité Radieuse, built by Le Corbusier at Marseille between 1945 and 1952 (*see also* TENEMENT BUILDING).

BIBLIOGRAPHY
V. Considerant: *Description du phalanstère et considérations sur l'architectonique* (1848)
N. R. Rianovsky: *The Teaching of Charles Fourier* (Berkeley, 1969)
B. Marrey: 'Saints-simoniens, fouriéristes et architecture', *Archvs Arch. Mod.* (1981)
J. Beecher: *Charles Fourier: The Visionary and his World* (London, 1986)
BERNARD MARREY

Fourmois, Théodore (*b* Presles, 14 Oct 1814; *d* Ixelles, nr Brussels, 16 Oct 1871). Belgian painter and lithographer. He grew up in poverty in Brussels and was employed from *c.* 1826 in the lithographic studio of the firm of De Wasme. There he became acquainted with various artists, including Paul Lauters (1806–1875), Jean-Baptiste Madou and François Stroobant. He was a student at the Académie Royale in Brussels from 1826 to 1829. Little is known about the remainder of his life. From 1831 he is believed to have lived in the house of the widow Meunier, where he must have known the future sculptor Constantin Meunier as a child. Fourmois married in 1854, after which he moved to the Brussels suburb of Ixelles, where he lived for the rest of his life.

Fourmois was initially active as a draughtsman and lithographer. He produced lithographs after Old Masters and he also provided original prints for albums and illustrated topographical books, such as *View of the Waterfall at Côo* (1839; Brussels, Bib. Royale Albert 1er). Fourmois's importance, however, is due to his being the first artist in Belgium to break with the tradition of academic landscape painting by painting, from the 1840s, *en plein air*. His carefully constructed landscapes, with farms and massive groups of trees, recall the Dutch landscape painters of the 17th century, as, for example, in *Landscape in Dauphiné* (1846; Ghent, Mus. S. Kst.). Within this traditional concept, Fourmois concentrated increasingly on the reproduction of atmosphere, making use of a livelier palette and greater freedom of brush technique. He was undoubtedly influenced by the work of John Constable and the Barbizon school. Fourmois painted in various parts of Belgium: the Kempen, the Ardennes and around Presles. He also worked in Switzerland and the Dauphiné region of France, where he painted many nature studies. Towards the end of his life he also worked around Tervuren, in the midst of the local colony of landscape painters.

BIBLIOGRAPHY
M. Maistriaux: 'Fourmois: Sa vie—son oeuvre', *Cah. A.*, vii (1961), pp. 2234–44
Het landschap in de Belgische kunst, 1830–1914 [The landscape in Belgian art, 1830–1914] (exh. cat., Ghent, Mus. S. Kst., 1980)
ROBERT HOOZEE

Fournier, Jacques. *See* BENEDICT XII.

Fournier, Pierre-Simon (*b* Paris, 15 Sept 1712; *d* Paris, 8 Oct 1768). French printer and publisher. He was born into a family of printers and type-founders. In 1729 he began to work at the celebrated Le Bé type foundry in Paris, of which his father was manager; he also studied drawing at the Académie de St Luc. In 1736 he started up as a professional type-founder, producing woodcut vignettes and some large-format type. In 1739 Fournier was formally registered as a typecutter. He made the first move towards the standardization of type sizes with a Table of Proportions (1737), although his method was supplanted by that of the Didot family. His first specimen book, *Modèles des caractères de l'imprimerie* (Paris, 1742), showed 4600 punches. Fournier's typographic skills lay in his modernization of type forms. His roman types increased the thin–thick stroke contrasts and used flat, unbracketed serifs; his italic has been described as the most legible of all. His interests also lay in the design of metalcut floral ornaments and in music cutting, for which he developed a more unified system than that previously possible. Fournier's technical improvements included moulds for the continuous casting of rules and leads that allowed for much longer rules. Having applied in 1757 for the status of Master Printer in order to print his own books, he was granted it in 1762, but it was soon annulled. His major late work was the *Manuel typographique* (Paris, 1764–6) comprising two of the intended four volumes and covering the cutting and founding of type and type specimens (*see* TYPOGRAPHY, fig. 2). His style fell from favour in the early 19th century but was rediscovered and re-evaluated by DANIEL BERKELEY UPDIKE in the 1920s.

BIBLIOGRAPHY
D. B. Updike: *Printing Types: Their History, Forms and Use*, 2 vols (Cambridge, MA, 1922)
H. Carter: *Fournier on Typefounding* (London, 1930)
A. Hutt: *Fournier: The Compleat Typographer* (London, 1972)
LAURA SUFFIELD

Fourth dimension. Term, widely used in early 20th-century art, signifying a higher dimension of space beyond immediate sensory perception. This concept enjoyed its greatest popularity between *c.* 1880 and *c.* 1920. It was an outgrowth of the 19th-century development of geometries of more than three dimensions (*n*-dimensional geometries), but by the end of the century the fourth dimension was discussed in philosophical and mystical terms as often as it was treated geometrically. Artists in nearly every major modern movement between 1900 and 1930 responded to it, making it one of the unifying themes of modernism. Despite the variety in the popular treatments of the subject, all of the artists interested in the fourth dimension before 1920 understood it as an aspect of space. Only after 1919 and the popularization of Einstein's General Theory of Relativity, with its space–time continuum, did the definition of the fourth dimension as time gain widespread acceptance.

Belief in the existence of a fourth spatial dimension, which might hold a reality truer than that of visual perception, encouraged artists to depart from visual reality and to reject completely such three-dimensional conventions as one-point perspective. The Cubists made the first artistic applications of a fourth dimension but did not abandon visual perception completely, whereas such other painters as Kupka, Malevich, Mondrian and van Doesburg found strong support in the idea for their creation of a totally abstract art. Artistic usages of the fourth dimension ranged from the geometrical approach of the Cubists and Duchamp (reinforced by the writing of the theoretical scientist Henri Poincaré) to the mystical, utopian visions of four-dimensional cosmic consciousness painted by Malevich, whose work was related to the writings of PYOTR USPENSKY. The fourth dimension also appealed to iconoclasts such as Duchamp as a subversion of long-standing 'truths' in the same way that non-Euclidean geometry (with its curved spaces) overturned the special status of Euclid's geometry.

The fourth dimension was also of interest within Italian and Russian Futurism, SUPREMATISM, Constructivism, De Stijl wartime synthetic Cubism and Dada, and it attracted American artists in the circles of Alfred Stieglitz and Walter Arensberg, as well as Bauhaus artists and Surrealists. Like van Doesburg, the artists in the last two groups sought in the 1920s to merge the new temporal fourth dimension of Einstein's space–time world with the earlier spatial fourth dimension. The argument that a new language was necessary to deal with four-dimensionality was also made by such composers as Edgard Varèse and by such writers as Aleksey Kruchonykh and Gertrude Stein.

See also MATYUSHIN, MIKHAIL.

BIBLIOGRAPHY
C. Bragdon: *A Primer of Higher Space (the Fourth Dimension)* (Rochester, NY, 1913)
L. D. Henderson: *The Fourth Dimension and Non-Euclidean Geometry in Modern Art* (Princeton, 1983) [extensive bibliog.]
——: 'Mysticism, Romanticism and the Fourth Dimension', *The Spiritual in Art: Abstract Painting, 1890–1985* (exh. cat., Los Angeles, CA, Co. Mus. A., 1986)
LINDA DALRYMPLE HENDERSON

Fowke, Captain Francis (*b* Ballysillan, Ireland [now in Northern Ireland], 7 July 1823; *d* London, 4 Dec 1865). Irish engineer. Educated at Dungannon College, Co. Tyrone, he entered the Royal Military College, Woolwich, in 1839 and was commissioned into the Royal Engineers in 1842. He served in Bermuda but came to notice in 1854 in Paris where he was put in charge of machinery at the Exposition Universelle 1855. In that year he became secretary to the British section, for which he was appointed Chevalier de la Légion d'honneur. He impressed Henry Cole, head of the British team and joint Secretary to the

Department of Science and Art. Fowke was appointed an Inspector in the Department in 1857, subsequently becoming its Architect and Engineer, when the Department created the South Kensington Museum (later the Victoria and Albert Museum and Science Museum). In that capacity Fowke's first building was the Sheepshanks Gallery, a windowless, top-lit building, designed with Richard Redgrave, and which survives within the Victoria and Albert Museum. Two years later Fowke designed a northern extension for the National Gallery of British Art, to house the Turner and Vernon Collections of the National Gallery in Trafalgar Square, also windowless and top-lit. They were both provided with gaslighting so that the public could be admitted in the evenings.

Following approval by a Select Committee of the House of Commons in 1860, Fowke prepared plans for permanent buildings for the South Kensington Museum, which included an unsupported iron and glass roof 33 m square (the North Court of the Victoria and Albert Museum) and an art school (later the Royal College of Art), to be built in stages, dependent upon grants from the Treasury. To assist with decoration, Cole and Fowke brought in three pupils of Alfred Stevens from Sheffield: Godfrey Sykes, James Gamble (1835–1911; designer, decorator and sculptor) and Reuben Townroe (1835–1911; designer and decorator).

For the Department of Science and Art, in 1858 Fowke designed the Royal Scottish Museum (now Royal Museum of Scotland), Edinburgh (begun 1861), and the enlargement of the National Gallery, Dublin. Also in 1858, with the architect Sydney Smirke (1798–1877), Fowke was commissioned by Prince Albert to design arcades round the Horticultural Society's gardens on the Great Exhibition Commissioners' land at South Kensington. He visited Paris to gather ideas, while Cole went to northern Italy and Rome, where he became an enthusiast for red brick, terracotta and mosaic (the South Kensington style; *see* TERRACOTTA, fig. 10), which, under the influence of Sykes, were first used in the Gardens (1861) and then in the Museum (from 1863). As Director of the South Kensington Museum's museum of construction, Fowke used the building as an exhibit.

Fowke designed the large, highly criticized building of the International Exhibition of 1862 in London. The Government bought the land but refused to buy the building, which was demolished in 1863–4, when a competition was held for a new museum on the site to house, among others, the natural history collections of the British Museum. Fowke won the competition to the fury of many architects who tried to influence the Government to overthrow the decision. Following Fowke's death, Alfred Waterhouse was asked to carry out Fowke's design but, after several years' delay, it was abandoned in favour of one by Waterhouse himself.

After Prince Albert's death (1861), Cole determined to build a concert hall to his memory and, following visits by himself and Fowke to Roman amphitheatres in France, a model of a large oval hall (the Royal Albert Hall) was approved by Queen Victoria in 1864. Before building began, Fowke died, and his designs were taken over by Lt-Col. (later Major-Gen.) Henry Young Darracott Scott (1822–83), appointed Director of New Works, South

Kensington Museum. Scott adapted Fowke's designs for the museum, the Royal Albert Hall and the School of Science. A vast iron and glass conservatory (destr. 1890s), built by Fowke in the Horticultural Gardens, was used as the Royal Albert Hall's southern entrance. Surviving elements of the arcades were destroyed in the 1950s to make way for the expansion of the Imperial College of Science and Technology. As Engineer to the Department of Science and Art, Fowke designed an enormous camera (1858) to take the first photographs of the Raphael Cartoons at Hampton Court, on glass plates 1 m square. He is also credited with inventing the camera bellows and a rudimentary vacuum cleaner for museum use.

BIBLIOGRAPHY

DNB
The Museums Area of South Kensington and Westminster, xxxviii of Survey of London (London, 1975)
J. Physick: The Victoria and Albert Museum: The History of its Building (London, 1982)
——: 'The South Kensington Museum', Influences in Victorian Art and Architecture, ed. S. Macready and F. H. Thompson (London, 1985)

JOHN PHYSICK

Fowler, Charles (*b* Cullompton, Devon, May 1792; *d* Great Marlow, Bucks, 7 Sept 1867). English architect. He was apprenticed to a builder and architect from Exeter, John Powning (1763–1832). He set up practice in London in 1818, after four years' experience in the office of David Laing (1774–1856), the architect of the new Custom House (1813–17), London. Four major buildings linked Fowler's reputation with the large new wholesale and retail markets that were soon to become a standard component of the 19th-century city: Hungerford Market (designed 1825; built 1831–3; destr. 1862 to make way for Charing Cross Railway Station), London; Covent Garden Market (1828–30), London; Lower Market (1835–7; destr. 1942), Exeter; and Higher Market (1835–8), Exeter, where he supervised construction after the death of George Dymond (*c.* 1797–1835). Of these, the multi-level Hungerford Market, on a long, narrow sloping site (142×38 m) with a 9.2-m drop between the Strand and the Thames, was the most complex and ambitious; not only did the initial design bring him the commission for Covent Garden, but the completed building also received much critical acclaim on the Continent, where it was well illustrated in Ludwig von Förster's *Allgemeine Bauzeitung* (1838–9, pls ccxlvi–cclii). Fowler's free-standing roof (1835) to the Lower Court of Hungerford was a delicate, double cantilevered construction in cast iron, a design that still appeals for its daring and structural grace. Of the same period as Covent Garden, the 85-m conservatory range (1827–30) for Syon Park, Middx, with its cast-iron structure and 11.6-m diameter glazed central dome, was another major work that helped to establish his reputation. In the following decade, Fowler's technical virtuosity was emphasized again by the fan-driven, ducted underfloor air distribution system that formed an integral part of his new London Fever Hospital (1848–9), Islington. Fowler's other important health care building, the Devon County Lunatic Asylum (1842–5), Exminster, was equally innovative; its semicircular plan with radiating wings overcame the inadequacies of the panopticon format, gave good centralized services and supervision and established a lucid planning principle; this ability to handle the planning needs of new building types has ensured his enduring reputation.

WRITINGS
'On Terrace Roofs', *Trans. RIBA*, i (9 May 1836), pp. 47–51 [illus. of laminated tile technique]
'Arrangement of Lunatic Asylums', *Builder*, clxxxi (25 July 1846), pp. 349–50, 354–5
'Some Remarks on Hungerford Market', *Trans. RIBA*, xiii (15 Dec 1862), pp. 54–7

BIBLIOGRAPHY
Colvin
J. C. Loudon, ed.: 'Hungerford New Market', *Archit. Mag.*, i (1834), pp. 56–62
——: 'Market of Covent Garden', *Archit. Mag.*, v (1838), pp. 665–77
T. L. Donaldson: 'Memoir of the Late Charles Fowler', *Trans. RIBA*, xviii (4 Nov 1867), pp. 1–15
J. Taylor: 'Charles Fowler: Master of Markets', *Archit. Rev.* [London], cxxxv (March 1964), pp. 174–82
——: 'Charles Fowler (1792–1867): A Centenary Memoir', *Archit. Hist.*, xi (1968), pp. 57–74
R. Thorne: *Covent Garden Market: Its History and Restoration* (London, 1980)
J. Taylor: *Hospital and Asylum Architecture in England, 1840–1914* (London, 1991)

JEREMY TAYLOR

Fowler, Orson Squire (*b* Cobocton, NY, 11 Oct 1809; *d* Sharon Station, CT, 1887). American social reformer. His interest in reform began while he was studying theology at Amherst College, MA. He wrote and lectured on the need to improve the built environment, discussing the question in *A Home for All* (1848), in which he called for economy in construction, better utilization of space and restrained architectural detailing. He justified his demands on the grounds of natural forms, claiming that nature 'appends only what is useful, and even absolutely *necessary*. . . . Nature's forms are mostly spherical. . .why not apply her forms to houses?'

During a trip to Milton, WI, in 1850, Fowler visited a six-sided concrete structure built by Joseph Goodrich (1844), which converted him to the use of concrete. Fowler's own home (1848; destr. 1897) in Fishkill, NY, was a starkly detailed concrete octagon that enclosed a greater area per length of wall than any other floor plan. With eight walls instead of four, more sunlight could be admitted; with less exterior wall surface allowing heat loss, it was easier to heat. To cool the house through natural ventilation, the sash window on the windward side could be opened to create a draught in concert with the central stair-hall door and cupola window. Sun or shade, breeze or protection were afforded by encircling porches. With each side essentially equal, site orientation was simple, allowing multiple views and maximum sunlight. Further, the materials for concrete were available everywhere and hence affordable to the average builder. Critics cited the high labour costs of construction and the difficulty of planning the interior room spaces. While the design was intended for the poor, clients were generally from the upper middle class. Perhaps the grandest of all octagon houses was the Moorish-revival plantation house known as Longwood, designed in 1861 for Dr Haller Nutt of Natchez, MS, by architect Samual Sloan of Philadelphia. Surviving examples of octagon houses include Armour–Carmer House (1860), Irvington, NY, and a house at Glen Aubrey, NY, built by George W. Smith in 1857.

Fowler's sponsorship of concrete was prophetic, though few used it at first because of the expense of binding cement. *A Home for All*, reprinted every year from 1848 to 1857, exerted an influence on American domestic architecture, as well as small-scale school and church design.

See also IRWIN, HARRIET MORRISON.

WRITINGS

A Home for All: or, The Gravel Wall and Octagon Mode of Building (New York, 1848); rev. as *The Octagon House: A Home For All*, with new intro. (New York, 1973)
The Octagon House (1853)

BIBLIOGRAPHY

C. F. Schmidt: *The Octagon Fad* (Scottsville, NY, 1958)
C. F. Schmidt and P. Parr: *More about Octagons* [Caledonia, NY, c. 1976]
A. Boulton: 'Age of the Octagon', *Amer. Her.*, xxxiv (Aug/Sept 1983), p. 13

KINGSTON WM. HEATH

Fox. English family of statesmen and patrons. The first notable figure in the family was Sir Stephen Fox (*b* Farley, Wilts, 27 March 1627; *d* Farley, Wilts, 28 Oct 1716), who sided with the Royalists in the English Civil War. After the Restoration of 1660 he achieved high office under Charles II, King of England, and succeeding monarchs. He built a villa at Chiswick, Middx, that was greatly admired by William III. His son Henry Fox, later 1st Baron Holland (*b* Chiswick, 28 Sept 1705; *d* London, 1 July 1774), became an important, if unscrupulous, politician and was accused of embezzlement. He rented Holland House (begun *c.* 1605), Kensington, London, from 1749, bought it in 1767 and spent much money on improvements. He transformed the long chamber on the first floor into a gallery for his picture collection, which included many works derived from the collection of the dukes of Richmond and Lennox through Fox's wife, Lady Caroline Lennox. He also acquired works by Joshua Reynolds, William Hogarth and Allan Ramsay.

The 1st Baron's third son was the distinguished prime minister Charles James Fox (*b* London, 24 Jan 1749; *d* Chiswick, 13 Sept 1806), who brought up his nephew Henry Richard Vassall Fox, 3rd Baron Holland (*b* Winterslow, Wilts, 2 Nov 1773; *d* London, 22 Oct 1840); the latter also began a career as a politician after travelling in Europe (1791–5). He inherited Holland House from his grandfather and with his wife, Elizabeth Vassall (1770–1845), established a brilliant circle of statesmen, writers and other celebrities there. The formal gardens created for Lord and Lady Holland by their librarian Buonaiuti in 1812 survive. Their eldest son, Charles Richard Fox (*b* 1796; *d* London, 13 April 1873), born before Lady Holland's divorce from her first husband, Sir Godfrey Webster, served in the army and the navy before becoming aide-de-camp to William IV. In 1820 he visited Greece and Asia Minor, which stimulated his interest in ancient coins, of which he formed a notable collection. It is described in his *Engravings of Unedited or Rare Greek Coins* (2 vols; London, 1856–62); at his death it consisted of 11,500 ancient Greek coins and now forms part of the Münzkabinett in the Bodemuseum, Berlin.

His younger brother, Henry Edward Fox, 4th Baron Holland (1802–59), made considerable alterations in the Italian style to the house in the mid-19th century, converting part of the 17th-century stables to the Garden Ballroom. After the death of the 4th Baron's widow in 1889, Henry Edward Fox-Strangways, 5th Earl of Ilchester (from a separate branch of the Fox family), took possession. Holland House was partly destroyed during World War II; the most notable surviving features are the gate piers (1629) in front of the house by Nicholas Stone (i) the elder, after a design by Inigo Jones.

DNB

BIBLIOGRAPHY

J. Friedlaender: 'Die Fox'sche Münzsammlung', *Archäol. Ztg* (1873), pp. 99–103
Giles Stephen Holland Fox-Strangways, Earl of Ilchester: *The Home of the Hollands* (London, 1937)
D. Hudson: *Holland House in Kensington* (London, 1967)

□

Fox, Charles (*b* Cossey, nr Norwich, 17 March 1794; *d* Leyton, Essex, 28 Feb 1849). English engraver. His father was steward to Lord Stafford, and his life was dominated by an interest in agriculture and floriculture. He judged for the Royal Horticultural Society and drew all the illustrations for *The Florist*. Charles Hodgson (*fl* 1802–25) of Norwich taught him drawing; the engraver William Camden Edwards (1777–1855) encouraged him to take up engraving. Fox later assisted the painter John Burnet in engravings after Sir David Wilkie; his chief work after this artist was *The Queen's First Council* (1846–7). Several plates after Wilkie were done for Robert Cadell's edition of Sir Walter Scott's novels (1830) and the illustrations to James Stark's *Scenery of the Rivers of Norfolk* (London, 1834). Among his engraved portraits are *Bishop Milner* (1822) after Georges Antoine Keman (1765–1830), *James Hogg* in Hogg's *Altrive Tales* (1832), *William Camden Edwards* and *John Burnet* after Stephen Poyntz Denning (1795–1864). In 1845 Henry Graves published Fox's engraving of *The Attack* after William Henry Hunt (*c.* 1834; priv. col., see J. Witt: *William Henry Hunt* (London, 1982), pl. 499). Also in 1845, he was reported to have received 1100 guineas for engraving the *Flight Interrupted* (1815–16; London, V&A) after William Mulready for the Royal Irish Art Union, but it was unfinished at his death.

BIBLIOGRAPHY

DNB; Thieme–Becker
A. J. [London] (1849), p. 105

BASIL HUNNISETT

Fox, E(manuel) Phillips (*b* Melbourne, 12 March 1865; *d* Melbourne, 8 Oct 1915). Australian painter and teacher. From 1878 to 1886 he trained at the National Gallery of Victoria Art Schools, Melbourne, and in 1887 left to study in Europe. In Paris he attended the Académie Julian and was taught by Jean-Léon Gérôme at the Ecole des Beaux-Arts and by the American artist T. Alexander Harrison (1853–1930). He was involved with the *plein-air* artists at Etaples, Pas-de-Calais, and in Brittany and also visited Giverny, where from 1883 Monet was living. By 1890 he had moved to England, to the artists' colony at St Ives, Cornwall. In 1892 he returned to Melbourne where he chiefly painted portraits and landscapes. He was a member of the Victorian Artists' Society, exhibiting with them between 1892 and 1900. In 1893 he established the lively

Melbourne Art School with Tudor St George Tucker (1862–1906). There an academic training coupled with a modified Impressionist technique was taught, as can be seen in Fox's painting the *Art Students* (1895; Sydney, A.G. NSW). In 1901 he left for London, having been commissioned by the Trustees of the National Gallery of Victoria to paint the *Landing of Captain Cook at Botany Bay* (Melbourne, N.G. Victoria). After his marriage in 1905 to the artist Ethel Carrick, he and his wife settled in Paris and remained there until 1913. His harmonious works celebrate the graceful languor of the Edwardian era, as in *Al fresco* (*c.* 1905; Adelaide, A.G. S. Australia). Although interested in depicting the effects of flickering sunlight on solid objects, he maintained an academic approach. He exhibited at the Société Nationale des Beaux-Arts, Paris, and at the Royal Academy, London.

BIBLIOGRAPHY

L. P. Fox: *E. Phillips Fox: Notes and Recollections* (Sydney, 1969)

B. R. Zubans: *Emanuel Phillips Fox: The Development of his Art, 1884–1913* (diss., U. Melbourne, 1979)

R. Zubans: 'Emanuel Phillips Fox: St Ives and the Impact of British Art, 1890–1892', *Australian Art and Architecture*, ed. A. Bradley and T. Smith (Melbourne, 1980), pp. 134–49

——: *E. Phillips Fox: His Life and Art* (Melbourne, 1995)

BARBARA B. KANE

Fox [née Carrick], **Ethel Carrick** (*b* Uxbridge, nr London, 7 Feb 1872; *d* Melbourne, 17 June 1952). Australian painter of English birth. She trained under the English painter Francis Bate (1858–1950) and from 1898 to 1902 she studied at the Slade School of Fine Art in London under Henry Tonks and Frederick Brown. She then went to the artists' colony in St Ives in Cornwall where she met Emanuel Phillips Fox, whom she married in 1905. The two painters then travelled around France, North Africa and Spain, visiting Australia in 1908 and 1913. In 1915 her husband died and she then travelled between Australia and Europe, running an art school for American and Australian students in Paris. She exhibited in Paris at the Salon d'Automne from 1904 to 1930 and at the Salon de la Société Nationale des Beaux-Arts from 1906 to 1937, and she was also a regular exhibitor in London. During the two World Wars she organized art unions for the relief of artists. In the 1930s she campaigned to persuade the Australian national art collections to buy works from modern French artists, such as Degas, Renoir and Toulouse-Lautrec. Her paintings were influenced by Post-Impressionism and were of genre, flower and landscape subjects, as in the *Quay at Dinard* (1942; Melbourne, N.G. Victoria).

BIBLIOGRAPHY

Catalogue of the National Gallery of Victoria (Melbourne, 1943), p. 61

A. McCulloch: *Encyclopedia of Australian Art*, i (Hawthorn, 1984), pp. 376–7

Fox, Revel (Albert Ellis) (*b* Durban, 20 Sept 1924). South African architect and urban planner. He studied architecture (1942–8) at the University of Cape Town, then worked (1951–2) for Ivar Tengbom in Stockholm. Fox returned to South Africa in 1952 and set up a variety of partnerships first in Worcester and later Cape Town. He first concentrated on domestic buildings that express a clear personal aesthetic, with their attention to detailing

and adaptation to the environment. The Wilson house (1954), Worcester, and La Cock house (1961), Cape Town, among others, are functional in nature but with visual references to the traditional domestic architecture of South Africa. His interest in housing traditions became the basis of his involvement in the restoration of Cape Dutch homes, for example Rust en Vreugd, Cape Town (1961). He also worked on housing projects, for example Montebello Apartments (1968), Newlands, and contributed to low-income, as well as emergency, shelter and core housing, for example Expandable Starter Units (1978), Valhalla Park, Cape Province. His larger public buildings, such as the BP Centre (1973), Cape Town, and Bank City (1994), Johannesburg, are notable for the same attention to detail as his domestic work, particularly with respect to function and environmental context. As an urban planner, Fox worked on a number of major projects, including the Durban Beach and City Redevelopment (1988), and as a consultant on urban and rural projects throughout Southern Africa. He received a number of architectural awards, including the Gold Medal of the South African Institute of Architects (1977), and he played an important role as a teacher and lecturer at universities in South Africa and abroad.

BIBLIOGRAPHY

CA

'Revel Fox: A Profile of the Architect and a Review of his Work', *Archit. SA*, 7 (1979), pp. 18–31

S. Trombley: 'Two Architects', *RIBA J.*, xci (1984), pp. 51–4

SUSAN DE VILLIERS

Fox, Sheldon. *See under* KOHN PEDERSON FOX.

Fox, Vincent. *See* VOLPE, VINCENT.

Foxing. Term for brown or yellow stains that appear on old paper in a scattered pattern of spots and blotches. It is caused by a type of mould and can be distinguished from iron or other brown stains by its continuous development in suitable conditions (*see* PAPER, §VI, 1). Foxing can be removed by using dilute bleach solutions.

RUPERT FEATHERSTONE

Fox-Strangways, W(illiam) T(homas) H(orner), 4th Earl of Ilchester (*b* 7 May 1795; *d* Melbury House, nr Dorchester, Dorset, 10 Jan 1865). English collector. He was educated at Westminster School, London, and at Christ Church, Oxford, before becoming a diplomat. He was posted to Italy several times, where he served as Secretary of Legation in Florence (1825–8) and then Naples (1828–32). He subsequently became Under-Secretary of State for Foreign Affairs (1835–40) and accepted further political appointments before retiring in 1866. He succeeded his half-brother as 4th Earl of Ilchester in 1858. He was fascinated by the architecture and literature of the Middle Ages and nurtured his interest in painting in Italy where, between *c.* 1827 and 1832, he assembled a pioneering collection of early Italian pictures. His whole collection numbered about 100 pictures and was particularly strong in Tuscan 'primitives', his most significant acquisition being Uccello's *Hunt in the Forest* (*see* UCCELLO, fig. 4). Surviving correspondence between the collector and his nephew, the photographer William Henry Fox Talbot, reveals that Fox-Strangways set out to form a collection that would illustrate the historical evolution of early Italian painting, and he bought from Italian collections that had been assembled on similar lines. His letters also provide a vivid insight into the Italian art market and the unparalleled opportunities then available to the British collector. In 1828 and 1834 he donated a total of 36 or 37 pictures to Christ Church and 41 pictures to Oxford University (Ashmolean Museum) in 1850. He retained the residue at Abbotsbury, Dorset (destr. 1913), although the bulk of the family collection was kept at Melbury House.

BIBLIOGRAPHY

Catalogue of Pictures Belonging to the Earl of Ilchester (privately printed, 1883)

F. Boase: *Modern English Biography*, ii (London, 1897/ *R* 1965)

J. Byam Shaw: *Paintings by Old Masters at Christ Church, Oxford* (London, 1967), pp. 9–10

C. Lloyd: 'Picture Hunting in Italy: Some Unpublished Letters, 1824–1829', *It. Stud.*, xxx (1975), pp. 42–68

——: *A Catalogue of the Earlier Italian Paintings in the Ashmolean Museum* (Oxford, 1977), pp. xv–xxv

G. S. Weinberg, '"First of All First Beginnings": Ruskin's Sketches of Early Italian Paintings at Christ Church', *Burl. Mag.*, cxxxiv, pp. 111–20

CHRISTOPHER LLOYD

Fox Talbot, William Henry. *See* TALBOT, WILLIAM HENRY FOX.

Foyatier, Denys (*b* Bussières, nr Lyon, 22 Sept 1793; *d* Paris, 19 Nov 1863). French sculptor. He began his career as a self-taught wood-carver, going on in 1813 to study sculpture in Lyon with Joseph Chinard and then with Joseph-Charles Marin. In 1817 he entered the Ecole des Beaux-Arts in Paris as a pupil of François-Frédéric Lemot. He first exhibited at the Salon in 1819 and from 1823 was in Rome for three years, his study of antique sculpture there confirming the stylistic predisposition of his Neo-classical training. In Rome he produced the model for his statue of *Spartacus* (marble; Paris, Louvre), which, when exhibited at the Paris Salon of 1830, aroused the enthusiasm of critics as well as of the public: the gladiator breaking his chains became the symbol of the revolution of that year. This success gained him many commissions for monumental sculpture, including marble statues of *Faith* (1830; Paris, Notre-Dame-de-Lorette), *Prudence* (1834; Paris, Pal.-Bourbon), *Cincinnatus* (1834; Paris, Jard. Tuileries) and *St Matthew* (1845; Paris, St Vincent-de-Paul). None of these figures has the epic spirit that animates *Spartacus*, and it was in small-scale works of more intimate character, such as the marble group *Young Girl Playing with a Kid* (1831; Lyon, Mus. B.-A.) and *Siesta* (marble, 1848; Paris, Louvre), and in his portrait busts that his talent was most apparent. The great work of the last years of his life is the monumental bronze equestrian statue of *Joan of Arc* in the Place du Martroi, Orléans (1855).

BIBLIOGRAPHY

Lami

Y. de La Genardière: *Denys Foyatier: Artiste statuaire, 1793–1863* (diss., Paris, Ecole Louvre, 1973)

Y. DE LA GENARDIÈRE

Foy Suzor-Coté, Marc-Aurèle de. *See* SUZOR-COTÉ, MARC-AURÈLE DE FOY.

Fra [Frate; It.: 'Brother']. For Italian names with this religious title, *see under* the surname where known or under the given name that follows the title.

□

Fracanzano. Italian family of painters. Alessandro Fracanzano (*b* Verona, 1567) was a late Mannerist painter who worked in Apulia in the early 17th century; his works include the *Assumption of the Virgin* (1607; Monopoli Cathedral) and the *SS Vitus, Modestus and Crescentia* (1621; Ruvo di Puglia, S Vito). His old-fashioned style was of little importance to his sons, (1) Cesare Fracanzano and (2) Francesco Fracanzano. Francesco, a more powerful artist than the more academic Cesare, made a major contribution to Neapolitan naturalism in the 1630s. Michelangelo Fracanzano (dates unknown), the son of Francesco, was also a painter, but no examples of his work have been identified.

(1) Cesare Fracanzano (*b* Bisceglie, *c.* 1605; *d* Barletta, 1651). His style was formed in Apulia, and his earliest works, such as the *Holy Family* and the *Education of the Virgin* (Barletta, S Gaetano), were influenced by the Mannerist painters Gerolamo Imparato, Ippolito Borghese (*d* 1627) and Fabrizio Santafede. In 1622 he went to Naples, and *c.* 1630 he and his brother worked in the studio of Ribera. Such works as the *St John the Baptist* (early 1630s; Naples, Capodimonte) were influenced by the master's use of colour, though not by his harsh realism. Between 1633 and 1635 Cesare worked in Barletta. He was interested in light and colour, and the graceful, Mannerist figures of the *Christ at the Column Comforted by Angels* (*c.* 1629–31; Naples, Pin. Girolamini) and the *St Michael* (*c.* 1635; Naples, Mus. N. S Martino) are painted in brilliant reds and ochres inspired by the glowing colours of van Dyck, whose influence was important in Neapolitan art in this period. After 1640 Cesare's art became more disciplined and academic, revealing the impact of Massimo Stanzione, as in the *Magdalene* (Andria, Palazzo Vescovile), and of Guido Reni, as in the *Crucifixion* (Bari, S Ferdinando). In 1640 he frescoed the vault of the nuns' choir in S Maria della Sapienza, Naples, with an *Assumption of the Virgin*, which suggests a response to Giovanni Lanfranco. This is close in style to the fresco cycle (*c.* 1650) of scenes from the lives and martyrdoms of SS Cosma and Damiano in the church at Conversano in Apulia, probably his last work. Carlo Rosa, Francesco Antonio Altobello and Nicola Glizi (*fl* 1658–80) were followers of Cesare.

(2) Francesco Fracanzano (*b* Monopoli, 1612; *d* Naples, ?1656). Brother of (1) Cesare Francanzano. He moved to Naples in 1622 with Cesare and like him entered Ribera's workshop. In 1632 he married Salvator Rosa's sister Giovanna. His early style remains obscure. Bologna (1958) attributed a group of paintings to him that show half-length figures against a predominantly dark background, painted in deep colours with loaded brushstrokes. These pictures, among them two versions of the *Prodigal Son* (Bari, Pin. Prov.; Naples, Capodimonte), are close to the style of Ribera and to that of the MASTER OF THE ANNUNCIATION TO THE SHEPHERDS (*see* MASTERS, ANONYMOUS, AND MONOGRAMMISTS, §I). Causa (1972) does not accept Bologna's conclusions and attributes most of these works to the latter artist. D'Elia's (1971) attribution to him of a series of works in Apulia has remained controversial.

The influence of Ribera dominates the two scenes from the life of St Gregory that Francesco painted in 1635: *St Gregory of Armenia Thrown into the Well* and a *Miracle of St Gregory of Armenia* (both Naples, S Gregorio Armeno). These pictures, with powerful, dramatic figures set against stormy skies, broadly handled with rich impasto, are key works in the development of Neapolitan painting in the 1630s. In the late 1630s there followed a group of paintings, among them the *St Catherine of Alexandria* (Rome, Ist. Previdenza Soc., see 1982 exh. cat., p. 84) and two versions of the *Triumph of Bacchus* (Naples, Capodimonte; Cambridge, MA, Fogg), that were more polished and refined in colour and texture, with slightly larger than life-size monumental figures. These works contain strong echoes of the art of Simon Vouet, Artemesia Gentileschi and Francesco Guarino.

After 1640 Francesco's art occasionally suggests a return to the style of Ribera and at other times displays a more classical manner. The *Ecce homo* (1647; New York, Morton B. Harris priv. col., see Spinosa, 1984, fig. 390) is close to Ribera in the broad brushstrokes and the harsh realism of the figures; the *Calling of St Matthew* (Rome, priv. col., see 1984 exh. cat., p. 288) is in a similar style and also suggests an awareness of French and Flemish Caravaggisti working in Rome. By contrast, the *Death of St Joseph* (1652; Naples, Santa Trinità dei Pellegrini) is a restrained and classical work.

BIBLIOGRAPHY

B. de Dominici: *Vite* (1742–5), p. 83
F. Bologna: *Francesco Solimena* (Naples, 1958), pp. 17, 19, 28 [Francesco]
R. Longhi: 'G. B. Spinelli ed i naturalisti napoletani del seicento', *Paragone*, xx/227 (1969), pp. 42–52 [Francesco]
M. D'Elia: 'Sulle orme dei Fracanzani in Puglia', *Studi di storia pugliese in onore di Nicola Vacca* (Galatina, 1971), pp. 117–30
A. Gamborta: 'La tela di San Vito di Alessandro Francanzano veronese', *Il rubastino*, 5 (1971)
R. Causa: 'La pittura del seicento a Napoli dal naturalismo al barocco' (1972), v of *Storia di Napoli* (Cava dei Tirreni, 1967–78), p. 933 [Francesco]
Painting in Naples from Caravaggio to Giordano (exh. cat., ed. E. Schleier; London, RA, 1982), pp. 162–3 [Francesco]; 272–3 [Cesare]
Restauri in Puglia, 1971–81 (exh. cat., ed. V. Pugliese; Bari, Pin. Prov., 1983), pp. 22–3 [Cesare]
N. Spinosa: *La pittura napoletana del '600* (Milan, 1984)
G. De Vito: 'Ritrovamenti e precisazioni a seguito della prima edizione della mostra del '600 napoletano', *Seicento napoletano* (Milan, 1984), p. 14 [Francesco]
Civiltà del seicento a Napoli (exh. cat., ed. S. Cassani; Naples, Capodimonte, 1984), pp. 143–6, 285–9 [Francesco]; 283–4 [Cesare]

ANNACHIARA ALABISO

Fragelli, Marcelo (Aciolly) (*b* Rio de Janeiro, 6 Oct 1928). Brazilian architect. He graduated in architecture from the Federal University of Rio de Janeiro in 1952 and went to work for M. M. M. Roberto, one of the early Modernist practices. Roberto was then attempting to develop structures that transcended the static forms of early functionalism but in a different direction from the sculptural forms of Oscar Niemeyer's experiments in Pampulha (1942–4). Fragelli assimilated these ideas but, when he formed his own practice in São Paulo (1961), he retained an individual approach to design; he also remained apart from the Brutalist style of João B. Vilanova Artigas that dominated São Paulo at that time. Fragelli's work was characterized by his skilful use of such materials as reinforced concrete, brick, timber and glass both in their natural state and in combination with each other, and by the delicate detail of his finishes; his buildings include houses for Tasso Fragoso Pires (1959), Rio de Janeiro, and Ernesto d'Orsi (1972), São Paulo. His best-known works include several stations on the northern section of the São Paulo Metro, especially those that are elevated and integrated with the structures of the supporting bridges, for example the Ponte Pequeña Metro Station (1973) where he also used cantilevered staircases. He also designed many residential, office and industrial buildings, including Edifício Converbrás (1980), Rio de Janeiro, and he received several awards including two honourable mentions in the 8th São Paulo Biennale (1963).

BIBLIOGRAPHY

'Modern Brazilian Architecture', *Process: Archit.*, 17 (1980), pp. 64–70 [special issue]
A. Xavier, C. Lemos and E. Corona: *Arquitetura moderna paulistana* (São Paulo, 1983)
A. Xavier, A. Britto and A. L. Nobre: *Arquitetura moderna no Rio de Janeiro* (São Paulo, 1991)

CARLOS A. C. LEMOS

Fragner, Jaroslav (*b* Prague, 25 Dec 1898; *d* Prague, 3 Jan 1967). Czech architect and teacher. He graduated in architecture (1922) from the Technical University, Prague. With his fellow students Vít Obrtel (1901–88), Evžen Linhart and Karel Honzík he formed the Four Purists, who sought to simplify architectural form as much as possible to geometric volumes. In 1923 he became a member of Devětsil, the avant-garde group centred on the figure of Karel Teige; he also joined the Architects' Club. Fragner's first independent work was the post-natal unit (1923–8) at Mukačevo, Ukraine, one of the first buildings in which Functionalist principles were applied. In 1927 he designed a garden city housing scheme (unexecuted) for Barrandov, Prague, with several types of suburban houses, based on the optimization of local features. These ideas were reflected in a number of other houses, for example in Kostelec nad Černými Lesy (1931–2) and Nespeky (1932–3), which also used various materials such as bare brickwork and natural stone to achieve harmony with the site. Between 1930 and 1941 Fragner worked on the vast industrial site of the ESSO power station at Kolín, where the main building in particular is a prime example of Functionalist architecture in its planning, geometric volumes and relationship with the environment. Another striking work is the Auto-Tatra showrooms (1932), Kolín, a two-storey building with an open display area with galleries on the ground floor and a separate flat above; the composition of large, uninterrupted glazed surfaces, complemented by an exterior staircase and terrace, has a polished appearance. In 1931 Fragner joined the Mánes Union of Artists, of which he was Chairman from 1940 to 1966. He was also a founder-member of the Union of Socialist Architects (1933). In 1949 he began to work at Stavoprojekt, the socialist design organization, and he produced a few works in the spirit of Socialist Realism. He became a professor at the Academy of Fine Arts, Prague (1949), and from the 1950s he worked mainly on the restoration of historic buildings, for example the reconstruction (1954–69) of the Karolinum in Prague.

BIBLIOGRAPHY

Jaroslav Fragner, 1898–1967 (exh. cat. by O. Nový, V. Růžička and E. Růžičková, Prague, Mánes Exh. Hall, 1969)

'Jaroslav Fragner', *Tschechische Kunst der 20er und 30er Jahre: Avantgarde und Tradition* (exh. cat. by R. Sedláková, Darmstadt, Ausstellhallen Mathildenhöhe, 1988–89), pp. 78–80

O. Nový and Z. Lukeš: 'Jaroslav Fragner', *Czech Architecture, 1988–89* (Prague, 1989), pp. 81–6

Devětsil: Czech Avant-garde Art, Architecture and Design of the 1920s and 1930s (exh. cat., ed. R. Švácha; Oxford, MOMA; London, Des. Mus.; 1990)

The Art of the Avant-garde in Czechoslovakia, 1918–1938 (exh. cat., ed. J. Anděl; Valencia-Ivan, 1993)

Prague 1891–1941 Architecture and Design (exh. cat., Edinburgh, City A. Cent., 1994)

Sorela-Česká architektura padesàtých let (exh. cat., ed. R. Sedláková; Prague, N.G., 1994)

RADOMÍRA SEDLÁKOVÁ

Fragonard. French family of artists. (1) Jean-Honoré Fragonard developed, from his beginnings as a pupil and follower of François Boucher, into the most brilliant and versatile artist in 18th-century France. He wielded brush, chalk and etcher's needle with extraordinary virtuosity, effortlessly varying his touch as he produced a succession of consummate masterpieces on themes from religion, mythology, genre and landscape. Uniquely, after promising beginnings as a history painter, he turned away from the Académie Royale and 'high art' and concentrated on lesser genres, more sympathetic to his spontaneous temperament. His independence of official circles led to a lack of securely datable projects, and much of his output can be dated, or even attributed, only tentatively. He had little direct influence on French painting, but his oeuvre shows many of the preoccupations of later artists with problems of style, subject-matter and conception. His only pupils of note were his sister-in-law Marguerite Gérard and his son (2) Alexandre Evariste Fragonard, who from an early age was noted as a draughtsman; during the Empire he began to work as a decorative painter and sculptor and also provided designs for the Sèvres porcelain factory. Subsequently he took up history painting, concentrating on Troubadour subjects. His son Théophile Fragonard (1806–76) also worked as a painter for Sèvres.

(1) Jean-Honoré Fragonard (*b* Grasse, 4 April 1732; *d* Paris, 22 Aug 1806). Painter, draughtsman, printmaker and museum official.

1. Life and work. 2. Posthumous reputation.

1. LIFE AND WORK.

(i) Early work and years in Italy, to 1761. (ii) Paris and official success, 1761–5. (iii) Work for collectors and decorative painting, 1766–72. (iv) Further travels and late works, 1773–88. (v) Final years, 1789–1806.

(i) Early work and years in Italy, to 1761. He was the only child of François Fragonard (1699–1781) and Françoise Petit, who both came from families of shopkeepers and glove-makers in Grasse. In 1738 the family moved to Paris, where, on the advice of François Boucher, Fragonard spent some time as a pupil of Jean-Siméon Chardin. He entered Boucher's own studio *c.* 1749 and probably remained there for about a year. Boucher was then at the height of his fame, and Fragonard doubtless assisted the overworked master on important commissions, such as large tapestry designs. He also made numerous copies after paintings by Boucher, such as *Hercules and Omphale* (untraced; C L62), and by Rembrandt, such as *Girl with Broom* (untraced; C L19). In 1752 Fragonard entered the competition for the Prix de Rome, relying on Boucher's influence to overcome the stipulation that all candidates had to be pupils at the Académie Royale. His winning entry, *Jeroboam Sacrificing to the Idols* (Paris, Ecole N. Sup. B.-A.), in fact shows little of Boucher's teaching but is rather painted in the grand manner of Carle Vanloo, whose influence can be seen in the colouring, the geometrical composition and the concern for expressive detail at this moment of high drama.

On 20 May 1753 Fragonard entered the Ecole Royale des Elèves Protégés, of which van Loo was Director. He remained there until 1756, and from this period two important paintings survive. The first, *Psyche Showing her Sisters Cupid's Presents* (1754; London, N.G.), has clear echoes of the prize painting but is more light-hearted, with great delight taken in the accessories, shimmering plate and jewels and billowing draperies of pink, white and gold. The second, *Christ Washing the Disciples' Feet*, was commissioned on 17 May 1754 by the Confrérie du Saint-Sacrement for their chapel in Grasse Cathedral (1755; *in situ*). It is austere in its setting and simple composition and reminiscent of van Loo's picture of the same subject (1742; Le Mans, Mus. Tessé).

In addition to these important history paintings, the years 1754–5 marked the beginning of Fragonard's career as a decorative painter. For an unknown patron, he executed four scenes from country life, on subjects painted many times by Boucher: *Harvester*, *Woman Gathering Grapes*, *Gardener* and *Shepherdess* (all Detroit, MI, Inst. A.). Boucher's influence is even more apparent in the mythological paintings from this period, such as the pendants *Jupiter and Callisto* and *Cephalus and Procris* (*c.* 1755; Angers, Mus. B.-A.).

In December 1756 Fragonard arrived in Rome. He remained there for five years, but little is known of his activities. He must have made a large number of copies; one of the few securely documented is *St Paul Regaining his Sight* (untraced), after Pietro da Cortona's painting in the church of the Cappuccini, Rome. He also made several large and sober red-chalk drawings of draped figures (e.g. the group in Montpellier, Mus. Atger) and painted his first amorous subject, the *Kiss Won* (*c.* 1759–60; New York, Met.), commissioned by the Bailli de Breteuil. Towards the end of 1758 he met Hubert Robert, who introduced him to new subjects and techniques: no doubt encouraged by Charles-Joseph Natoire, the two artists sketched constantly in the open air, and so similar in style are their many red-chalk drawings that their authors have often been confused. Fragonard spent the summer of 1760 at the Villa d'Este, as the guest of Robert's patron, the Abbé de Saint-Non, and he made a number of marvellously evocative red-chalk drawings of the park and gardens (e.g. ten sheets, Besançon, Bib. Mun.). In 1761 Fragonard accompanied Saint-Non and Robert on their tour of Italy, when they visited Naples and the north. Saint-Non described the journey in a diary (see Rosenberg and Brejon de Lavergnée), while Fragonard recorded the itinerary in

1. Jean-Honoré Fragonard: *Coresus and Callirhoë*, oil on canvas, 3.11×4.00 m, 1765 (Paris, Musée du Louvre)

copies of paintings and monuments in black or red chalk (71 of these drawings are in London, BM).

(ii) Paris and official success, 1761–5. After his return to Paris in 1761, Fragonard worked principally for collectors until he presented his *morceau d'agrément* to the Académie. Cuzin (1987) has suggested that he worked up a number of sketches made in Italy into oil paintings, a typical example being the *Gardens of the Villa d'Este* (*c.* 1762–3; London, Wallace), for which he made a preparatory drawing on the spot and an etching (see 1987–8 exh. cat., no. 66). Works of this period also show other Italian influences, notably that of Boucher's idol Giovanni Benedetto Castiglione, whose drawings Fragonard would have seen in Consul Smith's collection in Venice. He found a parallel source of inspiration in works by northern European artists, notably Jacob van Ruisdael, which resulted in a series of landscapes, among them the *Watering Place* (priv. col., C 110). During this period, perhaps *c.* 1763–4, he made two masterpieces: *Rinaldo in the Gardens of Armida* and *Rinaldo in the Enchanted Forest* (both priv. col., C 95–6). While ostensibly derived from Tasso's *Gerusalemme liberata*, these intensely operatic canvases were probably inspired by performances of Jean-Baptiste Lully's *Armide* in 1761 or 1764.

On 30 March 1765 Fragonard was approved (*agréé*) by the Académie Royale, on the strength of his painting *Coresus and Callirhoë* (Paris, Louvre; see fig. 1). The unusual subject, from Pausanias' *Description of Greece*, tells how the poet Coresus calls upon Bacchus to avenge his unrequited love for Callirhoë: the god spreads universal madness and as the price of calming the frenzy, demands Callirhoë's life. At the last moment, Coresus kills himself instead. Fragonard's mastery of composition, the expression of individual participants and the richness of colouring were all commended when the picture was exhibited at the Salon of 1765: Denis Diderot was ecstatic. It was bought by the Marquis de Marigny for the Crown, which also commissioned a pendant (never executed). Almost overnight, Fragonard came to embody the hopes of the French school and seemed to be about to restore the fortunes of history painting: Marigny announced to Natoire that 'on espère qu'il contribuera beaucoup à nous consoler de la perte de M. Deshays' (see 1987–8 exh. cat., p. 152).

(iii) Work for collectors and decorative painting, 1766–72. Fragonard was by now celebrated and, had he followed the traditional path of the history painter, might have become Premier Peintre du Roi and Director of the

Académie. Instead, he never sought to be received (*reçu*) at the Académie and seldom exhibited at the Salon, preferring the unofficial forum of the Salon de la Correspondance (1778–9, 1781–3, 1785–6). His contemporaries accused him of compromising his artistic integrity by pandering to the frivolous tastes of collectors. Certainly, he supplied an eager market with rapidly brushed paintings on a variety of themes. Even the few works he did show at the Salon of 1767, such as the *Swarm of Putti* (Paris, Louvre), probably intended as a ceiling decoration, and the *Head of an Old Man in Profile* (Muncie, IN, Ball State U., A.G.), were far from being *grandes machines*, as such critics as Diderot were quick to lament. The change in direction is symbolized in *The Swing* (1767; London, Wallace; see fig. 2), known from Nicolas de Launay's engraving as *Les hazards heureux de l'escarpolette*. It is a small painting, commissioned by the Baron de Saint-Julien to show his mistress being pushed in a swing by a bishop, while he himself looks on.

The *Head of an Old Man in Profile* heralded a completely new genre, the *figure de fantaisie*, of which some 15 by Fragonard survive, all dating from *c.* 1768–72. Although many of the sitters are identifiable, they are usually dressed in vaguely Spanish costume and are painted with such virtuosity that they are more fantasy than portrait. That of the *Abbé Richard de Saint-Non* (1769; Paris, Louvre; for illustration *see* SAINT-NON) was apparently painted from life, in only an hour, in long, fluent strokes of extraordinary boldness. Despite their technical brilliance, these pictures convey a wide variety of moods, from the studious concentration of the philosopher *Denis Diderot* (*c.* 1769;

Paris, Louvre) to the haughty flamboyance of the *grands seigneurs François-Henri, Duc d'Harcourt* (*c.* 1770; priv. col., C 176) and his brother *Anne-François d'Harcourt, Duc de Beuvron* (*c.* 1770; Paris, Louvre).

In addition to these easel paintings, Fragonard executed a number of decorative commissions for important patrons. The first of these (?1769–70; Paris, Carnavalet) was made in collaboration with Boucher and Jean-Baptiste Le Prince for a room in the hôtel particulier of the engraver Gilles Demarteau in Paris; another (1773–5; destr.) was for the dancer Marie-Madeleine Guimard (1743–1816). However, in scale and quality, the most important of these projects and the crowning achievement of Fragonard's career, indeed the greatest decorative ensemble produced in 18th-century France, was the *Progress of Love* (1771–2; New York, Frick). This series was commissioned by Mme du Barry for the salon en cul-de-four of her new pavilion at Louveciennes. Although described in 1772 as an 'hommage à l'amour', the precise sequence of the panels has never been satisfactorily explained: the principal scenes show *The Meeting*, *The Pursuit*, the *Lover Crowned* and *Love Letters*. The decorative scheme was completed by a ceiling panel simulating a cloudy sky by Jean-Bernard Restout and by four circular overdoors (untraced) by François-Hubert Drouais. Mme du Barry quickly rejected Fragonard's paintings: they may have referred too overtly to her amorous adventures; or their luxurious opulence of colour may have clashed with the elegant severity of Claude-Nicolas Ledoux's architecture. Certainly, by 1774 they had been replaced by ostensibly Neo-classical designs (two in Paris, Louvre and two in Chambéry, Préfecture) by Joseph-Marie Vien.

(iv) Further travels and late works, 1773–88. On 5 October 1773 Fragonard set off on his second journey to Italy, as artist-companion to the financier Jacques-Onésyme Bergeret de Grancourt, Saint-Non's brother-in-law. Fragonard drew constantly as the party travelled south through France and Italy, arriving in Rome two months later; he soon rediscovered his old haunts. He made landscapes, some in red chalk, but increasingly in brown wash, for example the *Umbrella Pines at the Villa Pamphili* (Amsterdam, Rijksmus.); and genre scenes and portraits, such as the *Woman of Santa Lucia* (New York, Mr & Mrs Eugene Victor Thaw priv. col., see 1987–8 exh. cat., no. 192). Fragonard also met the young François-André Vincent, whose work of this period resembles his own. Bergeret's caravan travelled to Naples in spring 1774 and continued to Vienna, Prague and the southern German states, arriving in Paris in September 1774. Unfortunately, the return was marred by a dispute with Bergeret over the ownership of Fragonard's drawings, which apparently led to an acrimonious court case.

In Paris, Fragonard continued to produce paintings and drawings of modest size for collectors, among them *figures de fantaisie*, genre and religious subjects and anecdotal scenes. He embarked on his religious paintings with as little seriousness as Boucher; and, apart from the early altarpiece at Grasse, none was commissioned by the Church or a religious foundation. Indeed, the most notable, the *Adoration of the Shepherds*, was hung as a pendant to the erotic subject *The Bolt* (both *c.* 1776; Paris, Louvre)

2. Jean-Honoré Fragonard: *The Swing*, oil on canvas, 830×650 mm, 1767 (London, Wallace Collection)

by the Marquis Louis-Gabriel de Véri. The only new departure in subject-matter was a series of decorative landscapes, the largest and most impressive of which is the so-called *Fête at Saint-Cloud* (*c.* 1775–80; Paris, Banque de France). These continued the tradition of Antoine Watteau's *fêtes champêtres* and stylistically mark a development of the leafy airiness of *The Swing* and the Louveciennes panels.

During the 1780s Fragonard became increasingly interested in mythological subjects, no longer painted in the manner of Boucher but in a smooth chiaroscuro, also favoured by Jean-Baptiste Greuze at this period. The heightened eroticism of such works as the *Fountain of Love* (*c.* 1785; London, Wallace) indicates that Fragonard was sensitive to the new mood of sentimental Neo-classicism that was becoming popular among Parisian collectors. Another theme that appeared with increasing frequency during these years was scenes of family life, perhaps reflecting his own domestic happiness, and portraits of his wife and children, in particular the enchanting and gently humorous *Alexandre-Evariste Fragonard Dressed as Pierrot* (*c.* 1785–8; London, Wallace). He had married Marie-Anne Gérard in 1769, and her sister Marguerite Gérard was his pupil and collaborated with him on a number of paintings, the identity of which is still debated. Fragonard's final notable activity of this decade was a series of book illustrations that are unique in the history of French art in being impossible to engrave satisfactorily. For whereas the final series of illustrations for La Fontaine's *Contes* (Paris, Petit Pal.) was commissioned by the publisher Pierre Didot, those for Ariosto's *Orlando furioso* (dispersed; see Mongan, Hofer and Seznec) and Cervantes's *Don Quixote* (dispersed; see 1987–8 exh. cat., pp. 508–9) are so rapidly drawn in black chalk, with brown wash so freely applied, that they were probably made for the artist's own pleasure.

(v) Final years, 1789–1806. For unknown reasons the Fragonard family left Paris at the end of 1789 and returned to Grasse, taking with them the *Progress of Love*, which was installed in the house of their cousin Alexandre Maubert. In 1790, in order to make the decoration fit into its new home, Fragonard added one large panel, the *Reverie*, five of cupids in various activities (e.g. *Love Pursuing a Dove*) and four of *Hollyhocks* (all New York, Frick). These were probably the last pictures he painted: after his final move to Paris in 1792, he seems to have confined himself to administrative tasks at the Palais du Louvre. During the French Revolution he successfully avoided both emigration and imprisonment and was appointed to various bodies formed to oversee the creation of a national museum in the Louvre. On the recommendation of Jacques-Louis David, he was appointed a member of the Conservatoire des Arts on 16 January 1794, becoming its president a year later. He was thus in charge of the new museum, which was rapidly expanding with paintings stolen from churches and private collections both in France and abroad. During the summer of 1797 Fragonard was given the title Inspector of the Transportation of Works of Art and oversaw the establishment of a new museum of the French school at Versailles. He continued in this post until 1800, and ended his life in relative obscurity.

2. POSTHUMOUS REPUTATION. Apart from Marguerite Gérard and his son, Alexandre-Evariste, Fragonard had no pupils of note. However, as the 19th century progressed, his preoccupations became the concerns of all intelligent artists: particularly the role of history painting, indeed the very notion of subject-matter, which came to take second place to considerations of conception and style. On his death, which was not widely reported, it was principally Fragonard's Neo-classical works that were most admired. However, during the 1840s, the stylistic freedom and imaginative supremacy of the Rococo were championed by left-wing critics and writers, such as Théophile Thoré. Fragonard's paintings and drawings were bought by young intellectuals for small sums: Hippolyte Walferdin, for example, formed a great collection of Fragonard paintings and drawings and in 1849 gave the *Music Lesson* (*c.* 1755; Paris, Louvre) to the Musée du Louvre, to stay there only as long as France remained a republic. However, the undemanding subject-matter and obviously attractive colours of the paintings soon brought them to the attention of the middle classes, especially bankers and financiers such as the Rothschilds, and they soon became the province of the rich. The taste for Fragonard followed closely that for Boucher and Watteau, and crossed the Atlantic, so that the *Progress of Love* now decorates a room in the Frick Collection in New York. Following the Goncourt brothers, scholarly interest in Fragonard has attempted to establish a chronology for his oeuvre, and, more recently, to distinguish his work from that of close associates and imitators.

BIBLIOGRAPHY

E. de Goncourt and J. de Goncourt: 'Fragonard', *Gaz. B.-A.*, xviii (1865), pp. 32–41, 132–62; also in *L'Art du dix-huitième siècle* (Paris, 1873, rev. 3/1882), pp. 241–342

R. Portalis: *Honoré Fragonard: Sa vie, son oeuvre* (Paris, 1889)

A. Tornézy: 'Bergeret et Fragonard: Journal inédit d'un voyage en Italie', *Bull. Soc. Antiqua. Ouest*, xvii (1894), pp. 1–431; as booklet (Paris, 1895)

P. de Nolhac: *J.-H. Fragonard, 1732–1806* (Paris, 1906) [includes cat. of paintings sold at auction between 1770 and 1805]

E. Mongan, P. Hofer and J. Seznec: *Fragonard Drawings for Ariosto* (London, 1945)

C. Valogne: '*Fragonard, mon grand-père*, par Théophile Fragonard', *Lett. Fr.* (17 Feb 1955), pp. 1, 9

G. Wildenstein: *Fragonard aquafortiste* (Paris, 1956) [complete illus. cat. of etchings]

F.-M. Biebel: 'Fragonard et Mme du Barry', *Gaz. B.-A.*, lvi (1960), pp. 207–26

G. Wildenstein: *The Paintings of Fragonard: Complete Edition* ([London, 1960])

A. Ananoff: *L'Oeuvre dessiné de Jean-Honoré Fragonard (1732–1806)*, 4 vols (Paris, 1961–70)

W. Sauerländer: 'Über die ursprüngliche Reihenfolge von Fragonards *Amours des bergers*', *Münchn. Jb. Bild. Kst*, n. s. 2, xix (1968), pp. 127–56

D. Wildenstein and G. Mandel: *L'opera completa di Fragonard* (Milan, 1972)

Drawings by Fragonard in North American Collections (exh. cat. by E. Williams, Washington, DC, N.G.A.; Cambridge, MA, Fogg; New York, Frick; 1978–9) [indispensable discussion of technique of drgs]

Fragonard (exh. cat. by D. Sutton, Tokyo, N. Mus. W.A.; Kyoto, Mun. Mus. A.; 1980)

Y. Cantarel-Besson: *La Naissance du Musée du Louvre*, 2 vols (Paris, 1981)

J.-P. Cuzin: 'De Fragonard à Vincent', *Bull. Soc. Hist. A. Fr.* (1981), pp. 103–24

Diderot et l'art de Boucher à David: Les Salons, 1759–1781 (exh. cat., ed. M.-C. Sahut and N. Volle; Paris, Hôtel de la Monnaie, 1984–5), pp. 204–16

J.-P. Cuzin: 'Fragonard dans les musées français: Quelques tableaux reconsidérés ou discutés', *Rev. Louvre*, 1 (1986), pp. 58–66

P. Rosenberg and B. Brejon de Lavergnée: *Panopticon italiano: Un diario di viaggio ritrovato, 1759–61* (Rome, 1986) [reproduces Fragonard's drgs made on journey]

J.-P. Cuzin: *Fragonard: Vie et oeuvre; Catalogue complet des peintures* (Paris, 1987; Eng. trans., New York, 1988) [C]

Fragonard (exh. cat. by P. Rosenberg, Paris, Grand Pal.; New York, Met.; 1987–8)

J.-P. Cuzin: 'Fragonard: Un Nouvel Examen', *Rev. A.*, 80 (1988), pp. 83–7

M. D. Sheriff: *Fragonard: Art and Eroticism* (Chicago and London, 1990)

J. H. Fragonard e H. Robert a Roma (exh. cat. by C. Boulot, J.-P. Cuzin and P. Rosenberg, Rome, Villa Medici, 1991)

Fragonard et le dessin français dans les collections du Petit Palais (exh. cat. by J.-L. de Los Llanos, Paris, Petit Pal., 1992–3)

COLIN HARRISON

(2) Alexandre-Evariste Fragonard (*b* Grasse, 26 Oct 1780; *d* Paris, 10 Nov 1850). Painter, sculptor and draughtsman, son of (1) Jean-Honoré Fragonard. Having been taught by his father and by David, he attracted notice at an early age and was considered the equal of Jean-Baptiste Isabey and of Hilaire Ledru (1769–1840) in his drawings. He made his début at the Salon of 1793 with *Timoleon Sacrificing his Brother* (drawing; untraced); later he exhibited genre subjects similar to those of J. A. Vallin (1760–after 1831) and Jean-Baptiste Mallet, which were frequently reproduced in prints. During the Revolution he produced several allegories, such as the *French Republic* (drawing; Grasse, Mus. Fragonard). He executed many drawings during the Consulate and the Empire; these are Neo-classical frieze compositions in which he made use of strongly contrasted lighting effects (e.g. the *Child Pyrrhus at the Court of Glaucias*, 1814; Paris, Louvre). He developed an official career as sculptor and painter during the Empire. He took part in a competition for the Peace of Amiens in 1801 (painting; Paris, Bib. Thiers), after which he received several commissions. He sculpted the pediment of the Palais Bourbon in Paris (destr. in the Revolution of 1830 and replaced by that of Jean-Pierre Cortot). Also for the Palais Bourbon, in 1810 he was commissioned to paint *trompe-l'oeil* grisailles to decorate the Salle des Gardes and the salon behind the peristyle

Alexandre-Evariste Fragonard: *Battle of Marignan, 14 September 1515*, 1836 (Versailles, Musée National du Château de Versailles et de Trianon)

(now destr. or hidden by the later false ceiling). In 1812 he was entrusted with the composition and execution of bas-reliefs for the obelisk that was to be built on the Pont Neuf, Paris, in memory of the Prussian campaign (not executed).

Fragonard also worked for the Sèvres porcelain factory during the Empire. He executed sketches (Sèvres, Mus. N. Cér.) for the column celebrating the German campaign (Versailles, Château). He produced models for the plinths of the Cordelier Vases in the Galerie d'Apollon in Saint-Cloud (1809), which were decorated with six plaques painted to resemble cameos and based on medals commemorating French victories in the Prussian campaign. He obtained further official commissions during the Restoration and was made Chevalier de la Légion d'honneur in 1817. He worked again in the Palais Bourbon, decorating the vault of the Salle des Séances with geometric motifs and allegories representing the 86 départements of France. (The Revolution of 1830 put an end to this project.) He made drawings for the *Coronation of Charles X* (Paris, Louvre) and received a commission to paint the ceilings of the Musée Charles X in the Louvre (*Francis I and Bayard*, 1819; *Francis I and Primaticcio*, 1827; both *in situ*).

In the 1820s Fragonard turned to history painting and became involved in the Troubadour movement. In contrast to the meticulous paintings of Jean-Antoine Laurent and Pierre Révoil, he achieved considerable freedom by means of a broader technique, a livelier touch and a vivid sense of setting. He brought the amplitude of history painting to such Troubadour themes as *Raphael Adjusting the Pose of his Model for the Virgin and Child* (1820; Grasse, Mus. Fragonard; *see* MODEL, ARTIST'S, fig. 3), *Bernard Palissy Burning his Furniture* (Sèvres, Mus. N. Cér.), the *Entry of Joan of Arc into Orleans* (1822; Orleans, Mus. B.-A.), the *Burghers of Calais* (exh. Salon 1822; Arras, Mus. B.-A.) and *Maria-Theresa Presenting her Son to the Hungarians* (exh. Salon 1822; Grasse, Mus. Fragonard).

Fragonard showed a taste for artificial and dramatic lighting, and he often repeated the motif of foreground figures silhouetted against and screening a background brightly illuminated by a diagonal fall of light. He usually chose subjects from the history of the French monarchy, but he also combined ancient and contemporary history to create a modern legend, as in *Vivant Denon Replacing the Bones of El Cid in his Tomb* (Saint-Quentin, Mus. Lécuyer), which celebrates Denon and the cultural policies of the Empire but is at the same time a meditation on medieval heroes. After the Revolution of 1830, lacking work, Fragonard submitted *Mirabeau before Dreux-Brézé* and *Boissy d'Anglas Saluting the Head of the Deputy Féraud* (both Paris, Louvre) to a competition for the decoration of the Salle des Séances in the Chambre des Députés (1830–31). He subsequently received a commission for the Musée Historique in the château of Versailles, the *Battle of Marignan, 14 September 1515* (1836; *in situ*; see fig.). Fragonard exhibited until 1842 and also executed a number of religious paintings (e.g. *Flight into Egypt*; Strasbourg Cathedral). He made many drawings for lithography, including several series for Baron Taylor's *Voyages pittoresques*.

WRITINGS
Recueil de divers sujets dans le style grec (Paris, 1815)
BIBLIOGRAPHY
J. Renouvier: *Histoire de l'art pendant la révolution* (Paris, 1863), pp. 197–200
P. Marmottan: *L'Ecole française de peinture, 1789–1830* (Paris, 1886), pp. 266–8
H. Béraldi: *Les Graveurs du XIXe siècle*, ii (Paris, 1889), pp. 160–62
P. Jary: 'Les Peintures murales du Palais-Bourbon', *Bull. Soc. Hist. A. Fr.* (1928), pp. 39–41
G. Wildenstein: *Fragonard aquafortiste* (Paris, 1956)
K. Simons: 'Vivant Denon et le romantisme: A propos d'un tableau d'Alexandre Evariste Fragonard', *Rev. Inst. Napoléon*, 132 (1976), pp. 55–65
M.-C. Chaudonneret: 'Le Concours de 1830 pour la Chambre des Députés: Deux Esquisses d'Alexandre Evariste Fragonard au Louvre', *Rev. Louvre*, 2 (1987), pp. 128–35
MARIE-CLAUDE CHAUDONNERET

Fraigevise, Frédéric. See FRÉGEVIZE, FRÉDÉRIC.

Fraikin, Charles-Auguste (*b* Herentals, 14 June 1817; *d* Schaerbeek, Brussels, 22 Nov 1893). Belgian sculptor. The son of a notary, he attended the Académie in Antwerp from 1829 to 1831 before receiving his diploma as a pharmacist in 1835. In 1836 he discovered the work of Guillaume Geefs and decided to abandon pharmacy for sculpture. Pierre Puyenbroeck (1804–84) noticed his talent and took him on in his studio. Fraikin was encouraged by François-Joseph Navez, the director of the Brussels Académie Royale des Beaux-Arts, and studied there under Louis Jéhotte (*c.* 1803–84). He exhibited for the first time in 1839 in Brussels where, six years later, his *Cupid Held Captive* won a gold medal and considerable success. Two versions in marble were ordered for the Musées Royaux des Beaux-Arts, Brussels, and the Hermitage, St Petersburg, and numerous copies of different sizes were circulated without his knowledge. He executed large numbers of engaging sculptures including *Psyche Calling Cupid to her Aid* (*c.* 1848; Brussels, Mus. A. Mod.) and the *Birth of Venus* (1861; Brussels, Pal. Royal). His brand of seductive classicism held sway in Belgium until the end of the 19th century; only his busts and the group portrait of the *Counts of Egmont and Hornes* (1864) in the Place du Petit Sablon, Brussels, diverge from this classicizing style. Constantin Meunier was among the pupils in his private studio. Fraikin had numerous titles and official duties, including membership of the Académie in Brussels from 1846 and service on the juries that governed education and the Salons. In 1888 he bequeathed his entire studio (now the Fraikin-Museum) to Herentals, his birthplace.

BIBLIOGRAPHY
E. Marchal: 'Notice sur Charles-Auguste Fraikin', *Annu. Acad. Royale Sci., Lett. & B.-A. Belgique* (1900), pp. 381–418
Museum Fraikin van Herentals (Herenthout, n.d.)
Hulde aan Karel-August Fraikin [Tribute to Charles-Auguste Fraikin], Herentals, Fraikin-Mus. cat. (Herentals, 1967)
Académie royale des beaux-arts de Bruxelles (exh. cat., Brussels, Musées Royaux B.-A., 1987), pp. 276–7, 295, 328–31
La Sculpture belge au 19ème siècle, ii (exh. cat., Brussels, Gén. de Banque, 1990), pp. 399–401
JACQUES VAN LENNEP

Fraile, Alfonso (*b* Marchena, Seville, 1930; *d* Madrid, 1988). Spanish painter. He studied at the Escuela Superior de Bellas Artes de San Fernando in Madrid and held his first one-man show in Madrid in 1957, exhibiting beautifully composed abstract pictures. After 1960 he and other painters who presented themselves under the name Nuevo

Espacialismo reintroduced the figure with a narrative emphasis, citing the Abstract Expressionist painter Willem de Kooning as one of their influences; Fraile was particularly interested at that time in the unflinching realism of Goya.

In his characteristic works of the 1970s Fraile presented monstrously distorted figures isolated against plain backgrounds or in quasi-theatrical settings. Their doll-like appearance, while recalling the works he admired by Klee and the Surrealists, lent them a savage and ironic critical edge, as found in his representation of an incapacitated *Superman* (1979; priv. col., see 1985 exh. cat., pl. 23). While the fine drawing and soft flesh tones emphasized the disjuncture of parts, the figures of the 1980s became more coordinated and active, and the use of colour became more luscious. This is particularly the case in mixed media drawings, such as *Marathon* (1983; see Calvo Serraller, p. 77), in which the construction of the heads of the repeated figures serves to isolate the dislocations.

BIBLIOGRAPHY
Alfonso Fraile, 1977–82 (exh. cat., Madrid, Gal. Theo, 1982)
F. Calvo Serraller: *Alfonso Fraile, 1982–1983* (Madrid, 1983)
Alfonso Fraile: Obra 1976–1985 (exh. cat., Madrid, Mus. A. Contemp., 1985)

F. MORENO CUADRO

Fraisinger, Caspar. *See* FREISINGER, CASPAR.

Frame. The role of the frame in the presentation of a picture fulfils some or all of the following functions: the protection of the painting; its display and physical attachment to the wall; the enhancement of subject and colour scheme while remaining subordinate to the picture; the definition of the picture's perimeter and the focusing of the spectator's attention on the subject; the provision of

1. European frames, 15th–19th centuries (Toronto, Royal Ontario Museum)

an area of transition between the real world and that of the picture; the creation of harmony with the surrounding interior decoration; and the isolation of the picture from a distracting background. It also exists as a pleasing ornamental object in its own right. The picture frame is the medium through which fine arts are merged with architecture and the decorative arts. Frames, often themselves works of art, have been designed by artists, architects (see fig. 1) and ornamentalists, and executed by highly skilled wood-carvers, gilders and craftsmen. Picture and frame are mutually dependent, the one incomplete without the other. They were generally conceived as a single stylistic entity, like the architectural mouldings surrounding frescoes or inset pictures, or a tapestry with its interwoven border; their fusion was commonplace in the Renaissance, when paintings and relief sculptures were integrated with architectural frames in wood or marble. Many paintings, however, have been separated from their original frames. This divorce rate, generally higher in proportion to the age of the picture, stems from various reasons. Because of the portability of unframed pictures, for instance, marriage with the frame has always been vulnerable. The act of framing is also a signal of ownership: pictures were reframed according to the tastes of new owners; to suit a prevailing style of interior decoration; or into a standard house or gallery frame.

The following survey charts the principal and most regularly used European and American frame designs and their stylistic development. The variety and interrelationship of patterns are clarified with diagrams and cross-sections drawn directly from archive photographs of frames containing their original or contemporary paintings, the majority of which may be seen in public collections. Captions indicate as accurately as possible frame opening sizes, followed by section width.

See also DISPLAY OF ART and MIRROR.

I. Introduction. II. Italy. III. France. IV. Britain. V. The Netherlands and Belgium. VI. Germany and Central Europe. VII. Scandinavia. VIII. Spain. IX. USA.

I. Introduction.

The types of frames may be broadly defined in three groups, governed by the picture's purpose, setting and owner. Ecclesiastical frames generally reflect the architectural style of their settings, reinforcing Catholic imagery or Protestant austerity. Court frames, commissioned by rulers and nobility, represent an essential, and long underestimated, component of the arts employed for propaganda purposes and as a status symbol, expressed through grandeur, luxury and sculptural magnificence; they may also have pictorial or family emblematic devices emphasizing subject and ownership. Secular frames, the greatest volume of production for domestic consumption, are often the standard and most economical 'pattern book' versions of court frames; their style and cost conformed to prevailing interior decoration and to the perceived significance of the painting. Within these main areas the style of the frame may also depend on the subject-matter of the picture: religious, mythological, historical, portraiture, genre, landscape, still-life or abstract. Two further factors determine the frame's character: whether it is a decorative element coordinating with contemporary furnishings; or whether it is solely the artist's responsibility, uncompromised by the taste of others and aesthetically integrated with the picture. Then it may be designed by the artist or painted directly on to the canvas, or projected in a *trompe l'oeil* extension of the picture on to the frame itself.

1. Form and function. 2. Stylistic overview. 3. Purpose. 4. Framemakers and reframing. 5. Historiography.

1. FORM AND FUNCTION. Viewers seldom 'see' the frame when contemplating a picture, and yet it occupies a substantial proportion of the picture/frame ensemble and, as such, inevitably has a significant peripheral influence on the painting within. Existing literature makes few references to the way in which the forms and functions of frames are achieved in their design or to the aesthetic relationship between a picture and its frame. The subject was summarized by Guggenheim (1897):

> The form and character of the frame are governed by the laws of aesthetics and of human sensation. The intention must be to engender a sense of harmony and to concentrate the beholder's attention on the painting. A frame constructed in accordance with a proper understanding of art and science will enliven the painting's colours, detach them from their surroundings and unite them into a harmonious and effective whole.

The frame and its functions can be assessed in terms of three fundamental and interrelated factors: overall shape or design, ornamentation and finish. The four component sides of the frame isolate the picture from the wall to a degree according to their scale and width. Its cross-section may be a flat border, a hollow moulding whose real depth enhances the picture's illusory perspective, or a bolection moulding projecting the subject forward from the wall surface. The contour of the frame is often broken by projecting corners and/or centres, as in the cartouches of Louis XIV and 17th-century Spanish frames and outset corners in the Palladian style, to create a play of diagonal and/or horizontal and vertical axes across the picture's composition. These projections, invariably employed in portrait frames, act as spatial coordinates; their axial geometry reinforces the pictorial composition and thereby focuses the viewer's attention on the sitter. At the same time this external contour, contrasting with the interior rectangle, assumes a distinctive and visible pattern on the wall. The elevations of virtually all frames share the common basic features of a narrow moulding adjacent to and delineating the boundary of the picture, echoed by another moulding nearest the wall and divided by a broader space between. The decoration of these surfaces determines the character and style of the frame and has been achieved over the centuries in countless ways, from the modest to the magnificent. Indeed the history of frames may be seen as a survey of the use of ornament (see fig. 2) throughout the ages, skilfully handled by designers to enhance and focus the subject without distraction.

In general there is a subtle balance and counterplay between mouldings and their decoration. The innermost

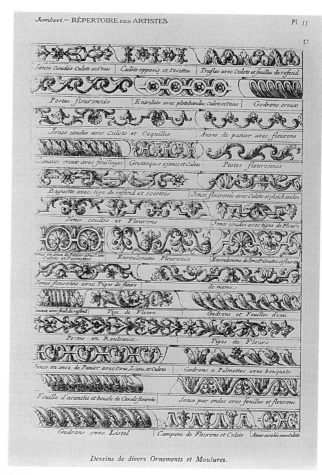

2. Ornament designs by Charles-Antoine Jombert; engraving from *Répertoire des artistes* (Paris, 1764), pl. 35

moulding, if decorated, is complemented by an adjacent plain frieze or hollow, the latter being a visual rest from the outer surface, more broadly decorated since further from the picture. Usually the scale of the painting's composition and detail is in proportion to that used for the ornament on the frame, such as the miniaturized techniques of Dutch works with fine ebony ripple mouldings, or the broader leaves and architectural motifs surrounding the bold draperies and settings of Baroque figure subjects. A powerful ornamental device employed to draw attention inwards is the use of a rhythmical series of raked lobing, usually running from centres to corners, known as gadrooning. Common in Mannerist (see fig. 14 below) and Baroque frames, this motif suggests a 360° sweep of lines radiating to and from the subject.

The third essential characteristic of the frame, as in all decorative art objects, is the colour and texture of its finish. The vast majority of frames are gilded or parcel-gilt; others are polychrome or of plain polished wood. From the earliest times gold has been employed in a multitude of ways to enhance the frame and therefore its content. Its glowing, reflective properties have endowed the frame with a special significance, literally highlighting the picture it contains as well as harmonizing with surrounding furnishings. Even more than the frame's form, the gilt finish uniquely isolates a work of art. Accustomed to constant, flat electric lighting, we tend to overlook the fact that paintings have been viewed for centuries by flickering candlelight. In the vast evening gloom of cathedrals and churches, altarpieces would seem to be surrounded by a pulsing 'halo' of light, and in palatial interiors or on domestic overmantels gilded frames were strong focal points regardless of the aesthetic merits of their pictures. Paintings on the four walls of parade rooms and galleries far outnumbered the furniture on the floor, and their impact was vastly enhanced by their gilded finish. Similarly, polychrome and parcel-gilt finishes were employed to great effect by medieval, Renaissance and Baroque decorators in Catholic countries. Church and court interiors were ablaze with colour, and frames were richly painted to coordinate simultaneously with their surroundings and to accentuate their pictures' colour schemes. Colour in frames heightened dramatic effect: painted and polychrome mouldings with flashing gold corners and centres animated portraits and accentuated the chiaroscuro drama within Spanish and Italian subjects.

The visual contrasts inherent in Classical architectural ornament, through its deployment of mouldings and enrichments, depended on an understanding of the properties of light. All those involved in the design of frames, especially architects, were skilled in the disposition and ornamentation of mouldings, as well as the interplay of their surface textures and varied finishes. The effectiveness of undecorated plain moulded frames depended on a careful juxtaposition of forms from the repertory of Classical mouldings to create a sequence of linear rectangles. From whatever viewpoint, there would then always be a series of facets whose gilded surface directed light. Paintings carrying deep, hollow profile frames would gain added luminosity by the light reflected on to them from the inside upper surfaces of the scotia.

The most sophisticated understanding and exploitation of the reflective possibilities of gold leaf are seen in French Baroque and Rococo frames, concurrent with Italian and English variants. Jean Berain I, Daniel Marot I and Juste-Aurèle Meissonnier, among others, designed sequences of ornament—shells, foliage and flowers linked by strapwork (see fig. 2)—to be carved and recut in the gesso in low relief against a background of textures: cross-hatching, punchwork and sanded and plain surfaces. All these components, when gilded, the raised areas burnished and contrasting with matt gold grounds (as in furniture mounts), created a complex orchestration of light that mirrored the paintings' broad or fine passages of brushwork, as well as ensuring that the frame was a decorative work of art in its own right, on a par with surrounding *objets d'art*.

The importance of the play of light on smooth and patterned surfaces governed the design of ebony and ebonized frames made by northern European cabinetmakers. Devoid of gold leaf or paint, and excepting examples veneered with tortoiseshell and luxury inlays, the aesthetic effect of such frames depended solely on their proportions, profile and a series of plain or finely decorated rectilinear mouldings that caught and fragmented the light. This

manipulation of light draws attention to the subject, whose colour scheme is also optically enhanced by the neutral surroundings of its black frame.

2. STYLISTIC OVERVIEW. Paintings and relief carvings have had borders from an early period—although this is a sophisticated development, defining the permanence and isolation of the image in contrast to the apparent transience of, for example, cave paintings, layered on a rough, unbounded surface. Stylized geometric margins appeared first on vase and tomb paintings between 2000 and 1000 BC, dividing narrative scenes and decorations into horizontal bands. Later, vertical divisions were added (e.g. Tomb of Sennefer, Luxor; *c.* 1453–1419 BC), while architectural frames were applied to wall carvings. A millennium later, in Classical Greece, the borders of mosaics became the organizing structure of the whole, arranging figures and scenes into an abstract pattern of circles and spandrels, squares and lozenges. Then, when images—devotional, memorial, didactic or aesthetic—began to be important in their own right and not merely adjuncts to walls and vases, the framing edge took on other functions. It became protective and emphatic, as with Byzantine and Carolingian ivory-carvings for book covers and diptychs, which would have architectural borders to safeguard them, and to provide focus and depth. On 11th- and 12th-century metalwork altars the frame was also protective, but, set with gems and other inlay, it symbolized the celestial glory of the Trinity and the saints. Even the decorative margins of illuminated manuscripts hint at the richness of heaven, reflect the imagery of the text or set up a tension with the text through grotesque details.

In the 12th and 13th centuries carved wooden frames appeared, the forebears of the modern movable frame. The first examples, like the engaged borders of the ivories and the metalwork altars, were in one piece with the painted ground. The panel had its surface lowered by gouging into a shallow box shape, the surrounding wall of which became the frame. The whole panel was then covered in gesso and gold leaf, the image being painted on the smooth, sunken surface. Patterns could then be punched into the gilded gesso to define robes, haloes, the junction of picture and frame, and the frame itself; so that, apart from the physical unity of both, there was a close identity of ornament and tone through the work. Larger altarpieces were developed, the painting ground formed of boards bonded together with transverse supports, dowels and glued linen layers, while separate mouldings, plain or simply carved, were laminated on to the outer edges to form the frame. This became increasingly elaborate: painted, carved or punched on its top edge, with auxiliary mouldings on either side. Finally, in Italy in the 14th and 15th centuries, the silhouette of the frame altered: at first a peaked pentagon imitating a basilica in cross-section, the altarpiece acquired tiers of painted images, each framed by a complex of inner decorative mouldings to simulate the nave, aisles, crypt and clerestory of a medieval church. The outer frame gained weight and solidity to support this edifice, with lateral buttresses in Italy, and was ornamented with architectural features: pinnacles, crockets, tabernacle work, cresting and niches. National variations of this style developed throughout

Europe. Eventually the increasing size of these great screens, especially in Spain, meant that they could no longer exist as independent structures; at a height of *c.* 9 m they had to be applied to the back wall of the church, often around an apse, as a pictorial panelling in which the frame was merely a separating device between each scene.

The cathedral silhouette continued as the form for free-standing altarpieces, but in the early Renaissance this outer contour became that of a Classical temple: a single frame, usually rectangular, around a single scene (the *sacra conversazione*, within a 'real' perspectival space). Neri di Bicci summed up the Renaissance aedicular frame as a squared form with predella, fluted lateral pilasters and architrave with frieze, cornice and foliage above; but it was soon as ornamental as the Flamboyant Gothic type, including decorative carving, pastiglia, painting and *sgraffito* on all surfaces, and added such features as modillions at the base. The architrave could expand into a triangular or segmental pediment, or the picture could be continued inside a broken pediment. Italy led in this evolution and in that of the non-aedicular frame, the *cassetta* and its variants, movable wooden case or moulding frames, applied from the 14th century to secular subjects and simpler religious images. Again, each country developed its own versions of the *cassetta*, and travel, trade and political connections all helped to spread framing motifs, mouldings and other influences from country to country. Renaissance designs, however, spread less quickly than the more florid High Gothic, Mannerist and Baroque styles.

With the Baroque period and the burgeoning of the great courts of Europe, the mainspring of patronage transferred from the church to the king, with his need for unparalleled public displays of wealth and power. The index of artistic leadership also began to move from Rome to Paris, and a golden age of framemaking began in France. This produced virtuosos of carving, gilding and recutting of gesso; creators of vast, three-dimensional sculptural frames for ceremonial portraits and Old Masters, coloured with a range of gold leaf; confectioners of delicate Rococo settings transcending the medium of carved wood, which were fitted to fantastic interior schemes of fretted *boiseries*. English and German carvers produced their own versions of Baroque and Rococo frames; and in England the Palladian idiom and Grecian style of Robert Adam spawned further integrated schemes, including ceilings, carpets, furniture and picture frames. Paintings were hardly more under this regime than elements in an abstract arrangement of objects, anchored to their setting by the correspondence of their frames with the ornamentations of surrounding objects.

A second wave of classical design in England and France during the late 18th century heralded a more uniformly international vocabulary of framemaking. With the Napoleonic Empire straddling Europe, the court style it promulgated could be reproduced both by craftsmen travelling with the Bonaparte rulers and by local carvers using patterns from Paris. In the early 19th century national differences tended to vanish, and the processes of the Industrial Revolution further homogenized and bastard-ized the art of making frames. Years of war and national debt meant that the carvers themselves were vanishing, unaffordable luxuries, and the first 40 years of the century

were marked by repetitious, standardized models, cheaply made of composition on a deal base and finished with ersatz base-metal 'gilding'. However, artists throughout Europe fought back sporadically by generating individually designed and carved frames. In the mid-19th century the Pre-Raphaelites revived old techniques of framemaking and ornamentation, experimented with geometric, natu-ralistic and symbolic motifs, and abandoned stock plaster patterns for original designs carved in oak and other 'honest' materials (see fig. 3). These practices were strongly influential in Europe, being diffused through the great international exhibitions of the late 19th century and by the mutual links of artists in different countries. Symbolist, classically inspired and Art Nouveau frames appeared, sometimes in striking admixtures. The Impressionists and Neo-Impressionists experimented with simple forms whose colouring was inspired by recently published scienti-fic studies of light and colour. Creative framemaking thus

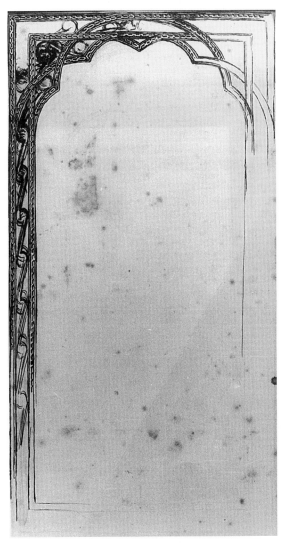

3. Frame design by William Holman Hunt, first design for frame of *Afterglow in Egypt*, pen and brown ink over pencil, 375×194 mm (private collection)

came almost wholly under the control of the artists themselves, rather than of master carvers who could design in their own right.

By the 20th century there were few remnants of original frame craftsmanship left. A handful of artists persevered in earnest re-creation of archaic methods, but Picasso and Braque subverted this approach, using the frame as a prop for *jeux d'esprits*: ropes became the setting for collages; painted and pasted borders replaced more formal designs; and fragments of frames were drawn around or appear in the background of paintings. Surrealists also treated the frame as a visual pun, or, like the Symbolists, as part of the work itself. There was little similar invention in the late 20th century; as in the early 19th there were few artists' frames but great reliance on mass-produced mouldings. The tendency was also to dispense completely with formal framing or to employ a minimalist technique of painted battens edging the stretcher, giving nominal protection without affecting the image.

3. PURPOSE. While the border was physically part of the work, as in early wall paintings and mosaics, its role was unquestioned because there could be no division of image and setting. With independent works, the purpose of the frame was increasingly to focus on and isolate the significant image; with the creation of large altarpieces, a symbolic dimension was added. The purposes of a Gothic altar frame are multiple. In the dimly lit churches of Spain and Italy, a gilded setting with faceted columns, buttresses and canopies could catch light and throw it on to the paintings within. The cathedral outlines and ever more complex architectural features meanwhile provided an analogue of the celestial Church, of which the actual church of brick and stone was a faint earthly echo. Such details as inset jewels, painted 'stained glass', gilded angels and the busts of prophets helped to magnify the glory of the central image, bringing a reflection of heaven to the poorest worshippers. Well-lit northern European churches did not require so much gold to illuminate their altarpieces, and although edge mouldings and pictorial grounds are usually gilded, the main frame area is painted in bands of colour, marbled, patterned, hung with donors' armorial bearings, inscribed or made precious with antique cameos and intricate mosaic work. These decorative techniques were again designed to reveal to the lay worshipper an analogue of Heaven, while inscriptions gave the educated spectator a further gloss on the painted scene, and coats of arms identified the gift both to God and to the Church.

Renaissance aediculae similarly create an allegorical pattern of the spiritual temple and imply the Classical concepts subsumed by Christianity, such as the Platonic ideal. Pure Renaissance examples are most common in Italy; they provide wide areas of reflective gold to compensate for the loss of the pictorial gilt ground. Secular Renaissance frames adapted the use of gold to illuminate; they also deploy complex relief patterns to animate the light given off by the frame. Depth and width are exploited to support the painted composition; and different types of carved or painted ornament reflect shapes within the picture. This relationship may reveal an abstract sense of pattern in the scene, undiscoverable without the original frame.

Besides provision of light and correspondence of pattern, the late medieval and Renaissance frame has another particular purpose. The early arched settings of small altarpieces suggest a church door opening on a spiritualized vision; the closeness of simple tabernacle forms and of the *cassetta* to an architectural opening reinforces the idea of the frame as a window, giving on to a world whose space and perspective are connected to those of the spectator. This architectural transition to the world of the painting is mirrored outwardly by the logical transition to the wall where it hangs, so there is no dislocation between a Flemish landscape and its embossed leather background or between a vision of Olympus and a Rococo boudoir. As paintings related less and less to their surroundings, this interval of passage became proportionately of greater importance. The decoration of the frame can enhance or modify this effect: in northern *trompe l'oeil* frames, where the painting is carried over the wooden moulding (for example a cloth or hand hanging down into the spectator's world), the window-like function is intensified, and the image given greater 'reality'. Carved architectural ornament, in sympathy with the outer and/or the painted worlds, also achieves a unity that is aesthetically coherent and that heightens the realism of the work. Ornament can also sustain a picture against the overwhelming opulence of a Baroque or Mannerist background: Louis XIV and Louis XV frames hold their own in Versailles, for instance, although it is also true that an over-elaborate design can itself swamp a small or subtle painting.

Further functions of setting can be seen in the trophy frame, which annotates and reveals the subject. Status and interests can be indicated for a portrait; hunting and battle scenes are given importance by appropriate motifs; and religious symbolism can be expanded. Ownership can also be proclaimed by the trophy frame, for example by the use of heraldic cresting. The trophy frame is related in some ways to the livery or gallery frame, which again proclaims ownership and links the painting as part of a collection to a single house or patron. Where the design is flexible and unassertive, the livery frame can bind a collection together or unify a roomful of disparate images; where it is contemporary with the pictures, it will usually harmonize naturally with the composition and with the wider architectural 'frame' of the interior. It can equally fragment this unity, however, where it is visibly anachronistic or aesthetically at odds with the image.

The idea of frame as window begins to break down when the abstract and decorative purposes of the picture consciously equal or surpass the representational elements. Arrangements of line and harmonies of colour, for example in the work of Dante Gabriel Rossetti, James McNeill Whistler and Albert Joseph Moore, are picked up in the geometric, carved and painted frames. Here, no attempt is made to contrive depth or spatial connection through the frame; instead, the choice of profile and ornament is aimed at flattening the pictorial image and emphasizing its decorative qualities. Symbolists and Secessionists followed this tendency, which also fed on their production of posters in flat, linear designs within ornamental borders. The loss of perspectival space within the picture and the importance given to flat patterning, colour and texture meant that the frame itself was increasingly unnecessary.

Stock plaster mouldings had long been the conventional way to provide a neutral frame that would not 'interfere' with the work, now that any alteration of the artist's vision began to be seen as undesirable, and the simultaneous wish for a Ruskinian honesty of presentation ended ironically in the 20th century in small strip frames, minimalist battens fastened to the stretcher sides and, finally, in no frame at all. This movement was bolstered by the architectural trend towards function and away from ornament. This provokes questions as to whether a frame is unnecessary interference with the artist's intention; whether this is only so in the case of abstract work; whether minimalist architecture and pictorial detail require minimal—or no—framing; whether the architecture itself provides sufficient frame; or whether, as Ortega y Gasset wrote, all pictures need frames for the image to cohere and avoid dissolution (see 1986 exh. cat.). Allied issues have been raised in the 20th century: the framing of heterogeneous museum collections; unsuitably framed individual pictures; institutional interpretation of the artist's assumed intentions; and the treatment of collectors' frames when they have a later date than the paintings they contain.

4. FRAMEMAKERS AND REFRAMING. The framemaker's relationship to artist, architect and patron is as relevant as historical knowledge of framing; especially the changing status of artist and carver, which illuminates the different values that have been set on the frame. Medieval altarpieces were executed by an equal team of carver, gilder and painter, in which the carver's wage might well be the highest. The painter had little say in the design, often receiving the carved, gilt panel only after the others had finished with it. Some early designs by artists do exist for a few works (e.g. by Dürer, Filippo Lippi, Lorenzo Lotto and Vittore Carpaccio); their rarity may be because few have survived or because they were uncommon. Even where contracts exist putting the painter in charge of the commission or requiring his design for a frame, the ornamentation may have remained the carver's province.

During the Renaissance dynasties of exceptional carvers flourished, particularly in Italy; these also enjoyed equal status with the artist and were often important architects/sculptors responsible for the interiors where the works would hang. A painting could still be commissioned when its frame was already complete, and there was little sense that the work of carving or gilding was inferior (e.g. Leonardo gilded the frame for his *Virgin of the Rocks*, 1480s; Paris, Louvre). Gradually, however, framing was left more in the artist's hands, and the 'name frames' began to emerge: these are designs associated with a particular painter, such as the 'Maratta', 'Canaletto', 'Longhi', 'Lely', 'Wright', 'Morland' and 'Whistler' frames. Distinct from the producers of these stock designs, however, a master carver was still socially on a par with the artist and was often engaged directly by the client to provide an exceptional frame. In France the master carvers, their workshops and the guilds became rich and influential; craftsmen began to stamp their frames with a studio mark; and dozens of pattern books were published and diffused throughout Europe. Sculptors, ornamentalists and cabinetmakers all produced frames that can be classed as

superb carvings, exquisite designs or precious pieces of furniture. The quality of these, residing not only in the original composition and carved detail but also in the application of layers of gesso, the recutting of the gesso and the use of toned gilding and part burnishing, was reflected in the high prices they commanded, although in the 16th, 17th and 18th centuries the cost of paintings rose proportionately faster than that of frames, and stock designs were relatively cheap.

Collectors tended to pay to frame their acquisitions suitably, as with the galleries built from the 16th to the 18th century to house specific collections, for which the architect would often design background hangings, decoration and frames. The jewels of a collection received settings approximating to their perceived worth. On the other hand, a Dutch patron of the 17th century or the early 18th would look to fashionable France rather than a native style when framing his most prized paintings, and French collectors of northern paintings would naturally do the same; from the time of their execution until quite a recent date, portraits by, for example, Rembrandt might be framed in French Baroque gilt frames, which can kill the contents.

The position of the framemaker crumbled, along with that of other luxury trades, because of the impoverishment and restraint caused by the revolutionary and Napoleonic wars of the late 18th century and the early 19th; and, with the advent of the Industrial Revolution, mass-produced products began to replace handmade goods. Machine-stamped lengths of moulding created cheap frames for the engravings churned out by new processes; framed pictures for the better-off middle and working classes became affordable; and there was a gradual infiltration into the higher end of the market and a consequent slump in demand for hand-carved frames. Other products of the mass market—composition and papier mâché, base metal instead of gold leaf—all fed this trend, and by 1813 the number of carvers had shrunk by almost nine-tenths. The artist's position remained unaffected: indeed, his status had changed from the artisan of the Middle Ages to the inspired creator of the Romantic Age, leaving the carver or framemaker reduced to the stature of mere craftsman. In the later 19th century the artist would become rich, titled and influential; but there was no equivalent place for the carver, just as there was no longer widespread demand for his skill. The design of any frame outside a production-line type was firmly in the artist's hands; and although the rarity of a tailor-made pattern executed by one of the few good carvers remaining meant that its price was comparatively high, still its maker would never be given the recognition, equal with the painter, that he had enjoyed five or six centuries earlier.

So little were good authentic frames valued that the early panel paintings shipped out of Italy in the 19th and 20th centuries were taken wholesale from their carved Gothic settings, and the latter were burnt to salvage the gold leaf. Museums in Europe and the USA reset the panels in pastiches of the original, with iron-like composition Gothic Revival ornament finished with drab oil-gilding and base leaf. Imitation French Baroque frames with stamped ornament were used on Italian Renaissance and Mannerist works; and original Louis XIV carved frames were stripped of their gilding, washed with subdued colour and used to marry Impressionist paintings to the Louis Revival interiors of their American purchasers. Soon this ubiquitous practice had fixed a generalized Louis XIV pattern in the public mind as the 'Impressionist frame'. Similarly, Turner's works lost their gilded hollow, 'Morland' or laurel frames, often ending in neutral greyish 1960s mouldings with inner hessian slips. Remedying this divorce of paintings from their contemporary settings began in earnest only in the late 20th century; the process is handicapped by the small number of original frames surviving and by the reluctance of institutions to spend on displaying authentically the pictures they have rather than on acquiring new ones. Curators may also baulk at hanging diverse styles of frame side by side, preferring to preserve a neutral pre-existing 'gallery' style or to create a new one. The loss of balance, colour and focus in many paintings is severe, and only the custom of illustrating art books with unframed reproductions could have blinded the spectator for so long to the effects of such misalliance. Some art history methodologies locate the work in its social and historical setting; it needs also to be appropriately sited in an immediate physical context that will take account of its original purpose and surroundings or subsequent place in a noted collection. It needs a frame.

5. HISTORIOGRAPHY. The dislocation of contemporary frames from their pictures has been a deterrent to art and furniture historians alike. The frame frustrates both disciplines and has long remained in a no-man's-land between the fine and the decorative arts. 99% of the illustrations in art histories exclude the frame, despite its crucial role in evoking its painting's milieu. This neglect has virtually eliminated the frame from the viewer's consciousness and critical appreciation. Since the early studies by Bode (1898–9), Roche (1931) and, later, Heydenryk (1963), recognizing the significance of frames, deeper exploration began in the last three decades of the 20th century and is gathering momentum. Grimm's broad and copiously illustrated survey *Alte Bilderrahmen* (1978) remains the standard work on the subject. Two important and beautifully illustrated books on the history of Italian frames, *La cornice italiana. . .* (1992) and *La cornice fiorentina e senese* (1992), together with studies by Mosco, are impressive successors to the pioneer works by Guggenheim and Morazzoni, placing Italy in the forefront of national frame history (*see* bibliography of §II below).

Appraisals of museum-frame collections have prompted exhibitions with excellent catalogues, exposing a new level of scholarship to an international audience: the Alte Pinakothek, Munich, undertook a detailed stylistic and regional analysis of its Italian frames in *Italienisch Bilderrahmen des 14.–18. Jahrhunderts* (1976); *Prijst de lijst* (Amsterdam, Rijksmus., 1984) is a meticulous account of 17th-century Dutch frames with their original pictures; *The Art of the Edge* (1986) surveys the role and development of the frame in the context of the Art Institute of Chicago's collection (and includes for the first time in English one of the few essays dealing with the conceptual issues of the frame, by José Ortega y Gasset); *Cadres de peintres* (Paris, Mus. d'Orsay, 1989) focuses on the integrity of 19th- and 20th-century artist-designed frames, a theme

that is developed by the catalogue *In Perfect Harmony* (Amsterdam, Rijksmus. van Gogh, 1995); and *Italian Renaissance Frames* (1990) is an in-depth catalogue of the frames and framemakers of the Renaissance paintings in the Lehman collection at the Metropolitan Museum of Art, New York. *The Art of the Picture Frame* (London, N.P.G., 1996) examines the portrait frame as it is affected by the input of patron, artist and framemaker; while *Frameworks* (London, Paul Mitchell, 1996), running in tandem with the National Portrait Gallery exhibition, analyses the frame within its larger setting. Permanent displays are far less common. The only museums showing (empty) frames as works of art have been the Musée des Arts Décoratifs, Paris, and the Dallas Museum of Art (Reves Collection), TX, both of which concentrate on 17th- and 18th-century French frames. Since 1995 these have been joined—and surpassed—by a private collection of 240 European frames donated to the Art Gallery of Ontario, Toronto (see fig. 1 above). This displays four centuries of the highest quality design and craftsmanship, and will become a focal centre for the study of frames. Alongside these institutional landmarks have appeared Mendgen's book (1991) and an increasing volume of specialized individual studies in leading art and museum journals, indicating the enormous depth of the subject's potential. An entire issue of the *Revue de l'art* (no. 76, 1987) was devoted to a stimulating overview of all the main contributions to frames, together with nine specialist articles and a comprehensive, indispensable bibliography. Two examples of frame studies being integrated with art-historical texts for the first time are the descriptive appraisal of frames in the picture guide of the Thyssen–Bornemisza collection (1989) and the essay on frames within an artist's monographic exhibition catalogue (*Wright of Derby*; London, Tate, 1990).

BIBLIOGRAPHY

H. Harvard: 'Cadre', *Dictionnaire de l'ameublement et de la décoration,* i (Paris, 1887), i, pp. 510–15
M. Guggenheim: *Le cornici italiane dalla meta del secolo XV allo scorio del XVI* (Milan, 1897)
W. von Bode: 'Bilderrahmen in alter und neuer Zeit', *Pan,* iv (1898–9), pp. 243–56
R. Thorel: *De l'influence du cadre dans les oeuvres d'art* (Paris, 1904)
F. Feneon: 'Les Cadres', *Bull. Vie A.* (Feb 1922)
W. Ayrshire: 'The Philosophy of the Picture Frame', *Int. Studio* (June 1926)
S. Roche: *Cadres français et étrangers du XVe siècle au XVIIIe siècle* (Paris, 1931)
F. S. Meyer: *A Handbook of Ornament* (Chicago, 1945)
J. White: *The Birth and Rebirth of Pictorial Space* (London, 1957)
A. Strange and L. Cremer: *Alte Bilderrahmen* (Darmstadt, 1958) [25 figs]
H. Heydenryk: *The Art and History of Frames* (New York, 1963) [100 figs]
M. Shapiro: 'On Some Problems in the Semiotics of Visual Art: Field and Vehicle in Image Signs', *Semiotica,* i (1969), pp. 223–42
P. Thornton and W. Reider: 'Pierre Langlois, ebéniste', *Connoisseur,* clxxviii/718 (1971), pp. 283–8; clxxix/720 (1972), pp. 105–12
J. Gloag: *Guide to Furniture Styles: English & French, 1450–1850* (London, 1972)
C. Grimm: *Alte Bilderrahmen: Epochen–Typen–Material* (Munich, 1978) [extensive bibliog.; 483 figs]; Eng. trans. as *The Book of Picture Frames* (New York, 1981) [with suppl. on American frames by G. Szabo; 30 figs, 489 pls] [G]
P. Thornton: *Seventeenth-century Interior Decoration in England, France and Holland* (New Haven and London, 1978)
W. Ehlich: *Bilderrahmen von der Antike bis zur Romantik* (Dresden, 1979)
G. Lacambre: 'Cadre', *Petit Larousse de la peinture* (Paris, 1979), pp. 258–60

P. Mitchell: 'The Framing Tradition', *Picture Framing*, ed. R. Wright-Smith (London, 1980), pp. 12–32 [9 colour pls]

T. Clifford: 'The Historical Approach to the Display of Paintings', *Int. J. Mus. Mgmt & Cur.*, i (1982), pp. 93–106

F. G. Conzen and G. Dietrich: *Bilderrahmen: Stil–Verwendung–Material* (Munich, 1983)

P. Cannon-Brookes: 'Picture Framing: A Neglected Art', *NACF Rev.* (1984), pp. 84–93 [12 figs]

S. Jervis: *The Penguin Dictionary of Design and Designers* (Harmondsworth, 1984)

P. Thornton: *Authentic Décor: The Domestic Interior, 1620–1920* (London, 1984)

S. E. Fuchs: *Der Bilderrahmen* (Recklinghausen, 1985) [146 figs]

P. Lewis and G. Darley: *Dictionary of Ornament* (London, 1986)

The Art of the Edge: European Frames, 1300–1900 (exh. cat., Chicago, IL, A. Inst., 1986) [incl. J. Ortega y Gasset: 'Meditations on the Frame', p. 21]

Rev. A., 76 (1987) [whole issue devoted to frames]

C. de Watteville: *Guide to the Exhibited Works in the Thyssen–Bornemisza Collection* (Lugano and Milan, 1989) [cat. entries on frames by P. Mitchell and L. Roberts, pp. 365–71]

Wright of Derby (exh. cat., London, Tate, 1990) [with essay on frames by P. Mitchell]

E. Mendgen: *Künstler rahmen ihre Bilder: Zur Geschichte des Bilderrahmens zwischen Akademie und Sezession* (Konstanz, 1991)

In Perfect Harmony: Picture and Frame, 1850–1920 (exh. cat., Amsterdam, Rijksmus. van Gogh, 1995)

The Art of the Picture Frame: Artists, Patrons and the Framing of Portraits in Britain (exh. cat., London, N.P.G., 1996)

Frameworks (exh. cat., London, Paul Mitchell, 1996)

II. Italy.

1. Precursors. 2. Pre-Renaissance. 3. Renaissance. 4. Mannerist. 5. Baroque. 6. Rococo. 7. Neo-classical and Empire. 8. 19th and 20th centuries.

1. PRECURSORS. The earliest decorative borders used in Italy to enclose paintings are probably those on Etruscan wall paintings (7th–2nd centuries BC). Though obviously not picture frames in the modern sense of a three-dimensional protective edging, they employ many of the motifs of Classical Greek architecture and vases as a setting for figurative scenes. Roman art was influenced equally by these Etruscan and Greek works; it also developed the Etruscan style of funerary portraiture, where the painting is 'framed' in architectural ornament. Other early types of border include those around mosaics and, later, the coarsened antique decoration of manuscript paintings. Panel painting—in the Byzantine tradition—was also well established in Italy as early as the 5th century AD, leading to the Western genre of altarpieces and also to the production of painted Crucifixes, the earliest of which is dated 1138. The latter were intended to ornament rood screens, to be hung from church ceilings or to be set on an altar, and they were invariably edged with a simple moulding, such as a taenia and an ogee or ovolo. From such decorative additions to the altar table came the paintings known as antependia or altar frontals. These are related to the carved sides of Roman sarcophagi with their Classical enrichments, as are metalwork frontals, such as the 11th-century Antependium of Basle with its scrolled foliate border and its architectural divisions. In these cases the work hardly counts as an independent, framed picture, but at the beginning of the 13th century the frontal was moved on to the top of the altar to become a dossal or free-standing retable, its frame gaining both decorative

and symbolic significance, and greater protective importance. Ensembles of both dossal and frontal exist, providing a large didactic area, which is unified by the decorative borders of each element.

The original method of framing panel paintings or early altarpieces was limited to gouging out a lowered painting surface within a traylike raised ledge. The surface of these remaining borders or engaged frames—often a painted or gilt band in the case of icons—gave an opportunity to apply the long tradition of sculpted and drawn ornament, already familiar through ivory and architectural carving, weaving, wall and manuscript painting, goldsmithing and mosaic. Punched and low-relief decoration was prevalent: a Sienese altarpiece of 1215, consisting of three tiered scenes on either side of a large *Christ in Glory* (Siena, Pin. N.), uses continuous runs of a star or daisy pattern, filling the whole width of each framing or separating band. A similar work by Margarito d'Arezzo, *Virgin and Child, Angels, Saints and Scenes from the Lives of SS John the Evangelist, Benedict, Catherine and Margaret* (mid-13th century; London, N.G.), has a deep outer gilt frame, ornamented with round bosses along its forward edges. Though Vasari credited Margarito with inventing these, they appear on other early frames and door-frames and are an antique device. Both bosses and daisies show an inventive use of gilded ornament some time before the appearance of complicated carved mouldings, as does the technique of *sgraffito*, applied to the overpainted flat surfaces of a frame to scratch out delicate arabesques and inscriptions from the gold beneath (e.g. Coppo di Marcovaldo: *Madonna del Bordone*, 1261; Siena, S Maria dei Servi).

2. PRE-RENAISSANCE. These first abstract, rectangular frames, closely related to Renaissance frames and their modern descendants, were soon overtaken by those with symbolic elements derived from architecture. The silhouette of the basilica, for example, with its gabled front shaped like an irregular pentagon, was imitated by some 13th-century altarpieces. The earliest dated version appeared in 1235, and examples were produced in the later 13th century by Duccio, Cimabue (*Virgin and Child*; Paris, Louvre) and Pacino di Bonaguida (the *Tree of Life*; Florence, Accad.). The borders of these gabled works follow the panel shape and are composed of variously complex flat, beaded and stepped mouldings fixed to the panels. They are gilt and polychrome, with elaborate panels of painted and *sgraffito* decoration on the flats; on the works by Duccio and Cimabue these are replaced with painted heads of prophets and saints inside roundels. Thus, painted visions of heaven were framed in representations of the spiritual Church, of which its earthly stone counterpart was a reflection. Gothic architecture, which made a later and less intense impact in Italy, was first reflected in art in these simple gabled frames.

The plain silhouette was elaborated within by trefoils, pointed arches or round arcading above rows of figures, as in Guido da Siena's *Virgin and Child Flanked by SS John the Baptist, John the Evangelist, Mary Magdalene and Francis* (1270s; Siena, Pin. N.) and *Madonna and Child Enthroned* (1275–80; Siena, Pal. Pub.). The arcading of the former is pierced beneath the gable by painted roundels, like rose windows; the gable of the latter rises in a pediment above the main panel and contains a representation of Christ as Judge. Both can be related to the Gothic façade (begun after 1215) of Siena Cathedral. Portable devotional pictures were being produced alongside such large altarpieces, for example the Magdalen Master's *Virgin and Child Enthroned with SS Peter and Paul* (*c.* 1265–70; New York, Met) and the *Crucifixion with SS Nicolas and Gregory* (*c.* 1310; Boston, MA, Mus. F.A.), attributed to Duccio, both of which are in the form of a triptych where two hinged panels fold across the main scene, like church doors giving access to a celestial world. The first is based on rectangular forms beneath a lintel; the second has segmental doors folding into the round arch of the Crucifixion scene, above which the peaked gable holds a *Christus Benedictus*. In a further development, Giotto's Badia Altarpiece (Florence, Mus. Opera Santa Croce) shows a large compartmentalized altarpiece, where the divisions echo the aisles and nave of a cathedral, separated by architectural piers, and pinnacles (untraced) rise between the five gables.

A final stage in the evolution of these altarpieces into images of the Church came with the building of the frame into a storeyed polyptych. At first there were two levels, representing the body and clerestory of the church, as in Pseudo-Jacopino's polyptych with the *Presentation of Christ in the Temple* (*c.* 1350–80; Bologna, Mus. Civ.). Here, a *Pietà* rises above the main scene, and there are two layers of saints. Next, the predella at the base, originating in the roundels and inscriptions of Giotto's altarpieces, was used to represent the 'crypt' of the church. The predella panels are embodied in the plinth supporting the major elements of the altarpiece and usually stand forward of these. As in architectural and sculptural plinths, they can be used for inscriptions, or for small-scale paintings (e.g. scenes from the life of a saint) fitting naturally beneath the vertical divisions of the upper scenes and framed by the pedestals of their pilasters and by the base and cornice of the plinth.

In the *Virgin and Child with Saints* (*c.* 1330; Bologna, Pin. N.) by Giotto's assistants, the painted architecture of the Virgin's throne reproduces the carved wooden frame, with its decorative crockets and square piers, and the interdependence of frame and painting is suddenly illuminated. This interdependence is also emphasized by the multiplying of levels in the more complex 14th-century polyptychs into a hierarchical arrangement of tiered saints and prophets, scenes from Christ's and the saints' lives, and pinnacled angels rising up and around a major scene (e.g. of the Virgin, the Coronation of the Virgin or the Crucifixion), to the highest image (of God the Father, Christ as Judge, Christ Blessing), as in Simone Martini's *St Catherine* polyptych (1319–20; Pisa, Mus. N. S Matteo). The spiritual world and the physical church, with its chapels, crypt and clerestory, were thus simultaneously represented.

The main outer frame, unbroken in 13th-century altarpieces, was fragmented in the 14th century into sloping-shouldered panels (bearing further panels above), ogee-arched and triangular gables, the vertical divisions hidden by thin Solomonic columns, the inner arches decorated with pendent fretted traceries (e.g. Niccolò di Pietro

Gerini, Spinello Aretino and Lorenzo di Niccolò's *Canonization of the Virgin*, Florence, Accad.). These altars are in the High Gothic idiom, which is architecturally far more northern European than Italian; yet they were developed, most importantly perhaps in Siena and Florence, by Italian craftsmen who worked closely with the painters, were paid sums that were a large proportion of (and could equal and even surpass) the cost of the picture and were sometimes commemorated by inscriptions on the altarpiece itself, their reputation and influence feeding back into the development of the northern European polyptych (see Gilbert, 1977).

In the 14th century and the early 15th polyptychs became so vast and elaborate that, at an early point, huge lateral buttresses were developed to support them and give additional emphasis. These were bolted on to the altar, but where the paintings have been removed in later periods through theft or sale, the buttresses have been lost, their clusters of pinnacles and abstract 'mosaic' decoration not valued equally with the pictures. Exceptions are Giovanni del Biondo's Rinuccini Altarpiece (1379; Florence, Santa Croce) and Taddeo di Bartolo's *Virgin and Child* (Volterra, Pin. Com.; see fig. 4), both ornate many-tiered polyptychs with decorative columns and pilasters hiding both the division between the painted panels and the physical joints of the planks forming the altar. These applied ornaments, like the arch traceries added after painting, show a shift in constructional processes, the earliest altarpieces having been painted only after all woodwork and gilding had been completed. Another work retaining its buttresses is Andrea di Cione's earlier Strozzi Altarpiece (1354–7; Florence, S Maria Novella), which is

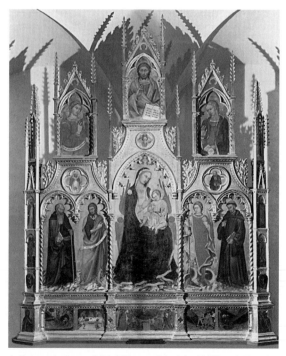

4. Polyptych frame, 3.26×2.71 m, original for Taddeo di Bartolo's *Virgin and Child*, 1411 (Volterra, Pinacoteca Comunale)

5. Engaged frame, 614×434 mm, original for Simone Martini's *Christ Discovered in the Temple*, 1342 (Liverpool, Walker Art Gallery)

important in that it shows the cell-like format of Biondo's altarpieces being swallowed by the expansion of the major scene into a single painted image. This prefigures the physically and metaphysically unified painting of the mid-Renaissance and indicates a move in the construction of the frame (which was now falling behind architectural development in Italy) towards the single containing frame of the 15th century.

The pure Gothic architectural frame, however, endured as late as the 1470s, as seen in the Venetian High Gothic altarpieces of Antonio Vivarini and Bartolomeo Vivarini (e.g. Venice, Accad.; Bologna, Pin. N.; *see* 1990 exh. cat., no. 10). These are works of striking flamboyance and intricacy, refining examples of the 14th century and the earlier 15th by the Veneziani and the Murani. Influenced by the Muslim objects entering Venice, Venetian metal-work and the filtering down to north Italy of the Northern High Gothic style, they turn the settings of the actual paintings into shimmering incrustations of pierced and undercut filigree. Conversely, plainer rectangular frames continued to appear alongside the soaring storeys and ornamental accretions of the major polyptychs, for example the large portable altarpiece of the *Virgin and Four Saints*, its five framed rectangular panels (1333–44; New York, Met.; Malibu, CA, Getty Mus.; priv. col.) attributed to Simone Martini and assistants. The frames, only one of which is an untouched original, consist of a flat painted with delicate arabesques and lozenges between stepped mouldings, united with the gold picture surface by a punched border. Here the protective role of the frame is most evident: a polyptych, originally over 2 m across and needing to be transported between various religious houses, required a setting that was both functional and decorative rather than a fragile fantasy of crockets and pinnacles.

Single rectangular panels also exist from an early period as independent works, looking towards the large 15th-century *quadro* and its aedicular or its *cassetta* frame (see §§3), for example Simone Martini's *Christ Discovered in the Temple* (1342; Liverpool, Walker A.G.; see fig. 5). Such panels might exist independently or as elements of small triptychs or diptychs, and while the panel might be elaborated with cusped and trefoiled arches, the frame might also be richly ornamented. On Paolo di Giovanni Fei's *Virgin and Child with Angels, Saints and Eve* (c. 1380–90; New York, Met.), the flat of the frame is decorated using the technique of *aggetti* (a compound of gesso pressed into a mould) or pastiglia with foliate scrolls and florets defined by punching, and inset polished glass cabochons. Within the frame, the picture surface is ornamented with a cusped arch, twisted colonnette and spandrel medallions painted with Gabriel and the Virgin Annunciate. A similar frame on Fei's *Virgin Suckling the Infant Christ* (New York, Met.) has additional inset plaques of *verre églomisé* decorated with heads, derived from the painted frame of Duccio's Rucellai *Madonna* (*see* DUCCIO, fig. 1).

3. RENAISSANCE.

(i) Early Renaissance. (ii) Aedicular frames. (iii) Craftsmen and workshops. (iv) *Cassetta* frames. (v) Tondo frames. (vi) Compound profile frames.

(i) Early Renaissance. The *quadro all'antica* proper—a rectangular picture in a classically inspired frame—had its first major expression in the work of Fra Angelico, who developed the *sacra conversazione* from its beginnings in Andrea di Cione's Strozzi Altarpiece, for example in the *Annunciation* (c. 1432; Cortona, Mus. Dioc.). The evolution of a single scene appearing to exist in 'real' time and 'real' space is thus intimately linked with the evolution of the frame as a 'window' on to that scene, rather than as a symbolic representation of the House of God with its many mansions. It is also linked to Brunelleschi's revival of Classical architecture and to the parallel development in painting of a Brunelleschian system of perspective, where the illusory pictorial space appears continuous with that of the 'real' world. The mediator between such a painted world and the spectator could no longer be the emblematic traceries of a Gothic frame, especially within the new classicizing buildings themselves, and so the aedicular frame was adopted, based on the Greek temple. In such early examples as Bicci di Lorenzo's *Annunciation* (Baltimore, MD, Walters A.G.), the frame of the *quadro* hesitates between the Gothic and Classical, but in the mature version the form is as described by Neri di Bicci (*see* §I, 2 above), with predella, pilasters and entablature. Interestingly, the influential fresco of the *Trinity* (1427) by Masaccio in S Maria Novella, Florence, with its perspectival recession based on the spectator's eye-level—the picture space appearing a continuation of 'real' space—uses Brunelleschian architectural forms to articulate the space and to frame the whole. (Brunelleschi may actually have designed this setting.)

The importance of 15th-century classically inspired sculptures and funerary monuments to the work of the framemaker should be stressed, and their influence is evident in a terracotta tabernacle frame of *c.* 1430–40 (see 1990 exh. cat., no. 6). Although frames were no longer engaged with the picture, tending towards an analogous separation of painter and wood-carver into artist and artisan, Renaissance artists were frequently polymaths capable of undertaking sculptural, painting and architectural projects, with a consequent overlapping of genres. Many trained as goldsmiths (Antonio Pollaiuolo, Andrea del Verrocchio, Brunelleschi) and had an intimate knowledge of decorative settings and ornamental fashions; while important sculptors and architects (Benedetto da Maiano, Giuliano da Maiano, Antonio di Ciaccheri Manetti, Giuliano da Sangallo) were also wood-carvers, designing and producing frames in their workshops for the foremost Renaissance painters, as well as the interiors in which the frames would hang. Equally the painter himself needed the ability to produce contractual drawings for both picture and frame if his client preferred to contract the whole work through him rather than the wood-worker.

The provenance of frame designs in the 14th and 15th centuries is obscure: there are cases where the patron obtained the wooden panel/frame (the *tavola*) from a wood-carver and would then contract an artist to paint it, the gap between operations allowing funds for the painting to be gathered; hence the altarpiece for S Francesco, Borgo San Sepulchro, was acquired from Bartolomeo the carpenter four years before Antonio da Anghiari was contracted to paint it in 1430 (see Gilbert, 1977). The wood-worker presumably designed the whole structure himself (or followed the client's rough sketch, or copied a pre-existing work). Alternatively, the wood-worker might be given a model; Jacopo Papero, for example, made the inner wooden frame for the *Madonna dei Linaiuoli* (Florence, Uffizi) after a model (1432) by Ghiberti. Fra Angelico then painted the image, and the next month Simone de Nanni Ferrucci (1402–69) was commissioned to carve the outer marble tabernacle, again after Ghiberti. The painter himself might commission the panel from his favoured wood-worker, as Neri di Bicci obtained his *tavole all'antica* from Giuliano da Maiano. Presumably, he supplied his own drawing for the frame, although Giuliano himself was of sufficient stature to undertake (as an artist would a picture) the whole design from a written specification. Again, the client might approach artist and wood-worker individually and draw up simultaneous contracts, probably requiring from the artist a preliminary design for the whole work, from which the wood-worker would copy the frame. Peramore di Bartolomeo undertook to make an altarpiece 'after the design given to him' the same day that Lorenzo Lotto agreed to paint it (as for the *Entombment, c.* 1512; Jesi, Pin. Civ.), Lotto being accustomed to providing such drawings of frames (see L. C. Matthew: 'New Evidence for Lotto's Career in Jesi', *Burl. Mag.*, cxxx (1988), pp. 693–7).

The move from engaged Gothic frame, constructed as one with the panel before gilding and painting began, to movable classical frame meant that control of the design generally passed from the wood-worker to the painter. More drawings of frames survive from this time, including those by such artists as Filippo Lippi, Vittore Carpaccio and Giovanni da Udine. The designs for the superb Venetian aedicular frames of Giovanni Bellini's Frari Triptych (Venice, S Maria Gloriosa dei Frari; see fig. 6) and Mantegna's *Virgin and Child with Saints* (1457–9; Verona, S Zeno) are attributed to the artists themselves. Both have used this control over the whole work to integrate its painted and carved architectural structures, as in Masaccio's *Trinity*, creating the illusion of the 'real' presence of heavenly visitants before the worshipper.

These two frames exhibit regional features in their construction and ornament. Even the earliest altarpieces display differing characteristics according to their place of origin—Sienese Gothic polyptychs tend to have truncated triangular tiers and inner depressed arches, Florentine altarpieces have elongated trefoil/pointed arches and more frequent painted roundels, and Bolognese frames are elaborate, with chunkier carving. The later aediculae and 16th- to 18th-century *cassetta* frames descended from them show these diversities too, but the continual movement of workers nationally means that, unless a painting framed by a local artisan and/or painted by a local artist has remained within the region or has a documented provenance for its frame, specific features cannot definitely be accredited to that region. However, certain points may be made, particularly regarding Venetian frames, notable from the 14th century for their richness, fineness of detail and the Moorish influence displayed in their use of pierced roundels and tracery. From the altarpieces (1320s–50s; Venice, Accad.) of Paolo Veneziano and Lorenzo Veneziano, encrusted with ornament and using blue and gilt

6. Aedicular frame made by Jacopo da Faenza, 1488, centre panel 1.84×0.79 m, original for Giovanni Bellini's Frari Triptych, 1488 (Venice, S Maria Gloriosa dei Frari)

shell-domed niches, through the polyptychs (e.g. 1443–4; Venice, S Zaccaria) of the Murano brothers, carved by Lodovico da Forlì, to the Late Gothic confections (1450s–70s) of the Vivarinis, decoration increasingly runs riot in a crescendo of lacework, fretted pinnacles, crockets carved into minute leaf sprays and overhanging pierced canopies.

(ii) Aedicular frames. With the flowering of Renaissance architecture and interior decoration, the picture frame took on a fully classical form. For altarpieces and devotional paintings this was the aedicula or tabernacle frame, for secular works the corresponding *cassetta*. As regional styles of structure and ornamentation modified each of these groups, a seemingly endless variety of frame patterns evolved; these multiplied as the language of the Renaissance was overtaken by that of Mannerism. This enormous productivity is in itself proof of the immense importance attached to the function and creation of frames during the Renaissance.

A celebrated example of the Renaissance aedicular frame, signed and dated 1488 by the carver Jacopo da Faenza, was created for Bellini's Frari Triptych (see fig. 6). This comprises a base with predella panels supporting two pairs of pilasters, each pair carrying an entablature linked by a broken segmental pediment, the whole carved with antique candelabrum patterns and scrolling foliage. Above

this are mounted actual candelabra between Roman sirens (functional candle-holders became a necessary part of the frame as the amount of gold leaf on the picture surface shrank: with gilding restricted to details of robes and haloes and then just to the frame itself, extra sources of light were needed to reveal the image). This repetition of motif, and of the frame's structure in the painted architecture, mean that frame and image are completely integrated. Aedicular frames were also used from the mid-15th century for the display of single panel altarpieces and smaller devotional works (see 1990 exh. cat.). As well as the façade of a Classical temple, the frame for Sano di Pietro's altarpiece, the *Virgin and Child with SS Mary Magdalene, James, Philip and Anne* (completed 1462; Pienza Cathedral), reflects that of Pienza Cathedral, for which it was commissioned. Its fluted pilasters support a triangular pediment, the tympanum decorated with the figure of Christ gazing on the Virgin and saints below. Also in Pienza Cathedral are late 15th-century works by Matteo di Giovanni and Giovanni di Paolo with segmental pediments, again on fluted pilasters.

A typical Venetian aedicula (see fig. 7a) in the same idiom as the Frari Triptych has low-relief pastiglia decoration on a punched ground, including foliate candelabra in the pilasters, and masks, dolphins and birds in the

7. Italian Renaissance aedicular frames: (a) Venetian frame with pastiglia decoration, opening 724×914 mm, original for Girolamo da Santacroce's *Virgin and Child with SS Augustine and Peter, c.* 1512 (Philadelphia, PA, Museum of Art); (b) Tuscan frame in parcel gilt walnut, opening 1943×1656 mm, probably original for Giuliano Bugiardini's *Virgin and St Mary Magdalene with St John the Baptist, c.* 1540 (New York, Metropolitan Museum of Art); (c) north Italian frame with fluted Corinthian columns, opening 1391×1168 mm, contemporary for Mantegna's *Virgin and Child with SS Mary Magdalene and John the Baptist, c.* 1490s (London, National Gallery)

predella frieze. Variations on pilasters and columns can be seen on the small devotional works by Bellini at Harewood House, W. Yorks, and there is another characteristically Venetian type (pastiglia decoration on a blue-black ground) on paintings also by Bellini in the Accademia di Belle Arti di Brera, Milan.

Aedicular frames in Tuscany reflect the region's more austere architectural style. Some carried low-relief antique ornament, others were in parcel gilt walnut or with grotesque decoration (7b) applied in gold to a *faux* walnut surface. Perhaps the most sumptuous surviving example in the Tuscan style—the design is attributed to the architect Giuliano da Sangallo—surrounds Domenico Ghirlandaio's *Adoration of the Shepherds* (1485; Florence, Santa Trìnita; *see* GHIRLANDAIO, (1), fig. 2); the artist's setting includes a corresponding triumphal arch and canopy with fluted pilasters. Columns were also used (7c), as noted above; this was more common in northern Italy and often echoed the pictorial architecture. Smaller aedicula from the Veneto sometimes used the distinctive twisted Solomonic column.

(iii) Craftsmen and workshops. The great altarpieces of the 14th to the 16th century were produced by famous carvers and sculptors who founded schools of craftsmen—in their workshops or indirectly—who propagated their styles in simpler types of frame. Some of these are known by name. The three men who created the Monte Oliveto Altarpiece (1384–5; Florence, Accad.) are commemorated equally on it: Aretino the painter, Cini the carver, Saracini the gilder; whereas in the case of Fra Angelico's *Madonna dei Linaiuoli*, the framemakers were subordinate, following designs by a prominent architect (see Gilbert). Titian's *Assumption of the Virgin* (Venice, Frari) was commissioned after the completion (1516) of its great marble aedicula by the master sculptor Lorenzo Bregno; Titian's work therefore—like a 13th-century panel painting—had to conform to a pre-existing frame. The painter Francesco Francia (a goldsmith and son of a wood-worker) designed aedicular frames for his work in the style of the Bolognese High Renaissance—with finely carved dense arabesques in parcel gilt on a dark ground—magnificently realized by the great wood-carver Andrea da Formigine (*c.* 1480–1559) (e.g. Francia's *Christ Enthroned and St Michael Subduing the Devil*; Bologna, S Domenico). The architect Manetti, even when promoted to *capomaestro* of Florence Cathedral, accepted the commission to frame Pesellino's altarpiece, the *Trinity with Saints* (London, N.G.); and Leonardo, when painting the *Virgin of the Rocks* (1480s; Paris, Louvre; two side panels by the brothers Giovanni Ambrogio de Predis and Evangelista de Predis), undertook himself to gild and colour the frame, which had been carved by Giacomo del Maiano.

Little differentiation was made between the 'fine art' of the painting and the 'applied art' of the frame: great men of whatever specialization seemed willing to design, carve or gild the precious settings for important works. Late in their lives, the successful sculptors and architects Giuliano da Maiano and Giuliano da Sangallo still undertook commissions for frames, the quality of which (e.g. Maiano's for Botticelli) indicates that these were not necessarily workshop products. Regarding secular items Vasari notes

that 'even the most excellent painters employed themselves. . .in painting and gilding. . .chests. . .beds, the backs of chairs, the frames and other ornaments of the rooms' (*Vite*, 1550, rev. 2/1568). The history and ornamentation of frames is thus intimately connected with the evolution of pictorial art, as it is with that of other furnishings; long panels painted by such artists as Piero della Francesca, let into the sides of cassoni between enriched mouldings, can equally be seen to stimulate or to derive from larger wall-hung paintings in similar mouldings. Likewise, picture and frame might become part of a complete decorative scheme. The bridal furnishings of the Casa Vecchia, Florence, possibly commissioned (1481) by Lorenzo the Magnificent for his ward Lorenzo di Pierfrancesco de' Medici, consisted in one room of pine furniture, a white-covered bed and a white wood frame around Botticelli's *Primavera* (*c.* 1478; Florence, Uffizi; see Foster and Tudor-Craig).

(iv) Cassetta frames. For the vast and increasing output of secular paintings, simpler rectangular frames were produced, the patterns and decoration of which were clearly

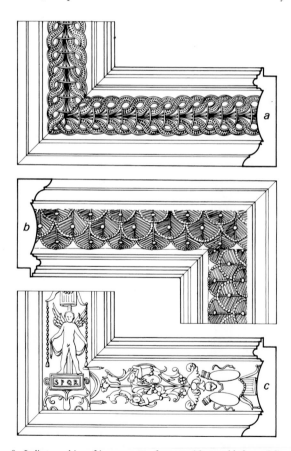

8. Italian cushion frieze *cassetta* frames with moulded pastiglia decoration, from the Veneto, late 15th century to mid-16th: (a) double guilloche pattern, contemporary for *Federigo II, Duke of Urbino*, school of the Marches (Florence, Museo Horne); (b) imbricated feather pattern, 380×305×88 mm, on Hans Schäufelein the elder's *Portrait of a Man*, 1507 (Washington, DC, National Gallery of Art); (c) grotesque pattern, 546×707×110 mm, contemporary for Mantegna's *Adoration of the Magi, c.* 1495–1505 (Malibu, CA, J. Paul Getty Museum)

9. Italian *cassetta* frames with continuous surface decoration, mid-16th century to mid-17th: (a) Roman plain gilt gallery frame, 910×1230×133 mm, early 17th century, original for Giovanni Girolamo Savoldo's *Lady with a Dragon Fur*, *c.* 1524–40 (Rome, Pinacoteca Capitolina); (b) marbled frieze, scrolled leaf-and-husk mouldings, 1330×1550×215 mm, adapted for Orazio Gentileschi's *Martha Reproving her Sister Mary*, *c.* 1520 (Munich, Alte Pinakothek); (c) gilt arabesque ornament in *sgraffito* on dark blue tempera, 711×2032×150 mm, mid-16th century, adapted for Piero di Cosimo's *Forest Fire*, 1488–1513 (Oxford, Ashmolean Museum); (d) engraved foliage on hazzled ground with ribbon moulding, 629×495×127 mm, late 16th century–early 17th, on Giovanni Bellini's *St Dominic*, *c.* 1515 (London, National Gallery); (e) Bolognese 'Albani' style frame with stylized flowers and foliage in punchwork, half-flowers and bay leaves, 368×444×100 mm, contemporary for Guercino's *Angels Weeping over the Dead Christ*, *c.* 1618 (London, National Gallery); (f) reverse profile frame with stylized leaf sight, 1676×1638×176 mm, early 17th century, adapted for Giovanni Cariani's *Seamstress Madonna*, 1524–8 (Rome, Palazzo Barberini); (g) ?Tuscan or Venetian frame with palmette and flower scrollwork in pastiglia on a punched ground, beaded and fluted mouldings, 1410×1080×167 mm, late 16th century–early 17th, adapted for Andrea del Sarto's *Holy Family*, 1515–16 (Paris, Musée du Louvre)

derived from contemporary altarpieces. The process of structural simplification that took place resulted in the disappearance of the pilasters, pediment and base of the altarpiece, leaving a simplified entablature profile, a decorated frieze between narrow mouldings. This became known as the *cassetta* frame, the basic theme, with infinite variations, of most 16th- and 17th-century Italian frame patterns. The *cassetta* itself is already present in some tabernacles as the surrounding inner frame (see fig. 7a). The intermediary phase consisted of an entablature minus the frieze—a combined cornice and architrave—to sit above a continuous decorated symmetrical frieze with

moulded borders, as on Bartolomeo Montagna's *Virgin and Child* (Worcester, MA, A. Mus.).

The *cassetta* frame was not so much a new development as a return to much older forms—the architectural borders of Classical doors and windows, the painted margins of frescoes, the decorative frames of manuscript illuminations—elaborated by Renaissance interest in ornament and varied by local virtuoso carvers. The section and borders of the *cassetta* or entablature frame were primarily architectural. Its frieze often echoing the decoration of an interior, the entire form was designed as a sophisticated play on the style and ornamentation of its intended setting. Regional variations were an obvious effect not only of the stylistic dialect of the craftsmen employed but also of the architectural vocabulary of the interior where the frame was to hang. The fact that the establishment of the locale and period of each pattern is speculative should be remembered in the following summary of stylistic, regional and chronological features.

The main *cassetta* patterns may most easily be charted by treating their continuous development over the 16th and 17th centuries before returning to the other principal concurrent frame styles of this period. The appearance of the *cassetta* frame is determined by two main factors: ornamental technique and finish, and the distribution of decoration. Although partially overlapping and not necessarily chronological, these characteristics may be divided into three groups: continuous surface decoration, with or without carved borders (see figs 8 and 9), 'Baroque' *cassettas* with corner and centre arabesques (see fig. 10) and fully architectural designs (see fig. 11). With few exceptions *cassetta* frames share the same underlying structure: a half-lapped back frame to which are applied mitred inner and outer mouldings. The decorative treatment of these mouldings and the frieze was endlessly varied according to region, function and cost.

Visually, the ancestor of the modern entablature frame in its basic oblong form is that type (late 13th century–14th) seen on Fei's work decorated in pastiglia (see §2 above). This was often engaged with the painted panel, however, and the earliest true movable *cassetta* appeared in the early 16th century in the Veneto, this being probably the first example of a mass-produced frame style (see fig. 8). The structure consists of a shallow convex frieze bordered by plain mouldings laminated on a flat back frame. Ornamental designs were applied to the frieze in thin strips of *aggetti*. These were usually cast in lengths between 125 and 150 mm, carefully joined to give a continuous pattern. The finish was all gilt or with the moulded section in polychrome. Of eight recorded patterns, three were most common, all deriving from antique Roman and earlier sources. The double guilloche (8a) was purely architectural, employed in Roman mosaic borders and in the decoration of ceilings (which often echo picture frames), pilasters, arches and such furnishings as cassoni. Layers of overlapping palm scales (8b) and Roman grotesque panels with winged putti, candelabra and SPQR tablets (8c) were also used. Others include undulating vines and trailing oak leaves with acorns. Intricately carved moulds facilitated the easy production of these low-relief

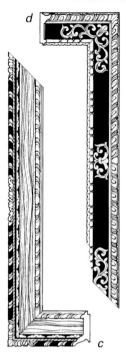

10. Italian *cassetta* frames with corner and centre surface and carved decoration, mid-16th century to mid-17th: (a) Tuscan reverse *cassetta* frame with gilt arabesques on black, striped convex sight moulding, 1080×1441×200 mm, mid-17th century, on Mattia Preti's *Draughts Players*, ?early 1630s (Oxford, Ashmolean Museum); (b) Florentine frame with carved gilt scrolled ornaments on red ground, beaded and fluted mouldings, 1110×1370×170 mm, late 16th century–early 17th, on Titian's *Virgin and Child with Saints*, *c.* 1503–10 (Paris, Musée du Louvre); (c) Tuscan parcel gilt frame with walnut frieze and gadrooned mouldings, 920×780×143 mm, contemporary for Titian's *St Dominic*, *c.* 1568 (Rome, Galleria Borghese); (d) Neapolitan or Tuscan frame with carved gilt scrolled ornaments on dark *faux-marbre* ground, raked stop-fluting, 1216×984×135 mm, contemporary for Ribera's *Philosopher*, *c.* 1637 (Hartford, CT, Wadsworth Atheneum)

surface decorations appropriate for small-scale works. Geometric ornaments were used for the secular portraits and mythological or allegorical subjects of the Renaissance, differentiating them from the aedicular shapes and often symbolic or naturalistic motifs associated with religious images. The purest form of *cassetta* with plain mouldings, all gilded, and found in Rome and Tuscany during the 16th and 17th centuries, was often employed as a 'gallery' frame—a streamlined, cost-effective pattern for framing whole groups of a collection, as at the Capitoline (9a) and Spada galleries, Rome. The *cassetta* frieze could also be painted to simulate marble and harmonize with a marble interior. *Faux-marbre* (9b) was more economical than gilding and a contrast to carved and gilt borders, as well as reinforcing the tonality of work painted in a chiaroscuro style.

The most elaborate and eye-catching surfaces were achieved by the application of Moresque and, later, arabesque ornament in *sgraffito* and mordant-gilt techniques (9c). Examples appeared throughout Italy, notably in the Veneto, the Marches and Tuscany. They derive from

painted borders—on illuminated manuscripts, on early engaged frames and even on the façades of Renaissance buildings, such as the Museo Horne and the Palazzo Medici–Riccardi (both Florence). The scrolling decoration was generally continuous in the 16th century but placed at corners and centres in the 17th (10a). Vertebrate candelabrum-based patterns were also used, springing from bottom centre to top centre of the frame. These designs were achieved in *sgraffito* by painting a layer of black or blue-black tempera (sometimes with other colours in combination) over the gilded frieze and scraping this away to reveal the design in gold. Such frames were an enduring and widely diffused type, involving finishes of extreme sophistication, which were allied to contemporary lacework and often based on the pattern books used by laceworkers (e.g. Giovanni Antonio Tagliente's *Essempio di recammi* (Venice, 1527), the earliest of such works and the first to publish Moresque designs).

The most frequently employed surface treatment of all-gilt frames was the execution of scrolling foliate patterns, either continuous or in panels, with punched work known as *bulinatura* (9e). The punching was done directly on to the gold surface, dimpling the gesso beneath it. It creates

11. Italian architectural *cassetta* frames with overall carved decoration, mid-16th century to mid-17th: (a) Tuscan parcel gilt frame with scrolling foliage on black, 978×1067×210 mm, first half of the 16th century, attributed to Antonio Barile (on loan from London, Victoria and Albert Museum), on Sebastiano del Piombo's *Holy Family with St John the Baptist and a Benefactor*, ?1517–20 (London, National Gallery); (b) Venetian fluted altarpiece frame, 2006×1346×228 mm, original for Titian's *St John the Baptist*, early 1540s (Venice, Galleria dell'Accademia); (c) Bolognese altarpiece frame with flowered guilloche, 4280×2240×500 mm, original for Francesco Albani's *Baptism*, second quarter of the 17th century (Bologna, Pinacoteca Nazionale); (d) north Italian frame with enriched flower chain, 2000× 1320×237 mm, second half of the 16th century, adapted for Tintoretto's *Christ in the House of Martha and Mary*, *c.* 1580 (Munich, Alte Pinakothek); (e) Venetian frame with flower chain frieze, brackets and gadrooning, 2057×1600×263 mm, contemporary for Veronese's *Mars and Venus United by Cupid*, second quarter of the 16th century (New York, Metropolitan Museum of Art)

subtle brocaded effects that alter as the light catches them and produce a sense of shimmering movement. The technique is directly descended from the punching of gilded areas on early panel paintings, when many different stamps were used to define anything from a halo to the pattern on a robe. Such panels often had, within their actual frames, an inner 'frame' or margin of ornamental punched lines on the gilded background of the painting, as in Simone Martini's *Annunciation* (Washington, DC, N.G.A.). It may also relate to glass- and metal-engraving. Less commonly, the contours could be engraved in a continuous line, contrasted with a background textured in zigzag chiselwork, known as hazzling (9d). Hazzle decoration occurs frequently as a means of highlighting the borders of later 17th- and 18th-century Italian and French frames. *Bulinatura* was a common technique throughout Italy but seems to have reached a high point in the central areas of Tuscany (especially Siena), the Marches and Emilia.

Late 16th- and early 17th-century Bolognese frames form a particularly coherent regional style (see Morazzoni, 1953). Many examples are found in the Pinacoteca Nazionale in Bologna and are notable for the finely rendered friezes of stylized blossom and foliage (e.g. Annibale Carracci: *Assumption of the Virgin*, 1592). Borders are generally foliate rather than architectural, with a distinctive outer bell-flower and inner running leaf band (9e). Occasionally the principal moulding forms the sight edge of the frame, projecting the picture plane forward, as on Giovanni Cariani's *Seamstress Madonna* (1524–8; Rome, Pal. Barberini; see fig. 9f): where the pattern is seen with a plain gilt frieze, with stylized leaves influenced by Bolognese examples.

As traditional as *sgraffito* and *bulinatura* was the use of pastiglia (see fig. 7a). Semi-liquid gesso is trickled through a cone (like cake icing) on to a design previously drawn on the frieze. The edges are sharpened while setting and, after gilding, the ground often punched to provide a contrasting texture, as on the frame of Andrea del Sarto's *Holy Family* (1515–16; Paris, Louvre; see fig. 9g). Far more easily created than by carving, this low-relief decoration, rounded by the surface tension of the drying gesso, yields a soft, flowing ornament, which on the del Sarto is set off by carved bead and fluted borders. Pastiglia ornament was particularly common in the Veneto, although found elsewhere in Italy. The technique dates back to the spandrels, borders and robes of 14th-century panel paintings, as well as to the decoration of 16th-century furnishings, notably the fronts of cassoni, and continues into mid-17th century *cassetta* frames.

16th- and 17th-century *cassetta* frames may generally be distinguished by the distribution of ornament. This was usually continuous in the Renaissance in accordance with antique sources (9c, d, g) but situated at the corners and centres in the Baroque period to correspond with pictorial movement. (For example, the vertical, horizontal and diagonal lines of Guercino's *Angels Weeping over the Dead Christ* (c. 1618; London, N.G.; see fig.9e) are subtly reinforced by the carved central flower motifs and corner rosettes, set on the finely punched frieze.) Ornamental techniques were similar in both centuries, and regional characteristics persisted. Peculiar to Tuscany was the use

of mordant-gilt corner and centre arabesques on black, sometimes with the main border finished in black and gold stripes (10a). These recall the blocks of alternating light and dark stone in Florentine window-frames and more strikingly on the façade of Siena Cathedral. The frame on Titian's *Virgin and Child with Saints* (Paris, Louvre; see fig. 10b) is characteristic of the more elaborate and formal Baroque *cassetta* from Florence or Rome, with straight fluted and beaded borders and, here, red tinted panels. The use of gadrooning was a typical Mannerist and Baroque device, giving a dynamic rhythm to the frame's structure and enhancing the focus on the subject. Typically Florentine (and also found in Venice) is the use of a plain walnut frieze with parcel-gilt gadrooned borders (10c). The prevailing Spanish influence in Naples as well as Florence is reflected in frames that combined—like the chiaroscuro of the paintings—boldly carved and gilt foliate scrolls on a black frieze with a gilt gadrooned outer rail (10d).

The decorative techniques so far discussed were generally for smaller-scale devotional and secular pictures seen at close range in intimate surroundings. *Cassetta* frames for larger-scale works—church altarpieces and historical and mythological subjects in palazzi—were more robustly decorated with carved architectural motifs reflecting the ornamentation of the building (ceilings, cornices and doorways), as well as larger pieces of furniture. For the purposes of classification, patterns formed from an underlying entablature profile may be termed architectural *cassetta* frames (see fig. 11). The luxuriantly carved Tuscan example on Sebastiano del Piombo's *Holy Family with St John the Baptist and a Benefactor* (?1517–20; London, N.G.; see fig. 11a) derives from the inner structure of the Renaissance altarpiece (of the type seen in fig. 7 above). The junctions of scrolling acanthus friezes on a blue-black ground form compartments, each containing a rosette and echoing the enriched beams and coffering of polychrome Renaissance ceilings. The ornamentation of the frieze, being the broadest element in the section, determines the character of the frame. Two large altarpieces bearing their original frames (11b and c) incorporate respectively fluting and a broad guilloche, the latter repeating contemporary Bolognese window-frames. Guilloche ornament frequently appears in the soffits of ceiling beams, as does the continuous chain motif enriched with flowers appearing on Jacopo Tintoretto's *Christ in the House of Martha and Mary* (c. 1580; Munich, Alte Pin.; see fig. 11d). This almost precisely repeats the ceiling decoration depicted in Veronese's frescoes in the Stanza dell'Olimpo at the Villa Barbaro, Maser, and is similar to the monumental frame on his *Mars and Venus United by Cupid* (second quarter of the 16th century, New York, Met.; see fig. 11e), with its five orders of carving. The stylized flattened flowers correspond with those in the Emilian 'Albani' pattern (see fig. 9e).

(v) Tondo frames. Beside oblong frames a peculiarly Tuscan form of setting developed: the circular frame for painted tondi, frequently of the *Virgin and Child*. This adapts the profiles and enrichments of the straight-railed frame, yet it is the descendant of much older forms. Circular wreaths and abstract bands of ornament are found in Greek vases

12. Renaissance tondo frame, diam. 890 mm, Tuscany, original for Girolamo del Pacchia's *Holy Family*, 1510–20 (Florence, Galleria dell'Accademia)

as early as the 6th century BC; set into Roman mosaic floors; carved on the 4th-century AD Arch of Constantine, Rome; on Byzantine and Carolingian ivory plaques; in Anglo-Saxon and Romanesque illuminated manuscripts; and around the windows of Gothic cathedrals. Painted roundels—with raised or punched edges—are used on altarpieces from the 13th century and feature in architectural sculpture and wall paintings of the early Renaissance. One of the most interesting forms, combining painted panel and gilded wooden border, is the birth tray (*desco da parto*) of the 14th and 15th centuries, on which food and gifts were presented to a new mother. At first twelve-sided, it became circular in the early 15th century, an example being the Medici birth tray of 1449 (sold, London, Sotheby's, 1995), ascribed to the Master of Fucecchio, the Master of the Adimari Cassone, or Scheggia, after Domenico Veneziano. Its flat is painted with coloured feathers, the emblem of Piero de' Medici, between cable and reeded mouldings—just as a *cassetta* would have been—and, except that it is painted on both sides, it is otherwise exactly the same as a contemporary framed easel picture.

Other influences on the tondo frame are sculptural: the tomb of *Leonardo Bruni* (*c.* 1444–51; Florence, Santa Croce) by Bernardo Rossellino popularized the stone 'Madonna tondo' in a plain circular moulding, and at the same time architectural roundels designed to hold carved or polychrome scenes appeared in Brunelleschi's interiors. The latter worked with Luca della Robbia, who produced enamelled terracottas for the simple round frames of the Pazzi Chapel, Santa Croce, Florence. Della Robbia tondi from the mid-15th century onwards have extravagantly moulded, colour-glazed frames in the form of fruit or flower garlands, almost overwhelming the modelled plaques. These usually show the Virgin or scenes from the Nativity, the circular frame being emblematic of eternity.

The garlands are also symbolic: della Robbia's *Adoration of the Shepherds* (London, V&A) is wreathed in roses, the Virgin's attribute; and the artist used various fruits on other examples—pomegranates or quinces for the Resurrection, grapes for the Eucharist, apples for the Fall and Salvation, citrons and pine for the Virgin again, and pears for Christ's love. These appear too on secular works: the circles of fruit between white architectural enrichments around the stemme or devices used to identify the palaces of prominent families (e.g. Stemma of René d'Anjou, *c.* 1470; London, V&A). Brilliantly coloured and observed, these fruits and vegetables express, besides their religious symbolism, various enthusiasms of the later Renaissance: the classical revival in which fruits were attributes of the Olympian gods; the concern with the natural world in the face of scientific discoveries; the recent obsession with gardens; and finally, the power of Neo-Platonic philosophy to interpret and transform, to cultivate the soul and make it bear fruit.

Such ideas encouraged a widespread use of gilded fruit-and-flower tondo frames in the late 15th century (e.g. on Francesco Botticini's *Virgin and Child* (the Benson Tondo); Cincinnati, OH, A. Mus.) and the early 16th (e.g. on the *Holy Family* (1510–20; Florence, Accad.; see fig. 12) by Girolamo del Pacchia (1477–1533)). The Botticini has a garland of many small fruits with flowers and leaves bound in a spiral ribbon and is a Florentine version found also on works by Ghirlandaio, Franciabigio and others. The Pacchia has a looser band of fruit and pine-cones, growing from two ribbon-bound urns at the base and meeting in a rose above the Virgin's head; this is a form used mainly by Sienese carvers but also by some Florentines (see 1990 exh. cat.). Both frames have *rais-de-coeur* enrichments and an outer scale pattern and, like the della Robbia wreaths, both employ fruit and flowers as attributes of the Virgin and Christ.

There are also architectural pastiglia and stucco tondo frames, closer to the *deschi da parto* and to ordinary *cassettas*; for example a 16-sided moulding frame with pastiglia scrolling of the flat on a Beccafumi *Virgin and Child Reading* (untraced; sold Nice) and a round flat border with multiple rows of cabling and raised flower patterns on a Florentine school *Virgin and Child with St John and an Angel* (16th century; London, N.G.). Like the garland frames, these are almost certainly original, the expense of replacing a circular frame being prohibitive, and are therefore good standards for comparisons of date and style with rectangular frames. In addition, there are rare examples that seem to transcend any relationship with the linear frame, such as the frame of the Doni Tondo. This was carved *c.* 1506–8 for the patron Agnolo Doni to frame Michelangelo's *Holy Family with St John the Baptist* (1506; Florence, Uffizi). Traditionally ascribed to the Sienese master carver Antonio Barile (1453–1516), it has been re-attributed to the Florentine family of del Tasso, who decorated the bridal suite where the picture hung (Cecchi, 1987; Baldi and others, 1992). It consists of a shallow cushion between antique ornaments and is gilded and decorated with richly carved vertebrate scrollings in which symbolic pelicans and winged bulls play. At five points, three-dimensional polychromed heads (of Christ, two prophets and two sibyls) emerge from roundels, possibly deriving from Ghiberti's heads on the east doors of the Baptistery, Florence, or even from the painted versions on frames by Cimabue and Duccio.

Even such a singular example of sculpture and design has a clear connection with the *cassetta* frame and can be traced through other tondo frames, such as those on Beccafumi's *Holy Family* (Florence, Mus. Horne) and Giuliano Bugiardini's *Holy Family with St John* (Turin, Gal. Sabauda). The latter has a central flat (decorated, like the Doni Tondo, with scrollings, pelicans and grotesques) and instead of square cassettes has analogous roundels with rosettes at four points equivalent to the corners of an oblong frame. Similar to both the Bugiardini and Michelangelo frames is that on the Beccafumi. This also has four roundels, from which spring heads like those on the Doni Tondo, possibly symbolizing the four quarters of the world. Once also attributed to Barile, it may now be dated 1533–5 and ascribed to the sculptor Lorenzo di Girolamo Donati (*fl* 1516–41), showing the influence of the Doni Tondo (see Cecchi).

Almost any profile or pattern might be adapted to a tondo frame. Two Florentine examples are related to those luxury rectangular frames with a pierced, undercut torus moulding, laid on a plain, painted ground: those on Filippo Lippi's *Virgin and Child* (1452–3; Florence, Pitti) and Botticelli's *Madonna of the Pomegranate* (*Virgin and Child with Six Angels*, 1487; Florence, Uffizi). Both have a central undulating leaf chain containing fleurs-de-lis on a blue ground. That on the Botticelli is ascribed to the workshop of Giuliano da Maiano (see Cecchi, 1987), who had, with the del Tasso brothers, decorated the Sala dei Gigli in the Palazzo Vecchio with the identical motif of lilies—an emblem of Florence since the early 14th century—in a leaf chain. The Botticelli and the earlier Lippi may both have hung in these chambers as part of an integrated decorative scheme reflecting the status and wealth of the city.

Tondi continued to be made, although less frequently after the late Renaissance. They revived in popularity during the 18th century, when oval forms became common for portraits, but otherwise circular frames are found as rare variants of particular styles. For example, those on Baldassare Franceschini's pair of allegorical figures (Florence, Mus. Bardini) are Mannerist frames, using tongued leaf ornaments boldly across the main cavetto to give the effect of a stylized daisy.

(vi) Compound profile frames. The entablature and torus profiles discussed form the basis of *cassetta* and tondi frames. Concurrently a number of patterns (see fig. 13) developed, based on the combination of enriched architectural mouldings—ogee, convex torus, concave scotia or cavetto etc—each creating different degrees of depth and movement. A typical Venetian 16th-century ogee profile frame (13a) has a ribbon-and-leaf sight with a continuous undulating pattern of bunches of fruit alternating with floral scrolls. The play of light is further enhanced by the flower heads projecting from the outside edge, enlivening the silhouette.

Veronese's gigantic canvas (2.4×4.1 m) of the *Supper at Emmaus* (*c.* 1560) has a classic architectural compound profile frame (13b) with a central raised torus of spiralling

13. Italian compound profile frames, 16th century: (a) Venetian frame with foliate scrolls, flowers and ribbon, 1800×2750×170 mm, contemporary for Tintoretto's *Raising of Lazarus*, *c.* 1558 (Minneapolis, MN, Institute of Art); (b) Venetian frame with shells and leaf spiral, 2410×4150×163 mm, contemporary for Veronese's *Supper at Emmaus*, *c.* 1560 (Paris, Musée du Louvre); (c) north Italian frame with strigillation, fruit torus and pierced leaf back, 965×813×185 mm, contemporary for Giovanni Battista Moroni's *A Man and a Boy*, *c.* 1570 (Boston, MA, Museum of Fine Arts); (d) Tuscan parcel gilt frame with cabled fluting, ribbon and egg-and-dart, 1200×927×185 mm, contemporary for Andrea del Sarto's *Charity*, *c.* 1528 (Washington, DC, National Gallery of Art)

leaves bordered by a leaf-carved ogee and, symbolically, an inner moulding of scallop shells, alternating face-up and face-down. In antiquity the scallop shell was the attribute of Venus (see Botticelli's *Birth of Venus*, 1484; Florence, Uffizi); but in Renaissance art it also identifies the pilgrim and is thus worn by Christ in Veronese's painting. The original frame for the *Last Supper* (*c.* 1530; Memphis, TN, Brooks Mus. A.) by Tommaso di Stefano (*c.* 1495–1564) is a Tuscan variant carved with shells in parcel-gilt walnut. Many Venetian frames have shells as a symbol of the maritime republic. A superb ogee moulding frame, with alternating shells and winged cherubs, surrounds Titian's *Education of Cupid* (Rome, Gal. Borghese).

The waveband ornament known as strigillation, deriving from 3rd-century AD Roman sarcophagi, was also employed in frames to great effect. The faceted surfaces of this near-abstract device provided a rapid and eye-catching movement of light; see, for instance, the frame (13c) on Giovanni Battista Moroni's *A Man and a Boy* (*c.* 1570; Boston, MA, Mus. F.A.). This striking ornament appealed to Mannerist designers and forms the entire surface decoration of a rare surviving example—original to the picture—on Francesco Salviati's *Portrait of a Man* (*c.* 1550–55; Malibu, CA, Getty Mus.).

4. MANNERIST. The development of the compound profile introduces a transitional stage between Renaissance and Mannerist forms as well as foreshadowing later

14. Florentine Mannerist bolection portrait frame with parcel gilt gadrooning, 920×720×140 mm, contemporary for Pontormo's *Portrait of a Halberdier*, ?1533–7 (Malibu, CA, J. Paul Getty Museum)

16th century are neither painted nor gilt but covered with vast swooping hooks and curved flutes. These echo Mannerist architecture, notably that by Michelangelo (stairs of the Biblioteca Laurenziana, *c.* 1524–34, completed 1550s), Bernardo Buontalenti (*trompe l'oeil* altar steps in S Stefano) and Bartolomeo Ammanati (façade of S Gaetano; all Florence). The deep volutes seen in these buildings reappear on frames, such as that now on Agnolo Bronzino's portrait of *Giovanni de' Medici* (1551; Oxford, Ashmolean). The raking, hooked outer moulding reinforces the diagonal lines implied between the grotesque masks in each corner and the cartouche 'frames' around the painted inset panels, both features of Mannerist architecture.

The creation of aedicular picture and mirror frames in the Mannerist style offered architects and designers endless opportunity for improvisation. As one-off architectural experiments in miniature, they became a fertile medium of expression, allowing more flexibility than the fixed frames in actual buildings. They developed mainly in Tuscany from around the 1540s and later in the Veneto and Lombardy. Florentine examples were generally walnut, parcel-gilt walnut or polychrome and often related to the stone pedimented windows set into the light stuccoed walls of Mannerist buildings, such as Michelangelo's

Baroque patterns. The structures and aims of Mannerism, subverting the classicism of the High Renaissance, are well expressed in the rich, energetic rhythms and imaginative use of ornament in the picture frame. The interior of the Palazzo Vecchio, Florence, partly decorated by Giuliano da Maiano, was a fertile source of Mannerist elements. The dramatic convex double flutes of the white and gold stucco frames set into the cove and walls of Francesco I de' Medici's *studiolo* there reappear on countless picture frames, such as a Tuscan parcel-gilt walnut frame (13d) with cabled fluting returning over a deep undercut scotia.

A superb example of the Mannerist interpretation of ornament for dynamic effect appears on the contemporary Tuscan frame now on Pontormo's celebrated *Portrait of a Halberdier* (*c.* 1537; Malibu, CA, Getty Mus.; see fig. 14). A reverse parcel-gilt walnut frame dating from the second quarter of the 16th century, it uses a theatrical enrichment of raking convex within concave tongues running from centre to corner of each rail. The effect is of a sharp spatial recession, pulling the eye towards the arrogantly poised head and abrupt foreshortening of the subject. Both painting and border play with the visual effects resulting from strong and opposed diagonals, in a typically Mannerist exaggeration of Classical motifs. Similar effects are seen in buildings and furniture of the time: the cornice of the Map Room in the Palazzo Vecchio features a gadrooned moulding in walnut. Tuscan cassoni of the mid- to later

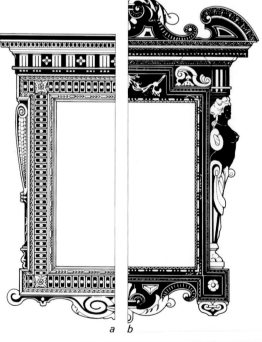

a   b

15. Italian Mannerist aedicular frames, 16th century: (a) Venetian or ?Lombard parcel gilt frame with eared corners and stop-fluted frieze, voluted apron, 967×832 mm, mid-16th century, on *Portrait of a Man*, Florentine school, late 15th century (Dublin, National Gallery of Ireland); (b) 'Sansovino'-style ?Tuscan parcel gilt frame with open double swan's-neck pediment and female caryatids, foliate apron, 656×521 mm, mid-16th century, on Cima da Conegliano's *St Jerome in a Landscape*, 1504–10 (London, National Gallery)

Biblioteca Laurenziana. This dramatic subversion of Classical structures is seen by comparing examples (see fig. 15) with their Renaissance predecessors (figs 6–8 above). Conventional pilasters, columns, capitals and bases have disappeared or become greatly simplified.

One of the finest surviving large-scale aedicular frames surrounds Rosso Fiorentino's *Dead Christ* (1525–6; Boston, MA, Mus. F.A.). Here the contrasts of parcel gilding and the eccentricity of the enrichments form a satisfyingly dramatic foil to the Mannerist use of colour and line in the painting; similarly the sensuous contours of the more curvilinear frame motifs echo the spiralling forms of Mannerist compositions. Drawings for frames designed by Ammanati for the Riccardi Library, Florence, in the style of that seen in figure 15b, show the open pediments, eared silhouettes, lateral volutes or caryatids and scrolled aprons that characterize the frame of Rosso's work, and also that on Michelangelo's *Entombment* (London, N.G.). Such frames negate the idea of the frame as window because of their great decorativeness; this rejection of illusion is repeated in contemporary paintings through the Mannerist artist's elimination of 'real' space and depth and the distortion of form in a search for ideal truth, pure emotion or dynamic composition. (The same denial of illusion appears in later Mannerist architecture: Michelangelo's Porta Pia (1561–4), Rome, incorporates blind first-storey 'windows' in eared frames with side volutes and pediments of combined swan's-neck and segmental form.)

(i) The 'Sansovino' frame. Jacopo Sansovino's work in Venice on the Libreria Sansoviniana (designed 1537), the façade of S Giuliano (1553) and other buildings became the focus for a group of Venetian artists whose style brought together certain elements of Mannerism, producing the most characteristic of Mannerist picture frames. Of these elements one is Sansovino's manipulation of architectural chiaroscuro; one is his use of such Mannerist features as the peltlike cartouches with scrolling clasps at S Giuliano. Another is the Moorish strapwork motif, which entered Europe *c.* 1500 via Venice; yet another is related to the Mannerist use of this motif by such designers as Baldassare Peruzzi. The exuberant stucco interiors of Giulio Romano (Mantua, Pal. Te, mid-1520s) were an influence, as was the work of Rosso and Francesco Primaticcio (Fontainebleau, from 1530), where stucco strapwork was first used three-dimensionally. These threads were woven together in Venetian interiors such as the Council Chambers of the Doge's Palace by, for example, the stuccoists Alessandro Vittoria and Marco del Moro, and the wood-carver Cristoforo Sorte. They can be seen in the vast stucco ceiling frames, with their geometrical parcel-gilt mouldings, the voluted clasps that curve across these mouldings and the curling, peltlike outer cartouches.

The 'Sansovino' picture frames that followed in Venice and Florence—the first to be identified by association with a name—date from the mid-16th century (see fig. 15b) and were at first a development of the Mannerist aedicule. Like this, they begin with a lateral symmetry but end, in their typical incarnation, as four identical rails. They became so popular in Venice as to be adopted as a 'gallery' frame. An example of the gilded aedicula frames Palma

16. Venetian Mannerist 'Sansovino' gallery frame, 1144× 992×115 mm, contemporary for Paris Bordone's *Knight in Armour*, *c.* 1540–45 (Raleigh, NC, North Carolina Museum of Art)

Vecchio's *Mars, Venus and Cupid* (priv. col., on loan to Southampton, C.A.G.); loaded with cherubs' heads, floral festoons and deep voluted bands that curl and clasp each other, it has the weight of a stonework cartouche. Other early examples, such as the adapted parcel-gilt frame now on Veronese's *Portrait of a Gentleman* (Malibu, CA, Getty Mus.), have the grotesquerie and inelegance of northern Mannerist furniture, with their caryatids and crammed surfaces. In the versions that are symmetrical on all four sides this inelegance is lost, and the heavy black scrolls with their gilded highlights and fanned rustication form the perfect complement to 16th-century portraits of men in gold-trimmed armour (see fig. 16). The elements of the 'Sansovino' frame were diffused through such engravings as Giulio di Antonio Bonasone's *Amori sdegni e gelosie di giunone* (1568) and Federico Zuccaro's *Recueils de divers cartels*.

(ii) Auricular and leaf frames. The interconnection of Mannerism and the Baroque, with all their oppositions and contradictions, is fully expressed in the AURICULAR STYLE and particularly in its application to frames. This style, a confection of melting cartilaginous and marine shapes, masks, leaves, scrolls and metamorphosing human forms, was developed by silversmiths in Holland and Bohemia *c.* 1600, and from the output of engraved Auricular designs, especially from the 1620s, it is reasonable to assume that frames in the style would have been produced in the first half of the 17th century. They would have formed appropriate settings for portraits of the prosperous bourgeoisie: for example merchants, particularly in Venice and Holland, whose connection with the sea is emblematized in marine forms. The earliest surviving Auricular

frames, however, date from 1654 and are Dutch (*see* §V below); it was not until the collective reframing by Cardinal Leopoldo de' Medici in the later 17th century of his works by Titian, Bronzino, Rembrandt and Caravaggio that Italian versions appear (Mosco, 1982, 1987). In the frames commissioned by Leopoldo the marine element is particularly emphasized: the broad frame on Dosso Dossi's *Rest on the Flight into Egypt* (Florence, Uffizi; see fig. 17) has a heavy reverse rabbet on which fishlike forms curl, dissolving into cartilage, conches and seaweed; the corners are set with pelts or amorphous masks, segmented tails and voluted eyes. There is also the amazing frame of pleated shell forms and spiny tails on Veronese's *Holy Family with St Barbara* (Florence, Uffizi), where putti holding the instruments of the Crucifixion emerge from corners carved with vertebrae and monstrous snouts. This develops from the Mannerist fondness for shell motifs and masks. (Buontalenti's work for the Medici in the later 16th century includes a grotto, as well as pre-Auricular ornament.)

Others of Leopoldo's frames—an early 'gallery' or 'livery' framing, lending unity to the collection—are related to early 17th-century Bolognese and Florentine leaf frames (G pls 100–103, 112–16). There is a fine collection of later versions in the Palazzo Davia–Barghellini, Bologna (see Sabatelli, Colle and Zambrano, 1992, pls 70–72). Leaf frames emerged from the Mannerist development of the 'moulding frame'; they have a looser, rolling style that is organic and Baroque rather than Mannerist and abstract. They are formed entirely of acanthus-derived foliage, cross-cut on a chunky reverse profile in the Bolognese style, or pierced and scrolling in the Florentine. Many of Leopoldo's larger frames are expanded into pierced foliate

17. Italian Mannerist Auricular gallery frame with sea creatures, 520×430×180 mm, 1660s–1670s, made for Cardinal Leopoldo de' Medici for Dosso Dossi's *Rest on the Flight into Egypt, c.* 1520 (Florence, Galleria degli Uffizi)

borders incorporating stylized aegricanes and mascarons, as on Dosso Dossi's *Stregoneria* (*c.* 1540; Florence, Uffizi) and Vasari's *Toilet of Venus* (Stuttgart, Staatsgal.). These are similar to Auricular cartouches by Stefano della Bella, who worked for the Medici in the 1630s, 1650s and 1660s.

Such frames are powerful settings for the Cardinal's Renaissance and Baroque paintings (more than half of which were Venetian). They glorify the patron, the picture and its surroundings but at the same time create a competition between picture and frame, which the latter often wins (see fig. 17). They could, however, very well hold their own in the Baroque painted and stuccoed interiors of the Palazzo Pitti, Florence, enlarged by Ammanati and Giulio Parigi and decorated by Pietro da Cortona. There are other styles connected both to the Medici and to the leaf frames, blending elements of Mannerism, Baroque and the Auricular, and feeding a generalized contemporary taste less eccentric than that of Cardinal Leopoldo. A weighty version of the *cassetta*, for instance, with plain rails, a leaf torus or multiple architectural mouldings, all enriched by corners and centres of Mannerist masks or scrolling Auricular cartouches, frames Botticelli's *Birth of Venus* (*c.* 1484; Florence, Uffizi) and Bernardo Strozzi's portrait of *Bishop Alvise Grimani* (Washington, DC, N.G.A.).

5. BAROQUE. Apart from these sophisticated Mannerist and Baroque openwork leaf frames with their irregular silhouettes, the majority of 17th-century Italian frames were straight-sided bolection mouldings, consisting of ogee, torus and astragal sections with varied leaf-and-bud enrichments (see fig. 18). In contrast to the earlier generation of flat section *cassetta* frames—which also continued into the 17th century—these reverse rebate profiles project the picture plane forward from the wall surface. The spectator's eye is then drawn into the illusory depth of the picture's composition. Such frames, with their evocation of three dimensions, rich decoration and focusing power, exemplify the Baroque style. Although the patterns in general appeared widespread, regional affinities can be detected. Probably in use in the earlier 17th century is pastiglia from north Italy (18a); and then gadrooning with outer leaf spiral from Rome or central Italy (18b); spiralled leaves, often with punchwork, from Emilia and the north (18c); and overall stylized acanthus with or without a leaf torus, from Tuscany and Emilia (18d). Large-scale Baroque pictures, such as altarpieces, were given corner and/or centre emphasis with bold acanthus cartouches, fine examples being found in Bologna (18e). By contrast, the basic bolection moulding was widely used in its most economical unadorned form (18g): either gilded, with or without punchwork, parcel-gilt or marbled. In the late 17th century it was applied, mainly all gilt, as a 'house frame' virtually throughout the Galleria di Palazzo Spinola and the Palazzo Rosso, both in Genoa, where it may be seen alongside a few versions enriched with fruit, leaves and husks (18f), which also occur in Lombardy.

The Baroque interiors for which these frames were designed expressed the splendour of the 17th-century Medici courts and the 'secularized' papal courts of Paul V, Urban VIII and Alexander VII, just as the courts of Charles I of England and Louis XIV of France were

18. Italian Baroque frames with bolection profile, 17th century: (a) north Italian frame with brushed pastiglia scrolling foliage on punched ground, leaves and ribbon, 165×93×13 mm, one of a pair adapted for Defendente Ferrari's *SS Jerome and Augustine* (Dijon, Musée des Beaux-Arts); (b) Roman frame with gadrooning and leaf spiral, 762×508×120 mm, original for Giovanni Battista Gaulli's *Christ and the Samaritan, c.* 1707 (Rome, Galleria Spada); (c) Emilian frame with leaf spiral, 950×810×109 mm, original for Giuseppe Maria Crespi's *Self-portrait,* 1710 (Bologna, Pinacoteca Nazionale); (d) Emilian frame with acanthus and laurel leaves, 1070×1455×178 mm, contemporary for the *Concert* by Mattia Preti and ?Gregorio Preti (*c.* 1603–1672), *c.* 1630 (Madrid, Museo Thyssen–Bornemisza); (e) Bolognese frame with laurel, cross-cut and corner acanthus leaves and punchwork, 2190×1440×223 mm, mid-17th century, made for Ludovico Carracci's *Madonna degli Scalzi, c.* 1590 (Bologna, Pinacoteca Nazionale); (f) north Italian frame with fruit, flowers and husks, 1238× 1460×130 mm, contemporary for Gioacchino Assereto's *Hagar and the Angel, c.* 1630–40 (Genoa, Galerie di Palazzo Rosso); (g) Genoese gallery frame, 1230×1000×140 mm, ?late 17th century-early 18th, made for Orazio de Ferrari's *Ecstasy of St Francis, c.* 1640 (Genoa, Galleria di Palazzo Rosso)

celebrated through a propagandizing art. Such patrons saw encouragement of the arts as an attribute of royalty and an enhancement of their prestige; for this reason, and because the Counter-Reformation had hobbled artistic freedom, artists were more in thrall than the great Renaissance artists had been to their employers, and the latter exerted more influence on the works created for them. Rudolf II of Bohemia and Leopoldo de' Medici both

influenced, to differing extents, the development and course of the Auricular style, Leopoldo more specifically with respect to frames. The Baroque was nurtured particularly at the papal courts, and the harnessing of all arts there to enhance prestige led both to a unity of style—painting, frame and setting were all of a piece—and to a versatility of talent: Bernini designed buildings, interiors, sculpture, silverwork, cartouches and occasional frame patterns (e.g. a richly carved, gilded frame with Baroque fluting and acanthus for a marble relief executed by his son Domenico Bernini). At the same time, the pressure of patronage moved the whole process—and thus the artistic centre—inexorably from Florence towards Rome and the Vatican, so that the great paintings and frames of the later Baroque period tend to be Roman rather than Tuscan or Bolognese.

The growing prestige of France was also important; as the national focus moved within Italy to Rome, so the international focus was increasingly moving from Italy to France. This is discernible in the French-derived frame profiles that appeared in northern Italy (Piedmont was actually ruled by France), where hitherto the influence had been all but exclusively the other way. French variants of Louis XIII and Louis XIV profiles appear in Italy in the late 17th century and early 18th, with a main torus and small ogee separated by a narrow scotia; they can be plain, engraved, enriched with strapwork on a hatched ground (also French) or naturalized with Baroque centre/corner cartouches. They were used for architectural mouldings as well as for frames. Examples of these types of frame can be found on Matthias Stom's *Adoration of the Shepherds* (Turin, Pal. Madama), Giovanni Benedetto Castiglione's *Hagar and the Angel* (Genoa, Pal. Rosso) and Jacopo Bassano's *Il piccolo mercato* (pair; Turin, Gal. Sabauda). The Galleria Sabauda in Turin has a large group of frames that are Italian interpretations of the later Louis XIV and Régence style; they amount almost to a house style. It also holds some enriched Piedmontese variants, in black and gold, or with gadrooned rails, as on Orazio Gentileschi's *Annunciation* (1622–3; Turin, Gal. Sabauda).

Similar to this 'Louis XIII' Piedmontese profile is perhaps the best known of the Italian frame types, most typical of the Roman Baroque in its richness, symmetry and classicism. Known as both the 'Salvator Rosa' and the 'Carlo Maratta' pattern, it has a severely linear pattern of stepped ogee and convex mouldings around a broad scotia. It dates from the late 17th century, remaining popular throughout the 18th and into the 19th. It is common in English interiors around paintings acquired on the Grand Tour, either in an original Italian version (as at Burghley House, Cambs) or as an English copy. It was the most versatile and widely produced pattern employed on all categories of work, from church altarpieces to miniatures. As might be expected, according to use and cost, the main theme had several variations, each with a regional change of key (see fig. 19).

In its purest form, where the moulding is entirely unenriched, the profile may be seen to derive from the section of the base of an Ionic or Corinthian column (19a). These plain versions were commonest from *c.* 1680 to *c.* 1750 in most of Italy, but especially in Rome, where the great papal collections were reframed en masse in the

19. Italian 'Salvator Rosa' frames, 18th century: (a) Roman plain moulding gallery frame, 1355×1665×130 mm, mid-18th century, for Caravaggio's *Rest on the Flight into Egypt*, *c.* 1596–7 (Rome, Galleria Doria-Pamphili); (b) Roman frame with acanthus-and-tongue sight, leaf spiral, stop-fluted back, 1200×900×115 mm, one of an original pair for Pompeo Batoni's *Peace and Justice*, *c.* 1750 (Montreal, Museum of Fine Arts); (c) ?Roman frame with acanthus-and-tongue in scotia, ribbon sight, egg-and-dart back, 1220×1980×140 mm, mid-18th century, adapted for Salvator Rosa's *Tobias and the Angel*, early 1660s (Hartford, CT, Wadsworth Atheneum); (d) central or north Italian frame with parcel gilding, raked stop-fluting, openwork corner and centre palmettes, 952×1118×155 mm, second quarter of the 18th century, adapted for Lambert Sustris's *St Jerome in a Landscape* (Oxford, Ashmolean Museum); (e) Roman frame with cabochon, leaf spiral, 775×500×107 mm, original for Jan Miel's *Veneration of St Lambert*, *c.* 1648 (Cambridge, Fitzwilliam Museum); (f) Neapolitan frame with imbricated leaves in lacquered silver, 1270×1016×100 mm, first half of the 18th century, adapted for Bernardo Cavallino's *St John the Evangelist*, late 1630s (private collection); (g) Bolognese *labbretto* frame, 570×475×63 mm, one of an original pair for Gaetano Gandolfi's *Head of an Old Man* and *Head of an Old Woman*, 1771 (Bologna, Cassa di Risparmio)

18th century. Here the 'Salvator Rosa' became the 'house frame' for the majority of pictures in the Barberini, Doria-Pamphili, Colonna, Spada and other collections. Most were gilded overall, but they are often found in silver leaf or—for contrast and economy—with the back edge and scotia painted in yellow ochre or raw sienna. Giovanni Paolo Panini, the great topographer of Roman views and interiors, faithfully depicted the Maratta frame in galleries crammed with paintings, as in the *Gallery of Cardinal Valenti-Gonzaga* (1749; Hartford, CT, Wadsworth Atheneum). Panini himself might have some claim to name the

pattern, his own canvases virtually all bearing 'Salvator Rosa' frames.

Many of the frames Panini illustrated show the most regular enriched version, having finely cut acanthus leaves alternating with tongues (or shields) on the sight edge, with a delicate ribbon or leaf spiral next to the outer rail (19b). The back edge could be a plain ogee, or carved with egg-and-tongue, or (as in 19b) with stopped-fluting and leaves, a motif generally found in works by Pompeo Batoni, the portraitist of the English Grand Tourist. The variant appears on the set of ten Evangelists painted for the Marenda family gallery at Forlì. The most elaborate variation, as popular in England as Italy (*see* §IV below), has an ogee moulding of acanthus set in the front scotia (19c). The combination of runs of carved leaf, ribbon, beading and egg mouldings alternating with plain gilt surfaces creates an opulent effect, wrapping the pictures in a rhythmical play of light.

Further patterns were developed by carving the upper convex moulding (19d–f). The most dynamic or Baroque effect employed gadrooning, often parcel gilt and occasionally combined with pierced scrolling foliage set at corners and centres of the scotia, usually for portraiture (19d). The use of cabochons set in C-scrolls alternating with flowers, together with complementary leaf and spiral mouldings, exemplifies the richness and exquisite detail that characterizes Roman Maratta frames (19e). At their most luxurious, these resemble metalwork more than wood-carving and were surely related to the design and production of ormolu frames and miniatures from such Roman workshops as that of the Valadier family. The tradition of pierced-gilt applied carving, or metalwork, on walnut mouldings dates to late 17th- and early 18th-century Roman and Genoese Baroque frames and furniture, examples being the exuberant mirror frame in the Minneapolis Institute of Arts and the showcase or *scarabattolo* in the Metropolitan Museum, New York. An example of this Baroque version of the Maratta, combining the pierced applied ornaments of (19d) with the cabochons in (19e) on a reverse profile, surrounds the *Flea Hunt* (Paris, Louvre) by Giuseppe Maria Crespi. The use of elaborately carved applied pierced foliage in the Maratta frame is seen to greatest effect in the spandrels for shaped canvases, such as Francesco Albani's lunette *Figures in a Classical Landscape* (Rome, Gal. Doria-Pamphili) and the eye-shaped modello by Giovanni Battista Gaulli of the *Adoration of the Lamb* (San Francisco, CA Pal. Legion of Honor) for a ceiling in the Palazzo Barberini, Rome. The third variant with a carved upper rail is generally associated with Neapolitan frames (19f). Here, overlapping leaves, running out from bound centres, are generally combined with inner acanthus-leaf and outer egg-and-dart ornaments, usually finished in lacquered silver leaf (*mecca*). This pattern, with its more distinctly Neo-classical motif, also appears in Germany and northern Europe.

In a delightful and typically Emilian treatment of the plain Maratta section, the sight edge is adorned with a shimmering motif known as *labbretto* ('little lip'). This scalloped effect, attributed to the Bolognese carver Pietro Roppa, is both decorative and simple, with a Rococo sense of movement. The pattern is found mainly on Emilian pictures: several can be seen in the Palazzo Davia–

Barghellini, Bologna, and many originals survive on works by Gaetano Gandolfi (19g). A fine undisturbed pair surround *Triumph* and *The Funeral* (both Nantes, Mus. B.-A.) by the Bolognese-trained painter Nicola Bertuzzi.

6. ROCOCO. This period of transition from the Baroque to the Rococo ended the primacy of Italian art; with the building of Versailles (from 1678), France had become the centre of European art, and art itself more homogeneous. The integrity of style begun in the Baroque period is evident in the continuing correspondence between frames, furniture and carved or stuccoed interior decorations, particularly in such centres as Parma, Venice, Florence, Bologna and Rome. Italian Rococo framing follows the general development of the style in the country. In Rome, which ignored the Rococo, the classical Maratta was the most common. It was in the north, with its nearness to France (particularly the Veneto), and in the extreme south that Rococo forms built on the tendencies preceding the style: elements of the Auricular, the curvilinear detailing of Francesco Borromini's and Guarino Guarini's architecture, the asymmetry of Giacomo Serpotta's work in Palermo, the use of C- and S-scrolls in early 18th-century Emilian carving, and so on. French strapwork ornament in the style of Jean Berain I and versions of Louis XV frames soon appeared, but Italian designs include an original and refined use of the style, with rocaille or flower carvings lighter than the most delicate French Rococo.

Three principal patterns developed in the Veneto that mark the progress to full Rococo style (see fig. 20). The simplest, which may be seen as a Venetian equivalent to the Bolognese *labbretto* frame, appears almost exclusively on the small-scale portraits and genre subjects by Pietro Longhi (20a). Invariably of a narrow ogee section with gadrooned back, a pierced scrolling acanthus leaf curls back from the sight edge. The pattern also occurs on works by the Guardi and as a shaped *boiserie*-like moulding in such works as Giambattista Tiepolo's ceiling decoration (*c.* 1755–60) for the Palazzo Mocenigo, Venice (reconstructed, Boston, MA, Mus. F.A.).

The most typical and versatile design—the so-called 'Canaletto' frame—dates from the first quarter of the 18th century (20b) and was developed from the same ogee section as the 'Longhi' pattern with a gadrooned back, having corner and centre sections carved in low relief with undulating stems and flowers on a punched ground. The remaining panels were burnished and are thus often described as mirrors. Simple in concept, the design created a pronounced movement of light around the subject and, when embellished with elaborate pierced rocaille carving at top and sides, became a standard frame for mirrors themselves, as in the example (*c.* 1725; New York, Met.) from the Palazzo Sagredo. The same motifs occur in the edges and aprons of contemporary console tables (for variations on these Venetian frames, see 1993 exh. cat.).

The flowering of Venetian Rococo can be seen in the frame now on Michele Giovanni Marieschi's *View of the Grand Canal with S Maria della Salute* (Madrid, Mus. Thyssen–Bornemisza; 20c). Although the inner edge and back recall the previous models, the surface here flows with peltlike rocaille panels bordered by continuously

20. Venetian Rococo frames, *c.* 1715–65: (a) 'Longhi' pattern frame with pierced leaf sight, gadrooned back, 610×500×50 mm, original for Pietro Longhi's *Merry Couple*, *c.* 1740 (Venice, Ca' Rezzonica); (b) 'Canaletto' frame with floral corners and centres, 660×470×70 mm, contemporary for Giovanni Battista Piazzetta's *Guardian Angel*, *c.* 1718 (Los Angeles, CA, County Museum of Art); (c) Rococo frame with asymmetric panels, 850×1270×125 mm, mid-18th century, adapted for Michele Giovanni Marieschi's *View of the Grand Canal with S Maria della Salute* (Madrid, Museo Thyssen-Bornemisza)

swept asymmetric scrolls retaining elements of earlier Auricular Mannerism. The liquid Venetian light is perfectly reflected in such melting sculptural borders. The apotheosis of the Rococo style is a magnificent frame (see Sabatelli, Colle and Zambrano, 1992, pl. 79) by the Venetian master carver Antonio Corradini. Commissioned *c.* 1775 by Count Perulli as a gift of gratitude to the Procurator Pietro Barberigo and gilded with two shades of leaf, this vast (*c.* 4.5×3.0 m) and flamboyant work is a compendium of Rococo ornament, given a peculiarly Italianate air by its use of slender swept rails and openwork. It looks back to earlier forms in the Barberigo device supported by putti at the crest, and in the figures of six Cardinal Virtues at the sides; but the delicacy and asymmetry is innately Rococo, while the treatment of the figures themselves anticipates Neoclassicism.

The Rococo style in northern Italy comprised a number of light-hearted, eccentric variations on the Louis XV frame, with engraved flowers on a hatched ground, wildly scrolling swept sides, striated rocaille hollows and asymmetric acanthus crests in the manner of Andrea Brustolon, as in the frame on Francisco Vieira Portuense's *Diana and her Nymphs* (Parma, G. N.). Such motifs are found in abundance in the great palaces of Piedmont and Liguria. The sumptuous interiors of the palazzi Reale, Stupinigi and Chiablese in Turin and the Palazzo Reale in Genoa combine superb shaped Rococo picture and mirror *boiseries* with corresponding independent frames, all flamboyantly carved in the French taste popular at the time of Charles Emanuel III (*reg* 1730–73).

7. NEO-CLASSICAL AND EMPIRE. The Neo-classical movement, although developed in and diffused from France, was actually catalysed in Italy. The Roman dislike of Rococo prettiness and frivolity, and the classical preferences that made the Maratta so popular there, encouraged in the 1740s the design of 'antique' ornament by students at the Académie de France in Rome (*see* §III below). The work of Piranesi was also influential, and the systematic excavations at Herculaneum and Pompeii from *c.* 1748 boosted interest in the Classical. In the last third of the 18th century, Italian furniture in the Neo-classical style began to appear; and then in northern Italy frames in the same, international, French-based design. Examples with characteristic oval format and architrave profile are found on the portrait of *Maria Luisa of Savoy* (Genoa, Pal. Reale) and on the portrait of *Giuseppe Placido, Son of Victor Amadeus III* (Piedmontese school, 1760; Stupinigi, Mus. A. & Ammobil.), which has a magnificent fluted trophy frame opulently carved by Giuseppe Maria Bonzanigo with an eagle, snake and sword festooned with laurel branches and garlands.

Because of the prolonged use of the Maratta frame, Neo-classical patterns (see fig. 21) developed later in Italy than France. A new standard section emerged, based on the Maratta but wider and more severely classical with a broader, deeper scotia and straight back edge. The upper step was invariably carved in egg-and-dart or leaf ornament, with a moulded bead sight edge (21a). Apart from this beading, the tradition of hand-carved ornament survived in Italian workshops far longer than in France and elsewhere. The contrast may be observed in the application of finely carved acanthus leaves in the scotia of some of the more de luxe gallery frames on works by Italian Old Masters in the Musée Condé, Château de Chantilly (see fig. 21b). More economical, the pattern in 22a was employed as a 'house style' for the set of ten *Battle Scenes* (Turin, Gal. Sabauda) by Jan Huchtenburgh (1647–1733). This profile is found predominantly in Lombardy (many examples in the Brera, Milan), Florence and Rome. Less frequent, and reminiscent of English frames, is the use of fluting with a feather or leaf moulding (see fig. 21c).

The *gusto greco* was briefly important; but although Italy was no longer giving contemporary leadership in style to Europe, it was fast becoming the European repository of archaeological references. Thus, when most of Italy was annexed by Napoleon in 1796–7, a Roman Neo-classicism triumphed and—in the form of the Consulate, Directoire and Empire styles—spread from the court of France back to that of Italy (*see* §III below). Examples of French-inspired Neo-classical-style gallery reframing are seen in two sets of four tondi by Francesco Albani. In the *Four Elements* (1625–8; Turin, Gal. Sabauda; 21d), the scotia profile is bordered with laurel, repeated in the spandrel

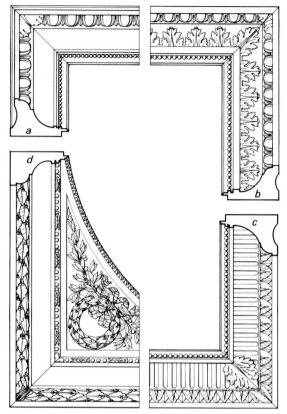

21. Italian Neo-classical and Empire scotia frames, late 18th century–early 19th: (a) with egg-and-dart, 2100×3050×173 mm, original for Gaspare Landi's *Three Marys at the Tomb*, *c.* 1812 (Florence, Palazzo Pitti); (b) with acanthus leaves and egg-and-dart, 1200×900×158 mm, *c.* 1780–1800, for Raphael's *Madonna of Loreto*, *c.* 1509–10 (Chantilly, Musée Condé, Château de Chantilly); (c) with fluted scotia and leaf tips, 1372×1000×125 mm, *c.* 1780–1800, one of a pair made for Salvator Rosa's *Raising of Lazarus* and *Tobias and the Angel*, *c.* 1660 (both Chantilly, Musée Condé, Château de Chantilly); (d) with circular aperture, diam. 1.80 m, and moulded spandrel ornament, 2255×2255 mm, *c.* 1800–10, for Francesco Albani's *Four Elements*, 1625–8 (Turin, Galleria Sabauda)

with a garland festooned with olive branches. Significantly, the ornament of this de luxe set is crisply moulded, showing the mastering of French techniques. The four *Loves of Venus and Diana* (*c.* 1617; Rome, Gal. Borghese) have French Empire frames with palmettes and similar olive-branch spandrels.

The ogee profile, with minimal applied composition corners (sometimes with centres or continuous decoration) of scrolling acanthus or palmettes, is typical of the Empire style, as seen in Mauro Gandolfi's *Self-portrait with a Lute* (Bologna, Pin. N.). It constitutes the vanguard of the mass-produced frame, used as a gallery-framing from the early 19th century (like the Medici Auricular frame in the 17th century and the Maratta frame in the 18th). It signals the rise of a bourgeois picture-buying public, given wealth by the industrial revolution but still unable to afford hand-carved frames for their paintings or prints. It is in some senses the nadir of framemaking in Italy, as elsewhere; the use of plaster or composition-moulded ornament caused a sharp diminution in the production of carved frames and the numbers of those making them. The boxwood moulds, exquisitely sculpted in reverse with the vocabulary of the ornamentalist, are among the more aesthetic products of this era.

8. 19TH AND 20TH CENTURIES. Recovery was gradual during the 19th century, but the trend for artist-designed frames, which began in Britain in the 1850s and on the Continent in the 1870s, slightly restored the situation, aided by the thrust for survival of the craft itself. Florence remained a centre for historicizing frames, which were often still hand-carved by such sculptors as Francesco Morini and Luigi Frullini (1839–97), who produced finely executed examples in the Renaissance Revival style (G pls 401–3). Neo-Mannerist and Neo-Baroque designs were also produced (e.g. the 20th-century version of a 16th-century Emilian eared frame; see Sabatelli, Colle and Zambrano, 1992, pl. 51). Nineteenth-century Baroque Revival patterns (see Baldi and others, 1992, pl. 172) can be seen, in the Palazzo Pitti, Florence, for example, in the pierced and undercut scrolling leaf frame on Giovanni Fattori's *Sheep Jumping*. In the 19th century British artists were also clients for a skill that had all but disappeared at home. For the last quarter of the century the 'second generation' Pre-Raphaelites, including John Melhuish Strudwick (*b* 1849), Roddam Spencer Stanhope, Evelyn De Morgan and G. F. Watts, imported carved Florentine frames in traditional patterns for their work. These were either *cassettas* enriched with candelabra and arabesques, or torus frames, the central, sometimes pierced, moulding surrounded by multiple rows of ornament.

The contemporary designs produced by 19th-century British and French artists had few counterparts in Italy, and there seems to have been little original native design in the 19th century until the arrival of Symbolism and Art Nouveau (known as the *Stile floreale* or *Stile Liberty* in Italy). *Liberty* designers were creating Art Nouveau interiors for Italy in the 1890s, and by 1899 the Esposizione Internazionale d'Arte Decorativa, Turin, finally mounted in 1902, was conceived, with entries by the British Walter Crane and Charles Rennie Mackintosh, the Belgian Victor Horta and such Italians as Eugenio Quarti and Carlo Bugatti. This stimulated the design of such frames as that on the portrait of *Signora Bruno Pagliano* (Florence, Pitti; see fig. 22) by Edoardo Gelli (1852–1933). Influenced by repoussé metalwork, such as Liberty's silver and pewter mirror frames, and almost certainly by the copper frame devised by William Holman Hunt for his painting *May Morning on Magdalen Tower* (1888–91; Port Sunlight, Lady Lever A.G.; *see* §IV below), Gelli's frame is typical of Art Nouveau design. Based on a *cassetta*-like form with a large flat, wider at the top and base than at the sides, it is decorated in relief with mermaids at the bottom, waterlilies along the top and swimming carp down the sides. The watery background is emphasized by being silvered, while the reliefs are picked out in gold. Here, the roots of Art Nouveau in the Auricular and Rococo styles are revealed. The frame's suitability to the society portrait it contains is less clear.

22. Italian Art Nouveau frame with mermaids, fish and waterlilies, 2.04×1.52 m, designed in Florence, 1904, contemporary with Edoardo Gelli's *Signora Bruno Pagliano*, 1904 (Florence, Palazzo Pitti, Galleria d'Arte Moderna)

Bugatti produced mirror and picture frames for his interiors, which moved from the *Stile Liberty* towards Art Deco and the Machine Age; an example of an Art Deco frame, with relief lozenges on a stained bare wood ground, can be seen on Giacomo Balla's *Borghetto Stream* (1938; Rome, G.N.A. Mod.). Balla also, like the Romanian Arthur Segal, used the frame as part of the picture surface, symbolically liberating his dynamic Futuristic images from the constraints of a retaining border (see 1995 exh. cat., pp. 228–9). Generally, however, 20th-century collections of contemporary Italian art—like French and British ones—display five main framing types. These are antique frames (often Louis XIV) or modern copies, frequently stripped of their gilding or colour-washed; 19th-century historicizing styles; late 19th- or 20th-century stained or polished wooden frames of austerely simple profiles; collectors' house frames; and modernist frames. The stained wooden frame is international, anonymous and basic to a degree; characteristic of the Bloomsbury Group in England, it can be found in all countries and settings of the period. It derives from the early Netherlandish wooden setting, with a profile composed of deep bevels and flats, or an ogee section, as can be seen, for example, on Elisabeth Chaplin's *Landscape* (1907; Florence, Pitti) and on works (Rome, G.N.A. Mod.) by Umberto Boccioni. It provides a plain, wide transitional border between picture and wall and is applied to all genres of work, from portrait to still-life. Examples of the collector's frame can be seen in the Mattioli private collection, Milan, on such paintings as Boccioni's *Materia* and Gino Severini's *Blue Dancer* (1912). Modernist frames include a hotch-potch of settings: late 20th-century mass-produced mouldings of wood, metal or perspex; and non-frames—strips of plywood nailed to the outer edge of the canvas solely as a protective measure, or shadow-boxes that reveal the entire naked canvas while still ironically isolating it from the spectator's world (e.g. Lucio Fontana: *Spatial Concept— Expectations*, 1959; Roberto Melli: *Composition*, 1918–19; both Rome, G.N.A. Mod.). Alberto Magnelli's *Workers on the Cart* (1914; Paris, Pompidou) is an instance of the frame surviving as a minuscule black moulding, outlining the painting in the way the flat areas of colours within the picture are themselves outlined and thus providing a last rare example of correspondence between the work of art and its setting.

BIBLIOGRAPHY

C. Cennini: *Il libro dell'arte* (MS.; *c.* 1390); ed. F. Brunellli (Vicenza, 1971); Eng. trans., ed. D. V. Thompson, as *The Craftsman's Handbook: Il libro dell'arte* (New Haven, 1933/R New York, 1960)

M. Guggenheim: *Le cornici italiane dalla meta del secolo XV allo scorio del XVI* (Milan, 1897)

W. von Bode: 'Bilderrahmen in alter und neuer Zeit', *Pan*, iv (1898–9), pp. 243–56

E. Bock: *Florentinische und venezianische Bilderrahmen* (Munich, 1902)

G. M. Ellwood and A. A. Braun: 'Italian Frames of the Fifteenth and Sixteenth Centuries', *Connoisseur*, lxxxiii (1929), pp. 205–11

M. Hauptmann: *Der Tondo: Ursprung, Bedeutung und Geschichte des italienischen Rundbildes in Relief und Malerei* (Frankfurt am Main, 1936)

G. Morazzoni: *Le cornici veneziane* (Milan, 1940)

—: *Le cornici bolognese* (Milan, 1953)

M. Cämmerer-George: *Die Rahmung der toskanischen Altarbilder im Trecento* (Strasbourg, 1966)

J. White: 'Measurement, Design and Carpentry in Duccio's *Maestà*', *A. Bull.*, lv (1973), pp. 334–66

E. Fahy: 'Les Cadres d'origines des retables florentins du Louvre', *Rev. Louvre*, 26 (1976), pp. 6–14

Italienische Bilderrahmen des 14.–18. Jahrhunderts (exh. cat., Munich, Alte Pin., 1976)

C. Gilbert: 'Peintres et menuisiers au début de la renaissance italienne', *Rev. A.*, 37 (1977), pp. 9–28 [18 figs]

M. Mosco: 'La Galleria Palatina: Il quadro e la cornice', *La città degli Uffizi* (exh. cat., Florence, Uffizi, 1982), pp. 71–83

F. G. Conzen and G. Dietrich: *Bilderrahmen: Stil—Verwendung—Material* (Munich, 1983)

P. Mitchell: 'Italian Picture Frames, 1500–1825: A Brief Survey', *Furn. Hist.*, 20 (1984), pp. 18–27 [30 figs]

T. J. Newbery: 'Towards an Agreed Nomenclature for Italian Picture Frames', *Int. J. Mus. Mgmt & Cur.*, iv (1985), pp. 119–28 [12 figs]

R. Foster and P. Tudor-Craig: *The Secret Life of Paintings* (London, 1986)

A. Cecchi: 'Les Cadres ronds de la renaissance florentine', *Rev. A.*, 76 (1987), pp. 21–24

M. Mosco: 'Les Cadres de Leopold de Medicis', *Rev. A.*, 76 (1987), pp. 37–40

Italian Renaissance Frames (exh. cat. by T. J. Newbery, G. Bisacca and L. Kanter, New York, Met., 1990) [108 figs]

Antiche cornici italiane dal cinquecento al settecento (exh. cat. by M. Mosco, Tokyo, Affari Cent. ICE, 1991)

R. Baldi and others: *La cornice fiorentina e senese: Storia e tecniche di restauro* (Florence, 1992)

F. Sabatelli, E. Colle and P. Zambrano: *La cornice italiana dal rinascimento al neoclassico* (Milan, 1992) [232 figs]

P. Mason: 'Smith's Picture Frames', *A King's Purchase: King George III and the Collection of Consul Smith* (exh. cat., London, Queen's Gal., 1993)

III. France.

1. Precursors and Gothic. 2. Late Gothic and early Renaissance. 3. Mannerist. 4. Louis XIII and Louis XIV. 5. Régence. 6. Rococo. 7. Transitional. 8. Neo-classical. 9. Directoire and Empire. 10. Bourbon Restoration. 11. Second Empire. 12. Mid-19th and 20th centuries.

1. PRECURSORS AND GOTHIC. The earliest examples of French frames are probably those on Carolingian ivories of the 9th–10th century (*see* CAROLINGIAN ART, §VI). These employed various types of ornament, which were related to those in illuminated manuscripts, as paintings and carvings often issued from the same religious houses; the borders of the manuscript illustrations were decorated with the same 'frames' of acanthus leaves, fillets, scrolled runs with *trompe l'oeil* gems, chains of rosettes and lozenges, vine leaves and columned niches, which are found around the ivories. In both cases, the format—if not the style—of the borders was a foretaste of the simpler Italian *cassetta* frames of the 16th century, while the use of ornament derived from Classical art was hardly less sophisticated than that of the 18th century. In France, as elsewhere in Europe, wooden picture frames did not appear until the 12th–13th century; they took, at first, the same forms of integral, raised border, with decoration greatly influenced by Italian models. The eponymous paintings (*c.* 1340; New York, P. Lehman priv. col.; Aix-en-Provence, Mus. Granet) by the Master of the Aix Panels, a member of the Sienese school in Avignon, show Italian influence in their delicate punched borders with chains of paterae between and inscribed on the gilded picture surfaces, and also in the grooved and reeded mouldings surrounding them. Because of the iconoclasm of the French Revolution, such survivals from the Gothic and Renaissance periods are rare; another is the French *Virgin and Child* (*c.* 1390–1400; New York, Frick; see fig. 23). This limits the punched border to a vestigial edging on three sides, but the frame itself is far more ambitious: the main hollow holds a carved run of scrolling vine leaves (an attribute of Christ), of the type seen carved in stone in Gothic cathedrals, offering a relatively early example of full-blooded undercutting. This frame stands out from, for example, Italian designs of the period but may be exceptional in having survived, rather than in its style. The simple flat/hollow/ogee moulding of the Wilton Diptych (1390s; London, N.G.; *see* DIPTYCH, fig. 2) represents a more mundane type of survival.

Gothic and Renaissance architectural frames are also rare, but enough remain to show how they resembled or differed from Mediterranean and northern European altarpieces. The earliest is probably the Carrand Diptych by the school of Paris (late 14th century; Florence, Bargello, see 1986 exh. cat., fig. 10). This resembles German and Netherlandish altarpieces in the wealth of carved architectural detail applied to the painted panels; its scenes are dwarfed beneath double aspiring gables with Flamboyant French crockets, finials, trefoiled arches and pendants. Unlike German and Flemish specimens, however, the outer frame of each panel is not rectangular but a slender irregular pentagon, a rectangle with a peaked top, recalling earlier Italian altarpieces, such as those of Cimabue and Duccio; the frame thus gives the impression of a soaring Gothic chapel in cross-section. It has the

23. Gothic frame with vine decoration, continuous with panel, 219×143×45 mm, French, probably Burgundian, for *Virgin and Child*, *c.* 1390–1400 (New York, Frick Collection)

steeply sloping bottom rainsill of northern works and, on the other rails, an inner run of decorative Flemish-type motifs. The Carrand Diptych is in size and shape more like a shrine than a monumental altarpiece; but even smaller devotional objects were produced for domestic use. The gold and enamel household triptych by the school of Paris (*c.* 1400) in the Rijksmuseum, Amsterdam, is very different. It has a simple rectilinear frame, with a trefoiled inner arch and a plinth; the cresting above depicts in gold the *Coronation of the Virgin*. This general form, apart from the crest, is representative of 15th-century French altarpieces, which tended to adopt the rectangular shape of northern works, often replacing their inner traceried gables and roses with an arcaded gallery of Gothic arches running above the painted panel, like a French cathedral façade. This band of 'windows' was often filled with a background glaze of red, blue or green over the gilding, imitating stained glass, a practice similar to contemporary Spanish works, where even more elaborate arcades and coloured rose 'windows' were common.

2. LATE GOTHIC AND EARLY RENAISSANCE. The international character of art at this period was demonstrated in France by the frequency of such stylistic exchanges. Among its sources was the work of sculptors from the provinces of Brabant and Flanders, which were then dependencies of the Duchy of Burgundy; influences such as these were more obvious in wood-carving even than in painting. Thus secular French paintings, such as portraits, tended, like Flemish and German portraits, to

be framed in moulded architrave or entablature profile frames, sometimes round-arched, sometimes with the northern rainsill (imitating a window) and often inscribed. An example is Jean Fouquet's portrait of *Charles VII of France* (*c.* 1444; Paris, Louvre). Its original flat, black frame with a slight hollow to the sight is butt-jointed and held with pins at each corner. The King is depicted between drawn white curtains within the frame, as though at a window; the inscription on the frame proclaims him as LE TRES VICTORIEUX ROY DE FRANCE on the top rail and CHARLES SEPTIESME DE LE NOM on the bottom rail. Examples of this type are found from the 15th century well into the 16th; in that time the only changes were the advent of the northern arched top and the use of more sophisticated mouldings.

Italian influences, already apparent in the Aix panels, were also important. The brothers of Charles V of France, Jean, Duc de Berry, and Philip the Bold of Burgundy, built up much of their collections through Italian dealers, while Genoa and Savona were in the protection of Charles VI. The result of Fouquet's visit to Rome *c.* 1455 can be seen in the splendidly classical aedicular 'frames' containing his miniatures of the Evangelists in the Book of Hours of Philippe de Commynes and also in his painting of *Guillaume Juvenal des Ursins* (*c.* 1460; Paris, Louvre; *see* FOUQUET, JEAN, fig. 2). The sitter's head is 'framed' by a *faux-marbre* panel held in carved and gilded Renaissance woodwork, with a classical cornice. The Italian campaigns of Louis XII and Francis I in the late 15th century and the early 16th also reinforced artistic connections with Italy. France of the Flamboyant Gothic period found the art of North Italy more sympathetic than the intellectual art of Florence; thus Renaissance motifs filtered into France via Piedmont and Lombardy, along with the decorative style of Venetian Gothic. The Genoese sculptor Jérôme Pacherot was employed by Cardinal Georges I d'Amboise at the château of Gaillon to carve a stone frame for Michel Colombe's relief altarpiece of *St George and the Dragon* (1508–9; Paris, Louvre): a pure Renaissance aedicula decorated with bucrania, flower scrolls and candelabra.

Wood-carvers were subject to the same influences, using the vocabulary of the Italian Renaissance alongside and even mingled with the Late Gothic idiom. For instance, a group of altarpieces (1519–25), commissioned by the Confrérie du Puy Notre-Dame d'Amiens for the cathedral, includes four elaborate High Gothic frames (G 253), and another—the earliest—with a range of Renaissance elements modified by Gothic (G 254). It has a Northern ogee-arched opening, surmounted by a curving canopied entablature in three double-ogee sections, with a frieze of medallion heads, horns and fabulous beasts sandwiched between classical mouldings. The side supports are neither classical pilasters nor Gothic colonnettes but a collection of Renaissance motifs, such as putti and medallions, stacked one above the other to give an impression of medieval grotesquerie. The four later frames are in full Flamboyant style, arched and gabled, with multiple finials and pendants in the French manner, although the canopy of one has a vestigial pediment, and another has urns and candelabra carved on the arched voussoir. This eclecticism echoes contemporary painting, where Late Gothic mannered realism shaded into Renaissance naturalism. The transition was encouraged around the end of the 15th century by the influx of Italian engravings by, for instance, Zoan Andrea and Nicoletto da Modena, and by Italian craftsmen capable of reproducing Renaissance ornament, although without a full understanding of Classical form and proportion. Until *c.* 1530 frames continued to be characterized by the combination of Gothic form with classical ornament (e.g. on the Burgundian school painting of *SS Peter and Malchus, c.* 1520; Dijon, Mus. B.-A.).

3. MANNERIST. Following the arrival in France of the Italian artists Rosso Fiorentino (1530) and Francesco Primaticcio (1532), and the institution of the Fontainebleau school, Mannerism became the leading style of the French court. It was probably Primaticcio who introduced at Fontainebleau a richly complex and individual method of framing wall paintings in stucco, a use that proved highly influential (*see* STUCCO AND PLASTERWORK, §III, 10(i)(b)). The pictures were held in gilt and painted stucco frames composed of classical mouldings, Renaissance ornament, della Robbia garlands and Rosso's fantastically shaped and scrolled strapwork. These were further enclosed in stucco and painted frames and surrounded by

24. French Italianate Mannerist aedicular frame, 420×293 mm, contemporary for Corneille de Lyon's *Portrait of a Man, c.* 1540 (Washington, DC, National Gallery of Art)

relief figures, grotesque masks and more strapwork cartouches, which were echoed in the panelling by the Italian wood-carver Scibec de Carpi. Strapwork frames, as Rosso developed them, were three-dimensional voluted panels or borders, derived from stylized animal skins and scrolls, Moorish and Gothic interlacing and earlier wooden frames, such as Florentine leaf and Sansovino frames (*see* §II above). They, too, were influenced by decorative engravings; their ancestry was Italian, Netherlandish, German and Hispano-Moresque, and variants were appearing in both northern and southern Europe during the 1520s, before the definitive form emerged at Fontainebleau. The decorative work there, such as Primaticcio's chimney-piece in the Chambre de la Reine (*c.* 1533–7; Fontainebleau, Château), plays with the frame itself as a work of art; the inset paintings are almost incidental to it and, in the spandrels, are actually part of it. Such work blurs the distinction between wooden movable frames, the painted borders of murals and architectural ornament, and it is hardly possible to say where the frame begins or ends.

In 1542 the collection of Francis I, set in suites of decorative frames, was hung in the withdrawing rooms of the Chambres des Bains at Fontainebleau: an early instance of the picture gallery as an emblem of monarchical power and prestige, in which opulent frames would emphasize the King's glory (*see* VALOIS, (14)). In the reign of Henry II there was a fashion for small portraits by François Clouet and Corneille de Lyon of courtiers and the royal family, placed in elaborate Mannerist aedicular frames (see fig. 24). These frames, called after these two artists and the first instance of French 'named' frames, derived from North Italian prototypes and were often made in Italy; they look like miniature versions of full architectural aediculae. They have broken or open pediments, free-standing lateral columns and deep friezes and plinths set with plaques of pietra dura, mother-of-pearl and tortoise-shell. The columns, which can be marbled, fluted and parcel-gilt, or ornamented with scagliola, use the Tuscan, Doric, Corinthian and Composite orders, and the body of the frame is painted black, with delicate gilt or coloured patterns. Pictures with frames of this type include Corneille's *Jean de Rieux* (Paris, Louvre); his *Duchess of Châtillon* (Indianapolis, IN, Mus. A.); and *Portrait of a Lady* in the style of Corneille (London, N.G.). The portraits, with their backgrounds of flat blues and greens, shine like icons in these settings, the costume details and women's headdresses echoed in the gilt-on-black ornamentation. They formed the basis of decorative schemes, variants on the formal picture gallery—such as Catherine de' Medici's 'portrait rooms' in the Hôtel de la Reine (later Hôtel de Soissons, 1572; destr.) in Paris, one combining paintings and Limoges enamels, the other portraits and mirror panels.

Schemes such as these underline the growing connection not only between picture, frame and room but also between frames and pieces of furniture. While Gothic reigned, furniture echoed architectural motifs pertaining to the frame as door or window; when cabinetmakers adopted a Renaissance vocabulary, it was the frame, now more a decorative object, that borrowed ornament from chest and armoire. This can be seen most clearly in provincial works, such as those by Hugues Sambin of

Dijon. In 1572 he published in Lyon *L'Oeuvre de la diversité des termes dont on use en architecture*, illustrated with 36 rich, Mannerist plates, which greatly influenced the local carvers of Dijon and Lyon. The effect of his decorative pieces may be seen by comparing those in the Musée des Beaux-Arts, Dijon, with a 16th- or 17th-century frame on a Tintoretto portrait in the Musée des Beaux-Arts, Orléans. The all-over shallow carving and the stylized leaf-and-dart runs are identical on furniture and frame, and demonstrate how the idiom of a provincial school might be used to integrate a painting with its surroundings. The influence here is still Italian, blended with the rich Renaissance style of the Burgundian court, as is generally true of French art and ornament at this period. Henry II and Henry IV had queens from the Medici family, who became patrons of architects and artists, and thus the influence of Italy permeated polite society.

4. LOUIS XIII AND LOUIS XIV. Marie de' Medici was Regent (1601–17) during the minority of Louis XIII, thus continuing the Italian influence into his reign. Consequently, the AURICULAR STYLE came to France from Italy, rather than from Utrecht and Bohemia, its places of origin. It can be seen architecturally in Marie de' Medici's additions (1615–25) to the chapel of the Trinity, Fontainebleau, and also in engraved frames to portraits, landscapes and scenes by artists of the first third of the 17th century. Claude Mellan, Jacques Callot, Daniel Rabel and Abraham Bosse all published prints 'framed' in varying degrees of Auricular ornament, Rabel's being particularly scrolly and cartilaginous. Bosse produced a sketch for painted panels in Auricular *boiseries* (London, V&A), but there are few, if any, known examples of actual picture frames in the style. By the mid-17th century, when Auricular frames had begun to appear on paintings in Holland, a coherent style (Louis XIII) had emerged in France: this modified Roman pattern, which overwhelmed other outside influences, led to the full-blown Baroque of Louis XIV and spread to Italy, Germany and England.

Early Louis XIII frames, of exceptional rarity, blend medieval and Renaissance sources in a highly complex sculptural interplay of stems, leaves and flowers, as on the frame of Raphael's *Baldassare Castiglione* (*c.* 1514–15; see fig. 25). This may be seen as a sophisticated version of the late 14th-century vine-leaf frame in fig. 23; the motif is fully developed with bunches of grapes and a front flowered guilloche moulding in another early Louis XIII frame, probably Burgundian, surrounding Titian's *Portrait of a Young Man* (London, N.G.; see Roche, pl. 3). Apart from such opulent examples, the two principal Louis XIII frame designs consist of straight-sided ogee, convex and torus profiles enriched with foliage, and decorative borders divided by hollows, friezes and fillets (see figs 26 and 27). In the first type, the convex profiles were carved with acanthus or leaves at right angles to the moulding ('crosscut') and, occasionally, projecting forward (26a). The leaves varied from broad and stylized (26b) to detailed and refined (26c). Greater movement was given by raking the leaves diagonally across the moulding from the centres of each side, here with alternating floral sprays (26d). Occasionally the leaves were carved only at corners and centres (26e). This more dynamic pattern was generally

25. Renaissance-style Louis XIII frame with rose branches and acanthus foliage, 820×670×200 mm, second quarter of the 17th century, on Raphael's *Baldassare Castiglione*, *c.* 1514–15 (Paris, Musée du Louvre)

used for portraits. Borders were usually ribbon, husks, leaf tips or guilloche; the last (26c), rarely seen, is the most conspicuously classical motif. These rhythmical borders clearly defined and contrasted with the broad band of luxuriant foliage between them, giving a rich play of light, heightened by the varied surface treatment—burnished hollows and cross-hatched and textured grounds. Although these designs and finishes were related in principle to Italian foliate frames, notably Bolognese and Florentine, they were nevertheless novel in their profiles, combining traditional ornament with refinement of execution.

The second, more common type of Louis XIII frame pattern (fig. 27) consists of a torus section enriched with garlands of laurel and/or oak leaves, bordered by ribbon, husks or leaf tips. This style developed during the middle third of the 17th century, in the train of French classicism, when the Roman-influenced style of Simon Vouet and the sober naturalism of Philippe de Champaigne were fashionable. The tension between line and ornament suited a reaction against the Baroque and could be adapted to both the Le Nain brothers' peasant scenes and the work of Nicolas Poussin. This is the most purely architectural of all French 17th-century frame patterns, deriving its form from Baroque ceilings and door-frames, such as those in the Hôtel de Lauzun, Paris. Transferred to a picture frame, its confined richness marries satisfyingly with classical paintings. It has little relationship to the furniture of the period; the latter, heavy and geometrical, has more in common with Northern pieces, while these frames, Italian in origin but already characteristically French in the floral

26. Louis XIII frames, second and third quarters of the 17th century: (a) bolection frame with acanthus, ribbon and husks, 900×560×102 mm, contemporary for Philippe de Champaigne's *Crucifixion*, 1655 (Kansas City, MO, Nelson–Atkins Museum of Art); (b) stylized acanthus-leaf frame, 1080×863×92 mm, (London, Paul Mitchell private collection); (c) convex frame with alternating leaves and buds, guilloche sight, 355×572×115 mm, 1640s–1660s, on Peter Paul Rubens's *Battle of Constantine and Licinius*, 1622 (Kansas City, MO, Nelson–Atkins Museum of Art); (d) convex frame with raking leaves and tendrils, ribbon sight, 1360×1950×132 mm, contemporary for Eustache Le Sueur's *Gathering of Friends*, 1640–42 (Paris, Musée du Louvre); (e) cushion frame with corner and centre leaves on cross-hatched ground, 788×642×80 mm (London, Paul Mitchell private collection)

detail introduced by Vouet, anticipate the ornamental designs of Charles Le Brun and the style of Louis XIV. The raised profile creates a strong feeling of depth around the subject, enhancing the picture's illusory perspective, and is appropriate for apsidal formats (27a); this arched-top pattern occurs also in the framing of carved Crucifixes. Large examples were sometimes bordered by a strong geometric ribbon contrasting with the leaves (27b). The frame for the Le Nain brothers' *Return from the Baptism* (signed and dated 1642; Paris, Louvre), densely carved with laurels and flowers, is exceptionally fine. A rare, early and beautiful southern French variation (27c), with ivy on a cross-hatched ground, recalls Gothic decoration.

Occasionally the characteristic ornaments of the two main styles, running acanthus leaves and burnished-leaf torus, are combined (see Roche, 1931, pl. 6). As with all basic patterns, both motifs are used unchanged on all sizes of frame, from the largest to the smallest, and are the first example of a national standardized pattern. However, the moulding can also appear without decoration (e.g. on

Paolo Veronese's *Martyrdom of St George*, Lille, Mus. B.-A.) or with textured mouldings and shallow-relief flowered panels between reposes, imitating armorial decoration (e.g. on Jacob van Loo's *Coucher à l'italienne*, *c.* 1650; Lyon, Mus. B.-A.). Louis XIII patterns were employed until the end of the century—as with all 17th- and 18th-century designs, which ran concurrently with earlier and later styles.

During the reign of Louis XIV there emerged two distinctive designs of frames (fig. 28) that may be considered transitional between Louis XIII and Louis XIV styles. The novel feature in both was the projecting corners and/or centres, which create a new dynamic Baroque interplay, diagonally as well as vertically and horizontally, with the pictures' composition. The more frequently produced in all sizes and formats was (28a), where the raised corners were carved with a profusion of flowers, often including the symbolic Louis XIV sunflower, with an artificial triple leaf in the corners in the form of a foliated, fanned lambrequin. Often the sight edge was carved, as here, to a corresponding length. The intermediary moulding, close in section to the Louis XIII convex patterns (fig. 26), was delicately incised with leaves and

27. Louis XIII frames with bunched-leaf torus: (a) arched-top frame with laurel leaves, 590×432×98 mm, *c.* 1640–70, original for Nicolas Chaperon's *Presentation of the Virgin*, 1639 (Houston, TX, Museum of Fine Arts); (b) bolection frame with laurel leaves and ribbon, 2080×1160×146 mm, original for Nicolas Mignard's *Judgement of Midas*, *c.* 1655–9 (Avignon, Musée Calvet); (c) southern French frame with trailing ivy engraved in scotia, 546×445×85 mm, mid-17th century, on Frans Pourbus the younger's portrait of *Louis XIII*, *c.* 1616 (Los Angeles, CA, County Museum of Art)

now carved with a complex but symmetrical rhythm of facing foliate C-scrolls (29a), linked with strapwork and flower heads on a cross-hatched ground, repeated in miniature on the sight and back edges, with corner acanthus leaves. Examples are found on Anthony van Dyck's *Judas* (Vienna, Ksthist. Mus.) and in the *grand luxe* frames on the Domenichino landscapes in the Guise bequest (Oxford, Christ Church Coll.). These patterns are echoed in Antoine Le Pautre's designs for friezes and carved ornament published in the 1650s (*Desseins de plusieurs palais*). The corner-and-centre frame that resulted from the addition of projecting cartouches to the straight-sided design (29b, c, d) became the most regularly employed type, synonymous with the Baroque style of Louis XIV; it became the dominant formula for portraiture. The cartouches contained shells, leaves, anthemia or fleurs-de-lis, accentuated by a broadly hatched ground (*quadrillage*). Earlier provincial patterns had a dentil sight edge (29b). Other examples include Philippe de Champaigne's *Good*

28. Louis XIII–Louis XIV frames, *c.* 1650: (a) convex frame with fanned lambrequins and flower corners and engraved reposes, 750×630×115 mm, second half of the 17th century, on Antoine Coypel's *Democritus*, 1692 (Paris, Musée du Louvre); (b) acanthus-spiral torus frame with corner and centre clasps, 1029×1130×116 mm, probably original for Laurent de La Hyre's *Allegorical Figure of Grammar*, 1650 (London, National Gallery)

flowers, to echo the corners. Such frames were used for Hyacinthe Rigaud's portrait of *Martin Desjardins* (1692; Paris, Louvre) and Georges de La Tour's *Cheat with the Ace of Clubs* (*c.* 1620–30; Fort Worth, TX, Kimbell A. Mus.). The other and rarer pattern (28b) appeared in *boiseries* and mirrors (see Roche, 1931, pl. 15). It was distinctly architectural and consisted of a torus over a flat base bordered by friezes and leaf tips. Unlike the bunched leaves of the Louis XIII model (fig. 27), this torus was enriched with spiralled leaves on strapwork and flowers, elegantly bound at corners and centres with clasplike cartouches, normally not projecting beyond the perimeter of the back edge. An example frames Thomas de Keyser's portrait of *Pieter Shout* (Amsterdam, Rijksmus.).

The most typical and widely produced frame patterns of the Louis XIV period (see fig. 29) developed countless variations, which may be broadly divided by their silhouettes into two types: straight-sided and with projecting cartouches. Although the underlying sections were basically the same as in the Louis XIII frame, they were decoratively quite different. The straight moulding was

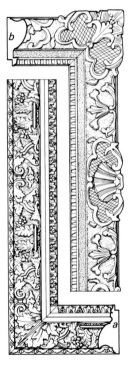

29. Louis XIII, Louis XIV and Régence style frames, *c.* 1650–1720: (a) Louis XIII–Louis XIV convex frame with acanthus corners, strapwork and flowers on cross-hatched ground, 908×720×153 mm, second half of the 17th century, on Nicolas Poussin's *Choice of Hercules*, late 1630s (Stourhead, Wilts, NT); (b) provincial Louis XIV convex frame with dentil front, foliate corners and shell centres on cross-hatched ground, 490×390×88 mm, second half of the 17th century, on Claude Lorrain's *Pastoral Landscape*, 1635 (Nancy, Musée des Beaux-Arts); (c) Louis XIV ogee frame with corner and centre cartouches linked by foliate scrolls and strapwork, 997×1429×115 mm, late 17th century, on Poussin's *Bacchanalian Revel before a Term of Pan*, mid-1630s (London, National Gallery); (d) Régence convex frame, foliate cartouches with gadrooned clasps and plain reposes, 970×1220×170 mm, 1720s, on Louis Le Nain's *Peasants Taking a Meal*, 1642 (Paris, Musée du Louvre)

Shepherd (Dijon, Mus. B.-A.) and Louis Le Nain's *Adoration of the Shepherds* (Dublin, N.G.). The main variation, heralding the Régence style (see fig. 30 below), had an ogee section and introduced a three-quarter round rail between the corners and centres (29c). This accentuated the projection of the cartouches, while giving a lighter effect. For large frames such as this, with elongated proportions, a demi-centre was introduced on the long sides to balance the distances between these accents.

As a later and distinguished counterpart to these patterns, there evolved a convex architectural section with a prominent hollow on the back edge extending to an outer rail of bound rods: the classical *fasces* moulding. This appears as a straight profile with alternating leaves and shells on Poussin's *Four Seasons* (Paris, Louvre) and occurs in *boiseries*, notably in Versailles and in the later decoration of choir-stalls at the cathedral of Notre-Dame, Paris, designed (*c.* 1790) by Robert de Cotte and carved by Jules Degoullons and others. Figure 29d shows how a contrasting pattern, modified with cartouches and plain rests in the Régence manner, could be derived from the same profile. The parentage of such specific designs is difficult to determine, for although elements appear in designs by Le Brun and Le Pautre, their use is different in tone—more grandiose, monumental and sober—from their use on frames. The same seems true of any relationship with silverware, often a source for framemakers, and with gilded wooden furniture. There may be a more direct link with designs by Pierre Mignard, who was, like Le Brun, a pupil of Vouet, and with precursors of André Charles Boulle, who evolved their own style from the vocabulary of mid-17th-century ornament. In the work of both, there is an overall effect reminiscent of early Louis XIV frames, one quite divorced from the 'antique' fixed borders of Louis XIV ceilings and wall paintings. Such frames were used in the 1670s style of interior decoration seen in Le Brun's Grands Appartements at Versailles. In the Salon de Mars and the Salon d'Abondance the walls were hung with velvet or silk according to the season; against these damasked materials the answering patterns of early Louis XIV frames formed the perfect transition from the jewelled and golden colours of works by Titian and Veronese to the opulent setting of the palace. The textured surfaces of these sophisticated frames, with their varied matt and burnished gilding, and the raised contours of convex and ogee mouldings, combined to catch light and throw it on the paintings, creating movement and animation. Simpler versions of such frames were also produced, of course, their patterns being governed by cost, suitability of setting or the status of the recipient. Anonymous *menuisiers* employed the same moulding profiles as the major carvers but cut costs by restricting decoration to the centres and corners; the 'rests' between these might be plain burnished gold or engraved with subtle patterns of flowers and foliage.

At the further extreme from such models the frames used for royal portraits and for the jewels of the King's art collection employ the full panoply of ornament in the mid- to late style of Louis XIV. They betray the influence of Jean Berain, Dessinateur du Cabinet du Roi from 1674, in their use of slender, grooved strapwork joining foliate C-scrolls, their lambrequin borders and panels of ornate

diapering, their light festoons of husks and flowers and their fantastic flourishes: tiny *têtes espagnolettes*, cornucopias etc. The style was again accommodated either to a convex or bird's-beak profile, as in the frames of Veronese's *Finding of Moses* (Orléans, Mus. B.-A.) and of Claude Lorrain's *Sunset Harbour and Village Fête* (Paris, Louvre), monogrammed with the entwined Ls of Louis XIV's cypher, or to an ogee. This style was also adapted to trophy frames, which, like the early inscribed frames, offered a gloss on their contents. Examples are the musical trophy frame of Veronese's *Mystic Marriage of St Catherine* (Oxford, Christ Church); the frame, appropriately carved with palm and olive branches, of Poussin's *Christ's Entry into Jerusalem* (Nancy, Mus. B.-A.); and that of Joseph Parrocel's *Hawking Party* (London, N.G.), one of a pair, with boars', rams' and dogs' heads in the centres and corners (these frames have been attributed to Philippe Cayeux (1688–1769)). Frames of the luxury class appeared more frequently in the 30 or so years following 1695, the date when the Surintendance des Bâtiments du Roi ordered two magnificent emblematic settings for Annibale Carracci's *Hunting* and *Fishing* scenes (Paris, Louvre).

5. RÉGENCE. During the last 20 years of Louis XIV's reign, framemakers had begun to emerge from their anonymity. Slightly earlier, Laurent van der Meulen (1645–1711), a carver from Mechelen, had been commissioned to make the frames in the Chambre du Roi, Versailles, but the accounts of the Bâtiments du Roi name a number of indigenous artists, such as Robert Lalande (*fl* 1679–1715) and Jean-Baptiste Pineau (1652–94). During the Régence and the subsequent reign of Louis XV, some two dozen carvers, including Edmé Chollot (*maître*, 1723), Jean Chérin (*maître*, 1760), Etienne-Louis Infroit (*maître*, 1768) and Joseph Cercueil (*maître*, 1787), are known from the stamps signing their frames. Even where the artists remain anonymous, it was in the *grand luxe* frames of the late Louis XIV and Régence period that a peak of the art was reached. The stages of making a frame multiplied. The rough body of a luxury frame was made by the *charpentier* or *menuisier*, but the carving was done by a *sculpteur*. Gesso was applied in many thin layers; when it had hardened, a *repareur* recut it to make the ornaments stand out in sharp and minute detail, adding cross-hatching, leaf veins and punchwork etc (see Shipounoff). Sand might also be applied to the gesso in the front frieze, thereby helping to separate visually the sight-edge carving from the textured body of the frame. After the application of a red and/or yellow bole as a ground tone for the gold, water gilding followed. Parcel burnishing, aided later in the 18th century by the application of gold leaf in two or more shades, produced still greater definition, illumination and splendour. The most stunning and majestic of all these great frames is that surrounding Poussin's *Adoration of the Golden Calf* (London, N.G.), owned by Philippe II, Duc d'Orléans, Regent during the minority of Louis XV. It offers the strongest argument for the retention of patrons' frames (where suitable or significant) as against the absolute of period framing. It measures over 1.5×2.0 m and is proportionately deep; its weight, sculptural detail and fine execution balance the tension of subject and

composition and set off the dancing rhythms and rich colouring.

Paradoxically, such objects were created in a time of decline and change. In the last years of Louis XIV's reign, court patronage had begun to decline; and the nouveaux riches and dealer–collectors who filled the gap tended to prefer small easel paintings, suited to the informal bourgeois room, to large-scale history paintings. Similarly, decorative taste was moving from the Baroque magnificence of Le Brun's Grands Appartements, through the lighter style of Jules Hardouin Mansart and Robert de Cotte, towards the Rococo. This is expressed in the engravings of Pierre Le Pautre, designer under Mansart for the Bâtiments du Roi. In his designs, verticals predominate: in tall chimney-glasses with delicate frames, and in pale and gilded panelling that increasingly diverges from the heavy geometrical mouldings of Le Brun's Versailles.

The change in frame styles was slower, and, as before, each was produced concurrently with its predecessor. Around 1710–20, Louis XIV ogee-profile patterns had a greater tendency towards straight top rails, with three main variations: continuous decoration along the ogee; corner and centre ornament only within the rail, as on Nicolas de Largillierre's *The Magistrate* (Amiens, Mus. Picardie); and corner and centre cartouches projecting through the rail with plain rests, as on Largillierre's *Self-portrait* (1711) and Hyacinthe Rigaud's *Self-portrait* (1716; both Versailles, Château). These blended into and overlapped with the RÉGENCE STYLE. Régence frames emphasize the same linear form on a large ogee or convex moulding; their decoration is less calligraphic and flowing, and uses panelled areas of ornament in the manner of Berain, while corners and centres acquire greater importance and sculptural weight—often overlapping the frieze to merge with the sight edge (e.g. Rubens's *Village Kermis*; Paris, Louvre). Elaboration of motif underlines this importance: centres and corners may have cabochons in shells, or both within a curving cartouche; fans, palmettes and diapered panels are held in C-scrolled borders of foliate, chain and egg carving (e.g. Louis Tocqué's *Marie Lecszinska*, 1740, and Jean Baptiste Nattier's *Duchesse de Chaulnes as Hebe*, 1744; both Paris, Louvre).

Such virtuosity of work was encouraged by the creation in 1705 of the Académie de St Luc as a school for the guild of painters and sculptors; its councillors included such prominent wood-carvers as Mathieu Legopuil, Nicolas Pineau and François Roumier; while the framemaker Guillaume Bouclet subsequently became its senior director. It provided a valuable training ground for such early 18th-century carvers and designers as Thomas Laîné (1682–1739), François-Antoine Vassé (1681–1736), Gilles-Marie Oppenord and Bernard Toro. Laîné and Toro both worked in Provence, in Avignon, Aix and Toulon, thus encouraging a diffusion of talent and style. So skilfully did Laîné execute both carving and gilding for the Crown at Versailles and Fontainebleau that even after his move to Avignon he was commissioned to carve an important cartouche frame for a painting of the young Louis XV with his court for a church in Paris. In 1740 he published in Aix-en-Provence a book of ornament that includes frames and mouldings with profiles; the ornament is in full Régence style, at once opulent and delicate. Laîné

was influenced by Toro, whose designs (published 1716–19) already display Rococo fantasy and asymmetry; Laîné's own carvings (1709–10) and those of Vassé (1714) in the chapel at Versailles developed the palm ornament so characteristic of later Rococo frames. Similarly, Oppenord's designs signal the early Rococo; they have the rough, hollowed shells that replaced the flat, stylized Louis XIV coquilles, as well as linked S-scrolls, and frames in which foliage and volutes begin to encroach on the framed surface. Two important designs for Régence interiors show these motifs emerging in transition to the full Louis XV style. One is Vassé's Galerie Dorée (1718–19) of the Hôtel de La Vrillière (now the Banque de France), Paris, with its curvilinear chimney-piece and tall, shouldered mirror, its pilaster plinths scrolled at the base in three dimensions, and its delicate, cartouche-shaped mural frames, with swan's-neck pediments and trophy bases. The other is Oppenord's scheme for the Palais Royal, Paris; particularly the designs for the Grands Appartements (1720), also with a curving fireplace and a chimney-glass, the slender mouldings of which rise to a great height to break out in a wealth of tendrils, diaperings and interlacings.

6. ROCOCO. With the flowering of the ROCOCO in the 1730s, the distinction between picture and frame became blurred. As integrated schemes of delicately scrolled and festooned panelling were devised, in a complex dance of pier and door, mirror, trumeau and overdoor, the room itself became the frame for decorative painted pastorals and *singeries*, which merged into the carved flowers and trophies that surrounded them. Early examples, both in Paris, are the Hôtel de Villars by Robert de Cotte and the Hôtel de Parabère designed by Anges-Jacques Gabriel and carved by Taupin, Degoullons and Legoupil of the Bâtiments du Roi; both show a Rococo integrity in which ornament hesitates between Régence and Louis XV. These were expensive works; the panelling of a room was charged not only by the panel or frame but also by the elements of each. Likewise, the cost of a picture frame was related to the complexity of the moulding; sometimes parallel runs of ornament were charged for separately, while additional decorations, such as centre or corner cartouches, diapered panels, festoons, masks, dragons and ribbons, were individually priced. It is therefore not surprising that attempts were made to reduce costs by replacing carved wood with moulded composition. In 1722 frames purchased as wooden from the framemaker André Tramblin (d 1742) and his son-in-law Pierre Delaunay (d 1774) were found to be of composition, and a case ensued in the criminal courts of Paris. In spite of opposition by the master carvers, the court decided that *ouvrages de composition* were legal products but must be labelled accordingly, and the Académie de St Luc voted to allow the use of 'compo' and varnished silver by its members. In 1727 this vote was rescinded, although *carton-bouillé* or *carton-pierre* had for a long time been accepted as a supplement to carved *boiseries* (see PAPIER MÂCHÉ, §2). Legality brought acceptance, however, and by mid-century Delaunay's compo frames were being recommended to aristocratic patrons.

François Roumier, who was a member of the Académie de St Luc, a sculptor in the Bâtiments du Roi and a creator of frames for pictures and mirrors, published in 1724 the *Livre de plusieurs coins de bordures*, which illustrates patterns for mouldings cut by the mitre (no profiles are given). The relationship of the designs to silverware is close, especially in the decoration of the title plate, where gadrooned C-scrolls appear with peapod ornament and with diapering, of which Roumier produced many elaborations. This is embryonic Rococo; tiny dragons and birds dart from the scrolls, but as yet there is no suggestion of asymmetry, which the royal framemakers seem to have adopted quite late, or of ROCAILLE. However, both appear in Roumier's next suite of plates, showing the trophies he carved (1723–5) in the Jacobin church (destr.) in the Faubourg St Germain, Paris. Seven of the nine trophies have extremely asymmetrical frames, while the *Crucifixion* scene is like a conch in section, surmounted by an irregular scallop shell. Artists worked in different styles for different patrons; and while the prevalence of the Régence frame may indicate the conservatism of framemakers, Roumier's trophies demonstrate, conversely, his awareness of contemporary style: as expressed, for example, by Juste-Aurèle Meissonnier, whose designs, instrumental in the development of the Rococo, also included frames. Meissonnier's engravings, published from 1723, show, in their asymmetry and use of rocaille, the clear tie, via Agostino Mitelli and Stefano della Bella, between the Auricular style (see §4 above) and this element of the Rococo. The classical linearity and order of the Régence style dissolved in the swirling Auricular-like curlicues of the full Rococo style in the late 1720s and 1730s, matured by the triumvirate of Meissonnier, Jacques de Lajoüe and Nicolas Pineau. All three produced specific patterns for frames. Lajoüe's *Nouveaux tableaux d'ornements et rocailles* shows the oblong outline of the frame breaking down into continuous double S-scrolls, enclosing bands of rocaille scattered with palm sprigs. He was influenced by François Boucher and Antoine Watteau, both painters who designed Rococo ornament, helping to annihilate the distinction between fine and applied art. Watteau's red-chalk drawing of two scorpion shells (Paris, Louvre) is symbolic of this annihilation, as is Boucher's tapestry design of *Venus in the Forge of Vulcan* (1757; Paris, Mus. A. Déc.). This has its original rocaille frame; the consonance of curving limbs with the swept outer rails of the frame, and of the vortical painted composition with the asymmetric corner shells, demonstrates the peculiarly intimate relationship of the Rococo picture to its setting.

Chinoiserie, an important element of Rococo style in furniture, tapestries, porcelain and mirror frames, does not seem greatly to have influenced the decoration of picture frames. Its only manifestation may be the enthusiasm for diapered panels noted in Régence and early Louis XV frames, such as those by Roumier. Diapered motifs are found in Greek, Persian, Byzantine and medieval ornament, but their 18th-century popularity may be traced to East Asian porcelain and the borders of lacquered furniture.

The Louis XV frames in the Musée des Arts Décoratifs, Paris, include a vast military trophy frame bearing the arms of Lorraine and carved with helmets, halberds and arrow sheaves, curled incongruously amid shell cartouches, and the ubiquitous Rococo palm. There is also a collection of small frames, disproportionately wide for their size, clotted with swirls of ornament similar to richly iced cakes, some with oval sights, all of which deny any pretence of modest enhancement of the painting. The period produced frames of greater variety and luxury than at any other time. Carvers were challenged to translate the most elaborate designs into three dimensions. At its best, the Louis XV frame was a piece of 'wall furniture' representing the ultimate in sculptural virtuosity, more than a match for any painting. Rococo frames demonstrate that style is invariably a function of cost; their patterns were dependent on status, hierarchy, the picture's intended location and the owner's purse, harmonizing with the court portrait or the modest still-life. The apparently bewildering variety of forms conceals a logical development and relationship of patterns.

The underlying common factor—often well-disguised—is the section or profile, consisting of a broad ogee rising to a top rail and leading to a back scotia. From this a variety of designs evolved, differing as to the degree of enrichment, the disposition of cartouches and the treatment of intervening spaces. Late Régence and early Louis XV patterns naturally overlap (see fig. 30a). Similar in surface design to the Nattier and Tocqué Régence frames referred to earlier (see §5 above), 30a nevertheless shares the section of the fully swept Rococo frame (30c). Figure 30b too has the same profile but presents another, radically different visual twist on the structure in its linear form, devoid of cartouches and surface decoration.

This ogee-sectioned form had three principal variants. The first and most economical either was completely plain or had gadrooning/fasces on the top rail and a leaf-tip sight. This was popular from the 1720s to the 1740s as a standard frame for portraits, pastels and still-lifes. The second, more luxurious version embellished the corners with richly carved cartouches, often to give more prominence and balance to larger compositions: identical examples are found on Boucher's *Rape of Europa* (exh. Salon 1747), Noël Hallé's *Dispute between Minerva and Neptune* (1747; both Paris, Louvre) and Carle Vanloo's *Silenus* (Nancy, Mus. B.-A.). These elaborate sculptural cartouches contrasted dramatically with the straight rails, giving weight and importance to the subject. Such dynamic corner accents could occasionally be transposed to great effect to emphasize the cardinal points of horizontal ovals, as on a figure subject (San Marino, CA, Huntington Lib. & A.G.) by Nicolas Lancret. In the third, frequently produced variant, the frame was surmounted by a single central cartouche known as a *fronton*, generally based on a cabochon or shell, flanked by pierced foliate scrolls and flowers (30b). Such frames appeared on domestic or court portraits of all sizes, pastels and oils. Adélaïde Labille-Guiard's small oval painting *Portrait of a Lady* (Paris, Mus. Cognacq-Jay) may be contrasted with the immense and superb winged *fronton* frame carved *c.* 1736 by Jacques Verberckt for Veronese's *Meal in the House of Simon the Pharisee* (Versailles, Château). Equally noteworthy is the exuberant crowned cartouche with triple fleur-de-lis on Alexis-Simon Belle's full-length portrait of *Queen Marie Leczinska and the Dauphin Louis* (Versailles, Château).

Swept frames, the silhouettes of which were composed of a series of curves (30c and d), have become the most

30. Late Régence and Louis XV frames, *c.* 1725–60: (a) Régence frame with foliate shell cartouches, gadrooned astragal and strapwork diapered reposes, 1130×1454×188 mm, *c.* 1725–30, on Jean-Siméon Chardin's *Attributes of the Arts and their Rewards*, 1766 (Minneapolis, MN, Institute of Arts); (b) Louis XV frame with rocaille *fronton*, 390×310×75 mm, *c.* 1730–35, one of a pair of originals for François Octavien's *Pierrot Disappointed* and the *Rehearsal in the Park* (Nancy, Musée des Beaux-Arts); (c) Louis XV frame with swept sides, foliate shell cartouches and strapwork cross-hatched reposes, 815×645×160 mm, *c.* 1740–50, on Jean-Honoré Fragonard's *The Warrior*, 1770s (Williamstown, MA, Sterling and Francine Clark Art Institute); (d) Louis XV frame with swept sides and foliate rocaille cartouches, 650×550×120 mm, original for Louis-Michel van Loo's *Marquis Edouard-Jean de Luker*, 1756 (Orléans, Musée des Beaux-Arts)

popular and characteristic frames of the Rococo period. The sophistication and complexity of their design and execution ensured that many such frames were seen as works of art in their own right; they were among the greatest creations of the decorative arts, complementing the finest furnishings. Of essentially the same section as the straight-railed patterns, the swept frame takes on a very different appearance by relaxing the top, and frequently the back, rail into a series of shallow curves. In the magnificent example in 30c, the straight foliate rail of 30b is curved between corners and centres to form 'demi-centres' with corresponding strapwork patterns in the panels. The recutting and texturing of the gesso are outstanding, and the panels have very fine cross-hatching. The outer fields of the cartouches, defined by a raised rail and incised, shaped line, carry punchwork; the frieze is sanded, and the ground for the sight-edge leaves is textured

with close straight incisions. Further contrasts are produced by burnishing the raised components after gilding, leaving the background matt gold. Thus the complex patterning of carved forms is given a dazzling vitality of finish. The overall effect is of a continual movement along the symmetrical swept rails and pierced cartouches, resonating with the irregular silhouette of the sitter within. Among the many variations on the Rococo frame, 30d has pierced cartouches with pear-shaped cabochons linked by continuous swept rails, with a sight edge of ribbed interlace.

Independent frames with shaped apertures were occasionally made as counterparts to their settings, a particularly fine example being the magnificent indented oval frames made, probably by Pineau, for Lancret's *Music Lesson* and *Innocence*, for the apartment in Versailles of the Duchesse de Chateauroux (see Mitchell, 1980, pl. 5). These are a sculptural *tour de force* in their own right: the ultimate in Rococo framing. Robbed of straight lines, the frame has dissolved into a complex counterpoint of arcs. The shaped sight is set off against the jaunty asymmetric silhouette; eight magnificent shell cartouches dominate the structure. Grandiose decorative schemes sometimes involved the commissioning of series of paintings that required similar specially designed frames: a celebrated example is the series of nine hunting scenes (Amiens, Mus. Picardie) ordered by Louis XV for the gallery of the Petits Appartements at Versailles and painted (1736–9) by Carle Vanloo, Boucher, Jean-François de Troy, Lancret and Parrocel. The magnificent frames, the work of Jacques Verberckt, have shaped openings and are sumptuously carved with figures, masks and rocaille cartouches against enriched diapering. Like the *grand luxe* Louis XIV frames, such luxury Rococo frames represent a high point in the wood-carver's art, and their cost now often approached that of the painting.

Large-scale glazing, which was relatively newly obtainable, affected the construction of frames, as well as expanding the number and types of works that might be framed. Previously, drawings, watercolours and prints had generally been stored mounted in albums or loose in portfolios; however, works that could be varnished with some sort of mastic preparation might be framed in a simple baguette or flat moulding. (The maps commonly seen in Dutch interiors may have been treated like this, and in the 1660s Samuel Pepys had had his engravings varnished and set in cheap black or gilt frames.) Pastels were particularly fragile, however, and it was only with the invention in France in 1687 of a process for producing large sheets of flawless plate-glass that they could be framed and hung like oil paintings. Frame patterns, repeated through every size and type of picture (portrait, landscape, altarpiece and miniature), often included drawing frames in a range of sizes; this indicates that works other than oils must have hung unglazed before the 1680s, or in glazing of the blown type. Examples of rocaille and Louis XV baguette mouldings, adaptable to drawings, overdoors (sometimes contained within more elaborate *boiseries*) and tapestries, may be seen in the Musée des Arts Décoratifs and the Musée Nissim de Camondo, Paris. The baguette often takes the form of ribbon-bound fasces, while rocaille motifs are used in the scotiae of simpler frames. Such frames demonstrate the wish for harmony among all the elements of an interior, and among works in all media. In the 1730s Boucher began to produce framed drawings; and from this period date the framed and glazed watercolours, gouaches, engravings and drawings that were to be found even in modest interiors.

The day-book of the 1750s of the marchand-mercier Lazare Duvaux notes the sale of two glazed cedar frames for drawings and a flowered frame for a print to the Marquise de Pompadour; he also sold her seven marquetry frames by one of the Oeben brothers, possibly also for drawings or prints. Far more elaborate frames, however, were supplied for pastels; these may have been made by Louis Maurisan (*d* 1773), who between 1744 and 1749 executed four frames for Maurice-Quentin de La Tour's pastels of the King, Queen, Dauphin and Dauphine, 'following M. Gabriel's designs and profiles'. Maurison was recommended in the mid-18th century as one of 'the best carvers of frames'.

7. TRANSITIONAL. The growth of Neo-classicism and rejection of Rococo were manifested in the picture frame by the creation of a distinctive and individual style, which amalgamated symmetrical Rococo cartouches with borders of classicizing ornament. Figure 31 illustrates its development from and relationship to the Neo-classical

31. Transitional and Louis XVI frames, *c.* 1760–85: (a) transitional Louis XV–Louis XVI oval frame with swept sides and back, oval sight, foliate rocaille cartouches, 740×650 mm, original for Jean-Honoré Fragonard's *Head of an Old Man, c.* 1770 (Amiens, Musée de Picardie); (b) Louis XV–Louis XVI frame with rocaille cartouches and fluting, 1025×1325×177 mm, original for Elisabeth-Louise Vigée Le Brun's *Peace Bringing back Plenty*, 1780 (Paris, Musée du Louvre); (c) Louis XVI entablature frame with acanthus leaves and guilloche back, 597×510×115 mm, *c.* 1765–85 (London, Paul Mitchell private collection)

patterns with which it co-existed. A prominent characteristic was that the outer edge—invariably a guilloche moulding—was swept, echoing the top rail (31a). The sight edge, here in a fully integrated oval, was consistently carved with perpendicular *rais-de-coeur* (leaf-and-tip ornament) adjacent to beading. Fine examples of the standard rectangular format are the frames of Boucher's *Marquise de Pompadour* and Claude's *View of the Campo Vaccino* and *Seaport with the Campidoglio* (all Paris, Louvre). A variant has an independent oval spandrel (e.g. as on Jean-Baptiste Greuze's *Mlle Montredon*; New York, Met.). This swept pattern, epitomized in the work of the master carver Jean Chérin (*fl* 1760–86), represented a disciplined balance between the organic and architectural forms of the Rococo and Neo-classical styles (see Mitchell, 1985). As in the previous generation of Louis XV frames (see fig. 30 above), curvilinear and straight versions developed. Thus the cartouches of the Claude pair are identical to those of 31b, where they are linked by a 'straightened' moulding of the same section, the scotia carved with fluting and an egg moulding. The same design was applied to Chardin's *The Ray-fish* (Paris, Louvre). Figure 31c shows the section carved with acanthus leaves, the Neo-classical frame having shed its Rococo embellishments. The transitional frames of the 1760s and 1770s thus echoed contemporary furnishings and interior decoration in blending two schools of ornament. The cartouche models (31a and b) exemplify the moderate Neo-classicism advocated by Jacques-François Blondel and agree with furniture of the period: chairs that retained a Rococo form along with classical ornament, as in Pierre Contant d'Ivry's scheme (late 1750s) for the Duchesse d'Orléans's apartments in the Palais-Royal, Paris. Figure 31c is in pure *goût grec*, as in a scheme of antique decoration designed by Victor Louis and executed in the 1760s by Brunetti for the church of Ste Marguerite, Paris.

The existence of these two types of early Neo-classical frame is explained by the persistence of a Rococo idiom for 20 years after the mid-century classical revival had begun. In 1757, the year in which Jacques-Germain Soufflot built the Neo-classical church of Ste Geneviève (now the Panthéon) in Paris, Beaumont carved for an important Carle van Loo portrait of *Louis XV* an asymmetrical swept frame with rocailles and C-scrolls; and in 1761, when frames *à la grecque* by Honoré Guibert (1720–91) appeared in the Salon on Louis-Michel van Loo's *Louis XV*, Alexander Roslin's portrait of the *Marquis de Marigny* and Greuze's portrait of *The Dauphin*, Gabriel de Saint-Aubin sketched them in his exhibition catalogue as though they were a unique group among a general Rococo manifestation. Many interiors were, of course, still in the Rococo style or contained Rococo furnishings with which newer objects had to blend. Thus the interiors of the house in Paris of Etienne-François, Duc de Choiseul, depicted by Louis-Nicolas van Blarenberghe in miniatures on the *Choiseul Box* (1770; Paris, Baron Elie de Rothschild priv. col.), have Neo-classical walls and floors, while most of the furniture is Rococo, and the picture frames range from Rococo through moderate to extreme Neo-classicism.

8. NEO-CLASSICAL. During the 1760s Neo-classicism grew rapidly in importance. Frames were designed in a multiplicity of styles, to play their part in harmonizing the presentation of pictures within the Neo-classical interiors and furnishings of the great Parisian hôtels particuliers. There was often little difference between the profiles of picture frames, mirror frames and the fixed frames surrounding doors, *boiseries*, fireplaces and chairs. A.-J. Roubo's encyclopedia, *L'Art de menuisier* (1768), which includes Louis XV patterns, also indicates, in several plates, the diversity of Neo-classical moulding profiles and decoration.

In the absence of framemakers' pattern books, analysis of an apparently bewildering spectrum of Neo-classical frames makes it possible to determine their underlying structure in terms of form, embellishment and use. Virtually all Neo-classical frames were generated by two basic sections (see fig. 32). The first was a flat section, which, in

its narrower form, may be termed the architrave profile (32a, b, c); when wider and more decorated, it may be called the entablature profile (32d, e, f). The second section was concave, with a frieze, referred to as a scotia profile; it was, in effect, the addition of a depth-enhancing scotia to the frieze of the architrave profile. In its unadorned and most economical form (32a), the architrave section consisted of a frieze bordered by an astragal, with adjacent fillet, and inner ogee. This type, linked by the term 'architrave' to the plain mouldings of doors, windows and *boiseries*, was used in varying widths from a narrow print frame, or baguette moulding, to frames for larger pictures. Carving this moulding with *rais-de-coeur* and pearls produced a classic Louis XVI frame (32b), widely employed for prints and pastels and, in its broadest section, for oils in both rectangular and oval formats. Oval frames, costlier than the rectangular, were seldom changed by later owners; the same was the case for those on pastels, owing

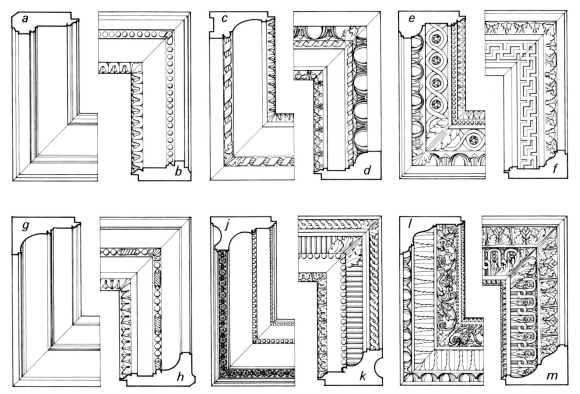

32. Louis XVI frames, *c.* 1760–1800: (a) plain moulded architrave frame, 706×620×87 mm, made for Jan van Ravesteyn's *Anna van Lockhurst*, 1634 (Paris, Musée du Louvre); (b) architrave frame with *rais-de-coeur* and beading, 432×596×60 mm, original for engraving of the *Palais de Justice of Paris*, signed AC, 1788 (Paris, Musée Nissim de Camondo); (c) architrave frame with ribbon-and-stave, 331×415×65 mm, original for Jean-Baptiste Lallemand's *Artist's Studio* (Dijon, Musée des Beaux-Arts); (d) entablature frame with egg-and-dart, 2.42×2.42 m, contemporary for Hubert Robert's *Interior of the Temple of Diana at Nîmes*, exhibited Salon 1787 (Paris, Musée du Louvre); (e) entablature frame with flowered interlace, made for Pieter Neeffs the elder's *Church Interior* (Aix-en-Provence, Musée Granet); (f) entablature frame with Greek key pattern, 875×1100×130 mm, original for *Etienne-François, Duc de Choiseul, Mme de Brionne and the Abbé Jean-Jacques Barthélemy* by Jacques Wilbaut (1729–1806) (Malibu, CA, J. Paul Getty Museum); (g) plain moulded scotia frame, 2127×6763×285 mm, made for Pierre Subleyras's *Supper at the House of Simon*, 1737 (Paris, Musée du Louvre); (h) scotia frame with triple bead and cabled bobbin, 2970×2010×175 mm, original for Joseph Vernet's *Gulf of Bandol*, 1754 (Paris, Musée de la Marine); (j) scotia frame with flowered interlace in composition, 1770×970×95 mm, original for Joseph Vernet's *Le Midi ou la calme* (Paris, Musée de la Marine); (k) fluted scotia frame with guilloche and *fronton*, 1143×876×126 mm, original for Elisabeth-Louise Vigée Le Brun's *Mme de la Châtre*, 1789 (New York, Metropolitan Museum of Art); (l) laurel scotia frame with scrolling foliage, 1460×1130×260 mm, altered, contemporary for Pierre-Paul Prud'hon's *Union of Love and Friendship*, 1770–90 (Minneapolis, MN, Institute of Arts); (m) cabled scotia frame with acanthus ogee, 1455×1120×204 mm, original for Jacques-Louis David's *Mme de Vergniac*, 1799 (Paris, Musée du Louvre)

to the latter's fragility; thus examples of both are often valuable documents of contemporary taste. The profile shown in 32b provides a restrained setting for an oval portrait, such as Louis-Michel van Loo's *Louis-Auguste of France* (1769; Versailles, Château). More elaborately, with acanthus-leaf ogee and a decorative ribbon-and-stave, it frames the oval tapestry portrait of *Louis XVI* (1744; Baltimore, MD, Walters A.G.) woven at the Gobelins factory. This original frame, with its rich festoon of flowers, its swagged apron, sceptre, crown and royal hand mounted above, is a remarkable and opulent example of a Neo-classical setting.

The more frequent appearance of oval portraits in this period may be due partly to the fact that matching Neo-classical borders were far less costly than their Rococo or Baroque counterparts; many were adorned with a cresting of flowers and/or ribbons, predominantly for female sitters. Fine examples surround François-Hubert Drouais's *Young Woman* (Paris, Mus. Cognacq-Jay), and *A Lady* by an unknown artist (*c.* 1780; Waddesdon Manor, Bucks, NT), which bears the stamp of its carver, Thomas Dumont. This was one of many instances of signed frames. Other contemporary framemakers who stamped their work include Françoise-Charles Buteux, Jean-Baptiste-Michel Dupuis, Paul Georges, Honoré Guibert (*c.* 1720–91), Claude Infroit, Andrew Lambert, Henri Lettone, Abraham or Antoine Levert, Pierre-François Milet, Claude Pepin, Nicolas Petit and J. S. Vasseur.

The *fronton* or decorative cartouche on the top rail of the frame was quite common in the de luxe Louis XVI architrave frame. Often these have outset or eared corners at the top or all round, as with an English Kentian frame (*see* §IV below), and are embellished with two to four runs of mouldings, which could include guilloche and *piastre* ornament. Such examples as Anton Raphael Mengs's portrait of *Charles IV of Spain* (Versailles, Château) have the *cordes à puits*, ropelike laurel festoons and pendants that characterize the early Neo-classical furniture of Le Lorrain in the 1750s. Other frames with fluted scotia (e.g. 32k), and those on Johann Ernst Heinsius's paired portraits of two of Louis XV's daughters (1785; Versailles, Château), carved by Buteux, have looser festoons and pendants of husks (as used by Robert Adam (i) and Thomas Chippendale (i)). Sometimes the festoons are floral, as on Jean-Siméon Chardin's *Bird-song Organ* (*c.* 1751; Paris, Louvre). The *fronton* varies from royal crests (Mengs and Heinsius), through a characteristic goffered bow (Chardin), to the stylized 'ram's-head' scroll with *piastre* decoration (32k). The *fronton* frame, especially with the goffered bow, was ideally suited to portraits; it softened the purity of the *goût grec* in accord with a gradual decrease of formality in the sitter, while dignifying the subject with a symbolic crown or canopy.

In a somewhat rarer variant of the architrave frame, the outer edge of the frieze gently curves up to a ribbon moulding (32c). Being centred, the ribbon gives a focus and a subtle rhythm to the subject. Expansion of the architrave to include the egg-and-dart moulding created the purest *goût grec* style (32d). This profile, at once sober and antique, lends the subject classical dignity and is employed most appropriately for scenes of Classical architecture, such as Hubert Robert's *Interior of the Temple of Diana at Nîmes* (exh. Salon 1787; Paris, Louvre; frame has been reduced). It is also effective on portraits, as in the oval (probably original) frame of Louis-Michel van Loo's portrait of *Joseph Vernet* (signed and dated 1768; Avignon, Mus. Calvet). The popularity of this style in the 1760s is borne out by two of Roslin's portraits, *A Man* (1766) and *Jean-François Marmontel* (1767; both Paris, Louvre). The most elaborate developments of the style covered the frieze with a pierced running ornament (32e and f). Entrelacs or interlace (32e) appeared in interiors on ceiling and wall mouldings, door entablatures, fireplace friezes, chair-frames and furniture mounts, all complemented by the picture frame. Notable examples, enriched with roses, surround Vigée Le Brun's *Bacchante* (*c.* 1785) and a grisaille panel (both Paris, Mus. Nissim de Camondo). One of the most distinctive ornaments of the Greek architectural vocabulary, the fret or key pattern, rarely seen in frames, appears, significantly, on a portrait (32f) of *Etienne-François, Duc de Choiseul*, one of the early champions of the authentic purity of the Neo-classical movement; it also occurs in architectural and furnishing contexts, without special reference to subject. Such frames, exquisitely carved, with the light shimmering between matt and burnished gilding, were an emphatic expression of the Neo-classical style.

The other section employed in the Neo-classical frame consisted of a frieze combined with an outer scotia (32g–m). This design approximates to the basic structure of the Classical entablature; the scotia represents the cornice, and the sight-edge moulding represents the architrave, the frieze being common to both. While the architrave profile, with its flatter section, is closer to the fixed mouldings in interiors, the scotia profile is an independent frame clearly projecting from the wall, its deep inward curve leading the eye into the subject. The effect is similar to its Louis XV counterpart, the plain ogee profile. The purity of its line is best seen in the unadorned moulding, often used, for the sake of economy and austerity, on large-scale canvases (32g). Further contemporary examples appropriately surround two major and severely classical works by Jacques-Louis David, the *Oath of the Horatii* (1783) and *Lictors Bringing Brutus the Bodies of his Sons* (exh. Salon 1789; both Paris, Louvre). The first degree of enrichment of the profile (32h) matches the architrave equivalent (32b) with the carving of two ornamental mouldings and is suitable for both intimate and large-scale works. The use of this pattern, and indeed of Neo-classical designs in general, must have been encouraged by its use in a major royal commission, the celebrated *Ports de France* series painted by Joseph Vernet. At least six of them were framed by Guibert, who was Vernet's brother-in-law. On this scale, the astragal was enlivened by a triple-bead and cabled bobbin moulding (32h), and emphasis was given by the integral title plaques carved at the top, with six pendant guttae. These relatively simple designs each cost about 815 livres, while Guibert's *goût grec* frame for van Loo's *Louis XV* (see §7 above) cost over 2098 livres before gilding. This was, however, a large trophy frame with a laurel-leaf garland around it, military motifs centred on each side and flags and a crowned crest at the top. Another early royal commission in the same extravagant style was René-Michel Slodtz's frame commissioned by the King for Carle

Vanloo's portrait of *Mlle Clairon as Medea* (Potsdam, Schloss Sanssouci); it was decorated with festoons of ribbon-tied bays and *rais-de-coeur*. The King's mistresses, Mme de Pompadour and Mme du Barry, also supported the *goût grec*, being customers of Poirier, the leading marchand-mercier dealing in Neo-classical objects.

An elegant and popular variation introduced a finely moulded decoration, usually interlace (32j) or piastres, into a channel in the top fillet. Small-scale decorative mouldings were made to match both the artist's painted details and, for instance, classical ormolu furniture mounts. Carving complete runs would have been prohibitively expensive, so these were cast in shorter lengths from boxwood moulds, a practice that started around the middle of the century. In this pattern, the outer ornaments were always moulded, and occasionally all of them were; however, the pearls were mostly hand-carved, possibly for durability or as practice for apprentice carvers. Many of the frames from the Infroit workshop were of this pattern, which was versatile and relatively economical and, although largely used on portraits, appeared on all categories of paintings. Examples surround Antoine Vestier's portrait of *Eugène-Joseph-Stanislas Foulon d'Ecotier* (1785; New York, Met.) and the *Elements of a Rustic Meal* by Henri Horace Ronald de la Porte (Paris, Louvre). A large-scale version with carved guilloche and outer moulded ribbon was appropriately severe and monumental for David's *Funeral of Patroclus* (*c.* 1779; Dublin, N.G.). The section might be further enhanced by enrichment of the scotia with flutes (32k) or laurel or acanthus leaves (32l and m); fluting was most frequently used, doubtless because of relative cheapness, the mitres being invariably covered with an acanthus leaf. This was the most conspicuously architectural of all the Neo-classical frames, matching interiors, furniture and silverware. The contrast of the matt flutes and burnished fillets gives a soft, vibrating light to the picture, while the geometric quality suits all genres of painting. An exquisite set of four frames and one further pair appear on small-scale works by Louis Lagrenée (all 1771; Stourhead, Wilts, NT). David's *Mme Pecoul* (1784; Paris, Louvre) is a fine portrait example, almost certainly original; while 32j, with inset interlace, echoes David's *Patroclus*.

One of the finest Neo-classical frames on public display (32l) demonstrates a further progression of the earlier *goût grec* style, now enriched across the whole face with the complete battery of antique ornamentation. The frieze is confidently carved with scrolling acanthus and flowers, the scotia with bay leaves. Although disguised, the section with its adjacent beading and *rais-de-coeur* is virtually identical to that of previous models (31b and c). The grandest of the architectural luxury frames have a frieze or shallow scotia carved with floral enriched cabling, adjacent to an ogee enriched with acanthus (32m). Examples of decorated or *grand luxe* Neo-classical frames with oval or round sights include those on Boucher's *Mme Baudoin* (1755–60; Paris, Mus. Cognacq-Jay) and Anne-Louis Girodet's portrait of *Mlle Lange as Danaë* (1799; Minneapolis, MN, Inst. A.). The Boucher has a frame not unlike van Loo's *Louis-Auguste* (see above), with a run of laurels on the top edge replacing a plain edge and pearls; however, between the oblong contour and the oval sight

there are spandrels ornamented with acanthus crosses pulled into long triangles. This is a variation on the corner emphasis of a Louis XV frame. The Girodet, the inset sepia-painted roundels of which puncture the spandrels of the main frame with their own small torus 'frames', achieves this emphasis through an opposition of the four roundels to the oval shape of the painting itself; the whole is given sculptural weight by an outer deep egg-and-dart moulding and by *rais-de-coeur* at the oval sight, while richness comes from foliate scrolls in the spandrels. This organized opulence suits the mannered classicism of Girodet's painting.

By the time of Louis XV's death in 1774, Neo-classicism had become so ubiquitous as to be attacked by Blondel for replacing the rounded 'human' contours of furniture with classical angularities. Only some small use of Rococo ornament remained, and some chairs with serpentine forms and curved legs were still being made in the 1780s. Hubert Robert's paintings (1770) of Mme Geoffrin's house show that by then all the pictures of this leader of fashion had Louis XVI frames. In the public field, the Comte d'Angiviller, who was appointed Directeur-Général des Bâtiments du Roi in 1774, organized the creation of a museum in the Grande Galerie of the Louvre, filling gaps in the royal collection and reframing much of it. He rejected the great carved Louis XIV and Louis XV frames for much simpler settings, incorporating a cartouche for title and artist, which were used for all types of pictures. In 1789, on the brink of the Revolution, overhead lighting was installed in the Salle Carrée, banishing some of the dimness that the burnish, projection and movement of Baroque and Rococo carved frames had been designed to pierce.

9. DIRECTOIRE AND EMPIRE. The French Revolution caused major changes in the administrative and political areas of the art world, such as the abolition of the guild system and the replacement, under the Directoire, of the Académie Royale by the Institut National. Change in taste was, however, less noticeable, since the DIRECTOIRE STYLE was descended from the ETRUSCAN STYLE, a severe form of Neo-classicism, which had first been introduced in the 1780s and continued into the Empire period. There was a close relationship at this time between frames (see fig. 33) and their surroundings (compare 33a with 33d). The finely moulded classical decorations, which reflect archaeological discoveries at Herculaneum and Pompeii, are reproduced on Directoire frames as single bands of anthemion ornament, alternating open and closed palmettes, or palmettes with honeysuckle. This can be seen in 33b and on David's *Self-portrait* (1794; Paris, Louvre). The profile of both frames is simple, with a scotia and ogee or double scotia, one plain and one enriched, usually trimmed with small runs of pearls and *rais-de-coeur*. Although Etruscan motifs predominated, the ubiquitous acanthus leaf continued to appear in Directoire and Empire frames. A typical example (33c) has a triple-bead and cabled bobbin moulding closely related to that of 32h above and to François-Joseph Bélanger's Salon in the Hôtel de Bourrienne, Paris (33a). The use of a frieze is reminiscent of Louis XVI patterns.

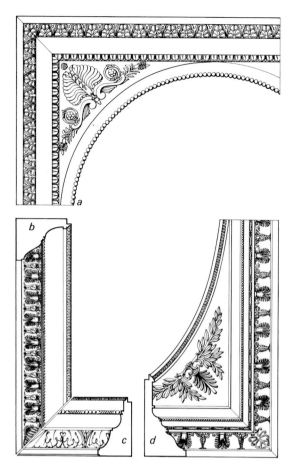

33. Directoire and Empire frames, c. 1795–c. 1820: (a) overdoor of the main salon of the Hôtel de Bourrienne (1792–1801), Paris, by François-Joseph Bélanger; (b) Directoire frame with palmettes, 1300×950×180 mm, one of a pair, originals for Jacques-Louis David's *Pierre Sériziat* and *Mme Pierre Sériziat and one of her Sons*, exhibited Salon 1795 (Paris, Musée du Louvre); (c) Empire frame with acanthus leaves, 410×720×90 mm, original for Pierre-Henri Valenciennes's *Landscape towards Mt Athos*, 1796 (Chicago, IL, Art Institute of Chicago); (d) Empire frame with oval sight and palmette spandrels, 1480×1220 mm, original for Jean-Auguste-Dominique Ingres's *Mlle Caroline Rivière*, exh. Salon 1806 (Paris, Musèe du Louvre)

These Directoire frames merged almost imperceptibly with those of the Empire (1804–15), when the motifs tended to be less closely set and more elaborately modelled, and where, as in David's portrait of *Pope Pius VII* (1805; Paris, Louvre), the profile often became richer and more complex. Many works from this period, particularly ovals, retain their original frames. The refined detail and flowing contours of 33d are perfectly matched by the exquisitely moulded palmettes, lotus buds and olive branches in the spandrels, which again echo the tympanum in the Hôtel de Bourrienne. The section of double scotia and ogee creates an appropriate depth and scale. However, at this period the ornament, even on frames for important works such as those commissioned by Napoleon and his family, was almost always made of applied composition. This great contrast with the carved luxury frames produced for the monarchies of Louis XIV, XV and Louis XVI resulted from several factors. One was the wish to remain politically aloof from the autocracies of the *ancien régime*, with their limitless expenditure on items of prestige; another, the comparative poverty of Napoleon's Empire. A further factor was the annexation of huge numbers of important paintings from galleries in the conquered Italian provinces and, subsequently, from Austria and Germany. Many of these works needed to be reframed quickly and at little expense, in the style that became the hallmark of Napoleon's reign. Finally, although abolition of the guild system in 1791 had removed restrictions on the movement of labour, artisans such as framemakers suffered severely during the years of wars and crises. The luxury market was all but suspended, and although Napoleon instigated schemes of redecoration in the Louvre and at Malmaison under Charles Percier and Pierre François Léonard Fontaine, neither the style nor the materials used for these gave such emphasis, as had been usual in the 18th century, to the art of carving. Paintings celebrating even the Emperor himself, such as David's *Coronation of Napoleon in Notre-Dame* (1805–7; Paris, Louvre), had austerely simple frames.

The rise of Napoleon thus stimulated the market for mass-produced frames, while severely curtailing the production of hand-carved work. The sculptor was now required to produce finely carved reverse moulds for casting ornaments for frames. Style and production methods mirrored each other and diffused throughout Europe. Repetitive hand carving of the small-scale complex detail of anthemion ornament, for example, would have been exceptionally laborious and costly; the enormous demand could be met only by mass-production techniques, which these craftsmen perfected, and the skills of which have been underestimated. The moulds, exquisitely worked in boxwood, which had the finest grain for accurate and smooth casting, gave detailed composition ornaments of very high quality. Far fewer skilled carvers were now needed, but the number of gilders was not reduced, especially as the same ornaments on a smaller scale were used in framing the vast contemporary output of prints. Among the standard patterns, special emblematic ornaments were created: the wide, slightly ogee outer moulding of the frame on Antoine-Jean Gros's portrait of *Maréchal Duroc* (Nancy, Mus. B.-A.) is decorated in composition with key-shaped, facing C-scrolls containing the bee motif adopted by Napoleon, interspersed with a species of lotus bud. The bee alludes to the emblem of early Frankish kings, while the lotus refers both to Napoleon's Egyptian campaign and, in its lily-like form, to the exiled French royal family. Napoleon, like the Bourbon monarchs, made political use of the arts; his choice of ornament can be seen as an assertion of his right to rule.

Percier and Fontaine were the main promulgators of this propagandist form of decoration; although there are few picture frames in their *Recueil de décorations intérieures* (Paris, 1801), there are numerous enrichments, such as Vitruvian scrolls, egg-and-dart, Greek frets, running anthemia etc, and many Napoleonic motifs, including eagles, bays and thunderbolts, all in a low-relief moulding, ideal for transferring to frames. A further influence on the Empire style was Vivant Denon, Directeur (1802–15) du

Musée Central des Arts (later the Musée Napoléon), who provided court artists with designs based on his researches in Egypt and Pompeii and supervised their work. The classic form of Empire frame survived into the third decade of the century on pictures of all scales, from small drawings and prints to such large canvases as the *Harbour of Cherbourg* (1822; Paris, Mus. Mar.) by Louis-Philippe Crépin (1772–1851) and the *Entrance of Charles X into Paris after his Coronation* (1825; Versailles, Château) by Louis-François Lejeune (1775–1848).

10. BOURBON RESTORATION. During this period, the compound profile frame of the Napoleonic era was generally superseded by frames having either a scotia or ogee section, with a variety of embellishments (see fig. 34).

34. Bourbon Restoration frames, *c.* 1815–50: (a) plain moulding scotia frame, 750×674×75 mm, *c.* 1820–50 (London, private collection); (b) scotia frame with *rais-de-coeur*, 1950×2950×215 mm, original for Nicolas-Toussaint Charlet's *Napoleon's Retreat from Russia*, 1836 (Lyon, Musée des Beaux-Arts); (c) scotia frame with Greek scrollwork corners and paterae centres, 597×1003×115 mm, original for Horace Vernet's *The Barouche*, 1836 (Paris, Musée Nissim de Camondo); (d) ogee frame with Greek scrollwork corners and centres and olive-branch frieze, 1410×2120×190 mm, original for Léopold Robert's *Arrival of the Harvesters in the Pontine Marshes*, 1830 (Paris, Musée du Louvre); (e) ogee frame with foliate scrolled and flowered corner cartouches, 2600×3250×225 mm, original for Eugène Delacroix's *Liberty Leading the People*, 1830 (Paris, Musée du Louvre)

In addition, some specialist designs, with more elaborate subject-related ornament, were created. The most economical forms of the regular profiles, often applied to prints of large pictures, were either undecorated (34a) or with a sight moulding of *rais-de-coeur* (34b). The section could be luxuriously transformed by applying an idiosyncratic corner motif (34c), a device based on a honeysuckle or palmette, from which curl tightly scrolled volutes holding rosettes, cornucopias or rams' heads—a motif occurring on contemporary furniture mounts. At the other end of the scale, the corner motif appears on the massive 400 mm-wide scotia frame for Théodore Gericault's masterpiece, *Raft of the Medusa* (exh. Salon 1819; Paris, Louvre), which was probably made when the painting was acquired by the State in 1824. In contrast to this relative sparseness of decoration, the frame in 34d, intended for a large canvas, achieves a more harmonious distribution of ornament in a variant of the ogee profile. The extra width required on this scale is achieved by means of a frieze inlaid with a continuous olive branch; the centres carry an elongated version of the corner palmette-and-rose motif, and the long side rests are punctuated by rosettes. This formula and its variants became clearly associated with the style of Louis-Philippe. One of the largest collections of such frames was made for the royal collection and is closely related to the interiors of the newly restored Versailles apartments.

Although straight-sided Neo-classical styles dominated the Empire and early Restoration periods, a few Rococo-based patterns, the projecting corners and centres of which provided a distinguished and contrasting silhouette (34e), emerged in the 1820s and 1830s. The three-dimensional, undercut and pierced cartouches, which combine late Régence and Rococo forms, have trailing, naturalistic floral sprays and represent an advance in mould-making from the low-relief Napoleonic styles. This design occurs on a number of works by Eugène Delacroix, including the *Massacres at Chios* (1824), *Liberty Leading the People* (1830; 34e) and *Women of Algiers in their Apartment* (1834; all Paris, Louvre). It seems probable that the artist selected these frames; his letters show his interest in framing, and his maternal grandfather was the framemaker Oeben. In the late 1820s Delacroix was using the framemaker Crozet and in the 1840s and 1850s P. Souty. In 1827 he wrote of *Still-life with Lobster* (Paris, Louvre): 'I have dug up a Rococo frame for it, which I have regilded and which will do for it splendidly.'

Louis-Philippe's transformation of Versailles into a museum followed this revivalist trend; the decoration, under the supervision of Frédéric Nepveu (1777–1862), included Rococo, Renaissance, Neo-classical, Louis XIV, neo-Gothic and oriental ornament. Only authentic picture frames, such as those by van der Meulen in the state apartments, were retained; otherwise, the paintings were set into *boiseries* or into painted frames by Jean Alaux (1786–1864), among others. The *horror vacui* of this type of decoration was then common in Europe; it appears in France in Duval's church decoration, and in England in the wall-to-wall Gothic of A. W. N. Pugin. The revivalist movement was fully exploited by the framemaking industry, the pattern books of which were expanded to include countless 'new' and skilfully reproduced designs (see fig. 35). Although collectively they appear to be an undisciplined mixing of decorative motifs, many were tailor-made to suit the pictures' subject and setting. Examples include the TROUBADOUR STYLE, a stylistic cocktail of quasi-Renaissance/Mannerist forms with corner busts, the frieze inlaid with masks and strapwork, all wrapped in a swept rocaille border (35a). Delacroix himself must surely have selected the frame, with its frieze of Moresque star patterns (35b), for his *Interior of a Dominican Convent in Madrid* (1831; Philadelphia, Pennsylvania Mus. of F.A.). Likewise, Jean-Léon Gérôme, many of whose works carry specialist frames, would have chosen—if not designed—the elegant architectural frame (35c) with its refined mouldings and delicately engraved fret pattern. Another frame notable for its innovative surface decoration is that of the portrait of *Achille Devéria* (exh. Salon 1837; Paris, Louvre) by Louis Verceil Boulanger (1806–67). Here the convex moulding, with Louis XIV-style corners, is covered with engraved vermiculation, a Renaissance architectural feature revived for 18th-century stonework.

The frames of Jean-Auguste-Dominique Ingres's paintings are exceptional for their individuality and quality. It is generally accepted that he participated in their design, and many have close stylistic links to their pictures. Those for *Cherubini with the Muse of Lyric Poetry* (1842; Paris,

36. Detail of Renaissance Revival frame with grapevine, birds, dragonflies and lizards, 1160×950×190 mm, attributed to Jean-Auguste-Dominique Ingres for his *Louis-François Bertin*, 1831 (Paris, Musée du Louvre)

35. Historical revival frames, c. 1830–60: (a) Troubadour-style frame, 984×750×170 mm, c. 1825–40 (Toronto, Royal Ontario Musuem); (b) entablature frame with Moorish decoration, 1660×1995×260 mm, original for Eugène Delacroix's *Interior of a Dominican Convent in Madrid*, 1831 (Philadelphia, PA, Museum of Art); (c) entablature frame with paterae on engraved frieze, 880×1500×280 m, original for Jean-Léon Gérôme's *Christian Martyr's Last Prayer*, 1863–83 (Baltimore, MD, Walters Art Gallery); (d) ogee frame with moulded flowers, 1194×914×177 mm, attributed to Jean-Auguste-Dominique Ingres for his *Mme Moitessier Seated*, 1856 (London, National Gallery)

Louvre) and of *Antiochus and Stratonice* (Chantilly, Mus. Condé) are appropriately Neo-classical in their use of Greek frets, Vitruvian scrolls and palmettes. The portrait of *Louis-François Bertin* (see fig. 36) has an elaborate band of undulating vines, decorated with birds, lizards and dragonflies, deeply moulded in composition and gilded with two shades of gold leaf. *Joan of Arc* (1854) and *The Source* (1856; both Paris, Louvre) have raised enrichments of vines; and the frames of *Princesse de Broglie* (New York, Met.) and of *Mme Moitessier Seated* (35d) are covered in deep relief garlands of many different flowers, the latter superbly matched to the sitter's dress.

11. SECOND EMPIRE. During this period (1852–71) and until almost the end of the century, the Salon endorsed the revival frame, especially for academic works. It was preferred by many artists and by curators, dealers and collectors, for reasons of economy and suitability (a Neo-classical style, for instance, being almost universally acceptable) and as a variously simple or opulent house style for large collections (see fig. 37). Straight-sided frames

predominated: these were invariably made in a wider section than their prototypes by the addition of a plain stepped frieze at the sight edge. The most popular Neo-classical style was the fluted scotia frame (37a; compare with original, 32k), which was applied to figure and landscape subjects and was often used as a uniform collector's/gallery pattern (e.g. Lavallard Col., Amiens, Mus. Picardie).

Later in the century appeared the Barbizon frame, associated with painters of that school, where the scotia became a complex profile of stepped flats and hollows, decorated in antique fashion with a steep acanthus ogee, *rais-de-coeur*, ribbon-and-stave, pearls etc, with a high outer laurel-leaf or oak-leaf torus (37c), all in composition. This novel style is rich, weighty and dignified, and at the same time economical enough for the new patrons of the 19th century. The pattern was produced in all sizes; for example, that for an upright landscape by Henri-Joseph Harpignies (*c.* 1875; Orléans, Mus. B.-A.) and a gigantic version (w. *c.* 300 mm) for Karl Daubigny's largest Salon landscape (1876; Frankfurt am Main, Städel. Kstinst. & Städt. Gal.). The deep, stepped profile, with its effect of perspectival recession, is admirably suited to landscapes.

Less generally appropriate, but popular as an indication of middle-class aspirations, are the skilfully moulded, plaster Louis XIV revival frames (37b), which proliferated from the mid-century. These were the main and more expensive alternative to the Barbizon frame. Their more random, undulating and deeply recessed foliage on a cross-hatched ground likewise suited landscapes, such as those by Henri Rousseau, Daubigny and Jean-François Millet in the Walters Art Gallery, Baltimore. Superb large-scale versions frame Edouard Manet's *Olympia* (1863; Paris, Mus. d'Orsay) and Gustave Courbet's *Deer in the Forest* (1868; Minneapolis, MN, Inst. A.). Established during the Second Empire, such patterns endured until the beginning of the 20th century: for example on the magnificent full-length frame of William Bouguereau's *Mother and Child* (1903; Richmond, VA Mus. F.A.). Equally opulent were the Régence and Louis XV revival patterns. The celebrated collection of Old Masters and 19th-century works in the Musée Condé, Chantilly, has a number of distinguished examples (37d).

The 19th-century artistic establishment had traditionalist inclinations (see P. A. Richebourg's 1860s photographs of the Salon hangings, held in the Musée d'Orsay Archives). The dealers' and moneyed collectors' preference was for nostalgic pastiche, in wood or composition, and the academic artists and curators of the various institutes favoured a small repertory of 17th- and 18th-century frame styles, with some anonymous plain mouldings, and mongrel frames built out of the framemakers' stock patterns. Moreover, the Salon made rules about the settings of pictures hung there: they must have a rectangular or square silhouette, even where the sight was round or oval; the width and depth of the moulding must be of a certain size; and, until the 1880s, the finish could only be gilt. Thus the frames were, at their worst, hackneyed, tawdry and cheaply made; at their best, the quality of the workmanship was betrayed by the bankruptcy of the invention.

12. MID-19TH AND 20TH CENTURIES. An inevitable reaction followed, in which the widespread influence in Europe of the Nazarene painters played a part. Several Nazarene painters designed the frames for their work (*see* §VI, below); although these were close in style to Gothic and Renaissance altarpieces, they had a contemporary quality, quite unlike the pastiches of Louis XIV frames. Nazarene frames probably catalyzed, through the work of William Dyce, the design of the Pre-Raphaelites' frames, and consequently those of the Symbolists and, indirectly, of the Impressionists and Post-Impressionists. In France, the Nazarene influence was already at work in the 1830s, on such artists as Victor Orsel, whose *Good and Evil* (1828–33; Lyon, Mus. B.-A.) is housed in a round-arched, polished wooden frame with a rainsill, halfway between medieval and Art Nouveau. It has an inner gilded and painted border with vignettes glossing the main scene and the lunette, and is linked to stained-glass design as much as to the altarpiece. The frame of Auguste Couder's *Scenes from 'Notre-Dame de Paris'* (1833; Paris, Mus. Victor Hugo) is even more retable-like, tripartite, with predella and medallions above; it celebrates Hugo's novel in eccentric swirls of gilded plaster, Renaissance ornament and strange voluted crockets (see 1990 exh. cat.). These are isolated creations, making no headway against the barrier of academic taste until reinforced in the 1860s and 1870s by the influence of English artist-designed frames (*see* §IV, 1 below). The interval was filled by a group of attributive Oriental picture frames, related to similar English types, which used the profile of a conventional

37. Second Empire frames, 1850s–1880s: (a) fluted scotia frame, 730×590×140 mm, original for Gustave Courbet's *Euphrasie Proudhon*, 1865 (Paris, Musée d'Orsay); (b) Louis XIV Revival frame, 832×1111×245 mm, original for Jean-François Millet's *Gleaners*, exhibited Salon 1857 (Paris, Musée d'Orsay); (c) deep ogee Salon frame with acanthus and laurel, 350×580×160 mm, original for Karl Daubigny's *Landscape at Sunset*, 1885 (Nancy, Musée des Beaux-Arts); (d) Rococo Revival frame, 1346×1676×188 mm, *c.* 1860, made for Nicolas Poussin's *Childhood of Bacchus*, *c.* 1630–35 (Chantilly, Musée Condé, Château de Chantilly)

Neo-classical frame, replacing the antique ornament with Egyptian motifs or Arabic script. An example is Gérôme's *Plain of Thebes, Upper Egypt* (1857; Nantes, Mus. B.-A.), with a scotia filled with papyrus and lotus buds and a band of hieroglyphics. These look back to the Egyptian Revival taste of the previous century and reflect the growing interest of many artists in the Middle and Near East. This interest also produced books on or including ornament of the region—the pattern books for furniture- and framemakers.

By the 1860s, however, a new source of ornament had appeared: Japan began to trade with the West. The simple shapes and plain grounds, craftsmanship, asymmetry and stylized organic decoration of its products appealed to those reacting against debased styles, poor workmanship and lack of invention. Exhibitions and imports fuelled the new enthusiasm, and the cult of JAPONISME began. In a series of four frames designed in 1864 by James McNeill Whistler (e.g on *La Princesse du pays de la porcelaine*; Washington, DC, Freer), there are flat borders, borrowed from early Pre-Raphaelite frames, incised with Japanese medallions in the corners and lateral centres, against an overall spiral patterning. The simple structure, type of ornament and obviously handmade decoration would have been startling in the Salon of 1865, where Whistler exhibited *La Princesse*, and where his fellow exhibitors, Manet, Edgar Degas, Camille Pissarro, Claude Monet, Auguste Renoir and Berthe Morisot, would have seen it. There was already a predisposition among the Impressionists to be interested in the framing of their works. In Degas's 1858–60 notebooks he sketched his *Bellelli Family* (1858–67; Paris, Mus. d'Orsay) in its frame, showing Neoclassical diapering and a laurel trim; and in 1864 Monet wrote to Frédéric Bazille that 'a picture gains 100% in a fine frame'. The cross-references in English and French painting around this time make it probable that there was some Pre-Raphaelite influence on French frame design; and many characteristics of Pre-Raphaelite frames can be discerned, in similar or related forms, in Impressionist designs.

Unfortunately, Impressionist frames are rare. Degas's works retain a number, and there are a putative Pissarro frame and gilt borders approved by the artists; otherwise little survives until the Neo-Impressionist/Symbolist frames of the 1880s and 1890s. Reviews of the group exhibitions and the artists' own letters reveal how startlingly different their frames were. The new designs probably first appeared *c.* 1873, when Whistler felt it necessary to claim painted frames as his invention, and when Degas reportedly framed his pastel *Ballet Rehearsal* in a moulding coloured 'soft dull grey and green'. Whistler may have been first but he continued to use gold leaf throughout his life, playing with different shades and restricting colour to the patterns painted on the flats. The Impressionists' innovation was the use of a solid colour or white to achieve a transition between their depictions of light and spontaneity and the walls on which these hung. Pissarro expressed in 1892 this striving for consistency with the setting, agreeing with Degas that a painted 'decoration' was 'an ornament. . .made with a view to its place in an ensemble. . .the collaboration of architect and

painter'. In the mid-1870s there is a gap in the documentation of Impressionist frames, during which Whistler's first one-man show took place in a London gallery painted grey and decorated with blue pottery, palms and flowers: a departure from conventional Pompeiian red. The records recommence with the third group exhibition of 1877, when both Degas and Pissarro apparently used white frames—neutral, as gold had been considered to be, but lacking the opulence and light-trapping qualities of gold.

From the same year, and continuing until 1883, Degas's notebooks contain sketches of frame profiles. They blend elements similar to Pre-Raphaelite designs into strong, imaginative forms completely different in type. Closest to an English model is the square section with four flutes outside a wide flat; this was eventually produced with three flutes and survives on at least five works, including the *Collector of Prints* (1866; New York, Met.) and *The Laundress* (1873; see fig. 38a). The latter frame is now gilded over, but that on *Dancer at Rest* (1879; priv. col.) is white with gold flutes, possibly the original finish. It is reminiscent of the plain wood chamfer with three gilt flutes used by Ford Madox Brown in the 1860s. Degas's other designs, which were completely original, greatly

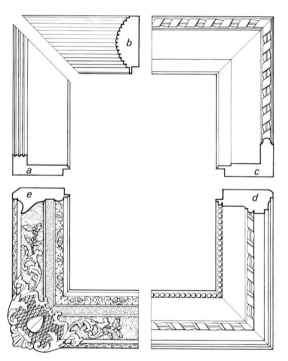

38. French artists' and dealers' frames, *c.* 1860–1900: (a) architrave frame with fluted edge, 543×394×100 mm, original for Edgar Degas's *Laundress (Silhouette)*, 1873 (New York, Metropolitan Museum of Art); (b) reeded cushion frame, 700×700×70 mm, original for Degas's *Two Bathers on the Grass*, *c.* 1896 (Paris, Musée d'Orsay); (c) architrave frame with ribbon-and-stave edge, 480×610×140 mm, original for Degas's *Cours de Gentlemen: Before the Start*, 1862 (Paris, Musée d'Orsay); (d) 'Durand-Ruel' Louis XVI Revival frame, 1360×980×75 mm, last quarter of the 19th century (private collection); (e) 'Durand-Ruel' Régence Revival frame, 670×940×115 mm, original for Camille Pissarro's *Stone Bridge in Rouen, Dull Weather*, 1896 (Ottawa, National Gallery of Canada)

influenced Whistler's frames of the 1890s. The first is a cushion profile, worked into as many as 21 tiny reeds along each rail (38b). Another Degas moulding had a zigzag section with stepped ogees, giving an effect of complex pleats and folds; a green one frames *Bather Lying on the Ground* (1886–8; Paris, Mus. d'Orsay). A more coarsely reeded torus moulding survives in at least four examples, in brown, green or white; in *After the Bath: Woman Drying the Nape of her Neck* (c. 1895; Paris, Mus. d'Orsay) it is brown. (It is worth noting that paintings joining the Louvre/Musée d'Orsay collections from the late 19th century tend to have retained their original frames.) All these designs are found, complete or in embryo, in Degas's sketches, together with the 'cockscomb' moulding, a smooth cushion worked into zigzags on one side. It has been suggested that Cluzel, a framemaker who worked for several Impressionists including Pissarro, helped Degas to realize this design. Both the profile and the colour of these frames are striking.

In 1879 Mary Cassatt used red as well as green, and in 1880 Pissarro's pictures were framed in colours complementary to the main shade of the painting. The colours of that year's exhibition rooms were equally striking; those of Pissarro's room, lilac, with a border of canary yellow, were echoed by the purple frames and yellow mounts of his prints. Such schemes, based on complementary or harmonizing colours, were extensions of the artist's frame to the whole setting, as a way of intensifying the focus on the paintings themselves. Decorative integrity was supremely important to Whistler, to Rossetti and, in different ways, to the Impressionists. Complete rooms, such as Pissarro's, were never replicated by his clients but had some effect on the design of commercial galleries. The Impressionists' immediate purchasers were mostly either bourgeois French or wealthy Americans, whose taste in art was discriminating but whose domestic surroundings were inevitably inclined towards the 19th-century Baroque and Rococo revivals; in such a setting, linear mouldings in pink or purple would have been inappropriate and tawdry. (The owner of a Degas recklessly changed its greygreen frame for gilt—only to have the canvas reclaimed by the artist.) The use of white frames was possibly an admission that the pictures' original setting could not be copied; they offered a less outré compromise. Artists used them for both aesthetic and economic reasons. Few remain, but knowledge of them is still associated with the pictures they framed, and they influenced the ways in which later schools would frame their art. In 1882 Berthe Morisot ordered a white frame for the seventh group exhibition as a matter of course, while in 1883 Pissarro complained that, after years of urging them on the dealer Durand-Ruel, he had been forced to give up. Yet two months later, Durand-Ruel showed Pissarro's pictures in white frames in London, and in May, Pissarro had 'two rooms full of white frames' in the Paris gallery. In 1887 he was attempting to circumvent the rules of the Exposition Internationale, forbidding white frames, with a design of white border, plain oak flat and gilt laurel trim. In 1887–8 Georges Seurat painted *The Models* (Merion Station, PA, Barnes Found.), which showed his *Sunday Afternoon on the Island of La Grande Jatte* (1884–6; Chicago, IL, A. Inst.) in its original broad white frame.

The Impressionists were, however, not solely devoted to white or coloured frames, nor totally dismissive of gilt. References in artists' letters reveal a use of gilt frames concurrently with the more innovative designs. Pissarro wrote (1889): 'The *Women with Pails*, placed in a fine new gilded frame, did admirably, with a heightening of the tone, a comforting warmth; very powerful and rich', and to Jean-Marie Fortuné Durand-Ruel (1892): 'You are right, the cost of frames in matt gold would be considerable; however, we could have three matt frames made for the three principal pictures.' In 1884 Monet asked Durand-Ruel for the address of Dubourg, the gilder, who was also used by Pissarro and Renoir. He ordered 12 frames for the 1891 exhibition of his *Haystack* series; two were white, and the rest presumably gold. Many Impressionist paintings depict gilded frames (e.g. Manet's *Eva Gonzales*, Henri Fantin-Latour's group portraits, Degas's interiors), while photographs of Monet's studio show the *Waterlilies* series in slender gilt mouldings.

It could be claimed that the archetypal Impressionist frames are neither the few surviving white or coloured artists' designs, nor the familiar stripped and colourwashed 18th-century frames beloved of dealers, but two contrasting types developed by their most tireless promoter and campaigner, Durand-Ruel. The first, a plain and elegant Louis XVI revival pattern (38d), was applied universally. In photographs of Impressionist exhibitions from 1905 to 1925 in the Durand-Ruel archives, the paintings are generally in these gilded frames; their burnished ribbon-and-stave mouldings can also be found on a related design (38c) framing Impressionist paintings in the Camondo collection (Paris, Mus. d'Orsay). The first style was found suitable for seascapes, figures, portraits, still-lifes and landscapes; it was presumably approved, even if grudgingly, by the artists. It appears on Degas's work, sometimes with an added white cuff (e.g. on *Ballet Rehearsal on Stage*; 1874); it framed a Pontoise landscape by Pissarro; Paul Signac's *Green Sail* (1904); and James Tissot's portrait of *Mme L. L.* (all Paris, Mus. d'Orsay). Its use may have been stimulated by Manet, many of whose oils and pastels have similar frames, in which they were exhibited at the Salon. The Camondo version, with its wide stepped flat and high traylike outer fillet surmounted by a ribbon-and-stave moulding, is even more spare and clean. It may have been specially designed as a 'livery' frame for Count Isaac de Camondo or have been developed from the Durand-Ruel type; the removal of the ribbon moulding to the outer edge creates a defining ripple of light around the whole.

An alternative pattern to 38d was a Régence-style frame (38e), some 25 of which have been recorded on works by Monet, Pissarro and Renoir, and most of which can be traced back to Durand-Ruel. It has moulded corner and centre cartouches on a cross-hatched ground, and front leaf-tip and shell ornament, in a dull bronze finish. Far more frames of this type survive than of the Neo-classical model, indicating collectors' preference for wider portrait-style frames with a more opulent finish; the curving lines of the decoration blended more happily than the severe geometry of 38d with the typical middle-class interior. These two dealer-selected patterns suggest that it was easier to sell Impressionist works with a traditional presentation than in their own ultra-modern frames, and that the artists themselves generally accepted this. Familiar frames enabled their radical work to be accommodated alongside older masters. Many pictures were given standard Second Empire Salon patterns, either through exhibition demands or to be acceptable to collectors. The versatile fluted scotia frame (37a above) appears on two snow scenes at Lausanne (1878; Paris, Mus. d'Orsay) and on Pissarro's *Versailles Road at Louveciennes* (1879; Baltimore, MD, Walters A.G.). The heavy Louis XIV style (37c above) is retained on several Monets (e.g. *Haystack (Sunset)* and *Haystack (Snow Effect)*; both 1890–91; Boston, MA, Mus. F.A.). It can be seen clearly in the studio photographs noted above, on paintings in the *Seine* and *Waterlily* series, while one of the latter, prominently displayed in two photographs, has a wide swept 18th-century-style setting—possibly the one Monet had in mind when he asked Octave Maus to take care of his 'old frames for which I have an especial regard'. As the studio photographs also show, Monet often preferred narrower frames, employing Louis XIII acanthus-leaf or torus patterns on such works as the *Rouen Cathedral* series (1892–3) in the Musée d'Orsay, Paris.

Another means of obtaining traditional framing was to use discarded *ancien régime* frames, which generally fitted without alteration, since canvases and the corresponding frames had remained standardized for over 200 years. Such hand-carved originals added authority and prestige; their deep patina, from the warm-coloured bole showing through distressed gilding, often harmonized with the subtle Impressionist palette better than new gold. The 810×650 mm portrait had been by far the most frequently produced size since the 17th century, and this may be the reason why so many Impressionist landscapes and seascapes were painted on figure-size canvases rather than the standard formats of landscapes (810×600 mm) or seascapes (810×540 mm). Renoir was firmly in favour of period Rococo frames, the curvilinear profile, C-scrolls and flowers of which enhanced his Boucheresque tendencies. Fine examples are the frames of his *Bouquet of Roses* (1879) and *Sketches of Heads (the Berard Children)* (1881; both Williamstown, MA, Clark A. Inst.), as well as *Gabrielle with a Rose* (1911; Paris, Mus. d'Orsay). (For an illustration of his sketch of a Rococo frame, see 1989 exh. cat., figs 6 and 7.) Thus the reframing of Impressionist and Post-Impressionist works is, perhaps, not so far as once was thought from the original artists' ideas. Their surviving frames are rare, and most galleries display their works in antique or reproduction Louis XIV, Régence and Louis XV styles, mainly applied by successive dealers and collectors. Many are impressive, others overwhelm. Excellent marriages occur with the use of 16th- and 17th-century Italian and Spanish frames; their broader, often coloured, sculptural forms harmonize well with the artists' composition and palette, as in the Bolognese 17th-century *cassetta* frame on Cézanne's *Still-life* (*c.* 1877; Paris, Mus. d'Orsay) and the boldly carved 17th-century Spanish leaf frame on Paul Gauguin's *Ia orana Maria* (1891–3; New York, Met.).

Vincent van Gogh (*see* §V, 6 below) and Gauguin introduced rather different artists' frames. Gauguin carved plaques, half flat decoration, half rounded forms, which reproduce the strange space of his paintings. His sequoia frame (1901–3; Paris, Mus. d'Orsay), picked out in red, which encloses the photograph of a Marquesan warrior, bridges the two media and echoes their decorative symbolism. It is conventional in structure, a broad sloping flat between two fillets; its treatment, with obvious chisel marks, relates it to the English Arts and Crafts Movement, its plainness to types of Neo-Impressionist frame and its motifs to the Symbolists. These links indicate the divergence and variety of French artists' frames, following the innovations of Impressionism. From the mid-1880s there was an upsurge in frames not only designed but constructed or decorated by artists, beginning with Seurat's experiments in Divisionism. He was highly sensitive to the frame's effect and used a more scientific approach than the Impressionists, working from ideas catalysed by, for example, Ogden Rood's treatise on light and colour. He applied the Divisionist technique of his paintings to his frames, using the point in shades of pure colour laid side by side to obtain an 'optical mix' at a distance, the constituent shades and—theoretically—the 'mix' itself being complementary to the adjacent canvas. He may have experimented with painted borders from 1886, although most date from 1889; by 1887 he was making painted frames, such as the painted flat of the fluted 'Degas' frame on *The Circus* (1890–91; Paris, Mus. d'Orsay), sometimes adding them to earlier pictures, such as *Honfleur* (1886; New York, MOMA).

Pissarro was impressed by Seurat's theories and in 1885–6 adopted the Divisionist technique. In 1888 he told Durand-Ruel that he wanted some of his Pointillist pictures included in the next Impressionist exhibition and 'will not be kept out because of my frames'. These were presumably decorated with some sort of coloured points, but none seems to have survived. The only apparently surviving painted frame on a Pissarro (*Garden at Pontoise*, 1881; Cambridge, Fitzwilliam), which may date from this period, is white with an ogee moulding between astragals and fillets, thickly textured on the ogee and splashed with green and blue. It is different enough from Seurat's frames to predate them, belonging, if original, to the Impressionist years. Seurat's frames also influenced those of his peers. Signac's *Women at the Well* (1892; Paris, Mus. d'Orsay) has a flat frame painted matt black with glossy blue squiggles, complementing the orange-gold points of the painting, while Théo van Rysselberghe used a blue-painted frame for his Divisionist *Man at the Helm* (1892; *see* §V below). These tone well with the pictures; it is questionable whether they would have been more effective than a white frame in creating the transition from painting to *fin-de-siècle* wall.

Other Post-Impressionists found different solutions. Henri Edmond Cross used a polished wooden frame on his Divisionist *Air of Evening* (1893–4; Paris, Mus. d'Orsay). Paul Sérusier's expressionistic *Breton Eve* (*c.* 1890; Paris, Mus. d'Orsay) also has a wooden frame, with a deep chamfer to the sight that acts as a focusing agent. Wooden frames like these have had many 20th-century successors; when harmonizing with the painting, they probably offer the best modern alternative to the traditional gold setting.

Symbolists and decorative artists adopted painted, patterned borders and frames that re-created in flat colours the carved ornaments of 17th-century Italian frames. In the 1870s Gustave Moreau produced watercolours of mythological scenes, edged with scrolling foliage and integral painted bands inside their conventional frames (see 1989 exh. cat., pl. 11). Maurice Denis translated this use of painted ornament to wooden plate frames, decorated by himself or his wife with patterns of flowers and leaves, as in his triptych of the *Mithouard Family* (1899; priv. col.; see 1990 exh. cat., pl. 41). In 1892 Pierre Bonnard executed the portrait of *Berthe Schaedlin* (New York, priv. col.) with a very similar frame, ornamented with coloured daisies. In both pictures the flat decorative quality of the painting is as important as the nominal subject and is enhanced by the ornamentation of the frames.

Bonnard's work was both decorative and Symbolist. In 1893 he sketched an overtly Symbolist frame for *Mother and Child*, a preparatory drawing for one of his illustrations to *Le Petit Solfège illustré* by his brother-in-law Claude Terrasse. This sketch also indicates the greater emphasis given to the decorative arts in Europe in the 1890s. The artists of the Nabis group all experimented with the applied arts, including framing, while from the 1880s Les XX of Belgium included decorative artists in their invitations to exhibit; they were in touch with the William Morris circle in England, and this connection, together with the decorative inclinations of Gauguin and the Nabis, aided the development of the Art Nouveau movement. Early Art Nouveau, combined with the literary Symbolism of Moreau and Jean Lecomte du Nouÿ, produced such settings as Marcel-Lenoir's aedicula for the *Coronation of Christ* (1890s; Montricoux, Mus. Marcel-Lenoir), a carved wooden structure with segmental pediment, fluted half-pilasters and a deep base; it has blunt rounded forms and is decorated with relief figures twined with looping organic lines. While the conception echoes the Renaissance Revival frames of Moreau's *Life* (1879–86; Paris, Mus. Moreau) or Lecomte du Nouÿ's *Homer as a Beggar* (1881; Grenoble, Mus. B.-A.), the treatment is drastically different and contemporary. Its religious symbolism derives from Gauguin's Pont-Aven school, and its decoration from the 'whiplash' line of Victor Horta and Henry Van de Velde; and it has some of the meltingly amorphous quality of the Auricular style. Art Nouveau picture frames are, however, rare; decorative paintings of the 1890s and 1900s in museums and private collections are most often hung unframed or in minimalist 20th-century strip mouldings. There remain, however, some mirror frames, which may be of carved, polished wood, repoussé copper or moulded metal; for example, the carved, wooden eared frame with vine and butterfly motifs by a student of William Morris (Paris, priv. col.). There are also interesting examples in the Musée de l'Ecole de Nancy, notably in polished oak, on portraits and landscapes with figures by Victor Prouvé. Otherwise there are decorative borders in the style, such as the bold painted leaf-and-flower motifs around a work by Paul Ranson: *Girl with Flowers* (c. 1890; Rome, Gal. Levante). These take up the picture's shapes and tones, using them as Bonnard did, to flatten the whole into an almost abstract decoration. Borders on Alphonse Mucha's posters attempt a similar abstraction but degenerate into mere prettiness of line.

These ideas appealed to Matisse; the *Red Studio* (1911; New York, MOMA) shows a decorative portrait in a frame painted like those of the Nabis, and a group of his pictures has integral painted borders. Georges Rouault, Matisse's fellow Fauve, produced similar works (*see* §V below). The various versions of Matisse's *Tahiti* (1936) have margins of flowers, very like the designs painted on to frames by Denis and Bonnard, but in this case painted on the canvas itself. The scene is composed as a window looking out on a seascape; it is bounded by a stylized lace curtain and by the flowery frame, but at the same time the illusion is undercut, partly by the flatness and abstraction of the artist's manner and partly by the frame itself, with its equally flat and decorative pattern. A pencil sketch of the scene and its border show that both were conceived together; and a photograph of 1940 shows Matisse working on the similar arrangement of *Verdure*, a landscape contained in a painted, scrolling margin, the whole framed in a simple moulding. Such a moulding is found on Matisse's portrait of *Sarah Stein* (1916; San Francisco, CA, MOMA), where a reverse-rebate triangular-sectioned frame emphasizes the severe geometry of the painting, and on his *Corner of Studio* (1912; Moscow, Pushkin Mus. F.A.), one of two of his works to have a grey-painted hollow frame. Even simpler are the narrow strips tacked around the stretchers of the Matisses in the Cone Collection, Baltimore Museum of Art (although these absolute reductions of the frame may have been imposed by a patron or curator). Both this minimalist form and the painted border undermine or subvert traditional notions of framing. The border defines the work as a decorative pattern with no depth, creating a tension with the realism, however stylized, of Matisse's interiors and landscapes. The minimal strip frame sets the painting directly against the wall, with only an outline to delimit its boundaries; there is no transitional area to rest the eye, no illusion of a window on other worlds. The canvas stands on its own merits, neither bound to its setting nor self-consciously separated from it.

Some of the Cubists, such as Picasso and Braque, returned to more traditional ideas by reproducing frames or elements of frames in their work, and by adding plain painted borders (*see* §VIII below). Others preferred wooden mouldings in the form of a completely unadorned white-painted torus, examples being Georges Valmier's *Five Senses* (1931; Paris, Mus. A. Mod. Ville Paris), Fernand Léger's *The Typographer* and Jean Gorin's *Composition No. 2* (1926; Nantes, Mus. B.-A.). This is an extremely satisfying solution to the problem of displaying a work that no longer obeys the conventions of representational art; the austerity of these monumental creations is repeated in the abstracted form of the frame. Similarly, the work of Hans Arp of the 1920s and 1930s was framed in basic, geometrically sectioned frames that indicate the large, abstract projecting forms in his paintings.

Surrealism, however, with its use of disturbing juxtapositions, continued the breakdown of the conventional frame, drawing it wholly or partially into the composition of the painting, or crossing it with elements of the central image. Early Renaissance artists had done this in order to heighten the illusionism of the whole; here (e.g. in works by René Magritte and Max Ernst) it was done to point out the ambiguity of the world portrayed. This has perhaps hastened the tendency of 20th-century artists to turn away from the frame or to demote it, using cheap stock mouldings as a gesture to delimitation and as a vestigial form of protection. Examples are Léger's *Tail of Comet on a Black Background* (*c.* 1931; Maeght priv. col.), a triptych with each panel in a simple gold border, and Amédée Ozenfant's *Large Still-life* (1926; Paris, Mus. A. Mod. Ville Paris). Only in a rare instance is the frame produced in tandem with the work or accorded any place in the artist's design, as in Serge Poliakoff's *Mural Composition* (1967; Paris, Pompidou). This is a composition of 13 panels inspired by icons, each framed in a painted border mimicking wood. In contrast, the diptych *Passage du bleu* (1977; Rennes, Mus. B.-A. & Archéol.) by Geneviève Asse (*b* 1923) is framed in a grey moulding designed and painted by the artist, which looks back to the simple northern European altar frames of the 14th and 15th centuries. These two examples show the diversity of the artists' frames that are still produced; there is no longer much sense of a coherent style, nor of a frame's purpose, but the individual designs that do appear are always eclectic.

BIBLIOGRAPHY

J.-F. Watin: *L'Art de faire et d'employer le vernis* (Paris, 1772); rev. as *L'Art du peintre, doreur, vernisseur* (Paris, 1776)

L. Deshairs: *Les Cadres de tableaux en France, de la fin du XVIe siècle au Premier Empire* (Paris, 1910–12)

H. Vial, A. Marcel and A. Girodie: *Les Artistes décorateurs du bois* (Paris, 1912)

F. de Salverte: *Les Ebénistes du XVIIIe siècle: Leurs oeuvres et leurs marques* (Paris and Brussels, 1927)

S. Roche: *Cadres français et étrangers du XVe siècle au XVIIIe siècle* (Paris, 1931)

L. Venturi: *Les Archives de l'Impressionnisme* (Paris, 1939)

J. Calmette: *Les Grands Ducs de Bourgogne* (Paris, 1949); Eng. trans. as *The Golden Age of Burgundy* (New York, 1962)

A. Blunt: *Art and Architecture in France, 1500 to 1700*, Pelican Hist. A. (Harmondsworth, 1957)

W. Graf Kalnein and M. Levey: *Art and Architecture of the 18th Century in France*, Pelican Hist. A. (Harmondsworth, 1972)

G. Bazin: *The Louvre* (London, 1979)

P. Mitchell: 'The Framing Tradition', *Picture Framing*, ed. R. Wright-Smith (London, 1980)

P. Cannon-Brookes: 'Robert Tournières, Lord Bateman and Two Picture Frames', *Int. J. Mus. Mgmt & Cur.*, iv (1985), pp. 141–5 [4 figs]

P. Mitchell: 'A Signed Frame by Jean Chérin', *Int. J. Mus. Mgmt & Cur.*, iv (1985), pp. 145–54 [8 figs]

B. Pons: *De Paris à Versailles, 1699–1736: Les Sculpteurs ornemanistes et l'art décoratif des Bâtiments du Roi* (Strasbourg, 1986)

The Art of the Edge: European Frames, 1300–1950 (exh. cat., Chicago, IL, A. Inst., 1986)

I. Cahn: 'Les Cadres impressionnistes', *Rev. A.*, 76 (1987), pp. 57–62

B. Pons: 'Les Cadres français du XVIIIe siècle et leurs ornements', *Rev. A.*, 76 (1987), pp. 41–50

I. Cahn: 'Degas's Frames', *Burl. Mag.*, cxxxi (1989), pp. 289–92

Cadres de peintres (exh. cat. by I. Cahn, Paris, Mus. d'Orsay, 1989) [37 figs]

Polyptyques: Le Tableau multiple du moyen âge au vingtième siècle (exh. cat., ed. C. Clément; Paris, Louvre, 1990)

D. Shipounoff: 'Picture Framing I: La Reparure', *Int. J. Mus. Mgmt & Cur.*, xiii (1994), pp. 431–4

For further bibliography *see* §I above.

IV. Britain.

1. Medieval. 2. Tudor and early Stuart. 3. Early Baroque. 4. Auricular. 5. Late Baroque. 6. Palladian. 7. Rococo. 8. Neo-classical. 9. Regency and early Victorian. 10. Pre-Raphaelite and Aesthetic Movement. 11. Late 19th and 20th centuries.

1. MEDIEVAL. Britain is comparatively less well-endowed with medieval altarpieces even than France, and the earliest stages of framemaking must be deduced from records and wall paintings. Antependia of gold, silver, ivory, silver gilt and precious stones are recorded from the 11th century; these would have been related to Germanic and other northern European examples. By the 12th century reredoses and altarpieces proper had appeared, and contemporary wall paintings indicate that geometric and mosaic patterns would have been used for frames. By the early 13th century the abbey at St Albans, Herts, boasted an altarpiece 'partly of metal, partly of wood' and another of two tiers. Arcading with gilt and painted mouldings and subject paintings in the niches appeared on church walls and was imitated in many wooden screens or free-standing reredoses, such as the 13th century example in the church of the Holy Innocents, Adisham, Kent, which was originally in Canterbury Cathedral. This has a Gothic architectural framework, like contemporary Italian altarpieces, with carved, gessoed, gilt and painted colonettes, trefoil arches and quatrefoils. Works such as these would probably have had the elaborately patterned decoration used for such architectural features as doors and window-frames: in the Painted Chamber at the Palace of Westminster, London, there were window mouldings gilded with black lines or painted red, green or blue. Similarly, in the 13th-century façades of such great Gothic cathedrals as Salisbury, Wells and Exeter there are mouldings, arcadings and colonettes that frame tiers of sculpted figures and are painted like the statues themselves, reproducing on a monumental scale an altar reredos with its pinnacled framework.

Techniques used for framing altarpieces were certainly transferred to buildings: fake enamelling, where panels of glass were gilded and painted on the reverse and then applied to wooden surfaces, was used on both the outside and inside of churches. The Westminster Retable (*c.* 1270–80; see fig. 39a) employs this method; it is in the bejewelled style of a reliquary and was much influenced by the interiors of the Sainte-Chapelle in Paris. Altarpieces in this reliquary style were extremely expensive in terms of the labour involved: in 1258 Peter of Spain received the huge sum of £80 for the Lady Chapel frontal and altarpiece in Westminster Abbey (including the frames); the Westminster Retable would probably have been even more expensive as it was the focal point of the whole abbey. The simple, oblong plate frame containing it is enriched with panels of *faux* enamel, beautifully worked with interlocking geometrical patterns and with 24 gessoed cameos of classical heads. Within are three panels with a micro-architectural framework (as in Spanish and northern European altarpieces), and two containing Saracenic eight-pointed medallions. These two types of inner frame are set against backgrounds, respectively, of further geometric and heraldic glass mosaics and of ultramarine glass panels painted with gilded vines and foliate scrolls. The inner

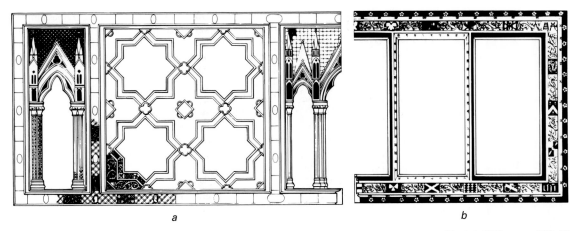

39. Medieval English gilt-wood and painted frames inset with glass panels: (a) on the Westminster Retable, 958×3335 mm, c. 1270–80 (London, Westminster Abbey); (b) on the Despenser Retable, 1124×2590mm, c. 1380–90 (Norwich Cathedral)

frames are also decorated, the architectural colonettes with painted pastiglia emblems and the star mouldings with *faux* enamel. The Westminster Retable links Anglo-French metalwork shrines and reliquaries with the great gilded and enamelled tombs of this period, the remains of which survive in the abbey. It also provided an archetype for such later and provincial altarpieces as the example (*c.* 1355) in St Mary's Church, Thornham Parva, Suffolk, and its antependium (*c.* 1355; Paris, Mus. Cluny); here, the architectural framework is simplified and brightly painted, the infill decoration is copied in gilt and painted, stamped pastiglia, and the outer frame with its enamel panels becomes a simple painted border.

In the Despenser Retable (*c.* 1380–90; Norwich Cathedral; see fig. 39b) the inner framework has disappeared, and the outer mouldings are now as subtle and varied as an early Italian *cassetta* frame. Two flats, an ogee and bevel are separated by gilded astragals and painted red or blue, apart from the large central flat. This combines 28 *faux*-enamel panels of glass silvered on the reverse and painted with armorial bearings in red and black, with gilded pastiglia panels of floral/foliate scrolling. The top rail and all four corners of the frame were replaced in 1958, and only three of the original glass panels remain, but skilful conservation has restored the decorative opulence contained by a severe linear form that characterizes the greatest frame designs. The gilt pastiglia work repeats the backgrounds of the paintings and echoes the curving forms of the figures within; it also sets organic, natural forms against the geometry of the heraldic motifs and the frame. The frame was apparently fixed to the panels before any gilding or painting was carried out, emphasizing the unity of picture and setting. Interest in a similar interplay of round, flat and ogee mouldings is illustrated by drawings in the Pepysian Sketchbook (Cambridge, Magdalene Coll.), the earliest parts of which are contemporary with the Despenser Retable. Two leaves show moulding sections, the comparative intricacy of which anticipates the more abstract architectural forms that would replace the Gothic style. They were possibly used by carvers of altarpieces and were probably current by the late 15th century. This was the date of the arrival in Britain of William Caxton.

The subsequent upsurge in production of printed pattern books influenced carving techniques, as did the simultaneous influx of Flemish carvers, who brought their own pattern books.

Very few Late Gothic British frames exist. The Swansea Triptych (second half of the 15th century; London, V&A) is the only remaining example in Britian of a type exported in quantities to the Continent. It is a large, single tier polyptych with seven carved alabaster panels in an oak frame. The latter is a simple linear structure with an inscribed predella, quoined mullions of stained oak and gilded pastiglia blocks, and canopies depending from the upper moulding. Otherwise, the decorative filigree frames of the International Gothic style have vanished, and must be extrapolated from such works as the great wood screen (*c.* 1480) in the church of St Edmund, Southwold, Suffolk, with its carved arcading and painted, gilded and pierced panels; this is itself a frame, designed to isolate and emphasize the drama of the liturgy.

2. TUDOR AND EARLY STUART. Renaissance altarpieces are almost non-existent in Britain, largely because Renaissance forms and principles were not properly assimilated in northern Europe until the 17th century. Secular paintings, however, required appropriate settings, and these derive paradoxically from the linear inner mouldings of a Renaissance *quadro*. A transitional example is the *Marriage Portrait of Edward IV and Elizabeth Woodville* (*c.* 1464; Northampton, Cent. Mus. & A.G.), a triptych similar to northern examples, with simple painted flat and hollow mouldings decorated with gilded guilloche. As the fashion for portraiture grew from the mid-15th century, so the numbers of these *cassetta* frames proliferated and became increasingly sophisticated. Their immediate predecessors, however, are northern rather than Italian, and they are related to the austere Flemish, Dutch or German ebonized or stained-wood frames. An example of this style of dark-wood portrait and genre frame surrounds *George Talbot, 6th Earl of Shrewsbury* (1580; Hardwick Hall, Derbys, NT; see fig. 40a). This is of half-lapped construction in a series of stepped ogees and flats that echo contemporary wainscoting. It shows the influence of the

40. Tudor and Stuart frames, 1540s–1680s: (a) ebonized parcel-gilt entablature frame, 570×432×64 mm, contemporary for English school: *George Talbot, 6th Earl of Shrewsbury*, 1580 (Hardwick Hall, Derbys, NT); (b) ebonized entablature frame with dentils and gilt Greek key pattern band, 1981×1727×178 mm, probably original for Marcellus Coffermans's *Adam and Eve*, 1543 (Hatfield House, Herts); (c) cushion frame with centre to corner palm leaves, 730×1168×64 mm, original for British school: *John Tradescant the Elder and his Wife Elizabeth, c.* 1638 (Oxford, Ashmolean Museum); (d) cushion frame with centre to corner stylized oak leaves, 717×1181×64 mm, original for British school: *John Tradescant the Younger and his Wife Hester*, before 1656 (Oxford, Ashmolean Museum); (e) cushion frame with centre to corner undulating leaves, 1016×1264×68 mm, contemporary for British school: *Denham Palace, Buckinghamshire, c.* 1695 (New Haven, CT, Yale Center for British Art); (f) Renaissance-style frame with gilt scrolling foliage on black, 1320×1490×140 mm, 1680s, made for Anthony van Dyck's *Lady Elizabeth Thimbelby and Dorothy, Viscountess Andover, c.* 1637 (London, National Gallery)

Flemish journeymen carvers who came to Britain from the 1470s. More elaborate versions, such as that in 40b with its bold run of dentils (the gilt fret may be a later addition), are similarly linked to 16th- and 17th-century architectural and furniture styles. Strong profiles with dentil mouldings can be found on ceiling cornices, chimney-pieces and door-frames in many of the great contemporary English houses (see Jourdain, 1950). Both frames and panelling of this period are generally of oak and were either painted or parcel gilt, illustrating their common genesis at the hands of the joiner-carver. Carved architectural ornament of this period is often northern in type, slightly grotesque, and based on strapwork, which was popular well into the 17th century. Engraved or painted frames often imitate this style, but picture frames tend not to, either because it was too heavy or oppressive when reproduced in wood or because it could less easily be used for large, continuous runs.

The patterns used by Inigo Jones in the 1620s and 1630s for ceilings, chimney-pieces and friezes were possibly adopted for picture frames at a relatively early stage,

in tandem with carved furniture etc. These frames employ Italianate motifs and Baroque versions of Classical forms. One type midway between this and the northern dark frame has an ebonized body with gilded corner decorations (examples, London, N.P.G.; Oxford, Ashmolean). Often of applied metalwork, these decorations might be abstract-/naturalistic foliate motifs or cherubim; they date from the middle third of the 17th century. A more common example of the full-blown style combines a flat 'ebonized' background with a continuous run of applied, pierced and gilded scrolling foliage. This pattern is a voluptuous Renaissance revival of a Classical motif, veering towards the Baroque and apparently developing from a more sparse pattern of the 1620s and 1630s. It came into its own in the hands of Restoration carvers during the third quarter of the 17th century and appears on the sides and aprons of chairs and overmantels. Examples can be seen on contemporary and also earlier works, for example, 40f by Anthony van Dyck. The style is especially associated with van Dyck and also appears with another modified version as a gallery frame at Althorp, Northants. It can be seen as the pure classical analogue of the Baroque 'Lutma' floral/foliate frame.

3. EARLY BAROQUE. Scrolled and lapping-leaf patterns were also common to a third contemporary frame type, the ubiquitous torus or cushion moulding; this simple, cheap but decorative design was employed for portraits, landscapes and subject pictures. It is a narrower, drawn-out version of a Classical pulvinated frieze, revived by such architects as Inigo Jones from decorative elements by Vittoria and Palladio. The use of overlapping bay leaves (40c), oaks or lobed half-flowers (40d), and spiralling leaves and peapods (40e) gives a varied rhythm and motion to a very basic structure— from a straight progression of oak leaves to the elongated elegance of undulating palms. The leaf centres and corners break these rhythms according to the usual Baroque pattern of crossed and diagonal focal lines. The frame (40c) for a double portrait sets each bust in its own painted oval bay-leaf torus.

Decorated cushion mouldings were ubiquitous in the 17th century. The Great Stairs at Chatsworth, Derbys, are carved on the stone undersides with a pattern-book variey of torus mouldings, while at Ham House, Richmond, there are ceiling and overdoor examples dating from the 1630s. French and Dutch variants are plentiful, the Dutch frames with their elaborate deep-cut bands of fruit, flowers and ruched ribbons coming very close to contemporary English examples. In both, the main torus is now supported by auxiliary mouldings—water-leaf, leaf-and-dart, husks, ribbons and hollows—and both derive first from Louis XIII prototypes, which themselves came from a Roman original. They are classical in their rich, linear form, reflecting the trends of French classicism under Poussin, although there could be dramatic breaks at centres and corners. A typical example surrounds a portrait of *Samuel Pepys* (1666; London, N.P.G.; see fig. 41a) with deep-cut curled-back leaves and flowers, and ribbon-and-leaf trims. This was silvered, as was the fashion (although silver frames were often later gilded). It cost 25 shillings, and the painting £14. It is very close to Dutch frames of the 1670s to 1690s and reflects the strong commercial link

41. British Baroque frames, 1660s–1710s: (a) Louis XIII-style fruit-and-leaf torus frame, 756×629×102 mm, original for John Hayls's *Samuel Pepys*, 1666 (London, National Portrait Gallery); (b) Louis XIII-style frame with undulating acanthus foliage and flowers, 2040×2619×134 mm, late 17th century, made for Orazio Gentileschi's *Joseph and Potiphar's Wife*, 1631–4 (London, Hampton Court, Royal Collection); (c) bolection frame with leaf-and-tendril torus, 1098×2710×126 mm, original for John Closterman's *Children of John Taylor of Bifrons Park*, ?1696 (London, National Portrait Gallery); (d) bolection frame with acanthus scrolls and floral sprigs, 2390×1570×152 mm, original for studio of Willem van de Velde II's *Man-of-War Firing a Salute*, late 17th century (Dublin, National Gallery of Ireland); (e) bolection frame with cross-cut acanthus leaves, 1067×1257×126 mm, *c.* 1660–90, on William Dobson's *Portrait of the ?Streatfield Family*, *c.* 1642–3 (New Haven, CT, Yale Center for British Art)

with Holland between 1651 and 1672. The effect of such frames is one of strong, flickering movement, achieved by bold undercutting; this supports the bravura technique of Restoration portraiture and echoes the broken glint of wigs and silk gowns. This type of frame was made to support the image against the new flock wallpaper (which Pepys mentioned), to echo costume and accessory details within the painting and to give decorative interest against a plainer setting. It is also used as an inset wall-frame and to outline elements of panelling (e.g. at Burghley House, Cambs). A rearrangement of the mouldings makes this a reverse rebate or bolection frame, pushing the picture plane forward, almost level with the torus, which is itself more dramatically cut (41c). Both the group portrait, with its swags of velvet and satins and rhythms of outstretched hands, and the frame with its spiral leaf torus broken by flower sprigs and its outer leaf-and-flower hollow, move the type from the Classical restraint of its Roman source to the dynamic unity of the Baroque.

In two styles of bolection frame developing from this, the profile of the moulding is smoothed from torus and hollow into a wide ogee moulding, with shallow relief decoration of undulating leaves and flower sprigs (41d) or cross-cut acanthus ('raffle leaves') (41e). These are typically Baroque: form and ornament support each other and gain drama from the play of light and texture on the frame.

They are also typical of the Louis XIV style in structure, with the ogee moulding that was the basis for different types of ornament through the second half of the 17th century. Figure 41d is also French-derived in its surface decoration, while 41e is a Baroque reworking of the more upright acanthus leaves seen, for example, on the cymatium of the Maison Carrée, Nîmes, and picked up by architects via Le Brun and Giovanni Francesco Romanelli to outline cornices, door-frames and panelling in the great houses of the later 17th century.

The other main type of profile at this time is based on a bird's-beak or quarter-round moulding and, like the Louis XIII garland torus of 41a, comes directly from France (41b). It is decorated with an alternating S-shaped scrolling leaf pattern, complex and intricately carved, and is one of the most sophisticated 17th-century English frames. Its source ultimately derives from Classical Roman friezes, although the leaf forms have been relaxed and the scroll rosettes removed. It would have been expensive to produce, given the density and detail of the ornament, and would have been reserved for the most precious work in a collection. Its linear form and regular, subtle patterning is again classical rather than Baroque, and it was designed to provide a subdued twinkle of light rather than a bold *chiaroscuro*.

4. AURICULAR. Along with these French-derived models, the later 17th century is notable for a completely different type of frame, which is Mannerist rather than Baroque or classical and is closely related to Dutch Auricular and 'Lutma' frames (*see* §V below). There were close links, both courtly and commercial, between Britain and the Netherlands at this time, and Dutch and Flemish carvers were well established in Britain. Those on the Grand Tour would also have seen the Auricular Medici frames in Florence (*see* §II, 4(ii) above). It was perhaps inevitable that a native form of the Auricular frame should be created, especially for portraits in the lush northern idiom of Lely and Godfrey Kneller (*see* AURICULAR STYLE). The English Auricular frame is called the 'Sunderland' after Robert Spencer, 2nd Earl of Sunderland, who employed it as a gallery frame at Althorp. It is naively carved on a shallow, flat carcass with an Italianate grotesque mascaron below and a cartouche above (see fig. 42). It is almost invariably gilded in a blond gold, which picks up the pale skin tones of the contemporary school of portraiture, while the curving forms echo draperies, coiffures and male wigs. It is a simple but highly theatrical shape, effectively isolating a painting from the dark walls of the period, which would be wainscoted or covered in tapestry or leather. The frame illustrated in figure 42 was carved by John Norris, 'frame-maker to the Court', who also supplied the frame shown in figure 41a to Samuel Pepys. Examples incorporating, like the Medici frames, such marine elements as cockleshells, conches, seahorses and fish heads are in the Manchester City Art Gallery and the National Portrait Gallery, London.

At this time Grinling Gibbons was developing the 'Lutma', with its flowers, fruits and cherubs, into an apotheosis of the carver's art. His first known frame was a wide torus carved with high-relief blossoms taken from contemporary Dutch flower paintings; John Evelyn valued

42. Auricular 'Sunderland' frame, 1655×1241 mm, early 1670s, one of a suite supplied by John Norris, original for school of Peter Lely: *John Maitland, 1st Duke of Lauderdale in Garter Robes, c.* 1650 (Ham House, Surrey, NT)

it at the large sum of £100. The super-realistic style was that of François Du Quesnoy via Artus Quellinus of the Netherlands; it spread through Europe but most particularly informed the Gibbons school in Britain, which included such carvers as Thomas Young, Jonathan Maine, Charles Oakey, Samuel Watson of Chatsworth, Edward Pearce, William Emmett, John Selden of Petworth, Joel Lobb and William Davis. Examples of frames and outer pendant wall-frames, carved in this ultra-realistic manner in lime- and pear-wood, can be seen at Windsor Castle; Badminton House, Glos; the Ashmolean Museum, Oxford; Ham House, Richmond; and Trinity College Chapel, Cambridge. These pale woods were to be seen against darker walnut, oak and olive-wood panelling. This was the period in which the carver took a central role in English decorative art (see Oughton). From 1691 until 1710 Gibbons was the major London employer of carvers at his Ludgate Hill workshops; in 1693 he succeeded Henry Philips as Master Sculptor and Carver in Wood to the Crown, and he worked on almost equal terms with Wren. At the same time the tradition was enriched by the tremendous influx of talented carvers from France, following the revocation of the Edict of Nantes (1685), while the economic stability of Britain meanwhile had been increasing since the Restoration (1660), giving scope for a vast output of ornamental carving—including pendent festoons and suites of frames—in large houses throughout the country.

5. LATE BAROQUE. In tandem with the work of Gibbons were the 'Lely' and 'Kneller' frames. These were of French derivation, developed from the torus and bird's-beak Louis XIII models, but with the sculptural decoration of the latter replaced by shallow calligraphic and flower-sprigged ornament. They represent the continental, Tory, Catholic taste in Britain as PALLADIANISM did the classical, Protestant, anti-Baroque Whiggish tendency. As with so many families of frame, the same profile appears in different guises, with a range of surface ornamentation. There is a plain version, the main torus/convex moulding surrounded by small astragals and hollows, edged by water-leaf, acanthus tip, ribbon-and-floret trims; and a panelled version (usually referred to as a 'Lely' (see fig. 43a, b and c). Here, convex reposes (often brilliantly burnished to act like mirrors) contrast with centres and corners of shallow-relief, scrolling, flowered *rinceaux*, gilded with a matt finish. Reverse rebate variations of both types exist (43b), as well as arched and oval frames, and there are more luxurious examples where the reposes are gadrooned (43c) or the whole central moulding is carved with an undulating lacy foliage pattern (43d). These latter styles, augmented with several rows of husk, leaf or ribbon moulding, and with a burnished gilt hollow providing definition, were obviously expensive in terms of labour and hence were often reserved for royal portraits (43c). The gadrooned panel design is peculiarly English, although parallel bands of gadrooning and floriation were used elsewhere in silverwork. The effect is rich and varied but at the same time—because of the shallow carving and refined detail—delicate and shimmering with light. More light was obviously thrown on to the picture surface by those frames with mirrored reposes, so these would be the choice for a more economical design or for a darker interior. Lely habitually used them, and the records of his posthumous sale of estate and studio contents detail the large number of such frames he kept on hand for completed paintings. Luxury versions of the same type, but continuously patterned with ornament in the style of Daniel Marot I, were made by Perry Malton for the great van Dyck paintings at Petworth House, W. Sussex.

Overlapping with the 'Lely' design and continuing through the Queen Anne period was a bolection frame (43e) carved with continuous centre to corner gadrooning. This form, peculiar to Britain, is a refined version of Italian Baroque models and is often referred to as the 'Kneller' frame; with its fast rhythm of centrally radiating lines, the gadrooning—reinforced by an outer leaf spiral—acts dramatically to focus on the sitter. The same profile, well disguised in ebonized pear-wood with only a carved and gilded sight edge, was an elegant and more economical alternative, its colour contrast combining the best of English and Dutch frames; an excellent example is on Kneller's portrait of *William Congreve* (Dublin, N.G.).

Developing from the Lely designs a range of 18th-century frames emerged, related to Louis XIV patterns, with the ogee profile of the latter. These generally have fairly wide, sculptural borders, in which the form is reflected by scrolling foliate ornament intertwined with

I, echoing his ceilings for the château of Chantilly, and the corner cartouches are similarly French (in 44c they are espagnolette ruffs derived from e.g. Du Cerceau's engravings).

Numerous variations on this style were possible: it lent itself to the trophy frame; for example, Charles Philips's portrait of *Frederick, Prince of Wales* (1731; New Haven, CT, Yale Cent. Brit. A.) has a central cartouche with the feathers of the prince's crest. There are also *grand luxe* models in the Louis XIV/early Régence style; these were made for the state apartments of great houses, sometimes in a design peculiar to the particular house (its 'livery frame' or house style), which was used indiscriminately for the paintings of whatever period or nationality that were acquired by the owner, often while on the Grand Tour. These frames, authentically French in both their

43. British Baroque frames, 1660s–1730s: (a) Louis XIII-style 'Lely' frame with leaf-and-flower corners and centres on punched ground, plain convex reposes, 1245×1029×122 mm, probably original for Willem Wissing's *John Cecil, 6th Earl of Exeter*, late 1680s (Chatsworth, Derbys); (b) bolection 'Lely' frame, 2184×1333×122 mm, original for Peter Lely's *Charles Stuart, 3rd Duke of Richmond and Lennox*, c. 1661 (Raleigh, NC, North Carolina Museum of Art); (c) bolection 'Lely' frame with gadrooned reposes, 2337×1429×133 mm, original for Godfrey Kneller's *Queen Anne as Princess of Denmark*, c. 1690 (Beningbrough Hall, N. Yorks, NT); (d) bolection 'Lely' frame with continuous scrolling foliage and gadrooning, 914×1054×83 mm, probably original for school of Lely: *Barbara, Duchess of Cleveland*, c. 1660–85 (Audley End, Essex); (e) Queen Anne bolection frame with gadrooning and leaf-and-flower back, 1080×800×100 mm, original for Godfrey Kneller's *Charles Dartiquenave*, 1702 (London, National Portrait Gallery)

strapwork (see fig. 44a and b). They are essentially Baroque and exploit contrasts of light and shade and texture in true Baroque style. The background 'hazzling', which gives basic variation of surface to the 'Lely' frame, becomes a more sophisticated sanded border (i.e. gold leaf applied to a drizzling of sand over size). This is set against matt and burnished water gilding, emphasizing the complex play of light over the different mouldings. The shallow decorative scrolling (44c) is closely related to designs by Jean Berain

44. British early Georgian French-style frames, 1720s–1760s: (a) straight Louis XIV-style frame with scrolling foliage and floral springs, 1295×990×100 mm, 1720s–1750s, on Daniel Mytens's *William Herbert, 3rd Earl of Pembroke*, before 1630 (Audley End, Essex); (b) Louis XIV-style frame with corner cartouches, 737×610×95 mm, original for Thomas Gibson's *George Vertue*, 1723 (London, Society of Antiquaries of London); (c) Régence style frame with shell corner/centre cartouches, 737×635×102 mm, original for William Hogarth's *William Cavendish, Marquess of Hartington*, 1741 (New Haven, CT, Yale Center for British Art); (d) straight Louis XV-style frame with gadrooning, 660×542×102 mm, original for Thomas Hudson's *Elizabeth, Wife of the Earl of Altamont*, 1752 (Westport House, Co. Mayo); (e) Louis XV-style frame with rocaille corner cartouches, 743×619×102 mm, original for Allan Ramsay's *The Artist's Second Wife, Margaret*, c. 1758–60 (Edinburgh, National Gallery of Scotland)

design and technique, were probably carved by Huguenot and Flemish immigrants. Peter Cousins and René Cousins, a framemaker and gilder respectively, came from the Low Countries in the 1670s with their apprentice Carée; René worked at Windsor Castle and Hampton Court Palace with Gibbons, and Peter for Charles, 6th Duke of Somerset, at Petworth. In the early 18th century Michael Hué (Huet) also made frames for Petworth, and Jean Pelletier did the same for Boughton House, Northants. Paul Petit and Henry Joris (Jouret) were employed by Frederick, Prince of Wales, in the 1730s, and William Thornton used the Huguenot craftsmen Jean Godier and Daniel Hervé at Wentworth Castle, S. Yorks, c. 1718–19. Luxury house frames in a pure Louis XIV style can be found at Chatsworth, Derbys, Stourhead and Corsham Court, Wilts; those at the last are identical designs, framing works by Reni, Rubens, Carlo Dolci, Bonifazio de' Pitati and William Dobson. The suitability of such a pattern to the Baroque classicism of Reni is questionable, but these frames were highly suitable for the backgrounds of cut velvet and the new flock wallpapers in use throughout the 18th century, and for the grained or painted wainscoting with its gradual accretions of *boiseries*.

Subject pictures and portraits tended to be given frames with centre and corner cartouches, as the focal lines between these points—diagonals and vertical crosses—emphasize the visual highlights of the single figure (face and hands), while the composition of a Baroque history painting or family portrait often utilizes the same focal lines. Marine scenes and landscapes, however, where the same qualities of movement, drama and emotional tension are not relevant, were usually given straight-sided frames with modest corners. Other variations include the mirrored reposes of a Lely frame between corner (sometimes also centre) panels of decoration in the style of Bérain; these were again more economical and gave stronger contrast of light and shade. In the portrait of *John Conyers* (c. 1747; New Haven, CT, Yale Cent. Brit. A.) by Francis Hayman, such a frame is visible in the background.

Throughout the 18th century these French-derived styles followed their continental precedents into the Régence type of frame: an ogee profile with straight sides defined by ovolo trim, fillets, ribbon-and-stick or gadrooning; larger centre and corner cartouches (with sunflowers, shells, espagnolette ruffs and knops); and linking trails of floral sprigs and *rinceaux*. The background of the ogee moulding was often given textural interest by engraved cross-hatching, and sanding could still be applied. The cabinetmaker Benjamin Goodison (d 1767) supplied Frederick, Prince of Wales, with a full-length portrait frame in the 1730s, which was 'carv'd & Guilt in Oyl Gold with a sanded ground ornamented with Shells £10.00' (see 1989 exh. cat.). This was a quick and economical version; by the 1750s Goodison was charging £74 and £72 15s. for Palladian frames (see §6 below) for Holkham Hall, Norfolk. The gadrooned sight edge then moved out to define the contour, giving richness and interest to a much more linear style. The trailing foliate decoration fell away from the rails, leaving stronger three-dimensional pierced corners contained by swooping, scrolled *rinceaux*, as the Régence style moved towards the Rococo. Examples of this can be seen on mid-18th-century portraits by Allan Ramsay (44e,

a favourite pattern for him), and Reynolds, and on Joseph Highmore's 12 paintings from *Pamela* (1744; Cambridge, Fitzwilliam; Melbourne, N.G. Victoria; London, Tate). The more economical, cornerless version of this gadrooned frame (44d) was often used for landscapes and large subjects where the corners would be too isolated to create focal emphasis.

6. PALLADIAN. The roots of the Palladian style (*see* PALLADIANISM) were fixed in the work of John Webb (i) and Inigo Jones, whose copy of Palladio's *Quattro libri dell'architettura* (1570) was bought in the 18th century by Richard Boyle, 3rd Earl of Burlington and 4th Earl of Cork, the patron of English Palladianism. In 1727 William Kent edited *The Designs of Inigo Jones* for Burlington, which inspired Kent to take up architectural design, including frames and overmantels. These were based on Jones's ideas, modified by what Kent had seen in Italy. The Palladian ideal was also moulded by Colen Campbell and his *Vitruvius Britannicus* (1715–25); his work and Kent's swiftly became the dominant style in Britain in the 1720s. Such simple, classical interiors as the Saloon elevations by Kent for Houghton Hall, Norfolk, epitomize this style: the eared overmantel with scrolled medallion drops is echoed by a cluster of sculptural egg-and-dart frames, the top rail of each rising in a graceful swan's neck. Kent indicated the contents of each frame, but it is clear that the pictures are subordinate to their places in the unified design.

The Palladian frame was unique to Britain, and it was a long-lasting style feeding into the later Neo-classicism of Adam and his followers. Its place in the articulation of an interior meant that it was ideally suited to the framing of a series of paintings, for example Kneller's forty Kit-Cat Club portraits (c. 1697–c. 1721; London, N.P.G., and Beningbrough Hall, N. Yorks, NT). These were painted for Jacob Tonson, the club's secretary, and were framed in a similar style to Kent's Houghton frames, with a heavy egg-and-dart, sanded flat and inner ribbon and flowers. The top and bottom rails are eared, with a foliate swan's-neck crest inset and a cartouche for the sitter's name at the bottom. They were made by Gerrard Howard, Carver and Gilder to the Royal Family, who framed the set in 1733 for two guineas each.

The frame in figure 45 is the opposite end of the range from this type of block framing; the eared structure defined by egg-and-dart moulding is similar, but the accumulated richly carved ornaments set this family portrait frame firmly in the luxury class. The sanded frieze is replaced by an enriched guilloche (or flowered interlacing), which appears in ceilings by Kent, frame designs by Isaac Ware and mirrors by the partnership of William Vile and John Cobb. It may also take the form of an enriched fret or a Vitruvian scroll. The corner paterae and shells, bay-leaf (sometimes oak-leaf) swags, acanthus clasps and lower cartouche with mascaron are characteristic of *grand luxe* luxurious Palladian frames, while the espagnolette head above, with its plaited hair, double shell and rioting palms and acanthus, lends a touch of Baroque drama. Similarly rich, movable frames are at Hampton Court Palace; Stourhead, Wilts; Audley End House, Essex; and Woburn Abbey, Beds; plainer eared frames set into complementary carved and panelled wall-frames at Temple Newsam, W. Yorks; and a suite of painted and gilt overmantel, full-length portrait frames, doorcases and frieze (1736–9), all by the architect Henry Flitcroft, at Ditchley Park, Oxon. Most full-scale Palladian interiors boasted work by immigrant Italian stuccoists, and there is a blurring of definition here between the plaster frame as extension of the wall and the separate carved wooden frame as supplied by the carver and gilder (*see* STUCCO AND PLASTERWORK, §III, 10(i)(c)).

7. ROCOCO. The Rococo was introduced in Britain *c.* 1721 with the arrival of George Michael Moser (i), a Swiss silversmith and pioneer of the style. Gibbons was succeeded in the same year by Kent's Palladian carver, James Richards. There was thus a considerable stylistic overlap, although the Rococo idiom took several years to become established after its full-blown emergence in France in the 1720s and—with Palladianism and, later, Neo-classicism to compete against—was never as strongly rooted in Britain as on the Continent. The Dining-room at Easton Neston, Northants, was decorated *c.* 1730 with integral plasterwork frames in which a Palladian swan's-neck and eared silhouette still underlie the exaggerated, scrolled contours and the infill of delicate Rococo *rinceaux.* These trophy frames, possibly by the stuccoist Charles Stanley, include such motifs as hunting horns and arrows around the inset paintings of hunting dogs. Further plaster trophies of bows, quivers and nets etc link pictures and frames to the walls and thus to the room as a whole, a unified approach to interior decoration that was shared by the Baroque, Palladianism and the Rococo.

Otherwise, Rococo picture frames only slowly infiltrated Britain: the first pattern book of ornament in the style, *Sixty Different Sorts of Ornaments,* by Gaetano Brunetti (*d* 1758), was not published until 1736, while at the same time classicism received another boost from the 1738 excavations at Herculaneum. The strong allegiance to French taste, however, continued through the influence of Huguenot carvers and gilders. Paul Petit, who was employed in 1731–2 on the Royal Barge (*see* BARGE, CEREMONIAL, fig. 1) designed by Kent and carved by James Richards, was working in a full Rococo style for the Prince of Wales by 1742 (see Buttery). His frame for John Wootton's group portrait of the *Prince and Friends out Hunting* (British Royal Col.) is again a trophy frame, with hounds' heads, dead snipe, powder flask, bow and arrows etc, surmounted by the Prince of Wales's feathers. Broken S-scrolls enriched with lambrequins or stylized fringes articulate the structure of the frame and echo the outstretched birds' wings, while rocailles and shells brimming with water enclose the swimming dogs' heads and sprout naturalistic bullrushes. Petit was paid £21 for this frame, but in 1739 he and Joris were paid £160 for a full-length Rococo trophy frame with military emblems for a portrait of the Prince. These are opulent, richly gilded, sculptural frames, the apogee of a rather short-lived style. Most Rococo frames date from 1745 to 1755, fewer from the early 1740s and 1760s. They are closely tied to furniture styles of the first half of the 18th century, while Palladian frames are related more to architectural interiors. An example of the relationship between Rococo furniture and

45. Palladian 'William Kent' trophy frame, 1916×1380 mm, original for Allan Ramsay's *Thomas, 2nd Baron Mansel of Margam, with his Half-brothers and Sister,* 1742 (London, Tate Gallery)

frames, and of Huguenot influence on both, is evident in the work of James Pascal, a Huguenot carver and gilder of Long Acre, London. He made picture frames for Sir Richard Colt Hoare for almost 20 years and in 1746 made a suite of gilded Rococo furniture for Temple Newsam House. These are in the sculptural manner of Petit's frames, including fanned lambrequins, rushes and rocailles.

The standard Rococo frame was far simpler, lighter and more economical—although the curving lines and embellishments gave a sense of luxury. A variety of basic types (see fig. 46), in use concurrently, ranges from the early C-scrolled corner and sanded flat (46a), developed from straight-sided Régence frames, to the sculptural rail with inner curved fillet (46f). Since the various elements—even in plainer versions (46b)—took time to produce, there would have been pressure on the framemakers to produce a continuous stream of stock patterns in standard sizes to supply the 'ready-made' end of the market. Variations include corners (with or without related symmetrical, asymmetrical or smaller centres) of rocailles, shells, espagnolette ruffs, fanned lambrequins, florets and sunflowers; pierced lambrequin moulding (46d); Gothick quatrefoils (46e); inner 'swept' fillets; gadrooned sights; textured grounds of sand; fluting or engraved diapering; and the very English use of trails of small five-petalled flowers.

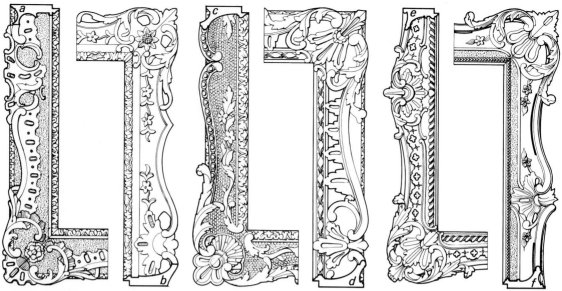

46. British Rococo frames, 1740s–1760s: (a) swept rocaille frame with sanded ground and cartouches, 905×705×108 mm, original for William Hogarth's *Frances Arnold*, one of a pair to *George Arnold*, *c.* 1738–40 (Cambridge, Fitzwilliam Museum); (b) swept frame with sanded frieze, flower and raffle-leaf cartouches, 768×635×89 mm, 1750s–1760s, on Sir Joshua Reynolds's *Mrs Abingdon*, 1771 (New Haven, CT, Yale Center for British Art); (c) swept ovolo frame with flower reposes on textured ground and corner shell cartouches, 527×650×89 mm, original for Edward Haytley's *Brockman Family and Friends at Beachborough Manor*, 1744–6 (Melbourne, National Gallery of Victoria); (d) swept openwork rocaille frame, husk sight, and leaf-and-shell cartouches, 565×876×80 mm, original for Richard Wilson's *The Thames near Marble Hill, Twickenham*, *c.* 1762 (London, Marble Hill House); (e) gadrooned sight frame with pierced quatrefoil rocaille reposes and raffle-leaf cartouches, 762×635×108 mm, probably original for Thomas Gainsborough's *Mr Clayton Jones*, *c.* 1744–5 (New Haven, CT, Yale Center for British Art); (f) frame with pearl sight, sanded band and trilobe-and-rocaille corner/centre cartouches, 750×622×120 mm, original for Francis Cotes's *Sir Richard Colt Hoare*, 1757 (Stourhead, Wilts, NT)

Many of these details appear in contemporary silverwork, for example in the work of the Huguenots Paul de Lamerie and Nicholas Sprimont; they derive from decorative metalwork of the previous generation and frequently have close connections with the designs of Daniel Marot I. They can also be found in furniture: for example in the designs *Six Sconces* (1744) and *Six Tables* (1746; both London, V&A) by Matthias Lock, the designs of Abraham Swan and the work of Thomas Johnson during the 1750s and 1760s. The second St Martin's Lane Academy (est. 1735), founded in London principally by Hogarth, helped stimulate much of this work and encouraged the exchange of decorative ideas between the different media.

Plasterwork was also closely connected with Rococo wood-carving; and although there are far fewer entire Rococo than Palladian interiors in Britain, the French fashion for an extension of the idiom through frames, *boiseries*, stuccowork and tapestries can be seen, for example, at Hagley Hall, Worcs, and in the work of the stuccoist Thomas Roberts at Rousham, Oxon. The latter demonstrates how the delicate later style of the 1760s could be a visual distraction from the pictures framed, and that while Rococo frames complement portraits by Arthur Devis and Gainsborough, and landscapes by Richard Wilson, they consort less comfortably with the bluff men and sober women portrayed by Benjamin West and Reynolds. This is especially true of later Rococo frames, where the carcass is attenuated and the silhouette broken

into fantastic flourishes under the influence of the chinoiserie and Gothick tastes of the 1760s summed up in Chippendale's pattern book *The Gentleman and Cabinet-maker's Director* (1754), and in which the blurring of elements between picture and looking-glass frames (often quite distinct in style) can be seen. These fragile, lacy structures would have been extremely expensive in terms of labour, and this catalyzed the use of a new medium for frames. In 1749 Mrs Delany wrote of the framemaker Joseph Duffour as 'the famous man for paper ornaments like stucco', and his trade-card proclaimed him as the 'Original Maker of Papier Machie'. Others rapidly copied this innovation and so during the late 18th century and the early 19th the mass-produced decoration of plain mouldings developed, spelling the end of the carved wooden frame. A fine suite of six papier-mâché Rococo frames was commissioned in the 1760s by Francis Mundy of Markeaton Hall (destr. 1964) for his set of portraits by Joseph Wright of Derby, an artist noted for the general supervision of his frames and their mainly Huguenot craftsmen (see 1990 exh. cat.).

8. NEO-CLASSICAL. During the phases of the Rococo, classical frames continued to be made: in the 1750s John Vardy designed Spencer House, London, and its furniture in a refined Kentian style, the frames probably being made by his carver–brother Thomas Vardy (*b* 1724); the latter also worked in the same idiom for Henry Flitcroft, as did Benjamin Goodison. But this was the tail end of the

Palladian style; this decade heralded the new classicists, as William Chambers returned from Rome in 1755 and Robert Adam from his Italian Grand Tour in 1758. Hagley Hall, Hereford & Worcs, was one of the last places to be decorated in the Rococo style (1759), and by 1761 the Italian stuccoists who had helped to promulgate the style had left the country. Neo-classicism was the new fashion, diffused through such archaeological studies as the Comte de Caylus's *Recueil d'antiquités*, Julien-David Le Roy's *Les Ruines des plus beaux monuments de la Grèce* (1758) and Stuart and Revett's *Antiquities of Athens* (1762–1816). As early as 1759, Sefferin Alken (1717–82), one of the major carvers of the next half century, was making five gilded frames to Adam's designs for the Breakfast Room at Kedleston Hall, Derbys, while Chambers was designing early Neo-classical furniture for the Society of Arts and also for Reynolds. The archetypal Neo-classical frame was introduced at around this time directly from Italy, where it had been current from the 17th century; this was the 'Carlo Maratta' or 'Salvator Rosa' frame (see fig. 47), which was used by the English for paintings acquired on the Grand Tour (*see* §II, 5 above). Authentic Roman versions were often brought back, such as the simple, undecorated type that was rarely produced in Britain. The characteristic 'Maratta' profile features an important scotia, surrounded by mouldings of a three-quarter round or deep ogee section (47a). The form is severely linear and classical, suitable for nearly every form of painting, and the straight lines were welcomed by those who were sated with the flamboyant curvaceousness of the Rococo. This severity, however, is mitigated by the enriched mouldings usually found on either side of the scotia (47a, b, c): egg mouldings, ribbon-and-stave, cross-cut acanthus or leaf-and-tongue, and gadrooning. It was the most widely used frame from the 1750s to the end of the century, surviving in its carved version to the 1820s, and beyond that in a plaster version. Reynolds used a 'Carlo Marat Frame' in preference to his other choice of Rococo ('French frames') during the 1760s; they were more economical and could be bought ready-made or quickly made to measure, as there were no complications of corner ornaments (see Penny and Gregory).

As with all other styles of frame, there were hierarchical gradations reflecting the subject-matter of the painting or its purpose, from a 'filler' for an important wall to a royal gift or collector's frame for an important Old Master. Thus minor landscapes or suites of pictures were often framed in 'Marattas' ornamented with only a small ribbon and beading or bead-and-bobbin (known as a 'semi Carlo'), while large portraits (47b and c) had all the convex mouldings enriched, giving a density of ornamentation and a consequent shimmer of light and movement. This undercuts the linear austerity of the contour and forms the perfect setting for depictions of men and women in the 'classical' poses and costumes of the later 18th century. An even more opulent or 'full Carlo' version (for a sitter shown full-length in robes of state) has the scotia filled with a deep ogee leaf-and-dart moulding (47d), and the celebratory marriage portrait of *Mr and Mrs John Custance* (1778; Kansas City, MO, Nelson–Atkins Mus. A.) has a leaf-and-shell ogee and enriched gadrooning on the outer rail (47e). This *grand luxe* frame confirms the status of the

47. British 'Carlo Maratta' frames, *c.* 1750–1800: (a) acanthus-and-tongue sight frame with ribbon-and-stave, 1270×1016×133 mm, original for Thomas Gainsborough's *Sir Christopher Whichcote, Bt*, 1775 (Burghley House, Cambs); (b) acanthus-and-tongue sight frame with ribbon-and-stave and gadrooning, 990×737×102 mm, original for Pompeo Batoni's *Sarah, Lady Fetherstonhaugh*, 1751 (Uppark, W. Sussex, NT); (c) acanthus-and-tongue sight frame with ribbon-and-stave and egg moulding, 2348×1650×114 mm, original for Johan Zoffany's *Mrs Woodhull*, *c.* 1770 (London, Tate Gallery); (d) husk sight frame with acanthus-and-tongue in scotia and ribbon-and-stave, 2375×1435×146 mm, original for Francis Cotes's *James Duff, 2nd Earl of Fyfe*, *c.* 1765 (Raleigh, NC, North Carolina Museum of Art); (e) frame with acanthus leaf-and-shell in scotia, ribbon-and-stave, enriched gadrooning and egg-and-dart back, 1498×2108×203 mm, original for Benjamin West's *Mr and Mrs John Custance*, 1778 (Kansas City, MO, Nelson–Atkins Museum of Art); (f) husk sight frame with pearls and fluted top rail, 1003×1245×102 mm, contemporary for Thomas Gainsborough's *Landscape with a Woodcutter*, *c.* 1763 (Houston, TX, Museum of Fine Arts); (g) husk sight frame with fluted scotia, acanthus corners and ribbon-and-stave, 1295×1473×121 mm, original for Angelica Kauffman's *Sappho*, 1775 (Sarasota, FL, Ringling Museum of Art); (h) ribbon-and-stave sight frame, plain and leaf fluting with acanthus corners and oak-leaf torus, 3188×3899×165 mm, on Sir Joshua Reynolds's *Marlborough Family*, 1778 (Blenheim Palace, Oxon)

artist Benjamin West, who in 1772 had been appointed Historical Painter to the King. All his subjects in the Picture Gallery at Buckingham Palace have retained this pattern. By contrast, a classical subject is emphasized by a fluted hollow (47g)—the trademark of the Neo-classical framemaker—which gives movement but also a geometrical purity (47h is an enriched example). Frames for pastels were made in identical mouldings but were glazed, as they had been in Rococo versions.

The 'Maratta' was ideally suited to the interiors of Adam. These already play geometrical shapes against each other, for example in the Music Room, Harewood House (1765–71), W. Yorks, with its ceiling and carpet of circles and fluted paterae, and walls articulated by a series of oblong stucco panels and picture frames. The Reynolds overmantel portrait and the large paintings of ruins by Antonio Zucchi were set in enriched gilded 'Maratta' frames as part of this overall design, which manages to achieve simultaneously clarity of line and richness of detail. The Saloon at Nostell Priory (1765–85), W. Yorks, is very similar, while in the Dining-room at Saltram House (1768–9 and 1780–81), Devon, Zucchi's paintings were set in white-painted carved wooden frames of unadorned 'Maratta' type. The interplay of straight and round was picked up in later oval-sight versions of the fluted 'Maratta', with rosette paterae or scrolled anthemia in the spandrels: a group of paintings of the 1780s by George Stubbs is framed in this way. Such frames are linked to Wedgwood's use of round and oval plaques and of cross-fluting, and also to Adam's use of painted medallions, for instance in the Glass Drawing-room (now London, V&A) of Northumberland House.

An extreme example of this play of form was expressed in the vogue at this time for print-rooms, where round, oval, square and oblong engravings with integral printed frames were glued in formal arrangements to the walls, interspersed with Neo-classical motifs of vines, festoons and drops of husks. Unframed prints would often be given printed borders imitating various architectural mouldings. In 1767 Chippendale decorated a room at Mersham-le-Hatch, Kent, in this way, and there are print-rooms at Castletown, Co. Kildare; The Vyne, Hants; Stratfield Saye, Hants; and Blickling Hall, Norfolk. A similar effect is seen in a designer's proposal for a wall elevation (workshop of John Linnell (i), 1778; London, V&A), where the oval and eared frames and their linking festoons are carefully drawn in to demonstrate how the arrangement of stucco or papier-mâché mouldings was to be made. An arrangement of mirrors and pictures in papier-mâché frames, with gilt trophies and pastoral groups, formed a scheme like this at Doddington Hall, Lincs, in the 1760s: fragments of the linking trophies survive, with the frames (as does a wallpaper printed with imitation framed engravings); these were probably all supplied by Peter Babel, who is recorded as sending two sanded and gilded frames and 70 ft of 'Paper machee Rich Border Gilt in Oil Gold' for £8 15s. Such schemes demonstrate the importance in the late 18th century of formal wall arrangements based on the size, shape and ornament of the picture frames, which overrode to a large extent the contents of the paintings within. This was a function of Augustanism, which had set the tone of the earlier 18th century with its restraint, formality and politesse.

Augustanism was diluted from the 1760s, however, by the romanticism and delicacy of touch introduced by Adam. The heavy classicism of the Palladians had disappeared, and although its forms (such as eared frames) were retained, they were much lighter and were softened by surrounding decorative motifs: by the 'grotesque, stucco & painted ornaments together with the flowing raunceau, with its fanciful figures & winding foliage', which

the Adam brothers claimed to have introduced. Thus Neo-classical frames were often made to be fitted into a scheme such as the one at Doddington Hall, where they would be linked by the ornamentation of the walls; and so a plain 'entablature' or *cassetta* form with a frieze of fluting, anthemia or enriched guilloche (see fig. 48a–f) became the centre for a carefully choreographed dance of stucco motifs. In the inset ceiling paintings by Angelica Kauffman in the Long Gallery, Harewood House, the superficial shape of a 'Maratta' has been retained, but the scotia has been flattened into a level frieze to conform to the architectural decoration of cornices, tables and chairs, pelmets and pier glasses. This development has been

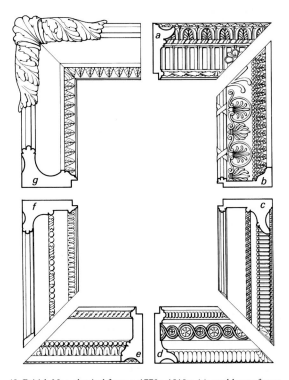

48. British Neo-classical frames, 1770s–1810s: (a) entablature frame with fluted frieze and corner paterae, 1780×2160×127 mm, original for Angelica Kauffman's *Sir Philip Tisdall and Family*, *c.* 1771 (Leixlip Castle, Co. Kildare); (b) Adam-style frame with moulded anthemia and palmettes, 1016×1619×114 mm, probably original for George Stubbs's *Mares and Foals in a River Landscape*, *c.* 1760–70 (London, Tate Gallery); (c) 'Romney' pattern frame with straight knulled rail, 2400×1480×133 mm, original for George Romney's *Sir Robert Gunning*, 1779–95 (Montreal, Museum of Fine Arts); (d) 'Romney' pattern frame with flowered guilloche, 2286×1290×120 mm, late 18th century, made for Anthony van Dyck's *Queen Henrietta Maria and her Dwarf, Sir Jeffrey Hudson*, *c.* 1633 (private collection); (e) 'Wright' pattern frame with *rais-de-coeur* and guilloche sight, 625×778×108 mm, original for Joseph Wright of Derby's *Dovedale by Moonlight*, exhibited 1785 (Oberlin, OH, Oberlin College, Allen Memorial Art Museum); (f) 'Raeburn' pattern frame with enriched bead-and-bobbin, 762×635×109 mm, original for Sir Henry Raeburn's *Rev. Robert Walker Skating on Duddington Loch*, 1778–84 (Edinburgh, National Gallery of Scotland); (g) Regency deep scotia frame with corner leaves and leaf-tip sight, 488×598×89 mm, probably original for John Constable's *Valley of the Stour (Dedham from Gun Hill)*, *c.* 1805–9 (London, Victoria and Albert Museum)

initiated (48a) in the use of shallow scotia, fluting and stiff-leaf decoration. In an archetypal Adam frame (48b), the 'Maratta' profile is subsumed by the entablature form, and a wide flat or frieze, replacing the scotia, is decorated with applied plaster or composition anthemia.

The use of composition burgeoned under Adam. By the 1770s it had begun to replace carved wooden ornament for frames, and for small ornate objects such as girandoles. Marble chimney-pieces and overmantels were often augmented with painted composition or replaced by painted wood and composition in minor rooms. James Wyatt employed scagliola for the first time in the Pantheon (1769–72; destr. 1937), Oxford Street, London, and ormolu was also used instead of gilded wood. A second generation of stuccoists flourished, mainly English and led by the important plasterer Joseph Rose jr (c. 1745–99); they had great influence on the use of moulded ornament for frames and furniture. This meant that unified schemes of great richness and complexity could be produced at a considerable saving and that large set-pieces could still be afforded through economies on serial frames and *boiseries*: for instance, the '2 very rich whole length Tabernacle Frames, carved, gilt, part burnished', made for £113 15s. by John Bradburn and William France in 1767. At first this did not have too much effect on English framemakers; the lack of guild restrictions compared with France meant that craftsmen were not bound to specialize in a single branch of work but could combine several, along with designing, dealing and entrepreneurial skills. They also achieved higher standing than on the Continent; John Gumley, who was cabinetmaker to the King, produced many Neo-classical frames; had a glassworks and acquired the Earl of Bath as a son-in-law; while Adam had a bank balance of £40,000 and became an MP. There was thus steady employment for such carvers as Sefferin Alken, who worked for Adam, Vile & Cobb and Sir William Chambers, producing frames for Croome Court, Worcs; Blenheim Palace, Oxon; and Kedleston Hall. Chippendale made and gilded frames for Nostell Priory, published designs for other craftsmen, including frames, and produced whole carved interiors at Harewood House and other Adam houses. John Linnell also worked for Adam but had inherited his father's important workshop together with an unusual amount of equipment; he produced frames for both pictures and mirrors. On the other hand, employment for such carvers as William Collett, a poor Huguenot, grew increasingly scarce because of the use of papier mâché. He must also have been affected by the tendency (48c, e, f) for ornament to drop away, leaving the simple entablature profile largely unadorned. These light, restrained designs are in the truest spirit of Neo-classicism and are admirably suited to landscape (Joseph Wright of Derby used 48e for his work in the early 1780s) or portraiture (Henry Raeburn used 48f as a standard frame). The type generally known as a 'Morland' frame (48g), after the painter George Morland, was also used for portraits, usually not with spiral acanthus corners as in the example shown, but in the plain version with a scotia and bound fasces moulding.

9. REGENCY AND EARLY VICTORIAN. At the end of the 18th century the wars with Revolutionary France interrupted a cosmopolitan life of patronage for the English aristocracy, cutting links with the artistic centres of Paris and Rome. At the same time the wars stimulated a fascination with French styles and taste: Henry Holland employed French craftsmen to work on Carlton House, London, and revived French gilding techniques. Holland's style was slightly heavier than the refined Neo-classicism of Adam, with ornament in Louis XVI style. The designs of Thomas Hope, an early English adherent of the Empire style, show very simple friezelike picture frames (see fig. 49a), decorated with stars, leaf-tip and bound fasces, and fitting in as one part of a more opulent whole, with draped walls, diapered ceilings, painted cornices and

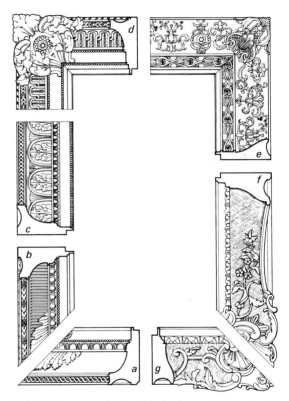

49. British Regency and early Victorian frames: (a) Empire style scotia frame, 2210×1676×153 mm, original for William Beechey's *Thomas Hope*, 1798 (London, National Portrait Gallery); (b) Empire style fluted scotia frame, 470×724×120 mm, possibly original for John Constable's *Hampstead Heath with a Rainbow*, 1836 (London, Tate Gallery); (c) Empire style scotia frame with arcade of acanthus leaves, 940×1194×190 mm, c. 1810–30, made for Nicolas Poussin's *Nurture of Jupiter*, c. 1636–7 (London, Dulwich Picture Gallery); (d) Empire style frame with enriched fluted/cabled scotia and corner acanthus cartouches, 279×336×152 mm, c. 1810–30, made for Jan van der Heyden's *Two Churches and a Town Wall*, 1660s (London, Dulwich Picture Gallery); (e) Regency 'Lawrence' frame with scrolling fleurons, 749×622×190 mm, original for Robert Scott Lauder's *Henry Lauder, the Artist's Brother*, c. 1827 (Edinburgh, National Gallery of Scotland); (f) Rococo Revival frame with floral springs, 317×495×93 mm, second quarter of the 19th century, made for John Constable's *Summer Evening*, c. 1811–12 (London, Victoria and Albert Museum); (g) Louis XIV Revival C-scrolled frame, 1127×2007×280 mm, original for J. M. W. Turner's *St Benedetto, Looking towards Fusina*, exhibited 1843 (London, Tate Gallery)

furniture in a rich but austere Grecian form. Similar frames, ornamented with bosses and ovolo mouldings, can be seen in Carlton House (49c resembles frames in the Crimson Drawing-room). In hollow frames, such as 49b and d, the wide Neo-classical flutes associated with Adam have narrowed in typical 19th-century style. These spring from the *goût grec* of late 18th-century France and have multiple rows of ornaments, including enriched fluting and peseta patterns, and huge corner cartouches. They are fussier than their originals and tend to accrete detail simply through the ease of applying composition mouldings. Because many of them are of composition, they appear to possess an iron-like hardness of edge and general brassiness (49e and g). They complement the great interiors of the late 18th century and the early 19th and were used as gallery frames (e.g. Apsley House, London), as they were in France in Napoleon's reframing of the Louvre, Paris.

Such frames, with their almost total use of moulded ornament, affected the wood-carving trade very badly. In addition sterling had been devalued by the Napoleonic Wars, materials and labour were more expensive, and the number of carvers in London was rapidly decreasing. By the early 19th century there were only 11 masters and about 60 journeymen in the capital (see Oughton). Wood-working machines were used to turn out lengths of plain mouldings with profiles, and these could then be ornamented in any fashion with corners and lengths of applied composition, shaped in box-wood reverse moulds, which were almost the only staple now required of the carver. This process was hastened by the interruption of the wood trade with France: the wars meant that easy-to-carve continental lime and fruitwoods were in short supply, and oak was requisitioned to make warships. Exotic woods from the colonies were easily obtainable for furniture but were unsuitable for carved and gilded frames as they were mainly hardwoods, notable for their beautiful colour and graining. This left only beech and deal, both of which were considered inferior and suitable only for the carcass of a frame, the ornament being supplied in composition. Frame-makers who had had 400 to 500 craftsmen working for them in the 18th century might now employ only one carver to produce moulds, which would then be in use for perhaps the next century. The firm of George Jackson, founded over 200 years ago, still holds its collection of moulds for architectural ornament, and the equipment and archive material of the firm of Joseph Green (est. 1801) survived well into the 20th century.

Composition frames in the Empire style and the *goût grec* of the French carver Chérin were followed by the adoption in Britain of other French revival styles (49f and g), including the calligraphic ornament and ogee profile of Louis XIV and Régence frames and the centre/corner cartouches of the latter. These were highly adaptable to the use of applied decoration and enabled large, ornate frames to be produced quite cheaply—the frames of Thomas Lawrence's and of Franz Xavier Winterhalter's portraits were in this form and were brilliantly gilded to take full advantage of the new gas lighting, which enabled extreme opulence at relatively small cost. This was also important for 19th-century methods of hanging, which from the early years of the century involved covering all available wall space with tiers of gilt-framed paintings—usually on a dark or patterned ground—between the equally ornate punctuation of door- and window-cases, overmantels etc. This method was used both in the domestic interior and for exhibitions. Reaction against such ubiquitous, brassy confectionery, however, set in quite early. By the 1830s A. W. N. Pugin was designing his own frames for St Mary's College, Oscott, Warwicks, and Alton Towers, Staffs, and such artists as Turner and Robert Huskisson produced one-off designs; the former framed an exhibition of marine paintings in lengths of ship's cable 'gilded' with yellow ochre.

10. PRE-RAPHAELITE AND AESTHETIC MOVEMENT. In 1845 Ford Madox Brown went to Italy, catalyzing not only the whole Pre-Raphaelite school of painting but also half a century of innovative frame design, which spread from Britain to most of Europe. He saw the settings of early Italian works and incorporated the idea of an arched triptych with colonnettes into the integral painted structure of *The Seeds and Fruit of English Poetry* (1845–51; Oxford, Ashmolean). By 1848 he was recorded working on the frame of *Wycliffe* (1848; Bradford, Cartwright Hall; since altered) and in the same year took as a pupil Dante Gabriel Rossetti, the other half of the Pre-Raphaelite partnership in frame design. Rossetti also travelled in Europe (1849), where he was struck by Flemish Old Master paintings and their frames. The Pre-Raphaelites were influenced not only in painting style by the predecessors of Raphael but also by the materials, construction and effect of medieval and early Renaissance frames. At first they took the Gothic–religious approach of the Nazarenes, who had encouraged Brown and were themselves interested in appropriate frames: arches, tondo inserts and inscriptions appear on Brown's and Rossetti's early works. As they became more fluent, abstract designs predominated, and motifs that attempted to shake off the classicizing tendencies of most 19th-century frames (see fig. 50a and b). One of their first innovations was the use of butt (or straight) joints to join the four rails of a frame, a technique copied from medieval plank frames; this had been the common type of joint until replaced in the 15th and 16th centuries by the Renaissance technique of mitring. Brown and Rossetti used this joint from at least 1851, at first with gessoed mouldings, but from c. 1861 on *cassetta* frames in which the central wide flat was gilded directly on the wood. This meant that an interesting, randomly textured effect was obtained from the oak grain showing through the gold leaf, an effect far removed from the uniform symmetry of stock composition mouldings. The butt joint was also clearly visible (50a), adding to the play of geometrical shapes on which these frames were built. Gilding on the wood was praised by such arbiters of taste as Charles Locke Eastlake and became part of the vocabulary of the Arts and Crafts Movement, appearing on frames in middle-class households everywhere. A similar naive or hand-crafted effect was given by the 'Oxford' frame, introduced at the same time. This 'light oaken frame, commonly called cruciform' (Eastlake: *Hints on Household Taste*, London, 3/1872), i.e. with mouldings crossed at the corners, was at first associated with religious pictures and then with prints and photographs. It was a

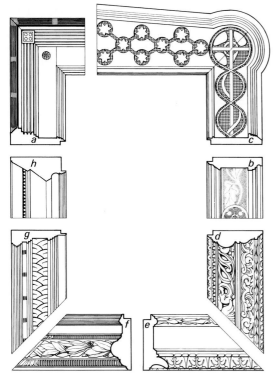

50. Pre-Raphaelite, Olympian and Aesthetic Movement frames: (a) Dante Gabriel Rossetti's and Ford Madox Brown's reed-and-roundel gilt on oak frame, with parcel gilt ebonized reeding at back, 1168×1321×165 mm, original of 1865 for Ford Madox Brown's *Jesus Washing Peter's Feet*, exh. RA 1852 (London, Tate Gallery); (b) Rossetti 'medallion' frame with punched foliate bevelled flat and 'fruit' roundels, 825×762×190 mm, original of *c.* 1873 for Rossetti's *The Beloved*, 1865–6 (London, Tate Gallery); (c) artist's gilt plate frame with shallow-relief symbolic motifs and inscribed ivory cuff, 857×1410×228 mm, 1859 original, for William Holman Hunt's *Finding of the Saviour in the Temple*, 1854–60 (Birmingham, City of Birmingham Museum and Art Gallery); (d) Renaissance Revival frame with pierced foliate/swan's-head torus, 1830×1092×170 mm, original for Edward Burne-Jones's *Beguiling of Merlin*, 1873–7 (Port Sunlight, Lady Lever Art Gallery); (e) 'Watts' pattern Italian *cassetta* with inner husk and butt-jointed flat, 648×521×160 mm, original for G. F. Watts's *William Morris*, 1870 (London, National Portrait Gallery); (f) Neo-classical frame with laurel leaves and fluting, 635×457×140 mm, original for Frederic Leighton's *Vestal*, 1883 (London, Leighton House Art Gallery and Museum); (g) artist-designed reeded frame painted with scale pattern, 2134×1092×153 mm, original of 1875 for James McNeill Whistler's *Symphony in White, No. 1: The White Girl*, 1862 (Washington, DC, National Gallery of Art); (h) artist-designed frame, reverse rebate with wide-stepped bevel and block-painted running triangles, 343×292×127 mm, original for Lawrence Alma-Tadema's *Priestess of Apollo, c.* 1888 (London, Tate Gallery)

cheap frame that escaped the tastelessness of mass-produced composition.

Figure 50a is a compendium of the motifs used by Brown and Rossetti. Together they invented the band of reeding that borders the oak flat and that was also carved in oak and gilded on the wood; and they designed the paterae that interrupt the reeding, playing square and circular shapes against each other. The flat is also inset

with small roundels, which are set against the straight lines of the frame and its joints. These two central elements comprise the archetypal 'reed-and-roundel' Pre-Raphaelite frame, which was copied by all their circle and continues to be the first choice of setting for late Victorian/Symbolist paintings, small portraits and drawings. Figure 50a also includes Brown's deep-fluted chamfer at the sight—often gilded and then scraped clean, leaving the flutes defined in gold against bare wood; and an answering outer bevel over which is laid Rossetti's parcel-gilt ebonized reeding. The whole effect is rich and decorative within the constraints of its linear and geometric forms, and it follows Ruskin's teaching of honesty in materials. It is superlatively well-suited to Brown's painting, with its warm mellow tones and composition of curves and straight lines, and is one of the high points of the 19th-century artist-designed frame.

Along with the reed-and-roundel frames of the early 1860s, Rossetti began to use a gilt-oak cuff with a triangular sectioned moulding indented on each side alternately with semicircular depressions. This was referred to by Brown as 'Rossetti's thumb-mark pattern', and he used it himself as an outer moulding. Rossetti employed it as an abstract border on a series of small decorative paintings of women. In the 1870s and 1880s these paintings grew larger and more voluptuous; full of a brooding eroticism, although still decorative, they required a bold, heavy frame to contain them. The design Rossetti chose had been used as a symbolic frame on his *Beata Beatrix* (1864–70; London, Tate), where a wide, canted flat, surrounded by small round and flat mouldings, was set with four circular medallions, their surface parallel to the picture plane. For the *Beatrix*, these medallions were decorated with shallow-relief representations of Platonic symbols. For the later decorative paintings (50b) they were carved with concentric circles in each quarter like fruit, the curving lines and seedlike shapes reflecting the compositions of the paintings and their symbolism underlying the sensuality of the subjects. The sloping flat of this frame is decorated with an early Renaissance punched foliate pattern, giving a brocade-like effect.

These frames were probably mainly produced by the firm of Foord & Dickinson, the principal framemakers for the Pre-Raphaelites in the last 30 years of the 19th century. Until *c.* 1867 Rossetti, Brown, John Everett Millais and William Holman Hunt had used the firm of Joseph Green, which in 1872 was taken over by W. A. Smith (and which continues to exist under the name of Bourlet). Green carved the reed-and-roundel (50a) and thumb-mark frames and Watts's frames (50e), and he framed Hunt's *Scapegoat* (1854–5; Port Sunlight, Lady Lever A.G.) with its symbolic motifs shallowly carved into a wide, flat torus. Foord & Dickinson was founded by George Foord, who was employed by the Society of Painters in Water-Colours (*c.* 1830–50), by Ruskin to frame his paintings by Turner, and by Turner himself. This firm later worked for Frederick Sandys, Frederic Leighton (fig. 51 below), Albert Joseph Moore and James McNeill Whistler (50g). Like Green, they were versatile, producing both stock patterns and hand-carved artist's designs; they were also called on to use such archaic techniques as butt-jointing, gilding on the wood and hand-painting some elements. They were, of course, expensive: in 1880 Rossetti was trying to get his patron William Graham to pay £100 for a frame, while in 1876 Hunt wrote that he may have found 'a carver who can work the pattern at less than £1000 per frame' (probably for the several large versions of the *Triumph of the Innocents*, which are carved with pomegranates; e.g. of 1876–87; Liverpool, Walker A.G.); at this time a stock frame from the firm of Agnew's, London, for one of Millais's Royal Academy paintings (1105×865×185mm) cost £13 15s.

Hunt's designs were, however, some of the most elaborate and labour intensive (see fig. 3 above). Except for his series of Near Eastern watercolours (and even these frames are not identical), he produced a unique setting for each subject. The frame (50c) for the *Finding of the Saviour in the Temple* (1854–60; Birmingham, Mus. & A.G.) has a suitably aedicular shape, outer mouldings crossing at the lower corners like the 'Oxford' frame and a wide flat carved in shallow sunk-work with symbolic motifs including Moses' rod and serpent on the left (Old Testament law) and Christ's cross with thorns and love-lies-bleeding on the right (New Testament law); above are the sun, moon and stars, and below heart's-ease for peace and daisies for 'humility and devotion'. Hunt described it as being 'designed by myself with ivory flat, in what I meant to be semi-barbaric splendour'. The very plain form, the wide expanse of gilding and the symmetrical patterning give a necessary area of transition from the exotic, detailed interior of the temple to the Victorian interior where it was to hang. The critic of the *Manchester Guardian*, in one of the first reviews to notice a picture frame, remarked on the way in which 'the symbols have overflowed the picture and expanded themselves all over the frame'.

Hunt's frame designs ranged from the symbolic bells for warning and marigolds for sorrow carved on the frame of the *Awakening Conscience* (1853–4; London, Tate) to the massive repoussé copper frames of 1889 made by C. R. Ashbee's Guild of Handicraft for *May Morning on Magdalen Tower* (1888–91; Port Sunlight, Lady Lever A.G.), and the aedicular frame of 1905 for *The Lady of Shalott* (Hartford, CT, Wadsworth Atheneum). Few of them were directly influential (except for the *May Morning* frames, which may have inspired Gustav Klimt's copper frames (*see* §VI, 7 below)), but they were all highly original, and this fifty-year period of lovingly designed, highly publicized frames was probably important in stimulating the great outflow of artists' frames in the late 19th century. The appropriateness and eclecticism of Hunt's frames were also important. The jury of selectors for the Great Exhibition of 1851 in London had attacked the degraded contemporary penchant for pointless decoration, for 'surrounding the frame of a pier glass with dead birds, game, shellfish, nets, and so on', and the various Victorian revival movements (Gothic, Rococo and Baroque) meant that there were a great many inappropriate horrors, easily produced in composition, waiting to cover a picture frame. Hunt and the other Pre-Raphaelites subverted this compulsion, using ornament imaginatively for decorative or symbolic ends. Millais's famous frame for Charles Allston Collins's *Convent Thoughts* (exh. RA 1851; Oxford, Ashmolean) sets three-dimensional plaster lilies on a plain

gilded plate frame with arched sight, a strikingly sophisticated design; and Millais and Arthur Hughes used wreaths of naturalistic ivy instead of classical bays and oaks. Noël Paton's fairy paintings are framed with Gothic tracery and diapering, and Sandys used a stylized 'window' effect, with Gothic rainsill and colonnettes, for his icon-like portraits of *femmes fatales*.

Many artists gave this inventive twist to traditional forms, without surrendering to the tawdriness of the different revivals. There was a time when late medieval and Renaissance Italian paintings, removed from their original settings by corrupt dealers and collectors, were being framed in 19th-century versions, with all the ungainly proportions, machined perfection and brassy finish of a deal and composition copy (examples, London, N.G.). Edward Burne-Jones used this type of cheap reproduction frame to some extent but he also appreciated craftsmanship and authentic design; he asked William De Morgan *c.* 1890 whether his framemaker could copy a Florentine frame, and in 1871 he wrote of his 'Giorgione', 'It is to have a glorious curly-wurly frame, a piece of wholesale upholstery round it to make it shine like a jewel as it is.' Burne-Jones adapted a carved late Renaissance Venetian frame, which he used for several of his more important works (50d). Formed of parallel bands of shallow, schematic classical mouldings, the design is given life and movement by the central pierced and undercut torus, which is set over a gilded hollow. The carving is based on intertwined foliate scrolls, among which swans' heads peer; the combination of this mythological emblem, the heavy opulence of the wide rail and the paradoxical grace given by gleams of light from the concealed hollow are suited to the subjects and style of Burne-Jones's paintings.

G. F. Watts was another creator of massive mythological works and, like Burne-Jones, used original and contemporary carved Florentine frames. The single design he is credited with, called a 'Watts' frame because it appears on 95% of his paintings, is a modest and workman-like *cassetta*, with a butt-jointed, gilt oak-veneered flat (50e). The only variations it was given are the replacement of the husk sight moulding by a chain of small leaves and the decoration of the flat with gilded gesso and a punched brocade pattern, just as Rossetti used for the enriched 'Watts' frame with black-and-gold reeding of *Monna Vanna* (1866, framed 1873; London, Tate). These frames are undatable, as Watts used them on paintings over 50 years, keeping a stock of standard sizes in his studio as Lely had done. The butt-jointed oak flat, however, indicates contact with Rossetti, and that they probably cannot pre-date 1861. Ideas, details and whole designs passed from artist to artist in the late 19th century; a variant of the thumb-mark moulding with triangular indentations was used by Sandys, reed-and-roundel frames by many of Rossetti's and Brown's circle (e.g. Sandys, Simeon Solomon, Maria Spartali Stillman) and derivative patterns by J. R. Spencer Stanhope, Val Prinsep, Robert Braithwaite Martineau etc. It is not surprising, therefore, to find Watts using a frame with one of Rossetti's and Brown's most striking innovations. It is given a completely different cast by the husk, bead-and-bobbin and acanthus mouldings that surround it—just as Watts aspired to be the great classical painter of the 19th century, so this is a compromise between a classical and a contemporary artist's frame. It is a successful compromise: it suits portraits, history, religious and subject paintings and is as ubiquitous as the reed-and-roundel frame.

Another artist influenced by the Rossetti–Brown circle was Whistler. He was in close contact with them from 1862, when he also met Burne-Jones and Sandys. The 1860s were fertile years for frame design: Brown and Rossetti were interchanging letters on frame patterns, and Sandys, Hunt, Hughes and Leighton were all designing their own frames. In 1864 Whistler produced a series of four simple carved wooden *cassettas* for the *Little White Girl* (London, Tate), *Purple Rose: The Lange Leizen of the Six Marks* (1863–4; Philadelphia, PA, Mus. A.), *La Princesse du pays de la porcelaine* (1863–4) and the *Golden Screen* (both Washington, DC, Freer). These Japonizing works were given eastern motifs on their frames: an Oriental fret and all-over spiral pattern, and incised sunlike medallions decorated with cherry blossom, potter's marks or leaves. The medallions are allied to Rossetti's use of them (fig. 50b) and to frames by Hunt, Leighton and Hughes. From 1865 Whistler was in close contact with Moore, and their aims at this time were very similar. Their attraction to the Aesthetic style led them in the late 1860s to similar arrangements of female figures in harmonies of colour, influenced by both Japanese and Classical ideals. They worked together and exchanged ideas, almost certainly including some reference to frames as inspired by Rossetti's circle. Also in 1865 Sandys exhibited *Gentle Spring* (1863–5; Oxford, Ashmolean), a single 'classical' figure close to Moore's later works. This was framed in a simple *cassetta*, with a plain central flat and outer and inner bands of reeding emphasizing the decorative cast of the painting; it was gilded directly on the oak. Deriving from the reed-and-roundel type, it seems to have been a seminal design for Moore and Whistler. The next year Moore exhibited *The Shulamite* (Liverpool, Walker A. G.), classicizing figures in harmonies of cream, tomato-red and apricot, in a frame composed of bands of reeds and fillets and small flats. Horowitz (1979–80) suggests that Whistler's first reeded frame dates from 1870–71, but it is possible that the example on *Symphony in White, No. 3* (1865–7; U. Birmingham, Barber Inst.) is the original, designed in tandem with that on *The Shulamite*.

Moore developed the reeded frame into a classical but modern design, keeping the flat oak carcass but having the reeds enriched with beading, bead-and-bobbin or stylized leaf forms, which complemented his decorative classical figures. Whistler took up the arrangement of mouldings of *The Shulamite* but with painted or incised patterned flats; figure 50g shows a wave or scale design coloured white to harmonize with the picture. He could have taken this motif from the East Asian porcelain he collected, but carved scale patterns were also used by Stanhope and Hunt. Whistler repeated it until at least 1879 and possibly into the 1890s, declaring *c.* 1873 that he had been the originator of a colour harmonization that included the painted frame (although Degas also used a coloured frame *c.* 1873; *see* §III, 12 above). It seems true that he did evolve the idea of a unifying scheme for his exhibitions, whereby curtains, carpets, walls, vases, attendants' livery etc were based on one or two colours, making a frame or

setting of the whole gallery; but the form of his frames is inseparably linked to his work with Moore and the influence of Rossetti and his followers. By 1891 the varied profile of the painted frames was exaggerated: the outer reeding was set on a large torus, and the flats diminished in size. This is the 'Whistler' frame, its projecting and stepped form and the linear effect of many tiny reeds no longer decoratively flattening, but creating a perspectival recession into the painting, emphasizing the space in which his figures now stood.

A similar effect was used by Lawrence Alma-Tadema, who developed his own distinctive profile for small pictures that did not warrant a grand, classical, pedimented setting. On his reverse rebate or bolection frames (50h), the parallel lines of the different mouldings and the painted decoration act like the reeding on a 'Whistler' frame to give a sense of depth and recession to the painting, and to intensify the focus on the subject in an almost theatrical way. This is an inventive design that breaks free from the banal reproductions of 17th- and 18th-century French styles, which formed the staple in the 19th-century framemakers' pattern books. It appears first on a work of 1869 but probably dates from 1874 when the picture was retouched. It has similarities to the triangular section of Rossetti's thumb-mark moulding—Alma-Tadema was close to Rossetti at least by 1871—but he had already shown an interest in frames, painting antique 'Roman' designs around the pictures in the background of the *Collector of Pictures* (1867; London, H. E. Finsness priv. col.). The geometrical moulding of figure 50h, with its echoing dogtooth design in black and gold, is one of Alma-Tadema's signature frames. It was used until his death in 1912 and after by his daughter Laura Alma-Tadema; without the painted decoration it was also used by such Newlyn school artists as Stanhope Forbes.

Alma-Tadema's larger works needed grandiose frames to complement their depictions of marble interiors and isolate them from the increasingly claustrophobic rooms of Victorian Britain. Photographs of these rooms, including Leighton's studio and the reception rooms of Rossetti's patron F. R. Leyland, show the busy backgrounds against which paintings were displayed (see Cooper, 1976). The answer to this problem was the revival of the Renaissance aedicular or tabernacle frame. This provided a wide boundary of gold leaf as an area of quarantine and a distinctive shape, which drew the eye, acting like a proscenium arch for the painting. But the copies of 15th-century aediculae with their mean plaster ornament, which lined the National Gallery, London, were the equivalent of Louis XIV reproductions to the classical revival or Olympian painters, and like the conventional moulding frame they had to be remade. Hunt had probably been the first to use an aedicular form with the pedimented silhouette of figure 50c and a modified beam, lintel and pilaster frame for *London Bridge* (1866; Oxford, Ashmolean). In the late 1860s Alma-Tadema used a more 'classical' version of the latter form for a *Roman Art Lover* (1868; New Haven, CT, Yale Cent. Brit. A.) and *Roman Interior* (Boston, MA, Mus. F.A.), refining them of imposed Renaissance ornament on the frieze, plinth and pilasters. The final step was to move completely away from the Italianate type of aedicule, with Corinthian or Composite order, and from the often horizontal format of the Renaissance.

From the late 1870s Alma-Tadema and Leighton both used aedicular frames, which were 'classical' in an archaeological sense rather than Renaissance revivals, and which were also peculiar to their own century and to the artists who designed them. Leighton's frames take two forms, the most idiosyncratic of which was in use from at least 1883 to 1885; the *Last Watch of Hero* (exh. RA, 1887; Manchester, C.A.G.; see fig. 51) is particularly interesting for the propriety of its use. It is in true 15th-century tabernacle form i.e. with an image or inscription relating to the dead person in a predella panel. Here, this takes the form of Leander's body painted in grisaille, highlighted by the stylized sideswept 'consoles' that also balance the elongated shape of the work. In the main panel an illusionistic window effect is reinforced by the way in which the architecture of frame and picture reflect each other and by the replacement of a gilt plinth by the marble sill in the painting. The effect of a refined, severe Greek classicism is supported by the clean, fluted pilasters and an important entablature; but the most striking feature is the domed Ionic capitals. Leighton took these from the 'unique Ionic order' of the Temple of Apollo at Bassai;

one capital had been brought to Britain in 1811 by C. R. Cockerell, who copied it in his Neo-classical buildings, such as the Ashmolean Museum and the Taylorian Institute, both in Oxford, and the Sun Fire Office, London. The last was an inspiration for Leighton, who visited it 'to revivify himself with...the beauty of Greek work'. The curving form is complementary to the curving lines of Leighton's statuesque women and their draperies. Leighton also used the Neo-classical frame (50f above); the equivalent of Alma-Tadema's (50h above), it appears along with 'Watts' frames, anthemion and lotus plaster patterns and painted or geometrical mouldings on small pictures and portraits of the 1860s and 1870s. Millais's paintings have the same frame, as on the *Order of Release* (1853; London, Tate) and *Black Brunswicker* (1860; Port Sunlight, Lady Lever A.G.). It is a good example of a stock composition moulding, which would suit most types of painting, be at home in many kinds of interior and be acceptable to all classes of patron as well as to the academic establishment. This is the type of frame found in Victorian and Edwardian pattern books, one of the staple frames of the last half of the century and a purer, more attractive form than the Louis XIV and Louis XV reproductions.

11. LATE 19TH AND 20TH CENTURIES. At the end of the 19th century there was a huge array of styles, from the Neo-classical stock frame through one-off trophy or attributive frames (now also often made of composition for economy) and types that had become conventionalized (aedicular frames in 'classical' or Renaissance style), to the rarer craftsman-made frame. The last included the rather naively carved and gilded frames brought from Florence by Watts, Evelyn De Morgan and John Melhuish Strudwick (1849–1937), and artists' frames such as those of Joseph Southall (1861–1944), who carved his own patterns and had them gilded by his wife (see fig. 52a). These frames were archaic survivals into the 20th century of an Arts and Crafts ideal; in the 20th century there was a rapid decrease in the numbers of tailor-made, historicizing or outré frames. In general they became much simpler (52b–g); even D. Y. Cameron's design (52b), an Art Nouveau interpretation of the 'Whistler' frame, shows a movement away from the general elaboration of 19th-century frames.

There was a minor fashion for chunky Spanish styles, which suited the bravura brushwork of John Singer Sargent, Glyn Philpott (1884–1937) etc, and which were adopted by the collectors of Picasso and Gauguin among others. These were probably either original frames, regilded and colour-washed, or carved on the Continent like the contemporary Florentine examples used by William and Evelyn De Morgan. During and after World War I carvers almost vanished, victims of the war, of economic constraints and of the new puritanism of design that succeeded *fin de siècle* opulence. The furniture of the 1920s and 1930s grew out of the plain, undecorated style of Charles Rennie Mackintosh, E. W. Godwin and the designers for Liberty's store, London; there was no place for carved enrichment, and frames were made to fit in with this minimalist tendency. Examples of this trend (52c and d) show the influence of Godwin's liking for machine-cut square-sections of wood, painted to tone with the pictures. They anticipate Le Corbusier's interiors and the minimalist

51. Artist-designed classical tabernacle frame with predella panel and Ionic capitals copied from the Temple of Apollo at Bassai, 2540×1448×127 mm, original for Frederic Leighton's *Last Watch of Hero*, exhibited Royal Academy 1887 (Manchester, City Art Gallery)

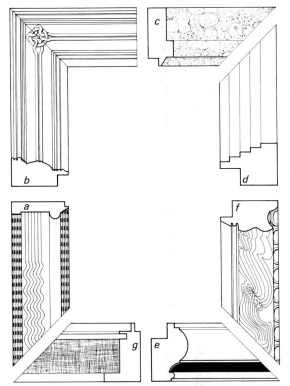

52. 20th-century British frames: (a) gilt architrave frame, wide flat with combed straight and wave enrichment, and front and back ripple mouldings, 262×349×70 mm, original for Joseph Southall's *The Botanists,* 1928 (Hereford, City Museum and Art Gallery); (b) Art Nouveau frame with Celtic knots at corners by Menzies & Son, Glasgow, 1330×1018×225 mm, original for D. Y. Cameron's *Nightfall, Luxor, c.* 1909–10 (Liverpool, Walker Art Gallery); (c) architrave profile painted frame, 505×406×126 mm, original for Nina Hamnett's *Osbert Sitwell, c.* 1918 (London, National Portrait Gallery); (d) stepped profile frame in silver finish, 610×762×90 mm, original for Christopher Nevinson's *Any Wintry Afternoon in England,* 1930 (Manchester, City Art Gallery); (e) cushion profile frame, 895×590×120 mm, original for Edward Wolfe's *Self-portrait,* 1920s (London, National Portrait Gallery); (f) comb-textured frame with stippled finish, 610×483×108 mm, original for Charles Ginner's *Punt in the Mill Stream,* 1933 (Cambridge, Fitzwilliam Museum); (g) box frame, white with fabric, 762×629×70 mm, original for Patrick Heron's *Thomas Stearns Eliot,* 1949 (London, National Portrait Gallery)

frames he used in the 1925 Paris Exhibition. The only decorative feature, apart from the painted finish, lies in the sculptural form, which generates its own chiaroscuro, so that the picture in each case is defined by the bold lines of shadow and highlight, creating a recessive effect similar to that of Whistler's and Alma-Tadema's more conventional gilt frames.

Machine-turned lengths of moulding were the only alternative to these extremely primitive shapes, as in the torus frame (52e) of Edward Wolfe's *Self-portrait* (1920s; London, N.P.G.). This exemplifies the commercial type used in the late 20th century, built of concave and convex sections and tied to the painting by discreet lines of colour or by a coloured wash. Classical in form and descent, it is

again suitable for nearly every sort of work and background. Machined finishes also created a trend in the first third of the century for Dutch ripple mouldings, used by Augustus John etc (fig. 52a is a hand-carved version of this). The geometrical patterns provide interest, texture and movement of light, which complement the work of the British Impressionists, and they were easily and relatively cheaply produced. They could also be painted by the artists themselves to give something of the hand-made, original finish that was no longer affordable or obtainable commercially in carved wood. Many frames of this type are coloured (52d) in white or grey to suit the new light interiors of the period. Figure 52f is a plain ogee frame where has the same type of effect, like a Dutch 'combed' moulding, has been achieved by literally combing a layer of gesso in random S-scrolls and then sponging on coloured paint. In this case, the colours chosen approximate to the antique gold finish of an original 17th- or 18th-century frame, but the textured surface is more suitable to the impasted technique of a modern painting.

There was a further reduction of form following World War II. Once more, light and shade are used for definition, and texture and colour to marry the frame to the painting (52g). The latter, held in gilded strips attached to the canvas edge, is sunk in an outer frame, the gap between the two providing a sharp boundary of shadow approximating to the emphatic black contours of the painting. The outer frame is traylike, recalling the earliest integral frames of panel paintings, the flat or cuff covered in hessian to tone with the picture. The two defining gilt mouldings are simple fillet shapes derived from earlier examples (52c and d), but the finish is more sophisticated, influenced by the inter-war luxury of the Art Deco movement. This type of frame is designed to bind the painting to its surroundings rather than to isolate it from them, as with some Pre-Raphaelite frames: the coloured hessian is important to this effect but had an unfortunate result in the hundreds of grey and oatmeal canvas inserts used in the 1960s, even for paintings by Turner in the Tate Gallery, where neither their colour nor their texture was appropriate.

Since World War II frames have generally been minimal or excised altogether. With no margin to focus the attention, to give the illusion of passage to a different world or to provide an area of rest for the eye, the work—particularly an abstract painting—risks reduction to a mere interruption or pattern on the wall surface. Some artists (Anthony Green etc) have clung to a vestigial frame of edging strips, like the inner frame in figure 52g; others have settled for commercial mass-produced mouldings, old or antique frames, or have tried to re-create their own setting peculiar to the work by painting some form of movable frame in harmony with the contents. Exceptionally, Howard Hodgkin painted a broad frame directly on the canvas, which in some works continues on to and envelops a surrounding frame moulding. Where the artist's imagination falls short of anything but a stock moulding, the long history of the frame remains as a rich quarry of allusion and visual play: for instance in the work of Michael Noakes, in the 1995 exhibition of the Royal Society of Portrait Painters, London, where two pendent portraits of the artist and his wife were shown, painted in integral *trompe l'oeil* frames from which the subjects break, like the Virgins and secular sitters of 15th-century Germany and Belgium. The modern carved frame, however, seems extinct as a costume for contemporary work, and certainty about the role of the frame has vanished, perhaps anticipating the broader introduction of holographic art, which will surround the spectator and will require no boundary.

BIBLIOGRAPHY

M. Jourdain: *English Interior Decoration, 1500–1830* (London, 1950)
R. Edwards: 'Picture Frames', *The Shorter Dictionary of English Furniture* (London, 1964) [29 figs]
J. Fowler and J. Cornforth: *English Decoration in the 18th Century* (London, 1974)
G. Beard: *Decorative Plasterwork in Great Britain* (London, 1975)
N. Cooper: *The Opulent Eye: Late Victorian and Edwardian Taste in Interior Design* (London, 1976)
J. Cornforth: *English Interiors, 1790–1848: The Quest for Comfort* (London, 1978)
F. Oughton: *Grinling Gibbons and the English Woodcarving Tradition* (London, 1979)
I. Horowitz: 'Whistler's Frames', *A. J.* [New York], xxxix (1979–80), pp. 124–131
Joseph Southall (exh. cat., Birmingham, Mus. & A.G., 1980)
G. Beard: *Craftsmen and Interior Decoration in England, 1660–1820* (Edinburgh, 1981)
H. Sandwith: 'National Trust Picture Frame Survey', *Int. J. Mus. Mgmt & Cur.*, iv (1985), pp. 173–8 [8 figs]
M. Tomlin: 'Picture Frames at Ham House', *Int. J. Mus. Mgmt & Cur.*, iv (1985), pp. 129–140 [21 figs]
The Quiet Conquest: The Huguenots in Britain (exh. cat., London, 1985)
L. Roberts: 'Nineteenth Century English Picture Frames', *Int. J. Mus. Mgmt & Cur.*, iv (1985), pp. 154–72 [24 figs]; v (1986), pp. 273–93 [25 figs]
N. Penny and M. Gregory: 'Reynolds and Picture Frames', *Burl. Mag.*, xi (1986), pp. 810–25 [61 figs]
D. Buttery: 'The Picture Frames of Paul Petit and Freerick, Prince of Wales', *Apollo* (1987), pp. 12–15
Designs for English Picture Frames (exh. cat., ed. P. Mason; London, Arnold Wiggins & Sons; London, Morton Morris & Co.; 1989) [68 figs]
P. Mitchell: 'Wright's Picture Frames', *Joseph Wright of Derby* (exh. cat., London, Tate, 1990)
M. Gregory: 'A Review of English Gilding Techniques: Original Source Material about Picture Frames', *Gilded Wood: Conservation and History* (Madison, 1991), pp. 109–18 [5 figs]
P. Mason: 'The Picture Frames', *Boughton House: The English Versailles*, ed. T. Murdoch (London, 1992), pp. 91–5
For further bibliography *see* §I above.

V. The Netherlands and Belgium.

1. Gothic. 2. Renaissance. 3. 17th century. 4. 18th century. 5. 19th century revival styles. 6. Late 19th and 20th centuries.

1. GOTHIC. From as early as the 10th and 11th centuries the Low Countries were able to support financially all aspects of the arts through the wealth built from their wool trade. In the 12th century Liège was a centre of cast-metal sculpture and ornament, and the archbishops of Cologne patronized goldsmithing in the Meuse Valley, where elaborate reliquaries with architectural frames and decorative borders were produced (e.g. the Stavelot Triptych, *c.* 1145; New York, Pierpont Morgan Lib.). Although the Low Countries were artistically dependent on France, there were strong local traditions and skills that were integral to the wood-carver's art; in the 13th century this Franco-Flemish exchange resulted in the production of carved wooden altarpieces. By the 14th century the dukes of Burgundy had absorbed the Low Countries into an enormous kingdom that extended as far as southern France; this meant that there was a constant interchange of ideas among artists patronized by the Burgundian court. Philip the Bold (*reg* 1363–1404) employed French and Netherlandish sculptors such as Jean de Marville and Claus Sluter, both of whom worked on the charterhouse of Champmol (*see* DIJON, §IV, 1(ii)). Philip also chose Jacques de Baerze, a south Netherlandish wood-carver, to produce intricate, sophisticated altarpieces for the charterhouse; these were then painted by Melchior Broederlam, also from the southern Netherlands, just as in Italy painter followed carver with no distinction between fine and decorative art. Philip's son, John the Fearless (*reg* 1404–19), employed the master cabinetmaker Jean de Liège (ii) to carve a crib (untraced), which was then painted and gilded by the court artist Bason. These two men probably collaborated on altarpieces as well. Many early Netherlandish works vanished when the Burgundian empire was broken up and when iconoclasm struck the northern Netherlands in the 16th century. Sculpture, however, flourished in the southern Netherlands, particularly in the 15th century; carved wooden altarpieces were exported throughout Europe up to the 16th century.

As in Italy, the earliest frames were integral with the picture panel, with raised ledges, as, for example, the oak ogee-shaped border surrounding the Master of St Veronica's *Christ, as the Man of Sorrows* (late 14th century; Antwerp, Kon. Mus. S. Kst.). Frames such as these gradually developed mouldings and decorations. However, as northern Europe absorbed the Gothic style in a manner unlike Italy, 15th-century Netherlandish frames took on a correspondingly different appearance. Instead of the Italian form of a simulated cross-section of a Gothic church (*see* §II, 2 above), Netherlandish altarpieces tended to have a linear simplicity with unbroken rectangular outlines and straight, arched or ogee tops (e.g. the Master of Flémalle's *Mérode Triptych*; *c.* 1425; New York, Cloisters). This simple moulding, with taenia, ogees and scotiae, is the precursor of later moulding frames and looks remarkably modern, except for the typically northern device of a sloping rainsill (akin to the *Wasserschlag* of a church window) that replaces the bottom moulding and gives an immediate sense of a window miraculously opening on to a celestial vision. This basic structure was sometimes elaborated by applied ornament, by the enthusiasm in northern Europe for coloured frames that echo the clear tones of the paintings, and by the development of intricate Gothic architectural tracery. These additions were either carved inside the frame or painted in the picture itself, creating the feeling of a gabled and pinnacled Italian altarpiece entirely within the oblong outer frame. The Norfolk Triptych (*c.* 1415; Rotterdam, Mus. Boymans–van Beuningen), commissioned by the Bishop of Liège, brother-in-law of John the Fearless, combines all these features. The scene has a background of painted Romanesque and Gothic niches, while on the frame carved daisies, symbolic of Christ's humility, were applied to the rainsill and corresponding upper mouldings, with a run of stylized vines painted along the outer edge. The blurring of roles here, where the artist painted his own inner 'frame', is mirrored in some altarpieces where the scene itself is carved, as in the triptych of the *Crucifixion* (1390–

99; Dijon, Mus. B.-A.) by Jacques de Baerze and Broederlam or *Descent into Limbo* (*c*. 1440; Amsterdam, Rijksmus.). Sculpted altarpieces from such centres as Liège, Antwerp and Brussels were sent mainly to Scandinavia, Germany and southern Europe. Jan Borman the elder was a later master of this art. His *St George* altarpiece (1493; Brussels, Musées Royaux A. & Hist.) is, like the *Crucifixion* by Jacques de Baerze, a confection of filigree tracery—niched, arched and galleried—framing dramatic three-dimensional scenes. Such altarpieces would have been stamped with their makers' marks.

Political ties with Spain may have had an effect on the style and intricacy of Netherlandish frames. (In the 1420s Jan van Eyck travelled with Burgundian delegations to Spain and Portugal.) The patronage of Italian merchants provided a further stylistic influence. An exceptional triptych frame (*c*. 1470; Brussels, Mus. A. Anc.) with a pinnacled churchlike silhouette reminiscent of a simplified Venetian altarpiece was made for Claudio de Villa; its rejection of the boxlike northern European outline signifies a potential openness of Netherlandish art to outside tastes. The frame carries a carved inscription on what corresponds to the predella panel at the base, exemplifying the use of inscription as another feature typical of early Netherlandish frames. The *Crucifixion* (*c*. 1428; New York, Met.; *see* EYCK, VAN, (2), fig. 1), a panel attributed to Jan van Eyck, is inscribed all round the simple border. Frames for his *Virgin and Child with SS Donatian and George and a Donor* (1436; Bruges, Groeningemus.) and *Man in a Red Chaperon* (traditionally known as the *Man in a Red Turban*; London, N.G.) also bear inscriptions. The latter has the artist's signature and the date of 21 October 1433 painted on the bottom rail and a proverb (*als ich kan*) on the top rail. Such inbuilt 'captions' were used to gloss or identify the contents (as in van Eyck's paintings) or else had a didactic purpose, as with biblical quotations that amplify a religious subject, generally to be found on early 16th-century altarpieces. The surround for the van Eycks' retable with the *Adoration of the Lamb* (or Ghent Altarpiece; begun after 1420; Ghent, Cathedral of St Bavo), pared down to an extremely simple flat plate frame with a tiny cavetto moulding at the sight, has didactic inscriptions, extending and echoing the quotations within the painting itself. These inscriptions are the sole ornament on the frame. It is generally true that, from the 15th century, frames around painted altarpieces—as distinct from those around sculpted altarpieces—are austerely plain in structure and are decorated only with quotations, *trompe l'oeil* stonework or bands of colour.

However, elements of the Flamboyant style and of Gothic sculptural decoration are seen in the inner parts of some frames painted to give the illusion of stone voussoirs and Gothic niches, as, for example, in Petrus Christus's *Annunciation* and *Nativity* (both 1452; Bruges, Groeningemus.) and Rogier van der Weyden's *Virgin and Child Enthroned* (Madrid, Mus. Thyssen–Bornemisza). The backs of the folding wings of many altarpieces also have painted architectural settings surrounding grisaille figures, as in the *Adoration of the Lamb*. The two panels by Christus might once have possessed vestigially architectural framings based on the window and rainsill, which—like Giotto's Bologna Altarpiece (*c*. 1330; Bologna, Pin. N.; *see* §II, 2

above)—would have emphasized the interdependence of picture and frame. The Netherlandish fascination with frames entirely in mock stonework or *faux-marbre* was not characteristic of France or Italy, where only such details as flats or columns would be rendered in this manner. In the northern and southern Netherlands clear light flooded through huge windows into the interiors of churches and secular buildings; thus, there was less need for the large gilded retable frames that reflected candlelight on to painted panels within dim, small-windowed interiors, as in Italy, or that provided definition within the colourful and elaborate settings of French churches. In southern Europe, gilt or parcel-gilt frames are common even for small devotional works, whereas the puritanical modesty of Jan van Eyck's small grisaille panel of the *Virgin and Child* (1437; Dresden, Gemäldegal. Alte Meister; *see* TRIPTYCH, fig. 1) within a painted stone frame is specifically northern European. South Netherlandish memorial portraits imitating either a church wall plaque or a tombstone also feature *trompe l'oeil* stonework. Van Eyck used painted marbling on the simple moulding of taenia, groove and ogee that frames *Margaret van Eyck* (see fig. 55a below) and for the frame of *St Barbara* (1437; Antwerp, Kon. Mus. S. Kst.), the latter simulating red marble with dark veins (*see* EYCK, VAN, (2), fig. 6). Similarly, the *Portrait of a Lady with a Pink* (55c below) by the Master of the Legend of St Ursula (i) has two clearly jointed marbled mouldings on each side alternating red and olive-grey. The Master of the Versten Portrait's *Louis de Gruuthuse* and several works by Hans Memling (all Bruges, Groeningemus.) are related; these are inscribed with the name and age of the sitter. They are also connected to Netherlandish round-arched and eared portrait frames (e.g. the triptych of *Charles of Ghent and his Sisters*; Vienna, Ksthist. Mus.), which (although not marbled) are tombstone-like in their form and probably originated in Germany. Portrait frames of this type are also linked to the convention of depicting the sitter within a stone window-niche or behind a marble sill (e.g. Jan van Eyck's *Portrait of ?Gilles Binchois*, 1432; London, N.G.). This is a means of enhancing the illusionism of the painting rather than being a symbolic device.

Imitation stone frames surrounding religious paintings, such as that on Jan van Eyck's grisaille *Virgin* in Dresden, have reference to the fabric of church architecture rather than, as in Italy, the church silhouette. This characteristic is also to be seen in Memling's triptych of the *Adoration of the Magi* (1479; Bruges, Memlingmus.), which has a simplified classical tabernacle frame, indicating the Italian influence introduced by such artists as van der Weyden. Its outer wings of *faux-marbre* enclose painted simulations of Gothic rainsill windows through which St John the Baptist and St Veronica are seen, as though through the windows of the Church, which metaphorically introduces the laity to such visions. The combination is eclectic yet decoratively and symbolically satisfying, and is effective in leading the spectator's eye into the miraculous scene. Memling reinforced the sculptural depth of his subjects by depicting them in arched stone niches, notably the figure of *St Anthony of Padua* painted in grisaille on the reverse of one panel of the diptych of the *Virgin and Child with a Donor* (1485–90; Chicago, IL, A. Inst.). On the front, *trompe l'oeil* was used, the donor's arm and prayer-book painted as though 'projecting' across the frame's sill.

Trompe l'oeil was a powerful device for engaging the spectator and was essential to both the illusory and didactic aspects of a painting, as seen in Simon Marmion's triptych with the *Virgin and Child* (1470; Madrid, Mus. Thyssen-Bornemisza), where the rainsill is overpainted with a carpet and with a cushion supporting the Child, as though he were actually within the spectator's space. Other examples are the portrait of *Engelbrecht II, Count of Nassau* (1482; 's Hertogenbosch, Noordbrabants Mus.) by Arnold van der Laar, which has the sitter's arm overlapping the frame; Memling's *Christ Blessing* (see fig. 53), where Christ's fingers rest on the upper edge of the sill; and a portrait of the Netherlandish school (*c.* 1520; Cologne, Wallraf-Richartz-Mus.), in which the male sitter's gloves are painted over the marbled frieze as though hanging towards the spectator. The use of *trompe l'oeil* has connections with Germany (see §VI, 1 below), but philosophically it is the equivalent of Brunelleschi's perspective system, in which the illusory pictorial space was made to seem continuous with the 'real' world. The Florentine origins of such *trompe l'oeil* devices are most evident in the frames on, for example, the *Deposition* after Petrus Christus and *Christ Blessing* by Gerard David, where the wide rainsill in both has been incised with criss-crossed lines imitating a pavement rapidly receding into the picture.

More south Netherlandish works of the period exist than do northern ones, and they tend to lack the monumentality of Italian altarpieces or Spanish retables. However, the Master of Alkmaar's *Seven Acts of Mercy* (1504;

53. Engaged polychromed and gilt frame, 346×254 mm, original for Hans Memling's *Christ Blessing, c.* 1481 (Boston, MA, Museum of Fine Arts)

Amsterdam, Rijksmus.) is a north Netherlandish work, and its scale surpasses even a relatively large painting such as Jan van Eyck's *Virgin and Child with SS Donatian and George and a Donor*. Its seven oblong panels, each 1 m high unframed, are mounted in a continuous unhinged casing—a huge, divided flat border with individual sight mouldings—made of polished wood and with an inscription beneath each panel. Similar to the rectangular five-panelled portable altarpiece of the *Virgin and Four Saints* (*c.* 1333–44; e.g. Malibu, CA, Getty Mus.; New York, Met.; priv. col.) attributed to Simone Martini (see §II, 2 above), the Master of Alkmaar's large work is interesting for its Netherlandish pedigree; its format, designed to be read from left to right with the viewer's eyes returning to Christ; the date of 1504 inscribed on it; its fabric and simple form; and the visible signs of its construction—butt joints secured with nails. Similar nails can be seen on south Netherlandish works by van Eyck and Memling, where, however, complex mouldings or a rainsill have dictated the use of mitred joints.

2. RENAISSANCE. More original Dutch frames and paintings seem to have survived from the later part of the 16th century than from the earlier, and by the mid-17th century they almost entirely supplanted Flemish works. Yet in the early 16th century there were still several important south Netherlandish artists, one of whom was Jan Gossart, who, stimulated by the increasing influence of Italian art on the Low Countries, visited Rome in 1508–9. The influence of such visits on the development of the frame can be seen not in any overt use of classical shape or ornament (which tended anyhow to be restricted to the settings of the paintings) but rather in forms and inscriptions, hitherto used for altarpieces or portraits, now being used for secular or mythological scenes. Gossart was known for his painting of moulded frames around many of his subjects (e.g. *Henry III, Count of Nassau-Breda, c.* 1516–17; Fort Worth, TX, Kimbell A. Mus.). By this device he underlined the importance of the frame's appearance and function in late 15th- and 16th-century Netherlandish painting. He employed inscriptions relating to the Virgin and donor on the frame of the Carondelet Diptych (1517; Paris, Louvre) but also used them on *Venus and Cupid* (1520; Brussels, Mus. A. Anc.; G pl. 66). The latter has a deep, round-arched frame with a complex arrangement of flat, concave and convex mouldings and a flat bottom shelf replacing the outer mouldings, which may be considered a 'Classical' analogue of the 'religious' rainsill. The central flat has an inscription with Venus' curse against men. Another secular yet didactic inscription, in imitation of the sacred quotations that would have embellished and glossed an altarpiece, appeared on the frame (untraced) of Quinten Metsys's *Moneychanger and his Wife* ('*Banker and his Wife*', 1514; Paris, Louvre).

Altarpieces of the 16th century are less likely to be inscribed, and, except for rectangular formats, they are shaped in a manner peculiar to the Low Countries. Unlike classically inspired Italian aediculae, which have single panels and horizontal architraves, Netherlandish altarpieces are usually triptychs, the central panel being either round or ogee-arched, or formed of a complex series of curves. The frame, with its combination of taenia, frieze, scotia, ogee and cavetto mouldings, faithfully follows these undulating outlines, which echo the curving gables of north Netherlandish architecture. A pair of triptychs by Ambrosius Benson and Quinten Metsys (both Antwerp, Mus. Mayer van den Bergh) exemplify the two main types of cross-section employed in oak mouldings. The frame on the Benson painting has a continuous flattish architrave profile with gilt frieze (possibly original) and black raised outer edges; the one on the Metsys painting (see fig. 54) has a similar finish with a shallow scotia profile running down to a rainsill.

A few altarpieces with crockets and finials survive. Examples are Jan Wellens de Cock's triptych of the *Crucifixion with Donors* (*c.* 1525; Amsterdam, Rijksmus.), the frame of which is integral with the painted panels; Jan Mostaert's *Portrait of a Man* (Worcester, MA, A. Mus.), possibly adapted; and Memling's portraits of *Tommaso Portinari* and his wife *Maria Maddalena Baroncelli* (both *c.* 1470; New York, Met.). Many frames, including the last two by Memling, have, however, lost their original finish, so that the present polished wood, full gilding or parcel gilding with black has little to do with the original conception of the framemaker, artist or patron. J. R. J. van

Asperen de Boer (see bibliography) has found that some frames were originally far more colourful: those of three north Netherlandish triptychs in the Stedelijk Museum De Lakenhal, Leiden, were repainted, probably in the 18th century or the early 19th. The frame surrounding the *Crucifixion* (*c.* 1517–22) by Cornelis Engebrechtsz., for example, was once russet-coloured on the outside and violet, green and gold inside, with a marbled predella frame. It has also lost its gilded crockets and finials. That of Lucas van Leyden's *Last Judgement* (1517) was originally lavender outside, and the mouldings inside—now black— were violet. It retains an inner run of blue between gold colonnettes, decorated with gilt flowers; this was originally painted with azurite, and since 1704 the decoration has been reproduced in modern Prussian blue. These altarpieces with coloured frames, and the earlier marbled frames, were the predecessors of more elaborately painted settings in the later 16th century and the early 17th. Examples include a frame painted with demons for the *Last Judgement* (1554; Brussels, Mus. A. Anc.) by Pieter Huys; an allegory (1600–20; Le Puy, Mus. Crozatier) by Frans Pourbus (ii) that is framed with painted scenes and inscriptions in cartouches; *Christ Carrying the Cross*

54. Engaged gilt and black ogee-arched frame, 1765×2210 mm overall, original for Quinten Metsys's triptych of the *Crucifixion with Donors*, *c.* 1520 (Antwerp, Museum Mayer van den Bergh)

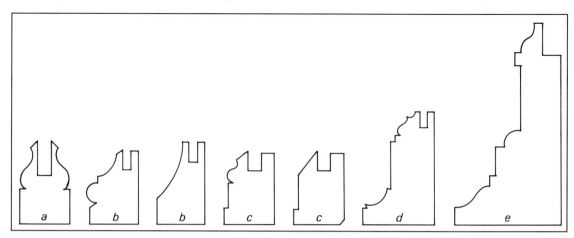

55. Flemish frame profiles, 15th and 16th centuries: (a) continuous ogee, polychrome, 323×257×45 mm, original for Jan van Eyck's *Margaret van Eyck*, 1439 (Bruges, Groeningemuseum); (b) cavetto with rainsill base, gilt and polychrome, centre panel 335×250 mm, sides and top 40 mm, base 45 mm, original for Goswijn van der Weyden's triptych of the *Abbé Antoine Tsgrooten*, 1507 (Antwerp, Koninklijk Museum voor Schone Kunsten); (c) frieze and ogee with rainsill base, polychrome, 240×200×40 mm, original for the Master of the Legend of St Ursula (i)'s *Portrait of a Lady with a Pink*, second half of the 15th century (Antwerp, Museum Mayer van den Bergh); (d) continuous entablature with cavetto, polychrome, centre panel 811×616×62 mm, original for Pieter Claeissins the elder's triptych of the *Crucifixion*, *c.* 1567–81 (Bruges, Groeningemuseum); (e) continuous entablature with ogee polychrome, 1095×1260×110 mm, original for the *Last Judgement*, 1578, by Jacob van den Coornhuuse (*fl* 1556–78) (Bruges, Groeningemuseum)

(*c.* 1578; Cologne, Wallraf-Richartz-Mus.) by Gillis Mostaert; and the *Crucifixion* (Ghent, Mus. S. Kst.) by Frans Francken (ii).

The evolution of 15th- and 16th-century Flemish frames and supports in the main artistic centres—Antwerp, Bruges, Brussels, Ghent, Leuven, Tournai and others—has been exhaustively explored, classified and illustrated by Hélène Verougstraete-Marcq and Roger van Schoute in *Cadres et supports dans la peinture flamande aux 15e et 16e siècles*. The book is essential for the study of the period and deals with craftsmen and the tools they used, various corporations, joinery and construction joints of frames, and cross-sections and finishes. It also discusses the five principal styles of moulding sections used, each having many regional variations (see fig. 55). These styles are based on combinations of Classical architectural mould-

56. Frans Francken II: *Cabinet of an Antwerp Amateur*, 477×777 mm, 1615–17 (Brussels, Musée d'Art Ancien)

ings such as cavetto, scotia, ogee, taenia (or band) and frieze. Ogee and scotia profiles, with or without sill (55a and b), were equally dominant in the second half of the 16th century, the scotia being the main section used in the first half of the 16th century. The architrave profile with ogee and sill (55c) is seen mainly in works of the second half of the 15th century. Entablature mouldings with outer cavetto (55d) or ogee (55e) both appeared in the first half of the 16th century and were used almost exclusively then, although in the second half of the 16th century the entablature with ogee was used twice as frequently, and it was the only one to survive into the early 17th century. As most of the sections indicate, the sides of the frames were grooved to fit around and stabilize the panel painting, being jointed with various forms of mortice-and-tenon and straight and mitred half-lap, and secured with dowels.

The display of 16th- and early 17th-century Flemish frames is documented—more comprehensively than at any time in the history of frames—in paintings of interiors of artists' studios and of the salons and galleries of noblemen and rich bourgeois collectors (*see* CABINET PICTURE). The vogue for this type of picture, showing the *kunstkamer*, was popularized chiefly by Frans Francken II and his circle. In *Cabinet of an Antwerp Amateur* (see fig. 56), for example, Francken pays homage to Rubens and other artists whose works can be identified. The walls of the room are shown covered with paintings in narrow ebonized or plain oak frames, all hung closely together in symmetrical groups. All types of subject-matter are displayed: landscapes, religious and mythological scenes, marine paintings and still-lifes.

The prosperity of the arts and their flowering in the Spanish Netherlands under Archduke Albert (*reg* 1620–21) and Archduchess Isabella are emphasized in a similar interior (Baltimore, MD, Walters A.G.) by Francken, painted in collaboration with Jan Breughel the elder, depicting the couple in a collector's cabinet. Such paintings are invaluable aids in authentic reframing; for example, the National Gallery in London, on acquiring Rubens's *Samson and Delilah* (*c*. 1609–10) in 1980, reproduced the original frame as it is seen in Francken's view of a room in the house of Nicolaas Rockox (*c*. 1630–35; Munich, Alte Pin.), the first owner of the Rubens painting (*see* FRANCKEN, (5), fig. 6).

Unlike the earlier shaped formats of religious paintings, few original frames surrounding secular or rectangular paintings have survived. Uniquely, oak frames with gilt sight edges have been retained on landscape scenes of the *Twelve Months* ('s Hertogenbosch, Noordbrabants Mus.), works of the Netherlandish school. The collection of the Rijksmuseum Het Catharijneconvent in Utrecht is relatively unaltered and is notable for the preservation of entablature frames with gilt arabesque decoration or inscriptions on the frieze. A few other frames of this type and period survive (see fig. 57a) and are in the Rijksmuseum, Amsterdam. The use of gilt ornament in the manner of Italian prototypes, although rare, is seen on two of the approximately 45 frames surrounding paintings in Francken's *Cabinet of Jan Snellinck* (Brussels, Mus. A. Anc.); and in the *Cabinet of an Antwerp Amateur* a pair of oak portrait frames carved with dentil decoration can be seen. Carved ornament is rare on Netherlandish frames, but dentils,

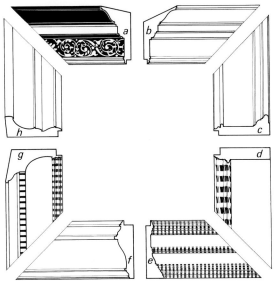

57. Belgian and Dutch frames, 16th and 17th centuries: (a) entablature frame, parcel gilt with scrolling foliage, 1040×880×103 mm, probably original for *Calvary*, *c*. 1510, by Jacob Cornelisz. van Oostsanen (*c*. 1470–1573) (Amsterdam, Rijksmuseum); (b) deep entablature frame in oak, 805×644×134 mm, original for Thomas de Keyser's *Portrait of a Lady*, 1630 (Rotterdam, Museum Boymans–van Beuningen); (c) ebony architrave frame, 440×382×100 mm, original for Pieter Codde's *Artist at his Easel*, second quarter of the 17th century (Rotterdam, Museum Boymans–van Beuningen); (d) ebony architrave frames with wave moulding, original pair for Hendrick Bloemaert's *Portrait of a Man* and *Portrait of a Woman*, 1647 (Baltimore, MD, Walters Art Gallery); (e) ebony entablature frame with wave mouldings, 740×600×130 mm, probably original for Bartholomeus van der Helst's *Portrait of a Lady*, 1656 (Frankfurt am Main, Städelsches Kunstinstitut und Städtische Galerie); (f) bolection frame in ebonized pear-wood, 535×460×70 mm, one of an original pair for Emanuel de Witte's *Portrait of a Man* and *Portrait of a Woman*, 1647 (Rotterdam, Museum Boymans–van Beuningen); (g) fruitwood scotia frame with wave mouldings, 745×605×112 mm, original for Nicolaes Maes's *Jacob de Witt*, 1657 (Dordrecht, Dordrechts Museum); (h) compound profile frame in ebonized fruitwood, 525×440×157 mm, one of an original pair for Jan Verkolje I's *William III* and *Mary Stuart*, after 1688 (Haarlem, Frans Halsmuseum).

first appearing on frames for 14th-century Italian Gothic altarpieces (examples, Florence, Accad.), are seen on the impressive pair of frames surrounding portraits of *William the Silent, Prince of Orange* and *Maurice, Prince of Orange* (both 1588; Arnemuiden, Raadhuis-Mus.; PL 1) by Daniel van den Queecborn (*c*. 1558–1641).

3. 17TH CENTURY.

(i) Introduction. (ii) Wood-finish frames. (iii) Carved and gilded frames.

(i) Introduction. Some types of frame and framing device were continued into the 17th century. The 'framing' of devotional paintings by a garland of flowers or a strapwork border painted on the canvas within the actual frame, as in Rubens's *Virgin and Garland* (Paris, Louvre) or Daniel Seghers's *Loyola* (Antwerp, Kon. Mus. S. Kst.), is similar to the effect created by the elaborately painted and highly coloured altarpieces of the late 16th century. Frames with entablature profiles (similar to those in 55e above and

57a) continued to be made in Flanders into the 1620s, overlapping with and becoming the basis of a new type of Dutch frame in the first quarter of the 17th century. There were no more innovations in framing in Flanders until the 19th century; characteristically Dutch styles were mostly used in the Low Countries in the 17th century, and regional variants of French types were fashionable in the 18th.

The archetypal 17th-century Dutch frame, leavened by the exotic addition of Auricular and Lutma designs and by trophy frames (see §(iii) below), has a black, occasionally parcel-gilt, moulding based on more sophisticated combinations of the flat- and round-sectioned mouldings in use from the early 15th century (see fig. 57). Its particular character depends on greater relative width and depth than before; on the use of broad, flat, cambered or shallow ogee and hollow areas; and on its finish, a veneer of ebony or other dark wood and an absence, or sparse use, of gilding. It is essentially a bourgeois style, designed not to assert its character within a court setting of gold, stucco and marble but rather to complement a domestic or municipal interior, with its light-coloured walls or tapestries, occasional linings of gilt leather, flooring of bare wooden boards or black-and-white tiles, and furniture of dark turned wood. Many factors contributed to the creation of this style of frame. A tax was levied on house frontages, resulting in small façades fronting long sequences of rooms, of which only the front and extreme back would receive direct natural light. Consequently, windows had to be large, and an ingenious arrangement of mirrors, open doorways, pale walls and light-coloured floors reflected cool, diffused light through the house, making such decoration as gold leaf unnecessary. In 1581 the Act of Abjuration had rejected Spanish sovereignty over the northern Netherlands, and in 1609 the Truce of Antwerp established the Dutch Republic. As a result, court culture and Catholicism were able to flourish only in the southern Netherlands. The north became progressively Protestant, its nobility dwindled and it cultivated a patrician, rather than a royal, style. The Protestant inclination was to design in a style inherently less ostentatious, less Baroque and smaller in scale than the Catholic; the black frames harmonize with this reduced scale, with locally made wooden furniture rather than French or Italian gilded pieces, and with the Protestant predilection for comfort rather than luxury. Dutch national pride also influenced the choice of frames. The northern Netherlands had a strong mercantile base, and in the late 16th century Amsterdam had superseded Antwerp to become the trade centre of Europe, importing valuable spices and rare woods from its colonies.

Although similar styles of framing would spread to Flanders, Austria and Germany, indigenous fruit woods or stained pine and oak would be used there, while Dutch frames are rich, for all their apparent austerity, in such woods as ebony and amboyna, and inlays of ivory, tortoiseshell and whalebone. In the late 16th century Antwerp was the centre of the craft of veneering and inlaying. Yet at this time, due to persecution by Spanish rulers, a great number of Flemish cabinetmakers emigrated to the northern Netherlands, re-establishing the craft in an area more able to support it. The wealthy Dutch middle and lower-middle classes bought pictures voraciously for pleasure and as an investment, having them framed in offcuts from the exotic woods that filled Amsterdam's saw-mills. An interest in the Dutch frame was also encouraged by the publication, probably in Wolfenbüttel around 1588, by Hans Vredeman de Vries of *Differents pourtraicts de menuiserie*. Considered to be the first pattern book for furniture, it was significant as a channel through which Renaissance classicism reached the Netherlands in the 1580s. In 1630, Hans's son Paul Vredeman de Vries (1567–after 1630) published *Verscheyden schrynwerck* (Amsterdam), another pattern book that included types of frames. Examples of 17th-century Dutch frames containing the original paintings can be found in the *Prijst de lijst* exhibition catalogue (1984; see bibliography) and are seen on the walls of many interiors in contemporary paintings by such artists as Vermeer, Nicolaes Maes, Gabriel Metsu, Jan Steen, Pieter de Hooch and Gerard ter Borch (ii). These 'paintings within paintings' provide information about styles of framing, methods of hanging and arrangements of pictures, and can confirm the date and provenance of a frame and its originality to the painting that it surrounds.

(ii) Wood-finish frames. From the early 17th century the parcel gilding of Dutch ebonized frames almost ceased. Their beauty now depended on an increasingly subtle interplay of stepped flat and curved surfaces, the edges of which catch light and create the effect of a receding perspectival vista; this is an especially effective focusing device for portraits but is also used for landscapes, still-lifes and allegories. Occasionally, the sight edge is ornamented with wave mouldings or ripple mouldings, but the use of such patterns over the whole frame is characteristic of Germany, Austria and Flanders. Dutch frames tend to rely on the silken sheen of ebony veneer acting as a foil for the paintings themselves. They also have a wide range of profiles, from a deep case frame, through a simple flat margin, to a reverse rebate. Contour is employed interestingly, with straight and curved lines played off one against the other. For example, van den Queecborn's five portraits of the van Wassenaer family (1627; Brussels, Château Duyvenvoorde; PL 12) have oblong black and gold frames with marbled circular spandrels painted on the canvas, while seven portraits of an unknown family (1632; Amsterdam, Rijksmus.; PL 15) have wide octagonal ebony frames with oval black slips.

The development of the principal profiles of 17th-century Dutch moulding frames is meticulously described and illustrated in *Prijst de lijst*. The following provides a précis of this work, augmented by unpublished examples of Netherlandish and Middle European frames. The Flemish entablature section in oak (55e above and 57a), popular from the 1550s to *c.* 1640, is deepened by the addition of a steep, narrow ogee back edge (57b), recorded as early as 1565. This treatment—like a perspective box—emphasizes the illusion of depth in a painting. The majority of small-scale pictures, as depicted in interior scenes, are framed with a narrow and shallower version of the entablature to create an architrave frame (57c). Here, the frieze is veneered in ebony, and inner and outer borders are moulded into sharply defined steps, reeds and hollows, the scale of which matches the artist's miniaturizing technique. More economical alternatives were pear- and other fruitwoods, which, because of their close grain, resemble ebony when stained black.

The decorative character of the plain wooden frame is greatly enhanced by the application of wave mouldings or ripple mouldings, made in ebony or stained hardwoods. The machine for producing these regular, closely spaced patterns is thought to have been developed first in the late 16th century in cabinetmaking workshops in Augsburg and Nuremberg (see §VI, 3 below); it then rapidly spread to Flanders, Spain and Italy. Relatively fewer wave-trimmed frames were produced in the Netherlands (57d, e, g), 17th-century Dutch pictures having been reframed in wave patterns in recent years. The ornaments were produced on a special milling machine by running straight-profiled strips of wood through shaped metal cutters mounted over a long, wave-shaped master template. Repeated movements of this jig cut successively deeper into the wood until a continuous undulating surface was achieved. The production of these increasingly sophisticated and varied mouldings enabled cabinet- and frame-makers to decorate their work without recourse to hand-carving. These fine, uniform wave mouldings create an even flicker of light, most effective as a subtle margin between the edge of a painting and its surround. In some cases the inner edge is gilded, and generally the effect is an opulent counterpart to the rarer and more expensive gilt frames produced by sculptors in wood. Ripple mouldings were used for furniture and on mirror frames, applied to the surrounds of cabinets and their doors, drawers and panels, and often inlaid with such materials as tortoiseshell, ivory or pearl. Frames for small Flemish, German and Italian pictures, relief sculptures and reliquaries closely resemble the fixed frames in cabinets and desks, the drawer-fronts and doors of which carry a series of paintings. An example is in the Rubenshuis, Antwerp, together with a tortoiseshell and wave moulding frame on Rubens's *Self-portrait.* The frame for Michiel Sweerts's *Young Man and the Procuress* (Paris, Louvre) is a superb and rare furniture-related pattern made in Flemish, German and Italian workshops and has pairs of pewter (or silver) stringing in the brown/black Macassar ebony frieze. The borders are Indian ebony inlaid with the same metal stringing and simultaneously machined into wave mouldings. Such luxury frames demonstrate that the enamel-like surface of oil paintings on copper or wooden panels is ideally matched by the density and opulent sheen of the hardest natural materials—ebony and tortoiseshell—combined with metal inlays. The frieze between the ebony wave edges is occasionally inlaid with rosewood and paler veneers to create a distinct colour contrast, as seen in the frame for Adriaen Brouwer's *Sense of Touch* (Munich, Alte Pin.).

The architrave profile was used in the Netherlands from the second quarter of the 17th century, either plain (57c) or with a rippled sight edge (57d). In the 1630s and 1640s a more elaborate, deeper section was developed, having two main veneered surfaces (the steep outside usually an ogee) separated by a flat and reeded moulding to the frieze, which is either an ogee or flat (PL inv. nos 24–5). This was a development from the earlier Netherlandish frame with deep entablature profile in oak (57a) and is invariably veneered in ebony and, exceptionally, in whalebone (PL 14). In the luxury version, three narrow reeded components were substituted for wave mouldings (57e). An intermediate pattern combines both, having wave moulding only on the inner edge (e.g. on Jan de Bray's *Portrait of a Man*; Rotterdam, Mus. Boymans–van Beuningen).

The reverse, or bolection, profile (57f) was in use in the Netherlands from the mid-1630s to the early 1670s and was a contrast to the inward-stepping frame. As with the other sections, it is veneered in ebony, palisander or an ebonized fruitwood (usually pear). Narrower than the entablature section, it frames all types of paintings (particularly rectangular or octagonal portraits) and reflects contemporary Italian and French Baroque frames in its projection of the picture plane forward from the wall surface.

From the mid-1640s until the end of the century the scotia profile and its variants became the dominant style of frame. Generally having straight mouldings in ebony or, more commonly, stained fruitwoods, they were used as surrounds for landscapes and portraits (PL 31, 51) and were occasionally enhanced with rippled components (57g). The warm, varied tones of Macassar ebony or palisander blend naturally with the warm pigments underlying landscape paintings (e.g. Aert van der Neer's *Landscape with Windmill*; Rotterdam, Mus. Boymans–van Beuningen). The optical enhancement of the colours of a painting is complemented by a focal emphasis, the width being increased by a forward-projecting ogee section, as in Willem Kalf's *Still-life with Orange* (Frankfurt am Main, Städel. Kstinst. & Städt. Gal.). A final development in the shape of the 17th-century Dutch wooden frame (57h) occurred from the mid-1640s to the mid-1670s, when a frieze was added to the scotia (e.g. on Jan de Bray's *Portrait of a Family*, 1667; Haarlem, Frans Halsmus.).

From the mid-1670s to the late 1690s the single or double ogee extension evolved to give additional weight and importance to portrait subjects (57h). The pair of frames on *Portrait of a Man* and *Portrait of a Woman* (1691; Amsterdam, Rijksmus.; PL 90) by Jan Verkolje I have some of the widest sections. The paintings' dimensions are each 570×490 mm, and the width of each rail of the frame is *c.* 210 mm. The surface area of each frame is therefore over $2\frac{1}{4}$ times that of the picture, reinforcing the frame's dominant role in focusing attention on the subject. The multiple reflections over the frame's many facets reinforce Verkolje's illusion of depth and space.

(iii) Carved and gilded frames. In the mid-17th century elaborate carved and gilded frames appeared, joining the infinite variations of the ebony moulding frame. They consist of three types: the Auricular frame, with carved marine, cartilaginous and skeletal forms; the Lutma frame (see LUTMA, (1)), with an Auricular base submerged beneath festoons of fruit and flowers; and the trophy frame, laden with attributes referring to the subject of the painting within. These luxurious frames are sumptuous expressions of Dutch Mannerism and of the skills of native wood-sculptors. Many show a skilful merging of fine art and decorative art, and serve as a renewed

endorsement of the supremacy of sculpture over painting in the Renaissance hierarchy of the arts. In the Netherlands no such type of frame can apparently be dated before 1652, the year of the trophy frame on Michiel van Mierevelt's portrait of *Jacob Cats* (Amsterdam, Rijksmus.; PL 32). The first Auricular example appeared the following year on the group portrait of *Capt. Dirck Veen and his Company* (Hoorn, Westfries Mus.; PL 33) by Abraham Liedt (*fl* 1653–9). This frame, however, is already sophisticated in its use of carving to create the melting marine forms that emblematize Dutch naval power.

The first Auricular frames have severely linear borders, but later versions allow the curving, sensuous shapes of shells, lobes and volutes to break across the outer edge and, more rarely, over the sight edge. Designs are softer and more flowing than the slightly later Italian counterparts commissioned by Cardinal Leopoldo de' Medici (*see* §II, 4(ii) above); the wood appears to have liquefied in a manner similar to the silverwork of the brothers Adam and Paulus van Vianen (*see* VIANEN, VAN, (1) and (2), and figs.). Auricular frames were more complicated and time-consuming to carve than even the best ebony frames and, because of their gold leaf, more expensive. They appear, as do ebony frames, in many 17th-century Dutch paintings of interiors, as surrounds for mirrors and all types of paintings but always as indicators of status and symbols of luxury. They are Mannerist in their refinement and distortions, Baroque in their flamboyant use of natural forms and anti-classical insofar as they are removed in concept from the Italian grotesques that were their inspiration. This lack of any classical reference may have made them acceptable to the newly independent Dutch Republic as alternatives to French and Italian frames. The style frequently appears in the backgrounds of the fashionable yet romanticized interiors painted by Gerard ter Borch (ii). '*Curiosity*' (*c.* 1660; New York, Met.), for example, depicts a chimney-piece with a gilded marine Auricular frame; gilt floral festoons surround it on the sides and face of the chimney and an elaborate cresting fronts it on the mantelshelf. Ter Borch's *Lady at her Toilet* (*c.* 1660; Detroit, MI, Inst. A.) shows the same chimney-piece painted white and with a white Auricular frame, while a similar silver mirror frame is on the toilet-table. White frames also appear in paintings by de Hooch and Jacob Ochtervelt, the light colour a possible influence from French stuccowork.

Lutma frames also have probable French influences. They are characterized by a wide Auricular band, like a softened strapwork cartouche: a linear shallow torus with Auricular corners. This is overlaid with such forms as swags of fruit and flowers, putti or grotesque masks. Fine examples frame Ferdinand Bol's *Self-portrait* (1660; Amsterdam, Rijksmus.), which is surmounted by a huge trophy-like sunflower, and Steen's *Feast of St Nicholas* (Amsterdam, Rijksmus.), the frame of which was originally made in 1661 for a portrait by Hendrick Berckman (1629–79; PL fig. 4). Lutma frames are also seen in Steen's portrait of the *Van Goyen Family* (Kansas City, MO, Nelson–Atkins Mus. A.), where one is set in an overmantel flanked by festoons, and in Emanuel de Witte's *Portrait of a Family* (1673; Lewis S. Fry priv. col.), surrounding a mirror. They denote a degree of modish luxury linked with a preference

in the 1670s for French fashion: in spite of his wars with France, William III, Prince of Orange, who became Stadholder in 1672, saw Paris as the cultural centre of Europe. The floral festoons of a Lutma frame had already been sanctioned in, for example, the gilt stuccowork of Louis Le Vau's Hôtel de Lauzun (1657) in Paris.

Both the Lutma and Auricular styles were to be influential for the development of English frames (*see* §IV, 4 above), especially through the work of the goldsmith Christiaen van Vianen, as was the trophy, the third type of Dutch carved frame. Trophy frames derived from Netherlandish altarpieces ornamented with the blazons of donors, as well as from Crucifixions where the frames are carved or painted with the instruments of Christ's Passion. These heraldic shields and holy 'weapons' were easily adapted to glorify such secular icons of 17th-century Dutch art as portraits of victorious sea-captains and paintings of naval battles. Superb examples of trophy frames surround a portrait of *Admiral Tromp* (*c.* 1655; Amsterdam, Ned. Hist. Scheepvaartsmus.; PL 37), the *Exodus of the Spanish Garrison from Breda, 10 October 1637* (*c.* 1663; Amsterdam, Rijksmus.; PL 50) by Hendrick de Meyer (*fl* 1637–83) and the *Battle of the Zuider Zee* (1668; Amsterdam, Rijksmus.; PL 59) by Jan Theunisz. Blanckerhoff (1628–69). The portrait of Tromp has a frame of polished fruitwood carved with Roman corselets, sheaves of arrows and tritons. The gilt lime-wood frame around Meyer's painting also has carvings of armour and arrows, as well as spears, halberds, cannon and shields in an intricate criss-crossed pattern, the whole surmounted by two bound figures. Blanckerhoff's frame (see fig. 58) is of bare wood but is a three-dimensional extravaganza against which the actual painting fades into misty mediocrity. Signed and dated *Johannes Kinnema 1668*, the frame took one-and-a-half years to create, Kinnema winning a bonus of 175 guilders over the commissioned price of 400 guilders; this represented 72% of the total cost of the painting, which was 800 guilders. It is an apotheosis of the framemaker's art but at the same time an empty exercise in virtuoso carving, as the function of a frame—to protect, highlight or gloss the picture—is subverted, the setting taking precedence.

Trophy frames seldom, if ever, appear in paintings of interiors, which reflect a more general and domestic taste. Because of their ornate form and celebratory nature, they were not displayed in the same manner as frames on other types of works. Mirrors, for example, were hung canted forwards and sometimes ornamented with a bow. Paintings might be covered with silk or velvet curtains and were hung from a wooden loop in the top rail or else were held by paired hooks or bolts at top and bottom. They were often ranged in tiers on the wall, some at a relatively low level (see Thornton, 1978, fig. 240).

By the end of the 17th century, the peculiarly indigenous flavour of Dutch furnishings, frames and interiors, as seen in the paintings of such artists as Vermeer and de Hooch, was overwhelmed by the popularity of the French taste. This is evident by a comparison of the interiors of two dolls' houses: one (last third of 17th century; Utrecht, Cent. Mus.) has a room hung with crested Lutma frames above mid-17th-century farthingale chairs; the other (1690; Amsterdam, Rijksmus.) has oval gilt frames and

58. Carved trophy frame by Johannes Kinnema (d 1673), signed and dated 1668, made for *Battle of the Zuider Zee*, 2.26×2.68 m, by Jan Theunisz. Blanckerhoff (1628–69) (Amsterdam, Rijksmuseum)

chairs with higher backs, all in the French manner. Although the latter interior is still *haut bourgeois* in general appearance, it reflects innovations brought by Daniel Marot I, a Huguenot who left France to take refuge in the Protestant Netherlands and who worked for William III and his wife Mary Stuart. He decorated William's palace of Het Loo in Apeldoorn and the Binnenhof in The Hague in the Louis XIV style. The Trêveszaal in the Binnenhof, with its late Baroque ceiling paintings and severely classical mouldings for the portraits set into the wall panels, shows how completely the French taste had been accepted in the Netherlands. From the late 1690s Marot published many designs, including those for a large group of chimney-pieces with doubled patterns for fireplace and overmantel. They depict various paintings (or niches for holding porcelain) within a choice of frames, thus reflecting an increasing desire that a room and its furniture and ornaments be unified in style. Marot's suites of engravings include designs for mirrors, cornices and picture frames. The first are torus mouldings decorated variously with all-over patterns, mirror-panels and corners-and-centres and have elaborate crestings of figures, masks and pendant festoons. Cornices and frames have a wide range of profiles and are rich in ornament deriving from Jean Berain I, Jean Le Pautre and Charles Le Brun, but are lightened by Marot's use of delicate key-shaped strapwork scrolls. The vast majority of carved and gilt frames seen today on 17th-century Dutch paintings are French in origin, fitted either by French collectors or by dealers in the course of trade. The French style of frame—popular both domestically and for the export market—was produced in the Netherlands, although it is now extremely rare. For instance, a richly carved pair of frames of bare wood (1696; PL 94) has a torus profile of bound leaves and fruit rendered in Louis XIII style (*see* §III, 4 above). Earlier examples occur from the mid-1670s, as do frames having centre cartouches with arms (e.g. Delft, Stedel. Mus. Prinsenhof; PL 72). The French Baroque corner-and-centre style may be distinguished as Dutch in origin by wider and indented strapwork in the cartouches, as seen framing the portrait of *Matthews van den Broucke* (1666; Dordrecht, Dordrechts Mus.) by Jacobus Levecq (1634–75).

4. 18TH CENTURY. Variations of French styles continued to be fashionable. For example, a frame in Régence style surrounds Judith Leyster's *Portrait of a Woman* (1635; Haarlem, Frans Halsmus.), and one with a distinctive undulating inner border in a bold Rococo style frames Nicolaes Maes's *The Dreamer* (Brussels, Mus. A. Anc.). Marot continued to work in the 18th century and designed (1734–9) the White Dining-room of the Huis ten Bosch in The Hague in *rococo hollandaise*. The room's stucco ceiling is covered with lambrequins, dancing strapwork and scrolled leaves. Symmetrical white frames with rocailles and ogee-arched tops provide settings for Jacob Eduard Witte's grisailles. Designers after Marot worked

first in a mature Rococo style and then in a Neo-classical Louis XVI style. Abraham van der Hart designed for Willem Philip Kops, a rich burgher from Haarlem, a room (1793; Amsterdam, Rijksmus.; *see* NETHERLANDS, THE, fig. 35) that includes gilt-framed panels and an overmantel of extreme restraint decorated only with leaf-and-dart and bead-and-bobbin trims. Adriaan de Lelie's *Art Gallery of Jan Gildemeester* (1794–5; Amsterdam, Rijksmus.) shows a room of a similar subdued green to the one designed by Hart and hung with three tiers of mainly 17th-century Dutch pictures, all of which are framed in simple linear gilt hollow or torus frames. In the later 18th century Italianate scotia patterns with moulded ornament were produced: the frame for Cornelis Troost's pastel *Figures in an Interior* (The Hague, Mauritshuis) has an outer triple laurel-leaf torus with bead-and-leaf sight. Frames with billowing ribbon *frontons* around Joseph-Benoît Suvée's *Self-portrait* (1771) and portrait of *Paul de Cock* (1779; both Bruges, Groeningemus.) are close imitations of oval frames in the Louis XVI style.

5. 19TH CENTURY REVIVAL STYLES. French frame patterns in moulded composition were the dominant styles in the Netherlands and Belgium for most of the 19th century. Empire frames have slight variations from their French prototypes in section and spacing of ornament. Fine examples with continuous scrolling foliage and honeysuckle survive on portraits (Haarlem, Frans Halsmus.) painted in 1823 by Drahounet. The Restoration style of moulded corner and centre ornaments on ogee and frieze is seen on Cornelis Kruseman's portrait of the *Romoudt Children* (1830; Utrecht, Catharijneconvent). From the 1840s to the 1890s Neo-classical, Louis XIII, Louis XIV, Régence and Rococo Revival patterns were produced. These followed their French Salon models (see fig. 35 above) and dates of currency closely; this suggests that many frames were made in France, where most Dutch and Belgian artists worked for some time, while others were by local framemakers or by Frenchmen working in the Netherlands or Belgium using French pattern books and techniques. Fluted scotia frames with acanthus leaves in the corners were favoured for landscape paintings of the 1840s and 1850s by such artists as Barend Cornelis Koekkoek (examples Dordrecht, Dordrechts Mus.) and Andreas Schelfhout (e.g. *Landscape*, 1850; Bruges, Groeningemus.). The frames for *Red Cabbages* (1883; Tournai, Mus. B.-A.) by Guillaume van Strydonck (*b* 1861) and *Aboard* (*c.* 1887; Amsterdam, Stedel. Mus.) by George Hendrik Breitner have broad, richly moulded convex profiles in a style between Louis XIII and Louis XIV with scrolling acanthus foliage and flowers. Paintings of the late 1890s by Jan Hendrik Weissenbruch and Maris (examples Dordrecht, Dordrechts Mus.) have Louis XIV style frames with projecting corners and centres and the artists' names moulded into the lower central cartouches. The most frequently selected standard pattern from the 1870s to the 1890s was the deep, wide, compound-profile, running-leaf frame (see fig. 37b above) favoured by the Barbizon school and found predominantly on landscapes and marine paintings by Dutch and Belgian artists. Notable examples in the Dordrechts Museum are Anton Mauve's *Fishing Boat on the Beach at Scheveningen* (1876), H. W. Mesdag's

Seascape (1879) and Bernard Blommers's *Beach Scene*. The effectiveness of this steep profile in leading the spectator's eye into the picture is demonstrated by the frame on a large-scale panorama of a stormy landscape (Bruges, Groeningemus.) by Joseph Théodore Coosemans (1828–1904).

Many hybrid Rococo frames with swept sides and elaborate cartouches were made for all types of 19th-century and Old Master paintings. One of the more ostentatious and distracting frames is the pseudo-Régence Rococo trophy frame with moulded quivers, torches and weirdly asymmetric titled *fronton* made for Rubens's *Prodigal Son* (Antwerp, Kon. Mus. S. Kst.). As in England, France and elsewhere in Europe, a number of more exotic and individual historical patterns were made, deviating from the usual pattern-book designs. Louis Gallait had the frames of his paintings decorated in the style and period of the subject-matter he depicted, as, for example, the huge canvas of the *Plague in Tournai in 1092* (1843; Tournai, Mus. B.-A.), where the massive frame has chevrons and cabled ornament in Romanesque style. An accurate interpretation of the Italian Renaissance style is seen in the frame surrounding Jan Frans Verhas's *The Schoolroom* (Ghent, Mus. S. Kst.), and a variation of a Baroque pattern is found on Liéven De Winne's portrait of *Paul De Vigne* (Ghent, Mus. S. Kst.).

6. LATE 19TH AND 20TH CENTURIES. Apart from isolated cases, Dutch and Belgian frames up to the 1880s have little originality. After the 1880s the influence of the Pre-Raphaelites—who had begun to design frames three decades earlier (*see* §IV above)—began at last to be felt in France and the Low Countries through such exhibitions as the Exposition Universelle of 1878 in Paris and those of Les XX and Libre Esthétique in Brussels. Pre-Raphaelite influence coincided with the rise of Symbolism and a growth in interest in the applied arts, of which framemaking was a part. An example of an early Symbolist frame surrounds *Virgin and Child* (1883; Bruges, Groeningemus.) by Théophile Lybaert (1848–1927). It is richly gilded and shaped like a tabernacle, and is one of the designs of the 1870s and 1880s based on the Biblical and literary themes popularized by the Nazarenes. It may have been directly influenced by the frame designed by John Everett Millais for Charles Allston Collins's *Convent Thoughts* (exh. RA 1851; Oxford, Ashmolean) with flat surface and arched sight (*see* §IV, 10 above), and the Art Nouveau designs used from the 1860s by Gustav Klimt (*see* §VI, 7 below) may also have been prototypes. With its expanse of gold, crenellated cornice and the deep rainsill (revived by the Pre-Raphaelites), Lybaert's frame is characteristic of embryonic Symbolist design. Frames in the mature Symbolist style have the same planar body, but their ornamentation tends to appear homespun and chunky.

Following these expressive Romantic attempts to bind the picture to its setting, and in the wake of the Impressionists' innovations (*see* §III, 12 above), van Gogh, who was interested in the presentation of his pictures, was stimulated to produce something more distinctive. His early letters to his brother Théo van Gogh are full of directions about the use of grey mounts; his drawings were to be set 'in a deep black frame', and oil studies to be mounted on gilt, black or red Bristol-board. His longest, most passionate statement (1885) on framing concerns the need to put the *Potato Eaters* (Amsterdam, Rijksmus. van Gogh) in a gold frame that would bring its blue tones to life by use of their complementaries, or at least to hang the painting on a corn- or ochre-coloured wall. Colour informed his ideas for frames: in 1888–9, while at Arles, he suggested one of royal blue and gold for the *Langlois Bridge* (Otterlo, Rijksmus. Kröller-Müller), a landscape painting of blues, greens and orange. Harmony and contrast in tone and texture were so crucial to him that he suggested that the frame, if not painted, could be faced with blue plush. He also suggested a 'warm creamy white' frame for a painting of a pink orchard, and for other works plain white frames, 'cold white and rough'. Later he had his own frames specially made in bare wood—oak, pine and walnut—for such works as the *Poet's Garden* and the *Poet's Head*, and he mentioned the use of chestnut-wood. As a further simplification, he and Gauguin nailed painted lathes to their stretchers, which approximated the borders on early medieval frames. Van Gogh then sketched an arrangement in which *La Berceuse* (Otterlo, Rijksmus. Kröller-Müller), in a red frame, would be placed between two paintings of sunflowers set in these painted lathes, the whole in the manner of a triptych. To Emile Bernard he described a further 'decoration' in which six paintings of sunflowers would be arranged on a wall, 'thin strips of wood painted with orange lead' framing each and heightening the backgrounds (which were 'palest malachite-green to *royal blue*'). The effect was to be like 'stained-glass windows in a Gothic church'. Such ideas show how the 19th-century manuals on colour theory by the chemist Michel-Eugène Chevreul and the physicist Ogden Rood influenced Post-Impressionist painters; they experimented not only with colour division but also with highlighting the picture by means of complementary colours on the frame (*see* NEO-IMPRESSIONISM). Economics was another important influence in the production of these primitive, coloured frames. Van Gogh's frames cost less than five francs as opposed to more than 30 francs for a gilt frame, and the Impressionists were similarly embarrassed. Théo van Gogh, on directions from Vincent, ordered frames painted white or of white woods, and Julien-François Tanguy, the Impressionists' dealer and colourman, seems to have produced some of these.

In the 1890s the influence of Seurat was strong among Belgian artists: Theo van Rysselberghe was one of the first to adopt the Divisionist technique. By the time he painted the portrait of *Maria Sèthe* (1891; Antwerp, Kon. Mus. S. Kst.), he was also producing integral painted borders and frames like Seurat's (*see* §III, 12 above). At the same time, Alfred William Finch painted a Divisionist border on *English Coast at Dover* (1891; Helsinki, Athenaeum A. Mus.), and Henry Van de Velde decorated the frame of *Garden at Kalmthout* (1891; Munich, Neue Pin.). Van de Velde's painting had already begun to move away from the Pointillist technique to a use of expressive lines influenced by van Gogh and Louis Anquetin. However, the wide cuff of the frame, inside its triple-reed and ovolo moulding, is painted with coloured 'points' complementary to the colours of the canvas. Van Rysselberghe was particularly interested in the applied arts and in the

construction of appropriate frames for his work. He also designed schemes for the exhibition rooms of Les XX and Libre Esthétique in Brussels. In 1892 he painted *Man at the Helm* in a Divisionist technique, putting it in a plate frame (presumably original) of strongly grained wood stained deep blue. This emulated the generally blue tint of many of Seurat's Pointillist frames and also produced the foil-like emphasis of a dark proscenium arch, an effect desired by Seurat. By 1890 Van Rysselberghe was apparently also using a version of the reeded 'Whistler' frame (*see* §IV, 10 above). One surrounds *Canal in Flanders* (priv. col.), its linear format suiting the increasingly expressionistic geometry of his compositions.

The combination of this interest in expressive line with the decorative Symbolism of late 19th-century French art, the growth of the applied arts, and Belgian connections with the English Arts and Crafts Movement, all put the Low Countries in the forefront of the development of Art Nouveau. In 1892–3 Victor Horta designed his first house, the Hôtel Tassel in Brussels, in a fully fledged Art Nouveau style, with curving tendrilled ironwork echoed by the painted walls and ceilings. He produced every item in the interior himself, including frames for mirrors and pictures. Jan Toorop exploited the sinuous patterns of Art Nouveau in his paintings and frames of the early 1890s. His Symbolist works, combining dense allegory with decoratively abstract surfaces, are among the few paintings since the time of the Gothic altarpieces (see §1 above) that are bound so inseparably to their settings. In *Song of the Times* (1893; Otterlo, Rijksmus. Kröller-Müller), for example, continuations of the linear patterns that decorate the painting itself are engraved across the wide flat frame and its deep bevel at the sight, while between and around them appear the shapes of a starry sky, sea, flowers, a skull and pickaxe. Here the frame also becomes the work of art, no longer merely an area of transition between painting and wall; at the same time, it is related to those medieval frames with motifs, inscriptions and crests that gloss the painting within and also delimit and protect it.

Symbolist ideas were also important for the Belgian Fernand Khnopff, who in the late 1870s had been influenced by the work of Burne-Jones, Millais and Gustave Moreau. His paintings became increasingly enigmatic portrayals of isolation and solipsism, related stylistically to the work of the Pre-Raphaelites. The frame around *I Lock my Door upon Myself* (1891; Munich, Neue Pin.) has an enriched chain moulding and a deep bottom cuff, similar to the differently sized rails used by Gustav Klimt and Franz von Stuck. With Khnopff, however, it creates a sense of unease and imbalance. The frame for *Brown Eyes and a Blue Flower* (see fig. 59) drastically crops the subject, emphasizing the claustrophobic intensity of the brown eyes; it is a reworking of the tondo frame, which looks forward to the minimalist ornament and machined finish of Art Deco objects of the 1920s. In the 1890s and early 1900s Khnopff executed several triptychs, one of which is *D'Autrefois* (1905; untraced; see R. L. Delevoy, C. De Croës and G. Ollinger-Zinque: *Fernand Khnopff: Catalogue de l'oeuvre* (Brussels, 1979), p. 345). In its structure and flat borders, the frame is reminiscent of the winged triptychs designed in the 1870s by the English artist Lawrence Alma-Tadema, with the addition of a classicizing

59. Gilt metal tondo frame with monogram, diam. 185 mm, original for Fernand Khnopff's *Brown Eyes and a Blue Flower*, 1905 (Ghent, Museum voor Schone Kunsten)

cornice and plinth. The Symbolists were attracted to retable-like forms; these gave importance to a painting and supported it decoratively and symbolically, while also enabling multiple images to be framed together. Often, as with *D'Autrefois*, there is no connection between the images save that forced by the frame itself, creating a sense of mysterious significance and poetic meaning.

Piet Mondrian's *Evolution* (1910; The Hague, Gemeentemus.), also a triptych but of three separate panels, is somewhat indebted to van Gogh's 'arrangements' in its minimal lathe-like frames and its form as a linked symbolic group. However, Mondrian's frames are mere delimiting lines, the 'frame' itself becoming the wall on which the paintings are hung.

In the course of the 20th century the frame has been demoted in importance and in some instances disappears entirely. However, its long history allows the artist to make visual play on its traditional role and conventional appearance. René Magritte's *L'Evidence éternelle* (1930; Houston, TX, Menil Col.), for example, is an 'arrangement' of five separate canvases that together form a type of 'polyptych'. Intended to be hung vertically, each shows a part of a naked female body as a lover would see it, in close-up. The whole thus becomes a memory of the beloved, reconstructed from those fragments, each of which is fractionally different in scale. The canvases cannot be assembled into a 'whole' woman, and their separate framing underlines this. The idea of the frame as a delimiting border has been converted into part of the message of the work. Generally, however, 20th-century frames play a strictly functional and undistinguished role. The flat or deeply cambered frames in stained wood or gold surrounding such paintings as Gustav De Smet's

Circus III (1924; Grenoble, Mus. Grenoble) and Rik Wouters's portrait of *Beeldhouwer Wynants* (Bruges, Groeningemus.) are repetitions of styles current in England, France and Italy in the early 20th century. Textured ogee mouldings are equally ubiquitous, as seen on frames around Frits Van den Berghe's *Dancers* (1925) and De Smet's *Married Couple with a Rose* (1932; both Bruges, Groeningemus.). Only Mondrian continued to play with form and function in frames for his later paintings. The austere linearity of the traylike frame around *New York City* (1942; Paris, Pompidou) matches the geometric latticework of painted lines within. The picture is set forward of the cuff so that its vestigial recession is reflected by that of the frame, which, like much of the painting, is white, thus making it 'disappear' against the pale walls for which it was designed. This manner of display is perhaps the 20th-century artist's ultimate comment on the purpose of a frame: to use it while dismissing it absolutely.

BIBLIOGRAPHY

W. Martin: *Alt. holländische Bilder (Sammeln/Bestimmen/Konservieren)* (Berlin, 1921)
S. Slive: 'Notes on the Relationship of Protestantism to 17th-century Dutch Painting', *A. Q.* [Detroit], xix (1956), pp. 3–15
W. Gaunt: *Flemish Cities: Their History and Art* (London, 1969); *R* as *The Golden Age of Flemish Art* (New York, 1983)
J. R. J. van Asperen de Boer: 'A Technical Examination of the Frame of Engebrechtsz.'s *Crucifixion* and Some Other 16th-century Frames', *Ned. Ksthist Jb.*, xxvi (1975), pp. 73–87
P. Thornton: *Seventeenth-century Interior Decoration in England, France and Holland* (New Haven and London, 1978)
The Complete Letters of Vincent Van Gogh, 3 vols (London, 1978)
The Stavelot Triptych: Mosan Art and the Legend of the True Cross (exh. cat., New York, Pierpont Morgan Lib., 1980)
Masters of 17th-century Dutch Genre Painting (exh. cat., ed. J. Landela Watkins; London, RA, 1984)
Prijst de lijst: De hollandse schilderlijst in de zeventiende eeuw [Praise/prize the frame: The Dutch picture frame in the seventeenth century] (exh. cat. by P. J. J. van Thiel and C. J. de Bruyn Kops, Amsterdam, Rijksmus., 1984) [PL]
P. J. J. van Thiel: 'Eloge du cadre: La Pratique hollandaise', *Rev. A.*, 76 (1987), pp. 32–6
A. Hoenigswald: 'Vincent van Gogh: His Frames and the Presentation of Paintings', *Burl. Mag.*, cxxx (1988), pp. 367–72
H. Verougstraete-Marcq and R. van Schoute: *Cadres et supports dans la peinture flamande aux 15e et 16e siècles* (Heure-le-Romain, 1989)
E. Mendgen: 'Der Bilderrahmen: Ein Randphänomen?', *Eur. J. A. Historians*, 4 (1992), pp. 258–66

For further bibliography *see* §I above.

VI. Germany and Central Europe.

1. Gothic. 2. Renaissance. 3. Baroque. 4. Rococo. 5. Neo-classical, Empire and Biedermeier. 6. 19th-century revival styles. 7. Late 19th and 20th centuries.

1. GOTHIC.

(i) Altarpieces. (ii) Small devotional and secular paintings.

(i) Altarpieces. The first German and Central European frames seem to have been most influenced by early illuminated manuscripts. In the 13th century, when simple architectural motifs were being introduced to the wooden borders of painted panels in Italy and France (*see* §§II, 2 and III, 1 above), German artists were treating their altarpiece panels like the flat sheets of vellum they were used to working on, and decorating the raised edges around the gouged-out picture surface with the motifs they would have painted, still in Byzantine style, in a Missal. The outside of the altarpiece wing known as the

Worms Panel (*c.* 1260; Darmstadt, Hess. Landesmus.) demonstrates this quite dramatically, the style of the martyred saint and his trefoil border coming very close to contemporary manuscript illustrations. The inside of the panel, with relief lobed quatrefoils on the frame, is also dissimilar to altarpieces of the time, in other countries. This way of regarding a retable frame as a decorative patterned margin influenced the development of subsequent altarpiece frames. The French Gothic style was slow to be accepted in Germany, and this meant that there were fewer alternatives than elsewhere to the evolution of richly patterned polychromed surface decorations as the defining boundaries of an image; mouldings existed but were subsidiary to these coloured motifs; and architectural structures were late in arriving in Germany and were adopted in different ways than in southern and western Europe. The Cologne Diptych with the *Virgin and Child* and the *Crucifixion* (see fig. 60) shows the development of this idiom, where dense, detailed abstract patterns of oblongs and lozenges in red and blue-black cover the flat of the two rectangular outer frames, and the small mouldings are swallowed up in this surface ornament. Roundels and lozenges are carved out between the painted motifs and would originally have been filled with relics or semi-precious stones; the precursors for this are not the more architectural large-scale frontals and dossals but smaller

reliquaries and book covers. A portable triptych with the *Life of Christ* (*c.* 1300–30; Cologne, Wallraf-Richartz-Mus.) still retains a band of semi-precious stones.

Byzantine influence was still important, especially when Prague emerged as an artistic centre—the setting for the court of the Holy Roman Empire—in the second half of the 14th century (*see* PRAGUE, §II, 1). Imperial influence stimulated such works as the decorative scheme in the chapel of the Holy Cross, Karlštejn Castle, where Master Theodoric painted 127 panels, some depicting saints (e.g. *St Matthew*, see Cutter, 1972, pl. 5). Here, the saints' painted heads are set, icon-like, against coloured grounds covered with decorative gilt-embossed patterns that flow out over the frame. At the same time, northern European *trompe l'oeil* techniques can be seen in the carrying of draperies etc on to the painted frame surface, rendering the image more immediate. In the 15th century this type of painted decoration became so standardized on one type of altar frame that the ornamented motifs were stamped rather than painted on to plain grounds. This was done either with opaque colours or with a type of mordant gilding such as that used for the patterns of robes within the picture. Among paintings that display this technique are the *Apocalypse* altarpiece (*c.* 1400; London, V&A; see Grimm, 1978 and 1981, pl. 26) from the workshop of Master Bertram, the altarpiece of the *Passion* (the Lempertz

60. German school: the Cologne Diptych with the *Virgin and Child* and *Crucifixion, c.* 1320–30 (Berlin, Bodemuseum)

61. Swiss school: *SS Stephen, Blaise, John the Baptist and Peter*, *c.* 1450 (Dijon, Musée des Beaux-Arts)

Altarpiece, *c.* 1420; Münster, see Fuchs, 1985, pl. 10) and the altarpiece with the *Coronation of the Virgin* and the *Ascension* (*c.* 1415–40; Cologne, Wallraf-Richartz-Mus.). The last has internal bands of painted pattern dividing the panel into quarters, and these bands are edged in pastiglia and have pastiglia rosettes, like vestigial carvings. The deep sight bevel of the altarpiece in Cologne also anticipates the rainsill (or *Wasserschlag*), which is copied from church windows and becomes such a feature of northern European retables (*see* §V above).

After a slow beginning the Rayonnant style spread swiftly in Germany and quickly took on the more elaborate elements characteristic of Gothic art in northern Europe. For example, the pierced lacework spire of the cathedral at Freiburg im Breisgau, the only one of its kind, illustrates the German fascination with fantastic attenuated fretwork that also characterizes German Rococo. Thus, altarpieces were produced that have simply moulded wooden stained, painted or parcel-gilt frames in the oblong or ogee-arched format of the northern and southern Netherlands, but that have been elaborated inside by flamboyant curlicued tracery painted on the picture surface. This is seen on the altarpiece of the *Trinity with Saints* (second half of the 16th century; Cologne, Wallraf-Richartz-Mus.), where a triptych-like effect has been given to an oblong panel painting by the imposition of Renaissance pillars and three round-headed arches filled with bushy foliate tracery. All

this is held in an ordinary, parcel-gilt, rectangular rainsill frame, giving a very rich effect extremely economically. The Master of Bodensee's ogee-arched Hakenlandberg Triptych (*c.* 1500; Karlsruhe, Staatl. Ksthalle) has a similar arrangement. Like Netherlandish altarpiece frames of the same period, the silhouettes of German, Austrian and Bohemian retables show little tendency to fragment into complex tiers of spires and pinnacles, as do the great Italian Gothic altars. Instead, possibly because of this technique of decorating the panel itself within a simple frame, Central European altarpieces preserve a rectangular outline, although complicated arrangements of tracery and elevation often appear within.

Stefan Lochner's *SS Mark, Barbara and Luke* (*c.* 1440s; Cologne; see Fucks, pl. 18) is framed in this way, in a flat, oblong format, with panels of carved pierced tracery applied at top and bottom to the picture itself. An altarpiece of the Swiss school (*c.* 1450; see fig. 61) has a whole carved microarchitectural gilded inner frame with tracery, gables, pinnacles, finials and crockets. The upper tier is set, as in Spanish altarpieces, against a painted background, like the night sky, full of praising angels; the whole work is set in a black-painted frame of determinedly anti-classical type, with a broad inscribed top rail. The outer, defining edge of the frame is a gilded rope moulding, which would not be found in a similar position on French or Italian altarpieces. The whole structure is of a vertical format, as Italian and Spanish retables—especially the latter—tend to be. German alters, however, are generally of one or, at most, two storeys, and are correspondingly very wide. The effect on the composition and arrangement of the picture panels is marked; in a Spanish or an Italian polyptych, the eye is drawn upward through a pyramid of focal lines, over the major narrative scene, to the celestial regions of the upper tiers inhabited by Christ in glory and God the Father. It is helped by the aspiring lines of the frame—by colonnettes, finials and pinnacles. With a German altarpiece, the eye is led from left to right, as in a book, before being pulled back to the central significant scene (which may occasionally rise a little above the others). This helps to underline the didactic elements in the painting and also softens the alien aspects of the soaring heavenly scenes. By keeping all the panels on the spectator's level, he is more easily involved, and the supernatural is rendered more immediate, everyday and comprehensible. The relative plainness of the frames also helps this reassuringly mundane presentation, as against the painted buttresses and broken silhouette of an Italian retable or the jewel-like patterns and gilding of a Spanish one. Examples of this drawn-out, horizontal structure include Lochner's triptych of the *Adoration of the Magi* (*c.* 1440–45; Cologne Cathedral), with internal cusped tracery applied to the panels (*see* LOCHNER, STEFAN, fig. 1); and the characteristically wide Güstrow Retable (1520; Güstrow Cathedral; see 1990 exh. cat., p. 38) and Michael Pacher's St Wolfgang Altarpiece (1471–81; St Wolfgang, Parish Church; see 1990 exh. cat., p. 38). Pacher's is unusual among German altarpieces in that it is crowned by a towering confection of lacey pinnacles; yet these do not grow out of a polyptych structure, as in a Venetian Gothic frame, but are planked on top of the basic horizontal oblong format (*see* PACHER, MICHAEL, fig. 1). Pacher was commissioned in 1471 to create the whole altarpiece himself, including two pairs of folding wings on each side, complete with two panel paintings to each shutter-surface, the Gothic crest, and the main scene; this is actually carved completely of wood, in a three-dimensional representation of the *Coronation of the Virgin*, to which the frame acts as a proscenium arch. Above the figures and dependent from the upper rail of the frame is a filigree elaboration of the tracery on Lochner's *Adoration of the Magi*—a forest of slender colonnettes and crocketed pinnacles, ogee arches and pendent drops. Pacher finished the work ten years later, signing the frame in 1481. He was paid 1200 guilders. The design, construction, painting, carving, gilding and colouring of the sculpted scene is a prodigious achievement. It is also striking for the combination of styles it represents. The painted panels have the recession and arrangement of figures that belong to Renaissance art, while the drama and movement are mannered—almost Baroque. The sculpted scene displays a Renaissance humanism and grace, but the differences of scale, the crowded space and especially the ornament are uncompromisingly Gothic. This is a demonstration of the enduring nature of Gothic decoration, in Germany and Central Europe just as in Venice, Spain, England and the Netherlands, and of the relative scarcity in these places of Renaissance ornament and frame designs.

(ii) Small devotional and secular paintings. The design of frames for small devotional and secular pictures follows very closely the prototypes established in the Netherlands from the 1430s, namely the van Eyck type (*see* §V, 1 above). Characteristic Gothic ogee mouldings with a flat outer section are found on a north German portrait of *c.* 1480 (Madrid, Mus. Thyssen–Bornemisza; G 42). This imitates the marbling on Jan van Eyck's portrait of *Margaret van Eyck* (1439; Bruges, Groeningemus.; see fig. 55a above). Occasionally, continuous moulding frames were produced in ebonized wood with multiple series of cavettos, ogees and steps that have the appearance of being distinctly German, rather than Netherlandish, in character. A rare surviving pair are those framing the double portraits of *Johan Stralenberg* and *Marguerite Stralenberg* (both Frankfurt am Main, Städel. Kstinst. & Städt. Gal.) by Conrad Faber Creuznach (1500–52/3). The most frequent design following south Netherlandish prototypes is the Gothic 'colonnette' moulding running on to a rainsill that often carries an inscription. An all-gilt example with inscribed sill frames the right half of a diptych (1493; Berlin, Gemäldegal.; see Grimm, pl. 45) by Hans Holbein the elder, originally part of a *Mater dolorosa*. An original polychrome and marbled version with inscription surrounds Holbein the elder's *Portrait of a Young Lady* (1516–17; Basle, Kstmus.), but, unlike Netherlandish examples, the sill is divided into two sections: a steeper bevel at the sight and a longer, shallow section below. The rainsill frame continued well into the 16th century, and occasionally examples are found that may be described as more individually German than Netherlandish: for example on Bernhard Strigel's portraits of *Hans Rott, a Patrician of Memmingen* and his wife *Margaret Volhin* (both 1527; Washington, DC, N.G.A.). These frames have abruptly stepped mouldings, strikingly finished in polychrome,

matching the sitters' costumes. The outer steps, continuous around the frames, are black, and the inner steps are brown; below, gilt ogee sections with brown fillets inside run down to brown painted sills that have inscriptions relating to the year in which the sitters were portrayed.

At least as frequently in Germany as in the Netherlands, the most popular style of frame for secular portraits had a shaped top, either an ogee or arch, providing a window-like focus on the sitter. The ogee-arched frame with rosettes (see fig. 62a) is reminiscent of Early Gothic frames, although the reverse ogee arch (62b) was more common in the 16th century. Curiously, many surviving arched frames in museum surveys are found on works by the Cologne artist Bartholomäus Bruyn the elder. The compact round-arched frame is generally favoured for smaller format pictures, such as the hinged diptych surrounding portraits of *Gerhardt Pilgrim* and his wife *Anna* (both *c.* 1525; Cologne, Wallraf-Richartz-Mus.). These are in black and gold, whereas the frame around Bruyn the elder's *Lady with a Carnation* (1540; Bonn, Rhein. Landesmus.) is polychrome, the outer surface enlivened with a painted spiralled leaf. For slightly larger three-quarter-length portraits painted about the mid-16th century, a reverse ogee arch was widened with the addition of hollow

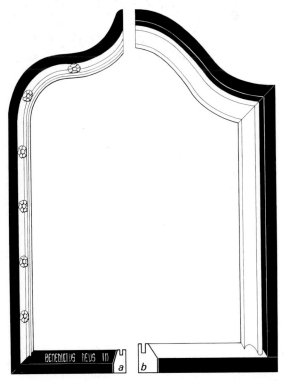

62. German secular frames, *c.* 1480–1550: (a) ogee-arched frame with vestigial colonnettes and rosettes on the arch, and a rainsill inscribed BENEDICTUS DEUS IN DOMS MEIS–1484, overall 909×598 mm, original for the Swabian Master's *Johann Gamspirsch*, 1484 (Heidelberg, Kurpfälzisches Museum); (b) reverse ogee-arched frame with colonnettes and rainsill, overall 470×350 mm, one of an original pair for Bartholomäus Bruyn the elder's *Christian von Cornersheim* and his wife *Elisabeth von Brauweiler*, both 1544 (Ottawa, National Gallery of Canada)

sections to each side—reminiscent of the centre panel of a Netherlandish triptych—as in Bruyn the elder's portraits of *Heinrich Salsburg* and *Helene Salsburg* (both 1549; Cologne, Wallraf-Richartz-Mus.).

A highly distinguished Gothic frame, the style of which is unrecorded elsewhere, surrounds Bruyn the elder's portrait of *W. Kannengieser* (1550; priv. col.). The upright portrait is framed in a rectangular Gothic structure of pilasters and finials with an elaborate sill. Within this, an ogee arch surmounts the portrait, the spandrels filled with flowers and foliage. Simple ogee or entablature profiles, often with inscriptions, were employed in the production of circular frames for miniature portraits, as, for example, Hans Holbein the younger's portrait of *Desiderius Erasmus* (1532; Basle, Kstmus.) and Bruyn the elder's portrait of *Dr Petrus von Clapis* (1537; Cologne, Wallraf-Richartz-Mus.). This treatment closely echoes the production of inscribed medals of rulers and miniatures in metal frames, and continued into the second half of the 16th century in works by Bartholomäus Bruyn the younger. Again the tradition for these relates to Netherlandish models found, for example, on works by Dieric Bouts I and Hans Memling. Occasionally, sitters were framed in rectangular entablature profile frames bearing biblical inscriptions on each side, as in Hermann tom Ring's portrait of *Domherrn Gottfried von Raesfeld* (1566; Münster, Westfäl. Landesmus.; F 25).

2. RENAISSANCE. The diffusion of Renaissance art, architecture and ideas throughout Germany was aided by the invention of printing in Germany in the mid-15th century. For the first time, representations of ornament and structure could be disseminated swiftly throughout Europe, and the effect was enormous. Ideas were also transmitted by Netherlandish artists who worked in Italy, as well as Germans who visited the country. Dürer had first visited Venice in 1494, and Hans Burgkmair I, the leading painter of the Augsburg Renaissance, was in Venice, and possibly in Lombardy, from 1507. Since no single school was established in Germany, numerous small centres arose instead where artists of individuality worked for the bourgeoisie or court patrons. In the last quarter of the 16th century the courts of Munich and Prague, whose rulers—dukes Albert V (*reg* 1550–79) and William V (*reg* 1579–98) of Bavaria and the Holy Roman Emperor Rudolf II (*reg* 1576–1612)—were devoted to art, attracted many talented artists from Italy and the Netherlands. Through Augsburg, which had been the traditional gateway to southern Germany from southern Europe, the Fugger and Welser families brought the first Italian artists to Germany. Several German artists, including Lambert Sustris, Friedrich Sustris and Hans Rottenhammer I, had themselves worked in Italy. Rudolf II's passion for collecting turned Prague into an international centre for the arts (*see* HABSBURG, §I(10)), and several German and Netherlandish artists arrived to work in the city, among them Bartholomäus Spranger, Hans von Aachen, Joseph Heintz (i), Roelandt Savery, Hans Vredeman de Vries and Paul de Vries (1567–after 1630). Having worked in Italy as well as in the Netherlands, these cosmopolitan figures would have been familiar with the types of frames found there and no doubt brought pattern books with them or

had artisans travelling in their entourages. The considerable number of engravings published by Hans Vredeman de Vries, including architectural interiors and the earliest furniture pattern book (*see* §V, 3(i) above), contributed to the production and decoration of frames employing Renaissance and Mannerist ornament.

Surviving frames made in Germany in the Renaissance style (see fig. 63) are exceptionally rare. A northern European form of the Italian *cassetta* frame, which may be

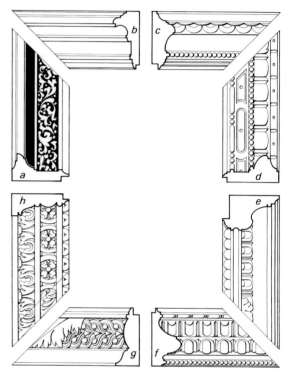

63. German Renaissance frames: (a) Italianate black-and-gold *cassetta* frame with continuous arabesques in *sgraffito*, 293×326×74 mm, possibly adapted, contemporary for Lucas Cranach the elder's *Portrait of a Man in a Fur Cap*, c. 1510–12 (Berlin, Gemäldegalerie); (b) entablature frame of stained and polished wood, 513×355×91 mm, contemporary for Lucas Cranach the elder's *Adam and Eve in Paradise*, 1531 (Berlin, Gemäldegalerie); (c) shallow scotia frame of stained and polished wood with scale decoration and beading, 559×381×78 mm, possibly original for Lucas Cranach the elder's *Portrait of a Woman*, 1559 (Washington, DC, National Gallery of Art); (d) knulled architectural frame of stained and polished wood with geometric panels, 537×385×70 mm, contemporary for Augsburg school: *Portrait of a Lady*, c. 1512 (Berlin, Gemäldegalerie); (e) reverse profile architectural frame of stained and polished wood with stop-fluting, 530×430×70 mm, contemporary for Ludger tom Ring the elder's *Portrait of an Architect*, c. 1540 (Berlin, Gemäldegalerie); (f) compound profile architectural frame of stained and polished wood with stop-fluting and knulls, 930×860×118 mm, mid-16th century, adapted for Jean Fouquet's *Etienne Chevalier with St Stephen*, c. 1452–3 (Berlin, Gemäldegalerie); (g) Italianate *cassetta* frame of stained and polished wood with double guilloche, 740×960×104 mm, possible original for Antonis Mor's *Two Canons*, 1544 (Berlin, Gemäldegalerie); (h) architectural frame of stained and polished wood with flowers and cross-cut acanthus foliage, 620×780×138 mm, mid-16th century, adapted for Joachim Patinir's *Rest on the Flight into Egypt*, c. 1520 (Berlin, Gemäldegalerie)

called an entablature profile, had long been popular in Germany, as in tom Ring's portrait of *Domherrn Gottfried von Raesfeld* bearing an inscription on the frieze (see §1 above). The same entablature profile frame appears on *Johannes Münstermann* (Münster, Westfäl. Landesmus.), also by tom Ring, but here with the frieze decorated in a continuous arabesque more Italianate in style. Foliage decoration in the frieze is also seen on the frame (63a) that is contemporary for Lucas Cranach the elder's *Portrait of a Man in a Fur Cap* (Berlin, Gemäldegal.). This profile, bordered by a painted cavetto with gilt mouldings, is in a style that must be considered more German than Italian. A similar Northern Renaissance *cassetta* frame, with multiple ribbed mouldings either side of a frieze, surrounds Dürer's *Portrait of a Clergyman* (Washington, DC, N.G.A.). The Italianate use of gilt ornament applied only at corners and centres of frames is equally rare, although it appears on two frames distinctly Germanic in character because of their stepped mouldings and the use of strapwork in the ornament. Both are contemporary with, and adapted to, their pictures: Wolfgang Huber's *Marggret Hundertpfundt* (1526; Philadelphia, PA, John C. Johnson Col.) and Cranach the elder's *Lamentation* (1538; Boston, MA, Mus. F.A.). One of the most distinguished northern European Renaissance frames—contemporary with, if not original to, the painting—is that on Hans Wertinger's portrait of *Duke Wolfgang of Bavaria* (first quarter of the 16th century). The upper edge is flat, painted black, with pronounced ogee and sharp mouldings reminiscent of Strigel's portraits (see §1 above). It is the decoration of the frieze that distinguishes this frame from any Italian precedents; the sides are painted with elaborate grotesques in black, the top and bottom with painted cartouches linked to the sides with elongated scrolls.

Due to the exceptional rarity of recorded German Renaissance altarpiece frames, knowledge is limited to the celebrated frame (Nuremberg, Ger. Nmus., see Grimm, pl. 64; drawing Chantilly, Mus. Condé) designed in 1508 by Dürer for the Landauer Altarpiece (1511; Vienna, Ksthist. Mus.) and carved in 1511 by Veit Stoss. The design—which follows Italian aedicular frames like that of Mantegna's San Zeno Altarpiece (1456–9; S Zeno, Verona)—has columns standing on a predella and supporting an entablature with figures and a segmental pediment. Although the structure is classical in form, the vine-leaf decoration of the predella, half columns and tympanum is more Gothic in feeling. The retable frames of the other great German Renaissance artist, Grünewald, are still more or less completely Gothic. The Isenheim Altarpiece (1512–15; Colmar, Mus. Unterlinden) has a simple outline frame of reeded mouldings and is parcel-gilt and marbled. The central sculpted scene and probably the pendent Gothic canopy were carved by Nikolaus Hagenauer.

Some of the earliest sources for Italian Renaissance decoration in Germany were the engravings of such furniture-makers and designers as Peter Flötner from Nuremberg, who visited Italy in 1520–21 and is regarded as one of the principal exponents of the Renaissance style in Germany. The effect on frames may be glimpsed only rarely and is characterized by what may be termed the compound profile architectural frame (63b–h). An impressive collection of such frames, unique in number and

quality, is in the Gemäldegalerie, Dahlem, Berlin, and they are occasionally found elsewhere. Although these are based on Italian models, the differences in their profiles, their pronounced carving and the fact that they are invariably of polished rather than gilded wood all suggest that they were made in workshops in northern Europe. These sharply defined wooden mouldings appear to demonstrate a German affinity with the purity of Tuscan architectural frames in natural wood, the austere forms of which accorded with the Protestant faith at this time of the Reformation. The undecorated form, typically Germanic in profile, has a deep scotia behind the frieze (63b), which could effectively be enriched by scale-and-bead carving (63c). The frieze may have geometric motifs reminiscent of furniture inlays (63d); here, the natural colour of the wood complements the blue-green background of the picture (as often found also in Cranach the elder's paintings). More Baroque in character is the forward-projecting fluted moulding (63e), surely more German than Italian and certainly an original variation. Frames with bold gadrooning and fluting (63f) are almost Mannerist in their definition, and those with interlacing (63g) recall Venetian and Tuscan prototypes. All-over carving (63h), recalling the ornamentation of interior—notably ceiling—architectural mouldings, is equally rare. The spirit of these mouldings is reflected in views of northern European interiors such as those painted by Bartholomeus van Bassen (e.g. in Darmstadt, Hess. Landesmus.). An unusual use of ornament—pointing to a German rather than Italian origin—is seen on Holbein the younger's *Portrait of an Unknown Falconer* (1542; The Hague, Mauritshuis), where the *cassetta*-style frame, with a natural wood finish, has a frieze inlaid with a Greek key pattern.

3. BAROQUE. Because Germany was divided into hundreds of small principalities—Catholic, Lutheran and Calvinist—no national Baroque style developed, as it had done in the centralized workshops of France. Italianate Baroque carved and gilt frames are rare in Germany, and in fact the dominant frame made here and in Austria from the late 16th century to the early 18th is the product of the cabinetmaker's workshop rather than that of the carver's and gilder's. The natural wood frame in all its forms, with inlaid and ripple decoration, is a product of the skilled craftsmen and designers in workshops in Nuremberg and Augsburg. The cabinets (examples Dresden, Kstgewmus. Staatl. Kstsamml.) they produced, exported in considerable numbers, demonstrate their astonishing technical skills in the use of veneers, inlays and semi-precious stones, filigree metal, tortoiseshell and ivory, with reeded and ripple mouldings. Equally luxurious frames, similar to those produced in Flanders, were demanded for pictures destined to hang in a KUNSTKAMMER (see fig. 64a). The frame for *Landscape with an Inn* (Munich, Alte Pin.; see Grimm, pl. 64) by Jan Breughel the elder is a rare example, with a tortoiseshell ogee outer edge and a veneered ebony frieze overlaid with elongated brass cartouches containing further tortoiseshell veneers. Occasionally, frames were inlaid with marquetry (e.g. Cranach the elder's *Christ and the Woman Taken in Adultery*, c. 1535; Ottawa, N.G.) or were of walnut with

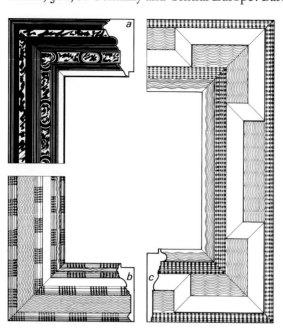

64. 17th-century German cabinet frames: (a) compound profile frame in ebony, veneered with tortoiseshell in geometric panels, with metal stringing, 220×280×97 mm, *c.* 1600, contemporary for Georg Flegel's *Still-life* (Munich, Alte Pinakothek); (b) reverse profile frame in ebonized fruitwood with wave and ripple mouldings, 552×434×158 mm, mid-17th century, adapted for Pieter Saenredam's *St Janskerk, Utrecht,* 1642 (Munich, Alte Pinakothek); (c) reverse profile frame in ebonized fruitwood with outset corners and wave and ripple mouldings, 285×251×127 mm, contemporary for Willem Drost's *Self-portrait, c.* 1652 (Cologne, Wallraf-Richartz-Museum)

marbled frieze (e.g. Holbein the younger's *Portrait of a Man with a Lute*; Berlin, Gemäldegal.).

These exotic inlaid frames are exceptional, the vast majority being in ebony or ebonized fruitwood. Some are plain mouldings, but most are decorated with various forms of wave and ripple enrichment. The development of the wave-moulding machine in Germany in the late 16th century enabled this form of decoration to spread thoughout Europe (*see* §V, 3(i) above); it was particularly prominent in Austria and Switzerland, being seen on frames, cabinets and other furniture, and indeed interiors (e.g. in the Swiss Period Room; New York, Met.), where wave mouldings were used to define the borders of panels. One of the earliest examples of this ornament is seen on an entablature profile frame for Pieter Bruegel the elder's *Sleeping Peasants* (1566; Munich, Alte Pin.). The section—essentially the same as in Late Gothic frames—appears transformed by the addition of ripple mouldings on the inner and outer edges, the whole being stained black. In southern Germany, Austria and Switzerland, increasing numbers of sophisticated wave and ripple ornaments were produced on jigs and distributed on picture and mirror frames in endless combinations (64b). These enrichments are aptly referred to as *Flammleisten* (Ger.: 'flame mouldings'), describing the effect caused by candlelight flickering across their surfaces. Such broad black frames would not interfere with the picture's colour scheme, and would successfully isolate the image from the surrounding wall

surface while also creating a shimmering focus. In comparison with their richly carved and gilt 'Catholic' counterparts, such frames achieve some of the most aesthetically satisfying presentations of paintings. For example, van Dyck's portrait of *Pieter Snayers* (Munich, Alte Pin.) is superbly set off by a forward-projecting, broad, undulating wave band adjacent to finer outer ripple mouldings. The distinctly Mannerist four-bead zigzag ornament in the frieze of the frame surrounding Pieter Bruegel the elder's *Head of an Old Peasant Woman* (Munich, Alte Pin.) is a more dramatic and rarer example—an inspiration for the frames designed by Franz von Stuck at the end of the 19th century.

In the later 17th century frames became heavier and were broader in width in relation to their aperture, having up to a dozen different sections and runs of ornament along each side. Zigzag or chevron ornament in miniature is combined with a novel basketweave moulding in the ebony frame surrounding Rembrandt's *Self-portrait* (1652; Vienna, Ksthist. Mus.). A more dynamic and Mannerist innovation is the use of outset or eared corners breaking the rectangular contour of the frame (64c). This device is seen in ceiling decorations and on the fronts of cabinets made in northern Europe, and was employed with either plain mouldings, as on Cranach the elder's *Eve* (Antwerp, Kon. Mus. S. Kst.), or with ripple mouldings.

Although apparently there are no recorded examples, frames in the AURICULAR STYLE, so popular in the Netherlands, must have appeared in Germany, evidenced by suites of engravings. Johann Matthias Kager published prints of ornamental frames in an Auricular style (see Jervis, 1984, p. 265) in the second edition of *Fuggerorum et fuggerarum imagines* (Augsburg, 1618). In the early 17th century Lucas Kilian, also a pioneer of the style, published a series of designs for Auricular ornaments, most of which were dedicated to goldsmiths (*see* KILIAN, (1)).

In the mid-17th century Italian influences introduced Baroque design to Germany: pietra dura craftsmen and cabinetmakers settled in Bohemia, Moravia, Prague, Würzburg, Salzburg and Vienna, drawn there by the Habsburg court, which encouraged Italian craftsmen to immigrate. In Munich, Schloss Nymphenburg was begun (1663) under the supervision of the Italian architect Agostino Barelli. Florentine influence touched the Palatinate and Baden-Baden, the rulers of which were connected with the Medici family through marriage. German craftsmen copied Florentine techniques of pietra dura and scagliola, ultimately influencing the production of luxury frames. The fashion for stucco decoration in Bavaria and Austria, introduced and fulfilled by Italian stuccoists (*see* STUCCO AND PLASTERWORK, §III, 10(i)(e)), also had its effect on the production of elaborate picture frames. Although the furniture in Schloss Weissenstein at Pommersfelden, Bavaria, is relatively sparse, picture frames in the collection (see fig. 65a) were profusely decorated with strongly accented cartouches in order to stand out against the surrounding abundance of gilded wood and plasterwork ornament. Pommersfelden frames—and there are a number of variations in the collection—are among the first examples of those series coming from the hands of the architect or interior designer. They needed to harmonize with the interior; and thus pictures of earlier dates and of

65. German gallery frames, c. 1700–45: (a) 'Pommersfelden' Baroque frame with pierced cartouches, 560×530×143 mm, c. 1700, made for Abraham Bloemaert's *Virgin and Child* (Toronto, Art Gallery of Ontario); (b) 'Effner' Régence style frame, 1170×940×155 mm, original for Joseph Vivien's *Self-portrait at an Easel*, 1730 (Munich, Alte Pinakothek); (c) 'Effner' late Régence style frame, 1370×1060×123 mm, probably original for Jean-Marc Nattier's *Marquise de Baglion as Flora*, 1746 (Munich, Alte Pinakothek)

different nationalities were reframed in a uniform style to suit the interior rather than the pictures themselves. Other examples from the Pommersfelden collection are Piedmontese in character, with a carved leaf sight edge and ogee moulding decorated with foliage and strapwork in the French manner. A similar example, on a larger scale and possibly executed by Italian craftsmen in French style, surrounds Adriaen van der Werff's *Entombment* (1703; Munich, Alte Pin.).

Baroque ornament, which may have influenced frame design, is found in engravings in the manner of the French designer Jean Le Pautre, published, according to Jervis (1984), by Joachim von Sandrart after he settled in Nuremberg in 1656. Designs for Italianate Baroque frames, crestings and brackets with rich acanthus ornament were published in *Neue romanische Ziehraten* (Augsburg, before 1686) by the architect and cabinetmaker Johann Indau. Similar acanthus frames, friezes and brackets were also included in designs published between 1690 and 1696 by the cabinetmaker Johann Unselt (*fl* 1681–96) from Augsburg (e.g. *Neues Zierrathen Büchlein*, 1690).

The various strands of Italian influence, however, were superseded in Germany by those of France during the late 17th century and the 18th. This was brought about by two events: first, the admission of 20,000 French Huguenot émigrés to Germany, under the Edict of Potsdam (1685). Among those who went were many craftsmen who worked for Frederick III of Brandenburg (*reg* 1688–1713) on the decoration of Schloss Charlottenburg, Berlin, and Schloss Oranienburg (interior destr. 1945), north of Berlin. Second was the return, in 1715, of Maximilian II Emanuel, Elector of Bavaria (*reg* 1679–1704; 1715–26), from exile in the Netherlands and France (*see* WITTELSBACH, §I(7)). He brought with him French and Dutch artists and craftsmen as well as first-hand knowledge of the château of Versailles. Among the most influential of the Germans whom he had taken with him to France was the architect JOSEPH EFFNER; from 1716 he was responsible for the enlargement of Schloss Nymphenburg in Munich and the completion of Schloss Schleissheim, near Munich. The so-called 'Effner' frame (65b) is characterized by highly decorative corners linked by straight, almost plain sides with an engraved surface, a feature common to the later Rococo frame. The corners serve to emphasize the diagonals and are essentially Régence in their formation of scrolling foliage and strapwork, inspired by Versailles but in a more 'mechanical' and rigid form. The refined quality of carving and gesso recutting is highlighted by the sparse surface between the corners. Produced in considerable quantity and in groups with different corner cartouches, either incised or fully carved, these gallery frames came to dominate and regularize the appearance of the picture collections at Nymphenburg and Schleissheim. A later variation (65c), between Régence and Rococo, surrounds a number of pictures; it has more freely carved cartouches with acanthus and palm foliage, and rocaille edges linked by ogee panels incised with strapwork compartments. Simplified and cruder versions of the 'Effner' frame, either all gilt or with gilt cartouches on straight black ogee sides, were produced in Austria in the 1720s (G 331–2). A similar formula with more elaborate cartouches, again on black rails, became an effective and economical Rococo frame in Austria in the 1740s (G 333).

4. ROCOCO. The Rococo style was enthusiastically adopted by the independent courts of Germany, each of which rivalled the others for architectural splendour, and soon spread to Austria and elsewhere in Central Europe. Although principally an aristocratic and moneyed style in France, it was taken up by the Church in Germany and Central Europe. This widespread and passionate adoption of Rococo decoration, combined with the innate German sense of uniformity, was embodied in the picture frame, which was produced in a series of elaborate standardized forms to harmonize with the display of entire princely collections. The finest of these were in Munich, Berlin, Potsdam and Dresden (see fig. 66). The exotic nature of the independent German Rococo frame, which pushed the elements of the style to its extreme, must be seen in the context of the fixed inset picture and mirror frames that were the ultimate expression of the frame in an interior. Most notable here is the Ahnengalerie (1726–31) in the Residenz in Munich. This masterpiece of German

66. German Rococo gallery frames, *c.* 1740–65: (a) 'Cuvilliés' frame with rocaille corner cartouches, 540×660×75 mm, made for Jean-Baptiste Pater's *Joys of Country Life, c.* 1735 (Munich, Alte Pinakothek); (b) Berlin and Potsdam gallery frame with rocaille corners, 780×630×66 mm, original for Antoine Pesne's *Frederick the Great as Crown Prince, c.* 1740 (Berlin, Gemäldegalerie); (c) Dresden gallery frame with oval sight and floral rocaille spandrels, 695×546 mm, width at centres 80 mm, *c.* 1765, made for Antoine Pesne's *Woman in a Turban, c.* 1710 (Dresden, Gemäldegalerie Alte Meister)

Rococo was one of the *Reichen Zimmer* of Elector Charles. The gallery contains a sequence of superbly carved and gilt frames with vases, flowers, allegorical figures, trophies and legendary beasts, produced by Wenzeslaus Miroffsky (*d* 1759). From 1730 to 1737 the room was converted to house 120 portraits of ancestors and relatives of the Wittelsbach dynasty. Hořín Castle, near Melnik, north of Prague, has a suite of Stone Rooms, decorated by the stuccoist Carlo Giuseppe Bessi and containing large landscape murals framed in the most delicate and attenuated style of middle European Rococo (see Jackson-Stops, 1990).

The interior designer FRANÇOIS DE CUVILLIÉS, his mastery of the decorative vocabulary learnt from over 40 years' Electoral service, was eminently capable of handling the picture frame. He was the central figure in the great flowering of the Rococo style in Munich from the 1720s. His imaginative interpretation of French Rococo was published (in *c.* 400–500 engravings) in such collections as *Livre de cartouche* (Munich, 1738), which included frames, ceiling and wall elevations with panelling, and furniture. Another series in 1745 covered many aspects of interior decoration and *objets d'art*, as well as picture frames. Among other designers whose prints helped to disseminate the Rococo style in Germany was the painter and engraver Georg Sigmund Rosch. In 1745 he engraved one of

Cuvilliés's suites of ornament, and later some 32 plates of his own designs were printed in Augsburg, including patterns for mirror frames and for general Rococo ornament. Rococo frames and cartouches also appear in some of the 40 plates published by Georg Michael Roscher (*fl* 1740–50) in Augsburg *c.* 1750. Perhaps the most influential Augsburger was Johann Esaias Nilson, however, whose 400 or so designs comprised allegorical figures in Rococo frameworks or cartouches, and in 1756 a Neoclassical mirror frame. Cuvilliés's well-balanced designs of frames (66a) for sequences of pictures, formerly in the parade rooms of the Residenz in Munich, both enhance and reinforce the painted compositions without disturbing them. Following the concept of the earlier 'Effner' frame (see §3 above; Cuvilliés had been Effner's draughtsman), elaborate rocaille ornament spills over the corners of the picture and is linked by delicately engraved sides bounded by a double-bead astragal on the outer edge. An important characteristic of this frame is the treatment of the scotia between the spectacular corners. This is carved in the gesso with a series of parallel grooves, interrupted by broader double burnished bands. These create a regular rhythm around the frame and could pick up and scatter candlelight freely. More prominence was given to these bands in versions where the scotia is wider; and they can take on an almost military appearance as in the frame on Louis Tocqué's *Frederick Michael of the Palatinate* (*c.* 1745; Munich, Alte Pin.). The creation of such frames—and of related furniture—was the responsibility of Miroffsky, Joachim Dietrich and Johann Adam Pichler (*fl* 1717–61), master carvers in the court workshop.

The rivalry between the various German princes is reflected in the astonishing frames created for Frederick William I of Prussia (*reg* 1713–40) for his son Frederick the Great (*reg* 1740–86) in his palaces of Schloss Charlottenburg, Berlin, the Stadtschloss (destr. World War II) and Schloss Sanssouci, Potsdam (66b); and later for Frederick-Augustus II, Elector of Saxony (*reg* 1733–63) at the Zwinger in Dresden (66c). Two flamboyant Rococo trophy frames, for example, were created for the pair of portraits (*c.* 1740; Stockholm, Drottningholm Slott) by Antoine Pesne of *Frederick William I* and his English queen, *Sophia Dorothea* (see fig. 67). This is virtuoso carving functioning as propaganda, celebrating and aggrandizing the power of the Prussian throne. The relatively simple, straight-railed carcass is transformed by characteristic German Rococo features: it has been overlaid by six huge cartouches, only the paired corners on each side matching; all are asymmetric, notably the great *fronton*, and all the central elements stray markedly on to the picture surface. The *fronton* combines the Prussian eagle, a shell cartouche with Frederick's monogram, his crown and a pendent order. Neither the pose of the tubby monarch nor the sober line and colour of his armour have the dynamism to transcend this Baroquely dramatic ornament; although the spectator's eye is certainly drawn to such an obtrusive frame, it does not necessarily leave it to dwell on the image of the King. This is a further example of the carver's mastery defeating his object, so that the frame, instead of protecting, enhancing, subtly annotating or isolating the image, smothers it. Even the interplay of lines between the cartouches is at odds with the compositional lines of the painting, and this disjunction is increased by the unintegrated relationship of rail and ornament—the *fronton* in particular appears like a large gaudy butterfly that has alighted on the frame.

The frames created for Frederick the Great's palaces are more successful versions of the same flamboyant genre. They have exceptionally broad, asymmetric rocaille cartouches at the corners, joined by slender straight mouldings at the sides (66b above). Here, however, this deliberate accentuation of the unequal scale of sides and corners gives the effect of 'floating' the picture off the wall. In many instances the sides are incised with scrolling foliage and flowers, a two-dimensional echo of the deeply sculpted corners. The designs for these frames are attributed to the King's architect Georg Wenceslaus von Knobelsdorff, working in collaboration with the 'Directeur des ornements' Johann August Nahl and the brothers Johann Michael Hoppenhaupt (i) and Johann Christian Hoppenhaupt. Having worked in Rome and Paris, Knobelsdorff—influenced by Cuvilliés and several French designers— introduced a novel and confident version of the Rococo style to Berlin. The design process is brilliantly captured in an anonymous sketch (1743–4; Berlin, Schloss Charlottenburg; G figs 24 and 25) from the so-called 'Knobelsdorff Sketchbook', showing corner and centre ornaments of picture frames. Frames for small works had only corner cartouches (66b above); centres were added for larger canvases: both formats combined perfectly with the interiors at the Schloss Sanssouci and Neues Palais, Potsdam. The more expensive swept-sided frames were much less common in German than in French Rococo and were not always as skilfully designed, as in that for *Breakfast* (1723; Berlin, Gemäldegal.) by Jean-François de Troy (ii).

Outside the princely collections fine German frames are rarely seen in public collections. A distinguished example surrounds the *Family of Graf von Fries* (1752; Düsseldorf, Kstmus.) by Johann Heinrich Tischbein I. The upper side of this novel frame has majestic asymmetric corner cartouches bearing the family arms, each surmounted by a crown, centred by an elaborate pierced *fronton*. There are minor centre flourishes at the sides running to rocaille corners, and an uninterrupted lower side. This apex formation of cartouches is beautifully echoed in the overdoor *boiserie* painted within. The pair of frames for Georges Desmarées's portraits of *Charles Theodore, Elector of Bavaria* and his wife (both Madrid, Mus. Thyssen-Bornemisza) are equally sumptuous, having asymmetric corners and centres, and finely engraved ogee sides. Smaller-scale versions of the Munich and Potsdam frame styles with narrow sides were favoured for conversation pieces and portraits exemplified in the pair by Georg Karl Urlaub (1749–1811) and a set of three by Johann Georg Ziesenis (all Frankfurt am Main, Städel. Kstinst. & Städt. Gal.).

The tradition in 18th-century Germany for framing entire collections in a Rococo style reached its zenith in the astonishing reframing programme in Dresden commissioned by Frederick-Augustus II. Hundreds of his paintings in this standardized frame style (66c above), each carrying the King's arms at the top and a crowned

67. Rococo trophy frame with pierced rocaille and flower corner cartouches, and asymmetric *fronton* with the arms, crest and crown of Prussia, one of an original pair for Antoine Pesne's *Frederick William I, King of Prussia and Sophia Dorothea, Queen of Prussia, c.* 1740 (Stockholm, Drottningholm Slott)

AR ('Augustus Rex') cipher at the base, hang in the now restored Gemäldegalerie Alte Meister. The design is fundamentally similar to the Cuvilliés pattern, with the back edge occasionally having an egg moulding. The frame was produced in countless formats and dimensions, from such large canvases as an Annibale Carracci (3.3×4.5 m) to miniatures by Jan Breughel the elder (each *c.* 130×90 mm). The apertures were brilliantly adapted within a rectangular contour to accommodate canvases of all formats—oval (66c above); ogee, arched top (e.g. *Adoration of the Magi* (*c.* 1516) by Joos van Cleve); octagonal (e.g. Carlo Dolci's *Head of St John the Baptist*) and arched top (e.g. Frans van Mieris the elder's *Music Lesson*). This reframing programme, unrivalled elsewhere in Europe, is a testament to the zeal and determination of Frederick-Augustus II to present his entire collection in a unified style, harmonizing with the interiors. The production of these frames, during a remarkably short time in the early 1760s, was the responsibility of the master wood-sculptor Joseph Diebel in his Dresden workshop. Diebel had worked for the court since 1740 and had introduced Rococo ornament to Dresden.

The display in the Gemäldegalerie Alte Meister of some 60 pastel portraits in Rococo swept-sided frames is equally remarkable. In contrast to the uniformly straight-sided frames on the oil paintings, these intimate portraits by Rosalba Carriera, Maurice-Quentin de La Tour, Jean-Etienne Liotard and others are presented in a sequence of frames, every one of which is different—with subtle variations in the design of cartouches and disposition of ornament—underlining the inexhaustible inventiveness and virtuosity of Diebel and his team of carvers and gilders. The centrepiece is a stunning pastel by Liotard—*La Belle Chocolatière* (*c.* 1744–5)—for which each cartouche on the frame is carved with such household objects as flower-baskets, keys, fans, sewing-bags, needles and balls of wool. Other pastels and oils by Liotard in museums in Geneva, Chicago, Cleveland, Detroit and Houston, have survived in superbly designed and carved Rococo frames, more German than French in character, which suggests that possibly Diebel or a Swiss framemaker was involved in their creation.

5. NEO-CLASSICAL, EMPIRE AND BIEDERMEIER. Court decorators were still working in the full Rococo style well into the 1770s, and it was not until *c.* 1780 that Neo-classical designs for furniture were published in Germany. Among the recorded engravings, including picture and mirror frames, appearing at this time were those by the designer Ignác Michal Platzer from Bohemia, who worked in a provincial Neo-classical style in the late 1780s and after. The classicism of the Louis XVI style never took hold in Germany to the extent that it did elsewhere, and it was soon overtaken by the Empire style, which spread quickly from France. The more precise use of antique ornament of the Empire style appealed to German taste, and frames were created to furnish entire galleries—as in the Rococo period—with a few individual patterns alongside. Probably the earliest livery frame was that created for the gallery of the Electors in Düsseldorf (the Kunstmuseum im Ehrenhof in Düsseldorf displays a number of them on Flemish, Dutch and Spanish pictures). The pattern (G 373) is a hybrid of late Baroque and Neo-classical forms, with furled leaf sight, frieze, ribbon moulding and broad outer torus of bound oak leaves and acorns, flanked on the outside by a garland of laurel. The torus resembles French Louis XIII frames, but noticeably Germanic—as in its Régence and Rococo predecessors (see §§3 and 4 above)—is the incision of fine striations over the carved areas, contrasting with the smooth frieze.

Another early Neo-classical frame is based on designs by the court architect Carl Albert von Lespilliez (1723–96), produced *c.* 1779 for the collection in the Hofgarten Galerie, Munich (G 374). This closely resembles contemporary French patterns, with leaf, frieze, beading and scotia. Instances of more specifically German Neo-classical frames are found on pictures from the Mannheim Collection, formed by the Electors Palatine. Two examples show the continuing fashion for recutting ornament in the gesso; the burnished shallow flutes (see fig. 68a) act as miniature light-catching mirrors, as in the Rococo frames—here set against a textured background with stylized lambrequin corners. Equally novel is the alternating frieze of smooth bands and reeds (68b) with an outer *fasces*

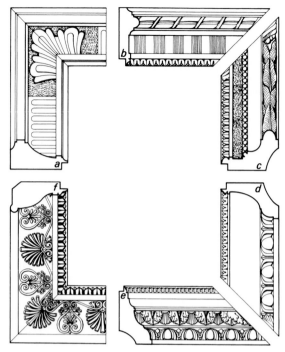

68. German Neo-classical and Empire style frames, 1790s–1820s: (a) fluted shallow scotia Mannheim Collection frame, 830×1410×100 mm, late 18th century, made for Esaias van de Velde's *Preaching of John the Baptist*, 1618 (Karlsruhe, Staatliche Kunsthalle); (b) entablature profile Mannheim Collection frame with striped frieze, 880×655×100 mm, late 18th century, made for *Old Man in Hussar's Uniform*, 1749, by Johann Georg Dathan (1701–49) (Karlsruhe, Staatliche Kunsthalle); (c) scotia frame with laurel torus, beading and water-leaves, 870×660×96 mm, original for *Herr and Frau Leutner, c.* 1800, by Josef Georg von Edlinger (1741–1819) (Düsseldorf, Kunstmuseum im Ehrenhof); (d) deep scotia frame with egg-and-dart and *rais-de-coeur*, 935×1175×157 mm, original for Joseph Anton Koch's *Bernese Oberland*, 1816 (Dresden, Gemäldegalerie Neue Meister); (e) Empire style frame with acanthus and egg mouldings, 740×619×116 mm, original for Julius Schnorr von Carolsfeld's *Virgin and Child*, 1820 (Cologne, Wallraf-Richartz-Museum); (f) ogee Empire style frame with running anthemia and palmette decoration, 1470×1016×176 mm, original for Friedrich Overbeck's *Virgin and Child with SS Elizabeth and John the Baptist*, 1825 (Munich, Neue Pinakothek)

moulding. Jean-Baptiste Perronneau's *Portrait of a Young Girl with a Kitten* (Karlsruhe, Staatl. Ksthalle) has similar regular shallow grooves recut into the frieze of the entablature profile frame. Bunched laurel leaves are the principal ornament in the frame made for Pompeo Batoni's state portrait of *Charles-Eugene, Duke of Württemberg* (1765; Stuttgart, Staatsgal.), and are also prominent on the frame for his portrait of *Emperor Joseph II and his Brother, Leopold I, Grand Duke of Tuscany* (1769; Vienna, Ksthist. Mus.; G 349).

More Italian than French in origin are the scotia profile frames. One version, current from the 1790s to the early 1800s, has textured laurel leaves and leaf tips separately carved and applied, with moulded beading (68c). Another—one of the most regularly produced classical patterns—is a frame with applied carved mouldings (68d); it is virtually identical to contemporary Italian models, more Greek than Roman in taste, appropriate to the inclinations of German architects. The frame around Gerhard von Kügelgen's *Saul and David* (1807; Dresden, Gemäldegal. Neue Meister) is a luxurious and rare embellishment of this design, having a scotia filled with a series of running foliate scrolls applied in pressed metal. Close imitations and variations of French Empire style patterns were produced extensively in Germany, several creative examples of which are on works by Joseph Anton Koch and Johann Christian Reinhart in the Städelsches Kunstinstitut und Städtische Galerie, Frankfurt am Main. A novel combination, contrasting refined acanthus leaves with heavier egg-and-flower moulding, provides an appropriate presentation for the Nazarene devotional picture (68e). Creative use of the imperial ornamental vocabulary—well suited to the purposes and themes of the Nazarene movement—is a feature of these frames, a fine example of which surrounds a Raphaelesque work by Friedrich Overbeck, one of the founders of the group (68f). The frame is distributed with broad palmettes and honeysuckle linked by undulating scrolls, all on a larger scale than contemporary French frames, which on this profile would have been decorated only at centres and/or corners. (For Nazarene frames *see also* §6 below.)

Doubtless encouraged by Napoleon I's programme of reframing in Empire style the pictures in the Musée du Louvre, the desire for streamlined presentation of paintings in German public collections was manifested in two major reframing programmes. As in the 18th century, leading architects were responsible, after whom these frames have been named. In Berlin, the architect Karl Friedrich Schinkel designed a standard gallery frame for the Altes Museum (1823–30; partially restored 1960s). Although having a number of variations, it is basically a broad ogee section decorated with moulded ornament in the form of regularly spaced palmettes on the sides, with much larger palmettes running into Greek scrollwork at the corners (G 370). In Munich Leo von Klenze, architect of the Alte Pinakothek, also provided designs for the frames, which were applied between 1830 and 1836. The section basically follows that of the French Empire-style patterns, with friezes, scotias and ogees, and the sight decorated with continuous patterns of anthemia and foliage (G 371).

French Empire-style patterns were closely imitated from about 1800 to the mid-1830s, but by far the most widely produced frames were influenced by the BIEDERMEIER style, produced for the newly prosperous middle classes in Austria and Germany as well as in Scandinavia. Frames, like furniture, were essentially simplified and popularized versions of the French Empire style (see fig. 69). Many paintings by Biedermeier Realists still retain original frames (e.g. Ferdinand Georg Waldmüller's *Portrait of the Artist's Son Ferdinand with a Dog*, 1836; Munich, Neue Pin.). Earlier Biedermeier designs were simple and sparse, reflecting the austerity of interiors, and were generally in styles closely following French Restoration models. The simplest were plain scotia or ogee mouldings. Five are depicted in the background of the *View from a Room in the Diana Baths* (1830; Vienna, Hist. Mus.) by the Viennese artist Nikolaus Moreau (1805–34). The sight

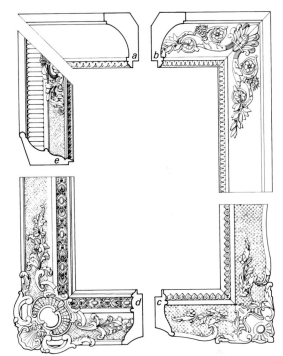

69. Biedermeier frames, *c.* 1815–50: (a) scotia frame with *rais-de-coeur* sight, 762×854×105 mm, original for Carl Begas the elder's *Begas Family*, 1821 (Cologne, Wallraf-Richartz-Museum); (b) scotia frame with Greek scrollwork corners, 270×222×67 mm, original for *Painter at the Easel with his Family*, 1838, by Wilhelm von Harnier (1800–38) (Cologne, Wallraf-Richartz-Museum); (c) swept Rococo style frame with lace panels, 241×206×96 mm, original for *Hussar and Sutler*, 1827, by Peter von Hess (1792–1871) (Cologne, Wallraf-Richartz-Museum); (d) straight Rococo style frame with lace panels, 768×630×128 mm, original for Alfred Rethel's *Philipp Jakob Passavant*, 1839 (Frankfurt am Main, Städelsches Kunstinstitut und Städtische Galerie); (e) fluted scotia frame with moulded cartouches on lace panels, 2300×2900×180 mm, original for Carl Friedrich Lessing's *Holy Grail*, 1836 (Düsseldorf, Kunstmuseum im Ehrenhof)

edge could be enhanced with leaf moulding (69a) and further with the addition of Greek scrollwork corners (69b). Biedermeier frames, as Empire, were relatively economical to produce, with their ornament in moulded composition. However, as they lacked the discipline of hand-carved frames, this occasionally led to an opulent tastelessness, especially in the revival Rococo patterns (69c, d, e). An innovation was the application of lace to the surface of the mouldings, giving a novel texture and linking the frame intimately to the fabrics of interior furnishings and to trimmings on clothing. The fine texture of lace was an effective and economical way of introducing surface contrast, previously achieved in hand-carved frames only by punch-work, the use of sand, and laborious recutting in the gesso. Occasionally the Biedermeier style was somewhat awkwardly adapted to the framing of large-scale canvases; the ogee profile frame (69e) on a painting by Carl Friedrich Lessing is augmented by three cartouches on the long sides and two on the short. Corner ornaments have also been added, as well as an outer scotia with continuous fluting. Other ornamental devices and techniques included the use of pressed metal mouldings. Good-quality print and drawing frames were produced in large quantities in mahogany or stained fruitwoods, often with stringing inlays and sometimes marquetry floral decoration.

6. 19TH-CENTURY REVIVAL STYLES. As elsewhere in Europe, framemakers in Germany and Austria responded to the various 19th-century revival styles by producing a wide diversity of frames. As well as standard First Empire styles in the first three decades of the century, many new patterns were created to correspond with the historical periods represented in paintings. Frames were sometimes tailor-made one-offs, as was the case for some of Caspar David Friedrich's works. *Cross in the Mountains* (see fig. 70) is a superb example of the 19th-century artist's frame, elaborating on the symbolic content of the picture. The arched palm branches allude to God's satisfaction with mankind. The base, which is analogous to the predella of a Gothic retable, carries the eucharistic symbols of wheat and vine branches. These form an arch over beams of light that echo the rays of the setting sun in the painting itself and that are centred on the Eye of God inside a triangle, symbolizing the Trinity. The frame was made by the sculptor Karl Kuhn from a sketch by Friedrich. Other Romantic landscapists, with their realistic approach to nature, employed equally individualistic frames (see fig. 71a). This example is a completely novel combination of Empire and Gothic styles, with its acanthus scotia and broad band of trailing ivy leaves.

70. Nineteenth-century artist-designed altarpiece frame by Karl Kuhn for Caspar David Friedrich's *Cross in the Mountains*, 1.15×1.10 m, 1808 (Dresden, Gemäldegalerie Neue Meister)

The Nazarenes, dedicated to the rejuvenation of German art in the Christian spirit of the Middle Ages, emphasized their links with 15th-century religious works by neo-Gothic and neo-Renaissance frames. The earliest example of a Nazarene frame, with a segmental arched setting enclosing two oblong panels in double lancet form, is on Franz Pforr's diptych *Shulamit and Maria* (1811; Schweinfurt, Samml. Schäfer, on loan to Nuremberg, Ger. Nmus.). These early frames, simple and severe, are relatively rare in public collections. One survivor surrounds Julius Schnorr von Carolsfeld's *Tribute Money* (1822; Düsseldorf, Kstmus.); its Gothic profile shows pronounced ribs overlapping at the corners. A more elaborate example (71b) has moulded paisley-like ornament running to quatrefoils in the corners. Victor Orsel's *Good and Evil* (exh. Salon 1833; Lyon, Mus. B.-A.; see 1990 exh. cat., no. 28) has a 19th-century polished wooden version of a Romanesque round-headed arch, with an inner painted border resembling a stained-glass window and illustrating episodes from the story dealt with in the picture; while a striking design is realized in the pair of Gothic lancet-shaped frames with moulded cusped ornament, echoing the architecture depicted in two views of Gothic churches by Carl Gustav Carus (both 1836; Munich, Neue Pin.). A more elaborate Gothic frame was designed for the Austrian Nazarene Joseph von Führich's *On the Road to Emmaus* (1837; Bremen, Ksthalle; G 389). Here, both inner and outer ribs cross at the corners. The deep scotia has continuous scrolling and counter-scrolling Gothic foliage painted in outline on the gilding, in a careful historicizing idiom that is both more attractive and truer to the painting than the neo-Gothic diapering used by both English and German Nazarenes.

Renaissance Revival frames are recorded intermittently from the 1820s to the 1880s on religious and classical subjects by the Nazarenes and others. Friedrich Overbeck's *Raising of Lazarus* (1822; Karlsruhe, Staatl. Ksthalle) is appropriately framed in a magnificent aedicule in the style of the Venetian Renaissance of the early 16th century, with Corinthian pilasters and entablature covered with scrolling foliage. Moritz von Schwind's *History of a Holy Fool* (untraced) is presented as a pedimented hinged triptych in the Renaissance style, while an intricately decorated upright arched-top frame, also Renaissance in type, was created for his *Symphony* (1852; Munich, Neue Pin.). Appropriately, Renaissance *cassetta* frames with punched scrolling foliage reminiscent of Bolognese examples (*see* §II above) and related to English patterns were the perfect counterparts to Anselm Feuerbach's depictions of classically inspired figures (71c). Similar frames are found on Arnold Böcklin's work, as are several deep foliate frames in an Italian Baroque style (see Mendgen, 1991).

In the 19th century the spread of artistic movements internationally was matched by an increasing variety of frame styles. Pattern books became somewhat standardized, each country producing virtually identical versions of a given style. Just as the First Empire patterns had become widespread, so too did those of the Second Empire frames favoured for paintings to be hung in the annual Salons. The skills and refinements of German framemakers were no less than those of the French, as is shown by an elegant frame in a late Baroque style with

71. Revival frames, 1830s–1890s: (a) Neo-Gothic/Empire frame with ivy and acanthus leaves, 1010×1360×173 mm, original for Ernst Fries's *Mountain Landscape near Massa di Carrara*, 1832 (Frankfurt am Main, Städelsches Kunstinstitut und Städtische Galerie); (b) Neo-Gothic frame with frieze of interlocked paisley motifs and quatrefoil corners, 260×340×78 mm, original for *The Visitation*, 1835, by Ernst Deger (1809–85) (Düsseldorf, Kunstmuseum im Ehrenhof); (c) Bolognese-style *cassetta* frame with scrolling foliage in punchwork, 1920×1140×275 mm, original for Anselm Feuerbach's *On the Seashore*, 1875 (Düsseldorf, Kunstmuseum im Ehrenhof); (d) Salonstyle frame with oak-leaf torus, 1650×2300×247 mm, original for Andreas Achenbach's *Mill on the River Erft*, 1866 (Düsseldorf, Kunstmuseum im Ehrenhof); (e) Neo-Baroque frame with fanned lambreguins or palmettes, 832×637×175 mm, original for Franz von Lenbach's *Russian Woman*, 1863 (Munich, Neue Pinakothek); (f) Neo-Baroque frame with scrolling acanthus foliage, 850×1135×213 mm, original for Hans Thoma's *View of Carrara*, 1886 (Frankfurt am Main, Städelsches Kunstinstitut und Städtische Galerie)

oak-leaf torus, finely beaded ribbon and—unlike the French version—leaf-tip back edge (71d) surrounding a landscape by Andreas Achenbach (1815–1910), a leading light of the Düsseldorf school. Almost the same versatile pattern appears equally successfully on Emanuel Gottlieb Leutze's portrait of *Ferdinand Lottner* (1852). These French Revival patterns seem to be current from the 1840s to the end of the century. Adolph von Menzel's *Sermon in the Old Monastery Church in Berlin* (1847; Dresden, Gemäldegal. Neue Meister), for example, has a frame with deeply undercut moulded scrolling acanthus leaves and flowers in a revival of the straight-sided Louis XIV style. The same design is seen on Fritz von Uhde's *Supper at Emmaus* (1884; Frankfurt am Main, Städel. Kstinst. & Städt. Gal.). A typical deep scotia fluted Neoclassical frame with laurel garland on the top rail is used successfully to enhance the perspective of *Cattle in an Alpine Landscape* (1871; Frankfurt am Main, Städel. Kstinst. & Städt. Gal.) by Anton Berger. Richer and

heavier versions of the deep ogee compound profile frame surrounding paintings of the Barbizon school, with laurel, acanthus, beading and water-leaves (*see* §III, 11 above), were produced in Germany, as seen on *Departure of the Emigrants* (1882; Dresden, Gemäldegal. Neue Meister) by Christian Ludwig Bokelmann (1844–94).

From the 1860s to the early 20th century Italianate Baroque frames were as popular as French Empire patterns. A number appear on works by Frans Xaver Winterhalter, including one with pierced openwork scrolling leaves and flowers for a study of a *Girl in Profile* (1862; priv. col.). Most designs resemble 17th-century Bolognese models, such as the spiralled leaf moulding on the frame for *Child with Doll* (1894; Düsseldorf, Kstmus.) by Arthur Kampf (*b* 1864) and the broad running stylized acanthus leaves on Max Liebermann's portrait of *Dr Frans Adickes* (1911; Frankfurt am Main, Städel. Kstinst. & Städt. Gal.).

A reaction to the standard pattern-book frames took place in Germany in the second half of the 19th century, as in France and elsewhere; and artists either used, commissioned or designed frames of greater individuality for their pictures. The highly popular portrait painter Franz von Lenbach preferred Italian-style frames, particularly antique examples. This taste was doubtless encouraged by his visits to Rome in the 1860s to make large copies of the Old Masters for the Munich connoisseur Adolph Friedrich, Graf von Schack. A number of Lenbach's portraits became visually associated with Old Masters through their frames. His portraits of *Alfred Oberlander* (*c.* 1888–90) and *Ludwig von Undzuder Tann-Rathsamhausen* (*c.* 1880; both Munich, Lenbachhaus; see Mendgen, 1991), for example, are set in Venetian Renaissance 'Sansovino' frames (*see* §II, 4(i) above). However, a number have modern interpretations of Baroque designs: *Russian Woman* is surrounded by a frame (71e) with conventional Baroque inner and outer mouldings but a completely new and striking fanned lambrequin motif running along the frieze.

7. LATE 19TH AND 20TH CENTURIES. As well as these historicizing Revival styles, there were many artists' frames, modern and innovative, that were produced for specific pictures. Hans Thoma designed highly individualistic frames. His romantic landscapes, classical subjects and symbolic portraits occasionally had the friezes of the frames painted overall by the artist. The *cassetta* frame that he painted for *Apollo and Marsyas* (1888; Bernheimer priv. col.), for example, is stained brown and painted in black, ochre and white with gold corners and centres, the lateral centres holding a bugle and violin as appropriate to the subject. Other frames for Thoma's work were equally and ingeniously novel in their use of ornament. *Landscape with Cattle Drinking by a Lake* (1885; Düsseldorf, Kstmus.) has a cushion profile frame with stylized lotus leaves, their tips interlocking and running towards the centre—a complete break with traditional patterns. So too is the sculptural handling of foliage—appropriately Italianate—for the frame surrounding a *View of Carrara* (71f). *Self-portrait* (1880; Dresden, Gemäldegal. Neue Meister), depicting Thoma in an apple orchard, has a gilt *cassetta* frame with a top frieze of children's heads representing the Fruits of

Life, and sides and base with naturalistically painted floral garlands. This type of symbolic portrait and emblematic frame is a descendant of the 17th- and 18th-century portrait in its trophy frame. Later 19th-century examples by other artists include Gustav Klimt's portrait of *Josef Pembaur* (1890; Innsbruck, Tirol. Landesmus.; G 408) in a wide, flat, gilded plate frame, with polychrome decoration in the style of an ancient Greek vase painting showing Apollo with his lyre, in honour of the sitter, a pianist.

A modern pattern-book frame that broke with tradition was the convex reeded frame (see fig. 72a), comparable to frames used by Whistler and Degas from the early 1870s to the late 1890s. The Art Nouveau stylization of traditional ornament is effectively employed in the picture frame and must have encouraged a revival of 17th-century wave and ripple mouldings (72b), which create a strong rhythmic pulse of light around the subject. Such a stock pattern surrounds *The Dinner* (1913; Munich, Neue Pin.) by the Munich Secessionist painter Franz von Stuck, who, being as much a student of the applied as the fine arts, had a

strong feeling for the decorative effect of frames, and designed many that give his work great individuality. The broad triple waveband (72c) with stylized egg moulding on the frame for *Head of a Young Girl* adds great potency to the image; the pattern derives ultimately from such 17th-century prototypes as that on Jan Breughel the elder's *Head of an Old Peasant Woman* (Munich, Alte Pin.)—but now has the added lustre of gilding. The same pattern appears again on the frame around Stuck's *Spring* (1912; Darmstadt, Hess. Landesmus.); here, the framemaker has been identified as Irlbacher (Mendgen, 1991, p. 323). Stuck employed an antique egg moulding in several other frames for classically inspired subjects, including *The Sphinx* (1904; Darmstadt, Hess. Landesmus.), where it is given the stylized and chunky treatment peculiar to Sessionist frames. The altar-like frame for *Sin* (1893; Munich, Neue Pin.; G 406) has the same solid presence. Heavy, baseless, fluted columns support an entablature incised with lotus leaf; the plinth mirrors the entablature, and its frieze inscribed with a cartouche containing the title. This theatrical presentation further dramatizes the shadowy, brooding figure in the painting and emphasizes her role as a femme fatale in the Symbolist canon. Along with Gustave Moreau's Salomes and vampires, the women painted by Fernand Khnopff, Stuck and even Dante Gabriel Rossetti have a sinister air, half-supernatural, underlined by the treatment of frames like this—primitive and temple-like.

Christmas (1910; Cologne, von Abercron; G 410) by Hans Pellar (1886–1971) has a 20th-century simplification of the classical aedicular frame; it is also a return to the engaged frame and panel of the Early Gothic altarpiece. The frame, part of the board on which the picture is painted, is made up of four straight, flat rails, with a shallow top, slightly broader sides and a deep base engraved with volutes and the picture's title—all bordered by gilt ripple moulding in the chunky Secessionist style. Similar ripple frames appear on other works by Pellar (G 409).

The Viennese Secessionist Gustav Klimt also set his paintings in stylized trabeate frames, with rails of unequal depth, shallow engraved ornament and inscriptions. Some of these were made by his brother Georg Klimt (*b* 1867) in repoussé sheet copper and are often gilded or silvered. A distinguished example surrounds *Judith I* (1901; Vienna, Belvedere; G 407), where abstract patterns have overflowed from the painting on to the frame (see Kosinski, 1993). The materials used may have been influenced by William Holman Hunt's repoussé copper frames for the two versions of *May Morning on Magdalen Tower* (see §IV, 10 above). Klimt was typical of Symbolist artists in his desire to unify the frame and its decoration with the picture's content; this was successfully achieved in such works as *Children Praying* (*c.* 1890; Vienna, Belvedere). A number of his metal frames are extremely narrow, with motifs and inscriptions, an elegant example surrounding the portrait of *Sonia Knips* (1898; Vienna, Belvedere), which is gold-plated, with the ornament in contrasting copperplate. These minimal frames were very effective, for instance the attenuated rails of steep arch-shaped section with continuous gilded ribbed moulding on Klimt's portrait of *Mada Primavesi* (1903; New York, Met.).

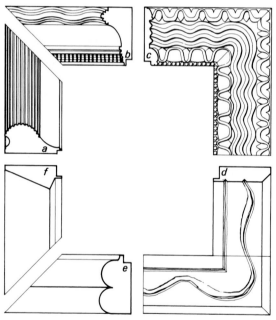

72. Art Nouveau and artist-designed frames, 1870s–1920s: (a) reeded cushion frame, 610×760×110 mm, original for Wilhelm Trübner's *Landscape*, 1876 (Frankfurt am Main, Städelsches Kunstinstitut und Städtische Galerie); (b) scotia frame with wave and ripple mouldings, 1370×1515×123 mm, original for Fritz von Uhde's *Portrait of the Artist's Daughter*, 1901 (Frankfurt am Main, Städelsches Kunstinstitut und Städtische Galerie); (c) artist's frame with broad wave moulding, 375×320×125 mm, original for Franz von Stuck's *Head of a Young Girl, c.* 1906 (Dresden, Gemäldegalerie Neue Meister); (d) artist's frame with undulating wave, 990×910×90 mm, original for Karl Schmidt-Rottluff's *Head of a Woman with Mask*, 1912 (Dresden, Gemäldegalerie Neue Meister); (e) artist's frame with double torus painted black, 840×950×78 mm, original for Ernst Ludwig Kirchner's *West Docks at Frankfurt*, 1916 (Frankfurt am Main, Städelsches Kunstinstitut und Städtische Galerie); (f) artist's frame with deep outer chamfer, 520×305×75 mm, original for *The Prayer*, 1919, by Gottfried Graf (1881–1938) (Dresden, Gemäldegalerie Neue Meister)

Frames in Germany in the 20th century, as elsewhere, are economical, geometric profiles—stained, gilded, painted with colour or bronze or in combinations of these finishes, generally to complement the picture's palette. Many Expressionist works retain their original frames, an exceptional example of which is on a painting by Karl Schmidt-Rottluff. It has a rudimentarily carved wave moulding adjacent to a straight line, finished in bronze (72d). Many original frames for Ernst Ludwig Kirchner's paintings are in the Städelsches Kunstinstitut und Städtische Galerie, Frankfurt am Main. The frame for *West Docks at Frankfurt* has a double cushion moulding (72e), echoing the arched spans of the bridge in the painting, and that for *Nude Woman with Hat* (1907) has a double stepped architrave, the outer gilt and the inner painted red. In Cubist paintings the lines of composition are emphasized by the angularity of the frame section (72f). The frame around Lyonel Feininger's *In Neubrandenburg* (1925; Karlsruhe, Orangerie) achieves this with a reverse profile with step and canted back finished in silver leaf. Arthur Segal, on the other hand, unified his work by treating a conventional plain frame moulding as part of the pictorial surface, undifferentiated from the canvas, so that 'the viewer's eye looks at everything equally' (see 1995 exh. cat., pp. 238–9). Kurt Schwitters ensured that the frames became integral parts of his collages by nailing strips of wood directly on to his compositions, as in *Little Seamen's Hostel* (1926; Düsseldorf, Kstsamml. Nordrhein–Westfalen). This procedure typified the attitude of many 20th-century artists to the frame and its historical function: it was a form to be reduced to a bare minimum or to be totally excised.

BIBLIOGRAPHY

C. D. Cutter: *Northern Painting* (New York, 1972)
F. G. Conzen and G. Dietrich: *Bilderrahmen: Stil–Verwendung–Material* (Munich, 1983)
S. Jervis: *The Penguin Dictionary of Design and Designers* (Harmondsworth, 1984)
S. E. Fuchs: *Der Bilderrahmen* (Recklinghausen, 1985) [F; 146 figs]
G. Jackson-Stops: 'Reviving Rich Ruins', *Country Life* (8 Nov 1990), pp. 98–105
Polyptyques: Le Tableau multiple du moyen âge au vingtième siècle (exh. cat., ed. C. Clément; Paris, Louvre, 1990)
E. Mendgen: *Künstler rahmen ihre Bilder: Zur Geschichte des Bilderrahmens zwischen Akademie und Sezession* (Konstanz, 1991)
——: 'Der Bilderrahmen: Ein Randphänomen?', *Eur. J. A. Historians*, 4 (1992), pp. 258–66
Gustav Klimt (exh. cat. by T. Stooss and C. Daswald, Zurich, Ksthaus, 1992)
D. M. Kosinski: 'Klimt in Zurich', *Apollo*, cxxxvii (1993), p. 59
E. Mendgen: 'Patinated or Burnished' and 'Art or Decoration', *In Perfect Harmony: Picture and Frame, 1850–1920* (exh. cat., Amsterdam, Rijksmus. van Gogh, 1995)

For further bibliography *see* §I above.

VII. Scandinavia.

1. Medieval. 2. Renaissance. 3. Mannerist. 4. Baroque. 5. Rococo. 6. Neoclassical. 7. Biedermeier and revival styles. 8. Late 19th and 20th centuries.

1. MEDIEVAL. The earliest picture frames in Scandinavia are associated with church art, and their structure, ornament and iconography are dependent on the countries through which Christianity was introduced—France, Germany and England. Christianity, however, also brought the world of Classical art to Scandinavia: Byzantine and Classical ornaments were added to the geometric and zoomorphic decorations of the Stave (carved wooden) churches, and influences from Flanders, Normandy and even the Lombard builders of Lund Cathedral in Sweden (from 1103) began to appear. French enamels were imported during the 12th and 13th centuries, and in Denmark such works as the Lisbjerg Altar, an embossed copper frontal and retable, were found, although this may have been imported. English art was very important in Norway and in turn influenced Denmark and Sweden; French art and architectural influence in Sweden were, however, greater. Hakon Hakonsen of Norway, a great patron and collector, started a school of Norwegian painting that was based on that of western Europe; he transformed his country in the same way, keeping close political links with England. When he was invited on a Crusade by Louis IX of France, the ambassador to his court was the English artist Matthew Paris of St Albans.

The earliest framed panel paintings that survive—thirty-one Norwegian antependia and one retable (most in Oslo, U. Oldsaksaml., and U. Bergen, Hist. Mus.)—are thus closely linked to contemporary English paintings and manuscript illuminations, with some influence from Flanders and northern France. Their frames continue the pre-Christian geometric style of decoration used for the interiors of the Stave churches, here applied to the graphic or relief representation of precious stones: a technique also found in the ornamentation of metalwork antependia from France and Germany, and in a work brought in the early 12th century from Byzantium by a Norwegian king. This style of decoration is particularly close to that of early Spanish antependia and retables. Variations in the style have been traced (Lindblom, 1916, p. 22), from the plain flat and deep bevel of, for example, the Heddal Church antependium (mid-13th century; Oslo, Nmus.), through the round and oval hollows and lozenges of the antependium of Skaun Church near Trondheim (*in situ*) to the painted square cassettes, oval bosses, contour lines and roundels of the St Olaf antependium (Copenhagen, Nmus.). The final variation adds carved or painted floral paterae, as on the Rijsby antependium (*in situ*) in Denmark and that from the church of Tresfjord, Norway (*in situ*; see fig. 73). These last ornaments probably originated in the neighbouring German states: stylistic influences were perpetually diffusing across the borders.

Very few of the early English altarpieces that seem to have inspired these Nordic versions survive; the latter, however, show what the missing English works would have been like. As in Spain, they seem to have survived partly because the ordinary parishes were not rich enough to replace their altars and antependia as artistic fashions changed. The impression of relative poverty is supported by an examination of the frames themselves: many have the shaped hollows, which mimic precious stones, but none has survived with an actual inlay of stone, painted glass or enamel. Moreover, the frames of Scandinavian altarpieces are rarely gilded; more often they are silvered or lacquered with a golden varnish, a trick that continued until the 19th century, when base-metal substitutes for gold leaf appeared. The Tresfjord antependium has been treated in this way.

The Black Death, which arrived in Norway in 1349, effectively diminished the number of potential patrons

73. Medieval Norwegian antependium with deep flat and bevelled frame, with painted undulating border and flowers, 988×755 mm, first half of the 14th century (Norway, Tresfjord Church)

and impoverished the Church. There are apparently no architectural frames in any of the Scandinavian countries; interior architectural settings are painted, and even as late as the end of the 14th century there seems to be no progression beyond the mid-13th-century style of flat moulding and deep bevel with coloured decorations. Prosperity began to return only with the Kalmar Union of Norway and Denmark in 1387 and Sweden (1389) under Margaret I of Denmark (*reg* 1387–1412). The huge political effort involved in this seems to have left little room for artistic patronage, however, and very little 15th-century Scandinavian art survives. A Norwegian antependium, from Volda Church, Sunnmore (*c.* 1500; Bergen, Vestlandske Kstindustmus.), has the same flat and bevel structure as the 13th-century antependia and was treated like a Flemish altarpiece, with a Gothic black letter inscription along the bottom rail, in white on gold. It is a native copy of the Netherlandish and Flemish altarpieces that were imported during the 16th century, together with wood-carvings from Antwerp. Flemish influence is also seen in the portrait of *Christian II of Denmark* (Copenhagen, Stat. Mus. Kst) by the Bruges-trained Michel Sittow, which has a round-arched frame in a simple half round or torus section, such as would be used in Flanders for a sitter of the middle or mercantile class.

2. RENAISSANCE. Although Christian II (*reg* 1513–23) had tried to introduce Renaissance ideas and art, the growth of Lutheranism and the coming of the Reformation proved more powerful. The Renaissance initially had little impact on the Nordic countries, and only folk art flourished, especially wood-carving and decorative painting. The end of the Union came in 1513 (although Norway merged with Denmark in 1537), and the upheavals this involved, together with the reorganization caused by Lutheranism, meant that it was not until *c.* 1550 that artistic interests and patronage began to increase. By this time many Scandinavian nobles were being educated in Italy, France and Germany and were learning of Renaissance art and architecture at first hand; they then brought foreign artists and craftsmen to build their houses and art collections. Such patrons as Frederick II of Denmark and Norway (*reg* 1559–88) and Eric XIV of Sweden (*reg* 1560–68) assisted this process. Work produced included Willem Boy's carved wooden relief of *Gustav I Vasa* (*c.* 1558; Mariefred, Gripsholm Slott), with its integral frame. Here the King stands in the full court dress of a Renaissance prince, gilded against a green ground and supported on a three-dimensional strapwork plinth. A small astragal and ogee moulding outlines the whole work, but the figure of the King is held in an inner gilt frame of a running flamelike motif with beading, and the top rail is a lambrequin canopy holding arms and a crowned G. It is a comparatively simple frame, but it illustrates the sudden late flowering of the Renaissance—principally at the court of Frederick II.

When Christian IV (*reg* 1588–1648) succeeded to the Danish throne in 1588, he was one of Europe's richest princes. However, as a patron he had no native tradition to build on; most artists and architects were still brought in from the south. Only the frames for these foreign artists' work were genuinely Scandinavian, because of the strong vernacular wood-carving skills; the royal cabinet-makers were the Danes Gregor Greuss (*fl* 1600–16) and Bertil Moller (1617–84), while the Court painters were Dutch. Architecture was also in the hands of Dutch or Flemish builders, and furniture and such items as frames were naturally affected by this contemporary 'Dutch Renaissance' style; they also acquired ornamental detail from such sources as the designs of Corbinian Saur of Bavaria, who was Court Goldsmith to Christian IV in Copenhagen from 1613. From the early 1590s, Saur had published refined engravings of jewellery, which set flowers and heraldic motifs within delicate strapwork designs.

Italian Renaissance ornament, entering Scandinavia via Germany and the Netherlands, can be seen in such frames as that on the relief plaque of Frederick II of Denmark and Norway (1589; Mariefred, Gripsholm Slott). The whole relief is given a complete frame with wide, complex gilt outer mouldings and a small answering moulding at the sight. Between is a black flat with fine scrolling foliate decoration in gold, Florentine or Bolognese in style and probably in *sgraffito*: very dense and Italianate. The two shutters fastened to the lateral mouldings are similarly decorated, on a much larger, coarser scale. The disparity of proportion in the two areas of decoration cannot be Italian and is probably a Danish response to a style that had still not been completely digested and was also 30 to 40 years out of date. A similar relic of an older style can be seen in the portrait of *Henrik Rantzau* (1598; Hillerød, Frederiksborg Slot). The sitter wanted to form a collection at his palatial manor house that would rival those of other late 16th-century princes; but his portrait with its inscribed sill mimics Flemish memorial pictures of 100 years earlier.

3. MANNERIST. In the early 17th century Christian IV devoted 20 years to the building of Frederiksborg Castle in Hillerød, making it the most splendid in contemporary Europe. Much of the castle and its contents were Mannerist in style: the oratory of his chapel (destr. 1859) was covered with a series of large paintings on the *Life of Christ*, framed in and interspersed with richly inlaid foliate and strapwork panels, as seen in a painting by Heinrich Hansen (Hillerød, Frederiksborg Slot). The panelling was articulated by tapered Mannerist pilasters, brackets and small caryatids or herms, and the paintings were held in bands of ebonized or stained-wood ripple moulding. The whole scheme was one of the earliest examples in Scandinavia of an interior in which paintings were integrated with their frames and with the surrounding decoration. The use of Mannerist motifs similar to this foliate and strapwork inlay, gilt or parcel-gilt ornament and grotesque caryatids can be found in contemporary furniture and also informs frames such as the original one on Reinholt Thim's *Ecce homo: Christian IV's Vision at Rothenburg Castle on 8 December 1625* (Copenhagen, Rosenborg Slot). This is a simple *cassetta* or entablature frame with oblong panels in the centre of each rail, the bottom one holding Christian IV's own summary of his vision, and each supported by shallow-relief strapwork motifs.

It is in a sombre style, however, untypical of Christian IV's reign. His castles were full of colour: pictures and their frames competed with walls hung with gilded leather or tapestries; ceilings of moulded or carved stucco or wood; furniture made from exotic woods; embroideries, hangings and upholstery. Against this rich background, paintings were hung in frames of equal colour and opulence. Following Netherlandish prototypes, a portrait of Christian IV's young second wife *Kirsten Munk* (c. 1615; Oslo, Kstindustmus., see 1988 exh. cat., no. 112) is set in a simple ogee frame, but of a startlingly vivid marbled tortoiseshell. An equally astonishing mirror frame in the style of a Mannerist tabernacle, with cresting, pedimented niche, scrolled apron and lateral brackets, was made in ebony, possibly by Greuss, and covered with runs of silver fretwork, snowflake motifs, winged cherubs and sculpted figures (all probably from Augsburg, see 1988 exh. cat., no. 725). These works are richer, more 'colourful' and slightly outré in effect compared to Mannerist works from Germany and the Low Countries. They are influenced both by the wealth of the commissioning patron and by

74. Danish Mannerist retable with storeyed aedicular trabeate structure in four tiers with crest, carved scenes from the *Life of Christ* and free-standing figures by Abel Schroder, oak, 1661 (Copenhagen, Holmens Church)

the opulence of their intended background. The flamboyance both of these frames and larger interior settings can be compared with those of medieval and Mannerist Spain; but the cause is probably a reaction to the long, black Nordic winters, as against the influence from the Moors in Spain. The use of polychrome decoration was as widespread in Scandinavia as in Spain: in the late 16th century and the 17th, for example, provincial frames were decorated with naively painted embellishments of stylized florets and leaves (examples can be seen in the Department of Modern Danish History, National Museum, Lyngby, near Copenhagen).

In the 1630s and 1640s, as the prosperity and eminence of Denmark declined, Sweden gained power, wealth and diplomatic prestige, and Queen Christina of Sweden (*reg* 1632–54) led a brilliant court. Foreign artists and architects were called to Sweden, and works of art were even more rapidly acquired when Prague was looted by the Swedes in 1648; it should be noted, however, that in the 16th and 17th centuries most paintings at Gripsholm Castle were hung unframed. By the second half of the 17th century such patrons and collectors as Carl Gustaf Wrangel had emerged. At his palace (*c.* 1650–70) at Skokloster he used German and Italian craftsmen; the German sculptor Markus Hebel carved a number of huge wooden chimney-pieces, mainly in a Flemish Mannerist style. They have open pediments, gilt, coloured and silvered high-relief trophies, coronets as crests and grotesque strapwork/Auricular cartouches of arms depending from these and covering the upper parts of the inset paintings. The paintings, from the *Metamorphoses*, have therefore much to contend with in their frames; the background areas are painted black, marbled in various colours and trimmed—especially along the carved sight edges of the paintings—with gilt mouldings.

Skokloster is a microcosm of the same exotic, highly coloured and over-ornamented world that emerged under Christian IV of Denmark and shows that Sweden too could absorb influences and styles from Germany, France and elsewhere and subsume them under the native tendency to ornament and accrete. Apart from the chimney-pieces, the 17th-century frames from Skokloster are mostly restrained copies of Dutch stained-wood or ebonized/parcel gilt examples, providing a rare place of rest for the eye among the general busyness. Only the Baroque mirror frames, many Spanish and dating from 1700 onwards, accord with the visual tumult. An instance of this *horror vacui* in a native carved altarpiece of the time is Abel Schroder's magnificently detailed oak retable (1661) for Holmens Church (see fig. 74). The 'frame' includes Solomonic columns, inner Auricular borders and dense background scrolling ornament reminiscent of the pre-Christian zoomorphic style. It is an extraordinary example of religious art in a Lutheran country and once more demonstrates a strange parallel with Spanish Baroque and Mannerist carvings.

4. BAROQUE. Thirteen years after the Holmens retable was completed, Burchardt Precht of Bremen settled in Stockholm. He was a skilled wood-carver, who also brought to Sweden the technique of decorating frames with metal foil (e.g. *c.* 1700; Stockholm, Skokloster Slott).

He set up a complete factory of mirrors and frames, supplying the aristocracy as well as the royal household with carved late Baroque styles. By 1700 he had created a virtual monopoly in his craft, especially in the production of glass frames for mirrors. These had panels of scrolling foliage in metal leaf or tinfoil and were then glazed or lacquered a transparent red. The finely detailed leafy flourishes were repeated on a coarser scale in the carved wooden crests of the frames. Precht also produced superbly carved picture frames, such as that for an oval portrait of *Karl XI* (Helsinki, Sinebrychoff A. Col.) by David Klöcker Ehrenstrahl (see fig. 75). An almost identical portrait with a very similar frame may also be by Ehrenstrahl or may be an assistant's copy; both frames have been attributed to Burchardt Precht and his workshop and may be after a design by Nicodemus Tessin (ii). Tessin had spent time in Rome, England and France, and influences especially from France and Italy are apparent in his work. This frame probably dates from after 1680, when he returned to live in Sweden, and is in the idiom of a full-blown, Baroque trophy frame. The complex ogee section of the main structure, and the prickly, parsley-like, cross-cut acanthus leaves that enrich it, are close to original Louis XIII patterns. The leaves are very finely carved, creating a tension of detail and texture with the rather large representation of the Swedish crown and the mask of Hercules's Nemean lion.

75. Swedish Baroque trophy frame with oval sight and ogee section in the Louis XIII style, 820×660 mm, original for David Klöcker Ehrenstrahl's *Karl XI*, after 1680; probably designed by Nicodemus Tessin (ii), carving attributed to the workshop of Burchardt Precht (Helsinki, Sinebrychoff Art Collection)

Many variants of Louis XIII profiles are found in Swedish frames—rectangular and oval. They feature main ogee or half-torus mouldings, carved with acanthus or bay leaves and supported by multiple small enrichments of leaves, beading, ribbon-and-stave, *rais-de-coeur* and hazzling. There are also Anglo-French variants of Louis XIII frames, with plain ogee mouldings and acanthus clasps, and Swedish copies of Dutch or English 'Lutma' frames, with their shallow carving of fruit, flowers and cherubs. Further Dutch influence appears in ripple frames—although these may be gilded rather than ebonized—showing the eclectic tendencies of Swedish craftsmen. Immigrant workers fostered this eclecticism: Huguenot carvers settled in Sweden, particularly after the 1685 Revocation of the Edict of Nantes.

Such men as Tessin were international in their manipulation of styles. Tessin likened the Royal Palace in Stockholm to a small château of Versailles, but its Baroque interiors show Italian and even Dutch influences. In the lavish Karl XI Gallery, the shaped ceiling paintings are framed in Louis XIII torus mouldings, cut into flowers and foliage; the walls are articulated by pilasters combining strapwork and arabesques; and the frieze and ceiling beams are supported by a mixture of large and small modillions. To achieve all this, a workshop of carvers and gilders was established from *c.* 1732, including the sculptor Jacques Adrien Masreliez (1717–1806) from 1748.

5. ROCOCO. The Rococo style was introduced into Scandinavia in the 1730s. Norway was susceptible to the colour, form and line of Rococo; the vernacular *rosemaling* (rose painting) technique, with its similar use of colours, floral designs and flourishes, had spread throughout the country, and the highly decorated interiors of French Rococo fitted into the existing tradition. France was allied with Sweden and subsidized Denmark, so that there was a continual commerce between all three countries; Christian VI of Denmark (*reg* 1730–46) began to build the palace of Christiansborg in Copenhagen, using both the popular Austrian Baroque style and the modern Rococo; and the Swedish architect Carl Hårleman, who was in Paris in 1732 and saw the flowering of the style, used his experience to reinvent Swedish architecture.

Hårleman returned to Sweden partly to help Tessin with the Royal Palace, but his own first large work was probably the palace of Svartsjö for Frederick of Sweden (*reg* 1720–51) in 1732. It was already in the full Rococo style and even went beyond its French sources by combining Rococo interiors with complementary exterior façades. Hårleman also worked at Drottningholm, producing a series of watercolour elevations for the various interiors (Paris, Inst. Tessin), which include Rococo overdoor frames, mirrors, picture frames and moulding sections. These are in the lightest and most delicate version of the style and are generally symmetrical. In the chapel in Drottningholm, which was built in the classical idiom of Tessin, Hårleman designed a frame for G. E. Schroder's altarpiece of the *Last Supper* that combines the dynamic movement of the Baroque with the curving asymmetry of the Rococo. It consists of a very simple linear ogee moulding with dark sculpted clouds swagged across it, and figures of angels at the sides and top giving a spiral

emphasis. The soft cloud shapes were repeated on the ceiling of the chapel, where this time Hårleman could impose more Rococo detail on the classical structure. They are used to frame and link the ceiling paintings, their soft forms echoing the marble banner above the eastern arch, the background of the altarpiece and the vibrant lines of the pulpit. They give a Germanic flavour to the chapel interior, set as they are against the white-and-gold diapered ceiling. Hårleman, however, was still primarily linked to a French perception of style: to help his craftsmen, lengths of French mouldings were imported to Sweden.

By the 1760s the Rococo style was thoroughly established in Scandinavia. Frames were made in a slender compromise between the French and German Rococo styles, with pronounced corners and *frontons* breaking from or applied to the narrow mouldings (see fig. 76). *Frontons* were more popular in Scandinavia than in France. The frame (76a) around the portrait of *Fru Werner* (Stockholm, Drottningholm Slott) is the most conventionally French in style. As on the similar frames surrounding the pastel portraits of *Count Tessin* and his wife (Stockholm, Nmus.), the corner cartouches are quite well integrated with the body of the frame. In the Danish example (76b), however, the huge asymmetric rocailles break suddenly from the rather severe torus mouldings in the dramatic fashion of a German Rococo frame. The effect on the portrait inside is not particularly flattering or enhancing as, although the shapes of the rocailles mirror the folds of drapery, fall of the hair, decoration of the dress etc, they are too large, too sculptural and too assertively close to the painted figure to do anything but

76. Scandinavian Rococo frames: (a) Swedish frame with shell corner cartouches and sanded panels, original for F. Keilhorn's *Fru Werner* (Stockholm, Drottningholm Slott); (b) Danish frame with pierced centre and corner cartouches, 905×760×71 mm, original for Johan Horner's *Portrait of an Elderly Lady*, 1752 (Copenhagen, Statens Museum for Kunst); (c) Swedish frame with rocaille cartouches, 590×490×47 mm, original for Lorens Pasch's *Portrait of a Lady*, *c.* 1770 (Helsinki, Sinebrychoff Art Collection)

77. Swedish Rococo frame with shell corner cartouches, *fronton* with arms and crown of Sweden, 2122×1562×146 mm, original to Swedish school: *Prince Gustav Aged 5*, 1751 (Stockholm, Drottningholm Slott)

overwhelm it. This is a case where the carver's virtuosity has produced a striking frame, but one that is detrimental to the work inside it.

The frame of *Prince Gustav Aged 5* (1751; Stockholm, Drottningholm Slott; see fig. 77) shows a more constructive use of the *fronton*, which is echoed by symmetrical shell and rocaille corners. Far closer in feeling to a French Rococo frame (save for the unusual profile with its sanded hollow and bound *fasces* moulding), this is a ceremonial setting for the full-length portrait of the Prince. The large and elaborate corners are controlled, first by a use of rigid symmetry, second by the width and plainness of the main structure and third by the relative proportions of the huge frame to the tiny figure of Gustav. The corners are used in the traditional Baroque manner, to set up diagonal lines of focus that converge on the head and hands of the figure; they also create an asymmetric play of lines with Gustav's head, a globe beside him and the sunburst above, each of which mirrors the shape of the carved corners. Such a complex set of relationships is certainly French in origin and may have been the creation of a Huguenot carver working with the finished painting. The *fronton* demonstrates the quality of the carving, with its rocaille cartouche, the three crowns of the Swedish arms and the

fragile sculpted coronet above. On a much smaller scale, the frame (76c) of *Portrait of a Lady* (*c.* 1770; Helsinki, Sinebrychoff A. Col.) shows similar compositional skill; the rounded acanthus corners above rocailles and C-scrolls are delicate and restrained, so that, although they are as close to the painting as in the Horner portrait (76b), they do not overwhelm the sitter. Instead, the correspondences between carved scrolls and drapery is fully integrated, and the diagonal lines between the corners hold and emphasize the face. The feeling here is of a Venetian Rococo frame, with its slender burnished panels, while the rounded sight corners with carved volutes trespassing on the picture surface are German rather than French.

Some highly successful Scandinavian Rococo frames were produced by French craftsmen for a set of 11 hunting pictures by Jean-Baptiste Oudry. These were commissioned by Tessin *c.* 1740 as a special installation (complete with overdoors etc) for the Royal Palace of Stockholm (*in situ*). They have the same nominal structure as figure 77: a straight-sided Régence type of frame, with corner cartouches and a *fronton*. The cartouches are based on irregular clam shells and contain the Swedish emblem of the Polar Star. The overdoors are lighter and more fanciful, the lateral rails wound with spiralling vines and the central crest wildly scrolling. The latter betrays some German influence, but the main hunting scene, with its chain-and-egg sight edge and asymmetric corners growing organically from the outer moulding, is definitely French. Bills in the palace archives confirm that these frames were carved in Sweden by French craftsmen; and it is interesting to see how the pure forms of the Rococo of Nicolas Pineau or Juste-Aurèle Meissonnier were adapted by the influences of place, time and other nations' variants of the same style.

Hårleman's influence on the Oudry installation would of course have been important; so perhaps would that of Jean Eric Rehn, who worked with Hårleman on the Royal Palace. He also designed a library (early 1760s) at Drottningholm in a mixture of Rococo and classical ornament, which included panelling, overdoor and overmantel mirror frames in the same delicate Rococo favoured by Hårleman. This co-existed with the flamboyant Germanic Rococo style of many frames at Drottningholm, and also with those in a heavy Louis XV style. Gripsholm Castle is also an important location for Rococo frames: many of these are in the straight-sided corner and *fronton* style favoured in Sweden, but the workmanship indicates that French carvers and gilders, or native craftsmen trained in France or by immigrant Huguenots, were involved (e.g. the frames of *Adolf Frederick* and *Louisa Ulrica*; Mariefred, Gripsholm Slott, workshop of Antoine Pesne). The second example shows a beautifully integrated design, with modest curved asymmetric flowery corners, plain, straight lateral rails and a symmetrical base cartouche balancing the crowned *fronton*. The rocaille corners and flower trails marry perfectly with the lace sleeves and inserts of the Queen's dress, while the straight rails reflect the internal architecture of the painting, with classical pilasters. A later painting of the Queen (also by Pesne) at Drottningholm, shows a much more typically Swedish interpretation of a ceremonial Rococo frame, where the huge rocaille corners jut into an eared silhouette, the *fronton* joins the top corners in a kind of Rococo 'pediment' and the rails are enriched with bold chain and stopped-flute gadrooning.

6. NEO-CLASSICAL. The transition to the Neo-classical style was perhaps already evident in Rehn's library at Drottningholm. Finland, like Sweden (to which it was annexed), came under this French-influenced stylistic shift; but Denmark, which still ruled Norway, was influenced by German art. In Sweden, Gustav III patronized all types of art (*see* GUSTAVIAN STYLE) and encouraged the links with France: he employed Louis-Jean Desprez and Rehn to create interiors for him. The White Drawing-room at Gripsholm, for example, was articulated by a series of round-arched window embrasures beneath a frieze of gilt modillions and bay-leaf swags (the *cordes à puit* of the French Neo-classical period). The effect is of a continuous triumphal arch, on the uprights of which are hung full-length portraits of reigning European monarchs. The frames are Neo-classical; their plain double torus rails and crowned *frontons* have evolved from the Rococo *fronton* frames in an assured and restrained evocation of classicism.

Both Drottningholm and the Prins Eugens Waldemarsudde, Stockholm, are filled with examples of Neo-classical furniture and mirror frames, which demonstrate the stylistic closeness of Sweden and France at this time. They also show a refinement of workmanship that is probably French: the corner paterae, bay leaves and enriched guilloches were recut in the gesso, giving a precision and sharpness of outline that is authentically Parisian, and there is gilding in red and yellow gold leaf. Swedish Neo-classicism is generally pure, but not heavy like early French *gout grec*; individual interpretations occurred, however, such as a giant piastre moulding on frames and panelling, which is only seen in miniature on French Louis XVI frames, and a fret or Greek key pattern, which is idiosyncratic and found only on Gustavian frames (see fig. 78).

Louis Adrien Masreliez (1748–1810), son of Jacques Adrien Masreliez, travelled extensively in France, Italy and Germany and imported the *style arabesque* to the Swedish court. From 1784 he was decorator to the King and the Swedish nobility and introduced his sophisticated brand of Neo-classicism. His watercolour designs for Gustav's pavilion at the castle of Haga have broad bands of ornament defining mural panels, articulated with medallions, and combining a range of classical architectural motifs to produce an impression of great richness and clarity. He designed furniture and interiors that marry, in a style analogous to the work of Robert Adam, decorated panelling, carpets, built-in and free-standing furniture, and inset frames, which are intended to bind certain set-piece paintings to the rooms containing them. Examples can be seen in Gustav's bedroom at Haga, where Masreliez was commissioned to incorporate Alexander Roslin's painting of *Sully at the Feet of Henry IV* (*in situ*) into the decoration; and in Prince Karl's Audience Chamber (1792) in the Royal Palace, Stockholm. In the latter, the whole room is a 'frame' for a series of pictures showing Swedish historical battles. The Roslin frame is in a chaste, fluted Neo-classical style subservient to the drama of the painting; but it is also 'framed' by the wall panels of gold on white, which

78. Swedish Gustavian *fronton* frame, with enriched fret pattern, laurel wreath and drops, original for Pehr Hilleström's *Princess Sofia Albertina* (Mariefred, Gripsholm Slott, Statens Porträttsamling)

use strong vertebrate scrolling ornaments between multiple bands of husks and beading. The latter are echoed by the carved husks and beading of the Neo-classical chairs and canape.

Apart from these inset frames, the typical Gustavian pattern is the rectangular *fronton* frame (fig. 78). These vary in type, from the extremely chaste, beaded versions found on portraits by Gustaf Lundberg and Angelica Kauffman in the Royal Palace and the Nationalmuseum, Stockholm, where a more purely French influence is apparent, to the more individual, native treatments, including a wide range of embellishment to the rectangular structure. Gustavian fret ornament is evident on the frame in figure 78 in an enriched version, with florets decorating alternate inlets of the pattern, and forms a suitable setting for the portrait. The related portraits of *Gustav III* and *Queen Sofia Magdalen* by Jacob Björk carry the lyrically decorative floral tone a stage further, replacing the staid Neo-classical bay-leaf pendants with trails of roses. The combination of this with the Neo-classical *fronton* form is bizarre but successful. An equally idiosyncratic version of the *fronton* style also frames Per Krafft's portrait of the musician and poet *Carl Michael Bellman* (Mariefred, Gripsholm Slott). This features a prominent ribbon-and-stave moulding and an arrangement of multiple enrichments rather like the classic 'Maratta' frame. The *fronton* takes the form of an attributive trophy, with mask, lyre and vines; the top of the trophy has a carved ribbon hanging and decorative paterae 'nail'. The sight edge of *rais-de-coeur* is carved with great refinement, as is the enriched guilloche around the lyre. Further examples of this enriched guilloche form the main ornament on full-length Neo-classical *fronton* frames on portraits of *Louis XV of France* by van Loo and *Catherine the Great of Russia* (Stockholm, Kun. Slott). These are similar to state portraits at the château of Versailles, and the frames may well have been made in France to complete the gift from Louis XVI of both works.

In Denmark the striking Rococo frames (76b above) in the Germanic fashion did not lead, as in Sweden, into a comparable great wave of Neo-classical artefacts. By the 1780s Denmark was at the height of one of its more prosperous periods, and patronage revived slightly. There were, however, no Neo-classical frames analogous to the individual, quirky type of the Swedish Gustavian style; Neo-classical frames in Denmark seem to have demanded nothing more original than the bound *fasces* moulding, which looks forward to the reeded artist's frames of later 19th-century Europe. Wilhelm Haffner's engraving of the *Family of the Prime Minister Hoegh Guldberg* (1782; Hillerød, Njaellandsk Flkmus.; see Praz, 1964, no. 135) shows the drawing-room of an illustrious and probably rich Danish man in the late 18th century; the furniture retains Rococo curves for comfort, but the setting—the medallion overdoors, the Classical statues and the symmetrical arrangement of pictures—is a product of Neo-classicism. The pictures have very simple *fronton* frames, with plain rectangular or oval contours, and decoration at the top of bay-leaf swags and a plain cartouche, or a coronet and foliage. The most notable aspect of this austere interior is the close grouping of the paintings on a single stretch of wall. This was to become a feature of 19th-century interiors, particularly in Denmark, when cramped symmetrical arrangements, often of miniature or very small pictures, would form a single decorative element. In this respect, the content of the painting becomes far less important than its size, shape and type of frame. Neo-classicism proper was introduced to Denmark in the late 18th century, mainly through the work of Nicolai Abraham Abildgaard, who in the mid-1790s designed rooms for Christian VII (*reg* 1766–1808) in a style varying from refined to extreme Neo-classicism; these included furniture.

7. BIEDERMEIER AND REVIVAL STYLES. During the 1790s the German Romantic artists Caspar David Friedrich and Philip Otto Runge arrived in Copenhagen. The type of frame they favoured was several stages removed from the strict Neo-classical style to the Empire or the Biedermeier type (see fig. 79); and so Abildgaard's influence did not generate a whole wave of Neo-classical framing in the idiom of the Swedish Gustavian style. The frames (79a and b) for the portraits of *The Merchant Joseph Raphael* (1824) and *Professor J. F. Schoun* (1836; both Copenhagen, Hirschsprungske Saml.) are both variants of the hollow frame with classical enrichment, which was an international style in the early 19th century. The heavy egg-and-dart, beading and *rais-de-coeur* of 79b became the predominant pattern in Denmark; it derives from an Italian source but probably arrived in Scandinavia via

79. Scandinavian Biedermeier, revival and early 19th-century artists' frames: (a) Danish Empire/Biedermeier scotia frame with oak leaves and acorns, 800×650×115 mm, original for C. W. Eckersberg's *The Merchant Joseph Raphael*, 1824 (Copenhagen, Hirschsprungske Samling); (b) Danish Neo-classical/Biedermeier scotia frame with egg-and-dart, 235×187×80 mm, original for Christian Albrecht Jensen's *Professor J. F. Schoun*, 1836 (Copenhagen, Hirschsprungske Samling); (c) Norwegian Empire/Biedermeier scotia frame with Greek scroll-work corners, 2000×2667×260 mm, original for J. C. C. Dahl's *View of Fortundalen*, 1836 (Oslo, Nasjonalgalleri); (d) Swedish Rococo Revival frame with asymmetric foliate corners (and crowned *fronton*), original for *King Leopold of the Belgians*, c. 1840s (Stockholm, Drottningholm Slott); (e) Danish artist-designed frame, 787×680×78 mm, original for Christen Købke's *Georg C. Hilker*, c. 1837, frame decorated by the sitter (Copenhagen, Statens Museum for Kunst)

German versions. It is extremely versatile, suitable for landscapes, portraits and still-lifes, although this particular example is perhaps overly heavy and wide for its painting. It is 'gilded' in metal leaf; virtually all Danish frames of the period use base metal rather than gold leaf—or, occasionally, lacquered silver. This is probably due to the impoverishment of Denmark and the loss of its colonial gold mines in the Napoleonic Wars; as in the Middle Ages, paint or an inferior metal replaced gilding. Another hollow classical frame (79c), a Norwegian version of the French Empire/Restoration frame, is decorated in the corners and along the small inner flat with applied composition ornament. Similar motifs were also used on Norwegian frames in the Rococo Revival style. A Swedish frame (79d) in the Rococo style is a slightly eccentric version of the original style, with scrolling foliage and flowers and a classical ormolu sight moulding. This pattern was applied en masse to the suite of portraits of heads of state in Drottningholm Slott, with individually made *frontons*.

Generally, however, the frames seen in ordinary homes of the 19th century were straight-sided hollow Empire/Biedermeier designs. Such types fitted into the low-ceilinged, informal Biedermeier room (see Thornton, 1984, no. 343), where a number of paintings in Empire frames, ranging from very large to very small, would be sandwiched between a decorative cornice and an elaborate carpet. In 19th-century Scandinavian interiors, paintings were often placed uncomfortably close to the ceiling, disrupting the internal balance even though careful ways of hanging (e.g. with ribbons, bows, sleeves hiding chains etc) were employed; they were also liable to the bunching already described. The interior in Peter Christian Thamsen Skovgaard's *Around the Tea Table at Vejby* (1843; Copenhagen, Stat. Mus. Kst.; Praz, 1964, no. 333) is a bareboarded, low-ceilinged living-room containing a bed, table and cupboard. On the walls are two groups of pictures, hung very close together in precise, symmetrical patterns. The frames are plain, rectangular or oval, and the paintings are indistinguishable, completely subordinated to the patterns made by their frames on the wall.

There was, however, an increasing reaction amongst artists against classicizing and Revival frames, and at an earlier point than in most European countries. But Denmark, because of its peripheral location, was influenced by the great centres of art, through visiting artists, while there is no evidence that they were in turn influenced by what they saw; although during the first 40 years of the 19th century, experiments were made with frames by Danish artists, these designs went unnoticed outside Scandinavia and had little impact within. This period includes most of the 'Golden Age' of Danish painting, characterized by its concern with light, colour and love of the country itself, qualities that were mirrored in the decorative arts by the use of bright colours and surface ornament, and pride in traditional skills such as woodcarving. These factors mingled most notably in the work of Christen Købke. He was a friend of the decorative painter Georg C. Hilker, and together they produced several frames for Købke's pictures that are innovative, attractive and yet still in the main tradition of Scandinavian ornamental painting. The frame (79e) on Købke's portrait of *Hilker* (c. 1837; Copenhagen, Stat. Mus. Kst) decorated by Hilker either to his own design or to that of Købke, has a painted gold border set between bands of black, with inner and outer gilt fillets. The border is embellished with a stylized run of elongated tulip-like flowers, set on an S-scrolled base and worked in a silver or greyish blue. It manages at once to reflect the Neo-classical style of the sculptor Bertel Thorvaldsen while rejecting the stock Empire moulding that was the descendant of the Neo-classical frame. It also follows on from the decorative borders seen in many Scandinavian interiors of the late 18th century and the early 19th on wall panels, ceramic stoves and friezes (see Thornton, 1984, nos 225, 230, 265, 306), which differ from other European painted borders in their stylized and slightly geometrical appearance. Købke and Hilker produced other frames together, notably the black and brown ornamental example for a *View of a Street in Copenhagen: Morning Light* (Copenhagen, Stat. Mus. Kst); and Købke also painted coloured borders on paintings that would otherwise have hung unframed (e.g.

the *Garden Steps at the Artist's Atelier* (c. 1841-5; Copenhagen, Stat. Mus. Kst). Constantin Hansen also painted borders on works that were not intended to be framed (e.g. *Kronborg Castle*, 1834; Copenhagen, Stat. Mus. Kst). This austere (and economic) approach to the frame fits with the bareness of Scandinavian interiors at this time. The comfort of the Biedermeier style was found mainly at the top of the social scale; and while relatively poor homes boasted collections of pictures hung in rather plain Empire frames, obviously the painted border was an acceptable alternative in keeping with the simple interior.

The middle classes rose with the growth in population of Norway, Denmark and Sweden, and they enthusiastically adopted the 19th-century revivals that were underway in Britain and France. The Rococo Revival was very important: the Swedish Rococo Revival style of the 1840s was a mainstream decorative trend throughout Scandinavia by the 1860s. The Amalienborg Slot of Christian IX (*reg* 1863–1906) in Copenhagen was decorated in the 1860s in the Danish version of the Rococo style; a contemporary drawing of the Blue Salon (see Thornton, 1984, fig. 3) shows gilt stucco palm and rocaille coving, Rococo Revival chairs and the original hanging of pictures. These still seem mainly to be in linear Empire frames, only one or two having corner decoration suggested. They are hung, however, in a typically Nordic arrangement: very symmetrically, in a formal pattern, and very close together. Two further illustrations (see Thornton, 1984, figs 409–10) show definite Rococo-style frames in a Swedish artist's house.

A couple of examples (see fig. 80a and b) illustrate the idiosyncratic and ornamental form this revival could take. Both have fundamentally linear, classical structures, but the earlier example (80b) has an upper swept Rococo moulding, which melts into a rounded rocaille corner with naturalistic lilies and roses, the sinuous lines of which anticipate the Art Nouveau style. The other (80a) is a hollow Empire profile with an important top moulding; the corners of this are embellished with realistic sunflowers, roses, convolvulus etc, all in the delicate idiom of a carved Rococo frame on a painted decoration by François Boucher. The style is very similar to frames by Ingres, apparently designed by the artist in the 1850s and 1860s; and to John Everett Millais's *Ophelia* (1851-2; London, Tate), which has a standard frame and corners of applied flowers extremely close to those featured in 80a. The flowers give a charm to the basic pine and composition carcass of the frame and suit the subjects of the period. A grandiose version of the style had also developed, as in the Hall of State, Drottningholm, for which Oscar I (*reg* 1844–59) ordered a new scheme of decoration in the 1840s beneath the original Baroque painted ceiling. This included diapered panels and overdoors and a suite of huge Rococo *fronton* frames (79d above) for a series of full-length portraits of contemporary monarchs; these gave rise to an outbreak of ceremonial portraits and frames that attempted to invest 19th- and 20th-century kings with the power and mystique of an absolute monarch (e.g. Oscar Björk's *Oscar II*, 1892, Stockholm, Drottningholm Slott). Both these ceremonial frames and the more charming, idiosyncratic flowered patterns reinforced the hold of revival Louis XIV and XV as fashionable styles. Salon

80. Late 19th-century Scandinavian frames: (a) Norwegian Neo-classical Revival frame with flower corners, 560×490×135 mm, original for Christian Krohg's *Braiding her Hair*, c. 1888 (Oslo, Nasjonalgalleri); (b) Finnish Rococo Revival frame with floral rocaille corners, 1130×1275×90 mm, original for Werner Holmberg's *Road in Hame: A Hot Summer Day*, 1860 (Helsinki, Athenaeum Art Museum); (c) Swedish bay-leaf torus frame, original for Ernst Josephson's *The Cheat*, 1886 (Stockholm, Prins Eugens Waldemarsudde); (d) Norwegian stylized leaf torus frame, 997×750×90 mm, original for Karl Lochen's *The Actor B. K.*, 1886 (Oslo, Nasjonalgalleri); (e) Norwegian Baroque Revival frame with gadrooning in bronze leaf, 910×736×110 mm, applied to Edvard Munch's *The Scream*, 1893 (Oslo, Nasjonalgalleri)

paintings in all the Scandinavian countries began to wear the brassy composition forms of these frames like a uniform; such works, from the 1850s to the 1890s, can be found in the national art galleries of the four chief Nordic countries. The relative ornateness of this type of frame encouraged a corresponding richness of ornament on the still-popular Empire type so that, from the 1870s to the 1890s, the profiles of linear hollow frames became a complex series of steps, fillets, astragals and cavettos, each of which is encrusted with a run of busy composition ornament. One Finnish frame (Helsinki, Sinebrychoff A. Col.) even has a small burnished hollow, only the corners of which are sanded.

Complex forms from Italian Baroque prototypes followed these eclectic French patterns in the 1880s, and even examples of the Spanish Herrera style (see §VIII, 4 below) were revived. From these were taken more simplified and attractive types that bear the mark of the artist. The frame (80c) for Ernst Josephson's *The Cheat* has a carved bay-leaf torus, with blurred contours and a calm

stolidity very different from the busy ornament of some Salon frames. It shows the influence of the English Arts and Crafts Movement and of the heavy Breton and primitive shapes that characterize Paul Gauguin's work in the 1880s. In a more sharply designed frame, however, it was a respectably conventional classical model, which was later used to reframe Munch's *Spring* (1889; Oslo, N.G.). This was first exhibited (1892) in a white-painted, plain moulding frame with a slight reverse rebate (see Rosenblum, fig. 9). Many of Munch's works were originally in simple white frames—flattened toruses, shallow hollows or slightly projecting ogee mouldings. Hung on dark gallery walls, these white frames emphasize the luminescent settings of Munch's early works and blend with the spare and modern interiors or the open northern landscapes depicted. They may well have been directly inspired by Seurat's white-painted frames (see §III, 12 above); Munch had visited Paris in 1885 and 1889 and may well have seen Seurat's paintings in their frames. Comparing *Spring* in the present gilt frame (above) with its own white frame, it is evident that Munch's choice is preferable. The gold frame is deadening and cannot illuminate a painting already saturated in light; its spiky pattern conflicts with the free brushwork and its classical references cannot expand on the inherent symbolism of the subject.

The most frequently used frame (80e) for Munch's work in the Nasjonalgalleri, Oslo, also appears on Christian Krohg's *Sick Girl* (1880–81) and Eilif Peterssen's portrait of *Locken* (1885) in the same museum. It is a chunky, simply cut, classical architectural pattern, suitable to most subjects and relatively straightforward to produce. The enriched gadrooning, with its roughly cut-out shapes, has an emphatic perspectival effect on any subject, giving depth and focal strength. It is particularly striking on Munch's *Ashes* (c. 1894) and the *Sick Child* (1885–6). In *The Scream* the violent diagonal recession and wild undulations of sea and sky gain nothing from the Mannerist rhythms of the frame, and one of Munch's flattened torus frames in black or dark blue might have been more suitable.

Another variation (80d) on the simple torus frame, popular in the 1880s throughout Scandinavia as a compromise between the artist's design and the Rococo Revival or Neo-classical pattern, is that surrounding Karl Lochen's *The Actor B. K.* (1886; Oslo, N.G.). The coarse, stylized cut has again something of the feel of an Arts and Crafts model. The portrait is loosely painted in tones of black, silver and gold; and it is unfortunate that, once again, the avoidance of real gold leaf has occasioned a clash between the subtle golden tones of the background and the unmodulated brassy glow of the frame.

8. LATE 19TH AND 20TH CENTURIES. During the 1880s and 1890s, Scandinavian artists were beginning to make their mark in international circles. Many Swedish painters, such as Ernst Josephson, Anders Zorn and Carl Larsson, worked in Paris and were influenced by Impressionism; and the Danes created their own equivalent to the artist community at Pont-Aven in the fishing village of Skagen, where Michael Ancher and Anna Ancher, P. S. Krøyer and the Norwegian Krogh painted *en plein air*. In 1890 Jens Ferdinand Willumsen met Gauguin at

Pont-Aven and under his influence experimented with wood-carving and various other crafts. He was also introduced to Symbolism and Synthetism, and one of the fruits of this was the extraordinary secular altarpiece, *Jotunheim* (1892–3; Frederikssund, Willumsens Mus.). The frame of polished carved wood, with stylized lateral columns, its plinths and capitals reduced to basic geometric forms, is more notable than the mountainscape in the painting. The lower edge of the 'entablature' projects down across the picture surface in a series of peaks, like the mountain-tops; these also reappear above the entablature in a painted metal silhouette mimicking the top range in the painting. On each side, the upper and lower rails jut out to support two pierced, enamelled copper panels decorated with symbolic personifications. The whole work, over 1 m high and 2.75 m across, is a strange, ornamental filigree of pattern, which manages to unite a high degree of abstraction with an esoteric allegory. It has something in common with the work of Jan Toorop (*see* §V, 6 above). Nothing like this colourful, cut-out, almost medievally decorative treatment of a frame seems to have been attempted before. A rather more restrained Willumsen frame (see fig. 81a) surrounds a painting showing the northern sun hanging over another desolate mountainscape. The frame, with its simple, two-tiered format, carved projecting E-shapes along the upper level and decorative, hand-gouged chequered effect, is self-consciously handmade in the Arts and Crafts style. It was possibly produced as well as designed by Willumsen and its hand-carved

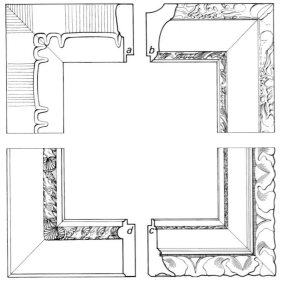

81. Scandinavian Art Nouveau and artists' frames: (a) Danish artist-designed frame with 'peaked' moulding and engraved 'sun-rays' decoration, original for Jens Ferdinand Willumsen's *Mountain Landscape with Rising Sun* (Oslo, Nasjonalgalleri); (b) Danish scotia profile frame, 435×616×95 mm, made by P. C. Damborg for Julius Paulsen's *Nocturne*, 1899 (Copenhagen, Hirschsprungske Samling); (c) Swedish stylized leaf frame, 768×577×140 mm, one of a pair, original for Anders Zorn's *Jacques Thiel*, 1890 (Stockholm, Thielska Galleri); (d) Danish artist-designed frame with shell ornament, 370×470×115 mm, original for P. S. Krøyer's *At the Grocer's Store when There Is No Fishing*, 1882 (Copenhagen, Hirschsprungske Samling)

roughness is more satisfying than the iron-like perfection of the revival frames (fig. 80 above). Another Willumsen frame, on his *After the Storm* (1905; Oslo, N.G.), is carved in the hollow with Art Nouveau poppies and broken lilies in ebonized and parcel-gilt shallow relief.

In contrast to Willumsen's icy suns and desolate landscapes is a tranquil, misty *Nocturne* (1899; Copenhagen, Hirschsprungske Saml.) by Julius Paulsen. The frame is similarly far from Willumsen's Arts and Crafts simplicity; it uses the new materials of the industrial age to create a contemporary style: a simple, machined and very smoothly 'gilded' hollow frame, to which two runs of composition ornament were applied (81b). The outer moulding was designed to reproduce the softened forms of aged or bluntly cut wood-carving, while the amorphous flower, pod and cloudlike shapes echo the rounded lines of the painting. Like Willumsen's frame, this shows a concern for unity of abstract form and appropriateness of mood, both of which are achieved by this composition frame. An analogous use of composition ornament to express a new style and complement the painting is evident in the frame (81c) for Anders Zorn's *Jacques Thiel* (1890; Stockholm, Thielska Gal.). It is not possible to say whether artist, owner or gallery was responsible for this pattern, which shows a stylized, Art Nouveau version of a leaf edge, versatile and appropriate to a range of subjects; but the marriage of portrait and frame is satisfyingly close in terms of resonance of form and tone. The use of composition for these Art Nouveau patterns in the 1890s shows how far from the conventional Empire frame choice had moved, and how stylistic innovations had been subsumed by the technological. Like Holman Hunt in England, who learnt from his carved wooden frame designs how to use composition constructively, the earlier one-off frames helped to revolutionize the designs used on mass-produced frames.

The Dane P. S. Krøyer was another artist-designer who, along with Willumsen, helped to achieve this. Examples of his work (81d, 82a and b) show the range of his decorative skill. His travels exposed him to a whole range of influences—the Impressionists and their *plein-air* techniques; the restricted colour harmonies of both Velázquez and Whistler; and the vast spectrum of artist-designed frames that were on display in London. One of his earlier frames (81d) is a broad, flat plate, 'gilded' on the wood, to which a wreath of composition shells has been applied around the sight. It may be of the same date as the painting or slightly later. It shares characteristics with early Pre-Raphaelite frames, such as Millais's flat plate frames with their olive-leaf, lily or ivy decoration, and is also similar to Arthur Hughes's flat, ivy-wreathed frames. The shells are attributes of the fishermen in the painting, providing an appropriate, if over-assertive, ornament. Krøyer's later frames are more successful, and he used runs of attributive shell ornament more subtly. A shamrock motif was favoured, for example painted in tones of brown on the flat of a conventional *cassetta* (82a). The stylized upright repeat pattern of the trefoil has affinities with the abstracted floral motifs of, for example, Charles Rennie Mackintosh and C. F. A. Voysey; it is also related to the stencil patterns used by Carl Larsson in his country house and later publicized in *A Home* (1899), his book of

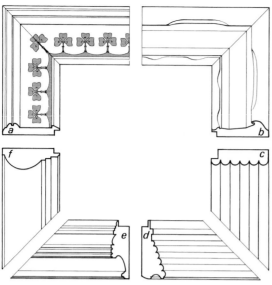

82. Scandinavian Art Nouveau and artists' frames: (a) Danish artist's frame painted with shamrocks, 394×500×100 mm, original for P. S. Krøyer's *Artist and his Wife with the Writer Otto Benzon, Skagen*, 1893 (Copenhagen, Hirschsprungske Samling); (b) Danish artist-designed frame with undulating mouldings, 1347×1867×150 mm, original for P. S. Krøyer's *Summer Evening at the Beach, Skagen*, 1899 (Copenhagen, Hirschsprungske Samling); (c) Swedish architrave profile reeded frame, 1568×1067×90 mm, original for Eugène Jansson's *City at Sunset*, 1897 (Stockholm, Thielska Galleri); (d) Swedish canted profile reeded frame, 1490×2007×93 mm, original for Eugène Jansson's *Nocturne*, 1901 (Stockholm, Thielska Galleri); (e) Swedish compound profile moulding frame, w. 127 mm, original for Oscar Björck's *Verner von Heidenstam*, 1900 (Stockholm, Prins Eugens Waldemarsudde); (f) Swedish cushion frame with stepped flat, 2100×1100×100 mm, original for Carl Larsson's *Signe Thiel*, 1900 (Stockholm, Thielska Galleri)

watercolours (originals in Stockholm, Nmus.). It is a cheap and effective way of producing a unique frame, and the hand-crafted aspects of the work are reinforced. Possibly Krøyer was aping Whistler's hand-painted signature frames, possibly just indulging the Danish tradition of painting every surface. Unfortunately, however, he did not use the very decorative result as Whistler or Maurice Denis would have used it: the effect of this type of ornament is inherently flattening; it is the reverse of a gadrooned moulding, which leads the eye into the painting and emphasizes depth and perspective. Krøyer's shamrocks need to be matched with a decorative, abstracted image in a shallow space, like Rossetti's or Denis's ornamented figures. The interior scene of 82a is too illusionistic to bear such a frame, and the effect is claustrophobic and busy. Krøyer's *Summer Evening at the Beach, Skagen* (1899; Copenhagen, Hirschsprungske Saml.), however, has an extremely successful plain-gilt *cassetta* frame (82b) with inclined central flat and raised ogee and torus mouldings. It has curved sections at intervals along the top outer torus moulding and the inner ogee, giving a rhythmic, undulating line to both and providing a more complex, faceted surface to catch and reflect light. The idea and something of the effect recall the wave-and-ripple mouldings of 17th-century Dutch frames and also the linear geometric

ornaments produced by Ford Madox Brown, Dante Gabriel Rossetti, Albert Moore and Whistler. The blond gilding echoes the cool gold of the sinking sun, the twilit sand and the clothes of the two figures, and the undulations of the moulding repeat the lines of the waves on the shore.

In the 1890s and in the early 20th century Swedish artists were also drawn to distinctive modern frames with no academic associations—often in the linear mould of Krøyer's design (82b). Many of the leading Swedish figures spent time in Paris, where they would have been exposed to the paintings and frames of the Impressionists and of Whistler. This is probably important for the genesis of the reeded frame in Sweden in the late 1880s and 1890s. Hollow reeded frames were used on works by Eugène Jansson: for example that on the *City at Sunset* (1897; Stockholm, Thielska Gal.; 82c) bears a great similarity to the reeded carcass of a Rossetti frame, but this may be coincidental. This was generally a fertile period for frame design in Scandinavia, and indirect influence from France may well have triggered many ideas fortuitously close to the sources of the Impressionists' ideas. Versions of Degas's reeded cushion frame appear, for example, on pictures by Louis Sparre and Gerhard Munthe. The solid bands of close linear mouldings (82c and d) are extremely simple and very effective. Although decorative, they do tend to enhance the illusionary space of a painting, since the effect of straight lines joined on four sides by mitred corners is of a perspective tunnel leading inwards. The result is very suitable for Jansson's 'blue' landscapes.

An unusual profile of half torus and quarter cavetto is outlined by a series of fillets and astragals, with three fillets as a central feature (82e). This mixture of small round and square mouldings is again reminiscent of frames by Brown and Rossetti and also of Albert Moore's earlier designs. It provides a strong setting with interesting light effects for Oscar Björck's portrait, a silhouette against a golden sunset sky, imitating both the chiaroscuro and the golden tones of the painting. The profile of the frame (82f) on a portrait by Carl Larsson has sloughed off all applied mouldings save for a restrained series of steps at the sight. The main section is a cushion with a stepped cavetto sight; this provides a bold, plain, barlike setting for the portrait. It has affinities with both Björck's frame and the flattened torus mouldings used by Munch. The columnar effect suits the classically conceived, full-length figure of Signe Thiel, whose static pose and fluted skirt suggest a kore; it also echoes the background of multiple vertical lines of the door, commode and wallpaper. This type of frame was one of the most satisfactory designs of the late 19th century and provided the basis for numerous subtle variations during the 20th. It is an international pattern and adapts to almost every genre of painting.

Larsson's works often contain internal evidence of domestic framing and hanging; the watercolour *A Home: Cosy Corner* from his book *A Home* shows his sitting-room, with white painted Gustavian furniture, a painted ceramic stove and a wall embellished with painted outline panels. On this wall is an original gilt *fronton* Gustavian mirror and a close-set group of two large, white-mounted prints in minimal gilt mouldings, two tiny, black-framed oval miniatures and another print in a close blue frame (the last three are hung from red ribbons). Between mirror and prints is a decorative painted panel beneath the window, edged in a border like the rest of the panelling, with a classical urn above trailing pendent ribbons. The combination of all these reflects the contemporary mixture of modern, antique, traditional and artist-designed frames, together with such typically Scandinavian techniques as ornamental painting and such customs as the close hanging of pictures (see 1986 exh. cat., no. 52a–d and 52h). Larsson's painting of his wife's bedroom contains one picture, a tiny flower painting in a wide gilt plate frame, totally unornamented and with rails the breadth of the picture. This type of frame, like the torus moulding on his portrait of *Signe Thiel* (82f), was widespread throughout Europe and provided an economic way of isolating a painting from its surroundings: instead of decoration, width was used. The finish was also economical, with gold leaf often applied directly to the wood in the style of the Pre-Raphaelites. Krøyer used this type of frame with one or two rows of applied ornament (e.g. with an outer run of palmettes and shells on *Arcanglone*, 1890; Copenhagen, Hirschsprungske Saml.). Zorn used separated square 'stud' or nailhead mouldings on his frame of an *Algerian Woman* (1887; Stockholm, Prins Eugens Waldemarsudde); he was one of the most travelled of Scandinavian artists and may well have been influenced in England by the many contemporary styles of frame being produced.

The Scandinavian artist to make greatest use of the Art Nouveau idiom was Akseli Gallen-Kallela. He had studied in Paris and spent a lot of time there during the 1880s. He was skilled at wood- and stone-carving, metalwork and painting, and in designing stained glass, architecture, furniture, graphic works and book illustrations. He also created cycles of frescoes, and for all his paintings designed decorative borders, wooden frames and ornamental mounts or inner frames. He may have produced the wooden frames himself. One of his earliest and most striking works is a secular triptych 'altarpiece' frame (see fig. 83a); this is for the second version of the so-called Aino Triptych (1891; Helsinki, Athenaeum A. Mus.), which depicts three stages of a Finnish myth or folk tale from the *Kalevala*, a collection of such tales made earlier in the 19th century. Gallen-Kallela had spent his honeymoon in Karelia, in the east of Finland, in search of the roots and settings of his national mythology; when he designed this second frame for the Aino story, the carved ornaments and symbols he used were those he saw as being 'Karelian', or purely Finnish, while the structure gave to a traditional myth the numinous mystery and power of a medieval retable. It is an extremely strong and effective frame, with its blocky rectangular forms and shallowly carved or gouged-out motifs. Two panels in the broad central mullions hold descriptions of the story, a device used by Holman Hunt, and (in the form of a poem attached to the frame) by Rossetti and Whistler.

In 1893 Gallen-Kallela painted the *Great Black Woodpecker (Wilderness)* (1891; Helsinki, priv. col.), set in a Karelian landscape; his technique was changing to a more decorative and textured style, and, like a tapestry, to which the picture was compared, the artist supplied it with an ornamental border (83b), further flattening and stylizing the scene. This border is made of a geometrically simplified running fir-branch pattern, sprinkled with white conelike

83. Scandinavian Symbolist frames: (a) left wing (detail) of artist-designed, inscribed triptych frame with folk art motifs, centre panel 1530×1530 mm, wings 1530×770 mm, w. 220 mm, by Akseli Gallen-Kallela for the Aino Triptych, 1891 (Helsinki, Athenaeum Art Museum); (b) Finnish integral frame painted with stylized pine branches, 1440×890×105 mm, by Akseli Gallen-Kallela for *Great Black Woodpecker (Wilderness)*, 1891 (Helsinki, private collection); (c) Finnish artist-designed frame with stylized leaves, 2700×1560×105 mm, by Akseli Gallen-Kallela for *Waterfall at Mäntykoski*, 1892–4 (Helsinki, private collection)

motifs, which eventually became almost emblematic of Finland. Interwoven with the branches, various animals pause and peer. The whole margin is given the stylization common to Symbolism and Art Nouveau at the end of the 19th century in a technique that is unmistakably of the period; the placing of the animals against the cruciform pine needles is, however, related to the densely painted borders of medieval illuminated manuscripts or, even further back, to Scandinavian zoomorphic carvings. The *Waterfall at Mäntykoski* (1892–4; Helsinki, priv. col.) is in the same half-Realist, half-decorative/Symbolist style as the *Great Black Woodpecker*. Still tapestry-like in its textured brushwork and slightly flattened space, the painting has been given a coloured frame (83c), decorated like a textile design by C. F. A. Voysey. The mystical force and music of the waterfall is expressed by five golden lines drawn from top to bottom of the picture, joining the two rails of the frame and making the entire subject into a decorative oblong harp. The frame itself is blue and is decorated with repeated leaf- or petal-like tassels in the style of Maurice Denis's painted flower frames, but through the agency of these 'golden wires' it becomes the wooden case of the harp, glossing the subject of the picture and supplying the Symbolist aspect that is otherwise merely suggested.

In 1916 Gallen-Kallela painted his *Self-portrait for the Uffizi Gallery* (Tarvaspää, Gallen-Kallela Mus.). His head and shoulders are like a classical bust, and the artist has enriched them in another retable-like or aedicular frame (see fig. 84a). With its greatly simplifed trabeate structure, tapered pilasters and anonymous order, it is like the monolithic entrance to an Egyptian tomb. Its memorial aspect is emphasized by the white paint and ebonized finish, and it is reminiscent of, and possibly influenced by, the aedicular frames used by Franz von Stuck (*see* §VI, 7 above). A large collection of Gallen-Kallela's drawings, including designs for frames, are held in the Gallen-Kallela Museum in Tarvaspää; they show his progression towards the classical restraint of his last frames. There are sketches of mouldings, corners of frames and numbers of profiles or sections, which surpass even Holman Hunt's sketches for frames in their thoroughness and accuracy.

A late example of a historicizing design (84b) was made in 1923 by Harald Slott-Møller for his portrait of *Sigrid Undset* (Oslo, priv. col.), the leading contemporary Norwegian author. In a letter to William Nygaard, Slott-Møller made it clear that he saw the design of the frame, with its revivalist zoomorphic and knot ornaments, as being in the same style as the portrait and as necessary to emphasize its character and composition. Similar pastiches of Viking ornament had been used in Britain on late 19th-century

scenes taken from Scandinavian history, but they fell out of fashion at the beginning of the 20th century. In Scandinavia, however, fashion and liking were tied to nationalism and the continuing struggle for independence. In this context, ancient indices of power and freedom became loaded with significance; hence the two bands of carved ornament on Slott-Møller's otherwise plain frame.

The Norwegian Gerhard Munthe was similarly infected with passion for his country's traditional styles; he studied the 18th-century art of *rosemaling* and produced numerous brightly tinted watercolours with integral painted borders based on the motifs and colours of old Norwegian art (Oslo, N.G.; see 1986 exh. cat., no. 63a–e). Otherwise 20th-century Scandinavian frames were much like those in the rest of Europe: very simple shapes such as flat plate frames, ogee, hollow, chamfered and flat *cassetta* frames. Finishes were also straightforward: dull gold, stained wood, coloured or white paint. Only rarely did an interesting example emerge, for example on Per Stenius's *Composition* (1951), a black plate frame overpainted with ochre squiggles.

BIBLIOGRAPHY

A. Lindblom: *La Peinture gothique en Suède et en Norvège* (Stockholm, 1916)

R. Hauglid and L. Grodecki: *Norway: Paintings from the Stave Churches* (New York, 1955)

M. Praz: *An Illustrated History of Interior Decoration from Pompeii to Art Nouveau* (London, 1964)

S. Sitwell: *Great Palaces* (London, 1964)

L. E. Plahter and U. Plahter: 'The Technique of a Group of Norwegian Gothic Oil Paintings', *Conservation of Paintings and the Graphic Arts: Lisbon, 1972*, pp. 131–8

V. Poulsen: *Danish Painting and Sculpture* (Copenhagen, 1976)

R. Rosenblum, ed.: *Edvard Munch: Symbols and Images* (Washington, DC, 1978)

L. Rangström, K. Skeri and E. Westin: *Skokloster: The Castle and Collections* (Balsta, 1980)

U. Plahter: 'Methods of Scientific Investigations and Art Historical Interpretations', *Safeguarding of Mediaeval Altarpieces and Woodcarvings in Churches and Museums*, ed. A. Andersson and P. Tångeborg (Stockholm, 1981), pp. 105–15

P. Thornton: *Authentic Decor: The Domestic Interior, 1620–1920* (London, 1984)

Danish Painting: The Golden Age (exh. cat., London, N.G., 1984)

J. Weibull, C. F. Palmstierna and B. Tarras-Wahlberg: *The Monarchy in Sweden* (Stockholm, 1986)

Dreams of a Summer Night: Scandinavian Painting at the Turn of the Century (exh. cat., London, Hayward Gal., 1986)

Speglar på Skokloster (Stockholm, 1987)

M. Malmanger: *One Hundred Years of Norwegian Painting* (Oslo, 1988)

K. Varnedoe: *Northern Light* (New Haven and London, 1988)

Agnes og Harald Slott-Møller (exh. cat., Copenhagen, Kstforen., 1988)

Christian IV and Europe (exh. cat., ed. S. Heiberg; Hillerød, Frederiksborg Slot, 1988)

U. G. Johnsson: *Gripsholm* (Stockholm, 1989)

P. Suhonen: *Designed by Gallen-Kallela* (Tarvaspää, 1989)

G. Alm, ed.: *Pictures from Drottningholm* (Stockholm, 1990)

Highlights in the National Gallery Collections (Oslo, 1990)

Stockholms Slott (Stockholm, 1991)

Walls, Walls: Give him Walls! (exh. cat., Tarvaspää, Gallen-Kallela Mus., 1991)

U. Plahter: 'Norwegian Altar Frontals: A Mediaeval Panel Construction Suitable for Dendrochronology?', *Dendrochronology and the Investigation of Buildings: Proceedings of an International Seminar at the Academy of Science and Letters: Oslo, 1992*, pp. 62–70

G. Alm: *Carl Hårleman och den Svenska rokokon* (Lund, 1993)

P. Cannon-Brookes: 'Picture Framing: A Swedish Baroque Frame in the Design of Nicodemus Tessin the Younger', *Int. J. Mus. Mgmt & Cur.*, xiii (1994), pp. 106–7

84. Scandinavian 20th-century frames: (a) Finnish artist-designed aedicular frame with tapering pilasters painted black and white, 660×596 mm, by Akseli Gallen-Kallela for *Self-portrait for the Uffizi Gallery*, 1916 (Tarvaspää, Gallen-Kallela Museum); (b) Danish carved wooden frame with lateral columns and bands of zoomorphic ornament, 930×1050 mm, by Harald Slott-Møller for *Sigrid Undset*, 1923 (Oslo, private collection)

Le Soleil et l'étoile du nord: La France et la Suède au XVIIIème siècle (exh. cat., ed. P. Grate; Paris, Grand Pal., 1994)

For further bibliography *see* §I above.

VIII. Spain.

1. Medieval. 2. Renaissance. 3. Mannerist. 4. Herrera style. 5. Baroque. 6. Rococo. 7. Neo-classical and early 19th century. 8. Late 19th and 20th centuries.

1. MEDIEVAL. Spain was conquered by the Muslims in AD 711; by the 10th century it had an Islamic majority (the north remaining Christian), and only in the 13th century did the Christians reverse the position, fully reconquering the country by 1492. The effect on the applied arts was particularly great, and for a long time borders of all sorts often displayed geometrical or Moresque elements, separate from the generally shared ornamental vocabulary of the rest of Europe.

(i) Early altar frontals. (ii) Gothic retables.

(i) Early altar frontals. The earliest framed panel paintings are identical in style and structure to those from the rest of Europe. They were at first altar frontals with the traditional arrangement of a central figure in a mandorla, flanked by two tiered panels of saints etc, each division marked by a decorative border. (For an example, late 11th–12th century, with zigzag scroll and flower decoration on flats, see Post, i, fig. 49.) While these first altarpieces were being produced, Byzantine and Carolingian ivories were imported in great numbers, and northern European influences came from goods entering the ports of Navarre, Castile and Asturias.

Spain was thus at a confluence of stylistic currents, including those of Islam and, from the 11th century, those brought by the Burgundian Cluniac orders and by Lombard artists. French ties became especially important: during the 12th century France was sovereign in Catalonia, while the House of Barcelona ruled Provence, and the pilgrim route from Gascony to Santiago de Compostela developed into a conduit of mutual influence. French or Rhenish altar frontals of enamel on silver and gold were imported by the Cluniac monasteries and copied in paint and gilt or silvered stucco by poorer foundations. These were given running Moresque decorations on their borders, including abstract ornaments and heraldic beast medallions, as in the frontals of S Climente de Taüll and Ginestarre de Cardós (both Barcelona, Mus. A. Catalunya) and of S Pere de Ripoll (Vic, Mus. Episc.). They also had Italianate motifs of bosses and rosettes, and scrolled decorations paralleling French manuscript illuminations. The frontals and their successors—the rear altar-rail supporting a Crucifix, which became first a predella to the Cross, and then a small retable behind it—were brilliantly coloured, like the enamels they mimicked. Such polychromy remained an important feature of both fine and applied art, seen for example in painted furniture, mosaics, statues and imported fabrics.

The same love of opulence resulted in the use of gilded, diapered grounds for panel painting in Spain well into the 15th century, when realistic backgrounds had long replaced them in the rest of Europe. This, together with the great size and intricacy of late medieval altarpieces, added enormously to their cost; perhaps because of it, retables

85. Integral frame for the Altar of Encamp, from Andorra, 13th century (Barcelona, Museu d'Art Catalunya)

of the 15th and 16th centuries especially, unlike other European altarpieces, have panel grounds or areas of the frame painted chrome yellow instead of gilt, particularly on shutters or the backs of free-standing examples. On frontals of the 12th and 13th centuries there are painted bands imitating precious stones as a similar economy. The centre/corner roundels that decorate the wide, flat frames are concave, rather than convex like those of 13th-century Italian frontals and retables, although they reproduce the cabochon jewels of the enamelled altarpieces (see Bazin, 1929, p. 47). Examples of both bands and roundels can be seen on the frontal of *St Andrew* from Sagós (late 12th century; Vic, Mus. Episc.) and the Altar of Encamp (13th century; Barcelona, Mus. A. Catalunya; see fig. 85). The latter is a true altar, with two lateral panels forming a box-shape with the frontal. It is illustrative of the enormous quantity of Spanish religious art that examples like this have survived, as they do nowhere else in Europe, except perhaps in Scandinavia.

(ii) Gothic retables.

(a) Establishment of the form. (b) Development.

(a) Establishment of the form. Though Spain continually trailed by a generation or so the stylistic evolution of the rest of Europe, Gothic architectural forms gradually appeared, at first in carved furniture decorations, with the adoption of arcading, clustered colonnettes, gables and lacey pierced geometrical designs that married Gothic tracery to abstract Islamic forms. Frames, like architecture, were slow to change, retaining a Romanesque style modified by Moorish elements. A late 13th-century frontal (Barcelona, Mus. A. Catalunya) shows the Romanesque three-part configuration with a central Christ in a mandorla, the flat border still combining four Moorish geometrical, heraldic and abstract floral motifs. It was not until the early 14th century that ogee-arched tops (e.g. the

Aragonese *St Peter Martyr*) and barbed quatrefoil medallions (e.g. *St Domingo*; both Barcelona, Mus. A. Catalunya) appeared on the same tripartite retables. Similarly, the peaked-gabled, pentagonal altarpiece of early 13th-century Florence and Siena did not appear in Spain until the 14th century, as in *St Christopher* (Castilian school; Madrid, Prado), where the flat frame is still painted with Arabic lions and castles (for León and Castile), and the inner divisions are scrolled in white on blue in Moorish style.

Even the established Gothic style was—especially outside Catalonia—not only late compared with its Italian and French equivalents, but also inseparably intermingled with Islamic motifs. The Reliquary of Piedra (1390; Madrid, Real Acad. Hist.) is a striking example of fully fledged Mudéjar ornament (or Muslim Gothic art produced under Christian rule): a shallow cupboard of triptych form, with low-relief carved borders beneath a deep cornice, it has eight-pointed Moresque stars and interlaced lozenges around painted panels in trefoil arches (comparable to the Westminster Retable; see fig. 39a above). In the cornice portraits of Christ, the Apostles and saints are framed by intricate Saracenic cusped arches, and the whole is picked out in gold and colour with bands of arabesques. Chests and other pieces of furniture are lavish with similar motifs, including pierced interlacing in the form of polygons, stylized daisies and abstract shapes of interlocking curves, which would be picked up and used in the fretwork canopies and tracery infills of the larger Gothic retables.

The gabled silhouette associated with Cimabue and Duccio probably arrived in Spain, if belatedly, through commercial and political connections with Tuscany. Florence had regular shipping lines to Mallorca, Barcelona and Valencia by the late 13th century, and as Barcelona grew as rich and influential as Bruges or Venice, so it adopted a form of the democratic Florentine political structure. Artistic and ornamental influences were intensified by such ties. The art of Barcelona was affected in the political aspects of production and patronage by the introduction of this alien democratic system. During the 14th century sculptors and woodworkers were simultaneously blended and divided into the guilds of carvers and cabinetmakers according to what they produced; rules of practice were enforced, as in the rest of Europe, and the hierarchical progression from apprentice through journeyman to master was set down. With the introduction of Florentine democracy, the middle classes moved rapidly to positions of power, and the newly reconstructed carvers' guild of Barcelona found their fellow guilds to be some of their richest and most influential patrons.

Enormous quantities of retables were commissioned for the chapels of the guildsmen's adoptive churches, a custom that was widespread in Europe but nowhere to the extent of the rich mercantile towns of Spain. The wealth of these bodies of artisans, as of the Church, whose power was backed by the Crown, provided a purse deep enough to finance the Spanish taste for frames of unbelievable flamboyance. Examples of altar frames commissioned by guilds (in both cases by the Guild of Cobblers for the chapel of St Mark, Barcelona Cathedral) surround the retable of *St Mark* (1437; Manresa, S María), attributed to Bernat Martorell, and a fragment of Jaume Huguet's Retable of the Shoemakers' Guild (see Post, vii, fig. 1).

These are also early types of the so-called trophy frame: the former has shoes painted in the pinnacles of the dividing pilasters, echoing the shoes woven into the saint's chasuble in the central panel of the altarpiece; the latter retains a gilt and stuccoed frame panel on each side of the surviving painting, interesting not only for the shoes painted in lozenges in the centres but also for the integration shown by the mid-15th century of Mudéjar motifs (Islamic bauble-shaped medallions with Gothic cusps). This is a long way from the Castilian *St Christopher* retable of the previous century (see above), where the Florentine silhouette was decorated with inappropriate and undigested Moorish emblems.

Italian connections began to supersede those with France in the 14th and 15th centuries—the Crown of Aragon ruled Sicily, Corsica, Sardinia and Naples and traded as frequently with Genoa as with Florence. The south-east corner of Spain grew extremely prosperous and was influenced artistically especially by Florence and Siena. Therefore, when Gothic frames finally ousted Romanesque, it was often in the Italian form seen on medieval Tuscan or Emilian altarpieces. A simple 14th-century gabled closing triptych in Tortosa Cathedral has leaflike crockets in the Italianate manner, while the altarpiece of *St Mark Manresa* (1346; Manresa, S María) by Arnau Bassa is an impressive tripartite polyptych, with painted figured pilasters ending in high pinnacles between its gables. The styles of these two altarpieces bring together, in the compass of a few years, half a century's evolution of Italian altar frames and show the eclecticism of choice possible in a country whose fashions continually trailed behind their neighbours'. Dilatoriness, and consequent imitation rather than innovation, do not mean that Spanish work lacked individuality. Spanish frames are almost always instantly recognizable as such, even where they copy. The Bassa Altarpiece, for instance, its body that of a typical Italian polyptych of the 1320s to 1340s, already has the square crockets on its gables and pinnacles and the wide blossom or flamelike finials characteristic of Spanish retables. In the second half of the 14th century, when Italian altarpieces were developing into cross-sections of High Gothic cathedrals (with predella or 'crypt', nave, aisles and upper tiers or 'clerestory'), the Spanish versions acquired their most idiosyncratic feature. As large and many-panelled as Italian retables, with arched and gabled outlines, crockets, pinnacles and finials like the most elaborate examples of International Gothic, they were now enclosed by carved, painted or stuccoed backboards and surrounded at the top and sides by a wide canted outer frame called a *guardapolvo* or dust guard. This combination protects the delicate filigree and varied silhouette of the upper retable; it also replaces the huge lateral buttresses needed to support the larger Italian polyptychs.

On account of the continued authority of the Catholic Church in Spain, upholding the sanctity of religious houses, preventing as far as possible the pillage of war and forbidding the sale of church treasures, and also because of the scale of patronage in Spain, many more of these retables, complete with both inner and outer frames, remain *in situ* than in other countries. Even where they have entered museums, the main structure with predella and *guardapolvo* nearly always remains intact, and only the ancillary elements are lost—the two lateral painted doors on either side of the altar, beneath the predella, and the altar frontal that 'joins' these two doors visually and stands forward of the plane of the retable itself. From the mid-14th century, however, antependia began to be replaced on the altar by panels of leather or embroidery.

A comparatively early example of the main structure is the Retable of Sigena (Barcelona, Mus. A. Catalunya), attributed to Jaime Serra and Pedro Serra, a characteristic example of the form from Catalonia, which is rich in such altarpieces. There are five vertical divisions, with a large central panel of the Virgin beneath the crowning image of (as almost always) a Crucifixion; the latter is often shaped, as here, in a stepped gable. (The top lateral panels are arched.) The divisions are separated vertically by plain wooden pilasters and horizontally on the side tiers by gilded geometrically patterned bands into which the pictures occasionally intrude. The predella has cusped segmental arches; the main arches and gables have enriched square crockets and square acanthus finials, and the pinnacles are slender with tiny crockets. Both *guardapolvos* and backboard are carved with stylized roses echoing those painted in the Virgin's hand, and the *guardapolvos* extend downward at the sides only to the moulding above the predella and are cut away there in a characteristic shouldered arch.

(b) Development. The Spanish love of opulence and ornament soon began to influence the retable, once the form outlined above was established. Other altarpieces by Pedro Serra (e.g. retables of the *Virgin and Child with Angels*, 1394, Manresa, S María, and of the *Virgin and All Saints*, monastery of Sant Cugat del Vallès) are elaborated by large three-sided columns painted with niched figures, and by a *guardapolvo* with gilded stucco leaves and coats of arms. In other examples enriched arcaded tracery fills the spandrels between the top of an arched panel and the bottom of the compartment above, and fantastic cusping fringes the inside of such arches, as in the Valencian triptych of *Bonifacio Ferrer* (after 1396; Valencia, Mus. B.A.), attributed to Lorenzo Zaragoza. The backboard may be covered in diapered stucco, painted arabesques or both, and the junctions of panels are concealed by ropelike plaits and twists, as in the retable of *St Michael* (1416–17; Girona, Mus. A.) by Lluís Borrassà.

Many foreign styles supplied this tendency to borrow and accumulate decorations. John I of Aragon (*reg* 1387–95) and his wife Yolande employed French and Flemish artists, initiating the relationship of Spanish and northern European art and reinforcing the inclination towards International Gothic; John II of Castile (*reg* 1406–54) collected works by Rogier van der Weyden and Jan van Eyck. These works stimulated the production of small panels in the naturalistic enamelled style of Flanders; the way they were assembled, however, is very different from the relatively sober scale of the north. In the 15th century the Spanish built them into immense towering structures, based on Sienese polyptychs with their many small panels, but vastly exceeding them in number and overall size. A retable of this period could be 9 m or more in height, rising up the apse of a church to the spring of the dome

86. Integral frame for the altarpiece of *St George* (detail) by the Master of the Centenar de la Pluma, 6.60×5.50 m, from Valencia, *c.* 1410–20 (London, Victoria and Albert Museum)

and curved around the inner wall of the east end—a reredos rather than an altarpiece.

This led to the development of three main types of retable. One was a grander, richer version of the Gothic polyptych frame with its outer *guardapolvos*, but still an altarpiece in dimension and scale. An example is the large altarpiece of *St George* (*c.* 1410–20; London, V&A; see fig. 86) by the Master of the Centenar de la Pluma, with numerous narrative scenes arranged in sixteen lateral and three central panels which tell the story of the saint's life. These are formed into a 'Gothic church' structure, supported by pinnacled columns containing painted niched figures, while the horizontal dividing bands are carved with quatrefoil roundels echoing furniture decoration of the late 14th century to the early 15th. The elaborate *guardapolvo* is also decorated with figures of the Apostles and a central image of the Holy Spirit, and with geometrical Moorish-influenced ornaments. The second type of retable was the reredos, where painted panels of identical size were set into a network of Gothic mouldings (and later, Baroque or Rococo ones) with little hierarchical gradation or centring of design, and the resultant honeycomb applied like wainscoting to the church wall. The third was a mixture of the two, ranging in size between altarpiece and reredos, but with sculpture replacing either completely or in part the painted panels.

Sculpture was important both inside and outside Spanish buildings and played a large part in the elaboration of surfaces, as can be seen, for example, from the riot of carved detail on the voussoirs of Romanesque portals. Lavishly sculpted altarpieces are, of course, also common in medieval Germany, but the carved retables found in Spain are as distinctive as the painted versions. The style of the carving was, however, often more up-to-date than that of contemporary painting and ornament. From the 15th century sculpted retables became more and more numerous and were frequently commissioned as offerings by the newly prosperous guilds or members of the middle class. Examples include the retable of *St Peter and the Virgin* sculpted by Pere Oller for Vic Cathedral and the vast alabaster retable of *St Tecla* (1426–36 and later) by Pere Johan (Pedro Juan de Valogona; *d* 1436) for Tarragona Cathedral. In the second, tiers of Flamboyant Gothic tracery dwarf even the life-size saints and Virgin and crush the shallow relief narrative scenes with their pygmy figures. Here the frame has completely taken over, to become not the cross-section of a church that frames the images in Italian altarpieces but the analogue of a cathedral façade, to which the carved scenes and figures are adjuncts. Also as on a Gothic cathedral, the carving is coloured and gilded, integrating even further the 'frame' and its contents.

The opulence of these works glorifies the rich guilds and city brotherhoods who commissioned them and who specified details of colour and gilding as well as layout on both sculpted and painted retables. In consequence, the work took so long to complete that contracts often name the inheritor of a commission in case of death, as happened with the retable of *St Tecla*: Pere Johan's assistant Guilermo de la Monta finished sculpting the retable after his master's death. This increasing elaboration and length of labour finally resulted in a reorganization of all the crafts involved. Until the 15th century partnerships of artists had taken it in turns to work on the framework or the painting of alternate altarpieces, their generalized training (including silversmithing) giving them the ability to carve ornament, gild, design and paint. However, during the first half of the 15th century three groups (of flesh painters, 'stuff painters' and gilders) were established by royal decree, while the manufacture of retable structures was broken down into architectural and figural elements. This meant that differentiated classes of framemakers, specializing in carving, gilding or decorating, at last began to emerge, and partnerships of specialist wood-carvers and painters are recorded, as in Italy from a much earlier period. For example, the altarpiece of *St Bernardino* (after 1455; Cagliari, Pin. N.) was carved by Raffaele Tomás (*fl* 1455–6) and painted, probably exclusively, by Juan Figuera.

With artists specializing in one type of work, there was an incentive to collaborate with different specialists and so progress more quickly on a single retable. There are frequent examples of mixed sculpted and pictorial retables where an artist, frame-carver, gilder and sculptor would

all have been involved. The commonest type is the so-called *remate* sculpture, where an ornamental Gothic canopy shelters a free-standing carved figure or group within the central section of a triptych, the shutters of which are decorated inside with tracery frames and painted scenes. Here the sculpture regains its importance, and the whole triptych structure is reduced again to a frame or backcloth. Examples include Nicolás Francés's triptych of the *Life of the Virgin* (after 1435; Tordesillas, Church of the Poor Clares) and his Triptych of Belchite (1439; Saragossa, parish church of Belchite), which has lost its central sculpture of the Virgin.

There is a northern European influence in these altarpieces, and it is notable how many artists were then travelling to and from Spain. Jan van Eyck came in 1429; the Bishop of Burgos imported Hans von Köln as his architect; Burgundian sculptors, along with Flemish and German, worked in Spain under the aegis of Philip the Good, 3rd Duke of Burgundy; Lluís Dalmau, court painter to Alfonso V of Aragon, was sent to Bruges in 1431; and such artists as Nicolás Francés and Jorge Inglés betray their origins in their names. Small devotional triptychs were produced in plain northern European moulding frames; and in both the framing structure and the International Gothic detail of the sculptured or *remate* Spanish altarpieces, Rhenish, Flemish and Burgundian styles and techniques can be seen.

The second type of retable mentioned above—the screen or reredos that covers the whole eastern end of the chancel—is more Italianate in its form and derivation. An example from 1445, the altarpiece of *Christ and the Virgin* (Salamanca, Old Cathedral), is actually by a Florentine, Dello Delli, known in Spain as Nicolás Fiorentino. This has 55 compartments, arranged in five tiers around the apse, of which only the central top panel breaks the overall identity by rising slightly higher. The symmetry has been marred by two bottom panels added by Fernando Gallego in 1500; otherwise each lower round-arched compartment has its own rectangular frame, while the top tier is crowned with a series of crocketed gables and pinnacles. Delli also frescoed the apsidal dome with a *Last Judgement*, edged with a decorative border imitating relief mouldings; while set into the bottom of the reredos, cutting the carved predella strip with its roundels of painted heads, is a niche holding a sculpted *Virgin and Child*. The coherence of this vast scheme, covering the whole interior of the apse, again makes it difficult to specify what is the frame: two parts of the whole lie outside the conventional wooden structure containing the painted panels, and three of the qualities that help to define a modern frame—that it is protective, discrete and technically movable—have no application here.

Apart from such imports as the Italian Delli, artistic influence in Castile was generally Flemish. In Catalonia, however, a native school was by then established and beginning to diffuse its style through western Spain. One of the most notable Catalan painters was Huguet, who left a number of important, mainly complete, retables; there are also surviving documents connected with his work that mention the frames. For instance, the Abbot of Ripoll contracted Huguet in 1455 to paint a predella, front and back, for a retable of the *Virgin*. The contract states that the back of the carved frames (*obra de talla*) shall be painted yellow in order to make the grisaille pictures stand out: this is an unusual reference to the use of yellow (noted above), which was also not as common in Catalonia as it was in Castile and Andalusia. The front of the predella was to be gilded, presumably because it was more frequently seen, and the backgrounds of the paintings tally in each case with the frames—yellow on the back and gold in front. In 1464 John II of Aragon (*reg* 1458–79) released Huguet and two wood-carvers, Durán and Prat, from military service, so that they could produce the Retablo del Condestable (1464–5; Barcelona, Real Capilla de S Agueda). This work, named for Don Pedro, Constable of Portugal, still retains the doors each side of the predella that enclose the altar, but it has lost the *guardapolvos* completely and for a long period was without the carved decoration of its wide, flat frame. The latter is painted red, and its twining chains of carved green foliage and gilded dragons have been restored. There is no internal 'church' silhouette or use of shaped panels, only the filigree canopy bands added above the upper tier and the tiny cusped fringing of each rectangular 'frame' remaining from the earlier Flamboyant Gothic phase. Elaborate carvings continued to be produced, but this altarpiece shows the first small movements away from Gothic.

2. RENAISSANCE. During the 15th century the influence of the Italian Renaissance began to percolate through Spain. The Italian *quadro all'antica*—the rectangular panel, with a Renaissance *cassetta* or an aedicular frame—was bound to affect the forms of Spanish paintings and their frames. As with other styles entering Spain, its influence was late and partial, but in the *Profession of St Vincent Ferrer* (after 1458; Paris, Mus. A. Déc.), from the school of Jacomart, a representation can be seen in the background of a retable showing SS Peter, Paul and Dominic. The scene is still not a naturalistic *sacra conversazione* as in Italy; but the use of an oblong panel in a single frame is significant, as is the outer gilt billet moulding on the black *guardapolvo*.

Spain remained eclectic in the use of styles: late 15th-century furniture in transition from the medieval to the Renaissance is decorated with arabesques, Gothic grotesques and Greco-Roman ornament, and figure sculpture veered more and more towards the style of the Renaissance; but such important painters as Bartolomé Bermejo used Gothic settings as late as the 1470s. As work on altarpieces had been divided among specialist craftsmen, it was also possible to find, in the late 15th century and well into the 16th, a Renaissance image, painted or sculpted, set in a Gothic architectural frame. Damián Forment's stone retables of the 1510s to 1530s show this disjunction of styles, as does Pedro Berruguete's painted retable of *St Thomas Aquinas* (c. 1500; Ávila, S Tomás). Berruguete's retable fills the east end of the church with several large scenes rather than the 55 small ones of Delli, and the painted compositions and overall format are definitely Renaissance rather than Gothic. However, their rich friezes of carved foliate tracery, although arranged between colonnettes in an approximation of a classical aedicule, are unashamedly Gothic, while a canopy in the form of a great spired cathedral crowns the central panel of St Thomas.

The Flamboyant Gothic vocabulary took almost as long to die out among painters as carvers and was probably prolonged by its popularity with patrons. Queen Isabella of Castile and León possessed more than fifty Flemish works and only two of the Italian Renaissance. When Spain achieved stability, unity and increased wealth in the 1490s under Ferdinand and Isabella, new riches from its American trade were used to build not in the Renaissance style but in the Northern Gothic. Juan Guas (*d c.* 1495) designed a presbytery for S Juan de los Reyes (1476–1503), Toledo, that epitomizes the Flamboyant style, modified by Moorish motifs. His drawing for it (pen and ink on parchment, 1.94×0.96 m; Madrid, Prado) includes a conventional tiered Gothic painted retable (never executed) with an inscribed *guardapolvo*; it is one of the few extant designs for Spanish altarpieces and could have been produced more than a century earlier. The same is true of the Great Retable of Toledo Cathedral, designed by a Burgundian and completed in 1505 by an army of craftsmen. Still in the Flamboyant style, this is Spain's largest retable, proclaiming Toledo's new position as the centre of Spanish art. In the early 16th century there was a gradual increase in the use of classical ornament and form, and as Toledo and the rest of Castile took over the artistic dominance of Aragon and Catalonia, the Renaissance replaced the Gothic. Initially there was a mixture of styles, as in the high altar retable (1499–1506) of Ávila Cathedral by Berruguete, Juan de Borgoña and Santa Cruz (*d* before 1508), in which each panel is framed by classical pilasters and topped by a Gothic canopy. The pilasters are carved with candelabra and foliate garlands, while the canopies feature cusped arches filled with delicate traceries in Mudéjar fashion.

Apart from the grandiose confections of retables and reredoses, there were other types of frame also. However, patronage in Spain was either more pious than elsewhere or found the baroque dramas of religious art more exciting than portraiture or history painting. Hence, though some portraiture of course existed, the main type of picture besides the great public altarpiece was the small devotional painting. The frames of these often took a northern European form (like the paintings themselves), with a simple moulding of scotias, astragals and fillets, sometimes with a rainsill at the bottom edge, as in Pedro Díaz de Oviedo's triptych of the *Nativity* (Madrid, Mus. Lazaro Galdiano). Northern influence also produced the same stained, veneered or painted black *cassetta* frames found in England, France and the Low Countries during the 15th and 16th centuries, and these were decorated with gilded pastiglia or *sgraffito* ornament derived from Italian models. Again, they show the diffusion of Renaissance motifs, which were spread in various ways, for example through Spanish nobles living in Italy, who transmitted back news of stylistic changes. Details can thus be found—such as the decoration of black frames—that may be traced to an Italian source; similarly, there are examples of whole decorative schemes, although rare in Spain, that originated in Renaissance Italy. These use the frame, sometimes in stucco, sometimes painted in *trompe l'oeil*, as one element of the whole, as in the chapter room and its antechamber in Toledo Cathedral. These were painted by the Burgundian Juan de Borgoña in 1509–11 for the prominent patron Cardinal Francisco Jiménez de Cisneros, Archbishop of Toledo. The antechamber uses *trompe l'oeil* architectural cornices, pilasters and niches in Renaissance style to mediate between an *artesonado* (a Mudéjar coffered ceiling), a painted garden and an ornamental door surround decorated with Moorish motifs. The chapter room itself includes several types of frame: illusionistic columns containing a large *Last Judgement* and scenes from the *Life of the Virgin*; painted pilasters and rails around a frieze depicting past archbishops; and gilt mouldings set into the wall to frame a group of prelates below. The design combines a gallery and didactic religious programme and is a rare instance of this type of scheme and also of the use of pure Renaissance ornament for frames. Both can be explained by the origins of the artist and by the faster adaptation to a new stylistic vocabulary in painting than in woodworking.

On account of the strong hold of late Flemish Gothic, architecture was also slower than painting to adjust to Renaissance proportion and decoration. One development of this staggered transition from style to style in different media is the PLATERESQUE STYLE of architecture, which uses a dense floral, foliate or candelabrum pattern on every panel, column, frieze or pilaster of a classical aedicula. Altarpieces in the Plateresque style were soon being

produced, such as the retable of an *Abbot with SS Cosmas and Damian* (16th century, Aragonese; Florida, John and Johanna Bass priv. col.). This has a segmental pediment with a head of Christ, decorated baluster columns and plinths and rather uncertain vertical and horizontal divisions that are neither classical pilasters nor Gothic canopies. Later in the 16th century sophisticated examples of the Plateresque can be seen, such as the frame on Pedro Machuca's retable of *St Pedro del Osma* (1546; Jaén Cathedral). Though still in the form of a towering screen-like reredos, the classical replaces the Gothic. Each of the nine panels is painted as a *quadro all'antica* and mounted in one cell of a flat ornamental border with moulding edges, based on the Italian *cassetta*. The friezes are carved with foliage and flowers like those on the façade of the University of Salamanca, and each corner and junction is mounted with a roundel holding a painted half-figure. The cresting consists of a tondo of *St Veronica* in the same friezelike border, supported by pierced grotesque scrolling designed to fill the round-arched niche behind the altar. The few large panels, against the many small ones of a Gothic retable, enable the whole to be read more easily; the arrangement is more lucid and the frame rich but less obtrusive.

3. MANNERIST. Mannerism flourished in the reign of Charles I, who in 1519 became the Holy Roman Emperor as Charles V. Italian political ties and artistic influence increased markedly during this period; already King of Naples and Sicily, Charles became King of Lombardy and was also crowned in Bologna in 1529, replacing the French hegemony in Italy by a Spanish one. Alonso Berruguete, who had brought Michelangelo's Mannerism to Spain, was made Pintor del Rey in 1518, and in 1526 Charles commissioned a Renaissance-style palace in the Alhambra, Granada, from Machuca. This proximity to Italy meant that Spain was quicker to absorb changes in style. Mannerism, like the Plateresque and Flamboyant Gothic, was more in accord with the Spanish love of drama and decoration than Renaissance ideals of proportion, restraint and balance. Mannerism was, therefore, almost immediately adopted in Spain, while examples of pure Renaissance form and ornament are comparatively rare.

Pedro Fernández and Gabriel Pou painted panels (1519–21) for the retable of *St Helena* (Girona Cathedral; see fig. 87), which are set in a frame so massive and ornamental that it is more like a metalwork reliquary than an altarpiece. Its elements are in High Renaissance style—the wide frieze and framing pilasters, with their raised gilt decoration of winged figures, urns and candelabra—as is its form, with trabeate structure and segmental pediment. However, familiarity with the Gothic *guardapolvos* caused the designer to add projecting canted sections to the entablature, predella and pilasters, supporting the jutting ends of the entablature on baluster columns of impressive and ornate complexity. The lateral canted panels are painted with aediculae containing figures and supported by atlantids, and the pediment is sheltered by a segmental coffered ceiling. The forward ends of the frieze hold a Platonic sun and moon, balanced on the predella by Mannerist cartouches. The internal divisions of the retable are marked horizontally by wide bands of scrolling foliage

87. Original Mannerist aedicular frame for the retable of *St Helena* by Pedro Fernández and Gabriel Pou, 1519–21 (Girona Cathedral)

and urns in the Plateresque style and vertically by slender balustered colonnettes. This vertical emphasis is Mannerist, as is the dramatic perspectival recession above the pediment. The density of ornament is almost more Gothic than Mannerist, however, and the whole frame shows how form and decoration were continually remade by Spanish craftsmen in their wish to glorify God (and the patron) through the enrichment of every surface. The paintings are dramatic and faintly Leonardesque, particularly the central large panel. Anything less positive would have been lost in the welter of surrounding decoration, yet the way the picture is forced to conquer the setting rather than gain support from it is peculiar to Spain, where, with the strong Moorish tradition, the idea of the frame merely enhancing the image was never as current as elsewhere.

A more refined Mannerism is demonstrated by the aedicular frame of Machuca's *Descent from the Cross* (*c.* 1547; Madrid, Prado). This has free-standing baluster columns, a deep pedestal with a hippogriff cartouche and a frieze of warring putti. The ground is coloured blue-black with the high-relief figures, masks and grotesques picked out in gold. There are none of the hooked volutes, raking flutes, clasps and peltlike forms that characterize Italian Mannerist frames, but the exaggerated vertical thrust of the columns, their ornate decoration and the powerful contrast of ground and gilt motif take this frame beyond both the purity of the High Renaissance and the coarser Mannerism of the *St Helena* retable. The painting, like that of the latter, is strong and dramatic, with an X-shaped composition, theatrical lighting and the elongations and distortions of Mannerism. The frame contains the image without subduing it, looking forward to the more Europeanized designs of the later 16th century and the 17th, and to a greater integration of picture and frame.

During the first half of the 16th century, Spanish commercial prosperity continued to increase. The colonies expanded to include Mexico, Peru and Chile, sending home gold and raw materials while providing a new market for manufactured goods. The wealth of the Church and the mercantile classes grew in proportion, as did the number and richness of the altarpieces they commissioned, epitomized by the Catalonian *St Helena* retable. In Castile, retables continued to be wholly or partly sculpted, as in the Middle Ages; painted works were for the less wealthy patron. An example of a part-sculpted, part-painted altarpiece is in the parish church of Fuentelaencina, Guadalajara. Begun in 1557, it is a transformation of the Gothic *remate* into a classical structure, magnifying it to the size of a reredos and filling the great arched niche behind the altar. Similar in design to the carved altarpiece of Burgos Cathedral, it lacks the latter's strict use of the orders and hierarchy of pediments. It is, in fact, a late Plateresque structure, built as a grid of entablatures and tall aediculae holding carved figures. These surround the central sculpted scenes and the lateral tiers of painted panels. Every section of the carved framework is crammed with ornament, from friezes to fretted, turned columns, and the central panels seethe with activity between decorated spandrels and pilasters. The top is crowned with a *Crucifixion* and two niches below a triangular pediment, and this is supported by tondi held in coral-like accretions of carving. At the extreme edges the vertical rails of a *guardapolvo* show, even at this late date. The team of six that executed it is recorded, the panels being painted by three artists. The framework is by Nicolas de Vegara the elder and Bautista Vasquez the elder, who also, along with Martin de Vandoma (*b* 1510/15), produced the sculptures. The framemakers thus in some sense defined the work; they produced the sculptures, the most valued element, and they fitted the whole to its site in the church. How much they influenced the design and its details is unclear, however; contracts often included a programmatic sketch setting out the client's wishes, so that the general shape and the sequence of the scenes could be followed. Probably the decoration was left to the carvers' discretion—the earlier incidence of Renaissance paintings in Gothic frames is otherwise hard to explain—but, again, those carvers would presumably have been chosen for the style as well as the competence of their work.

Italy dominated religious painting and carving, Spanish artists flocking there to study; but there was further Flemish influence too, through such immigrant painters as Antonis Mor, Peeter Kempeneer and others. Philip II, acceding in 1556, bought 15th- and 16th-century Flemish pictures and was left others by his aunt, Maria of Hungary. He also collected high-quality Italian works by Correggio, Raphael and Titian and employed followers of Pontormo and Andrea del Sarto to decorate the walls and altars of the Escorial. These two strains of influence appear in a charming, small altarpiece, the Tendilla Retable (*c.* 1555; Cincinnati, OH, A. Mus.). The paintings are both Flemish and Italianate, set in a carved and gilt-wood closing triptych with a semicircular broken pediment and predella. The ornament is rich but restrained, with delicate grotesques and candelabra; each panel is fringed at the top with pierced grotesque tracery, mimicking the canopies of a Gothic reredos. The predella frieze has an enriched floral chain, and the pediment a spiral ribbon holding fruit clusters and cherubs' heads. There are also two putti acroteria with armorial bearings, balancing a fruit-and-urn finial. Opinion is divided as to the altarpiece's origin: it may have been a northern import with tracery added to adapt it to Spanish taste, or it may be the product of one of the Flemish workshops established in Spain in the 16th century, such as that of the Beaugrant family. The inner shutter frames are plain, in the Flemish style; the floral chain is Italian, as are the Renaissance grotesques, while the proportion, chunky curved pediment and traceries are Spanish. Perhaps because of its small size, the frame, despite the variations of scale in the paintings, seems more window-like than on a towering reredos; this is especially true of the internal shutters, where the paintings of *Adam and Eve* and the *Sacrifice of Isaac* continue beyond the main panels, under their top rails and into the small upper segments, which close the broken pediment. Abraham's angel, particularly, seems to be fluttering behind a window bar. The Tendilla Retable, restrained in comparison with earlier altars, is nevertheless still richly decorated. Its tentative dating is symbolically one year before the accession of Philip II, who presided over Spain's Golden Age and also introduced the Spartan Herrera style.

4. HERRERA STYLE. Wealth poured into Spain from her colonies, and in celebration Philip II planned the

Palace of the Escorial (1563–84), designed in a sober Italianate style by Juan Bautista de Toledo and Juan de Herrera. Herrera expressed Philip's austere outlook, realizing the King's demands for 'simplicity of form, severity in the whole, nobility without arrogance, majesty without ostentation'. The chapel was at the centre of the palace, and the nucleus of that centre was the giant retable, also designed by Herrera (see *Sumario y breve declaración de los diseños y estampas de la fábrica de San Lorenço el Real del Escurial* (Madrid, 1589); engravings by Pedro Perret from the design). Here at last Spain belatedly found its own Renaissance style; paradoxically, in a land so attached to opulent decoration, it was one of an extremely pared-down classicism. The retable, over 26 m high, has four tiers, which apply the orders in strict sequence: Doric at the base, rising through Ionic and Corinthian to Composite on the top pedimented aedicula housing the *Crucifixion*. There is little other external decoration, save for the Doric frieze of metopes and triglyphs and the sculptures. Besides the internal group of the *Crucifixion* and the niched figures at the bottom, the frame has two figures with obelisks (the only Mannerist detail) supporting the Corinthian order and two more supporting the Composite order. It is a monument to Roman clarity and 'simplicity of form'; majesty is supplied by the materials: green jasper, red marble and gilding. It was executed by Jacopo da Trezzo I and Juan Bautista Comane (*fl c.* 1579–81), and the 15 gilt-bronze figures are by Pompeo Leoni. The combination of painting and sculpture in the retable relates it to Gothic *remate* altarpieces and gives it its Spanish character; its otherwise untypical austerity was to be influential in the 17th century.

The Escorial Chapel also features wall paintings set in architectural gadrooned mouldings; in the Library, which is richly painted and decorated, architectural entablatures and borders of Greek fret are used, echoing the classical severity of the furniture. The Library paintings also display important elements of the Herrera style as it was adopted by goldsmiths and other craftsmen: oblong framed panels and slender straps separated by cabochons or bosses. For goldsmiths and furniture-makers this style was important but specialized; for framemakers it had a much wider and longer-lasting significance. Moulding frames of this type proliferated throughout the 17th century; they combine Moorish ornaments and other geometrical motifs with the Herrera style and are characteristically Spanish. Instead of the swooping hooks and volutes of Italian Mannerism, the primary motifs include astragals (straight gadrooning or knulls) clasped round an outer torus, dentils, chain-and-egg mouldings, raked gadrooning, raised squares or lozenges like gems, chains of alternating short or stretched cabochons, dogtooth, frets and an extension of the astragal and torus that uses voluted clasps across a moulding (looking rather like a necklace of cotton reels). Some of these forms are Mozarabic, deriving from Islamic-influenced church architecture (e.g. a cotton-reel moulding and three types of dogtooth can be found above the portal of the Romanesque church of Lérida).

A compendium of these ornaments appears on the frame (see fig. 88a) of Johann Liss's *Satyr and the Peasants* (Washington, DC, N.G.A.). This has a hollow decorated with a fretlike pattern of flutes and fillets, undercutting an

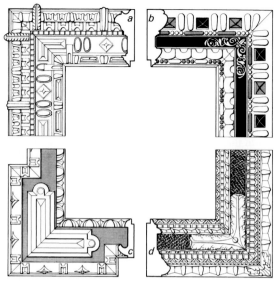

88. Spanish Herrera frames, 17th century: (a) with clasps and 'gemstone' decoration, 1333×1664×190 mm, contemporary for Johann Liss's *Satyr and the Peasants, c.* 1620 (Washington, DC, National Gallery of Art); (b) with paired knulls and 'gemstone' ornaments, parcel gilt and polychrome, 770×570×150 mm, on Joos van Cleve (i)'s *Christ and St John the Baptist as Children, c.* 1525–30 (Chicago, IL, Art Institute of Chicago); (c) outset corner frame, parcel gilt, blue painted frieze, 2.00×1.34 m, possibly original for El Greco's *Disrobing of Christ, c.* 1585–1608 (Munich, Alte Pinakothek); (d) with knulling, dentils and *sgraffito* scale decoration, 425×327×160 mm, late 16th century–early 17th, on the portrait of *Lady Lee* after Hans Holbein the younger, second half of the 16th century (New York, Metropolitan Museum of Art)

ovolo with a mirror-image fret, paired knulls and hooked cotton-reel clasps. In the flat below are raised cabochons, lozenges and oblongs outlined in black and red, set between dentils and another ovolo with clasps. Seen from a distance these motifs intermesh in a flickering pattern of uprights and crossbars, where multiple ornaments are restrained in a rigidly geometrical network. Other sources for the various motifs may be medieval book covers and early altars enamelled and set with gems. The cabochons and single knulls or astragals may be mixed with delicate gilt decoration, similar to the grounds of Herrera metalwork, as in the parcel-gilt black frame now on Velázquez's *Juan Calabazas* (*c.* 1644; Cleveland, OH, Mus. A.). Here the frame has found its ideal painting, setting off Velázquez's palette of cool greys and the geometrical patterns of stool and wall. On another type of frame the gilt-on-black decoration is reduced to centre and corner key shapes on a narrow black flat (88b). The flat is sunk between two bird's-beak mouldings, boldly carved with paired knulls and square 'gems', broad goffered knulls and bead-and-bobbin trims. The latter and the 'gems' are picked out alternately in red and blue and show how the long tradition of polychromy asserted itself in tandem with an elaboration of the Herrera style. An eared form (88c) of this Herrera frame exists; presumably the influence here is Palladian, although the effect is Mannerist, in keeping with the picture. The relatively slender rails, exaggerated by the chunky mouldings and the projecting corners, reinforce the vertical composition and El Greco's attenuated figures. Eared corners were also used as an element of the Plateresque style (e.g. the pair of carved doors from Seville, c. 1600–1700; Spanish Room, Philadelphia, Pennsylvania Mus. of F.A.). A further adaptation shows the separated knulls raised on faceted islands and arranged as raked gadrooning to give a strongly cabled effect that leads inwards to the painting. The frames now on Scarsellino's *Scene of Martyrdom* (Houston, TX, Sarah Campbell Blaffer Found.) and Mantegna's *Crucifixion* (Paris, Louvre) both have this dramatic outer gadrooning, above a flat set in rows of dentils.

These types of frame persisted throughout the 17th century, bridging the transition from Mannerism to Baroque. An example is the production of a Baroque corner or centre-and-corner emphasis through the application of a water-leaf or stiff-leaf motif. This ornament (both Gothic and Palladian) is doubled into a stretched, flower-like shape, and in appearance and use is somewhat like the Baroque half-flower of Bolognese frames (*see* §II, 5 above). It appears on the cabled frame now on Cosimo Rosselli's *Virgin and Child* (New York, Met.), which is reminiscent of the wall frames in the Escorial Library, and on the chunkily carved gadroon and dentil frames around Jacopo Tintoretto's *Portrait of a Young Man* (Detroit, MI, Inst. A.) and the portrait of *Lady Lee* (second half of the 16th century; New York, Met.), after Hans Holbein the younger. The last has a flat decorated with an engraved scale pattern (88d) and demonstrates how the accretion of ornament could transform the austere Herrera style into a flamboyant richness.

Another genre of frame that appeared in Spain during the 17th century and that harmonized with the severity of original Herrera patterns had a very different source. This is the family of stained or ebonized 'ripple' frames, directly related to the 17th-century Dutch type (*see* §V, 3(iii) above). Ties with the Netherlands were still close, although Holland was rebelling against the Spanish rule; ties with Catholic Flanders remained much stronger and formed a conduit for the interchange of artistic developments. In Protestant Holland the black frame was adopted as a bourgeois domestic fashion, in sympathy with cool, small-scale, well-lit interiors. In Spain, paradoxically, it became a royal style, associated with the grand unornamented scale of the Escorial, the 'majesty without ostentation' expressed by such court painters as Velázquez; it also suited the monastic art of the Counter-Reformation, produced by such men as Francisco Ribalta and Jusepe de Ribera. The inventory of the 1st Marqués de Leganés's pictures in 1630, when he owned a mere 17 (he died in 1655, owning more than 1300), records the frames of several: a portrait of *Philip IV* (c. 1628–9) by Rubens 'with an ebony frame carved in a wave-pattern'; a *Virgin and Child with SS Isabel and John* by Raphael, 1.7 m high, 'with a massive ebony frame with mouldings'; a very small portrait of *Erasmus* 'with an ebony setting'; a *Virgin and Child* by Titian 'with its ebony frame'; and the *Virgin and Child* (Madrid, Prado) by Rubens with a flower garland by Jan Breughel the elder, also 'with its ebony frame'. A later inventory notes two Riberas in black frames (see Volk, 1980).

Examples of Spanish ebonized frames can be found on Tintoretto's portrait of *Sebastiano Venier*, Rubens's portrait of *Albert VII of Austria* and its pendant *Isabella Eugenia* (both Vienna, Ksthist. Mus.), and Gillis van Coninxloo's *Landscape with Woods* (New York, Met.). The first is an adaptation of the parcel-gilt, black reverse rebate *cassetta*: the flat decorated with a coarse broken zigzag and the inner gilt moulding with broken ripple pattern. The Rubens portrait frames have more complex decoration and are altogether more sophisticated but also have a reverse rebate, projecting the image forward. This was presumably not a construction familiar to Spanish joiners, as the earlier Tintoretto frame uses it—like the surface pattern—somewhat awkwardly. The Vienna pair are more developed: they are decorated with repeated ripple patterns in the Dutch style, together with a wide band of gridlike points. They may well be in their original frames; the Tintoretto, however, must have been reframed. The male portraits are now especially well set off: both three-quarter figures, one clad in richly sober black and gold with white lace, the other in dark armour picked out in gold, they have an admirable foil in the black and gilt of the borders and the subtle flicker of light on the raised patterns. Van Coninxloo's landscape sketch is now in an unsuitable parcel-gilt ebonized frame with multiple ripple ornaments. Such a frame, scintillating with broken light over its entire surface and with even the usually plain central torus decorated with a gilded leaf-and-daisy pattern, shows the assimilation and elaboration of the style by Spanish-/Moorish craftsmen. Originally it would have housed a copper panel painted, possibly by a Dutch or Flemish artist, with a mythological or religious scene, miniaturized and brilliantly coloured. Such broad frames with concentric linear patterns emphasize the perspective recession of a scene, while the black veneer acts like a proscenium arch, heightening effects of light and colour.

5. BAROQUE.

(i) Variety of types. (ii) Development.

(i) *Variety of types.* Other Spanish frames of the 17th century seem to marry the chunky gilded carving of elaborated Herrera designs and the black and gold of a Dutch ebonized frame. With these is blended a third feature: the rolling forms of acanthus foliage, derived from early Baroque leaf frames and transmitted through the strong Spanish presence in Italy. In this respect, Ribera's *St Mary the Egyptian* (1651; Naples, Mus. Civ. Gaetano Filangieri) is interesting for its frame, which is possibly original. Here, Spanish, northern European and Italian influences are merged in the wide, lacy border of stained wood, ornamented across its width with bold classical mouldings and an acanthus band, and edged with a pierced egg-and-dart trim. It combines the Spanish lust for decoration with the sobriety of the contemporary mood, expressed in the naturalism, contemplativeness and tenebrism of Ribera's painting. Less complex products of these mixed influences are the early Baroque painted frames with slight reverse rebate and vigorous gilt leaf mouldings, which became common during the 17th century. Ribera's powerful Baroque style soon influenced his homeland, in spite of his residence in Naples; he was patronized by the Spanish viceroys there, and many of his works soon entered the royal collections. Naturalism such as his went hand-in-hand with a use of organic forms of ornament, and the craftsmen who had subverted the Herrera style into a lavish *mélange* of abstract motifs happily adopted the sculptural shapes of foliage, flowers and figures.

These expressive leaf-trimmed frames (see fig. 89) embody one of the most ubiquitous and recognizable of Spanish styles, which influenced and was influenced by Neapolitan and Bolognese styles of the 17th century. Simple examples can be seen on Giovan Battista Recco's *Still-life with Hare* (Munich, Alte Pin.), the anonymous *Portrait of a Woman* (Cincinnati, OH, A. Mus.; no. 1915.159) and Murillo's *Children Playing Dice* (*c.* 1665–75; Munich, Alte Pin.; 89a). Similar in profile and the use of parcel-gilt black, they employ a variety of Baroque leaf mouldings, from the rolled acanthus or petal torus of the Murillo and Recco to the saw-edged leaf of the Cincinnati painting. These are combined with back-edge trims of leaf ogee, ribbon or bay leaf. More exotic variations use polychromy and additional mouldings, as in the frame (89b) on Zurbarán's *Crucifixion* (1627; Chicago, IL, A. Inst.), where the inner torus with its cross-cut acanthus moulding has been expanded at the expense of the flat, gaining in substance and opulence by being picked out in

black and gold against a red ground. The flat remains black but is decorated by delicately scrolling centre and corner panels; the back trim is red and gold. Such a frame is, visually and symbolically, a powerful setting for the Caravaggist painting of the *Crucifixion* that it now holds. It also suggests the early Baroque interior where it would have hung, and where an increasing use of plastic form, chiaroscuro and colour began to draw painting and architecture closer together to create the unified, illusionary, dramatic effect of the later 17th century. One more example of this type looks back to the Dutch frame: between the gilt leaf mouldings, the flat is painted with panels of *trompe l'oeil* tortoiseshell on a black ground, mimicking the actual inlaid ebony and shell frames of 17th-century Spain and the Netherlands. Grimm shows (pl. 134) a related use of painted shell panels.

The simple black flat/reverse rebate with gilt leaf mouldings also forms the base of a centre/corner frame in full Baroque style. Here the focal ornaments are strong, gilded, foliate scrolls or key shapes applied to the dark flat (which may also be marbled or painted like tortoiseshell). This type lasted into the 18th century, and examples can be seen on Goya's *Portrait of a Prelate* (Louisville, KY, Speed A. Mus.) and Murillo's *Virgin of the Annunciation* (1670–80; Houston, TX, Mus. F.A.) and *Young Fruitseller* (*c.* 1670; Munich, Alte Pin.). The last has a prominent ogee moulding in *faux* shell replacing the inner-leaf torus; the central rosettes and corner leaf scrolls (89c) encroach on this ogee from their ground of red marble set with black marble roundels. The richness of the 'materials' together with the gilded edgings and carved, painted ornaments are counterbalanced by the subtle tones of red, cream and black, while the vigorous three-dimensional centres and corners set up a pattern of lines converging on the spiritualized face and delicate hands of the Virgin. Both the painting and frame exemplify Spanish Baroque.

Similar leaf mouldings around a central panel, with or without centres and corners, can also appear with a hollow profile, the flat being replaced by a painted scotia. Examples of this can be seen on Francesco Salviati's *Incredulity of St Thomas* (*c.* 1547; Paris, Louvre), *Still-life with Pears* (School of Zurbarán; Chicago, IL, A. Inst.), Antonio del Castillo's *Penitent St Peter* (*c.* 1635–40; Kansas City, MO, Nelson–Atkins Mus. A.) and Velázquez's *Don Pedro de Barbarana* (Fort Worth, TX, Kimbell A. Mus.; see fig. 90). Again, an eared-corner version of this exists, as seen on El Greco's *Trinitarian Monk* (Kansas City, MO, Nelson–Atkins Mus. A.). As the artist is relatively minor, the *Penitent St Peter* has almost certainly remained undisturbed in its original frame (89d), which is superb and elaborate, with wide edging ogee mouldings of rolled leaves, black marbled scotia and deeply cut floral and foliate centres and corners. Light, shade and plasticity are emphasized in this design by the broad central hollow, echoing the monumental form and dramatic lighting of the saint. The gilt leaf mouldings provide a shimmer of movement around the still image, and the centres and corners provoke an imaginary grid emphasizing the compositional lines. In the case of the Velázquez, the dramatic marbled panels—inner black scotia and outer red flat—may have been repainted at some time, although the scheme is probably original, echoing the black and red of the don's costume.

89. Spanish frames, 17th century: (a) architrave frame with gilded, stylized leaf mouldings and black painted frieze, 1400×1080×133 mm, contemporary for Bartolomé Esteban Murillo's *Children Playing Dice*, *c.* 1665–75 (Munich, Alte Pinakothek); (b) bolection leaf frame, parcel gilt and polychrome, 2860×1630×255 mm, first half of the 17th century, adapted for Francisco de Zurbarán's *Crucifixion*, 1627 (Chicago, IL, Art Institute of Chicago); (c) architrave frame with gilded stylized leaf mouldings and corner cartouches, black frieze, 1490×1130×140 mm, possibly original for Murillo's *Young Fruitseller*, *c.* 1670 (Munich, Alte Pinakothek); (d) bolection frame, parcel gilt with marbled scotia, leaves and fruit at corners and centres, 1194×914×170 mm, probably original for Antonio del Castillo's *Penitent St Peter*, *c.* 1635–40 (Kansas City, MO, Nelson–Atkins Museum of Art)

The flat or reverse rebate structure can be gilded overall instead of painted, with centres and corners and/or with decorated flats. A 17th-century frame like that now on Alessandro Magnasco's *Christ Attended by Angels* (18th century), with an enriched egg trim at the sight edge and a flat carved with a foliate strapwork chain, is essentially Spanish in its bold approach, curling leaf ends, beads and cabochons. However, 17th-century frames such as that on Goya's *Annunciation* (Boston, MA, Mus. F.A.), again carved throughout, show links with earlier Bolognese frames, both in their chunky technique and in their use of similar half-flower motifs. Where the frame is carved over the entire rail, this richness can be used to emphasize the status of the subject of a portrait, just as in the earlier retables where it enhanced the celestial qualities of the pictures, or to underline the importance of a work or its owner, as in the example (see fig. 91a) on Velázquez's *Sibyl with Tabula Rasa* (*c.* 1644–8; Dallas, TX, S. Methodist U., Meadows Mus. & Gal.).

There are Spanish versions of the Italian Baroque frame; these have more of a conventional entablature form and can be directly related to contemporary or earlier Italian types. For example, the frame (91b) on Niccolò Rondinelli's *Virgin and Child with an Angel Playing a Lute* (Atlanta, GA, High Mus. A.) has a raised sculptural inner moulding with scrolled leaf or petal forms, enriched on a wide flat, where they are linked by scrolling foliage. Such patterns can be found on Italian leaf frames and seem close to the lobed and voluted ornaments of Leopoldo de' Medici's frames in the Palazzo Pitti, Florence (*see* §II, 4(ii)

90. Spanish Baroque frame with foliate cartouches, parcel gilt with marbled panels, 1930×1092×175 mm, contemporary for Diego Velázquez's *Don Pedro de Barbarana*, 1631–3 (Fort Worth, TX, Kimbell Art Museum)

The gold centre and corner panels are flattened double flourishes, picked out with red hatched in gilt and black with gold stippling. The effect is grander than with the Castillo frame, richness of colour and detail substituting for lush carved borders and demonstrating the natural empathy of Spanish craftsmen for sculptural ornament, polychromy and decoration on decoration, even—perhaps especially—within the austerity of Philip IV's court.

The frame now on the Salviati has a similar Baroque richness; it is a hollow centre and corner frame, with a red-painted scotia that may be original. This is an example of the fortuitously happy liaisons between pictures and frames of different periods and countries that do emerge from the disastrously common lust to reframe. Salviati's Mannerist colours, contorted poses and diagonal lines are all served well by the analogous elements of the later frame. Less successfully, the *Still-life with Pears* is now in a marbled hollow frame with deeply carved projecting centres and corners. The sculptural weight of these heavy, voluted ornaments with their *cosse de pois* (peapod) centres is reminiscent of 'Sansovino' frames (*see* §II, 4(i) above) and would overwhelm the refined naturalism of the painted fruit and flowers were it not for their radiant lighting. The frame is carved at the corners with cherubs' heads, suggesting that the original painting was religious.

91. Spanish frames, 17th century : (a) Baroque frame carved with gilt scrolling foliage on black, 622×571×175 mm, contemporary for Diego Velázquez's *Sibyl with Tabula Rasa*, *c.* 1644–8 (Dallas, TX, Southern Methodist University, Meadows Museum and Art Gallery); (b) Mannerist frame with overall stylized scrolled leaves, 806×629×170 mm, mid-17th century, possibly made for Niccolò Rondinelli's *Virgin and Child with an Angel Playing a Lute* (Atlanta, GA, High Museum of Art)

above). A version of the *cassetta* form also appears and is continuously carved, with corners and centres, either gilded, or with painted flat and applied gold ornaments. An example of a corner-and-centre frame surrounds El Greco's portrait of *Jacomo Bosie* (*c.* 1600–10; Fort Worth, TX, Kimbell A. Mus.). The profile is again Italian, but the crinkled, dense form of the centre/corner ornaments on the flat is Spanish. A *cassetta* with gilt centres and corners and a painted flat can be found on El Greco's portrait of *Fray Hortensio de Paravicino* (*c.* 1610; Boston, MA, Mus. F.A.). The frame is probably slightly later than the painting (and is perhaps a modern reframing). It is an ornate setting for the ascetic theologian, and the ordered Baroque decorations do not respect the Mannerist composition; however, it is a splendid frame, showing the adaptation of the *cassetta* to indigenous style. The outer torus moulding has open crosscut bell-flowers between paired C-scrolls of flattened, clasplike form centred with cabochons, and these, like the prominent foliate scrolls applied to the black flat, are Spanish in style.

While these various types of modern, oblong frame—adaptable to portraits, still-lifes and history paintings as well as to religious works—were developing through the 16th and 17th centuries, there was still, surprisingly, a large demand for huge retable frames. In the rest of Europe the popularity of great polyptychs had died out by the end of the 16th century; they were replaced during the Baroque period by single panels mounted behind the altar, occasional triptychs and wall paintings that formed part of some integrated decorative scheme. In Spain, however, tiered retables were produced in quantity until the mid-17th century, although less frequently thereafter.

(ii) Development. In the 17th century Spain collapsed economically and as a world power, but this was the era of the Counter-Reformation: the Catholic Church was still immensely wealthy and used its wealth to propagandize its cause through art and architecture. The Crown was also rich, and, as wars impoverished Spanish industry and commerce, patronage moved from the guilds and bourgeois classes back to Court and Church. Craftsmen became dependent on these two sources of work, though they were more circumscribed than before by the clients' demands; and these craftsmen were now likely to be either native Spaniards or migrant Europeans, since in 1570 the Moors were expelled from Andalusia and in 1609 from the rest of Spain. This was done in the name of Counter-Reformation religious unity, but crafts and industries were consequently starved of skilled workers, and Spain grew even poorer.

An embryonic Baroque altarpiece is Ribalta's Retable of Santiago (1603; Algemesí, church of S Jaime Apostol). This preserves the screenlike structure of 15th- and 16th-century retables, filling the vaulted eastern end of the choir with a painted, sculpted polyptych five tiers deep and five across. The form is of a Renaissance or Mannerist altarpiece, elaborated with Solomonic columns (a particularly Baroque feature, anticipating by 20 years Bernini's baldacchino (1623–34) for St Peter's, Rome), horizontally divided panels, lantern-like acroteria and a Dutch gable-like crest. The whole creation, with the massive central sculpture of *St James*, dominates both the church and its own painted

panels. Much of this evangelizing art was exported to the Spanish colonies, where there were native Americans to convert and Protestant settlers to exorcize. Latin American frames are even more exotically ornate; the early 17th-century Retable of Metztitlán (Hidalgo, Mexico, church of the monastery of the Holy Kings; see de la Maza) is encrusted with ornament like a barnacled ship. It has swan's-neck pediments, Islamic stalactite drops and columns spiralled with vines. It is midway, in period and in its *horror vacui*, between 16th-century Plateresque and the Churrigueresque late Baroque of the early 18th century (see below).

Meanwhile in Spain itself, the growth of a purer Baroque style was helped by the accession (1621) of the great patron and collector, Philip IV. He installed Velázquez as Pintor de Cámara, commissioned tapestries and pictures from Rubens, sent Velázquez to Italy and employed the Neapolitan viceroys and Roman ambassadors to track down the finest pictures for the new Buen Retiro Palace (from 1630). He also instituted a royal workshop, which continued to produce furniture, including picture frames, into the 19th century. The first royal cabinetmaker was G. Campo. Against this background Zurbarán began his career, in the mid-17th century becoming painter to Philip IV. In 1638–9 he painted a retable for the Cartuja of Jerez de la Frontera (fragments; Grenoble, Mus. Peint. & Sculp.; New York, Met.; Cadiz, Mus. Pint.; for reconstruction see 1990 exh. cat., p. 46). This followed the earlier work of such artists as Berruguete in having several large-scale paintings arranged in three tiers of three. It was also, like Ribalta's altarpiece, an example of what *remate* had become—there was no longer any pretence of emulating the Gothic canopies that had named the genre, but the mixture of painting and sculpture that it now signified was still current, with carved figures of saints and a *Crucifixion* beneath a segmental pediment. The lowest saints were probably set against paired Solomonic columns, and there may have been triangular Baroque screens between the *Crucifixion* and the penultimate entablature.

In 1638–9 Zurbarán was commissioned to paint eight large (3.0×2.1 m) pictures devoted to 15th-century monks of the Hieronymite Order for the sacristy of the monastery at Guadalupe (*in situ*), and these were finished by August 1639 and sent unframed from Seville (see Cherry, 1985). They formed part of an opulent new interior, were set high on the walls between enriched Plateresque pilasters and decorative panels, and were framed, either under the direction of the architect or the influential Prior Diego de Montalvo, in striking examples of the elaborated Herrera style. They have an outer torus of 'cotton-reel' mouldings, crossed near the ends of each rail by pairs of giant hooked clasps, which appear to take a *trompe l'oeil* S-form and emerge from under an inner cotton-reel torus with the hook upwards, encroaching on the picture surface. Cartouches explaining the subjects are hung in smaller matching borders beneath each painting. These bold, peculiarly Spanish geometrical ornaments are reflected in the surrounding architectural mouldings that cover the walls and ceiling. Gemlike lozenges and cabochons are set in the cornice, and there are squared chains, segmented ovolos, metopes and triglyphs and huge chunky egg-and-dart mouldings, together with a large Vitruvian scroll. This ornamental extravaganza continues into the chapel of S Jerónimo beyond, for which Zurbarán painted an altarpiece and episodes from the *Life of St Jerome*. They hang in the same Herrera-type frames as those in the sacristy, and two of these frames have been set into the retable aedicula.

Typical of Counter-Reformation art in Spain, this theatrical use of varied ornamentation includes an insistence on native or Hispano-Moresque styles, as though they were identified with the purity of the Catholic tradition in the peninsula. It is far from an expression of the real political and economic state of the country, however. From 1635 to 1659 Spain was at war with France, and in 1639 Catalonia revolted and joined with France. During the 1640s, both Portugal and Naples rebelled; within Spain there was social unrest, an economy that government meddling had all but extinguished and, finally, plague. Patronage and connoisseurship, nevertheless, flourished against this grim background. Philip IV bought in quantity from Rubens's posthumous studio sale and from the collection of Charles I of England; he commissioned work from Claude and sent Velázquez to buy works by Jacopo Tintoretto and Veronese in Italy. The 7th Marqués del Carpio became chief minister, and his palace and art collection were one of the sights of Madrid. 16th-century Italian paintings—especially Venetian—were the most prized, but contemporary Baroque influence came through the acquisition of works by Guido Reni, Orazio Gentileschi and van Dyck, as well as Rubens.

A beneficiary of this hunger for art was the painter Francisco Rizi, who executed major decorative schemes for the Court and altarpieces for the Church. In 1655 he painted the *Martyrdom of St Peter* (Madrid, Fuente el Saz parish church), which has the naturalism, dramatic lighting, colour and action exemplified by such artists as Rubens. Its framework is solid and grand, reflecting the style of the paintings; it echoes their sense of movement by having the two lateral sections canted forwards, forming a tripartite bay, within which the two lower painted side panels are set back flush with the main surface. This imitates the illusion of dynamic movement found in architectural façades and the spatial complexity of Baroque wall paintings. Fluted Corinthian columns support the canted sections, and every moulding of the classical skeleton is enriched. Scrolling strapwork cartouches cross the entablature of the main *Crucifixion of St Peter*, crest the segmental pediment and form acroteria, set on large flattened volutes. Friezes and spandrels are set with roselike scrolled leaves (a common ornament on 17th-century Spanish moulding frames), and swags of carved fruit hang from the capitals of the upper tiers. The whole mass of carving is coloured and gilded, emphasizing the effects of light and movement. A year later Velázquez painted *Las Meninas* (1656; Madrid, Prado); the same Baroque illusionism describes complex effects of space and light within the painting, but colour and violent action are replaced by limited tones and subtle relationships. Around the depicted room, paintings hang in plain black northern European frames, which reflect the sombre austerity of the Court and harmonize with Velázquez's neutral tones. In this work, majesty is expressed in dignity of bearing rather than cloth of gold, and

the King and Queen reflected in the glass are also framed in a wide black border.

These oppositions of opulence and restraint make up Spanish Baroque. It is a style of painting and ornament rather than of architecture; the applied arts built on the basis of Mannerism, and Mannerist elements surfaced increasingly throughout the 17th century. Even on the façade (1667) of Granada Cathedral, with its Romanesque body and Herrera lines, small Mannerist flourishes appeared. Italian artists in Spain strengthened the High Baroque tradition: decorative schemes by, for example, Agostino Mitelli and Angelo Michele Colonna realized Mitelli's dynamic and soaring designs (he was also one of the precursors of the Auricular style). They probably influenced Rizi, whose illusionistic ceiling (1668) for S Antonio de los Portugueses, Madrid, painted with Juan Carreño de Miranda, has the same elongated niches shooting vertically away, the same scrolling pediments and the same foliate friezes that Mitelli used. Rich though Mitelli's ornament is, however, Rizi and Carreño surpassed it, adding segmental arches between swan's-neck pediments, replacing Ionic with spirally fluted Solomonic columns and breaking the inner 'frame' of the ceiling by lavish, slightly Auricular cartouches. A similar hint of the Auricular can be seen in Rizi's extraordinary illusionistic fresco (1678) for the chapel of the Miracle, convent of Descalzas Reales, Madrid. Here, a door opens on to another, imagined chapel, and above the painted door is a representation of the Annunciation, 'framed' in melting strapwork mixed with flowers and masks, such as would be seen in works by 18th-century followers of José Benito de Churriguera.

Increasingly busy decoration, multiplying Flemish Mannerist details on a Baroque structure and anticipating the Churrigueresque style (see below), is associated with the altarpieces of Claudio Coello. Coello knew Carreño and like him painted decorative schemes. Those in Toledo Cathedral repeat the native and large-scale classical ornaments that appear in the sacristy of the monastery of Guadalupe. Similarly, the retable (1668) by Coello, in the Benedictine church of S Plácido, Madrid, has a classically-inspired frame with such Baroque enrichments as fluted Composite columns, a frieze of roselike curling leaves, carved and painted masks facing three sides of supporting pillars, and quasi-Auricular cartouches. A sketch (Munich, Kleine Gal.) for or from this work, with integral painted frame, shows an even more voluptuous arrangement. Here, the round arch of the actual retable is given greater depth, hinting at a horseshoe Moorish arch, and is supported on Solomonic columns twined with vines. This may be a later replica, as the same motifs are reproduced in the work that brought together Coello and Churriguera: the retable of S Esteban, Salamanca (1692–3; see fig. 92).

Churriguera's three sons and such followers as Narciso Tomé, Francisco Hurtado Izquierdo and Pedro de Ribera took up his ornate Baroque vocabulary and elaborated it with Mannerist motifs into a fantasy of flowing multiple mouldings, *estípite* pilasters (broken into geometric panels and cartouches with several capitals) and ornaments taken from the picture frames he made (*see* CHURRIGUE-RESQUE). The resultant restless mass, picked out with gilding, was spread over every surface of an altarpiece and

92. Altarpiece frame (detail) by José Benito de Churriguera, h. *c.* 30 m, signed and dated 1693, for Claudio Coello's *Martyrdom of St Stephen* retable, 1692–3 (Salamanca, Monastery of S Esteban)

every wall of a church. When exported to the colonies, even more enrichment was added to impress native South Americans with the magnificence of their conquerors. The retable of S Esteban shows the first flourishes of the style. The frame, *c.* 30 m high, is a manifesto of Spanish High Baroque. The cornice, halfway up the frame, follows the receding and projecting planes of the three-niche plan in an echo of the Granada Cathedral façade, the rhythmic movement being supported below by eight Solomonic columns, paired one behind the other and twined with ornament like those in Coello's sketch. The centre of the cornice is broken by a Baroque shell, which protrudes into Coello's painting of the martyr above and is reflected in an immense crest, supported on a gigantic voluted clasp. Foliate roses, urns, margents and drooping bunches of carved and gilt flowers, angels and double *estípite* capitals are among the other enrichments. The frames of Spanish retables always tended to dominate the paintings, the strong colouring and emotional power of which perhaps developed in reaction to this. In this altarpiece the frame has triumphed, and the painting, pushed into the minor arch at the top, is completely overwhelmed—huge though it is—by the carving around and beneath it. The central niche is occupied by a great custodia; shaped like a Baroque domed cathedral, with colonnettes echoing the forest of Solomonic columns around it, it is also more insistent than Coello's painting of the *Martyrdom of St Stephen*.

Hurtado Izquierdo's altarpiece (1710s–20s) for the chapel of S José, Seville, takes this fantasy of carving to its extreme. Here there is no frame (or it is all frame); the architectural surround has dissolved into the frenetic ornamentation of every surface, giving no space for the

eye to rest. Free-standing sculptures, all different in scale, ropes of putti, inexplicable moulded brackets and cartouches, and *estípite* columns with multiple capitals fill the whole wall behind the altar with continuous, restless motion. This effect is increased by the Baroque use of lighting as a sculptural tool, so that artificially strengthened shadows lend a theatrical brilliance to the highlighted niches of the Virgin and Christ. Dramatic gestures and wind-torn robes give a further dynamism, and the sense of movement is heightened by a seemingly impossibly early appearance (given Hurtado Izquierdo's death in 1725) of Rococo in Spain. Asymmetric shells and rocaille cartouches jostle with serpentine strapwork, frame half-length sculpted saints, halo cherubs' heads and panel Christ's niche like a French boudoir.

France became an influence again in Spain when the Habsburg line died out on Charles II's death in 1700, and after the War of the Spanish Succession (1701–13), the Bourbon Philip V became the King of Spain. There was a greater emphasis on French artists: Philip's collection included work by Watteau, and he commissioned paintings from Michel-Ange Houasse and Jean Ranc. Spain's Italian possessions passed to the Holy Roman Empire, but Philip's second queen was Elisabeth Farnese of Parma, and the King employed such Italian artists as Andrea Procaccini and Francesco Solimena, so there was still stylistic contact with Italy. In the 1720s, however, ornamental art in Spain seemed little affected by these influences. Tomé's screen or Transparente (1720–32), backing on to the high altar of Toledo Cathedral, is characteristic of the period. Once more there is no means of separating frame and content as the architectural structure is so intimately related to the tiers of sculpted scenes. The Mannerist elements are similar to those of the S José Altarpiece—not *estípite* pilasters, but torn, *trompe l'oeil* leather sheaths on the lowest columns, curving entablatures and a strong vertical emphasis.

6. ROCOCO. By the time French ornamental influence took effect, it seemed to be out of date already: once more Spain was lagging behind the decorative currents of the east and north, unaffected by the aberration of Hurtado Izquierdo's early Rococo. In 1727 the 9th Conde de Aranda (*d* 1742) built a factory in Alcora producing faience to designs by Jacques Callot, who had died nearly a century before, and Jean Berain I, who had died in 1711. These designs confirmed the Baroque rut in which Spain was firmly set until the mid-18th century, merely varying it by Callot's inclinations to a pre-Auricular style and Berain's to a pre-Rococo. True Rococo ornament was introduced into Spain via the Real Academia de San Fernando, established by Ferdinand VI in 1752. Its director was Corrado Giaquinto of Naples, who helped Matteo Gasparini (*d* 1774) and José Canops with the decoration of the Palacio Real of Madrid (*see* SPAIN, fig. 29). The dressing-room of Charles III (after 1760) is in the extravagant asymmetrical Rococo manner developed decades earlier in France. All the elements of the full-blooded style are there: chinoiserie niches in the cove, carved and gilded looking-glasses, floral curlicued borders on the wall hangings and polychrome scrolling branches on the ceiling. Relatively few such interiors were produced in Spain,

possibly because of the long duration of Baroque there, as in Italy (with the exception of Venice). Rococo motifs appeared more frequently in the minor arts. The Conde de Aranda's factory began to produce earthenware plaques with integral moulded frames; these had high profiles, rocaille centre/corner cartouches and crests.

Rococo furniture was also produced in quantity, perhaps to rectify the lack of Rococo architecture; at first it was coarse and schematic, distinguishable from Baroque carving only by its asymmetry. Charles III halted the trade in French luxury furniture, and Crown and Court were forced to rely on native craftsmen—often not specialists as in Paris, but joiners and carvers of all work, who could produce anything from a retable to a girandole. They decorated everything in the same mixture of gilding and polychromy, and a sofa might display the same cartouches as an altarpiece. Similar motifs appeared on mirror frames (known as cornucopias because of their lavish fruit, flower and voluted ornaments) and especially on beds. These 18th-century beds illustrate the versatility of Spanish wood-carvers and bridge the gap between furniture and picture frames. They developed in the district around Girona and are furnished with huge decorative headboards that are really pictures with asymmetric Rococo frames. Made in one piece, and often free-standing from the bed or hung on the wall behind it, they are usually painted with religious scenes, angels, cherubs etc, or with family crests, and are surrounded with integral carved, sometimes gilded, borders of C- and S-scrolls, *rinceaux*, floral swags and rocailles, all in a vigorous but coarse native style. Examples can be seen in casas Ventós and Solà, Olot, and in the Museo Nacional de Artes Decorativas, Madrid.

Picture frames in the same style were produced, but for important paintings frames of a rather more French cast were used, either executed in Spain by French-influenced craftsmen or imported (as far as the King's restrictions allowed). On Luís Meléndez's *Still-life: The Afternoon Meal* (New York, Met.) is a straight-sided ogee frame (see fig. 93a) with sculpted Rococo corners and shallow-relief details. This is an example of Spanish craftsmen emulating an imported French style and endeavouring to assimilate it to the Baroque profile and ornaments they understood. Hence, an 18th-century work has a distinctly 17th-century air, the rocaille S-scrolls sitting oddly with the corner leaf clasps. From a distance, however, the Baroque form triumphs, and the solid profile and corner/centre focal points complement the curving lines and diagonal composition of Meléndez's picture. In contrast, the frame of François-Hubert Drouais's *Dauphin Louis, Son of Louis XV* (Madrid, Prado) is fully Rococo. It is comparatively restrained, with shells, flowers and a touch of asymmetry; there are even some early Neo-classical details. Its purity gives it a non-Spanish appearance: it is unlike the rustic vigour of the Rococo bedheads or the interior in Luis Paret's *Charles III Lunching before his Court* (c. 1770; Madrid, Prado), where the room is hung with tapestries enclosed in floral borders like polychrome carvings and where the asymmetrical mirror frame possesses a distinctly native character.

Charles III provided a background for the two versions of Rococo—sophisticated French and naive Spanish—as he moved his country from great impoverishment and

93. Spanish Rococo and Neo-classical frames, *c.* 1750–1820: (a) bolection frame with rocaille ornaments between corner and centre foliate volutes, 1060×1540×120 mm, possibly original for Luís Meléndez's *Still-life: The Afternoon Meal* (New York, Metropolitan Museum of Art); (b) gallery frame with leaves and ribbon, 1485×2038×100 mm, made for Antoine Coypel's *Susanna Accused of Adultery, c.* 1699 (Madrid, Museo del Prado); (c) fluted scotia frame with dentils, 1155×787×122 mm, original for Francisco de Goya's *Goya and his Doctor, Don Eugenio García Arrieta*, 1820 (Minneapolis, MN, Minneapolis Institute of Arts); (d) fluted 'pilaster' frame with corner roundels, 350×480 mm, late 18th century, made for Luís Meléndez's *Still-life with Plums, Figs, Bread, a Pitcher and Other Kitchenware*, 1760s (Madrid, Museo del Prado)

stagnation to a period of prosperity, such that Spain could support the complexity of full-blown Rococo. Two levels of craftsmen dealt with the dual styles. Firstly, designers and cabinetmakers such as the architects Ventura Rodríguez and José López (*c.* 1725–95), who ruled the royal workshops in the late 1760s and worked with the carver Tomás Castro, could reproduce French Louis XV frames or, equally, the Neo-classical frames and furniture that also appeared in the 1760s. Secondly, there were their lesser cousins, the craftsmen-joiners, who dealt competently with all types of artefact and gave each style a Hispanic flavour. (Native techniques were not abandoned even at the highest level, however: the royal workshops still employed a skilled polychromer.)

In the colonies, Rococo does not seem to have had a very strong impact; Churrigueresque Baroque had too great a hold. Works such as the retable of *Our Lady of Guadalupe* (late 18th century; Mexico City Cathedral; see de la Maza) show again how Rococo elements have been grafted on to the basic Baroque–Mannerist style. Shaped painted panels—ovals and eared ovals, with an ogee-topped panel above—are set in a round-arched structure and edged with light mouldings. There is no asymmetry, and Baroque volutes and a heavy central entablature compete with light floral scrolls.

7. NEO-CLASSICAL AND EARLY 19TH CENTURY. Neo-classicism was adopted more quickly than Rococo in

Spain; this was due partly to the historic influence of the classical Herrera style and partly to reaction against the long-enduring Baroque manner, which had lasted in Spain for more than a century and a half if Mannerism, the Churrigueresque and the Rococo are included. It was also due partly to the enthusiasm for the classical of the brothers Diego de Villanueva and Juan de Villanueva, who promulgated, both theoretically and practically, an alternative to the reign of the theatrical curve and volute. An early Neo-classical building is the Casita del Príncipe near Madrid, designed by Juan de Villanueva in 1784 for the future Charles IV. Juan's brother Diego had written on the revival of classicism in Spain, following interest in the excavations at Herculaneum and Pompeii, and the first experimental designs by the French Louis-Joseph Le Lorrain. Between Diego's theories and Juan's practice, however, the eternal Spanish craving for colour and decoration infected the classical ideals of spareness and clarity, and the interiors of the building are richly ornamented in Louis XVI style. Yet, although the cornices, dado rails, door-frames etc are pattern books of multiple architectural mouldings picked out in gold, the picture frames are quite plain. Mainly hollow or ogee in profile, they are either completely unornamented or touched with restrained geometrical decoration, possibly the simplest yet in the history of Spanish frames. They are evidently designed to mediate between the Baroque paintings they house and the floral silk wall hangings, resuming in this role the classic supportive function of a frame, which had been little apparent in Spain until now.

From around the same time comes another simple Neo-classical design (93d), which is also a gallery or 'livery' frame. A flat gilt border, it has three deep flutes along each rail and knobbed roundels mounted on squares at each corner (a 16th-century Italian motif). It was used in the last quarter of the 18th century to frame 45 still-lifes (most in Madrid, Prado) by Meléndez, which were assembled in a unified scheme to decorate the apartments of Charles IV's son Ferdinand in the palace at Aranjuez, near Madrid. The chunkiness and blown-up treatment of the ornament is typically Spanish; the oversized guilloche filling the whole flat on the frame of Anton Raphael Meng's *Maria Luisa of Parma* (Madrid, Prado) is similar.

Another Neo-classical gallery frame (93b) can be found on important paintings in the Prado (on those inventoried in the Madrid Alcázar in 1666, and those in Isabel de Farnesio's collection in 1746), which were probably re-framed between c. 1760 and c. 1790 on the orders of Charles III. This was to fit them to the new interiors of the Palacio Real, Madrid, which Charles's father had begun in 1738 and which was decorated in his own reign with both Neo-classical and Rococo rooms. These frames bridge the two styles, being in the transitional French taste of the late Rococo, when symmetry and classical ornament were reintroduced. They have an outer bird's-beak moulding, spiralled with acanthus leaves, a small ribbon moulding, plain hollow and an astragal bound with crossed ribbons. They can be found on Murillo's *Holy Family*, Nicolas de Largillierre's portrait of *Maria Anna Victoria de Bourbón* (1724), Veronese's *Venus and Adonis* (1582) and Titian's *Knight with a Clock* (all Madrid, Prado). The effect of the two larger mouldings, with enrichments

between plain reposes, is of a restrained spiralling geometry, underlined by the twisted ribbon, and of a slight shimmer of light. Obviously suitable to all genres of painting, it is perhaps not quite weighty enough for the larger works; in fact, it has an unusual delicacy for a Spanish frame. Richer designs followed later, employing a range of classical ornament, such as the cross-fluted hollow frame (93c), which manages to echo the Herrera style in its illusionistic tongued protrusion of fillets and double row of overlapping dentils. Pompeo Batoni's *William Hamilton* (?1770s; Madrid, Prado) also has a frame with a Hispanic air; double fillets down each rail hold runs of carved bay leaves, crossing at the corners to form cassettes holding paterae; further decorations include a prominent, enriched egg-and-dart trim and a bead-and-bobbin trim.

Charles IV ruled over this Neo-classical period in Spain; he was a collector (of Flemish and Italian Renaissance works as well as of paintings by Ribera); he also built the Pavilion of the Real Casa del Labrador, Aranjuez, for which Isidro González-Velázquez (c. 1765–after 1829) designed house, furniture and accessories, including frames, all in early 19th-century Neo-classical taste. Charles was a weak ruler and, having joined a coalition against France after Louis XVI's execution, in 1795 he was forced to ally with France. There was a reaction against French fashions and influence at this time, and the 'neutrality' of Neo-classicism aided its stylistic hold in Spain. In 1808 Charles was forced to give the crown to Napoleon's brother, Joseph Bonaparte, who began to suppress the religious orders and to sequestrate their goods. Fortunately, Spain was liberated in 1814 before the process had gone too far; one result might have been the splitting up of thousands of Spanish retables still *in situ* in churches and monasteries, the panels being sent to decorate the Louvre and the frames and settings being irretrievably lost, as has happened in Italy and France.

After the restoration of the monarchy (1814), the prevalent style during Ferdinand VII's reign (1814–33) had much in common with the French Empire style, in spite of the war with France and earlier reaction against its influence. Empire furniture was made in quantity in central and south-eastern Spain. Mirror frames were generally in the Empire taste, but picture frames tended to repeat 18th-century designs and were either Neo-classical or Baroque. This imitation increased through the 19th century, and under Isabella II (*reg* 1833–68) frames were a mixture of past Spanish styles and of anonymous 19th-century French stock patterns. Towards the end of Isabella's reign the country's prosperity began to increase again, and in 1876 Spain was made a constitutional monarchy under Alfonso XII (*reg* 1874–85). With greater wealth and political stability, the decrease in its artistic aloofness accelerated, and outside influences took more rapid root than ever before. William Morris was a model: the Proustian Room in the Villa Ocejo, Comillas, decorated for a visit of Alfonso in 1882, imitates Morris's wall coverings and friezes, although the frames are, characteristically, not yet part of this Arts and Crafts style, being Baroque, Neo-classical or replica 18th-century French.

8. LATE 19TH AND 20TH CENTURIES. By the 1880s, as in England and France, wealthy industrial barons wished

to confirm their own rise by investing in contemporary works of art. This coincided with the *modernismo* movement in Spain, which lasted from the 1880s to the 1910s, and which had much in common with Art Nouveau. It involved the use of new industrial processes in architecture and the applied arts, and the revival of a national style in a contemporary idiom. It swiftly took hold, encouraged by the new money waiting to support it, and by its expression through such designers as Antoni Gaudí. He was influenced by the Gothic vocabulary of Viollet-le-Duc and by the nationalistic spirit in his native Catalonia, where the medieval style of its prosperous days was also a defiant gesture to the classicism associated with Spain's oppression by France. Gothic was also more in tune than classicism with the Spanish love of colour and decoration. Islamic motifs and Rococo chinoiseries were sources for Gaudí's work, as was the current interest in organic forms of ornament; he developed the whiplash curve introduced by English designers, proclaiming the curved line as God's, the straight as Man's. He was also concerned to produce a 'complete' work, like the unified schemes of the Baroque period, where every item of an interior (furniture, floors, walls and frames) would reflect the same taste.

The *modernismo* movement lasted slightly longer in Spain than Art Nouveau in the rest of Europe, where it was already fading after its climax at the Exposition Universelle of 1900. One of Picasso's earliest works is a decorated picture frame (Barcelona, Mus. Picasso) and, influenced by the *modernismo* idea of the 'complete work', he also designed an interior scheme. The frame takes the form of a stripped Classical aedicula, with vestigial entablature and plinth; the top frieze is deeper than the other rails, and the whole is painted with symbolic motifs of a mother and child, fish, amphorae, flowers and an Olympian face. It follows in the line of artist-designed and decorated frames that were produced in quantity in Germany, Austria and England during the last decades of the 19th century, often in this pared-down classical style, and coincides with a term in Picasso's work in which he had still not broken from the Symbolism of the period. Picasso reworked this romanticized classical style and subject-matter in a series of decorative panels with integral 'frames' for the villa of La Mimoserie, Biarritz (1918; priv. col.). Here monumentality replaced Symbolism in representations of *L'Abondance*, *La Ronde* etc, and the 'frames' follow this, with scalloped borders around a deep plain margin or around a 'fillet' set with tiny roundels. Similar fillets bind the 'frames' to the room itself and its features, repeating the roundel motif along the skirting, around the windows and between the sections of panelling. The 'framed' images are set against a starry ground, which is echoed in negative shades on the ceiling. This concept of the 'complete' interior, although unfurnished, must have been influenced by Gaudí.

Picasso experimented with different types of frame, painted and applied, and also included frames and fragments of moulding within his pictures. Many of his canvases include integral painted borders, as in the black illusionist shaded frame painted around an abstract from the artist's own collection (see *Picasso's Picassos: An Exhibition from the Musée Picasso*, exh. cat., ed. D. Bozo, T. Hilton and R. Penrose; London, Hayward Gal., 1981).

Oval Cubist works of 1912 (e.g. the collage *Still-life with Chair-caning*; Paris, Mus. Picasso) were given actual frames of rope; Turner had framed marine paintings appropriately in ship's cable, but here the rope seems rather an aspect of the technique of collage. Some paintings of 1914 examine the idea of the frame within a frame and include *faux* frames—either painted imitation mouldings or applied borders, as in the scrolling leaf-and-berry wallpaper frieze on *Pipe and Sheet of Music* (Houston, TX, Mus. F.A.). Here Picasso's signature is set on a 'label' on the centre bottom 'rail', parodying museum labels as the frieze mimics a carved Neo-classical frame. Other works of the same year include segments of architectural frame mouldings as background, surround or simply part of a still-life, while several collages are mounted within shallow boxes that 'frame' them or within an actual frame. Joan Miró also used found frames, most notably in *Portrait* (1950; New York, Mr and Mrs Pierre Matisse priv. col.), using a 19th-century picture the frame of which reminded him of Gaudí's work as well as his own, and which he re-created as his own.

Juan Gris used frames within his paintings; like Picasso, he incorporated them as part of a still-life, while many of his portraits have reddish-brown integral borders that sometimes swell into the area of the actual picture. Again, Miró did this later on, and Picasso's late graphic works carry their own representations of three-dimensional carved wooden frames (see fig. 94). Such devices test the idea of what the work is and also circumvent the need for the real, movable frame at a time when frames were losing

94. Integral graphic border on Pablo Picasso's *Lady with a Ruff*, one of a pair of linocuts, 537×400 mm, 1963 (New York, Metropolitan Museum of Art)

much of their ornamental and crafted quality and becoming mass-produced functional elements of protection. They also provide, fortuitously, for the period later in the 20th century when curators unframed many modern works in order for the public to see them 'as the artist saw them'. Whether the artist would have countenanced this elimination of immediate context and necessary transition is rarely discussed, but where he has provided his own border—even as a joke or a parody—the role of the frame is clearly underlined and its acceptance by the maker of the image highlighted.

BIBLIOGRAPHY

R. R. Tatlock and others: *Spanish Art* (London, 1927)
G. Bazin: 'L'Art espagnol au Musée des arts décoratifs', *Gaz. B.-A.* (1929), pp. 46–53
C. R. Post: *A History of Spanish Painting*, 14 vols (Cambridge, MA, 1930)
F. de la Maza: 'Mexican Colonial Retablos', *Gaz. B.-A.*, 6th ser., xxv (1944), pp. 175–86
J. Folchi i Torres, ed.: *L'art catala*, 2 vols (Barcelona, 1957)
J. Claret Rubire and Marquis of Lozoya: *Muebles de estilo español des de el gotico hasta el siglo XIX* (Barcelona, 1962)
L. Feduchi: *El mueble español* (Barcelona, 1969)
F. J. Sánchez Cantón: *The Prado* (London, 1971)
R. Mulcahy: 'The High Altarpiece of the Basilica of San Lorenzo de El Escorial', *Burl. Mag.*, cxxii (1980), pp. 188–92
W. Rubin, ed.: *Pablo Picasso: A Retrospective* (New York and London, 1980)
M. C. Volk: 'New Light on a 17th-century Collector: The Marquis of Leganes', *A. Bull.*, lxii (1980), pp. 56–68
J. Claret Rubire: *Encyclopaedia of Spanish Period Furniture Designs* (New York, 1984)
P. Cherry: 'The Contract for Francisco de Zurbarán's Paintings of Hieronymite Works for the Sacristy of the Monastery of Guadalupe', *Burl. Mag.*, cxxvii (1985), pp. 374–81
E. Tufts: *Luís Meléndez: 18th-century Master of the Spanish Still-life* (Columbia, MO, 1985)
F. Davis: 'Not All Rapture', *Country Life*, clxxxii (19 May 1988), pp. 208–9
A. E. Pérez Sánchez and others: *The Prado* (London, 1988)
A. Mitchell and A. Garrido: *Spain: Interiors, Gardens, Architecture, Landscape* (London, 1990)
G. Worsley: 'La Casita del Principe, El Prado', *Country Life*, clxxxiv (20 Dec 1990), pp. 56–61
Polyptyques: Le Tableau multiple du moyen âge au vingtième siècle (exh. cat., ed. C. Clément; Paris, Louvre, 1990)
J. Brown: *The Golden Age of Painting in Spain* (New Haven and London, 1991)

For further bibliography *see* §I above.

PAUL MITCHELL, LYNN ROBERTS

IX. USA.

A distinguishing attribute of American picture frames is the extreme diversity of styles. Primarily influenced by European designs, American frames are a curious hybrid of many English, French, Dutch, Spanish, Italian and German styles. In spite of this cross-cultural barrage of influences from a variety of immigrant craftsmen, there has gradually emerged a basic characteristic of simplicity and strength of design. The reduction of complex ornamentation has been a common theme throughout the constantly changing styles of American frames. This simplification process also appears in the altering of the profiles or shapes of the mouldings. Such an approach was possibly due to the American craftsman's desire to design a new order. It could also have been caused by the lack of strict trade guilds, which allowed a greater latitude in pattern-making and a freedom that may have encouraged creativity. Shortage of traditional moulding profiles

and gilding materials may also have furthered this tendency towards rustic approaches to framing. Often, in rural areas, frames were finished with common house-paint. In some cases frames were marbled or grained to create a more refined appearance. The Decorative Arts Photographic Library at Winterthur, DE, the Museum of Early Southern Decorative Arts, in Winston-Salem, NC, and the International Institute for Frame Study (founded in the 1990s) in Washington, DC, are three major repositories of information on American framemakers and dealers of picture frames.

1. Before 1776. 2. 1776 and after.

1. BEFORE 1776. Although frames created by 18th-century craftsmen in such metropolitan areas as Boston, New York and Philadelphia echo more closely the sentiments of English taste, those produced in rural areas were more idiosyncratic and naive. Many framemakers in colonial America had been appprenticed in England or else used English pattern books for inspiration. Thomas Chippendale's *Gentleman and Cabinet-maker's Director* (London, 1754) was an influential and widely distributed manual of the decorative arts. Although in the major cities there were a few framemakers, picture frames were usually imported or made by a local craftsman out of window or door trim. The usual method of fabrication for these early frames was to hand-gouge the wood with a variety of curved, shaped, moulding planes. Methods of joinery are often an important clue in establishing a provenance for a frame. For example, the lap-joint or mortice-and-tenon construction method usually indicates a sophisticated European training. On the other hand, the simple 45%

95. American Rococo frame on John Singleton Copley's *Mrs John Scollay*, 889×686 mm, 1763 (New York, Kennedy Galleries Inc.)

mitre cut, joined with glue and nails, is more typically found in American-made frames. The splined corner, an elaborate technique often employed on large, highly embellished, carved European frames, made use of a compression joint. A piece of hardwood, tapered and chamfered, is inlaid into the back of the frame perpendicular to the mitred corner.

American framemakers in mid-18th-century Boston were considered to be inferior to and more expensive than their English counterparts. For example, the Boston selectmen were considering the purchase of a frame for a portrait of *Peter Faneuil* (Boston, MA, Mus. F.A.) by John Smibert. They stated that 'it could be got in London cheaper and better than with us.' In comparing the Rococo frames on two portraits by John Singleton Copley there is a marked difference between the frame on the painting of *Mrs John Scollay* (1763; New York, Kennedy Gals; see fig. 95) and the frame on *Mr Isaac Smith* (1769; New Haven, CT, Yale U. A.G.; see fig. 96). The profile on the earlier portrait is quite simple and consists of two flat boards that have been joined at an angle and later carved with typical foliate designs and piercing. The profile on the later portrait is an elaborately shaped deep scoop with a gadrooned sight edge. In addition to the dynamic carving of foliage and floral patterns, there is a separately carved and pierced shell at the top centre indicating a more sophisticated approach than the earlier, more rustic frame. Although there is no conclusive evidence as to who made either of these frames, it might be surmised that the simpler, more provincial frame on *Mrs Scollay* was made by a local craftsman influenced by Chippendale's *Director* rather than a highly trained London framemaker who was bound by a strict adherence to style and form. The analysis of wood type does not yield absolute proof, however, as north-east American white pine was exported to London during the 18th century.

2. 1776 AND AFTER. After the Revolution, Americans were inclined to produce frames on a large scale in their own manufacturing facilities rather than to import them. Taste in frame styles leant towards the Neo-classical patterns that were adopted via French influence. The simple restrained elegance of the Louis XVI style profile was easily adapted to the austere Yankee mentality. Charles Willson Peale's painting of *Henrietta Margaret Hill* (1790; Winston-Salem, NC, Mus. Early S. Dec. A.) illustrates the use of the classical ornamentation of egg-and-dart, lamb's tongue and twisted ribbonwork carved into a flat shallow profile. Peale, the first museologist in America, was adamant about frame styles chosen for clients, as evidenced by a letter he wrote in 1807 stating, 'A good picture deserves a good frame and a bad picture may sometimes preserve its place longer by having a handsome frame.' The Neo-classical taste continued into the first quarter of the 19th century, later evolving into the French Empire style of wide, deep-scooped mouldings ornamented with anthemion motifs in the corners. These were fabricated with low-relief composition or gesso putty.

Again, as in the previous century, the American penchant for design was one of simplification and reduction. In the 1830s, through the elimination of ornamentation, mouldings that were strong and simple yet elegant were

96. American Rococo frame on John Singleton Copley's *Mr Isaac Smith*, 1.27×1.02 m, 1769 (New Haven, CT, Yale University Art Gallery)

97. American raised cornerblock frame, 502×444 mm, 1830 (Washington, DC, Gold Leaf Studios)

98. American frame designs from a pattern book by Stanford White, published posthumously for Newcomb-Macklin Co., New York and Chicago, c. 1922

created. In rural areas frames were made using raised cornerblocks, and sometimes floral and foliate designs were stencilled on to the painted surface (see fig. 97). The most typical finish was to paint the frame black, although there were many regional variations that have yet to be catalogued and documented. During the 1850s, as mass production increased, individual expression and innovative frame designs were not typically pursued. Factories were producing larger amounts of heavily ornamented moulding, previously unavailable to the average consumer. Important centres of manufacturing fluctuated between such larger cities as Boston, New York, Philadelphia and as far south as Baltimore. Although Baltimore was by now considered to be one of the largest furniture manufacturing centres, in 1850 there were over 130 framemaking concerns in New York alone. Accelerated production created a stagnation in original designs, and the repetition of composition patterns was standard in the industry. Hand-carved frames were rare. Once a pattern was created, extrusion machines, embossing wheels and similar mass-production techniques were employed to make moulding by the length for national distribution.

Some innovations in design appeared in the 1870s. For example, a stencilling technique using glue and sand to create a textured effect similar to the patterning on a giraffe was used until the 1880s. Orientalist, Moorish, Gothic Revival and finally Renaissance Revival styles were popular during the last quarter of the 19th century. Most

of these frames were constructed with composition, which allowed for a greater number to be produced. James McNeill Whistler, active mainly in England, was among the first Americans to react to the Victorian penchant for superfluous ornamentation; his frame designs were to prove particularly influential (*see* §IV, 10 above). As a popular reaction to such ornamentation, frames were often made from a simple gilded plank of oak made from quarter-sawn wood. This style of frame became popular during the last quarter of the 19th century. Thomas Eakins often used this format to frame his work (e.g. *Professor Henry A. Rowland*; Andover, MA, Phillips Acad., Addison Gal.). For some of his portraits, he carved into the wood a design that related to the subject. On small works, he used a simple pine plank with no gilding. His use of this style of frame was caused by the ever-increasing influence of the Arts and Crafts Movement, which took hold in the USA at the end of the 19th century. Although the austerity of this approach was contrary to the opulence of the preceding generation, the simplicity appealed to the American sentiment.

Not all artists, however, used this simple type of frame. Many were inspired by the Renaissance Revival that was adopted by the architect Stanford White of McKim, Mead & White. His sphere of influence was widespread; he received many important commissions and was involved in the selection of paintings and their frames for several of his clients. He was friendly with many of the leading artists of the day and often designed frames for them. Abbott Handerson Thayer, for example, used White's designs for his paintings, as they were particularly well suited to his style of idealistic realism. Thayer painted women as angels to complement White's tabernacle frames. These frames were sometimes made by a leading framemaking company, Newcomb-Macklin Co., which had a showroom in New York and a factory in Chicago. Their pattern books show the wide diversity of styles available to artists and collectors alike (see fig. 98).

Arthur F. Mathews (1860–1945), a Californian artist and designer, made hand-carved, polychromed frames for his paintings. Many of the floral patterns carved into the frames were inspired from such indigenous flora as orange fruit and leaves. These images were also painted into the background of the painting, creating a harmonious and integrated combination of painting and frame. The tabernacle-style frames that he made were also polychromed and accented with an embellishment of gold leaf. These frames, often including such symbolic images as the swan, encompassed allegorical paintings and in some cases helped to convey subtle messages about the meaning of the painting. For his paintings in the Tonalist style, he created frames with subtle variations to accent the muted, sombre tones.

In Boston another Tonalist painter, Herman Dudley Murphy (1867–1945), started a framemaking concern called the Carrig-Rohane Shop, which had a wider sphere of influence than Mathews's work. Charles Prendergast (1869–1948) and Walfred Thulin (1878–1949) collaborated with Murphy to revolutionize framemaking in the USA. They made frames that were interpretations of European designs, hand-carved, carefully gilded and toned to harmonize with the paintings. Each frame was signed and dated on the *verso*. In New Hope, PA, during the first quarter of the 20th century, Fredrick Harer (1880–1948) designed and carved frames in the Carrig-Rohane manner. His apprentice, Bernard Badura (1896–1986), carried on the tradition of hand-carving and gilding, with each frame carefully wrought and chromatically keyed into the painting. The designs were distinctive and innovative, often made from hand-shaped wood. They reflected the new influences of Art Deco and other Modernist architecture.

Many artists were involved with the creation of frames for their own paintings. John Marin, for example, hand-crafted his frames with simple carving and painted the surfaces with whimsical colours to match the sentiment of his Abstract paintings. Marin used the frame as a device to integrate the flat surfaces of his abstractions. Henry Heydenryk (1905–94) was born in the Netherlands into a family of established framemakers, but he moved to the USA in the early 1930s to set up his own company and soon developed a reputation as one of the country's leading frame specialists. He popularized the rustic 'wormy chestnut' look in the 1940s and 1950s using mouldings that were angular and styled after the sweeping and streamlined look of contemporary Minimalist architecture. He also patented a self-lighting picture frame called the 'Heyden-Ray'; specially designed light bulbs were inserted into the deepened rabbet of the frame, illuminating evenly the surface of the canvas. Heydenryk's studio received many specialized commissions from artists, as well as making reproductions of classical designs. In 1960 Robert Kulicke (*b* 1924), an artist and designer, created the welded-corner metal frame for MOMA, New York. In 1964 he developed the Plexi-box frame and in 1967 he produced the first metal section frame for international distribution. Such abstract Expressionist artists as Willem De Kooning, Franz Kline and Robert Motherwell were among the first to use Kulicke's designs. The need for a new order of frame was more evident as these painters became the 'modern masters'. The thin strip of metal or plastic became the classic profile associated with their work, and Kulicke was the only frame designer who responded to their needs.

BIBLIOGRAPHY

H. Heydenryk: *The Art and History of Frames* (New York, 1963)
——: *The Right Frame* (New York, 1964)
The Art of Charles Prendergast (exh. cat. by R. Wattenmaker, New Brunswick, NJ, Rutgers U. A. Mus.; Boston, MA, Mus. F.A.; 1968)
R. Maryanski: *Antique Picture Frame Guide* (Niles, IL, 1973)
H. Jones: *Mathews: Masterpieces of the California Decorative Style* (Santa Barbara and Salt Lake City, 1980)
Herman Dudley Murphy (exh. cat. by W. Coles, New York, Graham Gal., 1982)
W. Adair: *The Frame in America, 1700–1900: A Survey of Fabrication Techniques and Styles* (Washington, DC, 1983)
A. Katlan: *American Artist's Materials Suppliers Directory* (Madison, CT, 1987)
The Art of the Frame: An Exhibition Focusing on American Frames of the Arts and Crafts Movement, 1870–1920 (exh. cat. by S. Smeaton, New York, Eli Wilner Gal., 1988)
W. Adair: 'Picture Framing, ii: Two Exhibitions of American Picture Frames', *Int. J. Mus. Mgmt & Cur.*, ix (1990), pp. 318–22
S. Mills: 'The Framemaker's Art in Early San Francisco', *A. CA* (Nov 1990), pp. 54–9
S. Burns: *Forgotten Marriage: The Painted Tin Type and the Decorative Frame* (New York, 1991)

For further bibliography *see* §I above.

WILLIAM B. ADAIR

Frampton, Sir **George (James)** (*b* London, 16 June 1860; *d* London, 21 May 1928). English sculptor and decorative artist. He began work in an architect's office before being apprenticed to a firm of architectural masons. Frampton studied modelling at Lambeth School of Art under W. S. Frith (1850–1924) and in 1881 entered the Royal Academy Schools, where he won a gold medal and travelling scholarship in 1887. This took him to Paris where he studied sculpture with Antonin Mercié and painting with P.-A.-J. Dagnan-Bouveret. He returned to London in 1889 having won a silver medal at the Salon for *Angel of Death* and *Christabel* (both untraced), the latter a polychromed plaster bust, which he claimed was modelled on those of Desiderio da Settignano and Antonio Rossellino. After returning to England he produced another bust, *Mysteriarch* (1892; exh. RA 1893; Liverpool, Walker A.G.), in which the influence of 15th-century Florentine art is combined with symbolism derived from the work of Edward Burne-Jones and Moreau Vauthier (1831–93). Frampton later further refined his conception of late Pre-Raphaelite imagery into the most ethereal and idealized of all his independent sculptures, *Lamia* (1900; London, RA), a life-size bust in bronze and ivory set with opals. It is one of the finest examples of polychromy in late 19th-century British sculpture and exists in a second version, in painted plaster (Birmingham, Mus. & A.G.).

Like Robert Anning Bell, with whom he shared a studio, Frampton was interested in bas-relief, which he developed in small panels in plaster or bronze, often employing colour, and in larger architectural schemes such as the nine silver-gilt panels depicting Arthurian heroines for the door of the Great Hall at Astor House, Westminster, London. Models for seven of these were shown at the Royal Academy in 1896. Frampton became a leading figure in the ARTS AND CRAFTS MOVEMENT, being a member of the Art Workers' Guild from 1887 and its Master in 1902. He also used *The Studio* to disseminate his views, contributing articles on the colouring of sculpture, jewellery and enamelling. Frampton made his greatest impact at the exhibition of the Arts and Crafts Society in 1896, where he showed an overmantel destined for a house in Germany designed by Charles Harrison Townsend, models for cabinet-door panels and a folding screen in leather decorated and inlaid with gold, aluminium, ivory, mother-of-pearl and enamels. He also showed in the first Viennese Secession exhibition in 1898 and with the Libre Esthétique in Brussels. He became Art Adviser to the London County Council and was, in part, responsible for the founding of the Central School of Arts and Crafts, of which he was joint head with W. R. Lethaby.

Frampton worked closely with a number of architects and contributed important groups of sculpture to the decoration of Glasgow Art Gallery (1898–1900), Electra House, Moorgate, London (1901–2), and the Victoria and Albert Museum, London (1905–7). But by far his most ambitious scheme of architectural sculpture was for the new premises of Lloyd's Registry of Shipping, Fenchurch Street, London (1898–1901), which resulted from close collaboration with the architect T. E. Collcutt. For this he carved a stone frieze of ethereal young women, reminiscent of his Arthurian heroines, holding model ships: these figures, depicting Trades, Commerce and Shipping, are arranged informally, and each group is contained between heavy columns above the ground-floor openings. Single figures in bronze, at the same height as the frieze, nestle between the columns at the corner of the building. Frampton was also much in demand for public sculpture and executed full-length statues of *Queen Victoria* for several cities including Calcutta, Winnipeg, St Helen's, Newcastle upon Tyne and Leeds, as well as of *Queen Mary* for the Victoria Memorial Hall, Calcutta, and Government House, New Delhi. He also made busts of *King George V* and *Queen Mary* for the Guildhall, London. His best-loved public sculpture, however, is undoubtedly *Peter Pan* (1910) given by the author J. M. Barrie to the children of London and erected in Kensington Gardens (*in situ*). Frampton was elected ARA in 1894 and RA in 1902; he was knighted in 1908. His wife Christabel [née Cockerell] (1863–1951) was a painter, as was their son Meredith (1894–1984).

DNB   BIBLIOGRAPHY
E. B. S.: 'Afternoons in Studios: A Chat with Mr George Frampton ARA', *The Studio*, vi (Jan 1896), pp. 205–13
F. Miller: 'George Frampton ARA: Art Worker', *A.J.* [London] (1897), pp. 321–4
M. H. Spielmann: *British Sculpture and Sculptors of To-day* (London, 1901), pp. 88–95
B. Read: *Victorian Sculpture* (New Haven, 1982)
S. Beattie: *The New Sculpture* (New Haven, 1983)
T. Stevens: 'George Frampton', *Patronage and Practice: Sculpture on Merseyside*, ed. P. Curtis (Liverpool, 1989)
B. Read and J. Barnes, eds: *Pre-Raphaelite Sculpture: Nature and Imagination in British Sculpture, 1848–1914* (1991)

PEYTON SKIPWITH

Français, François-Louis (*b* Plombières-les-Bains, Vosges, 17 Nov 1814; *d* Plombières-les-Bains, 18 May 1897). French painter and printmaker. After attending several courses in drawing in Plombières-les-Bains, he went to Paris at the age of 14 to study. He first worked as a copyist, produced caricatures and drew from models at the Académie Suisse. In 1831 he decided to study painting and completed his first landscapes, painting mainly in the environs of Paris and at Meudon with Paul Huet, who was his adviser for several years. In 1834 he entered the workshop of Jean Gigoux and met Henri Baron, who remained his faithful friend. He also studied at the Louvre where he developed a lifelong admiration for the work of Claude. From 1834 he lived at Barbizon, and after 1835 he often painted in the Forest of Fontainebleau, where he met Louis Cabat and also Corot, who became his adviser and introduced him to Théodore-Caruelle d'Aligny. Français also made the acquaintance of Narcisse Diaz and of the landscape painter Auguste-Paul-Charles Anastasi (1820–89), who became his friend. In 1837 he exhibited for the first time at the Salon in Paris, showing *Under the Willows* (1837; Tours, Mus. B.-A.), a composition in which the figures were painted by Baron. He exhibited regularly at the Salon until 1896. Between 1836 and 1840 his style was above all a skilful but eclectic mixture of various contemporary trends in landscape painting. He also took up printmaking early in his career, and in 1835 he produced some engravings for Jacques-Henri Bernardin de Saint-Pierre's *La Chaumière indienne* and for Alain-René Lesage's *Gil Blas*. After 1838 his lithographic production was considerable and included such important commissions as

that to illustrate Bernardin de Saint-Pierre's novel *Paul et Virginie*. With his friends Baron and Célestin Nanteuil (1813–73), he produced *Les Artistes anciens et modernes* (3 vols; 1848–62), a collection of lithographs after paintings by contemporary artists. Among the prints were those done after Corot's *Landscape, Sunset* (1840; Metz, Mus A. & Hist.), Diaz's *Bathers* (1847) and several of his own paintings.

From 1844 Français regularly visited Marly and Bougival, where, with Baron and Nanteuil, he acquired a boat nicknamed 'La Grenouillère' by the inhabitants of the area. Henceforth he signed his paintings *Français, élève de Bougival*. In 1846 he made his first journey to Italy and remained there for three years, although he had intended to stay for only a few months. He lived in Genoa (1846), Pisa (1846), Florence (1846–7), Rome (1846–9), Frascati (1847), Ariccia (1848) and Tivoli (1848–9). He executed mainly gouache studies in the Borghese Gardens and at Tivoli (e.g. *View of Tivoli*, 1850; Lille, Mus. B.-A.). During these years his style came to fruition, he began to paint in the closely set strokes that would be a feature of his later, better-known works, and his palette became more luminous, due probably to his work in watercolour (e.g. *Fountain at Ariccia*, 1848; Paris, Mus. d'Orsay). After returning to France, he travelled and painted in such regions as Marly, Vaux-de-Cernay, Saint-Cloud and Sèvres, where he painted with Constant Troyon. From 1850 he also frequented Honfleur and, with Corot, Courbet, Eugène Boudin and Johan Barthold Jongkind, painted the town and its environs (e.g. *Sunset near Honfleur*, 1859). In 1852 he travelled to Crémieu with Corot, Charles-François Daubigny and Auguste Ravier. At this time his preferred sites were Saint-Cloud, Plombières-les-Bains and the banks of the Loire, where he painted mainly forest interiors and scenes of riverbanks in a style more realistic than the classicism of his Italian period. Having acquired a passion for the light of the Mediterranean regions, he returned to Italy twice more, staying at Naples in 1858–9 and at Capri and Pompeii in 1864–5. In the 1850s and 1860s he also visited Alsace, Belgium, Switzerland and the Alps.

While Français always remained a much sought-after painter at the beginning of the 1860s, reviews of his work were much less favourable. His painting the *Sacred Wood* (Lille, Mus. B.-A.; see fig.) was exhibited at the Salon of 1864 in Paris and elicited hostile reactions. Although Corot admired it, Français's patron Alfred Hartmann, an industrialist from Alsace, compared it to 'a chicory dish seasoned with cream' (letter from Hartmann to Rousseau, 17 April 1864; Paris, Louvre, Cab. Dessins). The picture evokes an antique idyll and was painted after sketches done at Vaux-de-Cernay and Tivoli. Français executed other neo-classical landscapes in the same manner, in which mythological characters are introduced into realistic landscape settings painted from sketches made in Italy or France (e.g. *Orpheus*, 1863; Paris, Mus. d'Orsay). After 1873 he spent his winters in Nice, returning each spring to Vaux-de-Cernay and to Plombières-les-Bains in the summer. In 1875 he made a further trip abroad, visiting Algeria. In 1878, six years after he received the commission, he completed *Expulsion from the Garden* and the *Baptism*, painted decorative panels (*in situ*) for the font in La Trinité, Paris. At this time his work developed towards

François-Louis Français: *Sacred Wood*, oil on canvas, 1.09×1.34 m, 1864 (Lille, Musée des Beaux-Arts)

poetic naturalism. He executed a large number of self-portraits, some of them in pastels, and he also produced numerous pen-and-ink drawings, enhanced by sepia, that convey a certain melancholy. In the paintings of his later years (e.g. *View of Antibes*, 1895; Strasbourg, Mus. B.-A.) there is a return to a colouring similar to that present in his works *c.* 1858.

Throughout Français's career he retained a taste for detail inherited from his master Gigoux, and his works typically display a slightly mannered meticulousness. He rapidly acquired a considerable reputation and, once he had achieved financial success, he was much sought after. Outside France he also exhibited in Geneva (1857, 1858 and 1861) and at the two International Exhibitions of 1862 and 1874 in London. In 1890 he was appointed a member of the Institut de France. In 1901, four years after his death, a monument was erected to his memory at Plombières-les-Bains, and in 1905 his workshop, which he had presented to his native town, became the Musée Louis Français.

PRINTS
with H. Baron and C. Nanteuil: *Les Artistes anciens et modernes*, 3 vols (Paris, 1848–62)

BIBLIOGRAPHY
A. Gros: *François-Louis Français: Causeries et souvenirs par un de ses élèves* (Paris, 1902)

P. Miquel: *Le Paysage français au XIXe siècle, 1824–1874: L'Ecole de la nature*, iii (Maurs-la-Jolie, 1975), pp. 608–45
François-Louis Français, Plombières-les-Bains, 1814–1897: Illustrateur romantique (exh. cat. by R. Conilleau, Plombières-les-Bains, Mus. Louis Français, 1981)
Aquarelles, dessins et gravures de François-Louis Français (exh. cat., Région Lorraine, 1982–3)
Tradition and Revolution in French Art, 1700–1880: Paintings and Drawings from Lille (exh. cat., London, N.G., 1993)

LAURENCE PAUCHET-WARLOP

Francart [Franckaert; Francquart]**, Jacques** [Jacob] (*b* ?Antwerp, ?1583; *d* Brussels, *bur* 6 Jan 1651). Flemish architect, painter, draughtsman, engineer and writer. He was the son of an Antwerp painter, Jacques Francart (*b* before 1550; *d* 1601), and he was trained as a painter in Rome, where his father worked for some years. He greatly admired Michelangelo, Jacopo Vignola, Giacomo della Porta and Carlo Maderno. In 1599 the Flemish painter and architect Wenzel Coebergher married Francart's younger sister in Rome. After Coebergher had been appointed Court Engineer in 1605 to the Archduke Albert and Archduchess Isabella in Brussels, Francart likewise returned to the Low Countries in 1608 to begin a career as a painter and architect in the service of the Archduke, where he remained until the death of Isabella.

In 1622, influenced by his Roman sojourn, Francart published his *Premier livre d'architecture* in November 1616, a work of great importance to the development of the early Baroque style in the southern Netherlands. One month after its publication he was given the task of completing the Jesuit church in Brussels (destr. 1812), which had been begun by Hendrik Hoeimaker in 1606. This first building was of great importance both for Francart's career and for its influence on his contemporaries. Although it was built at the same time as the church of St Carolus Borromeus by Franciscus Aguilonius and Peter Huyssens in Antwerp, Francart's Jesuit church played a more important role in the evolution of Flemish early Baroque. It is to Francart's credit that he gave this Baroque church an indigenous character: although the front façade was influenced by the work of his Roman teachers, Francart's design also looks to the Flemish Late Gothic tradition (in part dictated by Hoeimaker's original design) in its preponderant verticalism and interior rib-vaulting. Tuscan columns carried the rib-vaults, decorated in the centre by escutcheons, a treatment of the nave that was echoed by many, including Huyssens at St Walburga's, Bruges.

In 1620 Francart built the Augustinian church in Brussels (*see* BELGIUM, fig. 5); the front façade, which was copied at the church of the Holy Trinity there, is similar to the Jesuit church and to Coebergher's Augustinian church in Antwerp. Lucas Faydherbe was also inspired by this façade for the church of Our Lady of Hanswijk in Mechelen. In June 1621 Francart designed the entire funeral procession of the Archduke Albert; the designs were published in 1623 as a series of prints. In 1629 he was commissioned to build the Béguinage Church in Mechelen (finished *c*. 1645 by Faydherbe), the interior of which is characterized by the round-arched arcades with Corinthian pilasters supporting an entablature, as in St Peter's (1629–*c*. 1719), Ghent, by Huyssens. Francart also rebuilt (1642–52) the church of Our Lady by the Dijle, Mechelen, by adding a choir chapel and two side chapels as a continuation of the 16th-century choir.

With Coebergher, Aguilonius and Huyssens, Francart was one of the most important church architects in the southern Netherlands in the early 17th century, pioneering the introduction and dissemination of the Roman early Baroque style. After Coebergher's death in 1632 Francart was appointed engineer to the Spanish king.

WRITINGS
Premier livre d'architecture de Jacques Francart, contenant diverses inventions de portes serviables à tous ceux qui désirent bastir et pour sculpteurs, tailleurs de pières, escriniers, massons et autres, en trois langues (Brussels, 1616)

PRINTS
Cent tablettes et escussons d'armes (Brussels, 1622)
Pompa funebris optimi potentissimusque principis Albert Pii, archiducis Austriae (Brussels, 1623)
Virorum illustrium ex ordini eremitarum D. augustini elogia cum singularum expressis ad virum iconibus (1630) [30 portraits engraved by Cornelis Galle (i) after drawings by Francart]

BIBLIOGRAPHY
BNB; Thieme–Becker
J. H. Plantenga: *L'Architecture religieuse dans l'ancien duché de Brabant depuis le règne des archiducs jusqu'au gouvernement autrichien, 1598–1713* (The Hague, 1926)

J. van Ackere: *Barok en classicisme in België* (Brussels, 1974)
L. Brouwers: *De Jezuïeten te Brussel, 1586–1773–1833* (Malines, 1979)

J.-P. ESTHER

Francastel, Pierre (*b* Paris, 8 June 1900; *d* Paris, 2 Jan 1970). French art historian. He was employed between 1925 and 1930 in the Service d'Architecture at the château of Versailles. This activity was crowned by the publication of *La Sculpture de Versailles* (1930), in which the subject, characterized by a triumph of classical discipline over the Baroque, is studied in the context of the general history of taste. This marked the beginning of the author's understanding of the way art functions in a given society and of the discipline that he termed 'sociology of art'. He gained his doctorate in 1930 and taught art history in Warsaw (at the Institut Français and the university) and, from 1937 to 1945, in Strasbourg and Clermont-Ferrand. In 1945 he was appointed cultural adviser to the French Embassy in Warsaw and organized exhibitions of French sculpture, painting and drawing. His first return from Warsaw to France was marked by the publication of *L'Impressionnisme* (1937), in which he described Impressionism as an artistic movement of lasting value and not a temporary fashion as its critics thought. In 1948 he gave the title 'Sociology of Art' to the studies he directed at the Ecole Pratique des Hautes Etudes in Paris. His major work was *Peinture et société* (1951), involving the direct comparison of two periods separated by four centuries, and the illuminating association of two apparently separate concepts, 'society' and 'space'. *Paris* (1968) is a remarkable application of sociological methods to the history of a great capital city. The *Etudes de sociologie de l'art* (1970) open with an introduction summing up Francastel's reflections after 20 years of research. The most significant articles were collected in the volumes *La Réalité figurative* (1965) and *L'Image, la vision et l'imagination* (1983).

WRITINGS
La Sculpture de Versailles: Essai sur les origines et l'évolution du goût français classique (Paris, 1930/*R* 1970)
L'Impressionnisme: Les Origines de la peinture moderne de Monet à Gauguin, Publications de la Faculté des Lettres de Strasbourg, seconde série, Les Belles Lettres, xvi (Paris, 1937)
Peinture et société: Naissance et destruction d'un espace plastique de la Renaissance au Cubisme (Paris and Lyon, 1951, 2/Paris, 1965, 3/1977)
La Réalité figurative: Eléments structurels de sociologie de l'art (Paris, 1965, 2/1978)
Paris: Un héritage culturel et monumental (1968); rev. as *Une destinée de capitale* (Paris, 1984) [with illus.]
Etudes de sociologie de l'art (Paris, 1970)
L'Image, la vision et l'imagination: L'Objet filmique et l'objet plastique (Paris, 1983)

GALIENNE FRANCASTEL

Francavilla, Pietro [Francheville, Francqueville, Pierre de] (*b* Cambrai, 1548; *d* Paris, 25 Aug 1615). Flemish sculptor. From a noble family, he learnt to draw in Paris in 1562–4. In 1565 he went to Innsbruck, presumably to assist Alexander Colin on the great tomb in the Hofkirche for the Holy Roman Emperor Maximilian I, and this is probably where he learnt sculpture. Archduke Ferdinand of Austria gave him a letter of introduction to Giambologna *c*. 1570, and he went to Florence, where he was sufficiently skilled at carving to become a partner of Giambologna, not merely an assistant. Francavilla's first important commission, for 13 marble statues of mythological subjects for the garden of a villa at Rovezzano, came from Abbot Antonio Bracci in 1574 and was delegated to him probably because Giambologna was heavily occupied. The earliest of these to be signed and dated, *Zephyr* (1576) and *Apollo* (1577; both London, Kensington Pal.), are obviously derivations of compositions by Giambologna. Four others (Windsor Castle, Berks, Royal Col., East Terrace Garden) are less indebted to the master, while the last in date is quite different from his style, showing *Venus with a Nymph and Satyr* arranged frontally, instead of spirally.

It is thought that Francavilla was responsible for the final carving of the marble version of Giambologna's group of *Florence Triumphant over Pisa* (Florence, Bargello), from a full-scale gesso model (1565; Florence, Accad.). The block of marble had reached Florence in 1569, and carving was finished in 1572, just after Francavilla had become available to assist. Next, he may have helped Giambologna with the Grimaldi Chapel in Genoa, as he later carved a pair of colossal statues of *Janus* and *Jupiter* (signed and dated 1585; Genoa, Gal. Pal. Bianco) for the Grimaldi Palace, and six allegorical statues for the Senarega Chapel in Genoa Cathedral. In Florence, he produced studies of *écorché* figures, for he is shown holding one in an anonymous portrait inscribed with his name and dated 1576. Bronze casts of this and two other *écorché* figures (Kraków, Jagiellonian U. Lib.) indicate that he was also interested in producing bronze statuettes, and several models have been attributed to him. He probably helped Giambologna with other great marble groups, such as the *Rape of a Sabine* and *Hercules Slaying a Centaur* (both Florence, Loggia Lanzi). They signed jointly the portrait statues of *Ferdinand I, Grand Duke of Tuscany* (Arezzo, Piazza Duomo; Pisa, Piazza S Nicola), both dating from 1594. The inscriptions state that he 'made' them from models by Giambologna. He also carved statues of *Cosimo I, Grand Duke of Tuscany* (1595; Pisa, Piazza Cavalieri) and *St Matthew* (1599; Orvieto Cathedral) from models by his colleague. Around 1585 he carved five statues, including *Moses* and *Aaron* (modelli; Florence, Bargello), for the Niccolini Chapel in Santa Croce, Florence (*in situ*). Other great marble works include *Orpheus and Cerberus* (1598; Paris, Louvre; see fig.) Towards the end of his career in Florence, *c.* 1600, he modelled four of the bronze narrative reliefs of New Testament scenes for the west doors of Pisa Cathedral.

In 1604 Francavilla signed a will in Florence. He then went to Paris, at the request of Marie de' Medici, Queen of France, to supervise the installation on the Pont Neuf of Giambologna's bronze equestrian statue of *Henry IV* (destr. 1796; fragments, Paris, Louvre). The statue was cast in Florence and shipped to France only in 1613. Francavilla was apparently responsible for modelling the four bronze *Slaves* (Paris, Louvre; *see* FRANCE, fig. 35) to decorate the angles of its pedestal, although they were cast only in 1618, after his death, by his son-in-law Francesco Bordoni. In France he also continued to carve statues in marble, such as *David with the Head of Goliath* (Paris, Louvre), which is still heavily indebted to Giambologna in compositional style. Known chiefly for his association with Giambologna, and not notably original as a sculptor,

Pietro Francavilla: *Orpheus and Cerberus*, marble, h. 2.5 m, 1598 (Paris, Musée du Louvre)

Francavilla on occasion succeeded in producing novel and quite exciting work.

BIBLIOGRAPHY
Thieme–Becker
F. Baldinucci: *Notizie* (1681–1728); ed. F. Ranalli (1845–7), iii, pp. 56–71
J. Pope-Hennessy: *Italian High Renaissance and Baroque Sculpture* (London, 1963, rev. 3/New York, 1985), pp. 90–91, pls 94–5
R. de Francqueville: *Pierre de Francqueville: Sculpteur des Medicis et du Roi Henri IV* (Paris, 1968)
H. Keutner: 'Pietro Francavilla in der Jahren 1572 und 1576', *Festschrift Ulrich Middeldorf* (Berlin, 1968), pp. 301–7, pls cxlii–cxlv
K. J. Watson: *Pietro Tacca: Successor to Giovanni Bologna* (New York and London, 1983), pp. 38–41
C. Avery: *Giambologna: The Complete Sculpture* (Oxford, 1987), pp. 225–7

CHARLES AVERY

France, Republic of [République Française]. Country in western Europe. It is bordered by Belgium and Luxembourg to the north-east; Germany, Switzerland and Italy

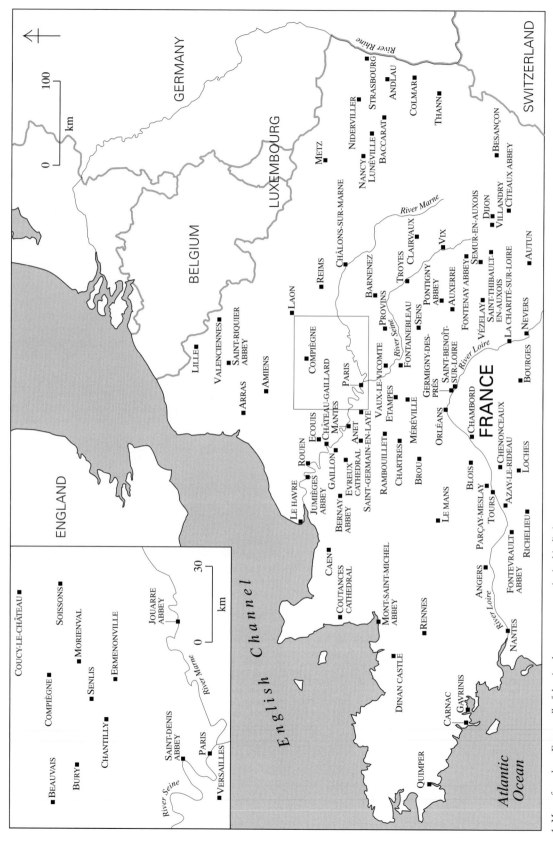

1. Map of northern France; all of the sites have separate entries in this dictionary

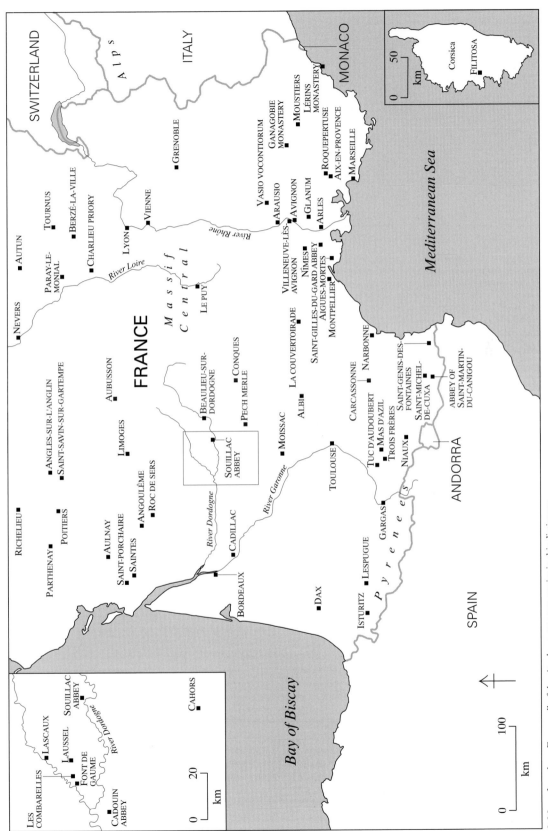

SWITZERLAND

ITALY

A l p s

MONACO

Corsica

Filitosa

km

0   50

Mediterranean Sea

GRENOBLE

VASIO VOCONTIORUM

GANAGOBIE
MONASTERY

MOUSTIERS

LÉRINS
MONASTERY

ROQUEPERTUSE

AIX-EN-PROVENCE

MARSEILLE

TOURNUS

BERZÉ-LA-VILLE

CHARLIEU PRIORY

VIENNE

LYON

ARAUSIO

AVIGNON

GLANUM

ARLES

River Rhône

AUTUN

PARAY-LE-
MONIAL

River Loire

M a s s i f
C e n t r a l

LE PUY

VILLENEUVE-LÈS-
AVIGNON

NÎMES

SAINT-GILLES-DU-GARD ABBEY

AIGUES-MORTES

MONTPELLIER

NEVERS

FRANCE

AUBUSSON

BEAULIEU-SUR-
DORDOGNE

CONQUES

PECH MERLE

LA COUVERTOIRADE

NARBONNE

SAINT-GENIS-DES-
FONTAINES

SAINT-MICHEL-
DE-CUXA

ABBEY OF
SAINT-MARTIN-
DU-CANIGOU

ANGLES-SUR-L'ANGLIN

SAINT-SAVIN-SUR-GARTEMPE

LIMOGES

ANGOULÊME

ROC DE SERS

MOISSAC

ALBI

CARCASSONNE

TUC D'AUDOUBERT

MAS D'AZIL

TROIS FRÈRES

NIAUX

RICHELIEU

PARTHENAY

POITIERS

AULNAY

SAINT-PORCHAIRE

SAINTES

CADILLAC

River Dordogne

River Garonne

TOULOUSE

GARGAS

LESPUGUE

ISTURITZ

P y r e n e e s

BORDEAUX

DAX

ANDORRA

SPAIN

Bay of Biscay

SOUILLAC
ABBEY

LES
COMBARELLES

LASCAUX

LAUSSEL

SOUILLAC
ABBEY

FONT DE
GAUME

CADOUIN
ABBEY

River Dordogne

CAHORS

km

0   20

km

0   100

2. Map of southern France; all of the sites have separate entries in this dictionary

to the east; Spain, Andorra and the Mediterranean Sea to the south; and the Atlantic Ocean to the west (see figs 1 and 2). One of the oldest and largest European nations, it covers an area of 551,000 sq. km. The country consists of the 96 départements of Metropolitan France, including Corsica, in the Mediterranean Sea; four overseas départements—French Guiana in South America; Guadeloupe and Martinique in the Caribbean Sea; and Réunion in the Indian Ocean; four overseas territories—French Polynesia, New Caledonia, Wallis and Futuna and the French Southern and Antarctic territories; and the 'territorial collectivities' of Mayotte in the Indian Ocean and Saint Pierre and Miquelon off the east coast of Canada. France has a population of 57,526,000 (1993 estimate), of which over one sixth lives in the capital, PARIS. This survey covers the art of the country from the medieval period. For a discussion of earlier developments in the art of France *see* PREHISTORIC EUROPE and ROME, ANCIENT.

I. Introduction. II. Architecture. III. Painting and graphic arts. IV. Sculpture. V. Interior decoration. VI. Furniture. VII. Ceramics. VIII. Glass. IX. Metalwork. X. Objects of vertu. XI. Textiles. XII. Patronage. XIII. Collecting and dealing. XIV. Museums. XV. Art education. XVI. Art libraries and photographic collections. XVII. Historiography.

DETAILED TABLE OF CONTENTS

I. Introduction.

Prior to the arrival of Julius Caesar in 58 BC, the region was peopled by the Celts, Ligurians and Iberians. After the collapse of the Roman Empire in the 5th century AD, the area of modern France was occupied by conflicting 'barbarian' peoples. The most successful of these were the Salian Franks, whose leader, Clovis I (reg AD 481–511), made Paris his capital in AD 508. The Merovingian dynasty, founded in AD 431 by Clovis's grandfather Merovius, was succeeded in AD 751 by the Carolingian dynasty (c. 747–987). Their greatest ruler was CHARLEMAGNE (reg 768–814), who gained an empire covering much of western Europe, and who was crowned Holy Roman Emperor in AD 800. His capital was Aix-la-Chapelle (now Aachen, Germany), where he built a magnificent palace, of which only the chapel survives.

After Charlemagne's death in AD 814, France suffered great instability. This lasted until the foundation in 987 of the Capetian dynasty (see CAPET), based in Paris, by Hughes Capet (reg 987–96). Despite the strengthening of the monarchy, the French nobles remained powerful, and in 1066 William, Duke of Normandy, conquered England and ascended to the English throne as William I.

During the 12th and 13th centuries French society was dominated by the prevailing religious enthusiasm of the period. This was reflected abroad in the Crusades, which brought contact with Italy and the Middle East, and at home in the establishment of numerous monasteries and other churches, which gave rise to new cultural expression. A particularly important development in the second half of the 12th century was the rise of the Gothic style in architecture, which then spread across Europe.

The 14th century was characterized by great upheaval in France, as in the rest of Europe. In 1348 the country fell victim to the Black Death. From 1337 to 1453 France was involved in the Hundred Years War with England. This conflict eventually led to the expulsion of the English from most of France. After the war's end the French kings concentrated on centralizing power and enhancing their own prestige.

In the early 16th century France reached a new level of cultural achievement under Francis I (*see* VALOIS, (14)), who brought from Italy leading Renaissance artists, including Rosso Fiorentino and Francesco Primaticcio. The second half of the century was marred by the Wars of Religion (from 1562), concluding with the Edict of Nantes (1598), which gave freedom of worship to the Protestant Huguenots. Despite this legislation, a policy of religious intolerance was again adopted by Armand-Jean du Plessis Richelieu (chief minister, 1624–42). Cardinal Richelieu's successor, Jules Mazarin (chief minister, 1643–61), successfully concluded the Thirty Years War (1618–48), but also provoked the civil war known as La Fronde (1648–59).

After Mazarin's death, Louis XIV (*see* BOURBON, §I(9)) greatly strengthened the absolute power of the monarchy, as well as constructing the magnificent palace at Versailles. During the reigns of Louis XIV and his predecessor Louis XIII (*reg* 1610–43), France became the most powerful nation in Europe and established a cultural hegemony that lasted more than a century. Louis XIV revoked the Edict of Nantes in 1685 and involved France in numerous wars, ending in the disastrous War of the Spanish Succession (1701–13).

Despite military setbacks and severe economic problems, the French Court remained a major cultural centre throughout the 18th century. Louis XV's mistress Mme de Pompadour was a particularly important patron, attracting such painters as François Boucher and Jean-Baptiste Greuze, as well as the philosopher Voltaire. However, these achievements could not rescue the *ancien régime* from catastrophe later in the century. The Revolution began in May 1789 with the meeting of the assembly of the Estates-General in Paris. In the following month the delegates of the third estate, representing the non-privileged classes, assumed the power to draw up a constitution, an act of defiance that was followed in July by the storming of the Bastille prison in Paris. As the situation worsened, Louis XVI and his wife, Marie-Antoinette, attempted to leave France in 1791, but were captured and executed two years later. Thousands were to lose their lives during the purges of the Terror (1793–4). The Revolution also led to the destruction of various religious and royalist monuments. Its events were commemorated in paintings by Jacques-Louis David.

The final years of the 18th century were marked by the dramatic rise of Napoleon Bonaparte, who became First Consul in 1799 and crowned himself Emperor in 1804 (*see* BONAPARTE, (1)). During the Napoleonic Wars, Bonaparte conducted an often brilliant campaign against the other leading European powers. However, his fortunes deteriorated after the disastrous invasion of Russia (1812), and in 1814 he was forced to abdicate and to retire to the island of Elba. Although Bonaparte returned triumphantly to France in 1815, he was decisively defeated at Waterloo soon afterwards and exiled to St Helena in the south Atlantic Ocean.

In 1815 the French throne was restored to the BOURBON dynasty, but the reactionary policies of Charles X led in 1830 to the July Revolution, which established the more liberal monarchy of Louis-Philippe. The new regime was also unable to satisfy the demands for political and social

reforms, and in 1848 the February Revolution established the Second Republic. In that year Napoleon's ambitious nephew Louis Napoléon became President, prior to seizing greater power through a coup d'état (1851) that made him Emperor Napoleon III. Artistically his reign was of great importance. Not only did he sanction the rebuilding of large areas of Paris by Baron Haussmann but he also set up the Salon des Refusés (1863), including paintings by such artists as Edouard Manet and Paul Cézanne, whose work had been refused by the jury of the official Salon in Paris.

Napoleon III's abdication in 1870, as a result of the disastrous Franco-Prussian War (1870–71), was followed by the establishment of the Third Republic. Over the next 50 years Paris was the centre of a series of remarkable artistic movements, including Impressionism and Cubism. This period was also marked by severe political and diplomatic crises, culminating in the catastrophe of World War I. While many avant-garde artists returned to classicizing styles in the 1920s and 1930s as part of a *rappel à l'ordre*, others joined radical movements such as Dada and its successor, Surrealism. In 1940 France was invaded by the German army, which occupied much of the country, while establishing the puppet Vichy government in southern France.

Following the country's liberation in 1944, the Fourth Republic was founded in 1946, and normal cultural life resumed. Gradually, however, Paris was replaced as the centre of avant-garde art by New York, partly due to the influx of European émigrés seeking exile from the war. In 1954 France became embroiled in the bitter Algerian War, which ended in 1962 with the granting of independence to Algeria. During the 1960s France was dominated by President Charles de Gaulle, who had brought in a new constitution in 1959, setting up the Fifth Republic. De Gaulle's autocratic style precipitated serious student unrest, leading to his resignation in 1969. He was succeeded by Georges Pompidou (1969–74), by Valéry Giscard d'Estaing (1974–81) and, from 1981 to 1995, by François Mitterand, who was responsible for prestigious cultural and architectural projects, as well as vigorously promoting the increased powers of the European Union. In 1995 Jacques Chirac was elected president.

BIBLIOGRAPHY
A. Michel: *Histoire de l'art*, 18 vols (Paris, 1905–29)
R. Fry: *Characteristics of French Art* (London, 1932)
F. Braudel: *L'Identité de la France*, 3 vols (Paris, 1986; Eng. trans., London, 1988–90)
R. Price: *A Concise History of France* (Cambridge, 1993)

CHRISTOPHER MASTERS

II. Architecture.

After the conquest of Gaul by Julius Caesar in 58–51 BC the Romans had introduced planned cities, large public buildings, temples and triumphal monuments, as well as the techniques of building in concrete, brick and stone masonry and the use of columns, piers, lintels, round arches, and barrel and groin vaults. Their monuments continued to inspire builders, and methods of construction introduced in antiquity were never completely forgotten. The numerous Roman remains in France include GLANUM (Saint-Rémy), NîMES, ARLES and ARAUSIO (Orange) in the south, and further north AUTUN, Langres, Reims and Paris (baths in the Musée de Cluny). For a discussion of architectural developments in France before the medieval period, *see* PREHISTORIC EUROPE, §IV, 2 and ROME, ANCIENT, §II, 2(ii)(a).

BIBLIOGRAPHY
P. Lavedan: *French Architecture*, Pelican Hist. A. (Harmondsworth, 1956)

1. Before *c.* 1500. 2. *c.* 1500–*c.* 1600. 3. *c.* 1600–*c.* 1814. 4. *c.* 1814–*c.* 1914. 5. After *c.* 1914.

1. BEFORE *c.* 1500.

(i) Early medieval, 5th–11th centuries. (ii) Romanesque and Gothic, 11th century to the late 15th.

(i) Early medieval, 5th–11th centuries. The architecture of the early medieval period, from the reign of Clovis (AD 482–511), first king of the Franks and a member of the Merovingian dynasty, to the earliest Capetians (*c.* 1000), is known mainly from documents and excavations. The style of secular buildings has been lost: rulers made use of Roman palaces and villas, while the rest of the population occupied modest structures of wood and cob. The tradition of building in more permanent materials survived, however, in church architecture. With the spread of Christianity from the 4th century and again after the baptism of Clovis in 496, churches initially took the form of Roman civic basilicas, often wooden-roofed, and baptisteries were built close to cathedrals, as at Aix-en-Provence and Poitiers (*see* POITIERS, §2(ii)). Oratories and funerary monuments were also constructed. Many churches had been built by the time of GREGORY, Bishop of Tours, writing at the end of the 6th century, when they were usually columnar basilicas with bell-towers. Surviving 7th-century crypts at JOUARRE ABBEY and St Laurent, Grenoble, show the reuse of antique columns and the continuity of Roman vaulting techniques (*see also* MEROVINGIAN ART).

There is more evidence for the Carolingian period (mid-8th century to early 10th; *see* CAROLINGIAN ART, §II). Excavations have revealed significant remains of the 8th-century churches of Saint-Denis Abbey (*see* SAINT-DENIS ABBEY, §I, 1), built under Pepin the Short (*reg* 751–68), and SAINT-RIQUIER ABBEY, erected by Angilbert, confidant of Charlemagne, as well as the 9th-century cathedral at Reims. Carolingian churches sometimes had intricate, vaulted crypts; that of St Germain, Auxerre (begun between 841 and 859; *see* AUXERRE, §2), the best preserved, consists of a complex of aisles, apses and passages, employing Roman construction techniques. The great churches have all been destroyed, but a few small monuments survive above ground, such as GERMIGNY-DES-PRÉS, the oratory of Theodulf, Bishop of Orléans at the time of Charlemagne. This is an entirely vaulted building, exceptional in its centralized plan, more characteristic in the compartmentalization of its interior and in its narrow, arched openings. The monastic pattern of buildings grouped around a cloister garth abutting the church was probably established in this period (*see* MONASTERY, §I).

(ii) Romanesque and Gothic, 11th century to the late 15th. The beginnings of Romanesque architecture are generally attributed to the years *c.* 1000; First Romanesque survived in places until *c.* 1080, and Second Romanesque continued

until the introduction of Gothic in the mid-12th century (*see* ROMANESQUE, §II). In the French Pyrenees the stone-vaulted churches of St Michel, Cuxa (*c.* 1009–40), and the abbey of SAINT-MARTIN-DU-CANIGOU (begun *c.* 997) are typical examples of First Romanesque architecture, but some wooden-roofed and partially vaulted buildings in other regions can also be considered as part of this tradition. In Burgundy the second abbey church at Cluny (948–81; *see* CLUNIAC ORDER, §III) had an east end with apses in echelon, while at ST PHILIBERT, TOURNUS, vaulting experiments were combined with the stylistic vocabulary of First Romanesque. In Champagne, St Remi at Reims (between 1007 and 1049; *see* REIMS, fig. 9) was built with an 11-bay nave with galleries and a projecting, aisled transept, heralding the arrangement of the great pilgrimage churches of the later 11th century, such as St Sernin, Toulouse (*see* TOULOUSE, fig. 2). Fulbert's crypt at Chartres Cathedral (after 1020) constitutes the first surviving example of a sanctuary with ambulatory and radiating chapels. Notre-Dame, Jumièges (1040–67), has the earliest great two-towered façade, while its nave has composite piers and wall shafts (*see* JUMIÈGES ABBEY, fig. 1).

At the end of the 11th century these scattered experiments resulted in a more mature Romanesque style, in which churches were entirely vaulted, with regular bays and wall surfaces articulated by shafts, compound piers and moulded arches. In Normandy churches remained wooden-roofed until the beginning of the 12th century, when the rib vault was adopted, as at Lessay Abbey. Three-storey elevations, with clearly defined bay divisions, predominated; and with the construction of St Etienne at Caen (*c.* 1066; *see* CAEN, fig. 1) the thick wall was pierced

3. Autun Cathedral, interior looking east, begun *c.* 1120

by a passage at clerestory level (*see* THICK-WALL STRUC-TURE). In Burgundy, in the third abbey church at Cluny (begun by 1088; destr.), pointed arches were preferred to round arches, both in the barrel vaults and the arcades. Its elevation was also three-storey, but a blind arcade replaced the Norman gallery, as can still be seen at Autun Cathedral (see fig. 3; *see also* AUTUN, §2(i)) and at PARAY-LE-MONIAL. In the Auvergne, where the volcanic stone is particularly hard, and in Languedoc, two-storey churches were more usual, with arcades and galleries but no clerestory. In south-west France, a source of plentiful soft limestone, churches with a single-cell nave spanned by domes are found from the Loire (e.g. FONTEVRAULT ABBEY) to the Garonne (e.g. the cathedrals of Angoulême and Cahors). A little further west (e.g. SAINT-SAVIN-SUR-GARTEMPE and Notre-Dame-la-Grande, Poitiers), aisles are almost as high as the central vessel in an arrangement that anticipates hall churches. Screen façades were covered with sculptural decoration, concealing the structure behind. Little secular architecture survives from this period: a few large, rectangular, stone donjons (e.g. *see* LOCHES, §1; Beaugency in Loiret) and some house façades. Gothic architecture appeared a little before the mid-12th century in the Ile-de-France (*see* GOTHIC, §II). In Abbot Suger's choir at Saint-Denis Abbey (1140–44; *see* SAINT-DENIS ABBEY, §I, 2 and fig. 3) rib vaults were combined with light, columnar supports, and the thin walls were pierced by large windows. The construction techniques, the twin-towered façades and the three-storey elevations of Romanesque Normandy were associated with much lighter walls and more open effects in such Early Gothic cathedrals as Senlis and Sens (*see* SENS, §1(i)). In north-east France attempts were made to combine the Norman thick-wall structure with the new aesthetic of lightness and luminosity, and four-storey buildings, with main arcades, galleries, triforium and clerestory, were erected at the cathedrals of Noyon and Laon and at St Remi, Reims (*see* LAON, fig. 2; REIMS, §IV, 3(i)). Notre-Dame, Paris, also had four storeys in the 12th century, but thin walls were maintained (*see* PARIS, fig. 31); its exceptional height could only be attained through the use of flying buttresses to stabilize the upper parts.

Early Gothic buildings built by the reformed monastic orders followed a separate development, which can be traced in the surviving 12th-century Cistercian churches at FONTENAY ABBEY and PONTIGNY ABBEY. Although sometimes monumental in scale, such churches are characterized by simplicity of design and austerity of detail, reflecting the precepts of the Order (*see* CISTERCIAN ORDER). The Cistercians also established a more systematic layout for their monastic buildings than the Benedictines and Cluniacs; this was caused partly by the Order's organization with its stress on conformity and partly by settlement on new, unrestricted sites close to water courses (*see* CLAIRVAUX ABBEY and MONASTERY, §I).

In the last decades of the 12th century, at the cathedrals of Chartres, Soissons and Bourges, a new phase of Gothic architecture, the so-called HIGH GOTHIC, was inaugurated (*see* CHARTRES, §I, 1; BOURGES, §II, 1(i); SOISSONS, §1). The mastery of flying buttresses permitted the suppression of galleries and the enlargement of openings—the clerestory windows at Chartres, the main arcades at Bourges—

in order to remove all partitioning and increase illumination. Strongly articulated thin walls and triforia created plastic effects. This style was developed at the cathedrals of Reims (begun 1211; *see* REIMS, figs 2–4), Rouen (begun after 1200; *see* ROUEN, figs 4 and 5), Le Mans (*see* LE MANS, fig. 1), Amiens (begun *c.* 1220; *see* AMIENS, figs 1 and 2) and outside France. Regional groups, however, preserved great originality, with wall passages incorporated into the elevations in Burgundy (e.g. Notre-Dame, Dijon, *c.* 1220–30) and Normandy (e.g. Bayeux Cathedral, begun *c.* 1230); and single-cell naves and hall churches in western France (e.g. St Serge, Angers; *see* ANGERS, §2(iii); Poitiers), where domical rib vaults were used instead of domes.

The RAYONNANT STYLE, which gradually came to dominate French architecture until the end of the 14th century, was introduced *c.* 1230–40. Appearing at Saint-Denis Abbey (begun 1231; *see* SAINT-DENIS ABBEY, fig. 4), at Troyes Cathedral (begun 1228; *see* TROYES, fig. 2) and in the choir of Amiens Cathedral (completed 1269; see fig. 4), this style reduced the supporting elements to very thin, linear structures. Openings were enlarged, window tracery became more complex, spreading also over wall surfaces, and triforia were glazed. The Sainte-Chapelle in Paris (*see* PARIS, fig. 34) constitutes a good example of these 'glass houses', although it is still sturdily built. Towards the end of the 13th century, arches became more pointed, support mouldings more undulating and embellished with fillets, and capitals less pronounced, as at St Urbain, Troyes (begun 1262; *see* TROYES, fig. 3).

The Hundred Years War arrested the building activity of most of the large workshops. Where work continued in the 14th century, as at St Ouen, Rouen (begun 1318;

4. Amiens Cathedral, east end, completed 1269

see ROUEN, fig. 7), late 13th-century formulae were retained. Architecture in the Midi was more innovative, notably in the use of brick in Languedoc; immense aisleless spaces were created at Albi Cathedral (begun *c.* 1277; for illustration *see* ALBI) and wide, squat hall churches at La Chaise-Dieu Abbey (Haute-Loire).

The first manifestations of the FLAMBOYANT STYLE, with its sinuous, flamelike tracery forms, appeared in buildings constructed by the royal entourage, for example at Jean, Duc de Berry's Sainte-Chapelle at Riom (Puy-de-Dôme; begun 1382), but it was not until the end of the Hundred Years War and the second half of the 15th century that this style spread throughout France: at the cathedrals of Albi and Lyon (Bourbon chapel); at Notre-Dame, Cléry (1429–83), on the Loire and at St Maclou, Rouen (1432–1531; *see* ROUEN, fig. 6); and in Picardy (the west nave chapels of Amiens Cathedral, Saint-Riquier Abbey and St Wulfram, Abbeville, begun after 1488). Arrangements are very diverse, storeys often being reduced to two, with wide proportions. Interiors are austere in the absence of capitals and in the treatment of the arch mouldings, which either continue those of the pier or 'die' into a smooth surface (as at St Germain, Auxerre, *c.* 1500, and St Séverin, Paris, after 1489). Decoration was reserved for windows and vaults, in which ribs and bosses multiplied, as in the cloister of CADOUIN ABBEY. On the exterior, the gables of portals overran façades; flying buttresses, parapets and the tops of towers became a pretext for ornamentation, creating very rich effects, as in the work of the CHAMBIGES family. Moreover, many cathedrals begun in the 13th century were finished only in the Flamboyant period (e.g. Rouen, Troyes and Tours).

More secular architecture survives from the later medieval period. In 1190 King Philip II Augustus brought the circular donjon into fashion at the Louvre in Paris. Cities such as Aigues-Mortes, Provins and Carcassonne were walled with flanking towers and monumental portals (*see* CASTLE, fig. 1), while the nobility built fortified castles and city palaces. From the 14th century comfort and domestic appointments were important even in castles, following the example of the Papal Palace in Avignon (*see* AVIGNON, fig. 1). In the 15th century sumptuous residences were built in Paris, Bourges and Dijon, and comfort prevailed over defence, as in the house (1443–51) of Jacques Coeur in Bourges (*see* BOURGES, fig. 6). The wealthier classes in towns built multi-storey houses, timber-framed in damp regions, for example at Dinan (Côtes-du-Nord), Rouen and Beaune (Côte-d'Or), and stone in the Loire Valley and the Midi. Buildings for communal use became more numerous: covered halls for markets, wash houses, fountains and bridges, as well as hospitals (e.g. Tonnerre, Yonne; the Hôtel-Dieu at Beaune; see fig. 5) and town halls (e.g. Compiègne, Oise; Arras, Pas-de-Calais).

5. Beaune, Hôtel-Dieu, begun *c.* 1443

H. E. Kubach: *Architecture romane*, Histoire Mondiale de l'Architecture (Paris, 1975)
L. Grodecki: *Architecture gothique* (Paris, 1979; Eng. trans., London, 1979)
M. Durliat: *L'Art roman*, A. Grandes Civilis. (Paris, 1982)
J. Bony: *French Gothic Architecture of the 12th and 13th Centuries* (Berkeley, Los Angeles and London, 1983)
A. Erlande-Brandenburg: *L'Art gothique*, A. Grandes Civilis. (Paris, 1983)
D. Kimpel and R. Suckale: *Die gotische Architektur in Frankreich, 1130–1270* (Munich, 1985)
X. Barral i Altet, ed.: *Le Paysage monumental de la France autour de l'an mil* (Paris, 1987) [incl. bibliogs for individual monuments]
C. Heitz: *La France pré-romane: Archéologie et architecture religieuse du haut moyen âge, IVe siècle–an mille* (Paris, 1987)
C. Wilson: *The Gothic Cathedral* (London, 1990)
E. Vergnolle: *L'Art roman en France* (Paris, 1994)

ANNE PRACHE

2. *c.* 1500–*c.* 1600.

French Renaissance architecture is the synthesis of two traditions: French medieval and Italian Renaissance. The legacy of the medieval period was rich: versatile masonry, colouristic use of materials, exuberant decoration and the basic forms of church and château. The basilican church with ambulatory long remained the norm in France, but the quadripartite vault with liernes and tiercerons proved less enduring. Until the 15th-century Valois rulers reconsolidated the power of the central monarchy, the relaxation of the defensive character of the French fort proceeded at an irregular pace to the Flamboyant-style château, with its large windows, elegant tracery, open and elaborate staircases, high and diversified roof line and varied masses of *corps de logis* and pavilions reflecting the old enceinte of walls punctuated with bastions. Outstanding examples include Rigny-Usse (Indre-et-Loire), Chaumont (Loire-et-Cher) and Meillant (Cher). From Italy, the French had begun to acquire a new repertory of antique decorative motifs before the end of the 15th century through the importation of books and engravings and the exportation of dynastic ambition to Naples and Milan. Predisposed towards the fecund, they were seduced by the brick and terracotta style of Lombardy, especially when translated into marble as for the façade of the Certosa di Pavia. Hardly less relevant to their aspirations was the lavish eulogy of Alfonso V of Aragon (later Alfonso I, King of

BIBLIOGRAPHY
L. Schürenberg: *Die kirchliche Baukunst in Frankreich zwischen 1270 und 1380* (Berlin, 1934)
K. J. Conant: *Carolingian and Romanesque Architecture, 800–1200*, Pelican Hist. A. (Harmondsworth, 1959, rev. 1966)
R. Branner: *St Louis and the Court Style in Gothic Architecture* (London, 1965)
J. Brosse, ed.: *Dictionnaire des églises de France*, 5 vols (Paris, 1966–71)
R. Sanfaçon: *L'Architecture flamboyante en France* (Québec, 1971)

6. Château of Azay-le-Rideau, entrance front and staircase pavilion, 1518

Naples), which provided the triumphal entrance to the Castelnuovo at Naples. Only gradually were they to understand and assimilate the intellectual essence of Florentine classicism: order and unity based on symmetry, the harmony of proportions enshrined in the Classical orders.

(i) Early Renaissance, *c.* 1500–*c.* 1540. (ii) Late Renaissance, *c.* 1540– *c.* 1560. (iii) Mannerism, *c.* 1560–*c.* 1600.

(i) Early Renaissance, c. *1500–*c. *1540.* The first phase of the French Renaissance effectively began with the Italian war (1494) of Charles VIII. It continued through Louis XII's reign till towards the end of that of Francis I. Its characteristics were inventiveness and structural virtuosity as, for instance, in the Hôtel Pincé (1523) by Jean de l'Espine at Angers, or the imposing staircases of the châteaux of Blois and Chambord (from 1519); agglomeration rather than coherent composition, betraying an obsession with the parts rather than the whole, as at the châteaux of Chenonceaux (1514–22), Fontainebleau (1528) or Valençay (*c.* 1540), Centre; and the skilful adaptation of misunderstood Classical detail to Flamboyant forms, as on the principal façade (1503) of the former Hôtel de Ville (now Hôtel des Créneaux) of Orléans, the chevet of St Pierre (1528) at Caen by Hector Sohier, the dormer windows of Francis I's wing (*c.* 1520) at Blois, the fantastic roof of Chambord (1537) or the interior façades of St Eustache in Paris, which, like Chambord, boasts an advanced sense of substance in occasional detail.

Its corner towers apart, the château of Bury (begun 1511), partly on the designs of Fra Giovanni Giocondo, marked a prophetic regularization of the medieval courtyard. In its principal façades, as in the garden façade at the

château of Azay-le-Rideau (1518–28; unfinished), an awareness of the importance of symmetry began to be apparent. Azay-le-Rideau was also precocious in adopting a three-dimensional order—albeit wildly uncanonical—to imply a distinction of vertical mass for the staircase pavilion of the entrance front (see fig. 6), which, as a major element for celebration, was inherited from the late Middle Ages. The bourgeois builders of these châteaux were instrumental in the comparable 'classicization' of the medieval town house, notably Florimond Robertet of Bury in the Hôtel d'Alluye (1498–1508) at Blois.

Francis I let irregular medieval foundations influence his wing of the château at Blois, although, in contrast to the flat planes of the inner façade, the deep recession of the superimposed window arcades overlooking the town (*c.* 1520) emulate Bramante's Cortile di S Damaso at the Vatican, Rome. In the great new building at Chambord (from 1519), however, the whole plan is an essentially symmetrical transformation of donjon and bailey, reputedly by the Italian Domenico da Cortona (*see* Château, fig. 1). In its detail, Flamboyant in form if antique in motif, Chambord is in direct line of descent from the fantasies of Jean, Duc de Berry's *Très Riches Heures* (1416). Indeed, the precedent for the habilitation of donjon and bailey was most persuasively set for the duke's brother, Charles V, at the château of Vincennes. There the King's rooms in the keep were superimposed on two storeys. At Chambord they were ordered horizontally, like the apartments of the Villa Medici (1485–94) at Poggio a Caiano, built by Cortona's master, Giuliano da Sangallo.

At the château of Gaillon (1502–10), built by both French and Italian craftsmen for Cardinal Georges d'Amboise, Archbishop of Rouen, perhaps the first attempt was made at unifying the disparate elements of the symbolic twin-towered postern by subjecting it to the elements of an order, in distant awareness of the Roman triumphal arch. Many great houses followed suit, including FON-TAINEBLEAU, its transformation for Francis I attributed to the master mason GILLES LE BRETON, with its slightly asymmetrical Porte Dorée (1528) recalling Luciano Laurana's superimposed loggias (1467–72) at the Palazzo Ducale, Urbino (for illustration see LAURANA, LUCIANO). With the notable exception of Le Breton's ordonnance at this monumental gateway, in the first half of Francis I's reign the ubiquitous pilaster was essentially decorative, interpolated ornaments usually denying it any virility. Nowhere is this more apparent than in the elegant tomb commissioned in 1516 by Francis I for *Louis XII and Anne of Brittany* at Saint-Denis Abbey (see SAINT-DENIS ABBEY, fig. 7). The chantry-like arcade sheltering the royal *gisants* is as uncanonical in its ordonnance as it is unconcerned with the symbolic significance of such antique forms as the triumphal arch, which was soon to inform the design of both portal and tomb. A fuller understanding of the correct form of the orders is apparent from the 1530s: three-dimensional columns, carefully spaced and proportioned, bear proper entablatures of architrave, frieze and cornice as in the Cour Ovale staircase (1531; destr. 1540) at Fontainebleau and the courtyard of the Hôtel d'Escoville (1538) at Caen by Blaise Le Prestre. The influence of the latter building was felt near by in the north wing of the château of Fontaine-Henri (from 1537), near Caen, where the three main blocks represent the three clearly defined phases of French late medieval and early Renaissance provincial architecture. The verticality in the disposition of these works was hardly less relevant to the problem of 'classicizing' medieval ecclesiastical forms—as at St Eustache (begun 1532), Paris, or on the west fronts of Angers Cathedral and St Michel, Dijon.

Also at this time French architects began to show a more coherent approach to planning and massing. A radical example was Francis I's Château de Madrid (1528; destr. 1792), near Paris, with twin square blocks of self-contained apartments surrounded by loggias and separated by grand salons. The loggias are notable for their Italianate regularity, and Girolamo della Robbia is sometimes credited with more than just the building's terracotta ornament. However, as Pierre Chambiges demonstrated in the courtyard of the château of SAINT-GERMAIN-EN-LAYE (1539–49; much altered), French master builders were now clearly aware of the importance in Roman High Renaissance design of three-dimensional relief, of the contrast between solid and void, light and shade and of the expression of weight in the enclosing fabric.

(ii) Late Renaissance, c. 1540–c. 1560. By the end of the reign of Francis I in 1547, Vitruvius and Italian theorists and commentators on him, especially Alberti, were being assiduously studied in France. Jacopo Vignola, SEBAS-TIANO SERLIO, ROSSO FIORENTINO and FRANCESCO PRI-MATICCIO came to France. Vignola stayed too briefly for much impact, but the others reproduced models from the High Renaissance school of Bramante and his followers, even transforming them with Mannerist virtuosity: Serlio's projects for the château of Ancy-le-Franc (1541–50), near

Tonnerre, and Primaticcio's wing of the Belle Cheminée (1568) at Fontainebleau and his Valois chapel project (c. 1563) for Saint-Denis Abbey represent the former; Rosso's Galerie François Ier (c. 1533) and the disputed Grotte du Jardin des Pins (c. 1543) at Fontainebleau, as well as Serlio's treatise on architecture, showed the way to the latter. France was producing theorists of her own too, such as Philibert de L'Orme and Jean Bullant. In this climate the first maturity of French classical architecture is apparent in the subjection of the parts to the whole, coordination of horizontals and verticals, emphasis on mass and volume, and comprehension of the importance of rational forms, of proportion and of the symbolic meaning and compositional value of the orders.

The demolition of Charles V's Louvre and the construction of a classical palace (1546–78; see PARIS, §V, 6(ii)), commissioned towards the end of his life by Francis I from PIERRE LESCOT, was the occasion for the first full expression of this maturity. Lescot's work in Paris in the mid-1540s is outstanding for the consistent application of canonical orders, as in the triumphal Fountain of the Innocents (1549), and rich sculptural detail executed by JEAN GOUJON, as in the courtyard of the Hôtel Carnavalet (from 1546). The Louvre project was resplendent in both respects. The expression of pavilions and *corps de logis* continued to provide the variety of forms that the French preferred in contrast to the Italians, but Lescot's superimposed Corinthian and Composite orders, scrupulous in their proportions and detail, were used in a way of crucial importance for the future: the progression from pilaster to column, with the projection of the mass of the pavilions from the body of the building, binding these disparate elements together, provided the basic means for the idiosyncratic French tradition to effect classical unity in the context of medieval variety.

Lescot's contemporary PHILIBERT DE L'ORME was born in Lyon, and his earliest surviving work there, the gallery (1535) of the Hôtel Bulliod, executed after his return from three years in humanist circles in Rome, admirably combines a scrupulously observed Ionic order and virtuoso masonry. Cardinal Jean Du Bellay (1492–1560), prominent among the French in Rome, brought de L'Orme to Paris c. 1540 to design a château at Saint-Maur-les-Fossés (begun c. 1541), Val-de-Marne. De L'Orme became principal architect to the Dauphin (later Henry II) and his mistress Diane de Poitiers from 1547. For Henry II he first produced the tomb of *Francis I and Claude de France*, canonical in its adaptation of the triumphal arch motif to a constrained site in Saint-Denis Abbey. De L'Orme's other main royal commissions were the Château Neuf at Saint-Germain (begun 1557) for Henry II (for illustration see SAINT-GERMAIN-EN-LAYE) and the Palais des Tuileries (from 1564; destr. 1871; see L'ORME, PHILIBERT DE, fig. 4), Paris, for the Queen Mother Catherine de' Medici. His varied responses to both were to be of huge importance. At Saint-Germain the single-storey main block with its four corner pavilions stood as a discrete entity, unencumbered by wings: the forecourt, square with a semi-circular recession to each side, was bordered only by low walls. For the vast, unfinished, Tuileries project the Queen

Mother prompted de L'Orme to develop a sumptuous new style that foreshadowed the decorative Mannerism of later 16th-century French practice and pattern books.

De L'Orme's main work for Diane de Poitiers was the château of Anet (1547–55). The entrance, its screen, one wing and the chapel remain on site, but the frontispiece from the central pavilion is preserved at the École des Beaux-Arts in Paris. At Anet, de L'Orme experimented with the disposition of the orders, not only to bind all the traditional parts of the château along horizontal lines, as he had earlier done at Saint-Maur, but also to cope with the stressed verticals of the pavilions. Another powerful variation on the theme of the triumphal arch, the composition of the entrance pavilion anticipates the dislocation and juxtaposition of elements in later 18th-century architecture. The chapel, an exercise in formal geometry preceded by de L'Orme's trefoil scheme for a chapel (1550s) at the château of Villers-Cottêrets, Aisne, inscribes a Greek cross in concentric circles, the inner one providing the domed rotunda (*see* L'ORME, PHILIBERT DE, fig. 2). Over a freely interpreted Corinthian order, defining the semi-circular façades of four overlapping triumphal arches, the virtuoso coffering of the dome spins the spiral pattern of the floor into three dimensions. De L'Orme's quotation of the triumphal arch motif was at its most literal on the main frontispiece, and the canonically superimposed Doric, Ionic and Corinthian orders produced a more profound gravitas than had yet been seen in France.

Scrupulousness in the expression of the orders, if not always sophistication in their handling, is apparent in contemporary or slightly later works in the provinces—especially in the south where antique remains and contiguous Italy provided more or less direct inspiration to complement the influence of the High Renaissance masters in Paris. Outstanding examples include the courtyard of the Hôtel Assezat (1552) by J. Castagné at Toulouse, with its three superimposed orders framing Serlian arcades; the two-storey arcaded screen on the courtyard of the château of Bournazel (*c.* 1550), Aveyron, by Guillaume de Lissorgues; the triumphal entrance arch (1571) of the château of La Tour d'Aigues, Vaucluse, where the principal *corps de logis* (*c.* 1560) follows Lescot's Louvre; and the Roman church front that provides the gable above the west façade (1562) of Rodez Cathedral by Guillaume Philander.

(iii) Mannerism, c. 1560–c. 1600. JEAN BULLANT, a younger contemporary of Lescot and de L'Orme, announced the end of this short-lived period of maturity in his work on the châteaux of ÉCOUEN (1556–78), Chantilly (*c.* 1560; *see* CHANTILLY, §1(i)) and La Fère-en-Tardenois (1552–62), Picardy. All were provided with frontispieces incorporating colossal orders, which were classical in attention to detail but unclassical in scale, and less interested in integration than in incident. These different characteristics may well derive from Bullant's detailed studies of antique buildings made in Rome in the early 1540s.

The architects of the late 16th century, inspired by the virtuosity of the Italian Mannerists but lacking their sophisticated grasp of licence in the Antique, reverted to an essentially decorative approach to articulation. Unlike the work of the earlier Renaissance, this was not the result of misunderstanding, but a conscious return to prolixity, often involving the wilful misuse of the orders as elements in a pattern of detail, masking rather than elucidating the structural realities of the building. These developments are generally associated with the dynasty of Jacques Androuet Du Cerceau the elder, who was particularly prominent as the editor of various suites of fantasies on Classical architectural themes and *Les Plus Excellents Bastiments de France* (Paris, 1576–9), which celebrated the achievement of French architects since the Renaissance (*see* DU CERCEAU, (1)). Providing an invaluable, if not always accurate, record of many masterpieces now lost, it constituted a pattern book for contemporary patrons and practitioners. The production of a pattern book and the elaboration of a decorative Mannerism were closely related, as the sumptuous illustrations of Du Cerceau's châteaux of Verneuil (1568), near Senlis, and Charleval (1570), near Rouen, amply demonstrate. Still prolix, if less bizarre, the Grande Galerie linking the Louvre and the Tuileries is generally associated with the names of various members of the Du Cerceau family and Louis Métezeau (*see* MÉTEZEAU, (1)).

The elder Du Cerceau built several houses in Paris that reflected the more practical contribution of his *Livre d'architecture* (1559) to the improvement of domestic planning, particularly in the provision of apartments of two or three rooms according to the rank of the patron. Other members of the dynasty were also prominent as builders of Parisian houses well into the next century, their now depleted legacy ranging from Baptiste Androuet Du Cerceau's Hôtel Lamoignon (1584; *see* DU CERCEAU, (2)) to Jean Androuet Du Cerceau's Hôtel de Sully (1624; *see* DU CERCEAU, (3)). Exuberant sculptural detail notwithstanding, with an impressive order of colossal Corinthian pilasters and assertive rustication respectively, neither of these works represents anti-classicism at its most florid. This was most evident in the provinces, particularly in the north where the influence of Flanders was pervasive; church, town house and château reflect this relapse into the flamboyant. Representative examples range from the Halle Echevinale (1593) at Lille by Jean Fayet, to the Maison Milsand (*c.* 1561) at Dijon by Hugues Sambin and the contemporary Hôtel de Beringuier-Maynier (Vieux-Raisin) in Toulouse.

BIBLIOGRAPHY

P. de L'Orme: *L'Architecture* (Paris, 1567)
J. A. Du Cerceau: *Les Plus Excellents Bastiments de France* (Paris, 1576–9)
S. Serlio: *Tutte le opere d'architettura e prospetiva di Sebastiano Serlio Bolognese* (Venice, 1619/R Farnborough, 1964)
J. Marot: *L'Architecture françoise* (Paris, [*c.* 1670]/R 1970)
J. Mariette: *L'Architecture française*, 5 vols (Paris, 1727–38/R 1927–9 in 3 vols)
J.-A. Piganiol de la Force: *Description de Paris* (Paris, 1736)
A.-N. Dézallier d'Argenville: *Voyage pittoresque de Paris* (Paris, 1749)
J.-F. Blondel: *L'Architecture françoise*, 8 vols (Paris, 1752–3/R 1904–5)
A.-N. Dézallier d'Argenville: *Voyage pittoresque des environs de Paris* (Paris, 1755, 2/1779)
——: *Vies des fameux architectes et sculpteurs* (1788)
P. du Colombier: *Le Style Henri IV–Louis XVIII* (Paris, 1941)
L. Hautecoeur: *Architecture classique* (1943–57)
E. de Ganay: *Châteaux de France*, 4 vols (Paris, 1948–53)
A. Blunt: *Art and Architecture in France, 1500–1700*, Pelican Hist. A. (Harmondsworth, 1953, rev. 4/1980/R 1988)
——: *Philibert de L'Orme* (London, 1958)

J.-P. Babelon: *Demeures parisiennes sous Henri IV et Louis XVIII* (Paris, 1965)

D. Thomson: *Renaissance Paris: Architecture and Growth, 1475–1600* (London, 1984)

CHRISTOPHER TADGELL

3. *c*. 1600–*c*. 1814. In the 17th and 18th centuries Paris and its galaxy of châteaux in the Ile-de-France began to rival Rome as the centre of architectural innovation in Europe. This was the result of a fortuitous convergence of patronage, artistic talent and the rapidly increasing power and prestige of the French monarchy under Louis XIII and Louis XIV (*see also* §XII below). This was sustained throughout the remainder of the *ancien régime* and the rule of Napoleon by a generally favourable economic climate for building, particularly in the private sector, the development of a system of architectural education through the establishment of the Académie Royale d'Architecture and a tradition of theoretical and critical writings on architecture, notable exponents of which included François Blondel, Claude Perrault, Jean-Louis de Cordemoy and Marc-Antoine Laugier (*see* TREATISE, §I). Although the architecture produced in and around Paris was highly influential, in the various French regions indigenous traditions of rural and urban vernacular buildings existed, along with a distinct high-style architecture, shaped by geographic, economic and cultural ties to other European centres (e.g. north-eastern France with Flanders; Lorraine with the Austrian empire; Provence with Genoa). The hôtels particuliers built in the 17th century in Aix-en-Provence (see fig. 7) consist of a massive rectangular block fronting the street and a modest rear

7. Jean Lombard: Hôtel de Maurel de Pontèves, Aix-en-Provence, 1647–51

garden rather than the *hôtel-entre-cour-et-jardin* layouts typical of Paris. The vitality of regional styles began to break down in the late 17th century as Parisian models, sometimes designed by Parisian architects, were introduced to such cities as Aix-en-Provence, as statements of fashion and as expressions of governmental policy.

RICHARD CLEARY

(i) Classicism, *c*. 1600–*c*. 1660. (ii) Louis XIV style, *c*. 1660–*c*. 1700. (iii) Régence and Louis XV styles, *c*. 1700–*c*. 1750. (iv) Neo-classicism, *c*. 1750–*c*. 1789. (v) Revolutionary period and Empire style, *c*. 1789–*c*. 1814.

(i) Classicism, c. *1600*–c. *1660.* The ground was laid for classicism during the regime of Henry IV (*reg* 1589–1610). By the beginning of the 17th century, though such works as the façade (1610) of St Etienne-du-Mont in Paris or the unfinished château of Brissac (1606), near Angers, were still common enough, the tide of ornament had turned, and it became typical for architects to rely simply on the contrast between rusticated quoins at the salient points of their structures and rendered or unrendered brick infill. This is nowhere better illustrated than in the relatively modest houses surrounding the Place Dauphine (1607–15; *see* PARIS, fig. 3) and the Place Royale (from 1605; now Place des Vosges), which Henry IV laid out in Paris as the nucleii for ordered development in the city. Monumental examples with a richer mixture of materials include the stable courtyard portal (1606) at Fontainebleau, which was inspired by Bramante's Belvedere niche in the Vatican, and the château of Grosbois (1597), Seine-et-Marne, both by Rémy Collin (*fl* 1597–1634).

In the second decade of the 17th century SALOMON DE BROSSE reasserted classical values, despite his training in the circle of the Du Cerceau family (*see* §2(iii) above) and his work at Verneuil. Starting with the château disposition of his master, de Brosse created a series of monumental works, embracing the châteaux of Coulommiers (begun 1613; destr. 1738), Seine-et-Marne, and Blérancourt (begun 1612; destr. World War I), Aisne; the Palais du Luxembourg (begun 1615) in Paris (*see* PARIS, §V, 8); and the Palais du Parlement (1618; now Palais de Justice) at Rennes. They show increased coherence in massing, clarity of volume, purity of line, control of detail and coordination of articulation. His debt to Jacques Androuet Du Cerceau the younger is apparent in his internal planning, with an apartment on each floor of the pavilions that invariably projected from the four corners of his main *corps de logis*. The square domes of Verneuil reappear at Blérancourt (for reconstruction drawing *see* CHÂTEAU, fig. 2), but, more consistent in height, de Brosse's roofs avoid asserting the parts at the expense of the coherence of the whole. Opposing obsession with anti-architectonic surface pattern, moreover, the lucidity of his ordonnance, progressing under sustained cornice lines from pilaster to column with the advance of the mass from *corps de logis* to pavilion, and the discreteness of his main block, derives from Lescot and de L'Orme. The difference between decorative whimsy and architectural imagination is nowhere better illustrated than in a comparison between the entrance pavilions of Verneuil and the Palais du Luxembourg (for illustration of the latter *see* BROSSE, SALOMON DE, fig. 1). De Brosse's contribution to the development of the hôtel was limited, but his contemporaries LOUIS SAVOT and

PIERRE LE MUET both furthered the genre. Savot produced a practical building manual, *Architecture françoise* (Paris, 1624), and Le Muet, in his *Manière de bastir pour toutes sortes de personnes* (Paris, 1623), took categorization in terms of social status even further than Du Cerceau had done. In practice, Le Muet's later Hôtel d'Avaux (1644), Paris, shows him to have been less fastidious than de Brosse—like most of his contemporaries. For example, the Hôtel Chalons-Luxembourg (*c.* 1623), Paris, by an unknown architect, retains the simple brick-and-stone style of Henry IV, but its entrance portal is a fantasy worthy of a latter-day Du Cerceau.

The main ecclesiastical work attributed to de Brosse is the west front of St Gervais–St Protais (1616; see fig. 8) in Paris. Clearly indebted to de L'Orme's Anet frontispiece, it illustrates well the application of his principles to the solution of the problem of providing a classical front to an essentially Gothic form of church. Nearby, the façade (1634) of St Paul–St Louis, less coherently articulated or controlled in detail, offers a constructive comparison. In the original projects for the church by ETIENNE MARTELLANGE and in the contemporary work of JACQUES LE MERCIER on the church (1631) at Richelieu, Indre-et-Loire, and the church of the Sorbonne (1635–48) in Paris, the architects consciously preferred a placid academic classicism to the recent French and current Flemish delight in lavish ornament, or the Roman Baroque conception of movement, both of which they considered licentious. At

8. Salomon de Brosse: west front of St Gervais–St Protais, Paris, 1616

the Sorbonne, the most original feature of the composition—the north façade, with its magnificent portico providing access to the college court—was Le Mercier's greatest success. Treated in the grandest manner, according to Blondel this façade was more 'regular' than that of any other church in Paris. Le Mercier's secular works have contributed less to his reputation. As Louis XIII's Premier Architecte he was commissioned (late 1630s) to quadruple the Cour Carrée at the Louvre, and he has been criticized by academic classicists ever since for the scale of the caryatids that he introduced to solve the problem of ordonnance in his new central pavilion at the Louvre, the Pavillon de l'Horloge (*c.* 1640). Working on a vast scale to meet Cardinal de Richelieu's pretensions at Richelieu, Le Mercier was unable to match de Brosse's conception of coherence. (For further discussion of both town and château at Richelieu, *see* RICHELIEU (i).)

The mantle of the early classical masters had passed to François Mansart (*see* MANSART, (1)) by the 1630s. In such works as the châteaux of Balleroy (1626), Calvados, and of Maisons (1642; *see* MANSART, (1), fig. 3), and in the wing he added to Blois (1635–9), he expressed those qualities generally associated with the French classical spirit of the 17th century: clarity combined with subtlety; restraint in ornament but richness in form; concentration by the elimination of inessentials; and obedience to a strict code of rules but flexibility within them. Although the planning of châteaux was conservative in retaining the traditional *enfilade*, his work at Blois is characteristic of his individualism in revealing a command of the Baroque techniques then being evolved in Rome: colossal scale, vigorous contrast in the contours of walls and the profiles of masses, alignment of varied spaces to provide rich vistas, vertical perspectives and dramatic lighting. His experiments in the latter were developed most influentially in his major ecclesiastical works (e.g. church of the Visitation (1632) and the Val-de-Grâce (1645), Paris, and the funerary chapel (after 1660) of the Bourbon family at Saint-Denis). The major works of LOUIS LE VAU, Mansart's younger rival, belong mostly to the rule of Cardinal Mazarin. But already in the 1640s Le Vau's flair for innovative planning was admirably demonstrated at the Hôtel Hesselin (1642), Paris. At the Hôtel Lambert, built from 1640 on the Ile Saint-Louis for the financier Jean-Baptiste Lambert, the curved court façade recalls Mansart and his sources, but the incoherent ordonnance is in marked contrast to that in Mansart's work. This inconsistent use of the orders can be seen at VAUX-LE-VICOMTE, one of Le Vau's most spectacular works, built for Nicolas Fouquet. Set in André Le Nôtre's splendid garden based on the principle, already developed by Mansart at Blois and Maisons, of placing the château at the climax of extended open vistas and decorated internally by Charles Le Brun after the style evolved earlier by Cortona at the Pitti, Florence, Vaux-le-Vicomte was the most startling ensemble of the day.

CHRISTOPHER TADGELL

Mansart, Le Mercier and Le Vau differed significantly in their approaches to planning, massing and the handling of the architectural orders, but each succeeded in adapting classical idioms to such distinctly French building types as the château and the Parisian hôtel (*see* HÔTEL PARTICU-LIER). They also synthesized Italian models of church design with French Gothic systems of proportion and masonry construction. Although different in appearance, their works observed the concept of *convenance*, the appropriateness of image to use, which became one of the guiding concepts of 17th- and 18th-century French architecture.

(ii) Louis XIV style, c. 1660–c. 1700. British and American historians writing about French architecture of the mid- to late 17th century commonly frame their discussions with the term Baroque, which invites comparison to Italy. In contrast, French scholars have preferred to reinforce nationalistic traits by using the term LOUIS XIV STYLE. Both points of view have merit. Through personal travels or graphic media, French designers were aware of the stylistic currents in Rome and other major Italian cities. Their approaches were also shaped by such local factors as conventional building types and construction techniques and the intentions of various French policy makers, such as Jean-Baptiste Colbert (*see* COLBERT, (1)), to establish cultural as well as political independence from the papacy.

Louis XIV (*see* BOURBON, §I(8)) and his powerful Directeurs des Bâtiments, Colbert (1661–83) and FRAN-ÇOIS MICHEL LE TELLIER LOUVOIS (1683–91), sought to fashion an architecture that would secure the monarch's reputation as the worthy successor of the Ancients. They conceived Paris as the new Rome, resplendent with public squares, triumphal gateways and such monumental buildings as the Hôtel des Invalides and the Louvre. In 1665 Colbert arranged for Gianlorenzo Bernini to travel to Paris to undertake the design of the east façade of the Palais du Louvre. Differences over cost, programme and style, coupled with parochial opposition from French architects, blocked Bernini's projects, and the Crown appointed a committee composed of Louis Le Vau, Claude Perrault (*see* PERRAULT, (2)) and CHARLES LE BRUN to resolve the issue. The resulting design presents an ordered, monumental elegance informed by imperial Roman architecture and French principles of façade composition. Since its construction (begun 1667), it has been a touchstone for what the *ancien régime* called the *grand goût* and what modern historians commonly refer to as French classicism.

Outside Paris, Louis XIV made use of Chambord, Fontainebleau and the other châteaux occupied seasonally by French monarchs, but he favoured Versailles (*see* VERSAILLES, §1). In the 1660s he commissioned Le Vau, Le Brun and ANDRÉ LE NÔTRE to enlarge and aggrandize the buildings and gardens built by his father, Louis XIII. In the late 1670s he commissioned Jules Hardouin Mansart (*see* MANSART, (2)) to undertake an even more ambitious expansion, which allowed him to transfer the seat of government to the château in 1682. The architecture, interiors and gardens of Versailles were conceived to provide a harmonious and fitting backdrop for Louis XIV's dazzling performance as the Sun King, and they served as a model for other European princes seeking to play similar roles. The Court style of Louis XIV was

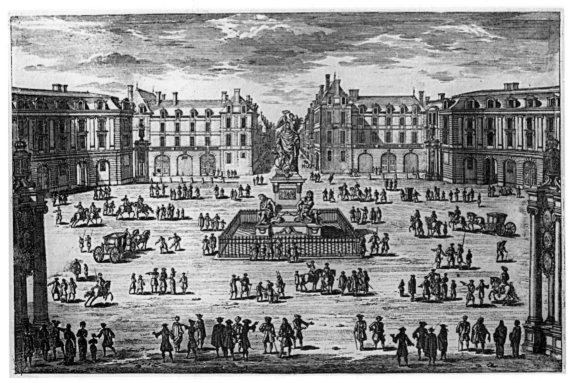

9. Jules Hardouin Mansart: Place des Victoires, Paris, 1685; from an 18th-century print

exported from Paris and Versailles to the French provinces in the designs of individual hôtels and governmental buildings and, on an urban scale, *places royales*, public squares with a statue of the reigning monarch framed by buildings with uniform façades. Conceived as a monument to royal power and grandeur, the *place royale* became a distinct urban form, following the designs of Hardouin Mansart for the Place des Victoires (1685; see fig. 9) and the Place Louis-le-Grand (1685; now Place Vendôme) in Paris (*see* MANSART, (2), fig. 3; *see also* PARIS, §II, 3). When planned in such provincial cities as Lyon and Dijon, they were typically commissioned by a courtier or royal administrator, funded by local revenues and designed by either Hardouin Mansart or another architect of the Bâtiments du Roi. A more austere strain of royal architecture was manifest in the work of the military engineer SÉBASTIEN LE PRESTRE DE VAUBAN, whose fortress towns (e.g. Neuf-Brisach, 1698; *see* MILITARY ARCHITECTURE AND FORTIFICATION, fig. 13) included civilian buildings as well as bastions.

(iii) Régence and Louis XV styles, c. *1700–c. 1750.* The architectural climate in France at the start of the 18th century was characterized by a decline in royal patronage, offset by an increase in the number of private commissions, the genesis of the ROCOCO decorative style and innovations in house planning by such designers as Armand-Claude Mollet (*see* MOLLET, (2)) and JEAN COURTONNE, who made comfort as important an objective as display. The use of the term Rococo to describe French architecture of the first decades of the century (French scholars typically use RÉGENCE STYLE and LOUIS XV STYLE) is perhaps misleading, for it brings to mind the sensuous curves and atectonic qualities of the decorative style, which was at its peak between the 1720s and 1750s. The massing and articulation of contemporary architectural exteriors, however, displayed few of these characteristics, except in the carving of keystones and other details. In general, building envelopes became simpler with unadorned string courses, panels and quoins replacing the architectural orders.

The two most prominent architects in the first half of the century were ROBERT DE COTTE, who refined the *grand goût* of the Louis XIV style in accordance with the programmatic and expressive requirements of the new era, and the highly inventive GERMAIN BOFFRAND. In such works as the projects for the château of Malgrange (1712), near Nancy, Boffrand synthesized and dramatically expanded on classical themes established by Le Vau, Hardouin Mansart and Palladio. Twenty years later, he created one of the masterpieces of the Rococo, the Salon Ovale (1735) of the Hôtel de Soubise in Paris (for illustration *see* LOUIS XV STYLE). Both architects enjoyed extensive practices and an international body of clients.

(iv) Neo-classicism, c. *1750–c. 1789.* Although Louis XV (*see* BOURBON, §I(10)) assumed personal rule in 1723, he did not establish himself as a patron of monumental architecture until he commissioned the Ecole Militaire (1750; completed to reduced plan, 1768) in Paris from Anges-Jacques Gabriel (*see* GABRIEL, (3)). Despite the absence of strong direction from the King, there was considerable interest in issues of public architecture and

urban planning among officers of the Crown, *philosophes* and the educated public. Under the banners of embellishment and utility, projects for street improvements, markets and governmental buildings were proposed throughout France, and new building types were developed, which became essential statements of civic pride. Among these was the monumental public theatre, exemplified by the Grand Théâtre (1773–80) in Bordeaux designed by VICTOR LOUIS.

The *grand goût* of Louis XIV remained the standard for such royal commissions as Gabriel's buildings facing the Place Louis XV (from 1753; now Place de la Concorde; *see* PARIS, fig. 6) in Paris and for the other *places royales* of Louis XV built in such provincial cities as Rennes, Bordeaux and Nancy. Questions of architectural style, however, provoked considerable debate, especially in the second half of the century. Popular enthusiasm for the Rococo waned, and it was replaced in the 1750s by the decorative fashion known as the GOÛT GREC, which was inspired by the archaeological discoveries at Pompeii, Herculaneum and Paestum. Alongside this fascination with the newly unearthed images of the ancient world were the more theoretical investigations of architectural composition, undertaken in Rome by an international community of architects influenced by Giovanni Battista Piranesi, a resurgent interest in the work of Palladio, and a body of rationalist criticism advocating a return to the more forthright structural expression of Gothic architecture, seen, for example, in the writings of MARC-ANTOINE LAUGIER. In this climate architects began to re-evaluate their handling of the orders and to experiment with a degree of freedom not seen since the first half of the 17th century. Buildings became manifestos, and among those of particular importance for their time were the church of Ste Geneviève (1757–90; now the Panthéon; *see* PARIS, §V, 9), designed by JACQUES-GERMAIN SOUFFLOT, in which the architect sought to synthesize classical design principles and Gothic structural economy (for illustration *see* RATIONALISM (i)), and the Ecole de Chirurgie (1771–86; now the Faculté de Medicine), Paris, by JACQUES GONDOIN, which integrated Greek, Roman and French forms in an architecture celebrating a noble simplicity, contrast and symmetry. Despite their different intentions and formal properties, both buildings are considered examples of French Neo-classicism, or the LOUIS XVI STYLE, a loosely defined term that has as its common denominator an approach to composition favouring discrete geometric shapes rather than compound or hybrid forms. In the planning of Ste Geneviève, Soufflot tested the strength of the stone to be used in the columns and piers in a well-publicized, if limited, step towards an understanding of the behaviour of structural materials, a growing area of research at this time. More systematic analysis became possible later in the century following the publication of such works as those of Charles-Auguste Colomb (1773) on statics and GASPARD MONGE on descriptive geometry (1795).

The foremost architect of the late 18th century was CLAUDE-NICOLAS LEDOUX, whose work exemplified the idea of *architecture parlante*, a 'literally' expressive architecture. He built fashionable town houses, a model saltworks and visionary projects that challenged social structures as well as the conventions of architectural expression. His inquiries in the latter realm just before and during the Revolution (1789–95) were paralleled by other architects, including ETIENNE-LOUIS BOULLÉE, who used drawings and writings to expand the realm of architectural design beyond the constraints of clients, cost and construction.

(v) Revolutionary period and Empire style, c. 1789–c. 1814. Few buildings of significance were built between the Terror (1793–4) and the Consulate (1799–1804). Among these was the Assembly Hall (1795–7) for the Conseil des Cinq-Cents (now the Chambre des Députés) at the Palais Bourbon in Paris, designed by Jacques-Pierre Gisors and others. Despite the lack of ready funds, the revolutionary governments looked towards the future and encouraged architects to address the symbolic and utilitarian needs of the new State by contemplating the adaptive reuse of historic buildings and the invention of building types.

The political and economic stability brought about by Napoleon Bonaparte's rule revived public and private investment in building. An ambitious public works programme throughout France produced a variety of urgently needed utilitarian structures, including warehouses, markets and slaughterhouses. Napoleon also planned ceremonial set-pieces intended to secure his place in the pantheon of great rulers (*see* PARIS, §II, 5). The completion of the Temple de la Grande Armée (renamed La Madeleine in 1845), Paris, begun in 1806 by ALEXANDRE-PIERRE VIGNON, was conceived as a monument to the French army. Its colossal temple form illustrates the more imitative aspect of French Neo-classicism in the early 19th century. By this time the teachings of the Académie regarding the primacy of the orders as the generators of form and the bearers of meaning were being challenged from a number of directions. In addition, the idea of Historicism had spread beyond the searches for the noble simplicity of antiquity and the principles of Gothic construction to a more general eclecticism. Napoleon's personal architects, CHARLES PERCIER and PIERRE-FRANÇOIS-LÉONARD FONTAINE, the virtual inventors of the eclectic EMPIRE STYLE, incorporated history with greater invention and subtlety and brought a sure sense of proportion and ornamentation to such diverse assignments as Fontaine's interiors of the château of Malmaison (*c.* 1800), Rueil-Malmaison, and Percier's façades of the Rue de Rivoli, Paris, begun in 1802 (*see* PARIS, fig. 7). Exotic imagery hitherto reserved for garden follies also began to appear in the city: thus, for example, the fashion for Egyptian imagery at the turn of the century inspired the construction in Paris of a commercial building faced with colossal Egyptian heads (2, Rue de Caire; 1799; see fig. 10).

10. Paris, 2, Rue de Caire, 1799; from a mid-19th-century drawing

BIBLIOGRAPHY
C. Perrault: *Vitruve: Les Dix Livres d'architecture* (Paris, 1673, rev. 1684/*R* 1979)
F. Blondel: *Cours d'architecture enseigné dans l'Académie Royale d'Architecture* (Paris, 1675)
C. Perrault: *Ordonnance des cinq espèces de colonnes selon la méthode des anciens* (Paris, 1683)
M. de Frémin: *Mémoires critiques d'architecture* (Paris, 1702)
J.-L. de Cordemoy: *Nouveau traité de toute l'architecture ou l'art de bâtir* (Paris, 1714/*R* 1966)
J.-F. Blondel: *Architecture françoise*, 8 vols (Paris, 1752–6/*R* 1904–5) [incl. original engravings from Mariette's *L'Architecture françoise*, 1727–38]
M.-A. Laugier: *Essai sur l'architecture* (Paris, 1753, rev. 1755/*R* 1978; Eng. trans., Los Angeles, 1977)
J.-F. Blondel: *Cours d'architecture*, 9 vols (Paris, 1771–7)

C. A. Coulomb: *Sur l'application des règles de maximis et minimis à quelques problèmes de statique relatifs à l'architecture* (MS., 1773); ed. in *Société Française de Physique: Collection de Mémoires relatifs à la physique*, i (Paris, 1884)
N. Le Camus de Mézières: *Génie de l'architecture* (Paris, 1780)
E.-L. Boullée: *Architecture: Essai sur l'art* (MS., *c.* 1788; Paris, Bib. N.); Eng. trans. as *Boullée's Treatise on Architecture*, ed. H. Rosenau (London, 1953)
G. Monge: *Géométrie descriptive* (Paris, 1795)
J.-N.-L. Durand: *Recueil et parallèle des edifices de tout genre, anciens et modernes* (Paris, 1801)
——: *Précis des leçons d'architecture données à l'Ecole Royale Polytechnique*, 2 vols (Paris, 1802–5)
J. Rondelet: *Traité théorique et pratique de l'art de bâtir*, 3 vols (Paris, 1802–30)
R. Blomfield: *History of French Architecture from the Death of Mazarin to the Death of Louis XV*, 2 vols (London, 1921)
A. Blunt: *Art and Architecture in France, 1500–1700*, Pelican Hist. A. (Harmondsworth, 1953, rev. 4/1980/*R* 1988)
F. Kimball: *Creation of the Rococo* (New York, 1964)
R. Coope: *Salomon de Brosse and the Development of the Classical Style in French Architecture, from 1565–1630* (London, 1972)
M. Gallet: *Stately Mansions: Eighteenth-century Paris Domestic Architecture* (New York, 1972)
W. G. Kalnein and M. Levey: *Art and Architecture of the Eighteenth Century in France*, Pelican Hist. A. (Harmondsworth, 1972)
A. J. Braham and W. P. J. Smith: *François Mansart* (London, 1973)
S. Eriksen: *Early French Neo-classicism* (London, 1974)
Piranèse et les Français, 1740–1790 (exh. cat., Rome, Acad. France, 1976)
F. Fichet: *Théorie architecturale à l'âge classique* (Brussels, 1979)
A. Braham: *Architecture of the French Enlightenment* (London, 1980)
J. M. Pérouse de Montclos: *Architecture à la française* (Paris, 1982)
A. Pérez-Gómez: *Architecture and the Crisis of Modern Science* (Cambridge, MA, 1983)

RICHARD CLEARY

4. *c.* 1814–*c.* 1914. In the most limited sense, the Restoration of the Bourbon dynasty in 1814 seemed to mark a turn away from the immense classical forms advocated by Napoleonic planning practices. The Restoration's stylistic preferences tended towards the TROUBADOUR STYLE, or early French classical forms, which sought to connect the Restoration with Valois and Bourbon forebears. Ironically, PIERRE-FRANÇOIS-LÉONARD

FONTAINE, Premier Architecte de l'Empereur, continued his practice during subsequent regimes, as evidenced in such explicitly Bourbon commissions as the Chapelle Expiatoire (1816–26) and the St Ferdinand Chapel (1842–3), both in Paris. Such projects dating from the Restoration and July Monarchy (1830–48) typified the growing desire of these regimes to memorialize a pre-Revolutionary past, to legitimate the political present by association with that past and visibly to subvert the authority of Napoleonic classicism. For the most part, large-scale construction in France ceased with the Restoration, due to the immense losses suffered by the French treasury during the Empire. Religious and private construction, however, continued.

(i) Basilical variants and private architecture at the Restoration. (ii) Academic classicism and Romanticism. (iii) Gothic Revival. (iv) New materials and the religion of progress. (v) Positivism and Eclecticism. (vi) The city-machine.

(i) Basilical variants and private architecture at the Restoration. When Catholicism was renewed as the State religion during the Restoration, church building became ideologically important and a prominent part of architectural practice. Despite the private, medievalizing preferences of the Bourbons, public churches related more to certain sanctioned pre-Revolutionary forms, less Neo-classical than Late Antique–Early Christian. The inescapable model was Jean-François Thérèse Chalgrin's St Philippe-du-Roule (1772–84; altered 19th century) in Paris, and it influenced such works as Notre-Dame-de-Lorette (1823–35; see fig. 11) by LOUIS-HIPPOLYTE LEBAS and particularly St Vincent-de-Paul (1832–45) by JACQUES-IGNACE HITTORFF, both placed in burgeoning northern—and middle-class—quarters of Paris. Although similar in plan, these churches have alternative strategies of façade articulation, thus intimating their architects' quite different

11. Louis-Hippolyte Lebas: Notre-Dame-de-Lorette, Paris, 1823–35

aesthetic positions. Lebas's building was a laconic reinterpretation of the Chalgrin basilical type, fronted by an apparently correct reconstruction of the early Roman Temple of Hercules at Cora (now Cori). Hittorff's building is also a basilica but differs from Lebas's austere and monochromatic exterior by overlaying the whole with colour. The main façade is a variant of a twin-towered Gothic cathedral coated with richly coloured paintings by Hippolyte Flandrin within, and polychrome terracotta panels designed by Pierre-Jules Jollivet in the exterior classical portico. The two attitudes towards form not only characterized practice but also came to shape the period's major architectural institution, the Ecole des Beaux-Arts (*see* PARIS, §VI, 3(iv)).

The period's attitude towards private city architecture is perhaps best illustrated by the quarters immediately surrounding the two churches. Both the Place St Georges, near Notre-Dame-de-Lorette, and the Place Charles X (now Place Lafayette), where St Vincent-de-Paul is located, were fronted with spare and continuous housing masses. The incised linearity of the façades and the simple classical language suggest housing typologies introduced by Charles Percier and Fontaine in their *Palais, maisons, et autres édifices modernes dessinés à Rome* (Paris, 1798) and schematized by JEAN-NICOLAS-LOUIS DURAND in his early Renaissance 'combinaisons verticales' from *Précis des leçons* (1802–5).

(ii) Academic classicism and Romanticism. The Bourbons revived several institutions, including the Académie Royale des Beaux-Arts, outlawed since 1793 (*see* PARIS, §VI, 3). The restored Académie called for a new official school for the instruction of art and architecture—the Ecole Royale des Beaux-Arts, as it was officially named in 1819 (*see also* §XV below). Despite the novelty of its name, the new school and its teachings were heavily dependent on the shapes of two earlier architectural institutions sanctioned by the Empire—Julien-David Le Roy's Ecole Privée d'Architecture and Durand's technical course at the Ecole Polytechnique. Together, these two streams of thought produced in the school an unstable, even volatile, admixture of Le Roy's Greek idealism with Durand's pragmatic typology, and they profoundly affected architectural theory and practice for the next century.

This discord, however, proved to be the aesthetic basis of the early Ecole, as well as the Académie, which selected the winner of the most prestigious of its awards, the PRIX DE ROME. It also accounted for much of the school's enduring energy. Winners during the first decade of the school often quoted directly from the themes of the school's aesthetics and practice. Henri Labrouste's Tribunal de Cassation project of 1824 merged the notion of a basic inscribed cross with an additive idea of functional bay construction and singularity of spatial type, the basilical planning deriving in this case from contemporary church construction (*see* LABROUSTE, (2)). This classic compositional scheme merited for him, as for many over the next 30 years, the Prix de Rome. Once at the Ecole de Rome, overseen by the Académie, Labrouste associated himself with other *pensionnaires*, specifically FÉLIX DUBAN, EMILE GILBERT and GUILLAUME ABEL BLOUET. The centre of much of the destabilization within the Ecole was, para-doxically, the Secrétaire Perpétuel of the Académie, AN-TOINE QUATREMÈRE DE QUINCY, who, in *Le Jupiter olympien* (Paris, 1815), had already begun to criticize the tendency to view classical architecture as pure, white and undecorated. His anti-purist diatribe found a responsive audience among the so-called Romantic generation: Félix Duban, Henri Labrouste, LOUIS DUC and Léon Vaudoyer (*see* VAUDOYER, (2)).

The resistance of this group to the Académie was set out in the annual *envois* that the *pensionnaires* sent back to Paris; even the basic archaeological *envois* were not im-mune to the emergent anti-classicism of the movement. One of these was the reconstruction of the Temple of Hercules at Cora, proposed in 1831 by Théodore La-brouste (*see* LABROUSTE, (1)) and quoted here not so much as type, as in Lebas's work, but as construction overlaid with polychromatic decoration, wherein resided the building's meaning. Henri Labrouste had expanded on this interpretation in his *envoi* of 1828–9—for the three hypaethral temples at Paestum—in which he sketched a historical development as a progression away from an ideal type. Labrouste's theories led him to refute both the documentation and conclusions of academic spokesman Claude-Mathieu Delagardette (1762–1805), whose *Ruines de Paestum* (1799) bore the Académie's imprimatur. As Labrouste assailed the canon, he also angered Quatremère de Quincy and his academic cohorts in Paris.

For most laureates architectural success was assured, as the Conseil Général des Bâtiments Civils commissioned them for major public works in Paris and elsewhere. Indeed, five of the six architects associated with early Romanticism were given their first major public commis-sions by this organization (all buildings illustrated under biographical entries): Gilbert, the Asile des Aliénés (1838–45) at Charenton; Duban, the Ecole des Beaux-Arts (1832–40); Duc, the Palais de Justice (1857–68) in Paris; Vau-doyer, the Conservatoire des Arts et Métiers (1838–72), Paris, and Marseille Cathedral (1845, 1852–93); Henri Labrouste was given no official work until 1838, when he was entrusted with the construction of the Bibliothèque Ste-Geneviève (1839–51), Place du Panthéon, Paris, ar-guably the period's single most important work (*see* §(iv) below).

(iii) Gothic Revival. Henri Labrouste was forced to find employment in another segment of the architectural pro-fession less influenced by the Académie, the Commission des Monuments Historiques, which was the first organi-zation officially to acknowledge the growing interest in medieval architecture. *Goût gothique* was fostered in France by such writings as François-René Chateaubriand's *Le Génie du christianisme* (1802). However, the spotlight was turned on to French medieval architecture by such Anglo-French writings as the works of Andrew Ducare (1713–85) and A. C. Pugin, who documented England's Norman architectural history. France then produced its own litera-ture, the most spectacular work being *Voyages pittoresques dans l'ancienne France* (from 1833) by Charles Nodier (1780–1844), Alphonse de Cailleux and Isidore-Justin-Séverin Taylor, the graphic style of which resembles Le Roy's *Ruines*. The draughtsmen involved included the

brothers Théodore Labrouste and Henri Labrouste, Jean-Baptiste-Antoine Lassus and EUGÈNE-EMMANUEL VIOL-LET-LE-DUC. Encouraged by the rigorous archaeological approaches of the English, French architects entered into a more analytical phase of their Gothic research, focusing first on stylistic categories, the subject of such works as ARCISSE DE CAUMONT's *Cours d'antiquités monumentales* (1830–41) and the periodical *Bulletin monumental* (from 1834). Research later turned to problems in structural systems and iconography as seen in the *Histoire de l'art monumental* (1845) by Louis Batissier (1813–82) and ADOLPHE-NAPOLÉON DIDRON's *Annales archéologiques* (from 1844), which published Lassus's articles on the human module and Viollet-le-Duc's early articles on Gothic construction. Institutions also arose from this interest—the first, the Société des Antiquaires de Norman-die, founded by Caumont, and then the Société des Edifices Religieux, headed by Didron, as well as the Commission des Monuments Historiques. The Commis-sion was founded to stave off future destruction of French architectural patrimony by inexpert or unsympathetic restorers, and to supervise the design and execution of harmonious restoration projects.

Two events were central to the history of the French GOTHIC REVIVAL during this period. Firstly, the fire that consumed Chartres Cathedral in 1836 gave particular impetus to the restoration movement. The architect in charge of restoration of the roof was Duban, and he was assisted by CÉSAR-DENIS DALY, a follower of Charles Fourier (1772–1837) and later the founder of the period's most important architectural journal, the *Revue générale de l'architecture et des travaux publics* (from 1839). The use of cast iron to form the roof structure was central to Duban's reconstruction, and he used it because of its fireproof properties and ease of erection. The second event to affect the course of the Gothic Revival was the construction of one of the most archaeologically accurate of all new Parisian churches, Ste Clotilde (1846–57) by Franz Chris-tian Gau. The responsibility for the ten-year design and construction was shared by two different ministries—Public Works and Interior—and two sub-organs of these, the Conseil des Bâtiments Civils and the Commission des Monuments Historiques, headed by Prosper Mérimée (1803–70) and encouraged by Didron and his journal. Merimée, Didron and the Commission finally won, but they were forced to bear full responsibility for the cloying form of this church.

From this moment on, archaeologically accurate church design was relegated to such works of restoration as Lassus's and Viollet-le-Duc's Notre-Dame (1844–64; *see* PARIS, §V, 1(i)), Paris. After this, there was a merger between Gothic and Romantic classicism—a *Néo-grec gothique*, in which Gothic vocabulary was attached to the muscular structuralism of such works as the Labroustes' Romantic *envois*. Indeed, while Viollet-le-Duc's St Denis-de-l'Estrée (1864–7), St Denis, or St Pierre (1864–70) at Petit-Montrouge by EMILE VAUDREMER alluded to an authentic parish-church type, they did so with a sense of sculptural form and structural gravity. These churches were far removed from the High Gothic of Lassus's Sacré-Coeur (from 1849) at Moulins, St Jean-de-Belleville (1854–9), Paris, or Gau's Ste Clotilde. Nineteenth-century innovations intruded still more aggressively into other churches, which were Gothic in name only, for instance ANATOLE DE BAUDOT's St Lubin (1865–9) at Rambouillet, with its exposed ironwork, or Louis-Auguste Boileau's almost wholly cast-iron St Eugène (1854–5), Paris (*see* BOILEAU, (1)).

(iv) New materials and the religion of progress. Although cast iron had been used in Empire architecture, it took on a distinctly ideological slant as it became a significant aspect in design teaching, first at the Ecole Polytechnique under JEAN-BAPTISTE RONDELET, who re-engineered Soufflot's unstable Ste Geneviève (1757–90; now the Panthéon; *see* PARIS, §V, 9). He was succeeded at the Ecole Polytechnique by LÉONCE REYNAUD, whose later *Traité de l'architecture* (Paris, 1850) interposed architectural with technological progress as spearheaded by Henri de Saint-Simon (1760–1825). Rondelet's rationalism was transferred to the teaching of the Ecole des Beaux-Arts by Blouet, who became the school's Professor of Theory, the first Romantic architect to be sanctioned by that institution.

Cast iron was used in church reconstruction from an early stage, because such use was considered essential to give the new material its ideological potency (*see* IRON AND STEEL, §II, 1). The first step in this progress was provided by Viollet-le-Duc in his reassessment of architecture as a clear distinction between structure and enclosure, as evidenced in his early articles in the *Annales archéologiques.* The next step entailed drawing a comparison between architectural and social structures along the lines described by such social engineers as the Saint-Simonian Reynaud and the Fourierist Daly. In short, structural progress came to be regarded by the utopians as a signifier of intellectual and social progress. This progress—for Saint-Simonians particularly—was conceived as a dialectic between organic and critical periods. Mixed structures in architecture came to signify a critical period for such theorists as Daly: the moment immediately before the advent of social unity and universal well-being.

Cast iron in churches was mostly hidden, particularly as it was used to restore historical form. Religion was regarded by the progressives as part of an earlier, historical and retrograde ideology. To a considerable degree, such organizations as the Commission des Monuments Historiques and the Service des Edifices Diocésains served to support the legitimacy of the Bourbon and Orléans governments by drawing useful visual parallels with a pre-Revolutionary past. It was therefore difficult to explore visible, innovative structural approaches in churches throughout the July Monarchy and Second Republic. It was only after the rise of Napoleon III that many architects were encouraged to explore the interplay of ancient and modern structural systems in church architecture. Despite the continued objections of such theorists as Daly, Viollet-le-Duc's challenge was soon met in such works as St Augustin (from 1862), Paris, by Victor Baltard (*see* BALTARD, (2)) and later, with the use of reinforced concrete construction, at Baudot's St Jean-de-Montmartre (1897–1907), Paris, during the Third Republic.

However, those places where new construction methods predominated were the institutions conceived as secular churches. These buildings were purveyors of a progressive ideology intent on transforming, even usurping, the traditional role played by religious institutions in society. Important examples included Vaudoyer's Conservatoire des Arts et Métiers and Henri Labrouste's Bibliothèque Ste-Geneviève. The Conservatoire was essentially a retrofitting of the 14th-century monastery of St Martin-des-Champs, which was common practice during the Revolutionary period (*see* VAUDOYER, (2), fig. 1). Nowhere is this recasting more apparent than in the monastery's refectory—a long space with twin naves divided by columns—which became a museum of machinery and thus came to sacralize the utilitarian. At the Bibliothèque Ste-Geneviève, Labrouste developed these processes, utilizing this type of religious space, thus transforming the library into a type of secular church (*see* LABROUSTE, (2), fig. 1). He emphasized the role of the library as modern institution, whose relation to contemporary society replicated that of the Church to the past, by using modern techniques, replacing masonry columns with cast iron. The Positivist agenda of this building was stressed on the façades, where the metal structure was identified externally by a range of cast-iron rondels, implicitly attached to the writing on the façades. This writing was a chronological list of the authors whose works were contained therein, and as a chronicle of great men it was intended to be an indicator of human progress, akin to that advanced by Auguste Comte (1798–1857). In its rhetorical use of spatial typology, structure and written text, the library was thereby transformed into the 'church' of Saint-Simonian 'New Christianity' or Comtian 'Religion of Humanity'.

(v) Positivism and Eclecticism. The Bibliothèque Ste-Geneviève did make manifest a new philosophical system—Positivism—which many hoped would create a new social order and usher in the new organic period that such utopians as Labrouste, Daly and Reynaud felt had been heralded by the Revolution of 1848. It conveyed a sense of promise that even Henri Labrouste's great Bibliothèque Nationale (1854–75), also in Paris, was unable to realize. The library's many formal ironies belied the comprehensive order that its written texts might have suggested, however. In architectural fact, this building appeared 'critical' and not 'organic', as authors writing after the collapse of the Second Republic were forced to admit.

From the sad realization that hybrid architecture represents society in flux emerged a fatalistic attitude towards architectural form that came to be termed 'Eclectic' by Daly in the mid-19th century (*see* ECLECTICISM). All major public works following the rise of Napoleon III and the Second Empire (1848–69) could more or less be termed eclectic. For instance, the Harlay façade of Louis Duc's Palais de Justice merely overlaid the Bibliothèque Ste-Geneviève with the idealistic colonnade of Louis-Pierre Baltard's Palais de Justice (begun 1834) in Lyon. At Marseille Cathedral, Vaudoyer combined Romanesque, Byzantine, late Florentine Gothic and Early Renaissance elements (*see* VAUDOYER, (2), fig. 2). Moreover, he did this while superimposing the whole on a vast urban ensemble of port-side warehouses, thereby intimating an unholy alliance between religion and commerce. Perhaps, most importantly, the Opéra (1860–75) by CHARLES

GARNIER in Paris revelled in the articulation of distinct spatial units, each generated by differing functions and systems of construction, while overlaying the whole plan with a classical cross-in-square (see fig. 12). This latter detail marked the project as radically different from the more Romantic project for the Opéra prepared by Viollet-le-Duc. It also marks Eclecticism's usurpation of the throne held by Romanticism until the reforms of 1863 at the Ecole, highlighted by the dismissal of Viollet-le-Duc from the post of Professor of Art and Aesthetics.

Eclecticism strove to conflate classical systems of comprehensive, formal order and Romantic distinctions of spatial parts, differences attributable to programme and varieties of structural system. Eclecticism in design was achieved only at the cost of aesthetic and ideological consistency. Despite the problems, this synthetic approach became the mainstay of academic theory from 1863 onwards, as evidenced in *Eléments et théorie de l'architecture* (Paris, 1901) by JULIEN AZAIS GUADET.

(vi) The city-machine. Despite the fact that positivistically inclined architects tended to think of the Second Empire as a transitional or critical period, former social utopians, many of whom then held significant posts in the government and economy, felt that their moment had arrived. Their belief was based on the fact that they encouraged the Emperor to regard Paris, and France as a whole, as an enormous productive machine. This argument was propelled along the lines of Fourier's psychoanalysis of society, subdivided into functional groupings on the basis of 'passional attraction'. It was also advanced by the architectural metaphors of complete social and political organization given shape by Fourierist Victor Considérant (1808–93), who described his social model in the autocratic terms of Louis XIV's Versailles. Productive capacity was thereby predicated on the bases of class differentiation and stratification. Saint-Simon and Comte described the pinnacle of this pyramidal social organization: productive society should be run by an enlightened élite, a priesthood of scientists.

These orderly schemes provided Napoleon III and his supporters (who included such bankers as LOUIS FOULD and such industrialists as the PÉREIRE brothers) with a new model for society, in which productive labour ought to be guided by those prescient few who know its end. This model was reflected within the gilded frame of Second Empire Paris (*see* PARIS, §II, 5(iii); *see also* SECOND EMPIRE STYLE). From 1853 Napoleon III set out his plans to make Paris the capital of the world. On the one hand, he completed the most important imperial project envisioned by Percier and Fontaine, as Louis-Tullius-Joachim Visconti, Hector-Martin Lefuel and Duban connected the Louvre to the Tuileries (1852–7) in the most flamboyant reinterpretation of mansarded Henri II style imaginable. On the other hand, Napoleon III and his planners—the most important being GEORGES EUGÈNE HAUSSMANN (see fig. 13)—sought to execute in Paris what Percier and Fontaine had termed the 'Grande Croisée'. This crossing was formed by the Rue de Rivoli and the Boulevard Sébastopol, and it crisscrossed the city, inscribing into it a typological form. Its endpoints coincided with four large city parks (Vincennes, Buttes-Chaumont, Montsouris,

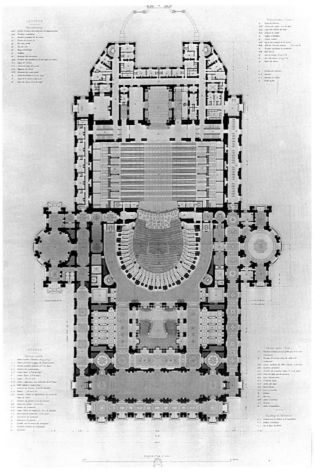

12. Charles Garnier: plan of the first floor of the Paris Opéra (1860–75); engraving from *Le Nouvel Opéra de Paris* (Paris, 1878)

Bois de Boulogne) the design and construction of which was overseen by ADOLPHE ALPHAND.

Napoleon III drew little from Restoration practice in architectural design. He did, however, appropriate many urban themes from work undertaken in Paris under Louis-Philippe, not the least of which was the ruler's admiration for the enlightened urban reforms of Napoleon (*see* ORLÉANS, House of, (5)). It was Louis-Philippe who completed the Rue de Rivoli (*see* PARIS, fig. 7) and who finally completed Napoleon's Arc de Triomphe de l'Etoile (Gilbert added a storey to Chalgrin's design, 1837; *see* PARIS, fig. 8), the Madeleine (formerly the Temple de la Grande Armée) and the Bastille Monument (Alavoine's Elephant was replaced, however, with Duc's Colonne de Juillet, 1831–40). It is significant that Louis-Philippe had set the stage for Second Empire city planning by considering new urban spaces as unified wholes; his grand urbanistic sense produced such projects as the gardens lining the Champs Elysées to the Place de l'Etoile, designed by Hittorff, which were bounded by architecture whose vaguely Renaissance forms recall Durand as well as Percier and Fontaine, and the Place de l'Opéra (1858–64) by Charles Rohault de Fleury (*see* ROHAULT DE FLEURY, (2)).

13. Georges Eugène Haussmann: Plan of Paris; from Adolphe Alphand: *Promenades de Paris*, ed. J. Rothschild (Paris, 1868) (Paris, Musée Carnavalet)

Louis-Philippe's schemes were also important for later urban planners, as he began a large-scale scheme of railway construction to link Paris with all parts of the country, producing possibly the period's most significant new architectural type—the railway station. The earliest of the great Parisian stations, the Gare du Nord (1846), with its broad, clear-span, cast-iron train shed, was built by Reynaud as the headquarters of the Chemin de Fer du Nord, developed by the Péreire brothers. The station as rebuilt by Hittorff (1861–4; *see* PARIS, fig. 9), now expressed the qualities of vaulted, interior space on the exterior—as did the Gare de l'Est (1847–52; *see* RAILWAY STATION, fig. 1) by François Duquesney (1790–1849)—while overlaying a colonnaded urban decoration that cast this building as urban monument.

The fire of Louis-Philippe's and Napoleon III's new productive machine, however, was stoked by the era's institutions of consumption. In this regard, the minimal structural expressions of the shopping arcade—for example, the Restoration Passage Choiseul (1825; between the Rue des Petits-Champs and the Rue St Augustin) by Tavernier, and the Louis-Philippe Galleries Jouffroy (1845; Boulevard Montmartre) by François-Hippolyte Destailleur (1787–1852), assisted by Romain de Bourge—became important to the capitalist life of France during the Second Empire. The Empire and Third Republic capitalized on the cast-iron framing of the arcade, translating it into the metal-framed department stores (e.g. the Bon Marché, Paris, 1867–76; for illustration *see* DEPARTMENT STORE) by Boileau and GUSTAVE EIFFEL and Frantz Jourdain's Art Nouveau La Samaritaine (1905–10), Paris. These buildings celebrated the new social ritual of shopping, taking it from the street into grand public foyers.

The celebration of consumption and concomitant production was perhaps shown best in Baltard's Halles Centrales de Paris (1854; for illustration *see* BALTARD, (2)) and by the Paris Expositions Universelles, from 1855 (*see* PARIS, §II, 6). These cast-iron, glass and, later, steel forms invariably signified the role of architecture as the middleman of capitalism, making Paris the market-place of the world. Perhaps the ultimate dignification of this kind of architecture occurred at the Exposition Universelle of 1889, where the Eiffel Tower (1887–9; for illustration *see* EIFFEL, GUSTAVE) on the Champ-de-Mars signalled entry into the Galerie des Machines (1888–9) by CHARLES-LOUIS-FERDINAND DUTERT, which was both factory and display pavilion, a great glass-and-steel cathedral complete with rose window, devoted to the cult of commerce (*see* IRON AND STEEL, fig. 4). The sublimation of the machine was completed, however, by the Exposition Universelle of 1900, not just with the outspokenly eclectic Grand and Petit Palais (1895–1900; for illustration of the Grand Palais *see* PARIS, fig. 10) by HENRI-ADOLPHE-AUGUSTE DEGLANE, CHARLES-LOUIS GIRAULT and others, but also with the Gare d'Orsay (1898–1900; now Musée d'Orsay), which was designed by VICTOR LALOUX to signify entry into the fair for those coming by rail from abroad.

BIBLIOGRAPHY

L. Hautecoeur: *Architecture classique* (1943–57)

H.-R. Hitchcock: *Architecture: Nineteenth and Twentieth Centuries*, Pelican Hist. A. (Harmondsworth, 1958, rev. 4/1977)

P. Lavedan: *Histoire de l'urbanisme à Paris: Nouvelle histoire de Paris* (Paris, 1975)

A. Drexler, ed.: *The Architecture of the Ecole des Beaux-arts* (Cambridge, MA, 1977)

D. Egbert: *The Beaux-arts Tradition in French Architecture, Illustrated by the Grands Prix de Rome* (Princeton, NJ, 1980)

R. Middleton and D. Watkin: *Neoclassical and Nineteenth-century Architecture* (New York, 1980)
Viollet-le-Duc (exh. cat., ed. B. Foucart; Paris, Grand Pal., 1980)
R. Middleton, ed.: *The Beaux-arts and Nineteenth-century French Architecture* (Cambridge, MA, 1982)
R. Becherer: *Science Plus Sentiment: César Daly's Formula for Modern Architecture* (Ann Arbor, MI, 1984)
D. Van Zanten: *Designing Paris: The Architecture of Duban, Labrouste, Duc and Vaudoyer* (Cambridge, MA, 1987)
J.-M. Pérouse de Monclos: *Histoire de l'architecture française* (Paris, 1989)
B. Schroeder-Gudehus: *Les Fastes du progrès: Le Guide des Expositions universelles, 1851–1992* (Paris, 1992)

RICHARD BECHERER

5. AFTER *c.* 1914. At the start of World War I, French architecture was facing some major issues: the search for new ideas on urban planning; progressive developments in the field of both concrete structures and steel frames; changes in terms of ornamentation and architectural forms. These were raised by such principal figures as Tony Garnier, the brothers Auguste Perret and Gustave Perret, Héctor Guimard and Anatole de Baudot. New conditions for development had occurred in the early years of the century: Cubism in the visual arts, psychology in the intellectual sphere, post-industrialism in social structure and thus in the creation of cities. The government had passed the first law concerning the protection of monuments in 1913, and the proposals of 1905 by EUGÈNE ALFRED HÉNARD for Paris were realized in Habitations à Bon Marché in 1919, called the 'Pink Belt' because the buildings were in brick. In the course of the 20th century Paris was to undergo major changes in terms of architecture (*see* PARIS, §II, 6).

(i) Purism, Cubism and the Modern Movement. (ii) Developments in Modernism and the great exhibitions. (iii) Post-war reconstruction. (iv) Post-modernism and the *Grands Projets*.

(i) Purism, Cubism and the Modern Movement. A link between the 19th and 20th centuries was provided by the ornamental style of ARTNOUVEAU, as seen in the entrances to the Paris Métro (for illustration *see* METRO STATION) designed by HÉCTOR GUIMARD, who was inspired by the theories of Viollet-le-Duc. His influence was countered by a reaction against ornament, seen in the writings of Adolf Loos. For the Salon d'Automne of 1912, Raymond Duchamp-Villon had designed the Maison Cubiste, decorated by André Mare, Jacques Villon, Marie Laurencin and Roger de la Fresnaye, which caused a scandal similar to that created by Marcel Duchamp's first ready-made. The influential ideas of Loos, Theo van Doesburg and Filippo Tommaso Marinetti were introduced to France in the Purist review *L'Esprit nouveau* (1920–25), created by LE CORBUSIER together with the painter Amédée Ozenfant and the poet Paul Dermée. Auguste Perret drew up designs for *ville-tours* (skyscrapers) in 1922, then in the following year for the basilica of Notre-Dame, Le Raincy, near Paris, in reinforced concrete (*see* PERRET, fig. 1). The engineer Eugène Freyssinet exploited innovations by FRANÇOIS HENNEBIQUE in reinforced concrete, designing long-span bridges and the large, reinforced-concrete dirigible hangars (1921) at Orly Airport, near Paris (for illustration *see* FREYSSINET, EUGÈNE). Watching these discoveries and inspired by Garnier, Le Corbusier conceived the 'Dom-Ino' houses (1914–15), which separated structural concrete columns and interiors, and in 1918, with Ozenfant, he published *Après le cubisme*, in which he assumed the role of introducing Modernism to France. Le Corbusier also investigated urban planning, both on a large scale with his controversial plan for a city of 3 million inhabitants (exh. Salon d'Automne, Paris, 1922), and on the scale of individual units, with his ideal standardized 'Maison Citrohan', a model raised on pilotis (slender piers) evoking the form of an artist's studio. In 1923 his book *Vers une*

14. Robert Mallet-Stevens: Villa Noailles, Hyères, 1923–6

architecture perfectly synthesized the ideal of De Stijl, the Bauhaus, Futurism, Russian Constructivism and the ideas of Garnier and Auguste Perret. Nautical images came from Viollet-le-Duc, Jules Verne or Victor Considerant (1809–93), whereas the concept of 'the house as a machine for living' pre-existed in the theories of Walter Gropius, Frank Lloyd Wright and Antonio Sant'Elia (*see also* MODERN MOVEMENT).

In 1917 Garnier had published the *Cité industrielle* (for illustration *see* GARNIER, TONY), and in 1919 Marcel Poète (1866–1950) created in Paris the first course in urban planning. These were followed in 1928 by the 'Loi Loucheur', which instigated the construction of 260,000 apartments in five years, generating major low-cost housing. The exhibition of 1916 in Paris of *La Cité reconstituée* had excited new interest in regional architecture and it was followed in devastated areas by the construction of such garden cities as Longueau, Reins, Lille, Tergnier and Stains Drancy, which highlighted new thoughts on healthy living, the main theme of the inter-war years. With the evolutionary dwellings in Pessac (1925–8), near Bordeaux, Le Corbusier materialized Garnier's concepts of housing associated with nature. In 1924 HENRI SAUVAGE was the first to create in Paris a residential unit with collective services. Adolf Loos, who lived in Paris from 1923 to 1928 and completed Tristan Tzara's house (1925–6; *see* LOOS, ADOLF, fig. 2), exerted a great influence on French architecture in terms of both theory and design, at the same time that André Breton was publishing *Le Surréalisme et la peinture* (1928).

CHARLES PLUMET, chief architect for the Exposition Internationale des Arts Décoratifs et Industriels Modernes, Paris (1925), celebrated the return of peace by bringing reconciliation between the modernists and the traditionalists. De Stijl and the Bauhaus were, however, voluntarily excluded. The Perret brothers participated with an area theatre (destr.), Garnier with the pavilions for Lyon and Saint-Etienne and Sauvage with the Pavillon du Printemps. Austria was represented by Josef Hoffmann, and Russia by Konstantin Mel'nikov. Cubist design in France was initiated by ROBERT MALLET-STEVENS with the Villa Noailles (1923–6) at Hyères (see fig. 14). He received two commissions for the exhibition, including the Pavillon du Tourisme. Le Corbusier's Pavillon de l'Esprit Nouveau displayed the Plan Voisin for Paris (*see* LE CORBUSIER, fig. 8), which incorporated urban concepts into the sphere of modern architecture.

(ii) Developments in Modernism and the great exhibitions. Opposing Le Corbusier's ideas, the American FREDERICK KIESLER designed the avant-garde Cité de l'Espace, which influenced urban-planning research until the 1960s. Considered a pioneer of Modernism, Henry Van de Velde nevertheless prefaced the catalogue of the exhibition of 1925 by praising those innovations that were rooted in the eternal laws of form. In the exhibition, ART DECO, often thought of as industrial art, appeared to be based on geometrical craft decoration, originating from the austere Functionalism defined by Gropius and represented in France by Le Corbusier and the partnership of EUGÈNE BEAUDOUIN and MARCEL LODS.

The ruptures in architecture were particularly exemplified by Frantz Jourdain (*see* JOURDAIN, (1)), who associated both cultural references to create innovative solutions, as in his highly decorated steel structure for the remodelling (1926–9) of his Art Nouveau La Samaritaine (1905–10) department store in Paris. Many architects tried to refrain from the use of such new materials as concrete, glass and steel. Traditional architects pursued personal standards, including JULES LAVIROTTE with his sculptural ceramic façades, and PIERRE LAPRADE, who, as well as designing buildings for the exhibition of 1925, published major sketchbooks after World War II, thus participating in a return to a taste for historicizing monuments. Other active architects included MICHEL ROUX-SPITZ, who adapted most of the modern concepts to major residential projects. The stands against the Modern Movement were often strong; in 1927 Le Corbusier was awarded equal first prize (with Richard Neutra and Hannes Meyer) in the competition for the League of Nations building, Geneva, against the views of Aristide Briand, who hated modern architecture; however the commission was given elsewhere, and this in part stimulated the foundation (1928) of CIAM (Congrès Internationaux d'Architecture Moderne), in which Le Corbusier played a dominant role.

Modern concepts (e.g. pilotis, strip windows, open plans) were further clarified by Le Corbusier with his projects for the Villa Savoye, (1929–31; *see* VILLA, fig. 10) Poissy, the Salvation Army Cité de Refuge (Paris; 1929–33), with its large, glass façade and air-conditioning, and the Pavillon Suisse (Paris; 1930–33). In 1931 Gropius was invited to Paris by the Salon des Artistes Décorateurs to represent the Deutscher Werkbund. In 1930 André Lurçat built the Ecole Karl Marx in Villejuif, Paris, giving an open-air image to the complex (*see* LURÇAT, (2)). In 1931 the Maison de Verre by PIERRE CHAREAU crystallized innovative modern interiors using steel and wood details (*see* GLASS, fig. 7). In 1936 Beaudouin and Lods, Jean Prouvé (*see* PROUVÉ, (2)) and VLADIMIR BODIANSKY designed the Maison du Peuple (completed 1939) at Clichy, using panels and steel components. In 1934 the UNION DES ARTISTES MODERNES (U.A.M.) published its manifesto, written by Louis Cheronnet, introducing the notion of 'Art social'. Members of the U.A.M. included Le Corbusier, Lurçat, Mallet-Stevens, CHARLOTTE PERRIAND, Chareau, GEORGES-HENRI PINGUSSON and Prouvé.

The great exhibitions, for example the Exposition Internationale des Arts et Techniques dans la Vie Moderne, Paris (1937), were occasions for such exceptional works as the extremely clear plan by JACQUES GRÉBER and also for the participation (typical of the pre-war period) of such architects as Albert Speer for Germany, Josep Lluís Sert for Spain, Alvar Aalto for Finland, Junzō Sakakura for Japan and Van de Velde for Belgium (for further discussion *see* EXHIBITION ARCHITECTURE).

(iii) Post-war reconstruction. After visiting New York (1935–6), and due to the distress of war, Le Corbusier concentrated on theoretical writings between 1937 and 1945. He published a number of works that, along with Gaston Bardet's *Problèmes d'urbanisme* (1941), became major

contributions to post-war reconstruction. The year 1945 opened with the Piet Mondrian retrospective at the Musée d'Art Moderne in Paris, which advanced a new abstraction. After World War II architectural thinkers turned to the broader problems of the reconstruction of their devastated country, moving from formalist concerns to more social preoccupations. With the war over, the pressing need for rebuilding stimulated a number of government commissions that progressively opened up a new method of planning schemes by multi-disciplinary teams comprised of urban developers, sociologists, engineers and architects. An important example was the multi-disciplinary group ATBAT set up by Le Corbusier and Bodiansky. Due to the exceptional demand for new construction, this post-war period placed France in the position of a real innovator in industrialized building.

The Perret brothers were assigned the reconstruction of LE HAVRE, for which Auguste first proposed a city on a horizontal slab, separating cars from pedestrians. Paris, however, remained the centre of thinking and the strength of both administration and the Académie. Lurçat, Pingusson, Beaudouin and Lods carried through the aesthetic of the International Style and introduced major architectural features into the design of large-scale projects. After obtaining the commission for 25 industrial houses in 1949, Prouvé led the development of prefabricated systems and integrated his pioneering technical views into several prototypical architectural directions, most notably housing at Meudon (1952) and the Pavillon d'Aluminium at the Centenary Exhibition of 1954 in Lille. Consulted in 1945 for the reconstruction of Saint-Dié and La Rochelle-La Pallice, Le Corbusier completed his first prototype of a Unité d'Habitation in 1952 at Marseille, with a pedestrian street at mid-height (for illustration *see* BRUTALISM). Several *unités* of similar design followed, all criticized by his peers. He also gave a new impulse to his work through a very sculptural use of concrete and, at a time when he was being called a Brutalist, by introducing shuttering that leaves motifs in low relief in the finished concrete; these developments can be seen in the chapel of Notre-Dame-du-Haut (1950–55) at Ronchamp (*see* LE CORBUSIER, fig. 6) and the monastery of Ste Marie de La Tourette (1953–9), Eveux-sur-l'Arbresle, on which André Wogenscky (*b* 1916) and Iannis Xenakis (*b* 1922) also participated. As Le Corbusier became extremely active towards the end of his life on commissions outside France, Brutalism was taken up principally by CLAUDE PARENT.

In 1956, dissent at the tenth meeting of CIAM resulted in the creation of TEAM TEN by Georges Candilis and Shadrach Woods (*see* CANDILIS-JOSIC-WOODS), Alison and Peter SMITHSON and ALDO VAN EYCK, among others, who sought more individual and humanistic principles of urban development and were critical of the rigid zoning and functionalism promoted by CIAM. In 1958 BERNARD ZEHRFUSS, MARCEL BREUER and PIER LUIGI NERVI together completed the Y-shaped UNESCO headquarters (from 1952) in Paris. During this period, a new generation of architects became active who were good builders but little concerned with grand principles. These included Xavier Arsène-Henri (*b* 1919), Louis Dubuisson (*b* 1914) and Luc Arsène-Henri (*b* 1923) and Maurice Novarina (*b* 1907), who developed and taught a new modernist

academic theory at the Ecole des Beaux-Arts, Paris. The growth of Paris was becoming hard to control, and the pre-war proposals of urban planner HENRI PROST were not put into practice. The idea thus came in 1955, influenced by English new towns, to build a second city—Parent's 'Paris-Parallèle'—to accommodate 3 million people. This opened up new capacities for extension and a new field for architectural experimentation. The planning teams involved major thinkers, but the result shows little coherence in terms of urban form and urban theory, except as an area containing individually innovative buildings. In the 1960s La Défense, the French version of an American high-rise commercial centre, was developed, providing Paris with a business district as an overspill; construction there continued during the 1980s and 1990s, with notable buildings including the Grande Arche (from 1983; see fig. 15) by Otto von Spreckelsen (1929–87).

Confident of the benefits of technology, YONA FRIEDMAN and PAUL MAYMONT, later joined by Xenakis and inspired by LOUIS I. KAHN, proposed an urban development and architecture based on space structures, as in the project for a 'Cosmic City' (Xenakis) of 1964. Chéréac designed juxtaposable living cells and Jean-Claude Bernard (*b* 1940) a 'Total City'. In 1965 the GEAM (Groupe d'Etude d'Architecture Mobile; est. 1957), founded by, among others, Friedman and Maymont, brought together new researchers who promoted new materials and movable designs, integrating cybernetics with the creation of new principles for the city. These architects, influenced by R. Buckminster Fuller and Kriesler, adopted the principles of geometry and organic growth. These movable structures

15. Otto von Spreckelsen: Grande Arche, La Défense, Paris, from 1983

could be erected quickly and without any real difficulties on the technical side, but they remained inconsequential on a socio-psychological level.

ANDRÉ MALRAUX, Minister of State for Cultural Affairs, gave an international impetus to French architecture by inviting to France such great foreign architects as Breuer. Above all, however, Malraux positioned himself as an ardent defender of ancient buildings and arranged numerous listings of monuments. In the old urban centres he set up a protection area of 500 metres around historic monuments, which served to fix the old centres of French cities while leaving room for innovation in the outskirts. Simultaneously, holiday architecture (e.g. resorts) really took off with the work of Jean Balladur and FRANÇOIS SPOERRY, who distinguished themselves in formalist projects; Spoerry was in his way a precursor of POST-MODERNISM.

(iv) Post-modernism and the Grands Projets. Post-modernist elements first appeared in French art around 1968; the movement led to a revolution in the spirit and structure of French society. This brought about the scuttling of the Ecole des Beaux-Arts and the dismantling of traditional studio teaching as it had existed for over a century. In the 1970s architecture found itself without any constructive philosophy, and it was the influence of such technological visionary schemes as Archigram that led to the construction of the Centre Georges Pompidou (1971–7; *see* PARIS, fig. 14) in Paris by RENZO PIANO and RICHARD ROGERS, an architecture of open planes said to be without any constraint. These liberating ideas were expressed in the opposite sense by the American Post-modernist movement, which included such formalist references to Neo-classicism as those expressed in housing schemes by Ricardo Bofill, for example the Arcades du Lac (1972–5) at the new town of Saint-Quentin-en-Yvelines and Les Espaces d'Abraxas (1978–83), Marne-la-Vallée (for illustration *see* BOFILL, RICARDO).

The return to acquired values, to the influence of memory, came also from Italy through the more intellectual TENDENZA movement, represented by ALDO ROSSI. This Neo-realism, with more modest ambitions regarding form, claimed to be more profound, with Antoine Grumbach and Bernard Huet as its sources of enlightenment. Architecture therefore distanced itself from great revolutionary ideas and at best aimed to satisfy the individual within his own community, which JEAN RENAUDIE, for example, attempted to achieve in his projects for star-shaped flats (1974–80) at Givors. The State, however, returned to display its power through impressive buildings initiated under the presidency of François Mitterrand: the *Grands Projets,* all executed in Paris. These included the Institut du Monde Arabe (1981–7) by JEAN NOUVEL; the remodelling (1982) of the Gare d'Orsay into the Musée d'Orsay by Pierre Colboc (*b* 1940) and Gae Aulenti; Spreckelsen's Grande Arche; the pyramidal extension (1985–9) to the Musée du Louvre (*see* PYRAMID, fig. 4) by I. M. PEI; the Cité des Sciences et de l'Industrie (1986) by Adrian Fainsilber and the surrounding Parc de la Villette (1983–6) by BERNARD TSCHUMI; the Opéra de la Bastille (1987) by Carlos Ott; the Ministry of Finance (1988; for illustration *see* CHEMETOV, PAUL); the Cité de la Musique

(1989) by Christian de Portzamparc; and the Bibliothèque Nationale (1991) by Perrault.

These public projects stimulated a strong development of architecture, and a new law established that all large schemes should be the subject of competitions, which in turn changed the nature of commissions. In the late 20th century French architecture was preoccupied with environmental issues, but by the 1990s had still not proposed any theory for the cities, where nostalgic movements tended to form, in order either to defend historical architectural landmarks and the status of the street in its most traditional form or to try to overrule urban planning in the interest of business. The modern city and the organization of its territory resulted from technocratic plans to link large cities, with each city hoping through its new rulers, the politicians, to build its own technopolis to attract business. A wide-open eclecticism resulted in which regional, sensitive, brutalist and international styles were apparently juxtaposed, while architecture retained its pivotal symbolic role in French national culture.

BIBLIOGRAPHY

Macmillan Enc. Architects
N. Pevsner: *An Outline of European Architecture* (Harmondsworth, 1942/*R* 1981)
P. Lavedan: *L'Architecture française* (Paris, 1944)
W. Pehnt, ed.: *Encyclopedia of Modern Architecture* (London, 1963)
J. M. Richards: *L'Architecture moderne* (Paris, 1968)
D. Amouroux, M. Crettol and J. P. Monnet: *Guide d'architecture contemporaine en France* (Paris, 1972)
R. Banham: *Theory and Design in the First Machine Age* (London, 1972)
A. Kopp, F. Boucher and D. Pauly: *L'Architecture de la reconstruction en France, 1945–1953* (Paris, 1982)
R. Jullian: *Histoire de l'architecture moderne en France: De 1889 à nos jours* (Paris, 1984)
K. Frampton: *Modern Architecture: A Critical History* (London, 1985)
Dictionnaire encyclopédique de l'architecture moderne et contemporaine (Paris, 1987)
J. Lucan: *France: Architecture, 1965–1988* (Paris and Milan, 1989)
W. Lesnikowski: *The New French Architecture* (New York, 1990)
G. Monnier, ed.: *Histoire critique de l'architecture moderne en France, 1918–1950* (Paris, 1990)
M. Ragon, ed.: *Histoire de l'architecture et de l'urbanisme modernes,* ii–iii (Paris, 1991)
C. Downey: 'Après les Grands Projets', *Archit. Rec.,* clxxxii/3 (1994), p. 13

MARC DILET

III. Painting and graphic arts.

The earliest paintings in France date from Paleolithic times, when early man recorded impressions of the animal and spiritual world in caves, in the area described as Franco-Cantabrian. Wall paintings with similar characteristics have been found at sites on the north coast of Spain (e.g. Altamira) and in south-western France, particularly in the Dordogne at LASCAUX (*c.* 15,000 BC). For further discussion of art of the prehistoric period *see* PREHISTORIC EUROPE. In the first millennium BC the Celtic peoples who occupied France ranged from Bohemia to Spain and the British Isles. The Celts are known primarily for intricate geometric ornament on metalwork but they also used paint, to decorate pottery and sanctuaries, such as those at ROQUEPERTUSE and Entremont on the Rhône estuary (*see also* CELTIC ART). With the Greek colonization of the southern coast of France (Massalia (now Marseille), *c.* 600 BC) and the Roman conquest of Gaul (1st century BC), the Celts and, later, the peoples from outside the boundaries of the Roman Empire were brought into contact with the vast cultural and artistic heritage of the Mediterranean. For further discussion of the art of this era, *see* MIGRATION PERIOD. The subsequent blending of the love of surface decoration, geometric ornament and stylized animal forms characteristic of these migrating peoples with the Greco-Roman tradition of depicting the human figure in space was a key factor in the art of northern Europe in the Middle Ages.

BIBLIOGRAPHY
B. Dorival: *La peinture française*, 2 vols (Paris, 1942)

1. Before *c.* 1450. 2. *c.* 1450–*c.* 1620. 3. *c.* 1620–*c.* 1715. 4. *c.* 1715–*c.* 1814. 5. *c.* 1814–*c.* 1914. 6. After *c.* 1914.

1. BEFORE *c.* 1450.

(i) Merovingian and Carolingian. (ii) Romanesque. (iii) Gothic.

(i) Merovingian and Carolingian. In the 5th and 6th centuries AD the Franks established dominion over a large area west of the Rhine. The Merovingian king Clovis I (*reg* 466–511) was baptized at Reims *c.* 503, and through his example the Frankish nation adopted the Christian faith. The Church then created its own geography in northern Europe. As monastic scriptoria became increasingly involved with the production and decoration of books, connections between monasteries, even though separated by great distances, help to explain the wide-ranging sources of ornament found in book illustration. An Irish monk, St Columban (*c.* 540–615), founded numerous abbeys on the Continent, such as Luxeuil in Burgundy, Corbie near Amiens and Bobbio in northern Italy. Illuminated manuscripts produced by these monasteries in the 8th century incorporate motifs derived from Insular illumination, Merovingian metalwork and Lombard ornament, and, less easily explained, Near Eastern textiles. The colourful designs of crosses, arches, birds, beasts and fish, executed primarily in orange/red, green, yellow and brown, that decorate pages of the Gelasian Sacramentary (Rome, Vatican, Bib. Apostolica, MS. Reg. lat. 316) are exuberant, lively and charmingly undisciplined.

At the end of the 9th century, under the leadership of Charlemagne (*reg* 768–814), the Frankish nation became an empire comprising Germany, France and north Italy. Charlemagne enthusiastically supported all the arts (*see* CAROLINGIAN ART). Wall painting and mosaic enriched church interiors and private chapels throughout the empire, although only fragments remain in France, such as the mosaics at GERMIGNY-DES-PRÈS and wall paintings in the crypt of St Germain, Auxerre (*see* AUXERRE, §2). The manuscripts were produced with a new seriousness of purpose, and their ornamentation become a high art. Important scriptoria were located at AACHEN, Charlemagne's capital; then, after his death in 814, when the empire was partitioned among his heirs, other centres developed throughout the Frankish provinces. During the time of EBBO, Archbishop of Reims (816–45), an important Psalter (816–34; Utrecht, Bib. Rijksuniv., MS. 32; *see* UTRECHT PSALTER) and a Gospel Book (Epernay, Bib. Mun., MS. 1; for illustration *see* AUTHOR PORTRAIT) were produced at the monastery of Hautvillers for the Archbishop. Under Emperor CHARLES THE BALD (*reg* 840–77),

the scriptorium at St Martin, Tours, undertook the production of large bibles (*see* TOURS, §2(i)), examples of which survive at Bamberg (Staatsbib., MS. Misc. class. Bibl. I), London (BL, Add. MS. 10546) and Paris (Bib. N., MS. lat. 1). The figure style of the Reims books is exuberant and sketchy, while that of Tours is more sober and restrained, but the artistic aims of both scriptoria perpetuated those set forth at Aachen, particularly in the close attention given to Late Antique models from Christian Rome. At Corbie, however, where connections with Ireland were long-standing, the artist of a 9th-century Psalter (Amiens, Bib. Mun., MS. 18) combined Insular ornament unexpectedly with Iranian motifs to create lively initials of human figures, beasts and geometric designs.

(ii) Romanesque. In the 10th century, centres of imperial power shifted to the Ottonians in the east. In the west Hugh Capet (*reg* 987–96), who ruled over an area west of the Rhône, Saône and Meuse rivers, gave his name to a dynasty of kings who, from the 12th century, resolutely consolidated political power around the royal domain. During the 11th century and the early 12th the arts flourished under the patronage of wealthy abbeys in Burgundy, Provence, Languedoc, Saintonge, Poitou and Normandy. Special interests, both local and distant, encouraged the development of regional styles, and regionalism is more significant in a discussion of the art of this period than statements characterizing it as French. In the south-west, manuscripts produced at Limoges and Moissac, and wall paintings at St Sernin, Toulouse, are best understood in the context of the pilgrimage routes to

16. Saint-Savin-sur-Gartempe, abbey church, nave with ceiling paintings, *c.* 1100

Santiago de Compostela in north-west Spain. A Sacramentary (Paris, Bib. N., MS. lat. 9438) from Limoges Cathedral contains illustrations that combine a brittle figure style influenced by the metalwork for which Limoges was famous with strident colours reminiscent of Spanish Apocalypses. In Burgundy, a region dominated by Cluny Abbey (*see* CLUNIAC ORDER, §III), the wall paintings at the abbot's retreat (*see* BERZÉ-LA-VILLE, PRIORY CHAPEL) show affinities with such Cluniac manuscripts as the Lectionary preserved in Paris (Bib. N., MS. nouv. acq. lat. 2246). The choice of colours in the paintings, particularly dark blue, and details in the treatment of the figures, are perhaps best explained by reference to the Italo-Byzantine art of Montecassino Abbey, which Abbot Hugh of Cluny (*reg* 1049–1109) visited in 1083.

In western France, especially Poitou and Touraine, regions that passed from French to English hands in the 12th century, a much lighter palette of earth colours is characteristic of many wall paintings, at Montoire, Le Liget, Tavant and SAINT-SAVIN-SUR-GARTEMPE, a church in which every available surface was painted with images or ornament (see fig. 16). Here the iconography of the nave frescoes (*c.* 1100) seems to depend on Anglo-Saxon

17. Pol, Herman and Jean de Limbourg: *Adoration of the Magi*; miniature from the Très Riches Heures, 290×210 mm, *c.* 1411/13–16 (Chantilly, Musée Condé, MS. 65, fol. 52*r*)

sources. Close connections with English scriptoria are evident in manuscripts produced in north-west France, such as a Gospel Book made at Liessies (Avesnes-sur-Helpe, Mus. Soc. Archéol.) during the time of Abbot Wedric (*reg* 1124–47). English influence even reached Burgundy. The illustrations in Gregory I's *Moralia in Job* (Dijon, Bib. Mun., MS. 129), a manuscript produced during the abbacy of the English monk Stephen Harding (*reg* 1109–33) at Cîteaux Abbey, reflect the English taste for coloured outline drawing.

(iii) Gothic. Under the leadership of Philip II Augustus (*reg* 1180–1223) and Louis IX (*reg* 1226–70), England's territories in western France were greatly diminished. Paris became the capital of strong centralized government. The development of a new style of architecture (now known as Gothic) in the Ile-de-France in the mid-12th century transformed all the arts. At SAINT-DENIS ABBEY, then at Sens, Laon, Paris, Soissons, Chartres, Bourges, Reims, Amiens and other urban centres in northern France, churches and cathedrals were rebuilt, attracting scores of artisans in wood, stone and glass. Large areas of painted glass created dazzling effects in translucent colour. The stylistic evolution of figures and ornament in stained glass parallels that of manuscript illumination, while the increasingly complex armatures in windows inspired more intricate framing devices in book decoration. The most exquisite example of the use of stained glass is perhaps the Sainte-Chapelle (1243–8), built by Louis IX to house precious relics (*see* PARIS, §V, 2(iii) and STAINED GLASS, colour pl. I).

Wealthy nobility, prosperous merchants, talented artisans and impoverished students were all attracted to Paris, where the cathedral school, famous for its scholars, developed into a university. Teachers and students needed books, and in the course of the 13th century secular scribes and artists set up shops on the Left Bank of the Seine to meet the demand. They also received commissions from wealthy patrons, and eventually these shops overshadowed monastic book production. French royalty became ardent patrons of the book arts. Manuscripts produced for Blanche of Castile, the mother of Louis IX, such as her Psalter (Paris, Bib. Arsenal, MS. fr. 1186) and the fragment of a Bible moralisée (New York, Pierpont Morgan Lib., MS. 240; *see* GOTHIC, fig. 72), show Parisian illuminators working with predominantly blue and red tonalities, and slender but rather awkward figures that derive from the earlier Transitional style found in manuscripts from England, Germany and northern France, such as the Psalter made for Ingeborg, wife of Philip II Augustus (Chantilly, Mus. Condé, MS. 1695; *see* TRANSITIONAL STYLE, fig. 2).

In the second half of the 13th century Parisian illuminators developed a distinctive style, best seen in a Lectionary commissioned for the Sainte-Chapelle (Paris, Bib. N., MS. lat. 8892). This exhibits a high level of craftsmanship, delicate, exquisitely controlled ornament and slender, swaying, almost mannered figures clothed in broad-fold drapery. A Psalter containing 78 full-page miniatures illustrating Old Testament subjects, which belonged to Louis IX himself (Paris, Bib. N., MS. lat. 10525), is the centrepiece of the style. The tonality is still predominantly blue and red, but the preciousness of the figures and the elaborate architectural backdrop against which they are placed is distinctive.

Stylistic advances were made at the end of the 13th century and in the first quarter of the 14th. Master Honoré possibly illustrated a Breviary (by 1296; Paris, Bib. N., MS. lat. 1023, fol. *v*; for illustration *see* HONORÉ, MASTER) for Philip IV, modelled drapery with white highlights adding dimension to the figures. Attributed to Jean Pucelle is the small Book of Hours, a miniature masterpiece (1325–8; New York, Cloisters, MS. 54.1.2; *see* GOTHIC, fig. 80) made for Jeanne d'Evreux (*d* 1371), wife of Charles IV. It contains sacred scenes and secular amusements modelled in light and shade in grisaille, while some of the figures are set in a tentative three-dimensional space, suggesting an awareness of the work of Duccio.

Paris remained a major centre of manuscript production throughout the 14th century, but in its last quarter two of the greatest of the royal bibliophiles, Charles V (*see* VALOIS, (2)) and his brother, Jean, Duc de Berry (*see* VALOIS, (3)), also employed accomplished painters from the southern Netherlands and Burgundy. Following the Italians, northern artists had become increasingly interested in creating the illusion of three dimensions—modelling drapery was not enough; architectural settings constructed with geometric perspective and landscapes with atmospheric perspective captured their attention. These interests, coupled with the patrons' taste for opulence, produced a brilliant period in French painting. Rich effects of colour and light, in costume and setting, are perhaps nowhere more accomplished than in Jean, Duc de Berry's TRÈS RICHES HEURES (*c.* 1411/13–16; Chantilly, Mus. Condé, MS. 65; *see* fig. 17). Here Pol, Herman and Jean DE LIMBOURG imbued even the scenes of Christ's life with royal luxury, surrounding the Virgin with ladies in fashionable dress, while Magi in gorgeous robes kneel before her, attended by a cavalcade of richly dressed servants and exotic beasts. By 1450 illusionism overwhelmed the small format of the book and the ancient tradition of surface embellishment, but by then the printing press had revolutionized the book industry (*see* PRINTING).

Church inventories reveal that paintings on wood—devotional pictures, altarpieces, ceilings and church furniture—were once abundant, but there are few surviving examples before the late 14th century. The patronage of Philip the Bold, Duke of Burgundy (*see* BURGUNDY, (1)), rivalled that of his brother, Charles V. Philip employed numerous panel painters, such as MELCHIOR BROEDERLAM, JEAN DE BEAUMETZ and JEAN MALOUEL, uncle of the Limbourg brothers. A large tondo of the *Pietà* (*c.* 1400–04; Paris, Louvre), attributed to Malouel and Henri Bellechose, exhibits on a larger scale the delicacy and refinement of the Limbourg brothers. During the 14th century, portrait painting, of which the image possibly representing *John II* (?before 1356; Paris, Louvre; *see* GOTHIC, fig. 66) is one of the earliest, heralded a new subject for painting and later sculpture. Although the reproductive arts, woodcuts and engraving, were developed in Germany and the Netherlands, the earliest-known woodblock, a fragment of a *Crucifixion* and *Annunciation*, is thought to have been produced in Burgundy at the end of the 14th century.

See also ROMANESQUE, §IV and GOTHIC, §IV.

BIBLIOGRAPHY

A. Hind: *An Introduction to a History of Woodcut, with a Detailed Survey of Work Done in the Fifteenth Century*, 2 vols (London, 1935/R New York, 1963)

J. Evans: *Art in Medieval France, 987–1498* (London, 1948)

G. Ring: *A Century of French Painting, 1400–1500* (London, 1949)

Abbé H. Breuil: *Four Hundred Centuries of Cave Art* (Montignac, 1952)

A. Leroi-Gourhan: *Treasures of Prehistoric Art* (New York, 1967)

M. Meiss: *French Painting in the Time of Jean de Berry*, 5 vols (New York and London, 1967–74)

J. Hubert, J. Porcher and W. F. Volbach: *Europe of the Invasions* (New York, 1969)

O. Demus: *Romanesque Mural Painting* (New York, 1970)

J. Hubert, J. Porcher and W. F. Volbach: *The Carolingian Renaissance* (New York, 1970)

C. R. Dodwell: *Painting in Europe, 800 to 1200*, Pelican Hist. A. (Harmondsworth, 1971)

R. Branner: *Manuscript Painting in Paris during the Reign of Saint Louis* (Berkeley, 1977)

B. Cunliffe: *The Celtic World* (New York, 1979)

The Last Flowering: French Painting in Manuscripts, 1420–1530, from American Collections (exh. cat. by J. Plummer and G. Clark, New York, Pierpont Morgan Lib., 1982)

M. Laclotte and D. Thiébaut: *L'Ecole d'Avignon* (Paris, 1983)

L. Grodecki and C. Brisac: *Gothic Stained Glass, 1200–1300* (London and Ithaca, 1985)

□

2. *c.* **1450–***c.* **1620.** After the period of stagnation from *c.* 1420 to *c.* 1440 following military defeat by the English at the Battle of Agincourt (1415), French painting experienced a rebirth from the middle of the century. New centres of art developed: Bourges and Tours, which had become royal capitals; Angers; from 1471, Aix-en-Provence, led by René I, Duke of Anjou (*reg* 1434–80); and at the end of the century Moulins, led by the dukes of Bourbon. Moreover, a new clientele was established in the clergy and particularly among such high-ranking officials of the monarchy as JACQUES COEUR, ETIENNE CHEVALIER and the JOUVENEL DES URSINS family. Most of the important painters who worked in France in the second half of the 15th century were either from northern Europe or were influenced by northern art. However, they were capable of translating the fundamental innovations of Netherlandish painting into the French style that was predominant at the time, characterized by simplicity, elegance, moderation and monumental proportions. This applies to illumination, as seen in the work of the MASTER OF KING RENÉ OF ANJOU (*see* MASTERS, ANONYMOUS, AND MONOGRAMMISTS, §I; possibly BARTHÉLEMY D'EYCK), who produced two of the most prestigious manuscripts of the 15th century: the *Livre du Cueur d'amour espris* (Vienna, Österreich. Nbib., Cod. 2597; for illustration *see* ANJOU, §II(4)) and the *Traité de la forme et devis d'un tournois* (or *Livre des tournois*; Paris, Bib. N., MS.fr. 2695). These characteristics are also present in the panel paintings of such artists as the MASTER OF THE AIX ANNUNCIATION (*see* MASTERS, ANONYMOUS, AND MONOGRAMMISTS, §I); Enguerrand Quarton (e.g. *Coronation of the Virgin by the Holy Trinity*, 1453–4; Villeneuve-lès-Avignon, Mus. Mun.; *see* QUARTON, ENGUERRAND, fig. 1); Nicolas Froment (e.g. triptych of the *Burning Bush*, completed 1476; Aix-en-Provence, St Sauveur Cathedral; for illustration *see* FROMENT, NICOLAS); and the MASTER OF MOULINS (Jean Hey; *see* MASTERS, ANONYMOUS, AND MONOGRAMMISTS, figs 1 and 2).

The Netherlandish example was not the only one that was followed. JEAN FOUQUET from Touraine, the most important painter of the period and one of the most outstanding French painters, visited Italy and was the only northern European painter to have fully understood the Florentine art of this period. It is surprising that in his miniatures he was able to achieve, in a personal manner, a sense of monumental authority, an epic spaciousness of narrative and a light range of colour more appropriate to the art of fresco painting, as seen in the Hours of Etienne Chevalier (begun *c.* 1452; Chantilly, Mus. Condé), the *Grandes chroniques de France* (*c.* 1460; Paris, Bib. N., MS. fr. 6465) and *Antiquités judaïques* (*c.* 1470; Paris, Bib. N., MS. fr. 247). Jean Bourdichon, also from Touraine, employed his knowledge of Milanese painting and of Perugino's work in a context directly stemming from the Gothic tradition (*see* BOURDICHON, JEAN, figs 1 and 2).

At the beginning of the 16th century French painting again experienced a lack of imagination and a decline in quality: 'After 1500, however, there are few signs of real activity in painting proper' (Blunt, p. 44). In this context Francis I (*reg* 1515–47) must be appreciated. From the beginning of his reign he endeavoured to collect works by the greatest Italian painters and to bring artists from Italy (*see* VALOIS, (14)). In 1516 or 1517, Leonardo da Vinci settled in Touraine, but his activity there—no doubt somewhat diminished due to age—is not widely known. Andrea del Sarto also visited Touraine but stayed only one year (1518–19). In the early 1530s the King succeeded in luring to France the Florentine ROSSO FIORENTINO, an admirer of Michelangelo and of the Mannerist art produced during the papacy of Clement VII (*reg* 1523–34), and the Bolognese FRANCESCO PRIMATICCIO, rival of Giulio Romano and of Parmigianino. These artists established contemporary Italian art as the official art of the French Court, especially at the château of Fontainebleau (*see* FONTAINEBLEAU, §1). There, Rosso, Primaticcio and the cabinetmaker Francisco Scibec de Carpi created lavish interiors that combined mural paintings, stucco framing, panelling and carved-wood ceilings. In the bedchamber of the Duchesse d'Etampes (see fig. 43 below) and the Salle du Bal, for example, Primaticcio's paintings were surrounded with stucco frames and figures, sometimes attributed to JEAN GOUJON. The interiors at Fontainebleau immediately acquired fame throughout Europe and gave rise to imitations. An engraving and etching studio was also set up at the château, from where Antonio Fantuzzi, Domenico del Barbiere, Jean Mignon, Pierre Milan, René Boyvin and Léon Davent spread the style of the FONTAINEBLEAU SCHOOL. The charm and strength of the school may largely be attributed to the differing personalities of Rosso and Primaticcio and to the contrast of Rosso's strange, harsh and tormented style with Primaticcio's lithe elegance. Following Rosso's death in 1540, Primaticcio, who had become a kind of Surintendant des Arts at the French court, continued work on the large-scale decoration at Fontainebleau. From 1552 he was assisted by NICOLÒ DELL'ABATE from Modena.

Although Italian artists predominated, northern European art continued to influence French painting. Around 1520 ANTWERP MANNERISM was introduced by the Master of Amiens, a south Netherlandish or northern French

painter who executed three large panels (1518, 1519 and 1520; all Amiens, Mus. Picardie) for the Puy de Notre Dame guild in Amiens, and the Netherlandish Godefroy le Batave, who illuminated the manuscript *Commentaries on the Gallic War* (1520; Chantilly, Mus. Condé, MS. 1139) for Francis I. The portrait painter Jean Clouet, who was probably born in the southern Netherlands and who settled in France *c.* 1516, also worked on this manuscript. It was he who most fully developed the method of drawing in black, red and sometimes white chalks, a technique originally used in preliminary studies for paintings, but which soon developed into a separate art form (*see* CLOUET, (1)). Although a Netherlandish element is perceptible in his rare paintings, his drawings (*crayons*) are reminiscent of such Italian Renaissance artists as Leonardo. His son François Clouet (*see* CLOUET, (2)) continued the technique, and in his Mannerist paintings he varied the ways in which the model was represented. At the same time, CORNEILLE DE LYON, a painter of north Netherlandish origin, worked more closely in the style of Jean Clouet, producing small, half-length portraits set against a plain background (see fig. 18).

Between 1540 and 1560 various centres were active independently of Fontainebleau and the Court. That in Paris centred around Jean Cousin le père and Charles Dorigny, and in Avignon around Simon de Mailly, while a school in Burgundy flourished under the patronage of the DINTEVILLE family. Important technical innovations in

18. Corneille de Lyon: *?Louise de Rieux, Dame d'Ancenis*, oil on panel, 170×130 mm, first half of the 16th century (Paris, Musée du Louvre)

stained-glass making allowed the art form to renew completely its forms and colours (ruby-red, grisaille and silver-stain; *see* STAINED GLASS, §I) and to utilize compositions by artists of the Fontainebleau school. This was also a productive time for book illustration, as seen in the engraved works of Bernard Salomon. JEAN DUVET, a little-known engraver, produced the *Apocalypse* (completed 1555), a visionary work that later inspired William Blake. Due in part to destruction caused by the Wars of Religion (1562–98), French painting in the last quarter of the century once again experienced a decline in quality. Antoine Caron, the official painter of the time, was a capable artist but produced works of low calibre. Jean Cousin le fils was principally a draughtsman and did not become well known. Only the art of drawing portraits in coloured chalks maintained its level of quality, with Etienne Dumonstier II and Pierre Dumonstier the elder.

Henry IV (*reg* 1589–1610) renewed the initiative of Francis I but engaged the services of Netherlandish artists rather than Italian ones (*see* BOURBON, §I(5)). Frans Pourbus the younger introduced the tradition of Netherlandish portrait painting to France. Ambroise Dubois from Antwerp, whose Mannerist art was based on a combination of Netherlandish elements and Italian styles, received commissions to decorate the château of Fontainebleau and the Palais du Louvre, Paris. Toussaint Dubreuil, greatly influenced by the works of Primaticcio, worked at Fontainebleau, the Louvre and the château of Saint-Germain-en-Laye (see fig. 19). Martin Fréminet, rival of the Cavaliere d'Arpino, trained in Rome, Venice and Turin. Unlike the first school of Fontainebleau, however, this second school did not command the same authority over the artistic evolution of the rest of the country. It was only in Nancy during the first two decades of the 17th century that a remarkable renewal of artistic activity took place. Foremost among those artists working in the city was Jacques Bellange, whose prints represent one of the pinnacles of late Mannerism.

19. Toussaint Dubreuil: *Toilet of Hyante and Climène* ('*Lady at her Toilet*'), oil on canvas, 1.07×0.97 m, *c.* 1600 (Paris, Musée du Louvre, on deposit at Fontainebleau, Musée National du Château de Fontainebleau)

BIBLIOGRAPHY
P. Gelis-Didot: *La Peinture décorative en France du XIe au XVIe siècle* (Paris, n.d.)
P. Rosenberg: *French Painting, 1500–1825; Les Primitifs français* (Paris, 1904)
A. Lerdy: *Evolution de la peinture française des origines à nos jours* (Paris, 1946)
G. Ring: *La Peinture française du XVe siècle* (London and Paris, 1949)
A. Blunt: *Art and Architecture in France, 1500–1700*, Pelican Hist. A. (Harmondsworth, 1953, 4/1980/R 1988)
O. Benesch: *The Art of the Renaissance in Northern Europe* (London, 1965)
C. D. Cuttler: *Northern Painting from Puccelle to Bruegel* (New York, 1968)
M. Meiss: *French Painting in the Time of Jean de Berry: The Limbourgs and their Contemporaries* (New York, 1974)
N. Reynaud: *Jean Fouquet*, Les Dossiers du département des peintures, 22 (Paris, 1981)
J. Snyder: *Northern Renaissance Art* (New York, 1985)

ANNE-MARIE LECOQ

3. *c.* 1620–*c.* 1715. During the reigns of Louis XIII (1610–43) and Louis XIV (1643–1715), France became the most powerful nation in Europe and established a cultural hegemony that lasted over a century. There were regencies at the start of both reigns but, thanks to a succession of able ministers—notably Richelieu (1624–42), Mazarin (1643–61) and Colbert (1661–83)—the monarchy became increasingly wealthy and secure. The growing strength of the Crown helped to create a national tradition in painting. At the start of this period the royal family commissioned important works from foreign artists, doing little to encourage the development of native French painting or graphic art; but by the time of Louis XIV's death (1715), relatively few foreign artists were working for the Court, and the Académie Royale de Peinture et de Sculpture was regulating and promoting the practice of the arts. French art in the 17th century was dominated by two developments. One was the institutionalization of painting in the service of the Crown. (For further discussion of the State in relation to art in 17th-century France *see* §XIII, 3 below; *see also* BOURBON, §I(9), 2; MAISON DU ROI, §II; and PARIS, §VI, 2.) The other development was the competition between rival schools (Flemish and Italian in origin) for the monopoly of the artistic authority that centralization had produced. The Flemish influence was mediated by Flemish artists working in France; the Italian influence by French artists studying, and sometimes also working, in Rome (*see* ROME, §III, 5).

(i) Mannerism and the influence of Caravaggio. (ii) Influence of Venice and Rome. (iii) Royal patronage and the Académie Royale.

(i) Mannerism and the influence of Caravaggio. During the early 1620s Frans Pourbus (ii) executed portraits for the Court; Rubens worked on the great cycle of the *Life of Marie de' Medici* (Paris, Louvre; *see* HISTORY PAINTING, fig. 2); and Philippe de Champaigne arrived in Paris. Also during this period young French artists, such as Claude Vignon, Simon Vouet, Nicolas Tournier and Valentin de

Boulogne, were working in Rome under the spell of Caravaggio and his followers (*see* BOULOGNE, VALENTIN DE, fig. 1). French artists and patrons had to look abroad simply because the indigenous tradition was weak. The Wars of Religion (1562–98) had interrupted patronage and isolated French artists from developments elsewhere in Europe. The prevailing style was a late form of Mannerism, which was strongest, not in France, but in the independent Duchy of Lorraine. There, its most notable exponents included the printmaker JACQUES CALLOT, who brought a taste for grotesque subjects and a technique of extraordinary refinement to such depictions of contemporary life as the *Miseries and Misfortunes of War* (*Les Misères et les malheurs de la guerre*); and Claude Deruet, who painted his masterpieces the *Four Elements* (*c.* 1640; Orléans, Mus. B.-A.) for Cardinal Richelieu; as well as Didier Barra and François de Nomé.

The absence of an established native tradition did not mean that the Caravaggesque style became dominant when its practitioners returned to France. It was rarely well received at Court, and the French artists who worked in Paris soon abandoned it: Vouet for a Baroque classicism, and Vignon for a version of Mannerism. It was in the provinces that the Caravaggesque style survived, in the work of NICOLAS TOURNIER in Toulouse, GUY FRANÇOIS in Le Puy, JEAN LECLERC in Lorraine, and TROPHIME BIGOT in Provence. The most original of the artists influenced by the Caravaggesque movement, GEORGES DE LA TOUR, may never have gone to Rome. He probably learnt from the example of Leclerc and the Dutch followers of Caravaggio, but in the small town of Lunéville in Lorraine, he was cut off from most of his contemporaries and gave to his subjects (e.g. *Job and his Wife*, *c.* 1635–50; Epinal, Mus. Dépt. Vosges & Mus. Int. Imagerie) a monumental stillness that was absent from his more theatrical models.

La Tour was by no means unrecognized in his lifetime, but his reputation died with him; the Court at Lorraine lost its significance after the French invasion of 1633, and during the ministry of Richelieu, Paris became the centre of artistic activity. The painter who profited most from the growth of royal and ecclesiastical patronage was Vouet, who not only produced numerous altarpieces, such as the *Presentation in the Temple* (1641; Paris, Louvre; see fig. 20), which Richelieu commissioned for the Jesuit Novitiate, but also executed several ambitious decorative schemes. To keep up with demand, he maintained a studio of assistants, many of whom made the journey to Rome and became accomplished painters in their own right (e.g. Pierre Mignard, François Perrier and Charles Le Brun). Few of them retained much trace of Vouet's style, but EUSTACHE LE SUEUR, who never went to Rome, was slow to shake off his master's influence, and it was not until the cycle of the *Life of St Bruno* (1645–8; Paris, Louvre), painted for the Carthusian monastery in Paris, that he moved decisively towards a delicate classicism inspired by Poussin and Raphael.

Vouet's chief rival in Paris was Philippe de Champaigne, a prolific painter of portraits and religious subjects. His early work betrayed Rubens's influence, but his compositions became increasingly severe; in later life, when he was

20. Simon Vouet: *Presentation in the Temple*, oil on canvas, 3.93×2.50 m, 1641 (Paris, Musée du Louvre)

associated with the Jansenists of Port-Royal (*see* JANSENISM), a connection celebrated in his famous *Ex-voto; Mother Catherine-Agnès Arnauld and Sister Catherine of Sainte-Suzanne Champaigne* (1662; Paris, Louvre; *see* CHAMPAIGNE, (1), fig. 4), his palette also became subdued. In the 1630s Champaigne executed several memorable portraits of *Richelieu* (e.g. London, N.G.), but it was his portraits of the intellectual bourgeoisie—the *noblesse de robe*—that were perhaps his most distinctive contribution to the art of the period, remaining influential for painters of the succeeding generation.

During the middle years of the century the upper levels of the bourgeoisie accounted for a significant proportion of the market for art (*see* §XII below), both in paintings and in prints. Painters sometimes doubled as etchers (e.g. CLAUDE LORRAIN) or engravers (e.g. LAURENT DE LA HYRE), but prints were usually the work of specialists, who might become successful artists in their own right. CLAUDE MELLAN, who while in Rome engraved after Vouet, made his name as an engraver of original portraits, as did the influential ROBERT NANTEUIL; he also engraved some of Champaigne's portraits and eventually became portrait engraver to the Court of Louis XIV. Printmakers produced not only portraits, however, but also genre scenes; some prints, such as the series *Mariage à la ville* and *Mariage à*

21. Louise Moillon: *Fruit and Vegetable Seller* (or *Mistress and Servant*), oil on canvas, 1.20×1.65 m, 1630 (Paris, Musée du Louvre)

la campagne by Abraham Bosse (the author of an early treatise on engraving), provide useful documentation of contemporary bourgeois life (see fig. 44 below).

The success of the three LE NAIN brothers, who all became founder-members of the Académie Royale in 1648, even though their work did not appear in any major collection, indicates that in painting, too, there was a significant demand for scenes of contemporary life. The Le Nains depicted rural but not necessarily peasant subjects; however, their market was in Paris, where they had moved from Laon in the late 1620s. Still-life painting also flourished in the capital. Louise Moillon (see fig. 21), Lubin Baugin and Jacques Linard appear to have worked in Paris for most of their careers; the flower painter JEAN-BAPTISTE MONNOYER remained there until *c.* 1690. Of the other outstanding painters of the 'lesser' genres, only SÉBASTIEN STOSKOPFF in Strasbourg had a regional base.

(ii) Influence of Venice and Rome. Although it sometimes inclined towards a naive realism, French genre painting of this period clearly owes much to Flemish and Dutch sources; the influence was, however, sometimes indirect, for some northern genre specialists worked in Rome, where Pieter van Laer (il Bamboccio) had created a vogue for low-life scenes. One of the Le Nain brothers may have visited Rome, and the battle painter Jacques Courtois

spent much of his career there. SÉBASTIEN BOURDON likewise imitated the Bamboccianti while in Rome in the mid-1630s, although for him this style was merely one of several that he could reproduce with fluency. On his way back to France he stopped in Venice, where he, like Jacques Blanchard before him, acquired a taste for 16th-century Venetian art, which he never wholly lost, even when he turned to portraiture. Although Venetian art was not the dominant influence in the work of any major French painter during this period, its importance should not be underestimated, for both Rubens and the young Poussin were captivated by Venetian colour; despite the Académie's official disapproval, it was the shared heritage of their otherwise irreconcilable followers in the second half of the century. Poussin had stopped in Venice on his way to Rome in 1624 and was also an admirer of Titian's *Bacchanals* (London, N.G., and Madrid, Prado), an enthusiasm clearly reflected in his paintings of the 1620s. When Poussin came to paint his own set of *Bacchanals*, the *Triumph of Pan* (London, N.G.; *see* POUSSIN, NICOLAS, fig. 2) and the *Triumph of Bacchus* (Kansas City, MO, Nelson–Atkins Mus. A.), commissioned by Richelieu in 1636 for his private collection, it was only the colour and the landscape that recalled his Venetian models; the arrangement of the figures revealed how much he had learnt, both from Raphael and the Bolognese artists of the late 16th-century school, and also from his study of the Antique.

In 1640 Poussin travelled to Paris to work on the decoration of the Grande Galerie of the Louvre. After two unfulfilling years he returned to Rome, but his brief stay was enough to establish his reputation as the leading painter of the day, and he continued to work for French patrons. He acquired some imitators, among them Le Sueur, Bourdon, Jacques Stella, Francisque Millet and Laurent de La Hyre, but came to be remembered as an exemplar of academic principles. Poussin's own artistic education had been haphazard, and he was not an outstanding draughtsman; yet his work might be seen to embody the aesthetic and moral values of classicism, for his handling of paint was exceptionally restrained; his compositions were carefully contrived to create a sense of balance (*see* PERSPECTIVE, colour pl. VII, fig. 2), which, as in the two sets of paintings of the *Seven Sacraments* (first series, Belvoir Castle, Leics, and Washington, DC, N.G.A.; second series, Duke of Sutherland priv. col., on loan to Edinburgh, N.G.), is sometimes so complete as to appear unnatural.

Although in some ways an isolated figure, Poussin shared his interest in landscape with other northern European artists working in Rome (*see* ITALY, §III, 5). His son-in-law, GASPARD DUGHET, with whom he worked closely in the 1630s, became one of the most successful landscape specialists in Rome; CLAUDE LORRAIN, who had accompanied Poussin on sketching expeditions in the countryside, became the acknowledged master of the ideal landscape (*see also* LANDSCAPE PAINTING, §II). Claude was a superb draughtsman who drew expertly from nature, but his highly finished compositional drawings and paintings are almost all of imaginary landscapes, in which genre elements, such as pastoral scenes or depictions of seaports, are combined with vague evocations of antiquity. Pictures such as the *View of Delphi* (Rome, Gal. Doria-Pamphili) and the *Seaport with the Embarkation of St Ursula* (1641; London, N.G.; *see* CLAUDE LORRAIN, fig. 3) were highly prized by wealthy patrons, but only about half of them were French; and Claude's work had little immediate impact on French painters, except for Pierre Patel (i) and La Hyre, who both mastered the decorative aspects of Claude's style without being able to reproduce his mysterious glowing light.

(iii) Royal patronage and the Académie Royale. Claude and Poussin spent almost their entire working lives in Rome, but of the next generation of French artists, few remained in Italy beyond their apprenticeship. The reasons for this included the decline of Rome as a centre for contemporary art, the dramatic growth in royal patronage during Louis XIV's reign and the establishment of the Académie Royale de Peinture et de Sculpture (*see* PARIS, §VI, 1). It was initially set up for the benefit of artists who wished to assert their independence from the guilds but later came under the control of Jean-Baptiste Colbert (*see* COLBERT, (1)), who changed its constitution in 1663, to make the Académie an agency of the State under the supervision of the Crown. The intention was not only to further the development of the arts for their own sake but also to promote pride in French artistic achievement and give to

artists a practical and theoretical training that would equip them to work on royal commissions.

From then on the Académie played a decisive role in artistic affairs; admission to its membership became the goal of artistic education. The Académie supervised important aspects of professional training, while the Académie de France in Rome (founded in 1666; *see* PARIS, §VI, 1) performed a similar function for the selected students sent to Italy; it was thus possible to require adherence to a single set of artistic standards. Until Colbert's death in 1683 the Académie was dominated by CHARLES LE BRUN, who ensured that it upheld the superior dignity of history painting, the primacy of drawing over colour and the superiority of Raphael and Poussin (the 'French Raphael') to the painters of Venice and Flanders. Le Brun was not unopposed, however, and in the Quarrel of Colour and Design (1671–2; *see* DISEGNO E COLORE), he had to put down the rebellion of a minority led by Gabriel Blanchard, which argued that colour was more important than line in the successful imitation of nature.

An accomplished draughtsman himself, Le Brun restrained his early taste for the Baroque after studying with Poussin in Rome and produced works of controlled elegance, such as the famous portrait of *Chancellor Séguier* (1661; Paris, Louvre; see fig. 22). When he was working on a large scale, however, as in the Galerie des Glaces (1678–84) at the King's new palace at Versailles, it was Rubens's example that he found most helpful. Le Brun was not the only painter to return to Rubens. The vast increase in the number and scale of decorative projects in the last quarter of the century put considerable strain on a theory in which perfection was epitomized by the work of Poussin, an artist who almost exclusively painted small canvases; many painters sought inspiration either from Rubens's *Medici* cycle or from the ceilings of the Italian Baroque. Indeed, from the time of the Quarrel of Colour and Design, artists divided into two camps: the advocates of POUSSINISME, who maintained the Academic orthodoxy, and those of RUBÉNISME, who argued in favour of colour and Venetian art.

Le Brun may not have been a pure Poussiniste; but the leader of the rival faction, Pierre Mignard (*see* MIGNARD, (2)), was hardly Rubéniste at all. He had the support of the Marquis de Louvois, Colbert's successor as Surintendant des Bâtiments, and in 1690 himself succeeded Le Brun both as Premier Peintre du Roi and as director of the Académie. He had spent over 20 years in Rome, where his models were Poussin and Giovanni Lanfranco, whose work he later imitated in the decoration of the cupola of the church of the Val-de-Grâce, Paris (completed 1666). The arguments that eventually led to the acceptance of the already pervasive influence of Rubens were provided by a theorist, ROGER DE PILES; he adopted ideas expressed in CHARLES DU FRESNOY's treatise *De arte graphica* (which he had translated in 1668) in his own *Dialogue sur le coloris* (1673) and *Dissertation sur les ouvrages des plus fameux peintres* (1681).

The triumph of the Rubénistes did not mean that painters drew their inspiration from a single artist. Rubénisme, unlike Poussinisme, allowed a fairly eclectic approach to tradition; the work of CHARLES DE LA FOSSE, a friend of de Piles who became director of the Académie

22. Charles Le Brun: *Chancellor Séguier*, oil on canvas, 2.95×3.57 m, 1661 (Paris, Musée du Louvre)

in 1699, exemplifies the range of sources being used by painters. For ceilings, such as the Dôme des Invalides in Paris (1702–5), La Fosse's model was Correggio, but for history painting he often turned to Venice (where he had spent three years in the 1660s), and for religious subjects, to Rubens. In contrast, JEAN JOUVENET, who also worked c. 1700 at Les Invalides, owed relatively little to Rubens and much to Le Brun, Poussin and the Carracci family. Even Antoine Coypel (*see* COYPEL, (2)), another friend of de Piles, gradually abandoned Rubens in favour of Italian models, especially the later Bolognese artists (who also influenced Bon Boullogne).

Artists working in the early years of the 18th century were united not so much by adherence to a particular theory as by a shared tendency to enhance the decorative aspects of any commission. In the case of the depiction of the *Ecstasy of St Teresa* by JEAN-BAPTISTE SANTERRE in the chapel of Versailles (1710; *in situ*), this involved neglecting the subject's religious significance in order to explore its erotic implications; in the work of Antoine Watteau (*see* WATTEAU, (1)) it meant eschewing overtly didactic themes in favour of the oblique morality of the theatre, a subject previously explored by Callot and by

Watteau's teacher Claude Gillot. Watteau had probably studied Rubens more closely than any of his contemporaries, yet there is little of Rubens's grandiloquence and energy in his paintings (and still less in his drawings); they suggest rather the refinement and whimsicality that were to become the commonplaces of the ROCOCO (*see* §III, 4 below).

The drift towards a Rococo sensibility did not extend to portraiture. Although Mignard painted a number of allegorical portraits, both the hierarchy of the genres and the increase in decorative projects had distanced history painting from portraiture, and it is revealing that one portrait painter, François Desportes, enjoyed greater success as a painter of animals (for illustration *see* DESPORTES, (1)). The leading portrait specialists of the new century were such artists as Nicolas de Largillierre and Hyacinthe Rigaud, who had not studied in Rome and who probably owed more to van Dyck than to any other artist. Largillierre, who trained in Antwerp and as assistant to Peter Lely in London, never lost a certain Baroque expansiveness, however; meanwhile Rigaud, who turned down the Académie's Prix de Rome in order to continue his career in Paris, derived from Champaigne's example a leaven of restraint. It was perhaps this that equipped him to capture in his portrait of *Louis XIV* (1701; Paris, Louvre; *see* RIGAUD, HYACINTHE, fig. 2) the peculiar mixture of extravagance and reserve that the King imposed on the Court in his later years, when he was under the influence of the devout Mme de Maintenon.

BIBLIOGRAPHY

Les Peintres de la réalité en France au XVIIe siècle (exh. cat., Paris, Orangerie, 1934)

R.-A. Weigert and M. Préaud, eds: *Inventaire du fonds français: Graveurs du XVIIe siècle*, Paris, Bib. N., Dept Est. cat., 9 vols (Paris, 1939–89)

A. Blunt: *Art and Architecture in France, 1500–1700*, Pelican Hist. A. (Harmondsworth, 1953, rev. 4/1980/*R* 1988)

R. Crozet: *La Vie artistique en France au XVIIe siècle* (Paris, 1954)

The Age of Louis XIV (exh. cat., London, RA, 1958)

B. Teyssèdre: *Roger de Piles et les débats sur le coloris au siècle de Louis XIV* (Paris, 1965)

I caravaggeschi francesi (exh. cat., Rome, Villa Medici, 1973)

M. Faré: *Le Grand Siècle de la nature morte en France* (Fribourg, 1974)

La Peinture en Provence au XVIIe siècle (exh. cat., Marseille, Mus. B.-A., 1978)

J. Bousquet: *Recherches sur le séjour des peintres français à Rome au XVIIe siècle* (Montpellier, 1980)

Claude Gellée et les peintres lorrains en Italie au XVIIe siècle/Claude Gellée e i pittori lorenesi in Italia nel XVII secolo (exh. cat., ed. J. Thuillier; Rome, Villa Medici, 1982)

La Peinture française du XVIIe siècle dans les collections américaines (exh. cat. by P. Rosenberg, Paris, Grand Pal.; New York, Met.; Chicago, IL, A. Inst.; 1982)

C. Wright: *The French Painters of the Seventeenth Century* (Boston, 1985)

M. Grivel: *Le Commerce de l'estampe à Paris au XVIIe siècle* (Geneva, 1986)

From Fontainebleau to the Louvre: French Drawing from the 17th Century (exh. cat. by H. T. Goldfarb, Cleveland, OH, Mus. A., 1989)

N. Heinich: *Du peintre à l'artiste: Artisans et académiciens à l'âge classique* (Paris, 1993)

Dessins français du XVIIe siècle dans les collections publiques françaises (exh. cat. by L. Piqueras, Paris, Louvre, 1993)

Grand Siècle: Peinture française du XVIIe siècle dans les collections publiques françaises (exh. cat. by M. Hilaire and P. Ramade, Montreal; Rennes; Montpelier; 1993)

A. Mérot: *La peinture française au XVIIe siècle* (Paris, 1994)

A. Schnapper: *Curieux du grand siècle: Collections et collectionneurs dans la France du XVIIe siècle* (Paris, 1994)

MALCOLM BULL

4. *c.* 1715–*c.* 1814. Although history painting was the primary art form during this period, portraiture, genre, still-life, landscape and religious art all flourished. The reign of Louis XV (1715–74) is often said to have produced a light, frivolous and superficial art that was created primarily to delight the eyes: the ROCOCO. Lack of finances frequently thwarted the State's grandiose plans to promote history painting. Under Louis XVI (*reg* 1774–93) more State funds were directed towards history painting to present an image of enlightened absolutism. This, coupled with the didactic aims of art as advocated by ENLIGHTENMENT critics, created a moral and serious art form: NEO-CLASSICISM. Neo-classicism was embraced as the official visual language of the Revolution, but the disappearance of royal and aristocratic patronage caused financial hardship for many artists. Napoleon saw the visual arts as an extension of statecraft and fully exploited their propaganda value. The violent upheavals of the Revolution and the Empire also changed the emotional register of art and led to the subjective tendencies of ROMANTICISM.

(i) Rise of the Rococo. (ii) Resurgence of history painting. (iii) Art of the Revolution and its aftermath.

(i) Rise of the Rococo. By the first decade of the 18th century the polemics of the previous century's debate on the primacy of line over colour (*see* §3(iii) above) were viewed as historical curiosities. The Académie Royale de Peinture et de Sculpture continued to be at the centre of French artistic life (*see* PARIS, §VI, 1), and history painters held a privileged position as practitioners of the most elevated category of painting. The sense of continuity also prevailed in the survival of many of Louis XIV's masters into the first decades of the century. In 1715 Antoine Coypel (*see* COYPEL, (2)) was named Premier Peintre to the new king, and he continued to produce rather stilted Baroque works based on the examples of Rubens, Domenichino and Correggio, for example *Aeneas Appearing before Dido* (*c.* 1715; Arras, Mus. B.-A.). In the space of six years the old guard of history painters disappeared, however, with the deaths of Charles de La Fosse in 1716, Jean Jouvenet and Bon Boullogne in 1717 and Coypel in 1722. History painting was in something of a crisis, and in 1727, as an encouragement, a competition was announced by the Duc d'Antin, Surintendant des Bâtiments du Roi. The winners were FRANÇOIS LEMOYNE with the *Continence of Scipio* and Jean-François de Troy (*see* TROY, (2)) with *Diana Resting* (both Nancy, Mus. B.-A.). None of the entrants, however, turned to the *grand siècle* exemplars of Poussin and Le Brun, being content to produce light and pleasing pictures. Lemoyne later undertook a major secular ceiling decoration for Louis XV, the *Apotheosis of Hercules* (1733–6) in the Salon d'Hercule at the château of Versailles, probably the best French example of an illusionistic ceiling painting. A great number of town houses (hôtels) were constructed in Paris in the first half of the century (*see* §II, 3 above) and these were decorated both with history paintings by such painters as Lemoyne and Charles-Joseph Natoire, and with ornamental arabesques and fantasies by Claude Gillot and Claude Audran III (for illustration *see* AUDRAN, (3)). Many works were designed to fit into wall panelling as part of an overall decorative ensemble. Natoire's series of the *Story of Psyche* (1737–9) in the Salon de la Princesse of the Hôtel de Soubise (now Archives Nationales), Paris, is a notable surviving example (for illustration *see* NATOIRE, CHARLES JOSEPH). The emergence of the Rococo style of decoration and the widespread use of carved panelling and mirrors devalued the traditional role of painting and threatened the status and position of history painting.

The lesser genres of painting advanced appreciably in the first half of the century, and Antoine Watteau occupied a special role in this process. An independent spirit, he was received into the Académie Royale in 1717 as a 'Painter of Fêtes Galantes' on the strength of his *Pilgrimage to the Isle of Cythera* (1717; Paris, Louvre; *see* WATTEAU, (1), fig. 3). His admission demonstrated both that the Académie Royale was flexible enough to recognize his talent (though not as a conventional history painter) and that it could not precisely define his art within the pictorial categories of the time. The study of nature lay at the root of Watteau's art, and to this he added a sense of fantasy, mystery and theatre. Although seemingly artificial, Watteau's work reveals a deep study of the human condition,

23. Jean-Baptiste Oudry: *White Dog with Dead Bustard*, oil on canvas, 1.45×1.18 m, 1724 (Stockholm, Nationalmuseum)

and he explored the complexities of life, death, love and the destiny of Man. The success of the new genre of the fête galante (for discussion *see* FÊTE CHAMPÊTRE) quickly attracted less gifted imitators, among them NICOLAS LANCRET and JEAN-BAPTISTE PATER. Watteau also contributed significantly to the draughtsmanship of the period, his favoured medium being *trois crayons*, black, white and red chalk on tinted paper, which gave a very painterly effect (*see* WATTEAU, (1), fig. 4 and DRAWING, colour pl. I, fig. 2). His work reached a wide audience due to the initiative of his friend JEAN DE JULLIENNE, whose *Recueil Jullienne* of 271 engravings after Watteau's work was published in 1734, with an additional 16 prints published from 1735 to 1739. The *Recueil* was a unique enterprise, being at once an illustrated catalogue of the paintings and drawings of a contemporary artist, a monument to the deceased painter and a commercial undertaking, albeit an unsuccessful one.

For a sophisticated and self-aware society, portrait painting was an important vehicle. HYACINTHE RIGAUD and NICOLAS DE LARGILLIERRE were the principal figures in the first half of the 18th century; both were capable of producing restrained and realistic portraits as well as grand ceremonial pieces that often had allegorical themes. Slightly later Jacques Aved and Jean-Marc Nattier introduced a vogue for less formal portraits, placing sitters in characteristic everyday poses: an example is Aved's *Mme Crozat* (1741; Montpellier, Mus. Fabre; for illustration *see* AVED, JACQUES). Maurice-Quentin de La Tour also enjoyed a high reputation for his penetrating character studies in pastel (*see* LA TOUR, MAURICE-QUENTIN DE, fig. 1 and

PASTEL, colour pl. V). Still-life, sporting and battle pictures were also popular. Such artists as François Desportes (animals, flowers and hunting scenes; *see* DESPORTES, (1)); JEAN-BAPTISTE OUDRY (still-life, hunting and game; *see* fig. 23); and Charles Parrocel (battles; *see* PARROCEL, (3)) made lucrative livelihoods from their specialized practices.

There were many different trends in the mid-18th century. In 1746 Mme de Pompadour (*see* POISSON, (1)) was installed as Louis XV's mistress, and she exercised a leading role in patronage of the arts. The foremost academic history painter was Carle Vanloo (*see* VANLOO, (3)), although the works of FRANÇOIS BOUCHER are more representative of the period generally. Boucher eschewed the Italianate decorative tradition in favour of a vibrant and luxurious approach. In 1753 he painted the *Rising of the Sun* and the *Setting of the Sun* (see fig. 24; both London, Wallace), clear manifestations of the spontaneity and *joie de vivre* of his art. Boucher benefited greatly from Mme de Pompadour's patronage, and his works were ideally suited to the Court and to the intimate interiors of Parisian hôtels. At the opposite end of the scale, Jean-Siméon Chardin produced beautiful still-lifes, the lowest-ranking of genres. Chardin's paintings reflect a static world of harmony and order, for example the *Jar of Olives* (1760; Paris, Louvre; *see* CHARDIN, JEAN-SIMÉON, fig. 4; *see also* STILL-LIFE, fig. 6). His works are direct and often executed with bravura brushwork and dense colour. Although visually very dissimilar, the works of Boucher and Chardin were often collected together, indicating that mid-century taste was not wholly partisan and could embrace artistic extremes. Landscape painting in the middle decades of the century is represented by Boucher's pastoral fantasies

24. François Boucher: *Setting of the Sun*, oil on canvas, 3.18×2.61 m, 1753 (London, Wallace Collection)

and the elegant topography of the series by Joseph Vernet (*see* VERNET, (1)) of the *Ports of France* (1755–65; Paris, Louvre and Mus. Mar.), one of the most important royal commissions of Louis XV's reign. These were engraved by Jacques-Philippe Lebas, one of the foremost reproductive engravers of the 18th century.

(ii) Resurgence of history painting. When calls were made for the reintroduction of serious moral content into painting, both Boucher and Chardin were victims of criticism. A body of critics emerged, including ETIENNE LA FONT DE SAINT-YENNE and DENIS DIDEROT, who were schooled in Enlightenment principles and who saw painting's function as didactic rather than hedonistic. After 1737 the Salon was a regular event in artistic life (*see* PARIS, §III, 3) and it became the focus for the critical exchanges of pamphleteers. Thus, in the 1740s, art criticism was born in France. Though the writings of the German Johann Joachim Winckelmann arrived in France in the 1750s, they had little impact compared to those of native authors. However, despite these critics, calls for virtuous subjects and a reformatory style, history painters themselves were content to satisfy the demands of private patrons for light mythologies. State intervention occurred in the guise of another competition in 1747, but little appreciable benefit accrued. In 1751 the Marquis de Marigny (*see* POISSON, (2)), brother of Mme de Pompadour, was appointed Directeur des Bâtiments du Roi and he instigated a policy for the rejuvenation of history painting. Unfortunately, the Ministry of Finance could not support his ambition, and Marigny actually achieved very little in the 1760s and 1770s. Even in 1765, when a number of historical works on virtuous subjects were commissioned for the royal château of Choisy from such painters as Noël Hallé and Joseph-Marie Vien, they were disliked by the King and were replaced by decorative tapestries. At this time history painters were seemingly incapable of producing works where style and subject-matter were consonant: a serious subject required a serious style. Artificially posed, pastel-coloured figures not studied from life and placed in non-naturalistic settings could not be used to convey a noble and elevated message. Ironically, it was a genre painter who provided the example of how history painters could acquire gravity and seriousness. With an awareness of Poussin, Jean-Baptiste Greuze constructed his works solidly as friezelike compositions, and their protagonists exchanged simple yet meaningful gestures. In the *Marriage Contract* (1761; Paris, Louvre; *see* GREUZE, JEAN-BAPTISTE, fig. 2), for instance, a rural nobility is present, and Diderot recognized that Greuze's work equalled that of the great history painters of the past. Classical antiquity was another frequently invoked element in painting in the 1750s and 1760s, and it became topical following the discoveries of HERCULANEUM (1738) and POMPEII (1748). Yet artists were unsure of exactly how to utilize antique sources, and for many it was simply a fashionable adjunct. Vien based the composition of his *Cupid Seller* of 1763 (Fontainebleau, Château; *see* VIEN, JOSEPH-MARIE, fig. 1) on an engraving after a wall painting in Herculaneum; but although the theme is antique, it is no more than a Rococo picture in classical fancy dress: the Neoclassical style was not fully formed until the 1780s.

In 1774 the new king Louis XVI appointed the Comte d'ANGIVILLER as Directeur des Bâtiments du Roi. From 1775 history paintings on moral themes were commissioned by the Crown. The first of these appeared at the Salon of 1777: six exemplary themes from ancient history painted by Louis-Jacques Durameau, Louis Lagrenée and Jean-Jacques Lagrenée, Hallé, Nicolas-Guy Brenet and Nicolas-Bernard Lépicié. At the same time, a lesser number of subjects from French history were also commissioned, the most famous being Brenet's *Death of Duguesclin* (1777; Versailles, Château; for illustration *see* BRENET, NICOLAS-GUY), indicating an interest in nationalism. Many of these works lacked stylistic coherence and simply appropriated and modified the unsuitable visual vocabularies of the recent past. However, in the later 1770s a number of artists, including FRANÇOIS-ANDRÉ VINCENT and PIERRE PEYRON (for illustration *see* PEYRON, PIERRE), looked to 17th-century French and Italian sources to invigorate their art and invest it with a seriousness of purpose. Perhaps the first true manifestation of a conjunction of a severe and noble style with serious subject-matter was *Belisarius Receiving Alms* of 1781 (Lille, Mus. B.-A.) by JACQUES-LOUIS DAVID. The debt to Poussin in this painting is obvious, but it is far more than a pastiche. David's economy of gesture and friezelike grouping imbued the painting with a deep sense of moral gravity. At this stage David was one of a number of artists concentrating on the creation of a virile and austere style capable of transmitting essential truths about morality and virtue. Drawing and the study of the life model played an important part in this development. Firm contours and outlines were adopted, and the technique of *trois crayons* was replaced by the use of a single chalk. Outline engraving was also studied and produced. With his painting the *Oath of the Horatii* (1784; Paris, Louvre; *see* DAVID, JACQUES-LOUIS, fig. 1), exhibited at the Salon of 1785, David moved into a position of stylistic dominance and set about disseminating his methods and techniques through his many pupils.

However pervasive David's influence was, the Rococo style was not immediately extinguished. Sober Neo-classicism was neither required for, nor suited to, domestic interiors, and the followers of Boucher continued to find adequate employment. In this period of transformation in French art Jean-Honoré Fragonard (see FRAGONARD, (1)) with his virtuosity and freedom of execution, occupied an individual but stylistically problematic position. From the 1750s to 1770s he was highly regarded as a painter of erotic mythological and genre scenes. During the 1780s his output declined, and in such works as *The Lock* (*c.* 1779–80; Paris, Louvre) he moved away from the erotic to the serious. Neither did landscape escape reform: Hubert Robert, influenced by Giovanni Paolo Panini, specialized in ruins and architecture—sometimes actual buildings in imaginary settings, sometimes pure fantasies—and added to them a literary and poetic content (*see* ROBERT, HUBERT, fig. 2). Pierre-Henri de Valenciennes, by way of a profound study of Poussin, developed an ideal and ennobled vision of nature (*see also* §5 below).

Both original and reproductive printmaking enjoyed great popularity. Cheap versions of popular pictures and illustrations of contemporary events were always in demand, and reproductive printmaking reached great heights of technical skill, especially in the hands of the pupils of Lebas. A number of new tools and techniques were developed, and Diderot's *Encyclopédie* (Paris, 1751–65) included detailed articles by engravers on the history and techniques of engraving and illustrations of tools and methods (*see* ENGRAVING, §II, 4, and fig. 7). Discriminating connoisseurs also sought original prints, and etching was a pastime among artistic amateurs including Mme de Pompadour and the Comte de Caylus. Methods of approximating the *trois crayons* process of draughtsmanship were discovered (*see* CRAYON MANNER), and in the period from mid-century to the Revolution colour-printing techniques became more sophisticated. Hand-colouring was replaced by the three primary-colour plate process refined by Jacques Gautier-Dagoty (*see* GAUTIER-DAGOTY, (1)), which aimed to imitate the appearance of oil paint (*see* PRINTS, §III, 6(ii) and GOUACHE MANNER, §2). Many gifted artists limited themselves to activities in draughtsmanship or illustration, particularly Charles-Nicolas Cochin (ii), Louis de Carmontelle and Gabriel de Saint-Aubin, the last an especially acute observer of Parisian society and the Salon. Book illustration also provided a welcome source of employment for artists, especially during hard times; such projects as the *Voyage pittoresque, ou description des royaumes de Naples et de Sicile* (1781–6) by the Abbé de SAINT-NON engaged large numbers of artists and draughtsmen. Saint-Non etched the plates for this project himself (*see also* BOOK ILLUSTRATION, §III).

(iii) Art of the Revolution and its aftermath. During the Revolution artists were exhorted to celebrate the glorious events or commemorate Republican martyrs (see fig. 25). Such highly topical scenes soon became outdated as the political situation changed, however. David's failure to complete the *Oath of the Tennis Court* (begun 1790; abandoned 1801; Paris, Louvre) is a notable case in point. There were surprisingly few depictions of the Revolution itself, and antique scenes were often used to convey lessons of heroism and civic virtue. Official and aristocratic patronage collapsed, and history painters in particular suffered. Some schemes and government competitions were organized but these were only partially successful. David became virtual dictator of the arts until the fall of Robespierre in August 1794. He succeeded in abolishing the Académie Royale in 1793, only for it to be replaced by the Beaux-Arts section of the Institut de France in 1796 (*see* PARIS, §VI, 1 and 3). Such revolutionary societies as the Commune des Arts were formed, but these were little more than gatherings of like-minded individuals rather than organizations with definite artistic programmes. For all their revolutionary rhetoric, artists were painting what they could sell, and the Salons (open from 1791) were full of portraits, genre scenes, still-lifes and landscapes.

The rise of Napoleon, first as Consul (1799) and then as Emperor (1804), provoked far-reaching changes in French art (*see* BONAPARTE, (1)). During this time there was a proliferation of portraits and paintings commemorating famous victories. As Premier Peintre to the Emperor, David was employed to immortalize the key events of the Empire in vast canvases, such as the *Coronation of*

25. Jacques-Louis David: *Jean-Paul Marat* (or *Death of Marat*), oil on canvas, 1.65×1.28 m, 1793 (Brussels, Musée d'Art Ancien)

Napoleon (6.21×9.79 m, 1805–7; Paris, Louvre; for detail *see* DAVID, JACQUES-LOUIS, fig. 4) where, in order to capture the Napoleonic pageant, strict Neo-classicism was abandoned in favour of a richer and more luxuriant treatment. David's commissions were, however, curtailed due to his exorbitant prices. His former pupils benefited from this situation, notably Antoine-Jean Gros, Anne-Louis Girodet and François Gérard. Gros was the preferred battle painter (e.g. *Nazareth*, 1800; sketch, Nantes, Mus. B.-A.; *Aboukir*, 1806; Versailles, Château; *Eylau*, 1808; Paris, Louvre) and he turned to the example of Rubens to infuse his scenes with dynamism and drama. Girodet's determination to be original often led to bizarre results, as with his allegorical *Apotheosis of French Heroes who Died for the Country during the War of Liberty* (or *Ossian and the French Generals*, 1800; Malmaison, Château N.; *see* GIRODET, ANNE-LOUIS, fig. 2). Gérard was the most favoured portrait painter, and his neo-Baroque images of Napoleon were multiplied on a large scale.

Artists were required to manufacture a Napoleonic myth, one that was free from monarchic associations but that also suggested parallels with Roman emperors and even with Christ. Not surprisingly, the responses to this task were extremely varied in style and vocabulary. *Napoleon I on the Imperial Throne* (1806; Paris, Mus. Armée) by JEAN-AUGUSTE-DOMINIQUE INGRES is a striking example of a deviation from traditional State iconography. This work, having the precession of van Eyck, is uncompromisingly direct in a format that is reminiscent of images of Jupiter or God the Father.

Although the style of David and his school continued to dominate history painting, challenges to the Davidian canon were presented in the first decades of the 19th century both by his former pupils and by such artists as PIERRE GUÉRIN and Pierre-Paul Prud'hon. The latter was the most successful history painter completely beyond David's sphere of influence. His erotically tinged, graceful and charming works led to him being called 'the French Correggio', although he also scored a notable success in serious history painting with *Justice and Divine Vengeance Pursuing Crime* (1808; Paris, Louvre; *see* PRUD'HON, PIERRE-PAUL, fig. 2). David and Prud'hon also differed considerably in their approach to draughtsmanship: David favoured an incisive linear style executed in black chalk, whereas Prud'hon produced shimmering nude studies in black and white chalks on grey or blue paper. Subjects of greater emotional intensity were sought out: Gros painted *Sappho at Leucadia* (1801; Bayeux, Mus. Gérard) and Jean Broc the *Death of Hyacinth* (1801; Poitiers, Mus. B.-A.). In both, moonlight is used to create glacial contours and unreal effects. The moral dimension of Neo-classicism, formerly an essential ingredient, became a lesser consideration, and antique scenes of terror, suffering and eroticism became fashionable. Formerly obsessed with the Greco-Roman world, French artists in the early 19th century began to turn to northern European sources for inspiration, such as the *Ossian* poems of James Macpherson and the English 'Gothick' novel. A taste for the French Middle Ages was also cultivated, as illustrated by the TROUBADOUR STYLE works of Fleury Richard, in which the degree of accuracy to the period attained rivalled the archaeological exactitude of orthodox Neo-classicism. Genre painting also prospered under Napoleon, particularly the intimate and anecdotal bourgeois scenes of Martin Drolling and Louis-Léopold Boilly, who were both inspired by 17th-century Dutch exemplars (*see* DRESS, fig. 49). Women artists, including MARGUERITE GERARD and Jeanne-Elisabeth Chaudet (*see* CHAUDET, (2)), also found success. The Salon of 1808 was called the 'Ladies' Salon', since 50 women artists participated.

With the fall of Napoleon, David went into exile in Brussels, but even before his departure there were signs that his work was out of step with the times. His last great Neo-classical painting, *Leonidas at Thermopylae* (1814; Paris, Louvre), was a static and contemplative work that was perceived as having little relevance to a nation traumatized by the retreat from Moscow of the French army and the end of the Napoleonic era. Théodore Gericault's *Wounded Cuirassier* (1814; Paris, Louvre), with its anonymous stumbling figure of a retreating soldier, reversed expectations of Napoleonic heroism, presenting instead an image redolent of defeat. Such a powerfully personal interpretation of history contrasts sharply with the universal goals and certainties of Neo-classicism; the diversity of artistic aspirations revealed in the works of this time demonstrates that no stylistic mode was truly dominant in French painting by the second decade of the 19th century.

BIBLIOGRAPHY

E. de Goncourt and J. de Goncourt: *L'Art au XVIII siècle* (Paris, 1859–75)
F. Benoît: *L'Art français sous la Révolution et l'Empire* (Paris, 1897)
A. Fontaine: *Les Doctrines d'art en France de Poussin à Diderot* (Paris, 1909)
J. Locquin: *La Peinture d'histoire en France de 1747 à 1785* (Paris, 1912/*R* 1978)
R. Rosenblum: *Transformations in Late Eighteenth-century Art* (Princeton, 1967)
W. Graf Kalnein and M. Levey: *Art and Architecture of the Eighteenth Century in France*, Pelican Hist. A. (Harmondsworth, 1972)
French Painting, 1774–1830: The Age of Revolution (exh. cat. by P. Rosenberg and others, Paris, Grand Pal.; Detroit, MI, Inst. A.; New York, Met.; 1974–5)
The Age of Louis XV (exh. cat. by P. Rosenberg, Toledo, OH, Mus. A.; Chicago, IL, A. Inst.; Montreal, Mus. F.A.; 1975–6)
M. Fried: *Absorption and Theatricality: Painting and the Beholder in the Age of Diderot* (Berkeley, 1980)
N. Bryson: *Word and Image: French Painting of the 'Ancien Régime'* (Cambridge, 1981)
P. Conisbee: *Painting in Eighteenth-century France* (Oxford, 1981)
D. Wakefield: *French Eighteenth-century Painting* (London, 1984)
Regency to Empire: French Printmaking, 1715–1814 (exh. cat. by V. Carlson and J. Ittman, Baltimore, MD, Mus. A.; Minneapolis, MN, Inst. A.; 1984)
T. Crow: *Painters and Public Life in Eighteenth-century Paris* (New Haven and London, 1985)
P. Bordes and R. Michel, eds: *Aux armes et aux arts! Les Arts de la Révolution, 1789–1799* (Paris, 1988)
M. Levey: *Painting and Sculpture in France, 1700–1789* (New Haven and London, 1993)

SIMON LEE

5. *c.* 1814–*c.* 1914.

(i) The search for a subject-matter. (ii) Romanticism, classicism and the development of *plein-air* painting. (iii) Influence of the studios. (iv) Realism and modern life. (v) Development and influence of Impressionism. (vi) The avant-garde and abstraction.

(i) The search for a subject-matter. After the restoration of the Bourbon monarchy (1814), paintings illustrating episodes in the life of Napoleon, commissioned from David and others, were removed from public view, and the subject was proscribed. There was an attempt to match these Napoleonic pictures with works celebrating the Bourbon monarchy commissioned to such artists as Horace Vernet (*see* VERNET, (3)), FRANÇOIS GÉRARD, LOUIS HERSENT and others, but these did not register in the public mind as strongly as the earlier works. Despite their removal, the propagandist pictures of the Napoleonic Empire, which combined modern subject-matter (the traditional concern of genre painters) and the heroism of the Antique, remained in the memory of artists throughout this period. Gericault's *Raft of the Medusa* (exh. 1819; Paris, Louvre; *see* GERICAULT, THÉODORE, fig. 3), *Liberty Leading the People* (1830; Paris, Louvre; *see* ALLEGORY, fig. 10) by EUGÈNE DELACROIX and a number of pictures illustrating the Greek War of Independence (1821–9) that were exhibited in the 1820s would not have been painted without the example of Antoine-Jean Gros's Napoleonic paintings (*see* GROS, ANTOINE-JEAN, fig. 1). In the later pictures, however, emphasis shifted from the hero placed at the centre of the composition to the common people who had earnt a new respect among all parties as a consequence of the Revolution. The search for heroic subjects in common life, for which there is little precedence in European art before 1789, inspired Gericault and LÉOPOLD ROBERT to look for a source of dramatic imagery in the life of the Italian peasants, and prepared artists in the 1830s to discover the heroism of ancient Rome among the Arabs of North Africa.

The demise of Napoleonic subjects encouraged artists to revert to traditional sources of inspiration. Mythological subjects depicted in an erotic manner, which had been favoured by collectors since the 18th century, increased in numbers as some of the older artists abandoned themes of modern life for subjects from Greek and Roman legends. David led the way, followed by Gros, but this tendency was associated above all with ANNE-LOUIS GIRODET, who had never been a very successful painter of modern life, and his pupils. Similarly, the so-called 'Troubadours', who combined the format of Dutch genre painting with subjects from national history, enjoyed even greater success in the reign of Louis XVIII (*reg* 1814–24) than they had during the Empire. Their preoccupation with the lives of the more illustrious French kings had endeared them to collectors at the imperial Court and attracted enthusiastic attention among former emigrés (*see* TROUBADOUR STYLE).

The reappearance of religious themes in art was the first significant novelty of the Restoration Salons. This revival was sustained by the need to supply French churches with altarpieces in place of those removed or destroyed during the 1790s. The Comte de Chabrol, the Préfet de Paris, commissioned dozens of large-scale paintings and distributed them to churches in Paris. The artists who painted them had little in the immediate past on which to base their work and turned for inspiration to Raphael's late work and to 17th-century precedents, as did the history painters of the Empire. These were also the sources of the religious pictures that restored Ingres's reputation in the 1820s, although his dependence on Raphael was more obvious than in the work of his colleagues (*see* INGRES, JEAN-AUGUSTE-DOMINIQUE, fig. 3). This attracted the attention of critics who were looking for an artist in the classical tradition who might replace David as an influence on young painters.

After the deaths of Girodet in 1824 and David in 1825, critics were anxious about the future of the French school, and this made them unusually sensitive to changes in art taking place at that time. They were reluctant to admit the debt that linked the work of artists of the 1820s with the principles of a previous generation. In retrospect, it is easier to understand that scenes of drama and violence painted by Pierre Guérin's pupils during the Restoration were largely chosen to allow them to demonstrate traditional skills in figure painting, chiaroscuro, gesture and expression. Sometimes these pictures illustrated ancient myth and history, as in Delacroix's *Death of Sardanapalus* (1827; Paris, Louvre; *see* ROMANTICISM, fig. 1), Xavier Sigalon's *Athalie Having her Children Massacred* (Nîmes, Mus. B.-A.) and Pierre Guérin's unfinished *Death of Priam* (Angers, Mus. B.-A.), but also themes from contemporary life, as in Vernet's *Massacre of the Mamluks* (Amiens, Mus. Picardie) and Gericault's *Raft of the Medusa*, which, despite their modern subjects, are essentially similar in detail and composition. Most of these paintings have a turbulence and diagonal emphasis not found in David's mature work; rather, they recall older conventions in favour before he became an influence.

(ii) Romanticism, classicism and the development of plein-air *painting.* The Paris Salon of 1824 marked a period of change. A number of practices associated with the Revolution and the Empire were abandoned by older artists, who might have been expected to sustain the tradition. The Troubadour style was no longer seen in exhibitions, although its exponents left a legacy of subjects that continued to inspire younger artists such as Delacroix, Paul Delaroche (*see* DELAROCHE, (2)) and RICHARD PARKES BONINGTON. Subjects taken from Greek and Roman literature, history and mythology rapidly lost popularity as artists, turning to more recent sources, took inspiration from a number of post-classical writers, particularly from Goethe, Shakespeare, Byron and Walter Scott, all of whom provided subject-matter for many French paintings in the following decades. However, in the critics' debate on styles that emerged from the Salon of 1824, subject-matter was not an issue of importance. In theory, experiments with technique were more contentious, although, in practice, critics' taste in this matter did not easily allow them to be neatly separated into classical and Romantic factions as they might have thought. For example, the proponents of Romanticism admired the work of Ingres, while those who admired classicism were attracted to the paintings of Eugène Devéria (*see* DEVÉRIA, (2)); all critics disliked Delacroix's *Death of Sardanapalus*, and hardly any favoured David's later followers and imitators (*see also* ROMANTICISM).

The sudden increase in paintings illustrating popular literature was linked to the growing market for prints, which encouraged painters to depict episodes from books and plays fashionable at the time through the recently developed technique of LITHOGRAPHY. Such literary pictures were easy to sell to dealers and collectors. Commercialization of art was also responsible for a steady increase in genre and landscape at the 19th-century Salons. The fashion for 17th-century Dutch art, which had established genre painting in late 18th-century France as a lucrative profession for a successful few, began to affect the practice of landscape painting in the 1820s. GEORGES MICHEL, whose landscapes were inspired by Philips Koninck, Ruisdael and Rembrandt, was little known for most of his life and was discovered by a younger generation of painters and their friends, who successfully exploited the conventions of Dutch landscape painting in the 1830s. While the taste for Dutch art was certainly important in promoting the art of THÉODORE ROUSSEAU, JULES DUPRÉ, Charles-François Daubigny (*see* DAUBIGNY, (1)) and other artists born in the decade after 1810 (*see also* BARBIZON SCHOOL), the most important contribution to the strength of landscape painting in 19th-century France came from the practice, associated with French painters at the Académie de France in Rome, of making *plein-air* studies. PIERRE HENRI VALENCIENNES, who in Rome learnt the importance of making oil sketches, established a school of landscape based on this practice when he returned to Paris. In 1817 he was instrumental in establishing a PRIX DE ROME for landscape painting. This gave it new status and provided new incentives to painters, although his goal, and that of the artists whom he trained, was to paint compositions in the tradition of Claude and Poussin based on studies made *en plein air* and organized like a stage set with trees and buildings flanking figures and serving as repoussoir devices. Studies did not have a high status as works of art but they were evidently popular with collectors and gave artists a taste for working in the open air, which they exploited profitably when the fashion for compositions in the style of Claude declined in the 1830s.

(iii) Influence of the studios. The variety of painting styles in the mid-19th century resulted from the many different private teaching studios that were an essential part of the system of education as it evolved around the life-drawing classes at the Ecole des Beaux-Arts in Paris (*see* PARIS, §VI, 3(ii)). The Ecole did not constitute a school of painting until 1863, and students wishing to study in the life class or to compete for the Prix de Rome had first to enrol with a private master. This gave private studios considerable importance as rival institutions with their own distinct traditions, although there were often cross-currents that brought the influence of Gros into Guérin's studio and the influence of Ingres into those of Delaroche and FRANÇOIS-EDOUARD PICOT. Tendencies were also passed from masters' studios to those of their pupils: for example from David's to Gros's, from Ingres's to that of Hippolyte Flandrin (*see* FLANDRIN, (2)) and from Picot's to that of ALEXANDRE CABANEL, thus ensuring a continuity over the years.

In the 1830s Ingres's role contributed to a tendency in studios to paint with a tighter finish and greater clarity, which combined in the work of his own pupils with an interest in 15th- and 16th-century Italian art. The result was a style of painting well-adapted to religious art, which in the early 1830s shifted from large, framed pictures exhibited at the Salons to wall paintings in oils, fresco or encaustic. This link with architecture encouraged a decorative element in French art, which was employed particularly in the more Gothic of Parisian churches: St Merri, St Germain-l'Auxerrois and the chancel of St Gervais–St Protais. However, the dominant painting style in chapels, otherwise associated with such artists as Alexandre-Jean-Baptiste Hesse, Michel-Martin Drolling and Emile Signol, was characterized by a sobriety and clarity of design based on a solid mastery of figure drawing. Important single commissions, representing either Flemish or Venetian tendencies, were also given to Delacroix, THÉODORE CHASSÉRIAU and THOMAS COUTURE. The failure of Vernet and of his son-in-law, Paul Delaroche, to participate in this enterprise suggested a reluctance by the authorities to admit into Parisian churches the artistic principles of the newly established Musée d'Historique at Versailles: Vernet had notoriously adapted the principles of historical realism to the portrayal of scenes from the Old Testament; Delaroche's commission in 1833 for a major scheme to decorate the nave of the Temple de la Grande Armée (or La Madeleine after 1845) in Paris was never realized. Both artists received important secular decorative commissions for the Musée du Louvre and the Ecole des Beaux-Arts, but despite the success of these works, these were exceptional commissions. By contrast, Delacroix was almost continually employed from the beginning of the July Monarchy (1830) until the 1850s, painting the ceilings of such major State buildings in Paris as the Palais Bourbon. Although he did not paint official portraits, he was

otherwise the most favoured official artist at the time, and his influence would unquestionably have been far greater if, like Ingres and several of his fellow academicians, he had been more interested in taking pupils.

Outside the realm of wall painting, Vernet's influence was unequalled. Although he was a pioneering member of a circle of painters grouped around Gericault during the Restoration, in the early 1830s he modified his lively manner of painting in favour of a sharper naturalism that appealed to Louis-Philippe (*reg* 1830–48) and that influenced younger artists, for whom exactitude and historical truth became major virtues. This tendency was taken up by Delaroche and by his best-known pupil, JEAN-LÉON GÉRÔME, the latter of whom imparted a photographic quality to his painting derived partly from his use of the camera. Gérôme, in turn, had an important influence on the many students who worked in his studio at the Ecole des Beaux-Arts in the last decades of the century. Like the landscape painters and the Realists of the 1850s, Vernet, Delaroche and Gérôme distrusted the conventions of the Académie des Beaux-Arts and turned instead to nature for alternatives. Delacroix and other artists who came to prominence in the 1820s were equally opposed to second-hand ideas and also took nature as their model, although they transformed it through the filter of their imagination, preferring fiction to fact.

(iv) Realism and modern life. Although Gérôme's work may often be described as realistic, in the 19th century Realism did not imply a detached style of painting but rather an attitude to contemporary themes. The preference of some artists for subjects from ordinary life was seen as a

26. Edouard Manet: *Nana*, oil on canvas, 1.54×1.15 m, 1877 (Hamburg, Hamburger Kunsthalle)

27. Alexandre Cabanel: *Birth of Venus*, oil on canvas, 1.30×2.25 m, 1863 (Paris, Musée d'Orsay)

deliberate attempt to downgrade the importance of subject-matter and undermine the objectives of 'high art'. Many critics mistook the detachment of GUSTAVE COURBET and EDOUARD MANET for indifference to the subject, although their aim was not to dispense with subject-matter but to find a technique through which they could assimilate a range of subjects taken from contemporary life, which had not previously been part of a painter's repertory. With Gérôme, ERNEST MEISSONIER and others, they stood back from their subject-matter and painted it with a deceptive detachment that, in the absence of the traditional rhetoric, at times makes it difficult to interpret meanings in their works. The importance that Courbet and Manet placed on modern subjects was linked to the Romantic idea that an artist should be true to his experience. In their writing both CHARLES BAUDELAIRE and ÉMILE ZOLA promoted a taste for subjects from modern urban life that was taken up by Manet and Degas from the early 1860s, although neither critic ultimately had much sympathy for Manet's apparently cool attitude towards his subjects, believing it to deny a role to the imagination (see fig. 26).

In the late 1840s artists from different backgrounds discovered contemporary urban and rural themes, and many turned their attention to images of labour and destitution. This tendency, also evident in contemporary English and German art, lasted until the early 1860s, at which time commercial pressures persuaded artists associated with these themes—for example Courbet, Alexandre Antigna, and Alfred Stevens (*see* STEVENS, (2))—to adopt more appealing subject-matter. WILLIAM BOUGUEREAU and ISIDORE-ALEXANDRE-AUGUSTIN PILS , who are not generally associated with this aspect of Realism, also dealt with such themes. This tendency was not, in itself,

controversial. Antigna's *The Fire* (1850; Orléans, Mus. B.-A.; for illustration *see* ANTIGNA, ALEXANDRE), depicting one of the hazards of urban poverty, was generally admired at the Salon of 1850 by the very critics who condemned Courbet's *Burial at Ornans* (1849–50; Paris, Mus. d'Orsay; *see* COURBET, GUSTAVE, fig. 1) at the same exhibition; they felt that Antigna, unlike Courbet, conveyed an obvious moral point through a traditional mastery of gesture, expression, chiaroscuro, figure drawing and composition. It was not Courbet's politics that made him controversial but rather his failure to make any apparent comment about a subject that was rich in social and dramatic possibilities. A more overtly socialist picture would certainly have provoked less outrage (for further discussion *see* REALISM).

Realism, in all its related forms, was only one of several approaches apparent in the Salons in the 1850s. During the July Monarchy a revival of interest in 18th-century art among collectors and designers encouraged a ROCOCO REVIVAL by French artists. This had already been evident by the late 1830s and had become an important element of commercial art in the following decade. At the beginning of their careers a number of artists, including Couture, JEAN-FRANÇOIS MILLET, NARCISSE DIAZ and Charles Muller (1789–1855), supplied the market with paintings in a Rococo taste at a time when this type of art had not yet become fashionable, but they eventually painted more ambitious themes. As the taste for the 18th century gained hold, it began to exercise a more lasting influence on academic artists, who found a ready sale for mythological subjects that combined an immaculate finish learnt from their teachers with compositions reminiscent of Boucher. Cabanel's famous *Birth of Venus* (see fig. 27) is, as critics pointed out at the Salon of 1863, composed in the manner

28. Elie Delaunay: *Plague at Rome*, oil on canvas, 1.31×1.76 m, 1869 (Paris, Musée d'Orsay)

of an 18th-century overdoor. Interest in Rococo art among artists of Cabanel's generation was encouraged by the prevailing taste for 18th-century furnishings. This gave artists the opportunity to paint murals and ceiling decorations in a similar style: PAUL BAUDRY, in his ceiling (1866–74) for the foyer of Charles Garnier's Opéra in Paris, combined a knowledge of 18th-century art with an awareness of earlier traditions. Baudry's later work (completed 1885) for Henri-Eugène-Philippe-Louis d'Orléans, Duc d'Aumâle, at his château at Chantilly, is more obviously Rococo in inspiration.

The paintings of single nude figures with allegorical and mythological titles, such as Cabanel's *Birth of Venus*, which were fashionable in the Second Empire (1852–70) and in the early decades of the Third Republic, were also influenced by the practice of the painted *académie*, the nude life study made in the studio. Ingres was the common inspiration for many of these pictures, painted by a generation of Prix de Rome winners who returned to Paris in the 1850s. These artists, including Bouguereau, Emile Lévy, Félix Giacomotti, Cabanel and Jules Lefebvre, were principally pupils of Picot, one of the most successful teachers of future Prix winners. Their influence on religious art, secular decoration and commercial painting was pervasive up to the 1890s, by which time their academic method of painting and their success in the Salons brought them into fashionable disrepute. Their successors in the 1860s, such as ELIE DELAUNAY (see fig. 28), PIERRE PUVIS DE CHAVANNES, Henri Léopold Lévy and GUSTAVE MOREAU, combined aspects of academic art with a debt to Delacroix and his followers and had their cult of 'style', so-named by critics, taken up by younger artists in the 1890s who were reacting against the mechanistic spirit of the age. Moreau, who did not win the Prix de Rome but in 1857 went to Rome at his own expense, escaped the growing critical suspicion that affected his fellow students at Picot's studio by treating traditional biblical and mythological themes in an eccentric manner. Like Puvis de Chavannes, who was discovered in the 1880s by younger artists who admired him as an important precursor of SYMBOLISM, Moreau was profoundly affected by the Romanticism of Chassériau and detested the Symbolists, for whom he was a venerated master.

(v) Development and influence of Impressionism. In the 1860s IMPRESSIONISM emerged from a combination of earlier landscape painting based on studies made *en plein air* and the newer interest in contemporary life. The Impressionists' reduction of subject to the depiction of light effects originated in the work of Corot and Daubigny, but whereas their predecessors had treated light in terms of tone, the Impressionists discovered that sunlight and shadow could be depicted by the contrasts of colour. Their use of colour

theories places them within a long tradition of artists who, since the time of Masaccio and Leonardo, had attempted to re-create the appearance of nature with the help of science. In the 1850s the use of archaeological motifs in the work of Gérôme and his fellow Néo-Grecs (*see* NÉO-GREC) had been inspired by a similar dependency on science in the interest of Realism, which, in all its varieties, was still the dominant tendency in the Salons of the 1870s. As one of three teachers of painting at the Ecole des Beaux-Arts, Gérôme had a pervasive influence among young students. The startling illusionism of Léon Bonnat's *Job* (Bayonne, Mus. Bonnat), which originated, as did the Realism of Manet, CAROLUS-DURAN and THÉODULE RIBOT in the example of Spanish art, was widely admired when the painting was exhibited in 1880. There were, however, already signs of change. The enthusiastic reception given by critics and collectors to Puvis de Chavannes's one-man show in 1881 marked his first success as a painter of easel pictures, the distinctive flatness and archetypal subject-matter of which became a major influence on the literary and mystical paintings of the 1890s. After an absence of several years, Moreau exhibited *Salomé Dancing before Herod* (Los Angeles, CA, Armand Hammer Mus. A.), *St Sebastian* and *Hercules and the Hydra of Lerna* (Chicago, IL, A. Inst.) at the Salon of 1876. This brought his visionary treatment of subjects dealing with suffering, mysticism and the *femme fatale* to the notice of a younger generation of writers and artists.

It is one of the paradoxes of 19th-century art that the Impressionists, who based their art on the Realist traditions of Manet, Corot and the Barbizon school, became, in the last years of the century, leading influences in the reaction against Realism. The manner in which the Impressionists used colour, which excited some contemporaries and enraged others, was adopted by many young artists in the 1880s and 1890s as an indication of how it could be used arbitrarily and expressively (*see* COLOUR, colour pl. III, fig. 1, IMPRESSIONISM, colour pls VI–VIII and OIL PAINTING, colour pls III and IV). VINCENT VAN GOGH, HENRI MATISSE, GEORGES SEURAT and PABLO PICASSO, who came to Impressionism from different backgrounds, were inspired to add to their paintings an element of colour that often had little to do with the purposes of Impressionism. This happened during a period of reaction against Naturalism (*see* NATURALISM, §2); in the 1880s, for example, AUGUSTE RENOIR looked back to the example of the Old Masters (e.g. *Bathers*, 1887; Philadelphia, PA, Mus. A.), while PAUL CÉZANNE and PAUL GAUGUIN, in keeping with a general tendency towards flatness and decorative effects in French art, developed more formal interests in surface pattern.

Flatness and pattern are characteristic of the reticent, domestic scenes of EDOUARD VUILLARD and the NABIS and of the more extrovert, late works of CLAUDE MONET that in retrospect became important for 20th-century artists who had more purely formal concerns. Reaction against illusionism led to an interest in surface effects, although this did not necessarily undermine the importance of subject-matter, which in some respects was reaffirmed by a return to essentials. The rules for the admission of works to the first exhibition of the Rose + Croix at the Galerie Durand in Paris in 1892, which

encouraged allegory, catholicism, mysticism and legendary themes and which proscribed all banal subjects, represented a general tendency that was intended to 'ruin realism, reform latin taste and create a school of idealist art' (*see* SALON DE LA ROSE + CROIX). Work of a mural and decorative character was favoured, while pictures in the style of Delaroche and Meissonier were not admitted to the exhibition.

(vi) The avant-garde and abstraction. The history of the avant-garde in France from NEO-IMPRESSIONISM to abstraction developed through small élites of artists and their friends, who were at the time on the margins of the art world and who acquired fame and influence only in retrospect. The success of the Impressionists encouraged them to experiment, and they were also supported by dealers and collectors who, having been given an incentive by the example of the Impressionist dealer Paul Durand-Ruel, invested in art that was 'difficult' or 'new'. Above all, it was through awareness of Impressionist colour that these artists gradually simplified the content of art and moved towards abstraction. In 1914 and 1915 Matisse painted views out of windows that dispensed entirely with the illusion of depth and reduced forms to a few elements of colour, although his work never became purely abstract. Cubism, as it developed after 1908 in the art of Braque and Picasso, was exceptional among these movements in that it concentrated on the representation of form and largely eliminated colour (*see* CUBISM, §1). Cubists employed such commonplace themes as portraits and still-life, which allowed them to take their art to the limit of representation while retaining a minimum of marks and clues to identify the subject. The introduction of printed letters and words into their paintings in 1912, followed by the invention of COLLAGE, further narrowed the gap between the method of representation and the object represented, although the first non-representational pictures, painted by VASILY KANDINSKY around 1910 and Robert Delaunay in 1912 (*see* DELAUNAY (ii), (1)), derived primarily from the expressive use of colour (*see* ABSTRACT ART).

The pursuit by French artists of new ways of expression in the 20 years after 1885 has become important through later consequences. It is unlikely that any contemporary account of art written before 1914 would have given prominence to Picasso or Delaunay, even though by this date they had painted some of their most important works. When Louis Dimier's *Histoire de la peinture française au XIXième siècle, 1793–1903* was published in 1914, it seemed obvious to him that both Naturalism and the traditions of the Ecole des Beaux-Arts were moribund. He mentioned Cézanne and van Gogh as artists in the circle of Gauguin, who attempted to reconcile the tension of the 19th century between Realism and the Ideal. However, he relegated them to a minor role and noted that none would have been known outside a circle of specialists without the intervention of dealers attempting to repeat Durand-Ruel's success with the Impressionists. Instead, Dimier associated the regeneration of French art at the end of the 19th century with such artists as Albert Besnard, Jacques-Emile Blanche, Charles Cottet, Walter Guy and Gaston La Touche, all of whom combined the effects of Impressionism with traditional styles and sub-ject-matter. As Henri Martin had already discovered, this was a fashionable formula that merged with older Rococo tendencies in the decorative art of Jules Chéret and Guillaume Dubufe (1853–1909) to create a style much favoured by officials and private patrons in the years before 1914. A history of French taste before 1914, therefore, should not end with Picasso but rather with Besnard, Jean-François Raffaëlli and others whose art represented the fashionable assimilation of Impressionism in France and elsewhere at a time when Paris was the world's capital of art.

BIBLIOGRAPHY

R. Muther: *The History of Modern Painting*, 3 vols (London, 1895)
L. Dimier: *Histoire de la peinture française au XIXième siècle, 1793–1903* (Paris, 1914)
L. Rosenthal: *Du Romantisme au réalisme* (Paris, 1914)
J. Rewald: *History of Impressionism* (New York, 1946, rev. London, 4/1973)
——: *Post-Impressionism from van Gogh to Gauguin* (New York, 1956, rev. 3/1978)
F. Novotny: *Painting and Sculpture in Europe, 1780–1880*, Pelican Hist. A. (London, 1960/R Harmondsworth, 1985)
A. Boime: *The Academy and French Painting in the Nineteenth Century* (London, 1971)
French Symbolist Painters (exh. cat., ACGB, 1972)
W. Vaughan: *Romantic Art* (London and New York, 1978)
H. Honour: *Romanticism* (London and New York, 1979)
The Realist Tradition (exh. cat., ed. G. Weisberg; Cleveland, OH, Mus. A., 1980)
R. Rosenblum and H. W. Janson: *Art of the Nineteenth Century* (New York and London, 1984)
T. J. Clark: *The Painting of Modern Life* (London, 1985)
M. Marrinan: *Painting Politics for Louis-Philippe* (New Haven and London, 1988)
Monet to Matisse: Landscape Painting in France, 1874–1914 (exh. cat. by Richard Thomson, Edinburgh, N. Gals, 1994)

JON WHITELEY

6. AFTER *c.* 1914.

(i) The *rappel à l'ordre*. (ii) Dada, Surrealism and abstraction. (iii) Art, society and politics. (iv) World War II and after.

(i) The rappel à l'ordre. World War I put an end to avant-garde and experimental art in France. Many artists were mobilized and fought on the battlefields, and those who had been participants in, for example, FAUVISM and CUBISM went their own separate ways. During the war and immediately after, there was a search for a new order in French art (the *rappel à l'ordre*). PABLO PICASSO was isolated in his search for inspiration in the art of the past. From 1915 he measured his own work against Ingres's and classical art and, after his visit to Italy from February to April 1917 and his designs in that year for the ballet production *Parade* by Erik Satie and Jean Cocteau (*see* PICASSO, PABLO, fig. 4), he began to paint still-lifes and generously proportioned figures, as well as the Cubist compositions in a more academic, draughtsman-like man-ner, often employing a Pointillist technique. His two versions of the *Three Musicians* (both 1921; Philadelphia, PA, Mus. A. and New York, MOMA; *see* PICASSO, PABLO, fig. 5), impressive and condensed expressions of Synthetic Cubism, were painted in the same year as the two versions of *Women at the Fountain* (both 1921; New York, MOMA, and Paris, Mus. Picasso). In these he made use of motifs from Poussin, Greek vase painting and antique statuary. On the other hand, *Bathers* (1918; Paris, Mus. Picasso)

and *Two Women Running on the Beach* (1922; Paris, Mus. Picasso) are both foretastes of the movement that would be known as Surrealism. For FERNAND LÉGER, the war served to strengthen his conviction that the machine age had to give rise to a new kind of beauty that would reflect the modern era. At this time he produced works on makeshift supports (e.g. *Soldier with Pipe*, 1916; Düssel-dorf, Kstsamml. Nordrhein-Westfalen) that are a combi-nation of contrasting forms and subjects taken from the hardships of the war years. After the war his work approached abstraction, but *Mechanical Elements* (1924; Paris, Pompidou) and other decorative mural paintings (e.g. *The City*, 1919; Philadelphia, PA, Mus. A.; *see* LÉGER, FERNAND, fig. 2) were part of an oeuvre that included paintings of *intimiste* subjects executed in a classically ordered style that reflected the Purist spirit of AMÉDÉE OZENFANT and Le Corbusier (*see* PURISM). In Léger's *Grand Déjeuner* (1921; New York, MOMA) and *Three Women on a Red Background* (1927; Saint-Etienne, Mus. A. Mod.), figures and objects were developed out of elements from the mechanical world and designs derived from Greco-Roman mosaics. This became the hallmark of his style, which in the 1940s and 1950s became even more monumental.

After demobilization in 1915, GEORGES BRAQUE re-turned to painting and became a leading figure of a 'modernist' school that claimed to be rooted in Roman-esque art. Preferring to be known as a craftsman, rather than a painter, he continued to use a Cubist grid in his works, thus ensuring a harmonious, multi-layered space within which to frame such objects as pieces of fruit, pitchers, chairs, dressers and billiard-tables, all of which are painted in thick, dark impasto. The rigour of Cubist composition allowed ALBERT GLEIZES to revive religious art in a modern and abstract idiom. Robert Delaunay glorified the modern world by painting in an abstract style (*see* DELAUNAY (ii), (1)); this culminated in 1937 with his decorative interiors for the aviation and railway pavilions (both destr.) for the Exposition Internationale des Arts et Techniques dans la Vie Moderne in Paris (*see* INTERNA-TIONAL EXHIBITION, fig. 2). Many French artists felt that their works, when placed as mural paintings in urban settings, would make more effective statements about art's relationship to society. Sonia Delaunay, however, pro-duced designs for textiles not so much because she sought to define a socially orientated order and behaviour but rather as a statement against contemporary fashion (*see* DELAUNAY (ii), (2); *see also* §XI, 2 below). The designs by RAOUL DUFY for the silk industry and for tapestries (see fig. 94 below) reflected the luxurious style of ART DECO, and the nimble style and cheerful colours of his paintings reflected a joy in 'typical French' life. The dark and stormy landscape of MAURICE DE VLAMINCK, on the other hand, expressed an 'anarchist' populism; his choice of subject-matter and style was in a sense an indication of his rejection of the deliberately reactionary modernism then prevalent. ANDRÉ DERAIN took an opposing view, working in a classical style of austere realism and drawing historical support from the exhibition *Peintres de la réalité au XVII siècle*, held in 1934 at the Musée de l'Orangerie, Paris. However, it was in the landscapes of ANDRÉ DUNOYER DE SEGONZAC—with their Arcadian images of a Provence spared by the Apocalypse—that the current poetic longing for a return to the land found its truest expression.

During the war years HENRI MATISSE executed a number of major works in which he refined Cubism almost to abstraction, and painting in its purest and most expressive manner was used to exalt colour in the very fullness of form. *Notre-Dame* (1914; New York, MOMA) is a scumble of colour with a few lines that suggest a perspective, and two towers flanked by black areas. The geometry of *The Moroccans* and *Piano Lesson* (both 1916, New York, MOMA) is calmer and firmer, and accentuates the intensity of the flat, uniform areas of colour. From 1917 to 1919 he alternated between works in which the language of painting overrode representation and those through which he expressed a certain nostalgia for a more peaceful and sensual style. With the example set by Derain, his influence formed a counterbalance to that of Picasso and to the interest in abstraction, which nevertheless remained essentially foreign to French art. When Matisse lived in Nice (from 1918), he was preoccupied with colour values, but his subjects at this time are never as *intimistes* as those of ALBERT MARQUET. Like PIERRE BONNARD, whose aim to express the ineffable beauty of the world by using a dusty light to dissolve forms in his middle-class park scenes and luncheons, Matisse was always more than a mere decorator.

(ii) Dada, Surrealism and abstraction. The 'return to order' was expressed in art in other ways. Indeed, when Cubism was reduced to an ensemble of nothing more than pure form, its designs readily lent themselves to the prettiness of Art Deco, and to 'modernist' pastoral scenes and decorous allegories of Progress, often found on the walls of public rooms of ocean liners. There was a great nostalgia behind such naive images of a France supposedly living and working according to the rhythm of the seasons, and some artists saw this type of art as symptomatic of a breakdown in society against which they had to react. The Dadaists felt that art could be used as a weapon against war and the stupidity of a bankrupt society and that DADA itself could be an act of protection. The celibate machines of Francis Picabia (see fig. 29) and Marcel Duchamp's earliest ready-mades (*see* READY-MADE) and such large works as *The Bride Stripped Bare by her Bachelors, Even* (*The Large Glass*, 1915–23; Philadelphia, PA, Mus. A.; *see* DUCHAMP, MARCEL, fig. 3) display the cynicism and irreverence of their creators and the absurdity of their conception. In the 1920s Dada was taken up in Paris by the writers TRISTAN TZARA, Philippe Soupault, LOUIS ARAGON and ANDRÉ BRETON. However, Breton was aware of its limits and in 1923 he broke with Tzara and with Dada. In 1924 Breton published the *Manifeste du surréalisme*, in which he advocated the use of automatic writing to break the constraints weighing so heavily on controlled, conscious thought (*see* AUTOMATISM). For him, art was a means to free the mind, to change people's lives and to achieve a proletarian revolution, not something with an autonomous existence. There was doubt whether painting could ever be truly Surrealist, yet SALVADOR DALÍ and YVES TANGUY gave SURREALISM its most convincing images of the unfamiliar. Tanguy's 'landscapes of the

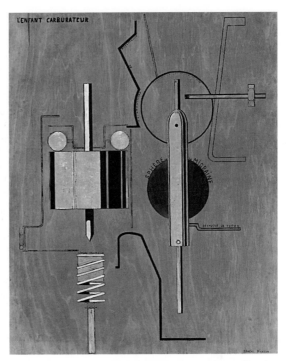

29. Francis Picabia: *Child Carburettor*, oil, enamel, metallic paint, gold leaf, pencil and crayon on stained plywood, 1.26×1.01 m, *c.* 1919 (New York, Solomon R. Guggenheim Museum)

mind' depict theatrical spaces in which cartilaginous and marbled forms cast their stony shadows (*see* SURREALISM, fig. 1). The 'paranoiac–critical' method that was Dalí's hallmark opened up 'the windows of the mind', and the extreme technical virtuosity and photographic precision of his painting captured the irrationality of the imaginative world in concrete form (*see* DALÍ, SALVADOR, fig. 1). The collages of MAX ERNST displace distant realities on to seemingly inappropriate planes, enabling them to illuminate the chance nature of objective fact. Like automatic writing, his *frottages* combine the power of dream images with a revelation of the unconscious. ANDRÉ MASSON followed the same path and, by working on his pictures from a vantage point directly above, expressed the free flow of his own inner tumult and allowed involuntary, elemental forms to emerge. JOAN MIRÓ retained no more of reality than an essential pictograph; Georges Bataille felt that his images were poetic signs ordered amid 'sunlit dust' in accordance with an 'inner model'. The artist most admired by the Surrealists, however, was Picasso, who in the 1920s produced paintings of libidinous, almost hallucinatory forms, as well as such works as *The Dance* (1925; London, Tate), full of dionysiac fury, which were a prelude to the more Surrealist-inspired *Crucifixions* (e.g. 1930; Paris, Mus. Picasso) and other works of an intense fearfulness (*see* DRAWING, colour pl. II, fig. 1). Surrealism dominated art life in France from 1925 to 1939, and in the *Second Manifeste du surréalisme* (1929) Breton set the agenda for the aesthetic debates of the 1930s by enlisting the movement in the cause of the Communist party. However, disputes, polemics, exclusions and passionate debates with the party weakened Surrealism, and the publication of the

Surrealist periodicals *Minotaure* and *Documents* hastened its drift towards anthropology. The work of Miró, Hans Arp, Masson, Ernst and Dalí, however, showed that formal invention could ultimately win out over orthodoxy.

The Surrealist uproar overshadowed another historical development that helped to confirm Paris as the premier international centre of the arts. Shortly after World War I many artists came as refugees from other countries. Establishing themselves in Montparnasse on the Left Bank in Paris, several formed a loosely constructed group known as the ECOLE DE PARIS. Among those who were part of the mythology of this cosmopolitan bohemia were AMEDEO MODIGLIANI, Tsugouharu Foujita and Moïse Kisling. CHAÏM SOUTINE, whose vehement art reflected his pain-filled life, and MARC CHAGALL, who peopled his tenderly poetic paintings with levitating figures, were also part of this group. Piet Mondrian's return to Paris from the Netherlands in 1918 was largely ignored at this time, as was the exhibition devoted to the Dutch movement De Stijl, organized in 1923 by the dealer Léonce Rosenberg. Abstraction was accepted in France only in the early 1930s, when Paris unwittingly became the international capital of abstract art after the Bauhaus in Berlin was closed down in 1933. Vasily Kandinsky settled in Paris, and Theo van Doesburg had been living there since 1929. With Jean Hélion, Otto G. Carlsund and Léon Tutundjian (1905–68), van Doesburg founded the CONCRETE ART movement in 1930. Its manifesto appeared that year, shortly after the first issue of *Cercle et carré*, the review launched by the writer Michel Seuphor and the Uruguayan painter Joaquín Torres García, and with support from Mondrian (*see* CERCLE ET CARRÉ). These ephemeral movements, opposed to Surrealism and to any form of realism, were supplanted in 1931 by the determinedly internationalist ABSTRACTION-CRÉATION group, who brought together all contemporary trends in non-figurative art, from the most rigorous geometric abstraction to the biomorphic works of HANS ARP and Willi Baumeister (*see* BIOMORPHISM).

(iii) Art, society and politics. The major debate after 1934, however, concerned art's political and social role. *Commune* magazine first questioned the role of writers and the future of painting, while Christian Zervos's *Cahiers d'art* called on artists to define the relationship of their art to society. Without necessarily adopting social realism as advocated by Aragon, many artists nevertheless believed that their purpose was no longer to decorate 'the palaces of the powerful with anodyne arabesques' but to use their art in the building of a new world. Edouard Georg (1893–1971), Henri de Waroquier (1881–1971) and MARCEL GROMAIRE were among many to explore a realism opposed to the imaginary world of the Surrealists and to the idealism of abstract art, the final passing of which was marked by Hélion's *Fallen Figure* (1939; Paris, Pompidou). The FORCES NOUVELLES group, including Henri Héraut (*b* 1894), Robert Humblot (1907–62), Jean Lasne (1911–46), Henri Jannot (*b* 1909), the Canadian Alfred Pellan, Georges Rohner (*b* 1913) and PIERRE TAL-COAT, called for a position to be taken against Impressionism and Expressionism by returning 'to drawing, to the conscientious craft of tradition, to the subject'. At this time Alberto

Giacometti (*see* GIACOMETTI, (3)) broke with Surrealism and asserted his allegiance to figurative work by painting *Still-life with Apple* (1937; priv. col.) in a sharp, 'scratched' style of drawing similar to that of Francis Gruber. ANDRÉ FOUGERON and EDOUARD PIGNON combined aspects of Cubism and Romanesque art in paintings that celebrated working-class struggles and the courage and suffering of those who fought in the Spanish Civil War (1936–9). The representation of everyday horrors gradually gave rise to the Théâtre de la Cruauté, and in 1937 the Galerie Billiet-Vorms in Paris held an exhibition, *L'Art cruel*, that included works by Masson, Picasso, Gérard Vuillamy (*b* 1909) and Dalí. This fascination with horror reached a paroxysm in 1943 with the *Hostages* series by JEAN FAUTRIER (e.g. *Head of a Hostage, No. 3*, 1943; Sceaux, Château, Mus. Ile de France). The strongest response to the horrors of the modern world was made by Picasso; his painting *Guernica* (1937; Madrid, Prado) is an allegory of universal terror, inspired by the German bombing of the Basque town of Guernica, that was described by Michel Leiris as a declaration of mourning for a dying world.

(iv) World War II and after. World War II was responsible for the decline of Paris as a major art centre, although the war and the German occupation did not entirely put an end to all art activity. Those who were nostalgic for a tradition that they believed had been corrupted by modern art now considered themselves victorious. Yet as early as 1941 an exhibition held at the Galerie Braun in Paris, *Vingt Jeunes Peintres de tradition française*, flaunted its opposition to the gerontocracy and to Maréchal's 'art and order'. It was followed in 1943 by *Douze Peintres d'aujourd'hui*, which included works by Pignon, Fougeron,

30. Maurice Estève: *Aquarium*, oil on canvas, 810×650 mm, 1944 (Paris, Pompidou, Musée National d'Art Moderne)

Jean Bazaine, Alfred Manessier, Maurice Estève and Charles Lapicque. Their art (for example see fig. 30), and that of Roger Bissière, with its universality, modernity and innovation, expresses the essence of reality by varying planes of pure colour within a palpable grid inherited from both Cubism and Romanesque stained glass. VIEIRA DA SILVA used such a grid to enclose small interior settings and landscapes containing dynamic symbols that suggested multiple perspectives, one held within another. SERGE POLIAKOFF filled his network of squares with saturated colour, and NICOLAS DE STAËL brought forms, almost completely purged of any links with reality, to the highest degree of tension, transforming his paintings into a vertical wall against which his dazzling shapes are framed.

Artists who attempted to recover a style that was quintessentially French were, with their liberated painting, expressing their faith in an illusory sense of community. However, by 1947 the Cold War had begun, and, after the expulsion of Communist ministers from the French government, the image of French art so closely associated with the Resistance movement during World War II, with Romanesque art and with Cubism, was beginning to be eroded. In 1948 works previously despised acquired greater visibility: for example, the paintings of Gruber and Bernard Buffet depicting characters in great misery. These figures bore witness to a tedious everyday existence that Gruber had in the 1930s called 'existential despair'. His nudes appear as if caged and placed in cramped rooms with tormented perspectives, not unlike Giacometti's solitary figures, who seem to shut themselves away in an atmosphere of hieratic enigma. BALTHUS combined discreet eroticism with his admiration for the Renaissance and Courbet. Fougeron, in *Parisian Women at the Market* (1948) and his publication *La Peintre à son créneau* (1948), militated for a realism in the style of Courbet or David. Several artists placed the question of style at the heart of the debate about commitment, including Léger with *The Builders* (1950; Biot, Mus. N. Fernand Léger), Pignon with his second version of *Dead Worker* (1952; Paris, Pompidou) and Picasso with *Massacre in Korea* (1951; Paris, Mus. Picasso). Picasso's *War* and *Peace* murals (1952, installed 1954; Vallauris, Mus. N. Picasso) and Matisse's designs for the Chapelle du Rosaire at Vence (1948–51) were both commissions for religious themes executed in a 'hedonist' style. In response to the debate about art's place in society, ART INFORMEL emerged, a group whose members advocated an art without tradition or future. WOLS, Fautrier, ANTONIN ARTAUD and HENRI MICHAUX were the precursors of this trend. Camille Bryen followed their example and expressed the driving urges of the unconscious mind in a style composed of hastily drawn lines. HANS HARTUNG produced works that had a lyrical style of drawing, while GEORGES MATHIEU, in his work, transformed these lines into an imperious and furious calligraphy. The unique style of PIERRE SOULAGES froze time and space in the sheer material quality of his 'black light'. Bram van Velde exorcised the absurd, keeping in check the movement of his sumptuous colours. Breton belatedly recognized the links between automatic writing and such abstract works, giving his support to Marcelle Loubchantsky (*b* 1917), Judit Reigl (*b* 1923) and SIMON HANTAÏ.

Surrealism exercised a profound influence on artistic creation at this time, leaving a heritage that included ART AUTRE (a term coined by writer and critic Michel Tapié), primitive and naive art, children's drawings and the art of the mentally ill. In 1948 Jean Dubuffet founded the Compagnie de l'Art Brut, assisted by Breton. From this came ART BRUT, in which artists 'trivialized' the figure in the manner of the writer Céline and painted in a style that constituted 'the inventive and respectful celebration of...materials, of serendipity, of the gestural'. *Cobra: Revue internationale de l'art experimental*, which appeared in 1948, was an avatar of Surrealism, yet challenged its tendency to be enthralled by the occult or Communist dogma. The magazine rejected the refined aesthetics of the type of art popular in Paris, instead favouring a kind of primitivism exemplified in the works of Jean-Michel Atlan, Etienne-Martin, Jacques Doucet and Gaston Chaissac, artists who produced drawings that plumbed the origins of untrammelled thought. Primitivism of this sort became most extreme with Wols and Michaux, whose work was, with Dubuffet's, at its furthest remove from 'cultured' painting.

In the late 1950s *Art informel* began to degenerate into formula, a vertiginous Tachism and a type of painting relying on sweeping clouds of colour that echoed Monet's late works. Such artists as Jean Degottex became interested in East Asian philosophies and religions, and created works relying heavily on Zen thought. Their quest for eternal nature was, in fact, a flight from a very different reality: that of an industrial society with its new products and cast-offs. From 1949 Jacques Mahé de la Villeglé (*b* 1926), François Dufrêne (1930–83) and RAYMOND HAINS, among others, began to replace collage with DÉCOLLAGE, in which torn posters and ready-mades created by anonymous hands figured prominently (for illustration *see* NOUVEAU RÉALISME). In the early 1950s YVES KLEIN painted his first monochromes. From 1957 he restricted them to International Klein Blue (IKB), the 'concentrate of poetic energy' and the manifestation of pure sensitivity. His mysticism, dealing with the immateriality of air, fire and emptiness, was counterposed by the plenitude of accumulation of ARMAN or the 'booby-trapped' paintings of the Swiss DANIEL SPOERRI, in which a kind of archaeology of urban life is presented. This same idea was celebrated by MARTIAL RAYSSE, who created paintings with seductive and cosmetic colours. In 1960 the critic Pierre Restany (*b* 1930) grouped these artists— as well as Mimmo Rotella, Jean Tinguely and Niki de Saint Phalle—under the heading of NOUVEAU RÉALISME. This movement closely paralleled American Pop art, which by 1964 was a dominant influence on French painting.

The exhibition *Le Mouvement*, held at the Galerie Denise René in 1955, revived the importance of geometric art. This was followed in 1960 by the founding of the GROUPE DE RECHERCHE D'ART VISUEL, which advocated collective activity and art as a form of play. Since the late 1940s ALBERTO MAGNELLI and CÉSAR DOMELA had introduced organic forms into their works to temper the rigours of abstraction, while VICTOR VASARELY systematically deployed abstraction in an optical play that successfully reflected the aesthetic preferences of an expanding society. FRANÇOIS MORELLET, for his part, placed abstraction at the service of chance and coincidence in a kind of 'minimalism' weighted with irony reminiscent of Duchamp (*see also* OP ART). Duchamp's 'assassination', played out by Gilles Aillaud (*b* 1928), Eduardo Arroyo and Antonio Recalcati (*b* 1938) in a series of paintings much like a film or cartoon, was an attempt to impose an art of intervention. The Figuration Narrative group was influenced by the Pop art of the Americans Andy Warhol and James Rosenquist and the Frenchmen Hervé Télémaque (*b* 1937), Bernard Rancillac (*b* 1931) and JACQUES MONORY, especially the last's *Murders* series (e.g. *Murder No. 20/1*, 1968; Paris, Pompidou) and *Velvet Jungle* series (e.g. *Velvet Jungle No. 10/2*, 1971; Amsterdam, Stedel. Mus.) and his use of an overall tone of Rembrandt blue to simulate photographic reproduction. The *Salle rouge pour le Vietnam* (1968), which included the artists of the Panique group, marked the limits of traditional anti-establishment commitment, while the left-wing group the Coopérative des Malassis exacerbated that tradition's 'critical realism'. The formal painting and analytical painting that dominated French art until the mid-1970s was fixed within this 'subversive' tradition and brought to it elements appropri-

ated from Nouveau Réalisme, accumulation and repetition, as well as from abstraction, gesture and line. In 1967 DANIEL BUREN, Olivier Mosset (*b* 1944), Michel Parmentier (*b* 1938) and Niele Toroni (*b* 1937) were at the very forefront of the avant-garde. Enthralled by the ideas of the American critic Clement Greenberg, they reduced painting to a simple visual utterance, using such interchangeable and infinitely reproducible elements as the circle, the vertical or horizontal band or the brushstroke repeated at regular intervals. Starting from this 'absolute zero', a number of artists, including the SUPPORTS-SUR-FACES group, André-Pierre Arnal (*b* 1939), Vincent Bioulès (*b* 1938), Louis Cane, Marc Devade (1943–83), Daniel Dezeuze (*b* 1942), Noël Dolla (*b* 1945), Toni Grand (*b* 1935), Bernard Pagès (*b* 1940), Jean-Pierre Pincemin (*b* 1944), Patrick Saytour (*b* 1935), André Valensi (*b* 1947) and Claude Viallat, went through a process in which the historical reality of a picture was analysed, so that its material elements could be concentrated upon. To this end, they used the large-scale formats and non-relational compositions of much contemporary American

31. Robert Combas: *Le Bebête à 'Roujeole' veut se taper la femme au corps de belle. Un Triangle se monte une pignolle, et le 'tueur de Folon' fait des poèmes sur 'tea-shirt' comme les habits de Castelbacouine*, oil, with rubber, on canvas, 1.64×2.07 m, 1984 (Paris, Pompidou, Musée National d'Art Moderne)

art and they also published a considerable number of texts articulating their theory and practices to denounce an alienating social order. After the publication of *Tel quel*, Sollers, Marcelin Pleynet (*b* 1933), Cane and Devade issued the review *Peinture, cahiers théoriques*. Christian Jaccard (*b* 1939), Jean-Michel Meurice (*b* 1938) and François Rouan, who succeeded in applying the method of deconstruction to the investigations of early Italian art, mirrored the subtle polemics of the other young theoreticians. Mosset painted geometric pictures similar to the American Robert Mangold; Buren adapted his stripes and lines to the architecture of the settings in which he exhibited; Toroni, imperturbable, continued to repeat his brushstrokes; Cane and Bioulès renewed their links with figurative painting; Viallat continued to paint forms, identifying them by marking gesture and line on supports without frames.

In the early 1970s a number of artists rejected this 'Matisse-like' painting and instead, as did BEN, drew inspiration for their combination of performance and installation from Duchamp and the FLUXUS group. In the same vein, Bertrand Lavier and Gérard Colin-Thiébault (*b* 1946) dealt with the concept of the ready-made as a way of questioning the whole idea of representation. Jean Le Gac (*b* 1936), in his narrative art, also questioned this idea, as did those who used the medium of photography in a systematic way. CHRISTIAN BOLTANSKI, in an archaeological search for that which history erases, also exploited the capacity of photography to embalm the subject. Sarkis (*b* 1938) used it to freeze memory, words and images into dramatically constructed scenes, while ANNETTE MESSAGER, SOPHIE CALLE, Jean-Louis Schoellkopf (*b* 1946), Georges Rousse (*b* 1947), Jean-Marc Bustamente (*b* 1952), Patrick Faigenbaum (*b* 1954) and Patrick Toscani were among many who were neither painters nor photographers, but who used photographs in their work. Around 1980 Gérard Garouste, Jean-Michel Alberola (*b* 1953), Alain Séchas (*b* 1955), Jean-Charles Blais (*b* 1956), Robert Combas (*b* 1957), Philippe Favier (*b* 1957), Denis Laget (*b* 1956) and Hervé Di Rosa (*b* 1959) produced finely crafted works that were inspired by Symbolist art or the savage violence of 'street culture' (see fig. 31). Other quite separate paths were taken: François Perrodin (*b* 1956) executed Minimalist works; Bernard Frize (*b* 1949) responded to Picabia by creating a scholarly and refined art; Fabrice Hybert (*b* 1961) dealt with 'ecological' dereliction; and Bernard Piffaretti (*b* 1955) chose as his theme the play on the reproduction of representation. From 1970 French art more or less followed trends first established in New York and Cologne; some considered that the increasing numbers of exhibition venues reduced painting to the level of merchandise, condemning it to represent itself.

BIBLIOGRAPHY
W. S. Rubin: *Dada and Surrealist Art* (New York and London, 1969)
J. Clair: *L'Art en France: Une Nouvelle Génération* (Paris, 1972)
——: 'Le Retour à l'ordre dans les arts plastiques et l'architecture, 1919–1925', *Actes du second colloque d'histoire de l'art contemporain de Saint-Etienne: Saint-Etienne, 1974*
'Art et idéologies: L'Art en occident, 1945–1949', *Actes du troisième colloque d'histoire de l'art contemporain de Saint-Etienne: Saint-Etienne, 1976*
Les Années 30 en France (exh. cat., Saint-Etienne, Mus. A. & Indust., 1979)
'L'Art face à la crise: L'Art en occident, 1919–1939', *Actes du quatrième colloque d'histoire de l'art contemporain de Saint-Etienne: Saint-Etienne, 1979*
J.-L. Daval: *Journal des avant-gardes, les années vingt, les années trente* (Geneva, 1980)
Paris-Paris, 1937–1957 (exh. cat., Paris, Pompidou, 1981)
B. Ceysson: *De l'invention de l'abstraction au surréalisme, 1910–1930*, iii of *La Grande Histoire de la peinture* (Geneva, 1982)
P. Daix: *Le Journal du cubisme* (Geneva, 1982)
J. Lassaigne: *Les Données de la figuration*, iv of *La Grande Histoire de la peinture* (Geneva, 1982)
P. Restany: *L'Aventure de l'art abstrait: De l'esthétique à l'éthique, 1945–1965*, v of *La Grande Histoire de la peinture* (Paris, 1982)
Aftermath, France, 1945–54: New Images of Man (exh. cat., London, Barbican A.G., 1982)
New French Painting (exh. cat. by J. Sans, Oxford, MOMA, 1984)
L. Bertrand-Dorléac: *Histoire de l'art, Paris, 1940–1944: Ordre national: Traditions et modernités*, preface M. Winock (Paris, 1986)
B. Ceysson and others: *Vingt-cinq ans d'art en France, 1960–1985* (Paris, 1986)
C. Millet: *L'Art contemporain en France* (Paris, 1987)
L'Art en Europe: Les Années décisives, 1945–1953 (exh. cat., Saint-Etienne, Mus. A. Mod., 1987)
Paris, 1937: L'Art indépendant (exh. cat., Paris, Mus. A. Mod. Ville Paris, 1987)
J.-P. Bouillon: *Journal de l'Art Déco, 1903–1940* (Geneva, 1988)
Les Années 50 (exh. cat., Paris, Pompidou, 1988)
L'Ecriture griffée (exh. cat., Saint-Etienne, Mus. A. Mod., 1991)
Paris Post-war: Art and Existentialism, 1945–1955 (exh. cat., London, Tate, 1993)

BERNARD CEYSSON

IV. Sculpture.

The tradition of stone sculpture appears to be very ancient in France, at least in the south, for some reliefs decorated with schematized figures, from Entremont (Aix, Mus. Granet) and Ensérune (Ensérune, Mus.; both 2nd century BC), for example, predate the arrival of the Romans in the mid-1st century BC. The Romans introduced monumental sculpture, as seen in the decoration of many triumphal arches, steles and statues, for example at ARAUSIO (Orange) and Arles (*see* ARLES, §1(i)). Votive objects in wood and terracotta were common, while bronzeworking is attested by figures of a local character. After the barbarian invasions of the 4th century AD, the practice of these crafts declined.

BIBLIOGRAPHY
L. Benoist: *La Sculpture française* (Paris, 1945)

1. Before *c.* 1500. 2. *c.* 1500–*c.* 1600. 3. *c.* 1600–*c.* 1700. 4. *c.* 1700–*c.* 1814. 5. *c.* 1814–*c.* 1900. 6. After *c.* 1900.

1. BEFORE *c.* 1500.

(i) Early medieval. (ii) Gothic.

(i) Early medieval. Under the Merovingians the marble workshops of the Pyrenean quarries continued to produce sculpted capitals and sarcophagi, for example at JOUARRE ABBEY. Generally, however, stone sculpture was confined to reliefs for screens, as in the mid-7th-century choir-screen from St Pierre-aux-Nonnains, Metz (now Metz, Mus. A. & Hist.), decorated mainly with ornamental interlace, foliate and geometric motifs, although occasionally biblical subjects and Christian symbols appear (*see* MEROVINGIAN ART). In the Carolingian period, stucco was also worked, for example at Germigny-des-Prés (*see* GERMIGNY-DES-PRÉS, §2).

The development of stone sculpture in the 11th century did not follow a uniform progression (*see* ROMANESQUE, §III, 1(ii)). Shortly before 1050, at Saint-Benoît-sur-Loire

32. *Pentecost* scene (or *Christ's Mission to the Apostles*), limestone, tympanum of the central nave portal, Ste Madeleine, Vézelay, *c.* 1120–50

sculptors carved foliate capitals close to the Corinthian form, which were sometimes enlivened by narrative scenes (*see* SAINT-BENOÎT-SUR-LOIRE, fig. 2). In Languedoc, apart from some early experiments in the Pyrenees, as at SAINT-GENIS-DES-FONTAINES, large-scale figure sculpture was developed only at the workshop of BERNARDUS GELDUINUS at St Sernin, Toulouse, at the end of the 11th century (*see* TOULOUSE, §2, (i)(b)). The question of the beginnings of Romanesque sculpture in France is complicated by the difficulties of dating related buildings in northern Italy, but the Italian developments in sculpture must have preceded those of France (*see* ITALY, §IV, 2). Cluny Abbey, however, by reason of its importance, must also have exercised a wide influence extending as far as Italy.

A monumental carving style first appeared on capitals. In Normandy and northern France, they were carved mainly with ornamental motifs, foliage, faces and interlace, then, towards the end of the 11th century, with geometric motifs. Elsewhere in France—on the Loire, in Burgundy and Languedoc—historiated capitals appear, but the first great sculptured portals are found only from *c.* 1100. One of the earliest, the Porte Miègeville at St Sernin, Toulouse, bears the *Ascension* on the lintel and tympanum (*see* TOULOUSE, fig. 3). The portal at St Pierre, Moissac (*see* MOISSAC, ST PIERRE, fig. 2) is subdivided by a carved trumeau (for illustration *see* COLUMN STATUE) and bears themes drawn from the Apocalyptic vision, with a deeper relief in the upper part to render the carvings more visible. The figures are placed hierarchically and are packed in to fill the surface. No attempts were made realistically to

represent proportion and expression, nor anatomy, draperies and perspective. Romanesque sculpture consists of highly schematized scenes, which respond to spiritual rather than to naturalistic concerns.

Sculptors' styles were remarkably varied, however, and there are great differences between the angular, agitated figures at Autun Cathedral in Burgundy (*see* AUTUN, fig. 2) and the more massive and static appearance of either the cloister figures at Moissac in Languedoc (*see* MOISSAC, ST PIERRE, fig. 1) or in the sculpture at Ste Foy, Conques, in the Rouergue (*see* CONQUES, STE FOY, fig. 2). Furthermore, large religious scenes on portals and capitals were mixed with a fantastic repertory of animals, monsters and hybrid figures, which reveal popular traditions, eastern influences and barbarian and pagan reminiscences. In Burgundy, sculpture from Cluny Abbey (the hemicycle capitals and fragments from the west portal; *see* CLUNIAC ORDER, figs 1 and 2) influenced the whole region. Its sense of relief, dynamism and attention to expression are seen also at the portals of Ste Madeleine, Vézelay (see fig. 32; for detail *see* VÉZELAY, STE MADELEINE, fig. 2), as well as at Autun, where the *Last Judgement* is, quite exceptionally, signed, by GISLEBERTUS. In western France, in Poitou and Saintonge, portals rarely have tympana but the archivolts and wall surfaces of façades are covered with reliefs and friezes, as at ST PIERRE, AULNAY, and Notre-Dame-la-Grande, Poitiers (*see* POITIERS, fig. 4). South-eastern France is characterized by sculpture of Classical inspiration at SAINT-GILLES-DU-GARD ABBEY and at St Trophîme, Arles (*see* ARLES, §2), where figures in high relief stand under architraves.

For carving in wood, lime, poplar and walnut were most popular. Some remarkable large-scale statues in wood were produced in this period: Virgin-reliquaries seated on thrones, for example at St Philibert, Tournus and Saint-Nectaire (Puy-de-Dôme), and coloured figures of the crucified Christ, as at St Pierre, Moissac, and Le Puy. These stylized and hieratic figures, with their simplified facial features, have a profoundly religious grandeur.

(ii) Gothic. Gothic sculpture originated in the Ile-de-France at the same time as the new architectural style, in the mid-12th century (*see* GOTHIC, §III, 1(i)), while Romanesque was still perpetuated in southern France. The portals of SAINT-DENIS ABBEY are mutilated, but the west ('Royal') portal of Chartres Cathedral exemplifies the new style (*see* CHARTRES, fig. 3). The hierarchical positioning of the figures and the stylized forms are Romanesque characteristics, but these are now combined with rigorous composition and the perfect adaptation of the sculptures to the architectural setting: column statues fit their embrasures exactly; tympana are less crammed with figures; reliefs are more vigorous and the iconographic programme is more coherent. This style was highly influential in the second half of the 12th century, with repercussions as far away as Santiago de Compostela Cathedral (Portica de la Gloria) in northern Spain.

Around 1200 the influence of Classical sculpture is suggested by attempts to represent more coordinated and supple forms, idealized facial types and fine, simple draperies (*see* MULDENFALTENSTIL). This style can be seen at Sens Cathedral (*see* SENS, §1(ii)) and, at the beginning of the 13th century, on the transept portals of Chartres Cathedral (see CHARTRES, fig. 4) and in the Visitation workshop on the west front of Reims Cathedral (see REIMS, §IV, 1(ii)). Iconographic themes had also evolved. The *Coronation of the Virgin*, represented for the first time at Senlis Cathedral (c. 1170; see SENLIS, §1), was connected with the Glorification of Christ and the Triumph of the Church. In the 13th century, additional subjects included local saints, biblical scenes and the illustration of scientific knowledge and daily life. The façade of Amiens Cathedral (see AMIENS, §1(ii)) constitutes a typical example of the monumental sculpture of the great cathedrals: the trumeau Christ (the 'Beau Dieu') and the *Last Judgement* on the central portal are flanked by portals dedicated to the Virgin and to diocesan saints. Figure sculpture was henceforth reserved for façades and abandoned on capitals.

Towards the middle of the 13th century, statuary on portals and in interiors became more independent of the architecture, at the cathedrals of Reims and Bourges, for example, and the Apostles in the Sainte-Chapelle (see PARIS, fig. 35). Later medieval portals show a development towards more ornamental forms: niches with tall canopies, pierced tympana and low-relief panels. Tombs were surmounted by effigies, and altarpieces, initially of modest size, grew increasingly larger.

The styles of sculpture also changed and reflected the evolution of contemporary thought. Figures were humanized and became more animated and expressive, as in the work of the JOSEPH MASTER (see MASTERS, ANONYMOUS, AND MONOGRAMMISTS, §I; and REIMS, fig. 5) at Reims Cathedral in the mid-13th century. Although verisimilitude of facial features and perspective were not predominant artistic concerns, effigies and donor statues demonstrate an increasing interest in portraiture. At the same time a style characterized by elegant, idealized figures with elongated proportions and sinuous forms was emerging, which can already be seen in the *Virgin* (c. 1250) on the north-transept portal of Notre-Dame, Paris. It has been associated with the tastes of princely patrons, and in the 14th century it was combined with artistic influences from Italy, notably through contact with Angevin Naples and the Avignon papacy, to form the so-called International Gothic, a courtly, refined and slightly unreal style, represented in such sculptures as the fireplace statues in the hall of Jean, Duc de Berry's palace in Poitiers (see GOTHIC, fig. 29). There was also more secular sculpture in the 14th century, the result of increasing lay patronage; and owing to the survival of royal and aristocratic accounts, the names of sculptors begin to be known, many revealing Netherlandish origins: JEAN PÉPIN DE HUY, JEAN DE LIÈGE (i), ANDRÉ BEAUNEVEU of Valenciennes and JEAN DE CAMBRAI.

From the end of the 14th century, a new stylistic tradition, characterized by agitated gestures and movements, and coarser, more sorrowful expressions, developed alongside this courtly style. Religious crisis, the misfortunes brought on by epidemics and war, and a more personal devotional emphasis have all been associated with its formation. New subjects were represented, first in eastern France: the *Virgin of Mercy*, the *Ecce homo* and the *Entombment*. The style is exemplified especially in the

work of CLAUS SLUTER, who arrived (c. 1385) at the Burgundian court in Dijon from the Netherlands. The statues of his ducal patrons for the portal and the prophets for the Well of Moses (see fig. 33) at the Charterhouse of Champmol (see DIJON, §IV, 1(ii)) introduced a new realism, which was combined with a lyrical vigour in the voluminous, deep and strongly shadowed draperies.

The influence of Sluter's honest and dramatic style is seen in all subsequent 15th-century sculpture. The Burgundian court at Dijon became an international centre, where Sluter's nephew, Claus de Werve from the northern Netherlands, Juan de la Huerta from Spain and Antoine Le Moiturier from France succeeded one another as ducal sculptors. A more elegant and sober style was maintained in the Bourbonnais and the Loire Valley with Jacques Morel, to whom is sometimes attributed the delightful alabaster effigy of *Agnès Sorel* (d 1450) in Loches Castle, and with Michel Colombe, sculptor of the funerary monument of *Francis II, Duke of Brittany, and his Wife, Marguerite de Foix* (1499–1507) in Nantes Cathedral (see §2 below and COLOMBE, (1)). The two influences spread, sometimes juxtaposed, as in the statues of the Albi Cathedral choir-screen (see ALBI, §I), or even combined, as in the *Entombment* (1496) in the Benedictine abbey church at Solesmes. The design of the *Entombment* shows, moreover, the arrival in France of Italian decorators, who executed the framing pilasters and introduced Renaissance

33. Claus Sluter: detail from the Well of Moses (1395–1405), limestone, Charterhouse of Champmol, near Dijon

motifs into France. The first wave of Italian influence was in Provence, geographically close to Italy, where Francesco Laurana was summoned from Naples by René I, Duke of Anjou, and where, in Avignon and Marseille, he worked until 1481. In Normandy, Cardinal Georges I d'Amboise, Archbishop of Rouen and Viceroy of Milan, brought Italian sculptors to the château of Gaillon, where they worked from 1502. In the Ile-de-France and the Loire Valley they were imported by Charles VIII (*reg* 1483–98) and Louis XII (*reg* 1498–1515) in the aftermaths of their campaigns in Italy. Guido Mazzoni was the first Italian Renaissance sculptor to work at the French Court, arriving from Naples in 1495. His major work, the tomb of *Charles VIII* in Saint-Deris Abbey, near Paris, sculpted after the King's death in 1498, was destroyed in 1798, but engravings show a sarcophagus, a kneeling king and four angels of a somewhat French pattern, with Italianate roundels along the sides.

BIBLIOGRAPHY

H. Focillon: *L'Art des sculpteurs romans* (Paris, 1931)
A. Gardner: *Medieval Sculpture in France* (Cambridge, 1931)
M. Aubert: *La Sculpture française au moyen-âge* (Paris, 1946)
E. Panofsky: *Abbot Suger on the Abbey Church of St Denis and its Art Treasures* (New Jersey, 1946)
L. Reau: *L'Art réligieux du moyen âge: La Sculpture* (Paris, 1946)
J. Evans: *Art in Medieval France* (London, 1948)
L. Lefrancois-Pillion: *L'Art du XIVe siècle en France* (Paris, 1954)
T. Muller: *Sculpture in the Netherlands, Germany, France and Spain, 1400–1500*, Pelican Hist. A. (Harmondsworth, 1966)
R. Branner: *Chartres Cathedral* (New York, 1969)
Y. Christe: *Les Grands Portails romans* (Geneva, 1969)
W. Forsyth: *The Entombment of Christ: French Sculptures of the XVth and XVIth Centuries* (Cambridge, 1970)
W. Sauerländer: *Gotische Skulptur in Frankreich, 1140–1270* (Munich and Paris, 1970; Eng. trans., London, 1972)
Les Fastes du gothique: Le Siècle de Charles V (exh. cat., ed. F. Baron; Paris, Grand Pal., 1981)
E. Vergnolle: *Saint-Benoît-sur-Loire et la sculpture du XIe siècle* (Paris, 1985)

ANNE PRACHE

2. *c.* 1500–*c.* 1600. At Cardinal Georges I d'Amboise's château at Gaillon the influence of Italian artists was felt initially through imported works of art, heralded by the arrival in 1506 of the Garden Fountain (dismantled 1759) carved specifically for the location by Antonio della Porta (*see* PORTA, DELLA, (1)) and his nephew Pace Gagini. The tomb of *Raoul de Lannoy and Jeanne de Poix* (1507–8) in the parish church of Folleville in Picardy (for illustration *see* GAGINI, (4)), also carved in Italy by della Porta and Gagini, is decorated along the face of the monument with roundels, flanked with putti, in a chastely simple manner that is characteristically Italian and oddly at variance with the richly ornamented Gothic niche in which the sarcophagus has been placed. In the Ile-de-France a series of royal tombs commissioned from Italian sculptors by Charles VIII (*reg* 1483–98), Louis XII (*reg* 1498–1515) and Francis I (*reg* 1515–47) introduced a national taste for the Italian manner, generally modified through the continuance of local traditions (*see* §1 above). The tomb commissioned in 1502 by Louis XII from Girolamo Viscardi of Genoa and other Italian sculptors in memory of the dukes of Orléans (ex-church of the Celestine, Paris; Saint-Denis Abbey) is derived from a French type, with a reclining figure on the sarcophagus. However, the tomb's most striking feature, the Twelve Apostles in classical niches along the sides of the sarcophagus, inserted in the place of the traditional weepers, has no precedent in French art. Louis XII's own tomb in Saint-Denis, commissioned by Francis I from Antonio Giusti (1479–1519) and Giovanni Giusti (1485–1549) and completed in 1531 (*see* SAINT-DENIS ABBEY, fig. 7), is even more frankly Italianate, translating the traditional French *gisants* into Italian statuettes and emphasizing the four sides of the monument with large statues of seated Virtues facing outwards, suggesting some knowledge of Michelangelo's designs for the tomb of *Julius II* (completed 1547; Rome, S Pietro in Vincoli).

The first French sculptor to imitate the Italians with equal skill was Michel Colombe, although his development is difficult to assess, since the earliest surviving sculptures with which his name is associated were made in the early 16th century when he was already in his sixties. The most elaborate is the funerary monument of *Francis II, Duke of Brittany, and his Wife, Marguerite de Foix* (1499–1507; Nantes Cathedral; for illustration *see* COLOMBE, (1)). It was originally attributed to Jérôme de Fiesole, who may have been responsible for some of the Italianate details, while the involvement of the painter Jean Perréal, who had a knowledge of contemporary Italian painting and who is accredited with the general design of the monument, must also explain some of the Italian influence in the ornament. Nevertheless, the conception of the tomb, flanked with the four Cardinal Virtues, is purely French and is derived from the vigorous tradition of Gothic sculpture in the area around Tours, where Colombe is recorded as being active from 1473. The result is a remarkably homogeneous fusion of influences. Colombe's relief altarpiece of *St George and the Dragon* (see fig. 34), carved within a frame of arabesques and bucrania by Jérôme Pacherot, was commissioned by Cardinal Georges I d'Amboise for the chapel at the château of Gaillon. It is more purely Italianate and probably reflects both the taste of the Cardinal and the concentration of work by Italian sculptors in Normandy in the period when it was carved.

During the early part of the 16th century most of the secular work inspired by Italian sources tended to be ornamental, while religious work tended to be figurative. This tendency was dramatically altered by the advent of the second generation of Italian sculptors in France, centred on Francis I's new château at Fontainebleau (rebuilding and enlargements begun 1528; *see* FONTAINEBLEAU, §1): ROSSO FIORENTINO arrived in 1530 to work there, and FRANCESCO PRIMATICCIO came in 1532. The Galerie François I in the château, with its rich combination of panels in fresco and stucco figures in high relief, marked the arrival of a wall-painting tradition deriving from the work of Raphael, Michelangelo and Giulio Romano, in which the element of sculpture was given a new emphasis. Although stone-carving played little part in the work at Fontainebleau, the elegant, elongated figures in stucco, which have an essential role in the overall aesthetic effect, had a lasting influence on the French tradition of sculpture in stone or bronze (see fig. 43 below; *see also* FONTAINE-BLEAU SCHOOL).

The development of this distinctively French variant of international MANNERISM was reinforced by the arrival of Benvenuto Cellini at the French Court in 1540. The two certain works that survive from his stay in France, the *Nymph of Fontainebleau* (*c.* 1542–3; Paris, Louvre) and the

34. Michel Colombe: *George and the Dragon*, marble relief, 1.75×2.72 m, 1508–9 (Paris, Musée du Louvre)

gold and enamel salt of Francis I (1540–43; Vienna, Ksthist. Mus.; *see* CELLINI, BENVENUTO, fig. 4), show a debt to Michelangelo's reclining allegorical figures on the Medici tombs (begun 1521) in the New Sacristy of S Lorenzo, Florence, transforming them into an elegant, decorative ideal that was much admired and imitated in France long after Cellini had returned to Italy in 1545. The style was developed by PIERRE BONTEMPS, who worked with Primaticcio at Fontainebleau; by JACQUIOT PONCE, who collaborated on the tombs of *Francis I* (1559–62) and *Henry II and Catherine de' Medici* (both Saint-Denis Abbey; *see* SAINT-DENIS ABBEY, fig. 8); by Jean Goujon, whose high-relief sculpture (1552–5; *in situ* but restored) on the Cour Carrée of the Palais du Louvre and reliefs (vertical ones *in situ*; horizontal ones Paris, Louvre; *see* GOUJON, JEAN, fig. 1) on the Fountain of the Innocents (1547–9; Paris, Place des Innocents; *see* FOUNTAIN, fig. 4) transposed the style of the Fontainebleau stuccoists to Paris; and by GERMAIN PILON, much of whose work derives from his early association with Primaticcio. Although Pilon's style shares a common source with Goujon's, the former's sculpture marks a break with the linear, elegant manner of the latter, adopting an expressive realism in his tomb sculptures for *Henry II* and *Chancellor René de Birague* (bronze, 1584–5) and *Valentine Balbiani* (marble, 1573–4; both Paris, Louvre). This realism was widely imitated by his followers, including Barthélemy Prieur in the bronze *Monument for the Heart of Constable Anne de* *Montmorency* (1571; Paris, Louvre) and the marble and bronze wall monument to *Christophe de Thou* (1582–5; Paris, Louvre; Saint-Denis Abbey) and Barthélemy Tremblay, Simon Guillain and Jean Warin, whose work continued the tradition of Pilon well into the 17th century.

BIBLIOGRAPHY
Lami
C. Martin: *La Renaissance en France: L'Architecture et la décoration* (Paris, 1910)
H. David: *De Sluter à Sambin: Essai critique sur la sculpture et le décor monumental en Bourgogne au XVe et au XVIe siècles: La Fin du moyen âge* (Paris, 1933)
F. Gébelin: *Le Style renaissance en France*, Arts, Styles et Techniques (Paris, 1942), pp. 21–30
P. Du Colombier: *L'Art renaissance en France*, Nouvelle Encyclopédie Illustrée de l'Art Français (Paris, 1945), pp. 51–74
A. Blunt: *Art and Architecture in France, 1500–1700*, Pelican Hist. A. (Harmondsworth, 1953, rev. 4/1980/R 1988)
W. H. Forsyth: *The Entombment of Christ: French Sculptures of the Fifteenth and Sixteenth Centuries* (Cambridge, MA, 1970)
L. Gillet: 'La Renaissance', *Histoire de l'art français*, i ([Paris], 1977), pp. 370–78
Description raisonnée des sculptures du Musée du Louvre: Renaissance française, intro. by J. Thirion, Paris, Louvre cat., ii (Paris, 1978)
A. Erlande-Brandenburg: *The Abbey Church of Saint-Denis*, Les Belles Eglises de Paris, ii (Paris, 1984)
Colloque de Fontainebleau organisé par l'Association Henri IV 1989 et le Musée national du château de Fontainebleau. Les Arts au temps d'Henri IV: Fontainebleau, 1989
Actes du colloque organisé au Musée du Louvre par le Service culturel. Germain Pilon et les sculpteurs français de la Renaissance: Paris 1990

3. *c.* 1600–*c.* 1700. As the importance of Fontainebleau declined in the early 1600s, portraiture became the most

35. Pietro Francavilla: *Slave*, bronze, h. 1.55 m, cast 1618 (Paris, Musée du Louvre); from the pedestal for the equestrian statue of *Henry IV* by Giambologna (destr. 1796)

was distinct from the Italian or Italo-Flemish manner prevalent in French sculpture during this period. For example, the robust elegance of the four bronze *Slaves* (see fig. 35), made by Pietro Francavilla for the base of the statue of *Henry IV* on the Pont Neuf but not cast until 1618, betrays the sculptor's training in the studio of Giambologna and is characteristic of the Mannerist tendency in French sculpture, which remained strong in Paris until the return of JACQUES SARAZIN from Rome in 1628. Sarazin had worked in Rome since 1610 and had acquired first-hand knowledge of the work of Carlo Maderno, Domenichino and François Du Quesnoy. Like Simon Vouet, who returned from Rome in the same period and became an important influence on the next generation of painters (*see* §III, 3 above), Sarazin established the classicizing ideals of early 17th-century Italian art in France through his many pupils. His quiet manner, combining solid academic forms, lightly idealized, with ample, well-modelled draperies, partly based on the Antique, adapted easily to different circumstances and was equally effective in the architectural sculpture on the Pavillon de l'Horloge of the Palais du Louvre (see fig. 36); in the four large stucco angels on the high altar of St Nicolas-des-Champs, Paris (*c.* 1629; *in situ*); or in the bronze groups designed by him for the *Monument for the Heart of Henri II de Bourbon, Prince de Condé* (1648–63; ex-St Paul–St Louis, Paris; Chantilly, Mus. Condé; for illustration *see* SARAZIN, JACQUES). These works are all characterized by a formal

36. Jacques Sarazin: stone caryatids on the Pavillon de l'Horloge of the Palais du Louvre (now Musée du Louvre), Paris, 1639–42

significant form of sculpture. The most important work of this period, Giambologna's bronze equestrian statue of *Henry IV* (destr. 1796), erected on the Pont Neuf in Paris in 1614, was the first in a line of equestrian portraits of successive monarchs from Henry IV (*reg* 1589–1610) to Louis XVI (*reg* 1774–92), all ultimately derived from the antique statue of *Marcus Aurelius* (2nd century AD; Rome, Mus. Capitolino). Apart from Bernini, whose brief visit to Paris in 1665 led to the production of an absurdly unsatisfactory equestrian statue of *Louis XIV* (1669–77), which was later altered by François Girardon but survives in the gardens at the château of Versailles, Italian sculptors were not, on the whole, employed by the French Court after 1614. However, Italian influences remained so strong in the early decades of the 17th century that it is difficult to distinguish a specifically French style of sculpture that beauty, combined with study from the model and a classical restraint, which dominated sculpture in the second half of the 17th century.

Contemporary Italian sculpture also influenced work in Paris, largely through the brothers François Anguier and Michel Anguier (*see* ANGUIER) and their younger contemporary PIERRE PUGET, who went to Italy long after Sarazin had returned and absorbed the later influences of Bernini, Alessandro Algardi and Pietro da Cortona. Puget, probably the most accomplished sculptor of the three, might have filled a role equal to that taken by Charles Le Brun in Court painting, but Jean-Baptiste Colbert's refusal to employ him in the team of sculptors at the château of Versailles limited his immediate influence. His *Milo of Crotona Attacked by a Lion* (marble, 1670–82; Paris, Louvre; *see* PUGET, PIERRE, fig. 1), which combined elements of Puget's work with a debt to the antique *Laokoon* (Rome, Vatican, Mus. Pio-Clementino), brought him a late celebrity when it was set up in the gardens at Versailles. However, he did not follow this with work of much significance, and his Italianate Baroque style was short-lived.

The huge enterprise at Versailles (*see* VERSAILLES, §§1 and 2), which became the focus of French sculpture in the second half of the 17th century, was dominated by Sarazin's pupils. The earliest sculptural work was commissioned for the gardens in the early 1660s, changing as the design for the château and the gardens became more ambitious. In the first instance the work was confined to decorative terms and a handful of statues, executed by Louis Lerambert II, the Anguier brothers, Thibault Poissant, Nicolas Legendre, Philippe de Buyster and others. However, when Colbert placed Le Brun in control of the overall planning in 1666, important commissions were awarded to Le Brun's protégés, the sculptors FRANÇOIS GIRARDON, Thomas Regnaudin, Gaspard Marsy, Balthazard Marsy and Jean Tuby.

In the same year Colbert sent Charles Errard le fils to Rome as the first director of the new Académie de France (*see* §XV below). Most of the great names among the sculptors of the succeeding generations (Nicolas Coustou, Robert Le Lorrain, Edme Bouchardon, Lambert-Sigisbert Adam (ii), René-Michel Slodtz and their successors) went to this academy, having won the Prix de Rome in France. This system made an institution from a practice common for nearly a century and ensured the continuing influence of contemporary Italian art and Classical sculpture on the work of French sculptors.

Like his many rivals, Girardon had been to Rome in the late 1640s. His debt to the classicizing style of Sarazin is evident in the marble group *Apollo Tended by the Nymphs*, commissioned from him in 1666 for the Grotto of Thetis at Versailles (moved to the Bosquet des Bains d'Apollon, 1774), which is replete with references to the Antique but is composed more like a painting than a sculpture (*see* GROTTO, fig. 2). Similarly, Girardon's relief of the *Bath of Nymphs* (lead, formerly gilded, 1668–70; *in situ*) for the gardens at Versailles is like a translation into sculpture of Domenichino's *Diana with Nymphs at Play* (1618; Rome, Gal. Borghese). His *Rape of Proserpina* (marble, 1677–99; Versailles, Château; *see* GIRARDON, FRANÇOIS, fig. 1) is derived from Bernini's group of the same subject (1621–

2; Rome, Gal. Borghese) but is tamed by a certain restraint that 17th-century French sculptors habitually imposed on the freer inventions of their Italian contemporaries.

Girardon remained the most prominent of the sculptors working at Versailles until he was eclipsed by ANTOINE COYZEVOX, whose lighter manner was more in keeping with the direction of Court taste after the fall of Le Brun than the formalized style of Girardon. Coyzevox's style derives from the same sources—Sarazin, Bernini and the Antique—but of these, the Antique was the least sustained. Unusually, he had not been to Italy, and he acquired his knowledge of Bernini at second-hand or through Bernini's portrait bust of *Louis XIV* (1665; Versailles, Château), which became the pattern for his own many portrait busts. His monuments for the tombs of *Cardinal Mazarin* (with Jean Tuby and Etienne Le Hongre; 1689–93; Paris, Chapel of the Inst. France; for illustration *see* COYZEVOX, ANTOINE) and *Jean-Baptiste Colbert* (with Tuby; 1685–93; Paris, St Eustache) include bronze figures that derive from Sarazin but have an added liveliness typical of the work that he executed for the Court and for private commissions.

Lami

BIBLIOGRAPHY

P. Francastel: *La Sculpture de Versailles: Essai sur les origines et l'évolution du goût classique en France* (Paris, 1930)
P. Du Colombier: *Le Style Henri IV–Louis XIII*, Arts, Styles et Techniques (Paris, 1941), pp. 86–92
C. Mauricheau-Beaupré: *L'Art au XVIIe siècle en France*, Nouvelle Encyclopédie Illustrée de l'Art Français, 2 vols (Paris, 1946–7)
P. Pradel: *L'Art au siècle de Louis XIV* (Lausanne, 1949)
A. Blunt: *Art and Architecture in France, 1500–1700*, Pelican Hist. A. (Harmondsworth, 1953, rev. 4/1980/R 1988)
P. Pradel: *La Sculpture du XVIIe siècle au Musée du Louvre* (Paris, 1958)
F. Gébelin: *L'Epoque Henri IV et Louis XIII*, Le Lys d'Or: Histoire de l'Art Français (Paris, 1969), pp. 35–54
V. Beyer: *La Sculpture française du XVIIe siècle au Musée du Louvre* (Bergamo, 1977)
L. Gillet: 'L'Art classique', *Histoire de l'art français*, ii ([Paris], 1977), pp. 36–8, 75–6
F. Souchal: *French Sculptors of the 17th and 18th Centuries: The Reign of Louis XIV*, 3 vols (Oxford, 1977–87); suppl. vol. (London and Boston, 1993)
A. Gibbon: *Bronzes français du grand siècle* ([Paris], 1985)
M. Martin: *Les Monuments équestres de Louis XIV: Une Grande Entreprise de propagande monarchique* (Paris, 1986)
F. Souchal: 'La Sculpture', *Le XVIIe siècle: Diversité et cohérence* (Paris, 1992), pp. 375–83
J.-R. Gaborit: *La Sculpture française*, Paris, Louvre cat. (Paris, 1993)

4. *c.* 1700–*c.* 1814. Sculpture, more than any other art in 18th-century France, depended on the patronage of the Crown, and with the suspension of the work at Versailles in the last years of the 17th century, the scope for new sculpture was restricted. The laying out of gardens (begun 1679) for the royal residence at the château of MARLY (1679–83; destr. 19th century) provided new opportunities for Antoine Coyzevox and for the younger generation of the Coustou brothers, Nicolas and Guillaume (*see* COUSTOU, (1) and (2)), and for RENÉ FRÉMIN and ROBERT LE LORRAIN. These sculptors followed the pattern of François Girardon and his contemporaries, making the obligatory trip to Rome and returning to France more ostensibly influenced by the work of Bernini and 17th-century painters than by the works of the Ancients. The sculptures commissioned for Marly are, in the main, light-hearted, following the example of Coyzevox's *Flora*, *Pan* and a

37. Edme Bouchardon: Fountain of the Four Seasons, marble, 1739–45, Rue de Grenelle, Paris

Hamadryad (all Paris, Louvre), commissioned in 1708 to form a group with Nicolas Coustou's seated marble figures of *Adonis*, the *Nymph with a Quiver* and the *Nymph with a Dove* (all 1708–10; Paris, Louvre). Nicolas Coustou's *Apollo* and Guillaume Coustou's *Daphne* (both 1711–14; Paris, Louvre) were directly inspired by Bernini's *Apollo and Daphne* (1622–4; Rome, Gal. Borghese). The pair of horse-tamers (marble, 1739–45; both Paris, Louvre; copies Paris, Place de la Concorde; for illustration *see* COUSTOU, (2)), sculpted by Guillaume Coustou towards the end of his life for Marly, seem, self-consciously, to mark his distance from Coyzevox, who had made a pair of horses earlier for the site, which were found to be too small (marble, 1701–2; both Paris, Louvre; copies Paris, Jard. Tuileries). Coyzevox's pair soar upwards, with figures of *Fame* and *Mercury* lightly perched on their backs. Coustou's pair are completely different in character, more in the heroic manner of Pierre Puget's work, which was admired in the 18th century and imitated in academic circles but was not, otherwise, taken as a model for public monuments, where charm and elegance were in higher favour. For most of Guillaume Coustou's life, the influence of Coyzevox was dominant. The work of Coyzevox's pupil Jean-Louis Lemoyne (*see* LEMOYNE, (1)) was a continuation of his master's style well into the 18th century, adding impressionistic effects that appear to have been inspired

by contemporary painting. His *Baptism of Christ* (1731; Paris, St Roch) is composed like a painting, with a frontal emphasis and unified, pictorial effect. This is also evident in Robert Le Lorrain's relief of the *Horses of Apollo* on the former stables of the Hôtel de Rohan, Paris (1736–7; *in situ*), which creates an effect of dramatic turmoil within a shallow space. This tendency was inspired, above all, by the example of Bernini, whose attempt to create a synthesis of painting, architecture and sculpture attracted imitators at the Académie de France in Rome. The work of René-Michel Slodtz (*see* SLODTZ, (4)) and also of Lambert-Sigisbert Adam sometimes depends directly on Bernini. Adam's *Neptune Calming the Waves* (Paris, Louvre), his *morceau de réception* for admission to the Académie Royale de Peinture et de Sculpture in 1737, was deeply marked by the bravura of Bernini's original, which Adam, with his brother Nicolas-Sébastien Adam, turned to again in the *Triumph of Neptune and Amphitrite* (lead, completed 1740) for the Bassin de Neptune in the gardens at Versailles (*in situ*; for illustration *see* ADAM (ii), (2)).

Adam's reputation did not survive the mid-century reaction against this style of sculpture, when the less theatrical manner of Edme Bouchardon (*see* BOUCHARDON, (1)) became fashionable among connoisseurs. Bouchardon had won the Prix de Rome in 1722 and accompanied his fellow prizewinner, Adam, to Italy in

1723. While Adam competed successfully for public commissions in Rome (he was the original choice as sculptor to execute the Trevi Fountain), Bouchardon made his reputation by making marble portrait busts. The fountain in the Rue de Grenelle (see fig. 37), the work that first brought him success in Paris, was commissioned by the city in 1739. Although not universally liked, it decisively marked the beginning of a reaction against Adam's style. The seated figure of the city of *Paris* at the centre of the group, reminiscent of the antique figure of *Rome* on the Capitoline Hill (*in situ*), is dwarfed by the large, severely simple base. The low reliefs of putti, representing the *Seasons*, on left and right of the main group, recall 17th-century prints by Charles Errard le fils and Jacques Stella, or François Du Quesnoy's famous relief of the *Bacchanale of Children* (1626; Rome, Gal. Doria-Pamphili) and suggest an inclination towards the art of the *grand siècle*, which underlies a number of aspects of the mid-century reaction against the Rococo. Much of Bouchardon's later work was not completed, and his reputation rested less on what he achieved and more on what he came to represent in the reaction against the Rococo that gathered strength in the 1750s. The fountain in the Rue de Grenelle closely anticipates the forms of architecture, sculpture and the decorative arts that became fashionable in the middle decades of the century through the efforts of Bouchardon's friends and admirers, the Comte de Caylus, Charles-Nicolas Cochin (ii) and the Abbé Jean-Bernard Le Blanc. The naturalism, smooth finish and simple, circular base of Bouchardon's *Cupid Cutting a Bow out of Hercules' Club* (marble, completed 1750; Paris, Louvre; *see* BOUCHARDON, (1), fig. 2) is an early example of the style of sculpture in high favour at Court in the 1750s, with the emergence of LOUIS-CLAUDE VASSÉ, Christophe-Gabriel Allegrain (*see* ALLEGRAIN, (2)), Guillaume Coustou (ii) (*see* COUSTOU, (3)), JACQUES-FRANÇOIS-JOSEPH SALY, Etienne-Maurice Falconet, Jean-Jacques Caffiéri (*see* CAFFIÉRI, (4)) and Jean-Baptiste Pigalle.

ETIENNE-MAURICE FALCONET, who characterized this reaction towards nature, simplicity and the Antique more than any other sculptor, was not obviously prepared for this role by his background. Taught by Jean-Baptiste Lemoyne (ii), the least 'antique' of French sculptors, he never visited Italy and took Puget's *Milo of Crotona Attacked by a Lion* (1670–82; Paris, Louvre) as his early model. However, he responded to the new 'Greek' taste of the 1750s, publicly despised the work of Bernini (which he could hardly have known) and produced figures of nymphs and bathers, smoothly finished with a sensuous elegance that is the equivalent in sculpture of Joseph-Marie Vien's classicizing naturalism in painting. These figures translated easily into porcelain statuettes that were produced at the Sèvres factory, where Falconet was appointed director of the sculpture studios in 1757. Through Sèvres the new style was popularized and was above all pioneered in interior decoration and the decorative arts, where the extremes of Rococo (*see* ROCOCO, §II) had always been much more visible than in the world of sculpture, which remained closely linked throughout to academic principles. Jean-Baptiste Pigalle was the frankest naturalist of this generation. The subject of his marble and bronze tomb of *Maurice, Maréchal de Saxe* (1753–76;

Strasbourg, St Thomas; *see* PIGALLE, JEAN-BAPTISTE, fig. 2) is Baroque in inspiration but transformed in every detail by the study of nature. Pigalle's marble statue of *Voltaire, Nude* (1770–76; Paris, Louvre; *see* fig. 38) represents the extreme instance of this tendency to rework traditional antique themes from nature.

The naturalism of Pigalle and his contemporaries found expression in portraiture, which was practised in the second half of the 18th century with new concentration by artists who produced some of its most memorable works. The series of sculpted portraits of the *Great Men of France* (the 'Grands Hommes'), inaugurated by the Comte d'ANGIVILLER in 1777, was the equivalent in sculpture of the paintings from national history that he commissioned in the hope that they would encourage virtuous emulation among the citizens of France. The commissions were distributed among the best and most promising sculptors: Clodion, PIERRE JULIEN, Caffiéri, JEAN-BAPTISTE STOUF, Charles-Antoine Bridan (*see* BRIDAN, (1)), LOUIS-PHILIPPE MOUCHY, Jean-Guillaume Moitte, AUGUSTIN PAJOU, Jean-Antoine Houdon and

38. Jean-Baptiste Pigalle: *Voltaire, Nude*, marble, h. 1.5 m, 1770–76 (Paris, Musée du Louvre)

others. Only 27 of the series were completed and they were never installed together as Angiviller had planned. Nevertheless, the enterprise, like a number of Angiviller's initiatives, had far-reaching consequences in the history of public statuary in France and elsewhere.

JEAN-ANTOINE HOUDON, whose early career in Rome seemed to promise a career in figurative sculpture, became a specialist in portraiture, sculpting a large number of marble busts and a smaller number of full-length figures—straightforward likenesses—to which he added a vitality and spontaneity that recall the pastels of Maurice-Quentin de La Tour. Apart from his *Flayed Man* (or *Ecorché au bras tendu*; plaster version, 1766–7; Gotha, Schloss Friedenstein; later and modified bronze version, Paris, Ecole N. Sup. B.-A.), which became a staple accessory in art classes throughout Europe, his remaining works, including *Winter* (*c.* 1783–5; Montpellier, Mus. Fabre) and his elegant *Diana the Huntress* (plaster version, 1776; Gotha, Schloss Friedenstein; later marble and bronze versions, Lisbon, Mus. Gulbenkian; Paris, Louvre; San Marino, CA, Huntington Lib. & A.G.; *see* HOUDON, JEAN-ANTOINE, fig. 2), are exercises in the graceful style of Falconet and his contemporaries, which Pajou and Pierre Julien practised successfully through the reign of Louis XVI (*reg* 1774–92) into the Revolutionary period.

The career of CLODION, Houdon's contemporary at the Académie de France in Rome, was established largely outside the world of official commissions by supplying the collectors' market with terracotta statuettes of nymphs, satyrs and putti derived from the types of Boucher's paintings and Falconet's statues and reduced to a pleasing formula (for illustration *see* CLODION). Before the Revolution, Clodion was involved in two major decorative schemes, supplying statues, along with Houdon and LOUIS-SIMON BOIZOT, for the dining-room of the Château de Maisons and reliefs on the façade of a courtyard in the Hôtel Bourbon-Condé in Paris. The reliefs of putti in the courtyard recall Bouchardon's reliefs in the Rue de Grenelle but, like Bouchardon, Clodion returned to the 17th century for his model, taking his ideas from Poussin and Du Quesnoy. On a superficial assessment, his art seems the type of frivolous decoration that might have been condemned by the taste of the Revolutionary era. Although Clodion survived unscathed, the loss of rich patrons was a severe blow to him, as it was to all artists; he responded by turning more intensively than ever to producing his terracotta statuettes, which were evidently popular throughout the Directory (1795–9) and the Consulate (1799–1804).

With the revival of public works in the Consulate and the First Empire (1804–14), Clodion received for the first time an important share in State commissions. The building works of the Empire, in particular, provided work for sculptors on an unprecedented scale: work on the Panthéon, the Palais du Luxembourg, the Louvre, the Vendôme column and numerous lesser monuments and buildings in Paris required the assistance of an army of sculptors. Series of portrait busts for the Senate in the Palais du Luxembourg and for the Palais des Tuileries (destr. 1871), and portraits of the Emperor Napoleon and his courtiers and their families made this a golden age for portrait sculptors. Despite the hostility of Jacques-Louis David, Houdon's portraits also survived the Revolution. On occasion, he showed a willingness to adapt to changing taste: in his terracotta herm bust of *Napoleon as Emperor* (1806; Dijon, Mus. B.-A.) he placed the subject on a rectangular base, undraped, like an ancient Roman emperor, in keeping with the fashionable simplicity of early 19th-century sculpture. His talent for such portraits was widely admired, but his *Diana* of 1776, of which he exhibited a bronze version in 1802, was criticized for lacking the 'ideal and severe character' that was expected from images inspired by myth and ancient history.

At the end of the 18th century, the Antique set a standard for judging and executing sculpture to an unprecedented extent. It had always been admired and used as a source of inspiration since the reign of Francis I (*reg* 1515–47) but did not become an exclusive source of ideas until the late 18th century, when Roman statues, above all, provided artists with a repertory of models. The contribution of Jean-Guillaume Moitte (*see* MOITTE, (2)) to Angiviller's series of the *Great Men*, his statue of *Jean-Dominique Cassini* (Paris, Mus. Observatoire) commissioned in 1787 represents the subject in the guise of an antique philosopher, barefoot and draped in a cloak that covers his knees like a toga. This work anticipated a host of statues, sculpted over the next two decades, which were similarly based on the work of the Ancients, sometimes to the point of pastiche. This tendency was appropriately seen in its purest form among the statues commissioned for the Senate in the Palais du Luxembourg, Paris, which included *Cincinnatus* (Paris, Pal. Luxembourg) by Antoine-Denis Chaudet, *Camillus* by Pierre-Charles Bridan and *Aristides* (plaster, exh. Salon 1804; untraced) by PIERRE CARTELLIER, all imitated from the free-standing statuary of ancient Rome. As a consequence, the nature and value of ancient sculpture were never more hotly debated than they were during this period, when the Antique became a measure by which all statuary was judged. The severity and heroism of ancient art was admired and imitated, but its grace and elegance, the qualities in which Clodion excelled, were equally admired, promoting a fashion for a smooth ideal that is as common in the paintings of Anne-Louis Girodet and his followers as it is in the sculpture of the First Empire. It was not the grace of Houdon's *Diana* that disturbed critics at the Salon of 1802 but the inappropriate realism and modernity of the figure. If Bernini was out of fashion in 1802, so too was the realism that succeeded his influence in French sculpture of the mid-18th century. In Italy Antonio Canova's art followed a similar path, from the early naturalism of *Daedalus and Icarus* (1778–9; Venice, Corter) to the polished Hellenistic ideal of *Cupid Awakening Psyche* (1783–93; Paris, Louvre; replica with variations, 1794–6; St Petersburg, Hermitage; *see* CANOVA, ANTONIO, fig. 1). In 1802 Canova was invited to Paris by Napoleon to sculpt his portrait, but his influence had preceded him. By this date he was the most famous living sculptor in Europe, and echoes of his work appear in numerous paintings and sculptures in France at the turn of the century. Canova's polished, graceful ideal is also found in Chaudet's *Cupid Playing with a Butterfly* (completed by Cartellier, exh. Salon 1817; Paris, Louvre), in François-Joseph Bosio's *Nymph Salmacis*, in Cartellier's *Modesty* (marble, exh. Salon 1808; Amsterdam, Hist.

Mus.), in *Psyche and Zephyr* (1814; Paris, Louvre) by Henri-Joseph Ruxthiel (1775–1837) and in Joseph Chinard's portrait busts of *Juliette Récamier* (marble, life-size, 1802; Lyon, Mus. B.-A.; for illustration *see* CHINARD, JOSEPH) and *Fanny Perrin with the Attributes of Psyche* (Clermont-Ferrand, Mus. Bargoin). The cult of the Antique brought the question of contemporary costume and the virtue of nudity more sharply into focus than ever before. The sculptors, supported by Canova's friend and admirer Quatremère de Quincy, insisted on the heroic ideal, in opposition to elements at Court who argued the case for modern dress. The Emperor's rejection in 1811 of Canova's monumental nude portrait (1803–6; London, Apsley House; bronze replica, 1809; Milan, Brera; for illustration *see* BONAPARTE, (1)) put an effective stop to this tendency, but it did not imply dismissal of all aspects of Canova's art, which was admired, as Girodet's paintings were, for some years after the fall of the Empire. Indeed, such sculptors as Jean-Pierre Cortot and the arch-classicist François-Joseph Bosio continued to practise Canova's ideals during the period of the Bourbon Restoration (1815–30), producing works that adapted the classical ideal of imperial allegory to serve the alliance of Monarchy and Church (*see* §5 below). Reaction against Canova and the sculptors of his generation finally came during the late 1820s and early 1830s in France.

BIBLIOGRAPHY

Lami

E. F. Dilke: *French Sculptors and Architects of the Eighteenth Century* (London, 1800)

F. Ingersoll-Smouse: *La Sculpture funéraire en France au XVIIIe siècle* (Paris, 1912)

M. Furcy-Raynaud: *Inventaire des sculptures exécutées au XVIIIe siècle pour la Direction des Bâtiments du Roi* (Paris, 1927)

French Painting and Sculpture of the XVIII Century (exh. cat., New York, Met., 1935)

E. Dacier: *Le Style Louis XVI*, Arts, Styles et Techniques (Paris, 1939), pp. 95–101

——: *L'Art au XVIIIième siècle en France: Epoques Régence–Louis XV, 1715–1760*, Nouvelle Encyclopédie Illustrée de l'Art Français (Paris, 1951), pp. 37–58

L. Réau: *L'Art au XVIIIième siècle en France: Style Louis XVI, 1760–1789*, Nouvelle Encyclopédie Illustrée de l'Art Français (Paris, 1952), pp. 54–82

L. Hautecoeur: *L'Art sous la Révolution et l'Empire, 1789–1815*, Nouvelle Encyclopédie Illustrée de l'Art Français (Paris, 1953), pp. 48–63

P. Pradel: *La Sculpture au XVIIIe siècle au Musée du Louvre* (Paris, 1958)

France in the Eighteenth Century (exh. cat. by D. Sutton, London, RA, 1968), pp. 136–9

W. von Kalnein and M. Levey: *Art and Architecture of the Eighteenth Century in France*, Pelican Hist. A. (Harmondsworth, 1972)

The Fire and the Talent: A Presentation of French Terracottas (exh. cat. by O. Raggio, New York, Met., 1976)

L. Gillet: 'La Réaction néo-classique', *Histoire de l'art français*, ii ([Paris], 1977), pp. 185–92

F. Souchal: *French Sculptors of the 17th and 18th Centuries: The Reign of Louis XIV*, 3 vols (Oxford, 1977–87); suppl. vol. (London and Boston, 1993)

G. Bresc-Bautier: *Sculpture française: XVIIIe siècle*, Notices d'Histoire de l'Art, 3 (Paris, 1980)

B. Rosasco: *The Sculptures of the Château de Marly during the Reign of Louis XIV* (New York, 1986)

Actes du colloque organisé au Musée du Louvre par le Service culturel. Clodion et la sculpture française de la fin du XVIIIe siècle: Paris, 1992

J.-R. Gaborit: *La Sculpture française*, Paris, Louvre cat. (Paris, 1993)

M. Levey: *Painting and Sculpture in France, 1700–1789*, Pelican Hist. A. (New Haven and London, 1993), pp. 61–157, 235–63

COLIN HARRISON

5. *c.* 1814–*c.* 1900.

(i) Influence of the Ecole des Beaux-Arts. (ii) Public statuary and the influence of government. (iii) Romanticism, academicism and 'national' sculpture. (iv) Challenges to Beaux-Arts classicism.

(i) Influence of the Ecole des Beaux-Arts. For the greater part of the 19th century French sculpture was dominated by the training of the Ecole des Beaux-Arts (*see* PARIS, §VI, 3(ii)). Although histories of painting in the period have largely dismissed the Ecole as retardatory and nugatory, for sculpture—always more dependent on 'official' support—it was crucial. Its hegemony was challenged by the more artisanal courses offered by the Ecole Gratuite de Dessin (or 'Petite Ecole'), especially after 1831 when Jean-Hilaire Belloc (1786–1866) took over the direction of this lesser rival, but up to the 1880s the history of French sculpture is preponderantly the history of the winners of the Prix de Rome: David d'Angers, François Rude, James Pradier, Jean-Baptiste Carpeaux, Henri Chapu, Alexandre Falguière, Louis-Ernest Barrias and Antonin Mercié.

By mid-century it was increasingly felt that the series of *concours* (competitions) punctuating the curriculum and culminating in the Prix de Rome were an outdated and inaccurate yardstick for gauging student potential. An attempt to reform the system in 1863 largely misfired, the reformers only partially succeeding in their aim of breaking the hold of the Institut de France over the Ecole, since most of the professors were members of both bodies (*see also* §XV below). They did, however, bring to an end the system of apprenticeship, in which students had learnt their craft in the private studios of their chosen masters, and sculpture studios were established within the Ecole itself. An attempt to modify the *concours* and the regulations affecting *envois* (works sent back from Rome by prizewinners) foundered against strong internal opposition. The rigours of the training in Paris, based on study from life and from antique models, were somewhat lessened when the successful student reached Rome; there is conspicuously greater variety in sculptors' Roman *envois* than in their Prix de Rome entries, the latter executed under duress within the precincts of the Ecole. These *envois* include some of the most striking works of the 19th century—Pradier's *Bacchante* (marble, exh. Salon 1819; Rouen, Mus. B.-A.), Guillaume's *Anacreon* (marble, exh. Salon 1852; Paris, Mus. d'Orsay), Carpeaux's *Ugolino and his Children* (version, bronze, 1857–63; Paris, Jard. Tuileries), Chapu's *Christ with Angels* (plaster, 1857; Le Mée-sur-Seine, Mus. Chapu), Mercié's bronze group *Gloria victis* (plaster version, exh. Salon 1874; Paris, Petit Pal.); although some of them met with doctrinaire strictures from members of the Institut or from the professors on the grounds either that their subjects were neither classical nor biblical or that their style was too personal, such departures were a common occurrence and were in most cases accepted as indications of the qualities expected of laureates. In the Ecole itself the range of source material was widened, particularly from the 1840s, to include a generous selection of casts of Quattrocento, High Renaissance and post-Renaissance works. Casts of Greek works up to the Early Classical period were also acquired. Concessions were thus made to eclecticism but none to the contemporary world. Modern subject-matter was formally proscribed for student *envois* in 1872, and to this has been ascribed the growing interest among Ecole-trained sculptors in allegory as a vehicle—however indirect—for commentary on modern life and events.

Government patronage, whether through a ministry, the Court or municipal or regional bodies, provided the most dependable source of employment for sculptors. The history of sculpture in this period is closely linked with changing political regimes and the projects that they initiated: the instability and transience of these regimes imposed on sculptors the necessity of adapting to new conditions in order to survive, a situation that brought into focus the question of the artist's social and political commitment. In the course of the century two sculptors in particular stood out for their refusal to compromise: DAVID D'ANGERS, during the July Monarchy (1830–48) and in the early years of the Second Empire (1852–70); and JULES DALOU, after the Commune of 1871. In both cases fidelity to Republican ideals earned them periods of exile.

(ii) Public statuary and the influence of government. Training in sculpture at the Ecole did not accord in detail with the requirements of public statuary. Intended to inculcate elevated precepts and aesthetic ideals, it provided in only a general sense a suitable rhetorical language for the polemical or propagandist aims of the State, which in practice often called for an ability to convey specific political messages, through portraits, scenes of recent history or allegory. Overt political propaganda is most evident in works produced between 1815 and 1848. The government of the restored Bourbons revived projects initiated under the *ancien régime* and embarked on a series of monuments expressing national expiation for regicide and the Reign of Terror. Jean-Pierre Cortot and François-Joseph Bosio returned to pre-Revolutionary types of allegory and apotheosis in the sculpture of the Chapelle Expiatoire in Paris (e.g. Cortot's *Marie-Antoinette Succoured by Religion*, marble, *c.* 1825) and in the commissions of Charles X's government for statues of *Louis XVI* (begun 1827; Paris, Place de la Concorde) by Cortot and of *Louis XVIII* (1826; Paris, Pal. Bourbon) by Bosio.

Following the Revolution of 1830 the new government of Louis-Philippe commandeered and adapted to its own ends schemes proposed in the previous decade, notably the decoration of the Arc de Triomphe du Carrousel and the Madeleine, both in Paris, and the Porte d'Aix in Marseille. The government also returned Ste Geneviève, Paris, to the secular function of the Panthéon, which it had enjoyed between 1791 and 1821, with a new pediment (1830–37) commissioned from David d'Angers (*see* DAVID D'ANGERS, fig. 2); undertook the sculptural embellishment of the Arc de Triomphe de l'Etoile; and instituted a programme of polemical decorations at the Palais Bourbon (*see* PARIS, §II, 5). Considered overall, this group of schemes was impressively orchestrated; it suppressed all that was anti-Revolutionary in the Restoration projects, acknowledging the existence of Napoleon as Emperor, while extolling the military prowess of Bonaparte as General, promoting a State-sanctioned Catholic morality (hardly recognized as such by Catholic critics), reassimilating Voltaire and Jean-Jacques Rousseau and a selected group of Revolutionary figures among the great men of the nation, and representing in staid allegories the moderate principles of constitutional monarchy.

(iii) Romanticism, academicism and 'national' sculpture. The climate of liberalism in the Salons of the early 1830s permitted younger sculptors, some of them affiliated with the Romantic tendency, to come before the public. Two Prix-de-Rome winners, FRANÇOIS RUDE and FRANÇOIS-JOSEPH DURET, created a precedent for moderate emancipation from classical canons in the treatment of the nude, exhibiting relaxed Neapolitan genre subjects (see fig. 39). Antoine-Louis Barye and Christophe Fratin (1800/02–64) launched what was to become another vogue, ANIMALIER SCULPTURE. Other forms of local colour—literary, geographical and historical—along with a colouristic handling of bronze emerged in the works of the Romantic sculptors Antonin-Marie Moine, Auguste Préault, Etienne-Hippolyte Maindron, Théodore Gechter, Jean-Bernard Du Seigneur (1808–66) and Jean-Jacques Feuchère (*see* ROMANTICISM). When Salon juries from 1836 began to suppress the more interesting work of this loose-knit school, some of its followers found alternative outlets in the expanding market for statuettes and decorative domestic sculptural ornament (*see* STATUETTE, §III). Another alluring feature of the statuette trade was its accommodation of fashion and topicality, in the caricatures of Jean-Pierre Dantan, for example, and in delicate portrayals of stage personalities by Jean-Auguste Barre and others. Neither was the classical repertory neglected in

39. François Rude: *Young Neapolitan Fisherboy Playing with a Tortoise*, marble, h. 765 mm, 1831–3 (Paris, Musée du Louvre)

this type of sculpture, the largest contribution coming from James Pradier, whose mythological themes were interspersed with modern erotic genre subjects (for illustration *see* PRADIER, JAMES).

Remaining aloof from such commercial endeavours, David d'Angers, Antoine Etex and Rude maintained an individualist concept of a 'national' sculpture that led them finally into opposition with the July Monarchy. David d'Angers increasingly turned his attention to the task of honouring great men in commemorative statues, tombs, busts and portrait medallions. The commissioning of such statues in France dated back to the years just prior to the Revolution (*see* §4 above). The restored Bourbon monarchy gave the activity a wider, national, base by erecting statues in the subjects' places of birth. David d'Angers's achievement was in bringing his personal initiative to bear in the choice of subject and location, stimulating local interest and sponsorship but sometimes giving his own labours free of charge.

The last major monument erected under the July Monarchy, the tomb of *Napoleon I* in the church of the Invalides, Paris, was characterized by an extreme aesthetic conservatism. The sculptors involved were Pradier (marble Victories, 1843–52), Duret (bronze allegories flanking door to the tomb, *c.* 1843) and Pierre-Charles Simart (marble allegorical reliefs and marble and bronze portrait statue, 1846–52). Such conservatism, which paradoxically the short-lived Second Republic (1848–52) did nothing to undermine, was inherited by the Second Empire (1852–70). The resurgence of academicism was accompanied by a comparative diffidence on the part of Napoleon III's government about political statements interpreted in monumental form. A lack of ideological content was compensated for by the sheer quantity of State commissions that were dedicated mainly to enlivening the surfaces of focal metropolitan buildings. 335 sculptors were employed between 1852 and 1857 on the restoration and extension of the Musée du Louvre, Paris; 131 sculptors worked from 1860 to 1875 on the Paris Opéra. Images of Napoleon III and of his imperial forebears appeared in the Louvre programme, but particular statements were swamped by an abundance of abstracted personifications and portraits of worthies. At the end of the 1860s the floridity of Charles Garnier's architectural conception of the new Opéra (*see* GARNIER, CHARLES, fig. 1) found in Carpeaux's allegorical group representing *Dance* (stone, 1866–9; *in situ*; *see* CARPEAUX, JEAN-BAPTISTE, fig. 1) a true sculptural counterpart, at least in the judgement of futurity: the immediate response from both the architect and the public was shock at what they deemed its excess and a demand for its removal.

During the July Monarchy the family of Louis-Philippe, notably Ferdinand-Philippe, Duc d'Orléans, had played its part, through personal patronage, in promoting the 'minor' Romantic genres in sculpture. Similarly, in the Second Empire certain sculptors received Court approval, which helped them to make their mark in both the private and the public domains. The florid styles of Carpeaux and ALBERT-ERNEST CARRIER-BELLEUSE were as much embedded in the tradition of decorative sculpture as in the traditions of the Ecole des Beaux-Arts. It was the support that both these sculptors received from the imperial household that in the later years of the Empire established their styles as a viable alternative to academic orthodoxy. Of the two, only Carpeaux succeeded in forging, from an eclectic grounding, a truly personal style that was excitable and impressionistic and that transcended its sources; Carrier-Belleuse, inventive enough in decorative composition, was usually content with a pastiche of the Renaissance or Rococo periods.

In certain cases, sculptors during the Second Empire were compelled to subordinate personal originality to the demands of archaeological reconstruction, since it was in the 1850s that Adolphe-Napoléon Didron and Eugène-Emmanuel Viollet-le-Duc introduced a more historically enlightened note into the restoration of such ancient monuments as Notre-Dame in Paris and the château of Pierrefonds in Oise. The erudite medievalism of Viollet-le-Duc's chief sculptural assistant, Geoffrey Dechaume (1816–92), is but one of the historicisms practised in this eclectic period.

In creating *Ugolino and his Children*, Carpeaux revitalized the sculpted nude, sharing this ambition with a group of young sculptors who took their inspiration from Michelangelo and the 15th century and subsequently became known as 'Les Florentins'. Two members of the group, Alexandre Falguière and Paul Dubois (i), studied in Rome in the early 1860s and were preoccupied with the youthful male figure and with anatomical characterization as opposed to the normative idealization encouraged by the Ecole. After 1870 ANTONIN MERCIÉ and Louis-Ernest Barrias (*see* BARRIAS, (2)) reinforced their early endeavours, and it was their emphasis on modelling and on emotive effects that informed much of the sculpture exhibited in the annual Salons between the Franco-Prussian War (1870–71) and the beginning of the 20th century. Rodin, in his early works, was clearly indebted to them, his *Age of Bronze* (version, bronze, 1875–7; London, V&A; *see* RODIN, AUGUSTE, fig. 1) and *St John the Baptist* (version, bronze, 1878; Copenhagen, Ny Carlsberg Glyp.) both finding their closest counterparts in the pieces exhibited by Mercié in the Salons of the early 1870s.

During the Third Republic (1871–1946), up to World War I, there was a tremendous increase in the number of commemorative statues being produced in Paris and the provinces, instigated mainly by the initiatives of regional and municipal governments, as for example the two monuments to the Republic commissioned by the City of Paris from Léopold Morice (1846–1920) (1883; Paris, Place de la République) and Jules Dalou (bronze, 1879–99; Paris, Place de la Nation; for illustration *see* DALOU, JULES). Societies also commissioned works from sculptors, as for example the Société des Gens de Lettres, which commissioned Rodin's monument to the writer *Honoré de Balzac* (plaster, exh. Salon 1898; rejected by the Société; bronze version erected 1939, Paris, intersection Boulevards Raspail and Montparnasse). In the case of war memorials or monuments of national interest a local contribution or a fund raised from public subscription might be augmented by funds from the central government. From this period the biggest concentration of sculpture within the City of Paris was a municipal project, the Hôtel de Ville, requiring the collaboration of 230 sculptors (see fig. 40). The building was embellished with

40. Façade of the Hôtel de Ville, Paris (begun 1874), embellished with work by 230 sculptors

many portraits of famous men and women of Paris, the sculptures combining costume pageantry with a new emphasis on realism.

In outdoor commemorative monuments of the last two decades of the 19th century, such as Dalou's monument to *Delacroix* (bronze, unveiled 1890) in the Jardin du Luxembourg, Paris, or Barrias's monument to *Victor Hugo* (inaugurated 1902; mostly destr. 1942) in the Place Victor-Hugo, Paris, elaborateness of composition and dramatic silhouette were the dominant trends. The variety of solutions proposed was a consequence of the increase in the numbers of such statues, as well as of the desire to educate through imagery. Here, as in the architecture of the same period, a total accommodation with the vocabulary of the Baroque was made. For David d'Angers, responsible for so many commemorations earlier in the century, the simple ingredients of a full-length portrait statue with subordinated attributes, an inscription and, optionally, reliefs on the pedestal illustrating incidents from the life of the subject, had been sufficient. To this type sculptors of the Third Republic added a wealth of allegory and of symbolic and anecdotal detail, such as had been used on tombs in the 17th and 18th centuries.

(iv) Challenges to Beaux-Arts classicism. The sculptural mood of the 1870s was elegiac, a response to France's defeat in the Franco-Prussian War (1870–71). After the establishment of the Third Republic, public statuary in particular entered an ebullient and ingratiating phase. Rodin's début as an exhibitor at the Salon coincided with the elegiac phase, and against a background of what he saw as the charlatanism and false poetry of most Salon

exhibits he pursued his own introverted researches in preparation for the unfinished *Gates of Hell* (bronze, 1880–1917; Paris, Mus. Rodin; *see* RODIN, AUGUSTE, fig. 3). Some of his projects for commemorative monuments take the allegorizing mode of his contemporaries to its furthest limit; others, like that to *Balzac*, incorporated symbolism in a single figure. However, he always made the monumental rhetoric his own, endowing it with a personal feeling above all for the language of the body itself, developed through his immense output of drawings and experimental models (*see* RODIN, AUGUSTE, fig. 4). At the same time he acknowledged his debt both to Michelangelo and to medieval sculptors, while retaining links with the more immediate traditions of the 19th century. This occurred at a time when, simultaneously with the erection of statues to great writers of the Romantic movement, a reassessment was underway of the achievement of earlier Romantic sculptors, some of whom were still active in Rodin's youth.

In the 1880s, within the Ecole, the innate conservatism of the more official sculptors made them ideal bulwarks of the establishment. In 1864 the post of Directeur of the Ecole des Beaux-Arts had been taken up by the sculptor Jean-Baptiste-Claude Eugène Guillaume; in 1878 it had passed to another sculptor, Paul Dubois (i), who retained it until his death in 1905, after which long-overdue reforms were finally introduced. However, in practice, the ascendancy of Rodin, who had been refused admission to the Ecole, and of Dalou, who had been a disappointed runner-up in the Prix de Rome, was an indication of the loosening of the grip of the Ecole on sculpture at large. Furthermore, at the Impressionist exhibition of 1881 EDGAR DEGAS showed his startlingly veristic wax sculpture of the *Young Dancer of Fourteen* (version, bronze, Rotterdam, Mus. Boymans–van Beuningen), a work closer in many ways to both contemporary and historic Italian sculpture than to anything then being produced in France. It took a critic of the originality of Joris-Karl Huysmans to appreciate the challenge being posed to the system. It was the first occasion in which an innovative painter–sculptor had cared to show his sculpture to the public at large; the vigorous modelling power of Théodore Gericault and Honoré Daumier remained a secret known only to frequenters of studios. After the *Young Dancer of Fourteen*, Degas, like them, chose not to exhibit his sculpture and turned exclusively to small-scale and experimental work in three dimensions.

A problem of the period that was brought into focus by Rodin in his marbles was that of authenticity. The deputing of the final execution of carved works to assistants or professional *praticiens* had been practised before the 19th century, but as the technical aspects of sculpture became more developed and the entrepreneurial systems facilitating the division of tasks became more sophisticated, a reaction set in, exacerbated by the virtuosic appearance at the Salons of a number of marble showpieces depicting mythological subjects by such sculptors as Denys Puech and Laurent-Honoré Marqueste (1848–1920). The reaction had already been registered by the Ecole, where classes in stone- and marble-carving were instituted in 1883, but it was in the exhibitions of sculpture at the Salons of the Société Nationale des Beaux-Arts during the 1890s that a more fundamental revision made its appearance, such Symbolist sculptors as Jean Dampt, Jean Carriès, Jules Desbois and Pierre Roche preferring the dual identities of poet and craftsman to the grandiose conception of *statuaire* and finding alternatives to marble in wood, pewter, ceramic, wax, gypsum, ivory, lead and combinations of these (*see* SYMBOLISM). Such experiments with mixed-media and polychromed sculpture were not practised exclusively by those who favoured an Arts and Crafts approach. Polychromy had been tentatively espoused by Neo-classical sculptors earlier in the century, after the publication in Paris in 1815 of Antoine Quatremère de Quincy's account of the ancient Greeks' use of colour in sculpture, *Le Jupiter olympien*, and experimentation of this kind had increased around mid-century. Sometimes the motive was archaeological, as with Simart's chryselephantine reconstruction of the *Athena Parthenos* (1846) for the château of Dampierre, Marne (*in situ*); sometimes it was to contribute to a work's voluptuous charge, as in Auguste Clésinger's *Woman Bitten by a Snake* (exh. Salon 1847; Paris, Mus. d'Orsay), in which the white marble of the subject's body was originally set off against a bed of tinted flowers. A more consistent commitment to coloured sculpture, exploiting gorgeous combinations of bronze, marbles and semi-precious stones, had been demonstrated from the mid-1850s by Charles Cordier in his busts of ethnic types, and in the final decade of the 19th century this ostentatious and materialistic polychromy was practised by Jean-Léon Gérôme and Barrias. Degas and Gauguin, the painter–sculptors connected with the Impressionist movement (*see* IMPRESSIONISM), both used

polychromy in their three-dimensional work; but although Gauguin's use of wood and ceramic and of colour to enhance the Symbolist import of his sculpture validates a comparison with the work of more conventional Symbolist sculptors, the hostile reception to such works as the polychromed wood reliefs *Soyez mystérieuses* (Paris, Mus. d'Orsay) and *Soyez amoureuses et heureuses* (Boston, MA, Mus. F.A.), which he showed in 1891 at the exhibition of Les XX (*see* <VINGT>, LES) in Brussels, and the rejection in 1895 of his stoneware statuette *Oviri* (1894; Paris, Mus. d'Orsay; *see* GAUGUIN, PAUL, fig. 5) from the Salon of the Société Nationale des Beaux-Arts, Paris, showed how far beyond the boundaries of Europe his primitivism had taken him, as opposed to the restricted European travels of other fellow sculptors.

In the 1890s two other, quite opposed, challenges to the closed world of Beaux-Arts classicism emerged. On the one hand, social-realistic representations in sculpture no longer had aesthetic and political inhibitions, as evidenced in the work of Jules Dalou, who led the way in the 1890s with his projects for a *Monument to Workers* (unexecuted; preparatory clay sketches, Paris, Petit. Pal.); on the other there was a fundamentalist classicism proposed by ARISTIDE MAILLOL. It was the latter—the line of least resistance, in a sense—that was to prove the more enduring, providing a link between the long tradition of classically inspired sculpture in France and the formalist researches of the 20th century.

BIBLIOGRAPHY
Lami
L. Benoist: *La Sculpture romantique* (Paris, 1928/*R* 1994 [with intro. by L.-J. Lemaistre])
P. Pradel: *La Sculpture du XIXe siècle au Musée du Louvre* (Paris, 1958)
G. Hubert: *Les Sculpteurs italiens en France sous la Révolution, l'Empire et la Restauration, 1790–1830* (Paris, 1964)
Pioneers of Modern Sculpture (exh. cat. by A. E. Elsen, London, Hayward Gal., 1973)
M. Agulhon: 'Imagerie civique et décor urbain', *Ethnol. Fr.*, v (1975), pp. 33–56
Metamorphoses in Nineteenth-century Sculpture (exh. cat., ed. J. Wasserman; Cambridge, MA, Fogg, 1975)
M. Agulhon: 'La Statuomanie et l'histoire', *Ethnol. Fr.*, viii (1978), pp. 145–72
B. G. Wennberg: *French and Scandinavian Sculpture in the Nineteenth Century* (Atlantic Highlands, NJ, and Stockholm, 1978)
The Romantics to Rodin: French Nineteenth-century Sculpture from North American Collections (exh. cat., ed. P. Fusco and H. W. Janson; Los Angeles, CA, Co. Mus. A.; Minneapolis, MN, Inst. A.; Detroit, MI, Inst. A.; Indianapolis, IN, Mus. A.; 1980–81)
A. Le Normand: *La Tradition classique et l'esprit romantique: Les Sculpteurs de l'Académie de France à Rome de 1824 à 1840* (Rome, 1981)
De Carpeaux à Matisse: La Sculpture française de 1850 à 1914 dans les musées et les collections publiques du nord de la France (exh. cat. by A. Pingeot and others, Calais, Mus. B.-A.; Lille, Mus. B.-A.; Arras, Mus. B.-A.; and elsewhere; 1982–3)
H. W. Janson: *Nineteenth-century Sculpture* (London, 1985)
La Sculpture française au XIXe siècle (exh. cat., ed. A. Pingeot; Paris, Grand Pal., 1986)
A. Le Normand-Romain: *Mémoire de marbre: La Sculpture funéraire en France, 1804–1914* (Paris, 1995)

PHILIP WARD-JACKSON

6. AFTER c. 1900.

(i) c. 1900–c. 1945. (ii) After c. 1945.

(i) c. 1900–c. 1945. At the beginning of the century Auguste Rodin still occupied a magisterial position in French sculpture, and his work dominated the annual

Salons. However, at the same time other, more experimental, sculptors were finding their inspiration in ethnographic collections and folk art and were becoming interested in direct carving as a form of expression. Two of the most famous, Jacob Epstein and Henri Gaudier-Brzeska, stayed for only a short time in Paris and worked principally in London, but their counterparts in France included not only Constantin Brancusi but also Paul Gauguin and ANDRÉ DERAIN. Indeed, some of the most intriguing, although isolated, of the experiments in sculpture at this time were made by painters. As Rodin's works were absent from the exhibition of the Société Nationale des Beaux-Arts of 1912, *Pénélope* (version, 1912; Otterlo, Rijksmus. Kröller-Müller) by EMILE-ANTOINE BOURDELLE occupied the place of honour. By the time of Rodin's death (1917), Bourdelle was prominent among a small group of French sculptors whom the press considered as worthy successors. Of the others—Albert Bartholomé, Henri Bouchard, Jean Boucher (1870–1939) and Aristide Maillol—it was in fact Bartholomé who eventually took over Rodin's presidency of the Société Nationale. Nevertheless, it was Bourdelle who was perhaps most consistently revered as the new leader of the French school during the following decade.

Rodin's death and the press's subsequent 'revelation' that some of his sculptures may have been the work of his team of *praticiens* produced a marked shift of opinion towards *taille directe*. There was a new interest in the authenticity of a piece, both in authorship and in material. Joseph Bernard was the figurehead for this movement, which proved triumphant at the Exposition Internationale des Arts Décoratifs et Industriels Modernes (1925), where the Douce France group (founded in 1913 in readiness for this exposition, which was originally planned for 1915) exhibited a pergola carved by Joachim Costa (1888–1971), Raoul Lamourdedieu, the twins Jan Martel and Joël Martel (both 1896–1966), L.-H. Nicot (1878–1944), P. C. Manès (1891/8–1963), Georges Saupique (1889–1961), François Pompon, Georges Hilbert (1900–82) and Ossip Zadkine. This fashion for direct carving wedded craftsmanship and decorative style; the work of Bernard and his colleagues was carried out predominantly in relief. There was evidence of a new awareness of medieval culture allied to a nationalism promulgated in terms of French Gothic art and the use of local stones; 'Frenchness' also extended to the use of colonial woods, and a recognizable colonial style developed. In the home, the ART DECO style was applied to domestic sculpture (and to a new bourgeois clientele), perhaps most notably in *animalier* pieces, of which Pompon, Mateo Hernández and Rembrandt Bugatti were the most notable exponents (*see* ANIMALIER SCULPTURE).

In 1914, shortly after the outbreak of World War I, there was already serious debate in artistic, journalistic and government circles about the regulation of forthcoming monumental commemoration. Such lively concern was due to the continuing glorification of the Franco-Prussian War (1870–71) in forms that many of these observers deplored. Contemporary journalists promoted sculptors whom they thought were worthy of creating monuments to honour the dead, for example Rodin, Bourdelle, Maillol, Boucher, Bouchard, Paul Landowski (1875–1961), Paul

Niclausse (1879–1958), Charles Despiau, L.-E. Drivier (1878–1951), Fernand David (1872–1927), Albert Marque and Pierre Roche. All these sculptors were to be involved in such commemoration (few outside the avant-garde were not), and some, such as Bouchard, who executed 22 war memorials, were highly successful. In addition, however, some of the most prolific sculptors of monumental works commemorating World War I, among them Charles Sarrabezoles (1888–1971), Maxime Real del Sarte (1888–1954), Saupique and Nicot, rose to prominence after 1918. The c. 38,000 war memorials that were erected in France provided much employment for sculptors over a relatively long period. Although most village memorials were in place by 1922, larger municipal monuments took much longer and were still being inaugurated considerably later. Pierre Poisson (1876–1953) and Charles Malfray were prominent exponents of such large-scale work.

In retrospect, there was a sharp contrast between the professional decorative sculptors (*statuaires*) who supplied these monuments and the avant-garde sculptors who made experimental work on a small, domestic scale and who were supported by a few dealers. While the professional sculptors were French, with Beaux-Arts training and were occasional winners of a Prix de Rome, the avant-garde were predominantly non-French and enjoyed none of the territorial fidelities that counted so strongly in the awarding of monumental commissions. CUBISM attracted many international followers: Henri Laurens stands out as the only French-born member of a group that included Jacques Lipchitz, Alexander Archipenko, Ossip Zadkine, Joseph Csáky and Pablo Gargallo. Since the beginning of the century artists from central and eastern Europe had been coming to Paris to study sculpture. In *La Jeune Sculpture française* (1919) André Salmon gave highest praise to the foreign artists at the Paris Salons and asserted that the federalism in Germany enabled the country to support both official and avant-garde sculpture. Salmon's book reveals a blurring of distinctions unimaginable later, and the surveys of sculpture that followed it in the 1920s and 1930s similarly confirm that modernity was perceived more variously at that time by the inclusion of Bourdelle, Despiau and Marcel Gimond (1894–1961) with Zadkine and the Cubist sculptors Laurens and Lipchitz.

However, the separate co-existence of two very different modes of sculpture, the monumental and essentially realist and the avant-garde, in a world that accorded each an equal, if differing importance, was already being broken down in the sculpture of the artists associated with SURREALISM in the 1920s. This contrasted strongly with previous modes in terms of its sources and its uncraftsmanlike facture. Marcel Duchamp, Salvador Dalí, Joan Miró and Meret Oppenheim made 'objects', the inspiration for which was primarily conceptual; Alberto Giacometti and Hans Bellmer reduced sculptural forms, and viewers' perceptions of these, to an instinctual, sexual plane. Pablo Picasso pursued the Surrealists' conceptualism and juxtaposition of various types of OBJET TROUVÉ and, by engaging Julio González to effect his arrangements (*c.* 1928–31), introduced forging and welding into fine art (*see* PICASSO, PABLO, fig. 8). Picasso then turned to the other extreme: modelling in mass. The bulbous heads produced in his studio at Boisgeloup after 1931 can be compared to contemporary work by Henri Matisse, Otto Freundlich and Jean Fautrier and even to Hans Arp's *Concretions*. Freundlich brought curvaceously swelling mass and texture into play with geometric Constructivism, and although Fautrier's monoliths are unmistakably human, while Arp gave priority to abstract form (*see* ARP, HANS, fig. 2), both used the force of mass as their vehicle.

Despite the revolutionary impact of Surrealism, however, two very distinct worlds came together in *Maîtres de l'art indépendant*, part of the Exposition Internationale des Arts et Techniques dans la Vie Moderne in Paris in 1937. The representation of sculptors is interesting: Maillol was pre-eminent with 61 works, followed closely by Despiau and Zadkine. Lipchitz, Laurens, Gargallo, Chana Orloff and Hernández all had between 25 and 36 pieces on show; next were Bourdelle and Rodin, with 15 and 14. The other sculptors, including Raymond Duchamp-Villon, Manolo, Robert Wlérick (1882–1944) and Drivier, were represented by fewer than six pieces. Outside the exhibition halls, however, it was the independent decorative sculptors rather than the avant-garde who triumphed: the Palais de Chaillot was adorned by such sculptors as Wlérick, Emmanuel Auricoste (*b* 1908), Henri Navarre (1885–1971), Paul Belmondo (1898–1982), Bouchard, Niclausse, Paul Cornet (1892–1977), Malfray and Sarrabezoles. Despiau was commissioned to design an *Apollo* to replace Bourdelle's *La France*, but delays meant that the latter was used once more, as it had been for the exhibition of 1925.

(ii) After c. *1945.* After World War II figures who had previously been identified with the avant-garde, such as Picasso, Zadkine, Giacometti, Miró and Max Ernst, took over as the Establishment, winning the prizes at the Biennales in Venice and São Paulo. Commemorative sculpture did not sustain its notable position after 1945: additions were simply made to the previous war's monuments. Public sculpture, however, flourished in the post-war period, enjoying the possibilities opened up by building schemes and new open-air sculpture parks. Welding was widely taken up and was used by such artists as Germaine Richier and César to make emaciated, distressed human and animal figures in wire and metals. The work of French sculptors at the Venice Biennale of 1952 also revealed a concern for the expressive value of gesture and a contemporary interest in the marriage of matter and memory, with the metal taking on a loaded, archeological role in evoking association. Richier was unusual among French sculptors of this period in making figurative work, although Giacometti had by now also returned to the figure in his search for the definitive human form.

The dominant French post-war aesthetic in sculpture developed the ideas of such precursors as ABSTRACTION-CRÉATION of the 1930s and the Salon des Réalités Nouvelles, established in 1946. This annual Salon, to which foreign artists also contributed, together with its magazine, *Art d'aujourd'hui*, helped establish a non-figurative hegemony despite continuing doubt within the movement as to the proper definition of the term 'abstract'. Much of the defining of 'abstract', 'concrete' and 'non-figurative' was effected through personal statements, group allegiances, and, perhaps most importantly, through 'homages' to pre-war figures, living and deceased. Naum

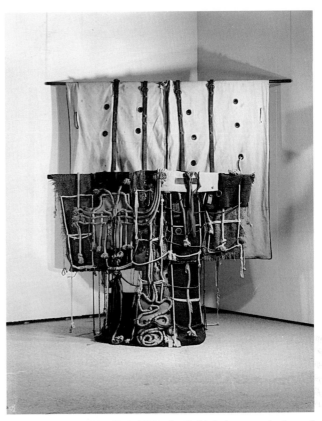

41. Etienne-Martin: *The Cloak (Habitation 5)*, fabric, lace, rope, leather and metal with canvas and leather cover, 2.0×1.6×0.3 m, 1962 (Paris, Pompidou, Musée National d'Art Moderne)

Gabo, Antoine Pevsner, Freundlich and Hans Arp were especially significant for younger sculptors. In particular, an intriguing bridge between Dada sculpture and Constructivism was provided by the work of Sophie Taeuber-Arp and Hans Arp, who showed that chance could be used not only as an anarchic principle but also as a mathematical one.

This trend towards abstraction soon allied itself to monumental sculpture and architecture: the expanses of space characteristic of post-war architecture suited sculpture on an equivalent scale, and such sculptors as André Bloc (1896–1966) (the editor of *Art d'aujourd'hui*) and Henri-Georges Adam took up the challenge, often using such modern materials as concrete. Adam became Professor of Monumental Sculpture at the Ecole Nationale Supérieure des Beaux-Arts in Paris in 1959. Etienne-Martin drew on such tendencies and extended them in his 'habitations' (see fig. 41), which are fusions of architecture and sculpture and which were echoed in Jean Dubuffet's 'walk-in' sculptures. Eugène Dodeigne's monoliths added expressive figuration to the archaeological surface of the work of Etienne-Martin and others. François Stahly was close to Etienne-Martin, and they collaborated on architectural commissions that reflect the influence of Léger's post-war teaching. Stahly's work, however, is more lyrical, like that of Etienne Hajdu (*b* 1907), blending the organic with the geometric. Both

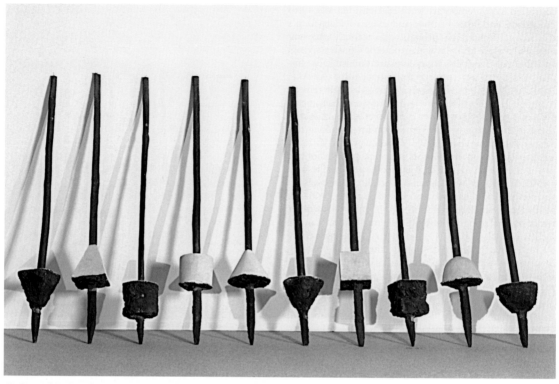

42. Bernard Pagès: *Stakes*, wood, earth and concrete, 10 components, each h. 300 mm, 1975 (Paris, Pompidou, Musée National d'Art Moderne)

were interested in the combination and orchestration of forms, although Hajdu used metals where Stahly employed wood and stone; both produced several public fountains. Jean Ipoustéguy combined the human figure with forms taken from architecture.

As earlier generations of foreign sculptors had come to Paris, drawn by the prestige of the academies or by possibilities of training or employment as *praticiens* in the studios of Rodin, Bourdelle and others, so this trend reappeared in the 1960s, with many South American artists interested in movement and light joining the OP ART and KINETIC ART movements in Paris, among them Jésus Soto and Julio Le Parc. Though basing their work on scientific laws of perception, their aim was often to reflect their perceptions of contemporary society. Their sources and materials made their work a natural ally of contemporary architecture. The Galerie Denise René, which held the exhibition *Le Mouvement* as early as 1955, was the focal point for these groups, to which the Danes Robert Jacobsen and Richard Mortensen may be added. By 1960 Op art and kinetic art, which were natural developments of the geometric abstraction movement, were established parts of the European exhibitions.

In 1960 the critic Pierre Restany (*b* 1930) sought to break with the past in announcing NOUVEAU RÉALISME. The painter Yves Klein spurred Restany to look beyond *Art informel* to a new generation, and although the critical definition of Nouveau Réalisme was never succinct, it was quickly identified with artists promoted by Restany: Klein, Jean Tinguely, Arman, César, Niki de Saint Phalle

and Christo. In the USA their work was exhibited with that of the American Neo-Dadaists or Pop artists, and Restany acknowledged the lineage in his exhibition *A 40° au-dessus de Dada* (1961), held at the Galerie J, Paris. Such artists as Tinguely and Takis had added a Dada element to kinetic sculpture, allowing it expressive, as well as structural power. César also used junk metals more blatantly and exhibited them, as did the other Nouveaux Réalistes, only slightly transformed (for illustration *see* CÉSAR). Arman and Martial Raysse collected small-scale domestic debris, presenting it in iconic form (for illustration *see* ARMAN).

The intellectual inquiry into the nature of painting, pursued around 1970 in France through the SUPPORTS-SURFACES group, had its counterparts in sculpture. Toni Grand (*b* 1935), Bernard Pagès (*b* 1940) and Patrick Saytour (*b* 1935) were initially associated with the Ecole de Nice, but Pagès was to distance himself after an exhibition in 1970 gave Supports–Surfaces its name. Despite the group's short life, all its members continued to examine the materials of sculpture, stripping them back to basics in a deconstructive effort to establish where sculpture begins and where it ends (see fig. 42).

Some of the most notable sculptural manifestations of the second half of the 20th century in France were for public sites. In Paris, Tinguely and Saint Phalle created their Stravinsky Fountain (1983) outside the Centre Georges Pompidou; in the courtyard of the Palais-Royal, Pol Bury installed two fountains (1985), while Daniel Buren in his work the *Two Plateaux* (1985–6) used his usual calculated formula of vertical stripes in sequences of cylindrical shapes of graduated size to engage the surrounding space. While Buren used stripes to reclaim and reshape space, on a smaller scale Jean-Pierre Raynaud (*b* 1939) used standard white ceramic tiles to expand Neo-plasticism into total environments. François Morellet used the simplest of means—lines on unhung canvases—to reassert underlying structures. In part, the contemporary French interest in 'site-specific' art stemmed from the enormous capital investment in art by the State in the 1970s and 1980s; new sites, or the reclamation of 'Le Patrimoine', demanded to be appropriated. To the fetishism and personal associations of Nouveau Réalisme Annette Messager and Christian Boltanski added the evocation of grief. In the stylized allusions of the work of Anne Poirier and Patrick Poirier there is a generalized nostalgia for a classical past. The new art of Bazile (*b* 1952), Bustamante (*b* 1952) and Jean-Luc Vilmouth (*b* 1952), which moved resolutely away from the art of evocation and memory, was at once clean, stylish, design-conscious and genuinely revelatory about our ways of seeing.

BIBLIOGRAPHY
A. Salmon: *La Jeune Sculpture française* (Paris, 1919)
A. Basler: *La Sculpture moderne en France* (Paris, 1928)
L. Benoist: *La Sculpture française* (Paris, 1945)
L. Gischia and N. Vedres: *La Sculpture en France depuis Rodin* (Paris, 1945)
P. Francastel: *Les Sculpteurs célèbres* (Paris, 1954)
A. M. Hammacher: *The Evolution of Modern Sculpture: Tradition and Innovation* (New York, 1969) [useful pls]
P. Kjellberg: *Le Guide des statues de Paris* (Paris, 1973)
Catalogues de sculptures des XIXe et XXe siècles dans les collections des musées de Poitiers et de la Société des antiquaires de l'ouest (exh. cat. by B. Chavanne and others, Poitiers, Mus. Poitiers, 1983)
A. H. Amann: *Catalogue des sculptures des XIXe et XXe siècles: Collections du Musée municipal de Mont-de-Marsan* (Mont-de-Marsan, 1985)
J.-L. Daval and others: *La Sculpture: L'Aventure de la sculpture moderne, XIXe et XXe siècles* (Geneva, 1986) [good pls]
A. Le Normand-Romain, A. Pingeot and L. de Margerie: *Musée d'Orsay: Catalogue sommaire illustré des sculptures* (Paris, 1986)
Qu'est-ce que la sculpture moderne? (exh. cat. by M. Rowell, Paris, Pompidou, 1986)
L'Epoque, la mode, la morale, la passion, 1977–87 (exh. cat. by C. David and others, Paris, Pompidou, 1987)
Coloniales, 1920-1940 (exh. cat. by E. Bréon and M. Lefrançois, Boulogne-Billancourt, Mus. Mun., 1990)

PENELOPE CURTIS

V. Interior decoration.

1. Before 1589. 2. 1589–1660. 3. 1661–1722. 4. 1723–1815. 5. 1816–*c.* 1890. 6. After *c.* 1890.

1. BEFORE 1589. The first effects of the Renaissance on French interior decoration were felt in the Loire Valley, where the French Court had retreated during the Hundred Years War (1337–1453). From his first Italian campaign in 1494, Charles VII brought back a team of architects, scholars and craftsmen, together with a considerable amount of looted booty. The furniture, pictures, works of art and textiles that had adorned the luxurious palaces of Italian princes brought a new magnificence to a way of life that had remained essentially medieval. This Italian influence (*see* ITALY, §V, 2) was first apparent in the 1490s at the royal château of Amboise, although none of the individual works of art nor the applied architectural decoration by such craftsmen as Bernadino da Brescia

(*fl* 1495) and Domenico da Cortona survives from this period. As a result of the subsequent Italian campaigns of Louis XII and Francis I between 1500 and 1525, the influence of northern Italy, particularly from Milan and Genoa, combined with the Late Gothic Flamboyant style, heightening the richness of detail and lavish effects of both architecture and furniture. The lifestyle of the nobility was peripatetic, and so most pieces of furniture were designed for easy transport, the chest (*coffre*) being the most important item in which to carry the folded ornamental textiles that were used to render the next residence comfortable, familiar and attractive. Tapestries with *millefleurs* designs, such as the *Lady and the Unicorn* series (*c.* 1490–1500; Paris, Mus. Cluny; *see* TAPESTRY, colour pl. I, fig. 1), evoke nostalgia for the courtly medieval world. The linenfold pattern used on the panels of seat furniture, *boiseries* and chests echoed the draped textiles used to adorn walls and beds. Bright reds, greens and blues were widely used, in dress as in tapestries. For the nobility, little had changed since Jean, Duc de Berry, was depicted at his table, sitting on a dais beneath a richly decorated canopy (*Très Riches Heures of Jean, Duc de Berry, c.* 1411–16 and *c.* 1485–6; Chantilly, Mus. Condé, MS. 65, fol. 1*v*; for illustration *see* VALOIS, (3)). The table is a simple plank on trestles covered with a patterned white cloth; all the colour in the scene is provided by the other textiles: the cloth of blue and gold covering the seat of the Duke, the brilliantly coloured tapestries of battle scenes that line the walls and the richly embroidered garments of the courtiers.

The new châteaux of the Loire Valley (*see* MAISON DE PLAISANCE), including Bury (1511–24), Chenonceaux (1514–22) and Azay-le-Rideau (1518–28), were built by private patrons in emulation of Italian pleasure villas and displayed a new regularity in plan as well as the use of architectural decoration of Classical inspiration, such as *rinceaux*, pilasters and profile heads. Nevertheless, interior decoration remained largely unchanged until the important building programme in the Ile-de-France started in 1525 by Francis I on his return from captivity in Madrid. 'Widowed of his dream, Italy', he set out to re-create it on French soil. The Sack of Rome in 1527 left many artists without patronage, and in 1530 Rosso Fiorentino was given the task of overseeing the decoration of the château of Fontainebleau (*see* FONTAINEBLEAU, §1), the King's favourite palace. Francesco Primaticcio, the assistant of Giulio Romano at the Palazzo del Te in Mantua, joined him in 1532; in addition to being a painter he was also a stuccoist. Working in the Italian Mannerist style, they revolutionized interior decoration in France during the second quarter of the 16th century (*see* FONTAINEBLEAU SCHOOL). Fontainebleau became, in Cellini's words, 'a new Rome'. The Galerie François I (1534–40), built by Gilles Le Breton and decorated by Rosso and Primaticcio, was the first manifestation of a truly northern Renaissance style. The architecture of the Galerie, northern in form, became the setting for an unprecedented decorative scheme that allied the Italian art of fresco to stuccowork executed in low and high relief. Divided evenly, the walls were covered in the lower part by wood panelling carved in cartouches containing the King's cipher by Francisco Scibec de Carpi. The upper part developed in 14 bays the didactic and scholarly theme of the sacred character of

43. High-relief stucco decoration by Francesco Primaticcio, 1541–4, in the bedchamber of the Duchesse d'Etampes, château of Fontainebleau, 1541–4; stairway added later

royalty and the greatness of the King, with a complex mythological iconography depicted in the livid colours and tormented forms of Italian Mannerist painting. The stucco decoration elaborated in inexhaustible three-dimensional variety the vocabulary of Raphael's grotesques and the nudes of Michelangelo, as well as the putti, garlands, satyrs and chimerae of the Classical world. Between the bays bronze reproductions of famous Classical statues from the Vatican collections were displayed, including the *Apollo Belvedere*, the *Laokoon* and the *Aphrodite of Knidos*. This grand reception room became the wonder of Europe, and designs of its innovative style of ornament were disseminated by such engravers as Antonio Fantuzzi. In 1541 Primaticcio began the decoration of the bedchamber of the Duchesse d'Etampes at Fontainebleau in the same manner, making extensive use of the motif of the elegant, elongated female nude that became characteristic of the Fontainebleau school (see fig. 43).

Textiles retained their importance, hung on walls and matching the bed-hangings and the new fixed upholstery of seat furniture (as opposed to the removable cushions of the Middle Ages). The mobility of furnishings became less important, although Francis I ordered several sets of tapestries woven in Brussels and another (Vienna, Ksthist. Mus.) with the exact designs of the Fontainebleau Galerie to adorn his apartments during his travels. The latter was woven in the Fontainebleau workshops and was given to the Austrian Emperor by Charles IX in 1547 as a wedding present on his marriage to Elisabeth of Austria. Richness

and luxury were reflected in the sumptuous colour schemes of black, orange, gold, violet, crimson and white. Spanish gilt leather became fashionable and was used on walls, furniture and cushions. Lavish and expensive Turkish carpets began to be used on the floors of small cabinets as well as for table-covers.

The second half of the century was characterized by a restrained classicism in interior decoration. The influence of Fontainebleau, still apparent when Ancy-le-Franc was built by Sebastiano Serlio in 1546 and decorated by Primaticcio and his assistant Nicolò dell'Abate, began to wane. The decoration of the king's bedchamber in the Palais du Louvre, Paris, supervised by Pierre Lescot in 1556, owed more to the Palazzo Massimo in Rome and to the influence of Philibert de L'Orme. De L'Orme brought a new, rigorously Classical spirit to the château of Anet (*see* ANET, §3), which he built (1547–55) for Diane de Poitiers. While the first part of the century had been dominated by Italian influence, in the second half there was a growing tendency towards a clearer, neater, more intellectual and archaeological use of forms and motifs. The publication of the designs of Jacques Androuet Du Cerceau the elder (*see* DU CERCEAU, (1)) was an important manifestation of this new spirit and nurtured the decorative arts of the last part of the century.

BIBLIOGRAPHY
L. Dimier: *Le Primatice: Architecte, peintre et sculpteur des rois de France* (Paris, 1900)
F. Gebelin: *Le Style renaissance en France* (Paris, 1951)

A. Blunt: *Art and Architecture in France, 1500–1700*, Pelican Hist. A. (London, 1953, rev. 4/1980/*R* 1988)
——: *Philibert de L'Orme* (Paris, 1958)
S. Béguin: *L'Ecole de Fontainebleau: Le Maniérisme à la cour de France* (Paris, 1960)
M. de Fayet: *Moyen-âge et Renaissance* (Paris, 1961)
L'Ecole de Fontainebleau (exh. cat., Paris, Grand Pal., 1972)
F. Robertet: 'Italianisme et Renaissance française', *Mélanges à la mémoire de Franco Simone*, vii (Geneva, 1983)

MONIQUE RICCARDI-CUBITT

2. 1589–1660. By the end of the 16th century, a more refined style of living had developed, characterized by harmonious, rich and comfortable settings. Contemporary letters, guides and gazettes serve as sources of information, and prints can also provide examples of interiors typical of this period (see fig. 44). Pierre Le Muet's *Manière de bien bâtir pour toutes sortes de personnes* (1623, 2/1647) and Louis Savot's *Architecture française des bâtiments particuliers* (1624; rev. 1673 by François Blondel), for example, were intended for both architects and builders, as were the *Livre d'architecture* (1632, 2/1641) by Jean Barbet (1591–before 1654) and *Pièces d'architecture* (1633) by Pierre Collot. Jean Cotelle II, an architect and painter to Louis XIII, compiled the *Livre des divers ornements pour plafonds* (*c.* 1640), and Jean Le Pautre and Jean Marot were responsible for numerous designs for fireplaces, ceilings, alcoves, beds, studies and candelabra.

The tone of this new manner of living was set by Henry IV, who commissioned leading experts to decorate and produce works for the royal residences. Rooms in the Palais du Luxembourg, Paris, refurbished after 1620 for Marie de' Medici, were sumptuously decorated. Others were to follow the King's lead, for example Cardinal de Richelieu, as seen in his magnificent castle in Poitou (nr Poitiers) and in the Palais Cardinal (1624–42; destr. 1763), Paris, the large study of which was praised by Henri Sauval as being 'for a long time the marvel and miracle of Paris'. Cardinal Mazarin's hôtel on the Rue de Richelieu (1635–45; now forming part of the Bibliothèque Nationale), Paris, was also richly decorated. These examples were in turn imitated by the wealthy bourgeoisie and by the lesser nobility who were keen to demonstrate their status by the erection of hôtels particuliers in Paris (*see* HÔTEL PARTI-CULIER). These were usually lavishly decorated and were located in the areas surrounding the Place Royale (now the Place des Vosges), in the Marais (for example, the Hôtel de Lamoignon, 1585–90, and the Hôtel de Sully, *c.* 1624–9), the Ile-Saint-Louis (Hôtel Lauzun, *c.* 1650–58) and in the Faubourg St-Honoré. Residences in the Ile-de-France were as richly decorated, most notably the château of Vaux-le-Vicomte, built and decorated from the late 1650s by Louis Le Vau, Charles Le Brun and André Le Nôtre for Nicolas Fouquet, Surintendant des Finances. The magnificent interiors at Vaux-le-Vicomte and those created for Anne of Austria at the Palais-Royal and the Palais du Louvre (1655) in Paris served as memorable examples to the young Louis XIV.

Domestic interiors were divided into three main sections: the formal rooms, the private apartments and the servants' quarters. The private lodgings generally comprised two apartments, one each for husband and wife.

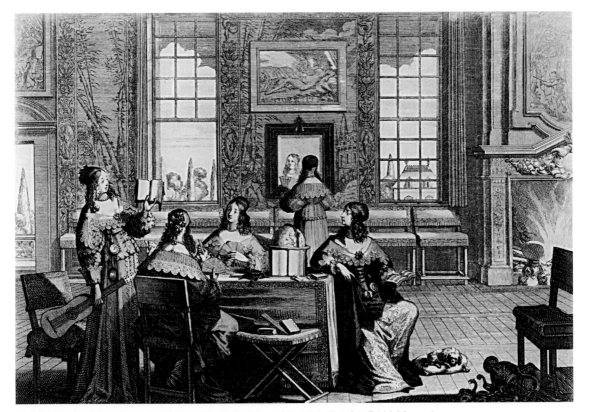

44. A Parisian interior; engraving by Abraham Bosse: *Les Vierges folles*, 1640s (London, British Museum)

Each apartment consisted either of one room containing a bed and an adjacent dressing-room or of the traditional enfilade of rooms, known as the *grands appartements*. Augustin-Charles d'Aviler pointed out in his *Cours d'architecture* that an apartment should have 'four rooms, namely an antechamber, a room, a dressing-room and a closet'. From 1640 plans indicate the presence of a dining-room, but it was rarely used as such, as meals could be served in any room; the terms *salle* or *salette*, however, were often employed to refer to a small-sized room in which meals were served. The taste for luxury and refinement was best exemplified in the study. Following the example of Mazarin in particular, this room held collections of large vases, ceramics, silverware, gems and rock crystals displayed in tortoiseshell or lacquer cabinets or on tables with pietre dure mosaic tops. Ornaments were also placed on small consoles, above which were mirrors, which rested against the walls.

The chimney-piece, ceiling and panelling were the principal features of each room. The chimney-piece *à la française*, which had been large, deep and heavily ornamented, lost its massive proportions from the middle of the 17th century. The fireplace had a smaller opening, the back of which was decorated with a sheet of cast iron known as a back-plate. By 1620 fire-dogs had become extremely large in size and fulfilled a purely decorative function. The size of the fire-dogs was later reduced as the result of a lowering of the opening of the fireplace. In the summer a wooden screen, iron panel or even a painted cloth screen was set in front of the fireplace to prevent draughts. Fireplaces were the main form of heating until *c*. 1650, when cast-iron or earthenware-tiled stoves and charcoal-pans were introduced.

Ceilings retained visible beams and joists, which were painted and decorated with gilt, or were made up of carved wooden panels, which acted as frames for inset paintings. These types of ceiling were replaced *c*. 1640–50 by flat ceilings with high arches. Ceilings in grand interiors were decorated with allegorical, mythological or history paintings enriched with carved and gilt stucco. These ceilings provided a harmony of decoration with the walls, as in the apartments of Anne of Austria at the Louvre by Giovanni Francesco Romanelli.

Walls had rectangular painted panels framed with moulding and often arranged one above the other; full-height wall panelling was rare before the end of the century. Landscapes, still-lifes, floral bouquets, arabesques and cartouches were depicted. The panels could also be painted in imitation of wood or stone. The upper section of the wall was decorated in a style still characteristic of the Renaissance period, as in the Study of Théagène and Chariclée at the château of Fontainebleau, decorated for Henry IV, and the gallery (*c*. 1631) of the château of Chessy for Henry de Fourcy. Towards the middle of the 17th century mural decoration became more homogeneous; walls could be flanked by narrow panels as at Vaux-le-Vicomte and by pilasters, often painted in white and gold, as at the Château de Maisons (1642–6). Sauval stated that the walls of the hôtel (1652) of the Abbé de La Rivière in Paris 'are made so brilliant by their gilding, that one would think that ingots had been used'. Nevertheless, a unified harmony of décor was only rarely achieved prior to Vaux-le-Vicomte.

During the reigns of Henry IV and Louis XIII luxuriousness was generally provided by textiles; tapestries, embroideries or gilt-leather hangings were fashionable, with paintings and mirrors hung over these coverings. A sense of harmony was achieved by *en suite* fabrics, for example having matching wall hangings, curtains, *portières*, bed-hangings and furniture upholstery. From the end of the 16th century this method of selecting fabrics was called *emmeublemen* and became standard practice after 1630. The celebrated Blue Room at the Parisian hôtel of the Marquise de Rambouillet was, in 1620, an excellent example of the use of colour coordination, the blue velvet curtains with motifs executed in gold *en suite* with the chair covers and table covering. Towards the mid-17th century larger bedrooms and studies could be fitted with Genoese velvet or with Venetian brocade in the winter and with damask or brocaded and painted satin in the summer. The use of two different materials of contrasting colours was fashionable.

Windows were made up of small lead squares, which allowed only a small amount of daylight to enter the room. It was extremely unusual for clear panes of glass to be used prior to 1660. Lighting was principally supplied from candlesticks or candelabra or by oil lamps. Wall lamps and brackets were introduced *c*. 1640. Projecting wall lamps were first to appear, followed by wall brackets enhanced by a mirror. Standard-lamps were made in Paris *c*. 1650, often sculpted in the form of a Moor, and called *guéridons*.

BIBLIOGRAPHY

M. Praz: *La filosofia dell'arredamento* (Milan, 1964, rev. 1982)

P. Thornton: *Seventeenth-century Interior Decoration in England, France and Holland* (New Haven and London, 1978/*R* 1981)

J. Féray: *Architecture intérieure et décoration en France des origines à 1875* (Paris, 1988) [with select bibliog.]

PASCAL-FRANÇOIS BERTRAND

3. 1661–1722. Just as the politics and military campaigns of Louis XIV dominated the history of Europe during the period 1661 to 1715, so the interior decoration of his Court at Versailles ruled fashion throughout France and the rest of Europe. Royal attention to every detail of furnishing was so explicit that this style was unequivocally identified with the *Roi Soleil*. Only magnificent surroundings could be expected for a ruler who turned his daily life into State ceremony. Louis's administrative obsession with control and centralization together with his philosophical penchant for logic forced structural clarity and physical symmetry on his interior spaces. The King's practice of assembling teams of specialists under a single artistic director and his reformation of French industries to better supply his palaces led to décor of striking unity (*see* MAISON DU ROI).

Louis's artistic sensibilities owed much to Anne of Austria (1626–62), his luxury-loving mother, whose tastes ran to brilliant and precious objects, and to his first minister, Cardinal Mazarin, whose grand style and extensive art collections excited admiration. However, it was the famous fête of 17 August 1661, when Nicolas Fouquet, Surintendant des Finances, celebrated the completion of his château of Vaux-le-Vicomte (*see* VAUX-LE-VICOMTE, §1), near Melun, that was the defining moment for the

King's design sense. The opulent interplay of stucco, painting and gilded wall panelling, designed by the painter CHARLES LE BRUN and based on Pietro da Cortona's Palazzo Pitti in Florence, dazzled the Court. Italian Baroque exuberance tempered by classicizing motifs and compartmentalized into distinct media immediately appealed to Louis. The best decoration of the previous decade, such as that at the Hôtel Lauzun (1650–58) in Paris, combined similar elements, but never before in France had all of these aspects coalesced so effectively. Only weeks after Fouquet's fête, the King arrested and imprisoned him, confiscated his property and brought the artistic team of Vaux-le-Vicomte to work on his own projects.

First among these was the rebuilding of the Galerie d'Apollon in the Palais du Louvre, Paris; Le Brun's painted ceiling was framed by high-relief stucco figures by Michel Anguier and other sculptors (see STUCCO AND PLASTERWORK, fig. 13). This gallery had the grace and sweep of Vaux but on an even grander scale. Although the gallery remained unfinished, Le Brun's concept is revealed by his commissions for blue-and-gold carpets from the Savonnerie factory in Paris, which were lushly ornamented with garlands, cornucopia and figural scenes mirroring the decoration of ceilings and walls. Two oversized cabinets conceived as Temples of Glory and Virtue (1681–3; Alnwick Castle, Northumb.; see GOBELINS, fig. 2), made of ebony and gilt-bronze by Domenico Cucci, would have emphasized the iconography of the King. The prominence of allegorical or emblematic references to the King as sculptural focus or pervasive motif became a hallmark of the LOUIS XIV STYLE.

Louis's personal taste becomes more apparent in his earliest decorated rooms (1662–8) at Versailles (see VERSAILLES, §1). Subsequent changes due to the gradual enlargement of the palace and the disappearance of furnishings over the years make it difficult to reconstruct the original appearance of these first rooms. Important information on the original project is provided by the *Inventaire général du mobilier de la Couronne*, such contemporary journals as the *Mercure galant*, visitors' memoirs and sets of engraved ornament design and architectural renderings. By all accounts, vivacious coloured marquetry, strikingly contrasting or complementary textiles and other lavish materials, notably silver, marked the emergence of the King's style. Furniture commissioned from the cabinetmaker Pierre Gole demonstrated Louis's penchant for inlaid woods, particularly floral marquetry, then popular in France and the Netherlands; the Salon's ceiling painted by Noël-Nicolas Coypel illustrates the continuing desire for ostentation in the grand Italian manner. Eighteen tabourets (stools), decorated in blue and gold with carved legs by the sculptor Philippe Caffiéri (i), reveal the predilection for sturdy, sculptural furniture supports, often emphasized through gilding. Yet Christopher Wren's comments, after his visit in 1665 to Versailles, characterizing the interiors as 'feminine' in contrast to 'the more masculine furnishings of the Palais Mazarin', suggest an air of delicacy in these rooms that was soon eclipsed by the ponderous solemnity of later decorations.

The sequence of rooms set a trend for *appartements*: a salon, an antechamber, the bedroom, a private room and closet. This order expresses the King's prescription for balance between private and social functions. In French *appartements* of the second half of the 17th century, such as these, doorways pierced the walls adjacent to the windows so as not to interrupt living spaces; chimneys, often of monumental carved stone, faced the entrances on the opposite walls. Major pieces of furniture dominated the rooms, particularly in newly fashionable bedroom alcoves, isolated by a balustrade and raised parquet floor (see fig. 45). Apart from beds, most furnishings lined the walls. Architects often designed a major suite of furniture for the conventionally shaped, rectangular rooms. The most characteristic ensemble of the period 1680 to 1700 is the CONSOLE TABLE surmounted by a mirror on a pier wall and flanked by *guéridons*.

Although Louis's palatial decorations emphasized grandeur, a secondary tendency prized novelty and surprise. A whimsical example was the Trianon de Porcelaine (1670–72; destr.), clad with blue-and-white tiles on the exterior and echoed inside by white stuccoed walls traced with blue or violet designs. It featured such remarkable furniture as a bed with a white taffeta canopy and panels embroidered with gold, silver and lilac. Private *appartements*, offering retreats from formality, stimulated design, which could in turn influence the principal rooms. The comfort found in these quarters, effected by upholstered furniture and screens against heat or draughts, was a major French contribution to décor, one that gradually infiltrated even formal rooms and determined 18th-century style.

With the King's decision in 1682 to install himself and his Court permanently at Versailles came the desire for more elaborate living quarters. The Grands Appartements became the most memorable expression of the Louis XIV style. These rooms' rich materials, bombastic sculptural weight and overt glorification of the monarch swept aside the lighter qualities of the earlier décor. Expanding the concept of the Galerie d'Apollon, the Galerie des Glaces (1678–84) and the Escalier des Ambassadeurs feature murals by Le Brun that praise the King's accomplishments (see LE BRUN, CHARLES, fig. 3). The mirrors facing the walls of the Galerie des Glaces were unprecedented in France and were made at the factory of Saint Gobain in Paris, which competed with Venetian production and introduced ever larger reflective surfaces into French interiors. Drawing on associations with Imperial Rome, stucco motifs of military trophies and bound slaves surrounded giant oval reliefs allegorically portraying Louis's battle victories in the antechambers of the Salon de la Guerre (see VERSAILLES, fig. 2) and the Salon de la Paix at either end of the Galerie des Glaces. The walls throughout the Grands Appartements varied from rectilinear geometrical patterns of coloured marbles to painted and gilt-wood panels to painted silks and patterned velvets from Lyon. Louis's painting collection hung against brocades, his antique and contemporary sculptures were placed on pedestals, and Delft planters were filled with citrus trees. Most of the floors were laid with parquet, some in elaborate radiating or arabesque marquetry; these were created by such outstanding *ébénistes* as André-Charles Boulle, who worked for the Grand Cabinet (1688).

Equally impressive was the furnishing, particularly the famous silver furniture (see §IX, 1(iii) below) and grand

45. Bedchamber of Louis XIV in the château of Versailles, late 17th century (restored)

cabinets. To supply such magnificent royal furnishings the minister Jean-Baptiste Colbert (*see* COLBERT, (1)) established the Manufacture Royale des Meubles de la Couronne in the Gobelins in 1662 (*see* GOBELINS). A wide variety of crafts was practised at this factory, not only tapestry-weaving and embroidery, but also wood-carving, veneering and gilding, metalwork and pietre dure. A royal charter protected the craftsmen from guild regulations and freed them to combine materials in wondrous and inventive ways. Cucci's magnificent pair of cabinets, supported by carved caryatids and incorporating colourful pietre dure scenes, suited the palatial interior while echoing painted and sculpted ceiling decoration. Such cabinetmakers as Gole and Boulle created inlaid veneers ranging from pewter and brass to tortoiseshell, mother-of-pearl and lapis lazuli, set against ebony or ivory; typically, these rich, natural materials completed many interiors of the period. Silver furniture, a feature at Versailles, was also in vogue in the wealthiest houses of the Ile-de-France. On a visit in 1687, the Swedish architect Nicodemus Tessin the younger counted 167 items of solid silver furniture in the State apartments. The effect of the large silver *guéridons* against the mirrors and crystal chandeliers in the Galerie des Glaces or the suite of silver furniture in the King's bedroom set against rich textiles is difficult to imagine due to the few surviving examples. Already by 1689 the financially disastrous war against the League of Augsburg forced the King to melt his and the nobility's silver furniture into bullion; five years later the Gobelins closed except for the tapestry-weaving studio.

The use of textiles in wall hangings, *portières*, bed-hangings, canopies, upholsteries and carpets continued to be an essential component of French interiors. Savonnerie carpets incorporating arabesques covered the floors of the wealthiest households (*see* CARPET, colour pl. I), while tapestries woven at Beauvais and the Gobelins combined allegorical scenes with grotesques after Jean Le Pautre and, later in the century, after the lighter designs of JEAN BERAIN I (*see also* TAPESTRY, colour pl. II, fig. 2). Versailles was a showcase for France's luxury production of silk ranging from lavish embroideries in the Grande Anti-chambre to the abundant silk hangings in the Grand Trianon (1687). Textiles also helped unify décor: the crimson velvet upholstery used for the King's bedroom suite (bed, armchairs, folding stools, floor cushions, table carpet and folding screen) was a dramatic focus of the room. Woven materials provided seasonal variety when the winter's heavy wool was exchanged—as was customary in many chambers—for light coloured silks in summer.

While interior decoration outside the Court should not be ignored, the primacy of Versailles as the centre of design is an inescapable fact. As the King gathered the nobility around the court, fewer châteaux were built in the last third of the 17th century. Building and decoration in Paris and the provinces closely followed designs by Le Brun or engraved ornament by Le Pautre or Berain; craftsmen trained in workshops supplying the Crown travelled to sites throughout the country. Stone or stucco might replace marble, painted decoration might imitate carved, but designs and conception from Parisian hôtel to country château tended to follow the royal example. Painted and gilt-wood panels in the Salon Doré (1687–8) in the Hôtel de Mailly, Paris, for example, simulated Le Brun tapestries, while the white-and-gold ceiling indicates the pervasive influence of Berain's symmetrical and vigorous patterns.

During the second half of Louis's long reign, style gradually evolved from heavy, sculptural forms to lighter, more purely ornamental ones. After the deaths of Colbert (1683) and Le Brun (1690) and the King's military and financial reversals, the huge scale and costly fabric of palace décor diminished. Typical of this development is the antechamber known as the 'Oeil de Boeuf' (1701) at Versailles, with a white ceiling and gilded stuccowork. The architect JULES HARDOUIN MANSART created variously shaped rooms and flatter wall definition. The walls of hôtels were often covered with *boiseries*, which featured grotesques in the style of Berain or were simply painted white. Chimneys became smaller, and white walls were lightened by the incorporation of mirrors. Furniture became more dynamic in shape, its overall form reinforced by continuity of ornament. The style of Boulle's inlaid metal and tortoiseshell furniture with its graceful arabesque patterns (*see* MARQUETRY, colour pl. VII) represents the ideal furniture to complement the interiors of this period. All of these tendencies merged into the distinctive Rococo style when Louis's great-grandson, Louis XV, reanimated Versailles on his accession to the throne in 1722.

BIBLIOGRAPHY
F. Kimball: *The Creation of the Rococo* (Philadelphia, 1943)
P. Levallois, ed.: *Le XVIIe Siècle français* (Paris, 1958)
A. Mairie: *Naissance de Versailles* (Paris, 1968)
——: *Versailles au temps de Louis XIV* (Paris, 1968)
G. Walton: *Louis XIV's Versailles* (Chicago and Harmondsworth, 1986)

For further bibliography see §2 above.

IAN WARDROPPER

4. 1723–1815. In the second quarter of the 18th century the sequence of rooms *en enfilade* was superseded by a more relaxed arrangement of smaller salons, cabinets (*see* CABINET (i), §4) and music rooms or libraries, as at the Hôtel de Matignon (1722–4), Paris, by Jean Courtonne (*see* HÔTEL PARTICULIER, §2). The new style was developed from the work of Gilles-Marie Oppenord and François-Antoine Vassé (1681–1736) and above all of Nicolas Pineau and Jean-Baptiste Leroux (e.g. antechamber in the Hôtel de Matignon, 1732, Paris) and represented the final departure from the Classical orders of the Louis XIV style. Columns and pilasters were no longer used. An architectural supporting frame for the wall articulation was omitted. In its place *boiserie* (wood panelling) became common; it gave rise to a delicate framework of *panneaux* (wall areas) into which twin-winged doors and tall windows were incorporated in the same way as projecting mantelpieces, glass-fronted bookshelves or large mirrors. Empty spaces were avoided. Delicate gilt *boiseries* covered the white fields of the *panneaux* and the areas just below the ceiling with asymmetrical, ornamental patterns (see fig. 46). Models for these were disseminated by the engravings of Jacques de Lajoüe, Juste-Aurèle Meissonier, Jean-Antoine Fraisse and Jean Mondon (*fl* 1736–45). Even painting was subordinated to this system; large-format ceiling paintings were little used.

The autonomous, exchangeable panel painting lost its place on the wall. Paintings and tapestries became decorative additions to *panneaux* or to the OVERDOORS (e.g. Cabinet de Singes, Hôtel de Rohan, 1749–52, Paris). Favourite subjects for the paintings were allegories, mythology, history, landscapes or hunting scenes, as well as Court feasts and masquerades by such artists as Jean-Baptiste Oudry, Jean-François de Troy (ii), Charles-Joseph Natoire, François Boucher and Carle Vanloo.

Fireplaces surmounted by mirrors often formed the centrepiece of a room's furnishings. They were tightly linked to the wall decoration and were complemented by fireplace furnishings (e.g. andirons and tongs), often formed entirely of rocaille scrolls of iron or bronze. The fireplace surround was usually of marble, but faience or porcelain tiles from Sèvres were also used. The firescreens were sometimes covered with a pastoral scene embroidered on silk and surrounded by a delicately carved frame.

Candle-holders had a special function in the room, either as candelabra (often from Venice) suspended from the ceiling, fixed to the wall as chandeliers (girandole) or standing on a table (*guéridon*). Numerically, the largest group of furnishing pieces, however, was the furniture, above all armchairs, chairs and tables. The Louis XV style had developed a considerable number of new pieces upon which to sit or recline, including the *fauteuil* with arms and backrest, the *bergère* with separately upholstered cushions and backrest, and the office chair with light wickerwork or solid leather upholstery. Curves in the backrests, seats and legs were intended to mask the effect of a weight-supporting structure, while close-fitting seat-shapes were developed to provide bodily comfort. The chaise longue was a combination of the armchair and *tabouret* (footstool), its design allowing the body to recline casually on soft forms and cushions, as seen in Boucher's painting *The Artist's Wife* (1743; New York, Frick). The upholstery of seat furniture could be exchanged in keeping with the seasons: taffeta in summer and velvet or brocade in winter. Tables were delicate and were usually intended for a specific purpose: the *table à jeu, table en chiffonnière, table de lit* and *table de nuit* (*see* §VI, 3 below). Convertible pieces, that might, for example, be transformed from a dressing-table into a writing-desk by letting down the mirror, were especially popular. Such musical instruments as harps, harpsichords or pianofortes were decorated like furniture, being richly embellished with inlays, marquetry and gilding. Sculptural mounts, as produced, above all, by Jacques Caffiéri, were popular not only for their decorative effect but also protected the elaborate veneers on the corners and feet of the furniture. CHARLES CRESSENT is regarded as one of the most important marquetry specialists in Paris at this time.

The range of accessories used to decorate the festive table extended from every kind of tableware, preferably of porcelain, through cutlery to the silver centrepiece (e.g. those by Meissonier) or porcelain figures (made at Sèvres). Vases were also used to decorate the table and, like mantelpiece clocks (*pendules*), were an important component of room decoration. Other popular decorative items were porcelain busts or small sculptures of lead, clay or biscuit porcelain (e.g. Etienne-Maurice Falconet's *Woman Bathing, c.* 1755–7; Sèvres, Mus. N. Cér.). Large sculptures were used in interiors only in isolated cases, and even then mainly in niches in staterooms or galleries (e.g. decoration in the Galerie Dorée, Hôtel de La Vrilliére (now the Banque de France), Paris, from 1718, by Vassé). Free-standing sculptures were occasionally situated on staircases.

Light was another fundamental component of the interior space of a room. Large french windows and crystal chandeliers illuminated the rooms. Carpenters used such light woods as citron-wood, amaranth or rose-wood, the polished surfaces of which reflected the light in the same way as the many mirrors and the shining parquet floors, an effect further heightened from the beginning of the 18th century by the use of East Asian lacquer (*see* LACQUER, §II, 1). Gold and silver ornaments gleamed against the white décor of the *panneaux* or the furniture surfaces. Mirrors created an illusion of endless suites of rooms and blurred the demarcations of spaces (*see* MIRROR, §VI, 2). Shadows and dark corners were avoided, and balustrades on staircases or balconies were replaced by light, delicate wrought-ironwork. The aim of this interior decoration was to create an impression of a seemingly intimate space combined with perspectives into imaginary pictorial realms by the use of mirrors and paintings, an example being Germain Boffrand's Salon Ovale in the Hôtel de Soubise (now the Archives Nationales; 1735–8), Paris, which is ornamented with paintings of the *Story of Psyche* by Natoire in the Salon de la Princesse

(for illustration *see* NATOIRE, CHARLES-JOSEPH) and stucco reliefs (*in situ*) by Jean-Baptiste Lemoyne (ii). This concept was disseminated by Jean-Baptiste Dubos, who contended that the reception of art was governed not by reason but by feeling (*Réflexions critiques sur la poésie et sur la peinture*, Paris, 1719).

For the bourgeoisie houses with several floors were increasingly built during the second quarter of the 18th century. They reflected the varying social ranks of the occupants by the arrangement of antechambers, main room, kitchen and smaller side-rooms; a large salon was generally not provided. Various designs make clear the intention to harmonize comfort, aesthetic form and the demands of the site or the building regulations. The furniture did not always conform to the fashionable trends of the leading social groups of the *ancien régime*. It often fell back on types common at the end of the 17th century. The curved legs and surfaces of chairs and tables were less elegant, and shapes and colours were heavier than in the fashionable pieces of the period, as seen in Jean-Siméon Chardin's *Saying Grace* (*c.* 1740; Paris, Louvre).

From about the mid-18th century a critical opposition provoked a debate on the decorative idiom of the Rococo style, led by such theorists as Charles-Nicolas Cochin (ii) in his article 'Supplication aux orfèvres, ciseleurs, sculpteurs en bois pour les appartements & autres par une société d'artistes' in the *Mercure de France* (Dec 1754, pp. 178–87). The imitation of nature and the reception of

46. Panelled room in the Bibliothèque de l'Arsenal, Paris, 18th century

47. Bathroom of Mlle Dervieux, by François-Joseph Bélanger, 1789, Paris; engraving by A. Detournelle, c. 1790 (Paris, Bibliothèque Nationale, Cabinet des Estampes)

antiquity underlay the new demands for a simple elegance and a strict symmetry. Forms were simplified, and decoration was again used to emphasize architectural structure and the boundaries of spaces. The interior walls of rooms, usually in light colours, were articulated by pilasters. The wall panels were decorated symmetrically with flower garlands, bows and medallions (e.g. Mlle Dervieux's bathroom, 1789, Paris; see fig. 47) or covered with patterned cloth. From about the mid-18th century wallpaper was also used, especially that from the factory of Jean-Baptiste Réveillon (see WALLPAPER, colour pl. IV, fig. 1). Panel paintings decorating the panelled, cloth- or paper-covered wall sections attempted to give an impression of realistic, natural scenes (e.g. those by Joseph Vernet and Jean-Honoré Fragonard). Armchairs, tables, commodes and writing-tables were decorated from c. 1760 with plant motifs, bows and ornamentation à la grecque. The forms had been disseminated by such collections of engravings as the Comte de Caylus's Recueil d'antiquités égyptiennes, étrusques, grecques, romains et gauloises (Paris, 1752–67) and Le antichità di Ercolano esposte (Naples, 1757–92), inspired by the excavations at Herculaneum (1738) and Pompeii (1748). Adapted to the fashion of the time, these engravings brought about an increasing severity in the ornamentation of marquetry and mounts (see NEO-CLASSICISM).

During the last quarter of the 18th century, in connection with a renewed vision of the ancient world, large sculptures were once again included in interiors, where, mounted on socles, they usually embodied allegories or ancient divinities, as seen in François Dequevauviller's engraving of a Gathering at a Concert (1783; Paris, Bib. N., cat. no. 63) after Niclas Lafrensen the younger. Chairs were given vertical backrests and fluted legs and were upholstered with Gobelins tapestry or silk damask (e.g. the private suite of Marie-Antoinette, château of Versailles, c. 1785).

In the years of the National Convention (1792–5) and the Directoire (Oct 1795–Nov 1799) the ground-plans of palaces increasingly took into account practical needs (see DIRECTOIRE STYLE). Ancient Roman decorative elements were combined with the heavy forms of French art of the 17th century (e.g. Château de Malmaison, interior furnishings, 1800; for illustration see FONTAINE, PIERRE-FRANÇOIS-LÉONARD). A closed, cubic outline was typical of the furniture of the Consulate period (1799–1804; see CONSULATE STYLE).

Napoleon Bonaparte's imperial pretensions created a heightened need for large rooms in which the demand for simplicity was combined with a desire for sumptuous furnishings (e.g. the interior decoration for the Grand Trianon and the château of Versailles). In the interiors of this period the decoration of bedrooms and studies could seem more important than that of salons or dining-rooms. An ideal example of this tendency was recorded by the architect Louis Martin Berthauld (1771–1823), who executed the designs of Charles Percier and Fontaine in the plans for the decoration of the bedroom of Mme Récamier in the Hôtel Necker, Paris (for illustration see EMPIRE

STYLE). In the Hôtel Necker the luxurious furnishings were strictly symmetrical and were subordinated to the functional lines of the building. The walls were covered in violet silk and divided up by very shallow articulation made up of socles, pilasters and cornices. A fireplace projected from the wall of one of the short sides of the room, matched by a mahogany secrétaire against the opposite wall, with a mirror over each. A dark mahogany door on one side was divided into six panels of light citron-wood, decorated with silver mounts. Just below the ceiling were frieze-like illustrations with motifs following Pompeiian models. On the long wall, opposite the two windows, stood a bed of reddish brown mahogany on a socle with two steps, with a canopy of white Indian fabric over it. To the right and left were jardinières and a night-table with an oil lamp. The individual pieces (now dispersed) of this furniture set, from the workshop of the Jacob brothers in Paris, were, like other utility objects of this time, based on the forms of furniture in antiquity. Apart from gold, the colours red, green and blue were predominant and often contrasted strongly with the colours of the wooden structures. In this way they not only emphasized a division between the different functional areas, but also set off the clear outlines of the strictly linear structures. Decorative objects were often based on patterns from Egyptian art, which had been disseminated after Napoleon's Egyptian Campaign (1798–9) in Percier and Fontaine's *Recueil de décorations intérieures* (Paris, 1812). Motifs included temples, pyramids, obelisks and sphinxes, combined with Roman armour, trophies and fasces (*see* EGYPTIAN REVIVAL).

While the ostentatious style of the Napoleonic era soon found its way into artistocratic and high-bourgeois circles, simpler forms were found in the interior decoration of less wealthy citizens. In the ground-plans and elevations of middle-class houses in Paris the need for simple room suites was predominant. Depending on social standing, doors and ceiling borders might have been decorated with ornamentation based on ancient models, or the fireplace surmounted by a framed mirror. Paintings were hung on the empty wall spaces, and the jardinière was a typical item of furniture.

BIBLIOGRAPHY

J. C. Krafft and N. Ransonette: *Plans, coupes et élévations des plus belles maisons et hôtels construits à Paris et dans les environs, an ix–x* (Paris, 1771–1802)
L. Hautecoeur: *Architecture classique* (1943–57)
J. Niclausse: *Thomire ciseleur (1751–1843): Sa vie, son oeuvre* (Paris, 1947)
F. Kimball: *Le Style Louis XV: Origine et évolution du Rococo* (Paris, 1949)
P. Francastel: *Le Style Empire du Directoire à la Restauration* (Paris, 1952)
H. Bauer: *Rocaille: Zur Herkunft und zum Wesen eines Ornament-Motivs* (Berlin, 1962)
M.-L. Biver: *Pierre Fontaine: Premier Architecte de l'Empereur* (Paris, 1964)
H. Honour: *Neoclassicism* (Harmondsworth, 1968/R 1984)
S. Eriksen: *Early Neo-classicism in France* (London, 1974)
A. Röver: *Bienséance: Zur ästhetischen Situation im Ancien Régime, dargestellt an Beispielen der Pariser Privatarchitektur* (Hildesheim, Zurich and New York, 1977)
H. Ottomeyer: *Das frühe Oeuvre Charles Perciers (1782–1800). Zu den Anfängen des Historismus in Frankreich* (Phil. diss., Munich, Ludwig-Maximilians U., 1981)
P. Thornton: *Authentic Decor: The Domestic Interior, 1620–1920* (London, 1984/R 1985)
P. Ariès and G. Duby, eds: *De la Renaissance aux Lumières* (1986), iii and *De la Révolution à la Grande Guerre* (1987), iv of *Histoire de la vie privée* (Paris, 1986–7)
S. Eriksen and G. de Bellaigue: *Sèvres Porcelain: Vincennes and Sèvres, 1740–1800* (London and Boston, 1987)
A. Pradère: *Les Ebénistes français de Louis XIV à la Révolution* (Paris, 1989)
——: *Die Kunst des französischen Möbels* (Munich, 1990)
H. Bauer and H. Sedlmayr: *Rokoko: Struktur und Wesen einer europäischen Epoche* (Cologne, 1991)

5. 1816–*c*. 1890. The fall of Napoleon and the Paris peace treaties of 1814 and 1815 gave rise to restorative tendencies of the most diverse kinds. These were supposed to reconcile the new society in post-Revolutionary France with the monarchy (Louis XVIII and Charles X). With the new Napoleonic nobility and the Bourbon aristocracy, the Church, too, regained importance; but after the accession of the bourgeois king Louis-Philippe and during the Second Republic (1848–52) it was above all the bourgeoisie, represented by entrepreneurs, artists and scientists, who gained ground. In the Second Empire (1852–71) and the Third Republic (1871) until the outbreak of World War I, industrialization emerged as the new force that set everything in motion. In the field of interior decoration the social changes linked to these transformations were expressed in an eclectic juxtaposition of different styles. While the Empire style and Asian and Middle Eastern fashions, as seen in Delacroix's the *Apartment of the Comte de Mornay* (1833; Paris, Louvre), and antique-style decoration, as in the Maison Pompéienne, Paris (1855; destr. 1891; project drawings and photographs; Paris, Bib. N.; Carnavalet; Mus. A. Déc.; see fig. 48), by ALFRED NICOLAS NORMAND for Prince Napoléon (*see* BONAPARTE, (10)), continued to exert an influence in the second half of the century, from *c*. 1830 the Gothic, Renaissance and Rococo revivals were preferred; towards the end of the century these tendencies called forth the reaction of the Art Nouveau style.

The revival of the Middle Ages brought about in interior decoration an increased use of neo-Gothic motifs, although in France this tendency was carried forward less by a Romantic enthusiasm for the Middle Ages than by a search for the constructional principles of the Gothic (*see* GOTHIC REVIVAL). About the middle of the century the Gothic style was even regarded, against the background of a Republican mood, as the *principe vrai*, as championed by Viollet-le-Duc; imitation of it was to embrace all branches of art and the crafts. Furniture was based on medieval forms and decorated with Late Gothic motifs; windows were embellished with stained glass, and paintings and small *objets d'art* were modelled on medieval patterns. The frequently flat ceilings of the usually rectangular living-rooms were decorated with applied groins and ribs, either painted or covered in dark varnish, as seen in the *Salon of the Princesse Marie d'Orléans in the Tuileries* (*c*. 1840; Paris, Mus. A. Déc.) by Prosper Lafaye (1806–83) and in the *Pink Room of the Château de Roquetaillade* (1868; Château de Roquetaillade, nr Mazères, Gironde) by EDMOND-CLÉMENT-MARIE-LOUIS DUTHOIT.

The renewed interest in the Renaissance (*see* RENAISSANCE REVIVAL), the artistic forms of which were prized as an expression of Italy's free city-republics of the 15th and 16th centuries, appeared through the increasing spread of the arts and crafts as an attribute of middle-class prosperity, as seen in Léger's *Scheme for a Room in the*

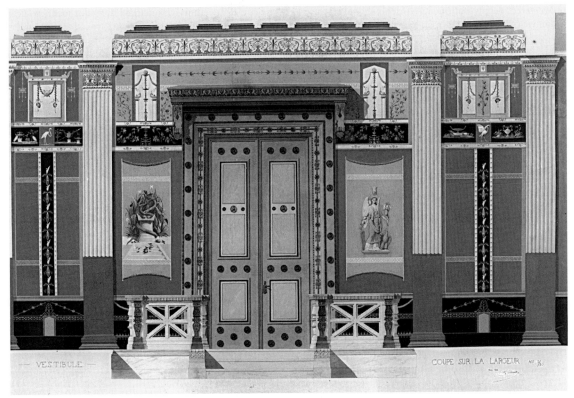

48. Maison Pompéienne, Paris, 1855; destr. 1891; commemorative drawing of the vestibule by Alfred Nicolas Normand, gouache, 0.74×1.15 m, 1862 (Paris, Musée des Arts Décoratifs)

Renaissance Style (1844; Paris, Mus. A. Déc.). But it was also seen as reflecting the splendour of the French royal courts under Francis I and Henry II, as seen in the *Room in the Parisian Hôtel of the Princesse Mathilde* (*c.* 1860; Paris, Mus. A. Déc.) by Eugène Giraud (1806–81).

The rounded, comfortable forms of the Rococo fell in with the desire for cozy domesticity (*see* ROCOCO RE-VIVAL). Furniture with rich ornamentation and gilt carvings, even if some were papier-mâché imitations, was subject to 18th-century contours no less than clocks, jewellery or fashionable dress. From *c.* 1840 Rococo Revival forms were used, especially for decorating salons or boudoirs. Imitations of the Louis XVI style came into fashion from *c.* 1860, although they were sometimes mixed with elements from the Louis XIV or Louis XV styles, as in the *Cabinet de Toilette and Cabinet de travail of the Empress Eugénie at Saint-Cloud* (1860; Compiègne, Château) by Fortuné Fournier (1798–1864).

Since the Rococo, like the Gothic, was seen as a genuinely French style, its imitation in 19th-century interiors fell in with nationalistic aspirations for art. In addition, the Rococo Revival, by reviving the decorative styles and manners of the *ancien régime*, was able to reflect the ideas of 19th-century French society. Accordingly, the revival was not limited to the aristocracy but soon penetrated the interiors of the nouveaux riches, who, lacking an artistic tradition of their own, hoped to ennoble themselves by this style of interior decoration.

In the second half of the 19th century this eclectic, historicizing style of living, especially among the *haute bourgeoisie*, took on more and more pompous forms. An antechamber had preferably to reflect Gothic or Renaissance idiom; a Gothic Revival dining-room might adjoin a Renaissance Revival or Baroque Revival salon. Windows were often leaded, while small *objets d'art* and ceramic wares in the Renaissance style of St Porchaire or Bernard Palissy by such artists as CHARLES-JEAN AVISSEAU adorned the mantelpiece. The rose-wood furniture of the bedroom might be decorated in the Rococo Revival style with marquetry and porcelain plaquettes made by Sèvres, as proposed by Oscar Edmond Ris-Paquot (*b* 1835) in *L'Art de bâtir, meubler et entretenir sa maison* (Paris, 1890). The movable furnishings of the salon, for which (despite machine production) the best materials, such as oak, walnut or exotic veneers, were used, could span the whole stylistic spectrum from the Henry II cupboard to the Louis XIV armchair, while indoor plants, especially palms, heavy velvet door curtains, East Asian carpets and wall decorations of wood, leather, tapestries from the Gobelins or painted wallpapers completed the decoration. For the colour scheme dark tones were preferred, as seen in Mihály Munkácsy's *Artist's Apartment in Paris* (1877; Budapest, N.G.) and *Interior Views of the Hôtel in the Rue de Berry* (*c.* 1882; Paris, Mus. A. Déc.) by François Schommer (*b* 1850). Apart from Ottoman-style sofas, a typical furniture piece of this period was the *crapaud*, a usually heavily upholstered, deeply buttoned and richly embellished low armchair (*see* UPHOLSTERY, colour pl. XV). In boudoirs the back wall of a niche and the vaulted base of the ceiling could be upholstered and padded to match luxuriously upholstered seats, as seen in V. Quetin's journal *Le Magasin de meubles* (Paris, 1865–7).

BIBLIOGRAPHY
L. Hautecoeur: *Architecture classique* (1943–57)
C. Duncan: *The Pursuit of Pleasure: The Rococo Revival in French Romantic Art* (New York and London, 1976)
L'Art en France sous le Second Empire (exh. cat., Paris, Réunion Musées N., 1979)
P. Thornton: *Authentic Decor: The Domestic Interior, 1620–1920* (London, 1984/*R* 1985)
P. Ariès and G. Duby, eds: *De la Révolution à la Grande Guerre* (1987), iv of *Histoire de la vie privée* (Paris, 1986–7)
C. Gere: *Nineteenth-Century Decoration: The Art of Interior* (London, 1989)

LUDWIG TAVERNIER

6. AFTER *c.* 1890. After the Exposition Universelle in Paris in 1889, the Union Centrale des Arts Décoratifs, influenced by the English Arts and Crafts Movement, joined with prominent politicians and cultural administrators to promote the reform of design in France and actively to create a new French style. The art dealer S. BING was pivotal to this enterprise, acting as consultant and emissary before setting up his shop, La Maison de l'Art Nouveau (est. 1895), the name of which encapsulated the movement (*see* ART NOUVEAU). French critics were, however, hostile to the movement, and at the time it was not a commercial success; they expressed more approval for the room-settings shown at the Exposition Universelle of 1900 in Paris. The interiors for Bing's pavilion, Art Nouveau Bing (destr.), were in an elegant, unified, Rococo-inspired style, using furniture created in Bing's workshops to designs by EUGÈNE GAILLARD, Edouard Colonna and Georges de Feure (*see* ART NOUVEAU, fig. 2). In Nancy EMILE GALLÉ created innovative glassware and furniture inlaid with marquetry. He in turn inspired the Daum brothers in their experimental glass production and Louis Majorelle to use his traditional furniture manufacture to subsidize a range of pieces in the new style. Despite the critical success of the 1900 exhibition, which marked the peak of the Art Nouveau style, it was never particularly popular: it appealed mainly to a social minority who could afford the individual craftsmanship, and to an intellectual élite who understood the literary and cultural references.

Designers, who during the late 19th century had emerged distinct from craftsmen, formed their first professional association, the Société des Artistes–Décorateurs (SAD), in 1901. They held annual salons and actively promoted reform and modernity in French design. Alarmed by the impact of the work of the Munich decorators (including Karl Bertsch, Bruno Paul, Richard Riemerschmid and Theodor Veil) shown at the Salon of 1910, they lobbied for another major exhibition to be held in Paris, and, after numerous postponements, this was eventually held in 1925 as the Exposition Internationale des Arts Décoratifs et Industriels Modernes, from which came the name ART DECO. This style was intended to reflect 'modern' life and embodied a strong reaction against the perceived decadence of Art Nouveau. It was shaped and influenced by a mixture of social and political developments as well as by art movements and cultural events.

The late 19th century was marked by major technological advances, such as the use of electricity, which was celebrated symbolically and practically at the 1900 Exposition Universelle in Paris. The rapid development of sophisticated machinery facilitated production and provided a new repertory of decorative symbols connected with power and speed, both natural and manmade. Such important groups of artists as the Fauves and the Cubists had made their mark in France by 1910. The 1909 visit of the Russian impresario Serge Diaghilev's Ballets Russes brought an explosion of colour to the Paris stage. French designers, lacking a national infrastructure for mass production, realized that their strength lay in creating unique pieces for the luxury market. An early experiment in marketing avant-garde art and design was the Maison Cubiste, exhibited at the 1912 Salon d'Automne, whose structure was designed by Raymond Duchamp-Villon. Its 'salon bourgeois', decorated and furnished by André Mare (1887–1932) with glass by Maurice Marinot, was hung with Cubist paintings by Marcel Duchamp, Léger and Jean Metzinger.

Other pioneer modernizers were the couturiers: in 1908 Paul Poiret employed Paul Iribe (1883–1935) to illustrate his deluxe album of dress designs in elegant room-settings, and in 1912 JACQUES DOUCET ordered his apartment in the Avenue du Bois, Paris, to be decorated and furnished by, among others, Eileen Gray and Iribe. Around 1911 Poiret set up the Atelier Martine, and Louis Süe (see

49. Drawing-room in the house of Helena Rubinstein, Paris, *c.* 1938; decorations by Louis Süe

50. Bedroom of Jeanne Lanvin in her house in the Rue Barbet-de-Jouy, Paris, designed by Armand Albert Rateau, 1922 (reassembled Paris, Musée des Arts Décoratifs)

fig. 49) founded the Atelier Français design group in Paris in 1912. They showed rooms hung with rich fabrics or wallpapers patterned with bold, Oriental-style designs inspired by Léon Bakst's Ballets Russes designs.

These developments came to an abrupt halt in 1914 with the outbreak of World War I, but many of the avant-garde ideas shown at the Salons of 1913 re-emerged, largely unchanged, in the early 1920s. Several important designers were appointed to head the newly established design studios at the major Paris department stores, for example Maurice Dufrène (1876–1955) at the Atelier Maîtrise in the Galeries Lafayette, Paris, in 1921, and Paul Follot to Le Bon Marché's Atelier Pomone, Paris, in 1922. Their use of bold, stylized patterns for textiles and wall-coverings and simply curved, or later geometric, furniture were marketed through catalogues and exhibited at the stores' pavilions at the 1925 exhibition and had a strong impact on public taste. Meanwhile, due to the growth of tourism, there was a new demand for traditional regional styles, including carved or painted dressers, chests and corner-cupboards from Brittany and multicoloured, printed textiles and folk pottery from Provence.

The 1925 exhibition served to clarify the divide that had emerged between the *ensembliers*, high-style, designer–decorators who used such luxury materials as ebony, ivory, shagreen and exotic woods and such laborious techniques as gilding and lacquering to create exquisite works of art for the élite, and the 'Functionalists', who believed in mass production and minimal decoration (*see* MASS PRODUC-TION). Pre-eminent among the *ensembliers* were Armand

Albert Rateau (1882–1938), who in 1922 had created jewel-like interiors for the couturier Jeanne Lanvin, full of decorative references to archaeological and Oriental sources (see fig. 50), and Jacques-Emile Ruhlmann, de-signer of the Hôtel d'un Riche Collectionneur, the most sophisticated of the pavilions at the 1925 exhibition. Furniture by Jean Dunand shown in the hôtel demon-strated the exquisite art of lacquering, which he had learnt from the Japanese master Seizo Sugawara. Dunand com-bined this laborious technique with decorative motifs drawn from African art; African-inspired pieces in fash-ionable interiors, such as Helena Rubinstein's Paris apart-ment, enhanced a neo-Baroque theme, and in Paul Ruaud's interiors of 1932 (which replaced those by Eileen Gray of 1919–22), designed for the milliner Suzanne Talbot, sur-faces were strewn with zebra and leopard skins and set with distinctively African-style stools by Pierre Emile Legrain.

The so-called 'engineers and constructors' favoured simple, white-painted or plain wood-panelled living-areas, rendered adaptable by the use of sliding panels, and built-in storage units, sparsely set with rectilinear furniture in bentwood, leather, glass, aluminium and, later, tubular steel. Flexible living-spaces furnished for easy maintenance reflected changes in the Parisian way of life; smaller family groups lived in smaller apartments, domestic help was scarce, and increasingly women worked outside the home. Effective plumbing, heating, food storage and hygiene were essential for the household to function efficiently. The most important Functionalist architect–designers were Le Corbusier, whose Cubist villa, Le Pavillon de L'Esprit Nouveau, the shocked organizers of the 1925 exhibition tried to suppress; the designer Francis Jourdain, who declared that 'you can most luxuriously install a room by unfurnishing it rather than furnishing it'; and Pierre Chareau, who designed the Maison de Verre (1928–32), Paris. Many of these designers became founder-members of the UNION DES ARTISTES MODERNES (est. 1929).

Such enlightened clients as Charles, Vicomte de Noailles, embraced both extremes; Robert Mallet-Stevens built an uncompromisingly modern villa for him at Hyères (1923–6; see fig. 14 above), while JEAN-MICHEL FRANK decorated de Noailles's Paris town-house, the Hôtel Bischoffscheim (*c.* 1929), with vellum-clad walls, bronze doors and furniture in shagreen and white lacquer. In 1930 Charles de Beistegui, a friend of de Noailles, commissioned a penthouse for a building on the Champs d'Elysées, Paris, from Le Corbusier but added some bizarre, Surrealist touches to the austere, modern interior, including a mirror-glass, theatre-curtain and a life-size Rococo-style porcelain *Negro* especially ordered from the Meissen Porcelain Factory. Outside, a fireplace surmounted with an ornate, empty mirror-frame was set into the low wall of the Roof terrace. At the Château de Groussay, near Versailles, de Beistegui abandoned such experiments and spent the 1930s painstakingly recreating historic interiors from different periods, a trend continued by others well into the 1950s.

The Exposition Internationale des Arts et Techniques dans la Vie Moderne of 1937 in Paris concentrated on economic and technological themes rather than design and decoration. The room-settings ranged from offices and board-room dining suites to formal domestic salons, functional bathrooms with wall-to-wall tiling and simple, austere bedrooms better suited to hotels and ocean liners—the major design commissions of the period—rather than the home.

After World War II the Functionalist designers assisted the Ministry of Reconstruction to rebuild bombed cities, while the more traditional decorators were commissioned to refurbish French embassies. Once again, the war had brought design developments to a sudden halt. Working in the modern idiom, designers such as Jean Royère (1902–81) allowed asymmetric, organic curves to soften the profiles of furniture they showed in the mid-1950s, which were otherwise little changed from the late 1930s.

The conservatism that characterized decoration in the 1950s and 1960s, with the revivals of historic styles, is attributable both to the after-shock of the war and the fact that official commissions for historic buildings did not permit the use of such new materials as steel or plastic. A few schemes along traditional lines allowed for some, often surreal, individual touches: painted *trompe l'oeil* wall decoration, imitation leopard-skin textiles and rugs and the display of unusual collections. In his house at Marnes-la-Coquette, the actor Jean Marais, for instance, had an alcove for a bed in his Chambre d'Hiver completely lined in red velvet, and in the dining-room the walls and ceiling were painted with *trompe l'oeil* wood panelling. After the war Madeleine Castaing (1895–1992) became the supreme exponent of decoration in the 19th-century style, combining the Second Empire, English Regency and Biedermeier

styles. She revived the use of bold, striped fabric and used it to create rooms with tented ceilings, recalling Napoleon's campaigns.

With the 'democratization' of taste in the 1960s, chunky, mass-produced plywood furniture, chairs, dining-tables and storage units became socially acceptable for the first time. In 1966 the chain-store Prisunic published a catalogue of affordable furniture, with many pieces in modular units, designed by Marc Berthier (*b* 1935) and Olivier Mourgue (*b* 1939). The magazine *La Maison de Marie-Claire* emphasized the informality and practicality of good, modern design.

By the 1970s eclecticism was well established at both popular and designer levels. Within white or neutral interiors, multicoloured textiles gave warmth and personality, particularly in bedrooms, where coordinated floral wallpapers and fabrics had always been popular, especially the renowned 18th-century printed cottons. The finest textiles were supplied by such designer–manufacturers as Pierre Frey and Manuel Canovas (*b* 1935), while the wallpaper firm Maunay (est. 1933) continued to produce the best hand-blocked wallpapers in traditional designs. In living-rooms, antique furniture was arranged next to modern pieces or to Modernist design-classics by Gray, René Herbst (*b* 1891) or Chareau reissued by Andrée Putman. Such contemporary decorators as François Catroux and Jacques Grange (*b* 1944) created provocative interiors for their own Paris apartments, juxtaposing works of art and objects from different geographic locations and periods.

In the 1980s modern design was actively promoted by the French government; in 1982 President François Mitterand commissioned Philippe Starck, the best known of the new wave of designers, to refurbish the private apartments of the Elysée Palace, Paris, with suites of high-tech, metal furniture by Ronald Cécil Sportes (*b* 1943), while Putman refurnished the 18th-century white and gilt-panelled office of the Minister of Culture, Jack Lang, with plain semicircular desks in blond wood made by the National Furniture Company. Concurrently with this sleek, ultra-modernity, a streak of neo-Baroque eccentricity was still evident in the exuberant furniture designs of Elizabeth Garouste (*b* 1949) and Mattia Bonetti (*b* 1952); their pieces use unusual materials and shocking colours, which appealed to the couturier Christian Lacroix (*b* 1951), whose showroom they designed in 1987. In keeping with the new environmental awareness of the 1990s, Starck promoted a self-build wooden house, the plans and philosophy of which are available through the mail-order catalogue Trois Suisses.

See also §VI, 6 below.

BIBLIOGRAPHY

M. Battersby: *The Decorative Twenties* (London, 1969, rev. 1988)
——: *The Decorative Thirties* (London, 1971, rev. 1988)
T. Zeldin: *France, 1848–1945*, 4 vols (Oxford, 1980)
G. P. Weisberg: *Art Nouveau Bing: Paris Style 1900* (New York, 1986)
M. Deschamps: 'Domestic Elegance: The French at Home', *L'Art de vivre* (London, 1989), pp. 107–43
D. Silverman: *Art Nouveau in Fin-de-siècle France: Politics, Psychology and Style* (London and Berkeley, 1989)
Y. Brunhammer and S. Tise: *The Decorative Arts in France: La Société des Artistes Décorateurs* (New York, 1990)

N. Troy: *Modernism and the Decorative Arts in France: Art Nouveau to Le Corbusier* (New Haven and London, 1991)

STELLA BEDDOE

VI. Furniture.

1. Before 1589. 2. 1589–1715. 3. 1716–93. 4. 1794–1848. 5. 1849–1914. 6. After 1914.

1. BEFORE 1589. *Mobilier*, the French word for furniture, reflects the peripatetic habits of medieval society. Feudal lords, the only owners of grand furniture, moved from château to château with their retinue and entire household according to seasons and because of epidemics, wars and crusades. The most versatile and important piece of furniture was the chest or *coffre*, as it was easy to transport and could be used in multiple ways for storage, as a travelling trunk, for seat furniture and even as a table. In northern France chests were primarily made of oak, while in southern France lime-, apple- and pear-wood as well as walnut and cypress were used. They were made by *huchiers* or *faiseurs de meubles* or *charpentiers de petite cognée* (carpenters of the small axe, as opposed to 'true' carpenters, or *charpentiers de grande cognée*). The guild system already existed in France by the 9th century, whereby the sons and relatives of craftsmen were given priority and hereditary privilege to follow their parents' trade. In the 12th century the guilds acquired powers of regulation that lasted until the system was abolished in 1791. The *aspirant* (apprentice) trained for about five years under a *maître*, whom he paid; he then became a *compagnon* and was paid for his work. He might then embark on a tour of France lasting three or four years in order to gain additional knowledge without breaking the guild's closed-shop rules. After this experience he was ready to re-enter the guild structure and prepare his *pièce de maîtrise*, which was judged by the *jurande* (a guild jury). He then became a *Maître de Corporation*, allowed to run his own workshop. Society became more settled and prosperous in the 13th century, and in 1254 the Provost of Paris, Etienne de Boileau, reorganized the guild system of *charpentiers* and *huchier-menuisiers* (coffermakers). These reforms were later ratified by a parliamentary decree in 1382 and were subsequently endorsed by Louis XI in 1467.

The oldest-known piece of movable furniture in France is a chest in the church of Aubazine in the Corrèze dating from the beginning of the 13th century, when elaborate French *coffres* set the fashion for the rest of Europe. Its plank construction, secured by mortice-and-tenon joints, is characteristic of the period. The decorative ironwork gave the structure added strength; wrought-iron was often used to create ornate scrollwork patterns recalling the design of cathedral doors, as in a chest of *c.* 1250–70 (Paris, Carnavalet). Built-in locker-type armoires in the form of wall niches fronted by doors were commonly used for storage. Some armoire doors from a château in Mont-Saint-Quentin in the Somme have a rich decoration of ivy and oak leaves in wrought-iron on a red-and-blue painted background (*c.* 1290–1320; Paris, Mus. A. Déc.). The development of tongue-and-groove construction was an important advance that enabled the *huchier-menuisier* to form panels within a framework held by wooden pegs or iron nails. These panels were sometimes pierced and

carved in relief, their ornamental designs inspired by Gothic styles of the great cathedrals. Native plants and animals, such fabulous or exotic creatures as griffins and monkeys, biblical figures and, later, such secular and courtly subject-matter as tournaments and jousting scenes were often framed within richly carved Gothic arches.

In the 15th century the *parchemin plié* or linenfold pattern first appeared. By this period a wider variety of furniture types had evolved. The *dressoir* or *buffet* is essentially a cupboard raised up on a stand. An example from the 15th century has double doors and two drawers underneath (Paris, Mus. A. Déc.), the doors featuring ornamental wrought-iron locks and hinges and the drawers carved with fleurs-de-lis framed by lozenges. The back of the stand has a linenfold pattern behind the arched columnar front. *Dressoirs* were used to display silver and gold plate and were often draped with rich textiles. Seat furniture was mostly derived from the bench, with or without a back, carved in the solid or with pierced Gothic tracery; these were termed a *banc*, *bancelle* or *archebanc* respectively. Seats of X-frame design inspired by classical prototypes were reserved for the nobility, while the *escabeau* or *tabouret* (a slab-end stool carved with linenfold) was more typical (e.g. in Paris, Mus. A. Déc.). In the early 15th century the high-back chair or *cathèdre*, so-called from its ecclesiastical origins, appeared, sometimes with a seat in the form of a chest that opened to reveal storage space. A *carreau* or removable cushion added comfort and colour, blue and red being common. At this date most tables were simple, consisting of wooden planks resting on trestles. Beds were of crude, boxlike construction but were dressed with costly textiles, including the bedspread, back cloth, tester and the *courtines* or bed-hangings. An exceptional example (late 14th century–early 15th; Paris, Mus. A. Déc.) survives from the château of Villeneuve-Lembon in Auvergne with a tester, carved headboard and barley-twist posts preserving traces of a gilt finish.

The influence of the Italian Renaissance was first felt in the Loire Valley after Charles VII returned from his Italian campaign in 1494. Furniture, works of art and foreign craftsmen introduced a new vocabulary of classical motifs promoted by the architect Fra GIOVANNI GIOCONDO, as well as Bernadino da Brescia (*fl* 1495) and Domenico da Cortona, both described as 'carpenter of all sorts'. *Rinceaux*, candelabra, profile medallion heads and classical architectural motifs were grafted on to older forms. At first the construction was of oak, and decorative techniques remained unchanged, the new repertory of ornament being applied solely as carved surface decoration; this phase lasted from *c.* 1500 to the 1520s, a *dressoir* from Joinville dated 1524 being a typical example (Paris, Mus. Cluny). Walnut gradually replaced oak and was used exclusively for luxurious furniture during the second half of the century; its smooth, close grain proved ideal for fine carvings emulating the perspective views and modelling of Italian painting and sculpture.

The return in 1525 of Francis I from captivity in Madrid heralded the beginning of the 'Second Renaissance', which lasted until 1589 and witnessed the triumph of Italianization brought about by Rosso Fiorentino and Francesco Primaticcio at the château of Fontainebleau in the Ile-de-France. Two elements remained unchanged: the mobility of furniture and its construction. The tradition of *meubles pliants* or *brisés*, folding furniture with hinges, perpetuated the medieval travelling custom. Brass replaced iron on these pieces, which unfortunately have not survived, although it is known that Catherine de' Medici carried *escabeaux de camp*, beds and tables on her travels. Furniture construction was still based on a system of rails and stiles secured by pegged mortice-and-tenon joints, framing tongue-and-groove panels. Dovetailing provided a neat finish for angle joints. Structural forms also remained much the same, although the chest was diminishing in importance. Seat furniture became lighter, open arms replacing solid arm supports in the *chaise à bras*, *caquettoir* or *caquetteuse* ('Gossip' chair).

Towards the end of the century a desire for increased comfort encouraged the use of fixed upholstery instead of the removable medieval *carreau*. The Gothic *dressoir* was further elaborated and transformed into the *buffet* or *meuble à deux corps*. This piece became the focus of new decorative techniques and designs until the end of the century when cabinets on stands appeared; Catherine de' Medici is recorded as having 'two cabinets of ebony and ivory veneer'. *Meuble à deux corps* could be carved, sometimes with gilt enrichments, or the walnut ground inlaid with light wood, ebony, ivory etc; sometimes marble or hardstone mosaics were inserted. Marquetry veneers were also used.

The names of some *marqueteurs* are recorded: in 1532 an Italian, Jehan Miquel Panthaleon, worked for Francis I, and in 1576 a Saxon, Hans Kraus, was Marqueteur du Roy. Regional differences in decoration appeared: in the Ile-de-France, under the Italianate influence of Fontainebleau, a Mannerist repertory of classical forms was used: broken pediments, cornices, pilasters and mythological scenes depicting nude figures. A *meuble à deux corps* (see fig. 51) in the Musée des Arts Décoratifs, Paris, is characteristic with its chest-on-chest form headed by a cornice and a broken pediment enclosing an aedicule with a Mannerist nude carved in high relief and gilded. The doors are decorated with panels in low relief, gilt and inlay of white and black marble. The twinning of the columns echoed in the top and bottom and the bun feet heralded a typical French form that was to be widely used in the early 17th century on cabinets with stands. To distinguish regional tastes in ornaments, the inventory (1596) of Fernand Gauthiot d'Ancier recorded some carved walnut pieces with columns as *façon de Paris*, as opposed to carved terms and figures, parcel-gilt or painted like bronze as *façon de Dijon*. One of the cabinets (1581) listed in the inventory is in the Musée du Palais Granvelle, Besançon.

French designers became important. Jacques Androuet Du Cerceau the elder (*see* DU CERCEAU, (1)) published *Petites Grotesques* in 1550; it was republished in 1562 together with several furniture designs. His ornamental repertory drew heavily on Italian Renaissance sources (especially following a stay in Italy) in the same manner as Philibert de L'Orme, architect of the château of Anet for Diane de Poitiers, who created a new French classicism. HUGUES SAMBIN, architect and wood-carver, was the author of *L'Oeuvre de la diversité des termes dont on use en architecture* (Lyon, 1572), which allied, in its fantastic herms

51. Walnut *meuble à deux corps*, 2.05×1.05×0.05 m, made in the Ile-de-France, *c.* 1585 (Paris, Musée des Arts Décoratifs)

and terms motifs, a full-blooded French provincial tradition to the grotesque designs of Netherlandish ornamentalists. New dormant tables followed the same decorative evolution as the *meuble à deux corps*, that is, richly carved with classical motifs and sometimes with *en éventail* (fanshape) feet after antique Roman models illustrated by Du Cerceau. Fantastically carved beds were also inspired by designs by the same artist. The Wars of Religion brought a slackening in the production of luxury furniture towards the end of the century.

BIBLIOGRAPHY
A. de Champeaux: *Le Meuble*, i (Paris, 1885)
G. Janneau: *Les Meubles*, i (Paris, 1949)
F. Gebelin: *Le Style renaissance en France* (Paris, 1951)
P. Verlet: *Styles, meubles, décors du moyen âge à nos jours*, i: *Du moyen âge à Louis XV* (Paris, 1972)
P. Eames: 'Furniture in England, France and the Netherlands from the Twelfth to the Fifteenth Century', *Furn. Hist.*, xiii (1977) [whole issue]
M. Burckhardt: *Mobilier moyen âge/Renaissance* (Paris, 1978)
J. Boccador: *Le Mobilier français du moyen âge à la renaissance* (Paris, 1988)

MONIQUE RICCARDI-CUBITT

2. 1589–1715.

(i) Louis XIII style. (ii) Louis XIV style.

(i) Louis XIII style. The Louis XIII style refers to the period from the accession of Henry IV (1589) to the accession of Louis XIV (1661). Characteristic of this transitional phase between the Renaissance and the Baroque is its internationality, made possible by the reception of Italian, Flemish and Spanish influences. These were transmitted by the immigration of such Netherlandish artists as Philippe de Champaigne, Gerard van Opstal and Philippe Vleughels (1619–94); the simultaneous emigration of such French artists to Italy as Simon Vouet, Nicolas Poussin and Claude Lorrain; and by the Italian artists working at the Court for Marie de' Medici and Cardinal Richelieu, and later for Cardinal Jules Mazarin and Anne of Austria.

After the end of the Wars of Religion (1598), France was economically ruined; trade and craft work were at a low ebb. To revive the economy and to reduce the outflow of capital abroad, Henry IV summoned craftsmen, including many cabinetmakers, from Flanders to Paris. In 1601, and again in 1608, he set up workshops for them below the Grande Galerie of the Louvre and in the Faubourg Saint Marcel, where they were able to work under the protection of the Crown, independent of the strict guild rules of the city. He had thereby created an important precondition for the development of French Baroque furniture, as the important 17th-century *ébénistes* were to emerge from these workshops.

The sober, severe style of furniture matched the poor economic situation of France at the beginning of the 17th century. Models developed in the Renaissance were mainly used, with simplified forms and decoration based on bourgeois interior decoration as recorded in the engravings of ABRAHAM BOSSE (see fig. 44 above). With the reign of Louis XIII, economic prosperity returned and with it interest in luxurious interior decoration. Decoration remained sober and sculptural motifs were largely omitted; *bois tourné* (lathe-turned wood) became the most important decorative element in furniture.

With the cabinet-type cupboards that had come into fashion, the techniques and materials used in furniture production multiplied towards the end of the reign of Louis XIII. Carved and turned furniture in solid wood was joined by lighter, veneered pieces; various woods were imported from the overseas provinces, as well as metal, tortoiseshell, ivory and mother-of-pearl for marquetry. The German Hans Kraus (*fl* 1576) and Jean Macé (*c.* 1620–72), a native of Blois who was recalled from Flanders by Marie de' Medici, founded the French tradition of ebony work with their cabinets (see fig. 52). The abundance of relief and the polychromy of the internal decoration of these ebony cabinets formed a contrast to the sober appearance of other Louis XIII furniture.

Most of the chairs and other seat furniture produced at the time of Louis XIII came from the workshops of the wood-turners, who had founded a separate guild at the end of the 16th century. The Renaissance chair with arms and backrest was followed from 1635 by the *fauteuil*, the actual armchair, although this was still distinguished by a low backrest tilted slightly backwards, with straight armrests. Like the chairs and tabourets (stools) also in common

52. Carved ebony cabinet, designed by Jean Macé, 2.00×1.60×0.53 m, *c.* 1640 (Paris, Musée des Arts Décoratifs)

use at the time, armchairs were firmly upholstered with leather and other costly materials. The simple construction of these seats contrasted to the artistically made, H-shaped frame of turned supports, twisted or like beads on a string (*en torsade* or *en chapelet*). Carved motifs at the ends of the armrests were usually in the form of lions' heads or paws, as well as busts.

The forms of tables were less differentiated; they were based on Renaissance models, but the number of legs, linked by rails, was reduced. To achieve greater harmony, tables and chairs were fabricated together and decorated with the same turned motifs. Cupboards and walnut *buffets à deux corps*, which were being increasingly used in bourgeois households, most fully embodied, with their geometrical, diamond-shaped, relief-like ornamentation, the principles of architectonic strictness and the sober décor of the age of Louis XIII.

(ii) Louis XIV style. With the reign of Louis XIV (*see* BOURBON, §I(9)), a unified, national art style began to develop for the first time, taking on an exemplary character for other European countries. Art, placed programmatically in the service of the absolutist system, made visible the sovereign's claim to power by the splendour and luxury of the Court décor, as realized from 1682 in the opulent

53. Cabinet-on-stand, ivory veneer and marquetry, by Pierre Gole, 1.26×0.84×0.39 m, *c.* 1662 (London, Victoria and Albert Museum)

placed in the service of the King (*see* GOBELINS). Like the workshops in the Louvre founded by Henry IV, the Manufacture Royale was exempted from the strict guild regulations, and this was of enormous importance for the stylistic development of French Baroque furniture until well into the 18th century. The guild system protected the interests of the established artisan caste and thus allowed neither free competition nor the foundation of workshops by foreign craftsmen. In addition, there were strict rules governing which work could be done by which craftsman, inhibiting technical and stylistic innovation. At the Manufacture Royale, by contrast, the collaboration of goldsmiths, painters, cabinetmakers, metal-casters and sculptors inspired new inventions and combinations of materials, in which such foreign traditions as the Italian pietre dure technique and flower-marquetry, originating from Flanders, all converged. Through the fame of such *ébénistes* working at the Court as PIERRE GOLE, who specialized in ivory marquetry (see fig. 53), and DOMENICO CUCCI, who was known for his pietre dure works (*see* GOBELINS, fig. 1), veneered furniture took on increasing importance beside carved furniture. The high point of this development, towards the end of the 17th century, was the creations of ANDRÉ-CHARLES BOULLE, who perfected the technique of brass, pewter and tortoiseshell marquetry (boullework) with unbelievable precision, combining it with gilt-bronze mounts (*see* MARQUETRY and colour pl. VII).

The furniture of this period was distinguished by a classical, majestic appearance, expressed in the robust, right-angled forms and architectural elements such as the *pied de balustre*. The decoration consisted of reliefs incorporating mythological scenes, arabesques, large acanthus leaves, lions' paws, female masks and bearded heads. Formally, this furniture still shows elements of the Louis XIII style, but its size, richness of ornamentation and stronger colours gave a more sumptuous effect.

Until the death of Colbert (1683), the official artistic style fostered by the King was dictated by Charles Le Brun, who, as director of the Académie Royale and the Manufacture Royale des Meubles, conceived the entire output of art at Court and strictly supervised its execution. His designs affected both the large furnishing programmes at Versailles and in the Louvre and the details of furniture, tapestries and stuccowork. With his balanced compromise between the Italian Baroque, which he had studied in Rome, and the classical French tradition, he created an atmosphere of grandeur exactly attuned to the pretensions of the young Louis XIV.

The Court art of Louis XIV undoubtedly had its richest manifestation in the furnishings at Versailles, with tables, candelabra and seats of solid silver, designed by Le Brun and fashioned by such outstanding silversmiths of the time as Claude Ballin, René Cousinet, Alexis Loir I and Pierre Germain. This opulent silver furniture (designs in Stockholm, Nmus.) was melted down in 1689 and in 1710 in an attempt to restore the devastated State finances caused by the war against the League of Augsburg (*see also* §IX, 1(iii)(a) below).

With Colbert's death Le Brun lost his central position and thus his influence on artistic style. At the same time the King, aged by his political and financial setbacks,

furnishings of the château of Versailles. The economic and political consolidation of the country reinforced these efforts, contributing to a considerable accumulation of capital among the lesser nobility and bourgeoisie; they in turn tried to imitate the Court splendours. The regional styles previously detectable were smothered by this trend, and the dictates of the Court style took control everywhere.

In furniture, a shift of emphasis from the functional to the decorative can be observed. The individual pieces now formed a unity with the whole interior decoration of a room, with the purpose of expressing the power and prestige of the patron, a purpose that went hand in hand with a higher valuation of the products of arts and crafts. The sumptuous furniture of princes, the *meuble d'apparat*, was a means of representation and also served as a vehicle for Court ceremonial, as can be seen in the development of the *lit de parade* (bed of state; see fig. 45 above) and in the allocation of seat-types to people in accordance with their social rank.

With the foundation in 1667 of the Manufacture Royale des Meubles de la Couronne by Jean-Baptiste Colbert, the King's Surintendant et Ordonnateur Général des Bâtiments, Arts et Manufactures, more than 250 artisans were showed himself tired of the ceremonial he had established. The Grand Trianon was built as a place of private refuge, which signalled the end of artistic dirigisme. JEAN BERAIN I took over as director of the State workshops and, with his designs, gave French furniture a greater lightness and grace. In the field of ornamentation, above all, he transcended the preceding heaviness of form, replacing it by imaginative inventions harking back to Raphael's grotesques, which he further enriched with figural motifs in exotic profusion (e.g. monkeys, smiling masks and Chinese dancers; *see* CHINOISERIE). Through the dissemination of his designs in ornamental pattern books he influenced art production throughout Europe. His influence is most clearly seen in the marquetries of Boulle. The structure of furniture also changed towards the end of the 17th century. Forms became softer and, with console feet, the curved line became more widespread.

Louis XIV seat furniture was formally derived from the models of the preceding epoch. The *fauteuil*, made of walnut, differed from these by its substantially higher backrest, curved arms and legs in baluster form. Chairs of richly sculpted oak and beech with the characteristic diagonal rails were directly influenced by the Court of Versailles. With the multiplicity of kinds of seats, from the chair with arms through the padded armchair to the *placet* (higher tabouret stool) and the *ployant* (folding chair), different levels of comfort were established. In addition, the first seats for resting and reclining came into being in the form of the *bergère* (wing armchair) and the *lit de repos* (couch), a forerunner of the 18th-century chaise longue. Seat furniture was covered in such expensive materials as silk, damask and tapestries, which, with the wall coverings, gave the rooms their polychrome character.

With its sumptuous decoration, carved wooden furniture took over the role of the display pieces from the melted-down silver furniture. Above all, monumental tables of oak or beech-wood with heavy marble tops, four-cornered, pillar-like legs and diagonal cross-pieces meeting like volutes adorned the vestibules, salons and galleries of the nobles' palaces, in conjunction with console tables fixed to the walls and monumental candelabra. The positioning of the console table below a large mirror between two doors or windows gave the interior decoration its rhythmical character (*see* CONSOLE TABLE).

In the second half of the 17th century the height of fireplaces was reduced, while at the same time mirrors took on monumental proportions, made possible by technical developments in the workshops for mirror production founded by Colbert in Nevers, Paris and Saint-Gobain (*see* MIRROR, §VI, 2). Mirrors were given richly sculpted frames, while the firescreen of carved wood, covered in silk or tapestry, was set in front of the fireplace. The sumptuous impression given by the carved furniture was further underlined by lavish gilding.

Such large cupboards as *armoires* or *buffets* for clothing and tableware played a subordinate role, since they were mostly used in country houses and smaller Paris properties. Probably made by carpenters (*menuisiers en bâtiment*) rather than cabinetmakers, their architectonic structures are closer to the wall coverings and doorways of the period. Walnut, used in the period of Louis XIII, was now

54. Commode, ebony marquetry with gilt-bronze mounts, one of a pair by André-Charles Boulle, 0.89×1.31×0.65 m, 1708–9 (Versailles, Musée National du Château de Versailles et de Trianon)

replaced by solid oak. Carved medallions and pilasters with figural motifs served as decorative elements.

The cabinet, however, remained the most typical piece of furniture of the 17th century. With various, sometimes hidden, compartments and drawers it evolved from the feminine dressing-table into a collector's piece. Initially still veneered with black ebony, the decoration became more refined, and the diversity of materials increased: in the second half of the 17th century polychrome marquetry with flower, bird or leaf motifs of Dutch origin predominated. The development of its appearance can best be seen in the various types of feet. Simple columnar or baluster legs were increasingly replaced by fluted pilasters and finally by goats' feet or caryatids. These cabinets were made by the best-known veneer specialists of the time including Gole, Cucci (*see* GOBELINS, fig. 1), Gilles-Marie Oppenord, Auburtin Gaudron, Jacques Sommer, Philippe Poitou (*c.* 1640–1709) and Boulle.

The so-called *bureau Mazarin*, a kind of writing-table with side drawers and a niche for the legs, was very probably developed by Gole. The first examples were very ornate, having eight scroll legs linked by rails; subsequently the dimensions and the number of legs were reduced, and the angular basic form was made more vibrant with convex and concave surfaces. The lighter *bureau plat* (a writing-table without drawers and only four legs), which developed from it, came into fashion only after Louis XIV's death and really belongs to the RÉGENCE STYLE.

The most important invention at the end of Louis XIV's reign was the COMMODE (chest-of-drawers), a rectangular piece of storage furniture with drawers, rich marquetry decoration and metal mounts (see fig. 54), which in the 18th century superseded the cabinet. Although the shape of the commode had existed previously, its dissemination should be seen in connection with the work of Boulle, who supplied several other European princely houses apart from the French Court and nobility.

With the decline of ceremonial and the increasing emphasis on private comfort, traditional furniture types were made more functionally specific. Apart from the different table variants (card-, writing- and dressing-tables), *c.* 1700 library cupboards with latticed glass doors and various small corner cupboards (*écoignures*) were created.

At the end of Louis XIV's reign, furniture design was shaped above all by the output of the Boulle workshop in Paris. With the help of his 20 assistants, Boulle developed the technique of marquetry made of tortoiseshell and metal to the highest perfection and disseminated ornamental decoration, to designs by Berain, in countless variations. Initially for reasons of robustness, Boulle reinforced his furniture with ormolu (gilt-bronze) mounts, which later took on a purely decorative character, emphasizing the charm of the multicoloured surfaces. With the change in furniture shapes to the lighter structures and rhythmical curved surfaces of the Rococo, the Boulle workshop made an important contribution in the transition from the severe splendour of the 17th century to the more relaxed luxury of the 18th.

BIBLIOGRAPHY
Inventaire de tous les meubles du Cardinal Mazarin [1653] (London, 1861/R Genf, 1973)
C. Dreyfus: *Musée du Louvre: Le Mobilier français* (Paris, 1921)
P. Du Colombier: *Le Style Henri IV–Louis XIII* (Paris, 1941)
Louis XIV: Fastes et décors (exh. cat., Paris, Mus. A. Déc., 1960)
J. Viaux: *Bibliographie du meuble (Mobilier civil français)*, 2 vols (Paris, 1966–88)
G. Janneau: *Le Mobilier français*, 2 vols (Paris, 1967–74)
P. Verlet: *Styles, meubles, décors, du moyen âge à nos jours*, i: *Du moyen âge à Louis XV* (Paris, 1972)
S. Jervis: *Printed Furniture Designs before 1650* (Leeds, 1974)
A. Gonzales-Palacios: *Europäische Möbelkunst: Frankreich, 16.–18. Jahrhundert*, i (Munich, 1975)
P. Kjellberg: *Du moyen âge à Louis XV* (1978), i of *Le Mobilier français* (Paris, 1978–80)
J.-P. Samoyault: *André-Charles Boulle et sa famille* (Genf, 1979)
D. Alcouffe: 'Dal rinascimento al Luigi XIV', *Il mobile francese* (Milan, 1981)
T. H. Lunsingh Scheurleer: 'Pierre Gole: Ebéniste du roi Louis XIV', *Burl. Mag.*, cxxii (1984), pp. 380–94
A. Pradère: *Die Kunst des französischen Möbels: Ebenisten von Ludwig XIV. bis zur Revolution* (Munich, 1990)
P. Verlet: *Le Mobilier royal français: Meubles de la couronne conservés en Europe et aux Etats-Unis* (Paris, 1990)
Le Meuble régional en France (exh. cat., Paris, Réunion Musées N., 1990–91)

CHANTAL ESCHENFELDER

3. 1716–93. The period from 1716 to 1793, which spans the reigns of Louis XV and Louis XVI, is the golden age of French furniture. New furniture types were introduced (commodes, corner-cupboards, secretaries, *bergères*), and there was a constant experimentation with form and decoration, with a systematic exploitation of richer materials (e.g. gilt bronze, exotic woods, lacquer, porcelain, painted sheet metal and pietra dura) along with innumerable technical innovations.

The consolidation and increased security achieved in France during the reign of Louis XIV resulted in an increasingly sedentary population. Furniture ceased to be another item of luggage to be moved from place to place but became an intrinsic part of the household. The arts of the tapestry-maker and the upholsterer gave way to the more fragile arts of sculpted wood and delicate marquetry. The role of furniture in interior decoration became dominant, while the decoration of the building fabric itself (floors, ceilings, walls and fireplaces) became relatively

impoverished; furniture-makers appropriated the technical resources previously associated with interior architecture, such as painting, gilding etc.

From the wars pursued under Louis XV and the upheavals of the Régence emerged a newly enriched bourgeoisie that promoted comfort, intimacy and discretion in the area of interior decoration, against the more ostentatious luxury favoured by the aristocracy. The large interior spaces of the previous century gave way to smaller rooms, each with a specific purpose (e.g. *salon de campagnie*, *cabinet de travail*, library and bathroom), as well as to the interconnecting spaces such as corridors and mezzanines.

(i) New furniture types. (ii) Expansion of cabinetmaking. (iii) Woods and techniques.

(i) New furniture types. While only the cabinet, chest, bureau and table, with its two pedestal tables (*guéridons*), were known in the 17th century, in the 18th century new furniture types proliferated. A new piece of furniture was invented for every function (card-playing, writing, reading, working, needlework, snacks), and sometimes even seats for different body postures. The game-tables were covered in green fabric or, for the more luxurious examples, green velvet and were completed by a removable leather cover. As these tables were purely functional, only brought into the salon for playing, they were quite simple, usually of cherry-wood, and often folding. Even those for royal residences, supplied by Antoine-Robert Gaudreaus between 1740 and 1751, were simply veneered in king-wood or Brazilian rose-wood. In the same way, those supplied by GILLES JOUBERT to Marie-Antoinette for the Petit Trianon at the château of Versailles were simple cherry-wood tables with king-wood fillets. The most popular was the *tric-trac* table, first made in ebonized wood or with a plain king-wood or satin-wood veneer. The model became more refined during the reign of Louis XVI; the *tric-trac* table, generally of mahogany, had two small drawers to store the pieces, dice and dice boxes. From the 1730s innumerable small tables appeared in addition to game-tables. In the inventories of such *ébénistes* as MATHIEU CRIARD or Pierre Roussel (1732–82), references are made to *tables mignonettes*, *en limaçon*, *à l'anglaise*, *à la Dauphine*, *à patins* and *à trois fins*. The most widely used were writing-tables, comprising a velvet- or leather-lined top, a side drawer fitted with an inkwell, a sand sprinkler and a sponge box. Unlike the game-tables, which were purely functional, these small tables placed in intimate rooms were often elaborate. It is beside one of these tables, made by Bernard van Risamburgh (ii), that the Marquise de Pompadour is seated in a painting by Boucher (1756; Munich, Bayer. Hypo-Bank, on loan to Munich, Alte Pin., see DRESS, fig. 45). The fantasy of the makers was limitless: there were needlework-tables, *vide-poches*, *chiffonnières*, tables *à la bourgogne* and *à déjeuner*—for taking a small morning snack. These tables are rectangular or kidney-shaped and are supported on two feet with stretchers joined by a stretcher. *Guéridons*, formerly tall, fragile structures of giltwood or marquetry used as lampstands, became lower, multi-purpose tables. The tripod base and round top were retained, but the top could now be raised on a shaft or pivoted, as in the case of the mahogany *tables à thé* inspired from 1780 by English models. With 'anglomania' came the fashion for mahogany dining-room tables, which after

1780 began to replace the traditional pine boards resting on trestles in antechambers. To do away with service at intimate suppers, small individual sideboards, called *tables servantes* or *rafraîchissoirs*, were invented, with trays for plates and tubs for cooling the wine. The *ébéniste* François-Gaspard Teuné (*b* 1726) made these in a triangular shape in rose-wood for the Comte d'Artois, but most of these sideboards were mahogany and rectangular with rounded corners and legs inspired by English models. Canabas [Joseph Gegenbach] (1712–97) specialized in these tables. Another trace of anglomania is seen in rectangular mahogany tables with folding legs called *à l'anglaise* and made *c*. 1778 by the *ébéniste* PIERRE GARNIER and his imitators; they were inspired by gate-leg tables from England.

During the Régence (1715–23) there was a fashion for tables *en cabaret*, fitted with a top in Chinese lacquer or French polish that was placed on a stand of gilt-wood or red or black lacquer to match the top. These tables were carried by the servants like simple trays holding refreshments. About 1750 such MARCHANDS-MERCIERS as LAZARE DUVAUX sold porcelain tea-sets and trays (*cabarets*) with tables to support them, decorated with complementary marquetry or lacquer.

This gave rise to the idea of integrating the porcelain *cabaret* with the table, and *c*. 1760 the first porcelain tables, by van Risamburgh and ROGER VANDERCRUSE, were made for the *marchand-mercier* Simon-Philippe Poirier (?1720–85). The *table de nuit* comprised two marble top sections and often a side drawer; in order to move them from the alcove to the wardrobe they were often fitted with handles at the sides. Around the end of the 18th century toilet-cabinets were made and, at the same time, toilet-tables, usually of walnut, fitted with mirrors and compartments with faience or porcelain utensils. JEAN-FRANÇOIS OEBEN and his imitators produced *c*. 1760 two new table types that had lasting success: the *table mécanique*, the top of which slides back as the drawer is opened (see fig. 55), and the *table à gradin*, which under Louis XVI became the *bonheur du jour*, a very fashionable item of furniture.

The secrétaire, a piece of furniture combining a table and writing-desk, emerged *c*. 1725; it was also called the *secrétaire en pente* and remained in fashion throughout the reign of Louis XV. Such *ébénistes* as PIERRE MIGÉON II, who sold more than 100 (almost all in marquetry) between 1726 and 1731, and JACQUES DUBOIS, who made the finest of them with japanning or *vernis Martin*, specialized in them. Another type of secrétaire, the *secrétaire à abattant*, called *en armoire* at the time, appeared during the 1750s (for illustration *see* RIESENER, JEAN-HENRI). The first secrétaire of this type bought by the Crown was delivered by Gaudreaus in 1747. During the 1760s Oeben introduced the *secrétaire à cylindre*, which supplanted the *secrétaire en pente* as the fashionable piece of furniture (see fig. 56).

The commode, however, was the most successful piece of furniture in the 18th century. Introduced *c*. 1695, it was first called *table en bureau* or *bureau* and remained a rare item until the end of the reign of Louis XIV (1715). The Princess Palatine was obliged as late as a letter of 24 March

55. *Table mécanique* stamped by Jean-François Oeben, oak veneered with mahogany, king-wood, tulip-wood and marquetry woods, gilt-bronze mounts, h. 698 mm, *c*. 1761–3 (New York, Metropolitan Museum of Art)

1718 to explain:

> The present that Madame de Berry gave my daughter is very galant. She gave her a commode. A commode is a large table with large drawers and the top is very fine, with gilt ornaments. In these drawers were all sorts of things *à la mode*: shawls, coiffures, *andriennes*, ribbons, stockings, everything that is *à la mode*, certainly worth a thousand pistoles, and very pretty gloves, fans …

For a time the commode continued to be used as a bureau, with a veneered or marquetry top; the commodes delivered

56. *Secrétaire à cylindre* stamped by Jean-Henri Riesener, sycamore and amaranth veneers and gilt-bronze mounts, 1.05×1.13×0.64 m, 1784 (Paris, Musée du Louvre)

57. *Commode à la régence* attributed to Etienne Doirat (with the stamp of Pierre Migéon II) veneered with *bois satiné*, gilt-bronze mounts, 0.84×1.53×0.66 m, *c.* 1720–25 (Paris, Musée Carnavalet)

by Hécquet for Queen Maria Leszczyńska (1703–68) at the châteaux of Fontainebleau and Marly in 1725 still had veneered tops. At the same time, the commode's primary use as a store for clothing often made it a purely functional piece of furniture in the 1720s, made of walnut or pine and relegated to the wardrobe. The inventory (1744) of Louis-Alexandre, Comte de Toulouse (1678–1737), is revealing in this respect. In his vast hôtel in Paris (now the Banque de France) there were only two walnut commodes and even they were banished to the wardrobe. A contrasting situation was found at the château of Rambouillet, near Paris, where the furniture was more modern and to which Louis de Bourbon, Duc de Penthièvre (1725–93), had made some modifications. There, although a good number of commodes were confined to the wardrobe, some were also beginning to be found in the large staterooms. From the 1730s, the tops were made of marble from French, Belgian or Italian quarries (e.g. commode by Charles Cressent, *c.* 1730; Waddesdon Manor, Bucks, NT; for illustration *see* RÉGENCE STYLE). The most widely used was *rouge de Rance*, known as Flanders marble, rivalled on fine furniture by Sarrancolin from the Pyrenees and Brèche d'Alep from Italy or Provence. Under Louis XVI white marble, grey St Anne

marble, *bleu Turquin*, Spanish Brocatelle and Italian *griotte* were fashionable. From the mid-18th century the commode was established as an indispensable item in any bedroom. When the château of Villarceaux, near Paris, was furnished between 1755 and 1759, purchases of cabinetwork were limited to about ten commodes with as many writing-tables and night-tables. Gradually the commode became a prestigious item, which after 1770 occupied a prominent place in bedrooms and even salons and boudoirs. The commode could have three rows of drawers (*en tombeau*) or two rows of drawers perched on tall legs, a form called *à la Régence* (see fig. 57). More rarely it had a single drawer and was then called *en console*. At first the drawers were separated by a fixed rail, which the *ébénistes* contrived to conceal around 1750, retaining only a thin partition between the drawers. About 1760 Oeben developed a three-part form of commode for the Marquise de Pompadour, called *à la grecque*, with three central drawers slightly projecting in front of side cupboards. The idea was to lock the whole piece by a single turn of the key in the central lock. The form was much repeated, and the break-front remained the hallmark of Transitional and Louis XVI furniture. About 1780 a three-panelled form of commode, particularly suited to showing off japanned or mahogany panels, became dominant. This type of piece was produced by Adam Weisweiler, BERNARD MOLITOR, Conrad Mauter (1742–1810) and GUILLAUME BENEMAN.

A special form of commode—the *commode à encoignures*—produced during the Régence by Charles Cressent and ANTOINE-ROBERT GAUDREAUS (e.g. commode by Gaudreaus, 1739; London, Wallace; for illustration *see* COMMODE), with doors at the sides, came back into fashion under Louis XVI. These pieces could be open, with marble or lacquered shelving used to display objects, and were called *à l'anglaise*. Sometimes associated with the commode are one or two *encoignures* with matching decoration; thus, the blue-lacquered commode of Mlle de Mailly at the château of Choisy-le-Roi, near Paris, was complemented by a corner-cupboard decorated in the same way, just as Gaudreaus's medal cabinet (1738; Versailles, Château) is flanked by a pair of corner-cupboards by Joubert in the cabinet of Louis XV at Versailles. In Duvaux's day-book (published Paris, 1873) there are several references to commodes supplied with matching corner-cupboards: for example, 'a corner-cupboard of old lacquer very finely embellished with gilt bronze' supplied to the Marquise de Pompadour in August 1753, at the same time as a commode with the same lacquer; or 'a commode veneered in red varnish with pagodas' supplied to Mme de Mirepoix in June 1753 with two matching corner-cupboards. The fashion for corner-cupboards culminated with the Rococo, which banished right angles and simple geometric forms.

The tendency to associate corner-cupboard and commode was not, however, constant, as the corner-cupboard was often a functional piece used in wardrobes. In the Régence, the corner-cupboard tended to be a two-part piece called an *encoignure en armoire*, with two curved doors at the bottom and tiered shelves at the top. Later, in the *tablette d'encoignure*, the upper rack of shelves was reduced in size and separated from the bottom. It was hung from the wall above the corner cupboard and had matching decoration. The 18th-century fashion for the commode and all forms of secrétaire coincided with increasing disaffection for the storage furniture—cabinet, chest and armoire—popular in the 17th century. After having practically gone out of production in Paris after 1700, the cabinet came back into fashion in the form of variants devised after 1760 by *marchands-merciers*, such as the *cabinets à bijoux* on stands by Bernard van Risamburgh (ii) (*see* RISAMBURGH, VAN) or the *secrétaires en cabinets* by Vandercruse, Martin Carlin and Weisweiler. In the same way, the *coffre de toilette*, sumptuous examples of which were supplied by André-Charles Boulle around 1700, returned to fashion in the form of the porcelain chests made by MARTIN CARLIN (*see* CERAMICS, colour pl. I, fig. 3) to the order of the *marchands-merciers* Poirier and Daguerre.

The armoire continued to exist in the Régence in the form of a cupboard of low or medium height, the most sumptuous models being created by CHARLES CRESSENT and Boulle. One of these models, a lower version of the cupboards (Paris, Louvre) from Hamilton Palace, Strathclyde, was so successful that the Boulle workshop almost mass-produced it, and the *marchand-mercier* CLAUDE-FRANÇOIS JULLIOT had it copied by Philippe-Claude Montigny (1734–1800) in the 1760s. The existence of

these Neo-classical copies shows clearly that the armoire was by then a thing of the past, linked to nostalgia for the pomp of the Louis XIV period. In rural areas at the same time, however, the armoire remained the most important piece of storage furniture, as is attested by the countless extant examples and by the richness of their carved decoration.

The *bureau plat*, which also originated at the beginning of the 18th century, underwent considerable development (*see* BUREAU). Its shape, designed by Boulle *c.* 1710–20, evolved very little during the 18th century, with a central drawer slightly set back from the front and flanked by two shaped drawers (e.g. of 1759 by Joubert; New York, Met.; *see* LACQUER, colour pl. I, fig. 2); at most, the curved contours were replaced after 1760 by straight lines. Here too, the splendour of Boulle's examples made them the undisputed models, and even late in the century prominent people, ministers or financiers, sought out Boulle bureaux.

In the 18th century the bed remained the principal and most expensive piece of furniture. In the Régence a variety of enclosed bed called *en tombeau* was fashionable. Posts of unequal height (tall at the head, low at the foot) gave the canopy a fairly steep slope. Such beds can be seen in the engravings by J. Dumont illustrating Paul Scarron's *Roman comique* (1727). A bed *à l'impériale* had a dome-shaped canopy evoking the imperial crown. On the bed *à la duchesse* there were no posts at the foot, so that the canopy, with its side strips and curtains the length of the bed, had to be fixed to the wall by brackets and attached to the ceiling. In the second half of the 18th century, beds of diverse shape appeared in increasing numbers. One of the most widespread, the bed *à la polonaise*, which appeared at the time of Maria Leszczyńska, had two and sometimes three bed-heads and four columns extended by curved iron rods supporting a central dome (*see* BED, fig. 2). This bed was placed along the wall, as was the *à la turque* model, a bed with two or three scroll-shaped heads and without posts (see fig. 58); the dome was fixed to the wall to hold the curtains, which fell each side of the bed-heads. Under Louis XVI a variant called *en chaire à prêcher* or *à la romaine* had two straight backrests with two columns on the rear uprights and curved iron rods joined together to support a canopy fixed to the wall. While the woodwork of the enclosed beds of the 17th century was generally chamfered and without ornament, the new beds were sumptuously carved. Under Louis XVI, such ornamentalists as Jean-Charles Delafosse and Paul Ranson vied to invent new models of beds *à la chinoise*, *à l'italienne* or *à la Dauphine*, which were not always made. During the 18th century the wood-carver's art generally gained considerable ground at the expense of that of the upholsterer, and this applied to beds as much as to couches, chairs and the gilt-wood mouldings surrounding wall hangings. Another category of bed, combining elements of the couch and the armchair, was the *lit de repos*. Without curtains and generally placed against the wall or in a niche, they had two scrolled rests at the sides with cylindrical bolsters and cushions resting against the wall.

Sometimes, these *lits de repos* had a third backrest on the long side, so that they became reminiscent of sofas. Then they were called beds *à l'anglaise*. At the end of the reign of Louis XIV and deriving from the *lit de repos* the

58. Bed *à la turque* attributed to Jacques-Jean-Baptiste Tilliard, gilded beech, 1.74×2.65×1.88 m, *c.* 1750–60 (Malibu, CA, J. Paul Getty Museum)

chaise longue emerged. It had a backrest sometimes fitted with wings, armrests and legs joined by a crossrail. The chaise longue could have a cane bottom or be fully upholstered, but mostly it had a mattress like a bed. It could be made of two interlocking parts, in which case it was called a *duchesse brisée* (e.g. *c.* 1730; Paris, Carnavalet). From 1740, it was often made in three interlocking parts: a main section in the form of a high-backed *bergère*, a middle part and an end section shaped like a small rounded *bergère* with a low back. The *canapé* or sofa, which emerged at the end of the 17th century, also derived from the *lit de repos*. At the height of the Rococo a sofa called *en corbeille* emerged, with armrests continuing the back in a sinuous movement. The sofa *à confidents* is a large sofa flanked by corner seats, which may be fixed or detached. Small sofas with asymmetrical backs, called *méridiennes* or *veilleuses*, also served as *lits de repos*, with higher backs surrounding one side.

Of all seats, the *fauteuil* was the most diverse and underwent the most profound changes. Very few documented or dated examples exist from the first half of the 18th century but they can be studied in paintings of interiors by Jean-François de Troy (ii) (e.g. *At the Dressing Table*, 1727; Kansas City, MO, Nelson–Atkins Mus. A.; *see also* UPHOLSTERY, colour pl. XIV, fig.1) or prints. The high-backed, fully upholstered Louis XIV chair with console legs evolved to a lower armchair with a back framed by carved wood and armrests trimmed with lace

covers and sinuously carved like the legs. Gradually, the legs lost their stretchers, and the armrests were set back and became increasingly sinuous. In addition to these seats with flat backs, called in the inventories old armchairs *à la reine* or *meublants*, as they were placed against the wall, small chairs with curved backs called *courants*, as they were light and easily moved to the centre of the room, were invented. Great quantities, at least 20 or more, of these chairs could be found in French drawing-rooms, facilitating mobility and the art of conversation. For card games the *voyeuses à genoux* were invented, which allowed ladies encumbered with voluminous panniers to follow the game. For men, *ponteuses* were invented, with horseshoe seats astride which one sat to watch the game with one's elbows resting on the back. For comfort, the *bergère* was invented, a wide, low armchair with full, padded sides. Some especially wide *bergères*, now called *marquises*, were called *confidents* or *tête-à-tête* at the time. Sometimes, an especially high, enveloping back turned them into *bergères en confessional*. Some models, called *fauteuils en bergères* at the time, were shaped like armchairs in outline, with the wood of the armrests showing on the inside but covered in material on the outside as in *bergères*. Two other varieties of armchair, those *de toilette* and *de cabinet*, were very similar to each other and are now almost always called *fauteuils de bureau*. They had cane-bottomed seats, sometimes with thin leather upholstery, with a central leg at the front (e.g.

fauteuil de cabinet by Etienne Meunier, 1735; Malibu, CA, Getty Mus.).

(ii) Expansion of cabinetmaking. The history of furniture in the 18th century is one in which *ébénistes* progressively nibbled away at the traditional specialities of the *menuisiers*. While cabinetmaking in the 17th century was confined in content to a few types of precious furniture (such as cabinets, bureaux or some tables), it gradually encroached on storage furniture (chests, commodes, armoires, bookcases), tables, *guéridons*, *torchères*, console tables and even armchairs, which by the end of the 18th century were made using cabinetmaking techniques. The craze for cabinetmaking was such that by the end of the reign of Louis XV it had supplanted joinery. The carved wooden console table was from now on often made of mahogany or satin-wood, or was replaced in salons by commodes, which until then had been confined to the bedroom. About 1780 the banker Laborde furnished the salon of his Paris hôtel with four mahogany console tables made by Carlin, while the Duchesse d'Arenberg furnished the salon of her hôtel in the Rue de la Ville l'Evêque, Paris, with two mahogany half-moon console tables made by Roussel. For the *salon des jeux* at the château of Saint-Cloud, Marie-Antoinette ordered (1788) two mahogany half-moon console tables from Daguerre, while in 1786 Louis XVI had two amaranth console tables made by Beneman for his powder-room at Fontainebleau. At Versailles, Daguerre supplied a mahogany console table and a console-commode in satin-wood for the Duchesse d'Harcourt in 1787, the latter being made by Claude-Charles Saunier (1735–1807). In the end, the taste for luxury was such that even beds (like the one sold from the collection of Leroy de Senneville in 1784), support frames for baths or fire-screens such as that supplied by Jean-Henri Riesener for M. de Fontanieu in 1773 were produced by *ébénistes*.

(iii) Woods and techniques. Menuisiers used only indigenous woods: beech and walnut were used to make armchairs and beds in Paris and most regions except the west, where armchairs were sometimes made of oak, and in some regions where rarer woods were used (ash, cherry-wood, elm, acacia). Beech, with a less attractive natural appearance, was preferred for chairs that were to be painted or gilded. By contrast, walnut, with its beautiful grain and warm colours, was better suited to waxing in its natural colour, especially in the Rhône Valley and at Grenoble, where fine walnut trees were available. Woods were often patinated in natural colour (called patina *à la capucine*); in the case of beech this was done to give it the colour of walnut, whereas with walnut it was done on chairs to unify various pieces of walnut, which often had too disparate grains and colours. The *à la capucine* patina, so fashionable under the Régence and Louis XV, tended to flake with time and has often been removed in modern restorations; examples are consequently rare. From the 1780s joiners started using such cabinet-work woods as mahogany, satin-wood and amaranth to make chairs. These woods were used as veneer on the horizontal parts of the seat, and in solid form for other parts (legs, arm-rests), which were thus suitable for carving.

The console table, generally made at the same time as the *boiserie* for rooms by builders' carpenters was made of the same wood as that used for chairs (beech and walnut) with an extensive use of oak during the reign of Louis XVI. For some parts intended to be more intricately carved such softwoods as lime were sometimes used. In the provinces, where luxury cabinet work was far less widespread than in Paris, other furniture (cupboards, tables, commodes, sideboards, dressers) was generally made of solid wood using joinery techniques. The woods used were principally walnut, which lends itself well to carving, and oak, but cherry and pear were also used. In some regions, joiners used such local woods as olive in Provence, chestnut in Périgord, pine in Auvergne, and elm or ash in conjunction with other woods in Burgundy, Bresse and Saintonge. In the east, *menuisiers* embellished their furniture with inlaid motifs on a walnut base, a rudimentary version of marquetry. In the 17th century, walnut and ebony were the noble woods *par excellence*; they tended to be replaced on fine furniture during the 18th century by veneers of exotic woods and to be used increasingly on utility or provincial furniture.

Regarding the assembly techniques for chairs, beds or other cabinet work, the plates in the *Encyclopédie* (1751–72), by Diderot and d'Alembert (1717–83), are very detailed (*see* PARIS, fig. 28). For chairs, the woods were first cut by handsaw, then the different parts were cut to size using templates. Mouldings or carvings were then cut into the various pieces of wood. For intricate carving, the pieces had to be passed to a wood-carver, the *menuisier* confining himself in theory to carving simple reliefs and mouldings. The pieces were then assembled using mortise-and-tenon joints, held in place by wooden pegs (on chairs) or long iron screws (on beds). Then chairs were passed to the gilder. The wood was covered with a size with a base of glue and gesso applied in five or six successive coats and then sanded down. This size was then worked and carved to reveal and heighten the carving. This important operation, called the *reparure*, gave full relief to the sculpture. The wood was then covered with *assiette*, a preparation with a base of yellow- or red-coloured glue, which fixed the gold leaf. For *ébénistes* the joining was done with tongue-and-groove for panels, with some elements assembled by mortise-and-tenon, while drawers and sometimes top panels were assembled using dovetail joints. The quality of assembly and of the woods used for the carcass improved throughout the 18th century until, with the great *ébénistes* of the 1780s—Riesener, JEAN-FRANÇOIS LELEU and ADAM WEISWEILER—it reached a level of perfection that was hardly surpassed in the 19th century. In the Régence the carcass was still made of pine and was rudimentary but with very carefully made drawers in polished walnut. It is surprising to find this very casual form of pine construction in commodes by Cressent, the base panels being made of simple, horizontal boards. On some Régence furniture part-oak, part-walnut drawers are found, or a combination of walnut, and a white wood (e.g. poplar). Gradually the structures were perfected: pine was replaced by oak for the carcasses (*c.* 1730s), and oak gradually replaced walnut for drawers. Pine, however, continued to be used on side panels or panels between drawers, or shelves covered in leather. In fine pieces by JEAN-PIERRE LATZ and van Risamburgh the bottoms were made of very carefully chamfered panels. In pieces by van

Risamburgh walnut drawers had strips of wood acting as slides at the corners. Furniture finished in VERNIS MARTIN was often made of fruit-tree wood (pear or walnut) or sycamore, which held the paint better than oak. Sometimes, when a japanned object had parts or links in *vernis Martin*, they were made of pieces of soft wood or sometimes even thin sheets of pear-wood glued to the oak body, as is the case with the commode (Paris, Louvre) by van Risamburgh for Maria Leszczyńska at Fontainebleau in 1737. Despite all these improvements, it is surprising to find in a good number of 18th-century Parisian pieces carelessly made carcasses or unexpected woods. Roubo explained in *L'Art du menuisier* (1769–74) that it had to do with the practice of some *ébénistes* of having the bodies of their furniture made at low cost by *menuisiers* whose speciality it was. Even if Roubo probably exaggerated the scale of the phenomenon, it does explain the faults observed on some otherwise fine pieces as well as the often-practised habit of double-stamping. Once the body was finished, the *ébéniste* set about gluing sheets of wood more than 2 mm thick, which might be for a plain veneer or for parquetry or marquetry.

In Paris (*see* PARIS, §IV, 3) the only indigenous veneer woods used were cherry (used on the inside of doors) and olive, which was very fashionable between 1720 and 1735, as is indicated by numerous commodes of olive-wood with compartments of king-wood supplied to the royal furniture depository by the *ébéniste* Hécquet (*fl c.* 1715–26), then by Gaudreaus. All other veneer woods were exotic woods coming from the West Indies, South America, Madagascar and East Asia. The most widely used were tulip-wood, amaranth-wood, *bois satiné* and rose-wood. Mahogany and satin-wood were well established after 1780. The use of these woods variedly greatly during the course of the 18th century, depending on fashion and fluctuations in a sometimes erratic supply. About 1720 the fashion was for dark, plain veneers: ebony, Brazilian rose-wood and king-wood lent themselves to beautiful effects in plain veneers. In the absence of ebony, many utility pieces were made of blackened wood, usually stained pear. Apart from plain veneer, the fashion between 1720 and 1740 was for parquetry effects or for leaves, butterfly wings or diamonds. Violet-wood, with its vivid grain, was excellent for these effects. The fashion for it culminated in Paris between 1735 and 1740, when its price was higher than those for other woods. Cressent used a variety of *bois satiné* called *bois de cayenne*, with which he produced shimmering effects. Only after 1740 did tulip-wood begin to be used (it is first mentioned in supplies by Gaudreaus to the royal family in 1745). Gradually it became established as the most widely used wood for veneers. Another innovation of the 1740s was the return of flower marquetry. Until that date, inventories describe only furniture with 'plain veneer' or 'lozenge compartments' or 'mosaic veneer', and the term *marqueterie* referred only to Boulle marquetry (*see* MARQUETRY, colour pl. VII). In the journal of the Garde Meuble Royal, which records in detail all deliveries of furniture and their dates, the first mention of flower marquetry appears in 1745, with the supplies of the *marchands-merciers* Thomas-Joachim Hébert (*d* 1773) and Pierre Lebrun (*d* 1771) for the Dauphin and Dauphine at Versailles. These first marquetries were both sprays of flowers in end-cut wood (as seen on the two pieces by van Risamburgh at Versailles) and polychrome flowers as on 'the *bois satiné* bureau with flower veneer in different colours' supplied by Lebrun for the Dauphin's library at Versailles. The two styles of floral marquetry were to exist concurrently during the Rococo. Such leading *ébénistes* as van Risamburgh, JOSEPH BAUMHAUER and Dubois, followed by Martin-Etienne Lhermite and Jean-François Dubut (*d* 1778) produced only end-cut marquetry, which went out of fashion at the end of the 1760s. With the second technique designs were treated in a more realistic manner using a mosaic of pieces of wood stained with natural tints. Between 1760 and 1770 some *ébénistes* created pictures in wood depicting landscapes and ruins, chinoiseries or trophies (e.g. *secrétaire à cylindre* by Riesener, *c.* 1775; Waddeson Manor, Bucks, NT). Apart from the great workshops of famous *ébénistes* that had their own specific style, a good number of *ébénistes* called on *ébénistes* who specialized in marquetry, such as CHARLES TOPINO, Guillaume-Joseph Lepage and André-Louis Gilbert (1746–1809), who sold them ready-made marquetry pictures. It is known that Topino sold numerous marquetry pieces to his brother Jean-Baptiste Topino (*d* 1801), an *ébéniste* in Marseille. This practice explains why the same marquetry pictures are found on furniture stamped by different *ébénistes*.

The workshop of ANDRÉ-CHARLES BOULLE underwent its greatest expansion between 1715 and 1725; this is confirmed by inventories compiled in these years, when *c.* 30 workers were employed. Much of the furniture now attributed to Boulle is datable to between 1710 and 1720. Between 1715 and 1730 many Parisian workshops continued to produce furniture featuring Boulle marquetry. It is known that Joseph Poitou (*c.* 1680–1718), van Risamburgh, Nicolas Sageot (*d* 1731) and Noël Gérard (*b* before 1690; *d* 1736) were familiar with this technique. Again precise identifications are difficult, as it has been discovered that families of such independent marquetry workers as Toussaint Devoyes (*d* 1753) and his son François Devoyes (*fl c.* 1750) worked for such different *ébénistes* as Sageot, Gérard or Pierre Moulin, between 1710 and 1720. Later, Toussaint Devoyes's son-in-law Jacques Sellier, also a marquetry worker, worked for Latz.

It is difficult to identify at what time Boulle marquetry went out of fashion; in 1745 the stock of such a *marchand-mercier* as Pierre Rougeux (*fl* 1740–60), who had premises close to the Mint, still contained several items by Boulle, including a *bureau plat* and a Boulle commode. It is probable, however, that the period when the Rococo was at its height (1745–60) corresponds to the time when this type of Boulle furniture went out of production. From the 1760s, with the beginnings of Neo-classicism, Boulle furniture came back into fashion. Such cabinetmakers as ADRIEN FAIZELOT DELORME, Philippe-Claude Montigny (1734–1800), René Dubois and Nicolas-Pierre Séverin (1728–98) restored furniture half a century old for a generation of new collectors (e.g. *secrétaire à abattant*, 1770–75; Malibu, CA, Getty Mus.). Such *marchands-merciers* as Julliot specialized in the resale of this furniture, which sometimes had to be modified to match the taste of the period. Cupboards, too tall for the décor of the 1770s and considered outdated, were often dismantled and used to make low cupboards. At the same time pastiches were produced, especially at the instigation of Julliot, and made by ETIENNE LEVASSEUR, Montigny and JOSEPH BAUMHAUER, whose production lasted with this fashion until *c.* 1800.

BIBLIOGRAPHY

L. Courajod, ed.: *Livre-journal de Lazare Duvaux, marchand-bijoutier ordinaire du roy, 1748–1758*, 2 vols (Paris, 1873)

H. Havard: *Dictionnaire de l'ameublement et de la décoration*, 4 vols (Paris, 1887–9)

E. Molinier: *Le Mobilier au XVIIIe siècle*, iii of *Histoire des arts appliqués à l'industrie* (Paris, [*c.* 1900])

H. Vial, A. Marcel and A. Girodie: *Les Artistes décorateurs du bois*, 2 vols (Paris, 1912–22)

F. de Salverte: *Les Ebénistes du XVIIIe siècle: Leurs oeuvres et leurs marques* (Paris, 1923, rev. 5/1962)

P. Verlet: *Le Mobilier royal français: Meubles de la couronne conservés en France*, 4 vols (1945–94)

——: *Les Meubles français du XVIIIe siècle*, 2 vols (Paris, 1956, rev. 1982)

F. Watson: *Furniture*, London, Wallace cat. (London, 1956)

P. Verlet: 'Le Commerce des objets d'art et les marchands-merciers à Paris au XVIIIe siècle', *Annales* (1958), pp. 10–29

F. Watson: *Louix XVI Furniture* (London, 1960)

C. Dauterman and J. Parker: *Decorative Art from the Samuel Kress Collection* (Oxford, 1964)

P. Verlet: *La Maison du XVIIIe siècle en France* (Fribourg and Paris, 1966)

F. Watson: *The Wrightsman Collection*, 3 vols (New York, 1966–70)

A. Boutemy: *Meubles français anonymes du XVIIIe siècle* (Brussels, 1973)

G. de Bellaigue: *The James A. de Rothschild Collection at Waddesdon Manor*, 2 vols (Fribourg, 1974) [multi-vol. cat. of the col. at Waddesdon Manor]

S. Eriksen: *Early French Neo-classicism* (London, 1974)

H. Ottomeyer and P. Pröschel: *Vergoldete Bronzen: Die Bronzearbeiten des Spätbarock und Klassizismus*, 2 vols (Munich, 1986)

B. Pallot: *L'Art du siège au XVIIIe siècle en France* (Paris, 1987)

P. Verlet: *Les Bronzes dorés français du XVIIIème siècle* (Paris, 1987)

A. Pardailhé-Galabrun: *La Naissance de l'intime* (Paris, 1988)

A. Pradère: *Les Ebénistes français de Louis XIV à la Révolution* (Paris, 1989)

T. Dell: *Furniture in the Frick Collection*, 2 vols (New York, 1992)

D. Alcouffe: *Le Mobilier du Musée du Louvre*, 2 vols (Dijon, 1993)

A. PRADÈRE

4. 1794–1848. During this period French furniture underwent a complete transformation. The generation of cabinetmakers, carvers and designers that had ensured continuity between the reigns of Louis XV and Louis XVI was disappearing, and the taste of customers changed. Under the *ancien régime* well-designed and crafted furniture had been largely reserved for the wealthy classes; by 1848, however, many more citizens could afford to furnish their homes.

Among the most important cabinetmakers before 1815 were Georges Jacob and his sons Georges Jacob II and François-Honoré-Georges Jacob-Desmalter (*see* JACOB (ii)), MARTIN-GUILLAUME BIENNAIS, Guillaume Beneman, BERNARD MOLITOR and ADAM WEISWEILER. By the late 1790s the revival of antique styles was being applied to contemporary furniture, and cabinetmakers often executed the designs supplied by painters or architects. The poor economic climate that followed the Revolution meant that ostentatious parade furniture and elaborately shaped pieces ceased to be made, and indigenous woods were preferred. The trend in design was towards multi-purpose pieces with geometric shapes, straight lines and simple curves. Ornament was kept strictly controlled and not used to conceal structure. The palmette, first adopted *c.* 1785, became a favourite motif. Diamond shapes, inlaid or painted, were frequently the only decoration on panels.

Palmettes and diamonds also adorned chairs at their joints. The uprights of chests-of-drawers, writing-desks and tables took the form of colonnettes, pilasters or plinth figures. Chimeras, classical figures, swans, griffins and sphinxes enriched the most expensive pieces (e.g. bureau of Josephine Bonaparte, designed by Percier and Fontaine and made by the Jacob brothers, in the form of a triumphal arch with winged Victories at the corners, 1796–1803; Malmaison, Château N.). But a great part of the ornamental vocabulary reflected political events and included such Revolutionary emblems as Phrygian bonnets, clasped hands, trees of liberty etc. Napoleon's expedition to Egypt in 1798 led to the use of pyramids, caryatids, lotus flowers and scarabs inspired by the engravings of VIVANT DENON. After 1799 military attributes taken from ancient Rome came into fashion.

Although few new design types were introduced, the terminology of furniture changed. According to the engravings of Pierre de La Mésangère, published in the *Journal des dames et des modes* between 1802 and 1835, a small chest-of-drawers was called a *chiffonnier*, a lady's writing-desk or *bonheur-du-jour* became a *gradin* and a wash-stand became an *athénienne* and so forth. Comfortable chairs gave way to a type of chaise longue called a *méridienne*, while the gondola chair replaced the *bergère*. The legs of chairs were often square in section and curved in the form of sabres; the backs were of openwork in various forms that included struts, a network of spread cords, palmettes, hour-glasses and confronted sphinxes.

The transitional style of the early period, sometimes called Directoire, was succeeded by the EMPIRE STYLE around 1804. Napoleon commissioned CHARLES PERCIER and PIERRE-FRANÇOIS-LÉONARD FONTAINE to create the decorative effect of his imperial regime, based on the art of antiquity and the desire for homogeneous, coherent interior schemes. The Emperor had a liking for magnificence; consequently there was a tendency to create heavy furniture of enormous proportions and excessive richness for the Court. The originality of Empire furniture lies more in its form than in its decoration. Its dimensions ceased to be on a human scale, and everything was designed to produce an austere, heroic atmosphere worthy of a generation of warriors. Chests-of-drawers fall into two types: those with short legs and three drawers, and examples enclosed by double doors faced to look like drawers. *Bureaux plats* continued to be made, most often in mahogany. They were often huge in size, decorated with finely chased bronze mounts with matt gilding and resting on complex monopod supports of composite animals. Writing-desks with cylinder-tops or fall-fronts were adorned with bronze mounts of the same type; alternatively, stylized foliage served as a framework for crowned Victories mounted on a triumphal chariot (see fig. 59) or for Greek dancing girls. Ornamental console tables had an identical monumental structure.

The *psyché* or cheval-glass, a new item of furniture, consisted of a heavy base and sturdy uprights with a full-length mirror fixed between them on pivots. Designed as outsize *guéridons*, pedestal tables were generally heavy. On luxurious models the thick wooden top was replaced by marble, porphyry, mosaic or malachite. Certain types of small items of furniture continued to be made without the

59. Fall-front desk with a central gilt-bronze mount of Apollo's chariot, mahogany veneer with a white Carrara marble top, made in Paris, c. 1804 (Paris, Musée du Louvre)

use of monstrous supports: work-tables, game-tables, tea-tables and dressing-tables. The night-table usually took the form of a cylindrical *somno* in massive mahogany. The number of chairs in each room became fewer. The armchair, of vast proportions, was no longer designed for intimate conversation; it had a fixed place along the wall. The front legs were often adorned with swans, eagles, lions or chimeras that form a straight line from the armrests to the floor. In typical models the feet are cylindrical, fluted, turned or tapered and encased in bronze sabots. The gondola type continued to be in favour. Beds were of two types, those with straight posts in the form of columns decorated with bronze mounts, or *en bateau*. In the latter, two ends of equal height, either curved inwards or scrolled back, are linked by a low curving vase (for illustration *see* EMPIRE STYLE).

After the restoration of the French monarchy in 1815, rulers no longer set the policy for artistic creation; the Court ceased to be the crucible in which new styles were refined. Louis XVIII was content to have the letter N and the Napoleonic bees removed from his predecessor's furniture and replaced by L and fleurs-de-lis. During the short reign of Charles X, the neo-Gothic style of furniture became more widespread. It had originated unobtrusively at the end of the Empire; before 1813 Jacob-Desmalter had made Gothic-style chairs in gilt-wood for the Comtesse d'Osmond. The nouveaux riches preferred the showy and pretentious designs produced by such ornamentalists as Bance and Muidebled. The most elegant ensembles

were commissioned by émigrés who needed to refurnish their homes. Among members of the bourgeoisie, common sense and a taste for the practical and comfortable led them to furnish their somewhat cramped apartments with a quantity of well-constructed furniture of small dimensions, made of native woods and therefore relatively inexpensive. Mahogany continued in fashion until 1820, but after the Exposition des Produits de l'Industrie of 1823 in Paris, certain cabinetmakers introduced luxury furniture in maple-wood and walnut. Striking decorative effects were also achieved by using pink ash, speckled thuya, mottled plane tree, gnarled elm, pale sycamore and amber maple. Richly figured timbers were also used for veneers, and the vivid patterns of roots and burls were fully exploited. A light and charming repertory of garlands, pearls and other motifs was employed for marquetry, inlay or gilt-bronze mounts, giving life to furniture. Writing-desks of all shapes and sizes became highly complicated and heavy. Dining-tables still used the vocabulary of the preceding period. A multitude of little occasional tables, elegantly and ingeniously designed, began to clutter up apartments, although the *psyché*, the *somno*, wash-basins and console tables were slow to abandon a certain imperial heaviness. Chairs became lighter, more mobile and more comfortable. Armchairs and chairs with stuffed backs, upright or slightly curved, still had chimeras or winged genies for their supports, but very early on straight backs dropped from fashion. Gondola chairs continued to enjoy an extraordinary vogue (e.g. armchair of maple-wood inlaid with purple-wood, c. 1830; Paris, Mus. A. Déc.). The *méridienne* and sofa in very distinctive shapes were made of native woods and ornamented with inlaid palmettes and garlands as bronze mounts gradually became rarer.

The period between 1830 and 1848 marked a break with the production practices of the *ancien régime*. The replacement of handcraft by machines threw traditional workshops into disarray, although Jacob-Desmalter continued in business until 1847. The introduction of new processes became essential to meet the demands of a new market: a larger, more prosperous bourgeoisie found it necessary to equip its domestic surroundings without the aid of furniture acquired by inheritance. The machines exhibited for the first time in Paris at the Exposition des Produits de l'Industrie of 1839 made mass production possible. Originality declined as furniture from earlier periods was copied. By drawing on collections of engravings, such ornamentalists as Aimé Chenavard produced albums (e.g. *Nouveau recueil d'ornements*, 1833–5) to assist cabinetmakers in concocting furniture in the neo-Egyptian, neo-Gothic and neo-Renaissance styles. An example is a *commode-secrétaire* in the neo-Renaissance style by Guillaume Grohé and Jean-Michel Grohé (*fl* 1829–61) in palisander, ebony and palm with plaques of marble (1839; Paris, Louvre). For ordinary furniture light woods were abandoned, and there was a return to ebony, rose-wood, mahogany, oak and, after 1827, native woods blackened by chemicals. Ingenious combinations were developed for small apartments: chests-of-drawers could be transformed into writing-desks, dressing-tables or, by adding an upper stage with glass doors, into bookcases. The *semainier*, a tall and narrow chest-of-drawers, proliferated. The wardrobe with mirrors, often with an enormous, thinly veneered drawer at its base and headed by a deeply moulded cornice, became an essential item in the bedroom. Tables were round with a single bulbous pedestal, often turned and grooved. Little tables in the form of dessert-tables, work-tables, knitting- or sewing-tables and the *vide-poche* with hidden compartments continued in popularity. Chairs became more comfortable but hardly more elegant; for example, the Voltaire armchair was low and deeply upholstered with a high back. Small squat armchairs and huge sofas with their frames completely covered stood alongside gondola armchairs and rows of light side chairs.

BIBLIOGRAPHY

Y. Brunhammer and M. Ricour: 'Le Style empire, le style restauration: Louis XVIII et Charles X', *Jard. A.*, 37 (1957), pp. 53–7; 38 (1957), pp. 121–4

——: 'Le Mobilier Louis-Philippe', *Jard. A.*, 42 (1958), pp. 388–91

S. Granjean: *Empire Furniture, 1800–1825* (London, 1966)

J. Viaux: *Bibliographie du meuble (Mobilier civil français)*, 2 vols (Paris, 1966–88)

5. 1849–1914. Napoleon III left all artistic initiative in the hands of the Empress and his ministers. However, wishing to have a sumptuous court and to encourage the development of all branches of industrial art, he brought in a number of distinguished cabinetmakers to work for the Crown: GUILLAUME GROHÉ, Henri Fourdinois (1799–1871) and Alfred Beurdeley (1808–82). Two new concepts gained currency: furniture in different styles could now stand side by side in the same room; and there was also a considerable increase in the density of furniture in rooms. It is not possible to list all the types of furniture available during the Second Empire, since so many hybrids were created and a plethora of chairs of all sorts invaded the domestic interior (*see* UPHOLSTERY, colour pl. XV). Traditional forms, transformed by castors, upholstery and braiding, became barely recognizable; many varieties of wood were used, as well as iron, painted cast iron, cane, bamboo, papier mâché and even boiled cardboard. In regard to style, chairs designed for comfort were the most important. They were upholstered and skirted with no part of the frame in evidence; squat armchairs, called *crapauds*, sofas and pouffes had fringes reaching to the ground. The *borne* was an enormous round pouffe. *Confidentes à deux places* and *indiscrets à trois places* were settees with S-shaped backs for two or three occupants. The structure of furniture became heavier with columns of octagonal section, metal feet turned in spirals and bronze mounts of tormented shapes emphasizing massive cornices. Precious woods were used for the exteriors and enriched with inlays of silver, tin, copper, mother-of-pearl, ivory and tortoiseshell; plaques of porcelain, marble and pietre dure were set into dark wood. The interiors of case furniture were often veneered in light woods or lined with mirrors or padding of luxurious fabrics. Tables were of all shapes and sizes, dimensions and styles. Table-tops folded away in a variety of ways; they were sometimes covered with marquetry or inlay, plates of glass placed over dried flowers, mosaics, *verre églomisé*, tooled leather or textiles.

Two main stylistic trends became evident. The first, the more creative but less widespread, drew its inspiration from the vogue for history painting with literary references. The most striking example is the Médaillier de Mérovée

by the cabinetmaker Charles Guillaume Diehl (1811–85) and the sculptor Emmanuel Fremiet (see fig. 60). Exhibited at the Exposition Universelle (1867) in Paris, this medal-cabinet was inspired by the *Récits des temps mérovingiens* (1840) by Augustin Thierry. The second trend drew on furniture dating from the reigns of Louis XIV and Louis XV. These designs inspired those artists whose work was restricted to creating imitations, such as Mme Perrier's dressing-table (1867; Paris, Mus. A. Déc.) by Paul Christofle (1838–1907), Gustave-Joseph Cheret (1838–94) and ALBERT-ERNEST CARRIER-BELLEUSE, a console table supported by bronze figures in the Italian Baroque style (*c.* 1865; Paris, Mus. A. Déc.) by Jules Dalou and the neo-Renaissance cabinet made by A. Kneib for the Hôtel de la Païva in Paris (*c.* 1865; Paris, Mus. A. Déc.). These pieces foreshadowed a period of nearly 40 years during which similar decorative formulae would be exploited. The Second Empire thus had a profound influence on the art of furniture, creating such superbly unified ensembles as that made for the Ministry of Finance in Paris. Sumptuousness and brilliant colours were characteristic of these reinterpretations of earlier styles.

At the beginning of the Third Republic (1871–1940), a slow transformation began to take place that laid the foundation for a new concept of furniture. The general

60. Médaillier de Mérovée by Charles Guillaume Diehl, cedar-wood, ebony and ivory, with sculptural mounts and a relief panel by Emmanuel Fremiet in silver-plated bronze and copper, 2.38×1.51×0.60 m, 1867 (Paris, Musée d'Orsay)

public, however, was unaware of these developments, and mainstream commercial furniture, based on the revival of historic styles, changed little between 1870 and World War I. The fashion for pastiche, resulting from intensive industrial production, the conventions of bourgeois taste and a lack of interest in the art of furniture among the intellectual élite, made it difficult for a new style to emerge. Even so, within the world of imitation, such artists as François Lincke and Joseph Zwiener achieved quite astonishing feats using styles from the past. Nevertheless, certain critics had long been unhappy about contemporary taste. E. Guichard, who reported on the furniture section of the Exposition Universelle of 1867 in Paris, wrote: 'we lack invention; we are very good at copying, but that is not enough'. The leaders of the renewal that resulted in the ART NOUVEAU movement were architects, painters, sculptors and designers, but not cabinetmakers. The influence of such artists as EUGÈNE GRASSET and EMILE GALLÉ on furniture styles owed more to their overall work in decorative art, their writings and their pupils than to the small number of their original works.

The Art Nouveau movement in France was assisted by developments in neighbouring countries: in England, William Morris created Arts and Crafts furniture that became well known in Paris within a few years. In Belgium, two progressive architects, HENRY VAN DE VELDE and Victor Horta, attempted to furnish the homes they built for themselves with furniture noteworthy for the logical use of materials and carefully thought-out design. By the turn of the century, French artists were also influenced by JAPONISME, a fashion due in part to the publication of *Le Japon artistique* (6 vols; 1888–91) by S. BING.

Art Nouveau reflected the individualism of its creators, but all of them had in common a desire to interpret nature. Grasset, author of *Méthode de composition ornementale* (1905), taught his pupils to analyse plants and incorporate them in ornament. Gallé, who had founded the Ecole des Arts Décoratifs de Nancy in 1895, expressed similar ideas in an article entitled 'Le Mobilier contemporain orné d'après nature' (1900). However, although the natural structure of plants was often accurately rendered in Art Nouveau ornament, the equilibrium of mass and the correct distribution of volume were sometimes ignored. Grasset's table decorated with kitchen herbs, or a table, the top of which is in the shape of a water-lily leaf (Paris, Mus. A. Déc.), or a bookcase in walnut and cast iron (1890; Paris, Mus. d'Orsay) by RUPERT CARABIN are typical of this style, as is the gilt-bronze bed designed by Edouard Lièvre for Mme Valtesse de la Bigne (Paris, Mus. d'Orsay). Héctor Guimard, who had been influenced by Horta and was responsible for the décor and furniture at the famous Maxim's restaurant in Paris, was commissioned in 1894 to design, decorate and fit out the Castel Béranger, a block of flats in Paris. The furniture, with its subtle structures and sinuous shapes, showed great originality.

The Exposition Universelle of 1900 in Paris provides a good opportunity to take stock of the achievements of Art Nouveau. The Union Centrale des Arts Décoratifs (founded 1882) commissioned Georges Hoentschel (1855–1915) to fit out three rooms at the exhibition. The dense, over-abundant floral decoration was wonderfully executed but disconcertingly diverse. There was no overall

coherency to Art Nouveau since all its great exponents, including ALEXANDRE CHARPENTIER, LOUIS MAJORELLE (see fig. 61), Gallé, H. J. F. Bellery Desfontaines (1867–1909), Tony Selmerheim (1871–1971) and CHARLES PLUMET, were highly competitive in respect of ingenuity, skill and individuality. The Art Nouveau pavilion, where Bing had organized a harmonious and sophisticated exhibition, was much more homogeneous. He assigned the six rooms of an apartment to different artists: the antechamber, dining-room and bedroom went to EUGÈNE GAILLARD, whose curving furniture in moulded and carved native woods was decorated with discreet floral ornament. EDOUARD COLONNA's furniture for the sitting-room was somewhat flimsy, while GEORGES DE FEURE produced an ensemble of subtle, sinuous lines that lent feminine grace to the boudoir and bathroom (*see* ART NOUVEAU, fig. 2).

In reaction to Art Nouveau, some artists produced furniture in simpler and more robust shapes, functionalism being seen as more important than preciousness. Maurice Dufrène (1876–1955), a founder-member in 1901 of the Société des Artistes-Décorateurs (SAD), inaugurated a range of furniture in very dark native wood and defended the use of mechanical processes and mass production. In 1910 the Deutscher Werkbund, which brought together

61. Armchair designed and manufactured by Louis Majorelle, carved walnut stained green (with reproduction upholstery), h. 1.1 m, exhibited in Paris at the Exposition Universelle of 1900 (London, Victoria and Albert Museum)

artists, decorators and craftsmen, exhibited at the Salon at the Grand Palais. Although derided by the Parisian public, their style impressed the French organizers, who appreciated that excessive individualism is inimical to the birth of a new style and that team work is essential for creating a coherent, functional environment, adapted to the requirements of modern life. To this end PAUL POIRET, the fashion designer, opened the Atelier Martine in 1911 with the goal of producing very simple furniture inspired by Cubism, in white wood painted in vivid colours. In 1912 LOUIS SÜE set up the Atelier Français, a boutique of modern decorative art. In the same year the department store Au Printemps called on René Guilleré (1878–1931), another founder of SAD, to take over the direction of L'Atelier Primavera, and Dufrène was appointed head of Les Galeries Lafayette. Francis Jourdain (see JOURDAIN, (2)) declared his hostility to the naturalist style and founded the Ateliers Modernes in 1912 with the object of designing furniture for workers. Gradually such artists as PAUL FOLLOT, Paul Iribe (1883–1935), Léon-Albert Jallot (1874–1967), Clément Mère (1870–after 1925) and André Mare (1885–1932) developed a new style. They sought to adapt form to use and replaced elaborate asymmetrical floral ornament with delicate stylized motifs in a very light relief, but these efforts were temporarily curtailed by the outbreak of war.

BIBLIOGRAPHY
P. Olmer: *La Renaissance du mobilier français, 1895–1927* (Paris, 1927)
J. Viaux: 'Le Mobilier Napoléon III', *Rev. Ameublement* (1965), March, pp. 191–7; April, pp. 175–81; May, pp. 123–9
——: *Bibliographie du meuble (Mobilier civil français)*, 2 vols (Paris, 1966–88)
C. B. Heller: *Art Nouveau meubles* (Paris, 1991)

6. AFTER 1914. Following the disruption of World War I, in 1919 the Société des Artistes-Décorateurs (SAD) declared its goals: to help the devastated regions by producing simple industrial furniture; to obtain the agreement of commerce and industry to assist artists in creating a modern style; and to promote this style among the broad public. Dining-rooms and bedrooms in prefabricated elements were designed by Théodore Lambert (1857–after 1910), and ensembles in lacquered poplar wood with geometric decoration were produced by LOUIS SÜE and André Mare. Subsequently, the Compagnie des Arts Français (1919–28) of Süe and Mare published a trade catalogue from which clients could order the furniture of their choice. In 1919 René Joubert (d 1931) joined with Georges Mouveau to set up Décoration Intérieure Moderne (DIM) and in 1924, with the collaboration of Philippe Petit (d 1945), they began to commission mass-produced furniture of robust construction and very restrained decoration. André Domin (1883–1962) and Marcel Genevrière (b 1885) established the Maison Dominique (1922–70) to produce furniture inspired by Cubism that was both comfortable and elegantly veneered in precious woods. The department stores also participated: in 1923 Le Bon Marché appointed Paul Follot to direct its design studio, Atelier Pomone, and Etienne Kohlmann (1903–after 1945) and Maurice Matet (1870–after 1945) presided over the Studium at the Grands Magasins du Louvre. These ateliers implemented the goals of SAD. Despite these efforts, the Salons held immediately after the war concentrated on one-off pieces fabricated by specialist artisans.

The style called *Style moderne* at the time and ART DECO since the 1960s was the final phase of a long process of development and defies precise definition. Its foundations had been laid well before 1913, when such artists as Clément Mère (1870–after 1925) and Paul Iribe (1883–1935) had exhibited furniture that qualifies as Art Deco. This movement assimilated such diverse and contradictory influences as Cubist, Constructivist and Futurist painting, the Ballets Russes, the arts of Africa and Asia, and haute couture. There were a few underlying principles: form must derive from function, and decoration must be an integral part of structure. Furniture must suit the conditions of modern life, which meant simple and functional furnishings with easy upkeep. The principal room in an apartment, newly christened the living-room, was required to serve as the drawing-room, dining-room, bedroom and study; among various items of built-in furniture, it also contained low tables, ingenious little writing-desks and bookcases fitted into the wall above the sofa.

Art Deco furniture designers can be divided into three different categories. There were the traditionalists who remained faithful to the ideal of elegant, luxurious furnishings: JACQUES-EMILE RUHLMANN (see ART DECO, fig. 2) combined ivory with exotic woods, Follot worked with sycamore and padouk, and André Groult (1884–1967) designed furniture in oak and shagreen mosaic, enriched with rose-wood colonettes inlaid with ivory. The modernists, on the other hand, subscribed to a rigid functionalism from which ornament was virtually banished: Jacques Adnet (1900–after 1959) designed a dining-room in 1928 with lacquered burr-walnut in restrained forms, while André-Léon Arbus (1903–69) produced furniture veneered in sycamore and Gabon ivory, with pure lines and virtually no ornament. Louis Sognot (1892–1970), who was greatly influenced by Cubism, specialized in metal and mirror furniture. Finally, a number of individual designers and decorators developed an eclectic approach: thus PIERRE-EMILE LEGRAIN was attracted by the massive, robust furniture of Africa (see fig. 62), while Eugène Printz (1889–1948), one of the few professional cabinet-makers, produced unornamented pieces in wood with complicated forms inspired by the Baroque. The variety of materials used was virtually infinite. Black ebony, greatly prized by Ruhlmann, rapidly vanished from the market, to be replaced by veined macassar-ebony. All the exotic woods that had long been known came back into fashion, with the addition of woods recently introduced from Africa: bubinga, paroba, okoumé and zingana. Legrain even attempted to make use of the rugged timber of the palm-tree. Nor was the beauty of native species neglected. This extraordinary range was augmented by the lacquer furniture of JEAN DUNAND and EILEEN GRAY. Leather was frequently replaced by such precious skins as tinted shagreen, glazed or painted, or even pony skin. Ivory, tortoiseshell, mother-of-pearl, parchment, straw, wicker and such metals as silver, copper, bronze, tin and zinc also made their appearance. The vogue for wrought-iron by Edgar Brandt (1880–1960) and Raymond Henri Subes (1893–1970) and the introduction of plate-glass panels into furniture were also significant.

In 1925 the Exposition Internationale des Arts Décoratifs et Industriels Modernes in Paris became the field on

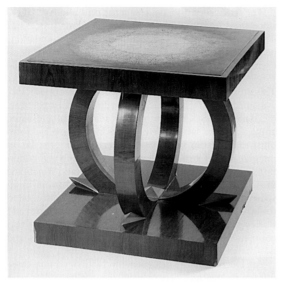

62. Table by Pierre-Emile Legrain, palisander veneer, the top painted to simulate eggshell lacquer, 1923 (Paris, Musée des Arts Décoratifs)

which all the schools of furniture design encountered each other. It exacerbated the rivalries among the decorators, but as a result certain trends emerged. First and foremost, the exhibition finally dispelled the lingering prejudice against machinery and promoted the development of modern production methods. The word *ensemblier* was born, implying the need for a mastermind to coordinate the work of the architect, designer and cabinetmaker: the term *décorateur* also expressed this development. Furniture was no longer merely the concern of cabinetmakers. Instead, it was first conceived by a designer and then produced on machines by different artisans. It is significant that between the wars there were only 5 or 6 professional cabinetmakers, compared to 80 or 90 furniture designers.

The exhibition was an immense success. Each of the ateliers of the department stores designed and furnished its own pavilion. The Pavillon de l'Esprit Nouveau by LE CORBUSIER was poorly received by the general public, as his 'machine for living in' was a concept too advanced for his time. The pavilion of the Compagnie des Arts Français, called the Musée d'Art Contemporain, exhibited furnishings by Süe and Mare with powerful curves, enveloping shapes, luxurious materials and bold colours. The Hôtel d'un Collectionneur, designed by the architect Pierre Patout, was devoted to the work of Ruhlmann, both as a furniture designer and as an interior decorator of great sophistication. Ruhlmann was also responsible for a room in the Pavillon d'un Ambassadeur, where SAD displayed the work of its members. Pierre Selmesheim (1869–1941) and Henri Rapin (1873–1939) were responsible for the architecture and overall presentation. There were vast differences between the luxurious and voluptuous room prepared for Madame by Groult and the austere quarters for Monsieur designed by Léon-Albert Jallot (1874–1967). The sophisticated luxury of the office-library designed by Pierre Chareau contrasted with the stark simplicity of the hall by Robert Mallet-Stevens.

The exhibition did not put an end to the rivalry among the schools. The UNION DES ARTISTES MODERNES came into existence in 1929. Such founders and members of the movement as Francis Jourdain (*see* JOURDAIN, (2)), Chareau, Le Corbusier and René Herbst (1891–1982) were followers of a Spartan functionalism, but for some members the geometrization of forms did not mean abandoning precious materials and decorative refinements. The debate on modern furniture broadened and was no longer confined to the professionals. The Art Deco style persisted, evolving gradually, until the end of World War II and beyond. Some modifications were due to the introduction of new materials, especially metals. Initially, metal furniture imitated wooden furniture but it became liberated from this model and acquired its own aesthetic (e.g. dressing-table in chromed steel and mirror by René Herbst, 1930; priv. col., see Duncan, colour pl. 34). Duralumin tubes, chromium-plated steel, lacquer or enamel, zinc veneer, aluminium and patinated bronze were all used to make small tables, office furniture and other pieces that could be easily combined. Metal was often finished with glass; glass slabs, whether painted or not, transparent or opaque and sometimes engraved, were in common use as table-tops. In 1938 experiments were made with armchairs in safety glass.

After World War II, French furniture entered a period of decline. The idea that there was a characteristic French style in the 1950s is of recent origin; in fact there was nothing exclusively French since all European furniture was characterized by an internationalism drawn from American originals. French production at this time was depressingly banal and subsequently inspired by Scandinavian modernism. From 1960 to 1965 wood disappeared almost completely from prestigious furniture made commercially by famous firms and by the few cabinetmakers in business. Gradually, however, a reaction came about, and between 1975 and 1990 a new generation of artists emerged, following the example of PHILIPPE STARCK, Xavier Mantegot, Guy de Rougement and Marc Berthier. Linked with French traditions of quality, their creativity was expressed in the search for new forms and the return to the use of elegant materials, including various species of wood. Thus P. Deltombes used maple and sycamore scribbled with pastel colours. These developments began during the presidency of Georges Pompidou (1969–74), who commissioned contemporary furniture for his private apartments in the Palais de l'Elysée, Paris, and have since been encouraged by annual orders from the Garde Meuble National.

BIBLIOGRAPHY

J. Viaux: *Bibliographie du meuble (Mobilier civil français)*, 2 vols (Paris, 1966–8)
Y. Amic: *Le Mobilier français, 1945–1964* (Paris, 1983)
G. de Bure: *Le Mobilier français, 1965–1979* (Paris, 1983)
A. Duncan: *Art Deco Furniture: The French Designers* (London, 1984)
P. Kjellberg: *Art Déco: Les Maîtres du mobilier, le décor des paquebots* (Paris, 1986)
Y. Brunhammer and G. Delaporte: *Les Styles des années 30/50* (Paris, 1987)
K. J. Sembach, G. Leuthäeur and P. Gössel: *Le Design du meuble au XXe siècle* (Cologne, 1989)
Y. Brunhammer and S. Tise: *Les Artistes décorateurs, 1900–1942* (Paris, 1990)

JACQUELINE VIAUX

VII. Ceramics.

1. Pottery. 2. Porcelain.

1. POTTERY.

(i) Before 1600. (ii) 1600 and after.

(i) Before 1600.

(a) Lead-glazed. Lead-glazed pottery was produced during Gallo-Roman times around Vichy and Saint-Remy-en-Rollat, where a brilliant green was obtained from the addition of copper oxide to the glaze. During the early Middle Ages, however, this technique was lost, and burial grounds dating from the 9th century to the 13th in the Ile-de-France yielded very few fragments of glazed earthenware; the funerary pottery consisted of fairly rough clays decorated in relief. The first manifestation of renewed production of lead-glazed pottery appears to have been for paving tiles in churches; some green-glazed tiles at Sainte-Colombe-les-Sens could date from as early as the 9th century.

During the 12th century glazed earthenware tiles incised with simple geometric designs in green or brown glazes were produced in quantity in the provinces of Bourgogne and Champagne for the Cistercian abbeys. This tradition was continued in other parts of France: for example, Saint-Denis Abbey, in the suburbs of Paris, was paved during the time of Abbot Suger with small, glazed tiles in the manner of a mosaic. The early 13th-century tiled pavement in the form of a rosette at Saint-Pierre-sur-Dives Abbey in Normandy is an early example of the use of slip, which was applied to the surface of the tile and inlaid with designs of a contrasting colour. This technique was dispersed to other parts of France by peripatetic potters who travelled with their moulds; such areas as Normandy, Beauvaisis and Burgundy therefore used similar designs.

During the 13th century heraldry was used extensively in these decorative tile schemes: stylized animals and mythical beasts inspired by Near Eastern motifs, introduced through the Crusades, were combined with such French motifs as fleurs-de-lis, birds and flowers in Gothic trefoils and quatrefoils surrounded by lozenges, chevrons or chequers. The ornamental quality of the tiles, exploiting the contrast of light and dark clay to the best advantage, is further emphasized by the rosettes composed of four tiles or multiples of four.

The use of the human figure in decorative schemes appeared during the 13th century, but in the 14th and 15th centuries contemporary scenes, reminiscent of tapestries, were depicted on tiles and included scenes of hunting, musicians or entertainers. Mottoes were also used: in the Hôtel-Dieu, founded in Beaune in 1443 by Nicolas Rolin, Chancellor to Philip the Good, 3rd Duke of Burgundy, paving tiles in the chapel are inscribed with the initials of Rolin and his wife, Guigonne de Salins, and the motto *Seulle*. Tin-glazed tiles later replaced lead-glazed tiles, although the old moulds continued to be used for some time.

Useful wares including jugs, bowls and boxes dating from the 14th century were excavated on the Paris Left Bank on the site of the old city wall (1183) built by Philip II Augustus. Around the Ile-de-France and in the regions of Beauvaisis, Saintonge, Normandy, Alsace and Provence, the same type of polychrome pottery with low-relief decoration was produced (e.g. yellow-glazed jugs; Paris, Louvre), some of which was similar in style and technique to the wares of Flanders and southern England, possibly due to itinerant craftsmen. In the 13th century there were already some important workshops in the Beauvaisis, namely at Beauvais, Savignies and Lachapelle-aux-Pots. The inventory of Charles VI (1399) mentions 'a pottery beaker from Beauvais mounted in silver'. A large range of luxury and useful wares was produced, including plates, bowls, jars, flagons and bottles, in addition to such religious objects as ex-voto plaques or 'Passion' dishes, for example the green-glazed earthenware dish (1511; Sèvres, Mus. N. Cér.) decorated with the coat of arms of Charles VIII and his wife, Anne of Brittany, the monogram of Christ and the words *Ave Maria*. A hard, fine greyish clay was used at Beauvais, decorated with relief or incised with geometric, floral, animal and human motifs inscribed with Gothic script. Roof finials to adorn gables were also made, for example in Normandy, and usually depicted riders and musicians. In the Pré-d'Auge, Normandy, other useful wares (e.g. paté dishes) were also made; in the Sarthe regions fountains and religious wares were a speciality (e.g. holy-water stoup, ?1550–75; London, Wallace); while potteries in the Alsace concentrated on statues and earthenware stoves. SAINT-PORCHAIRE pottery (end of the 15th century–*c.* 1570) is mentioned several times in contemporary inventories, which attests to its value. Wares, which included tazze, bowls and candlesticks, were made from a fine clay inlaid with brown-and-black slips and covered in a transparent, colourless lead glaze. Some items were decorated with masks, arabesques and Vitruvian scrolls (e.g. tazza, *c.* 1540; London, V&A), while others displayed high-relief reptiles, such as those used by BERNARD PALISSY on his *rustiques figulines*.

Palissy was first recorded as working at Saintes in 1539 as a portrait painter, glass painter and draughtsman. The Saintonge was a renowned pottery area in La-Chapelle-des-Pots; production included jugs and such pilgrim-flasks

63. Lead-glazed earthenware dish with moulded snake, lobsters, frog and lizard by Bernard Palissy or a follower, 371×493 mm, from the Saintonge, second half of the 16th century (London, Wallace Collection)

64. Faience plate depicting *Aaron's Rod Changing into a Snake*, after an engraving by Salomon Bernard, diam. 415 mm, from Lyon, 1582 (London, British Museum)

as the green-glazed example (mid-16th century; Paris, Louvre) decorated in low-relief with the coat of arms and motto *A Planos* of the Constable of France, Anne de Montmorency. The inventory (1556) of the Constable from his Paris hôtel recorded several items of Saintes earthenware. The Constable became Palissy's patron and in 1556 commissioned a rustic grotto for the château of Ecouen; it was, however, never completed. In 1563 Palissy, who was a Huguenot, was arrested as a heretic; he was finally released after a royal decree from the queen, Catherine de' Medici, appointed him Inventeur des Rustiques Figulines du Roi. In 1567 he began work on a grotto for the Jardin des Tuileries in Paris for the Queen. The grotto was covered with moulded, lead- and tin-glazed reptiles, fish, plants and shells in the same manner as his *rustiques figulines*, the most famous of which are the oval dishes covered in moulded and glazed mosses, ferns, crustaceans, snakes and shells, which are attributed to him or a follower (see fig. 63). Palissy also made *terres jaspées* (marbled grounds) based on the designs of such sculptors from the Fontainebleau school as Jean Goujon. The influence of Palissy was widespread, and at the pottery in Avon, near Fontainebleau, directed by Barthélemy de Blénod, lead-glazed figures and groups were later produced in the Palissy style. Similar-style figures and groups (e.g. boy with a dog, early 17th century; Paris, Louvre) were also made at Manerbe in Normandy.

(b) Faience. Faience, which came to France through Italy and Moorish Spain, was introduced in the 14th century. Both Spanish and Italian potters are recorded as working in France during this period. Between 1332 and 1338 Jehan de Valencia is recorded as working as a potter in Bourges and Poitiers. In Narbonne Spanish Muslims

produced the characteristic green and purple wares typical of Mediterranean faience; this style was also made in Avignon in the potteries of Italian and Spanish artists. In Lyon Italian potters, from Genoa or Florence, are mentioned in a document of 1512 (*see* LYON, §3(i)); in 1570 Pezaro from Genoa was granted a charter to produce faience, while his brother was appointed Potier du Roi. Such artists as Guillaume Tardessire (*fl* 1574) and Giulio Gambin (?1552–?1620) from Faenza joined them and produced *istoriato* albarelli and dishes in the style of maiolica from Urbino. The painting on a plate (1582; London, BM; see fig. 64) of *Aaron's Rod Changing into a Snake* was based on a woodcut by Salomon Bernard (1506/10–61), which was used to illustrate *Quadrins historiques de la Bible* (Lyon, 1553) by Claude Paradin and published by Jean de Tournes. Some of these Italian craftsmen possibly collaborated on the production of the faience tile pavement in the choir of the priory church at Brou, Bourg-en-Bresse, Burgundy, which Margaret of Austria, Duchess of Savoy, built as a mausoleum (1504) in memory of her third husband, Philibert II, Duke of Savoy (1480–1504). François de Canarin (*fl* 1552) is recorded in relation to the tiles on which male profile heads *all'antica* are surrounded by stylized foliage on a blue ground in the style of Faenza. In 1528 the Florentine potter Girolamo della Robbia was working on the decoration of the Château de Madrid in the Bois de Boulogne, Paris, for Francis I. He may have taught Masséot Abaquesne (*fl* 1526–59), who established the manufacture of faience at Rouen *c.* 1525. Abaquesne also worked on decorative tiled schemes at the château of Ecouen in 1542 and at the Château de La Bâtie d'Urfé (1551). In Nîmes the Huguenot potter Antoine Syjalon (1524–90) made faience plates, pilgrim-flasks and albarelli in the Italian style from 1544 in a range of such high-temperature colours as blue, yellow and orange (e.g. pilgrim-flask, 1581; New York, Met.). Syjalon depicted subjects in a satirical manner. In Montpellier, where the oldest medicine faculty in France was based, production included albarelli by such potters as Pierre Estève in the 1570s and the Ollivier and Favier families at the beginning of the 17th century. Nevers also owed its faience production to the Italian masters; production began in 1588 under the brothers Augustin Conrade (*fl* from 1585), Baptiste Conrade and Dominique Conrade from Albisola with Giulio Gambin, who had worked at Lyon. They were supported by Ludovico Gonzaga, who became Duke of Nevers on his marriage to Henriette de Clèves in 1565.

(c) Stoneware. Stoneware was produced in the Beauvaisis from the fine local clay towards the end of the Middle Ages. Wares were decorated in relief with a bluish glaze and were of a very high quality; a dish (beginning of the 16th century; Paris, Louvre) is decorated in low relief with the arms of Villiers de L'Isle Adam, Bishop of Beauvais (1497–1521), and fleurs-de-lis. In the Berry region hard, grey, salt-glazed stonewares were also produced during the 16th century.

(ii) 1600 and after. In 1603 Henry IV granted the Conrade brothers (*see* §(i)(b) above) a 30-year monopoly for the production of faience. The *istoriato* plates, vases and ewers

are very similar to those made in Lyon. Some early Baroque sculptural works in the style of the della Robbia potters was produced in the Conrade workshop (e.g. *Virgin and Christ*, 1636; Nevers, Mus. Blandin). After the Conrades' monopoly expired (1633), other factories were established in Nevers by such potters as Berthélemy Bourcier and Nicolas Estienne (*see* NEVERS, §1). The Italianate *istoriato* production was continued, in addition to a more French style inspired by the paintings of such contemporary artists as Poussin and Vouet and the engravings of François Chaveau (e.g. plate depicting the *Rape of Europa*, *c.* 1675; Paris, Louvre). A Franco-Nivernais style developed after 1660, which reflected the taste for pastorals described in such contemporary novels as the prose romance *L'Astrée* (1607–27) by Honoré d'Urfé.

Towards the end of the 17th century Nivernais potters were influenced by a rich variety of styles: East Asian decoration was applied to forms inspired by contemporary French silverware. About 1670 the celebrated *bleu persan* ground was introduced by adding cobalt oxide to the glaze. The use of blue and yellow grounds was inspired by wares from East Asia, Venice and Savona; these were decorated with sprays of flowers and fantastic birds in yellow, blue, orange and white (e.g. flowerpot, *c.* 1670; London, V&A). Through the trade of the French East India Company opened by Jean-Baptiste Colbert, potters were able to copy imported Chinese Transitional wares (1620–44), the so-called blue-and-white (e.g. ewer, *c.* 1660; Saumur, Mus. A. Déc.). This style spread to the other factories, which may have been started by Nivernais potters.

A patented letter (25 Nov 1644) granted a 30-year monopoly (later extended to 50 years) to Nicolas Poirel, Sieur de Granval, 'to produce in the province of Normandy all sorts of useful tableware in white faience or painted in coloured enamels'. When this licence was registered at the parliament in Rouen (29 Feb 1648), it was recorded as having been contracted to Edmé Poterat (1612–87), whose son Michel Poterat succeeded him in 1673 and whose eldest son Louis Poterat obtained a new licence (1673) for his own factory (*see* ROUEN, §III). At first forms and decoration imitated those of Nevers and later Delft, until Louis Poterat developed the style most characteristic of Rouen, the so-called *style rayonnant* in blue *en camaïeu* (blue monochrome), often picked out in a brownish-red (see fig. 65). Because the Sumptuary Edict of 1689 prohibited the use of silver tablewares, Rouen producers could manufacture large 'services'. Between *c.* 1720 and 1740, due to the proximity of Dieppe (one of the ports used by the East India Company), polychrome chinoiserie decoration emulated Chinese porcelain Kang Xi wares (1661–1722) using the *famille verte* (green, yellow, blue, iron-red and purple) palette. Jean-Baptiste Guillibaud (*d* 1739) is particularly associated with this style of decoration. Between 1725 and 1750 sculptural items including busts and celestial and terrestrial globes were also produced. The Rococo style was introduced *c.* 1740, and wares were decorated with pastorales, *fêtes galantes* and chinoiseries. During the French Revolution some *faïence parlante* with revolutionary or royalist mottoes was produced at Rouen and Nevers.

65. Faience ewer with underglaze-blue decoration, h. 247 mm, from Rouen, *c.* 1700–10 (London, Victoria and Albert Museum)

The success of Rouen encouraged the establishment of such other northern factories as those in Lille (*see* LILLE, §3(i)) and Sincency (est. 1734). In the south of France, two important factories were established in the 18th century: Moustiers and Marseille. The first pottery in MOUSTIERS was established *c.* 1679 by Pierre Clérissy (1651–1728). Wares were painted with armorial devices, historical scenes and hunting scenes (e.g. oval dish, *c.* 1700; Sèvres, Mus. N. Cér.) inspired by the engravings of Antonio Tempesta and painted by François Gaspard Viry (1682–1750). Towards the end of the 17th century and the beginning of the 18th, wares were decorated in blue-and-white with lambrequin borders and strapwork in the style of Jean Berain I (e.g. dish, *c.* 1710; London, BM). The factory in Marseille (*see* MARSEILLE, §2) was established in 1679 in the suburb at Saint-Jean-du-Désert by Joseph Clérissy (*c.* 1649–84), Antoine Clérissy (*d* 1743) and François Viry. Wares produced were very similar to those of Moustiers: blue-and-white hunting scenes, coats of arms and Berain-inspired decoration. After 1740 both Marseille and Moustiers abandoned blue-and-white decoration for a high-temperature palette of blue, green, orange-yellow and purple. Moustiers developed a more refined painting technique of miniatures in round medallions surrounded by wreaths with borders of swags and festoons. At Marseille from *c.* 1740 Joseph Fauchier (*d* 1751) produced richly decorated wares with mythological scenes and bold Rococo borders in polychrome enamels. Moustiers and Marseille encouraged the development of such other southern factories as those in Montpellier, Toulouse and Montauban.

The second Sumptuary Edict (1709) encouraged the establishment of more faience factories. By 1721 Charles François Hannong (1669–1739) was producing faience in

66. Faience dish with enamelled floral decoration by Joseph-Adam Hannong, diam. 250 mm, from Strasbourg, 1762–80 (London, Victoria and Albert Museum)

Strasbourg (*see* STRASBOURG, §II, 2). At first blue-and-white faience was made, inspired by the wares of Rouen. From 1737 Hannong's son Paul Antoine Hannong (1700–60) was in charge of both the Strasbourg factory and another factory in Haguenau (est. 1724). At first high-temperature colours were employed, but *c.* 1740 enamelling was introduced and thus a greater range of colours was used, including 'Purple of Cassius' (a rich crimson). Enamels were used for the new *fleurs des Indes* inspired by East Asian designs, which were replaced *c.* 1769 under Joseph-Adam Hannong (1734–after 1790) by the more naturalistic *fleurs fines* or *fleurs de Strasbourg* (see fig. 66). The faience factory in NIDERVILLER was directly linked to the Strasbourg factory; its founder, Baron Jean-Louis de Beyerlé, was the Directeur de la Monnaie in Strasbourg and attracted such artists from Strasbourg as François-Antoine Anstett (*b* 1732). Wares were usually decorated with delicately painted enamels, with an emphasis on a wide range of reds from light pink to deep purple. The factory was particularly famous for its *décor bois* ground (a *trompe l'oeil* form of decoration imitating wood grain), superimposed with 'printed' landscapes on white paper. Well-modelled figures and figure groups were also produced.

About 1728 a faience factory was established in Lunéville by Jacques Chambrette (1705–58), who produced Rococo-style faience (*see* LUNÉVILLE, §2). Factories in Marseille also used enamelling, and the local academy of painting and sculpture (est. 1753) provided training for faience painters. Such directors of Marseille faience factories as La Veuve Perrin (*d* 1793), Joseph Gaspard Robert (*c.* 1750–93) and Antoine Bonnefoy (1762–1815) produced some of the best Rococo faience. Wares were lightly decorated with landscapes, genre scenes, sprays of flowers,

fish and seascapes, and chinoiseries derived from designs by Jean Pillement. Coloured grounds in yellow and turquoise were used together with green, blue and pink monochrome. At Sceaux, near Paris, a faience factory was developed under the patronage of Louise, Duchesse du Maine (1670–1753), between 1735 and 1748 and directed by Jacques Chapelle (*b* 1721). Wares, which included dinner-services, potpourris and vases, were decorated in enamels in the Strasbourg style with chinoiseries and *trompe l'oeil* designs (e.g. tureen and stand, *c.* 1780; Paris, Louvre). In 1772 the factory was bought by Richard Glot, who in 1790 was to petition the Assemblée Nationale on the poor state of the French faience industry following the trade contract signed with England in 1786.

English creamware (cream-coloured earthenware) was seriously undermining faience, as it was both cheap and suitable for popular Neo-classical designs. Creamware based on English patterns was therefore produced by such French factories as the Pont-aux-Choux factory in Paris, which in 1772 proclaimed itself to be the 'Royal Manufacturer of French earthenware in the imitation of that of England'. English craftsmen worked at the factories in both Creil and Montereau from 1774, while Staffordshire potters opened factories at Douai and La-Charité-sur-Loire. By 1786 *faïence fine* (creamware) was produced at Chantilly, Apt and Lunéville.

During the 19th century pottery was produced industrially, and many wares were decorated with transfer-printed designs (for example *see* BORDEAUX, §3). Transfer-printing was an English technique, which was pioneered in France at the associated factories in Creil and Montereau. At an exhibition of 1839 in Paris printed wares were exhibited by the factories of De Boulen in Gien and Fouque Arnoux in Valentine. Various revival styles encouraged the use of such older techniques as salt-glazing at Beauvais *c.* 1840. Palissy-style wares and copies of Saint-Porchaire wares were made by CHARLES-JEAN AVISSEAU of Tours *c.* 1850; he exhibited his wares at the international exhibitions in Paris and London. At Rubelles, near Melun, Baron A. du Tremblay invented *c.* 1844 the technique called *émaux ombrants* (impressed pottery covered with translucent, coloured enamels), which imitated the effect of enamelling (e.g. dish, *c.* 1850; London, V&A).

Towards the end of the 19th century artist–potters produced wares that were clearly inspired by East Asian ceramics, particularly those of Japan (*see* JAPONISME). JOSEPH-THÉODORE DECK was one of the most important artist–potters; some of his decorative earthenwares were painted by such artists as Félix Bracquemond (*see* BRACQUEMOND, (1)) and Eléonore Escallier (e.g. plate, 1867; Paris, Mus. A. Déc.). In the early 1870s the studio potter ERNEST CHAPLET introduced the use of barbotine (a method of decorating with slips under the glaze) at the Auteuil studio in Paris, run by the Haviland Co. in Limoges. From 1882 he worked in the studio in Vaugirard, Paris, run by the same company, and it was there that he was introduced to PAUL GAUGUIN, with whom he collaborated on a series of decorated earthenware pots. The studio potter André Methey (1871–1920) organized a group of artists including Renoir, Bonnard, Maurice de Vlaminck, André Derain and GEORGES ROUAULT to paint a series of plates at his studio in Asnières; these were exhibited at the

Salon d'Automne in 1907. In the 20th century many painters, including PABLO PICASSO and FERNAND LÉGER, experimented with ceramics.

BIBLIOGRAPHY

F. Girard: *Les Faïences parlantes du XVIIIe siècle* (Paris, 1938)
E. Lane: *French Faience* (London, 1948)
Y. Brunhammer: *La Faïence française* (Paris, 1959)
G. Fontaine: *La Céramique française* (Paris, 1965)
M. Ernoult-Gandouet: *La Céramique en France au XIXe siècle* (Paris, 1969)
Céramiques de France du moyen-âge à la Révolution (exh. cat., Montreal, Mus. F.A., 1971)
Faïences françaises du XVIe au XVIIIe siècle (exh. cat., Paris, Grand Pal., 1980)
J. Fréal: *Les Pots d'apothicaire en France du XVIe au XIXe siècle* (Paris, 1982)
A. Lajoix: *La Céramique en France, 1925–1947* (Paris, 1983)

MONIQUE RICCARDI-CUBITT

2. PORCELAIN.

(i) Before 1800. (ii) 1800 and after.

The history of the manufacture of porcelain in France and the products made may be divided into three distinct and significant phases: the period from the 1670s to 1769, dominated by the manufacture of soft-paste (*pâte tendre*) porcelain in and around Paris; from 1769 to 1848, notable for the earliest hard-paste ('true') wares; and from 1849 to the present day. Ancillary to these major fields of activity, but more reflective of developments across the Rhine, is the output of the factories in Strasbourg and Niderviller in Alsace. Unlike the porcelain manufacturers in East Asia and Germany, French porcelain manufacturers did not initially have access to kaolin (china clay), an essential element in the successful manufacture of hard-paste porcelain. The earliest wares made in France were therefore of soft-paste porcelain. The discovery in 1769 of deposits of kaolin at Saint-Yrieix in Limousin made the production of hard-paste porcelain possible by *c.* 1772. This technical improvement, which coincided with the end of the reign of Louis XV and a shift to the Neo-classical style, was to prove of doubtful benefit. In the Paris area production continued under Court patronage until the end of the reign of Louis-Philippe (1848). During the third period the Court no longer served as a source of patronage; industrialized methods were introduced, and the main centre of production shifted from Paris to Limoges, which was much closer to the raw materials required for production.

(i) Before 1800.

(a) Soft-paste. (b) Hard-paste.

(a) Soft-paste. Although the first successful porcelain factory was started in Meissen, Saxony, in 1709, the first porcelain actually produced in Europe—since the brief production in Florence (*c.* 1575–83) under the patronage of the Medici—was French. Production took place in Rouen *c.* 1673 when a factory was established by Louis Poterat (1641–96). Porcelain from Rouen is rare, and those pieces that can be attributed to the factory with absolute certainty are few. Attributed wares are decorated with blue in the prevailing Louis XIV style; many of the pieces

67. Soft-paste porcelain teapot with applied prunus blossom decoration, h. 122 mm, made at Saint-Cloud, *c.* 1700–20 (London, Victoria and Albert Museum)

tentatively given to this short-lived factory, which would seem to have closed by about 1698, are probably in fact early products from the factory in Saint-Cloud.

At Saint-Cloud (*see* SAINT-CLOUD, §3), just outside Paris, soft-paste porcelain was claimed to have been manufactured from 1672, and production continued under Berthe Coudray, widow of the founder Pierre Chicaneau (*d* 1677), and her second husband, Henri-Charles Trou (*d* 1700). Porcelain was manufactured under the Chicaneau and Trou families at Saint-Cloud until it closed in 1766, making it the first successful French porcelain factory and the first therefore to produce an identifiable corpus of products. The paste of Saint-Cloud is creamy-white with a greenish tinge, and the wares are heavily potted with wide foot rims. The factory seems to have encountered severe technical difficulties, as very few flatwares would seem to have been successfully fired. As at Rouen and many other factories, the earliest wares were decorated in blue and white. The shapes of mustard pots, trencher salts, spice-boxes and pomade pots were clearly derived from contemporary metalwork forms, and decorative motifs were inspired by the designs of Jean Berain I. The earliest whitewares (see fig. 67) were directly inspired by Chinese *blanc de chine* porcelains from the Dehua kilns in the province of Fujian, which had been imported in large quantities throughout the second half of the 17th century. The factory also developed its own range of relief patterns, including an imbricated pattern inspired by artichoke leaves and late Baroque scrollwork. The earliest polychrome wares combined underglaze blue with a limited range of enamels and gilding. Chinese-inspired figures were made (e.g. Chinese man, *c.* 1720; Hamburg, Mus. Kst & Gew.). Saint-Cloud was a pioneering producer of one of the most delightful aspects of early French porcelain: *objets de galanterie*. These small luxury objects, generally mounted in silver or silver gilt, ranged from snuff-boxes to handles for canes, knives and forks and assumed all sorts of human and animal forms.

68. Soft-paste porcelain snuff-box with Kakiemon-style decoration, h. 44 mm, made at Chantilly, c. 1740–50 (Hamburg, Museum für Kunst and Gewerbe)

Objets de galanterie were also made at Chantilly (*see* CHANTILLY, §2(i)). This factory was founded in 1725 by Louis-Henri de Bourbon, Prince de Condé (1692–1740), under the direction of Ciquaire Cirou (*d* 1751). The early wares were unusual in being covered in an opaque white tin glaze, which created a most attractive result. The Prince had a substantial collection of porcelain from the Japanese Arita kilns, which provided the inspiration for the early wares decorated in the Kakiemon palette (iron-red, blue, yellow and blue-green), known as the *décor coréen* (see fig. 68). At first, designs were distinctly Japanese or were based on Meissen designs; however, a synthesis of French and Japanese form and decoration soon emerged. The decoration was also gradually adapted to French taste, and only the Kakiemon palette survived. Whitewares and figures can be distinguished from similar Saint-Cloud pieces due to the use of the tin glaze. The polychrome figures and groups, clockcases and animals were also decorated in enamels derived from the Kakiemon palette, with an extensive use of aubergine. Knife handles are among the most original porcelain productions from the

69. Soft-paste porcelain sugar bowl, made at Mennecy, c. 1770 (London, Victoria and Albert Museum)

factory. During the 1740s it employed floral decoration reminiscent of wares from Meissen and blue enamelled decoration, of which the 'Armorial' service made for the Prince himself is the outstanding example. Although the factory continued production until the 1800s, the dominance of Vincennes and Sèvres (see below) from the 1740s effectively stopped any significant achievement at Chantilly during the later years.

In 1748 a factory that had been established in 1734 in the Rue de Charonne in Paris under the patronage of François-Louis de Neufville, Marquis de Villeroy (1695–?1765), was denied the right to build a kiln for the production of soft-paste porcelain; it was therefore moved to Mennecy (*see* MENNECY PORCELAIN FACTORY). It was managed by François Barbin (?1689–1765), his son Jean-Baptiste Barbin (*d* 1765) and his son-in-law Louis Evrard des Pitons (*d* 1754). Wares are noted for their naive charm rather than for sophistication or originality of output. Mennecy paste is creamy-white, and the enamel decoration is characterized by the predominance of a rose-pink, which was frequently used on the rims of the wares as a substitute for gilding, which was allowed only at Vincennes. Decoration included floral sprays, with occasional figures and birds. Production included such small items as custard cups and covers, vases, pedestals and bowls (see fig. 69). Potpourri vases and lids covered in blossoms were a successful model. Some early Chinese figures made at Mennecy are quite excellent, modelled with charm and decorated in soft colours. European figures were also produced, and the pink used extensively on the wares was also used on these. Mennecy also produced *objets de galanterie*, notably snuff-boxes in the shape of baskets, commodes, trunks and bowls of flowers. In 1773 the factory was moved to Bourg-la-Reine, where an inferior version of earlier products was made by the new owners, Joseph Jullien (*d* 1774) and Charles-Symphorien Jacques (*d* 1798) from the faience factory at Sceaux.

All of these factories suffered irretrievable damage because of the various privileges acquired by the factory of Vincennes (*see* VINCENNES, §2). This was founded in 1740 when Jean-Henri-Louis Orry de Fulvy (1703–51), half-brother of Philibert Orry, Comte de Vignory, Contrôleur Général des Finances, provided space for a workshop in a disused part of the royal château of Vincennes for Gilles Dubois (1713–after 1760) and his brother Robert Dubois (1709–59), former employees of Chantilly. The factory was directed by Claude-Humbert Gérin (1705–50) and later François Gravant (c. 1715–64), both of whom were also from Chantilly. In 1745 Orry de Fulvy obtained a royal privilege that granted the factory a 20-year licence to produce porcelain in the manner of Meissen, 'painted and gilded', and to produce figures and flowers. Initially the factory's most successful product was small porcelain flowers, which were sold to such *marchands-merciers* as LAZARE DUVAUX to be mounted on ormolu stems (e.g. of 1749; Dresden, Porzellansamml.). The early wares were decorated in imitation of Meissen porcelain with stylized flowers and landscapes within cartouches; the shapes on which this decoration was deployed were, however, distinctly French and closely related to the wares of Chantilly.

Despite a gradual increase in production, the finances of the factory were poor, and in 1745 Orry de Fulvy approached Jean-Baptiste Machault d'Arnouville (1701–94), who had succeeded his brother as Contrôleur Général des Finances, to obtain support from the King. The company, however, was unable to remain self-sufficient and was dissolved in 1752.

A new company was organized, partly owned by Louis XV and complemented by the growing patronage of Mme d'Etiolles, later the Marquise de Pompadour. The political and monopolistic situation of the factory was the background to an enhanced artistic performance derived from the combined technical skills of the goldsmith Jean-Claude Chambellan Duplessis (see DUPLESSIS), employed from 1748, and the chemist Jean Hellot (1685–1766), who was appointed in July 1751 to expand the palette of colours and improve the pastes. Figures were produced and were based on the designs of such artists as François Boucher. Initially glazed and very rarely coloured, these figures were more frequently produced in matt biscuit porcelain. These groups or pairs of figures were often used as table decoration.

Hellot's research into colour gave rise to the use of ground colours. The tradition of solid ground colours was derived from East Asian porcelain and had been copied at Meissen. However, the soft-paste porcelain of Vincennes was far more sympathetic to this than the hard-paste of Meissen, and the colours produced displayed an extraordinary depth and richness. Various colours were produced: *bleu lapis*, a rich, dark blue, and *bleu céleste* were introduced in 1753, *jaune jonquille* and *vert pomme* in 1756 and a violet in 1757. Combined with Rococo honey gilding, these colours were used to produce decorative effects of truly luxurious splendour. The colours were employed on services for Louis XV, including one with a *bleu céleste* ground (examples in Duke of Buccleuch priv. col.), and were used on numerous services either given to or ordered by other European royalty. In 1756 the factory was moved to new premises at Sèvres, which was conveniently situated between Paris and Versailles near the Marquise de Pompadour's château at Bellevue (see SÈVRES PORCELAIN FACTORY). In 1759, owing to continuing financial problems, the factory was taken over by the Crown, and Louis XV became solely responsible for its outgoings. The most exotic pieces were those made for the Marquise de Pompadour decorated with pink, blue and green grounds (examples in Malibu, CA, Getty Mus.; New York, Met.; Paris, Louvre; see also CERAMICS, colour pl. I, fig. 3).

(b) Hard-paste. Hard-paste porcelain was first made at Sèvres after kaolin had been discovered in 1769 at Saint-Yrieix. Much of the factory's finest production during the reign of Louis XVI, however, continued to be made in soft paste, including the King's service (1783–92; Brit. Royal Col.), and figures continued to be made in biscuit. In 1782, in keeping with the splendour of the factory's clientele and aspirations, the King commissioned a series of biscuit figures called the 'Grands Hommes', which were based on sculptures of famous French men, including Descartes, Molière, Corneille, Racine, Turenne and Vauban. They were not, however, commercially very successful. Hard-paste porcelain was used for some Neo-classical

wares, although jewelling, another of the factory's inventions, which used enamels on gold leaf, continued to be applied to soft-paste porcelain.

By the time of the French Revolution (1789), the royal privileges at Sèvres had been lifted, and the factory was in poor financial shape, particularly as the King, its principal client, had not paid for many of his purchases. It was also suffering increasing competition from the numerous small factories that had been established in and around Paris, all of which were producing hard-paste Neo-classical wares. Many of these factories were under the protection of other members of the royal family and therefore had such titles as the Manufacture de la Reine, the Manufacture du Comte d'Artois and the Manufacture du Duc d'Angoulême (see PARIS, §IV, 2).

In Strasbourg hard-paste porcelain was first produced in 1751 at the faience factory of Paul Antoine Hannong (1700–60). Due to the restrictions caused by the Vincennes privilege, however, production had to be moved to Frankenthal in Germany in 1755. In Niderviller the faience factory established c. 1754–5 by Baron Jean-Louis de Beyerlé, Directeur de la Monnaie in Strasbourg, also began to make hard-paste porcelain c. 1760–65 (see NIDERVILLER). The figures produced closely resemble those made in Ludwigsburg and are similar in style to those made in Zurich. Wares are usually in the Neo-classical style. Production continued at Niderviller until the then proprietor, Adam-Philippe, Comte de Custine (1740–93), was executed in 1793. The factory, however, remained active after the Revolution until well into the 19th century.

The only other significant areas of production before the Revolution were at Marseille and Limoges. In Marseille, Joseph Robert, a faience maker of some renown, developed a hard-paste body in the late 1760s. His production was limited, and the only significant pieces were wares decorated with figures in landscapes in the Meissen tradition. The town of Limoges is conveniently situated near the kaolin deposits of Saint-Yrieix. In 1771 the old faience factory, which had belonged to the Massié family, was turned over to the production of hard-paste porcelain by Joseph Massié in partnership with the chemist Nicolas Fournérat and the merchants Pierre Grellet (d 1774) and Gabriel Grellet. After a decade of undistinguished production, however, the factory was bought by Louis XVI to supply hard-paste blanks for decorating at Sèvres (see LIMOGES, §2). All the hard-paste wares of the Louis XVI period, whether produced in the Paris area or elsewhere in France, are characterized by a very white body and standardized decoration.

(ii) 1800 and after. Production at Sèvres was almost non-existent after the French Revolution until Napoleon Bonaparte recreated the necessary social conditions for the manufacture and sale of such expensive materials as porcelain. Napoleon, assisted by Charles Maurice, Duc de Talleyrand-Périgord (1754–1838), and other members of the imperial Court, commissioned services, vases and pieces of furniture decorated with porcelain plaques in keeping with the grand style that Sèvres handled with such skill. The most outstanding work of this period is the Egyptian service (1808; Stratfield Saye House, Hants), made for Napoleon and later given to Arthur Wellesley,

70. Hard-paste porcelain bulb-vases, made at the Jacob-Petit factory, Paris, c. 1840 (New York, Metropolitan Museum of Art)

1st Duke of Wellington, by Louis XVIII; with its centre-piece formed as Egyptian temples and obelisks, it echoes the spirit of the great services made during the reign of Louis XV. Such major artists as Jean-François Swebach-Desfontaines and Etienne Leguay (1762–1846) were employed to paint landscapes, portraits and allegorical subjects generally on richly gilded and coloured grounds.

The other Parisian factories also catered for the same tastes and often employed the same artists as Sèvres. The workshops of Nast (1781–1834), Dihl & Guérhard (1781–1828) and Darte (1795–1833) were the most successful factories producing high-quality work in the Empire style. Much of the blank porcelain from Paris was exported for decoration in Naples and in the workshop of Louis Cretté (d 1813) in Brussels. After the Restoration of the Bourbons in 1815, the tradition of producing State services continued at Sèvres. Other Paris factories continued to produce wares in a diluted Empire style, while the factory of Jacob-Petit (1796–1868) made richly decorated and encrusted ornaments, inkstands and vases in an early Victorian style (see fig. 70). Throughout the 19th century the numerous factories in Limoges produced tablewares on an industrial scale using industrial techniques. Also throughout the century there was a continuous production in Paris of wares purporting to be of earlier date, depicting celebrities of the past on jewelled, royal-blue grounds in the 18th-century Sèvres style. To these were added large vases, often mounted with poor-quality, imitation ormolu.

The 18th century was so overwhelmingly successful that French manufacturers have mostly preferred to recycle old ideas rather than seeking a new vocabulary. The last Parisian porcelain factory closed in 1922. Production at Sèvres, however, continued in the 20th century, and the factory was particularly successful at the Exposition Internationale des Arts Décoratifs et Industriels Modernes of 1925 in Paris, exhibiting wares that were strong in both form and colour. Limoges remained the most important centre for the production of French porcelain in the late 20th century.

BIBLIOGRAPHY
W. B. Honey: *French Porcelain of the Eighteenth Century* (London, 1972)
R. de Plinual de Guillebon: *Paris Porcelain* (London, 1972)
S. Eriksen and G. de Bellaigue: *Sèvres Porcelain: Vincennes and Sèvres, 1740–1800* (London and Boston, 1987)
R. Savill: *The Wallace Collection Catalogue of Sèvres Porcelain*, 3 vols (London, 1988)
T. Préaud and A. d'Albis: *La Porcelaine de Vincennes* (Paris, 1991)

HUGO MORLEY FLETCHER

VIII. Glass.

1. Before 1600. 2. 1600 and after.

1. BEFORE 1600. The earliest glass to have been found in France, in the form of beads, dates from the Chalcolithic period (c. 2000 BC). The production of such beads continued during the Bronze Age and the Iron Age (see PREHISTORIC EUROPE, §§V, 8 and VII, 7). Roman glassware was present in Gaul from the late 1st century BC to the early 5th century AD (see ROME, ANCIENT, §VIII, 2). The sodium-dominated composition of the glass produced, using nitre from the Near East, remained astonishingly consistent over a period of four centuries and lasted into part of the Merovingian period. The Merovingian glass of

the north-western part of France is quite well known owing to the practice of including glass in graves, a custom that continued until the end of the 7th century. There was a degree of continuity with the glass produced during the late Empire period, but glassware nevertheless became increasingly rare and the range of forms became more restricted. Some new types of glass appeared, such as cone beakers, bell-shaped beakers and 'claw' beakers, sometimes decorated with opaque-white trails. The glass of southern France is less well known due to the absence of grave goods but comes within the Mediterranean sphere (e.g. stemmed goblets, lamps etc). No Carolingian glass has been found in any tombs, and it is known in France only from a small number of urban excavations (Saint-Denis, near Paris; Tours). Both soda and potash glass was made at this time.

The glass of the 12th and 13th centuries did not differ much in form: phials for holy water in the south, ribbed glasses with the foot in the form of a truncated cone in the north. Some regional characteristics did, however, develop towards the end of the 13th century and during the 14th; the northern half of France tended to produce wine glasses on a tall, slender stem, such as the famous Verre des Augustins (14th century; Rouen, Mus. Ant.; see fig. 71) and a number of examples found recently in Chevreuse, Metz, in Toulouse and Besançon (e.g. wine glass, first half 14th century; Besançon, Mus. B.-A. Archaeol.). The people of the Midi appear to have preferred footless goblets and small, shallow dishes in colourless glass sometimes decorated with trailed blue glass. Workshops multiplied in the forest areas (e.g. Argonne, Normandy), where they were near a source of fuel. In the north potassium obtained from fern or beech ash tended to replace soda as the alkali in the manufacture of *verre de fougère* (forest glass), although the latter continued to be used along the Mediterranean coasts where salicornia (glasswort) was cultivated. Enamelled goblets *à la façon de Venise* are almost wholly absent.

The glassmaking industry developed spectacularly at the end of the 15th century and during the 16th with the arrival of a large number of Italian glassmakers. Regional features tended to disappear, and there was a noticeable trend towards uniformity in production throughout the whole country. Drinking glasses became common, and there was a general return to sodic glass, which relegated *verre de fougère* to only the most everyday items (e.g. medicine glasses and small stoppered bottles). Only the east of France stood out from the rest of the country, with the production of the Germanic forms, the most widespread of which were the *Krautstrunk* and the *Stangenglas*. A large number of 16th-century texts contain references to famous glassmakers originally from Murano, Mantua or Altare who settled in Poitou, Argonne, Nevers or Saint-Germain-en-Laye (this last workshop was patronized by Henry II and Catherine de' Medici). In 1565 Ludovico Gonzaga (1539–95) became Duke of Nevers through his marriage to Henrietta of Cleves and soon after brought over members of the Saroldi family from Altare. They were responsible for much of the extant enamelled and gilded glass of this period (e.g. goblet, after 1565; London, Wallace).

BIBLIOGRAPHY

Morin-Jean: *La Verrerie en Gaule sous l'empire romain* (Paris, 1913/R 1977)

J. Barrelet: *La Verrerie en France de l'époque gallo-romaine à nos jours* (Paris, 1953)

C. Landes: *Verres gallo-romains*, Paris, Mus. Carnavalet (Paris, 1983)

V. Arveillez-Dulong: *Le Verre d'époque romaine au Musée archéologique de Strasbourg* (Paris, 1985)

G. Sennequier: *Verrerie d'époque romaine: Collections des Musées départementaux de la Seine-Maritime* (Rouen, 1985)

D. Foy: *Le Verre médiéval et son artisanat en France méditerranéenne* (Paris, 1988)

M. Feugère, ed.: *Le Verre préromain en Europe occidentale* (Montagnac, 1989)

Ateliers de verriers de l'antiquité à la période pré-industrielle. Actes des 4èmes rencontres de l'Association française pour l'archéologie du verre: Rouen, 1989

A travers le verre, du moyen âge à la renaissance (exh. cat., ed. D. Foy and G. Sennequier; Rouen, Mus. Ant., 1989)

Vitrum: Le Verre en Bourgogne (Autun and Dijon, 1990)

'Verrerie de l'est de la France, XIIIe–XVIIIe siècle: Fabrication-consommation', *Rev. Archéol. E. & Cent.-E.*, ix (1990)

S. Gaynor: 'French Enameled Glass of the Renaissance', *J. Glass Stud.*, xxxiii (1991), pp. 42–80

Verre et merveille: Mille ans de verre dans le nord-ouest de la Gaule, Guiry-en-Vexin, Mus. Archéol. Dépt. (Guiry-en-Vexin, 1993)

71. Verre des Augustins goblet, h. 178 mm, 14th century (Rouen, Musée des Antiquités)

Le Verre de l'antiquité tardive au moyen-âge, IVe–VIIIe siècles: Filiations et innovations. Actes des 8èmes rencontres de l'Association française pour l'archéologie du verre: Guiry-en-Vexin, 1993

2. 1600 AND AFTER. During the 17th century, French luxury glassmaking was still influenced by Venice. This imported fashion, however, took root in France with the continued settlement and ennobling of Italian glassmakers. One of them, Bernard Perrot (1619–1709), settled in Orléans in 1662 under the protection of Philippe I, Duc d'Orléans, brother of King Louis XIV. Perrot invented a new process for making flat glass panels by casting (patented in 1688) and explored techniques unknown in France for making *porcelaine en verre* (opaque white glass) and *rouge des anciens* (transparent red glass). Such other centres of production as Paris and Nantes contributed to the expansion of French glassworks producing glass *à la façon de Venise*. The use of coal as fuel for the furnaces was developed for the first time in France at Rouen.

The repertory of forms created in imitation of 16th-century Venetian pieces is practically impossible to distinguish from one French province to another because of the common provenance and itinerant Italian workers. From this confusion, however, there emerged some typical local products such as small glass figures made in Nevers, known as *verre filé de Nevers* (e.g. *Louis XIV*, late 17th century; London, BM).

The Italian influence, confined to luxury glass, did not weaken traditional French production for general use: *verre de fougère* continued to be made in the forest regions and soda glass in the coastal regions. The industry supplied the population with a large quantity of forms ranging from

72. Acid-etched glass vase by Maurice Marinot, h. 170 mm, 1934 (Corning, NY, Museum of Glass)

drinking glasses, flasks and bottles to lamps and holy-water stoops.

The production of flat glass was the major French economic undertaking in the 17th century. From 1665 Louis XIV and his minister Jean-Baptiste Colbert concentrated production on plate-glass hitherto imported at great expense from Italy. In 1665, on their recommendation, a plate-glass company was set up in the Paris suburb of Saint-Antoine employing Italian workers, which supplied mirrors for the Galerie des Glaces installed in the château of Versailles between 1678 and 1683 (*see* VERSAILLES, fig. 2). With the same royal authority a new company, the Manufacture Royale des Grandes Glaces, was set up in 1693 at Saint-Gobain in Picardy. In 1695 this company was combined with the Saint-Antoine establishment and run under the title Manufacture Royale des Glaces de France.

At this time glass in the Bohemian style, available in France since 1690 and characterized by cut and engraved decoration, became established in northern and eastern France. These blown shapes were cut like rock crystal, with a wheel, before being polished; this type of glass was already known as 'crystal'. English-style glass also became increasingly popular as it was supremely suitable for cutting: this new material, 'English crystal' or lead glass, contained a high proportion of lead oxide and had been invented by George Ravenscroft in 1676. The conversion of French glassworks over to the production of English lead glass was at its height after 1750: it was made at Chaumont-sur-Loire from 1772, at Villeneuve-Saint-Georges near Paris from 1779, at Rouen and Romesnil in Normandy from 1783 and at Bordeaux from 1787. It was in Lorraine and Paris, however, that this tendency was most highly developed: the firm of BACCARAT (est. 1764) switched to the production of lead glass in 1772, and Saint-Louis, near Bitche (est. 1767), known as the Verrerie de Münzthal, in 1781; the Manufacture de Cristaux et Emaux de la Reine, established at Sèvres near Paris, changed over to lead glass in 1783, before moving to Creusot in 1784.

The Revolution of 1789 obliged glassmakers to surrender their special rights to burning wood in their furnaces and other exemptions and to be subject again to general laws. This upheaval caused workshops to close, ownership to change hands and firms to be reorganized and relocated. In the production of utility glassware, new centres of production emerged at coal-bearing sites supplied by canals or railways. These upheavals were stimulated by major technical innovations such as artificial probes, gas generators and blowing by compressed air, which induced firms to replace their existing equipment. About 1820 such factories as Saint-Louis adopted the American technique of press-moulding, an industrial process of mechanical fabrication used for cheap, mass-produced wares.

About 1820, after a period of uncertainty, output became increasingly diversified, and production increased to the point of overproduction. The absence of a specific style resulting from the multiplicity of stylistic references (Etruscan, medieval, Renaissance, Chinese) was compensated by a widening of techniques including the rediscovery of *millefiori* glass and inlay, opaline, flashed and cameo glass, enamelling, gilding and engraved inscriptions etc. Technical expertise improved, as did its application to fantastic, purely decorative objects. This flowering, brilliant but dispersed, rested mainly on the work of four glassworks before the advent of the Second Empire (1852–70): CHOISY-LE-ROI (1821–51), Baccarat, Saint-Louis and Clichy (est. 1837), around which other small and more or less ephemeral glass workshops gravitated.

It is generally agreed that the development of lead glass had ended by 1850; the techniques had been mastered and the scope for expression more or less explored. Neither the pomp of the Second Empire, the prestige of the great international exhibitions nor the exotic sources of inspiration (notably Islamic and Japanese art) and some technical innovations were enough to enliven an output that was increasingly infected by an industrial conservatism devoid of creative impulses.

At the end of the 19th century a reconvergence of glass and art resulted from initiatives by independent glassmakers. For *c.* 50 years France became the undisputed leader in the international history of glass. In this development, first as part of the ART NOUVEAU movement, the contribution of glassmaking workshops is clearly seen: those of the glassmaker and ceramicist François-Eugène Rousseau (1827–91) from 1867 in Paris, and EMILE GALLÉ in Nancy from 1874; and then from *c.* 1890 contributions of the DAUM family, also at Nancy, and RENÉ LALIQUE.

Between 1892 and 1900 the sculptor Henri Cros perfected the technique of *pâte de verre*, which was taken up by Georges Despret (1862–1952) at Jeumont, François Emile Décorchemont (1880–1971) at Conches and Gabriel Argy-Rousseau (*b* 1885). In the field of mould-blown glass, the outstanding personality was MAURICE MARINOT; about 1911 this painter from the Fauve group abandoned painting for glass. Until 1937 he produced a quantity of pieces, heavy items such as bottles and sometimes vases, which were deeply acid-etched (see fig. 72) or enhanced by deliberate internal effects, in his workshops in the Viard Glassworks at Bar-sur-Seine. Like Cros, Marinot increasingly considered his vases as sculptures sometimes entirely without utilitarian function. This new way of looking at glass inaugurated an era of independent expression. World War II put an end to this artistic upsurge, confining glasswork to the factories, the most important of which—Baccarat, Saint-Louis, Lalique and Daum—continued to operate in the late 20th century.

The opening of a workshop for blown glass at Biot by Eloi Monod and his family in the 1950s, and the establishment of the Dieulefit Centre by Claude Morin in the 1970s, created an active centre of glassmaking in southern France and laid the foundation for a glass revival within an international context, in which all modes of expression, from blowing and moulding to thermo-forming and engraving, were encouraged. Industrial sheet glass assembled in combination with other materials is one area of research, as are monumental forms made of moulded blocks. The combination of materials and techniques allows non-glassmaking artists access to glass, opening the way to the most liberated forms of expression in contemporary art.

Industrial design is one of the strong areas of contemporary French glass, in the creation of replicated objects, furniture and interior decoration features. Previously confined to bottles, tableware and light fittings, glass has become the leading material in all spheres of functional design.

BIBLIOGRAPHY

J. Barrelet: *La Verrerie en France . . .* (Paris, 1953)
J. Bloch-Dermant: *L'Art du verre en France, 1860–1914* (Lausanne, 1974)
D. Klein: *This History of Glass* (London, 1984)
J. Bellanger: *Verre d'usage et de prestige: France, 1500–1800* (1988)
S. Frantz: *Contemporary Glass* (New York, 1989)
C. Vaudour: *L'Art du verre contemporain* (Paris, 1992)

CATHERINE VAUDOUR

IX. Metalwork.

1. Gold and silver. 2. Base metals.

1. GOLD AND SILVER. Marking of French silver began in the 13th century, when a town mark was introduced at Tours (1275). Makers' marks appeared in Paris by 1313, when the fleur-de-lis was instituted as the device identifying the city. (Silversmiths in provincial towns frequently incorporated similar devices representing their towns into their marks.) A date letter system was in irregular use from 1427 and was made obligatory for the entire country in 1506. In 1549 the standard of silver was fixed at 95.8% or 11 *deniers*, 2 *grains*. In 1672 a system of tax marks was instituted throughout France; from that year each piece of silver had to be marked with two tax marks, struck before and after completion and changed approximately every six years, as well as a maker's mark and the date letter, which was struck by the warden of the guild and changed annually in Paris. (Date letters did not change as regularly in provincial cities.) The goldsmiths' guild and the system of tax marks were abolished in 1791, and a new system of marking was introduced in 1798. The date letter system was also discontinued, and two standards of silver, 95% and 80%, were permitted. Silver was struck with assay and new tax marks that were in use for terms of about nine years until 1838, when the last marks were registered.

CLARE LE CORBEILLER

(i) Before *c.* 1450. (ii) *c.* 1450–1599. (iii) 1600–1789. (iv) After 1789.

(i) Before c. *1450.* Examples of early medieval goldsmiths' work from France are the 5th-century ornamental brooches, buckles and sword hilts of gold and silver set with precious gemstones, as in the sword ornaments (Paris, Bib. N., Cab. Médailles) from the tomb of King Childeric (*d* 481), in which garnets are set in symmetrical patterns delineated by gold cloisons. Also from this period is a fragment of the Cross of St Eligius (*c.* 600; Paris, Bib. N., Cab. Médailles), once set above the main altar in Saint-Denis Abbey. Ornament and figural work in low relief is found in the earliest Christian reliquaries of the 7th and 8th centuries (e.g. the gilded-copper reliquary casket of St Mummolus, early 8th century; Saint-Benoît-sur-Loire Abbey). Some works of this kind also have decoration of interlaced ornament, such as the 7th-century gilded-copper reliquary in the parish church of Saint-Bonnet-Avalouze. Low-relief decoration continued in the early Carolingian period, as in the earliest part of the Pepin Reliquary (Conques, Trésor Ste Foy; *see* CAROLINGIAN ART, §V). The places of origin of Carolingian metalwork are much

disputed. During the reign of Charles the Bald, Saint-Denis, Reims and perhaps also Metz were centres of metalwork production, but there is much controversy as to what can be attributed to these places. Works of this period possibly made at Saint-Denis or Reims include the cover of the CODEX AUREUS OF ST EMMERAM (Munich, Bayer. Staatsbib., Clm. 14000), the front cover of the Lindau Gospels (New York, Pierpont Morgan Lib., MS. M. 1) and the Arnulf Ciborium (Munich, Residenz). In these examples, the figures are in relatively high relief and are surrounded by jewelled frames with gems set in elaborate raised mounts. The figures are close in style to those in manuscripts of the Reims school, such as the Utrecht Psalter (Utrecht, Bib. Rijksuniv., MS. 32). Some of the ivories of the Metz school were set in gold and jewelled frames with filigree ornament and served as book covers for Gospel books made at Metz. The cover of the Gospels (Paris, Bib. N., MS. lat. 9383) also has cloisonné enamels set between the gems, a rare example of the use of enamel in the Carolingian period. (For a discussion of this enamel technique and those mentioned below *see* ENAMEL, §2.)

Few examples of 10th- and 11th-century French goldsmiths' work survive. It was probably in the 10th century that the first cult image of St Faith (Conques, Trésor Ste Foy) was made, although the figure has work added at later periods (*see* CONQUES, STE FOY, §2). From the late 10th century or the 11th is the large half-length figure of *St Baudime* (Saint-Nectaire, Priory Church), the head and hands of which were restored in the 12th century. An almost unique surviving example of liturgical vessels of the period are the chalice and paten (Nancy, Trésor Cathédrale) of the second half of the 10th century, given by St Gauzelin to his foundation of Bouxières-aux-Dames Abbey (935). The decoration of the paten incorporates enamels, gems and filigree ornament.

At the end of the 11th century, the art of the goldsmith again began to flourish, and numerous works survive from the 12th century. Although the same techniques of filigree, relief and gem-setting continued, it is in the extensive use of enamelling that 12th-century French metalwork differs markedly from that of the preceding periods. The technique of champlevé enamel, which had been used in northern Europe in pre-Roman times, was rediscovered *c.* 1100, probably in southern France. It was used in the plaques with busts of saints on the portable altar of *St Faith* (*c.* 1100) and in the circular medallions on a reliquary chest of the early 12th century (both Conques, Trésor Ste Foy). By the second quarter of the century, champlevé enamel was being used in the Limousin region (*see* ROMANESQUE, fig. 77), in such works as the Bellac Reliquary (Bellac, Parish Church). By the middle years of the century Limoges (*see* LIMOGES, §1) was emerging as the major centre of enamel production in France, supplying other regions and countries in competition with centres in northern Spain, the Meuse Valley in Belgium and the Rhineland and Lower Saxony in Germany. Book covers, small reliquary chasses, crosses, ciboria, eucharistic doves and other liturgical objects were made in Limoges. Shrines such as that of St Calmine (Mozac, Parish Church) were also decorated with Limoges enamels. This production continued throughout most of the 13th century but is of variable quality. In the second quarter of the 12th century SUGER, ABBOT OF SAINT-DENIS, employed Mosan metalworkers to make the enamel cross (destr.) for his abbey. The chalice (Washington, DC, N.G.A.), ewers (Paris, Louvre) and vases (Paris, Louvre) made for the abbey under his patronage do not, however, have enamel decoration but incorporate antique vessels of crystal, onyx, porphyry and sardonyx and are set in 12th-century gold or silver-gilt mounts, enriched with gems and filigree decoration.

Champlevé enamel decoration gave way in the first quarter of the 13th century to niello decoration or elaborate filigree work combined with jewels, for example on the reliquary crosses of Clairmarais (Saint Omer Cathedral), Blanchefosse (Parish Church) and Eymoutiers (St Etienne). During the reign of St Louis, three-dimensional relief figures were favoured for shrines and reliquaries. The silver statuette of *St Blaise* (Namur, Mus. Dioc.) may be from this period but it has also been dated to the early 14th century. High-relief and three-dimensional figures set in an elaborate architectural framework can be seen in the shrine of St Taurin (Evreux, St Taurin) of *c.* 1240–55. From the same period are the covers (Paris, Bib. N., MSS lat. 8892, 9455, 17326) of the Evangeliaries of the Sainte-Chapelle, Paris, decorated with silver-gilt figures in high relief and with niello. Parisian works with silver-gilt figures from the latter part of the century include the reliquary of the Holy Tunic (Assisi, S Francesco) and the Pamplona Reliquary representing the *Three Marys at the Tomb* (Pamplona, Cathedral Treasury).

Basse taille (translucent) enamel decoration dominated goldsmiths' work of the 14th century. Early examples of this technique are the reliquary of the Holy Blood (Boulogne, St François de Sales) and the Crown reliquary of the Paraclete (Amiens, Trésor de la Cathédrale Notre Dame). Several chalices, crosses, liturgical vessels and triptychs of the first half of the century are decorated with *basse taille* enamels, for example the Copenhagen Ewer (Copenhagen, Nmus.; see fig. 73), the Namur Triptych (Namur, Mus. Dioc.), the triptychs in Seville (Cathedral Treasury) and Milan (Mus. Poldi Pezzoli), the polyptych of Thomas Bazin (New York, Pierpont Morgan Lib.) and the Osnabrück and Wipperfurth (St Nicolas) chalices. The reliquary statuette of the *Virgin and Child* (Paris, Louvre; *see* GOTHIC, fig. 86) incorporates both translucent enamels and silver gilt and was given by Joanna of Evreux (1310–71) in 1339 to Saint-Denis Abbey.

During the reign of Charles V several objects of goldsmiths' work can be connected directly with the patronage of the King. The Royal Gold Cup (*c.* 1380–90; London, BM; *see* ENAMEL, colour pl. III, fig. 1) is decorated with scenes from the *Life of St Agnes* in translucent enamel and shows the extreme refinement that had been achieved in that technique by the second half of the century. Equally notable are the cantor's staff (Paris, Bib. N., Cab. Médailles) and Gospel cover (Paris, Bib. N., MS. lat. 8851) given by the King to the Sainte-Chapelle, his coronation sceptre (Paris, Louvre) and the enamelled and jewelled gold bridal crown of Queen Blanche of England (Munich, Residenz), which was probably produced in Paris.

Around 1400 a new technique was introduced in which enamel is applied to three-dimensional forms. Probably

73. The Copenhagen Ewer, silver gilt and *basse taille* enamel, h. 225 mm, made in Paris, *c*. 1320–30 (Copenhagen, National-museum)

from *c*. 1425 to *c*. 1500. Some reliquaries present the relic in a dramatic fashion, as in the reliquary of the Veil of St Aldegonde (1469; Maubeuge, St Aldegonde), in which elegant kneeling angels in silver gilt and enamel hold up the relic in a glass cylinder, above which, in enamel *en ronde bosse*, is the figure of the saint under a pinnacled tabernacle receiving the veil from heaven.

BIBLIOGRAPHY

T. Müller and E. Steingräber: 'Die französische Goldemailplastik um 1400', *Münchn. Jb. Bild. Kst*, n. s. 2, v (1954), pp. 25–79

U. Middeldorf: 'On the origins of "Email sur ronde bosse"', *Gaz. B.-A.*, lv (1960), pp. 233–44

P. Lasko: 'The Thorn Reliquary: The Art of Parisian Goldsmiths of about 1400', *Apollo*, lxxvi (1962), pp. 248–57

E. Steingräber: 'Beiträge zur gotischen Goldschmiedekunst Frankreichs', *Pantheon*, xx (1962), pp. 156–66

M.-M. Gauthier: 'Le Trésor de Conques', *Rouergue roman*, ed. G. Gaillard and others (La Pierre-qui-vire, 1963), pp. 98–184

Les Trésors des églises de France (exh. cat., ed. J. Taralon; Paris, Mus. A. Déc., 1965)

J. Taralon: *Les Trésors des églises de France* (Paris, 1966)

E. Steingräber: 'Nachträge und Marginalien zur französisch-niederländischen Goldschmiedekunst des frühen 15. Jahrhunderts', *Anz. Ger. Nmus.* (1969), pp. 29–39

M.-M. Gauthier: 'Les Couvertures précieuses des manuscrits à l'usage de la Sainte-Chapelle', *Septième centenaire de la mort de Saint Louis. Actes des colloques de Royaumont et de Paris, 1970*, pp. 141–64

——: *Emaux du moyen âge occidental* (Fribourg, 1972)

E. Kovacs: 'Problèmes de style autour de 1400: L'Orfèvrerie parisienne et ses sources', *Rev. A.*, xxviii (1975), pp. 25–33

R. W. Lightbown: *Secular Goldsmiths' Work in Medieval France: A History* (London, 1978)

D. Gaborit-Chopin: 'Orfèvrerie et émaillerie', *Les Fastes du gothique: Le Siècle de Charles V* (exh. cat., Paris, Grand Pal., 1981), pp. 220–75

——: 'Les Emaux translucides parisiens dans la première moitié du 14e siècle', *Archéologia*, clxii (1982), pp. 32–7

J. Taralon: 'La Châsse de Saint Taurin d'Evreux', *Bull. Mnmtl*, cxl (1982), pp. 41–56

D. Gaborit-Chopin: 'Suger's Liturgical Vessels', *Abbot Suger and Saint-Denis*, ed. P. L. Gerson (New York, 1986), pp. 282–94

H. Tait: 'Email en ronde bosse', *Catalogue of the Waddesdon Bequest in the British Museum*, i (London, 1986), pp. 22–58

M.-M. Gauthier: *Emaux méridionaux: Catalogue international de l'oeuvre de Limoges: L'Epoque romane* (Paris, 1987)

J. Cherry: *Goldsmiths* (London, 1992)

NIGEL J. MORGAN

Parisian in origin, it is often referred to as enamel *en ronde bosse*. Charles VI and the dukes of Anjou, Berry and Burgundy seem to have favoured this technique and commissioned luxurious objects in which the method was used. An image of the *Virgin and Child* (Toledo, Cathedral Treasury) was made for Jean, Duc de Berry, before 1402, and the reliquary cross in Esztergom (Cathedral Treasury) was given in that same year by Margaret of Flanders to her husband, Philip the Bold of Burgundy. Perhaps the most famous surviving example of the technique, the Goldenes Rössl (1403–4; Altötting, St Philip & Jakob, Schatzkam.; *see* GOTHIC, fig. 95), was made for Charles VI. Also from the first decade of the 15th century in enamel *en ronde bosse* is the elaborate reliquary of the Holy Thorn (London, BM).

After these works of exceptional quality of the International Gothic, French goldsmiths' work of the rest of the 15th century comes as rather an anticlimax. Much of what survives is in the form of reliquary busts, reliquaries in a variety of forms and liturgical vessels. The dating of these objects is controversial, as in the case of the reliquary in silver gilt showing St Margaret emerging from the dragon (Luceram, Parish Church), where the dating ranges

(ii) c. 1450–1599. Knowledge of secular gold and silver dating before the mid-16th century is based almost entirely on accounts and inventories, as few examples have survived. Plate made for René of Anjou was of gold in accordance with his rank and would have included beakers, spoons and a *drageoir* (sweetmeat bowl). He is also known to have commissioned glass and 'porcelain' mounted in gold and silver, and he and his wife, Queen Joanna, used basins, écuelles and thin plates (*tranchoirs*) of plain silver.

A single extant example representing Court goldsmiths' work *c*. 1450 is an agate salt (Paris, Louvre) mounted in gold and raised on an architectonic stem with a gabled filigree foot, the whole resting on a polygonal arcaded and battlemented base. A salt (untraced) made in 1453 for René of Anjou was described as boat-shaped and set with precious gemstones, and another, made in the same year for Jacques Coeur, was in the form of a stag. Enamelled decoration on late medieval Court silver is chiefly in the champlevé and *basse taille* techniques, but painted pictorial enamelling was recorded from 1420, and a covered goblet (untraced), dating from *c*. 1460 and entirely enamelled with hawking scenes, is known from a 17th-century drawing (Oxford, Bodleian Lib.).

Some pieces of elaborate goldsmiths' work were made in Paris, but both King René and Queen Joanna commissioned plate from silversmiths in Angers, Avignon and Saumur. Paris was not the exclusive royal seat until the reign of Francis I, and, during the 15th century and the early 16th, goldsmiths flourished in a number of provincial towns, especially those where monarchs temporarily resided or visited. Goldsmiths in Troyes, for example, are known to have made beakers and *pots* (small ewers) for the entry of Charles VIII in 1486. In 1493 the city of Lyon presented Queen Anne of Brittany with the figure of a gold seated lion, and Lyonnais goldsmiths also executed a covered vase in the Renaissance style for Queen Eleanor, wife of Francis I, in 1533.

Utilitarian plate of this period had little decoration, although there are records of hammered decoration that would have produced highly faceted, textured surfaces. Utilitarian forms recorded in the 15th century include écuelles, *tasses* (drinking bowls), beakers, spoons, basins, platters of various sizes and mustard pots of barrel form. Bowls were plain, shallow hemispherical forms, with raised or engraved bands of decoration around the rim. In a Franco-Burgundian variant, popular in the second half of the 15th century, the base of the bowl was domed and ornamented with a pattern of shallow, concave circles. Beakers were of tapered cylindrical form, sometimes footed, and were decorated with an engraved or moulded band around the middle of the body.

Church plate of the late 15th century and the early 16th is chiefly represented by reliquaries and chalices, both Parisian and provincial. Reliquaries are of varied form: a reliquary (c. 1460; Reims, Cathedral Treasury; *see* PARIS, fig. 25) of almost secular elegance by Guillaume Lemaître (*fl* 1458) of Paris is composed of a rock-crystal covered standing-cup with painted enamel decoration and gold mounts set with gems. A basic design of sculptural reliquary consists of a horizontal casket flanked or supported by angels. One made in Valenciennes of rock crystal, silver gilt and enamel (Maubeuge Church) has unusually strong Gothic elements for its date of 1469. Another common type of reliquary from this period has an arm shape, composed of sheets of silver attached to a wooden core and sometimes set with gemstones. Reliquary busts were similarly constructed or were entirely of silver and enamelled (e.g. early 16th century; Saint Lizier Cathedral). Another example of this type is the reliquary bust of *St Ursula* (Reims, Cathedral Treasury) by an unidentified silversmith of Tours. Made of gold, silver and enamelled copper, it was apparently altered from its original form about 1505.

Chalices retained the Gothic form of plain bowl, knopped stem and foot. The knop is generally faceted, with engraved or enamelled roundels, a treatment borrowed for the stems of monstrance-reliquaries, ciboria and processional crosses. A knop of polygonal, architectonic form was introduced in the 16th century, the niches filled with arches or small sculptures. The foot is multi-lobed, sometimes alternating with pointed elements. A common, simple type of decoration is a radial pattern of chased,

flamelike lappets encircling the bowl and foot. An exceptionally lavish variant from the early 16th century is a chalice and paten (Saint Jean-du-Doigt, St Jean-Baptiste) by Guillaume Floch (*fl* 1515–46) of Morlaix, chased with symmetrical panels of foliage and cornucopia.

The architectonic forms of late 15th-century French secular silver survived well into the 16th century. A related group of silver pieces illustrates the form and style of Court silver c. 1530–35. It includes two caskets, one dated 1532–3 (priv. col.) and another 1533–4 (Mantua Cathedral), and an unmarked ciborium (Paris, Louvre) and salt (London, Goldsmiths' Co.), all linked by such common features as scrolled brackets, portrait medallions and claw-and-ball feet. Associated with this group is the Burghley Nef (1527–8; London, V&A; see fig. 74), a salt designed as a ship resting on the back of a mermaid, supported on a platform in the form of waves and raised on claw-and-ball feet.

About 1530, however, the Mannerist style was introduced and promoted by Francis I, who imported Italian craftsmen to provide the decorations for the château of Fontainebleau. The most influential was Rosso Fiorentino, whose designs were widely circulated through prints, which from this period until the end of the 18th century were a dominant medium for the dissemination of style. Rosso was described by Vasari as having designed plate for the King, and this work is probably represented in engravings by René Boyvin of ewers, salts and other items composed of complex sculptural and strapwork elements.

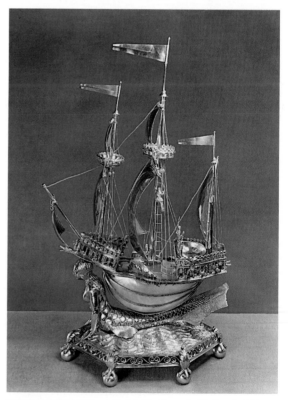

74. The Burghley Nef, nautilus shell and parcel-gilt silver, h. 352 mm, Paris, 1527–8 (London, Victoria and Albert Museum)

The engraved designs of Jacques Androuet Du Cerceau the elder and the work of French-born goldsmiths, however, were more restrained. Du Cerceau's formal style is discernible on the enamelled gold mounts and dolphin feet of an agate-covered standing-cup (c. 1550; Paris, Louvre).

The footed standing-cup or tazza, with a deep bowl and set on a baluster or sculptural stem, the latter typically in the form of three linked figures, was introduced in the mid-16th century. Repoussé pictorial decoration began to appear on tazze and basins after c. 1555. Several examples are listed in the 1556 and 1568 inventories of the plate of Anne de Montmorency, Constable of France. Dated examples, embossed and chased with allegorical or battle subjects, some derived from prints by Etienne Delaune and Du Cerceau, date from the 1560s to the 1580s (e.g. basin; Cambridge, Fitzwilliam; see fig. 75). There are also records from the mid-16th century of goldsmiths producing items for buffets. These were ensembles composed of a variable number of basins, vases and cups intended to display the wealth and status of the owner.

By the late 16th century, the Mannerist style had become more restrained. On the mounts of an onyx ewer (1569–70; Vienna, Ksthist. Mus.) by Richard Toutain the younger (d 1579), Rosso's bold strapwork was translated into an enamelled band of elegant Moresques. A naturalistic use of enamelling during this period is indicated by a green enamelled candlestick in the form of a tree recorded in the inventory (1589) of the plate of Catherine de' Medici.

Silver produced from c. 1530 outside Court circles is generally simple in form and decoration. Tazze with plain bowls and lightly chased or embossed baluster stems were made throughout France (as late as 1608 in Besançon). The Montmorency inventories record undecorated silver-gilt basins, as well as écuelles and platters for kitchen use. An inventory (1532) of châteaux in the Franche-Comté region lists a plain silver-gilt nef, cups with gadrooned borders, ewers, candlesticks, flagons and a sweetmeat bowl, all silver gilt. A common form of ewer has a long cylindrical body with a shallow lip, low stepped foot and squared handle. Decoration is generally limited to an engraved band around the body and a cast foot rim. Plate (Paris, Louvre) made between 1579–80 and 1584–5 for the chapel of the Order of St Esprit, Paris, is of this simple character, although the large, plain surfaces of a pilgrim flask and ewers in this set are enlivened by hammered surfaces.

BIBLIOGRAPHY
Les Trésors des églises de France (exh. cat., ed. J. Taralon; Paris, Mus. A. Déc., 1965)
C. Hernmarck: *The Art of the European Silversmith, 1430–1830*, 2 vols (London and New York, 1977)
R. W. Lightbown: *Secular Goldsmiths' Work in Medieval France: A History* (London, 1978)

(iii) 1600–1789.

(a) 17th-century forms and styles. (b) 18th-century forms and styles. (c) Provincial styles and the dissemination of designs in the 18th century.

(a) *17th-century forms and styles.* No Court silver of the early 17th century has survived. The inventory (1643) of the plate of Cardinal Richelieu, however, illustrates the growing repertory of objects. The nef, ewer and basin,

75. Silver-gilt basin with decoration after designs by Jacques Androuet Du Cerceau the elder, diam. 455 mm, Paris, 1560–83 (Cambridge, Fitzwilliam Museum)

écuelle and sweetmeat container continued in use, although candelabra, platters, cadinets, baskets and matching spoons and forks were also used. A gold casket on claw-and-ball feet (c. 1645; Paris, Louvre), entirely embossed with a dense symmetrical arrangement of flowerheads and foliage, has traditionally been associated with Anne of Austria, wife of Louis XIII. Sculptural decoration in relief is evident on Parisian secular and church plate from c. 1625 to 1650, notably on a large ewer and basin (1649; Moscow, Kremlin, Armoury), the decoration of which combines features of the Dutch Auricular style with elegant stylized figures in the Fontainebleau manner. Flat-chased patterns of broad strapwork also continued to form part of the Parisian and provincial decorative vocabulary c. 1650.

The little surviving utilitarian silver made before c. 1680 is mostly provincial. Ewers and beakers retained their simple profiles and decoration, and écuelles of this period are plain in form and fitted with shaped, openwork lug handles. Dining forks with two tines and square-topped shafts appeared c. 1620, although three-tined forks were made by 1650. Casters for pepper or sugar were cylindrical or polygonal with domed covers and either plain or with engraved decoration.

In the second half of the 17th century, many new forms were introduced. The inventories of Cardinal Mazarin (1653–61) and Anne of Austria (1666) record silver andirons, braziers, candlestands and a balustrade, but the production of silver furniture did not become significant until the reign of Louis XIV. Large-scale pieces designed for the furnishing of the château of Versailles, mostly cast of solid silver, were executed at the Manufacture des Gobelins, Paris, under the direction of Charles Le Brun. Inventories made between 1671 and 1705 record silver tables, benches, mirror-frames, andirons, *brancards* (stands for trays), vases for orange trees, large ewers and basins and candlestands. Most were probably designed by Le Brun, but some may have been designed and executed by Alexis Loir I (*see* LOIR, (2)). Other goldsmiths who produced silver furniture for Versailles were Claude BALLIN (i), René COUSINET, Nicolas de Launay (*fl c.* 1682–?1709), Thomas Merlin (*fl c.* 1665–89), Jean de Viaucourt (*fl* 1657–?1675) and Claude de Villers (*fl c.* 1665–?1702). All of this silver was melted down in 1689, but its appearance is known from drawings (Stockholm, Nmus.) by and attributed to Le Brun, Ballin and de Launay. The massive scale and sculptural character of this silver furniture, indicated by the drawings, is evident in a single surviving piece: a baptismal font (Stockholm, Kun. Slottet) made in Stockholm by the Parisian silversmith Jean-François COUSINET in the shape of a shell-form basin supported by three caryatid putti on a triangular base.

Filigree silver was itemized in the inventory of the plate of Louis XIV, but it is uncertain whether it represented work from the late 17th century or was a collection inherited from his mother, Anne of Austria, and therefore dating from the mid-17th century. One of the most important innovations of this period was the matching dinner service, used at the Court by 1673. The style of tableware used at the Court of Louis XIV is known from designs, acquired by the Swedish court in 1702, by Nicolas-Ambroise COUSINET and JEAN BERAIN I. The forms represented are conspicuous for clarity of profile, solidity and methodical decoration. Ornamental motifs include medallions with profile heads in a classical style, bands of lambrequins (plain or flat-chased with diapered or strapwork patterns) encircling the lower parts of ewers and casters and gadrooned, guilloche and strapwork borders. These elements appear on a long-necked ewer (1696–7; Poitiers Cathedral) by Nicolas de Launay with a springing-leopard handle that marks the transition in tableware from the vigorous Italianate style to the controlled French Late Baroque style.

Other new forms were used both at and outside the Court. Toilet services were introduced by 1660 and included a mirror, ewer and basin, candlesticks, boxes for jewels, powder, roots and toothpicks and often snuffers and an écuelle. The individual pieces are usually stylistically consistent but were often made over several years by different silversmiths (e.g. set of 1658–76; Copenhagen, Rosenborg Slot; see fig. 76). One mirror (Paris, Louvre) and two toilet services made in Paris between 1659–61 and 1677 are richly decorated with palm fronds, acanthus and other foliage; the forerunner of these was the gold casket of *c.* 1645 mentioned above. One service (1669–71; Chatsworth, Derbys) is by Pierre Prévost (*fl c.* 1670; *d* 1716), the other (1672–7; Edinburgh, Royal Mus. Scotland) possibly by the tentatively identified Pierre Flamand. These designs influenced those of ecclesiastical plate: an ensemble (1666–7; Troyes, Trésor Cathédrale) by Nicolas Dolin (*fl* 1647–95) differs from contemporary embossed and chased basins and toilet services only in the religious subject-matter of the pictorial decoration.

Other new objects that first appeared between *c.* 1670 and 1700 were teapots, the earliest examples of which (1699–1700; New York, Met.), made in Paris, are low and

76. Silver toilet service, Paris, 1658–76 (Copenhagen, Rosenborg Slot)

spherical, coffeepots and chocolatepots, circular tureens for *olio* (a stew of Spanish origin), dish covers, soap- and sponge-boxes, sauceboats, cooking vessels and coffee and ice-cream cups. The centrepiece or *surtout* was developed by 1692 as an adjunct of the table service and originally consisted of a tureen-like vessel for fruit or flowers surrounded by casters, cruets and boxes for salt and spices, all arranged on a stand with candle-holders.

(b) 18th-century forms and styles. Between *c.* 1700 and *c.* 1730 forms were regular and balanced with clear profiles occasionally enlivened by stepped or convex mouldings with ovolo, guilloche or gadrooned bands. Common forms were beakers, ewers and basins, spice-boxes, candlesticks, écuelles, sugar casters, cruet-frames, eggcups and mustard pots. The surfaces of these items are either plain, apart from bands of chasing or applied or engraved lambrequins, or are entirely covered with intricate patterns of lightly chased and engraved strapwork and foliage. Candlesticks, which had been of clustered columnar form in the 1660s and 1670s, developed into the baluster type by 1700. Pepper and spices were contained in single or double boxes with hinged covers. These forms, as well as cruet-frames, are commonly oval or polygonal and rest on low, scrolled feet. Scalloped or polygonal dishes with moulded or gadrooned rims were common in Paris during this period and continued to be used in the provinces until *c.* 1745. The lug handles of écuelles were superseded by solid cast ones, and the covers, which between *c.* 1670 and 1700 had been flat with ring handles, became increasingly

domed, with knob, calyx or berry finials. Footed cylindrical mustard pots with hinged covers, curved handles and bands of lambrequins were common in Paris between *c.* 1700 and 1720, and in the provinces until *c.* 1750. The type was succeeded *c.* 1740–50 by the barrel form of medieval origin. A spouted pear-shaped vessel with hinged cover and curved handle and generally with a spirally fluted body appears to have served as either a mustard pot or a milk pot. Few teapots were made except in northern France. *Surtouts* gradually became more elaborate: in an example by Claude BALLIN (ii) (1727–8; St Petersburg, Hermitage), the tureen was omitted in favour of a frame with free-standing figures. In the first third of the 18th century there was also a fashion in Paris for fitting Japanese Imari porcelain with silver or silver-gilt mounts. Marked examples (Paris, Mus. A. Déc.; Malibu, CA, Getty Mus.) date from 1717 to 1737.

The Rococo style made an early and vigorous appearance in a wine-cooler (1727–8; Paris, Louvre) by Thomas Germain (*see* GERMAIN, (1)) with a twisting profile, worked surfaces and naturalistic plant ornament. The repertory of objects in the 1730s and 1740s remained mostly unchanged, but from *c.* 1730 to *c.* 1760 forms became softer and more fluid, and much use was made of spiral fluting after *c.* 1735. The helmet-shaped ewer was succeeded by a pear-shaped form with a single- or reverse-scrolled handle and hinged cover. After *c.* 1740 the handles of écuelles became more asymmetrical in outline and were composed of more naturalistic scrollwork and foliage. Sauceboats began to appear *c.* 1735 and by *c.* 1740 were double-lipped with opposing handles, a form that was retained in Paris until *c.* 1765 and in the provinces somewhat later.

Teapots made in Paris between 1730 and 1780 are commonly pear-shaped with long spouts curved upwards from the base and terminating in a bird's or dog's head. Baluster-shaped sugar casters were not produced in Paris after *c.* 1730 but were made in provincial towns until *c.* 1740. They were replaced from *c.* 1740 to *c.* 1780 by covered bowls and sugar spoons with pierced hemispherical bowls. By 1736 the *surtout* was chiefly ornamental, and one made that year by Jacques Roettiers (Paris, Louvre) is entirely sculptural, designed as a stag hunt on a rockwork arch.

By the mid-18th century compositions of fully sculptural animals, fish and vegetation were significant in the decoration of Rococo tureens and dish covers. Early examples include two tureens (1735–8; Lugano, Col. Thyssen-Bornemisza; Cleveland, OH, Mus. A.) by Henry Adnet (*fl* 1712–45) and Pierre François Bonnestrenne (*fl* 1714–*c.* 1738), designed and signed by Juste-Aurèle Meissonnier, the covers of which are piled with forms of shellfish and vegetation (for illustration *see* MEISSONNIER, JUSTE-AURÈLE). Later examples of this style include tureens (e.g. of 1757–8; New York, Met.) by Edmé Pierre Balzac (*fl* 1739–*c.* 1781), their covers modelled with figures of hounds attacking a stag. Figures of children and putti feature in the work of Antoine-Sebastien Durand (*fl* 1740–*c.* 1785) and François-Thomas Germain from *c.* 1750 to 1765, notably in a pair of mustard pots (1750–51; Lisbon, Mus. Gulbenkian) in barrows propelled by children, made for Mme de Pompadour by Durand. The only large-scale

sculptural work in 18th-century French silver, a set of 16 figures of dancers (1757–8; Lisbon, Mus. N. A. Ant.) made as table decoration by Ambroise-Nicolas COUSINET, also dates from this period.

From *c.* 1730 to *c.* 1770 numerous dinner services, chiefly in the Rococo style, were produced in Paris for the French and foreign courts and aristocracy. Six were made for Louis XV between 1727 and 1766, although none has survived. The earliest known extant service is one (1735–8; sold London, Sotheby's, 16 June 1960) made by Jacques Roettiers. The most notable silversmiths engaged in the production of these elaborate services during the mid-18th century were Thomas Germain and his son, François-Thomas Germain, Edmé Pierre Balzac and Antoine-Sebastien Durand. All these silversmiths, except François-Thomas Germain, contributed to an assembled service (1727/8–1758/9; Paris, Louvre; New York, Met.; priv. cols) ultimately acquired by Louis-Philippe, King of the French. François-Thomas Germain executed services for the courts of Portugal and Russia (1756–62 and 1756–9; both dispersed; examples in Lisbon, Mus. N. A. Ant.; Philadelphia, PA, Mus. A.; New York, Met.). Another service in Portugal by Germain (*c.* 1757; Lisbon, Mus. N. A. Ant.), commissioned by Joseph, King of Portugal, shows the development of the mature Rococo style, in which form is defined by a continuous movement of scrolls and naturalistic plant ornament. Few surfaces are left plain, and the sinuous bodies of tureens, coffeepots and ewers in this service are ribbed or almost entirely covered with relief decoration. Other silversmiths working in the same manner in the 1750s were François Joubert (*fl* 1749–*c.* 1793) and Charles Spire (*fl* 1736–*c.* 1788).

Simpler utilitarian pieces from the mid-18th century have bodies of curvilinear profile, flat-chased and engraved with bands of rocaille scrolls and shellwork. The finials of écuelles from *c.* 1750 to 1760 are typically a single fruit or artichoke rising from a leaf base. The bodies of ewers are plain, although often with chased decoration of marine subjects below a band around the middle of the body, and the scrolled handles commonly incorporate rippling waves and shellwork. The bodies of cruet-frames, which from *c.* 1710 had been solid, were gradually reduced by *c.* 1765 to footed trays supporting openwork frames composed of vines or foliage. Candlesticks and candelabra from *c.* 1745 to 1765 are of baluster form. The shafts are generally sinuous, often spiralled and ribbed and further decorated with cartouches, scrolls and layered panels of rippling (e.g. by Michel Delapierre II, 1747–8; New York, Met.). About 1760 the handles of sauceboats were asymmetrically opposed, and the sauceboat was raised on a foot and sometimes provided with a footed stand. The Rococo style was also popular for ecclesiastical work, for example a chalice of 1756–7 (Landes, St Sever Abbey).

From *c.* 1730 to the Revolution, the main types of goldwork included jewelled and enamelled snuff-boxes (*see* §X, 2 below) and such related accessories as châtelaines, shuttles and notebooks. Articles in rock crystal for the dressing-table were often mounted in gold (examples of 1728–30; New York, Met.), as were some pieces of Vincennes and even Meissen porcelain (e.g. bowl of *c.* 1730 with gold handles of 1734; New York, Met.). Some gold tableware was also made, particularly in the mid-18th

77. Silver tureen by Jacques-Nicolas Roettiers, h. 298 mm, Paris, 1775–6 (New York, Metropolitan Museum of Art)

century. Between 1748 and 1758 the Parisian *marchand bijoutier* Lazare Duvaux provided Louis XV and Mme de Pompadour with several gold coffeepots and gold coffee spoons, usually as part of ensembles with porcelain cups and saucers. Duvaux also supplied platters (1758; untraced) and a sculptural gold salt and pepper box (1753; untraced). Some goldsmiths specialized in the production of gold mounts and others in the manufacture of gold cutlery, tableware or boxes.

Neo-classicism began to appear in Parisian silver *c.* 1760 but co-existed with Rococo elements until the 1770s. In this transitional stage smooth profiles and solid forms were combined with formal, symmetrical arrangements of Neo-classical ornament, in which geometric panels, rosettes, guilloche forms, laurel and leaf-tip borders are dominant. Figure sculpture for candelabra and tureens, for example those by Robert-Joseph AUGUSTE (1767–8; New York, Met.) and Louis Lenhendrick (*fl* 1747–83) (1769–70; St Petersburg, Hermitage), continued to be used. A more austere style was practised, beginning with a table service (1770–73), known as the Orloff Service (St Petersburg, Hermitage; New York, Met.), made by Jacques-Nicolas Roettiers for Catherine II of Russia. Roettiers's distinctive use of guilloche mouldings and fluting appears in a tureen of 1775–6 (New York, Met.; see fig. 77).

Neo-classical features also appear in utilitarian wares from the last third of the 18th century. After *c.* 1765 the double-lipped sauceboat was replaced by a boat-shaped model with a single, upturned handle. The écuelle disappeared from the repertory of Parisian silversmiths *c.* 1765 but continued to be produced in some provincial cities in the 1780s (e.g. made in Strasbourg, 1784; ex-Hallé priv. col., see Dennis, i, p. 339). It was superseded by a covered bowl of similar size with loop handles, sometimes naturalistically modelled as leaf stems or twigs. From *c.* 1750 to 1775 the sugar bowl was of an inverted circular or oval pear-shaped form, with handles, feet and cover with a berry finial and accompanied by a matching tray. Sugar bowls, mustard pots and cruet-frames from *c.* 1775 to 1789 are usually in the form of silver frames, formed of vertical pilasters connected by festoons, enclosing dark-blue glass liners. Mustard pots of this period are cylindrical and footed, with hinged covers and spoons. In the late 18th century a form of long-bodied, pear-shaped coffeepot on three curved legs, with the handle at right angles to the spout, was also common. This model was also used for chocolatepots. A new form, introduced *c.* 1765, was the wine-glass cooler or monteith of English origin. The earliest extant examples are by Robert-Joseph Auguste (of 1776–8, ex-Baron Robert de Rothschild priv. col.; e.g. of 1779, sold, Paris, Pal. Galliéra, 8 Dec 1969). An example of Neo-classical ecclesiastical silver is a chalice (1779; London, V&A) by the Imlin workshop of Strasbourg.

After *c.* 1785 the deep, bowl-shaped tureen resting on low feet was replaced by a shallower, tapered form raised on a pedestal foot. New types of small tureens or covered dishes appeared, and wine-bottle coolers became common. Angular handles first appeared *c.* 1786–7 in the work of Henri AUGUSTE (e.g. covered dish, 1786–90, ex-David-Weill priv. col.; tureen, 1787, sold Geneva, Christie's, 20 Nov 1979). Surfaces became plainer, and decoration was increasingly limited to rims, handles and finials, although vase-shaped ewers of this period often incorporate figural handles (e.g. by Jean Baptiste François Chéret (1728–*c.* 1790), 1784–5; New York, Met.).

(c) Provincial styles and the dissemination of designs in the 18th century. Despite the numerous changes in style throughout the 18th century, there was considerable repetition of decorative elements and forms by both Parisian silversmiths and provincial silversmiths copying Parisian styles. Some provincial silversmiths are known to have worked in Paris before attaining the status of master in their native towns, and, while inventories of plate in provincial collections rarely specify the origin of silver, it has been suggested that in Grenoble in 1720 a substantial amount of silver in use was of Parisian manufacture.

Such basic forms as the small spiral-form mustard or milk pot were made with little variation throughout the 18th century, in this case by numerous silversmiths in Paris between 1740–42 (e.g. Paris, Mus. A. Déc.) and 1768–9 (e.g. New York, Met.). Handles of identical design recur on écuelles made by different Parisian makers and by provincial silversmiths. Variations of a shell-form salt-cellar on a double scroll base were produced in 1745–6 in Paris and until 1771 in Toulouse (examples in New York, Met.). Such repetition of designs reveals the widespread use of pattern books; among the widely circulated designs for silver were those of Pierre Germain (*fl* 1744–83) (*Eléments d'orfèvrerie*, 1748) and J. R. Lucotte (*fl* 1760–84).

The influence of Parisian silver did not preclude the development of regional characteristics and types of objects. Large pear-shaped teapots, often ribbed and with long spouts, were common to Lille and its surrounding towns. 'Marriage-cups'—shallow, two-handled bowls on chased ring feet—were produced in the region around Rennes. Wine tasters were in wide production, and their place of manufacture was often indicated by the form of handle, for example a serpent, kidney-shape, strap or another type. Silver made in Strasbourg was almost always gilded, according to German custom, and a form specific to Strasbourg was the flattened, lobed beaker (e.g. by Johann Jacob Erhlen (*fl* 1728–?1750), 1736–50; Paris, Mus. A. Déc.). Exaggerated decoration is characteristic of silversmiths in Toulouse, notably in work by the Landes and Samson families in the Rococo style (e.g. écuelle and plate by Louis Landes, 1774; New York, Met.; see fig. 78), and from *c.* 1760 to *c.* 1775 curvilinear forms were often completely ribbed or channelled and swathed in floral swags and garlands.

BIBLIOGRAPHY
G. Bapst: *Les Germain* (Paris, 1887)
H. Bouilhet: *L'Orfèvrerie française aux XVIIIe et XIXe siècles*, i (Paris, 1908)
Les Trésors de l'orfèvrerie de Portugal (exh. cat., Paris, Mus. A. Déc., 1955)
F. Dennis: *Three Centuries of French Domestic Silver*, 2 vols (New York, 1960)
Les Grands Orfèvres de Louis XIII à Charles X (Paris, 1965)
La Table d'un roi: L'Orfèvrerie du XVIIIe siècle à la cour de Danemark (exh. cat., ed. J. P. Babelon; Paris, Mus. A. Déc., 1987–8)
Versailles: The View from Sweden (exh. cat., ed. E. E. Dee and G. Walton; New York, Cooper-Hewitt Mus., 1988)
F. Buckland: 'Silver Furnishings at the Court of France, 1643–1670', *Burl. Mag.*, cxxxi (1989), pp. 328–36
L. d'Orey: *The Silver Service of the Portuguese Crown* (Lisbon, 1991)
Versailles et les tables royales en Europe, XVIIème–XIXième siècles (exh. cat., Versailles, Musées N., 1993–4)

(iv) After 1789. Little silver was made between the Revolution and 1800. The goldsmiths' guild was abolished in 1791, and many silversmiths known to have been working before that date were no longer recorded. Some continuity of style was provided by the work of Henri Auguste and by JEAN BAPTISTE CLAUDE ODIOT, both of whom worked before and after the Revolution. Odiot acquired many designs by Jean-Guillaume Moitte for silver by Auguste.

Forms and decoration from *c.* 1800 to 1820 were based on classical and Egyptian sources. Chased and engraved decoration was abandoned in favour of smooth and plain surfaces, commonly ornamented with cast elements attached by means of rivets. There were two main types of decoration. The work of MARTIN-GUILLAUME BIENNAIS is densely ornamented with friezes of anthemion, scrollwork, sphinxes, sea-horses, classical figures and swans, the emblem associated with the Empress Josephine, often based on designs by Percier and Fontaine. The bodies of pieces produced by Auguste and Odiot, however, are simple and massive, with plain surfaces and stylized foliate borders, and are dominated by figure sculpture used as supports or handles. Other silversmiths active in this period were Philippe-Jean-Baptist Huguet (*fl c.* 1798–1810), Marc Jacquart (*fl c.* 1797–1829) and Jean-Charles Cahier (1772–after 1849). The last executed both secular and ecclesiastical plate, and his work shows the transition between the Empire and Renaissance Revival styles.

Most silver made during the Empire period is gilded. Teapots became common at this time, and new objects included the tea-urn and a covered sugar bowl on a high stand rising above a circular frame, in which spoons are held vertically. The *nécessaire*, a travelling case in which dozens of table or toilet articles are fitted, was a speciality of Biennais. There was also a revival of silver furniture, for example the cradle of the King of Rome by Odiot

78. Silver écuelle and plate by Louis Landes, w. of écuelle 295 mm, Toulouse, 1774 (New York, Metropolitan Museum of Art)

(1811; Vienna, Ksthist. Mus.), elaborate table services and ceremonial objects, for example the nef (1804; Malmaison, Château N.) made by Auguste for Napoleon.

The Restoration (1815) inaugurated a period of revival styles that lasted until *c.* 1890, while the Empire style lingered until *c.* 1825. Its austere forms were retained, but the smooth profiles were broken up by increasingly rich sculptural and foliate ornament, anticipating the development of the Renaissance Revival style of the mid-19th century. This transitional manner is exemplified by the silver-gilt plate (Reims, Cathedral Treasury) made by Cahier for the coronation (1824) of Charles X and by a massive sculptural silver-gilt vase (1830–35; Los Angeles, CA, Co. Mus. A.) by Jacques-Henri Fauconnier (1776–1839) commemorating the Marquis de Lafayette. Another style, influenced by English silverwork and characterized by soft Rococo forms and profuse scrollwork, was introduced *c.* 1826 by Charles-Nicolas Odiot (1789–1869), who had worked in London for the firm of Garrard. This style was later developed by Odiot into a naturalism in which tableware is partly or entirely formed of branches and leaves (e.g. tea-urn, *c.* 1840; Paris, Louvre). The Moorish style is apparent in the work (*c.* 1845–55) of Marrel Frères, Frédéric-Jules Rudolphi (*fl* 1844–55) and FERDINAND BARBEDIENNE. Rudolphi's skilful eclectic style integrates Islamic forms with silver tracery work, inlaid ivory and gemstones, usually on a ground of oxidized silver.

By 1840 a major part of silver production was controlled by large family firms, principally those of Odiot, Christofle and Froment-Meurice, utilizing modern technological innovations to reach an expanding middle-class market. Odiot concentrated on the production of tableware in a succession of Rococo Revival, Renaissance Revival, Islamic and 18th-century styles. The firm founded by Charles Christofle (1805–63) also produced silver in revival styles, made widely accessible by his introduction of electroplating into France in 1842. François-Désiré Froment-Meurice (1802–55) worked in a romantic medieval-Renaissance idiom, producing a wide variety of silver- and goldsmiths' work, ranging from jewellery to furniture.

The complex compositions of Renaissance Revival style reinstated a need for specialist designers, sculptors and

79. Coffret from a dressing-table ensemble by François-Désiré Froment-Meurice and others, parcel-gilt silver, gilt-copper, enamel, glass and gemstones, h. 420 mm, Paris, 1847–51 (Paris, Musée d'Orsay)

chasers, and by 1840 many were working independently and/or for one or more firms. Although Froment-Meurice designed most of his own work, he and other silversmiths occasionally employed the sculptors Jean-Jacques Feuchère and Jean-Baptiste-Jules Klagmann (1810–67) for models that were executed by Antoine Vechte (1799–1868) or Jules Wièse (1818–90). LOUIS-CONSTANT SÉVIN designed items for Froment-Meurice, Jean-Valentin Morel (1794–1860) and Barbedienne, and Albert-Ernest Carrier-Belleuse provided sculptural models for Jacques-Henri Fauconnier, the brothers Auguste Fannière (1818–1900) and Joseph Fannière (1820–97) and Christofle.

80. Soup tureen and plate by Jean Puiforcat, silver with quartz handles, 360×200 mm, Paris, 1925 (Paris, Musée des Arts Décoratifs)

The Renaissance tradition of composite goldsmiths' work was revived in the 1840s and 1850s, chiefly by Froment-Meurice and Morel. An agate cup (known as a *coupe des vendanges*; Paris, Louvre) on a sculptural base of silver and silver gilt, and enamelled and set with pearls, was designed by Froment-Meurice and executed *c.* 1844 by Vechte and Wièse. A tall cup (1855; London, Walter Godny col.), inspired by the Baroque style, its bowl of carved jasper with dramatic sculpture and enamelled gold mounts, was made by Morel to a design by Sévin.

The prominence given to sculptural silver encouraged the development of a new repertory of large-scale forms from *c.* 1840 to *c.* 1880. Monumental centrepieces composed of numerous allegorical sculptural groups were produced by Froment-Meurice and Christofle, and the production of silver furniture was revived. Froment-Meurice, with the collaboration of several sculptors and enamellers, executed a dressing-table (1847–51; Paris, Mus. d'Orsay; see fig. 79) with a mirror and accompanying items in a predominantly Gothic style, and in 1867 the firm of Christofle exhibited a dressing-table (Paris, Mus. A. Déc.) in the Louis XVI manner. Trophies and other presentation pieces were also common. In 1869 the Fannière brothers executed a large nef (Paris, Mus. A. Déc.) with allegorical figures commissioned by the Empress Eugénie for presentation to Ferdinand de Lesseps.

From *c.* 1850 to *c.* 1880 the resurgence of the manufacture of church plate based on Gothic traditions was led by Placide Poussielgue-Rusand (1824–89) in Paris and by Thomas-Joseph Armand-Calliat (*fl c.* 1862–81) in Lyon. Poussielgue-Rusand was influenced by the work of the architect Eugène-Emmanuel Viollet-le-Duc, who secured many commissions for him and provided numerous designs for his work, which is precise and simple in form but enlivened by graceful foliate ornament (e.g. reliquary, *c.* 1855–60; Paris, Notre-Dame Cathedral Treasury). Armand-Calliat's style is more eclectic and more linear (e.g. ciborium, 1867; Paris, Mus. A. Déc.).

The interest of Napoleon III in ancient Greek and Roman art stimulated a *néo-grec* fashion in silver from *c.* 1862 to 1870. The most important works in this style include cups and tableware, often enriched by naturalistic foliage in relief, by Christofle and Barbedienne. Charles Rossigneux (1818–1907) designed such items for Christofle, and Sévin and Désiré Attarge (*c.* 1820–78) designed and chased many of Barbedienne's pieces (e.g. ewer, 1862; New York, Met.).

The exhibition of the work of Louis Comfort Tiffany at the Exposition Universelle of 1878 in Paris reinforced the popularity of Japonisme and the emerging Art Nouveau style. The production of monumental sculptural silver continued, but these forms were gradually modified by a greater harmony between form and decoration and an emphasis on naturalistic plant ornament. Proponents of the Art Nouveau style, which, after *c.* 1890, eclipsed most of the heterogeneous revivals, were Christofle, LUCIEN FALIZE, Ernest Cardeilhac (1851–1904), Jules Brateau (1844–1923) and, for ecclesiastical plate, Maurice Poussielgue-Rusand (*fl c.* 1885–1900). Falize, however, was also active in the revival of medieval enamelling techniques. In 1896 he made a gold beaker (Paris, Mus. A. Déc.) for the Union Centrale des Arts Décoratifs with a pictorial frieze on a densely patterned ground of grapes and leaves incorporating a variety of enamels. Fernand Thesmar (1843–1912) executed gold bowls and cups with *plique à jour* enamel from 1888 to *c.* 1903, and in 1898 the jeweller Eugène Feuillâtre (1870–1916) exhibited silver pieces enamelled with naturalistic decoration in translucent colours.

The Art Nouveau style lasted until 1914 and was only slightly modified by the more angular forms popular in Germany. After World War I, however, a new Modern Movement style in silver was led by JEAN PUIFORCAT, who, by 1925, had mastered a style based on rounded geometric shapes that he used for bowls, tureens (see fig. 80) and tea sets with plain surfaces, their simplicity dramatized by the frequent use of ivory, wood or hardstones for handles or finials. Others working in a similar idiom were Jean Tétard (*b* 1907) and the firms of Aucoc and Christofle.

BIBLIOGRAPHY
P. Burty: *F.-D. Froment-Meurice* (Paris, 1883)
H. Bouilhet: *L'Orfèvrerie française aux XVIIIe et XIXe siècles*, ii–iii (Paris, 1910–12)
S. Grandjean: *L'Orfèvrerie du XIXe siècle en Europe* (Paris, 1962)
The Second Empire, 1852–70: Art in France under Napoleon III (exh. cat., Philadelphia, PA, Mus. A., 1978)
H. Bouilhet: *Christofle: Silversmith since 1830* (Paris, 1981)
S. Jervis and others: *Art and Design in Europe and America, 1800–1900* (London, 1987)
J.-M. Pinçon and O. Gaube du Gers: *Odiot l'orfèvre* (Paris, 1990)
CLARE LE CORBEILLER

2. BASE METALS.

(i) Before 1450. (ii) 1450–1599. (iii) 1600–1800. (iv) After 1800.

(i) Before 1450. From the 6th and 7th centuries AD in the Aquitainian, Burgundian and Frankish Merovingian regions, copper alloys (usually described as bronze) were extensively used for buckles, fibulae and brooches and to ornament leather objects (e.g. purses). The decoration on such objects consists of plain interlace, interlaced animals and birds or isolated fantastic animals, as on the bronze buckle decorated with figures of animals in medallions (Troyes, Mus. B.-A. & Archéol.) and decorative bronze purse ornaments (Brussels, Musées Royaux A. & Hist.) from Wingles, Pas-de-Calais. Some wooden objects with low-relief bronze sheet decoration, sometimes gilded, have Christian motifs and served either as liturgical vessels or relic containers. Examples include the 6th-century tankard with scenes of the *Life of Christ* (Saint-Germain-en-Laye, Mus. Ant. N.) and a number of reliquary caskets, such as the gilded-copper example at Saint-Bonnet-Avalouze, the casket of St Mummolus (*see* §1(i) above), and one that shows the *Virgin and Child with SS Peter and Paul* (8th century; Paris, Mus. Cluny).

Little copper-alloy metalwork survives from the Carolingian period. Some scholars claim that the celebrated early 9th-century bronze throne of Dagobert from Saint-Denis Abbey (now Paris, Bib. N., Cab. Médailles), now generally considered to have been produced probably in Aachen, was made in Saint-Denis in the late 9th century. The small bronze equestrian statuette of an emperor (Paris, Louvre) is thought to have been made perhaps in Metz *c.* 850–75 and may represent Charles the Bald.

Many more works of bronze or gilt-bronze survive from the 11th and 12th centuries. These include lion doorknockers of the mid-11th century (Saint-Omer Cathedral and Bourbourg, parish church) and of the late 11th century (Brioude, St Julien; Ebreuil, St Léger; and Le Puy, Mus. Crozatier); the fragments of the shrine of St Babolinus (*c.* 1100; Le-Coudray-Saint-Omer, Parish Church); the candlestick bases of *c.* 1125–50 at Reims (Reims, Mus. Vieux-Reims); several aquamanilia perhaps from Lorraine, in the form of griffins, dragons or lions (e.g. of *c.* 1130, London, V&A; of *c.* 1150–75, St Petersburg, Hermitage; two of *c.* 1150–1200, Florence, Bargello); the seated figures that personify the Four Elements (*c.* 1180; Munich, Bayer. Nmus.); the figures of *Moses* and a *Prophet* (late 12th century; Oxford, Ashmolean); and three cross bases from Lorraine (Amsterdam, Rijksmus.; Basle, Hist. Mus.; Brussels, Musées Royaux A. & Hist.). The French origin of these pieces is determined by parallels with Romanesque and Early Gothic stone sculpture and by their stylistic difference from the larger groups of surviving contemporary bronzes from the Mosan region and Germany.

Few Gothic bronze effigies survive of the many that must once have existed. That of *Evrard de Fouilloy, Bishop of Amiens* (*d* 1222) in Amiens Cathedral is a rare example of the Early Gothic style. Gilt-bronze was used for several head reliquaries, such as those of *St Valeria* and *St Essentia* (late 13th century and early 14th) at St Martin, Brive, and that of *St Ferreolus* (1346) at Nexon, Haut Vienne, and for such statuette reliquaries as that of *St John the Baptist* (14th century) at the parish church of Brienne-le-Château, Aube. The two prophets (Cleveland, OH, Mus. A.; Paris, Louvre) from the shrine (1409) of St Germanus of Paris are also of gilt-bronze. Many of the commonly found bronze objects of the later Middle Ages, such as buckles, candlesticks, door-knockers, lecterns and lavers, seem to have been fabricated in the Mosan region, Flanders and Germany and imported into France. However, some gilt-copper croziers, altar and processional crosses and certain liturgical vessels of French manufacture survive.

Most medieval objects in tin, lead or pewter (e.g. flagons, cups and plates) served purely functional purposes and were rarely decorated. Tin chalices with the *cuppa* gilded were allowed for poor churches and for burial chalices for ecclesiastics (e.g. in Paris, Boucaud priv. col.; see Boucaud and Frégnac, fig. 21); several are mentioned in historical sources, but few survive. Lead was used for fonts and pilgrim badges, of which many examples exist (e.g. from the shrine of Our Lady of Boulogne; London, Guildhall). The best known of the lead fonts include the 12th-century example at Saint-Evroult-de-Montfort, Orne, which is decorated with the Labours of the Months and saints and those in the parish churches at Berneuil, Somme, and Espeaubourg, Oise, which are both decorated with figures of saints and foliage. Ten 13th-century fonts survive (e.g. in Aubin, Aveyron), as do five from the 14th century (e.g. in the former Lombez Cathedral, Gers) and the 15th.

As in England, iron was used for locks, grilles and railings, and to decorate wooden doors and chests. In the 12th century openwork, deeply grooved foliage or ornamental patterns of iron were set on wooden doors without emphasizing the hinge bars, with pieces not welded together but attached separately (e.g. in Angers Cathedral and Le Puy Cathedral). The decoration of early 13th-century doors (e.g. that of the south portal of the west façade of Notre-Dame, Paris) is characterized by similar deeply grooved foliage stems, with additional elaboration of foliage in regular coils, occasionally inhabited with birds, and with stamping made using moulded dies and punches. Stamping ceased later in the 13th century in favour of working the iron cold using file and saw. There was a parallel development in the techniques used to make iron grilles from that of the 12th century at Le Puy Cathedral, through the early 13th-century example from the former Ourscamp Abbey, to the Rouen Cathedral choir gates of c. 1300 (both Rouen, Mus. Le Secq des Tournelles). Many 14th- and 15th-century window grilles survive that have repeated pattern designs, for example the hearts on the grille (c. 1450) from the Maison Jacques Coeur (now Rouen, Mus. Le Secq des Tournelles). Also from that period are iron door-locks with elaborate pierced tracery designs (examples in London, V&A). A rare example of a fine 13th-century iron candlestick decorated with animal heads is at St Martin, Brive, Corrèze.

BIBLIOGRAPHY

R. Bordeaux: *Serrurerie du moyen-âge: Les Ferrures de portes* (Oxford and Paris, 1858)
E. Viollet-le-Duc: *Dictionnaire raisonné de l'architecture française du XIe au XVIe siècle*, 10 vols (Paris, 1858–68), vi, pp. 54–81; viii, pp. 288–368
G. Bapst: *Les Métaux dans l'antiquité et au moyen âge: L'Etain* (Paris, [c. 1885])
C. Enlart: *Manuel d'archéologie française*, 3 vols (Paris, 1902–16), ii, p. 887; iii, pp. 273–94, 302–8, 353–64
H. Lüer and M. Creutz: *Geschichte der Metallkunst*, i (Stuttgart, 1904)
J. Tavernor-Parry: *Dinanderie: A History and Description of Mediaeval Art Work in Copper, Brass and Bronze* (London, 1910)
H. R. d'Allemagne: *Ferronnerie ancienne: Rouen, Le Musée Le Secq des Tournelles* (Paris, 1924)
J. S. Gardner: *Ironwork*, i (London, 1927/R 1978)
O. Hoever: *An Encyclopaedia of Ironwork* (London, 1927); rev. as *A Handbook of Wrought Iron* (London, 1962)
O. von Falke and E. Meyer: *Romanische Leuchter und Gefässe: Giessgefässe der Gotik* (Berlin, 1935)
Les Trésors des églises de France (exh. cat., ed. J. Taralon; Paris, Mus. A. Déc., 1965)
J. Taralon: *Les Trésors des églises de France* (Paris, 1966)
H. Swarzenski: *Monuments of Romanesque Art* (London, 1967)
J. Hubert, J. Porcher and W. F. Volbach: *Europe in the Dark Ages* (London, 1969)
M.-N. Delaine: *Ferronnerie médiévale du centre de la France* (Clermont-Ferrand, 1975)
P. Boucaud and C. Frégnac: *Les Etains des origines au 19e siècle* (Fribourg, 1978)
U. Mende: *Die Türzieher des Mittelalters* (Berlin, 1981)
P. Springer: *Kreuzfüsse* (Berlin, 1981)

NIGEL MORGAN

(ii) 1450–1599. During the late 15th century base metals were used concurrently with precious metals and rivalled them in popularity. Artisans in France continued to use a flamboyant Gothic repertory. Until this period wrought-iron was used essentially for practical purposes, in the construction of buildings and for furniture, kitchen utensils and fire-irons; now it also assumed a decorative function. Strap hinges, hinges and locks (e.g. Rouen, Mus. Le Secq des Tournelles; London, V&A) fitted to the surfaces of furniture were decorated with ogives and intricate and skilfully pierced pinnacles or, occasionally, fantastic animals or figures in the round. These motifs also appear on

andirons, lamps and, more rarely, kitchen utensils and fire-irons. Few objects made of pewter have survived from this period, and those that do are mainly such utilitarian items as dishes and plates. About 15 pewter pot-bellied pitchers (e.g. London, V&A; Paris, Mus. A. Déc.) are now known. These were most probably used as measures and thus serve as important cultural evidence of the customs of the time. There are, however, some pewter liturgical objects—monstrances (e.g. Paris, Louvre), pyxides, chalices and baptismal fonts—occasionally decorated with pinnacles and Gothic arches in a manner similar to other contemporary metalwork items. Bronze and brass were widely used in the production of kitchen utensils, lamps and ecclesiastical objects and were decorated in a Late Gothic style. This period was dominated by the influence of workshops on the Meuse, particularly those of Dinant (*see* BELGIUM, §IX, 2(i)–(ii)). Paris, Toulouse, Lyon and Strasbourg, the main centres of metalworking, produced such ecclesiastical items as chalices, monstrances, pyxides and censers (e.g. Paris, Mus. Cluny; London, V&A) made of brass or copper and embellished with applied relief ornament, which could subsequently be engraved, silver plated or gold plated; apart from this, copper does not seem to have been widely used for making decorative objects.

In the 16th century the school of Fontainebleau provided a wide decorative repertory for metalworkers. Wrought-iron locks (e.g. Rouen, Mus. Le Secq des Tournelles), latches and flat bolts were decorated with grotesques, grotesque masks, strapwork arabesques and knotwork; occasionally even the emblem of the sovereign was included. Decoration was executed in the repoussé technique or by means of engraving or etching, and objects were sometimes gold-plated. Pierced and engraved iron and steel keys (see fig. 81) became veritable works of art in themselves. Such forms as caskets, boxes and scissors appeared and were similarly ornamented. Kitchen utensils and fire-irons became much more ornate and were often engraved and embellished with grotesque masks and bronze or brass rosettes.

The production of pewter reached great heights of excellence during the 16th century, as pewterers competed successfully with other metalworkers. Inventories show that a considerable amount of display pewter was produced at this time, to be shown on sideboards and dressers, probably as a substitute for expensive plate. Display pewter consisted of large basins and ewers richly decorated with cast, low-relief ornament comprising figures surrounded by densely packed Mannerist ornament, decoration similar to contemporary goldsmiths' work. Figurative themes were borrowed from antiquity or the Bible. This type of pewter was probably produced in Lyon from the mid-16th century, and the most notable pewterer of the time was FRANÇOIS BRIOT (*see also* PEWTER, fig. 2).

Bronze and brass were still used for numerous domestic objects, including lamps, torches and candelabra, decorated with grotesque masks, foliage and arabesques. Brass and copper could be beaten into very fine leaves, enabling the production of items that could be decorated by repoussé and engraving. Spouts and ears were sometimes attached later. Many dishes and basins (examples in Paris,

81. Steel key, l. 115 mm, ?late 16th century (London, Victoria and Albert Museum)

Mus. A. Déc.; London, V&A), referred to as 'offerings', survive; these usually served as reflectors of light. The decoration could comprise a central medallion with a secular symbol (flowered vase, Sibyl or, less commonly, a coat of arms) or a religious scene, around which can run several friezes, usually swaged or stamped.

BIBLIOGRAPHY

G. Bapst: *Les Métaux dans l'antiquité et au moyen âge: L'Etain* (Paris, [*c.* 1885])
H. R. d'Allemagne: *Histoire du luminaire* (Paris, 1891)
H. Demiani: *François Briot, Caspar Enderlein und das Edelzinn* (Leipzig, 1897)
J. Tavenor-Perry: *Dinanderie* (London, 1910)
H. R. d'Allemagne: *Ferronnerie ancienne* (Paris, 1924)
E. Franck: *Petite ferronnerie ancienne* (Paris, 1948)
A. J. G. Verster: *Tin door de eeuwen* [Pewter throughout the ages] (Amsterdam, 1954)
P. Boucaud and C. Fregnac: *Les Etains des origines au 19e siècle* (Fribourg, 1978)

PHILIPPE BOUCAUD

(iii) 1600–1800.

(a) Gilt-bronze. (b) Other.

(a) Gilt-bronze.

Introduction. The use of gilt-bronze in furnishings during the 17th and 18th centuries was one expression of the resurgence of a more refined lifestyle that developed during the 17th century. Its use became widespread during

the reign of Louis XIV and contributed to the sumptuous and luxurious décor in grand interiors of the time. The essential quality that made bronze so attractive as a medium was that it formed a perfect base for gilding (*see* GILDING, §§I, 3 and II, 4) or, more rarely, silvering. Gilt-bronze was used in every aspect of interior furnishings and replaced ironwork. *Bronzes d'ameublement* comprised clocks, mirrors, fire-dogs, wall-lights, candelabra and chandeliers; ormolu mounts were applied to furniture, porcelain and hardstones. Gilt-bronze was also used for door furniture, to ornament chimney-pieces, staircases, *boiseries* and marble and was even used to adorn watches. One motive behind this increased use of gilt-bronze can be found in the many sumptuary edicts issued by Louis XIV, in which he forbade the use of precious metals in furnishings. These measures had a serious, though temporary, effect on the type of work carried out in precious metals, but the edicts did not prevent makers from resorting to gilding or silvering in order to create objects considered indispensable not only for the pomp, glory and majesty of the Crown itself but also for the luxurious surroundings demanded by the French nobility. Items that had previously been executed in silver and silver gilt were now re-created in gilt–bronze, for example the *surtout de table* (Toledo, OH, Mus. A.) made for Louis de Bourbon, the Grand Dauphin, by Nicolas de Launay (1647–1727).

During the reign of Louis XIV a precise distinction was drawn between the two trades of the *fondeurs-fondants* (metal-casters and founders) and the *fondeurs-ciseleurs* (metal-casters and chasers or engravers), both of which belonged to the same guild. Gilding and silvering were the exclusive domain of a separate guild, that of the *doreurs-ciseleurs* (gilders and chasers or engravers); it was not until 1776 that these two guilds merged. The *fondeurs-fondants* confined themselves to the single activity of casting, while the job of designing and creating models for bronze work was the responsibility of the *fondeurs-ciseleurs*. Most of the latter group were also sculptors, for example André-Charles Boulle, Domenico Cucci, Jean-Joseph de Saint-Germain and Pierre-Philippe Thomire, and such members of the Académie Royale de Sculpture et de Peinture or the Académie de Saint-Luc as Sébastien Slodtz and his sons, François-Antoine Vassé, Jacques Caffiéri, Philippe Caffiéri (ii), Etienne Martincourt (?1735–after 1791) and Jean-Louis Prieur. All were experts in chasing and engraving, the skill that gave bronze its value prior to gilding. Towards the end of the 18th century such gilders as Pierre Gouthière and François Rémond were celebrated for the techniques of matt and burnished gilding. Gilders, for example Louis-François Gobert (*d* 1772), often used their own models, which would have first been cast in bronze by the *fondeurs-fondants*, later chased or engraved and gilt. Sculptors, furniture-makers and watchmakers also had their own models, to which they had exclusive rights as long as the casting and gilding was carried out by qualified master craftsmen.

Baroque and Rococo. In the early 17th century gilt-bronze was not used for furnishings to any great degree except in the case of ornament in church choirs, for example chandeliers and lecterns. It then began to make an appearance in domestic interiors, as in the pedestals

(1641) for the Palais du Louvre, Paris, and the capitals and bases (1653–5) of the columns of the baths in Anne of Austria's winter apartments, also in the Louvre. Although Cucci and Boulle both bore the title of Ebéniste et Ciseleur du Roi, the use of gilt-bronze in furniture was generally confined to the edges of table-tops, the capitals of columns and the ferrules placed around the posts or uprights. Cucci delivered candelabra (Paris, Mus. A. Déc.) to the Marquise de Seignelay in 1693, and Boulle also executed candelabra in 1699 for the private apartments of the Grand Dauphin at Versailles. Stylistically, however, this range of objects was no different from the identical models executed in gold or silver.

The use of gilt-bronze came into its own at the end of the 17th century. A move away from the Baroque can be seen in two of Boulle's chandeliers, the chandelier with the figure of Renown (Paris, Louvre) and the Dolphin Chandelier (Malibu, CA, Getty Mus.), and in the Four Hours of the Day Clock by Jean Berain I, Pierre Le Nègre (*fl* 1680–1711) and Sébastien Slodtz, of which only the design is extant (Stockholm, Nmus.). This development was more strongly marked in such other works by Boulle as the commode for the King's Chamber in the Trianon (1708; Versailles, Château) and his Venus Marine Clock (London, Wallace), in which the wood is effectively a secondary material. Other examples that point towards a fundamental change in the use of materials include the terminal busts of *Zephyrus* and *Flora* (1713) that Vassé attached to the mantel of a chimney-piece intended for the Duchesse de Berry at Versailles.

Gilt-bronze lent itself admirably well to the expression of the Rococo style. Boulle introduced Rococo elements into a number of his works, for example some wall-lights with dragons (Paris, Mme Grog-Carven priv. col.), which matched the similarly inspired wall-lights designed by Jean Berain II (1674–1726) and Sébastien Slodtz in 1720 for Maximilian II Emanuel, Elector of Bavaria (Munich, Schloss Nymphenburg, destr.). Vassé in turn modelled a dragon in triumphant pose holding candle-nozzles in its jaw and on its wings (Lisbon, Mus. Gulbenkian). The major casters and founders working in gilt-bronze in the Rococo style included Jean Le Blanc (*fl c.* 1730–60), the brothers Jean-Baptiste and Nicolas Barthélemy Fuzellier (*fl c.* 1710–50), Nicolas Vassoult (*fl c.* 1710–65), Thomas Germain, Jacques Confesseur (*c.* 1690–1759) and Charles Cressent. Others whose work was especially fashionable were Jacques Caffiéri, Saint-Germain and Jean-Claude Duplessis, who made an astonishing brazier (Istanbul, Topkapı Pal. Mus.) in 1742 on the orders of Louis XV as a gift for Mahmud I, Sultan of Turkey. Asymmetrical Rococo was to reach its apogee in the pieces executed in the 1750s by François-Thomas Germain, for example the wall-lights for the Palais-Royal, Paris (Malibu, CA, Getty Mus.), and the mantelpiece in the Bernsdorf Palace, Copenhagen.

The gilt-bronze mounts used in furniture were on occasion so overwhelming that many pieces appeared to be no more than a mere support for the extravagance of the mounts. This can be seen in the medal-cabinet (Versailles, Château) executed for Louis XV by Antoine-Robert Gaudreaus and the Slodtz brothers, in the series of commodes decorated with hunting scenes (Dresden,

Schloss Pillnitz; Malibu, CA, Getty Mus.) executed by Bernard van Risamburgh II for Frederick-Augustus II, Elector of Saxony, and in the regulator clocks (Dresden, Altes Schloss, possibly destr.) in the form of life-size palm-trees, decorated with girandoles, which were executed by Jean-Pierre Latz and intended for the same sovereign.

Another new use for gilt-bronze was that of creating mounts for hardstones, marble or porcelain. The practice spread on an unparalleled scale owing to the impetus given by *marchands-merciers* and collectors. Porcelain vessels were transformed into potpourris, ewers, fountains, clocks or perfume burners. Two greyhounds were modelled keeping watch at the foot of a celadon water-basin with reservoir and tap (Versailles, Château), delivered to Louis XV in 1742, for example, and a terrace complete with balustrade, staircase and gilt-bronze trophy served as a plinth for a massive Sèvres flower vase (Dresden, Zwinger). The most prominent artists specializing in this technique included Louis Paffe (*fl* 1733–70), Duplessis, Saint-Germain, Vassoult and Edme-Jean Gallien (1720–after 1781), although no work by them is signed. From 1745 onwards the Rococo style went through a more sober phase, an example of which is the well-known astronomical clock (Versailles, Château) made by Passement and the Caffiéris.

Neo-classicism. Jean-Jacques Caffiéri was foremost among those working in *le goût grec* and was renowned after 1757 for the bronzes he executed to adorn Ange-Laurent de La Live de Jully's furniture (Chantilly, Château), as was Edme Roy (*fl* 1745–80), who made the famous clock with a figure of Study for Mme Geoffrin; the figure

82. Gilt-bronze case enclosing the Avignon Clock by Pierre Gouthière after a design by Louis-Simon Boizot, h. 679 mm, 1771 (London, Wallace Collection)

on the clock was modelled by Laurent Guiard (1723–88). Robert Osmond (1713–89) designed a clock adorned with a vase and lions' heads (Cleveland, OH, Mus. A.), and Saint-Germain created not only the Spirit of Denmark Clock (Copenhagen, Amalienborg) but also a number of astonishing candelabra with tripod bases terminating in lions' paws. Etienne Martincourt designed the Astronomy and Geography Clock (Malibu, CA, Getty Mus.). Prieur sent his candelabra with eagles to Warsaw (now in Detroit, MI, Inst. A.), while Claude-Quentin Pitoin delivered numerous wall-lights and lamps to the Garde Meuble de la Couronne. Rather than being particularly original, however, these works presented a rigid interpretation of Neo-classicism.

The Etruscan style can be seen in the wall-lights executed by Prieur for the palace ballroom in Warsaw (now in Paris, Mus. Nissim de Camondo), in those made for the high altar in Embrun Cathedral by Jean-Baptiste Allnet (*fl* 1766–86) and in the clock (St Petersburg, Hermitage) with allegorical figures that Prieur made for the marriage of Louis XVI after a design by François Boucher. This style was fully developed in the Four Seasons Candelabra (London, Buckingham Pal., Royal Col.) executed by Philippe Caffiéri (ii), in the Three Graces Clock (Toronto, Royal Ont. Mus.) by François Vion (1737–after 1790), in the Ship Clock (ex-Roberto Polo priv. col., New York) by Nicolas Bonnet (1740–after 1790) and in the Avignon Clock (London, Wallace; see fig. 82) by Gouthière and Louis-Simon Boizot. The artists, designers and craftsmen who were responsible for developing this vision of the 'grand style' included Boizot, François-Joseph Belanger, Gilles-Paul Cauvet, Charles-Louis Clérisseau, Nicolas Ledoux, Jean-Démosthène Dugourc and Jean-François Forty (*fl c.* 1760–90). Such talented sculptors as Jean-François Houdon and Augustin Pajou also contributed, as did Prieur, Martincourt, Louis-Gabriel Feloix (1730–after 1790), Jean-Claude-Thomas Duplessis the younger, Gouthière, Rémond and Thomire.

Imaginary and exotic animals, for example the kneeling camels that appear on Gouthière's lamps (Paris, Louvre), were often used to form a support for monumental compositions, as seen in the candelabra with ostriches (Versailles, Château) by Rémond and the clocks with Vestal virgins carrying the sacred fire (Minneapolis, MN, Inst. A.) by Thomire, where rams' heads were used as handles for the vases and eagles' heads were used to support the candle-nozzles. Duplessis and Thomire, who succeeded one another as modellers and designers at the Sèvres factory, were renowned for the quality of their mounts for porcelain and hardstones. Such mounts can also be seen in works by Gouthière (e.g. in Paris, Louvre), Rémond and Antoine-Louis Pajot (*c.* 1730–81), where the refinement of these artists' imaginations vied with the equally remarkable perfection of their chasing. After *c.* 1780 gilt-bronzes incorporated into furnishings began to display exaggeration, as in some work by Jean-Henri Riesener, Martin Carlin, Adam Weisweiller and Guillaume Beneman. A typical example of this development can be found in the gilt-bronze mounts on the jewel-cabinet made for Marie-Antoinette by Jean-Ferdinand-Joseph Schwerdfeger (Versailles, Château; see fig. 83), which were executed by Boizot, Martincourt and Thomire.

83. Gilt-bronze mounts by Louis-Simon Boizot, Etienne Martincourt and Pierre-Philippe Thomire on a jewel-cabinet by Jean-Ferdinand-Joseph Schwerdfeger, 1787 (Versailles, Musée National du Château de Versailles et de Trianon)

The French Revolution offered new subject-matter for bronzeworkers, although such symbols as the lictors' fasces were already part of the visual vocabulary prior to 1789, as in the commode from Louis XVI's apartments at Saint-Cloud (Malibu, CA, Getty Mus.). The success of the novel *Paul et Virginie* (Paris, 1787) by Bernardin de Saint-Pierre influenced works, including clocks and candelabra, executed *au nègre*. A considerable number of subjects remained fashionable, such as the nymph Erigone and the numerous variations executed on the theme of love, as seen in such sculptures by Philippe-Laurent Roland (1746–1816) as the *Chariot of the Seasons* (Madrid, Pal. Real) and the *Pledge of Love* (St Petersburg, Hermitage), which were cast by Thomire, and in such work by François-Nicolas Delaistre (1746–1823) as *Friendship Led by Love and Crowned by Hymen* (New York, Mr and Mrs Frank Richardson III priv. col.). By the end of the 18th century, the most brilliant period in the execution of works in gilt-bronze in France drew to a close.

BIBLIOGRAPHY

D. F. Lunsingh-Scheurleer: *Chinesisches und japanisches Porzellan in europäischen Fassungen* (Brunswick, 1980)

H. Ottomeyer and P. Pröschel: *Vergoldete Bronzen: Die Bronzearbeiten des Spätbarock und Klassizismus*, 2 vols (Munich, 1986)

P. Verlet: *Les Bronzes dorés français du XVIIIème siècle* (Paris, 1987)

G. Bresc-Bautier: 'Problèmes du bronze français: Fondeurs et sculpteurs à Paris, 1600–1660', *Archvs A. Fr.*, n. s., xxx (1989), pp. 11–50

JEAN-DOMINIQUE AUGARDE

(b) Other. During this period wrought-iron was relegated to the ranks of mere ironmongery inside furniture. Locks (e.g. in Rouen, Mus. Le Secq des Tournelles), the mechanisms of which grew increasingly complicated, were sometimes very finely engraved, while keys were always very ornate, chased and engraved. Caskets made of polished iron were often engraved with simple foliage and were made for keeping important papers and jewellery. Kitchen and household implements and andirons, which were produced in great numbers, remained simple in design, with their shafts turned to form balusters, sometimes embellished with volutes or more rarely with bronze or brass motifs. Pewter, hardy and inexpensive, was the only material capable of meeting the enormous domestic, commercial, religious and medical demands. On the whole, pewter objects of this period are simple, without decoration (they were for daily use and needed to be easy to clean). The most representative examples were the candlestick *à la financière* (Paris, Mus. A. Déc.), the shaft of which represents a bundle of small, interconnected candles, and the broad-rimmed charger *à la cardinal* (Paris, Mus. A. Déc.), so called because it was introduced into France by Cardinal Jules Mazarin. Decoration in relief was abandoned, with only a few plates engraved with designs and even then it was often a simple coat of arms. Bronze, brass and copper continued to be used for the manufacture of kitchen and household implements, and for candleware, where models with shafts turned to form balusters and triangular bases predominated.

Louis XIV's penchant for grandiose decorative arts was to have repercussions in the use of base metals during the 18th century. Wrought-iron was often relegated to a utilitarian role—handles of kitchen or household implements, and andirons—in objects the visible and ornamental parts of which were made of bronze or brass, which was often gilded. There were, however, some extremely fine examples of locks engraved and chased with designs and also often embellished with gilt-bronze or brass motifs. In the building trade, railings and gratings, balconies, banisters and lanterns were decorated with volutes and foliage, which were most often gilded. The most famous 18th-century French ironmonger was Jean Lamour (1698–1771), who designed the wrought-iron decoration of the Place Stanislas in Nancy, constructed between 1752 and 1756.

During Louis XIV's wars of conquest pewter was the most important metal. Indeed, in order to reanimate completely depleted finances, Louis XIV ordered gold and silver plate to be melted down, setting the example himself at Versailles. The pewterers thus offered the customer 'silver-style' objects equal in quality and decorative appearance to those lost in the melting pots. Ewers with lids, soup bowls, terrines (examples in Paris, Mus. A. Déc.), candlesticks, salt cellars etc were decorated with cartouches, friezes and lambrequins, which made them a perfect replacement for the silverware that had disappeared. Their relatively low cost facilitated their broad distribution, and their use continued beyond the mid-18th

century. Every sizeable town included several workshops; the larger centres having dozens where veritable dynasties worked at their craft: Antheaume, Boicervoise, Samain in Paris, Morand in Lyon, and Isenheim in Strasbourg. Unfortunately for the pewter industry, the continued development of tin-glazed earthenware and later the creation of European porcelain were to deal it a fatal blow. From the mid-18th century, pewterers struggled to survive, often working only for religious communities and hospitals.

Melted bronze and brass continued to be the privileged materials for the manufacture of kitchen and household implements, and for candleware, which played an important role in interiors. The decorative repertory, initially constituting rows of gadroons and lambrequins, later turned to Rococo motifs and wreathed sides, then, towards the end of the 18th century, to pearls and 'antique-style' masks. The objects are mostly parcel-gilt or silver-plated, and it was in the area of furnishings that the industry achieved the greatest quality. Sheet brass and copper, without special decoration, were still used for the manufacture of a variety of vessels. Warming pans, decorated with various motifs, were manufactured in Normandy (examples in Villedieu-les-Poêles; Mus. Poêlerie) or in the Massif Central.

BIBLIOGRAPHY
H. R. d'Allemagne: *Histoire du luminaire* (Paris, 1891)
——: *Ferronnerie ancienne* (Paris, 1924)
E. Franck: *Petite ferronnerie ancienne* (Paris, 1948)
P. Boucaud and C. Fregnac: *Les Etains des origines au début du 19e siècle* (Fribourg, 1978)
P. Schiffer, N. Schiffer and H. Schiffer: *The Brass Book* (Exton, 1978)
P. Hornsby: *Pewter of the Western World, 1600–1850* (Exton, 1983)

(iv) After 1800. In the 19th century wrought-iron was primarily utilized for the production of domestic objects, particularly those for heating and cooking, and thus its use declined with the progressive rejection of open-hearth fires. At the beginning of the 20th century Héctor Guimard designed architectural ironwork in the Art Nouveau style (e.g. panel for a balcony, c. 1900; London, V&A), and several French glassmakers and potters used wrought-iron frames for goblets, lamps and chandeliers (examples in Paris, Mus. d'Orsay; Paris, Mus. A. Déc.). It was not until the 1930s, however, that there was a major revival of wrought-iron in decorative art, in the form of railings, staircases, tables, frames and lights. Edgar Brandt (1880–1960), who worked in Paris, designed a series of wrought-iron and tin-plate panels (c. 1922–8; London, V&A; Mus. London) in the Art Deco style for the lifts of Selfridges department store, London. Other notable ironworkers during the early to mid-20th century included Raymond Subes (1893–1970) and Gilbert Poillerat (1902–88).

The use of copper was restricted to kitchen utensils until the 1930s, when a number of French artists and designers, including JEAN DUNAND and Claudius Linossier (1893–1953), revived the traditional techniques of hammering and repoussé. They produced goblets, vases and dishes that often incorporate brass or silver inlay patterns in the Art Deco style (e.g. of 1925; Lyon, Mus. B.-A.; see fig. 84) and are sometimes patinated or lacquered. In the late 20th century such craftsmen as Maurice Perrier (*b* 1925) and Guy Lommé (*b* 1947) produced both traditional patinated vessels and anthropomorphic forms in copper.

The use of pewter, which had been superseded by that of ceramics in the 18th century, was revived from the beginning of the 19th century. The simple techniques and relatively low cost of manufacturing pewter enabled the production, mainly in Paris, of series of inexpensive sculptures and decorative objects (e.g. Paris, Mus. A. Déc.). The most notable craftsmen working in pewter in the late 19th century included Jules Brateau (1844–1923), Jules Desbois, Jean Baffier (1851–1921) and Raoul Larche. In the 1930s another traditional technique, pewter dinanderie, was used for numerous objects in the Art Deco style. Repoussé and hammering enabled the production of bold, unadorned forms. Apart from Dunand, other craftsmen using this technique included Maurice Daurat (1880–1960) and Jean Desprès (1889–1980).

In the Empire and Restoration periods there was a proliferation of decorative bronzework, often gilt, particularly for furniture. Among the most important works are those of PIERRE-PHILIPPE THOMIRE and Martin-Guillaume Biennais (*see also* §(iii)(a) above). Small bronze pieces in the form of animals became popular before the mid-19th century; towards the end of the century these were produced by such sculptors as Antoine-Louis Barye and Pierre-Jules Mène. Around 1900 the firms of Barbedienne, Susse Frères, Rudier and Siot-Decauville manufactured small, decorative bronze as well as pewter pieces after designs by Jean Baffier, Raoul Larche and many others. In the same period Guimard designed furniture fittings, such as handles, knobs and bell-buttons. Small bronze objects and decorative items continued to be produced during the Art Deco period by such craftsmen as Demeter Chiparus (1888–1950), known for his sculptures (Paris, Mus. d'Orsay; Paris, Mus. A. Déc.) that combine metals with ivory, and Armand-Albert Rateau (1882–1938), who is also justly famous for his original furniture creations in bronze (e.g. Paris, Mus. A. Déc.).

BIBLIOGRAPHY
Le XIXème Siècle français, Connaissance des Arts (Paris, 1957)
Tardy [H. G. E. Lengellé]: *Les Etains français* (Paris, [1958])
P. Schiffer, N. Schiffer and H. Schiffer: *The Brass Book* (Exton, 1978)
Jules Brateau et le renouveau de la poterie d'étain (exh. cat. by P. Boucaud, Paris, 1986)
P. Kjellberg: *Les Bronzes du XIXème siècle* (Paris, 1989)
D. Forest: *La Dinanderie en France, 1900–1950* (in preparation)
PHILIPPE BOUCAUD

X. Objects of vertu.

1. Enamel. 2. Gold boxes. 3. Jewellery. 4. Hardstones. 5. Ivory and bone.

1. ENAMEL. Enamel techniques (*see* ENAMEL, §2) were employed by French goldsmiths as early as the Carolingian period (*see* §IX, 1(i) above). In the 12th century Limoges emerged as an important centre of production for devotional articles in champlevé (*see* LIMOGES, §1 and ROMANESQUE, §§VI, 2 and VII), and by the 14th century *basse taille* enamel was perfected by goldsmiths in France to embellish gold and silver vessels and plaques. The Royal Gold Cup (*c.* 1380–90; London, BM; *see* ENAMEL, colour pl. III, fig. 1), made in Paris undoubtedly for Charles V, is

84. Dish by Jean Dunand, patinated copper inlaid with silver, diam. 610 mm, 1925 (Lyon, Musée des Beaux-Arts)

a rare surviving example of the outstanding pieces made at this period (*see* GOTHIC, §§V, 2 and VI).

In the 16th century the leading enamel painter, LÉONARD LIMOSIN, worked for the Court at the château of Fontainebleau, and it was while the Florentine Benvenuto Cellini was employed there that he executed the celebrated gold salt decorated with *basse taille* enamel (1540–43; Vienna, Ksthist. Mus.; *see* CELLINI, BENVENUTO, fig. 4; *see also* ENAMEL, colour pl. IV, fig. 1). In the 17th century in Paris *basse taille* remained the principal enamel technique practised by goldsmiths. At this time champlevé was generally confined to heraldic motifs and to border decorations. Champlevé in the style of an incised linear reserve cut (*taille d'épargne*) was used for foliate patterns on the inner covers of watches and for monograms. Raised surface effects were produced with the glaze, with drops of high-fusing enamel applied to the ground (*émail à la goutte*) to imitate tiny cabochon stones or split pearls. In another technique, white enamel was trailed over a black ground and fused to form a raised pattern. Relief enamels were otherwise made by thinly glazing a chased gold surface (*émail en ronde bosse*). The method, employed for Renaissance jewellery, was adapted in the 17th century for watches and lockets to produce raised scrolls and floral emblems (*see* §3 below). The type of enamel known as *en résille sur verre* was adopted by Parisian makers during the period 1600 to 1640 for decorating watches and lockets.

In Blois, a centre of watchmaking, enamel painting methods were refined, and a particular style suitable for miniatures was developed for the decoration of watchcases. The goldsmith Jean Toutin (1578–1644) introduced *c.* 1630–32 a wider range of vitrifiable pigments derived from minerals with metal oxides as the main ingredients and a technique involving painting on an enamelled ground with these colours mixed with oil of lavender and applied with a pointillé method, which enabled miniatures to be created with greater naturalism than previously. Enamel miniatures were painted in this manner with amatory, allegorical and devotional themes. Henry Toutin (1614–83) added such painted decorations to watches signed by Blaise Foucher (*d* 1662) of Blois (see fig. 85) and Goullons of Paris. Jacques Vauquer (1621–86), the leading designer of the Blois school, published engravings for the use of ornamentalists featuring the rose, the carnation and the daisy. With enamels such motifs took the form of brightly coloured floral designs against black or white grounds. A fashion also existed for watchcases glazed with cerulean blue enamel, with raised floral motifs on the exterior and pastoral scenes painted in a simple style on the interior.

During the reign of Louis XIV small paintings were set into box lids (*boîtes à miniature*). Those with portraits (*boîtes à portrait*) had flattering miniatures of the King, prominent noblemen and ladies of the Court. JEAN PETITOT, born in Geneva of French descent, improved on Toutin's technique for portraiture and was the leading artist in enamel portrait miniatures, producing such works as the miniature of Louis XIV in a frame after a design by Gilles Légaré (24×21 mm; London, V&A). He worked for Louis XIV from *c*. 1650 to *c*. 1684.

During the 18th century, when the demand in France for elaborate and exotic decoration reached its height, enamel lent richness and variety to the work of a number of leading goldsmiths. Enamels continued to be closely associated with the watchmaking industry, which flourished in France. Family businesses continued for several generations, and fine watches with painted enamels were made during the 18th century by the firms of Le Roy, Lenoir and Jean Romilly in Paris.

Goldsmiths specializing in the making of gold boxes (*see* §2 below) offered larger pieces for table display from the 1730s, with the sides and bases decorated as well as the lids. Both *basse taille* and painted enamels remained in vogue for these. The colourful floral themes of the 1730s were replaced in the next decade by a preference for stylized figural groups, including chinoiserie subjects, enamelled in translucent blue or green. *En plein* enamelling of box lids began to be superseded in the 1740s, when cagework snuff-boxes (*tabatières à cage*) became fashionable. For these, enamelled panels were made as separate components and set into the gold framework; by 1755 this form of decoration predominated, enamellers being able to replace the panels and thus alter the ornament to suit changing fashions. Enamellers and enamel painters generally supplied more than one boxmaker, and consequently similar designs may be found on articles bearing the marks of different goldsmiths. The enamel panels were often reset into mounts of a later period.

Enamel paintings in the 18th century featured floral motifs, religious and Classical subjects and interiors after David Teniers (ii), as well as idealized pastoral, romantic and erotic scenes after François Boucher and other popular artists. *En camaïeu* painting came into vogue in the 1770s. This gave the illusion of relief, with shaded white enamel applied over a sepia, pink, green or blue ground. Among 18th-century Parisian goldsmiths who incorporated enamel in their snuff-boxes were Jean Ducrollay (*fl* 1734–61), Jean George (*fl* 1752–65), Noël Hardivilliers (*fl* 1729–71), Michel-Robert Hallé (Hallet; *fl* 1737–54; see fig. 86) and Jean-François Breton (Lebreton; 1713–*c*. 1791; see fig. 88 below). Adrien-Jean-Maximilien Vachette (1753–1839), who was appointed enameller to the emperor Napoleon I, continued to work in the principal styles of the Louis XVI period well into the 19th century.

From 1768 the type of *basse taille* known as guilloche came to the fore. This involved a mechanical method of cutting in patterns with special lathes and superseded hand-engraving (flinking) for larger surfaces; it was used to create geometric designs, including various types of sunrays, waves, concentric circles, moiré effects and interlacing straight cuts. Translucent enamels fused over such a surface, especially over silver, produce luminous colours; with opalescent enamels the iridescent, or *changeant*, effects are increased. Guilloche plaques flanked miniatures, were inset into châtelaines or formed the ground for jewelled monograms. Copper-gilt as well as gold watchcases were decorated with guilloche in the 1790s by such firms as Vaucher of Paris. Guilloche was widely used to produce a brilliant ground for superimposed miniature paintings. A variation, initiated in Geneva, was achieved by fusing small, low-relief emblems stamped from gold foil (*paillons*) or silver (*clinquants*) into the guilloche glaze (*see* SWITZERLAND, §X). The *paillons*, shaped as dots, stars, crescents and bows, were used to add sparkle or to enrich borders. Simulated engraved designs were created with *paillons* in such shapes as fountains and birds. Joseph-Etienne Blerzy (*fl* 1768–1806) of Paris decorated his boxes (e.g. oval snuff-box, 1787–9; London, V&A) in this manner in the 1780s.

85. Painted enamel watchcase attributed to Henry Toutin, diam. 66 mm, Blois, *c*. 1640–50; movement by Blaise Foucher (London, British Museum)

During the 19th century designers and manufacturers introduced new styles of enamelling and researched long-neglected techniques. The firms of Charles Christofle (1805–63) and Ferdinand Barbedienne were the most successful and prolific in making vessels in copper gilt using various enamelling techniques. Jean Valentin Morel (1794–1860) was one of several French craftsmen who produced large vessels with figures *en ronde bosse* in the Renaissance manner. Enamel painting as practised in Limoges in the 16th century was rediscovered in the 1840s, and the medieval style of champlevé was also revived there in the 19th century. Louis Bourdery (1859–1901) became the best-known artist working in the former manner, making plaques and large urns in grisaille. (For an illustration of an enamel plaque (1865) by Claudius Popelin, *see* BONAPARTE, (8).) Emile Samson (1837–1913) produced excellent copies of 18th-century enamels made at Battersea (*see* ENGLAND, §X, 2) in his factory at Montreuil. From the late 19th century Eugène Feuillâtre (1870–1916) was the leading maker of larger pieces of *plique à jour* for box lids (e.g. silver box with domed lid, *c.* 1902; London, BM) and exhibition plates. Fernand Thesmar (1843–1912) made cloisonné designs and delicate *plique à jour* bowls. Outstanding enamelled ecclesiastical pieces were still made in the early 20th century, for example the Crown of the Virgin (1929; Paris, Trésor Cathedrale Notre-Dame) by Boucheron, with *plique à jour* and opalescent enamels. At the Exposition Universelle in Paris in 1900, Peter Carl Fabergé exhibited exquisitely enamelled work made by his craftsmen in St Petersburg, including some of the series of Imperial Easter Eggs made for the Russian court; this introduced a fashion for larger, shaped articles decorated with guilloche in limpid colours.

A quantity of high-quality enamels continued to be made in the late 19th century and up to 1914 in *basse taille*, usually guilloche on silver, or as painted enamels with floral motifs, or designs in the style of Watteau or one of his contemporaries. These traditional enamelling techniques were used to ornament clockcases, mirror- or picture-frames, watches, cigarette cases, powder boxes, perfume bottles, opera glasses and articles for the dressing-table and drawing-room, as well as jewellery. Such objects formed part of the stock of the leading French retailing goldsmiths and were also exported all over the world. By the late 1920s, enamelling was less widely employed for objects of vertu, but some production continued. Camile Fauré (1872–1947) and Alexandre Marty (1876–1943) made vases (Limoges, Mus. Mun.) of copper covered with foils and translucent enamels in the Art Deco style. In the late 1980s and early 1990s, Alain Duban (*b* 1952) produced enamelled bowls, boxes, vases and table ensembles for Porcelaines Bernardaud, Limoges (examples in Limoges, Mus. Mun.).

BIBLIOGRAPHY
H. Clouzot: *La Miniature en France* (Paris, 1925/6)
H. Ricketts: *Objects of Vertu* (London, 1971)
A Thousand Years of Enamel (exh. cat., London, Wartski, 1971)
R. W. Lightbown: *Secular Goldsmiths' Work in Medieval France: A History* (London, 1978)
H. Tait and C. Gere: *The Jeweller's Art* (London, 1978)
Princely Magnificence: Court Jewels of the Renaissance, 1500–1630 (exh. cat., London, V&A, 1980–81)
H. Tait: *The Waddesdon Bequest* (London, 1981)

86. *Basse taille* enamelled gold snuff-box by Michel-Robert Hallé, 80× 36.8×59.7 mm, Paris, 1750 (London, Victoria and Albert Museum)

S. Bury: *Jewellery Gallery Summary Catalogue,* London, V&A cat. (London, 1983)
A. Somers Cocks and C. Truman: *The Thyssen-Bornemisza Collection: Renaissance Jewels, Gold Boxes and Objets de Vertu* (London, 1984)
G. Neret: *Boucheron: Four Generations of a World-renowned Jeweller* (New York, 1988)
E. Speel: 'Enamel Portrait Miniatures', *Ant. Colr*, lviii/12 (1988), pp. 54–7
——: 'Enamelled Opera Glasses' *Ant. Colr*, lx/12 (1989), pp. 54–9
K. A. Snowman, ed.: *The Master Jewellers* (London, 1990)
Trésors d'émail: Catalogue des acquisitions, 1977–1992, Limoges, Mus. Mun. cat. (Limoges, 1992)

For further bibliography *see* §2 below.

ERIKA SPEEL

2. GOLD BOXES. The production of gold boxes in France extended from the first quarter of the 18th century to the mid-19th, and those designed and made in Paris at this time are unsurpassed in quality or variety. The manufacture of gold boxes eventually developed into a specialization of goldsmithing. The number of makers was relatively small, as the membership of the goldsmiths' guild in Paris at any one time was limited to 300, as decreed by Francis I in 1543. Decorative work was farmed out to enamellers, chasers, engravers and lapidaries. A number of preparatory drawings (Paris, Mus. A. Déc.; London, V&A) for gold boxes by such designers as Gabriel de Saint-Aubin and Gravelot survive.

As Louis XIV disliked snuff (and those who snuffed), the *boîte à portrait*, a type of flat gold box, usually with an enamelled portrait of either a member of the royal family or the nobility or a loved one, set either in the box or on the cover and used to confer royal favour or as a gift, was invented in the late 17th century. No snuff-boxes from the reign of Louis XIV are extant. The most elegant gold boxes were made after Philippe II, Duc d'Orléans, became Regent in 1715. He employed such artists as Gilles-Marie Oppenord, Juste-Aurèle Meissonnier, Antoine Watteau and Charles Cressent, who rejected the sombre magnificence of the Baroque style in favour of the light-hearted

Rococo. The makers of snuff-boxes began to incorporate depictions of flowers, birds, insects, shells and rocaille elements into their work.

To accommodate these motifs, a new design of snuff-box was developed, either shell-shaped or based on asymmetrical, scrolling Rococo forms, as exemplified by the designs (1727–31) of Meissonnier, which inspired the popular snuff-boxes of Daniel Gouers (Govaers; *fl* 1717–48; see fig. 87). His work is signed *Gouers à Paris*, and some of his pieces are characterized by the use of strips of diamonds to define scrollwork. He also produced some of the earliest surviving *boîtes à portrait* (1720s; Paris, Louvre; St Petersburg, Hermitage), set with portraits of Louis XV and Marie Leczyńska. Only one gold and lapis lazuli snuff-box (Geneva, J. Ortiz Patino priv. col., see Snowman, pl. 146) by Meissonnier survives: it is signed and dated 1728.

During the 1740s the manufacture of gold boxes in Paris developed into a well-organized industry involving a number of specialized trades. This is exemplified by the introduction of *tabatières à cage* or *en cage*, which are some of the most attractive French gold boxes (*see* SHELL, colour pl. I, fig. 2). These consist of a slender framework of gold fitted with panels of hardstone, mother-of-pearl, valuable Japanese lacquer, *vernis Martin* or such other materials as *poudre d'écaille*, a composition of powdered tortoiseshell dyed to the required tint. The gold cagework would be chased or engraved by a *ciseleur*, the most celebrated being Gérard Débêche (1706–after 1777), who signed his work. Some boxes were assembled in the shops of *marchands-merciers*, who also supplied panels and sometimes commissioned designs.

Snuff-boxes that are generally rectangular with panels of mother-of-pearl or hardstone, decorated with small, encrusted figural subjects in hardstone that are northern European in character, were made from *c.* 1745 to 1750. It is possible that these panels were composed in a German workshop controlled by the Meissen master Johann Martin Heinrici (1711–86) and exported to France and other European countries. Heinrici also specialized in inlay work

on lacquer, with various richly coloured and glinting materials, for example shell, tinted mother-of-pearl and tiny, bright squares of gold mosaic. This technique is known as *lac burgauté*.

During the 1740s the restless pattern of the Rococo was replaced by a far simpler form of rectangular, circular or oval box, with areas of flat-chased or engraved gold or carved mother-of-pearl, hardstone or lacquer panels held in cagework mounts and decorated with enamelled motifs. In the mid-18th century enamelling became the dominant method of decorating gold boxes. Initially painted enamel bouquets or lines of flowers or scrollwork covering all surfaces were featured; *en plein* enamels were also introduced at this time; popular themes included mythological subjects in the style of François Boucher (see fig. 88), as well as floral designs. Jean Moynat (*fl* 1745–61) specialized in the production of snuff-boxes decorated with flowers, possibly enamelled by Louis-François Aubert (*c.* 1721–55). Carved reserved areas with opaque enamel scenes or motifs, a popular decoration for Louis XV style boxes, are described as being enamelled *en plein sur fond réservé*. Gold boxes with blue or green *basse taille* enamels, particularly with designs of exotic birds or foliage (see fig. 86 above), were also fashionable.

The art of combining several colours of gold in a decorative scheme, known as *quatre-couleur* work, reached its peak in the mid-18th century in Paris. The properties of the metal added to the gold (usually in the proportion of 3.75 parts in the case of 20.25 carat gold used in France from 1721 to 1789) determines the colour of the resultant alloy. The addition of copper or silver produces red or green gold respectively. Blue or grey gold can be made by adding arsenic or steel filings. Many subtle shades are possible as the composition of the alloy is varied.

Panels painted in miniature or chased in coloured golds, reproducing paintings (or details from paintings) by fashionable artists or Renaissance masters, were employed on gold boxes in the late 1750s. Those represented most frequently are the French painters of *bergeries* or *scènes galantes*, for example Watteau, Boucher, Jean-Honoré Fragonard, Jean-Baptiste Greuze and Nicolas Lancret. Genre subjects by David Teniers (ii) and Jean-Siméon Chardin, as well as still-lifes and scenes from French and Dutch landscape paintings, were also popular. Jean Ducrollay (*fl* 1734–61) produced a number of boxes with decoration of this type.

Another prominent maker of gold boxes in the mid-18th century was Jean George (*fl* 1752–65), who, apart from his outstanding skills as a goldsmith, was also an adept businessman and had the acumen to buy all the flat, gold-mounted tortoiseshell patch-boxes made in Paris some 30 years earlier. Having engraved them with his firm's name, he sold them profitably as 'Georgettes' in the 1760s. These patch-boxes were much shallower than snuff-boxes, so that the patches, which were worn by men, as well as women, could be plucked out with ease.

Due to the gradual development of the Neo-classical style in the late 1750s and the 1760s, the wavy line, so characteristic of the flanges, decoration, cartouches and structure of gold boxes from the first half of the 18th century, was superseded by the ordered decoration and straight lines of the Louis XVI style. Each panel, whether

87. Red gold snuff-box by Daniel Gouers with a yellow gold *sable* belt round the waist, 86×27×60 mm, made in Paris, 1732–8 (New York, private collection)

above or below the opening of a box, had independent decoration, often including a wreathed medallion in the centre. The most striking characteristic is the use of designs inspired by Neo-classical architecture, often emphasized by such motifs as pilasters, capitals and pediments.

In the 1760s and 1770s gouache miniatures were set in gold cagework (for illustration *see* CHOISEUL, (1)). LOUIS-NICOLAS VAN BLARENBERGHE and Jacques Charlier (1720–90) were the outstanding painters in this field. During the same period Jacques-Joseph de Gault (*c*. 1738–1812) is said to have invented the technique of enamel painting in grisaille. Panels with classical scenes in this technique, including tiny figures that appear to have been carved from ivory or stone, were set into gold boxes. The most prolific makers of gold boxes in the third quarter of the 18th century were Charles Le Bastier (*fl* 1754–83), Pierre-François Drais (*fl* 1763–88), Pierre-François Mathis de Beaulieu (*fl* 1768–91), Jean-Marie Tiron (*fl* 1748–81) and Noël Hardivilliers (*fl* 1729–71).

The enamelling technique most commonly employed by the makers of Louis XVI style gold boxes consisted of a simple method involving the use of translucent enamel. Large, slightly sunken fields, usually rectangular, oval or circular, following the contours of the box, were engraved or more often engine-turned in patterns of wavy lines or circles and then enamelled *en plein* with several layers of translucent flux, allowing the patterns to be seen clearly. In the 1770s the most popular colours of enamel were red, dark blue and dark green and from *c*. 1780 midnight blue and purple. An opalescent effect was produced by using one layer of opaque or semi-opaque enamel. Painted scenes in coloured enamels, covered by a further layer of translucent enamel, were also popular. Borders with pearl and leaf designs were enamelled in white and green.

From about 1770 gold boxes for comfits or sweetmeats that had been termed *drageoirs* were known as *bonbonnières*. Examples in rock crystal were known as *boîtes à bonbons* because they enabled the brightly coloured sweets to be clearly seen. During the 1770s and 1780s mythological and allegorical subjects in enamel set in medallions were used on snuff-boxes, and portraits were rarely employed. One of the most prominent goldsmiths at this time was Adrien-Jean-Maximilien Vachette (1753–1839), who continued working in the Empire period.

After the Revolution, not surprisingly, the demand for gold boxes declined rapidly. *Tabletiers* (dealers in fancy goods and novelties) sold modest substitutes, for example boxes of wood, ivory, composition, shell or horn, that are of no great value. Charlotte Corday, Marat, Robespierre, the Bastille and even the guillotine are the subjects of the decoration on many of these boxes. Napoleon, however, approved of snuff-boxes, both as containers for the snuff he so enjoyed (he is reputed to have used no less than seven pounds a month at one point in his career) and as carefully chosen gifts to help a diplomatic campaign. Most of the boxes produced in the Napoleonic period, therefore, are *boîtes à portrait*, decorated with either a portrait of the Emperor (e.g. of 1809–14; London, V&A) or his monogram set in diamonds. Although it had become fashionable for women to take snuff in the Régence period, this custom was probably still prevalent in the Napoleonic era, as it is recorded that a type of small snuff-box, known as

88. Gold snuff-box by Jean-François Breton, enamelled *en plein* with subjects after François Boucher, the cover depicting *Apollo with his Lyre* and set with diamonds, 79×36×58 mm, 1753–4 (Los Angeles, CA, Rosalinde and Arthur Gilbert Private Collection)

a *demi journée*, was popular at this time. In the mid-19th century the production and quality of gold boxes declined sharply; most examples of this date are in the style of those of the 1760s and 1770s.

BIBLIOGRAPHY
L. Courajod ed.: *Livre–journal de Lazare Duvaux, marchand–bijoutier ordinaire du roy, 1748–1758*, 2 vols (Paris, 1873)
A. Maze-Sencier: *Le Livre des collectionneurs* (Paris, 1885)
H. Nocq: *Le Poinçon de Paris*, 5 vols (Paris, 1926)
E. Beuque and M. Frapsauce: *Dictionnaire des poinçons de-maîtres: Orfèvres français du XIV siècle à 1838* (Paris, 1929)
H. Nocq and C. Dreyfus: *Tabatières, boîtes et étuis* (Paris, 1930)
L. Carré: *A Guide to Old French Plate* (London, 1931)
H. Berry-Hill and S. Berry-Hill: *Antique Gold Boxes* (New York, 1960)
C. Le Corbeiller: *European and American Snuff Boxes, 1730–1830* (London, 1966)
J. Helft: *Le Poinçon des provinces françaises* (Paris, 1968)
D. Nyberg: *Meissonnier: An Eighteenth Century Maverick* (New York, 1969)
S. Grandjean, K. Aschengreen Piacenti, C. Truman and A. Blunt: *Gold Boxes and Miniatures of the Eighteenth Century: The James A. De Rothschild Collection at Waddesdon Manor* (Fribourg, 1975)
K. Blakemore: *Snuff Boxes* (London, 1976)
C. Le Corbeiller: *The Wrightsman Collection: Gold Boxes* (New York, 1977)
J. Helft: *Nouveaux poinçons* (Paris, 1980)
S. Grandjean: *Les Tabatières du Musée du Louvre* (Paris, 1981)
A. Somers Cocks and C. Truman: *The Thyssen-Bornemisza Collection: Renaissance Jewels, Gold Boxes and Objets de Vertu* (London, 1984)
A. K. Snowman: *Eighteenth Century Gold Boxes of Europe* (London, 1990)

A. KENNETH SNOWMAN

3. JEWELLERY. By the late Middle Ages gold- and silverwork, which included jewellery, was a thriving trade and was regulated through the guilds. Rings, *fermails* (clasps), brooches, pins and belts, which had been produced throughout the preceding centuries, continued to be made by craftsmen working primarily in Paris. By 1270 the *Livre des métiers* of Etienne Boileau, Provost of Paris, describes 120 corporations under his jurisdiction including gold- and silversmiths and 'cristalliers et perriers de pierre

89. Gold necklace with blue and white enamel, set with diamonds and hung with a pearl and a cabochon sapphire, l. 365 mm, *c.* 1670 (London, Victoria and Albert Museum)

naturelle'. Collars, which had become unfashionable in the 10th century, were worn again in the 13th, encouraged by Queen Margaret of Provence (1221–95), wife of Louis IX. He instigated the fashion for gold shoulder chains for men, which led (from the second half of the 14th century) to the tradition of the collars of the various orders of chivalry. Jewellery was extremely popular during the reign of the Valois kings, and in 1332 an edict was issued to protect the trade against paste imitations. The height of production was during the reign of Charles V (1364–80). Gemstones and pearls were increasingly used, while the techniques of engraving, chasing and, most brilliantly, the enamelling techniques of *basse taille* and *en ronde bosse*, a new technique that was developed in France and Burgundy in the late 14th century, were refined (*see* ENAMEL, §2(iii) and (iv); GOTHIC, §V, 2). Royal inventories record cameos, seals and intaglios, and Charles V presented an antique sardonyx cameo of Jupiter to the cathedral of Notre-Dame in Chartres after having it engraved with the first verse of the Gospel according to St John (now in Paris, Bib. N.). The Princes des Fleurs de Lys (royal princes) vied with the king in the magnificence and value of their jewellery; for example, Charles the Bold (*reg* 1467–77), Duke of Burgundy, owned the renowned 'Rose' and 'Plume' parures (15th century; untraced), later taken by the Swiss after the defeat of the House of Burgundy. Ornate bracelets became a love token worn by both sexes in the 15th century, and contemporary portraits (e.g. *Elisabeth of Austria* by François Clouet; Paris, Louvre)

reveal that pearls continued to be used in abundance; they were sewn on to the clothes of men and women, caught in the gold mesh of a *carcan* (large collar), *fronteau* (headdress) or *tressoir* (hairnet) and diadems for the women, and on crowns, belts, paternosters and clasps of all types for both men and women.

In the 16th century the French campaigns in Italy influenced the use of classical forms. Jewels and objects of vertu were brought back, and Italian goldsmiths worked at the French Court. For example, Matteo del Nassaro (*fl* 1515–47), an intaglio-carver from Verona, settled in Paris in 1515, where he cut a portrait of *Francis I* in grey agate (Paris, Louvre), and Benvenuto Cellini moved to Paris in 1537. The second Fontainebleau school promoted such French designers as René Boyvin and Jacques Androuet Du Cerceau the elder, as well as such Flemish designers as Hans Collaert and Cornelis Floris; their engraved designs led to the use of motifs of the nude and grotesques in both metalwork and gem-engraving, as well as to the renewed taste for pearls, which were worn by men as earrings, in the Spanish tradition, during the reign of Henry III (*reg* 1574–89). After the Treaty of Madrid in 1527, Francis I reorganized the administration of the crown jewels: La Chambre des Comptes was in charge of the royal treasure, which included three great rubies, the Côte de Bretagne (Paris, Louvre), L'A Romain and L'Oeuf de Naples (both untraced), which became the cornerstones of the royal wealth and were repeatedly pawned to raise funds. They appeared in the inventory of Louis XIV and made the royal jewels one of the first treasures of Europe whose settings would be changed according to fashion, a trend that influenced other European courts.

In the 17th century classicism superseded the Italianate Mannerism of the Fontainebleau style, and the art of the lapidary was developing more than that of the goldsmith. Diamonds became highly fashionable and remained so for two centuries owing to the increase in supplies following the discovery of new mines from 1650 to 1660. The rose-cut was introduced, giving greater brilliance to the stone than the former table-cut; the settings were also improved to give greater prominence to the stones. Designs by Gilles Légaré in his *Livre des ouvrages d'orfèvrerie* (Paris, 1663) illustrated this new tendency, together with the use of the bow (see fig. 89) and girandole (independent drop) shaped ornaments, which continued to be used until the 19th century. Although such traditional techniques as enamelling continued to be used (see fig. 89), it was the pearls, gemstones and diamonds that were brought back from Asia by Jean-Baptiste Tavernier (1605–89) in 1666 and J. Chardin in 1670 and 1677 that were most prized in jewellery. The inventory of the royal treasure of 1691 records a chain made for Louis XIV as well as 45 of the largest diamonds of the royal treasure, including the 18 Mazarin diamonds, which had been bequeathed to the Crown at the death of the minister in 1661. In 1665 the King had bought the 33-carat diamond known as Le Guise and in 1669 he wore the Diamant Bleu (now the Hope Diamond, Washington, DC, N. Mus. Nat. Hist.) at a reception for the Grand Turc. The Regent Diamond was bought by the Regent, Philippe II, Duc d'Orléans, for the coronation of Louis XV in 1722 and was displayed on the crown together with the Sancy Diamond (both Paris,

Louvre). Louis XVI had them recut to suit the new fashion; this disfiguring of historical pieces was a trend that continued after the Revolution.

During the reign of Louix XV the *à jour* or open setting was used, which lightened the design and gave more brilliance to the stones themselves. The pastoral fashion led to a new realism in jewellery design; sprays and feathers tied elegantly with bows and ribbons became popular (*see* JEWELLERY, fig. 5), while classical cameos and intaglios were also fashionable again; Mme de Pompadour was taught how to carve them by the expert carver Jacques Guay from 1752. In 1790 the royal treasure was given to the Assemblée Nationale; it was stolen in 1792 while stored in the Garde-Meuble Royal. Only the Regent and the Sancy diamonds were recovered, which the Directoire pawned in the former royal manner. Napoleon I had the Regent Diamond fitted on his sword-guard in 1811 and, enthused by the current taste for the Antique, had 24 cameos from the Imperial Library mounted by F. R. Nitot and Etienne Nitot (1750–1809) for the empress Josephine (1763–1814). Aquamarines, peridots and topazes were used in addition to other, more precious stones in settings inspired by the Antique. The extravagant expenditures of Napoleon (6 million francs for himself and his wife Marie-Louise) were matched only by those of the empress Eugénie from 1852 to 1870; her love of jewellery encouraged the fashion for gemstones, with designs that were heavily influenced by the past.

In 1894 RENÉ LALIQUE produced pieces of jewellery that broke with past tradition and heralded a new concept in design and style. Reacting against the emphasis given to gemstones, his designs incorporated hardstones, ivory and horn in brilliantly enamelled gold; he used motifs of the female form and such natural forms as flowers, insects and birds to create a sensuous setting on asymmetrical lines (*see* JEWELLERY, colour pl. II, fig. 1). This Art Nouveau style influenced such other artists and designers as Eugène Feuillatre (1870–1960), Eugène Gaillard and Georges Fouquet (1862–1957), for whom Alfonse Mucha produced many designs. Mucha was inspired by his favourite muse and model, the actress Sarah Bernhardt, for whom Lalique designed the Lotus Jewel (London, Garrick Club), which she wore as a hair ornament in the play *Yseyl* in 1894. These pieces were termed *bijoux pour le théâtre* because of their association with actresses and for their large size and exotic forms. The Exposition Universelle of 1900 in Paris marked the climax of the Art Nouveau style, with jewellery taking on an *objet d'art* quality, often with a Symbolist undertone, for example the 'Kiss' brooch of 1900 (Lisbon, Fund. Gulbenkian). At the Exposition Internationale des Arts Décoratifs et Industriels Modernes of 1925 in Paris such jewellery firms as Boucheron, founded in 1858, and Cartier, founded in 1897, were acclaimed for their exhibits, which used coloured stones, particularly rubies, in a new setting without cloisons between the stones. This technique created a seemingly effortless flow of light over the glittering gems and formed the basis of most luxury jewellery of the 20th century, with its renewed emphasis on the brilliance and value of the gemstones (*see* JEWELLERY, colour pl. II, fig. 3). During the second half of the 20th century there was a reaction to this trend with the

'artists' jewels', which were valued for their aesthetic qualities rather than for their intrinsic value. Jean Lurçat, a painter and tapestry designer, collaborated in 1959 with Patek Philippe to produce a range of brooches with a design of the moon and the sun (Paris, Pompidou), while in 1963 Braque exhibited 133 pieces of jewellery (Paris, Pompidou) he had realized together with Baron Henry-Michel Hegu de Lowenfeld. These were based on Classical myths and were executed in a Cubist style.

BIBLIOGRAPHY

J. Androuet Du Cerceau: *Bracelets, agraphes et pendants d'oreilles* (*c.* 1560–80/*R* Paris, 1979)

R. Boyvin: *Le Livre de la bijouterie de René Boyvin* (*c.* 1575/*R* Paris, 1979)

G. Légaré: *Livre des ouvrages d'orfèvrerie fait par Gilles l'Egare, orfèvre du roy* (Paris, 1663/*R* 1979)

A. Decle: *Historique de la bijouterie française* (Paris, 1889)

A. Lejard: *La Tradition française: L'Orfèvrerie, la joaillerie* (Paris, 1942)

E. Coche De La Ferte: *Bijoux du haut moyen-âge* (Lausanne, 1961)

Dix Siècles de joaillerie française (exh. cat., Paris, Louvre, 1962)

The Jewellery of René Lalique (exh. cat. by V. Becker, London, Goldsmiths' Co., 1987)

MONIQUE RICCARDI-CUBITT

4. HARDSTONES. As early as the 13th century there existed in Paris a guild of rock crystal- and hardstone-carvers. From the late 13th century onwards there was a notable development in the production of hardstones in France, based on a widespread interest in Court circles for gemstones, hardstones and cameos. French glyptic production in the Middle Ages, which favoured antique themes and unusual subject-matter, took firm hold, especially in Burgundy, until the 15th century, when production became the special province of Italian craftsmen. Linked to the renowned Franco-Burgundian production of the 15th century is a large onyx cameo in a later mount, carved with the figure of the dead Christ held by an angel (Florence, Pitti). Numerous examples of hardstone vases are listed in the inventories of Charles V, Jean, Duc de Berry, Louis I of Anjou, Philip the Bold, René, Duke of Lorraine, and Charles the Bold. A rock crystal goblet (Vienna, Ksthist. Mus.) that was owned by Philip the Good is decorated with circular designs, mounted in enamelled gold and set with diamonds, rubies and pearls.

Several Italian craftsmen were active in France from 1515 to 1547. Matteo del Nassaro (*fl*1515–47) of Verona, for example, worked at the Court of Francis I and executed several portraits of the King (e.g. Paris, Louvre) and oval onyx reliefs depicting hunting scenes and battles. The art of hardstone-carving during the 16th century reached its peak in the work of Olivier Condoré, Guillaume Duoré and Julien de Fontenay. During this period pendants were also produced, comprising a bust or torso hardstone relief mounted in enamelled gold and set with gemstones (e.g. agate cameo of a Moor; Madrid, Mus. Thyssen-Bornemisza).

The international Mannerist taste particularly suited the production of carved vases with gold mounts, as seen for example in the onyx ewer with gold mounts set with emeralds, rubies and diamonds (Vienna, Ksthist. Mus.) given by Charles IX to Archduke Ferdinand of Austria, Count of Tyrol (*reg* 1564–95), in 1570. Hardstone vases formed an important part of the great collection of Louis XIV, many of which can now be seen in the Musée du Louvre, Paris. An outstanding example is the ewer of sardonyx, lapis lazuli and agate, with mounts of enamelled gold and featuring a wide variety of motifs (see fig. 90). This bears the mark of a Parisian goldsmith, Pierre Delabarre, who was active in the first half of the 17th century. Cardinal Jules Mazarin was a particularly renowned collector of hardstones and possessed ebony cabinets with inlaid panels of Florentine pietre dure (see FLORENCE, §III, 2(i)). His copious correspondence with the Florentine abbot Luigi Strozzi is evidence of his constant interest in hardstone work. The demand for works of this type at the French Court was not matched by the presence of skilled craftsmen capable of executing hardstone pieces of similar quality to those produced in Florence. In 1668, seven years after the death of Mazarin, documentary evidence reports the existence in Paris of three Florentine craftsmen, Ferdinando Migliorini (c. 1638–83), Orazio Migliorini (c. 1643–78) and Filippo Branchi (c. 1638–99), who were active in the Gobelins workshops (see GOBELINS, §3). They were joined in 1670 by Gian Ambrogio Giachetti.

Objects of vertu employing hardstones continued to be produced well into the 18th century, especially snuff-boxes and *étuis*. Notable examples of hardstone carving could

be seen in the work of Jacques-Joseph de Gault (c. 1738–1812), Adrien-Jean-Maximilien Vachette (1753–1839) and Louis Siries, who moved to Florence in 1746. Hardstone carving was popular in the Neo-classical period, and vases carved in jasper, amethyst or polychrome marble with elaborate gilt-bronze mounts were fashionable. Pierre Gouthière was one of many who produced mounts for hardstone vases and tazze (e.g. pair of jasper perfume-burners; London, Wallace). In the mid-19th century hardstone work was highly reminiscent of Renaissance production, as, for example, the agate 'grape harvest' goblet, mounted in silver gilt, made in 1844 by the goldsmith François-Désiré Froment-Meurice (1802–55). His son, Emile Froment-Meurice (1837–1913), also produced works in rock crystal, among which is a *surtout de table* of silver and rock crystal made for Napoleon III in 1867 (Paris, Mus. A. Déc.). Vases, table decorations and small statuettes of polychrome marble and hardstone were widespread during the 19th century. The sculptor Charles-Henri-Joseph Cordier blended different materials in his exotic works, as in *Negro of the Sudan* (1857; Paris, Mus. d'Orsay), which has a bronze head but a bust and turban of onyx. Louis-Ernest Barrias also delighted in combining such coloured materials as marble, onyx and lapis lazuli, as can be seen in his *Nature Revealed to Science* (1899; Paris, Mus. d'Orsay).

BIBLIOGRAPHY

Y. Hackenbroch: 'Commessi', *Bull. Met.*, xxiv (1966), pp. 212–24
H. R. Hanloser: 'Début de l'art des cristalliers aux pays mosan et rhénan', *Mnmts Hist. France*, 1–2 (1966), pp. 19–23
D. Alcouffe: 'Le collezioni francesi di gemme del XVI secolo', *A. Illus.*, vii/59 (1974), pp. 264–78
——: 'The Collection of Cardinal Mazarin's Gems', *Burl. Mag.*, cxvi (1974), pp. 514–26
Y. Hackenbroch: *Renaissance Jewellery* (London, 1979), pp. 56–104
D. Alcouffe: 'Les Emailleurs français à l'Exposition Universelle de 1867', *Antol. B.A.*, iv/13–16 (1980)
A. Gonzalez-Palacios: 'La manifattura dei Gobelins a Parigi', *Mosaici e pietre dure: I quaderni dell'antiquariato* (Milan, 1981), pp. 35–50
D. Alcouffe: 'Le "Maître au dragon": Les Créations de l'orfèvre parisien Pierre Delabarre', *Rev. A.* (1988), pp. 47–56

ANNA MARIA MASSINELLI

5. IVORY AND BONE. Walrus, narwhal and elephant tusks were carved in France, as were bones of horses, oxen or whales, according to availability. In the Roman Empire, walrus tusks were used mostly for the carving of such small objects as sword guards and combs, which combined the classical style with the later use of animal and stylized vegetal forms (e.g. Sens, Trésor Cathédrale). In the Carolingian period a school of ivory-carvers, the Liuthard group, developed a naturalistic style (e.g. the *Miracle of Cana*, c. AD 875; London, BM). Another school, the Court school of Charlemagne (formerly known as the Ada group), worked in a more stylized manner, reminiscent of Near Eastern art and contemporary Italian wall-paintings.

11th- and 12th-century French ivory sculpture was mostly influenced by Eastern models, for example the Reliquary of St Cassien (12th century). In the north of France an English influence can be detected at Saint Omer, among other towns, where the 'Winchester' style was emulated. Few ivory-carvings have survived from between 1180 and 1260. Etienne Boileau, Provost of Paris, described ivory-carving in his *Livre des métiers* (c. 1261–70)

90. Ewer, sardonyx, lapis lazuli and agate, with enamelled gold mounts, by Pierre Delabarre, h. 280 mm, c. 1630 (Paris, Musée du Louvre)

as part of the sculptors' organization. During the late 13th century and the 14th the ivory trade between Asia, Africa and Europe grew steadily. There was such a great demand for ecclesiastical and secular objects that, despite the abundance of ivory, bone of various types was also used to produce polyptychs and statuettes, as well as such useful wares as caskets, mirror-cases (e.g. of the 14th century; Paris, Mus. Cluny; *see* MIRROR, fig. 8) and knife-handles. The addition of polychromy and gilding emphasized the mannered elegance of these objects in the French Gothic style, as in the *Coronation of the Virgin* group (*c.* 1250–60) and the *Virgin and Child of Sainte Chapelle* (*c.* 1250–60; both Paris, Louvre). Secular objects were often decorated with scenes of courtly love. Some carvers are mentioned by name: Jean le Braellier is noted in Charles V's inventory, and Berthelot Héliot (*fl* 1393) in the service of Philip the Bold, Duke of Burgundy.

A separate guild of ivory-carvers was recognized in 1507. Production had declined in the 15th century, but the quality remained high. In the 16th century only tusks were used, bone having been abandoned. Hanaps, drinking horns, powder horns, combs and boxes were among the items produced at this time. Jean Goujon and Jean Cousin (i) are mentioned as ivory-carvers, although better known as sculptor and painter respectively. In the 17th century JEAN MAUGER, Graveur de Medailles to Louis XIV, carved an ivory medallion depicting the King triumphing over heresy and set in an oval frame (*c.* 1700; Paris, Louvre). Jean-Baptiste Guillermin (1643–99) signed the *Christ of the Black Penitents* on a misericord (1659; Avignon, Mus. Calvet). Jean Milet, known as Francisque (1644–81), was in the service of Louis II, Prince de Condé in Flanders, and JEAN CAVALIER, a French carver resident in England, carved an ivory portrait of Queen Mary of England in 1686 (London, V&A).

At the end of the 17th century and the beginning of the 18th Dieppe became an important centre of ivory-carving. Seven carvers are recorded, among whom were Cointre, who specialized in statuettes of 'Gueux', beggars in the manner of Jacques Callot, Pierre Bienaymé, famous for his carvings of Christ, and Jean-Antoine Belleteste (1731–1811), who carved in ivory the *Four Seasons* at Versailles (Grand Trianon). Pierre Mariette's *Abecedario* gives the name of Joseph Villerme (*d* Rome, 1720), known for 'several crucifix of ivory and holly'. In the 19th century ivory-carvers in Dieppe imitated the finely pierced ivory fans imported from China. Alphonse Baude was renowned for this technique. Ivory was used in jewellery by Paul Vever (1851–1915) and Henri Vever (1854–1942) and René Lalique (the 'Kiss' brooch, 1900; Lisbon, Fund. Gulbenkian). Chryselephantine statuettes were made in the 19th century. Augustin Moreau-Vauthier (1831–93) exhibited *Fortune with Children* (destr.) at the Salon of 1881; it had an onyx base set with gold and precious gemstones supporting an enamelled sphere on which rested the ivory group. The fashion for this type of piece culminated in the 1920s and 1930s with work by Claire Jeanne Roberte Colinet (*fl* 1913–40), who specialized in statuettes of women in ballet poses, Henry Fugére (*b* 1872; *fl* until 1927) and Demeter Chiparus (1888–1950), a Romanian artist who produced erotic nudes and female figures in a manner influenced by the Ballets Russes.

BIBLIOGRAPHY

Lami
E. Bosc: *Les Ivoires* (Paris, 1889)
L. Grodecki: *Ivoires français* (Paris, 1947)
Tardy: *Les Ivoires: Evolution décorative du 1er siècle à nos jours*, 2 vols (Paris, 1972–7)
V. Arwars: *Art Deco Sculpture: Chryselephantine Statuettes of the 20's and 30's* (London, 1975)
D. Gaburit-Chopin: *Ivoires du moyen-âge* (Paris, 1978)

MONIQUE RICCARDI-CUBITT

XI. Textiles.

1. Tapestry. 2. Silk. 3. Embroidery. 4. Printed cotton. 5. Lace. 6. Carpets.

1. TAPESTRY.

(i) Before *c.* 1420. (ii) *c.* 1420–*c.* 1530. (iii) *c.* 1530–1657. (iv) 1658–1800. (v) After 1800.

(i) Before c. *1420.* The origins of tapestry in France are rather obscure. No satisfactory definition has been provided for *tapissiers sarrasinois*, a term first used in the *Livre des métiers* (*c.* 1261–70) of Etienne Boileau. It would seem, however, to allude to the Arabic origins of the technique of tapestry production, which was supposedly passed on to Westerners at the time of the invasion of Spain, or during the Crusades. The more specific term 'high warp' appeared shortly thereafter in Paris (1303) and Arras (1313).

During the first half of the 14th century production was limited. There are few references to the purchasing of tapestries, and designs appear to have been geometric patterns, emblems, birds and small animals. No works from this period survive: they were probably made with cheap materials, such as hemp warps. Around 1360 there was a change in design, including the introduction of figurative scenes. The use of tapestry increased in the courts of Europe, prompted, it would seem, by Louis I, Duke of Anjou, and soon followed by the other princes of the French royal family. There has been much speculation on the rapid development of the Parisian workshops at the end of the 14th century and on their sudden disappearance during the 15th. Lestocquoy (1978) noted that Paris was first and foremost a commercial centre, dominated by the important merchants NICOLAS BATAILLE, Jacques Dourdin (*d* 1407) and Pierre de Beaumetz (*fl* late 14th century; *d* 1411). Their accounts reveal that they ordered many of their supplies from Arras, and, after the death of Beaumetz, there were few traces of 'Parisian tapestry', although some sales of tapestries were recorded there in the second half of the century.

From *c.* 1340 until the mid-15th century the main centre of tapestry production was indisputably the town of Arras, which was patronized by the Dukes of Burgundy (*see* ARRAS, §2). Although relevant literature reveals that production was substantial, it is difficult to evaluate its artistic contribution as there are so few extant works. Except for the *Apocalypse* tapestries (1378–9; Angers, Château, Col. Tap.; *see* ANGERS, fig. 4), the remaining fragments of the *Nine Worthies* wall hanging (New York, Cloisters; *see* GOTHIC, fig. 114), as well as those of the *Presentation in the Temple* (Brussels, Musées Royaux A. & Hist.), can be dated to the end of the 14th century. While recognizing the influence of French illustrated manuscripts, it is essential to bear in mind that the disappearance of wall paintings of the time renders stylistic interpretation very difficult. The *Story of Jourdain de Blaye* (*c.* 1385; Padua, Mus. Civ.), of a more realistic nature, is innovative, as more importance is given to the landscape, into which the artist attempted to incorporate the characters. Among the well-known hangings are the *Battle of Roosbeek* (destr.) executed for Philip the Bold, Duke of Burgundy, in 1382, and the *Jousts of St Denis* (destr.) commissioned by Charles VI in 1397. These wall hangings were very imposing in size and were mainly used for civil or religious ceremonies.

Tapestries were also used for everyday decoration and were the main furnishings of the period. The exquisite *Annunciation* (*c.* 1400; New York, Met.; *see* TAPESTRY, fig. 5), which can be linked to the Late Gothic style, is an example of this highly refined art. In the *Offering of the Heart* (*c.* 1400; Paris, Mus. Cluny), elegant, dreamy-faced characters are set against a highly ornate *verdure* ground; this work and the tapestries *Scenes from Romances* (Paris,

Mus. A. Déc.), among others, reflect the courtly ideal of the end of the medieval period, which provided weavers with many popular themes.

For bibliography *see* §§(iii) and (v) below.

ISABELLE DENIS

(ii) c. 1420–c. 1530. The history of tapestry in France in the 15th century and at the beginning of the 16th is extremely complex, due to a lack of evidence. At this time painters, cartoon-makers and weavers moved from town to town; designs were sent to various disparate weaving centres and were often borrowed from engravings; a number of examples attest to the reworking of sometimes very old cartoons; and weavers inevitably imposed their own interpretation on designs. Attribution cannot therefore be based on stylistic criteria, and only written evidence (which is very scarce and rarely refers to surviving works) can be considered reliable.

91. Tapestry depicting *Winged Stags*, wool and silk, 3.47×3.80 m, *c.* 1450–60 (Rouen, Musée des Antiquités)

There was an abundance of commissions, both ecclesiastical and secular, at this time, but problems in establishing the origin and provenance of the works make it difficult to attribute them with any certainty. For example, the hypothesis of the 'Loire' workshops has been abandoned owing to a lack of documentary evidence. Flanders was undoubtedly important, especially such centres as Brussels, whose significance has recently been established, and Tournai. The role attributed to France has thus been undermined (see BELGIUM, §XI, 1). Although Parisian workshops had been prosperous at the end of the 14th century, there is evidence of only two tapestry makers in 1421, three in 1423 and none at all fifteen years later. Even so, in 1460–61 the chapter of the cathedral of St Maurice in Angers bought tapestries in Paris, and in 1484 the magistrate of Tournai bought a 'room' of tapestries for a seigneur of the French Court. But the suppliers of these may well have been simply merchants. The mainstream of work came from the powerful workshops of Arras, with such individuals as Jean Walois (d 1452) and Guillaume au Vaissel; these workshops were in operation during the first half of the 15th century but continued to produce until the end of the century. There were also craftsmen in many towns in the region, for example in Lille, Valenciennes and Saint-Omer. There were others elsewhere, notably in the central regions of France. At Felletin, near Aubusson in the province of La Marche, tapestries were being produced from the end of the 15th century at the latest, as many tapestries from this area appear in the inventory of the estate of Charlotte d'Albret, Duchesse de Valentinois, made after her death in 1514.

In the absence of sources, with a few exceptions, it is perhaps best to consider design and weaving separately, in order to characterize the diversity of French tapestry at the end of the Middle Ages. The artists who designed the delicately balanced *Winged Stags* (c. 1450–60; Rouen, Mus. Ant.; see fig. 91) and Charles VII's *Baillée de Roses* (New York, Met.) probably worked for the royal family. The tradition of symbolic and heraldic tapestries continued into the 16th century, as is shown by the set of hangings (1488–1515; Boston, MA, Mus. F.A.) bearing the arms and emblems of Louise of Savoy (1476–1531) and Charles, Comte d'Angoulême (1459–96), which already shows some Italian influences. Tapestries with religious subjects were very common. These were vast compositions or choir wall hangings of reduced height to fit over choir-stalls. According to contemporary critics, many of these reveal a Flemish taste, for example the *Life of St Stephen* (c. 1500; Paris, Mus. Cluny) commissioned c. 1490 by Jean Baillet, Bishop of Auxerre, or the *Life of St Peter* (untraced) made for Beauvais Cathedral in 1460; the latter was reminiscent of the style of Jacques Daret, who worked in Arras between 1446 and 1458. On the other hand, the *Life of the Virgin* (1500; *in situ*), made for the church of Notre-Dame in Beaune, must have been produced locally, since it was based on 21 scenes (untraced) by PIERRE SPICRE, a Burgundian painter, also made for the choir in Notre-Dame, in 1474–5. This cannot have been by any means the only example of commissions to local artists. In fact many hangings suggest similarities with illustrations in *Livres de piété* printed at this time in Paris, of which the most remarkable are the *Life of the Virgin* and the *Life of*

St Remigius given, respectively, to the cathedral of Notre-Dame and to the church of St Rémi in Reims by Archbishop Robert de Lenoncourt in 1530 and 1531 (see REIMS, §III). Historical subjects are also well represented, although such pastorals as the *Seigneurial Couple* (c. 1420–30; New York, Met.), which was inspired by Parisian courtly mannerism, were particularly in vogue c. 1500. With *millefleurs* backgrounds, they are considered some of the finest tapestries but are also particularly problematic to date and attribute with any certainty. The *Lady with the Unicorn* (c. 1490–1500; Paris, Mus. Cluny; see TAPESTRY, colour pl. I, fig. 1), a particularly outstanding example of this genre, may well have been designed in Paris, and the origins of the *Seigneuriale* (Paris, Mus. Cluny) or *Narcissus* (Boston, MA, Mus. F.A.) are also uncertain. Their controlled elegance and refinement are, however, entirely in keeping with the French tradition.

For bibliography see §§ (iii) and (v) below.

HERVÉ OURSEL

(iii) c. *1530–1657*. Numerous documents reveal the increasing activity of tapestry workshops in many French towns from c. 1530. Because tapestries were not marked, however, it is difficult to match surviving tapestries and known commissions, and it is virtually impossible to accredit tapestries to specific centres of production. Apart from the workshop in Fontainebleau, established by Francis I c. 1540 (see FONTAINEBLEAU, §2), there were also such weavers in Paris as Pierre Blasse and Jacques Langlois (*fl* 1537–55), who in 1543 were commissioned by Cardinal de Givry, Bishop of Langres, to work on eight hangings depicting the *Life of St Mammès* (two in Langres Cathedral; one in Paris, Louvre; for illustration see COUSIN, (1)) based on cartoons by Jean Cousin (i). Although still archaic in composition, using a series of episodes juxtaposed in a single work, these tapestries nevertheless show the influence of the Renaissance: the frames consist of strapwork motifs, and the style of architecture represented is Classical. Stylistic and technical similarities allow for a comparison of these tapestries to the *Story of Diana* series (Château of Anet; Rouen, Mus. B.-A.; New York, Met.), the cartoons of which were provided by painters of the Fontainebleau school; they are even more innovative in their increased sense of perspective, as well as in their repertory of decorative borders directly inspired by Classical design.

Finely executed warping and cursive writing, setting off grey-monochromed motifs against a coloured background, are the main features of such grotesque tapestries as *Cybele* (Paris, Mobilier N.), which is marked with the initials of Henry II and Diane de Poitiers, or the *Death of Joab* (c. 1566–85; Paris, Mobilier N.), made for the Marshal of La Châtre. Jacques Androuet Du Cerceau the elder, Nicolò dell'Abate and Francesco Primaticcio are names associated with the design of these works, but the weaving cannot definitely be attributed to Fontainebleau.

From 1551 the Atelier de la Trinité, located in a hospital in the Rue St Denis, Paris, taught orphans the high-warp technique. Of the *Life of Christ*, commissioned from this workshop in 1584 for the church of St Merri, Paris, only two rather coarsely woven fragments remain (Paris, Mobilier N. and Mus. Cluny), as well as 27 drawings (Paris, Bib. N.) attributed to Henri Lerambert (1550–1609). There were also workshops at this time in such provincial towns as Charleville, Reims and Toulouse. The most important area, however, was the Creuse, where workshops in Aubusson and nearby Felletin became very productive in the second half of the 16th century. The production of this region was rather rustic in style and mainly restricted to *verdures* and hunting scenes; they are also difficult to distinguish from similar tapestries woven in Flanders. Eventually, however, the subject-matter was broadened to include romances and the lives of saints. They were often copied from engravings and were created in a limited range of colours (blues, yellows, browns) with quite thick wool.

Paris, however, increasingly rose to prominence at this time as the most important centre of French tapestry production. In 1597 Henry IV decided to bring together the various independent workshops in and around Paris to form a factory capable of competing with the more successful Flemish workshops. A high-warp workshop was initially set up in the former Jesuit establishment in the Faubourg St Antoine and then in the Galeries du Louvre. The factory continued to function until c. 1660 under the management of Girard Laurent (d 1616) and Maurice Dubout (d 1611) and their successors. The most important event, however, in the history of Parisian tapestry production was the establishment in 1607 of a workshop in the Hôtel des Gobelins in the Faubourg St Marcel. The workshop was run by two Flemish weavers, Marc de Comans (d 1644) and François de La Planche (van den Plancken; 1573–1627), and was given many privileges. In return the workers had to mark their low-warp tapestries and keep 80 looms in use—60 in Paris, the rest in Tours (see TOURS, §2(ii)) and Amiens (see AMIENS, §2(ii)). The products of the new factory were largely embellished with silk and gold thread. They rapidly acquired international acclaim and were exported all over Europe. The workshop of de La Planche's son Raphaël de La Planche (fl 1625–61) was transferred to the Faubourg St Germain in 1633 and long remained known for the exceptional workmanship and outstanding quality of its tapestries.

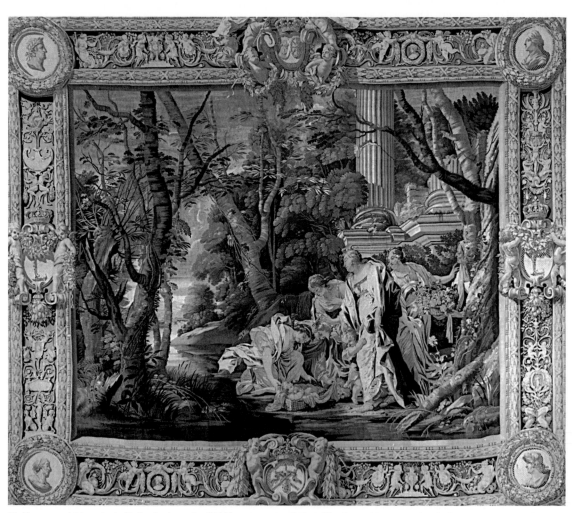

92. Tapestry of *Moses in the Bullrushes* from the *Old Testament* series designed by Simon Vouet, wool and silk, 4.95×5.88 m, made at the Galeries du Louvre, Paris, c. 1630–40 (Paris, Musée du Louvre)

Until *c.* 1625 Parisian wall hangings were greatly influenced by earlier designs. For the *Story of Diana*, Toussaint Dubreuil was inspired by the tapestries of Diane de Poitiers, while the *Story of Artemisia*, in the style of Antoine Caron, was taken from a manuscript given to Catherine de' Medici in 1562. Both works were very popular and were copied numerous times. Although the series the *Story of Constantine* (*c.* 1623–5; Philadelphia, PA, Mus. F.A.; *see* TAPESTRY, fig. 9), designed by Rubens and made in the St Marcel workshop, did not seem to exert any influence on Parisian tapestry at this time, the return of SIMON VOUET to Paris from Italy in 1627 marked an important turning-point. Such wall hangings as the *Old Testament* (see fig. 92), *Renaud and Armide* and the *Story of Ulysses*, which were produced from his cartoons, employed a new spatial layout. Instead of using a basic gradation of colours, Vouet introduced a dynamic use of light. Wide, oblique rays of light created a series of contrasting scenes, which were arranged like a theatre set. Vouet's new range of bright colours, used to dye the silk thread, was a further innovation. Vouet also employed deep frames filled with putti, medallions, foliage and arabesques set against yellow and blue grounds. Vouet carried out these works with the help of a team of specialists including Justus van Egmont, Pierre Patel (i) and Jean Cotelle I (1607–76).

Vouet's style was continued by some of his students, including Eustache Le Sueur and Michel Corneille (i), whose use of bright colours and uncluttered compositions were aspects of Vouet's work and long influenced the style of Parisian tapestries. However, the works of Georges Lallemant, Claude Vignon, Philippe de Champaigne, Laurent de La Hyre and Sébastien Bourdon exhibit extremely different pictorial tendencies, favouring the lyrical and monumental aspects of an art that was frequently represented in painted galleries at the time.

ISABELLE DENIS

BIBLIOGRAPHY
J. Guiffrey: 'La Tapisserie aux XIVe et XVe siècles', *Histoire de l'art*, ed. A. Michel, iii/1 (Paris, 1909), pp. 343–74
L. Deshairs: 'La Tapisserie au XVIe siècle', *Histoire de l'art*, ed. A. Michel, v/2 (Paris, 1913), pp. 887–920
G.-J. Demotte: *Tapisserie gothique*, 2 vols (Paris, 1924–6)
Le Seizième Siècle européen: Tapisseries (exh. cat., ed. G. Viatte; Paris, Mobilier N., 1965–6)
Chefs d'oeuvre de la tapisserie gothique du XIVe au XVIe siècle (exh. cat., ed. F. Salet and G. Souchal; Paris, Grand Pal., 1973–4)
J. Lestocquoy: *Deux siècles de l'histoire de la tapisserie, 1300–1500* (Arras, 1978)
F. Joubert: 'La Tapisserie au XIVe siècle', *Les Fastes du gothique* (exh. cat., Paris, Grand Pal., 1981–2), pp. 388–93
——: *La Tapisserie médiévale au Musée de Cluny* (Paris, 1987)
F. Salet: 'Remarques sur le vocabulaire ancien de la tapisserie', *Bull. Mnmtl*, cxlvi (1988), pp. 211–29
I. Denis: 'L'Histoire d'Artémise, commanditaires et ateliers: Quelques précisions apportées par l'étude des bordures', *Bull. Soc. Hist. A. Fr.* (1991), pp. 21–36
A. S. Cavallo: *Catalogue of the Medieval Tapestries in the Metropolitan Museum*, 2 vols (New York, 1993)
La Chasse au vol au fil des temps (exh. cat., Gien, Mus. Int. Chasse, 1994)
For general bibliography *see* §(v) below.

ISABELLE DENIS, HERVÉ OURSEL

(iv) 1658–1800. This was the most important period in the history of French tapestry production, when some of the most outstanding European tapestries were made. French tapestry manufacturers seized the markets, which had previously been dominated by the Flemish factories, and became the most important producers of hangings in Europe. In 1658 NICOLAS FOUQUET, King Louis XIV's Surintendant des Finances, set up a workshop in Maincy outside Paris, in order to provide furnishings for his nearby château of Vaux-le-Vicomte. The painter CHARLES LE BRUN was director of this private concern and he was assisted by *c.* 25 Franco-Flemish weavers under the management of the Parisian Loys Blamars. The workshop produced such sets as the *Famous Men* and the eight-piece *Story of Constantine*. After the arrest of Fouquet in 1661, the tapestry workshop and the château were confiscated by the Crown. Jean-Baptiste Colbert (*see* COLBERT, (1)) took this opportunity to reform the tapestry industry in France by bringing the workshop in the Hôtel des Gobelins (*see* §(iii) above) in Paris under the directorship of Le Brun. The Gobelins (*see* GOBELINS, §2) was opened in 1663 and it was given the official title of Manufacture Royale des Meubles de la Couronne in 1667. The workshop was intended to supply luxury furnishings for the royal palaces and contribute to the image of French cultural supremacy, which Colbert and Louis XIV were keen to promote. This image was so important to French propaganda policy that Colbert was directly involved in the Gobelins workshop, and in 1664 he was given the official title of Surintendant des Bâtiments et Ordonnateur Général, Arts et Manufactures. There were *c.* 250 workers under Le Brun who were organized to work in one of the three high-warp workshops run by Jean Lefèbvre (1600–75), Henri Laurent and Jean Jans (*fl* 1662–8) or in the one low-warp workshop, which was managed by Jean de La Croix and Jean-Baptiste Mozin (*fl* 1667–93). There were also groups of painters, dyers and *c.* 60 apprentices. Such painters as Jean-Baptiste Monnoyer and Gilbert de Sève were employed to work up cartoons based on Le Brun's designs; cartoons from Maincy were also used at the Gobelins.

The Gobelins tapestries were of a very high standard and were strictly reserved for the Crown. Several copies of a set were often woven and presented as royal gifts abroad. It was not just the quality of the tapestries that enhanced the image and reputation of the French Crown but also the subject-matter, which was specifically chosen by Le Brun to glorify Louis XIV: for example in *The Seasons* (Paris, Mobilier N.), designed in 1664, royal palaces are depicted in the distance, while in the now famous *Story of the King* (1665–78; Versailles, Château), designed in 1662, Louis XIV is shown carrying out various functions, such as visiting the Gobelins where he is surrounded by all the luxurious items made for him in the factory (*see* GOBELINS, fig. 1). *The Months* (*see* TAPESTRY, colour pl. II, fig. 2), or the *Royal Households* (1676; Paris, Mobilier N.), realistically depicts such châteaux as Versailles and Blois, set in verdant landscapes with elaborate architectural frames, which provided an image of the wealth of the French Crown.

Colbert was also responsible for organizing a tapestry workshop at Beauvais in Picardy in 1664 (*see* BEAUVAIS, §2). This was established in conjunction with the tapestry dealer Louis Hinart (*d* 1697), who was the first director. Although the workshop had royal protection, it remained an independent concern, and its clients were mainly courtiers and wealthy individuals. The factory, however,

93. Tapestry hanging from the series *Victories of Charles V* designed by Jean-Baptiste Martin I and Jean-Louis Guyon, 4.30×8.05 m, 1711–18 (Vienna, Kunsthistorisches Museum)

struggled under Hinart, and the King became the sole owner in 1684, at which time Philippe Béhagle (Behaegel; *fl* 1684–1704), a Flemish tapestry merchant from Oudenaarde, was put in charge of production. In anticipation of the lighter, more frivolous style of 18th-century tapestry, the factory produced such sets as *The Grotesques* on a yellow ground (1685–1720; four in London, V&A), which was designed by Monnoyer based on engravings by Jean Berain I.

As well as the Gobelins and Beauvais, there were other, smaller tapestry factories in production in the 17th century. In 1665 Colbert made enquiries into the workings of the workshops of Aubusson and Felletin on the banks of the River Creuse in the province of La Marche (*see* AUBUSSON, §1). These workshops had probably been in operation since the 14th century, but the work was of rather poor quality and was made only for local use. Colbert, however, recognized their potential, reorganized them and gave them a royal charter. Throughout the 17th century weavers were mainly forced to copy cartoons and engravings from other workshops, and on the whole production was limited to mythological scenes and *verdure* tapestries. It was not until the 18th century that the standard of production really improved when Aubusson finally received its own designer in 1732.

Lille became a centre of tapestry production of some importance after the Flemish weaver Georges Blomaert set up a workshop there in 1680 (*see* LILLE, §3(ii)). André de Pannemaker and François de Pannemaker, members of a weaving family from Brussels, ran a small workshop producing *verdures* in Lille for over 50 years. More important than both of these establishments, however, was that set up in 1688 by Jean de Metten, a weaver from Brussels,

who was succeeded in 1701 by his son-in-law Guillaume Waerniers (Wenier; *d* 1738). By 1713, 21 looms were in operation, producing such high-quality tapestries as the *Story of Don Quixote* after Antoine Coypel and the *Marriage Feast at Cana*. After Waerniers's death, the workshop was of little importance, although production continued until *c*. 1775.

In 1698 Leopold, Duke of Lorraine (*reg* 1698–1729), reopened a workshop that had been established in Nancy in the early 17th century and had been closed during the Thirty Years War (*see* NANCY, §3). In order to commemorate the memory of his father, Charles V, nominal Duke of Lorraine, Leopold commissioned a series of hangings called the *Victories of Charles V* (1703–10) after cartoons by Charles Herbel and woven by Charles Mité; this first set was not altogether satisfactory, and the Duke commissioned another set from cartoons by Jean-Baptiste Martin I in collaboration with Jean-Louis Guyon, from which were woven the 'large hanging' of the *Victories of Charles V* (1711–18; Vienna, Ksthist. Mus.; see fig. 93). Continued problems at the workshop, however, forced some workers to go to the new workshop set up in the nearby town of Lunéville in 1718, under the leadership of Josse Bacor and Sigisbert Mengin. In 1723 Bacor left Lunéville and set up another workshop in the château of La Malgrange on the outskirts of Nancy. Other regional centres of tapestry production were Amiens, Tours and Valenciennes.

In April 1694 the Gobelins was forced to close because of the continuing wars and for financial reasons; many of the weavers left and returned to Flanders or went to Beauvais. The factory was, however, reopened in January 1699 and almost immediately began production of tapestries in a lighter style, which set the trend for the 18th century. The first of these were the eight *Portières des dieux* and the twelve *Grotesque Months* designed by Claude Audran III. One of the most popular sets from the Gobelins was the *Story of Don Quixote* (1714; Rome, Pal. Quirinale; Stockholm, Kun. Husgerådskam.) designed by Charles-Antoine Coypel, which was the first series of tapestries to feature *à alentours* borders; these were deep, elaborately decorated frames comprising such motifs as ribbons, floral swags, putti, trophies and birds surrounding a central cartouche.

In keeping with the Rococo style, tapestries in the 18th century were conceived as purely ornamental; they were expected to imitate paintings, and the weaver was obliged to reproduce the cartoon exactly. A much wider colour range was introduced so that more subtle shades, reminiscent of the range of colours possible in paintings, could be achieved. Colbert's regulations of 1671, which had forbidden the use of non-fast (*petits teints*) colours, were ignored, and many new dyes were developed; for example, the *Legate's Audience* (1680; Paris, Mobilier N.) designed by Le Brun used only 79 shades, while *The Bloodhound* (1740) employed 364. The subject-matter of 18th-century tapestries was also very different from the more grandiose subjects of the late 17th century. There was a strong reaction against the mythological and historical subjects and grand themes typical of the Baroque style. Lighter and more frivolous Rococo subjects, including pastoral and genre scenes, chinoiseries and grotesques, were particularly popular and were more suitable forms of decoration for the smaller, more intimate apartments in Parisian hôtels and at Versailles.

One of the most influential tapestry designers of the 18th century was JEAN-BAPTISTE OUDRY. In 1726 he became the chief draughtsman at Beauvais and was instrumental in reviving the flagging reputation of the factory. Oudry specialized in animal and pastoral subjects, and his most famous works include the sets the *Hunts of Louis XV* (Florence, Pitti) and *Rural Pleasures*. Oudry was also known for his designs for tapestry-woven upholstery; a set of designs illustrating the *Fables of La Fontaine* formed the basis for sets of chair-covers woven in Beauvais and other centres. In March 1734 Oudry became director of Beauvais and quickly brought in the painter FRANÇOIS BOUCHER as factory painter. Boucher was hugely successful at Beauvais and designed some of the factory's most successful series. His early work includes the two sets called *Fêtes italiennes*, the first of which was designed in 1736 and woven by 1739, while the second was woven from 1742 (e.g. of *c.* 1762; New York, Met.; *see* BEAUVAIS, fig. 5). Boucher's next series were the *Story of Psyche* (1741–2; Rome, Pal. Quirinale; Stockholm, Kun. Husgerådskam.), which was designed in 1739, and the *Loves of the Gods* (e.g. in London, Osterley Park House, NT; *see* TAPESTRY, fig. 10), designed in 1747 and woven from 1749; the latter was also later made at the Gobelins. After Oudry's death in 1755, Boucher went to the Gobelins, where he became the Inspecteur sur les Ouvrages, and stopped supplying designs for Beauvais.

In keeping with the taste for the exotic, such tapestries as the *Chinese Hangings*, designed by Boucher for Beauvais in 1742, and the *New Indies* (Vienna, Ksthist. Mus.), designed by François Desportes in 1735 and made at the

Gobelins, were also popular; the latter consists of eight subjects, including *The Elephant*, the *Combat of Animals* and the *King Borne by Two Moors*. The set called the *Turkish Costume*, designed by Amédée van Loo and woven in 1777 at the Gobelins, also exploits this taste.

The 18th century was a particularly prosperous period for Aubusson and Felletin. In 1732 the painter Jean Joseph Du Mons gave the factory new impetus as he provided the weavers with new cartoons. The dyer Firmazeau, who was sent to Aubusson from the Gobelins, provided the necessary technical help. During the 18th century large quantities of tapestry hangings and furniture coverings were produced at Aubusson, mainly with pastoral scenes. Cartoons used at Beauvais and the Gobelins were also copied, with typical Rococo-style subject-matter.

During the second half of the 18th century, Neoclassical tapestries were produced at Beauvais, Aubusson and the Gobelins. The French Revolution, however, destroyed the market on which the tapestry trade largely relied, and, although production did continue, it was on a much reduced scale.

BIBLIOGRAPHY
M. Block: *François Boucher and the Beauvais Tapestries* (Boston, 1930)
European Tapestries of the 18th Century (exh. cat., Detroit, MI, Inst. A., 1930)
Charles Le Brun: Premier directeur de la Manufacture royale des Gobelins (exh. cat., ed. M. Florisoone; Paris, Mus. Gobelins, 1962)
For general bibliography *see* §(v) below.

DIANA FOWLE

(v) After 1800. The history of tapestry in France after 1800 concerns mainly the factories of the Gobelins, Beauvais and Aubusson. During the First Empire (1804–14), following the turmoil of the French Revolution, the Gobelins turned to the production of historical scenes based on cartoons by Antoine-Jean Gros, David and Carle Vernet. New tapestries were made depicting 13 scenes from the *Story of Marie de' Medici* using cartoons by Rubens. During the Second Empire (1852–70), a number of historical portraits were woven, together with those of Napoleon III and his wife, the empress Eugénie, which were based on the paintings of Franz Xaver Winterhalter. Tapestries based on the compositions of Paul Baudry and Diéterle were also made. In addition weavers continued to copy such Old Masters as Boucher. At Beauvais production was concentrated on the manufacture of furnishings for the royal palaces between 1800 and 1819, and during the Second Empire it produced very little apart from work for the Emperor's household.

The most important factory in Europe during the 19th century, however, was Aubusson. While the other factories had encountered enormous difficulties during the French Revolution, Aubusson was more adaptable, and the successful production of moquette—a velvety piled fabric—enabled the factory to continue production right through into the 19th century. The most important factories in Aubusson were those run by Rogier, Debel and, particularly during the Restoration, Sallandrouze de la Mornaix. Between 1812 and 1842 carpet production at Aubusson became increasingly important (*see* AUBUSSON, §2).

Although revival styles became increasingly popular in the decorative arts during the mid-19th century, tapestry production was, despite some attempts by Fernand Maillaud Flandrin, quite unaffected. Throughout the 19th century there was an increasing demand for tapestries for upholstery purposes, including seat-covers, for chairs and sofas, and curtains, from all the important French factories. All types and qualities were made, and the trend continued into the 20th century. After World War I such artists as RAOUL DUFY, Leonetto Capiello, Gaudissart and Valtat were employed to design furnishing tapestries for Beauvais. From 1922 an interesting experiment was attempted by the collector Marie Cuttoli: such artists as Fernand Léger, Miró, Braque, Lucien Coutaud (b 1901) and Dufy (see fig. 94) were encouraged to reproduce their paintings in tapestry at Aubusson. The experiment was only moderately successful, for artists were not as directly involved in the production of the tapestries as they might have been.

Despite the serious economic difficulties encountered by the tapestry industry at the end of the 1920s, a new and exciting period began during the 1930s, and the painter Jean Lurçat (see LURÇAT, (1)) was to prove instrumental in this revival. In 1936 he was commissioned by the Gobelins to produce the *Illusions of Icarus* (1936; The Hague, Kon. Huisarchf). In 1937 he went to Aubusson, where he studied the techniques employed in medieval tapestries and introduced new working methods, which enabled more efficient and cheaper production. Together with Marcel Gromaire and Pierre Dubreuil (1891–1970) he produced the *Four Seasons* tapestries (1939; Paris, Mobilier N.).

In 1945 Lurçat set up the Association des Peintres-Cartonniers de Tapisserie at Aubusson. The group included the artists Robert Henry, Vincent Guignebert,

Jacques Lagrange, Denise Majorel, Jean Picart-le-Doux (1902–81), Marc Saint-Saëns (b 1903) and Robert Wogensky, and its aim was to reproduce the work of famous painters in tapestry. At the same time the Adnet brothers, under the name Compagnie des Arts Français, produced tapestries based on designs by such artists as Coutaud, Rohner and Despierre.

The movement to encourage the production of new tapestries was so successful that both private dealers and public collections began to show an interest in purchasing tapestries. At La Galerie La Demeure, established by Majorel, French tapestries were exhibited and gained an international reputation. The artist Pierre Baudouin (1921–70) introduced such famous artists as Henri-Georges Adam (1904–67), Braque, Alexander Calder, Charles Lapicque, LE CORBUSIER and Picasso to the art of tapestry production, and their work was woven at Aubusson, where the Gobelins had moved in 1939. Outside Aubusson many tapestry workshops were established, for example by Jacqueline D'rrbach, Yvette Cauquil-Prince and Marie Moulinier, and in Angers and Saint-Cyr. In the late 20th century the interest in tapestry production continued in France, and new working methods and art forms were developed. At the factories works designed by such contemporary artists as Pincemin, Hartung and Rouan were woven.

BIBLIOGRAPHY
J. Lurçat and others: *La Tapisserie française: Muraille et laine* (Paris, 1946)
                                    MARTINE MATHIAS

GENERAL
A. Jubinal: *Les Anciennes Tapisseries historiées, ou collection des monuments les plus remarquables de ce genre qui nous soient restés du moyen âge, à partir du XIe siècle au XVIIIe siècle inclusivement*, 2 vols (Paris, 1818–39)
J. J. Guiffrey, E. Müntz and A. Pinchart: *Histoire générale de la tapisserie*, 3 vols (Paris, 1878–85)
J. Deville: *Recueil de statuts et de documents relatifs à la corporation des tapisseries depuis le moyen âge jusqu'à nos jours* (Tours, 1886)
M. Fenaille: *État général des tapisseries de la manufacture des Gobelins depuis son origine jusqu'à nos jours, 1600–1900*, 5 vols (Paris, 1903–23)
W. G. Thomson: *A History of Tapestry* (London, 1906, rev. Wakefield, 3/1973)
J. Badin: *La Manufacture des tapisseries de Beauvais depuis son origine jusqu'à nos jours* (Paris, 1909)
H. Göbel: *Wandteppiche*, 3 vols (Leipzig, 1923–34; Eng. trans. of vol. i, New York, 1924)
J. J. Marquet de Vasselot and R.-A. Weigert: *Bibliographie de la tapisserie, des tapis et de la broderie en France* (Paris, 1935)
G. F. W. Digby: *French Tapestry from the 14th to 18th Century* (London, 1951)
R.-A. Weigert: *La Tapisserie française* (Paris, 1956; Eng. trans., London, 1962)   □

94. Tapestry of *Mozart's House* designed by Raoul Dufy, 1.38×1.13 m, 1934 (private collection)

2. SILK. Silk has been woven in France from at least the 14th century, but most of the centres, including Aix-en-Provence, Avignon, Lyon, Marseille, Montpellier, Nîmes, Orange, Paris, Reims, Rouen, Tours and Troyes, made plain or narrow fabrics largely for local sale (see SILK). Until the late 17th century the European silk industry was dominated by Spain and Italy, although a French factory had been established at Avignon, when the Papal Court moved there in 1309. Avignon was known for its *popeline* (poplin), a mixed silk and wool fabric, and, although its importance dwindled when the popes returned to Rome (1377) and was later overshadowed by other centres, it was again prosperous in the 16th century, when

it specialized in velvet production; it survived as a centre until the late 18th century.

During this early period, most silks were imported into France from Italy and the Near East. Lyon was well placed geographically on the main trade route from the Mediterranean to northern Europe and it had long been a centre for the distribution of imported Italian silks (*see* LYON, §3(ii)). Purchase of these Italian silks, however, resulted in a large outflow of cash, which the Crown was eager to avoid in an attempt to build up the economy. Louis XI was therefore keen to foster the French silk industry and create a rival to the Italian centres of production. Louis's first attempt in 1466 to establish a silk-weaving industry in Lyon was strongly resisted, however, by merchants who had a vested interest in the importation of foreign silks, and the industry was instead set up at Tours in 1470. Tours was well placed, being on the River Loire within reach of both Paris and Orléans and having many important families living in the surrounding area. Tours was granted many privileges by the King, including various tax exemptions, and by 1490 there were *c.* 100 looms in operation. The success of the industry in Tours presented a threat to Lyon; it petitioned for and was granted comparable privileges in 1536. In addition it was given the sole rights over the import of raw silk, on which all other French centres of production were obliged to pay a substantial duty. Nevertheless the industry in Lyon was slow to develop, and throughout the 16th century the city's very simple silks were unable to compete with the imported Italian figured silks. In the north of France, Paris, Orléans and Rouen (which received its permit in 1543) also became important centres of silk production.

The 17th century was an increasingly prosperous period for the French silk industry; the accession of Henry IV in 1589 and the resulting peace marked the beginning of a period of stability and economic reconstruction. The King was keen to encourage the French textile industries, and he and his minister Baron de Rosny (from 1606 Duc de Sully) were determined to build up the domestic silk industry to such a position that it would rival that of Italy. As an initial boost to the trade, the importation of all foreign silks was prohibited for one year in 1599. Of lasting importance was the introduction of widespread sericulture in southern France in an effort to achieve self-sufficiency in the raw material. Barthélemy de Laffemas supervised the planting of ten million mulberry trees in the Venaissin in Provence and wrote a treatise encouraging landowners to plant such trees; the King led the way by planting *c.* 100 km of trees around the Tuileries in Paris.

Efforts were also made to encourage the diversification of types of weaves. French weavers mainly produced plain silks, while the Italians specialized in elaborate figured silks and velvets, which dominated the top end of the market. An edict of 1599 authorized the weaving of silks in the Italian manner, in an attempt to encourage the French weavers to copy the more accomplished Italians. This was not very effective as the French lacked the technical skill of the Italians. In order to rectify this the Milanese weaver Claude Dangon was brought to Lyon in 1604–5 to make adjustments to the draw loom; by 1610 there were 19 looms in the city producing complex silks and polychrome velvets. Throughout the 17th century the French silk industry, with the protection of the Crown, became increasingly powerful. A sumptuary law of 1614 was designed to encourage the sale of rich silks, and in 1665 Jean-Baptiste Colbert, Surintendant et Ordonnateur Général des Bâtiments et Manufactures (*see* COLBERT, (1)), introduced new codes of practice and regulations regarding the production of silk. In 1667 the import of foreign silks was prohibited once again.

During this period Tours was the main centre of silk production, closely rivalled by Lyon. Many smaller factories were established in such towns as Reims, Troyes and Miaux. One of the most important new centres was the royal factory set up by Marcelin Charlier in Saint-Maur-les-Fossés, near Paris, probably during the mid-17th century. The silks produced there were of a very high standard and were woven specifically for the Crown. The high regard in which they were held is demonstrated by the fact that in 1686 brocaded silks produced in Saint-Maur were given by Louis XIV to the King of Siam. The factory probably closed after the death of Charlier, and unfortunately there are no documented surviving products.

By the end of the 17th century the French silk industry had successfully achieved its aim of rivalling the Italians. From *c.* 1680, however, the industry in Tours began to decline. The reasons for this were numerous: foreign markets were lost during the wars of the late 17th century and the early 18th; many of the workers who were Huguenots left Tours after the revocation of the Edict of Nantes (1685) and emigrated to more tolerant countries. The competition from Lyon, which had the advantage of the customs monopoly on raw silk, proved to be too much

95. Brocaded silk damask, probably made in Lyon, *c.* 1715 (London, Victoria and Albert Museum)

for Tours, and Lyon gradually took over all the markets previously dominated by Tours. Despite its distance from Paris, the well-organized Lyonese industry maintained close links with the Court, providing it with high-quality figured silks. The city also increased its range of half-silks and plain silks including brocaded damasks (see fig. 95). In the 1650s *taffetas lustré* had been developed, which became famous throughout Europe.

Other silk-producing centres in France during the 17th and 18th centuries were mainly in the south. Nîmes profited from the plague of 1722 that ruined Avignon, and specialized in inexpensive narrow-width fabrics with small patterns. Satins were produced at Marseille. Aix-en-Provence, Narbonne and Perpignan were smaller centres. Also at this time the ribbon-weaving industry in Paris flourished.

The dominant position of the French silk industry during the 18th century was due to the exquisite silks produced. Louis XIV had succeeded in making France the leader of European taste, with the result that French designs and fashions were in great demand abroad. Lyon increased in importance and became the most important centre of silk production in Europe. The establishment of the Lyon School of Design in 1756 encouraged the creation of new designs and patterns.

Although furnishing silks were conservative in style and changed only slowly throughout the 18th century, dress silks changed annually. The extraordinary silks produced at the beginning of the 18th century combined elements of Indian, Chinese, Japanese and European ornament and are known as BIZARRE SILKS. By the 1710s the designs were becoming more symmetrical and densely filled with foliage and in the 1720s they were decorated with diaper-filled bands, which have been called 'lace-patterned' silks. During the early 1730s increasingly naturalistic designs were introduced, which were made possible by the shading technique, *point rentré*, invented by the designer Jean Revel (1684–1751). From the 1740s the designs reflected the Rococo style and therefore became increasingly asymmetrical (see fig. 96); C-shaped scrolls and delicate floral sprays set on plain white grounds became popular. Meandering floral trails, thin ribbons and finally solid bands became an increasingly notable feature of the designs in the 1750s and 1760s. Trails of fur, reputedly introduced by PHILIPPE DE LASALLE in 1763, remained popular into the 1770s. By that time, however, the influence of the Neo-classical style was leading to the reduction of surface pattern. The designs for dress fabrics became steadily smaller and simpler: sprigs, rosettes, lattices and stripes. Elaborate fabrics brocaded with metal and coloured silk were replaced by plain, slight fabrics. The only exception was in the field of furnishing silks: during the 1770s and 1780s fanciful chinoiserie designs in the style of Jean Pillement and large-scale patterns, designed by de Lasalle, composed of life-sized birds and floral swags, mixed with fanciful architectural motifs, were produced.

The French Revolution severely damaged the silk industry, and work ceased in 1793. A commission for furnishing silks from Charles IV, King of Spain, however, led to a revival in 1795. These superb silks in the Classical and Etruscan styles were made by Jean-Démosthene Dugourc and the firm of Camille Pernon in Lyon. Further

96. Brocaded silk by Philippe de Lasalle, probably made in Lyon, *c*. 1770 (London, Victoria and Albert Museum)

commissions came from Spain and from Napoleon. Bonaparte was concerned both with promoting French industries and with displaying his power and position, and the design links with ancient Rome emphasized his importance as Emperor. After 1815 patronage was once more in the hands of the Crown, first under Louis XVIII and then Charles X (*reg* 1824–30). Some samples of the superb silks woven at this time are preserved in the Mobilier National in Paris.

During the second half of the 18th century there had been many attempts to improve the draw loom, which culminated in the loom attachment of 1804 by JOSEPH-MARIE JACQUARD. This used a punch-card system to control the warp threads and made the assistant, known as the drawboy, unnecessary (*see* TEXTILE, §II, 1(ii)). Due to the simplicity of most patterns at the time, however, it was not widely taken up until the 1830s. Other technical innovations, new fabrics and new textile items were adopted in the early 19th century; they included shawls (in imitation of those coming from India), crêpe de chine, tulle (a silk knitted net), brocaded muslin and plush. Philippe de Lasalle had been the first to weave (in the 1770s) portraits in imitation of those made at the Gobelins in the 1760s; these were popular in the early 19th century. Vestments became an increasingly important part of the industry in Lyon and continued as such throughout the 19th century.

Despite riots in Lyon against the introduction of the Jacquard loom in 1831 and 1834, it was increasingly used as large patterns came back into fashion, and an eclectic style based on a variety of historical patterns developed, reaching its peak in the 18th-century revival style of the Second Empire (1852–70). The industry was stimulated from the early 19th century by a series of industrial exhibitions, but the silks shown at the international exhibitions in the 1850s and 1860s led to a reassessment of the state of French silk design. Methods of teaching industrial design were reformed, and in 1889 the Musée Historique des Tissus was established in Lyon.

Despite the vagaries of the industry in the late 19th century, which were aggravated by the collapse of French sericulture, the Lyon industry continued to produce very fine silks. Some, like the woven books produced by the Maison Henry in the 1860s, were a technical *tour de force*, others showed the growing influence of Japanese design, as in the spectacular silks with naturalistic flowers starkly placed on black grounds shown at the Exposition Universelle of 1889 in Paris. Reproduction silks continued to play a large part in the French industry, which was not influenced by the Art Nouveau style of the late 19th century. Following the success of his work for the Ballets Russes, however, Paul Poiret influenced the designs of many silks of the mid-1910s and early 1920s. The work of Raoul Dufy and Michel Dubost was also very influential on Lyon silks during the early 20th century. Quite different was the influence of the Union des Artistes Modernes, in particular of Sonia Delaunay, who in the 1920s designed a series of geometric silk patterns, related to avant-garde paintings, which made a major impact at the Exposition Internationale des Arts Décoratifs et Industriels Modernes of 1925. During the 1920s the mechanization of the industry was completed, and synthetic silk and other fibres were introduced. Silk remained, however, a speciality of the industry in Lyon at the end of the 20th century.

BIBLIOGRAPHY

J. de L'Hiberderie: *Le Dessinateur pour les fabriques d'étoffes d'or, d'argent et de soie* (Paris, 1764)
O. van Falke: *Decorative Silks* (London, 1936)
J. K. Tilton: *Empire Silks* (New York, 1953)
P. Thornton: 'The Bizarre Silks', *Burl. Mag.*, c (1958), pp. 265–70
——: *Baroque and Rococo Silks* (London, 1965)
Soieries Empire (exh. cat., ed. J. Coural; Paris, Mobilier N., 1980)
M. Carlano and L. Salmon: *French Textiles: From the Middle Ages through the Second Empire* (Hartford, 1985)
S. Anderson Hay, ed.: *A World of Costume and Textiles: A Handbook of the Collection*, Providence, RI Sch. Des., Mus. A. cat. (Providence, 1988)
Ancien Régime–Premier Empire, 1785–1805 (exh. cat. by A. Gruber, Riggisberg, Abegg-Stift., 1989)
Soieries de Lyon: Commandes royales au XVIIIe siècle, 1730–1800 (exh. cat., Lyon, Mus. Hist. Tissus, 1989)
P. Arizzoli-Clémentel: *Le Musée des tissus de Lyon* (Paris, 1990)
N. Rothstein: *Silk Designs of the Eighteenth Century in the Collection of the Victoria & Albert Museum* (London, 1990)
P. Arizzoli-Clémentel: *Lyon en 1889: Les Soyeux à l'Exposition universelle de Paris* (Lyon, 1991)

DIANA FOWLE

3. EMBROIDERY. Medieval literature shows that embroidery was made in France in the Middle Ages, but the examples that have survived are extremely rare (e.g. tunic, 7th century; Chelles, Mus. Alfred Bonno) and very damaged, with the exception of the famous Bayeux Tapestry (1066–97; Bayeux, Mus. Tap.), which is very probably English. 13th-century French embroidery is very similar to contemporary English embroidery (*opus anglicanum*) but it lacks the mastery and richness. Some liturgical vestments in collections in France, Sweden and Italy are generally accepted as being French; they are embroidered with silk and gold thread in underside couching (*point couché*) and split stitch and illustrate scenes from the life of Christ and the saints (e.g. cope of *c.* 1274; Uppsala Cathedral). Scholarly clerics would often have been involved in the choice of the iconography.

Some superb antependia date from the 14th and 15th centuries. Images of saints or sacred scenes are depicted under arcades of gold couched work and silk split stitch (e.g. of early 15th century; Lyon, Mus. Hist. Tissus). A few rare episcopal mitres from the same period decorated with river pearls and jewels have also survived. The alms purses known as *sarrazinoises* (Saracen purses) could well have been a speciality of Parisian workshops. These purses, which were embroidered with lively scenes of romances or imaginary animals, provide an image of the medieval courtly embroidery used to decorate hangings and clothes that was very popular in the royal and princely courts in Paris, the Touraine and Burgundy (e.g. of 14th century; Troyes Cathedral).

Far more documentation has survived from the 16th and 17th centuries. The favoured techniques in France at this time were *or nué* (shaded gold), *petit point* (raised work) or *gros point* (canvas work) and *lacis* (darned net). Non-figurative embroidery, particularly with floral decoration, was widespread, but figurative embroidery was very often still made, frequently based on engravings and pattern books. Although professional embroiderers worked for the royal Court in Paris and at the château of Versailles, as well as for the church and the nobles, amateur embroidery also developed. At this time, however, religious embroidery no longer dominated to such an extent. Small masterpieces were nonetheless produced, exhibiting incredible virtuosity due to the subtlety of the *or nué* technique.

Bedcovers were often richly embroidered with appliqué, creating a robust decoration of geometric and vegetal knotwork on velvet or satin; alternatively they were delicately decorated with grotesques worked in silk or in *petit* or *gros point* work, imitating tapestry-work and illustrating courtly scenes or biblical stories in a rather rustic style. The bedcovers (destr.) and other furnishings for Louis XIV's bedchamber at Versailles (see fig. 43 above), which were embroidered by Simon Delobel (*fl c.* 1685) over a 12-year period, were a sumptuous ensemble of high-relief gold embroidery. The *petit* or *gros point* was a technique that was more accessible to amateurs. Some of these 'amateur' pieces are of professional quality, such as the hangings (see fig. 97) made for Versailles by the orphans of the Couvent de St Joseph, Paris, which were based on drawings by the Court painter Charles Le Brun.

Embroidery in the 18th century was profoundly affected by two factors: the development of quasi-industrial techniques and the pre-eminent role of textile designers. During this period Lyon was the main centre of silk production in France, and the designers working there were highly skilled (*see* §2 above). By 1780 more than 6000 embroiderers were employed in Lyon, and they practically monopolized the production of high-quality liturgical vestments, such as the rich *ornement* (set of embroidered

vestments) made for the coronation of the Emperor Charles VII (*reg* 1742–5).

Embroidered hangings were used in royal and imperial palaces. These were woven in Lyon and embroidered there or in Paris with garlands, fruit, flowers, musical instruments and trophies in a bold Rococo style. This was gradually replaced towards the end of this period by the Neoclassical style and then in the early 19th century by the Empire and Egyptian revival styles. Such textile designers from Lyon at this time as Philippe de Lasalle, Jean-Démosthène Dugourc and Jean-François Bony (1754–1825) were internationally famous and were commissioned by the courts in Russia and Spain to provide upholstery fabrics, which were often embroidered. Even dress embroidery was organized on a commercial basis. Sumptuous and charming men's waistcoats and jackets in particular were produced in Lyon (e.g. waistcoat of *c.* 1780; London, V&A).

In the 19th century the demand for embroidered textiles grew more than ever and extended to all social classes. Industrialization of production, due to the invention of the embroidery machine (1828), meant that, by the mid-19th century, large quantities of goods could be produced at moderate costs; hand-embroidery, however, was still widely practised. Clothes, underwear, bedclothes, table-linen and upholstery were decorated with either one or the other type of embroidery. Peasant costumes became popular for a short period during the 19th century and were decorated with folk designs using both manual and machine embroidery. Needlework was considered an indispensable part of a young girl's education, whatever her class. A large amount of literature on the subject was published in the form of magazines and manuals, which gave advice and patterns in every style and technique. Around 1890 an interest in the Arts and Crafts Movement encouraged the production of hand-embroidery. The painter Emile Bernard and the sculptor Aristide Maillol among others created embroidery designs.

From the beginning of the 20th century, however, embroidery was considerably less popular than it had been. Nevertheless, a few studios in Lyon and Paris continued production. In Lyon a few firms produced good-quality machine-embroidery. In Paris many of the important dress designers embroidered their designs in-house or arranged for it to be done elsewhere. Some Parisian studios specialized in the superb skill of restoring embroidered hangings from historic palaces (e.g. those from the bedchamber of Marie-Antoinette at Versailles; *in situ*). In the late 20th century embroidery was also still practised by a certain number of amateurs and textile artists.

97. Embroidered hanging of *Air*, with Louis XIV as Jupiter, from the *Elements* series, wool and silk tent stitch on canvas, 4.45×2.84 m, made at the Couvent de St Joseph, Paris, late 17th century (London, Victoria and Albert Museum)

BIBLIOGRAPHY

L. de Farcy: *La Broderie du XIème siècle à nos jours d'après des spécimens authentiques et les anciens inventaires*, 3 vols (Paris, 1890), 2 suppls (Angers, 1900–19)

J. J. Marquet de Vasselot and R.-A. Weigert: *Bibliographie de la tapisserie, des tapis et de la broderie* (Paris, 1935)

M. Schuette and S. Müller-Christensen: *The Art of Embroidery* (London, 1964)

C. Lubell, ed.: *France*, iii of *Textile Collections of the World* (London and New York, 1975–7)

H. Bridgeman and E. Drury, eds: *Needlework: An Illustrated History* (New York and London, 1978)

M. Carlano: 'Embroidery', *French Textiles: From the Middle Ages through the Second Empire*, ed. M. Carlano and L. Salmon (Hartford, 1985), pp. 71–114

MONIQUE KING

4. PRINTED COTTON. Indian printed cottons were imported into France at least as early as 1587. By the 1650s they were widely available for both dress and furnishings. The first recorded European attempt to print cottons was made in Marseille in 1648, and in the 1650s and 1660s factories that experimented with Indian dyeing and printing processes were established. The popularity of printed cottons continued to increase until pressure from other textile trades contributed to legislation in 1686 and 1687 banning the importation and domestic production of printed textiles, and in 1790 their wearing and use.

Although the prohibition halted the early development of the French industry, printed cottons were obtainable through smuggling and were openly used at Court. By the 1740s restrictions were being relaxed, and in 1759 the authorization to print cloth was granted. For some decades the French industry thrived; between 1750 and 1775 there were 120 cotton-printing workshops in France. Printed-textile factories had been established in 1744 in Marseille and in 1757 at Orange. The first factory in Nantes was founded in 1758. During this period much research was carried out into fast dyes, and the area around Rouen became a centre for turkey-red dyeing. In the town of Mulhouse, then in the republic of Mulhouse in Upper Alsace, which became French territory in 1798, the factory of Koechlin, Schmaltzer & Cie was established in 1747 and under various changes of ownership and direction helped to bring the textile-printing industry in Alsace to prominence.

The manufacturer who made the greatest single contribution to the development of cotton printing in France was CHRISTOPHE-PHILIPPE OBERKAMPF, in his factory at Jouy-en-Josas, near Versailles. He started production in 1760, and his printed cottons led the fashionable market for these in France until the end of the 18th century (*see* TEXTILE, colour pl. X, fig. 1). In the 1760s woodblock printing was the only technique used at Jouy, but copper-plate printing began to be introduced elsewhere in France (e.g. Amiens, 1760; Sèvres, 1763; Corbeil, 1766). Copper plates, initially used almost exclusively for furnishing textiles, were in use at Jouy by 1770 and in Nantes by 1780. The quality of production possible encouraged the commissioning of artists to produce designs, most notably the classical and genre scenes for Oberkampf by Jean-Baptiste Huet I. By the late 1780s workshops were experimenting with engraved copper rollers, particularly in Alsace, and the first copper-roller printing machine in France was in service at Jouy in 1797.

After 1800 the industry in Mulhouse developed considerably, but elsewhere in France the industry declined. Jouy's production fell away after 1805; Oberkampf refused to compromise the quality of his printed cottons in order to compete with cheaper goods. The factory at Jouy and the factory of Petitpierre & Cie in Nantes eventually closed in the 1840s, while printers in Rouen continued to concentrate on the cheaper end of the market. Such ports as Marseille and Bordeaux, suffering through the loss of overseas markets, did not survive as important textile

centres. The introduction of mechanization became for many manufacturers the means of survival, saving labour costs and reducing the price of the finished article. Legislation in 1815 banning imported yarn and cloth encouraged domestic production using power-assisted spinning, and French cotton fabric became abundant. Between 1815 and 1825 important technical discoveries were made in France, including the first chrome dyes, which laid the foundations for the modern dyestuffs industry. Fashions in printed textiles at this time were marked by new colours as well as by new patterns. Although the printing industry in Alsace continued to flourish, with such firms as Dollfus-Mieg and Thierry-Mieg dominating, the annexation of Alsace by Germany in 1871 meant that France lost its important centre of printed-textile manufacture. Rouen grew increasingly strong and became the centre of the French cotton industry, mechanizing extensively and developing its spinning and weaving.

During the early 20th century there was a continued progress in the commercial production of printed cottons in Rouen and Alsace, which was returned to France after World War I, and invigorating change through the involvement in printing of artist–designers, particularly Sonia Delaunay and Raoul Dufy; the latter profoundly influenced the production of printed textiles in his work for Bianchini-Férier between 1912 and 1928, including his hand-blocked furnishing fabrics produced at Tournon. Alongside these innovations and the development of screenprinting in the 1920s, traditional patterns maintained their popularity, and the reproduction of historic designs continued to be a considerable part of the industry, which in its diversity retained such techniques as block-printing alongside technical progress.

BIBLIOGRAPHY

H. Clouzot: *La Manufacture de Jouy et la toile imprimée au XVIIIe siècle* (Paris, 1926; Eng. trans., New York, 1927)
S. D. Chapman and S. Chassagne: *European Textile Printers in the Eighteenth Century: A Study of Peel and Oberkampf* (London, 1981)
J. Brédif: *Toiles de Jouy* (Paris, 1989); Eng. trans. as *Toiles de Jouy: Classic Printed Textiles from France, 1760–1843* (London, 1989)
M. Schoeser and K. Dejardin: *French Textiles from 1760 to the Present* (London, 1991)

CLARE WOODTHORPE BROWNE

5. LACE. In the second half of the 16th century large quantities of cutwork (*point coupé*; *see* LACE, §1) were imported into France from Flanders and Italy; the Italian style was promoted by Catherine de' Medici, who brought the designer Federigo de Vinciolo (*fl* 2nd half of 16th century) to Paris. Cutwork and *lacis* (darned netting), which was very popular, were also made in France itself at this time, while the important silk and metal-thread bobbin lace industry likewise got under way. In the 17th century the principal areas of lacemaking in France became more clearly defined. They included Normandy, the region around Arras and the Auvergne, with centres for silk and linen bobbin lace at Le Puy and Aurillac. Metal-thread laces were made at Aurillac, Lyon and in the Paris area, which also produced cheap thread laces and large amounts of black silk lace.

Despite numerous prohibitions, enormous amounts of lace continued to be imported, particularly needle lace from Venice. In the 1660s Jean-Batiste Colbert, Louis

XIV's Surintendant des Bâtiments et Ordonnateur Général, Arts et Manufactures, decided that the only way to stop this drain on the economy was to establish a government-sponsored lace industry in France. By a royal proclamation of 1665 a company was set up in Paris to run the industry, and lacemakers were brought from Venice and Flanders to work in the towns of Le Quesnoy, Arras, Reims, Sedan, Château-Thierry, Loudun, Alençon and Aurillac. All the lace was then called *point de France*, a name now given only to the needle lace produced around Alençon in Normandy. By the time the official company ceased operation in 1692 *point de France* had achieved a distinctive style of its own and entered the brief but glorious period when designs were inspired by the work of Jean Berain I (see fig. 98).

The French needle lace industry inevitably suffered during the early 18th-century slump but began to revive *c.* 1710. In 1708 the first lace business was established at Argentan, which from that time shared a virtual monopoly of the needle lace industry with nearby Alençon. The distinctive types of lace known by these place names emerged in the 1720s, but both types were probably made in both towns.

The French bobbin lace industry, however, was still heavily dependent on Flanders at this time. Le Puy continued to produce straight laces of the Antwerp type, while the lace industries at VALENCIENNES and Lille—ceded to France in 1678 and 1668 respectively—remained

closely linked to developments in Flanders after the revival of the 1720s. Valenciennes lace was also made in Normandy, while Brussels and Mechelen laces were imitated elsewhere in France. The silk lace produced around Paris was particularly successful after the mid-18th century due to the fashion for *blonde*—undyed silk lace with geometric patterns on a mesh ground. *Blonde* was also made in Le Puy from the 1740s and by the end of the century in Normandy as well.

The French Revolution and its aftermath were disastrous for the French lace industry—apart from *blonde*. It was, however, during this period that machine lace was introduced. Point net machines were taken to Lyon in 1786 and developed to produce the net known as tulle, which soon gave rise to an embroidered net industry at Lyon, Nîmes and Courdrieu. Later, machines were also brought from England, and in 1816 the advent of the first pusher machine inaugurated the industry in the Pas-de-Calais, which was to become Nottingham's most serious rival from the 1850s.

The spectacular revival of the hand lace industry by the mid-19th century began with an increased production of *blonde*, which spread from Chantilly and Caen to Bayeux. In 1829 the lace business in Bayeux was taken over by August Lefébure. When *blonde* went out of fashion in the 1840s, Lefébure switched to the black silk lace still called Chantilly, introducing the method of making large pieces by joining narrow strips (*see* CHANTILLY, §2(ii)). In the

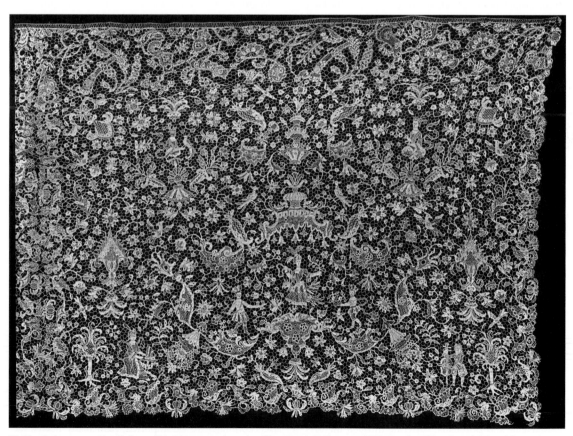

98. Needle lace cravat (detail), linen, 330×864 mm, in the style of Jean Berain I, France, *c.* 1700 (London, Victoria and Albert Museum)

1850s he began producing Alençon and a revived Venetian lace. The other great company of Verdé-Delisle Frères in Paris also assisted the revival. Cheaper varieties of Valenciennes lace continued to be made in Normandy, and Lille and Arras laces flourished, while in Le Puy and Mirecourt very versatile industries were developed, which produced both novelties and cheaper versions of the classic laces.

The fall of the Second Empire in 1871 was disastrous for the hand lace industry, and this time recovery was only partial. Fine laces were still produced into the early 20th century, but machine lace had won the day; World War I marked the end of any significant hand lace industry. After World War II attempts at a revival were made, notably at Le Puy, but only on a very small scale.

BIBLIOGRAPHY

G. Despierres: *Histoire du point d'Alençon depuis son origine jusqu'à nos jours* (Paris, 1886)
E. Lefébure: *Broderies et dentelles* (Paris, 1887)
H. Hénon: *L'Industrie des tulles et dentelles mécaniques dans le département de Pas-de-Calais, 1815–1900* (Paris, 1900)
A. Lefébure: *Dentelle et guipure* (Paris, 1904)
L. de Laprade: *Le Point de France et les centres dentelliers aux XVIIe et XVIIIe siècles* (Paris, 1905)
A. Maletot: *La Dentelle de Valenciennes* (Paris, 1927)
R. Gounot: *L'Evolution de l'art de la dentelle du Puy au XIXe siècle* (Le Puy, 1978)
B. de Buffévent: *L'Economie dentellière en région parisienne au XVIIe siècle* (Pontoise, 1984)

PATRICIA WARDLE

6. CARPETS. Parisian medieval guild regulations distinguished between *tapissiers* producing coarse, woollen covers, and tapestry-weavers working *en haute lice* and *tapissiers sarrazinois*, the latter being taken to be weavers of pile fabric in imitation of Middle Eastern carpets. Pile carpets feature in later inventories, including those of Francis I, where two are described as *faict en France* and *oeuvre de Tours*. Individual weavers continued this old tradition well into the 18th century, but the French carpet industry that obtained international renown started only in the early 17th century.

Henry IV and his successors, Louis XIII and Louis XIV, sought to by-pass the guilds, tackle the problem of excessive expenditure on imported goods and enhance their own position and grandeur by establishing royal workshops under their direct patronage. It was for this purpose that Henry IV had special quarters built beneath the Grande Galerie of the Louvre, Paris, in which Pierre

99. Tapestry-woven carpet, 3.98×4.56 m, made in Aubusson, late 1820s to early 1830s (London, Victoria and Albert Museum)

Dupont (1577–1640), formerly an illuminator and embroiderer, had set up a carpet-weaving workshop by 1608. Other entrepreneurs developed a site at Chaillot, just outside Paris, where Marie de' Medici had founded an orphanage; the first venture, a soap factory (Savonnerie), was abandoned, as was a linen factory, but in the mid-1620s one of Dupont's apprentices, Simon Lourdet (d 1671), set up another carpet workshop making use of cheap labour from the orphanage. Royal pressure forced the two men into an uneasy partnership, and the Council of State granted them joint rights to manufacture 'tout sortes de tapis, autre emmeublemens et ouvrages de Levant' for 18 years from July 1627.

Separate workshops were maintained at the Louvre and the Savonnerie by the two men and their sons until 1671, when Philippe Lourdet died and Louis Dupont moved his workshop to Chaillot. The greatest achievements of the SAVONNERIE were reached through the patronage of Louis XIV and Jean-Baptiste Colbert, from the mid-1660s to the 1690s. By that time the factory (encompassing both workshops) was famous for its thick, soft-piled carpets, no longer made in imitation of Eastern models but decorated with designs in keeping with the French Baroque style and showing the influence of Charles Le Brun and subsequent official designers (see CARPET, fig. 9 and colour pl. I). Almost the entire output was commissioned for the Crown, either for personal use or for gifts. In addition to carpets, the workshops produced bench and tabouret covers, screen panels and canopies, *portières*, pictures and, less commonly, chair and sofa covers.

The royal decrees by which their businesses were established had instructed Dupont and Lourdet to found workshops in other cities, and their apprentices were free to do the same. In reality such competition was forestalled by restricting the number of apprentices and by pursuing through the courts any that did seek independence. This created a virtual monopoly for the Savonnerie and forced a number of French carpet weavers to set up their workshops in such other countries as Germany, England and Sweden. The only centres to break this tight control were at Aubusson and nearby Felletin in central France, where tapestry-woven and pile carpets began to be produced on a small scale during the mid-18th century. A great flowering followed the reorganization of Aubusson in 1743 and of Felletin in 1768 (see AUBUSSON, §2). The reforms concentrated on improvements in design and technique and also on the creation of a marketing outlet in Paris. By copying the designs and effect of Savonnerie carpets, but at a cheaper price, the two centres filled a real gap in the market created by the declining interest in Eastern carpets and the growing demand for European models. The royal tapestry factory at Beauvais also responded to this demand; from 1780 it was run by de Menou, one of the men responsible for developing Aubusson, and in the years before the French Revolution a substantial proportion of the workers were employed on weaving both tapestry and pile carpets (see BEAUVAIS, §2).

During the 18th century a form of loop-pile carpeting, known as Moquette, was woven at Lille, Tournai, Abbeville and Rouen; it was considered good enough for use in secondary rooms and for upholstery. Some loom-woven

Brussels carpeting was manufactured at Aubusson, which also produced embroidered carpets.

The Revolution interrupted production at all the centres, but, under the Consulate (1799–1804), work restarted at the Savonnerie, which was made an imperial factory by Napoleon. During the first quarter of the 19th century magnificent carpets and other furnishings were woven in the Neo-classical style. Although the workshops were transferred to the Gobelins factory in 1826, they continued to function independently into the late 20th century. Pile carpet production at Beauvais stopped at the Revolution, with designs and equipment being sold to the Savonnerie workshop, but tapestry-woven carpets were again produced during the Empire. It was Aubusson, however, that became the dominant centre for tapestry-woven carpets during the 19th century. It produced a very large number, mostly in delicate, soft colours with designs based on those of the Louis XVI and Empire styles (see fig. 99).

BIBLIOGRAPHY

M. Jarry: *The Carpets of the Manufacture de la Savonnerie* (Leigh-on-Sea, 1966)
——: *The Carpets of Aubusson* (Leigh-on-Sea, 1969)
P. Verlet: *The James A. de Rothschild Collection at Waddesdon Manor: The Savonnerie* (London, 1982)

SANTINA M. LEVEY

XII. Patronage.

The history of patronage in the territory that is modern France begins with the domination of creations for devotional use, first pagan and later Christian. Ecclesiastical patronage reached its high point in the 12th century, although the institutions of the Catholic Church continued as patrons with varying degrees of activity until the Revolution (1789–94), when church properties were seized and the Church suppressed. Although re-established and sustained by State assistance with constructions in the 19th century, the wealth of the episcopacy was gone forever. From the late Middle Ages, regional court patronage rose in importance and from the 16th century was gradually eclipsed by royal patronage. From then until the Revolution royal and State patronage were synonymous. Civic patronage emerged from feudal links between communities and lords who were secular, ecclesiastical or royal. The guilds who dominated in each locality cooperated with their feudal liege in providing the benefits of social order and common meeting places and services. Over time the civic bodies gained great autonomy that was often linked to regional parliamentary power. Private patronage emanated from aristocratic wealth derived from feudal dues and lands, and later from association with the Court and venal offices. Middle-class wealth was derived from legal or parliamentary services to the State, or from contracting, banking and tax collection as concessions from the Crown. By the 18th century private patronage rivalled royal patronage in sustaining artists and establishing aesthetic standards. In the 19th and 20th centuries the centralization of the old government bureaucratic system was retained through often rapidly shifting political regimes. State patronage declined steadily in prominence in the fine arts with significant consequences for the prestige of French art internationally. At the same time social and economic change dictated a decline in religious and private patronage. Much private wealth in the 19th and 20th centuries found its way into the allied activity of collecting (*see* §XIII below). Only corporate and private architectural patronage and important State urban and historic preservation projects were exceptions to this general decline.

1. Before the 12th century. 2. 12th–15th centuries. 3. 16th and 17th centuries. 4. 18th century and Revolutionary period. 5. 19th and 20th centuries.

1. BEFORE THE 12TH CENTURY. The construction of temples, civic buildings and villas by the Romans at Nîmes, Narbonne and elsewhere are reflections of Roman rather than Gallic patronage (*see* ROME, ANCIENT, §I, 3), although they did provide models of building types. There was a Gallo-Roman industry specializing in carving sarcophagi for Early Christian use. The 4th-century AD decorations of the cemetery of Les Alyscamps at Arles represent some of the earliest Christian-sponsored art in Gaul. By the Merovingian and Carolingian periods the Church supported an active textile industry, which had survived since Gallo-Roman times and which made goods for private consumption, in its creation of church-hangings and vestments. Similarly, with the rise in the creation of reliquary and ritual vessels, goldsmithing and jewellery-making flourished. All of the Merovingian and Carolingian monarchs required splendid metalwork in personal ornament, plate and coronation and ceremonial regalia (*see also* MEROVINGIAN ART and CAROLINGIAN ART): Chilperic I (*reg* 523–84) was said to have been very proud of the gold plate he commissioned. With the exception of the Carolingian Court, the most significant institutions of architectural patronage before the 10th century were ecclesiastical. The principal pattern in the troubled period from the 6th to 8th centuries was the reuse of Roman structures for Christian purposes: in AD 596 St Gregory instructed the monk Augustine not to destroy the constructions of the pagans but only their religious idols.

The principal forms of artistic expression were associated with religious practice, either for church decoration or funerary monuments. The sponsors were archbishops and bishops and, more rarely, ducal families. For example, in the 6th century Bishop GREGORY of Tours ordered the mural decoration in fresco of the churches of St Martin and of St Perpétue, neither of which has surviving paintings. From the 4th century St Jerome (*c.* 342–420) had commended the copying of manuscripts as an appropriate activity for the cenobitical clergy. Some monasteries actively sponsored manuscript illumination. CHARLEMAGNE (*reg* 768–814) was the first important royal patron in the history of northern Europe. His capital at Aix-la-Chapelle (now AACHEN) was renowned for its architecture and as a centre of the arts. In particular he sponsored monastic institutions where painted illumination was practised and deserves much credit, albeit indirect, in the achievements of the schools of St Gall (in Switzerland), Reims, Metz, Orléans (i), Moissac, Cluny and Languedoc. Charlemagne's direct patronage in the Ile-de-France went to Saint-Denis Abbey to build the second church, consecrated in 754; in 782 he also had built the monastery church at Aniane, near Montpellier, and during the 790s the monastery of St Riquier, near Abbeville.

France was freed from the Holy Roman Empire in 841. The early kings controlled little territory, however, and

were, consequently, relatively poor, hence the absence of significant royal patronage. Ducal courts were often wealthier than the royal Court, and in the distant parts of the territory not controlled by the kings of France, the Church provided the only stable organization co-existing with the myriad feudal fiefdoms into which the land was divided. The dioceses of France had been convened for the first time at the Council of Arles in 314 and were organized in ecclesiastical provinces corresponding to the civil provinces of Roman Gaul. The cathedrals already had their treasures and relics. While bishops and archbishops were important in rebuilding many metropolitan churches, much stylistic innovation during the Romanesque period was achieved by the patronage dispensed by the abbots of the great monasteries using endowments such as those bequeathed by Charlemagne to Cluny Abbey or by Queen Bathilde to found Jumièges Abbey in 654, and also from gifts by laymen. (For further discussion *see* ROMANESQUE, §II, 1(i).)

In the 10th century, after the depredations of the wars and invasions of the 5th to the 9th centuries, monastic growth (especially of the BENEDICTINE ORDER), the rise of the cult of relics and the gradual emergence of more stable princely courts, particularly after Hugh Capet's coronation in 987, led to a dramatic period of building and rebuilding. By the end of the 10th century there were 474 abbeys and collegiate churches in the territory from the Pyrénées to Normandy. The foundation of Cluny Abbey in 910 and the subsequent wave of reformation led by Abbot Odo (*reg* 927–44) were important in the soundness and growth of the Benedictines, which were supported by Hugh Capet. The wealth of the orders came from several sources. Endowments from royal and noble families represented an indirect means of patronage of scriptoria and building works. Direct royal and noble patronage came in the form of reliquary statues, magnificent sculpted tombs or gifts of goldsmiths' work for liturgical use. From their Court at Dreux, King Robert (*reg* 996–1031) and Queen Constance made an offering of a golden sculpted reliquary figure of *St Savinien* to Sens in the early 11th century. Another form of patronage comprised the gifts brought by every pilgrim to the shrine of a saint's or martyr's relic. Many of these were of gold, but in some cases the pilgrim paid for a small part of the construction, as is attested, for example, by the inscription on a capital at the Benedictine pilgrimage abbey at Volvic showing the commoner Guillaume de Bez handing to the abbot both the column and capital that he had paid for.

2. 12TH–15TH CENTURIES. The consecration in the 1140s of Abbot Suger's new royal abbey church at Saint-Denis marked the high point of monastic art and architecture. SUGER was the single most important patron of the 12th century, though it is doubtful that he was himself the inventor of the coherent programme of iconography and artistic form found in his church and expressed in the interplay of architectural space and coloured light through stained-glass windows and in linked imagery in glass, statuary, reliquary and liturgical objects (*see* GOTHIC, fig. 1; *see also* SAINT-DENIS ABBEY, figs 2, 3 and 5). As a royal mausoleum, Saint-Denis continued to receive significant

royal gifts, such as Charles VI's sculpted reliquary for *St Charlemagne*, long after the monastic orders declined in importance. From the accession of Louis VII in 1146, universal taxes to support the Crusades began to drain away the relative wealth of the orders. The loss of bequests to monasteries through the ascendancy in education of the secular clergy over the monastic clergy by the mid-12th century and the rising wealth and safety of cities further shifted the centre of patronage from monastery to cathedral, a trend later to be reinforced by the gradual decline of pilgrimage. It was increasingly under the patronage of metropolitan bishops that the architectural innovations of the Early Gothic style were made. As secular domestic architecture increased in importance, it affected monastic architecture, as at Mont-Saint-Michel Abbey in the early 13th century. By the 14th century the great abbeys had neither the wealth nor the need to build new churches. Two exceptions were the papal gifts of Clement VI and Gregory XI to build the Benedictine church of La Chaise-Dieu, near Le Puy, in 1344–78, and the exceptional deviation from the austerity of Cistercian architecture in the splendid royal funerary church of Royaumont in the Val-d'Oise, founded by St Louis (Louis IX; *reg* 1226–70) in 1228. Monasteries that served as mausolea for the great families of France continued, however, to receive richly sculpted tombs into the 16th century.

The individuals whose patronage shaped architectural development in the period from the 12th to the 14th centuries were members of the episcopate who represented the separate sees comprising the bureaucracy of church government. Some important cathedral cities, such as Noyon, Soissons, Laon, Reims and Amiens, were centres of trade and agriculture. Laon, Tours, Chartres, Orléans and Paris added the presence of cathedral schools to their prosperity from other sources. Nevertheless, despite the wealth of the cathedrals, local government was often disputed between the cathedral chapters and the town authorities. The chapters had been reorganized as colleges of Augustinian canons with chapter houses and cloisters at each cathedral. Bishops were often members of the feudal nobility as well as princes of the Church. General prosperity had increased their private fortunes and seigneurial revenues. The benefaction of a bishop sometimes took the form of buying land personally from the local duke, as, earlier, Bishop Geoffrey de Mountbray did to create the new cathedral at Coutances, consecrated in 1056. More often, the bishop would spend the wealth of the cathedral chapter and make the decisions to initiate a vast undertaking, as did Abbot Hugues III, Archbishop of Rouen, who returned from the dedication of Abbot Suger's Saint-Denis Abbey inspired with zeal to exceed his rivals in rebuilding Rouen Cathedral.

Some cathedrals rivalled the Benedictine abbeys as pilgrimage shrines. Indeed, the chapters of Chartres and Laon refused to have the wealth and benefits of the cult of relics go entirely to the monastic orders, and they established deliberate policies to develop their cathedrals as pilgrimage churches. In 1112, the chapter of Laon developed the clever fund-raising device of a travelling exhibition of their relics. The old cathedral was reconstructed after a fire in that year and was replaced by Bishop Gautier de Mortagne's project less than 50 years later.

Chartres was rebuilt after the fire of 1194 as a pilgrimage shrine for the relic of the tunic of the Virgin. As the work progressed, important parts of the decoration, such as the carved portals or the stained-glass windows, were paid for by individual donors, from kings to canons. Iconographic and stylistic links among such cathedrals as Chartres and Bourges, or between cathedrals and Benedictine usages, were less a result of the direct influence of individual donors than of theological or artistic evolution guided by the bishops or the masters of the works. Churches were often draped with elaborate embroideries, the most important surviving example of which is the so-called BAYEUX TAPESTRY, said to have been made in the late 11th century as the gift of William the Conqueror's half-brother Odo, Bishop of Bayeux, to be displayed in Bayeux Cathedral on the feast day of St John.

The rebuilding or replacing of cathedrals was often due to destruction by fire. Also, urban cathedrals, almost always situated in organic proximity to market-places, needed to be enlarged as the towns' populations grew. One constant principle in French urban planning has been the willingness to demolish older monuments to make way for new projects. The Bishop of Paris, Maurice de Sully (*c.* 1120–96), and his five successors showed no hesitation in demolishing a Merovingian and a Carolingian church and in cutting into the Gallo-Roman ramparts in order to build Notre-Dame on the Ile-de-la-Cité. A significant development of the cathedral plan in the 13th, 14th and 15th centuries resulting directly from patronage was the addition of small chapels along each side of the nave to serve as chantry chapels or chapels dedicated to the vast number of newly forming confraternities. In these, as in chapels built for chivalric orders, the imagery reflected the iconography of the patron rather than conforming to a larger programme.

The development of private patronage by ecclesiastics in the relative prosperity of the later medieval period was dramatic and tended to be identified with AUGUSTINIAN CANONS who were allowed by their rule to own property. A canon in a cathedral close could own many alabaster statuettes, Limoges candlesticks and wall hangings depicting religious scenes, and even have a small library. Bishops' palaces were of a feudal rather than a monastic type, reflecting the resident's status as a baron giving and receiving oaths of loyalty. A bishop in his city palace lived every bit as splendidly as the lay upper nobility, as is evidenced by the 12th-century episcopal residences at Auxerre and Meaux. Tapestry was an art form especially prized by bishops from the 12th to the 16th centuries, and tapestries were found in private chapels and entertaining rooms in both town houses and country houses of members of the episcopate (*see* TAPESTRY, §II, 1). Other orders, vowed to poverty, evolved their own architectural styles. These included the Knights Templar, related to the Cistercians, the Knights Hospitaller, associated with the Augustinians, and the foreign mendicant Franciscan, Dominican and Carmelite orders. St Louis (*see* CAPET, (2)) and the popes in Avignon supported the CARTHUSIAN ORDER, among others. The Charterhouse of Champmol, outside Dijon, founded in 1383 by Philip the Bold, Duke of Burgundy (*reg* 1363–1404; *see* BURGUNDY, (1)), became the repository of one of the greatest medieval collections of paintings and sculpture of the French, Flemish and

Burgundian schools and retains the greatest works of CLAUS SLUTER (*see also* DIJON, §IV, 1).

Medieval secular architecture had developed around the fortified castle that was the essential element in every seigneur's fief. From the 10th century to the late 13th century many design considerations were dictated by the requirements of defence. In the 12th century town houses larger than ordinary citizens' houses began to be built by seigneurs: in 1120–25 Archambaud de Saint-Antonin built a house in Saint-Antonin in which the windows of the main floor were ornamented with columns with carved capitals and separated by piers with sculpted figures.

The prestige of Paris was based on the importance of the royal presence in the capital. The Capetians, notably Philip II Augustus (*reg* 1180–1223) and St Louis, established an indissoluble tie between Paris and the Crown, challenged only in the 1470s when Louis XI attempted to make Tours the capital. The Capetians used the palace on the Ile-de-la-Cité (site of the present Palais de Justice) as the centre of government, and it was there that St Louis built the Sainte-Chapelle (*see* PARIS, §V, 2) as a castle chapel to house the relic of the Crown of Thorns, acquired in 1239. Philip II Augustus built the château of Vincennes and in 1204 began a castle on the present site of the Musée du Louvre. The Valois kings, who acceded to the throne in 1328, continued to embellish the Palais du Louvre and to add to the fabric of Paris. Charles V (*reg* 1364–80; *see* VALOIS, (2)) added to the security of Paris when he built the Bastille in collaboration with civic authorities. He also formed a superb royal library with many illuminated manuscripts, and his brother Louis, Duke of Anjou (1339–84), amassed a large collection of over 3500 items. The Palais du Louvre as it is depicted in the magnificent illuminated manuscript the Très Riches Heures (Chantilly, Mus. Condé, MS. 65, fol. 10*v*) reflects its appearance under Charles VI (*reg* 1380–1422), whose uncle Jean, Duc de Berry (*see* VALOIS, (3)), one of the most prolific patrons of the later Middle Ages, commissioned the illuminations from the LIMBOURG brothers. In spite of the outbreak of the Hundred Years War in 1337, the French courts approved of the display of wealth as a sign of security and stability. Charles VI (*see* VALOIS, (4)) was the first to have established the pattern of the large MAISON DU ROI (royal household) that included artists and workmen and provided a lavish and expensive setting for the monarch. This pattern was expected to be repeated on a lesser scale by dukes of the royal house and the greatest of the lords of the realm, and commensurately more modestly as the scale of the orders of chivalry was descended. The patronage of the houses of Artois, Anjou and BOURBON, and of the dukes of ORLÉANS, BURGUNDY and Berry, reflected the royal Court's love of tapestry, stained glass, plate, furniture and jewellery, along with the performing arts. These great nobles often set stylistic trends more sophisticated, or, at any rate, different from those of the royal Court. The wealthy bourgeoisie also emulated this taste, as in the case of JACQUES COEUR, a merchant of Bourges who held great power at the Court of Charles VII. His house in Bourges, built between 1443 and 1451, is the most perfect example of a wealthy middle-class mansion of the 15th century (*see* BOURGES, §II, 4). Private patronage grew in importance in the 14th and 15th centuries, in part to support domestic religious practice. Artists were called upon to make illuminated Psalters and Books of Hours, furniture for chapels, portable altarpieces and family tombs.

By the early 12th century many of the old Roman towns had had their communal rights recognized by the bishops, feudal lords or the king. Many new cities were founded in the 12th and 13th centuries and were integrated into the feudal system. Louis VII (*reg* 1137–80), who founded Villeneuve-le-Roi (now Villeneuve-sur-Yonne, nr Sens), was required to build walls and gates, a church and market hall and to set up a forge and baking oven. Older towns received improvements and grew accordingly. Paris was administered by the Prévot des Marchands, the most powerful of whom was Etienne Marcel, who built the new walls of the city between 1356 and 1358. Throughout its history Paris, as a royal city, collaborated with the Crown in making improvements, and it was replanned with wider streets. Houses grew in height as space became precious. As wealth increased, houses ornamented with Gothic windows and chimneys became fashionable. In the 15th century some fine mansions in the Marais quarter, including the Hôtel des Archevêques de Sens, were built.

By the mid-13th century trade guilds were established in Paris. Some were also confraternities, which pre-dated guilds, but all had some religious basis. The goldsmiths' guild supported five confraternities, each with a designated good work as its goal: the confraternity of St Eloi maintained a hospital. All guilds and confraternities were patrons of the arts as they were able; at the least, they would sponsor a chapel with a statue of their patron saint, where their community could hear Mass. Wealthier guilds might give stained-glass windows incorporating the symbols of the guild. The guilds and confraternities of the Passion who built elaborate sets for their mystery plays also had a great influence on the visual arts. The *échevins* or magistrates of a town were organized as guilds or corporations that embodied communal authority and were responsible for constructing a communal belfry and an hôtel de ville in their particular town. In the late Middle Ages the hôtel de ville of any town was a larger and more magnificent example of the mansion architecture of the wealthier merchants. Such communal buildings as hospitals were most often private donations, while the municipality might build market halls and university buildings.

3. 16TH AND 17TH CENTURIES. The introduction of the classicizing motifs of Italian Renaissance art and architecture into France was gradual in the 16th century and was associated with the rise of royal and secular patronage. France's kings had been exposed to north Italian art during the military campaigns that made Milan French territory on and off in the last years of the 15th century and the first quarter of the 16th. French institutions were weakened after the disasters of the 14th and 15th centuries—the Hundred Years War and the Black Death—and more susceptible to foreign influence. The Concordat of 1516 gave Francis I (*reg* 1515–47; *see* VALOIS, (14)) the right to nominate bishops and many abbots, ending the great period of the Gallican Church and of French church architecture. With a court dominant over the Church, it was natural that a more secular emphasis and more

humanizing style should supersede the medieval styles so intimately reflecting ecclesiastical values. The Council of Trent (1545) virtually ended the development of medieval imagery in the Reformed Catholic Church.

Under Francis I the French State took on the character of personal absolutism and centralization that distinguished the *ancien régime* down to the Revolution. As the Crown was the central political authority, so the Court became the arbiter of taste in the arts. Francis's intention was to form a court that would rival the cultural sophistication of the Italian states. The new wing of the château of Blois and the château of Chambord (from 1519) were built as a direct result of royal policy, and it was a part of this policy to attract Italian artists to France, as Francis did with Leonardo da Vinci, Francesco Primaticcio, Rosso Fiorentino, Benvenuto Cellini and Nicolò dell'Abate (*see also* §III, 2 above). Early in his reign the Court was itinerant, as it had been for much of the Middle Ages. The Loire Valley had been favoured by the aristocracy for its hunting, salubrious climate and, in troubled times, relative security and prosperity. In the early 16th century great noble families were joined by the rich bourgeoisie in building country houses in the areas around Blois and Tours. One of the most captivating of these and among the first to use elements of the Renaissance style was the château of CHENONCEAUX (1514–22), built by the bourgeois Bohier family. The new Italianate motifs were also used in ecclesiastical settings, as in the Benedictine abbey at Fécamp in Normandy and in such civic commissions as the Hôtel de la Vieille Intendance in Orléans. Later in Francis's reign the Court centred itself on Paris, where the King built several châteaux in the vicinity, including Saint-Germain-en-Laye (1539–49; much altered) and Madrid (begun 1528; destr. 1792). The château of Fontainebleau (1528) became the most complete expression of Francis's conception of culture in the arts, combining new groundplans and painted and sculptural decoration with allegorical and pagan iconographies that were novel for France (*see* FONTAINEBLEAU, §1). In addition to creating the FONTAINEBLEAU SCHOOL, formed of Italian masters and the French and Flemish artists they trained or influenced in every form of fine and decorative art, Francis sent Primaticcio to Italy either to buy or have copied for his collection well-known antique statues and Italian Renaissance paintings. These were added to the growing royal collection housed at Fontainebleau or incorporated into the extensive gardens designed in the Italian mode. The building, its gardens and its royal collection of modern and antique works of art exercised a profound influence on French artists well into the 17th century, as evidenced by Père Dan's publication in 1642 of the royally financed *Le Trésor des merveilles de la maison royale de Fontainebleau*. One exception to Francis's passion for the Italianate was in portrait painting, in which Flemish naturalism became a part of French portrait conventions. Jean Clouet, François Clouet and Corneille de Lyon were the most sought-after portrait painters of the first half of the 16th century.

In constructing a new Hôtel de Ville, Francis I assisted with improvements to Paris made by the *échevins*, who undertook two other innovative urban projects in the 16th century: the construction of terraced houses on the new Pont Notre-Dame (1508–12) and on the Ile-de-la-Cité

between the Petit Pont and the Hôtel-Dieu (1552–4). These houses with uniform façades represent the beginning of the history of urbanism in Paris. Ecclesiastical patronage, with the exception of a few abbeys, tended to follow the Gothic style of additions and alterations to existing churches. The one notable new ecclesiastical construction, St Eustache in Paris (begun 1532), used Gothic plan and structure with Renaissance decoration.

Henry II (*reg* 1547–59; *see* VALOIS, (15)) and the ministers who ruled France for him, Anne, Duc de Montmorency, and the Guise family, directly supported the emergence of a genuinely French classicizing style and continued to support the policies of Francis I and to patronize his artists, notably Primaticcio and Sebastiano Serlio. Henry II interested himself personally in the improvements to the Palais du Louvre, where Jean Goujon worked as sculptor and Pierre Lescot as architect. He also left his mark in the fields of bookbinding and armour. His mistress DIANE DE POITIERS took an active part in art patronage and commissioned Philibert de L'Orme to build the château of Anet (1547–55) and to make additions to Chenonceaux, which she acquired. Serlio's château of Ancy-le-Franc (1541–50), near Tonnerre in Burgundy, created the prototype for the 'classic' château and his Grand Ferrare at Fontainebleau for Cardinal Ippolito II d'Este (i) the model for the essential urban mansion.

The Wars of Religion (1560–98) were extremely disruptive to society and to the institutions that patronized the arts. Of the few important works of the second half of the 16th century, Constable ANNE DE MONTMORENCY employed Jean Bullant as architect at the châteaux of ECOUEN (1556–78), Chantilly and La Fère-en-Tardenois (1552–62), Picardy, and Catherine de' Medici (*see* VALOIS, (16)), widow of Henry II, used him to build the Hôtel de Soissons in Paris, with its distinctive observatory in the form of a colossal column. Catherine also sustained the theoretical publications of Jacques Androuet Du Cerceau the elder.

Henry IV (*reg* 1589–1610; *see* BOURBON, §I(5)) restored the crown's stability and made numerous innovative improvements to the city of Paris in urban planning and architectural style, notably in the Place Royale (from 1605; now Place des Vosges) and the Place Dauphine (1607–15; *see* PARIS, fig. 3). Private development was encouraged. In 1608 the entrepreneur–contractor Christophe Marie acquired from the King the right to develop the Ile Notre-Dame (now Ile-de-la-Cité), in exchange for which he built the Pont-Neuf. From the late 1590s Henry IV continued the renovations, decorations and additions to the château of Fontainebleau, using such artists as Toussaint Dubreuil, Ambroise Dubois and Martin Fréminet, who have come to be known as the Second School of Fontainebleau. After Henry's death Marie de Medici (*see* BOURBON, §I(6)) served as regent and had Salomon de Brosse build the Palais du Luxembourg (begun 1615) in Paris (*see* BROSSE, SALOMON DE, fig. 1). The Duc de Sully, minister to Henry IV, had a private hôtel (1524) built in Paris that bears his name and is one of the most elegant of the period.

Although Lorraine was an independent duchy until its annexation by France in 1634, its culture was predominantly French. The active patronage of the dukes Charles

III (*reg* 1545–1608) and his son Henry II (*reg* 1608–24) (*see* LORRAINE) supported a distinctive form of late Mannerist art inspired by the Second School of Fontainebleau and including some of France's most important printmakers, including Jacques Callot and Jacques Bellange.

The youth of the two successive monarchs of the 17th century, Louis XIII (*reg* 1610–43) and Louis XIV (*reg* 1643–1715), resulted in power being concentrated in the hands of strong ministers, first Cardinal de Richelieu (*see* RICHELIEU (ii), (1)) and later Cardinal Mazarin (*see* MAZARIN, (1)), both of whom were the most powerful patrons and collectors of their day. During the period 1630–61, which ended in the beginning of the personal reign of Louis XIV, France grew as an international power and became a wealthier, more unified nation, albeit at the cost of several periods of open conflict against the nobility and religious dissenters at home and wars against Spain and the Holy Roman Empire. The prominence of ecclesiastics in the management of the State and, naturally, in the acquisition of personal wealth assisted a florescence of important church and philanthropic building and decoration in Paris, including Jacques Le Mercier's church of the Sorbonne (1635–48), François Mansart's Val-de-Grâce (begun 1645; *see* MANSART, (1), fig. 2) and Louis Le Vau's Collège des Quatre Nations (begun 1662; now the Institut de France). Powerful figures also built private hôtels in Paris and estates in the country symbolizing their station: Richelieu commissioned Le Mercier to build the Palais Cardinal (now Palais Royal) and the château and new town at Richelieu; RENÉ DE LONGUEIL, Marquis de Maisons, commissioned François Mansart to build the château of Maisons (now Maisons-Laffitte), near Paris (*see* MANSART, (1), fig. 1). Wealthy members of the bourgeoisie commissioned hôtels in the most refined expression of the new Baroque style, such as Jean-Baptiste Lambert's hôtel (begun 1635), designed by Le Vau (*see* LE VAU, (1), fig. 2) and decorated by Charles Le Brun (*see* LAMBERT, (1)). One of the most sophisticated examples of the maturity of the French school and the integration of the arts, architecture and landscape design was the château of Vaux-le-Vicomte (1656–61), created for the great patron but ill-fated minister of finance NICOLAS FOUQUET, who assembled Le Vau, Le Brun and André Le Nôtre to build it.

Louis XIV (*see* BOURBON, §I(8)) and his minister Jean-Baptiste Colbert (*see* COLBERT, (1)) crystallized the institutions of patronage (the Bâtiments du Roi; *see* MAISON DU ROI, §II), academic training (the Académie Royale de Peinture et de Sculpture and the Académie Royale d'Architecture) and arts manufactures (the GOBELINS), which made French arts pre-eminent among nations, supplanting the supremacy formerly reserved for Italian craft, art and architecture. Prestige was attached to being a royal artist by the gift, beyond the income from commissions, of annual stipends for life and special perquisites for members of the royal academies. Colbert adopted the aspiration for a monumental royal presence in the capital in pursuing the grand design for the Cour Carrée of the Palais du Louvre, begun by Le Mercier and Le Vau. After many aborted attempts, this project produced one of the most celebrated monuments in French architecture, the vaunted colonnade by Mansart, Le Vau and Claude Perrault (*see*

PARIS, §V, 6(ii)), which was abandoned by Louis XIV and left incomplete in favour of the reconstruction (1660s) of the château of VERSAILLES as the centre of government and the Court outside the capital. After the death of Colbert in 1683 and up to his own death in 1715, Louis XIV directed his commissions increasingly to the splendour and luxury of the royal palaces, creating a pattern of expensive daily living that kept the aristocracy seeking preferments constantly occupied with the hermetic life at Versailles, the Grand Trianon and the château of Marly. Jules Hardouin Mansart was Louis XIV's principal architect and director of works, not only for such great Court projects as the church of Nôtre-Dame at Versailles (from 1684) but also for the Dôme of the Invalides (*see* MANSART, (2), fig. 1) and the Place Louis-le-Grand (now Place Vendôme; *see* PARIS, fig. 4) and Place des Victoires in Paris.

Civic patronage underwent a renewal in the more prosperous circumstances of the 17th century. A number of provincial capitals and other towns, including Rennes, Marseille and Toulouse, undertook ambitious urban plans that provided work for painters and sculptors as well as architects. In Paris the *échevins* commissioned *ex-votos* and official portraits. From 1630 until 1708 the Paris goldsmiths' corporation commissioned annually a devotional painting for Notre-Dame: this became one of the most sought-after commissions for rising artists (*see* MAY OF NOTRE-DAME DE PARIS).

4. 18TH CENTURY AND REVOLUTIONARY PERIOD. The more self-referential the Court became in the late reign of Louis XIV, the more independent of aesthetic domination were members of the Parisian *noblesse de robe* and business classes. The contractors, bankers and tax farmers who made private fortunes in the 17th and 18th centuries, and who intermarried with the old *noblesse d'épée* and were ennobled in their turn, were prominent new patrons of the later years of the *ancien régime*. The banker Pierre Crozat (*see* CROZAT, (1)), for instance, had an important residence in Paris built by one of the architects who worked for the King; he also supported Charles de La Fosse of the Académie Royale, as well as Antoine Watteau, whose career had no royal support whatsoever. Members of the old nobility, such as the Comte d'Evreux (Crozat's son-in-law) and Philippe II, Duc d'Orléans (*see* ORLÉANS, House of, (3)), built splendid urban residences for use when they wished to escape the formality of Court life. The standard of taste for decorative arts—furniture, interiors, porcelain, metalwork and textiles—that was established by private patrons in 18th-century Paris reached the very greatest heights.

Crown patronage in the first half of the century was greatly diminished, the royal treasury having been severely depleted by the wars at the end of Louis XIV's reign. Royally sponsored civic projects were rare and often paid for by the municipal authorities rather than the Crown, as was the case with Edme Bouchardon's fountain in the Rue de Grenelle, Paris. Louis XV (*reg* 1715–74; *see* BOURBON, §I(10)) proved in his first maturity to have good, though unchallenging taste, given to the natural accuracy of the sporting and still-life painters Jean-Baptiste Oudry and Jean-Jacques Bachelier, and the portraits of Jean-Marc

Nattier. The King's personal patronage and the commands given by his mistress the Marquise de Pompadour (*see* POISSON, (1)), using the monies she received from the King, followed established Parisian taste in the decoration of the châteaux of Bellevue, Champs, Choisy-le-Roi and Crécy-Couvé, all of which had paintings and sculpture by François Boucher, Carle Vanloo, Jean-Baptiste Pigalle, Etienne-Maurice Falconet and Joseph-Marie Vien. Louis XV's preference for classicizing architecture is reflected in Anges-Jacques Gabriel's designs for the Pavillon Français and the Petit Trianon at Versailles. His appointment of ABEL-FRANÇOIS DE VANDIÈRES, Marquis de Marigny (*see* POISSON, (2)), the brother of Mme de Pompadour, as Directeur des Bâtiments du Roi signalled an important renewal of ambitious public-spirited royal commissions. In Paris, Marigny revived Colbert's project for the completion of the Louvre and commissioned Jacques-Germain Soufflot to build the church of Ste Geneviève (now the Panthéon; *see* SOUFFLOT, JACQUES-GERMAIN, fig. 3) and Gabriel the Place Louis XV (now Place de la Concorde; *see* PARIS, fig. 6); he commissioned Joseph Vernet's series of paintings of the *Ports of France* (Paris, Louvre and Mus. Mar.) and made efforts to revive history painting and the Gobelins tapestry works.

Louis XVI (*reg* 1774–92) continued the policies of his grandfather, supporting worthwhile civic projects and such factories as Sèvres. Jacques-Louis David's *Oath of the Horatii* (exh. Salon 1785; Paris, Louvre; *see* DAVID, JACQUES-LOUIS, fig. 1) was a royal commission to provide new models for the Gobelins, and Louis XVI's Directeur des Bâtiments, the Comte d'ANGIVILLER, continued the impetus begun by Marigny with his ambitious commissions for statues of the *Great Men of France* (1776; *see* §IV, 4 above). Both of these commissions were given in keeping with the royal policy that a public museum would be created and that the works of art made for inclusion in it would convey patriotic or uplifting moral values (*see* §XIV below). The King (*see* BOURBON, §I(11)) indulged his intimates discreetly in exquisite small-scale private settings, as, for example, Queen Marie-Antoinette's Petit Hameau (1782–5) by Richard Mique and Hubert Robert in a remote corner of the park at Versailles. The patronage of some members of the royal family, such as the Comte d'Artois (later Charles X; *see* BOURBON, §I(14)), was more innovative than that of the Crown and frequently as costly. Increasingly, as the century progressed, artists as different as Jean-Honoré Fragonard and Jean-Baptiste Greuze were able to fashion their careers almost exclusively from private rather than royal patronage: the wealthy Court official ANGE-LAURENT DE LA LIVE DE JULLY, for instance, was not only one of Greuze's most constant patrons but also commissioned from Louis-Joseph Le Lorrain a splendid and influential suite of Neo-classical furniture.

The Revolution institutionalized iconoclasm and demolitions where no replacement use was envisaged, as in the destruction of the Bastille and of royal monuments and the vandalism or seizure of church valuables and images. More positively, the revolutionary government succeeded in realizing a public museum in the Louvre (*see* §XIV below) and created a new and rapidly changing iconography of public pageants, many associated with

JACQUES-LOUIS DAVID. The temporary pieces of architecture, sculptures, banners and chariots made for these festivals occupied much of the artistic energy and financial resources of the central government. Art was used almost exclusively as a political device by the State and interest groups. New forms, such as popular imagery and satire, rose to levels of prominence new in history.

5. 19TH AND 20TH CENTURIES. There were significant continuities between the royal patronage of the *ancien régime* and the State patronage of the 19th and 20th centuries. There were, however, significant new admixtures in the overall patterns of patronage after 1800 stemming from the general decline in aristocratic and private patronage, the continuing secularization of society and the increasing acquisition of art through a market rather than by commission (*see* §XIII below).

While Napoleon (*reg* 1804–14; *see* BONAPARTE, (1)) was not privately an important patron of the arts, during the First Empire the French State undertook ambitious urban projects and revived the fine and decorative arts, after their decline with the loss of their patrons during the Revolution. In Paris, Napoleon ordered the extension and regularization of the Rue de Rivoli (begun 1802; *see* PARIS, fig. 7), construction of the Arc de Triomphe du Carrousel and the Arc de Triomphe de l'Etoile, the Temple de la Grande Armée (renamed the Madeleine in 1845) and additions to the Louvre (then housing the Musée Napoléon). As the Imperial family and new nobility became wealthier and more prominent, they built rapidly and acquired furnishings. They favoured the Neo-classical style, and the imagery of Roman myth, Egyptian gods and Napoleonic conquests appeared widely in Sèvres porcelain, Lyon silks and furniture (*see* EMPIRE STYLE).

Whereas the *ancien régime* had commissioned paintings and sculpture for the royal collection with or without a particular site in mind, the post-Revolutionary State provided direct support to artists by buying existing works for inclusion in a museum or by making a direct commission for a particular site. Once a national system of museums was created, acquisition by the State of contemporary art became a controversial issue, having political overtones in the frank preference for acceptable styles and subject-matters over aesthetic experiment and social commentary. Though this function is more directly linked to the history of the Salon system (*see* PARIS, §VI, 3(iii)) than to patronage, the importance in terms of financial support and professional recognition was identical, as far as the artist was concerned. The governments of the monarchy of Louis-Philippe (*reg* 1830–48; *see* ORLÉANS, House of, (7)) and the Third Republic (from 1870) favoured descriptive styles depicting heroic and virtuous actions drawn from ancient sources or modern French history; the Bourbon restoration monarchs Louis XVIII (*reg* 1814–24) and Charles X (*reg* 1824–30) and the First and Second Empires (1804–14; 1852–70) sponsored work of ideological and political cast, sustaining the dynastic and religious values of the regimes (*see* BONAPARTE, (8)). Relative to the *ancien régime*, in the 19th century there was a paucity of State expenditure on culture.

Throughout the century there were artists who succeeded in working for the State or for civic bodies, churches and social organizations that gave commissions for decorations or public monuments. Among these were Napoleon I's propagandists—David and Antoine-Jean Gros—and the artists who worked for the monarchies of Louis XVIII, Charles X or Louis-Philippe—Jean-Auguste-Dominique Ingres, Eugène Delacroix, Pierre Guérin, François-Joseph Heim, Hippolyte and Paul Flandrin, Paul Delaroche, François Rude, Théodore Chassériau and Thomas Couture—and in the second half of the century the pillars of the Académie des Beaux-Arts—Léon Bonnat, William Bouguereau, Emmanuel Fremiet, Jules Dalou and Jean-Baptiste Carpeaux—and some, such as Auguste Rodin, who achieved commissions after enduring mistreatment early in their careers. The history of the avant-garde, from Théodore Gericault to such apolitical landscape painters as Jean-Baptiste-Camille Corot, Gustave Courbet, Edouard Manet and the Impressionists and later artists, is one of finding middle-class private collectors, receiving an occasional commission (usually a portrait) and attempting to receive support from a new breed of art dealer. Some private collectors, such as ALFRED BRUYAS, played important roles in supporting artists as different as Delacroix and Courbet. There were still a few important aristocratic patrons, such as the Duc de Luynes, who commissioned the architect Félix-Jacques Duban and the artists Rude and Ingres to restore his château of Dampierre (Yvelines).

Architectural patronage, however, functioned much as before with the State and civic bodies the foremost, but by no means the exclusive, sponsors of innovation. Vast urban growth of the 19th century created opportunities for architects to fill the need for new types of specialized buildings: hospitals, prisons, schools, railway terminals, museums, libraries, factories, department stores and pavilions. Henri Labrouste's Bibliothèque Ste-Geneviève (1839–51) built for the Ministère de l'Education Publique et des Cultes (see LABROUSTE, (2), figs 1 and 2) and Charles Garnier's Opéra (1860–75; see GARNIER, CHARLES, fig. 1) were two seminal buildings created in Paris as government commissions. Eugène-Emmanuel Viollet-le-Duc was a pioneer in the restoration of medieval churches and castles for government and private patrons. In the former spirit of demolishing the old toward creating the new, Napoleon III's urban projects under the direction of Baron GEORGES-EUGÈNE HAUSSMANN transformed Paris into a model of a modern capital. Massive investment by private companies in railways and services and the building of modern blocks of flats by developers opened up entire new quarters of French cities to the burgeoning upper middle class.

Except in the case of commissions for public monuments, the pattern of patronage in the 20th century was centred on the preservation of certain institutions—such as the Gobelins in the form of the Mobilier National, which continued to serve the State—and reliance on the museum system and public exhibition programmes as the mainstay of public culture; a domain that also came to incorporate such former royal properties as the châteaux of Fontainebleau and Versailles. Private patronage depended on small clusters of people, frequently foreigners, who actively supported art made in France, again often by foreigners. Early in the century the principal buyers of works by Henri Matisse, Georges Braque and Pablo Picasso were Gertrude Stein and her circle (see STEIN, (3)) and the newly wealthy Russian collectors Sergey Shchukin (see SHCHUKIN, (1)) and Ivan Morosov. The Peau de l'Ours group around André Level collected the works of Picasso and others before World War I and proselytized for modern art. By far the most interesting new commissions both in art and architecture came from private sponsors or the Church. Auguste Perret pioneered the use of reinforced concrete in private houses in Paris and Boulogne-sur-Mer in the early years of the century (see PARIS, fig. 12) and later did such civic and State commissions as the Théâtre des Champs-Elysées (1911–13), Paris, Notre-Dame at Le Raincy (1922–3; see PERRET, fig. 1), near Paris, and the Mobilier National complex (1934) and the Musée des Travaux Publics (1937), both in Paris. Le Corbusier's career in France reflects the same pattern, with houses built for private clients that allowed the architect opportunities for experimentation: the Cook House (1926), Boulogne-sur-Seine; Villa Savoye, Poissy (1929–31; see VILLA, fig. 10); the Unité d'Habitation (1945–52), Marseille; and Notre-Dame-du-Haut, Ronchamps (1950–55; see LE CORBUSIER, fig. 6). After World War II there was increased activity in the building and decoration of churches. Fernand Léger, Georges Rouault, Jacques Lipchitz, Matisse and Jean Lurçat collaborated in the parish church at Assy (Haute-Savoie), which was designed by Maurice Novarina and sponsored by the Dominican M.-A. Couturier (1897–1954), publisher of L'Art sacré. Another important ecclesiastical commission was the Chapelle du Rosaire of the Dominican nuns at Vence, decorated by Matisse from 1948 to 1951.

The Fourth Republic (1946–58) instituted a policy of cultural devolution with a more even distribution of new construction and civic improvements throughout the country. During the Fifth Republic (from 1958), this policy led to the creation of the system of 'Maisons de la Culture' under the direction of the new Ministère des Affaires Culturelles (1959), entrusted initially to ANDRÉ MALRAUX. This ministry is responsible for museums, historic monuments, all performing arts, visual arts, literature, cinema and cultural development. The Fifth Republic made the preservation and restoration of national monuments and the development of museums a priority. For the fine and plastic arts, the ministry established three agencies for giving commissions and financial aid to artists or for making direct purchases: the Réunion des Musées Nationaux; the Délégation à la Création aux Métiers Artistiques et aux Manufactures (DCMAM), created in 1979; and the Centre National d'Art et de Culture Georges Pompidou. The annual budget in the mid-1980s was 12 million francs, representing around 5% of the budget of the ministry. Through these funds André Masson was commissioned to decorate the ceiling of the Théâtre de l'Odéon (1965) and Marc Chagall to paint the new ceiling for the Paris Opéra (1964). France also allocated 1% of the cost of construction of public buildings to State commissions for their decoration. From 1981, under the Socialist government of François Mitterrand, the budget for the Ministère des Affaires Culturelles increased dramatically, with special emphasis being placed on the film industry and television. Yet, for all the prominence of some 20th-century presidencies, there was little sign of a comprehensive policy on patronage of the arts. President Charles de Gaulle (1944–6; 1958–69) did not have any coherent programme for the arts but rather projected French political superiority by using Malraux to promote the prestige of French culture as an ideological weapon. The negative pattern of State art patronage changed, beginning with the formula begun by President Georges Pompidou (1969–74) of initiating major new museum projects to serve as his monument: the Centre Georges Pompidou (1971–7) by Richard Rogers and Renzo Piano (*see* PARIS, fig. 14), housing the Musée Nationale d'Art Moderne; the Musée d'Orsay by Pierre Colboc and Gae Aulenti (*b* 1927), begun by President Valéry Giscard d'Estaing (1974–81), and the Grand Louvre project centred around I. M. Pei's Pyramide (*see* PYRAMID, fig. 3), a project of President Mitterrand. It is noteworthy that these schemes used foreign architects. President Pompidou also breached the traditions of urban planning in Paris by advocating the construction of the 200 m high Tour Montparnasse in central Paris and demolishing Les Halles market without having a coherent project to build on the site. Mitterrand and his government pursued a policy of using culture as a symbol of their Socialist programme. The ambitious State support for the constellation of Grands Projets or Grands Chantiers built in Paris and throughout the country in the 1980s and 1990s (*see* §II, 5(iv) above) was particularly reminiscent of the French royal tradition of augmenting the *gloire de la patrie* through the creation of grand public monuments.

BIBLIOGRAPHY

J. Locquin: *La Peinture d'histoire en France de 1747 à 1785* (Paris, 1912/R 1978)
J. Evans: *Art in Medieval France, 987–1498* (London, 1948)
A. Blunt: *Art and Architecture in France, 1500 to 1700*, Pelican Hist. A. (Harmondsworth, 1953, rev. 4/1980/R 1988)
J. Park, ed.: *The Culture of France in our Time* (Ithaca, 1954)
H.-R. Hitchcock: *Architecture: Nineteenth and Twentieth Centuries*, Pelican Hist. A. (Harmondsworth, 1958, rev. 4/1977)
K. J. Conant: *Carolingian and Romanesque Architecture, 800–1200*, Pelican Hist. A. (Harmondsworth, 1959, rev. 1966)
J. Evans: *Monastic Architecture in France from the Renaissance to the Revolution* (Cambridge, MA, 1964, rev. New York, 1981)
W. S. Stoddard: *Monastery and Cathedral in France* (Middletown, 1966); *R* as *Art and Architecture in Medieval France* (New York, 1972)
J. Tulard: *Le Consulat et l'empire, 1800–1815*, Nouvelle Histoire de Paris (Paris, 1970)
R. Cazelles: *Nouvelle histoire de Paris de la fin du règne de Philippe Auguste à la mort de Charles V, 1223–1380*, Nouvelle Histoire de Paris (Paris, 1972)
W. G. Kalnein and M. Levey: *Art and Architecture of the Eighteenth Century in France*, Pelican Hist. A. (Harmondsworth, 1972)
La Collection de François Ier (exh. cat. by S. Béguin and J. Cox-Rearick, Paris, Louvre, 1972)
L'Ecole de Fontainebleau (exh. cat., ed. S. Béguin; Paris, Grand Pal., 1972)
J. Favier: *Paris au XVe siècle, 1380–1500*, Nouvelle Histoire de Paris (Paris, 1974)
A. Chastel, ed.: *Colloque international sur l'art de Fontainebleau: Paris, 1975*
M. Ozouf: *La Fête révolutionnaire, 1789–1799* (Paris, 1975); Eng. trans. as *Festivals and the French Revolution* (Cambridge, MA, 1988)
D. Thomson: *Renaissance Paris: Architecture and Growth, 1475–1600* (Berkeley, 1984)
C. Lord: *Royal French Patronage of Art in the Fourteenth Century: An Annotated Bibliography* (Boston, 1985)
R. Mousnier and J. Mesnard, eds: *L'Age d'or du mécénat, 1598–1661* (Paris, 1985)
M. Dennis: *Court and Garden: From the French Hôtel to the City of Modern Architecture*, Graham Foundation Architecture Series (Cambridge, MA, 1986)
M. Andrault and P. Dressayre: 'Government and the Arts in France', *The Patron State*, ed. M. C. Cummings and R. S. Katz (Oxford, 1987)
J. Forbes: 'Cultural Policy: The Soul of Man under Socialism', *Mitterrand's France*, ed. S. Mazey and M. Newman (London, 1987)
D. Wachtel: *Cultural Policy and Socialist France* (New York and London, 1987)
M. Marrinan: *Painting Politics for Louis-Philippe: Art and Ideology in Orléanist France* (New Haven, 1988)
M. Green: *Symbol and Image in Celtic Religious Art* (London and New York, 1989)
E. Kennedy: *A Cultural History of the French Revolution* (New Haven, 1989)
D. J. Sherman: *Worthy Monuments: Art Museums and the Politics of Culture in Nineteenth-century France* (Cambridge, MA, and London, 1989)
M. C. FitzGerald: 'Skin Games', *A. America*, lxxx (1992), pp. 70–83, 139–41

ALDEN R. GORDON

XIII. Collecting and dealing.

1. 14th and 15th centuries. 2. 16th century. 3. 17th century. 4. 18th century. 5. 19th century. 6. 20th century.

1. 14TH AND 15TH CENTURIES. The earliest well-documented secular collections of the Middle Ages are those formed by Charles V (*reg* 1364–80; *see* VALOIS, (2)) and his brothers Jean, Duc de Berry (*see* VALOIS, (3)), Philip the Bold, Duke of Burgundy (*reg* 1364–1404; *see* BURGUNDY, (1)), and Louis I, Duke of Anjou (*reg* 1360–84; *see* ANJOU, §II(1)), all admirers of beautifully illuminated books. They bought from booksellers and picture dealers but commissioned their most celebrated works of art directly: sculptures by Claus Sluter, for example (see fig. 33 above; *see also* DIJON, fig. 4), at Philip the Bold's Charterhouse of Champmol (*see* DIJON, §IV, 1), and the Duc de Berry's manuscript illuminations by the Limbourg brothers (*see* LIMBOURG, DE, figs 1–4 and TRÈS RICHES HEURES). The Duke of Burgundy also benefited from the flourishing art market in the southern Netherlands, which lay within his domain. The inventory of the library of Charles VI (*reg* 1380–1422; *see* VALOIS, (4)), drawn up at the request of John, Duke of Bedford, reveals the continuing enthusiasm for collecting books and manuscripts. There are some records of an incipient art trade between France and Italy, encouraged by the establishment of the Papacy at Avignon (*see* AVIGNON, §§1, 2 and 3(ii)). FRANCESCO DI MARCO DATINI, a merchant from Prato, set up business in Avignon in 1350 and received commissions for works that he then ordered from painters in Florence, the first consignment arriving on 8 February 1371. At the same time he was engaged in exporting fine French enamels to Italy. In these dealings names of painters are rarely mentioned, but on 6 March 1386 four panel paintings (none identified) by Jacopo di Cione are recorded as arriving in Avignon.

As a result of the beginning of the Hundred Years War (1337–1453), political instability and factional quarrelling among the Valois princes led to a decrease in the royal demand for artefacts. However, the Court of René I became an important artistic centre in the mid-15th century (*see* ANJOU, §II(4)), and by the time of the Italian campaigns of Charles VIII (*reg* 1483–98) and Louis XII (*reg* 1498–1515), works of art from Italy became freely available in France. Louis XII (*see* VALOIS, (13)) assembled a small collection of Italian pictures; the Cardinal Georges I d'Amboise, his chief minister and Viceroy of Milan (*see*

AMBOISE, (1)), built up a collection of sculpture commissioned from artists in Milan and Genoa to decorate his château of Gaillon (Eure). In 1498 the Maréchal de Gié requested the Signoria of Florence to send to France seven Roman busts that had belonged to Lorenzo the Magnificent of the Medici family and a copy (untraced) of Donatello's statue of David (bronze, begun 1459; Florence, Bargello) executed by Michelangelo. The copy was acquired not by de Gié but by his successor at the Court of Louis XII, Florimond ROBERTET, for whom in 1501 Leonardo painted the *Virgin and Child*, later known as the *Virgin of the Yarnwinder* (untraced; version, Duke of Buccleuch priv. col.).

2. 16TH CENTURY.

Early in his life Francis I (*reg* 1515–47; *see* VALOIS, (14)) showed a love of Italian art, particularly Florentine painting. From his father-in-law, Louis XII, he inherited several Italian paintings, including a version of Leonardo's *Virgin of the Rocks* (Paris, Louvre). By 1525 Francis's collection was already rich in Italian works, and, in addition to his own purchases, he received gifts from Pope Leo X and Lorenzo II de' Medici, among which were Raphael's *Holy Family* (1518) and *St Michael* (1518; both Paris, Louvre). On his release from captivity in Spain following his defeat at Pavia in 1525, Francis must have found consolation in adding to his collection, which was soon to decorate a former hunting-lodge at Fontainebleau, where he began making improvements in 1528 (*see* FONTAINEBLEAU, §1). This was to become the most distinguished and refined decorative ensemble of a period in which the building and decoration, in the Italian taste, of many châteaux in Touraine, Normandy and the Ile-de-France took place. The great distances involved compelled Francis to make use of agents for his later dealings with Italian artists. They included Giovan Battista della Palla, a member of the anti-Medici faction, who had made his home in France, and Pietro Aretino. After 1540 Francis, with the assistance of Francesco Primaticcio (and perhaps on his advice), began to satisfy a new-found passion for antique sculpture. He obtained bronze casts of a number of celebrated pieces, including the *Laokoon* and the *Apollo Belvedere* (both Rome, Vatican, Mus. Pio-Clementino), from the collections of the Vatican, thus inaugurating a fashion that was to be widely imitated. In addition to the magnificent works of art he assembled, he owned a cabinet of curiosities, which may have been maintained until the Wars of Religion (1560–98) but which probably disappeared in the looting of 1590. Towards the end of his reign, Henry IV (*reg* 1589–1610; *see* BOURBON, §I(5)) began to re-create such a cabinet and also made improvements to Fontainebleau and the Palais du Louvre, but the new Salle des Antiques in the Louvre was barely completed at the time of his assassination. During the late 16th century the most interesting of the royal collectors was Henry II's wife, Catherine de' Medici (*see* VALOIS, (16)), who had an abiding interest in portraits. She set up a gallery that contained hundreds of portraits of historical figures and that was modelled after Paolo Giovio's museum in his house on Lake Como, Italy. Partly through her influence, portrait galleries became common in France in the 16th century and the early 17th.

3. 17TH CENTURY.

In France, as elsewhere in Europe in the early 17th century, there was a surge of collecting activity, for which collections of curiosities, such as that formed by Francis I, had provided a precedent. Such collections, frequently of encyclopedic range, were based on the German *Wunderkammer* (*see* KUNSTKAMMER) and frequently included pictures, particularly if they were painted on such unusual supports as plaster, shell, copper or jasper. Such collecting was not dominated by Court taste, nor was it confined to Paris. NICOLAS-CLAUDE FABRI DE PEIRESC, Conseiller au Parlement de Provence, an antiquary and friend of Rubens, remains one of the best-known *curieux*, as they were called. His library, which was an important part of his collection, was kept in rooms also filled with statues, vases, portraits and mathematical instruments, as well as an odd assortment of mummies and stuffed animals. Such collections could be found in many provincial towns, particularly in the south; Montpellier, Aix-en-Provence, Arles, Lyon, Nîmes and Avignon, localities rich in antique remains, were obvious centres. Such collections of shells, flowers and natural curiosities frequently included medals and inscriptions.

Although learned collections of this kind may have been the rule, there were collectors who were mainly interested in paintings. At Lyon, where there was a rich middle class, whose fortunes were based on banking and the silk industry, there were several important collectors of Poussin's work, though Pointel (*d* 1660), the most celebrated, moved to Paris *c.* 1641. Jacob Spon, an antiquary from Lyon, listed several collectors in Paris who acquired nothing but paintings, and differentiated between those who collected contemporary works and those—including Charles de Blanchefort de Créquy, Duc de Lesdiguières (*see* LESDIGUIÈRES, CHARLES DE BLANCHEFORT, (2)), and Everard Jabach, probably the best-known collectors of the early 17th century—who bought both contemporary and older works.

Marie de Medici (*see* BOURBON, §I(6)), on her arrival in Paris in 1601, immediately began to improve her surroundings by buying works of art. Her most important commission was that given to Rubens for a series of paintings (from 1622–5) to decorate the newly built Palais du Luxembourg (begun 1615). Her son Louis XIII (*reg* 1610–43; *see* BOURBON, §I(7)) continued the interest in the revival of Italian art. Although not as active a collector as his brother, Gaston Bourbon, Duc d'Orléans (*see* BOURBON, §I(8)), Louis nevertheless acquired works by a number of Venetian Old Masters, as well as several by such contemporary French painters as Claude Lorrain and Georges de La Tour. The dispersal of several Italian collections, in particular that of the Gonzaga family in Mantua followed by the paintings in the collection of Charles I of England and his court in 1649–53, led to the formation of collections on a scale never before possible. Armand-Jean du Plessis, Cardinal de Richelieu (*see* RICHELIEU (ii), (1)), his protégé and successor Cardinal Jules Mazarin (*see* MAZARIN, (1)) and EVERARD JABACH, the German-born banker and financier who resided in Paris, were the three men, all admirers of Italian art, who profited most from this situation. Jabach, through the agency of the dealer Oudancour, was the most important buyer at the sale of Charles I's paintings. He developed a love of drawings at an early age and also admired the work of Netherlandish and German artists: Hans Holbein the younger's portrait of *Anne of Cleves* (1539–40; Paris, Louvre) belonged to him, as did Titian's *Man with a Glove* (*c.* 1523; Paris, Louvre), bought from the Gonzagas, and the *Fête champêtre* (*c.* 1511; Paris, Louvre; formerly attributed to Giorgione), the latter two of which are perhaps the most admired from his collection. Jabach also bought paintings by such contemporary Italian artists as Domenichino, Giovanni Lanfranco, Domenico Fetti and Pietro da Cortona. Richelieu, on the other hand, showed no interest in contemporary Italian work until late in life. He owned antiquities and replicas of antique statues, with which, like Mazarin and NICOLAS FOUQUET, he decorated his houses. He also collected paintings by such earlier artists as Leonardo, Perugino and Mantegna, and among contemporary artists preferred the work of Poussin and Philippe de Champaigne. However, his interest in Italian painting may have influenced the collecting tastes of LOUIS PHÉLYPEAUX DE LA VRILLIÈRE, whose hôtel (parts survive as the Banque de France) once contained the most splendid gallery of 17th-century Italian painting in Paris. La Vrillière preferred contemporary Italian art, though of an austere and heroic kind, more characteristic of 17th-century French art than the refined mythologies preferred by Mazarin, whose tastes had been formed in Italy.

By the late 17th century, however, the royal collection had become unrivalled, as Louis XIV's minister Jean-Baptiste Colbert attempted to restore the splendour of Fontainebleau (*see* COLBERT, (1)). The collection absorbed—at least in part—most of the private ones of the period, including that of the disgraced Fouquet and much of Jabach's, especially his large collection of over 5500 drawings. The Duc de Richelieu, who had inherited much of the collection of Cardinal de Richelieu, his great-uncle, and added to it a number of works by Poussin, lost it at a game of tennis with Louis XIV as the result of a rash bet (*see* RICHELIEU (ii), (2)). However, as Jabach and Mazarin had done on previous occasions, he built up a new collection with the help of the critic Roger de Piles and became one of the first important collectors of the work of Rubens, an artist not as yet much admired in France in spite of Marie de Medici's commissions from him. Works by masters of the Venetian High Renaissance were introduced into the royal collection for the first time through the acquisition of Jabach's pictures in particular. Louis XIV's celebrated policy of acquiring originals of fine antique sculpture or copies of them was not, as far as can be deduced, the expression of a private taste but rather an ambitious attempt at magnificent public display in which didactic intentions played a part, since he planned to provide the newly established Académie de France in Rome with a set of casts of the best antique statues. The pupils of the Académie assisted in the programme of making casts and copies, and the director took advantage of opportunities to acquire original pieces from great family collections in Rome (*see* §XV below). In 1685, for example, Louis XIV acquired the *Cincinnatus* and the *Germanicus* (both Paris, Louvre), which were the first two celebrated antique statues to enter his collection, purchasing them from Prince Savelli, who had inherited them from the Peretti family.

Dealers played a limited role in the formation of the great collections of the 17th century. Mazarin, who rented the Hôtel d'Estrées in Paris for the purpose of holding auctions there, bought Raphael's portrait of *Baldassare Castiglione* (1514–15; Paris, Louvre) through Alfonso López, a Spanish dealer. In 1682 Louis XIV bought from the dealer Alvárez 33 pictures of remarkable consistency of taste by Bolognese artists and northern European artists working in Italy, of which 18 of the 29 identified were landscapes. The following year Alvárez sold two paintings by Poussin to the King. However, such diplomatic agents as Luigi Strozzi, who represented France at the court of the dukes of Tuscany, or the Abbé ELPIDIO BENEDETTI, who was based in Rome, were more important than dealers in forming great collections. Painters, among them Gabriel Blanchard, Jacques Stella, Claude Vignon and Charles Le Brun (the last of whom almost certainly advised Colbert), also bought and sold the work of other artists. Print collectors probably relied rather more on dealers, since there was a flourishing print trade in Paris in the 17th century. The Abbé MICHEL DE MAROLLES, the best known print collector of his day, bought a large part of his collection at the sale of Delorme (possibly Charles de l'Orme, *d* 1655) but was also a customer of Pierre Mariette (ii). The large number of print-dealers working in Paris then—some of whom, like the Mariette family, played an important part in the development of the market in the 18th century—suggests that customers were plentiful.

4. 18TH CENTURY. The earliest and most splendid of 18th-century collections was that of Philippe II, Duc d'Orléans (*see* ORLÉANS, House of, (3)), whose artistic adviser was the painter Antoine Coypel. The collection was assembled by methods not fundamentally different from those of the great 17th-century collectors; thus, a number of pictures arrived as gifts from those anxious to secure the Duke's favours. From a dealer in Rotterdam, Abbé Guillaume Dubois obtained for the Duke a series of *Seven Sacraments* (Duke of Sutherland priv. col., on loan to Edinburgh, N.G.) that Poussin had painted for Paul Fréart, Sieur de Chantelou. The Duke owed his most spectacular success to the skill of the banker Pierre Crozat (*see* CROZAT, (1)), who acquired for him most of the collection of Christina, Queen of Sweden, much of which had belonged previously to the Gonzaga family in Mantua. During these negotiations Crozat built up a collection for himself, and on his return to Paris his generous and attractive hospitality did much to spread a taste for art, particularly for drawings: Pierre-Jean Mariette (*see* MARIETTE, (4)) and the Comte de Caylus were among his regular visitors. In the early 18th century sale catalogues, as yet relatively few in number, were inaccurate and full of misspellings. Mariette, whose purchases at Crozat's sale in 1741 laid the foundations of his own extraordinary collection, wrote the catalogue for the sale, which set entirely new standards of scholarship. This procedure was consciously emulated by EDMÉ-FRANÇOIS GERSAINT when he prepared the catalogue for Quentin de Lorangère's sale in 1744.

After 1750 Mariette's methods became standard, and they were taken up by Pierre Rémy (*d* ?after 1787), who added a note of unashamed commercialism and exaggerated enthusiasm to the description of the lots. Auction sales increasingly became the focus of the art trade; the most prominent dealers wrote the catalogues and acted as experts. These men were often artists, though better remembered as dealers: Rémy, Gersaint, Pierre-François Basan, Françoise Joullain, Gabriel Huquier, the engraver Boileau, Alexandre-Joseph Paillet and Jean-Baptiste Glomy (*d c.* 1786). Members of the Académie Royale de Peinture et de Sculpture were forbidden to deal in pictures; artists who did so were expected to belong to the Académie de Saint-Luc, which tried to retain a monopoly of the trade. JACQUES AVED, who was not a member, was censured for excessive dealing in other artists' works. Dealers helped to form collections: Boileau advised Louis-François, Prince de Conti; Gersaint went to The Hague in 1745 with a commission from Augustin Blondel de Gagny; the banker Nicolas Beaujon relied on Rémy when he formed his collection in the 1780s. They often bought at auction: for example Rémy, Basan, Joullain, Paillet and Jean-Baptiste-Pierre Le Brun all made large purchases at the sale of the government official Paul Randon de Boisset's collection in 1777, presumably sometimes with commissions from clients but also for their own stock.

Picture collecting, no longer dominated by Court taste, was now chiefly associated with moneyed aristocracy, particularly bankers and tax farmers. Bolognese, Dutch and Flemish art was the mainstay of these collections, although a small number of collectors, of whom ANGE-LAURENT DE LA LIVE DE JULLY in the 1760s was one of the first, began to concentrate particularly on French painting. Others included Louis-Gabriel, Marquis de Véri; Joseph-Hyacinthe, Comte de Vaudreuil; the Abbé Joseph-Marie Terray; and the financier Laurent Grimod de la Reynière. Many collectors added galleries to their hôtels in Paris, and these could be visited on application, much like English country houses. Works of the Dutch school became popular at this time through the activities of Gersaint, who preferred Italian art but frequently bought pictures while travelling in the Netherlands. The dealers Paillet and Jean-Baptiste-Pierre Le Brun were particularly associated with Dutch art.

The art market in Paris became increasingly international: Frederick the Great of Prussia, Catherine the Great of Russia and Gustav III of Sweden all bought pictures in France through transactions in which painters and critics played significant roles. For example, it was through the combined efforts of Diderot, Etienne-Maurice Falconet and Melchior Grimm that Catherine the Great was able to buy the major part of the Crozat collection, now in the State Hermitage, St Petersburg. At a rather less grand level, there is the example of the English writer William Beckford, whose love of French books and art caused him to linger in Paris after the onset of the French Revolution, moving into ever more splendid houses as the owners fled and buying up the residue of their possessions.

The Revolution and the wars that followed resulted in losses, of which the most dramatic was the sale, by Louis-Philippe-Joseph, Duc d'Orléans (Philippe Egalité), of the great collection of the Orléans dynasty. Within a few years, however, such Napoleonic emissaries, diplomats, scholars and soldiers as Vivant Denon, François Cacault and Maréchal Soult brought back from other parts of Europe paintings that were to open up new fields of collecting in the areas of Spanish art and 13th- and 14th-century Italian art. The sense of the past, acutely rendered by the events of the Revolution, did much to stimulate the collection of medieval and early Renaissance artefacts; the example of Alexandre Lenoir (*see* LENOIR, (1)) was followed by that of ALEXANDRE DU SOMMERARD (whose collection now forms the Musée de Cluny, Paris), while an outstanding, slightly later example is the collection of Jules Soulages (now in the Victoria and Albert Museum, London).

5. 19TH CENTURY. The taste for Dutch and Flemish art established in the 18th century continued during the Empire. It was shared by several members of the Imperial family and was often accompanied by a liking for contemporary French painting that shared some of the characteristics of Dutch art, such as the work of the Troubadour artists. The number of dealers increased, and a new phenomenon emerged of the dealer specializing entirely in contemporary painting. One of the first 19th-century collections devoted entirely to modern art was that of GIOVANNI BATTISTA SOMMARIVA, whose Neo-classical tastes prolonged an interest in that style well into the Romantic period. He formed his collection by dealing directly with artists, but collectors came increasingly to rely on dealers, whose activities dominated artistic life by the end of the century. By 1830 it was possible to associate certain dealers with particular trends in contemporary art: Alphonse Giroux specialized in Gothic ruins; CLAUDE SCHROTH and JOHN ARROWSMITH in English art and the young French Romantics; Paul Durand-Ruel supported landscape artists (*see* DURAND-RUEL, (2)). It was not until the 1840s that the sale of collections devoted entirely to modern pictures became standard; that of the Duchesse d'Orléans in 1852 has been taken as a watershed for the value of pictures by Ingres, Delacroix, Ary Scheffer and Paul Delaroche. Thereafter, auction sales were to play a significant role in increasing the value of dealers' stock. This brought about a change in status for many artists; the artist 'homme du monde', exemplified by Ernest Meissonier, was a phenomenon of the Second Empire, and the activities of the dealer ADOLPHE GOUPIL brought large financial rewards for the artists he promoted. Speculation, as ever, must have been a factor encouraging the frequent dispersal of collections of modern pictures at the Hôtel Drouot. Some of the most celebrated, those of LAURENT-RICHARD, Khalil-Bey and Alfred Edwards, sold during the 1860s and 1870s, closely resembled one another; their owners had drawn on the advice and expertise of two dealers, Paul Durand-Ruel and HECTOR BRAME.

There was a small group of collectors of 18th-century French art who were part of an increasing trend towards collecting contemporary paintings. They included Richard Seymour-Conway, 4th Marquess of Hertford, the Marquis de Cypierre, Eudoxe Marcille (1814–90) and Camille Marcille (1816–75), all of whom lent pictures to an exhibition held in Paris in 1860 at the premises of the dealer Louis Martinet and organized by Francis Petit. Shortly after, the value of 18th-century art rose steeply; by the end of the century it once again became the province of a financial aristocracy, and the general shift in taste away from collections of Old Masters brought rich rewards for some of the living artists whose work was in the greatest demand. Paul Durand-Ruel's exhibitions of Impressionist paintings in the USA in the late 1880s marked a further important expansion of the transatlantic market already explored by Adolphe Goupil when he promoted the works of Jean-Léon Gérôme, William-Adolphe Bouguereau and Alexandre Cabanel in the 1860s.

6. 20TH CENTURY. Dealers who had specialized in Impressionist paintings at the end of the 19th century continued to supply a rich international clientele in the early years of the 20th century. Collecting on a grand scale was not confined to the American market; Alexandre Berthier, Prince de Wagram (1883–1918), for example, owned a large collection of Impressionist paintings that the dealer Roland Knoedler bought after his death. Some collectors, among them the couturier JACQUES DOUCET, acquired at different times 18th-century paintings and Impressionist works. René Gimpel and his sometime associate Nathan Wildenstein sold 18th-century and Impressionist paintings largely to an American market, where a growing taste for interior decoration provided dealers with further scope. The dealer most closely associated with the avant-garde, particularly the Cubist movement, was DANIEL-HENRY KAHNWEILER. Like Durand-Ruel, his habit was to buy from young artists whose reputations had yet to be established. Among his early customers were ROGER DUTILLEUL, whose collection was inherited by the textile manufacturer Jean Masurel of Roubaix, and Sergey Shchukin (see SHCHUKIN, (1)), much of whose collection is now in the Pushkin Museum of Fine Arts, Moscow. Until 1939 the market for contemporary art in New York was dominated by Paris dealers and their agents, but from World War II a market for American painting displaced French art. From 1945 Paris became much less important as an international centre for art sales, largely owing to extremely strict legislation governing the export of works of art and the monopoly that allowed only the *Commissaires-Priseurs*, appointed by the French government, to hold auctions. Such sales were rarely specialized, unlike those held by the English auction houses in Monaco, and were therefore less attractive to prospective clients. In the late 20th century the French government attempted to protect the national heritage and to stimulate the art market; for example, the law of 1968 governing *dation* (comparable with the English *in lieu* system) was extended to cover gifts, division of estates *inter vivos* (from one living person to another) and wealth tax, thereby making possible such acquisitions as that by the Louvre in 1990 of a collection of porcelain, jewellery and furniture from Baron Edmond Adolph Maurice Jules Jacques de Rothschild (*b* 1926). In 1990 a new law was passed allowing insurance companies to invest in works of art through unquoted companies. One of the first acquisitions of this sort was Titian's *Allegory of Marriage*, incorrectly known as *Allegory of Alfonso d'Avalos* (*c.* 1530–35; Paris, Louvre; *see* ALLEGORY, fig. 6), sold by the Marquis Hubert de Ganay, who had inherited it from his aunt the Comtesse de Béhague.

Unlike London, Paris retained its strong indigenous market for works of art. It seemed likely that the relaxing in 1993 of some restrictions governing auctions and exports would eventually result in a re-emergence of Paris's importance as an international centre. From 1970 the reassessment of the reputation of many 18th- and 19th-century French artists was accompanied by the emergence of dealers with a specialized interest in these areas, able to supply private collectors and museums with what they wanted.

BIBLIOGRAPHY

A.-N. Dézallier d'Argenville: *Voyage pittoresque de Paris* (Paris, 1749)
C. F. Joullain: *Réflexions sur la peinture et la gravure, accompagnées d'une courte dissertation sur le commerce de la curiosité, et les ventes en général* (Metz, 1786)
L. V. Thierry: *Guide des amateurs et des étrangers voyageurs à Paris*, 2 vols (Paris, 1786–7)
E. Piot: *Cabinet de l'amateur et de l'antiquaire*, 4 vols (Paris, 1842–6)
C. Blanc: *Le Trésor de la curiosité*, 2 vols (Paris, 1857)
L. Courajod, ed.: *Livre-journal de Lazare Duvaux, marchand–bijoutier ordinaire du roy, 1748–1758*, 2 vols (Paris, 1873)
A. Bertolotti: 'Objets d'art transportés de Rome en France du 16e au 19e siècle, 1541–1864', *Nouv. Archvs A. Fr.*, n. s. 1, ii (1880–81), pp. 57–82
P. Eudel: *L'Hôtel Drouot et la curiosité* (Paris, 1881–)
E. Bonnaffé: *Dictionnaire des amateurs français au XVIIe siècle* (Paris, 1884)
C. Stryienski: *La Galerie du régent, Philippe d'Orléans* (Paris, 1913)
J. Alazard: *L'Abbé Luigi Strozzi, correspondant artistique de Mazarin, de Colbert, de Louvois et de La Teulière* (Paris, 1924)
R. Brun: 'Notes sur le commerce des objets d'art en France et principalement à Avignon à la fin du XIVe siècle', *Bib. Ecole Chartes*, cv (1934), pp. 327–46
R. Brimo: *L'Evolution du goût aux Etats-Unis* (Paris, 1938)
I. Origo: *The Merchant of Prato, Francesco di Marco Datini* (New York, 1957)
P. Verlet: 'Le Commerce des objets d'art et les marchands–mercier à Paris au XVIIIe siècle', *An. Econ. Soc. Civilis.* (1958), pp. 10–29
G. Wildenstein: 'Pasithée, Maréchale de Retz et ses collections', *Gaz. B.-A.*, n. s. 6, lii (1958), pp. 209–18
R. Gimpel: *Journal d'un collectionneur marchand de tableaux* (Paris, 1963)
E. Duverger: 'Réflexions sur le commerce d'art au XVIIIe siècle', *Theorien und Probleme*, iii of *Stil und Überlieferung in der Kunst des Abendlandes* (Berlin, 1967)
R. Moulin: *Le Marché de la peinture en France* (Paris, 1967)
Apollo, xcvii (1973) [issue devoted to 18th-century French collections]
F. Haskell: *Rediscoveries in Art* (London, 1976)
M.-F. Pérez: 'Collectionneurs et amateurs d'art à Lyon au XVIIIe siècle', *Rev. A.* [Paris], 47 (1980), pp. 43–52
F. Arquié-Bruley: 'Les Commissaires–priseurs parisiens avant 1870', *Rev. A.* [Paris], 54 (1981), pp. 85–9
F. Haskell and N. Penny: *Taste and the Antique* (New Haven and London, 1981)
M. Grivel: *Le Commerce de l'estampe à Paris au XVIIe siècle* (Geneva, 1986)
A. Brejon de Lavergnée: *L'Inventaire Le Brun* (Paris, 1987) [about Le Brun's manuscript 'Inventaire des tableaux du Cabinet du Roy']
K. Pomian: *Collectionneurs, amateurs et curieux, Paris, Venise, XVIe–XVIIIe siècle* (Paris, 1987)
A. Schnapper: *Le Géant, la licorne et la tulipe: Collections et collectionneurs dans la France du XVIIe siècle* (Paris, 1988)
Les Donateurs du Louvre (exh. cat., ed. M.-A. Dupuy; Paris, Louvre, 1989)
C. Wainwright: 'In Lucifer's Metropolis', *Country Life*, clxxxvi (1 Oct 1992), pp. 82–9
C. B. Bailey: *Patrons or Clients: Collecting Contemporary Art in Paris at the End of the 'ancien régime'* (in preparation)

LINDA WHITELEY

XIV. Museums.

1. Origins, 16th–18th centuries. 2. Early museums in Paris, late 18th century. 3. Distribution to provincial museums, early 19th century. 4. The Palais du Luxembourg and Musée Historique. 5. Museum policy from the July Monarchy to the early years of the Third Republic. 6. Museum management, late 19th century and 20th.

1. ORIGINS, 16TH–18TH CENTURIES. Jean-Baptiste Boisot, abbot of St Vincent in Besançon, is usually given

credit for establishing the first museum in France by bequeathing his collection of coins, medals, books and works of art, assembled from the relics of the collection of Cardinal Antoine Perrenot de Granvelle (1530–86), to the Benedictine Order in St Vincent on condition that it be made available twice weekly to anyone who wished to study there. The museum was intended primarily as a place for scholarship, like the cabinets of curiosities associated with a number of early museums. Religious houses provided a good basis for scholarly collecting. The cabinet of antiquities preserved in Ste Geneviève Abbey since 1675 and based on the famous collection of NICOLAS-CLAUDE FABRI DE PEIRESC, was probably very similar to the museum in Besançon and might have a better claim than Granvelle's cabinet as the earliest museum in France. Monastic collections and private cabinets were, however, sometimes very like museums in character, and it is probably unwise rigidly to insist on the differences between the institutional museums and the collections from which they developed in the 17th century.

Art galleries evolved from a different basis and, with the notable exception of the museum in the Palais du Louvre, Paris, were associated with the growth of public art schools. Original paintings by Old Masters, copies, contemporary paintings, drawings and engravings were valued as examples to inspire and instruct students. The oldest of these collections, assembled at the school of the Académie Royale de Peinture et de Sculpture in Paris, consisted largely of MORCEAUX DE RÉCEPTION submitted by artists to the Académie in the 17th and 18th centuries. One of the earliest recorded collections outside Paris was bequeathed in 1752 to the art school at Reims by a former director, Ferrand de Monthelon, who acquired his paintings in Germany and Italy. From 1783 François Devosges III, director of the art school at Dijon, purchased works of art with a grant from the Etats de Bourgogne and in 1787 he assembled them, as well as copies of Italian works painted by the school's students, in a museum sanctioned by the Etats. Apart from the museum at Dijon and a few others, including the art schools in Aix-en-Provence and Valenciennes, collections assembled before the Revolution were probably very modest. They form part of the history of French museums only because they provided the foundations on which provincial museums developed in the 1790s, when an unexpected wealth of art was released into the keeping of the municipal councils after the Revolution.

After the decree of the Assemblée Nationale of 2 November 1790 that nationalized the property of the clergy, a commission was nominated to organize a series of storehouses in the provinces to hold works of art confiscated from the clergy and the émigrés. As the municipalities were responsible for administering these stores, the impetus in founding and maintaining public galleries of art passed from the art schools to the municipal councils. Within a few years the most important art schools' collections had been absorbed into the structure of the new municipal museums. The Musée des Beaux-Arts in Grenoble, established by the drawing-master in 1798 and opened to the public in 1800, was taken over by the local council in 1807. By 1812 these municipal stores, frequently situated in disused monasteries, had become the basis of museums in Tours, Nancy, Angers, Avignon, Bordeaux, Toulouse, Caen, Rouen, Le Mans, Rennes, Lille, Niort, Marseille, Grenoble, Montpellier and Nantes; existing museums in Aix-en-Provence, Valenciennes, Dijon and Reims were transformed by the spoils of the Revolution.

The policy of confiscating the property of the Church, largely inspired by a long-standing desire to conserve and classify the national heritage, became more urgent in August 1792 with the widespread destruction of monuments and works of art associated by the mob with religion and the monarchy. Although the *députés* were concerned by the effects of vandalism, they did not take effective measures until October 1793, when a decree of the Assemblée outlawed the destruction of the 'signs of feudalism and royalty' and called for their preservation in museums. The reaction after the fall of Maximilien Marie Isidore Robespierre consolidated the movement to create museums by linking the disgraced Jacobins with the vandalism in Paris and the provinces.

2. EARLY MUSEUMS IN PARIS, LATE 18TH CENTURY. The history of the Musée des Monuments Français, which opened in 1795 in converted premises in the monastery of the Petits-Augustins in Paris, mirrored changing attitudes towards the conservation of the national heritage. After the fall of the Jacobins, Alexandre Lenoir (*see* LENOIR, (1)), founder of the museum, represented himself as saving historical monuments from imminent destruction, although the museum had originated as a consequence of the Decree of 1790 before vandalism had become a serious threat. Nevertheless, the zeal with which he transferred tombs and monuments to the Petits-Augustins exceeded the simple need for preservation. Lenoir laid out the rooms in his museum with a sense of the theatric and an affection for the works of art that helped to give them an aesthetic value that the antiquaries who had previously studied them had not felt so keenly. The monuments assembled in the museum and its garden contributed to extending the taste for national history of all periods, especially the Middle Ages, among French writers and artists, including the so-called Troubadours, a group of Royalist and Catholic painters who studied in the museum in the early 19th century (*see* TROUBADOUR STYLE). However, the presence of the royal tombs from Saint-Denis Abbey indicated the museum's implicit part in the desecration of French churches; this was intolerable to the clergy, who staged a reaction in 1815.

The Musée Central des Arts (also known as the Musée de la République), which opened in 1793 in the Grande Galerie of the Palais du Louvre, was to an even greater extent heir to ideas and proposals associated with the *ancien régime*. In keeping with a tendency among 18th-century European monarchs to put State collections on public view, the Directeur des Bâtiments du Roi assembled 96 paintings from the royal collection and placed them in the Palais du Luxembourg, where from 1750 to 1779 they were visible to the public two days a week. The gallery, which included works by Leonardo, Raphael, Poussin, Veronese, Titian, Correggio and Andrea del Sarto, was probably designed as the precursor to a more ambitious installation in the Louvre. The pictures were evacuated when the Palais du Luxembourg became the official residence of the Comte de Provence, but financial difficulties and structural problems involving the arrangement of the windows in the Grande Galerie of the Louvre delayed progress until after the fall of the monarchy (1792), when the royal proposal was immediately adopted as the policy of the Revolution. Jean-Marie Roland, Minister of the Interior, nominated a commission to put the long-delayed conversion of the Grande Galerie in hand, and, despite opposition from Lenoir, who feared the new museum would undermine his own ambitions for the Petits-Augustins, the museum opened on 10 August 1793.

Unlike Lenoir's museum, the display of paintings in the Louvre confirmed conventional ideas of what constituted great art. The majority was taken from the royal collection, while most of the others were religious paintings by well-known 17th-century artists and had been removed from churches in Paris and the environs after 1790. The existence of the museum, being based on confiscated works of art, encouraged an extension of its policy to include works from states conquered by France where the argument for conservation was not applicable. The process began in the Netherlands after the victory of Fleurus (1794), when the commissioners appointed to remove works of art sent many Flemish pictures back to Paris. A few 15th-century paintings, of which Hubert van Eyck's *Adoration of the Lamb* (*c.* 1423–32; Ghent, St Bavo; for illustration *see* EYCK, VAN, (1)) was the most conspicuous, were included but these were the exceptions in a collection that was otherwise based on a conventional taste for the work of Rubens and his contemporaries. These paintings were the precursors of even better-known sculptures and paintings taken during Napoleon Bonaparte's first Italian campaign and brought to Paris in convoys from 1796 to 1798.

3. DISTRIBUTION TO PROVINCIAL MUSEUMS, EARLY 19TH CENTURY. The policy of expanding the Louvre through confiscation and peace treaties put extreme pressure on the storehouses in Paris and Versailles, which by 1801 contained over 1600 paintings. A consular decree of 1 September 1801 authorized a distribution of over half of these paintings to the départements, provided that the municipalities would pay the costs of transport, restoration and installation in an adequate museum. This decree, inspired by a need to dispose of a surplus of paintings, involved 12 towns in France: Lyon, Bordeaux, Strasbourg, Marseille, Rouen, Nantes, Dijon, Toulouse, Caen, Lille, Rennes and Nancy, as well as Brussels, Mainz and Geneva, three towns in the occupied territories; the following year Tours and Montpellier were added at the request of the town councils. Grenoble, inexplicably overlooked, became a major recipient of State generosity after a similar request. In 1811 a further 209 paintings were distributed to Lyon, Grenoble, Brussels, Toulouse, Caen and Dijon. By this means a number of spectacular works of art by Perugino, Rubens, Veronese and others found their way into provincial museums.

At the time, however, some of the directors of the museums responded with disappointment; the Musée des Beaux-Arts in Bordeaux, according to its director Pierre Lacour, received only 'wretched copies passed off as originals or originals still more wretched'. Although, in retrospect, this statement appears a harsh judgement, it probably seemed a justifiable comment at the time, as distribution to the provinces was chiefly devised as a convenient way to dispose of unwanted works of art that included, almost by accident, a few masterpieces by artists who were already well represented at the Louvre.

After the fall of Napoleon, most works of art that had been taken from the Netherlands, Italy and the German states were returned, despite a campaign of delayed tactics by VIVANT DENON, who, as director of the Louvre since 1802, had been chiefly responsible for creating the Musée Napoleon. The provincial museums were also requested to return works taken from the conquered states, but the directors of the museums stalled, and the foreign owners, for the most part, abandoned their efforts to recover their plundered heritage. In any case, most works in the provincial museums had come from French collections, although the quantity of paintings by Rubens removed from Flanders ensured a rich distribution of his art to regional museums where they mostly remained after several of his more famous works from Mechelen and Antwerp, allocated to the Louvre, had been returned to the Netherlands.

4. THE PALAIS DU LUXEMBOURG AND MUSÉE HISTORIQUE. With the loss of so many treasures from the Louvre, Rubens's cycle of paintings for Marie de' Medici (1622–5; Paris, Louvre; *see* HISTORY PAINTING, fig. 2), Eustache Le Sueur's series of the *Life of St Bruno* (from 1645; Paris, Louvre) and Joseph Vernet's and Jean-François Huë's *Ports of France* (begun 1753; Paris, Louvre, Mus. Mar. & Pal. Luxembourg; Cherbourg, Mus. B.-A.) were transferred from the Palais du Luxembourg to fill the void. The empty gallery in the Palais du Luxembourg was transformed into a museum of contemporary French art, which opened to the public on 24 April 1818. The works of art in the new museum, assembled from various sources, were increased by purchases made chiefly at the annual Salons. By 1822 the collection contained 103 paintings, including major works by David, Anne-Louis Girodet, Pierre Guérin and their pupils, which generally were transferred to the Louvre after an artist's death to make room for work by younger artists. This was only a partial solution to the overcrowding at the Luxembourg, a problem that has continued to affect museums of contemporary art.

The removal of Napoleonic battle paintings to the Musée Historique, which opened to the public in 1837 in the château of Versailles, partly eased the problem of space at the Luxembourg. The Musée Historique, which included many 17th- and 18th-century paintings representing modern history, was not intended to be a museum of contemporary art, although it acquired this character through the scale of commissions given by Louis-Philippe to many of the leading artists of the day. However, its holdings did not attract enthusiastic reviews from most art critics, and when the King fell from power in 1848, the museum lost its political purpose.

5. MUSEUM POLICY FROM THE JULY MONARCHY TO THE EARLY YEARS OF THE THIRD REPUBLIC. As well as purchasing works for the Luxembourg, the governments of the July Monarchy and successive regimes increasingly purchased paintings at the annual Salons for distribution to the municipal museums. This coincided with a phenomenal expansion in the number of regional museums, which from 1830 until 1914 increased at the rate of several a year. Learned societies in the provinces were particularly instrumental in establishing museums of archaeology in Avranches (1835), Béziers (1839), Langres (1846), Montbéliard (1832), Saint-Lô (1859), Saint-Dizier (1881) and elsewhere. These were directly related to an increased interest in archaeology in France in the first half of the 19th century, which received national recognition when Napoleon III founded the Musée des Antiquités Nationales in Saint-Germain-en-Laye in 1855. Sociétés des Amis des Arts, which also proliferated in France in the same period, were founded and managed by one or two museums but they were of little importance compared to the gifts and bequests from artists and collectors that enriched many existing museums and on which many new museums were founded after 1830.

The wealth of Old Master paintings in provincial museums was increased by the distribution of works of art from the collection of the disgraced Italian administrator GIAMPIETRO CAMPANA. These had originally been purchased by Napoleon III as the basis of an industrial museum on the model of the South Kensington (now Victoria and Albert) Museum in London but were ultimately dispersed throughout France after opposition from the Louvre. The 14th- and 15th-century Italian works from Campana's collection enriched the holdings of museums that already had many works by painters of a later date. However, this distribution was not dictated by concern for the provincial museums but by a desire to escape from an embarrassing impasse, in which Napoleon III found himself caught between the administrators of the Louvre, who feared opposition from a rival institution, and the curators of the Campana collection and the artists at the Académie Royale, who supported the proposed museum. Consequently no national museum of industrial design was established until 1877, when the Union Central des Arts Décoratifs founded the Musée des Arts Décoratifs in a wing of the Louvre. In 1872 a second major distribution of Old Master paintings took place, also as a measure of convenience and which included many large or damaged pictures for which the Louvre had neither space nor use.

Despite the sporadic influx of Old Master paintings, most of the provincial museums concentrated in the hundred years after 1815 on the acquisition of contemporary art. The system of distributing State purchases of Salon paintings to the municipal museums (which took the place of the Old Master paintings that had been dispersed during the First Empire) brought a wealth of 19th-century French art into the regions. This tendency was rooted in the provincial museums' origins in regional art schools and academies. The development of regional collections from works of art confiscated in the 1790s was almost everywhere entrusted to either the director of the local art school or other artists in the locality. The best known of these artist–administrators—Pierre Lacour in

Bordeaux, L.-J. Jay in Nancy, François Devosges III in Dijon, and Le Carpentier and Lemonnier in Rouen—were conscious chiefly of the needs of local artists in selecting and displaying works of art. Jean-Antoine Chaptal also explicitly favoured towns where there was a community of artists capable of taking advantage of the works of the Old Masters that he distributed. The curators of the municipal museums that were established throughout France in the 19th century were usually, like their predecessors in the 1790s, practising artists with a preference for the work of their contemporaries. They were assisted by the distribution of Salon paintings purchased in increasing numbers by the government in Paris for the benefit of a growing network of museums that by 1900 numbered more than 300. The scale of State largess varied from the works sent to the Musée des Beaux-Arts in Lille and the Musée de Picardie in Amiens, both of which received over 200 paintings mostly by contemporary artists, to the Musée Municipal in Parthenay (Deux-Sèvres), where four Sèvres vases deposited by the State constituted the entire museum. Landscapes and still-lifes formed an increasing part of the works distributed during the Second Empire and after, corresponding to the wishes of many museum directors, who, like directors of collections of contemporary art at that time and later, found themselves increasingly encumbered by works that were not old enough to be of historic interest nor new enough to be fashionable. The curator of the Musée des Beaux-Arts at Béziers, who in the mid-1890s told the government inspectorate that he would willingly exchange any of the State deposits for paintings by Renoir, Degas, Monet, Gauguin, Rodin, Toulouse-Lautrec, Cézanne, Camille Pissarro, Odilon Redon, Maurice Denis, Vuillard or Bonnard, was exceptional in his choice but voiced a not uncommon dissatisfaction with the accumulated effects of a policy that had enriched the provincial museums with numerous works by artists who had become unfashionable.

Copies, which in the 18th century were sometimes preferred to second-rate originals, fell into disfavour in the course of the 19th century. In 1792 Devosges included 26 copies among the 37 Italianate pictures that he selected from the confiscated property of the clergy and émigrés for his new museum in Dijon. Like plaster casts and reproductive engravings, copies had an important place in the best-equipped art schools. In 1834 Adolphe Thiers set up a Musée des Etudes at the Ecole des Beaux-Arts that was the first of its kind, although heir to a tradition originating in the Court of Francis I (*reg* 1515–47). The more ambitious Musée des Copies, which opened in Paris in 1871 when CHARLES BLANC was director of the Bureau des Beaux-Arts, attracted much hostility and was closed down in 1873 by his successor (*see* COPY).

6. MUSEUM MANAGEMENT, LATE 19TH CENTURY AND 20TH. In the 19th century the majority of French museums were funded and managed by the municipalities. However, there was almost no legislation to govern the conduct of these institutions. The committee of enquiry set up in 1905 by the Minister of Education could find only two significant pieces of legislation: a decree of 1794 establishing the need to isolate museum premises from industrial furnaces, and a clause in the decree of 1852 concerning administrative decentralization that gave local prefects the right to nominate museum directors without reference to central government. To this could be added the more significant ruling of 22 February 1859 preventing the sale or dispersal of books and medals from public libraries that was used, on doubtful grounds, to prevent regional museums from selling works of art. The thousands of works sent to provincial museums by the government, however, gave the State a claim on a significant part of the regional collections and a right to appoint the curators of the more prominent museums, who increasingly came from the Ecole du Louvre.

The central government, by sending works of art to the many provincial museums, assumed a sort of control over their operations, whereby it established its right to approve the nomination of curators in any museum that had ten works or more on deposit. This right was strengthened by the law of 10 August 1941 that brought the curators of 20 provincial museums under the direct control of the State and limited the municipal right to propose acquisitions. The law also created an office for administering provincial museums, which after 1945 gave the government authority to reorganize museums throughout France. This included a long and difficult scheme to retrieve, through negotiated exchanges, the early Italian paintings from the Campana collection and install them in 1976 in a new museum, the Musée du Petit Palais, in Avignon. It also made possible expensive programmes of refurbishment in museums in Lyon, Marseille, Grenoble, Rouen, Lille and Amiens with substantial funding from central government.

The state of the national collection of contemporary art, transferred in 1886 from the Palais du Luxembourg to the Musée de l'Orangerie in Paris, was a matter of concern in the early 20th century. After 1914 the importance that had been given to art by 19th-century regimes diminished, to be further reduced by the economic problems of the 1930s. The Palais du Luxembourg, established as a museum where contemporary art would be displayed before it moved to more permanent locations, could not function without renewed funds. A reliance on gifts and loans, which changed the character of the institution as a *musée de passage*, put increased pressure on the small space available at the Musée de l'Orangerie. This led to the transfer of the collection to the Palais de Tokyo, used during the Exposition Internationale des Arts et Techniques dans la Vie Moderne in 1937; there it was formally established as the Musée National d'Art Moderne with its own permanent collection. The same premises then housed the Musée d'Art Moderne de la Ville de Paris, after the national modern art collection moved (see below).

The decline of central government as a patron of the museums was partly compensated for by the increasing role of the City of Paris in developing and managing collections. In addition to the studios of artists that it acquired by gift or bequest (Musée Jean-Jacques Henner, Musée Hébert, Musée Gustave Moreau, Musée Auguste Rodin, Musée Delacroix and Musée Renan-Scheffer) and the private collections for which it became responsible (Musée Jacquemart-André, Musée Marmottan and Musée Cognacq-Jay), the city council took possession of the structure built by Charles-Louis Girault for the Exposition Universelle of 1900 and brought together the dispersed works belonging to the City to form the collection of the Musée du Petit Palais. Art of the 19th century was particularly well represented in these collections, despite a weeding out in the mid-1930s when the more academic works were put into storage.

The accumulated effects of the policy of 19th-century governments in buying contemporary art, combined with the decline of the Palais du Luxembourg, left a heritage of 19th-century paintings in the storehouses of the Louvre and in provincial museums, as well as an inadequate provision for 20th-century art in Paris. The appointment in 1959 of ANDRÉ MALRAUX as Minister of State for Cultural Affairs marked the beginning of a renewed interest in the importance of museums by successive presidents, who responded to years of neglect with a succession of *Grands Projets*. The first of these ambitious schemes, the Centre Georges Pompidou, opened in 1977 and provided a grandiose home for the collections of the Musée National d'Art Moderne along with a library, an exhibition space and a centre for contemporary music (*see* PARIS, fig. 14). In 1973 President Georges Pompidou had taken up a suggestion that the disused Gare d'Orsay in Paris might be a suitable building for a gallery for 19th-century works of art that had been dispersed to provincial museums and that were in the reserves of the Louvre and the Musée du Jeu de Paume, in Paris. The Musée d'Orsay, opened in 1986, contains not only popular Impressionist and Post-Impressionist paintings but also 19th-century sculptures and paintings that had fallen from fashion in the early 20th century, but which in the 1970s were in the process of rediscovery and re-evaluation. The third of these great projects, undertaken by President François Mitterand, was the expansion of the Louvre to provide more space for its immense collections. Like the two earlier schemes initiated by President Pompidou, it was undertaken in response to inherited problems and was tackled with a scale of public funding for the arts unequalled since the Second Empire.

See also MUSEUM, §I.

BIBLIOGRAPHY
L. Clément de Ris: *Les Musées de province*, 2 vols (Paris, 1859–61)
P. de Chennevières: *Souvenirs d'un directeur des beaux-arts*, 5 vols (Paris, 1883–9)
L. Hautecoeur: *Les Musées de province* (Paris, 1908)
H. Lapauze: *Les Musées de province* (Paris, 1908)
C. Gould: *Trophy of Conquest* (London, 1965)
Le Musée du Luxembourg en 1874 (exh. cat. by G. Lacambre, Paris, Grand Pal., 1974)
F. Haskell, ed.: *Saloni, gallerie, musei e loro influenza sullo sviluppo dell'arte dei secoli XIX e XX* (Bologna, 1981)
P. Angrand: *Histoire des musées de province au XIXe siècle*, 4 vols (Les Sables d'Olonne, 1984–6)
E. Pommier: *Le Problème du musée à la veille de la Révolution* (Montargis, 1989)
D. J. Sherman: *Worthy Monuments: Art Museums and the Politics of Culture in Nineteenth-century France* (Cambridge, MA, and London, 1989)
For further bibliography *see* MUSEUM, §§I and II.

JON WHITELEY

XV. Art education.

Art education in France may be divided into two periods. Up to the middle of the 17th century the guild system offered its apprentices technical instruction in the practice of art, without recourse to theory. After the foundation in

Paris of the Académie Royale de Peinture et de Sculpture in 1648, followed by the Académie Royale d'Architecture in 1671, art education took on the essentially academic form that it retained into the late 20th century. Students were educated in specialized schools in the discipline of fine art through courses designed to promote an awareness of its theoretical aspects. Although provincial academies of art and schools of design flourished in the later 18th century and the 19th, they were generally subordinate to the institutions in Paris. By the 19th century they were as much concerned with teaching draughtsmanship to apprentices in industry as with teaching the fine arts. For the ambitious student they were only a first step to training in Paris at the Ecole des Beaux-Arts and, for the few, the winning of a scholarship to the Académie de France in Rome, the institutionalized culmination of the traditional artistic education. To a significant degree, therefore, art training in France since the 17th century has been the concern of government, which evolved a centralized institutional structure and a highly developed career path.

1. The guild system. 2. The Académie Royale de Peinture et de Sculpture and the Académie de France. 3. The Ecole Royale des Elèves Protégés. 4. Architectural education before the Revolution. 5. The Revolutionary period and its aftermath. 6. The Ecole des Beaux-Arts and teaching studios in the 19th century. 7. The reforms of 1863. 8. 20th-century developments.

1. THE GUILD SYSTEM. The guild or Communauté des Maîtres Peintres et Sculpteurs de Paris (commonly called the Maîtrise) was the earliest form of professional association in the arts and trained artisans (craftsmen skilled in the mechanical arts) in the technique, or 'art', of painting and sculpture. There were two kinds of guild apprentice (trainee or student): the *apprentis-privé*, who, as the son or relation of a master, was favoured with easy access to the guild; and the *apprentis-étranger*, who had to buy an apprenticeship and undergo a long period of training. The guild statutes of 1391 stipulated that an apprentice must engage for eight years and pay four livres per year or engage for ten years without a fee. Traditionally, the guild was familial, mercenary and secretive. Tuition was workshop-based and skills learnt through assisting the workshop master, who handed down studio recipes and formulae to his apprentices. Towards the end of the reign of Louis XIV (*reg* 1643–1715), the guild was allowed to open a school, given the official name of the Académie de Saint-Luc from 1723, for its own members and their children. While the Académie Royale de Peinture et de Sculpture (*see* §2 below) introduced a radical form of art training antagonistic to guild practices, it would not finally win uncontested superiority over the guild until 1776, when the latter was abolished by royal decree along with all corporations.

2. THE ACADÉMIE ROYALE DE PEINTURE ET DE SCULPTURE AND THE ACADÉMIE DE FRANCE. When the Académie Royale was founded (1648) in emulation of the academies of Florence and Rome, it was held that the superiority of Italian art was due to the academic training that its students received. This was mistaken: most of Italy's artists trained in workshops under the tuition of a studio master. The Académie Royale, which aimed for the professional and social advancement of its members as

practitioners of a liberal art, signalled a shift in art education away from technical instruction in a craft to a theoretical understanding of fine art. The success of its instruction was largely due to its prerogative to teach life drawing, a privilege denied the guild's Académie until 1705. As the making of art was now seen as the application of theoretical understanding (catered for by lectures on geometry, perspective, anatomy, history, geography and literature), the menial aspects of workshop practice (including the application of paint) were not taught. The Académie's 12 professors, who each taught one month per year, taught only drawing as the proper means to express the artist's conception. Young artists continued, however, to be attached to the studio of a painter, sculptor or engraver, where they were able to learn the practical aspects of their art. The strength of the Académie Royale's training (backed up by the authority of the monarchy) was such that students who did not become academicians could still enter the guild after three years' instruction. In the 18th century there was a call for more public drawing schools, but the Académie regarded any competition as a challenge to its monopoly and a threat to its doctrines. Nevertheless, successful provincial drawing schools were founded, such as those in Bordeaux and Dijon, the latter established in 1765 by FRANÇOIS DEVOSGES, III. In 1766 the academician Jean-Jacques Bachelier opened a successful drawing school in Paris for apprentices of manufacturing; this won official approval and in 1767 became the Ecole Royale Gratuite de Dessin (the 'Petite Ecole'). Further education for craftsmen in the applied arts was offered by the Ecole des Gobelins and the Ecole Royale de Dessin at Sèvres. In these schools emphasis was placed on the drawing of ornament and pattern-making for the realization of decorative projects.

In 1666 the Académie de France in Rome was created. This provided the students of the Académie Royale de Peinture et de Sculpture, and later of the Académie Royale d'Architecture (*see* §4 below), with an opportunity to study at first hand the art of Classical antiquity and the Renaissance. Such an exposure had been an aspiration of French artists since the previous century, and many had travelled to Italy at their own expense or that of a patron. Henceforth, the experience was absorbed into the institutions of State-sponsored art education. In the 18th century the authorities of certain regions also established Rome scholarships. That of the Etats de Bourgogne was first awarded in 1776, to Bénigne Gagneraux.

The laureate of the Rome Académie's PRIX DE ROME (suspended 1792–7, 1914–18 and 1940–41) received a scholarship that varied between three and five years. Until the 20th century the programme for painters and sculptors was based around study of the art of Classical antiquity and the Renaissance. It included the making of compositional sketches, drawings from the Antique and, in the fourth year, a full-scale painted or sculpted copy of an important example of the art of the past. Only in the last year was the student permitted to execute a finished work of his own invention. Likewise in architecture, the student was expected to study the Classical tradition through the measurement and drawing of approved monuments of antiquity and the Renaissance. This orientation continued well into the 20th century. For most students, the Rome

Académie offered both a recompense for their years of application in Paris and an interlude before their professional careers began. In 1863 reforms to the Prix de Rome system were made that fixed the length of scholarships at three years and that were, in part, designed to broaden students' training (*see* §7 below).

For a history of the Académie Royale *see* PARIS, §VI, 1; for its relationship to similar institutions *see* ACADEMY; for a history of the Académie de France *see* PARIS, §VI, 1.

3. THE ECOLE ROYALE DES ELÈVES PROTÉGÉS. In 1749, in recognition that the education offered by the Académie Royale did not furnish its Prix de Rome winners with the necessary technical skills to profit from their scholarship, Charles-Antoine Coypel, Director of the Académie, supported by Charles-François Le Normand de Tournehem, Directeur des Bâtiments du Roi, opened the Ecole Royale des Elèves Protégés in Paris, a 'finishing' school for six laureates, four of whom were painters and two sculptors. It was directed first by Carle Vanloo and later by Louis-Michel van Loo and was housed in the Place du Vieux-Louvre, at the eastern end of the Palais du Louvre. Instruction lasted three years and it was based on the life model, supplemented with classes in literature, history and geography. Students also copied in the Cabinet du Roi and in the Galerie d'Apollon in the Palais du Louvre, where cells (*loges*) were constructed for their use. The regulations recognized the special difficulties of the sculptor and allowed students to help their teachers occasionally in the execution of suitably edifying work. To some in the Académie Royale, the new school implied a lack of confidence in the Académie's teaching: in 1775 Jean-Baptiste Pierre, Premier Peintre du Roi and current director of the Académie, forced its closure. That the attack was politically motivated is clear from the fact that the Académie opened an Ecole des Elèves Artistes in imitation of its rival, but this failed and closed in 1790.

4. ARCHITECTURAL EDUCATION BEFORE THE REVOLUTION. Traditionally, the techniques of building were learnt in the workshops of their practitioners—masons, carpenters, bricklayers, glaziers and plumbers—and on the building site (*see* MASON (i), §II, 2). Stereotomy, the geometry of stone-cutting, remained one of the fundamental components of architectural education, linking the classically inspired architecture of the *ancien régime* with medieval practice. In the later 16th century, as a division began to open between those who designed a building and those who constructed it, the emphasis began to shift from the workshop to the studio or drawing office. There, not only could the primary skill of drawing be learnt but also the new architectural treatises and pattern books studied. In 1671 the Académie Royale d'Architecture (*see* PARIS, §VI, 2) was inaugurated under the patronage of Louis XIV. Unlike the Académie Royale de Peinture et de Sculpture, it was not a professional body with many members but a royal council. Its one professor lectured publicly twice a week. The first was FRANÇOIS BLONDEL, whose teaching, like that of many of his successors, was concerned with theoretical issues, and who sought to establish universally valid principles based on the best examples of Classical architecture. Regular deliberations

on Vitruvius and the treatises of Italian and French Renaissance authors fostered a climate of discourse. Practical training and exercises designed to lead to success in the Académie's annual student competitions (1720–1968) continued to take place in the private office of an architect or, for some, in the drawing offices of the Bâtiments du Roi (*see* MAISON DU ROI, §II). In the course of the 18th century the Grand Prix of the Académie Royale d'Architecture gradually became the Prix de Rome, but under the *ancien régime* the annual architectural prize did not automatically carry the right to a place at the Académie de France in Rome. The Directeur des Bâtiments du Roi often chose to select his own candidate to send to Italy to complete his education.

Because of the limitations of the teaching of the Académie Royale d'Architecture, other institutions concerned with architectural training were established in the mid-18th century. In 1742 Jacques-François Blondel (*see* BLONDEL, (2)) established the Ecole des Arts in Paris, the first school of architecture in France that was independent of the Académie. His academic ideas, including the notion of *caractère*, and their emphasis on the importance of 17th-century French architecture as a model, as well as that of Classical Rome and the Italian Renaissance, are recorded in his books *L'Architecture française* (1752–6) and *Cours d'architecture* (1771–7), the latter a revised version of lectures given in 1750. In 1762 he was appointed professor at the Académie Royale d'Architecture, where he lectured on practical as well as theoretical issues and introduced new student competitions. In 1747 the Corps des Ponts et Chaussées, the royal department of civil engineering, established the Ecole des Ponts et Chaussées (*see* PARIS, §VI, 4), under the direction of Jean-Rodolphe Perronet, to serve the needs of the engineers who played an important role in urban and architectural design and the building of bridges, main roads and canals. Jacques-François Blondel and Etienne-Louis Boullée were among those who taught architectural courses there.

5. THE REVOLUTIONARY PERIOD AND ITS AFTERMATH. The advent of the Revolution signalled the end of art training within the two royal academies as a privilege dependent on the monarchy. ANTOINE QUATREMÈRE DE QUINCY, in *Considerations sur les arts du dessin en France* (Paris, 1791), advocated a public school of art separate from the Académie Royale; political events, and the zeal of Jacques-Louis David, overtook him. David was elected to the Convention Nationale in 1792, and his attacks on academic art education resulted in the abolition of the royal academies in August 1793. The Ecole des Beaux-Arts, no longer royal, reopened on 28 September 1793 without modifying its educational principles. In 1795 this became the Ecole Spéciale de Peinture, Sculpture et Architecture (most commonly referred to as the Ecole des Beaux-Arts), which combined the teaching functions of the two previous academies. The teaching strength was increased to 39—9 painters and 3 deputies; 9 sculptors and 3 deputies; 4 architects and 4 deputies; 2 teachers of construction; and one each of ornament, geometry, anatomy, perspective and history (including antiques and costume). At this time the school occupied the Salle des Antiquités in the Louvre, opening at 7 a.m. (9 a.m. in

winter) and closing at 2 p.m. Also in 1795 the Ecole Centrale des Travaux Publics opened in Paris. In the same year its name was changed to the Ecole Polytechnique, one of the functions of which was the teaching of architecture to prepare students for entry to the Ecole des Ponts et Chausées. It remained active into the late 20th century.

In 1805 the Institut de France (created 1795), one section of which had assumed many of the non-teaching functions of the old academies of painting and sculpture and architecture (*see* PARIS, §VI, 3(i)), moved to the Collège des Quatre-Nations in Paris, and the Ecole Spéciale de Peinture, Sculpture et Architecture moved with it. In 1816 the school moved again, this time to its present site in the former monastery of the Petits-Augustins on the Rue Bonaparte. An *ordonnance du roi* of 1819 provided its legal foundation as an independent institution under State control, but in practice the Académie des Beaux-Arts retained monopoly over the Académie de France in Rome; furthermore, students who trained in private studios and who wished to enter the competition for the Prix de Rome had to succeed in the term competitions controlled by the Académie des Beaux-Arts. The Ecole Gratuite de Dessin continued in existence, having dropped its royal appellation (in 1877 it became the Ecole Nationale des Arts Décoratifs).

6. THE ECOLE DES BEAUX-ARTS AND TEACHING STUDIOS IN THE 19TH CENTURY. Students who enrolled at the Ecole des Beaux-Arts had often received elementary instruction in the provinces, either from local artists or in regional Ecoles de Dessin, such as those at Dijon, Rouen, Valenciennes and Lyon. Equally, it was the goal of ambitious students at the Petite Ecole to gain entry to the Ecole des Beaux-Arts. This institution, which did not charge fees, admitted students (many of whom were foreigners), aged between 15 and 30 years, by means of tests in figures drawn from nature and from the Antique, anatomical drawing, perspective, history and architectural drawing. Between 500 and 600 students registered annually, advancement being made through weekly, monthly or term *concours*, such as those of drawing, and sketch competitions for history painting (instituted 1816), landscape (1822), perspective and torso (1784), anatomy and *tête d'expression* (instituted in 1760 by the Comte de Caylus). At 7 a.m. (in winter 8 a.m.) the model took up the pose; there were additional classes in drawing from 4 p.m. to 6 p.m. daily; anatomy and perspective twice weekly; and in history and archaeology, general history, literature, and history of art once each week. In theory, the goal for all students was the annual Prix de Rome competition; but the proportion of possible prize winnners to students was small. Many did not compete for the Grand Prix; many who won did so only after several attempts. Similarly, from 1819, students of the architectural section of the Ecole progressed through a series of monthly competitions, towards the Prix de Rome. The subjects of the monthly competitions usually reflected pragmatic concerns—schools, public baths or railway stations—while those for the Prix de Rome were of a more grandiose kind (*see* BEAUX-ARTS STYLE). Such was the prestige of the system that for decades the appellation 'ancien élève de l'Ecole des Beaux-Arts' served as a highly prestigious form of architectural qualification in France, even for those who failed to win, or even to take part in, the Prix de Rome competition.

As with the academies of the *ancien régime*, the primary function of the Ecole des Beaux-Arts was to provide drawing classes, give theoretical lectures and provide an institutional framework for advancement through competitions. The practice of the arts continued to be taught in the artist's studio or the architect's drawing office. Increasingly, however, teaching studios were separate from an artist's working studio. A system of *ateliers privés* grew up, each often paid for and administered by the students themselves, the artist or *patron* calling regularly to inspect and correct the work. Among painters, the studios of David, Antoine-Jean Gros, Pierre Guérin, Jean-Auguste-Dominique Ingres, Léon Cogniet, Paul Delaroche, Charles Gleyre and Jean-Léon Gérôme offered a tradition of teaching that prepared the student, through elementary drawing practice and studio competitions, for the *concours de places* of the Ecole des Beaux-Arts and, ultimately, the Prix de Rome. The sculptors Pierre Cartellier, David d'Angers, François Rude, James Pradier and François Jouffroy also ran notable *ateliers privés*, as did the architects Félix-Jacques Duban, Eugène-Emmanuel Viollet-le-Duc, Henri Labrouste and Victor Laloux. Within the architecture ateliers, the younger members learnt much from assisting their seniors, particularly during the four months each year when the Prix de Rome competition was in progress, and all members would assist in the preparation of the competition drawing. The students who succeeded tended to come from the studios of academicians.

Many students, on arriving from the provinces, enrolled in the painting studios; for example Jean-François Millet with Delaroche or Paul Baudry with Michel-Martin Drolling. Both of these younger artists had begun their training under provincial teachers who set them to copy engravings and to study in the local museums; both were awarded municipal grants to continue their studies in Paris. The studios were open from 7 a.m. or 8 a.m. until noon, when the students went on to the Louvre to make copies after antique sculptures or Old Master paintings, in particular those of Raphael and Poussin, although some teachers advocated the study of such colourists as Rubens and Veronese. From 4 p.m. they attended the Ecole des Beaux-Arts. Baudry, for example, trained in the morning in Drolling's atelier, spent the afternoon copying in the Louvre and from 4 p.m. worked at the Ecole. The student of painting, for instance, progressed from copying engravings—Ingres had his pupil Eugène-Emmanuel Amaury-Duval copy Marcantonio Raimondi's engravings of Raphael as an induction—to drawing *après la bosse* (after plaster casts), an intermediary stage leading to drawing from life. The next step was the actual painting, in which the student graduated from copying or painting parts of the figure to painting the ensemble (*see* COPY). This reliance on the copying of approved works of art was followed, *mutatis mutandis*, by architectural students, who were expected, like their 18th-century predecessors, to study the buildings of Classical antiquity (which now included Greek as well as Roman models), of the Italian Renaissance and of 17th-century France. Medieval architecture was only grudgingly admitted as an officially acceptable field of study after the mid-19th century. Even so, Viollet-le-Duc's brief tenure in 1864 of the professorship of Art History and Aesthetics at the Ecole was unpopular with both the establishment and the students of the classically orientated institution.

For the young artist who had no ambition to compete for entrance to the Ecole des Beaux-Arts or for the Grand Prix, the studios of such independent artists as the painter THOMAS COUTURE offered a similarly rigorous training without directing students towards the Grand Prix. Similarly, the success of such well-known studios as the Académie Suisse, the Académie Colarossi and the Académie Julian was based on independence from the studios of the academicians. Rodolphe Julian (1839–1907) had opened the Académie Julian in 1873, and, by 1889, 600 students were enrolled in five studios. His 'academy' offered the opportunity to work from the model from 8 a.m. daily. After four years Julian appointed visiting professors with major reputations who attended twice weekly to offer criticism: William Bouguereau, Tony Robert-Fleury, Gustave Boulanger, Jules Lefebvre, and for the sculpture studio, Henri Chapu. Other independent studios in Paris followed, inspired by the Académie Julian and by the early example of Gustave Courbet's Atelier Libre: the Atelier Benjamin Constant in Montmartre, and those of Fernand Cormon (in whose studio Vincent van Gogh and Henri de Toulouse-Lautrec studied), Léon Bonnat and Carolus-Duran in Pigalle.

Some studios were reserved for women, such as one run by Julian in the Passage des Panoramas, where Mariya Bashkirtseva enrolled at the age of 17. Women students followed a path similar to that of men, although the great disadvantage was that until the end of the 19th century they were denied access to the life class at the Ecole des Beaux-Arts, which effectively excluded them from many important competitions that offered access to the basic form of academic art practice: history painting. Many teachers, such as Ingres, reported that Marie Bracquemond, wife of Félix Bracquemond, expected women to specialize in such minor genres as still-life. The few women who succeeded in surmounting this prejudice were, for the most part, personally related to their teachers. Such artists included Constance Mayer, who having begun her training with Joseph-Benoît Suvée and Jean-Baptiste Greuze, embarked on a professional and personal liaison with Pierre-Paul Prud'hon; Rosa Bonheur, who began her training with her father Raymond Bonheur (*d* 1849); and Marie-Amélie Cogniet (1798–1869), who was a student of her brother Léon Cogniet.

For a history of the Ecole *see* PARIS, §VI, 3.

7. THE REFORMS OF 1863. By the 1860s it was recognized that the Ecole des Beaux-Arts did not offer a balanced education. The professors were all members of the Académie and many were out of touch with new developments—Ingres was over 80 and had been a professor since 1829. This incestuous system engendered mannerism, formulae and studio recipes. The Ecole was accused of stifling progress through its system of competitions and of defining 'fine art' too narrowly. In 1863 a

major restructuring of the Ecole took place, led by Viollet-le-Duc with support from Napoleon III and his government. The Ecole was to become independent of the Académie, and the Académie was to lose much of the power it had enjoyed for the past 70 years. The reforms of 13 November resulted in a director being nominated for five years; the Prix de Rome for historical landscape being abolished; and the age limit of competitors for the Grand Prix being lowered from 30 years to 25 years and the duration of the scholarship to four years (only two of which needed to be spent in Rome). The Académie had its right to organize competitions taken away, and it was no longer allowed to direct the Académie de France in Rome. Most importantly, the daily drawing classes and many of the competitions were abolished in favour of teaching studios for painting, sculpture and architecture (*ateliers officiels*) to be administered by the Ecole, and where admission was by invitation of the teacher. The Académie reacted with indignation: Ingres, speaking for many, claimed that procedures need not be taught in the art school, as the application of paint, for example, could be learnt in a week. The Académie believed, naively, that Napoleon III had been deceived by his advisers Prosper Mérimée (1803–70), Viollet-le-Duc (who, as a student, had not been enrolled at the Ecole) and the Comte de NIEUWERKERKE, Surintendant des Beaux-Arts. The Emperor, however, had taken a personal interest. The reforms largely failed; with hindsight, Viollet-le-Duc believed that government oppression of the arts replaced that of the Académie. In architectural education a more significant long-term innovation was the introduction by the Ecole in 1867 of a diploma, to be awarded to an unlimited number of winners of an annual competition. This was to be a sign of architectural proficiency less exclusive than the Prix de Rome. By the end of the 19th century it had become the goal of most students of architecture. Another innovation in the field of architectural studies was the introduction of *ateliers préparatoires*, which, from the 1880s, prepared beginners for admission to the Ecole by teaching mathematics, drawing and architectural design.

In 1871 the situation as it had existed before 1863 was largely restored when CHARLES BLANC, an academician since 1868 and head of the Bureau des Beaux-Arts, rescinded the reforms, once again placing the Académie in control of the Prix de Rome and, by extension, of the Académie de France in Rome. The official studios of painting, sculpture and architecture remained, however, running in tandem with the outside studios, which only went into serious decline with increasing costs after World War I. There was, however, little difference to be discerned between the teaching of the *ateliers officiels* and those *ateliers privés* run by academicians or geared to the needs of the Ecole des Beaux-Arts.

8. 20TH-CENTURY DEVELOPMENTS. The history of official art education in France from 1914 to 1968 was fraught with difficulties. The conservatism of the academic system was increasingly at odds with developments in art, while growing numbers of students and rising costs of education led to the gradual breakdown of the old system of *ateliers privés*. There was inadequate expansion of official provision to counteract this. Many teachers remained

excessively Francocentric in their views, at a time when many innovations in painting, sculpture and architecture were coming from central Europe and, later, the USA. The reforms resulting from the widespread student protests of May 1968, which have been interpreted as a condemnation of the centralization of French education and a movement for educational and institutional autonomy, radically restructured art education in France (although many of the reforms, as in 1863, were later reversed). On 6 December 1968, André Malraux, Minister of State for Cultural Affairs, abolished the system of studios and *patrons* in the fine arts and architecture at the Ecole Nationale Supérieure des Beaux-Arts (as the Ecole des Beaux-Arts had become). It was replaced with a series of dispersed and autonomous units called Unités Pédagogiques (not all of which were in Paris), each free to establish its own curriculum. On 16 September 1970, the Ministry reorganized the Académie de France in Rome and abolished the Grand Prix; henceforth, selection of candidates would be decided by a committee appointed by the Ministry. Thus, all power over the Académie in Rome was effectively removed from the Académie des Beaux-Arts. From 1981, under the Socialist government of François Mitterand, the Ministry of National Education began to offer greater vocational training in tertiary art education; this move towards professional, as opposed to academic, training echoes, however distantly, the practices of guilds before the academies formulated their radical definition of the activity proper to the artist.

BIBLIOGRAPHY
L. Courajod: *L'Ecole royale des élèves protégés* (Paris, 1874)
L. Vitet: *L'Académie royale de peinture et de sculpture: Etude historique* (Paris, 1880)
Règlement de l'Ecole nationale et spéciale des beaux-arts, Ministère de l'instruction publique et des beaux-arts (Paris, 1884)
G. Pinet: *Histoire de l'Ecole polytechnique* (Paris, 1887)
A. Lemaistre: *L'Ecole des beaux-arts, dessinée et racontée par un élève* (Paris, 1889)
H. Guédy and E. Muntz: *L'Enseignement à l'Ecole nationale et spéciale des beaux-arts* (Paris, 1900)
E. Delaire: *Les Architectes élèves de l'Ecole des beaux-arts, 1793–1907* (Paris, 1907)
A. Fontaine: *Les Doctrines d'art en France: Peintres, amateurs, critiques, de Poussin à Diderot* (Paris, 1909/R Geneva, 1970)
J. Guiffrey: 'Histoire de l'Académie de Saint-Luc', *Archvs A. Fr.*, n. s., ix (1915) [whole issue]
L. Hourticq: *Ecole nationale supérieure des beaux-arts* (Paris, 1937)
L. Hautecoeur: *Histoire de l'architecture classique en France*, 7 vols (Paris, 1943–57)
R. Taton, ed.: *Enseignement et diffusion des sciences en France au XVIIIe siècle*, Histoire de la Pensée, xi (Paris, 1964)
A. Boime: *The Academy and French Painting in the Nineteenth Century* (London, 1971)
——: 'The Teaching Reforms of 1863 and the Origins of Modernism in France', *A. Q.* [Detroit], n. s. i/1 (1977), pp. 1–39
R. Chafee: 'The Teaching of Architecture at the Ecole des Beaux-Arts', *The Architecture of the Ecole des Beaux-Arts*, ed. A. Drexler (London, 1977), pp. 61–109 [with a summary of architectural training from the foundation of the Académie Royale d'Architecture]
D. Egbert: *The Beaux-Arts Tradition in French Architecture*, ed. D. van Zanten (Princeton, NJ, 1980) [illustrated by the Grand Prix de Rome]
A. Wagner: 'Learning to Sculpt in the Nineteenth Century', *Romantics to Rodin: Nineteenth-century French Sculpture in North American Collections* (exh. cat., ed. P. Fusco and H. W. Janson; Los Angeles, CA, Co. Mus. A., 1980), pp. 9–19
N. Heinich: *La Constitution du champ de la peinture française au XVIIe siècle* (diss., U. Paris, Ecole des Hautes Etudes en Sciences Sociales, 1981)
A. Brunot and R. Coquand: *Le Corps des ponts et chaussées* (Paris, 1982)
R. Middleton, ed.: *The Beaux-Arts and Nineteenth-century French Architecture* (London, 1982)
A. Le Normand-Romain: 'Comment fait-on un sculpteur? II: Formation', *La Sculpture française au XIXe siècle* (exh. cat., ed. A. Pingeot; Paris, Grand Pal., 1982), pp. 28–57
J. Laurent: *Arts et pouvoirs en France de 1793 à 1981: Histoire d'une démission artistique* (Saint-Etienne, 1983)
Les Concours d'esquisses peintes, 1816–1863 (exh. cat. by P. Grunchec, Paris, Ecole N. Sup. B.-A., 1986)
Le Grand Prix de Peinture: Les Concours des Prix de Rome de 1797 à 1863 (exh. cat. by P. Grunchec, Paris, Ecole N. Sup. B.-A., 1986)
J. Laurent: *A propos de l'Ecole des beaux-arts* (Paris, 1987)
J. Milner: *The Studios of Paris: The Capital of Art in the Late Nineteenth Century* (New Haven and London, 1988)

PAUL DURO

XVI. Art libraries and photographic collections.

Although specialist art libraries are a relatively recent development, some of the oldest French libraries and archives contain collections of artistic importance. The most significant of these is the Bibliothèque Nationale, Paris, which developed from the French royal collections and which has been on its present site at the Rue de Richelieu since 1721. As well as its books, this institution also contains over 300,000 volumes of manuscripts, 15 million prints and photographs, 650,000 maps and plans and 300,000 coins and medals. Unique primary sources are possessed by the Archives Nationales, Paris, founded in 1789, whose contents are outlined in *Les Sources de l'histoire de l'art aux Archives nationales*. Since this guide's publication in 1955, other important documents have entered the archive's collections, including the papers from 1793 to 1920 of the Ecole Nationale des Beaux-Arts. The pre-revolutionary archives remain in the possession of the Ecole (formerly the Académie Royale de Peinture et de Sculpture), whose library also includes prints, drawings and photographs. Like the Archives Nationales, the Musée du Louvre was also established in Paris during the revolutionary period: it contains an important library, now called the Bibliothèque Centrale des Musées Nationaux. Other venerable French institutions of artistic importance include the Bibliothèque Inguimbertine, Carpentras (founded 1745), which contains a collection of drawings and prints, and the Bibliothèque Municipale d'Étude et d'Information, Grenoble (founded 1772). In the 19th century artists and designers began to appreciate the need for a specialist art library, leading to the foundation of Bibliothèque Forney, Paris, in 1886. As well as its 135,000 volumes, the library has special collections of 19th- and 20th-century drawings of furniture and fabrics, and 15,000 French posters.

While these are all important institutions, one of the greatest art libraries in France is the Bibliothèque d'Art et d'Archéologie (the Fondation Jacques Doucet), based on the gift made by Jacques Doucet to the University of Paris in 1917. Doucet had acquired a magnificent art collection, which he complemented by creating a library of 100,000 printed books, 500 volumes of manuscripts, 10,000 prints and 150,000 photographs. Doucet had in fact opened this collection to the public before he gave it to the university. This gift was followed by the bequest of the Bibliothèque Littéraire, whose volumes were beautifully bound by Pierre-Emile Legrain and Rose Adler (1890–1989). Since

Doucet's original gift, the Bibliothèque d'Art et d'Archéologie has expanded to include 400,000 books.

Further notable additions to the art libraries of France were made after World War II, particularly in the form of museum libraries, such as that at the Musée d'Aquitaine (founded 1960) and, more importantly, the Documentation du Musée National d'Art Moderne (founded 1955), now housed in the Centre Georges Pompidou in Paris. Other institutions include the Bibliothèque de l'Institut d'Art Moderne (founded 1963) in Aix-en-Provence, which also contains a large quantity of slides. Important photographic collections also exist in the Bibliothèque de la Direction de l'Architecture, the Service Photographique de la Réunion des Musées Nationaux and the Maciet collection at the Bibliothèque des Arts Décoratifs, all in Paris. Like Doucet, Maciet acquired an enormous number of photographs (between 1880 and 1911), which has not grown significantly since its donation to a public institution. More specialized collections include the Service d'Etude et de Documentation du Département des Peintures du Louvre, which includes images of works in the Louvre, and the photographic library of the Centre d'Etudes Supérieures de Civilisation Médiévale, established in Poitiers in 1954.

BIBLIOGRAPHY

M. Dormoy: *Jacques Doucet* (Abbeville, 1931)
M. Rambaud: *Les Sources de l'histoire de l'art aux Archives nationales* (Paris, 1955)
——: 'Les Sources de l'histoire de l'art dans les archives de France', *Bull. Soc. Hist. A. Fr.* (1972), pp. 353–68
Repertoire des collections photographiques en France, Documentation Française (4/1972)
Collections photographiques des administrations et établissements publics: Paris et agglomération parisienne, Documentation Française (1974)
P. Lelievre: 'La Bibliothèque d'art de Jacques Doucet', *Bull. Biblioph.* (1980), pp. 39–46

CHRISTOPHER MASTERS

XVII. Historiography.

Although the study of the history of French art has been marked since its origins by a strongly nationalist bias, it has always been open to foreign influences, and foreign scholars have made a very significant contribution. Indeed, the first substantial discussions of French artists appear in the writings of Giorgio Vasari, Bellori and Sandrart. Apart from Michel de Marolles, whose *Livre des peintres et graveurs* (1677) is hardly more than a catalogue of his own collection in verse, the first extended work of French art history was André Félibien's *Entretiens sur les vies et sur les ouvrages des plus excellens peintres anciens et modernes* (1666–85). Naturally, this was heavily influenced by the Italian writers named in his preface, Vasari, Carlo Ridolfi, Giovanni Baglione and Raffaello Borghini; while the dialogue form of the work was imitated from Borghini's *Il riposo* or from Aretino's *Dolce*, Félibien's ultimate model was Vasari's *Vite*. Unlike such works of his contemporaries as Roland Fréart de Chambray's *Idée de la perfection de la peinture* (1662) or Roger de Piles's *Dissertation sur les ouvrages des plus fameux peintres* (1681), the interest of Félibien's text lies not so much in theoretical considerations as in the bibliographical details and charm of the narrative, which, as Félibien hoped, have become an important source of information on major and minor French artists of the 17th century. Félibien's *Entretiens*

became a model for the numerous obituaries read to the Académie in the 18th and 19th centuries, and for A.-J. Dezallier d'Argenville's *Abrégé de la vie des plus fameux peintres* (1745–52), Bernard Lépicié's *Vies des premiers peintres du roi* (1752), Charles Blanc's monumental *Histoire des peintres de toutes les écoles* (1850–60) and Théophile Silvestre's *Les Artistes français* (1855–6). The strictly monographic element of Félibien, coupled with strong documentary research, persisted into the 20th century with the monographs by Etienne Moreau-Nélaton, Charles Clément and Marius Vachon, among others, which represent the Vasarian tradition in French art-historical writing.

Pierre Monier's precocious attempt to write an *Histoire des arts qui ont rapport au dessein* (1698) spanning the millennia, from ancient Assyria to the Renaissance, is characteristic of the intellectual ambitions of artists and their associates at the Académie Royale de Peinture et de Sculpture (founded 1648), who wrote most of the earliest art-historical works in France. However, the scope of Monier's book sets it apart from other 17th-century writings, which are either theoretical or biographical. In general, the study of the history of art, as opposed to the study of artists' lives, was an 18th-century development, inspired by the work of antiquaries, who were, in the first instance, more concerned with the context of art than with the works themselves. The monumental *L'Antiquité expliquée et représentée en figures* by Dom Bernard de Montfaucon, and its sequel, *Les Monuments de la monarchie françoise* (1729–33), were compiled principally to illustrate literary and historical texts, and, although the chronological sequence of illustrations in the second work gives it the semblance of a history of French art, this was not Montfaucon's intention. The work of antiquaries like Montfaucon, however, provoked an interest in early artefacts, from which the discipline of art history developed. The antiquary the Comte de Caylus, in his *Recueil d'antiquités* (1752–67), concentrated on the art of antiquity, intending, as Caylus explained in his preface, to provide an illustrated history of taste or a survey of 'l'histoire des arts', which he hoped would have a beneficial effect on contemporary French painters and sculptors. His strictly empirical approach, which he compared to the work of a physician, was, however, less influential than that adopted by the German scholar Johann Joachim Winckelmann in his *Geschichte der Kunst des Alterthums* (Dresden, 1764), of which the first of several French translations appeared in 1766. Winckelmann's speculative, lively and structured account of the development of ancient art, and in particular the framework that he proposed for Greek art, divided into separate periods of birth, maturity and decay, became a model for several French art historians, including Pierre Chaussard (1766–1823), Claude-Henri Watelet (1718–86), Toussaint-Bernard Emeric-David (1755–1839) and Antoine Quatremère de Quincy, adapting it to the history of French art.

Although it is common to oppose the *philosophes*, like Winckelmann, to the *érudits*, like Caylus, the two approaches were not mutually exclusive. Jean-Baptiste Séroux d'Agincourt's *L'Histoire de l'art* (1823) was initially inspired by the idea of continuing Winckelmann's history of ancient art through the Middle Ages to the 16th century;

the sense of his work is suggested by its title. He was also motivated by his early friendship with Caylus, whose concern with authenticity and accuracy he shared. However, by the time his work finally appeared in 1823, the idea of providing an illustrated account of the decadence of art in the Middle Ages had been overtaken by a radical change in the sympathies of scholars. Alexandre Lenoir, whose Musée des Monuments Français (opened 1795) in Paris was the visual equivalent of Séroux's text and heir to the work of Montfaucon and Caylus, was, also, in the first stages, deeply influenced by Winckelmann. He originally intended to save historical monuments from imminent destruction, and, like Séroux, to illustrate the rise and fall of art as the Antique declined into barbarism, revived in the Renaissance and declined again in the 17th century to recover under David; the final impact of his work was, however, completely different. The works of art displayed in Lenoir's museum (see §XIV above) and his artistic method of displaying them did more than any other source in the early 19th century to bring about a reassessment of the art of the Middle Ages. The division of the museum, one room per century, encouraged the growth of a cultural history, divided into centuries and focusing not on individual artists but on questions of style. Indeed, the first notable use of the term 'Renaissance', in the title of the seventh volume of Jules Michelet's *Histoire de France* (Paris, 1855), was probably inspired by Michelet's memory of Lenoir's museum.

The link between art history and archaeology in France was confirmed when a course for art historians was created at the Ecole des Chartes in Paris in 1846 for the study of medieval artefacts. The first professor was the archaeologist Jules Quicherat (1814–82), best remembered for his documentary account of Joan of Arc's trial, followed by Robert de Lasteyrie (1849–1921), author of classic texts on the Romanesque and Gothic. In 1863, as part of general reforms at the Ecole des Beaux-Arts in Paris, a course in the history of art was introduced at the suggestion of Viollet-le-Duc, although the hostility of the students prevented him from giving classes. The post was then given instead to Hippolyte Taine, whose rigorous determinism made him a curious choice as tutor for practising artists. Taine's attempt to explain art in terms of climate and geography, which derived from the 18th-century scholars Charles-Louis de Secondat, Baron de Montesquieu and the Abbé du Bos, influenced the direction of art history in France and elsewhere, allied sometimes to a vigorous nationalism.

Much of the most interesting work of this period was, however, empirical and detached. Influenced by the work of the Ecole des Chartes, the study of art history in 19th-century France became largely the study of documents. The work of generations of archivists was published in a succession of periodicals, of which the first was the austere and unillustrated *Revue universelle des arts* (1853–66). The founding of the Société de l'Histoire de l'Art Français in 1854, with its own bulletin for the publication of inventories, letters and documents of all kinds concerning the history of French art, was intended for the same scholarly readership. Its best-known publication, P.-J. Mariette's rewriting of Orlandi's *Abécédario*, appeared serially from 1851 to 1860, but the importance of work published by

the society in the *Archives de l'art français* and the *Bulletin de la Société de l'histoire de l'art français* lies in the accumulation of thousands of less glamorous documents. The generation of scholars who contributed in the early years (Anatole de Montaiglon, Jules Guiffrey, Maurice Fenaille, Furcy-Raynaud, the Comte Léon de Laborde and the Marquis de Chennevières) made their name by publishing materials for the use of others, rarely interpreting and rarely commenting on quality.

These writers personified the closer relationship between the development of art history in France and the evolution of museums, as a new administrative class of art historians moved into museum posts previously reserved almost exclusively for artists. The Ecole du Louvre, founded in Paris in 1882 to train the new curators, was based on the model of the Ecole des Chartes, which had been founded in 1821 to train archivists. The best known of the early teachers at the Ecole du Louvre, Louis Courajod (1840–96), had been trained at the Ecole des Chartes, and in 1867 he joined the staff of the Cabinet des Estampes at the Bibliothèque Nationale, where he studied the administration of the arts in the 18th century. This was a field of special interest to the archivists of his generation, but, unlike them, Courajod was a ferocious polemicist who detested the Académie Royale and its influence on 17th-century art, and who traced the origins of the French genius in art not to the influence of the Italians, whom he deplored, but to its Franco-German roots in the Middle Ages. His fiercely nationalistic standpoint derived from a reaction among several art historians of the mid-century, including Théophile Thoré, who turned to the tradition of northern Realism, from Fouquet to Courbet, as being anti-Italian and anti-academic. A parallel tendency towards the study of the history of popular imagery, associated especially with Champfleury's research in ceramics and prints and his work on the art of the Le Nain brothers, consolidated a rejection of all forms of academic art in certain scholarly circles. Moreover, as the fortunes of David and his school declined, scholars and collectors paid increasing attention to 18th-century painting, giving Boucher and his contemporaries a somewhat undeserved glory as champions of the anti-academic faction; the articles published by the Goncourt brothers as 'L'Art au XVIII siècle' (1859–75) are, for example, strongly marked by their refusal to take account of the Académie Royale in the development of French art.

One consequence of this movement was that art historians looked for, and found, a school of French painting before the age of Fontainebleau, with which accounts of French painting had conventionally begun. The culmination of their research was the *Exposition des primitifs français*, organized chiefly by Henri Bouchot, curator of the Cabinet des Estampes, and held in 1904 at the Musée des Arts Décoratifs, Paris. In his introduction to the catalogue, Georges Lafenestre claimed that art in France, and painting in particular, had been sustained without interruption since the days of the Gauls, even through the period of the 'brutal divorce brought about by fashion and pedantry', when Francis I imported Italians to Fontainebleau, and when only Clouet and Corneille de Lyon kept alive the spirit of French art. This argument provoked a vigorous response from Louis Dimier (1865–1943), who in his *French Painting in the XVI Century* (1904) demolished the mythical 'French School of 1500' with vindictive relish, pointing out Clouet's origins in the Netherlands and reasserting the value of the art of Fontainebleau. His rejection of artistic nationalism, strikingly at variance with his commitment to the Action Française, took strength from his thesis on Primaticcio, completed in 1900 and published in abridged form in 1928.

Dimier belonged to a generation of art historians who emerged from the universities at the end of the 19th century with a taste for writing revisionist theses, aided by the research of the archivist–scholars, such as Courajod, whom Dimier admired. Although the Sorbonne in the 1890s offered a course in the history of art, the subject was not fully integrated until 1898, when the suppression of theology at the Sorbonne, following the separation of Church and State, released funds for a course in the history of medieval religious art. Emile Mâle, whose *L'Art religieux du XIIIe siècle en France* appeared in 1898, was appointed to the post that was converted to a chair in 1912. This gave studies in Paris a certain bias towards the Christian Middle Ages, which was less pronounced at the University of Lyon, where art history had been taught since 1876. The creation of a chair at Lyon in 1902 maintained a strong tradition that persisted into the late 20th century. The early incumbents included Léon Rosenthal, author of the classic defence of French Romanticism, *Du Romantisme au réalisme* (1914); and Henri Focillon, who wrote a superb account of *La Peinture du XIXe siècle* (1927–8). Focillon specialized in his early years in the art of the 19th century but turned to the Middle Ages following his appointment to the chair at the Sorbonne.

The strength of the French tradition by this date, combined with hostility in the aftermath of the Franco-Prussian War (1870) and World War I, perhaps explains French indifference towards the study of imagery as it developed in Germany. Pierre Francastel, who approached the study of the context of art from a solid background in factual art history and might have bridged the gap between France and Germany, was hostile to such study, while his followers moved from the study of art as such, into sociology and semiotics. Against this background, André Chastel took an exceptional interest in applying the methods of the Warburg Institute of London to a wide, cosmopolitan range of subjects.

By the late 20th century documents and connoisseurship still formed the basis of art history in France; it remained for foreign scholars, notably British and American, to adapt methods from other disciplines to propose new ways of looking at French art and its context. Most scholarly syntheses of French art published since World War II have been written in English, notably those in the Pelican History of Art series, supplemented by accounts of Impressionism and Post-Impressionism by John Rewald. The exception is Louis Hautecoeur's magisterial survey of the classical tradition of French architecture. Knowledge of the art of the 17th and 19th centuries has been concentrated in a series of monographic exhibitions, almost invariably organized by museum curators. However, the re-evaluation of 19th-century artists and the

attempt to question the traditional notion of an *avantgarde* has also been promoted by a series of exhibitions in France, notably *French Painting 1774–1830: The Age of Revolution* (1974–5) and *Le Musée du Luxembourg en 1874* (1974; Paris, Grand Pal.), and culminated in the opening of the Musée d'Orsay in Paris in 1986. Unfortunately, the enormous budget lavished by the State in the Mitterand era on French museums, both national and provincial, did not make it easier for French scholars to publish their work, and almost all works are catalogues published for exhibitions, while monographs on major French artists generally continued to be written by foreigners and published outside France.

BIBLIOGRAPHY

R. Fréart de Chambray: *Idée de la perfection de la peinture* (Paris, 1662)

A. Félibien: *Entretiens sur les vies et les ouvrages des plus excellens peintres anciens et modernes*, 5 vols (Paris, 1666–85); rev. as 6 vols (Trévoux, 1725/R Farnborough, 1967)

M. de Marolles: *Le Livre des peintres et graveurs* (Paris, 1677); ed. G. Duplessis (Paris, 1855; rev. Paris, 1872)

R. de Piles: *Dissertation sur les ouvrages des plus fameux peintres* (Paris, 1681)

P. Monier: *Histoire des arts qui ont rapport au dessin, divisée en trois livres, où il est traité de son origine, de son progrès, de sa chute et de son rétablissement* (Paris, 1698; Eng. trans., London, 1699)

J.-F. Félibien: *Recueil historique de la vie et des ouvrages des plus célèbres architectes* (Paris, 1687; Trévoux, 1725/R Farnborough, 1967)

B. de Montfaucon: *L'Antiquité expliquée et représentée en figures*, 15 vols (Paris, 1719–24)

——: *Les Monumens de la monarchie françoise*, 5 vols (Paris, 1729–33)

A.-J. Dézallier d'Argenville: *Abrégé de la vie des plus fameux peintres*, 3 vols (Paris, 1745–52); rev. as 4 vols (Paris, 1762; Ger. trans., Leipzig, 1767–8)

Comte de Caylus: *Recueil d'antiquités égyptiennes, étrusques, grecques et romaines*, 7 vols (Paris, 1752–67)

B. Lépicié: *Vies des premiers peintres du roi, depuis M. Le Brun jusqu'à présent*, 2 vols (Paris, 1752; Ger. trans., Halle, 1769)

A.-N. Dézallier d'Argenville: *Vies des plus fameux architectes et sculpteurs depuis la renaissance des arts* (Paris, 1788)

C.-H. Watelet and P.-C. Levesque: *Dictionnaire des arts de peinture, sculpture et gravure*, 5 vols (Paris, 1792/R Geneva, 1972)

S. d'Agincourt: *L'Histoire de l'art par les monumens depuis sa décadence au IVe siècle jusqu'à son renouvellement au XVIe siècle*, 6 vols (Paris, 1823)

C. Blanc: *Histoire des peintres de toutes les écoles*, 14 vols (Paris, 1850–60)

P.-J. Mariette: *Abécédario de P.J.M. et autres notes inédites*, ed. P. de Chennevières and A. de Montaiglon, 5 vols (Paris, 1851–60)

G. Guillet de Saint-Georges: *Mémoires inédites sur la vie des membres de l'Académie* (Paris, 1854)

T. Silvestre: *Les Artistes français* (Paris, 1855–6)

E. de Goncourt and J. de Goncourt: *L'Art au XVIII siècle* (Paris, 1859–75)

E. Mâle: *L'Art religieux du XIIIe siècle en France* (Paris, 1898)

L. Dimier: *French Painting in the XVI Century*, trans. H. Child (London, 1904)

Exposition des primitifs français (exh. cat., intro. G. Lafenestre; Paris, Mus. A. Déc., 1904)

A. Fontaine: *Les Doctrines d'art en France: Peintres, amateurs, critiques, de Poussin à Diderot* (Paris, 1910/R Geneva, 1970)

L. Rosenthal: *Du Romantisme au réalisme* (Paris, 1914)

J. Schlosser-Magnino: *Die Kunstliteratur* (Vienna, 1924); Fr. trans. as *La Littérature artistique* (Paris, 1984)

H. Focillon: *La Peinture du XXe siècle* (Paris, 1927–8)

French Painting, 1774–1830: The Age of Revolution (exh. cat. by P. Rosenberg and others, Paris, Grand Pal.; Detroit, MI, Inst. A.; New York, Met.; 1974–5)

F. Haskell: *History and its Images: Art and the Interpretation of the Past* (London and New Haven, 1993)

☐

Francés, Nicolás (*fl* 1434; *d* León, before 2 Nov 1468). ?Spanish painter, illuminator and sculptor. Although his name implies he was French, all pertinent documentation refers to León. He is first mentioned in 1434 in a document relating to a painted life-size wooden statue that he made for the knight Suero de Quiñones, where he is cited as the author of the 'rich retable' of León Cathedral. The immense Retablo Mayor of León Cathedral must have been an imposing work. Descriptions of it, before its replacement by a Baroque altarpiece in 1740, describe a polyptych, which followed the configuration of the cathedral's Capilla Mayor, with eighteen large panels arranged in tiers of four (except at the centre, where two paintings surmounted a sculpted effigy of the *Virgin*). The panels had scenes from the *Life of the Virgin* and the *Life of St Froilan*. Dividing these vertical tiers were *entrecalles*, vertical strips of a large number of smaller saints' effigies. Of the paintings, five large and twenty small images survive and have been recombined with other, later panels into the present high altar retable and episcopal chair.

If Master Nicolás was cited in 1434 as having painted the Retablo Mayor, it was probably complete by this time. The style of the surviving panels is typical of work of the Late Gothic period. In the scene of the *Purification of the Virgin*, for example, the Virgin ascending the staircase to the altar is shown in minute scale in comparison to her companions, and the stair itself tilts towards the viewer, while the Gothic colonnettes in front of them are cut at mid-height so as not to obstruct the view.

Similar conventions are seen in the panel of *St Froilan in the Desert*, with its small slender trees, large, carefully observed flowers and simultaneous narrative. In this painting, as in the other, space is arbitrary. While there is nothing specifically French in these panels, and some art historians have detected Italian influence, the frames are nevertheless typical of Castilian-Leónese retables of this period.

Nicolás Francés: retable of the *Life of the Virgin and St Francis*, tempera on panel, 5.57×5.58 m, from the chapel of Esteba de las Delicias, La Bañeza, *c.* 1435–45 (Madrid, Museo del Prado)

The surviving panels of the Retablo Mayor are the basis for attributing two other altarpieces to Master Nicolás. One, in the chapel of Fernando López Saldaña (treasurer to King John II of Castile-León) in the convent of S Clara, Tordesillas, is a north European type triptych with a sculpted centre and painted wings showing scenes from the *Life of the Virgin*. The other is a retable (Madrid, Prado; see fig.), also dedicated to the Virgin, from an estate chapel at Esteba de las Delicias near La Bañeza (León). The narrative scenes and frames of both these works are similar in style to the León Cathedral retable, as is a miniature of the *Nativity*, signed *Ns.*, from a choir-book (León, Mus.–Bib. Real Colegiata S Isidoro). These works are generally believed to date from the 1430s and 1440s.

While on the regular payroll of León Cathedral, Francés made banners, gilded images and other similar commissions between 1445 and 1460. In 1451, he was given the commission for wall paintings in the cathedral cloister, a task that was to occupy him until 1461. Although many of these paintings, which illustrate the *Passion*, have severely deteriorated, those that survive, for example the *Ecce homo*, suggest a move towards larger figures and more proportional settings, although strict perspective is generally ignored. The exact place of Nicolás Francés in contemporary Leónese painting, however, is difficult to determine, owing to the dearth of surviving works.

BIBLIOGRAPHY

F. J. Sánchez Cantón: 'Maestre Nicolás Francés, pintor', *Archv Esp. A. & Arqueol.*, i (1925), pp. 41–65
C. R. Post: *A History of Spanish Painting*, iii (Cambridge, MA, 1930), pp. 262–96
F. Alvarez: 'La Pulchra-leonina y su retablo de la Capilla Mayor', *Archvs Leoneses*, xii (July–Dec 1952)
F. J. Sánchez Cantón: *Maestre Nicolás Francés* (Madrid, 1964)

JUDITH BERG SOBRÉ

Francesca, Piero della. *See* PIERO DELLA FRANCESCA.

Franceschini, Baldassarre [il Volterrano] (*b* Volterra, 1611; *d* Florence, 1690). Italian painter and draughtsman. He was the son of Guasparri Franceschini, a sculptor in alabaster, and studied first with the local artist Cosimo Daddi (*d* 1630) then, from 1628, in Florence with Matteo Rosselli. His first works, which are still in Volterra, are the *Purification of the Virgin* (1630; Volterra, S Agostino), *Elijah and the Angel* (1631; Volterra, S Giusto Abbey Church) and the *Assumption of the Virgin* (1631; Volterra, Archv Capitolare); they reveal the influence of Rosselli and elements of Mannerism.

After working briefly in Florence with Giovanni da San Giovanni and Vincenzo Manozzi, Franceschini attracted the patronage of Don Lorenzo de' Medici, who in 1636 commissioned him to paint a cycle of frescoes on the history of the Medici family for the courtyard of the Villa Petraia; Franceschini painted the scenes depicting the deeds of Catherine de' Medici and her children, of Leo X, Clement VII, Francesco I, Giuliano and Lorenzo de' Medici, Maria de' Medici and Alessandro de' Medici. The cycle was not completed until *c.* 1648, for Franceschini interspersed the work with other projects. In 1639 he painted *St Michael Overcoming Lucifer* in the parish church of Castello, Florence, and between 1639 and 1640 *St Catherine and the Crucifixion* (Florence, Uffizi). In 1640 he made a trip to northern Italy, visiting Bologna, Ferrara, Venice and Parma and then almost certainly coming south to Rome. His response to this journey is evident in the fresco and stucco decoration (1642) of the chapel of the Orlandini in S Maria Maggiore, Florence, where many motifs are inspired by Correggio's dome in Parma and by the Roman works of Michelangelo and Raphael.

The 1640s were highly creative years, and in 1644 Franceschini executed the *Glory of St Cecilia* in the chapel of S Ansano in the SS Annunziata, Florence, a cycle of exceptional Baroque splendour. The ceiling depicting *Vigilance and Sleep* in the Villa di Castello, where the influence of Pietro da Cortona unites with echoes of Correggio, also dates to around this period. In 1650 Franceschini executed *Christ Comforted by Angels* for the refectory of the convent of S Teresa in Prato (Prato, Mus. Pitt. Murale).

Franceschini completed the Petraia cycle in 1648 and was thus enabled to commit himself more fully to other important commissions. From the early 1650s he executed many oil paintings, frescoes on tile and a fresco cycle for the Palazzo Galli Tassi. His most significant commission of the period was the frescoed decoration of the vault and pendentives of the Colloredo Chapel (dedicated to St Lucy) in the SS Annunziata, Florence, with the *Glory of St Lucy* and *Four Virtues* (1650–52). The decoration reveals

Baldassarre Franceschini: *Mystic Marriage of St Catherine*, oil on canvas, 2.04×1.86 m, 1650s (Prato, Cassa di Risparmio)

an obvious familiarity with the latest work of contemporary Roman masters, above all Pietro da Cortona and Bernini. This suggests that Franceschini visited Rome in the period 1651–2 to bring himself up to date. It must have been at this time that he frescoed an *Aurora* in the Palazzo del Bufalo (*in situ*).

On his return to Florence, he painted frescoes in the Palazzo della Gherardesca, the Palazzo Guadagni (later called the Palazzo di S Clemente) and the Palazzo Niccolini (*in situ*). He also executed some beautiful cabinet paintings of mythological subjects, for instance *Orpheus and Eurydice* (Florence, Pucci priv. col.) and *Venus and Cupid* (Stockholm, Nmus.). In 1655 he delivered an altarpiece depicting *St John the Evangelist* (Volterra, Pin. Com.) to the nuns of the convent of S Chiara for their church. Towards the end of the 1650s he worked on a series of commissions for Vittoria della Rovere, for whom he painted the ceiling of the Sala delle Allegorie in the Palazzo Pitti (*c.* 1657–8), a *Mystic Marriage of St Catherine* (Prato, Cassa di Risparmio; see fig.) and *St Mary Magdalene Supported by Angels* (Florence, Pitti), which was intended for the ceiling of a room in the villa at Poggio Imperiale.

In 1661 Franceschini completed a grandiose cycle of frescoes (begun 1653) decorating the dome and the pendentives of the Niccolini Chapel in the SS Annunziata, Florence. Here in an airy space that harks back to Pietro da Cortona, angels and biblical figures witness the coronation of the Virgin by the Holy Trinity, while in the pendentives four colossal sibyls wonder at and discuss the event. By this date Franceschini was an established artist, and he accompanied Archduke Ferdinand Charles of Austria on a trip to the north of Italy. He was also employed at around this time by Cardinal Giovanni Carlo de' Medici to paint the latter's portrait (Florence, Pitti) and to provide him with many cabinet pictures (some Florence, priv. col.; others untraced).

The 1660s were also marked by a series of important commissions, such as the *Alms of St Louis of France* for the church of the Ospedale di S Maria Nuova, Florence, the allegorical *Glory of Louis XIV* (Versailles, Château) and the vast undertaking of the decoration of the vault and cupola of the tribune of the SS Annunziata, with an *Assumption of the Virgin* and *Virgin in Glory* (1670–83). This was a demanding commission, which forced the elderly Franceschini to work on scaffolding at dizzying heights and in an uncomfortable and badly lit environment, yet he also completed other works at the same time; a large canvas of the *Assumption of the Virgin* (Vallombrosa, Monastery Church), a *St Filippo Benizi in Glory* for the SS Annunziata and a *Virgin with Saints* for the Certosa di Pisa at Calci. Illness slowed this frenetic activity, yet the artist continued to work until his death, though without the same ease of brush that he had formerly possessed (Baldinucci).

BIBLIOGRAPHY

F. Baldinucci: *Notizie* (1681–1728); ed. F. Ranalli (1845–7), v, pp. 141–98

Il seicento fiorentino: Arte a Firenze da Ferdinando I a Cosimo III, 3 vols (exh. cat., ed. A. Parronchi and A. Brook; Florence, Pal. Strozzi, 1986), iii, pp. 188–93 [with full bibliog.]

M. Gregori and E. Schleier, eds: *La pittura in Italia: Il seicento* (Milan, 1988, rev. 1989), pp. 920–21

M. Gregori, ed.: *Cappelle barocche a Firenze* (Milan, 1990)

MARCO CARMINATI

Franceschini, Marcantonio (*b* Bologna, 5 April 1648; *d* Bologna, 24 Dec 1729). Italian painter and draughtsman. He was a leading master of his time. He painted altarpieces and cabinet pictures and was exceptionally skilled at large-scale fresco decoration, in which capacity he was widely active. He was the pupil of Carlo Cignani, himself the most distinguished pupil of Francesco Albani, and thus traced his artistic lineage directly back to Bolognese classicism. He interpreted the principles fundamental to this style with a rigour unequalled by any contemporary Italian master, being rivalled in this only by such French classicists as Eustache Le Sueur. Many artists were trained in his studio in Bologna and at his summer villa at Belpoggio. His closest follower was Giacinto Garofalini (1661–1723). Pupils of greater distinction included Giacomo Antonio Boni and Giuseppe Marchesi.

1. Life and work. 2. Working methods and technique.

1. LIFE AND WORK.

(i) Training and work as Cignani's assistant, 1665–80. Franceschini's father, Giacomo Franceschini, and mother, Giulia Maffei, were of Bolognese origin. He received the conventional education of that time in the humanities and at the age of 17 entered the studio of Giovanni Maria Galli-Bibbiena, a follower of Albani and the progenitor of a celebrated dynasty of theatre scenery painters. Franceschini's training in this studio, although thorough, would seem to have had little influence on the formation of his style. On his master's death in 1665, Franceschini 'resolved to follow the school of Albani' (Bologna, Bib. Com., MS. B4067) and entered the studio of the most renowned Bolognese artist of the day, Carlo Cignani, through whom he came to study the work of earlier Bolognese classicists such as Domenichino, Guido Reni and Albani himself. Eighteenth-century commentators invariably characterized Franceschini as Cignani's favourite pupil. Certainly Cignani proposed that Franceschini should marry his cousin, Teresa Quaini, who was also the sister of another studio assistant, Luigi Quaini (1643–1717). Thus the association of the three painters took on the character of a family enterprise.

During the 1670s Franceschini worked as Cignani's principal assistant. The finest product of their collaboration, carried out between 1678 and 1680, was the lovely mural cycle of mythological scenes, among them the *Bacchus and Ariadne* and the *Rape of Europa*, in the Palazzo Giardino, Parma (see Roli, pl. 20, a, b, c). Franceschini and Quaini, working under Cignani's supervision and to his cartoons (London, Hampton Court, Royal Col.), were largely responsible for the execution of the murals, which completed an earlier scheme (1600–02) by Agostino Carracci left unfinished on his death.

(ii) First independent works, c. 1680–90. In the early 1680s Franceschini developed his independent practice. He made a brilliant début as a fresco painter with two ceiling decorations, *Fortuna and the Seasons* in the Palazzo Ranuzzi, now the Palazzo Giustizia, Bologna (1680; see Roli, pl. II) and the *Allegory of Felsina* in the Palazzo Marescotti–Brazzetti, Bologna (1682; see Roli, pl. 24a), both executed in collaboration with the *quadratura* painter Enrico Haffner. The *Fortuna and the Seasons*, lyrical in spirit and

1. Marcantonio Franceschini: *Birth of Adonis*, oil on copper, 485×690 mm, c. 1700 (Dresden, Gemäldegalerie Alte Meister)

painted in lustrous blond tones, is among the most arresting ceiling decorations of its period. Franceschini was more brilliant in invention and execution than the slower and more meticulous Cignani and had a particular gift for conveying the elegant and poetic. He developed this skill in a gallery of the Palazzo Monti, now the Palazzo Brazzetti, Bologna, where he executed fresco decorations (1682; see Miller, 1960, figs 43, 44, 45) in which the figures are more elongated and the contours softer than in his previous work.

In this period Franceschini also established his reputation as a painter of altarpieces and cabinet pictures. He was commissioned to paint altarpieces for churches in Bologna and as far afield as Piacenza and Rimini; these include the *Almsgiving of St Thomas of Villanueva* (1687; Rimini, S Agostino) and the *Virgin with SS John the Baptist, Luke and Peter Celestine* (1688; Bologna, S Giovanni Battista dei Celestini). Between 1686 and 1687 Franceschini, with Haffner, carried out sumptuous fresco decorations in the Monti Chapel in the church of Corpus Domini in Bologna; in August 1686 Giovanni Giacomo Monti commissioned him to paint the *Death of St Joseph* for the altar of this chapel (*in situ*). The painting is severe and unadorned in composition yet soft and tender in the expression of emotion, and it is Franceschini's best-known religious work.

The artist's account book, preserved in the Biblioteca Comunale at Bologna (MS. B 4), indicates that during this decade, primarily under the influence of Albani's exquisite

poesia, Franceschini had begun to paint pastoral mythologies such as the *Birth of Adonis* (Dresden, Gemäldegal. Alte Meister; see fig. 1) or *Venus Discovering the Dead Adonis* (untraced; both pictures commissioned in 1686). He interpreted the Ovidian themes with a distinctive poetic charm and a clean elegance of figure style and colouring, with landscape settings of Arcadian serenity. Such pictures became the principal basis for Franceschini's popularity with a patrician clientele outside Italy, especially his princely patrons in the German-speaking lands, such as Count Kaunitz-Rietburg, Johann Wilhelm Wittelsbach, Elector Palatine, or Johann Adam, Prince of the House of Liechtenstein at Vienna.

(iii) Major decorative works, 1690–c. 1710. By 1690 Franceschini had become one of the most sought-after fresco decorators of his time. Between 1690 and 1696, with Haffner and Quaini, he undertook the fresco cycle illustrating scenes from the *Life of St Catherine of Bologna* on the cupola, pendentives and vault of the convent church, the Corpus Domini (heavily damaged in 1943), of the saint's order in Bologna; the cycle ranks as one of the most ambitious church decorations of the age. Franceschini painted the *Communion of the Apostles* (see fig. 2) for the high altar of the same church. Three huge frescoes in the choir of S Bartolomeo, Bologna, were also painted around this time by Franceschini, again with Quaini's assistance; they depict *St Bartholomew Destroying a Pagan Idol*, the *Martyrdom of St Bartholomew* and *St Bartholomew Exorcising a Woman Possessed by Devils* (1690–91). A

2. Marcantonio Franceschini: *Communion of the Apostles* (1690–96), high altar painting, and pendentive frescoes, Corpus Domini, Bologna

ceiling decoration, the *Coronation of Bradamante* (1696), in the reception hall in the Palazzo Ducale at Modena presents a stirring celestial vision, a richly-figured allegory eulogizing Rinaldo II d'Este and his bride Carlotta on the occasion of their marriage. It is another good example of Franceschini's mature style and has also survived intact. A vast cycle of scenes eulogizing the Republic of Genoa (1702–4; destr. 1777), painted by the artist in the Sala del Maggior Consiglio in the Palazzo Ducale, Genoa, was another extensive project.

Between 1691 and 1709 Franceschini's main patron was Prince Johann Adam of the House of Liechtenstein, for whom he undertook an ambitious decorative project for a suite of rooms and a gallery in the Prince's summer residence outside Vienna, the Gartenpalais Liechtenstein in der Rossau, just then in process of construction. The rooms, overlooking the palace garden, called for the sort of Arcadian idyll for which Franceschini was so renowned. The Prince required scenes for the walls and ceilings of two rooms in the left wing of the building, one dedicated to Diana, one to Venus. Between 1692 and 1700 Franceschini painted and sent to Vienna twenty-six huge canvases illustrating episodes from the myths of the two goddesses. The second phase of the commission involved large ceiling paintings for the adjacent gallery and for two rooms in the right wing of the palace (*in situ*). The undertaking occupied Franceschini for nearly 20 years and is one of the most extensive unified groups on a mythological theme of its period by an Italian artist. The paintings also comprehensively demonstrate Franceschini's elegant classical idiom, particularly in the polished, highly distilled beauty of his figure types, which are reminiscent of those of Reni and Albani yet are quite distinct from them. The forms are compact, suavely rounded, with flesh tones of a pearly luminescence. Figure poses were developed only after careful consideration as to the means of obtaining an ideal grace and formal balance. Resilient fresh and pure colour was applied to enhance the clarity and articulation of the figures. Deep blues and resonant crimsons and yellows form the dominant motifs: the blue especially is often delicately rose-tinted in the drapery highlights to give a fine roseate effect. Unusual colours, such as lilac, magenta, coral, reddish orange and slate blue-grey, were also employed, the pigment thinly applied on a carefully primed canvas, with occasional moderately impasto passages.

The commission stimulated a lengthy correspondence (preserved in the family archive at Vaduz) between patron and painter, determining subjects and settling methods of shipment and payment etc. There is also interesting material relating to Franceschini's activities as the Prince's Bolognese agent for the acquisition of pictures. Altogether the letters make an illuminating record of contemporary princely patronage.

(iv) Late works, 1711–29. In 1711 Franceschini was called to Rome by Pope Clement XI to provide cartoons for the mosaic decoration of the lunettes and cupola of the Cappella del Coro in St Peter's. He remained in Rome for a year and was knighted by the Pope, who later also made him a Cavaliere di Gesù Christo. His last major undertaking as a fresco decorator was the beautiful *Assumption of St Filippo Neri and his Presentation to the Virgin* (1714), in the vault of S Filippo Neri at Genoa; the work is especially impressive for its colouring and for the rosy light that suffuses the vast scene. During his last years Franceschini created some of his finest pictures, such as the series of the *Four Seasons* (1716; Bologna, Pin. N.) commissioned by Victor Amadeus II, Prince of Carignano, and a cycle of oil paintings, scenes from the *Life of Diana*, painted for Stefano Pallavicini's palace, now the Palazzo Podestà, in Genoa (1715–21; see Miller, 1957, pls 22–4). These works are pastoral idylls similar to the mythological pictures for the Gartenpalais Liechtenstein.

During this period of his life Franceschini was for a time (1719–22) director of the Accademia Clementina, Bologna's first official art academy. He had been a founder-member in 1709 and had since acted as vice-director under Cignani. The secretary of the Accademia, Giovan Pietro Zanotti, included a biography and an engraved portrait of Franceschini in his *Storia dell'Accademia Clementina*. To enable him to write this, a member of the artist's family—possibly his son, the painter and prelate Giacomo Franceschini—provided Zanotti with notes, which survive today (Bologna, Bib. Com.), on Franceschini's career. Further documentation from 1682 is provided by Franceschini's account book (Bologna, Bib. Com., MS. B 4) and by a register of his principal works, which was originally drawn up by the artist himself and is today preserved in a transcription (Bologna, Bib. Cassa di Risparmio).

2. WORKING METHODS AND TECHNIQUE. In nearly all of his fresco commissions Franceschini was assisted by Quaini, who painted the settings for the figures and, in large-scale works in any medium, sometimes blocked in the composition. Franceschini made many preparatory drawings, several of which survive: there is an important group in the Cooper-Hewitt Museum, New York, and there are two bound volumes of figure studies, one in the Accademia Carrara, Bergamo, the other in the Palazzo Rosso, Genoa. As a draughtsman Franceschini is best known for his pen-and-wash compositional drawings, such as the *Birth of Adonis* (New York, Met.) made for the painting of 1686. He worked in the Bolognese classical tradition, making precise studies of details of figures from the live model, usually in red chalk heightened with white. Among such studies is the *Right Hand Clutching a Torch; A Left Arm Extended; A Partially Draped Foot* (Bergamo, Accad. Carrara B.A.) made for the *Allegory of Felsina* (1682).

BIBLIOGRAPHY

Thieme–Becker

G. P. Zanotti: *Storia dell'Accademia Clementina di Bologna* (Bologna [1739]), pp. 219–48

A. Arfelli: 'Marcantonio Franceschini, 1648–1729', *Com. Bologna*, xiii (1933), pp. 2–10

O. Kürz: *Bolognese Drawings at Windsor Castle* (London, 1955), pp. 101–8

D. Miller: 'L'opera di M. A. Franceschini nel duomo di Piacenza', *Boll. A.*, xli (1956), pp. 318–25

——: 'Franceschini and the Palazzo Podestà, Genoa', *Burl. Mag.*, xcix (1957), pp. 231–4

Maestri della pittura del seicento emiliano (exh. cat., Bologna, Pal. Archiginnasio, 1959), pp. 179–87, nos 87–91

D. Miller: 'An Early Series of Decorations by Franceschini in the Palazzo Monti, Bologna', *Burl. Mag.*, cii (1960), pp. 32–5

E. Feinblatt: 'An Unnoticed Ceiling by Franceschini', *Burl. Mag.*, ciii (1961), pp. 312–13

D. Miller: 'Important Drawings by Marcantonio Franceschini at Cooper Union', *A. Bull.*, xliii/2 (1961), pp. 133–4

P. Torriti: 'Marcantonio Franceschini's Drawings for the Frescoes in the Sala del Maggior Consiglio, Ducal Palace, Genoa', *Burl. Mag.*, civ (1962), pp. 423–8

D. Miller: 'Addenda to Franceschini's Lost Decorations in the Ducal Palace, Genoa', *Burl. Mag.*, cvi (1964), p. 374

——: 'Two Early Paintings by Marcantonio Franceschini; A Gift of the Bolognese Senate to Pope Clement XI', *Burl. Mag.*, cxii/807 (1970), pp. 373–8

Painting in Italy in the Eighteenth Century: Rococo to Romanticism (exh. cat., ed. J. Maxon and J. J. Rishel; Chicago, IL, A. Inst.; Minneapolis, MN, Inst. A.; Toledo, OH, Mus. A.; 1970), pp. 126–7, no. 50

D. Miller: 'Some Unpublished Drawings by Marcantonio Franceschini and a Proposed Chronology', *Master Drgs*, ix (1971), pp. 119–38

R. Roli: *Pittura Bolognese, 1650–1800: Dal Cignani ai Gandolfi* (Bologna, 1977)

S. Rudolph: 'The Gran Sala in the Cancelleria Apostolica: A Homage to the Artistic Patronage of Clement XI', *Burl. Mag.*, xvi (1978), pp. 593–601

D. Miller: 'Franceschini's Decorations for the Cappella del Coro, St Peter's: Bolognese and Roman Classicism of the Later 17th Century', *Burl. Mag.*, cxxiv/953 (1982), pp. 487–92

——: 'An Album of Drawings by Marcantonio Franceschini in the Accademia Carrara, Bergamo', *Master Drgs*, xxl (1983), pp. 20–32

Liechtenstein: The Princely Collections (exh. cat., New York, Met., 1986), pp. 8–22, nos 3–10

DWIGHT C. MILLER

Francesco I, Grand Duke of Tuscany. *See* MEDICI, DE', (16).

Francesco, Domenico di. *See* DOMENICO DI MICHELINO.

Francesco, Giovanni di. *See* GIOVANNI DA PISA (i).

Francesco, Guido. *See* FRANÇOIS, GUY.

Francesco da Cotignola. *See* ZAGANELLI, FRANCESCO.

Francesco d'Antonio (di Bartolommeo) (*b* Florence, before 1393; *d* Florence, after 1433). Italian painter. He was a minor Florentine master whose work follows the shift in Florentine painting from the style of Lorenzo Monaco through that of Gentile da Fabriano, Masaccio and Masolino in the 1420s to that of Fra Angelico at the beginning of the 1430s. His artistic personality was differentiated by Longhi from that of an artist now identified as Masaccio's brother Giovanni di Ser Giovanni, called SCHEGGIA. Francesco enrolled in the Arte dei Medici e Speziali in 1409 and was recorded as a member of the Medici e Speziali guild on 21 November 1429. His earlier phase is represented by his only signed and dated work, a triptych with the *Virgin and Child and Two Saints* (1415; Cambridge, Fitzwilliam), and by the signed frescoes (*c.* 1420) of the *Annunciation* and the *Coronation of the Virgin* in S Francesco at Figline Valdarno. These paintings confirm Vasari's statement that Francesco, whom he referred to as 'Francesco Fiorentino', was apprenticed to Lorenzo Monaco. In the next phase of Francesco's stylistic development, his manner is closer to the late Gothic style as exemplified by Gentile da Fabriano and is evident in *Virgin and Child* (London, N.G.) and *St Ansano* (Florence, S Niccolò sopr'Arno). His later, broader and more realistic style, perhaps reflecting the influence of Masaccio transmitted through Masolino, is seen in four organ shutters (Florence, Accad. Dis.) with the *Evangelists* on one side and singing angels on the other, which he delivered to Orsanmichele in 1429, a fresco of the *Virgin and Child*

with Two Saints (Montemarciano, S Giovanni Valdarno, Oratory of the Madonna delle Grazie), a *Virgin and Child with Four Saints* (Florence, tabernacle in Piazza S Maria Novella), a dossal (Florence, Sopr. Gal.) commissioned after 1427 by Bernardo Quaratesi for S Niccolò sopr'Arno in Florence, the perspective composition of the *Healing of the Lunatic Boy* (Philadelphia, PA, Mus. A.), reminiscent of the circle of Masaccio and sometimes attributed to Masaccio himself, and the Rinieri Altarpiece of the *Virgin and Child with SS Jerome and John the Baptist* (Avignon, Mus. Petit Pal.). This last was executed at the beginning of the 1430s and shows movement towards Fra Angelico typical of many painters like Francesco who were associated with the late Gothic current.

BIBLIOGRAPHY

G. Vasari: *Vite* (1550, rev. 2/1568); ed. G. Milanesi (1878–85)

O. Sirén: *Don Lorenzo Monaco* (Strasbourg, 1905), pp. 162–3

M. Salmi: 'Francesco d'Antonio fiorentino', *Riv. A.*, xi (1929), pp. 1–24

G. Gronau: 'Francesco d'Antonio pittore fiorentino', *Riv. A.*, xiv (1932), pp. 382–5

R. Longhi: 'Fatti di Masolino e di Masaccio', *Crit. A.*, v (1940), pp. 186–7

F. Zeri: 'Note su quadri italiani all'estero', *Boll. A.*, xxxiv (1949), pp. 22–6

L. Berti: 'Note brevi su inediti toscani', *Boll. A.*, xxxvii (1952), pp. 175–7

C. Shell: 'Francesco d'Antonio and Masaccio', *A. Bull.*, xlvii (1965), pp. 465–9

The Great Age of Fresco (New York, 1968), pp. 122–5

R. Freemantle: *Florentine Gothic Painters* (London, 1975), pp. 425–32

J. Beck: 'Una prospettiva . . . di mano di Masaccio', *Studies in Late Medieval and Renaissance Painting in Honor of Millard Meiss* (New York, 1977), pp. 48–53

——: *Masaccio: The documents* (New York, 1978), p. 51

E. Biag: *Francesco d'Antonio* (diss., U. Siena, 1983)

E. Rice: 'St Jerome's Vision of the Trinity: An Iconographical Note', *Burl. Mag.*, cxxv (1983), pp. 151–5

E. Biag: 'Francesco d'Antonia di Bartolommeo', *La Maddalena tra sacro e profano: Da Giotto de Chirico* (exh. cat., ed. M. Mosco; Florence, Pitti, 1986), pp. 47–8

F. Ciani Passeri: 'La Madonna Assunta di Loppiano di Francesco d'Antonio', *O.P.D.*, iii (1988), pp. 102–7

CECILIA FROSININI, HELLMUT WOHL

Francesco d'Antonio (Zacchi) da Viterbo [il Balletta] (*b* ?Viterbo, *c.* 1407; *d* ?Viterbo, before 1476). Italian painter. His workshop was at his home in Piazza S Maria Nuova, Viterbo, where he is documented as active between 1430 and 1464. Two polyptychs form the stylistic core of his attributed oeuvre. The first, signed and dated 1441 and depicting the *Virgin and Child Enthroned with Saints*, was painted for S Giovanni in Zoccoli, Viterbo, the second, signed only and depicting the *Virgin and Child Enthroned with SS Rose and Catherine of Alexandria*, for S Rosa, Viterbo. On the evidence of the dated work Volpe recognized Francesco as the contemporary, rather than the son of the painter Antonio da Viterbo (*fl c.* 1450–*c.* 1480). Untouched by the advent of the Renaissance, his compositions remain firmly entrenched within the traditions of the Gothic style and display great affinity with the Late Gothic painting of Pisa and, especially, Siena. His early work reflects the enduring influence of Bartolo di Fredi and Taddeo di Bartolo, both active generations before Francesco himself. From them he adopted not only the parallel alignment of his figures with the picture plane but also the sumptuous tooling of their clothing and the conical and tubular cascades of their lavish drapery. This trend in Francesco's oeuvre reaches its first climax in the triptych depicting *Christ Enthroned*, formerly in S Maria

Maggiore, now in S Lorenzo, Tuscania. The later polyptychs in S Giovanni in Zoccoli, Viterbo, and S Rosa, Viterbo, show a reduction in the effusive drapery of their saints and a relaxation of the consistently parallel alignment of the figures with the picture plane. Facial features take on a new distinctiveness, and richly coloured garments are preferred. In the use of these devices they bear remarkable resemblance to the works of Ottaviano Nelli, but are closest to the style of the Sienese painters Luca di Tommé and Turino di Vanni. In the predella scenes of the S Giovanni in Zoccoli polyptych, which include scenes from the life of St John the Evangelist, the animated, almost playful narrative style is fully consistent with the language of the waning Late Gothic style as employed by Nelli and Jacopo Salimbeni. In Francesco's later works, after the middle of the 15th century, a new tendency towards the dramatic emerges. In the fresco of the *Crucifixion* (Viterbo, S Maria Nuova, chapel of S Ambrogio) the Virgin and St John the Evangelist grieve passionately over the dead Christ. Their anguished faces and dramatic gestures clearly reflect similar treatments of the subject by Matteo Giovanetti and Salimbeni. In 1464 Francesco was commissioned to paint and gild a coat of arms for Pope Calixtus III for the Castello of Viterbo. Other works include a fresco depicting the *Virgin and Child Enthroned with a Goldfinch* (ex-S Maria in Gradi, Viterbo; Viterbo, Mus. Civ.), a fresco of the *Virgin and Child Enthroned* (Tuscania, S Biagio), and a panel depicting *St Ambrose* (Viterbo, S Ambrogio). Attributed works are in the Walters Art Gallery, Baltimore, MD, and S Maria Poggio, Viterbo. Francesco's son Gabriele (*fl* 1473–83) was also a painter.

BIBLIOGRAPHY

G. Signorelli: 'I più antichi pittori viterbesi', *Boll. Mun., Viterbo* (Oct 1934), pp. 6ff
La pittura viterbese (exh. cat., ed. I. Faldi and L. Mortari; Viterbo, Mus. Civ., 1954); review by F. Zeri, *Boll. A.*, xl (1955), pp. 85–91
C. Volpe: 'Una ricerca su Antonio da Viterbo', *Paragone*, xxii/253 (1971), pp. 44–52
F. Zeri: *Italian Paintings in the Walters Art Gallery* (Baltimore, 1976)
A. M. Corbo: 'Documenti: Chiese ed artisti viterbesi nella prima metà del sec. XV', *Commentari*, n. s. xxviii/1–3 (1977), pp. 162–71
A. M. Pedrocchi: 'Francesco d'Antonio Zacchi, detto il Balletta', *Il quattrocento a Viterbo* (exh. cat., ed. R. Cannatà and C. Strinati; Viterbo, Mus. Civ., 1983), pp. 137–46
A. Sibrilli: 'Il Balletta, Francesco d'Antonio Zacchi', *La pittura in Italia: Il quattrocento*, ed. F. Zeri, ii, (Turin, 1987), pp. 570–71

JOHANNES TRIPPS

Francesco de' Franceschi (*b* ?1425; *fl* 1443–68). Italian painter. His most important known work is the 12-part polyptych of *St Peter* (1447; Padua, Mus. Civ.), formerly in S Pietro, Padua. The largest panel, *St Peter Enthroned*, shows the saint in full papal regalia. In smaller flanking panels are standing figures of *St Christopher*, *St Paul* and *St John the Baptist*, as well as the *Archangel Michael*, depicted trampling the demon. In yet smaller panels, perhaps originally placed above, are half-length figures of *St Francis*, *St Mary Magdalene*, *St Clare* (*?Scholastica*) and *St Prosdocimo* (*?Benedict*). The top panel, a *Crucifixion*, is flanked by the two narrowest panels, both of an *Angel Praying*. The polyptych was long attributed to Antonio Vivarini and Bartolomeo Vivarini, or Michele Giambono, but in 1904 Moschetti proved that it was painted by Francesco, whose name once appeared on its frame.

While the polyptych of *St Peter* is Francesco's only securely dated and attributed work, Fiocco's attribution to him of the *St Mamas* panels is convincing. The cult of this martyr was particularly popular in Lombardy. There are seven known panels, the largest of which is of *St Mamas and the Lion*, with the flanking *Angel Gabriel* and *Virgin Annunciate* (all Verona, Castelvecchio); the others are in Venice (Correr) and New Haven, CT (Yale U. A.G.). Fiocco considered them much inferior to the work of Giambono; while Francesco's perspective had advanced somewhat beyond Giambono, Fiocco noted that he could not depict expression. He believed the *St Mamas* panels to be from a cassone, but Sandberg-Vavalà (1927) identified them as parts of a polyptych. She also wrote more favourably of the painter, whom she found a poor draughtsman but a 'vigorous colourist', whose rendering of drapery was 'large and plastic' and who was 'careful and rich in his ornament'. She pointed out that in contrast to Giambono, whose figures have 'little tactile reality', those of Francesco, if uncouth in form, suggest mass and volume. Unlike that of Antonio Vivarini, Francesco's drapery is 'settling down to the restraint and plasticity of the early Renaissance'. Giambono's drapery, by contrast, is 'characteristic of the most flowery virtuosity of the Gothic movement'. In her further research (1940) Sandberg-Vavalà added to his oeuvre two panels depicting full-length, standing figures of *Mary Magdalene* and *St Catherine* (both Oxford, Ashmolean). Of other attributions to Francesco she accepted only the *Virgin and Child* (Venice, Ca' d'Oro) and the panels of *St Catherine*, *St Clare*, *St Mary Magdalene* and *St Lucy* (all Budapest, Mus. F.A.).

Thieme–Becker   BIBLIOGRAPHY

A. Moschetti: 'Un'ancona di Francesco de' Franceschi pittore veneziano del secolo XV', *Boll. Mus. Civ. Padova*, vii/4 (1904), pp. 70–77
G. Fiocco: 'Due Madonne di Michele Giambono', *Dédalo*, v (1924), pp. 443–55
E. Sandberg-Vavalà: 'Michele Giambono and Francesco dei Franceschi', *Burl. Mag.*, li (1927), pp. 215–21
——: 'Additions to Francesco de' Franceschi', *Burl. Mag.*, lxxvi (1940), pp. 155–6
I capolavori dei musei veneti (exh. cat. by R. Pallucchini, Venice, Correr, 1946), pp. 45–8
G. Mariacher: *Il Museo Correr di Venezia: Dipinti dal XIV al XVI secolo* (Venice, 1957), pp. 80–81
C. Seymour jr, ed.: *Early Italian Paintings in the Yale University Art Gallery: A Catalogue* (New Haven, 1970), pp. 242–3

ALEXANDRA HERZ

Francesco del Borgo [Francesco del Cereo di Borgo San Sepolcro] (*b* Borgo San Sepolcro, Tuscany; *d* Rome, 1468). Italian architect, illuminator and papal functionary. He is first mentioned in 1450 as a member of the financial staff of the Apostolic Chamber and of the secret treasury of Nicholas V, and he rose quickly through the levels of the financial bureaucracy at the papal court. He is known to have illustrated manuscripts of Latin translations of Archimedes, Euclid, Ptolemy and Muhammad al-Qazwini [Kazwini], some of which were decorated at his behest in 1457–8. Mixing in humanist circles at the court, Francesco may have been taught architecture and engineering by Leon Battista Alberti.

Alberti may also have recommended Francesco to Pius II, who commissioned him to design the benediction loggia in front of St Peter's and the reshaping of the Piazza

S Pietro. Francesco planned to replace the temporary wooden pulpit in front of the old atrium, from which the earlier popes had blessed the crowd, by a two-storey marble loggia of eleven bays. Its elevation recalled the exterior of Roman theatres. Instead of half columns, however, antique marble shafts articulated the arcades. It was the first faithful imitation of Roman Imperial architecture and the first forum building *all'antica* erected since antiquity, and it was probably inspired by Alberti's *De re aedificatoria* (1452). In contrast with the formal Tuscan language of Bernardo Rossellino's contemporary piazza in Pienza, Francesco's loggia marks the beginning of an autonomous Roman Renaissance, the architectual expression of the new imperial aspirations of the papacy. Work on the loggia was continued until *c.* 1510 but was never finished, and the structure was destroyed in 1600. Other works that Francesco probably designed for Pius II are the surviving tabernacle near Ponte Milvio in Rome on the spot where Pius received the skull of St Andrew in 1462; a chapel in the outer left aisle of Old St Peter's with a two-storey tabernacle for the skull of St Andrew; and the fortress of Tivoli (1461–2).

In 1465 Francesco received a commission from Pius's successor, Paul II, to enlarge the palace that Paul had begun while Cardinal Piccolomini; it became the new papal residence (now the Palazzo Venezia). Although Superintendent of the Works, Francesco's exact role is uncertain, but by the time of his death the irregularly shaped 9th-century basilica of S Marco incorporated in the south side of the Palazzo Venezia had been transformed into a symmetrical church, featuring columns that supported vaulted aisles, semicircular chapels, transepts ending in exedrae, an elevation articulated in the nave by half columns and, in the aisles, by pilasters, and a rich coffered ceiling roofed with gilded lead tiles. For the old portico, a two-storey benediction loggia was substituted; it had only three bays but was similar to the one Francesco built for Pius II at St Peter's. In front of the S Marco loggia a regular piazza was laid out, one side of which was defined by the new Palazzetto Venezia (dismantled 1911 and re-erected further west). This was a hanging garden for the Pope, surrounded by porticos. The tripartite entablatures in both storeys and the exquisite proportions of the sober exterior are all attributable to Francesco. The Palazzetto was incorporated in the east wing of the papal palace; new halls of enormous size were added, together with a vestibule containing a coffered barrel vault and staircases. The huge corner tower was built after Francesco's death, and the two large portals and fragmentary courtyard date from after Paul II's death.

Francesco's activities as a financial expert and architect are documented in a well-preserved series of account-books for the papacy. As an architect, his achievement lies between Alberti's revival of Roman Imperial architecture and the more conservative language of Michelozzo di Bartolomeo and Bernardo Rossellino. Francesco's use of antique prototypes and his somewhat abstract detailing are a result of the influence of the humanist circles in Rome. His many followers dominated Roman architecture for the next decades and were superseded only by Donato Bramante's arrival in 1499.

BIBLIOGRAPHY

E. Müntz: *Les Arts à la cour des papes pendant le XVe et la XVIe siècle*, ii (Paris, 1879), pp. 23–4
I. P. Dengel, M. Dvořák and H. Egger: *Der Palazzo Venezia in Rom* (Vienna, 1909)
G. Zippel: 'Paolo II e l'arte', *L'Arte*, xiii (1910), pp. 241–58
I. P. Dengel: *Palast und Basilika San Marco in Rom* (Rome, 1913)
G. Zippel: 'Ricordi romani dei Cavalieri di Rodi', *Archv Soc. Romana Stor. Patria*, xliv (1921), pp. 169–205
P. Tomei: *L'architettura a Roma nel quattrocento* (Rome, 1942), pp. 72–3
R. Olitsky Rubinstein: 'Pius II's Piazza S Pietro and St Andrew's Head', *Essays in the History of Architecture Presented to Rudolf Wittkower* (London, 1967), pp. 22–3
J. Ruysschaert: *Enea Silvio Piccolomini Papa Pio II* (Siena, 1968), p. 263
A. Spotti Tantillo: 'Inventari inediti di interesse libario', *Archv Soc. Romana Stor. Patria*, xcviii (1975), pp. 77–94
Palazzo Venezia: Paolo II e le fabbriche di S Marco (exh. cat. by M. L. Casanova Uccella, Rome, Pal. Venezia, 1980)
C. L. Frommel: *Der Palazzo Venezia in Rom* (Opladen, 1982)
——: 'Francesco del Borgo: Architekt Pius' II. und Pauls II. Teil I', *Röm. Jb. Kstgesch.*, xx (1983), pp. 107–54
——: 'Francesco del Borgo: Architekt Pius' II. und Pauls II. Teil II', *Röm. Jb. Kstgesch.*, xxi (1984), pp. 71–164
J. R. Banker: 'Piero della Francesco, il fratello Don Francesco de Benedetto e Francesco dal Borgo', *Prospettiva* [Florence], 68 (1992), pp. 54-6

CHRISTOPH LUITPOLD FROMMEL

Francesco del Cossa. *See* COSSA, FRANCESCO DEL.

Francesco di Antonio del Chierico [Cherico] (*b* 1433; *d* 27 Oct 1484). Italian illuminator and goldsmith. The creator of some of the liveliest miniatures of the 15th century, his manuscripts are rich in stylistic innovation and thematic invention, sometimes elaborated in a very limited space. He worked for the most important patrons in Italy and abroad, beginning his artistic career under Cosimo il Vecchio and Piero I de' Medici, and continuing it under Lorenzo the Magnificent. Vespasiano da Bisticci was his contact with patrons outside Florence, who included Federigo II da Montefeltro, Ferdinand I, King of Naples, Louis XI of France and Matthias Corvinus, King of Hungary. Francesco decorated texts of all kinds—literary, historical, scientific, religious—and of all sizes, from small Books of Hours to huge choir-books. Amid this variety of subjects his studies of the human figure and his introduction of portraits was innovative; he also established his own approach to landscape, with results similar to those of Antonio Pollaiuolo. His inventions, however, were reserved for privately commissioned books of small size. He created a new kind of book illustration and interpretation with his miniatures for Petrarch's *Triumphs* and *Apollo and Daphne*, the latter almost all in the form of drawings or tinted drawings (e.g. Rome, Vatican, Bib. Apostolica, MS. Chigi L. IV 114, fol. 10*r*; Venice, Bib. N. Marciana, MS. it. IX. 431, fol. 9*r*; and Boston, MA, Pub. Lib., MS. C 4269B, fol. 1*r*, all with variants). For the works of Ptolemy and Pliny he invented the image of the Humanist in his study (e.g. Naples, Bib. N., MS. V. A. 3 and Vienna, Österreich. Nbib., Cod. lat. 2).

Francesco's miniatures show a subtle understanding of the Antique, acquired through an interpretation of Classical texts and through his knowledge of, for example, ancient cameos and sarcophagi. All his work shows an experimental, anti-academic approach. Even the borders of his decorated pages show a high level of creativity: in the innumerable putti, the arrangements of flowers and elegant candelabra. A concentration of bizarre details and innovative images appears in the Book of Hours of Lorenzo the Magnificent and Clarice Orsini (Holkham Hall, Norfolk, MS. 41), with its astrological apparatus linked with dates significant for the patrons, in a Breviary and Pontifical (Florence, Bib. Medicea-Laurenziana, MSS Plut.17.28 and 23.1) and in a Petrarch manuscript (Florence, Bib. Riccardiana, MS. 1108). His manner of drawing is vibrant, his colouring light, sometimes using an expressive sketchy technique with watercolour (e.g. the Florence Pontificale).

Francesco is documented from 1452 as a goldsmith and was enrolled as a lifelong member of the Compagnia di S Paolo in Florence. This activity has not been reconstructed, but there is evidence of it in the high quality of his drawings, visible in unfinished miniatures. His many works are documented from 1456, the date of his first extant Petrarch manuscript (Paris, Bib. N., MS. ital. 545). In 1457 he began work on Bishop Donato Medici's project for choir-books for Pistoia Cathedral, with collaborators executing the minor decoration. Francesco's work includes the *Exorcism of St Zeno* (Pistoia, Pal. Vesc., Corale L, fol. cxliii*r*).

Francesco's work for Piero de' Medici began in 1458 with his miniatures for Pliny's *Natural History* (Florence, Bib. Medicea-Laurenziana, MS. Plut. 82.3). Here he introduced the theme of *Two Young Lovers*, with mythological figures in the borders (fol. 4*r*). In another manuscript (Florence, Bib. Medicea-Laurenziana, MS. Plut. 82.4), illustrated by Ser Ricciardo di Nanni, Francesco illuminated the title page and signed it in Greek. His signature appears again in Piero's Plutarch (Florence, Bib. Medicea-Laurenziana, MSS Plut. 65.26–7), with a miniature of *Theseus and the Minotaur in the Labyrinth* (fol. 2*r*). Extraordinarily rich

in miniatures is the Breviary (Florence, Bib. Medicea-Laurenziana, MS. Plut. 17.28) with subtle details in homage to Lorenzo de' Medici. Francesco's most important Petrarch manuscript (Paris, Bib. N. MS. ital. 548) has a rare theme of a *Shipwreck* (fol. 1*v*)—an allegory alluding to Lorenzo, who commissioned it. The iconography of the other miniatures follows that of the 1456 Petrarch; the same designs were to return enriched in other Petrarch *Triumphs* (e.g. Milan, Castello Sforzesco, MS. 905).

The miniatures for the choir-books of the Badia of Fiesole (Florence, S Lorenzo, Archv Capitolare, B 201, C 202, D 203, E 204, F 205, H 207, I 208, K 209), to which he contributed from 1461, had the financial support of Cosimo il Vecchio. The large size of these volumes offered scope for original experimentation comparable to that enjoyed by painters in other media. This is demonstrated especially in the *St Michael and the Dragon* (K 209, fol. 46*r*), *David and Goliath* (F 205, fol. 1*r*), *Tobias and the Angel* (F 205, fol. 92*r*) and the *Birth of John the Baptist* (H 207, fol. 76*r*). In these miniatures a new vocabulary of imagery and a new artistic vision, enhanced by literary and theological experience were created: for example in the *Three Marys at the Tomb* (E 204, fol. 2*v*), or in the *Communion of the Apostles* (fol. 169*r*), where the arrangement of the figures and the biblical scenes are similar to the drawing and painting of Antonio Pollaiuolo.

The next set of choir-books Francesco illustrated was for Florence Cathedral (Florence, Bib. Medicea-Laurenziana, MSS Edili 148–51). This grandiose project, originally assigned to Zanobi Strozzi, was begun in 1463 but not completed until 1474. It was carried out by a whole workshop, which included such painters as Cosimo Rosselli and Domenico Ghirlandaio, as well as such young

Francesco di Antonio del Chierico: *Exodus*; miniature from the Urbino Bible, 275×178 mm, 1477–8 (Rome, Vatican, Biblioteca Apostolica, MS. Urb. lat. 1, fol. 27*r*)

illuminators as Attavante Attavanti and the Master of the Hamilton Xenophon. Here Francesco's miniatures all have a monumental quality, both in the figures and the landscapes, whose luminosity is reminiscent of Domenico Veneziano's work. In these choir-books the narration extends to the tondi in the borders. Among the most important miniatures are the *Baptism* (MS. Edili 148, fol. 15*r*), the *Martyrdom of St Reparata* (MS. Edili 150, fol. 56*v*), with its Verrocchio-like touches, the bold perspective foreshortening of the *Nativity* (MS. Edili 150, fol. 72*v*) and a *Procession* (MS. Edili 149, fol. 75*r*), with its effective group portraits. His other numerous works for important religious orders include the choir-books for the Opera dell'Annunziata (1471–2).

Francesco's collaboration with other painters (e.g. Domenico and Davide Ghirlandaio) reached its high point in the Bible for Federigo da Montefeltro (1477–8; Rome, Vatican, Bib. Apostolica, MSS Urb. lat. 1–2). This work shows further interest in the human figure in motion, as well as in landscape and antiquity, with compositional inventions in the frames of the tondi (e.g. scenes from *Genesis*). The copies by Francesco Rosselli in the Origen manuscript (Modena, Bib. Estense, MS. lat. 458) suggest a direct connection with the drawings of Francesco del Chierico. Among Francesco's light-filled scenes are the scene from *Exodus* (MS. Urb. lat. 1, fol. 27*r*; see fig.), the *Tobias and the Angel* (MS. Urb. lat. 1, fol. 213*v*), and *Judith Killing Holofernes* (MS. Urb. lat. 1, fol. 218*r*). Vespasiano da Bisticci, who served as agent for the court at Urbino, procured a precious library for the Duke, which included such works by Francesco as the *De varietate fortune* (Rome, Vatican, Bib. Apostolica, MS. Urb. lat. 224), with putti playing at the foot of the page and the portrait of *Poggio Bracciolini* (fol. 2*r*), the *Disputationes Camaldulenses* (Rome, Vatican, Bib. Apostolica, MS. Urb. lat. 508) with a full-page portrait of *Federigo da Montefeltro with Landino* (single leaf), and the great *Vision of St Bernard* (Rome, Vatican, Bib. Apostolica, MS. Urb. lat. 93, fol. 7*v*).

The most recent critical studies on Francesco have revealed his authorship of numerous works that D'Ancona had assigned to Francesco Rosselli, an artist who as an illuminator owes much to Francesco del Chierico's work. The latter also had a profound influence on the development of Attavante and the Master of the Hamilton Xenophon, as well as on such other lesser-known artists as the Master of the Decads and Bartolomeo di Domenico di Guido.

BIBLIOGRAPHY

G. Vasari: *Vite* (1550, rev. 2/1568); ed. G. Milanesi (1878–85)
P. D'Ancona: *La miniatura fiorentina dall'XI al XVI secolo*, 2 vols (Florence, 1914)
S. De Ricci: *A Handlist of Manuscripts in the Library of the Earl of Leicester at Holkham Hall* (Oxford, 1932)
P. R. Taucci: 'I corali miniati della SS Annunziata a Firenze', *Studi Stor. Ordine Servi Maria*, i (1933), pp. 150–53
M. Levi D'Ancona: *Miniatura e miniatori a Firenze dal XIV al XVI secolo* (Florence, 1962)
J. J. G. Alexander and A. C. De La Mare: *The Italian Manuscripts in the Library of Major J. R. Abbey* (London, 1969)
A. Garzelli: 'Antico e Nuovo Testamento nei codici miniati della Biblioteca Laurenziana: I e II', *Crit. A.*, 143–4 (1975), pp. 19–38, 25–41
——: *La bibbia di Federico da Montefeltro: Un'officina libraria fiorentina, 1477–1478* (Rome, 1977)
——: 'Zanobi Strozzi, Francesco di Antonio del Chierico e un raro tema astrologico nel libro d'ore', *Renaissance Studies in Honor of Craig Hugh Smyth*, ii (Florence, 1985), pp. 237–44
——: *Miniature fiorentine del Rinascimento: Un primo censimento*, 2 vols (Florence, 1985)
——: 'Note su artisti nell'orbita dei primi Medici: Individuazione e congetture dai libri di pagamento della Badia Fiesolana, 1440–1485', *Stud. Medi.*, xxvi (1985), pp. 435–64
——: 'I miniatori fiorentini di Federico da Montefeltro', *Atti del convegno: Federico di Montefeltro: Lo stato, le arti, la cultura: Roma, 1986*
M. Levi D'Ancona: 'Appunti d'archivio: L'anagrafe di Francesco di Antonio del Chierico', *Miniatura*, (1988), pp. 145–7
The Painted Page: Italian Renaissance Book Illumination, 1450–1550 (exh. cat., ed. J. J. G. Alexander; London, RA, 1994)

ANNAROSA GARZELLI

Francesco di Bartolomeo Alfei. See ALFEI, FRANCESCO DI BARTOLOMEO.

Francesco (Maurizio) di Giorgio Martini (Pollaiolo)
[Francesco di Giorgio] (*b* Siena, *bapt* 23 Sept 1439; *d* Siena, *bur* 29 Nov 1501). Italian architect, engineer, painter, illuminator, sculptor, medallist, theorist and writer. He was the most outstanding artistic personality from Siena in the second half of the 15th century. His activities as a diplomat led to his employment at the courts of Naples, Milan and Urbino, as well as in Siena, and while most of his paintings and miniatures date from before 1475, by the 1480s and 1490s he was among the leading architects in Italy. He was particularly renowned for his work as a military architect, notably for his involvement in the development of the BASTION, which formed the basis of post-medieval fortifications (*see* MILITARY ARCHITECTURE & FORTIFICATION, §III, 2(ii) and 4(ii)). His subsequent palace and church architecture was influential in spreading the Urbino style, which he renewed with reference to the architecture of Leon Battista Alberti but giving emphasis to the purism of smooth surfaces. His theoretical works, which include the first important Western writings on military engineering, were not published until modern times but were keenly studied in manuscript, by Leonardo da Vinci among others; they foreshadowed a number of developments that came to fruition in the 16th century (*see* BALDASSARE PERUZZI and SEBASTIANO SERLIO).

1. Architecture. 2. Painting and drawing. 3. Sculpture.

1. ARCHITECTURE.

(i) Buildings and projects. (ii) Theory and writings.

(i) Buildings and projects. In Francesco di Giorgio's baptismal record his grandfather's occupation is given as a poultry farmer, which explains the traditional account of his rise from a humble background to become a great artist whom Vasari considered second only to Brunelleschi in establishing Renaissance architecture. Research has shown, however, that Francesco's father was a civil servant in the commune of Siena, and through him Francesco was able to meet Mariano Taccola, a Sienese notary and student of mechanics. As a boy Francesco had access to Taccola's library, from which he drew both technical knowledge and inspiration, as demonstrated by the *Codicetto* (Rome, Vatican, Bib. Apostolica, MS. Urb. lat. 1757), a small book full of notes and drawings taken from Taccola's books. Francesco was possibly apprenticed to the painter Francesco di Bartolomeo Alfei, and his first documented payment as an independent artist was in 1464.

1. Francesco di Giorgio Martini: fortress of Sassocorvaro, begun 1476–8; with partial 18th-century remodelling

Although there is no documentary evidence that Francesco studied under il Vecchietta, both are known to have been present in 1470–72 at the Ospedale della Scala, where Francesco worked as a painter and where he is also thought to have given advice on the hospital's new church, S Maria della Scala (*see* SIENA, §III, 2). Francesco's first professional involvement with building was in the field of civil engineering: in 1469 he was appointed, along with Paolo d'Andrea, as Operaio dei Bottini (conduit master) for Siena. This was an important post, as the two men undertook to increase by a third the city's water supply, which was delivered through long subterranean conduits (*bottini*). Francesco continued to work on the construction and maintenance of the conduits for most of his life, accumulating much experience of hydraulics and construction. In 1472 he was replaced by Berto d'Antonio, but in 1492 he was again in charge of the works, assisted by Berto's sons. As there is no evidence that Francesco took part in the rebuilding of Pienza, this work on the conduits appears to have been his most important formative experience in architecture and engineering in his Sienese training.

The only architectural work that can be attributed to Francesco in Siena before he went to Urbino is the church of the Osservanza, begun just outside the city in 1474 and improved, possibly by himself, in 1476. Although its plan, with an aisleless nave, sail vaults, dome and choir, displays Florentine accents and is a type that never recurs in Francesco's later work, the simplification of the parts and the use of a broken entablature over the pilasters between the side chapels, which so often characterized his later architecture, suggest that Francesco not only completed the church but also actually planned it. If so, he might previously have been called to Urbino by the Franciscan Observants, for whom he completed the friary of S Bernardino (see below).

Francesco may have met Federigo da Montefeltro (Count and from 1474 Duke of Urbino; *reg* 1444–82) and been invited to Urbino as early as 1472, after leaving his post as Operaio dei Bottini in Siena. He was possibly involved in the construction of the new fortress at Volterra, which Federigo built with the Florentines after his victorious siege of the city. On becoming Duke of Urbino in 1474 Federigo needed an architect to replace Luciano Laurana (who had left for Naples in 1472) and to complete

his palace and build the cathedral and fortresses. Having broken off his partnership with the painter Neroccio de' Landi in 1475, Francesco was certainly living in Urbino from at least 1476, and by May 1477 he was already in the full confidence of the Duke and the Duke's close friend, Ottaviano Ubaldini. He represented them in negotiating some contracts in Gubbio, one of which cites him as the designer of decorations for a room that was being built in the Palazzo Ducale there, perhaps the *studiolo* emulating that in Urbino. Another document mentions him as planner and director of works on the ravelin of Costacciaro. At about this time Francesco produced the *Opusculum* (London, BL, Harley MS. 3281, Cod. 197 *b* 21). This codex, without text except for the dedication to Federigo, was illustrated with drawings of machines and fortresses; Francesco may have presented it to the Duke on his arrival in Urbino, with the aim of promoting his engineering talents. In November 1477 Francesco declared himself resident in Urbino in the service of Federigo, and in 1478 he was accredited by two letters of Federigo for diplomatic missions at Siena.

Military architecture was prominent among Francesco's first documented works for Federigo. In particular, the ravelin of Costacciaro, with its angular form, met the new need for an architecture that could withstand gunfire and could be defended by grazing fire. It shows similarities to the ravelin of Volterra. The contemporary fortress of Sassocorvaro is only apparently far removed from this choice of new defensive forms. On the town side it survives in its original, circular form, but on the other side a casemate built by Francesco in the new pointed form was replaced by a rampart between two towers probably in the 18th century (see fig. 1). An important element of the Sassocorvaro fortress is the quadrangular courtyard with arches on piers, which already shows clearly the simplified, concise architectural language Francesco later developed in Urbino.

Francesco's most important works in Urbino were the completion of the Palazzo Ducale, the new cathedral, the church and cloister of S Bernardino and the convent of S Chiara. The loss of most of the city archives has made secure attributions and datings impossible. In the palace, which Vasari wrongly attributed entirely to Francesco, he completed what had already been started by Laurana, probably beginning with the courtyard, where he set the inscription in honour of Duke Federigo into friezes on the ground and first floors. In addition, it seems that Francesco added the Giardino Pensile garden terrace together with the adjacent wing that connects the main range (north wing) of the palace with the Castellare (a building abutting the cathedral; *see* URBINO, §4 and figs 3 and 4). He built a spiral ramp towards the garden in the connecting wing and installed a complex system of service rooms and catchment chambers in the basement. This included Federigo's antique-style bathroom in the western part of the main range, between the towers and below the Cappella del Perdono and the Tempietto delle Muse (both possibly to his own design) on the ground-floor. The bathroom comprises a series of small rooms on various levels unified by a simple architectural order, an interesting example of Francesco's ability to link irregular spaces in a coherent way. Some decorative elements inside the palace are also attributable to Francesco. These include the design of an intarsia panel of the *studiolo* (1476), depicting a squirrel against the background of an arch flanked by pilasters, which recalls Francesco's portal leading from the ramp to the garden terrace (*see* STUDIOLO, fig. 1).

Francesco's ability to create unity from diverse elements is also shown by his design of the palace's 'Facciata ad Ali', which, together with the cathedral, forms a square closed on three sides and open towards the city. In this case Francesco used a more ornate architectural vocabulary. On the ground-floor he set the doors and windows in flat rusticated stone between large pilasters, with a base in the form of a bench, its back decorated with a frieze of the *Arts of War*. The large first-floor windows, probably designed by Laurana, are not aligned with the doors below; this was a novel and disconcerting feature, but it resolved the problems of design unity created by the asymmetrical main elevation of the palace facing the city. The attribution to Francesco of the wing with arches on pilasters facing the Cortile del Pasquino remains uncertain. Francesco also built the Data, a long stable block for, at most, 300 horses to the west of the palace, and he constructed a bastion with a large spiral ramp inside (rest. 1977 by Giancarlo De Carlo) that gave access to the Data from the level of the palace and controlled the walls that extended to the Mercatale, a market square at the foot of the hill.

From *c.* 1480–81 Francesco built the new cathedral, on the site of the previous one opposite the palace. Compared with the ornate language of the palace façade, Francesco's solutions for the cathedral were simplified and austere. The sides of the nave show links with forms used by Alberti on the side of S Francesco, Rimini, and the still incomplete façade has elements of Alberti's design for S Andrea, Mantua, which was then under construction. After the earthquake of 1781 the church was restored by Giuseppe Valadier and others, who changed the architectural decoration but retained the main structure. From his survey drawings (1789), Francesco's church appears to have had a nave covered by a barrel vault on arches supported by piers without bases, aisles, projecting transepts and a large choir flanked by two chapels. Light was admitted mainly through the dome, which stood on an octagonal drum; the perimeter walls had curved chapels, where they are framed like the ends of the transepts by arches similar to the one Francesco designed for the palace *studiolo*. The unity of the whole was ensured by a pair of entablatures that encircled the whole interior, matched (as far as can be reconstructed) by external entablatures at the same height.

Francesco's architectural language was characterized by clearly defined volumes made up of plane surfaces, with horizontal articulation encircling the structure without interruption and thus unifying the whole. This was derived not only from his Sienese training and Romanesque

2. Francesco di Giorgio Martini: S Bernardino, Urbino, begun *c.* 1480–82

tradition but also from his own interpretation of ancient architecture. This original interpretation, close to the reality of the ruins then visible in Rome and elsewhere in Italy, was also expressed in his other church at Urbino, S Bernardino, which he began *c.* 1480–82. Together with its cloister it was built to complete the friary of the Franciscan Observants and to form Federigo's mausoleum, where indeed he was later buried. Set on a hill facing the city, the church had an aisleless nave ending in a wider square space with four columns at the corners supporting the dome, as in an ancient mausoleum. The solid volume, lined by string courses and entablatures inside and out, is ornamented with columns, windows in the nave with alternating segmental and triangular pediments (then a very new feature) and a trabeated portal with dolphin capitals (see fig. 2).

Also around 1482–3 Francesco must have begun work on the convent of S Chiara, Urbino, commissioned by Elisabetta, Federigo's daughter and the widow of Roberto Malatesta. The church is situated on a slope and gives on to S Bernardino with a two-storey elevation flanked by porticoed wings. Here, too, the arches on pilasters echo the simplified motif of the order continued up to the entablature above. This seems to be the first appearance of the winged façade, and it served as a model for Pope Innocent VIII's Belvedere (1484–92) at the Vatican (*see* ROME, §V, 14(iii)(2)). The convent church, built on a circular plan and surmounted by a dome, was not altered in its basic form by 17th-century modifications.

The Palazzo Ducale at Gubbio, donated by the city in 1480 to Duke Federigo, was probably also designed by Francesco, who was there for several years from 1477. The Gubbio palace is modelled on that at Urbino, but it is built on substantial earlier structures, incorporating an ancient square for the courtyard and using the medieval Palazzo della Guardia as the main body of the lower section. For this reason it is full of asymmetries, most visibly in the courtyard. The latter has four unequal sides, three of them porticoed with arches on columns and one with a series of hanging arches. The corners are similar to those at Urbino but adapted to follow the trapezoidal form of the courtyard and emphasized by the different widths of the pilasters that make up the main order, showing a very different conception from that of Laurana. The palace at Gubbio also repeats the urban scale of the palace at Urbino, allowing for the different context, as the Gubbio palace housed the municipal waterworks and was linked via an open space to the adjacent castle keep, which was renovated from 1480 in the latest defensive style. In view of the chronology as well as the architectural features, it is likely that this, too, was the work of Francesco di Giorgio, as was the ravelin at the Porta del Marmoreo, built downhill from 1486.

Francesco worked on numerous fortifications in other parts of the duchy of Montefeltro, and he discussed some of them in the *Trattati*, where he illustrated the castles of Sassofeltrio, Tavoleto and Serra S Abbondio (all *c.* 1478–86; destr.), that of Cagli (*c.* 1480–85; partly destr.), and two built between 1483 and 1490 or later for Giovanni della Rovere: Mondavio (incomplete but in good condition) and Mondolfo (destr. 1864–95). Modernizations of the castles of S Leo and Fossombrone can also be

attributed to Francesco as they reflect the defensive criteria he expounded and the forms he used. Although Francesco probably remained constantly in Urbino in the first years of his employment by Federigo, he was still interested in Sienese projects.

In the years following Federigo's death in 1482 Francesco was able to accept fairly large commissions elsewhere. One of these was for the church of S Maria del Calcinaio at Cortona, in which he was invited to participate by Luca Signorelli, who went to see Francesco in Gubbio on 17 June 1484. The first stone of the church was laid in 1485, and the building followed the drawing and the wooden model for which Francesco was paid in 1484. The church corresponds well to some of the drawings in Francesco's *Trattati*. It has a barrel-vaulted, aisleless nave and an octagonal dome (built in 1508 by the Florentine Pietro di Domenico di Norbo) on squinches over the crossing (see fig. 3). The essence of the design is revealed in the semicircular chapels set in the thickness of the walls at ground-level and in the aedicule windows on the first floor, framed by superimposed orders with pilaster strips below and separated by a narrow string course from pilasters above. This corresponds with the exterior design in both elevation and plan, so that the divisions of the external surface are visibly unequal. Francesco thus gave priority to architectural consistency based on structural rather than visual regularity. This was also clearly conveyed through the use of *pietra serena* for the orders on the white plastered walls of the interior, which, together with the proportions and the variety of capitals and cornices, makes

3. Francesco di Giorgio Martini: S Maria del Calcinaio, Cortona, interior looking east, begun 1485

the church a fine example of Francesco's mature architecture.

Francesco is thought to have been in Naples in 1484, although there is no documentation to confirm this. Although in 1485 the Sienese commune began asking him to return to his native city and appointed him to help repair the bridge at Maciareto, he was still evidently involved with projects in Urbino, near which in 1486 he bought a farm with a house at Villa Rancitelli. In the same year the contract was signed to build the Palazzo della Signoria at Jesi, following the model designed by Francesco and carved in wood by Domenico d'Antonio Indivini. This is a three-storey, isolated and compact building, with a rectangular plan incorporating a courtyard, a tower and a large hall with a vault on central piers at ground-floor level, over which on the first floor is the great meeting-hall. The courtyard is rather small, with arcaded loggias on piers on the ground-floor and arches on columns on the second; these, however, were built after the design of Andrea Sansovino, who in 1519 was summoned to complete it. The exterior features large Guelph windows (but lacking the lower mullion) on the first and second floors. This building represents a revival of the traditional type of the medieval Tuscan and Umbrian town hall. Its features, severe and yet modern, recall the spare language formerly used by Francesco in Urbino. Links have also been suggested with the inner ground-floor loggia of the Palazzo degli Anziani in Ancona, also attributed to Francesco, but the documentary evidence to confirm this is incomplete.

It was around this time that Francesco returned to Siena, where in 1487 he completed the bridge at Maciareto. He was appointed to design the fortress at Casole d'Elsa and to survey the territory between Chianciano and Montepulciano to settle a border dispute between the two communes. At the same time, however, Federigo's successor Guidobaldo I (reg 1482–1508) still referred to Francesco as 'his' architect. His return to Siena was confirmed in 1488, when he was engaged on projects for the city, but his assistant Giacomo Cozzarelli was still in Urbino, and in January 1489 Francesco again wrote home from Gubbio to give news of political events and troop movements.

In 1490 a new period began in Francesco's life. After returning to Siena he was sought for projects and consultations all over Italy. At the request of Galeazzo Maria Sforza he went to Milan in June 1490 to prepare a scheme for the lantern of the cathedral (together with Giovanni Antonio Amadeo and Giovanni Giacomo Dolcebuono) and in the same month he was in Pavia with Leonardo da Vinci for a consultation concerning the construction of the cathedral. The journey was important from the point of view of exchanges with Milanese architects, especially Bramante and Leonardo. That November he designed fortresses with Virginio Orsini at Campagnano and Bracciano and in Abruzzo. In January 1491 he was in Florence, where he entered the competition held by Lorenzo the Magnificent, Lord of Florence (reg 1469–92), for the cathedral façade. After visiting Naples in early 1491 he returned to Siena, but in 1492 he was again in Naples, where he spent between six and eight months before being recalled to Siena to repair the dam on the River Bruna. He spent the whole of 1495 in Naples and was again back

there in 1497 to plan the new outer defences (modified 16th century; destr.) of the Castelnuovo, in polygonal form with towers at the corners, which were begun in 1494 and continued by his assistant Antonio Marchesi da Settignano (1451–1522). Francesco probably also worked on the new west walls of the city and on a new fortress at Castel Sant'Elmo, which was subsequently built (1537–46) in a different form by Pedro Luís Scrivá. He also participated in inspections for the Kingdom of Naples, while the fortresses of Otranto, Gallipoli and Taranto, as well as the modernization of that at Monte Sant'Angelo, are probably linked with his designs, as are numerous other fortifications in the region (Ortona, Matera).

Even during the years when Francesco was documented in Naples he continued his activity in Siena, especially in the field of military architecture. In 1491 he was called to Sesta della Berardenga and to Cerreto Ciampoli to build fortifications (destr.), as well as to Lucca to work on the city's defences. In 1493 he was in Castelluccio di Montepulciano to inspect the model for the fortress; he was there again in 1496 and 1498, to demolish a bridge and a fort. In 1499 he was again in Urbino, and in 1500 he gave advice on buttressing the dome of S Maria di Loreto, and he perhaps designed the aqueduct and new fortifications in Loreto (built 1518–21). No civic architecture by Francesco is documented in Siena during his last years, but the design (c. 1492) of a new building for the Sapienza and two important buildings ascribed to his followers were probably planned by him. The church of S Sebastiano in Vallepiatta, begun after 1493, was built on a Greek cross plan with apses at the sides and ends of the arms. The Villa Chigi at Le Volte, near Siena, was built (c. 1496–1505) with projecting wings, a form that was later used by Baldassarre Peruzzi in Agostino Chigi (i)'s villa (1505–11; now the Villa Farnesina) in Rome.

(ii) Theory and writings. The *Trattati* is the title conventionally given to Francesco di Giorgio's collected writings, comprising essays on the role of the architect in relation to the new Renaissance interests in techniques and ancient buildings, studied through ruins and literary sources. The text is illustrated with numerous drawings and clear examples of architecture and machines. The *Trattati* have remained in manuscript form, surviving in several versions in different codices: the text was written by copyists, while the drawings are at least partly by Francesco's hand. Only Francesco's translation of Vitruvius in the Magliabechiano Codex (Florence, Bib. N. Cent., MS. Magl. II.I. 141, pt 2) is entirely autograph, but this has only seven folios with drawings. The Saluzziano Codex (Turin, Bib. Reale, MS. Saluzziano 148, pt 1) contains numerous autograph corrections by Francesco and a section on antique monuments connected with his survey drawings (Florence, Uffizi, MS. 318–37A).

Various hypotheses have been suggested to explain the work's complex evolution, and various dates have been proposed for the different versions. After the first main studies (Promis, 1841; Salmi, 1947; Maltese, 1969), the codices produced directly by Francesco were subdivided into two groups, the first (datable to before 1486) comprising the Laurenziano Codex (Florence, Bib. Medicea-Laurenziana, MS. Ashburnham 361) and the Saluzziano Codex, and the second (datable to 1485–92) consisting of the Siena Codex (Siena, Bib. Com. Intronati, MS. S. IV.4) and the Magliabechiano (pt 1). Maltese dated the *editio princeps* of Vitruvius's *On Architecture* by the philologist Sulpicio da Veroli to 1486 and placed it between the two groups. This chronology was generally accepted, although still the subject of discussion among scholars, but, following a re-examination of the material by Mussini (1991), it appears that the first group of codices dates from around 1487–9, although many parts incorporated in it had been prepared and collected by Francesco over many years previously. Thus, Francesco's treatises were put in order only after, and not before, his experiences as an architect, and he was able to work on the successive versions only after returning to Siena (?after 1496).

The first version of the *Trattati* begins with the programme of the new military architecture, which called for fortresses built low to the ground, with defences based on the broken perimeter, to permit flanking with the use of firearms, and on the moat. The latter was to be defended by embrasures set low in the castle walls and by covered gun stations inserted in the counterscarp. Francesco favoured sharp-angled walls facing the enemy, although in many cases these were protected by towers at the corners. This, together with the anthropomorphic fortress and the rhomboid type, which he considered perfect, represents the pentagonal form of bastion that influenced military architecture for many centuries (and which Francesco was credited with inventing by early 19th-century authors). This form, which he used more properly in ravelins and advanced bulwarks, can be considered a geometric rationalization of experiments tried in embryonic form in the fortresses of Fano (1439–45) and Cesena (1452–66) built by Matteo Nuti. Above all, Francesco laid great stress in his writings on the necessity of adapting to the conditions of the site and taking advantage of its defensive possibilities, sometimes using concentric circles of walls and detached forward defences.

The order of topics changes in the second version of the *Trattati*, in which a broad range of religious and civic architecture, subdivided by types is presented. Following Alberti, the civic architecture is classified according to the social standing of the intended occupant. The drawings, detailed and original, offer multiple solutions for each theme and are full of rich and realistic architectural invention, ready for further elaboration into final designs. They include drawings that have been linked to projects realized and knowledge accumulated by Francesco after 1490. The part of the *Trattati* devoted to the architectural orders is also set out in an original way. Despite its shortcomings, which include the insistent application of anthropomorphism and some misunderstandings, it was considered sufficiently up to date to be almost plagiarized by Luca Pacioli in *De divina proportione* (Venice, 1509). The treatises are supplemented with drawings of civil and military machines, which are often based on Francesco's early notes from Taccola's books. Francesco continued his activities until his death, which explains why his last architectural projects and the final reorganization of his

treatises were interrupted. As late as 1501 he is documented as making a tour of inspection of Sienese defences.

FRANCESCO PAOLO FIORE

2. PAINTING AND DRAWING. Francesco di Giorgio is generally thought to have studied with the painter and sculptor Vecchietta, although this is undocumented. The dating and even the attribution of several of his paintings and manuscript miniatures is controversial. Probably dating from the early 1460s are three cassone panels with scenes from the Old Testament: *Joseph Sold into Slavery*, *Joseph and Potiphar's Wife* and *Susanna and the Elders* (all Siena, Pin. N.). In style these are close to the work of il Vecchietta, as is the cassone front showing the *Triumph of Chastity* (Malibu, CA, Getty Mus.). Numerous other cassoni (e.g. Florence, Mus. Stibbert; London, V&A; New York, Met.) dating from the end of the 1460s show Francesco's interest in narrative and are early examples of a renewed interest in antiquity in Siena. This tendency can also be seen in the fragment of a headboard illustrating an episode from the *Story of Psyche* (*c.* 1465; Florence, I Tatti)—not the *Rape of Helen*, as previously supposed. All these paintings reveal the artist's taste for the classically inspired representation of architecture and cities. The painted book cover of records of the Sienese Biccherna, depicting the *Virgin of the Earthquake* (1467–8; Siena, Archv Stato, inv. 51), is also close to the fabulous and still 'courtly' style of Vecchietta (generally attributed to Francesco, this painting is also credited by Angelini in Bettosi, 1993 exh. cat., no. 51, to an assistant, 'Fiduciario di Francesco', representing one of his earliest works). Datable soon after (*c.* 1473–4) is the so-called *Bianca e Siena* (Florence, Bib. N. Cent., MS. Palatino 211, fol. 1*r*), which also has characteristic city views, based on real places but interpreted in terms of Classical antiquity.

Francesco's first securely dated works are a group of miniatures in dated manuscripts. The earliest extant miniature represents an *Allegory of Chastity* accompanied by an illustration of the *Three Labours of Hercules*, in a manuscript of Albertus Magnus's *De animabilis* (Siena, Mus. Castelli, inv. 3, fol. 1*r*), which is dated 1463. Although it has been considered contemporary with the manuscript, the miniature may date to *c.* 1470 (Neerman, see 1982 exh. cat.). Other miniatures of around this date include the *Allegory of Theology* in a manuscript dated 1466, *Alphonsi summi theologi ordine S Augustini* (Siena, Mus. Castelli) and a *Nativity* in an initial from an Antiphonal (Chiusi Cathedral, Cod. B, fol. 3*r*). Payments for the Antiphonal were made to Lorenzo Rosselli (*b* 1390) between 1458 and 1461, although Francesco's work may have been executed later, perhaps completing illumination left unfinished by Rosselli. During this early period, Francesco came into contact with Liberale da Verona (in Siena from 1467) and with Girolamo da Cremona (in Siena from 1470) and was strongly influenced by them. Indeed, certain drawings and paintings have been variously attributed to one or all three of these artists; for instance the panel with *Youths* (Florence, I Tatti) has been attributed by Berenson, Weller and Pope-Hennessy (1947) to Francesco, but is believed by Zeri (1950) to be by Girolamo, and by Longhi and Laclotte to be by Liberale. The latter's influence can be seen in the first important large-scale work by Francesco (probably assisted by a pupil; see De Marchi Bellosi, 1993 exh. cat., no. 56), the *Coronation of the Virgin* (1472–4; Siena, Pin. N.) and, above all, in the gable representing *God the Father*. The style is elaborate, but overburdened and contrived, the composition derived from a niello engraving (Florence, Bargello), which in its turn is derived from a drawing attributable to Maso Finiguerra or Pollaiuolo. The work reveals Francesco's attempt to incorporate innovations from contemporary Florentine painting, particularly the work of Verrocchio. For example, the figures are monumental and brought into the foreground, and there is also an attempt to soften the linear quality typical of Sienese painting. This may reflect the influence of Botticelli, although since Botticelli was still young the reverse is also possible (Yuen).

Close in date to the *Coronation* is a large detached fresco of *Fidelity* (Los Angeles, CA, Norton Simon A. Found.). Conceived as an illuminated page, the painting shows not only the rhythmic qualities of Botticelli but also signs of the influence of Neroccio de' Landi, who moved in the same artistic circles as Francesco from 1469 and worked with him until 1474. Various paintings of the Virgin, paralleling works by Filippino Lippi and Giovanni Boccati, date from this period, for instance two panels of the *Virgin and Child* (Siena, Pin. N. and ex-Pini priv. col., Bologna), the latter attributed to Francesco by Pope-Hennessy (1939) but ascribed by Longhi to 'someone close to Boccati'. Other versions of the *Virgin and Child* (e.g. Avignon, Mus. Petit Pal.; Madrid, Mus. Thyssen-Bornemisza; Coral Gables, FL, U. Miami, Lowe Art Gal.) are more archaizing in style and probably earlier. After 1475 Francesco's style became more naturalistic, both in terms of human form and in the use of light. This is evident in his only signed work, a *Nativity* (*c.* 1475–6; Siena, Pin. N.) from the monastery at Monte Oliveto; serene and sentimental, its typology is Verrocchian.

From 1477 to 1487, Francesco was in Urbino, working at the court of Federigo da Montefeltro. Vasari cited a medal by Francesco of *Duke Federigo I*, which has been convincingly identified with a surviving medallion portrait (*c.* 1478; London, BM). Another portrait of the Duke appears in a manuscript (Rome, Vatican, Bib. Apostolica, MS. Urb. lat. 508, fol. 1*v*), together with a painting once believed to be the only known self-portrait of Francesco (the miniature is now attributed to Botticelli, and the subject is identified with Cristoforo Landini; see Bellosi, 1993 exh. cat., fig. 88). After his stay in Urbino, Francesco's pictorial style underwent a further transformation, with his figures becoming increasingly 'abstract', almost symbolic, if not 'proto-Mannerist', anticipating the *figura serpentinata* of the 16th century. This is evident, for example, in the figure drawings that accompany the second version (*c.* 1495) of Francesco's *Trattati* (*see* §1(ii) above). The stereometric figure drawings (whose autography has been questioned), quite different from the more naturalistic ones in the first version of the treatise, combine the legacy of Urbino's perspective culture and that of Piero della Francesca with the lofty concept of the 'science of drawing', the perfect equal of the other liberal arts, arithmetic and geometry; it is here that the artist's most significant contribution to the Italian Renaissance is evident. The attribution of some late painted works to

Francesco is controversial. The grisaille frescoes of *c.* 1490–94, uncovered in the Bichi Chapel in S Agostino, Siena, have in the past been attributed to him. Their execution and style, however, argues against this, particularly since they were painted at a time when Francesco was often absent from Siena and, as with some of his sculptural works (*see* §3 below), had to leave the execution of certain of his works to his pupils. Another work that has been removed from Francesco's oeuvre is the *Disrobing of Christ* (Siena, Pin. N.), which is probably the work of a later follower, *c.* 1500–03 (Seidel, 1979), of Baldassare Peruzzi (Frommel) or of 'Fiduciario di Francesco' (S. Santoro in Bellosi, 1993 exh. cat., no. 108).

3. SCULPTURE. There is little stylistic link between Francesco's paintings and sculpture, the latter being generally far more sophisticated. He worked in wood, bronze and terracotta, and he also made medallions and plaquettes; there is some evidence that he also worked in stone (e.g. *Virgin and Child*, Berlin, Staatl. Museen; see Bagnoli in Bellosi, 1993 exh. cat., no. 25). His first securely

4. Francesco di Giorgio Martini: *Deposition*, bronze relief, 860×750 mm, 1474–7 (Venice, S Maria del Carmine)

datable sculpture is a life-size wooden polychrome figure of *St John the Baptist* (1464; Siena, Mus. Opera Duomo), made for the Compagnia di S Giovanni Battista della Morte, and evidently influenced by Donatello, who worked in Siena from 1457 to 1461. No other sculptural work of Francesco's can be positively dated before *c.* 1474. While in Urbino, Francesco produced the bronze relief of the *Deposition* (Venice, S Maria del Carmine; see fig. 4), originally from the oratory of Santa Croce in Urbino, and which can be firmly dated between 1474 and 1477. This relief, formerly attributed to Leonardo, reveals a lively concern for the rendering of forms by using light and shadow and suggests the influence of Donatello, even if only indirectly (Schubring, 1907; Pope-Hennessy, 1985; Luchs). More straightforward references to Donatello's work emerge in Francesco's bas-relief of the *Flagellation* (Perugia, G.N. Umbria), also formerly attributed to Leonardo as well as to Verrocchio and Bertoldo di Giovanni and almost certainly executed in Urbino around 1480–85 (only Del Bravo dates it to 1490–95). It is remarkable for the extremely skilful perspectival rendering of buildings, and for its rough finish, which gives the material a delicate quality and creates fine effects of light: this is one of the masterpieces of Renaissance sculpture, drawing directly on Classical art in a highly dramatic way, as already evident in the slightly earlier Venice *Deposition*. The great painting representing the *Nativity* (*c.* 1495; Siena, S Domenico) belongs to this late period of activity, and it is consistent stylistically with the two great bronze *Angels* in Siena Cathedral, with their undulating motion and light-filled modelling. These two *Angels*, which document Francesco's late style so well, are dated 1489–92, and documents indicate that they were cast under the direction of Francesco's pupil Giacomo Cozzarelli (*see* COZZARELLI, (2)).

PIETRO C. MARANI

UNPUBLISHED DRAWINGS

London, BL, Harley MS. 3281, Cod. 197 *b* 21 [*Opusculum*]

WRITINGS

Il Codice Ashburnham 361 della Biblioteca Medicea Laurenziana di Firenze: Trattato di architettura de Francesco di Giorgio Martini (MS.; *c.* 1490); ed. P. C. Marani, 2 vols (Florence, 1979)

Trattato di architettura civile e militare di Francesco di Giorgio Martini, architetto senese del secolo XV (MS.; *c.* 1490); ed. C. Promis, 3 vols (Turin, 1841)

Francesco di Giorgio Martini: Trattati di architettura ingegneria e arte militare (MS.; *c.* 1490–1500); ed. C. Maltese, 2 vols (Milan, 1967)

G. Scaglia, ed.: *Il 'Vitruvio Magliabechiano' di Francesco di Giorgio Martini* (Florence, 1985)

L. Michelini Tocci, ed.: *Das Skizzenbuch des Francesco di Giorgio Martini, Vat. Urb. lat. 1757* (Zurich, 1989)

BIBLIOGRAPHY

EARLY SOURCES

G. Santi: *La vita e le geste di Federico di Montefeltro, Duca d'Urbino* (MS.; *c.* 1492); ed. L. Michelini Tocci, ii (Rome, 1985), pp. 418, 419, 424, 670, 675, 742

G. Vasari: *Vite* (1550, rev. 2/1568), ed. G. Milanesi (1878–85), iii, pp. 69–79

MONOGRAPHS

A. S. Weller: *Francesco di Giorgio, 1439–1501* (Chicago, 1943)

R. Papini: *Francesco di Giorgio, architetto*, 3 vols (Florence, 1946)

C. Maltese: *Francesco di Giorgio*, I Maestri della Scultura (Milan, 1966)

P. Rotondi: *Francesco di Giorgio nel Palazzo Ducale di Urbino* (Novilara, 1970)

R. Todelano: *Francesco di Giorgio Martini: Pittore e scultore* (Milan, 1987)

F. P. Fiore and M. Tafuri, eds: *Francesco di Giorgio, architetto* (Milan, 1993–4)

ARCHITECTURE AND ENGINEERING

C. Promis: *Biografie di ingegneri militari italiani dal secolo XV alla metà del XVIII* (Turin, 1874)

W. Lotz: 'Eine Deinokratesdarstellung des Francesco di Giorgio', *Mitt. Ksthist. Inst. Florenz*, v (1937–40), pp. 428–33

C. Maltese: 'Opere e soggiorni urbinati di Francesco di Giorgio', *Studi artistici urbinati* (Urbino, 1949), pp. 57–83

P. Rotondi: 'Contributi urbinati a Francesco di Giorgio', *Studi artistici urbinati* (Urbino, 1949), pp. 85–135

M. Salmi: 'Il Palazzo Ducale di Urbino e Francesco di Giorgio', *Studi artistici urbinati* (Urbino, 1949), pp. 9–55

P. Sanpaolesi: 'Aspetti dell'architettura del '400 a Siena e Francesco di Giorgio', *Studi artistici urbinati* (Urbino, 1949), pp. 137–68

P. Rotondi: *Il Palazzo Ducale di Urbino*, i–ii (Urbino, 1950–51)

G. H. Fehring: *Studien über die Kirchenbauten des Francesco di Giorgio* (Würzburg, 1956)

C. Maltese: 'L'attività di Francesco di Giorgio Martini, architetto militare nelle Marche attraverso il suo "Trattato"', *Atti del XI congresso di storia dell'architettura: Marche, 1957*, pp. 281–328

M. Dezzi Bardeschi: 'Le rocche di Francesco di Giorgio nel ducato di Urbino', *Castellum*, viii (1968), pp. 97–140

P. Marconi: 'Una chiave per l'interpretazione dell'urbanistica rinascimentale: La cittadella come microcosmo', *Quad. Ist. Stor. Archit.*, 85–90 (1968), pp. 53–94

G. H. Hersey: *Alfonso II and the Artistic Renewal of Naples, 1485–1495* (New Haven and London, 1969)

H. Burns: 'Progetti di Francesco di Giorgio per i conventi di S Bernardino e Santa Chiara di Urbino', *Atti del congresso internazionale. Studi Bramanteschi: Milano, Urbino, Roma, 1970*, pp. 293–311

P. Rotondi: *Francesco di Giorgio nel Palazzo Ducale di Urbino* (Novilara, 1970)

M. Dezzi Bardeschi: 'L'architettura militare del '400 nelle Marche con particolare riguardo all'opera di Francesco di Giorgio', *Stud. Maceratesi*, 9 (1975), pp. 137–49

R. Pane: *Il rinascimento nell'Italia meridionale*, i, ii (Milan, 1975–7)

G. Martines: 'Il Palazzo Ducale di Gubbio: Un brano sepolto della città medievale, un'ipotesi per Francesco di Giorgio', *Ric. Stor. A.*, 6 (1977), pp. 89–110

A. Bruschi: 'Pareri sul tiburio del duomo di Milano: Leonardo, Bramante, Francesco di Giorgio', *Scritti rinascimentali di architettura* (Milan, 1978), pp. 320–86

G. Martines: 'Francesco di Giorgio a Gubbio in tre documenti d'archivio rinvenuti e trascritti da Pier Luigi Menichetti', *Ric. Stor. A.*, 11 (1980), pp. 67–9

P. C. Marani: 'Leonardo, Francesco di Giorgio e il tiburio del duomo di Milano', *A. Lombarda*, 62 [1982], pp. 81–92

——: 'A Reworking by Baldassarre Peruzzi of Francesco di Giorgio's Plan of a Villa', *J. Soc. Archit. Historians*, xli/3 (1982), pp. 181–8

F. P. Fiore: 'Francesco di Giorgio e il rivellino "acuto" di Costacciaro', *Quad. Ist. Stor. Archit.*, n. s., 1–10 (1983–7), pp. 197–208

D. Gallavotti Cavallero: 'Francesco di Giorgio di Martino, architetto, ingegnere, scultore, bronzista per la SS Annunziata di Siena', *Paragone*, xxxvi/427 (1985), pp. 46–56

M. Agostinelli and F. Mariano: *Francesco di Giorgio e il Palazzo della Signoria di Jesi* (Jesi, 1986)

F. P. Fiore: 'Francesco di Giorgio a Gubbio', *Federico di Montefeltro: Le arti* (Rome, 1986), pp. 151–70

——: 'Francesco di Giorgio e le origini della nuova architettura militare', *L'architettura militare veneta del cinquecento* (Milan, 1988), pp. 62–75

——: 'Le residenze ducali di Urbino e Gubbio: "Città in forma di palazzo"', *Archit. Stor. & Doc.*, 1–2 (1989), pp. 5–34

R. Schofield: 'Amadeo, Bramante and Leonardo and the Tiburio of Milan Cathedral', *Achad. Leonardi Vinci: J. Leonardo Stud. & Bibliog. Vinciana*, ii (1989), pp. 68–100

M. S. A. Dechert: 'The Military Architecture of Francesco di Giorgio in Southern Italy', *J. Soc. Archit. Historians*, xlix/2 (1990), pp. 161–80

P. C. Marani: 'Francesco di Giorgio a Milano e a Pavia: Consequenze ed ipotesi', *Prima di Leonardo: Cultura delle macchine a Siena nel rinascimento* (Milan, 1991), pp. 93–104

P. Matracchi: *La chiesa di S Maria delle Grazie al Calcinaio presso Cortona e l'opera di Francesco di Giorgio* (Cortona, 1991)

M. Mussini: *Il trattato di Francesco di Giorgio Martini e Leonardo: Il Codice Estense restituito* (Parma, 1991)

THEORY

E. Berti: 'Un manoscritto di Pietro Cataneo agli Uffizi e un codice di Francesco di Giorgio Martini', *Belvedere*, vii (1925), pp. 100–03

P. Fontana: 'I codici di Francesco di Giorgio Martini e di Mariano di Iacomo detto il Taccola', *XVIe Congrès international d'histoire de l'art 1936: Résumés des communications présentées en section. Actes du Congrès: Berne, 1936*, i, pp. 102–5

H. Millon: 'The Architectural Theory of Francesco di Giorgio', *A. Bull.*, xl (1958), pp. 257–61

L. Reti: 'Francesco di Giorgio Martini's Treatises on Engineering and its Plagiarists', *Technol. & Cult.*, iv/3 (1963), pp. 287–98

P. Marconi, F. P. Fiore, G. Muratore and E. Valeriani: *La città come forma simbolica: Studi sulla teoria dell'architettura nel rinascimento* (Rome, 1973)

L. Reti, ed.: *Leonardo da Vinci: I codici di Madrid* (Florence, 1974)

R. J. Betts: 'On the Chronology of Francesco di Giorgio's Treatises: New Evidence from an Unpublished Manuscript', *J. Soc. Archit. Historians*, xxxvi/1 (1977), pp. 3–14

S. Pepper and Q. Huges: 'Fortification in Late 15th-century Italy: The Treatise of Francesco di Giorgio Martini', *Brit. Archaeol. Rep., Suppl. Ser.*, 41 (1978), pp. 541–60

R. Feuer-Tóth: 'Un Traité italien du XVe siècle dans le Codex Zichy de Budapest', *Actes du colloque. Les Traités d'architecture de la Renaissance: Tours, 1981*, pp. 99–113

L. Lowic: 'The Meaning and Significance of the Human Analogy in Francesco di Giorgio's *Trattato*', *J. Soc. Archit. Historians*, xlii (1983), pp. 360–70

F. P. Fiore: 'La traduzione da Vitruvio di Francesco di Giorgio: Note ad una parziale trascrizione', *Archit. Stor. & Doc.*, 1 (1985), pp. 7–30

C. Kolb: 'The Francesco di Giorgio Material in the Zichy Codex', *J. Soc. Archit. Historians*, xlvii/2 (1988), pp. 132–59

M. Mussini: *Il 'Trattato' di Francesco di Giorgio Martini e Leonardo: Il Codice Estense restituito* (Parma, 1991)

G. Scaglia: *Francesco di Giorgio: Checklist and History of Manuscripts and Drawings in Autographs and Copies, from c. 1470 to 1687, and Renewed Copies, 1764–1839* (Bethlehem, London and Toronto, 1992)

DRAWINGS

C. Gamba: 'A proposito di alcuni disegni del Louvre', *Rass. A.*, ix/3 (1909), pp. 37–40

C. Brandi: 'Disegni inediti di Francesco di Giorgio', *Arte*, xxxvii (1934), pp. 45–57

B. Degenhart: 'Francesco di Giorgios Entwicklung als Zeichner', *Z. Kstgesch.*, iv (1935), pp. 103–26

——: 'Unbekannte Zeichnungen Francesco di Giorgio', *Z. Kstgesch.*, viii (1939), pp. 117–50

M. Salmi: 'Disegni di Francesco di Giorgio nella collezione Chigi Saracini', *Quad. Accad. Chigiana*, xi (1947), pp. 7–45

A. E. Popham and P. M. R. Pouncey: *Italian Drawings in the Department of Prints and Drawings in the British Museum, XIV–XV Centuries* (London, 1950), pp. 32–8

T. Buddensieg: 'Die Kostantinsbasilika in einer Zeichnung Francescos di Giorgio und der Marmorkolossos Kostantins des Grossen', *Münchn. Jb. Bild. Kst*, xiii (1962), pp. 37–48

L. Michelini Tocci: 'Disegni e appunti autografi di Francesco di Giorgio in un codice del Taccola', *Scritti di storia dell'arte in onore di Mario Salmi* (Rome, 1962), ii, pp. 203–12

A. Forlani Tempesti: *Disegni italiani della Collezione Santarelli, sec. XV–XVII* (Florence, 1967)

C. L. Ragghianti: 'Note ai disegni di Francesco di Giorgio', *Crit. A.*, xiv/89 (1967), pp. 38–53

C. Maltese: 'Il protomanierismo di Francesco di Giorgio Martini', *Stor. A.*, iv (1969), pp. 440–46

F. P. Fiore: *Città e macchine del'400 nei disegni di Francesco di Giorgio Martini* (Florence, 1978)

E. Beltrame Quattrocchi: *Disegni toscani e umbri del primo rinascimento dalle collezioni del Gabinetto Nazionale delle Stampe* (Rome, 1979)

C. H. Ericsson: *Roman Architecture Expressed in Sketches by Francesco di Giorgio Martini: Studies in Imperial Roman and Early Christian Architecture* (Helsinki, 1980)

G. Scaglia: 'Autour de Francesco di Giorgio Martini ingénieur et dessinateur', *Rev. A.*, xlviii (1980), pp. 7–25

A. Parronchi, ed.: *Baldassarre Peruzzi: Trattato di architettura militare* (Florence, 1982)

S. Szabo: *Masterpieces of Italian Drawing in the Robert Lehman Collection, the Metropolitan Museum of Art*, no. 14 (New York, 1983)

M. Morresi: 'Francesco di Giorgio e Bramante: Osservazioni su alcuni disegni degli Uffizi e della Laurenziana', *Atti del convegno. Il disegno di architettura: Milano, 1988*, pp. 117–24

G. Scaglia: *Francesco di Giorgio: Checklist and History of Manuscripts and Drawings in Autographs and Copies, from c. 1470 to 1687, and Renewed Copies, 1764–1839* (Bethlehem, London and Toronto, 1992)

P. C. Marani: 'L'Amadeo e Francesco di Giorgio Martini', *Atti del convegno: Giovanni Antonio Amadeo: Scultura e architettura del suo tempo. Milano, 1993*

PAINTING

P. Schubring: *Cassoni: Truhen und Truhenbilder der italienischen Frühenrenaissance* (Leipzig, 1915), nos 462–7

A. McComb: 'The Life and Works of Francesco di Giorgio', *A. Stud.* (1924), pp. 3–32

A. Venturi: 'Per Francesco di Giorgio Martini', *Arte*, xxviii–xxx (1930), pp. 51–8

J. Pope-Hennessy: 'Francesco di Giorgio Martini, Neroccio: Two Madonnas and an Altarpiece', *Burl. Mag.*, lxxv (1939), pp. 229–35

——: *Sienese Quattrocento Painting* (Oxford, 1947)

C. Brandi: *Quattrocentisti senese* (Milan, 1949)

F. Zeri: 'Una pala d'altare di Gerolamo da Cremona', *Boll. A.*, xxxv (1950), p. 39

E. Carli: *La pittura senese* (Milan, 1955)

M. Laclotte: *De Giotto à Bellini* (Paris, 1956)

R. Longhi: 'Un familiare del Boccati', *Paragone*, xiii/153 (1962), pp. 60–64

F. Russoli: *La raccolta Berenson* (Milan, 1962)

F. Zeri: 'Un intervento su Francesco di Giorgio Martini', *Boll. A.*, xlix (1964), pp. 41–4

T. Yuen: 'New Aspects of Botticelli's Late Works: A Suggestion for the Dating of the Dante Illustrations and Francesco di Giorgio's Influence', *Marsyas*, xii (1966), pp. 22–33

C. L. Frommel: 'Baldassarre Peruzzi als Maler und Zeichner', *Röm. Jb. Kstgesch.*, xi (1967–8)

B. Berenson: *Central and North Italian Schools*, i (1968), pp. 140–41

B. Fredericksen: *The Cassone Painting of Francesco di Giorgio* (Los Angeles, 1969)

M. Salmi: 'Una precisazione su Francesco di Giorgio', *Commentari*, xxii/4 (1971), pp. 335–6

F. Bisogni: 'Risarcimento del *Ratto di Elena* di Francesco di Giorgio', *Prospettiva*, vii (1976), pp. 44–6

P. Torriti: *La Pinacoteca Nazionale di Siena: I dipinti dal XII al XV secolo* (Genoa, 1977)

M. Seidel: 'Die Fresken des Francesco di Giorgio in S Agostino in Siena', *Mitt. Ksthist. Inst. Florenz*, xxiii (1979), pp. 3–108

L. Vertova: 'Cupid and Psyche in Renaissance Painting before Raphael', *J. Warb. & Court. Inst.*, xlii (1979), pp. 104–21

Mostra di opere d'arte restaurate nelle province di Siena e Grosseto (exh. cat. by M. Seidel, Siena, Pin. N., 1979), pp. 152–9

Codici liturgici miniati dei Benedettini in Toscana (exh. cat., Florence, Cent. Incon. Certosa, 1982), pp. 269–83 [contribution by G. Neerman]

A. Garzelli: 'Un'inedita allegoria di Francesco di Giorgio Martini', *Paragone*, xxxvi/427 (1985), pp. 124–34

J. Pope-Hennessy: [review of P. Anselm Riedl and M. Seidel: *Die Kirchen von Siena* (Munich, 1984)], *Burl. Mag.*, cxviii (1986), pp. 512–13

Renaissance Painting in Siena (exh. cat. by K. Christiansen, L. Kanter and C. Strehlke, New York, Met., 1988), pp. 316–27

Francesco di Giorgio e il rinascimento a Siena, 1450–1500 (exh. cat., ed. L. Bellosi; Siena, S Agostino, 1993), pp. 19–89, 284–9, 290–316, 420–86

SCULPTURE

P. Schubring: *Plastik Sienas im quattrocento* (Berlin, 1907)

G. F. Hartlaub: 'Zur Würdigung des Francesco di Giorgio als Maler und Bildhauer', *Pantheon*, xxv (1940), pp. 87–92

J. Pope-Hennessy: *Italian Renaissance Sculpture* (London, 1955, rev. Oxford, 3/1985), pp. 61–3, 246, 307–9

G. Eimer: 'Francesco di Giorgios Fassadenfries am Herzogpalast zu Urbino', *Festschrift Ulrich Middeldorf*, i (Berlin, 1968), pp. 187–98

C. Del Bravo: *Scultura senese del quattrocento* (Florence, 1970)

E. Carli: *Scultori senesi* (Milan, 1980)

F. Fumi: 'Nuovi documenti per gli angeli dell'altar maggiore del duomo di Siena', *Prospettiva*, xxvi (1981), pp. 9–25

G. Bernini Pezzini: *Il fregio dell'arte della guerra nel Palazzo Ducale di Urbino: Catalogo dei rilievi*, Urbino, Pal. Ducale cat. (Rome, 1985)

A. Luchs: 'Francesco di Giorgio Martini', *Donatello e i suoi: Scultura fiorentina del primo rinascimento* (exh. cat., ed. A. Phipps Darr and G. Bonsanti; Florence, Forte Belvedere, 1986), pp. 225–9

F. PAOLO FIORE, PIETRO C. MARANI

Francesco di Giovanni di Domenico. *See* BOTTICINI, FRANCESCO.

Francesco di Pietro della Biada. *See* BENAGLIO, FRANCESCO.

Francesco di Stefano. *See* PESELLINO.

Francesco di Valdambrino (*fl* 1401; *d* Siena, 20 Aug 1435). Italian sculptor. He is best known as the friend and occasional collaborator of Jacopo della Quercia in Lucca and Siena, but he already had a considerable reputation before his association with della Quercia. In 1401 Francesco was invited to participate in the competition for the second set of bronze doors for the Florentine Baptistery together with Lorenzo Ghiberti, Filippo Brunelleschi, Niccolò di Piero Lamberti, Niccolò d'Arezzo, Simone da Colle and Jacopo della Quercia. His first dated work is a polychromed wooden statue of the standing *Virgin and Child* (1403), in S Andrea, Palaia (Burresi). Both the delicate *Virgin and Child* and the rigidly iconic *St Peter* (Montalcino, Mus. Dioc. A. Sacra) are in the Late Gothic style then current in Pisa, and show the influence of Nino Pisano in particular.

Francesco was in Lucca in 1405–7, when Jacopo della Quercia was carving the tomb of *Ilaria del Carretto* (Lucca Cathedral) with its classicizing frieze of putti carrying garlands. Francesco is believed to have executed the frieze on the north side of the sarcophagus, where the figures are less robust and less spatially ambitious (although Freytag has suggested the frieze is the work of Matteo Civitali's workshop). Francesco may also have contributed to the design of the colossal heads on the exterior of the cathedral. A statue of *St Nicholas of Tolentino* (Lucca, S Maria Corteolandini) has also been attributed to Francesco (Paoli).

By 1409 Francesco had returned to Siena, where he is documented carving four wooden statues of the city's patron saints. Three bust-length fragments of *St Vittorio*, *St Savino* and *St Crescenzio* (all Siena, Mus. Opera Duomo) survive, and they reveal an artist with a refined and sensitive manner best seen in the delicate treatment of the facial features. Francesco helped Jacopo della Quercia to buy marble for the Loggia di Mercanzia (Loggia di San Paolo), Siena, and it has also been suggested that he contributed to the decoration of the Fonte Gaia; the *Rhea Silvia* (*c.* 1416–18) has been attributed to him. He may have also aided Quercia in his capacity as the official (1409–22) in charge of the water pipes that service the fountains of Siena. Francesco held several political offices including *gonfaloniere* and *consigliere* (1411 and 1412) and was elected to the Priore in 1415 and 1435.

Although a capable marble worker, Francesco's best works are polychromed wooden sculptures, a medium that enjoyed a considerable vogue among Sienese sculptors. *St Stephen* (Empoli, Mus. S Andrea) and *St Ansano* (Lucca, SS Simone e Guida) are both depicted as pensive, introspective figures. A number of wooden Annunciation groups have been attributed to Francesco (San Quirico, S Maria in Vitaleta; Munich, Bayer. Nmus.; Amsterdam, Rijksmus.); the most accomplished in the emotional interaction of the figures and their fluid linear rhythms and grace are the *Virgin Annunciate* and the *Angel Gabriel* (Asciano, Mus. A. Sacra). It has been suggested that an equestrian statue of *St Ansano* (San Cassiano in Controne,

Pieve) was either a collaborative work between Quercia (horse) and Francesco (saint; see Freytag) or the work of Quercia alone (Middeldorf). A date of the mid-1420s (Del Bravo) seems more plausible than the traditional dating of 1406–7.

BIBLIOGRAPHY

Thieme–Becker

G. Milanesi: *Documenti per la storia dell'arte senese*, 3 vols (Siena, 1854–6)
P. Bacci: *Francesco di Valdambrino: Emulo del Ghiberti* (Siena, 1936)
C. L. Ragghianti: 'Su Francesco di Valdambrino', *Crit. A.*, iii (1938), pp. 136–43
E. Carli: *Scultura lignea senese* (Milan, 1951)
C. Del Bravo: *Scultura senese del quattrocento* (Florence, 1970)
C. Freytag: 'Beiträge zum Werk des Francesco di Valdambrino', *Pantheon*, xxix (1971), pp. 363–78
A. Bagnoli: 'Francesco di Valdambrino', *Jacopo della Quercia nell'arte del suo tempo* (Florence, 1975), pp. 120–35
U. Middeldorf: 'Due problemi quereschi', *Jacopo della Quercia fra gotico e rinascimento* (Florence, 1977), pp. 147–9
E. Carli: *Gli scultori senesi* (Milan, 1980)
M. Paoli: 'Un nuova opera documentata di Francesco di Valdambrino', *Paragone*, xxxii (1981), pp. 66–77
M. Burresi: 'Incrementi di Francesco di Valdambrino', *Crit. A.*, 4th ser., I/6 (1985), pp. 49–59

ELINOR M. RICHTER

Francesco di Vannuccio (*fl* 1356–89). Italian painter. He was listed with his contemporaries Paolo di Giovanni Fei and Bartolo di Fredi in Sienese civic records of 1356 and is continually recorded in the city until after 1389. He was probably dead by 1391. Francesco's only signed work dates from his maturity, and there is no agreed body of early work. The small triptych of the *Virgin and Child with Saints*, the *Annunciation* and the *Crucifixion* (Siena, Pin. N., 183), often but not universally attributed to an early phase of his development, suggests some contact with such painters as the Ovile Master and Naddo Ceccarelli. The elongated figures also broadly recall Paolo di Giovanni Fei and other painters of the mid-century. But stylistic affinities between this triptych and the signed and dated double-sided processional image, with the *Virgin and Child with Saints* on one side and the *Crucifixion and Saints* on the other (1380; Berlin, Gemäldegal.), are hardly overwhelming. The style of the Berlin *Crucifixion* suggests a connection with a more overtly expressive area of the Sienese tradition and with the late style of Simone Martini in particular. The intense twisting figures of *St John* in the Berlin panel and in another *Crucifixion* (ex-Kaulbach Col., Munich) clearly recall the *Joseph* of Simone's *Christ Returning from the Temple* (Liverpool, Walker A.G.) or the standing figures of the frontispiece to Petrarch's edition of Virgil (Milan, Bib. Ambrosiana). The beetle-browed and distinctly fleshy faces of Francesco's figures, expressive almost to the point of caricature, may ultimately derive from such models as the mourning women of Simone's *Entombment* (Berlin, Gemäldegal.) or the figures in the Master of the Codex of St George's panels. The composition of the Annunciation on a diptych with an *Annunciation and Two Donors* and the *Assumption* (Cambridge, Girton Coll.) derives directly from Simone.

The proportions of the figures in this group of works are squatter and less consciously elegant than those of the Siena triptych or those in the paintings of most of Francesco's contemporaries. An intense and original sensibility, a searching concern for the inner drama behind outward gesture, is revealed throughout Francesco's work, and his reworking of earlier Sienese models is in response to an expressive drive markedly stronger than those of other backward-looking painters of his time. This is most evident in the Berlin and ex-Munich *Crucifixions*, where the dialogue between the figures is supported by their emotional gestures and expressions. Marginal areas of larger works reveal this intensity too, as in the small busts of the gesticulating *Virgin* and *St John* flanking a *Man of Sorrows* on a reliquary (ex-R. Von Kaufmann Col., Berlin), contrasting with the cooler *Madonna of Humility* of the main panel.

BIBLIOGRAPHY

R. van Marle: *Italian Schools*, ii (1924), pp. 531–3

C. Brandi: 'An Unpublished Reliquary of Francesco di Vannuccio', *A. America*, xx (1931), pp. 38–48

R. Offner: 'The Works and Style of Francesco di Vannuccio', *A. America*, xxi (1932), pp. 89–114

C. Brandi: 'Francesco di Vannuccio e Paolo di Giovanni Fei', *Bull. Sen. Stor. Patria*, n. s., iv (1933), pp. 25–42

B. Berenson: *Central and North Italian Schools*, i (1968), p. 145

P. Torriti: *La Pinacoteca Nazionale di Siena: I dipinti dal XII al XV secolo* (Genoa, 1977, 2/1980), pp. 162–3

Il gotico a Siena (exh. cat., ed. M. Boskovits; Siena, Pal. Pub., 1982), pp. 282–6, nos 105 and 106

JOHN RICHARDS

Francescuccio da Fabriano. *See* GHISSI, FRANCESCUCCIO.

Frances Sibyl Augusta, Margravine of Baden-Baden. *See* ZÄHRINGEN, (1).

Francés y Sanchez-Heredero, José [Lago, Silvio] (*b* Madrid, 1883; *d* Madrid, 1963). Spanish critic and writer. He is noted for his documentation of artistic life in Spain, particularly in Madrid, in annual compilations of reviews of the previous season's artistic events published from 1916 to 1925–6 as *El año artístico*; these constitute an invaluable source for the study of the period. As a critic for reviews such as *La Esfera* and *Nuevo Mundo* he wrote both under his own name and occasionally under the pseudonym of Silvio Lago, gradually adopting a more conservative and even traditional aesthetic. In 1923 he became a member of the Academia de Bellas Artes de San Fernando and shortly afterwards its permanent secretary. He was innovative in promoting caricature as a fine art, notably in Salones de Humoristas held in Madrid for several years from 1916 and in books such as *El mundo ríe* (1921) and *El arte que sonríe y que castiga* (1924). He was also involved in the publication of a collection of monographs on artists under the imprint of Biblioteca Estrella; these represented one of the first serious attempts to publicize some of the most important Spanish painters and sculptors of the century. In addition he translated the works of Edgar Allan Poe and Charles Baudelaire into Spanish and wrote novels and short stories.

BIBLIOGRAPHY

J. A. Gaya Nuño: *Historia de la crítica de arte en España* (Madrid, 1975), pp. 308–9, 314, 324

M. DOLORES JIMÉNEZ-BLANCO

Franchi, Alessandro (*b* Prato, 15 March 1838; *d* Siena, 29 April 1914). Italian painter. He first studied in Prato. In 1853 he was urged by Cesare Guasti (1822–89), the Purismo theorist, to study under Luigi Mussini in Siena in order to absorb a French brand of Purism that was allied to the teaching of Ingres and Hippolyte Flandrin rather than to the rigid purist principles of the Nazarenes. Franchi became Mussini's favourite pupil and was praised for his exceptional talent, his assiduousness and the purity of his forms. His first public commissions—*St Elizabeth of Hungary, St Louis of France* (both 1860–61; Prato, S Domenico) *St George* (1863; Prato, oratory of S Giorgio)—were strongly influenced by the contemporary style of Mussini, who was working on *St Crescentius* for Siena Cathedral. Following the example of Antonio Ciseri, Franchi later developed his own style, adding gentle elegiac forms, usually religious, to compositions of an arid and puristic simplicity. From 1873 to 1876 he executed frescoes (e.g. *Expulsion from Paradise*, 1876) for the Cappella Vinaccesi in Prato Cathedral. After painting *Virgin and Child Enthroned with Saints* for S Pier Forelli in Prato, he designed some of the cartoons (1875–8) for the floors of the cathedrals of Siena and Prato. Many of his most notable works of the 1880s were produced for buildings in Siena: the mythological frescoes of the *Four Elements* in the loggia of the Palazzo Bichi Ruspoli, the frescoes for the chapels of the Misericordia Cemetery, and the frescoes of the *Virgin in Glory with St Simon Stock* (1884) for the oratory of S Teresa. He also collaborated with such artists as Cesare Maccari and Pietro Aldi (1852–88) on the decoration of the Sala Vittorio Emanuele in the Palazzo Pubblico (e.g. *Italy Triumphant*, 1891).

BIBLIOGRAPHY

N. Mengozzi: *Lettere intime di artisti senesi* (Siena, 1908)

L. Franchi Mussini: *Alessandro Franchi e le sue opere* (Siena, 1915)

N. Mengozzi: 'Il pittore Alessandro Franchi: Notizie biografiche', *Bull. Sen. Stor. Patria*, xxii (1915), pp. 3–108

P. Rossi: 'L'opera artistica di Alessandro Franchi', *Rass. A. Sen.* (1915), pp. 3–14

C. Del Bravo: 'Per Alessandro Franchi', *An. Scu. Norm. Sup. Pisa*, n. s. 2, ii (1972), pp. 737–59

A. Natali: 'Gli affreschi di Alessandro Franchi nel Duomo di Prato', *Ant. Viva*, 6 (1975), pp. 43–9

R. Agresti: 'Alessandro Franchi', *Siena tra Purismo e Liberty* (exh. cat., ed. M. Batazzi; Siena, Pal. Pub., 1988), pp. 138–52, 250–56

GIOVANNA UZZANI

Franchi, Antonio [il Lucchese] (*b* Villa Basilica, nr Lucca, 14 July 1638; *d* Florence, 18 July 1709). Italian painter and theorist. After training in Lucca with Domenico Ferrucci, he settled for 12 years (1655–67) in Florence, where he studied with Felice Ficherelli and Baldassare Franceschini. His style unites classical and Baroque elements and reflects his study of the art of Reni, Cortona and Rubens. He returned to Lucca in 1668: most of his early work is to be found there or in the surrounding area (e.g. *Saints Worshipping the Trinity*, 1665; Lucca, S Maria dei Servi, and *SS Lucy, John the Baptist, Francis Xavier and Others, c.* 1670; Montecarlo, S Andrea). In 1674 he established himself in Florence, first under the patronage of the Strozzi family and later under the Medici. The *Temple of Love* and *The Sacrifice* (both Florence, Gal. Corsini) were probably painted in that year for the Marchese Pier Francesco Rinuccini and are among his most accomplished works, inspired by Cortona's romantic vision of the ancient world. In 1683 he was admitted to the Accademia del Disegno, and in 1684 he painted various biblical and mythological scenes for Prince Ferdinando de' Medici, all untraced except for the *Garden of Love* (Rome, Pal. Montecitorio).

In 1686 the Grand Duchess Vittoria della Rovere appointed Franchi as her official portrait painter. He was inspired by the tradition of court portraiture established by such French artists as Pierre Mignard yet brought to it a new informality and a sharper sense of character. Among his portraits are *Lucrezia Rinuccini Corsini* (1681; Florence, Gal. Corsini), the seven portraits of *Anna Maria Luisa de' Medici* made at the time of her marriage (1691), and a series of portraits of ladies (1690–91) painted for the private apartment of Violante of Bavaria (Florence, Depositi Gal.). Franchi's religious works include *Joseph's Vision* (Florence, S Giovannino degli Scolopi), the *Madonna of the Rosary* (Pescia, Prepositura), both dating from 1694, and the frescoes depicting scenes from the *Life of St John the Baptist* (1699–1701; Florence, S Frediano in Cestello).

Apart from painting, Franchi had scholarly interests: he studied philosophy and worked on scientific inventions. His treatise on painting, *Trattato della teorica pittoresca*, was completed shortly before his death but left unpublished until 1739, when Giuseppe Rigacci (*fl* 1740) oversaw its publication, dedicated it to the Florentine collector and biographer Francesco Maria Niccolò Gabburri and even provided it with a new title: *La teorica della pittura*. Rigacci may also have altered the structure and contents of the treatise. A few days before his death, Franchi described his 'little treatise' to the painter and theorist Ludovico David, whose *L'amore dell'arte* had influenced him: the first section was to have four chapters of general introduction, followed by five chapters on the forms of painting (chiaroscuro; reflected colour and colour harmony; perspective; colours in shadows; foreshortening) and finally four chapters on particular artistic problems (reflections on water; drapery folds; painting cupolas). Franchi's contemporary biographers said that he was a follower of the great colourists, and this interest is reflected in his concern for colour and light. Although he described two aspects of *disegno* (perspective and foreshortening), others, such as anatomy, proportion and the study of antiquity, were omitted. He ignored the literary basis of painting (invention), although there is mention of it in the published work (chaps 19–20, 23). Despite his Venetian sympathies as a artist, as a critic and pedagogue he found that his contemporaries painted too quickly and too abundantly. The second section was planned as a miscellaneous collection of topics relating to connoisseurship and artistic taste (e.g. 'How to distinguish good from bad pictures'; 'What people mean when they say a picture is well brushed'; 'It is shown that speed in painting is incompatible with perfection'). The published work has a more traditional pedagogic format that depends largely upon Giovanni Paolo Lomazzo.

WRITINGS

La teorica della pittura ovvero: Trattato delle materie più necessarie per apprendere con fondamento quest'arte (Lucca, 1739)

BIBLIOGRAPHY

F. S. Baldinucci: *Vite* (1725–30); ed. A. Matteoli (1975), pp. 41–52
S. Bartolozzi: *Vita di Antonio Franchi lucchese pittor fiorentino* (Florence, 1754)
L. Lanzi: *Storia pittorica della Italia*, i (Bassano, 1809), pp. 244–5
The Twilight of the Medici: Late Baroque Art in Florence, 1670–1743 (exh. cat., ed. S. F. Rossen; Detroit, MI, Inst. A.; Florence, Pitti; 1974)
M. Gregori: 'Ricerche per Antonio Franchi', *Paradigma*, i (1977), pp. 65–89
F. Nannelli: 'Antonio Franchi e la sua "vita" scritta da Francesco Saverio Baldinucci', *Paradigma*, i (1977), pp. 317–69 [documentary study of Franchi's life based on Bartolozzi and Baldinucci]

MARGHERITA PALATUCCI, PHILIP SOHM

Franchi, Rossello di Jacopo (*b* ?Florence, 1377; *d* Florence, 10 Aug 1456). Italian painter and illuminator. He was possibly a pupil of Mariotto di Nardo, matriculating in the Guild of St Luke in 1424. He filed a joint tax return with his brother Giunta di Jacopo (*b* 1379) in 1427 in which he claimed that he was not practising his art since he had 'nothing to do'. He was documented in 1429 as involved in illumination. In 1433 he painted 12 figures of apostles for Florence Cathedral with Bicci di Lorenzo and Lippo di Corso (1357–1404). He worked with Ventura di Moro (*fl* 1416–56) on scenes from the *Life of St Peter Martyr* (1445–6; Florence, Mus. Bigallo). Franchi's dated works include *St Blaise Enthroned* (1408; Florence Cathedral), the *Coronation of the Virgin* (1420; Florence, Accad. B.A. & Liceo A.) and the signed and dated *Coronation of the Virgin* (1439; Siena, Pin. N.), the last showing an interesting iconographical development with the figures of Christ and the Virgin seated as if in a tomb. He was typical of many of the prolific artists of the early 15th century catering for the Florentine art market in producing compositions based on those of the better-known masters of his day. His style is close to that of Bicci di Lorenzo and Lorenzo Monaco, although his drapery is slightly more agitated and he does not carry through Monaco's sophisticated treatment of space. His quite strongly modelled figures are often set against flat, decorated backgrounds that negate their plasticity. However, the strongly illusionistic frescoes of a *Male Saint* and *St Lucy* (both Florence, S Miniato al Monte) are more powerful.

BIBLIOGRAPHY

C. Pini and G. Milanesi: *La scrittura di artisti italiani (sec. XIV–XVII): Riprodotta con la topografia da Carlo Pini e correda di notizie da Gaetano Milanesi* (Florence, 1876)
U. Procacci: 'Di Jacopo di Antonio e delle compagnie di pittori del corso degli Adimari nel XV secolo', *Riv. A.*, xxxv (1960), pp. 3–70 (52 n. 99)
B. Berenson: *Central and North Italian Schools* (1968)
R. Fremantle: *Florentine Gothic Painters from Giotto to Masaccio: A Guide to Painting in and near Florence, 1300 to 1450* (London, 1975)

ANABEL THOMAS

Franchini [Francini]. *See* LAFRANCHINI.

Franchoys. Flemish family of artists. Lucas Franchoys I (*b* Mechelen, 23 Jan 1574; *d* Mechelen, 16 Sept 1643) was a portrait and figure painter from an old Mechelen family. He was dean of the Guild of St Luke six times between 1603 and 1640. He probably trained both his sons, (1) Pieter Franchoys and (2) Lucas Franchoys II, as well as Nicolas Smeyers (*d* 1645), Antoon Imbrechts and Eloi Bonnejonne (*d* 1695), who married one of his daughters.

(1) Pieter [Peeter] **Franchoys** (*b* Mechelen, 20 Oct 1606; *d* Mechelen, 11 Aug 1654). Painter. After studying in Antwerp (where, according to de Bie, he was trained by Gerard Seghers) and visiting Paris, he returned to Mechelen in 1635 and established himself as a painter of portraits and religious subjects. Only a few portraits have survived, for example *Man Holding a Wine-glass* (1639; Brussels, Mus. A. Anc.). Stylistically they are related to his brother's portraits: like Lucas II, Pieter represented his sitters with a sense of calculated informality. In this respect he was influenced by Anthony van Dyck. He enjoyed a considerable reputation, as is evidenced by the interest taken in his work by Archduke Leopold William.

(2) Lucas Franchoys II (*b* Mechelen, 28 June 1616; *d* Mechelen, 3 April 1681). Painter and etcher, brother of (1) Pieter Franchoys. Like his brother, Lucas probably underwent further training in Antwerp after initial studies with his father. De Bie said that Rubens was his master for many years, though there is no other evidence for this. He is first mentioned as a painter in 1649 in connection with commissions for churches in Tournai, where he lived for some years. Works executed in this period include the *Adoration of the Shepherds* (1650; Tournai Cathedral). Cornelius de Bie mentioned a six-year stay in France, perhaps a confusion arising from Tournai's proximity to the French border. He returned to Mechelen by 1654 and painted altarpieces and other religious compositions for many of the churches, monasteries and convents there (e.g. the *St Roch* altarpiece, *c.* 1671; Mechelen, St Janskerk). One of his patrons was Archbishop Alphonse de Bergues, whose portrait he painted.

Franchoys's many monumental altarpieces make him one of the most important painters of the Counter-Reformation, both in Tournai and in Mechelen. These works are linked stylistically to the later works of Anthony van Dyck, after which he made several etchings. In general Franchoys worked within the trend of late 17th-century Flemish painting, with its emphasis on a more emotional interpretation of religious iconography, for which van Dyck's work provided a better starting-point than that of Peter Paul Rubens. There is a definite stylistic evolution between his early paintings done in Tournai, with their cramped composition and robust figures, and his later works painted in Mechelen, with the figures more effectively disposed and their poses more expressive. Franchoys's later work shows strong similarities with the painting of Pieter Thys, who was also influenced by van Dyck. Thys and Franchoys undoubtedly exchanged ideas on artistic matters. In his portraits, Franchoys adopted van Dyck's calculated informality. His self-portrait, known from an engraving by Coenrad Waumans (*b* 1619), is extremely close in style to the engraved artist portraits in van Dyck's *The Iconography* (*c.* 1632–44).

BIBLIOGRAPHY

Thieme–Becker
C. de Bie: *Het gulden cabinet* (1661), pp. 152–4, 374–6
J. S. Held: 'Sketches by Lucas Franchoys the Younger', *A.Q.*, xiv (1951), pp. 45–55
Le Siècle de Rubens (exh. cat., Brussels, Mus. Royaux A. & Hist., 1965), p. 83 [Pieter]
F. de Saligny: 'Lucas Franchoys', *Mus. Royaux B.-A. Belgique: Bull.*, xvi (1967), pp. 209–32
M. L. Hairs: *Dans le sillage de Rubens: Les Peintres d'histoire anversois au XVIIe siècle* (Liège, 1977), pp. 184–8
H. Colsoul: 'Lucas Franchoys de jonge (1616-1681)', *Hand. Kon. Kring Oudhdknd., Lett. & Kst Mechelen/Bull. Cerc. Archéol., Litt. & A. Malines*, xcii (1988), pp. 117–283; xciii (1989), pp. 197–257

HANS VLIEGHE

Francia [Raibolini]. Italian family of painters and goldsmiths. They worked mainly in and near Bologna. (1) Francesco Francia was the son of a carpenter. He had two sons, (2) Giacomo Francia and Giulio Francia (*b* Bologna, 20 Aug 1487; *d* Bologna, 22 Jan 1545).

(1) Francesco Francia [Raibolini] [il Francia] (*b* Bologna, *c.* 1450; *d* Bologna, 1517). He turned to painting *c.* 1485, and his first works already testify to the considerable technical accomplishment and gentle religious sensibility that remained constants of his art. His major surviving paintings are altarpieces, mostly images of the Virgin and saints, initially done for Bologna and later for nearby centres, notably Parma, Modena, Ferrara and Lucca. He also painted many small-scale devotional works and a few portraits. The apochryphal anecdote reported by Vasari that Francia died on seeing Raphael's altarpiece of *St Cecilia* (Bologna, Pin. N.) is emblematic of the change in taste that suddenly made his art—like that of Perugino—look old-fashioned.

1. Before 1500. 2. 1500–06. 3. After 1506.

1. BEFORE 1500. Francia trained as a jeweller and goldsmith. Unlike other 15th-century artists who trained as goldsmiths, such as Ghiberti and Verrocchio, he did not use this craft apprenticeship simply as a step towards artistic work of higher status. He signed his pictures *Aurifex* (goldsmith) to the last and frequently served as an officer of the goldsmiths' guild. He was also in charge of the Bolognese mint under the Bentivoglio and later under Pope Julius II. A number of coins designed by him survive, as do niello paxes of the *Crucifixion* (*c.* 1488–90) and the *Resurrection* (*c.* 1500; both Bologna, Pin. N.), which are adorned with the coats of arms of prominent families and appear to commemorate marriages. The *Crucifixion* was probably a wedding present from Giovanni II Bentivoglio to his bride, Ginevra Sforza; the *Resurrection* must date from *c.* 1481, the year Bartolomeo Felicini married Dorotea Ringhieri. A third silver pax (untraced) was executed at immense expense for Giovanni Sforza and his wife, Lucrezia Borgia.

In his generally well-informed account of Francia's life, Vasari stated that his first painting was the altarpiece of the *Virgin and Child* (main panel and *Pietà*, Bologna, Pin. N.; *Nativity*, Glasgow A.G. & Mus.; *Baptism*, Lisbon, Fund. Gulbenkian; *St Francis*, London, Colnaghi's) painted in 1490 for the chapel of Bartolomeo Felicini in S Maria della Misericordia, near Bologna. However, stylistic evidence suggests this is not the case, and the work is now dated 1494. (The picture was retouched and the figures of SS Proculus and Monica added, possibly by (2) Giacomo Francia.) A sharper, more chiselled style is evident in three small-scale paintings, which may be earlier. All appear to have belonged to the Bolognese humanist Bartolomeo Bianchini (*b c.* 1480; *d* before 1528). The first, the *Crucifixion with SS John the Evangelist and Jerome* (Bologna, Pal. Com.), shows a high degree of influence from the work of Ercole de' Roberti and perhaps that of Francesco del Cossa but is already highly personal in style. Since Francia's paintings were praised by Angelo Michele Salimbeni (*Epitalamii pro nupitali . . .*, Bologna, Bib. U., MS. no. 1491) as early as 1487, a date of *c.* 1485 is plausible.

The portrait of *Bartolomeo Bianchini* (see fig. 1) and the *Holy Family* (Berlin, Gemäldegal. Alte Meister) inscribed with Bianchini's name, which may have formed a diptych, cannot be significantly later in date. They reveal the same precision of modelling in the figures and a surface almost like enamel; as with Francia's use of oil paint, which is noted by Vasari, this suggests awareness of Northern painting.

Francia painted another altarpiece, the *Virgin Enthroned with Child, Saints and Two Angels*, c. 1494 for the chapel of Giovanni II Bentivoglio in S Giacomo Maggiore, Bologna (*in situ*). Close in style to the works of Lorenzo Costa (i), who executed frescoes for the chapel, it shows Francia's taste for sweet characterization and balanced composition within a classicizing—but not authentically classical—setting, into which the figures are tightly crowded. The altarpiece of the *Virgin and Child with SS Paul, Francis and the Infant John the Baptist* (Bologna, Pin. N.), which was commissioned by Giovanni Battista Scappi for S Maria della Misericordia, Bologna, must date from soon after 1494; Francia also painted a portrait of *Evangelista Scappi* (Florence, Uffizi). Another Bentivoglio commission of about this date was the *Adoration of the Child* (1498–9; Bologna, Pin. N.) for the high altar of the Misericordia, which originally had Costa's *Adoration of the Magi* (Milan, Brera) as its predella. It depicts the Virgin kneeling and flanked by St Augustine and the patron, Anton Galeazzo Bentivoglio (1472–1525). The standing

shepherd sporting a laurel wreath is probably Anton Galeazzo's brother, Alessandro, a poet. A later, simplified version of the composition (Forlì, Pin. Civ.) was painted for Francia's friend Paolo Zambeccari, for whom he also executed frescoes in his palace in Bologna and a *Virgin and Child with St Francis*, dated 1503 (all untraced). The *Virgin and Child with Saints* (Bologna, Pin. N.) for the Manzuoli chapel in the Misericordia, which shows a more open prospect than its precursors, probably also dates from the last years of the 15th century.

One of Francia's most important commissions for the Bentivoglio, his frescoes for the family palace in Bologna, were destroyed (1507) at the time of their fall. Vasari, who cannot have seen the frescoes, describes a fictive bronze *Disputation of Philosophers* and a *Judith and Holofernes*. A drawing on vellum of *Judith* (best version, New York, Pierpont Morgan Lib.), clearly inspired by Andrea Mantegna's treatments of the theme, may be related, but it does not seem to be for a many-figured composition such as Vasari described. Rather, like a number of mythological and allegorical sheets by Francia (New York, Pierpont Morgan Lib.; Oxford, Ashmolean; Vienna, Albertina) and Mantegna's drawing of *Judith* (1491; Florence, Uffizi), it was probably intended as a work of art in its own right. A fresco fragment (Bologna, Pin. N.) from the site of the Bentivoglio palace supports a date c. 1495–1500 for the decoration.

2. 1500–06. Francia's style around 1500 is displayed in the *Virgin and Child with SS Lawrence and Francis* (1500; St Petersburg, Hermitage), with its charming angel musicians. It was painted for the Calcina family as the high altarpiece of S Lorenzo, Bologna. Perugino's *Virgin and Child with Saints* (Bologna, Pin. N.) must have arrived in S Giovanni in Monte around this time, although Francia probably already knew of Perugino's art, since their styles are especially close in this period. Also signed and dated 1500 is the high altarpiece (Bologna, Pin. N.) for Santissima Annunziata. It portrays an unusually static Virgin Annunciate receiving the swooping Angel Gabriel's salutation, while above, in a mandorla, is the figure of the Christ Child holding a cross. The Virgin is flanked by SS Francis and Bernardino and SS John the Evangelist and George. The scale of the figures is more monumental than before, and there is a new expansiveness. A variant of the central motif occurs in another altarpiece, the *Virgin with SS Jerome and John the Baptist* (Bologna, Pin. N.), originally in S Girolomo de Miramonte, Bologna. The *St Roch* (see fig. 2), for the Compagnia dei Morti, Bologna, is more animated, but the expressive language is still confined to the hand raised in supplication and the eyes rolled heavenwards. A votive fresco in the Palazzo Comunale, Bologna, dated 1505, the *Madonna del Terremoto*, shows the Virgin hovering over a topographically accurate view of the city.

Before their fall, the Bentivoglio helped to fund frescoes for the oratory of S Cecilia, next to their parish church, S Giacomo Maggiore. The most prominent local artists of the period were involved, notably Lorenzo Costa (i) and Amico Aspertini, and each appears to have contributed two frescoes: Francia painted the *Marriage* and the *Burial* of St Cecilia c. 1504–6. The figure of St Cecilia in the

1. Francesco Francia: *Bartolomeo Bianchini*, oil on panel, 565×405 mm, c. 1485 (London, National Gallery)

2. Francesco Francia: *St Roch*, tempera on panel, 2.17×1.50 m, 1502 (New York, Metropolitan Museum of Art)

Burial is based on the figure of Christ in Mantegna's engraving of the *Entombment*, but Francia's approach to narrative is otherwise understated and undramatic. This is equally apparent in such works as the altarpiece of the *Baptism of Christ* (1509) and the predella panel of the *Adoration of the Magi* (after 1500; both Dresden, Gemäldegal. Alte Meister). At this time Francia continued to work predominantly for Bolognese patrons, but his fame had spread, and he was in demand elsewhere for both secular and ecclesiastical commissions. Isabella d'Este was unsuccessful in persuading him to produce a painting for her *studiolo* in the Palazzo Ducale at Mantua. One of his paintings of *Lucretia* (three versions, Dresden, Gemäldegal. Alte Meister; Dublin, N.G.; York, C.A.G.) may be that recorded by Vasari as commissioned for Francesco Maria I della Rovere, Duke of Urbino. For the same patron he also executed a pair of saddles (untraced) representing a *Forest Fire*, which, as described by Vasari, seem uncannily similar to Piero di Cosimo's *Forest Fire* (Oxford, Ashmolean). Francia's *Annunciation* (Milan, Brera) is documented as in progress in the will of Antonio de Grado of 23 August 1505. Commissions for such private devotional works were increasingly important in the final decade of Francia's career.

3. AFTER 1506. With the overthrow of the Bentivoglio in 1506, Francia was obliged to seek work outside Bologna. Vasari noted three altarpieces he painted soon afterwards for Modena. The *Virgin and Child with Saints* (ex-Berlin,

Kaiser-Friedrich Mus., destr.), however, was signed and dated 1504, and the *Annunciation with St Albert* (Chantilly, Mus. Condé) is not dated; so only the *Baptism* (1509; Dresden, Gemäldegal. Alte Meister) is definitely dated after the fall of the Bentivoglio. (A fourth Modenese commission is the *Madonna of the Rose-hedge*; Munich, Alte Pin.) The *Annunciation* has a Carmelite connection, as do the *Baptism* (London, Hampton Court, Royal Col.) and the *Entombment with St Hilarion* (Turin, Sabauda).

Francia's other important monastic patrons were the Benedictines of the Congregation of S Giustina, Parma. According to Vasari, his first commission for them was the *Lamentation* (Parma, G.N.) for S Giovanni Evangelista, Parma, allegedly once dated 1510, followed by a *Virgin with Saints* (untraced) for their house in Reggio Emilia and finally by the *Circumcision* (Cesena, Madonna del Monte). The Reggio Emilia altarpiece may be the *Virgin and Child with the Infant John the Baptist and Benedictine Saints* (1515; Parma, G.N.) which must have been painted for a Benedictine church. It is often suggested that (2) Giacomo Francia and Giulio Francia collaborated on this altarpiece and other late works. These include the *All Saints* (Ferrara Cathedral) and two altarpieces for Lucca, an *Immaculate Conception* based on one by Vincenzo Frediani (1502–3; Lucca, Villa Giunigi) and the *Virgin and Child with St Anne and Saints* (London, N.G.). In addition to these commissions Francia continued to be in demand in his native Bologna. This is evidenced by such works as the portrait of Isabella d'Este's son, *Federico Gonzaga* (1510; New York, Met.), painted in Bologna while the boy was *en route* to Rome as a papal hostage. If the portrait of *Bishop Altobello Averoldi* (Washington, DC, N.G.A.) dates from 1513, when the sitter served his second term as governor and vice legate of Bologna, it reveals Francia's sustained high reputation. After Francia's death his sons continued the family business but do not appear to have felt bound to complete paintings he left unfinished. The fascinating hybrid, the *Presentation of the Virgin* (Rome, Pal. Barberini), bears an inscription stating that what Francia left unfinished was completed by Bartolomeo Passarotti.

BIBLIOGRAPHY

G. Vasari: *Vite* (1550, rev. 2/1568); ed. G. Milanesi (1878–85), iii, pp. 533–64

C. G. Malvasia: *Felsina pittrice* (1678); ed. G. Zanotti (1841)

J. A. Calvi: *Memorie della vita e delle opere di Francesco Raibolini detto il Francia* (Bologna, 1812)

G. C. Williamson: *Francesco Raibolini, Called Francia* (London, 1901)

M. Carmichael: *Francia's Masterpiece* (London, 1909)

G. Lipparini: *Francesco Francia* (Bergamo, 1913)

B. Berenson: *Central and North Italian Schools* (1968)

R. Rossi Manaresi and J. Bentini: 'The Felicini Altarpiece by Francesco Francia: Contribution of Technical Analyses to the Solution of a Chronological Problem', *Atti del XXIV Congresso Internazionale di Storia dell'Arte: Bologna, 1979*, pp. 395–409

J. Cartwright: *Mantegna and Francia* (London, 1981), pp. 63–114

Leonardo: Il Codice Hammer e la Mappa di Imola presentati da Carlo Pedretti—Arte e scienza a Bologna in Emilia e Romagna nel primo cinquecento (exh. cat., Bologna, Pal. Podestà, 1985)

C. Dempsey: 'Malvasia and the Problem of the Early Raphael and Bologna', *Stud. Hist. A.*, xvii (1986), pp. 57–70

S. Stagni: 'Francesco Francia', *Pittura bolognese del cinquecento*, ed. V. Fortunati Pietrantonio, i (Bologna, 1986), pp. 1–28

Bologna e l'umanesimo, 1490–1510 (exh. cat., ed. M. Faietti and K. Oberhuber; Bologna, Pin. N., 1988)

Colnaghi Master Paintings, 1400–1850 (exh. cat., London, Colnaghi's, 1991), pp. 24–7, no. 5

DAVID EKSERDJIAN

(2) Giacomo Francia [Raibolini] (*b* Bologna, *c.* 1486; *d* Bologna, 3 Jan 1557). Son of (1) Francesco Francia. He was trained by his father in painting and goldsmithing. In 1517, the year of his father's death, he and his brother, Giulio, assumed responsibility for the family business and together executed many altarpieces, identifiable by the initials (I I) of their latinized names (Iacobus and Iulius). Giacomo's earliest known work is the *Virgin in Glory with SS Peter, Mary Magdalene, Francis, Martha and Six Nuns* (after 1515; Bologna, Pin. N.). In this painting, as in the *SS Jerome, Margaret and Francis* (1518; Madrid, Prado) and the *Nativity* (1519; Parma, S Giovanni Evangelista), both dated and signed by both brothers, there appear, in addition to the influence of their father, echoes of the monumental style of Raphael.

In the early 1520s Giacomo painted, again in collaboration with Giulio, the *Deposition* (Bologna, Pin. N.), the *Crucifixion* (Bologna, S Stefano) and *God the Father with Angels* (Bologna, S Petronio). During this period Giacomo probably went to Florence and perhaps to Rome. He was also influenced by contemporary Ferrarese painting, especially in the imaginary landscape backgrounds to several of his works from this period, such as the *Virgin and Child with SS Paul, Mary Magdalene and the Infant John the Baptist* (Bologna, Pin. N.) and *St Michael with SS Dominic and Francis* (Bologna, S Domenico). The Ferrarese influence is also evident in works from the same period executed with his brother. The fresco depicting the *Nativity* (Bologna, SS Vitale e Agricola) also dates from this period. With these works of the 1520s Giacomo reached his full artistic maturity.

Another altarpiece signed by both brothers, depicting *St Frediano with SS James, Lucy, Ursula and a Blessed Person* (*c.* 1530; Bologna, Pin. N.), repeats the compositional structure of Raphael's *St Cecilia in Ecstasy* (Bologna, Pin. N.) and conveys a certain severity in the powerful monumentality of the figures. The same grandiose modelling characterizes a slightly later work, by Giacomo alone, the *Virgin and Child with the Infant St John the Baptist, SS Francis, Dominic, Mary Magdalene and Agnes* (Berlin, Gemäldegal.), but here the greater elegance of the elongated figures with their balanced, graceful movements was inspired by the refined style of Parmigianino, who was in Bologna from 1527 to 1530. It is significant that at this point Giacomo abandoned the Ferrarese landscapes typical of his works of the early 1520s.

A banner depicting the *Virgin and Child with SS Sebastian, Joseph and the Infant St John the Baptist* (1535; Fuipiano, near Bergamo, parish church) concludes the experimental phase when Giacomo was open to the influence of the dominant artistic trends. Thereafter he limited himself to the reworking of old-fashioned and well-used designs and forms, probably as a consequence of the spread of the difficult Mannerist style. He produced compositionally repetitive works (e.g. *Virgin and Child with SS Gervasio, Protasio, Catherine, Justine and Four Nuns*, 1544; Milan, S Maria di Piazza) based on the centralized Raphaelesque type, combined with an archaizing return to the style of his father. A document of 8

Giacomo Francia: *Virgin and Child with the Infant St John the Baptist*, oil on panel, diam. 880 mm, 1540s (Baltimore, MD, Walters Art Gallery)

October 1545 records Giacomo as a member of the council of the Compagnia delle Quattro Arti.

Among Giacomo's late works are the *Nativity* (1551; Bologna, S Cristina). In addition to large altarpieces, Giacomo also executed numerous smaller panels for private female convents. Compositionally, these are conventional works that reflect the religious requirements of the patrons. Two of the best examples are the tondo depicting the *Virgin and Child with the Infant St John the Baptist* (Baltimore, MD, Walters A.G.; see fig.) and the *Virgin and Child with SS Lawrence and Gregory* (Philadelphia, PA, Mus. A.). Though a prolific artist, many of his works have been destroyed or lost and are known only from documentary sources.

BIBLIOGRAPHY

Thieme–Becker
G. Vasari: *Vite* (1550; rev. 2/1568); ed. G. Milanesi (1878–85)
C. C. Malvasia: *Felsina pittrice* (1678); ed. G. Zanotti (1841)
——: *Le pitture di Bologna* (Bologna, 1686); ed. A. Emiliani (Bologna, 1969)
A. Venturi: *Storia* (1901–40), VII/iii, pp. 952–73
E. Jacobsen: 'I seguaci del Francia e del Costa in Bologna', *L'Arte*, viii (1905), pp. 81–93
A. Emiliani: *La Pinacoteca Nazionale di Bologna* (Bologna, 1967)
N. Roio: 'Giacomo e Giulio Raibolini detti i Francia', *Pittura bolognese del cinquecento*, ed. V. Fortunati Pietrantonio, i (Bologna, 1986), pp. 29–57

NICOSETTA ROIO

Francia, (François-)Louis(-Thomas) (*b* Calais, 21 Dec 1772; *d* Calais, 6 Feb 1839). French painter and engraver. The son of the director of the Military Hospital in Calais, Francia was intended for the legal profession; his talent as an artist was recognized early, and he was permitted to attend the local drawing school where, at the age of 16, he was awarded all of the prizes. He retained a passionate loyalty to Calais and to its art school, vigorously protesting in 1835 against plans to exclude pupils under ten years of age from the drawing class; such crusades were characteristic of this energetic man.

Because of the political upheavals of 1790, Francia chose to go to London rather than to Paris. There he found employment as a drawing-master in a Hampstead school. Although he spoke no English, he was befriended by Joseph Charles Barrow (*fl* 1789–1802) who, when he opened his own drawing school in 1792, appointed Francia as an assistant. Francia soon became a member of the group of young artists including Turner and Thomas Girtin who worked in the evenings at Dr Thomas Monro's Academy. He was a founder-member of the sketching society named the Brothers. Its origins, membership and purpose ('establishing by practice a school of Historical Landscape, the subjects being original designs from poetick passages') are recorded in Francia's hand and signed by him in the minutes of the first meeting, 20 May 1799, on the reverse of a watercolour *Landscape Composition—Moonlight* (London, V&A). He exhibited with the Associated Artists in Water-Colours, a rival organization to the Old Water-Colour Society, from its foundation in 1808.

While his earliest work was either topographical illustration or picturesque scenery in the manner of Girtin (whose dot-and-dash technique is much in evidence in *Cottages in a Valley*, 1805; London, V&A), Francia quickly developed a facility in the dramatic rendering of light effects by broad washes, placing the best of his work on a par with that of Cotman. Francia's original and liberal approach to current aesthetic theory can be gauged from the interesting series of aquatints that he published in 1810 in 'imitation' of his own and other artists' landscape sketches, entitled *Studies of Landscape by T. Gainsborough, J. Hoppner RA, T. Girtin, Wm. Owen RA, A. Callcott, A. S. Owen, J. Varley, J. S. Hayward and L. Francia, Imitated from the Originals by L. Francia* (1810).

In 1817 Francia returned to Calais; he had already established himself as a marine painter exhibiting regularly at the Royal Academy. He concentrated on this genre (almost exclusively in watercolour) for the latter part of his life. Francia was employed briefly as secretary to the British Consul in Calais. His home became a port of call for visiting British artists; he found a patron in the expatriate Beau Brummell (1778–1840) and gathered around him a group of artists, including Eugène Isabey, Jules Collignon (*d* 1850), Louis Tesson (*fl* 1841–67) and his own son, Alexandre Francia (1813–84), also an accomplished professional landscape and marine artist. His most celebrated protégé, Richard Parkes Bonington, was in Calais for only a brief period but remained a close friend. Francia was undoubtedly instrumental in passing to a whole generation of French watercolourists a fluency in watercolour and, at his best, a crispness and confidence in composition. The tension between sharply defined hulls and riggings and the liquid squiggles that suggest the lazy recessive lines of rutted cart tracks in the *Banks of a Canal* (London, V&A), and the combination of transparent washes and brilliant dashes of gouache, are typical of Francia's most influential work. By 1830, however, his style of representing the coastline between Calais and Le Havre and his records of spectacular shipwrecks must have seemed outdated. In his last years he lacked patronage and, while retaining his acerbic humour, he died a disappointed and harassed man.

BIBLIOGRAPHY
E. Le Beau: *Notice sur Louis Francia* [*c.* 1839–40] [mem. by a contemp.]
Louis Francia 1772–1839 and his Son Alexandre (exh. cat. by A. Reed and S. Smith, London, Anthony Reed Gal., 1985)
M. Pointon: *The Bonington Circle: English Watercolour and Anglo-French Landscape, 1790–1855* (Brighton, 1985)
——: *Bonington, Francia and Wyld* (London, 1985)
Louis Francia (exh. cat., Calais, Mus. B.-A., 1989)

MARCIA POINTON

Franciabigio [Francesco di Cristofano Giudicis] (*b* Florence, 30 Jan 1484; *d* Florence, 14 Jan 1525). Italian painter. The son of a Milanese linen-weaver, he had completed his apprenticeship, in Florence, by 18 October 1504. His earliest documented works, for example a *Pietà* (1506) for S Pancrazio, Florence, have not survived. According to Vasari, Franciabigio trained with Mariotto Albertinelli, in whose last work, the signed and dated *Crucifixion* (1506; Florence, Certosa del Galluzzo, Pin.), he painted the angels (Shearman). In December 1508 the names of Franciabigio and Andrea del Sarto, who sometime between autumn 1506 and 1509 set up a joint workshop, were entered in the registration book of the Arte de' Medici e Speziali, to which painters were required to belong. The *Portrait of a Young Man* (Paris, Louvre) dates from this period. The work, which was later enlarged, shows the subject half-length, leaning pensively against a balustrade, with strong areas of shadow around the eyes. This is the first in a series of male portraits typical of Franciabigio: the subjects, each of whom wears a hat, are mostly placed in front of a landscape, with their gaze fixed meditatively or piercingly on the onlooker. The religious works from this period, such as the *Virgin and Child* (1509; Rome, Pal. Barberini), also show a movement away from the style of Albertinelli and Raffaellino del Garbo and begin to reveal instead the influence of Leonardo, Michelangelo and, especially, Raphael. Yet Franciabigio's connection with Andrea del Sarto was the determining factor in his career. When in 1509 it was del Sarto who received the commission to complete the fresco cycle in the atrium of SS Annunziata, Florence, their relationship altered significantly. They had been regarded as equals, but thereafter del Sarto developed into the more successful and also the more innovative painter, and Franciabigio, who had begun to absorb elements from del Sarto's style, remained in his shadow.

Around 1511 del Sarto and Franciabigio's joint workshop moved to the vicinity of SS Annunziata, and many young artists were associated with it. Franciabigio nonetheless trained two of his brothers, among others, in a separate workshop. In 1513 he finally received a commission for a fresco in the atrium of SS Annunziata, the *Marriage of the Virgin*. In this work he had to compete directly with del Sarto's creations. Vasari described how the affair took a disastrous course when Franciabigio damaged sections of his finished fresco, including the Virgin's face. The monumental conception of the work was new in Florentine art. The temple vestibule in the background, a classical triumphal arch, takes up half the surface of the painting, but Franciabigio failed to relate it satisfactorily to the figure groups in the foreground. The overall appearance of the work has led to the assumption that Franciabigio was in Rome shortly before (*c.* 1511–12).

The *Portrait of a Young Man* (*c.* 1513; Detroit, MI, Inst. A.), signed with initials, reinforces this supposition. The subject looks back over his shoulder at the onlooker, a pose that by 1513 was already very popular. Perfected by Giorgione in Venice, it had been brought to Raphael in Rome via Sebastiano del Piombo. The signed and dated *Portrait of a Young Man* (1514; Florence, Uffizi) and the *Portrait of a Knight of St John* (London, N.G.) are very similar in terms of composition. The subject of the latter may be Giulio de' Medici, later Pope Clement VII, and the work can be connected with a commission from the Maltese sisters of S Giovanni della Calza, Florence, whose abbess was also a Medici. For the refectory of this convent, Franciabigio painted a *Last Supper* (1514), whose illusionistic windows depicting views of the convent's surroundings are an interesting feature. In the signed and dated panel depicting the *Virgin Enthroned with St John the Baptist and Job* (1516; Florence, Uffizi), the figure of St John, according to Vasari, is a self-portrait by Franciabigio. This panel is very close to del Sarto's style.

From 1515 Franciabigio executed several pictures of the Virgin that echo his own early work, for example the *Madonna del Pozzo* (*c.* 1517–18; Florence, Accad. B.A. & Liceo A.). In 1518–19, with del Sarto away in France, Franciabigio executed two grisailles for the Florentine Chiostro dello Scalzo. He may, however, have followed pre-existent designs for these. He carried out several commissions for the Medici after their return to Florence from exile in 1513. The last of these was for decorations to celebrate the marriage in 1518 of Lorenzo de' Medici, Duke of Urbino. When Pope Leo X arranged for the magnificent interior decoration of Poggio a Caiano, the villa his father Lorenzo the Magnificent had bought in 1479, Franciabigio was employed to decorate the ceiling in the *salone* in collaboration with the stuccoist Andrea Feltrini. Franciabigio followed this with a fresco of the *Triumph of Cicero* (*c.* 1520–21), one of his major works, a theme related to Medici rule and one well suited to exploit his inclinations towards drama and rhetoric.

Franciabigio had probably made a second visit to Rome *c.* 1519 in connection with this commission. At any rate, the portrait of *Jacopo Cennini* (London, Hampton Court, Royal Col.; see fig.), signed with a monogram, is contemporary with the frescoes at Poggio a Caiano and shows the influence of Roman portraiture of the period. The sitter was identified by Vasari as a steward of the Medici, and the picture itself offers several pointers to this, notably the coat of arms, the keys and the laurel. The broken laurel stem probably alludes to the deaths of Giuliano de' Medici, Duc de Nemours (1516), and Lorenzo, Duke of Urbino (1519), which suggests a date of composition after May 1519. The steward, shown in a neglected state with an open collar, pauses at the beginning of a new line and looks out of the picture with a worried expression.

The *Story of Bathsheba* (1523; Dresden, Gemäldegal. Alte Meister) is Franciabigio's best-known late work. The main point of interest resides in the unusual bathing scene. The bath is shown as a baptismal font, which fits with the pose of the serving girl to the right of Bathsheba. The daring pose of the figure on the left at the edge of the fountain recalls Michelangelo's *Ignudi* and the prophet Jonah from the Sistine Chapel ceiling. Franciabigio's last

Franciabigio: *Jacopo Cennini*, oil on panel, 650×489 mm, *c.* 1520 (London, Hampton Court, Royal Collection)

work, according to Vasari, was a *Noli me tangere* (before 1525; Florence, Mus. Horne) frescoed for the house of a friend who was a linen-weaver. After this, Vasari stated, he died of an illness brought on by plague fever.

Thieme–Becker

BIBLIOGRAPHY

G. Vasari: *Vite* (1550, rev. 2/1568); ed. G. Milanesi (1878–85), v, pp. 189–200
S. J. Freedberg: *Andrea del Sarto*, 2 vols (Cambridge, MA, 1963)
J. Shearman: *Andrea del Sarto*, 2 vols (Oxford, 1965)
B. Berenson: *Central and North Italian Schools* (1968)
M. Winner: 'Cosimo il Vecchio als Cicero: Humanistisches in Franciabigios Fresko zu Poggio a Caiano', *Z. Kstgesch.*, xxxiii/4 (1970), pp. 261–97
S. Regan McKillop: *Franciabigio* (Berkeley, Los Angeles and London, 1974)
L. Pagnotta: 'Franciabigio', *La pittura in Italia: Il cinquecento*, ed. F. Zeri, ii (Milan, 1987) [lists pubns since 1974]
S. Padovani: 'Andrea dell Sarto: Ipotesi per gli inizi', *A. Crist.*, lxxii (1988), pp. 197–216

ANDREW JOHN MARTIN

Francin, Claude(-Clair) (*b* Strasbourg, Bas-Rhin, 5 June 1702; *d* Bourg-la-Reine, Hauts-de-Seine, 18 March 1773). French sculptor. He was the son of the sculptor François-Alexis Francin (*b* before 1670, *d* before 1726) and nephew on his mother's side of Nicolas Coustou and Guillaume Coustou (i); he was also the latter's pupil. He married the daughter of Pierre Le Pautre (ii). After spending six years at the Académie de France in Rome, he lived from 1737 to 1747 in Paris, where he was much in demand for work in such churches as St André-des-Arts, the Oratory of St Honoré and particularly St Roch, which still has his two stone *Angel-musicians*, situated under the organ loft and executed in a light and charming style. For Louis XV he sculpted a nude *Ganymede* (Baltimore, MD, Walters A.G.), a marble work of extreme delicacy that remained unfinished. He often exhibited his work at the Salon.

In 1748 the sculptor Jacques Verberckt, whom Anges-Jacques Gabriel had put in charge of the sculptural decoration related to the urban renovation of Bordeaux, recommended Francin to carry on this work, and the artist settled in Bordeaux until 1765. In particular, he was responsible for the sculptural decoration of three stone pediments of the Bourse, representing the *Greatness of Princes, Neptune Protecting Commerce* and the *Meeting of the Garonne and the Dordogne*—works full of vivacity and agility. He also produced a stone relief, *Time Revealing Truth*, surrounding the clock on the staircase; the *Chariot of the Sun* (stone), located over the entrance to the Bordeaux Academy (now in Rue Judaïque); a stone figure of *Liberality* on the central pavilion of the Place Royale; and the decoration for the Porte Digeaux, Porte d'Aquitaine, Porte Royale and Porte Tourny. Finally, he was responsible for the marble pedestal of the bronze equestrian statue of *Louis XV* (destr.) by Jean-Baptiste Lemoyne (ii), with its trophies representing the *Four Continents* and its two minutely detailed marble bas-reliefs of the *Battle of Fontenoy* and the *Capture of Port-Mahon* (both now Bordeaux, Mus. Aquitaine), in which he succeeded in combining historical accuracy with correct composition.

On his return to Paris, Francin was received (*reçu*) by the Académie Royale de Peinture et de Sculpture in 1767, on presentation of a rather cloying marble statuette of *Christ at the Column* (Paris, Louvre). His work is in general distinguished by its vivacity, elegance and gentleness. Claude Francin's son Guillaume Francin (1741–1830) was a sculptor specializing in busts: his work included retrospective portraits, such as that of *Jean Goujon* (1796; Paris, Louvre), and portraits of his contemporaries, such as *Jean Le Rond d'Alembert* and *Christoph Willibald Gluck* (both before 1799; Paris, Louvre).

Jal; Lami
BIBLIOGRAPHY
C. Marionneau: 'Documents inédits sur les travaux des sculpteurs Verberckt et Francin pour la Place Royale de Bordeaux de 1733 à 1757', *Réun. Soc. B.-A. Dépt.* (1883), pp. 184–93
——: 'Les Travaux à Bordeaux du statuaire Francin, 1748–1765', *Réun. Soc. B.-A. Dépt.* (1890), pp. 546–62
F. Thomas: 'Le Séjour à Bordeaux de Claude Francin', *Rev. Philom. Bordeaux & Sud-Ouest* (May/June 1915), pp. 16ff, 95ff
P. Courteault: *Archives historiques du département de la Gironde* (Paris and Bordeaux, 1918), pp. 100–13
——: 'La Place Royale de Bordeaux', *Archvs A. Fr.*, xii (1922), pp. 1–451
M. Furcy-Raynaud: 'Les Sculptures exécutées au XVIIIe siècle pour la direction des Bâtiments du roi', *Archvs A. Fr.*, xiv (1927), pp. 148–51
X. Védère: *Le Palais de la Bourse à Bordeaux* (Bordeaux, 1955), pp. 72–8, 81; pl. 27–31
H. Haug: 'Une Oeuvre retrouvée', *Cah. Alsac. Archéol., A. & Hist.*, v (1961), p. 156
F. C. Pariset: 'L'Eglise de Cantenac', *Rev. Hist. Bordeaux & Dépt Gironde*, xii (1963), pp. 208–10
FRANÇOISE DE LA MOUREYRE

Francione [Francesco di Giovanni] (*b* 1428; *d* Florence, 25 July 1495). Italian carpenter and architect. Most of his work was in Florence or on Florentine territory, although he may have worked on the tomb of *Pope Calixtus III* (*reg* 1455–8) at St Peter's, Rome. He was responsible for intarsia decorations for interiors such as Pisa Cathedral (1461–74), where he also worked on the coffered ceilings (destr. 1595) and the audience chamber in the Palazzo Vecchio, Florence (1475–80).

Francione also made architectural models (all untraced). Vasari mentioned one for the villa at Poggio a Caiano, which was ultimately built (*c.* 1483) to a design by Francione's pupil Giuliano da Sangallo. Francione also made a model of SS Flora and Lucilla (1470), Arezzo, with Giuliano da Maiano and one for the competition for the façade of Florence Cathedral (1491). His model (1493) for the vaulting in the vestibule of S Spirito, Florence, was done to the design of Giuliano da Sangallo and Cronaca. As a military architect, Francione contributed to the development of the bastion. He served at the sack of Volterra (1472) and was subsequently responsible for rebuilding sections of the fortress, where his large, low, round bastions show an early architectural response to cannon. He was later active as military architect at Pietrasanta (1484–5), Sarzana (1487) and Sarzanello (1492–5), where he mixed round and polygonal bastions.

Francione's workshop on the Via de' Servi, Florence, was a training ground for some of the most important architects, engineers and woodworkers of the time. Among his pupils and collaborators were Giuliano and Antonio da Sangallo (i), Baccio Pontelli, Baccio d'Agnolo, La Cecca (1447–*c.* 1488) and Giuliano and Benedetto da Maiano.

BIBLIOGRAPHY
Thieme–Becker
G. Marchini: *Giuliano da Sangallo*, 2 vols (Florence, 1942)
P. Voit: 'Una bottega in Via dei Servi', *Acta Hist. A. Acad. Sci. Hung.*, vii (1961), pp. 197–228
J. R. Hale: 'The Early Development of the Bastion: An Italian Chronology *c.* 1450–*c.* 1534', *Europe in the Late Middle Ages*, ed. J. R. Hale, J. R. L. Highfield and B. Smalley (London, 1965), pp. 466–94
NICHOLAS ADAMS

Franciosino, il. *See* CORDIER, NICOLAS.

Francis, Prince of Anhalt-Dessau. *See* ANHALT-DESSAU, FRANCIS, Prince of.

Francis I [François], King of France. *See* VALOIS, (14).

Francis I, 7th Duke of Brittany. *See* BRITTANY, (1).

Francis I style. *See* FRANÇOIS Ier STYLE.

Francis II, 10th Duke of Brittany. *See* BRITTANY, (3).

Francis, John F. (*b* Philadelphia, PA, 13 Aug 1808; *d* Jeffersonville, PA, 15 Nov 1886). American painter. Beginning as an itinerant portrait painter in rural Pennsylvania, he produced works including flattering, colourful portraits of his sisters in the style of Thomas Sully, often incorporating small still-life details (e.g. *Three Children*, 1840; Boston, MA, Mus. F.A.). He abandoned portraiture after 1850 to concentrate exclusively on still-life subjects in the tradition of the PEALE family.

Francis's still-lifes fall into three main types: luncheon, dessert and fruit-basket. *Luncheon Piece* (Newark, NJ, Mus.), a fine example of the first type, shows a porcelain vessel overflowing with grapes, nuts and fruit, which dominates the centre of the well-balanced composition. Ranged horizontally on the linen-draped table are bottles of wine, goblets, a wedge of cheese with biscuits and an elaborate china pitcher, all set against a dark background in the Dutch manner. The dessert pieces, such as *Strawberries and Cake* and *The Dessert* (both 1860; New York, Richard York Gal.), feature fruits, cakes, china, silverware and linen and often include a landscape detail. Basket compositions are simpler, concentrating on fruits, sometimes cut open, and nuts spilling onto a linen cloth (e.g. *Still-life*, 1859; Boston, MA, Mus. F.A.). Francis painted over a hundred variations on these themes. He worked in a broad, painterly style, emphasizing the individuality of the objects, which he rendered in bright colours alternating with subtle tonalities. Francis was one of the most accomplished mid-19th-century American still-life painters and his work established a link between the tradition of the Peales and the innovations of William Michael Harnett.

BIBLIOGRAPHY
A. Frankenstein: 'J. F. Francis', *Antiques*, lix (1951), pp. 374–7
Catalogue of Paintings by John F. Francis (exh. cat. by G. L. Hersey, Lewisburg, PA, Bucknell U., 1958)
W. H. Gerdts and R. Burke: *American Still-life Painting* (New York, 1971)
A Suitable Likeness: The Paintings of John Francis (1832–1879) (exh. cat. by D. W. Dunn, Lewisburg, PA, Packwood House Mus., 1986)

GERTRUDE GRACE SILL

Francis, Sam(uel Lewis) (*b* San Mateo, CA, 25 June 1923; *d* Santa Monica, CA, 4 Nov 1994). American painter and printmaker. Following an accident leading to spinal tuberculosis while serving in the US Army Air Corps, he started to paint for distraction in 1944, studying privately under David Park in 1947. He subsequently relinquished his earlier medical studies in favour of painting, completing his BA (1949) and MA (1950) at the University of California at Berkeley. During this period he experimented with different styles of painting, notably Surrealism and the Abstract Expressionism of Jackson Pollock, Mark Rothko and particularly Clyfford Still. His own style emerged in 1949–50; in *Opposites* (1950; Tokyo, Idemitsu Mus. A.), for example, dripping, corpuscular shapes painted in fluid red circulate freely around the canvas, indicating what was to become a perennial concern with 'ceaseless instability'. With its sensitivity to sensuous colour and light, Francis's work was already showing very different concerns from the expressive iconography and energy of many of the Abstract Expressionists.

In 1950 Francis moved to Paris, where he attended the Atelier Fernand Léger and met Jean-Paul Riopelle, who remained an important influence. At first restricting his palette to muted greys and whites, he soon produced monochromatic paintings made up of transparent layers of colour. Exposure to the work of Bonnard and Matisse, and especially to Monet's *Waterlilies* in the Musée de l'Orangerie in Paris, reinforced his early predisposition to the qualities of light and colour. These interests came to the fore in paintings such as *Big Red* (1953; New York, MOMA), a vibrant and energetic painting of intense hue. Such works led to his identification with ART INFORMEL and to his inclusion in important group shows of this tendency, but he remained wary of being associated with any movement. By the end of 1955, the characteristic colour cells were beginning to break asunder, and empty space was opened up on the canvas. A visit to Japan in 1957 on his first tour around the world coincided with an even bolder use of white space and an increasingly asymmetrical composition, as in *The Whiteness of the Whale* (1957; Buffalo, NY, Albright–Knox A.G.). His acquisition of a larger studio in Paris and his experience of making mural-sized works led him to increase the dimensions of his paintings. His first commissions for large-scale paintings included a triptych intended for the Kunsthalle in Basle but not installed (e.g. *Basel Mural 2*, oil on canvas, 4.25×6.08 m, 1956–8; Amsterdam, Stedel. Mus.), a painting measuring *c.* 8 m in width for Sogetsu School of Flower Arrangement in Tokyo (*Tokyo Mural*, 1957) and a large mural for the Chase Manhattan Bank in New York (*Chase Manhattan Mural*, oil on canvas, 2.37×11.79 m, 1959; see Selz, p. 71).

Between 1960 and his return to California in 1962, the colour blue became dominant in Francis's work, for example in the *Blue Balls* series, in which rounded, organic shapes occupy the edge of the canvas. Making his home in the Los Angeles suburb of Santa Monica, he reverted to combinations of bright, but now harder and colder, colours that were less modulated than before, reflecting his increasing concern with lithography (see Lembark). In 1964 he was included in an exhibition, organized by Clement Greenberg (Los Angeles, CA, Co. Mus. A.), that gave its name to a new tendency in abstract art, POST-PAINTERLY ABSTRACTION, although Francis was again resistant to being bracketed in this way with other artists. His work became more austere and silent in the late 1960s, echoing his interest in oriental simplicity and coinciding with certain trends in American Minimalism. In such paintings as *Mako* (1966; artist's col., see Selz, p. 104) a large central space, comparable in the artist's view to a great white sail, is framed by bright bands of colour placed at the periphery of vision. Critics noted the fascination for the void and the existential absence of colour in his work at this time.

Francis's contact in 1971 with a Jungian psychiatrist renewed his early interest in dreams and alchemy and led him to produce a series of paintings reminiscent of *maṇḍala*s, with centrally placed squares, rectangles and circles. By 1977, however, Francis felt the need for a more severe structure and made paintings comprised of spattered perpendicular grids. These began to loosen during the 1980s in favour of letter- or snakelike configurations, covered with arabesque webs and drips of a brilliant hue. Exuding an explosive energy, Francis's later work continued to reveal the sensuous and often hedonistic celebration of human emotion that was a dominant feature of his art.

BIBLIOGRAPHY
Sam Francis (exh. cat. by G. Duthuit, Paris, Gal. Rive Droite, 1955)
Sam Francis (exh. cat. by J. J. Sweeney, Houston, TX, Mus. F.A.; Berkeley, U. CA, A. Mus.; 1967)
Sam Francis: Paintings, 1947–1972 (exh. cat. by R. T. Buck, F. Meyer and W. Schmied, Buffalo, NY, Albright–Knox A.G.; Washington, DC, Corcoran Gal. A.; New York, Whitney; Dallas, TX, Mus. F.A.; 1972–3)
P. Selz: *Sam Francis* (New York, 1975, rev. 1982)
Sam Francis: The Litho Shop, 1970–1979 (exh. cat., New York, Brooke Alexander, 1979)
A. Parinaud: 'Sam Francis: La Création est une méditation courte et ardente', *Gal. Jard. A.*, 199 (1980), pp. 31–5 [interview]
M. Waldberg: *Sam Francis: Métaphysique du vide* (Paris, 1986)
Y. Michaud: 'Sam Francis: Paris années 50, *Art Press*, 127 (July–Aug 1988), pp. 18–21 [interview]

Sam Francis Now: Paintings, 1989–1990 (exh. cat. by B. Hare and A. Patrizio, Glasgow A.G. & Mus.; U. Edinburgh, Talbot Rice Gal.; 1990)

Sam Francis: Blue Balls (exh. cat. by P. Selz, New York, Larry Gagosian Gal., 1991)

Sam Francis: Edge Paintings (exh. cat. by W. Hopps and N. Wilder, Santa Monica, CA, James Corcoran Gal., 1991)

C. W. Lembark: *The Prints of Sam Francis: A Catalogue Raisonné, 1960–1990*, 2 vols (New York, 1992)

Y. Michaud: *Sam Francis* (Paris, 1992)

M. D. Plant: *The 'Second Occupation': American Expatriate Painters and the Reception of American Art in Paris, 1946–58* (PhD diss., Providence, RI, Brown U., 1992)

Sam Francis (exh. cat. by A. Mousseigne, Y. Michaud, M. R. Rubinstein and P. Guyotat, Labege-Innopole, Cent. Rég. A. Contemp. Midi-Pyrenées, 1992)

P. Hulten: *Sam Francis* (Stuttgart, 1993)

J. F. Lyotard: *Sam Francis: Lesson of Darkness Like the Paintings of a Blind Man* (Venice, CA, 1993)

ANNA MOSZYNSKA

Francis-Joseph, Emperor of Austria and King of Hungary. *See* HABSBURG-LORRAINE, (2).

Francis Joseph [Franz Josef] **I**, Prince of Liechtenstein. *See* LIECHTENSTEIN, house of (5).

Franciscan Order [Order of Friars Minor]. Religious order founded in 1209 by St Francis of Assisi. In its broader sense the name encompasses two other organizations that he founded: the ORDER OF POOR CLARES and the Tertiaries (founded 1221), lay brothers who were affiliated to the Franciscans but usually lived in the world. The Franciscans were active in Italy from the early 13th century, but they spread rapidly and eventually became a worldwide movement; they were wealthy and influential patrons of art and architecture.

I. Introduction. II. Iconography. III. Patronage.

I. Introduction.

St Francis (1181/2–1226), born Giovanni Bernardone, was the son of a wealthy cloth merchant and was encouraged to spend money freely and enjoy a pleasure-seeking life. In 1205 he began experiencing 'visitations' and withdrew to meditate and pray. He began to show a keen interest in the poor that went beyond the giving of alms and led to his associating himself with them. Another 'divine visitation' came to him in the ruined church of S Damiano, just outside Assisi, when a painted wooden crucifix spoke, telling him to repair God's church, which was crumbling. Francis took these words literally and began raising money by selling bales of cloth from his father's shop for the purchase of building materials. At the instigation of his father he was summoned before the Bishop of Assisi, where Francis took off his clothes and laid them with all the money he had at the feet of the bishop, declaring that he was not only renouncing earthly goods but his earthly father as well. After this dramatic display Francis wandered alone, enduring much hardship, before returning to Assisi to repair three ruined churches: S Pietro, S Damiano and the Porziuncola. He financed these repairs and his own subsistence by begging. By 1209 Francis had been joined by three other men, and for their use he drew up a simple Rule based on the Gospels, advocating such ideals as charity and the renunciation of possessions. In the same year, while in Rome with 12 companions, Francis obtained the approval of his Order from Pope Innocent III (*reg* 1198–1216). The friars followed very strict ideals of poverty and humility, wishing to emulate the life of Christ and his Apostles. They led extremely deprived lives and were itinerant preachers, active in Umbria and Tuscany, gathering followers and leaving brethren to continue the mission. Francis even went as far as Syria, where he attempted to convert the sultan of Egypt: he offered to demonstrate the power of his faith by walking through fire. In 1223, to commemorate his pilgrimage to Bethlehem, Francis recreated a Christmas crib at Greccio and thus instituted a great tradition. He often spent days in prayer and solitude, and on one such occasion, in the summer of 1224 on Mt La Verna, Francis experienced a vision that left him with marks identical to Christ's wounds imprinted on his hands, feet and side. This event, known as the stigmatization, was kept secret until after Francis's death on 3 October 1226, when it was revealed and hailed as a great miracle. Less than two years later, on 16 July 1228, Francis was canonized by Pope Gregory IX (*reg* 1227–41).

The first officially approved Rule of 1221 best expressed the spirit of Francis's mission. Of primary importance was the obedience he pledged to the papacy; the other brethren were to obey St Francis and his successors. Equally important was the vow to live in obedience, chastity and poverty. A postulant was expected to leave his family and to sell all his possessions, giving any money he thus raised to the poor. He was forbidden to touch money and had to beg for his subsistence. In 1223 a more precise formulation was drawn up and approved by Pope Honorius III (*reg* 1216–27). It retained the three vows, but took into account the increasing numbers of friars and the larger area in which they were active. It took on a new meaning, however, when Francis wrote his testament in 1226, in which he prohibited any glosses and changes to the Rule. In the testament Francis reiterated his beliefs and made a few contradictory allusions to art: as he was devoted to the Eucharist, he demanded that it should be honoured and venerated and that the place in which it was kept should be preciously adorned. Manuscripts, because they contained the words of God, were also to be honoured and venerated. At the same time, he warned the friars not to receive, under any pretext, churches, humble homes or anything built for them, if this went against the Rule; he asked his brethren to stay in such buildings as passers-by and pilgrims. Friars were also forbidden to solicit privileges for any of their churches or convents.

Even before the death of Francis, the Order had divided into two branches: those (later called Spirituals) who wished to observe the Rule literally and to continue as a group of itinerant friars, working in the fields and begging, and the Conventuals, who wanted the Order to become more monastic and who accepted modifications to the requirement of poverty. In 1230 Pope Gregory IX attempted to resolve the impasse by declaring that St Francis's testament was no longer binding upon his followers. To bypass the clause in the Rule that stipulated that friars must live without property, he decreed that they could use property owned by the papacy or the cardinal-protector of the Order. This was confirmed by Pope Martin IV (*reg* 1281–5) in 1283, who also granted the third party full administrative powers over Franciscan property, including the right to buy, sell, exchange or sue and was appointed or dismissed by the friars; thus the Franciscans became owners of what they used in all but name. Many irregularities and abuses were subsequently committed, causing bitter divisions within the Order. In 1312 Pope Clement V (*reg* 1305–14) sought to tackle the issue in a bull that also carried implications for buildings and furnishings. Churches were not to be excessive in size or number. Liturgical vessels were required to be adequate but were not to be of great value or have any untoward embellishment. It was, however, left up to the guardian of a friary or his superior to interpret this statement, and, not surprisingly, Clement's decree did not resolve the internal problems of the Order. They were, in fact, exacerbated by the bull issued by Pope John XXII in 1322, which denied the validity of the distinction between use and ownership in Franciscan practice; henceforth the Franciscans became 'owners' of property rather than just 'users'.

The 14th century was characterized both by the moral and spiritual decline of the Order and by renewed attempts at its revival as the ideal of evangelical perfection through close adherence to the Rule. In an effort to resolve the new internal conflict of the Franciscans, John XXII (*reg* 1316–34) branded the Franciscans heretics in 1323. Nevertheless, a new reform movement, the so-called Observants, was founded in 1368. It became extremely powerful by the end of the century and was officially recognized at the Council of Constance in 1415. The Observants found a great leader, vigorous reformer and charismatic preacher in St Bernardino of Siena (1380–1444), who helped make the branch so successful. By 1415 they were allowed to settle in the Porziuncola at Assisi, on the condition that their income was passed on to the main house of S Francesco. The Observants' strength and influence grew rapidly, and in 1517 they were separated from the Conventuals by papal decree. More reformed branches were formed in the 16th century; the most important of these, the CAPUCHINS, played an important role in the Counter-Reformation. The Franciscans continued to expand until the mid-18th century and were prominent and successful as missionaries, most notably in the Spanish and Portuguese colonies of South America. The fragmented groups of Observants were reunited in 1897, since when they have been known as the Order of Friars Minor, a separate group from the other main branch of Franciscans, the Conventuals.

BIBLIOGRAPHY

V. Facchinetti: *S Francesco nella storia, nella leggenda, nell'arte* (Milan, 1926)
M. Bihl: 'Statuta generalia ordinis edita in capitulis generalibus celebratis Narbonae an. 1260, Assisii an. 1279 atque Parisiis an. 1292', *Archv Franciscanum Hist.*, xxxiv (1941), pp. 13–94, 284–358
R. B. Brooke: *Early Franciscan Government* (Cambridge, 1959)
M. D. Lambert: *Franciscan Poverty: The Doctrine of the Absolute Poverty of Christ and the Apostles in the Franciscan Order, 1210–1323* (London, 1961)
J. R. H. Moorman: *A History of the Franciscan Order: From its Origins to the Year 1517* (Oxford, 1968)
M. Habig, ed.: *St Francis of Assisi: Writings and Early Biographies: English Omnibus of the Sources for the Life of St Francis* (Chicago, 1973)
D. Nimmo: *Reform and Division in the Medieval Franciscan Order: From Saint Francis to the Foundation of the Capuchins* (Rome, 1986)
C. Frugoni: *Francesco: Un'altra storia* (Genoa, 1988)

II. Iconography.

The feature that distinguishes Franciscan friars is the full-length grey, brown or occasionally black habit and cowl. The habit is drawn at the waist by a rope knotted three times to symbolize the vows of poverty, chastity and obedience. In the early 13th century the friars were depicted barefoot, while in the 14th and 15th centuries they were sometimes shown wearing sandals.

1. St Francis. 2. Other Franciscan saints.

1. ST FRANCIS. The founder of the Order can be recognized by the stigmata, the visual proof of his special status as imitator of Christ; they were represented by a red mark on both hands and feet (or a hole in more realistic depictions of the 15th century) and an open wound in the chest on his right side, visible through a slit in the habit. In the 13th century he was represented with an emaciated face, a tonsure and a short beard; later he was often shown beardless. His most common attributes are the crucifix, lily and occasionally a book (as, for example, in Andriolo de' Santi's carved figure of *St Francis* of *c.* 1342–5, above the portal of S Lorenzo, Vicenza). (For 16th-century iconography and attributes see below.)

The earliest known image of St Francis is a wall painting dated 1228 in the Benedictine church of Sacro Speco, Subiaco. This full-length painting is inscribed *Frater Franciscus* and depicts the Saint with a beard, a cowl on his head and no halo; it is thought to commemorate his visit to Subiaco in 1218. During the 13th century St Francis was the subject of many painted narrative cycles that illustrated events from his life. Initially, these were based on his first biography, the *Vita prima*, written *c.* 1230 to a papal commission by Tommaso de Celano (*c.* 1190–1260). This straightforward account may have been based on the documents of the canonization process and was more like a papal chancery document than a memorial. Intimate and familiar aspects of St Francis's life were exploited for the benefit of the Church. Much insistence was placed on the Saint's virtue and on his submission to the Holy See. Since not all 150 chapters of the *Vita prima* could be depicted, patrons, advisers or painters selected the most appropriate scenes. The most complete cycle of the *Life of St Francis*, the Bardi *St Francis* (*c.* 1240; Florence, Santa Croce), was based on this source. The Saint is shown standing, surrounded by 20 episodes illustrating his life and posthumous miracles. Each scene is delineated by a rich border, with half-length images of Franciscans at the intersection of the borders. The depiction of the *Stigmatization*, which was given much emphasis in the *Vita prima*, is clearly based on that account. It corresponds closely with Celano's description of St Francis's vision of a man standing above him, looking like a seraph with six wings, arms extended, feet joined together and fixed to a cross. St Francis was the subject of several other paintings of this type, known as *vita retables*, but invariably they showed a reduced cycle of scenes from his life. (For illustrations of two slightly earlier examples see BERLINGHIERI, (2) and GIUNTA PISANO.)

In 1244 the Chapter General commissioned a revised biography, which was to take into account the reports of eye-witnesses. The *Vita secunda* (1247), also by Celano, was divided into two parts: the first described the conversion of St Francis, while the second was a character study of the Saint and followed no chronological order. By the time it was written, the Order was much divided; the *Vita secunda* supported the views of the Spirituals (*see* §I above) and inspired the now fragmentary fresco cycle (?1260) by the St Francis Master in the Lower Church of S Francesco, Assisi (*see* ASSISI, §II, 2). Fifteen years after its appearance it was thought necessary to replace the second biography with an account that would bring concord in the Order. The *Legenda maior* (for reading in the refectory) and *Legenda minor* (for liturgical use) were written in 1263–6 by the Minister General of the Order, St Bonaventure (*c.* 1217–74). By carefully rewriting the works of Celano, St Bonaventure presented St Francis as the founder of an order that was now working for the Church. The *Legenda maior* was to be the official biography of St Francis, and a decree was passed in 1266 that all earlier accounts should be destroyed. This had tremendous consequences for the development of Franciscan iconography. After 1266 painters gradually abandoned Celano's writings in favour of St Bonaventure's, to which they adhered in their depictions of the life of St Francis. The cycle became more conventionalized and hagiographical and presented the view that the Order had moved away from its earlier standards of simplicity and poverty. Events from St Francis's life were adapted to resemble the life of Christ or of Old Testament figures, and in visual representations the two were often paralleled. Like Christ, St Francis was shown to have had twelve disciples, by one of whom he was rejected; St Francis was also tempted by demons, and in emulation of Christ's suffering on the cross he received the stigmata. He was sometimes shown bringing water forth from a rock, like Moses, or being carried to heaven in a chariot of fire, like Elijah (*see* GOTHIC, fig. 77). His life was also modelled on those of Early Christian and contemporary saints. St Francis rolled in snow as St Benedict had rolled in thorns to resist temptations of the flesh; he saw Christ detached from the cross as St Bernard had done and gave his cloak to the poor in the manner of St Martin. Finally, St Francis shouldered the crumbling Lateran basilica in emulation of St Dominic (*see* DOMINICAN ORDER, fig. 1). The influence of St Bonaventure's writings is best seen in the 28 scenes from the *Life of St Francis* (*see* ASSISI, §II, 2) in the Upper Church of S Francesco at Assisi, painted around the turn of the 14th century, as well as in the Bardi Chapel frescoes of *c.* 1320 in Santa Croce, Florence. In particular, the *Stigmatization* and the *Recognition of the Stigmata* relied heavily on Christian iconography to support Francis's Christ-like status. In order to enable the reader and ultimately the viewer to see St Francis as the imitator of Christ, St Bonaventure modified Celano's account and described the instrument of St Francis's stigmatization as Christ crucified with six wings in the manner of a seraph. This provided the iconography for subsequent renderings, for example that by Giotto in the Bardi Chapel (see fig. 1).

Several popular scenes from the life of St Francis are based on other sources, for example the *Fioretti* or *Little Flowers of St Francis*, a collection of legends about the Saint, dating from *c.* 1375. This is the source of the image of *St Francis Preaching to the Birds* (e.g. in the Bardi *St Francis*) and of *St Francis and the Wolf of Gubbio*, the

1. *Stigmatization of St Francis* (*c.* 1320), fresco by Giotto, Bardi Chapel, Santa Croce, Florence

subject of a panel (London, N.G.) from Sassetta's polyptych (1437–44; dispersed; for locations *see* SASSETTA) painted for S Francesco, Borgo San Sepolcro. The latter scene was often depicted and referred to St Francis's miraculous taming of the wolf that had terrorized the town of Gubbio. Personifications of the three Franciscan vows of Poverty, Chastity and Obedience appear in the early 14th-century frescoes of *Franciscan Allegories* in the vault over the high altar of the Lower Church, S Francesco, Assisi, together with the *Apotheosis of St Francis*. One of the scenes shows St Francis placing a ring on the finger of Poverty, who is wearing tattered clothes. (For a later example of the *Mystic Marriage of St Francis see* SASSETTA, fig. 3.) This iconography was subsequently rare, although it was popular with the Observants in the 15th century and was represented in two panels (Munich, Alte Pin.) by Domenico Veneziano. For St Bernardino of Siena, leader of the Observants, obedience was the most important of the Franciscan virtues. It was often symbolized by an older friar, frequently St Bernardino himself, placing a yoke of obedience around the neck of a younger friar.

The Franciscans had a special devotion to the cross, to which many of their churches (e.g. Santa Croce, Florence) were dedicated. Two principal iconographic themes are associated with the cross and were often adopted in Franciscan decoration. The Legend of the True Cross recounted the history of the wood from which Christ's cross was made (for fuller explanation *see* CALVARY) and was the subject of several fresco cycles, including the one by Agnolo Gaddi in Santa Croce, Florence (*c.* 1388–93; *see* GADDI, (4), fig. 1) and the celebrated cycle (1453–4) by Piero della Francesca in S Francesco, Arezzo (see fig. 2). The other theme relates to the Tree of Life and is derived from St Bonaventure's devotional work *Lignum vitae*. Interesting illustrations of it by Taddeo Gaddi (*c.* 1360;

2. *Invention and Recognition of the True Cross* (*c.* 1450s), fresco by Piero della Francesca, S Francesco, Arezzo

Florence, Santa Croce) and PACINO DI BONAGUIDA show Christ crucified not on a cross but on a tree, with 12 medallions hanging like fruit from 12 branches. Inscriptions and pictures allude to the Creation and Fall of Man, and the life, death and glorification of Christ.

3. *St Francis Comforted by an Angel*, by Francisco Ribalta, oil on canvas, 2.04×1.58 m (Madrid, Museo del Prado)

In late 16th-century Italy, at the time of the Counter-Reformation and especially following the decisions of the Council of Trent (1545–67), St Francis became one of the most popular and widely venerated saints. A totally new Franciscan iconography evolved as it was the Saint's mystical and visionary experiences rather than the story of his life that were considered capable of transforming the spectator and that captured the imagination, becoming the focus of devotion. The only one of the early scenes that retained its validity was the stigmatization, and the Saint was also often shown alone, meditating on a crucifix or skull. A 16th-century expansion of the former iconography shows St Francis being embraced by the crucified Christ and is typical of the period in emphasizing the Saint's empathy with Christ and his meditation on Christ's agony. Another important and widespread theme, which developed in the 16th century, is that of St Francis being consoled by one or more musician angels and sometimes simultaneously experiencing a vision of Christ. A variant of this theme shows St Francis in ecstasy and being supported by angels. This often has visual echoes of the iconography of the *Pietà*, no doubt a deliberate reminder of St Francis's status as imitator of Christ.

Once established in Italy, the new Franciscan iconography spread rapidly across Europe. It had an enormous impact in Spain, where it was introduced by El Greco and later taken up by numerous painters, including Zurbarán and Francisco Ribalta (see fig. 3). The Catholic Netherlands was also enormously receptive to the subject, and Rubens's prolific rendering of Franciscan iconography was both a response to demand and an inspiration to followers.

2. OTHER FRANCISCAN SAINTS. A number of Franciscan friars became very famous during their lifetime and were later canonized. Biographical accounts celebrated their lives and usually also their posthumous miracles.

These saints were adopted as patrons of many Franciscan churches, and their iconography was widely used. St Anthony of Padua (*b* Lisbon, 15 August 1195; *d* nr Padua, 13 June 1231; *can* 30 May 1233) was the Order's second most important saint. He was usually depicted as a bald, corpulent friar, older than St Francis and often holding a book. From the beginning of the 14th century he holds a lily and later a flame or a heart, as in the 15th-century fresco (S Francesco, Deruta) by an Umbrian artist. Despite St Anthony's popularity, the fact that a large basilica, Il Santo, was built in Padua (*see* PADUA, §4(i) and fig. 3) to enshrine his relics and a Franciscan province was named after him, he never reached the same status as St Francis in terms of iconography. The earliest of the existing cycles that illustrate his life and miracles appears in the early 14th-century stained glass of the St Anthony Chapel in the Lower Church of S Francesco, Assisi. In the mid-15th century DONATELLO produced the bronze relief panels (1445–50) of the high altar in Il Santo, Padua, with scenes from the *Life of St Anthony*, while 16th-century marble narrative reliefs with similar scenes by Tullio Lombardo, Jacopo Sansovino and Girolamo Campagna decorate the walls of St Anthony's Chapel, the Cappella del Santissimo.

St Louis of Toulouse (*b* Toulouse; *d* Brignoles, 19 August 1297; *can* 1317), another important Franciscan saint, was the elder brother of King Robert of Naples, in whose favour he had renounced the crown in order to become a Franciscan. He is usually represented as a Franciscan bishop wearing a mitre, a cope over a Franciscan habit and sometimes holding a crozier. In some renderings, for example that of 1317 by Simone Martini (*see* GOTHIC, fig. 78), St Louis gives the earthly crown to his brother, while two angels place the crown of heaven on St Louis's head; scenes from his life are presented on the predella.

St Bernardino of Siena joined the Franciscan Order in 1402 and was frequently represented in Franciscan art, especially after his canonization in 1450. He is commonly depicted as an elderly, clean-shaven, ascetic friar, and his usual attribute is a round or square disc bearing the letters IHS, as he had a particular devotion to the sacred name of Jesus. The earliest images of St Bernardino, which probably also represent his likeness, are two panels (1444; Siena, Osservanza and Siena, Pin. N., 203) painted by Pietro di Giovanni d'Ambrogio. The Saint was also sometimes depicted with three episcopal mitres at his feet, as in the fresco dated 1451 by Sano di Pietro in the Palazzo Pubblico, Siena. The mitres symbolized the three bishoprics he refused: Siena, Ferrara and Urbino. Although he never quite reached the level of popularity attained by St Francis, he had a great following, and a few narrative cycles illustrating his life survive, including a predella (Arezzo, Gal. & Mus. Med. & Mod., 23) by Neri di Bicci, a fresco cycle by Pierantonio Mezzastris in S Francesco, Montefalco, and one by Bernardino Pinturicchio in S Maria d'Aracoeli, Rome.

III. Patronage.

One of the greatest areas of Franciscan patronage was architecture. Some months before St Francis's canonization in 1228, the construction of a large basilica in Assisi was already planned, and it became the mother house of the Order on 22 April 1230 (*see* ASSISI, §II, 1). Elsewhere the Franciscans usually settled outside the city walls, and they moved into town centres only from 1230 onwards. Although traditional accounts suggest that either St Francis of Assisi or St Anthony of Padua founded the early settlements, laid the first stone or were associated with the first donor, it appears that the first buildings and churches used by the friars were usually not built by them. Most sites were pre-existing and received from a local bishop, the Benedictine Order or a lay benefactor. These early churches were extremely small. It is known, for example, that during the processions surrounding the funeral of St Anthony of Padua in S Maria Mater Domini, Padua, candles had to be trimmed before entering for fear of fire. The first purpose-built Franciscan churches were slightly bigger and usually comprised a single nave ending in an apse and covered with a wooden roof. They were quickly outgrown, in the case of Padua as early as the 1260s, and were rebuilt on a larger scale in a new architectural style.

In 1260, during a meeting of the General Chapter at Narbonne, specific building regulations were laid down concerning Franciscan architecture and art. The Constitutions of Narbonne prescribed that vaults were permitted only over the high altar; there was to be no superfluous decorative painting on columns or window surrounds; bell-towers were not to be built as separate structures; historiated glass was allowed only behind the high altar and could show only Christ on the cross, the Virgin, St Francis or St Anthony. No altarpieces or other objects were permitted on an altar; no church was allowed such excesses as censers, crucifixes and gold or silver vessels, with the exception of a crucifix with relics, or vessels for the host. The chalice was to be simple, and the number of chalices was not to exceed the number of altars, save an extra one for use in the convent. These prohibitions were very rarely observed, as is clear from such richly decorated churches as S Francesco in Assisi, Il Santo in Padua and Santa Croce in Florence (*see* FLORENCE, fig. 18).

A mendicant type of architecture did, however, develop and was shared by Franciscans and Dominicans and later Carmelites and Servites. It consisted of either an aisleless nave with three apses at the east end, or an aisled church with a transept ending in a number of apsidal chapels. The ceilings were wooden in the earlier churches, but later they were sometimes replaced by vaulting. Apart from sharing these very general characteristics, as well as the principle of simplicity, Franciscan churches were often quite dissimilar. A few examples, such as S Chiara, Assisi, were influenced by the mother church, but elsewhere they represent the fusion of Gothic architecture with local building styles.

By the middle of the 13th century the Franciscans had firmly established themselves throughout Italy and beyond, with churches for example in Ulm (1250) and Paris (Ste Marie-Madeleine, 1255–62; destr.), while by *c.* 1300 Franciscan friaries were ubiquitous in almost all of Europe and totalled some 1400 houses. (For a discussion of Franciscan Gothic architecture in Italy, Germany and Spain *see* GOTHIC, §II.) The standardized 'mendicant' plan adopted by both Franciscans and Dominicans provided not only an ideal preaching environment, thanks to its vastness and openness, but also an uninterrupted wall surface suitable for large-scale decoration. The preferred type of visual representation in Franciscan churches was the narrative, from the early examples of panel painting (*see* §II above) to such 15th-century wall-painting cycles as the 12 scenes from the *Life of St Francis* (1452) by Benozzo Gozzoli in the choir of S Francesco, Montefalco. The first painted cycles, such as those illustrating the Old and New Testament and the *Life of St Francis*, in the Upper and Lower Churches of S Francesco, Assisi, used the didactic values of narrative wall painting to disseminate the Order's official teachings, to correlate the lives of Christ and St Francis and to encourage the devotion of both friars and the laity. They were also technically innovative and were among the first experiments in fresco in Umbria. In the 14th century such cycles as Giotto's Bardi Chapel frescoes (*c.* 1320; Florence, Santa Croce) illustrate the *Life of St Francis*, while those illustrating the *Life of St John the Evangelist* in the neighbouring Peruzzi Chapel are an example of a non-Franciscan iconography in a Franciscan church. By contrast, Domenico Ghirlandaio's fresco cycle of the *Life of St Francis* (commissioned 1478–9; Florence, Santa Trinita) was painted in a church that was not Franciscan.

The Franciscan Order has sometimes (especially in the 19th century) been credited with artistic and literary innovations. Studies have, however, shown that in the majority of cases the friars had little say in the artistic commissions found on their premises and that communes, families, ecclesiastics, confraternities and individuals were the real patrons. It is therefore not surprising to find that there is much individuality in Franciscan churches. There are, nevertheless, documented cases of friars who were involved in some aspects of the arts. Brother Elias of Cortona is, for example, credited with the supervision of building operations at S Francesco, Assisi. He was no doubt helped by Philip of Campello, a friar whose name appears in documents as *magister ecclesiae* and *prepositus.* Franciscan supervisors were also found on other building sites, and in Il Santo in Padua two of the *murari* were members of the Order. Brother Clarello, also from Padua, was asked to carve a tomb in 1292; another friar, Nicola *talapiera*, occasionally helped with the carving of the façade portal (1342–5) of S Lorenzo, Vicenza, and helped the guardian, Pace da Lugo, to supervise the work.

Lay patrons contributed to the fabric of Franciscan churches and all aspects of their decoration. They were not constrained by neighbourhood loyalties, nor were they tied to the patronage of any single order. Wealthy individuals frequently financed whole sections of a church, as was the case at S Fermo Maggiore, Verona, or endowed a chapel, established a chantry or financed narrative wall-painting cycles. Cheaper alternatives included votive paintings, sculpture and altar furnishings such as retables, chalices, hangings and vestments. A minimum investment was not required by the friars, which meant that almost every member of the laity could patronize the arts in one way or another. No doubt this was one of the factors that made the Order so appealing during the Middle Ages. Perhaps owing to its apparent lack of control over commissions, the Order was open to much artistic experiment. All forms of art were commissioned, including

monumental wall and panel paintings, such large sculptural works as tombs, and architectural as well as free-standing sculpture. There are a great many examples of stained glass both in S Francesco, Assisi, and elsewhere. For example, the 14th-century stained glass in the Franciscan church of Königsfelden, Switzerland, includes scenes of *Pope Innocent III Confirming the Rule, St Francis Preaching to the Birds*, the *Stigmatization* and the *Death of St Francis.* There are also many examples of Franciscan embroidery, for example the 14th-century silk and gold altar-cloth (Toulouse, Mus. St-Raymond) commissioned for a Franciscan convent, which features the *Life of St Francis* paralleled with the *Life of Christ*. Examples of metalwork include a quadrilobe phylactery (*c.* 1230; Paris, Mus. Cluny) that shows St Francis standing and receiving the stigmata.

With the exception of a cluster of Umbrian and Tuscan Franciscan churches that in the 14th century modelled their decoration on the Upper and Lower Churches of S Francesco, Assisi, the rest of the Order did not attempt to make their churches look 'Franciscan'. Indeed, no doubt owing to the mechanisms of patronage, it cannot be said that Franciscan churches conform to any set programmes of decoration. Privately endowed public chapels such as S Giacomo Maggiore (1372–9; now S Felice) and S Giorgio (1377–84) in Il Santo, Padua, are the best documented areas of that church and, significantly, areas where Franciscan participation was at its lowest. The donors commissioned the workshops themselves, handled all payments and even chose paintings that reflected the family's taste rather than the friars'. It is most difficult to attempt to explain the reasons behind the lack of Franciscan participation in artistic projects. Perhaps this may have been the case only in privately endowed commissions, or perhaps it reflected a wish on the friars' part not to be involved in the complicated legal processes of artistic commissions. It is also possible that in this way the Franciscans expressed a deliberate stand against the uses of property.

BIBLIOGRAPHY

L. da Pietralunga: *Descrizione della basilica di S Francesco e di altri santuari di Assisi* (*c.* 1570–80; Assisi, Bib. Com., MS. 148); ed. P. Scarpellini (Treviso, 1982)
H. van Thode: *Franz von Assisi und die Anfänge der Kunst der Renaissance in Italien* (Berlin, 1885)
E. Bertaux: 'Les Saints Louis dans l'art italien', *Rev. Deux Mondes*, clviii (1900), pp. 616–44
L. Gillet: *Histoire artistique des ordres mendiants* (Paris, 1912)
P. L. Bracaleoni: *L'arte francescana* (Todi, 1924)
V. Facchinetti: *Iconografia francescana nella vita e nella storia di settecento anni* (Milan, 1924)
G. Kaftal: *Iconography of the Saints in Tuscan Painting* (Florence, 1952)
R. Wagner-Rieger: 'Zur Typologie italienischer Bettelordens Kirchen', *Röm. Hist. Mitt.*, ii (1957–8), pp. 266–98
L. Réau: *Iconographie de l'art chrétien*, 3 vols (Paris, 1958)
K. W. Humphreys: *The Book Provisions of the Medieval Friars, 1215–1400* (Amsterdam, 1964)
G. Kaftal: *Iconography of the Saints in the Central and Southern Italian Schools of Painting* (Florence, 1965)
H. Dellwing: *Studien zur Baukunst der Bettelorden im Veneto: Die Gotik der monumentalen Gewölbebasiliken*, Kunstwissenschaftliche Studien, xliii (Munich, 1970)
J. Gardner: 'The Early Decoration of Santa Croce in Florence', *Burl. Mag.*, cxiii (1971), pp. 391–3
A. Smart: *The Assisi Problem and the Art of Giotto* (Oxford, 1971)
H. van Os: 'St Francis of Assisi as a Second Christ in Early Italian Painting', *Simiolus*, vii (1974), pp. 115–32
G. Ruf: *Franziskus und Bonaventura* (Assisi, 1974)

H. Maginnis: 'Assisi Revisited: Notes on Recent Observations', *Burl. Mag.*, cxvii (1975), pp. 511–17

J. Poeschke: *Die Kirche San Francesco in Assisi und ihre Wandmalereien* (Munich, 1975)

G. Kaftal: *Iconography of the Saints in the Painting of North East Italy* (Florence, 1978)

P. Scarpellini: 'Note sull'iconografia antoniana nel San Francesco di Assisi', *Il Santo*, xix (1979), pp. 595–601

L. Tintori and M. Meiss: *The Painting of the Life of St Francis in Assisi, with Notes on the Arena Chapel* (Ann Arbor, 1980)

J. Gardner: 'Some Franciscan Altars of the Thirteenth and Fourteenth Centuries', *The Vanishing Past: Studies of Medieval Art, Liturgy and Metrology Presented to Christopher Hohler*, ed. A. Borg and A. Martindale, Brit. Archaeol. Rep., Int. Ser., 3 (Oxford, 1981), pp. 29–38

G. Ruf: *Das Grab des heiliges Franziskus: Die Fresken der Unterkirche von Assisi* (Freiburg im Breisgau, Basle and Vienna, 1981)

H. van Os: 'The Earliest Altarpieces of St Francis', *Atti del Primo Convegno di studi per l'VIII centenario della nascità di S Francesco, 1182–1982: Assisi, 1981*, i, pp. 333–8

J. L. Cannon: 'Dating the Frescoes by the Master of S Francesco at Assisi', *Burl. Mag.*, cxxiv (1982), pp. 65–9

P. Scarpellini: 'Iconografia francescana nei secoli XIII e XIV', *S Francesco: Storia e Arte* (exh. cat., ed. R. Rusconi; Assisi, S Francesco, 1982)

J. Gardner: 'The Cult of a Fourteenth-century Saint: The Iconography of Louis of Toulouse', *Società internazionale di studi Francescani. I Francescani nel Trecento. Atti del XIV convegno internazionale: Assisi, 1986*, pp. 169–93

R. Goffen: *Spirituality in Conflict: Saint Francis and Giotto's Bardi Chapel* (London, 1988)

H. Dellwing: *Die Kirchenbaukunst des späten Mittelalters in Venetien* (Worms, 1990)

R. Hatfield: 'The Tree of Life and the Holy Cross: Franciscan Spirituality in the Trecento and the Quattrocento', *Christianity and the Renaissance: Image and Religious Imagination in the Quattrocento*, ed. T. Verdon and J. Henderson (Syracuse, NY, 1990), pp. 132–60

L. Bourdua: 'Committenza francescana nel Veneto', *La pittura nel Veneto: Il Trecento*, ed. M. Lucca (Milan, 1992), pp. 463–79

——: 'Friars, Patrons and Workshops at the Basilica del Santo, Padua', *Stud. Ch. Hist.*, xxviii (1992), pp. 131–41

LOUISE M. BOURDUA

Francisco, Juan (*b* Alcalá de Henares, *c.* 1500; *d* Alcalá de Henares, 1579–80). Spanish silversmith. He was the son of the silversmith Juan Faraz, who worked for the Colegio Mayor de S Ildefonso in Alcalá de Henares. Francisco was apprenticed to his father and continued to work for him until the death of the latter. He made use of Renaissance-style baluster structures in his pieces, although the grotesque ornamentation on other pieces is close to Mannerism. Several of his silver objects are preserved, for example parts of the cross of Miraflores de la Sierra (1549; London, V&A), with a stand fashioned by Antonio Fernández Cantero in 1715; the cross of El Casar de Talamanca (before 1546; Madrid, Mus. N. A. Dec.); the processional crosses of Mondéjar (1545) and Buitrago (1546); the *macollas* of El Casar (before 1546; Jaén Cathedral) and Pastrana (1552); the receptacle for unconsecrated hosts (*c.* 1554; Madrid, C. Y. Col.); a chalice (1560–64; parish church of Viñuelas, Guadalajara); and a splendid bowl with a border of medallions (London, V&A). About 20 documented pieces by Francisco made between July 1538, when he was commissioned to execute the cross of Rascafría (his first known piece) and his execution of the cross of Pezuela de las Torres, which was paid for in 1579, have not survived. His brother Antonio Faraz (*b* Alcalá de Henares, *c.* 1510; *d* 1576) produced works that are different in form and decoration from those of Juan Francisco. Antonio Faraz made the processional crosses of Caspueñas, La Mierla and Pioz. His monstrance

for Balconete is the earliest-known radial type of monstrance in Spain.

For illustration of work *see* SPAIN, fig. 51; for bibliography *see* SPAIN, §IX, 1.

JOSÉ MANUEL CRUZ VALDOVINOS

Franciscus Italus [Franciscus Florentinus; Francesco Fiorentino] (*fl c.* 1502–16; *d* Kraków, 16 Oct 1516). Italian architect and sculptor, active in Poland. Franciscus Italus, who has been incorrectly identified as Francesco della Lora, joined the court in Kraków of Prince Sigismund (later Sigismund I; *see* JAGIELLON, (2)), whom he had probably met in Hungary, in 1502. His first work, which was also the earliest Renaissance work in Poland, was the tomb (1502–5) of *King John I Albert* (*d* 1501) in Wawel Cathedral, Kraków. This work was related to the Florentine type of arcaded wall tomb. Bas-relief arabesques, which cover even the architectural articulation of the tomb, derive from the early Renaissance decorations by Ambrogio d'Antonio Barocci in the palace in Urbino. Related in style are the decorative bow window and window of the west wing of Wawel Castle in Kraków, executed by Franciscus in 1504–6. In connection with the rebuilding of the castle following the accession of Sigismund I (1506), Franciscus travelled to Buda in Hungary (1507 and 1510) to engage Italian and German workmen for his workshop. Consequently, the north wing (1507–16) of the castle exhibits combined Gothic and Renaissance features. The question of whether the present three-storey arcades can be identified with those added to the wing at this time remains open; their forms resemble the style of Bartolomeo Berrecci, Franciscus's successor on the project, but they are less developed and more decorative.

BIBLIOGRAPHY
PSB; SAP

S. Komornicki: 'Franciszek Florentczyk i pałac wawelski' (Franciscus the Florentine and the Wawel Palace), *Przegląd Hist. Sztuki*, i (1929), pp. 57–69

B. Przybyszewski: 'Muratorzy i kamieniarze zajęci przy budowie zamku królewskiego na Wawelu, 1502–1536' [Bricklayers and stone masons engaged on the construction of the Wawel royal castle, 1502–36], *Biul. Hist. Sztuki*, xvii (1955), pp. 149–61

A. Fischinger: 'Nagrobek Jana Olbrachta i początki rzeźby renesansowej w Polsce' [The tomb of John Albert and the beginnings of Renaissance sculpture in Poland], *Renesans: Sztuka i ideologia* [Renaissance: art and ideology], ed. T. S. Jaroszewski (Warsaw, 1976), pp. 451–66

——: 'Pałac Króla Aleksandra na Wawelu', *Roc. Kraków.*, 56 (1990), pp. 79–93

ADAM MIŁOBĘDZKI

Franck, Hanns. *See* LÜTZELBURGER, HANS.

Franck [Frank; Franckh], **Hans** [Hanns; Johannes] **Ulrich** (*b* Kaufbeuren, *c.* 1590–95; *d* Ausburg, ?autumn 1675). German painter, draughtsman, printmaker and organist. He was apprenticed to his father, the Kaufbeuren painter and town architect Daniel Erbe ('Franckh'; *b* 1573; *fl* 1603). In 1630 he painted *SS Cosmas and Damian* (Kaufbeuren, Kirche bei Kauf), which he signed as a 'painter and organist'. By 1637, at the latest, he had moved to Augsburg: on 30 October 1638 he acquired citizenship there and a work permit as a retailer. His early career in Augsburg was devoted mainly to portraits, both drawings and paintings, but one painting depicts the *Baptism of St Augustine* (1638; Beuerberg, Augustines-Chorherrenstift). His later work includes drawings of *Foxhunting* (1645) and *Artists and Connoisseurs* (*c.* 1665; both Berlin, Kupferstichkab.) and the painting *Jacob's Reconciliation with Esau* (1660; Warsaw, N. Mus.).

The best-known example of Franck's graphic work is a sequence of 25 engravings (1643–56), possibly inspired by Jacques Callot's *Misères de la guerre* series (1633), in which he portrayed war from the standpoint of its victims. He also produced designs for goldsmiths and silversmiths, such as the pattern, elaborated in the painting *Jacob's Reconciliation with Esau*, for a showpiece plate (1645; Moscow, Kremlin) by the Augsburg goldsmith Hans Jakob Baur I. This reached Moscow in 1647 as a gift from Christina, Queen of Sweden, to Alexei, Tsar of Moscow (*reg* 1645–76). Franck had links, both personal and stylistic, with Johann Heinrich Schönfeld, and it is possible that he was familiar with Dutch painting in the style of Jacob Duck and Maerten Stoop (*c.* 1620–47).

BIBLIOGRAPHY

ADB; Thieme–Becker; Hollstein: *Ger.*

A. Andresen: *Der deutsche Peintre-graveur* (Leipzig, 1864–78)

A. Hämmerle, ed.: *Die Radierungen des Hanns Ulrich Franckh, Malers aus Kaufbeuren, 1613/1675* (Augsburg, 1923)

T. Muchall-Viebrock: *Deutsche Barockzeichnungen* (Munich, 1925), p. 33

J. Michałkowa: 'Nouvelles acquisitions du département de la peinture européene, 1958–1962', *Bull. Mus. N. Varsovie/Biul. Muz. N. Warsaw.*, iv/6 (1963), p. 103

Augsburger Barock (exh. cat., Augsburg, Rathaus, 1968), pp. 105–6, 181–7

Augsburger Stadtlexikon (Augsburg, 1985), p. 113

R. Biedermann: *Hanns Ulrich Franck: Das zeichnerische Werk* (in preparation)

JOSEF Č. MANCAL

Franck, Pauwels. See FIAMMINGO, PAOLO.

Francke, Master (*fl* Hamburg, *c.* 1424–36). German painter. 'Mester Francke(nn)' was named in an entry (1541) in the memorial book of Hamburg's England Traders' Association, quoting a lost contract of 1424 commissioning a *Passion* altarpiece (remnants, Hamburg, Ksthalle), then still located in the Johanniskirche, probably having been set up in the south chapel soon after it came into the Association's possession in 1436. It is thought that 'Mester Francke' was the 'fratre Francone Zutphanico' or 'fratre Francone' named in *Anabaptistici furoris monasterium evertentis historica narratio* (1573), in which Hermann von Kerssenbroich (1517–85) reported that pictures by that artist in Hamburg Cathedral had been profaned by Anabaptists. *Die Ordnung der Wiedertäufer in Münster*, based on a 1534 report by Hermann Ramert, mentioned the pictures of Brother 'Frantz von Sudfeld': Graf Otto von Hoya, Bishop of Münster (*reg* 1409–20), had unusually close ties with the Dominicans in Zutphen. It may thus be inferred that 'mester Francke', 'fratre Francone Zutphanico' and 'Franz von Sudfeld' were the same person. He may also have been the 'black' (i.e. Dominican) monk in Hamburg who painted the altar shrine that Hans Kinkelow, a joiner and carver from Reval [Tallinn], was commissioned in 1424 to make for the Dominicans of that city. (The completed work, with the *Trinity* as its main picture, was installed in 1436 but destroyed in 1537.) This evidence combines to suggest that after an initial period as a Dominican novice and monk at Zutphen, Francke moved to the Dominican monastery in Hamburg after 1420; there is no sign of him after 1429.

Although undocumented, the *St Barbara* altar (Helsinki, N. Mus.; ex-Nykyrko Parish Church) is ascribed to Master Francke; it is thought to have been commissioned by Bishop Magnus II Tavast of Turku for a St Barbara's chapel he installed in Turku Cathedral in 1415. From one aspect the double-winged altar shows eight scenes from the *Legend of St Barbara* and from another a large central shrine with a carving of the *Death of the Virgin*, accompanied on the wings by two reliefs from the *Life of the Virgin*, which were the work of a carver strongly influenced by Master Francke. The figures, colouring, architectural elements and contours of the landscape indicate that the painter had visited northern France and Burgundy as a journeyman, and the influence of the Boucicaut Master is seen in, for example, the contrasting of richly clothed Orientals (cf. the Khan's Palace with three guards in the *Livre des merveilles du monde*, 1413; Paris, Bib. N.) with the smooth walls of the buildings. However, Master Francke exaggerated the size of the people in the pursuit scene to suggest overwhelming danger. The judgement scenes (fragments) are arresting for the vivid, mean faces of the bailiffs, surprising for the period and already foreshadowing Late Gothic realism. A similar impact is created in the smaller of his two paintings of the *Man of Sorrows* (*c.* 1415–24; Leipzig, Mus. Bild. Kst.), in which Christ almost glowers straight at the onlooker.

The *Man of Sorrows* was depicted again in the *Passion* on the altar of the England Traders' Association (1424; remnants, Hamburg, Ksthalle). An engraving in the *Historia ecclesiae Hamburgensis diplomatica* (Hamburg, 1723) by Nicolaus Staphorst (1679–1731) shows the altarpiece as it originally looked it its second position, including the support with *Christ and the Twelve Apostles*. A fragment of a large *Crucifixion* on the central panel and the reverse faces of the inner wings indicate that the third position was devoted to the Passion. The second position showed four scenes from the *Life of St Thomas Becket* along the top; along the bottom were four scenes from the *Life of the Virgin*. The two outer wings and support are untraced, while the untraced centre panel of *Mount Calvary* is recorded in a weak altar-wing (Copenhagen, Kstindustmus.) by a follower. There is a rich variety in the figures, for example the way in which St Mary Magdalene turns markedly to the Virgin and St John anxiously clings to her. Other scenes from the *Passion* are outstanding examples of Master Francke's rich inventiveness, for example the *Flagellation* (see fig.) with its complicated overlapping of objects and people grouped together below a broad, shallow arch. Christ is heartbreakingly depicted—in a way prefigured in representations from the north Netherlands and Westphalia. In the *Entombment* Master Francke's back view of a female figure in black seemingly frozen in grief is quoted from Giotto's fresco (1503–5) in the Arena Chapel in Padua, which must have been familiar to him from Italian book illuminations seen in France. The *Resurrection* marked a peak in his bold disregard for the iconographical rules then in force, with the risen Christ making off into the wilds, his back half-turned to the viewer.

The last painting so far known to be by Master Francke is another *Man of Sorrows* (?1423; Hamburg, Ksthalle, ex-Johanniskirche), a three-quarter-length figure of Christ

Master Francke: *Flagellation*, from the altarpiece of the England Traders' Association, panel, 990×889 mm, 1424 (Hamburg, Hamburger Kunsthalle)

with his right hand going to the wound in his side. Despite his mild expression, he gains monumentality through his isolation—the background angels are of purely secondary importance. Except in the use of motifs—even as late as *c.* 1500 in an altar in Hannover by Hinrik van dem Kroghe (*fl* 1471–1503/4)—Master Francke did not attract any imitators.

BIBLIOGRAPHY
B. Martens: *Meister Francke* (Hamburg, 1929)
T. Rensing: 'Über die Herkunft des Meister Francke', *Wallraf-Richartz-Jb.*, xxix (1967), pp. 31 ff
Meister Francke und die Kunst um 1400 (exh. cat., ed. H. W. Grohn and others; Hamburg, Ksthalle, 1969)

HANS GEORG GMELIN

Francke, Paul (*b* Weimar, 1538; *d* Wolfenbüttel, 1615). German architect. From 1573 he worked as architectural administrator in the service of the Dukes of Brunswick-Wolfenbüttel: Julius (*reg* 1568–89), Henry Julius (*reg* 1589–1613) and Friedrich Ulrich (*reg* 1613–34). From 1580 until his death Francke was entrusted with the supervision of all the building work carried out for the dukes. He

supervised the alterations and extension of the city fortifications at Wolfenbüttel, which formed part of the town
building programme of Duke Julius. As well as the partial
rebuilding of Erichsburg in Einbeck (1604–12), his major
works are the new university at Helmstedt, known as the
Juleum (1592–7), and the main Protestant church, dedicated to the Blessed Virgin Mary, at Wolfenbüttel (begun
1608). The Zeughaus (arsenal) at Wolfenbüttel (1613; *see*
WELF, (5), fig. 2) and the reconstruction of the castle
tower at Wolfenbüttel (1612–13) are also attributed to
him. A church he designed for Hornburg in the Harz
(1613) was not executed. The Juleum at Helmstedt is a
two-storey, five-bay building with a high saddle roof. Its
main features are the sumptuous ornamentation of the
tower containing the spiral staircase, the two end gables
and five dormer gables, the two portals and the window
tracery, which are evidence of Francke's personal and
sometimes unconventional style. The Auditorium Maximum on the ground floor is a two-aisled hall in four bays,
with a flat roof supported by three term-piers, a form that
was hitherto unparalleled. The same characteristic features
are also found in the Marienkirche at Wolfenbüttel, which
is a hall church with nave and aisles in five cross-rib-
vaulted bays, a false transept and a one-bay chancel
terminating in five sides of an octagon. Francke translated
the structural elements of the traditional forms and ornament of a Gothic church into the language of the late
Renaissance. An early design included term-piers as supports for the vaults. The executed octagonal piers have
square capitals, richly ornamented, which bear no direct
relationship to the Vitruvian orders. The dormer gables
are characterized by the use of term-pilasters and strapwork. Probably the greatest of Francke's designs is that
for the church tower (unexecuted), with gallery, curved
roof and pointed spire.

The ornamental forms at the Juleum and Marienkirche
(including orders, scrollwork and strapwork) are typical of
this period but remain Francke's own independent inventions. The interaction of cubic building and tower, of wall
surface and opening, and of the articulation of the decoration, reveal an assured feeling for balanced proportions.
His sense of harmony and his fertile imagination make
Francke one of the most important Renaissance architects
of north Germany.

BIBLIOGRAPHY
Macmillan Enc. Architects
F. Thöne: *Wolfenbüttel, Geist und Glanz einer alten Residenz* (Munich,
1963)
H. H. Möller: 'Das Juleum in Helmstedt', *Niedersächs. Dkmlpf.*, vi (1965–
9), pp. 204–21
W. Kelsch and W. Lange: *Predigt der Steine: Der Bildschmuck der Turmfas-
sade an der Hauptkirche Beatae Mariae Virginis in Wolfenbüttel* (Wolfen-
büttel, 1984)
H. G. Möller, ed.: *Die Hauptkirche Beatae Mariae Virginis in Wolfenbüttel*
(Hannover, 1987)
WOLFGANG CILLESSEN

Francken. Flemish family of artists. The fact that the
same Christian names occurred in three generations of
painters who used identical signatures has caused a great
deal of confusion in attributing their various works. It is
still not possible to distinguish between all members of
the family reliably, as signed and dated works are not
available for some of the family members. Several of them
were also active in France. Nicholas Francken (*b* Herentals,
c. 1510/20; *d* Antwerp, 12 March 1596) moved to Antwerp
with his family in the early 1560s; he taught three of his
sons to paint, (1) Hieronymus Francken I, (2) Frans
Francken I and (3) Ambrosius Francken I, who were also
apprenticed to Frans Floris in Antwerp *c*. 1560. In the next
generation, all the sons of Frans Francken I were artists:
Thomas Francken (*b* Antwerp, 28 Feb 1574; *d* Antwerp,
c. 1625), for whom only one altarpiece (1617/18; Aartse-
lar, St Leonardus) is now known; (4) Hieronymus
Francken II; (5) Frans Francken II, the best-known and
most talented member of the family; and Ambrosius
Francken II (*b* Antwerp, *c*. 1590; *d* Antwerp, *bur* 8 Aug
1632), who painted landscapes and peasant scenes. The
sons of Frans Francken II followed in their father's
footsteps, but were weaker artists: (6) Frans Francken III,
the best of the youngest generation; Hieronymus Francken
III (*b* Antwerp, *bapt* 1 Aug 1611; *d* after 1661), who
specialized in religious subjects; and Ambrosius Francken
III (*b* Antwerp, *c*. 1614; *d* Antwerp, 1662). There is a
portrait of the *Francken Family* (*c*. 1580; Le Puy, Mus.
Crozatier) by Herman van der Mast.

BIBLIOGRAPHY
Hollstein: *Dut. & Flem.*; Thieme–Becker
F. J. Van den Branden: *Geschiedenis der Antwerpse schilderschool* (Antwerp,
1883)
J. Gabriels: *Een Kempisch schildersgeslacht: De Franckens* (Hoogstraaten,
1930)
C. Van de Velde: 'Le *Portrait de la famille Francken*: Une Oeuvre de
Herman van der Mast', *Studia Ioanni Białostocki sexaguario dicata*
(Warsaw, 1981), pp. 341–8
E. Larsen: *17th-century Flemish Painting* (Freren, 1985), pp. 52–3, 64–5

(1) Hieronymus Francken I (*b* Herentals, *c*. 1540; *d*
Paris, 1 May 1610). Painter. It is uncertain, after his training
in Antwerp, whether he went to Italy, as seems to be
suggested by his *Venetian Carnival* (1565; Aachen, Suer-
mondt-Ludwig-Mus.), a remarkable picture with a graceful
company of dancers portrayed against the scenery props
of the *commedia dell'arte*. Such a subject would be quite
exceptional for Antwerp at such an early date, lending
further support to the idea that he spent some time in
Italy in the mid-1560s. There is no question, however, that
from 1566 to 1572 he was in France. In 1568 Cornelis
Floris, the Antwerp master builder, sent his son to Paris
to serve his apprenticeship with Hieronymus I, who was
back in Antwerp again for a short period in 1574. From
1578 until his death his presence at the French court at
Fontainebleau can be documented. In 1585 Hieronymus
I painted an *Adoration of the Shepherds* with donor portraits
of the Thou family for the Parisian church of the Cordeliers
(now Ste Ursule-de-la-Sorbonne), which remains *in situ*.
In the same year he was married in Paris and completed,
undoubtedly in collaboration with his brother Ambrosius
I, a triptych with scenes from the *Life of St Eloi, Bishop of
Noyon* for the altar of the Blacksmiths' Guild in Antwerp
Cathedral (Antwerp, Kon. Mus. S. Kst.). In 1594 Hieronymus I was appointed Peintre du Roi to the French king.
As well as religious commissions, which were idealistic in
character and completely in accordance with 16th-century
taste, he painted groups of dancers at court (e.g. Vienna,
Ksthist. Mus.), which anticipate the development of this
type of composition in the 17th century, particularly in the
work of his nephew, Frans Francken II. A *Self-portrait* by

Hieronymus I is also preserved (Aix-en-Provence, Mus. Granet).

BIBLIOGRAPHY

J. Guiffrey: *Artistes parisiens des XVI et XVIIe siècles* (Paris, 1915), pp. 25–44 [inv. of his estate]

J. Gabriels: *Bijdrage tot de geschiedenis van het Nederlandsche romanisme: De kunst der Nederlanden*, i (Brussels, 1930), pp. 57–64, 96–101

L. Colliard: 'Tableaux représentant des bals à la cour des Valois', *Gaz. B.-A.*, n. s. 5, lxi (1963), pp. 147–56

P. M. Auzas: 'L'Adoration des bergers, 1585, de Hierosme Francken', *Bull. Soc. Hist. A. Fr.* (1967), pp. 61–4

——: *Hirosme Francken dit Franco: Peintre du roi Henri III et du roi Henri IV* (Brussels, 1968)

U. Härting: *Frans Francken II* (Freren, 1989), pp. 18–20

(2) Frans Francken I (*b* Herentals, 1542; *d* Antwerp, 2 Oct 1616). Painter, brother of (1) Hieronymus Francken I. He became a master in the Antwerp Guild of St Luke in 1567 and a deacon in 1587. Together with Marten de Vos and Frans Floris, Frans I and his brother Ambrosius I were the most important painters in Catholic Antwerp during the Counter-Reformation. After the Iconoclastic Fury, the brothers received a number of ecclesiastical commissions to replace works destroyed in the churches in and around the city (e.g. for the St Waltrudiskerk, Herentals, and the St Maartenskerk, Aalst). Huge altar-pieces, such as the *Last Judgement* for Herentals, with the figures ranged in rows as in a frieze, with very little depth or breadth, illustrate Frans I's hieroglyphic style. His earliest surviving works are two panels of a triptych of the *Last Supper* (1581; Ghent, Mus. S. Kst.) painted for the high altar of the cathedral of St Bavo in Ghent. His masterpiece, a triptych of *Christ among the Scribes* for Antwerp Cathedral (1587), remains *in situ*: its figures with their reticent gestures are rather wooden in effect, but the heads indicate the artist's skill for portraiture. Frans I's hand has been recognized in some court portraits (see Van de Velde, 1962–3), which account for his talent in this area. As well as large-scale commissions, Frans I also painted small-scale cabinet pictures (e.g. *Belshazzar's Feast*, Stockholm U., Kstsamml.), a genre continued and perfected by his sons Frans II and Hieronymus II. However, *Christ Carrying the Cross* (1597; Dresden, Staatl. Kstsamml.) is so far the only known signed and dated cabinet picture by Frans I.

BIBLIOGRAPHY

K. Langedijk: 'Ein Bildnis Frans Franckens I gemalt von Frans Pourbus dem Jungeren in den Uffizien zu Florenz', *Mitt. Ksthist. Inst. Florenz*, ix (1959–60), pp. 259–64

J. Bruyn: 'Francisco Frutet or Frans I', *Jb.: Kon. Mus. S. Kst.* (1962–3), pp. 56–74

C. Van de Velde: 'Portretten van Frans Francken den oudere', *Jb.: Kon. Mus. S. Kst.* (1962–3), pp. 175–86

——: *Frans Floris* (Brussels, 1975), pp. 175–85

E. Duverger: *Kunstinventarissen uit de zeventiende eeuw*, i (Brussels, 1984), pp. 389–94 [inv. of the artist's estate drawn up on 15 Feb 1617]

U. Härting: *Frans Francken II* (Freren, 1989), pp. 20–21

(3) Ambrosius Francken I (*b* Herentals, *c.* 1544; *d* Antwerp, 16 Oct 1618). Painter and draughtsman, brother of (1) Hieronymus Francken I. In 1569 he was in the service of the Bishop of Tournai, then in 1570 he is recorded at Fontainebleau, where he may have had the chance to study the works of Rosso Fiorentino and Francesco Primaticcio. By 1573–4 Ambrosius I was back in Antwerp, and at about that time he became a master in the Guild of St Luke; he was appointed an associate deacon of the guild in 1581 and a deacon in 1582. Between 1594 and 1605 he employed four apprentices. Such large altarpieces as the *Miracle of the Loaves and Fishes* (1598) for Antwerp Cathedral, the *Martyrdom of St Jacob* (1608) for the St Jacobskerk and the *Last Supper* for the St Joriskerk in Antwerp (all Antwerp, Kon. Mus. S. Kst.) are stiffly composed of rather muscular figures based on Classical prototypes. The artist's debt to Marten de Vos can be seen in the opulently draped robes and other details. These huge altarpieces influenced ecclesiastical taste, and Ambrosius I's many surviving works attest to his popularity in his own day; he had a considerable impact on his contemporaries.

Some grisailles mentioned in inventories under the name 'Ambrosius Francken' are partly his work, but some are also by his nephew, Ambrosius II. The *Women of Weinsberg* (1600; Weinsberg, Burg Weibertren), a painting by Ambrosius I in shades of red-brown, is notable for the muscular bodies shown in harmonious contrapposto. Of his once copious drawings, only a few preliminary drawings for various print series by Philip Galle, Hans Collaert and the Wierix brothers have survived. The drawings of scenes from the *commedia dell'arte* that are ascribed to Ambrosius I by Mielke and van Tatenhove are also interesting and unusual, showing plays that he may have seen at Fontainebleau in the 1570s.

BIBLIOGRAPHY

N. de Poorter: 'De kunstwerken van het Antwerpse barbier: Een chirurgijnsambachten', *Liber memorialis: 350 jaar Collegium medicum Antverpiense* (Antwerp, 1970), pp. 123–36

H. Mielke: 'Antwerpener Graphik in der 2. Hälfte des 16. Jahrhunderts: Der *Thesaurus veteris et novi testamenti* des Gerard de Jode (1585) und seine Künstler', *Z. Kstgesch.*, xxxviii (1975), pp. 29–83

C. Van de Velde: *Frans Floris* (Brussels, 1975), p. 115

J. van Tatenhove: [review of M. Schapelhouman: *Oude tekeningen in het bezit van de Gemeentemusea van Amsterdam* (Amsterdam, 1979)], *Oud-Holland*, xcvi (1982), pp. 191–7

U. Härting: *Frans Francken II* (Freren, 1989), p. 19

(4) Hieronymus Francken II (*b* Antwerp, *bapt* 12 Sept 1578; *d* Antwerp, 17 March 1623). Painter, son of Frans Francken I. He probably trained with his father and in 1605 was apprenticed to his uncle, Ambrosius I. Hieronymus II became a master of the Antwerp Guild of St Luke in 1607 and was apparently in Paris in 1609. The similarity of style in the figures in the groups of dancers by Frans II and Hieronymus II may possibly be explained by their both having spent some time training in Paris with Hieronymus I, who had already earlier produced variations on this theme. Hieronymus II's signed painting of *Jan Snellinckx's Studio* (1621; Brussels, Mus. A. Anc.) is the starting-point for other ascriptions to him of such pictures of art galleries as the *Art Gallery with the Archdukes Albert and Isabella* (Baltimore, MD, Walters A.G.). The staffage in these interiors is sometimes by as yet unidentified figure painters. Hieronymus II's subject-matter and his figure style have such affinities with works by Frans II that his paintings (e.g. the *Seven Wise and the Seven Foolish Virgins*, Warsaw, N. Mus.) have often been ascribed to his younger brother. The scale of Hieronymus II's figures is sometimes awkward, as in his signed and dated *Horatius Cocles at the Sublicius Bridge* (1620; Antwerp, Kon. Mus. S. Kst.) and his monogrammed gouache drawing of *David and Goliath* (sold Amsterdam, Sotheby's, 25 April 1983, lot 26, as by

Hieronymus Francken I). Hieronymus Francken II also made a speciality of still-lifes, developed from the contrast of the signed painting of the *Rich and the Poor at Table* (1604; Antwerp, Kon. Mus. S. Kst.).

BIBLIOGRAPHY
S. Segal: 'De keus in de kunst: Over de betekenis van zeventiende eeuwse stillevens', *Tableau*, viii/5 (April 1986), pp. 56–60
U. Härting: *Frans Francken II* (Freren, 1989), pp. 167–82

(5) Frans Francken II [the younger] (*b* Antwerp, *bapt* 6 May 1581; *d* Antwerp, 6 May 1642). Painter, son of (2) Frans Francken I. Of all the members of the Francken family, Frans II is the most important and still the most widely known. There are paintings by him in all large public collections in Europe. Besides altarpieces and painted furniture panels, he produced mainly small cabinet pictures with historical, mythological or allegorical themes. Frans II's rank as an artist is not so much derived from his extensive output as from his innovative subject-matter: his depictions of luxuriously decorated *Kunstkammern* and art galleries (*see* CABINET PICTURE, §2; *see also* FRAME, fig. 56) influenced Jan Breughel (i), Rubens and David Teniers (ii), while his early paintings of 'monkeys' kitchens' (allegorical scenes of human vice, such as smoking and gluttony, enacted by monkeys) set the direction for Jan van Kessel and Teniers.

Frans the younger introduced many other unusual themes that later became popular, such as the *Triumphal Procession of Amphitrite* (Brunswick, Herzog Anton Ulrich–Mus.) and *Croesus and Solon* (Vienna, Ksthistmus.). Although all these subjects required either landscape or interior settings, Frans II was only really skilled as a painter of small figures, and his own backgrounds are generally inferior to his figures. Works of a high overall standard tend to be collaborative efforts between Frans II and specialist painters such as the landscapists Abraham Govaerts, Josse de Momper II and Tobias Verhaecht, and the architectural painters Bartholomeus van Bassen, Pieter Neeffs (i) and (ii), Hendrick van Steenwijck (i) and Paul Vredeman de Vries (1567–after 1630). For a long time the work of Frans II was inflated by unsubstantiated ascriptions, but in 1983 Härting used stylistic criteria to propose a revised chronology of his work and to remove many falsely attributed pictures.

1. EARLY CAREER, BEFORE *c.* 1620. Frans II presumably served his apprenticeship in the studio of his father, but it is probable that he also trained in Paris with his uncle Hieronymus I, perhaps at the same time as his brother, Hieronymus II. In 1605 Frans II became a master in the Antwerp Guild of St Luke, of which he served as deacon in 1616. Records show that he worked directly for the art dealer Christian van Immerzeel, who sold paintings to Spain. In van Immerzeel's lists of works for sale, replicas and copies as well as originals of works by Frans II are mentioned. The attribution of weaker works is thus made even more difficult by the existence of innumerable contemporary works from his studio. Frans II registered only one apprentice, but in addition to his own sons he certainly employed his sons-in-law and other apprentices and must have been absolved from registering them.

It is still difficult to form a clear idea of Frans II's early work, as there are no dated works before 1600. Few signed

1. Frans Francken II: *Kunstkammer of Nicolaas Rockox*, oil on panel, 623×965 mm, 1630–35 (Munich, Alte Pinakothek)

2. Frans Francken II: *Israelites after Crossing the Red Sea*, oil on panel, 605×1050 mm, 1621 (Hamburg, Hamburger Kunsthalle)

paintings can be dated before the turn of the century on stylistic grounds. Among the exceptions is the *Crucifixion* (Hannover, Niedersächs. Landesmus.), based on a missing *Crucifixion* by Pieter Breughel (i). With the *Abduction of Helen*, formerly on the French art market (ex-Gal. A. St Honoré, Paris, 1986), Frans II tackled a completely different subject, again basing his work on a model, this time a drawing by Nicolò Dell'Abate. Both of these early examples of Frans II's work carry the abbreviated signature *den jon F. Franck*, meaning 'the younger'. (He sometimes used the signature *d. o. Franck*, meaning 'the elder', from *c.* 1621, rather than from 1616, the year of his father's death, as was previously supposed.) In his early work Frans II showed a predilection for depicting the nude, as can be seen in the *Last Judgement* (Stuttgart, Staatsgal.). His unusual scenes of a *Witches' Sabbath* (e.g. 1606; London, V&A) were a speciality of the first two decades of the 17th century. Frans II and his brother Hieronymus II seem to have been the only two painters who translated this subject, previously known only in the graphic arts, into painting.

Frans Francken II was also the inventor of the composition known as the 'monkeys' kitchen'; this genre, which was subsequently widely disseminated by Teniers, was already fully developed in Francken's work in the first decade of the 17th century, for example the *Monkeys Playing Draughts* and *Monkeys at the Barber's* (both before 1610; Schwerin, Staatl. Mus.).

Frans II's earliest paintings of art collections date from 1612 or before; a typical example shows an interior with numerous paintings and scholars sitting before them in discussion (1612; sold Sotheby's, London, 19 April 1967, lot 112, see Härting, no. A376). Such pictures of interiors usually contain a moralizing message, which is conveyed by means of the subjects of the 'pictures within the picture'.

In one example, the *Interior of a Gallery with Iconoclastic Donkeys* (e.g. *c.* 1615–18; Rome, Pal. Barberini; *see* CABINET PICTURE, fig. 2), connoisseurs of art are juxtaposed with the idiots who destroy art; in others the *vita voluptuosa* is contrasted with the recognition of Christian redemption, but the paintings depicted are always used didactically to point to the meaning of the picture. It is rare that the collection depicted was one that actually existed; one exception is the *Kunstkammer of Nicolaas Rockox* (see fig. 1), but even here there is an allusion to humanistic discrimination in collecting, as reflected in the realistic reproduction of the objects and the representation of the Five Senses. A moralizing purpose was also intended in Frans II's depictions of companies of dancers, like those earlier portrayed by his uncle Hieronymus I. Frans II's masked dancers or pictures of conflagrations were meant to warn against the wickedness of pleasure and of the inevitable outcome of such dissipation.

2. MATURE CAREER, *c.* 1620 AND AFTER. Frans II's early palette of green, olive and red-brown shades was replaced from the 1620s by a bright, cool colour spectrum. There was also a change in his method of applying colour. While he had previously used a thick impasto, from *c.* 1630 he changed to using a glaze composed of more fluid binding oils, and several transparent layers, sometimes of different colours, were superimposed, giving the garments worn by his small figures a gauzy sheen. The *Israelites after Crossing the Red Sea* was a favourite subject that appeared

in a variety of compositions, some of which were subsequently often copied. The most subtle version of the subject was executed in collaboration with the landscapist Tobias Verhaecht (1621; see fig. 2). The *Meeting of Jacob and Joseph* (Essen, priv. col., see Härting, no. A9), which has a landscape background by Abraham Govaerts and animals by Hans Jordaens III, is nonetheless a competent work. Francken's figures animate the landscape on a natural scale: for once they are not tiny staffage adjuncts but rank on equal terms with the landscape. The variety of the garments, materials and textures and the harmony of the colours, in relation both to each other and to the landscape, compensate for the artist's stock repertory of faces. Isocephaly (where all the figures are of roughly the same height) is typical of Frans II's multi-figured scenes. Another hallmark are his rather well-modelled horses, with their animated eyes.

Frans II remained productive during the last decade of his life, and he also continued to treat a great variety of subjects until late in his career, though more briefly than in the narratively rich compositions of the 1620s. In the paintings executed during and after the 1630s the moralizing messages ceased to be apparent, and he gave a noticeably stronger emphasis to genre elements. At the same time his colours became more subdued, with ochre predominating, and the brushstrokes more fleeting. One unusual technique that he employed late in his career, following in the footsteps of Gillis Mostaert, occurs in compositions with painted grisaille scenes within the main picture, giving the work the appearance of an illuminated manuscript, as in the *Last Judgement* (Stuttgart, Staatsgal.) and the *Prodigal Son* (1633; Paris, Louvre).

BIBLIOGRAPHY
S. Speth-Holterhoff: *Les Peintres flamands de cabinets d'amateurs* (Brussels, 1957), pp. 65–96
F. C. Legrand: *Les Peintres flamands de genre au XVIIe siècle* (Brussels, 1963), pp. 25–39
H. Vlieghe: 'Een drieluik en twee beschilderde sacristiedeuren van Frans Francken', *Jb.: Kon. Mus. S. Kst.* (1968), pp. 157–76
M. Díaz Padrón: 'Frans Francken II en la catedral de Sevilla: Algunas consideraciones a su obra en España', *Goya*, 129 (1975), pp. 168–75
Rubens e la pittura fiamminga del seicento (exh. cat. by D. Bodart, Florence, Pitti, 1977), pp. 126–35
Le Siècle de Rubens dans les collections publiques françaises (exh. cat., Paris, Grand Pal., 1977–8), pp. 88–93
U. Härting: *Studien zur Kabinettbildmalerei des Frans Francken II: Ein repräsentativer Werkkatalog* (Hildesheim, 1983) [with extensive bibliog. and illus.]
J. Müller Hofstede: 'Non saturatur oculus visu': Zur *Allegorie des Gesichts* von Peter Paul Rubens und Jan Breughel I', *Wort und Bild in der niederländischen Kunst und Literature des 16. und 17. Jahrhunderts* (Erftstadt, 1984), pp. 243–89
U. Härting: *Frans Francken II* (Freren, 1989)
——: 'Fragen an eine "Kreuzerrichtung"—mit dem heiligen Bavo?', *Niederdt. Beitr. Kstgesch.*, xxx (1991), pp. 97–118
——: 'Doctrina und pietas, über frühe Galeriebilder', *Jb.: Kon. Mus. S. Kst.* (1993), pp. 95–133

(6) Frans Francken III (*b* Antwerp, 1607; *d* Antwerp, *bur* 4 Sept 1667). Painter, son of (5) Frans Francken II. He was elected a master in the Antwerp Guild of St Luke only in 1639 and became a deacon in 1656–7. Like his father, he signed his pictures with the abbreviation *den jon*, so that style is the only basis for distinguishing between the two artists. Frans III was said to have been given the nickname 'Rubens-Francken' by his contemporaries, although the oldest record of this nickname is 1883 (Van

den Branden). However, it is quite inappropriate as Frans III was merely an inferior imitator of Frans II. Even though his work must be assessed mainly on the basis of the staffage figures he painted for the church interiors of Pieter Neeffs (i), the nickname is misleading as any influence of Rubens is undetectable. The signed *Scene with Company* (Salzburg, Residenzgal.) shows compositional borrowings from his father and elements of Dutch genre painting; the figures, however, are less skilful and solid than those of his father and more coarsely executed. Frans III's lack of success is demonstrated by the fact that in 1656 he had to sell the house he had inherited from his father and move into lodgings in Antwerp. Some church interiors previously ascribed to Frans II (e.g. London, Wallace) are actually collaborative works by Frans III and Neeffs.

BIBLIOGRAPHY
F. J. Van den Branden: *Geschiedenis der Antwerpse schilderschool* (Antwerp, 1883), p. 614
URSULA HÄRTING

Franckenberg, Conrait von. *See* KUENE VON DER HALLEN, KONRAD.

Franckenstein, Goll van. *See* GOLL VAN FRANCKENSTEIN.

Franco, (Giovanni) Battista [Baptista Veneziano; il Semolei] (*b* Venice, ?1510; *d* Venice, 1561). Italian painter, engraver and draughtsman. Giorgio Vasari, who knew Franco well and who is the chief source for his life, claimed that Franco was born in 1498; however, later writers placed his birth in 1510, and the latter date seems more likely. Although Venetian by birth, by the age of 20 Franco was in Rome, where he devoted himself to making drawings after the Antique and particularly after the works of Michelangelo; he was one of the first to copy the frescoes in the Sistine Chapel. At this date he invariably worked in pen and made no original drawings. However, he subsequently made his own, more spontaneous studies, such as the *Man in a Cloak* (*c.* 1557–61; London, BM), in pen and wash over black chalk, and a total of about 100 drawings by his hand are now known. He also made many prints, often combining etching with engraving, as in *St Jerome* (*c.* 1554), printed from an enormous single plate (872×480 mm), showing an energetic, muscular saint at his devotions. Luigi Lanzi claimed that Franco was the master of Federico Barocci.

Franco first started to paint when Raffaelle da Montelupo secured him a commission to paint decorations on the Ponte Sant'Angelo for the triumphal entry of Emperor Charles V into Rome on 5 April 1536. At the same time he frescoed the Porta San Sebastiano with scenes of ancient Roman history in grisaille. Later the same month he travelled to Florence to work on decorations for the Emperor's entry there; he also collaborated with Vasari on the decoration of Palazzo Medici for the arrival of Margaret of Austria, the future wife of Duke Alessandro de' Medici, in June 1536. While making drawings after Michelangelo's Medici tombs in S Lorenzo, Florence, he met Bartolomeo Ammanati, who later housed Franco and Bartolommeo della Gatta at Urbino.

After Duke Alessandro's assassination (1537), his successor, Cosimo de' Medici, made Franco his personal painter and commissioned him to paint a triple portrait of *Pope Clement VII, Cardinal Ippolito de' Medici and Duke Alessandro de' Medici* (untraced). Franco based the likenesses on portraits by Sebastiano del Piombo, Titian and Jacopo Pontormo respectively (Vasari). He also made a painted copy (Florence, Casa Buonarroti) after Michelangelo's cartoon of *Noli me tangere* (untraced), then in the Medici collection. Also for Cosimo he painted the *Allegory of the Battle of Montemurlo* (Florence, Pitti), a badly organized composition, with figures directly copied from Michelangelo's design of the *Rape of Ganymede*. In June of 1539 he decorated a triumphal arch (destr.) at the Porta al Prato, Florence, for the wedding of the Duke to Eleonora of Toledo. Together with Ridolfo Ghirlandaio and Michele Tosini, he frescoed the cloister of the Madonna delle Vertighe near Monte Sansavino in the Valdichiana with scenes from the *Life of St Joseph* in grisaille.

By 1541 Franco was back in Rome, where he copied Michelangelo's *Last Judgement* soon after its unveiling in October. He also frescoed the loggia of the palace (destr.) of Cardinal Francesco Cornaro. His fresco of the *Arrest of St John the Baptist* (*c.* 1541–5) in S Giovanni Decollato, Rome, was described by Vasari as ill-proportioned and badly coloured. It is composed of elements taken from Michelangelo's works combined without thought of context or dramatic significance.

In 1545–6 Franco frescoed the vault of the choir of Urbino Cathedral with the *Assumption of the Virgin* (destr.); the work disappointed Guidobaldo II della Rovere, Duke of Urbino, because it failed to equal the quality of Franco's preparatory drawings, and he delayed its payment. Thinking Franco's skills were better suited to working on a small scale, the Duke commissioned him to make designs for maiolica produced at Casteldurante; a typical example is a plate with *Moses Striking the Rock* (London, V&A).

On 15 September 1547, Franco was commissioned to paint 14 small panels of scenes from the *Life of Christ* for Osimo Cathedral; although heavily dependent on Michelangelo, he tried to create dramatic effects through his use of light. In early 1548, Franco made decorations for the entry into Urbino of Guidobaldo and Vittoria Farnese after their wedding (Feb 1548); he then painted a Raphaelesque altarpiece of the *Virgin and Child with Saints* for S Venanzio, Fabriano (*in situ*); after returning to Rome with Ammanati, *c.* 1549, he painted scenery for the company of actors of the poet Giovanni Andrea dell'Anguillara. In 1550, with Girolamo Siciolante, he decorated the façade of the palace of Cardinal Federico Cesi with the coat of arms of Julius III (destr.); the same year he painted a fresco cycle of scenes from the *Life of the Virgin*, figures of Prophets and sibyls, and the *Crucifixion* in S Maria sopra Minerva.

After another period in Urbino, Franco returned to his native Venice, probably *c.* 1552, certainly by 1554. There he rapidly assimilated Venetian techniques in his use of light and colour while retaining something of the monumental figure style of Michelangelo. Although Vasari considered Franco to be an important exponent of Roman

disegno in Venice, his influence on local painters was not very strong. The altarpiece of the *Baptism* (see fig.) was painted for the family chapel of Ermolao Barbaro, the Patriarch of Aquileia, in S Francesco della Vigna. The large scale of the figures and their rhetorical gestures still owe something to Michelangelo, but the use of line is less harsh than in his earlier works; in two preliminary drawings (both Edinburgh, N.G.) he used a soft chiaroscuro to create light effects. Several other Venetian works, including a *Virgin and Child* in S Giobbe, have been lost.

Franco also did decorative painting in Venice: he painted the stuccowork designed by Alessandro Vittoria on the Scala d'Oro (destr.) in the Doge's Palace; and for the Libreria Marciana from 1556 onwards, he painted ceiling tondi of allegorical subjects and two *Philosophers* on the walls, for which the British Museum *Man in a Cloak* may have been a study. He also painted 48 panels on the ceiling of the Sala dell'Estate (destr.) of the Fondaco dei Tedeschi (6 preserved, Venice, Correr) and the Sala delle Mariegole in the Procuratie Nuove. A lunette in the *salone* of the Palazzo Grimani at S Maria Formosa is also attributed to him. Finally, he decorated several buildings designed by Andrea Palladio, including the Palazzo Chiericati, Vicenza, and the Villa Malcontenta. His last work,

Battista Franco: *Baptism*, oil on panel, 3.4×1.9 m, *c.* 1555 (Venice, S Francesco della Vigna)

like the Villa Malcontenta left unfinished at his death, was the decoration of the Grimani Chapel in S Francesco della Vigna, Venice, for the Patriarch Giovanni Grimani; there he frescoed the vault with Virtues and angels in geometric compartments divided by elaborate stucco decoration, a selfconsciously Roman, classicizing work. The decoration was completed by Federico Zuccaro.

BIBLIOGRAPHY

Bolaffi; Thieme–Becker
G. Vasari: *Vite* (1550, rev. 2/1568); ed. G. Milanesi (1878–85), vi, p. 571
B. Berenson: *The Drawings of the Florentine Painters*, 2 vols (London, 1903, rev. 2/Chicago, 1938)
M. Pittaluga: *L'incisione italiana nel cinquecento* (Milan, 1930)
W. R. Rearick: 'Battista Franco and the Grimani Chapel', *Saggi & Mem. Stor. A.*, ii (1958–9), pp. 105–39
N. Ivanoff: 'La Scala d'Oro del Palazzo Ducale di Venezia', *Crit. A.*, viii (1961), pp. 27–41
L. S. Richards: 'Drawings by Battista Franco', *Bull. Cleveland Mus. A.* (1965), pp. 107–12
S. J. Freedberg: *Painting in Italy, 1500–1600*, Pelican Hist. A. (Harmondsworth, 1971, rev. 2/1983), pp. 484–6, 494, 539, 632, 714
L. Grumiero Salomoni: 'Battista Franco nelle Marche', *A. Ven.*, xxvi (1972), pp. 237–45
J. Lessman: 'Battista Franco disegnatore di maioliche', *Faenza*, ii (1976), pp. 27ff
H. Zerner: *Italian Artists of the Sixteenth Century: Palma, Rota, School of Fontainebleau*, 33 [XVI/ii] of *The Illustrated Bartsch*, ed. W. Strauss (New York, 1978–9), pp. 156–258
Palladio e la Maniera (exh. cat. by V. Sgarbi, Vicenza, S Corona, 1980)
J. A. Gere and P. Pouncey: *Italian Drawings in the Department of Prints and Drawings in the British Museum: Artists Working in Rome, c. 1550 to c. 1640*, London, BM cat., 2 vols (London, 1983), pp. 80–94

MARIA SICA

Franco, Giacomo (*b* Verona, 11 Feb 1818; *d* Venice, 28 June 1895). Italian architect. The self-taught son of wealthy parents, he drew the buildings of old Verona while working in an architectural studio there, and contributed illustrations to Jules Gailhabaud's *L'Architecture du Ve au XVIIe siècle* (Paris, 1858–9). In his practice he demonstrated fluent use of early Christian to late Renaissance styles. He achieved regional fame for his public buildings, including the restoration of the Loggia del Consiglio (1871–91) in Verona, and the monumental Ossario (1879) at the battlefield site (1866) in neighbouring Custoza, a massive obelisk atop an octagonal chapel housing the remains of the war dead. He also designed villas on the Adriatic and on Lake Garda. His best-known work was the cathedral at Lonigo (1875–95), near Venice, a restrained but thoroughly 19th-century integration of Romanesque Lombardic elements that recalls the 12th-century church of S Zeno Maggiore at Verona. Camillo Boito praised it as the best design of its time and place. In 1865 Franco was made an honorary member of the Accademia di Belle Arti in Florence. Late in his life he taught at the Accademia in Venice and became director of it shortly before his death.

BIBLIOGRAPHY

Thieme–Becker
E. Lavagnino: *L'arte moderna dai neoclassici ai contemporanei* (1956), v of *Storia dell'arte classica e italiana* (Turin, 1926–56), pp. 565ff

GRETCHEN G. FOX

Franco dei Russi [Rossi] (*b* ?Mantua; *fl c.* 1453–82). Italian illuminator. Although he may have been in Ferrara as early as 1453, he is first unambiguously recorded in 1455, in the contract for the sumptuously decorated Bible of Borso d'Este (1455–61; Modena, Bib. Estense, MS.

V.G. 12, lat. 422–3). Este court records refer to Franco 'da Mantova', but it is not obvious where he received his earliest training. His early style, in the Bible illuminations, reveals a certain courtly quality and naturalism of detail associated with a Lombard background, but these characteristics are tempered by a degree of sobriety. Figures tend to be large-scale, their heavy garments falling in long, straight patterns or gathered into broader, broken folds. Landscapes are schematic and airless, often marked by relatively dense foliage and wavelike hills. His palette is cool and opaque. It is generally agreed that Franco left Ferrara early in the 1460s to work in the Veneto, where he remained until 1471 or 1472. During this decade his style changed decisively, taking on the humanistic tone, crispness of figural definition, colour saturation and hardness of landscape forms typical of Andrea Mantegna. While working in the Veneto, Franco may also have played a role in the development of the architectural frontispiece. This motif appears in a copy of Bernardo Bembo's *Oratio gratulatoria* for Doge Cristoforo Moro (London, BL, Add. MS. 14787, fol. 6*v*). Autograph images that most clearly define Franco's style in the 1460s and very early 1470s include a cutting representing the triumph of a scholar or humanist (London, BL, Add. MS. 20916, fol. 1*v*) and the frontispiece of a copy of the Bible in Italian printed in Venice in 1471 by Vindelinus de Spira (Wolfenbüttel, Herzog August Bib., Cod. Slg 151, 2°, vol. i, fol. 1*v*). In the early 1470s Franco moved to Urbino; he has been identified as the illuminator 'maestro francho da ferara' recorded as a member of the household of Federigo II da Montefeltro in a list prepared after the Duke's death in 1482. Franco was probably one of the illuminators of a copy of Dante's *Divine Comedy* executed for Federigo between 1474 and 1482 (Rome, Vatican, Bib. Apostolica, MS. Urb. Lat. 365).

BIBLIOGRAPHY

M. Bonicatti: 'Aspetti dell'illustrazione del libro nell'ambiente padovano del secondo "400"', *Riv. A.*, xxxii (1957), pp. 107–49
M. Levi D'Ancona: 'Contributi al problema di Franco dei Russi', *Commentari*, xi (1960), pp. 33–45
G. Mariani Canova: *La miniatura veneta del rinascimento, 1450–1500* (Venice, 1969)
The Painted Page: Italian Renaissance Book Illumination, 1450–1550 (exh. cat., ed. J. J. G. Alexander; London, RA, 1994)

CHARLES M. ROSENBERG

François, Claude [Frère Luc] (*b* Amiens, 1614; *d* Paris, 17 May 1685). French painter. He trained in the studio of Simon Vouet after 1627 and in 1634 travelled to Rome, where he was influenced by the work of Raphael and Guido Reni and by such artists as Girolamo Muziano. In 1635 he painted a copy (Longeau, parish church) of Jacopo Bassano's *Assumption* (Rome, S Luigi dei Francesi). He returned to Paris in 1639 and worked for Pierre Sublet de Noyers and Anne of Austria on decorative schemes at the Louvre and elsewhere. In 1641 he joined the reformed Franciscan order of the Recollects in Paris, taking his vows as Frère Luc in 1645. From this point on François's works were largely confined to subjects taken from the life of St Francis, painted for Recollect monasteries in Paris, Melun, Rouen, Châlons-sur-Marne, Sézanne and elsewhere. Those that survive show François to have been an honest, if not particularly inventive artist, who had memorized what he had seen in Italy. Among his more successful works are *Christ Granting St Francis Partial Indulgence*, *The Death of St Francis* (both 1679; Paris, St Jean–St François) and *Pope Nicholas V Discovering the Tomb of St Francis* (Sézanne, Hosp.).

Early in 1670, for unknown reasons, François travelled to Quebec, where he painted a number of pictures with religious themes, such as the *Assumption* (Quebec, Gen. Hosp.) and the *Guardian Angel* (Quebec, Mus. Qué.). He also worked as an architect, rebuilding the monastery of Quebec and drawing up plans for the Quebec seminary. He returned to France late in 1671. His last known painting is *Our Lady of the Rosary*, painted in 1680 for the chapel of the Salpêtrière, Paris (*in situ*). His pupils included Roger de Piles, Claude Saint-Paul [Simpol] (1666–1716), and Arnould de Vuez.

BIBLIOGRAPHY
G. Morisset: *La Vie et l'oeuvre du Frère Luc* (Quebec, 1944)
F.-M. Gagnon and N. Cloutier: *Premiers Peintres de la Nouvelle-France*, i (Quebec, 1976), pp. 55–115
M.-T. Laurelhe: 'Le Frère Luc (1614–1685): Récollet, peintre de saint François', *Bull. Soc. Hist. A. Fr.* (1982), pp. 49–57

THIERRY BAJOU

François, Guy [Francesco, Guido] (*b* Le Puy, Haute-Loire, *c.* 1578; *d* Le Puy, 1650). French painter. He is documented (under the Italian form of his name) in Rome in 1608, both in the archives of the Accademia di S Luca and in parish records. He presumably returned to France before 1613, for at that date he executed a painting (untraced) for the church of St Pierre, Montpezat, Tarn-et-Garonne. From 1614 to 1616 he is documented as working on paintings (untraced) for St-Pierre-de-Monastier in Le Puy. His earliest surviving painting is the *Virgin and Child with Two Saints* (1615; Le Puy, Mus. Crozatier). There are two signed and dated paintings of 1619, both in Le Puy: the *Virgin of the Rosary* in St Laurent and a *Crucifixion with Two Marys and St John* in the church of the Collège; the former church also has François's the *Incredulity of St Thomas*. By *c.* 1620 he had established a busy workshop with many apprentices. At some point between 1623 and 1626 he was in Toulouse; he is recorded again in Le Puy in 1627–8, 1636 and 1638. In 1630 he was in Riom and in 1633–4 in Montpellier. Many signed and dated paintings by François survive from the years 1619–46, all of them large altarpieces. Apparently official painter to the Jesuits in Le Puy, he also worked regularly for other religious orders in the region. His style is similar to that of Caravaggio, tempered with the influence of Guido Reni and Carlo Saraceni, whose studios he must have frequented in Rome: the influence of Saraceni is particularly evident in the gentle lighting of his paintings, as well as in the female facial types and the focus on anecdotal detail. Nicolson reattributed Saraceni's famous *St Cecilia* (Rome, Pal. Corsini) to François; and Rosenberg (see 1982 exh. cat.) similarly gave a *Holy Family in St Joseph's Workshop* (Hartford, CT, Wadsworth Atheneum), previously attributed to Saraceni, to François. He was one of a number of French painters who established a form of Caravaggism in the provinces.

BIBLIOGRAPHY
Guy François (Le Puy, 1578?–1650) (exh. cat., ed. M.-F. Pérez; Le Puy, Mus. Crozatier; Saint-Etienne, Mus. A. & Indust.; 1974)
M.-F. Pérez: 'Deux Nouvelles Attributions à Guy François (1578?–1650)', *Inf. Hist. A.*, xx/5 (1975), pp. 220–24
D. Ternois: 'Guy François (Le Puy, Saint-Etienne 1974)', *Inf. Hist. A.*, xx/3 (1975), pp. 137–45
M. Pettex Sabarot: 'Le Puy, Musée Crozatier, Guy François: Attributions et propositions à propos d'un ensemble de toiles franciscaines', *Rev. Louvre*, 5–6 (1979), pp. 414–26
B. Nicolson: *The International Caravaggesque Movement* (London, 1979); rev. as *Caravaggism in Europe*, ed. L. Vertova (Turin, 1990)
La Peinture française du XVIIe siècle dans les collections américaines (exh. cat., ed. P. Rosenberg; Paris, Grand Pal.; New York, Met.; Chicago, IL, A. Inst.; 1982), pp. 246–7

François, Jean-Charles (*b* Nancy, 4 May 1717; *d* Paris, 22 March 1769). French engraver and publisher. After studying painting at Nancy, he started work in 1733 in Dijon as an engraver of coats of arms. From 1740 to 1748 he worked as an engraver in Lyon with the publisher Robert-Menge Pariset, who in 1748 brought out his *Principes de dessein faciles et dans le goût du crayon* (Pognon and Bruand, nos 1–12). François then established himself in Paris, where he published (1751–3) volumes of engravings by the architect Emmanuel Héré (PB 227–91) of the châteaux in Lorraine belonging to Stanislav I, King of Poland. François was a skilled and inventive printmaker, who is best known for being the first in France to practise engraving in the crayon manner (*see* CRAYON MANNER, §2) in order to imitate chalk drawings. To achieve this, he employed, in turn, the burin to make double or triple lines (1740–48); a plate prepared by the use of a mezzotint rocker (1756); etching on top of a varnish ground prepared with various tools (1757); and soft-ground etching re-worked with tools (1758). In the *Rape of Ganymede* (1758; PB 107), after François Boucher, he also experimented with a tonal process known as *lavis*, a precursor of the aquatint. He made, after old or contemporary masters, more than 300 plates, most of which were teaching examples. The engraving that François made in 1767 of the portrait of *Dr François Quesnay* (PB 108), after Jean-Martial Frédou (*c.* 1711–95), combined all his techniques and epitomizes his expertise. Although he received little support from official circles, he finally obtained in 1757 a pension and the post of Graveur des Desseins du Cabinet du Roi. He worked for a time with his rival Gilles Demarteau; Louis-Marin Bonnet was his pupil.

PRINTS
Principes de dessein faciles et dans le goût du crayon (Lyon, 1748)

BIBLIOGRAPHY
J. Hérold: *Gravure en manière de crayon: Jean-Charles François* (Paris, 1931)
——: 'Supplément au catalogue de Jean-Charles François', *Louis-Marin Bonnet* (Paris, 1935), pp. 1–2
E. Pognon and Y. Bruand: *Inventaire du fonds français: Graveurs du XVIIIe siècle*, Paris, Bib. N., Cab. Est. cat., ix (Paris, 1962), pp. 293–354 [PB]

MADELEINE BARBIN

François, (Pierre-)Joseph(-Célestin) (*b* Namur, 29 March 1759; *d* Brussels, 13 March 1851). Flemish painter and draughtsman. He learnt drawing in Charleroi from Pierre-Balthasar de Blocq (1729–95), who later sent him to Antwerp to study with Andries Cornelis Lens. François also attended the Antwerp academy (1773–6), where he was taught by Guillaume-Jacques Herreyns. After leaving the academy, he received portrait commissions and also cooperated with Lens on a *History of Bacchus* series (Brussels, Mus. A. Anc.) for the Salon Stevens.

François was in Italy from 1778 to 1781; there he studied the work of Raphael, Annibale Carracci, Guido Reni, Domenichino and Guercino. In 1780 he visited Naples and saw the ruins of Paestum, and the following year he travelled to Vienna, where he spent six months. He returned to the southern Netherlands in 1782, sometime after which he executed a series of four paintings, the *History of Venus*, for Baron de Vinck. Three red-chalk studies for this series are known (ex-art market, Paris, 1974; see exh. cat., p. 124). In 1789 he again visited Rome. His journal records about a hundred sketches from nature, of which only four are known. He also painted landscapes such as *Bridge at Teverone* (?1790; Brussels, priv. col., see exh. cat., p. 265).

In 1792 François returned to Brussels, where he completed his most important painting, *Marius Seated in the Ruins of Carthage* (*c.* 1791–4; Brussels, Mus. A. Anc.), which reflects his interest in Neo-classicism, tempered by naturalism, and his liking for forms with distinct outlines and a definite physical presence. He became Professor of Drawing at the Ecole Centrale du Département de la Dyle. He also taught at the Académie des Beaux-Arts in Brussels, where his pupils included François-Joseph Navez. Among the portraits of this period are his *Self-portrait* and that of his wife, *Marie-Françoise François* (both 1799; Brussels, priv. col., see exh. cat., p. 408). During the period of French rule in the southern Netherlands, he painted a series of somewhat sickly and insipid miniatures of mythological subjects and executed a number of drawings for engravings of political allegories; it seems likely that he visited France at this period. François's last works include small devotional paintings inspired by 17th-century Flemish work, and drawings and paintings of sites and monuments around Brussels. In 1810 he was a founder-member of the Société pour l'Encouragement des Beaux-Arts in Brussels. His son Ange François was also a painter.

UNPUBLISHED SOURCES

Brussels, Bib. Royale Albert 1er [MS. journal: *Deuxième Livret, ou suite à la note des tableaux que j'ai peints depuis mon premier voyage d'Italie, c'est-à-dire depuis l'année 1782*]
Brussels, priv. col. [MS.: *Notes pour servir à mon second voyage en Italie en 1790*]

BIBLIOGRAPHY

M. S. Van der Burght and R. Van der Burght: *Joseph François, peintre belge: Emule de David, 1759–1851* (Brussels, 1948)
B. Issaverdens: 'Pierre-Joseph-Célestin François', *1770–1830: Autour du Néo-classicisme en Belgique* (exh. cat., Brussels, Mus. Ixelles, 1985–6), pp. 120–33, 265, 408

BERNADETTE THOMAS

François, Lucien (*b* Brussels, 22 June 1894; *d* Brussels, 23 March 1983). Belgian architect, furniture designer and teacher. He was self-taught and acquired most of his knowledge in the architectural office of Fernand Bodson. In 1919 he went to Sicily under the auspices of the Belgian company that was installing the tramway in Palermo and built a dozen villas on the Mondello Lido. Upon his return to Belgium, he was asked by Louis Van der Swaelmen and Jean-Jules Eggericx to take part in the construction of the garden cities Le Logis and Floréal at Watermael-Boitsfort, Brussels, where he built some 50 houses (1921–2). François became one of the principal representatives of the lyrical tendency in the modern movement in Belgium. He entered and won a number of competitions, including one that led to his commission to build a workers' village (1922–4) for a granite company in Saint-Pierre de Plesguen in Brittany, France, that was based on regional inspirations. His mature work was devoted mainly to building private houses in Brussels and Brabant, some of which were strongly influenced by Frank Lloyd Wright, for example the villa of Dr Libbrecht (1927) at Rixensart. At the same time he was involved with furniture design and in 1939 he succeeded Antoine Pompe at the Institut Supérieur des Arts Décoratifs de la Cambre, Brussels, where he taught the furniture course for 20 years. His last major work was the design of a district of an old city for the Exposition Universelle et Internationale (1958) in Brussels. He drew inspiration for this project from the most interesting old streets, squares and buildings in Belgium.

BIBLIOGRAPHY

A. Van Loo: 'Lucien François, au-delà de l'intimité', *Archvs Archit. Mod.*, 12 (1977), pp. 41–61

ANNE VAN LOO

François, Maître (*fl c.* 1460–80). French illuminator. He was one of the leading artists of the school that dominated book illumination in Paris during the second half of the 15th century. His only documented work—and thus the basis for the reconstruction of his oeuvre—is a two-volume French translation of St Augustine's *City of God* (*c.* 1469–73; Paris, Bib. N., MSS fr. 18–19) bearing the arms of Charles de Gaucourt, Governor of Amiens and appointed Lieutenant General of Paris in 1472. Robert Gaguin, a noted scholar and general of the order of the Trinitarians, wrote to de Gaucourt in August 1473:

> We gave to the excellent painter Franciscus the outlines of the pictures and the schemes of images which you ordered to be painted for the books of the *City of God*, and he has finished the work as he began it with the most perfect craftsmanship. Indeed, he is such an accomplished artist that Apelles would rightly have taken second place to him.

A reference to a 'Maître François enlumineur' found by de Laborde in the inventory dated 1473 of the household of Charles II, Comte du Maine, has led to Gaguin's Franciscus becoming known as Maître François. While Franciscus worked for patrons in the Maine region, there is no conclusive evidence that he is identical with Charles II's resident illuminator, who is also recorded in the Comte's service in Provence in 1481. This seems to indicate a long-serving member of the household, a position incompatible with large scale book production in Paris (Reynauld, 1993 exh. cat.).

Maître François, the illuminator of de Gaucourt's *City of God*, can be distinguished from two other artistic personalities within this Parisian school: his predecessor the MASTER OF JEAN ROLIN (*see* MASTERS, ANONYMOUS, AND MONOGRAMMISTS, §I), active *c.* 1440–65, and the later chef d'atelier (*fl.c.* 1480–95), variously called the Chief Associate of Maître François, Jacques de Besançon or the MASTER OF JACQUES DE BESANÇON (*see* MASTERS, ANONYMOUS, AND MONOGRAMMISTS, §I). Some 50 manuscripts illuminated by Maître François are extant, two-thirds of which are Books of Hours; he also illuminated liturgical books and executed large and detailed illustrative

Maître François: *Tower of Babel*, 245×237 mm, miniature from St Augustine: *City of God, c.* 1469–73 (Paris, Bibliothèque Nationale, MS. fr. 19, fol. 81*v*)

programmes for Classical, theological and moral texts, usually in French translation. He was much patronized by members of the court and aristocracy in Paris, and by the courts of Anjou and Maine. His commissions include: a *Compendium historial* (Paris, Bib. N., MS. fr. 9186) for Jacques d'Armagnac, a French translation of the *Memorabilia* by Valerius Maximus (London, BL., Harley MSS 4373–5) for Philippe de Commynes, a French translation of Jacopo da Voragine's *Golden Legend* (Paris, Bib. N., MSS 244–5; with the Master of Jacques de Besançon) for Antoine de Chourses and Katherine de Coëtivy and a *City of God* (Paris, Bib. S-Geneviève, MS. 246) for Mathieu Beauvarlet.

Maître François inherited from the Master of Jean Rolin compositional patterns and iconography developed by the Bedford Master in Paris earlier in the century. Certain Netherlandish elements in Maître François's work, some of which have been thought to be reminiscent of Dieric Bouts (Spencer, 1974), were possibly also mediated through the Master of Jean Rolin, since it is thought that this artist came to Paris either from the north or from Burgundy, where he may have worked for Cardinal Jean Rolin II in a milieu influenced by Netherlandish artists (Sterling; Reynaud, 1993 exh. cat.). Maître François's style is distinguished from that of the Master of Jean Rolin by the firm modelling of his figures and the clarity of their pose and gestures; even in crowded scenes there is an emphasis on dramatic interaction (see fig.). The more devotional scenes in Books of Hours are sometimes enlivened by allusions to contemporary drama, such as the mystery play by Arnoul Gréban.

Maître François's compositions are systematically and lucidly structured. While his interior settings are based on many of the conventions of the Bedford Master's workshop, he uses such features as framing coloured marble columns, views of vaulted ceilings, balustrades with pierced openings and stretches of green tiled floors, bounded by brown walls hatched in black, to create a sense of space within which objects and figures are clearly positioned and related to one another. Landscape and external settings are characterized by their stratification of planes into near, middle and far distance. Maître François often used a somewhat strident palette of intense blues, greens, oranges and reds combined with muddy violets, pinks and browns and surfaces liberally highlighted with gold. Sometimes, however, this colour range is strikingly modified by the use of white and grisaille, especially for garments, with shades of white finely modelled in pale mauves and violets. This more restrained and sensitive use of colour reflects the influence of the Touraine panel painter and illuminator Jean Fouquet although there is no proof for the suggestion that he was Fouquet's son François (Thuasne).

The calendars of a group of Books of Hours illuminated by Maître François in the early 1470s, which employ this grisaille technique, indicate that they were made for patrons in the diocese of Angers and Le Mans. They include the Wharncliffe Hours (Melbourne, N.G. Victoria, MS. Felton 1; London, BL, Egerton MS. 2045; New York, Pierpont Morgan Lib., MS. M. 73) and the Hours of René II of Lorraine (Lisbon, Gulbenkian Mus., MS. L.A. 147). The scribe of the Wharncliffe Hours has been identified as Jehan Dubrueil, who copied and signed the text of the Hours of Jacques de Langeac (also illuminated by Maître François; Lyon, Bib. Mun., MS. 5154) in Paris in 1465. Similar grisaille techniques are also present in the work of the Master of Jean Rolin and his contemporary the Master of Coëtivy.

BIBLIOGRAPHY
Thieme–Becker

P. Durrieu: *Un Grand Enlumineur parisien au XVe siècle: Jacques de Besançon et son oeuvre* (Paris, 1892)
L. Thuasne: 'François Fouquet et les miniatures de la *Cité de Dieu* de Saint Augustin', *Rev. Bib.*, viii (1898), pp. 33–57
L. Thuasne, ed.: *Roberti Gaguini epistolae et orationes* (Paris, 1903), i, p. 225
G. F. Warner: *Valerius Maximus: Miniatures of the School of Jean Fouquet* (London, 1907) [for pls]
A. de Laborde: *Les Manuscrits à peintures de la 'Cité de Dieu' de Saint Augustin* (Paris, 1909), ii, p. 401
R. Beer: 'Les Principaux Manuscrits à peintures de la Bibliothèque impériale de Vienne', *Bull. Soc. Fr. Repr. MSS Peint*, ii (1912), pp. 18–19, 48
H. Y. Thompson: *Illustrations from One Hundred Manuscripts in the Library of H. Y. Thompson* (London, 1915), v, pls XLII–XLVI
S. de Ricci: 'Les Manuscrits de la Collection Henry Yates Thompson', *Bull. Soc. Fr. Repr. MSS Peint.*, x (1926)
E. P. Spencer: *The Maître François and his Atelier* (diss., Cambridge, MA, Harvard U., 1931)
——: 'L'Horloge de sapience', *Scriptorium*, xvii (1963), pp. 277–99; xix (1965), pp. 104–8
M. Manion: *The Wharncliffe Hours: A Study of a Fifteenth-century Prayerbook* (Sydney, 1972)
O. Pächt and D. Thoss: *Französische Schule* (1974), I/i of *Die illuminierten Handschriften und Inkunabeln der österreichischen Nationalbibliothek* (Vienna, 1974–), pp. 80–93, 152–61, figs 142–59, 327–65
E. P. Spencer: 'Dom Luis de Busco's Psalter', *Gatherings in Honor of Dorothy E. Miner* (Baltimore, 1974), pp. 227–40
——: 'Le Lectionnaire du Cardinal Charles II de Bourbon', *Doss. Archéol.*, xvi (1976), pp. 124–9
M. Manion: *The Wharncliffe Hours* (London, 1981) [excellent facs. pls]
The Last Flowering: French Painting in Manuscripts, 1420–1530, from American Collections (exh. cat. by J. Plummer, New York, Pierpont Morgan Lib., 1982), pp. 65–71
M. Manion and V. Vines: *Medieval and Renaissance Illuminated Manuscripts in Australian Collections* (London, 1984), pp. 187–98, pl. 41, figs 214–18
J. Marrow: 'Miniatures inédites de Jean Fouquet: Les Heures de Simon de Varie', *Rev. A.* [Paris], lxvii (1985), pp. 7–32
C. Sterling: *La Peinture médiévale à Paris, 1300–1500*, ii (Paris, 1990)
Les Manuscrits à peintures en France, 1440–1520 (exh. cat. by F. Avril and N. Reynaud, Paris, Bib. N., 1993)
J. H. Marrow: *The Hours of Simon de Varie* (Malibu, 1994)

MARGARET M. MANION

François Ier style [François Premier style; Francis I style; Fr. *Style François Ier*]. Term used to describe the architecture and sculpture of the first phase of the French Renaissance, which coincided with the late rule of Louis XII and the early rule of Francis I (1515–*c*. 1530). The style was revived in the 19th century (*see* RENAISSANCE REVIVAL) for architecture and the decorative arts. In architecture it is a hybrid style characterized by an overlay of imperfectly understood Italian ornamentation on traditional Gothic forms. An important early example is the château of GAILLON (1508–10) built by Cardinal Georges I d'Amboise (*see* AMBOISE, D', (1)); others, built mainly for courtiers and patricians, are the châteaux (or parts of them) at Oiron, Vendeuvre, CHENONCEAUX, BURY, AZAY-LE-RIDEAU and elsewhere. These works feature an adoption of the decorative vocabulary of Milanese Quattrocento architecture, an ornamented mode of pilasters, medallions and grotesques, to which French architects trained in the Flamboyant style readily responded. This style was continued in Francis I's châteaux in the Loire valley, such as BLOIS, where the wing that bears his name (1515–24) has novel Renaissance-style elements: a monumental staircase and double-tiered loggias based on Bramante's at the Vatican. CHAMBORD (1519–1550) has a more Italianate character and monumentality, but its roof has turrets, chimneys and dormers of differing designs in the spirit of Flamboyant style but adorned with Italian architectural motifs. In sculpture the François Ier style was also a highly ornamented hybrid style, exemplified by Girolamo Viscardi's sculptures at the abbey church of La Trinité Fécamp Abbey (1507–8), which is Late Gothic in structure but Italianate in its carved decoration. Major tombs in this style are the tomb of *Louis XII and Anne of Brittany* (1516–31) by Antoine Giusti (1479–1519) and Jean Giusti (1485–1549) in Saint-Denis Abbey (*see* SAINT-DENIS ABBEY, fig. 7), where the disposition of the elements, with the kneeling king and queen above and the *gisants* in an arcaded enclosure, follows tradition, but the tomb's Virtues and Apostles show Florentine influence; and the tomb of *Georges I d'Amboise and Georges II d'Amboise* (begun 1515; Rouen Cathedral; for illustration *see* AMBOISE, D', (1)) by Roulland Le Roux, whose abundant ornamentation and mixture of modes epitomizes the François Ier style.

BIBLIOGRAPHY

A. Blunt: *Art and Architecture in France, 1500–1600*, Pelican Hist. A. (Harmondsworth, 1971, rev. 1982)

W. Prinz and R. G. Kecks: *Das französische Schloss der Renaissance: Form und Bedeutung der Architektur, ihre geschichtlichen und gesellschaftlichen Grundlagen* (Berlin, 1985)

J. Guillaume: 'La Première Renaissance, 1495–1525', *Le Château en France*, ed. J. P. Babelon (Paris, 1986)

JANET COX-REARICK

Francucci, Innocenzo. *See* INNOCENZO DA IMOLA.

Frangk, Jacoff. *See* HAYLMANN, JACOB.

Frank, Jean-Michel (*b* Paris, 1895; *d* New York, March 1941). French designer. He studied at the Lycée Janson de Sailly, Paris, from 1904. In 1915 his two brothers were killed in World War I, followed by his father's suicide and his mother's death in a mental institution. As a result, in 1920 Frank found himself with a substantial family inheritance, enabling him to travel extensively and to move in the élite circles of fashionable Paris. In 1927 he commissioned the French designer–craftsman Adolphe Chanaux (1887–1965) to decorate his apartment, an event that spurred a partnership based on shared viewpoints. Chanaux and Frank accepted several commissions for furniture and interior design, including a spare, all-white apartment interior (1927) for the couturier Elsa Schiaparelli (1890–1973). Frank's fame as an arbiter of French taste spread abroad, and in the same year he decorated the hall and salon of the San Francisco apartment of American businessman Templeton Crocker, in liaison with Jean Dunand, who designed the décor of the remaining rooms. The interiors were featured in the February 1927 issue of American *Vogue* (see Duncan, fig. 82). Frank was a keen judge of scale, form and texture, designing clean-lined, cubic furniture in an array of exotic veneers, including straw marquetry, snake- and sharkskin, undressed kid,

vellum, parchment, cane and gypsum (e.g. armchair veneered in sharkskin, *c.* 1927–9; New York, Barry Friedman priv. col., see Duncan, fig. 78). He advocated uncluttered rooms with neutral colour schemes (earth tones, ochres, cream) and parchment-lined walls, the use of precious woods, hand-sewn leather upholstery and such materials as ivory, rock crystal, quartz or alabaster for sculptural lamp bases and sconces. His interiors were based on classical proportions, stripped of relief ornamentation but enhanced with sumptuous finishes, and Baroque Revival objects modified by Surrealism, notably his moulded plaster wall sconces in the shape of hands holding Roman torches. He commissioned an illustrious group of artists and craftsmen to contribute a range of designs, working with Alberto and Diego Giacometti (table bases, andirons, light fixtures of bronze or plaster), Salvador Dalí (screens and furniture), the architect Emilio Terry (furniture and interior layout) and Christian Bérard (carpet designs). Cabinetmaking, veneering and varnishing were carried out in Paris at Chanaux's workshop on the Rue Montauban with showrooms for display at 140 Faubourg Saint-Honoré. In 1939 Frank left Paris for a brief sojourn in Buenos Aires and from there travelled to New York, where he was offered a lectureship at the School of Fine and Applied Arts. The Paris operation was closed down and later ransacked by the Nazis. In 1941, in a state of depression, he jumped to his death from a New York building. Led by American decorator Billy Baldwin (1903–83), Frank's work was rediscovered by a new generation of interior designers in the late 1970s and 1980s.

BIBLIOGRAPHY

A. Duncan: *Art Deco Furniture: The French Designers* (London, 1984)

P. Bayer: *Art Deco Interiors: Decoration and Design Classics of the 1920s and 1930s* (London, 1990)

Frank, Josef (*b* Baden, nr Vienna, 15 July 1885; *d* Stockholm, 8 Jan 1967). Austrian architect, interior designer, teacher and writer. He studied architecture at the Technische Hochschule, Vienna, and then worked for a year with Bruno Möhring in Berlin. After a study visit to Italy he established himself as an independent architect in Vienna in 1910, building in the period before World War I a number of single-family houses distinguished by highly simplified forms and balanced proportions; examples include the Villa Hoch (1912) and Villa Wassermann (1914), both in Vienna. After the war he taught at the Kunstgewerbeschule, Vienna (1919–25), and collaborated with Adolf Loos and others in the Viennese garden city movement, which was based on English models. He took a leading role in the construction of cooperatively run garden suburbs and also contributed five residential buildings, several storeys high, to Vienna's communal housing scheme, for example Winarskyhof (1924). Frank played a significant role in the propagation of artistic innovation in the early 20th century. As a member of both the Deutscher Werkbund and Österreichischer Werkbund, he took part in many exhibitions, including those at the Weissenhofsiedlung (1927) in Stuttgart and at the Werkbund colony (1932) in Vienna. As Vice-President (1928–32) of the Österreichischer Werkbund he argued for the *Neues Bauen* movement in traditionalist Austria, while warning against exaggerated forms and industrialized techniques of the new doctrine in Germany—a view that was at odds with some of the more dogmatic theories of CIAM, Le Corbusier and the Bauhaus. As an interior designer he created numerous fabric designs, characterized by brightly coloured motifs drawn from a variety of cultures. In 1925 he founded an interior furnishing business, Haus und Garten, in Vienna (*see* AUSTRIA, §VI, 4). In 1933, as a result of increasing politicization in Austria, he settled in Sweden, and worked for the rest of his life for the interior design firm Svenskt Tenn. His fabric and furniture designs contributed to the development of the new Swedish furnishing style that became known internationally as 'Swedish modern'. From 1941 to 1946 he was a teacher at the New School for Social Research, New York. Frank was also a writer, contributing to many journals; for a photograph of him *see* CIAM.

WRITINGS

Architektur als Symbol: Elemente deutschen Neuen Bauens (Vienna, 1931)
ed.: *Die internationale Werkbundsiedlung Wien, 1932* (Vienna, 1932)

BIBLIOGRAPHY

Josef Frank, 1885–1967 (exh. cat. by J. Spalt, H. Czech and E. A. Plischke, Vienna, Hochsch. Angewandte Kst, 1981)

WILFRIED POSCH

Frank, Robert (*b* Zurich, 9 Nov 1924). American photographer and film maker of Swiss birth. He emigrated to New York City in 1947, having worked in the studios of various Swiss photographers and film makers, including that of Michael Wolgensinger (*b* 1913). The small, handmade book, *40 Fotos* (artist's col.) prompted Alexey Brodovitch (1898–1971) of *Harper's Bazaar* to hire the young, unknown photographer. The book included examples of a wide variety of his work and provided evidence of his early skill at juxtaposing images and creating photographic sequences.

Until 1951 Frank remained a regular contributor to *Harper's Bazaar*, where he met the photographer Louis Faurer (*b* 1916), but he also did freelance work for magazines such as *Look*, *Life* and *Fortune*; for his own pleasure he recorded New York with a newcomer's vision, creating images of uncanny insight and poetic spareness. These qualities would remain hallmarks of later work that critics found to be a harsh and unpalatable judgement of prosperous, post-war America. *Macy Parade* (1947; artist's col.), like his other photographs of the late 1940s, demonstrates a clear-cut documentary approach that is still closer to European formalism than to American photography of the period.

While at *Harper's Bazaar*, Frank began a series of photographic journeys that lasted for more than a decade. In 1948 he visited Peru and Bolivia, creating a highly sympathetic portrait of rural Indian life that he presented to Brodovitch, once again in the form of a handmade book. Selections from the series were later printed in the French magazine *Neuf* (1952) and in *Indiens pas morts* (Paris, 1956), both published by Robert Delpire. In 1950 his work was exhibited for the first time at the Museum of Modern Art in New York.

From 1951 until 1953 Frank lived abroad, and his visits to Switzerland, Spain, London and Wales provided new settings for images that were documentary yet at the same time increasingly informal and intimate in approach; one particularly compassionate series is devoted to Welsh miners. He disliked the photojournalistic habit of creating a distinct visual narrative and preferred in all of his series to allow the flow and content of the images to speak for themselves. On his return to the United States in 1953, Frank met Walker Evans whose influence, along with that of Bill Brandt, he has widely acknowledged.

From 1955 to 1956, as the first foreign photographer to receive a Guggenheim fellowship, he criss-crossed the USA, creating thousands of negatives from which, in 1957, he selected, printed and arranged in sequence the 83 images for the book he proposed. Unable to find an American publisher, he approached Delpire, who published it in France as *Les Américains*, with text by Alain Bosquet (Paris, 1958). The following year it was published with an introduction by Jack Kerouac, as *The Americans* (New York, 1959, rev. 1978). The dark, shadowed, seemingly casual, grainy glimpses of American popular culture—endless highways, cars, parades, flags, jukeboxes and political gatherings (see fig.)—unleashed a bitter torrent of criticism. The pictures were labelled 'neurotic' and 'sick' by those who little noticed or understood that the book, which in its structure paid homage to Walker Evans's *American Photographs* (New York, 1938), was a brilliantly conceived and sequenced work. The style, in part a result of his use of a 35mm Leica camera, was loose, fast and

Robert Frank: *Political Rally, Chicago*, photograph, 1956 (Houston, TX, Museum of Fine Arts)

cinematic. The vision that shaped *The Americans* was one shared by Frank's friends and contemporaries who gave birth to the Happenings, Pop Art, junk or street art, beat generation poetry and new cinema that energized the avant-garde of the late 1950s.

After completing two more short projects, including the *Bus* series (1958; see 1986 exh. cat.), Frank renounced photography for film-making in 1959. Of the six films created between 1959 and 1969, *Pull my Daisy* (1959), made with American painter Alfred Leslie (*b* 1927), became a classic of American sub-culture. In 1969 Frank left New York and settled in Mabou, Nova Scotia, with his second wife, the artist June Leaf (*b* 1929). A commission to film the Rolling Stones 1972 tour resulted in the controversial drug culture saga *Cocksucker Blues*. Frank's other films include a musical *About me* (1971), *Keep Busy* (1975), *Energy and How to Get it* (1981) and *This Song for Jack* (1983). In 1980 he made the film *Life Dances on* in tribute to his daughter Andrea, who died in a plane crash in 1974.

Reclusive and increasingly self-referential in his work, Frank completed *Lines of my Hand* (New York, 1972), a 25-year retrospective of his photography. This revived his interest in still images and in 1974 he began to make new photographs, often concerned with language, such as *Words, Nova Scotia* (1977; Ottawa, Can. Mus. Contemp. Phot., see 1986 exh. cat., p. 3), and handwritten messages, such as *Sick of Goodbys* (1978; Houston, TX, Mus. F. A., see 1986 exh. cat., p. 69). Personal confrontations with death and despair are explored in collages, Polaroid composites and multiple images linked with scratchy inscriptions. They record, beyond Frank's Nova Scotia, a personal landscape that is felt as much as seen.

BIBLIOGRAPHY
G. Arnaud: 'Indiens des hauts-plateaux', *Neuf*, 8 (1952), pp. 1–35
Robert Frank (exh. cat., intro. P. Katz; New York, Sidney Janis Gal., 1979)
Robert Frank: Photographer/Film-maker, Works from 1945–1979 (exh. cat. by P. Brookman, Long Beach, CA, Mus. A., 1979)
Walker Evans and Robert Frank: An Essay on Influence (exh. cat. by T. Papageorge, New Haven, CT, Yale U., A.G., 1981)
Robert Frank: New York to Nova Scotia (exh. cat., ed. A. Tucker; Houston, TX, Mus. F.A., 1986)
CONSTANCE W. GLENN

Franke, Günther (*b* Berlin, 29 Oct 1900; *d* Munich, 5 Oct 1976). German art dealer and collector. In 1923 he took over the Graphisches Kabinett, a Munich subsidiary of the Berlin art dealer J. B. Neuman, whose associate he had been since 1918. He immediately exhibited contemporary artists, such as Erich Heckel, Max Beckmann, Emil Nolde, Otto Mueller, Franz Marc and Ensor, already revealing his predilection for German Expressionism. In 1926 he moved to Briennerstrasse. He was particularly supportive of Beckmann's work and later that of Ernst Wilhelm Nay. During the Nazi period he continued to safeguard their works and to act for them and other banned artists, mostly under the cover of early 19th-century exhibitions, keeping their paintings in a backroom in the gallery and in the cellar.

In 1946 Franke resumed his gallery work in the former sculptors' studio in the Villa Stuck, moving in 1963 to 50 Prinzregentenstrasse, and in 1966 to 22 Maximilianstrasse.

He put on a great number of one-man exhibitions, mostly involving German artists, but he concentrated on Beckmann and Nay. Beside his work as a dealer, he built up an extensive private collection in his house in Munich; five rooms there were open to the public once a week. The core of the collection consisted of numerous works by Beckmann; in 1975 Franke donated 29 oil paintings and a sculpture by him to the Bayerische Staatsgemäldesammlungen in Munich, including *Baden-Baden Dance-hall* (1923), *Carnival* (1930) and *Self-portrait with Sculpture* (1941; all now Munich, Staatsgal. Mod. Kst). Franke's collection also included prints and drawings by other artists whose work he had shown in his gallery, such as Xaver Fuhr (1898–1974), Erich Heckel, Otto Mueller, Christian Rohlfs and Alfred Kubin.

BIBLIOGRAPHY
Sammlung Günther Franke (exh. cat., Munich, Lenbachhaus, 1960)
D. Schmidt, ed.: *Briefe an Günther Franke: Porträt eines deutschen Kunsthändlers* (Cologne, 1970)
Hommage à Günther Franke (exh. cat., Munich, Villa Stuck, 1983)
ACHIM SOMMER

Frankenthaler, Helen (*b* New York, 12 Dec 1928). American painter and printmaker. She studied with Rufino Tamayo while at Dalton School, New York, with Paul Feeley (*b* 1910) at Bennington College, VT (1946–9), and privately with Wallace Harrison in 1949 and Hans Hofmann in 1950. In that year she met Clement Greenberg, David Smith, Jackson Pollock, Lee Krasner, Willem de Kooning and others. Like several of the exponents of ABSTRACT EXPRESSIONISM she was concerned with the forms and energies latent in nature. In the mythology of technical breakthrough that was part of the culture of the New York School, her work *Mountains and Sea* (1952; artist's col.; see fig.) has an established place. Extending Pollock's method of painting on unprimed canvases on the floor, she allowed thinner pigments to soak directly into the canvas. This created a closer relationship between image and surface, the weave of the raw canvas being visible within the painted image. At the same time the visibility of the canvas beneath the painted surface negated the sense of illusion and depth. It was a device that called attention to both the material and the nature of the medium. The technique also generated a new range of liquid-like atmospheric effects reminiscent of the watercolours of John Marin. Morris Louis and Kenneth Noland, the leading figures of a group sometimes known as the WASHINGTON COLOR PAINTERS, were among several painters who saw *Mountains and Sea* in 1953 and developed its implications in their own work. Louis in particular pursued the possibilities of the technique of 'staining' colour into the canvas.

There is a strong sense of technical play in Frankenthaler's works, which are often meditations on the divisions and ambiguities of space. One of her subtlest and most abstract pieces of this kind is *Seven Types of Ambiguity* (1957; artist's col., see Rose, p. 65), in which, without major shifts in colour values, she explored depth and perspective in witty homage to the English literary critic William Empson, after whose book (London, 1930) of densely-layered criticism the painting is named. In 1958 she married Robert Motherwell. About 1957 she began to

Helen Frankenthaler: *Mountains and Sea*, oil on canvas, 2.2×2.98 m, 1952 (artist's collection, on loan to Washington, National Gallery of Art)

explore relationships between linear skeins and small sun-like shapes in serial works. This in turn gave way in the early 1960s to single stains and blots. Her next phase involved an expansion of form and the use of richer colours with acrylics, as in *Cape (Provincetown)* of 1964 (*see* UNITED STATES OF AMERICA, fig. 18). Throughout the late 1960s and 1970s she continued this larger scale of work in a conscious exploration of large abstract forms and their shifting relationship to the framing edge, as in *Mauve District* (1966; New York, MOMA), and she executed sequences of paintings in which she alternately emptied and filled the centre spaces, such as *Stride* (1969; New York, Met.).

Throughout her career Frankenthaler experimented with both form and materials, exhibiting sculpture in the mid-1970s and working with woodcuts and colour printing as in *Essence Mulberry* (woodcut, 1977; see 1980 exh. cat., p. 49). In the 1980s her work became calmer, the gesture less energetic, her range of colours more sombre.

BIBLIOGRAPHY
Helen Frankenthaler (exh. cat. by E. C. Goossen, New York, Whitney, 1969)
B. Rose: *Helen Frankenthaler* (New York, 1970)
Helen Frankenthaler, Prints: 1961–1979 (exh. cat., ed. J. Aaron, S. Lyons and C. Evans; Williamstown, MA, Clark A. Inst., 1980)
Frankenthaler: The 1950s (exh. cat., text C. Belz; Waltham, MA, Brandeis U., Rose A. Mus., 1981)
Frankenthaler: Works on Paper, 1949–1984 (exh. cat. by K. Wilkin, New York, Guggenheim, 1985)
J. Elderfield: *Helen Frankenthaler* (New York, 1987)

CHRISTOPHER BROOKEMAN

Frankenthal Porcelain Factory. German ceramics factory. Although Paul Antoine Hannong (1700–60) had succeeded in producing hard-paste porcelain with Joseph Jakob Ringler (1730–1804) at his faience factory in Strasbourg in 1751, he was forbidden to produce porcelain because of the exclusive privilege granted to the royal factory in Vincennes. In 1755 Hannong transferred the business to Frankenthal, but he himself stayed in Strasbourg, employing his son Charles-François Hannong (*d* 1757) to manage the concern. In 1757 he replaced him with his younger son Joseph Adam Hannong (1739–after 1800). In 1761 the factory was sold to the Elector Palatine Charles Theodore of Sulzbach (*reg* 1742–99). Adam Bergdoll (1720–97) was made technical director and was succeeded in 1775 by the outstandingly competent Simon Feilner (1726–98). The unusual colour-sample plate (1775; London, BM), decorated with 60 small posies of flowers, is by Feilner, who presented it to the Elector Palatine as proof of his superb technical expertise.

From the beginning the factory employed such outstanding artists as the model-designer Wilhelm Lanz (*fl* 1755–61), who was brought by Paul Antoine Hannong from Strasbourg; other artists included Johann Martin Heinrici (1711–86), the brothers Johann Friedrich Lück (1727–97) and Carl Gottlieb Lück (*d* 1777) from Meissen and the painting-foreman Gottlieb Friedrich Riedel (1724–84), who went to Ludwigsburg in 1759. A combination of deep crimson, rich-green, carmine and later shades of grey and brown are characteristic Frankenthal colours. Outstanding artists included: the 'Amerindian' flower painter Johann Nicolaus Mittmann (1715–84); the European flower painters Carl Haussmann (1742–*c.* 1802) and Andreas Handschuh (*d c.* 1778); the animal and bird painter Riedel the painter of *commedia dell'arte* characters and figures after Watteau and Boucher, Andreas Philipp Oettner; the painter of Dutch genre scenes, after David Teniers (ii), Christian Winterstein (*fl* 1757–95); the figure painters Johann Bernhard Magnus (*c.* 1745–98) and Franz Joseph Weber (*fl* 1760–84); and the flower and fruit painter Georg Konrad Rahner (1745–after 1800). Jakob Osterspey (*c.* 1730–82) painted beautiful landscapes and mythological figures after Boucher (e.g. breakfast-service, 1765–70; Frankfurt am Main, Mus. Ksthandwk; *see* GERMANY, fig. 56). Wares were also decorated by Michael Glöckle (1751–*c.* 1802) with *décor bois* (a *trompe l'oeil* form of decoration imitating grained wood) imposed with representations of engravings inspired by wares from Niderviller or with the 'golden star' pattern on a purple ground by Michael Appel (1724–85). Flowers in four tones of gold on a royal-blue ground were a particular speciality. Patterns based on brocades or wallpapers in the Louis XVI style were adopted from Sèvres; crimson and gold flowers painted over gilt-striped grounds were among the most popular patterns of the 1770s and 1780s (e.g. plate, 1770–75; Munich, Bayer. Nmus., Neue Samml.). The influence of Sèvres is also evident in the broad borders and rims; they were more luxuriant and wider at Frankenthal than in other German factories. There are, however, very few examples of purely Neo-classical motifs.

In the production of figures, Frankenthal was second only to Meissen. In an inventory made at the end of the 18th century 200 groups and 600 single figures, including allegories of the Senses, Seasons and Elements, hunting scenes, pastoral scenes, figures from the *commedia dell'arte* and Chinese figures, are listed. The chief modeller was the sculptor Johann Wilhelm Lanz (*fl* 1755–61) from Strasbourg, who was succeeded by Johann Friedrich Lück, the sculptor Konrad Lick (1730–93), Lück's brother Carl Gottlieb Lück, Adam Bauer (*c.* 1743–*c.* 1780) and from 1779 the sculptor Johann Peter Melchior (1742–1825), who produced Neo-classical figures mainly in biscuit porcelain (e.g. *Apotheosis of the Electoral Pair*, 1792; Berlin, Schloss Charlottenburg).

In 1794 the factory was requisitioned by French Revolutionary troops and sold to Peter van Recum; with the help of Bergdoll, the former technical director, van Recum renewed production but only for a short period. After being requisitioned for a second time the factory was closed in 1799.

BIBLIOGRAPHY

F. H. Hoffmann: *Frankenthaler Porzellan* (Munich, 1911)
L. W. Böhm: *Frankenthaler Porzellan* (Mannheim, 1960)
A. Maus and L. Steinemann: *Die Künstler und Fabrikanten der Porzellan-manufaktur Frankenthal* (1961)

WALTER SPIEGL

Frankenthal school. Term used to refer to a group of landscape artists living in Frankenthal, Germany, from *c.* 1586 to the 1620s. In 1562 the Elector Palatine Frederick III established an asylum for Protestant refugees at Frankenthal. By *c.* 1586 the growing community included a number of landscape painters, chiefly émigrés from Flanders and Brabant, who had fled religious persecution after the fall of Mechelen and Antwerp to the Spanish in 1585. Sponsel and Plietzsch proposed that there was actually a 'colony' of painters, a 'Frankenthal school'; however, more recent research (Krämer, 1975) suggests that the small, shifting group of landscape painters—of which Gillis van Coninxloo III (*see* CONINXLOO, VAN, (2)) was the most important member—may not have counted more than a few artists at any one time.

Even with the possibility of marginal employment by compatriot tapestry-weavers active there, Frankenthal did not offer a very fertile environment for painters. The Electors Palatine were not noted patrons, in contrast to many contemporary princes. Van Coninxloo, who had arrived in Frankenthal by 1587, was probably urged to come by family members already there. The three other important landscape painters known to have stayed there are PIETER SCHOUBROECK, ANTOINE MIROU and Hendrik Ghysmans (before 1560–1611). Schoubroeck was the son of a Protestant clergyman who settled in Frankenthal in 1586. In the 1590s, Kramer affirms that he travelled to Rome and then worked in Nuremberg, moving to Frankenthal in 1600 to collect an inheritance. Mirou came to Frankenthal with his pharmacist father, who was there by 1586. Ghysmans, already a master in Antwerp in 1581, was in Frankenthal by 1586; he is recorded as supplying several paintings to the courts in Brussels and Dresden, though his known oeuvre consists of only a few signed drawings reflecting his Mechelen origins.

General characteristics associated with the Frankenthal school can be seen from a comparison of van Coninxloo's only known painting datable to his stay in Frankenthal, *Landscape with the Judgement of Midas* (1588; Dresden, Gemäldegal., Alte Meister), with the representative compositions by Schoubroeck, *Wilderness with Travellers* (1604; Munich, Alte. Pin.), and Mirou, *Forest with the Temptation of Christ* (1607; Munich, Alte Pin.). These have wide views full of variety and contrasts, with hilly open spaces and sometimes thrilling rock formations or a distant river, all structured in planes of light and shadow and framed by dense woods. The whole is animated by tiny villagers or hunters, depicting some mythological moment of truth or an edifying biblical scene. The works delight the viewer by offering a fantasy of myriad resting-points for the eye rather than by recording a unified experience of nature. This break-up of the surface is counteracted in the work of van Coninxloo by his freer brushstrokes but increased in the others' work by minute handling.

Some anonymous works, especially drawings, assigned to this 'school' may be by painters known only as names in church records (such as Jan van Bossche or Daniel de Weerdt), by followers of van Coninxloo in Holland after 1595 or by other Flemish artists who joined the diaspora and who may (or may not) have stopped in Frankenthal. The paintings of Schoubroeck and Mirou show affinities to those of Jan Breughel the elder, who must have passed through the region on many occasions. Other landscape artists who fled Mechelen or Antwerp and whose work shows similar stylistic and iconographic interests include Pieter Stevens, who worked for the Holy Roman Emperor Rudolf II in Prague, or the peripatetic Frederick van Valckenborch. The notion that early landscapes painted by Adam Elsheimer in Frankfurt were influenced by the Frankenthal school has been discarded due to the reattribution of these works to the Antwerp landscape painter Adriaen van Stalbemt.

BIBLIOGRAPHY

J. L. Sponsel: 'Gillis van Coninxloo und seine Schule', *Jb. Kön.-Preuss. Kstsamml.*, x (1889), pp. 57–71

E. Plietzsch: *Die Frankenthaler Maler: Ein Beitrag zur Entwicklungsgeschichte der niederländischen Landschaftsmalerei* (Leipzig, 1910/R Soest, 1972)

Die Frankenthaler Maler (exh. cat., Mannheim, Städt. Reiss-Mus.; Frankenthal, Staatl. Gym.; 1962)

H. G. Franz: *Niederländische Landschaftsmalerei im Zeitalter des Manierismus*, 2 vols (Graz, 1969)

M. Krämer: *Pieter Schoubroeck: Maler in Frankenthal* (diss., U. Hamburg, 1975)

——: 'Die Probleme einer Malerschule in Frankenthal', *Zeichnung in Deutschland, deutsche Zeichner 1540–1640* (exh. cat. by H. Geissler and others, Stuttgart, Staatsgal., 1979)

JOANEATH A. SPICER

Frankfort, Henri (*b* Amsterdam, 24 Feb 1897; *d* London, 16 July 1954). Dutch archaeologist and cultural historian. After studying at the University of Amsterdam and under FLINDERS PETRIE at University College, London, he directed the Egypt Exploration Society's excavations at Akhenaten's city of EL-AMARNA and elsewhere (1925–9). He was Field Director of the Iraq Expedition of the Oriental Institute of Chicago from 1929 to 1937 and conducted excavations at the Assyrian site of KHORSABAD and in the DIYALA REGION; the latter made an important contribution to knowledge of the art of the SUMERIANs, particularly of their architecture and of the Early Dynastic period (*c*. 2900–2500 BC). He held professorships at Chicago, Amsterdam and London and was Director of the Warburg Institute from 1949 to 1954. In 1954 he was elected a Fellow of the British Academy and he was also Corresponding Member of the Royal Dutch Academy of Sciences.

Frankfort was a scholar of immense range, insight and artistic sensibility, with an abiding concern for the interrelations of the cultures of the ancient Aegean, Egypt and Mesopotamia, and he was instrumental in defining a structure for the integrated study of early Near Eastern civilizations. It was characteristic of his approach to see artefacts as works of art that could lead to a deeper understanding of ancient cultures, rather than merely as sources of historical data: his *Cylinder Seals* was sub-titled *A Documentary Essay on the Art and Religion of the Ancient Near East*. Frankfort's monumental *Art and Architecture of the Ancient Orient* was published posthumously.

WRITINGS

ed.: *The Mural Painting of El-'Amarneh* (London, 1929)

with A. de Buck and B. Gunn: *The Cenotaph of Seti I at Abydos*, 2 vols (London, 1933)

with J. D. S. Pendlebury: *The City of Akhenaten*, ii of *The Excavations at Tell El-Amarna during the Seasons 1926–32* (London, 1933)

Cylinder Seals: A Documentary Essay on the Art and Religion of the Ancient Near East (London, 1939)

Sculpture of the Third Millennium BC from Tell Asmar and Khafajah, Oriental Institute Publications, xliv (Chicago, 1939)

More Sculpture from the Diyala Region, Oriental Institute Publications, lx (Chicago, 1943)

with others: *The Intellectual Adventure of Ancient Man: An Essay on Speculative Thought in the Ancient Near East* (Chicago, 1946); as *Before Philosophy* (Harmondsworth, 1949 [abridged])

Stratified Cylinder Seals from the Diyala Region, Oriental Institute Publications, lxxii (Chicago, 1955)

'The Dying God', 'Heresy in a Theocratic State', 'The Archetype in Analytical Psychology and the History of Religions', *J. Warb. & Court. Inst.*, xxi (1958), pp. 141–78

'The Last Predynastic Period in Babylonia', *Early History of the Middle East*, ed. I. E. S. Edwards, C. J. Gadd and N. G. L. Hammond, Cambridge Anc. Hist., i/2 (London, rev. 2/1968), pp. 71–92

The Art and Architecture of the Ancient Orient, Pelican Hist. A. (London, 1954, rev. Harmondsworth, 4/1969)

BIBLIOGRAPHY

J. Vindenas: 'Bibliography of Henri Frankfort', *J. Nr E. Stud.*, xiv (1955), pp. 4–13

L. GLYNNE DAVIES

Frankfurt am Main. German city on the River Main *c.* 32 km east of its confluence with the Rhine. It is the largest city in the state of Hessen, constituting an administrative district of its own. It has a population of *c.* 630,000. Its name, originally Frankonovurd (ford of the Franks), probably dates from when it became a Frankish possession with a royal court, following the expulsion of the Alemanni (*c.* AD 500), although an early documentary mention is in a record from AD 794 that refers to the arrival of Charlemagne at the 'Villa Franconovurd' to open an imperial diet and synod. In 1992 a document was found in which Frankfurt is mentioned as already being in existence before 741. As in all the large cities in the late medieval period, trade was an important element in the economic development of Frankfurt, which later became a major financial centre. The commitment of the citizens and industry to cultural development survived into the late 20th century.

1. History and urban development. 2. Art life and organization. 3. Centre of metalwork production.

1. HISTORY AND URBAN DEVELOPMENT. Remains of settlements from all prehistoric cultures existing in the Rhine–Main region since the Neolithic period have been found at Frankfurt. The core of all settlements was the Domhügel, which has been occupied uninterruptedly since the middle Bronze Age. Under Roman rule a fortress was first built in the present district of Höchst. Roman buildings also indicate the presence of a military camp. A Frankish royal court was later established on the ruins of the Roman baths. Both the royal palace built in 822 by Louis I, the Pious (*reg* AD 814–40), and Frankfurt's strategic position in the eastern part of the empire, assured the importance of the site. From 843 it became the capital of the East Frankish kingdom. The palace settlement was fortified under the Ottonians before 1000. A market settlement was then developed on the site, which was enclosed by a wall in the mid-12th century, and which had grown into a town by 1200. Frederick Barbarossa was elected king in Frankfurt in 1152. Subsequently 23 kings were selected and, from 1562, crowned in Frankfurt. Hohenstaufen emperors (*reg* 1138–1256) founded a new moated castle, the Saalhof, on the riverbank and laid out a town with a regular street-plan around the Domhügel, forming the basis for further development in the Middle

Ages. The Main bridge was built *c.* 1200, and in 1221 a settlement of the Teutonic Order was founded on the southern bridgehead.

In the 13th and 14th centuries Frankfurt developed into a trading centre, hosting fairs of international importance; an autumn fair is mentioned in 1227 and a spring fair from 1330. Frankfurt joined the first confederation of Rhineland towns in 1254. As the town prospered its area grew: the extensive Neustadt embraced Zeil and Rossmarkt and the square on the Hauptwache; by 1387 the inhabitants numbered almost 1387. In 1343 the Neustadt was enclosed by a strongly fortified wall, reinforced with ramparts and bastions during the Thirty Years War (1618–48). This was demolished in 1804–9, but its trace remains in the ring of lawns around the centre. The left (north) bank of the Main became the centre of trade and crafts, while market gardeners, vintners and fishermen lived in Sachsenhausen on the opposite bank. In 1372 Frankfurt became an autonomous city. The town's Jewish community, which had suffered heavy persecution in 1241 and 1349, was forced in 1462 to occupy a ghetto by the old town wall.

While the city's cathedral of St Bartholomew remained loyal to Roman Catholicism, the city adopted Lutheranism in 1535. Frankfurt allied itself with the Protestant princes in the Schmalacadic League. A more moderate constitution was introduced with the emperor's agreement in 1716. In 1792 and 1796 Frankfurt was occupied by the French, and when the Holy Roman Emperor Francis II abdicated in 1806, the town lost its status as an imperial city. In 1815 it became capital of the German Confederation created by Napoleon I, the population numbering *c.* 40,000 inhabitants. From 1816 until its incorporation in Prussia in 1866, it remained an independent Free City. With the national assembly at the Pauluskirche in 1848, the city moved to the centre of the movement towards German unification. The dissolution of the German Confederation and annexation to Prussia (1866) meant that the stock exchange and Frankfurter Bank (founded 1854) lost their pre-eminence to Berlin. Nevertheless Frankfurt rapidly developed as a commercial and industrial city. Construction of the railway, enlargement of the eastern and western docks, the canalization of the Main and the opening of the Rhine–Main airport reinforced its position as a centre of trade and communications.

The cathedral of St Bartholomew was built between 1250 and 1269 as the successor to the Carolingian palace chapel (840–47). In 1315 a chancel was added to the original hall with a nave and side aisles, and a wide transept built from 1346 as a place for imperial election. The west tower, built in 1414 to plans by Madern Gerthener, was

1. Frankfurt am Main, Leonhardskirche, begun 1219; from a pre-World War II photograph

completed only in the 19th century, and, at 94.75 m high, it came to dominate the city's skyline (for illustration *see* GERTHENER, MADERN). The Magdalenenkapelle contains a monumental devotional group donated by Frank von Ingelheim of the *Entombment* (1442), the earliest figural group of this kind in Germany. The second oldest church in the city is the Leonhardskirche (see fig. 1), a basilica with nave and side aisles and towers above the side chancels at the east end. It was begun in 1219 and dedicated to St Leonhard in 1323. The slender high chancel with stellar vaulting was begun by Madern Gerthener in 1425 and consecrated in 1434. In 1507–36 the basilica was substantially remodelled by H. von Bingen into a Late Gothic hall with five aisles. The Salvator Chancel (1508) features a suspended vault with a central pin and boss. The tympanum of the south porch has a relief with the Three Kings (1425) by Gerthener. The Nikolaikirche, first mentioned in 1264, was consecrated as a chapel to the imperial court in 1290 and was probably connected to the neighbouring Hohenstaufen Palace in the Saalhof. It became the church of the city council in the second half of the 15th century.

Other churches of interest include the Liebfrauenkirche; originally a Gothic chapel of the Virgin (1310–20) it was converted in the 14th century into a hall structure, which still survives, despite the church's destruction in 1944 and rebuilding in 1954. The Katharinenkirche (1344–6), in terms of physical and historical prominence, is the Protestant counterpart to the Catholic cathedral. In 1522 Martin Luther's pupil Hartmann Ibach preached the first Protestant sermon here. It was rebuilt by Melchior Hessler (?1643–85) in 1678–81 and was again rebuilt in 1953–4. The Pauluskirche (1270) was originally the church of the barefooted Franciscan friars but became Lutheran in 1529. In 1787 plans for a new building were drawn up by Johann Andreas Liebhardt (1713–88); these were only implemented in 1833, giving rise to a Protestant hall church on an oval ground-plan with a square tower. The rotunda has a domed roof *c.* 30 m high; the interior has a gallery running round the entire building, seating *c.* 2000 people. The German National Assembly was held there in 1848–9. After the destruction of the war, the church was rebuilt by 1948 by Rudolf Schwarz and renovated in 1987–8. In the foyer is a mural (l. 35 m, 1987–9) by Johannes Grützke, depicting the *Procession of the Parliamentarians* of 1848. The Dominikanerkloster and the Heiliggeistkirche (formerly St Maria) originally constituted a 13th-century Dominican monastery complex, sometimes used in the Middle Ages for the election of the emperor. St Maria was consecrated in 1259. In 1470–72 the chancel was raised with reticulated vaulting. The church of St Maria in Sachsenhausen was built in 1221 by the Teutonic Order. It has a single-nave hall and was consecrated in 1309. A Baroque façade was built by Ferdinand Kirchmeyer (*b* before 1725; *d* after 1751) in front of the existing one in 1747–51.

The architectural and historic centre of Frankfurt is the Römerberg. In the Middle Ages it was the market-place and the site for fairs. It is an irregular complex of squares, containing the Fountain of Justice and dominated by civic houses, the Nikolaikirche and the stepped gable façade

(1610) of the Rathaus or Römerhaus, originally a 14th-century dwelling, which became the council building in 1405. In 1984 the historic row of timbered façades on the east side of the square was restored. The Goethehaus on the Grosser Hirschgraben, where Johann Wolfgang von Goethe was born in 1749, was remodelled in 1755–6 by Johann Friedrich Uffenbach (1687–1769) and rebuilt in 1949 after destruction in the war, complete with those furnishings that survived; it also contains a collection of 400 paintings and 16,000 graphic works, many of which are by Goethe, as well as around 30,000 manuscript pages by Goethe and his circle. Also from the 18th century the Holzhausenschlösschen, commissioned by J. H. von Holzhausen, was built as a moated castle by Louis-Rémy de La Fosse in 1727–8. A notable building of the 19th century is the opera house (1873–88) by Richard Lucae, built in a Renaissance Revival style and financed by donations from local citizens. Ruined in World War II, it was rebuilt in 1976 and was reopened in 1981 as a concert hall and congress centre. Expressionist architecture of the early 20th century is exemplified by the entrance hall of the Höchst AG building by Peter Behrens, built in clinker brick.

During World War II a third of the city's buildings suffered severe damage, and the old town was totally destroyed. After the war Frankfurt again developed into a financial centre and reasserted its leading position as a centre for commercial fairs. Between the 1980s and 1990 a series of 13 buildings (some reconstructed, some new) designed by prominent architects were built along the Sachsenhausen bank of the Main to form the Museumsufer (*see* §2 below). By the late 20th century the city's skyline was dominated by imposing high-rise buildings in the style of North American cities. The Messeturm (h. 256.5 m, 1989–91) by Helmut Jahn is one of the tallest buildings in Europe. The Post-modernist Torhaus (1983–4) by Oswald Mathias Ungers is flanked by Ungers's Galleria (1980–83) built in the same style. Other prominent buildings in the centre include those of the banking quarter, dominated by the twin towers (h. 155 m) of the headquarters of the Deutsche Bank (1979–84), the 80 floors of which contain an important collection of modern art. In front of the building is the sculpture *Continuity* (granite, h. 5 m, 1983–6) by Max Bill.

2. ART LIFE AND ORGANIZATION. Frankfurt's cultural development was carried forward from the Middle Ages by a proud citizenry led by wealthy patricians, merchants and self-confident artisans organized in guilds. In the 15th and 16th centuries the urban crafts flourished, above all bronze-casting, goldsmiths' work and book printing, while in the 17th and 18th centuries faience production developed. Until its secularization (1803) the Heiliggeistkirche remained richly furnished with such works as an altarpiece (1501) by Hans Holbein (i), which incorporated one of the largest early German winged altarpieces (parts of which are now housed in the Städelsches Kunstinstitut und Städtische Galerie, or 'Städel'); the main painting from the altar of St Thomas, the *Assumption of the Virgin and her Coronation by the Holy Trinity* (1507–9) by Albrecht Dürer was destroyed, but a copy by Jobst Harrich is in the Historisches Museum, as

is the altarpiece *Holy Kinship* (*c.* 1503) by the MASTER OF FRANKFURT (*see* MASTERS, ANONYMOUS, AND MONOGRAMMISTS, §I). Two wooden figures of the Teutonic Order's patron saints, St George and St Elizabeth, by Cornelius Andreas Donnett (1682–1748), survive from the former Baroque high altar of the church of St Maria in Sachsenhausen. The important altarpiece showing the *Assumption of the Virgin* (1736) was requisitioned by French troops in 1796 and is now in the Musée du Louvre, Paris. A number of other artistic figures are associated with the city, including the natives Adam Elsheimer and Joachim von Sandrart. In 1624 the engraver Matthäus Merian (i) from Basle took over the de Bry publishing house. Johann Conrad Seekatz painted genre scenes and nature studies in the circle of Goethe's father, Johann Caspar von Goethe. Gustave Courbet may have worked in the city in 1858–9. The Kronberg painters' colony flourished near by in the 19th century.

The founding of the first museums in the 19th century was due to the patronage of the middle classes, who left their collections to the municipality at a relatively early date. The earliest museum historically is the Städelsches Kunstinstitut und Städtische Galerie (or 'Städel'; 1816), founded by the banker and merchant JOHANN FRIEDRICH STÄDEL, whose collection of *c.* 500 paintings (mainly by German and Netherlandish artists of the 17th and 18th centuries) forms the basis of the museum. The collection of contemporary art built up by the Städtische Galerie suffered irreplaceable losses under the Nazis. In 1878 a new museum was built on the Schaumainkai by Oskar Sommer; in late 1990 a new wing for 20th-century art was completed by Gustav Peichl. Attached to the building since 1874–7 is the Staatliche Hochschule für Bildende Künste, where such celebrated artists as Johann David Passavant, Moritz von Schwind and Max Beckmann all taught. Beckmann lived in the city from 1915 to 1933, and his works include the *Iron Footbridge* (1922; see fig. 2), which depicts commercial activity along the Main.

One of the best specialist museums in Frankfurt is the Liebighaus (Museum Alter Plastik), which houses a collection of sculpture spanning 4500 years. It occupies the former villa of Baron H. von Liebig, built shortly before 1900. The house was sold to the city on the condition that it would be used as a museum of sculpture. An annexe was completed in 1990. The Deutsches Architekturmuseum houses temporary exhibitions and plays a part in contemporary urban-planning projects. It also contains a collection of architectural models by such architects as Mies van der Rohe. The building was remodelled in 1984 by Oswald Matthias Ungers as a Post-modernist monument comprising a 'house within a house', since it encloses a neo-classical villa of 1912. The Museum für Kunsthandwerk, originally the Villa Metzler but with a noteworthy new wing (1982–4) by Richard Meier, offers exhibition space for about two-thirds of its *c.* 30,000 works of European and Asian art and craft. Other museums on the Schaumainkai are the Deutsches Postmuseum, the Deutsches Filmmuseum (opened 1984) and the Museum für Völkerkunde, for which a new building designed by Richard Meier was under construction in the 1990s.

The Jüdisches Museum has been housed since 1988 in the Rothschildpalais (1821) on the Unter-Mainkanal;

2. Max Beckmann: *Iron Footbridge*, oil on canvas, 1205×845 mm, 1922 (Düsseldorf, Kunstsammlung Nordrhein–Westfalen)

owned by the Rothschild banking family since 1846, it was built by Johann Friedrich Christian Hess (1785–1845) and remodelled in 1988 by Ante Josip von Kostelac. It is an important centre of documentation on the history of the Jews in Germany. Its collection includes devotional artefacts, manuscripts and historical documents. The Museum für Vor- und Frühgeschichte is housed in the former Karmeliterklosterkirche (completed 1310, enlarged 15th–16th century; addition by Josef Paul Kleihues, 1988–9). The Archäologisches Museum (housed in the Arkadenkreuzgang of the late 15th-century monastery complex) has an important cycle of wall paintings (1514–17; rest. 1980–84) by Jerg Ratgeb of the *Fall of the Rebel Angels*, the *Last Judgement* and the story of *Elias*. In 1991 the Museum für Moderne Kunst opened, housing the collection of the Darmstadt industrialist Karl Ströher, in which Pop art and Minimalist art are well represented. The building was designed by Hans Hollein (see fig. 3).

The Frankfurter Kunstverein (founded 1829) is one of the oldest art associations in Germany. It is based in the Steinernes Haus, a patrician dwelling of 1464. An important exhibition venue is the Schirn Kunsthalle Frankfurt, which was opened in 1986, and in 1989 the first 'Art Frankfurt' fair was held, adding to the city's reputation as an art metropolis. The presence of wealthy banks and firms willing to purchase art works stimulated the art market, which is also supported by the Ars Antique fair. There are also branches of such auction houses as Christie's, Sotheby's, Arnold, Döbritz and Zimmermann.

3. Frankfurt am Main, Museum für Moderne Kunst, by Hans Hollein, 1991

BIBLIOGRAPHY
H. S. Hüsgen: *Nachrichten von Franckfurter Künstlern und Kunst-Sachen* (Frankfurt am Main, 1780)
B. Bothe: *Geschichte der Stadt Frankfurt am Main* (Frankfurt am Main, 1913)
E. Keyser: *Hessisches Städtebuch* (Stuttgart, 1957)
G. Vogt: *Frankfurter Bürgerhäuser des 19. Jahrhunderts* (Frankfurt am Main, 1970)
H. Tilton: 'Naked City', *Connoisseur*, ccxiii/859 (Sept 1983), pp. 90–97
H.-E. Haverkampf and R. Burgard: 'Museums in Frankfurt am Main', *Int. J. Mus. Mgmt & Cur.*, v/1 (March 1986), pp. 13–18
B. Klemm: *Kulturstadt Frankfurt* (Frankfurt am Main, 1990)
Frankfurt am Main: Die Geschichte der Stadt, Frankfurter Historische Kommission (Sigmaringen, 1991)

PETRA SCHNIEWIND-MICHEL

3. CENTRE OF METALWORK PRODUCTION. Silver, iron, pewter and copper items were produced in Frankfurt from the Middle Ages. The first ordinances of the pewterers' guild were established in 1514, although pewter was made in the city before that date. A standard of four units of tin to one of lead was initially adopted, but pewter with a higher tin content was later produced. In the 18th century Frankfurt was an important centre for the production of pewter flatware and of what is known as 'wrythen' pewter, a term used to describe a fluted or swirling design. In this period one of the prominent families active in the pewter trade was the Klingling family (*see* GERMANY, §IX, 2).

Between 1460 and 1520, 110 silversmiths are recorded as having worked in the city, and there were 300 in the 17th century. Notable 16th- and 17th-century silversmiths included the de Brys and Birckenholtz families. The silversmiths of Frankfurt marked their work with a splayed, crowned eagle until the early 19th century, when a standard mark was established that continued in use until 1888, following the adoption in 1884 of a uniform system of marking for silver made throughout Germany. Almost all the makers' marks used consist of monograms and names, but devices were occasionally used.

See also GERMANY, §IX, 1.

BIBLIOGRAPHY
Das Ratssilber der Stadt Frankfurt am Main (exh. cat., Frankfurt am Main, Mus. Ksthandwk, 1963)

PETER HORNSBY

Frankish art. *See* MEROVINGIAN ART.

Frankl, Paul (*b* Prague, 1879; *d* Princeton, NJ, 30 Jan 1962). American art historian. He first trained as an architect but, in his early thirties, he turned to the study of art history and in 1911 submitted his doctoral dissertation at Munich University on 15th-century stained glass in southern Germany. Under the influence of his teacher,

Heinrich Wölfflin, Frankl soon attempted a systematic definition of the formal principles underlying Renaissance and post-Renaissance architecture. His first theoretical work, *Die Entwicklungsphasen der neueren Baukunst* (1914), was strongly influenced by the visual formalism and philosophical idealism of German art history in the decades before World War I. It isolated four main categories of analysis, which were fundamental to much of his later investigations: spatial composition, treatment of mass and surface ('corporeal form'), treatment of light, colour and other optical effects ('visible form'), and the relation of design to social function ('purposive intention'). His emphasis on spatial analysis as a determinant of style relied heavily on August Schmarsow's works on Baroque and Rococo architecture. His concept of 'visible form' (sometimes called 'optical form'), which presupposes that viewers derive their experience of a building kinetically, as the mental synthesis of many images from different viewpoints, owed much to late 19th-century theories of perception, in particular to Konrad Fiedler's and Adolf von Hildebrand's emphasis on the physiological and psychological processes of seeing, and to Alois Riegl's notion of 'haptic' and 'optic' forms. Frankl's principal debt, however, lay in his adoption of Wölfflin's quasi-Hegelian model of style as a predetermined, supra-individual force, impelled onwards by its own immanent laws, and evolving from one art-historical period to another through the action and counter-action of 'polar opposites': the underlying formal principles of a style are diametrically antithetical to those of the styles preceding and succeeding it.

Frankl was appointed to the chair of art history at Halle University in 1921 and turned his attention to medieval architecture, which was to be his lifelong interest, applying his method with a rigour and tenacity unmatched by any of his contemporaries. As analysed in *Die frühmittelalterliche und romanische Baukunst* (1926), the essential formal principles of Romanesque architecture may be seen as the polar opposites of Gothic. Early medieval churches are 'additive' (composed of separate areas) rather than having the 'partial' spaces of Gothic (conceived as a subdivided whole); their forms are 'frontal' (shaped or arranged at angles of 90°) rather than 'diagonal' (to be seen diagonally or in recession); and their whole appearance is 'structural' (their elements keep, or seem to keep, each other in balance under pressure and counter-pressure) rather than 'textural' as in Gothic, where forms lose their structural function and become decorative coverings. In 1934 he was dismissed from the university by the Nazis. For the next four years he prepared his treatise on the phenomenology and morphology of art history, *Das System der Kunstwissenschaft* (1938; see STYLE); ponderous and unwieldy, it achieved instant obscurity.

Frankl emigrated to the USA in 1938, where he held a research position at the Institute of Advanced Study, Princeton, until his death. He applied the methods of *Das System* to the problems of Gothic architecture. His monumental *The Gothic: Literary Sources and Interpretations through Eight Centuries* (1960) and *Gothic Architecture* (1962) are complementary halves of a single quest for what he believed to be the essence of the Gothic style, as revealed by writings on the subject from the 12th to the 20th century, and exemplified in the buildings themselves.

The latter book employed such Wölfflinian stylistic concepts as partiality, diagonality and the textural to establish the degree of 'Gothicness' in later medieval architecture, but also extended Wölfflin's formalism with a long section on social function and religious meaning ('purposive intention'), without, however, integrating it with the history of style.

Frankl's single-minded Hegelian quest to relate the formal roots of style with function and culture by uncovering a generating spiritual essence at the centre of the historical process had no influence on mid-20th century art history, which was predominantly positivist; but his emphasis on spatial analysis made a deep impression on such German architectural historians as Sigfried Giedion and Nikolaus Pevsner; his concept of diagonality was developed by Jean Bony (*b* 1908) and his interest in social function may lie behind the researches into architectural meaning and purpose by his most distinguished pupil, Richard Krautheimer.

WRITINGS
Die Glasmalerei des fünfzehnten Jahrhunderts in Bayern und Schwaben (Strasbourg, 1912)
Die Entwicklungsphasen der neueren Baukunst (Leipzig and Berlin, 1914); Eng. trans. as *The Principles of Architectural History: The Four Phases of Architectural Style, 1420–1900* (Cambridge, MA, and London, 1968/*R* 1973)
Die frühmittelalterliche und romanische Baukunst (Potsdam, 1926)
Das System der Kunstwissenschaft (Brno, 1938)
The Gothic: Literary Sources and Interpretations through Eight Centuries (Princeton, 1960)
Gothic Architecture, Pelican Hist. A. (Harmondsworth, 1962)

BIBLIOGRAPHY
R. Krautheimer: Obituary, *A. J.* [New York], xxii/1 (1962), p. 167
Obituary, *Wallraf-Richartz-Jb.*, xxiv (1962), pp. 7–14 [complete writings list]

PAUL CROSSLEY

Franks, Sir Augustus Wollaston (*b* Geneva, 20 March 1826; *d* London, 21 May 1897). English museum curator and writer. (All objects mentioned are in London, BM.) He spent his early years abroad, mainly in Geneva and Rome, and was then educated at Eton College in Berkshire (1839–43) and Trinity College, Cambridge (1845–9), where he was a founder-member of the Cambridge Architectural Society and a member of the Antiquarian Society. In the year of his graduation he published *A Book of Ornamental Glazing Quarries*, on medieval glazing patterns. After leaving Cambridge he became involved with the recently founded Royal Archaeological Institute and was honorary secretary to the Committee for its medieval exhibition of 1850. In 1851 he was appointed an assistant in the British Museum, London, with special charge of the British and medieval collections, which he started to expand with tenacious energy. At the sale of the Ralph Bernal Collection in 1855, he bought some of the best works, including the famous Lothair Crystal, with £4000 that he had managed to obtain from the Treasury. The following year, after hard negotiation, he acquired the collection of antiquities that had been unearthed in London and were owned by Charles Roach-Smith (1807–90).

In 1866 Franks became Keeper of the Department of British and Medieval Antiquities which, since the reorganization of the Museum in 1860, was within the Department of Oriental Antiquities. From this time he had to rely almost entirely on donations to expand the collection, many of them—including the 8th-century Northumbrian whalebone casket that bears his name—made by himself. He also used his widespread contacts to secure numerous bequests, for example the collections of Felix Slade (1790–1868), William Burges and Octavius Morgan (1803–88). The ethnographic collection of Henry Christy (1810–65), a museum in its own right, came to the British Museum through Franks's influence as one of its trustees. His greatest coup, however, was to acquire the Royal Gold Cup (*see* ENAMEL, colour pl. III, fig. 1) that, in 1391, had been a gift from Jean, Duc de Berry, to Charles VI of France. This he bought with his own money, retrieving most of the outlay by public subscription and, finally, Treasury funds. From 1886 to his retirement in 1896, he was Senior Keeper of the Museum. In the course of his career his interests widened enormously, which is evident from the numerous articles he wrote on various subjects for *Archaeologia* and the *Proceedings of the Society of Antiquaries*, of which society he was twice Director (1858–67; 1873–80). His few books include *Examples of Oriental Art in Glass and Enamel* (1858) and *Himarytic Inscriptions from Southern Arabia* (1863), and, with R. G. Latham, he edited J. M. Kemble's *Horae Ferales* (1863). On his death the remainder of his own collection, which includes the Treasure of the Oxus and 80,000 bookplates, was donated to the British Museum.

WRITINGS

A Book of Ornamental Glazing Quarries (London and Oxford, 1849)
Examples of Oriental Art in Glass and Enamel (London, 1858)
Himarytic Inscriptions from Southern Arabia (London, 1863)
ed. with R. G. Latham: J. M. Kemble: *Horae Ferales or Studies in the Archeology of the Northern Nations* (London, 1863)

BIBLIOGRAPHY

DNB
M. Caygill: *The Story of the British Museum* (London, 1981), pp. 41–4
D. M. Wilson: *The Forgotten Collector: Augustus Wollaston Franks of the British Museum* (London, 1984)

☐

Franque, François (*b* Avignon, 1710; *d* ?1793). French architect. He was the son and pupil of Jean-Baptiste Franque (1683–1758), from a distinguished family of architects who practised in the south of France. In 1730 he moved to Paris, and from 1733 to 1736 he studied at the French Academy in Rome. He became a member of the Académie Royale d'Architecture in 1755 and a royal architect. He is best known for his ecclesiastical buildings and small town houses (hôtels) and for successfully upholding the principles of classical purism practised by the Mansart family. Jacques-François Blondel dedicated several plates in both his *Cours d'architecture* (Paris, 1771–7) and the *Encyclopédie* (Diderot–d'Alembert; Paris, 1751–65) to Franque's work, praising the 'regularity of his planning' and the 'commendable simplicity of his taste'. Franque's Hôtel de Villefranche (*c.* 1740), Avignon, was considered by Blondel to be a masterpiece of planning. The irregular urban site meant that only the main rooms and courtyards could retain clearly defined geometrical shapes; the remaining rooms were accommodated in the left-over spaces. A residential building (*c.* 1750) in the Rue Coq Saint-Honoré, Paris, with an arcaded ground-floor and four severe storeys above, was regarded by Blondel as a model of urban architecture.

Among the ecclesiastical buildings worked on by Franque were the abbeys of Corbie (*c.* 1740), near Amiens; Saint-Benoît-sur-Loire (1746), near Orléans; Prémontré (1757), near Laon, where the three main blocks each have a rounded central pavilion with a curved pediment resembling a mitre; and Villers-Cotterêts (1765), where he used geometrically shaped rooms to reconcile the various alignments of the existing buildings. Franque's designs for the rebuilding of the Abbaye Royale de Pentémont (now the Ministère des Anciens Combattants), Paris, were based on Jules Hardouin Mansart's church of Les Invalides (1676–1706) near by; Franque's design was executed (1749) by Pierre Contant d'Ivry in a more Neo-classical manner. Franque was also involved with the design of the Peyrou promenade in Montpellier, developed around the new aqueduct. His recommendations for the layout (1765) were incorporated into the final work, which was executed by Jean-Antoine Giral in 1767–72.

WRITINGS

'Eloge de J.-F. Blondel', *J. B.-A. & Sci.*, i (1774), pp. 559–70

BIBLIOGRAPHY

Diderot–d'Alembert, i, 'Architecture'
J.-F. Blondel: *Cours d'architecture*, iii (Paris, 1773)
L. Hautecoeur: *Architecture classique*, iii, iv (1950–52)
W. G. Kalnein and M. Levey: *Art and Architecture of the Eighteenth Century in France*, Pelican Hist. A. (Harmondsworth, 1972)
P. Pinon: 'Architectural Composition and the Precept of Regularity from Peruzzi to Franque', *Daidalos*, v (1985), pp. 57–70

ZILAH QUEZADO DECKKER

Franque, Jean-Pierre (*b* Le Buis, Drôme, 11 Aug 1774; *d* Paris, 28 March 1860). French painter. He and his twin brother, Joseph-Boniface Franque (1774–1833), who was also a painter, were the sons of a modest farmer and, according to a local story, their youthful talent was such that the provincial government paid for them to study in Grenoble. They enrolled at the Ecole Gratuite in Grenoble and stayed for about two years (1786–8), training to become engravers. During the revolutionary period, the twins' education was taken over by the Département de la Drôme. In 1792 their case was discussed at the National Assembly in Paris, which placed them in David's atelier and provided a pension for four years. David agreed to educate them but refused payment, writing to the President of the Assembly, 'I am overjoyed to be chosen to be the first teacher of these youths who could be called children of the nation since they owe everything to her.' The two brothers were considered very promising students, and David asked Jean-Pierre to assist him in the execution of the *Intervention of the Sabine Women* (1796–9; Paris, Louvre). Jean-Pierre also became involved with LES PRIMITIFS and the mysterious Maurice Quaï (1779–1804), who reacted against Davidian principles and advocated a return to 'primitive' 15th-century Italian art. Franque demonstrated his independence from David in the selection of the subject for his 1806 Salon début, the *Dream of Love Induced by the Power of Harmony* (destr.). In the spring of 1807 he was one of the 26 painters who entered a sketch (untraced) for the competition for a large painting representing Napoleon on the battlefield of Eylau, a competition won by Gros. In 1810 Franque produced *Allegory of the Condition of France before the Return from Egypt* (Paris, Louvre). This complex picture is a peculiar mixture of the allegorical, symbolic and historical, and depicts a seated Napoleon implored by a personification of France to come to her aid. An inscription within the work reads, 'France, suffering under an unhappy government, summons from the bosom of Egypt the hero on whom her destiny depends.' With its crystalline light effects and imaginative composition, this work is related to the Ossianic subject-matter of Girodet and Gérard. Franque's work is often reminiscent of the brilliant polished finish of Gérard's paintings.

Franque continued with large-scale religious and mythological pictures that tend to be very emphatic with exaggerated poses and glossy colour, for example the *Conversion of St Paul* (exh. Salon 1819; original untraced, version in Dijon, Mus. B.-A.) and *Jupiter Sleeping in the Arms of Juno on Mount Ida* (exh. Salon 1822; Montauban, Mus. Ingres). After 1830 he became involved with the restoration of the Musée d'Histoire, Versailles, and painted many bland historical portraits that did nothing to enhance his reputation. (More than sixty of these are at the château of Versailles.) For his services he was rewarded with the Légion d'honneur in 1836, and he continued to work on official projects until his death.

The Franque brothers sometimes collaborated on works (e.g. *Hercules and Alcestis*, exh. Salon 1814; untraced), but their careers diverged after 1812, when Joseph went to Italy as the protégé of Napoleon's sister Elisa Bacciochi, becoming professor of drawing at the Carrara academy in 1814. With the fall of Napoleon he went to Naples and there became director of the academy until his death in November 1833. He was a portrait painter of considerable ability, often portraying the Bonapartes and Bacciochis, for example the very tender *Marie-Louise Watching the Sleeping King of Rome* (exh. Salon 1812; Versailles, Château). Even when in Italy he continued to work for French patrons, for example the *Duc de Berry* (Naples, Accad. B.A.). His last Salon exhibit was *Scene during the Eruption of Vesuvius* (1827; Philadelphia, PA, Mus. A.), a frantic depiction of panic, with figures climbing over one another to escape the lava.

BIBLIOGRAPHY
French Painting, 1774–1830: The Age of Revolution (exh. cat., Paris, Grand Pal.; Detroit, MI, Inst. A.; New York, Met.; 1975–6), pp. 419–22
D. Rosenthal: 'Joseph Franque's *Scene during the Eruption of Vesuvius*', *Bull. Philadelphia Mus. A.*, lxxv/324 (1976), pp. 2–15
G. Levitine: *The Dawn of Bohemianism: The Barbu Rebellion and Primitivism in Neoclassical France* (University Park, PA, 1978)

SIMON LEE

Frantz. German family of architects active mainly in Silesia and Greater Poland. Marcin Frantz (*b* Rewahl [now Tallinn, Estonia], 1679; *d* Legnica, 6 Nov 1742) trained under his stepfather, the builder Jerzy Winkler, and later travelled to Sweden and Pomerania. After returning to Silesia he was commissioned by the Protestant community to build a church in Landeshut (now Kamienna Góra, Poland) in 1709–20, which he based on St Catherine's, Stockholm. Around 1710 he completely rebuilt the palace in Peterswaldau (now Pieszyce), and in 1728–32 that in Kotzenau (now Chocianów). His work was influenced by the early 18th-century palace style of Vienna and Prague. Marcin's son, Karol Marcin Frantz (*b* Liegnitz [now Legnica, Poland], before 1 Oct 1712; *d* Rydzyna, 6 Nov

1755) was educated within the artistic circle of Kilian Ignaz Dientzenhofer, whose work influenced his first independent commission, the parish church in Seitsch (now Siciny; 1736–40). During this period he was appointed architect to the Polish king Augustus III and in 1742 he was brought to Rydzyna in Greater Poland by Aleksander Józef Sułkowski, minister of the Saxon court. He worked there from 1742 to 1750, restoring Pompeo Ferrari's palace and building the annexes and a church, thereby creating one of the most magnificent late Baroque architectural ensembles in Poland. The church at Rokitno was built (1746–56) to his plans. Karol Marcin Frantz was one of the most outstanding architects working in Silesia and Greater Poland during the first half of the 18th century. Developing the type of church that originated in Bohemia in the early 18th century, he created a distinctive, dynamic type of composition featuring aiseless naves with plans based on interpenetrating circles and ellipses.

BIBLIOGRAPHY
G. Grundmann: *Die Baumeisterfamilie Frantz* (Breslau, 1937)
K. Kalinowski: *Architektura doby baroku na Śląsku* [The architecture of the Baroque period in Silesia] (Warsaw, 1977)

ANDRZEJ ROTTERMUND

Franz-Dreber, (Karl) Heinrich. *See* DREBER, HEINRICH.

Franzone [Franzoni]. Italian family of administrators and patrons. In 1678 Malvasia noted that one Agostino Franzone (i), son of Tommaso Franzone, had a collection of paintings by the Bolognese artists Annibale and Ludovico Carracci, Guido Reni and Francesco Albani. Agostino was probably the owner of the Palazzo Franzone at 23 Piazza Luccoli, Genoa, and also wrote a book on the Genoese nobility. He may also have owned two marble busts of *St Peter* and *St Paul* (priv. col., see Montagu, ii, cat. nos 200, 201) by Alessandro Algardi. One of the most distinguished members of the family was Agostino's nephew Giacomo Franzone (*b* Genoa, 25 Dec 1612; *d* Rome, 1696–7), who moved in 1636 to Rome, where he managed the papal finances in a variety of offices until he became a cardinal in 1660. He played a leading role in supervising the execution of the artistic projects in Rome commissioned by Innocent X (*see* PAMPHILI, (1)) and Alexander VII (*see* CHIGI, (3)). These included the sculptural decoration of the interiors of St Peter's (and the commissioning from Algardi of the *Leo and Attila* relief), of S Agnese in Piazza Navona and of S Giovanni in Laterano, where *c.* 1653 Franzone succeeded Virgilio Spada as Superintendent of Works. As Treasurer-General, Franzone was a member of the special committee of the Fabbrica of St Peter's formed by Alexander VII in 1657 to oversee income and expenditure on the building, and consequently he made the acquaintance of the principal sculptors in Rome and became a patron in his own right. Among his acquisitions were sculptures by Algardi. In the inventory of Algardi's studio made after the sculptor's death in 1654 appears the name of another Agostino Franzone, possibly Giacomo's uncle but probably his brother, who died in Genoa in 1705. Agostino Franzone (ii) was a Genoese senator who bequeathed four reliefs attributed to Algardi to his nephew Stefano Franzone. Agostino (ii) acquired a chapel, the Cappella del Crocefisso, in the Carmelite church of S Carlo (now SS Vittore e Carlo) in Genoa. The principal sculptural decoration of the chapel, including the marble busts of the brothers Franzone, a bronze Crucifix and bronze busts of saints, has traditionally been attributed to Algardi. The quality of these works, as well as the death of Algardi in 1654, however, have led them to be partly reattributed to Domenico Guidi, who perhaps worked from terracotta models by Algardi.

BIBLIOGRAPHY

G. P. Bellori: *Vite* (1672); ed. E. Borea (1976), pp. 404, 414–15
C. C. Malvasia: *Felsina pittrice* (1678); ed. G. Zanotti (1841), i, pp. 355, 358; ii, pp. 65, 197
G. O. Corazzini: *Memorie storiche della famiglia Franzoni* (Florence, 1879)
M. Labò: *I palazzi di Genova di P. P. Rubens e altri scritti d'architettura* (Genoa, 1970), pp. 150–55 [incl. app.: 'La cappella dell'Algardi nei Santi Vittore e Carlo a Genova', pp. 37–40]
J. Montagu: *Alessandro Algardi*, 2 vols (New Haven and London, 1985), i, pp. 93, 212–13, 234, 265; ii, pp. 330, 340, 353, 359–60, 376–7, 385, 473, 477

JANET SOUTHORN

Frascati. Italian hill town near the ancient settlement of Tusculum, about 21.5 km south-east of Rome, noted for its many fine 16th- and 17th-century villas. Tusculum was an ancient town in the Alban Hills occupied by the Romans in 381 BC. Towards the end of the Republican period the vicinity of Tusculum was the site of numerous villas of famous Romans, including Cato, Lucullus and Cicero; the latter's *Tusculan Disputations* is set at his villa there. Tusculum was destroyed in 1191 under Pope Celestine III, and Frascati, set below it at the foot of the Alban Hills, subsequently became the favourite location for *villeggiatura* or country living for the urban Romans. In 1537, during the reign of Pope Paul III, the papacy reacquired feudal rights to the territory of Tusculum from the Colonna family. From 1538 to 1545 the papal architect Jacopo Melighino renovated the walls, piazzas and streets of Frascati, and in 1549 the Pope issued a medal inscribed *Tuscolo rest[ituto]* in honour of the renovation. As a result of Paul III's enjoyment of summer stays at Frascati, having visited it every year since the spring of 1536, his courtiers soon emulated him, buying or renting country houses or vineyards there. In May 1548 Monsignor Alessandro Rufini, Bishop of Melfi, bought land where he built the Villa Rufina, also commemorated on the papal medal of 1549. The building, designed by Nanni di Baccio Bigio,

was originally designed as a symmetrical, four-tower structure with loggias on the ground floor between the corner towers on two sides; it was later remodelled by Francesco Borromini as the Villa Falconieri (see below). The loggia on the north side looked out over the flat plain of the Campagna below the hillside with a magnificent distant view of Rome. This siting is typical of later villas in the area.

Soon after 1551 Nanni began another, more modest villa, the Villa Ricci (later Villa Tusculana), east of the town for Cardinal Giovanni Ricci of Montepulciano (1497–1574). Cardinal Ranuccio Farnese began in 1560 to purchase land near the Villa Ricci and in 1562 added the villa itself to his holdings with the intention of developing a large estate there. Meanwhile, in 1560 Pier Antonio Contugi, physician to Pius IV, acquired land west of the Villa Rufina and erected a small villa, Villa Contugi, which later became the nucleus of the splendid Villa Aldobrandini (see below). Similarly, Annibal Caro in 1563 bought land west of Frascati that he claimed was the site of the ancient Roman villa of Lucullus. There Caro built a small casino, the Caravilla (later Villa Torlonia), and personally laid out a small ornamental garden.

Bishop Rufini sold the Villa Rufina in 1563 to the Cenci family and in the following year began a new casino on land given to his family just above his former residence. It was named the Villa Rufinella and was acquired in 1581 by Cardinal Guido Ferreri. The scarcity of water that plagued all these villas during the 16th century is illustrated by the violent reaction of Ferreri's neighbour, Paolo Sforza, to the small fountains Ferreri created for his gardens. Convinced that Ferreri had diverted water from the Sforza holdings, Sforza ordered that the Ferreri fountains be destroyed. Gregory XIII resolved the argument by ordering Sforza to restore the fountains under the threat of a heavy fine.

A more expansive building campaign began at Frascati following the purchase in 1567 by Cardinal Marcus Sitticus Altemps (1533–95), nephew of Pius IV, of the Villa Ricci. Jacopo Vignola enlarged the old villa in 1569, more than doubling its interior space by giving it a large central salon flanked by two smaller identical apartments. It was renamed the Villa Tusculana and was regularly visited by Gregory XIII. In order to provide increased accommodation for the papal entourage, Cardinal Altemps acquired more land above his villa and employed Martino I Longhi to erect a larger villa (1573–4). It was named Mondragone in honour of the Pope, whose coat of arms featured a dragon. The new building, like the earlier ones, faced north with a distant prospect of Rome from the terraces in front of it. The interior repeated Vignola's arrangement at the Villa Tusculana, with a large central salon—in this case, two storeys in height—flanked by two apartments, one on the east side for the Pope and another on the west for the Cardinal, each with its own private garden. Altemps also had a small palace, called the Retirata, built in 1574–9 behind the Villa Mondragone for his son. Gregory XIII visited the Villa Mondragone every year of his reign except the last, between four and twelve times a year.

Following his election in 1592, Clement VIII gave the Villa Contugi to Cardinal Pietro Aldobrandini (see ALDOBRANDINI, (2)), his nephew and secretary of state, in 1598.

1. Frascati, Villa Aldobrandini, water-theatre and cascade, 1603–21; engraving from Giovanni Battista Falda: *Fontane di Roma* (Rome, 1675), part 2

In 1601 Giacomo della Porta was commissioned to expand and redecorate the small 16th-century casino. The new Villa Aldobrandini, topped by a mammoth broken pediment and roof-top belvedere, looms over the rear of the town of Frascati. The vaults of the principal rooms were frescoed (1602–3) by the Cavaliere d'Arpino with scenes from the Old Testament. The principal element of the new work, however, was the great water-theatre (see fig. 1). Although probably part of della Porta's original plan, it was executed to the designs of Carlo Maderno and Giovanni Fontana (iii). Behind the villa a large arcaded exedra at the foot of the hill frames waterworks, and a cascade plunges down the hillside, rushing through the central arch of the exedra into a large basin. Two large, spiral columns that stand above the cascade represent the Columns of Hercules at the limits of the Classical world. They symbolize the expansion of the Catholic Church under Clement VIII and Aldobrandini. From 1615 to 1621 the rooms at both ends of the exedra were lavishly decorated, the one on the left being a chapel dedicated to St Sebastian and that on the right a temple of the arts, the Room of Apollo, containing an artificial Mt Parnassus with the winged horse Pegasus in a water-basin below it. On the mount were wooden automata of *Apollo* and the nine *Muses* playing their musical instruments accompanied by a water-organ beneath, all operated by hydraulic power. The walls of the Room of Apollo were frescoed (1616–18; four panels *in situ*; six London, N.G.) with scenes from the *Life of Apollo* by Domenichino.

The election of Paul V in 1605 encouraged his nephew Cardinal Scipione Borghese to emulate the building activities of his predecessor, Cardinal Aldobrandini. In 1607 Borghese purchased the casino of Caravilla begun by Annibal Caro in the 16th century, and he employed Flaminio Ponzio from 1607 to 1612 to create a magnificent cascade similar to that at the Villa Aldobrandini but accompanied by staircases that curve around the broad cascade, which is composed of several basins. Unlike the Aldobrandini cascade, it is not aligned with the villa but serves as a backdrop to the gardens at one side. In 1613 the Borghese obtained the Villa Mondragone from the Altemps family. The main villa and the Retirata were connected by a long wing on the west side, while on the east side a large garden was laid out with a raised water-theatre at the south end (see fig. 2) and an arcaded garden loggia at the other end; Giovanni Vasanzio worked on this project. Cardinal Borghese also purchased the Villa Tusculana and renamed it the Villa Vecchia. It was severely damaged in World War II but survives rebuilt in a similar form. In 1614 Cardinal Borghese increased his holdings at Frascati by acquiring a villa just east of the Villa Mondragone and the Villa Vecchia. Originally built in 1604–5 by Monsignor Ferdinando Taverna, governor of Rome under Clement VIII, the building became known as the Villa Borghese and was enlarged after plans attributed to Girolamo Rainaldi. Rusticated porticos, which flank the north front, and a semicircular staircase leading to the formal garden were built. In the 1730s frescoes were added to some of the interiors by Ignaz Heldmann (*d* 1751), Giuseppe Valeriani (*d* 1761) and Domenico Valeriani (*d* 1771).

2. Frascati, Villa Mondragone, garden and water-theatre, 1613; engraving from Giovanni Battista Falda: *Fontane di Roma* (Rome, 1675), part 2

On the election of Gregory XV in 1621, his nephew Cardinal Ludovico Ludovisi purchased the Caravilla, and Maderno increased the water effects by adding a long wall with 22 niches of water jets at the base of the existing cascade. At the end of the 17th century the garden was enlarged into a wooded park, and wings were added to the original building. The Villa Ludovisi, known as the Villa Torlonia from the late 19th century, was destroyed in World War II, but the gardens were subsequently restored. The major work at Frascati in the late 17th century was at the Villa Rufina, acquired in 1628 by Orazio Falconieri and entirely transformed *c.* 1667–8 to designs attributed to Francesco Borromini. The existing villa was incorporated into a grander scheme, consisting of a central block, recalling Pietro da Cortona's Villa Sacchetti (1625–9), near Rome, and two long side wings. The building, renamed the Villa Falconieri, was completed in the late 1660s by Ciro Ferri, who was also responsible for frescoes in the interior, including *Spring* and *Autumn* (*c.* 1680; for illustration *see* FERRI, CIRO). Additional frescoes were executed in the 1670s by Carlo Maratti and Giovanni Francesco Grimaldi. Although severely damaged during World War II, the villa was restored, as was the Villa Rufinella. The latter had been purchased in 1740 by the Jesuits of the Collegio Romano, Rome, as a summer retreat. It was rebuilt (1741–5) for them by Luigi Vanvitelli, who, as well as providing additional accommodation, added a small oval chapel.

During the 19th century many of the villas at Frascati were neglected. Some were further damaged and several completely destroyed during World War II, although some restoration work later took place. The original appearance of the town and its surrounding villas can best be appreciated in Matthäus Greuter's large print of Frascati published in 1620. Giovanni Battista Falda later depicted many of the beautiful gardens in part 2 of his *Fontane di Roma* (Rome, 1675; see figs 1 and 2 above).

BIBLIOGRAPHY

R. Lanciani: 'La riedificazione di Frascati per opera di Paolo III', *Archv Soc. Roman. Stor. Patria*, xvi (1893), pp. 517–22

F. Grossi-Gondi: *La villa dei Quintili e la villa di Mondragone* (Rome, 1901)

C. L. Franck: *Die Barockvillen in Frascati* (Munich, 1956; Eng. trans., 1966)

P. Portoghesi: 'L'opera del Borromini nel palazzo della villa Falconieri', *Quad. Ist. Stor. Archit.*, xv (1956), pp. 7–20

K. Schwager: 'Kardinal Pietro Aldobrandinis Villa di Belvedere in Frascati', *Röm. Jb. Kstgesch.*, ix–x (1961–2), pp. 289–382

C. d'Onofrio: *La villa Aldobrandini a Frascati* (Rome, 1963)

M. Fagiolo dell'Arco: 'Villa Aldobrandini Tusculana', *Quad. Ist. Stor. Archit.*, lxii–lxvi (1964), pp. 61–92

R. M. Steinberg: 'The Iconography of the Teatro dell'Acqua at the Villa Aldobrandini', *A. Bull.*, xlvii (1965), pp. 453–63

G. M. Andres: 'Cardinal Giovanni Ricci: The Builder from Montepulciano', *Il pensiero italiano del rinascimento e il tempo nostro: Atti del V convegno internazionale del centro di studi umanistici: Firenze, 1970*, pp. 306–8

I. Belli-Barsali and M. G. Branchetti: *Ville della campagna romana* (Milan, 1975)

D. R. Coffin: *The Villa in the Life of Renaissance Rome* (Princeton, 1979)

A. Tantillo Mignosi: *Villa e paese* (Rome, 1980)

DAVID R. COFFIN

Frasconi, Antonio (*b* Buenos Aires, 28 April 1919). Uruguayan printmaker and illustrator of Argentine birth. The son of Italian parents who settled in Montevideo when he was two weeks old, he first exhibited drawings in 1939 at the Ateneo in Montevideo and studied printmaking with various artists, while also working as a political caricaturist in the weekly publications *Marcha* and *La Línea Maginot.* His diverse influences included German Expressionism, José Guadalupe Posada, the Taller de Gráfica Popular and woodcuts by Japanese artists such as Katsushika Hokusai and Kitagawa Utamaro.

Frasconi visited the USA in 1945 on a grant from the Art Students League, New York, and later taught extensively at the New School in New York. His illustrated edition of *Twelve Fables of Aesop* (New York, 1954), published by MOMA, was chosen as one of the 50 Books of the Year by the Institute of Graphic Arts, and in 1960 he won the Grand Prize at the Venice Film Festival for his film *The Neighbouring Shore*, based on more than 100 woodcuts. His work as a printmaker encompassed political themes, as in the series *Those who Have Disappeared* (see 1987 exh. cat.), as well as portraits of jazz musicians such as *Duke Ellington* (1976), *Bessie Smith* and *Charles Mingus* (1973), and of the American 19th-century poet *Walt Whitman* (1981) (see 1985 exh. cat.). In 1969 he was named a National Academician by the New York Academy of Design.

BIBLIOGRAPHY

N. Hentoff and C. Parkhurst: *Frasconi—Against the Grain* (New York and London, 1974)

Antonio Frasconi: Un clásico de la xilografía (exh. cat., ed. A. Kalenberg; Montevideo, Mus. N.A. Plást., 1985)

Involvement: The Graphic Art of Antonio Frasconi (exh. cat., Los Angeles, UCLA, Wight A. G., 1987), pp. 46–7

ANGEL KALENBERG

Fraser, Alexander (*b* Edinburgh, 7 April 1786; *d* London, 15 Feb 1865). Scottish painter. He studied at the Trustees Academy in Edinburgh, where he was a contemporary of David Wilkie. He first exhibited at the Associated Society of Artists in Edinburgh in 1809 and at the Royal Academy in London in 1810. From 1813 he worked as an assistant to Wilkie in London and he later specialized in painting the still-lifes in such larger compositions by Wilkie as the *Irish Whiskey Still* (1840; Edinburgh, N.G.). Fraser also painted in his own right, producing such small-scale, genre pictures as *Scotch Fair* (*c.* 1834; Dundee, McManus Gals). Characterized by the high quality of the still-life detail, these paintings were directly derived from Wilkie's early

work in theme, though in execution they reflect the increased richness of his later style.

DNB

D. Macmillan: *Scottish Art, 1460–1990* (Edinburgh, 1990), pp. 181–4

DUNCAN MACMILLAN

Fraser, Charles (*b* Charleston, SC, 20 Aug 1782; *d* Charleston, 5 Oct 1860). American lawyer, painter, writer and orator. With the exception of a few trips north, Fraser rarely left Charleston. He showed artistic talent early and began his brief formal training with drawing lessons from the engraver and landscape painter Thomas Coram (1757–1811). He was befriended by the painters Edward Greene Malbone, Washington Allston and Thomas Sully. With his fellow student Sully, he drew lively stage sets and made sketches of comical characters. Fraser's sketchbooks from this period also contain copies after travel-book illustrations and views of historic Charleston and its environs. Despite his artistic inclinations, his family encouraged him to study law, which he practised between 1807 and 1818, while also establishing a reputation as a miniature painter. Several aspects of Fraser's style and working technique remained constant throughout his career. His miniatures were usually signed or initialled and dated on the reverse of the backing card. Between 1818 and 1846 they were documented in a record book (Charleston, SC, Gibbes A.G.). The sitter's eyelid is formed by a dark curved stroke to suggest the crease about the eye. The backdrop to the sitter is generally rendered with dark, blue-grey hatching that is deepest in colour near the shoulders, lightening noticeably towards the side to which the head is turned. Fraser's early miniatures, often small ovals, show the strong influence of Malbone, who worked in Charleston in 1801, 1802 and 1806. In one of Fraser's best and earliest miniatures, *James Pringle Reid* (1803; Charleston, SC, Gibbes A.G.), the influence of Malbone's light palette and his modelling technique of hatching and crosshatching is readily apparent. Later, Fraser's brushwork became characterized by a carefully detailed pattern of stippling. Fraser enjoyed a long, active and distinguished career, depicting Charleston's leading citizens and visiting dignitaries. In 1857 he was honoured by his friends and patrons with a major retrospective of his work including 319 portrait miniatures and 139 landscapes, still-lifes and sketches.

BIBLIOGRAPHY

A. R. Huger Smith and D. E. Huger Smith: *Charles Fraser* (Charleston, 1924/*R* 1967)

A. R. Huger Smith: 'Charles Fraser', *A. America*, xxiii (1935), pp. 22–34

R. P. Tolman: 'The Technique of Charles Fraser, Miniaturist', *Antiques*, xxvii (1935), pp. 19–22, 60–62

M. R. Severns and C. L. Wyrick jr: *Charles Fraser of Charleston: Essays on the Man, his Art and his Times* (Charleston, 1983)

DALE T. JOHNSON

Fraser, Furness & Hewitt. *See under* FURNESS, FRANK.

Fraser, John Arthur (*b* London, 9 Jan 1838; *d* New York, 1 Jan 1898). English painter, active in North America. He received some artistic training in England before emigrating to British North America in 1858 and settling in Quebec. While sketching in the Eastern Townships during the 1860s and 1870s, he developed a preference for depicting landscape. In 1860 William Notman employed

Fraser in his Montreal photography firm to tint portrait photographs, and in 1868 Fraser became a full partner in the Toronto branch. This early contact with photography greatly influenced his painting. He was a founder-member of the Society of Canadian Artists, Montreal, in 1867, of the Ontario Society of Artists, Toronto, in 1872 and a charter member of the Royal Canadian Academy in 1880. In 1883 he dissolved his partnership with Notman and by 1885 lived in Boston, MA, where he became a member of the Boston Art Club and the Boston Watercolor Society. Early in 1886 Sir George Stephen, President of the Canadian Pacific Railway, commissioned him to paint some views of the Rockies for London's Colonial and Indian Exhibition. Fraser based these on photographs by Alexander Henderson, given to him by Sir William Van Horne. In Fraser's watercolour *Summit Lake near Lenchoile, Bow River, Canadian Pacific Railway* (1886; Ottawa, N.G.), the cropped composition, telescoped space and schematic rendering of the distant mountains and foreground shore, juxtaposed with a more focused middle ground, clearly reveal its photographic source.

In the summer of 1886 Fraser travelled to the West Coast. While the works from this sketching trip are more emphatic and direct in interpretation, the treatment of colour and space in *Fraser River Line of Canadian Pacific Railway* (1886; Hamilton, Ont., A.G.) also implies a photographic source. Fraser was in Britain in 1888 and late 1889. The fluid planar recession and low-keyed, more evenly valued colour of the *Heart of Scotland* (c. 1889; Toronto, A.G. Ont.) represent a stylistic change. He returned to New York in 1889 and continued to paint and exhibit in Canada and the USA. He also produced some illustrations after photographs for *Century Magazine*.

BIBLIOGRAPHY
D. Reid: *Our Own Country Canada: Being an Account of the National Aspirations of the Principal Landscape Artists in Montreal and Toronto, 1860–1890* (Ottawa, 1979)
Fact and Fiction: Canadian Painting and Photography, 1860–1900 (exh. cat. by A. Thomas, Montreal, McGill U., McCord Mus., 1979); as book (Montreal, 1982)
D. A. Pringle: *Artists of the Canadian Pacific Railroad, 1881–1900* (diss., Montreal, Concordia U.,1983)
John Arthur Fraser (1838–1898): Watercolours (exh. cat. by K. L. Kollar, Montreal, Concordia U., Williams A. Gals, 1984)
KATHRYN L. KOLLAR

Frassinelli, Gian Piero. *See under* SUPERSTUDIO.

Fratellini [née Marmocchini Cortesi], **Giovanna** (*b* Florence, 1666; *d* Florence, 18 April 1731). Italian painter. After training with Livio Mehus and Pietro Dandini she was appointed lady-in-waiting to Vittoria della Rovere, dowager Grand Duchess of Tuscany, who had her instructed in painting and music. She studied painting in miniature with Ippolito Galantini (1627–1706) and in pastel with Domenico Tempesti (c. 1655–1737). She also learnt to paint in enamel and she finished her studies with Anton Domenico Gabbiani. Grand Duke Cosimo III, Grand Prince Ferdinando and his consort Violante Beatrice of Bavaria and numerous other members of the nobility commissioned portraits from her. The oval-shaped miniature enamel *Portrait of a Young Man* (Baltimore, MD, Walters A.G.) perhaps depicts Cosimo III's son Gian Gastone de' Medici. Fratellini married in 1684,

and her unidealized *Self-portrait* (Florence, Uffizi) shows her painting a portrait of her son Lorenzo. She also painted fables, bacchanals and historical subjects, such as the *Death of Lucretia* (untraced). The painter Violante Beatrice Siries (1709–83) was her pupil.

BIBLIOGRAPHY
Bryan; Thieme–Becker
M. C. Ross: 'An Enamelled Portrait by Giovanna Fratellini', *Burl. Mag.*, lxxxix (1947), pp. 314–17
G. Greer: *The Obstacle Race: The Fortunes of Women Painters and their Work* (London, 1979), pp. 27, 253, 276

Fratina [Fratino], **Giovanni.** *See* DEMIO, GIOVANNI.

Freake Painter. *See* MASTERS, ANONYMOUS AND MONOGRAMMISTS, §I.

Fréart. French family of administrators, writers and collectors. The brothers (1) Roland Fréart, Sieur de Chambray, and (2) Paul Fréart, Sieur de Chantelou, were active in the administration of the fine arts in France in the middle decades of the 17th century, being the cousins of François Sublet de Noyers, the Surintendant des Bâtiments du Roi, and they played a role in the return to Paris from Rome of Nicolas Poussin. Chambray went on to publish an important contribution to the academic debate on the relative importance of drawing and colour in painting. Chantelou was one of Poussin's most faithful patrons.

BIBLIOGRAPHY
H. Chardon: *Les Frères Fréart de Chantelou* (Le Mans, 1867)
J. von Schlosser: *Die Kunstliteratur* (Vienna, 1924); Ital. trans. as *La letteratura artistica* (Florence, 1956/R 1977)

(1) Roland Fréart, Sieur de Chambray (*b* Le Mans, 13 July 1606; *d* Le Mans, 11 Dec 1676). In 1630 he travelled to Italy, where he remained until 1635. He studied the architecture in Rome and associated with collectors, for example Cassiano dal Pozzo, and with artists, among them Poussin. In 1639 Chambray travelled to Rome with his brother (2) Paul Fréart, Sieur de Chantelou, principally to convey the king's invitation to Poussin to return to France as Premier Peintre du Roi. While in the city the brothers took casts of bas-reliefs from Trajan's Column and of antique capitals and medals. In 1640 they accompanied Poussin to Paris, but the death of Cardinal Richelieu and the consequent dismissal in 1643 of the Fréarts' cousin Sublet de Noyers temporarily brought an end to Chambray's public role, and he devoted himself to writing. In particular he took an interest in the principles of architecture. He translated Palladio's *I quattro libri dell'architettura* (1651) and Euclid's *Perspective* (1663). His own writings on art reflect a love of geometry and mathematics. In 1650 Chambray wrote the *Parallèle de l'architecture antique et de la moderne* with an important preface on the superiority of ancient over modern artists. In 1651 he published for the first time Leonardo's treatise on painting as the *Traitté de la peinture de Léonard de Vinci*, which was regarded by Charles Le Brun and the Académie Royale de Peinture et de Sculpture as an authoritative text on art theory. Chambray stressed the primacy of drawing and, in particular, of linear perspective over colour in painting. He vehemently disliked the work of the majority of modern painters and associated the use of colour with decadence and with mannerism. His ideas on art were crystallized in the *Idée de la perfection de la peinture*, published in 1662. Chambray intended this as a rule book for art and a guide for contemporary painters. He emphasized the importance of strict, rigorous geometry as truth in art. The *Idée* served as a manifesto against the sensual and the purely visual, as opposed to intellectual, in painting. Chambray was devoted to the art of Poussin, in which he saw the perfect realization of the classical ideal. He strongly criticized Michelangelo for what he considered extravagant and capricious compositions; he also condemned Rubens, Caravaggio, Tintoretto and Veronese for encouraging a libertine art. In 1666 Colbert gave Chambray the task of examining the projects and designs for the new east façade of the Palais du Louvre. Chambray remained committed to the classical ideal in art; in the QUARREL OF THE ANCIENTS AND MODERNS he was the relentless champion of the Ancients. His portrait by Charles Errard is in the Musée du Louvre.

WRITINGS

Parallèle de l'architecture antique et de la moderne (Paris, 1650)
Traitté de la peinture de Léonard de Vinci (Paris, 1651)
Idée de la perfection de la peinture démontrée par les principes de l'art (Paris, 1662)

BIBLIOGRAPHY

DBF
B. Teyssèdre: *Roger de Piles et les débats sur le coloris au siècle de Louis XIV* (Paris, 1957) pp. 56–62

AMAL ASFOUR

(2) Paul Fréart, Sieur de Chantelou (*b* Le Mans, 25 March 1609; *d* ?1694). Brother of (1) Roland Fréart, Sieur de Chambray. In 1638 he became secretary to his cousin, François Sublet de Noyers, and it was in this capacity that he visited Italy (where he may already have spent some time with Roland) in 1639 and 1640. On the latter occasion he brought Poussin back to Paris and, although Poussin's subsequent period as Premier Peintre du Roi was not a success, it marked the beginning of a long friendship between him and Chantelou. After the death of Richelieu, and the dismissal of Sublet de Noyers in 1643, Chantelou declined a post as intendant of buildings and continued to serve his cousin until 1645, when he became secretary to the Duc d'Enghien (later Prince de Condé). In 1647 he became a royal steward. When Bernini moved to France in 1665 to work for Louis XIV, Chantelou was instructed by Jean-Baptiste Colbert to act as his guide and companion. During the five months he spent with the artist, he kept a diary, which remains a valuable document. In 1675 he retired from public service.

Chantelou was not a man of exceptional literary or intellectual gifts, but he had a genuine enthusiasm for art. His diary provides a detailed picture of Bernini's personality and opinions and useful documentation of the commission for the well-known bust of *Louis XIV* (Versailles, Château). It also reveals something of Chantelou's own views, which seem to have been uncomplicated and practical: Correggio, he remarked, could produce the same effects as Leonardo, and in only a fraction of the time. A collector of paintings rather than drawings (about the authenticity of which he feared being misled), he owned, at the time of Bernini's visit, copies of works by Domenichino, Annibale Carracci and Raphael, as well as original paintings by Poussin and Jean Lemaire (1597–1659). Chantelou's patronage of Poussin had begun in 1639 with the *Israelites Gathering Manna* (Paris, Louvre). Other works by Poussin in his possession included the *Ecstasy of St Paul* (1643; Sarasota, FL, Ringling Mus. A.), commissioned as a pendant to a *Vision of Ezekiel*, then believed to be an original Raphael; a series of the *Seven Sacraments* (Edinburgh, N.G.), a theme Poussin had already treated for Cassiano dal Pozzo, and a *Self-portrait* (Paris, Louvre) completed in 1650.

The correspondence between Chantelou and Poussin began in 1639 and ended only with the artist's death. Poussin's letters alone survive. They deal almost exclusively with practical matters, notably the delay in the completion of work that Chantelou had commissioned. Chantelou appears to have been jealous of another of Poussin's French patrons, Jean Pointel (*d* 1660); it was to reassure him that Pointel was not receiving work of higher quality that Poussin wrote in 1647 the letter in which he expounded his theory of 'modes', explaining that it was inappropriate to make direct comparisons between paintings of disparate moods. The two friends also looked after one another's business interests: Poussin acted as his patron's agent in Rome, arranging the dispatch of items for his collection, and Chantelou was the executor of the painter's will in 1665. After Chantelou's own death his collection was dispersed.

WRITINGS

L. Lalanne, ed.: *Le Journal du voyage du cavalier Bernin en France* (Paris, 1885/*R* Aix-en-Provence, 1981; Eng. trans., Princeton, 1985)

BIBLIOGRAPHY

C. Jouanny, ed.: *Correspondance de Nicolas Poussin* (Paris, 1911/*R* 1968)

MALCOLM BULL

Freddie, Wilhelm [Carlsen, Frederik Wilhelm (Christian)] (*b* Copenhagen, 7 Feb 1909). Danish painter and sculptor. He studied briefly at technical college and at the school of graphic arts of the Kunstakademi in Copenhagen, but he was largely self-taught. Freddie painted his earliest abstracts in 1926, but in 1929 he became acquainted with André Breton's periodical *La Révolution surréaliste*. The following year he introduced Surrealism to Scandinavia with the painting *Liberty, Equality and Fraternity* (priv. col.), which he showed at *Kunstnernes Efterårsudstilling* ('Artists' Autumn Exhibition'). In 1934 he met the painters Harry Carlsson and Vilhelm Bjerke-Petersen. Through Bjerke-Petersen, Freddie became involved with the international Cubist-Surrealist exhibition at *Den Frie* (the Free Exhibition) in Copenhagen in January 1935. Freddie exhibited there along with Magritte, Man Ray, Arp, Miró, Dalí, Yves Tanguy and others. He also participated in later large international Surrealist exhibitions.

Freddie became one of the most important Surrealists in Denmark, and his work caused scandals from the beginning. When, in March 1937, he opened his exhibition *Sex-surreal: Træk gaflen ud af øjet på sommerfuglen* ('Sexsurreal: pull the fork out of the eye of the butterfly'), it was denounced as a danger to public morals. Three of his major works, the paintings *Psychophotographic Phenomenon: The World War's Fallen* (Silkeborg, Krtmus.) and the *Legionnaires of Pleasure* (priv. col.), and the object *Sexparalysis Appeal* (Ålborg, Nordjyllands Kstmus.), a painted plaster bust from the 1890s, equipped with a painted-on penis, among other things, ended up in the Criminal

Museum in Copenhagen and Freddie was imprisoned. In 1961 he provoked a re-opening of the case when he exhibited copies of the works. Freddie, along with the works of art, was cleared of the obscenity charge in May 1963, and the case led to a revision of the Danish pornography laws, including the abolition of censorship. Freddie's work commented both on sexual morality and on politics. During the German occupation of Denmark he was classified as *entartet*, and the appearance of the painting *Meditation on Anti-Nazi Love* (Ålborg, Nordjyllands Kstmus.), in which Hitler appears, enforced his flight to Sweden in 1944. He stayed there for six years. After his trial in 1963 Freddie became well known and accepted in Denmark, especially with the purchase by Statens Kunstfond in 1965 of the painting *Venetian Rock'n'Roll* (1960; Copenhagen, Stat. Mus. Kst). He then received some decorative commissions, including Egholm School in Vallensbæk (1970). Between 1973 and 1979 he was a professor at the Kunstakademi in Copenhagen.

Freddie remained an anarchic social commentator all his life, but his forms of expression changed. Such artists as Ernst, Tanguy and Dalí inspired his paintings of the 1930s, which display his mastery of the illusionistic devices of the academic tradition. After a number of paintings with powerful chiaroscuro effects, he abandoned 'classic' Surrealism in the 1940s. What emerged can be seen, for example, in the *Moon's Fiancé* (1947; Humlebæk, Louisiana Mus.), in which illusionistic form is replaced by concatenated parts of human bodies, markings, geometric shapes and machine-like fragments. Around 1955 his work became more abstract, with elements of collage and assemblage, and often including photographic fragments. On the whole his work is united by the presence of mainly female eroticism. Freddie, who regarded Surrealism as a spiritual state rather than a philosophy or artistic style, also worked in film (e.g. two short Surrealist films made with Jørgen Roos, *The Definitive Refusal of Permission for a Kiss*, 1949, and *Eaten Horizons*, 1950) and ballet design (e.g. for *Kærlighedens triumf: Surrealistisk intermezzo*, 'The triumph of love: Surrealist intermezzo', 1940). He also designed clothes and took part in Surrealist demonstrations. He was a prolific graphic artist and, as a member of the international group PHASES, he was highly active in international exhibitions.

BIBLIOGRAPHY

V. Bjerke-Petersen: *Wilhelm Freddie* (Copenhagen, 1935)

S. Colding: 'Wilhelm Freddie', *The Studio* (1948)

G. Luca and others: *Wilhelm Freddie* (Copenhagen, 1962) [Dan., Ger. and Fr. text]

E. Jaguer: *Wilhelm Freddie—Pilene fra den elektriske bue* [Wilhelm Freddie—the arrows from the electric arc] (Copenhagen, 1969) [Dan., Ger. and Fr. text]

E. Fischer: *Wilhelm Freddie: Tegninger, collager, grafik* [Wilhelm Freddie: drawings, collages, graphics] (Copenhagen, 1973)

P. Schmidt: *Wilhelm Freddie—Den evige oprører* [Wilhelm Freddie—the eternal insurgent] (Copenhagen, 1976)

Freddie (exh. cat., ed. B. Raben-Skov; Copenhagen, Stat. Mus. Kst, 1989–90) [cat. rais.]

VIDEOS AND FILMS

O. Braunstein: *Vil de køre med frøken?* [Will you drive with the lady?] (broadcast 2 April 1968) [TV film]

P. Kirkeby: *Wilhelm Freddie* (1972) [film]

BIRGIT HESSELLUND

Frédeau, Ambroise (*b* Paris, ?*c.* 1589; *d* Toulouse, 1673). French painter and sculptor. He joined the Augustinian monastery in Toulouse in 1640; an inventory of his goods drawn up at this time shows him to have painted a variety of subjects, including such religious and mythological works as *St John the Baptist* and *Female Satyr Carrying her Young* (both untraced), and to have been a sculptor, producing, among other pieces, a *Virgin and Child* (untraced). From 1640 to 1652 he ran a busy studio at the monastery, supplying numerous religious paintings to the clergy of Toulouse and the surrounding area, as well as to private patrons. After 1652 his production declined, because of eye problems possibly suffered as a result of the plague of that year.

Only a handful of Frédeau's works are extant, all of religious subjects. They include *St Augustine Offering his Heart to the Virgin* (*c.* 1640; Toulouse, Mus. Augustins), *Jesus Appearing to his Mother* (before 1653; Toulouse, St Pierre), *St Roch Tended by the Angel* (1650; L'Isle-sur-Tarn, parish church) and the *Blessed William of Toulouse Tormented by Demons* (1657; Toulouse, Mus. Augustins). Frédeau typically crowded his figures to the foreground plane of his pictures, which display hardly any sense of depth and are constructed in accordance with strict geometric layouts. One drawing by him is known to survive: the *Death of St Joseph* (1647; Toulouse, Mus. Dupuy). None of his sculptures remains, though the records of the monastery in Toulouse mention such works as a relief of the *Massacre of the Innocents* (1642) and a wood model for a silver statue of *St Nicholas of Tolentino* (1647).

BIBLIOGRAPHY

P. Saliès: 'Ambroise Frédeau, religieux augustin du couvent de Toulouse, peintre, sculpteur et miniaturiste', *Mém. Acad. Sci., Inscr. B.-Lett. Toulouse*, n. s. 14, cxxiii (1961), pp 123–45

Jean Chalette, Ambroise Frédeau, peintres à Toulouse (exh. cat. by A. Mousseigne, Toulouse, Mus. Augustins, 1974), pp. 13–57

THIERRY BAJOU

Fredensborg. Danish castle *c.* 40 km north-west of Copenhagen. The summer residence of the Danish court, it was originally a hunting seat, built in 1719–22 for Frederick IV (*reg* 1699–1730) by JOHAN CORNELIUS KRIEGER. It comprised a *corps-de-logis* and an octagonal forecourt surrounded by single-storey buildings. The *corps-de-logis*, the nucleus of the layout, is a centralized building with a square hall in the middle, two storeys high and surmounted by a four-sided cupola. The plan of the building is derived from the Palladian villa type, but the shape of the cupola gives the exterior a French rather than Italian appearance. The central hall is undoubtedly inspired by a similar room in the Palazzo Albergati in Bologna, attributed to Baldassare Peruzzi, which Frederick visited twice. An unexecuted project (1708; Washington, DC, Lib. Congr.), which the King commissioned from FRANCESCO MUTTONI in Vicenza, could have been influential, despite its megalomaniac appearance, in the choice of the Palladian central plan and some of the stuccowork in the cupola room. It remains, however, an original design. Krieger also laid out the semicircular garden directly in front of the building.

The original building was gradually enlarged by the addition of other structures, for example a chapel wing placed between an orangery and a guest house connecting the *corps-de-logis* with the stables. This wing was erected from 1742, together with ten smaller buildings that flanked the entrance to the castle. In 1741 the second storey of the *corps-de-logis* was raised, and the four minaret-like chimneys built. From 1754 to 1756 the main building was augmented with four pavilions at the corners, with a link building between two of them. The final alteration took place in 1774–6, when C. F. Harsdorff raised the forecourt buildings by one storey, removed the wing directly in front of the main building and flanked the resulting open space with pavilions.

BIBLIOGRAPHY

J. Steenberg: *Fredensborg Slot: Monumenter og Minder* [Fredensborg Castle: Monuments and relics], 2 vols (Copenhagen, 1969–79) [Eng. summary]

L. Puppi: 'Un progetto di Francesco Muttoni per Federico IV di Danimarca', *Veltro: Riv. Civiltà It.*, xxv/1–3 (1981), pp. 281–91

H. Lund: 'Frederik IV's italienske tegninger' [Frederick IV's Italian designs], *Architectura: Arkithist. Aaskr.*, x (1988), pp. 45–55

HAKON LUND

Fréderic, Léon (Henri Marie) (*b* Brussels, 26 Aug 1856; *d* Schaarbeek, 27 Jan 1940). Belgian painter and draughtsman. He studied briefly under Charle-Albert before attending the Académie Royale des Beaux-Arts, Brussels, where he became a pupil of Jules Vankeirsbilck (1833–96) and Ernest Slingeneyer (1820–94), also working in the studio of Jean-François Portaels. In 1878 he went to Italy with the sculptor Julien Dillens; he stayed there for over a year, making numerous studies after the artists of the Quattrocento. In 1878 he made his début at the Triennial Salon in Brussels and became a member of the group of Realist painters known as L'ESSOR. The very early work still shows the influence of E. Wauters (1846–1933), with whom he collaborated on the *Panorama of Cairo* (untraced).

In 1882 Fréderic was awarded his first medal at the Triennial Salon in Brussels for the triptych *Chalk Sellers* (Brussels, Mus. A. Mod.). The objective, realistic style and the smooth painting technique are characteristic of his work; also typical is the elaboration of one theme over several large canvases. The bleak and melancholy atmosphere of the expanding suburbs inspired him to paint tramps and a series of *Women in Rags* (1882–3). In 1883 he went to stay in Nafraiture, a rural village in the Ardennes, where he was to return repeatedly and which from that time became his chief source of inspiration. In Nafraiture he painted a number of landscapes but felt primarily drawn towards the villagers. He rendered the peasants' simplicity and resignation in paintings such as the *Farmer's Life*, a series of five canvases (1885–8; Brussels, Mus. A. Mod.) and *Two Walloon Peasant Children* (1888; Antwerp, Kon. Mus. S. Kst.).

Fréderic maintained his realistic approach towards his subjects, for example the series of 11 large charcoal drawings *Flax, Corn and Earth* (1888), in which he represented the necessities of life, including the *Making of the Linen* (1.15×1.0 m, 1888; untraced, see Legrand, pl. 109). He travelled to England and Germany and moved to Schaarbeek in 1889. In 1893 he received an invitation from the progressive Brussels group Les XX and in 1896 he joined the Art Idéaliste group. In these years he painted large allegorical scenes in which he expressed his ideals of social harmony and unity with nature. These works are purely symbolical, without any reference to reality, and reveal the influence of the English Pre-Raphaelites. They are crowded with figures and show an abundance of plants and flowers: for example, *Nature (Fertility)* (1897) and the triptych called *The River* (1890–99; both Brussels, Mus. A. Mod.). Certain symbolic motifs in these paintings, such as that of the swan, are conceivably related to Art Nouveau. Fréderic also painted a number of portraits, for example *Elodie Lambotte* (1893; priv. col., see Legrand, pl. 53); his detailed, precise manner of painting and arrangement of the figure create a dreamy atmosphere that has strong similarities with Symbolism.

BIBLIOGRAPHY

BNB

F. C. Legrand: *Het symbolisme in België* (Brussels, 1971)

L. Fréderic (exh. cat., St Joost-ten-Node, Charlier-Hôtel, 1973)

D. CARDYN-OOMEN

Frederici, Paolo di Giovanni. *See* PAOLO DI GIOVANNI FEI.

Frederick, Emperor of Germany. *See* HOHENZOLLERN, (14).

Frederick (Louis), Prince of Wales. *See* HANOVER, (1).

Frederick I [Barbarossa], Holy Roman Emperor and King of Germany. *See* HOHENSTAUFEN, (1).

Frederick I, King of Prussia. *See* HOHENZOLLERN, (4).

Frederick II, Holy Roman Emperor and King of Sicily. *See* HOHENSTAUFEN, (2).

Frederick II, King of Denmark and Norway. *See* OLDENBURG, (1).

Frederick II, King of Prussia. *See* HOHENZOLLERN, (7).

Frederick [Friedrich] **II**, Landgrave of Hesse-Kassel. *See* HESSE-KASSEL, (3).

Frederick III, Elector of Brandenburg. *See* HOHENZOLLERN, (4).

Frederick III, Elector of Saxony. *See* WETTIN, (3).

Frederick III, Holy Roman Emperor. *See* HABSBURG, §I(2).

Frederick III, King of Prussia. *See* HOHENZOLLERN, (14).

Frederick-Augustus I, Elector of Saxony. *See* WETTIN, (7).

Frederick-Augustus II, Elector of Saxony. *See* WETTIN, (8).

Frederick Henry, Stadholder and Prince of Orange. *See* ORANGE NASSAU, (3).

Frederick the Great, King of Prussia. *See* HOHENZOLLERN, (7).

Frederick William, Elector of Brandenburg. *See* HOHENZOLLERN, (3).

Frederick William I, King of Prussia. *See* HOHENZOLLERN, (5).

Frederick William II, King of Prussia. *See* HOHENZOLLERN, (9).

Frederick William III, King of Prussia. *See* HOHENZOL-LERN, (10).

Frederick William IV, King of Prussia. *See* HOHENZOL-LERN, (11).

Frederiksborg Castle. *See* HILLERØD, FREDERIKSBORG CASTLE.

Fredi, Bartolo di. *See* CINI, (1).

Frediani, Vincenzo (di Antonio) [Master of the Immaculate Conception] (*fl* Lucca, 1481–1505). Italian painter. The discovery of the contract for a large painting of the *Immaculate Conception* (Tazartes, 1987) has identified Frediani as the painter of a group of paintings formerly attributed to the Master of the Immaculate Conception (Symeonides). He was probably trained in Lucca but in the 1480s fell under the influence of Ghirlandaio, Filippino Lippi and Botticelli. In 1481 he painted an altarpiece (untraced) for the Lucchese merchant Paolo di Serfederigi for his altar in S Agostino, Lucca. The *Virgin and Child Enthroned with SS Nicholas, Dominic, Vincent, Peter Martyr and Two Angels* (ex-Kaiser-Friedrich-Mus., Berlin; destr.) was ordered by Domenico del Voglia in 1482 for his chapel in S Romano, Lucca, and finished before 1485. This painting was previously attributed to another anonymous master, the Buonvisi Painter, and it is possible that other paintings attributed to that Master may be the work of Frediani.

In the 1490s Frediani had an important workshop in Lucca. The *Virgin and Child with Saints* (Lucca, S Eustachio di Montignoso) is dated 1495, and in 1496 he executed paintings (untraced) in the Palazzo degli Anziani, Lucca. The *Virgin and Child with SS Peter and Andrew* (church of Tempagnano di Lunata) and frescoes and an altarpiece for the chapel of the Tertiary Franciscans (Lucca, S Francesco; both destr.) all dated from 1497. In 1502 the Tertiary Franciscans ordered a second, large, altarpiece of the *Immaculate Conception* (Lucca, Villa Guinigi) for S Francesco, Lucca. It was finished in 1503. Its complex iconography, a remarkable piece of Franciscan propaganda, was stipulated in the contract. The *Coronation of the Virgin with Saints* (Lucca, Villa Guinigi), formerly in S Lorenzo ai Servi, almost certainly dates from the same period. The large altarpiece of the *Death and Assumption of the Virgin* (San Maria a Colle, nr Lucca, parish church), dating from the beginning of the 16th century, is stylistically close to Michelangelo di Pietro. In 1505 Frediani started to paint a *Virgin and Child* for S Gennaro at Capannori that was left unfinished at his death and completed by Ranieri di Leonardo da Pisa.

BIBLIOGRAPHY
S. Symeonides: 'An Altarpiece by the Lucchese Master of the Immaculate Conception', *Marsyas*, viii (1957–9), pp. 55–65
E. Fahy: 'A Lucchese Follower of Filippino Lippi', *Paragone*, clxxxv (1965), p. 16
M. Ferretti: 'Percorso lucchese', *An. Scu. Norm. Sup. Pisa*, n.s. 2, v/3 (1975), pp. 1041–3
——: 'Di nuovo sul percorso lucchese', *An. Scu. Norm. Sup. Pisa*, n.s. 2, viii/3 (1978), pp. 1245–7
M. Natale: 'Note sulla pittura lucchese alla fine del quattrocento', *Getty Mus. J.*, viii (1980), pp. 49–51
M. Tazartes: 'Anagrafe lucchese, i: Vincenzo di Antonio Frediani "pictor de Luca": Il Maestro dell'Immacolata Concezione', *Ric. Stor. A.*, xxvi (1985), pp. 4–17
——: 'Nouvelles perspectives sur la peinture lucquoise du quattrocento', *Rev. A.*, lxxv (1987), pp. 29–36
C. Baracchini and others: 'Pittori a Lucca tra '400 e '500', *An. Scu. Norm. Sup. Pisa*, n.s. 2, xvi (1986), pp. 743–824

MAURIZIA TAZARTES

Free Classic Style. *See* QUEEN ANNE REVIVAL.

Freed, James Ingo. *See under* PEI, I. M.

Freed, Leonard (*b* Brooklyn, NY, 23 Oct 1929). American photographer and film maker. He was mainly self-taught in photography but studied briefly under Alexey Brodovitch (1898–1971). In 1958 he became a freelance photojournalist, working for such publications as the *Sunday Times Magazine*, the *New York Times Magazine*, *Der Stern* and *Geo*. Freed worked primarily in 35 mm black and white in the tradition of 'concerned photography', typical of the Magnum agency, which he joined in 1970. Through such images as *Harlem, New York* (1967; see 1985 exh. cat., p. 124) he showed his interest in social groups, for example Black and Jewish communities. His works have been published in a number of collections (see photographic publications). Freed's films explore similar themes, for example *Dansende vromen* ('Dance of the pious'; 1963) about Hasidic Jews, and *The Negro in America* (1966), both made for Netherlands Television.

PHOTOGRAPHIC PUBLICATIONS
Black and White America (New York, 1968)
Made in Germany (New York, 1970); rev. as *Leonard Freed's Germany* (London, 1971)
Police Work (New York, 1980)
La Danse des fidèles (Paris, 1984)

BIBLIOGRAPHY
Contemp. Phots
The Spectre of Violence (exh. cat. by S. Davies, London, Phot. Gal., 1973)
American Images: Photography, 1945–1980 (exh. cat., ed. P. Turner; London, Barbican A.G., 1985)

VIRGINIA DODIER

Freedman, Barnett (*b* London, 19 May 1901; *d* London, 4 Jan 1958). British painter, lithographer, illustrator and designer. He was the eldest son of poor Russian–Jewish immigrants in London's East End and spent much of his childhood in hospital. At 15, Freedman's talent for drawing led to jobs as a draughtsman for a monumental mason, then for an architect. After five years' evening study at St Martin's School of Art, London, he won a scholarship to the Royal College of Art (1922–5), where he later became a teacher himself. As a painter, Freedman was neither reactionary nor avant-garde; traditional subject-matter, in a subdued but contemplative manner, gave little hint of his ebullient personality. He is remembered chiefly as a pioneer of colour autolithography for machine production at the Curwen and Baynard presses, which he achieved by transferring drawings on stone to offset plates. Books illustrated in this way include *Lavengro* (1936), *War and Peace* (1938), *Henry IV, Part I, Oliver Twist* (both 1939), *Wuthering Heights* (1941), *Jane Eyre* (1942) and *Anna Karenina* (1950); most were published by New York limited edition clubs. Freedman autolithographed some 40 book jackets and numerous posters and played a leading role in the production of large-scale colour prints for

Contemporary Lithographs (1937), Lyons (1947, 1951, 1955) and Guinness (1956). He staged plays at the Scala, Little and Fortune theatres, designed the Silver Jubilee stamp in 1935 and tackled ephemera with consummate professionalism. An official war artist, first with the British Expeditionary Force in France, then with the Admiralty until 1946, Freedman won the CBE for his work. This included large-scale paintings, portraits of entire ships' crews and the notable lithograph *15-inch Gun Turret in HMS Repulse*. Examples of his work are in the Tate Gallery, Victoria and Albert Museum and Imperial War Museum, London, as well as in numerous provincial British galleries. After the war, he became a rumbustious TV and radio personality.

UNPUBLISHED SOURCES

Manchester, Met. U., All Saints Lib. [archive of letters and ephemera]

WRITINGS

'Lithography: A Painter's Excursion', *Signature*, ii (March 1936), pp. 10–15

'Every Man his own Lithographer', *The Listener* (9 June 1938), pp. 1227–9

'Autolithography or Substitute Works of Art', *Penrose Annu.*, xciv (1950), pp. 62–3

BIBLIOGRAPHY

J. Rothenstein: 'Barnett Freedman', *Studio Int.*, ix/109 (Feb 1935), pp. 90–93

J. Mayne: *Barnett Freedman*, English Masters of Black-and-White (London, 1948)

Barnett Freedman, 1901–1958 (exh. cat., intro. by Sir S. Tallents, London, ACGB, 1958)

P. Gilmour: 'Barnett Freedman', *Artists at Curwen* (exh. cat., London, Tate, 1977), pp. 66–74, 121–2

——: 'Unsung Heroes: Barnett Freedman', *Tamarind Pap.*, viii/1, 2 (1985), pp. 15–24

PAT GILMOUR

Freer, Charles Lang (*b* Kingston, NY, 25 Feb 1856; *d* New York, 25 Sept 1919). American manufacturer and collector. Born into poverty, he left school at the age of 14 to work, first in a cement factory and then as a clerk in a store. Soon afterwards, Frank J. Hecker, manager of the Kingston & Syracuse Railroad, noticed the young man's business acumen and made him paymaster of the railroad. In 1880 the two men became partners and opened the first railway carriage factory in the Midwest, the Peninsular Car Works. However, by the age of 44, Freer was compelled to retire because of his frail constitution; already a wealthy man, he was on his way to becoming a major collector. He initially collected art to embellish his home in Detroit, built by Wilson Eyre in 1890 and decorated by the American painters Dwight W. Tryon, Thomas Wilmer Dewing and Abbot Handerson Thayer in exchange for advice on investments. Freer valued the moral character of these artists' work and shared their vision of pure and noble womanhood found in such paintings as Thayer's *Virgin Enthroned* (Washington, DC, Freer). Freer soon developed an interest in prints and in 1887 he discovered the etchings of James McNeill Whistler, which he thought the highest expression of his aesthetic. His passion for the artist's work was instant and enduring and, by 1890, when collector and artist met in Paris, Freer owned more than 80 etchings by Whistler. His collection eventually numbered over 1000 prints, pastels and paintings and included *Harmony in Blue and Gold: Peacock Room* (1876–7; Washington, DC, Freer), a dining-room designed for Liverpool shipowner F. R. Leyland by Thomas Jeckyll and radically revised by Whistler.

Whistler became Freer's close friend and, together with Ernest Francisco Fenollosa, introduced him to the splendours of East Asian art, long before his fellow American collectors became interested in it. As early as 1887 he had purchased a Japanese fan attributed to Ogata Kōrin (later to a follower). Then, on his friends' advice, he bought Japanese and some Chinese prints and later added fine Korean examples. On four trips to East Asia between 1895 and 1911 he visited the major private and public collections and made important purchases. When he returned from his last Asian trip Freer owned over 8000 Asian works. These included numerous examples of Chinese ceramics, especially from the early Han, Tang and Song periods. From his Japanese collection he especially cherished some thirty sketches by Katsushika Hokusai and two Kamakura-period paintings of the *bodhisattva* Jizō.

In December 1904 Freer offered the contents of his collection to the Smithsonian Institution in Washington, DC. This was the first significant bequest of art ever made to the US government by a private citizen, but it was only accepted following the efforts of Theodore Roosevelt. The Freer Gallery of Art finally opened to the public in 1923 (*see* JAPAN, fig. 255). Later it was enhanced by the addition of a fine Japanese and Chinese collection belonging to Freer's great friend Agnes Meyer (1887–1970).

BIBLIOGRAPHY

The Freer Gallery of Art, 3 vols (Tokyo, n.d.)

A. E. Meyer: *Charles Lang Freer and his Gallery* (Washington, DC, 1970)

N. Clark: 'Charles Lang Freer: An American Aesthete', *Amer. A. J.*, 11 (Oct 1979), pp. 54–68

Apollo, cxvii/258 (1983) [issue ded. to Freer]

P. Pal, ed.: *American Collectors of Asian Art* (Bombay, 1986)

KATHRYN BONOMI

Frégevize [Fraigevise; Frégévise], **Frédéric** [Friedrich] (*b* Geneva, 1770; *d* Geneva, 9 Oct 1849). Swiss painter. He began by painting on enamel, at which he became very proficient, producing portraits, landscapes and flower pictures. Moving to Berlin, from where his family had originated, he devoted himself to painting in oil on canvas and became a member and professor of the Berlin Akademie. He specialized in landscape painting but produced some genre paintings and portraits. The best-known of his landscapes are those that reproduce effects of moonlight. In 1823 he was made an honorary member of the Société des Artistes, Paris. In 1829 he returned to Geneva. His paintings are notable for their careful technique, probably deriving from his early experience of working on enamel. He was the father of Edouard Frégevize (*b* 1840), a lithographer and painter.

BIBLIOGRAPHY

SKL

☐

Frei, Hans (*b* Basle, 30 April 1868; *d* Basle, 14 March 1947). Swiss medallist, goldsmith and sculptor. He began a three-year engraving apprenticeship at the age of 14 and first worked as an engraver and medallist in Vienna, attending the Goldschmied- und Ciseleurschule while also continuing to study goldsmithing and engraving in Germany. In 1893 he attended classes in sculpture and engraving at the Ecole des Arts Industriels and the Ecole des Beaux-Arts in Geneva, and in 1894–6 he studied at the Ecole Nationale Supérieure des Arts Décoratifs in Paris, coming into contact with the medallist Oscar Roty. In 1896–7 he studied sculpture at the Académie Julian in Paris, also undertaking work for jewellery manufacturers in his Paris studio from 1896. He returned to Basle in 1898 and set up on his own, achieving an international reputation. The major part of his output consisted of over 400 medals and plaques commemorating jubilees, festivals, dedications and foundations. The most interesting examples were portrait medals, which he executed in a simple style (e.g. *Jakob Burckhardt*, tin, 1898; Basle, Hist. Mus.), and self-portraits (e.g. in 1896 and 1928, silver; Basle, Hist. Mus.). He also created sculptures in the round such as figures for fountains and funerary monuments, including the tomb of *Albert Anker* (1912; *in situ*) in Ins, as well as cast and embossed plates for tombs, cups and mugs, pieces made in gold and a large number of seal dies.

BIBLIOGRAPHY
H. Aeppli: *Der Schweizer Medailleur Hans Frei* (Basle, 1933)
Hans Frei (exh. cat. by H. Krattiger, Riehen, Gemeindehaus, 1968)
Albert Ankers Antlitz (exh. cat. by S. Kuthy, Pfäffikon, Schwyz, Seedamm-Kultzent., 1991)

F. FORTER

Freiberg. German city in Saxony with a population of *c.* 51,600. The city, which grew rich from silver mining after the discovery in 1168 of a silver deposit in the village of Christiansdorf, developed in several stages at the end of the 12th century and the beginning of the 13th. The Wettin margraves of Meissen granted 'free', or unregulated, mining privileges ('Bergbaufreiheit') to the miners, most of them from the Harz mountain region, who streamed into the area, and for this reason the city was named 'Freiberg'. Four large parish churches were built in the Romanesque period; among them was the Marienkirche, which later became the cathedral (*see* §1 below). At the beginning of the 13th century, the Oberstadt (upper town) received its regular layout with a large, square market-place. The cultural activity of the city reached its peak in the late 15th century and the 16th. The parish churches were rebuilt in Late Gothic style, and the impressive Rathaus and patrician residences were built in stone. The Wettins enlarged (1566–79) their castle into a Renaissance palace, Schloss Freudenstein. The city suffered a reversal of fortune in the 17th and 18th centuries, owing to the decline of the mining industry and to the destruction caused by wars and fires. From 1711 the organ-builder Gottfried Silbermann (1683–1753) had his workshop in Freiberg. The city later became a centre for mining technology; the Bergakademie (mining academy), Europe's first technical institute, was founded in 1765.

BIBLIOGRAPHY
M. Unger: *Stadtgemeinde und Bergwesen Freibergs im Mittelalter* (Weimar, 1963)
H. H. Kasper and E. Wächtler, eds: *Geschichte der Bergstadt Freiberg* (Weimar, 1986)

1. CATHEDRAL. The Marienkirche was built in the last quarter of the 12th century as the parish church of Freiberg, and it is chiefly notable for its sculpture. To the Late Romanesque basilica were added two important works of sculpture after 1225: the 'Golden Portal', erected

between the west towers, and the pulpitum. The church was rebuilt following its elevation (1480) to cathedral status, and after a fire in 1484 the pulpitum was broken up, while the Golden Portal was moved to the south side of the new Late Gothic hall church. The construction of the pulpitum and the Golden Portal is undocumented, but circumstantial evidence suggests that both were commissioned by the margrave of Meissen or his advocates, and that the iconographic programme was created by Ludeger, abbot of the Cistercian monastery of Altzella, which held the patronage of the churches at Freiberg. The Golden Portal is the earliest splayed portal in Germany to have figures on the jambs and archivolts (*see also* GOTHIC, §III, 1(iii)(b)). It is of Grillenburg sandstone and had polychrome decoration, traces of which survive. The two-storey pulpitum, also of sandstone, had a central ciborium and a pulpit and was surmounted by an oak *Crucifixion* group (now on a beam within the chancel arch), which retains its original paintwork. The latter is an important example of 13th-century central German crucifixes of the three-nail type. The ground-plan of the pulpitum has been excavated, and six relief panels (damaged) are preserved in the cloister. The dating of the sculptures (*c.* 1225–40) is based only on stylistic comparisons. Although French influences can be detected in the typology, motifs and iconography, there is a stylistic affinity with the 'Lower Saxon' style, especially that of Halberstadt. Byzantine painting provided another important stimulus. The Freiberg sculptures are related to those of Wechselberg (*see* WECHSELBURG, SCHLOSSKIRCHE). Henry, Duke of Saxony and other members of his family were buried in the cathedral, which led, in the second half of the 16th century, to its becoming one of Europe's grandest family mausolea (*see* WETTIN, (4)).

BIBLIOGRAPHY
A. Goldschmidt: *Die Skulpturen von Freiberg und Wechselburg* (Berlin, 1924)
E. Hütter and H. Magirius: 'Studien zur Goldenen Pforte', *Kunst des Mittelalters in Sachsen: Festschrift Wolf Schubert* (Weimar, 1967), pp. 179–231
H. Magirius: *Der Freiberger Dom: Forschungen und Denkmalpflege* (Weimar, 1972)

HEINRICH MAGIRIUS

Freiburg im Breisgau. German cathedral city in Baden-Württemberg, on the River Dreisam between the Black Forest and the Rhine Valley about 30 km south-west of Stuttgart. Many of its older buildings, evidence of its historical importance as a cultural centre from the 12th century, were destroyed during World War II, but the cathedral (*see* §2 below) escaped damage.

1. History and urban development. 2. Cathedral.

1. HISTORY AND URBAN DEVELOPMENT. The town was founded in 1120 by Berthold III, Duke of Zähringen (*d* 1122), deriving its name from the wide-ranging freedoms granted to the citizens by successive dukes. In 1218 Freiburg passed to the Urachs, then in the 14th century to the Habsburgs. It was built according to one of the earliest known medieval regular plans: the line of the original town walls still exists in the form of a ring road surrounding the Old Town, the layout of which is bisected by a main

thoroughfare (today the Kaiser Josephstrasse). The medieval growth and prosperity of the town were based on silver mining and crafts and were reflected in the numerous building campaigns, each financed by the citizens, that expanded the parish church (now the cathedral).

In the late Middle Ages the Albert-Ludwigs-Universität (founded 1457) underwent a period of growth, and the number of religious orders that built churches in Freiburg greatly increased. These included the Franciscans, whose church of St Martin, founded in 1262, was freed of later additions by the restoration of 1953 to reveal its Early Gothic sobriety. During the reign of Maximilian I, Holy Roman Emperor, who held the Imperial Diet in Freiburg in 1498, numerous mansions and town houses were built, most of which were destroyed in 1944. Notable among them is the Basler Hof on the Kaiser Josephstrasse, built in 1494–1505 (partly destr. 1944; rest.). Its magnificent façade displays three Gothic oriels and two sculptured Renaissance portals. A vulnerable outpost of Austrian Habsburg power, Freiburg was attacked many times during the Thirty Years War (1618–48) and lost two thirds of its population. When France eventually gained control over the town (1677–97), Vauban built fortifications intended to make it less vulnerable in future conflicts, but these were dismantled in 1748 at the Peace of Aix-la-Chapelle. Again under Austrian control, Freiburg was an administrative centre in the 18th century but was incorporated into Baden in 1805. The see of Konstanz was moved to Freiburg in 1827, and the growth of the city in the 19th century is reflected in efforts to remove sections of the walls in order to assist expansion, while the rebuilding programme that took place after the end of World War II allowed much of the city to be modernized.

BIBLIOGRAPHY

L. A. Ricker: *Freiburg: Aus der Geschichte einer Stadt* (Freiburg im Breisgau, 1982)

H. Keller: 'Die Zähringer und die Entwicklung Freiburgs zur Stadt', *Die Zähringer: Eine Tradition und ihre Erforschung*, ed. K. Schmid (Sigmaringen, 1986), pp. 17–29

2. CATHEDRAL.

(i) *Architecture.* The former parish church of Unserer Lieben Frau, which became the cathedral in 1827, is built in red sandstone quarried locally at Freiburg and Tennenbach. The earliest surviving parts are the typically upper Rhenish 'cock towers' (*Hahnentürme*), with treasury and archive rooms, the non-projecting transept and the crossing dome. Stylistically related to Basle Minster, this work is associated with Berthold V, Duke of Zähringen (*d* 1218), on the grounds that the next phase, comprising the two eastern bays of the nave, can be linked to his successor, the Urach Egon, Duke of Freiburg. These are in an Early Gothic style related to the nearby Cistercian abbey of Tennenbach, where Egon's brother was abbot. Structural problems in the vaults seem, however, to have dictated another change in architect, and the remaining four nave bays were built according to a High Gothic plan related to Strasbourg Cathedral. The west tower is thought on the basis of style to have been built by a series of Strasbourg builders from the later 13th century to the mid-14th; but the aesthetically superior, if impractical, openwork spire is without comparison in Strasbourg or anywhere else.

Freiburg has perhaps the earliest and most influential example of the single-towered west end. The *Hahnentürme* were redecorated to harmonize with the west tower.

An inscription in the Late Gothic choir indicates that it was begun in 1364; the designer was almost certainly Johann Parler von Gmünd (*see* PARLER, (2)). The five-bay choir has flanking chapels, six radiating chapels and a net vault. Although political and economic difficulties brought building to a halt in 1380, the original plan was carried through by HANS NIESENBERGER from 1471. Work was still continuing in 1532, but the choir must have been in use by 1513, when it was consecrated.

BIBLIOGRAPHY

H. Reinhold: *Der Chor des Münsters zu Freiburg und die Baukunst der Parlerfamilie* (Strasbourg, 1929)

W. Noack: 'Neue Ergebnisse zur Baugeschichte der Münster von Strasbourg und Freiburg', *Forsch. & Fortschr.*, xxiv (1948), pp. 35ff

——: 'Das Langhaus des Freiburger Münsters', *Schau-ins-Land*, lxxvii (1955), pp. 18–48

V. Osteneck: 'Die romanischen Bauteile des Freiburger Münsters, und ihre stilgeschichtlichen Voraussetzungen', *Studien zur spätromanischen Baukunst am Oberrhein* (Bonn, 1973)

W. Hart: *Das Freiburger Münster* (Freiburg im Breisgau, 1978)

F. Vellguth: *Der Turm des Freiburger Münsters* (Tübingen, 1983)

R. Liess: 'Der Rahnsche Riss des Freiburger Münsterturms und seine Strassburger Herkunft', *Z. Kstwiss.*, xlv (1991), pp. 7–66

(ii) *Sculpture.* Freiburg Cathedral is richly decorated inside and out with sculpture dating almost exclusively from the 13th and 14th centuries. At the west end, the usual French cathedral façade programme on the theme of *Salvation* is condensed on to a single portal and amplified on the walls of the adjoining narthex. There are five levels of sculpture on the west tower for which no overall iconographic scheme has been identified. The north and south nave buttresses are decorated with figures in tabernacles depicted mainly in pairs. These figures, including Old Testament kings, apostles and bishops, have been interpreted as symbolic buttresses of the church, analogous to the real buttresses on which they stand. Apostles also appear on the nave piers, but here they are arranged according to their popularity, thus suggesting their practical role in medieval daily life as models and intercessors. The 14th-century sculpture at the east end is largely confined to two portals. On the north portal the *History of Salvation* is depicted again but recast, emphasizing the contrast between the *Fall of Man* and the *Crucifixion*. The south portal is devoted to the *Death and Coronation of the Virgin*.

The sculptural campaigns are closely related to the cathedral's architectural history. The early work of the transepts can be related to Basle Minster, and the east nave buttress sculpture has been related to Cistercian work. These are dated respectively to just before and just after 1218, when the shift of power to the Urach dukes may explain the major change of building plan. Much of the mid- and late 13th-century sculpture of the nave buttresses and the two lower levels of the west tower has been related to work at Strasbourg Cathedral.

The sculptures of the west portal and narthex form one of the most elaborate ensembles of High Gothic sculpture in Germany. The sculptors, who had all been influenced by French Gothic work, also executed the apostles in the nave and much of the work on the third level of the west tower. The tower sculptures are dated by the installation of the tower clock in 1280, and those of the nave by the

Freiburg im Breisgau Cathedral, *Prophet with a Headcloth*, sandstone, h. 2.93 m, from the west tower, after 1310 (Freiburg im Breisgau, Augustinermuseum)

proportions, in garments with soft folds. The place in the iconographic programme of the unusual pair of figures personifying evil, positioned near the outer door, is uncertain. The seductive nude 'Woman of the World' (or *Voluptas*) is accompanied by the 'Prince of the World' (or 'Flattering Seducer'), who is well dressed on one side but riddled with worms crawling through his body on the other. The ten (formerly eleven) prophets of the fourth level of the tower (see fig.) were studied and photographed during restoration work after World War II. They are now seen to be one of the most important sculptural achievements of the 14th century. They are closely related to the somewhat later *Tomb of Christ* inside the cathedral, and both campaigns have been linked in turn to earlier sculpture from the transept of Rouen Cathedral (France), generally dated 1300–10. Their flattened, elongated bodies reinforce the intensely expressive qualities of their faces.

The choir portals are dated after 1354 and are attributed to Johann Parler von Gmünd and his associates. The figures are carved with the short, plump bodies, dramatic gestures and especially wide heads, with small round eyes, characteristic of the Parler school. The figure of St Christopher beside the south portal, standing on a leafy console, beneath a tower tabernacle and supporting the Christ child on his back, is particularly finely carved. The *Annunciation* and *Adoration of the Magi* reliefs on the outer and inner lintels respectively of the sacristy portal are in the same style as the portals. They have been related stylistically and iconographically to the portals of the Holy Cross Church, Schwäbisch Gmünd (1351), and also to sculpture in Ulm and Augsburg, suggesting the importance of south German work for the origin of the Parler sculptural style.

BIBLIOGRAPHY

O. Schmitt: *Gotische Skulpturen des Freiburger Münsters*, 2 vols (Frankfurt am Main, 1926)

G. Münzel: *Der Skulptur in der Verhalle des Freiburger Münsters* (Freiburg im Breisgau, 1959)

F. Kobler: *Der Jungfrauzyklus der Freiburger Münstervorhalle* (Bamberg, 1970)

W. Hart: *Die Skulpturen des Freiburger Münsters* (Freiburg im Breisgau, 1975)

P. Kurmann: 'Skulptur und Zackenstil: Eine Gruppe der Strebepfeilerapostel am Langhaus des Münsters in Freiburg im Breisgau', *Z. Schweiz. Archäol. & Kstgesch.*, xl (1983), pp. 109–114

(iii) Stained glass. Except for some white glass in the nave clerestory, the cathedral is almost completely glazed with medieval stained glass. This includes the high choir and choir chapels, the transepts and the nave aisle windows. A large proportion of the original glass is preserved, although much is no longer *in situ*; medieval glass from other churches has been incorporated to supplement the original glass.

Nine medallions from the *Tree of Jesse* (*see* STAINED GLASS, fig. 3), now in the south transept, are preserved from the choir of the Romanesque building and can be dated before 1218. From the Early Gothic period are three mid-13th-century medallions (Freiburg im Breisgau, Augustinmus.) from the south transept rose, attributed to an Upper Rhenish workshop, perhaps from Basle. The north transept windows (*in situ*) have been related to the Strasbourg workshop that built the west end of the nave.

transfer of responsibility for the church to the citizens in 1311. The coats of arms of Freiburg's patrician patrons found beneath the nave apostles that they commissioned could have appeared only after that date. Several works of the narthex are particularly skilful in execution: the free-standing sculptures of the *Wise and Foolish Virgins*, saints and the female personifications of the *Liberal Arts*, which stand between the arches above the arcades of the north and south walls, are depicted in the round with naturalistic

The Strasbourg glaziers also made the eastern nave windows, of which only the *Martyr* window and the tracery of the *Tailors* window (*c.* 1280) are preserved in the cathedral. The western nave windows were glazed by a local workshop influenced by glass in the Freiburg Dominican church. Images of their patrons, largely local guilds, help to date them between 1320 and 1340. The western clerestory windows were also made *c.* 1340; four segments remain, with standing figures beneath tabernacles, and mining scenes.

The rest of the glazing was not done until considerably later. The original axial window of the west tower was probably commissioned by the Freiburg knight Rumprecht von Graben in 1480 and can be attributed to Peter Hemmel von Andlau. It was removed in the 19th century, and the surviving fragments, including the *Crucifixion* and donor's panels, are now in the Badisches Landesmuseum, Karlsruhe. The choir glazing (now replaced by copies of the originals, of which some are in the Augustinermuseum) began after the completion of the vaults in 1511 and proceeded under Hans Gitschmann von Ropstein (*d* 1564) until 1528. Hans Baldung Grien is believed to have designed the St Anne window for Ropstein with figures set in grisaille glass (1515), as well as windows for the Stürzel and Blumenegg chapels.

Windows were destroyed during a French attack in 1744 and in the late 18th century, when stained-glass panels of the nave clerestory and the lower parts of the nave aisles were replaced with white glass. In the early 19th century, however, a taste for medieval glass led to the installation of old glass obtained from other buildings, including Freiburg's Dominican church and Konstanz Cathedral. The choir glass was damaged by a restoration attempt in 1869–83, when the original paint of eight chapel windows and one and a half high choir windows was removed by the restorers Helmle-Merzweiler and redone following sketches of the originals.

The attempt to recreate a medieval appearance was systematized between 1917 and 1925 by Fritz Geiges, although his methods were also problematic, including the creation of new glass and overpainting; the overpaint was removed only during the restoration of 1970–82. Geiges's new tracery glass was destroyed by bombing during World War II, but his Himmelsbach and Clothiers' windows remain. Coloured interlace compositions, reconstructed from old fragments, have been set in the four eastern clerestory windows.

BIBLIOGRAPHY

F. Geiges: *Der mittelalterliche Fensterschmuck des Freiburger Münsters* (Freiburg im Breisgau, 1931)
I. Krummer-Schroth: *Glasmalereien aus dem Freiburger Münster* (Freiburg im Breisgau, 1967)
Glasfenster aus dem Freiburger Münster: Ihre Erhaltung und Sicherung (exh. cat., intro. R. Becksmann; Freiburg im Breisgau, Augustinmus., 1975)
R. Becksmann: 'Das Jessefenster im Freiburger Münster: Eine Stiftung des letzten Zähringer?', *Die Zähringer: Eine Tradition und ihre Erforschung* (Sigmaringen, 1986), pp. 135–49

VIRGINIA ROEHRIG KAUFMANN

Freisinger [Fraisinger], **Caspar** (*b* Benedictine lands at Ochsenhausen, nr Biberach, *c.* 1550–55; *d* Ingolstadt, 1599). German draughtsman, painter, miniaturist and etcher. According to an allegorical *Self-portrait* drawing (Budapest, Mus. F.A.), he was in Ingolstadt by 1581. He acquired citizenship there and his master's certificate in 1583 and married soon after. His style suggests a sojourn in Italy, presumably before 1581, as proposed by Stange. Thöne's idea that he was trained in Munich by Christoph Schwarz cannot be justified on stylistic grounds. The question of Freisinger's artistic origins revolves around his approximately 70 drawings, often fully signed and dated; these are, however, except for the *Self-portrait*, all later than 1589. Benesch drew attention to the influence of Parmigianino and later of Jacopo Bassano, but the predominant influence seems central Italian—the Zuccaro brothers, Cesare Nebbia etc. Freisinger must also have been familiar with the art of Venice. From the mid-1590s there are occasional traces of Rudolfine influence. The emphasis on landscape, the emotional expression of the figures and the liking for narrative embellishment seen, for instance, in *Christ Being Led forward* (*c.* 1592; Stuttgart, Staatsgal.; see fig.) are, on the other hand, traits typical of southern Germany and Bavaria. There is an unmistakable echo of the style of the Danube school—Altdorfer and Melchior Feselein.

Apart from the drawings, Freisinger's extant work consists of just two panel paintings, the *Raising of Lazarus* (1591; Ingolstadt, Pfarrkirche) and the *Coronation of the Virgin* (1594–5; Eichstätt-Wintershof, Catholic church); wall paintings in the Spitalkirche, Ingolstadt; a few miniatures in the records of Munich (then Ingolstadt) University; and five etchings. Untraced but documented works include the former high altar of the Ingolstadt Jesuitenkirche (1595). In his day Freisinger was the most notable painter in Bavaria and a considerable draughtsman. His influence extended to Eichstätt, Freising, Abensberg and Moosburg. Anonymous copies after drawings by him and a considerable number of pupils and followers—notably Georg Kopp (1570–1622)—indicate the high esteem in which he was held.

Caspar Freisinger: *Christ Being Led forward*, pen and ink and grey wash, 160×163 mm, *c.* 1592 (Stuttgart, Staatsgalerie)

BIBLIOGRAPHY

H. Kuhn: 'Die Alt-Ingolstädter Maler', *Sammbl. Hist. Ver. Ingolstadt*, lvi (1938), p. 32

F. Thöne: 'Caspar Freisingers Zeichnungen', *Z. Dt. Ver. Kstwiss.*, vii (1940), pp. 39–63

A. Stange: 'Eine Zeichnung von Caspar Freisinger', *Albertina-Stud.*, ii (1964), pp. 106–9

Zeichnung in Deutschland, 1540–1640 (exh. cat., ed. H. Geissler; Stuttgart, Staatsgal., 1979), ii, pp. 163–5

HEINRICH GEISSLER

Fremiet, Emmanuel (*b* Paris, 6 Dec 1824; *d* Paris, 10 Sept 1910). French sculptor and stage designer. He was born into a poor though well-connected family and from the age of 12 contributed to the domestic funds by doing a variety of unskilled jobs. In 1838 he started evening classes at the Petite Ecole (Ecole Gratuite de Dessin), Paris, and between 1842 and 1844 worked in the studio of the sculptor François Rude, who was his uncle. The impact of Rude's training method, combining the inspirational with an emphasis on the study of natural proportions and structure, was reinforced for Fremiet by the lessons he learnt in his first artistic enterprises: working with the painter and naturalist Jean-Charles Werner (*fl* 1830–60) at the Musée National d'Histoire Naturelle, Paris, on a compendium of comparative anatomy; helping Dr Mateo Orfila (1787–1853) assemble the specimens for his anatomical museum; and adding artistic touches to embalmed corpses at the Paris Morgue.

Fremiet made his Salon début in 1843 with a plaster statuette of a *Gazelle* (version, Paris, priv. col., see 1988–9 exh. cat., p. 74), and animal statuettes in bronze formed the bulk of his early commercial output. Between 1855 and 1872 he personally cast and marketed bronzes from his own models. He began an impressive series of state commissions modestly with a *Marabou Stork and Cayman* (bronze, 1850; Paris, Mus. d'Orsay), designed to support a porphyry table, part of the Egyptian display in the Louvre. Around 1853 he received an extensive if unlucrative commission, made in person by Napoleon III, for 50 statuettes (ultimately there were 72) showing *Figures from the Army of the Second Empire* (destr. 1871; bronze replicas, Dijon, Mus. B.-A.). These scrupulous renderings of character and costume were carried out in a variety of materials for maximum verisimilitude. Fremiet's documentary and educational ambitions in sculpture were shared by such contemporaries as Charles-Henri-Joseph Cordier and Louis Rochet, and on a number of occasions he insisted on the archaeological and anatomical veracity of his natural-historical and historical re-creations. His notorious groups representing confrontations between humans and animals needed such claims to be maintained in the face of controversy. Because it was considered to echo Darwin's views on the origins of man (though this had not been Fremiet's intention), the *Female Gorilla Carrying off a Negress* (plaster) was refused by the jury of the Salon of 1859 but exhibited behind a curtain on the authority of the Surintendant des Beaux-Arts; it was destroyed by vandals in 1861 but is known from an old photograph (see 1988–9 exh. cat., p. 99). In his historical reconstructions, documentary study was enlivened by substantial imaginary input, whether the presentation was dramatized, as in the relief of the *Triumph of Merovée* (silver-plated bronze and copper, 1867; Paris, Mus. d'Orsay; *see* FRANCE,

fig. 60) and the *Stone Age Man* (bronze, 1872; Paris, Parc Zool.) or static, as in the *Gallic Chief* and *Roman Horseman* (both bronze), which were executed in 1866 for the Musée des Antiquités Nationales at Saint-Germain-en-Laye (*in situ*).

The adaptation of horse to rider in imaginary portraits had already been of concern to Fremiet in his army models, and in the groups for Saint-Germain-en-Laye he treated it on a larger, though still not monumental, scale. From the mid-1870s onwards the equestrian theme came to predominate over other subjects. His *Joan of Arc* (bronze, 1874; Paris, Place des Pyramides), despite criticisms of the disproportion of horse to rider, almost immediately assumed symbolic status as an emblem of France resurgent after defeat in the Franco-Prussian War (1870). Fremiet's extreme sensitivity on the subject of proportion led him to modify the statue in 1899 to conform with a second version he had done for Nancy (bronze, 1889–90). In its final form, and gilded, the *Joan of Arc* in the Place des Pyramides shares a Symbolist preciosity of style with two other major works by Fremiet from the 1890s, *St George Defeating the Dragon* (bronze, 1891; Barentin, Mus. Mun.) and *St Michael* (bronze, 1896; Mont-Saint-Michel Abbey; replica, Paris, Mus. d'Orsay).

Fremiet continued to maintain his preoccupation with natural history, in 1872 proposing to Charles Blanc the setting up at the Palais du Trocadéro in Paris of an educational sculpture park incorporating models of prehistoric creatures. The project was not realized in the form proposed (an earlier state commission for a statue of a plesiosaurus, in 1852, had equally come to nothing), but a more decorative and allegorical version (some statues, Paris, Mus. d'Orsay) was carried out by a large number of sculptors, including Fremiet, for the Exposition Universelle of 1878 held at the Trocadéro. Fremiet's position as leading national animalier sculptor was confirmed when, in 1875, he succeeded Antoine-Louis Barye as professor of zoological drawing at the Musée National d'Histoire Naturelle in Paris. In 1876 he designed the costumes for Alexandre Mermet's opera *Jeanne d'Arc* at the Paris Opéra (designs, Paris, Bib. N.). In 1887 he exhibited at the Salon a variant of his destroyed *Gorilla* group of 1859, *Gorilla Carrying off a Woman* (plaster; Nantes, Mus. B.-A.), and in 1895 his assistant Henri Greber (1854–1941) carried out in marble his group of an *Orang-utan and Native of Borneo* (Paris, Mus. N. Hist. Nat.). Apart from the many works in public collections in Paris the most extensive representation of Fremiet's work is in the Musée des Beaux-Arts, Dijon, consisting of a bequest made in 1955 of the master bronzes for Fremiet's statuettes used by the Barbedienne foundry.

See also ANIMALIER SCULPTURE.

BIBLIOGRAPHY

Lami

T. H. Bartlett: 'Emmanuel Fremiet', *Amer. Architect & Bldg News*, xxxi (1891), pp. 72–3, 101–3, 134–7, 172–4, 201–4; xxxii (1891) 24–8, 70–72, 113–15, 129–31

J. de Biez: *Un Maître imagier: E. Fremiet* (Paris, 1896)

——: *Emmanuel Fremiet* (Paris, 1910)

P. Fauré-Fremiet: *Emmanuel Fremiet* (Paris, 1934)

The Romantics to Rodin: French Nineteenth-century Sculpture from North American Collections (exh. cat., ed. P. Fusco and H. W. Janson; Los Angeles, Co. Mus. A.; Minneapolis, Inst. A.; Detroit, Inst. A.; Indianapolis, Mus. A.; 1980–81)

La Sculpture française au XIXe siècle (exh. cat., ed. A. Pingeot; Paris, Grand Pal., 1986)

Emmanuel Fremiet: 'La Main et le multiple' (exh. cat. by C. Chevillot, Dijon, Mus. B.-A., 1988–9)

PHILIP WARD-JACKSON

Frémin, René (*b* Paris, 1 Oct 1672; *d* Paris, 17 Feb 1744). French sculptor. A pupil of François Girardon and Antoine Coyzevox, he won the Prix de Rome in 1694 and spent the years 1695–9 in Rome, where he contributed two elegant Baroque bronze bas-reliefs, from drawings by Andrea Pozzo, to the sculptural ensemble of the altar of S Ignazio in Il Gesù (*in situ*). On his return to France he was approved (*agréé*) by the Académie Royale in 1700 and received (*reçu*) as an academician the following year on presentation of the bas-relief *Time Unveiling Truth* (marble; frags, Paris, Ecole N. Sup. B.-A.). At the Salon of 1704 he exhibited an ambitious stone group of *Hercules Abducting Deianera* (Chantilly, Château, park), which recalls the great groups of Giambologna and Gianlorenzo Bernini as well as the sculpture of Versailles.

Frémin was much employed by the Bâtiments du Roi on sculptural projects at the French royal palaces. At Versailles he carved allegorical figures and trophies in bas-relief in the chapel (1707–9; *in situ*), while for the gardens at the château of Marly, Yvelines, he created some of his most important works, including the lively and graceful statue of *Flora* (marble, 1706–9; Paris, Louvre) for the Cascade Champêtre, which with its gracefully asymmetrical pose and extreme refinement of execution belongs to the new relaxed style introduced by Coyzevox in opposition to the classicizing grandeur of French sculpture at the height of the Louis XIV period. The running statue of a *Nymph* (marble, 1714–17; Paris, Louvre) contributed by Frémin to the series of 18 statues of *Companions of Diana* planned for the gardens at Marly similarly represents the new proto-Rococo style, as does the monumental marble group of *Zephyr and Flora* for the gardens at Trianon (completed by Jacques Bousseau; Paris, priv. col., see Souchal, i, p. 59), begun in 1713 in collaboration with Philippe Bertrand but abandoned by Frémin when he was called to Spain in 1721.

From 1719 to 1721 Frémin was employed on the decoration of the chapel of Cardinal de Noailles, Notre-Dame, Paris, where he executed a gilt-bronze bas-relief of the *Assumption* (destr. 1790s). But in 1721, in response to an invitation from Philip V of Spain, he went, together with Jean Thierry, to work on the sculptural decoration of the park at La Granja de S Ildefonso, near Segovia. As director of the project Frémin helped to create one of the most remarkable surviving ensembles of garden sculpture of the 18th century (for illustration *see* SAN ILDEFONSO). The statuary at La Granja, in both lead and marble, was clearly inspired by the experiences of working at Versailles and especially in the more light-hearted setting of Marly. Although it is sometimes difficult to distinguish between the works of Frémin and Thierry, some of which were executed later by Bousseau, Hubert Dumandré and Pitué (e.g. the Latona Basin and the Fountain of the Renommée), a number of the principal works can be attributed to Frémin himself, including the flamboyant Fountain of Perseus and Andromeda, the *Abduction of Pandora by Mercury* and some groups showing struggles between animals and children playing (all lead). In addition, he either carved or supplied models for numerous free-standing marble statues (e.g. the sinuous *Milon of Crotona* or a *Companion of Diana*) and vases after drawings by Gilles-Marie Oppenord.

Frémin was also an accomplished portrait sculptor, producing busts of, among others, *Philip V* and *Elizabeth Farnese* (both marble, *c.* 1721; Madrid, Pal. Real) that combine the grandeur of Baroque formal portraiture with lively and alert characterization. In 1733 he was created First Sculptor to the King of Spain and granted patents of nobility. He returned to Paris with a fortune in 1738 and ended his very successful career as rector of the Académie Royale.

BIBLIOGRAPHY

Lami; Souchal

J. Digard: *Les Jardins de la Granja et leurs sculptures décoratives* (Paris, 1934), pp. 421–35, 450, 571–3, 575–80

Y. Bottineau: *L'Art de cour dans L'Espagne de Philippe V, 1700–1746* (Bordeaux, [1962], rev. Paris, 1993)

B. Pons: 'Oppenord and the Granja de San Ildefonso', *Burl. Mag.*, cxxxi (1989), pp. 337–41

GUILHEM SCHERF

Fréminet, Martin (*b* Paris, 23 Sept 1567; *d* Paris, 18 June 1619). French painter. He first studied with his father, Médéric Fréminet (*fl* 2nd half of the 16th century), who is thought to have taught also Toussaint Dubreuil. Martin Fréminet painted a *St Sebastian* (untraced) for the church of St Josse in Paris before leaving for Italy around 1587. In Rome he became a friend of the Cavaliere d'Arpino, took an interest in the painting of Caravaggio and, above all, studied the work of Michelangelo. A number of untraced paintings that he executed in Rome were recorded in the form of engravings by Philippe Thomassin and published between 1589 and 1592: they included the *Holy Family* (1589), the *Annunciation* (1591) and the *Baptism* (1592). These Italian works revealed him to be one of the individuals who, alongside the Cavaliere d'Arpino, contributed to the renewal of Roman Mannerism that dominated the end of the century (Thuillier, pp. 670–71). Among Fréminet's works was a *Flagellation* engraved by Thomassin (1590–92), which closely resembled and may have been the model for the Cavaliere d'Arpino's *Flagellation*, engraved by Aegidius Sadeler II (1593).

Fréminet spent some time in Venice and in Turin, where he worked for Duke Charles Emanuel I of Savoy. Henry IV summoned him back to France after the death of Dubreuil, who had been working for the King, and when Etienne Dumonstier II died in 1603, Fréminet became Peintre et Valet de Chambre du Roi. In 1606 he painted the Dauphin (the future Louis XIII), to whom he was also drawing-master, and in 1615 he received the Order of St Michel. The King also commissioned him to execute the decorations for the chapel of the Trinity at the château of Fontainebleau, following an iconography inspired by the Jesuit Louis Richeôme (1544–1625). From 1606 Fréminet painted the vault (see fig.) and the piers and supplied designs for the stuccoes executed by Barthélemy Tremblay, as well as for the high altar. Fourteen oval paintings (replaced, 18th century) representing scenes from the *Life of Christ* occupied the spaces between the windows; six oil sketches (Paris, Louvre) for these have

Martin Fréminet: vault paintings, chapel of the Trinity, château of Fontainebleau, *c.* 1606

recently been attributed to Fréminet (Cordelier). He died before completing work at the chapel.

Other works by Fréminet in France include eight large canvases (2.4×1.0 m; Orléans, Mus. B.-A.) representing the four Doctors of the Church and the four Evangelists, which were apparently painted in accordance with an earlier design for the décor of the chapel of the Trinity. Fréminet's *Oath of Hannibal* is in the Musée Magnin in Dijon, while the Musée Départemental in Gap has his *Adoration of the Shepherds*, which was brought there from the hospice at Montgenèvre and was probably painted in northern Italy. Fréminet's drawings and engravings are also to be found in a number of other institutions, including the Louvre, the Ecole des Beaux Arts and the Bibliothèque Nationale in Paris, Christ Church Library in Oxford, the Hessisches Landesmuseum in Darmstadt and the Nasjonalgalleriet in Oslo.

Fréminet enjoyed a high reputation among his contemporaries in Italy and France. His French works seem to be more monumental and tauter than those he executed in Italy, but their composition is essentially the same: two large figures in the foreground, one on either side, with almost the whole of the picture occupied by overlapping figures turned in on themselves in a highly dynamic spiral-like movement. These figures are depicted as powerfully muscular and are often clothed in flying draperies that add to the dramatic character of the scenes. It was probably

this impression of heightened strength that earned Fréminet the nickname of the 'French Michelangelo'. He married the widow of Ambroise Dubois; their son, Louis Fréminet (1616–51), became keeper of the paintings in the chapel of the Trinity. He was also a painter, though none of his work is known.

BIBLIOGRAPHY
K. von Mander: *Schilder-boek* ([1603]–1604)
G. Mancini: *Considerazioni sulla pittura* (MS. *c.* 1621), ed. A. Marucchi, 2 vols (Rome, 1956–7)
P. Dan: *Le Trésor des merveilles de la maison royale de Fontainebleau* (Paris, 1642)
S. Béguin: *Fontainebleau: Le maniérisme à la cour de France* (1960)
C. Samoyault-Verlet: 'Précisions iconographiques sur trois décors de la seconde école de Fontainebleau', *Actes du colloque international sur l'art de Fontainebleau: Fontainebleau and Paris, 1972*, pp. 241–7
L'Ecole de Fontainebleau (exh. cat., Paris, Grand Pal., 1972), pp. 113–15
J. Thuillier: 'Histoire de la création artistique en France, II: Peintres Français en Italie au XVIIe siècle, Martin Fréminet, Louis Brandin, Jean Boucher', *Annu. Coll. France: Résumé Cours & Trav.*, lxxix (1978), p. 670
D. Cordelier: 'Martin Fréminet, "aussi sçavant que judicieux"', *Rev. A.*, lxxxi (1988), pp. 57–72
De Niccolo dell'Abate à Nicolas Poussin: Aux sources du classicisme (exh. cat., Meaux, Mus. Bossuet, 1988)

CELIA ALEGRET

French, Daniel Chester (*b* Exeter, NH, 20 April 1850; *d* Stockbridge, MA, 7 Oct 1931). American sculptor. Essentially self-taught, he studied briefly in the 1870s with John Quincy Adams Ward, William Rimmer, William Morris Hunt and Thomas Ball. In 1873 he was awarded the substantial commission for the life-size *Minute Man* (bronze, 1874) erected in Minute Man National Historical Park, Concord, MA, to commemorate the Battle of Concord. In what became one of his best-known pieces, he adapted the Classical *Apollo Belvedere* (Rome, Vatican, Mus. Pio-Clementino) for his New England farmer to create a sturdy image that forcefully characterizes the determined patriotism of the men who defended their land. After two years in Italy (1874–6) French worked in Washington, DC, and Boston, MA, executing architectural sculpture and a number of portraits, including a distinguished marble bust of *Ralph Waldo Emerson* (1879; Cambridge, MA, Harvard U.).

French's next major commission, the seated statue of *John Harvard* (bronze, 1884; Cambridge, MA, Harvard U.), received creditable reviews; however, he still had not reached artistic maturity. While in Paris in 1886–7 he improved his modelling technique and absorbed current French tendencies. A comparison of *John Harvard* and the *Thomas Gallaudet* memorial (bronze, 1888; Washington, DC, Gallaudet Coll.) reveals the enormous benefit that French derived from his stay in France. Not only is the pose of *Gallaudet* more relaxed than that of *Harvard*, but French handled his medium with a greater degree of ease and confidence. If the shirt in *Harvard* has stiff repetitive folds, in *Gallaudet* it hangs in a more realistic fashion.

French settled in New York and opened a studio from which he established a reputation—alongside Augustus Saint-Gaudens—as the leader of American sculpture. He was selected to contribute works that were placed prominently in such large collaborative projects as the World's Columbian Exposition of 1893 in Chicago, the bronze doors (1904) at the Boston Public Library and *The Continents* (marble groups, 1907) at the US Customs House in New York. More private in location and content, and superior in composition and spirit, are the *Angel of Death and the Sculptor* (bronze, 1891; Jamaica Plain, MA, Forest Hills Cemetery), a memorial to the sculptor Martin Milmore (1844–83), and the *Melvin Brothers* memorial (marble, 1908; Concord, MA, Sleepy Hollow Cemetery), two funerary monuments that are among the sculptor's finest achievements. French's interest in landscape architecture led him to collaborate with the architects to integrate the sculptures with their sites harmoniously. The masterfully conveyed meaning of these two works makes them especially profound and affecting statements about death.

The over life-size, seated and meditative *Abraham Lincoln* for the Lincoln Memorial (marble, ded. 1922; Washington, DC), French's most famous piece, became a national icon and crowned the artist's long and celebrated career. He continued to sculpt until his death at Chesterwood, his summer home and studio in Stockbridge, MA, which subsequently opened as a museum in his memory.

A chronicler of American heroes and themes, French brought his works from sketch, quarter-size, half-size and occasionally full-size model to completion with the precise, disciplined and measured qualities that were a trademark of his personality. The advent of abstraction cast a shadow over his academic BEAUX-ARTS STYLE; nevertheless, well into the 20th century, he continued in the same mode that had brought him acclaim.

BIBLIOGRAPHY

Mrs D. C. French: *Memories of a Sculptor's Wife* (Boston, 1928)
A. Adams: *Daniel Chester French, Sculptor* (Boston, 1932)
M. Cresson: *Journey into Fame: The Life of Daniel Chester French* (Cambridge, MA, 1947)
W. Craven: *Sculpture in America* (New York, 1968, rev. Newark, 2/1984)
Daniel Chester French (exh. cat. by M. Richman, New York, Met., 1976/R Washington, DC, 1983)

KATHRYN GREENTHAL

French, Leonard (*b* Brunswick, Melbourne, 10 Oct 1928). Australian painter and designer. With encouragement from Victor Greenhalgh, he attended evening classes at the Royal Melbourne Institute of Technology from 1944 to 1947. He studied from 1949 to 1951 in England, Belgium and Ireland where his interest in Celtic art increased. With the aid of a travelling scholarship in 1960–61, he studied the Eastern art of Asia, and in 1965 went to the USA on the Harkness Fellowship. His travels were often responsible for his series' themes. Literary images and social injustices were frequently used, as in *Iliad* (1952), *Edmund Campion* series (1963), the *Death of a Revolution* (on South America, 1974–6), and South African-inspired works in the mid-1980s. French carefully constructed his images which are based on formal patterns and shapes, for example in *Death and Transfiguration* (1957; Melbourne, Joseph Brown Gal.). Using simple, easily recognizable symbols, he portrayed a powerful bluntness and honesty. After studying enamelling techniques in the 1960s, French's paintings became known for their thick glowing layers of enamel on different textual levels, at times with gold leaf added. Apart from paintings and murals, he was known for his stained glass projects,

mosaics, tapestries, etchings and lithographs. He was commissioned by the National Gallery of Victoria to create the biggest stained-glass ceiling in the world (1962–8; *see* AUSTRALIA, fig. 20).

BIBLIOGRAPHY

K. Dunstan: 'French Glass', *Sydney Morning Herald* (5 April 1986) ['The Good Weekend']
The Jack Manton Prize 1987: Recent Works by Fourteen Australian Artists (exh. cat. by B. MacAulay, Brisbane, Queensland A.G., 1987)

CHRISTINE CLARK

French Antilles. *See under* ANTILLES, LESSER.

French Guiana [Guyana; Fr. La Guyane]. French department on the north-east coast of South America, bordered by Surinam to the west and by Brazil to the south and east (see fig. 1). The capital city, Cayenne, is located on a small estuary island and holds two-thirds of the total population of *c.* 100,000. The department occupies *c.* 90,000 sq. km. The interior is almost entirely covered by Amazonian forest, bordered and traversed by rivers and empty of people. The swamp forest and the plains towards the coast are relatively densely populated. The first French settlement was established in the region in 1604; despite the greed of the various European powers in the 16th and 17th centuries, French Guiana remained a French colony until 1946, when it became an overseas department.

This article discusses art and architecture since colonization. For a discussion of Pre-Columbian arts in French Guiana, *see* SOUTH AMERICA, PRE-COLUMBIAN, §V.

1. Map of French Guiana

I. Introduction. II. Architecture. III. Traditional and other arts. IV. Art life and institutions.

I. Introduction.

In the 16th century there were over 30 ethnic groups of *c.* 30,000 people in total, spread out between the Mana and Maroni rivers. The economy, established at the time of colonization, rested on the trade in African slaves. However, removed from main trade currents, the region remained underpopulated. Economic activity was based on the cultivation, using servile labour, of plantations of sugar cane, annatto, indigo, cotton and spices. In 1676 Cayenne was occupied by the Dutch for one year, and the Portuguese later occupied the city from 1808 to 1817. In 1982 French Guiana became a completely separate region governed by two local assemblies. Conceived primarily as a logistical support for the French Antilles, the colony of French Guiana has only rarely been considered for its intrinsic interest, and different French governments have always hesitated between developing the region for general habitation or just exploiting its natural resources; by the late 20th century French Guiana remained an underdeveloped country.

The extensive variety of ethnic groups is the result of successive immigrant waves of varying origins. The predominant groups are Asians and African-European mulattos; there remain, in reduced numbers, the original Amerindian inhabitants, as well as European settlers and blacks descended from African slaves who escaped from Surinam. Creole society serves as the region's administrative and political pillar, although in the 20th century there was a greater involvement of tribal Amerindians and people of African descent in this area. Additional groups included French convicts sent to Devil's Island and other penal colonies, and gold prospectors who came in the mid-19th century.

II. Architecture.

With its grid layout, the city of Cayenne is typical of 18th-century colonial towns, which were built on flat ground. The centre is occupied by administrative offices and businesses. The urban network, proposed in a fully preserved layout drawn up by Etienne François de Turgot, Governor of Guiana, in 1764, was executed between 1821 and 1842. The Place des Palmistes, graced by royal palm trees, is surrounded by traditional colonial buildings that have been restored. The colonizers, wishing to protect themselves from foreign incursions and from the hostilities of the Caribbean Indians, built such forts as Cépérou fort (*c.* 1679) in Cayenne. Its upper parts preserve some of the old layout, and its enclosing wall shows former ramparts. To the south of Cayenne is the brick Diamant fort (1848), comprising a battery, vaulted barracks and triangular courtyard; restoration, begun in 1985, has saved the fort from the encroaching tropical vegetation. Soldiers and sailors played a role in the stylistic development of domestic architecture. Navy carpenters from the French provinces taught their techniques, and a craftsmen's guild

2. Creole house, Mana, French Guiana

was formed. Some models of European houses and churches were copied and adapted to the climatic conditions. However, frequent fires, coupled with the use of poor materials, have meant that there are no significant remains of these buildings. Dutch and French influences were allied with local Guianese techniques in improvements made to the homes of wealthy city dwellers. Creole houses (see fig. 2), built in the early 19th century, are interesting for their adaptation to the climate, using vast roof spaces, high ceilings and openings to ensure passive air circulation. Often two storeys high, the houses were sometimes surrounded by canopies with balconies on the main façade. The steeply sloping roofs had large overhangs. Particular care was taken with houses, mainly for rich merchants, built between the late 1880s and the 1930s, using brackets of wrought or cast iron and iron guard rails and floors. Examples are found in the Bar des Palmistes and Rue Mollé, Cayenne. For country houses, which were to proliferate after the abolition of slavery, plaited wood, knotted in an earthen mortar, and laths and planks were used. Gardens were planted around the houses.

Of all the convict prison sites, only those of Saint-Laurent-du-Maroni, Saint-Jean and the Iles du Salut, off the coast of Kourou, still preserve some of the elements of the prison and its organization. This architecture reveals a surprising unity considering that it was created by many unpaid labourers. The quarters for the administrators and directors were given a degree of comfort; the building complexes were surrounded by low brick walls; wide passageways isolated the living quarters; and finally the washrooms and kitchens were linked by covered galleries. The Saint-Laurent buildings were subsequently used as offices for the administration of the sub-prefecture. The hospital and town hall have retained their uses, as have many of the buildings occupied by civil servants. Conservation and renovation projects were under way in the 1990s: some buildings were classified as historic monuments, such as the church of Iracoubo (1887–97).

III. Traditional and other arts.

From both Western and Creole points of view it is possible to make fairly arbitrary distinctions in French Guianese artistic production between the fields of arts and crafts, the latter being confined more (although not exclusively) to the tribal population. In the late 20th century there were only six Amerind peoples (c. 3200 individuals) in French Guiana, belonging to different linguisto-cultural groups. The Galibi (or Kalina), Wayana, Palikur, Arawak, Wayampi and Emerillon were the outcome of a complex dynamic in which the Amerinds were either in opposition to or took part in the formation of the colony, although the polarization of French Guiana by gold and convicts hardly affected them. These societies have maintained contact with each other through commercial, festive or matrimonial exchanges. Their artistic creation is closely linked to the value attached to material objects and group activities, essentially revolving around feasts and dances. The forest environment, hunting and fishing are the principal inspirations for creation and imagery. Boat-building has a strong tradition, and vessels are typically brightly painted. Body art includes extensive face and body painting and tattooing. Feathers are used for head-dresses and general adornment (see fig. 3), with live birds often being plucked and injected with pigment to produce new coloured feathers. Beads are made from shells, glass, seeds and stones for use in necklaces and armlets that portray animal forms or that are arranged in geometric patterns. Basketwork is traditionally practised by men, and animal or geometric images are made either by weaving different materials or by using coloured elements. Pottery is also made, but with the exception of the red, white and black ware made for sale to tourists by the Arawak, its decoration is not of particular interest. Diversity of artistic creation increased when these societies came into contact with the West. In 1967 the French administration proposed French citizenship, and therefore French rights, to the Amerinds and to the population of African descent, in an effort to regulate through assimilation the problem of their identity. Between 1967 and 1969, c. 65% of the six ethnic groups of Amerinds became French, but the groups were not all in contact with the West to the same degree; the Galibi and Palikur were used to contact with Europeans through temporary work on the coast, but the Wayampi and Wayana in the interior were ill-prepared for the dependence that would follow.

Groups of people of African descent began to escape from coastal plantations in the latter part of the 17th century, moving inland, while others started to settle on the banks of the Maroni River from the late 18th century.

3. Wayana festive headdresses, Twenké, French Guiana, 1984

They adopted many traits of the way of life and techniques of their Amerindian neighbours, in particular boat-building. The Aluku, who number *c.* 3000, are French citizens and are integrated into the dominant economic and political system; the Samaraka (also *c.* 3000 in number) settled on the coast at Kourou and Saint-Laurent and work seasonally, selling sculpted images to tourists. The Aluku and Ndjuka groups provided transport for miners during the goldrush in the late 19th century, which allowed them to introduce many changes into their way of life. The history of the art of these peoples is remarkable for the ease with which ideas and shapes moved from one region to the other and from one medium to another. Wood-carving and sculpture, often bearing painted decorations, carving on gourds, patchwork and embroidered clothing have been the traditional artistic activities. The style of Aluku artefacts, as well as those of other groups of African descent, developed in the context of cultural exchanges based on rituals and marriage between groups. Among the artefacts some relatively constant traits can be seen: notions of colour contrast, syncopated symmetry and curvilinear script, based on globally African concepts but related principally to West African tribal art.

Innovation and invention are visible where Amerind and European contributions mix, ensuring that black Guianese art possesses constantly changing qualities, adapted to new forms and techniques. The result is a synthesis that bears witness to the Afro-American cultural process. Decorative sculpture and painted wood-carving started to develop from the latter part of the 19th century and blossomed and evolved over the following century. Until the late 20th century all Aluku men carved and sculpted objects, principally utilitarian, which they offered to their wives or girlfriends. These objects were characterized by skilled low-relief work and frequently by sexual imagery personal to the couple. However, the wealth of artistic production is now mainly to be seen only in museums and private collections, and despite the various attempts to safeguard the artistic traditions, the quality of the artefacts has declined. Since the division of the Aluku's Inini territory into three parts in 1968 and the regionalization of 1982, deep social and cultural changes have taken place, such as the dispersal of clans, growing monetarization and lower levels of artistic activity. Living areas, painted decoration, furniture and everyday utensils have taken on a Western appearance; the painting formerly associated with carving ceased to be practised by all but a handful of individuals. Gourds, traditionally decorated by women, have been practically abandoned in favour of plastic and glass crockery; the few remaining gourds are kept for funerary purposes or for sale to tourists. The same applies to hand-sewn and embroidered patchwork clothes, which have been replaced by ready-made garments generally bought through catalogues. The social role of *objets d'art* as gifts between spouses has almost disappeared. Only boat-building has continued to thrive. Music remained the most significant marker of ethnic identity, with drums still being made for community rituals and festivals.

The influence of the Amerinds and groups of African descent on Creole society was largely material. It was among the Guianese Creoles that the first qualified craftsmen in jewellery were recruited; French businessmen and entrepreneurs were to introduce to the colony a taste for adornments and jewels that the Creole élite adopted at the end of the 19th century. Jewellery became a symbol of the wealth acquired in gold nuggets, and gold had a monetary value until the eve of World War II. Following the influx of migrants from the Antilles in the late 19th century and early 20th, Guianese jewels were often inspired by Antilles models, such as convicts' chains and choker necklaces. It was, however, principally the Chinese, acting as intermediary merchants at the gold-prospecting sites, who inspired a style favouring gold of different colours and the mixture of gold and precious stones. A later foreign group that established itself in French Guiana was the Hmong community from Laos, who arrived from 1977. They achieved successful economic integration largely through the agricultural sector, but their traditional craftwork of embroidered wall hangings with cloth appliqué work, produced mainly by women, was sold at markets close to their villages.

The convict population included a number of artists: François Lagrange painted the chapel of the Ile Royale (1938–41) in oil and produced works on canvas after he was freed. His portraits and scenes from a convict's life and of Guianese people brought him a degree of renown, and although the chapel painting has deteriorated considerably, some of his canvases have been preserved in Cayenne. In the early 20th century the former convict Pierre Huguet painted scenes in the church of Iracoubo (1887–97), which connect episodes from the New Testament to friezes and decorative motifs of mock marble and sky, sometimes executed in stencil. Huguet's work is reminiscent of popular paintings that are naive in style. Some Galibi artists, including Fritz St Jura, Thérèse Josselin, Mayipulo and Kiliman, became integrated into contemporary society by painting scenes of traditional life in a naive style on canvases and by selling stools in animal forms. It is among the youngest generation of French Guianese, born to immigrant parents, that one can see a real emergence of Western-style plastic arts. John Lie A Fo (*b* 1945), a Surinam artist who settled in French Guiana, had exhibitions in the Caribbean, Venezuela and the Netherlands. His expressionistic style of painting incorporates *figuration libre* (abstracted figuration) and elements of graffiti. José Legrand (*b* 1947), one of the founders of the Formsens arts centre, exhibited in Paris and introduced innovative practices into French Guiana, such as works on urban sites and displays concerned with the problems of the colonized Creole. The work of Roseman Robinot (*b* 1944), Frank Doriac, Raymond Désiré and Thierry Tian Sio Po (*b* 1964) expresses their Guianese identity while also revealing connections to international art.

IV. Art life and institutions.

The Musée de Cayenne, which houses natural history and ethnographic exhibits, was established in 1901. In late 20th-century French Guiana the need began to be felt to rediscover cultural and historic reference points, searching for identity by making overtures to indigenous people rather than to European traditions. From 1986 the Wayana association, Caway, ensured that Amerindian artefacts, intended largely for sale to tourists, displayed the same qualities as in the past. An association to preserve the national artistic heritage of the Alukus, called Mi Wani Sabi ('I want to know'), was founded in 1989 to supervise the continuation of ancestral forms; that same year it organized the exhibition *Regards sur l'art Boni aujourd'hui*. In addition to organizing exhibitions, the association republished old works and created a documentary archive. There is, however, an undercurrent of assimilation into Creole society. A planned regional museum would offer the chance not only to preserve old artefacts still available from indigenous peoples but also to reflect the recognition of Guianese Creoles.

Two artists' associations, the Association des Artistes de Guyane (ADAG, founded 1979) and Association des Artistes Peintres (AAP, founded 1980), concentrate on the avant-garde and are represented by students whose work developed in Europe, the Antilles and North America. In 1979 the first group exhibition of young painters living in French Guiana was held. In 1983 the AAP, and in particular José Legrand, created Formsens, which was, until 1988, an exhibition space, meeting place, loan library and video library. In 1984 an exhibition of contemporary European artists was organized (see 1984 exh. cat.). On the whole, Guianese artists have been frustrated by the absence of a structure for exhibiting and by the difficulty of establishing a market for local art. Between 1985 and 1987, some 15 exhibitions took place in Cayenne, in hotels, office buildings and restaurants.

In 1989 the dozen or so artists grouped around Serge Goudin-Thebia, a Guianese living in Martinique, founded an association called Mitaraka. In its manifesto the group stated its commitment to 'revealing the specific forms of the relationship between art and the sacred and between the sacred and art, through flora and fauna, manners and customs, and the mythology of the Creole and traditional cultures of French Guiana'. Mitaraka also published a periodical by the same name; the first issue (Feb 1992) included poetry, art criticism and interviews with local painters. Although Mitaraka seemed innovative in its inclusion of members from beyond French Guiana, notably the Antilles and Venezuela, non-Creole artists have had to adopt Creole and generally Western techniques to express their Guianese identity; only when assimilated into the prevailing Creole ambience are non-Creoles able to give voice. In the late 20th century a dialectic existed between an imitative tradition and the search for an artistic expression of Guianese identity, and this represented more than a simple split between learned and popular art. The emergence of questions of identity and the questioning of ties with France have turned the plastic arts and literature of French Guiana into a forum for collective commitment to those forgotten by history, whose voice has not been heard.

BIBLIOGRAPHY
J. Hurault: *Africains de Guyane* (Paris, 1970)
P. Grenand and F. Grenand: 'Les Amérindiens de Guyane Française aujourd'hui: Eléments de compréhension', *J. Soc. Américanistes*, lxvi (1979), pp. 361–82
S. Price and R. Price: *Afro-American Arts of the Suriname Rain Forest* (Berkeley, 1980)
Du réel à l'imaginaire (exh. cat., Cayenne, Hôtel de la Préfecture, 1984)
K. M. Bilby: *The Remaking of the Aluku: Culture, Politics, and Maroon Ethnicity in French South America* (diss., Baltimore, MD, Johns Hopkins U., 1989)
Regards sur l'art Boni aujourd'hui (exh. cat. by M.-P. Jean Louis and S. Anelli, Cayenne, Cons. Reg. Guyane, 1989)
'Des Blancs et des Indiens', *Phréat., Lang. & Création*, liii (1990), pp. 9–17
D. Bégot: 'Le Système des beaux arts dans le monde créole', *La Grande Encyclopédie de la Caraïbe*, x (Guadeloupe, 1990), pp. 26–47
M.-J. Jolivet: 'Entre autochtones et immigrants: Diversité et logique des positions créoles guyanaises', *Etud. Créoles*, xiii/2 (1990), pp. 11–32
J.-P. Klingelhofer, ed.: *Culture, Artisanat Wayana*, Caway Association (Cayenne, 1990)
'Les lianes d'Ariane', *Phréat., Lang. & Création*, liii (1990), esp. pp. 9–17, 47–60, 94–100 [special issue on French Guiana]
'Cultures de la Guyane et des Caraïbes: Arts de la terre, poétique du monde', *Mitaraka* i (1992) [whole issue]

MICHELE BAJ STROBEL

French Somaliland. *See* DJIBUTI.

French Sudan. *See* MALI.

Frenzel, Johann Gottfried Abraham (*b* Dresden, 1 Jan 1782; *d* Dresden, 6 Nov 1855). German printmaker, draughtsman and writer. He studied drawing under Cajetan Toscani (1742–1815) and Mietsch at the Dresden Akademie der Bildenden Künste. Later, as a student of Johann Adolph Darnstedt (1769–1844), he became involved with engraving, especially landscape subjects. In 1809 he began work at the Dresden Gallery of Engravings and Drawings, established by Christian Gottlieb Dolst (1740–1814); on Dolst's death in 1814, Frenzel took over the running of the gallery. During this time he established a considerable reputation as an innovative printmaker, and his engravings, notable for their technical virtuosity, painterly effects and fidelity to the model, entered royal collections in Dresden. His main subjects were 17th-century landscapes by such artists as Claude and Ruysdael. Frenzel also contributed five large plates for the album *Dresden mit seinen Prachtgebäuden und schönsten Umgebungen* (1808) and produced a succession of individual prints of architecture and landscapes. The best-known example of his book illustration is Maximilian Prinz zu Wied-Neuwied's *Reise nach Brasilien in den Jahren 1815–1817* (Frankfurt, 1820).

Although primarily occupied by engraving, Frenzel was also active as a draughtsman and etcher. In later years he became increasingly involved in writing about printmaking, a subject that had been little explored.

WRITINGS
Sammlung der Kupferstiche und Handzeichnungen . . . des Herrn Grafen F. V. Sternberg-Manderscheid, 6 vols (Dresden, 1836–42)
Die Bekehrung der Paulus, ein dem A. Dürer zu zueignendes bis jetzt unbekanntes Kupferblatt aus des Meisters frühester Periode in lithographirtem Facsimile (Leipzig, 1854)
König Friedrich August als Kunstfreund und Kunstsammler dargestellt (Dresden, 1854)
Die Kanzel in der Domkirche zu Freiberg (Leipzig, 1856)

BIBLIOGRAPHY
Seubert; Thieme–Becker
H. Singer: *Künstlerlexikon* (1814), p. 476
G. K. Nagler: *Monogrammisten* (1858–1920)

Frère, (Pierre) Edouard (*b* Paris, 10 Jan 1819; *d* Ecouen, 20 May 1886). French painter. At the age of 17 he entered the atelier of Paul Delaroche at the Ecole des Beaux-Arts in Paris. He exhibited regularly at the Salon in Paris from 1842 to 1886 and at the Royal Academy in London from

1868 to 1885. He was the younger brother of the Orientalist painter Théodore Frère (1814–88) and, unlike many other 19th-century artists, preferred not to live in Paris but in Ecouen.

Edouard Frère is known mainly for his peasant scenes, showing daily life in the country, which gained him popularity with the middle class during the Second Empire. He depicted childhood in such paintings as the *Little Cook* (1858; New York, Brooklyn Mus.), showing an interest in the traditional activities of the poor, a novel idea at that time. He specialized in small-scale genre paintings in warm colours and adhered to a narrative approach to dramatic subject-matter that was softened by a sometimes rather affected sentimentality.

Following Frère's association with the dealer Ernest Gambart in 1854, an exhibition of his work was organized in London, where the mediation of fellow artist and critic John Ruskin, who admired him, was a guarantee of success. From the 1880s his work was popular with American collectors. His pupils included George Boughton (1833–1905).

BIBLIOGRAPHY
W. D. Conway: 'Edouard Frère and Sympathetic Art in France', *Harper's Mthly*, xliii (1871), pp. 801–14
The Realist Tradition: French Painting and Drawing, 1830–1900 (exh. cat., ed. G. P. Weisberg and others; Cleveland, OH, Mus. A.; New York, Brooklyn Mus.; Glasgow, A.G. & Mus.; 1980–81)
The Nineteenth-century Paintings in the Walters Art Gallery (exh. cat. by W. R. Johnston, Baltimore, MD, Walters A.G., 1982)
A. DAGUERRE DE HUREAUX

Fréron, Elie-Catherine (*b* Quimper, 20 Jan 1718; *d* Montrouge, nr Paris, 10 June 1776). French writer. A mainstay of the French academic tradition, Fréron is best known as the opponent of the Philosophes, notably Voltaire and the Encyclopédistes. He expressed his interest in art through his critiques of the Salons and his reviews of books on the fine arts. Educated by the Jesuits, from 1739 to 1743 he collaborated with Abbé Pierre-François-Guyot Desfontaines (1685–1745), editor of *Observations sur quelques écrits modernes*. He went on to direct his own publications, including the *Journal étranger* and the better-known periodical *Année littéraire*.

The sheer volume of Fréron's work forced him to seek collaborative help. Jacques-François Blondel and Pierre Patte were among those who assisted on architectural matters, while Charles-Nicolas Cochin II and, to a lesser extent, Michel-François Dandré-Bardon, were involved in articles on painting and sculpture. In the *Journal étranger* in 1756, Fréron introduced Johann Joachim Winckelmann's writings to French readers; on the subject of architecture he defended the classical tradition. From 1761 to 1771 Fréron's reviews of the Salons were written under Cochin's influence, on occasion directly from his reports. Fréron remained a staunch defender of rules and supporter of the Ancients (*see* ANCIENTS AND MODERNS, QUARREL OF THE), reticent with regard to any metaphysical speculations on Beauty.

BIBLIOGRAPHY
Voltaire: 'Anecdotes sur Fréron' [1761], *Mélanges* (Paris, 1961), pp. 385–92
J. Balcou: *Fréron contre les philosophes* (Geneva, 1975)
J. Biard-Millérioux: *L'Esthétique d'Elie-Catherine Fréron, 1739–1776: Littérature et critique au XVIIIe siècle* (Paris, 1985)
CHRISTIAN MICHEL

Freschel, Daniel. *See* FRÖSCHL, DANIEL.

Fresco. Wall painting technique in which pigments are dissolved in water only and then applied to fresh, wet lime plaster (the *intonaco*). As the wall dries, the calcium hydroxide of the plaster combines with carbon dioxide in the atmosphere to form calcium carbonate. During this process the pigments become an integral part of the wall, forming a fine, transparent, vitreous layer on its surface. Fresco is particularly vulnerable to damp and for this reason is suitable only for dry climates. This article discusses the technique as systematized in Italy from the 14th century; for its history, development and variations elsewhere, as well as the conservation of fresco, *see* WALL PAINTING, §§I and II.

Fresco painting was technically demanding and was usually carried out on a large scale, so the painter had to be accurate in drawing up his composition and capable of organizing a team of skilled hands, from the masons to the assistant painters who were assigned the less important parts of the work.

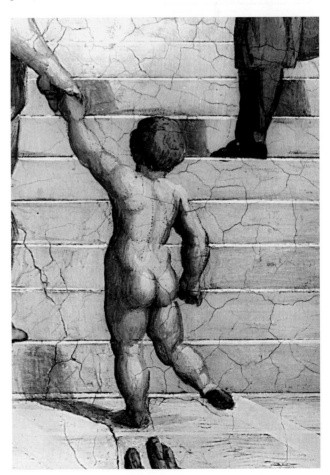

1. Fresco of the *Fire in the Borgo* (1517) by followers of Raphael, Stanza dell'Incendio, Vatican, Rome; detail showing pouncing

2. Fresco of the *Apotheosis of St Clement* (1600) by Giovanni and Cherubino Alberti, vault of the Galleria Clementina, Vatican, Rome; detail showing incised outlines

1. PREPARATION OF THE WALL. The wall was first carefully brushed and dampened. A layer of coarse plaster with a rough finish (the *arriccio*) was then applied. This could be done several years before the *intonaco*, though if the *arriccio* was old it had to be well brushed and wetted before the *intonaco* was applied. Usually the painting was carried out on the *intonaco* (*see* §4 below), but occasionally a further layer, an *intonachino*, was applied as a base for the paint. This can be found in Roman frescoes but rarely in Renaissance ones.

The plaster of the various layers was composed of slaked lime and an inert filler, such as sand, ground marble or pozzolana (a baked clay of volcanic origin). The proportions were the same for the *arriccio* and the *intonaco*, although for the *arriccio* the aggregate, or filler, was coarse grained, while for the *intonaco* it was fine grained. There were two standard mixes: strong or fat mortar, which was composed of one part lime to two parts filler and tended to crack as it dried, and lean mortar, which had one part lime to three of filler. If a lean mortar contained pozzolana, the proportion could be one part lime to 1.75–2 parts pozzolana. The lime is obtained by firing calcareous rocks, composed largely of calcium carbonate ($CaCo_3$), at a temperature of 850–900 °C. By adding water to the resulting quicklime (CaO), slaked lime (calcium hydroxide, $Ca(OH)_2$) was obtained.

Good slaked lime underwent a long maturing process in vats or pits covered with water—the Romans allowed their lime to mature for at least three years. Microcrystalline limestones produced lean lime, which required less water in its manufacture, while cryptocrystalline or compact limestones produced fat lime, which required more water. The sand (silicon dioxide) had to be sharp sand obtained from a quarry or river, not from the seashore, where it contains salt; the individual grains had to be angular, not rounded, to encourage bonding with the lime. Pozzolana is found as a natural rock in the regions surrounding Rome and Naples. Violet or black in colour, it produced a compact plaster superior to that obtained from sand or ground marble.

The appearance of the finished fresco depended on the way in which the *intonaco* was applied. Until the 15th century it was worked with a trowel to obtain an almost smooth surface, while from the 16th century, in an attempt to emulate painting on canvas, a rougher texture was created by working up the surface with short strokes of a brush.

2. LAYING OUT AND TRANSFERRING THE COMPOSITION. The vertical, horizontal and diagonal lines of the composition were laid out on the *arriccio* with cords pulled tight and pressed hard against the plaster. The rest of the composition was sketched out in charcoal, which enabled the artist to make corrections as necessary. The definitive

3. Fresco of the *Apotheosis of St Clement* (1600) by Giovanni and Cherubino Alberti, vault of the Galleria Clementina, Vatican, Rome; detail showing incised squaring

design, the SINOPIA, was brushed in and served as a guide for the final execution of the painting. The whole composition was drawn full scale on a CARTOON, which was cut up into sections of varying sizes so the painting could be done piecemeal (*see* §4 below). As each section of the *intonaco* was applied, the design was transferred from the cartoon by POUNCING (see fig. 1) or by running a stylus over the outlines. (In the 14th century the design was transferred by pouncing and then painted in yellow ochre, so the artist could make any necessary adjustments before proceeding.) The lines of painted frames and architectural forms were often incised (see fig. 2) directly on to the plaster without a cartoon, with the aid of compasses, rulers, set squares and cords pulled taut.

Another method of transfer, used especially in the 17th century for vast ceiling frescoes, was squaring (see fig. 3), which replaced the time-consuming and costly cartoon technique. The small-scale compositional drawing was squared, as was the surface to be painted, sometimes with the aid of cords or shadows projected from a light source covered by a wire mesh. In each new square the painter copied the lines contained in the corresponding smaller square in the drawing.

3. PIGMENTS. The range of colours for fresco was restricted to those that could withstand the alkaline action of the lime. Other colours could be used *a secco*, but a good fresco painter used secco colours as little as possible, since they were less durable. Fresco colours included vine black, black earth, ivory black; red ochres (particularly those rich in haematite), cinnabar (which is mixed with white to give a pink flesh colour); yellow ochre, yellow earth, Naples yellow, green earth, umber, raw and burnt sienna; *bianco sangiovanni*; and finally, smalt. All the other traditional colours, including ultramarine, azurite, malachite and erinite, were not suitable for fresco and were therefore applied *a secco*.

The pigments had to be finely ground in water. They could not be mixed on the palette because in drying they altered in tone and intensity and so could not be easily repeated. Instead, the whole range of colours in their various tonal gradations was prepared in advance in sufficient quantities to complete the composition. The colours were then kept in jars of water called *mestiche*. While the work was in progress the colours for each *giornata* (*see* §4 below) were taken from the jars as necessary.

4. APPLICATION OF THE PIGMENTS. The composition was divided into sections that could be worked in one day, called *pontate* or *giornate*. *Pontate* were used in Roman, Byzantine and 13th-century frescoes; they followed the arrangement of the scaffolding (It.: *ponteggio*), so were rectangular in shape and usually fairly large. *Giornate* were occasionally used in Roman murals but only became widespread from the 13th century. They followed outlines in the composition and so were irregular in shape; they were usually applied from top to bottom and from left to right.

Once the design or guidelines of a *giornata* had been traced, work could begin on the painting and could continue for several hours, depending on the climate and

4. Fresco of the *Fire in the Borgo* (1517) by followers of Raphael, Stanza dell'Incendio, Vatican, Rome; detail, in raking light, showing the plaster sliced away at the edge of a *giornata*

the season. The best time to begin painting was two or three hours after the laying down of the *intonaco*; conditions for work were optimum for at least two hours, after which the plaster began to form its crust of calcium carbonate. Work then became increasingly difficult, and the results correspondingly disappointing as the pigment was no longer absorbed. If the plaster was sprayed with water, work could continue for another hour, but during this stage only liquid colours could be used. Finally, when those colours that are mixed with the white pigment *bianco sangiovanni* began to dry and turn whitish in an irregular fashion, work had to cease, and the unpainted plaster was removed with an oblique cut (see fig. 4). This was the moment when highlights were applied, an operation that required experience and dexterity because colours with a green or black base became lighter as they dried, while those containing iron oxides became darker.

Any areas that could not be painted in fresco were done later, when the composition was completely finished and the plaster thoroughly dry. These included colours incompatible with fresco and figurative motifs that overlapped several *giornate* (lances, festoons, ribbons etc). This operation was carried out *a secco* with pigments bound in adhesive. For each colour, a complementary undercoat was prepared *a fresco*: white for the blues, with shadows in yellow ochre for drapery, and black, red ochre or grey–blue for monochrome backgrounds. Metal leaf enamel—either gold or tin glazed with yellow to imitate gold—was also applied *a secco*, most frequently for armour and decorative motifs. Some gold areas, such as haloes or crowns, may have been raised in relief with a doughy mortar (not too moist) worked with a spatula, a mixture of flour and varnish worked with the tip of a paint brush or a mixture of warm beeswax and resin.

Fresco required no protective or enhancing finish like the varnish that was applied to canvas or panel paintings. Indeed, this would have prevented the formation of the transparent, glassy layer of calcium carbonate that gives fresco painting its characteristic force and beauty, as well as its resilience. Easily subject to decay or change, the organic substances in any such varnish would have compromised both the appearance and the preservation of the painting.

See also LIME SECCO, SECCO, SGRAFFITO and WALL ?PAINTING.

BIBLIOGRAPHY

EARLY SOURCES

C. Cennini: *Il libro dell'arte* (*c.* 1390); Eng. trans. and notes by D. V. Thompson jr as *The Craftsman's Handbook: 'Il libro dell'arte'* (New Haven, 1933/R New York, 1954)
G. Vasari: *Vite* (1550, rev. 2/1568); ed. G. Milanesi (1878–85)
G. B. Armenini: *De' veri precetti della pittura* (Ravenna, 1587)
A. Pozzo: 'Breve istruttione per dipingere a fresco', *Prospettiva de' pittori ed architetti* (Rome, 1692)

SPECIALIST STUDIES

R. La Montagne St Hubert: *The Art of Fresco Painting* (Paris, 1923)
R. Mayer: *The Artist's Handbook* (New York, 1940, rev. 4/1982/R London, 1987)
Frescoes from Florence (exh. cat. by V. Procacci and others, London, Hayward Gal., 1969)
U. Procacci and L. Guarnieri: *Come nasce un affresco* (Florence, 1975)
G. Botticelli: *Tecnica e restauro delle pitture murali* (Florence, 1980)
G. Ronchetti: *Pittura murale* (Milan, 1983)
E. Borsook and F. Superbi Gioffredi, eds: *Tecnica e stile*, 2 vols (Milan, 1986)

GIANLUIGI COLALUCCI

Fresnaye, Roger de la. *See* LA FRESNAYE, ROGER DE.

Fret. *See* MEANDER.

Fretwork. Ornamental openwork pattern consisting of strips of wood cut with a fret saw.

☐

Freud, Lucian (*b* Berlin, 8 Dec 1922). British painter and draughtsman. He was the son of the architect Ernst Freud (1892–1970) and the grandson of SIGMUND FREUD. His family moved to England in 1932, and in 1939 he became a naturalized British subject and enrolled at the East Anglian School of Painting and Drawing, Dedham, run by Cedric Morris. Apart from a year in Paris and Greece, Freud spent most of the rest of his career in Paddington, London, an inner-city area whose seediness is reflected in Freud's often sombre and moody interiors and cityscapes. In the 1940s he was principally interested in drawing, especially the face, as in *Naval Gunner* (1941; priv. col., see Gowing, pl. 22), and occasionally using a distorted style reminiscent of George Grosz, as in *Page from a*

Sketchbook (1941; priv. col., see Gowing, pl. 17). He began to turn his attention to painting, however, and experimented with Surrealism, producing such images as the *Painter's Room* (1943; priv. col., see Gowing, pl. 26), which features an incongruous arrangement of objects, including a stuffed zebra's head, a battered chaise longue and a house plant, all of which survived his Surrealist phase and appeared separately in later paintings. He was also loosely associated with Neo-Romanticism, and the intense, bulbous eyes that characterize his early portraits show affinities with the work of other artists associated with the movement, such as John Minton, whose portrait he painted in 1952 (London, Royal Coll. A.). He established his own artistic identity, however, in meticulously executed realist works, imbued with a pervasive mood of alienation. He was dubbed by Herbert Read 'the Ingres of existentialism' (*Contemporary British Art*, Harmondsworth, 1951, rev. 1964, p. 35) because of such images as those of his first wife, Kitty (the daughter of Jacob Epstein), nervously clutching a rose in *Girl with Roses* (1947–8; London, Brit. Council).

Two important paintings of 1951 established the themes and preoccupations that dominated the rest of Freud's career: *Interior in Paddington* (Liverpool, Walker A.G.) and *Girl with a White Dog* (London, Tate). In the former an archetypal 'angry young man' figure (the sitter was photographer Harry Diamond who would pose again for Freud), in dishevelled raincoat, cigarette in one hand, the other fist clenched, is placed in claustrophobic proximity to a meticulously executed man-sized potted plant in an anonymous interior space. *Girl with a White Dog* is a virtuoso handling of fabrics and textures, juxtaposing the smooth hairs of the bulldog, the wool of the sitter's dressing-gown and the silk bedspread on which she sits, but of more enduring interest is the expressive, staged quality of the composition, the way the model supports an exposed breast on her wrist and stares resolutely beyond her canine companion. Both paintings demonstrate an eagerness to establish a highly charged situation, in which the artist is free to explore formal and optical problems rather than expressive or interpretative ones. Later poses of comparable theatricality include *Naked Man with Rat* (1977; priv. col., see Gowing, pl. 175) and *Naked Girl with Egg* (1980–81; London, Brit. Council; *see* ENGLAND, fig. 24).

By the late 1950s Freud had lost interest in achieving a meticulous sheen on the surface of his pictures: brushmarks became spatial as he began to describe the face and body in terms of shape and structure, for example in *Pregnant Girl* (1960–61; priv. col., see Gowing, pl. 90), and often in female nudes the brushstrokes help to suggest shape. By the time of the tautly modelled *Reflection (Self-portrait)* (562×512 mm, 1985; priv. col., see 1987 exh. cat., pl. 82), attention to tonal detail had become so acute, however, that paint was built up in concentrations devoid of any compositional function. Throughout his career Freud's palette remained distinctly muted.

A close relationship with sitters was often important for Freud. His mother sat for an extensive series in the early 1970s after she was widowed, and his daughters Bella and Esther modelled nude, together and individually. Such artists as Frank Auerbach and Francis Bacon, and such patrons as Lord Goodman and Baron Thyssen-Bornemisza, sat for portraits. The performance artist Leigh Bowery posed for an extensive series of nude pictures in the early 1990s. Although the human form dominated his output, Freud also executed cityscapes, viewed from his studio window, and obsessively detailed nature studies, such as *Two Plants* (1977–80; London, Tate). The 1980s and early 1990s were marked by increasingly ambitious compositions in terms of both scale and complexity, such as the *Large Interior, W11 (After Watteau)* (1.86×1.98 m, 1981–3; priv. col., see 1991 exh. cat., p. 64), which involves five sitters, including family members and his then mistress, the artist Celia Paul (*b* 1959), arranged in homage to Watteau's *Pierrot Content* (1712; Lugano, Col. Thyssen-Bornemisza).

BIBLIOGRAPHY

J. Rothenstein: *Modern English Painters* (London, 1974), iii, pp. 192–200
Lucian Freud (exh. cat., intro. J. Russell; London, Hayward Gal., 1974)
L. Gowing: *Lucian Freud* (London, 1982)
Lucian Freud: Paintings (exh. cat., intro. R. Hughes; Washington, DC, Smithsonian Inst.; Paris, Pompidou; London, Hayward Gal.; W. Berlin, N.G.; 1987)
Lucian Freud: Works on Paper (exh. cat., intro. N. Penny; Oxford, Ashmolean; Edinburgh, Fruitmarket Gal.; Hull, Ferens A.G.; and elsewhere; 1988)
Lucian Freud: Paintings and Works on Paper, 1990–91 (exh. cat., texts B. Mantura and A. Cook; Milan, Castello Sforzesco; Liverpool, Tate; 1991)
C. Lampert: *Lucian Freud: Recent Work* (London, 1993)
C. Hartley: *The Etchings of Lucian Freud: A Catalogue Raisonné, 1946-1995* (London and New York, 1995)

DAVID COHEN

Freud, Sigmund (*b* Freiberg, Moravia [now Příbor, Czech Republic], 6 May 1856; *d* London, 23 Sept 1939). Austrian psychoanalyst and collector. After studying at the University of Vienna and working first in histology, then in neurology, he spent the winter of 1885–6 in the clinic of the great French pathologist, Jean-Martin Charcot (1825–93). From Charcot Freud learnt that every hysterical symptom is ideogenic, in other words an idea plays a crucial part in its genesis. The bodily extent of the symptom corresponds not to any neuro-physiological unit but to what the idea denotes, and the symptom may be alleviated through talking out the idea, for example under hypnosis. The pathogenic idea is invariably unconscious, or inaccessible to consciousness. Over the years Freud, while maintaining a clinical practice in Vienna, elaborated and transformed this hypothesis, and out of it psychoanalytic theory emerged.

First, Freud extended the scope of the hypothesis from symptoms to bungled actions, slips of the tongue, dreams, jokes, and eventually the neurosis. Secondly, he recognized that the idea, originally held to be the core of a memory, represented a desire. Thirdly, Freud concluded that the idea was unconscious because the mind had defended itself against something unacceptable. For many years he equated defence with repression but he then admitted other mechanisms of defence, such as projection, introjection, denial and splitting. Fourthly, Freud identified the desires that provoked repression as being, ultimately, infantile and sexual. Having conceded infantile sexuality he gradually worked out an account of psychosexual development, consisting of the oral, anal, phallic and genital stages, complicated by regression. Freud's theory

of the 'Oedipus complex', a crucial occurrence in this development, postulated that the child, seeking the undivided sexual attentions of one parent, comes to desire the annihilation of the other, and its 'dissolution' through the introjection of the hated, hence feared, parent, led to a greater attention to the structure and internal functioning of the mind. In *Das Ich und das Es* (Leipzig, 1923; Eng. trans. as *The Ego and the Id*, London, 1927; *Standard Edition*, xix) he formulated his structural theory with its division into ego, which is the controlling agency, super-ego, or internalized parent, and id, which is the reservoir of instinct. Already, in *Jenseits des Lustprinzips* (Leipzig, Vienna and Zurich, 1920; Eng. trans. as *Beyond the Pleasure Principle*, London, 1922; *Standard Edition*, xviii), he had postulated, alongside sexuality, the Death Instinct, recognizable in its outgoing form as aggression. Throughout his career Freud worked at constructing a metapsychology, in which ordinary psychological notions such as desire, emotion and belief would be superseded and explained by shifts in psychic energy. This energy was either free-floating or bound to an idea.

Freud had great reverence for the arts, and his writings on them consist partly of general, rather sketchy, accounts of what art is, which belong very largely to the first part of his career and are uninfluenced by either the structural theory or the postulation of aggression, and partly of much fuller studies of particular artists or works of art (Leonardo da Vinci, Michelangelo's *Moses*, Dostoyevsky). However, these latter works are, despite their brilliant aperçus, mostly illustrations of some fragment of psychoanalytic theory (*see* PSYCHOANALYSIS AND ART). In 'Der Moses des Michelangelo' (*Imago*, iii/1, 1914, pp. 15–36; Eng. trans. *Complete Works*, xiii, pp. 209–38) Freud said that he found himself almost incapable of gaining pleasure from a work of art unless he could explain what its effect was due to: the art he collected seems not to confirm this.

Freud took virtually no interest in contemporary art, though the Surrealists tried to gain his approval for their special appropriation of his views (*see* SURREALISM and AUTOMATISM). In his famous meeting with Salvador Dalí in London in 1938, Freud is said to have wryly remarked that it was Dalí's conscious mind that interested him. Freud had a passion for ancient art and was an avid collector, acquiring most works from dealers in Vienna. He brought his collection, which included Etruscan pieces, ancient Roman pots, heads, figurines and glassware, ancient Greek pots, heads and figurines, and ancient Egyptian figurines and fragments of wall painting, to London when he fled Vienna after the Nazi occupation in 1938, and it is now housed in the Freud Museum, London. Freud professed to have read more archaeology than psychology, and over the decades he used archaeology as a metaphor for the psychoanalytic process. He visited many archaeological sites in Europe, and a lifelong friend was Emanuel Löwy (1857–1938), a professor of archaeology in Rome and later in Vienna.

Freud's son Ernst Freud (1892–1970) was an architect practising in London, and Ernst's son was the painter LUCIAN FREUD.

WRITINGS

J. Strachey, ed.: *Standard Edition of the Complete Psychological Works of Sigmund Freud*, trans. J. Strachey and A. Freud, 24 vols (London, 1953–74)

H. Nunberg, ed.: *Minutes of the Vienna Psychoanalytic Society* (New York, 1962–7)

BIBLIOGRAPHY

E. Jones: *Sigmund Freud: Life and Work*, 3 vols (London, 1953–7)
R. Wollheim: *Freud* (London, 1971)
J. J. Spector: *The Aesthetics of Freud* (New York, 1972)
R. Wollheim: 'Freud and the Understanding of Art', *On Art and the Mind* (London, 1973), pp. 202–19
P. Gay: *Freud: A Life of our Time* (New York, 1987)
E. H. Gombrich: 'Freud's Aesthetics', *Reflections on the History of Art* (London, 1987), pp. 221–39
L. Gamwell and R. Wells, eds: *Sigmund Freud and Art: His Personal Collection of Antiquities*, intro. P. Gay (New York and London, 1989)

RICHARD WOLLHEIM

Freudenberger, Sigmund (*b* Berne, 16 June 1745; *d* Berne, 13 Aug 1801). Swiss painter, draughtsman and engraver. In 1761 he went to work for the portrait painter Emanuel Handmann in Basle, where he stayed for three years. In 1765, with Adrian Zingg (1734–86), he left for Paris, where he trained with Jakob Schmutzer (1733–1811) and frequented the studio of Jean Georges Wille, the celebrated engraver. He worked as a book illustrator during this period. The work of Boucher, whom he met, and of Greuze and Fragonard had a significant influence on his artistic development. Freudenberger returned in 1773 to Berne, where he undertook several portraits. He became friendly with Johann Ludwig Aberli, with whom he travelled the countryside, which he recorded in numerous drawings, watercolours and engravings. He specialized in genre scenes, rustic still-lifes and portrayals of Bernese peasant life, which became very popular. In some works, such as a red chalk drawing of *A Woman Playing the Harp* (1778; Zurich, Schweizer. Landesmus.), he continued the gallant style he had learnt from Boucher. His watercolours were frequently engraved, either individually or in series, and hand-coloured. His style is characterized by detailed and careful execution and by an intimate, narrative approach, although he tended to idealize his rustic subject-matter. His work was significant in introducing genre subjects in Switzerland, where artists had tended to concentrate on pure landscape. He ran a large studio where Daniel Lafond (1763–1831), Niklaus König and Georg Mind (1768–1814) were pupils. The French Revolution was disastrous for his art and his business and clouded the last years of his life. After his death Mind coloured his engravings.

SKL

BIBLIOGRAPHY

E. Gradmann and A. M. Cetto: *Schweizer Malerei und Zeichnung im 17. und 18. Jahrhundert* (Basle, 1944), p. 66
M. Huggler: *Sigmund Freudenberger: Der Berner Kleinmeister, 1745–1801* (Berne, 1976)

JEANNE-MARIE HORAT-WEBER

Freudenstadt. Popular health resort in Baden-Württemberg, Germany. It was formerly a fortified town in the northern Black Forest, laid out with strict regularity according to Renaissance ideals. It owes its origin both to the silver and copper mines in nearby Christophstal and to its position on an important trade route, the Kniebis-strasse. Strategic factors also played a part in the foundation of the town by Duke Frederick I of Württemberg (*reg* 1593–1608): it was designed to protect the route to his possessions on the Upper Rhine and provide a fortress against the hostile bishopric of Strasbourg.

Duke Frederick entrusted the planning to his architect Heinrich Schickhardt II, already experienced in urban planning, who, in his inventory of possessions and plans up to 1632, reported on the two main designs of 1599 (Stuttgart, Hauptstaatsarchv). The first scheme shows an ideal town on a square plan. Comparable in structure to a Roman *castrum*, the *cardo* and *decumanus* lead from the gates at the centre of each one of the sides to a central square. Other streets intersecting at right angles divide the area into nine blocks, the central one a square with the town hall. The castle and church squares are diagonally opposite each other. Where they serve to fortify the bastion, the houses are in rows; elsewhere they are laid out around courtyards and gardens. This project displeased Duke Frederick and was modified in line with his wishes. The castle was moved to the centre of the plan, and the houses were aligned uniformly around it in place of the courtyard layout. In Schickhardt's second plan, which was half realized, the streets are arranged in the form of concentric squares crossed by intersecting lines drawn from the corners and the middle of each side. Four rows of houses were aligned concentrically about the square on which the public buildings were situated. At the corners were the church (1601–14), the town hall and the staple house (1602–9, destr. 1945) and a hospital (destr. 1632) on L-shaped ground-plans. A four-winged castle was set diagonally in the middle, its angles touching the centre of the square's sides. In the case of the church, the wings of the L were constituted by two naves, one for men and one for women, with the altar and pulpit at the angle. To fortify the town, old-fashioned round bastions were planned. Other designs show up-to-date ramparts.

In actual execution the square was lined with arcades, though the castle remained unbuilt, and up to the second half of the 17th century a wooden enclosure served for fortification. Religious refugees from Austria and local miners settled in the town. Between 1599 and 1612, 287 houses were built on the lines planned, though 188 sites remained bare. On Duke Frederick's death in 1608 the building programme stagnated; state funds were withdrawn, and the tax concessions to citizens were rescinded. In addition, mining proved unprofitable and the adjoining land infertile. After epidemics of plague (1610, 1635), a fire that destroyed the town (1632) and the turmoils of war, Freudenstadt had only 72 residents in the mid-17th century. In 1667–74 the town was converted by Matthias Weiss (1636–1707) into a fortress, the gates and walls of which were razed in the 19th century when the town became a health resort. After the catastrophic fires of 1945, Freudenstadt was rebuilt on a simplified plan by Ludwig Schweizer from 1949 to 1955. Instead of the timbered houses with gabled frontages shown on a presentation coin of 1627, solidly constructed terraced houses line the somewhat widened streets today, and the market square has been cleared of its gardens.

Numerous models are cited for Freudenstadt's layout: the suburb with hospital and tournament ground at Stuttgart, the cities of Ferrara and Livorno, which Schickhardt had visited, and the French new towns of Vitry-le-François and Nancy. Finally, parallels to the ground-plan and fortifications are to be found in architectural treatises by Albrecht Dürer (*Etliche Underricht zu Befestigung der*

Stett, Schlosz und Flecken, Nuremberg, 1527), Daniel Speckle (*Architectura von Vestungen*, Strasbourg, 1584) and Jacques Perret. Dürer's design for a royal city on a square ground-plan is closest to the layout that was executed. Clearly, Schickhardt's designs no longer corresponded with the urban planning ideal of his time, whereby fortified towns had streets leading radially from a central square. In his conception for Freudenstadt, it seems, he consciously made use of earlier forms to give the town a venerable appearance. Apart from the town's ground-plan, the projected castle, the church and the fortifications show reminiscences of Gothic and early Renaissance forms— all, no doubt, at the behest of Duke Frederick, for Schickhardt always protested that Freudenstadt had not been built as he had intended.

BIBLIOGRAPHY

J. Baum: *Forschungen über die Hauptwerke des Baumeisters Heinrich Schickhardt in Freudenstadt, Mömpelgard und Stuttgart, sowie über die Schlösser in Weikersheim und Aschaffenburg*, Stud. Dt. Kstgesch., 185 (Strasbourg, 1916)

Die Renaissance im deutschen Südwesten (exh. cat., Heidelberg, 1986)

DIRK JONKANSKI

Freudweiler, Heinrich (*b* Zurich, 16 Oct 1755; *d* Zurich, 1 Dec 1795). Swiss painter. He first trained with the Zurich landscape painter Heinrich Wüest; he then studied the 17th-century Dutch and Flemish masters, as well as the works of Hogarth, in Düsseldorf and Mannheim. In 1784 with his friend Konrad Gessner he visited Dresden, where he received instruction in portrait painting from Anton Graff, and Berlin, where he became a close friend of Daniel Chodowiecki, a draughtsman and engraver. In 1785 he settled in Zurich as a landscape, portrait and genre painter. Influenced by the Dutch Little Masters and Hogarth and Chodowiecki, and on the basis of his own observation, Freudweiler developed an unpretentious, true-to-life style, painting small landscapes, contemporary genre and family conversation pieces, generally on wood. He was a co-founder of the Kunstgesellschaft (1787) in Zurich. From 1786 he became successful in Swiss bourgeois circles with his portrait-like *Trauerallegorien* (e.g. *A Mother's Solicitude in Eternity*, 1786; Zurich, Ksthaus), full-length portraits of people who had died, with allegories relating to death and resurrection. These were the pictorial counterparts of the mourning odes or elegies on the death of family members or friends that were popular at the time. In these works Freudweiler's style approached a sentimental classicism, although he continued to paint conversation pieces in an ornamental and decorative Rococo style. His historical compositions were less successful, although his painting *The Abbot of Engelberg Pardoning the Ringleaders of the Rebellious Valley Dwellers* (1795; Zurich, Ksthaus) is noteworthy.

BIBLIOGRAPHY

SKL

Zürcher Kunstgesellschaft: Katalog der Sammlung von Gemälden und Bildwerken im Kunsthaus (Zurich, 3/1910), pp. 34–5

W. Hugelshofer: *Schweizer Kleinmeister* (Zurich, 1943), p. 16

E. Gradmann and A. M. Cetto: *Schweizer Malerei und Zeichnung im 17. und 18. Jahrhundert* (Basle, 1944), pp. 31, 72–3

P. Wescher: *Die Romantik in der schweizer Malerei* (Frauenfeld, 1947), pp. 92–3

Von Gessner bis Turner: Zeichnungen und Aquarelle von 1750–1850 im Kunsthaus Zürich Graphische Sammlung (exh. cat. by B. von Waldkirch, Zurich, Ksthaus, 1988), pp. 17–19

INGRID SATTEL BERNARDINI

Freund, Gisèle (*b* Berlin, 19 Dec 1912). French photographer and writer of German birth. She studied sociology and art history before becoming an international freelance photojournalist in 1935. She took documentary photographs covering social issues and portraits of writers, artists and intellectuals, for example *Simone de Beauvoir* (see Freund, 1985, pp. 140–41). Her work was published by *Life*, *Weekly Illustrated*, *Picture Post*, *Paris-Match* and many other magazines, and exhibited internationally. During World War II she fled to southern France, and to Argentina and Chile, where she worked with the Louis Jouvet Theatre Company. She spent a brief period in Mexico (1950–52) but was based in France from 1946. A pioneer of 35 mm photo-reportage, in both black and white and colour, she revealed in her work a preoccupation with the role of photography in society, culminating in her pioneering study, *Photographie et société* (1977).

WRITINGS

La Photographie en France au dix-neuvième siècle (Paris, 1936)

Le Monde et ma caméra (Paris, 1970; Eng. trans. as *The World in My Camera*, New York, 1975)

Gisèle Freund, Photographer (New York, 1985)

PHOTOGRAPHIC PUBLICATIONS

Mexique précolombien (Neuchâtel, 1954)

James Joyce in Paris: His Final Years (New York, 1965)

Photographie et société (Paris, 1977; Eng. trans., Boston, 1980)

BIBLIOGRAPHY

Gisèle Freund: Fotografien, 1932–1974 (exh. cat. by K. Honnef, Bonn, Rhein. Landesmus.; Kassel, Fotoforum Gal.; 1977)

VIRGINIA DODIER

Freund, Hermann Ernst (*b* Uthlede, nr Bremen, 15 Oct 1786; *d* Copenhagen, 30 June 1840). Danish sculptor and decorative artist of German birth. After training as a smith and die-cutter, he studied (1805–17) at the Kunstakademi in Copenhagen. In 1817 he won a medal for his relief *Abraham Expels Hagar and Ishmael* (1817; Copenhagen, Kon. Dan. Kstakad.), and then received the academy's travel scholarship. He travelled through Berlin, Dresden and Prague to Vienna, and then via Venice and Florence to Rome, where he arrived in April 1818. His meeting with the sculptor Bertel Thorvaldsen had profound and ultimately unhappy consequences for his career. He worked in Thorvaldsen's studio, assisted him in the execution of several works and became increasingly dependent on him, even as he attempted to sculpt independently. Freund's first sculpture in Rome was *Chloe* (plaster, 1818; destr.; marble version begun 1824; ex-Copenhagen, Christiansborg Slot, destr. 1884; see Oppermann), a statue of a young girl, symbolizing innocence, helping a lamb to drink. This work has some similarities with Thorvaldsen's sculpture but is more reminiscent of that of German sculptors working in Rome, such as Ridolfo Schadow. In Freund's portrait busts various styles are to be found. In the bust of the portrait painter *Christian Albrecht Jensen* (1818; Copenhagen, Ny Carlsberg Glyp.), Freund simplified and idealized the sitter; in the bust of the poet *B. S. Ingemann* (1818; Copenhagen, Ny Carlsberg Glyp.) the treatment is more naturalistic. It is possible that

Thorvaldsen helped Freund with this work. (In return, Freund helped Thorvaldsen with the bust of the Norwegian painter *J. C. C. Dahl* (1821; Bergen, Billedgal.).) During Thorvaldsen's visit to Denmark in 1819–20, Freund took charge of his Roman studio.

Before his departure from Denmark, Freund had obtained the commission for a series of statues of the *Apostles* for C. F. Hansen's Church of Our Lady in Copenhagen and had begun work on one of them. The commission, however, was subsequently offered to Thorvaldsen, who accepted it on condition that Freund be given other work. Freund was therefore asked to provide four statues of the *Evangelists* for the church of Christiansborg Slot, and some statues for the palace itself. The cancellation of the first commission, however, was a considerable blow, and it soured Freund's relations with both Thorvaldsen and Hansen. He completed only one of the figures (plaster, 1823; placed in church 1891) of the *Evangelists*.

Freund discovered his real strength in the presentation of Nordic gods and myths. Statues of *Loke* and *Odin* (both 1822; Copenhagen, Ny Carlsberg Glyp.) are the first examples. With its vigorous movement and expressive face, *Loke* is unique among contemporary Neo-classical sculpture. Freund's *Odin* was subsequently reworked (1825–6) and cast in bronze (Copenhagen, Ny Carlsberg Glyp.). At the same period Freund prepared the models for the work usually recognized as his masterpiece, the relief frieze of *Ragnarok* ('Twilight of the Gods') for Christiansborg Slot. The frieze presented episodes from Nordic mythology with figures such as Hel (Loke's daughter, the goddess of the underworld), as well as dwarfs, elves, trolls and men. The frieze was finished and installed after Freund's death but was destroyed in the fire of 1884. A copy (Copenhagen, Stat. Mus. Kst) was made by his nephew Georg Christian Freund (1821–1900). Freund's last years in Rome were fraught with problems and he returned to Denmark on foot, travelling via Paris and Berlin and arriving in Copenhagen in the autumn of 1828. In the following years he was occupied with the preparation of funerary monuments, many with inset reliefs. These memorials, clearly inspired by Greek stelae, constitute an important contribution to Danish Neoclassicism, in some cases incorporating polychrome decoration in the ancient Greek manner.

Freund was also an influential designer of interiors and fittings. Appointed professor at the Kunstakademi in 1829, he received an apartment with the post and decorated it in the Pompeian style (*see* DENMARK, §V, 2 and fig. 15). In spite of its evident Classical inspiration, Freund's design was perceived as particularly Danish, and it influenced later Danish interiors. Freund also designed his own furniture and utensils and in this way too established a tradition for the decoration of a Danish artist's home. Among Freund's later sculptures were a bust of the architect *C. F. Hansen* (1830; Copenhagen, Kon. Dan. Kstakad.) and a fountain sculpture of a boy with a swan (1837; Copenhagen, Rosenborg Slot). In his later years Freund suffered from heart disease and occasionally from the fits of melancholy that had dogged his whole life and had prevented him from completing more major works.

BIBLIOGRAPHY

DKH

N. Høyen: *Forklaring af H. Freunds frise, Ragnarok* [Explanation of H. Freund's frieze, *Ragnarok*] (Copenhagen, 1857)

V. Freund: *Hermann Ernst Freunds levend* [Hermann Ernst Freund's life] (Copenhagen, 1883)

T. Oppermann: *Billedhuggeren Hermann Ernst Freund* [The sculptor Hermann Ernst Freund] (Copenhagen, 1916)

Omkring Loke: Arbejder af Hermann Ernst Freund [Around Loke: works by Hermann Ernst Freund] (exh. cat., ed. H. E. Nørregård-Nielsen; Copenhagen, Ny Carlsberg Glyp., 1986)

Ragnarokfrisen af H. E. Freund [The *Ragnarok* frieze by H. E. Freund] (exh. cat., ed. K. Monrad; Copenhagen, Stat. Mus. Kst, 1986)

BJARNE JØRNÆS

Freundlich, Otto (*b* Stolp [now Stupsk, Poland], 10 July 1878; *d* Maidanek concentration camp, nr Lublin, 9 March 1943). German painter, sculptor, stained-glass designer and writer. He studied art history (1903–4) in Berlin and Munich. After a visit to Florence (1905–6), he began to experiment with sculpture and studied with Lothar von Kunowski (*b* 1866) in Berlin (1907–8). He spent 1908–9 in Paris, where he met Picasso, Braque and Gris. Between 1910 and 1914 he divided his time between Paris, Berlin and Cologne: from 1910 he participated in the exhibitions of the Berlin Secession and from 1913 had contacts with the Sturm-Galerie in Berlin. His expressive early works included both sculptures and flat, geometric paintings (e.g. *Composition with Figure*, 1911; Pontoise, Mus. Pontoise). Having spent World War I in Cologne, from 1918 to 1924 he lived in Berlin, where he was one of the founder-members of the Novembergruppe in 1918, and contributed to the radical newspaper *Die Aktion: Zeitschrift für Freiheitliche Politik und Literatur Aktion*. In 1920 Walter Gropius tried to make him a teacher with the Bauhaus, but this was opposed by the faculty. In 1924 he moved to Paris but maintained his German contacts, writing in 1929 as a correspondent for the newspapers published by the artists' group Die Progressiven in Cologne. In 1931 he was one of the first members of the group Abstraction–Création in Paris, where he then opened his own private academy.

From the early 1920s Freundlich developed a Constructivist style characterized by interlocking cellular forms, which was more elastic, rhythmic and colourful than his previous painting. Such compositions as *My Sky is Red* (1933; Paris, Pompidou) are based on an orthogonal framework, in which the right angles are twisted irregularly. The paintings contain elaborate systems of colour modulations, which create complementary harmonies and degrees of spatial illusionism. The application of impastoed paints also creates a three-dimensional effect. Freundlich's paintings also expressed his political views: his belief in 'cosmic Communism', for example, is associated with the colours in *My Sky is Red*. Freundlich's work with stained glass from the early 1920s is closely linked with his abstract paintings, and indeed it had the greatest influence on the development of his style. In 1924 Freundlich received permission to set up as a stained-glass painter in France, although he did not subsequently receive any commissions. His admiration for the stained glass in Chartres Cathedral inspired him to produce numerous small abstract gouaches and pastels, which were essentially designs for imaginary stained glass. In the few surviving examples of his glass, the pieces, joined by narrow pieces of lead, are mainly irregular, usually within a square frame: like the paintings, they form complicated colour systems.

In Freundlich's sculpture the constituent parts of the work are transformed by their interrelationship, as in *Ascension* (bronze, 1.93×1.04×1.03 m, 1929; e.g. Paris, Pompidou). The importance given to the organization of the individual forms is linked with Freundlich's collectivist social theories, while his spiritual aspirations are expressed in the work's title. *Ascension* also shows affinities with the biomorphism of Picasso's sculptures of the early 1930s, and with Constructivist concepts of architectural sculpture. Freundlich was led towards working on monumental sculpture in towns and the countryside by what he saw as the closeness of such forms to architecture and 'collective' values. He designed an unexecuted *Lighthouse of the Seven Arts* (plaster model, *c*. 1936; Pontoise, Mus. Pontoise), which was meant to stand at the intersection of two vast streets with sculptures, running through Europe and finishing in Auvers-sur-Oise near Paris. The concept of the monumental 'sculpture architecturale' was intended to inspire community building of centres of communication: Freundlich proposed such landmarks as concrete towers, 30 m high, menhirs and illuminated towers for aeroplanes in *Skulpturenhügel* (1936, published Paris, 1959).

Although his Utopian ideals were unrealized, Freundlich achieved some success as one of the abstract painters who contributed to the Parisian salon Réalités Nouvelles (founded 1939), alongside Kandinsky, Mondrian, Robert and Sonia Delaunay and František Kupka. In Germany, however, his work was condemned by the Nazis: indeed the publication accompanying the exhibition of ENTAR-TETE KUNST in Munich in 1937 had on its cover an illustration of Freundlich's plaster sculpture the *New Person* (1912; destr.). During World War II Freundlich fell a victim of the Holocaust, even though he fled to the Pyrenees after a group of artists, including Picasso, managed to arrange his release from internment. He was arrested and deported in February 1940 and later died in a concentration camp.

WRITINGS

U. Bohnen, ed.: *Otto Freundlich: Schriften* (Cologne, 1982)

BIBLIOGRAPHY

F. Kaiser, ed.: *Entartete Kunst: Führer durch die Ausstellung* (Munich, 1937)
G. Aust: *Otto Freundlich* (Cologne, 1960)
La Donation Freundlich au Musée de Pontoise: Vingt-deux oeuvres (exh. cat., Association les amis d'Otto Freundlich; Pontoise, Mus. Pontoise, 1974)
J. Heusinger von Waldegg: *Otto Freundlich (1878–1943)* (Cologne, 1978)
Hommage à Otto Freundlich (exh. cat., ed. Y. Fischer; Jerusalem, Israel Mus., 1978) [Fr., Eng. and Hebrew]
J. Heusinger von Waldegg: *Otto Freundlich: 'Ascension', Anweisung zur Utopie* (Frankfurt am Main, 1987)

GOTTLIEB LEINZ

Frey, Albert. *See under* KOCHER AND FREY.

Frey, Dagobert (*b* Vienna, 23 April 1883; *d* Stuttgart, 13 May 1962). Austrian art historian. In 1911, after completing a course of study in architecture at the Technische Hochschule, Vienna, he became assistant to Max Dvořák at the office for the preservation of national monuments. On Dvořák's advice Frey began studying art history, producing a dissertation on Bramante's design for St Peter's and its apocrypha. The architecture of the Renaissance, the Baroque and the modern period became focal points of his research, although he also produced numerous contributions on Austrian art. He was appointed Professor of Art History at the University of Breslau (now Wrocław, Poland) in 1931 and extended his interests to the problems of art in north-eastern Europe. In 1945 he returned to Vienna and resumed his work at the office responsible for monuments. In addition, he published on theories of art and methodological questions. In 1951 he moved to Stuttgart, where he was Professor of Art History at the Technische Hochschule. In his last years he wrote on such great creative figures as Giotto, Titian, Michelangelo and Rembrandt. Frey's methodological position is a synthesis of the procedure of the Vienna School, based on the study of historical development through sources, and the unorthodox system of Josef Strzygowski, which transcended subject boundaries. The work of Julius von Schlosser and, above all, that of Dvořák, based on intellectual history, were of fundamental importance to Frey. In keeping with Strzygowski's comparative approach, he also showed an intense interest in neighbouring disciplines, an interest in science and a regard for artistic questions outside his own region, particularly those of Eastern Europe. Frey's unfulfilled intention was to unite the different components of his work into a comprehensive philosophy of art.

WRITINGS

Bramantes St-Peter-Entwurf und seine Apokryphen (Vienna, 1915)
Gotik und Renaissance als Grundlagen der modernen Weltanschauung (Augsburg, 1929)
Englisches Wesen in der bildenden Kunst (Stuttgart, 1942)
Kunstwissenschaftliche Grundfragen: Prolegomena zu einer Kunstphilosophie (Vienna, 1946, rev. Darmstadt, 1972)
Grundlegung zu einer vergleichenden Kunstwissenschaft (Vienna, 1949/R Darmstadt, 1970)
'Dagobert Frey', *Österreich. Geschwiss. Gegenwart Selbstdarstell.*, ii (1951), pp. 47–77 [autobiography]
G. Frey, ed.: *Manierismus als europäische Stilerscheinung: Studien zur Kunst des 16. und 17. Jahrhunderts* (Stuttgart, 1964)
——: *Bausteine zu einer Philosophie der Kunst* (Darmstadt, 1976)

BIBLIOGRAPHY

Kunstgeschichtliche Studien: Dagobert Frey zum 23. April 1943 von seinen Kollegen, Mitarbeitern und Schülern (Breslau, 1943)
'Dagobert Frey zum 70. Geburtstag', *Z. Ostforsch.*, ii/4 (1953) [whole issue]
O. Demus: 'Dagobert Frey', *Alm. Österreich. Akad. Wiss.*, cxiii (1962), pp. 389–400
Dagobert Frey, 1883–1962: Eine Erinnerungsschrift (Kiel, 1962)
'Dagobert Frey: Verzeichnis seiner Werke', *Österreich. Z. Kst & Dkmlpf.*, xvi (1962), pp. 154–7
H. Sedlmayr: 'Dagobert Frey', *Jb. Bayer. Akad. Wiss.* (1963), pp. 176–9
U. Gensbaur-Bendler: *Dagobert Frey: Lebensphilosophische Grundlagen seiner Kunsttheorie* (diss., U. Innsbruck, 1986)
——: 'Dagobert Frey: Lebensphilosophische Grundlagen seiner Kunsttheorie', *Wien. Jb. Kstgesch.*, xlii (1989), pp. 53–79

EDWIN LACHNIT

Frey, Johannes Jakob (*b* Basle, 27 Jan 1813; *d* Frascati, Rome, 30 Sept 1865). Swiss painter. He was taught first by his father, the painter and lithographer Samuel Frey (1785–1836). He studied in Paris in the early 1830s, and then in Munich (1834); thanks to the sponsorship of Emilie Lindner, a patron of the arts, he was able to move on to Rome where he specialized in landscape painting (*Mountains in the Roman Campagna*, Basle, Kstmus.) At the end of the 1830s he moved to Naples, travelling to

Sicily and to Spain. In 1842 he set out for Egypt with the Royal Prussian Expedition led by Richard Lepsius but had to return to Italy, settling finally in Rome. Frey was very productive and his studio attracted many visitors. He had especially close links with the Prussian court, where his Italian landscapes found a ready market. According to F. Noack he had considerable ability as a colourist, but there were some weaknesses in his draughtsmanship. The Kunstmuseum in Basle has a collection of his paintings.

BIBLIOGRAPHY

Bénézit; *SKL*; Thieme–Becker

F. Noack: *Deutsches Leben in Rom, 1700 bis 1900* (Stuttgart and Berlin, 1907)

CHRISTINA STEINHOFF

Frey, Johann Jakob, I [the elder] (*b* Lucerne, 17 Feb 1681; *d* Rome, 11 Jan 1752). Swiss draughtsman and printmaker, active in Italy. He was the son of the sculptor in wood Hans Heinrich Frey (*fl* 1650–80). With support from Franz Josef Meyer von Schauensee he went to Rome in 1702. For several months he was a pupil of the Flemish engraver Arnold van Westerhout, and then the painter Carlo Maratti. Maratti's influence was decisive, as he drew Frey's attention to the picturesque qualities of etching. Thereafter Frey combined etching and engraving in most of his prints. His very precise and accurate reproductive engravings after 17th- and 18th-century Old Masters, for example the *Aurora* (1722) after Guido Reni and the *Flight into Egypt* (1735) after Maratti, are his most important works. The most complete collection of his graphic works is in the Zentralbibliothek in Lucerne. In 1726 he returned briefly to Switzerland; he was also commissioned to design the ceiling fresco for the nave of St Jost Church at Blatten, Lucerne.

UNPUBLISHED SOURCES

Lucerne, Zentbib. [MS. autobiography]

BIBLIOGRAPHY

SKL

A. Reinle: *Die Kunstdenkmäler des Kantons Luzern*, vi (Lucerne, 1965), pp. 298, 455

JEANNE-MARIE HORAT-WEBER

Frey, Karl [Carl] (*b* 1857; *d* March 1917). German art historian. He studied at the University of Berlin, writing his dissertation on the Loggia dei Lanzi in Florence. 16th-century Florentine art and historiography became his field of specialization. In 1884 he prepared an edition of Vasari's *Vite* and, in the early 1890s, following the publication by the Hungarian scholar Cornelius von Fabriczy of the *Codice dell'Anonimo Gaddiano* (1893) and the *Libro di Antonio Billi*, two 16th-century documents in the Biblioteca Nazionale Centrale at Florence that offered evidence of art-historical writing in Florence before Vasari, Frey published his own extensively annotated editions of both documents.

Towards the end of the 1890s he began to work on Michelangelo, publishing the first critical edition of the artist's letters. In 1907 it was revised and republished together with *Michelagniolos Jugendjahre*; Frey hoped to produce a parallel series of studies on Michelangelo's life and career. However, they were the only two volumes to appear. Two years later he published a book on the artist's drawings, returning at the same time to an ambitious programme of publications on Vasari's writings and influence. Frey's work, unfinished at the time of his death, was completed for publication by his son Hermann-Walther Frey.

WRITINGS

ed.: *Sammlung ausgewählter Biographien Vasaris*, 4 vols (Berlin, 1884–7)

Die Loggia dei Lanzi zu Florenz: Eine quellenkritische Untersuchung (diss., U. Berlin, 1885)

ed.: *Il Libro di Antonio Billi esistente in due copie nella Biblioteca Nazionale di Firenze* (Berlin, 1892)

ed.: *Il Codice Magliabechiano contenente notizie sopra l'arte degli antichi e quella de' fiorentini da Giotto a Michelangelo, scritte da Anonimo* (Berlin, 1892)

Le vite di Michelagniolo Buonarroti (Berlin, 1897)

ed.: *Die Dichtungen des Michelagniolo Buonarroti* (Berlin, 1897, rev., Berlin, 3/1964)

ed.: *Sammlung ausgewählter Briefe an Michelagniolo Buonarroti* (Berlin, 1899/rev., ed. H.-W. Frey, 3/1961)

Michelagniolos Jugendjahre, 2 vols (Berlin, 1907)

Die Handzeichnungen Michelagniolos Buonarroti (Berlin, 1909–11; 1925)

ed.: *Die literarische Nachlass Giorgio Vasaris*, 3 vols: i (Berlin, 1909–11); ii (1930); iii (1940)

ed.: G. Vasari: *Le vite de' più eccellenti pittori, scultori ed architetti. Mit kritischem Apparate herausgegeben von Dr Karl Frey* (Munich, 1911)

ed.: *Il carteggio di Giorgio Vasari* (Munich, 1923)

ed. with H. W. Frey: *Il carteggio di Giorgio Vasari dal 1563 al 1565* (Arezzo, 1941, rev. 3/1961)

JANET SOUTHORN

Freyssinet, Eugène (*b* Objat, Correze, 13 July 1879; *d* Saint-Martin-de-Vesubie, nr Nice, 8 June 1962). French engineer and theorist. He attended the Ecole Polytechnique and the Ecole des Ponts et Chaussées, Paris, where he studied with Jean Résal (1854–1919), Paul Séjourné (1851–1939) and Charles Rabut (1852–1925), the latter being one of the pioneers of reinforced concrete. In his first post as a government engineer in Moulins (1907–13) Freyssinet built a number of reinforced-concrete bridges, including that at Prairéal-sur-Besbre (1907), where for the first time the centring was struck by the use of jacks, creating a thrust at the crown. For the contractor François Mercier he built several works under state supervision. In 1910–12 he undertook to build three three-arch concrete bridges over the River Allier for the cost of one masonry bridge. The first, at Le Veurdre (1910; destr. 1940), was designed with a flat, lightly reinforced three-hinged arch with horizontal jacks at mid-span that raised the arch for decentring. The arch sank by 130 mm during the winter of 1910–11 due to deformation of the concrete, and Freyssinet raised the jacks to induce stresses that would counteract the downward deflection, an idea that provided the basis for his later development of prestressed concrete. His second bridge over the River Allier, at Boutiron (1912), constructed by Claude Limousin's building company, was designed on similar principles.

In 1914 Freyssinet left government service and became Technical Director of Société Limousin. During World War I he constructed industrial buildings in several towns including Dole, Saint-Etienne, Bourges, Montluçon, Bergerac and Moulins, as well as building bridges and some early aircraft hangars. He then went into partnership with Limousin (1918–28). During this period Freyssinet built several railway bridges and industrial buildings, as well as some world-record-breaking long-span concrete structures: the viaduct (designed 1914; constructed 1919; span *c.* 100 m) at Villeneuve-sur-Lot had the largest span for unreinforced bridges; the Seine Bridge (1919–23; destr. 1940, rebuilt 1946), Saint-Pierre-du-Vauvray, where the deck is suspended below the arches, had the longest spanning arches (132 m) for bridges of any type; and his airship hangars (1921; destr. 1944; see fig.) at Orly were then the largest-spanning (88 m) concrete buildings. The latter were designed as a series of slender, hollow-section parabolic arches connected by thin slabs to create the appearance of a corrugated shell. His finest work of the 1920s was the three-span bridge (1924–30) that crosses the Elorn estuary at Plougastel, near Brest, where each arch is a hollow box with a span of 188 m. The scale of these works led Freyssinet to study closely the behaviour of concrete, particularly its deformation or 'creep' under loading and its weakness in tension. In 1928 he patented his theory of permanent prestressing using high-strength steel cables stretched to induce high initial compressive stresses in the concrete: earlier experiments by others using low-strength steel had failed.

At the end of 1928 Freyssinet left Limousin—who was unconvinced of the potential of the new theory—and went into business in Montargis producing prestressed concrete electricity poles, but the venture failed in 1933. He was then invited to assist with the new transatlantic marine terminal at Le Havre, which was sinking in some places at a rate of 26 mm per month. By reinforcing the foundations with new beams, the whole being prestressed by external tie-rods, he succeeded in halting the subsidence and proving the effectiveness of prestressing. In 1935 Freyssinet signed an exclusive contract in Paris with the firm of Campenon–Bernard. After working on contracts for dams in Algeria, he invented (1939) the conical wedge anchorage for prestressing. In 1941 he began construction of the Marne Bridge at Luzancy but, because it was during the Occupation and materials were scarce, the timber was rotten and the centring began to give way. Freyssinet then had the idea of prefabricating the voussoirs, positioning them with shear legs, then reinforcing and prestressing them. The bridge was completed in 1946: a further five bridges over the Marne followed (1947–51), with spans averaging about 75 m and thicknesses of about 1 m at the crown. In 1943 Edmé Campenon created the Société Technique pour l'Utilisation de la Précontrainte. Freyssinet's subsequent work using prestressing included three motorway viaducts (1951–3; span 150 m) between Caracas and La Guaira in Venezuela; the subterranean basilica of St Pius X (1956–8; with Pierre Vago) at Lourdes; the skewer bridge (1958) for the N10 road at Orly; and the Saint-Michel Bridge (1959–62) over the Garonne at Toulouse, completed shortly before his death.

Freyssinet was one of the most brilliant designers in reinforced concrete, creating beautiful forms that reflected his belief that 'When calculations do not balance with my intuition, I simply redo the calculations.' He also developed techniques that subsequently came into widespread use around the world. His technical innovations came from a direct understanding of the behaviour of concrete gained through experience in construction as well as design.

Eugène Freyssinet: airship hangar, Orly, 1921 (destr. 1944)

Les Grandes Constructions (Paris, 1930)
Une Révolution dans les techniques du béton (Paris, 1936)
H. Lemoine and P. Xercavins, eds: *Un Amour sans limite* (Paris, 1993)

BIBLIOGRAPHY
A. Kirkwood Dodds: 'The Freyssinet Process of Prestressing Concrete', *Architect & Bldg News* (1942)
'A Half Century of French Prestressing Technology', *Travaux* (1966) [whole issue]
Y. Guyon: 'L'Homme et l'oeuvre', *L'Ingenieur-constructeur*, cxxxiv (1969), pp. 89–96
D. P. Billington: 'Historical Perspective on Prestressed Concrete', *J. Prestressed Concr. Inst.*, xxi/5 (1976), pp. 48–71
J. A. Fernandez Ordonez: *Eugène Freyssinet* (Barcelona, 1979) [Fr. and Eng. text]

BERNARD MARREY

Frézier, Amédée-François (*b* Chambéry, 1682; *d* Brest, 1773). French engineer and theorist. He moved from Savoy to Paris at an early age and was educated at the Collège de France, where he studied theology for three years and then mathematics as a pupil of Philippe de La Hyre (1640–1718), the disciple of Gérard Desargues. Frézier subsequently travelled to Italy, and in 1707 he published the *Traité des feux d'artifice pour le spectacle*. In the same year he enrolled in the Corps de Génie, in which he remained until his retirement in 1764. In 1712 he departed on a two-year mission to South America, and in 1719 he was posted to Santo Domingo (Dominican Republic) to maintain fortifications. On his return in 1727 he was made chief engineer and, after a brief spell in Phalsbourg (nr Strasbourg), he was placed in charge of military fortifications in Landau (now Germany). In the ten years he spent there he executed his only major building, the military hospital, and published (1737–9) his monumental treatise on stereotomy, a summation of contemporary knowledge on the subject. An abbreviated version, *Eléments de stéréotomie*, was produced (1760) for the pupils of Jacques-François Blondel's school. In his mathematics Frézier emerged as a follower of Desargues's theory of conic sections, though not of his geometric method known as the *manière universelle*. The rigorous organization and encyclopedic nature of this collection of stereotomic case studies is remarkable, especially for the inclusion of an unusually lucid account of Gothic vaults.

It is, however, the *Dissertation sur les ordres d'architecture* (1738) appended to the third volume of the treatise that is of greatest interest to the architectural historian. In this

WRITINGS
'L'Amélioration des constructions en béton armé par introduction de déformations élastiques systématiques', *Génie Civ.*, xciii/11 (1928), pp. 254–7

Frézier continued his polemic against Jean-Louis de Cordemoy, which had begun in the journal *Mémoires de Trévoux* (1709 and 1711). In all things Frézier was a rationalist and a relativist. He attacked Cordemoy's liking for mansard roofs, on the grounds that the change in pitch was illogical, and singled out for special attack his advocacy of arcades. Frézier himself objected vehemently to the combination of arcade and columnar screen because it reduced the Classical architectural orders to a superfluous decorative role. He believed that the smallness of stones available in France, necessitating the use of flat arches in entablatures, meant that colonnades were often inappropriate. He yearned for the effect of lightness achieved in Gothic churches, as opposed to the superfluity of material in contemporary construction, and he recommended the primitive hut as a paradigm for its economy and utility— an ideal he probably realized in his baldacchino (destr.) for the church of St Louis, Brest, constructed from four antique columns. In this suggestion he did not go quite as far as his later adversary, Abbé Marc-Antoine Laugier. Their polemical exchanges, conducted in the journal *Mercure de France* (1754), are misleading in that they highlight minor differences in opinion. As much as anything else it was the amateur status of Cordemoy and Laugier that Frézier objected to, for the three were united in their censorship of the extravagance of the Rococo style and the irrationality of contemporary French architecture.

WRITINGS

Traité des feux d'artifice pour le spectacle (Paris, 1707, 2/1747)
La Théorie et la pratique de la coupe des pierres et des bois pour la construction des voûtes, 3 vols (Strasbourg and Paris, 1737–9); rev. as *Eléments de stéréotomie* (Paris, 1760)
Dissertation sur les ordres d'architecture (Strasbourg and Paris, 1738) [appended to vol. iii of *La Théorie et la pratique*]

BIBLIOGRAPHY

P. du Colombier: 'Amédée-François Frézier', *Festschrift für Karl Lohmeyer*, ed. K. Schwingel (Saarbrucken, 1954)

RICHARD JOHN

Friano, Maso da San. *See* SAN FRIANO, MASO DA.

Friars Minor. *See* FRANCISCAN ORDER.

Friars Preachers. *See* DOMINICAN ORDER.

Frias. Portuguese family of artists. (1) Nicolau de Frias, the son of a Vizcayan sculptor, founded a dynasty of architects who were active for four generations through the 17th century directing official architectural training in Lisbon: his son Teodósio de Frias (*d* 1634) was Master of Royal Works, designer of the austere doorway in the style of the Escorial at the monastery of S Maria, Belém (*in situ*), and of the Flamengas convent at Alcântara, where members of his family were buried until 1715. Other family members included Eugenio de Frias, Luis de Frias, Valeriano de Frias, Teodósio de Frias the younger, who specialized in making gardens, and two military engineers, (2) Francisco de Frias da Mesquita, who had a distinguished career in Brazil, and Sebastião de Frias (*d* 1671).

(1) Nicolau de Frias (*b* Lisbon, 1537; *d* Lisbon, 11 July 1610). Architect. He taught draughtsmanship while working as a wood-carver in his youth, becoming well-known for building wooden and hydraulic constructions.

He was recognized as an accomplished architect by the church authorities in Lisbon and had planned the dormitory of the convent of S Domingos (destr. 1755) in Lisbon on a cruciform plan by the time he accompanied King Sebastian as a siege engineer on the ill-fated campaign of Alcazarquivir (1578). He was taken prisoner, but after a year he was ransomed by Philip II and thereafter had a successful career at court. In 1587 he was appointed the first Master of Works in the city of Lisbon, Master of Royal Works in 1592 and, on the death of Filippo Terzi in 1597, Master of the Royal Paço da Ribeira, with the obligation to teach architecture. His designs for churches in Lisbon, later modified, were for S Marta (1583), the Chelas Monastery (1589) and S Engrácia (1606); and he was responsible for the carved wood interior of S Catarina (1586; destr.). His report (1596) on a water supply for Lisbon may have been compiled with Francisco de Holanda. Frias was made a Knight of the Order of Christ in 1598. At this time he worked at the convent of the Order of Christ, Tomar, where one of his daughters married the court painter Domingos Vieira Serrão.

Although little of his work has survived, Frias is an interesting figure because of his versatility and for his gradual move in architecture from the Portuguese 'plain' style to the style, more in the Spanish tradition, developed by Juan de Herrera at the Escorial. He attained prestige as a new type of architect–designer.

RAFAEL MOREIRA

(2) Francisco de Frias da Mesquita (*b* 1578; *d* after 1645). Military engineer, active in Brazil. From 1598 onwards he was in receipt of a royal pension as the pupil of his relative (1) Nicolau de Frias. As a Master Engineer in Brazil between 1603 and 1635, he played an important role in setting an architectural style for the colony. Numerous civil and ecclesiastical buildings were made his responsibility. He played an important part in the dissemination of the Mannerist architecture of the period. Working during the Spanish domination over Portugal (1580–1640), he had the opportunity to execute projects by Tiburzio Spanocchi, architect to Phillip II, such as the Forte da Lage (1606) in Recife and the Forte do Mar (1609–12) in Salvador, Bahia. In 1614 he planned and began the construction of his principal work, the Forte dos Reis Magos, in Natal, Rio Grande do Norte. In the same year he took part in the reconquest of Maranhão, where he planned the Forte de Quaxenduba in São Luis. In 1617 he travelled south to build the Fortaleza de São Mateus in Cabo Frio; in the same year he planned the Mosteiro dos Benetinos in Rio de Janeiro. As a soldier, he took part in the expulsion of the Dutch from Salvador (1624–5), constructing fortifications during this war. He is last recorded in 1645 as an elderly, retired man, living in Portugal.

BIBLIOGRAPHY

Viterbo
J. Gomes de Brito: 'Convento das flamengas em Alcântara e os arquitectos Frias', *Rev. Arqueol.* [Lisbon], ii (1888)
C. Silva-Nigra: 'Francisco de Frias de Mesquita, engenheiro-mor do Brasil', *Rev. SPAHN*, ix (1945), pp. 9–84
A. de Carvalho: *D. João V e a arte do seu tempo*, ii (Lisbon, 1962), pp. 49–50, 140–41
V. Serrão: *Bol. Cult. Assembl. Distr. Lisboa*, cxxxiii (1977), p. 42; cxxxvi (1980), p. 4

C. A. C. LEMOS

Frías Escalante, Juan Antonio de. *See* ESCALANTE, JUAN ANTONIO DE FRÍAS.

Fribourg [Ger. Freiburg]. Swiss city on the River Saane (Fr. Sarine), capital of the canton of Fribourg, with a population of 37,400. It was founded in 1157 by Duke Berchtold IV of Zähringen (*reg* 1152–86). In 1218 the Zähringens were succeeded by the Counts of Kyburg. From 1277 to 1452 the city was ruled by the Habsburgs and subsequently by the House of Savoy. Fribourg's ring of defensive works, built between the 13th and 15th centuries, forms the greatest complex of surviving medieval fortifications in Switzerland. In parts, steep cliffs above the river made walls unnecessary. Fourteen towers, a bulwark and about 2 km of the original city walls remain.

The Bourg quarter (see fig.), the oldest part of the city, occupies the site of the Zähringen Fortress (destr. 15th century). Shortly after the city's foundation, the Auge quarter was developed, and later in the 13th century the Neuveville (Ger. Neustadt) quarter was added. These areas have generally retained their medieval structure, including entire rows of Gothic houses (e.g. Rue de la Neuverville) unique in Switzerland.

In the Middle Ages the city's economy centred on drapery and tanning. Textile production reached a peak between 1430 and 1450 and collapsed in the mid-16th century, forcing the canton to concentrate on dairy farming. As Fribourg's territory expanded, the city's political influence grew, and by 1478 it was made a free imperial city. In 1481 the canton of Fribourg joined the Swiss Confederation, since when its history has generally paralleled that of Switzerland.

During the Reformation Fribourg remained Roman Catholic. As a result, several religious orders settled in the city, notably the Jesuits, who formed their first college there in 1580 (see below). The city became a Counter-Reformation centre, and in 1613 the Bishop of Geneva chose Fribourg as his new residence after being driven away from Lausanne. In 1889 the first Roman Catholic university was founded, transforming the city into the most important Catholic ecclesiastical centre of Switzerland. Because of this, the city has many notable religious buildings, above all St Nicolas Cathedral (a church until 1924), built in four campaigns between 1283 and 1490. It is a High Gothic pillared basilica with a façade tower (h. 76 m; see fig.). Its choir, originally rectangular, was rebuilt in polygonal form (1627–31). The main portal is surmounted by a tympanum depicting the *Last Judgement*, framed by archivolts with angels, Prophets and Patriarchs. The cathedral has a unique collection of *Jugendstil* stained-glass windows (1895–1934) by JÓZEF MEHOFFER. Other interesting churches and convents include the Franciscan church (before 1281; altered 18th century) and monastery (1281; altered 18th century); the 13th-century Cistercian abbey church and convent (rebuilt 1660–66) of Notre-Dame de la Maigrauge; and the church (1604–13; altered 18th century) and former Jesuit college of St Michel, built in a Late Gothic style with Rococo decoration. The centrally planned church of Notre-Dame des Visitandes (1653–6) is by JOHANN FRANZ REYFF (*see also* SWITZERLAND, §II).

Fribourg, view of the Auge and Bourg quarters from the south, showing the tower of St Nicolas Cathedral

The most important secular buildings are the town hall and the Hôtel Ratzé. The town hall (from 1501), on the site of the Zähringen Fortress, is Late Gothic in style. The ground-plan is trapezoidal, and it was originally a granary. The three-storey Hôtel Ratzé (1581–5; now Mus. A. & Hist.) by Jean Fumal has a rectangular ground-plan, a hip roof, pavilions and a staircase tower connecting it to an elaborate three-storey gallery. Fribourg has numerous 16th-century fountains, for example, the Fountain de la Force (1549–50; original Fribourg, Mus. A. & Hist.) by Hans Gieng (*d* 1562). These great basins with columns in the middle, surmounted by biblical or allegorical figures, originally served as a source of drinkable water. They were made of limestone, but, due to shifting traffic patterns, most have been repositioned and replaced by copies. In the 20th century Jean Tinguely designed the mechanically operated Tinguely Fountain (1984).

Of the many bridges spanning the Saane, the oldest is the Berne Bridge, a covered, wooden bridge dating from the 17th and 18th centuries. The famous Zähringen Suspension Bridge (1832–5) by Joseph Chaley (1795–1861) was replaced by an iron and concrete design in 1922–4. Twentieth-century buildings include the Université Miséricorde (1938–41) and the church of Christ-Roi (1951–3), both designed by Denis Honegger and Fernand Dumas. The Banque de l'Etat (1977–82) was designed by Mario Botta.

BIBLIOGRAPHY

M. Strub: *La Ville de Fribourg*, Kstdkml. Schweiz, xxxvi, Les Monuments d'art et d'histoire du canton de Fribourg, ii (Basle, 1956–9)
F. Deuchler: *Schweiz und Liechtenstein*, Reclams Kstführer (Stuttgart, 1979), pp. 281–303
Kunstführer durch die Schweiz, Gesellschaft für schweizerische Kunstgeschichte, iii (Wabern, 1982), pp. 658–846
Inventar der neueren schweizer Architektur (INSA), 1880–1920, Gesellschaft für schweizerische Kunstgeschichte, iv (Berne, 1982), pp. 165–247

HEIDI NAEF

Frick, Henry Clay (*b* West Overton, PA, 18 Dec 1849; *d* New York, 2 Dec 1919). American industrialist and collector. (All works mentioned are in New York, Frick.) He was born into a well-to-do family of German descent engaged in the distillery business in western Pennsylvania. By clever financing through the Mellon banking interests and by his own business acumen, he developed the coke-mining industry in the environs of Pittsburgh, PA, and by 30 had become a millionaire. Joining forces in 1889 with Andrew Carnegie, he reorganized the steel industry by using railroad connections between coke and steel mills, improving management and exploiting immigrant labour. In 1901, in collaboration with J. Pierpoint Morgan and Elbert Gary, Frick formed the US Steel Corporation, at the time the largest industrial conglomerate in the world. He emerged from this effort a multimillionaire.

While resident in Pittsburgh, Frick began collecting paintings, primarily of the Barbizon school. He owned a particularly fine collection of Millet drawings, in which he took great pride. By 1901, however, his taste had changed. In that year he bought paintings by Turner and Vermeer as well as a Monet landscape. These were followed by works by Hobbema, Aelbert Cuyp and Gerard ter Borch and the leading 18th-century British portrait painters. When Frick moved to New York in 1904 and rented the Vanderbilt house at the corner of Fifth Avenue and 51st Street, he sold most of his Barbizon works and concentrated instead on Old Masters.

Around 1912 Frick commissioned Thomas Hastings (1860–1929) of Carrère & Hastings to design a home on 70th Street that would eventually serve as a gallery 'for the use and benefit of all persons whomsoever'. He embarked on an intensive course of collecting, seeking works of the highest quality with no concern for price. Most critics agreed that he had a 'keen sense for really important pictures', and that he was 'a fastidious and cautious' collector. Occasionally, however, he let his acquisitions be guided by intermediaries such as Roger Fry, Knoedler & Co. and Joseph Duveen. Frick's 1916 catalogue of paintings lists 116 works from the Dutch, Flemish, Spanish, German, Italian and British schools, a few Impressionist works (Degas, Manet, Renoir) and a small collection of American art, including four portraits by Whistler and Gilbert Stuart's *George Washington*. Among the most important works included were Rembrandt's *Self-portrait* of 1658, six portraits by Anthony van Dyck, three by Hals, Titian's *Pietro Aretino* and Velázquez's *Philip IV of Spain at Fraga*. Frick acquired three of the thirty-two Vermeers then known to exist, and four panels from Fragonard's series of the *Progress of Love* (1773) from the J. P. Morgan Collection, for which he is said to have paid £1,250,000; the latter hang in a room decorated in 18th-century taste. The paintings were augmented by a fine collection of statuary, enamels, bronzes, porcelain and precious furniture.

The Frick house and collection were left to Frick's wife and daughter for their use until 1933, when they were bequeathed to the City of New York. Frick left an endowment of £15,000,000, primarily for the upkeep of the gallery, but also for further acquisitions. Designed to demonstrate that art is not 'a lifeless thing', the Frick Collection evokes the atmosphere of a millionaire's private home in early 20th-century New York; as such, it stands as a monument to its founder. The Frick Art Reference Library, adjacent to it, is one of the major visual reference resources in the United States. It is possible that Frick, sensitive about criticism of his labour policies, hoped that his fabulous gift to the public would improve his image in American history. Whatever his motives, there is no question that the collection is one of the greatest private galleries in the world.

BIBLIOGRAPHY

F. Levy: 'The Frick Art Gallery', *Evening Post Mag*. [NY] (6 Dec 1919)
F. J. Gregg: 'The Frick Collection', *New York Herald* (7 Dec 1919)
G. B. Harvey: *Henry Clay Frick, the Man* (New York, 1928, rev. 1936)
The Frick Collection: An Illustrated Catalogue, 2 vols (Princeton, 1968)
N. Burt: *Palaces for the People: A Social History of the American Art Museum* (Boston, 1977)

LILLIAN B. MILLER

Friday Club. British group of painters, active 1905–22. Vanessa Bell conceived of and created the Friday Club in the summer of 1905. She was inspired by her experience of Parisian café life and the artists introduced to her in Paris by Clive Bell, and she hoped to create in London a similar milieu in which artists and friends could meet to exchange ideas. The Club met for lectures and held regular exhibitions in rented rooms, one taking place in Clifford's Inn Hall in 1907, another at the Baillie Gallery in 1908. Its members were oddly assorted: Vanessa Bell drew upon students from the Royal Academy Schools and the Slade School of Fine Art, as well as her own family and family friends. Lecturers included Clive Bell, Basil Creighton, Walter Lamb and Roger Fry. Virginia Woolf remarked that in its early stages the Club was split: 'one half of the committee shriek Whistler and French Impressionists, and the other are stalwart British'. In 1913 Essil Elmslie replaced Vanessa Bell as secretary to the Club, and meetings and discussions outside the annual exhibitions ceased. However, between 1910 and 1914 its exhibitions included young artists of talent, among them J. D. Innes, Derwent Lees (1885–1931), John Currie (*c.* 1890–1914) and Henry Lamb, and drew much comment from the press. Despite this, the history of the Club remains shadowy because no minutes of its meetings exist and not all its exhibition catalogues can be traced.

BIBLIOGRAPHY

Catalogues of the Friday Club belonging to P. G. Konody are in the Victoria and Albert Museum, London
R. Shone: 'The Friday Club', *Burl. Mag.*, cxvii (1975), pp. 279–84
For further bibliography *see* BELL, VANESSA.

FRANCES SPALDING

Friðfinnsson, Hreinn (*b* Dalir, west Iceland, 19 Feb 1943). Icelandic painter, sculptor, photographer and conceptual artist, active in the Netherlands. He studied at the Myndlista- og handíðaskóli Íslands (Icelandic School of Arts and Crafts), Reykjavík (1958–60), in Rome (1966–7) and in Limoges (1970–71), after which he moved to the Netherlands. He was one of the founding members of the Icelandic avant-garde group SÚM and he took part in its first exhibition in 1965. His early work consists of emblematic abstract paintings, enlivened with three-dimensional elements such as nails or rope (e.g. *Painting*; 1966, Reykjavík, N.G.). When he developed an interest in conceptual art, Friðfinnsson began to use photography as a medium for concretizing his ideas, which derive from Icelandic myth and folklore as well as from dreams and poetry.

Friðfinnsson's *House Project* (1974) was suggested by a story by the Icelandic writer Thórbergur Thórðarson about an old man who wanted to build an inside-out house. Friðfinnsson built a house that fitted this description at a secret venue in Iceland and then photographed it (see 1987 exh. cat.). Through such displacements and subtle contrasts Friðfinnsson evolved a complex visual structure, which bore some resemblance to the introspective nature of Icelandic poetry during the 1970s, in which the concept of time is also important. In the early 1980s Friðfinnsson began to assemble three-dimensional works out of disparate materials such as wood, perspex, marble, stainless steel and wire netting, which were placed in contrast with flat elements such as drawings, photographs and gold leaf (e.g. *Untitled*; 1985–6, Reykjavík, N.G.). This served both to widen the references in his work and to render them more oblique and evocative, underlining his poetic sensibility.

BIBLIOGRAPHY

Sleeping Beauty—Art Now, Scandinavia Today (exh. cat., essays P. Hultén and Ö. Hjort; New York, Guggenheim, 1982)
A. Ingólfsson: 'Iceland', *Northern Poles* (Copenhagen, 1986), pp. 62–7
Hreinn Friðfinnsson (exh. cat., Grenoble, Magasin-Cent. N. A. Contemp., 1987) [contains an interview with the artist]
Hreinn Friðfinnsson (exh. cat., intro. L. Helgadóttir; Helsinki, Nord. A. Cent., 1988)
B. Nordal: *Hreinn Friðfinnsson* (Reykjavik, 1993) [Icelandic and Eng. text]

AÐALSTEINN INGÓLFSSON

Fridlyand, Semyon (Osipovich) (*b* Kiev, 28 Aug 1905; *d* Moscow, 14 Feb 1964). Russian photographer of Ukrainian birth. He worked as a shoemaker from the age of 14 but was invited to Moscow to work as a photographic laboratory assistant for *Ogonyok*, the first Soviet illustrated weekly, by his cousin Mikhail Koltsov (1898–1942), the renowned journalist. He began to take photographs in 1925, becoming a professional photojournalist working for the agency Unionfoto (later Soyuzfoto) from 1930 to 1932, the magazine *SSSR na stroyke* (1932) and *Pravda* (from 1933). He later headed the photographic department at *Ogonyok*.

Fridlyand played a major part in the development of photojournalism in the USSR, which became a leading means of disseminating information and propaganda following the revolution of 1917. He cultivated social themes concerned with the aftermath of the revolution, for example *At a Hostel, Moscow* (1926; see exh. cat., p. 26), and with the period of reconstruction, for example *Builders of the Town Komsomolskaya on the Amur* (1934; see Morozov and Lloyd, p. 189). He contributed numerous articles to photographic magazines concerning photojournalistic theory and practice and he fostered in particular the development of the photo–essay. During World War II he was a war correspondent.

BIBLIOGRAPHY

Early Soviet Photographers (exh. cat. by D. Mrázková and V. Remeš, Oxford, MOMA, 1982)
S. Morozov and V. Lloyd, eds: *Soviet Photography, 1917–1940: The New Photojournalism* (London, 1984)

KEVIN HALLIWELL

Fridrihsons, Kurts (*b* Riga, 7 Sept 1911; *d* Riga, 31 Jan 1991). Latvian painter. He served as both inspiration and reproach to Latvian artists who pursued their vocations in blind accordance with prevailing styles, whether the dull decorativism of the 1930s or later the pedantry of Socialist Realism. Dating from his studies in Paris before World War II, Fridrihsons's correspondence with Edvard Munch and association with André Derain and André Gide were misconstrued by Stalinist authorities as subversive, and he was one of the members of the French Group tortured and condemned to the gulag. After his rehabilitation and return to Latvia in 1956, Fridrihsons began exploring a highly idiosyncratic style, characterized by flattened, attenuated form, striated line and saturated colour. With Olǵerts Jaunarājs (*b* 1907), he was a pioneer of abstraction in Latvia, using the properties of watercolour and architectonic subjects as occasions for non-figurative painting. Having little in common with either the national or Soviet traditions, Fridrihsons was rarely included in the official circuit of exhibitions, publications and commissions during the Khrushchev and early Brezhnev periods, but by the 1970s he had gained broad recognition for his powerful, large-scale watercolours, provocative stage designs and book illustrations. His ink-on-paper *Composition X* (1967; New Brunswick, NJ, Rutgers U., Zimmerli A. Mus.) is a bleak, colour-field miniature; its laconic mood and countervailing, calligraphic linework (singular within Latvian art of the time) was sustained and developed further by ILMĀRS BLUMBERGS. Fridrihsons died immediately after completing a painting series devoted to Soviet military repression of the Latvian independence movement.

BIBLIOGRAPHY

M. Čaklais: 'Kurta Fridrihsona pierniņai' [To the memory of Kurts Fridrihsons], *Lit. & Māksla* (1991)
I. Ziedonis: *Kurts Fridrihsons* (Riga, 1985)
G. Repše: *Kurts Fridrihsons* (in preparation)

MARK ALLEN SVEDE

Friedeberg, Pedro (*b* Florence, 11 Jan 1937). Mexican painter. The son of German Jewish parents, he arrived in Mexico at the age of three. Having shown an early inclination for drawing and reading, he studied architecture at the Universidad Iberoamericana, where he was profoundly influenced by the teaching of Mathías Goeritz. Although his paintings, filled to overflowing with surprise, were sometimes described as examples of Surrealism or fantastic realism, they are not easily definable in terms of conventional categories. He used architectural drawing as the medium through which he created unusual compositions in series such as *Pure and Impure Architecture*; *Animals, People, Idiots, Philosophers*; *Sublime Perspectives*; and *Unclassifiable Lucubrations*. Friedeberg also designed furniture and useless objects, admitting that his artistic activity was rooted in boredom. This sense of irony and surfeit imparted to his pictures, through the hallucinatory repetition of elements, an asphyxiating formal disorder.

BIBLIOGRAPHY

I. Rodríguez Prampolini: *Pedro Friedeberg* (Mexico City, 1973)

JULIETA ORTIZ GAITÁN

Friedeberger, Klaus (*b* Berlin, 23 Aug 1922). British painter of German birth. He left Germany in 1938, reaching England in 1939 and Australia in 1940. His first works were in a Surrealist manner, for example *Shopping Centre* (1942; Canberra, N.G.). From 1944 Friedeberger exhibited with the Contemporary Art Society in Australia. He then studied painting at East Sydney Technical College (1947–50). After returning to England (1950) he produced a series of brilliantly coloured paintings, mainly of children at play, characterized by a formalized expressionist intensity. For some years he combined painting with work as a graphic designer and a part-time teacher (Central School of Arts and Crafts, London College of Printing). In 1963 his first one-man show was held (London, Hamilton Gals). In the late 1960s Friedeberger's work changed; figurative representation and the use of colour were eventually abandoned altogether. His new monochrome paintings (exh. 1986, London, Warwick A. Trust) are quite heavily impastoed and exploit the manifold possibilities of black/grey/white. They present an expressive, convincing reality of their own, independent of allusions to anything not inherent in the process and the painting itself. Tonality provides illusionistic scope to create forms and space. A large retrospective (1942–92) was held at Woodlands Art Gallery, London, in 1992. Examples of Friedeberger's work are in the National Gallery of Australia, Canberra.

BIBLIOGRAPHY

Klaus Friedeberger (exh. cat. by C. Spencer, London, Hamilton Gals, 1963)
Surrealism: Revolution by Night (exh. cat. by C. Chapman, Canberra, N.G., 1993)

JULIE FRIEDEBERGER

Friedhoff, Gijsbert (*b* Rotterdam, 1892; *d* Haarlem, 1970). Dutch architect. He trained at the Technische Hogeschool in Delft. His first projects, from the 1920s, showed a conservative design approach that he would follow throughout his career. Apart from W. M. Dudok, Friedhoff's chief model in the 1920s was the National Romanticism of contemporary Scandinavian architects, and he was among those architects sometimes referred to by their contemporaries as the 'Swedes'. This is particularly visible in the Raadhuis (1930–33) in Enschede, whose design won a competition in 1929. It refers directly to Ragnar Ostberg's town hall in Stockholm in its large closed brick wall planes with small, high windows, in its vertical proportions and curved lower edges, and in its refined siting and detailing. Friedhoff's other work before World War II included a Christian Science church (1937) in south Amsterdam in an extremely plain traditional style. After the war Friedhoff was able to display his monumental style in several large government office buildings, of which the best known is the Rijksbelastingkantoor (1956–8) in Amsterdam; it has axial symmetry, a classicizing façade and detailing, and a composition of large closed volumes. Although Friedhoff has been regarded as one of the conservative architects of the DELFT SCHOOL (ii), his entirely personal, sober and refined formal language, his great sensitivity in harmonizing a building with its surroundings and his subtle use of light and shadow in both interior and exterior save his work from being simply historicist.

BIBLIOGRAPHY

J. J. Vriend: *De bouwkunst van ons land* [The architecture of our country] (Amsterdam, 1938)

A. Boeken and others: *Nederlandse architectuur: Uitgevoerde werken van bouwkundige ingenieurs* [Dutch architecture: executed works by architectural engineers] (Amsterdam, 1956)
J. J. Vriend: *Nieuwere architectuur* (Bussum, 1957)
G. Fanelli: *Architettura moderna in Olanda, 1900–1940* (Florence, 1968; Dut. trans., The Hague, 1978, 2/1981)

J. P. BAETEN

Friedlaender, (Gotthard) Johnny (*b* Pless, Upper Silesia, 21 June 1912). German etcher and painter. He studied under Otto Mueller at the Kunstakademie, Breslau (now Wrocław, Poland), and then moved to Dresden, where he was a member of the Assoziation Revolutionärer Bildender Künstler Deutschlands (ASSO). In 1935 he went to Ostrava, Czechoslovakia [now Czech Republic], to escape the Nazis. In 1937 he moved to The Hague, where he held his first exhibition of prints and watercolours, before settling in Paris. His etchings of the 1930s combine an intensely worked line, drawing on the German printmaking tradition, with realistic subject-matter, as in *Dead Horse* (1933; see 1987 exh. cat., no. 50). During World War II he lived in Marseille and worked with the French resistance movement. After the war an atmosphere of mystery, similar to the automatist Surrealism of André Masson, became more marked in his etchings, for example *Fish and Birds I* (1947; see 1987 exh. cat., no. 53). Animals and human figures remained his principal subjects until the mid-1950s, when they gave way to more elegant, abstract colour compositions that, in their combination of delicate forms and symbols, maintain landscape associations. In the 1960s he began producing works that suggested musical modes of organization in their tonality, rhythmic structures and harmonization of colours. The titles of many of the etchings suggest musical associations, such as *Prelude* (1965; priv. col., see 1987 exh. cat., no. 122), while in others recurrent echo-forms provide an analogy with the field of acoustics, as in *Migrating Birds* (1966; see 1987 exh. cat., no. 125). In many etchings of the 1970s Friedlaender paid homage to eminent musicians, such as *For Luciano Sgrizzi at the Harpsichord* (1976; priv. col., see 1987 exh. cat., no. 151), while plants, including thistles, herbs and *Poppies* (1981; see 1987 exh. cat., no. 160), were another recurrent theme.

BIBLIOGRAPHY

Friedlaender in het Frans Halsmuseum (exh. cat. by H. L. C. Jaffé, Haarlem, Frans Halsmus., 1977)
Johnny Friedlaender (exh. cat. by F. R. Schmückings, Dresden, Kupferstich-kab., 1980)
Johnny Friedlaender: Zeichnungen, Radierungen, Aquarelle, Gemälde, Alben und Mappenwerke (exh. cat., ed. R. Blaum and S. Salzmann; Bremen, Ksthalle, 1987)

SIEGFRIED SALZMANN

Friedlaender, Walter (*b* Berlin, 10 March 1873; *d* New York, 6 Sept 1966). German art historian. Originally a Sanskrit scholar (diss., Berlin, Humboldt-U., 1898), he studied art history from 1903 to 1906. His first important publication, *Das Kasino Pius des Vierten* (Leipzig, 1912), showed an inclination for identifying and researching key areas of late Renaissance and Baroque art that had hitherto been dismissed as mere byways. He was instrumental in reviving the reputation of Poussin and published his first monograph on the artist, *Nicolas Poussin: Die Entwicklung seiner Kunst*, in Munich in 1914. He took up the challenge of the French Romantics in *Von David bis Delacroix* (Bielefeld, 1930; Eng. trans. by R. Goldwater, Cambridge, MA, 1952). He was on the verge of retirement from Freiburg University when he left Nazi Germany and began a new career, in 1935, at the Institute of Fine Arts, of New York University. He did much to encourage the increasing popularity of art history in the American graduate school, through his gifts for compositional and iconological analysis, perhaps above all through his ability to communicate a passionate regard for the sensual qualities in works of art.

WRITINGS
Caravaggio Studies (Princeton, 1955)
Mannerism and Anti-Mannerism in Italian Painting (New York, 1957)
Nicolas Poussin: A New Approach (New York, 1964)

BIBLIOGRAPHY
G. Kauffmann and W. Sauerländer, eds: *Walter Friedlaender zum 90. Geburtstag* (Berlin, 1965) [full bibliog.]

JAMES DAVID DRAPER

Friedlander, Lee (*b* Aberdeen, WA, 14 July 1934). American photographer. He first became interested in photography in 1948, and from 1953 to 1955 he studied under Edward Kaminski at the Art Center of Los Angeles. In 1956 he settled in New York and supported himself by producing photographs of jazz musicians for record jackets, for example *Count Basie* (1957; see Malle, pl. 39). He also produced photographs influenced by Eugène Atget, Walker Evans and Robert Frank and, like his subsequent works, these were all in black and white. In 1958 he discovered the work of the little-known photographer E. J. Bellocq from whose gelatin dry-plate negatives of the brothels of New Orleans he took prints, which were included in the exhibition *E. J. Bellocq: Storyville Portraits* at MOMA in New York in 1970. In 1960, 1962 and 1977 Friedlander was awarded Guggenheim Memorial Foundation grants, and his works began to appear in such periodicals as *Esquire*, *Art in America* and *Sports Illustrated*. He had his first one-man show in 1963 at the International Museum of Photography at George Eastman House in Rochester, NY. From the 1960s Friedlander started taking photographs of the 'social landscape' of the USA, detached images of urban life which, like Pop art works, captured the feel and look of modern society, though often with depressing effect. *Newark, New Jersey* (1962; see Friedlander, 1978, pl. 2) is characteristic of these and includes shop-window reflections, posters and signs, which tend to compress spatial depth. In atmosphere and subject-matter these works have affinities with the work of Friedlander's friend Garry Winogrand. Friedlander's collaboration with Jim Dine further emphasized his links with Pop art, and in 1969 they published *Works from the Same House*. This included etchings by Dine and photographs by Friedlander, so arranged that examples of each faced one another, creating a suggestive juxtaposition of imagery.

Other works by Friedlander in the 1960s included the series of works that appeared in *Self-portrait* (1970). Contrary to the tradition of the genre Friedlander only appears in the photographs in the most oblique way, in reflections in mirrors and glass or merely as a shadow. Urban themes also proved a dominant theme in the 1970s, leading to such bleak images as *Albuquerque* (1972; Chicago, IL, A. Inst.), showing an undistinguished expanse

of deserted city. One of his most notable projects of this decade was the work for *The American Monument* (1976) for which he photographed over 100 public monuments. These included a whole range of memorials to war dead, local officials and figures from American history. Through this curious diversity of images Friedlander provided a fragmentary view of the nation's values and heroes.

In 1979 Friedlander was commissioned by the Akron Art Museum to produce a photographic documentary of the industrial areas of the Ohio river valley, the results of which appeared in *Factory Valleys: Ohio and Pennsylvania* (1982). It consisted of photographs of the urban industrial landscape and of the factory labourers at work. The dour landscape and alienating, monotonous work routines present a cold picture of the underside of developed, industrial society. From the late 1970s and into the 1980s Friedlander took numerous photographs of the landscape in Japan, some of which appeared in *Cherry Blossom Time in Japan* (1986). A similar spirit pervaded the series *Flowers and Trees* (1981). In contrast to his urban works these stress the beauties of nature, although in the context of his other works they acquire a nostalgic, exotic aura. *Portraits* (1985) ranged chronologically from 1958 to 1983, while for *Nudes* (1991) Friedlander photographed his subjects in unusual poses, using novel framing to revitalize a traditional subject. Many of his photographic books were published by his own firm, the Haywire Press of New City, NY.

PHOTOGRAPHIC PUBLICATIONS
Works from the Same House (London and New York, 1969) [incl. etchings by Jim Dine]
Self-portrait (New City, 1970)
The American Monument (New York, 1976)
Lee Friedlander: Photographs (New City, 1978)
Flowers and Trees (New City, 1981)
Factory Valleys, afterword by L. G. Katz (New York, 1982)
Lee Friedlander: Portraits, text by R. B. Kitaj (Boston, 1985)
Cherry Blossom Time in Japan (New City, 1986)
Nudes, text by I. Sischy (London and New York, 1991)

BIBLIOGRAPHY
L. Malle: *Lee Friedlander* (Paris, 1987; Eng. trans., New York, 1988)

□

Friedländer, Max Jacob (*b* Berlin, 5 June 1867; *d* Amsterdam, 11 Oct 1958). German art historian and museum director. The son of the court jeweller in Berlin, he studied in Munich, Florence and Leipzig, where he wrote a dissertation on Albrecht Altdorfer. After practical training in Berlin and his first, brief activity at the Wallraf-Richartz-Museum in Cologne, he became an assistant at the Gemäldegalerie der Staatlichen Museen, Berlin, in 1896. He became Deputy Director in 1904 and Director in 1924; from 1908 he was head of the Kupferstichkabinett. With Wilhelm von Bode he systematically increased the holdings of the Berlin museums and donated a number of important works to the Gemäldegalerie and Kupferstichkabinett. In 1933 he left museum service and in 1939 emigrated to Amsterdam. Friedländer, who had a strongly positivistic education, was regarded as a severe critic of Giovanni Morelli's method of art analysis, most notably represented in German-speaking countries by Franz Wickhoff. Friedländer wrote over 600 books and articles, especially on early German and early Netherlandish art, and a monograph on Max Liebermann, whose works he collected, as well as those of Max Slevogt and the French

Impressionists. His most important work, *Early Nether-landish Painting*, which has been published in various versions and editions since the German original appeared in the 1920s, is a comprehensive survey of art in the Netherlands in the 15th and 16th centuries and is regarded as a standard work on the period. Friedländer wrote of the process of understanding a work of art *(Erinnerungen und Aufzeichnungen*, 1967, p. 38):

> Anyone who 'understands' a work of art—to use that all-embracing word—is, in relation to the one who has produced it, a reproducer. He stands in relation to the producer as the actor does to the dramatist or the pianist to the composer. Painted canvas becomes a work of art only when it has the effect of a work of art. The onlooker enjoying the work creates it as the pianist awakens the composer's work, by empathizing with it, being borne along by it.

WRITINGS

Albrecht Altdorfer der Maler von Regensburg (Leipzig, 1891)
Von van Eyck bis Bruegel: Studien zur Geschichte der niederländischen Malerei (Berlin, 1916)
Albrecht Dürer (Leipzig, 1921)
Der Holzschnitt (Berlin, 1921, 4/1970)
Pieter Bruegel (Berlin, 1921)
Albrecht Altdorfer (Berlin, 1923)
Die niederländischen Maler des 17. Jahrhunderts (Berlin, 1923)
Die altniederländische Malerei, 11 vols (Berlin, 1924–33); 3 further vols (Leiden, 1935–7); Eng. trans. as *Early Netherlandish Painting*, 16 vols (Leiden, 1967–76)
Lucas van Leyden (Leipzig, 1924)
Max Liebermann (Leipzig, 1924)
Matthias Grünewald: Die Zeichnungen (Berlin, 1927)
On Art and Connoisseurship (London, 1942); in Ger. as *Von Kunst und Kennerschaft* (Berlin, 1946)
Essays über die Landschaftsmalerei und andere Bildgattungen (The Hague, 1947)
Über die Malerei: Essays über die Landschaftsmalerei und andere Bildgattungen (Munich, 1963)
R. M. Heilbrunn, ed.: *Erinnerungen und Aufzeichnungen* (Mainz and Berlin, 1967)
with J. Rosenberg: *Die Gemälde von Lucas Cranach*, ed. J. Schwartz (Basle, 1979)
Von van Eyck bis Bruegel: Studien zur Geschichte der niederländischen Malerei, ed. G. Busch (Frankfurt am Main, 1986)

BIBLIOGRAPHY

LK; NDB
L. Blumenreich: *Max J. Friedländer: Verzeichnis der Schriften* (Berlin, 1927)
Festschrift für Max J. Friedländer: Zum 60. Geburtstag (Leipzig, 1927)
Aan Max J. Friedländer 1867–1942 aangeboden door enkele vrienden en bewonderaars van zijn werk [Offered to Max J. Friedländer 1867–1942 by several friends and admirers of his work] (The Hague, 1942)
Max J. Friedländer ter ere van zijn negentigste verjaardag [Max J. Friedländer in honour of his 90th birthday] (Amsterdam, 1957)
U. Kultermann: *Geschichte der Kunstgeschichte: Der Weg einer Wissenschaft* (Munich, 1990)

ANDREAS KREUL

Friedman, André. *See* CAPA, ROBERT.

Friedman, Yona (*b* Budapest, 5 June 1923). French architect of Hungarian birth. He studied architecture at the Technical University, Budapest (1943), but he left Hungary in 1945, completed his training at the Technion, Haifa (Dip. Arch., 1948) and subsequently taught. In 1956 he attended CIAM X in Dubrovnik, which confirmed his belief that requirements generated by technological progress and demographic growth were too great to be solved by traditional social, urban and architectural values and structures. In 1957 he settled in Paris and founded the Groupe d'Etude d'Architecture Mobile (GEAM) with

Paul Maymont, Frei Otto, Eckard Schultze-Fielitz, Werner Runhau and D. G. Emmerich. The group's manifesto was Friedman's *L'Architecture mobile* (1958), in which he rejected the idea of a static city. In contrast he developed the principle of 'infrastructure', a skeletal metal 'space-frame grid' of several levels, on which mobile lightweight 'space-defining elements' would be placed. He proposed to adapt these ideas for large cities by superimposing this grid on the existing fabric of London, Tunis and New York, or by allowing commercial facilities to be built over the network of high speed roads in Los Angeles.

Friedman's ambition was 'to help the inhabitant to become master of his own design', the sub-title of *L'Architecture mobile*, and to encourage architects to become less self-important and to gain an awareness of how they could be useful to their client. Applications of his participatory concepts were used in an unexecuted project for the CDC headquarters in Ivry-sur-Seine (1976) and the Lycée David d'Angers, Angers (1978–80). His ideas, conveyed by simple diagrams and cartoons, gained a significant popular appeal. His exhibition *Une Utopie réalisée* drew a record attendance at the Musée d'Art Moderne de la Ville de Paris in 1975 and it later toured Latin America, sponsored by the French government.

A gifted self-promoter, Friedman wrote and lectured extensively, and in the early 1960s his ideas began to be discussed worldwide, especially in Japan where they were adopted by Kenzo Tange and exponents of 'metabolist' architecture (*see* METABOLISM). Many urban planners, architects and critics found his concepts too simplistic and objected that occupants would never accept the state of being disconnected from ground level. In *Pour une architecture scientifique* (1970), Friedman attempted to prove that his visions were based on careful reasoning. After 1976 he enlarged the scope of his activities, adapting his theories to the needs of developing countries. In 1981 he began work with Eda Schaur (*b* 1945) on a museum where techniques and methods for self-reliance would be demonstrated to disadvantaged people, resulting in the Museum of Basic Technology, Madras, India.

WRITINGS

L'Architecture mobile (Paris and Tournai, 1970)
Pour une architecture scientifique (Paris, 1970; Eng. trans., Cambridge, MA, 1975)
Une Utopie réalisée (exh. cat., Paris, Mus. A. Mod. Ville Paris, 1975)

BIBLIOGRAPHY

M. Ragon: 'Yona Friedman: De l'habitat évolutif à l'autoplanification', *Urbanisme*, xliii/143 (1974), pp. 75–7
R. Banham: *Megastructure: Urban Features of the Recent Past* (New York, 1976), pp. 60, 62
A. Hill: 'Yona Friedman', *RIBA J.*, lxxxiii/3 (1976), p. 105

ISABELLE GOURNAY

Friedrich, Caspar David (*b* Greifswald, 5 Sept 1774; *d* Dresden, 7 May 1840). German painter, draughtsman and printmaker. Along with Phillip Otto Runge, he was the leading artist of the German Romantic movement, notable especially for his symbolic and atmospheric treatment of landscape.

1. Life and work. 2. Working methods and technique. 3. Critical reception and posthumous reputation.

1. LIFE AND WORK. After receiving a general education with a private tutor, Friedrich studied drawing and etching

from 1790 to 1794 with Johann Gottfried Quistorp (1755–1835), drawing teacher at the university in Greifswald. From 1794 until 1798 he studied at the Akademi for de Skønne Kunster in Copenhagen, where his most important teachers were Nicolai Abraham Abildgaard, Jens Juel, Christian August Lorentzen (1749–1828) and Johannes Wiedewelt (1759–1802). The influence of Danish painting, especially that of Juel and Abildgaard, was strong and is evident even in his later years; Juel's landscapes were notable for their clarity of composition and Abildgaard encouraged Friedrich's enthusiasm for the mythology and history of the Scandinavian and Germanic peoples. Friedrich swiftly developed a confident and disciplined manner, as seen in the pen-and-wash drawing *Landscape by Moonlight with a Ruined Watermill* (c. 1795; Copenhagen, Stat. Mus. Kst), and facility in handling both pen, line and watercolour as seen in the *Landscape with Garden House* (1797; Hamburg, Ksthalle).

In May 1798 Friedrich left Copenhagen and, after a short stay in Berlin, settled in Dresden, where he remained, except for visits to central Germany and Bohemia, for the rest of his life. He studied life drawing at the Hochschule der Bildenden Künste in Dresden, and in 1799 some of his works were shown for the first time at the Hochschule exhibition. Following the Dresden tradition, Friedrich drew intensively from nature, producing his first landscape etchings using largely symbolic motifs such as paths, bridges, rivers, trees, distant hills and views of cities. These works made marked use of contrast, itself symbolic,

between lit and shadowed passages. Many sketches and etchings appear to be variants of each other, for example those of c. 1799–1800 (e.g. *Landscape with Bridge*, etching, 1799; gouache sketch, 1800, Dresden, Kupferstichkab.).

From spring 1801 until July 1802 Friedrich stayed in Greifswald. While in the north he visited the island of Rügen, and from sketches made there he created some large sepia landscapes comparable with the work of Adrian Zingg (1734–1816), a master of the Dresden sepia tradition. His sepia sketches and portraits drew admiration and, encouraged by Johann Wolfgang von Goethe, he submitted two drawings to the Weimarer Kunstfreunde exhibition in 1805 (e.g. *Summer Landscape with Dead Oaktree*; Weimar, Schlossmus.) and won a prize. Friedrich also produced figure studies; such drawings as *Woman Sitting on a Rock next to a Dying Tree Wound with Ivy* (1801; Dresden, Kupferstichkab.) point to the emergence of an approach to landscape determined by both emotional and spiritual response. The association of particular landscape views with the times of day, the seasons or the ages of man, was a dominant theme in Friedrich's work in Dresden during the next ten years or so. Figures would often be combined with landscape, or elements such as trees might stand in for them. The influence on Friedrich of Philipp Otto Runge is likely in this connection. The two artists had met in Greifswald in 1801–2, and from 1803 to 1805 Runge was living in Dresden and working on his own *Times of Day* cycle. Like Runge, Friedrich expressed his ideas on the times of day in words as well as

1. Caspar David Friedrich: *Mountain Landscape with a Rainbow*, oil on canvas, 700×1030 mm, 1810 (Essen, Museum Folkwang)

images, producing four religiously inspired poems in 1803–4 (see Hinz, 1968).

In 1807 Friedrich began painting in oils, possibly motivated to adopt the technique by a commission from Graf F. A. von Thun-Hohenstein (1786–1873) for an altarpiece for the chapel of Děčín (Ger. Tetschen) Castle in Bohemia (now in Czech Republic). The painting *Cross in the Mountains* (1807–8; Dresden, Gemäldegal. Neue Meister) represents in surprising monumentality and purity Friedrich's conception of religious landscape. The work fulfils the Romantic requirement of creating a new devotional image in a depiction of landscape. This corresponded with panentheistic belief, developed from Lutheran Protestantism, of the kind espoused by the theologian Daniel Friedrich Schleiermacher and the poet Gottfried Ludwig Kosegarten (1750–1818), in which God manifests himself in nature and man views the widening landscape as an act of devotion. Friedrich had met Schleiermacher in Greifswald, and Kosegarten had lived in the nearby Baltic port of Wolgast from 1785 to 1792. Friedrich portrayed this concept in his second powerful picture, the *Monk by the Sea* (1809–10; Berlin, Schloss Charlottenburg), in which the oppressive gloom of the stormy sky and the lone figure of the monk endow landscape with an ability to express fears and emotions not naturally invested in it. Both paintings received vehement criticism, as well as enthusiastic approval from the Romantics.

The *Monk by the Sea* and a picture devised to accompany it, *Abbey in an Oakwood* (1809; Berlin, Schloss Charlottenburg), were exhibited in 1810 at the Akademie in Berlin, of which Friedrich was a member, and the *Abbey in an Oakwood* was bought by the Prussian Crown Prince, later Frederick William IV. The painting includes one of Friedrich's principal motifs: the ruin, which symbolizes the vanished Christian Church of the Middle Ages. The oaks symbolize the pagan world. The procession of monks with the coffin leads across the graveyard, past the empty grave, through the portal with the cross to a distant light, which indicates an altar, on which God appears in the word of the gospel. The bright sky with the waxing moon at the right could signify evening or morning, evening suggesting death and the grave, morning suggesting hope for resurrection. Friedrich's landscapes from this point are increasingly dominated by motifs of sublimity, which gives them a special distinction. The *Mountain Landscape with a Rainbow* (1810; Essen, Mus. Flkwang; see fig. 1) is striking in its sombre and disturbing storm light; and the serene, unworldly sea of misty peaks in *Morning in the Riesengebirge* (1810–11; Berlin, Schloss Charlottenburg) make this work the most intensely spiritual of Friedrich's mountain views from this time. The painting was exhibited in Weimar in 1812, and it was bought by Frederick William III of Prussia.

In 1813, during the French occupation of Dresden, Friedrich stayed in the Elbsandsteingebirge; in March 1814 he took part in the patriotic exhibition celebrating the liberation of Dresden. An expression of patriotic fervour is to be found in the defiant presentation of figures in traditional German costume, as in *On the Sailing Ship* (1813–14; St Petersburg, Hermitage) and *Two Men Contemplating the Moon* (1819; Berlin, Tiergarten, N.G.). These costumes had been adopted as part of the fight against Emperor Napoleon Bonaparte. Students with republican and anti-feudalist leanings, some of whom had just returned from the war, dressed in the 'old German' style as early as 1815, and by 1818 this fashion was widespread among students, artists and writers. When reaction set in in 1819 these republicans were prosecuted as 'demagogues'; the costume was banned. It recurs, however, in Friedrich's pictures after this time, indicating that he was a republican.

During the years from 1818 to 1820 Friedrich began to vary the symmetrical principle of order in his paintings and to introduce asymmetries. He began to lay new emphasis on figures, as, for example, in *Wanderer above a Sea of Fog* (c. 1818; Hamburg, Ksthalle) and *Woman at a Window* (1822; Berlin, Tiergarten, N.G.; *see* SYMBOL, fig. 3). A strain of irony tends to undermine the more positive side of Friedrich's work from this time. In the *Chalk Cliffs at Rügen* (1818; Winterthur, Samml. Oskar Reinhart; see fig. 2), the apparent significance of the three large foreground figures and their relation to each other is immediately called into question by their precarious foothold in the dramatic setting. Return visits to Greifswald resulted in naturalistic landscape views, painted from life, such as *Meadows near Greifswald* (c. 1820–22; Hamburg, Ksthalle).

In 1823 the Norwegian landscape painter Johann Christian Dahl moved into a flat in Friedrich's house, and for some time the two painters worked and exhibited together. The close friendship with Dahl probably contributed to a new openness and willingness to experiment, which also

2. Caspar David Friedrich: *Chalk Cliffs at Rügen*, oil on canvas, 900×700 mm, 1818 (Winterthur, Sammlung Oskar Reinhart)

3. Caspar David Friedrich: *Stages of Life*, oil on canvas, 730×940 mm, *c.* 1835 (Leipzig, Museum der Bildenden Künste)

extended his range of colours. However, the more naturalistic approach to landscape prompted by Dahl was invariably supplemented by symbolic meaning in Friedrich's paintings, incorporating such ideas as the transience of life, death and rebirth.

In 1824 both Dahl and Friedrich had received chairs at the Akademie der Bildenden Kunst in Dresden, but Friedrich failed to succeed Johann Christian Klengel as landscape painting teacher, after his death in 1824. A period of illness in 1825–6 followed this severe disappointment. This experience set the predominant tone of Friedrich's last 15 years, one of sadness and resignation. Among the rather sombre works carried out in the late 1820s, however, were some of great power. *Snowed-up Hut* (*Hut in the Snow, c.* 1827; Berlin, Tiergarten, N.G.) is remarkable for its intense mood and restrained colour scheme.

In *Äusserung bei Betrachtung einer Sammlung von Gemälden von grösstenteils noch lebenden und unlängst verstorbenen Künstlern*, written in 1830, Friedrich commented negatively on his era as well as on its artists, criticizing the idealistic aims of the Nazarenes, the petty preoccupations of the artists of the Biedermeier tendency, all manner of artistic modishness, the claims of the academies and the pretensions and power of the critics. He clearly felt pushed into isolation. However, the paintings the *Great Enclosure*

(*c.* 1832; Dresden, Gemäldegal. Neue Meister) and *Stages of Life* (*c.* 1835; Leipzig, Mus. Bild. Kst.; see fig. 3) are two of his most beautiful and impressive works, and his treatment of symbols of transience and death in the latter painting has a marked liveliness.

In 1835 Friedrich suffered a stroke that prevented him from painting; in his last years he returned to the technique of sepia. Although his late works reveal his frailty, there were several aspects in which he devised very strong images, as in his series of symbolic works showing owls and graves, which seem to be meditative preparations for death in the hope of resurrection, for example *Coffin by a Grave* (*c.* 1836; Moscow, Pushkin Mus. F.A.). In 1838 his last works were exhibited at the academy in Dresden.

2. WORKING METHODS AND TECHNIQUE. It was while working on his *Times of Day* cycle that Friedrich fully developed his idea of landscape mirroring human experience and emotions; at the same time he perfected his sepia drawing technique, eliminating every element of sketchiness and completely covering all underdrawing, exploiting the transparency of the medium to incorporate the full impact of the brightness of the paper. The details of Friedrich's landscape drawings were invariably symbolic in a religious and philosophical sense, although it was

4. Caspar David Friedrich: *Winter Landscape with Church*, oil on canvas, 330×430 mm, 1811 (London, National Gallery)

often for their technique rather than their content that such works were praised. As the abstract meaning he sought to convey grew in importance for him, so did his tendency to pair and group several pictures as complementary presentations of the same notion. A pair of sepia views from his studio in Dresden, with the river and the far bank seen through the window (both 1805–6; Vienna, Ksthist. Mus.), shows this device at its most straightforward, although, for Friedrich, these apparently simple scenes were freighted with symbolic meaning—the dark interior, signifying the present earthly life, being deliberately contrasted with the bright 'divine' realm of the view beyond. The formal device of sharp and symbolic contrast between foreground and background is also to be found—in the landscape drawing style that Friedrich was bringing to full development—in several works produced after another journey to the island of Rügen in 1806.

Before he began painting in oils in 1807, Friedrich had defined both his symbolic language and the character of his images, which confront a limited foreground with an infinite distance, immense closeness with transcending remoteness, the interior with the exterior, this world with that to come. The middle ground is eliminated. This double layered picture space is accentuated by the symmetrical arrangement of the objects, as in the painting *Cross in the Mountains.* Friedrich undertook thorough preparations for this work, making a great many studies of individual landscape details such as pine trees and of

the general character of the Bohemian landscape near Tetschen. The extent of his concern for the design of the frame indicates a new level of engagement both with the work itself and with his patrons.

From 1810 Friedrich's paintings reveal an increasing recurrence of Gothic architectural elements, evidence of the extent to which his more worldly concern, in the form of intense patriotism, was evoked by the rigours and fears of the period of struggle against Napoleon. Gothic architecture was associated not only with the forms of nature but with the German spirit in particular. This suggests that such features as the Gothic cathedral rising like a vision in the background of *Winter Landscape with Church* (1811; London, N.G., see fig. 4; version, Dortmund, Mus. Kst & Kultgesch.) were designed to allude to a specifically German interpretation of the life beyond the grave. Friedrich's preoccupation with Gothic architecture persisted into peacetime. The commission in 1817 for internal decoration in a 'Gothic' style for the Marienkirche in Stralsund was given to Karl Friedrich Schinkel and Friedrich, thus suggesting that the cultivated public firmly associated him with this style. As it appears in Friedrich's paintings at this time, however, Gothic architecture is invariably presented as part of an ideal realm, the heavenly city glimpsed beyond a real landscape or seascape setting. This is the case, for example, in *Neubrandenburg in the Morning Mist* (c. 1816–17; Bielefeld, priv. col.; version, Kiel, Stift. Pommern) in which two male figures in the deeply shaded foreground look on as the sky flames into brilliant yellows and pinks behind the silhouetted towers and spires.

Motivation derived by Friedrich from the work of other artists was important in the process of forming his own views on art, both as recorded in notes and letters and as expressed in pictures that were themselves criticisms or adaptations of other artists' themes. Thus Friedrich's view of the mountain peak *The Watzmann* (1825; Berlin, Neue N.G.), based on a watercolour by August Heinrich (1794–1822), was a comment on the approach to such scenes in the work of both Ludwig Richter (as a mere 'vedutist') and Josef Anton Koch (as a mere 'geologist'). Friedrich's *Woman at a Window* was an acknowledgement of the achievements in this genre of Georg Friedrich Kersting, whom Friedrich had visited in Meissen the year before, and a demonstration that scenes of this kind could go further, as allegory or symbol, than Kersting himself had allowed.

While recuperating from a period of illness in 1824, Friedrich produced landscape views without symbolic significance: 37 pen and watercolour scenes painted in Rügen, probably planned as the basis for subsequent prints, although the plan was never carried out (Börsch-Supan and Jähnig, 1973, nos 324–6). In the late 1820s his painting revealed a renewed readiness to observe both form and colour in the natural world. This is especially clear in a series of detailed and highly finished watercolour studies made on a sketching trip to Bohemia in 1828 (ibid., nos 377–8), and also in paintings evincing a great interest in subtle and intricate effects of light, as in the combination of moonlight and firelight in the beach scene *Evening by the Baltic* (1830; Dresden, Gemäldegal. Neue Meister). Friedrich's interest in light effects also encouraged his development of landscape scenes for viewing in a diorama-type device (*see* DIORAMA), as in the double-sided *Mountain Landscape with River* (*c.* 1830–35; Kassel, Neue Gal.).

3. CRITICAL RECEPTION AND POSTHUMOUS REPUTATION. Friedrich was the most important Romantic painter in Germany, and the critical reception of his work reveals the singularity of his position. In Dresden he met a circle of individuals—intellectuals, university lecturers and artists—who in part originated and developed and in part embodied and disseminated Romantic ideas. They were a group of individuals from the 'educated classes', who corresponded frequently with their friends in Jena, Berlin, Heidelberg, Hamburg and Greifswald (Rügen). They also visited each other regularly. This was the class that sustained German Romanticism, which never became a popular movement reaching the wider ranks of German society. This factor determined the success of Friedrich's work: respected by this small circle and adored by a few people, his fame only lasted about ten years, from 1808 (*Cross in the Mountains*) to about 1820, when several of his works were bought by Tsar Nicholas I. His appointment as honorary professor at the academy in Dresden in 1824 was his last mark of public esteem and, at the same time, his failure to secure the appointment as landscape painting teacher was an almost humiliating rejection of the artist by official opinion. After 1825 his work was generally considered to be gloomy and strange and was only marginally recognized, a fact unaffected by good sales of his pictures and some spectacular visits by important artists and noblemen. When Friedrich died, his oeuvre was unrecognized by official art criticism. When his old friend Carl Gustav Carus (1789–1869) wrote his obituary he gave the impression that Friedrich's work belonged to a distant past. His work was rediscovered by Norwegian art historian Andreas Aubert (1851–1913), who came across Friedrich's work while researching the oeuvre of Johann Christian Dahl. Aubert ensured that Friedrich was represented with 32 paintings in the *Deutsche Jahrhundert-Ausstellung* in 1906 in Berlin. The public, with expectations schooled by Impressionism, had regained a taste for the depiction of twilight, sunsets and moonlight. Moreover, the Symbolist movement prepared the ground for an understanding of Friedrich's symbolic language. Since then his painting has been popular in Germany, being generally, and superficially, understood as painting of mood. Friedrich and his art were held to be a symbol of the spirit of German nationalism during the era of Nazism. His art received wide recognition from inclusion in *The Romantic Movement* exhibition at the Tate Gallery in London in 1959, and since that time his work has become accepted as the most important German contribution to European Romanticism.

WRITINGS

Äusserung bei Betrachtung einer Sammlung von Gemälden von grösstenteils noch lebenden und unlängst verstorbenen Künstlern (1830; MS.), Dresden, Kupferstichkab.; ed. S. Hinz in *Caspar David Friedrich in Briefen und Bekenntnissen* (E. Berlin, 1968/R Munich, 1974), pp. 84–134

BIBLIOGRAPHY

A. Aubert: 'Der Landschaftsmaler Friedrich', *Kunstchronik*, vii (1895–6), pp. 282–93
——: 'Caspar David Friedrich', *Gott, Freiheit und Vaterland*, ed. G. J. Kern (Berlin, 1915)
W. Wolfradt: *Caspar David Friedrich und die Landschaft der Romantik* (Berlin, 1924)
H. von Einem: *Caspar David Friedrich, der Landschaftsmaler: Ein Volksbuch deutscher Kunst* (Leipzig, 1940)
K. W. Kästner, L. Rohling and K. F. Degner: *Caspar David Friedrich und seine Heimat* (Berlin, 1940)
The Romantic Movement (exh. cat., London, Tate, 1959)
W. Hofmann: 'Bemerkungen zum Tetschener Altar von C. D. Friedrich', *Christ. Ksthl.*, 100 (1962), pp. 50–52
G. Eimer: 'Caspar David Friedrich und die Gotik: Analysen und Deutungsversuche: Aus Stockholmer Vorlesungen', *Balt. Stud.*, 49 (1962–3), pp. 39–68
R. Rosenblum: 'Caspar David Friedrich and Modern Painting', *A. & Lit.*, 10 (Autumn 1966), pp. 134–46
W. Sumowski: *Caspar David Friedrich-Studien*, Wiesbaden, 1970)
Caspar David Friedrich, 1774–1840: Romantic Landscape Painting in Dresden (exh. cat., ed. W. Vaughan, H. Börsch-Supan and H. J. Neidhardt; London, Tate, 1972)
W. Geismeier: *Caspar David Friedrich* (Vienna and Munich, 1973)
H. Börsch-Supan and K. W. Jähnig: *Caspar David Friedrich: Gemälde, Druckgraphik und bildmässige Zeichnungen* (Munich, 1973) [cat. rais.; contains extensive bibliog.]
——: *Caspar David Friedrich: Das gesamte graphische Werk* (Munich, 1974) [with cat. of drgs by S. Hinz]
Caspar David Friedrich, 1774–1840 (exh. cat., ed. W. Hofmann; Hamburg, Ksthalle, 1974)
G. Eimer: *Caspar David Friedrich: Auge und Landschaft: Zeugnisse in Bild und Wort* (Frankfurt am Main, 1974)
J. C. Jensen: *Caspar David Friedrich: Leben und Werk* (Cologne, 1974; rev. 8/1988; Eng. trans., New York, 1981)
H. J. Kunst: 'Die politischen und gesellschaftlichen Bedingtheiten der Gotikrezeption bei Friedrich und Schinkel', *Krit. Ber.*, ii/5–6 (1974), pp. 120–29
P. Maerker: *Geschichte als Natur: Untersuchungen zur Entwicklungsvorstellung bei Caspar David Friedrich* (diss., Kiel, Christian-Albrechts U., 1974)

Caspar David Friedrich und sein Kreis (exh. cat., Dresden, Gemäldegal. Neue Meister, 1974–5)

B. Hinz and others: *Bürgerliche Revolution und Romantik: Natur und Gesellschaft bei Caspar David Friedrich* (Giessen, 1976)

G. Fiege: *Caspar David Friedrich in Selbstzeugnissen und Bilddokumenten* (Reinbek bei Hamburg, 1977)

G. Eimer: *Zur Dialektik des Glaubens bei Caspar David Friedrich* (Frankfurt am Main, 1982)

G. Fiege: *Caspar David Friedrich: Linien und Transparenz* (Paris, 1984)

P. Betthausen and others, eds: *The Romantic Spirit: German Drawings, 1780–1850, from the Nationalgalerie, Berlin, and the Kupferstichkabinett, Dresden* (New York and London, 1988)

H. Börsch-Supan: *Die deutsche Malerei von Anton Graff bis Hans von Marées, 1760–1870* (Munich, 1988)

Casper David Friedrich to Ferdinand Hodler: A Romantic Tradition (exh. cat., ed. P. Wegmann; Berlin, Alte N.G.; Los Angeles, CA, Co. Mus. A.; New York, Met.; London, N.G.; 1993–4)

The Romantic Spirit in German Art, 1790–1890 (exh. cat., ed. K. Hartley and others; Edinburgh, Royal Scot. Acad. and Fruitmarket Gal.; London, Hayward Gal.; Munich, Haus Kst; 1994–5)

JENS CHRISTIAN JENSEN

Friedrich, Nikolaus (*b* Cologne, 17 July 1865; *d* Berlin, 6 Feb 1914). German sculptor. He came from a family of artisans and first attended an art school in Cologne. Between 1891 and 1893 he found his first scope for sculptural activity when he produced decorations for the World's Columbian Exposition in Chicago. After 1893 he underwent academic training in Berlin. The Prix de Rome of the Akademie in Berlin enabled him to make a study trip to Italy in 1896–7. On his return to Berlin, he joined Reinhold Begas's studio as a pupil (1897–1901). The influence of this important sculptor is visible in his first known work, *Figure Fastening a Sandal* (1897; Berlin, Alte N.G.). His next works were also influenced by the neo-Baroque, as shown by *The Falconer* (untraced) presented at the Grosser Kunstausstellung in Berlin in 1898.

In 1899 Friedrich joined the Secession and he was regularly represented at their exhibitions until 1911. The works that he produced from this date lost the picturesque style of his teacher Begas in favour of a reduction of content and form. Outwardly they drew near the archaizing idiom of Adolf von Hildebrand's Neo-classicism. *Archers* (1904; Berlin, Alte N.G.) and *Shot-putters* (1907; Berlin, Skulpgal.) are works conveying a universal message. The only known publicly exhibited work by Friedrich was the monumental figure of a *Tug-of-war Competitor* at the Rheinhafen in Cologne, which was unveiled in 1911. In it, as in other works by Friedrich, such as *Boccia Players* (1909; Cologne, Wallraf-Richartz-Mus.), a powerful plasticity is combined with a tendency to thrust outwards into space.

BIBLIOGRAPHY

P. Bloch and W. Grzimek: *Das klassische Berlin* (Berlin, 1978), p. 317

Berlin und die Antike, intro. P. Bloch (Berlin, 1979)

P. Bloch and B. Hüfler: *Rheinland-Westfalen und die Berliner Bildhauerschule des 19. Jahrhunderts* (Berlin, 1984)

W. Hansmann: 'Der *Tauzieher* am Kölner Rheinauhafen', *Denkmalpflege im Rheinland* (Cologne, 1989)

SIBYLLE EINHOLZ

Friedrich-Augustus I, Elector of Saxony. *See* WETTIN, (7).

Friedrich-Augustus II, King of Poland. *See* WETTIN, (8).

Friedrich of Villach (*fl c.* 1415–55). Austrian painter. A citizen of Villach from 1415 at the latest, he was the founder and for many years the leader of a painters' workshop based there, producing primarily wall paintings but also some panel paintings. Through the art of south Germany and the Alpine region he came into contact with Parisian illumination of *c.* 1400 and was also familiar with Bohemian painting of *c.* 1400–10. A skilful eclectic, he drew on these and sometimes also on traditional Italian influences in developing a late soft style, linear and two-dimensional in effect, which was typical of Carinthia. His paintings and those closely connected with him are characterized by their rich, unusual landscapes and the slightly accentuated expressions of the heads, for example in the *Legend of St George* and the *Imago Pietatis* (*c.* 1421; Mariapfarr, parish church) and in the scenes of the *Passion* (1428; Millstatt, Ernst-Kapelle). Wall paintings depicting the *Childhood of Christ*, the *Passion* and *St George* (*c.* 1435–40; Sankt Gandolf, Glan Valley, parish church) include a *Procession and Adoration of the Magi*, which is deemed the best and most representative of the products of his workshop. In later wall paintings the hand of his son and pupil JOHANNES OF LJUBLJANA can also be detected. Only one panel painting has been attributed to Friedrich: a *Virgin and Child with Four Standing Saints* (*c.* 1435; Villach, Mus. Stadt).

BIBLIOGRAPHY

W. Frodl: *Die gotische Wandmalerei in Kärnten* (Klagenfurt, 1944), pp. 35–7

J. Höfler: *Die gotische Malerei Villachs*, i (Villach, 1981), pp. 15–60

JANEZ HÖFLER

Friend, Donald (Stuart Leslie) (*b* Warialda, NSW, 6 Feb 1915; *d* Sydney, 17 Aug 1989). Australian illustrator, painter and writer. He studied under Dattilo Rubbo (1871–1955) in Sydney before travelling to London to work (1935–6) under Mark Gertler and Bernard Meninsky (1891–1950). Extensive travel through Africa on his return journey to Australia helped develop his love of the exotic and an interest in non-Western art. In the early 1940s he worked in close association with Russell Drysdale, making a reputation as a talented figure and landscape draughtsman and colourist. He enlisted in the Australian army in 1942 and in 1945 he was commissioned as an Official War Artist, working in New Guinea and Borneo in the last months of World War II. He published two illustrated wartime memoirs, *Gunner's Diary* (Sydney, 1943) and *Painter's Journal* (Sydney, 1946), which strengthened his reputation as a writer and illustrator of great wit and charm.

After a period working in the small country town of Hill End, Friend left Australia for more than 20 years, living and working first in Sri Lanka and then for an extended period in Bali. Within Australia his work was associated with the SYDNEY GROUP of Neo-Romantics, nicknamed the 'Charm school' by critics. His lavishly illustrated books, exemplified by the extravagant *Bumbooziana* (Melbourne, 1978), brought him considerable success and notoriety. Forced to leave Bali in 1980, he returned to Australia and continued to work despite rapidly declining health. The charm and decorative qualities of his work denied him wide critical acclaim but in turn provided him with a loyal and popular following.

WRITINGS

A Collection of Hillendiana (Sydney, 1956)
Donald Friend in Bali (Sydney, 1972)
The Adventures of Blue-eyed Patty (Melbourne, 1979)
Crogan's Gully (Melbourne, 1979)

BIBLIOGRAPHY

R. Hughes: *Donald Friend* (Sydney, 1970)
G. Fry and C. Fry: *Donald Friend: Australian War Artist, 1945* (Melbourne, 1981)

GAVIN FRY

Friends, Religious Society of [Quakers]. Body of radical Protestants that originated in 17th-century England, during the Civil War and the Commonwealth (1642–60). Quakers emphasize the importance of man's inner experience of God, and of living according to the 'inward light'. There is no creed, no clergy nor any sacraments. In meetings for worship Quakers sit together in silence until a member of the meeting is moved to speak or pray.

Foremost among the founders of Quakerism was George Fox (1624–91), whose early proclamations of the 'light within' often led to persecution and imprisonment for blasphemy. In 1652 he met a particularly receptive community of Seekers in Westmorland and north-west Lancashire, and from that point the movement gathered momentum. Quaker meetings were established throughout England, in Cromwellian Ireland (1650s) and in the North American colonies—including Pennsylvania, which William Penn (1644–1718) founded as a Quaker colony in 1682. Friends continued to grow in number until the end of the century, although thousands were imprisoned or fined for their beliefs.

Following the 1689 Toleration Act in England, the Quakers were able to build meeting-houses and meet for worship with greater freedom from persecution. The 18th century was marked by quietism, although Friends' social concerns (most notably pacifism, prison reform and the abolition of slavery) were widely influential. During the 19th century Quakerism was affected by the evangelical movement and in North America separate 'Friends' Churches' were created, with hymn-singing and sermons not unlike those of other Protestants. In the 20th century the different branches of the Society grew closer together, and Quakerism developed in Africa.

Friends' meeting-houses are often praised for their plainness and dignity. Without need for altar, pulpit, choir or vestry, a characteristic meeting-house has only an arrangement of benches around the room, with a raised 'stand' or elders' bench along one side. Sometimes further accommodation is provided by a gallery, and in large buildings an extra room for the once separate women's meeting may be found. The meeting-house of 1688 at Jordans, Bucks, is a good rural example from the early period. Urban examples have often been of greater size and sophistication, as is suggested by the Neo-classical Friends' Meeting House (1828–30) in Manchester, by Richard Lane. In the resolute simplicity of Quaker worship there is no role in a meeting-house for paintings, statues or stained glass, and even the symbolism of the cross is eschewed.

Early Quakers distrusted portraiture as well as religious art, and George Fox encouraged Friends to remove all images from their houses. Some 18th-century Friends did allow themselves to be painted, however, and in America particularly silhouette portraits were permitted. BENJAMIN WEST came from a Quaker community in Pennsylvania and never repudiated Quakerism, although he was not a member. His portrayal of *William Penn's Treaty with the Indians* (1771–2; Philadelphia, PA Acad. F.A.) is the most famous depiction of Quaker history. During the 19th century some active Quakers painted regularly, including the English landscape painter Samuel Lucas (1805–70) and the American Edward Hicks (*see* HICKS, (1)) (1780–1849), renowned for his visionary portrayals of the *Peaceable Kingdom* (e.g. *c.* 1825–30; New Haven, CT, Yale U. A.G.).

Although painting was generally excluded from the Quaker experience, architecture was admitted. The atmosphere of the Friends' meeting-house must sometimes have kindled a wider interest in buildings. Thomas Rickman, the historian of English Gothic architecture, was a member of the Society of Friends, although he designed many buildings for the Church of England, and the Victorian architect Alfred Waterhouse came from a Quaker family. Quaker patronage was responsible for several important precursors of the Garden City, including that commissioned by GEORGE CADBURY at Bournville, near Birmingham (begun 1894 and continued with the appointment of W. Alexander Harvey as architect in 1897), and by the ROWNTREE family at New Earswick, N. Yorks (begun 1902 by Raymond Unwin).

Joseph Edward Southall: *St Dorothea and her Two Sisters Refusing to Worship the Idol*, tempera on canvas, 624×584 mm, 1901–2 (private collection)

After about 1860 Friends' opposition to art came to seem increasingly hidebound, and a more tolerant attitude developed as part of the general reaction against 'drab' Quakerism. An indication of the change is provided by the Birmingham painter and graphic artist Joseph Edward Southall (1861–1944), whose work includes landscapes, portraits of fellow Quakers and figure compositions of pacifist themes. *St Dorothea and her Two Sisters Refusing to Worship the Idol* (1901–2; priv. col.; see fig.) may be read as his defence against possible accusations of idolatry. By 1925 the 'social and spiritual value' of art was officially recognized by Friends, and individual Quakers appeared more frequently as patrons of contemporary art. Through the creation of the Quaker Fellowship of the Arts in 1954 and several subsequent publications, the Society has come to re-examine its own inheritance and to reconcile the artistic impulse and the 'inward light'.

BIBLIOGRAPHY

W. C. Braithwaite: *The Beginnings of Quakerism* (London, 1912, rev. Cambridge, 2/1955)
——: *The Second Period of Quakerism* (London, 1921, rev. Cambridge, 2/1961)
A. Ford: *Edward Hicks: Painter of the Peaceable Kingdom* (Philadelphia, 1952)
H. Lidbetter: *The Friends Meeting House* (York, 1961)
F. J. Nicholson: *Quakers and the Arts* (London, 1968)
J. O. Greenwood: *Signs of Life* (London, 1978)
Joseph Southall, 1861–1944: Artist–craftsman (exh. cat., Birmingham, Mus. & A.G.; London, F.A. Soc.; 1980)
K. C. Barnes: *Integrity in the Arts* (York, 1984)

CHRISTOPHER WAKELING

Fries. German family of artists. Three sons of a prosperous banker and manufacturer in Heidelberg all worked in that city for part of their careers, as well as in Munich, Karlsruhe, Düsseldorf, Geneva and Rome. They were all principally painters, working in a Romantic style, although the eldest, (1) Ernst Fries, was also a lithographer. Wilhelm Fries (*b* Heidelberg, 1819; *d* Konstanz, 29 March 1878) lived in the area of Lake Constance for most of his life and painted landscapes of that region, the Bavarian Alps and northern Italy. The youngest son, (2) Bernhard Fries, was also a landscape painter.

BIBLIOGRAPHY

Heidelberger Maler der Romantik (exh. cat., ed. K. Lohmeyer; Heidelberg, Kurpfälz. Mus., 1919)
K. Lohmeyer: *Heidelberger Maler der Romantik* (Heidelberg, 1935)
A. von Schneider: *Badische Malerei des neunzehnten Jahrhunderts*, Forschungen zur Deutschen Kunstgeschichte, ix (Berlin, 1935, rev. Karlsruhe, 2/1968)
J. C. Jensen: *Aquarelle und Handzeichnungen der deutschen Romantik* (Cologne, 1978)

(1) Ernst Fries (*b* Heidelberg, 22 June 1801; *d* Karlsruhe, 11 Oct 1833). Draughtsman, painter and lithographer. He received his first drawing lessons from the university drawing master in Heidelberg, Friedrich Rottmann (1768–1818), the father of the painter Carl Rottmann. In 1815–18 he studied drawing and watercolour painting in Karlsruhe, landscape and figure drawing at the Akademie in Munich, and optics and perspective in Darmstadt. In about 1817 he started producing lithographs based on his own drawings or on works by other artists. Around 1820 he made his first attempts at oil painting. During the years 1819–23, Fries often went on sketching

trips, alone or with friends, both in the area near his home and further afield, for example in Switzerland. Throughout this period he sought to develop a personal style out of diverse influences: his teachers, his father's collection of Dutch 17th-century works, and the contemporary painters Georg Augustus Wallis (1768–1847), Carl Kuntz and Joseph Anton Koch. Fries's wash drawings reveal a measure of independence in their light touch and free execution, and in the attempt to reproduce light and variety of tone.

Fries spent the years 1823 to 1827 in Italy, where he gradually freed himself from these influences. Under the guidance of Koch in Rome in 1824 and Wallis in Massa di Carrara in 1825, he perfected his oil painting technique. In Rome he also made friends with Ludwig Richter and his circle from Dresden, from whom he learnt much about drawing in landscape, and with the Frenchmen Edouard Bertin and Camille Corot. With Rome as a base, he travelled through the surrounding countryside and extensively to other Italian locations. The watercolour *From the Park of the Villa Chigi in Ariccia* (1824; Karlsruhe, Staatl. Ksthalle) reveals the characteristics of Fries's art, already fully expressed both in drawing and colouring. The foreground is fleetingly indicated, the middle ground precisely drawn and the background gently indicated. In the colouring there is a prevalence of green and brown tones. The later works from this period eventually do away with the pencil underdrawing to become pure watercolours. The paintings of the first years in Italy were certainly carried out with lighter colours, although they adhere to the example of Carl Kuntz in the precision of the execution and the smooth application of paint (e.g. *Landscape in the Latin Mountains*, 1825; Karlsruhe, Staatl. Ksthalle). In 1826 Fries produced a large number of masterly watercolours marked by the predominance of a variety of green tones. The *Pons Augustus near Narni* (Heidelberg, Kurpfälz. Mus.) is also notable for incorporating the translucent effect of the white paper in the colouring. In addition, Fries raised the viewpoint of his landscape scenes, giving them a more emphatic effect of depth. The large drawings also give the impression of space, depth and plasticity by making use of pencils of different hardness and by frequently varying the direction of the hatching (e.g. *Civita Castellana*; Heidelberg, Kurpfälz. Mus.). This highpoint in Fries's work can be traced back to his knowledge of the Italian landscape paintings of French artists, especially Corot.

In spring 1827 Fries returned to Heidelberg, and in 1829 he settled in Munich. He was then appointed court painter to Leopold, Grand Duke of Baden, and moved to Karlsruhe, where he committed suicide. In the smaller paintings of Fries's final period (1827–33), Italian influences persisted, as shown by the predominance of tones of green and brown, pastel colours and the use of light and shade to model the landscape and create a strong sense of plasticity (e.g. *Neuberg Monastery near Heidelberg*, 1828; Heidelberg, Kurpfälz. Mus.). Fries's easel paintings (predominantly commissioned works) generally depicted idealized Italian landscapes, painted in a smooth, conservative manner, for example *Mountain Landscape near Massa di Carrara* (1832; Frankfurt am Main, Städel.

Kstinst. & Städt. Gal.). Fries maintained his high standard in watercolour, although using tones that were rather more subdued.

BIBLIOGRAPHY

C. Gravenkamp: *Ernst Fries, 1801–1833: Sein Leben und seine Kunst* (diss., U. Frankfurt am Main, 1925)

——: 'Ernst Fries: Ein Beitrag zur Bildkunst der Romantik', *Der Cicerone*, xvii (1925), pp. 1069–81

Ernst Fries: Landschaftsmaler aus Heidelberg (exh. cat., ed. K. Lohmeyer and C. Gravenkamp; Heidelberg, Kurpfälz. Mus., 1927)

K. Lohmeyer: *Heidelberger Maler der Romantik* (Heidelberg, 1935), pp. 283–307

S. Wechssler: *Ernst Fries: Gemälde, Aquarelle und Zeichnungen im Besitz des Kurpfälzischen Museums Heidelberg* (Heidelberg, 1974)

E. Bott: *Ernst Fries, 1801–1833: Studien zu seinen Landschaftszeichnungen* (Cologne, 1978)

SIGRID WECHSSLER

(2) (Jacob Daniel Georg Gottlieb) Bernhard Fries

(*b* Heidelberg, 16 May 1820; *d* Munich, 21 May 1879). Painter and draughtsman, brother of (1) Ernst Fries. In his youth he was inspired by the paintings in his father's collection by his elder brother Ernst and by Carl Rottmann and the Scottish painter George Augustus Wallis (1770–1847), who was active for some time in Heidelberg. Bernhard Fries studied figure drawing in Karlsruhe with the Nazarene painter Carl Koopmann (1797–1894), and in 1835 he entered the Akademie der Bildenden Künste in Munich, leaving two years later to pursue landscape painting in Italy, where he stayed intermittently until 1846. He was trained in the traditions of Neo-classicism and Romanticism but developed a greater realism in his work through his study at the Staatliche Kunstakademie, Düsseldorf, from 1840 to 1843 with Johann Wilhelm Schirmer and Andreas Aschenbach (1815–1910). In 1848 Bernhard Fries went to Geneva, due to the political situation in Germany, and became acquainted with Alexandre Calame. As he was a Democrat, Bernhard was banned from Bavaria, and on his return to Germany in 1852 he therefore lived again in Heidelberg, developing a free style in small, intimate landscapes of the region of the Neckar River (e.g. *Farmhouses at Schlierbach*, 1852; Heidelberg, Kurpfälz. Mus.). In 1853–4 he was again in Rome and then moved back to Munich, where, influenced by Rottmann's landscape murals (1830–33) in the arcade of the Hofgarten, he planned and partly executed a series of paintings with Italian views, such as the *Oreto Valley, Palermo* (Munich, Schack-Gal.). Due to the loss of his assets, Fries had to take into account public taste; these works, therefore, are an often unsuccessful combination of fresh impressions of nature and Rottmann's luminism. Fries's later paintings give greater evidence of his own style, combining realistic elements and atmospheric values.

BIBLIOGRAPHY

ADB; *NDB*; Thieme–Becker

Obituary, *Kunstchronik*, xiv (1879), pp. 638–40

F. von Boetticher: *Malerwerke des neunzehnten Jahrhunderts*, i/1 (Leipzig, 1891/*R* 1948), pp. 351–2

Bernhard Fries: Ein Heidelberger und Münchener Maler, 1820–1879 (exh. cat., ed. K. Lohmeyer; Heidelberg, Kurpfälz. Mus., 1922)

R. Pérard: *Bernhard Fries: Ein Maler des Uebergangs im neunzehnten Jahrhundert, in seinem Leben und künstlerischen Werk* (Darmstadt, 1930)

JÖRN BAHNS

Fries, Adriaen de. *See* VRIES, ADRIAEN DE.

Fries, Hans (*b* Fribourg, *c.* 1460–62; *d* ?Berne, after 1518). Swiss painter and draughtsman. The most important painter of religious art in early Renaissance Switzerland, he was a product of the late 15th-century school of the Bernese CARNATION MASTERS (*see* MASTERS, ANONYMOUS, AND MONOGRAMMISTS, §I), a school that operated within the Late Gothic tradition of South Germany. The son of a Fribourg baker and town councillor, Fries presumably trained as a painter in Berne with the 'Carnation Master' Heinrich Bichler (Büchler; *fl* 1466–97). He may well have substantially contributed to Bichler's *Battle of Morat* (1480; ex-Fribourg Town Hall, until 1563). When this picture—commissioned by the town of Fribourg to commemorate a Swiss victory over the Burgundians—was handed over, he was presented with an expensive garment. In 1487–8 and 1497 he is recorded as living in Basle, but he most probably also travelled about during these years, presumably visiting Alsace (Colmar) and almost certainly Augsburg and the Tyrol. His landscape work is influenced by Netherlandish painters, his figure work by Augsburg painters (Hans Holbein the elder and Hans Burgkmair) as well as by Michael Pacher.

From *c.* 1499 Fries was again in Fribourg, where he was paid a salary for ten years from 1501. Most of his surviving works (which are mainly in excellent condition) were produced during this period—painted panels of altar retables for the churches and monasteries in Fribourg, some bearing clear signatures, which suggests the artist's self-assured attitude. Two panels of a small Lady altar from 1501 (Munich, Alte Pin.) show *St Anne with the Virgin and Child*, the *Martyrdom of St Sebastian*, the *Vision of St Bernard* and the *Stigmatization of St Francis*. Also in 1501 Fries started work on panels showing the *Last Judgement*, with the *Resurrection of the Blessed* on the left and the *Descent of the Damned into Hell* on the right (Munich, Alte Pin.). In 1502 he painted, most probably for the church of the Antonites in Berne, a *Christ Collapsing under the Burden of the Cross* (not signed but dated; Berne, Kstmus.). After this, in 1503, come altarwings showing *St Christopher* and a scene from the *Life of St Barbara* (Fribourg, Mus. A. & Hist.) and, of like style and therefore probably period, a winged picture showing the *Adoration of the Magi* (Zurich, Ksthaus). The altarpiece of *St John the Evangelist* (Zurich, Schweiz. Landesmus.; see fig. for left wing, *St John on the Island of Patmos*), a work of great quality, was probably painted *c.* 1505 for St Nicholas (now Fribourg Cathedral). During the same period Fries painted two altar-wings for the church of Attalens near Vevey, showing *St Margaret* and *St Nicholas* (Fribourg, Mus. A. & Hist.), as well as the wings of another altarpiece for St Nicholas (later taken to Bugnon Castle, therefore known as the Bugnon Altar; Fribourg, Mus. A. & Hist.), with the *Acts of Charity* on the two outer panels and, on the inside, the *Dispersion of the Apostles* and the *Descent of the Holy Ghost*. Another of Fries's principal works remains in the Fribourg Franciscan church that commissioned it in 1506; its scenes from the *Life of St Antony of Padua* bring the artist's narrative talent to the fore. The dense series of works from the Fribourg period is concluded by an *Allegory of Christ's Death on the Cross* (ex-Cugy, nr Fribourg; Fribourg, Mus. A. & Hist.).

Hans Fries: *St John on the Island of Patmos*, left wing of the *St John the Evangelist* altarpiece, oil on panel, each panel 1.30×0.31 m, *c.* 1505 (Zurich, Schweizerisches Landesmuseum)

Four drawings supplement the Fribourg series, two signed and two firm attributions. An exact pen-and-wash drawing, probably a design for a stained-glass window (1505; Fribourg, Franciscan church; on dep. Fribourg, Mus. A. & Hist.) depicts *St Clare Carrying a Monstrance*. In contrast to its precision stand three drawings of the *Virgin*, probably of later date, of great skill and intrinsic artistic value. One uses black ink with white highlights on reddish-brown, primed paper (Basle, Kstmus.); the others (Munich, Staatl. Graph. Samml.; Basle, Kstmus.) use pen with sepia wash, and black chalk. Fries also worked as a miniaturist in the illustration of Peter von Molsheim's (*c.* 1420–*c.* 1490) *Chronicle of the Burgundian War* (1478; illustrated by Fries; ed. A. Büchi, Berne, 1914; Fribourg, Bib. Cant. & U.).

In 1509 or 1510 Fries seems to have settled in Berne, where, as in Fribourg, he received substantial commissions. In 1512 he produced the panels of a large Lady altar of which nine sections survive (six, Basle, Kstmus.; two, Nuremberg, Ger. Nmus.; one, Hamburg, Ksthalle). Whereas earlier works had given an impression of immediacy, this work gives an impression of traditionalism. The same applies to the wings of an altarpiece showing *St John the Baptist* and *St John the Evangelist* (1514; Basle, Kstmus.), painted by Fries for the commanders of the Order of St John of Jerusalem in Fribourg.

Like the Basle painter Hans Herbst, Hans Fries stands directly between the Gothic and Renaissance traditions, always inclining towards the traditional rather than the progressive. His work is not free of a certain narrative and popular coarseness—as in the Lady altar of 1512 and the altar of St Antony—yet at the same time he rises to achievements that bear comparison with the paintings of Hans Baldung and Bernhard Strigel (he has much in common with the latter). Fries is masterful in his use of colour and in the compositional techniques by which he sets individual figures and groups in expressive interrelation. The striking use of stance and gesture sometimes (as in the Munich *Stigmatization*) lends his figures an air at once mystical and fanatical. His work is characterized by the use of gold backgrounds or high horizons; the use of light to increase plasticity; by monochrome, sharply coniform rocks, white water surfaces; and above all by the treatment of isolated figures as if they were painted wooden sculptures. This last feature suggests that Fries was familiar with the art of wood-carving—a supposition supported by a wooden statue of *Christ Ascending into Heaven* that is probably by Fries (Fribourg, Mus. A. & Hist.). Fries's small but unified oeuvre marks a solitary climax of Swiss painting of the early 16th century. The great Swiss painters who follow—Hans Leu the younger, Niklaus Manuel and Urs Graf—consistently dissociated themselves from his Late Gothic style.

BIBLIOGRAPHY

Bénézit; *NDB*; *SKL*; Thieme–Becker.

E. His: 'Hans Fries', *Jb. Kstwiss.*, ii (1869), pp. 51–9

A. Kelterborn-Haemmerli (and A. Büchi): *Die Kunst des Hans Fries* (Strasbourg, 1927)

W. Hugelshofer: *Schweizer Handzeichnungen des XV. und XVI. Jahrhunderts*, i of *Die Meisterzeichnung* (Freiburg im Breisgau, 1928), p. 15, pls 9, 10

H. Rott: *Quellen und Forschungen zur südwestdeutschen und schweizerischen Kunstgeschichte im XV. und XVI. Jahrhundert*, iii of *Der Oberrhein, Text* (Stuttgart, 1938), pp. 145–6, 215, 233, 251–2; *Quellen ii (Schweiz)* (Stuttgart, 1936), pp. 44, 242, 278

G. Schmidt and A. M. Cetto: *Schweizer Malerei und Zeichnung im 15. und 16. Jahrhundert* (Basle, n.d. [1940]), pp. 19–22, vii, xx–xxii

E. Dominique and M. Moullet: 'Un Dessin inédit de Hans Fries', *Z. Schweiz. Archäol. & Kstgesch.*, iii (1941), pp. 50–53

P. L. Ganz: 'Der Marienaltar von Hans Fries', *Z. Schweiz. Archäol. & Kstgesch.*, xiii (1952), pp. 103–11

J. Gantner and A. Reinle: *Kunstgeschichte der Schweiz*, iii (Frauenfeld, 1956), pp. 53–6

M. Strub: *Les Monuments d'art et d'histoire du canton de Fribourg*, ii (Basle, 1956), pp. 21, 148–9, 242, 244–5; iii (Basle, 1959), pp. 48–51, 87, 91, 309, 427–9, 434–5

A. Stange: *Kindlers Lexikon der Malerei*, ii (Zurich, 1965); iv, index (Munich, 1967)

Swiss Drawings: Masterpieces of Five Centuries (exh. cat. by W. Hugelshofer, Smithsonian Inst. Trav. Exh. Serv., 1967–8), p. 21

L. H. Wüthrich: *Spätgotische Tafelmalerei: Aus dem schweizerischen Landesmuseum*, 23 (Berne, 1969), pp. 19–20

H. Landolt: *100 Meisterzeichnungen des 15. und 16. Jahrhunderts aus dem Kupferstichkabinett* (Basle, 1972), pp. 36–7, pls 44, 45

M. Roethlisberger: *Schweizer Malerei: Vom Mittelalter bis 1900*, ed. F. Deuchler (Geneva, 1975), pp. 48–50

Niklaus Manuel Deutsch: Maler, Dichter, Staatsmann (exh. cat., ed. C. Menz and H. Wagner; Berne, Kstmus., 1979), pp. 19–21, 57, 61, 205–6 [articles by H. Wagner and W. Hugelshofer]

LUCAS WÜTHRICH

Fries, Moritz, Graf von (*b* Vienna, 6 May 1777; *d* Paris, 26 Dec 1826). Austrian collector, patron and bibliophile. He inherited the estate of his brother Josef von Fries (1765–88); the latter had begun collecting during a tour of Italy (1785–7), where he became friendly with Goethe, who reported that he had often been duped into buying fakes. As a student in Leipzig (1794–7), Moritz von Fries acquired valuable prints and studied the arts. He was an enthusiastic collector and greatly expanded the collection, which was housed in his palace in the Josephplatz in Vienna; the palace was also the site of the Congress of Vienna (1815) and a meeting-place for artists and intellectuals. (For a discussion of the palace and the Fries tomb monument *see* ZAUNER, FRANZ ANTON.) He was also a patron of Ludwig van Beethoven and a business acquaintance of Franz Schubert, as well as an honorary member of the Akademie der Bildenden Künste and one of the original members of the Wiener Musikverein.

His collection included over 16,000 books (mostly large, illustrated works of the 18th century), 300 paintings and 100,000 drawings and prints representing all schools. He particularly sought to collect complete suites of prints, acquiring such works as the projects of Heinrich Füger for the *Messiade* (1740s–1773) of the poet Friedrich Gottlieb Klopstock. The signature of Moritz von Fries's curator—Franz Rechberger—appears on the majority of his drawings and prints, which were mounted on a special yellowish paper known as 'Fries paper'. Although no catalogue of the collection exists, travellers' accounts, reproductive prints and sales catalogues refer to works by such artists as Raphael (portrait of the *Queen of Sicily*), van Dyck (e.g. the *Dead Christ*), Rembrandt (*Vertumnus and Pomona*), Dürer (the *Dying Mary of Burgundy*), Isaack van Ostade (*Winter Landscape*) and Andrea del Sarto (*Virgin and Child*), as well as to those by contemporary Viennese artists; there were also copies of Italian paintings. Moritz von Fries bought paintings abroad as well as in Vienna and commissioned works from such artists as Karl Agricola (1779–1852), Adam Bartsch and Canova. Angelica Kauffman, Johann Baptist Lampi (i), Agricola and Füger are known to have executed portraits of him and his family. In addition to paintings, drawings, prints and books, he collected coins, minerals and antique and contemporary sculpture, including Canova's life-size group *Theseus and Centaur* (1804–19; Vienna, Ksthist. Mus.).

Financial difficulties, followed by the bankruptcy of his firm in 1826, forced Fries to sell his collection privately and publicly in Vienna (Artaria, from 5 April 1824 and 26 April 1826), Amsterdam (Roos & Engelberts, from 21 June 1824; de Vries, from 24 June 1824), London (Christie's, 26 June 1824) and Paris (Henry, Laneuville, 19–20 and 24–27 April 1826). After his death further sales were held in Vienna (e.g. Artaria, from 7 Jan, from 4 Feb and from 3 March 1828). Among the drawings that were sold were eight studies of heads by Raphael. Some of his finest drawings entered the Graphische Sammlung Albertina; 150 were acquired by Thomas Lawrence. Fries's collection of over 22,000 portraits, which Johann Kaspar Lavater had used for his writings on physiognomy, was acquired for the private library of Emperor Francis II (*reg* 1804–35). Among the paintings from his collection were a

portrait of *Martin Schongauer*, attributed to Hans Burgkmair I (Munich, Alte Pin.), Rachel Ruysch's *Still-life with Fruits, Flowers and Insects* (1716; Florence, Pitti; for illustration *see* RUYSCH, RACHEL) and Luca Giordano's *Prometheus* (Vienna, Akad. Bild. Kst.). Other works are in public collections in such cities as Prague and Paris.

BIBLIOGRAPHY
'Zur Geschichte der gräflich Friesschen Gemäldesammlung', *Bl. Gemäldeknd*, iv (1908), pp. 176–80
'Beiträge zur Geschichte der Galerie Fries in Wien', *Bl. Gemäldeknd*, v (1909), pp. 89–91
T. von Frimmel: *Lexikon der Wiener Gemäldesammlungen*, i (Munich, 1913), pp. 408–39
F. Lugt: *Marques* (1921), pp. 535–6

BLKO

Friesz, (Emile) Othon (*b* Le Havre, 6 Feb 1879; *d* Paris, 10 Jan 1949). French painter. He began his training in Le Havre in 1896 under the enlightened teaching of the French painter Charles Lhuillier (1824–99) and continued in Paris under Léon Bonnat until 1904 at the Ecole des Beaux-Arts. In 1903, however, he decided against an academic career and started showing his work at the Salon des Indépendants and, from 1904, at the Salon d'Automne. At this stage he was working in an Impressionist style (for illustration *see* LE HAVRE). Following the emergence of FAUVISM at the infamous Salon d'Automne of 1905 and a painting trip with Georges Braque to Antwerp in 1906, he adopted the bright, anti-naturalistic palette of the Fauves, for example in his *Fernand Fleuret* (1907; Paris, Pompidou). He became closely associated with Matisse, renting a studio in the same building as him in Paris from 1905 to 1908. In the summer of 1907, however, painting with Braque in La Ciotat, in the Midi, Friesz began to turn to the example of Cézanne, seeking to emphasize a strong sense of pictorial construction that he felt had been sacrificed to Fauvism's colouristic excesses. The Arcadian subject-matter of much of his subsequent work up to 1914 was also indebted to Cézanne, especially to his *Bather* compositions, as in *Spring* (1908; Paris, Mus. A. Mod. Ville Paris). Like Cézanne, Friesz was anxious to re-establish connections between contemporary, avant-garde painting and the classical tradition, a quest enhanced by a trip to Italy in 1909, where he was particularly struck by the work of Raphael and Giotto, and by his frequent studies in the Louvre. In 1911 Friesz went to paint in Portugal where, echoing Cézanne's remarks, he said, 'You can see Poussin remade according to nature' (Brielle, p. 14). As a result, despite close connections with the Cubist circle of artists and writers, Friesz never renounced a realistic figurative style.

After World War I, during most of which he undertook studies for aerial camouflage for the War Ministry, Friesz's fame and reputation grew, marked by the publication of a short book on him by André Salmon. Two years later he was instrumental in creating the Salon des Tuileries, an enterprise designed to encourage rapprochement between academic and avant-garde artists. With the award of the Carnegie Institute prize in 1925 and his instatement as Chevalier du Légion d'honneur in 1926, Friesz became a central figure in the French art establishment's tardy acceptance of the avant-garde. In 1926 one of his paintings was hung in the Musée du Luxembourg. Following the publication of an album of reproductions of his works in 1928 and a large one-man show in Paris in 1929, after which his works were bought by museums in Dresden, Grenoble and Stockholm, his status as a major European painter was secure; Raoul Dufy, like Braque an old friend from Le Havre, described him in 1934 as 'the most gifted painter of our generation' (Gauthier, p. 125). Having painted sets for a production of Georges Duhamel's play *La Lumière*, staged in 1912 at the Théâtre de l'Odéon in Paris, from the 1920s he involved himself in private decorative commissions, for example for *Rouen* (Paris, 1929) by André Maurois. These were followed by a tapestry cartoon, *Peace* (oil on canvas, 600×730 mm, see Gauthier, pl. 105), for the Gobelins in 1932 and by a large decorative mural, *The Seine* (3.5×12 m, 1937), for the Palais de Chaillot in Paris. He taught from 1929 at the Académie Scandanive and from 1941 to 1944 at the Académie de la Grande Chaumière, both in Paris, and in 1938 he served on the jury for the Carnegie Institute in Pittsburgh. In 1933 he was made Officier du Légion d'honneur and in 1939 Commandeur du Légion d'honneur. During and after World War II, Friesz continued to paint in Paris, concentrating on still-lifes.

BIBLIOGRAPHY

G. Burgess: 'The Wild Men of Paris', *Archit. Rec.*, xxviii, 5 (1910), pp. 401–14
A. Salmon: *Othon Friesz* (Paris, 1920)
F. Fels: *Propos d'artistes* (Paris, 1925)
F. Fleuret, C. Vildrac and A. Salmon: *Friesz: Oeuvres, 1901–1927* (Paris, 1928)
R. Brielle: *Othon Friesz* (Paris, 1930)
F. Olivier: *Picasso et ses amis* (Paris, 1933)
Retrospective Othon Friesz (exh. cat., Paris, Gal. Charpentier, 1950)
M. Giry: *La Jeunesse d'Othon Friesz* (diss., U. Lyon lettres & droit, 1951)
M. Gauthier: *Othon Friesz* (Paris, 1957)

TOM PARSONS

Frie Udstilling [Dan.: 'Free Exhibition']. Danish association founded in 1891 in Copenhagen as an exhibiting society for progressive young Danish artists in revolt against official state institutions. Founder-members of the Frie Udstilling included its initiator, Theodor Philipsen, Johan Rohde, Jens Ferdinand Willumsen, Vilhelm Hammershøi, Harald Slott-Møller, Agnes Slott-Møller, Joakim Skovgaard, Niels Skovgaard, Kristian Zahrtmann, Peder Severin Krøyer and Julius Paulsen. Although they did not share a common aesthetic, these artists were united in their opposition to the conservative Kongelige Danske Akademi for de Skønne Kunster and its restrictive annual exhibition at the Charlottenborg, and in their promotion of international avant-garde painting.

The first exhibition organized by the association was held in March 1891 at Valdemar Kleis gallery at Vesterbro in Copenhagen. The critic Karl Madsen (1855–1938), a champion of the association, reported the exhibition's success in the radical cultural review *Tilskueren*. The organization moved into a temporary building designed by Thorvald Bindesbøll in the city's Hømarked in 1893, and among its achievements was the inclusion of major works by van Gogh and Gauguin in its exhibition of 1893. The association relocated to its permanent building, designed by Willumsen, in 1898 and moved again in 1914 to its current location, also designed by Willumsen, opposite Østerport station.

For illustration *see* COPENHAGEN, fig. 3.

BIBLIOGRAPHY

K. Madsen: 'Den frie udstilling', *Tilskueren* (April–May 1891), pp. 323–43
Fra den frie udstillings barndom: Festskrift til Franz Wendt (Copenhagen, 1975)
B. Lindwall: 'Artistic Revolution in Nordic Countries', *Northern Light: Realism and Symbolism in Scandinavian Painting, 1880–1910* (exh. cat., ed. K. Varnedoe; New York, Brooklyn Mus., 1982), pp. 35–42
J. F. Willumsen og den frie udstillings første år, 1891–1898 (exh. cat. by L. Krogh, Frederikssund, Willumsens Mus., 1982)
Gauguin og van Gogh i København i 1893 (exh. cat., essay by M. Bodelsen; Copenhagen, Ordrupgaardsaml., 1984)
B. Scavenius: *Den Frie Udstilling for Kunst* (Copenhagen, 1991)

PATRICIA G. BERMAN

Frieze. In the Classical orders of architecture, a horizontal member in an entablature that is above the architrave and below the cornice (*see* ORDERS, ARCHITECTURAL, §I). The word has also come to be used in various contexts for horizontal bands of ornamental or figural decoration.

1. ENTABLATURE FRIEZE. In each of the five Classical orders of architecture the form of the frieze follows fairly strict conventions, with some variation. The Doric frieze (see fig. 1) was an essential part of the Doric order from its earliest development in mainland Greece in the 7th century BC; it is separated from the architrave on which it rests by a narrow projecting strip called the taenia. The frieze itself is composed of alternating triglyphs and metopes. Aligned with each triglyph of a Doric frieze, below the taenia, is a thin horizontal strip, the regula, with a series of small truncated cones, the guttae, on its underside. Above each triglyph and above each metope on the underside of the cornice is a thin slab, a mutule, also carved with guttae (*see also* GREECE, ANCIENT, §II, 1(i)(a)).

Early Greek temples built in stone may have derived their details from earlier buildings of wood, imitating structural elements that were essential in wood but that became decorative details in stone. The frieze area would correspond to the place where the wood beam ends rest on the lintel (the architrave) and support the eaves (the cornice). Triglyphs would represent the beam ends, the metopes the spaces between, faced with plain, sculpted or painted tiles, and the guttae the pegs used to hold the beams in place. Whether the elements derive directly from wood construction or not, the visual effect of a Doric frieze is one of repeated structural modules, sometimes with decoration added in the metopes (for further illustrations *see* THERMON and SELINUS, fig. 2). In many Doric buildings triglyphs were placed one over each column and one over each intercolumniation. At the corners of the building it was necessary to alter the spacing slightly in order to end the sequence with a triglyph and yet evenly distribute the weight of the load above to the column below (*see also* ORDERS ARCHITECTURAL, §I, 2(i)(a)). Sometimes, however, especially in buildings of larger scale, an intercolumniation might accommodate two or three sets of triglyphs and metopes, though one triglyph would still be aligned with each column.

When the Ionic order was developing in the 6th century BC on the west coast of Asia Minor, its entablature had no

1. Outer frieze (Doric) and inner frieze (Panathenaic) from the west entrance of the Parthenon, Athens, 447–432 BC

frieze. Above the architrave were mouldings and a continuous series of projecting blocks called dentils, which created a strong contrast of alternating light and dark beneath a prominent cornice. (Dentils, like triglyphs, might have had a distant connection with the ends of beams in earlier wood structures.) As the Ionic order spread west to mainland Greece and eventually throughout the Greco-Roman world, the area between the architrave and cornice sometimes contained a row of dentils and sometimes a blank frieze. Most commonly, however, Ionic buildings employed a frieze filled with a continuous band of figured relief sculpture as, for example, on the Siphnian Treasury at Delphi (*c.* 525 BC; *see* GREECE, ANCIENT, fig. 53), one of the first Ionic buildings to appear in mainland Greece. The frieze on the Temple of Apollo at BASSAI (*c.* 430–*c.* 400 BC; *see* GREECE, ANCIENT, fig. 41), which depicts an *Amazonomachy*, is exceptional for being on the inside wall of the cella. The visual effect of an Ionic frieze is one of uninterrupted horizontality, which may be enlivened by complex, non-architectonic, sculpted forms.

Entablature friezes became important fields for figured sculpture, thus providing examples of the development of narrative techniques in Greek art. A continuous strip, for example, is ideal for representing processions: one figure after the other, all proceeding in one direction, induce the viewer to follow visually and to participate by walking with the figures in order to see what comes next. A famous example appears on the inner frieze of the Parthenon (fig. 1), where the figures depicted recall the great Athenian festival, the Panathenaic procession. The viewer is drawn to follow the figures, as the procession itself would have moved, from the west end of the building around either

long side and then to the central east door, where the narrative and the actual procession both culminated in the ceremony of providing a new robe for the statue of Athena.

The Corinthian and Composite orders, used prodigiously in Roman architecture, employed an entablature similar to the Ionic, though more varied in treatment, often richer in embellishment and often combined with the use of arches and ressauts (projections of an entablature out from its course to top an unengaged column on a pedestal). The frieze component might be blank, or might be sculpted with decorative features such as garlands or with continuous figural compositions, or might be carved with an inscription, as on the Pantheon in Rome, where the inscription refers to an earlier structure of the late 1st century BC. The Tuscan order, native to the Italian peninsula, might be either friezeless or have a blank or decorated frieze. (For further discussion *see* ROME, ANCIENT, §IV, 1(iv)(b).)

The subsequent history of the entablature frieze is the history of survivals and revivals of Classical architecture. Wherever columns are used and are topped by a flat lintel, there are likely to be elements resembling an architrave, frieze and cornice. This combination of forms has been valued, not only by the ancients but also from the Renaissance to the present, for providing a successful and satisfying balance between strong verticals and repeated but varied horizontals. In medieval architecture horizontals were often marked by string courses or corbel-tables, while in Early Christian architecture columns more often supported arches than lintels, and in Gothic architecture vertical forms were allowed predominance.

2. Frieze from the palace gates at Balawat (detail; h. 270 mm), bronze, mid-9th century BC (London, British Museum)

2. OTHER FRIEZES. The word frieze is commonly used today to describe a horizontal band of ornament in any architectural context, including non-Classical contexts, for example with reference to the bands of figured relief cut into the rock at the Hittite complex of YAZILIKAYA (i), which date from the mid-2nd millennium BC. The word is also used to describe an area over 3 m high that is filled with sculpted ornament across the long width of the Maya Palace of the Governors at UXMAL in Mexico (c. 7th century AD). In addition to relief sculptures, any band of painting or decoration that runs horizontally along a wall, including a stencilled or wallpaper pattern (see WALLPAPER, colour pls IV, fig. 3 and V, fig. 2), may be called a frieze, whether it contains a figural composition or just repeats a simple decorative motif. Horizontal strips of ornament on furniture and other objects, though they are most often referred to by such terms as band ornament or band patterns, may be called friezes if they occur below a projection resembling a cornice, as is often seen in furniture that adopts Classical architectural forms in miniature. The term frieze may also refer to virtually any figural composition in a long horizontal field. Examples of this broad usage include the Assyrian reliefs from the palace gates at Balawat (see fig. 2). These are worked on sheets of bronze that were affixed to wooden doors, and the reliefs would have appeared as numerous horizontal registers, one below the other, depicting scenes of conquest. Another broad application of the term is evident in the expression 'capital frieze' used with reference to sculpture at Chartres Cathedral (see CHARTRES, §I, 2). On the Royal Portal embrasures of the west façade (c. 1160), a series of shaft capitals is carved with figural scenes in deep relief, and their format can be read either as continuous bands that project, recede and turn to follow the complexity of the numerous shafts, or as individual figured capitals lacking rigid boundaries between them.

BIBLIOGRAPHY

W. B. Dinsmoor: *The Architecture of Ancient Greece: An Account of its Historical Development* (London, [1927]/*R* 1950)
B. S. Ridgway: 'Notes on the Development of the Greek Frieze', *Hesperia*, xxxv (1966), pp. 188–204
B. Ashmole: *Architect and Sculptor in Classical Greece* (London, 1972), pp. 116–91

ELMA SANDERS

Frigidarium. *See under* BATH (ii), §1.

Friis, Ewert [Ewerdt] (*b* Bredstedt, 1619; *d* Gävle, 10 Nov 1672). German wood-carver, active in Sweden. He executed pulpits (*c.* 1656) and altarpieces (1669) in the Christina Church in Falun, Dalarna, the Trinity Church in Gävle (1657–62) and the parish church in Askersund, Närke (1660). In the Christina Church Friis was responsible for the tall altarpiece in the choir and for the pulpit, the choir screens (part destr.; painted and gilded 1906) and the organ façade (destr.). The towering altarpiece combines Baroque detailing and a Gothic surge in its proportions, in harmony with the monumental post-Gothic choir in which it stands. It is raised on a socle and divided into four storeys, which diminish in height and width upwards, giving the whole its vertical thrust. In the socle and in the separate storeys are placed central panels with paintings on canvas (from bottom to top): the *Last Supper*, the *Crucifixion*, the *Resurrection*, the *Ascension* and the *Last Judgement*, the depiction of the latter being unique in Sweden. The paintings are framed by ornate columns and statuettes of apostles, evangelists and putti, carved by Friis. The composition culminates in a standing figure of *Christ Carrying the Orbus mundi*. The pulpit is decorated with similar ornamentation and also has low reliefs with scenes from the *Life of Christ*. It was originally carried by a standing angelic atlantid (removed in 1906 to the church museum). The choir screens have slender balusters and carry statuettes of the Virtues, angels' heads and scrolls.

Friis's Baroque scrolls represent his best work, whereas his figure sculptures are a little stiff, notwithstanding a certain Mannerist elegance.

BIBLIOGRAPHY

SVKL

H. Rabén: *Träskulptur och snickarkonst i Uppsverige under renässans och barock* [Wood sculpture and wood-carving art in Upper Sweden during the Renaissance and the Baroque] (Stockholm, 1934)

R. Haupt: 'Ewert Friis aus Holstein', *Nordelbingen*, 13 (1937)

'Kristine kyrka', *Sveriges kyrkor: Dalarna Falun* (Stockholm, 1941)

I. L. Ångström: *Altaravlor i Sverige under renässans och barock: Studier i deras ikonografi och stil, 1527–1686* [Altarpieces in Sweden during the Renaissance and the Baroque: Studies in their iconography and style, 1527–1686] (diss., Stockholm, 1992)

TORBJÖRN FULTON

Friis, Knud (*b* Skanderborg-Stilling, 12 March 1926). Danish architect. In 1957, having worked for C. F. Møller, he established a practice with Elmar Moltke Nielsen (*b* 1924). Friis, one of the few Danish architects to give rise to an identifiable school, had a decisive influence on Danish architecture during the 1960s and 1970s. He combined elements taken from Brutalism and Japanese domestic wooden architecture with traditional Danish components to create robust and exuberant buildings. Among his early family houses was his own in Århus (1958) and the houses at Permelillevej (1962), Århus. To Friis, the interaction of architecture and landscape was vital; in two summer houses at Helgenaes, rusticity is emphasized with rough concrete walls and turf roofs.

Friis's interest in originality of design and concern for the honest use of materials are apparent in the hotels Lakolk on the island of Rømø (1966), Stavreby Forest (1968) near Middelfart, in the education centre Scanticon (1969), Århus, and in Skjoldhøj College (1973). For a series of secondary schools, including those at Risskov (1969), Århus, and Viborg (1974), he developed a school complex in which the traditional school corridors became internal streets and squares used by students in free periods: the buildings are, in effect, small towns. On a larger scale, the headquarters of the Jutland Telephone Company (1971), Århus, were built on the same principle. Friis also planned the further education centres for the Siemens company near Munich (1974) and in Princeton, NJ (1981). He was professor at the School of Architecture in Århus (1967–70) and was made honorary fellow of the American Institute of Architects in 1983.

BIBLIOGRAPHY

'Knud Friis et Elmar Moltke Nielsen: Habitation individuelle à Brabrand, près d'Århus, Danemark', *Archit. Aujourd'hui*, 88–93 (1960), pp. 54–5

'Lakolk Hotel in Rømø Island: Knud Friis and E. Moltke Nielsen, Architects', *Archit. Aujourd'hui*, 134 (1967), pp. 54–9

NILS-OLE LUND

Frink, Dame Elisabeth (*b* Thurlow, Suffolk, 14 Nov 1930; *d* Blandford Forum, Dorset, 18 April 1993). English sculptor and printmaker. She studied at the Guildford School of Art (1946–9) and with Bernard Meadows at the Chelsea School of Art (1949–53). She was linked with the post-war school of British sculptors, including Reg Butler, Bernard Meadows and Eduardo Paolozzi, though her work is distinguished by her commitment to naturalistic forms and themes. Frink's range of subjects included men, birds, dogs, horses and religious motifs. *Bird* (1952;

London, Tate), with its alert, menacing stance, characterizes her early work. She concentrated on bronze outdoor sculpture with a scarred surface created by repeatedly coating an armature with wet plaster; each coating is distressed and broken, eliminating detail and generalizing form. In the 1960s Frink's continuing fascination with flight was evident in a series of falling figures and winged men. While living in France from 1967 to 1970, she began a series of threatening, monumental, goggled male heads. On returning to England, she focused on the male nude, barrel-chested, with mask-like features, attenuated limbs and a pitted surface, for example *Running Man* (1976; Pittsburgh, PA, Carnegie Mus. A.). Frink's sculpture, and her lithographs and etchings created as book illustrations, drew on archetypes expressing masculine strength, struggle and aggression.

BIBLIOGRAPHY

E. Mullins: *The Art of Elisabeth Frink* (Park Ridge, NJ, 1973)

B. Robertson and others: *Elisabeth Frink, Sculpture: Catalogue Raisonné* (Salisbury, 1984)

E. Lucie-Smith: *Frink: A Portrait* (London, 1984)

Elisabeth Frink (exh. cat., London, RA, 1985)

Elisabeth Frink, Sculpture and Drawing, 1950–1990 (exh. cat., Washington, DC, N. Mus. Women A., 1990)

ELISABETH ROARK

Frisch, Johann Christoph (*b* Berlin, 9 Feb 1738; *d* Berlin, 28 Feb 1815). German painter, draughtsman and etcher. He was taught by his father, Ferdinand Helfreich Frisch (1707–58), and by Christian Bernhard Rode (1725–97), supplementing this training by copying pictures in the royal gallery at Sanssouci in Potsdam. He travelled with Jean-Baptiste de Boyer, Marquis d'Argens (1704–71), to Provence and Rome, where from the spring of 1765 he made studies of antiquities and studies after Raphael, Annibale Carracci and Guido Reni. On his return to Berlin in 1768, he undertook commissions mainly for monumental and historical paintings. He executed wall and ceiling paintings in several Potsdam palaces: the Berliner Schloss (1789), the former Niederländisches Palais (before 1779), the Neues Palais (1768, *c.* 1795), the Neue Kammern at Sanssouci (1774) and the Marmorpalais (1790), and in the Schloss auf der Pfaueninsel (*c.* 1796). He also produced easel paintings of mythological and historical subjects primarily relating to Frederick II, King of Prussia, and more than 30 known portraits, among them *Frederick the Great, King Frederick William II*, Prussian ministers and generals, fellow artists and representatives of the Enlightenment, including *Immanuel Kant, Gotthold Ephraim Lessing* and *Moses Mendelssohn*. Many of these paintings are in the Schloss Charlottenburg and Märkisches Museum, Berlin, and the Neues Palais, Potsdam, and drawings for them are in the Kupferstichkabinett, Berlin. Frisch had considerable influence as a teacher at the Berlin Akademie der Künste, being appointed rector in 1786 and director in 1805.

UNPUBLISHED SOURCES

Berlin, Kstbib. & Mus. [E. Berckenhagen: *Die Malerei in Berlin vom 13. bis zum ausgehenden 18. Jahrhundert*, cols 88–93, pls 292, 293, 305, 393, 405, 441, 442, 492]

BIBLIOGRAPHY

NDB; Thieme–Becker

H. Borsch-Supan: *Die Kunst in Brandenburg-Preussen* (Berlin, 1980), nos 98, 140

Friedrich der Grosse (exh. cat., Berlin, Geh. Staatsarchiv Preuss. Kultbes., 1986); iv, nos 12c, 23a; viii, nos 10c, 22c

E. Berckenhagen: 'Johann Christoph Frisch und Friedrich der Grosse', *Die Weltkunst*, lxi (1991), pp. 2200–01, fig. 4

EKHART BERCKENHAGEN

Frisius [de Vries], **Simon (Wynhoutsz.)** (*b* Harlingen, *c.* 1580; *d* The Hague, 1629). Dutch printmaker and merchant. He must have trained in Amsterdam before establishing himself in 1598 as a printmaker in Paris, where his accurate handling of the etching needle in imitation of the engraver's burin proved to be highly suitable for illustrating the books of French calligraphers. He is important for the reintroduction of etching to Holland in the early 17th century. He made prints to illustrate Jan II van de Velde (i)'s *Spieghel der Schrijfkonste* ('Mirror of calligraphy'; Rotterdam, 1605). From 1611 he was in The Hague, where in 1614 he became a member of the Guild of St Luke. His wide-ranging oeuvre comprises 230 or more prints of high quality, mainly etchings. Apart from the calligraphic illustrations there are prints after the early Dutch masters Jan Gossart and Lucas van Leyden, prints of historical subjects, the series of 68 portraits of artists, *Pictorum aliquot celebrium praecipue Germaniae inferioris effigies* (1610), which he produced for the publisher Hendrik I Hondius (ii), as well as topographical views, birds and butterflies and, most importantly, landscapes. Although in two series dated 1611 and 1614 Frisius was still working after the landscape compositions of artists such as Matthijs Bril, whose schematic designs (e.g. *Landscape with Travellers and a Church*) were by then old-fashioned, he had earlier been the first to turn Hendrick Goltzius's innovative drawings of pure landscape (e.g. *Mountainous Landscape*, 1608) into successful graphic reproductions. His 53 etched portraits of the *Counts of Friesland* (1622), in contrast, are still archaic in feel. The estate of Frisius's wife mentioned a painting by him (untraced), while Welcker ascribed a boldly hatched pen drawing of *St Jerome* (1624; Amsterdam, priv. col., see Welcker, 1936, fig. 5) to him on the basis of a presumed signature and date on the verso. Through his business activities, his position as Dutch agent for foreign rulers and his artistic productivity, he built up a large estate, including a considerable amount of property.

BIBLIOGRAPHY

A. J. Welcker: 'Simon Wynhoutsz. Frisius: konstryck plaetsnyder' [Simon Wynhoutsz. Frisius: ingenious engraver], *Oud-Holland*, xliii (1926), pp. 107–11; liii (1936), pp. 219–56

H. Miedema: 'De yllustraerjes fan Simon Frisius foar Winsemius' Chronique', [The illustrations by Simon Frisius for Winsemius's chronique], *It Baeken* [The beacon], xviii (1956), pp. 110–17

——: 'De yllustraejes by de apokrife skiedskriuwing', [The illustrations to the apocryphal stories], *It Baeken* [The beacon], xxii (1960), pp. 60–72

N. M. Orenstein: *Hendrik Hondius (Duffel 1573–The Hague 1650) and the Business of Prints* (New York, 1992)

CHRISTIAAN SCHUCKMAN

Frit. Term used in glass technology to describe a mixture of sand and fluxes heated together to form a semi-vitrified mass as a first stage in the production of glass. This material is then pulverized and may be used in the manufacture of glass or ceramic glazes. The term is also applied to moulded, unglazed, sintered-quartz bodies. At the site of el-Amarna in Egypt cakes of differently coloured frits were found in a workshop of the 14th century BC. Particularly fine frit beads, objects and vessels were produced in ancient Egypt (e.g. London, BM; *see* EGYPT, ANCIENT, §XVI, 5). In a coloured frit the colour runs throughout, whereas in faience (a glazed sintered-quartz body often wrongly described as a frit; *see* ANCIENT NEAR EAST, §II, 5) only the glaze may be coloured. The terms 'glass paste' or '*pâte de verre*' were often applied indiscriminately to frit and opaque glass.

BIBLIOGRAPHY

P. R. S. Moorey: *Materials and Manufacture in Ancient Mesopotamia: The Evidence of Archaeology and Art—Metals and Metalwork, Glazed Materials and Glass*, Brit. Archaeol. Rep., Int. Ser., ccxxxvii (Oxford, 1985)

DOMINIQUE COLLON

Frith, Francis (*b* Chesterfield, Derbys, 1822; *d* Cannes, 25 Feb 1898). English photographer. He is noted for his studies of the Middle East and for establishing the largest photographic publishing firm in the 19th century. He was born into a Quaker family and spent five unrewarding years apprenticed to a cutler in Sheffield, suffering a nervous breakdown in 1843. After two years recuperative travel he became a successful businessman, first in wholesale groceries and later in printing. His involvement with photography began at this time. He was one of the founder-members of the Liverpool Photographic Society in 1853 and he exhibited portraits and landscapes to much critical acclaim.

The sale of Frith's printing firm in 1854 financed the expeditions to Egypt and the Holy Land that were to establish his pre-eminence among early travel photographers. He made three trips between 1856 and 1860. On the first, he sailed up the Nile to the Second Cataract, recording the main historic monuments between Cairo and Abu Simbel. On the second, he struck eastwards to Palestine, visiting Jerusalem, Damascus and other sites associated with the life of Christ. The final expedition was the most ambitious, combining a second visit to the Holy Land with a deeper southward penetration of the Nile. His photographs of the temple at SOLEB, 800 miles south of Cairo, represent a genuinely pioneering achievement (see fig.). Unlike many travel photographers of this period, Frith used the wet collodion process in preference to the more convenient paper-based calotype (*see* PHOTOGRAPHY, §I). Because it involved chemically sensitizing the glass plates on site, this process posed particular problems in a climate dominated by heat, dust and insects. Commenting sardonically on how his chemicals often boiled on contact with the glass, he nevertheless produced negatives that are remarkable for their consistently high technical standard. His equipment included standard full-plate (200×250 mm), mammoth (400×500 mm) and stereoscopic cameras.

Although Frith was not the first European photographer to visit Egypt, his work was wider in its geographical scope and more systematic in its coverage than that of, for example, Maxime Du Camp. Frith photographed most of the key monuments several times, combining general views with close studies of their significant details and broader views of their landscape environment. The clarity

Francis Frith: *Temple of Soleb, Upper Egypt*, wet collodion photograph (New York, Public Library)

of his images proved to be of immense value to archaeologists. The photographs are also often powerfully composed, revealing an understanding of the poetic qualities of light that gives them lasting aesthetic value. Frith's earlier experience as a printer proved useful in the commercial exploitation of his photographs. They were exhibited widely, sold through print dealers and issued in serial form to subscribers. In 1858–60 he published *Egypt and Palestine Photographed and Described by Francis Frith*, the first of a series of magnificent albums containing mounted albumen prints accompanied by letterpress commentaries. In 1862 he also produced a limited edition of *The Queen's Bible*, illustrated with his photographs of the Holy Land. He had set up his own publishing firm in Reigate in 1859 and he specialized in picturesque scenes for the rising tourist market. Travel remained an obsession, but books such as *The Gossiping Photographer at Hastings* (1864) reveal a change of tenor from the heroic Egyptian work. Through his shrewd exploitation of the picture postcard the firm quickly became the largest of its kind in the 19th century. The business remained in the Frith family after his death and was wound up in 1971. Material salvaged from the premises was later reissued as the Francis Frith Collection.

PHOTOGRAPHIC PUBLICATIONS

Egypt and Palestine Photographed and Described by Francis Frith, 2 vols (London, 1858–60)
The Queen's Bible (London and Glasgow, 1862)
The Gossiping Photographer at Hastings (Reigate, 1864)

BIBLIOGRAPHY

B. Jay: *Victorian Cameraman: Francis Frith's Views of Rural England, 1850–1898* (Newton Abbot, 1973)
J. van Haaften: *Egypt and the Holy Land in Historic Photographs* (New York, 1980)
J. Talbot: *Francis Frith* (London, 1985)
D. Wilson: *Francis Frith's Travels: A Photographic Journey through Victorian Britain* (London, 1985)

RAY McKENZIE

Frith, William Powell (*b* Aldfield, nr Ripon, N. Yorks, 9 Jan 1819; *d* St John's Wood, London, 2 Nov 1909). English painter. His parents were in domestic employment before taking a hotel in Harrogate in 1826. They encouraged him to become an artist, despite his own desire to be an auctioneer. While at school in Dover, Frith sketched caricatures and copies of Dutch genre scenes (Dover Mus.) that betray his disposition to narratives. His taste did not accord with the academic training he received at Henry Sass's Academy in London (1835–7) and at the Royal Academy Schools (1837). Frith began his career as a portrait painter, using members of his family as models. He first exhibited at the British Institution in 1838, and during the 1840s he established himself with his entertaining historical and literary subjects in the popular tradition of C. R. Leslie, William Mulready and Sir David Wilkie. He was a member of THE CLIQUE, which included Richard Dadd, Augustus Egg, Henry O'Neil and John Phillip. His friendship with Charles Dickens began with commissions for paintings of *Dolly Varden* (London, V&A) and *Kate Nickleby* (untraced) in 1842.

Frith's first exhibit at the Royal Academy of 1840, *Malvolio before the Countess Olivia* (untraced), was followed by other subjects from Scott, Sterne, Goldsmith, Shakespeare, Dickens and Molière. A scene from Goldsmith, the *Village Pastor* (priv. col., see *A. J.* [London], Aug 1956), clinched Frith's election as ARA in 1845. Some of his more ambitious works in this group, such as *English*

Merrymaking a Hundred Years Ago (exh. RA 1847; oil sketch, London, V&A) and *Coming of Age in the Olden Time* (1849; priv. col., see Strong, pl. vi), show his detailed study of historic costume, furniture and architecture. In 1852 he was elected RA. His mediocre diploma picture, a self-portrait in his studio, known as the *Sleeping Model* (1853; London, RA), underlines the variable quality that characterizes his output.

The few pictures that made Frith's reputation are of contemporary subjects. These started, tentatively, with a picture of a servant girl (*c.* 1853), which was engraved with the saleable title of *Sherry Sir?* Encouraged by his friend John Leech and perhaps stimulated by the example of his *Punch* illustrations, as well as by a visit to Ramsgate in 1851, Frith produced his first ambitious modern-life subject: *Life at the Seaside* (or *Ramsgate Sands*, exh. RA 1854; London, Buckingham Pal., Royal Col.; see fig.). Despite Frith's doubts about attempting a subject never depicted before, it was a great success. Its purchase by Queen Victoria encouraged Frith to produce the equally popular *Derby Day* (exh. RA 1858; London, Tate) and the *Railway Station* (1862; Egham, U. London, Royal Holloway & Bedford New Coll.). Both paintings proved to be successful speculative ventures: Frith received £1500 for *Derby Day* from Jacob Bell and £5250 for the *Railway Station* (including copyright and exhibiting rights) from LOUIS VICTOR FLATLOW, and the sale of engravings from each was to provide far greater sums for the subsequent owners of the copyright, the dealer Ernest Gambart and the printseller Henry Graves. In *Derby Day* Frith painted a representative section of the huge crowd which gathered annually on Epsom Downs, introducing every familiar human type and social class associated with the races; he employed ROBERT HOWLETT to provide photographs on which he based his group studies. He chose Paddington as the setting for his *Railway Station* crowd, incorporating nearly 100 figures. Frith's self-confessed interest in the

city crowd, its physiognomy and expression inspired both subjects. His aptitude for the dramatic grouping of large numbers of people into coherent units, his eye for the anecdotal and his unabashed inclination to appeal to sentiment are all fully exploited and enhanced by his precise technique.

Frith's agreement to paint the *Marriage of the Prince of Wales* (1865; Windsor Castle, Berks, Royal Col.) led to the abandonment, at the sketch stage, of a commission from Gambart to paint the *Times of Day*, a set of three contemporary London scenes including *Morning: Covent Garden, Noon: Regent St* and *Night: The Haymarket* (priv. col.). These sketches and the painting of *Charles II's Last Sunday* (exh. RA 1867; priv. col., see Strong, p. 95) are among the last of Frith's compositions to display the fluent composition and inventiveness of character and incident associated with his best works.

Although Frith's *Salon d'Or, Homburg* (Providence, RI Sch. Des., Mus. A.), a sensation-seeking view of the notorious gambling hall at Homburg, proved a success at the Royal Academy of 1871, the composition is comparatively stiff, and his touch and characterization less precise. These faults are increasingly evident in later works, notably in the *Private View of the Royal Academy, 1881* (exh. RA 1883; priv. col.), where the only interest derives from the inclusion of contemporary characters such as Oscar Wilde and Anthony Trollope.

Frith painted two series of five paintings, the *Road to Ruin* (1878; priv. col., see Lister, pls 16–20) and the *Race for Wealth* (1880; Vadodara, Mus. & Pict. Gal.), which depict the contemporary vices of gambling and dishonest speculation, respectively. The format enabled Frith to circumvent the difficulties intrinsic to large-scale composition, but despite their popularity these scenes inevitably lack the dramatic interest that Frith had previously focused into a single powerful image. Frith's homespun and transparently opportunist moralizing was out of date and

William Powell Frith: *Life at the Seaside* (or *Ramsgate Sands*), oil on canvas, 0.76×1.53 m, 1854 (London, Buckingham Palace)

lacked the satirical sting that Hogarth had injected into his works on similar themes.

Frith retired as an RA in 1890 but continued to exhibit until 1902. His greatest success in later life came from his books, *Autobiography and Reminiscences* (1887) and *Further Reminiscences* (1888), in which he showed himself as much a literary as an artistic raconteur, and in which he assessed his career with winning modesty and irony. Other writings include *John Leech: His Life and Work* (1891) and articles in which he invariably voiced his protests against all modern developments in art.

UNPUBLISHED SOURCES
London, V&A [corr.]

WRITINGS
Autobiography and Reminiscences, 2 vols (London, 1887)
'Crazes in Art', *Mag. A.*, xi (1888), pp. 187–91
Further Reminiscences (London, 1888)
John Leech: His Life and Work, 2 vols (London, 1891)

BIBLIOGRAPHY
'British Artists: xvii, W. P. Frith', *A. J.* [London] (1856), p. 237
T. Taylor: *The Railway Station Painted by W. P. Frith, Esq.* (London, 1862)
W. W. Fenn: 'William Powell Frith, RA', *Mag. A.* (1880), p. 82
H. Quilter: *Preferences in Art* (London, 1892)
W. Frith: 'A Talk with my Father', *Cornhill Mag.* (May 1906), pp. 597–607
——: 'Small Talk with my Father', *Cornhill Mag.* (Dec 1907), pp. 802–10
Obituary, *The Times* (3 Nov 1909)
An Exhibition of Paintings by W. P. Frith, RA, 1819–1909 (exh. cat. by J. Mayne, London, Whitechapel A.G., 1951)
R. Lister: *Victorian Narrative Paintings* (London, 1966)
J. Maas: *The Prince of Wales's Wedding: The Story of a Picture* (London, 1977)
R. Strong: *When Did you Last See your Father?* (London, 1978), pp. 90–95
Great Victorian Pictures (exh. cat. by R. Treble, ACGB, 1978)
J. Chapel: *Victorian Taste* (London, 1982)
M. C. Cowling: *The Artist as Anthropologist: The Representation of Type and Character in Victorian Art* (Cambridge, 1989)

MARY COWLING

Fritsch, Elizabeth (*b* Whitchurch, Salop, 11 Sept 1940). Welsh potter. She studied harp and piano at the Royal Academy of Music, London (1958–64), but inclined towards the plastic arts and in 1968 took a three-year course at the Royal College of Art, under Hans Coper. She worked at the Bing & Grøndahl factory (now merged with the Royal Porcelain Factory), Copenhagen (1972–3). The Crafts Advisory Council/British Council, London, organized her first solo exhibition in 1974 since when her work has been shown extensively in Britain, Europe and Japan. Her stoneware, earthenware and porcelain pots are coil built, then scraped and smoothed and painted with softly coloured slip in geometric designs inspired by musical rhythms and notation ('Saxophone and Piano Duo', 1978; London, V&A) and influenced by Pre-Columbian and African art. Although her pots are vessels, they are not functional. Early pots were designed to be picked up and held in the hand; more recent ones are meant to be viewed from one or two angles like abstract still-lifes. For an example of her stoneware pots, *see* ENGLAND, fig. 67.

BIBLIOGRAPHY
P. Dormer: *Elizabeth Fritsch in Studio* (London, 1985)
——: *The New Ceramics: Trends and Traditions* (London, 1986, 3/1989)
Elizabeth Fritsch: Vessels from Another World (exh. cat.; London, Crafts Council, 1993)

Fritsch, Theodor (*b* 1853; *d* 1933). German writer and political theorist. He first came to prominence in Germany as the author of nationalist and anti-Semitic propaganda. His *Handbuch der Judenfrage*, first published in 1887, reached 29 editions by 1923 and 49 editions by 1944. In 1896 he published *Die Stadt der Zukunft*. Although it received little attention at the time in Germany, Fritsch's plan is notable for anticipating by two years the publication of Ebenezer Howard's first Garden City tract: *Tomorrow: A Peaceful Path to Real Reform*. While it is unlikely that Howard knew of Fritsch's proposal, the two schemes have several features in common. Both are based on circular plans subdivided by radial axes and ring roads. In both cases the centre of the town is devoted to public and commercial functions, with housing running away from the centre in concentric bands, according to a declining scale of status. The cheapest housing is located on the periphery of both towns, flanked by a band of factories and workshops. In contrast to Howard's scheme, however, half of Fritsch's circular plan is designated as parkland. This reflects Fritsch's ultra-conservative political standpoint, which admitted that cities were essential to a modern, industrial society, but insisted that the true course of all social and moral values remained the land. In his city plan Fritsch incorporated many genuinely novel concepts, including superblocks with communal gardens and playgrounds, split-level circulation, underground service tubes carrying gas, electricity, water, sewage and pneumatic postal services, and satellite industrial estates. He did not develop these ideas further, however, and devoted his later years to writing virulent anti-Semitic propaganda.

WRITINGS
Die Stadt der Zukunft (Leipzig, 1896)

BIBLIOGRAPHY
K. Bergmann: *Agrarromantik und Grosstadtfeindschaft* (Meisenheim am Glan, 1970)
K. Hartmann: *Deutsche Gartenstadtbewegung: Kulturpolitik und Gesellschaftsreform* (Munich, 1976)

IAIN BOYD WHYTE

Frizzoni, Gustavo (*b* Bergamo, 11 Aug 1840; *d* Milan, 10 Feb 1919). Italian art historian. His family was of Swiss Protestant origin and had collected paintings for generations. His parents, Giovanni Frizzoni (1805–49) and Clementina Reichmann (1815–1904), were connoisseurs and collectors. His elder brother Teodoro shared undergraduate lodgings with Jacob Burckhardt and was a celebrated philanthropist, while his uncle Federico Frizzoni (1807–93) owned the outstanding Frizzoni-Salis collection, housed in his family villa at Bellagio. Giovanni Morelli became Gustavo's mentor and was responsible for his art historical education. Despite his extreme modesty and his devotion to Morelli's ideas and methods, Gustavo's writings have an independent viewpoint, as exemplified in his collected essays, *Arte italiana del Rinascimento*. He made significant contributions to the literature on Baldassare Peruzzi and the Lombard followers of Leonardo da Vinci, and to the study of Venetian painting with his excellent edition of Marcantonio Michiel's *Notizie d'opere di disegno* (Bologna, 1884). He was an impeccable connoisseur with a truly discerning eye, and was much concerned with the formation and installation of national European collections. One of his best articles (much indebted to the manuscripts he inherited from Morelli, as were other of his later writings) is his account of the Italian paintings in the National Gallery, London. He knew many Italian restorers, especially Giuseppe Molteni and Luigi Cavenaghi, and his experience of their work makes his writing an important source on the early condition of works of art and their provenances. He was an active trustee of the Poldi Pezzoli Museum at Milan and of Morelli's collection in the Accademia Carrara, Bergamo. On his death his library and collection of photographs went to the Accademia di Brera, Milan.

WRITINGS

Collezione di quaranta disegni scelti della raccolta del Senatore Giovanni Morelli (Milan, 1886)
Arte italiana del rinascimento: Saggi critici (Milan, 1891)
G. Morelli, ed.: *Kunstkritische Studien über italienische Malerei: Die Galerie zu Berlin* (Leipzig, 1893) [incl. his account of Morelli's life, pp. xi–lxiii]

BIBLIOGRAPHY

A. Locatelli-Milesi: 'Gustavo Frizzoni: Vita e bibliografia', *Boll. Civ. Bib. Bergamo*, xviii (1924), pp. 135–45
M. C. Rodeschini Galati: 'La dispersione della collezione Morelli', *I disegni della collezione Morelli*, ed. G. Bora (Bergamo, 1988), pp. 21–30

JAYNIE ANDERSON

Frølich, Lorenz (*b* Copenhagen, 25 Oct 1820; *d* Hellerup, 25 Oct 1908). Danish painter and draughtsman. He studied drawing under Martinus Rørbye and painting under Christen Købke and C. W. Eckersberg, also visiting the studio of Thomas Couture in Paris (1852–3). He travelled extensively abroad, living in Germany (1845–6), Italy (1846–51) and Paris (1851–75), also spending time in Denmark (1854–7) and London (1870–71). The various European artistic trends he encountered, ranging from German Romanticism and French *plein-air* and Salon painting (a rare combination) to English Pre-Raphaelitism, all combined with his Danish Golden Age background to produce a truly eclectic spirit. Frølich's best work is in the graphic arts. Among his most important illustrations are those for Adam Fabricius's *Danmarks historie, I* (Copenhagen, 1854), P. J. Stahl's *La Journée de Mademoiselle Lili* (Paris, 1862) and Hans Christian Andersen's fairy tales, in a three-volume edition entitled *Nye eventyr og historier* (Copenhagen, 1870–74); his illustrations for Musaeus's *The Loves of Hero and Leander*, intended to accompany Edmond FitzGerald's translation (1859), were partly published as a separate book, *Hero og Leander* (Copenhagen, 1899). His ability to capture children in movement made him a congenial children's book illustrator, although he was criticized for the satirical strain in his interpretation of Andersen. In his work on Classical subjects he was influenced by Greek vase painting, the reliefs of Bertel Thorvaldsen and Herman Wilhelm Bissen, as well as the drawings of Asmus Jakob Carstens and John Flaxman. He was commissioned to paint two large canvases to decorate the Court of Appeal in Flensburg: *Valdemar II Giving the Jutlandic Law in Vordingborg 1240* (Flensburg, Landgericht) and *Frederick IV Receiving the Oath of Allegiance by the Estates of the Realm in Gottorp 1721* (1854–7; Kiel, Landesgesch. Samml. der Schleswig-Holsteinischen Landesbib.). Among his best paintings, however, are his landscapes from the woods of Fontainebleau, such as *From Fontainebleau* (1859; Copenhagen, Ny Carlsberg Glyp.), in which the intensity of colour shows the effects

of *plein-air* painting. He also executed designs for furniture, and in his later years took up pottery under Jens Ferdinand Willumsen.

WRITINGS

F. Hendriksen, ed.: *Lorenz Frølich, 1820–25. Oktober–1920: Egne optegnelser og breve til og fra hans slægt og ungdomsvenner* [His own reminiscences and letters to and from relatives and friends of youth], 2 vols (Copenhagen, 1920–21)

BIBLIOGRAPHY

Lorenz Frølich: Tegninger og illustrationer [Drawings and illustrations] (exh. cat., ed. H. Westergaard; Copenhagen, Thorvaldsens Mus., 1968)
Lorenz Frølich, 1820–1908: Malerier, møbler, tegninger, grafik [Paintings, furniture, drawings, graphic work] (exh. cat., ed. H. Westergaard; Copenhagen, Stat. Mus. Kst, 1971)

JENS PETER MUNK

Frölicher, Otto (*b* Solothurn, 5 June 1840; *d* Munich, 2 Nov 1890). Swiss painter. He was taught drawing at school by Gaudenz Taverna (1814–78), and in 1859 he went to Munich to study with the landscape painter Johann Gottfried Steffan. He moved to Düsseldorf to study under Oswald Achenbach from 1863 to 1865. After a period in Switzerland he returned to Munich at the end of 1869. He was interested in both Dutch landscapes of the 17th century and contemporary French painting, and the influence of Jacob van Ruisdael, Meindert Hobbema and the Barbizon painters, such as Jules Dupré and Charles-François Daubigny, can be seen in his views of the open landscape around the city. Agitated cloudy skies over a deep horizon as in *Landscape with Tree* (*c.* 1877–8; Aarau, Aargau. Ksthaus) are characteristic of his painting at this time. He was a friend of Hans Thoma, Adolf Bayersdorfer (1842–1901) and the Swiss painter Adolf Stäbli (1842–1901) and was involved with the group of artists around the landscape painter Adolf Lier (1826–82), who were all influenced by French work. In 1876 he stayed with Dupré in Paris, and in the summer of 1877 he visited Barbizon, which made a strong impression on him. The detailed and distinct naturalistic style of his earlier paintings gave way to a softer manner of depicting forms. His atmospheric studio compositions such as *Early Spring* (1890; Solothurn, Kstmus.) were based on *plein-air* studies consisting of small oil sketches in which he established colours and spatial relations.

BIBLIOGRAPHY

H. Uhde-Bernays: *Otto Frölicher: Sein Leben und Werk* (Basle, 1922)
G. Wälchli: *Otto Frölicher* (Solothurn, 1950)

SEPP KERN

Froment(-Delormel), (Jacques-Victor-)Eugène (*b* Paris, 17 June 1820; *d* Paris, 1 March 1900). French painter, designer and printmaker. He was a pupil of Jules Jollivet, Pierre Lecomte and Eugène-Ammanuel Amaury-Duval, for whom he also acted as executor. From 1857 to 1885 he worked mainly as a designer for the Sèvres manufactory. He exhibited regularly at the Paris Salon from 1842 to 1880; from 1864 he could exhibit his works at the Salon without having to undergo selection by the jury. Heavily influenced by the style of Ingres's pupils, and especially Amaury-Duval, Froment painted a *Virgin* (1846; Autun, St Jean) that recalls the contemporary work of Ingres for the stained-glass windows in the chapel of St Ferdinand at Dreux. In the same year he painted *St Peter*

Healing a Lame Man at the Door of the Temple in the church at Pégomas.

Froment's genre scenes, with their pleasant, decorative symbolism, are often close to the works of Jean-Léon Gérôme and Jean-Louis Hamon, or his friend Henri-Pierre Picou (1824–95). He did many engravings to illustrate such works as Louis Ratisbonne's *La Comédie enfantine* (Paris, 1860) and Victor Hugo's *Livre des mères* (Paris, 1861). He also did some mural decorations in the chapel of St Joseph in Autun Cathedral, as well as decorating the chapel of St Martin-les-Autun at the seminary at Autun, in collaboration with Alfred de Curzon, in 1855–6.

BIBLIOGRAPHY

J. Rerolle: 'Eugène Froment: Artiste peintre, sa vie, son oeuvre', *Mém. Soc. Eduenne*, xxviii (1900), pp. 339–47

La Tradition d'Ingres à Autun (exh. cat. by G. Vuillemot, Autun, Mus. Rolin, 1971)

G. Vuillemot: 'Carnets d'Eugène Froment et album romain d'Amaury-Duval', *Rev. Louvre*, 6 (1972), pp. 497–8

A. DAGUERRE DE HUREAUX

Froment, Nicolas (*fl c.* 1460; *d* before 23 Dec 1484). French painter and draughtsman. Although first mentioned in Uzès (Languedoc) in 1465, he probably originated from Artois or Picardy, where he acquired his early training, subsequently working in the southern Netherlands. His first documented work, signed and dated 18 May 1461, is a triptych of the *Raising of Lazarus* (Florence, Uffizi). Executed on oak panels, it is distinctive for its grimacing, gesticulating figures and intense realism (e.g. the prominent fly on the tablecloth). It is painted in a style largely dependent on Rogier van der Weyden and Dieric Bouts, but also on the illuminator Loyset Liédet and other artists at the court of Burgundy whose work was of a graphic nature. The figure at the far left in the central panel may be a self-portrait of Froment. The altarpiece was commissioned by Francesco Coppini, Bishop of Terni and Papal Legate, who is depicted on the exterior of the wings praying to the Virgin. The prelate, who was recorded in the southern Netherlands in 1459–62, probably ordered the triptych as a political gift for Cosimo de' Medici. The latter, in turn, presented the work in 1462–3 to the Franciscan convent of Bosco ai Frati, Mugello. To Froment's period in the southern Netherlands have also been ascribed, in collaboration with Jacques Daret of Tournai, cartoons for tapestries produced in 1460 for Guillaume de Hellande, Bishop of Beauvais (Beauvais Cathedral; Boston, MA, Mus. F.A.; Paris, Mus. Cluny). Attributable to Froment and in a related style are a *Mourning Virgin*, a fragment on oak of a larger panel (USA, priv. col.), and a drawing with the upper part of a *Transfiguration* (Berlin, Kupferstichkab.).

In 1462–5 Froment settled in Provence, as did several other contemporary northern artists. He was in Avignon in February 1468 and by January 1474 had purchased several properties, no doubt a measure of his success. In 1470 he was commissioned by Catherine Spifami, widow of Laugier Guiran, to paint an altarpiece (untraced) of the *Death of the Virgin with SS Mary Magdalene and Catherine*, with donors on the wings, for a chapel appended to Notre-Dame-de-Consolation in Aix-en-Provence. Around that time Froment probably also painted the *Martyrdom of St*

Mitre (Aix-en-Provence, St Sauveur). It was commissioned by Mitre de la Roque, a merchant, for his funerary chapel. Roque figures in the foreground with his wife and their (probably added) children. The work shows a new concern for space as well as an increased interest in monumentality (especially the executioner). In 1471–2, on commission of the spice merchant Pierre Marin, Froment produced a window of the *Annunciation* for the choir of St Pierre at Avignon. In 1473 he designed the embroideries for the uniforms of Avignon's couriers and props for *tableaux*, including the *Temple of Jerusalem*, erected for the entry of the papal governor, Charles II of Bourbon. In 1476 Froment painted 204 shields that included the arms of the Papal Legate Giuliano della Rovere. The following year the city ordered from the artist 14 'échafauds' for the feast of Corpus Christi, including scenes of the *Temptation of Christ*, the *Annunciation* and the *Story of Gideon*.

Froment was soon noticed by René I, Duke of Anjou, who used his services regularly in 1475–9. At times the artist is referred to as 'peintre du roy de Secille', although he did not draw a steady stipend but was remunerated project by project. Froment was again in Aix-en-Provence, where he produced his major work, the triptych of the *Burning Bush*, for which he received final payment in 1476. Until 1794 the altarpiece was on the altar of a chapel in the Carmelite church in Aix-en-Provence, which was planned as the burial site for René's entrails; after 1804 the triptych was transferred to the city's cathedral. The central panel depicts the *Annunciation to Joachim*. In the upper field the Virgin appears in the burning bush (depicted as a pyracantha, a species native to Provence), an association, apparently formulated by René himself, of Moses's vision with the Immaculate Conception. On the inner wings are vivid portraits of *René* and his second wife *Joanna of Laval* as orants. Froment here reassessed his Netherlandish training, increasing the monumental and solemn effects and including a panoramic landscape and, on the outer wings, *trompe-l'oeil* grisaille sculpture (see fig.) developed by van der Weyden.

In 1477 Froment was paid by René for 'certain paintings which the said lord had devised' and was employed in the new residence that the Duke had purchased and considerably enlarged in Avignon. From that summer until November, Froment executed with his helper a wall painting in the main gallery showing a naval battle between Turks and Christians; he later painted the arms of René and Joanna in the spandrels of the portal. In 1477 Froment also painted a lance and plate armour for a horse. In September 1478 he enlivened a banner for the trumpet of the court minstrels and in October painted an *Annunciation*, for which he received only the modest sum of 3 écus. In January 1479 Froment was responsible for glass panes brought from Lyon, for shields with the arms of Joanna, and for other decorative works. In the autumn he produced 'draps de paincture'—painted linen that resembled tapestries. The portraits of *René of Anjou* and *Joanna of Laval* on the Matheron Diptych (poplar; Paris, Louvre) are so close to those on the *Burning Bush* altarpiece that the work must be by Froment and date to *c.* 1479, since the Duke is depicted as older. The last mention of Froment in René's accounts is in November 1479; the Duke died in the following year.

Nicolas Froment: *Annunciation*, exterior wings of the triptych of the *Burning Bush*, oil on panel, 410×305 mm, completed 1476 (Aix-en-Provence, St Sauveur Cathedral)

In 1481–2 Froment, with the painter Thomas Grabuset, received commissions from the Avignon municipality related to another processional entry of Giuliano della Rovere: shields and *tableaux* of the *Triumph of King Arthur* with nymphs, zodiacal signs, a monkey and a fountain. Froment is referred to on 21 March 1483 as 'peintre emina[nt]' in the records of Paulet Heydini, treasurer of grain in Avignon, but is mentioned as no longer alive by 23 December 1484, when one of his former properties changed hands. Froment is primarily considered a master of the realist tendency in Avignon. His influence has been noted both in the south Netherlands (e.g. the Master of the View of St Gudule) and in Provençal painting, primarily in the altarpiece of the Pérussis family (New York, Met.), painted in 1480 for the charterhouse of Bonpas.

BIBLIOGRAPHY
L.-H. Labande: 'Notes sur quelques primitifs de Provence, II: Nicolas Froment', *Gaz. B.-A.*, 6 ser. ix (1933), pp. 85–103
M. Spears Grayson: 'The Northern Origin of Nicolas Froment's *Resurrection of Lazarus* Altarpiece in the Uffizi Gallery', *A. Bull.*, lviii (1976), pp. 350–57
C. Sterling: 'Nicolas Froment, peintre du nord de la France', *Etudes d'art médiéval offertes à Louis Grodecki* (Paris, 1981), pp. 325–36
M. Laclotte and D. Thiébaut: *L'Ecole d'Avignon* (Paris, 1983)
F. Joubert: 'Jacques Daret et Nicolas Froment: Cartonniers de tapisseries', *Rev. A.* [Paris], 88 (1990), pp. 39–47
C. Sterling: 'Tableaux français inédits: Provence', *L'Oeil*, 425 (Dec 1990), pp. 46–53

PATRICK M. DE WINTER

Fromentin, Eugène(-Samuel-Auguste) (*b* La Rochelle, 24 Oct 1820; *d* Saint-Maurice, 27 Aug 1876). French painter and writer. The wide skies and sweeping plains of his native Charente region left him with a love of natural beauty for which he later found affinities in Algeria and the Netherlands. From his youth he showed academic intelligence, literary talent and artistic aptitude. In 1839 he was sent to Paris to study law, but he became increasingly interested in drawing. Although his father, a skilled amateur artist who had studied with Jean-Victor Bertin, never became reconciled to his son's desire to pursue painting as a career, Fromentin was sent to study with the Neo-classical landscape painter Jean-Charles-Joseph Rémond (1795–1875); however, he preferred the more naturalistic Nicolas-Louis Cabat. Fromentin developed slowly as an artist and began to show real promise as a landscape draughtsman only in the early to mid-1840s. He published his first important piece of criticism on the Salon of 1845.

From 3 March to 18 April 1846, Fromentin made a secret visit to Algeria, to attend the wedding of the sister of the painter Charles Labbé (*fl* 1836–85). The following year he made his debut in the Salon, showing a view of the countryside near La Rochelle (England, priv. col.) and two Algerian scenes, which herald his lifelong devotion to Eastern subjects. He returned to Algeria twice for longer stays (24 September 1847 to 23 May 1848, 5 November 1852 to 5 October 1853). Between these journeys he began to establish himself as an Orientalist, exhibiting 11 Algerian works in the 1850–51 Salon. He also made a lively but abortive effort to paint Provençal peasants on his honeymoon in 1852. Fromentin used the notes and sketches made on his second and third Algerian visits not only in paintings but also in his two travel books, *Un Eté dans le Sahara* (1857) and *Une Année dans le Sahel* (1859). His twin talents significantly enhanced his critical renown, and he became acknowledged as a leading Orientalist. At the Salon of 1859 he received a first-class medal and the Légion d'honneur, as well as praise from such avant-garde critics as Baudelaire and the young Degas.

During the 1860s Fromentin achieved considerable success. In 1863 he published his only novel, *Dominique*, in which the doomed love of the eponymous hero for a married woman reflects events in the author's own youth. The vigorous rough impasto of his early Algerian paintings, inspired by Decamps, Diaz and Marilhat, and expressing his immediate excitement, was replaced with the softer mature style of his most familar works, in which the filtering process of memory combined with his increasing technical facility. However, Fromentin was not satisfied with his successful pictorial synthesis and, in the late 1860s, made several attempts first to inject greater drama into his work, then to alter his subject-matter. *Oriental Battle Incident* (1867; Dublin, N.G.), *Land of Thirst* (*c.* 1869, Paris, Mus. d'Orsay) and *Fantasia* (1869; Poitiers, Mus. B.-A.) all have antecedents in his own travel-books a decade earlier; but in both painting and writing Fromentin's strength lay in the still evocation of place and atmosphere rather than in the representation of action. A series of centaur paintings of 1868, inspired by a decorative commission for Prince Paul Demidov's Hôtel Païva in Paris, was greeted with critical incredulity. Fromentin subsequently shifted to painting scenes in Venice and then in Egypt, where he was invited as part of the French delegation for the opening of the Suez Canal. Lack of critical or popular enthusiasm persuaded him to return to the subjects that had made him famous. At the 1874 Salon he exhibited two accomplished works, both entitled *Algeria Remembered* (Dublin, N.G.; Kansas City, MO, Nelson–Atkins Mus. A.).

In 1875 Fromentin made his only trip to the Low Countries, for whose art he had always felt deep empathy. The following year he published *Les Maîtres d'autrefois*, an eloquent and involved visual examination of Flemish and Dutch painting. Fromentin neglected areas then out of fashion, such as early Netherlandish art and Vermeer, concentrating on the 17th century, to which he brought the technical knowledge of a painter and an extremely refined critical intelligence. Influenced by the philosophy of Hippolyte Taine, he sought to relate the achievements of Dutch artists to their way of life and surrounding landscape, although he was equally receptive to the intangible power of Rembrandt's portraits. In 1876 Fromentin exhibited at the Salon two pictures inspired by his trip to Egypt and wrote an anonymous critique of the 1876 Salon, which was published in *Bibliothèque universelle et revue suisse* in Lausanne. He died suddenly the same year from cutaneous anthrax.

The discernment that informed Fromentin's criticism often had a crippling effect on his own art, and his letters poignantly document his self-conscious struggle with a double muse. Fromentin's refined critical sense and his high classical ideals caused him to adjudge his own pictorial efforts a failure; but his romantic persistence in the struggle to produce significant work marks him out as an interesting figure. Like Gustave Moreau and Puvis de Chavannes, Fromentin was an enlightened, established artist, who did not fit the stereotyped repressive academic mould and who was just as opposed as the radical Impressionists to the Salon norms of slick finish and anecdotal content.

WRITINGS
Les Maîtres d'autrefois (Paris, 1876; Eng. trans., Boston, 1882; London, 1913)
P. Blanchon, ed.: *Eugène Fromentin: Lettres de jeunesse* (Paris, 1909)
——: *Eugène Fromentin: Correspondance et fragments inédits* (Paris, 1912)
B. Wright and P. Moisy, eds: *Gustave Moreau et Eugène Fromentin: Documents inédits* (La Rochelle, 1972)
G. Sagnes: *Eugène Fromentin: Oeuvres complètes* (Paris, 1984)
B. Wright, ed.: *Fromentin: Correspondance générale* (in preparation)

BIBLIOGRAPHY
L. Gonse: *Eugène Fromentin: Peintre et écrivain* (Paris, 1881; Eng. trans., Boston, 1883)
P. Dorbec: *Eugène Fromentin* (Paris, 1926)
Fromentin: Le Peintre et l'écrivain, 1820–1876 (exh. cat., La Rochelle, Mus. B.-A., 1970)
B. Wright: *Eugène Fromentin: A Bibliography* (London, 1973)
J. Thompson and B. Wright: *La Vie et l'oeuvre d'Eugène Fromentin* (Paris, 1987)

JAMES THOMPSON

Fromiller, Josef Ferdinand (*b* Oberdrauburg, 1693; *d* Klagenfurt, 9 Dec 1760). Austrian painter, draughtsman and printmaker. After a short apprenticeship with his father, he trained from 1708 to 1713 under Ferdinand Stainer (*d* 1725). In 1716 he completed his first major work as a fresco painter in Schloss Trabuschgen in Obervellach. In 1733 he was appointed a 'landscape painter of Carinthia'; this enabled him to secure all the major commissions in the province, where he worked almost exclusively. From 1740 he worked on frescoes depicting historical scenes in the Landhaus in Klagenfurt and in the former Stiftkirche Maria Himmelfahrt at Ossiach, as well as on numerous altarpieces in churches and monasteries throughout the province—for example *St Nicholas in Glory* (*c.* 1747; Strassburg im Gurktal, S Nikolaus). Fromiller was chiefly influenced by artists of the 16th and 17th centuries, such as Titian and Veronese, Annibale Carracci, Carlo Maratti, Pietro Testa, Andrea Pozzo, Simon Vouet and Rubens. Lacking both an academic training and the travel in Italy usual for artists at this time, he probably became familiar with major works of late Renaissance and Baroque art through prints. He was little influenced by his contemporaries, although he undertook a careful study of works by Johann Georg Bergmüller. From 1750 onwards he devoted himself increasingly to still-life and genre paintings. He also produced over 300 drawings and prints.

BIBLIOGRAPHY
H. Thaler: *Josef Ferdinand Fromiller, 1693–1760: Ein Beitrag zur Barockmalerei in Kärnten* (diss., U. Vienna, 1978)
——: 'Die Arbeiten Josef Ferdinand Fromillers im grossen und im kleinen Wappensaal des Klagenfurter Landhauses', *Österreich. Z. Kst & Dkmlpf.*, xxxv (1981), pp. 115–24

HERFRIED THALER

Frómista, S Martín. Former Benedictine monastery in Palencia province, Castile, Spain. It was founded before 1066 by Doña Mayor, Condesa de Castilla and widow of Sancho the Great of Navarre. Through St Zoil of Carrión, the monastery became affiliated to the Cluniac Order in 1118. The church was begun before 1090 and is an early example of Romanesque on the pilgrimage route to Santiago de Compostela. It has an aisled and barrel-vaulted nave with an octagonal lantern tower, transepts and three eastern apses; the façade is flanked by a pair of circular towers. It was drastically restored at the beginning of the 20th century, when many capitals and corbels were replaced.

A talented sculptor was involved in the church's decoration; one of the apse capitals, for example, bears a daring composition that is derived from the Orestes sarcophagus that was then housed in the neighbouring church of S María de Husillos (now in Madrid, Mus. Arqueol. N.). Along the route from Toulouse to Santiago, and particularly at Jaca, there are numerous examples of the influence of the imagery from this sarcophagus, providing evidence of the work of this master and his assistants. A probable Gascon connection seems confirmed by other capitals at Frómista, bearing the story of the *Fall*, in which the hand of the master who worked at Saint-Gaudens (Garonne) can be recognized. A third group of capitals, carved with smooth leaves surmounted by balls, is related to capitals in Burgos Cathedral (begun 1079) and San Pedro de Arlanza (1080). The use of fables is precocious: the fox and raven, and the monkey and fox, are allegories of greed and pride and probably relate to the *Chastising of the Miser* and the *Fall*, which are represented near by. The narrative capitals tend to be concentrated on the arcades nearest the entrances, as if they were conceived as interior portals. Themes related to ecclesiastical censure of civil violence are depicted on the capitals nearest the south door. On the corbels from the exterior (some of them at Palencia, Mus. Arqueol. Prov.) are represented the basic repertory of grotesques typical of the later Spanish Romanesque.

BIBLIOGRAPHY

M. Gómez-Moreno: *El arte románico español* (Madrid, 1934), pp. 84–9
G. Galliard: *Les Débuts de la sculpture romane espagnole: León, Jaca, Compostelle* (Paris, 1938), pp. 145–55
M. A. García Guinea: *El arte románico en Palencia* (Palencia, 1961, rev. 1975)
S. Moralejo: 'Sobre la formación del estilo escultórico de Frómista y Jaca', *Actas del XXIII congreso internacional de historia del arte: Granada, 1973*, i, pp. 427–33
——: 'The Tomb of Alfonso Ansúrez (†1093): Its Place and the Role of Sahagún in the Beginnings of Spanish Romanesque Sculpture', *Santiago, Saint-Denis and Saint Peter: The Reception of the Roman Liturgy in León-Castile in 1080*, ed. B. F. Reilly (New York, 1985), pp. 63–100
——: 'San Martín de Frómista en los orígenes de la escultura románica europea', *Jornadas sobre el románico en la provincia de Palencia* (Palencia, 1985), pp. 27–37

S. MORALEJO

Frommel, Carl Ludwig (*b* Birkenfeld, Rheinland-Pfalz, 29 April 1789; *d* Ispringen, nr Pforzheim, 6 Feb 1863). German painter and printmaker. From 1805 to 1809 he studied under Jakob Becker and the engraver Christian Haldenwang (1770–1831) at the Staatliche Akademie der Bildenden Künste, Karlsruhe. In 1809 he went on a study trip to Paris, where Empress Josephine commissioned him to paint a series of 12 landscapes in watercolour. In 1813 he went to Rome on a scholarship, remaining there until 1817 and becoming, with Friedrich Gmelin (1760–1820), part of the Nazarene circle. He also visited Sicily with the architects Friedrich Gärtner and Daniel Ohlmüller. After his return to Karlsruhe he became Professor of Painting and Engraving at the Akademie in 1817. He executed numerous etchings (e.g. *Ponto Lupo in Tivoli*, 1815), engravings and paintings from his drawings and watercolours of the Italian landscape, and many of these were published in such folios as *Arriccia* (1820), *Tivoli* (1822), *Ätna* (1824) and *Vesuv* (1832). In them he adopted a classical style of landscape somewhat influenced by the work of Johann Christian Reinhart. In 1824 he visited London and became acquainted with the technique of steel-engraving. That year, with the English printmaker Henry Winkles (*fl* 1815–32), he opened a studio for steel-engravers in Karlsruhe. It published numerous collections of steel-engravings produced under Frommel's direction, including *30 Ansichten Griechenlands* (1830), *Carl Frommels pittoreskes Italien* (1840) and *Baden und seine Umgebungen* (1843). In 1830 he was appointed Director of the Gemäldesammlung in Karlsruhe and in 1834 he was granted a stay of several months in Italy to gather up-to-date information about gallery layout and planning. In 1837 he instigated the decision to rebuild the Staatliche Kunsthalle, and he became its director until 1858, which left him little time for his own work. His son Otto Frommel (1835–61) was a landscape painter and lithographer.

PRINTS

Arriccia (Mannheim, 1820)
Tivoli (Karlsruhe, 1822)
Ätna (Karlsruhe, 1824)
30 Ansichten Griechenlands (Karlsruhe, 1830)
Vesuv (Karlsruhe, 1832)
Carl Frommels pittoreskes Italien (Leipzig, 1840)
Baden und seine Umgebungen (Karlsruhe and Baden-Baden, 1843, rev. London, 1870; suppl. 1877)

BIBLIOGRAPHY

Thieme–Becker
A. von Schneider: *Badische Malerei des 19. Jahrhunderts* (Karlsruhe, 1968)
M. Fuss: 'Carl Ludwig Frommel, 1789–1863: Maler und Kupferstecher', *Badische Heimat*, ed. Ekkhart (1970), pp. 95–100

S. TRÄGER

Fronte Nuovo delle Arti. Italian group of artists. It was founded by Renato Birolli in 1946 as the Nuova Secessione Artistica Italiana and renamed in 1947. The manifesto of 1946 was signed by Giuseppe Santomaso, Bruno Cassinari, Antonio Corpora, Renato Guttuso, Ennio Morlotti, Armando Pizzinato (*b* 1910), Giulio Turcato, Emilio Vedova and the sculptors Leonardo Leoncillo (1915–68) and Alberto Viani. During the first group exhibition, which was held at the Galleria della Spiga in Milan in 1947, Cassinari resigned, and the sculptors Pericle Fazzini and Nino Franchina (*b* 1912) joined. This was the vanguard of Italian painters and sculptors who, in the wake of the fear and stagnation brought on by World War II, endeavoured to revitalize Italian 20th-century art, which they felt had died with Futurism and Pittura Metafisica. Although the artists were stylistically very different, ranging from abstraction to naturalism, they were united by left-wing politics and by their wish, as stated in their manifesto, to give their 'separate creations in the world of the imagination a basis of moral necessity'. While the group also shared an admiration for Picasso, the polarization of the abstract formalists and the realists became increasingly evident during the Venice Biennale of 1948. That year the Communist journal *Rinascita* published an article highly critical of works exhibited in Bologna by Fronte Nuovo members. The assumption that the Communists had no artistic preferences was shattered and this helped to destroy the group. Its stylistic diversity is indicated in a comparison of Guttuso's powerfully figurative *Mafia* (1948; New York, MOMA) with Turcato's *Revolt* (1948; Rome, G.N.A. Mod.); the latter evokes the resistance to German repression in near abstract forms derived from Picasso's *Guernica* (Madrid, Prado). The group had disintegrated by 1952, when Birolli, Corpora, Turcato and Vedova were among the abstract painters gathered together in Lionello Venturi's GRUPPO DEGLI OTTO PITTORI ITALIANI.

BIBLIOGRAPHY

20th-century Italian Art (exh. cat., ed. J. T. Soby; New York, MOMA, 1947)
Italian Art in the 20th century (exh. cat., ed. E. Braun; London, RA, 1989)

□

Frontier art. *See* WILD WEST AND FRONTIER ART.

Frontinus, Sextus Julius (*b c.* AD 30; *d* 104). Roman administrator and writer. He was a senatorial aristocrat. During his early career he served as governor of Britain (AD 74–8). His conquest of Wales led to the establishment of Caerleon and Chester as permanent legionary fortresses. He was probably responsible for initiating the programme of Roman urban development in Britain for which Tacitus (*On the Life of Agricola* xxi) gave credit to his father-in-law, Agricola, who succeeded Frontinus as governor. In AD 97 Frontinus was commissioned to reorganize Rome's water supply and in 100 was awarded the unusual distinction of a third consulship.

Frontinus wrote on the aqueducts of Rome, surveying, the art of war, stratagems and farming. In *De aquis urbis Romae* (On the water supply of the city of Rome) he showed his appreciation of the management of Rome's aqueducts and revealed a typical Roman pragmatism; he contrasted the practicality of the great Roman system with 'the idle Pyramids and the useless but famous works of the Greeks' (*De aquis urbis Romae* I.16). This treatise survives complete, full of invaluable and detailed information about the aqueducts that supplied Rome, including their names, sources, construction, capacity and maintenance, and the regulation of public and private distribution of water. His other writings were all on practical or technical subjects, showing the versatility of capable men of his class; of these works the *Strategemata* is the only substantial remnant.

WRITINGS

The Stratagems and the Aqueducts of Rome, Eng. trans. by C. E. Bennett (London, 1925)

BIBLIOGRAPHY

C. Herschel: *Frontinus and the Water Supply of the City of Rome* (Boston, MA, 1899, rev. London, 2/1913) [text and Eng. trans. with commentary]
T. Ashby: *The Aqueducts of Ancient Rome* (Oxford, 1935)

T. F. C. BLAGG

Fröschl [Flosche; Freschel; Fröschlein; Frossley], **Daniel (von)** (*b* Augsburg, 7 May 1563; *d* Prague, 16 Oct 1613). German draughtsman, painter and antiquary. He was a significant figure in the Prague court of Emperor Rudolf II. The son of an Augsburg advocate, by 1580 he is documented as a fully trained miniaturist. He may have worked for Ulisse Aldrovandi in Bologna before taking service (1597–1604) with the Grand Duke of Tuscany. In 1601 he was summoned to the court of Rudolf II in Prague on the recommendation of Hans von Aachen, and he was confirmed in the post of miniaturist there on 28 December 1601. After returning to Italy he continued to work for Rudolf II and was eventually appointed court miniaturist in 1603, though he does not seem to have settled in Prague until 1604. In 1607 Fröschl was appointed court antiquary: between then and 1611 he drew up the inventory (Vaduz, Samml. Liechtenstein) of Rudolf II's Kunstkammer, listing works belonging to the categories of nature (*Naturalia*), arts and crafts (*Artefacta*) and science (*Scientifica*). Philipp Hainhofer's account in 1610 claims that this left him hardly any time for painting. After the Emperor's death in 1612 Fröschl was accused of misappropriating items from the Kunstkammer, and of political meddling.

Very little of Fröschl's work as a painter has been preserved. He was famous for his miniatures, especially nature studies that undoubtedly owed much to the Prague work of Roelandt Savery. However, Fröschl's studies of birds, drawings with 'perspective spheres' and still-lifes of flowers are known only from written sources. Otherwise Fröschl often borrowed subject-matter from other works of the Rudolfine court, where the inspiration for many pictures can be traced back to the personal ideas of the Emperor. Amorous encounters between the gods and mythological couples, episodes from the Turkish wars and the glorification of the Emperor can be found in his work. *Adam and Eve* (*see* MINIATURE, fig. 4), one of his earliest works for Rudolf II, is a copy after a drawing (sold London, Christie's, 8 July 1975, lot 87) by Bartholomeus Spranger. A frog beside the monogram D. F. makes a subtle play on the artist's surname. One of the favourite

Daniel Fröschl: *Mercury and Psyche*, watercolour and bodycolour on parchment, 134×86 mm, *c.* 1606 (Vienna, Kunsthistorisches Museum)

themes of Rudolfine art, the female nude viewed from behind, recurs in Fröschl's watercolour *Zeus and Antiope* ('*Two Satyrs and a Nymph with Putto*'; Edinburgh, N.G.), which also refers back to Spranger's *Eve*. The miniature *Mercury and Psyche* (Vienna, Ksthist. Mus.; see fig.) seems an allegory of peace after the Turkish wars ended in 1606, with the divine couple suspended above a view of Prague with Hradčany Castle. However, a second level of interpretation is also conceivable: Psyche, the personification of the human soul, is raised to immortality by the god of knowledge.

Two of Fröschl's compositions draw on Dürer, whose work was also represented in Rudolf's collection. The watercolour *Virgin with Child and a Portrait of Dürer* (Vienna, Ksthist. Mus.) draws on two drawings by Dürer (both Vienna, Albertina). The *Virgin with Child and Bunches of Grapes* (Prague, Loreto Treasury), based on a drawing by Dürer related to his *Virgin and Child with the Pear* (1512; Vienna, Ksthist. Mus.), is one of Fröschl's few miniature oil paintings to have been preserved.

BIBLIOGRAPHY

Thieme–Becker
O. Doering, ed.: *Des Augsburger Patriciers Philipp Hainhofer Beziehungen zum Herzog Philipp II von Pommern-Stettin*, n. s. vi of *Quellenschriften für Kunstgeschichte und Kunsttechnik des Mittelalters und der Neuzeit* (Vienna, 1894)

E. Neumann: 'Das Inventar der rudolfinischen Kunstkammer von 1607/1611', *Analecta Reginensia I: Queen Christina of Sweden, Documents and Studies* (Stockholm, 1966), pp. 262–5

E. Fučíková: 'Künstler am Hofe Rudolf II und ihre Beziehungen zum Werk Albrecht Dürers', *Umění*, xx (1972), pp. 149–66

Zeichnung in Deutschland: Deutsche Zeichner, 1540–1640, i (exh. cat., Stuttgart, Staatsgal., 1979–80), no. B28

T. daCosta Kaufmann: *L'Ecole de Prague: La Peinture à la cour de Rodolphe II* (Paris, 1985; rev. and Eng. trans. Chicago and London, 1988)

Prag um 1600: Kunst und Kultur am Hofe Kaiser Rudolfs II, i (exh. cat., Vienna, Ksthist. Mus., 1988), nos. 116–19, 196–7, 402

L. Tongiorgi Tomasi: 'Daniel Fröschl before Prague: His Artistic Activity in Tuscany at the Medici Court', *Beiträge zur Kunst und Kultur am Hofe Rudolfs II. Symposium, Prag 1987* (Freren, 1988)

C. HÖPER

Frost, A(rthur) B(urdett) (*b* Philadelphia, PA, 17 Jan 1851; *d* Pasadena, CA, 22 June 1928). American illustrator and painter. After a short apprenticeship to a wood-engraver and several years in a Philadelphia lithographic shop, he achieved recognition as a comic illustrator with the publication of *Out of the Hurly Burly* (London, 1874) by Max Adeler (the pseudonym of C. H. Clarke). Shortly thereafter he joined the staff of Harper and Brothers, New York, where, along with such artists as Edwin Austin Abbey and Howard Pyle (1853–1911), he contributed pen-and-ink and wash illustrations to the books and journals published by the firm.

During the last quarter of the 19th century, a period often characterized as the 'golden age of American illustration', Frost's humorous, homely subjects and comic caricatures appeared regularly in American magazines such as *The Century Illustrated* and *Collier's* as well as those of the Harper group. Best remembered are his illustrations for Joel Chandler Harris's stories, particularly *Uncle Remus: His Songs and his Sayings* (London, 1895). Frost's use of a sequential format in the presentation of many of his comic drawings, as seen in his books *Stuff and Nonsense* (London, 1884) and *The Bull Calf and Other Tales* (London 1892), was influential in the development of the American comic strip.

Though hampered by colour-blindness, Frost's study of painting, begun in 1882 under Thomas Eakins and resumed in the late 1890s with William Merritt Chase, resulted in a series of sporting and shooting scenes painted in the 1890s, which achieved wide popularity through lithographic reproduction: Scribner's published a portfolio of twelve (1903), and four others were issued posthumously by the Derrydale Press (1933–4). His son, Arthur Burdett Frost jr (1887–1917), was a painter and exponent of Synchromism.

BIBLIOGRAPHY

H. Reed: *The A. B. Frost Book* (Rutland, VT, 1967)

Arthur Burdett Frost: Artist and Humorist, 1851–1928 (exh. cat., Chadds Ford, PA, Brandywine River Mus., 1986)

ANNE CANNON PALUMBO

Frost, Charles Sumner. *See under* COBB, HENRY IVES.

Frost, Terry (*b* Leamington Spa, 13 Oct 1915). English painter. Encouraged to paint in a prisoner-of-war camp by fellow prisoner and artist Adrian Heath, he moved to ST IVES in Cornwall after the war, studying at the St Ives School of Painting. From 1947 to 1950 he attended Camberwell School of Art, which, with Heath's studio, was the focal point of Constructivist tendencies in England. Frost followed their concern for proportion and systematic procedures but he soon rejected their historicist notions of a necessary development towards abstraction from two to three dimensions and the potential relationship between painting, architecture and design. Frost's paintings relied upon the division of the painted rectangular canvas but the arcs in his work, generated by golden section proportions, were reminiscent of the rocking of boats, as in *Movement—Green, Black and White* (1951; London, Tate). His period at Leeds University as Gregory Fellow in painting (1954–6), which followed his first one-man show in London at the Leicester Galleries (1952), led to paintings that evoked the features of the Yorkshire countryside and harsh snowy winters. He returned to St Ives in 1956 but spent the decade from 1964 teaching at Reading University, before settling back at Newlyn in 1974.

Frost favoured shapes based on the circle or half-circle, such as wedges and crescents, while he increasingly used saturated colour in intertwining loops and arcs, half-circles and bands. Rather than giving predominance to either colour, form or facture, and thereby establishing a single-minded thrust of development, he made these formal elements interact in a composite and loosely evocative abstraction.

BIBLIOGRAPHY

L. Alloway: *Nine Abstract Artists* (London, 1954)

Terry Frost: Paintings, Drawings and Collages (exh. cat., ACGB, 1976)

D. Lewis, ed.: *Terry Frost* (Aldershot, 1994)

VIDEO RECORDINGS

Terry Frost, Arts Video, AVA/6 (London, 1980) [videotaped interview]

ADRIAN LEWIS

Frost, William Edward (*b* London, Sept 1810; *d* London, 4 June 1877). English painter. His earliest training was with a gifted amateur neighbour. About 1825 William Etty advised him to study with Henry Sass (1788–1844) and to draw in the British Museum. In 1829 he entered the Royal Academy Schools, London, and between *c.* 1830 and *c.* 1845 he painted more than 300 portraits. The success of *Prometheus Bound by Force and Strength* (exh. RA 1840; untraced), *Una and the Satyrs*, which won a £100 premium in the competition to decorate the New Palace of Westminster (1843), and *Christ Crowned with Thorns* (exh. RA 1843; untraced) led him to concentrate on mythological and historical subjects. He regularly used Spenser and Milton as source material but also enjoyed bacchanalian scenes, which allowed him to combine landscape and female nudes in such paintings as the *Disarming of Cupid* (exh. RA 1850; Brit. Royal Col.).

Frost's work was popular with all levels of society, and engravings after his paintings were circulated widely. He shared several patrons with Etty, whose example he followed more closely as his career progressed; one obituarist suggested that Frost's works surpassed those of Etty. He was elected an ARA following the success of *Diana and Actaeon* (exh. RA 1846; Ponce, Mus. A.), and in 1870 he became an RA; his diploma work was *Nymphs and Cupid* (exh. RA 1872; London, RA).

BIBLIOGRAPHY
W. Sandby: *The History of the Royal Academy*, ii (London, 1862), pp. 219–21
Great Victorian Pictures (exh. cat. by R. Treble, ACGB, 1978), pp. 38–9

PHILIP McEVANSONEYA

Frosterus, Sigurd (*b* Asikkala, nr Lahti, 4 June 1876; *d* Helsinki, 2 March 1956). Finnish architect and writer. He became known as an aggressive opponent of the National Romantic style in architecture, which had begun as a reform movement, taking its inspiration from the English Arts and Crafts Movement. In Finland, however, where its most important representatives were Eliel Saarinen and Lars Sonck, the movement's picturesque and romantic manifestations achieved great popularity. In 1904 Frosterus made his famous attack on romanticism with GUSTAF STRENGELL, with whom he also collaborated on some building projects. In connection with the competitions for the railway stations for Helsinki and Viipuri, the friends published a number of newspaper articles, collected into a pamphlet and furnished with handsome typography, which held that romantic architecture was at its worst and most anachronistic in designs for station buildings that were clearly 'modern' design tasks. Saarinen, who won both competitions, suffered their bitterest criticism but was persuaded to take a serious interest in Rationalist architecture, a change that had a lasting and, it is generally held, positive, effect on his work. Frosterus participated in both competitions with progressive and handsome projects. However, the jury thought them 'imported' and did not award them prizes. Frosterus had indeed worked on his entries while in Henry Van de Velde's office in Weimar in 1903–4, and Van de Velde's influence can be seen in the ornamentation and in the Rationalism of the general conception.

Frosterus who, like Strengell, had gained an honours degree in addition to his architectural qualification, espoused ideals in direct opposition to romanticism: rationality, internationalism and a positive orientation towards industrial methods of production. These characteristics remained apparent when he began to execute his own commissions: his best-known work is the Stockmann department store (1924–31) in the centre of Helsinki, which won second prize in a competition (1916).

Frosterus wrote essays and books not only on architecture and painting but also on literature, his travels and on such 'modern' subjects as lawn tennis and new weapons and fighting techniques. In 1935 his philosophical views were published in *Stålålderns janusansikte* [The Janus-face of the steel age], a book that has been compared with Spengler's *Decline of the West* (1918–22) as an analysis of its time.

WRITINGS
Arkitektur: En stridskrift vara motståndare tillägnad af Gustaf Strengell och Sigurd Frosterus [Architecture: a challenge to our opponents by Gustaf Strengell and Sigurd Frosterus] (Helsinki, 1904); Eng. trans. by A. Salokorpi, *Abacus*, iii (1983), pp. 67–81 [with commentary]

BIBLIOGRAPHY
A. Salokorpi: *Sigurd Frosteruksen tilataiteelliset lähtökohdat* [Fundamentals of Sigurd Frosterus's spatial art], *Arkkitehti/Arkitekten*, 6 (1962), pp. 138–44

ASKO SALOKORPI

Frothingham, Benjamin (*b* Boston, MA, 6 April 1734; *d* Charlestown, MA, 19 Aug 1809). American cabinetmaker. He was the son of a Boston cabinetmaker of the same name and set up a shop in Charlestown, MA, in 1756. He served as a major in the American army during the American War of Independence (1775–83) and after the war joined the Society of the Cincinnati, a fraternal organization of American officers who had served during the war. In 1789 he was visited by President George Washington, a fellow member and past president of the society. Known for his block-front and serpentine-front case furniture with corkscrew flame finials, Frothingham also worked in other styles: he made a *bombé* secrétaire (1753; Washington, DC) and later in the century a sideboard (sold American Art Association, 2–4 Jan 1930, lot 417) and table (ex-Joseph Kindig III, York, PA, 1974) in the style of Hepplewhite. Most of his known pieces are labelled, the Boston silversmith Nathaniel Hurd (1729–77) engraving his label. Frothingham's eldest son Benjamin Frothingham III (1774–1832) also became a cabinetmaker.

BIBLIOGRAPHY
M. M. Swan: 'Major Benjamin Frothingham, Cabinetmaker', *Antiques*, lxii (1952), pp. 392–5
R. H. Randall, jr: 'Benjamin Frothingham', *Boston Furniture of the Eighteenth Century*, ed. W. Whitehill (Boston, 1974), pp. 223–49

JULIA H. M. SMITH

Frottage [from Fr. *frotter*: 'to rub']. Technique of reproducing a texture or relief design by laying paper over it and rubbing it with some drawing medium, for example pencil or crayon. Max Ernst and other Surrealist artists incorporated such rubbings into their paintings by means of collage. It is also a popular method of making rubbings of medieval church brasses and other ancient monuments and inscriptions.

Frottis. Thin transparent or semi-transparent layer of pigment lightly rubbed into the ground during the early stages of a painting.

☐

Frowinus [Frowin], Abbot of Engelberg (*d* Engelberg, Obwalden, 27 March 1178). ?Swabian ecclesiastic, writer and ?illuminator. He took his vows at St Blasien (Swabia) and, probably after a period at Einsiedeln Abbey, went on to Engelberg. From 1147 until his death he was the Abbot of Engelberg, to which he brought spiritual and economic prosperity. He founded the extensive library and the writing school there and himself wrote learned treatises. Despite differences in script, the manuscripts that survive from Frowinus's period form a unified group, especially in their illustrations; a strict graphic effect, a confident but reserved use of colour and many original touches are typical of the pen drawings that are preserved, with initials decorated with animals and human figures. It is impossible to ascertain whether Frowinus made a personal contribution to the manuscripts that name him as their originator. Durrer believed that Frowinus was actively involved in the decoration of these manuscripts, suggesting that he worked as a book illuminator; but Bruckner thought this unlikely, as medieval scholars virtually never also worked as scribes or illuminators. He traced the unity back to strictly observed guidelines in the scriptorium and believed that the early work of Frowinus's period is in keeping with the development of Swabian illumination, suggesting that other monks from St Blasien worked in the Engelberg scriptorium while Frowinus was abbot. Many manuscripts bearing his name or showing the unmistakable signs of his school are preserved, of which about thirty are in Engelberg itself (including the outstanding Frowinus Bible), about six in Einsiedeln and one at St Paul, Lavanthal (Carinthia).

SKL

BIBLIOGRAPHY

R. Durrer: *Die Kunstdenkmäler des Kantons Unterwaldens* (Zurich, 1899–1928), pp. 188–200 [with inv. of Frowinus's MSS in Engelberg]

——: 'Die Maler- und Schreiberschule von Engelberg', *Anz. Schweiz. Altertknd.*, n. s., iii (1901), pp. 42–55, 121–76

A. Bruckner, ed.: *Schreiberschulen der Diözese Konstanz: Stift Engelberg*, Scriptoria medii aevi helvetica, viii (Geneva, 1950)

F. FORTER

Frueauf. Austrian family of painters. (1) Rueland Frueauf (i) and his son (2) Rueland Frueauf (ii) executed religious paintings in southern Germany and Austria.

(1) Rueland Frueauf (i) (*b c.* 1440–50; *d* Passau, 1507). The family coat of arms (an owl) has led to the surmise that he came from Obernberg am Inn. Mentions in Salzburg archives between 1470 and 1480 show that he stayed there long after his training. He is documented as painting frescoes of *SS Christopher and Nicholas* in Passau in 1481, also completing frescoes (destr.) in the Rathaus, begun by Ruprecht Fuederer in 1471. In 1484 Salzburg city council appointed him as an adviser to Michael Pacher in executing the altar of the Stadtpfarrkirche (now Franziskanerkirche). He subsequently reacquired citizenship of Passau.

Four split panels of a dismantled winged altarpiece from Salzburg (1490–91; Vienna, Belvedere) are the only work securely attributed to Frueauf, being initialled several times by him. Attributions such as the *Crucifixion* from Salzburg, with five figures (*c.* 1470; Vienna, Belvedere), and the *Man of Sorrows* from Piding (*c.* 1500; Munich, Alte Pin.) mark out the framework of his stylistic development. The early *Crucifixion*, before a brocade ground and on a shallow landscape stage, is still in the Salzburg tradition. The increasingly expressive narrative element in the later Salzburg altarpiece exploits the mobility of idealized figures, which take on greater substance and are harmonized with the sparingly used landscape perspectives. His spatial conceptions are modified in late works such as the *Man of Sorrows* or the *Virgin of the Ears of Corn* (*c.* 1495; both Salzburg, Mus. Carolino Augusteum), probably under the influence of Pacher. The MASTER OF GROSSGMAIN (*see* MASTERS, ANONYMOUS, AND MONOGRAMMISTS, §I) is thought to have been Frueauf's pupil.

(2) Rueland Frueauf (ii) (*b* ?Salzburg, 1470s; *d* Passau, after 1545). Son of (1) Rueland Frueauf (i). He acquired citizenship of Passau through marriage, not later than 1497. Almost all the works securely attributed to him through the monogram 'RF' are owned by the Augustinian foundation of Klosterneuburg; of these, the wing paintings of an altar of *St John* are dated 149(9), those of an altar of *St Leopold* 1505 and a single panel of *St Leopold* 1507 (see

Rueland Frueauf (ii): *St Leopold with Anna Selbdrill*, oil and tempera on panel, 705×465 mm, 1507 (Vienna, Belvedere, Museum Mittelalterlicher Kunst)

fig.). The *St Anne, the Virgin and the Christ Child* in the Belvedere, Vienna, is dated 1508. A *Crucifixion* of 1496, the attribution of which has recently been contested, showing the Nikolauskirche of Passau in the background, is generally regarded as the earliest work that can be attributed to Frueauf. It has also recently been suggested that he collaborated on the *St Vitus* Altar (1487; Nuremberg, Ger. Nmus.) in Nuremberg, but this can be ruled out on grounds of age (for a different view *see* MASTERS, ANONYMOUS, AND MONOGRAMMISTS, §I: MASTER OF THE AUGUSTINIAN ALTAR).

The strong increase in the element of landscape (or architecture) in Frueauf's compositions, together with the more frequent inclusion of small mobile figures carrying the narrative element, make Frueauf a forerunner of the so-called Danube school. The high degree of expressiveness that distinguishes his landscapes is achieved by his ability to reduce natural models to large-scale abstract curves, which heighten the pictorial content, often through a concentric composition.

BIBLIOGRAPHY

L. Baldass: *Conrad Laib und die beiden Rueland Frueauf* (Vienna, 1946), pp. 5–60, pls 58–109

A. Stange: *Deutsche Malerei der Gotik*, x (Berlin, 1960), pp. 38–44, 104, 176, pls 62–9

E. Baum: *Katalog des Museums mittelalterlicher Österreicher Kunst*, i of *Kunst der österreiche Galerie Wien* (Vienna and Munich, 1971), p. 79

A. Rohrmoser, ed.: *Spätgotik in Salzburg: Die Malerei, 1400–1530* (exh. cat., Salzburg, Mus. Carolino Augusteum, 1972), *Jschr. Salzburg. Mus. Carolino Augusteum*, xvii (1972), pp. 119–24, pls 46a, 51

E.-M. Zimmermann: *Studien zur Frueauf-Problem (Rueland Frueauf der Ältere und der Meister von Grossgmain)* (diss., U. Vienna, 1975)

ALBIN ROHRMOSER

Fruhtrunk, Günter (*b* Munich, May 1923; *d* Munich, 12 Dec 1982). German painter. He first studied architecture (1940–41), and in 1950 completed a five-year apprenticeship with the painter William Straube (1871–1954). In 1952 he began working in Fernand Léger's studio, in Paris. Like Léger, he found inspiration in modern technology although Fruhtrunk sought to free human thought from the influence of the machine rather than pay it tribute. From the outset his search for an original, non-representational pictorial structure led him to charge his paintings with intense energy. Initially, he achieved this through basic geometrical forms, positioned diagonally. In their expression of movement, they contradicted the Constructivist principles that had been Fruhtrunk's starting-point. From 1955 his work showed the influence of Hans Arp, in whose studio he was working at this period. Fruhtrunk used stripes to give his compositions more tension, for example the *Mathematics of Intuition, Study No. 5 (Homage to Arp)* (acrylic on chipboard, 1960–63; Bonn, Städt. Kstmus.). It was not until the mid-60s, however, that he began to interrelate stripes and formal sections in a taut system extending across the whole pictorial surface. In the following years, Fruhtrunk further intensified this surface energy by breaking up the apparent rhythmic regularity using bands of colour of varying breadth; he extended this device to monumental works during the late 1960s and 1970s, for example *Cobalt V* (acrylic on canvas, 1.5×1.5 m, 1978–9; Munich, Staatsgal. Mod. Kst.). In these works the pictorial rhythm harmonizes with the colour to create tonal chords. In some of his works of the 1980s he modified the homogeneously, anonymously applied colour of previous paintings by brushing separate stripes visibly more freely.

BIBLIOGRAPHY

E. Gomringer, M. Imdahl and G. Steiner: *Fruhtrunk* (Starnberg, 1978)

D. Honisch: *Neue Malerei in Deutschland* (Munich, 1982), pp. 35–42

Günter Fruhtrunk (exh. cat., Brunswick, Kstver., 1983)

BEATRICE V. BISMARCK

Frunze. *See* BISHKEK.

Fruosino, Bartolomeo di. *See* BARTOLOMEO DI FRUOSINO.

Fruytiers, Philip (*b* Antwerp, 10 Jan 1610; *d* Antwerp, 21 June 1666). Flemish painter, illuminator and printmaker. He is one of the rediscovered minor masters of the 17th-century Flemish school. He was educated in the humanities at the Jesuit college in Antwerp, but it is not known with whom he studied painting. In 1631–2 he was enrolled as a master in the Guild of St Luke in Antwerp.

Until the 1960s Fruytiers was known only as the author of a few excellent miniature portraits in watercolour and gouache on paper or vellum. One of the earliest, *Family on a Terrace* (1638; sold, London, Sotheby's, 25 Feb 1959,

lot 15), includes a painter at work, which may be a self-portrait. The best-known miniature, *Four Children of Rubens and Hélène Fourment with Two Servants* (1638; Windsor Castle, Berks, Royal Col.), is probably the portrait of the children mentioned in the inventory of Rubens's estate in 1641, on which the costs of the frame and glass were still owing.

According to de Bie, Fruytiers also painted altarpieces, but no examples were known until the intertwined monogram *PHF* on three large canvases representing saints (one dated 1652; all Antwerp, Kon. Mus. S. Kst.), which had been attributed to a hypothetical painter P. H. Franck, was identified as Fruytiers's signature (see Baudouin, 1967). The same signature was then found on another altarpiece (*c.* 1659) in the parish church in Zundert, north Brabant (now the Netherlands). This led to the attribution to Fruytiers of other paintings in museums in Brussels, Antwerp and Madrid, and in the parish church of Gistel, West Flanders (now Belgium). Drawings for altarpieces are in Antwerp (Stedel. Prentenkab.), New Haven, CT (Yale U., A.G.) and Berlin (Kupferstichkab.). Fruytiers also painted large-scale portraits such as those of *David Teniers the Younger* (1655; sold London, Christie's, 16 July 1972, lot 43) and of *Three of Rubens's Children* (*c.* 1639; ex-Koetser Gal., London, 1975). An expressive portrait drawing of *Joannes Tollenaere* (after 1643; New York, Pierpont Morgan Lib.) is a preliminary study for an engraving. Fruytiers also made designs for the engraved illustrations of devotional books and for other religious prints by Cornelius Galle the younger, Conrad Lauwers and other Antwerp engravers. Among these is the frontispiece of the *Imago primi saeculi Societatis Jesu* (1640), celebrating the 100th anniversary of the Jesuit Order. Fruytiers's own etched portraits of *Father Innocentius Calatayerone* and of the mathematician and astronomer *Godfried Wendelen* are some of the best Flemish portrait etchings of the 17th century. Fruytiers's style is much closer to the refinement and delicacy of van Dyck than to the more monumental art of Rubens, whom he must have known personally.

BIBLIOGRAPHY

Hollstein: *Dut. & Flem.*

C. de Bie: *Het gulden cabinet* (1661)

P. Colman: 'Seize cuivres de l'*Imago primi saeculi Societatis Jesu*', *Bull. Inst. Royal Patrm. A.*, iv (1961), pp. 187–97

J. S. Held: 'Two Drawings by Philip Fruytiers', *A. Q.* [Detroit], xxvii (1964), pp. 265–73

F. Baudouin: 'Een Antwerp schilder uit Rubens' omgeving: Philip Fruytiers, de monogrammist PHF', *Jb.: Kon. Mus. S. Kst.* (1967), pp. 151–85

——: 'Nog een toeschrijving an Philips Fruytiers' [Another attribution to Philip Fruytiers], *Mus. Royaux B.-A. Belgique: Bull.*, (1968), pp. 161–9

C. Van de Velde: 'Another Drawing by Philip Fruytiers', *Master Drgs*, xxi (1983), pp. 163–6

Flemish Drawings in the Age of Rubens (exh. cat. by A.-M. Logan, Wellesley Coll., MA, Davis Mus. & Cult. Cent., 1993–4), pp. 162–3

FRANS BAUDOUIN

Fry, E(dwin) Maxwell (*b* Wallasey, Ches, 2 Aug 1899; *d* London, 3 Sept 1987). English architect and writer. After serving in the King's Regiment at the end of World War I, he entered the University of Liverpool School of Architecture in 1920. He spent a vacation working in New York in the office of Carrère & Hastings, and in 1924 he graduated and went to London in search of work. He first joined the office of Adams & Thompson, specialists in urban planning, then worked from 1927 to 1930 as Chief Assistant in the Architects' Department of Southern Railways in London; he returned to Adams & Thompson as a partner from 1930 to 1934. During this time he contributed many articles and drawings to architectural journals. Fry's early works included a garden village (1929) at Sittingbourne, Kent, and a house (1932) at Wentworth, Surrey, in the neo-Georgian style typical of the Liverpool School in the 1920s. He was introduced to the Modern Movement through his membership of the Design and Industries Association; his Modernist convictions were strengthened after he met Wells Coates in 1932, and in 1933 he became a founder-member of the MARS Group in support of the Modern Movement.

Fry's first Modernist work was a showroom (1933; destr.) for Westminster Electric Supply Corp. in Victoria Street, London. He also designed several blocks of low-cost flats in London in the 1930s, which reflect his concern to link Modernism with social reform. Sassoon House (1934), Peckham, used a portal truss system (engineer Kirkwood Dodds) and incorporated separate bathrooms, an unusual feature at the time. Kensal House (1936), North Kensington, was a much larger scheme sponsored by the Gas Light and Coke Co. to demonstrate the use of coal gas, and Fry was one of a team of architects, with Robert Atkinson and Grey Wornum, working with housing consultant Elizabeth Denby. Kensal House included several blocks of flats, recreational facilities, shops and a nursery school and playground. Fry's design (see fig.)

E. Maxwell Fry: Kensal House Flats, North Kensington, London, 1936

included separate staircases for each pair of flats instead of a common balcony access, and the flats were spacious, well planned and carefully detailed. In both schemes he paid great attention to standardizing construction and completing the projects as cheaply as possible so they could be rented economically at low rents. In the later 1930s he designed some notable houses in the International Style, for example Sun House (1936), Frognal Lane, Hampstead, and Miramonte (1937), Kingston upon Thames; both have horizontal windows, white walls and projecting balconies.

In 1934 Fry was involved in the emigration to England of Walter Gropius, and they were subsequently in partnership together until 1937 (see GROPIUS, WALTER, §3). During this time, although their work was credited jointly, they ran largely separate jobs. Perhaps the most important product of the partnership was Impington Village College (1936–9), Cambs, designed by Gropius and reworked by Fry to reduce its costs. A highly distinctive example of school design, it combines functional clarity with human scale and the integration of the building and site. After Gropius left for the USA in 1937 Fry continued in practice alone; other works of this period included a timber house (1935) at Chipperfield, Herts; an electrical showroom (1937) in Regent Street, London; flats (1938) at 65 Ladbroke Grove, London; and Cecil House (1940), a hostel for women students in Gower Street, London, which shows an interest in a variety of materials. Fry was closely involved with the exhibition *New Architecture* (1938) mounted by the MARS Group, and as a member of its Town Planning Committee he was also involved with the MARS Group's Plan of London proposal of 1942.

Fry served in the Royal Engineers in World War II, spending part of his service in West Africa, where he became Town Planning Adviser to the resident minister, together with JANE B. DREW, whom he had married in 1942. In 1946 they formed Fry, Drew & Partners, later joined by Lindsay Drake and Denys Lasdun (from 1951 to 1958) and then Frank Knight and Norman Creamer (from 1960). The West African experience of Fry and Drew led to a long period of large-scale projects in Africa, mostly for educational buildings. In Ghana they built Aburi School and College, Adisadel College and Accra Community College (all 1946) and Ashanti Secondary School for Boys (1950), Kumassi; in Togoland (now Republic of Togo), Amedzoffe College (1946); and in Nigeria, teachers' training colleges at Wudil and Kano (1958), University College (1959), Ibadan, and several schools in Lagos (1960), as well as office buildings and housing (see NIGERIA, §IV, 2). Their African work was based on a thoroughly researched approach to the problems of building in the tropics; they were among the first British architects to work overseas and their books became standard texts on the subject of tropical building. Their designs adapted Modernism to local conditions, incorporating local materials and traditional elements such as decorative pierced screen walls. Their work in England during this period included Passfield Flats (1949), Lewisham, and the Riverside Restaurant (1951) at the South Bank Exhibition, London, for the Festival of Britain, which incorporated a mural painted by Ben Nicholson, one of many works of modern art commissioned by Fry for his buildings.

In 1951 Fry and Drew were appointed Senior Architects to the project to build a new capital city for the Punjab at Chandigarh and Fry was influential in the selection of Le Corbusier and Pierre Jeanneret to join the project. Fry and Drew stayed in India for three years, working mainly on housing within Le Corbusier's master plan. Fry also built the Legislative Assembly (1966) at Port Louis, Mauritius. English works from the later years of Fry's career included the Head Office of Pilkington Glass (1965), St Helens, Lancs, a late-Miesian design, the Mid-Glamorgan Crematorium (1969) and the Breakspear Crematorium (1975), Northwood, Middx, which were more organic in form and materials. Critics found these later works disappointing compared to the pre-war designs that had made his reputation as a pioneer of the Modern Movement in Britain. Fry continued his interest in urban planning with the redevelopment of Hatfield Old Town (1972), Herts. He was awarded the Royal Gold Medal of the RIBA in 1964 and retired from practice in 1973.

WRITINGS

with J. Gloag: *The Need for Planning Town and Countryside* (London, 1933)
English Town Hall Architecture (London, 1934)
Fine Building (London, 1944)
with J. B Drew and H. L. Ford: *Village Housing in the Tropics* (London, 1947)
with J. B. Drew: *Tropical Architecture in the Humid Zone* (London, 1956)
——: *Tropical Architecture in the Dry and Humid Zones* (London, 1964)
Art in a Machine Age (London, 1969)
Autobiographical Sketches (London, 1975)

BIBLIOGRAPHY

U. Kultermann: *New Directions in African Architecture* (London, 1969)
S. Hitchins, ed.: *Fry, Drew, Knight, Creamer* (London, 1978)
D. Dean: *The Thirties: Recalling the English Architectural Scene* (London, 1983)

ALAN POWERS

Fry, Roger (Eliot) (*b* London, 14 Dec 1866; *d* London, 9 Sept 1934). English theorist, critic and painter. He was educated at Clifton College, Bristol, and King's College, Cambridge, where he studied natural sciences. He was descended on both sides of his family from seven generations of Quakers, but he abandoned Christian beliefs on reaching adulthood. The legacy of Quakerism, however, continued to influence the direction of his career in his willingness to stand apart from mass opinion and from established authority, and in his distrust of all display.

On leaving Cambridge, he trained as a painter, first under Francis Bate (1853–1950), then for two months at the Académie Julian in Paris. He regarded the activity of painting as central to his life and continued to paint and exhibit throughout his career. Although critical opinion has never been high, his art stands out consistently for its intellectual clarity of construction. However, Fry also soon established a reputation as a scholar of Italian art. He made his first visit to Italy in 1891 and in 1894 began lecturing on Italian art for the Cambridge Extension Movement. He published the book *Giovanni Bellini* in 1899 and a series of major articles on Italian art in the *Monthly Review* in 1900–01. He enjoyed friendship with Bernard Berenson, Herbert Horne and other connoisseurs and collectors, becoming part of an international network of scholars. In 1903 he helped found the *Burlington*

Magazine and between 1901 and 1906 wrote art criticism for *The Athenaeum*, a leading literary periodical. In this way his name became known in the USA, and in 1906 he was appointed Curator of Paintings at the Metropolitan Museum of Art in New York. The following year his position was altered to that of European Adviser. In both of these roles he acquired paintings and drawings for the museum, some of them notable additions to the collection.

Fry's life and career underwent abrupt changes in 1910. His position at the Metropolitan was suddenly terminated after a dispute with the chairman of the trustees, J. Pierpont Morgan. On medical advice his wife, Helen Coombe, was certified and committed to an asylum after several years of mental illness. In November of the same year, following his return to London, he opened the exhibition *Manet and the Post-Impressionists* at the Grafton Galleries. This, with the Second Post-Impressionist Exhibition, held in the winter of 1912–13, effectively brought the British public up to date with developments in art that had taken place in France over the previous 30 years, and radically altered Fry's reputation. From 1910 he was regarded in England as the apostle of modern art. He was involved with various artists' groups and was the prime mover behind the Omega Workshops, which flourished between 1913 and 1919. In founding the Omega Workshops, Fry's aim was to introduce the fresh sense of design, colour and proportion inspired by Post-Impressionism into the applied arts. He therefore commissioned young artists to decorate furniture and other objects and to design fabrics, rugs, carpets and marquetry. Rich colour and pattern challenged the sobriety formerly upheld by the Arts and Crafts Movement, for the aim was to display neither good taste nor correct thinking but rather the artist's delight in the act of creating, given the free play of sensibility. The anarchic style of the Omega Workshops and Fry's unbusinesslike methods did not suit all the artists involved, notably Wyndham Lewis, who left after a public row, taking a handful of artists with him and setting up the Rebel Art Centre in competition.

With the appearance in 1920 of *Vision and Design*, a collection of articles and essays, Fry's influence as a critic and arbiter of taste was further extended. To a lay audience this book offered a seemingly simple directive: to look at form. This cut through the apparent confusion surrounding modern art and, as Fry demonstrated, could also be applied to the art of any age or culture. Its essays on native American Indian and African-American art had a crucial influence on the young sculptor Henry Moore and, by expanding the range of artistic interest, it contributed in general to the breakdown of the hegemony of the Greco-Roman tradition over Western art.

Fry's second collection of essays, *Transformations* (1926), was less influential than his monograph on *Cézanne* (1927). The latter was both the first comprehensive account of this artist's career and the first to notice the influence of Cézanne's watercolours on his post-1885 oils. Fry's three subsequent books on French, Flemish and British art brought together lectures written in connection with exhibitions held at the Royal Academy in London. These lectures, given under the auspices of the National Art Collections Fund, increased Fry's success and left him, for the rest of his life, a public figure much in demand.

Fry's most significant contribution was the introduction of Post-Impressionism into Britain and his promotion of a formalist aesthetic that encouraged its appreciation. He was also a discerning and provocative critic, opening up new areas of interest and making widely accessible subjects that had previously been the preserve of an educated or moneyed élite. His work as critic and exhibition organizer was for some time regarded as an innovative and advantageous influence upon modern art in Britain. However, opinion subsequently viewed his legacy as restrictive and unsupportive of British traditions. Ironically, this man who did much to expand the audience for art came to be criticized for his exclusiveness, for insisting on a formalist approach at the expense of historical and sociological enquiry.

WRITINGS

Giovanni Bellini (London, 1899)
Vision and Design (London, 1920)
Transformations (London, 1926)
Cézanne: A Study of his Development (London, 1927)
Flemish Art (London 1927)
Characteristics of French Art (London, 1932)
The Arts of Painting and Sculpture (London, 1932)
Reflections on British Painting (London, 1934)
Last Lectures, intro. by K. Clark (Cambridge, 1939)
Regular contributions to *Athenaeum, Nation & Athenaeum* and *New Statesman & Athenaeum* (1901–34) and to *Burl. Mag.* (1903–34)

BIBLIOGRAPHY

D. A. Laing: *Roger Fry: An Annotated Bibliography of the Published Writings* (New York, 1979)
J. V. Falkenheim: *Roger Fry and the Beginning of Formalist Art Criticism* (Ann Arbor, MI, 1980)
F. Spalding: *Roger Fry: Art and Life* (London, 1980)
——: 'Roger Fry and his Critics in a Post-modernist Age', *Burl. Mag.*, cxxviii (1986), pp. 489–92

FRANCES SPALDING

Fry, Thomas (*b* in or near Dublin, *c.* 1710; *d* London, 2 April 1762). Irish painter, mezzotint-engraver and porcelain manufacturer, active in England. He probably trained in Dublin, benefiting from the example of the portrait painter James Latham. However, there were few opportunities for portrait painters in Dublin, and by 1735 he had moved to London. He was sufficiently established by 1736 to be commissioned by the Saddlers' Company, London, to paint a full-length portrait of *Frederick, Prince of Wales* (destr.; version, Windsor Castle, Berks, Royal Col., see Millar, no. 543). Frye engraved this portrait himself in mezzotint (1741; see Chaloner Smith). He also worked as a miniature painter, both in oil and in pencil. He quickly matured into a confident and assured portrait painter and could undoubtedly have made a greater name for himself, but he chose to join Edward Heylyn (1695–after 1758) in the attempt to produce porcelain at the Bow Factory, London. In 1744 they took out a patent for a new method, using china clay brought to England from the North American colony of Georgia by Andrew Duché, a potter. After a period of experimentation Frye took out a further patent on 17 November 1749. Under his direction the Bow Porcelain Factory, in which Frye and Heylyn were joined by two other partners, produced a variety of well-received soft-paste figures and vessels. However, Frye's health apparently suffered from work among the furnaces, and he retired in 1759. His importance at Bow

may be gauged from the fact that the works did not long survive his departure.

After 15 years during which he had painted very little, Frye resumed work as an artist. He painted a number of portraits, including that of the young *Jeremy Bentham* (1760; London, N.P.G.), and exhibited portraits with the newly established Society of Artists (1760–61). However, the main achievement of his remaining years was the series of powerful mezzotints by which he is now chiefly remembered. In the *Public Advertiser* of 28 April 1760 he announced a subscription of 'Twelve Mezzotinto Prints, from Designs in the Manner of Piazetta, drawn from Nature and as large as life' at two guineas a set, to be closed when 200 sets had been taken. The result was a novel series of varied portrait studies, unnamed except for a *Self-portrait* (CS 6); their striking poses, and Frye's successful use of the dramatic light effects that mezzotint could supply, made an immediate impact and had an influence on other artists, notably Joseph Wright of Derby. Although Frye's ill-health delayed publication, he produced a second set, representing *Six Ladies, in Picturesque Attitudes, and in Different Dresses of the Present Mode*, announced in the *Public Advertiser* of 4 April 1761. A number of related drawings have survived. Frye also made drawings, reputedly sketched in the theatre, of *George III* and *Queen Charlotte*; a mezzotint of the former by Frye (CS 1) was published shortly after his death from consumption. The companion plate (CS 17) was signed by his pupil William Pether, whose help had no doubt been crucial in enabling Frye to produce so many prints in such a short time. A document shown in Frye's portrait of *John Ellis* (1761; priv. col.), which Pether later engraved, indicates that Frye took him into partnership on 21 April 1761.

BIBLIOGRAPHY

DNB; Strickland; Thieme–Becker
J. Chaloner Smith: *British Mezzotinto Portraits*, ii (London, 1879), pp. 516–22 [CS]
A. Graves: *The Society of Artists of Great Britain (1760–1791): The Free Society of Artists (1761–1783)* (London, 1907), p. 96
Bow Porcelain, 1744–1776: A Special Exhibition of Documentary Material to Commemorate the Bi-centenary of the Retirement of Thomas Frye (exh. cat. by H. Tait, London, BM, 1959)
O. Millar: *Pictures in the Royal Collection: Tudor, Stuart and Early Georgian*, 2 vols (London, 1963)
Irish Portraits, 1660–1860 (exh. cat. by A. Crookshank and the Knight of Glin, London, N.P.G.; Dublin, N.G.; Belfast, Ulster Mus.; 1969), pp. 16, 42–4, 78
M. Wynne: 'Thomas Frye (1710–1762)', *Burl. Mag.*, cxiv (1972), pp. 79–84 [incl. list of Frye's most important known works]
——: 'A Pastel by Thomas Frye, *c.* 1710–62', *BM Yb.*, ii (1977), pp. 242–5
E. Adams and D. Redstone: *Bow Porcelain* (London, 1981, rev. 1991)

DAVID ALEXANDER

Fu Baoshi [Fu Pao-shih; *ming* Fu Ruilin] (*b* Xinyu, Jiangxi Province, 1904; *d* 1965). Chinese painter and art historian. He was one of the last great literati or scholar–amateur painters in China and formed a link between the traditional élite literati painters and the new artists of the 20th century. He also combined traditional methods with Western techniques and concepts, which earned him the respect of admirers of the classical tradition, as well as popularity with those of modern outlook. For the support he received from the new regime, Fu Baoshi reciprocated by, among other things, painting pictures that made reference to the poems of Mao Zedong. Fu is particularly renowned for his landscape paintings, in which he introduced new methods of depicting mountains, and for his images of people.

Fu grew up in very poor circumstances, but with the help of friends of the family he managed to receive a little education. From an early age he began to concentrate on the art of seal-carving and on copying the pictures of old masters, especially Daoji. From 1921 in preference to his name (*ming*) he called himself Baoshi: *bao* means 'to embrace', *shi* stands for Daoji, whose style name (*zi*) was Shitao. In 1933 he went to Japan, where he studied at the Imperial Art College in Tokyo, coming into contact with Western concepts that had just found their way into Japan. At that time he also immersed himself in the study of Chinese painting theory through books that were available in Japan.

His mature style, which was remarkable particularly for its fusion of technical mannerism and realism, was formed during his stay in Japan. His later work also combined a method of very expressive abstract painting, used, for example, in his depiction of landscapes, with painstakingly executed details, such as figures. He did not confine himself to painting unspoilt scenery and often depicted landscapes very realistically, although his representations of people were traditional. His paintings were also characterized by subdued colours, which he continued to use (unlike some of his contemporaries) in a traditional Chinese way. Chinese ink, with its countless nuances, provided the foundation for creating the maximum effect of colour with the minimum of paint.

Many of his pictures were painted on *pizhi* ('skin paper'), robust paper that contains long fibres. Fu took successful advantage of its qualities to introduce some new effects. He was particularly skilled at painting scenes of rain-covered mountains, waterfalls and other landscapes, which were done very quickly but exude much charm. Atmospheric effects were achieved by letting the ink spread through the porous surface of the paper. To redeem a landscape that was perhaps too grand in scale or too abstract, he might place a figure or group of figures, depicted in the finest detail, in a critical spot. The viewer's eye would be drawn to the figure or group of figures, and the rather lifeless area of the picture would then be experienced merely as a pleasant background. Occasionally critics have reproached him for this calculated placement of figures to compensate for the less successful parts of a work and for not thinking out the composition mentally in advance. They call his mountains 'skin without bones', the 'bones' being the structural lines, which are often wholly absent from Fu's paintings, and the 'skin' being the visible surface.

In 1938 Fu Baoshi returned to China, where the artist and teacher Xu Beihong secured a post for him in the Art Department at the Central University of Nanjing, Jiangsu Province. His career as a painter then took a steep upturn. His greatest successes from 1936 to 1938 were exhibitions in Sichuan and Yunnan provinces and the publication of works on Chinese art. In 1937, just before the outbreak of the Sino–Japanese war, he moved to Chongqing in Sichuan, where the Nationalist government had its headquarters; after the war he returned to Nanjing. Posts he held included that of professor in the Department of Fine Arts at Nanjing Teachers' College, head of the Jiangsu Academy of Traditional Chinese Painting and Vice-chairman of the National Artists' Association.

In the 1950s, with the support of the communist government, he and other painters travelled extensively. He visited the most famous states in China and travelled throughout Romania and Czechoslovakia. From all his journeys he brought back sketchbooks full of impressions, which he used in a great variety of ways, in the 1960s turning some of them into traditional paintings, others into works that demonstrated strong Western influences. His largest composition (5.5×9 m), entitled *Such is the Beauty of our Mountains and Streams* after a line in Mao Zedong's poem *Xue* ('*Snow*'), hangs in the Great Hall of the People, Tiananmen Square, Beijing.

WRITINGS
Shi Tao shangzen niampu [The chronology of Shi Tao] (1948)
Zhongguo gudai shanshuihuashi de yanjiu [Studies in the history of ancient landscape painting] (Shanghai, 1960)

BIBLIOGRAPHY
M. Sullivan: *Chinese Art in the Twentieth Century* (Berkeley and Los Angeles, 1959)
Chu-tsing Li: *Trends in Modern Chinese Painting* (Ascona, 1979)
Wu Linsheng: 'Fu Baoshi's Contribution to Traditional Chinese Painting', *Chin. Lit.*, 1 (1980), pp. 58–67

FRIEDRICH ZETTL

Fuchigami, Hakuyō (*b* Kumamoto, 14 Dec 1889; *d* Tokyo, 8 Feb 1960). Japanese photographer. He learnt photographic techniques at Nagasaki and opened a photographic portrait studio in Kōbe in 1918. He was interested not only in portraiture but also in other photographic genres. His photograph *Village Bathed in Evening Sun* won first prize in the first All-Kansai Photography Competition. In 1922 he founded the monthly photography magazine *Hakuyō*, publishing not only his own works but those of photographers Sunao Morita, Gesshū Ogawa (1891–1967), Yasuzō Nojima and Seiyō Sakakibara in high-quality collotype. In November 1922 the Japanese Photographic Art Association (Nihon Kōga Geijutsu Kyōkai) was founded, mainly from the subscribers to the magazine, and an annual exhibition was organized. From *c.* 1925 Fuchigami and a group of photographers, known as Kōsei-ha ('Constructivist school'), moved away from soft-focus photographs of nature and began to treat the picture surface as an abstract work. The European Futurist and Dadaist movements exerted some influence on the group, particularly on the work of Kikuji Nishi, Jun Tsusaka and Saigorō Matsuo. In 1928 Fuchigami went to the Japanese colony of Manchuria to run the railway advertising and information service, and the Japanese Photographic Art Association dissolved. In 1934 he set up the Manchurian Photographers Association.

BIBLIOGRAPHY
K. Iizawa: *Art Photography in Japan, 1900–1930* (Tokyo, 1986), pp. 1–119
T. Ozawa, ed.: *The Heritage of Art Photography in Japan*, Complete Hist. Jap. Phot., ii (Tokyo, 1986), pp. 161–4
Art Deco Photography in Japan (exh. cat. by R. Kaneko and J. Takeba, Nagoya, City Mus., 1992), pp. 5–14

KOHTARO IIZAWA

Fu-chow. See FUZHOU.

Fuchs, Bohuslav (*b* Všechovice, Moravia [now Czech Republic], 24 March 1895; *d* Brno, 18 Sept 1972). Czech architect. He studied architecture at the Academy of Fine Arts, Prague, under Jan Kotěra, in whose office he also worked. Between 1921 and 1923 he shared a studio in Prague and carried out some works with Josef Štěpánek; he then settled in Brno where he worked in the Brno Municipal Construction Office (1923–9) before setting up his own practice. Fuchs was a member of the Mánes Union of Artists, the Czechoslovak delegate to CIAM and vice-president of the International Federation of Housing and Town Planning, and he became a leading representative of modern architecture in Czechoslovakia. His early work was influenced by Czech Cubism and the brick-based Rationalist architecture of the Netherlands. In the mid-1920s he developed his own specific style of Functionalism, which emphasized the emotional qualities of interior space and its dynamic, plastic expression. He often stressed the space-forming role of the staircase, which he considered to be the heart of the whole building and the element from which the spatial effects of other functions were derived. This design approach was evident in his own house (1927–8) and was particularly striking in the Avion Hotel (also 1927–8), both in Brno. In the latter he used a clever arrangement of the staircase and galleries to produce a magnificent play of views through four storeys of the building, which was constructed on a narrow elongated site (8.4×34 m).

In the second half of the 1930s Fuchs began to enrich his dynamic concept of architecture by exploiting the effects of natural materials in a way that responded to the rural or urban environment, which took his work a step closer to the organic architecture of Hans Scharoun or Hugo Häring. An example of this approach is the Green Frog Thermal Baths (1935–6) at Trenčianské Teplice. Fuch's extensive career covered all areas of architecture including regional and urban planning, and he was also involved in furniture and interior design. After World War II he became a professor at the Technical University, Brno (1945–58), and he directed his energies towards the reconstruction of historic town centres and the theory of urban planning. His winning entry in the competition for the extension of the National Theatre in Prague in the 1960s renewed the tradition of Modernism in Czechoslovak architecture.

BIBLIOGRAPHY

Z. Rossmann: *Architekt Bohuslav Fuchs, 1919–1929* (Basle, 1930)
J. Dvořák: 'Bohuslav Fuchs: Contribution de la Tchécoslovaquie', *Archit. Aujourd'hui*, 113–14 (1964), pp. 140–41
Z. Kudělka: *Bohuslav Fuchs* (Prague, 1966)
V. Šlapeta: 'Bohuslav Fuchs, 24.3.1895–18.9.1972', *Bauwelt*, lxiii (1972), pp. 1760–61
——: 'Brno: Una capitale dell'architettura moderna', *Parametro*, 114 (1983), pp. 12–14
The Brno Functionalists (exh. cat. by V. Šlapeta, Helsinki, Mus. Fin. Archit., 1983)

VLADIMÍR ŠLAPETA

Fuchs, Emil (*b* Vienna, 9 Aug 1866; *d* New York, 13 Jan 1929). Austrian sculptor, medallist and painter. He studied at the Akademie der Bildenden Künste, Vienna, and at the Berlin Akademie. He travelled to Rome before settling in London in 1897, exhibiting at the Royal Academy the following year. His sculptural oeuvre consists of large groups, portrait busts, statuettes and memorials in marble, bronze and silver. The bronze statue *La pensierosa* (New York, Met.) is a good example of his contemplative style, and the marble *Mother-love* (exh. London, RA, 1898; untraced, see autobiography, opp. p. 28) of his liking for melodramatic allegory; his memorials include *The Sisters* (marble; Liverpool, Walker A.G.). His paintings are mostly portraits, in a flashy style that owes much to his friend John Singer Sargent (e.g. *Sir Joseph Duveen*, 1903; London, Tate). Both his painted and sculpted portraits were immensely fashionable in Britain at the turn of the century, and he was taken up by the royal family, modelling a number of medals that were struck for Queen Victoria, portraying Princess Alexandra as the *Princess of Pity* (silver, 1900; London, BM) and executing a coronation medal for Edward VII (silver and bronze, 1902). He brought to the British medal the soft-edged decorative style then popular in Austria, to which he always remained faithful. He designed the postage stamps of Edward VII, but after World War I he moved to New York, where he continued working until his suicide.

WRITINGS

With Pencil, Brush and Chisel: The Life of an Artist (New York, 1925) [autobiography]

BIBLIOGRAPHY

Forrer; Thieme–Becker
M. Jones: 'Emil Fuchs in England', *Medal*, vi (1985), pp. 23–9
The Beaux-Arts Medal in America (exh. cat. by B. A. Baxter, New York, Amer. Numi. Soc., 1988)
P. Attwood: *Artistic Circles: The Medal in Britain, 1880–1918* (London, 1992), pp. 44, 47–8

PHILIP ATTWOOD

Fuchs, Ernst (*b* Vienna, 13 Feb 1930). Austrian painter, printmaker, sculptor and stage designer. He received his first training in painting and sculpture at Frohlich's painting school (1943–5), Vienna, and then at the Akademie der Bildenden Künste in Vienna; there he met Albert Paris Gütersloh's pupils, Erich Brauer, Wolfgang Hutter (*b* 1928) and Anton Lehmden (*b* 1929), who together developed a style that came to be known as PHANTAS-TISCHER REALISMUS. Fuchs was also a founder-member of the Art-Club (1946), as well as the group that set up in opposition to it in 1951, the Hundsgruppe, with Fritz Hundertwasser and Arnulf Rainer. His work of this period was influenced by the art of Gustav Klimt and Egon Schiele and then by Max Pechstein, Heinrich Campendonck, Edvard Munch, Henry Moore and Picasso; he also sought to achieve the precise techniques of such artists as Albrecht Altdorfer, Albrecht Dürer, Matthias Grünewald and Martin Schongauer.

Between 1950 and 1961 Fuchs lived mostly in Paris but made repeated journeys to the USA and Israel. In 1958 he founded his own gallery in Vienna to support the younger painters of the Phantastischer Realismus school; he likewise inaugurated the Pintorarium with Hundertwasser and Rainer. Following his conversion to Catholicism (1956) he produced a number of important works on religious themes, including the *Cycle of the Rosary* (1958–61) triptych, for the Rosenkranzkirche in Hetzendorf, Vienna, and *Moses and the Burning Bush* (1956–7; Vienna, Belvedere). He also dealt with contemporary issues in his paintings (*Psalm 69*, 1949–60; see Fuchs, 1978, p. 53).

In 1961 Fuchs returned to Vienna, where he had the vision of what he called the 'verschollener Stil', the theory of which he set out in *Architectura Caelestis: Die Bilder des verschollenen Stils* (Salzburg, 1966); the work reveals the influence of Symbolism as well as of ancient civilizations. Fuchs also produced several cycles of prints, such as *Unicorn* (1950–52), *Samson* (1960–64), *Esther* (1964–7) and *Sphinx* (1966–7; all illustrated in Weis). From 1970 Fuchs made sculptural works, such as *Large Esther* (h. 2.63 m, 1972), located outside the artist's house in Huettelbergstrasse, Vienna; the house later became a museum. From 1974 he became involved in opera and the work of Richard Wagner, designing stage sets and costumes.

WRITINGS
R. P. Hartmann, ed.: *Fuchs über Ernst Fuchs: Bilder und Zeichnungen von 1945–1976* (Paris, 1977)
Im Zeichen der Sphinx: Schriften und Bilder (Munich, 1978)
Planeta Caelestis (Berlin and Munich, 1987)

BIBLIOGRAPHY
Die Wiener Schule des Phantastischen Realismus (exh. cat., Hannover, Kestner-Ges., 1965)
H. Weis, ed.: *Ernst Fuchs: Das graphische Werk* (Vienna, 1967)
R. P. Hartmann, ed.: *Ernst Fuchs: Das graphische Werk, 1967–1980* (Munich, 1980)

INGEBORG KUHN-RÉGNIER

Fuchs, Peter (*b* Mülheim, nr Cologne, 27 Sept 1829; *d* Cologne, 31 July 1898). German sculptor. From 1844 to 1849 he was an apprentice mason in the Cologne Dombauhütte and for the next two years worked as a mason for St Nicolai in Hamburg and in the studio of Vincenz Statz in Cologne. From 1851 to 1854 he worked in Speyer with the sculptor Gottfried Renn (1818–80) and in Frankfurt am Main with Eduard Schmidt von der Launitz (1797–1869) and Eduard Jakob von Steinle. In 1855 Fuchs returned to Cologne, where he created such large sandstone reliefs and statue groups as the *Four Prophets* (1858) for the Mariensäule in the Gereonsdriesch and the life-size figures of *SS Dionysius and Reinold* (1866–71) for the west front of St Mauritius. From 1865 to 1881 he produced some 700 life-size and slightly over-life-size sculptures for Cologne Cathedral, mostly reliefs and seated and standing figures depicting scenes from the Bible and lives of the saints. Many of these are to be found on the columns and walls of the south transept (1866–72), the west towers (1871), the west front and the north front (1879–81) and the Petersportal (1881). Several preliminary drawings (1879–80) for uncompleted sculptures are located in the Dombauarchiv. Influenced by the Nazarenes, after 1870 Fuchs lengthened his figures and encased them in garments with sharp-edged, graphic folds. He was also influenced by the work of contemporary German sculptors working in the monumental style, as can be seen in the rendering of naturalistic heads and pathetic expression and in the isolation of the figures from each other. The reliefs and statues of Old and New Testament prophets (1895–8) from the tympanum and the bronze doors of the west front of Bremen Cathedral, with their attenuated stances and pronounced folds of drapery, show his debt to the figures in Ghiberti's *Gates of Paradise* (Florence, Mus.

Opera Duomo) and to the sculptures of the BEURON SCHOOL of the last third of the 19th century.

BIBLIOGRAPHY
E. Trier and W. Weyres, eds: *Kunst des 19. Jahrhunderts im Rheinland*, iv (Düsseldorf, 1980)

WALTER GEIS

Füchsl, Alfréd. *See* FORBÁT, FRED.

Fude no Ayamaru. *See* KITAGAWA UTAMARO.

Fuente, Enrique Yañez de la. *See* YAÑEZ, ENRIQUE.

Fuga, Ferdinando (*b* Florence, 11 Nov 1699; *d* Naples, 7 Feb 1782). Italian architect. He was one of the most successful Italian architects of the 18th century. In his long career serving popes and Charles III, King of Naples (*reg* 1734–59), he tackled building commissions covering every aspect of architecture, both ecclesiastical and secular. As the son of a court official in service to Ferdinand de' Medici, Grand Prince of Tuscany, who acted as his godfather, Fuga's connections enabled him to move with great diplomatic skill at court.

1. Training and early career in Rome, before 1748. 2. Naples, 1748–82.

1. TRAINING AND EARLY CAREER IN ROME, BEFORE 1748. At the age of 12 Fuga entered the studio in Florence of the court sculptor and architect Giovanni Battista Foggini in order to study architecture. Foggini concentrated on familiarizing his students with the works of Florentine artists of the Cinquecento, including Michelangelo, Bartolomeo Ammanati and Bernardo Buontalenti, and Foggini's Baroque interpretations of the decorative motifs used by Buontalenti proved influential for Fuga.

In 1718 Fuga went to Rome to continue his training, probably at the Accademia di S Luca. He attempted to establish himself in Rome, helped by his connections with Tuscan diplomats. His first competitive designs, for the façade (1722) of S Giovanni in Laterano (the Lateran Basilica), the Fontana di Trevi (1723) and the façade (1725) of S Maria sopra Minerva, were unsuccessful, although he did attract the patronage of Cardinal Niccolò del Giudice, who commissioned him to build a chapel (1726–7) in the Palazzo Cellamare, Naples. In 1729 he was appointed engineer to the Sicilian Board of Works, for which he built a large bridge (1729–30; destr.) over the River Milicia. In his early designs Fuga displayed an almost unsettling stylistic versatility. The pluralism of the artistic scene in Rome is confidently reflected in his work, even in the details; for example, late Baroque academic classicism is evident in his scheme for the Fontana di Trevi, and flowing Rococo curves and Mannerist façade ornament, derived from Florence and the work of Buontalenti, are evident in his projects at S Giovanni in Laterano and S Maria sopra Minerva. Fuga seems to have drawn inspiration in Rome from the synthesis of motifs from the work of Francesco Borromini and Bernini, which are associated more directly with the work of their pupil Filippo Juvarra, as well as from Foggini, although no dependency can be demonstrated. In both the Lateran project and the Cellamare Chapel the influence of Andrea Pozzo's scenographic architectural designs, with their lively sculptural breaching of forms and the powerful chiaroscuro effects that result, is also clear.

In 1730, following the election of the Florentine Lorenzo Corsini as Pope Clement XII (*reg* 1730–40), Fuga returned to Rome, where he was appointed architect to the papal palaces. In this position he was entrusted with many projects as part of the intensive building activity that typified the pontificate of Clement XII, beginning in 1731 with the extension of the papal residence, the Palazzo Quirinale. After adding to the so-called *manica lunga*, the wing for the papal *famiglia*, the papal stables on the Piazza del Quirinale, begun in 1721 by Alessandro Specchi, were extended (1731); and in 1732 work began on the construction of the Palazzo della Consulta (see fig. 1) opposite the papal residence, an administrative palace intended to house two ministries. Fuga's ambitious, richly articulated first design for the façade was rejected, the client insisting on a simpler building. The façade constructed thus has a completely flat appearance with strictly linear articulation and limited ornamentation: its 13 bays of equal width are framed on both floors by light-coloured pilaster strips. Fuga's adaptability is also evident in his ingenious arrangement of the building on the exceptionally difficult site, using a trapezoidal ground-plan. The courtyard of the palazzo offers only a semblance of regularity; everything is based on slanting or irregular lines, but the overall effect works. Fuga showed extraordinary skill in resolving the difficult inner partitioning of the building, enabling it to be used by the two ministries, their equal status suggested by the bold double staircase leading to them both from the main entrance.

Fuga employed a more conventional vertical articulation, using a colossal order of pilasters above a plinth storey in the manner of Bernini's Palazzo Chigi (begun 1664), in the façade he designed (before 1737) for the enlargement of Conte Alessandro Petroni's palazzo (now Palazzo Cenci-Bolognetti). Fuga's other main works in Rome at this time, S Maria dell'Orazione e Morte (1733–7) in Via Giulia and the Palazzo Corsini (1736–58), demonstrate a similar reduction in formal splendour in the course of the design stage, attributable not so much to Fuga as to the client. In both cases Fuga produced a brilliant solution for the ground-plan. He fitted the church into a narrow gap between buildings as an elongated oval with undulating contours, in order to reconcile the boundaries of the plot, while the palace was designed in three sections in order to respect existing buildings, with the grand, effectively integrated staircase (1751–3) added as an afterthought.

The early stage of Fuga's career caused a crisis in his stylistic development. Clement XII, influenced by his own architect Alessandro Galilei and represented by Cardinal Neri Corsini, promoted an architectural programme that was inimical to the Baroque, in pursuance of a quite deliberate cultural policy. This imposed limits on Fuga's self-confident handling of the tradition-based repertory he had acquired and obliged him to respect the straight line, the right angle and strictly subordinated ornamentation. His capacity to adapt to the wishes of his patron was demonstrated once again. From the mid-1730s Fuga's oeuvre shows stylistic continuity, and although he reverted to a more scenographic style during the pontificate of Benedict XIV (*reg* 1740–58), he never again resorted to curvilinear projections or Rococo decoration.

Fuga's designs for the atrium (1741) of S Cecilia in Trastevere, effectively created as a framing vista, and

1. Ferdinando Fuga: Palazzo della Consulta, Rome, 1732–7

2. Ferdinando Fuga: façade of S Maria Maggiore, Rome, 1741–3

particularly the façade (1741–3) for the basilica of S Maria Maggiore (see fig. 2), intended to be a showpiece when viewed from a distance, demonstrate his extraordinary ability to achieve the maximum effect in an existing context. The design for the portico of S Maria Maggiore (*see* ROME, §V, 20), which had been started in 1735, required that the new façade be integrated with existing buildings on either side and that the medieval mosaic on the old façade be preserved. Fuga adopted the articulation of the buildings on either side as a basic pattern, accentuated by the use of columns and pediments. The bays of both storeys are open to their full height and width, so that the façade becomes transparent, achieving its effect through chiaroscuro within a formal, unified framework. Sculptural decoration is subordinated to architecture. The upper storey, consisting of the benediction loggia built against the old façade, takes up the rhythm of the portico and raises it to a level of monumentality. Rhythmically articulated and pervaded with light, the façade has a festive air, and it may be regarded as Fuga's masterpiece in Rome.

One of Fuga's most charming buildings is the Coffee House (1741–3), a U-shaped pavilion with a restrained classical exterior and elegant interior decoration, constructed in the garden of the Palazzo Quirinale for Pope Benedict XIV. Other work of this period included the extension of the Ospedale di Santa Spirito (1742–4; destr.), where Fuga adhered to the functional articulation of the 15th-century building; and a design for the small hospital cemetery (1745; destr.) on the Janiculum, which demonstrates that he was also able to find convincing solutions for utilitarian buildings, with slender means and good proportioning. Fuga repeated this design on a larger scale in Naples for the Cimitero del Tredici (1763). Fuga's initial

proposals for rebuilding the church of the German Jesuit college in Rome, S Apollinare (1742–8), were rejected at the instigation of Cardinal Alessandro Albani. In the accepted scheme, however, Fuga skilfully sited a chapel of mercy at the end of the nave as an elegant vestibule, but the design of the façade and the interior is rather monotonous, as is the college building constructed in 1745 near the church. Fuga's church and convent (1739–44) for the Ursuline nuns at Calvi d'Umbria, although only partly realized, shows greater inventiveness.

Fuga was a highly successful architect with an established social position. In 1736 he was accepted as an honorary member of the Accademia di S Luca, Rome, and in 1754 he was elected its head. Fuga held an abundance of offices in Rome: as well as his position at the papal court, he was a member of the cameral administration as Architetto del Tribunale delle Strade from 1740 and Architetto del Popolo Romano from 1747. Besides enjoying the patronage of Cardinal Neri Corsini, Fuga owed the unbroken continuity of his career in Rome mainly to Cardinal Trojano Acquaviva (*d* 1747), the representative of the Spanish crown in Rome. He had been instrumental in procuring for Fuga the post of architect to the Roman possessions of Charles III, King of Naples, as early as 1737. In this capacity, Fuga was responsible for the festive decorations on the Piazza di Spagna in Rome in September 1738 on the occasion of the King's marriage. After the death of the two Neapolitan court architects, Domenico Antonio Vaccaro in 1745 and Ferdinando Sanfelice in 1748, Charles III summoned Fuga and Luigi Vanvitelli to Naples to assume responsibility for his major building projects. As the economic situation in Rome ruled out any further large-scale projects there, Fuga resolutely set about building a new career for himself in Naples. He was not appointed royal architect, however, until 1759, when he moved permanently to Naples and relinquished the offices he held in Rome.

2. NAPLES, 1748–82. Fuga's main work in Naples was the Albergo dei Poveri, which was intended to provide shelter and workshop employment for 8000 orphans and homeless people. The building needed to be on a colossal scale. In 1748–9 Fuga first designed a square complex grouped around four courtyards following the tradition of such hospital buildings as the Albergo dei Poveri (1654) in Genoa by Stefano Scaniglia (*fl* 1654), with the main façade punctuated by a domed church. The building had to be relocated for structural reasons, and the topography of the new site meant that only an elongated complex of buildings was possible. Fuga thus placed the courtyards in line and in the middle of the complex located the church, with a circular plan and four aisles radiating from the centre, providing separate accommodation for women, girls, boys and men. The overall length of the hospital was intended to be 600 m, but the huge building, begun in 1753 after prolonged preparatory work on the site, overtaxed the kingdom's financial resources, and by 1819 only two of the courtyard complexes had been built, while the church was still not completed. Nevertheless, the project provided further proof of Fuga's talent for working out a plan and for the carefully studied proportioning even of large-scale blocks, although the unarticulated façades are

monotonous. Another such project was the complex of huge grain stores (begun 1779; destr.) at the harbour.

Despite many varied commissions for the court and nobility in Naples, Fuga's creative talent gradually declined. The façades (*c.* 1780) of the neighbouring Caramanico and Giordano palazzi consist of an array of individual motifs that are no longer linked structurally and therefore remain isolated. Even the Villa Favorita (completed *c.* 1768) in Resina, near Naples, built for Stefano Regio Gravina, Principe di Aci, did not display the stringency of Fuga's earlier buildings. The alterations to Palermo Cathedral, which were proposed in 1767, were also merely conventional. In the elegant façade (*c.* 1780) of the church of the Gerolomini in Naples, however, Fuga reverted at the end of his life to the style of his early works. The reference to motifs from the Florentine late Baroque was already evident in the charming little court theatre in the Palazzo Reale in Naples, established in 1768. The developments leading to Neo-classicism had passed Fuga by, leaving no trace.

From the beginning of his career, Fuga was not so much a theorist as an exceptionally talented pragmatist, which was why he was so accomplished at functional planning. Confronted with difficult problems relating to the site or the complex uses of the intended building, he solved them ingeniously precisely because he was not compromised by ideological principles. Much of his work displays an unerring sense of proportion and rhythm, although he was particularly successful as an architect of utilitarian buildings, which are characterized by their formal reticence. The flatness on his buildings, often imposed by urban-planning factors, is skilfully counteracted by vertical articulation, particularly with the use of pilaster-strips, the spacing of which could be adjusted with some flexibility as they were not directly related to the overall proportions of the order. In his later work he manipulated a virtual repertory of prefabricated components, which were variously combined for each project: an economical way of working, but one that ran the risk of monotony. This is most evident in the ornamentation he used; even after his repertory of form had been consolidated in the mid-1730s, he tended to use a selection of pre-established decorative motifs. His change of style in the 1730s did not arise, however, from an intention on his part to form a new style or to give expression to new requirements, but seems to have been based primarily on complying with the wishes of his patrons. Significantly, Fuga had no pupils who carried on his style; even by the second half of the 18th century, his work had ceased to arouse any interest.

BIBLIOGRAPHY

F. Milizia: *Memorie degli architetti antichi e moderni*, ii (Bassano, 1785), pp. 287–91
G. Matthiae: *Ferdinando Fuga e la sua opera romana* (Rome, 1952)
Disegni di Ferdinando Fuga e di altri architetti del settecento (exh. cat. by L. Bianchi, Rome, Gab. N. Stampe, 1955)
R. Pane: *Ferdinando Fuga: Con documenti a cura di R. Mormone* (Naples, 1956)
A. Agosteo and A. Pasquini: *Il Palazzo della Consulta nella storia e nell'arte* (Rome, 1959)
H. Hager 'Die Kirche Santa Maria dell'Orazione e Morte von Ferdinando Fuga', *Röm. Qschr.*, lvii (1962), pp. 126–45
G. Pane: 'Ferdinando Fuga e l'Albergo dei Poveri', *Napoli Nob.*, 3rd ser., v (1966), pp. 72–84
C. Mancini: *S Apollinare* (Rome, 1967)
G. E. Rubino: 'La sistemazione del Museo Borbonico di Napoli nei disegni di Fuga e Schiantarelli (1777–79)', *Napoli Nob.*, 3rd ser., xii (1973), pp. 125–44
J. Garms: *Il Bambin Gesù* (Rome, 1979)
D. Garstaing: 'Ferdinando Fuga and the Convent of the Stimmate in Palermo', *Burl. Mag.*, cxxv (1983), pp. 749–50
J. Pinto and E. Kieven: 'An Early Project by Ferdinando Fuga for the Trevi Fountain in Rome', *Burl. Mag.*, cxxv (1983), pp. 746–9
E. Kieven: 'Rome in 1732: Alessandro Galilei, Nicola Salvi, Ferdinando Fuga', *Light on the Eternal City: Observations and Discoveries in the Art and Architecture of Rome*, Papers in Art History from the Pennsylvania State University, ii (University Park, 1987), pp. 255–75
Ferdinando Fuga e l'architettura romana del settecento (exh. cat. by E. Kieven, Rome, Gab. N. Stampe, 1988)
A. Guerra: *L'Albergo dei Poveri di F. Fuga a Napoli* (doctoral thesis, U. Venice, 1992)

ELISABETH KIEVEN

Fūgai Ekun [Dōjin] (*b* Hijishio, Kanagawa Prefect., 1568; *d* Lake Hamana, Shizuoka Prefect., 1654). Japanese Zen monk, painter and calligrapher. He entered the Shingon-sect temple Kansōji at the age of four or five, transferring to the Sōtō-sect Zen temple Chōgenji a few years later. Around the age of 16 he moved to the leading Sōtō temple in eastern Japan, Sōrinji. After completing his Zen training, perhaps in 1596, Fūgai spent two decades on pilgrimage. In 1616 he became abbot of Jōganji in Sagami Province (now part of Kanagawa Prefect.), but after only a few years he gave up his position to live in mountainside caves, which earned him the nickname Ana Fūgai ('Cave Fūgai'). This practice may have been in emulation of Bodhidharma (Jap. Daruma, the first Zen patriarch), who was reputed to have meditated in front of a wall for nine years; but such rejection of temple life was rare for a 17th-century Japanese monk. While living in the Kamisoga Mountains, Fūgai is said to have made ink paintings of Daruma, which he would hang at the entrance to his cave, so that farmers could leave rice for the monk and take the paintings home. Many such works remain, darkened by incense, in farmhouses of the region. After some years Fūgai moved to a small hut in the village of Manazuru, south of Odawara, where he continued his ink painting and calligraphy. Besides Daruma, he also depicted the wandering monk Hotei (Chin. Budai; one of the Seven Gods of Good Fortune) and occasionally brushed self-portraits and landscapes in ink on paper.

Fūgai's most characteristic paintings, however, are of themes such as *Bodhidharma Crossing the River Yangzi on a Reed* (see 1979 exh. cat., no. 27). The personal intensity of his life is expressed in his paintings, in which black accents enliven grey ink tones to emphasize the eyes, nostrils and mouths of the figures. Fūgai often added his own poetry to his paintings, usually quatrains about Daruma or Hotei, in bold, swirling cursive script (Jap. *sōsho*), such as the following:

> This wall-gazing old barbarian monk
> Has eyes that exceed the glow of the evening lamp;
> His silence has never been challenged—
> His living dharma extends to the present day.

In 1651 the Daimyo of Odawara, Inaba Masanori (1623–96), invited Fūgai to live at his castle. The old monk did not find the extravagant life of the daimyo to his taste, however, and soon left to wander in Izu Province, living for a time at Chikukei'in in Baragi. According to legend,

Fūgai died in 1654 standing up in a grave he had asked village labourers to dig for him by the shore of Lake Hamana. Although he accepted no disciples and founded no school, Fūgai was one of the most dynamic producers of *Zenga* (painting and calligraphy by Zen monks; *see* Japan, §VI, 4(vii)) of the Edo period (1600–1868) and beyond.

BIBLIOGRAPHY

S. Takase: *Fūgai Ekun Zenshi to sono sakuhin* [The Zen master Fūgai Ekun and his art works] (Hiratsuka, 1960)

Bokubi [Ink arts], 101 and 104 (1960, 1961) [both issues dedicated to Fūgai Ekun]

Song of the Brush: Japanese Paintings of the Sansō Collection (exh. cat., ed. J. Rosenfield; Seattle, WA, A. Mus., 1979)

Fūgai Dōjin ibokuten [Exhibition of remaining works of Fūgai] (exh. cat., Odawara, Shōei Mem. Hall, 1982)

S. Addiss: 'The Life and Art of Fūgai Ekun', *E. Buddhist*, xix/1 (1986), pp. 59–75

——: *The Art of Zen: Paintings and Calligraphy by Japanese Monks, 1600–1925* (New York, 1989)

STEPHEN ADDISS

Füger, Heinrich Friedrich (*b* Heilbronn, 8 Dec 1751; *d* Vienna, 5 Nov 1818). German painter. At the age of eight he was already painting miniature portraits. In 1764 he entered the Hohe Karlsschule in Stuttgart and received drawing lessons from Nicolas Guibal. Overawed by the great historical paintings in the ducal gallery, he lost heart and moved to Halle to study law; but in 1771 public demand for his miniatures encouraged him to return to painting, and in that year he moved to Leipzig, to the school of Adam Friedrich Oeser, where he became acquainted with Classical art. Returning from this two-year training, he was introduced to the works of the Italian Renaissance by Guibal. His fresh and natural miniature portraits on ivory remained in demand; portraits of his parents (1774; Vienna, Akad. Bild. Kst.) also date from these years. During a stay in Dresden, Füger met the British Ambassador, Sir Robert Murray Keith (1730–95). In 1774 he followed him to Vienna, where Keith organized numerous portrait commissions at the Austrian court.

Füger was awarded a two-year travel scholarship to Italy and left for Rome in 1776. In Rome he studied Classical art and the works of Raphael and Anton Raphael Mengs. The extension of his grant enabled him to stay in Italy for seven years, during which time he came in contact with Mengs, Jacques-Louis David, Angelica Kauffman and Gavin Hamilton. In his two years in Naples, Füger painted a portrait of *Queen Caroline* (1781; Caserta, Pal. Reale) and the four great allegories of the *School of Athens*, *Envy*, *Wealth* and the *Rebirth of the Arts* (tempera and oil; before 1783) in the library of the Palazzo Reale in Caserta. These paintings provide the most mature expression of early Neo-classicism in Naples. Figure studies from 1777–81 (notably Vienna, Akad. Bild. Kst.) in the style of Annibale Carracci, Raphael and Mengs, such as the oil painting *Apollo among the Muses* (*c.* 1780; Berlin, Neue N.G.), bear witness to his stay in Rome. The theme of self-contemplation in the arts, as it is treated in this painting and those in Caserta, occupied Füger throughout his life; the representation of female figures also shows his art at its best.

Rejecting an invitation to St Petersburg, Füger returned in 1783 to Vienna, where he became vice-director of the Akademie der Bildenden Künste (director in 1795). As court painter he remained the most popular portrait artist until *c.* 1798, when an eye ailment prevented his painting miniatures. Among his most important large-scale paintings are the portrait of the *Princess Galitzine* (1799; Berlin, Alte N.G.) and historical paintings of the *Death of Germanicus* (1815), *Death of Virginia* (1816; both Vienna, Belvedere) and *Antiochus and Stratonice* (*c.* 1790; Stuttgart, Staatsgal.). Füger's oeuvre has the eclectic character of the transitional stage between academic and mature Neo-classicism, showing influences from antiquity, the High Renaissance and classical elements of the Baroque, as well as of British portraiture, such as that of Joshua Reynolds, probably mediated in Rome by Angelica Kauffman.

In 1806, already loaded with honours of many kinds, Füger exchanged his post as director of the Akademie for the directorship of the imperial gallery, motivated partly by anxieties about the war with Napoleon, partly by internal tensions at the Akademie, where the attacks of the rising anti-academic movement were directed mainly at Füger, who was criticized for lacking both sensitivity and a direct study of nature and life.

BIBLIOGRAPHY

NDB; Thieme–Becker

Österreichische Künstler und Rom: Vom Barock zur Secession (exh. cat., Vienna, Akad. Bild. Kst.; Rome, Pal. Braschi; 1972), pp. 5–6, 53–4, 123–5, nos 89–96, figs 6, 7, 68, 69

H. von Einem: *Deutsche Malerei des Klassizismus und der Romantik* (Munich, 1978), p. 30

A. M. Schwarzenberg: *Heinrich Friedrich Füger* (diss., U. Vienna, 1978)

INGRID SATTEL BERNARDINI

Fugger. German family of merchants, bankers, patrons and collectors.

(1) Jakob Fugger II [the Rich] (*b* Augsburg, 6 March 1459; *d* Augsburg, 30 Dec 1525). He was the grandson of Hans Fugger (*d* 1408), the founder of the family cloth business, and with his two elder brothers, Ulrich Fugger (1441–1510) and Georg Fugger (1453–1506), built one of Europe's first great international mercantile firms. Through privileges granted by the Holy Roman Emperors Frederick III (*reg* 1440–93) and Maximilian I (*reg* 1493–1519), the brothers amassed fortunes in banking and later mining, including a near monopoly on European copper. At his death, Jakob's wealth was estimated to be almost two million gulden.

Although an ecclesiastical career was originally planned for Jakob, he was sent to the firm's offices in Venice and Rome in 1477–8. In 1485 he became director of the branch in Innsbruck that oversaw the mining of silver in nearby Schwaz. The international character of his company is evident in a portrait of Jakob in the *Kostümbiographie des Matthäus Schwarz* (Brunswick, Herzog Anton Ulrich-Mus.), begun in 1520, in which he stands before the desk of Schwarz, his accountant. The wall behind is filled with drawers, each labelled with the location of one of Jakob's trading branches, including Rome, Venice, Budapest, Kraków, Milan, Innsbruck, Nuremberg, Antwerp and Lisbon.

Jakob Fugger II is best known for erecting the Fugger Chapel (1509–13; consecrated 1518) in the Carmelite monastery of St Anna and the Fuggerei in Augsburg. The Fugger Chapel was the first significant Renaissance-style burial project in Germany. Although the names of the architect and decorators are undocumented, much of the sculptural decoration has been attributed to Sebastian Loscher (*fl* 1510–48) and Hans Daucher. The most notable works are the four marble reliefs against the western wall. Albrecht Dürer designed *c.* 1510 the central pair representing the *Resurrection*, with the shrouded corpse of Ulrich below, and, to the right, *Samson and the Philistines*, with the effigy of Georg. The outer pair honouring Jakob are more Italianate in their architectural features, possibly due to the involvement of Hans Burgkmair I, the leading painter in Augsburg. The sculptural decoration also included marble putti on the balustrade; the free-standing marble *Lamentation* and three limestone reliefs adorning the altar; and elaborate wooden choir-stalls (destr. 1832), ornamented with 16 pear-wood busts of male and female worthies (3 in Berlin, Bodemus.). Jörg Breu the elder painted the wings of the large and small organs, the former depicting the *Ascension* and the *Assumption of the Virgin*, the latter *Allegories on the Invention of Music*, that dominate the upper western wall. The splendour of the chapel is still evident despite the repeated removal of art from 1818 and the bomb damage of 1944.

As the chapel was nearing completion, Jakob Fugger II initiated his second major project, the Fuggerei. Located in the St Jakob's district of Augsburg, this was the most ambitious urban social project of the period in Germany. Although the concept may have been inspired by almshouses and retirement homes, the Fuggerei was designed as a charitable community for working families. It was constructed between 1517 and 1523 by Thomas Krebs (*fl* 1513–23), Augsburg's master builder, and consisted of 52 terraced houses with their own streets and wells; the chapel of St Markus was built later (1581–2).

Other than these projects, Jakob's patronage was somewhat limited. Unlike many of his later relatives, he was never a great collector of art, although he did purchase jewellery and commission portraits. In 1506 he acquired four famous jewels from the city of Basle that the Swiss had captured from Charles the Bold, 4th Duke of Burgundy, at the Battle of Grandson (1476). He later sold two of these to Emperor Maximilian I, Charles's son-in-law. The jewels have not been traced (drawings in Basle, Hist. Mus., nos 1916/475-8 and see Deuchler, 1963). Jakob also ordered portraits of himself and his wife, Sibylla Artzt, from various artists, including Thoman Burgkmair and Hans Burgkmair, Hans Holbein the elder and Dürer. Particularly significant is the chiaroscuro woodcut portrait (*c.* 1511) by Hans Burgkmair and Jost de Negker. This provided the model for numerous other likenesses of Jakob, including Hans Schwarz's bronze medal (1518), one of the earliest German examples. In 1522 Jakob commissioned Giulio Romano to paint the *Holy Family with SS James, John the Baptist and Mark* (*in situ*; *see* GIULIO ROMANO, fig. 2) for the family chapel in the newly rebuilt S Maria dell'Anima, the German church in Rome.

(2) **Anton Fugger I** (*b* Augsburg, 10 June 1493; *d* Augsburg, 14 Sept 1560). Nephew of (1) Jakob Fugger II. He was the son of Georg Fugger, and, with his elder brother Raymund Fugger (1489–1535), he directed the family firm following the death of his uncle. Anton soon assumed control of the company, since Raymund was far

more interested in scholarly pursuits, and he was one of the first great German collectors of ancient coins, bronzes and marbles (see Lieb, 1958 and Busch, 1973). Anton trained at various branches of the company, and between 1517 and 1522 he ran the office in Rome, where in 1519 Pope Leo X knighted him and made him a count of the papal court. As Protestantism gained strength in Augsburg in the 1530s, he remained a staunch Roman Catholic. Through his close ties to the Holy Roman Emperor Charles V, to whom he repeatedly lent money, his firm expanded into the Americas. In 1532 he had a grant to part of Chile and South Peru; by 1536 he was trading in slaves.

Although Anton Fugger made artistic donations to various churches, including St Moritz and the Fugger Chapel in St Anna in Augsburg, S Maria dell'Anima in Rome, Antwerp Cathedral and S Salvator in Almogro, his major project was the embellishment of his house in the Weinmarkt in Augsburg. Between 1512 and 1515 Jakob Fugger had joined his residence with his mother-in-law's, with a massive façade in emulation of an Italian palazzo. Anton and Raymund each received half. During the Imperial Diet of 1530, when Charles V resided in Anton's house (no. 36), Beatus Rhenanus described it as being filled with paintings, but no inventory of Anton's holdings survives. The interior was sumptuous; the marble columns were decorated in the antique style, the chimneypieces were also of imported marble and the ceiling gilt. In the early 1530s the western wing (Damenhof) was rebuilt in emulation of the courtyard of the ducal Residenz in Landshut. Anton engaged Jörg Breu the elder between 1532 and 1536, though the artist's autobiography fails to specify the type of paintings done. The chapel dedicated to St Sebastian was also renovated.

Anton used his wealth to buy property in and around Augsburg, throughout Swabia and also in Alsace and Hungary. The most significant of the Swabian country seats was Babenhausen, purchased in 1539, to which the architect Quirin Knoll (*fl* 1527; *d* 1552/3) added a new west wing in 1543. Elaborate gardens, a bathhouse and a hunting-lodge are mentioned in the inventory of 1557. Although later partially altered, Babenhausen now houses the Fugger-Museum.

(3) **Hans Fugger** (*b* Augsburg, 4 Sept 1531; *d* Augsburg, 15 April 1598). Son of (2) Anton Fugger I. He shared little of his father's enthusiasm for business. With the firm's bankruptcy in 1563 and the formation of a new company by his elder brother Marx Fugger (1529–97), Hans turned increasingly to his interest in art. In 1566–7 he began avidly collecting ancient sculpture and coins, often purchased through such agents as David Ott in Venice and Jacopo Strada. Foremost among his holdings was the *Amazon* sarcophagus (4th century BC; Vienna, Ksthist Mus.), which was found near Athens and brought to Augsburg in November 1568. Hans prided himself on his knowledge of antiquity and his ability to spot fakes. He frequently commissioned such sculptors as Girolamo Campagna of Venice to repair his damaged statues and such sculptors as Alexander Colin to make modern copies of ancient busts. He took an active interest in German

excavations for Roman remains, especially those conducted around Strasbourg.

In 1566 Marx and Hans split Anton's house, which they had been sharing since 1560, and Hans received the west or rear half, which he decided to renovate in order to provide a suitable setting for his burgeoning collections. Between 1568–9 and 1575 a loggia, perhaps decorated with illusionistic architectural murals, was constructed in the courtyard; an elaborate marble fountain in the form of a grotto was set in the courtyard wall; and the bath and library rooms were redecorated. An elaborate great hall, a smaller room, known as the 'Emperor's Chamber', and a chapel were added to the first floor. Hans lured a talented team of artists to Augsburg, including the designer Friedrich Sustris, who was assisted by the fresco painter Antonio Ponzano (d 1602) and the stuccoist Carlo di Cesari del Palagio. Hans's renovations were destroyed during World War II, except for portions of the most significant, the two-room library, where most of Hans's antiquities were stored. This room was damaged (1944) and has been heavily restored. The walls and ceilings were decorated with grotesque paintings, depicting classicizing landscapes, *Apollo and the Muses*, maidens holding musical instruments, which alluded to the library's secondary function as a concert hall, *Fortuna* and personifications of the months and seasons. Inspired by the paintings in the Casa Aurea of Nero in Rome, Sustris created the first Roman-style decorative programme in Germany; both rooms of the library were also lined with marble busts of Roman emperors set in niches.

Although Hans inherited and acquired numerous estates, his primary residence outside Augsburg was at Kirchheim an der Mindel, where he erected a new palace. Constructed between 1578 and 1583 by Jakob Eschay (d 1606), the complex consists of a large square, with a church set in the middle of the western wing. Its Great Hall is the best preserved of the major late Renaissance examples in Germany and Austria. Wendel Dietrich's intricate ceiling (for illustration see DIETRICH, WENDEL), made with six different types of wood, was completed in 1585. Carlo di Cesari del Palagio and Hubert Gerhard added the 12 over life-size terracotta statues of emperors and illustrious women that adorn the west and east walls of the Great Hall. In 1587 Gerhard also contributed the terracotta figures of *Mars, Venus, Vulcan* and two putti that adorn the large chimneypiece. In the 1580s, to decorate the dining-room and other chambers, Hans acquired market scenes by Vincenzo Campi, landscapes and allegories by Paolo Fiammingo and portraits by Nicolas Juvenel I. The palace chapel, which also served as the parish church, contains the *Virgin with SS Peter and Paul* altar (c. 1580) by Alexander Paduano and Hans Fugger's marble tomb (1584–7), designed by Gerhard and carved by Alexander Colin. Alessandro Vittoria executed the bronze *Annunciation* altar (1580–83; Chicago, IL, A. Inst.) for the upper chapel. In the courtyard originally stood Gerhard's huge bronze fountain group of *Mars and Venus Playing with Cupid* (1584–94; Munich, Bayer. Nmus.). The formal gardens were laid out between 1584 and 1586 by Benedikt Faktour. Despite the subsequent sale of various works of art and the destruction of the north wing and the north part of the western wing in 1852,

Kirchheim remains one of the finest Renaissance palaces and a testament to Hans's refined tastes, as well as his ability to attract talented masters from across the Continent.

(4) Octavian Secundus Fugger (b Augsburg, 17 Jan 1549; d Augsburg, 31 Aug 1600). Great-nephew of (2) Anton Fugger I. Together with his older brother Philipp Eduard Fugger (1546–1618), in 1564 he studied at the Collegium Germanicum in Rome, where he met Petrus Canisius, the famed Jesuit. This encounter strongly influenced his devotion to the Roman Catholic Church and the Jesuit Order. In 1579 the brothers were instrumental in establishing the Jesuit College of St Salvator (destr. 1773) in Augsburg. They purchased houses and a garden on Kohlergässlein in 1580, and the new complex was constructed between 1582 and 1584. Octavian Secundus also donated money and art to the college. He gave 100 gulden for an *Apostles* altar in 1584 and 500 gulden for a tabernacle in the following year. His deep personal piety also prompted him in 1586–7 to renovate the chapel of his house at 40 Weinmarkt. He commissioned an *Agnus Dei* altar (Nuremberg, Ger. Nmus.) from Hans Kastner and 12 terracotta statues of *Apostles* by Hans Steinmüller (c. 1554–1619; untraced). His small collection of holy relics, now in St Markus in the Fuggerei, Augsburg, was displayed here.

Of all of Octavian Secundus's projects, only his burial chapel in SS Ulrich and Afra in Augsburg survives largely intact. In 1583 he initiated the renovation of the chapel of St Benedict. Christoph Schwarz was commissioned to design the altar in 1585, but, on his death in 1592, Peter Candid was employed to paint the *Virgin and Child with SS Benedict and Francis* (in situ). Wendel Dietrich created the altar-frame, which includes standing wooden statues of *SS Peter and Paul* by Christoph Murmann the younger (1564/5–1630). In 1590 Jakob Dietrich (fl 1580s–90s) made the tall grille enclosing the chapel.

Besides his business activities, Octavian Secundus held various civic offices, including that of city building master in 1585 and superintendent of buildings from 1594 until his death. It was during his tenure that the three monumental bronze fountains in Augsburg (all in situ)—Hubert Gerhard's *Augustus* in front of the town hall (1588–94; in situ) and Adriaen de Vries's *Mercury* (completed 1599) and *Hercules* (1597–1602)—were conceived.

BIBLIOGRAPHY

NDB

G. Lill: *Hans Fugger (1531–1598) und die Kunst: Ein Beitrag zur Geschichte der Spätrenaissance in Süddeutschland* (Leipzig, 1908)

G. Freiherr von Pölnitz: *Jakob Fugger: Kaiser, Kirche und Kapital in der oberdeutschen Renaissance*, 2 vols (Tübingen, 1949–51)

Fugger und Welser: Oberdeutsche Wirtschaft, Politik und Kultur im Spiegel zweier Geschlechter (exh. cat., Augsburg, 1950)

N. Lieb: *Die Fugger und die Kunst im Zeitalter der Spätgotik und frühen Renaissance* (Munich, 1952) [first major study of Fugger patronage]

——: *Die Fugger und die Kunst im Zeitalter der hohen Renaissance* (Munich, 1958)

G. Freiherr von Pölnitz: *Anton Fugger*, 4 vols (Tübingen, 1958–71)

F. Deuchler: *Die Burgunderbeute* (Bern, 1963), pp. 120–5

H. Habel: *Landkreis Mindelheim*, xxxi of *Bayerische Kunstdenkmale* (Munich, 1971), pp. 168–87

R. von Busch: *Studien zu deutschen Antikensammlungen des 16. Jahrhunderts* (diss., U. Tübingen, 1973), esp. pp. 85–99

H. Dressler: *Alexander Colin* (Karlsruhe, 1973), pp. 103–5, 182

Hans Burgkmair, 1473–1973: Das graphische Werk (exh. cat., Stuttgart, Staatsgal., 1973), pl 91

B. Wind: 'Vincenzo Campi and Hans Fugger: A Peep at Late Cinquecento Bawdy Humor', *A. Lombarda*, xlvii–xlviii (1977), pp. 108–14

M. Baxandall: *The Limewood Sculptors of Renaissance Germany* (New Haven, 1980), esp. pp. 132–5, 296–8

N. Lieb: *Octavian Secundus Fugger (1549–1600) und die Kunst* (Tübingen, 1980)

Welt im Umbruch: Augsburg zwischen Renaissance und Barock, 3 vols (exh. cat., Augsburg, Rathaus and Zeughaus, 1980), esp. iii, pp. 66–81, 151–7 [superb survey of 16th-century Augsburg and its art]

H. R. Hitchcock: *German Renaissance Architecture* (Princeton, 1981), esp. pp. 7–21, 124–5, 269–71

M. Tietz-Strödel: *Die Fuggerei in Augsburg: Studien zur Entwicklung des sozialen Stiftungsbaus im 15. und 16. Jahrhundert* (Tübingen, 1982)

F. Herre: *Die Fugger in ihrer Zeit* (Augsburg, 1985)

D. Diemer: 'Hubert Gerhard and Carlo Pallago als Terrakottaplastiker', *Jb. Zentinst. Kstgesch.*, iv (1988), pp. 19–141, esp. pp. 19–53

B. Bushart: *Die Fuggerkapelle bei St Anna in Augsburg* (Munich, 1993)

JEFFREY CHIPPS SMITH

Fugitive. Term used to describe pigments or dyes that fade or change colour due to the action of light. (It does not refer to colour changes caused by chemical reactions with the atmosphere or surrounding materials.)

RUPERT FEATHERSTONE

Führich, Joseph Ritter von (*b* Kratzau, N. Bohemia, 9 Feb 1800; *d* Vienna, 13 March 1876). Bohemian painter, printmaker and teacher. Until he was 18 he was trained by his father, Wenzel Führich, a painter and mason. In 1819, at the academy exhibition in Prague, he made his début with two history paintings. Their success enabled him to study in Prague. Dürer was the first powerful influence on his style; on a visit to Vienna in 1822, medieval and Renaissance art made a similar impression. His illustrations for Ludwig Tieck's *Leben und Tod der heiligen Genoveva* (1824–5) attracted the interest of Prince Metternich, who helped him obtain a scholarship to study in Italy. On his arrival in Rome in 1827, Führich made contact with Friedrich Overbeck and other German artists there. He met Joseph Anton Koch (1768–1839) and was commissioned to complete the Tasso room (1827–9) in the Casino Massimo. In Rome he was impressed by Italian Renaissance works, particularly Raphael's frescoes in the Vatican. On the return journey to Vienna, he admired Fra Angelico's paintings and the frescoes in the Camposanto in Pisa. After a period in Prague, Führich obtained a teaching post in Vienna in 1834, becoming professor of historical composition at the Kunstschule in 1840. Such works as *Jacob and Rachel at the Well* (1836; Vienna, Belvedere) and the *Legend of St Isidore* (1839; Mannheim, Städt. Ksthalle) made him the leading representative of Nazarene-style painting in Austria. In 1844–6 he produced a monumental cycle of the *Stations of the Cross* for the church of Johann-Nepomuk and in 1850 completed the cartoons for the frescoes in the Altlerchen Church, Vienna. His late work consists largely of prints and drawings with a religious content, which brought him great popularity.

BIBLIOGRAPHY

Thieme–Becker

M. Dreger: *Joseph Führich* (Vienna, 1912)

H. von Wörndle: *Joseph Führichs Werke* (Vienna, 1914)

SEPP KERN

Fujayra. See under UNITED ARAB EMIRATES.

Fujii, Hiromi (*b* Tokyo, 23 Aug 1935). Japanese architect. He graduated in architecture from Waseda University, Tokyo, in 1958. He also studied and worked in both Milan and London (1964–8) before establishing his office in Tokyo in 1968. His highly intellectual and conceptual architecture evolved with the development of the Japanese New Wave in the 1970s (*see* JAPAN, §III, 5). His works were influenced by European Constructivism and Neoplasticism, and by Rationalist architects such as Giuseppe Terragni, as well as by American Minimalist art. They also allude to the modular dimensioning and layering of space seen in traditional Japanese architecture. His aim was a 'quintessential architecture' wherein references to everyday life were minimalized. He attempted to neutralize routine and conventional patterns of perception, in order to generate meaning on a purely existential basis. Such an approach indicated his structuralist interpretation of architecture in his early designs. He completed relatively few buildings; the first ones, including the Miyajima House (1973), Shinjuku, Tokyo, and Todoroki House (1975), Ichikawa, Chiba Prefecture, are all small cubic structures of unfinished reinforced concrete. His outstanding works of the 1980s include the Ushimado International Arts Festival Centre (1985) in Okayama, the Second Gymnasium (1985) of the Shibaura Institute of Technology in Omiya, Saitama Prefecture, and the Project Mizoe No. 1 (1988) in Iizuka City, which move away from the previously closed, inward-oriented compositions and, following a course of 'deconstruction', are largely defined by the unique application of two-dimensional layers of walls.

WRITINGS

'Architectural Metamorphology', *Japan Architect*, lv/283–4 (1980), pp. 15–23

'Quintessential Architecture and Suspended Form', *Japan Architect*, lv/283–4 (1980), pp. 25–7

BIBLIOGRAPHY

A New Wave of Japanese Architecture (exh. cat., ed. K. Frampton; New York, Inst. Archit. & Urb. Stud., 1978)

H. Yatsuka: 'Hiromi Fujii's Vision-reversing Machine', *Oppositions*, 22 (1980)

B. Bognar: *Contemporary Japanese Architecture: Its Development and Challenge* (New York, 1985)

K. Frampton, ed.: *The Architecture of Hiromi Fujii* (New York, 1987)

B. Bognar: *The New Japanese Architecture* (New York, 1990)

——: *The Japan Guide* (New York, 1995)

BOTOND BOGNAR

Fujinoki Tomb. Japanese tomb in Ikaruga-chō, Nara Prefecture. Excavated in 1985, it was probably a late 6th-century AD keyhole-shaped mound (*zenpōkōenfun*; *see* JAPAN, §III, 2(ii)), in which the stone passageway and chamber were orientated south-south-east. The mound had been built of soil from earlier tombs. The burial chamber is unusually high (4.1 m); this is a feature of tombs of the Nara and Kyoto areas. It contains a large, red-painted, house-shaped sarcophagus (*iegata sekkan*) made of Mt Nijō tufa; the Mt Nijō quarry provided stone for many sarcophagi in the region. The body and lid are each one slab, and the shape of the sarcophagus—wide and raised at the north-eastern end to accommodate head and shoulders—follows an old Chinese style that was quite rare in Japan. It is now thought that the coffin was installed after the floor of the tomb was laid and before the wall slabs were erected (it is only 800 mm from the back wall).

In 1988 the sarcophagus was opened, to reveal the bones of two human occupants and a rich array of personal possessions.

Haji earthenware (see JAPAN, §VIII, 2(i)(c)) and Sue stoneware (see JAPAN, §VIII, 2(ii)(a)) were discovered at the entrance to the burial chamber. All the metal grave goods, some wrapped in cloth, were stacked behind the sarcophagus; these included about 1000 slats of iron armour, numerous iron arrows, arrowheads, bronze horse trappings and other gilt-bronze objects. Except for the iron objects, it is believed that all the metal pieces were made in Korea, indicating close cultural ties between Japan and Korea at this time. Fujinoki has yielded the most extensive and ornate collection of horse trappings of the Kofun period (c. AD 300–710) so far found. Two gilt-bronze saddle bows with palmette, animal and bird motifs set in hexagonal frames are particularly noteworthy because of their unique compositional arrangement; notable also are flank ornaments (gyōyō), stirrups and tail or rump ornaments. The patterns on the latter consist of palmettes and real and imaginary birds and beasts and were probably drawn from Chinese sources from before the Tang period (AD 618–907).

The quantity and quality of the grave goods, the adjusted dating of the tomb in the light of excavations, the state of the bones of the taller occupant and the other material in the sarcophagus, and documents referring to the tomb combine to suggest that Fujinoki was the burial place of the assassinated Emperor Sushun (reg AD 587–92).

BIBLIOGRAPHY
Ikaruga Fujinoki kofun [Ikaruga Fujinoki tomb], Ikaruga-chō Kyoiku Iinkai [Ikaruga-chō Education Committee] (1986)
J. E. Kidder jr: 'The Fujinoki Tomb and its Grave-goods', Mnmt Nipponica, xlii/2 (1987), pp. 57–87
——: 'The Fujinoki Sarcophagus', Mnmt Nipponica, xliv/4 (1989), pp. 415–60
'Fujinoki kofun to sono jidai' ten [Exhibition on 'Fujinoki tomb and its period'] (exh. cat., Kashihara, Archaeol. Res. Lab. and NHR Serv. Cent., 1989)
J. E. Kidder jr: 'Saddle Bows and Rump Plumes: More on the Fujinoki Tomb', Mnmt Nipponica, xlv/1 (1990), pp. 75–85
J. EDWARD KIDDER JR

Fujishima, Takeji (b Kagoshima, 18 Sept 1867; d Tokyo, 19 March 1943). Japanese painter. After studying Nihonga (modern Japanese-style painting), in 1884 he went to Tokyo, where he became the pupil of the Shijō-school artist Kawabata Gyokushō (1842–1913). He changed to Yōga (Western-style painting) in 1890, studying with Yukihiko Soyama (1859–92) and Hōsui Yamamoto (1850–1906). When the course in Yōga was established at the Tokyo School of Fine Arts (now Tokyo University of Fine Arts and Music) in 1896, he was made an assistant professor on the recommendation of Seiki Kuroda (1866–1924), at the same time becoming a member of the Hakubakai (White Horse Society). Through his contact with Kuroda he was introduced to plein-air painting, but he was soon influenced by Art Nouveau and other European fin-de-siècle styles.

From 1900 Fujishima produced cover illustrations for the magazine Myōjō ('Venus'); oil paintings such as In Praise of the Tenpyō Era (1902; Kurume, Fukuoka Prefect., Ishibashi A. Mus.) and Butterflies (1904; priv. col., see Kumamoto, pl. 1) boosted his reputation. The decorative qualities visible in these works and his affinity for the forms of Art Nouveau were linked with his study of Nihonga; this is also evident in later works in which the simplification of nature enhances the decorative quality. From 1905 to 1909 he was in Europe under the auspices of the Japanese Ministry of Education and studied with Fernand Cormon in Paris and Carolus-Duran in Rome. His interest in Impressionism led to one of his finest works, the Black Fan (1908–9; Tokyo, Bridgestone A. Mus.). Also, in early Renaissance painting he identified a sense of calm similar to the Asian spirit of tranquillity, a perception that crystallized in Orchid (1926; priv. col., see Kumamoto, pl. 21), a half-length portrait of a woman in Chinese dress.

After his return to Japan, Fujishima became a professor at the Tokyo School of Fine Arts, where he not only provided guidance for the younger artists but also participated in the organization of official exhibitions. In the 1930s he produced a succession of paintings, including Surging Waves at Daio Point (1932; Tokyo, Eisei Bunko) and Terraced Fields (1938; Kurashiki, Ōhara Mus. A.), in which the Japanese landscape is depicted with clear, crisp and bold brushwork.

BIBLIOGRAPHY
M. Kawakita: Fujishima Takeji, iii of Nihon kindai kaiga zenshū [Complete collection of modern Japanese painting] (Tokyo, 1963)
K. Kumamoto: Fujishima Takeji (Tokyo, 1967)
Y. Kamon: Fujishima Takeji, xxxi of Kindai no bijutsu [Modern art] (Tokyo, 1975)
TORU ASANO

Fujita, Tsuguharu. See FOUJITA, TSUGOUHARU.

Fujiwara (i) [Fujiwarakyō; Fujiwara no miya; Shinyaku no miyako]. Japanese site, south of the city of Nara in the city of Kashihara, Nara Prefecture, in what was once Yamato Province. It is traversed by the Asuka River and surrounded by mountains in the north, east and west. Historical sources such as Nihon shoki (Chronicle of Japan; AD 720) and Shoku Nihongi (Chronicle of Japan, continued; AD 797) record that Fujiwara was the seat of the ancient Japanese monarchy and central government from AD 694 to 710. Empress Jitō (reg 686–97) ordered the construction of a new capital at the site of Fujiwara in 690, in part to fulfil an earlier desire expressed by her husband Tenmu (reg 672–86). The site chosen was an area in northern central Yamato Province that was bounded by four ancient regional highways. The word Fujiwara is not a variation on a royal or palace title (or on the ideographs thereof), as was usual in the Asuka-Hakuhō period (552–710). Scholars therefore believe that it was either adapted from a local place name—Fuji ga hara—or assigned in connection with burgeoning Fujiwara family influence at court. In 694 Jitō moved her government north to Fujiwara, abandoning the old capital at nearby Kiyomigahara in Asuka.

Although the Fujiwara site was excavated intermittently after 1934, much remains unclear. The city seems, however, to have measured approximately 2.6×1.7 km and to have been laid out in a grid pattern (see JAPAN, fig. 44). It may have marked the first adaptation in Japan of a Chinese model, possibly one developed at Luoyang in the Northern Wei (386–535) or Sui (581–618) periods, for construction of a royal 'palace city' (*tojō*) (*see* JAPAN, §IV, and PALACE, §VI, 3). The city consisted essentially of two sectors: the Daidairi ('palace compound') in the north, and the city proper. The city proper was traversed by eight boulevards (*ōji*) on a north–south axis and twelve avenues (*jō*) on an east–west axis; sectors formed by the intersection of boulevards and avenues were called *bō* (blocks). The main north–south boulevard was Suzaku Ōji, which led north from Fujiwara's southern main gate to the Daidairi.

The walled Daidairi consisted of four sections aligned on a south–north axis: the Chōshūden or Chōshūdō ('assembly compound'), a waiting area where courtiers gathered; the Chōdōin ('ministries compound'), an administrative precinct where the business of government was conducted in 12 buildings called Chōdō (Court Chambers or Ministries); the Daigokuden (Great Hall of State), the audience hall where the sovereign presided; and the Dairi (Inner Palace), where the sovereign and his family lived. At Fujiwara the Daidairi was entered from the south via a gate called Suzakumon, which opened on the Chōshūden, to the east and west of which was an assembly hall. To the north of the Chōshūden was the middle gate (*chūmon*), which gave on to the Chōdōin, with its six court chambers on each side. Further north was the Daigokuden, which was approached via the palace's formal inner gate (*seimon* or *kōmon*). The Daigokuden, which became a fixture of the Daidairi elsewhere after Fujiwara was built, is believed to have been a transformed version of the Chōdō Seiden (Formal Hall of State) earlier seen in the Dairi of palaces such as that at Naniwa (*see* OSAKA, §I, 2). The Dairi at Fujiwara possibly extended north from the Daigokuden compound.

BIBLIOGRAPHY

Prince Toneri: *Nihon shoki* [Chronicle of Japan] (AD 720); Eng. trans. by W. G. Aston as 'Nihongi', *Trans. & Proc. Japan Soc., London*, suppl. (1896) [whole issue]

Shoku Nihongi [Chronicle of Japan, continued] (AD 797)

M. Ueda: 'Miyako no shutsugen to chiiki no bunka' [Regional culture and the emergence of capital palace cities], *Asuka, Hakuhō, Zusetsu Nihon bunka no rekishi* [An illustrated history of Japanese culture]; ed. M. Ueda and others, ii (Tokyo, 1979), pp. 45–64

K. Tsuboi: *Kinkihen* [The home provinces], Zusetsu hakkutsu ga kataru Nihonshi [An illustrated history of Japan as revealed through excavations], iv (Tokyo, 1985)

MIMI HALL YIENGPRUKSAWAN

Fujiwara (ii). Japanese family of courtiers, regents (*sesshō*, *kanpaku*) and artists. They wielded enormous power during much of the Heian period (AD 794–1185) and played a leading role in the regency government (*sekkan seiji*; AD 967–1068). The years 894–1185 are often referred to as the Fujiwara period. The Fujiwara clan was founded by Nakatomi no Kamatari (614–69), who had assisted Prince Naka no Oe (later Emperor Tenji, *reg* 661–72) in the coup of 645 that eliminated the rival Soga family. In 669 Tenji bestowed on Nakatomi the name Fujiwara ('wisteria field'). The Fujiwara reached the height of their power with the regent Fujiwara no Michinaga (966–1028), after whose time Fujiwara dominance at court began to decline. The family also produced a number of skilled calligraphers who were instrumental in establishing or influencing styles of aristocratic Japanese-style (*Wayō*) calligraphy, such as those of the Sesonji and Hosshōji schools (*see* JAPAN, §VII, 2(ii)). (1) Fujiwara no Sari and

(2) Fujiwara no Kōzei, along with ONO NO MICHIKAZE, were renowned as the Sanseki ('three brush traces'; Three Masters), so designated because of their accomplishments in both Chinese- and Japanese-style calligraphy, but several other members of the family also achieved fame as calligraphers or painters. Two great legacies of the Fujiwara period and monuments to Fujiwara taste are the Hōōdō (Phoenix Hall) of BYŌDŌIN at Uji, south-east of Kyoto, and a sculpture installed within it of *Amida* (Skt Amitabha) by JŌCHŌ.   □

(1) Fujiwara no Sari [Fujiwara no Sukemasa] (*b* AD 944; *d* 998). Calligrapher. He joined the court nobility in 978, attaining the high rank of Senior Third in 984. In 991 he was appointed Deputy Governor (Dazai Daini) of Dazaifu in Kyushu. According to records, Sari created many important calligraphies, including name plaques for the imperial palace buildings and gate, and for the Rokuharamitsuji, a Buddhist temple in Kyoto; for these plaques his calligraphy would have been copied in carving by craftsmen. The earliest extant calligraphy by Sari is the *Shikaishi* (priv. col.), a poem written on a *kaishi* (jotting paper), believed to have been composed by him in 969 during a poetry party held at the residence of his grandfather, Fujiwara no Saneyori. It is also thought to be the oldest extant example of handwritten calligraphy on a *kaishi*. A spontaneous piece, in Chinese characters, it exhibits Sari's mastery of the tradition of the influential 4th-century Chinese calligrapher Wang Xizhi (*see* WANG (i), (1)) and of the style of Ono no Michikaze. The irregular spacing of the characters and the eccentric diversity of ink tone reveal Sari's forceful and impetuous temperament. He is considered a less 'dignified' calligrapher than Michikaze, less 'elegant' than Kōzei and more individualistic and unconventional than both, in his writing style as in his life. The remaining genuinely attributable extant works by Sari are such letters as the *Kyokajō* ('Avoiding summer'; see Tamura, pl. 30), probably written between 983 and 985, the *Rirakujō* ('Leaving the capital', *c.* 991; Tokyo, Hatakeyama A. Mus.), written to his nephew Fujiwara no Sanenobu on the way to Dazaifu, and the *Tōnobenjō* (see Tamura, pl. 31), a letter of enquiry to the Head Chamberlain probably written in 998, four months before Sari's death. Sari's letters were all written in great haste and display an emphatic linearity unusual in Japanese-style (*Wayō*) calligraphy. The sharply angled turns where the brush changed direction were characteristic.

BIBLIOGRAPHY

H. Onoue: 'Sanseki ni tsuite' [About the 'three brush traces'], *Shodō zenshū* [Complete collection of calligraphy], ed. K. Shimonaka, xii (Tokyo, 1954), pp. 22–9, 169–72; pls 52–64

Y. Nakata, ed.: *Sho* [Calligraphy] (Tokyo, 1970–73); Eng. trans. as *The Art of Japanese Calligraphy* (New York and Tokyo, 1973)

S. Iijima, ed.: *Shodō jiten* [Dictionary of calligraphy] (Tokyo, 1975), pp. 683–5

E. Tamura, ed.: 'Sanseki: Michikaze, Sari, Kōzei' [The 'three brush traces': Michikaze, Sari, Kōzei], *Nihon No Bijutsu*, cxxii/7 (1976) [whole issue]

Y. Nakata, ed.: *Ono no Tōfū: Fujiwara no Sari* [Ono no Michikaze and Fujiwara no Sari] (1977), xvi of *Shodō geijutsu* [Art of calligraphy] (Tokyo, 1975–7, rev. 1979–82)

Tokubetsuten nihon no sho [Special Exhibition: Japanese calligraphy] (exh. cat., Tokyo, N. Mus., 1978)

(2) Fujiwara no Kōzei [Fujiwara no Yukinari] (*b* AD 972; *d* 1027). Calligrapher. His style was free from marked idiosyncrasy and easy to emulate, and it became a standard writing style inherited by the Sesonji school (*see* JAPAN, §VII, 2(ii) and fig. 122), which enjoyed an authoritative position for five centuries before it eventually declined into mannerism. Kōzei is known as a master of *kana* (Japanese phonetic script). However, of the 30 or more *kana* calligraphies associated with his name and written in the gently flowing style thought to be typical of his work (see *Shodō zenshū*, xiii (Tokyo, 1954), pls 29–42), none has been positively attributed to him. The extant works most likely to be from his hand were written entirely in *mana* (Chinese characters used as units of meaning), in Chinese running (Jap. *gyōsho*; Chin. *xing shu*) and in cursive (Jap. *sōsho*; Chin. *cao shu*) scripts, but skilfully adapted to the Japanese taste for grace and delicacy.

He was raised by the Regent Koretada, his grandfather, after his father Yoshitaka's premature death. Kōzei rose high at court: to Senior Second Rank and to the post of Provisional Major Counsellor (*gon-dainagon*). Kōzei was probably the most popular calligrapher of his time and was favoured with the patronage of the great statesman and court official Fujiwara no Michinaga (AD 966–1027), and of emperors, court aristocrats, shrines and temples. *Gonki* ('Diary of the counsellor'), a transcript of the diary kept by Kōzei, illustrates his busy schedule of completing title characters for *sūtra*s, inscriptions for temple bells, calligraphies of poems to be mounted on decorative folding screens or made up into presentation books, final copies of court documents and literary works. Kōzei also executed the names of palace buildings, to be copied in carving on wooden plaques hung at the building entrances.

Surviving works include some masterly poem fragments (*Honnōji-gire*) written on paper decorated with phoenix (Kyoto, Honnōji; see Tamura, pl. 46); a scroll of poems by the Tang-period (AD 618–907) poet Bo (or Bai) Juyi (AD 772–846), written when Kōzei was 47 (Tokyo, N. Mus; see Tamura, pls 14 and 44), a representative work although he himself found it wanting; and a letter written two years later announcing his promotion to Provisional Major Counsellor, which exhibits to the full the grace and decorum of his Japanese style (Tokyo, priv. col.; see Tamura, pl. 11).

Kōzei was talented as well as diligent. He studied the works of Michikaze and, according to the *Gonki*, a *Sōgokuhen* (a character dictionary of the fastest script). His court position enabled him to borrow at least six Chinese calligraphic copybooks from the Imperial Repository (Gi-yōden), including the famous *Treatise of Warrior Yue Yi* and the *Huang ting jing* (the 'Yellao court scripture') attributed to the 4th-century calligrapher Wang Xizhi (*see* WANG (i), (1)). Kōzei was a devout Buddhist and a disciplined man, slow to anger yet quick-witted, qualities that seem to have been reflected in his calligraphy and that perfectly suited the courtly mood and taste of the time. Kōzei's son Yukitsune (1013–50) was also a calligrapher and headed the Sesonji school after Kōzei, but few works are reliably attributed to him. Kōzei no Musume (1006–21), Kōzei's cherished fourth daughter, who was married to the son of Fujiwara no Michinaga, evidently inherited her father's talent. Work she did before the age of 14 served some students as a calligraphic text.

BIBLIOGRAPHY

H. Onoue: 'Sanseki ni tsuite' [About the 'three brush traces'), *Shodō zenshū* [Complete collection of calligraphy], ed. Y. Shimonaka, xii (Tokyo, 1954), pp. 22–9, 173–9, pls 66–90

Y. Haruna: 'Fujiwara no Kōzei', *Bokubi* [Beauty of ink], cxxx (1963)

Y. Nakata, ed.: *Sho* [Calligraphy] (Tokyo, 1970–73); Eng. trans. as *The Art of Japanese Calligraphy* (New York and Tokyo, 1973)

S. Iijima, ed.: *Shodō jiten* [Dictionary of calligraphy] (Tokyo, 1975), pp. 667–78

Y. Nakata, ed.: *Fujiwara no Kōzei* (1975), xv of *Shodō geijutsu* [Art of calligraphy] (Tokyo, 1975-7, rev. 1979–82)

E. Tamura, ed.: *Sanseki: Michikaze, Sari, Kōzei* [The 'three brush traces': Michikaze, Sari, Kōzei], *Nihon No Bijutsu*, cxxii/7 (1976) [whole issue]

SADAKO OHKI

(3) Fujiwara no Sadanobu (*b* 1088; *d* between 1151 and 1156). Calligrapher, fifth direct descendant of (2) Fujiwara no Kōzei. He was the son of Fujiwara no Sadazane (?1076–1120), grandson of Fujiwara no Korefusa (1030–96) and fifth-generation head of the Sesonji school of calligraphy (*see* JAPAN, §VII, 2(ii)). Unlike a number of his illustrious forebears, he did not have a flourishing government career; however, he was recognized for his calligraphic skills at an early age. A number of his dated works survive on petitions and screens and in the form of calligraphies to be copied in carving for plaques over gates and temple doors. Sandanobu also brushed calligraphies for poetry anthologies, such as the 39-volume transcription, *c.* 1112, of the *Sanjūrokunin kashū* ('Collection of the 36 master poets'), a compilation of representative Japanese verse made by Fujiwara no Kintō (966–1041). The *Sanjūrokunin kashū* transcription was executed by 20 different calligraphers, including Sadanobu (e.g. page from *Ishiyama-gire* ('Poems of Ki no Tsurayuki'); Seattle, WA, A. Mus.; *see* JAPAN, §VII, 1(i) and fig. 117). He is particularly well known, however, for his copy of the Buddhist *sūtra*s, *Hannya rishukyō* and the *Issaikyō* (the whole Buddhist canon). He began copying the *Issaikyō* when he was 42 and persevered for 23 years until he had copied all 5048 volumes. For this major accomplishment he was accorded the special respects of the Minister of the Left, Fujiwara no Yorinaga (1120–56). Such was the quality of his work that when Sadanobu sent a poem to Saigyō (1118–90), the famous Buddhist priest 30 years his junior, Saigyō rewarded him with the unusual favour of a poem in return. Sadanobu also added the postscript (*okugaki*) to the famed *Byōbu dodai* ('Draft for inscription on a folding screen') attributed to ONO NO MICHIKAZE. Probably because of the speed with which Sadanobu wielded the brush, there is a slight upward slant to the right in his script. His writing represented a fluid interpretation of the Sesonji style.

BIBLIOGRAPHY

Y. Nakata, ed.: *Sho* [Calligraphy] (Tokyo, 1970–73); Eng. trans. as *The Art of Japanese Calligraphy* (New York and Tokyo, 1973)

M. Kotani: 'Heian jidai no sho' [Calligraphy of the Heian period], *Nihon no Bijutsu*, clxxx/5 (1981) [whole issue]

Masters of Japanese Calligraphy, 8th–19th Century (exh. cat. by Y. Shimizu and J. M. Rosenfield, New York, Japan House Gal., 1984)

(4) Fujiwara no Tadamichi (*b* 1097; *d* 1164). Calligrapher and poet. At the early age of 19 he was appointed to a high government office. After a political and military conflict with his father, Tadazane (1078–1162), and his brother Yorinaga (1120–56), which also included the issue of succession to the throne, Tadamichi emerged triumphant and served as regent for 38 years near the end of the Heian era (794–1185). When he was taken by his father at the age of six for an audience with Emperor Horikawa (*reg* 1087–1107), he is said to have been given a calligraphy textbook by ONO NO MICHIKAZE, one of the Sanseki ('three brush traces'; Three Masters) of calligraphy of the early Heian period. Soon recognized for his writing skills, he began creating calligraphies for plaques, religious petitions (*ganmon*) and on large square poem cards (*shikishi*). Tadamichi based his style on that of (2) Fujiwara no Kōzei, another of the Sanseki, but developed a more deliberate, vigorous, stronger stroke, less elegant and smooth than the styles of the early Heian-period court calligraphers, and more appropriate to the tastes of the warrior classes, which were then in the ascendancy. After his son Motozane became regent, he retired to the temple of Hosshōji, where he died. His calligraphic style, which therefore became known as the Hosshōji style, flourished for many years. Tadamichi was also celebrated as a poet, writing in Japanese and Chinese. Of the works brushed by him, drafts of 29 letters are extant, but none of his poetry has survived.

BIBLIOGRAPHY

M. Kotani: 'Heian jidai no sho' [Calligraphy of the Heian period], *Nihon no Bijutsu*, clxxx/5 (1981) [whole issue]
Masters of Japanese Calligraphy, 8th–19th Century (exh. cat. by Y. Shimizu and J. M. Rosenfield, New York, Japan House Gal., 1984)

CECIL H. UYEHARA

(5) Fujiwara no Shunzei [Fujiwara no Toshinari; Shakua] (*b* 1114; *d* 1204). *Waka* poet, literary theorist and critic, calligrapher. He was born into a branch family of the Fujiwara clan and, like many of his family, became a court official. In 1167, upon his elevation to Senior Third Rank at court, he changed his given name from Akihiro to Toshinari. In 1172, he rose to his highest office, the relatively modest post of chamberlain of the empress dowager's household, from which he retired owing to illness. He took the tonsure and the Buddhist name Shakua in 1177. Despite his relatively low rank, Shunzei was highly regarded as a literary critic and arbiter of poetry competitions. Shunzei's deeply felt Buddhism and practice of meditation were reflected in his poetry, which for him was a serious, almost religious vocation. His poetic ideal may be described as *yūgen* ('mystery and depth') and *sabi* ('loneliness'), which together enabled a poet to express the transience of human experience and of the beauty of nature. In 1183, Emperor GoShirakawa (*reg* 1155–8) commissioned him to compile the seventh imperial anthology of classical Japanese poetry, the *Senzaiwakashū* ('Collection of a thousand years').

The political turbulence and violent shift of power from aristocratic courtiers to warriors during the late Heian (794–1185) and early Kamakura (1185–1333) periods naturally influenced Shunzei's life and are clearly revealed in his handwriting as well as in his poetic conception. Shunzei did not develop a truly individualistic style until he was in his fifties. Only about a dozen of Shunzei's calligraphies are extant, mostly letters, copies of imperial poetry anthologies or copies of his own poems. The earliest extant piece is a fragment of the *Kokinwakashū* ('Anthology of ancient and modern Japanese verse';

commissioned *c.* 905), commonly referred to as the *Akihiro-gire* ('Akihiro fragment'; see Kuso, pl. 37). It dates from about 1143 and is written in an orthodox *kana* (Japanese phonetic script) style of smooth brushwork typical of the then prevailing Hosshōji school of calligraphy (*see* (4) above).

The record (Tokyo, Maeda Ikutoku Found. Lib.; see Kuso, p. xviii, pl. 37) of a poetry competition held in 1172 at Hirotasha, a Shinto shrine (now in Hyōgo Prefect.), reveals a marked change of style in his work: a pronounced angularity where the brush changed direction and conspicuous 'nail-heads' or thickening from pressure on the brush at the end of horizontal strokes. These distinctive characteristics became more pronounced in Shunzei's later life. The *Hino-gire Senzaishū* (Tokyo, Dai Tōkyū Mem. Found.; see Kuso pl. 41), a fragment of the *Senzaiwakashū*, written in 1188 when Shunzei was 74, exhibits even more markedly angular turns and spiky strokes, as well as wire-thin strokes without much 'flesh'. The calligraphies of his last decade were less wiry, but the distinctive sharply angled turns remained. Shunzei was outwardly a gentle and courteous man, but his individualistic calligraphic style reveals disciplined inner strength. He was the father of the famous poet and calligrapher (7) Fujiwara no Teika.

BIBLIOGRAPHY

S. Kuso: 'Fujiwara no Shunzei', *Shodō zenshū* [Complete collection of calligraphy], ed. K. Shimonaka, xviii (Tokyo, 1956), pp. 34–46, 173–8, pls 37–46
S. Morita, ed.: 'Fujiwara no Shunzei', *Bokubi* [Beauty of ink], cdiii (1965)
Y. Nakata, ed.: *Sho* [Calligraphy] (Tokyo, 1970–7); Eng. trans. as *The Art of Japanese Calligraphy* (New York and Tokyo, 1973)
S. Iijima, ed.: *Shodō jiten* [Dictionary of calligraphy] (Tokyo, 1975), pp. 686–90
Y. Nakata, ed.: *Saigyō: Fujiwara no Shunzei; Fujiwara no Teika* (1977), xvi of *Shodō geijutsu* [Art of calligraphy] (Tokyo, 1975–7, rev. 1979–82)
Masters of Japanese Calligraphy, 8th–19th Century (exh. cat. by Y. Shimizu and J. M. Rosenfield, New York, Japan House Gal., 1984), pp. 11–16, 46–50, 96–7

SADAKO OHKI

(6) Fujiwara no Takanobu (*b* 1142; *d* 1205). Painter and poet, stepson of (5) Fujiwara no Shunzei. Born into an aristocratic literary family, he was known by his peers to be a skilled artist and an accomplished poet. However, as a courtier, for whom painting was an avocation rather than a profession, Takanobu remained outside the purview of the Edokoro (Bureau of Painting), instead becoming one of the amateur painters with professional skills who were emerging at that time.

Together with his son (8) Fujiwara no Nobuzane, Takanobu is credited with the development of an indigenous form of Japanese portraiture called *nisee* ('likeness painting; see JAPAN, §VI, 3(iii)). During the Heian period (794–1185), idealized facial features appear to have been preferred in secular portraits of aristocrats. Using the convention of *hikime kagihana* ('line for an eye, hook for a nose'), such portraits gave a rather stereotyped depiction of their subjects. By contrast, court records and personal diaries show that Takanobu was skilled in painting realistic faces in a way contemporary viewers found shocking. In 1173 the minister Kujō Kanezane (1149–1207) noted his good fortune at not having been present for the three imperial pilgrimages illustrated on the walls of the Saishō-kōin at the temple Hōjūji in Heian-Kyō (Kyoto): he had thus avoided becoming the subject of one of Takanobu's extremely naturalistic depictions of the courtiers in attendance.

Only three portraits at the Jingoji in Kyoto are now associated with Takanobu, although the attribution is unconfirmed. Originally part of a set of five, which included a portrait of retired Emperor GoShirakawa (reg 1155–8), the extant paintings depict Minamoto no Yoritomo (1147–99; see JAPAN, §VI, 3(iii) and fig. 87), Taira no Shigemori (1138–79) and Fujiwara no Mitsuyoshi (1132–1183).

BIBLIOGRAPHY

T. Mori: 'Minamoto Yoritomo zō ni tsuite' ['On the portrait of Minamoto Yoritomo'] *Bijutsushi*, 2 (1950), pp. 28–39

M. Graybill: *Kasen-e: An Investigation into the Origins of the Tradition of Poet Pictures in Japan*, i and ii (diss., Ann Arbor, U. MI, 1983)

NICOLE FABRICAND-PERSON

(7) Fujiwara no Teika [Fujiwara no Sadaie; Myōjō] (*b* 1162; *d* 1241). Poet, editor and calligrapher, son of (5) Fujiwara no Shunzei. He inherited his talents as a *waka* (Japanese classical) poet from his father, whom he eventually exceeded. Unlike his genial father, however, he was aloof, hot-tempered and obstinate; consequently his advancement as a court official was slow, although he did, in 1232, reach the rank of Provisional Middle Counsellor. He took the tonsure in 1233 and assumed the priestly name Myōjō but continued literary work until his death.

Teika played a leading role in preserving the classical poetry tradition of the Heian period (794–1185) in the face of an emerging warrior culture. He was appointed one of six people to compile the eighth and most influential imperial anthology, the *Shinkokinwakashū* ('New collection of ancient and modern Japanese verse'; completed 1205), although he quarrelled with Emperor GoToba over the choice of poems for inclusion. He was also sufficiently respected in government circles to be appointed poetry tutor to the young shogun Minamoto no Sanetomo (1192–1219) and sole compiler of the *waka* anthology *Shinchokusenwakashū* ('New imperial collection of Japanese verse'; completed 1235), commissioned by Emperor GoHorikawa (reg 1221–32).

Teika was an exacting editor, collator and copyist of earlier Heian-period literature, and the standard editions of many classics, such as the *Genji monogatari* ('Tale of Genji'; *c.* 1005) and the *Sarashina nikki* ('Sarashina diary'; *c.* 1060), are based on his texts. His own poetry was characterized by emotional intensity and evocative power. His compilations, such as *Eiga taigai* ('General rules of poetic compilations'; *c.* 1222), had a tremendous impact on later poets. His taste largely defined what are recognized as the Heian-period classics.

Teika's calligraphic style was extremely individualistic. The works of his twenties, possibly still influenced by the then prevailing Hosshōji school (see (4) above), display a flowing movement created by the elongation of each character and considerable vertical linking of characters. Even these early works were marked by heavy accentuation of lines, especially of the verticals, a feature that endured in his calligraphy throughout his life. Some time before he turned 40 he began to produce densely spaced calligraphic phrases with distinctive, squat character shapes. The works of his mid-forties are represented by a fragment of his own *waka* poems, known as *Eisō-gire* ('Eisō fragments',

1207; Tokyo, Maeda Ikutoku Found. Lib., see Murayama, pl. 3). It exhibits a long sweep of rushing brushwork; the characters are remarkably squat and close together as if to economize on space. Teika's concern was not excellent writing but accurate recording. His characters were therefore heavily inked and rather lacking in variation for each phonetic script.

From his sixties onwards a telling feature of Teika's work was that the characters were written independently. Probably because of failing eyesight and general physical frailty, Teika could no longer write with his accustomed vigour in his late years. Extant works from this period include the famous *Ogura no shikishi* ('Ogura poem cards', *c.* 1235; priv. col., see Murayama, fig. 23 and pl. 1) and the *Sarashina nikki* ('Sarashina Diary', *c.* 1237; Imperial Household Col., see Murayama, pl. 7). The weighty vertical lines and the almost arbitrary accentuation of wide brushstrokes are clearly evident in these works.

Teika was not considered an important calligrapher until the late 16th century, when his style came to be venerated, principally by practitioners of the tea ceremony, who hung prized examples in the *tokonoma* (decorative alcoves) of their teahouses. Teika's second son, Tameie (1198–1275), was also an accomplished, if more orthodox, calligrapher, as were Tameie's sons, such as Tameuji (1222–86).

BIBLIOGRAPHY

S. Murayama: 'Fujiwara Teika', *Nihon: Kamakura II* [Japan: Kamakura II], ed. Z. Kanda and others, *Shodō zenshū* [Complete collection of calligraphy], xix (Tokyo, 1957), pp. 12–19, 141–7, pls 1–9

Y. Haruna: *Fujiwara no Teika*, Bokubi [Beauty of ink], cxxix (Kyoto, 1963), pp. 17–29

Y. Nakata, ed.: *Sho* [Calligraphy] (Tokyo, 1970–73); Eng. trans. as *The Art of Japanese Calligraphy* (New York and Tokyo, 1973)

S. Iijima, ed.: *Shodō jiten* [Dictionary of calligraphy] (Tokyo, 1975), pp. 693–703

Y. Nakata, ed.: *Saigyō, Fujiwara no Shunzei, Fujiwara no Teika* (1977), xvi of *Shodō geijutsu* [Art of calligraphy] (Tokyo, 1975–7, rev. 1979–82)

S. Shimizu and J. Rosenfield: *Masters of Japanese Calligraphy: 8th–9th Century* (New York, 1984), pp. 11–16, 46–50, 96–7, pl. 13

Word in Flower: the Visualization of Classical Literature in 17th-century Japan (exh. cat., ed. C. Wheelwright; New Haven, CT, Yale U. A.G., 1989)

SADAKO OHKI

(8) Fujiwara no Nobuzane (*b* 1176; *d* ?1265). Painter, son of (6) Fujiwara no Takanobu. Taught by his father, he became a prominent court painter in Kyoto during the Kamakura period (1185–1333). Like his father, Nobuzane brought a heightened naturalism to court portraiture, especially compared with the conventionalized pictorial style (*Yamatoe*; see JAPAN, §VI, 3(iii)) of the Heian period (794–1185). Facial features that had been rendered with little more than a slanting stroke for the eye and a hook for the nose now exhibited much more individualized detail. Though only slightly truer to life than their forerunners, these works by Nobuzane were called *nisee* ('likeness pictures').

Few surviving works can be assigned with assurance to Nobuzane. Usually associated with his name are a portrait (hanging scroll, ink and light colour on paper, 1221; Osaka, Minase Shrine) of *Retired Emperor GoToba* (reg 1183–98) and two series of imaginary portraits of 36 famous poets and poetesses of the Nara (710–94) and Heian periods (*Sanjūrokkasene*; part of a broader tradition of pictures of poetic immortals called KASEN'E). These two handscroll compositions are known as the Satake, after the name of a former owner, and the Agedatami, in reference to the fact that each poet is seated on a raised (*age*) mat (*tatami*). Extant fragments, painted in ink and colour on paper and now mounted as hanging scrolls, are preserved in a number of collections (e.g. Osaka, Fujita Mus. A.; Tokyo, Gotoh Mus.; Washington, DC, Freer; and Cleveland, OH, Mus. A.).

BIBLIOGRAPHY

T. Minamoto: *Yamatoe no kenkyū* [*Yamatoe* studies] (Tokyo, 1976)
T. Mori: *Sanjūrokkasene* [36 immortal poets] (1979), xix of *Shinshū Nihon emakimono zenshū* [Complete collection of Japanese handscrolls, new edition], ed. I. Tanaka (Tokyo, 1976–81)
M. Graybill: *Kasen'e: An Investigation into the Origins of the Tradition of Poet Pictures in Japan* (diss., Ann Arbor, U. MI, 1983)
Court and Samurai in an Age of Transition: Medieval Paintings and Blades from the Gotoh Museum, Tokyo (exh. cat., New York, Japan Soc., 1990)

JOAN H. O'MARA

Fujiwara no Sadaie. *See* FUJIWARA (ii), (7).

Fujiwara no Sukemasa. *See* FUJIWARA (ii), (1).

Fujiwara no Toshinari. *See* FUJIWARA (ii), (5).

Fujiwara no Yukinari. *See* FUJIWARA (ii), (2).

Fukami Gentai. *See* KŌ TEN'I.

Fukase, Masahisa (*b* Hokkaido, 25 Feb 1934). Japanese photographer. He graduated in 1956 in photography at Nihon University in Tokyo and worked as a commercial photographer. His first exhibition, the one-man show *Buta wo kurose* ('Kill the pigs'; Tokyo, Ginza A.G., 1961), was a surrealistic fantasy set in a slaughterhouse. The photographs in this exhibition were later gathered in the collection *Yūgi* ('Play'; Tokyo, 1971). He established his individual style in the series *Yōko* (Tokyo, 1978), which records with bitter humour his daily life with Yōko, his wife from 1964 to 1976. After his divorce from her, his work became more abstract, and flocks of ravens, suggestive of human mortality, were chosen as graphic symbols. In 1977 the series *Karasu* ('Ravens'; Tokyo, 1986) received the Ina Nobuo Prize. His viewpoint became increasingly introspective, characterized by the expression of a concern with the more profound aspects of life and death. Shortly after publishing his book *Chichi no kioku* ('Memories of father'; Tokyo, 1991) he was seriously injured in an accident.

BIBLIOGRAPHY

New Japanese Photography (exh. cat. by J. Szarkowski and S. Yamagishi, New York, MOMA, 1974), pp. 68–73
Japanese Photography Today and its Origin (exh. cat. by A. Colombo and I. Doniselli, Bologna, Gal. A. Mod.; Milan, Pal. Reale; Brussels, Pal. B.-A.; London, ICA; 1979), pp. 156–7
Black Sun: The Eyes of Four (exh. cat. by M. Holborn, Oxford, MOMA; London, Serpentine Gal.; Philadelphia, PA, Mus. A.; 1985), pp. 49–64

KOHTARO IIZAWA

Fukashijō. *See* MATSUMOTO CASTLE.

Fukuda, Heihachirō (*b* Ōita, 28 Feb 1892; *d* Kyoto, 22 March 1974). Japanese painter. He graduated in 1918 from the Kyoto Municipal Professional School of Painting and participated in such official exhibitions as the New Bunten, the Teiten and the Nitten. Initially he studied the realism

of the Chinese Song (960–1279) and Yuan (1279–1368) periods and the traditional Japanese Maruyama–Shijō school (*see* JAPAN, §VI, 4(viii)), experimenting exhaustively with the depiction of the subject. However, in the 1930s Fukuda simplified the forms of his subjects and established a traditional Japanese painting style (*Nihonga*; *see* JAPAN, §VI, 5(iii)), using fresh observation and decorative composition in such works as *Ripples* (1932; priv. col.). Subsequently his principal interest was in combining decorative and realistic elements. His important works include *Rain* (1953; Tokyo, N. Mus. Mod. A.). In 1947 he became a member of the Japan Art Institute, and in 1961 he received the Order of Cultural Merit.

BIBLIOGRAPHY

Fukuda Heihachirō (Tokyo, 1976)

YOSHIKAZU IWASAKI

Fukuhara, Shinzō (*b* Tokyo, 25 July 1883; *d* Tokyo, 29 Sept 1946). Japanese photographer. The son of the head of Shiseido pharmaceutical company, he went to the USA in 1908 to study pharmacology at Columbia University. He graduated in 1913 and, on his way back to Japan, he spent six months in Paris, where he took many photographs, mainly of the banks of the Seine, reminiscent of sketches by Degas; these were later published as *Pari to Sēnu* ('Paris and the Seine'; Tokyo, 1922) and were highly regarded as examples of Japanese pictorial photography.

In 1921 he founded the Photographic Art Association (Shashin Geijutsu-sha) with Isao Kakefuda (1886–1953), Motō Ōtaguro (1893–1979) and Rosō Fukuhara (1892–1946), and began to produce the magazine *Shashin geijutsu* ('Photographic art'). In it he outlined his influential philosophy, which emphasized the visual impression of the subject, 'light with its harmony', transferred to the photographic surface. His later collections included *Hikari to sono kaichō* ('Light with its harmony'; Tokyo, 1923), *Seiko fūkei* ('Scenes of Seiko'; Tokyo, 1931) and *Matsue fūkei* ('Scenes of Matsue'; Tokyo, 1935). In 1924 he founded, and subsequently advised, the Japanese Photographic Association (Nihon Shashin-kai).

BIBLIOGRAPHY

K. Iizawa: *Art Photography in Japan, 1900–1930* (Tokyo, 1986), pp. 91–7
T. Ozawa, ed.: *The Heritage of Art Photography in Japan*, Complete Hist. Jap. Phot., ii (Tokyo, 1986), pp. 33–42
Shinzo of Roso Fukuhara (exh. cat. by H. Chandès and K. Iizawa, Paris, 1994)
The World of Shinzo Fukuhara: Poetics of Light (exh. cat. by Y. Fukuhara and others, Tokyo, 1994)

KOHTARO IIZAWA

Fukuzawa, Ichirō (*b* Fukuoka, Gunma Prefect., 18 Jan 1898; *d* Tokyo, 16 Oct 1992). Japanese painter. In 1918 he entered the literature department of Tokyo University; however, a liking for sculpture made him turn his attention to fine art. Travelling to France to research European art (1924) caused his interest to shift from sculpture to painting. From *c.* 1929 he was influenced by Surrealism and, stimulated by the collages of Max Ernst, he produced such works as *Another's Love* and *Science Blinds Beauty* (both 1930; Takasaki, Gunma Prefect. Mus. Mod. A.). In 1931, shortly before his return to Japan, he sent 37 *Yōga* (Western-style) paintings to the first exhibition of the Dokuritsu Bijutsu Kyōkai (Independent Art Society). The ironic, witty and sharp punning nature of these pieces had hitherto not been seen in Japanese painting. Their display caused a great sensation in *Yōga* circles.

Although the influence of Surrealism had already begun to permeate Japanese art circles, Fukuzawa's return in summer 1931 stimulated widespread interest in Surrealism. He gathered together a group of painters influenced by Surrealism, leading to the formation of the Bijutsu Bunka Kyōkai (Art Culture Society) in 1939. The work *Oxen* (1936; Tokyo, N. Mus. Mod. A.) is characteristic of this period, with a distinctive irony and allegorical meaning. However in 1941, due to arrests resulting from suspicion of a link between Surrealism and Communism, he ceased to create his Surrealist works freely and at one point even painted war pictures. After World War II, Fukuzawa produced such paintings as *Group Defeat* and *Collapse* (both 1948; Takasaki, Gunma Prefect. Mus. Mod. A.), which dealt with the theme of a country defeated in war, while demonstrating his renewed creativity. In 1952 he travelled again, touring Europe and countries in Latin America, and after his return to Japan in 1954 he developed an expressionistic style with strong colours and animation, seen for example in *Burial* (1957) and *Black Spiritual* (1962; both Tokyo, N. Mus. Mod. A.).

BIBLIOGRAPHY

T. Hijikata and others: *Fukuzawa Ichirō gashū: 'Kani no yokobai'* [The paintings of Fukuzawa Ichirō: 'The crab crawling'] (Tokyo, 1969)

T. Uemura and others: *Fukuzawa Ichirō sakuhinshū* [A collection of works by Fukuzawa Ichirō] (Tokyo, 1987)

TORU ASANU

Fulani [Fulbe; Peul]. Fulfulde-speaking people, numbering more than six million, scattered across West Africa. Most of the Fulani live in the savannah and semi-desert of the Sudanic belt, with population concentrations in Senegal, the Middle Niger region of Mali, southern Niger, northern Nigeria and northern Cameroon. Their pre-eminent visual arts are the decoration of gourd containers (mostly by pastoral groups in Niger, Nigeria and Cameroon), the weaving of wool blankets (exclusive to the settled artisan castes living in the Middle Niger region of Mali) and body decoration (reflecting a preoccupation with physical beauty shared by all Fulani). Fulani architecture ranges widely from the transient homesteads of nomadic herders to the Hausa-inspired permanent structures of Islamicized urban residents (Prussin). Pottery techniques and styles are in general adopted from neighbouring groups. Some pastoral Fulani women produce coiled fibre mats as lids for gourds, and some other minor arts are also practised. A number of museums in the USA (e.g. Los Angeles, UCLA, Fowler Mus. Cult. Hist.), Europe (e.g. Tampere, Pyynikinlinna) and Africa (e.g. Bamako, Mus. N.) have significant collections of Fulani arts, especially textiles. There are a number of well-illustrated publications, as well as films and video recordings, featuring Fulani arts (see bibliography).

1. Cultural history. 2. Gourds. 3. Textiles. 4. Body arts.

1. CULTURAL HISTORY. Although they prefer to call themselves Fulbe, they are known by several different names by the peoples among whom they live. They are, for example, known as Fulani by the Hausa, Peul by the Wolof and by French writers, Fula by the Bamana and Felaata by the Kanuri. The names Bororo and Wodaabe refer specifically to a small Fulani sub-group, most of whom live in Niger and northern Nigeria and who maintain a rigorously nomadic lifestyle. Owing to their origins as cattle herders, the Fulani have dispersed widely across West Africa, travelling in constant search of pasturage and water through regions largely inhospitable to agriculture. Although the site of their earliest occupation is contested, there is some agreement that they originated in the Fouta Toro region of Senegal. In about the 12th century they began moving southward into Guinea and progressively eastward across the savannah. The first records of a pastoral Fulani presence among the Hausa of Nigeria date from the 15th century. In modern times the Fulani comprise populations whose lifestyle has remained pastoral as well as those who have settled in towns and cities, abandoning their once nomadic existence and living closely with sedentary agriculturalists. These latter, settled Fulani are mostly Muslim and have closer relations with their fellow town-dwellers than with the nomadic Fulani whose way of life they disparage. The pastoral Fulani, who also have largely adopted Islam, resent the sedentary Fulani for having given up cattle herding.

The pastoral Fulani are the largest nomadic group in Africa. Their lifestyle is structured around an annual transhumant cycle, and the number and kinds of material goods they possess are both limited and defined by their frequent movements and temporary homesteads. Pastoral Fulani men are responsible for the herds, and their socio-economic status is based on the number of cattle they own. Their wives have exclusive milking rights and market the resultant dairy products. Settled Fulani groups are found across West Africa, with the greatest concentrations of population in Senegal, Guinea, the Middle Niger and northern Nigeria. Their history includes periods of political and military aggression against their non-Fulani neighbours. Jihads were launched in the mid-18th century against the 'pagans' of Fouta Djallon, and another was initiated in the Middle Niger in the mid-19th century. The most famous of the Fulani conquerors, however, was Uthman dan Fodio who led a holy war in northern Nigeria in the early 19th century and brought under Fulani control a vast area called the Sokoto Caliphate, which exerted religious, political and cultural domination until colonial times. The settled Fulani became the ruling class among the Hausa, the Nupe and the northern Yoruba of Ilorin, as well as among the diverse ethnic groups of Adamawa province in north-east Nigeria, where they continued to constitute the minority élite into the 1990s. Both nomadic and sedentary Fulani groups have adopted some of the arts of the peoples with whom they live or bought what they need from people who often produce artefacts specifically for them.

2. GOURDS. Among the pastoral Fulani gourd containers constitute not only a woman's essential milking equipment but also her primary possessions. A young woman receives her first gourds from her mother and mother-in-law after the birth of her first child, and the gourds she proceeds to accumulate are indicators of her success as wife and mother. There are, in fact, conventions for the

1. Fulani woman's collection of gourds, baskets, coiled-fibre mats and mirrors displayed at the annual Worso festival, Niger; from a photograph by Carol Beckwith, 1982

ways gourds are kept and accumulated. Aside from those used as daily household equipment, others—usually decorated—are nested together in sets of ten and encased in tightly woven basketry. The encased bundles of gourds are held together with an intricate network of rope or leather thongs, which may be ornamented with silver studs and other decorative objects. Supported on two wooden poles, this elaborate portable assemblage (*kaakol*) is taken from site to site on the back of a pack ox and set up beside its owner's bed every time a new temporary homestead is established. The time and energy lavished on the *kaakol* and its presentation reflect its importance as an indicator of a woman's changing economic position. When a girl is born, for example, more decorated gourds are added to the pack in anticipation of those her mother will give to her when she marries.

The contents of the *kaakol* are unwrapped and carefully arranged for public display annually at a communal festival known as Worso, when members of Fulani lineages gather together to celebrate the year's births and marriages. The elaborate displays, set up on long, low tables in the open air, contribute an important aesthetic component to such celebrations, while at the same time allowing women to proclaim publicly their successes (see fig. 1).

Although the sheer number of gourds a woman accumulates (which can reach into the hundreds) refers to the size of her household and her reproductive achievements, Fulani women also take great pride in the decoration of individual containers. The gourds in the *kaakol* of the Wodaabe Fulani of southern Niger, as well as the gourd bowls regularly used for holding milk, are decorated with a technique known as pressure-engraving, in which an iron tool with an awl-like blade is pulled across the surface while pressure is applied. Although this technique is laborious and painstaking, it is also well suited to the nomadic lifestyle as it requires only one tool, and a woman can start and stop working at will. Wodaabe gourds are distinguished by having a wide band of outer shell carved away from around the rim, providing a thin handling edge and a frame for the design. Deeply carved sunburst patterns are then worked at four points around this frame,

with other finely incised geometric patterns along the sides. The Wodaabe Fulani rub the worked areas with kaolin, which adheres to the incisions, its whiteness contrasting with the deep gold of the gourd shell. With handling and the regular application of butter, such gourds may achieve a warm, lustrous patina. Pastoral Fulani women in northern Nigeria also decorate large, hemispherical gourd containers used to transport milk and other foodstuffs. Complex patterns of fine lines are impressed into the surface, the pressure-engraved areas then filled in with a mixture of butter and ashes, resulting in patterns of black designs against the background of the gourd shell. As with Wodaabe gourds, motifs tend to be worked around the outer edge so that they are visible when the gourd is inverted and carried on the head.

Although gourds and their decoration are important for all Fulani, it is in north-eastern Nigeria and northern Cameroon that the Fulani art of gourd decoration has reached its most elaborate expression. Whereas the pastoral Fulani here, as elsewhere, use a pressure-engraving technique, their settled neighbours use pyro-engraving, a process that has technical advantages and the potential for greater aesthetic diversity. Heated iron tools are used to burn lines directly into the gourd shell, with variations being achieved by altering the shape of the knife, the part of the blade used for burning and the amount of pressure applied. A complex gridwork is burnt across the design field, its structure defined by the strips of shell left unblackened. A common variation involves dyeing the gourds red after engraving by immersing them in a dye compound made by mixing the leaves and outer sheaths of the sorghum plant and the leaves of the indigo plant in boiling water. An oily paste may also be applied to areas of the gourd before dyeing, resulting in a tessellated polychrome pattern. The most elaborate gourds decorated with this combined pyrogravure/resist-dye technique have glowing, saffron yellow areas of shell protected by the paste and bright, deep red dyed areas: both colours contrasting with the black, engraved lines, which often form complex interlace patterns (for illustrations see 1986–8 exh. cat., p. 20, pls 18, 19). *See also* AFRICA, §V, 11.

Carried atop a woman's head, the embellished gourd is an extension of the Fulani woman's preoccupation with her appearance (*see* §4 below). In the past, the decorative patterns on gourds were associated with particular lineage groups (Dupire, 1962). Although the meanings of designs have largely been forgotten, certain groups favour particular motifs. There are stylistic relationships between the markings on gourds and the scarifications on pastoral Fulani women's faces, and in certain cases the same names have been ascribed to both. By the early 1990s manufactured enamel bowls had begun to replace decorated gourd bowls among some Fulani.

3. TEXTILES. The Fulani weaving industry in the Middle Niger area of Mali is the exclusive prerogative of a caste of professional weavers renowned throughout the region for the production of elaborately patterned wool blankets, made for sale in local markets or produced on commission. The men of the caste are the weavers, and their wives are potters, while other Fulani women spin, dye and reel the wool threads. The weavers are best known for their blankets (*kaasa*), woven of handspun sheep's wool and sold in public markets. Several different varieties of *kaasa* are woven, primarily for pastoral Fulani men who use them during the dry-season months to keep out the cold and the mosquitoes. At the end of the season, the blankets are often sold to local traders, who then sell them at markets, especially in the cloth market in Mopti. *Kaasa* are woven on narrow-strip looms; six strips, each 200 mm wide, being sewn together, selvage to selvage, to create a blanket 1.8–2.5×1.2 m. Whereas the simplest versions are plain white, other *kaasa* have weft-float patterns in red, yellow or black, usually taking the form of lozenges, triangles, chevrons and lines. The patterns woven on the strips all line up when they are sewn together. The distinctive motifs have been said to refer to elements of the environment through which the nomadic Fulani move, for example black horizontal lines refer to their transhumant paths (Imperato, 1973).

The second category of Fulani woollen textile is the *arkilla*, the largest and most expensive blanket produced in the Middle Niger region. There are three types, all of which are hung by a bride next to her marriage bed. The *arkilla amunga* is made for Songhai women, the *arkilla jenngo* is made for Tuareg women and the *arkilla kerka* is made for the Fulani nobility. As with the *kaasa*, the practical function of such blankets is to protect against mosquitoes. In addition, however, its presence in a couple's sleeping room serves symbolically to sanction their marriage: traditionally, marriage among the Fulani nobility was impossible without an *arkilla*.

Like the *kaasa*, the *kerka* is woven in strips sewn together edge to edge. Its size corresponds to that of the Fulani bed, measuring approximately 4.8×2 m (see fig. 2). When hung, the six strips that make up the blanket are aligned horizontally; sometimes there is a seventh band at the top, used for suspension. The colours of the *kerka* are essentially the same as those of the *kaasa*, with red rather than white predominating. Weaving a *kerka* can take from

2. Fulani *arkilla kerka* blanket suspended over a marriage bed, near Tonka, northern Mali; from a photograph by Bernard Gardi, 1980

three to eight weeks, because of its size and the complexity of its weft-float patterns. Many of the designs have names. The central motif of the blanket, for example, is *leruwel* ('the moon surrounded by stars'). Its significance may be multivalent. The red background may refer to the fact that each time the centre of a strip is reached (i.e. when this motif is woven) the person who has commissioned the blanket must slaughter a young sheep. It may also refer to the blood shed by a young bride on her wedding night. The moon in the design may symbolize Islam, often represented by a crescent moon and star.

Traditionally, a settled Fulani woman's prized possession was a *kerka*, equivalent to the nomadic Fulani woman's collection of gourds. Handwoven textiles are gradually being replaced by the manufactured types available in markets: mosquito nets replacing woven wool blankets. By the early 1990s few specialists wove the expensive *kerka*, and the numbers of sheep necessary for the production of the threads had been reduced by drought in Mali. Commercial cotton thread is being substituted for wool, with a subsequent loss in status for the caste weaver who, in working with cotton, joins the ranks of other non-professional weavers. Although cotton textiles are woven with designs that recall the traditional *kerka*, new colours and motifs have been introduced, reflecting the syncretism characteristic of modern life in Africa.

4. BODY ARTS. Much of the artistic energy expended by Fulani is lavished on the human form itself, particularly during youth. Among Fulani women, hair design is particularly elaborate, varying with age, location and social standing, and consisting of different combinations of braids, coils and crests of hair. The Fulani manipulation of hair has been regarded as a form of sculpture (Delange). Some Fulani women in Futa-Djallon, Guinea, are known for a style called *dyubade*, in which their upper hair is stretched into an elaborate crest by fixing it to a high, arched strip of bamboo. The Fulani practice of wearing richly patterned cloths and a profusion of ear, arm, neck, ankle and hair ornaments distinguishes them from their more modestly adorned neighbours. Particularly distinctive in the Middle Niger region are the large gold earrings and amber ornaments worn by Fulani women. Among some nomadic Fulani groups, facial scarification has continued to be practised into the 1990s. Small cuts were made with a razor blade and the incisions rubbed with charcoal, the cuts healing in patterns of dark blue, closely placed, raised lines. The first marks are cut during infancy at the corners of the mouth (Beckworth and Van Offelen), and as a child grows designs are worked in stages—at the temples, on the forehead and along the cheekbones. Such scarifications identify their bearers as Fulani and constitute part of the Fulani aesthetic of female beauty.

The Fulani emphasis on physical appearance is nowhere more evident than during the Gerewol festival held each year at the end of the rainy season. Gerewol is essentially a beauty contest, in which the most handsome young men of two lineages compete. They participate in hours of uninterrupted dancing every afternoon and evening for seven days. On the last day, ten or more of the dancers are selected by a group of female elders as finalists. Then, three of the most beautiful maidens choose the most handsome. The participants invest considerable energy in their appearance, aiming to achieve the highest standards of Fulani beauty. For the men this involves lightening their faces with a pale yellow ochre; blackening their lips and the rims of their eyes to enhance the whiteness of their teeth and the whites of their eyes; painting a line down the centre of the forehead, nose and chin to lengthen the nose; shaving the hairline to elongate the forehead; and painting the corners of the mouth and the cheeks with motifs reminiscent of women's facial scarifications. They then wrap their heads in white turbans, don elaborately embroidered dark blue cloth tunics and add an array of jewellery of brass, silver, beads, leather and cloth. The young women also pay special attention to their dress, wearing indigo-dyed, handwoven wrappers covered in multicoloured embroidery, carrying on their heads pieces of folded, brightly coloured cloth shot through with gold or silver threads and a mass of ornaments around their necks, in their ears and on their wrists, forearms and ankles. Though also true of men's ceremonial dress, women's costume especially reveals the strong Fulani penchant for accumulations of decorative elements: seven to ten large metal hoops through each ear, rows of narrow metal bracelets and strands of small, multi-coloured beads around the neck, in the hair or hanging at the side of the face. This annual collective celebration of endurance and survival should be understood in the context of the itinerant, largely solitary existence of the pastoral Fulani.

BIBLIOGRAPHY

F. W. de St Croix: *The Fulani of Northern Nigeria: Some General Notes* (Lagos, 1944/*R* Westmead, 1972)

D. J. Stenning: *Savannah Nomads: A Study of the Wodaabe Pastoral Fulani of Western Bornu Province, Northern Region, Nigeria* (London, 1959)

M. Dupire: *Peuls nomades: Etude descriptive des Wodaabe du Sahel nigérien*, Travaux et Mémoires de l'Institut d'Ethnologie, lxiv (Paris, 1962)

J. Delange: *Arts et peuples de l'Afrique noire* (Paris, 1967; Eng. trans., New York, 1974), pp. 140–51

African Textiles and Decorative Arts (exh. cat. by R. Sieber, New York, MOMA; Los Angeles, CA, Co. Mus. A.; San Francisco, CA, de Young Mem. Mus.; Cleveland, OH, Mus. A.; 1972–3)

P. J. Imperato: 'Wool Blankets of the Peul of Mali', *Afr. A.*, vi/3 (1973), pp. 40–47, 84

R. Gardi: *Indigenous African Architecture* (New York, 1974), pp. 19–27

P. J. Imperato: 'Kereka Blankets of the Peul', *Afr. A.*, ix/4 (1976), pp. 56–9, 92

L. Prussin: 'Fulani–Hausa Architecture', *Afr. A.*, x/1 (1976), pp. 8–19, 97–8

T. J. H. Chappel: *Decorated Gourds in North-eastern Nigeria* (Lagos, 1977)

C. Seydou: *Bibliographie générale du monde Peul*, Etudes nigériennes, 43 (Niamey, 1977)

J. Picton and J. Mack: *African Textiles: Looms, Weaving and Design* (London, 1979, rev. 1989)

C. Beckwith and M. van Offelen: *Nomads of Niger* (New York, 1983)

J. Africanistes, lv/1–2 (1985) [issue devoted to Worso Festival]

C. O. Adepegba: *Decorative Arts of the Fulani Nomads* (Ibadan, 1986)

The Essential Gourd: Art and History in Northeastern Nigeria (exh. cat. by M. C. Berns and B. R. Hudson, Los Angeles, UCLA, Wight A.G.; Honolulu, HI, Acad. A.; New York, Cent. Afr. A.; Washington, DC, N. Mus. Afr. A.; 1986–8)

K.-F. Schaedler: *Weaving in Africa South of the Sahara* (Munich, 1987)

R. Dognin: 'Les Calebasses des Peuls du Cameroun: Fonction symbolique et décor gravé—les limites de l'explication anthropologique', *Anthropologie de l'art: Formes et significations—arts de l'Afrique, de l'Amérique et du Pacifique*, ii, ed. L. Perrois and C.-F. Baudez (Paris, 1989), pp. 89–104

B. Gardi and C. Seydou: '*Arkilla kerka*: La Tenture de mariage chez les Peuls du Mali', *Man Does Not Go Naked: Textilien und Handwerk aus afrikanischen und anderen Ländern*, ed. B. Engelbrecht and B. Gardi, Basler Beiträge zur Ethnologie (Basle, 1989), pp. 83–106

Arkilla Kerka: Tekstilleja Lansi-Afrikasta (exh. cat. by. E. Kivekäs, B. Gardi and U. Pallasmaa, Tampere, Pyynikinlinna, 1991–2) [Fin. and Fr. text]

FILMS AND VIDEO RECORDINGS

R. Gardner: *Deep Hearts* (1979) [film, 16 mm]

L. Woodhead: *The Wodaabe*, Disappearing World (Manchester, 1988) [TV documentary/video]

MARLA C. BERNS

Fulda. Town in Hessen, Germany, the site of a former Benedictine monastery and of the shrine of St Boniface, apostle to the Germans. The abbey church, which became a cathedral in 1752, was a prime architectural example of the Carolingian renaissance before its rebuilding in the 18th century. The monastic complex included the surviving funerary chapel, dedicated to St Michael. The monastery was secularized in 1803. The town was also a notable centre for the production of faience in the 18th century.

1. CATHEDRAL. The monastery was founded in 744 by Sturm, a Bavarian disciple of the Anglo-Saxon missionaries, under the direction of St Boniface. The site was chosen for its remoteness from the warlike and still pagan Saxons and was described as being 'in the wilderness', although Sturm gave his bishop an encouraging report on its potential fertility and the adequacy of the water supply. Excavations have shown that the site had previously been surrounded by a rampart and ditch, enclosing some apparently domestic buildings of late or post-Roman date

on a different alignment from that adopted for the monastery (see fig.).

The earliest church was dedicated to St Saviour and St Mary. It appears to have been built to a standard plan-type of aisled nave with eastern apse, measuring *c.* 40×22 m overall. Immediately to the west lay a building at least 17.5×11.0 m in size, with a sunken floor, which possibly formed the atrium of Sturm's church, although Lobbedey has implied that it may have been a massive sepulchre or feretory within the later church.

A grandiose rebuilding programme was begun *c.* 790, with a final dedication in 819. Sturm's church was replaced on a slightly larger scale; a major extension was then added to the west end, more than doubling the length of the church. The new building comprised a large nave with side aisles and an apse at its east end, but the architectural and liturgical emphasis was at the west end, where there was a massive transept with screened-off ends. A western apse is implied by a concentric foundation further to the west, which was part of the claustral complex, belonging either to a cloister walk or to a 'paradise' of the St Gall type (*see* ST GALL ABBEY, §2). Crypts were constructed just before the dedication below both the western choir and the eastern apse. The remains of St Boniface, who had been buried at the west end of the earlier church in 754, were translated to the western choir; over his original grave, in the centre of the new nave, was erected the Holy Cross altar with an elaborate reliquary tower (*requiem*)

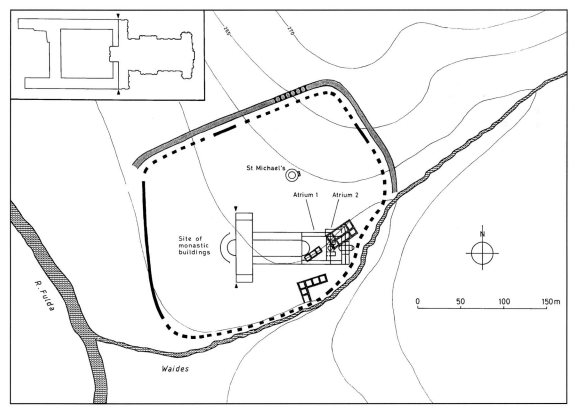

Fulda, plan of enclosure showing abbey church, pre-monastic buildings and (inset) plan of Baroque cathedral, begun *c.* 1704; drawing by David Parsons

behind it. An atrium was built to the east of the church and further extended in the 10th century, and the claustral buildings were moved from the south to the west side of the church.

The dependence of this complex on Roman models is clear. The church itself was based on Old St Peter's in Rome, in particular the vast continuous western transept and apse, the reverse orientation, the use of crypts and the focus on the principal saint's resting place. The Fulda church was not, however, a slavish imitation of St Peter's. In form the hall crypts were quite unlike the corridor crypt of St Peter's, and the eastern apse was a feature inherited from the original church; also there is no evidence for double aisles at Fulda. The atrium may have been inspired by the famous example at St Peter's, although this was a common feature of Early Christian architecture. The placing of the cloister and monastic buildings to the east of the church can be paralleled at S Giovanni in Laterano, and Candidus in his contemporary *Vita Eigilis* explained this position as 'following Roman custom . . . on account of the proximity of the martyr' (*Romano more . . . propter vicinitatem martyri*; see MGH, Scriptores, xv/1, Hannover, 1887, p. 231).

It is clear from drawings made in the 16th and 17th centuries that the church and its ancillary buildings remained substantially unchanged throughout the Middle Ages. At some stage twin towers were built, flanking the eastern apse of the church; in 1120–21 one of these collapsed, and both were rebuilt. There was also a tower over the western choir. All of this was swept away in the early 18th-century 'modernization' of Fulda, which included a massive landscaping programme in the town centre and the replacement of many of the buildings in the Baroque style. A new abbey church, designed by Johann Dientzenhofer, was built between 1704 and 1712. It consists of a domed central bay with shallow transepts and a sanctuary bay to the west, behind which is the former monks' choir. The nave has arcades on irregularly spaced piers, again a Roman quotation, from the Baroque wall elevation of S Giovanni in Laterano, and a twin-towered east façade. The towers incorporate masonry from their medieval predecessors and the plan of two projecting chambers at the west end is determined by the surviving walling of the Carolingian transept.

2. ST MICHAEL. The former funerary chapel was dedicated in 822. The east end of the surviving building (*see* SEPULCHRE CHURCH, fig. 1), comprising a rebuilt rotunda and apse over the original crypt, to which a west tower and two-storey nave were later added, gives some impression of the architect's original intentions, which according to Candidus were symbolic as well as practical. For example, the eight columns supporting the rotunda represented the Beatitudes, and the circular form eternal life. On the basis of the altar inscriptions provided by Hrabanus Maurus (Abbot 822–42) it is generally assumed that the plan was also influenced by the Anastasis Rotunda (church of the Holy Sepulchre) in Jerusalem, probably via Arculf's 7th-century account in Adamnan's *De locis sanctis*, a copy of which was in the Fulda library (though Ellger disputes the Anastasis interpretation and argues that the sepulchre was not introduced until 1092). St Michael's

contained a representation of the Holy Sepulchre, perhaps a stone reliquary/replica, and one of its major relics was earth from the Holy Land.
See also EIGIL and RATGAR.

BIBLIOGRAPHY

R. Krautheimer: 'The Carolingian Revival of Early Christian Architecture', *A. Bull.*, xxiv (1942), pp. 1–38
F. Oswald, L. Schaefer and H. R. Sennhauser: *Vorromanische Kirchenbauten*, Veröff. Zentinst. Kstgesch. München, iii (Munich, 1960–70), pp. 84–9
L. Pralle: *Fulda: Dom und Abteibezirk*, Die blauen Bücher (Königstein im Taunus, [1974])
H. Hahn: 'Eihloha: Sturm and das Kloster Fulda', *Fulda. Geschbl.*, lvi (1980), pp. 50–82
D. Parsons: 'Sites and Monuments of the Anglo-Saxon Mission in Central Germany', *Archaeol. J.*, cxl (1983), pp. 280–321
U. Lobbedey: 'Zu eingetieften Räumen in früh- und hochmittelalterlichen Kirchen', *Frühmittelalt. Stud.*, xx (1986), pp. 390–413 (402–4)
O. Ellger: *Die Michaelskirche zu Fulda als Zeugnis der Totensorge* (Fulda, 1989)
W. Jacobsen, ed.: Veröff. Zentinst. Kstgesch. München, (1991), pp. 132–3 [suppl. vol.]

DAVID PARSONS

3. CENTRE OF CERAMICS PRODUCTION. In 1741 a faience factory was founded in Fulda by Amadeus von Buseck, Prince-Bishop of Fulda. Production included candlesticks, vases and tureens (e.g. tureen, *c.* 1745; London, V&A). Despite the high quality of the wares, production was discontinued in 1768. Many of the skilled faience workers found employment in the porcelain factory founded in 1764 by Heinrich VIII, Prince-Bishop of Bibra. In the late 1760s the modeller Johann Valentin Schaum (1714–71) began reproducing figures from the factory in Frankenthal. After initial problems Abraham Ripp (*c.* 1737–96) became director in 1770. Schaum was succeeded by the Bohemian Wenzel Neu (*c.* 1708–74), whose sculptural talent is most beautifully expressed in the boldly conceived *commedia dell'arte* figures in the style of Jacques Callot's *Balli di Sfessania* engravings (1621–35) and in a *Madonna Immacolata on the Globe* (e.g. of *c.* 1775; Hamburg, Mus. Kst & Gew.). It is not clear whether he also collaborated on the figures of children, ladies, cavaliers and officers reminiscent of figures from the factory in Höchst or on the groups with hunters and shepherds on flat sparsely decorated bases. In 1774 Neu was succeeded by Georg Ludwig Bartholomae (*c.* 1744–88), who placed his graceful gardeners and wine-growers, musicians and dancers on mound rocaille bases. Fulda tableware is distinguished by the quality of the white paste and by the fine, smooth glaze. Shapes are in a simple Louis XVI style; only handles, feet and spouts are subtly accentuated. Wares are painted in delicate shades or bright colours and decoration included *en camaieu* landscapes in iron-red, birds in crimson or grisaille medallions. A popular motif was the black portrait silhouettes surrounded by foliate borders. The factory closed in 1789.

BIBLIOGRAPHY

H. H. Josten: *Fuldaer Porzellanfiguren* (Berlin, 1929)
E. Kramer: 'Fuldaer Porzellan in hessischem Staatsbesitz', *Keramos*, 13 (1961), pp. 9–18

WALTER SPIEGEL

Fuller, George (*b* Deerfield, MA, 17 Jan 1822; *d* Brookline, MA, 21 March 1884). American painter. The son of a farmer, he was partly self-taught. In 1842 he studied drawing in Albany, NY, with the sculptor Henry Kirke Brown (1814–86). Later that year he moved to Boston, where he attended drawing classes at the Boston Artists' Association and admired the dreamy, imaginative paintings of Washington Allston. After 1847 Fuller was based in New York but he made three extended journeys to the South before 1859 in search of portrait commissions.

As a portrait painter Fuller attained little distinction in the 1850s; his style was realistic, dark and somewhat dry. He executed several landscape studies and paintings, strongly reminiscent of the dominant Hudson River school manner in their clarity and tight brushwork. His most interesting earlier works are his many acutely observed sketches of black slave life in Montgomery, AL, where he lived in the winter of 1857–8.

When his father died in 1859, Fuller returned to Deerfield, MA, to manage the family farm, but before doing so, he made his only voyage to Europe, a six-month tour of the museums of Britain and the Continent. He continued to paint but had virtually no contact with the art worlds of Boston and New York until 1875 when, close to bankruptcy, he took some of his recent paintings to Boston. Favourable criticism and several sales followed, and he became one of the Boston artistic and literary circle. By 1877 Fuller was exhibiting regularly in both Boston and New York, and his reputation soared.

During his farming years Fuller changed his style from literal realism to reticent mystery. He painted fewer portraits, concentrating instead on quiet, dreamy landscapes and imaginary figures. He drew on memories of Allston, Rembrandt and the romantic, bucolic paintings of such Barbizon school artists as Jean-François Millet and Jean-Baptiste-Camille Corot. The paintings of Fuller's last decade were progressively more nebulous, with blurred outlines and muted atmosphere, using a limited range of dim, muffled tones in amber, green or tan. These evocative compositions were acclaimed by contemporary critics as the quintessence of pictorial poetry.

Fuller was best known for his paintings of young, pensive country women, such as *Winifred Dysart* (1881; Worcester, MA, A. Mus.); critics praised them not as images of the body but as materializations of pure, virginal souls. His paintings of melancholy racial outcasts also have a spiritual quality, as in *The Quadroon* (1880; New York, Met.), in which the lovely maiden sits wearily in a cotton field. Fuller's landscapes are similarly nebulous and moody: some are quiet Deerfield farm scenes, but more interesting are Southern scenes based loosely on Fuller's memories and sketches of slave life but in the colours used by the Barbizon school. *Turkey Pasture in Kentucky* (1878; Norfolk, VA, Chrysler Mus.), with its black turkey herders, its dim, green atmosphere and pervasive bucolic tranquillity, represents an almost perfect fusion of regional idiom and Barbizon sentiment.

Like other American Barbizon followers, Fuller followed William Morris Hunt's lead in rejecting the realism and provincialism of pre-Civil War American painting. His combination of idealism with soft focus and twilight established him as a significant forerunner of TONALISM, the refined, poetic style perfected by late 19th-century aesthetes. Fuller was no aesthete, however, but rather an artist obsessed with the problem of communicating spiritual truths through the crude medium of paint. In this last respect, he was comparable to the *fin-de-siècle* visionaries George Inness and Albert Pinkham Ryder. Fuller's importance was unassailed until the 1920s but several decades of neglect followed before he was reassessed in the 1980s.

BIBLIOGRAPHY

J. B. Millet, ed.: *George Fuller: His Life and Works* (Boston, 1886)
S. Burns: 'A Study of the Life and Poetic Vision of George Fuller (1822–84)', *Amer. A. J.*, xiii (1981), pp. 11–37
——: 'George Fuller: The Hawthorne of our Art', *Winterthur Port.*, xvii (1983), pp. 125–45
——: 'Images of Slavery: George Fuller's Depictions of the Antebellum South', *Amer. A. J.*, xv (1983), pp. 35–60
George Fuller: At Home (exh. cat., ed. S. L. Flynt; Deerfield, MA, Mem. Hall Mus., 1984)
S. Burns: 'Black, Quadroon, Gypsy: Women in the Art of George Fuller', *MA Rev.*, xxvi (1985), pp. 405–24

SARAH BURNS

Fuller, Isaac (*b c.* 1606; *d* London, 17 July 1672). English painter. He was renowned in his day for large historical, mythological and biblical subjects but was also a very able portrait painter. According to Vertue, he studied under François Perrier in France *c.* 1630, and in 1644 he is documented as working in Oxford, at the same time as William Dobson. There he painted altarpieces, including a *Resurrection* for All Souls College (a wild imitation of Michelangelo, which John Evelyn considered 'too full of nakeds for a chapel'), a *Last Judgement* for Magdalen College and a *Last Supper* for Wadham College. None of these works is known to survive. He also copied Dobson's *Beheading of John the Baptist*, substituting the heads with portraits of his friends. On moving to London, Fuller worked on decorative schemes for churches, taverns and private houses and continued to paint portraits. In 1654 he published a drawing book, *Un libro di disegnare*, with 15 etched plates, but there are no known copies. Much of his decorative work was destroyed in the Great Fire in 1666, including that in the Painters' Hall and St Mary Abchurch. Vertue admired his erotic life-size Bacchic figures in the Mitre Tavern in Fenchurch Street. Five crudely painted canvases commemorating the *Adventures of Charles II after the Battle of Worcester in 1651* (London, N.P.G.) are his only surviving decorative works. Fuller's reputation as a painter rests mainly on three variants of a Rembrandtesque *Self-portrait* (1670; Oxford, Bodleian Lib.; Oxford, Queen's Coll.; and London, N.P.G.) and a *Portrait of an Unknown Man* inscribed John Cleveland (1644; London, Tate), in which the unrestrained poses and gestures, bold brushwork and coarse surface texture all reflect the independence of a lively artist who was not bound to the conventions of contemporary portraiture. Lely lamented that 'so great a genius should besot or neglect so great a talent', a reference to Fuller's carefree, boisterous lifestyle.

BIBLIOGRAPHY

C. H. Collins Baker: *Lely and the Stuart Portrait Painters*, i (London, 1912), pp. 124–9
'The Note-books of George Vertue', *Walpole Soc.*, xx (1932), p. 128
E. Waterhouse: *Painting in Britain, 1530–1790*, Pelican Hist. A. (Harmondsworth, 1953, 4/1978), pp. 89–90
M. Rogers: 'Isaac Fuller and Charles II's Escape from the Battle of Worcester', *Connoisseur* (July 1979), pp. 164–9

Drawing in England from Hilliard to Hogarth (exh. cat. by L. Stainton and C. White, London, BM, 1987), pp. 102–3

JOHN SHEERAN

Fuller [née Warrick], **Meta Vaux** (*b* Philadelphia, PA, 9 Jan 1877; *d* Framingham, MA, 1968). American sculptor. Her long career anticipated and included the period of the Harlem Renaissance of the 1920s and early 1930s (*see* AFRICAN AMERICAN ART, §2). She studied at the Pennsylvania Museum and School for Industrial Art, Philadelphia, from 1893 to 1899. This was followed by a period in Paris (1899–1902) at the Ecole des Beaux-Arts and the Académie Colarossi. She exhibited regularly at the Pennsylvania Academy of Fine Arts. Her early work, with themes of death and sorrow, was characterized by a powerful expressionism. At the Tercentennial Exposition (1907) she was awarded a gold medal for the Jamestown Tableau, a fifteen-piece sculpture that recorded the settlement of the black community of Jamestown in 1607. In 1909 she married and settled in Framingham, MA. After the loss of her early work in a fire of 1910, she built a new studio where she executed sculptures on the subject of racial division, for example *Ethiopia Awakening* (1914; New York, Pub. Lib., Schlomberg Cent. Res. Black Cult.) and *Talking Skull* (1937; Boston, MA, Mus. Afro-Amer. Hist.). A retrospective of Fuller's work was held at the Danforth Museum of Art, Framingham, in 1973.

BIBLIOGRAPHY
J. A. Porter: *Modern Negro Art* (New York, 1943)
P. Dunfold: *A Biographical Dictionary of Women Artists in Europe and America since 1850* (Philadelphia, 1989; Hemel Hempstead, 2/1990)
C. S. Rubinstein: *American Women Sculptors* (Boston, 1990)

□

Fuller, R(ichard) Buckminster (*b* Milton, MA, 12 July 1895; *d* Los Angeles, 1 July 1983). American architect and inventor. He was known as 'the Wizard of the Dome' (Rosen, 1969) because of the phenomenal success of his geodesic domes, of which more than 250,000 have been built all over the world. Fuller broached the principal social and environmental problems of the 20th century and linked the ideas of a fertile mind with a mathematical and engineering bent to the drive of a man of action in implementing and disseminating them. His work ranged from the invention of dynamic map projections, through designs for mass-housing compatible with industrial production methods, to new structural systems for building domes of almost any conceivable diameter—viable economical systems of space-enclosure capable of execution by unskilled labour. In addition he was a mystic and man of letters, distinguished enough to be appointed Charles Elliot Norton Professor of Poetry at Harvard University, Cambridge, MA (1962).

1. Early years, to *c*. 1927. 2. The Dymaxion projects. 3. Development of the domes. 4. Later career.

1. EARLY YEARS, TO *c*. 1927. He was born into a family with a background in letters and the law, and it was to the experience of boats and shipbuilding during holidays on the coast of Maine that he attributed his earliest creative urges. In 1913 he went to Harvard but he had been dismissed twice by 1915, having spent a year or so in Canada between these dates as a machine-fitter apprentice.

He then worked for Armour and Company in New Jersey and New York and rose from meat porter to assistant cashier.

In 1917 he married Anne Hewlett, daughter of James Monroe Hewlett (1869–1941), a distinguished architect, mural painter and stage designer, a future president of the American Institute of Architects (1928) and Director of the American Academy in Rome (1932–5). The Hewlett connection was a second major formative influence until World War I led him to join the US Navy; he was discharged as a lieutenant in 1919. Many of his later ideas relating concepts of time and space, energy production, utilization and self-sufficiency stem from his experience of maritime engineering and navigation: motifs and images in his designs are reminiscent of ships and rigging.

Fuller worked in industry again before joining his father-in-law in setting up a company known as the Stockade Building System to exploit an invention of Hewlett's, a fibrous concrete building block. This was in 1922, shortly before the death of his first daughter, an event that was to have significant effects upon Fuller, who associated it with the societal failure symbolized by war. Working at the operational end of the building industry, assessed by Fuller himself as '. . . the most prodigious of men's fumbling activities' (McHale) and in stark contrast to the wartime mobilization of effort and efficiency seen in the Navy, after five years Fuller was probably not unhappy when a change in financial control of the company left him high and dry in 1927. Fortuitously it came a little after the birth of his second daughter and this, together with the release from commercial pressures, brought a regeneration of optimism. He determined to pursue what he described as the 'art and science of generalised and anticipatory design competence'.

2. THE DYMAXION PROJECTS. The 4D and 4D Timelock essays, outlining the conceptual bases of much that was to follow, were published almost immediately and Fuller set up the 4D Company. Proposals for a Ten Deck building were published before the end of 1927. The floors were supported from a central mast-like core (over 55 m high), the whole assembly light enough to be carried under a 275 m airship and placed wherever in the world they were required. Like a battleship each building was to be self-supporting for considerable periods of time. The design was associated with Fuller's World Town Plan (also 1927), which postulated the building of 2000 million new homes over the ensuing 80 years. The better-known single-family version of these dwellings, the Minimum Dymaxion Home, was a hexagonal duralumin one-storey unit suspended above ground-level by cables from what is described on the schematic drawing as a 'central supporting mast . . . [which also] contains power unit and services . . . ' (see fig.). It was to be demountable and easily transportable. In 1929 it was labelled the Dymaxion House, linking together words often used by Fuller, 'dynamism', 'maximum' and 'ions'. It electrified architects and the public alike, and Fuller found he had an audience for futuristic designs. He spent a year in research at the Pierce Foundation (1931), and the first Dymaxion Corporation succeeded 4D in 1932. Three models of the Dymaxion car (in Fuller's eyes a part of the continuing study of

transportation in relation to Dymaxion buildings) were produced between 1930 and 1934, and his interest in vehicle design continued until 1948 when he published designs for a car developed a few years earlier for the Kaiser Corporation. The Dymaxion bathroom (1937), a prefabricated pressed metal combined unit, begun at the Pierce Foundation, was not developed until he joined the Phelps Dodge Corporation as Assistant Director of Research (1936–8). A year studying world economic and material resources as a consultant to *Fortune* magazine followed, before he set up the second Dymaxion company in 1941 and produced the Dymaxion Deployment Units in association with the Butler Manufacturing Company. He used elements of the company's corrugated metal grain-storage bins to make single and double circular units. It was the first of Fuller's designs to be mass-produced (1000 units per day at one stage) and, ironically, it was again for wartime purposes—hospitals, radar stations and many other uses.

In a wartime appointment in the Board of Economic Welfare (1942–4), Fuller suggested that after the war aircraft factories be turned over to house-production, but a shortage of accommodation before the war ended motivated rapid prototype development. The result was the Wichita House of 1945–6, produced by the Beech Aircraft Corporation in their Wichita factory using aircraft-building techniques. It was another circular aluminium single-unit dwelling, suspended on cables from a slender stainless-steel mast. Despite high praise for the product, it was not put into production: the war came to an end and the capacity of the industry was diverted elsewhere.

3. DEVELOPMENT OF THE DOMES. Again Fuller was freed from industrial responsibilities, and it was in the 10 years up to 1954 in Wichita, first in another Dymaxion Company (1944–6) and then as chairman of his own research foundation, that he was to reach the culmination of his inventiveness, the GEODESIC DOME. In it over a period of years he synthesized his engineering, geological and cartographic design skills into an artefact with truly universal space-enclosing application. Its development was helped through its early stages by students in numerous schools of architecture, where he rapidly became a popular figure whose altruistic aims chimed with a growing student awareness of world social problems. Early examples were constructed in the late 1940s, including one at Black Mountain College, NC, where he taught for a while, but it was not until 1953 that the breakthrough came with the commission from the Ford Motor Company to cover the courtyard—*c.* 28 m in diameter—of the Rotunda building at their River Rouge Plant, Dearborn, MI.

A further development, Tensegrity domes, soon followed, and first Synergetics Incorporated (1954–9), then Geodesics Inc. and Tetrahelix Inc. were formed and continued in operation until 1983. Success was confirmed when the US Marine Corps accepted Fuller's dome in 1956, and his radomes of the same date for use in the Arctic were further justification of the principles he had expounded a quarter of a century earlier, namely light, air-transportable structures capable of efficient operation in any climate.

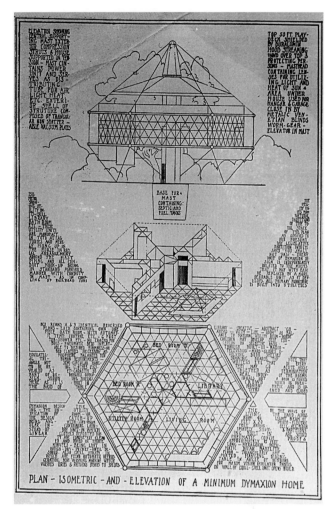

R. Buckminster Fuller: design for Minimum Dymaxion Home (4D House), 1927–32 (Los Angeles, CA, Buckminster Fuller Institute)

4. LATER CAREER. Fuller always courted fame: in the 1960s he became a peripatetic entrepreneur and teacher on a global scale, delivering lectures that lasted between three and six hours. He formed an architectural partnership with Shoji Sadao (*b* 1927) in 1979 and other professional associations in England and the USA. His international status grew as his domes were used to fulfil prestigious commissions, the largest at the Baton Rouge Union Tank Car Company plant in Louisiana (115 m diameter) in 1959, for the United States Pavilion at Expo '67 in Montreal (for illustration *see* GEODESIC DOME), the Weatherdome (1973) on Mt Fuji, Japan, and the Spaceship Earth dome (1982) in Disneyworld at Orlando, FL.

Fuller was an uncompromising exponent of the machine aesthetic. His work provides a reference point for the definition of Functionalism in architecture. For example, Le Corbusier's block in the Weissenhofsiedlung, Stuttgart (1927), looks most unlike 'a machine for living in' by comparison with Fuller's exactly contemporary Dymaxion house. He helped in no small measure to define the attitude, for so long common amongst Modernists, that architecture was primarily a technological discipline but he saw this attitude fade in the 1970s. He found a new audience, however, among the exponents of environmentalism who were quick to espouse his principles relating to the use of nature's systems and his concepts of self-sufficiency: his domes, much used for scientific, industrial and especially military purposes, were at last seen as the means of facilitating worldwide environmental control and resource management for ecological purposes in ways he had propounded for over half a century.

WRITINGS

4D Timelock (Chicago, 1928/*R* Albuquerque, 1972)
Nine Chains to the Moon (Philadelphia, 1938, New York, 1963)
with R. W. Marks: *The Dymaxion World of Buckminster Fuller* (New York, 1963/*R* 1973)
Ideas and Integrities (New Jersey, 1963)
Operating Manual for Spaceship Earth (New York, 1968)
J. Meller, ed.: *The Buckminster Fuller Reader* (London, 1970)
Earth Inc. (New York, 1973)
with E. J. Applewhite: *Synergetic Explorations in the Geometry of Thinking* (New York, 1975)
——: *Synergetics 2: Further Explorations in the Geometry of Thinking* (New York, 1979)

BIBLIOGRAPHY

J. McHale: *R. Buckminster Fuller* (New York, 1962), p. 13
'The Dymaxion American', *Time* (10 Jan 1964), pp. 46–51
S. Rosen: *Wizard of the Dome—Buckminster Fuller, Designer for the Future* (Boston, 1969)
'The World of Buckminster Fuller', *Archit. Forum*, ccxvi (1972), pp. 49–96
H. Kenner: *Bucky: A Guided Tour of Buckminster Fuller* (New York, 1973)
R. W. Donaldson: *Mind's Eye of Buckminster Fuller* (New York, 1974)
A. V. Lord: *Pilot for Spaceship Earth* (New York, 1978)
M. Vance: *Richard Buckminster Fuller: A Bibliography* (Monticello, IL, 1980)
E. J. Applewhite, ed.: *Synergetics Dictionary: The Mind of Buckminster Fuller* (New York, 1985)
J. Ward, ed.: *The Artefacts of Buckminster Fuller*, 4 vols (New York, 1985)
L. S. Sieden: *Buckminster Fuller's Universe: An Appreciation* (New York, 1989)
M. Pawley: *Buckminster Fuller/Martin Pawley* (London, 1990)

RICHARD GUY WILSON

Fuller, Thomas (*b* Bath, 8 March 1823; *d* Ottawa, 28 Sept 1898). Canadian architect of English birth. He was trained in Bath under James Wilson (1816–1900), who specialized in the design of Nonconformist churches, usually in the Gothic style, and schools. Fuller's earliest-known independent commission was the rebuilding (1845–8) of the Anglican cathedral in Antigua, which had been destroyed in an earthquake. He produced an elaborate design for a cruciform building with an Italianate stone exterior, an earthquake-proof interior timber frame, and a richly panelled classical interior. However, because it failed to conform to the prevailing Gothic Revival style, it was criticized by the progressive English architectural press.

Back in England by 1847, Fuller formed a partnership with William Bruce Gingell (1819–1900), also a pupil of Wilson's, who is known chiefly for his later designs in Bristol in a massive Byzantine style. Fuller & Gingell, who had offices at Bath and possibly Bristol, followed Wilson in their preference for commissions of a public and institutional character, usually rendered in the fashionable Italianate style. By this time, however, Fuller was keenly interested in the Gothic Revival and is said to have assisted Raphael (1817–77) and J. Arthur Brandon (1821–47) in

their publications on English medieval architecture, such as *An Analysis of Gothick Architecture* (1844).

Around 1851 James Wilson took Fuller as his partner. The arrangement cannot have lasted long, however, since by 1855 Fuller was in practice on his own and in or about that year he is known to have designed the town hall of Bradford-on-Avon, Wilts. This was his most important English commission in the assertive High Victorian manner that later characterized his work in Canada.

In 1857 Fuller emigrated to Canada, establishing himself in Toronto, Canada West (now Ontario), a flourishing small city. There he came into contact with other Gothic Revival architects including Frederic William Cumberland (1820–81), who with his partner William George Storm (1826–92) was then embarked on building University College, Toronto, in an eclectic High Victorian manner. It is possible that Fuller assisted them in this project. In 1858, with the civil engineer Chilion Jones (1835–1912) as his partner, Fuller designed the handsome suburban parish church of St Stephen-in-the-Fields, Toronto, the first of a series of small, mostly Anglican, churches in Ontario modelled on the village churches of medieval England and arranged according to the dictates of the Ecclesiological Society in England. Particularly representative of his work in this vein, though its design was altered by an assistant, King Arnoldi, during construction, is the church of St Alban the Martyr, Sandy Hill, Ottawa (1866–77).

The commission for which Fuller is best known, the Canadian Parliament Buildings at Ottawa (see fig.; *see also* OTTAWA, §2), was won in competition in 1859. Fuller & Jones's design grafted eclectic Gothic detail upon a mansarded body of formal ceremonial plan; in so doing it responded to the latest developments in the English Gothic Revival and came to serve as a stylistic prototype for the public architecture of Canada, which was just then emerging as a nation.

In 1863, while the Canadian Parliament was under construction, Fuller & Jones won the competition to design a new Capitol at Albany for the State of New York. Though nothing came of this project, another competition four years later resulted in Fuller, who in the meantime had split up with Jones, being asked to collaborate with Arthur D. Gilman (1821–82) and Augustus Laver (1834–98) on a definitive scheme for a State Capitol. Their joint design, which had the two legislative chambers elevated on a *piano nobile* astride a central court, and a grandly pavilioned Second Empire exterior that was to climax in a colossal tower and dome, was followed until 1875 when, with the third storey already reached, construction was stopped and an Advisory Board formed. Major changes were recommended in plan and style, and Fuller was dismissed, to be replaced by Leopold Eidlitz and H. H. RICHARDSON, who added two upper storeys in the Romanesque style. The 'Battle of the Styles' fought at Albany became a professional *cause célèbre* epitomizing the struggles and uncertainty in American architecture in the 1870s.

Fuller remained in the USA, winning with Laver in 1871 the commission to design the San Francisco Town Hall & Law Courts (destr. 1906). The complex was in a heavily decorated Boroque Revival style. Ten years later, however, he accepted the invitation of the Canadian Government

Thomas Fuller: Houses of Parliament, Ottawa, entrance façade and departmental blocks, 1859–66; photograph by Samuel McLaughlin, c. 1880; only the library building survived a fire in 1916

to return to Ottawa as Chief Architect of the Department of Public Works. He served in this capacity until his retirement in 1896, and designed or was responsible for the design of about 140 federal buildings, principally post offices and customs houses. Such buildings assumed a particular importance across the far-flung Dominion as representatives of the new federal government established in 1867. For these structures Fuller devised a striking blend of functional planning and bold, towered silhouette suggestive at times of the High Victorian Gothic of Parliament itself. Excellent examples of post offices designed under Fuller survive at Almonte (1889–91), Brockville (1883–6) and Cambridge (1884–7), three Ontario communities. Related to these in style, but a great deal larger, is the Langevin Block, Wellington Street, Ottawa (1883–9), a federal office building opposite Parliament Hill. Fuller's experience in the USA with large public buildings notable for their functional planning and plain yet picturesque massing was especially useful when he came to design the Langevin Block.

The high standard of design and efficient office organization developed under Fuller and his distinguished predecessor, Thomas Seaton Scott (1826–95), continued to influence the Chief Architect's branch until well into the 20th century. This was partly due to the presence there of Fuller's son, Thomas William Fuller (1865–1951), who was Chief Architect from 1927 to 1937. The Fuller architectural dynasty helped establish and maintain in Canadian federal architecture a maturity and integrity surprising for such a youthful country.

DCB

BIBLIOGRAPHY

The Builder, iii (1845), p. 603, vii (1849), p. 595 [St John's Cathedral, Antigua]

Sess. Pap. Parl. Dominion Canada, i–xxxii (1867/8–1989) [appendices, annual reports of the Minister of Public Works]

Amer. Architect & Bldg News, i (1876), pp. 82–3, 106–7 [NY State Capitol]

Obituaries, *Ottawa Evening J.* and *Ottawa Citizen* (29 Sept 1898); *Amer. Architect & Bldg News*, lxii (1898), p. 37; *The Builder*, lxxv (1898), p. 366; *Can. Architect & Bldr*, xi (1898), p. 168

H. Kirker: *California's Architectural Frontier: Style and Tradition in the Nineteenth Century* (San Marino, 1960, rev. Santa Barbara, 1973), pp. 97–8 [San Francisco Municipal Buildings]

W. Langsam: *The New York State Capitol at Albany: Evolution of the Design, 1866–1876* (diss., New Haven, CT, Yale U, 1968)

——: 'Thomas Fuller and Augustus Laver: Victorian Neo-Baroque and Second Empire vs. Gothic Revival in North America', *J. Soc. Archit. Historians*, xxix (1970), p. 270

M. MacRae and A. Adamson: *Hallowed Walls: Church Architecture of Upper Canada* (Toronto, 1975), pp. 159–61

C. A. Thomas: 'Architectural Image for the Dominion: Scott, Fuller and the Stratford Post Office', *J. Can. A. Hist.*, iii/1, 2 (Autumn 1976), pp. 83–94

——: 'Dominion Architecture: Fuller's Canadian Post Offices' (diss., U. Toronto, 1978) [the most comprehensive source of Fuller's career]

——: 'Thomas Fuller (1823–98) and Changing Attitudes to Medievalism in Nineteenth-century Architecture', *Soc. Stud. Archit. Canada: Sel. Pap.*, ii (1978), pp. 103–47

C. A. Thomas and A. J. Thomas: 'Canadian Showcase, Chicago, 1893', *Racar*, v (1978–9), pp. 113–15

D. Owram: *Building for Canadians: A History of the Department of Public Works, 1840–1960* (Ottawa, 1979)

J. Coolidge: 'Designing the Capitol: The Roles of Fuller, Gilman, Richardson and Eidlitz', *Proceedings of the New York State Capitol Symposium: Albany, 1983*, pp. 21–7

M. Archibald: *By Federal Design: The Chief Architect's Branch of the Department of Public Works, 1881–1914* (Ottawa, 1983)

C. A. Young: '*Odawah': The Competition of 1859 for the Canadian Parliament Buildings*, (MPhil thesis, U. Toronto, 1988)

H. Kalman: *A History of Canadian Architecture*, 2 vols (Toronto, 1994)

CHRISTOPHER A. THOMAS

Fuller Russell, John. *See* RUSSELL, JOHN FULLER.

Füllmaurer, Heinrich (*fl* Herrenberg, nr Tübingen, 1526–46). German painter and draughtsman. He was a close friend of the Reformation theologian Kaspar Gräter, who later became a Lutheran court preacher; in 1537 Gräter dedicated a catechism to him. Füllmaurer is documented as having worked with Albrecht Mayer and Marx Weiss the younger (1536–80) on the painted decoration of the ducal apartments in Stuttgart. He also collaborated with Mayer on a series of over 500 coloured drawings (Vienna, Österreich. Nbib.) for the two herbals written by the botanist Leonhard Fuchs, *De historia stirpium commentarii* (Basle, 1542) and *Neu Kreuterbuch* (Basle, 1543), and in addition completed hundreds of drawings for a sequel, which was never published (the majority of the wood blocks are in Tübingen, U. Botanisches Inst.). One of the woodcuts includes portraits of Füllmaurer and Mayer, as well as a portrait of the Strasbourg woodblock-carver Veit Speckel (*d* 1590), clearly based on a drawing by Hans Baldung.

Füllmaurer's major work is the Mömpelgarder altar (Vienna, Ksthist. Mus.). This has long been attributed to Matthias Gerung, although Fleischhauer has plausibly related it to payments to Füllmaurer for an unidentified work, made in 1539–40 by George I, Graf von Mömpelgard (1498–1558), who was residing in Montbéliard (Mömpelgard). The large, six-winged altar is an example of early Protestant iconography, with scenes from the *Life of Christ* according to the Evangelists and the Acts of the Apostles and with passages from Luther's translation (1522) of the Bible. Bright, colourful and clear, these scenes are evidently the work of an experienced illustrator. In Schloss Friedenstein, Gotha, there is a modified version supposedly created for Ulrich VI, Duke of Württemberg, for a church or chapel in Stuttgart.

BIBLIOGRAPHY

H. Rott: *Alt-Schwaben und die Reichsstädte* (1934), ii of *Quellen und Forschungen zur südwestdeutschen und schweizerischen Kunstgeschichte im XV. und XVI. Jahrhundert.* (Stuttgart, 1933–8), pp. lv–lvii, lxviii

W. Fleischhauer: *Renaissance im Herzogtum Württemberg* (Stuttgart, 1971), pp. 154–9

Die Renaissance im deutschen Südwesten (exh. cat., Karlsruhe, Bad. Landesmus., 1986), p. 154, nos C 14, C 14a, E 19

KURT LÖCHER

Fulton, Hamish (*b* London, 21 July 1946). English photographer and conceptual artist. He studied sculpture at St Martin's School of Art, London, from 1966 to 1968, at the same time as Jan Dibbets, Barry Flanagan, Gilbert and George, John Hilliard, Richard Long and Bruce McLean, and at the Royal College of Art, London, from 1968 to 1969. Basing his work on long-distance walks lasting from one day to several weeks, Fulton recorded his physical and emotional experience of the landscape by photographing it in black-and-white with a 35 mm camera; in typical works such as *Slioch Hilltop Cairn/Circling Buzzards* (2 photographs, each 118.1×87.6 mm, 1980; London, Tate), he then presented a single photograph or sequence of photographs, usually printed on a large scale and in a rich tonal range, often in conjunction with printed captions. These texts sometimes describe prosaic matters, such as the length, duration or date of the walk or the weather conditions under which the walk was made; in other cases a sequence of words evokes a poetic mood particular to the walk, enabling the spectator to bring to the work his or her own feelings, glimpses, memories and encounters with landscape. While his work has been linked both to conceptual art and land art, Fulton saw himself as heir to British traditions of landscape painting. His work was perhaps most widely disseminated in his books.

PHOTOGRAPHIC PUBLICATIONS

Hollow Lane (London, 1971)
Skyline Ridge (London, 1975)
Song of the Skylark (London, 1982)
Horizon to Horizon (Londonderry, 1983)
Four Nights Camping in a Wood (Neuss, 1987)

BIBLIOGRAPHY

M. Auping: 'Hamish Fulton: Moral Landscapes', *A. America*, lxxi/2 (Feb 1983), pp. 87–93

R. White: 'Hamish Fulton: Interview, 1981', *View*, iv/2 (1983) [whole issue]

PAULINE BULLARD

Fulvio, Andrea (*b* ?Palestrina, *c.* 1440; *d* Rome, 1527). Italian antiquary and writer. His early career is obscure. A precocious disciple of Pomponio Leto's Academy, he quickly joined the circle of Roman antiquaries. Fulvio is probably to be identified with 'Andreas Praenestinus', who composed a short epigram appended to Thomas Ochsenbrunner's *Priscorum heroum stemmata* (1494, 2/1510). Another of Fulvio's youthful poems prefaced Francesco Albertini's *Opusculum de mirabilibus novae et veteris urbis Romae* of 1510. Albertini relied heavily on Fulvio ('vir doctissimus') for archaeological and epigraphic matters.

Fulvio's first independent tracts, the *Ars metrica* and *Epistola nova*, published some time between 1510 and 1512, bear the cognomen 'Sabinus', reflecting his new status as Roman citizen. While serving as *maestro regionario* in his neighbourhood of S Eustachio, he composed a description of Rome's ruins in Virgilian hexameter. Dedicated to Leo X and published a few months after his election in 1513, the *Antiquaria urbis* was an encomium to both the ancient and the modern city. In discussing the Capitoline Fulvio cites the famous antiquities restored to the Comune by Sixtus IV; in closing he praises the Roman Gymnasium (Sapienza) founded under Eugenius IV and promoted by Alexander VI. It is ironic that a poem by Gianfrancesco Pico della Mirandola (1469–1533) exhorting the Pope to remove his collection of pagan deities from the sculpture garden in the Belvedere courtyard was also published in 1514 and by the same press of Giacomo Mazzocchio. Around 1515 Fulvio wrote an epigram in homage to Andrea Sansovino's marble group of *St Anne, the Virgin and Child* (1512) in S Agostino. This sculpture, and Raphael's fresco of *Isaiah* on the pier above, had been commissioned by Johannes Goritz in 1512 and became the meeting-point each year of a circle of humanists dedicated to the cult of St Anne. An anthology of their verses, entitled the *Coryciana* (1524), includes two of Fulvio's poems. In 1517 he completed *Illustrium imagines*, a historical compendium of famous men illustrated with profiles taken from the obverses of ancient Roman coins, but his facsimiles reflected little interest in the burgeoning field of numismatics. In a prefatory letter to Jacopo Sadoleto (1477–1547), Mazzocchio implies that Fulvio took on this commission as a professional 'antiquarius'.

Around 1518 Fulvio probably began advising Raphael on Leo X's commission for a series of reconstructed views of ancient Rome. A letter dated 1514, in which Raphael refers to 'Fulvio nostro, chol quale siamo iti di questo dì ciercando le belle anticalie', is generally considered fake. However, in the preface to his guidebook *Antiquitates urbis* (1527), Fulvio mentions accompanying Raphael around the city only a few days before the artist's death (1520). Fulvio frequently took part in excavations and contributed to the *Epigrammata antiquae urbis*, edited by Mariangelo Accursio and Mazzocchio the following year. Yet he conceived the *Antiquitates* from the perspective of a historian, not that of an architect ('non modo geographice, sed ethymologice cum rerum causis'). This work was sponsored by Clement VII, for whom Fulvio had two years earlier composed a poetic ode in celebration of the papal jubilees, entitled *Saecularis: Sive Iobilaevs*. (Their origin is traced back to the *ludi saeculares* of imperial Rome.)

WRITINGS

Ars metrica (?1510/12)
Epistola nova (?1510/12)
Antiquaria urbis (1514)
Aegloga de ortu Servatoris (?1514/15)
Illustrium imagines (Rome, 1517)
Epigrammata antiquae urbis Romae (Rome, 1521)
Andreae Fulvii Antiqvarii Ro. Saecularis: Sive Iobilaevs Annvs ad Clementem VII. Pont. Max. (1525)
Antiquitates urbis per Andream Fulvium nuperimme Aeditae (Rome, 1527)

BIBLIOGRAPHY

R. Weiss: 'Andrea Fulvio antiquario romano (*c.* 1470–1527)', *An. Scu. Norm. Sup. Pisa, Lett., Stor. & Filos.*, ser. ii, 28 (1959), pp. 1–44
F. Ascarelli: *Gli annali topografici di Giacomo Mazzocchi* (Florence, 1961), pp. 41–2
F. Castagnoli: 'Raphael and Ancient Rome', *The Complete Works of Raphael* (New York, 1969), pp. 569–84
V. A. Bonito: 'The Saint Anne Altar in Sant'Agostino: Restoration and Interpretation', *Burl. Mag.*, 124 (1982), pp. 268–80
P. Jacks: *The Antiquarian and the Myth of Antiquity: The Origins of Rome in Renaissance Thought* (Cambridge, 1993), pp. 180–84

PHILIP J. JACKS

Fumiani, Giovanni Antonio (*b* Venice, *c.* 1645; *d* Venice, 1710). Italian painter. He trained in Bologna under Domenico degli Ambrogi, a specialist in architectural perspective, but by 1668 he was in Venice, where he painted a *Virgin and Saints*, characterized by a monumentality reminiscent of the Carracci, in S Benedetto. He was influenced by Bolognese artists, particularly Ludovico Carracci and Alessandro Tiarini, and soon also became interested in the work of Veronese, so that he started to use elaborate architectural settings and brighter colours. This is apparent in the *Virgin Appearing to Pius V* (1674; Vicenza, S Lorenzo), whose monumentality foreshadows Tiepolo, whereas mosaics in S Marco, created in 1677 from Fumiani's cartoons, are closer to the idiosyncratic art of Pietro della Vecchia. He contributed to the decoration of S Rocco (1675, 1676, 1678), where he painted a large canvas of the *Charity of St Roch* on the ceiling of the nave, and afterwards the decoration of S Pantaleone with scenes from the *Life of St Pantaleon* (completed 1704). Here he painted canvases to cover a large ceiling (25×50 m), an ambitious undertaking, both in its scale and in the harmony and unity of the magniloquent images, that parallels Andrea Pozzo's decoration of S Ignazio, Rome. Fumiani was still inspired by Bolognese *quadratura* decoration, enriched by elements derived from Veronese, most notably the female figures. In his smaller paintings, however, such as the *modelli* (Florence, Uffizi) painted for the Grand Prince Ferdinand of Tuscany, for whom he worked for a long time, with Niccolò Cassana acting as intermediary, Fumiani revealed a lively decorative sense and a taste for animated, sensual subjects that produced works of great quality. His last work, the large lunette depicting *Frederick III Visiting St Zachary's Convent in the Company of the Doge* (Venice, S Zaccaria), is still dominated by architecture inspired by Veronese; the composition of the work is complex and the colours rich.

BIBLIOGRAPHY

N. Ivanoff: 'La sacra rappresentazione di G. A. Fumiani', *Emporium*, cxxxv/810–16 (1962), pp. 249–55
The Twilight of the Medici: Late Baroque Art in Florence, 1670–1743 (exh. cat., ed. S. Rossen; Detroit, MI, Inst. A.; Florence, Pitti; 1974), pp. 234–7
P. Rossi: 'La Scuola Grande di S Rocco: Committenti e artisti (Antonio Smeraldi, Enrico Merengo, Antonio Molinari, Giovanni Antonio Fumiani, Ambrogio Bon, Santo Piatti', *A. Ven.*, xxxix (1985), pp. 194–203
V. Sgarbi: 'Fumiani', *F.M.R. Mag.*, xi/43 (1986), pp. 40–42
U. Ruggeri: 'Aspetti della fortuna di Paolo Veronese nella pittura veneziana del seicento', *Atti del convegno sulla fortuna di Paolo Veronese: Venice, 1989*

UGO RUGGERI

Fumihiko Maki. *See* MAKI, FUMIHIKO.

Functionalism. Term applied to architecture in which the form of a building is derived from the function it is intended to fulfil. As employed by such historians as Nikolaus Pevsner and Siegfried Giedion, the term became generally identified with early 20th-century Modernism, for, like many of their architect contemporaries, they used it in justifying that style. It would, however, be hard to substantiate the claim that modern architecture is truly more functional than that of many other periods, particularly as it was impregnated with aesthetic and social concerns that sometimes conflicted directly with the requirements of use.

Even in the realm of theory modernists cannot claim any monopoly on functionalist ideas: A. W. N. Pugin claimed in his *True Principles of Pointed or Christian Architecture* (1841) that 'there should be no features about a building which are not necessary for construction, convenience or propriety', defining propriety as the appropriate reflection of the internal arrangements in the exterior. Even though he applied them to Gothic examples, he drew his ideas from the French Neo-classical tradition, while the French reiterated theories borrowed from the Italian Renaissance. Thus functionalist ideas can be found in *De re aedificatoria* (Florence, 1485) by Leon Battista Alberti if one chooses so to read them, and these derive from the theories of Vitruvius. Many studies of vernacular architecture are also susceptible to a functionalist interpretation.

If its superficial use as a stylistic tag is rejected, Functionalism becomes a complex issue, for it concerns the relationship between use and meaning, disputed since the days of Aristotle. The predominance of the term in architecture in the 20th century reflects a broader cultural tendency, for it was also used in other fields, notably social anthropology, where its leading theorist was Bronislaw Malinowski (1884–1942; *see* ANTHROPOLOGY AND ART). The decisive influence in both areas of knowledge was the rise of science and the associated ideology of Positivism, which gives primacy to the physical world, naively discounting all the philosophical difficulties of interpretation. Crucial, too, was Charles Darwin's theory of natural selection, which seemed to explain nature in terms of strict adaptation to purpose: Nature was demonstrated to be no longer static but in a state of flux, its great and hitherto inexplicable diversity reduced to a single process. Even if the mechanism was and still is in dispute, the evidence for the theory of evolution was overwhelming.

The importance of the Darwinian revolution cannot be overestimated. The natural world was put into a new perspective, and the same principles were applied to many aspects of human culture. Nature, the traditional yardstick for aesthetic criteria, took on a new interpretation: flowers were no longer beautiful for the sake of our enjoyment, but merely in order to attract pollinating insects; all was purposeful. The impact on architecture coincided with a crisis of meaning precipitated by the proliferation of 'styles' borrowed from buildings all over the world and thus

rapidly devalued. Heroic attempts to create a new 'style' in the form of Art Nouveau also proved fruitless. The way was thus open for a return to what were seen to be fundamental principles: logical structure and construction, economic use of materials and a close attention to the requirements of use.

The formulation of an 'organic architecture' by the American architect LOUIS SULLIVAN was directly influenced by evolution theory. He was responsible for the much quoted phrase 'form follows function', advocating a renunciation of ornament as early as 1892 and producing a series of buildings notable for their expressed structure. Sullivan reflected a tendency in American thinking that can be traced back to the Transcendentalism of Henry Thoreau (1817–62) and Walt Whitman (1819–91), and to the prophetic ideas of Horatio Greenough (*see* GREENOUGH, (1)). Primarily a sculptor, Greenough is better known today for his writings: as early as 1843 he advocated 'a scientific arrangement of spaces and forms to function and to site' (Greenough, 1947), and considered that 'character is the record of function', ascribing the beauty of a sailing frigate to its close response to the pressure of wind and wave. The concept of organic architecture was extended by Frank Lloyd Wright, who worked in Sullivan's office (1888–93); he stressed the idea that a building should grow in response to site and circumstances. Wright's revolutionary architecture was published in Berlin in 1910, and proved influential (*see* WRIGHT, (1)).

European Modernists were greatly outnumbered by traditionalists even in the 1920s, and they soon discovered the value of solidarity, concealing their sometimes considerable differences of approach behind a common front. Functional or pseudo-functional arguments were their best ammunition against their conservative rivals and were widely and uncritically accepted. The appearance of the new architecture, cubic and white, was read as functional because of its simplicity and a then unusual lack of ornament, even if its organization was often based on abstract geometric composition. Its authors often sincerely believed their functionalist arguments, but found in practice that the pressures of use were insufficient to dictate form. Moreover, when they turned to the question of construction, they found a craft industry geared to traditional designs. Thus, although they spoke of machine production, their works were often constructed by hand, and the 'machine aesthetic' was dictated not so much by machinery itself as by an anticipation of what it might bring. The desired simplicity of detail, however, and the compulsive use of crude flat-roof technologies resulted in technical failures and maintenance problems: 'Functionalist' architecture often functioned badly.

As well as these shortcomings there were some direct contradictions: Le Corbusier is widely remembered for his statement in *Vers une architecture* (Paris, 1923) that 'A house is a machine for living in', yet around the same time he also proclaimed that 'architecture is the masterly, correct and magnificent play of masses brought together in light'. He, more than any other individual architect, was responsible for the development of the 'white architecture', derived directly from Purism, a movement led by him. Perhaps the secret of Le Corbusier's success lay in his ability to justify the impressive forms resulting from his

1. Johannes Duiker: Open-air School, Amsterdam, 1929–30 (under construction)

Purist aesthetic on the basis of a supposed Functionalist programme, but the contradiction was noted at the time by perceptive critics and still haunts architecture today.

The texts written in the 1920s by many supposedly Functionalist architects tend to be contradictory or inadequate. Johannes Duiker's apologia for his Open-air School (1929–30; see fig. 1) in Amsterdam, for example, seems to present it as a machine for sunning children. Most other functions go unmentioned, including many preoccupations of the architect visible in the building. Although interesting as evidence of the architect's attitude, such a document does not constitute an adequate description of work or theory. Perhaps architects are generally too close to their work to view it objectively, and too busy to undertake the difficult task of reflective analysis. Some architect-theorists, however, do struggle to define basic principles, and among those active in the 1920s two stand out in contrasting positions: HANNES MEYER, who represents a positivistic functionalism, and HUGO HÄRING, the father of organic functionalism (*see* ORGANIC ARCHITECTURE).

Meyer's manifesto 'Bauen', published in the Bauhaus magazine in 1928, the year he became director of the Bauhaus, was a statement of aims for the school and it remains a landmark in architectural theory. It opens with a denial of art, claiming that everything is a product of the formula 'function times economy'. He lists the 12 functions of a dwelling, claiming them as the only motives when building a house, and explains how the measurements—psychological as well as physical—that affect function are to be made; he asserts that 'building is nothing but organization: social, technical, economic, psychological organization'.

In spite of his functionalist polemic, Meyer's work fails to exemplify his theories. His description of his and Hans Wittwer's League of Nations project (1926–7; see fig. 2) is almost self-contradictory, opening with a denial of symbolic connotations, then going on to discuss what the building represents. Even at the level of the 'functional criteria' the arguments do not hold. The oval hall, for example, is supposed to answer acoustic requirements, but no account is taken of the concentrated reflections that the curved surfaces would produce. His ideas nevertheless influenced the reorganization of architectural education after World War II, when departments of architecture were renamed departments of environmental design, history was dethroned and attempts were made to turn architecture into an objective science. This approach proved woefully inadequate, for it depended on the assumption that all aspects of building lent themselves to measurement, and it tried to turn qualities into quantities. Measurable aspects were taken into account while unmeasurable ones, such as the value of a view from a window, were omitted. The reductiveness of such a programme resulted in cultural impoverishment that is widely felt, and remains a prime cause of the so-called crisis of Modernism in architecture.

A qualitative rather than a quantitative strand of functionalism was pursued by Hugo Häring, secretary of the Berlin organization Der Ring. He saw the Modernist revolution as a liberation from academic formalism, an opportunity to allow new forms to develop in response to

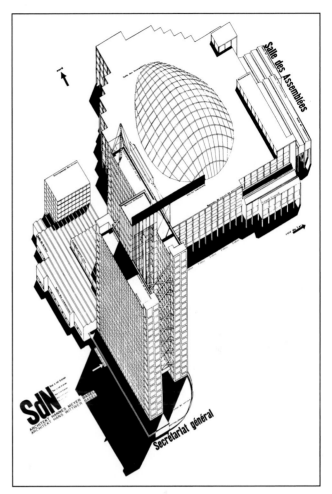

2. Hannes Meyer and Hans Wittwer: preliminary study for the Palace of the League of Nations, Geneva, 1926–7; axonometric view

the requirements of life, and he rejected the formal vocabulary of Le Corbusier in the 1920s as representing a return to geometry. If forms were evolved to fulfil performance requirements, he claimed, they would develop their own character in relation to the role they play: 'We should not express our own individuality, but rather the individuality of things, their expression should be identical with their being.' A well-known example of his organic functionalism is his farm at Garkau (1924–5) near Lübeck. The barn was given a lamella roof, an unusual construction that takes the structural shape of a pointed arch. Häring gave credible explanations for various planning decisions, but of special interest is the hierarchical relation of parts, culminating in the pear-shaped cowshed that relates the cows to the bull. Here he went beyond use itself towards the expression of use, thus linking the pragmatic with the symbolic. He foresaw the dangers of a purely technical approach and never allowed technique to dominate his own work. Although he built little, he provided the inspiration for a continuing tradition of German architecture that gained impetus in the 1950s and

1960s from his friend and colleague HANS SCHAROUN. Alvar Aalto held a similar theoretical position, and more recently ALDO VAN EYCK and RALPH ERSKINE have both claimed to pursue Functionalism at this more elevated level.

In the 1970s Functionalism came under attack—from Post-modernists, because it seemed to deny all symbolic content, and from Italian Rationalists, because they chose to emphasize architectural type and monumentality at the expense of response to immediate conditions. Both tendencies have since run into difficulties through ignoring the relationship between use and meaning. A door handle is as much an invitation to open a door as the means of doing so, while space is still organized hierarchically in ways we take for granted; it is no accident, for example, that the judge sits on axis in a law court, and in the highest, most decorated seat. It was precisely in this relationship between the arrangement of space and the habits and conventions of society that the form–function question in architecture was pursued most fruitfully in the late 20th century.

See also RATIONALISM (ii) and MODERN MOVEMENT.

BIBLIOGRAPHY

A. W. N. Pugin: *The True Principles of Pointed or Christian Architecture* (London, 1841)
H. Häring: 'Wege zur Form', *Die Form*, 1 (1925), pp. 3–5; Eng. trans. in *Form and Function*, ed. T. Benton and D. Sharp (Milton Keynes, 1975)
H. Meyer: 'Bauen' (1928), *Hannes Meyer: Bauen und Gesellschaft: Schriften, Briefe, Projekte*, ed. K.-J. Winkler (Dresden, 1980), pp. 47ff
H. Greenough: *Form and Function*, ed. H. A. Small (Berkeley, 1947)
E. R. De Zurko: *Origins of Functionalist Theory* (New York, 1957)
G. Baird: 'Karel Teige's Mundaneum, 1929, and Le Corbusier's In Defense of Architecture, 1933', *Oppositions* (1974), no. 4
J. Posener: 'Critique of the Criticism of Functionalism', *Lotus Int.*, 11 (1976), pp. 5–11
P. Steadman: *The Evolution of Designs: Biological Analogy in Architecture and the Applied Arts* (Cambridge, 1979)
P. B. Jones: 'Hugo Häring', *Archit. Rev.* [London] (April 1982), pp. 40–47
——: 'Implicit Meanings', *Archit. Rev.* [London] (June 1985), pp. 34–9

PETER BLUNDELL JONES

Fünfkirchen. *See* PÉCS.

Fungai [Fongario; da Fonghaia; Fungari], **Bernardino** (Cristofano di Nicholo d'Antonio di Pietro) (*b* Siena, *bapt* 14 Sept 1460; *d* Siena, 1516). Italian painter. He is recorded in 1482 as Benvenuto di Giovanni's *garzone* at work on the monochrome frescoes decorating the drum of the cupola of Siena Cathedral. Most scholars have accepted Benvenuto as Fungai's teacher but stress the greater influence of Matteo di Giovanni; other proposals have included Giovanni di Paolo and, following the reattribution of paintings traditionally ascribed to Giacomo Pacchiarotti, Pietro Orioli. Fungai depended heavily on the preceding generation of Sienese painters and was considerably influenced by the contemporary activity of Pietro Perugino, Luca Signorelli and Bernardino Pinturicchio in and around Siena. His works are characterized by the docility of the figures, a keen decorative sensibility in the use of colour and the treatment of drapery and landscape, and a pleasantly engaging narrative skill. Although identification of works from his early career is problematic, a sizeable oeuvre has been ascribed on the basis of a signed and dated altarpiece executed for S

Niccolò al Carmine depicting the *Virgin and Child Enthroned with SS Sebastian, Jerome, Nicholas and Anthony of Padua* (1512; Siena, Pin. N.).

Fungai's style first appears definitively in the *Stigmatization of St Catherine of Siena* (completed by Nov 1497; Siena, S Caterina in Fontebranda). The lunetted panel is dominated by the elongated figure of the saint kneeling at the left with brightly lit palms, face upturned towards a crucifix at the right. Above, a half-length Virgin and Child accompanied by saints and angels witness the miracle. The foreground sanctuary opens entirely on to a panorama of graceful buildings, gentle hills and tall, feathery trees that lead to an extensive sea defined by a blue-toned, undulating coastline and enlivened with small boats. This landscape, with its Umbrian influences, persists as a key element throughout Fungai's repertory. The contrast between the solid, hard-edged and hieratic figures in the lunette and the small background and predella figures with dancelike poses and freely moving, sketchy drapery is also typical. The apogee of this hieratic style is the *Coronation of the Virgin* (completed 1501; Siena, S Maria dei Servi). The aggrandized central figures and static, formally ranked saints and angels fill the plane. Bright, cool tones prevail. Four scenes from the *Legend of St Clement* (Strasbourg, Mus. B.-A.; York, C.A.G.) may have formed part of the predella. Lyrical landscape and narrative charm similarly characterize Fungai's decorative, secular panels, notably in his stories of Scipio Africanus (ex-Agnew's, London; St Petersburg, Hermitage) and of a young woman pushed overboard from a ship and rescued from the water (Houston, TX, Mus. F.A.). Fungai's fascination with landscape and study of Pinturicchio are paramount in the altarpiece of 1512. His later works, for example the *Assumption* (Siena, Pin. A.), tend to be dry and overtly eclectic.

Fungai may have used an oil technique in the 1512 altarpiece to create fluid passages that anticipate Domenico Beccafumi (see Cole). Fungai's abundant use of gold is noteworthy in sumptuous damasks and in painted areas incised to reveal gilding. Commissioned in 1494 to decorate ceremonial banners with gold and azure and in 1499 to gild the organ case for the cathedral, he may have had a reputation for his adept handling of expensive materials. Other works attributed to him include frescoes (Siena, Monte Paschi and Ist. Sordomuti) and devotional panels (London, N.G.; Siena, Pin. N.).

Judging the altarpieces still in Siena, early scholars disparaged Fungai for a perceived lack of originality and for succumbing to Umbrian influences. His reputation rose with the attribution of other works (see Perkins, Berenson, Borenius), especially the narrative paintings on cassone panels (publicized by Schubring). Bacci published Romagnoli's fundamental text and all documents, establishing the date and Fungai's connection with the S Maria dei Servi *Coronation*. Refinement of attribution (anticipated by Vertova) and a full reassessment of chronology (attempted only by van Marle) are in order.

BIBLIOGRAPHY

Thieme–Becker
G. Vasari: *Vite* (1550, rev. 2/1568); ed. G. Milanesi (1878–85), vi, p. 416
F. M. Perkins: 'Alcuni dipinti senesi sconosciuti o inediti', *Rass. A.*, xiii (1913), pp. 121–6
P. Schubring: *Cassoni* (Leipzig, 1915), pls CXXIV–CCXV

T. Borenius: 'Unpublished Cassone Panels: III', *Burl. Mag.*, xl (1922), pp. 189–90

B. Berenson: 'Quadri senza casa: Il quattrocento senese II', *Dedalo*, ii (1931), pp. 735–67

F. M. Perkins: 'Pitture senesi poco conosciute', *La Diana*, vii (1932), pp. 179–94, 236–46

A. Venturi: *Storia*, x (1932), pp. 319–30

R. van Marle: *Italian Schools*, xvi (1937), pp. 465–85

P. Bacci: *Bernardino Fungai pittore senese (1460–1516)* (Siena, 1947)

E. Carli: 'Dipinti senesi nel museo Houston', *Ant. Viva*, ii/4 (1963), pp. 15–25

B. Berenson: *Central and North Italian Schools* (1968), i, pp. 149–52; ii, pls 927–40

L. Vertova: 'Il Maestro della Pala Bagatti Valsecchi', *Ant. Viva*, viii/1 (1969), pp. 3–14

P. Torriti: *La Pinacoteca Nazionale di Siena: I dipinti dal XV al XVIII secolo* (Genoa, 1981), nos 431–41

L. Vertova: 'Cicli senesi di virtù: Inediti di Andrea di Niccolò e del Maestro di Griselda', *Scritti di storia dell'arte in onore di Federico Zeri* (Milan, 1984), pp. 200–12

B. Cole: *Sienese Painting in the Age of the Renaissance* (Bloomington, 1985), pp. 142–4

Painting in Renaissance Siena, 1420–1500 (exh. cat., ed. K. Christiansen, L. Kanter and C. Strehlke; New York, Met., 1988), pp. 352–9

CAROLYN C. WILSON

Funhof [Fonhave; Funghoff], **Hinrik** (*fl* Hamburg, 1475; *d* 1485). German painter. He first appears in Hamburg records in 1475, marrying the widow of Hans Borneman and taking over this painter's workshop. At the same time municipal payments for painted signs and paintings are recorded, as they are in 1480, 1481 and 1483. From 1479 to 1484 Funhof received larger payments for an altarpiece in St Georg, his parish church. In 1484 he received a payment from the Brotherhood of Our Dear Ladies' Coronation for a work in the cathedral. Of these works in Hamburg only the small panel of the *Virgin with the Ears of Corn* (Hamburg, Ksthalle), from the convent of St Mary Magdalene, remains. The church register of St Georg, however, also notes Funhof being paid in 1482 for a journey to Lüneburg. The registers of St Johannis in Lüneburg connect this with a commission for four large panels for its high altar, final payments for which were made to Funhof's widow in 1485, when his name is also recorded in a Hamburg register of deaths. The four large panels (*in situ*), on the altarpiece's second view, show the legends of *St Cecilia*, *St John the Baptist*, *St George* and *St Ursula*.

A dependence on Netherlandish models has always been observed in Funhof's paintings. The *Virgin with the Ears of Corn* is undoubtedly his earliest surviving work, probably from the end of the 1470s. The closed church interior shown in earlier renditions of this image is broken up, opening up landscape views to the sides of the closed rear wall—a constructional device learnt from work of the young Hans Memling in Bruges (e.g. the *St Catherine* triptych, *c*. 1474; Hospital of St John). This stylistic influence shows also in Funhof's Lüneburg pictures, but here the Westphalian painter achieved a decisive modification of effect. With their wealth of cool colours (light blue, red and green), psychological depth of event and profusion of cultural-historical details (gamblers, meals, clothing on the *St Cecilia* panel, for example), Funhof's pictures, after Bernt Notke's, represent the peak of Late Gothic panel painting in north Germany.

BIBLIOGRAPHY

K. Koppmann: *Kämmereirechnungen der Stadt Hamburg*, iii: *1471–1500* (Hamburg, 1878); iv: *1482–1500* (Hamburg, 1880)

C. G. Heise: *Norddeutsche Malerei* (Leipzig, 1918), pp. 107ff, 162ff, notes 31–4

F. Stuttmann: 'Hinrik Funhof, sein Verhältnis zu den Niederlanden und seine Stellung in der niedersächsischen Kunst', *Pantheon*, xxvii (1936), pp. 75ff

K. Zuhorn: 'Zur westfälischen Herkunft des Hamburger Malers Hinrik Funhof', *Westfäl. Forsch.*, xvii (1963), p. 79; *Westfalen: Aft. Gesch., Kst & Vlksknd.*, xlii (1964), p. 428

P. Pieper: 'Fragen um Hinrik Funhof', *Jb. Hamburg. Kstsamml.*, xiv/xv (1970), pp. 85–104

HANS GEORG GMELIN

Funi, Achille [Virgilio Socrate] (*b* Ferrara, 26 Feb 1890; *d* Appiano Gentile, nr Como, 26 July 1972). Italian painter and teacher. He attended the Scuola Municipale d'Arte Dosso Dossi, Ferrara (1902–5), and studied under Cesare Tallone at the Accademia di Belle Arti di Brera, Milan (1906–10). Influenced by meeting Umberto Boccioni and Carlo Carrà, he formed the Gruppo Nuove Tendenze with Anselmo Bucci (1887–1955) and Leonardo Dudreville (1885–1975) and the architects Antonio Sant'Elia and Mario Chiattone. Funi adopted Boccioni's and Carrà's dynamic style (e.g. *Man Getting Off a Tram*, 1914; Milan, Gal. A. Mod.) and in 1915 volunteered to serve in World War I with other Futurists. This interruption allowed him to reassess Futurism. Influenced by the circle of Fascist intellectuals around Margherita Sarfatti, he developed an allusive realism (e.g. *Self-portrait*, 1918; priv. col., see 1973 exh. cat., fig. 7), which, in the manifesto *Contro tutti ritorni in pittura* (1920), he and Mario Sironi distinguished from the prevalent archaism. In 1922, with Sironi, Bucci, Dudreville and others, he formed the Sette Pittore del Novecento, exhibiting at the Galleria Pesaro, Milan, in 1922. The following year the Sette Pittore developed into the NOVECENTO ITALIANO, and further shows were held at the Galleria Pesaro, and in 1924 at the Venice Biennale. Funi treated contemporary subjects with an idealizing Renaissance realism, as in *Maternity* (1921; Turin, priv. col., see 1973 exh. cat., fig. 16).

Such classical nudes as Funi's *Venus in Love* (1928; Milan, Gal. A. Mod.) anticipated his mature didactic mural painting, which began with the *Aeneid* murals (destr.) at the Triennale in Monza in 1930. Using preparatory studies from life, he was admirably equipped for the monumentality and swiftness that fresco technique demanded. The mural *Italian Athletic Games* (1933; destr.), painted for the fifth Triennale of Milan, encapsulated the aspirations of the *Manifesto della pittura murale* (1933), signed with Sironi, Carrà and Massimo Campigli, by paralleling ancient and modern images. This led to his most important cycle, the *Myth of Ferrara* (1934–7) in the hall of the Palazzo Comunale, Ferrara (*in situ*). Although commissioned by the radical Fascist Italo Balbo, the themes were taken from Renaissance epic poems: Torquato Tasso's *Gerusalemme liberata* and Ludovico Ariosto's *Orlando furioso*. Assisted by Felicità Frai (*b* 1914), Funi matched the drama of these writings to a dynamic realism recalling Pompeiian and Ferrarese precedents. Balbo also commissioned from Funi his triumphalist *Entry of 'il Duce' into Tripoli* (1937–9; Tripoli, Governor's Pal.; destr.) while Funi was already in Libya working on the Giottesque cycle of the *Life of St Francis* (1936–9) for S Francesco, Tripoli (*in situ*). Despite his support for the regime of Mussolini, *Moses with the Tablets of the Law* (1937–9; Milan, Pal. Giustizia) was attacked for its Jewish subject. During World War II he was unable to finish the *Myth of Rome* (1942–3) for Adalberto Libera's Palazzo dell'Esposizione (1937–40) in the Città Giardino EUR, near Rome, and in 1949 these were covered by removable panels done by Severini. In 1945, after a year as Director of the Accademia di Brera in Milan (where he had taught since 1940), he was forced to resign because of his appointment by the Fascists. He moved to the Accademia Carrara di Belle Arti in Bergamo (1946–53) but returned to the Brera in 1948, working concurrently at both institutions and eventually being reinstated as Director at the Brera (1957–60). Despite retaining his classicism for such paintings as those (1962–3) in S Antonio dei Frati Minori, Rimini, he encouraged students as diverse in approach as Gianni Dova and Valerio Adami.

BIBLIOGRAPHY

Achille Funi (exh. cat. by R. De Grada, Milan, Pal. Permanente, 1973)
Achille Funi (exh. cat. by A. Negri and Z. Birolli, Ferrara, Gal. Civ. A. Mod., 1976)
L. Scaudino: *Achille Funi e il mito di Ferrara* (Ferrara, 1985)
Achille Funi: Dal Futurismo alla maniera grande (exh. cat. by R. De Grada, G. A. Dell'Acqua, G. Mascherpa and N. Colombo, Milan, Brera, 1987)
Achille Funi: Itinerari di un affrescatore, 1930–1943 (exh. cat. by C. Cazzaniga, F. Dangor, V. Mazzarella and I. Sacco, Rome, Gal. Serpenti, 1988)
La scuola di Funi (exh. cat., ed. L. Somaini; Mendrisio, Mus. d'A., 1988)

MATTHEW GALE

Funj. *See under* NUBIA, §VII.

Funk, Hans (*b* Zurich, *c.* 1470; *d* Zurich, *c.* 1539–40). Stained-glass painter. He was mentioned before 1489 in court records in Zurich, where relatives were also active as stained-glass artists at the beginning of the 16th century. He settled *c.* 1499–1500 in Berne, living from 1509 in the Kirchgasse (now Münstergasse), and in 1519 he was appointed a member of the cantonal parliament (Grosser Rat). He received many commissions throughout the Swiss Confederation, above all in Berne and Fribourg, and his work exercised a significant influence on the other stained-glass artists of Berne. The earliest records of work by Funk come from the treasury accounts of Fribourg and Berne in 1504 and 1505: in 1505 he executed a series of windows (destr.) depicting the estates of the Alte Orte for Fribourg Town Hall. Earlier than this, however, is a window (*c.* 1501; Berne, Hist. Mus.) with both a signature and the monogram HFG ('Hans Funk Glasmaler'). The quality of Funk's art may be seen in the expressive characterization of the halberdiers holding the arms of Bremgarten and the Confederation, and in the combination of exact detail and liveliness in the fine gold work.

Following these works are a window of 1510 depicting *SS Nicholas and Mary Magdalene* (Berne, Hist. Mus.); one of 1512 showing *Duke Bertold V*, founder of Berne, lying in a meadow with a tree behind him bearing the arms of the city offices (Mulhouse, Mus. Hist.); and five windows of *c.* 1520 at Uerkheim Pfarrkirche, Aargau, depicting the *Virgin* with crescent moon and *SS Leodegar, Vincent and Maurice* with the arms of the estates of Berne. The border work here contains columns and foliate ornamentation, a mingling of Gothic and Renaissance motifs characteristic of the period. About 1522 Funk produced a series of armorial windows for Utzenstorf Pfarrkirche, showing the arms of Berne and Solothurn accompanied by the patron saints of the estates; their lavish upper sections are in the Bernisches Historisches Museum. Further armorial windows are in the Chapelle St Barthélémy, Fribourg (1526), and the Hôtel de Ville de la Palud, Lausanne (*c.* 1528).

Funk's window of *c.* 1532 entitled *The Old and the Young Citizen* (Berne, Hist. Mus.) has become, through its artistic quality and the importance of its content, the best-known stained-glass window of the 16th century in Switzerland. Above is seen the Battle of Novara (1513); below stand the representatives of two generations. On flanking scrolls, on either side, the young citizen asks where the older generation found its good fortune, while the older citizen accounts for the generational difference in terms of different lifestyles. The later window for the Gesellschaft zum Affen (1539; Berne, Hist. Mus.)—a work ascribed to Funk and his workshop that displays the Gesellschaft's symbol of a crouching ape looking at itself in a mirror—was the cause of a quarrel between Funk and the glazier Simprecht Baumeister. In 1539 Funk was banished from Berne after being accused of the murder of Baumeister. He died shortly afterwards.

Attributed to Funk are some carefully drawn designs for windows that are often close to the works of Niklaus Manuel Deutsch or go back to other models. A sketch for an armorial window (*c.* 1525–30; Vienna, Albertina) depicts the coat of arms of the town of Grüningen; another of 1532 (Zurich, Ksthaus) shows the arms of Jakob May flanked by a halberdier and a junker.

BIBLIOGRAPHY

H. Lehmann: 'Die Glasmalerei in Bern am Ende des 15. und Anfang des 16. Jahrhunderts', *Anz. Schweiz. Altertknd.*, n. s. 16 (1914), pp. 306–24; 17 (1915), pp. 45–65, 136–59, 217–40, 305–29; 18 (1916), pp. 54–74, 135–53, 225–43
B. Anderes: 'Die spätgotische Glasmalerei in Freiburg i. Ü.', *Freiburg. Geschbl.*, 51 (1962–3), pp. 105–22, 175–81
F. Bächtiger: 'Erörterungen zum *Alten und jungen Eidgenossen*', *Jb. Bern. Hist. Mus.* (1969–70), pp. 35–70
Niklaus Manuel Deutsch: Maler, Dichter, Staatsmann (exh. cat., Berne, Kstmus., 1979), passim

E. LUTHER

Funke, Jaromír (*b* Skuteč, 1 Aug 1896; *d* Prague, 22 March 1945). Czech photographer and theorist. Together with Josef Sudek and Jaroslav Rössler he was one of the most important representatives of Czech avant-garde photography of the 1920s and 1930s. He studied medicine, law and philosophy at Charles University in Prague and at the University of Bratislava but did not graduate. As an amateur photographer from 1920 he promoted 'pure' photography instead of traditional refined prints resembling the graphic arts and painting. A professional freelance photographer from 1922, he was a leader of the young opposition movement in photography, who founded the Czech Society of Photography (1924) and who wanted photography to fulfil new social functions. In his work Funke managed to combine some of the leading tendencies of European photography between the two World Wars, uniting Constructivism and Functionalism with Surrealism and social commentary. At the same time he managed to retain traditional Czech lyrical qualities. His work was rational, communicative, inventive in design and emotionally effective. A typical feature is his use of the dynamic diagonal.

Funke made a number of photographic series (e.g. *The Composition, Time Lasts, Unsaturated Earth, Bad Housing*), believing that only through the interaction of parts could a theme be fully covered and made accessible. He taught photography at the School of Arts and Crafts in Bratislava in 1931–5 and, from 1935 to 1944, at the School of Graphic Art in Prague. Together with the latter's Director, Ladislav Sutnar, he published *Fotografie vidí povrch* (1935). He spent several years as an editor of the journal *Fotografický Obzor*, in which he published a number of articles, among them 'Od fotogramu k emoci', which serves as his manifesto. Towards the end of the Nazi occupation of Czechoslovakia he was forced to work as a labourer.

WRITINGS

with L. Sutnar: *Fotografie vidí povrch* [Photography sees the surface] (Prague, 1935)
'Od fotogramu k emoci' [From the photogram to emotion], *Fot. Obzor*, 11 (1940); repr. *Rev. Fot.*, xx/1 (1976), pp. 64–5

BIBLIOGRAPHY

L. Linhart: *Jaromír Funke* (Prague, 1960)
L. Souček: *Jaromír Funke: Fotografie* (Prague, 1970)
Czechoslovakian Photography—Jaromír Funke, Jaroslav Rössler (exh. cat., London, Phot. Gal., 1982)
D. Mrázková and V. Remeš: *Tschechoslowakische Fotografen, 1900–1940* (Leipzig, 1983)

DANIELA MRÁZKOVÁ

Fu Pao-shih. *See* FU BAOSHI.

Fūrai Sanjin. *See* HIRAGA GENNAI.

Fures y Muñoz, Gerónimo (*b* Aragón; *fl* early 17th century). Spanish collector. He was a dilettante artist who held high offices in the court of Philip IV as Gentilhombre de la Boca, a member of the Consejo Supremo de Italia and the Conservador of the royal patrimony in the Kingdom of Naples, Sicily and Milan. These posts made it possible for him to assemble a fine collection of drawings by Italian painters and sculptors. He also had a collection of paintings, which was visited by Charles I, then Prince of Wales, on his visit to Madrid in 1623 for negotiations for the Spanish marriage. Fures y Muñoz presented him with eight paintings of his choice (although they were never sent) and presents of fine swords, broadswords, arquebuses and crossbows.

One of Fures y Muñoz's interests was the devising and painting of emblems (*emblemas morales*), whose lofty content made their invention a favourite occupation of Spanish courtiers and gentlemen. They had become popular from 1581, when Juan de Borja published his *Empresas morales* in Prague, and were given new vogue by the publication of the *Emblemas morales* of Sebastián de Covarrubias Orozco (Madrid, 1610). One of Fures y Muñoz's devices is described by Vicente Carducho in 1633: a ship whose sails are blown by a prosperous gale, with the motto 'Ne credas tempori' (Trust not the weather). Fures y Muñoz was a typical late Renaissance virtuoso in his interest in weapons, pictures, drawings and in amateur painting.

BIBLIOGRAPHY

V. Carducho: *Diálogos de la pintura* (1633); ed. F. Calvo Serraller (Madrid, 1979), pp. 421–2
R. W. Lightbown: 'Some Notes on Spanish Baroque Collections', *The Origins of Museums*, ed. O. Impey and A. Macgregor (Oxford, 1985), pp. 137–8

R. W. LIGHTBOWN

Furini, Francesco (*b* Florence, 1603; *d* Florence, 19 Aug 1646). Italian painter. He was one of the leading Florentine painters of the first half of the 17th century, famous for the ambiguous sensuality and *sfumato* effects of his many paintings of female nudes. He first studied with his father, Filippo Furini, nicknamed Pippo Sciamerone and described by Baldinucci as a portrait painter, and he completed his apprenticeship in the studios of Domenico Passignano and of Giovanni Bilivert. Inspired by an admiration for Classical sculpture, which he studied in the Medici collection in Florence, and for Raphael, he travelled to Rome, which he reached as early as 1619 (Gantelli, see 1972 exh. cat.). Here he came into contact with Bartolomeo Manfredi and with Giovanni da San Giovanni. In 1623 he assisted the latter on the frescoes of the *Chariot of the Night* in the Palazzo Bentivoglio (now Pallavicini-Rospigliosi), commissioned by Cardinal Guido Bentivoglio, and also perhaps on the lower paintings (1623–4) in the apse of the church of SS Quattro Coronati, Rome. His first dated work is the *Crucifixion of St Bartholomew* (1623; Todi, S Bartolomeo).

On his return to Florence *c.* 1624, Furini worked with Matteo Rosselli. The romantic mythological painting *Cephalus and Aurora* (Ponce, Mus. A.), which includes, in the bottom right, a vividly naturalistic putto reminiscent of Manfredi, may date from 1623–4, and in 1626 Furini signed and dated *Painting and Poetry* (Florence, Pitti), which reveals the legacy of his stay in Rome. The picture was commissioned by the Accademia del Disegno, and in its theme, which illustrates Horace's famous dictum 'Ut pictura poesis', and in its Renaissance composition, it demonstrates Furini's interest in the classicism of Raphael. His veneration for Classical sculpture is also evident in his many mythological and allegorical paintings of the late 1620s and 1630s. His images are drawn from the Antique yet reinterpreted through an intense study of nature (he made many life studies, particularly from the female model). They are also endowed with a lyrical poetry that suggests the artist's admiration for Gianlorenzo Bernini's mythological works and his study of Leonardo da Vinci. Furini possessed a copy (Modena, Bib. Estense, Cod. Campori) of Leonardo's *Trattato della pittura* that he himself illustrated. Works of the period include the *Death of Adonis* (Budapest, Mus. F.A.), the *Glorification of the House of Salviati* (1628; Salviati priv. col., see Gregori and Schleier, p. 270), *Acis and Galatea* (Munich, Alte Pin.), *Hylas and the Nymphs* (1630; Florence, Pitti; see fig.) and *Deianeira and Nessus* (1631; untraced), painted for the Riccardi family. With *Acis and Galatea*, which established his fame, Furini created a highly individual and morbidly sensual style. The handling is refined, the touch light, almost ephemeral, and the soft flesh tones of his female nudes are rendered in ultramarine. His increasingly sweet, *sfumato* style suggests that, by 1629, he had made a journey

Francesco Furini: *Hylas and the Nymphs*, oil on canvas, 1.1×1.3 m, 1630 (Florence, Palazzo Pitti)

to Venice (Barsanti). It also suggests an interest in Florentine painting of the early 16th century, such as, for example, the work of Andrea del Sarto.

By 1633 Furini had become the priest of S Ansano in the Mugello, but this did not diminish his interest in female beauty. In *Lot and his Daughters* (*c.* 1634; Madrid, Prado), the figure viewed from behind is based on the Medici *Venus* (Florence, Uffizi; Gregori, 1989), and the work again illustrates the artist's use of antique models, reinforced by the study of nature. His biblical heroines, such as *Judith* (Rome, priv. col., see Gregori and Schleier, p. 278), convey the passionate abandon that made the theme of Mary Magdalene particularly dear to him. His earliest treatment of this (Vienna, Ksthist. Mus.) introduced the extreme sensuality that he developed in many later variants. In 1638 he made a documented visit to Venice, and in 1639, through the support of the Marchese Giulio Vitelli, he won the commission for the lunettes in the Sala Terrena in Palazzo Pitti, Florence (now Mus. degli Argenti), which had remained unfinished on the death of Giovanni da San Giovanni in 1636. Furini contributed *Lorenzo the Magnificent and his Artists* and the *Death of Lorenzo*. At the Palazzo Pitti he came in contact with Pietro da Cortona, who had completed the frescoes in the Sala della Stufa, an encounter that encouraged Furini to develop a more Baroque style, which nonetheless retained

an emotional, Venetian character, as in the *Judith and Holofernes* (1642; Rome, Pal. Barberini) and the *St Sebastian* (Schleissheim, Neues Schloss). He again visited Rome in 1645, shortly before his death.

BIBLIOGRAPHY

F. Baldinucci: *Notizie* (1681–1728); ed. F. Ranalli (1845–7), iv, pp. 629–44

E. Toesca: *Francesco Furini* (Rome, 1950)

Disegni di Francesco Furini (exh. cat., ed. P. Bigongiari; Florence, 1968)

G. Corti: 'Contributi alla vita e alle opere di Francesco Furini', *Ant. Viva*, x/2 (1971), pp. 14–23

Disegni di Francesco Furini e del suo ambiente (exh. cat. by G. Cantelli, Florence, Uffizi, 1972)

A. Barsanti: 'Una vita inedita del Furini', *Paragone*, xxv/289 (1974), pp. 67–86; xxv/291, pp. 79–99

——: 'Ancora sul Furini', *Paragone*, xxv/294 (1974), pp. 54–72

M. P. Mannini: 'Allegorie profane del Furini', *Paragone*, xxx/353 (1979), pp. 48–61

G. Cantelli: *Repertorio della pittura fiorentina del seicento* (Fiesole, 1983), pp. 88–9, figs 415–59

Il seicento fiorentino: Arte a Firenze da Ferdinando I a Cosimo III, 3 vols (exh. cat., ed. A. Parronchi and A. Brook; Florence, Pal. Strozzi, 1986), i, pp. 264–78, 279–81; ii, pp. 248–52; iii, pp. 93–4

M. Gregori and E. Schleier, eds: *La pittura in Italia: Il seicento* (Milan, 1988, rev. 1989), i, pp. 315–16 [essay by M. Gregori]; ii, pp. 748–9 [essay by A. Barsanti]

Pittura del seicento: Ricerche in Umbria (exh. cat., Spoleto, Chiesa di S Nicolo, 1989), pp. 274–7 [article by B. Toscano]

FRANCESCA CAPPELLETTI

Furner, A(rthur) Stanley (*b* 1911; *d* Haenertsburg, Northern Transvaal, 19 July 1971). South African architect, writer and teacher of British birth. He worked first as junior partner in the firm Kallenbach, Kennedy and Furner (from 1928; later Kennedy, Furner, Irvine-Smith and Joubert). His early work included the Plaza chain of cinemas in Pretoria, Johannesburg and Cape Town (1930–31), and the Arundel Court and Heath's Building flats (before 1934), both Johannesburg. These pioneer modern buildings, elegant and restrained, were perhaps closer to Austrian architecture than to the European avant-garde. The later work of his firm included many landmarks of Johannesburg, such as the railway station complex. Furner's reputation was also built on the significant role he played in the development of modern architecture in South Africa as a writer and teacher. He gave the Transvaal Group its initial impetus and its sense of direction. He became a senior lecturer in architecture at the University of the Witwatersrand under G. E. Pearse in 1925. He immediately made his mark as a gifted and influential teacher and a contributor, and later editor, of the *South African Architectural Record*. His tenure in official positions was brief, ending when he entered practice in 1928, but his influence was enduring and vital. His important article 'The Modern Movement in Architecture' (1925) was among the first anywhere to see the various strands of development as a comprehensive whole.

WRITINGS

'The Modern Movement in Architecture', *S. Afr. Archit. Rec.*, 12 (1925), pp. 87–9; 3 (1926), pp. 6–8

BIBLIOGRAPHY

'Stanley Furner: An Appreciation by a Student', *S. Afr. Archit. Rec.*, 12 (1928), p. 224
'Notes on the Plaza Kinema, Johannesburg', *S. Afr. Archit. Rec.*, 12 (1931), pp. 117–19
G. Herbert: 'Furner: A Pioneer Commentator on the Modern Movement', *Plan*, lvii/12 (1972), pp. 7–8, 23
——: *Martienssen and the International Style: The Modern Movement in South African Architecture* (Cape Town, 1975)

GILBERT HERBERT

Furnerius, Abraham (*b* Rotterdam, *bapt* 14 March 1628; *d* Rotterdam, *bur* 6 May 1654). Dutch draughtsman and painter. He was the son of Dr Johannes Claesz. Furnerius (*d* 1668), a Rotterdam surgeon and collector of drawings, prints and art books, and the brother-in-law of the painter Philips Koninck (who married his sister Cornelia). Abraham was also related to Gerrit van Battem, whose mother was a Furnerius and who may have trained with him in Rotterdam between 1648 and 1654. Abraham was himself apprenticed to Rembrandt in Amsterdam in the early 1640s, according to Samuel van Hoogstraten, who was a fellow pupil at the time. Van Hoogstraten remarked of Furnerius that he 'later [i.e. after his apprenticeship] was quite good in his landscapes'. If the writer was referring to paintings, these are known only from the 1673 estate inventory of items belonging to Maria, another of Abraham's sisters.

Furnerius is now remembered only as a draughtsman, especially of landscapes, many of which were formerly ascribed to Rembrandt. Some drawings (e.g. sheets in Dresden, Kupferstichkab.; Cambridge, Fitzwilliam; St Petersburg, Hermitage; and Oxford, Ashmolean) are inscribed with his name in an old hand (previously thought to be signatures); most of these drawings, which may have come from his father's estate (auctioned in 1668), bear a previously unidentified 17th-century collector's mark (see Schatborn) that is written in the same ink as the inscriptions and may well be that of the father. Two of the inscribed drawings (Oxford and Cambridge) depict distant views of Amsterdam, which were inspired by Rembrandt's etched *View of Amsterdam from the North-west* (*c.* 1640; B. 210). Furnerius also produced other important topographical views of the northern and southern Netherlands. Among those previously attributed to Rembrandt are several views of Amsterdam that now are recognized to be by Furnerius: the *Bastion Rijzenhoofd* (Amsterdam, Hist. Mus.), the *Bastion 'De Rose'* (Haarlem, Teylers Mus.) and the *View of the Grimnesse-Sluis* (Paris, Louvre). These can be dated *c.* 1647, the year inscribed on a related drawing of a *Lock and Bridge in Amsterdam* (Hamburg, Ksthalle). A later drawing by Furnerius, representing the *Ruins of the Old Amsterdam Stadhuis after the Fire of 7 July 1652* (Haarlem, Teylers Mus.), shows that Furnerius's style was rather naive.

BIBLIOGRAPHY

S. van Hoogstraten: *Inleyding tot de hooge schoole der schilderkunst* [Introduction to the high school of painting] (Amsterdam, 1678)
P. Schatborn: 'Van Rembrandt tot Crozat: Vroege verzamelingen met tekeningen van Rembrandt' [From Rembrandt to Crozat: early collections with drawings by Rembrandt], *Ned. Ksthist. Jb.* (1981), pp. 1–51 (17–20)
W. Sumowski: *Drawings of the Rembrandt School*, iv (New York, 1981), nos 984–1051a
Rembrandt en tekenaars uit zijn omgeving [Rembrandt and draughtsmen from his surroundings] (exh. cat. by B. Broos, Amsterdam, Hist. Mus., 1981), pp. 130–33
J. Giltay: 'Abraham Furnerius en Gerrit van Battem', *Essays in Northern European Art Presented to Egbert Haverkamp-Begemann* (Doornspijk, 1983), pp. 97–101

B. P. J. BROOS

Furness, Frank (*b* Philadelphia, PA, 12 Nov 1839; *d* Wallingford, PA, 30 June 1912). American architect. His work celebrated American individualism and represented a commitment to the present while denying the European past, establishing a peculiarly American sensibility. His buildings, frequently in red brick, are unmistakable in their visceral directness of expression. Severely criticized after the 1880s, they have won new appreciation in the second half of the 20th century.

1. LIFE AND WORK.

(i) Early training, until 1870. Furness was strongly influenced by his father, the Rev. William Henry Furness (1802–96), a transplanted Bostonian whose closest friend from childhood was Ralph Waldo Emerson (1801–82). Through Emerson, the family was drawn into the wider circle that shaped American culture, including Henry David Thoreau (1817–62) and Walt Whitman (1819–92). It was an intellectually stimulating environment, in which a copy of John Ruskin's *The Seven Lamps of Architecture* was in the household by 1849, the year of its publication. Frank's oldest brother, William Henry Furness jr (1827–61), became a talented German-trained portrait painter; his other brother, Horace Furness (1833–1912), became renowned as editor of the *Variorum Shakespeare*. In 1857

Frank travelled to New York to enter the newly formed architectural studio of Richard Morris Hunt. There, with George B. Post, Charles Gambrill (1830–80) and William Robert Ware, Furness was exposed to the foundations of Victorian eclecticism: drawing from nature and design based on the proportions of Classical architecture, flavoured by a pragmatic approach to theory that permitted great flexibility. Guided by Hunt, Furness became a forceful designer and a splendid draughtsman, skilfully emulating Hunt's light pencil, a style that he passed on to Louis Sullivan when he worked briefly in the office of Furness and Hewitt.

Furness's studies were interrupted in 1861 by military service in the cavalry during the Civil War; in 1864 he returned to Hunt's office for more than a year. Then, instead of going to Paris for study, Furness opened a practice in Philadelphia. In 1867 he formed a partnership with John Fraser (1825–1906), who had an established practice, and with George Watson Hewitt (1841–1916), a former member of John Notman's office. At the outset Fraser, Furness & Hewitt were unsuccessful in a number of architectural competitions, but by 1870 they were established as the rising young architects for élite Philadelphia with several important church and institutional commissions to their credit.

(ii) Professional success, 1871–90. In 1871 while Fraser was in Washington, DC, pursuing government work, Furness and Hewitt, without their senior partner, entered and won the competition for the Pennsylvania Academy of the Fine Arts in Philadelphia (completed 1876). Their overlaid polychromatic Gothic details on a building whose main façade was French with a projecting central pavilion crowned by a mansard roof and flanked by stridently coloured wings. Some elements, notably the triglyph-like blocks on the front, recalled the Néo-Grec that Hunt had learnt and taught in the 1850s. The eclectic fusion of classicism and medievalism in Furness's early masterpiece demonstrated his continuing debt to Hunt, but the strikingly asymmetrical composition of the side elevation in which interior functions were expressed on the exterior denoted an original approach. Simultaneously the firm became the favourite for the banking industry of Philadelphia; the office's violently proportioned and strangely detailed designs reflected the commercial role of the façade as the identifying symbol of the bank. The monochromatic Néo-Grec Northern Savings Fund (1871) at 6th and Spring Garden streets, the polychromed Venetian Gothic Guarantee Trust and Safe Deposit Company offices (1873; destr. 1956) and later the contentiously over-scaled Provident Life and Trust Company offices at Fourth and Chestnut streets (1876; destr. 1959; see fig. 1) demonstrated how far commercial design could be pushed in the Darwinian environment of American commerce. It is those buildings of the 1870s that have fascinated and horrified historians and critics, leading to the reputation of Furness as the most extreme, and least relevant, of late 19th-century American architects.

By 1876 the partnership of Furness & Hewitt was dissolved; five years later draughtsman Allen Evans (1849–1925) became a partner in Furness & Evans, the name which, with minor modifications reflecting additions to

1. Furness & Hewitt: Provident Life and Trust Company Building, Philadelphia, Pennsylvania, 1876; destr. 1959

the partnership, remained until the firm's dissolution long after Furness's death. Despite the modest staff of six or eight, which permitted Furness to stamp his personality on most of the designs, the firm was remarkably prolific with more than 600 commissions between 1881 and 1912. This was made possible by the repetitive nature of many of the projects, among them nearly 200 railway stations in the 1880s alone. It was also the result of a clear and rational approach that represented each function in directly expressed construction, which made his work stand out against the increasingly derivative character of western architecture.

That Furness's vigorous and original architecture was accepted by his clients, many of whom were drawn from his father's congregation or were otherwise linked to the Philadelphia social reform movement, suggests that it meant more than mere fashion. Indeed, his strongly expressed, functionally expressive buildings of red brick contrasted with the fashionable marble-clad architecture of the day. But, guided by Emerson's perception that America should find her own cultural forms and live in the present, and not the past, Furness also avoided the brick historicism available to him, both the Colonial and Queen Anne revivals. The resulting buildings of the 1880s, including the Undine Barge Club (1881), the Gravers Lane Station (1881) for the Reading Railroad, the National Bank of the Republic (1883; destr.) and the Baltimore and Ohio terminal (1886; destr.) in Philadelphia, were particularly successful. Irregular fenestration, bold naturalistic ornament, the direct use of iron and steel and the juxtaposition of volumes each shaped to a particular use, divorced these designs from historicism and anticipated the free composition of the 20th century.

The most remarkable of these commissions was the library for the University of Pennsylvania (1888–91; restored Venturi, Scott Brown Associates, 1986–91). There Furness juxtaposed the cultural form of the cathedral for the public spaces with the glass-roofed industrial form of the train shed for the book stack in a red palette of brick, terracotta, sandstone and tile (see fig. 2). This colour scheme came to stand for the political and cultural values of the old Whig élite of Philadelphia, who contrasted the red brick of Quaker meetings and Independence Hall with the marble-clad, palatial mansions of the *nouveau riche* and the vast bulk of the new City Hall then rising in the centre of the city. In the case of the University Library, the colour and the forms were astonishing, but the plan was a model of logic. A large entrance porch opens into an immense stair-tower, which provides access to all of the public spaces. The five-storey high, skylighted reading room serves as a giant light well, while the glass-floored and glass-roofed book stack was expandable to meet the needs of the growing collection.

(iii) Later years, 1891–1912. Furness's style was more successful in small-scale buildings than in the larger scale office towers and institutions permitted by modern construction methods. His architecture remained fundamentally sculptural, only rarely exploring the new spatial possibilities of steel, save for the vast train sheds of his railway buildings. In 1892 Furness recalled the Gothic detail of George Gilbert Scott's St Pancras Station (1865), London, for the massive extension to the Pennsylvania Railroad's Broad Street Station (destr. 1952). Three years earlier, in an extension of the Provident Bank offices, he had demonstrated that Victorian complication, with varicoloured bands and a multi-storey and dormered roof, were incompatible with the scale of modern buildings. As Louis Sullivan would later point out (1924), H. H. Richardson's large, simple buildings better met the requirements of the large building; by the 1890s Furness's expressive eclecticism was displaced by Richardson's Romanesque and the classicism of the Beaux-Arts. For another decade, however, Furness remained faithful to his red brick, strongly formed and anti-historical architecture, establishing the visual character of Philadelphia.

By 1905 even Furness was forced to modify his personal style, when he adapted the Roman Pantheon for the offices of the Girard Trust Company on Broad Street just south of City Hall. Although the client had stipulated a scheme in the modern classical style in place of his architect's customary brick, Furness still managed to transform the style into a personal statement contrasting a soaring sail-vaulted interior with the hemispherical and squat exterior. It is a worthy successor to the light-filled stair-hall of the Pennsylvania Academy of the Fine Arts and the great banks of the 1870s. In this building Furness demonstrated most directly that his architecture depended not on the

2. Furness, Evans & Co.: Furness Building, formerly the Library of the University of Pennsylvania, Philadelphia, 1888–91

extrinsic issue of style but on the intrinsic factors of proportion, character and scale, qualities that typify great architecture in any age.

2. INFLUENCE. Unlike Richardson in Boston or Hunt in New York, Furness never established a national practice; instead his work remained centred in Philadelphia and extended from that city only along the routes of the railways that were based there. Nor did Furness ever establish a consistent proportion-based theory that could be reduced to academic dogma. After 1885 few of his designs were published and, apart from 'Hints to Designers' (*Lippincourt's Magazine*, 1878), he wrote little. In the Centennial Exhibition in Philadelphia (1876), when many of his contemporaries exhibited their drawings, Furness restricted his efforts to showing his prize dogs in the agricultural department. By the 1880s and 1890s, when the national taste had changed towards a more accurate use of the historical styles, his work, rooted in the issues of Emerson's demand for the present and the representation of Philadelphia political reform, was incomprehensible to out-of-town critics. They characterized it as 'the Furnessic reign of architectural terror' and worse, singling his buildings out to criticize the architecture of his native city. The violence of the criticism suggests how far Furness—and Philadelphia—had moved from the American mainstream.

Furness should not be categorized as an American eccentric; he was trained in the values of social individualism that were tolerated in Quaker and anglophile Philadelphia and, more than any other American architect, was exposed to the ideas of his culture. Many of the best young architects in Philadelphia, including John Stewardson and Joseph Huston (1866–1940), trained in his office; of greater import however were those in whom Furness kindled his sense of an American architecture. These included Louis Sullivan, who recalled in his autobiography that Furness 'made buildings out of his head'. In a similar vein, Albert Kelsey, a student a generation later, claimed Furness was 'determined America should create an art of its own making and opposed to copying European styles of ancient or modern design'. William L. Price and George

Howe, who worked in the office shortly after Furness's death, also absorbed the Furness method and his values. After World War II many of Furness's most original buildings were demolished, but their tough brick vitality, expressive force, ironic wit and style and strength of character stimulated the so-called Philadelphia school, one which could equally be called the Furness school.

BIBLIOGRAPHY

L. Sullivan: *The Autobiography of an Idea* (New York, 1924)

The Architecture of Frank Furness (exh. cat. by J. F. O'Gorman, G. Thomas and H. Myers, Philadelphia, PA, Mus. A., 1973)

Drawing towards Building: Philadelphia Architectural Graphics, 1732–1986 (exh. cat. by J. O'Gorman and others, Philadelphia, PA Acad. F.A., 1986), pp. 128–9, 135–8, 172

G. Thomas and others: *Frank Furness: The Complete Works* (New York, 1991)

GEORGE E. THOMAS

Furniture, vernacular. Term used to describe items of furniture made in local rather than cosmopolitan traditions of design and construction, and intended for everyday use. It is made in countries throughout the world, for use by nomadic and settled peoples, in rural and urban communities. Essentially such furniture reflects the direct needs of ordinary people's domestic and non-domestic lives. Vernacular furniture is thus part of the culture of communities, and its place and function achieve meaning as a direct reflection of the context and use for which it was made. No one descriptive framework can adequately encompass the rich variety of disparate traditions that made up national or regional codes of design, and it is within this notion of regionality that a sense of the coherence of vernacular furniture emerges, reflecting history, geography and, particularly, economy.

Since vernacular furniture is the product of local rather than cosmopolitan design traditions, it generally owes little to the fashionable forms that emanated from metropolitan centres. The essence of the true vernacular is based on a complex interaction between localized design, construction techniques, available materials and the particular ergonomic and social needs of the community. Some vernacular furniture does, however, incorporate classical motifs, absorbed and redefined within the vernacular form. In some traditions, too, there is an indebtedness to fashionable cabinetmakers of the 18th and 19th centuries. Where these influences appear, the vernacular is often less able to synthesize these in new or original ways, and naive and undeveloped motifs and styles appear that are quasi-vernacular, as a result. However, vernacular designs have also influenced some forms of 18th- and 19th-century furniture design, from sophisticated interpretations of 'rustic' furniture during the 18th century to the 'idealized' rural forms adopted by the Arts and Crafts Movement (e.g. oak, rush-seated chair by C. F. A. Voysey, c. 1905; London, V&A).

The role of furniture-makers also differed between fashionable and vernacular traditions. Cabinetmakers and other specialists were usually distanced from the clients, who were seen as the architects of style, the makers being deemed to be merely 'conduits' of others' taste. In contrast, makers and the clients who bought vernacular furniture were usually from the same class. In this way, the makers were also to a greater or lesser degree the designers of

furniture, often adapting designs and decorative treatments in the light of the customer preference, and with particular uses in mind. There is also a strong convention in some communities for individuals to make their own furniture. Such traditions abound worldwide and range from the seating made in the Scottish Highlands, which was essentially fashioned with an axe from two cleft sections of a naturally shaped branch, joined by hand-shaped cross-spindles and supported on four simple legs (see fig.), to the furniture made in Newfoundland, Canada, by skilled boat builders, who used fir felled in the surrounding forests and incorporated motifs from their early immigrant roots.

Although some cultures have for many centuries maintained their traditional furniture designs, as seen in the bed and couch forms used in the Middle East and Asian countries, other more recent cultures, fashioned by immigrants from a number of cultural groups, have synthesized different traditions to form a new vernacular furniture tradition. This is evident, for example, in the 18th-century regional furniture designs of the USA.

Vernacular furniture is often characterized by its parsimonious and restrained use of materials; attempts to decorate furniture or to create fashionable designs were less evident and resulted in the adoption of functional forms, with the skilled and restrained use of tools and

Chair, oak frame and cross spindles, alder seat, 760×420×330 mm, from Caithness, Scotland, 19th century (Edinburgh, National Gallery of Scotland)

reliance on habit of technique being adopted to create items quickly in the face of economic constraints. Vernacular furniture is also typically made from locally grown hard- and soft-woods and does not usually involve the use of imported exotic woods. However, in the more affluent, industrial regions of many countries imported mahogany, in particular, was used often in a limited way, for cross-banding or veneers.

In many countries the makers of vernacular furniture were not specialists but made furniture as part of a repertory of other woodwork including house joinery and carpentry. During this work they developed a sense of architectural space that was reflected in the furniture dimensions; for example, furniture for single-storey dwellings was often made to make use of the wall rather than floor space, with tall pieces being common. This furniture was often decorated with fretted devices, painting and simulation techniques.

For a history of individual furniture types, *see* BED, CHAIR, CUPBOARD, SOFA and TABLE.

BIBLIOGRAPHY
J. Gauthier: *Le Mobilier des vieilles provinces de France* (Paris, n.d.)
I. Plath: *The Decorative Arts of Sweden* (New York, 1966)
J. S. Stewart: *The Folk Arts of Norway* (New York, 1972)
V. Chinnery: *Oak Furniture: The British Tradition* (Woodbridge, 1979)
N. Loughman: *Irish Country Furniture* (Dublin, 1984)
B. D. Cotton: *Cottage and Farmhouse Furniture in East Anglia* (1987)
——: 'Irish Vernacular Furniture', *Reg. Furn. Soc. J.*, iii (1989), pp. 1–26
——: *The English Regional Chair* (Woodbridge, 1990)
C. Gilbert: *English Vernacular Furniture, 1750–1900* (London, 1991)
C. Kinmouth: *Irish Country Furniture, 1700–1950* (Yale, 1993)

B. D. COTTON

Furse, Charles Wellington (*b* Staines, 13 Jan 1868; *d* Camberley, 6 Oct 1904). English painter. He studied at the Slade School of Art from 1884, at the Académie Julian, Paris, and the Westminster School of Art. He exhibited regularly at the Royal Academy (1888–1904), where his portraits brought him widespread fame, and from 1891 at the New English Art Club. The possible influences of Holl and Whistler can be seen in such sombre half-length works as *John Murray* (*c.* 1891; London, N.P.G.). In 1892 Furse took a studio in Tite Street (near to that of John Singer Sargent), where he worked on his monumental equestrian group portrait of *Lord Roberts* (3.4×4.54 m, 1893–5; London, Tate; unfinished). In later figure paintings such as the *Return from the Ride* (1902; London, Tate) an outdoor background with a horse and/or dogs is a dominant theme. Furse's free brushstrokes together with lighter colour and strong highlights show Sargent's influence. In 1900 Furse married Katharine, daughter of John Addington Symonds, the model for his most celebrated work, *Diana of the Uplands* (1903–4; London, Tate). He painted murals of dockside working scenes in the town hall in Liverpool (1899–1901). In 1904 he was elected ARA; later that year he died of tuberculosis, and a memorial exhibition was held at the Burlington Fine Arts Club in 1906.

DNB
BIBLIOGRAPHY
Illustrated Memoir of Charles Wellington Furse ARA, Burlington Fine Arts Club (London, 1908)
K. Furse: *Hearts and Pomegranates: The Study of Forty-five Years, 1875 to 1920* (London, 1940)

SARAH WIMBUSH

Fürstenberg, Pontus (*b* Göteborg, 5 Oct 1827; *d* Göteborg, 10 April 1902). Swedish collector and patron. He came from a Jewish merchant family in Göteborg where he managed a textile company with his brother Arthur and cousin Ludwig. He was also active in liberal politics. His art gallery (*c.* 1885), designed by Adrian Petterson (1835–1912) and installed in the attic of his house, was open to the public, in accordance with his democratic principles. His collecting was in part a way to achieve social acceptance. During the 1870s he bought such conventional works as those by the artists of the Düsseldorf school of genre painting, including Bengt Nordenberg's *In the Organ Loft* (1868; Göteborg, Kstmus.). Although an honorary member of the Kungliga Akademi för de fria Konsterna, in the 1880s he actively supported the modernist group Opponenterna (The Opponents), led by Ernst Josephson, who disagreed with the practices of the Akademi. He brought Carl Larsson to Göteborg to teach non-traditional methods of drawing and painting at the Göteborgs Museum's school (now the Valands Målarskola) and he commissioned from him such large paintings as the triptych *Renaissance, Rococo, Modern Art* (1888–9; Göteborg, Kstmus.) for his gallery. His collection of approximately 260 works of contemporary art was Sweden's largest private collection at the time. Canvases by lesser-known artists, for example *Summer* (1884; Göteborg, Kstmus.) by Raphaël Collin (1850–1916), were interspersed with those by such major ones as Gauguin (e.g. *Winter Landscape*, 1888; Göteborg, Kstmus.). In the 1880s and 1890s the collection acquired its Nordic character as he purchased such works as Josephson's *Old Woman Spinning* (1887; Göteborg, Kstmus.). He donated his collection to the city of Göteborg. After his death it was transferred to the city's museum in the Ostindiska Kompani (East India Company). In 1925 the collection was installed in the newly built Konstmuseum (1923) in the Götaplats.

UNPUBLISHED SOURCES
Göteborg, Ubib.; Stockholm, Kun. Bib.; Uppsala, Ubib. [lett., photographs, plans, visitors' bks, inventories, notes and pap.]
BIBLIOGRAPHY
G. Pauli: 'Fürstenbergska galleriet', *Ord & Bild*, x (1902), pp. 337–54
J. Runnqvist: *Mecenaten Pontus Fürstenberg* [The patron Pontus Fürstenberg] (diss., Uppsala U., 1953)
L. Vogel: *Konstsamlaren och konstmecenaten Pontus Fürstenberg* [The art collector and art patron Pontus Fürstenberg] (diss., Stockholm U., 1987)
L. Waern: 'Pontus Fürstenberg som samlare' [Pontus Fürstenberg as collector], *Ksthist. Tidskr.*, v/3–4 (1988), pp. 22–31
J. Gavel: 'Carl Larsson och Pontus Fürstenberg', *Carl Larsson* (exh. cat., ed. T. Gunnarsson; Göteborgs Museer; Stockholm, Nmus.; 1992)

JONAS GAVEL

Fürstenberg Porcelain Factory. German ceramics factory. Charles I, Duke of Brunswick-Wolfenbüttel, founded a porcelain factory in Fürstenberg in 1747. Attempts, however, to produce hard-paste porcelain were unsuccessful until after the arrival of the arcanist Johann Kilian Benckgraff (1708–58) from Höchst in 1753. Despite difficult economic circumstances and great technical problems—often the wares became misshapen and cracked during firing, and the glaze was a greyish-yellow—production was extensive from the beginning. Modellers included Simon Feilner (1726–98), Johann Georg Leimberger

(1711–63), Anton Carl Luplau (1745–95), Johann Christoph Rombrich (1731–94), Christian Gottlieb Schubert (*fl* 1735) and the sculptor Desoches from the Académie Royale de Peinture et de Sculpture in Paris, who arrived in Fürstenberg in 1769. He created 45 groups of figures, including mythological scenes, allegorical groups of the seasons, Chinese men, and children, including the much copied *Family at a Coffee Table* (1771; Bremen, Focke-Mus.), as well as vases and candlesticks.

In 1756 the first great table-service (the Seckendorff Service) was produced, but generally production concentrated on coffee-, tea- and chocolate-services, vases, incense-burners, kettles, centrepieces, tureens, cachepots and clockcases. The inspiration for these wares came from Meissen, Berlin, Sèvres and from the factory of Josiah Wedgwood. Shapes and decoration followed the stylistic trends of the period: first the late Rococo style, with ozier borders, piercing, flowers and relief motifs; later the Louis XVI style, with clean outlines and sparse decoration; and finally the Neo-classical style, employing straight lines and tectonic forms. During the Empire period, in addition to flower and fruit designs, borders of acanthus, ivy, oak, laurel and vine leaves were introduced. During the Biedermeier period (1815–48) wares were decorated with colourful sprays of flowers.

During the second half of the 19th century production was dominated by historicist styles. Towards the end of the century *Jugendstil* wares were created by E. J. Kruse, Paul Eberlein, Anton Zentner and Hermann Gradl. The 1930s were dominated by the designers Wilhelm Wagenfeld, Siegfried Müller, Walter Nitzsche and F. A. Sundermann. In the late 20th century the factory produced contemporary-style wares in addition to reproductions of such old figures as those by Feilner or designs by Rombrich.

BIBLIOGRAPHY

Fürstenberger Porzellan aus drei Jahrhunderten (exh. cat. by C. Mosel, Hannover, Kestner-Mus., 1956)
G. Spies: *Fürstenberger Porzellan: Empire-Gegenwart* (Brunswick, 1972)
S. Ducret: *Fürstenberger Porzellan*, 3 vols (Brunswick, 1973)
Fürstenberger Porzellan vom Rokoko bis zum Historismus (exh. cat. by H. W. Haase, Bremen, Focke-Mus., 1986)
Weisses Gold aus Fürstenberg: Kulturgeschichte in Spiegel des Porzellans, 1747–1830 (exh. cat., Brunswick, 1988)

WALTER SPIEGL

Furtmeyr, Berthold (*fl c.* 1460; *d* after 1501). German illuminator. He spent most of his career in Regensburg, and his workshop comprised the only group of painters of significance operating there at that time. The influences from which he formulated his style were from Nuremberg (Michael Wolgemut), Vienna (Martinus 'opifex' of the Austrian court school, who worked for a time in Regensburg) and the Netherlands. His hand is found in 14 manuscripts (*c.* 1465–1500), including illustrated copies of the Old Testament, missals and an astronomical manuscript. His style is characterized by somewhat bland facial expressions and calm figure compositions with little sense of movement. He used vibrant coloured contrasts and set the scenes and figures in verdant landscapes with hills and mountains. Rich decorative borders incorporate flowers, fruit and foliage ingeniously adapted as framing devices for the miniatures.

Among Furtmeyr's main works are two illustrated copies of the Old Testament (*c.* 1465–70; Munich, Bayer. Staatsbib., Cgm 8010a; Augsburg, Ubib. 1.3.2°.III and IV), made for members of the family of Stauff zur Ehrenfels; each has over 350 pictures set as small framed scenes in the text. His masterpiece is the five-volume missal (*c.* 1478–89; Munich, Bayer. Staatsbib., Clm. 15708–12) of Bernhard von Rohr, Archbishop of Salzburg (*fl* 1468–87), one of the most luxuriously decorated missals of the Middle Ages. It contains 22 complete missal texts for the great feasts of the Church year with 30 full-page miniatures, plus 18 full-page *Crucifixions* at the beginning of the canon prayer and 84 historiated initials; the full-page miniatures have rich decorative borders of the type in which Furtmeyr excelled.

BIBLIOGRAPHY

Thieme–Becker
A. von Rohr: *Berthold Furtmeyr und die Regensburger Buchmalerei des 15. Jahrhunderts* (Bonn, 1967)
Regensburger Buchmalerei (exh. cat., ed. F. Mütherich and K. Dachs; Munich, Bayer. Staatsbib.; Regensburg, Museen Stadt; 1987), pp. 111–23
R. Kahsnitz: 'Die Handschrift und ihre Bilder', *Die Furtmeyr-Bibel in der Universitätsbibliothek Augsburg*, ed. J. Janota (Augsburg, 1990), pp. 65–135

NIGEL J. MORGAN

Furttenbach [Furtenbach; Furttembach]**, Josef** [Joseph], the elder (*b* Leutkirch, 30 Dec 1591; *d* Ulm, 12 Jan 1667). German merchant, architect and writer. He received his commercial training in Italy, where he lived between 1608 and 1620, mainly in Genoa and Florence but also visiting other important cities in northern and central Italy and travelling as far south as Rome. During these years he acquired a wide knowledge of architecture, engineering and mathematics. In Genoa he learnt fortification design under Paolo Rizio and gunmaking and pyrotechnics with Hans Veldhausen of Augsburg. He encountered Galileo Galilei in Florence and also made contact there with the architect Giulio Parigi, who had a decisive influence on him, awakening his lifelong interest in the building and decoration of theatres. His travel journal *Newes itinerarium Italiae* (1627) became a standard guide for travellers.

In 1620 Furttenbach returned to Leutkirch but settled in Ulm the following year, working as a merchant until his death. In 1623 he was made a citizen of Ulm, where he was admitted to the Ulm guild of merchants in 1624 and later appointed to various public offices. As a deputy in charge of the municipal building office (1631), Furttenbach supervised public building construction and the fortifications of Ulm and was involved in urban planning. The buildings erected in Ulm to Furttenbach's designs were mostly of a functional character; they were later much altered or were destroyed in 1944. Recorded in his treatises, they include the reinforcement of the Danube banks (1631); the Brechhaus (1634), a hospital designed to Italian models for plague victims; the Am Seelgraben waterworks (1638; extant); and the German school known as In der Eich. Furttenbach also accepted private commissions. The Theater im Binderhof (1641, enlarged 1650) incorporated the Italian concepts of a foreshortened stage and backdrop, but unlike contemporary Italianate court theatres north of the Alps, it was intended for a middle-class audience and could seat 1000 people.

Furttenbach's historical significance is due to his many influential and widely read publications on architecture and engineering. His aim was to import Italian ideas into Germany, and his main interest lay in the appropriateness of a building to its purpose, rather than in its aesthetic dimension. His ideas were alien to the tradition of German architectural thinking, which adhered to the five Classical orders as described in the works of Hans Blum, Wendel Dieterlin and Jacopo Vignola. In Furttenbach's books, which follow the pragmatic tradition of architectural theory represented by Sebastiano Serlio and Alvise Cornaro, the text is limited to a commentary on the projects illustrated: their functions and spatial division are described in minute detail. While his works lack a theoretical exposition of the rules of 'good' architecture, they do demand that the points of the compass, lighting and climate should all be respected in the arrangement of rooms—a Vitruvian concept of *decor naturalis*. The illustrations are of paramount importance, particularly the ground-plans, which usually follow a rigidly schematic layout. The same simple geometrical figures are used time and again for the most diverse purposes: a square four-winged building around a courtyard; a U-shaped three-winged layout; a cruciform layout set in a square. The few façade elevations derive their forms from the Italian late Renaissance and show a monotonous accumulation of window bays and applied orders. With their emphasis on individual areas of architecture and building technique, Furttenbach's treatises constitute a valuable and comprehensive record of the public, private and sacred buildings required by south German society in the 17th century. His writings represent part of the development of architectural theory away from Vitruvius and the great treatises of the Renaissance towards a more specialized approach in which such topics as civil and military architecture are treated separately (*see* TREATISE, §I). *Architectura civilis* (1628) deals primarily with secular architecture for all classes, from the prince's palace to the burgher residence, with additional examples of church buildings and hospital designs. Furttenbach takes Italian buildings as his starting-point, using their principles of symmetry, axiality and the enfilade sequence of rooms (particularly praised by Furttenbach and a feature of which he was the first exponent in Germany), to develop his own designs. *Architectura navalis* (1629) is devoted to shipbuilding and *Architectura martialis* (1630) to military architecture. The examples of fortifications in *Architectura universalis* (1635) are drawn from his own work in Ulm, municipal buildings and ordnance. *Architectura recreationis* (1640) has as its theme the private house: castles and burgher country houses with extensive gardens were intended at that period as places of recreation and symbols of peace after the turmoil of the Thirty Years War (1618–48). Furttenbach's own house (destr.; see fig.) in Ulm, an adaptation of an older structure on an irregular site, exemplifies his maxims for secular building in *Architectura privata* (1641), which advocates good lighting and ventilation, a convenient layout of rooms and staircases and the alignment of rooms with the points of the compass. The book also describes his famous and much-visited private collections, including models of buildings and machines, mechanical devices, weapons, books and architectural drawings.

Josef Furttenbach: design (1638) of his house in Ulm, engraved by J. J. Campanus, 370×295 mm; from *Architectura privata* (Augsburg, 1641), pl I

After the Peace of Westphalia (1648) Furttenbach went on to publish a series of small treatises, often in the name of his son Josef Furttenbach the younger (*b* Ulm, 7 Nov 1632; *d* Ulm, 1655). Each of these simple projects, intended to cover all areas of civil architecture and to serve as guidelines for the rebuilding after the war, illustrates a single building problem with a model design. They include writings on Protestant church architecture, school building, farm buildings, a scheme for a free commercial town and designs for town gates, sundials, a cemetery, a hospital and a public building for the celebration of burgher weddings. Since the younger Furttenbach frequently stressed in the text that the designs used are based on his father's material, his own role must have been primarily that of an editor. He also worked as a painter: the portrait of *Joseph Furttenbach the Elder* (1647; Ulm, Ulm. Mus.) and a diptych showing a firework display designed by his father (1645; Nuremberg, German. Nmus.) are attributed to him.

WRITINGS

Newes itinerarium Italiae (Ulm, 1627/*R* Hildesheim and New York, 1971)
Architectura civilis (Ulm, 1628/*R* Hildesheim and New York, 1971)
Architectura navalis (Ulm, 1629/*R* Hildesheim and New York, 1975)
Architectura martialis (Ulm, 1630/*R* Hildesheim and New York, 1975)
Architectura universalis (Ulm, 1635/*R* Hildesheim and New York, 1975)
Architectura recreationis (Augsburg, 1640/*R* Hildesheim and New York, 1971)
Architectura privata (Augsburg, 1641/*R* Hildesheim and New York, 1971)
Mechanischer Reiss Laden (Augsburg, 1644)
Mannhaffter Kunst-Spiegel (Augsburg, 1663)

Furttenbach the younger produced 11 of a planned series of 14 works on civil architecture, mainly using projects by his father: *Kirchen-Gebäw* (1649); *Teutsches Schul-Gebäw* (n.d.); *Mayer-Hoffs-Gebäw* (1649); *Gewerb-Statt-Gebäw* (1650); *Pass Verwahrung* (1651); *Von Sonnenuhren* (1652); *Gotts-Ackhers Gebäw* (1653); *Hospittals-Gebäw* (1655); *Feriae architectonicae* (1662); *Hochzeit-Hauss-Gebäw* (1662); *Garten-Pallästlins Gebäw* (1667).

BIBLIOGRAPHY
M. Berthold: 'Joseph Furttenbach, Architekt und Ratsherr in Ulm', *Ulm & Oberschwaben*, xxxiii (1953), pp. 119–79

E. Forssman: *Säule und Ornament: Studien zum Problem des Manierismus in den nordischen Säulenbüchern und Vorlageblättern des 16. und 17. Jahrhunderts* (Uppsala, 1956), pp. 193–7

Architekt und Ingenieur: Baumeister in Krieg und Frieden (exh. cat., Wolfenbüttel, Herzog August Bib., 1984)

H.-W. Kruft: *Geschichte der Architekturtheorie* (Munich, 1985), pp. 193–5

'*Vom Schönen gerührt . . .': Kunstliteratur des 17. und 18. Jahrhunderts aus Beständen der Bibliothek Oettingen-Wallerstein, Universität Augsburg* (exh. cat., Harburg, Schloss, 1988), pp. 13–17, 57–61

HANS H. AURENHAMMER

Furtwängler, (Johann) Adolf (Michael) (*b* Freiburg im Breisgau, 30 June 1854; *d* Athens, 10 Oct 1907). German archaeologist. His pioneering work transformed the study of Greek art from dependence on literary sources into a discipline based on a comprehensive knowledge of artefacts. Furtwängler was descended from a Black Forest family of peasants, wood-carvers and clockmakers; he attended Freiburg school, where his father was headmaster, studied Classics at Freiburg and Leipzig, and Classical archaeology under Heinrich Brunn (1822–94), the first professor of the subject at Munich. At the newly established Deutsches Archäologisches Institut at Rome (1877–8), he acquired mastery of the vast quantity of Greco-Roman sculpture in Italian collections. In Greece (1878–9) he studied original Greek artefacts, plentifully unearthed in recent excavations. He and Georg Loeschke (1852–1915) classified and published the pottery excavated by HEINRICH SCHLIEMANN at Mycenae. Furtwängler's work on 14,150 small bronzes from Olympia culminated in his authoritative fourth volume of the German excavation reports (1890). As museum assistant in Berlin (1880–94), he visited every European museum and handled innumerable Greek artefacts. His catalogue of the Berlin vases (1885) laid the foundations of the history of Greek vase painting. His influential *Meisterwerke der griechischen Plastik* (1893; Eng. trans., 1895) followed the hypothesis—now challenged—that the multifarious sculptures of the Roman period were copies of Classical Greek masterpieces, lost but attested in literature. His work on ancient gems (1900), based on examination of over 50,000 dispersed items, clarified a previously intractable subject. Succeeding Brunn as professor in Munich (1894), he also ran three museums there, including the Glyptothek, where he recognized the erroneousness of Bertel Thorvaldsen's reconstruction (1830) of the pedimental sculpture from the Temple of Aphaia on Aigina (Munich, Glyp.; *see* AIGINA, fig. 2 and GREECE, ANCIENT, fig. 54): Furtwängler's excavations on Aigina (1901–7) enabled him to reconstruct the pediments correctly. He died of dysentery contracted on Aigina. The conductor Wilhelm Furtwängler (1886–1954) was his son.

WRITINGS

with G. Loeschke: *Mykenische Thongefässe* (Berlin, 1879)

Beschreibung der Vasensammlung im Antiquarium (Berlin, 1885)

with G. Loeschke: *Mykenische Vasen* (Berlin, 1886)

Die Bronzen und die übrigen kleineren Funde von Olympia (1890), iv of *Olympia*, ed. E. Curtis and F. Adler (Berlin, 1890–97)

Meisterwerke der griechischen Plastik (Berlin, 1893); Eng. trans. and ed. by E. Sellars as *Masterpieces of Greek Sculpture* (London, 1895)

Die antiken Gemmen: Geschichte der Steinschneidekunst im klassischen Altertum, 3 vols (Berlin, 1900)

with K. Reichhold: *Griechische Vasenmalerei*, 3 vols (Munich, 1904–32)

with E. Fiechter and H. Thiersch: *Aegina: Das Heiligtum der Aphaia*, 2 vols (Munich, 1906)

Die Aegineten der Glyptothek König Ludwigs I nach Resultaten der neuen bayerischen Ausgrabung (Munich, 1906)

NDB

BIBLIOGRAPHY

L. Curtius: *Torso, zerstreute und nachgelassene Schriften* (Stuttgart, 1957), pp. 213–14

E. Buschor: *Geist und Gestalt: Biographische Beiträge zur Geschichte der bayerischen Akademie der Wissenschaften*, i (Munich, 1959)

THOMAS BRAUN

Furuta Oribe (*b* Mino Prov. [now part of Gifu Prefect.], 1544; *d* Osaka, 1615). Japanese samurai and master of the tea ceremony. He strongly influenced the development of tea aesthetics in the late 16th century and early 17th (*see* JAPAN, §XIV, 1). He was reportedly born into the Kuwahara family and then adopted by Yoshida Shigesada (*d* 1598). He became known as Oribe after his appointment as a military official, Oribe no Kami, of Mino Province in 1585, at which time he became commander of Nishigaoka Castle at Yamashiro, near Kyoto. Oribe distinguished himself in the service of the military dictators ODA NOBUNAGA and TOYOTOMI HIDEYOSHI and through them met SEN NO RIKYŪ, the foremost practitioner of the *wabicha* tea ceremony, which was based on the concept of *wabi* ('simple, austere natural beauty'). By 1590 Oribe was one of Rikyū's most promising disciples, and the two exchanged poetry and attended tea ceremonies together. Remarkably, Rikyū chose Oribe as his successor in preference to his own sons; similarly, when Rikyū died in 1591, Hideyoshi chose Oribe to replace him as tea master. After Hideyoshi's death, Oribe became close to the first Tokugawa shogun, Ieyasu (1542–1616), and in 1605 was appointed tea ceremony instructor to Ieyasu's son, the powerful second shogun, Hidetada (1579–1632). In the next decade Oribe enjoyed great prestige, but in 1615 he was accused of spying against Ieyasu and forced to commit suicide.

Although Oribe recorded Rikyū's rules of *wabicha* in the *Oribe hyakkajō*, he himself turned away from *wabi* ideals and developed a more elaborate style, probably in response to the growing class consciousness of his patrons, the newly empowered military. Discarding Rikyū's egalitarian attitudes, he deliberately distinguished among his guests by social status, seating those of higher rank closer to the *tokonoma* (decorative alcove) on *tatami* mats and those of lower rank further from the *tokonoma* on the bare plank floor.

Oribe's style of tea also affected the design of the ceramic vessels used in the ceremony and of the buildings and gardens. Although it is not clear to what extent Oribe actually designed utensils or supervised their design and production, it is certain that during his ascendancy in the world of tea many new shapes, colours and decorative patterns became enormously popular. Whereas Rikyū had preferred to serve tea using everday utensils in simple shapes and neutral or sombre hues, Oribe favoured utensils made especially for tea, artfully shaped, vividly coloured and audaciously patterned. These ceramic wares are called *Oribe yaki* (Oribe ware; *see* JAPAN, §VIII, 3(i) and SETO). Oribe liked forms that were distorted, such as shoe-shaped (*kutsugata*) teabowls, assertively distinctive, such as irregular serving dishes with bail handles, or positively whimsical, such as the candlesticks shaped like Portuguese sailors. The colour schemes include an unmistakable copper-green glaze, often combined with cream-coloured glaze and iron-red or brown underglaze designs. The decorative patterns are bold and often abstract; frequently one piece bears several seemingly unrelated designs. By expanding the range of utensils acceptable in the tearoom, Oribe encouraged his patrons to compete with each other for innovative ways of serving tea.

Oribe made some of his greatest changes in the tea-room and tea house garden. Whereas Rikyū had built tea-rooms with few or no windows, so that the environment within would seem divorced from the world outside, Oribe added windows and skylights to frame an outdoor view or to bring special lighting effects into the space. He is most famous for the *shikishi mado*, a window made of squares of translucent paper (as, for example, in En'an, rebuilt at Yabunouchi School, Kyoto); one such window would be placed above another but slightly offset. He also hung flowers in a window so that the petals would glow in the light. Woods of different colours and textures were juxtaposed so as to highlight their unique qualities. While the tea-room used by Rikyū was only about 2 m sq. (two *tatami* mats), Oribe preferred a larger room and often combined the tea ceremony in a three-and-three-quarter-mat tea-room with a dinner party in a spacious *shoin*-style ('book hall' or 'study'; *see* JAPAN, §III, 4(ii)(a)) chamber. In the garden, Oribe added stone lanterns of his design (Oribe *dōrō*) to light the path and used both naturally shaped stepping-stones and cut-stone paving to make interesting walkways to the tea-room. Such emphasis on visual effects delighted the new patrons of the tea ceremony. Together with his notable pupil KOBORI ENSHŪ and his other immediate successors, Oribe greatly changed Japanese preferences in architecture and garden design, bringing a refined elegance to the plain rusticity of *wabicha* championed by Rikyū.

BIBLIOGRAPHY

T. Hayashiya, K. Yokoi and T. Narabayashi, eds: *Nihon no chasho*, i, Tōyō Bunkō [The Oriental library], cci (Tokyo, 1971)

S. Nakamura: 'Furuta Oribe and Ennan', *Chanoyu Q.*, 17 (1977), pp. 9–19

K. Isao: 'Kan'ei Culture and Chanoyu', *Tea in Japan*, ed. P. Varley and K. Isao (Honolulu, 1989), pp. 135–60

BRUCE A. COATS

Fusajirō. *See* KITAŌJI, ROSANJIN.

Fuseli, Henry. *See* FÜSSLI, (3).

Fu Shan [*zi* Qingzhu; *hao* Selu] (*b* Taiyuan, Shanxi Province, 12 July 1607; *d* Songzhuang, Shanxi Province, 23 July 1684). Chinese calligrapher, painter, poet and scholar–official. He was born in northern China to a scholarly family. When he was only 15 he passed the local examination, the first of three stages in the civil service examination ladder, to receive his *xiucai* degree and in 1625 became a stipendiary. Following his failure in the next stage—the provincial examinations—he went to study at the San Li Academy in Taiyuan. There he gained a reputation as a man of high moral character, in part because of his aversion to widespread official corruption in the late part of the Ming period (1368–1644); this may have hindered his advancement to an official career. After the Manchu conquest and the subsequent establishment of the Qing dynasty (1644–1911), Fu Shan's loyalty to the

Fu Shan: *Landscape*, hanging scroll, ink on silk, 1703×425 mm, 17th century (Berkeley, CA, Ching Yuan Chai Collection)

preceding dynasty led to his imprisonment and torture. In 1655, however, his students secured his release, and he began a period of travel in the northern provinces, visiting famous mountains, including Mt Hua in Shaanxi Province and Mt Tai in Shandong Province. During this period he worked as a physician and won renown as a poet.

At the age of 72, Fu Shan was urged to take the *boxue hongci* examination, which Qing officials hoped would bring eminent scholars into the administration. He refused but was compelled nonetheless to journey to Beijing to pay his respects to the court. When he reached the city gates Fu Shan would go no further, throwing himself to the ground in protest. His action was interpreted as a gesture of obeisance, and he was allowed to return to Shanxi with the title of Secretary of the Grand Secretariat, an honour which he never acknowledged. He spent his later years in Songzhuang, south of Taiyuan, and died there.

As a calligrapher, Fu Shan is regarded as one of the most original talents of his time; he favoured deliberately misshapen characters and once avowed that he preferred 'deformities to slipperiness, the spontaneous to the premeditated'. A similar inclination is seen in his paintings, which are mostly of pines and rocks, bamboo or landscapes. An undated landscape (see fig.) represents a river valley winding among cliffside houses and leafy trees. Thin, even brushstrokes define the form of the rock groupings and provide texture; the thickly wooded foreground landscape becomes increasingly light and barren as the valley yields to distant peaks, and zigzag movements create a sense of depth. In the centre of the painting an overhang merges confusingly with adjacent cliffs so that there is no clear sense of which rock face precedes another. Like WU BIN, Fu Shan also painted fanciful or fantastic landscapes. Some examples of this kind on album leaves depict flamelike peaks and pinnacles, meandering streams and waterfalls. These visionary landscapes are quite different from the plain riverscapes of the SOUTHERN SCHOOL artists of the Jiangnan region and the more conservative works of the NORTHERN SCHOOL landscapists.

See also CHINA, §IV, 2(vi) and fig. 102.

BIBLIOGRAPHY
A. W. Hummel, ed.: *Eminent Chinese of the Ch'ing Period, 1644–1912* (Washington, DC, 1943–4), pp. 260–62
Traces of the Brush: Studies in Chinese Calligraphy (exh. cat. by Shen Fu and others, New Haven, CT, Yale U. A.G.; Berkeley, U. CA, A. Mus.; 1977), p. 96
J. Cahill: *The Distant Mountains: Chinese Painting of the Late Ming Dynasty, 1570–1644* (New York, 1982), pp. 163–5
VYVYAN BRUNST, with JAMES CAHILL

Fushimi (*b* 1265; *reg* 1287–98; *d* 1317). Ninety-second emperor of Japan, calligrapher and poet. The second son of Emperor GoFukakusa (*reg* 1246–60), he abdicated in favour of his son GoFushimi (*reg* 1298–1301) in 1298 and later retired to a monastery. He was one of the most talented calligraphers among Japanese emperors and indeed one of the outstanding calligraphers of the Kamakura period (1185–1333). Instead of following the then popular calligraphy styles, he emulated those of the 10th-century masters, ONO NO MICHIKAZE and Fujiwara no Sari (*see*

FUJIWARA (ii), (1)), two of the Sanseki ('three brush traces'; Three Masters). He was regarded as a greater calligrapher than even the celebrated Fujiwara no Kōzei (*see* FUJIWARA, (ii), (2)) of the later part of the Heian period (794–1185). Fushimi's calligraphy eschewed strong, vigorous strokes and was instead clear, graceful and elegant. He developed a *Wayō* (native) style, which now bears his name and which differed from the Sesonji style (*see* JAPAN, §VII, 2(ii)) practised by his court calligrapher, Tsunetada (1247–?1320), in that it referred to styles current in Song-period (960–1279) China. During the Muromachi (1333–1568) and Edo (1600–1868) periods Fushimi's calligraphy style was popular as an instructional model. Many of Fushimi's calligraphies are extant in poetry collections, as fragments (*gire*) of *kana* (Japanese syllabic) calligraphy in his even and fluid style, for example the *Hirosawa-gire* (Kyoto, Nishi Honganji) and the *Chikugo-gire*, and in collections of calligraphies by emperors. His sons GoFushimi, Prince SON'EN and Emperor Hanazono (*reg* 1308–18) were also noted calligraphers.

BIBLIOGRAPHY
Z. Kanda, K. Korezawa, K. Sakurai and others: *Nihon: Kamakura II* [Japan: Kamakura II] (1957), xix of *Shodō zenshū* [Complete collection of calligraphy] (Tokyo, 1954–68)
Emperor Fushimi, ii of *Nihon meiseki sōkan* [Library of famous calligraphies] (Tokyo, 1976–)
CECIL H. UYEHARA

Fusina, Andrea da (*fl* 1486; *d* Milan, 1526). Italian sculptor and mason. In 1486 he entered Giovanni Antonio Amadeo's workshop at the Certosa di Pavia, and in 1506 he went with Amadeo on one of his visits to work at Milan Cathedral. He was commissioned in 1495 by the Ospedale Maggiore in Milan to execute the marble tomb of *Daniele Birago, Archbishop of Mitilene* and his brother *Francesco Birago* (completed *c.* 1500; Milan, S Maria della Passione), which depicts Daniele Birago guarded by four putti, reclining on his funeral bier, supported on two sarcophagi placed in tiers. An exuberant example of Lombard classical decorative ornament, it illustrates his debt to the repertory of decoration he would have learnt at Pavia. In 1497 he was paid for a figure for Milan Cathedral, which has been identified as the *Judas Maccabeus*, whose pose and antique armour suggest that Fusina was familiar with the Lombardo family's works in Venice and Padua. A figure of the *Magdalene* (Milan, cathedral) may be the one that Lomazzo recorded that Fusina made for the cathedral; the overtly classicizing personification suggests that it formed a pendant to the *Judas Maccabeus*.

In 1508 Fusina requested permission from the workshop of Milan Cathedral to go to Rome and Loreto. By February 1510 he had returned to Milan as architect at the cathedral, although later that year he was working at the Certosa di Pavia. He also started work on the tomb of *Bassiano da Ponte* (completed 1517; Lodi, cathedral), an austere design in which da Ponte is shown reclining on his side, his head resting on his hand, a device used by several Lombard sculptors at this period. For the tomb (1519; Milan, Castello Sforzesco; formerly S Maria della Pace) of *Bishop Battista Bagarotti* (?1437–1522), Fusina reverted to an earlier Lombard style, with the sarcophagus and bier supported on bulging candelabra columns and characterization of the figure secondary to decorative detail, which is executed in deeply undercut relief. A number of undocumented works are attributed to him, including a relief of *Francis I* of France (Milan, Castello Sforzesco; see Malaguzzi-Valeri), the tomb of *Stefano Varisio* (1521; Monza, cathedral) and several epitaphs in Milanese churches.

BIBLIOGRAPHY

G. P. Lomazzo: *Trattato dell'arte della pittura* (Milan, 1584)

F. Malaguzzi-Valeri: 'Note sulla scultura lombarda del rinascimento: Il Caradosso e il Fusina', *Rass. A.*, v (1905), pp. 169–73

S. Vigezzi: *La scultura lombarda nel cinquecento* (Milan, 1929), pp. 47–55

A. Pettorelli: 'Il monumento del vescovo Bagaroto', *Boll. Stor. Piacent.*, iii (July–Sept 1933), pp. 97–101

G. Agosti: *Bambaia e il classicismo lombardo* (Turin, 1990), pp. 173–94

ANTONIA BOSTRÖM

Füssli [Fuseli]. Swiss family of artists and writers. (1) Johann Caspar Füssli, descended from a long-established Zurich family of metalworkers, combined the practice of art with art-historical work in the mid-18th century, being followed in both by his eldest son, (2) (Johann) Rudolf Füssli, who worked mainly in Austria and Hungary. Johann Caspar's younger son Johann Heinrich Füssli left Zurich to travel in Germany, England and Italy, styling himself (3) Henry Fuseli after he settled in London in 1779. There, through his strikingly original paintings and drawings and the influence of his teaching and writing, he remained a prominent figure in English art circles until his death in 1825. Johann Caspar's other children, Hans Caspar Füssli (1743–86), Elisabeth Füssli (1744–80) and Anna Füssli (1749–72), were botanical and entomological illustrators. A later Füssli of Zurich, Wilhelm Heinrich Füssli (1830–1916), also practised as a painter.

(1) Johann [Hans] **Caspar Füssli** (*b* Zurich, 3 Jan 1706; *d* Zurich, 4 May 1782). Writer, painter, draughtsman, collector, publisher and teacher. He probably acquired basic skills from his father, the painter Hans Rudolf Füssli. From 1724 he trained in Vienna under the influence of the work of Martin van Meytens and was introduced to antique masterpieces through plaster casts by Daniel Gran. After he had carried out several commissions as a portrait painter at the court of Baden in Rastatt (e.g. *Princess Wilhelmina of Prussia* (1731) and *Cardinal Damian Hugo von Schöborn* (1732)), other commissions took him as far away as Düsseldorf. Later he entered the service of Eberhard-Ludwig, Duke of Württemberg. From 1733 until his return to Zurich in 1736 he stayed in Nuremberg, Augsburg and Munich, where he met the painters Jan Kupecký, Georg Philipp Rugendas (i) and Johann Elias Ridinger, as well as Franz Joachim Beich and Georges Desmarées. From Zurich he kept in close touch with the most famous German, French and Italian artists and writers, among them Friedrich Gottlieb Klopstock, Anton Raphael Mengs, Hyacinthe Rigaud, Francesco Solimena and Johann Joachim Winckelmann. His portraits were executed with craftsman-like skill and close attention to detail and realism, for example the portraits of *Councillor Hans Caspar Bodmer* (1746) and *Johann Jakob Bodmer* (1753; both Zurich, priv. col.). His primary importance, however, lies not in his activities as a painter and teacher of drawing—his sons (2) Rudolf Füssli and (3) Henry Fuseli were probably his most notable pupils—but in his role as writer and collector of prints and 16th- and 17th-century Swiss drawings.

WRITINGS

Geschichte und Abbildung der besten Mahler in der Schweiz, 2 vols (Zurich, 1755–7); rev. as *Geschichte der besten Künstler in der Schweiz, nebst ihren Bildnissen*, 5 vols (Zurich, 1769–79)

Leben der berühmten Maler Rugendas und Kupetzky (Zurich, 1758)

Gedanken über die Schönheit und den Geschmack in der Malerei (Zurich, 1765)

Raisonnierendes Verzeichnis der vornehmsten Kupferstecher und ihrer Werke (Zurich, 1771)

Thieme–Becker

BIBLIOGRAPHY

G. K. Nagler: *Neues allgemeines Künstlerlexikon*, v (Leipzig, 1905), p. 207

G. Schiff: *Johann Heinrich Füssli, 1745–1825* (Zurich, 1973), pp. 23, 28, 50, 52, 73, 84, 124, 324

Y. Boerlin-Brodbeck: 'Johann Caspar Füssli und sein Briefwechsel mit Jean-Georges Wille: Marginalien zu Kunstliteratur und Kunstpolitik in der 2. Hälfte des 18. Jahrhunderts', *Jb. Schweiz. Inst. Kstwiss.* (1974–7), pp. 77ff

(2) (Johann) Rudolf Füssli (*b* Zurich, 1737; *d* Vienna, April 1806). Administrator, painter, draughtsman and etcher, son of (1) Johann Caspar Füssli. While training in his father's workshop he etched 37 vignettes for the *Geschichte und Abbildung der besten Mahler in der Schweiz* (1755–7). He tried to continue his education in Vienna from 1759 but was unsuccessful and so became a secretary to the counts of Pallasch in Pressburg (now Bratislava). After a brief revisit to Zurich, he worked in Hungary from 1770, eventually becoming president of the tax commission for the Syrmier district in 1786. The death of Emperor Joseph II in 1790 left him without a job, but he was shortly afterwards summoned to Vienna to become court draughtsman. The knowledge of art shown in the writings he then produced led to his being appointed to set up and direct the Kupferstichkabinett and library of the Akademie der bildenden Kunste in 1800.

WRITINGS

Kritisches Verzeichnis der allerbesten Kupferstiche, die nach den berühmtesten Malern aller Schulen gestochen worden sind, 4 vols (Zurich, 1798–1806)

Annalen der bildenden Künste für die österreichischen Staaten, 2 vols (Vienna, 1801)

Thieme–Becker

BIBLIOGRAPHY

G. K. Nagler: *Neues allgemeines Künstlerlexikon*, V (Leipzig, 1905), pp. 207–9

G. Schiff: *Johann Heinrich Füssli, 1741–1825* (Zurich, 1973), pp. 24, 79, 145

Y. Boerlin-Brodbeck: 'Johann Caspar Füssli und sein Briefwechsel mit Jean-Georges Wille: Marginalien zu Kunstliteratur und Kunstpolitik in der 2. Hälfte des 18. Jahrhunderts', *Jb. Schweiz. Inst. Kstwiss.* (1974–7), pp. 77ff

GEORG PAULA

(3) Henry Fuseli [Johann Heinrich Füssli] (*b* Zurich, 6 Feb 1741; *d* Putney Hill, nr London, 16 April 1825). Painter, draughtsman and writer, active in England, son of (1) Johann Caspar Füssli. He spent most of his working life in England, where he established himself as the most original history painter and draughtsman of his generation. Renowned for his treatment of bizarre and psychologically penetrating subjects, he was also a prolific writer and, from 1779, Professor of Painting at the Royal Academy.

1. Life and work. 2. Working methods and technique. 3. Writings and lectures.

1. LIFE AND WORK. Fuseli received rigorous art-historical training from his father, becoming acquainted with the Neo-classical ideas of Johann Joachim Winckelmann and Anton Raphael Mengs: his godfather was the poet and artist Salomon Gessner. The Anglophile scholars

Johann Jacob Bodmer and Johann Jacob Breitinger introduced him to Classical philology and to Homer, Dante, Shakespeare, Milton and the *Nibelungenlied*. This training impressed upon Fuseli the affinity of painting and poetry and the power of poetic imagery in defining human experience.

Although Fuseli started to draw when he was eight, copying engravings in his father's collection, he was ordained into the Zwinglian ministry in 1761. However, the following year he and his close friends Johann Kaspar Lavater and Felix Hess published an attack on a corrupt Zurich magistrate. As a result, they were unofficially advised to leave the city for a while, and in 1763 they toured Germany. They visited the mathematician and art theorist Johann Georg Sulzer in Berlin, the Protestant theologian Johann Joachim Spalding in Barth, Pomerania, and the poet Friedrich Klopstock at Quedlinburg. Fuseli returned to Berlin that year to assist Sulzer with his *Allgemeine Theorie der schönen Künste*.

At this time Fuseli's interests were primarily in literature and moral philosophy, and when he visited London in 1764 it was chiefly to explore English literature and to forge links between English and German writers. He travelled with the English *chargé d'affaires* in Berlin, Sir Andrew Mitchell, through whom he met the publisher Joseph Johnson (1738–1809) and made many influential friends in his circle. In London Fuseli began to take a serious interest in art and was drawn to literary and theatrical life, particularly David Garrick's performances. Encouraged to become a painter by Joshua Reynolds, whom he met in 1767 or 1768, Fuseli finally abandoned theology and philosophy, though never literature. He had

been making drawings sporadically since boyhood and had produced illustrations for Tobias Smollett's *Peregrine Pickle* (1769) and Dr Willoughby's *Practical Family Bible* (1766–70), but his greater ambitions drove him to Rome in 1770 to devote himself to high art.

Fuseli reached Rome, via Genoa and Florence, at the end of May. His eight-year stay was broken only by visits to Venice in 1772, to recuperate from fever, and to Naples in 1775. Although brought up on Winckelmann's idealization of Greek art and condemnation of Michelangelo, Fuseli found himself overwhelmed not only by the grandeur and scale of Roman sculptures—as expressed in his powerful drawing of *The Artist in Despair over the Magnitude of Antique Fragments (the Right Hand and Left Foot of the Colossus of Constantine)* (*c.* 1778–80; Zurich, Ksthaus; see fig. 1)—but also by the heroic drama of Michelangelo's Sistine Chapel frescoes. Rejecting the excessively pure archaism of Winckelmann and Mengs, Fuseli developed his own fusion of the linear and compositional discipline of Roman relief sculpture with the more dramatically expressive rendering of the human form achieved by Michelangelo and such Mannerist artists as Parmigianino and Rosso Fiorentino. Fuseli's art was concerned uniquely with the human figure seen in tragic or violent situations drawn from Aeschylus, Homer, Dante and especially Shakespeare (e.g. *The King of Denmark is Poisoned by his Brother while Sleeping*, 1771; Zurich, Graph. Samml. Eidgenöss. Tech. Hochsch.). His choice of subjects, dramatic composition and rapidly developing mastery of stylized form soon made him the most original artist then working in Rome and the focus of an international circle of followers and friends, including Johann Tobias Sergel, Nicolai Abildgaard, John and Alexander Runciman, Thomas Banks, George Romney, James Barry and James Northcote. His reputation spread beyond Italy, and his literary friends in Germany acclaimed his work as the visual counterpart of their own *Sturm und Drang* movement.

In 1778 Fuseli returned to Zurich, where he began painting an episode from Swiss history, the *Oath of the Rütli* (completed 1780), for the Rathaus. This was based on a drawing executed in his last days in Rome. Although reunited with Lavater and other old friends in Zurich, he was bitterly nostalgic for Rome and torn between emotional attachments to Magdalena Hess and to Lavater's niece Anna Landolt. The rejection of his suit by Anna's father so upset him that he returned to London in 1779, where he rejoined his old friends around Joseph Johnson and widened his circle to include the bankers Thomas Coutts (1735–1822) and William Roscoe of Liverpool and William Lock (1732–1810) of Norbury, all of whom were to become important patrons. From this period he styled himself Fuseli and dedicated himself to history painting on a grand scale, transferring to canvas the bold and disturbing imagery and massive, heroic abstraction of his Roman drawings. His deficient technique provoked hostile reactions at first, but in the Royal Academy exhibition of 1781 he had his first great success with *The Nightmare* (Detroit, MI, Inst. A.; see fig. 2), a remarkable evocation of a mood and moment of terror in a rhythmic composition that is also dependent on motifs from Hellenistic sculpture. This picture—perhaps an attempt to exorcise Fuseli's

1. Henry Fuseli: *The Artist in Despair over the Magnitude of Antique Fragments (the Right Hand and Left Foot of the Colossus of Constantine)*, red chalk and sepia wash, 420×352 mm, *c.* 1778–80 (Zurich, Kunsthaus, Zürich)

2. Henry Fuseli: *The Nightmare*, oil on canvas, 1.02×1.27 m, 1781 (Detroit, MI, Institute of Arts)

bitterness against Anna Landolt by punishing her with a dream—was to be followed a decade later by a more distanced and rational reworking of the theme, in which the symptoms of disturbed sleep were given almost clinical description (Weimar, Goethe-Nmus. Frauenplan).

Shakespeare's plays continued to provide subjects for Fuseli in major pictures including the *Three Witches* (1783; Stratford-upon-Avon, Royal Shakespeare Mus.) and *Lady Macbeth Sleepwalking* (1784; Paris, Louvre; see fig. 3). These established beyond doubt his claim to rank alongside Reynolds and Benjamin West as a history painter and to surpass them in emotional force to the extent that his work appeared antithetical to their sober classicism. They also assured his position as one of the originators, and possibly a proposer while still in Rome, of John Boydell's Shakespeare Gallery. Up to the first exhibition of the Gallery in 1789, most of Fuseli's energies were devoted to this project. The critical success of his pictures contributed largely to his reputation and to his election as Associate of the Royal Academy in 1788 and full Academician in 1790, despite the opposition of Reynolds. Fuseli's contributions to the Shakespeare Gallery were the most numerous and indeed, including work such as *Titania and Bottom* (completed 1790; London, Tate; see fig. 4), the most original;

despite this he initially received less for his paintings than Reynolds, West or James Barry.

This lack of financial recompense and a resentment that Boydell was more concerned with profit than the promotion of history painting prompted Fuseli to venture a scheme over which he could retain total control. In 1790 he began his own Milton Gallery, working against a stormy emotional background. In 1788 he had married Sophia Rawlins, who had been an amateur artist's model and would often feature in his work. The following year, however, he met the writer Mary Wollstonecraft, a friend of William Blake, whom Fuseli had known and admired since *c.* 1787. Her infatuation with Fuseli led her in 1792 to propose that the three of them go to Paris to witness the Revolution, but this suggestion was dropped when Fuseli's wife put a stop to the association. He meanwhile persuaded his friends, including Coutts, Lock, Johnson and Roscoe, to underwrite the Milton Gallery by regular subscription, thus providing an annual income while work progressed on such pictures as the *Creation of Eve* (1793; Hamburg, Ksthalle). The exhibitions of the 47 paintings in 1799 and 1800 were not, however, an unqualified success, and the second had to be promoted by an Academy banquet in Fuseli's honour. Print sales did not

3. Henry Fuseli: *Lady Macbeth Sleepwalking*, oil on canvas, 2.21×1.60 m, 1784 (Paris, Musée du Louvre)

redeem the time expended on the large paintings, and once again Fuseli gained more respect than remuneration. In the end his Milton Gallery was a heroic and instructive failure, admired by Fuseli's colleagues but rejected by the public.

Both the Shakespeare and Milton subjects gave rein to Fuseli's interests in the supernatural, fairy mythology and demonic superstition—concerns that matched the trend of contemporary thought, which was moving away from the rational scepticism of the Enlightenment. While the two large projects occupied most of his attention up to 1800, he also found time for other themes that gave scope for his obsessions. *Thor Battering the Midgard Serpent* (1788; London, RA) was the forerunner of a series of paintings and drawings illustrating Nordic poets and legends, while Dante was another favourite source. Throughout his career Fuseli also produced countless images of women, from portraits of his wife and other models wearing the latest fashions of clothes or hairstyles to erotic and disturbing depictions of courtesans and *femmes fatales* (e.g. *Symplegma*, 1809–10; London, V&A; *see also* EROTIC ART, fig. 7).

In 1799 Fuseli was elected the Academy's Professor of Painting, a post he held until 1805; he was made Keeper in 1804. He was re-elected Professor in 1810, and the statutes were changed to enable him to retain the Keepership as well. Real financial security came to him only at this time. His regime at the Academy was liberal and eccentric, but his eye for talent was unerring, and his pupils

included most of the leading names of the next generation, notably John Constable, Edwin Landseer, William Mulready, Charles Robert Leslie and Benjamin Robert Haydon. By 1814 Haydon had turned against Fuseli, offended by his irreverent ideas and by his failure to recognize the worth of the Elgin marbles. The last quarter of Fuseli's life was occupied largely with writing, teaching and formulating his art-historical ideas. In 1802, during the brief Peace of Amiens, he visited Paris with Joseph Farington to see the Musée Napoléon, and in the following years he published extensively. His later paintings were often reworkings of earlier themes but became more dramatic and mysterious than ever through a bolder and more painterly execution, as in the transparent paintwork of *Garrick and Mrs Pritchard in Macbeth* (1812; London, Tate). He died at the country home of his friend, the Countess of Guildford, and was buried in St Paul's Cathedral, London.

2. WORKING METHODS AND TECHNIQUE. Throughout his career Fuseli maintained an extremely practical and professional approach to his art that can seem at odds with its wayward subject-matter. In his earliest days he took pains to demonstrate his versatility as an illustrator and portrait painter as well as a historical painter; in later years he was among the first London artists to exhibit in the provinces. In addition he was always anxious to oversee, and secure an adequate return from, the reproduction of his work through prints. An early massacre of Fuseli's illustrations for the French edition of Lavater's *Physiognomische Fragmente* (1781–6) put him on his guard against incompetent reproductive engravers, and he was happy to secure some help from Blake, who had worked for Johnson since 1779. But Blake was too much immersed in projects of his own to give the unstinting personal service Fuseli thought desirable, and Boydell's Shakespeare Gallery had proved clearly that in most cases it was the publisher, not the original artist, who reaped the profits from reproductive prints. This explains in part Fuseli's concern to retain complete control of his own Milton Gallery, as well as his appointment in 1803 of Moses Haughton as his personal engraver, boarding and employing him until 1819 to engrave and publish his work and keeping a fair share of the proceeds for himself.

From the outset Fuseli's art proceeded from drawings, and most of its formal, tonal and iconographical characteristics were first worked out on paper. He had no academic or conventional training as a painter and was in effect self-taught; many of his canvases have deteriorated badly as a result of faulty or experimental techniques. Even early drawings such as *Lear and the Dead Cordelia* (1774; Zurich, Ksthaus) establish the key features of his art: the setting of monumental figures—whose extremely expressive attitudes are defined by tense linear strokes of pen or chalk—against vague, receding darkness washed in grey or purple. The same presentation of figures against void and shadow occurs constantly in his paintings, where the literal definition of space is of no concern. However, his use of chiaroscuro was not exclusive; he claimed he had courted colour all his life as a despairing lover would a disdainful mistress. Pale muted tones are often contrasted with passages of vivid local tint to produce a sparkling

4. Henry Fuseli: *Titania and Bottom*, oil on canvas, 2.16×2.74 m, 1790 (London, Tate Gallery)

effect. His painting technique did not change materially until after *c.* 1810, when it became much broader and more impressionistic.

Fuseli's drawing styles meanwhile had diversified, ranging from sharp essays in pen and ink, with or without his characteristic washes of greys, mauves and ochres, to softer and more subtly modulated use of unaccompanied pencil or black chalk. His later drawings tend to be more suggestive than assertive and achieve an almost ghostly effect, in contrast to the vigorous linearity of earlier work. These technical changes in both drawings and paintings accompanied developments in his approach to composition. The highly wrought and strained schemes of his Roman and post-Roman phases gave way in the 1790s to simpler and perhaps more consciously classical arrangements that suggest analogies with antique reliefs and John Flaxman's line engravings. These patterns in turn yield to more shadowed—and sometimes nocturnal—groupings, in which outline is cloaked by tone.

3. WRITINGS AND LECTURES. Fuseli's writings, which include poetry, translation, journalism, theory and history, in retrospect appear scarcely less influential than his art. His earliest publications, an English translation (1765) of Winckelmann's *Reflections on the Paintings and Sculptures*

of the Greeks and *Remarks on the Writings and Conduct of J.-J. Rousseau* (1767; the first unfavourably reviewed and the second largely ignored), are based on initial enthusiasms that he later qualified. Fuseli also worked in London on a *History of German Poetry* in 1769 (MS. destr. 1770), but suspended literary activities while in Rome. On his return to England he reviewed books and Academy exhibitions in Johnson's *Analytical Review* (with no hesitations about praising his own work). He also continued to translate, producing a free rendering of Lavater's *Aphorisms on Man* in 1788 and contributing to Johnson's edition of his friend's *Physiognomische Fragmente* (1792).

Fuseli's reviews are significant barometers of his own thinking. Writing of Murphy's *Tacitus* in 1793, he revealed a change of heart over the French Revolution, having, like most moderate intellectuals, been turned against it by the Terror. Although he rejected his early enthusiasm for Rousseau's ideas as Utopian, Fuseli adopted his belief that art is both the product of, and a threat to, corrupt society. Yet far from rejecting art, Fuseli proceeded to the more radical conclusion that art and morality were distinct, an idea that underpinned the amoral and exceptional character of his own work. In a review of the Rev. R. A. Bromley's *Philosophical and Critical History of the Fine Arts* (1793) he uncompromisingly stated that the 'moral usefulness' of the arts 'is at best accidental and negative' (*Analytical Review*, xvi (1793), pp. 242–3). Thus he saw nothing blasphemous in making Satan the real hero of his Milton series, presenting him as a rebellious figure with whom he could identify as an artist, while his lack of specific faith by this stage of his life (or perhaps a residual puritanism) made him reluctant to depict God except on his own secular terms.

Discussing Reynolds's last *Discourse* (1791), Fuseli challenged his fellow painter's theory of imitation with the view that, while only a mind equal to Michelangelo's could profit by copying him, such a mind would never 'condescend' to do so. However, he shared Reynolds's opinion that artistic excellence was only to be acquired through study and selection from nature, thus differing from Blake, who believed the artist should look beyond the visible world and seek out genius in his own innate ideas. Although Fuseli declared Blake 'damned good to steal from', he was not sympathetic to the visionary side of Blake's art, believing that it displayed more of 'fancy' than true 'imagination'. Historians have tended to exaggerate the proximity of the two artists: nevertheless Fuseli was prepared to support the publication of Blake's designs and in 1796 contributed an unsigned introduction to Blake's edition of Edward Young's *Night Thoughts*.

Fuseli's ultimately classicist ideas on artistic education crystallized in his Academy lectures, begun in 1801. These were splendidly unprejudiced and never promoted the character or claims of his own art; indeed his dismissal of personal eccentricities, his condemnation of violent or frightening themes and his attacks on the Italian Mannerists are strongly at variance with it. His belief in excellence through selection from nature and in the absolute superiority of classical art, followed in the hierarchy by Roman and Florentine painting, were essentially unoriginal. More interesting are his asides on the history of art and on his contemporaries, which display his wide knowledge and his conviction—this at least being consistent with his own work—that expression, as found in such artists as Rembrandt and Caravaggio, constituted a higher state of art than the ideal beauty advocated by Winckelmann. Fuseli's art-historical erudition was further expressed in a widely revised edition of Matthew Pilkington's *A General Dictionary of Artists* (1805) and in his own 'History of Art in the Schools of Italy', projected from 1808 (see Knowles). His *Aphorisms, Chiefly Relative to the Fine Arts*, which he had noted since 1788, perhaps in emulation of those of his friend Lavater, were published in 1818.

WRITINGS

trans.: *Reflections on the Paintings and Sculptures of the Greeks* (London, 1765)

Remarks on the Writings and Conduct of J.-J. Rousseau (London, 1767, rev. Zurich, 1962)

Aphorisms, Chiefly Relative to the Fine Arts (London, 1818)

The Collected English Letters of Henry Fuseli, ed. D. H. Weinglass (New York, 1982) [complete edn: excellent annotations and concise biogs of correspondents and friends]

BIBLIOGRAPHY

A. Cunningham: 'Henry Fuseli', *The Lives of the Most Eminent British Painters, Sculptors and Architects*, ii (London, 1830)

J. Knowles: *The Life and Writings of Henry Fuseli, Esq.*, 3 vols (London, 1831) [comprehensive early biog. with col. of Fuseli's pubns and lectures and transcription of the 'History of Art in the Schools of Italy']

A. Federmann: *Johann Heinrich Füssli: Dichter und Maler, 1741–1825* (Zurich, 1927)

P. Ganz: *The Drawings of Henry Fuseli* (New York, 1949)

E. C. Mason: *The Mind of Henry Fuseli: Selections from his Writings with an Introductory Essay* (London, 1951)

N. Powell: *The Drawings of Henry Fuseli* (London, 1951)

F. Antal: *Fuseli Studies* (London, 1956)

G. Schiff: *Johann Heinrich Füsslis Milton-Galerie*, Schweizerisches Institut für Kunstwissenschaft, iv (Zurich, 1963) [fullest study of this crucial aspect of Fuseli's career]

M. Pointon: *Milton and English Art* (Manchester, 1970) [incl. concise account of Fuseli's career, with selection of pls]

N. Powell: *Fuseli: 'The Nightmare'* (London, 1972)

P. Tomory: *The Life and Art of Henry Fuseli* (London, 1972)

G. Schiff: *Johann Heinrich Füssli: Oeuvrekatalog* (Zurich, 1973)

Henry Fuseli (exh. cat. by G. Schiff; London, Tate; Hamburg, Ksthalle; 1975) [good pls and chronology; strong emphasis on psychological interpretation of Fuseli's iconography]

The Fuseli Circle in Rome: Early Romantic Art of the 1770s (exh. cat. by N. L. Pressly, New Haven, CT, Yale Cent. Brit. A., 1979)

Füssli e Dante (exh. cat., ed. C. Gizzi; Pescara, Casa Dante, Torre Passeri, 1985)

DAVID BLAYNEY BROWN

Fustat, al-. *See under* CAIRO.

Fusuma. Paper-covered, sliding door panel, used to separate spaces inside a Japanese dwelling. It is properly known as *fusuma shōji* (*see* SHŌJI) in Japanese. Panels may be removed when larger spaces are needed. While the *shōji* has a thin covering of paper on one side only, the *fusuma* is covered on both sides for greater privacy and so serves not only as a sliding door but also as a wall to the enclosure. *Fusuma* were commonly painted as part of a room decoration. Many examples of these painted panels may be found in temple complexes in Japan. Like multi-panel folding screens (*byōbu*), the *fusuma* were painted so that the scene extended from panel to panel. Handsome printed paper and gold leaf were also used to adorn the sliding doors. In many cases doors had decorated, indented metal handholds to permit opening and closing. In most structures three or four *fusuma*, each about 900 mm wide, were placed in a track between load-bearing posts. Above them there would commonly be a structural section called *ranma* reaching from the lintel to the support beams for the roof. The *ranma* could be opened or left closed. *Fusuma* are still found in modern Japanese homes. As modular units the *fusuma* can be moved from room to room. When damaged it can be re-papered by gluing new paper on the latticework underneath.

BIBLIOGRAPHY

Kodansha Enc. Japan, 'Architecture, traditional domestic'

ROBERT W. KRAMER

Futurism. Italian movement, literary in origin, that grew to embrace painting, sculpture, photography and architecture, which was launched by the publication on 20 February 1909 of 'Le Futurisme' by Filippo Tommaso Marinetti in the Paris newspaper *Le Figaro*. Marinetti's intention was to reject the past, to revolutionize culture and make it more modern. The new ideology of Futurism set itself with violent enthusiasm against the weighty inheritance of an art tied to the Italian cultural tradition and exalted the idea of an aesthetic generated by the modern myth of the machine and of speed.

I. Painting, graphic arts and sculpture. II. Architecture.

I. Painting, graphic arts and sculpture.

1. Foundations and first manifestos of Futurism, 1909. 2. First Futurist works, 1910–11. 3. International manifestations of Futurism, 1912–13. 4. Futurism during World War I. 5. Post-war developments.

1. FOUNDATIONS AND FIRST MANIFESTOS OF FUTURISM, 1909. Marinetti laid the foundations of the new literary poetics in his first manifesto, written in late 1908. Every new creation or action, he wrote, was now based on the 'beauty of speed'; museums, libraries, 'venerated' cities and academies had to be destroyed, as they belonged to traditional culture. An art born of progress was now to take the place of all the artistic forms of the past, even the most recent ones, because they were stale and static. These words were immediately taken up by a group of young painters based in Milan—Umberto Boccioni, Luigi Russolo and Carlo Carrà—who declared their enthusiastic support for Marinetti's ideas and offered to extend the same revolutionary polemic to figurative art. The *Manifesto dei pittori futuristi*, issued as a pamphlet dated 11 February 1910, was signed by Gino Severini and Giacomo Balla. This document, dashed off after their first meeting with Marinetti, expressed the new artistic ideals in violently aggressive words:

> We want to fight ferociously against the fanatical, unconscious and snobbish religion of the past, which is nourished by the evil influence of museums. We rebel against the supine admiration of old canvases, old statues and old objects, and against the enthusiasm for all that is worm-eaten, dirty and corroded by time; we believe that the common contempt for everything young, new and palpitating with life is unjust and criminal.

This first manifesto of Futurist painting was followed on 11 April 1910 by a more specific statement entitled *La pittura futurista: Manifesto tecnico*. The group declared their break with traditional and realistic painting and proclaimed the advent of a new awareness, which they labelled the 'dynamic sensation'. They claimed that the spatial conceptions of the past were smashed and that 'space no longer exists.' In their view, 'The construction of pictures is stupidly traditional. Painters have always depicted the things and persons placed before us. We shall place the spectator at the centre of the picture' (Drudi Gambillo and Fiori, i, 1958, pp. 65–6). A new theory of colour was proposed (ibid., p. 57):

> How can we still see a human face as pink, while our lives are undeniably doubled by night-time activity? The human face is yellow, it is red, it is green, it is blue, it is violet. The pallor of a woman looking into a jeweller's window is more iridescent than all the prisms of the jewels that fascinate her. Our pictorial sensations cannot be expressed in whispers. We make them sing and shout in our canvases, which ring out with deafening triumphal fanfares.

2. FIRST FUTURIST WORKS, 1910–11. Despite these strong affirmations, the young artists continued to work along the lines of divisionism and complementarity of colour; only from 1911 can one speak of real Futurist painting. Until the end of 1910 Boccioni was still oscillating between an exasperated Expressionism influenced by

Munch and a divisionism reminiscent of Seurat; Carrà was torn between an 18th-century kind of academicism and the new theories of colour; Russolo remained tied to Symbolist ideas; and Severini, working in Paris, was strongly attracted by French Post-Impressionist painting. The first Futurist works, painted in 1910, were still closely derived from Marinetti's literary images; they included Russolo's *Perfume* (1910; sold London, Sotheby's, 1990, see Martin, fig. 45), Boccioni's *Controluce* (1910; priv. col., see M. Calvesi and E. Coen, *Boccioni*, Milan, 1983, p. 304) and Carrà's *Swimmers* (1910; Pittsburgh, PA, Carnegie Mus. A.) and *Funeral of the Anarchist Galli* (1910–11; New York, MOMA; for illustration *see* CARRÀ, CARLO).

During the first year of Futurist activity the manifestos were frequently publicized by provocative declamations at evening performances; these irritated the public, which responded by throwing fruit and other objects. Turin, Naples and Milan were the first cities to be touched by the impetuous violence of Futurism. It was only in April 1911 that Futurist paintings were presented in Milan at the *Mostra d'arte libera* organized in the former workshops of the Ricordi record factory. In this large exposition— open, according to the invitation, to 'all those who want to assert *something new*, that is to say far from imitations, derivations and falsifications'—a small section was devoted to the Milanese Futurists Boccioni, Carrà and Russolo. Among the paintings shown by Boccioni was *Work*, retitled *The City Rises* (1910–11; New York, MOMA), a picture with a Symbolist flavour, representing human and animal tension in a vortex of colour fragmented in oblique threadlike brushstrokes. In *Mourning* (1909; priv. col.) the figures and gestures are multiplied and elongated in an Expressionist manner, producing a profoundly emotive sensation, while in *The Laugh* (1911; New York, MOMA), the tangle of figures is emphasized by intense bands of light. Carrà and Russolo presented works inspired by the new expression of form, adhering, as Carrà later wrote, 'to the symphonic concept of masses, weight and volume, of a general movement of forms determined by the modern sensibility'. The public and the critics reacted to the exhibition in very different ways. The most unexpected attack came from the young Florentine painter and writer Ardengo Soffici, who was close to French literary and artistic circles and very open to the avant-garde experiences of Cubism. Irritated by his violent review, the Futurists organized an expedition to Florence to punish Soffici. The quarrel was quickly settled, and the two groups were soon united under the banner of Futurism.

During this period Marinetti decided to spread propaganda abroad to make the Futurist movement known in other countries. An exhibition was planned in Paris at Bernheim-Jeune, and in autumn 1911 Boccioni and Carrà briefly joined Severini there, seeing Cubist works for the first time. The exhibition, which took place in February 1912, consisted of works by Boccioni, Carrà, Russolo and Severini. In the preface to their catalogue the artists emphasized their divergence from Cubism because of its static expression; they claimed to be searching for 'a style of movement', in opposition to the analytical view of the French painters. In this text their theoretical position was newly clarified: 'To make the spectator live at the centre of the picture, as our manifesto says, the painting must be the synthesis of what is remembered and what is seen.' They affirmed (Apollonio, 1970, p. 92):

> If we paint the phases of an uprising, the crowd bristling with fists and noisy cavalry assaults will be translated on the canvas into bands of lines corresponding to all the forces in conflict, following the painting's laws of general violence. These lines of force must envelop the spectator and carry him away; he himself must be in some way obliged to grapple with the figures in the picture. All the objects, according to physical transcendentalism, tend towards the infinite through their force-lines, to bring the work of art back to true painting. We interpret nature by presenting these lines on the canvas as the origins or prolongations of the rhythms which the objects impress on our sensibilities.

A more aggressive and individual figurative programme now corresponded to the ideas expounded by the Futurists in their manifestos. In Boccioni's work, in fact, form and space were blended into a universal synthesis with colour, analysed in new combinations of complementary hues, tonal contrasts and Expressionistic deformations. The broken, fragmented and refracted representation was recomposed into a vortex of luminosity with a strong ascending tension. Impressionist and Post-Impressionist components were undoubtedly mixed with elements of Cubism. The decomposition of the subject, however, was not intended to create a new dimensionality. Nor did Boccioni seek to construct a reality that would preserve only the memory of the object. Rather, the artist aimed to expand space through formal elements, which could emphasize the dynamic tension of the subject in relation to the surrounding environment.

In the second version of a set of three paintings entitled *States of Mind* (New York, MOMA and Civ. Mus. A. Contemp.), painted in autumn 1911 after his trip to France, Boccioni was searching for a style in which to translate sensations and emotions into images. The lines became a dynamic projection of the subject's state of mind, an objectivist transposition of a perception. In *The Farewells* the vision seems confused and chaotic; a locomotive is wedged into a tangled network of undulating and horizontal lines that suggest the chaos of departure and emotional embraces. In *Those who Go* (*see* BOCCIONI, UMBERTO, fig. 1) the bullet-like speed of the rushing train is underlined by very rapid oblique brushstrokes, while in *Those who Remain* the vertical line of stasis prevails.

In works from this period by Carrà, space is defined by more accentuated linear rhythms, and the formal structure

1. Giacomo Balla: *Swifts: Paths of Movement+Dynamic Sequences*, oil on canvas, 673×1251 mm, 1913 (New York, Museum of Modern Art)

of the object is given more depth. The colours are quieter than those used by Boccioni, attenuated so as to make the painting cohere as a uniform whole. Carrà creates a magical equilibrium of forms and colours, giving special attention to the composition and thus creating a sensation of suspended movement. In the *Gallery of Milan* (1912; Milan, priv. col., see 1986 exh. cat., p. 159) the forms follow one another in a dynamic rhythm that tends to override the mere visual data; figuration is eliminated to bring out the vibrant energy of the material.

In Russolo's works of this time the Symbolist energy that pervaded his earlier paintings had lost none of its force. *Memory of a Night* (1911; priv. col., see 1986 exh. cat., p. 204) depicts an apparition, a dream in which spectral figures move in a deserted city. Among the Futurists Russolo was the artist who gave most space to imagination and fantasy, through his linear description of colours and lights, in a surreal play of movements. In *The Revolt* (1911; The Hague, Gemeentemus.; for illustration *see* RUSSOLO, LUIGI) and *Dynamism of an Automobile* (1912–13; Paris, Pompidou) the composition is simplified into a succession of triangular forms that simulate the movement of a crowd or a motor-car.

Balla's early Futurist experiments are quite different. He represented movement with a more analytical approach, contemplating the spatial displacement of the object in time. In *Dynamism of a Dog on a Lead* (1912; Buffalo, NY, Albright-Knox A.G.) or the *Hand of the Violinist* (1912; London, priv. col., see 1961 exh. cat., p. 59) Balla captures the successive movements of the dog's lead, legs and wagging tail or the musician's left hand on his instrument, as in a sequence of superimposed and slightly off-register photographic images. The overpowering effect of physical sensations, particularly when exaggerated by modern machinery and inventions associated with speed such as the automobile, was taken as the subject for paintings such as *Speed of an Automobile+Lights+Noise* (1913; Zurich, Ksthaus; for illustration *see* BALLA, GIACOMO). It was his long-standing interest in photography that suggested to him this episodic reading of the transformation of movement into a vision of reality that was still persuasive in naturalistic terms. Paintings such as *Swifts: Paths of Movement+Dynamic Sequences* (1913; New York, MOMA; see fig. 1), with their calculated rendering of the stages of an action, suggest an awareness of the sequential photographic studies of Eadweard Muybridge and the chronophotography of Etienne-Jules Marey. Balla also encouraged the 'photodynamic' experiments of his friend Anton Giulio Bragaglia, which used long exposures to fix the fluidity of action. Bragaglia's attempts to establish these images as works of art, however, were scorned by the Milanese Futurists.

Of all the Futurists, Severini came closest to the experiments of the Neo-Impressionists. He constructed his images through the fragmentation of colour and form, unifying them through the harmony of the composition as a whole. Visual impressions appear to be broken down into many small coloured elements, as in a mosaic, and then regrouped to create a kaleidoscopic effect. In his early Futurist paintings, such as *Voices of my Room* (1911; Stuttgart, Staatsgal.), he proposed a simultaneity of plastic forms and sensations. As he declared in his manifesto of

1913, 'Le analogie plastiche del dinamismo: Manifesto Futurista': 'Now in our age of dynamism and simultaneity, no reality can be separated from those memories, affinities and plastic aversions which its expansive action evokes simultaneously in us, and which are equally abstract realities, if one is to realize the total action of the reality in question.'

3. INTERNATIONAL MANIFESTATIONS OF FUTURISM, 1912–13. Through the tireless propagandist activity of Marinetti, the Futurist movement spread abroad very rapidly in 1912. Exhibitions in Paris, Berlin, London, Brussels and other major European capitals propagated the new aesthetic of speed in different cultural environments. The aggressive character of the group gave rise to the most extreme reactions. In Germany and France in particular the intellectual and mercantile classes either closed ranks in defensive positions or gave the Futurists their enthusiastic support.

In Italy Marinetti tried to break through the general distrust by lining up with the Tuscan literary group of *La voce* and by transforming the magazine *Lacerba* into an organ for the diffusion of Futurist poetics. Every issue contained theoretical articles or polemical replies, as well as reproductions of drawings and paintings. The alliance with the Florentine group renewed the combative and aggressive spirit of Futurism. On the occasion of the first Futurist exhibition in Rome in 1913, at the Teatro Costanzi, Giovanni Papini and Ardengo Soffici also participated in the opening festivities. The latter, converted to the Futurist spirit, also exhibited various works with a strong formal accent, although they were based on the decomposition of planes.

Lacerba published a polemic between Boccioni and Guillaume Apollinaire on the idea of simultaneity, while in its pages new manifestos appeared. These included Marinetti's 'L'immaginazione senza fili e le parole in libertà' (i/12, 1913, pp. 121–4), Apollinaire's 'L'Antitradition futuriste' (i/18, 1913, pp. 202–3), Carrà's 'La pittura dei suoni, rumori e odori' (i/17, 1913, pp. 185–7), Marinetti's 'Il teatro di varietà' (i/19, 1913, pp. 209–11) and 'Il programma politico futurista' (i/20, 1913, pp. 221–2), signed by the group. On 1 August 1914 *Lacerba* also printed the contents of a pamphlet by Antonio Sant'Elia, 'Manifesto dell'architettura futurista' (repr. in Drudi Gambillo and Fiori, 1958, pp. 81–5), which had first appeared a month previously (*see* §II below). The alliance between the Futurists and *Lacerba* represented by these texts was soon destroyed by ideological differences, and at the end of 1914 their paths diverged.

As the number of followers of Futurism increased, so did the number of their exhibitions. At the end of 1913 an exhibition entitled *Lacerba* took place at the Libreria Gonnelli in Florence, and in Rome Giuseppe Sprovieri's new Galleria Permanente Futurista held a show of sculpture by Boccioni, previously exhibited in France. While Marinetti's activity reached out towards Russia and arrived in England with the support and encouragement of Christopher Nevinson, in Italy Futurism welcomed a number of new artists into its ranks: the poet Francesco

Cangiullo (1888–1977), Fortunato Depero, Enrico Pram-polini, Ottone Rosai, Giorgio Morandi, Mario Sironi and Arturo Martini.

Within the original group of painters, individual posi-tions emerged more and more strongly from 1913. With the publication of his manifesto 'L'arte dei rumori' (Apol-lonio, 1970, pp. 126–33) Russolo abandoned his interest in painting to devote himself to music and the construction of new instruments, seeking to create harmonic modula-tions and chords that would give the 'sensation of the pulsating agitated life' of the metropolis. Carrà for his part elaborated theories about synaesthesia in 'La pittura dei suoni, rumori e odori', asserting that sounds, noises and smells must penetrate into the pictorial whole and give plastic expression to those sensations: 'To obtain this *total painting*, which demands the active cooperation of all the senses, *painting: plastic state of mind of the universal*, one must paint in the way that drunkards sing and vomit, sounds, noises and odours!' (Apollonio, 1970, p. 166). In his paintings these ideas were expressed by a more and more profound abstraction of forms in a dynamic sense. But Carrà did not deny the three-dimensional view of the whole, accompanied by a search for more material solidity.

Around 1913 Severini's paintings, given an intense vitality of colour and light, were also tending towards a simplification of structure, as can be seen in his manifesto, written during the same period: 'It is *essentially important* to destroy the principle of light, local tones and shadows which painters before us have used to render the action of light on bodies, which belongs to the relativity of luminous, momentary and accidental phenomena' (Apol-lonio, 1970, p. 176). The study of movement and speed led Severini to emphasize intensity and luminous radiances in a sparkling colouristic abstraction. The subject of dance and of ballerinas already evident in works such as *Dynamic Hieroglyphic of the Bal Tabarin* (1912; New York, MOMA; for illustration *see* SEVERINI, GINO) brought out the decomposition of light and the fragmentation of lines, synthesized into joyous vortices of pure colours.

2. Umberto Boccioni: *Unique Forms of Continuity in Space*, bronze, 1175×876×368 mm, 1913 (London, Tate Gallery)

4. FUTURISM DURING WORLD WAR I. At the out-break of World War I the subject-matter of Futurist painting assumed more importance and became more overtly aggressive, with images of armoured trains, tunnels and cannons, as in Severini's *Plastic Synthesis of the Idea 'War'* (1915; Munich, Staatsgal. Mod. Kst). Their preferred colours also changed, becoming metallic. These images of war were the last studies of movement and formal com-position within the Futurist movement; Severini, in fact, changed his painting in the direction of a formal purity of line and a classicism based on mathematical formulae.

Boccioni's use of complementary colours and dynamic intersecting planes created considerable spatial complexity in the image. His studies on dynamism led him, as early as 1912, to broaden his interests to sculpture, heralded by his publication in that year of his technical manifesto of Futurist sculpture, 'La scultura futurista' (Drudi Gambillo and Fiori, i, 1958, pp. 67–72). In his sculptures he sought to synthesize the impulses of a movement made by an object or by a figure, as in *Unique Forms of Continuity in Space* (1913; London, Tate; see fig. 2), in terms of the absolute movement of the universe, extending the planes

of the represented image in space. In his paintings Boccioni also developed his manner of figuration in the direction of abstraction, although this did not obliterate the subject, which remained recognizable thanks to the lines of its dynamic tension. Nevertheless, in the works of that period, such as *Dynamism of a Footballer* (1913; New York, MOMA) and *Dynamism of a Human Body* (1913–14; Milan, Civ. Mus. A. Contemp.), one can see the possibility of a return to a formal analysis.

The predominance of purely formal concerns in Boc-cioni's painting re-emerged at the end of 1914 through a meditation on volumes and masses inspired by the work of Cézanne. This was the basis on which, from 1916, his Futurist works went beyond the original poetics of the movement. In the new images, linked to a different spatial conception, the preoccupation with motion and speed was reabsorbed in a renewed interest in the subject itself. Divisionism now reappeared, amplified by more rapid brushstrokes to the point where they suggested a Cubist type of figuration, while colour was crystallized in violent chromatic juxtapositions.

Balla around 1913 moved from the veristic rendering of objects to a bold total abstraction of lines and colour. His series of *Iridescent Interpenetrations*, for example *Radial Iridescent Interpenetration: Prismatic Vibrations* (1913–14; Turin, Gal. Civ. A. Mod.), represent the extreme schematization of his studies of light and movement. In this work, coloured triangles, lined up in accord with optical affinities, create abstract and analytical visual textures. *Mercury Passing before the Sun, Seen through a Spyglass* (1914; Vienna, Mus. 20. Jhts) marks the artist's passage from the *Interpenetrations* to a true synthesis of forms. In Balla's paintings of 1915 simultaneity, which in Boccioni arose from the interpenetration of forms, was rendered through prismatic geometric schemes.

It was this particular conception of form and colour that influenced Depero, who joined the Futurist movement in 1914. Along with Balla he signed a manifesto on the *Ricostruzione futurista dell'universo* (Rome, 1915), in which they proclaimed themselves Futurist abstract artists and sang the praises of a joyous universe, 'brightly coloured and full of light' (Apollonio, 1970, pp. 254–8). They created multimedia 'plastic complexes' from the most diverse elements, in accord with their abstract imaginative sensibilities. Balla's artistic experiments now extended to the theatre and to toys, chairs, benches, screens, divans and lampshades, mostly in green and yellow; huge Futurist flowers in scintillating colours rose from the floor, generated by an artificial nature.

Even in the preceding years Balla had amused himself by applying his theories on visual perception to realities outside painting itself. In his manifesto *Vestito antineutrale* (Apollonio, 1970, pp. 192–6), dated 11 September 1914, he described the style of an 'antineutral costume' to be worn in the demonstrations supporting Italy's entry into World War I: 'Since *neutrality is the synthesis of all that belongs to the past*, we Futurists today flaunt these antineutral, festively warlike clothes.' Balla himself enjoyed scandalizing the public with his eccentric dress.

5. POST-WAR DEVELOPMENTS. With the end of World War I and the deaths of Boccioni and Sant'Elia, Marinetti's movement lost its subversive character, and its centre moved from Milan to Rome. Balla, who emerged as the key artist of the movement, pursued his experiments with a new vein of spirituality, almost mysticism. Around him Prampolini bordered on Surrealism with his multimedia images, while Depero crystallized his figures in a mechanistic kind of schematization. With Marinetti's *Manifesto del tattilismo* (Drudi Gambillo and Fiori, i, 1958, pp. 56–61), dated 11 January 1921, a new and more playful phase of Futurism became official: 'The ends of Tactilism must be tactile harmonies, simply; and it must collaborate indirectly towards the perfecting of spiritual communications between human beings, through the epidermis.' These were years of great fervour in all fields, from dance to theatre, politics, cinematography and photography. In addition to the work made during this period by the movement's three senior artists—Balla, Prampolini and Depero—a new generation emerged, led by the mechanistic works of Gerardo Dottori and including also the geometric abstractions of Bruno Munari. This 'second

Futurism', as it became known, was reinforced by the foundation of the Turin Futurist group by FILLIA in 1923.

AEROPITTURA, a new phase of Futurism that attempted to revitalize the movement through a new cosmic idealism, was announced in 1929 by the publication of the *Manifesto dell'Aeropittura*, signed by Balla, Benedetta (Marinetti's wife, the painter and writer Benedetta Cappa, 1897–1977), Depero, Dottori, Fillia, Marinetti, Prampolini, the painter and sculptor Mino Somenzi (1899–1948) and the painter Tato (pseud. of Guglielmo Sansori, 1896–1974). In it they proposed a new theory of spiral dynamism. The heroic, dramatic transgressiveness of Futurism was thus transformed into a more imaginative and lyrical synthesis of the movement. Although in its strictest sense Futurism was confined to Italy, almost from its inception it had repercussions in other countries, leading notably to VORTICISM in England and to CUBO-FUTURISM and RAYISM in Russia.

For further illustrations *see* SANT'ELIA, ANTONIO and SIRONI, MARIO.

WRITINGS
F. T. Marinetti: *Le Futurisme* (Paris, 1911); rev. and ed. G. Lista (Milan, 1980)
M. Drudi Gambillo and T. Fiori, eds: *Archivi del futurismo*, 2 vols (Rome, 1958 and 1962/*R* Rome, 1986) [anthol. of pubd and unpubd lett. and doc. and illus. cat. of works by major artists]
F. T. Marinetti: *Teoria e invenzione futurista*, ed. L. De Maria (Milan, 1968)
L. Scrivo, ed.: *Sintesi del futurismo: Storia e documenti* (Rome, 1968)
U. Apollonio, ed.: *Futurismo* (Milan, 1970); Eng. trans. as *Futurist Manifestos* (London, 1973)
G. De Marchis and M. Carrà: *Lacerba* (Milan, 1970) [facs. of edns pubd 1913–15]
L. Caruso, ed.: *Manifesti, proclami, interventi e documenti teoretici del futurismo*, 4 vols (Florence, 1980)
C. Carrà: *La mia vita* (Milan, 1981)

For further writings *see* MARINETTI, FILIPPO TOMMASO.

BIBLIOGRAPHY
G. Ballo: *Preistoria del futurismo* (Milan, 1960)
R. Carrieri: *Futurismo* (Milan, 1961)
R. T. Clough: *Futurism, the Story of a Modern Art Movement: A New Appraisal* (New York, 1961)
E. Crispolti: *Il secondo futurismo: 5 pittori e 1 scultore, Torino, 1923–1938* (Turin, 1961)
Futurism (exh. cat. by J. C. Taylor, New York, MOMA, 1961)
G. Acquaviva: *Futurismo* (Milan, 1962)
M. Calvesi: *Il futurismo*, 3 vols (Milan, 1967)
M. Martin: *Futurist Art and Theory* (Oxford, 1968)
M. Verdone: *Cinema e letteratura del futurismo* (Rome, 1968)
E. Crispolti: *Il mito della macchina e altri temi del futurismo* (Trapani, 1969; rev. 1971)
M. Kirby: *Futurist Performance* (New York, 1971; rev. 1986)
L. De Maria: *Marinetti e il futurismo* (Milan, 1973)
G. Lista: *Futurisme* (Lausanne, 1973)
Futurism: A Modern Focus (exh. cat., New York, Guggenheim, 1973)
J. P. Andreoli de Villers: *Futurism and the Arts: A Bibliography* (Toronto, 1975)
C. Tisdall and A. Bozzolla: *Futurism* (London, 1977)
P. Pacini, ed.: *26 Esposizioni futuriste, 1912–1918* (Florence, 1978) [repr. of Futurist exh. cats]
——: *Esposizioni futuriste, 1912–1931 (seconda serie)* (Florence, 1979) [repr. of Futurist exh. cats, with intro.]
G. Lista: *Arte e politica: Il Futurismo di sinistra in Italia* (Milan, 1980)
Futurism and the International Avant-garde (exh. cat. by A. d'Harnoncourt and G. Celant, Philadelphia, PA, Mus. A., 1980)
F. Roche-Pézard: *L'Aventure futuriste, 1909–1916* (Rome, 1983)
The Futurist Imagination: Word and Image in Italian Futurist Painting, Drawing, Collage and Free-word Painting (exh. cat., ed. A. C. Hanson; New Haven, CT, Yale U. A.G., 1983)
Futurismo a Firenze: 1910–1920 (exh. cat., Florence, Pal. Medici–Riccardi, 1984)
C. Salaris: *Storia del futurismo* (Rome, 1985)

I futuristi e la fotografia: Creazione fotografica e immagine quotidiana (exh. cat. by G. Lista, Modena, Musei Civ., 1985–6)

E. Crispolti: *Storia e critica del futurismo* (Rome, 1986)

M. Perloff: *The Futurist Moment* (Chicago, 1986)

Futurismo & futurismi (exh. cat., ed. P. Hultén; Venice, Pal. Grassi, 1986)

A. D'Elia: *L'Universo futurista, una mappa: Dal quadro alla cravatta* (Bari, 1988)

C. Salaris: *Bibliografia del futurismo, 1909–1944* (Rome, 1988)

ESTER COEN

II. Architecture.

In the first five years or so after the inception of Futurism by Filippo Tommaso Marinetti in 1909, architecture figured only by implication in the polemic of the manifesto writers of the Futurist movement, in the verses of its poets and in such Cubist-influenced paintings as Umberto Boccioni's the *Street Came into the House* (1911; Hannover, Kstmus). The Futurist's denunciation of historic precedent as a basis for design, their near-religious belief in science and technology and their emphasis on dynamism as an end in itself presented more intractable problems in architecture than in the other arts. Thus the earliest Futurist manifesto specifically to deal with architecture did not appear until 29 January 1914, in the Roman newspaper *Il piccolo giornale d'Italia* (Apollonio, ed., 1970, pp. 181–3). 'Aerostruttura, basi per un'architettura futurista', illustrated with drawings of two hypothetical projects, was by Enrico Prampolini, an associate of the Futurist group surrounding Giacomo Balla in Rome. It owes much to ideas on form and space already advocated by Boccioni (*see* §I, 2 above), who also wrote, but did not publish, his

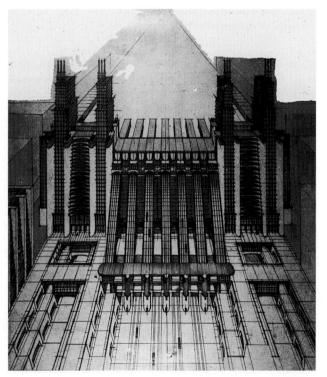

3. Futurist central railway station and airport; drawing by Antonio Sant'Elia from his series *Città nuova*, black ink and black and blue crayon on tracing paper, 500×390 mm, 1914 (Como, Museo Civico Storico G. Garibaldi)

views on architecture early in 1914 (first pubd 1972; repr. Godoli, pp. 185–7), attempting to relate the dynamic principles of Futurist painting and sculpture to architecture. This delay, followed by the outbreak of World War I, produced an architectural movement that operated solely through the medium of published and exhibited drawings and manifestos.

In 1912 the Milan-based architect ANTONIO SANT'ELIA, working in the popular northern Italian *Stile Liberty* and influenced by the review *Die Wagner Schule*, made the first of several hundred drawings of hypothetical buildings. These drawings constitute the main body of work on which the visual images associated with architectural Futurism are based. In examples executed in 1912 the *Stile Liberty* manner is still apparent, but by March 1914 it had virtually disappeared in the vivid perspective pencil and crayon sketches in the series *Città nuova* exhibited by Sant'Elia at the Prima Mostra dell'Assocazione degli Architetti Lombardi (Milan, Pal. Permanente). Among these, the earliest developed subjects of the Futurist architectural canon, were designs for a hydroelectric power station with battered walls (Como, Mus. Civ. Stor. Garibaldi) and stepped-back buildings with curved lift-towers (for illustration *see* SANT'ELIA, ANTONIO). Sant'Elia had recently become a member of the Nuove Tendenze, a moderate Milanese Futurist group, and showed his *Città nuova* series again in May–June 1914 at an exhibition of the group's work (Milan, Famiglia A.). He also contributed to the catalogue a 'Messagio' above his own signature, although he may have been helped in its composition by the art critic and journalist Ugo Nebbia (1880–1965). It contains no reference to Futurism *per se*, but the tenor of its contents and its format closely resemble earlier Futurist manifestos. Two months later, approached by Carlo Carrà, Sant'Elia joined the Futurist movement, and on 11 July 1914 some of the same drawings, now labelled *La Città futurista*, and a modified and extended version of the 'Messagio' were published as a pamphlet under the title *Manifesto dell'architettura futurista*, appearing in *Lacerba* a month later. The fully developed drawings depicted non-rhetorical, soaring forms—visionary scenographic representations of Utopian but feasible urban development, as in the high-speed transit system at several levels, served by an airstrip at roof level (1914; Como, Mus. Civ. Stor. Garibaldi; see fig. 3). They express the apotheosis of new technologies and the dynamic energy of urban living, as advocated in the foundation manifesto. Moreover, as Banham pointed out, by affirming in the 'Messagio' that architecture remains an intuitive art, Sant'Elia '... anticipates ... the anti-Functionalist mood of Le Corbusier and Gropius in the Twenties ...' (1960, p. 130). Mario Chiattone, with whom Sant'Elia shared a studio, exhibited drawings in a similar though more earthbound style in the Nuove Tendenze exhibition. Futurist drawings and polemic were vigorously distributed by Marinetti to avant-garde groups in northern Europe, but the movement lost much of its vigour with the deaths in action of Boccioni and Sant'Elia in 1916.

After World War I Virgilio Marchi (1895–1960) acknowledged himself a follower of Sant'Elia in his own 'Manifesto dell'architettura futurista: Dinamico, stato d'animo drammatica', published in *Roma futurista* (29 Feb

1920), but added little to pre-war positions. His drawings range from the unadventurous towers and arched bridges of the proto-Rationalist *Metropoli futurista* to the incomprehensible contorted confections with titles such as *Visione architettonica* (both 1919–20), most of them published in his book *Architettura futurista* (Foligno, 1924). Mario Chiattone, who had not joined the Futurist movement, reverted to a nondescript Neo-classical manner, while Fortunato Depero and Prampolini, members of long standing, resorted to the device of using giant letters of the alphabet to form exhibition stands. In spite of Marinetti's efforts at revival (*Manifesto dell'architettura aerea*, 1934, with Angiolo Mazzioni and Mino Somenzi), in the 1920s and 1930s Futurist architecture merged with *Razionalismo* and European Expressionism.

Because of the association of Marinettian Futurism with Fascism, and as the *Città nuova* drawings were completed and exhibited before Sant'Elia joined the movement, attempts were made after World War II, especially by Bernasconi (1956) and Zevi (e.g. 1975, p. 177), to dissociate the work from the movement. Architectural influences other than Futurism have been adduced, such as the stepped-back apartments by Henri Sauvage, Rue Vavin, Paris (1912–14) and Harvey W. Corbett's vision of the future New York, reproduced in the *Illustrazione italiana* (Feb 1913). Etlin (1991) regarded Sant'Elian Futurism as one of several lines of development towards Italian Modernism between the wars, while Banham maintained that, as a turning-point in modern theories of design, its qualities were 'primarily ideological and concerned with attitudes of mind'. Whatever its origins, Sant'Elia's imagery retains its Futurist name and chimes with the popular conception of the architecture of the European modern movement in the inter-war years.

BIBLIOGRAPHY

B. Zevi: *Storia dell'architettura moderna* (Turin, 1955, rev. 2/1975)
G. Bernasconi: 'Il messaggio di Antonio Sant'Elia del 20 maggio 1914', *Rev. Tec. Svizzera It.* (July 1956), pp. 145–52
P. R. Banham: *Theory and Design in the First Machine Age* (London, 1960), pp. 98–137 [contains a complete Eng. trans. of the 'Messagio']
Z. Birolli, ed.: *Umberto Boccioni: Altri inediti e apparati critici* (Milan, 1972)
Fillia [L.Colombo]: 'Futurismo e Fascismo', *L'architettura in Italia, 1919–1943: Le polemiche*, ed. L. Patteta (Milan, 1972), pp. 257–60
U. Apollonio, ed.: *Futurismo* (Milan, 1970); Eng. trans. as *Futurist Manifestos* (London and New York, 1973)
E. Godoli: *Guida all'architettura moderna: Il futurismo* (Bari, 1983)
E. Crispolti: *Attraverso l'architettura futurista* (Modena, 1984)
L. Caramel and A. Longatti: *Sant'Elia: L'opere completa* (Milan, 1987; Eng. trans., New York, 1988)
D. P. Doordan: *Building Modern Italy: Italian Architecture, 1914–1936* (New York, 1988), pp. 19–44
B. Zevi: 'Lines of Futurism', *A. & Des.*, v/11–12 (1989), pp. ix–xvi
R. A. Etlin: *Modernism in Italian Architecture, 1890–1940* (Cambridge, MA, and London, 1991), pp. 53–100

JOHN MUSGROVE

Fux, Johann [Hanns] **Georg** (*b* Ausserpfitsch, nr Sterzing, Tyrol, 1661; *d* Straubing, Bavaria, 1706). German sculptor. He was first apprenticed to Hans Wild (*fl* 1678), an armourer in the Tyrol; he is next recorded in 1693 in Straubing, where he became a master and citizen in 1695. Much work by him in Straubing is extant: in St Veit's church he was responsible for the wooden herms of angels on the pulpit, the angels on the pulpit sound-board and the wooden putti and herms on the side altars, as well as

allegorical stucco figures of *Ecclesia* and *Bavaria* and the angels on the arch of the choir. The epitaph of the patrician *Stöger* family on the north wall of St Peter's church (1693) shows that he also worked in stone. Fux's most important work, however, is in ivory, for example a group of the *Crucifixion with St Mary Magdalene* in the Carmelite monastery in Straubing. His masterly carvings of Crucifixes and figures of saints, such as the *Virgin and St John the Evangelist* (1683; Munich, Bayer. NMus.), *Virgin and Child* (Hamburg, Mus. Kst & Gew.) and *St Sebastian* (1690–1700; Hamburg, Mus. Kst & Gew.), are executed with exquisite workmanship and are distinguished by the delicacy and formal variety of the modelling of garments and by the unpretentious naturalness of the faces and gestures. Drawings found in Straubing reveal that Fux acted as adviser in the rebuilding (*c.* 1702) in the Baroque style of the tower of St Veit.

BIBLIOGRAPHY

L. Möller: 'Bildwerke in Stein, Holz, Ton, Elfenbein, 1600–1800', *Jb. Hamburg. Kstsamml.*, v (1960), pp. 233–74
E. von Philippovich: *Elfenbein* (Brunswick, 1961, rev. Munich, 1982)
H. R. Weihrauch: *Hanns Georg Fux: Elfenbeinschnitzer und Bildhauer in Straubing* (Straubing, 1968)
K. Tyroller: 'Neue Arbeiten von Joh. Georg Fux', *Jber. Hist. Ver. Straubing & Umgeb.*, lxxvii (1974), pp. 115–29

CAROLA WENZEL

Fuyō Kō. *See* KŌ FUYŌ.

Fuzhou [Foochow; Fu-chou]. Capital city of Fujian Province in China, a coastal port on the northern section of the Min River delta. The history of the city goes back to the Han period (206 BC–AD 220). It became the provincial capital in the Tang (AD 618–907) and during the Five Dynasties period (AD 907–60) was the capital of the kingdom of Min (909–46), which extended from Zhejiang Province in the north to Guangdong Province in the south. When the region came under the control of the Song (960–1279), Fuzhou was a flourishing trading port from which ships sailed to Indonesia, the Philippines and South-east Asia. At this time the city was a thriving centre of Buddhism; most of the numerous large temples were dominated by the Chan (Jap. Zen) Buddhist school. There was also a Muslim population; in the Tang period Arab traders had settled in Fuzhou, and many local people converted.

In the Yuan (1279–1368) and Ming (1368–1644) periods Fuzhou was a major port from which tea, silk, porcelain and ceramics were exported to markets in South-east Asia, Japan, West Asia, Europe and elsewhere. During the 19th century it was one of China's main centres for the export of tea and was also important for trade in lacquerware and camphor. At the end of the Second Opium War (1856–60), the city was opened as one of the five treaty ports (*see* CHINA, §I, 4(ii)), and a foreign community of traders was established on Nantai Island in the Min River. With the decline of the tea trade towards the end of the 19th century, Fuzhou became less important as a trading port.

Remains of artistic interest at Fuzhou include Buddhist temples dating from the Five Dynasties period onwards. Although many of these were demolished or converted into schools or factories after 1949 under Communism, most of the important ones have been reconstructed or renovated since 1980. The few traditional buildings left within the city include the renovated White Pagoda (Baita) and surrounding temple, the Chongfu Temple (Chongfu si) and the Kaiyuan Temple on the shore of West Lake (Xi hu). The latter, of which only some buildings remain, is a reconstruction of the Ming period, with flat, sloping roofs in green tiles and high gables. Approximately 2 km outside the western city gate is the Xi Chan gu Temple, originally built during the Tang period. It was severely damaged during the Japanese occupation of China (1937–45) and the Cultural Revolution (1966–76) and restored in the 1980s. The temple houses various relics and treasures relating to the local history of Buddhism, including stone pagodas, stelae and a collection of calligraphy.

On Mt Gu to the east of Fuzhou is the oldest and largest Buddhist temple in the province, the Yongquan Temple. Founded in AD 908, it has several large buildings and a magnificent garden. The oldest structures are the main hall, which dates from 1022, and the Thousand Buddha Stupa, built in 1082; most of the buildings date from the Ming period. The temple surrounds a paved courtyard in which a rectangular area of water is crossed by a broad, flat bridge. The statues and other Buddhist paraphernalia in the temple are mostly products of the later part of the Qing period (1644–1911). The garden is in Ming style, with rock arrangements, paved walkways and various types of gates, including circular moon gates. The most impressive features are the extensive areas of large rocks and vertical cliff faces carved with calligraphy. The inscriptions, some dating from the Song period, include poetry, prose and Buddhist texts.

To the west of Fuzhou is Mt Niaoshi, where there once stood several temples. Only a stone pagoda dating from the Five Dynasties period remains, built in the same style as the twin pagodas at Quanzhou. About 60 km to the south of Fuzhou is the Wanfu Temple, associated with the Ōbaku school of Japanese Zen Buddhism. The founder of the school, Yinyuan Longqi (Ingen Ryūki), was the abbot of this temple, who, as a staunch Ming loyalist, emigrated to Japan after the rise of the Qing and established the famous MANPUKUJI in Uji, to the east of Kyoto. The temple consists of two large buildings, a Dharma Hall and a Monks Hall, both of which date from the 16th–17th century.

Fuzhou is also known for the 13th-century brick tomb of the young woman Huang Sheng, discovered in the suburbs in 1975. The tomb contained a coffin with the remains of Huang Sheng and over 436 funerary objects, including lacquerware, silk clothes, ornaments and bronze mirrors. The clothing is of special significance because of its variety, high quality and distinctive local style (*see also* CHINA, §XIII, 8(iii)).

BIBLIOGRAPHY

E. Boerschmann: *Baukunst und Landschaft in China* (Berlin, [*c.* 1920]); Eng. trans. by L. Hamilton as *Picturesque China, Architecture and Landscape: A Journey through Twelve Provinces* (New York, [1923]); rev., with intro by Wang-go Weng, as *Old China in Historic Photographs* (New York, 1982), pls 166–77

Lu Xiang, ed.: *Fujian*, Zhongguo zhishi congshu [China knowledge series] (Hong Kong, 1977)

Chugoku bukkyō no ryo [A journey of Chinese Buddhism], iv (Kyoto, 1980), pp. 83–120

Fuzhou Nan Song Huang Sheng mu [Southern Song tomb of Huang Sheng in Fuzhou], Fujian Prov. Mus. (Beijing, 1982) [archeological report]

Fanhui: *Xi Chan gu si* [The Ancient West Chan temple] (Fuzhou, 1987)

HENRIK H. SØRENSEN

Fyodorov-Davydov, Aleksey (Aleksandrovich) (*b* Moscow, 18 March 1890; *d* Moscow, 6 June 1969). Russian art historian. He dedicated most of his writing to a single theme, landscape painting in the context of Russian culture from the 18th century to the early 20th, and was instrumental in the formation and definition of the Marxist-based, social approach to art history that evolved during the Soviet period. He studied at the History and Philology Faculty of Kazan' University (1919–23) before entering the Moscow Institute of Archaeology and Art Studies to conduct research (1923–8) into Russian art of the industrial capitalist era. Simultaneously he headed the Fine Arts Section of Narkompros's Glavnauk Art Department, appeared as an art critic for the periodical *Pechat' i revolyutsia* and published his ideas concerning dialectical materialism in art in his first book (1925). In 1931 he was put in charge of the New Russian Art department of the Tret'yakov Gallery, a post he held until 1934. From 1944 he was professor of art history at Moscow University and the Moscow Institute of Applied and Decorative Art, becoming head of department in both. From the late 1930s Fyodorov-Davydov concentrated on Russian landscape painting, publishing monographs on individual artists. His theory, which sought to establish the ideological content of landscape, and which remained largely unchanged until his death, was that it had developed in two fundamental directions: the first as rational analysis, from Ivan Shishkin to Vitol'd Bialynickahy-Birula (Byalynitsky-Birulya; 1872–1957), and the second as 'romantic' perception, as evident in the work of Mikhail Lebedev, Arkhip Kuindzhi and, finally, Arkady Rylov. The second, lacking absolute ideological reliability, was termed 'progressive-realist landscape' by Fyodorov-Davydov. On this basis he was able to read into the landscapes of Isaak Levitan, for example, an artist to whom he devoted particular attention in his later career, criticism of the injustices and inequalities of his surroundings.

WRITINGS

Marksistskaya istoriya izobrazitel'nogo iskusstva [A Marxist history of fine art] (Moscow, 1925)

Russkoye iskusstvo promyshlennogo kapitalizma [Russian art of industrial capitalism] (Moscow, 1929)

Sil'vestr Feodosiyevich Shchedrin, 1745–1804 (Moscow, 1946)

Russkiy peyzazh XVIII–nachala XIX veka [Russian landscape of the 18th century to the early 19th] (Moscow, 1953)

Fyodor Yakovlevich Alekseyev (Moscow, 1955)

Fyodor Aleksandrovich Vasil'yev (Moscow, 1955)

Isaak Il'ich Levitan: Zhizn' i tvorchestvo [Isaak Il'ich Levitan: life and work] (Moscow, 1966)

ed.: *Isaak Il'ich Levitan: Pis'ma, dokumenty, vospominaniya* [Isaak Il'ich Levitan: letters, documents, reminiscences] (Moscow, 1966)

Russkiy peyzazh vtoroy poloviny XIX–nachala XX veka [Russian landscape of the second half of the 19th century to the early 20th] (Moscow, 1974)

BIBLIOGRAPHY

K. Miskaryan, ed.: *Aleksey Aleksandrovich Fyodorov-Davydov: Russkiy peyzazh XVIII–nachala XX veka* [Aleksey Aleksandrovich Fyodorov-Davydov: Russian landscape of the 18th century to the early 20th] (Moscow, 1986)

JEREMY HOWARD

Fyt [Fijt], **Jan** (*b* Antwerp, *bapt* 15 June 1611; *d* Antwerp, 11 Sept 1661). Flemish painter, draughtsman and etcher.

1. LIFE AND WORK. He was apprenticed in Antwerp in 1621–2 to Hans van den Berch [Berghe] (not to be confused with Jan van den Bergh of Alkmaar) and probably completed his training with Frans Snyders. In 1629–30 Fyt became a master in the Antwerp Guild of St Luke, but he continued to work for Snyders until 1631. In 1633 and 1634 he was in Paris. According to his biographers, he then went to Italy; an Italian journey is confirmed by the fact that in 1650 he joined the Antwerp Guild of Romanists (exclusive to those who had visited Rome), of which he became the dean in 1652. He apparently worked in Rome, where he joined the Schildersbent and was given the nickname 'Goudvink' (Dut.: 'goldfinch'). In Venice, according to Orlandi, Fyt worked for the Sagredo and Contarini families. He is also thought to have visited Naples, Florence and Genoa, and Orlandi stated that he also went to Spain and London. By 5 September 1641 Fyt was back in Antwerp, where, apart from a brief trip to the northern Netherlands in 1642, he apparently remained for the rest of his career. However, Jan-Erasmus Quellinus stated that he again travelled to Italy in the 1650s, a claim supported to some extent by the mention in 1671 of a *Self-portrait* (untraced) supposedly painted some 20 years earlier in Venice (see 1977 exh. cat.).

The archives of the Antwerp Guild of St Luke include the names of two of Fyt's students: in 1643 Jeronimus Pinckaert, who worked for Fyt for five years before moving to the Netherlands, and in 1649–50 Jacob van de Kerckhoven, the more important of the two. Although Pieter Boel is not mentioned by name, he was also apparently taught by Fyt. Fyt's name also appears frequently in the Antwerp archives as someone involved in disputes and lawsuits over money: against Erasmus Quellinus (ii) (1642), against his brother Peter (1648), his sister Anna (1651), the city of Antwerp (1652), his father-in-law Boudewijn van den Zande (1654–9) and the art dealer Frans Diericx (1656). The painter was apparently a rather rapacious man.

Fyt's oeuvre is extensive: Greindl (1956) listed 287 still-lifes, 166 of which are signed. A large number of these are hunting still-lifes (e.g. *Feathered Game, Mushrooms and Vegetables*, Brussels, Mus. A. Anc.). In addition, there are flower-pieces and numerous scenes with live animals, such as hunts (including those in Munich, Alte Pin.), animal fables and scenes from the poultry-yard. Many of his paintings are dated: development is easy to chart, since work survives from almost every year between 1638 and 1661. There are often replicas (apparently completed by assistants) that date later than the original version of the composition. For example, the best version of the *Bird's Concert* (Vaduz, Samml. Liechtenstein) is dated 1658, while other versions are dated 1661.

Fyt's earliest work, which is not known, was presumably fairly close to that of Snyders, and several hunting-pieces from Snyders's circle have been hypothetically ascribed to Fyt (Robels). The earliest works attributed to Fyt with a greater degree of certainty already show Italian influence: abandoning Snyders's use of local colour, Fyt adopted a tonal palette determined by a dirty brown, grey or moss-green ground. Fyt's approach was emphatic, becoming freer as he developed. The same tendency towards increasingly greater movement can be seen in the choice of dynamic motifs and in the treatment of profiles and contours. The compositions also bear witness to an increasingly daring but always balanced asymmetry (e.g. *Vase of Flowers in a Landscape with a 'Noli me tangere'*,

Jan Fyt: *Vase of Flowers in a Landscape with a 'Noli me tangere'*, oil on canvas, 1.18×1.97 m, *c.* 1660 (Brussels, Musée d'Art Ancien)

c. 1660; Brussels, Mus. A. Anc.; see fig.). The structure of the composition is frequently established by a hierarchy of differently accentuated sections, conveying the feeling of a view that is either in or out of focus. The use of a toned ground allowed Fyt to combine unexpected colours without the result becoming busy or clashing. Fyt's drawings include studies of dogs and hunting scenes, generally executed in pen and wash. A few can be linked directly to finished paintings; for example, the *Still-life with a Man and a Dog* (Düsseldorf, Kstmus.) is repeated in a painting in the Kunsthistorisches Museum, Vienna.

2. CRITICAL RECEPTION AND POSTHUMOUS REPUTATION. Fyt was one of the most prosperous artists in Antwerp, and he had good contacts among the important collectors and patrons of the period. His work is frequently mentioned in 17th-century Antwerp inventories; for example, Erasmus Quellinus (ii) and Johannes Philips Happart each owned half a dozen of Fyt's works, including various oil sketches. In 1649 Fyt appeared as a witness in a case against J. H. Eversberck, who was acting as a purchasing agent for the Governor of the Spanish Netherlands, Leopold William, in whose inventory of 1659 several of Fyt's works can also be found. Among his foreign patrons was Carlo Guasco, Marqués de Solerio, to whom he dedicated a series of etchings of dogs (1642; B. 9–16). He probably had other foreign clients, which would help to explain the subsequent distribution of his works outside the southern Netherlands. Four paintings now in the collection of the Duque de Alba (Madrid, Pal. Liria, Col. Casa Alba) may have belonged to Luis Méndez de Haro y Guzman, 6th Marqués del Carpio, in the 17th century, and the inventory of José Francisco Sarmiento, Conde de Salvatierra, mentions seven that may have come from the collection of Juan, 7th Conde de Monterrey (Governor of the Spanish Netherlands in 1670–75). Isabella Farnese bought various works by Fyt (Madrid, Prado) for her palace at La Granja. Prince Clemens Augustus of Cologne (1700–61) owned some 25 of Fyt's paintings (some now Munich, Alte Pin.).

Fyt occasionally collaborated with colleagues in Antwerp, such as Erasmus Quellinus (ii), Thomas Willeboirts Bosschaert (1614–54; e.g. *Diana at Rest*, Vienna, Ksthist. Mus.), Pieter Thijs and possibly also Jacob Jordaens. A document from 1660 mentions that Jan Breughel the younger, Erasmus Quellinus and Jan Peeters (*b* 1624; *d* before 1680) were at that time prepared to pay Fyt the large sum of 18 guilders a day, which they considered fitting for a painter 'whose work was bought primarily by princes and counts'. Fyt had a tremendous influence on still-life painting in Flanders and the Netherlands as well as Italy. There are at least 13 Flemish painters who can be characterized as followers of Fyt (Greindl, 1956), and their work, particularly that of Pieter Boel and David de Coninck (1636–99), is still sometimes ascribed to him. Fyt's influence in Italy is due not only to his travels there but also to the fact that several of his followers worked there for a time.

BIBLIOGRAPHY

Hollstein: *Dut. & Flem.*; Thieme–Becker; Wurzbach

P. A. Orlandi: *Abecedario pittorico* (1704, rev. 2, ed. P. Guarienti, Venice, 1753), p. 250

A. von Bartsch: *Le Peintre-graveur* (1803–21) [B.]

F. J. Van den Branden: *Geschiedenis der Antwerpsche schilderschool*, 2 vols (Antwerp, 1883), ii, pp. 1085–92 [standard biog.]

W. von Bode: *Die Meister der holländischen und flämischen Malerschulen* (Leipzig, 1917); rev. by E. Plietzsch (Leipzig, 9/1958), pp. 560–66

R. Oldenbourg: *Die flämische Malerei des XVII. Jahrhunderts* (Berlin, 1918, rev. 1922), pp. 193–5

G. Glück: *Rubens, Van Dyck und ihr Kreis*, Gustav Glück Gesammelte Aufsätze, i (Vienna, 1933), pp. 343–8, 362–4

E. Greindl: 'Jan Fyt, peintre de fleurs', *Miscellanea Leo van Puyvelde* (Brussels, 1949), pp. 163–5

M.-L. Hairs: *Les Peintres flamands de fleurs au XVIIe siècle* (Brussels, 1955, rev. 3/1985), pp. 313, 372–6

E. Greindl: *Les Peintres flamands de nature morte au XVIIe siècle* (Brussels, 1956, rev. 1983), pp. 95–107, 348–54 [list of works and useful pls]

D. Bodart: *Les Peintres flamands des Pays-Bas méridionaux et de la principauté de Liège à Rome au XVIIe siècle*, 2 vols (Brussels and Rome, 1970), i, p. 473

C. G., Herzog zu Mecklenburg: *Flämische Jagdbilder von Franz Snyders und Jan Fyt*, Die Jagd in der Kunst (Hamburg and Berlin, 1970), pp. 22–7

G. Keyes: 'Still-life Drawings by Fyt and Snyders', *Burl. Mag.*, cxix (1977), pp. 311–12

Rubens e la pittura fiamminga del seicento nelle collezioni pubbliche fiorentine (exh. cat. by D. Bodart, Florence, Pitti, 1977), p. 325

J. K. Müllenmeister: *Meer und Land im Licht des 17. Jahrhunderts, II: Tierdarstellungen in Werken niederländischen Künstler A-M* (Bremen, 1978), pp. 67–8, pls 144–50

S. A. Sullivan: *The Dutch Gamepiece* (Totowa and Montclair, NJ, 1984), pp. 19–21

A. Balis: 'Fabeluitbeeldingen in de 17de-eeuwse Vlaamse schilderkunst' [The representation of fables in 17th-century Flemish painting], *Zoom op zoo: Antwerp Zoo Focusing on Arts and Sciences*, ed. C. Kruyfhooft (Antwerp, 1985), pp. 263, 265–6

J. P. De Bruyn: 'De samenwerking van Peter Boel en Erasmus II Quellinus', *Jb.: Kon. Mus. S. Kst.* (1985), pp. 286–7

H. Robels: *Frans Snyders: Stilleben- und Tiermaler, 1579–1657* (Munich, 1989)

A. Balis: 'Pieter Thijs, Maarten Pepijn en een derde pseudo-Boeckhorst', *Jan Boeckhorst, 1604–1668: Medewerker van Rubens* (exh. cat., Antwerp, Rubenshuis; Münster, Westfäl. Landesmus.; 1990), pp. 98–9

ARNOUT BALIS

G

Gabae. *See* ISFAHAN.

Gabal al-Silsila. *See* GEBEL EL-SILSILA.

Gabashvili, Georgy [Gigo] **(Ivanovich)** (*b* Tiflis [now Tbilisi], 22 Nov 1862; *d* Tsikhisdziri, 28 Oct 1936). Georgian painter. He studied at the St Petersburg Academy of Arts, where he was influenced by Gotfrid Villeval'de (1818–1903), painter of battle-scenes, and he held his first exhibition in 1891. He was also well acquainted with the Wanderers, and his *Three Townsmen* (1893; Tbilisi, Mus. A. Georg.) displays his aspirations towards Critical Realism. Seeking new sources of inspiration Gabashvili travelled to Central Asia where studies and sketches similar to the work of Vasily Vereshchagin resulted in *Bazaar in Samarkand* (1896; Tbilisi, Mus. A. Georg.; another version, 1897), in which a mastery of drawing is combined with commonplace colouring and weak composition. He also travelled to Munich but was not impressed by the modernism of German painters. In 1895, IL'YA REPIN received a gold medal for his *Zaporozhe Cossacks Write a Letter to the Turkish Sultan* (main version 1880–91; St Petersburg, Rus. Mus.), a painting that greatly influenced Gabashvili, who from 1898 made trips around Georgia for his 'khevsur' cycle (e.g. *Drunken Khevsur*, 1899; Tbilisi, Mus. A. Georg.), which is reminiscent of the psychological portraits of Frans Hals. Under the influence of Repin, Gabashvili painted the multi-figured composition *Alaverdoba* (1898; Tbilisi, Mus. A. Georg.). He devoted the latter part of his life to his students, founding an art studio in 1897, and from 1900 teaching at the school of drawing at the Caucasian Society for the Promotion of the Arts, where he later became Director. From 1922 to 1930 he was the head of the art studio at the Academy of Art in Tbilisi. He remained a staunch realist and made known his opposition to left-wing art.

BIBLIOGRAPHY
G. Gabashvili (exh. cat., Tbilisi, Mus. A. Georg., 1951)
M. Duduchava: *Gigo Gabashvili* (Tbilisi, 1958)
I. A. Urushadze: *Gigo Gabashvili* (Tbilisi, 1958)
Gabashvili, Gigo, 1862–1968 (exh. cat. by K. Bagratishvili, Tbilisi, Mus. A. Georg., 1963)

SERGEY KUZNETSOV

Gabbiani, Anton Domenico (*b* Florence, 13 Feb 1652; *d* Florence, 22 Nov 1726). Italian painter. He first trained with the Medici court portrait painter Giusto Suttermans and then with the painter Vincenzo Dandini. On 20 May 1673 he arrived in Rome, where he studied for three years under Ciro Ferri and Ercole Ferrata at the Accademia Fiorentina. He responded in particular to the paintings of Pietro da Cortona and Carlo Maratti who were both to be important influences on him. Though not precocious, Gabbiani became one of the most noted painters from the Accademia. After a period in Venice (1678–9) with the portrait painter Sebastiano Bombelli, he was in Florence in 1680. By 1684, the year in which he executed an *Annunciation* (destr.) for the Palazzo Pitti, he was an independent painter. His first important public commission, the *St Francis de Sales in Glory* (1685) for the church of SS Apostoli, Florence (*in situ*), shows the influence of Maratti in its grandiose composition and that of Dandini in the treatment of figures. In Prince Ferdinando de' Medici Gabbiani found a particularly loyal patron, and he painted his portrait, *Ferdinando de' Medici and his Musicians* (*c.* 1685; Florence, Pitti). One of the works executed for Ferdinando was possibly a portrait of his sister, which Chiarini has identified with the painting of *Anna Maria Luisa de' Medici* (*c.* 1685; Florence, Pitti). Further works from this period are the group portrait of *Three Musicians* (Florence, Pitti) at Ferdinando's court and a *Group of Courtiers* (1685–90; Florence, Uffizi).

After the marriage in 1689 of Ferdinando to Violante of Bavaria, Gabbiani continued to receive commissions. In December 1690 he returned from a five-month stay in Vienna, where he had gone to paint a portrait of the Habsburg Emperor Leopold I and his son Joseph, King of Bohemia, but had been unable to carry out the commission owing to illness. On his return to Florence, he painted frescoes at Poggio a Caiano (1691; destr.) and in the Prince's apartments in the Palazzo Pitti (1692–3), as well as a decoration (destr.) representing *Parnassus* for the Teatro della Pergola (see Hugford). Gabbiani executed a number of fresco cycles of Classical and mythological subjects in Florentine palaces and villas, including the palazzi Strozzi–Ridolfi (1694), Gerini (1694–5), Corsini (1695), Medici–Riccardi (1690–97) and Orlandini del Beccuto (1697). A large number of preparatory drawings survive for these decorative schemes (Florence, Uffizi). While employed at the Palazzo Corsini he was approached to execute work in the Palazzo Ducale, Genoa, but was prevented from undertaking this commission by Ferdinando. In 1698 he again worked at Poggio a Caiano, executing a fresco of the *Apotheosis of Cosimo il vecchio* (see fig.) for which he was paid 400 scudi. Several of the frescoes executed during this period (e.g. Palazzo Gerini) include beautifully realized landscape views reflecting his

Anton Domenico Gabbiani: *Apotheosis of Cosimo il vecchio* (1698), fresco, Sala da Pranzo, Villa Medici, Poggio a Caiano

personal observation from journeys to Rome and Venice and anticipating the treatment of landscape by Marco Ricci and Sebastiano Ricci.

Possibly at Ferdinando's suggestion, Gabbiani travelled again to Venice in 1699 to study the works of the great Venetian colourists in an attempt to enliven his somewhat monochromatic palette. Between 1702 and 1718 he executed the fresco of the *Assumption of Mary Magdalene* in the cupola of S Frediano in Cestello, Florence (*in situ*). Ferdinando so admired his *Rest on the Flight into Egypt* (1704; Florence, Depositi Gal.) that it was put on public view in the Piazza del Duomo on the Feast of Corpus Domini. After Ferdinando's death in 1713 Gabbiani continued to receive important commissions from the Medici. The *Christ Giving Communion to St Peter of Alcantara in the Presence of St Teresa of Avila* (1714; Schleissheim, Neues Schloss), which shows the influence of Sebastiano Ricci, was possibly commissioned by Cosimo III for his daughter Anna Maria Luisa de' Medici. There were also religious commissions, such as those for the *Assumption of the Virgin* and the *Virgin and Child with the Symbols of the Passion* (both 1720–22; Florence, Uffizi). These and many of his later works reflect both the paintings of Sebastiano Ricci and the classicism of Maratti. At his death, Gabbiani left incomplete a fresco of the *Feast of the Gods* in the Palazzo Incontri, Florence. His funerary monument was erected in S Felice in Piazza, Florence.

There are two *Self-portraits* by Gabbiani of 1685 and *c.* 1715 (both Florence, Uffizi), the latter produced for Cosimo's portrait gallery in the Uffizi.

BIBLIOGRAPHY
I. E. Hugford: *Vita di Anton Domenico Gabbiani pittor fiorentino* (Florence, 1762)
A. Bartarelli: 'Anton Domenico Gabbiani', *Riv. A.*, xxvii (1951–2), pp. 107–30
M. Chiarini: 'Antonio Domenico Gabbiani e i Medici', *Kunst des Barock in der Toskana* (Munich, 1976), pp. 333–43
M. Gregori and E. Schleier, eds: *La pittura in Italia: Il seicento*, ii (Milan, 1988, rev. 1989), p. 749
                                                                          □

Gabburri [Gaburri]**, Francesco Maria Niccolò** (*b* Florence, 16 Jan 1676; *d* Florence, 1742). Italian art historian and collector. He was the son of the Florentine poet Odoardo Gabburri and of Virginia del Becuto. After receiving a good education in music, literature and languages, he studied painting under Onorio Marinari (1627–1715). In 1697 Gabburri married Camilla Bonacossi (*d* 1702), with whom he had three daughters. Grand Duke Cosimo III de' Medici entrusted him with several diplomatic missions, but he soon devoted all his time to collecting and the study of art history. Among contemporary artists to whom he gave encouragement was AGOSTINO CORNACCHINI, who decorated his Palazzo Giuntini, Florence. Pierre-Jean Mariette's visit to Florence in 1719 stimulated Gabburri to begin an ambitious ency-clopedic dictionary of artists' lives, from the primitives to his contemporaries. The entries in the *Vite*, modelled on those of Pellegrino Antonio Orlandi's *Abecedario pittorico* (Bologna, 1704), have remained in manuscript form (Florence, Bib. N. Cent.). Gabburri belonged to a circle of distinguished European connoisseurs, which included the Comte de Caylus and Pierre Crozat. He corresponded frequently with Mariette and was a friend of Jonathan Richardson the elder, Padre Sebastiano Resta, Antonio Balestra and Anton Maria Zanetti the elder. Between 1706 and 1737 he lent 284 works from his collection to exhibitions organized by the Accademia del Disegno, which were held regularly at SS Annunziata, Florence. In 1725 he made what was perhaps his most spectacular purchase: 600 drawings by Fra Bartolommeo found in the convent of S Caterina of Siena and previously owned by Sister Plautilla Nelli (1523–88), who had inherited them. These he bound into three volumes (two of figure studies, now Rotterdam, Mus. Boymans–van Beuningen; one with landscapes, now dispersed, sold Sotheby's, London, 20 November 1957). The catalogue of Gabburri's entire collection of drawings (1722; MS. Florence, Bib. N. Cent.) bears witness to his taste in this field: he possessed numerous pastels and no fewer than 400 drawings by CECCO BRAVO. In 1743 Horace Walpole, 4th Earl of Orford, purchased drawings from Gabburri's collection, acquiring two examples of each artist's work. Most of the rest of the collection of drawings was sold by Gabburri's heirs to the English dealer William Kent in 1758 or 1759.

BIBLIOGRAPHY

G. G. Bottari and S. Ticozzi: *Raccolta di lettere sulla pittura, scultura ed architettura*, 8 vols (Milan, 1822–5), ii, pp. 324–71 [Gabburri's corr. with Mariette and others]

F. Borroni Salvadori: 'Francesco Maria Niccolò Gabburri e gli artisti contemporanei', *An. Scu. Norm. Sup. U. Pisa*, iv/4 (1974), pp. 1503–64

——: 'Le esposizioni d'arte a Firenze dal 1674 al 1767', *Mitt. Ksthist. Inst. Florenz*, i (1974), pp. 1–166

N. Turner: 'The Gabburri/Rogers Series of Drawn Self-portraits and Portraits of Artists', *J. Hist. Col.*, v/2 (1993), pp. 179–216

CATHERINE MONBEIG GOGUEL

Gabetti, Roberto. *See under* NEO-LIBERTY.

Gabla. *See* BYBLOS.

Gable, decorative. Ornamental treatment of the upper part of a wall at the end of a building with a pitched roof. An architectural feature prominently employed in northern Europe in the 16th and 17th centuries, it is one of the very few stylistic inventions of the Renaissance that did not originate in Italy. The earliest recorded use of a Renaissance gable proper was in the Netherlands at the palace (*c.* 1530) of Margaret of Austria at Mechelen. Between the date of this building and that of the masterpiece of the Netherlandish Renaissance, Antwerp Stadhuis (1561–5; *see* ANTWERP, fig. 9), with its vast, classicizing central gable, the foundations were laid for the adoption of gable forms that were to affect architectural development throughout the region. Surviving examples in Ghent, Bruges, Antwerp and other towns bear testimony to the scale of experimentation that took place at this time as the new idiom was grafted on to the traditional stock of Gothic forms.

The decorative gable found its fullest expression in secular architecture. A typical solution was to subdivide the entire façade of a narrow-fronted, well-fenestrated building into smaller units by means of a regular grid of pilasters and cornices. Storey-high bands thus created were 'stacked' in tiers that narrowed progressively upwards to form the gable. The richest decoration was reserved for the parapet protruding beyond the roof-line. Here a variety of ornamental motifs, freely drawn from the classical and Gothic repertories, provided linkages between the 'steps' of the gable as well as a fitting culmination to the vertical emphasis it gave to the entire façade. This simple but effective formula allowed ample scope for individual expression while maintaining the all-important link with the fashionable world of the Renaissance. In the hands of two master designers, Cornelis Floris and, in particular, Hans Vredeman de Vries (see fig.), the system was transformed into STRAPWORK, an even more readily transmittable decorative medium that had a lasting influ-ence in northern Europe after the 1560s.

Gables remained dominant features in both the north-ern and southern Netherlands until the 18th century. In Holland the stepped gable predominated—no fewer than eight varieties were used in Amsterdam alone during the first half of the 17th century—even though the format was sometimes stretched almost beyond recognition, as in the famous neck-gable (*halsgevel*) of Philips Vingboons, where the top storey of the gable is articulated by a full-height central bay, capped by a pediment and linked by scrolls to low-rise flanking bays.

In the southern Netherlands the scrolled gable (*pignon en cloche* or *pignon chantourné*) prevailed during the 17th

Decorative gable designs by Hans Vredeman de Vries, from his *Architectura* (Antwerp, 1563), pl. 146

century. This type, which formed a harmonious transition between the often bizarre configuration of early Netherlandish gables and the formal disposition of the classical front, came in two basic varieties: an aedicule flanked by scrolls, and an ordinary scrolled gable with or without a pediment. The former type, which provided the most direct link with Italian traditions, was first introduced by Alessandro Pasqualini (i) at Buren Castle (*c.* 1540; destr.). The ordinary scrolled gable was probably derived from northern Gothic variants and had a particular attraction for Baroque architects. It flourished during the Jesuits' great church-building campaign in the southern Netherlands in the first quarter of the 17th century. Here too, however, the gable tradition had lost much of its vigour by the end of the century: the magnificent examples erected in Brussels after the French bombardment of 1695 proved to be its swansong.

The Renaissance and Baroque gables of the German-speaking countries paralleled and in some respects surpassed those of the Netherlands. The transformation of the Late Gothic German vernacular also began in the early 16th century, but the arrival of Renaissance ideas via an eastern route as well as a western one brought different interpretations. This was countered from the mid-century by strong Netherlandish influences, especially through the publications of Vredeman de Vries, such as *Architectura* (Antwerp, 1563; see fig.). Consequently the gable tradition that emerged here, while quite distinct from that of the Netherlands, shared many of its characteristics, such as the ornamentation used and the layered design. Differences in appearance arose chiefly from the German gables being generally broader, with a lower window-to-wall ratio and fewer subdivisions. They are also more often found in detached or corner locations rather than in a terrace. This gives them a more 'restful' appearance than their Netherlandish counterparts, a characteristic further enhanced by an early preference for the gentler outline of curvilinear gable forms.

The latter format remained central to gable development in Germany during the 17th and 18th centuries, from the serious-minded efforts of Elias Holl in Augsburg to the exuberant finale of the S-contoured Rococo gable, such as that on the Helblinghaus (*c.* 1730) in Innsbruck. One gable type produced in the region for which there is no counterpart in the Netherlands is the so-called *welsche Gebel*, which is characterized by a large semicircular feature or lunette that caps the façade (*see* WESER RENAISSANCE). This lunette motif probably came from northern Italy, where it may be found on the Scuola Grande di S Marco (1487), Venice. The *welsche Gebel* made its first appearance in Anhalt Saxony and Thuringia in the 1520s and from there spread as far north as Sweden.

Germany and the two Netherlands remained the natural home of the decorative gable throughout the Renaissance and Baroque periods, although it was also adopted by some adjoining countries. Denmark was the most receptive of the Scandinavian countries to influences from its southern neighbours, but no lasting gable tradition was established, despite the example set by Dutch masters during the reign of Christian IV (*fl* 1588–1648). Similarly, no independent style emerged in eastern Europe, although gables similar to those in the German states were used in Silesia, Bohemia, Moravia, Poland and Hungary. Instead, emphasis was placed on the development of a decorative parapet to hide the sunken roof behind. A cross between the two traditions in Bohemia and Moravia, as on the town hall (1537–9) of Litoměřice, produced solutions that rivalled the achievements of contemporary gable designers in the West.

Only in England did the decorative gable receive anything like the attention it was given in its countries of origin. Since there was no precedent for its use in English Gothic architecture, it was probably imported from the Continent in the 16th century. Its subsequent development, however, took an independent course: although there are parallels between English gables and those of other countries, borrowings were rarely literal and no consistent pattern of foreign influence can be identified. At the end of the 16th century the stepped gable was widely abandoned in favour of the curvilinear type. As elsewhere in northern Europe, it would appear that the designs of Vredeman de Vries were significant in determining the format adopted in England, for example at Kirby Hall (*c.* 1570–75), Northants. The decorative gable became an important motif in the formal vocabulary of Jacobean builders, and in a classicized version, as the misnamed 'Dutch gable' with pediment and scrolls, it featured prominently in the English proto-Baroque or Artisan Mannerist phase, as at Swakeleys (1638), Middlesex. Early in his career even Inigo Jones flirted briefly with the use of scrolled gables, for example in his design (1608; Oxford, Worcester Coll.), for the New Exchange, London. The decorative gable retained its popularity longest, however, in the vernacular of the east coast of England, which shared a common building material (brick) and close cultural and trading links with the Continent; it remained in use there until the early 18th century. English gable forms tend to be simpler than those on the Continent. Despite many local variations, a few basic themes were adhered to, notably the ogee contour, which linked up with local Gothic practice.

Decorative gables were also a dominant feature of Dutch colonial architecture, especially in South Africa in the 18th and 19th centuries (*see* CAPE DUTCH STYLE). In Europe, however, changing tastes and the rise of Neoclassicism from the mid-18th century led to a sharp decline in their popularity. Despite serious attempts to reintroduce them, especially during various historicist revivals in the 19th century, decorative gables never again became part of an organic architectural tradition.

For further illustrations *see* MASON, figs 3 and 4.

BIBLIOGRAPHY

C. Buls: *L'Evolution du pignon à Bruxelles* (Brussels, 1908)
C. L. Cudworth: 'The Dutch Gables of East Anglia', *Archit. Rev.* [London], lxxxv (1939), pp. 113–18
P. Müller: 'Die "welschen Gewels": Ein Stil-element der deutschen Renaissance-Architektur', *Minden. Heimatbl.*, xxxiii (1961), pp. 121–39
J. van der Meulen: *Die europäische Grundlage der Kolonialarchitektur am Kap der Gute Hoffnung* (diss., Marburg, Philipps-U., 1962)
G. Hogewood: *De Amsterdamse trapgevel in de zeventiende eeuw* (diss., U. Amsterdam, 1969)
C. Thiels: 'Krulgevels in het Maasland', *Ned. Ksthist. Jb.*, xxii (1971), pp. 41–174
E. Unnerbäck: 'Welsche Giebel: Ein Renaissancemotiv und seine Verbreitung in Mittel- und Nordeuropa', *Antikva. Arkv*, 42 (1971), pp. 1–75

J. Białostocki: *The Art of the Renaissance in Eastern Europe: Hungary, Bohemia, Poland* (Oxford, 1976)

H.-R. Hitchcock: *Netherlandish Scrolled Gables of the Sixteenth and Early Seventeenth Centuries* (New York, 1978)

——: *German Renaissance Architecture* (Princeton, 1981)

H. J. Louw: 'Anglo-Netherlandish Architectural Interchange, *c.* 1600–*c.* 1660', *Archit. Hist.*, xxiv (1981), pp. 1–23

J. Schellekens: 'Scrolled Gables of the Sixteenth and Seventeenth Centuries in the Low Countries', *J. Soc. Archit. Hist.*, li (1992), pp. 430–35

HENTIE LOUW

Gabo, Naum [Pevzner, Naum (Borisovich)] (*b* Klimovichi, Belarus, 5 Aug 1890; *d* Waterbury, CT, 23 Aug 1977). American sculptor of Belorussian birth. He was brought up in the Russian town of Bryansk, where his father owned a metallurgy business. Early paintings display his romantic and literary spirit, for example *Self-portrait* (*c.* 1907–10; artist's family priv. col., see 1986 exh. cat., pl. 128), but in 1910 he went to the University of Munich to study medical and scientific subjects (1910–12), then philosophy and history of art (1912–14). The lectures of Heinrich Wölfflin and the writings of Henri Bergson were significant influences on him at this time. Gabo also studied engineering at the Technische Hochschule, Munich (1912–14), where there was a large collection of mathematical models. During World War I he took refuge in Norway (1914–17) and started working with his 'stereometric method' of construction, one of several techniques he adopted from such models, and through which he made a significant contribution to the development of the language of Constructivism. This enabled him to make images from sheet materials such as cardboard, plywood and galvanized iron, incorporating space in the body of the work and thereby denying the solidity of matter. Around this time he adopted the surname Gabo to distinguish himself from his brother, the artist ANTOINE PEVSNER.

Gabo's first constructed works were figurative (e.g. *Constructed Head No. 2*, 1916; London, artist's family priv. col., see 1986 exh. cat., p. 92), but following his return to Russia in 1917 he started to make non-figurative reliefs and towers from transparent plastic and glass. *Column* (144 mm; London, Tate), his most important architectonic sculpture of this period, was conceived in the winter of 1920–21 as a celluloid model. As he intended with most of his works, Gabo enlarged this construction several times. (There is a 1.05 m version in New York, Guggenheim, and a 1.93 m version in Humlebæk, Louisiana Mus.; both measurements include an integral base.) In 1920, in conjunction with an open-air exhibition on Tverskoy Boulevard, Gabo, together with his brother, published his *Realistic Manifesto*, summarizing his views on art. As with all Gabo's writings this manifesto is poetically forceful and was highly influential. Rejecting Cubism and Futurism Gabo called for an art for a new epoch, a public art recognizing space and time as its basic elements and espousing construction and kineticism. These ideas are embodied in *Kinetic Construction (Standing Wave)*, 1919–20; London, Tate, see fig.).

In 1922 Gabo travelled to Berlin in connection with the *Erste Russische Kunstausstellung*, held at the Van Diemen Gallery, in which he was well-represented with about ten works. There he met Katherine S. Dreier, his first important patron, and he soon came into contact with many

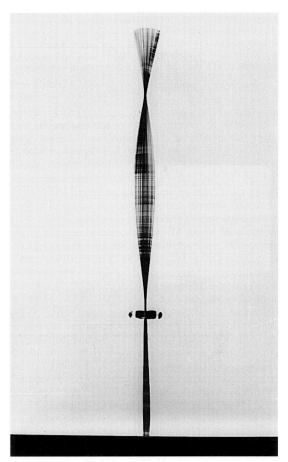

Naum Gabo: *Kinetic Construction (Standing Wave)*, mobile, h. 616 mm, 1919–20 (London, Tate Gallery)

artists and architects, such as Hans Richter, Kurt Schwitters, Hugo Häring, the brothers Hans and Wassili Luckhardt and artists of the Bauhaus. Throughout the 1920s Gabo continued to employ glass, metal (sometimes painted black or white) and plastics in his works, which remained architectonic or monumental in conception (for illustration *see* PLASTIC). He also designed a stage set for Diaghilev's ballet *La Chatte* (model in London, Tate), first performed in Monte Carlo in 1927, and in 1931 he submitted plans to the competition for the Palace of the Soviets in Moscow. In 1930 he had an important one-man show at the Kestner-Gesellschaft in Hannover, and in 1931 he became a member of the group Abstraction–Création in Paris.

By 1933 Gabo had moved to Paris, but in 1935 he made a brief visit to London, where he settled in 1936. There he made friends with Herbert Read, and with Leslie Martin and Ben Nicholson, with whom in 1937 he edited *Circle*. Through Dr John Sisson, Gabo was introduced to perspex, the new plastic developed by Imperial Chemical Industries that he employed in some of his best-known works, such as *Translucent Variation on Spheric Theme* (1937; New York, Guggenheim) and *Spiral Theme* (1941; London, Tate). Gabo made over 20 free-standing variations on the basic 'spheric' theme, differing in size and materials. More elaborate developments include *Model for 'Spheric Construction: Fountain'* (1937/8; London, artist's family priv. col.), *Bas-relief on a Circular Surface, Semi-spheric* (1938; Paris, priv. col.) and *Construction in Space, with Net* (1952; London, artist's family priv. col.). During World War II Gabo lived in Cornwall (1939–46), and there he started using nylon monofilament as in his works entitled *Linear Construction in Space* (e.g. *Linear Construction in Space No. 1 (variation)*, 1942–3; London, Tate). Materials were in short supply during the war, but Gabo was able to continue to paint and carve. In 1943 he was commissioned through the Design Research Unit to design a car for the Jowett Car Company. In 1946 Gabo moved to the USA, where he became a close friend of Lewis Mumford. Following a major exhibition of his works in New York in 1948, he began to receive commissions for public projects. The first of these, for the Esso Building at the Rockefeller Center (1949), New York, remained unexecuted, but in 1951 he completed his *Construction Suspended in Space* for the Baltimore Museum of Art. There followed an important commission for the *Bijenkorf Construction* in Rotterdam (h. *c.* 25 m, 1956–7), through which Gabo intended to celebrate the reconstruction of the city following World War II. Ultimately related to the 'spheric theme', this work was developed directly from his entry to the international competition for which he submitted a *Model for a Monument to the Unknown Political Prisoner* (410 mm, 1952; London, Tate), which gained one of the five second prizes. In the early 1950s Gabo took up wood-engraving, which he used until the mid-1970s to explore the same concepts as his sculpture (see 1986 exh. cat., p. 190).

Gabo's work does not fit simply into the machine aesthetic. As he wrote in 1957: 'Not the Machine—the creative spirit of man is my inspiration'. An artist of diverse interests, Gabo was fascinated and influenced by scientific and mathematical images, whether visually or verbally described, and particularly by the enigmas of science. While he valued supremely the autonomy of the artist, he also sought to integrate not only sculpture, architecture and design but also art and science. Thus he felt that his 'constructive idea' could serve as a philosophy not only for art but for life in general.

WRITINGS

with Antoine Pevsner: *Realistichsekiy Manifest* [Realistic manifesto] (Moscow, 1920)
with J. L. Martin and B. Nicholson, eds: *Circle: International Survey of Constructive Art* (London, 1937) [incl. two essays by Gabo]
Gabo: Constructions, Sculpture, Paintings, Drawings, Engravings (London, 1957) [contains essays by Herbert Read and Leslie Martin and a selection of Gabo's writings]
Of Divers Arts: The A. W. Mellon Lectures in Fine Arts, National Gallery of Art, Washington, DC, 1959, Bollingen Series, xxxv/8 (Princeton, 1962, 2/1971)

BIBLIOGRAPHY

Alexei Pevsner: *A Biographical Sketch of my Brothers: Naum Gabo and Antoine Pevsner* (Amsterdam, 1964)
C. Lodder: *Russian Constructivism* (New Haven, 1983)
Naum Gabo: Sixty Years of Constructivism (exh. cat., ed. S. A. Nash, J. Merkert and C. Lodder; Dallas, Mus. A., 1986) [incl. cat. rais. of constructions and sculptures and extensive bibliog. comp. C. C. Sanderson]
Naum Gabo: Monoprints (exh. cat., ed. G. Williams; U. Cambridge, Kettle's Yard, 1987)

COLIN C. SANDERSON

Gabon [République Gabonaise]. Country on the Atlantic coast of western equatorial Africa, bordered by Equatorial Guinea and Cameroon to the north and by the Republic of Congo to the east and south. Gabon became independent in 1960. Its capital is Libreville and French is the national language.

1. GEOGRAPHY AND CULTURAL HISTORY. Gabon's heavy rainfall and warm temperatures mean that much of the country's total area of *c.* 267,667 sq. km is covered by tropical rainforest. Its population (*c.* 1,113,000; UN estimate, 1989) is increasingly concentrated in urban areas, leaving the interior plateau sparsely inhabited. Pygmies occupied the dense Gabonese rainforest from *c.* 5000 BC, followed by migrating Bantu-speaking peoples from *c.* AD 1000. The first European contact was made in the 1470s by Portuguese maritime explorers, and slaves and ivory were major exports until the mid-19th century. European merchants, missionaries and officials established permanent settlements, and the Fang peoples began a migration from their homeland near Cameroon to these commercial centres. By the 1880s the country was one of the four territories of French Equatorial Africa, becoming the French Congo in 1890 and then Gabon (within the French Congo) in 1903. Independence from French colonial rule was secured on 17 August 1960.

This entry covers the art produced in the area since colonial times. For the art of the region in earlier periods *see* AFRICA, §VII, 5. *See also* FANG and KOTA (ii).

2. CONTINUING TRADITIONS. Traditional Gabonese art is used by indigenous associations for education and adjudication, anti-witchcraft therapy and ancestral commemoration. It includes masks, reliquaries, religious architectural elements, musical instruments, costumes, accessories and body decoration.

The Ogowe River style of white-face masks continue to be danced publicly in quasi-traditional contexts. These feminine clay-whitened masks include full, rounded, naturalistic representations (belonging to the Punu, Lumbo, Vili, Vungu, Varama, Ngove, Myene, Eshira and Galwa peoples); flat, graphic, abstract forms (of the Vuvi, Sango, Sangui, Ondumbo and Njabi peoples); and those combining face and helmet forms, different planes and masses, and variations of white and red colours (employed by the Fang, Kota, Kwele, Obamba, Wumbu, Ndassa, Enenga, Aduma, Adjuma, Apindji and Wundji peoples).

Bwiti religion and its offshoot, Mbiri, perpetuate both classical and more modern interpretations of traditional Gabonese art. Bwiti originated as the centre of the religious and social life of the Tsogo people, and its Fang form combines Tsogo and Christian sources with similar, pre-existing Fang religious and artistic conceptions. Bwiti art forms include such interior elements as painted posts, lintels, bark walls, stools, reliquaries, *ngombi* figurated harps and *obango* drums. Other mainstays of traditional art are basketry and the *sinkhosi* reliquaries of southern Gabon. In basketry, whole stalks and raffia, as well as rattan strips of palm, bamboo, reed, liana, pandanus and bark, are handwoven into the armature and roofing of traditional wattle-and-daub architecture, workaday baskets, boxes, bags, furniture, mats, nets, traps, bands and loincloths, as well as the essential fringe and costume of traditional masks.

3. POPULAR ARTS. Gabon has had one highly successful form of tourist art, known as Mbigou sculpture, which is named after one of the two villages in Ngounie Province, south-central Gabon, where the tradition originated. At first the tradition comprised only utilitarian pipes, vases and jars, fashioned from the greenish-grey or reddish-brown serpentine found in hills surrounding the village of Mbigou. After extraction the serpentine was carved with adzes and knives and given a lustrous patina by heating and rubbing with palm oil. Between 1927 and 1930 the

Mbigou Basket Carrier (*porteuse*) by Massala, steatite, h. 280 mm, from the Alibadeng workshop, Libreville, Gabon, 1978 (USA, private collection)

local French colonial administrators encouraged the carvers to expand their repertory to create souvenir sculptures based on traditional masks and figures. The revamped craft was established and spread through the work of such carvers as Moulaloukou (*d* 1962), Tanga (*d* 1954), Tsamba and Baupaul. In the 1960s and 1970s production was taken over by such younger carvers as Massala, Lossangoye and Makambo in the Alibadeng workshop near Libreville Airport and the Village de Lumière workshop in Lambaréné. One of the successes of the modern reinterpretation of indigenous art, Mbigou sculpture represented Gabon in the FESTAC world festival of African culture held in 1977 in Lagos, Nigeria.

In general, Mbigou sculpture may be seen as a reinterpretation in stone of traditional Gabonese art forms. Traditional stylistic features include eyes shaped like cowrie shells and bun coiffures, while traditional subjects include such village archetypes as the Mother and Child, the Basket Carrier, the Drummer, the Harp Player and the Cook. The Mbigou Basket Carrier or *porteuse* (see fig.) represents a common traditional form while also offering a reinterpretation of this frequent subject of traditional Punu/Lumbo pendant miniatures. The posture, eyes, heart-shaped face and patina are classically Gabonese, while the *pagne*-skirt is a more recent innovation.

The most visible domestic popular art form comprises the fabrics that are tailored into the formal shirts and dresses worn on such national holidays as the Fête de la Jeunesse. Consistent design features are the national colours (blue, yellow and green) and the heraldic device of an escutcheon framing a black-and-white photographic portrait of Gabon's second president, El Hadj Omar Bongo.

4. FINE ARTS. Painting in Gabon is represented by such artists as Koumba Gratien (*b* 1965). In 1989 he won a prize at the 1989 Centre International des Civilisations Bantu (CICIBA) Biennale while also working as a sign painter and attending the Ecole Nationale des Arts et Manufactures (ENAM). Another painter, Marcellin Minkoe-Minze (*b* 1953), a professor at ENAM, developed a nationalistic style, exemplified by an untitled, symbolist oil painting in which two expressionistic reclining nudes may be seen as the focus of a cyclical, layered history of Gabon. The convergence and metamorphosis of opposites are symbolized by the Ogowe River style white-face masks worn by the nudes and by a half-moon pendant.

Modern Gabonese sculpture is represented by the decorative wood-carving commissioned in 1967 for the interior of the Catholic church, St Michael of Nkembo, Libreville, from the self-taught Zephyrin Lendogno (*b c.* 1930) and his assistants, and carried out over 17 years. The varnished, low-relief carving of 31 pillars, the pulpit and a baptismal font translates traditional sculptural forms into languid narrative compositions (for illustrations see exh. cat., p. 103).

Classically Bantu visual forms are also combined with Western idioms in architecture, as exemplified in the Libreville headquarters of CICIBA, designed by the Gabonese architect A. G. Mangala. The parallel front and rear buildings of the low-lying, H-shaped ground-plan are connected by an atrium and a central, longitudinal corridor, ending in an arboretum-flanked plaza.

5. ART LIFE AND ORGANIZATION. Since independence, contemporary popular art and fine art have played major roles in defining and communicating Gabon's ethnic and national identity. Indigenous and Western materials, markets and technologies have been successfully combined. New works of traditional art have continued to be commissioned for ritual purposes by such religious groups and associations as Bwiti and Mbiri (*see* §2 above), while older works have been collected by ethnologists and dealers for the Musée des Arts et Traditions, Libreville, and for Western museums and private collectors. The export market in fakes and replicas of traditional Gabonese art is centred in Douala, Cameroon.

Most of Gabon's fine artists live in the capital, where there is maximum potential for exhibition and patronage. Faced with cramped, multifunctional studio space (see exh. cat., p. 190) and expensive materials in limited supply, artists support themselves and their families by the exhibition and sale of fine art while crossing back and forth into commercial art. Although contemporary fine art is increasing in production in Gabon, it has yet to establish a market in the West. CICIBA is its largest patron in Gabon, followed by many of the foreign, African and national governmental offices, hotels, banks and businesses. The popular arts of Mbigou sculpture and national fabrics (*see* §3 above) are patronized respectively, though not exclusively, by foreigners and native Gabonese.

CICIBA was established in 1983 by Gabon's President Bongo and has ten member nations: Angola, the Central African Republic, Comoros, the Republic of Congo, Equatorial Guinea, Gabon, Rwanda, São Tomé and Principé, Zaïre and Zambia. Gabonese fine art has been included in the first three biennales of contemporary art organized by CICIBA, held in 1985 and 1989 in Libreville and in 1987 in Kinshasa. The Musée des Arts et Traditions in Libreville was founded in 1963 and directed by the French until 1975. Its permanent collection of ethnographic and folk art material has been acquired through fieldwork.

Art education is provided by the Ecole Nationale des Arts et Manufactures, Libreville, where sculpture in various materials, easel painting, fresco painting and decorative ceramic painting are taught. At a less advanced level, basketry is a mandatory subject in primary schools.

BIBLIOGRAPHY

H. Kayser, ed.: *Gabun: Gestern und Heute* (Hildesheim, 1973)

M. W. Mount: *African Art: The Years since 1920* (Bloomington, IN, 1973)

B. Allainmat and A. Guyon: *Pierres de M'bigou* (Paris, 1977)

M. Rémy: *Le Gabon aujourd'hui* (Paris, 1977)

J. Anquetil: *L'Artisanat créateur au Gabon* (Paris, 1983)

Badi-Bangwa Ne Mwine: *Art contemporain Bantu: Deuxième biennale du CICIBA, Kinshasa, juillet 1987*

B. Allainmat Mahine and B. Arenant: *Art contemporain Bantu* (Libreville, 1989) [on 3rd CICIBA biennale]

S. Peters and others, eds: *Directory of Museums in Africa/Répertoire des musées en Afrique* (London and New York, 1990)

Africa Explores (exh. cat., ed. S. Vogel; New York, Cent. Afr. A., 1991)

N. Guez: *L'Art africain contemporain/Contemporary African Art: Guide Edition 92–94* (Paris, 1992) [directory of artists and art institutions]

S. Njami, ed.: 'Libreville–Gabon', *Rev. Noire*, v (1992), pp. 1–31

Sculpture gabonaise contemporaine (exh. cat., Paris, Mus. N. A. Afr. & Océan., 1992–3)

D. FRANCINE FARR

Gaboury, Etienne-Joseph (*b* Bruxelles, Manitoba, 24 April 1930). Canadian architect. He was educated at St Boniface College (BA, 1953) and the University of Manitoba in Winnipeg (BArch, 1958). He won a French government scholarship to attend the Ecole des Beaux-Arts in Paris (1958–9). Following an apprenticeship in Winnipeg, he entered into partnership with Denis Lussier (1938–75) and S. F. J. Sigurdson (*b* 1935). From 1976 he was principal of Gaboury Associates Incorporated. Gaboury was strongly influenced by the later work of Le Corbusier, in particular the chapel of Notre Dame du Haut at Ronchamp with its mystical light-filled interior and sense of immeasurable space. His work always reflected a deep concern and a personal search for the regional influences on architecture as manifested by the landscape, climate and the vivid quality of the Canadian prairie sunlight.

One of Gaboury's important early projects was the Eglise du Précieux Sang in St Boniface, Manitoba, a strikingly mystical space employing a double helical structure. Another important commission was the St Boniface Cathedral project (1972) in which a smaller, modern basilica was inserted within the ruined walls of the original structure, which had been damaged by fire in 1968. The Canadian Embassy in Mexico City (1981) is an example of Gaboury's interest in contextualism. Exterior materials and textures defer to Mexico's Mayan past while the interior atrium is filled with Canadian references reflecting an increasng concern with the metaphorical aspects of architecture. He holds numerous Canadian architecture and heritage awards and is a member of the Royal Canadian Academy and a Fellow of the Royal Architectural Institute of Canada.

WRITINGS

'Towards a Prairie Architecture', *Prairie Forum*, v/2 (1980), pp. 237–47

BIBLIOGRAPHY

C. W. Thomsen: 'Etienne Gaboury: Architektur in der Prairie', *Parnass* (May/June 1985), pp. 46–53

R. DOUGLAS GILLMOR

Gabrawi, Dayr al-. *See* GEBRAWI, DEIR EL-.

Gabriel. French family of architects. Jacques I Gabriel (*b* Argentan) was sufficiently prominent before the end of the first decade of the 17th century to be called upon to provide Rouen with a Hôtel de ville. His sons Maurice I Gabriel (*b* 1602; *d* 1649) and Jacques II Gabriel (*b* 1605) practised architecture in Normandy and Touraine respectively. Maurice's sons Jacques III Gabriel (*b* 1637; *d* 1697) and Maurice II Gabriel (*b* 1639; *d* 1693), practised in Paris, where they were eclipsed in importance by Jacques II's son (1) Jacques IV Gabriel. Jacques IV's second son, (2) Jacques V Gabriel, also became an architect, but the most distinguished member of the family was Jacques V's son (3) Ange-Jacques Gabriel.

(1) Jacques IV Gabriel (*b c.* 1637; *d* 1686). He married the great-niece of François Mansart in 1664 and thereby allied the Gabriel family to Jules Hardouin Mansart, the future Premier Architecte du Roi. Active in Paris on royal works (including the Pont Royale) and the Hôtel de Condé, Jacques IV was a founder member of the Académie Royale d'Architecture. He collaborated with Jules Hardouin Mansart at Versailles and Clagny and, as Architecte Ordinaire du Roi, was one of the principals in the office of the Premier Architecte at Versailles. He was responsible in particular for the château of Choisy for Mlle de Montpensier from 1680. Clearly related to Clagny in its clear-cut horizontal lines, countered only by the tall rectangular windows and light rustication to the slight projections at salient points, its sparing use of the Orders and its sculptural detail, Choisy marks Jacques IV Gabriel as a major progenitor of the 'noble simplicity' that the school of Jules Hardouin Mansart inherited from such late Parisian works of François Mansart as the Hôtel Guéné-gaud in the Rue des Archives.

(2) Jacques V Gabriel (*b* ?Paris, 1667; *d* Fontainebleau, 1742). Son of (1) Jacques IV Gabriel. His mother bought him the office of Contrôleur Général des Bâtiments et Jardins du Roi on the death of its incumbent, Jules Hardouin Mansart's brother Michel Hardouin (1647–87). Thereafter Jacques V was trained in the Premier Architecte's office with Robert de Cotte; the two, lifelong friends and colleagues, visited Italy together in 1689–90. Gabriel was active in the bureau of the Bâtiments du Roi from the mid-1690s and rapidly became Jules Hardouin Mansart's principal assistant after Robert de Cotte. He was admitted to the Académie Royale d'Architecture in 1699, ennobled in 1704, made Architecte Ordinaire and Contrôl-eur des Dedans du Château de Versailles in 1709 (the year after de Cotte succeeded Jules Hardouin Mansart as Premier Architecte) and became Premier Ingénieur des Ponts et Chaussées in 1716. He succeeded de Cotte as Premier Architecte and Director of the Académie Royale d'Architecture in 1734 and 1735 respectively.

Jacques V's career as a principal officer in the Bâtiments du Roi coincided with a period of comparative inactivity. However, he was extensively employed by private patrons and on public works in the provinces. His name is associated with several Paris houses, most plausibly the former Hôtel Varangeville in Rue St-Dominique (1704), the Hôtel de Blouin in Faubourg St-Honoré (1718) and the Folie de Gramont at Issy (1714); he worked for the financier John Law and speculated on his own behalf in and around the Place Vendôme. One of the first public works attributable to him is the bishop's palace at Blois, probably designed in 1698 while he was Contrôleur of Chambord. After the heavily encumbered medieval bridge at Blois was swept away in 1716, he was responsible for the construction of its replacement over the following decade. From 1725 he supervised the rebuilding of Rennes after the fire of 1720, laying out the Place du Palais des Etats before Salomon de Brosse's great building and the Place Neuve before his own clock tower and monument to Louis XV flanked by twin buildings for the Présidial and the Hôtel de Ville (1730). From 1732 he worked for the Compagnie des Indes at Lorient, providing projects for the directors' building among administrative and commercial complexes. As a major element in the modernization of Bordeaux he was entrusted in 1729 with the construction of the Place Royale framing an equestrian

monument to Louis XV. The scheme was enlarged to embrace a building for the Bourse, plans for which were finalized in 1741, but the pressure of other work, including the urgent need to rebuild the Chambre des Comptes in Paris after a fire of 1737, distracted Gabriel, and the completion of the Bordeaux complex was left to his son, (3) Ange-Jacques Gabriel. In 1724 he was called on to complete the scheme for a Place Royale and the reform of the ancient Palais des Estates at Dijon, evolved by Mansart and Cotte after 1683: he was responsible in particular for the pedestal of the equestrian statue of Louis XIV that the hemicyclical place was to frame, the west wing of the Palais with its sumptuous portal and staircase leading to the Salle des Etats (1731, 1735) and the embellishment of the Chapelle des Elus (1737). He designed the cathedral of La Rochelle in 1741 but left its completion to his son. He designed choir stalls for the cathedral of Orléans in 1702 and contributed to the completion of the Neo-Gothic west front there from 1723.

For Louis XV, Jacques V's first concern was with the small pavilion of La Muette in the Bois de Boulogne, which the child king had been given as his own in 1719, and in 1737 he laid down the lines upon which it was to be transformed over the following decade. In the later 1730s he was also commissioned to expand the accommodation for the King's entourage at Compiègne and Fontainebleau: the Compiègne work was absorbed and eclipsed by the comprehensive rebuilding of the château after 1747, and the Louis XV wing at Fontainebleau, begun in 1738, was finished in several stages after Jacques V's death by Ange-Jacques, who had collaborated on the project from its inception. From 1735, too, the Premier Architecte was responsible for adding to and redecorating the King's private rooms at Fontainebleau. After the return of the court to Versailles in 1722, the first major campaign of redecoration was concentrated on the queen's apartments for Marie Leczinska in 1725, and, as Contrôleur des Dedans du Château, Jacques V no doubt contributed to it. Louis XV's extended campaign of work on the expansion of his own apartments began effectively the year after Jacques V became Premier Architecte with the great series of rooms that constituted the private apartment along the northern side of the Cour de Marbre. Here and in the contemporary work on the queen's private apartments, Jacques was assisted by his son Ange-Jacques, who had succeeded him as Contrôleur de Versailles.

As a principal in Jules Hardouin Mansart's office, Jacques V Gabriel shared the responsibility for the evolution of the Rococo style of interior decoration, but the precise scope of his contribution is impossible to determine, despite his association with major examples of work in the genre from the choir stalls at Orléans to the *Petits Appartements* at Versailles. Developed from the beginning of the century to meet new requirements of comfort in small rooms, the non-monumental, anti-architectonic Rococo, with its unstable masses, ambivalent spaces, vigorous contours and free-ranging repertory of ornament, was not allowed fundamentally to affect exteriors. However, Jacques V and his colleagues used restrained curves and refined Rococo detail in both stone and wrought iron to modulate the lucid, harmonious Academic Classicism inherited from Jules Hardouin Mansart and the contemporaries of Jacques IV.

(3) Ange-Jacques Gabriel (*b* Paris, 1698; *d* Paris, 1782). Son of (2) Jacques V Gabriel. Presumably educated in the circle of the Premier Architecte, he was a member of the Académie Royale d'Architecture by 1728 and was assisting his father on the Place Royale at Bordeaux in 1729. Ange-Jacques does not seem to have followed in his father's footsteps to Italy or to have shared his private career. Preoccupied from the outset with work on royal buildings, under his father, he developed a special relationship with Louis XV, who had a sophisticated appreciation of architecture. He became Contrôleur de Versailles in 1734 and succeeded Jacques V as Premier Architecte and Director of the Académie Royale d'Architecture in 1742. In these capacities he was responsible for all the major royal projects of the reign, and Louis XV's full maturity as a patron coincides with Ange-Jacques's period as Premier Architecte. He gave up that office in March 1775, within the first year of the new reign, but retained the honorary title and the directorship of the Académie until his death.

Under him—and a king obsessed with privacy, comfort and change—there was incessant reorganization of the royal apartments in the major châteaux: Versailles, Fontainebleau, Compiègne and Choisy. Change was impelled by Gabriel's capacity to meet the King's costly desire for redecoration in accordance with transformations in taste that must be accounted among Europe's most refined. Decorum was a major consideration too, but convenience was certainly no less important. Antique warrens of communications were rationalized, with new corridors and staircases conveniently related to new covered entrances. Rooms were regularized and enlarged, and new facilities, such as dining rooms and bathrooms, installed. The King's bedroom and Council Chamber at Fontainebleau (1751–4) are among the most spectacular legacies of all this change. However, the process may be marked at Versailles by the elegant Rococo rooms of the King's private apartments (begun under Jacques V) and the Dauphin's establishment (1746–7); the still richer rooms of Mme Adelaide (1752) and the sumptuous Council Chamber (1755) respectively succeeding and preceding the King's first-floor private suite; the tectonic scheme for the King's dining room (1753) off the *enfilade*, which was itself 'modernized' in 1755, and successive changes to the still more private accommodation on the floors above; and, finally, the new ground-floor rooms for Mesdames and the last additions to the King's first-floor suite (from the late 1760s), extremely refined Rococo in the main but culminating in the essentially architectonic King's library (1774).

Beyond internal changes, Gabriel worked throughout his career on schemes for renovating and enlarging Versailles, Fontainebleau, Compiègne, La Muette, Choisy and Bellevue: the first three, the King's principal residences, were transformed. In 1742–3 he produced a comprehensive project for replacing unsound building, including the inconveniently placed Ambassadors' Staircase, and for upgrading the decorum of the Cour Royale at Versailles. This project was modified in 1749, revised in 1754 and

1. Ange-Jacques Gabriel: interior of the Opéra, Versailles, 1748–70

1759 and partially realized in 1772–5. The early versions translated Jules Hardouin Mansart's Ionic garden front into Doric, recommended for entrances by Academic theory, but Gabriel's interest in the Louvre, particularly in Giovanni Lorenzo Bernini's third project, was predominant from 1759. At Fontainebleau, schemes for the Cour du Cheval Blanc and the Cour de la Fontaine responded to the revised Gros Pavillon (1749–50) between them. Their monumental transformation in the early 1770s incorporated alternative ideas for a triumphal entrance arch, which acknowledged the mastery of Philibert de L'Orme at Anet. The project evolved from 1747–50, for Compiègne's rebuilding was consistent in style with the Louis XV wing at Fontainebleau, but the revisions of the 1760s—altered in execution by Gabriel's pupil Ledreux—echo the impact of the Louvre on the project for Versailles.

All Louis XV's châteaux were to have theatres: that embraced by Gabriel's comprehensive project for Versailles and begun in 1748 was to be one of Europe's masterpieces. A Rococo scheme was developed in the 1750s under the influence of the Teatro Reggio in Turin. The precedents set for the French court by Gaspare Vigarani in the 17th century were not forgotten in architectonic revisions of the 1760s, and from 1765 the scheme was transformed with reference to Andrea Palladio into the essentially Neo-classical Opéra completed in 1770 for the wedding of the future Louis XVI to Marie-Antoinette (see fig. 1).

To cater for the King's desire to retreat from court with the Marquise de Pompadour, hermitages were built at each of the main châteaux. The one at Fontainebleau and the simpler Pavillon Français at Trianon (1749–50) were the first. In 1754 another was built in the gardens of Compiègne and a much more substantial example added at Choisy. If the latter followed the Grand Trianon, though on an intimate scale, the château of Marly provided the model for the Petit Trianon (see VERSAILLES, §4), the culminating masterpiece of the series. The nearly-cubical block resolved the conflicting axes and levels of the entrance and the formal garden leading to the Grand Trianon, while subtle variations on the use of the Corinthian order coped with aspects ranging from entrance court and formal garden to the various facilities of an important botanical garden.

Variations on the theme of the hermitage provided hunting lodges in the forests around Versailles and Saint-Germain-en-Laye. In 1750 at Le Butard near Vaucresson, and again in 1766 at La Muette near Saint-Germain, the elegant order of a garden retreat was replaced by virile rustication. In 1755 the same approach was expanded for Saint-Hubert near Rambouillet; over the next 20 years this developed into an extensive château, Gabriel's only known unconstrained exercise in that genre.

Gabriel does not appear to have had a private practice beyond work done at the King's behest for members of the royal circle, particularly at Ménars for the Marquise de Pompadour and at Louveciennes for the Comtesse Du Barry. However, in his capacity as Premier Architecte he was responsible for a number of important public works. He completed the cathedral at La Rochelle and the Place Royale at Bordeaux, begun by his father, and he was

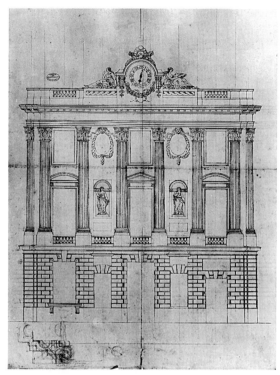

2. Ange-Jacques Gabriel: Aile du Gouvernement, Versailles, elevation of the end pavilion and sketch (below) of alterations, pen and ink, 720×480 mm, 1771 (Paris, Archives Nationales)

heavily involved in other schemes for Bordeaux, substantially revising a local project for the Place de Bourgogne in particular (1751). He demonstrated his abilities as a town planner in Paris but did not work on a great metropolitan church in France: the two most important Parisian commissions in the field, for the rebuilding of the Madeleine and St Geneviève, went to Pierre Contant d'Ivry and Jacques-Germain Soufflot respectively. Frederik V of Denmark called on him to revise a local scheme for the Frederikskirchen (1754) in Copenhagen, but he was superseded there by Nicolas-Henri Jardin, and, apart from the splendid chapel of the Ecole Militaire in Paris (late 1760s), his executed work in the ecclesiastical field was limited to the parish church and presbytery of Choisy (1748 and 1764).

Begun in 1750, the vast project for the Ecole Militaire was conceived to provide professional training for potential officers in the light of France's experience in the War of the Austrian Succession. In both its original form, rivalling in extent the neighbouring Invalides, and the much reduced revisions of 1768, Gabriel modelled his main façade on the two 17th-century schemes executed for the south front of the Louvre. The pre-eminence accorded to the Louvre by the Académie, over which he presided, was also acknowledged by Gabriel in his other Parisian public work: his entry for the inconclusive competition of 1748 for the Place Louis XV and the synthesis he was required to provide of all that the King found best in the entries to the second competition of 1753. This was specifically concerned with the site provided by the King at the foot of the Tuileries gardens: Gabriel's moats, ballustrades and sentry boxes (sadly omitted in the 19th-century transformation of the Place de la Concorde) responded to the King's stipulation that the views of the gardens, river and Champs Elysées were not to be obstructed. The palaces that form the backdrop to the square reveal the influence of the scheme of Claude Guillot-Aubry (1703–71) and the chapel at Versailles as much as Gabriel's own academic interest in the Louvre. This last interest, from 1754, turned to practical preoccupation with the completion of the Square Court to house the royal academies and a Grand Council Chamber.

Gabriel gave practical expression to the Academic Classical principles elaborated by Jacques-François Blondel and his predecessors. In particular, he was guided by the ideal of emulation—of aspiring to transcend canonical example. Propriety recommended certain models: the colonnade of the Louvre, the garden front of Versailles, the châteaux of Marly and Maisons. Genius could transform them by the original application of compositional techniques also stamped with the authority of the masters. From the mainstream of the French classical tradition, brought to its highest degree of sophistication by Mansart, Gabriel derived the ability to unify and simultaneously accent his masses—whether complex, as in the projects to rebuild Versailles (see fig. 2), or compact, as in the Gros Pavillon at Fontainebleau—by varying the plasticity of a consistently applied order in response to variations in the plane of the wall. In solving specific design problems he was more flexible than the theoretician Blondel and revived Mannerist techniques or resorted to Roman High Baroque ones in lieu of French classical orthodoxy. An example of the first is the interpenetration of forms to assert the small sentry boxes that played a major role in defining the Place Louis XV. An example of the second, inspired by Bernini's third Louvre project, is the 1759 scheme for Versailles, where the wall is confronted with an order conceived of as an independent, rather than merely articulating, agent. Further, the juxtaposition of wings and contrasting main block, as in the Ecole Militaire or the presbytery of Choisy, recalls Bernini's Palazzo Chigi.

Sixteenth-century Italian and French examples, too, inspired Gabriel c. 1750 to adopt a repertory of decorative detail that was more architectonic than that favoured by his immediate predecessors. In line with the work of the most advanced of his contemporaries, Soufflot in particular, this was complemented with strictness of line, firmness of form and simplicity of contour to correct prevailing French practice: the sumptuousness of projects like those from the 1740s for rebuilding Versailles, La Muette and Compiègne gave way to 'noble simplicity' resulting from the restriction of ornament to the articulating members of a building—above all the order and the frames of doors and windows, as at Saint-Hubert (1756) or the Petit Trianon. Reversing the tentative spread of free-ranging Rococo ornament from interiors to exteriors in the primarily domestic practice of the early years of Louis XV, Gabriel was among the first to bring the architectonic approach to bear on the transformation of interior decoration when unconstrained by existing work—for instance, in the Pavillon Français (1749; see fig. 3) and at Saint-Hubert.

3. Ange-Jacques Gabriel: interior of the Pavillon Français, Trianon, Versailles, 1749

Because much of his career was spent avoiding disparity between new and existing work, as propriety required, Gabriel may be seen as conservative, but to characterize him as such is to ignore the radical implications of his unconstrained works. Early among these, the Choisy project of 1746 shows his preference for clear-cut masses; the architectonic repertory of detail, the juxtaposition and confrontation of contrasting forms, anticipated at the end of the 1740s in Le Butard, are fully developed by the mid-1760s for Compiègne and the Choisy presbytery. Gabriel's mature achievement leads directly to the hard-edged, rationalist forms and collage-like compositions of the most radical among the second generation of French Neo-classicists.

BIBLIOGRAPHY

E. Fels: *Ange-Jacques Gabriel* (Paris, 1912; rev. 1924)
C. Tadgell: 'Gabriel's Grands Projets for Versailles', *Archit. Rev.*, clvii/937 (March 1975), pp. 155–64
——: *Ange-Jacques Gabriel* (London, 1978) [extensive bibliography]
M. Gallet and Y. Bottineau: *Les Gabriel* (Paris, 1982) [bibliography]

CHRISTOPHER TADGELL

Gabriël. Dutch family of artists.

(1) Paulus Joseph Gabriël (*b* Amsterdam, 11 July 1784; *d* Amsterdam, 1 Jan 1834). Sculptor. He was the son of a sculptor and ornamental mason. From 1805 to 1807 he trained as a miniature painter and draughtsman in Paris before turning to sculpture in 1807. In that year he received financial support from Louis-Napoleon to remain in Paris, where he worked in the workshop of Pierre Cartellier and from 1810 studied at the Ecole des Beaux-Arts. Although he did not win the Prix de Rome, he was allowed to go to Rome, staying in the Villa Medici with other Dutch artists. Gabriël established a close friendship with Antonio Canova, who became his artistic mentor; the period he spent in Rome was to have a lasting influence on his later development. In 1813 he returned to Cartellier's workshop in Paris; shortly afterwards William I asked him to become Royal Sculptor. In 1814 he was also appointed City Sculptor of Amsterdam on condition that he returned to the Netherlands, which he subsequently did.

Gabriël achieved considerable success early in his career with sculptures that were mostly Classical in inspiration. His portrait busts were particularly successful, notably those of *Cornelis Apostool* (*c.* 1815; Amsterdam, Rijksmus.) and *P. C. Hooft* (1817; Amsterdam, Trippenhuis). In addition he made a number of funerary sculptures: among the finest is the monument (1819; Amsterdam, Nieuwe Kerk) to *Vice-Admiral J. H. van Kinsbergen* (1735–1819), who had been a great admirer and generous patron of Gabriël. In 1820 Gabriël was appointed Director of the sculpture department at the Koninklijke Academie van Beeldende Kunsten in Amsterdam. He held the post until his death, but his partly classical, partly eclectic work brought him no followers.

FRANSJE KUYVENHOVEN

BIBLIOGRAPHY
Scheen
J. de Vries jr: 'Paul Joseph Gabriël: Nederlandsch beeldhouwkunstenaar', *Alm. Schoone & Goede* (1847), pp. 140–68
P. K. van Daalen: *Nederlandse beeldhouwers in de negentiende eeuw* [Dutch sculptors in the 19th century] (The Hague, 1957), pp. 85–96

GEERT JAN KOOT

(2) Paul Joseph Constantin Gabriël (*b* Amsterdam, 5 July 1828; *d* Scheveningen, 23 Aug 1903). Painter, son of (1) Paulus Joseph Gabriël. He received his first training not from his father, who died when he was only five years old, but at evening classes at the Amsterdam Academie (1840 and 1843). Later he was instructed by the architect Louis Zocher (1820–1915), and *c.* 1844 he was sent to the private art school of the landscape painter Barend Cornelis Koekkoek in Cleves. However, after a year he returned to the Netherlands because Koekkoek thought he had too little talent to be a painter. Gabriël then went to live briefly in Haarlem, where he copied works in the Welgelegen pavilion, which then housed the nation's modern art collection, and earned his living drawing portraits. In Haarlem he met Anton Mauve, with whom he was to have much contact later on. In 1853 Gabriël went to Oosterbeek, the Dutch Barbizon. This was a period of intense activity and discussion with other painters, including Gerard Bilders. From 1856 to 1859 he lived in Amsterdam, where he suffered severe financial difficulty because his paintings failed to sell. In 1860 he moved to Brussels and stayed there with brief interruptions for the next 24 years. In Brussels he received support and advice from the Dutch artist Willem Roelofs, who had been living in the city since 1847. In 1866 he became a member of the Société Belge des Aquarellistes, and in 1867 he married. One well-known

work dating from his early years in Belgium is *In Groendendaal near Brussels* (*c.* 1866–7; The Hague, Rijksmus. Mesdag), which was the first painting to show his artistic independence from Jean-Baptiste-Camille Corot and the Barbizon painters, as well as from the Dutch artists working in the Romantic tradition.

Apart from landscapes Gabriël painted mainly flower-pieces, which gradually brought him increasing appreciation in Belgium; in 1875 he received the Belgian Order of Leopold. His most influential pupil in Brussels was Willem Bastiaan Tholen, with whom he made many visits to the Dutch polders. In 1884 Gabriël left Belgium to establish himself in Scheveningen. He stayed there until his death, although he also spent much time working outside The Hague (Voorschoten, Oosterbeek, Kinderdijk and Heeze). Artistic recognition came only gradually in the Netherlands: in 1890 the Gemeentemuseum in The Hague acquired his large canvas *Peat Cutting at Kampen*, which Gabriël probably painted shortly beforehand, following one of his excursions with Tholen.

Gabriël belonged to the third and last generation of the Hague school, although his fondness for sunny polder landscapes painted in fairly bright colours set him somewhat apart from the other Hague school artists. He was an original artist who avoided the successful formula of the Hague school — the atmospheric landscape in grey tones. Yet he was perfectly capable of rendering an atmospheric landscape, as can be seen from his *Train in a Landscape* ('*Il vient de loin . . .*') (1887; Otterlo, Kröller-Müller). Gabriël placed the recording of reality above interpretation. His work tended to be geometrical in conception and almost mathematical in structure, something for which he was much admired by Piet Mondrian, who copied his *In the Month of May* (Amsterdam, Rijksmus.). H. W. Mesdag was another painter who was deeply interested in Gabriël and bought his paintings. Although he achieved considerable fame in Belgium and France during his lifetime, Gabriël never received much attention in the Netherlands and even after his death remained relatively obscure among Hague painters, due partly to his long stay in Brussels and partly to his independent position.

FRANSJE KUYVENHOVEN

BIBLIOGRAPHY
Scheen
M. Rooses, ed.: *Het schildersboek: Nederlandsche schilders der negentiende eeuw, in monographieën door tijdgenoten* [The book about painters: Dutch painters of the 19th century, in monographs by contemporaries], i (Amsterdam, 1898), pp. 211–36
Schilderijen en tekeningen van P. J. C. Gabriël (exh. cat., Amsterdam, Larensche Ksthandel, 1911)
H. E. van Gelder: 'Brieven uit P. J. C. Gabriël's Brusselschen tijd' [Letters from P. J. C. Gabriël's period in Brussels], *Oud-Holland*, xlii (1925), pp. 178–80
H. F. W. Jeltes: 'Brieven van Gabriël', *Oud-Holland*, xliii (1926), pp. 117–27
W. J. de Gruyter: *De Haagse School*, i (Rotterdam, 1968), pp. 76–89 [with Eng. summary]
The Hague School: Dutch Masters of the 19th Century (exh. cat., The Hague, Gemeentemus.; London, RA, 1983), pp. 181–5
De Haagse School: De collectie van het Haags Gemeentemuseum (exh. cat., The Hague, Gemeentemus., 1988)
The Age of Van Gogh: Dutch Painting, 1880–1895 (exh. cat., ed. R. Bionda, C. Blotkamp and others; Glasgow, Burrell Col.; Amsterdam, Van Gogh Mus.; 1990–91)

GEERT JAN KOOT

Gabriel, Albert(-Louis) (*b* Cérisières, 2 Aug 1883; *d* Bar-sur-Aube, 23 Dec 1972). French architectural historian and archaeologist. He obtained a diploma in architecture at the Ecole des Beaux-Arts, Paris, and from 1908 to 1911 he was attached to the French School at Athens, where he participated in the publication of the school's excavations at Delos and studied the medieval buildings of Rhodes. During World War I he was an interpreter in Syria. He earned his license-ès-lettres at the University of Paris in 1921 with theses on the ramparts of Rhodes and the excavations at Fustat (Old Cairo). This double education as an architect and archaeologist shaped his later works on the Islamic monuments of medieval Anatolia, Iraq and Iran. He visited Syria and Cilicia in 1922 and Syria again in 1925; he taught at the universities of Caen (1923), Strasbourg (1925–46) and Istanbul (1926–30). From 1930 to 1955 he directed the Institut Français d'Archéologie in Istanbul. In 1933 he was elected to the Académie des Inscriptions et Belles-Lettres and in 1946 to the Collège de France.

WRITINGS

with A. Bahgat: *Fouilles d'al-Foustât* (Paris, 1921)
La Cité de Rhodes, 2 vols (Paris, 1921–3)
Monuments turcs d'Anatolie, 2 vols (Paris, 1931–4)
Voyages archéologiques dans la Turquie orientale et les provinces d'au delà du Tigre, 2 vols (Paris, 1940)
Châteaux turcs du Bosphore (Paris, 1943)
with E. Hospels: *La Cité de Midas*, 3 vols (Paris, 1952–5)
Une Capital turque: Brousse, Bursa, 2 vols (Paris, 1958)

BIBLIOGRAPHY

P. Boyancé: Obituary, *Acad. Inscr. & B.-Lett.: C. R. Séances* (Jan 1973), pp. 1–2

Gabrieli, Gabriel de' (*b* Roveredo, nr Bellinzona, 1671; *d* Eichstätt, 21 March 1747). Italian master builder and architect. In the early 1690s he was a master builder at the court of Prince John Adam of Liechtenstein in Vienna, where he worked at the Liechtenstein town palace, firstly under Domenico Martinelli and later (1705–6) completing it to his own plans, the staircase showing his influence most strongly. Gabrieli was summoned to Ansbach in 1694 by Markgraf Georg Friedrich to submit plans for rebuilding the palace there, and while the Margrave deliberated, Gabrieli took on other commissions in Ansbach. He built a garden house (1697–9; now the Prinzenschlossen) for Privy Counsellor Georg Christian Seefried above the palace quarter. Less well preserved is his summer-house (1696–1701) for Lieutenant-Colonel Jahnus in Pfaffengreuth. Gabrieli began work on the Ansbach Palace in 1705, after the Margrave's death. A fire in 1709 facilitated a complete remodelling, and Gabrieli, who was promoted to court architect and Director of Building in 1709, now had to incorporate his own building, which had been spared by the fire, and some old walls into the new project. This caused awkward problems in the interior and led to a breach between patron and architect. In 1714 Gabrieli left Ansbach and entered the service of Prince-Bishop Konrad of Eichstätt. The palace in Ansbach was completed by the VON ZOCHA brothers from 1723. Gabrieli's first work in Eichstätt was the remodelling (1716–18) of the façade of the west choir of the cathedral. From 1735 to 1737 Gabrieli built the Residenz of the prince bishop; in his design of the ambient space, informality notably prevails over Baroque pomp. The site is bounded by palace buildings, the simplicity of which is interrupted only by the rich ornamentation of the portal and pediment zones. Gabrieli's works helped to shape the rest of Eichstätt. Important buildings by him include the Ostein–Riedheim canons' house, the Schönbornhof and the Weldenpalast. About 1730 he remodelled the bishop's palace at Hirschberg to form a three-winged Rococo complex by symmetrically unifying the previous buildings. Gabrieli's buildings demonstrate his originality and show the influence of Johann Bernhard Fischer von Erlach. His work combines Austrian architectural sensibility with the discipline of Roman palazzo style.

BIBLIOGRAPHY

T. Neuhofer: 'Gabriel de Gabrieli: Ein Barockbaumeister', *Zwiebelturm*, vii (1952), pp. 162–7
K. Pilz: 'Der Architekt Gabriel de Gabrieli in Ansbach und Eichstätt', *Frankenland* (1959), pp. 77–85
T. Neuhofer: 'Beiträge zur Kunstgeschichte Bayerns', *Sammbl. Hist. Ver. Eichstätt*, lxii (1967–8), pp. 8–101
B. Appel: 'Gabriel de Gabrieli: Ausstellung des Diözesanarchivs Eichstätt', *Sammbl. Hist. Ver. Eichstätt*, lxxi/lxxii (1978–9)

BIRGIT ROTH

Gaceta del arte. An international monthly cultural review that was published in Tenerife, Canary Islands, from February 1932 to June 1936. Its editor-in-chief was Eduardo Westerdahl (1902–80), and its editors included the writer Domingo Pérez Mink. The proclamation of the Second Republic in Spain in 1931 created an atmosphere of liberalization, and national and international avant-garde periodicals of the previous decade such as *Esprit*, *Cahiers d'art*, *Die Brücke* and *Revista de Occidente* reappeared. The very character of the islands and the emphasis on international tourism favoured the *Gaceta del arte*'s publication. Its viewpoint was dependent on Westerdahl's European travels, which put him in contact with such contemporary avant-garde movements as Functionalism, Rationalism, Surrealism and many others. His programme was to disseminate the most progressive styles and ideas emerging in Europe, from aesthetics and ethics to fashion. From the outset, *Gaceta del arte* maintained connections with the Rationalist movement in architecture. Its contacts with Surrealism emerged later through Oscar Domínguez. The *Gaceta del arte* always maintained its independence, however, although there was a Surrealist faction among the magazine's editors, represented chiefly by Domingo López-Torres and Pedro Garcia Cabrera. Domínguez exhibited in Tenerife in 1933 and the review devoted a special issue to Surrealism. The *Exposición internacional del Surrealismo* was held in Tenerife in 1935 and included works by De Chirico, Duchamp, Dalí, Max Ernst, Domínguez and Giacometti among others; André Breton visited the island for the occasion. The *Gaceta* continued as a platform for the discussion of new ideas from Europe and from Spain. Its contributors included some of the most important artists of the day, such as Miró, Kandinsky and Angel Ferrant. It was always well received, particularly in liberal circles in Madrid and Barcelona. When the Spanish Civil War loomed in 1936, the review took a position against the war and against Fascism, but events caused its disappearance in June 1936.

BIBLIOGRAPHY

D. Pérez Mink: *Facción española surrealista de Tenerife* (Barcelona, 1975)

E. Westerdahl: *Gaceta del arte: Revista internacional de cultura* (Madrid, 1981)

PILAR BENITO

Gachet, Dr Paul(-Ferdinand) [Van Ryssel] (*b* Lille, 30 July 1828; *d* Auvers-sur-Oise, Val d'Oise, 9 Jan 1909). French doctor, collector, painter and engraver. In 1848 he began to study medicine in Paris, where he frequented the Bohemian circles of AMAND GAUTIER, Gustave Courbet and Champfleury. In 1857 he visited Montpellier, where he met the great collector Alfred Bruyas; it was probably through him that he came to know Paul Guigou, Adolphe Monticelli and Auguste Cézanne, Paul Cézanne's father. In 1858 Gachet was awarded a doctorate by the University of Montpellier for his thesis *Etudes sur la mélancolie*. On his return to Paris he established a medical practice; among his patients were the engraver Charles Meryon and Rachel Pissarro, mother of Camille Pissarro. The turning-point in his life came when in 1872 he bought a property at Auvers-sur-Oise; his house there became a haven for the Impressionist painters.

In the same year Gachet began to collect seriously, buying 18 small paintings by Guigou at the latter's studio sale. He acquired many works from his painter friends and lent Cézanne's *A Modern Olympia* (?1873; Paris, Mus. d'Orsay) to the First Impressionist Exhibition of 1874. He eventually owned about 30 works by Cézanne, including several floral still-lifes that the artist painted at his house from bouquets arranged by Mme Gachet. At Pissarro's instigation, Vincent van Gogh went to live at Auvers in 1890 and consulted Gachet about his deteriorating mental health. They struck up a friendship, and van Gogh painted two portraits of *Dr Gachet* (Paris, Mus. d'Orsay; sold New York, Christie's, 15 May 1990, lot 21, now Japan, priv. col.) and made his only etching, another portrait of *Dr Gachet*, under his direction. Gachet therefore had the distinction of being one of the first collectors of works by the Post-Impressionists. His son Paul Gachet (1873–1962) donated important works from his father's collection to the Louvre in 1949, 1951 and 1954.

BIBLIOGRAPHY

J. Adhémar and J. Lethève: *Inventaire du fonds français après 1800*, Paris, Bib. N., Cab. Est. cat., viii (Paris, 1954), pp. 294–300

P. Gachet: *Deux amis des impressionnistes: Le Docteur Gachet et Murer* (Paris, 1956)

P. Gachet, ed.: *Lettres impressionnistes au Dr Gachet et à Murer* (Paris, 1957)

S. Monneret: *L'Impressionnisme et son époque: Dictionnaire international*, i (Paris, 1987), pp. 257–9

A. Distel: *Les Collectionneurs des impressionnistes: Amateurs et marchands* (Paris, 1989), pp. 195–205

☐

Gadamer, Hans-Georg. *See under* HERMENEUTICS.

Gadányi, Jenő (*b* Budapest, 28 March 1896; *d* Budapest, 29 Feb 1960). Hungarian painter. He graduated from the College of Fine Arts, Budapest, in 1923. The influence of his teacher, János Vaszary (1867–1939), is clearly visible in such early works as *Blue-eyed Girl* (1927; Budapest, N.G.). He was also attracted to the avant-garde, mainly under the influence of Károly Kernstok. In 1927 he travelled to Paris and studied the work of Picasso and Matisse, and Surrealist and abstract painters. His early period (late 1920s to mid-1930s) is characterized by subjective works combining Constructivist, Cubist and Surrealist techniques (e.g. *Horses*, 1932; Budapest, N.G.). From the mid-1930s depictions of natural objects were filtered through memory. *Fantastic Landscape* (1948; Budapest, N.G.), a combination of the real and unreal, sums up his attempts to use Constructivism and Expressionism.

Gadányi produced most of his work between 1948 and 1953 when he withdrew to the countryside. He painted numerous monumental symbolic figure compositions (e.g. *Seer*, or *The Thinker*, 1950; Budapest, N.G.). Still under the influence of early Cubism, his work had the scope of classical allegorical paintings. *Woman with a Rooster* (*c*. 1952 ; Budapest, N.G.), of which he made several versions, best demonstrates the expressive and monumental character of his paintings. Gadányi exhibited regularly (*c*. 1930) with the New Society of Fine Artists (Képzőművészek Új Társasaga: KÚT) and the Association of New Artists (Új Művészek Egyesülete). Between 1946 and 1949 he taught at the School of Applied Arts in Budapest and was a member of the EUROPEAN SCHOOL (Európai Iskola) (1945–8).

BIBLIOGRAPHY

Jenő Gadányi (exh. cat., intro. E. Kállai; Budapest, Ernst Mus., 1948)

E. Körner: 'Jenő Gadányi', *Művészettörténeti Értesítő* (1960), no. 4, pp. 304–13

Jenőné Gadányi: *Így történt* [This is how it happened] (Budapest, 1965) [Memoirs by the artist's wife]

I. Rácz: *Gadányi* (Budapest, 1965)

ZSUZSANNA BAKÓ

Gaddi (i). Italian family of painters. Three generations were active in Florence. (1) Gaddo Gaddi, who established a thriving workshop, was a contemporary and apparently a friend of Giotto. His son (2) Taddeo Gaddi is believed to have been trained by Giotto. Taddeo was a highly successful painter, and tax records show that he enjoyed a comfortable financial position in the last two decades of his life. His four sons were mentioned in a lost tax record (1376) from the neighbourhood of S Pier Maggiore in Florence. Three of them were painters: (3) Giovanni Gaddi, (4) Agnolo Gaddi, the most productive and successful, and Niccolò Gaddi, of whom very little is known. Taddeo's fourth son, Zanobi Gaddi (*d* 1400), does not appear to have followed the same profession.

(1) Gaddo (di Zanobi) Gaddi (*fl* 1312–30). He is recorded in the rolls of the Arte dei Medici e Speziali between 1312 and 1320. According to other documents, now lost, he was still alive in 1327 and 1330. Despite his connection with two of the most important painters in 14th-century Florence, Giotto and his own son Taddeo Gaddi, virtually nothing is known about Gaddo's work. Whether he collaborated with Jacopo Torriti and Andrea Tafi (*fl* 1300–25), as Vasari stated, is impossible to determine; attempts to reconstruct his work around a group of wall paintings in S Francesco, Assisi, where Torriti worked, are thus conjectural. An alternative interpretation of Gaddo's oeuvre, based on another Vasarian attribution, the *Coronation of the Virgin* mosaic on the entrance façade of Florence Cathedral, is also conjectural but more credible. Around this latter work has been grouped a small number of panels, in style strongly reminiscent of Cimabue, including an exceptional *Virgin and Child* in S Remigio, Florence.

BIBLIOGRAPHY

G. Vasari: *Vite* (1550, rev. 2/1568); ed. G. Milanesi (1878–85), i, pp. 345–52

F. Mather jr: *The Isaac Master: A Reconstruction of the Work of Gaddo Gaddi* (Princeton, 1932)

M. Boskovits: *Cimabue e i precursori di Giotto* (Florence, 1976)

A. Tartuferi: *La pittura a Firenze nel duecento* (Florence, 1990), pp. 49–50, 105–6

(2) Taddeo Gaddi (*fl* ?mid-1320s; *d* 1366). Son of (1) Gaddo Gaddi. He was a pupil of Giotto and one of the most inventive and influential painters in 14th-century Florence. According to Cennini, Taddeo stayed with Giotto for 24 years. Although the exact length of their association is unverifiable, it probably ended only with the latter's death in 1337. Taddeo probably occupied a still undefined but doubtless important position in Giotto's workshop during the master's busy last years, but such responsibility did not prevent him undertaking work on his own as early as the 1320s.

1. EARLY WORK, BEFORE *c.* 1340. Taddeo's earliest works, a fragmentary *Virgin and Child* (Castelfiorentino, Mus. S Verdiana) and a *Stigmatization of St Francis* (Cambridge, MA, Fogg), are both datable to the mid-1320s, and demonstrate the close derivation of his style from Giotto, whose compositions he adopted and revised. These works also initiated Taddeo's lifelong connection with the Franciscan Order, for which he and his shop became the leading painters in Florence. An important early commission, a polyptych with the *Man of Sorrows with Saints* (ex-Bromley-Davenport Col., Macclesfield), originally in the Lupicini Chapel in Santa Croce, reveals that despite the influence of his training, Taddeo was open to other styles, in this case Sienese.

The great project of Taddeo's youth and one of the most remarkable monuments of early Italian painting is the series of frescoes in the Baroncelli Chapel in Santa Croce, Florence (see fig. 1). This is probably to be dated soon after 1328, the date of an inscription on the funerary monument. The importance of the project is also indicated by the presence in the chapel of a now underappreciated *Coronation of the Virgin* signed by Giotto and attributed to his workshop. This has given rise to speculation that Giotto played a decisive part in the design of the chapel decoration, but the evidence of the frescoes gives eloquent testimony to Taddeo's own role. Although dependent on Giotto's ideas, as expressed in the Bardi and especially the Peruzzi chapels in the same church, the Baroncelli frescoes also show a departure from them. In these works Taddeo explores with great vigour his interest in dynamic spatial play, powerful foreshortening, animated narrative and dramatic effects of light. His complex and playful architectural constructions, notably the temple in his famous and much copied *Presentation of the Virgin* (see fig. 1, lower left), which inspired such 15th-century painters as the Limbourg brothers, are so ingenious that first Filippo Villani then Vasari promoted the myth that Taddeo was a practising architect. The ebullient spirit of his work reaches its height in the *Marriage of the Virgin* (see fig. 1, lower right), the iconography of which may reflect contemporary marriage customs. Yet Taddeo was also capable of expressing sincere spirituality, as may be seen in the light-filled scenes on the window wall of the chapel. In form, content and in effect the chapel is a remarkably unified whole that presents themes of ancestry and revelation.

The first documentary mention of Taddeo is *c.* 1330, when he matriculated into the Arte dei Medici e Speziali. During the 1330s Taddeo undertook to produce for the sacristy of Santa Croce a series of panels (Berlin, Gemäldegal.; Florence, Accad.; Munich, Alte Pin.) paralleling the lives of Christ and St Francis. He was also at work elsewhere in Santa Croce, in the Bardi di Vernio Chapel begun by Maso di Banco. Although Taddeo apparently specialized in large-scale paintings, during these years he also produced small works for private devotion, notably his splendid triptych of 1334 (Berlin, Gemäldegal. 1079–81) and a damaged but exquisite *Virgin Enthroned* (Berne, Kstmus.). Another major work, now known only through a badly damaged fresco fragment and some tantalizing stained glass, must have been the decoration of another chapel in Santa Croce, which is datable by an inscription and by a documentary bequest to around 1335.

2. MATURE WORK, *c.* 1341–66. After his great teacher's death, Taddeo is documented in 1341 and 1342 for partially extant work in the crypt of S Miniato al Monte, Florence. According to a letter dated 7 September 1342 and traditionally associated with him, Taddeo was in Pisa working for the Gambacorti family and accepted another commission from one of the Strozzi in Florence. During the 1340s his abilities are evident in the subtle yet effective perspective and in the restrained yet intense expressiveness that he developed once he had absorbed the influence of Maso di Banco's work. His artistic maturity is visible above all in a fragmentary *Lamentation* (Florence, Mus. Santa Croce), which he painted for Santa Croce as a pendant to a *Coronation of the Virgin* by Maso.

Taddeo was not the rigid imitator he has often been portrayed but an artist responsive to the artistic culture around him. This is apparent even in his late work, produced after the plague of 1348 in which many painters of his generation died. The situation that resulted was dramatically different, and Taddeo responded with an approach that sought to reconcile the lessons of his training with Giotto and the aims of younger artists led by Orcagna. In 1348, after the onset of the Black Death, Taddeo was included in a list of the leading painters available to complete a *Virgin and Child* already begun and left unfinished by Alesso di Andrea (*fl* 1341–7) for S Giovanni Fuorcivitas in Pistoia, and in 1353 Taddeo received payments for that work (*in situ*). Two years later he signed a *Virgin and Child* (Florence, Uffizi), which he undertook for the Segni family and which stood in S Lucchese, Poggibonsi. Taddeo's new approach is also evident in a *Virgin Enthroned* (1355; Florence, Uffizi), in a *Virgin and Child* at S Lorenzo alle Rose, near the Certosa del Galluzzo, near Florence, and especially in his enormous fresco of the *Tree of Life, Lives of the Saints and Last Supper* (see fig. 2; for detail see MONASTERY, fig. 11) *c.* 1360 in the former refectory of Santa Croce. The latter painting, which displays his abiding interests in illusionism and light but which also corresponds to the darker tone typical of works

1. Taddeo Gaddi: scenes from the *Life of the Virgin* (*c.* 1328), fresco, Baroncelli Chapel, Santa Croce, Florence

2. Taddeo Gaddi: *Tree of Life, Lives of the Saints and Last Supper* (*c.* 1360), fresco, former refectory of Santa Croce, Florence

after the mid-century, must be considered one of the most moving and powerful images of Taddeo's oeuvre. Even toward the end of his long life and even given a theme as potentially dry as S Bonaventura's treatise on the Tree of Life, he was able to produce an image that was direct and accessible. In that sense, he was always a true and worthy pupil of Giotto.

Tax records, particularly his holdings in the Monte Comune and various payments, which throughout his life locate Taddeo in the quarter of Santa Croce in the Via S Maria (now Via Michelangelo), suggest that he was financially comfortable in the last two decades of his life. Moreover, his advisory service for the Cathedral Works between 1355 and 1366 reflects his professional status. The only other documented work by him is a *Resurrection* in S Maria Nuova, Florence, for which the painter received payment on 9 March 1365, in the year before his death and burial in the second cloister of Santa Croce.

BIBLIOGRAPHY

G. Vasari: *Vite* (1550, rev. 2/1568); ed. G. Milanesi (1878–85), i, pp. 571–86
R. Longhi: 'Qualità e industria in Taddeo Gaddi ed altri', *Paragone*, x (1959), no. 109, pp. 31–40; no. 111, pp. 3–12
E. Borsook: *The Mural Painters of Tuscany from Cimabue to Andrea del Sarto* (London, 1960, rev. Oxford, 1980), pp. 42–3
J. Gardner: 'The Decoration of the Baroncelli Chapel', *Z. Kstgesch.*, xxxiv (1971), pp. 89–113
R. Offner and K. Steinweg: *Corpus*, suppl.; ed. H. B. J. Maginnis (1981), pp. 67–71
A. Ladis: *Taddeo Gaddi* (Columbia and London, 1982)
A. Rave: *Christiformitas: Studien zur franziskanischen Ikonographie des Florentiner Trecento am Beispiel des ehemaligen Sakristeischrankzyklus von Taddeo Gaddi in Santa Croce* (Stuttgart, 1984)
A. Ladis: 'An Old Picture in Florence', *Source*, vii (1987), pp. 1–5

(3) Giovanni Gaddi (*fl* 1362–85). Son of (2) Taddeo Gaddi. He undoubtedly trained in his father's shop, where he must have assumed an important position before the latter's death in 1366. He appears to have had a role in running his father's affairs during the last years of Taddeo's life when, beginning in 1363, he is mentioned as making tax payments for him, while from 1362 he had a separate account with the Florentine Monte Comune, in which he had invested almost as much as his father. He is first recorded as a painter in 1369, when he was working in the Vatican in the company of Giovanni da Milano and one 'Iocti', identified as Giottino. By then, as the heir to his father's shop, Giovanni must have had a certain prominence. Nevertheless, he enrolled in the Arte dei Medici e Speziali only on 5 April 1372. His name, usually along with those of his brothers, appears in Florentine tax records of 1378, 1379 and 1385.

In the absence of any signed or documented works by Giovanni, his oeuvre remains a matter of speculation. An attempt to identify him as the author of a group of his father's late works has rightly been challenged, even though their collaboration during the 1360s is likely. More promising, but as yet unproved, is a hypothesis that identifies him as the so-called Master of the Misericordia, a painter active during the 1370s and 1380s and named after a panel depicting the *Madonna of Mercy* (Florence, Accad.). The work of this artist, which is known only from panels, anticipates Agnolo yet also recalls Taddeo, from whom he frequently adopted motifs and to whom his works (predella panels with *Life of St Eligius*, Madrid, Prado) have been erroneously attributed.

BIBLIOGRAPHY

L. Marcucci: *Gallerie Nazionali di Firenze: I dipinti toscani del secolo XIV* (Rome, 1965), pp. 133–6
M. Boskovits: *Pittura fiorentina alla vigilia del rinascimento* (Florence, 1975), pp. 62–5, 215, n. 79
A. Ladis: *Taddeo Gaddi* (Columbia and London, 1982), pp. 15, 76, 262–3

(4) Agnolo Gaddi (*fl* 1369; *bur* 16 Oct 1396). Son of (2) Taddeo Gaddi. Through both his brother Giovanni and his father, Agnolo was heir to the Giottesque tradition and to a successful family enterprise, which he directed with enormous success up to the turn of the 15th century. He is first mentioned as a painter in 1369, when he assisted his brother Giovanni and Giovanni da Milano in decorations for Urban V (*reg* 1362–70) in the Vatican. Although he probably did not assume full responsibility for the workshop until his brother Giovanni's death, he must have begun accepting his own commissions as early as the 1370s. The nature of his early work and whether it included

an altarpiece dated 1375 (Parma, G.N., 435), however, remains a matter of debate. Logical or likely though it may be, the notion that this early activity developed out of his brother Giovanni's still little-known art is hypothetical. Whereas the works grouped around Giovanni's name are all small panels, Agnolo was an artist who, like his father, excelled in wall painting. Indeed, three monumental fresco cycles (see below), in the Castellani Chapel (painted *c.* 1384) and the choir (painted *c.* 1388–93) of Santa Croce, Florence, and the chapel of the Sacra Cintola (doc. 1393–5) in Prato Cathedral, constitute the artist's most notable surviving works and offer a basis for reconstructing the content and chronology of his oeuvre.

Both the size and, consequently, the character of Agnolo's genuine production remain matters of scholarly discussion. Around the core of monumental works, some scholars have added a large and disparate group of paintings varying widely in craftsmanship and quality. As the head of an established shop, Agnolo probably did not lack commissions or sales and, like his father, he may not have exercised tight control over all the works produced under his name. The large body of paintings associated with his workshop cannot be dismissed, for it is an indication of his industry and the success of his enterprise, but it perhaps also tends to obscure his individual contribution.

A fair amount is known about Agnolo's activity in the 1380s from the various documents that survive. In 1380 he painted an *Annunciation* (untraced) for the Florentine hospital of the Bigallo. On 8 February 1381 he was considered for communal office, and in the following year

1. Agnolo Gaddi: *Finding of the True Cross* (*c.* 1388–93), fresco, Santa Croce, Florence

his name appears in a scrutiny for the position of councillor of the Arte dei Medici e Speziali; he was again considered for communal office nine years later. In 1383 a letter from Agnolo, recommending potential painters to Francesco di Marco Datini, marks the beginning of a long and sometimes difficult relationship with the wealthy Pratese merchant. Datini, who also employed the painter's brother Zanobi Gaddi, became Agnolo's principal private patron. In a letter dated 22 January 1384 the painter Tommaso del Mazza (*fl* 1375–91) tells Datini that Agnolo will judge the value of his work for Datini.

At the same time as he was working in Prato, Agnolo enjoyed a busy and prominent career in Florence. In addition to the frescoes (*c.* 1384) painted for the Castellani Chapel, Santa Croce, he contributed designs to and gave advice on the sculptural decoration of the Loggia della Signoria (or Loggia dei Lanzi) between 1383 and 1386: on 27 June 1383 he received payment for the designs for two sculptures eventually carved by Jacopo di Piero Guidi (*fl* 1379–1405); on 11 February and 12 August of the following year he received payment for additional designs of *Virtues*; on 27 December 1385, together with other artists, he gave his opinion on the completed parts of the sculptural decoration; on 27 March 1386 he received payment for designs for the figures of *Prudence* and *Charity*, eventually carved for the Loggia by Giovanni d'Ambrogio and Jacopo di Piero Guidi respectively. In 1387, the same year in which he enrolled in the Guild of St Luke, he began his long association with Florence Cathedral. In that year he is documented as receiving payment for the design of the figure of an *Apostle* to be carved by Piero di Giovanni Tedesco (*fl* 1386–1402) and to be placed on the façade.

Agnolo's work is remarkable for its rapid development. Such early paintings as the frescoes in the Castellani Chapel, a *Coronation of the Virgin* (London, N.G., 568), and a polyptych of the *Virgin and Child Enthroned with*

2. Agnolo Gaddi: *SS Julian and Nicholas with Scenes from their Lives*, tempera on panel, 248×285 mm, *c.* 1395 (Munich, Alte Pinakothek)

Angels and Saints (Berlin, Bodemus., 1039) reveal strong debts to Agnolo's father and to the more brittle forms of Niccolò di Pietro Gerini. Toward the end of the 1380s, however, in such works as a *Coronation of the Virgin* (Washington, N.G.A.) and especially his vast fresco cycle of the *Legend of the True Cross* (see fig. 1) in the choir of Santa Croce in Florence, he developed his own distinctive formal language. The latter cycle was one of the most ambitious, inventive, daring and impressive monuments of the entire century, and it became the iconographic model for later treatments of the theme, including that of Piero della Francesca in Arezzo. Its expansive spatial constructions, dynamic compositions and richly varied surfaces have an irresistible decorative appeal. Yet, in this work of gorgeous complexity, capriciousness and fantasy, Agnolo managed to balance artifice with penetrating observation of nature and humanity, the latter evident notably in the portrait-like treatment of some of his figures. The cycle is also of capital importance for its still inadequately investigated intellectual content, which reflects contemporary Franciscan thought.

Agnolo continued to work for various patrons both in Florence and Prato in the 1390s. On 23 March 1390 he gilded and painted two statues (untraced) of *St John the Baptist* and *St John the Evangelist* by Piero di Giovanni Tedesco for the façade of Florence Cathedral. In the same year, and together with Pesello, he produced the design for a wooden sculpture to be placed over the door leading from the cathedral to the campanile. By 22 January 1392, after having worked in the Palazzo Datini in Prato from 19 September until 21 December of the previous year, Agnolo and two other artists, including Niccolò di Pietro Gerini, were petitioning Datini to be paid, a demand not met until 6 May 1394. In the interim he began his work for the chapel of the Sacra Cintola in Prato Cathedral, since payments for the series of frescoes of the *Life of the Virgin* and the *Legend of the Sacra Cintola* commenced on 19 June 1392. Actual work probably began only in November 1393, when Agnolo's patron Datini lent him bedding, and continued until 25 May 1395, when payments ended. The start of this work coincided with a legal imbroglio resulting from taxes Agnolo owed the Florentine commune. When a tax-collector broke down the door of his house, Agnolo responded by assaulting the official, an act that resulted in a large fine of 600 lire imposed on 7 October 1392. The following November a Florentine official, with the aid of local police, sought to arrest him in Prato Cathedral, but the painter escaped thanks to the aid of friends, who helped start a brawl; he later avoided the fine by pleading poverty. While safe in Prato, Agnolo painted a fresco of the *Assumption of the Virgin* (untraced) on the façade of the cathedral, for which he received payment on 28 June 1395. He was perhaps overburdened with work, because in a letter of 24 January 1396 Datini begs that Agnolo complete a panel of *St Peter*, a *Crucifix* and 'other things'.

Meanwhile, Agnolo's work for Florence Cathedral continued: on 6 August 1394 he was commissioned to design two stained-glass windows, and on 23 December 1395 he received a payment for cartoons for another window made by Antonio da Pisa, author of a treatise on stained glass; perhaps related to these projects is a payment on 7 April

1396 for painting a window splay and another payment on 16 June 1396 of money owed to him by a glass painter. During this period he continued to provide other services to the cathedral. On 21 October 1395 he received payment for designs for four statues, and on 2 December 1395 he and Pesello were given the important commissions of designing monuments to *John Hawkwood* (untraced) and *Pietro Farnese* (fragmentary, Florence, Mus. Opera Duomo). His public commissions did not preclude other projects, for in 1394 and 1395 he received payments for an important altarpiece for S Miniato al Monte. On 16 October 1396 he was buried in the family sepulchre in Santa Croce. Final payment for the altarpiece of S Miniato went to Agnolo's brother Zanobi in the same year.

By the mid-1390s Agnolo's work, exemplified by a *Madonna of Humility* (Jacksonville, FL, Cummer Gal. A.), *SS Julian and Nicholas with Scenes from their Lives* (Munich, Alte Pin.; see fig. 2), his little-studied stained glass in Florence Cathedral, and especially the frescoes in the chapel of the Sacra Cintola in Prato Cathedral, show an increasing sweetness, delicacy, grace and lightness, both in form and colour, while remaining within the Giottesque tradition. Indeed, his last works, completed while he was still relatively young, raise the interesting question of what his position might have been had he lived longer. In any case, his work, which proved decisive for a generation of artists at the end of the century, at once anticipated the flamboyant Gothic of Lorenzo Monaco and, in its human content, offered inspiration to artists of the emerging early Renaissance.

BIBLIOGRAPHY

G. Vasari: *Vite* (1550, rev. 2/1568); ed. G. Milanesi (1878–85), i, pp. 635–46
G. Poggi: 'La Cappella del Sacro Cingolo nel duomo di Prato', *Riv. A.*, xiv (1932), pp. 356–76
R. Salvini: *L'arte di Agnolo Gaddi* (Florence, 1936)
L. Bellosi: 'Da Spinello Aretino a Lorenzo Monaco', *Paragone*, xvi (1965), no. 187, pp. 18–43
M. Boskovits: 'Some Early Works of Agnolo Gaddi', *Burl. Mag.*, cx (1968), pp. 209–15
——: *Pittura fiorentina alla vigilia del rinascimento* (Florence, 1975), pp. 117–24, 295–304
B. Cole: *Agnolo Gaddi* (Oxford, 1977)
M. Boskovits: 'In margine alla bottega di Agnolo Gaddi', *Paragone*, xxx (1979), no. 355, pp. 54–62
M. Eisenberg: *Lorenzo Monaco* (Princeton, 1989)
A. Ladis: 'Un'ordinazione per disegni dal ciclo della vera croce di Agnolo Gaddi a Firenze', *Riv. A.*, xli (1989), pp. 153–8

ANDREW LADIS

Gaddi (ii). Italian family of patrons and collectors.

(1) Giovanni de' Gaddi (*b* Florence, 1493; *d* Rome, 19 Oct 1542). The son of Taddeo Gaddi and Antonia Altoviti, he was a prominent member of his family and is given ample attention by Vasari and Cellini. Throughout his life he sponsored artists and writers, and in his houses in Rome and Florence he collected works of art and rare books. He spent his youth in Florence, where he lived in the Palazzo Gaddi, which stands adjacent to the Piazza di Madonna. In these Florentine years, according to Vasari, he was friendly with Jacopo Sansovino, Niccolò Tribolo, Giovanni Francesco Rustici and Andrea del Sarto, who all produced important works of art for him (e.g. *Madonna and Child* by Andrea del Sarto; Rome, Gal. Borghese). Gaddi moved to Rome in 1525 and became clerk of the chamber to Pope Clement VII. He continued his patronage of Sansovino, collecting his terracotta models and perhaps commissioning him to build the palazzo that stands in Via del Banco di Santo Spirito. He was also friendly with Sebastiano del Piombo, Michelangelo and Benvenuto Cellini. He collected antiques and, according to Vasari, owned some antique pieces that had belonged to Ghiberti, including the relief sculpture of *Amor and Psyche*, known as the *Bed of Polycletus* (untraced). His interests were literary as well as artistic. Annibal Caro was his secretary in Rome for many years, and other poets and writers also found hospitality in his house. It was thanks to his interest that Machiavelli's *Il principe* (1513) and *Discorsi* (1513–21) were published in Rome.

BIBLIOGRAPHY

G. Vasari: *Vite* (1550, rev. 2/1568); ed. G. Milanesi (1878–85)
B. Cellini: *La Vita* (1558–66); ed. P. d'Ancona (Milan, 1925)
P. Litta: *Famiglie celebri italiane* (Florence, 1862), ii, pp. 83–4
A. G. Mansuelli: 'Il torso Gaddi nella Galleria degli Uffizi', *Boll. A.*, xliii (1958), pp. 1–11

(2) Niccolò Gaddi (*b* Florence, 12 Oct 1537; *d* Florence, 14 June 1591). Nephew of (1) Giovanni de' Gaddi. He was the son of Sinibaldo Gaddi and Lucrezia Strozzi and he was one of the most important collectors in Florence in the second half of the 16th century. He was close to the Medici and held important political posts as ambassador to Ferrara in 1569 and as part of the entourage of Eleonora de' Medici on her bridal journey to Mantua in 1584. His collection, which he kept in the Florentine palazzo in Via del Giglio, is known through a detailed inventory. It reflected the artistic and scientific interests of the court of Francesco I de' Medici, being a mixture of *naturalia* and *artificialia* typical of late 16th-century collections. In addition to works of art, antiques and natural curiosities, Gaddi collected a rich library and a vast collection of drawings, five volumes (bought in 1574) being from Giorgio Vasari's collection (*see* VASARI, (1) §IV). Before that time drawings had not been greatly esteemed by collectors.

To increase his collection and his botanical garden, Gaddi corresponded with many artists and dealers, not only on his own behalf but also on that of Francesco I de' Medici. Early sources often praise him not only for his collection but also for having commissioned the Gaddi Chapel in S Maria Novella in Florence, which was designed by Giovanni Antonio Dosio (1575–6); Giovanni Bandini made marble relief panels of the *Presentation of the Virgin* and the *Marriage of the Virgin* for the chapel in the 1570s and Alessandro Allori painted the frescoes of the dome. Gaddi was in constant contact with this artist and in fact may himself have been an amateur architect. In 1579 he was appointed lieutenant of the Accademia dell'Arte e Disegno. He was a friend of Federico Zuccaro and contributed to the polemics over the frescoes for the dome of Florence Cathedral. With his death the Gaddi family became extinct, and Niccolò's collections were inherited by his Pitti nephews.

BIBLIOGRAPHY

G. de' Ricci: *Il priorista* (Florence, 1595)
S. Ammirato: 'Lettera al Cardinal Ferdinando de' Medici', *Opuscoli* (Florence, 1637–42), ii, pp. 55–7

J. Gaddi: 'Elogio di Niccolò Gaddi', *Elogi storici in versi e in prosa* (Florence, 1639), p. 271

G. G. Bottari and S. Ticozzi: *Raccolta di lettere sulla pittura, scultura e architettura* (Milan, 1822), iii, pp. 262–327

C. Valone: 'A Note on the Collection of Niccolò Gaddi', *Crit. A.*, xlii (1977), pp. 151–207

C. Acidini Luchinat: 'Niccolò Gaddi collezionista e dilettante del cinquecento', *Paragone*, xxxi (1980), no. 359–61, pp. 141–75

DONATELLA PEGAZZANO

Gaddiano, Anonimo. *See* MAGLIABECHIANO, ANONIMO.

Gadō. *See* ONO GADŌ.

Gaertner, Eduard (*b* Berlin, 2 June 1801; *d* Zechlin, Brandenburg, 22 Feb 1877). German painter and lithographer. His father was a master carpenter and his mother a gold embroiderer, and he had his first drawing lessons in 1811 in Kassel, where he had gone with his mother after the occupation of Berlin. After returning to Berlin he became in 1814 an apprentice painter at the Königliche Porzellanmanufaktur; and from 1821 he studied under Carl Wilhelm Gropius (1793–1870), then engaged as a painter of stage sets at the Königliches Theater in Berlin and also known for his townscapes. Here Gaertner developed skill in the rendering of perspective. He first exhibited at the Akademie der Künste, Berlin, in the following year. In 1824–5 he was commissioned to paint interior views of Berlin Cathedral (see fig.) and the chapel of the Schloss Charlottenburg (both Berlin, Schloss Charlottenburg). In return, he was granted funds to enable him to spend three years in Paris, where he studied under François Bertin. Gaertner's views of Paris already show his gift for lighting and use of staffage. His special ability lay in his understanding of the character of a city as the work of its inhabitants.

Eduard Gaertner: *Interior View of Berlin Cathedral*, oil on canvas, 770×620 mm, 1824 (Berlin, Schloss Charlottenburg)

After his return to Berlin he swiftly established himself as the leading painter of urban views, which he regularly showed at Berlin Akademie exhibitions. Interest in this genre grew along with the spate of building activity in Berlin after the end of the wars against Napoleon. There was a fresh interest in paintings of new buildings in particular, intended for a local rather than a visitors' market. Two large views of the former Berlin Schloss, *The Schlüterhof* and *The Eosanderhof* (both 1831; Potsdam, Neues Pal.), show Gaertner's bold use of light and shadow. With the six-part panorama *View over Berlin from the Roof of the Friedrich-Wedersche Church* (1834; Berlin, Schloss Charlottenburg) Gaertner showed the spread of the city by this time. After painting a replica of this work for the Prussian king's daughter Alexandra Feodorovna, Empress of Russia, in 1835–6 (St Petersburg, Hermitage), Gaertner visited Russia in 1837, and again from 1838 to 1839, staying in both St Petersburg and Moscow. He completed a large number of city views, including a three-part view of *The Kremlin* (1839; Berlin, Schloss Charlottenburg), commissioned by Frederick William III. With the death of the Prussian king in 1840, Gaertner lost his most powerful patron and interest in his work began to wane as it came to seem too stiff and objective to Romantic sensibilities. Gaertner tried to adapt to the change in taste, adopting a more painterly approach; in particular, he paid attention to effects of lighting. The vogue for city views had passed its peak, however, and Gaertner turned to landscape painting. Journeys to Prague in 1841–2, through West and East Prussia in 1845–6, and to Silesia in 1848–51 introduced new subjects; but it was architecture rather than setting that most engaged Gaertner's attention. At this period he occasionally also invented ideal landscape settings for real buildings, as in the *Ruined Monastery of Lehnin in an Imaginary Mountain Landscape* (Berlin, Schloss Charlottenburg). Gaertner also produced watercolours of interiors and lithographs of both landscape and city views; but after the middle of the century his productivity in all respects dwindled. (An example of his work from this period is his oil painting of the *Bauakademie and Friedrich-Wedersche-Kirche* in Berlin (1868; Berlin, Tiergarten, N.G.; *see* SCHINKEL, KARL FRIEDRICH, fig. 2).) The rise of photography appeared to be making the architectural painter redundant.

Thieme–Becker

BIBLIOGRAPHY

W. Kiewitz: *Eduard Gaertner: Verzeichnis seiner Originallithographien* (Berlin, 1928)

Eduard Gaertner (exh. cat., ed. I. Wirth; W. Berlin, Berlin Mus., 1968)

Eduard Gaertner, 1801–1877 (exh. cat., ed. U. Cosmann; E. Berlin, Märk. Mus., 1968)

I. Wirth: *Eduard Gaertner: Der Berliner Architekturmaler* (Frankfurt am Main, 1978)

E. Trost: *Eduard Gaertner, 1801–1877* (Berlin, 1991)

HELMUT BÖRSCH-SUPAN

Gaertner, Peter. *See* GERTNER, PETER.

Gaetano, il. *See* PULZONE, SCIPIONE.

Gafar, Melchiorre. *See* CAFFA, MELCHIORRE.

Gagarin, Grigory (Grigor'yevich) (*b* St Petersburg, 11 May 1810; *d* Châtellerault, 30 Jan 1893). Russian painter, draughtsman and writer. In 1823–4 he studied in Rome under the Russian painter Karl Bryullov, but he otherwise lacked any formal artistic training. From 1832 Gagarin was in the diplomatic corps, and from 1841–64 he was in military service, mainly in the Caucasus, where he took part in fighting. Gagarin developed his talents by practice in drawing and painting. He worked as an illustrator, and his scenes for Sollogub's story *Tarantas* (St Petersburg, 1845) give a very realistic picture of Russian provincial life and expose the ugly truth behind the elegant façade of the Russian empire of the period. Several of Gagarin's lithographs are well-known, including a series of portraits and also a title page for Pushkin's poem *Ruslan and Lyudmila* in which Gagarin attempted to move away from making decorative vignettes to conveying the content of the literary work.

While in the Caucasus, Gagarin carried out a great deal of sketching, skilfully depicting battle scenes, military life and exotic landscapes. He also produced many portraits. In the 1840s he began to work in oils. His most famous oil paintings are: *Karagach: The General Headquarters of the Nizhegorodskiy Regiment* (*c.* 1840; St Petersburg, Rus. Mus.), the *Meeting of Shamil' with General Klyukke von Klyugenau* (1849; Moscow, Tret'yakov Gal.) and *Battle at Akhatla 8 May 1841* (*c.* 1840; St Petersburg, Rus. Mus.). In 1854 Gagarin was summoned to St Petersburg to work at the Academy of Arts; from 1859 to 1872 he was its Vice-president. At the Academy he organized a museum of Byzantine and Russian antiquities. For the last 20 years of his life he was a full member of the Russian Archaeological Society, publishing albums of ornaments and articles about Russian art.

WRITINGS

Sobraniye vizantiyskikh, gruzinskikh i drevnerusskikh ornamentov i pamyatnikov arkhitektury [A collection of Byzantine, Georgian and old Russian ornaments and architectural monuments] (St Petersburg, 1897–1903)

Vospominaniya Knyazya G. G. Gagarina o Karle Bryullove [Grand Duke G. G. Gagarin's recollections of Karl Bryullov] (St Petersburg, 1900)

BIBLIOGRAPHY

A. Savinov: *Grigory Grigor'yevich Gagarin, 1810–1893* (Moscow, 1951)

G. A. PRINTSEVA

Gage, George (*b* ?Firle, Sussex, *c.* 1592; *d* London, 1638). English diplomat and connoisseur. As early as 1616 he was involved in negotiations with Rubens on Sir Dudley Carleton's behalf and came to know the artist better than any other Englishman. During the 1620s Gage acted as an agent for English collectors, especially Charles I. In 1629 Gage was in Rome, where he obtained moulds, including one of the Borghese *Gladiator* (Paris, Louvre) owned by Cardinal Scipione Borghese and kept at the latter's villa, which enabled Hubert Le Sueur to cast copies in bronze (Windsor Castle, Berks, Royal Col.) for Charles I. Gage's own home (destr.) in Queen Street, Westminster, London, was 'a palace adorned with lascivious pictures . . . which the statue of a golden queen adornes'—presumably a reference to a cast of Le Sueur's bust of *Queen Henrietta Maria*. Gage, who was the architect of the house (destr.) built nearby in St James's Park for Alathea Howard, Countess of Arundel, is the chief individual depicted in van Dyck's *Portrait of a Man with Two Attendants* (London, N.G.), probably painted in Italy in the early 1620s.

BIBLIOGRAPHY

W. Prynne: *Rome's Master-peece* (London, 1643), p. 24

W. N. Sainsbury: *Original Unpublished Papers Illustrative of the Life of Sir Peter Paul Rubens* (London, 1859)

Van Dyck in England (exh. cat. by O. Millar, London, N.P.G., 1982)

D. Howarth: *Lord Arundel and his Circle* (London and New Haven, 1985)

DAVID HOWARTH

Gagini [Gaggini; Gazini; Gazzini]. Italian family of sculptors, masons and architects. One branch of the family, which came from Bissone, Ticino, was active in Genoa from the 15th century. (1) Domenico Gagini initially worked there, as did his nephew (2) Elia Gagini and their relation (3) Giovanni Gagini. In the early 16th century Giovanni's brother (4) Pace Gagini collaborated with Antonio della Porta (*see* PORTA, DELLA, (1)), his and Giovanni's uncle, on work that included French and Spanish commissions. The Gagini workshop was organized along medieval lines: they produced works in collaboration, combining the skills of mason and sculptor. Their work was chiefly of a decorative and ornamental nature, figurative sculpture being of secondary importance. They remained active in Genoa until the 19th century.

Domenico, one of the most innovative members of the family, settled in Sicily between 1458 and 1463 and founded a separate branch that remained active until the 17th century. Domenico's son (5) Antonello Gagini was an outstanding sculptor: later generations, including Antonello's son Fazio Gagini (1520–67), merely copied earlier designs and produced derivative works. So far, it has only been possible to reconstruct the genealogy of the Sicilian branch of the family.

BIBLIOGRAPHY

Thieme–Becker

F. Alizeri: *Notizie dei professori del disegno in Liguria dalle origini al secolo XVI*, iv (Genoa, 1876)

G. di Marzo: *I Gagini e la scultura in Sicilia nei secoli XV e XVI*, 2 vols (Palermo, 1880–83)

A. Venturi: *Storia* (Milan, 1901–40), vi

L. A. Cervetto: *I Gagini da Bissone: Loro opere in Genova ed altrove* (Milan, 1903)

H.-W. Kruft: *Domenico Gagini und seine Werkstatt* (Munich, 1972)

——: *Antonello Gagini und seine Söhne* (Munich, 1980)

(1) Domenico Gagini (*b* Bissone, *c.* 1425–30; *d* Palermo, 29–30 Sept 1492). Filarete referred to a 'Domenico from the lake of Lugano, disciple of Pippo di Ser Brunelleschi' (*Trattato di architettura*, Milan, 1461–4), and it seems probable that Domenico was apprenticed to Brunelleschi, although there is no documentary evidence. As a sculptor, Domenico was most influenced by Donatello. Domenico's first major commission was the façade of the chapel of S Giovanni Battista in Genoa Cathedral, on which he worked from 1448 until 1456–7 (see fig.). This façade is reminiscent of the porch of Brunelleschi's Pazzi Chapel in Florence and also reflects a knowledge of Donatello's work. Stylistically, however, it remains a product of the Lombard early Renaissance decorative style; probably many Lombard assistants were involved. Other works by Domenico that date from *c.* 1455 include an overdoor relief of *St John the Baptist in the Wilderness* (Lawrence, U. KS, Spencer Mus. A.), a statuette of the *Virgin and Child* (ex-Berlin, Staatl. Museen; destr.) and another statuette of the *Virgin and Child* in the sacristy of Torcello Cathedral.

Domenico was first recorded in Naples in January 1458. With Isaia da Pisa, Antonio Chellino (*fl* 1446–60), Pietro

Domenico Gagini: panels showing the *Life of St John the Baptist*, marble, 1448–56/7 (Genoa Cathedral, Chapel of S Giovanni Battista)

di Martino da Milano, Francesco Laurana and Paolo Romano, he undertook to complete the triumphal arch of the Castelnuovo. Only the group of wind-players to the far right of the triumphal frieze and the figure of *Temperance* on the upper tier can be ascribed to him. The lively procession of musicians is deeply undercut, with some figures carved almost in the round. Of the four Virtues set in niches, *Temperance* is the most graceful. Her head is inclined, and her cloak is arranged in a diagonal sweep falling heavily over her feet. While in Naples, Domenico also produced a portal with a double-sided overdoor relief in the Sala dei Baroni at the Castelnuovo (largely destr. 1919) and a recess containing a statuette of the *Virgin and Child* (Naples, Capodimonte) in the former sacristy of the chapel of St Barbara in the Castelnuovo. The relief of the *Adoration of the Christ Child* (Washington, DC, N.G.A.) probably also dates from this period. Stylistically, all these works show a fluidity of line more characteristic of painting than of sculpture.

Shortly after the death of Alfonso of Aragon in 1458, Domenico seems to have moved to Sicily, although he was first documented there in 1463. His first work there was probably the restoration of the 12th-century mosaics in the Cappella Palatina in Palermo. In 1463 Pietro Speciale, at that time Praetor of Palermo, commissioned him to make a tomb for his son Antonio. The recumbent figure, in S Francesco d'Assisi, Palermo, was rediscovered in 1948 (there is some controversy about whether to ascribe the work to Domenico or to Francesco Laurana). He was probably commissioned at the same time to make

the portrait bust of *Pietro Speciale* dated 1468 (Palermo, Pal. Speciale-Raffadali). From 1463 Domenico carried out several commissions in Palermo and for patrons in other parts of Sicily and in Mallorca. In 1465 he paid a brief visit to Genoa on business. Thereafter he appears never to have left Sicily.

Works of a particularly high quality include *St Julian* (c. 1463; Salemi, Chiesa Madre); an allegorical overdoor relief of *Ferdinand of Aragon Enthroned* (after 1473; Los Angeles, CA, Co. Mus. A.); the reliquary of *Gandolfo da Binesco* (1482; Polizzi Generosa, Chiesa Madre); the tomb of *Bishop Giovanni Montaperto* (*d* 1485) in Mazara del Vallo Cathedral; and the monument to *Panormus* (the base of which is probably by Gabriele di Battista; Palermo, Municipio). These examples show how Domenico's agitated but elegant style, in which he breaks down the contours, gradually lost its vigour. While in Sicily Domenico left an increasing amount of work to his studio assistants, with a consequent fall in the artistic standard. Much of the work became stereotyped, and his studio continued to reproduce a number of items, such as Madonnas, in a standardized manner—even after the artist's death.

Domenico also traded in sugar and owned a property business. In 1487 he was a leading signatory among the *marmorarii* and *fabricatores* of Palermo when they petitioned for independent legal status.

BIBLIOGRAPHY
S. Bottari: 'Per Domenico Gagini', *Riv. A.*, xvii (1935), pp. 77–85
W. R. Valentiner: 'The Early Development of Domenico Gagini', *Burl. Mag.*, lxxvi (1940), pp. 76–87
S. Bottari: 'Nuovi studi su Domenico Gagini', *Siculorum Gymnasium*, n. s., ii (1949), pp. 324–30
M. Accascina: 'Sculptores habitatores Panormi', *Riv. Ist. N. Archeol. & Stor. A.*, n. s., viii (1950), pp. 269–313
——: 'Aggiunte a Domenico Gagini', *Boll. A.*, xliv (1959), pp. 19–29
E. Arslan, ed.: *Architetti e scultori del quattrocento* (Como, 1959), i of Arte e artisti dei laghi lombardi
S. Bottari: 'Un'opera di Francesco Laurana', *Boll. A.*, xlv (1960), pp. 213–16
F. Meli: 'Francesco Laurana o Domenico Gagini?', *Nuovi quaderni del Meridione*, iii (1965), pp. 305–15
B. Patera: 'Sull'attività di Francesco Laurana in Sicilia', *Annali del Liceo Classico 'G. Garibaldi' di Palermo*, ii (1965), pp. 526–50
M. Donato: *Domenico Gagini nel periodo pre-siciliano* (Acireale, 1968)
M. Accasiana: 'Inediti di scultura del rinascimento in Sicilia', *Mitt. Ksthist. Inst. Florenz*, xiv (1970), pp. 251–96
H.-W. Kruft: 'Die Madonna von Trapani und ihre Kopien', *Mitt. Ksthist. Inst. Florenz*, xiv (1970), pp. 297–320
——: 'La cappella di San Giovanni Battista nel duomo di Genova', *Ant. Viva*, ix/4 (1970), pp. 33–50
G. L. Hersey: *The Aragonese Arch at Naples, 1443–1475* (New Haven, 1973)
H.-W. Kruft and M. Malmanger: 'Der Triumphbogen Alfonsos in Neapel', *Acta Archaeol. & A. Historiam Pertinentia*, vi (1975), pp. 213–305
H.-W. Kruft and F. Negri Arnoldi: 'Postille a Domenico Gagini', *Boll. A.*, lx (1975), pp. 242–4
F. Negri Arnoldi: 'Revisione di Domenico Gagini', *Boll. A.*, lx (1975), pp. 18–29
B. Patera: 'Scultura di rinascimento in Sicilia', *Stor. A.*, 24/25 (1975), pp. 151–8
R. Pane: *Il rinascimento nell'Italia meridionale*, ii (Milan, 1977), pp. 302–7

(2) Elia Gagini [Elia de Bissone] (*fl* 1441–89). Nephew of (1) Domenico Gagini. He has often been confused with other sculptors called Elia (such as Elia di Bartolomeo da Ponte Lombardo, active in Città di Castello). No works can be securely attributed to him. In 1441, and again between 1450 and 1454, he worked on the Loggia Comunale in Udine. On 8 March 1457 he was named as Domenico Gagini's representative for work undertaken and accounts due in connection with the chapel of S Giovanni Battista in Genoa Cathedral. It is not clear how much he contributed to the chapel's façade. In 1465 Domenico Gagini took a six-year lease on a house in Genoa for his nephew Elia. In 1472 Elia undertook to make a number of columns and transport them to Seville. In 1478 he paid rent on a studio in Genoa. In 1512 a report compiled by Romerio da Campione (*fl* 1508–19) mentions the late Elia Gagini's contributions to the decoration of a chapel of the Madonna delle Rose in S Maria di Castello, Genoa, but it is impossible to identify surviving fragments in this church with the chapel decorations.

BIBLIOGRAPHY

L. Filippini: 'Elia Gaggini da Bissone', *L'Arte*, xi (1908), pp. 17–29
C. Someda: 'Architetti e lapicidi lombardi in Friuli nei secoli XV e XVI', *Architetti e scultori del quattrocento*, ed. E. Arslan, i (Como, 1959), pp. 309–42, i of Arte e artisti dei laghi lombardi
H.-W. Kruft: 'La cappella di San Giovanni Battista nel duomo di Genova', *Ant. Viva*, ix/4 (1970), pp. 33–50

(3) Giovanni Gagini (*fl* Genoa, 1449–1514; *d* Mendrisio, *c.* 1517). Relation of (2) Elia Gagini. He was the son of Beltrame Gagini (*d* before 1476). His earliest surviving work is the rose window in S Michele, Pigna, Liguria, which is inscribed and dated 1450. Giovanni's later architectural works continue to show the influence of the Lombard Late Gothic style, already clearly apparent here. In 1451–2 Giovanni and Leonardo Riccomanno (*fl* 1431; *d* after 1472) jointly executed a portal in the sacristy of S Maria di Castello, Genoa. In 1457 Giovanni was commissioned to make the portal of the Palazzo Doria-Quartara, Genoa. The ornamental doorframe supports a rectangular marble overdoor relief of *St George and the Dragon*. The scene is flanked by two shield-bearing soldiers, reverses from a single design. This portal establishes the design for the decoratively unified Genoese portal type. *St George and the Dragon* became the principal and most important theme for Genoese portals during the 1450s and 1460s, partly because of the old devotion to St George in Genoa and partly due to the Banco di S Giorgio, to which the city owed its economic prosperity. Other Genoese portals by Giovanni or his studio are those in the Palazzo Brancaleone Grillo, where he may also have helped construct the courtyard, and at the Palazzo Valdettaro–Fieschi. There are also two overdoor reliefs in the Victoria and Albert Museum, London. In 1487–8 he delivered overdoor reliefs of *St George* to Lerici, Liguria, and to Bastia, Corsica. Other reliefs produced in his studio found their way to Chios. Characteristic of all these works is an ornamental, decorative style that betrays little individuality. In 1461 Giovanni was in charge of the construction of the Ponte S Zita, Genoa.

In 1465, when Giovanni was in Genoa, Domenico Gagini declared himself in Giovanni's debt for deliveries of marble. In the same year Giovanni was commissioned by Matteo Fieschi and Giacomo Fieschi to decorate their family chapel in Genoa Cathedral: the tomb of *Cardinal Giorgio Fieschi* (*d* 1461) and the entrance arch still survive. In 1475 Giovanni and Michele d'Aria (*fl* 1446–1502) were commissioned by Francesco Spinola to construct a marble

fountain and a marble screen adorned with angels for the chapel of S Vincenzo in S Domenico, Genoa. In 1488 Giovanni agreed to build a chapel in S Maria delle Vigne, Genoa, and to decorate it. Neither work survives. In 1504 Giovanni authorized his nephew Antonio Barosino to collect outstanding debts, especially from his brothers Antonio Gagini (*fl* 1504; *d* between 1526 and 1532) and (4) Pace Gagini. In 1506 he acquired from Bernardo Forno da Campione a stock of marble and *pietra nera* (slate). From 1507 Giovanni lived in Mendrisio, and a votive relief in the cloister of the Servite monastery in Mendrisio is dated 1514. In 1517 he made his will.

SKL

BIBLIOGRAPHY

E. Gavazza: 'Ricerche sull'attività dei Gagini architetti a Genova', *Architetti e scultori del quattrocento*, ed. E. Arslan (Como, 1959), pp. 173–84, i of Arte e artisti dei laghi lombardi
J. Pope-Hennessy and R. Lightbown: *Catalogue of Italian Sculpture in the Victoria and Albert Museum*, i (London, 1964), pp. 386–91
H.-W. Kruft: *Portali genovesi del rinascimento* (Florence, 1971)
E. Poleggi: *Santa Maria di Castello e il romanico a Genova* (Genoa, 1973), p. 141
H.-W. Kruft: 'Alcuni portali genovesi del rinascimento fuori Genova', *Ant. Viva*, xvii/6 (1978), pp. 31–5

(4) Pace [Pasio] **Gagini** (*fl* 1493–1521). Brother of (3) Giovanni Gagini. Pace was trained in the masons' lodge at the Certosa di Pavia. Initially he worked for his uncle Antonio della Porta (see PORTA, DELLA, (1)) as a *piccatore lapidum*. On 6 November 1493 he signed a four-year contract with his uncle Antonio to work as a *scultor et magister figurarum marmoris*. Pace's collaboration and partnership with his uncle lasted until 1513. In 1501 Francesco Lomellini commissioned them to construct a family chapel in S Teodoro, Genoa. After the church's destruction in 1870, the altar retable, depicting the *Adoration of the Christ Child*, and the monument to Lomellini were incorporated into the present church. In 1504 Pace undertook to supply two marble columns for the main doorway of the monastery church of the Certosa di Pavia. Before 1513 Pace and della Porta worked on the right-hand tabernacle in the choir of the Certosa, which had probably been commissioned from Francesco Briosco (*fl* 1500–11) in 1511.

From 1506 Gagini and della Porta undertook a number of commissions for France, including a fountain (dismantled 1759) for the château of Gaillon, near Rouen, which is recorded in a drawing (*c.* 1575; London, BM) and engraving by Jacques Androuet Du Cerceau the elder, and the tomb of *Raoul de Lannoy and Jeanne de Poix* in the parish church of Folleville, Picardy, on which the recumbent effigy of *Raoul de Lannoy* (see fig.), the French Governor of Genoa, bears Pace's signature. The tomb relief of mourning putti, attributable to Pace alone, shows a classical influence. A statuette of the *Virgin and Child*, which both della Porta and Pace signed, is in the parish church of Ruisseauville, Pas-de-Calais. In 1508 both sculptors were paid for the seated figure of *Francesco Lomellini* in the Palazzo S Giorgio, Genoa, although only Pace signed the work. In all these works Pace's individual style is hard to define, since the sculptor always collaborated with his uncle.

In 1520 Pace and Girolamo Viscardi, among others, signed a petition addressed to the municipality of Genoa

Pace Gagini: tomb of *Raoul de Lannoy*, marble, 1507–8 (Folleville Church, Picardy)

asking for the sculptors to be released from their dependence on the *antelami* and given separate legal status. On 1 April 1521 Pace appointed the sculptor Francesco de' Brocchi to be his representative in Genoa. This is probably connected with his departure for Seville. In 1520 Pace seems to have been commissioned by Don Fadrique de Henríquez de Ribera to make the tomb of his mother, Doña Catalina Ribera. No documentary record for this commission exists. The tomb, which Pace signed, was erected in the charterhouse of Seville and is now in the university church. It consists of two arches raised on a high base, the outer supported on piers, the inner on highly decorated columns, with niches containing figures of saints. The recess is decorated with rectangular reliefs of *Christ in Limbo* and *Christ Carrying the Cross* beneath a lunette of the *Adoration of the Shepherds*. The recumbent effigy lies on a bier supported by winged, sphinx-like figures. The tomb combines classical details, such as flying victories and putti, with the surface decoration typical of Lombard sculpture. The design follows the pattern of a typical 15th-century Roman tomb set into a wall, such as the tomb of *Paul II* (ex-St Peter's, Rome; fragments Rome, Grotte Vaticane, and Paris, Louvre) by Giovanni Dalmata and Mino da Fiesole. Pace himself can only have been responsible for a small part of its execution.

Pace Gagini is important in the dissemination of Lombard Renaissance sculpture into France and Spain. His style is very difficult to isolate since it is bound up with traditional studio methods then current in Genoa.

BIBLIOGRAPHY

C. Justi: 'Lombardische Bildwerke in Spanien', *Jb. Kön.-Preuss. Kstsamml.*, xiii (1892), pp. 3–22, 68–90 [repr. in C. Justi: *Miscellaneen aus drei Jahrhunderten spanischen Kunstlebens*, i (Berlin, 1908)]
C. Magenta: *La Certosa di Pavia* (Milan, 1897)
L. Beltrami: 'Pasio Gaggini di Bissone alla Certosa di Pavia', *Rass. A.*, iv (1904), pp. 26–8
——: 'Le opere di Pasio Gaggini in Francia', *Rass. A.*, iv (1904), pp. 58–62
R. Maiocchi: *Codice diplomatico artistico di Pavia dall'anno 1330 all'anno 1550*, 2 vols (Pavia, 1937–49)
R. Bossaglia: 'La scultura', *La Certosa di Pavia* (Milan, 1968), pp. 39–80
H.-W. Kruft: 'Antonio della Porta genannt Tamagnino', *Pantheon*, xxviii (1970), pp. 401–14
——: 'Genuesische Skulpturen der Renaissance in Frankreich', *Actes du XXII congrès international d'histoire de l'art: Budapest, 1972*, pp. 697–704
——: 'Pace Gagini and the Sepulchres of the Ribera in Seville', *Actas del XXIII congreso internacional de historia del arte: Granada, 1977*, pp. 327–38
C. R. Morschek jr: *Relief Sculpture for the Façade of the Certosa di Pavia, 1473–1499* (New York, 1978)

(5) Antonello [Antonio] **Gagini** (*b* Palermo, 1478–9; *d* Palermo, between 31 March and 22 April 1536). Son of (1) Domenico Gagini. He was the leading representative of the Sicilian branch of the family. He was trained as a sculptor in the studio of his father. Between 1504 and 1506 he appears to have been in Calabria and Rome, where he briefly worked as Michelangelo's assistant on the tomb of *Julius II* (relief on the left-hand socle of the *Rachel* niche, S Pietro in Vincoli). His early work shows the influence of Francesco Laurana, Michelangelo and Andrea Sansovino. Antonello built up a large studio, and for decades he was able to monopolize all the major sculptural commissions in Sicily and, to some extent, Calabria. However, the large scale of his studio led to artistic and stylistic stagnation. Antonello's work as an architect still needs further research.

From 1498 to 1508 Antonello based his studio in Messina and produced statues of the Virgin and Child, altar retables and tombs. In 1507 he received his most important commission: to provide sculptures for the chancel of Palermo Cathedral. Work went on until 1574, long after his death. This, one of the largest ensembles of sculptures produced in the Renaissance, was arranged on two levels, with pilaster strips dividing the 42 statues, reliefs and friezes. The whole ensemble combines both Italian and Spanish stylistic and compositional elements. While the cathedral was being restructured along classical lines (1781–1801) the ensemble was broken up, but most of the figures survive (the figures of *Christ* and the *Apostles* are on the altar in the chancel), and it has been possible to reconstruct it in a drawing (Kruft, 1980). In some of these figures Antonello achieved a simple monumentality.

Antonello undertook many commissions for Sicily, Calabria and Malta, some of which he had to delegate to other studios. He worked mainly in marble, but sometimes also in a mixture of plaster and a papier mâché (*mistura*), terracotta and bronze. Other works of especially high quality include a marble arch and altar retable (1503–17; Palermo, S Zita); *St John the Baptist* (1521–2; Castelvetrano, S Giovanni Battista); the *Annunciation* (1525; Erice, Mus. Civ. Cordici); the altar retable of *St George* (1526; Palermo, S Francesco d'Assisi); and the tomb of *Antonio Scirotta* (*c.* 1527; Palermo, S Zita). Stylistically, Antonello's works are striking both for their high degree of technical expertise and for a sentimentality of expression that gives them common appeal. He was highly respected and from 1517 was consul of the sculptors' guild of Palermo. Antonello also had dealings in agriculture and trade, and he acquired numerous properties. Artistically and socially he appears to have identified himself with the artisan milieu in which he moved.

Antonello's five sons, Giandomenico (*b* 1503; *fl* until 1560), Antonino (*b* before 1514; *fl* until 1574), Giacomo (1517–98), Fazio (1520–67) and (Giovan) Vincenzo (1527–95), were also sculptors. They were all employed in their father's large workshop. Although they never achieved Antonello's high standard, each son developed a fairly individual style, and the following pieces can be attributed thus: a marble arch by Antonello, Antonino, Giandomenico and Giacomo (1531–9; Trapani, Santuario della SS Annunziata); the *Transfiguration* by Antonino (*c.* 1537; Mazaro del Vallo Cathedral); and the reliefs on the arch of the Cappella del Crocifisso (1557–65; Palermo Cathedral) by Fazio and Vincenzo. This last was dismantled in the 18th century, but there is a sketched reconstruction in Kruft (1979, 1980).

BIBLIOGRAPHY

V. Auria: *Il Gagino redivivo, o'vero notitia della vita, ed opere d'Antonio Gagino* (Palermo, 1698)
A. Gallo: *Elogio storico di Antonio Gagini* (Palermo, 1860)
F. Meli: *Matteo Carnilivari e l'architettura del quattro- e cinquecento a Palermo* (Rome, 1958)
V. Regina: *Antonello Gagini e sculture cinquecentesche in Alcamo* (Palermo, 1969)
H.-W. Kruft: 'Die Cappella del Crocifisso im Dom von Palermo: Ein Rekonstruktion', *Pantheon*, xxxvii (1979), pp. 37–45
——: *Antonello Gagini und seine Söhne* (Munich, 1980)

HANNO-WALTER KRUFT

Gagliardi, Rosario (*b* Syracuse, ?1682; *d* Noto, ?1762). Italian architect. He was already living in Noto in 1708 and remained there for most of his life. The old town on Monte Alveria, 7 km to the north-west, had been destroyed by an earthquake in 1693, and Gagliardi's career was mostly spent in the construction of the new town (*see* NOTO). In 1713 he began work on plans for S Maria dell'Arco, in which he showed a traditionalist tendency. By then he had already acquired the title of Magister, and he reached the status of *architetto* in 1726. He was later appointed municipal architect, a greatly coveted position involving special commissions from the municipality. He also seems to have collaborated on the planning, construction and supervision of the most important religious buildings in Noto. As well as S Maria dell'Arco, the churches of S Chiara (1748), S Domenico (1727; façade 1732–6) and SS Crocifisso are now known to be his work, while others are attributed to him (S Carlo, S Nicolò, SS Salvatore). As 'architect of the city of Noto and its valley', Gagliardi also worked in Syracuse, Modica, Ragusa, Caltagirone and Comiso. An excellent example of his spatial inventiveness can be seen in the plan for S Giorgio (1744), Ragusa Ibla, where he revealed his mastery of façade design with a campanile in the Sicilian style. His use of this element, together with his strong interest in the scenic setting of his buildings, was something he shared with other architects working in 18th-century Europe. That model, with its transformation of the central part of the campanile into a tower, had a widespread influence on the buildings constructed in the Val di Noto; in Gagliardi's own work the Austrian-style central tower may be seen again at Noto Cathedral (S Nicolò) and at S Giorgio (1738), Modica. In 1762, by then in poor health, Gagliardi appointed his nephew Vincenzo Sinatra, already his collaborator, as his proxy and successor. After that date Gagliardi's name disappears from all documents, so that 1762 is thought to be the year of his death. Recent research has revealed Gagliardi to have had a considerable influence on his contemporaries in Noto. His work shows the strong imprint of the Italian Baroque tradition, mediated by his knowledge of basic Renaissance concepts and his familiarity with the treatise literature.

BIBLIOGRAPHY

L. di Blasi and F. Genovesi: *Rosario Gagliardi: Architetto dell'ingegnosa città di Noto* (Catania, 1972)
C. G. Canale: *Noto: La struttura continua della città tardo-barocca* (Palermo, 1976)
S. Tobriner: *The Genesis of Noto* (London, 1982)

LUCIA TRIGILIA

Gagneraux, Bénigne (*b* Dijon, 24 Sept 1756; *d* Florence, 18 Aug 1795). French painter and engraver. He was one of the most important artists to emerge from François Devosge's school of art in Dijon. His reputation, like that of his fellow Dijonnais artist Pierre-Paul Prud'hon, is based on a number of Neo-classical works of a pleasingly poetic character, which Devosge had encouraged. In 1776 he became the first artist from the Dijon art school to win the Prix de Rome with his painting of an uplifting moral subject, *Manius Curius Dentatus Refusing the Presents of the Samnites* (Nancy, Mus. B.-A.). The Dijon academy was very quickly recognized as one of the most important outside Paris. As a student there Gagneraux was directed towards examples from antiquity, the Italian Renaissance and the work of Poussin. During his four-year study period in Rome (1779–81) he worked on a copy (Dijon, Pal. Justice) of Raphael's *School of Athens* (Rome, Vatican, Stanze Raffaello) to fulfil his obligation to the States of Burgundy which sponsored him. He spent most of his life in Italy, working in the company of Anton Raphael Mengs, Johan Tobias Sergel and Henry Fuseli in the 1770s and with Antonio Canova, Gavin Hamilton, Goethe and Jacques-Louis David in the 1780s. In 1784 he was recognized as an artist of exceptional talent by Gustav III of Sweden, who visited Gagneraux's studio and bought the large painting *Blind Oedipus Commending his Family to the Gods* (Stockholm, Nmus.; see fig.). This subject, which was subsequently taken up by many painters, was unusual for its time. David, however, had produced *Blind Belisarius Begging for Alms* (Lille, Mus. B.-A.) in 1781, which was similar in subject, sentiment and style. In common with contemporary history painters in Paris, Gagneraux showed an interest in dramatic subjects, clear and legible gestures and expressions and stark, austere settings. *Oedipus* was a

turning-point in his career. As a direct consequence of the picture's success, he began to receive commissions from the King of Sweden and members of the court circle. One of the first of these was for a group portrait commemorating the meeting between Gustav III and Pope Pius VI in the Vatican (Stockholm, Nmus.). It was completed in 1785 and a copy (Prague, N.G., Šternberk Pal.), commissioned by the Pope, was done in 1786. It displayed Gagneraux's competence as a portrait painter and his ability to mass a large group on a grand scale. He took certain liberties with the architecture in an attempt to idealize it and with the positions of the main figures, which imitated those of the most revered antique statues shown in the background. This imaginative reconstruction of a solemn occasion, in which there was no attempt at absolute historical accuracy, was characteristic of Gagneraux's approach. Sandström pointed out the duality in Gagneraux's works, showing how disciplined studies from Egyptian statues and Greek vases in his notebooks were given as much attention as the paintings of more imaginative, fantasy subjects, such as the *Magician* (1790–95; Milan, Ambrosiana) or *Phaethon Terrified by the Sign of the Lion* (1790–95; Mâcon, Mus. Mun. Ursulines). The *Phaethon* is interesting not only for the surprisingly dynamic movement and rich, intense colouring but also for the unusual experimental technique employed. It is painted on gilded

Bénigne Gagneraux: *Blind Oedipus Commending his Family to the Gods*, oil on canvas, 1.22×1.63 m, 1784 (Stockholm, Nationalmuseum)

paper and laid down on panel, producing exciting light effects in certain areas.

In the last decade of his life Gagneraux showed an impressive range of subjects and great versatility in technique. He produced two large paintings of the *Battle of Senef* (1787–8) and *Crossing the Rhine* (1789–90). These were commissioned by the States of Burgundy and intended as the first in a series of six to decorate the ducal palace in Dijon in homage to the governor and his ancestors (now reinstalled in Dijon, Mus. B.-A., Salon Condé). These turbulent, confused battle scenes, influenced by those of Leonardo da Vinci, Raphael and Le Brun, were unrivalled until Napoleon commissioned similar scenes at the turn of the century. In 1787 Gagneraux painted a ceiling in the Villa Borghese, Rome, with *Jupiter and Antiope* (Rome, Gal. Borghese, room 18), which was at the time considered to be one of his best works and of which he painted a replica (untraced) in 1789 during his stay in Naples. He was most at ease with such mythological or allegorical subjects, and they dominated his works of the late 1780s and early 1790s. Examples include *Psyche Awakened by Love*, painted for the Palazzo Altieri, Rome (1790; *in situ*, Sala Pompeiana), and *Psyche Carried by Zephyrs to the Palace of Love* and *Hebe Giving Drink to the Eagle of Jupiter* (both 1792; Norrköping, Löfstad Slott), which were commissioned by Baron Evert Taube, a member of the King of Sweden's retinue. For this type of subject Gagneraux chose cool pastel colours and gave the figures softer forms and sweeter expressions, more appropriate to the textual source. This was the story of Cupid and Psyche from Apuleius' *Golden Ass*, which was popular among artists in the second half of the 18th century for decorative and easel painting alike. In 1792 he received a commission for *Soranus and Servilia* (Dijon, Mus. B.-A.) from the daughters of Louis XV; this unusual subject marked a return to his earlier type of history painting. Finally, in 1792, he published a collection of 18 of his own line-engravings, some recording his own earlier paintings, others original works. They were among the first of such collections, pre-dating the engravings made by Tommaso Piroli (*d* 1824), after John Flaxman's illustrations for the *Iliad*, by one year. Flaxman and Gagneraux knew each other and both studied Greek vases and engravings of antiquities, for example the *Antichità di Ercolano* (1757–96) and those in the collection of Sir William Hamilton.

The last years of Gagneraux's life were troubled by illness and by the Italians' hostility towards the French in Rome during the aftermath of the French Revolution. His studio was ransacked and his brother Claude was hounded out of Rome. Gagneraux himself eventually left in February 1793, intending to go to Sweden. He stopped in Florence, where he was made an 'accademico professore' and in 1794 he was appointed History Painter to the King of Sweden. He died in Florence after falling from a window. This was regarded as suicide rather than accident. In 1796 his brother mounted an exhibition of his work in Dijon.

BIBLIOGRAPHY

H. Baudot: 'Eloge historique de Bénigne Gagneraux', *Mém. Acad. Sci., A. & B.-Lett. Dijon*, liii (1845–6, rev. 2/1889), pp. 173–219

P. Quarré: 'Les Artistes bourguignons à Rome au XVIIIe siècle', *Société française de littérature comparée, Actes du troisième congrès national: Dijon, 1959*, pp. 19–26

S. Laveissière: *Dictionnaire des artistes et ouvriers d'art de Bourgogne* (Paris, 1980), pp. 222–5

B. Sandström: *Bénigne Gagneraux (1756–1795): Education, inspiration, oeuvre* (diss., Stockholm U., 1981)

Bénigne Gagneraux (1756–1795): Un Peintre bourguignon dans la Rome néo-classique (exh. cat., ed. S. Laveissière; Rome, Acad. France; Dijon, Mus. B.-A.; 1983)

HELEN WESTON

Gagnon, Charles (*b* Montreal, May 1934). Canadian painter and photographer. After studying briefly in Montreal, he moved to New York in 1956 and enrolled at the Parsons School of Design. He later studied painting at the New York School of Design (1957) and at New York University. He first exhibited in 1958 at the Galerie Artek in Montreal and the following year had his first one-man show there. He was in New York until 1960 and the paintings executed during this period clearly show the influence of Abstract Expressionism, for example *Untitled* (1956; see 1978 exh. cat., p. 128).

After returning to Montreal Gagnon made a series of collage works using newspaper and other printed matter, similar to those of Rauschenberg. These were followed in 1961 by a series of landscape paintings in which the paint was applied in a spontaneous, Expressionist manner, as in *Landscape* (1961; Ottawa, N.G.). During 1961–2 he worked on a number of shallow box constructions containing various objects and materials. In 1965 he was commissioned to provide designs for the Agricultural, Christian and Hydro-Québec pavilions at Expo 67 in Montreal (1967). In the late 1960s he produced paintings that were almost monochrome except for subtle colour variations, such as *(Steps) December* (1968–9; Montreal, Mus. F.A.). The later paintings employ a wider palette of broadly and spontaneously brushed colour, still showing the influence of Abstract Expressionism, as in *Cassation/Open* (1976; Ottawa, N.G.). Throughout his career he also worked with photography and film. His photographs often deal with the bleakness of urban life, as in *Men's Room, Union Station, Toronto* (1970; see 1978 exh. cat., p. 209).

BIBLIOGRAPHY

A. Paradis: *16 Quebec Painters in their Milieu* (Quebec, 1978), pp. 37–46

Charles Gagnon (exh. cat. by P. Fry, Montreal, Mus. F.A., 1978)

Gagnon, Clarence (Alphonse) (*b* Montreal, 8 Nov 1881; *d* Montreal, 5 Jan 1942). Canadian painter, printmaker and illustrator. His mother fostered his early talent for drawing and painting, and despite his father's wishes that he enter business he studied drawing and painting under William Brymner at the Art Association of Montreal (1897–1900). Through the patronage of the Montreal businessman and collector James Morgan, he was able to travel to Europe, studying from 1903 to 1905 at the Académie Julian, Paris, under Jean-Paul Laurens. Gagnon returned to Canada in 1909, settling in Baie-Saint-Paul (near Montreal), which became his preferred sketching area. His affection for French-Canadian life is evident in his anecdotal series of depictions of habitant life, a theme to which he returned throughout his career (e.g. *Horse Racing in Winter, Quebec, c.* 1927; Toronto, A.G. Ont.). He became an associate of the Royal Canadian Academy in 1910 and a full member in 1922. From 1911 to 1914 he moved between Canada,

France and Norway, always working up sketches he had done in Quebec. He ground his own paints, and from 1916 his palette consisted of pure white, reds, blues and yellows; his paintings are distinguished by their brilliancy of colour and simple, decorative design. From 1924 to 1936 Gagnon lived in Paris, where he illustrated in coloured woodblocks L. F. Pouquette's *Le Grand Silence blanc* (Paris, 1926) and Louis Hémon's story of Canadian frontier life, *Marie Chapdelaine* (Paris, 1933; original paintings in Kleinburg, Ont., McMichael Can. A. Col.). Gagnon thumbprinted the back of his canvases to ensure against forgeries.

BIBLIOGRAPHY

A. H. Robson: *Clarence Gagnon, R.C.A., LL.D.* (Toronto, 1938, rev. 1948)

The Prints of Clarence Gagnon (exh. cat. by I. M. Thom, Victoria, BC, A.G. Gtr Victoria, 1981)

Marie Chapdelaine: Illustrations (exh. cat. by I. M. Thom, Kleinburg, Ont., McMichael Can. A. Col., 1987–8)

ALEXANDRA PEL

Gagny, Augustin Blondel de. *See* BLONDEL DE GAGNY, AUGUSTIN.

Gahō. *See* HASHIMOTO GAHŌ.

Gahona, Gabriel Vicente. *See* PICHETA.

Gai, Antonio (*b* Venice, 3 May 1686; *d* Venice, 4 June 1769). Italian sculptor. His father, Francesco, was a wood-carver, and Gai qualified as a master wood-carver in 1710. The geometric precision and subtle rhythm of his later work remained indebted to this early training. In 1733 he undertook the execution of the portal of the Loggetta in Venice; this was an important public commission and demonstrates his high local standing, which was confirmed in 1764 when he was elected president of the Venetian Accademia. He was admired by Consul Joseph Smith, who commissioned many works on behalf of English clients. Carl Gustave Tessin recorded in 1736 that these commanded a high price and that Gai was hailed as a new Michelangelo.

Today Gai's importance has been brought into perspective, but he remains one of the most interesting Venetian sculptors of his time. He belongs to the classical current, and his work demonstrates an affinity with Giuseppe Mazza, and above all with Antonio Corradini and Giuseppe Torretti. For the Villa Soderini, Nervesa, Treviso, he completed a series of sculpted groups, figures and vases (mostly destr. 1914–18) in collaboration with Torretti. Giambattista Tiepolo had painted a fresco cycle at the Villa, and in 1738 Gai, together with Tiepolo, gave evidence on the inheritance of Gherardo Sagredo (1691–1738), Zaccaria Sagredo's nephew and heir.

In 1738 Gai also executed the stone statues of *Sight* and *Hearing* for the steps of the Villa Giovanelli, Noventa Padovana. Their geometric and rhythmic abstraction, combined with a spontaneous quality, is distinctive of Gai's art. Two marble allegorical statues on the staircase of the Conservatorio Benedetto Marcello, Venice, can be attributed to him on the basis of their stylistic similarity to those at Noventa. Another interesting series of stone statues was for the garden of the Palazzo Vecchia (now Romanelli), Vicenza, representing the *Four Seasons*. These

are now in the Parco Querini, Vicenza. Also by Gai are the two stone statues placed on the spiral columns of one of the grand gateways of the Villa Pisani, Stra.

In 1751 Gai executed the *lavello* in the sacristy of St Mark's, Venice. He competed with Giovanni Marchiori in 1753 for the commission for statues to be placed on the high altar of S Maria della Pietà, Venice; in the event Marchiori made the statue of *St Peter* and Gai that of *St Mark*. The marble statues of *Faith* and of *Fortitude*, for the high altar of S Vitale, Venice, probably belong to the same period. Among Gai's other works are: the marble low relief of the *Agony in the Garden* (Dolo, Arcipretale); the marble *SS Peter and Paul* (Scaltenigo, parish church); the stone statues of saints, allegorical figures, putti and the arms of the Dolfin family on the portal of S Antonio Abate, Udine; and the figures of *St Lorenzo Giustiniani* and the *Blessed Gregorio Barbarigo* (1765–8) on the crowning parts of the façade of S Rocco, Venice.

Gai's two sons, Francesco (*fl* 1769–89) and Giovanni Maria, collaborated with him on the execution of the Loggetta and probably also in other works. No biographical information survives for Giovanni Maria, but his works include a marble *St John the Baptist* (Bassano, Villa Rezzonico); two marble busts, of *Nicolo Sagredo* and *Alvise Sagredo* (Venice, S Francesco della Vigna); and the bust of *Teofilo Folengo* (Campese, Parrocchiale). Although no works attributable to Francesco Gai remain, he is recorded from 1769, when he was required to replace his father as a member of the Accademia in Venice, until 1789.

BIBLIOGRAPHY

T. Temanza: *Zibaldon*, ed. N. Ivanoff (Venice and Rome, 1963)

C. Semenzato: *La scultura veneta del seicento e del settecento* (Venice, 1966)

CAMILLO SEMENZATO

Gaignat, Louis-Jean (*b* Le Nivernais, 1697; *d* Paris, April 1768). French collector. He sought consolation for the early loss of his wife and daughter in his collections of paintings and books, which contained extremely rare editions. He insisted that on his death the collections be sold item by item, in order to give collectors the opportunity to acquire individual works that they prized. His paintings included a *Virgin* by Murillo, which was acquired by Empress Catherine II of Russia.

BIBLIOGRAPHY

G.-F. Debure: *Supplément à la Bibliographie instructive* (Paris, 1769), 2 vols [includes cat. of Gaignat's library]

□

Gaignières, (François-)Roger de (*b* Entrains-sur-Nohain, Nièvre, 30 Dec 1642; *d* Paris, 27 March 1715). French historian and collector. Descended from a bourgeois family in Lyon that had recently been raised to the nobility, he first entered the service of the House of Guise. There he began to gain a reputation as a virtuoso, with a particular interest in genealogy. Although of modest financial means Gaignières enjoyed powerful support, which he put to use in building up his collection. In 1680 he received a pension from the royal exchequer; and after the death of Marie de Guise in 1688, he became the protégé of Anne-Marie d'Orléans, Duchesse de Montpensier, the cousin of Louis XIV, and his favourite, Françoise Athénaïs de Rochechouart, Marquise de Montespan. For several years Gaignières was one of the private tutors to Louis XIV's grandson Louis, Duc de Bourgogne (1682–1712), with the task of teaching him history through pictures.

For almost 20 years Gaignières travelled in France in search of historical documents, aided by his valet, Barthélemy Rémy, who was responsible for transcribing the inscriptions they encountered, and a draughtsman, Louis Boudan (*fl* 1687–1709). The Benedictine monks, of the congregation of Saint-Maur in particular, with whom Gaignières worked on a history of Brittany, opened their monasteries to him. His extensive collection of books, documents, paintings, drawings and prints was designed to illuminate European, and especially French, history from the Middle Ages onward. In 1703 the minister of state Louis Phélypeaux de Pontchartrain suggested to the King that Gaignières be assigned the task of cataloguing France's historical monuments; the project, however, was not realized.

At the request of the Duc de Bourgogne, in 1711 Gaignières gave the whole of his collection to the Crown in return for a personal pension from the King and compensation for his heirs. After Gaignières's death it was entrusted to Pierre de Clairambault (1651–1740), who brought about the collection's dispersal in 1717. Clairambault transferred the drawings of costumes and funerary monuments, the geographical documents and topographical charts and the 7700 drawn or engraved portraits to the Bibliothèque Royale (now Bib. N.). The remaining prints (*c.* 16,000), printed books and all the historical portraits (over 1000) were sold at auction the same year at the Place des Victoires, Paris. The King kept only the 14th-century profile portrait painted in tempera on panel of *Jean II, Le Bon* (Paris, Louvre).

Gaignières's collection was a rare example of specialization in the 17th century. He attempted to approach history in a systematic manner, both during his searches for original documents and in the course of classifying them for other users. Among his admiring visitors was Bernard de Montfaucon, who borrowed heavily from the collection for his *Monuments de la monarchie française* (1729). Few (around 10%) of the portraits formerly in Gaignières's collection are now in French public collections; examples that are include *Henri de Lorraine, Duc de Guise* and *François II de la Rochefoucauld* (both Versailles, Château). They and others can be identified by the seal of Jean-Baptiste Colbert de Torcy, nephew of the deceased minister to Louis XIV, Jean-Baptiste Colbert, placed on the reverse for the sale in 1717. The vestiges of Gaignières's collection (that in the Bibliothèque Nationale is dispersed among various departments) remain a unique source of information on the portraiture, iconography, architecture and political history of France from the Middle Ages to the early 18th century. Those items that record buildings and sculptural monuments subsequently destroyed or altered are among the most valuable to scholars.

BIBLIOGRAPHY

L. Delisle: *Le Cabinet des manuscrits de la Bibliothèque impériale* (Paris, 1868), i, pp. 335–56
H. Bouchot: *Inventaire des dessins exécutés pour Roger de Gaignières*, 2 vols (Paris, 1891)
C. de Grandmaison: *Gaignières, ses correspondants et ses collections de portraits* (Niort, 1892)
J. Adhémar and G. Dordor: 'Les Tombeaux de la collection Gaignières à la Bibliothèque nationale', *Gaz. B.-A.*, n.s. 5, lxxxiv (1974), pp. 1–192 [Medieval tombs]; lxxxvii (1976), pp. 1–128 [17th-century tombs]
C. Chardigny: 'The Seal of Colbert de Torcy: Roger de Gaignières' Historical "Museum"', *Apollo*, cxxviii (1988), pp. 171–5
M. Polonovski: 'Deux Dessins inédits exécutés pour R. de Gaignières concernant l'église abbatiale de Saint-Denis', *Bull. Soc. N. Antiqua. France* (1988), pp. 348–56

CHRISTIANE CHARDIGNY

Gailde [Guayde], **Jean** [Jehan] [Grant Jehan le Masson] (*fl* 1490; *d* before 1519). French architect. He was one of the leading masons in the very active and artistically fertile milieu of Troyes in the decades around 1500. In the 1490s he was employed by the municipality on the magnificent Belle Croix and on various fortification projects, especially on the city-gate known as the Beuffroi, for which he prepared the *protretz*, or project drawings, designed the sculptural programme and served as Master of the Works. After the completion of the Beuffroi (1507), Gailde worked on other city-gates, including the Comporté and the Croncels, and also on the new choir-screen of the parish church of the Madeleine, Troyes, begun *c.* 1508 and finished by 1515. This screen, Gailde's only surviving work, secures his status among the most creative masons of French Flamboyant. It bridges the opening between the eastern crossing piers in a single span divided into three bays, without any visible support. This sleight of hand was achieved by means of radial voussoirs, the joints of which are disguised by the prolific sculptural decoration. Gailde probably also designed the choir of the Madeleine, constructed in the last years of the 15th century, and he was also involved as visiting expert (in 1506) in the start of work on the new west front of Troyes Cathedral. In the last years of his life he carried the title 'Maistre Maçon pour le Roy nostre sire à Troyes'. He was buried under his choir-screen in the Madeleine.

BIBLIOGRAPHY

Bauchal
A. Lance: *Dictionnaire des architectes français* (Paris, 1872)
R. Koechlin and J.-J. M. de Vasselot: *La Sculpture à Troyes et dans la Champagne méridionale au XVIe siècle* (Paris, 1900/R 1966)
B. Collet: 'Jehan Guayde, maître-maçon, au service de la ville de Troyes (1492–1518)', *Vie Champagne*, 366 (1986), pp. 3–8; 367 (1986), pp. 9–16
——: 'Jehan Gailde, maître d'oeuvre du jubé de la Madeleine', *Vie Champagne*, 379 (1987), pp. 13–20
——: 'Les Compagnons de Jehan Gailde au jubé de la Madeleine', *Vie Champagne*, 380 (1987), pp. 9–13

STEPHEN MURRAY

Gailhoustet, Renée (*b* Oran, Algeria, 15 Sept 1929). French architect and teacher. She moved to France in 1947 and after study at the Sorbonne and the Ecole des Beaux-Arts, Paris, she opened her own practice at Ivry-sur-Seine, near Paris. During the 1970s and early 1980s she was involved primarily with social housing, most of her projects being located in densely populated urban centres. She advocated bringing nature into urban housing, through the use of garden-balconies and courtyards. Many of her projects have been extremely large in scale, such as the social housing and community development (1968–87; with Jean Renaudie) at Ivry-sur-Seine, comprising 800 flats and maisonettes, together with shops, nursery, medical centre and library. Between 1975 and 1986 she designed 180 balcony flats at Saint-Denis, which betray formal ties to Le Corbusier; a severe, planar geometry is relieved only by the outwardly jutting triangular balconies and cylindrical columns raising the flats above a lower level of shops. Gailhoustet later moved away from urban social housing, frustrated with the restrictions of zoning rules and other regulations. In the late 1980s and after she was involved in housing projects outside France. One of the most ambitious is a housing development (1986–9) on Ile de la Réunion, Indian Ocean. Along with housing, the development includes schools and a shopping centre built on a steeply sloping site. Gailhoustet also lectured at various architectural schools in France and was a professor at the International School of Architecture, Sofia.

BIBLIOGRAPHY

J. Nouvel and others: 'Loger? Ou bien réinventer le monde?', *Archit. Aujourd'hui*, 252 (1987), pp. 21–3

C. Lorenz: *Women in Architecture: A Contemporary Perspective* (New York, 1990)

I. Scalbert: 'Ivry-sur-Seine Town Centre', *AA Files*, 23 (1992), pp. 44–8

WALTER SMITH

Gaillard, Eugène (*b* 1862; *d* 1933). French designer. He was a barrister by profession, and his legal training is perhaps reflected in his furniture designs, which are solid in construction, each part being carefully conceived to relate to the whole. He published his theories about avant-garde furniture and became established as an advocate of the modern school. Although known almost exclusively for his furniture, he also designed a wide range of objects and decorative schemes in an elegant Art Nouveau style.

Early in his career Gaillard collaborated in S. Bing's fashionable Art Nouveau shop in Paris. Together with Georges de Feure and Edouard Colonna he created interiors and furniture for Bing's pavilion, Art Nouveau Bing (destr.), at the Exposition Universelle of 1900 in Paris. Under Bing's direction these artists carried out an aesthetic programme that laid claim to 'the old French tradition' infused with 'a lively spirit of modernity'. Gaillard was responsible for three rooms in the pavilion: the vestibule, dining-room and bedroom. French precedents, especially elements from the Rococo style, were freely used as a source of inspiration. In the vestibule Gaillard installed a mosaic floor, bold pink draperies and a stencilled frieze that effectively set off a walnut portemanteau with mirrored back and shelves. The dining-room was furnished in walnut, ornamented with scrolled foliage and panelled wainscot, beneath a mural painted by the Spanish artist José María Sert (1876–1945). His buffet for the dining-room (Copenhagen, Kstindustmus.) expresses the spirit of his creations in its fondness for abstract features inspired by naturalistic forms. The critic Gabriel Mourey wrote about the bedroom that 'Everything in this room is soft, delicate and caressing, without, however, any eccentricity or weakness.'

Later in his career Gaillard designed deeply moulded furniture with sharply curved corners displaying carved decoration; he consistently favoured sinuously flowing, carved panels and ormolu drawer pulls. His chairs, which were very popular, do not exhibit excessive ornamentation, being of a plainer, heavier construction, often with leather seats instead of decorative upholstery fabrics.

About 1903 Gaillard ended his collaboration with Bing and established his own firm, which produced furniture of similar designs. By 1907 Gaillard had simplified his designs significantly; his furniture became lighter in contrast to the rather ponderous style of earlier pieces, and the decoration was less strident. He claimed in *A propos du mobilier* (1906) that his approach to furniture design was based on five rules: a piece of furniture should express its function as far as possible; the nature of the material must be respected; no unnecessary constructive elements should be included; in wood an arch is only to be regarded as a decorative element; and ornament should be abstract. Even in pieces where the abundance of carved ornaments is excessive, Gaillard's furniture possesses a constructive logic. In the furniture made between 1900 and 1914 Gaillard attempted to 'invest the most humble object with an undeniable artistic character' and to 'furnish beautiful prototypes of all kinds for the so-called art industries'. Gaillard's designs developed from stylized naturalism to full abstract decoration and ultimately to a phase of simplification with the introduction of clearly defined planes and curved lines. Little is known about the later phase of his career.

WRITINGS

A propos du mobilier: Opinions d'avant-garde, technique fondamentale, l'évolution (Paris, 1906)

BIBLIOGRAPHY

G. Mourey: 'Round the Exhibition: The House of the "Art Nouveau Bing"', *Int. Studio*, xx (1900), pp. 164–81

H. F. Lenning: *The Art Nouveau* (The Hague, 1951)

S. T. Madsen: *Sources of Art Nouveau* (New York, 1955)

A. Duncan: *Art Nouveau Furniture* (New York, 1982)

G. P. Weisberg: *Art Nouveau Bing* (New York, 1986)

D. Silverman: *Art Nouveau in Fin-de-siècle France: Politics, Psychology and Style* (Berkeley, 1989)

LIANA PAREDES-AREND

Gaillon, château of. French château on the River Seine *c.* 95 km north-west of Paris, in the département of Eure. A medieval fortress, owned from 1263 by the archdiocese of Rouen, previously stood on the site, built around a quadrilateral courtyard. It was ruined during the Hundred Years War (1337–1453) but was substantially repaired (1454–63) by Cardinal Guillaume d'Estouteville. Of his work there remain only the turret bearing his name and the entrance pavilion (Renaissance decoration added 1508–10). The château was rebuilt (from 1502; see fig.) in the Renaissance style—its earliest manifestation in France—by Georges I d'Amboise (*see* AMBOISE, D', (1)), Cardinal–Archbishop of Rouen, who had served as governor of Milan. His first master masons were royal employees: Guillaume Senault (*fl* 1495–1509) for the lower chapel (rest. 1989) in the tower of the Grant'Maison, and Colin Biart, who built an open gallery in the typical Loire style (rest. 1982–5) between the Grant'Maison and the Tour de la Syrène, overlooking the Seine valley. To divide the base-court from the *cour d'honneur*, Cardinal d'Amboise started building another gallery (begun 1505; reassembled 1985–7) supported by the Estouteville turret on one side and the Grant'Vis of the Grant'Maison on the other. The capitals are decorated with dolphins; the ermines and fleur-de-lis of Anne of Brittany, wife of King Louis XII (removed during the French Revolution and since replaced), decorated the columns. The work was

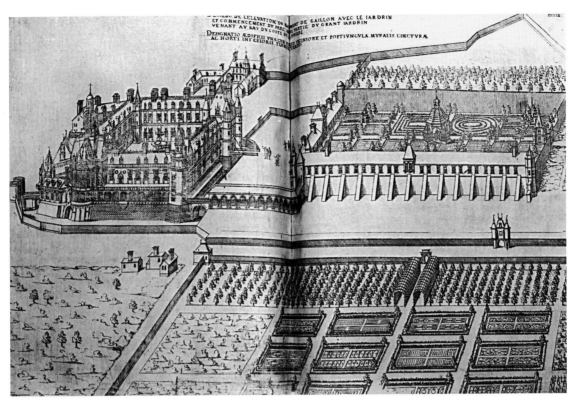

Gaillon, view of the château and gardens, rebuilt from 1502 (dismantled after 1797; rest. from 1975); from J. A. Du Cerceau: *Les Plus Excellents Bastiments de France* (Paris, 1576–9)

increasingly influenced by Italian masons, who collaborated from 1506 with PIERRE DELORME and Pierre Fain (*fl* 1501–22) to transform the *cour d'honneur*. The gallery adjoining the Grant'Maison (rebuilt 1988) is evidence of the aesthetic changes and of the exceptional refinement of this skilful combination of Flamboyant and Renaissance sculpture. The courtyard façades were decorated with medallions of Roman emperors and of Mars and Minerva. There were also statues of *King Louis XII* (now Paris, Louvre), *Georges I d'Amboise*, and his nephew, another Cardinal–Archbishop of Rouen, *Georges II d'Amboise* (both untraced). In the centre of the court stood a large fountain (1506; erected 1508; now at Charentes, Château de la Rochefoucauld) by Antonio della Porta (*see* PORTA, DELLA, (1); *see also* FOUNTAIN) and his nephew Pace Gagini, which was a gift from the Republic of Venice.

For Jacques-Nicolas Colbert, Archbishop of Rouen from 1691 to 1707, Jules Hardouin Mansart extended the Orangery, but of his work only the west wing survives. The château was confiscated (1797) by the Revolutionary authorities and sold to a M. Darcy, who dismantled it and sold architectural elements piecemeal in Paris until 1809. Parts were bought by Alexandre Lenoir for his short-lived Musée des Monuments Français, Paris. After its closure, the Gaillon fragments were re-erected in 1834 by (Jacques-) Félix Duban in the main courtyard of the Ecole des Beaux Arts, Paris. From 1975 they were returned to Gaillon as part of an extensive restoration programme.

The first garden at Gaillon, the Lydieu (1502–6), stood on the western side of the château and contained a lake, a fishpond, a heronry and bowers surrounding a chapel, and several buildings used as lodgings during construction. Closer to the château, the Upper Garden (1504–9) was very similar to the gardens at Amboise and Blois, designed by the same Neapolitan garden designer, Pacello da Mercogliano (*d* 1534). It consisted of 24 squares arranged around an octagonal pavilion that housed a fountain, and two rectangles, one a maze and the other displaying coats of arms. The plan of the maze was probably inspired by the famous *Hypnerotomachia Poliphili* (1499). In the park Cardinal Charles I de Bourbon (1523–90) built several basins with a hermit's cave (*see* HERMITAGE), and the Maison Blanche (1566; destr.), a sumptuous casino in the High Renaissance Mannerist style that has been attributed to Jacques Androuet Du Cerceau (i). Finally, Cardinal de Bourbon enlarged the planted area by creating the large Lower Garden in the valley, at present partially encroached on by building lots. He also added the large Latin inscription—HIC JUNGITUR UTILE DULCI—carved on the entrance pavilion to honour the work of his predecessors. The gardens were redesigned (1691–2) by André Le Nôtre and only the terraced site of the Upper Garden and the park, with its star-shaped pattern of pathways converging on a central circle where the pavilion marks the centre, now survives.

BIBLIOGRAPHY

A. Deville: *Compte de dépenses de la construction du château de Gaillon* (Paris, 1850)

L. Courajod: *Alexandre Lenoir: Son Journal et le Musée des monuments français*, ii (Paris, 1886), pp. 74–131

W. H. Ward: *French Châteaux and Gardens in the XVIth Century: A Series of Reproductions of Contemporary Drawings hitherto Unpublished by Jacques Androuet Du Cerceau* (London, 1909)

A. de Beatis: *Voyage du Cardinal d'Aragon (1517–18)* (Paris, 1913), pp. 145–54

F. Gebelin: *Les Châteaux de la Renaissance* (Paris, 1927), pp. 107–13

E. Chirol: *Un Premier Foyer de la Renaissance en France: Le Château de Gaillon* (Rouen, 1952)

R. Weiss: 'The Castle of Gaillon in 1509–1510', *J. Warb. & Court. Inst.*, xvi (1953), pp. 1–12

E. Chirol: 'Heurs et malheurs du Château de Gaillon', *Précis Acad. Rouen*, 1982/83 (Fécamp, 1984)

W. Prinz and R. G. Kecks: *Das französische Schloss der Renaissance* (Berlin, 1987), pp. 481–8

J.-P. Babelon: *Châteaux de France au siècle de la Renaissance* (Paris, 1989), pp. 86–93

Y. Lescroart and B. Mouton: 'Le Château de Gaillon', *Mnmts Hist.*, clxv (1989), pp. 36–42

ELISABETH CHIROL

Gainsborough, Thomas (*b* Sudbury, Suffolk, *bapt* 14 May 1727; *d* London, 2 Aug 1788). English painter, draughtsman and printmaker. He was the contemporary and rival of Joshua Reynolds, who honoured him on 10 December 1788 with a valedictory *Discourse* (pubd London, 1789), in which he stated: 'If ever this nation should produce genius sufficient to acquire to us the honourable distinction of an English School, the name of Gainsborough will be transmitted to posterity, in the history of Art, among the very first of that rising name.' He went on to consider Gainsborough's portraits, landscapes and fancy pictures within the Old Master tradition, against which, in his view, modern painting had always to match itself. Reynolds was acknowledging a general opinion that Gainsborough was one of the most significant painters of their generation. Less ambitious than Reynolds in his portraits, he nevertheless painted with elegance and virtuosity. He founded his landscape manner largely on the study of northern European artists and developed a very beautiful and often poignant imagery of the British countryside. By the mid-1760s he was making formal allusions to a wide range of previous art, from Rubens and Watteau to, eventually, Claude and Titian. He was as various in his drawings and was among the first to take up the new printmaking techniques of aquatint and soft-ground etching. Because his friend, the musician and painter William Jackson (1730–1803), claimed that Gainsborough detested reading, there has been a tendency to deny him any literacy. He was, nevertheless, as his surviving letters show, verbally adept, extremely witty and highly cultured. He loved music and performed well. He was a person of rapidly changing moods, humorous, brilliant and witty. At the time of his death he was expanding the range of his art, having lived through one of the more complex and creative phases in the history of British painting. He painted with unmatched skill and bravura; while giving the impression of a kind of holy innocence, he was among the most artistically learned and sophisticated painters of his generation. It has been usual to consider his career in terms of the rivalry with Reynolds that was acknowledged by their contemporaries; while Reynolds maintained an intellectual and academic ideal of art, Gainsborough grounded his imagery on contemporary life, maintaining an aesthetic outlook previously given its most powerful expression by William Hogarth. His portraits, landscapes and subject pictures are only now coming to be studied in all their complexity; having previously been viewed as being isolated from the social, philosophical and ideological currents of their time, they have yet to be fully related to them. It is clear, however, that his landscapes and rural pieces, and some of his portraits, were as significant as Reynolds acknowledged them to be in 1788.

1. Life and work. 2. Working methods and technique.

1. LIFE AND WORK. Gainsborough's father, John Gainsborough, a clothier and crêpe-maker, was declared bankrupt in 1733, after which he became the local postmaster. He had three other sons and four daughters; the family was a close one. Gainsborough's low-church background was always important to him; unlike Reynolds, he would never work on the Sabbath.

(i) Early years and training in London, to 1748. (ii) Sudbury, 1748–51. (iii) Ipswich, 1752–*c*. 1759. (iv) Bath, *c*. 1759–73. (v) London, 1774–88.

(i) Early years and training in London, to 1748. Gainsborough was an artistic prodigy; legend has it that he would play truant from school to go out drawing in the countryside, forging excusatory notes supposedly from his father. He seems to have received some training from one Francis Wynantz (who probably hailed from the Low Countries), Charles Jervas and Francis Hayman, all of whom were working in Suffolk in the 1730s. Around 1740 Gainsborough went to London, where he trained with Gravelot, the French draughtsman and engraver, and apparently also with Hayman; there is circumstantial evidence that he studied at the St Martin's Lane Academy, which Hogarth had set up in 1735. Gravelot and Hayman were engaged on a variety of artistic enterprises; Gainsborough contributed decorative surrounds to the engravings of heads that Gravelot was making (1741–3) after Jacobus Houbraken for Thomas Birch's *Heads of Illustrious Persons of Great Britain*, while Hayman was supervising the decoration of the supper-boxes (completed by 1742) at Vauxhall Gardens, London, a project in which Gainsborough is believed to have been involved. Since he was able to earn an independent living from the time of his arrival in London, it is possible that, like Hayman, he was employed on scene-painting for the theatre.

Gravelot was intimately acquainted with the works of Watteau, and his own drawings display a dexterity and ease that Gainsborough readily adopted. Hayman painted in the Anglo-French manner usually associated with Hogarth, and he taught Gainsborough lessons in both the handling of paint and systems of colouring compositions. The St Martin's Lane Academy, like Slaughter's Coffee House, supplied a forum in which artists could discuss and argue issues. Hogarth's was the dominant personality in these debates, and Gainsborough must have been affected by this lively atmosphere. It is thought that he set up independently after Gravelot's return to Paris in October 1745, although the prospect of marrying Margaret Burr, who had £200 a year settled on her, may also have entered into his calculations; the marriage took place in July 1746. His first surviving dated work portrays the bull-terrier *Bumper* (1745; priv. col., see Hayes, 1982, ii, pl. 1a) and is inscribed on the back: 'A most Remarkable Sagacious Cur'. The dog stands on a mound next to a tree trunk, the scene being closed by a line of forest. The setting is comparable with a number of small landscapes of that period in which Gainsborough showed arrangements of woodland scenery (e.g. *Wooded Landscape with Peasants Resting*; London, Tate), stylistically demonstrating a good understanding of the art of Jan Wijnants and Jacob van Ruisdael; at this time he was also involved in restoring Dutch landscapes. Gainsborough's talents were recognized. William Woollett made engravings after his drawings, and on at least one occasion Hayman employed him to fill in the landscape background to one of his own portraits. His contemporaries appreciated his gifts; his roundel of *The Charterhouse* (1748; London, Foundling Hosp.) stands out in comparison with the paintings of London hospitals that Edward Haytley and Samuel Wale contributed to Hogarth's project of decorating Thomas Coram's Foundling Hospital with works by British artists (*in situ*). Gainsborough concentrated less on describing the architecture than on demonstrating an expertise in perspective, and the whole composition is unified through a striking chiaroscuro, proper to the sky of thick cumulus that illuminates the scene. Like Richard Wilson, who pictured both *St George's Hospital* and the *Foundling Hospital* (both *in situ*), Gainsborough understood his subject as supplying the material for an artistic composition, not simply as being there to be illustrated. That at the age of 21 he was invited to contribute to these decorations is a measure of the respect in which he was held by his fellow artists—a respect that was not, however, translating itself into commissions.

(ii) Sudbury, 1748–51. Gainsborough could sell his landscapes to dealers only at 'trifling prices', and in 1748, when his father died, he returned to Sudbury, presumably expecting to shine more brightly in a provincial setting. The painting known as *Cornard Wood* (or *Gainsborough's Forest*; London, N.G.) had been begun before Gainsborough had left for London and was completed in 1748. This remarkable picture (*see* LANDSCAPE PAINTING, fig. 8) shows how, to a far greater degree than anyone except Wilson, Gainsborough had not just assimilated the lessons of other landscape painting but could utilize them in evolving a style directed towards communicating the appearance of contemporary landscape. He likewise adapted the lessons of Gravelot and Watteau to the representation of the East Anglian proletariat, examples of which are scattered through the work. The composition was mediated through Ruisdael's *Wooded Landscape with a Flooded Road* (Paris, Louvre; pencil copy by Gainsborough, U. Manchester, Whitworth A.G.), adapted to an arrangement of woodland scenery typical of the Sudbury region. A track winds through the trees towards what may be the village of Great Cornard. In the forest a woodman, a labourer and a milkmaid are working or resting, to show that the rural economy is based on a bountiful and providential nature, while travellers, entering the scene, link it with the more general landscape of Britain. Gainsborough's painted imagery matches that evoked by such poets as James Thomson in celebrating the glories of their country; it stresses that hard work and enlightened land management, together with good government and the Protestant religion, are the bases of that material prosperity that alone can foster the virtues of civilization. Particular

1. Thomas Gainsborough: *Mr and Mrs Andrews*, oil on canvas, 698×1194 mm, *c.* 1748–50 (London, National Gallery)

motifs communicate a popular iconography; Gainsborough's oak trees bring to mind ships and hence the military and mercantile naval supremacy that underpinned Britain's greatness. That some of the figures work while others dally fits the poets' celebration of Britain's nature, which gave its bounty unstintingly. Gainsborough's 'Dutch' style would have been associated with the representation of 'common' nature recognized by all; it thus stressed the documentary element in this illusion of a scene in an East Anglian woodland lit by a huge and rolling sky.

There was more money to be made, however, in portraiture. In *Mr and Mrs Andrews* (*c.* 1748–50; London, N.G.; see fig. 1), the most celebrated of Gainsborough's early efforts, the wealthy young landowner Robert Andrews with his wife Frances are placed to the side of a prospect of their estate, with Sudbury and the Suffolk hills closing the vista. This was an exercise in a mode of showing figures in landscapes that was initially adapted from Watteau by Hogarth and had become the stock-in-trade of Arthur Devis and was also often used in Hayman's paintings. Andrews, dressed for shooting and nuzzled by a brown-and-white pointer, leans against the arm of a smart green bench on which is perched his bride, simpering gracefully in a fine sky-blue gown; behind her rises the trunk of an oak. The rest of the picture catalogues their possessions and sets them, in a carefully descriptive style, in the wider world of East Anglia. The corn stooks witness Andrews's enlightened husbandry, lines of stubble indicating his pioneering use of the seed drill. Flocks of sheep graze in folds set against plantations of oaks, to the left of which cattle and horses browse. The composition was designed to flatter young Mr Andrews by presenting him in the role of a good landowner; the painting must have been shaped largely by the patron's demands, for Gainsborough never painted such imagery again. Much like Hayman, he preferred to set his sitters at their leisure in a rather more general landscape.

(iii) Ipswich, 1752–c. 1759. Gainsborough, like any astute businessman, had various formulae for attracting clients and, like many of his contemporaries, produced heads and half-lengths, in addition to full-length portraits and painting and drawing landscapes. Sudbury, however, provided limited opportunities, and in 1752 the Gainsboroughs moved to the larger town of Ipswich. As a trading port and market town, it supplied a larger pool of prospective clients, and a good many portraits date from the 1750s. However, in 1758 Gainsborough wrote to a Colchester patron, Robert Edgar: 'I thought I should have been at Colchester by this time. . .but business comes in and being chiefly in the Face way, I'm afraid to put people off when they are in the mind to sit', showing that making a living could be a precarious business. At Ipswich he fell in with a cultured and mildly eccentric coterie and became an enthusiastic member of a musical club. His close friendship with John Joshua Kirby (1716–74), Hogarth's agent in Ipswich and author of *Dr. Brook Taylor's Method of Perspective Made Easy* (1753), to which Hogarth contributed a spoof frontispiece, would have kept Gainsborough abreast of the latest developments in the metropolitan art world. Factions were forming among the artists; some, Hayman being prominent among them, were attempting to form themselves into an academy, a development that Hogarth strenuously opposed.

Gainsborough himself was not isolated from the wider world, receiving a commission in 1755 from Francis Russell, 5th Duke of Bedford, for two landscapes for Woburn Abbey, Beds (*in situ*). One, *Wooded Landscape with Peasant Boy*, showing haymaking, a green scene drenched in a liquid and golden light, describes farm labour as an almost indolent occupation; it contrasts with its pair, *Wooded Landscape with Woodcutter*, in which—to the left—a ploughman, labouring on enclosed land, counterpoints—to the right—the flirtation of a woodcutter and a milkmaid on common ground, with the whole closed by a distant view of Ipswich. Both landscapes maintain a georgic iconography and both deploy an imagery common in contemporary writing and picture-making. Gainsborough responded to the scenery around Ipswich by expanding his range in landscape; certain views along the Orwell later became associated with him, as in *Wooded River Landscape* (*c.* 1754–6; priv. col., see Hayes, 1982, ii, no. 56). His paintings and drawings also included estuary scenes and studies of individual figures, shepherds or ploughmen, secure in their own worlds. This was a selective view of a reality that evidently gave the artist great pleasure; he began to paint it in increasingly sophisticated ways, his style becoming more fluent and his paraphrases of or references to other artists more wide-ranging and subtle. However, he found it as hard as ever to sell landscapes.

In portraiture, too, Gainsborough's wit and ambition became increasingly evident. In 1753 Philip Thicknesse (1719–92), later to become his biographer, disparaged Gainsborough's three-quarter length of *Admiral Edward Vernon* (London, N.P.G.) and claimed that it was his own commission for the painting of *Landguard Fort* (untraced), which Thomas Major engraved a year later, that had really set Gainsborough on his professional way. In reality, Vernon was portrayed in the same idiom as Thomas Hudson's *Admiral Byng* (1749; London, N. Mar. Mus.), and Gainsborough by then had access to a variety of poses to suit different sitters. *John Plampin* (1753; London, N.G.), for example, finely dressed in a blue suit, reclines on a mound in the foreground of an extensive and fluently painted landscape. This pose had a complex history: it had originated in Watteau's *Antoine de la Rocque* (untraced but known from an engraving) and was adapted by Hogarth to the figure of the drunken rake in the tavern scene (*The Orgy*) from the *Rake's Progress* (London, Soane Mus.). Hayman used it for his portrait of *Philip Thicknesse* (1750s; St Louis, MO, A. Mus.), and both he and Gainsborough may have meant to communicate an intimate and ironic view of their sitters. Besides painting portraits in landscape, Gainsborough was also figuring his sitters in interiors; he represented *William Wollaston* (*c.* 1759; Ipswich, Christchurch Mansion), later MP for Ipswich, seated in a contemplative, relaxed mood with his flute and sheets of music, and also at full-length, leaning on a fence in front of his house, Finborough Hall (priv. col., see Hayes, 1975, pl. 44). The sitter is recognizably the same person in each portrait, attesting to Gainsborough's famed exactness in taking a likeness.

(iv) Bath, c. *1759–73.* Although he was getting commissions, Gainsborough failed to make a good living in Ipswich. In 1758–9 he had begun travelling as an itinerant portrait painter in Buckinghamshire and elsewhere, and in 1759 he moved to Bath. This elegant spa was a perfect place for a portrait painter, for it served a wealthy but constantly changing population of visitors. William Hoare was already established as a portrait painter there, but the fact that Gainsborough felt able to raise his prices considerably soon after his arrival, and again between 1770 and 1772, indicates that the supply of sitters was plentiful. He seems to have gained a reputation initially by word of mouth. Around this time he began to change his style under the impact of Anthony van Dyck, pictures by whom he saw at Wilton House, Wilts.

Gainsborough could be impatient with his patrons, and some portraits of this period communicate an impression that the artist was doing the bare minimum, in contrast with other portraits that are extraordinary and brilliant. One such painting is that of *Ann Ford* (1760; Cincinnati, OH, A. Mus.), who in 1762 became Philip Thicknesse's wife; it is a masterly demonstration of the artist's powers. In colour, the scarlet of the curtain is set off against the silver-white of the dress, with its canary ribbons. The virtuosity of its handling was beyond any of Gainsborough's contemporaries. While the figure is set in Hogarth's three-dimensional serpentine line of beauty, the presence of musical instruments imbues the composition with something of the iconographical complexity traditionally found in pictures of musicians. Ann Ford was a talented amateur musician, who had caused scandal by performing in public. Gainsborough pictured her as he later did the musicians *Johann Christian Bach* (1766; Bologna, Mus. Bib. Musicale) and *Carl Friedrich Abel* (exh. RA 1777; San Marino, CA, Huntington A.G.) in an attitude of thought. In contrast to other artists, notably Reynolds, who could not visualize women as socially active and creative, but only as passive and domesticated or else fictionalized into goddesses, Gainsborough, following Hogarth's lead, was able to picture them leading their real lives, however incompatible this might be with perceived notions of the proper ordering of society. He was, however, equally capable of representing them as cosmetically beautiful objects, to be gazed on and admired; such full-lengths as *Mary, Countess Howe* (1763–4; London, Kenwood House), in which the sitter poses, clad in shimmering pink, against a broadly brushed landscape, and, later, the *Honourable Mrs Thomas Graham* (1777; Edinburgh, N.G.; see fig. 2), have contributed to subsequent misconceptions of the later 18th century as an era of glamour and elegance. Rather than dramatize his male sitters or place them, as Reynolds did, in invented circumstances, Gainsborough tended to represent them straightforwardly: thus *John, 10th Viscount Kilmorey* (1768; London, Tate) stands four-square, gazing unblinkingly out of the canvas. The cumulative effect of the Bath portraits is to produce the image of a class that was both hard-headed and extremely self-confident.

Gainsborough continued to paint landscapes. He handed over some of his remaining Suffolk scenes to Panton Betew, a silversmith and art dealer in London who subsequently had them engraved. His new pictures showed

2. Thomas Gainsborough: the *Honourable Mrs Thomas Graham*, oil on canvas, 2.37×1.54 m, 1777 (Edinburgh, National Gallery of Scotland)

an immediate, if general response to the hillier and more wooded countryside of Somerset. The influence of Rubens became marked, particularly in lighting effects, while he continued to show rustic figures going about their rural business. A major shift occurred around 1767: in the *Harvest Wagon* (U. Birmingham, Barber Inst.; see fig. 3) the landscape of woodland, tracks and ponds with a church in the distance, first used in *Cornard Wood* (many of Gainsborough's landscapes were based on a very limited repertory of compositional schemata), was virtually dematerialized through transparent glazes of paint. Instead of contributing a narrative logic to the composition, Gainsborough's wagon appears halted for no reason, and a discrepancy is displayed between the labourers' rags and the finery of the women (for whom his daughters served as models). The figures paraphrase respected pictorial sources, from *Alexander and Bucephalus* in the Piazza del Quirinale, Rome, to Rubens's *Deposition* (Antwerp Cathedral), but Gainsborough adapted them incongruously to a scene of low nature and denies them any unambiguously elevated function. In various ways the *Harvest Wagon* appears to be a pivotal work. Important experiments in landscape were to develop from it, and it made a crucial contribution to a contemporary aesthetic debate on the proper relevance of the Old Masters and history painting in a modern world.

3. Thomas Gainsborough: *Harvest Wagon*, oil on canvas, 1.21×1.45 m, 1767 (Birmingham, University of Birmingham, Barber Institute of Fine Arts)

Although based in Bath, Gainsborough maintained close links with London. He exhibited at the Society of Arts from 1761 and was a founder-member of the Royal Academy in 1768, a step that involved alienating Kirby, then President of the Society of Artists, thus measuring the importance that Gainsborough attached to the institutional management of his career. He appears to have been acutely aware of the kind of Italianate academic art that Reynolds was striving to promote and that he himself was against by training and inclination. In 1767 he wrote to William Jackson of history pictures being 'tragicomic' and demonstrated the tragicomedy in the *Harvest Wagon*, where historical sources were used to pictorially incoherent ends. A year later he was attempting to realize a painting of *Shakespeare between Tragedy and Comedy*. This was challenging Reynolds, who in 1762 had exhibited *Garrick between Tragedy and Comedy* (priv. col., see 1985–6 exh. cat., no. 42), at his own game and even raising the stakes. Gainsborough thought he had failed; Postle (1991) discovered that this composition had been overpainted with the fine portrait of *Johann Christian Fischer* (exh. RA 1780; London, Buckingham Pal., Royal Col.). In 1771

Gainsborough engaged in a correspondence with William, 2nd Earl of Dartmouth, who had insisted that a portrait of *Lady Dartmouth* (Sudbury, Gainsborough's House) should be draped in the indeterminate manner that Reynolds so strongly promoted. Gainsborough resisted this, because it damaged his attempt to get a likeness. 'I have that regard for truth, that I hold the finest invention as a mere slave in comparison', he wrote, adding, 'I never could have patience to read Poetical impossibilities, the very food of a Painter.'

Gainsborough's claimed pragmatism did not prevent him from attempting a deeply serious kind of modern painting, in the manner of Hogarth's modern moral subjects. A picture of labourers and children in *Going to Market* (*c.* 1769–71; London, Kenwood House) appears to show a beautiful, tranquil evening scene. The procession moves along a track, winding through trees, past a pond, with a cottage where figures relax against a sunlit wall in the left distance; these motifs had so often made previous appearances in drawings and paintings that this landscape type might be considered to represent some ideal England. Here this appearance is deceptive, for the mounted figures, possessing quantities of food, are denying their charity to an old woman and girl almost sunk into a shaded foreground, while their own travelling implies migration and dispossession. It is likely that Gainsborough was reacting to the disruption that the enclosure and engrossing of land were creating. He incorporated this serious content into his paintings through an imagery that all who cared to look might recognize, although it seems that few did.

In 1772 Gainsborough took as his apprentice his nephew, GAINSBOROUGH DUPONT, who graduated to being a studio assistant and helped to paint the subordinate parts of some pictures. On the whole, however, Gainsborough preferred to paint the entire picture himself.

(v) London, 1774–88. By 1774 Bath was supplying fewer portrait sitters, and Gainsborough moved to London with his family, settling in Schomberg House, Pall Mall. The previous year he had quarrelled with the Royal Academy over the hanging of his pictures and did not exhibit there again until 1777. Gainsborough was not alone in having uncomfortable relationships with the institution, being ambivalent in adapting his art to academic conventions. His drawings, featuring the same motifs as his paintings,

were increasingly complex. He mixed media (*see* §2 below), and so his work defied definition, blurring those boundaries between drawing and painting that preserved a propriety in the use of media, and thus undermining the validity of any system of academic laws. Landscapes of low subjects could assume an inappropriate gravity, while portraits could be either superficial or sophisticated (e.g. *Morning Walk*, 1785; London, N.G.; *see* DRESS, fig. 47). The late portrait of *Mrs Richard Brinsley Sheridan* (1785; Washington, DC, N.G.A.) almost blends the sitter into the wildly fanciful landscape that surrounds her, setting up a dialectic between notions of the female and of nature. Gainsborough's men, on the other hand, seldom seemed to attain such fictional elevation.

It is not clear what Gainsborough meant to signify by giving similar landscape backgrounds to portraits of real people and to pictures of invented themes. He increasingly began to picture his rural subjects in mountainous settings or in such a way as to place them within a tradition of landscape painting. The *Watering Place* (exh. RA 1777; London, N.G.) was adapted from the Rubens's picture of the same title (London, N.G.), setting itself in deliberate

4. Thomas Gainsborough: *Diana and Actaeon*, 1.58×1.88 m (London, Buckingham Palace, Royal Collection)

rivalry with it. He also made a soft-ground etching of this subject (c. 1776–7; London, BM; for illustration see ETCH- ING, SOFT GROUND) that was published by John Boydell in 1797. In the slightly earlier *Rocky Wooded Landscape with Rustic Lovers and Cattle at a Watering Place* (c. 1773– 4; Viscount Camrose priv. col.), the lighting recalls Claude and the hilly wooded terrain Gaspard Dughet. In the foreground is a group of cattle and to the right a youth addressing a seated girl. This imagery of dalliance and peace looked back to Gainsborough's earliest paintings. His figures continued to migrate from picture to picture, and his themes were repeated: the *Harvest Wagon* of 1784–5 (Toronto, A.G. Ont.), which the Prince of Wales (later George IV) bought, was a variation on the earlier painting of that title.

Gainsborough experimented increasingly. He tried etching in soft ground and in 1781 planned to publish three prints on coloured paper, looking deceptively like drawings. He painted on glass (e.g. London, V&A), the pictures to be lit from behind in a special box; the subjects covered his range in landscapes, including the seascapes and coastal scenes he had begun to try. He attempted mythological subjects, as in *Diana and Actaeon* (London, Buckingham Pal., Royal Col.; see fig. 4). At the same time he was also tackling literary and biblical themes, as well as apparently subjectless pictures, such as *The Mall in St James's Park* (1785; New York, Frick). In 1784 he had a final rupture with the Royal Academy, after it had refused to hang a group of royal portraits so that they might be seen at exhibition.

From the late 1770s Gainsborough was painting larger- scale pictures of the rural poor in a famous series of 'fancy pictures'. Among other things these inverted his relation- ship with his sitters, as he gave money to the poor from whom he selected his models for these works. The *Cottage Door with Children Playing* (1778; Cincinnati, OH, A. Mus.) strangely contrasts the stooped and haggard figure of the faggot-gatherer with the healthy hordes of women and children cascading from a cottage scarcely large enough to contain them. Contemporaries reacted with sentimental complacency to other fancy pictures that have come to seem harrowing; there is nothing cheerful about the ragged and isolated *Cottage Girl with Dog and Pitcher* (1785; Dublin, N.G.; for illustration see FANCY PICTURE). Perhaps in the rural poor Gainsborough saw the one subject that might convey simple but serious ideas. His *Two Shepherd Boys with Dogs Fighting* (exh. RA 1783; London, Kenwood House) adapted its composition from prints after Titian's *St Peter Martyr* (destr.), also referring to Titian in its colouring. The subject, originating in Hogarth's engravings of the *Four Stages of Cruelty*, was presented as a grand anti-pastoral, for shepherd boys should not neglect their flocks, nor should their dogs fight, and thus the painting took on a serious morality. Subse- quent 'cottage door' paintings buried their subjects of domestic harmony deep in woodland, perhaps to associate this ideal with a state of nature and accordingly to measure it against the unnaturalness of fashionable urban existence. Gainsborough was proudest of *The Woodman*, a single, contemplative figure, and on his deathbed he begged Reynolds to come to view it. This painting, sold in 1798,

was subsequently destroyed in a fire but is known from an engraving by Pierre Simon (before 1750–1810).

2. WORKING METHODS AND TECHNIQUE. Gains- borough was one of the most technically proficient and, at the same time, most experimental artists of his time. His oil technique was extremely sound—Francis Wynantz may have instructed him in traditional methods of oil painting—and he was adept in the uses of glazes and scumbling. In the course of his career his handling of oil paint became progressively looser and more suggestive, and because he was so expert in working oils he could attempt the experimentation evident in late works. Al- though he occasionally lapsed into the use of bitumen, his technical competence makes a notable contrast with that of Reynolds and, to a lesser degree, of many of his contemporaries. According to Reynolds, 'he occasionally made copies from Rubens, Teniers, and van Dyck, which it would be no disgrace to the most accurate connoisseur to mistake, at the first sight, for the works of those masters'. Gainsborough understood enough of the traditions of oil painting to be able to replicate earlier work and to develop those traditions in his own paintings. Hence, draperies are handled with a brilliance that ac- knowledges van Dyck, while some later landscapes are represented in a manner that looks back to Rubens but goes beyond him.

Reynolds also gave some information on Gainsbor- ough's working practices. He appears to have been con- stantly observing his surroundings, noting what was exceptionally interesting. He scanned faces keenly and would take people to his studio to be drawn or painted; this happened with the beggar children who were the models of the later fancy pictures. Apparently it was imperative for him to use models; when painting the *Cottage Girl with Pigs* (1782; Castle Howard, N. Yorks), using the same girl as in the *Cottage Girl with Dog and Pitcher*, legend has it that the pigs were running wild in the studio. A similar condition applied to landscapes: Reynolds said that Gainsborough was in the habit of dragging bits of trees and vegetation into his studio, and he 'framed a kind of model of landskips on his table; composed of broken stones, dried herbs, and pieces of looking glass, which he magnified and improved into rocks, trees, and water'. He is said to have used candles to cast light, broccoli for vegetation, and lumps of coal for rocks; this practice can be confirmed by a close scrutiny of his late landscapes.

Gainsborough made compositional drawings for both portraits and landscapes but was not regular in this practice. Reynolds remarked on Gainsborough's liking to paint at night by candlelight—he seems to have been a compulsive worker—and on his habit of 'forming all the parts of his picture together' rather than finishing off one part at a time. An unfinished portrait, such as the small one of *Edward, Duke of Kent* (c. 1786–7; New Haven, CT, Yale Cent. Brit. A.), shows how every part of a picture would be brought to an equal degree of finish as it progressed towards completion. It also confirms that Gainsborough painted very thinly; he used longer and broader brushes than anyone else. In *Nollekens and his Times* (1828) John T. Smith wrote of Gainsborough:

I was much surprised to see him sometimes paint portraits with pencils [brushes] on sticks full six feet in length, and his method of using them was this: he placed himself and his canvas at a right angle with the sitter, so that he stood still and touched the features of his picture exactly at the same distance at which he viewed his sitter.

Such a system must have been extremely tiring, particularly as Gainsborough always stood to paint, and it raises the question of where he put the palette. Almost certainly he liked to work under subdued light in order to obliterate superfluous detail. The Rev. Henry Scott Trimmer described Gainsborough's palette as comprising 'yellow ochre, Naples yellow, yellow lake. . .a preparation of orpiment, raw sienna, vermillion, light red, Venetian, and the lakes. . .burnt sienna, cologne earth (this he used very freely and brown pink the same). . .a great deal of terre verte, which he used with his blues, generally with ultramarine. Latterly he used Cremona white.'

Gainsborough liked to experiment. He enjoyed Philippe Jacques de Loutherbourg's miniature theatre, the *Eidophusikon* (1781), and about the same time painted a series of landscapes, representative of the range of his work in that genre, on glass transparencies. These were designed to be placed in a box, candle-lit from behind, to present the spectator, viewing from a distance of about one metre through an aperture fitted with a lens, with an approximation of actual lighting effects. In his eagerness to stretch the boundaries of art, he was particular about the means. He admired the paper on which the *New Bath Guide* was printed in 1766 and in 1767 wrote to ask for some but was sent the wrong kind:

> The mischief of that you were so kind as to enclose is not only the small wires but a large cross wire. . .which the other has none of, nor any impression of the smallest wire. I wish, Sir, that one of my landskips, such as I could make you upon that paper, would prove a sufficient inducement for you to make further inquiry.

He also often used coloured paper for his drawings.

Gainsborough was an expert draughtsman in graphite or chalk and could also handle watercolour with consummate skill. From an early stage in his career he was willing to mix his media. By the 1760s he was mixing pencil, watercolour and gouache, or chalk and watercolour, and varnishing the resulting drawing. He soon progressed to mixing chalk, washes and oil paint, again fixing the drawing with a varnish. His most extraordinary experiments were the drawings (e.g. *Rocky Wooded Landscape with Drovers and Cattle*; Buscot Park, Oxon, NT) in imitation of oil paintings that were exhibited at the Royal Academy in 1772. He was secretive about the techniques he used for these but sent a complex account of his procedures to his friend William Jackson. Sheets of paper were glued together; the composition was then established, using India ink and Bristol white lead, and fixed in skimmed milk, before the paper was placed in a frame to be stretched. Once this was dry, colours were added to complete the picture, and then water, to which gum Arabic had been added, was floated over the whole. Once it was dry, the picture was varnished three times.

In the 1770s Gainsborough developed an interest in the relatively new techniques of aquatinting and soft-ground etching. Both were extremely pictorial systems of printmaking; in each he rendered his characteristic landscape compositions and in 1781 was preparing to publish three soft-ground etchings: *Wooded Landscape with Two Country Carts and Figures*; *Wooded Landscape with Peasant Reading Tombstone, Rustic Lovers and Ruined Church*; and *Wooded Landscape with Herdsman Driving Cattle over a Bridge, Rustic Lovers and Ruined Castle* (pubd 1797 by Boydell; see Hayes, 1971, pp. 62–77). Printed on coloured paper, these actually look like chalk drawings rather than prints, which is entirely consistent with an artist who had tried to pass off watercolours as oil paintings and who had no truck with the restrictive effects of academic rules in a swiftly changing world.

UNPUBLISHED SOURCES

London, RA [MS. of O. Humphry: *Biographical Memoir*, i of *Original Correspondence of Ozias Humphry, R.A.* (*c.* 1802)]

WRITINGS

M. Woodall, ed.: *The Letters of Thomas Gainsborough* (London, 1961, rev. 1963)

BIBLIOGRAPHY

P. Thicknesse: *Sketches and Characters of the Most Eminent and Most Singular Persons now Living* (London, 1770)
J. Reynolds: *Discourses on Art* (London, 1778); ed. R. R. Wark (London, 1959/R New Haven and London, 1975) [14th discourse]
P. Thicknesse: *A Sketch of the Life and Paintings of Thomas Gainsborough, Esq.* (London, 1788)
J. Farington: *Diaries* (1793–1821); ed. K. Garlick and A. Mackintyre (i–vi) and K. Cave (vii–xvi) as *The Diaries of Joseph Farington*, 16 vols (New Haven and London, 1978–84)
W. Jackson: *The Four Ages* (London, 1798)
E. Edwards: *Anecdotes of Painters* (London, 1808), pp. 129–43
G. W. Fulcher: *Life of Thomas Gainsborough* (London, 1856)
W. T. Whitley: *Thomas Gainsborough* (London, 1915)
E. K. Waterhouse: *Gainsborough* (London, 1958)
J. Hayes: *The Drawings of Thomas Gainsborough*, 2 vols (London, 1970)
——: *Gainsborough as Printmaker* (London, 1971)
——: *Gainsborough: Paintings and Drawings* (London, 1975)
R. Paulson: *Emblem and Expression: Meaning in English Art of the Eighteenth Century* (London, 1975)
Gainsborough and his Musical Friends (exh. cat. by L. Stainton, London, Kenwood House, 1977)
M. Pointon: 'Gainsborough and the Landscape of Retirement', *A. Hist.*, ii (1979), pp. 441–55
J. Barrell: *The Dark Side of the Landscape: The Rural Poor in English Painting, 1730–1840* (Cambridge, 1980)
Gainsborough (exh. cat. by J. Hayes, London, Tate, 1980–81)
J. Lindsay: *Thomas Gainsborough: His Life and Art* (London, 1981)
J. Hayes: *The Landscape Paintings of Thomas Gainsborough*, 2 vols (London, 1982)
Gainsborough Drawings (exh. cat., ed. J. Hayes and L. Stainton; Washington, DC, Int. Exh. Found., 1983)
A. Corri: *The Search for Gainsborough* (London, 1984)
Reynolds (exh. cat., ed. N. Penny; Paris, Grand Pal.; London, RA; 1985–6), pp. 114, 205
A. Bermingham: *Landscape and Ideology: The English Rustic Tradition, 1740–1860* (Berkeley, Los Angeles and London, 1986)
Gainsborough in Bath (exh. cat. by A. Sumner, Bath, 1988)
M. Postle: 'Gainsborough's "Lost" Pictures of Shakespeare: "A Little out of the Simple Portrait Way"', *Apollo*, cxxxiv (1991), pp. 374–9

MICHAEL ROSENTHAL

Illustration Acknowledgements

We are grateful to those listed below for permission to reproduce copyright illustrative material and to those contributors who supplied photographs or helped us to obtain them. The word 'Photo:' precedes the names of large commercial or archival sources who have provided us with photographs, as well as the names of individual photographers (where known). It has generally not been used before the names of owners of works of art, such as museums and civic bodies. Every effort has been made to contact copyright holders and to credit them appropriately; we apologize to anyone who may have been omitted from the acknowledgements or cited incorrectly. Any error brought to our attention will be corrected in subsequent editions. Where illustrations have been taken from books, publication details are provided in the acknowledgements below.

Line drawings, maps, plans, chronological tables and family trees commissioned by the *Dictionary of Art* are not included in the list below. All of the maps in the dictionary were produced by Oxford Illustrators Ltd, who were also responsible for some of the line drawings. Most of the line drawings and plans, however, were drawn by the following artists: Diane Fortenberry, Lorraine Hodghton, Chris Miners, Amanda Patton, Mike Pringle, Jo Richards, Miranda Schofield, John Tiernan, John Wilson and Philip Winton. The chronological tables and family trees were prepared initially by Kate Boatfield and finalized by John Johnson.

Ferrara *1* Photo: Archivi Alinari, Florence; *2* Photo: Christine Verzar; *3* Fototeca, Musei Civici d'Arte Antica, Ferrara

Ferrari de': (1) Gregorio de' Ferrari *1* Archivio Fotografico, Soprintendenza per i Beni Artistici e Storici del Piemonte; *2* Gabinetto Fotografico, Soprintendenza per i Beni Artistici e Storici, Florence

Ferrari, Defendente Museo Civico d'Arte Antica, Turin

Ferrari, Gaudenzio Archivio Fotografico, Soprintendenza per i Beni Artistici e Storici del Piemonte

Ferrari, Luca Galleria e Museo Estense, Modena/Soprintendenza per i Beni Artistici e Storici di Modena e Reggio Emilia

Ferrata, Ercole Photo: Archivi Alinari, Florence

Ferretti, Giovanni Domenico Photo: Bridgeman Art Library, London

Ferri, Ciro Photo: Gabinetto Fotografico Nazionale, Istituto Centrale per il Catalogo e la Documentazione, Rome

Ferrucci: (1) Francesco di Simone Ferrucci Photo: Archivi Alinari, Florence

Ferrucci: (2) Andrea di Piero Ferrucci Board of Trustees of the Victoria and Albert Museum, London

Ferstel, Heinrich von Bildarchiv, Österreichische Nationalbibliothek, Vienna

Fête champêtre *1* Photo: Giraudon, Paris; *2* Fine Arts Museums of San Francisco, CA (Mildred Anna Williams Collection; no. 1977.8); *3* Trustees of the National Gallery, London

Fetti, Domenico *1* Photo: © RMN, Paris; *2* Photo: Gabinetto Fotografico Nazionale, Istituto Centrale per il Catalogo e la Documentazione, Rome

Feuchtmayer: (3) Joseph Anton Feuchtmayer *1–2* Photo: Ulrich Knapp

Feuerbach, Anselm Staatliche Kunsthalle, Karlsruhe

Fez Photo: Nadia Erzini

Fiammingo, Paolo Kunsthistorisches Museum, Vienna

Fiasella, Domenico Photo: M. Newcome Schleier

Fibre art Photo: Sheila Hicks, New York

Fibreglass Tate Gallery, London

Figini and Pollini Architectural Association, London/Photo: W.A.C. White

Figino, Ambrogio Galleria dell'Accademia, Venice

Fiji *1* Trustees of the British Museum, London; *2* Museum of Archaeology and Anthropology, Cambridge University

Filarete *1* Photo: Archivi Alinari, Florence; *2* Photo: British Architectural Library, RIBA, London

Fildes, Luke Royal Holloway and Bedford New College, University of London, Egham, Surrey

Filla, Emil Moravian Museum, Brno/Photo: František Krejčí

Filonov, Pavel Picture Gallery of Armenia, Erevan

Finiguerra, Maso Photo: Archivi Alinari, Florence

Finland *2* Museum of Finnish Architecture, Helsinki; *3* Photo: P.O. Welin, Åbo; *4* Museum of Finnish Architecture, Helsinki/Photo: Ingervo; *5* Photo: Kalevi Pöykkö; *6* Art Museum, Turku; *7* Amos Anderson Museum of Art, Helsinki; *8* Provincial Museum, Turku/ Photo: Lars Saari; *9* Provincial Museum, Turku/Photo: Pekka Kujanpaa; *10* Ateneum, Helsinki/Central Art Archives, Helsinki; *11, 16* National Museum of Finland, Helsinki; *12* National Archives, Helsinki; *13–14* Board of Trustees of the Victoria and Albert Museum, London; *15* Photo: Dr Sirkka Kopisto

Fioravanti, Aristotele Photo: VAAP, Moscow

Fiorenzo di Lorenzo Soprintendenza per i Beni Ambientali, Architettonici, Artistici e Storici di Perugia

Fireplace furnishings Photo: Jerry Hardman-Jones, Leeds

Firuzabad Photo: G. Herrmann

Fischer, Johann Michael *2* Photo: Bavaria-Verlag, Munich

Fischer von Erlach: (1) Johann Bernhard Fischer von Erlach *1* Photo: Overseas Agenzia Fotografica, Milan; *2* Bildarchiv, Österreichische Nationalbibliothek, Vienna

Fischer von Erlach: (2) Joseph Emanuel Fischer von Erlach Bildarchiv, Österreichische Nationalbibliothek, Vienna

Flags and standards *1* British Library, London (Add. MS. 45131); *2* Metropolitan Museum of Art, New York; *3* Master and Fellows of Corpus Christi College, Cambridge; *4* Egyptian Museum, Cairo; *5* Trustees of the British Museum, London; *6* Abbey Library, St Gallen (Cod. Sang. 22); *7* Bodleian Library, Oxford (MS. Arch. Selden.A.1, fol. 64*r*)

Flamboyant style Photo: Arch. Phot. Paris/© DACS, 1996

Flanagan, Barry Tate Gallery, London/© Barry Flanagan

Flandrin: (2) Hippolyte Flandrin Art Museum, Princeton University, Princeton, NJ (Museum purchase, Caroline G. Mather Fund)

Flaxman, John *1* Photo: Anthony Kersting, London; *2* College Art Collections, University College, London

Flémal, Bertholet Photo: © ACL Brussels

Flinck: (1) Govaert Flinck *1–2* Rijksmuseum, Amsterdam

Florence *1–2, 4, 6, 9, 11–20, 22–4* Photo: Archivi Alinari, Florence; *3, 5, 7–8* Photo: Scala, Florence; *10* Photo: Bardazzi Fotografia, Florence; *21* Photo: Conway Library, Courtauld Institute of Art, London; *25* Photo: Z. Waźbiński

Floris: (1) Cornelis Floris II Photo: Flemming G. Rasmussen

Floris: (2) Frans Floris I *1* Photo: © ACL Brussels; *2* Museo de Arte de Ponce, San Juan/Luis A. Ferré Foundation Inc., San Juan

Flötner, Peter Germanisches Nationalmuseum, Nuremberg

Flower painting *1* Statens Museum for Kunst, Copenhagen; *2* Musées Royaux des Beaux-Arts de Belgique, Brussels; *3* Trustees of the Wallace Collection, London; *4* National Gallery of Scotland, Edinburgh; *5* Trustees of the National Gallery, London; *6* Photo: Giraudon, Paris

Foggini, Giovanni Battista Photo: Archivi Alinari, Florence

Fohr, Carl Philipp Kurpfälzisches Museum, Heidelberg

Foley, John Henry Photo: Conway Library, Courtauld Institute of Art, London

Folly British Library, London (no. 34.f.11)

Fomin: (1) Ivan Fomin Photo: Verlag der Kunst, Dresden

Fon Photothèque du Musée de l'Homme, Paris

Font *1* Photo: Dr Marina Falla Castelfranchi; *2* Photo: Anthony Kersting, London; *3* Photo: Conway Library, Courtauld Institute of Art, London

Fontaine, Pierre-François-Léonard Archives d'Architecture du XXe siècle de l'Institut Français d'Architecture, Paris

Fontainebleau *1* Trustees of the British Museum, London; *2* Photo: Arch. Phot. Paris/© DACS, 1996

Fontainebleau school *1* Bildarchiv, Österreichische Nationalbibliothek, Vienna; *2* Photo: AKG Ltd, London

Fontana (ii): (2) Lavinia Fontana Photo: Scala, Florence

Fontana (iv): (2) Domenico Fontana *1* Photo: Bibliotheca Hertziana, Rome; *2* British Library, London (no. AC 3032, 3rd series, vol. V 53, CUP 1250.d.1/6)

Fontana (v): (1) Carlo Fontana *1* Photo: Prof. Helmut Hager; *2* Photo: Archivi Alinari, Florence; *3* Royal Collection, Windsor Castle/© Her Majesty Queen Elizabeth II

Fontana, Annibale *1–2* National Gallery of Art, Washington, DC

Fontana, Lucio Civico Museo d'Arte Contemporanea, Palazzo Reale, Milan

Fontanesi, Antonio *1* Cabinet des Estampes, Musée d'Art et d'Histoire, Geneva; *2* Museo Civico d'Arte Antica, Turin/Galleria Civica d'Arte Moderna e Contemporanea, Turin

Font de Gaume Photothèque du Musée de l'Homme, Paris

Fontebasso, Francesco Dallas Museum of Art, Dallas, TX (Gift of Colonel C. Michael Paul; no. 1964.110)

Fontevrault Abbey Photo: Anthony Kersting, London

Foppa, Vincenzo *1* Photo: Electa, Milan; *2* Metropolitan Museum of Art, New York (Theodore M. Davis Collection/Bequest of Theodore M. Davis, 1915; no. 30.95.293)

Forain, Jean-Louis Southampton City Art Gallery/© DACS, 1996

Forbes, Stanhope City Museum and Art Gallery, Plymouth

Ford, Edward Onslow Tate Gallery, London

Forgery *1* Museum Boymans–van Beuningen, Rotterdam; *2* Board of Trustees of the Victoria and Albert Museum, London; *3* Courtauld Institute Galleries, London; *4* Library, Leeds University (Brotherton Collection)

Fort Center Florida Museum of Natural History, Gainesville, FL

Fortuny: (1) Mariano Fortuny y Marsal *1* Real Academia Catalana de Bellas Artes de San Jorge, Barcelona; *2* Museu Nacional d'Art de Catalunya, Barcelona/Photo: MNAC Photographic Service (Calveras/Sagristà)

Forum Architectural Association, London/Photo: Belinda Durbridge

Foster, Myles Birket Yale Center for British Art, New Haven, CT

Foster, Norman Photo: Ian Lambot

Fountain *1, 3, 5* Photo: Archivi Alinari, Florence; *2* Photo: Bildarchiv Foto Marburg; *4* Photo: Arch. Phot. Paris/© DACS, 1996; *6* Photo: © RMN, Paris; *7* Photo: © Norman McGrath, New York, 1978; *8* Öffentliche Kunstsammlung Basel, Kunstmuseum, Basle

Fountains Abbey *1–2* Photo: Conway Library, Courtauld Institute of Art, London

Fouquet, Jean *1* Staatliche Museen zu Berlin, Preussischer Kulturbesitz; *2* Photo: © RMN, Paris; *3* Photo: Giraudon, Paris; *4* Bayerische Staatsbibliothek, Munich

Fouquier, Jacques Musée des Beaux-Arts, Nantes/Photo: Patrick Jean

Fragonard: (1) Jean-Honoré Fragonard *1* Photo: Giraudon, Paris; *2* Trustees of the Wallace Collection, London

Fragonard: (2) Alexandre-Evariste Fragonard Photo: © RMN, Paris

Frame *1* Art Gallery of Ontario, Toronto; *2–3, 42, 86* Board of Trustees of the Victoria and Albert Museum, London; *4, 6* Photo: Scala, Florence; *5* Board of Trustees of the National Museums and Galleries on Merseyside, Liverpool/Walker Art Gallery, Liverpool; *12, 22* Photo: Bardazzi Fotografia, Florence; *14* J. Paul Getty Museum, Malibu, CA; *16* North Carolina Museum of Art, Raleigh, NC; *17, 25, 36* Photo: Paul Mitchell; *23* Frick Collection, New York; *24* National Gallery of Art, Washington, DC (Ailsa Mellon Bruce Fund); *39* Photo: RCHME/© Crown Copyright; *45* Tate Gallery, London; *51* Manchester City Art Galleries; *53* Museum of Fine Arts, Boston, MA (Bequest of William A. Coolidge); *54* Museum Mayer van den Bergh, Antwerp; *56* Musées Royaux des Beaux-Arts de Belgique, Brussels; *58* Rijksmuseum, Amsterdam; *59* Museum voor Schone Kunsten, Ghent; *60* Staatliche Museen zu Berlin, Preussischer Kulturbesitz/Photo: Jörg P. Anders; *61* Musée des Beaux-Arts de Dijon/Photo: Hugo Maertens; *67, 77–8* Statens Konstmuseer, Stockholm; *70* Staatliche Kunstsammlungen Dresden; *73* Riksantikvaren, Oslo; *74* Nationalmuseum, Copenhagen; *75* Museum of Foreign Art, Sinebrychoff/Antell Collection, Helsinki/

Central Art Archives, Helsinki/Photo: Jukka Romu; *85, 87, 92* Photo: Ampliaciones y Reproducciones MAS, Barcelona; *90* Kimbell Art Museum, Fort Worth, TX; *94* Metropolitan Museum of Art, New York (Gift of Mr and Mrs Charles Kramer, 1979; no. 1979.664.1); *95* Photo: Kennedy Galleries Inc., New York; *96* Yale University Art Gallery, New Haven, CT; *97–8* Photo: Mr William Adair

Français, François-Louis Musée des Beaux-Arts, Lille

Francavilla, Pietro Photo: © RMN, Paris

France *3, 5, 15, 40* Photo: Conway Library, Courtauld Institute of Art, London; *4, 32–3* Photo: James Austin, Cambridge; *6* Photo: Christopher Tadgell; *7* Photo: Henry Ely, Aix-en-Provence; *8, 11, 14* Photo: Arch. Phot. Paris/© DACS, 1996; *9–10, 46–7* Bibliothèque Nationale de France, Paris; *12* Bibliothèque et Musée de l'Opéra, Paris/Photo: Bibliothèque Nationale de France, Paris; *13* Musée Carnavalet, Paris/Musées de la Ville de Paris/© DACS, 1996; *16* Photo: Zodiaque, St-Léger-Vauban; *17, 19, 21, 27–8, 34, 36–8* Photo: Giraudon, Paris; *18, 20, 22, 39, 43, 45, 54, 56, 59–60, 79, 90, 92* Photo: © RMN, Paris; *23* Statens Konstmuseer, Stockholm; *24, 63, 82* Trustees of the Wallace Collection, London; *25* Photo: © ACL Brussels; *26* Hamburger Kunsthalle, Hamburg; *29* Solomon R. Guggenheim Museum, New York (no. FN 55.1426)/Photo: Robert E. Mates; *30–31, 41–2* Musée National d'Art Moderne, Paris; *35* Photo: Giraudon/© RMN, Paris; *44, 64, 85* Trustees of the British Museum, London; *48, 51–2, 62, 80* Musée des Arts Décoratifs, Paris; *49* Photo: Philippe Garner; *50* Musée des Arts Décoratifs, Paris/Photo: Laurent Sully Jaulmes; *53, 61, 65–7, 69, 74, 81, 86, 89, 95–9* Board of Trustees of the Victoria and Albert Museum, London; *55* Metropolitan Museum of Art, New York (Jack and Belle Linsky Collection, 1982; no. 1982.60.61); *57* Musée Carnavalet, Paris/© DACS, 1996; *58* J. Paul Getty Museum, Malibu, CA; *68* Museum für Kunst und Gewerbe, Hamburg; *70* Metropolitan Museum of Art, New York (Gift of Henry G. Marquand, 1894; no. 94.4.228,.229); *71, 91* Musée Départemental des Antiquités, Rouen; *72* Corning Museum of Glass, Corning, NY; *73* Nationalmuseum, Copenhagen; *75* Syndics of the Fitzwilliam Museum, Cambridge; *76* Kunstindustrimuseet, Copenhagen/Rosenborg Slot, Copenhagen; *77* Metropolitan Museum of Art, New York (Gift of Mrs Reginald McVitty and Estate of Janet C. Livingston, 1976; no. 1976.357.1ab); *78* Metropolitan Museum of Art, New York (Bequest of Catherine D. Wentworth, 1948; no. 48.187.7ab.8); *83* Photo: RMN, Paris/© DACS, 1996; *84* Musée des Beaux-Arts de Lyon; *87–8* Photo: Wartski Jewellers Ltd, London; *93* Kunsthistorisches Museum, Vienna; *94* Photo: Bridgeman Art Library, London

Francés, Nicolás Photo: Ampliaciones y Reproducciones MAS, Barcelona

Franceschini, Baldassarre *1* Cassa di Risparmio e Depositi, Prato

Franceschini, Marcantonio *1* Gemäldegalerie Alte Meister, Dresden; *2* Photo: Archivi Alinari, Florence

Francesco di Antonio del Chierico Biblioteca Apostolica Vaticana, Rome

Francesco di Giorgio Martini *1* Photo: Conway Library, Courtauld Institute of Art, London; *2* Photo: James Austin, Cambridge; *3* Photo: Archivi Alinari, Florence; *4* Photo: Osvaldo Böhm, Venice

Francia: (1) Francesco Francia *1* Trustees of the National Gallery, London; *2* Metropolitan Museum of Art, New York (Gift of George R. Hann, 1965; no. 65.220.1)

Francia: (2) Giacomo Francia Walters Art Gallery, Baltimore, MD

Franciabigio Royal Collection, Windsor Castle/© Her Majesty Queen Elizabeth II

Franciscan Order *1–2* Photo: Archivi Alinari, Florence; *3* Museo del Prado, Madrid

Francke, Master Hamburger Kunsthalle, Hamburg

Francken: (5) Frans Francken II *1* Bayerische Staatsgemäldesammlungen, Munich; *2* Hamburger Kunsthalle, Hamburg

Franco, Battista Photo: Osvaldo Böhm, Venice

François, Maître Bibliothèque Nationale de France, Paris

Frank, Robert Pace/MacGill Gallery, New York

Frankenthaler, Helen National Gallery of Art, Washington, DC (Collection of the artist)

Frankfurt am Main *1* Photo: Bildarchiv Foto Marburg; *2* Kunstsammlung Nordrhein-Westfalen, Düsseldorf/© DACS, 1996; *3* Museum für Moderne Kunst, Frankfurt am Main/Photo: Rudolf Nagel

Frascati *1–2* British Library, London (no. 559.d.12)

Freiburg im Breisgau Städtische Museen, Freiburg

Freisinger, Caspar Staatsgalerie, Stuttgart

Fréminet, Martin Photo: Arch. Phot. Paris/© DACS, 1996

French Guiana *2–3* Photo: Michèle Baj Strobel

Fresco *1–4* Vatican Museums, Vatican City, Rome